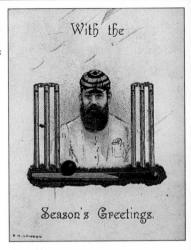

130TH YEAR

WISDEN

CRICKETERS' ALMANACK

1993

EDITED BY MATTHEW ENGEL

PUBLISHED BY JOHN WISDEN & CO LTD

A COMPANY JOINTLY OWNED BY
GRAYS OF CAMBRIDGE (INTERNATIONAL) LIMITED
AND
BOWATER PLC

SOFT COVER EDITION £19.50   CASED EDITION £22.50

ISBN
Cased edition 0 947766 20 0
Soft cover edition 0 947766 21 9

John Wisden & Co Ltd
25 Down Road
Merrow
Guildford
Surrey
GU1 2PY

Computer typeset by Spottiswoode Ballantyne Ltd, Colchester
Printed in Great Britain by William Clowes Limited, Beccles

PREFACE

In the November of 1991 I was at Eden Gardens in Calcutta, along with approximately 90,000 other people, reporting the first-ever international between India and South Africa for *The Guardian*. There was considerable debate at the time as to exactly how approximate that figure of 90,000 was and whether the figure might have beaten the 90,800 recognised as the record attendance for a day's cricket.

I tried to weigh the evidence on both sides, failed to reach a definite conclusion and told my readers that the editor of *Wisden* had better sort it out. Had I foreseen what was to happen next I would have kept quiet. Five months later I was the editor of *Wisden*, to my own and no doubt many other people's astonishment. Calcutta unfortunately is still Calcutta and the number of people in any given place at a given time is generally a matter for conjecture. The balance of evidence was that it was not a record. Most importantly, for the purposes of this almanack, there was no absolute evidence that it was.

The most revered tradition of *Wisden* is its accuracy and I feel as bound to uphold that as if on oath. Inevitably, a volume of this size, produced under pressure, must contain some mistakes. Any editor lives in terror that he will pick up the finished copy and discover a horrific one: *WIDSEN* on the front cover, maybe. All one can say is that the effort put into eliminating errors is as exhaustive (and exhausting) as the combination of the fallible human brain and the even more fallible computer can achieve.

There are other traditions that are just as sacred: *Wisden's* continuity and its independence from cricket's ruling bodies so that it remains free to comment robustly on the issues the game faces. Whoever temporarily carries the torch has to maintain these. Cricket provides entertainment for millions of people. The satisfaction the game gives is enhanced immeasurably because of the importance it attaches to its past (sometimes it cares less about the future, which is another matter) and to the integrity of its records and statistics. This may be a triviality but, as the horse racing sage Phil Bull said of his sport, it's a great triviality.

Wisden is also surrounded by an aura of myth. One myth is that the Almanack somehow never changes. Anyone who owns a large number of volumes knows that *Wisden* has changed enormously over the years, just as the game has. For the most part – and rightly – it has done so slowly, organically, almost stealthily, mutating a good deal more carefully than cricket itself. In 1938, when Wilfrid H. Brookes was editor, the Victorian look and layout were transformed instantly into something recognisably like the modern *Wisden* and, with luck, no future editor will ever again need to attempt anything as revolutionary as that.

What I have tried to do is to make the book clearer and more accessible to new readers without disturbing the rhythm understood by those who already know and love it. To do that, I have actually gone back to a couple of pre-1938 ideas. One is the inclusion of a proper table of contents, the absence of which has always struck me as one of *Wisden's* dafter customs. The other is the division of the book into different parts, which is mainly a formalisation of the existing ordering.

The improved Contents means the Index moves to its more logical position at the back and becomes an Index to Cricketers. Many of the other changes are additions to *Wisden's* service: the back-of-the-book articles on the year's developments in various ancillary departments of the game; something closer to proper recognition for domestic club cricket; and, as the game spreads, news from 20 different ICC member-countries, far more than ever before.

Some other changes have been forced by events. In 1992, MCC did not play any first-class cricket, thus making its long-established positioning in front of the first-class counties completely anachronistic. The Other Matches at Lord's section also seemed to have outlived its usefulness and the games recorded there in the past have now been moved to their logical positions: Oxford v Cambridge under Universities, Eton v Harrow under Schools and so on.

The death of John Arlott in 1991 saddened us all. It also left a gap in *Wisden*. With just a two-year break, John had been the Almanack's book reviewer since the section began in 1950. There was no one else with the stature to take on the task in quite the same way and it seemed to me proper to turn outside the enclosed world of cricket writing to find a reviewer. From now on, *Wisden's* book reviews will be written by someone different each year: a reviewer with a literary reputation first and a separate enthusiasm for cricket. I was honoured that J. L. Carr agreed to inaugurate what I hope will become a tradition.

Of more ancient traditions, the most famous has been maintained as before. The Five Cricketers of the Year are Wasim Akram and Alec Stewart, for their performances in Test cricket; Ian Salisbury, for his stunning success with leg-spin in county cricket; Martyn Moxon, both for his batting and for displaying qualities of leadership that enabled Yorkshire to raise their ancient bar on outsiders with a minimum of fuss; and Nigel Briers, for showing how a captain with character can help transform a team.

The choice became mine because my predecessor, Graeme Wright, after six years as editor and eight as assistant editor before that, decided last year that he needed a change. My admiration for his achievement has grown by the week. He is, more than any other one person, the creator of the modern *Wisden* and he has been generous in his help whenever I needed it. Luckily, I inherited the magnificent team that Graeme built, headed by Harriet Monkhouse, the in-house editor, and Christine Forrest, the production editor. If *Wisden* has survived a year under a tyro (sometimes tyrannical) and error-prone editor, it is primarily due to them, and to Roy Smart, our computer expert, Gordon Burling, our proofreader, Marcus Williams, who gave editorial support and encouragement, and Peter Bather and Mike Smith at Spottiswoode Ballantyne, our typesetter.

I would also like to mention Bill Frindall and John Kitchin, for their work on the statistics and obituaries respectively. Our correspondents are listed after the Contents. It is not a full list of everyone who played a part. Administrators at Lord's and elsewhere were unfailingly patient with enquiries. My colleagues on *The Guardian* – Mike Averis above all – and in the press box were helpful and supportive in all kinds of ways. My most special thanks go to my wife Hilary, who made many vital editorial contributions and tolerated my moods with wondrous good humour, and to my son Laurie, whose first year had to compete with *Wisden's* 130th. The most important task for everyone involved in cricket is to ensure that Laurie's generation will in time get the same pleasure out of the game that we do.

MATTHEW ENGEL

Newton St Margarets,
Herefordshire,
January 1993

CONTENTS

Part Four: Overseas Cricket in 1991-92

Part Five: Administration and Laws

Part Six: Miscellaneous

LIST OF CONTRIBUTORS

The editor acknowledges with gratitude the assistance afforded in the preparation of the Almanack by the following:

Colin Ackehurst	G. S. Gordon	Dudley Moore
Graham Allen	Russell Grant	Graham Morris
Jack Arlidge	Gul Hameed Bhatti	Gerald Mortimer
David Armstrong	David Hallett	David Munden
Chris Aspin	Maurice Hankey	Mike Neasom
Philip Bailey	David Hardy	Qasim E. Noorani
Mark Baldwin	Peter Hargreaves	David Norrie
Jack Bannister	Bob Harragan	Francis Payne
Colin Bateman	Norman Harris	S. S. Perera
June Bayliss	Les Hatton	Matt Pritchett
Brian Bearshaw	Murray Hedgcock	S. Pervez Qaiser
Sir William Becher	Michael Henderson	Qamar Ahmed
Michael Berry	Frank Heydenrych	Andrew Radd
Scyld Berry	Eric Hill	David Rayvern Allen
Edward Bevan	Clive Hitchcock	Nick Richmond
J. Watson Blair	Lt-Col. K. Hitchcock	Barry Rickson
Robert Brooke	Philip Hoare	Amanda Ripley
Gordon Burling	Derek Hodgson	Rex Roberts
C. R. Buttery	Dr Grenville Holland	Dicky Rutnagur
John Callaghan	Gerald Howat	Carol Salmon
John Campbell	Simon Hughes	Geoffrey Saulez
Mark Campkin	Ken Ingman	Derek Scott
J. L. Carr	Jai Kumar Shah	Mike Selvey
David Collins	David James	Roy Smart
Andrew Collomosse	John Jameson	Bill Smith
Terry Cooper	Kate Jenkins	Karen Spink
Geoffrey Copinger	Tom Jenkins	Rob Steen
Ted Corbett	Martin Johnson	Richard Streeton
Tony Cozier	Peter Johnson	E. W. Swanton
John Cribbin	Ihithisham Kamardeen	John Thicknesse
Brian Croudy	Abid Ali Kazi	Stephen Thorpe
Jon Culley	John Kitchin	Jan Traylen
Noah Davidson	Chris Lane	Chris Turvey
Geoffrey Dean	Ken Lawrence	Sudhir Vaidya
Chris Douglas	Stephanie Lawrence	Gerry Vaidyasekera
Patrick Eagar	Alan Lee	David Walsh
Ken Farmiloe	David Llewellyn	Marilyn Warnick
John Featherstone	David Lloyd	Tim Wellock
Brian Fell	Nick Lucy	Geoffrey Wheeler
Paton Fenton	Steven Lynch	Steve Whiting
Don Ferguson	Bryan McAllister	Richard Whittingdale
T. J. Finlayson	John MacKinnon	Marcus Williams
Bill Frindall	Roger Mann	Mark Williams
David Frith	A. R. May	Margaret Wilson
Nigel Fuller	Allan Miller	Donald Woods
Simone Gambino	R. Mohan	Peter Wynne-Thomas
Ghulam Mustafa Khan	Chris Moore	

Thanks are accorded also to the following for checking the scorecards of first-class matches:
M. R. L. W. Ayers, L. Beaumont, G. R. Blackburn, Mrs C. Byatt, L. V. Chandler, W. Davies, B. T. Denning, J. Foley, B. Hunt, V. H. Isaacs, B. H. Jenkins, D. Kendix, A. C. Kingston, D. A. Oldam, S. W. Tacey and R. D. Wilkinson.

PART ONE: COMMENT

NOTES BY THE EDITOR

When you lie awake at four o'clock on a winter's morning, it is always the little things that are so damn bothersome. I sometimes wonder what would happen if, as is statistically probable some day soon, a cup final at Lord's ended with both teams having the same number of runs and wickets. Would they really give the trophy, as the rules insist, to the team with most runs after thirty overs? What on earth is the difference between a run scored off the last ball of the thirtieth over and the first ball of the thirty-first?

And why do they now announce Test teams any old day instead of on Sunday morning, which was part of the warp and weft of an English summer? One would hear the England selectors' latest enormity and go out and vent one's frustrations by mowing the lawn or murdering the weeds. Has this tradition vanished because the few people in the know, so secretive when it suits them, cannot be trusted not to leak the names to their favourite Sunday newspaper? And why, if you ask in a sports store for a pair of cricket flannels, will the assistant only offer something made in a material resembling sandpaper but without the softness? If this is what professional cricketers wear, does it explain why they are so keen to play as little as possible?

With luck, it is eventually possible to go back to sleep and worry about something else the next night. But cricket does keep creeping back. There is something insidious about the game. Its glory is that it works on so many levels: well-briefed spectators will think they know what is going on even though the contest taking place in the middle may be full of all kinds of private sub-plots. It does not matter. Other spectators may be more detached, conscious only of white-clad (usually) figures in a summer's landscape; they might have found even the last over of the 1992 Lord's Test match a restful backdrop to reading a book or doing their knitting.

Cricket can appeal to the athlete and the aesthete alike; it can veer between lyric poetry, differential calculus and Thai kick-boxing. No game has such range, such depth. But it is all extremely fragile. Editors of *Wisden* have been worrying about the game in these pages for most of the Almanack's existence. It has always been in crisis of one sort or another.

A game of two halves

Last year the crisis moved into an acute phase. It was nothing to do with ball-tampering, dissent, TV umpiring, coloured clothing nor any of the other issues that dominated the cricketing press in 1992, nor even to do with the manufacture of flannels. Cricket, at the highest level, has acquired a unique and insoluble problem by turning itself into two separate sports. There is traditional cricket, a game that has stood the test of time as a satisfying pastime and way of life but which finds it increasingly hard to get an audience. And there is one-day cricket, which is popular among spectators but is regarded with varying degrees of contempt by the professionals forced to play it, administrators forced to stage it and journalists forced to report it.

It distorts cricket's skills and produces a mutant game which, while it might on occasion be tense, is essentially shallow.

The winter of 1992-93 has produced some wonderfully vivid Test cricket, in Australia particularly. There have been huge crowds in Melbourne and Calcutta. But with the Indian authorities frightened even to schedule a full Test series, these still look like upward blips on a downward graph. The highest form of the game may have reached the point county cricket was at in the 1950s when its audience began to find other things to do.

The autumn of 1992 brought the first Tests in South Africa for 23 years and the first ever in Zimbabwe (to be reported fully in the 1994 *Wisden*). This should have been a glorious time for cricket. The village-sized attendances in Harare and Bulawayo may have been inevitable; there is no cricket-watching base in Zimbabwe. But what happened in South Africa? The crowds at Durban, for their first-ever Test against India, were actually lower than the low figures put out by the ground authority. The idea that the longest-awaited cricket match in history would attract just 5,000 people on its opening day would have been regarded throughout the years of boycott as insane.

All this is gradually ceasing to be a surprise. Players and administrators appear to have forgotten that Test cricket was ever meant to be a public entertainment. The boring passage of play, the possibility of the draw, the long block – all these have their place in cricket tactics. But when they become the entire strategy, the effects are disastrous.

The series between South Africa and India, which was desperately important to the future of the game, was played throughout at a level that might have been carefully designed to repel the casual spectator. Zimbabwe's inaugural Test in Harare against India was screamingly dull. A little boy sitting behind me (one of a couple of hundred spectators) asked his mother impatiently: "Who's winning?" "Sssh," she said, "nobody." She was right too. Do you think he will be clamouring for a ticket next time there is a Test match? The Zimbabwe coach John Hampshire defended his team (406 for five after two days) by saying they had to learn – in which case they should do so in private. There are very few books to buy in Harare these days and I had no knitting. But the South Africans and Indians, with no excuses, were even worse. The scoring-rate over five days in the Test at Cape Town was 1.83 an over. It was an affront to a beautiful setting.

In the 1960s cricketers were enjoined to play "brighter cricket". At the start of every tour, like politicians promising better times, captains said they would play it. Now they would probably regard such an idea as insulting. Brighter cricket? Entertainment? We do all that in the one-dayers.

Fortunately, cricket is a resilient game. One great match (like West Indies' one-run win over Australia in Adelaide), one victory (India over England in Calcutta) can galvanise the local public and wipe out the memory of many wretched days. But if Test cricket is to thrive, as well as survive, there have to be many more Adelaides than Harares.

Standing alone

The forces of darkness, or at any rate floodlit cricket, may be taking over the world but England for the moment is safe. This summer brings England v Australia, and the game's treasurers are licking their lips. Test cricket in this country has avoided the trends elsewhere for various reasons: the great series of 1981 persuaded a new generation that Test cricket could be thrilling; the Test and County Cricket Board has not allowed the fact that the public seem to want one-day internationals to sway them into staging many; the London Tests have established themselves, more than ever, as social occasions; the rhythm of the English summer helps push the series along, at least in years when there is only one touring team; and TV and, above all, radio commentary have insinuated themselves into the life of the nation.

So far, the canker afflicting Test cricket elsewhere has spread furthest here into county cricket. This year the English three-day county game is replaced by the four-day game, much admired by those who sit in offices and plan cricket, much disliked by those who still go and watch it, especially at the Festival Weeks. The arguments for and against the change are given by some very distinguished antagonists elsewhere in the Almanack. One pauses here simply to speculate that the system chosen for 1993 will not last three years, as planned. There are too many empty spaces on the programme. The counties may well force the restoration of the zonal Benson and Hedges games, though there would be more merit in having 18 rather than 17 four-day matches, nine home games each, with counties playing their traditional rivals twice. In theory, cricketers want to play less; in practice, someone will want to try and make money somehow.

Whatever your views, you must admire the cunning of the TCCB officials who have ground down the opposition to the four-day game by making three-day cricket, over a period of years, seem ridiculous. Since 1989 they have forced the counties to play their three-day games on four or five-day pitches: any miscalculation in favour of result wickets has been punished by the threat of the 25-point deduction. Teams winning the toss this summer, aided by the four-day format, two runs for no-balls and the general climate in favour of batsmen, may well consider themselves failures if they are out before mid-afternoon on the second day for anything less than 450. The games may look neater in the 1994 *Wisden* than ever before. But if they contain any fun and entertainment for the spectator it is likely to happen only by accident; and no doubt someone at the Board will change the rules next winter to make sure that gets eliminated.

For the time being, everyone has to give the new system a chance, coloured clothing on Sunday and all. I have no profound objections to this gimmick – and the players should have had their names on their backs in all professional cricket years ago. If, however, the counties are planning to change their colours every year to exploit children and make them buy up-to-date gear at rip-off prices, which is what happens in football, then they are taking the road to hell.

Silence and Lamb

The 1992 Test series between England and Pakistan really did produce exciting cricket, largely because two brilliant fast bowlers, Wasim Akram and Waqar Younis, produced a method of attack that, after years when the only way of fighting the bias against batsmen was by aiming to knock their heads off, restored the focus of the game to the stumps. There is *prima facie* evidence that part of their method of doing so involved breaking the Laws of Cricket. This produced material that filled the papers with weeks of argument, 99 per cent of it ignorant. Jack Bannister's article on the subject in this year's *Wisden* is designed to slice through the misinformation. It is typical that the facts should have been so hard to ascertain. Only English humbuggery could produce a scale of values by which Allan Lamb was fined more for exposing alleged cheating than Surrey were for actually doing it. Only in cricket could Aqib Javed's behaviour towards umpire Roy Palmer at Old Trafford quickly be overtaken by the fact that the manager, Intikhab Alam, defended him. If a manager cannot defend his players who on earth can? But two of the eight provisions of the ICC Code of Conduct are designed to stop anyone saying anything to the press.

The obsession, especially at Lord's, with keeping things quiet gets worse all the time, though it never succeeds. The £750 fine on the Derbyshire chairman in 1991 for a mild criticism of the England manager was one preposterous example; the endless (and completely ineffective) censorship of players' opinions goes on to no discernible purpose; the chairman of selectors refuses to offer any explanation for the omission of David Gower from the tour party; the secretary of ICC refuses to say anything whatever about the reason for the ball being changed in a one-day international at Lord's; when county officials drop players for "internal disciplinary" reasons, they think it is none of their members' business. Those of us close to the game know that cricket is run by very nice, hard-working, intelligent and, in many cases, forward-thinking people. They seem entirely unaware that they sometimes give the impression to those further away of having served an apprenticeship under one of the less enlightened Romanovs.

Of umps and refs

> "Chaos umpire sits,
> And by decision more embroils the fray."
> Paradise Lost, Book II 907-8

It was clear to anyone watching the England–Pakistan series that the relationship between the Pakistanis and English umpires had, as they say in the divorce courts, "irretrievably broken down". As in a marriage, not all the blame can be heaped one way. Pakistani cricketers are indeed paranoid but that does not mean people are not out to get them. However hard umpires try to be fair, years of niggling from one country's team must start to affect their subconscious judgment.

The world umpiring system is now a shambles. ICC has willed a solution, an international panel of umpires, but has refused to will the means, i.e. how to pay for it. Instead, with great solemnity, they have created the completely irrelevant system of referees. It is very nice that so many affable and deserving former Test players not at the time employed in television are able to take part in this make-work scheme. But they can serve only one purpose; indeed their terms of reference, shorn of ICC jargon, boil down to only one purpose: to reinforce the authority of the umpires.

Competent Test match umpires do not need anyone to reinforce their authority; they already possess enough. However, because the game has refused to rid itself of the 19th-century delusion that a system of home-country officials can function effectively, Test match umpires round the world have been (all too frequently) incompetent or (just occasionally) corrupt. Even men supremely good at giving out and not out have not been in a strong enough position to run against the prevailing local culture, such as the West Indian notion that endless intimidation of batsmen is an acceptable form of play.

There are practical problems in setting up the panel. The longer people persist in believing there is a sensible alternative the harder it will get. The situation is not helped by the umpires themselves. English umpires have argued that such a panel would diminish their career prospects, when in fact it would enhance them immeasurably. They also persist in being dog-in-the-manger about repeating the experiment which enabled overseas officials to get experience in English cricket. One Test umpire told me he has begged for years for a chance to stand in a few Championship matches and never had the courtesy of a reply from Lord's. Overseas associations are just as obstructive in a different way, by doing far too little to encourage former first-class players to join them. Everyone should now be aware that the empirical skills, instincts and sheer nous acquired playing first-class cricket are a far better preparation for top-level umpiring than years spent passing exams. Yet still some umpires' unions prefer recruits who can recite the law on seam-picking word-perfectly instead of someone who knows how it is done.

Into the current vacuum have come various nonsenses: first, the turn-and-turn-about three-umpire matches tried in Zimbabwe and South Africa; and then, South Africa's unique contribution, the TV umpire. This involves an official sitting in the stand to adjudicate on run-outs and, if they still exist, stumpings, by watching the replay if requested by the umpire in the middle. As a stunt, it gave the Durban Test a little publicity, not that it helped the attendance much. It also sowed the first harmless-looking seed of something that could grow to be thoroughly pernicious.

If cricket has contributed anything to society as a whole, it is the notion that the umpire's decision is final and that cricketers do not argue with it. Anything else is not cricket. The idea is completely foreign to, for instance, baseball. Wise professional cricketers have always known that the good decisions and the bad ones balance out over time. Wise selectors, who presumably exist somewhere, do not ruin a player's career for one bit of bad luck. And above all cricket teaches us that, in the end, whether you are in or out does not matter much. What matters most is the ability to accept the decision. As a rule of thumb, cricketers should have that firmly understood by the age of 11.

This only works at a professional level if (see above) umpiring is recognised as fair-minded, competent and authoritative. That, however, is considered too expensive, though it is hardly more expensive to fly umpires round the world than to fly the referees round and have a man paid to sit and watch television on the off-chance. Only the tiniest percentage of cricket matches would ever be able to have TV umpiring. Yet the doubt and dissent will spread to every English village, every corner of the Bombay maidan and the Port-of-Spain savannah. If Steve Bucknor is called idiotic, as he was in Johannesburg, for giving someone not out without calling for the replay, how can old Fred from Middle Snoring make such a decision? Proponents said TV umpiring worked in American football. News travels slowly to South Africa. The National Football League had just decided to scrap it all and go back to basics.

The Gower affair

The finishing touches are being put to these notes as England go down to defeat in the Calcutta Test, a few days after the members of MCC held a special general meeting and rejected, by 6,135 votes to 4,600, a motion of no confidence in England's Test selectors proposed by 286 dissident members against the strong opposition of the MCC committee. The vote in the hall, as opposed to the postal ballot, was in favour of the motion by 715 to 412, and it would have been clear to a neutral, fair-minded observer, if one was present, that the proponents won the debate as well.

The meeting was called because the selectors had left out Gower and, only slightly less controversially, Jack Russell and Ian Salisbury from the tour of India; Salisbury, who had flown out to act as a net bowler, was later asked to join the tour. Ted Dexter's refusal to give the reasons for Gower's omission was widely seen as arrogant; Keith Fletcher, the new England manager, did offer an explanation – that too many batsmen would have been in their mid-30s – which was quite incredible. One expects managers to lie, fib or obfuscate when they have a record to defend; it was a shock for it to happen on Fletcher's first day. Gower's omission created a furore not seen in 25 years since the selectors left out Basil D'Oliveira, with consequences that went far beyond the loss of a Test match or two, from a tour of South Africa.

Since MCC no longer directly controls English cricket it was not a logical forum for public discontent, but it was a very effective one. The club committee made it their business to defend, if not the selection, then at least the selectors' right to do as they wanted without hindrance – so it was some-times implied – from the ignorant masses. At various times, the committee and their supporters suggested that it was wrong to criticise selectors before the team had played, because that was pre-judgment; it was wrong to criticise during the tour, because that constituted disloyalty to the England team; and of course it was wrong to criticise afterwards, because that meant hindsight, and any fool can have that. The use of the word disloyalty is particularly interesting in this context. We will come back to that in a moment.

There was no sustainable cricketing case for the omission of Gower from a Test series against India. No one seriously made one. Selectors have always had their own secret agenda: prejudices against certain players considered to be unsuitable tourists. In the old days men were sometimes omitted because they did not buy their round at the bar; these days they are more likely to be left out because they do.

Many players throughout history have had their Test careers aborted or curtailed because of these personal defects, real or perceived. It is, however, entirely bizarre that those defects should suddenly be discovered in the cricketer who has played more Test matches for England than anyone in history.

There are many criticisms that can legitimately be made of Gower as a cricketer and, above all, as a captain; Graham Gooch's period of captaincy since 1989 has been marked by a dedication and determination that have often been quite magnificent. But the English cricket public, as I was saying earlier, have remained loyal to their Test team in a manner unmatched elsewhere in the world. The modern player who has most reciprocated that loyalty has been Gower. Between 1978-79 and 1986-87 he went on nine successive winter tours. The following year, understandably, he asked for a break. Since then he has been willing to play for England any time, anywhere, even to the point of something close to public humiliation by Gooch in Antigua in 1990. He did not go on any rebel tour nor is there any evidence (as there is for some other players who subsequently trumpeted their loyalty) that he seriously contemplated it. The contrast with Gooch – his decision to go to South Africa in 1981-82, his refusal, for understandable family reasons, to tour Australia in 1986-87, his need to have Donald Carr fly out to Antigua in 1986 to persuade him to stay because some politician had criticised him, the fact that he planned to skip the (abandoned) India tour of 1988-89 until he was offered the captaincy, even his insistence on not going to Sri Lanka this year – is very stark.

This party for India was chosen last September at a moment when reconciliation was being offered all round, to John Emburey for instance. Now Emburey is a fine cricketer and a nice man. But he is the only person in the whole shabby history of these enterprises who actually signed up for rebel tours to South Africa on two separate occasions. Short of standing on the square at Lord's on the Saturday of a Test match and giving a V-sign to the Long Room, it is hard to imagine how anyone can have shown greater unconcern about whether he plays for England or not. For him, forgiveness was instant. For Gower, there was none. The whole business reflected badly on English cricket; the dissidents were right to make themselves heard.

A first-class mess

Before the First World War, my predecessor Sydney Pardon must have been able, as he wrote his Notes (presumably with a quill pen rather than a word processor), to sit back and reflect at leisure on the season just gone and contemplate the one ahead. *Wisden's* role is to celebrate cricket as well as to indulge in anguished analysis of it. I was hoping to finish these Notes in an appropriately spring-like fashion: summer's coming, the Australians are coming, there are some very fine young players breaking into county cricket. It's still a beautiful game. Last year I saw two of the best days' cricket I have ever seen in my life: the Sunday of the Lord's Test and, in improbably blistering heat, the last day of Durham's game against Northamptonshire at Stockton-on-Tees.

I was starting to ruminate happily on these memories when news came through that the secretary of ICC had announced that he did not think the matches played on the rebel tours in South Africa before 1991 were first-class, which put many of the statistics in this and every other existing record book in doubt. His view was endorsed by the full ICC in the very week *Wisden* went to press. There was no time to alter the statistics in this edition; indeed a full year will hardly be enough.

I have never wavered in my view that the rebel tours were immoral. However, first-class status in cricket does not imply a moral judgment; in any case it is outrageous to make that judgment 11 years after the event. The matches palpably fitted ICC's own definition of what constitutes first-class cricket and *Wisden* strongly opposes any change in their status. Cricket's rulers did little to stop the tours when they were taking place. Now, when they are history, they have responded with a piece of vindictiveness that has a minimum effect on the players involved and a maximum effect on the integrity of the game's statistics. Do such details matter? I think so.

But anyway, as I was saying, it's the little things that are really bothersome...

PAKISTANI BOWLING – FAIR OR FOUL?

By JACK BANNISTER

Wasim Akram and Waqar Younis achieved two things in the English summer of 1992. They perfected the first genuine fast bowling innovation since overarm bowling was legalised in 1864. They also provoked repeated controversy and unproven charges alleging that their success was entirely dependent upon illegal tampering with the ball.

True or false? Fair or foul? Trick or treat? The facts first. Bowlers throughout history have bowled as fast as the Pakistani pair, and other bowlers have achieved a similar amount of late swing, but never in living memory have two bowlers achieved so much late movement through the air at such a pace . . . and usually with the old ball.

Their series statistics are impressive enough: nine games between them, in which they bowled 334.5 overs for 1,019 runs and 43 of the 71 wickets taken. They took a wicket every 46.72 balls. Furthermore, of the 43, 26 were bowled or lbw, and 14 more caught in the arc from wicket-keeper to gully. The fingers started to point because a second new ball was invariably refused by the Pakistan captain, Javed Miandad, and because there were five astonishing collapses by England when, from positions of relative prosperity, their batsmen were swept away by Wasim and Waqar with a ball well over fifty overs old.

It started in the Lord's Test, when England went from 197 for three to 255 all out and 108 for two to 175. At Headingley, the genies rubbed their old lamps to even greater effect, with England collapsing from 270 for one to 320 all out. At The Oval, they went from 182 for three to 207 all out and, in the second innings, from 153 for five to 174 all out. That is an aggregate of 221 runs for the loss of 36 wickets, with the two fast bowlers taking 24 of those wickets. The carnage happened, not at the start of an innings when, traditionally, the brand new ball is a fast bowler's most lethal weapon but three or four hours later, when the ball was older, softer, and with a less prominent seam.

All the men who have revolutionised bowling in the past have been spinners: Bosanquet with the googly, Grimmett and Benaud with the flipper, and Iverson, Ramadhin and Gleeson, who all baffled batsmen with a freakish grip. Of course there have been great swing and swerve bowlers throughout the 20th century – George Hirst, Fred Root and Bob Massie for example. But they were not genuine fast bowlers. Nor did they become more penetrative as the ball got older. It is this crucial difference which sets Wasim and Waqar apart from all other bowlers, because their methods go against all previously established principles, most of which have a sound scientific basis.

Traditionally, swing bowlers have obtained their movement through the air by maintaining the seam in a near-upright position to act as a rudder, with one polished side of the ball providing less resistance than the rougher side, with the result that swing is induced in the opposite direction. But bowlers have often found practice harder than theory, especially at the optimum speed for late movement in the ball's flight path. And there has never been a satisfactory logical explanation why one ball swings more than another, or for the relevance of humidity.

Wind tunnel experiments have established the vital importance of the seam. If the ball had no seam, it could swerve but not swing. As dimples on a golf ball make it fly further, so the seam of the cricket ball energises the air, reducing the resistance on one side and making swing bowling possible. Experiments at the University of Sydney have established that a bigger seam makes the ball swing more, and that new balls swing more than old. A team of scientists from Imperial College, London decided that optimum swing was achieved at around 60 mph with the seam at 20 degrees from the line of flight. Nobody argued with the boffins, because the theories fitted the facts and vice versa, but Wasim and Waqar have achieved violent and late swing at 80 mph despite ignoring three basic principles.

1. They do not swing the ball while it is new, yet obtain extravagant movement after three or four hours of use.

2. They do not rely on one side being highly polished.

3. Particularly in the case of Waqar, the ball is not held loosely by the first two fingers and a thumb, but often wedged firmly into the palm of the hand, baseball pitchers' fashion.

The loose grip has always been thought to give a bowler the best chance of keeping the ball in its own vertical axis. Richard Hadlee, with a classic upright hand action, could hit the seam more often and had the chance to swing the ball, whereas Greg Thomas, for instance, who had a tight grip, often found the ball rotating through the air laterally, which reduced the chance of getting the movement he wanted. So, the suspicion was, since the Pakistanis swung the old ball an unusual amount, and late, it must have been treated illegally.

What did happen is that the Pakistanis avoided the traditional method of keeping one side highly polished. Instead, by keeping one side smooth and allowing the other to roughen with use, they converted the normal evenly-weighted cricket ball into one with bias: i.e. the smooth side would be wet with sweat and spit and would become heavier than the dry, rough side. The net effect makes the ball behave like a bowl which is officially weighted to produce bias.

The wetting of a ball is legal, providing only natural properties are used, and so is a natural roughening. But that alone will not turn an ordinary bowler into a devastating one. Remember that Wasim and Waqar have played in county cricket, but no other Lancashire or Surrey bowler has suddenly developed the ability to swing the old ball so much – although Surrey have been reported several times for illegal interference with the ball. Even more significantly, the Pakistan support bowler Aqib Javed has not benefited anything like as much from any so-called doctoring. It is one thing to prime a hand grenade; the trick is knowing how and when to pull the pin.

To get the right effect, the ball needs to be held correctly and, in order to generate late swing, propelled fast and at near-yorker length. This calls for a degree of ability and control which is beyond most bowlers, who are neither quick enough nor accurate enough to bowl yorkers at more than 80 mph. The length is crucial. Neither Pakistani fast bowler swings good-length deliveries simply because, at their pace, the bias of the weighted ball cannot come into play until the ball slows down. It is not in the air long enough when it travels the good length distance of about 45 feet. It is only when the ball travels the extra distance into yorker territory that the subsequent slight decrease in pace allows the bias to work. The principle is the same as in golf, where a long putt breaks more as the ball loses speed towards the hole, and in bowls, where the bias of the bowl is more pronounced towards the end of its journey.

The key to all this is the position of arm and hand. Neither Wasim nor Waqar has a high arm, and the violent in-swing of Waqar is complicated by the dropped right arm and his point of delivery, which is close to the stumps. He thus has the ability to start his line outside the right-hander's off stump, and it is against that angle that the late and pronounced swing becomes virtually unplayable. Most revolutionary of all is Waqar's grip, which uses most of the hand and fingers. According to the Imperial College theory, if the seam is canted 20 degrees to leg side and the smooth polished half faces the off side, the result is an in-swinger. Waqar reverses this by holding the ball so that the smooth, damper half faces leg side and, because it is heavier, drags the ball that way. Hence the phrase "reverse swing". The skill still lies in the ability to bowl fast at yorker length. Imran Khan claims he could reverse-swing the ball in England from mid-July onwards when most of the county squares became hard and worn. He quotes the Lord's Test in August 1982 as an example of his ability to move the ball when the England bowlers, using conventional methods, achieved no movement in the air at all.

So fair or foul? It is perfectly legal to make one side of the ball heavier by sweat and spit (as opposed to Vaseline or sun cream), therefore reverse swing itself is legal. It only becomes illegal if the bowlers are hastening the process by making the rough side lighter and gouging bits out. That is the element that brought the cries of "Cheat". There is, in my view, a strong case for widening Law 42.5 to allow a reversion to the practice permitted before 1980, of rubbing the ball on the ground to let bowlers, usually spinners, get a better grip. If sweat and spit are permissible to shine or dampen one side of a ball, why should the other side not be rubbed in the ground? The balance of cricket has shifted so far in favour of the batsmen that treatment of the ball should be permitted, as long as umpires can control it and there is no alteration of the condition of the ball, i.e. no tearing away at the surface until strips of leather are removed.

Only bowlers with the ability to bowl fast and with the control to bowl yorkers, such as Wasim and Waqar, would benefit – as would the game of cricket. Bouncers were hardly used in 1992 by two bowlers who are to be congratulated for producing some of the most spectacular bowling that spectators in England have ever seen. Any genuine innovation in sport is fascinating to watch. Wasim Akram and Waqar Younis won the series for Pakistan on superior ability. A minor change in Law 42.5 will ensure that neither they, nor future successful imitators, need have their feats clouded by controversy.

Jack Bannister is cricket correspondent of the Birmingham Post *and a BBC commentator. He played for Warwickshire between 1950 and 1968 and took 1,198 first-class wickets.*

AFRICAN SUNRISE

By DONALD WOODS

In 1992 cricket's prodigal son, South Africa, came back fully to the game's global family through the World Cup competition and the first-ever Test matches against West Indies and India. After decades of isolation from real international competition the South African cricketers had two main points to prove – that South Africa was still among the top cricketing nations and that its team represented a new South Africa, in which apartheid was replaced with positive action to make up for past wrongs.

In theory the new South Africa ought to develop even stronger teams than the powerful combination which crushed Australia in seven of the last nine Tests before the curtain of isolation dropped in 1970, when the batting was so strong that Mike Procter went in as low as eight or nine. The hope is that the new South Africa will in time draw its Test stars from all the cultural groups of the nation instead of only the English-speaking whites, who number no more than six per cent of the total population. Until comparatively recently most of the whites, the Afrikaners, were so alienated from cricket that those few making it to Test level were regarded as "anglicised" and somehow not truly of the Volk. So great was the cultural chasm between the two white groups that when Springbok captain Dudley Nourse introduced his players to the Afrikaner Prime Minister Dr Daniel Malan on the eve of the 1951 tour to England, Malan told the astonished Nourse that he hoped the team would enjoy their visit to South Africa.

Batsmen such as Andre Bruyns of Stellenbosch, who would probably have been a Springbok captain had there been no isolation, led a new wave of young Afrikaner cricketers to prominence in the mid-1970s. Their deeds in the domestic Currie Cup competition caused such a spread of cricket popularity among Afrikaans schools that by the time of the 1992 World Cup no fewer than four members of the South African team, Cronje, Bosch, Wessels and Donald, came from Afrikaans-speaking homes.

But the main recruitment in the new South Africa will have to come from those previously excluded from all hope of representing their country at cricket: the 84 per cent of South Africans formerly classified under the apartheid lexicon as "non-white", the Africans, so-called "Coloureds" and "Indians" – until recently subjected to 317 racial laws. If the nation's cricket comes to represent its demography accurately, this black majority of some thirty millions will in due course supply about threequarters of future South African teams. Fortunately for the future of South African cricket there is among this black majority a longer tradition and greater depth of cricket involvement than there was for many years among the Afrikaner whites, so that the integration of black players into the national playing structures should be a somewhat easier process than the integration of Afrikaners. As far back as the turn of the century there was a black fast bowler, Krom Hendricks, good enough to be chosen for South Africa against England, and his omission was the first of many surrenders by white South African cricket administrators to the racial considerations of their political leaders. This system of meddling was described as "keeping politics out of sport".

[*Patrick Eagar*

Above: Mohammad Azharuddin, the Indian captain, releases one of 13 doves of peace at Kingsmead, Durban before the country's first-ever Test against South Africa in November 1992, part of what was called "The friendship tour". *Below:* The South African fielders appeal for a run-out against Sachin Tendulkar in the Durban Test, a decision which square-leg umpire Cyril Mitchley referred, for the first time in history, to a colleague watching a TV replay. Karl Liebenberg gave Tendulkar out from the pavilion.

[*Patrick Eagar*

During the years of segregation young white South Africans idolised their cricketing heroes from Faulkner and Schwarz to the Pollocks and Richards, while young blacks in the country preferred to identify with Nicholls, Salie, Roro, Majola, Malamba, Ntikinca, Barnes, D'Oliveira, Bhamjee, Ntshekisa and Ebrahim – all black players as unknown to their white compatriots as they were to the cricket world at large. They may not have been national figures but they were local and regional heroes, especially in the Cape Province. All the time many whites liked to assume blacks were not interested in cricket. Meanwhile, the only white cricketers cheered on by black cricket fans were those playing *against* South Africa. When Neil Harvey played his epic match-winning innings of 151 not out for Australia against South Africa at Durban in 1950, every scoring stroke he made was cheered from the seating area reserved for blacks, not least by a young lawyer named Nelson Mandela.

How good were the black players of those years? D'Oliveira was the only one given the international opportunity to prove himself, but there is evidence that a number of them were worth Springbok places. Taliep Salie was a googly bowler regarded by Clarrie Grimmett as good enough for any Test team in the world. Among the Africans were Frank Roro, who scored 20 centuries in black inter-provincial cricket, Khaya Majola, Ben Malamba, Edmund Ntikinca and Sam Ntshekisa, all of whom showed skills far above average despite adverse pitches and playing conditions. Tiffie Barnes and Baboo Ebrahim would have been stars in any first-class cricket arena, and as wicket-keepers "Chicken" Bhamjee and C. J. Nicholls were regarded by some sound judges as being at least as good as their counterparts in the white cricket world. So there was a lot to be sorry for in South Africa's cricketing past; a lot of lost time and opportunity and a lot of wrong to acknowledge and put right as the first-ever South African team chosen consciously on merit only was assembled for the World Cup in Australia and New Zealand.

On performance grounds alone the South Africans had a good World Cup, reaching the semi-final after beating teams as powerful as West Indies, Australia, India and the eventual winners, Pakistan, and in their first Test matches thereafter they were far from outclassed, despite the long years of isolation. More importantly, however, they showed an intelligent level of acknowledgment of the point of the boycott in a manner which their rugby compatriots failed to emulate. The key to this acknowledgment was the trust developed between Dr Ali Bacher, managing director of the then South African Cricket Union, and Steve Tshwete, chief spokesman on sport for the African National Congress. Their relationship was the tip of an iceberg of more widespread commitment throughout South African cricket. It was also expressed through what had become a genuine commitment to the development of cricket among black children in the townships. Initially the Township Development Programme had been a limited and exploratory project which, if not entirely window-dressing, was nevertheless paternalistic, lagging well behind the desired return to international cricket in the priorities of most of the white cricket administrators.

The catalyst for real change was the last rebel tour, led by Mike Gatting in 1990. The extent of the opposition to it stunned many people in the SACU, who had ignored the warnings of anti-apartheid activists and expected the tour to pass off as peacefully as the previous six. But there were indications even beforehand that some formerly blinkered administrators had begun to realise that the kids in the townships were showing exciting abilities and that the best priority for South African cricket was the mission to black youth. The tour was something of a throwback. Suddenly, almost without realising the transition, Bacher and his colleagues were thinking as real South Africans for the first time in their lives. This was all that Tshwete and his associates had been waiting for, and they responded with generous enthusiasm. From the moment white officials began to view the youth scheme rather than tours as the main priority, the ANC made the tours possible again.

Soon the SACU merged with its old rival, the South African Cricket Board, the new United Board was admitted to ICC and South African cricket began to be riven instead by the same disputes that characterise the game elsewhere, mostly over the eccentricities of the selectors. This argument reached its peak when Jimmy Cook and Clive Rice were left out of the World Cup squad. But Cook, Rice, Kepler Wessels and Peter Kirsten are all in or approaching their cricketing old age. There is a new generation of stars to find as representatives of the new South Africa. It was significant that Bacher and his colleagues were now bandying about names like Masemola, Mahuwa and Mabena. These are black cricketers still in their teens, but already showing talent to excite their elders. Walter Masemola is a fast bowler of rare pace and promise, Kenneth Mahuwa is a left-handed opening batsman and Billy Mabena is another exciting batting prospect. As the township coaching scheme develops and spreads wider afield such prospects will presumably multiply.

What else will come out of Africa? Perhaps Namibia will develop surprises for other cricket countries as it has already for some rugby countries. And Zimbabwe? After years of going it alone with dwindling supply sources the embattled Zimbabwean cricket administrators suddenly acquired a valuable fan of the game with unusual influence. President Robert Mugabe was excited at the prospect of how cricket development could help both national unity and the international regard for Zimbabwe. The growth of the game in Zambia and Kenya also serves as a reminder of the probability that a future political federation of southern and central African states could bring in its wake a further development of cricket as a subcontinental sport there. Whether South Africa will offer the cricket world new stimuli other than television umpiring remains to be seen. But political reconciliation in Southern and Central Africa could yet give cricket its greatest geographical boost. As young blacks increasingly excel at the game, and as growing numbers seek to emulate them, we may yet see Test matches one day played as far afield as Lusaka and Luanda.

On a final conservationist note, here is a suggestion to save the Springbok emblem. If the blacks are generous enough to let the previously white symbol remain, the whites should be imaginative enough to add black to the green-and-gold Springbok colours. Green-gold-black are the traditional colours of the African National Congress, the Pan Africanist Congress and the original Inkatha-kaZulu and black liberation groups generally. They also happened to be the colours of the rugby Springboks up until the mid-1920s. Useful change allied to tradition makes a powerful claim.

Donald Woods is a London-based writer and broadcaster. He was editor of the Daily Dispatch *in South Africa until he was arrested for anti-government activities in 1977. At the time he was the only white member of the governing council of the South African Cricket Board. He fled the country in 1978.*

FROM GRAVESEND TO THE GRAVE

THE DECLINE AND FALL OF THREE-DAY CRICKET

By JOHN THICKNESSE

Scores of retired cricketers and most spectators over 40 will be convinced there can never be a game as good as three-day county cricket. But the version that was laid to rest in August 1992 was a burlesque of the one they loved. Three-day cricket had been dying, slowly, since the winter meeting of the Test and County Cricket Board in 1980, when the switch to full covering was made. Imperceptibly at first, but unmistakably by the end of the decade, pitches lost the individuality that had made the English game unique.

The irony of full covering – that is, the protection of pitches during breaks of play through rain or bad light as well as overnight – is that it has had precisely the opposite effect from the one that was intended: the improvement of England's performance at Test level through a Championship programme played, in theory, on surfaces comparable to those in use for Tests. Uncovered pitches, it was argued, gave bowlers too much help: eliminate the weather factor, putting potential England bowlers on the same footing as their opposite numbers overseas, and they would have to brush up on their control and extend their armoury to go on taking wickets. That it has not worked like that, and seems little more likely to in four-day cricket, is primarily because English pitches lack the bounce of pitches overseas, particularly those of Australia and the West Indies. Deprived of the rain that made the Championship a game of such variety, and one which required such a diversity of skills, the surfaces went dead.

Derek Underwood was one of the leading actors in the most exhilarating day's cricket I have seen, taking seven for 103 while Rohan Kanhai miraculously made 107 in a Warwickshire total of 204, on a kicking, turning Gravesend pitch in 1970. Underwood would have been a freak if by 1987, the season he retired at the age of 42, he had not lost some zip; but he was no slower through the air than he had been in his prime, and he was still, by some way, Kent's best spinner. But he was depressed and disillusioned: in 600 overs the quickest "slow" left-armer in the game (his stock pace was brisk slow-medium) had had three batsmen caught at slip, of whom one fell to his faster ball. "The snick just doesn't carry any more," he said regretfully. "Slip has become a luxury position. Covering came in to limit the effectiveness of seamers bowling on green pitches, but it has handicapped the spinners more." Five years further down the line, statistics leave no doubt that he was right. In the 12 seasons before full covering (1969-80) there was always at least one spinner in the top ten of the bowling averages, and in 1971 there were five. By contrast, in 12 seasons of full covering, seven have passed without a spinner among the leading ten, counting only those bowlers with 20 or more wickets. When Underwood's successor in the Kent team, Richard Davis, finished sixth last season, he became the first English spinner to win a top ten place since John Childs and Jack Simmons in 1986.

If Underwood ran out of wickets, little wonder lesser bowlers floundered. Despite the uneven pitches of the later 1980s and, until 1990, seams so pronounced that with strong thumb and finger-nails it was possible to pick a ball up by the seam and lob it several feet, captains of all but the best teams had nearly given up trying to win games by bowling the opposition out. To meet the requirements of the third-day run-chase, bowling of a lower standard than that of serious 12-year-olds became accepted practice.

In the eyes of many county cricketers, the three-day game had become near enough a farce, unwinnable in most circumstances except through junk bowling, leading to a declaration and a run-chase, the terms of which the captains had negotiated. Played as it had been since the mid-1980s, even many of its greatest admirers were content to see it go. But the duration of the matches was not the cause of its demise. It was covered pitches. And because of the bat's ascendancy – in which umpires' liberal interpretation of "benefit of doubt", lack of bounce and pace in pitches and, not least, MCC's failure to restrict the weight of bats all play a part – it would be no surprise to me if by the end of the decade the unacceptable features of three-day cricket have begun to reappear.

In the 12 seasons up to 1980, there were 97 instances in *Wisden's* first-class averages of batsmen averaging 50 and upwards. In 12 subsequent seasons, the number soared to 189. And by no means all those "extra" runs have come when the fielding side have not been trying.

Such statistics firmly suggest that the switch to covered pitches in 1981 was based on a false assumption – that the techniques of English professionals would improve only in conditions favouring the bat. Yet there are as few outstanding English bowlers now as at any time since 1946, when counties were short of players following World War Two. And since today's players are twice as fit, practise harder and in cricket terms are playing for hefty sums of money, the conclusion that the more conditions vary the higher the standard of play is a hard one to resist.

Largely because of Underwood, who through his pace and great accuracy was uniquely destructive on drying pitches, the myth has grown in English cricket that batting was more or less a lottery after rain, with the ball turning square for the spinners and flying off a length for the faster bowlers. In reality, the bowlers' advantage was seldom as great as is supposed. Unless sunshine followed rain, the pitch would often stay a pudding, on which anything underpitched sat up asking to be hit; and even when the surface crusted – the "sticky dog" – it might have been only for an hour that the ball turned and bounced unpredictably in height and pace. Those were the conditions Kanhai faced that day at Gravesend, and his response was breathtaking in its opportunism and audacity. Correctly divining that attack was the best if not only method of defence, he straight-drove Underwood's first ball to him for six, and went on to make his 107 out of 177, scoring 54 in boundaries with three sixes and nine fours. Unless the ball was full enough to drive, he made no attempt to score off Underwood, taking many balls on the thighs and upper body and, with six or seven fieldsmen clustered within feet of him, used the bat as infrequently as possible.

Underwood bowled 36 successive overs – and on a pitch on which the bounce varied between knee and shoulder-high, Alan Knott did not allow a single bye. It was cricket of a stunning standard. Warwickshire went on to win by 93 runs. But though the ball turned on all three days – Underwood taking seven wickets in the second innings too – Lance Gibbs of the West Indies, then possibly the best dry-wicket off-spinner in the world, came out of it with four for 136 for Warwickshire. Bowling on wet pitches was a specialised art, as was batting, and learning those arts was regarded as an essential part of a player's education. It can hardly be a coincidence that Graham Gooch and Mike Gatting, who have become the most prolific batsmen in the country, started their careers when pitches were left open to the elements.

The counties were suspicious enough of the effect of four-day cricket to trim two years off the Murray Committee's recommendation that the experiment should last five years. That was primarily for commercial reasons: secretaries were unsure they could find satisfactory sponsorship for games whose third day was a Saturday, and whose tempo was likely to be slow. By 1995, however, the cricketing defects of the format may be unmistakable.

One chance was lost in 1987, when for a season pitches were left uncovered during the hours of play. This half-hearted experiment failed, largely because the run-ups were still covered and, in a year of green pitches, the spinners never got on often enough to prove the point either way. There was another missed opportunity in 1992; before the change, there should have been a season when four-day games were interspersed with three-day games on uncovered pitches, just to try it out. Perhaps then England's Test record might really have started to improve. It is a salutary thought that since 1981, in 120 Tests, there have been half again as many defeats as wins, 43 to 28; while between 1969 and 1980, in 114 Tests, victories outnumbered losses 38 to 26.

John Thicknesse has been cricket correspondent of the Evening Standard *since 1967.*

THE MURRAY REPORT

Three-day county cricket ended in 1992 because the Test and County Cricket Board voted on May 19 to accept the recommendations of the Structure Working Party (The Murray Report). The main points in the Report were:

1. From 1993 each team in the County Championship should play the other 17 teams just once in four-day games – almost all matches to have Thursday starts, continuing on Friday, Saturday and Monday.

2. The 55-overs-a-side Benson and Hedges Cup to be played as a straight knockout competition with no zonal games.

3. The Sunday League to be played as 50 overs a side with no restrictions on run-ups. The TCCB had already agreed to the introduction of coloured clothing, a white ball and black sightscreens.

It was agreed that the changes should last at least three years rather than the five originally suggested in the Report.

The committee was chaired by M. P. Murray, the chairman of Middlesex. Other members were: B. G. K. Downing, chairman of the TCCB marketing committee; Sir Ian MacLaurin, chairman of Tesco; E. Slinger, vice-chairman of Lancashire; C. J. Tavaré, captain of Somerset; L. A. Wilson, chairman of Northamptonshire; and C. A. Barker, TCCB accountant.

W. R. F. Chamberlain, A. C. Smith and T. M. Lamb, chairman, chief executive and cricket secretary of the TCCB, also attended meetings.

THE MURRAY REPORT

THE CASE IN FAVOUR

By ALAN LEE

By 1992, the county fixture list, bedrock of English cricket, had degenerated into an unholy mess. With each new year, it seemed, the schedulers were adopting baffling new variations with the glee of a creator of crossword puzzles producing heinously cryptic clues. It had become ever more obvious that the counties were playing too much cricket, most of it badly scheduled and designed to depress standards and discourage excellence.

This was the cause of the working party, under Mike Murray. The effect is the most radical set of reforms the county game has ever seen. In welcoming almost all the conclusions of the working party, I believe I am only mirroring a relief, within the game, that the cluttered chaos of recent years will now give way to an ordered symmetry, the emphasis on improving quality at the expense of quantity.

Four-day cricket in the County Championship is inevitable and overdue. But for the voluble dissent of a number of county administrators, doubtless expressing the views of their older and more reactionary members, it would have been adopted long ago. Now, though it may cynically be seen as only the outcome of players' disrespect for the three-day game, there are many more advantages to the change than that. Five seasons of experimentation with a mixed programme of three and four-day games have been revealing. A substantially higher proportion of the longer games produced a positive result and, what is more, did so without recourse to the wearisome spectacle of "joke bowling" which has brought three-day cricket into increasing disrepute. Spin bowling has been encouraged by the extra day and there is compelling evidence to support the theory that the better team will usually prevail.

The scheduling of almost all Championship games from Thursday to Monday is not ideal, as continuity can be lost by the intrusion of a Sunday League game. But it does give members the Saturday championship cricket they desire, and it does give the fixture list a symmetry which has been missing for too long. At last, those who follow the game will understand exactly when a game is due to start, and over what period it will be played.

The argument of lost revenue and lost festivals has always seemed to me a shallow one. It will take only a measure of refocusing and a positive attitude for counties to market the four-day game successfully; as for festivals, those worthy of support will all continue, albeit in a slightly revised form. Retaining all three limited-overs competitions smacks, to me, of marketing expediency getting the better of cricketing sense, but at least the abolition of the unloved group stages of the Benson and Hedges Cup allows the early part of the season to be dominated, as it always should be, by the Championship.

Mike Murray has served the game admirably. His working party consulted extensively throughout the game, and there is so much logic behind their conclusions that they are fully worthy of their three-year trial.

Alan Lee is cricket correspondent of The Times.

THE CASE AGAINST

By E. W. SWANTON

The Murray Report was a dangerously plausible document. I say so, because it was lucidly presented, and will have seemed reasonable to many who do not have the background and experience to realise its wide implications. Over the last few years, the TCCB executive has spared no effort to maximise revenue to the centre, chiefly by focusing all attention on the England team and acceding to every demand of its management; hence "loyalty bonuses", and the two-day rest before Tests which threw the pattern of county fixtures into a hopeless confusion. This muddle of their own creation they now intend to rescue by the desperate remedy of truncating the Championship.

Although all are agreed that players are worn down by too much one-day cricket, the 1993 programme will increase the ratio of limited-over as against "proper" cricket. There will be less Championship cricket and surely duller, slower cricket. Let me list some considerations and perhaps expose a few fallacies.

1. Three-day cricket on uncovered pitches produced outstanding county teams, and great England cricketers for a century or more, until full pitch-covering was introduced in 1981. In these conditions, it could still fulfil that role *granted the will of the captains*.

2. First-class cricket must entertain by positive attacking play. A four-day diet encourages a workaday grimness, putting initiative and variety at a discount. It is all of a piece with the defensive philosophies of Messrs Stewart and Fletcher.

3. "Other countries cover their pitches, so we should." No. In England, experience on different surfaces refines technique and often makes for intriguing, sometimes heroic, cricket.

4. In 1992 the 18 counties played on 66 grounds. With the inevitable concentration on the main centres, I estimate that at least 20 grounds will eventually be lost to county cricket.

5. Festival weeks. For several counties the heart of their summer. Few will survive, certainly, if made to start on a Thursday.

6. Countrywide interest in county cricket has always been the life-blood of our game. The proposed 1993 programme will mean that the vast reading public will be deprived for more than 30 days of the season of any active match reporting.

7. Of the 20 four-day periods in 1993, seven will coincide with Tests or one-day Internationals. So members and public will see their top players in only five or six home Championship matches a season.

8. Early batsmen used to average around 38 or 40 first-class innings. Now it will be, say, 30. Correspondingly fewer chances then for young cricketers.

9. Current players favour the 17×4 scheme. Well, they would, wouldn't they? Less "work", less travel.

10. Is all-play-all a "fairer" way of determining the champions, as is alleged? Arguable. The more matches the less will be the influence of the weather.

Famous players, of all vintages, bar the present, have the deepest misgivings. It is a tragic dichotomy.

From 1946 to 1975 E. W. Swanton was cricket correspondent of the Daily Telegraph, *which originally published a fuller version of this article.*

[*Mander and Mitchenson Collection*

Robertson Hare as Gilbert Augustus Pegson, captain of England, and Ralph Lynn as
Dandy Stratton in *A Bit of a Test*, by Ben Travers, at the Aldwych Theatre in January 1933.

THE ROAR OF THE GREASEPAINT –
THE SMELL OF THE LINSEED

By DAVID RAYVERN ALLEN

"All the world's a stage", wrote somebody qualified by birth to play for Warwickshire; and no part of it is more theatrical than a cricket field. The parallels are many and obvious.

Enter Stage Left: A leading batsman. Warm applause. Expectant hush. The dialogue begins. A battle of wills ensues. Crafty strokes are made. Advantage swings this way and that. Decisive points are reached. *Longueurs* are experienced. Pre-arranged intervals are taken. The denouement arrives. Ovation as bows are taken from the pavilion balcony.

That, of course, is just a framework. Michael Billington, the theatre critic of *The Guardian*, has a complementary view: "The instant, one-day game is rather like a one-act play, whereas a five-day Test corresponds to Elizabethan five-act drama with its swift reversals of fortune and cumulative tension."

The allegiance of the theatre and its players to the summer game may well go back to the days when knights were bold and their attendants merely dismissed. However, leaving aside a casual reference in Thomas D'Urfey's 1693 play *The Richmond Heiress*, the first connection can be picked up at Norwich in 1744, when one Geo. Alexander Stevens assumed the character of a cricketer in part of an epilogue to a play "desir'd by the Gentlemen Cricketers of Barrow":

> "Of all the Joys our Parents did Partake,
> From Games Olympic, down to Country Wake;
> To one more noble they cou'd ne'er resort,
> Than Cricket! Cricket! ever active Sport."

The noble joy was referred to only in passing by the playwrights of the late 18th and 19th centuries. Cricket lovers in the audiences at the Theatre Royal, Covent Garden, for the comedies of Thomas Morton, John O'Keeffe and George Colman the younger, had to make do with lines such as, "Stay – here's Kent, fertile in pheasants, cherries, hops, yeomen, codlings and cricketers". But Kent had the rite of the annual cricket week, which mixed the sporting and dramatic. Tom Taylor of the I Zingari club appeared on stage there in August 1842 to deliver a prologue. He was wearing full cricketing apparel with bat in hand.

> "Hearing they played to-night in the cause of cricket
> I thought I'd come and se'em, that's the ticket!
> (*Producing a ticket for the Play*)
> But scarcely had I reached the play-house door,
> When three chaps rushed upon me, with a roar,
> 'We've found a Prologue!' 'Here, you sir', says one,
> 'Just clear your throat, shoulder your bat, and on.'
> 'On where?' says I. 'Why on the stage, at once!'
> And here they've left me, looking like a dunce,
> To speak a Prologue – Heaven knows what upon."

Theatres and cricket clubs often worked in harness in the 19th century to mount gala benefits for local professionals. And for a period, roughly between the demise of the various professional touring teams like All-England and the early days of the County Championship, troupes of Clown Cricketers entertained the public. The cricket was of a farcical nature with balls disappearing through trick bats and caught on hats. The players did celebratory somersaults when wickets fell. After a game in an afternoon the troupe would decamp to a nearby theatre to give a stage performance in the evening. W. R. Gilbert of Gloucestershire, and Tom Emmett and Edmund Peate of Yorkshire were three of several first-class cricketers who turned out under assumed names.

The only time that county cricketers as a team have played the game on the West End stage was when the impresario Sir Oswald Stoll mounted a variety spectacle for his winter season of 1908 at the Coliseum. The billing read *Surrey v Middlesex*, with four professionals from The Oval captained by Alan Marshal, against the same number from Lord's led by Albert Trott. J. T. Hearne and 19-year-old "Patsy" Hendren were in the Middlesex side. The audience were given a scorecard to keep tabs on the official scorer who was on the stage itself. The painting on the backcloth was of a village green surrounded by trees, depicting a pastorally idyllic summer's day. The pitch was restricted to 15 yards and adapted rules applied; for instance, a hit meant a run had to be attempted. The runs scored at each performance were cumulative and each morning the revised score was posted outside the theatre. At one performance, the net which protected orchestra and audience from the four-ounce ball could not be raised for some reason and the game proceeded with those in the stalls acting as extra fielders. Fortunately, no one was hurt. At the end of a week, Middlesex just managed to beat Surrey.

Several theatrical eminences of the era were great enthusiasts. A small boy, calling himself W.G., appeared in *Walker, London*, J. M. Barrie's first really ambitious play. Barrie, who led his own team, The Allahakbarries, often to resounding defeat, also collaborated with Arthur Conan Doyle in a musical called *Jane Annie*, which contained a cricket number. The show flopped.

Sir Frank Benson, one of the old school of actor-managers and best remembered for his Shakespearian touring company, maintained the most balanced view of all between cricket and the stage. When he needed a replacement he reputedly wired: "Urgent – send a slow left-arm bowler to play Cassius." Benson's casting arrangements were simple – all he wanted was a reasonable eleven to take on sides at each of the stops on the tour. Sheridan Morley recalls that his first question to aspiring actors at auditions would be "Position?", which apparently did not have present-day overtones.

In Benson's company for some years was Oscar Asche, lyricist of the oriental musical fantasy *Chu Chin Chow*, which ran in London for many years. Asche, whose real name was John Stanger Heiss, was born in Australia of Scandinavian descent; he liked to describe himself as "a rotund striker". On the night of one Eton and Harrow match he wanted all the robbers in *Chu Chin Chow* to carry miniature cricket bats on to the stage. He detested slow cricket and his invective was once turned against a labouring J. T. Hearne at Lord's: "How I would like that fellow to play

[*Tom Jenkins*, The Guardian
Botham at Bournemouth: The Pavilion Theatre, not Dean Park.

Desdemona to my Othello, because I should enjoy strangling the life out of his carcass."

Any mention of cricket and threatre catches up eventually with the England captain turned actor, C. Aubrey Smith, who before fostering the game in Los Angeles had founded a theatrical cricket club in England called The Thespids. They sported the same colours as the suffragettes – green and white with purple stripe – and were good enough to play a match against London County, captained by the real W.G. They had a number of well-known actors in their ranks, including H. B. Warner, H. H. Ainley, Gerald du Maurier and Basil Foster, one of the seven Foster brothers who played for Worcestershire. In a production of *The Dollar Princess* at Daly's Theatre, his understudy was another cricketer, Surrey and England fast bowler N. A. Knox. Over the years, The Thespids had several off-shoots and successors, notably The Actors, The Stage and The Concert Artists Association. The CAA XI at various times included David Nixon, Jack Warner, Cyril Fletcher and Jimmy Cutmore, who, when opening the batting for Essex, generally refrained from using his fine baritone voice.

During the 1930s, stage offerings on cricket included R. C. Sheriff's *Badgers Green*, Herbert Farjeon revues and *A Bit of a Test* by Ben Travers, which featured Robertson Hare as captain of an MCC side touring Australia. In more recent times the threads between pitch and boards have become even stronger as cricket continues to exercise an ever greater hold on the imagination of dramatists. Perhaps it is because the game contains an element of concealment, an unspoken sub-text, part of what that cricket-loving playwright Harold Pinter meant when he referred to "a hidden violence".

"This thing here," says writer/hero Henry holding his cricket bat in Tom Stoppard's play *The Real Thing*, "which looks like a wooden club, is actually several pieces of particular wood cunningly put together in a certain way so that the whole thing is sprung, like a dance floor. It's for hitting cricket balls with. If you get it right, the cricket ball will travel two hundred yards in four seconds, and all you've done is give it a knock like knocking the top off a bottle of stout, and it makes a noise like a trout taking a fly . . ."

Other contemporary pieces involving cricket either intrinsically or incidentally include *Outside Edge*, Richard Harris's comedy parading sexual mores in the pavilion, which starred Julia McKenzie and Maureen Lipman in an early cast at the Hampstead Theatre; *Underwood's Finest Hour* by Terry Jones and Michael Palin, in which Derek Underwood's unlikely six over the Vauxhall stand to win the Test with three minutes remaining cues the birth of a child in a maternity ward; *Close of Play* by Simon Gray; Alan Ayckbourn's *Time and Time Again* and some of his *Intimate Exchanges* – "They've started this filthy floodlit cricket with cricketers wearing tin hats and advertisements for contraceptives on their boots." Modern dramatic invention is high on linseed.

A previous generation saw Nobel prize-winning all-rounder Samuel Beckett and batsman Terence Rattigan – Dublin University and Harrow respectively – retire from playing "at the height of their promise". Googly-bowling critic Kenneth Tynan, who was much troubled by cartilage strain, had "a very good leg glance". Trevor Howard would insist that any work contract should contain a clause allowing time off for Tests. And Peggy Ashcroft, who is supposed to have secreted a small portable radio under her wig in the Stratford run of *The Wars of the Roses* in order to listen to commentary on the Test match, captained the Lancastrians against the Yorkists, led by Donald Sinden. "Her team had Cyril Washbrook as honorary captain and mine had Len Hutton," Sinden recalled. "You need to know your history to appreciate why Brewster Mason as the Earl of Warwick was the umpire. Politically the result of the match had to be a draw."

The West Indian philosopher C. L. R. James declared: "Cricket is first and foremost a dramatic spectacle. It belongs with the theatre, ballet, opera and the dance". Sir Laurence Olivier once said: "I have often thought how much better a life I would have had, what a better man I would have been, how much healthier an existence I would have led, if I had been a cricketer instead of an actor." On the other hand, Ian Botham gave up the chance of a Test match in New Zealand because he was playing the king in *Jack and the Beanstalk* in Bournemouth. The grass is always greener.

David Rayvern Allen is a BBC radio producer and the author of 20 books on cricket.

[Patrick Eagar

Back row: Mushtaq Ahmed, Rashid Latif, Zahid Fazal, Naved Anjum, Aqib Javed, Inzamam-ul-Haq, Ata-ur-Rehman, Waqar Younis, Aamir Sohail, Moin Khan, Eric Johnson (physiotherapist). Front row: Asif Mujtaba, Wasim Akram, Intikhab Alam (cricket manager), Javed Miandad (captain), Khalid Mahmood (tour manager), Salim Malik (vice-captain), Ramiz Raja, Shoaib Mohammad.

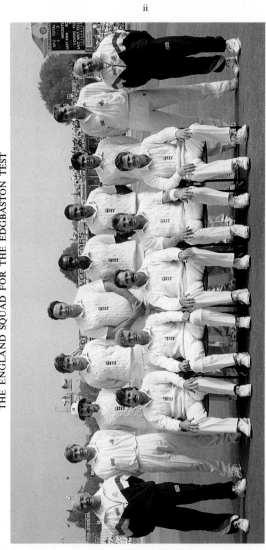

THE ENGLAND SQUAD FOR THE EDGBASTON TEST

[*Patrick Eagar*]

Back row: M. J. Stewart (*manager*), I. D. K. Salisbury, R. C. Russell, G. A. Hick, D. R. Pringle, C. C. Lewis, P. A. J. DeFreitas, M. R. Ramprakash, T. A. Munton, L. Brown (*physiotherapist*). *Front row*: A. J. Lamb, A. J. Stewart, G. A. Gooch (*captain*), I. T. Botham, R. A. Smith.

TRIUMPH IN MELBOURNE

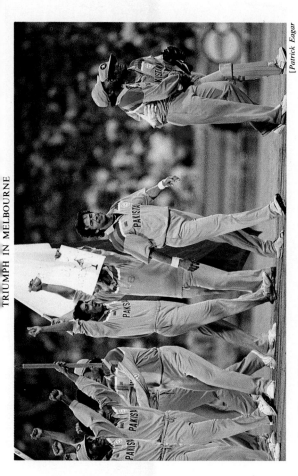

[*Patrick Eagar*

Imran Khan, the Pakistan captain, leads the celebrations after his team beat England in the World Cup final.

RECORD MOMENT

[*Patrick Eagar*

David Gower hits Aqib Javed for four at Old Trafford to overtake Geoff Boycott's total of 8,114 and become England's leading run-scorer in Test cricket. Two months later, to widespread astonishment and criticism, Gower was left out of the tour party for India.

[*David Munden*]

A scene from Zimbabwe's first-ever Test match, against India in October 1992, with the jacaranda trees in bloom at the Harare Sports Club.

CHAMPION AGAIN

Essex, county champions in 1992 for the sixth time in 14 years, still manage to savour the moment with the customary frivolities.

[*Graham Morris*

DRESSING UP FOR SUNDAYS

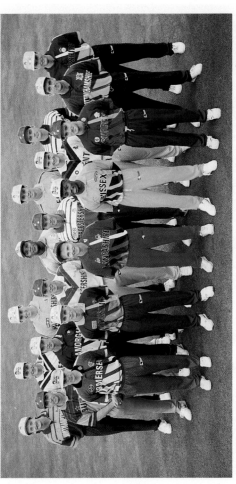

[*Graham Morris*]

Representatives of each first-class county pose at The Oval in the uniforms their teams will wear in the Sunday League in 1993. *Back row:* David Capel (Northamptonshire), John Emburey (Middlesex), Tim Munton (Warwickshire), Devon Malcolm (Derbyshire), Neil Foster (Essex), Tony Wright (Gloucestershire), Paul Terry (Hampshire). *Middle row:* Phil Bainbridge (Durham), Matthew Maynard (Glamorgan), James Whitaker (Leicestershire), Neal Radford (Worcestershire), Mark Ealham (Kent), Paul Pollard (Nottinghamshire), Mark Lathwell (Somerset), Richard Blakey (Yorkshire), Neil Fairbrother (Lancashire), Carlos Remy (Sussex), Graham Thorpe (Surrey).

FIVE CRICKETERS OF THE YEAR

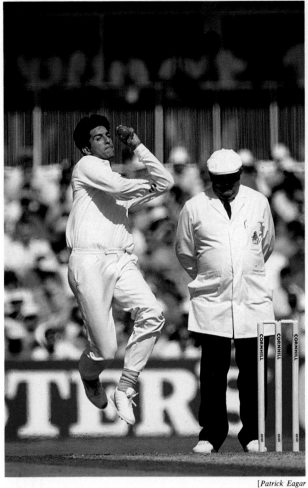

[*Patrick Eagar*

WASIM AKRAM

FIVE CRICKETERS OF THE YEAR

[*Patrick Eagar*

MARTYN MOXON

FIVE CRICKETERS OF THE YEAR

[*Jan Trayler*

IAN SALISBURY

FIVE CRICKETERS OF THE YEAR

[*Patrick Eagar*

ALEC STEWART

FIVE CRICKETERS OF THE YEAR

[*David Munde*

NIGEL BRIERS

FIVE CRICKETERS OF THE YEAR

NIGEL BRIERS

ven those bookmakers still wincing at the memory of the third-degree
nger burns sustained at Headingley '81 were willing to quote Leicester-
ire in telephone numbers at the start of last summer. In the manner of
sino owners when a high roller hits town, or a candidate on a wet election
ay, they would probably have sent a car round for anyone in Aylestone or
shby-de-la-Zouch who fancied a punt on their team in 1992. "Leicester-
ire for the Championship? Certainly, sir. What odds would you like?"

In the event, they would have kept their money, but not without the odd
ervous tic along the way. Leicestershire, widely fancied for the wooden
oon, mounted a serious challenge for the County Championship until
vaporated when Essex ran away with it in the closing weeks; and by
eating Essex in the semi-final of the NatWest Trophy at Grace Road, they
warded their supporters, who had been waiting for the opportunity to
ead south for a September Cup final at Lord's since the Gillette Cup
egan and the road to London was the sort on which people pulled the
Morris Oxford into a lay-by for a picnic.

Considering that there had been rather more activity at the player-exit
ate than the spectator-entrance turnstile in recent years, these were
npressive achievements. Since Leicestershire won the Benson and Hedges
up in 1985, the combination of steadily declining morale and a failure to
tract players from outside their own modest resources had made them one
f the softer touches on the circuit. The 1992 renaissance was, by general
onsent, a tribute to the determination of their 37-year-old captain to pull
is county out of an apparently endless rut by the application of old-
ashioned virtues such as hard work and team spirit.

Three years previously, NIGEL EDWIN BRIERS, born in Leicester
n January 15, 1955, had taken charge after David Gower left to join
ampshire, and the county's declining fortunes did not improve for the
ext two summers under the care of the Australian coach, Bobby Simpson.
riers then decided that enough was enough. He called the players together,
ointed out that the club had done nothing with so-called "star" names in
e dressing-room, and that here was the chance for everyone to start
ulling together. Anyone who did not could expect regular invitations to
rn out for the Second Eleven.

Briers insisted on punctuality and smartness, reasoning that a side that
cked discipline off the field was unlikely to have much on it, and he
imself became a much more positive captain out in the middle. Having
itially led the side in the absences of Gower and Peter Willey, he had
een understandably more concerned about not losing matches than
inning them, but after a hesitant first year as official captain, gradually
enerated more confidence both in himself and his team. Briers had been
armarked by Ray Illingworth as a potential leader in the mid-1970s, and
hen he finally took charge, he became the first home-grown captain of the
ub since Maurice Hallam was replaced by Illingworth in 1969.

He had been groomed for leadership both with Leicestershire Schools
d England Youth teams, and might have inherited the job earlier but for
o things. Leicestershire were such a strong side when Briers became a

regular member of the playing staff in 1975 that it was no easy tas
establishing himself as a fixture in the team. He also chose, after becomin
the club's youngest ever débutant in 1971 (aged 16 years, 103 days), t
spend the next four years establishing employment credentials in teachin
Educated at Lutterworth Grammar School and Borough Road College
Isleworth, he now teaches PE and history at Ludgrove School i
Wokingham.

By the end of 1983, Briers would have been an ideal choice as captain
However, Gower was chosen to succeed the sacked Roger Tolchard and fc
the next three years Briers suffered a series of personal setbacks. He los
both his form and his confidence in 1984 and 1985, and in 1986 his forearr
was so badly broken in a game at Hove that he was almost forced to retire
However, after further unsatisfactory periods under the captaincy of Wille
and, for a second time, Gower, Briers was chosen to take over in 1990, an
despite the distractions of a benefit season, responded with his best eve
season and scored 1,996 first-class runs.

In many ways, this was no surprise, as Briers thrives on hard work. A
cliché it may be, but he is the "model pro"; first into the nets, a stickler fc
practice, and almost irritatingly neat, tidy, and well-ordered with his ki
Furthermore, he has not missed a Leicestershire game since 1987, and ha
played some of his best cricket for the club since inheriting the captaincy i
his mid-30s. An elegant, predominantly front-foot batsman, Briers remain
a very fine fielder in the covers, but perhaps his greatest quality is h
undiminished enthusiasm for the game.

He is also a good communicator (although perhaps less so to his battir
partner when he is looking for a single to get off the mark) and togethe
with the new coach, Jack Birkenshaw, has restored harmony and stabili
to the side. Last summer, he also completed 1,000 runs for the sixt
summer running (ninth in all) and was rewarded with a new contract tha
will take him into his 41st year. "When you are losing all the time, it do
get to you," says Briers, "which is why last year was so rewarding. I don
know how long I can go on, but whenever I do finish, it is my dearest wis
to leave behind a damn good side." – Martin Johnson.

MARTYN MOXON

Some cricketers are born great, others achieve greatness and an unfortuna
few have greatness thrust upon them. Len Hutton obviously belongs in th
first category, Geoffrey Boycott in the second. Any heir to county cricke
burnish'd throne, the Yorkshire opener's spot, must bear the weight a
tradition that comes with the last curse.

Although he has come closer than a good many predecessors to realisi
a youthful potential which brought unwarranted comparisons with the ric
lineage of Yorkshire batsmanship, no one could say Martyn Moxon is
great player. However, the county's captaincy is an office great enough
snap the resolve of anyone ill-prepared for the club's frequent outbreaks
self-flagellation; in that respect he has done the state some service.

If he was not fully versed in the committee-room squabbles which mal
a Sicilian village resemble a model of harmony, he is now. The thr
seasons of his captaincy, unsuccessful in terms of winning trophies, ha
nevertheless steeled him for the years ahead and strengthened his positio

Without an obvious challenger in the dressing-room, he will preside over the short to medium-term future of the world's most celebrated competitive cricket club. Detractors have suggested it is a club with a glorious future behind it, but Yorkshire have learned to live with such jibes. Craig McDermott, had he been available as expected, might have made a big difference to their bowling last season. When the Cricket Academy at Bradford gets into a full, productive swing, the committee should have more encouraging matters to discuss.

Despite the arrival of Sachin Tendulkar, in McDermott's stead, the sans-culottes proved reluctant to storm Headingley's ramparts. Only a few Yorkshiremen, of the public variety, ripped up their membership cards in protest against the inclusion of an outsider, and flounced off to watch Durham. In common with many more significant amendments of law and common law, Yorkshire's repeal of their non-native policy met with general acquiescence. That self-erected barrier, and the financial crisis which threatened to engulf the club, provided the backdrop to the situation Moxon inherited. Stripped of their exclusive birthright, the modern Yorkshire side is much like Essex or Northamptonshire, only less successful. The longed-for revival has yet to take shape.

MARTYN DOUGLAS MOXON was born in Barnsley on May 4, 1960, two years before Boycott took his first steps as a Yorkshire cricketer. He joined the ranks in June 1981 as Boycott's locum, making 116 on his first-class début against Essex at Headingley (the first Yorkshire batsman for 60 years to do so). Batsmen often have difficulty finding their range and repertoire. This is particularly true of opening batsmen, who must always remember Picasso's maxim, "liberty within order". It took Glenn Turner the better part of his career to throw off the shackles and, although Moxon's flowering has been less obvious, he is certainly a freer player now than he was five years ago, even if he gets bowled too often, front leg buckled.

In 1992 he stood apart from his team-mates, as a serious captain should. The dropping of Ashley Metcalfe, his regular opening partner for five years, showed that reputations would no longer take precedence over the team's better interests. After missing four Championship matches with a broken finger, Moxon himself returned to make the business runs that betokened a batsman at the flood of his talent, and he ended the season with 1,385 at 53.26. He made them attractively, excelling in the drives through cover and mid-wicket, but when the call came for an opener to accompany Graham Gooch it went to Michael Atherton. In every era there are batsmen whose ability is more commonly recognised by their peers than by the selectors: in the 1970s it was Trevor Jesty of Hampshire. It must now be uncertain whether anyone, including Moxon himself, will ever know his true measure. In Yorkshire they have watched in stupor as others, less gifted and less constant, have got the nod: at almost 33 he is not ideally placed to resume a Test career that brought ten caps between 1986 and 1989.

Injuries may have played too prominent a part. In 1984 a cracked rib deprived him of an appearance against West Indies at Lord's, delaying his début for two years. In 1991-92 he was due to lead the England A team but broke a thumb in a beer match in Bermuda on the first day of the tour. Even when he seemed well set for a century at Auckland in 1987-88 he joined the 99 Club instead. Overlooked for the senior team the past two winters despite convincing claims on paper, he faces opposition from younger, more favoured players when Gooch retires from Test cricket. Two of the favoured share the same dressing-room. Moxon, to his great credit, greeted Richard Blakey's promotion to the England one-day side, and subsequently to the touring party for India, with kind words, while he had to make do with taking the A team to Australia. It must have been harder to accept the call-up for Paul Jarvis graciously, given the bowler's record of injuries, moods and rebellion. Moxon was eight when Yorkshire won their last Championship. Since then a generation has grown up more familiar with discord than the club's glorious pageant. Whether he likes it or not the honour invested in his job obliges him, as the club's figurehead, to remind the next generation of that tradition. – Michael Henderson.

IAN SALISBURY

If last summer's leading candidate for the time capsule was the elegant cover drive David Gower unfurled at Old Trafford to become the leading English Test match run-scorer, the most consistently evocative delight came courtesy of another south coast anachronism. In the course of taking 87 first-class wickets with his leg-breaks, moreover, Ian Salisbury of Sussex became the first specialist leg-spinner to play for England in 21 years. On that same Thursday morning in June, odd-looking birds with snouts and curly tails were reportedly sighted flying over St John's Wood.

The spinner, or so decrees one of cricket's Ten Contemporary Commandments, emergeth not from the chrysalis until he hath entered his fourth decade. Philip Tufnell first defied the law in 1990, and in 1992 there was blasphemy aplenty: no fewer than seven slow men from the shires aged between 22 and 28 took 50 first-class victims or more. High of arm, supple of wrist and boundless of spirit, IAN DAVID KENNETH SALISBURY was one of the youngest and the most productive.

He is a rarity in more senses than one, belonging to the exclusive quintet of Northamptonshire-born players who have represented England (after C. T. Studd, Arthur Mold, George Thompson and David Capel). Born in Northampton on January 21, 1970, the slim, flaxen-haired Salisbury attended Moulton Comprehensive, where cricket had no place on the curriculum, leaving him to learn the rudiments at his father's village club in Brixworth. He played soccer in midfield for the Northamptonshire School team but, urged on by John Malfait, a local man and a staff coach at Lord's, he also found himself picked for the County Second Eleven in 1987 as a batsman.

At the time he bowled a few leg-breaks as a sideline and he was encouraged to bowl more in the nets by Andy Roberts, another local boy who was already on the staff as a leg-spin specialist. But Roberts's presence meant that Northamptonshire had no special reason to encourage Salisbury or – when his batting failed to develop significantly – take him on as a full timer. Instead, he joined the MCC groundstaff. It was there, under the wing of Don Wilson, that his bowling improved enough to win him a contract with Sussex. They also had another leg-spinner, Andy Clarke. But Clarke was essentially a defensive bowler, and this time it was Salisbury who survived. At Hove Norman Gifford advised him how to adapt to different pitches; and when he spent the winter of 1989-90 playing club cricket in Zimbabwe, the sleepy surfaces of the Harare Sports Club made Salisbury learn the value of precise line and length and variety of attack.

Recognition was remarkably swift. He was picked for the England A team in the next two winters, improved steadily and in the West Indies in early 1992 was regularly dismissing front-line batsmen. Unafraid to entice the eager-footed forward, he doubled as stock and strike bowler from a gentle bobbing approach. Even so, his inclusion in the 13 for the first Test against Pakistan three months later was decried in certain quarters as a marketing gimmick rather than a statement of intent, all the more so when the selectors dropped him from the final eleven, after the opening day was washed out and they changed their stated plans. To their credit, they really did pick him for the next Test at Lord's and Salisbury flourished before an enchanted Saturday gallery. When Javed Miandad, arguably the world's finest player of spin, groped at a perfectly pitched leg-break, the ball looped up to kiss the shoulder of the bat and Ian Botham brought off a spectacular slip catch. It was not so much a feather in a new cap, exulted Scyld Berry in the *Independent on Sunday*, as "a head-dress to grace Hiawatha". It was the first time a specialist wrist-spinner had taken a wicket for England since Robin Hobbs held Rohan Kanhai's return drive at Port-of-Spain in January 1968.

After bemusing Wasim Akram with a googly, then a sparingly deployed part of his armoury, the débutant despatched Salim Malik, Aamir Sohail and Moin Khan on the Sunday to spur a depleted attack to within two wickets of an improbable victory. The reunion with terra firma was immediate, Miandad himself taking the long handle to this uppity young pup at Manchester. Salisbury now harked back to his cricketing roots, and his resilient half-century dispelled the threat of the follow-on.

He is blessed with the requisite mix of optimism and realism demanded of one who plies such a precarious trade, and it would have been out of character had he felt bitter at his initial exclusion from the senior party to India; he was added to the squad after being sent out only as a net bowler. Sussex's last two Championship engagements nevertheless produced the aggressive riposte of a man spurned: six for 29 and five for 54 against Lancashire, then seven for 54 (a career-best) and five for 84 against Yorkshire. Opponents were frequently flummoxed by a faster ball. He also felt confident enough to bowl the googly more often. He finished with more wickets than anyone except Courtney Walsh.

Deservedly named Young Cricketer of the Year by the Cricket Writers' Club, Salisbury, together with his Pakistani counterpart Mushtaq Ahmed, had instigated a romantic revival. If the ailing Bill O'Reilly was reading the scoreboards in the *Sydney Morning Herald* in the weeks before he died, he would have been content in the knowledge that, against the odds, his art lived on. – Rob Steen.

ALEC STEWART

It was at Lord's, midway through the morning session of the fourth one-day international last summer, that it was spotted. Alec Stewart, England captain for the day, opening batsman some days, floating middle-order batsman other days, infielder, outfielder, shake-it-all-aboutfielder and wicket-keeper, was standing behind the bowler's stumps, quietly buffing the ball on his flannels as, with a wave here and a flourish there, he set the field. "Omigod," said someone, "I think he's going to bowl."

He didn't, of course, but it is testament to the image that he has created that the possibility even fleetingly crossed the mind. Through sheer honest endeavour, schoolboyish "me sir, please sir" enthusiasm and a willingness to fit into any role in any circumstance, Stewart first of all made his versatility a reason to select him over others. Then, having got into the England side, he made himself indispensable. Brisk and polished, he became the very model of a modern professional. One day, perhaps, an Italian club will buy him for five million quid.

The rise of ALEC JAMES STEWART – born in Merton on April 8, 1963 – to the position of England vice-captain, acting-captain and genuine Test-class batsman has surprised many. It is not that the pedigree was absent: the fact that Micky Stewart, the recently retired England manager and former Test player and Surrey captain, is his father is unknown only to recent returnees from the planet Jupiter. That in addition his mother, Sheila, was a top netball and hockey player is less well-documented. It was a family environment conducive to the production of a young sportsman.

His cricket progress was through the ranks: Tiffin School, junior Surrey sides, Surrey second team during his final school year, and finally, when he left school at 18, actually on to the Surrey staff – Micky was manager – where he has been since 1981. Simultaneously, he began an association with Australian grade cricket, playing season after season with the Midland-Guildford club in Perth. If his batting skills were learned at The Oval, it was the Aussie school of hard knocks that instilled in him a mental toughness, a desire to give as good as he got, to mix it verbally. So when, on his first tour, and playing only his second Test, he crossed swords with Desmond Haynes at Trinidad, Haynes by no means got the better of him. And if sometimes – as in the 'ere-we-go atmosphere of the World Cup – his behaviour panders uncomfortably to the yob element in the crowd, then at least he has spark.

No one can say that success has come easily. He has always appeared to be a well-organised, busy, bat-twirling player, perky as a parrot, capable of making entertaining runs, but lacking, apparently, the commitment to register the big scores that get noticed: the first ten years of his career had brought him just 16 first-class centuries. Had he not developed his wicket-keeping he might even now not have received the chance in international cricket.

Yet even having made the squad it was not easy to establish himself. Time after time, he played fluently and well, getting set at the crease, only to waft once too often and depart, muttering to the sky, aware that no capitalising on good form is a criminal offence in cricket, for the bad times are only just around the corner. It was, then, to his credit that he worked so hard to eliminate from his game his vulnerability to the slip cordon, and became greedy for greater things. Dropped after the disastrous tour of Australia in 1990-91, he was recalled, much to his surprise, to keep wicket in the final Test against West Indies that summer. It was an opportunity he could not afford to miss; and he took it. England won memorably. Two weeks later he scored his first Test century, against Sri Lanka, and in the 17 Test innings after his return he scored 952 runs at an average of 68.00. There is an air of authority about his cricket.

Now he is also free of the shackle – real or perceived, media figment or not – of being the son of the England manager. It is a relationship that has always created debate. Nepotism, some have cried, has smoothed his progress. Nonsense, say others, if any one has been held back it has been Alec because of Micky's need to be seen to be scrupulously fair to others. Father and son, for their part, have always gone out of their way to eliminate the whole issue, with Micky insisting that, in cricketing terms, he has not had a son, and referring to Alec simply as "Stewie", while Alec has attempted to divorce himself from it by calling his father "manager" even at home. At times it was too much, synthetic almost.

Micky was there in Jamaica when Alec walked out to bat for the first time as an England player, and when he scored his first century. He was there when Alec, under considerable pressure to succeed, held the catches behind the wicket that helped beat the West Indies at The Oval. But never once was there a public acknowledgment of father's pride in his son. Are they really such a dispassionate family? Of course not. "He's been absolutely delighted for me," said Alec, "and he's told me so. But he was never going to show it publicly, was he? I think he always felt it could be misinterpreted, and that was the last thing he wanted. He's done nothing but treat me fairly." So now we know. Besides which it is no longer an issue. Alec Stewart has long since been his own man. – Mike Selvey.

WASIM AKRAM

Whatever the controversy surrounding their methods – and this is detailed elsewhere in *Wisden* – there is no question that in 1992 Wasim Akram and Waqar Younis were the most successful cricketers in the world. Opening the bowling for Pakistan, they had a variety and aggression that made them as potent a pair as the game has seen.

In the Test series in England, Wasim took 21 wickets in four Tests. In the other tour matches he was even more devastating and finished with 82 first-class wickets in all at 16.21 each. He had already made his name as a batsman of sometimes astonishing power. In January 1993 he was suddenly appointed to succeed Javed Miandad as Pakistan's captain, with Waqar as his deputy. Few cricketers were so obviously destined for the game's aristocracy, but his elevation came even sooner than his admirers had expected. As captain he will be recognised more clearly and more widely as head of state than whichever general or politician holds the nominal office in Islamabad.

None of this was obvious in his boyhood. WASIM AKRAM was born in Lahore on June 3, 1966, to a moderately affluent middle-class family, in which his father was mostly concerned with his son's happiness rather than his success. His mother was the more ambitious for him, but her thoughts hardly embraced professional sport. They sent him to the fee-paying Cathedral School in Lahore, where all the lessons, other than Urdu, were conducted in English. In the tradition of the English public school, the Cathedral's scholars were expected to play games. Wasim, dreaming of the feats of Zaheer Abbas, Asif Iqbal and Mushtaq Mohammad, needed no urging to play cricket.

At 12 he was opening the bowling and batting for the school team. At 15 he was captain, his whole life consumed by cricket, at school, in nets at home, in the garage with his brother, and in street games played with a tennis ball. These matches were played of an evening in the lanes of old Lahore. As many as ten or more teams would compete in a tournament, each side contributing an entry fee, the eventual winners scooping the pool. It was fast, intensely competitive, as much a test of eyesight, reactions and stamina as ability. Wasim was so outstanding that local clubs took notice. When he took four wickets for Ludhiana against Lahore Gymkhana, including those of Ramiz Raja and Intikhab, he won nomination to the talent camp, a summer examination of Lahore's best 100 young players, promoted by the Pakistan Board.

He was then 18 and his big in-swing and formidable hitting attracted attention. In his class were Ramiz Raja, Mohsin Kamal and Ijaz Ahmed, and he won further nomination to the Pakistan Under-19 camp in Karachi. There the sight of this tall, lively left-armer offering so much promise delighted Pakistan's former fast bowler, Khan Mohammad, who soon taught him to lift his arm in the delivery stride, adding pace.

By sheer chance Javed Miandad, seeking practice, took a turn in the Under-19 net. He was so impressed by the youngster's ability to move the ball at speed, while retaining control, that he insisted Wasim be included in a squad of 14 for a three-day Patron's XI match against the New Zealanders at Rawalpindi. Wasim, again at Miandad's insistence, displaced the better-known Tahir Naqqash in the final selection and fewer first-class débuts have been more impressive: seven for 50 in the first innings, two more wickets in the second. His scalps included John Wright, Bruce Edgar and John Reid. In such circumstances a Pakistani newspaper's description of Wasim as "a sensation" was restrained.

He then made his international début in a one-day match against New Zealand at Faisalabad and, only two months after his entry at Rawalpindi, he was chosen to tour New Zealand. According to Miandad, he did not even realise the Pakistan Board would pay him. In his second Test, at Dunedin, he took ten for 128. It was early 1985 and he was 18 years old.

His reputation soon reached England and Lancashire began tracking him almost immediately. Advised by Imran Khan to seek experience of English conditions before Pakistan's 1987 tour, he spent a summer with Burnopfield in the Durham League, where he remembers a tiny, freezing flat, wet grounds, and playing on in the rain. Wasim signed an unparalleled six-year contract for Lancashire, in secret, on the first night of the 1987 tour. His burst on English cricket the following summer with a maiden first-class century in his second Championship match, against Somerset, and a performance of Sobers-like proportions against Surrey at Southport. There he took five for 15 including a hat-trick, made a half-century in the first innings and then, with Lancashire struggling, scored 98 off 78 balls. The scores were level when he was last man out, caught on the boundary.

In conversation later that summer he emphasised the point made by so many overseas professionals: "You try to play too much first-class cricket. You sacrifice quality for quantity." Wasim expressed himself much more happily in the one-day competitions where he became, probably, the most feared opponent, able to turn a one-day game, with bat or ball, in two or three overs. Championship cricket, on Old Trafford's improving square, he found to be frustrating, culminating in an outburst in 1991 that led to a umpires' report and a £1,000 fine by the county club. For weeks there were rumours, as Wasim struggled with a recurring groin strain, that he would not return. The situation was resolved by a new contract that may have made Wasim the world's best-paid cricketer until, that is, Surrey came to settle with Waqar.

Meanwhile, his reputation as a Test cricketer was growing all the time. At Adelaide in 1989-90, he had a partnership with Imran Khan that saved Pakistan from what looked like imminent defeat and took them to the edge of victory. Wasim's driving to the long, straight boundary of the Adelaide Oval was as powerful as anything ever seen on the ground. Imran was the junior partner. For some time Imran had been saying that Wasim was the world's greatest all-rounder. Here was the evidence.

After 1992, it is possible to say more than that. He stands at the moment as perhaps the fastest and most destructive left-arm bowler the world has seen. – Derek Hodgson.

FIVE CRICKETERS – PAST CHOICES

The following players who played first-class cricket in Britain in 1992 were ineligible for consideration for Five Cricketers of the Year because they had been chosen before. The years refer to the date of the *Wisden* rather than the season. A full list of Cricketers of the Year from 1889 to 1988 can be found in the 1989 *Wisden*.

C. E. L. Ambrose (1992); M. A. Atherton (1991); P. Bainbridge (1986); K. J. Barnett (1989); I. T. Botham (1978); A. R. Butcher (1991); J. H. Childs (1987); P. A. J. DeFreitas (1992); A. A. Donald (1992); R. M. Ellison (1986); J. E. Emburey (1984); N. A. Foster (1988); M. W. Gatting (1984); G. A. Gooch (1980); D. I. Gower (1979); C. G. Greenidge (1977); D. L. Haynes (1991); G. A. Hick (1987); Javed Miandad (1982); D. M. Jones (1990); Kapil Dev (1983); A. J. Lamb (1981); M. D. Marshall (1983); P. A. Neale (1989); N. V. Radford (1986); D. W. Randall (1980); I. V. A. Richards (1977); R. B. Richardson (1992); R. T. Robinson (1986); R. C. Russell (1980); Salim Malik (1988); R. A. Smith (1990); F. D. Stephenson (1989); C. A. Walsh (1987); Waqar Younis (1992); M. E. Waugh (1991); J. J. Whitaker (1987).

A CANNY FIRST SEASON

By SIMON HUGHES

Durham began their first season as a first-class county with a bang and ended it with a whimper. In between, the experience was rather like a novice's round of golf – some booming early drives and the odd good hole but plenty of double bogeys. By September, injuries to key batsmen and a lack of really incisive bowlers relegated the team to bottom place in the Championship, and there they finished. There was plenty to be proud of, though.

We are supposed to live in John Major's classless society, so he would have been pleased that for much of the season a team managed by a Cook also contained a Jones, a Smith and a Brown. Durham was a magnet for players from all corners of the country, many disillusioned with their previous counties after years trudging the same path. At first, the public school accents of some recruits jarred uneasily against the Potteries jargon and north-eastern lingo of others, but the humour and goodwill of everyone proved the catalyst. What the team lacked in pace bowling and depth, it adequately made up for with determination and charisma. It could not, however, replace Dean Jones's expertise and panache once he departed for Australia in late July.

Well as men like Larkins, Parker and Bainbridge played, they were unable to mask the overall inexperience of the team and, as injuries took their toll, the youthful Durham aspirants were cruelly exposed. Geoff Cook himself observes in his book, *The Narrow Line*: "Nothing in cricket ever begins to compare with the intense psychological rupture involved in moving from a county second eleven to the first eleven." The gulf in standards is far wider than anything they have had to cross in the past, or will in the future; even the climb to Test cricket is less precipitous. This meant that new names like Mark Briers and Stewart Hutton were suddenly thrust into the front line and, after promising beginnings, found the sheer intensity of full-time professionalism too onerous, and the spindly body of the left-arm seamer Simon Brown eventually buckled under the strain of endless days in the field. John Wood and Paul Henderson would not yet have played any first-team cricket in more established squads. All are well ahead of schedule in their own careers, as is the 18-year-old Jimmy Daley who recorded two accomplished eighties in the last week of the season.

The remarkable thing about Durham cricket is the indomitable support. It is a common misconception that the area is typified by reclaimed slag heaps upon which people live in poky houses and eat pease pudding for tea. In fact, the county is characterised by stupendous views and a loyal, optimistic population. They soon idolised favourite members of the team and revelled in the new identity. Importantly, the team won its first competitive game – a nailbiting Sunday encounter against Lancashire – giving it immediate credibility. There were two Championship victories to follow – one by an innings – and a mid-table position in the Sunday League. Losing to Leicestershire in the quarter-finals of the NatWest was easily the low point of the season.

The problems of setting up a new county are manifold. How would the various club wickets stand up to four-day cricket? What size might the crowds be? How many toilets would need to be installed? Many of the logistics had to be judged on a trial and error basis, and one or two home matches were lost through unfamiliarity with the pitch. Volunteers were lured to help erect marquees or drag hoardings about, and there was a touching family atmosphere about the whole venture. This effectively eliminated any barriers there might have been between players and supporters, adding to the refreshing informality of the grounds themselves. Teams and administrators mingled happily together at lunchtimes, and everywhere there were special welcomes and receptions.

The extent of regional interest in the new adventure was emphasised by eight-page pull-outs in local newspapers, grounds crawling with TV crews and a membership closed at 6,500 in early July. The county has a vast hinterland, stretching from Middlesbrough to Sunderland and from the industrial Teesside coast right across the Pennines. The players' problem was never going to be attracting spectators to the grounds but finding their own way to them. Within a complex network of wide roads various individuals became lost *en route* to one of the less familiar clubs like Jesmond, Hartlepool or Gateshead Fell.

Behind the scenes, Durham were quick to avoid the cumbersome infra-structure that has so stifled the advance of the county game. Instead of delegating responsibility to a catalogue of committees, Durham established a limited company controlled by a board of directors. Thankfully, the board did not meddle with team selection, which was exclusively the domain of Cook and David Graveney. Floodlit matches were organised, and leading players like Botham and Jones placed at the disposal of clubs and businesses. And when the new stadium at Chester-le-Street is completed in 1995, Durham will be endowed with the best facilities in the land.

For the participants, the County Championship had become a treadmill, as teams of weary players lurched from one venue to the next along well-worn tracks. Playing for Durham was more like an expedition, taking unfamiliar routes, touring new areas of cricketing enthusiasm. Everywhere there were fresh and not always pleasant discoveries – the biting wind off the moors at Gateshead Fell, the thieves at the Racecourse, Chester-le-Street's shirtfront wicket, the perilous scorers' crow's nest in Stockton's pavilion. At Hartlepool the backdrop of industrial effluent and petro-chemical plants contrasted drastically with the leafy ambience of the ground.

There were players' habits and methods to evaluate too. Paul Parker liked a rigorous pre-match net, while Wayne Larkins preferred to disappear into a corner of the dressing-room in a cloud of nicotine; this seemed to happen less when the match was not sponsored by Benson and Hedges. Some batsmen paced about anxiously if they were due in next, others had to be disturbed from a post-lunch snooze. The wicket-keeper Andy Fothergill had no idea how far back to stand when Botham was bowling. As a convenient departure from the norm, no unnecessary demands were made on the playing staff – they were required to report only an hour before the start rather than be forced to idle away hours completing crosswords, as most sides do.

This particularly appeased Botham – not what you could call an early morning sort of person – and, until injuries materialised, his name on the team sheet provided the ideal launching pad. Not only was his reputation still intact on the field but his mere presence lured an extra throng through the turnstiles. So, even at the end of the season when the team had not won a match for a month, home Sunday games were sold out, and there were ample crowds even on a wet Thursday in Darlington.

The first Championship win, at Cardiff, and the elimination of Middlesex from the NatWest represented the highlights of the season. Both were wholehearted team efforts and decisive victories. Glamorgan were beaten by an innings as first Larkins and Jones then Parker battered the bowling into submission on an unreliable wicket, which was then wickedly exploited by Brown with the new ball. Larkins's innings were regularly entertaining but always fraught with danger; Parker was less exciting but slightly more reliable. This was illustrated in the Middlesex match when, pursuing 260 against a less than fearsome attack, Larkins mishooked in the first over and was out for a duck – it was left to Parker and a restrained Botham to engineer victory. That such a fine performance should have been squandered by inept batting in the next round at Leicester was a travesty. On that occasion, Graveney, the captain, looked as downcast as a man can be, while Cook, though dejected, pondered the future of the team, thinking of his five-year-plan like Mao-Tse-Tung.

The long journeys to away matches and the lack of success took their toll on the players, but the extraordinary enthusiasm of the Durham faithful maintained the spirit level. To the sports fanatics of the north-east mere participation in the County Championship is a revelation, and though the end results were disappointing, they were not disheartened. At the conclusion of the last match, many came on to the field to shake each player personally by the hand. "Eet's been a canny first season," they said, "and we canner wait for the next." With the area's record of producing pedigree players, an astute management and the foundations laid in Chester-le-Street for England's first purpose-built Test match arena, there should be plenty more for them to shout about in future. Rome wasn't built in a day, either.

Simon Hughes played for Middlesex from 1980 to 1991 before signing for Durham, where he went to university. He writes a regular summertime column for The Independent.

PART TWO: RECORD SECTION

TEST CRICKETERS

FULL LIST FROM 1877 TO AUGUST 9, 1992

These lists have been compiled on a home and abroad basis, appearances abroad being printed in *italics*.

Abbreviations. E: England. A: Australia. SA: South Africa. WI: West Indies. NZ: New Zealand. In: India. P: Pakistan. SL: Sri Lanka.

All appearances are placed in this order of seniority. Hence, any England cricketer playing against Australia in England has that achievement recorded first and the remainder of his appearances at home (if any) set down before passing to matches abroad. Although the distinction between amateur and professional was abolished in 1963, initials of English professionals before that date are still given in (brackets). The figures immediately following each name represent the total number of appearances in *all* Tests.

Where the season embraces two different years, the first year is given; i.e. 1876 indicates 1876-77.

ENGLAND

Number of Test cricketers: 556

Abel (R.) 13: v A 1888 (3) 1896 (3) 1902 (2); *v A 1891 (3); v SA 1888 (2)*
Absolom, C. A. 1: *v A 1878*
Agnew, J. P. 3: v A 1985 (1); v WI 1984 (1); v SL 1984 (1)
Allen (D. A.) 39: v A 1961 (4) 1964 (1); v SA 1960 (2); v WI 1963 (2) 1966 (1); v P 1962 (4); *v A 1962 (1) 1965 (4); v SA 1964 (4); v WI 1959 (5); v NZ 1965 (3); v In 1961 (5); v P 1961 (3)*
Allen, G. O. B. 25: v A 1930 (1) 1934 (2); v WI 1933 (1); v NZ 1931 (3); v In 1936 (3); *v A 1932 (5) 1936 (5); v WI 1947 (3); v NZ 1932 (2)*
Allom, M. J. C. 5: *v SA 1930 (1); v NZ 1929 (4)*
Allott, P. J. W. 13: v A 1981 (1) 1985 (4); v WI 1984 (1); v In 1982 (2); v SL 1984 (1); *v In 1981 (1); v SL 1981 (1)*
Ames (L. E. G.) 47: v A 1934 (5) 1938 (2); v SA 1929 (1) 1935 (4); v WI 1933 (3); v NZ 1931 (3) 1937 (3); v In 1932 (1); *v A 1932 (5) 1936 (5); v SA 1938 (5); v WI 1929 (4) 1934 (4); v NZ 1932 (2)*
Amiss, D. L. 50: v A 1968 (1) 1975 (2) 1977 (2); v WI 1966 (1) 1973 (3) 1976 (1); v NZ 1973 (3); v In 1967 (2) 1971 (1) 1974 (3); v P 1967 (1) 1971 (3) 1974 (3); *v A 1974 (5) 1976 (1); v WI 1973 (5) v NZ 1974 (2); v In 1972 (3) 1976 (5); v P 1972 (3)*
Andrew (K. V.) 2: v WI 1963 (1); *v A 1954 (1)*
Appleyard (R.) 9: v A 1956 (1); v SA 1955 (1); v P 1954 (1); *v A 1954 (4); v NZ 1954 (2)*
Archer, A. G. 1: *v SA 1898*
Armitage (T.) 2: *v A 1876 (2)*
Arnold (E. G.) 10: v A 1905 (4); v SA 1907 (2); *v A 1903 (4)*
Arnold, G. G. 34: v A 1972 (3) 1975 (1); v WI 1973 (3); v NZ 1969 (1) 1973 (3); v In 1974 (2); v P 1967 (2) 1974 (3); *v A 1974 (4); v WI 1973 (3); v NZ 1974 (2); v In 1972 (4); v P 1972 (3)*
Arnold (J.) 1: v NZ 1931
Astill (W. E.) 9: *v SA 1927 (5); v WI 1929 (4)*
Atherton, M. A. 21: v A 1989 (2); v WI 1991 (5); v NZ 1990 (3); v In 1990 (3); v P 1992 (3); *v A 1990 (7)*
Athey, C. W. J. 23: v A 1980 (1); v WI 1988 (1); v NZ 1986 (2); v In 1986 (2); v P 1987 (4); *v A 1986 (5) 1987 (1); v WI 1980 (2); v NZ 1987 (1); v P 1987 (3)*
Attewell (W.) 10: v A 1890 (1); *v A 1884 (5) 1887 (1) 1891 (3)*

Bailey, R. J. 4: v WI 1988 (1); *v WI 1989 (3)*
Bailey, T. E. 61: v A 1953 (5) 1956 (4); v SA 1951 (2) 1955 (5); v WI 1950 (2) 1957 (4); v NZ 1949 (4) 1958 (4); v P 1954 (3); *v A 1950 (4) 1954 (5) 1958 (5); v SA 1956 (5); v WI 1953 (5); v NZ 1950 (2) 1954 (2)*

Bairstow, D. L. 4: v A 1980 (1); v WI 1980 (1); v In 1979 (1); *v WI 1980 (1)*

Bakewell (A. H.) 6: v SA 1935 (2); v WI 1933 (1); v NZ 1931 (2); *v In 1933 (1)*

Balderstone J. C. 2: v WI 1976 (2)

Barber, R. W. 28: v A 1964 (1) 1968 (1); v SA 1960 (1) 1965 (3); v WI 1966 (2); v NZ 1965 (3); *v A 1965 (5); v SA 1964 (4); v In 1961 (5); v P 1961 (3)*

Barber (W.) 2: v SA 1935 (2)

Barlow, G. D. 3: v A 1977 (1); *v In 1976 (2)*

Barlow (R. G.) 17: v A 1882 (1) 1884 (3) 1886 (3); *v A 1881 (4) 1882 (4) 1886 (2)*

Barnes (S. F.) 27: v A 1902 (1) 1909 (3) 1912 (3); v SA 1912 (3); *v A 1901 (3) 1907 (5) 1911 (5); v SA 1913 (4)*

Barnes (W.) 21: v A 1880 (1) 1882 (1) 1884 (2) 1886 (2) 1888 (3) 1890 (2); *v A 1882 (4) 1884 (5) 1886 (1)*

Barnett (C. J.) 20: v A 1938 (3) 1948 (1); v SA 1947 (3); v WI 1933 (1); v NZ 1937 (3); v In 1936 (1); *v A 1936 (5); v In 1933 (3)*

Barnett, K. J. 4: v A 1989 (3); v SL 1988 (1)

Barratt (F.) 5: v SA 1929 (1); *v NZ 1929 (4)*

Barrington (K. F.) 82: v A 1961 (5) 1964 (5) 1968 (5); v SA 1955 (2) 1960 (4) 1965 (3); v WI 1963 (5) 1966 (2); v NZ 1965 (2); v In 1959 (5) 1967 (3); v P 1962 (4) 1967 (3); *v A 1962 (5) 1965 (5); v SA 1964 (5); v WI 1959 (5) 1967 (5); v NZ 1962 (3); v In 1961 (5) 1963 (1); v P 1961 (2)*

Barton (V. A.) 1: *v SA 1891*

Bates (W.) 15: *v A 1881 (4) 1882 (4) 1884 (5) 1886 (2)*

Bean (G.) 3: *v A 1891 (3)*

Bedser (A. V.) 51: v A 1948 (5) 1953 (5); v SA 1947 (2) 1951 (2) 1955 (1); v WI 1950 (3); v NZ 1949 (2); v In 1946 (3) 1952 (4); v P 1954 (2); *v A 1946 (5) 1950 (5) 1954 (1); v SA 1948 (5); v NZ 1946 (1) 1950 (2)*

Benson, M. R. 1: v In 1986

Berry (R.) 2: v WI 1950 (2)

Binks, J. G. 2: *v In 1963 (2)*

Bird M. C. 10: *v SA 1909 (5) 1913 (5)*

Birkenshaw J. 5: *v WI 1973 (2); v In 1972 (2); v P 1972 (1)*

Bligh, Hon. I. F. W. 4: *v A 1882 (4)*

Blythe (C.) 19: v A 1905 (1) 1909 (2); v SA 1907 (3); *v A 1901 (5) 1907 (1); v SA 1905 (5) 1909 (2)*

Board (J. H.) 6: *v SA 1898 (2) 1905 (4)*

Bolus, J. B. 7: v WI 1963 (2); *v In 1963 (5)*

Booth (M. W.) 2: *v SA 1913 (2)*

Bosanquet, B. J. T. 7: v A 1905 (3); *v A 1903 (4)*

Botham, I. T. 102: v A 1977 (2) 1980 (1) 1981 (6) 1985 (6) 1989 (3); v WI 1980 (5) 1984 (5) 1991 (1); v NZ 1978 (3) 1983 (4) 1986 (1); v In 1979 (4) 1982 (3); v P 1978 (3) 1982 (3) 1987 (5) 1992 (2); v SL 1984 (1) 1991 (1); *v A 1978 (6) 1979 (3) 1982 (5) 1986 (4); v WI 1980 (4) 1985 (5); v NZ 1977 (3) 1983 (3) 1991 (1); v In 1979 (1) 1981 (6); v P 1983 (1); v SL 1981 (1)*

Bowden, M. P. 2: *v SA 1888 (2)*

Bowes (W. E.) 15: v A 1934 (3) 1938 (2); v SA 1935 (4); v WI 1939 (2); v In 1932 (1) 1946 (1); *v A 1932 (1); v NZ 1932 (1)*

Bowley (E. H.) 5: v SA 1929 (2); *v NZ 1929 (3)*

Boycott, G. 108: v A 1964 (4) 1968 (3) 1972 (2) 1977 (2) 1980 (1) 1981 (6); v SA 1965 (2); v WI 1966 (4) 1969 (3) 1973 (3) 1980 (5); v NZ 1965 (2) 1969 (3) 1973 (3) 1978 (2); v In 1967 (2) 1971 (1) 1974 (1) 1979 (4); v P 1967 (1) 1971 (2); *v A 1965 (5) 1970 (5) 1978 (6) 1979 (3); v SA 1964 (5); v WI 1967 (5) 1973 (5) 1980 (4); v NZ 1965 (2) 1977 (3); v In 1979 (1) 1981 (4); v P 1977 (3)*

Bradley, W. M. 2: v A 1899 (2)

Braund (L. C.) 23: v A 1902 (5); v SA 1907 (3); *v A 1901 (5) 1903 (5) 1907 (5)*

Brearley, J. M. 39: v A 1977 (5) 1981 (4); v WI 1976 (2); v NZ 1978 (3); v In 1979 (4); v P 1978 (3); *v A 1976 (1) 1978 (6) 1979 (3); v In 1976 (5) 1979 (1); v P 1977 (2)*

Brearley, W. 4: v A 1905 (2) 1909 (1); v SA 1912 (1)

Brennan, D. V. 2: v SA 1951 (2)

Briggs (John) 33: v A 1886 (3) 1888 (3) 1893 (2) 1896 (1) 1899 (1); *v A 1884 (5) 1886 (2) 1887 (1) 1891 (3) 1894 (5) 1897 (5); v SA 1888 (2)*

Broad, B. C. 25: v A 1989 (2); v WI 1984 (2) 1988 (2); v P 1987 (4); v SL 1984 (1); *v A 1986 (5) 1987 (1); v NZ 1987 (3); v P 1987 (3)*

Brockwell (W.) 7: v A 1893 (1) 1899 (1); *v A 1894 (5)*

Bromley-Davenport, H. R. 4: *v SA 1895 (3) 1898 (1)*

Brookes (D.) 1: *v WI 1947*

Brown (A.) 2: *v In 1961 (1); v P 1961 (1)*

Brown, D. J. 26: v A 1968 (4); v SA 1965 (2); v WI 1966 (1) 1969 (3); v NZ 1969 (1); v In 1967 (2): *v A 1965 (4); v WI 1967 (4); v NZ 1965 (2); v P 1968 (3)*

Brown, F. R. 22: v A 1953 (1); v SA 1951 (5); v WI 1950 (1); v NZ 1931 (2) 1937 (1) 1949 (2); v In 1932 (1); *v A 1950 (5); v NZ 1932 (2) 1950 (2)*

Brown (G.) 7: v A 1921 (3); *v SA 1922 (4)*

Brown (J. T.) 8: v A 1896 (2) 1899 (1); *v A 1894 (5)*

Buckenham (C. P.) 4: *v SA 1909 (4)*

Butcher, A. R. 1: v In 1979

Butcher, R. O. 3: *v WI 1980 (3)*

Butler (H. J.) 2: v SA 1947 (1); *v WI 1947 (1)*

Butt (H. R.) 3: *v SA 1895 (3)*

Calthorpe, Hon. F. S. G. 4: *v WI 1929 (4)*

Capel, D. J. 15: v A 1989 (1); v WI 1988 (2); v P 1987 (1); *v A 1987 (1); v WI 1989 (4); v NZ 1987 (3); v P 1987 (3)*

Carr, A. W. 11: v A 1926 (4); v SA 1929 (2); *v SA 1922 (5)*

Carr, D. B. 2: *v In 1951 (2)*

Carr, D. W. 1: v A 1909

Cartwright, T. W. 5: v A 1964 (2); v SA 1965 (1); v NZ 1965 (1); *v SA 1964 (1)*

Chapman, A. P. F. 26: v A 1926 (4) 1930 (4); v SA 1924 (2); v WI 1928 (3); *v A 1924 (4) 1928 (4); v SA 1930 (5)*

Charlwood (H. R. J.) 2: *v A 1876 (2)*

Chatterton (W.) 1: *v SA 1891*

Childs, J. H. 2: v WI 1988 (2)

Christopherson, S. 1: v A 1884

Clark (E. W.) 8: v A 1934 (2); v SA 1929 (1); v WI 1933 (2); *v In 1933 (3)*

Clay, J. C. 1: v SA 1935

Close (D. B.) 22: v A 1961 (1); v SA 1955 (1); v WI 1957 (2) 1963 (5) 1966 (1) 1976 (3); v NZ 1949 (1); v In 1959 (1) 1967 (3); *v A 1950 (1)*

Coldwell (L. J.) 7: v A 1964 (2); v P 1962 (2); *v A 1962 (2); v NZ 1962 (1)*

Compton (D. C. S.) 78: v A 1938 (4) 1948 (5) 1953 (5) 1956 (1); v SA 1947 (5) 1951 (4) 1955 (5); v WI 1939 (3) 1950 (1); v NZ 1937 (1) 1949 (4); v In 1946 (3) 1952 (2); v P 1954 (4); *v A 1946 (5) 1950 (4) 1954 (4); v SA 1948 (5) 1956 (5); v WI 1953 (5); v NZ 1946 (1) 1950 (2)*

Cook (C.) 1: v SA 1947

Cook, G. 7: v In 1982 (3); *v A 1982 (3); v SL 1981 (1)*

Cook, N. G. B. 15: v A 1989 (3); v WI 1984 (3); v NZ 1983 (2); *v NZ 1983 (1); v P 1983 (3) 1987 (3)*

Cope, G. A. 3: *v P 1977 (3)*

Copson (W. H.) 3: v SA 1947 (1); v WI 1939 (2)

Cornford (W. L.) 4: *v NZ 1929 (4)*

Cottam, R. M. H. 4: *v In 1972 (2); v P 1968 (2)*

Coventry, Hon. C. J. 2: *v SA 1888 (2)*

Cowans, N. G. 19: v A 1985 (1); v WI 1984 (1); v NZ 1983 (2); *v A 1982 (4); v NZ 1983 (2); v In 1984 (5); v P 1983 (2)*

Cowdrey, C. S. 6: v WI 1988 (1); *v In 1984 (5)*

Cowdrey, M. C. 114: v A 1956 (5) 1961 (4) 1964 (3) 1968 (4); v SA 1955 (1) 1960 (5) 1965 (3); v WI 1957 (5) 1963 (2) 1966 (4); v NZ 1958 (4) 1965 (3); v In 1959 (5); v P 1962 (4) 1967 (2) 1971 (1); *v A 1954 (5) 1958 (5) 1962 (5) 1965 (4) 1970 (3) 1974 (5); v SA 1956 (5); v WI 1959 (5) 1967 (5); v NZ 1954 (2) 1958 (2) 1962 (3) 1965 (3) 1970 (1); v In 1963 (3); v P 1968 (3)*

Coxon (A.) 1: v A 1948

Cranston, J. 1: v A 1890

Cranston, K. 8: v A 1948 (1); v SA 1947 (3); *v WI 1947 (4)*

Crapp (J. F.) 7: v A 1948 (3); *v SA 1948 (4)*

Crawford, J. N. 12: v SA 1907 (2); *v A 1907 (5); v SA 1905 (5)*

Curtis, T. S. 5: v A 1989 (3); v WI 1988 (2)

Cuttell (W. R.) 2: *v SA 1898 (2)*

Dawson, E. W. 5: *v SA 1927 (1); v NZ 1929 (4)*

Dean (H.) 3: v A 1912 (2); v SA 1912 (1)

DeFreitas, P. A. J. 31: v A 1989 (1); v WI 1988 (3) 1991 (5); v NZ 1990 (2); v P 1987 (1) 1992 (2); v SL 1991 (1); *v A 1986 (4) 1990 (3); v WI 1989 (2); v NZ 1987 (2) 1991 (3); v P 1987 (2)*

Denness, M. H. 28: v A 1975 (1); v NZ 1969 (1); v In 1974 (3); v P 1974 (3); *v A 1974 (5); v WI 1973 (5); v NZ 1974 (2); v In 1972 (5); v P 1972 (3)*

Denton (D.) 11: v A 1905 (1); *v SA 1905 (5) 1909 (5)*

Dewes, J. G. 5: v A 1948 (1); v WI 1950 (2); *v A 1950 (2)*

Dexter, E. R. 62: v A 1961 (5) 1964 (5) 1968 (2); v SA 1960 (5); v WI 1963 (5); v NZ 1958 (1) 1965 (2); v In 1959 (2); v P 1962 (5); *v A 1958 (2) 1962 (5); v SA 1964 (5); v WI 1959 (5); v NZ 1958 (2) 1962 (3); v In 1961 (5); v P 1961 (3)*

Dilley, G. R. 41: v A 1981 (3) 1989 (2); v WI 1980 (3) 1988 (4); v NZ 1983 (1) 1986 (2); v In 1986 (2); v P 1987 (4); *v A 1979 (2) 1986 (4) 1987 (1); v WI 1980 (4); v NZ 1987 (3); v In 1981 (4); v P 1983 (1) 1987 (1)*

Dipper (A. E.) 1: v A 1921

Doggart, G. H. G. 2: v WI 1950 (2)

D'Oliveira, B. L. 44: v A 1968 (2) 1972 (5); v WI 1966 (4) 1969 (3); v NZ 1969 (3); v In 1967 (2) 1971 (3); v P 1967 (3) 1971 (3); *v A 1970 (6); v WI 1967 (5); v NZ 1970 (2); v P 1968 (3)*

Dollery (H. E.) 4: v A 1948 (2); v SA 1947 (1); v WI 1950 (1)

Dolphin (A.) 1: *v A 1920*

Douglas, J. W. H. T. 23: v A 1912 (1) 1921 (5); v SA 1924 (1); *v A 1911 (5) 1920 (5) 1924 (1); v SA 1913 (1)*

Downton, P. R. 30: v A 1981 (1) 1985 (6); v WI 1984 (5) 1988 (3); v In 1986 (1); v SL 1984 (1); *v WI 1980 (3) 1985 (5); v In 1984 (5)*

Druce, N. F. 5: *v A 1897 (5)*

Ducat (A.) 1: v A 1921

Duckworth (G.) 24: v A 1930 (5); v SA 1924 (1) 1929 (4) 1935 (1); v WI 1928 (1); v In 1936 (3); *v A 1928 (5); v SA 1930 (3); v NZ 1932 (1)*

Duleepsinhji, K. S. 12: v A 1930 (4); v SA 1929 (1); *v NZ 1929 (4)*

Durston (F. J.) 1: v A 1921

Edmonds, P. H. 51: v A 1975 (2) 1985 (5); v NZ 1978 (3) 1983 (2) 1986 (2); v In 1979 (4) 1982 (3) 1986 (2); v P 1978 (3) 1987 (5); *v A 1978 (1) 1986 (5); v WI 1985 (3); v NZ 1977 (3); v In 1984 (5); v P 1977 (2)*

Edrich, J. H. 77: v A 1964 (3) 1968 (5) 1972 (5) 1975 (4); v SA 1965 (1); v WI 1963 (3) 1966 (1) 1969 (3) 1976 (2); v NZ 1965 (1) 1969 (3); v In 1967 (2) 1971 (3) 1974 (3); v P 1971 (3) 1974 (3); *v A 1965 (5) 1970 (6) 1974 (4); v WI 1967 (5); v NZ 1965 (3) 1970 (2) 1974 (2); v In 1963 (2); v P 1968 (3)*

Edrich, W. J. 39: v A 1938 (4) 1948 (5) 1953 (3); v SA 1947 (4); v WI 1950 (2); v NZ 1949 (4); v In 1946 (1); v P 1954 (1); *v A 1946 (5) 1954 (4); v SA 1938 (5); v NZ 1946 (1)*

Elliott (H.) 4: v WI 1928 (1); *v SA 1927 (1); v In 1933 (2)*

Ellison, R. M. 11: v A 1985 (2); v WI 1984 (1); v In 1986 (1); v SL 1984 (1); *v WI 1985 (3); v In 1984 (1)*

Emburey, J. E. 60: v A 1980 (1) 1981 (4) 1985 (6) 1989 (3); v WI 1980 (3) 1988 (3); v NZ 1978 (1) 1986 (2); v In 1986 (3); v P 1987 (4); v SL 1988 (1); *v A 1978 (4) 1986 (5) 1987 (1); v WI 1980 (4) 1985 (4); v NZ 1987 (3); v In 1979 (1) 1981 (3); v P 1987 (3); v SL 1981 (1)*

Emmett (G. M.) 1: v A 1948

Emmett (T.) 7: *v A 1876 (2) 1878 (1) 1881 (4)*

Evans, A. J. 1: v A 1921

Evans, T. G.) 91: v A 1948 (5) 1953 (5) 1956 (5); v SA 1947 (5) 1951 (5) 1955 (5); v WI 1950 (3) 1957 (5); v NZ 1949 (4) 1958 (5); v In 1946 (1) 1952 (4) 1959 (2); v P 1954 (4); *v A 1946 (4) 1950 (5) 1954 (4) 1958 (3); v SA 1948 (3) 1956 (5); v WI 1947 (4) 1953 (4); v NZ 1946 (1) 1950 (2) 1954 (2)*

Fagg (A. E.) 5: v WI 1939 (1); v In 1936 (2); *v A 1936 (2)*

Fairbrother, N. H. 7: v NZ 1990 (3); v P 1987 (1); *v NZ 1987 (2); v P 1987 (1)*

Fane, F. L. 14: *v A 1907 (4); v SA 1905 (5) 1909 (5)*

Farnes, K. 15: v A 1934 (2) 1938 (4); *v A 1936 (2); v SA 1938 (5); v WI 1934 (2)*

Farrimond (W.) 4: v SA 1935 (1); *v SA 1930 (2); v WI 1934 (1)*

Fender, P. G. H. 13: v A 1921 (2); v SA 1924 (2) 1929 (1); *v A 1920 (3); v SA 1922 (5)*

Ferris, J. J. 1: *v SA 1891*

Fielder (A.) 6: *v A 1903 (2) 1907 (4)*

Fishlock (L. B.) 4: v In 1936 (2) 1946 (1); *v A 1946 (1)*

Flavell (J. A.) 4: v A 1961 (2) 1964 (2)

Fletcher, K. W. R. 59: v A 1968 (1) 1972 (1) 1975 (2); v WI 1973 (3); v NZ 1969 (2) 1973 (3); v In 1971 (2) 1974 (3); *v A 1970 (5) 1974 (5) 1976 (1); v WI 1973 (4); v NZ 1970 (1) 1974 (2); v In 1972 (5) 1976 (3) 1981 (6); v P 1968 (3) 1972 (3); v SL 1981 (1)*

Flowers (W.) 8: v A 1893 (1); *v A 1884 (5) 1886 (2)*

Ford, F. G. J. 5: *v A 1894 (5)*

Foster, F. R. 11: v A 1912 (3); v SA 1912 (3); *v A 1911 (5)*

Foster, N. A. 28: v A 1985 (1) 1989 (3); v WI 1984 (1) 1988 (2); v NZ 1983 (1) 1986 (1); v In 1986 (1); v P 1987 (5); v SL 1988 (1); *v A 1987 (1); v WI 1985 (3); v NZ 1983 (2); v In 1984 (2); v P 1983 (2) 1987 (2)*

Foster, R. E. 8: v SA 1907 (3); *v A 1903 (5)*

Fothergill (A. J.) 2: *v SA 1888 (2)*

Fowler, G. 21: v WI 1984 (5); v NZ 1983 (2); v P 1982 (1); v SL 1984 (1); *v A 1982 (3); v NZ 1983 (2); v In 1984 (5); v P 1983 (2)*

Fraser, A. R. C. 11: v A 1989 (3); v In 1990 (3); *v A 1990 (3); v WI 1989 (2)*

Freeman (A. P.) 12: v SA 1929 (3); v WI 1928 (3); *v A 1924 (2); v SA 1927 (4)*

French, B. N. 16: v NZ 1986 (3); v In 1986 (2); v P 1987 (4); *v A 1987 (1); v NZ 1987 (3); v P 1987 (2)*

Fry, C. B. 26: v A 1899 (5) 1902 (3) 1905 (4) 1909 (3) 1912 (3); v SA 1907 (3) 1912 (3); *v SA 1895 (2)*

Gatting, M. W. 68: v A 1980 (1) 1981 (6) 1985 (6) 1989 (1); v WI 1980 (4) 1984 (1) 1988 (2); v NZ 1983 (2) 1986 (3); v In 1986 (3); v P 1982 (3) 1987 (5); *v A 1986 (5) 1987 (1); v WI 1980 (1) 1985 (1); v NZ 1977 (1) 1983 (2) 1987 (3); v In 1981 (5) 1984 (5); v P 1977 (1) 1983 (2) 1987 (3)*

Gay, L. H. 1: *v A 1894*

Geary (G.) 14: v A 1926 (2) 1930 (1) 1934 (2); v SA 1924 (1) 1929 (2); *v A 1928 (4); v SA 1927 (2)*

Gibb, P. A. 8: v In 1946 (2); *v A 1946 (1); v SA 1938 (5)*

Gifford, N. 15: v A 1964 (2) 1972 (3); v NZ 1973 (2); v In 1971 (2); v P 1971 (2); *v In 1972 (2); v P 1972 (2)*

Gilligan, A. E. R. 11: v SA 1924 (4); *v A 1924 (5); v SA 1922 (2)*

Gilligan, A. H. H. 4: *v NZ 1929 (4)*

Gimblett (H.) 3: v WI 1939 (1); v In 1936 (2)

Gladwin (C.) 8: v SA 1947 (2); v NZ 1949 (1); *v SA 1948 (5)*

Goddard (T. W.) 8: v A 1930 (1); v WI 1939 (2); v NZ 1937 (2); *v SA 1938 (3)*

Gooch, G. A. 99: v A 1975 (2) 1980 (1) 1981 (5) 1985 (6) 1989 (5); v WI 1980 (5) 1988 (5) 1991 (5); v NZ 1978 (3) 1986 (3) 1990 (3); v In 1979 (4) 1986 (3) 1990 (3); v P 1978 (2) 1992 (5); v SL 1988 (1) 1991 (1); *v A 1978 (6) 1979 (2) 1990 (4); v WI 1980 (4) 1985 (5) 1989 (2); v NZ 1991 (3); v In 1979 (1) 1981 (6); v P 1987 (3); v SL 1981 (1)*

Gover (A. R.) 4: v NZ 1937 (2); v In 1936 (1) 1946 (1)

Gower, D. I. 117: v A 1980 (1) 1981 (5) 1985 (6) 1989 (6); v WI 1980 (1) 1984 (5) 1988 (4); v NZ 1978 (3) 1983 (4) 1986 (3); v In 1979 (4) 1982 (3) 1986 (2) 1990 (3); v P 1978 (3) 1982 (3) 1987 (5) 1992 (3); v SL 1984 (1); *v A 1978 (6) 1979 (3) 1982 (5) 1986 (5) 1990 (5); v WI 1980 (4) 1985 (5); v NZ 1983 (3); v In 1979 (1) 1981 (6) 1984 (5); v P 1983 (3); v SL 1981 (1)*

Grace, E. M. 1: v A 1880

Grace, G. F. 1: v A 1880

Grace, W. G. 22: v A 1880 (1) 1882 (1) 1884 (2) 1886 (3) 1888 (3) 1890 (2) 1893 (2) 1896 (3) 1899 (1); *v A 1891 (3)*

Graveney (T. W.) 79: v A 1953 (5) 1956 (2) 1968 (5); v SA 1951 (1) 1955 (5); v WI 1957 (4) 1966 (4) 1969 (5); v NZ 1958 (4); v In 1952 (4) 1967 (3); v P 1954 (3) 1962 (4) 1967 (3); *v A 1954 (2) 1958 (5) 1962 (3); v WI 1953 (5) 1967 (5); v NZ 1954 (2) 1958 (2); v In 1951 (4); v P 1968 (3)*

Greenhough (T.) 4: v SA 1960 (1); v In 1959 (3)

Greenwood (A.) 2: *v A 1876 (2)*

Greig, A. W. 58: v A 1972 (5) 1975 (5) 1977 (5); v WI 1973 (3) 1976 (5); v NZ 1973 (3); v In 1974 (3); v P 1974 (3); *v A 1974 (6) 1976 (1); v WI 1973 (5); v NZ 1974 (2); v In 1972 (5) 1976 (5); v P 1972 (3)*

Greig, I. A. 2: v P 1982 (2)

Grieve, B. A. F. 2: *v SA 1888 (2)*

Griffith, S. C. 3: *v SA 1948 (2); v WI 1947 (1)*

Gunn (G.) 15: v A 1909 (1); *v A 1907 (5) 1911 (5); v WI 1929 (4)*

Gunn (J.) 6: v A 1905 (1); *v A 1901 (5)*

Gunn (W.) 11: v A 1888 (1) 1890 (2) 1893 (3) 1896 (1) 1899 (1); *v A 1886 (2)*

Haig, N. E. 5: v A 1921 (1); *v WI 1929 (4)*

Haigh (S.) 11: v A 1905 (2) 1909 (1) 1912 (1); *v SA 1898 (2) 1905 (5)*

Hallows (C.) 2: v A 1921 (1); v WI 1928 (1)
Hammond, W. R. 85: v A 1930 (5) 1934 (5) 1938 (4); v SA 1929 (4) 1935 (5); v WI 1928 (3) 1933 (3) 1939 (3); v NZ 1931 (3) 1937 (3); v In 1932 (1) 1936 (2) 1946 (3); *v A 1928 (5) 1932 (5) 1936 (5) 1946 (4); v SA 1927 (5) 1930 (5) 1938 (5); v WI 1934 (4); v NZ 1932 (2) 1946 (1)*
Hampshire, J. H. 8: v A 1972 (1) 1975 (1); v WI 1969 (2); *v A 1970 (2); v NZ 1970 (2)*
Hardinge (H. T. W.) 1: v A 1921
Hardstaff (J.) 5: *v A 1907 (5)*
Hardstaff (J. jun.) 23: v A 1938 (2) 1948 (1); v SA 1935 (1); v WI 1939 (3); v NZ 1937 (3); v In 1936 (2) 1946 (2); *v A 1936 (5) 1946 (1); v WI 1947 (3)*
Harris, Lord 4: v A 1880 (1) 1884 (2); *v A 1878 (1)*
Hartley, J. C. 2: v SA 1905 (2)
Hawke, Lord 5: *v SA 1895 (3) 1898 (2)*
Hayes (E. G.) 5: v A 1909 (1); v SA 1912 (1); *v SA 1905 (3)*
Hayes, F. C. 9: v WI 1973 (3) 1976 (2); *v WI 1973 (4)*
Hayward (T. W.) 35: v A 1896 (2) 1899 (5) 1902 (1) 1905 (5) 1909 (3); v SA 1907 (3); *v A 1897 (5) 1901 (5) 1903 (5); v SA 1895 (3)*
Hearne (A.) 1: *v SA 1891*
Hearne (F.) 2: *v SA 1888 (2)*
Hearne (G. G.) 1: *v SA 1891*
Hearne (J. T.) 12: v A 1896 (3) 1899 (3); *v A 1897 (5); v SA 1891 (1)*
Hearne (J. W.) 24: v A 1912 (3) 1921 (1) 1926 (1); v SA 1912 (2) 1924 (3); *v A 1911 (5) 1920 (2) 1924 (4); v SA 1913 (3)*
Hemmings, E. E. 16: v A 1989 (1); v NZ 1990 (3); v In 1990 (3); v P 1982 (2); *v A 1982 (3) 1987 (1) 1990 (1); v NZ 1987 (1); v P 1987 (1)*
Hendren (E. H.) 51: v A 1921 (2) 1926 (5) 1930 (2) 1934 (4); v SA 1924 (5) 1929 (4); v WI 1928 (1); *v A 1920 (5) 1924 (5) 1928 (5); v SA 1930 (5); v WI 1929 (4) 1934 (4)*
Hendrick, M. 30: v A 1977 (3) 1980 (1) 1981 (2); v WI 1976 (2) 1980 (2); v NZ 1978 (2); v In 1974 (3) 1979 (4); v P 1974 (2); *v A 1974 (2) 1978 (5); v NZ 1974 (1) 1977 (1)*
Heseltine, C. 2: v SA 1895 (2)
Hick, G. A. 11: v WI 1991 (4); v P 1992 (4); *v NZ 1991 (3)*
Higgs, K. 15: v A 1968 (1); v WI 1966 (5); v SA 1965 (1); v In 1967 (1); v P 1967 (1); *v A 1965 (1); v NZ 1965 (3)*
Hill (A.) 2: *v A 1876 (2)*
Hill, A. J. L. 3: *v SA 1895 (3)*
Hilton (M. J.) 4: v SA 1951 (1); v WI 1950 (1); *v In 1951 (2)*
Hirst (G. H.) 24: v A 1899 (1) 1902 (4) 1905 (3) 1909 (4); v SA 1907 (3); *v A 1897 (4) 1903 (5)*
Hitch (J. W.) 7: v A 1912 (1) 1921 (1); v SA 1912 (1); *v A 1911 (3) 1920 (1)*
Hobbs (J. B.) 61: v A 1909 (3) 1912 (3) 1921 (1) 1926 (5) 1930 (5); v SA 1912 (3) 1924 (3) 1929 (1); v WI 1928 (2); *v A 1907 (4) 1911 (5) 1920 (5) 1924 (5) 1928 (5); v SA 1909 (5) 1913 (5)*
Hobbs, R. N. S. 7: v In 1967 (3); v P 1967 (1) 1971 (1); *v WI 1967 (1); v P 1968 (1)*
Hollies (W. E.) 13: v A 1948 (1); v SA 1947 (3); v WI 1950 (2); v NZ 1949 (4); *v WI 1934 (3)*
Holmes, E. R. T. 5: v SA 1935 (1); *v WI 1934 (4)*
Holmes (P.) 7: v A 1921 (1); v In 1932 (1); *v SA 1927 (5)*
Hone, L. 1: *v A 1878*
Hopwood (J. L.) 2: v A 1934 (2)
Hornby, A. N. 3: v A 1882 (1) 1884 (1); *v A 1878 (1)*
Horton (M. J.) 2: v In 1959 (2)
Howard, N. D. 4: *v In 1951 (4)*
Howell (H.) 5: v A 1921 (1); v SA 1924 (1); *v A 1920 (3)*
Howorth (R.) 5: v SA 1947 (1); *v WI 1947 (4)*
Humphries (J.) 3: *v A 1907 (3)*
Hunter (J.) 5: *v A 1884 (5)*
Hussain, N. 3: *v WI 1989 (3)*
Hutchings, K. L. 7: v A 1909 (2); *v A 1907 (5)*
Hutton (L.) 79: v A 1938 (3) 1948 (4) 1953 (5); v SA 1947 (5) 1951 (5); v WI 1939 (3) 1950 (3); v NZ 1937 (3) 1949 (4); v In 1946 (3) 1952 (4); v P 1954 (2); *v A 1946 (5) 1950 (5) 1954 (5); v SA 1938 (4) 1948 (5); v WI 1947 (2) 1953 (5); v NZ 1950 (2) 1954 (2)*
Hutton, R. A. 5: v In 1971 (3); v P 1971 (2)

Iddon (J.) 5: v SA 1935 (1); *v WI 1934 (4)*
Igglesden, A. P. 1: v A 1989

Ikin (J. T.) 18: v SA 1951 (3) 1955 (1); v In 1946 (2) 1952 (2); *v A 1946 (5); v NZ 1946 (1); v WI 1947 (4)*

Illingworth (R.) 61: v A 1961 (2) 1968 (3) 1972 (5); v SA 1960 (4); v WI 1966 (2) 1969 (3) 1973 (3); v NZ 1958 (1) 1965 (1) 1969 (3) 1973 (3); v In 1959 (2) 1967 (3) 1971 (3); v P 1962 (1) 1967 (1) 1971 (3); *v A 1962 (2) 1970 (6); v WI 1959 (5); v NZ 1962 (3) 1970 (2)*

Illingworth, R. K. 2: v WI 1991 (2)

Insole, D. J. 9: v A 1956 (1); v SA 1955 (1); v WI 1950 (1) 1957 (1); *v SA 1956 (5)*

Jackman, R. D. 4: v P 1982 (2); *v WI 1980 (2)*

Jackson, F. S. 20: v A 1893 (2) 1896 (3) 1899 (5) 1902 (5) 1905 (5)

Jackson (H. L.) 2: v A 1961 (1); v NZ 1949 (1)

Jameson, J. A. 4: v In 1971 (2); *v WI 1973 (2)*

Jardine, D. R. 22: v WI 1928 (2) 1933 (2); v NZ 1931 (3); v In 1932 (1); *v A 1928 (5) 1932 (5); v NZ 1932 (1); v In 1933 (3)*

Jarvis, P. W. 6: v A 1989 (2); v WI 1988 (2); *v NZ 1987 (2)*

Jenkins (R. O.) 9: v WI 1950 (2); v In 1952 (2); *v SA 1948 (5)*

Jessop, G. L. 18: v A 1899 (1) 1902 (4) 1905 (1) 1909 (2); v SA 1907 (3) 1912 (2); *v A 1901 (5)*

Jones, A. O. 12: v A 1899 (1) 1905 (2) 1909 (2); *v A 1901 (5) 1907 (2)*

Jones, I. J. 15: v WI 1966 (1); *v A 1965 (4); v WI 1967 (5); v NZ 1965 (3); v In 1963 (1)*

Jupp (H.) 2: *v A 1876 (2)*

Jupp, V. W. C. 8: v A 1921 (2); v WI 1928 (2); *v SA 1922 (4)*

Keeton (W. W.) 2: v A 1934 (1); v WI 1939 (1)

Kennedy (A. S.) 5: *v SA 1922 (5)*

Kenyon (D.) 8: v A 1953 (2); v SA 1955 (3); *v In 1951 (3)*

Killick, E. T. 2: v SA 1929 (2)

Kilner (R.) 9: v A 1926 (4); v SA 1924 (2); *v A 1924 (3)*

King (J. H.) 1: v A 1909

Kinneir (S. P.) 1: *v A 1911*

Knight (A. E.) 3: *v A 1903 (3)*

Knight (B. R.) 29: v A 1968 (2); v WI 1966 (1) 1969 (3); v NZ 1969 (2); v P 1962 (2); *v A 1962 (1) 1965 (2); v NZ 1962 (3) 1965 (2); v In 1961 (4) 1963 (5); v P 1961 (2)*

Knight, D. J. 2: v A 1921 (2)

Knott, A. P. E. 95: v A 1968 (5) 1972 (5) 1975 (4) 1977 (5) 1981 (2); v WI 1969 (3) 1973 (3) 1976 (5) 1980 (4); v NZ 1969 (3) 1973 (3); v In 1971 (3) 1974 (3); v P 1967 (2) 1971 (3) 1974 (3); *v A 1970 (6) 1974 (6) 1976 (1); v WI 1967 (2) 1973 (5); v NZ 1970 (1) 1974 (2); v In 1972 (5) 1976 (5); v P 1968 (3) 1972 (2)*

Knox, N. A. 2: v SA 1907 (2)

Laker (J. C.) 46: v A 1948 (3) 1953 (3) 1956 (5); v SA 1951 (2) 1955 (1); v WI 1950 (1) 1957 (4); v NZ 1949 (1) 1958 (4); v In 1952 (4); v P 1954 (1); *v A 1958 (4); v SA 1956 (5); v WI 1947 (4) 1953 (4)*

Lamb, A. J. 79: v A 1985 (6) 1989 (1); v WI 1984 (5) 1988 (4) 1991 (4); v NZ 1983 (4) 1986 (1) 1990 (3); v In 1982 (3) 1986 (2) 1990 (3); v P 1982 (3) 1992 (2); v SL 1984 (1) 1988 (1); *v A 1982 (5) 1986 (5) 1990 (3); v WI 1985 (5) 1989 (4); v NZ 1983 (3) 1991 (3); v In 1984 (5); v P 1983 (3)*

Langridge (James) 8: v SA 1935 (1); v WI 1933 (2); v In 1936 (1) 1946 (1); *v In 1933 (3)*

Larkins, W. 13: v A 1981 (1); v WI 1980 (1); *v A 1979 (1) 1990 (3); v WI 1989 (4); v In 1979 (1)*

Larter (J. D. F.) 10: v SA 1965 (2); v NZ 1965 (1); v P 1962 (1); *v NZ 1962 (3); v In 1963 (3)*

Larwood (H.) 21: v A 1926 (2) 1930 (3); v SA 1929 (3); v WI 1928 (2); v NZ 1931 (1); *v A 1928 (5) 1932 (5)*

Lawrence, D. V. 5: v WI 1991 (2); v SL 1988 (1) 1991 (1); *v NZ 1991 (1)*

Leadbeater (E.) 2: *v In 1951 (2)*

Lee (H. W.) 1: *v SA 1930*

Lees (W. S.) 5: *v SA 1905 (5)*

Legge G. B. 5: *v SA 1927 (1); v NZ 1929 (4)*

Leslie, C. F. H. 4: *v A 1882 (4)*

Lever, J. K. 21: v A 1977 (3); v WI 1980 (1); v In 1979 (1) 1986 (1); *v A 1976 (1) 1978 (1) 1979 (1); v NZ 1977 (1); v In 1976 (5) 1979 (1) 1981 (2); v P 1977 (3)*

Lever, P. 17: v A 1972 (1) 1975 (1); v In 1971 (1); v P 1971 (3); *v A 1970 (5) 1974 (2); v NZ 1970 (2) 1974 (2)*

Leveson Gower, H. D. G. 3: *v SA 1909 (3)*

Levett, W. H. V. 1: *v In 1933*

Lewis, A. R. 9: v NZ 1973 (1); *v In 1972 (5); v P 1972 (3)*

Lewis, C. C. 14: v WI 1991 (2); v NZ 1990 (1); v In 1990 (2); v P 1992 (5); v SL 1991 (1); *v A 1990 (1); v NZ 1991 (2)*

Leyland (M.) 41: v A 1930 (3) 1934 (5) 1938 (1); v SA 1929 (5) 1935 (4); v WI 1928 (1) 1933 (1); v In 1936 (2); *v A 1928 (1) 1932 (5) 1936 (5); v SA 1930 (5); v WI 1934 (3)*

Lilley (A. A.) 35: v A 1896 (3) 1899 (4) 1902 (5) 1905 (5) 1909 (5); v SA 1907 (3); *v A 1901 (5) 1903 (5)*

Lillywhite (James jun.) 2: *v A 1876 (2)*

Lloyd, D. 9: v In 1974 (2); v P 1974 (3); *v A 1974 (4)*

Lloyd, T. A. 1: v WI 1984

Loader (P. J.) 13: v SA 1955 (1); v WI 1957 (2); v NZ 1958 (3); v P 1954 (1); *v A 1958 (2); v SA 1956 (4)*

Lock (G. A. R.) 49: v A 1953 (2) 1956 (4) 1961 (3); v SA 1955 (3); v WI 1957 (3) 1963 (3); v NZ 1958 (5); v In 1952 (2); v P 1962 (3); *v A 1958 (4); v SA 1956 (1); v WI 1953 (5) 1967 (2); v NZ 1958 (2); v In 1961 (5); v P 1961 (2)*

Lockwood (W. H.) 12: v A 1893 (2) 1899 (1) 1902 (4); *v A 1894 (5)*

Lohmann (G. A.) 18: v A 1886 (2) 1888 (3) 1890 (2) 1896 (1); *v A 1886 (2) 1887 (1) 1891 (3); v SA 1895 (3)*

Lowson (F. A.) 7: v SA 1951 (2) 1955 (1); *v In 1951 (4)*

Lucas, A. P. 5: v A 1880 (1) 1882 (1) 1884 (2); *v A 1878 (1)*

Luckhurst, B. W. 21: v A 1972 (4); v WI 1973 (2); v In 1971 (3); v P 1971 (3); *v A 1970 (5) 1974 (2); v NZ 1970 (2)*

Lyttelton, Hon. A. 4: v A 1880 (1) 1882 (1) 1884 (2)

Macaulay (G. G.) 8: v A 1926 (1); v SA 1924 (1); v WI 1933 (2); *v SA 1922 (4)*

MacBryan, J. C. W. 1: v SA 1924

McConnon (J. E.) 2: v P 1954 (2)

McGahey, C. P. 2: *v A 1901 (2)*

MacGregor, G. 8: v A 1890 (2) 1893 (3); *v A 1891 (3)*

McIntyre (A. J. W.) 3: v SA 1955 (1); v WI 1950 (1); *v A 1950 (1)*

MacKinnon, F. A. 1: *v A 1878*

MacLaren, A. C. 35: v A 1896 (3) 1899 (4) 1902 (5) 1905 (4) 1909 (5); *v A 1894 (5) 1897 (5) 1901 (5)*

McMaster, J. E. P. 1: *v SA 1888*

Makepeace (J. W. H.) 4: *v A 1920 (4)*

Malcolm, D. E. 21: v A 1989 (1); v WI 1991 (2); v NZ 1990 (3); v In 1990 (3); v P 1992 (3); *v A 1990 (5); v WI 1989 (4)*

Mallender, N. A. 2: v P 1992 (2)

Mann, F. G. 7: v NZ 1949 (2); *v SA 1948 (5)*

Mann, F. T. 5: *v SA 1922 (5)*

Marks, V. J. 6: v NZ 1983 (1); v P 1982 (1); *v NZ 1983 (1); v P 1983 (3)*

Marriott, C. S. 1: v WI 1933

Martin (F.) 2: v A 1890 (1); *v SA 1891 (1)*

Martin, J. W. 1: v SA 1947

Mason, J. R. 5: *v A 1897 (5)*

Matthews (A. D. G.) 1: v NZ 1937

May, P. B. H. 66: v A 1953 (2) 1956 (5) 1961 (4); v SA 1951 (2) 1955 (5); v WI 1957 (5); v NZ 1958 (5); v In 1952 (4) 1959 (3); v P 1954 (4); *v A 1954 (5) 1958 (5); v SA 1956 (5); v WI 1953 (5) 1959 (3); v NZ 1954 (2) 1958 (2)*

Maynard, M. P. 1: v WI 1988

Mead (C. P.) 17: v A 1921 (2); *v A 1911 (4) 1928 (1); v SA 1913 (5) 1922 (5)*

Mead (W.) 1: v A 1899

Midwinter (W. E.) 4: *v A 1881 (4)*

Milburn, C. 9: v A 1968 (2); v WI 1966 (4); v In 1967 (1); v P 1967 (1); *v P 1968 (1)*

Miller, A. M. 1: *v SA 1895*

Miller, G. 34: v A 1977 (2); v WI 1976 (1) 1984 (2); v NZ 1978 (2); v In 1979 (3) 1982 (1); v P 1978 (3) 1982 (1); *v A 1978 (6) 1979 (1) 1982 (5); v WI 1980 (1); v NZ 1977 (3); v P 1977 (3)*

Milligan, F. W. 2: *v SA 1898 (2)*

Millman (G.) 6: v P 1962 (2); *v In 1961 (2); v P 1961 (2)*

Milton (C. A.) 6: v NZ 1958 (2); v In 1959 (2); *v A 1958 (2)*

Mitchell (A.) 6: v SA 1935 (2); v In 1936 (1); *v In 1933 (3)*

Mitchell, F. 2: *v SA 1898 (2)*

Price (W. F. F.) 1: v A 1938
Prideaux, R. M. 3: v A 1968 (1); *v P 1968* (2)
Pringle, D. R. 30: v A 1989 (2); v WI 1984 (3) 1988 (4) 1991 (4); v NZ 1986 (1); v In 1982 (3) 1986 (3); v P 1982 (1) 1992 (3); v SL 1988 (1); *v A 1982 (3); v NZ 1991* (2)
Pullar (G.) 28: v A 1961 (5); v SA 1960 (3); v In 1959 (3); v P 1962 (2); *v A 1962 (4); v WI 1959* (5); *v In 1961 (3); v P 1961* (3)

Quaife (W. G.) 7: v A 1899 (2); *v A 1901* (5)

Radford, N. V. 3: v NZ 1986 (1); v In 1986 (1); *v NZ 1987* (1)
Radley, C. T. 8: v NZ 1978 (3); v P 1978 (3); *v NZ 1977* (2)
Ramprakash, M. R. 9: v WI 1991 (5); v P 1992 (3); v SL 1991 (1)
Randall, D. W. 47: v A 1977 (5); v WI 1984 (1); v NZ 1983 (3); v In 1979 (3) 1982 (3); v P 1982 (3); *v A 1976 (1) 1978 (6) 1979 (2) 1982 (4); v NZ 1977 (3) 1983 (3); v In 1976 (4); v P 1977 (3) 1983* (3)
Ranjitsinhji, K. S. 15: v A 1896 (2) 1899 (5) 1902 (3); *v A 1897* (5)
Read, H. D. 1: v SA 1935
Read (J. M.) 17: v A 1882 (1) 1890 (2) 1893 (1); *v A 1884 (5) 1886 (2) 1887 (1) 1891 (3); v SA 1888* (2)
Read, W. W. 18: v A 1884 (2) 1886 (3) 1888 (3) 1890 (2) 1893 (2); *v A 1882 (4) 1887 (1); v SA 1891* (1)
Reeve, D. A. 3: *v NZ 1991* (3)
Relf (A. E.) 13: v A 1909 (1); *v A 1903 (2); v SA 1905 (5) 1913* (5)
Rhodes (H. J.) 2: v In 1959 (2)
Rhodes (W.) 58: v A 1899 (3) 1902 (5) 1905 (4) 1909 (4) 1912 (3) 1921 (1) 1926 (1); v SA 1912 (3); *v A 1903 (5) 1907 (5) 1911 (5) 1920 (5); v SA 1909 (5) 1913 (5); v WI 1929* (4)
Richards, C. J. 8: v WI 1988 (2); v P 1987 (1); *v A 1986* (5)
Richardson (D. W.) 1: v WI 1957
Richardson (P. E.) 34: v A 1956 (5); v WI 1957 (5) 1963 (1); v NZ 1958 (3); *v A 1958 (4); v SA 1956 (5); v NZ 1958 (2); v In 1961 (5); v P 1961* (3)
Richardson (T.) 14: v A 1893 (1) 1896 (3); *v A 1894 (5) 1897* (5)
Richmond (T. L.) 1: v A 1921
Ridgway (F.) 5: *v In 1951* (5)
Robertson (J. D.) 11: v SA 1947 (1); v NZ 1949 (1); *v WI 1947 (4); v In 1951* (5)
Robins, R. W. V. 19: v A 1930 (2); v SA 1929 (1) 1935 (3); v WI 1933 (2); v NZ 1931 (1) 1937 (3); v In 1932 (1) 1936 (2); *v A 1936* (4)
Robinson, R. T. 29: v A 1985 (6) 1989 (1); v In 1986 (1); v P 1987 (5); v SL 1988 (1); *v A 1987 (1); v WI 1985 (4); v NZ 1987 (3); v In 1984 (5); v P 1987* (2)
Roope, G. R. J. 21: v A 1975 (1) 1977 (2); v WI 1973 (1); v NZ 1973 (3) 1978 (1); v P 1978 (3); *v NZ 1977 (3); v In 1972 (2); v P 1972 (2) 1977* (3)
Root (C. F.) 3: v A 1926 (3)
Rose, B. C. 9: v WI 1980 (3); *v WI 1980 (1); v NZ 1977 (2); v P 1977* (3)
Royle, V. P. F. A. 1: *v A 1878*
Rumsey, F. E. 5: v A 1964 (1); v SA 1965 (1); v NZ 1965 (3)
Russell (A. C.) 10: v A 1921 (2); *v A 1920 (4); v SA 1922* (4)
Russell, R. C. 31: v A 1989 (6); v WI 1991 (4); v NZ 1990 (3); v In 1990 (3); v P 1992 (3); v SL 1988 (1) 1991 (1); *v A 1990 (3); v WI 1989 (4); v NZ 1991* (3)
Russell, W. E. 10: v SA 1965 (1); v WI 1966 (2); v P 1967 (1); *v A 1965 (1); v NZ 1965 (3); v In 1961 (1); v P 1961* (1)

Salisbury, I. D. K. 2: v P 1992 (2)
Sandham (A.) 14: v A 1921 (1); v SA 1924 (2); *v A 1924 (2); v SA 1922 (5); v WI 1929* (4)
Schultz, S. S. 1: *v A 1878*
Scotton (W. H.) 15: v A 1884 (1) 1886 (3); *v A 1881 (4) 1884 (5) 1886* (2)
Selby (J.) 6: *v A 1876 (2) 1881* (4)
Selvey, M. W. W. 3: v WI 1976 (2); *v In 1976* (1)
Shackleton (D.) 7: v SA 1951 (1); v WI 1950 (1) 1963 (4); *v In 1951* (1)
Sharp (J.) 3: v A 1909 (3)
Sharpe (J. W.) 3: v A 1890 (1); *v A 1891* (2)
Sharpe, P. J. 12: v A 1964 (2); v WI 1963 (3) 1969 (3); v NZ 1969 (3); *v In 1963* (1)
Shaw (A.) 7: v A 1880 (1); *v A 1876 (2) 1881* (4)

Sheppard, Rev. D. S. 22: v A 1956 (2); v WI 1950 (1) 1957 (2); v In 1952 (2); v P 1954 (2) 1962 (2); *v A 1950 (2) 1962 (5); v NZ 1950 (1) 1963 (3)*

Sherwin (M.) 3: v A 1888 (1); *v A 1886 (2)*

Shrewsbury (A.) 23: v A 1884 (3) 1886 (3) 1890 (2) 1893 (3); *v A 1881 (4) 1884 (5) 1886 (2) 1887 (1)*

Shuter, J. 1: v A 1888

Shuttleworth, K. 5: v P 1971 (1); *v A 1970 (2); v NZ 1970 (2)*

Sidebottom, A. 1: v A 1985

Simpson, R. T. 27: v A 1953 (3); v SA 1951 (3); v WI 1950 (1); v NZ 1949 (2); v In 1952 (2); v P 1954 (3); *v A 1950 (5) 1954 (1); v SA 1948 (1); v NZ 1950 (2) 1954 (2)*

Simpson-Hayward, G. H. 5: *v SA 1909 (5)*

Sims (J. M.) 4: v SA 1935 (1); v In 1936 (1); *v A 1936 (2)*

Sinfield (R. A.) 1: v A 1938

Slack, W. N. 3: v In 1986 (1); *v WI 1985 (2)*

Smailes (T. F.) 1: v In 1946

Small, G. C. 17: v A 1989 (1); v WI 1988 (1); v NZ 1986 (2) 1990 (3); *v A 1986 (2) 1990 (4); v WI 1989 (4)*

Smith, A. C. 6: *v A 1962 (4); v NZ 1962 (2)*

Smith, C. A. 1: *v SA 1888*

Smith (C. I. J.) 5: v NZ 1937 (1); *v WI 1934 (4)*

Smith, C. L. 8: v NZ 1983 (2); v In 1986 (1); *v NZ 1983 (2); v P 1983 (3)*

Smith (D.) 2: v SA 1935 (2)

Smith, D. M. 2: *v WI 1985 (2)*

Smith (D. R.) 5: *v In 1961 (5)*

Smith (D. V.) 3: v WI 1957 (3)

Smith (E. J.) 11: v A 1912 (3); v SA 1912 (3); *v A 1911 (4); v SA 1913 (3)*

Smith (H.) 1: v WI 1928

Smith, M. J. K. 50: v A 1961 (1) 1972 (3); v SA 1960 (4) 1965 (3); v WI 1966 (1); v NZ 1958 (3) 1965 (3); v In 1959 (2); *v A 1965 (5); v SA 1964 (5); v WI 1959 (5); v NZ 1965 (3); v In 1961 (4) 1963 (5); v P 1961 (3)*

Smith, R. A. 36: v A 1989 (5); v WI 1988 (2) 1991 (4); v NZ 1990 (3); v In 1990 (3); v P 1992 (5); v SL 1988 (1) 1991 (1); *v A 1990 (5); v WI 1989 (4); v NZ 1991 (3)*

Smith (T. P. B.) 4: v In 1946 (1); *v A 1946 (2); v NZ 1946 (1)*

Smithson (G. A.) 2: *v WI 1947 (2)*

Snow, J. A. 49: v A 1968 (5) 1972 (5) 1975 (4); v SA 1965 (1); v WI 1966 (3) 1969 (3) 1973 (1) 1976 (3); v NZ 1965 (1) 1969 (2) 1973 (3); v In 1967 (3) 1971 (2); v P 1967 (1); *v A 1970 (6); v WI 1967 (4); v P 1968 (2)*

Southerton (J.) 2: *v A 1876 (2)*

Spooner, R. H. 10: v A 1905 (2) 1909 (2) 1912 (3); v SA 1912 (3)

Spooner (R. T.) 7: v SA 1955 (1); *v In 1951 (5); v WI 1953 (1)*

Stanyforth, R. T. 4: *v SA 1927 (4)*

Staples (S. J.) 3: *v SA 1927 (3)*

Statham (J. B.) 70: v A 1953 (1) 1956 (3) 1961 (4); v SA 1951 (2) 1955 (4) 1960 (5) 1965 (1); v WI 1957 (3) 1963 (2); v NZ 1958 (2); v In 1959 (3); v P 1954 (4) 1962 (3); *v A 1954 (5) 1958 (4) 1962 (5); v SA 1956 (4); v WI 1953 (4) 1959 (3); v NZ 1950 (1) 1954 (2); v In 1951 (3)*

Steel, A. G. 13: v A 1880 (1) 1882 (1) 1884 (3) 1886 (3) 1888 (1); *v A 1882 (4)*

Steele, D. S. 8: v A 1975 (3); v WI 1976 (5)

Stephenson, J. P. 1: v A 1989

Stevens, G. T. S. 10: v A 1926 (2); *v SA 1922 (1) 1927 (5); v WI 1929 (2)*

Stevenson, G. B. 2: *v WI 1980 (1); v In 1979 (1)*

Stewart, A. J. 22: v WI 1991 (1); v NZ 1990 (3); v P 1992 (5); v SL 1991 (1); *v A 1990 (5); v WI 1989 (4); v NZ 1991 (3)*

Stewart (M. J.) 8: v WI 1963 (4); v P 1962 (2); *v In 1963 (2)*

Stoddart, A. E. 16: v A 1893 (3) 1896 (2); *v A 1887 (1) 1891 (3) 1894 (5) 1897 (2)*

Storer (W.) 6: v A 1899 (1); *v A 1897 (5)*

Street (G. B.) 1: *v SA 1922*

Strudwick (H.) 28: v A 1921 (2) 1926 (5); v SA 1924 (1); *v A 1911 (1) 1920 (4) 1924 (5); v SA 1909 (5) 1913 (2)*

Studd, C. T. 5: v A 1882 (1); *v A 1882 (4)*

Studd, G. B. 4: *v A 1882 (4)*

Subba Row, R. 13: v A 1961 (5); v SA 1960 (4); v NZ 1958 (1); v In 1959 (1); *v WI 1959 (2)*

Sugg (F. H.) 2: v A 1888 (2)

Sutcliffe (H.) 54: v A 1926 (5) 1930 (4) 1934 (4); v SA 1924 (5) 1929 (5) 1935 (2); v WI 1928 (3) 1933 (2); v NZ 1931 (2); v In 1932 (1); *v A 1924 (5) 1928 (4) 1932 (5); v SA 1927 (5); v NZ 1932 (2)*

Swetman (R.) 11: v In 1959 (3); *v A 1958 (2); v WI 1959 (4); v NZ 1958 (2)*

Tate (F. W.) 1: v A 1902

Tate (M. W.) 39: v A 1926 (5) 1930 (5); v SA 1924 (5) 1929 (3) 1935 (1); v WI 1928 (3); v NZ 1931 (1); *v A 1924 (5) 1928 (5); v SA 1930 (5); v NZ 1932 (1)*

Tattersall (R.) 16: v A 1953 (1); v SA 1951 (5); v P 1954 (1); *v A 1950 (2); v NZ 1950 (2); v In 1951 (5)*

Tavaré, C. J. 31: v A 1981 (2) 1989 (1); v WI 1980 (2) 1984 (1); v NZ 1983 (4); v In 1982 (3); v P 1982 (3); v SL 1984 (1); *v A 1982 (5); v NZ 1983 (2); v In 1981 (6); v SL 1981 (1)*

Taylor (K.) 3: v A 1964 (1); v In 1959 (2)

Taylor, L. B. 2: v A 1985 (2)

Taylor, R. W. 57: v A 1981 (3); v NZ 1978 (3) 1983 (4); v In 1979 (3) 1982 (3); v P 1978 (3) 1982 (3); *v A 1978 (6) 1979 (3) 1982 (5); v NZ 1970 (1) 1977 (3) 1983 (3); v In 1979 (1) 1981 (6); v P 1977 (3) 1983 (3); v SL 1981 (1)*

Tennyson, Hon. L. H. 9: v A 1921 (4); *v SA 1913 (5)*

Terry, V. P. 2: v WI 1984 (2)

Thomas, J. G. 5: v NZ 1986 (1); *v WI 1985 (4)*

Thompson (G. J.) 6: v A 1909 (1); *v SA 1909 (5)*

Thomson, N. I. 5: *v SA 1964 (5)*

Titmus (F. J.) 53: v A 1964 (5); v SA 1955 (2) 1965 (3); v WI 1963 (4) 1966 (3); v NZ 1965 (3); v P 1962 (2) 1967 (2); *v A 1962 (5) 1965 (5) 1974 (4); v SA 1964 (5); v WI 1967 (2); v NZ 1962 (3); v In 1963 (5)*

Tolchard, R. W. 4: *v In 1976 (4)*

Townsend, C. L. 2: v A 1899 (2)

Townsend, D. C. H. 3: *v SA 1934 (3)*

Townsend (L. F.) 4: *v WI 1929 (1); v In 1933 (3)*

Tremlett (M. F.) 3: *v WI 1947 (3)*

Trott (A. E.) 2: *v SA 1898 (2)*

Trueman (F. S.) 67: v A 1953 (1) 1956 (2) 1961 (4) 1964 (4); v SA 1955 (2) 1960 (5); v WI 1957 (5) 1963 (5); v NZ 1958 (5) 1965 (2); v In 1952 (4) 1959 (5); v P 1962 (4); *v A 1958 (3) 1962 (5); v WI 1953 (3) 1959 (5); v NZ 1958 (2) 1962 (2)*

Tufnell, N. C. 1: *v SA 1909*

Tufnell, P. C. R. 10: v WI 1991 (1); v P 1992 (1); v SL 1991 (1); *v A 1990 (4); v NZ 1991 (3)*

Turnbull, M. J. 9: v WI 1933 (2); v In 1936 (1); *v SA 1930 (5); v NZ 1929 (1)*

Tyldesley (E.) 14: v A 1921 (3) 1926 (1); v SA 1924 (1); v WI 1928 (2); *v A 1928 (1); v SA 1927 (5)*

Tyldesley (J. T.) 31: v A 1899 (2) 1902 (5) 1905 (5) 1909 (4); v SA 1907 (3); *v A 1901 (5) 1903 (5); v SA 1898 (2)*

Tyldesley (R. K.) 7: v A 1930 (2); v SA 1924 (4); *v A 1924 (1)*

Tylecote, E. F. S. 6: v A 1886 (2); *v A 1882 (4)*

Tyler (E. J.) 1: *v SA 1895*

Tyson (F. H.) 17: v A 1956 (1); v SA 1955 (1); v P 1954 (1); *v A 1954 (5) 1958 (2); v SA 1956 (2); v NZ 1954 (2) 1958 (2)*

Ulyett (G.) 25: v A 1882 (1) 1884 (3) 1886 (3) 1888 (2) 1890 (1); *v A 1876 (2) 1878 (1) 1881 (4) 1884 (5) 1887 (1); v SA 1888 (2)*

Underwood, D. L. 86: v A 1968 (4) 1972 (2) 1975 (4) 1977 (5); v WI 1966 (2) 1969 (2) 1973 (3) 1976 (5) 1980 (1); v NZ 1969 (3) 1973 (1); v In 1971 (1) 1974 (3); v P 1967 (2) 1971 (1) 1974 (3); *v A 1970 (5) 1974 (5) 1976 (1) 1979 (3); v WI 1973 (4); v NZ 1970 (2) 1974 (2); v In 1972 (4) 1976 (5) 1979 (1) 1981 (6); v P 1968 (3) 1972 (2); v SL 1981 (1)*

Valentine, B. H. 7: *v SA 1938 (5); v In 1933 (2)*

Verity (H.) 40: v A 1934 (5) 1938 (4); v SA 1935 (4); v WI 1933 (2) 1939 (1); v NZ 1931 (2) 1937 (1); v In 1936 (3); *v A 1932 (4) 1936 (5); v SA 1938 (5); v NZ 1932 (1); v In 1933 (3)*

Vernon, G. F. 1: *v A 1882*

Vine (J.) 2: *v A 1911 (2)*

Voce (W.) 27: v NZ 1931 (1) 1937 (1); v In 1932 (1) 1936 (1) 1946 (1); *v A 1932 (4) 1936 (5) 1946 (2); v SA 1930 (5); v WI 1929 (4); v NZ 1932 (2)*

Waddington (A.) 2: *v A 1920* (2)
Wainwright (E.) 5: v A 1893 (1); *v A 1897* (4)
Walker (P. M.) 3: v SA 1960 (3)
Walters, C. F. 11: v A 1934 (5); v WI 1933 (3); *v In 1933* (3)
Ward, A. 5: v WI 1976 (1); v NZ 1969 (3); v P 1971 (1)
Ward (A.) 7: v A 1893 (2); *v A 1894* (5)
Wardle (J. H.) 28: v A 1953 (3) 1956 (1); v SA 1951 (2) 1955 (3); v WI 1950 (1) 1957 (1); v P 1954 (4); *v A 1954* (4); *v SA 1956* (4); *v WI 1947* (1) 1953 (2); *v NZ 1954* (2)
Warner, P. F. 15: v A 1909 (1) 1912 (1); v SA 1912 (1); *v A 1903* (5); *v SA 1898* (2) 1905 (5)
Warr, J. J. 2: *v A 1950* (2)
Warren (A. R.) 1: v A 1905
Washbrook (C.) 37: v A 1948 (4) 1956 (3); v SA 1947 (5); v WI 1950 (2); v NZ 1937 (1) 1949 (2); v In 1946 (3); *v A 1946* (5) *1950* (5); *v SA 1948* (5); *v NZ 1946* (1) *1950* (1)
Watkin, S. L. 2: v WI 1991 (2)
Watkins (A. J.) 15: v A 1948 (1); v NZ 1949 (1); v In 1952 (3); *v SA 1948* (5); *v In 1951* (5)
Watson (W.) 23: v A 1953 (3) 1956 (2); v SA 1951 (1) 1955 (1); v NZ 1958 (2); v In 1952 (1); *v A 1958* (2); *v WI 1953* (5); *v NZ 1958* (2)
Webbe, A. J. 1: *v A 1878*
Wellard (A. W.) 2: v A 1938 (1); v NZ 1937 (1)
Wharton (A.) 1: v NZ 1949
Whitaker, J. J. 1: *v A 1986*
White (D. W.) 2: *v P 1961* (2)
White, J. C. 15: v A 1921 (1) 1930 (1); v SA 1929 (3); v WI 1928 (1); *v A 1928* (5); *v SA 1930* (4)
Whysall (W. W.) 4: v A 1930 (1); *v A 1924* (3)
Wilkinson (L. L.) 3: *v SA 1938* (3)
Willey, P. 26: v A 1980 (1) 1981 (4) 1985 (1); v WI 1976 (2) 1980 (5); v NZ 1986 (1); v In 1979 (1); *v A 1979* (3); *v WI 1980* (4) *1985* (4)
Williams, N. F. 1: v In 1990
Willis, R. G. D. 90: v A 1977 (5) 1981 (6); v WI 1973 (1) 1976 (2) 1980 (4) 1984 (2); v NZ 1978 (3) 1983 (4); v In 1974 (1) 1979 (3) 1982 (3); v P 1974 (1) 1978 (3) 1982 (2); *v A 1970* (4) *1974* (5) *1976* (1) *1978* (6) *1979* (3) *1982* (5); *v WI 1973* (3) *1982* (5); *v NZ 1970* (1) *1977* (3) *1983* (3); *v In 1976* (5) *1981* (5); *v P 1977* (3) *1983* (1)
Wilson, C. E. M. 2: *v SA 1898* (2)
Wilson, D. 6: *v NZ 1970* (1); *v In 1963* (5)
Wilson, E. R. 1: *v A 1920*
Wood (A.) 4: v A 1938 (1); v WI 1939 (3)
Wood, B. 12: v A 1972 (1) 1975 (3); v WI 1976 (1); v P 1978 (1); *v NZ 1974* (2); *v In 1972* (3); *v P 1972* (1)
Wood, G. E. C. 3: v SA 1924 (3)
Wood (H.) 4: v A 1888 (1); *v SA 1888* (2) *1891* (1)
Wood (R.) 1: *v A 1886*
Woods S. M. J. 3: *v SA 1895* (3)
Woolley (F. E.) 64: v A 1909 (1) 1912 (3) 1921 (5) 1926 (5) 1930 (2) 1934 (1); v SA 1912 (3) 1924 (5) 1929 (5); v NZ 1931 (1); v In 1932 (1); *v A 1911* (5) *1920* (5) *1924* (5); *v SA 1909* (5) *1913* (5) *1922* (5); *v NZ 1929* (4)
Woolmer, R. A. 19: v A 1975 (2) 1977 (5) 1981 (2); v WI 1976 (5) 1980 (2); *v A 1976* (1); *v In 1976* (2)
Worthington (T. S.) 9: v In 1936 (2); *v A 1936* (3); *v NZ 1929* (4)
Wright, C. W. 3: *v SA 1895* (3)
Wright (D. V. P.) 34: v A 1938 (3) 1948 (1); v SA 1947 (4); v WI 1939 (3) 1950 (1); v NZ 1949 (1); v In 1946 (2); *v A 1946* (5) *1950* (5); *v SA 1938* (3) *1948* (3); *v NZ 1946* (1) *1950* (2)
Wyatt, R. E. S. 40: v A 1930 (1) 1934 (4); v SA 1929 (2) 1935 (5); v WI 1933 (2); v In 1936 (1); *v A 1932* (5) *1936* (2); *v SA 1927* (5) *1930* (5); *v WI 1929* (2) *1934* (4); *v NZ 1932* (2)
Wynyard, E. G. 3: v A 1896 (1); *v SA 1905* (2)

Yardley, N. W. D. 20: v A 1948 (5); v SA 1947 (5); v WI 1950 (3); *v A 1946* (5); *v SA 1938* (1); *v NZ 1946* (1)
Young (H. I.) 2: v A 1899 (2)
Young (J. A.) 8: v A 1948 (3); v SA 1947 (1); v NZ 1949 (2); *v SA 1948* (2)
Young, R. A. 2: *v A 1907* (2)

AUSTRALIA

Number of Test cricketers: 352

a'Beckett, E. L. 4: v E 1928 (2); v SA 1931 (1); *v E 1930 (1)*
Alderman, T. M. 41: v E 1982 (1) 1990 (4); v WI 1981 (2) 1984 (3) 1988 (2); v NZ 1989 (1); v P 1981 (3) 1989 (2); v SL 1989 (2); *v E 1981 (6) 1989 (6); v WI 1983 (3) 1990 (1); v NZ 1981 (3) 1989 (1); v P 1982 (1)*
Alexander, G. 2: v E 1884 (1); *v E 1880 (1)*
Alexander, H. H. 1: v E 1932
Allan, F. E. 1: v E 1878
Allan, P. J. 1: v E 1965
Allen, R. C. 1: v E 1886
Andrews, T. J. E. 16: v E 1924 (3); *v E 1921 (5) 1926 (5); v SA 1921 (3)*
Archer, K. A. 5: v E 1950 (3); v WI 1951 (2)
Archer, R. G. 19: v E 1954 (4); v SA 1952 (1); *v E 1953 (3) 1956 (5); v WI 1954 (5); v P 1956 (1)*
Armstrong, W. W. 50: v E 1901 (4) 1903 (5) 1907 (5) 1911 (5) 1920 (5); v SA 1910 (5); *v E 1902 (5) 1905 (5) 1909 (5) 1921 (5); v SA 1902 (3)*

Badcock, C. L. 7: v E 1936 (3); *v E 1938 (4)*
Bannerman, A. C. 28: v E 1878 (1) 1881 (3) 1882 (4) 1884 (4) 1886 (1) 1887 (1) 1891 (3); *v E 1880 (1) 1882 (1) 1884 (3) 1888 (3) 1893 (3)*
Bannerman, C. 3: v E 1876 (2) 1878 (1)
Bardsley, W. 41: v E 1911 (4) 1920 (5) 1924 (3); v SA 1910 (5); *v E 1909 (5) 1912 (3) 1921 (5) 1926 (5); v SA 1912 (3) 1921 (3)*
Barnes, S. G. 13: v E 1946 (4); v In 1947 (3); *v E 1938 (1) 1948 (4); v NZ 1945 (1)*
Barnett, B. A. 4: *v E 1938 (4)*
Barrett, J. E. 2: *v E 1890 (2)*
Beard, G. R. 3: *v P 1979 (3)*
Benaud, J. 3: v P 1972 (2); *v WI 1972 (1)*
Benaud, R. 63: v E 1954 (5) 1958 (5) 1962 (5); v SA 1952 (4) 1963 (4); v WI 1951 (1) 1960 (5); *v E 1953 (3) 1956 (5) 1961 (4); v SA 1957 (5); v WI 1954 (5); v In 1956 (3) 1959 (5); v P 1956 (1) 1959 (3)*
Bennett, M. J. 3: v WI 1984 (2); *v E 1985 (1)*
Blackham, J. McC. 35: v E 1876 (2) 1878 (1) 1881 (4) 1882 (4) 1884 (2) 1886 (1) 1887 (1) 1891 (3) 1894 (1); *v E 1880 (1) 1882 (1) 1884 (3) 1886 (3) 1888 (3) 1890 (2) 1893 (3)*
Blackie, D. D. 3: v E 1928 (3)
Bonnor, G. J. 17: v E 1882 (4) 1884 (3); *v E 1880 (1) 1882 (1) 1884 (3) 1886 (2) 1888 (3)*
Boon, D. C. 63: v E 1986 (4) 1987 (1) 1990 (5); v WI 1984 (3) 1988 (5); v NZ 1985 (3) 1987 (3) 1989 (1); v In 1985 (3) 1991 (5); v P 1989 (2); v SL 1987 (1) 1989 (2); *v E 1985 (4) 1989 (6); v WI 1990 (5); v NZ 1985 (3) 1989 (1); v In 1986 (3); v P 1988 (3)*
Booth, B. C. 29: v E 1962 (5) 1965 (3); v SA 1963 (4); v P 1964 (1); *v E 1961 (2) 1964 (5); v WI 1964 (5); v In 1964 (3); v P 1964 (1)*
Border, A. R. 130: v E 1978 (3) 1979 (3) 1982 (5) 1986 (5) 1987 (1) 1990 (5); v WI 1979 (3) 1981 (3) 1984 (5) 1988 (5); v NZ 1980 (3) 1985 (3) 1987 (3) 1989 (1); v In 1980 (3) 1985 (3) 1991 (5); v P 1978 (2) 1981 (3) 1983 (5) 1989 (3); v SL 1987 (1) 1989 (2); *v E 1980 (1) 1981 (6) 1985 (6) 1989 (6); v WI 1983 (5) 1990 (5); v NZ 1981 (3) 1985 (3) 1989 (1); v In 1979 (6) 1986 (3); v P 1979 (3) 1982 (3) 1988 (3); v SL 1982 (1)*
Boyle, H. F. 12: v E 1878 (1) 1881 (4) 1882 (1) 1884 (1); *v E 1880 (1) 1882 (1) 1884 (3)*
Bradman, D. G. 52: v E 1928 (4) 1932 (4) 1936 (5) 1946 (5); v SA 1931 (5); v WI 1930 (5); v In 1947 (5); *v E 1930 (5) 1934 (5) 1938 (4) 1948 (5)*
Bright, R. J. 25: v E 1979 (1); v WI 1979 (1); v NZ 1985 (1); v In 1985 (3); *v E 1977 (3) 1980 (1) 1981 (5); v NZ 1985 (2); v In 1986 (3); v P 1979 (3) 1982 (2)*
Bromley, E. H. 2: v E 1932 (1); *v E 1934 (1)*
Brown, W. A. 22: v E 1936 (2); v In 1947 (3); *v E 1934 (5) 1938 (4) 1948 (2); v SA 1935 (5); v NZ 1945 (1)*
Bruce, W. 14: v E 1884 (2) 1891 (3) 1894 (4); *v E 1886 (2) 1893 (3)*
Burge, P. J. 42: v E 1954 (1) 1958 (1) 1962 (3) 1965 (4); v SA 1963 (5); v WI 1960 (5); *v E 1956 (3) 1961 (5) 1964 (5); v SA 1957 (1); v WI 1954 (1); v In 1956 (3) 1959 (2) 1964 (3); v P 1959 (2) 1964 (1)*

Burke, J. W. 24: v E 1950 (2) 1954 (2) 1958 (5); v WI 1951 (1); *v E 1956 (5); v SA 1957 (5); v In 1956 (3); v P 1956 (1)*

Burn, K. E. 2: *v E 1890 (2)*

Burton, F. J. 2: v E 1886 (1) 1887 (1)

Callaway, S. T. 3: v E 1891 (2) 1894 (1)

Callen, I. W. 1: v In 1977

Campbell, G. D. 4: v P 1989 (1); v SL 1989 (1); *v E 1989 (1); v NZ 1989 (1)*

Carkeek, W. 6: *v E 1912 (3); v SA 1912 (3)*

Carlson, P. H. 2: v E 1978 (2)

Carter, H. 28: v E 1907 (5) 1911 (5) 1920 (2); v SA 1910 (5); *v E 1909 (5) 1921 (4); v SA 1921 (3)*

Chappell, G. S. 87: v E 1970 (5) 1974 (6) 1976 (1) 1979 (3) 1982 (5); v WI 1975 (6) 1979 (3) 1981 (3); v NZ 1973 (3) 1980 (3); v In 1980 (3); v P 1972 (3) 1976 (3) 1981 (3) 1983 (5); *v E 1972 (5) 1975 (4) 1977 (5) 1980 (1); v WI 1972 (5); v NZ 1973 (3) 1976 (2) 1981 (3); v P 1979 (3); v SL 1982 (1)*

Chappell, I. M. 75: v E 1965 (2) 1970 (6) 1974 (6) 1979 (2); v WI 1968 (5) 1975 (6) 1979 (1); v NZ 1973 (3); v In 1967 (4); v P 1964 (1) 1972 (3); *v E 1968 (5) 1972 (5) 1975 (4); v SA 1966 (5) 1969 (4); v WI 1972 (5); v NZ 1973 (3); v In 1969 (5)*

Chappell, T. M. 3: *v E 1981 (3)*

Charlton, P. C. 2: *v E 1890 (2)*

Chipperfield, A. G. 14: v E 1936 (3); *v E 1934 (5) 1938 (1); v SA 1935 (5)*

Clark, W. M. 10: v In 1977 (5); v P 1978 (1); *v WI 1977 (4)*

Colley, D. J. 3: *v E 1972 (3)*

Collins, H. L. 19: v E 1920 (5) 1924 (5); *v E 1921 (3) 1926 (3); v SA 1921 (3)*

Coningham, A. 1: v E 1894

Connolly, A. N. 29: v E 1965 (1) 1970 (1); v SA 1963 (3); v WI 1968 (5); v In 1967 (3); *v E 1968 (5); v SA 1969 (4); v In 1964 (2); 1969 (5)*

Cooper, B. B. 1: v E 1876

Cooper, W. H. 2: v E 1881 (1) 1884 (1)

Corling, G. E. 5: *v E 1964 (5)*

Cosier, G. J. 18: v E 1976 (1) 1978 (2); v WI 1975 (3); v In 1977 (4); v P 1976 (3); *v WI 1977 (3); v NZ 1976 (2)*

Cottam, W. J. 1: v E 1886

Cotter, A. 21: v E 1903 (2) 1907 (2) 1911 (4); v SA 1910 (5); *v E 1905 (3) 1909 (5)*

Coulthard, G. 1: v E 1881

Cowper, R. M. 27: v E 1965 (4); v In 1967 (4); v P 1964 (1); *v E 1964 (1) 1968 (4); v SA 1966 (5); v WI 1964 (5); v In 1964 (2); v P 1964 (1)*

Craig, I. D. 11: v SA 1952 (1); *v E 1956 (2); v SA 1957 (5); v In 1956 (2); v P 1956 (1)*

Crawford, W. P. A. 4: *v E 1956 (1); v In 1956 (3)*

Darling, J. 34: v E 1894 (5) 1897 (5) 1901 (3); *v E 1896 (3) 1899 (5) 1902 (5) 1905 (5); v SA 1902 (3)*

Darling, L. S. 12: v E 1932 (2) 1936 (1); *v E 1934 (4); v SA 1935 (5)*

Darling, W. M. 14: v E 1978 (4); v In 1977 (1); v P 1978 (1); *v WI 1977 (3); v In 1979 (5)*

Davidson, A. K. 44: v E 1954 (3) 1958 (5) 1962 (5); v WI 1960 (4); *v E 1953 (5) 1956 (2) 1961 (5); v SA 1957 (5); v In 1956 (1) 1959 (5); v P 1956 (1) 1959 (3)*

Davis, I. C. 15: v E 1976 (1); v NZ 1973 (3); v P 1976 (3); *v E 1977 (3); v NZ 1973 (3) 1976 (2)*

Davis, S. P. 1: *v NZ 1985*

De Courcy, J. H. 3: *v E 1953 (3)*

Dell, A. R. 2: v E 1970 (1); v NZ 1973 (1)

Dodemaide, A. I. C. 8: v E 1987 (1); v WI 1988 (2); v NZ 1987 (1); v SL 1987 (1); *v P 1988 (3)*

Donnan, H. 5: v E 1891 (2); *v E 1896 (3)*

Dooland, B. 3: v E 1946 (2); v In 1947 (1)

Duff, R. A. 22: v E 1901 (4) 1903 (5); *v E 1902 (5) 1905 (5); v SA 1902 (3)*

Duncan, J. R. F. 1: v E 1970

Dyer, G. C. 6: v E 1986 (1) 1987 (1); v NZ 1987 (3); v SL 1987 (1)

Dymock, G. 21: v E 1974 (1) 1978 (3) 1979 (3); v WI 1979 (2); v NZ 1973 (1); v P 1978 (1); *v NZ 1973 (2); v In 1979 (5); v P 1979 (3)*

Dyson, J. 30: v E 1982 (5); v WI 1981 (2) 1984 (3); v NZ 1980 (3); v In 1977 (3) 1980 (3); *v E 1981 (5); v NZ 1981 (3); v P 1982 (3)*

Eady, C. J. 2: v E 1901 (1); *v E 1896 (1)*

Eastwood, K. H. 1: v E 1970

Ebeling, H. I. 1: *v E 1934*
Edwards, J. D. 3: *v E 1888 (3)*
Edwards, R. 20: v E 1974 (5); v P 1972 (2); *v E 1972 (4) 1975 (4); v WI 1972 (5)*
Edwards, W. J. 3: v E 1974 (3)
Emery, S. H. 4: *v E 1912 (2); v SA 1912 (2)*
Evans, E. 6: v E 1881 (2) 1882 (1) 1884 (1); *v E 1886 (2)*

Fairfax, A. G. 10: v E 1928 (1); v WI 1930 (5); *v E 1930 (4)*
Favell, L. E. 19: v E 1954 (4) 1958 (2); v WI 1960 (4); *v WI 1954 (2); v In 1959 (4); v P 1959 (3)*
Ferris, J. J. 8: v E 1886 (2) 1887 (1); *v E 1888 (3) 1890 (2)*
Fingleton, J. H. 18: v E 1932 (3) 1936 (5); v SA 1931 (1); *v E 1938 (4); v SA 1935 (5)*
Fleetwood-Smith, L. O'B. 10: v E 1936 (3); *v E 1938 (4); v SA 1935 (5)*
Francis, B. C. 3: *v E 1972 (3)*
Freeman, E. W. 11: v WI 1968 (4); v In 1967 (2); *v E 1968 (2); v SA 1969 (2); v In 1969 (1)*
Freer, F. W. 1: v E 1946

Gannon, J. B. 3: v In 1977 (3)
Garrett, T. W. 19: v E 1876 (2) 1878 (1) 1881 (3) 1882 (3) 1884 (3) 1886 (2) 1887 (1); *v E 1882 (1) 1886 (3)*
Gaunt, R. A. 3: v SA 1963 (1); *v E 1961 (1); v SA 1957 (1)*
Gehrs, D. R. A. 6: v E 1903 (1); v SA 1910 (4); *v E 1905 (1)*
Giffen, G. 31: v E 1881 (3) 1882 (4) 1884 (3) 1891 (3) 1894 (5); *v E 1882 (1) 1884 (3) 1886 (3) 1893 (3) 1896 (3)*
Giffen, W. F. 3: v E 1886 (1) 1891 (2)
Gilbert, D. R. 9: v NZ 1985 (3); v In 1985 (2); *v E 1985 (1); v NZ 1985 (1); v In 1986 (2)*
Gilmour, G. J. 15: v E 1976 (1); v WI 1975 (5); v NZ 1973 (2); v P 1976 (3); *v E 1975 (1); v NZ 1973 (1) 1976 (2)*
Gleeson, J. W. 29: v E 1970 (5); v WI 1968 (5); v In 1967 (4); *v E 1968 (5) 1972 (3); v SA 1969 (4); v In 1969 (3)*
Graham, H. 6: v E 1894 (2); *v E 1893 (3) 1896 (1)*
Gregory, D. W. 3: v E 1876 (2) 1878 (1)
Gregory, E. J. 1: v E 1876
Gregory, J. M. 24: v E 1920 (5) 1924 (5) 1928 (1); *v E 1921 (5) 1926 (5); v SA 1921 (3)*
Gregory, R. G. 2: v E 1936 (2)
Gregory, S. E. 58: v E 1891 (1) 1894 (5) 1897 (5) 1901 (5) 1903 (4) 1907 (2) 1911 (1); *v E 1890 (2) 1893 (3) 1896 (3) 1899 (5) 1902 (5) 1905 (3) 1909 (5) 1912 (3); v SA 1902 (3) 1912 (3)*
Grimmett, C. V. 37: v E 1924 (1) 1928 (5) 1932 (3); v SA 1931 (5); v WI 1930 (5); *v E 1926 (3) 1930 (5) 1934 (5); v SA 1935 (5)*
Groube, T. U. 1: *v E 1880*
Grout, A. T. W. 51: v E 1958 (5) 1962 (2) 1965 (5); v SA 1963 (5); v WI 1960 (5); *v E 1961 (5) 1964 (5); v SA 1957 (5); v WI 1964 (5); v In 1959 (4) 1964 (1); v P 1959 (3) 1964 (1)*
Guest, C. E. J. 1: v E 1962

Hamence, R. A. 3: v E 1946 (1); v In 1947 (2)
Hammond, J. R. 5: *v WI 1972 (5)*
Harry, J. 1: v E 1894
Hartigan, R. J. 2: v E 1907 (2)
Hartkopf, A. E. V. 1: v E 1924
Harvey, M. R. 1: v E 1946
Harvey, R. N. 79: v E 1950 (5) 1954 (5) 1958 (5) 1962 (5); v SA 1952 (5); v WI 1951 (5) 1960 (4); v In 1947 (2); *v E 1948 (2) 1953 (5) 1956 (5) 1961 (5); v SA 1949 (5) 1957 (4); v WI 1954 (5); v In 1956 (3) 1959 (5); v P 1956 (1) 1959 (3)*
Hassett, A. L. 43: v E 1946 (5) 1950 (5); v SA 1952 (5); v WI 1951 (4); v In 1947 (4); *v E 1938 (4) 1948 (5) 1953 (5); v SA 1949 (5); v NZ 1945 (1)*
Hawke, N. J. N. 27: v E 1962 (1) 1965 (4); v SA 1963 (4); v In 1967 (1); v P 1964 (1); *v E 1964 (5) 1968 (2); v SA 1966 (2); v WI 1964 (5); v In 1964 (1); v P 1964 (1)*
Hazlitt, G. R. 9: v E 1907 (2) 1911 (1); *v E 1912 (3); v SA 1912 (3)*
Healy, I. A. 36: v E 1990 (5); v WI 1988 (5); v NZ 1989 (1); v I 1991 (5); v P 1989 (3); v SL 1989 (2); *v E 1989 (6); v WI 1990 (5); v NZ 1989 (1); v P 1988 (3)*
Hendry, H. S. T. L. 11: v E 1924 (1) 1928 (4); *v E 1921 (4); v SA 1921 (2)*
Hibbert, P. A. 1: v In 1977

Higgs, J. D. 22: v E 1978 (5) 1979 (1); v WI 1979 (1); v NZ 1980 (3); v In 1980 (2); *v WI 1977 (4); v In 1979 (6)*

Hilditch, A. M. J. 18: v E 1978 (1); v WI 1984 (2); v NZ 1985 (1); v P 1978 (2); *v E 1985 (6); v In 1979 (6)*

Hill, C. 49: v E 1897 (5) 1901 (5) 1903 (5) 1907 (5) 1911 (5); v SA 1910 (5); *v E 1896 (3) 1899 (3) 1902 (5) 1905 (5); v SA 1902 (3)*

Hill, J. C. 3: *v E 1953 (2); v WI 1954 (1)*

Hoare, D. E. 1: v WI 1960

Hodges, J. R. 2: v E 1876 (2)

Hogan, T. G. 7: v P 1983 (1); *v WI 1983 (5); v SL 1982 (1)*

Hogg, R. M. 38: v E 1978 (6) 1982 (3); v WI 1979 (2) 1984 (4); v NZ 1980 (2); v In 1980 (2); v P 1978 (2) 1983 (4); *v E 1981 (2); v WI 1983 (4); v In 1979 (6); v SL 1982 (1)*

Hohns, T. V. 7: v WI 1988 (2); *v E 1989 (5)*

Hole, G. B. 18: v E 1950 (1) 1954 (3); v SA 1952 (4); v WI 1951 (5); *v E 1953 (5)*

Holland, R. G. 11: v WI 1984 (3); v NZ 1985 (3); v In 1985 (1); *v E 1985 (4)*

Hookes, D. W. 23: v E 1976 (1) 1982 (5); v WI 1979 (1); v NZ 1985 (2); v In 1985 (2); *v E 1977 (5); v WI 1983 (5); v P 1979 (1); v SL 1982 (1)*

Hopkins, A. J. Y. 20: v E 1901 (2) 1903 (5); *v E 1902 (5) 1905 (3) 1909 (2); v SA 1902 (3)*

Horan, T. P. 15: v E 1876 (1) 1878 (1) 1881 (4) 1882 (4) 1884 (4); *v E 1882 (1)*

Hordern, H. V. 7: v E 1911 (5); v SA 1910 (2)

Hornibrook, P. M. 6: v E 1928 (1); *v E 1930 (5)*

Howell, W. P. 18: v E 1897 (3) 1901 (4) 1903 (3); *v E 1899 (5) 1902 (1); v SA 1902 (2)*

Hughes, K. J. 70: v E 1978 (6) 1979 (3) 1982 (5); v WI 1979 (3) 1981 (3) 1984 (4); v NZ 1980 (3); v In 1977 (2) 1980 (3); v P 1978 (2) 1983 (3) 1983 (5); *v E 1977 (1) 1980 (1) 1981 (6); v WI 1983 (5); v NZ 1981 (3); v In 1979 (6); v P 1979 (1) 1982 (3)*

Hughes, M. G. 37: v E 1986 (4) 1990 (4); v WI 1988 (4); v NZ 1987 (1) 1989 (1); v In 1985 (1) 1991 (5); v P 1989 (3); *v E 1989 (6); v WI 1990 (5)*

Hunt, W. A. 1: v SA 1931

Hurst, A. G. 12: v E 1978 (6); v NZ 1973 (1); v In 1977 (1); v P 1978 (2); *v In 1979 (2)*

Hurwood, A. 2: v WI 1930 (2)

Inverarity, R. J. 6: v WI 1968 (1); *v E 1968 (2) 1972 (3)*

Iredale, F. A. 14: v E 1894 (5) 1897 (4); *v E 1896 (3) 1899 (3)*

Ironmonger, H. 14: v E 1928 (2) 1932 (4); v SA 1931 (4); v WI 1930 (4)

Iverson, J. B. 5: v E 1950 (5)

Jackson, A. 8: v E 1928 (2); v WI 1930 (4); *v E 1930 (2)*

Jarman, B. N. 19: v E 1962 (3); v WI 1968 (4); v In 1967 (4); v P 1964 (1); *v E 1968 (4); v In 1959 (1); 1964 (2)*

Jarvis, A. H. 11: v E 1884 (3) 1894 (4); *v E 1886 (2) 1888 (2)*

Jenner, T. J. 9: v E 1970 (2) 1974 (2); v WI 1975 (1); *v WI 1972 (4)*

Jennings, C. B. 6: *v E 1912 (3); v SA 1912 (3)*

Johnson I. W. 45: v E 1946 (4) 1950 (5) 1954 (4); v SA 1952 (1); v WI 1951 (4); v In 1947 (4); *v E 1948 (4) 1956 (5); v SA 1949 (5); v WI 1954 (5); v NZ 1945 (1); v In 1956 (2); v P 1956 (1)*

Johnson, L. J. 1: v In 1947

Johnston W. A. 40: v E 1950 (5) 1954 (4); v SA 1952 (5); v WI 1951 (5); v In 1947 (4); *v E 1948 (5) 1953 (3); v SA 1949 (5); v WI 1954 (4)*

Jones, D. M. 49: v E 1986 (5) 1987 (1) 1990 (5); v WI 1988 (3); v NZ 1987 (3) 1989 (1); v I 1991 (5); v P 1989 (3); v SL 1987 (1) 1989 (2); *v E 1989 (6); v WI 1983 (2) 1990 (5); v NZ 1989 (1); v In 1986 (3); v P 1988 (3)*

Jones, E. 19: v E 1894 (1) 1897 (5) 1901 (2); *v E 1896 (3) 1899 (5) 1902 (2); v SA 1902 (1)*

Jones, S. P. 12: v E 1881 (2) 1884 (4) 1886 (1) 1887 (1); *v E 1882 (1) 1886 (3)*

Joslin, L. R. 1: v In 1967

Kelleway, C. 26: v E 1911 (4) 1920 (5) 1924 (5) 1928 (1); v SA 1910 (5); *v E 1912 (3); v SA 1912 (3)*

Kelly, J. J. 36: v E 1897 (5) 1901 (5) 1903 (5); *v E 1896 (3) 1899 (5) 1902 (5) 1905 (5); v SA 1902 (3)*

Kelly, T. J. D. 2: v E 1876 (1) 1878 (1)

Kendall, T. 2: v E 1876 (2)

Kent, M. F. 3: *v E 1981 (3)*

Kerr, R. B. 2: v NZ 1985 (2)

Kippax, A. F. 22: v E 1924 (1) 1928 (5) 1932 (1); v SA 1931 (4); v WI 1930 (5); *v E 1930 (4) 1934 (1)*

Kline L. F. 13: v E 1958 (2); v WI 1960 (2); *v SA 1957 (5); v In 1959 (3); v P 1959 (1)*

Laird, B. M. 21: v E 1979 (2); v WI 1979 (3) 1981 (3); v P 1981 (3); *v E 1980 (1); v NZ 1981 (3); v P 1979 (3) 1982 (3)*

Langley, G. R. A. 26: v E 1954 (2); v SA 1952 (5); v WI 1951 (5); *v E 1953 (4) 1956 (3); v WI 1954 (4); v In 1956 (2); v P 1956 (1)*

Laughlin, T. J. 3: v E 1978 (1); *v WI 1977 (2)*

Laver, F. 15: v E 1901 (1) 1903 (1); *v E 1899 (4) 1905 (5) 1909 (4)*

Lawry, W. M. 67: v E 1962 (5) 1965 (5) 1970 (5); v SA 1963 (5); v WI 1968 (5); v In 1967 (4); v P 1964 (1); *v E 1961 (5) 1964 (5) 1968 (4); v SA 1966 (5) 1969 (4); v WI 1964 (5); v In 1964 (3) 1969 (5); v P 1964 (1)*

Lawson, G. F. 46: v E 1982 (5) 1986 (1); v WI 1981 (1) 1984 (5) 1988 (1); v NZ 1980 (1) 1985 (2) 1989 (1); v SL 1989 (1); *v E 1981 (3) 1985 (6) 1989 (6); v WI 1983 (5); v P 1982 (3)*

Lee, P. K. 2: v E 1932 (1); v SA 1931 (1)

Lillee, D. K. 70: v E 1970 (2) 1974 (6) 1976 (1) 1979 (3) 1982 (1); v WI 1975 (5) 1979 (3) 1981 (3); v NZ 1980 (3); v P 1972 (3) 1976 (3) 1981 (3) 1983 (5); *v E 1972 (5) 1975 (4) 1980 (1) 1981 (6); v WI 1972 (1); v NZ 1976 (2) 1981 (3); v P 1979 (3); v SL 1982 (1)*

Lindwall, R. R. 61: v E 1946 (4) 1950 (5) 1954 (4) 1958 (2); v SA 1952 (4); v WI 1951 (5); v In 1947 (5); *v E 1948 (5) 1953 (5) 1956 (4); v SA 1949 (4); v WI 1954 (5); v NZ 1945 (1); v In 1956 (3) 1959 (2); v P 1956 (1) 1959 (2)*

Love, H. S. B. 1: v E 1932

Loxton, S. J. E. 12: v E 1950 (3); v In 1947 (1); *v E 1948 (3); v SA 1949 (5)*

Lyons, J. J. 14: v E 1886 (1) 1891 (3) 1894 (3) 1897 (1); *v E 1888 (1) 1890 (2) 1893 (3)*

McAlister, P. A. 8: v E 1903 (2) 1907 (4); *v E 1909 (2)*

Macartney, C. G. 35: v E 1907 (5) 1911 (1) 1920 (2); v SA 1910 (4); *v E 1909 (5) 1912 (3) 1921 (5) 1926 (5); v SA 1912 (3) 1921 (2)*

McCabe, S. J. 39: v E 1932 (5) 1936 (5); v SA 1931 (5); v WI 1930 (5); *v E 1930 (5) 1934 (5) 1938 (4); v SA 1935 (5)*

McCool, C. L. 14: v E 1946 (5); v In 1947 (3); *v SA 1949 (5) v NZ 1945 (1)*

McCormick, E. L. 12: v E 1936 (4); *v E 1938 (3); v SA 1935 (5)*

McCosker, R. B. 25: v E 1974 (3) 1976 (1) 1979 (2); v WI 1975 (5) 1979 (1); v P 1976 (3); *v E 1975 (4) 1977 (5); v NZ 1976 (2)*

McDermott, C. J. 36: v E 1986 (1) 1987 (1) 1990 (2); v WI 1984 (2) 1988 (2); v NZ 1985 (2) 1987 (3); v In 1985 (2) 1991 (5); v SL 1987 (1); *v E 1985 (6); v WI 1990 (5); v NZ 1985 (2); v In 1986 (2)*

McDonald, C. C. 47: v E 1954 (2) 1958 (5); v SA 1952 (5); v WI 1951 (1) 1960 (5); *v E 1956 (5) 1961 (3); v SA 1957 (5); v WI 1954 (5); v In 1956 (2) 1959 (5); v P 1956 (1) 1959 (3)*

McDonald, E. A. 11: v E 1920 (3); *v E 1921 (5); v SA 1921 (3)*

McDonnell, P. S. 19: v E 1881 (4) 1882 (3) 1884 (2) 1886 (2) 1887 (1); *v E 1880 (1) 1884 (3) 1888 (3)*

McIlwraith, J. 1: *v E 1886*

Mackay, K. D. 37: v E 1958 (5) 1962 (3); v WI 1960 (5); *v E 1956 (3) 1961 (5); v SA 1957 (5); v In 1956 (3) 1959 (5); v P 1959 (3)*

McKenzie, G. D. 60: v E 1962 (5) 1965 (4) 1970 (3); v SA 1963 (5); v WI 1968 (5); v In 1967 (2); v P 1964 (1); *v E 1961 (3) 1964 (5) 1968 (5); v SA 1966 (5) 1969 (3); v WI 1964 (5); v In 1964 (3) 1969 (5); v P 1964 (1)*

McKibbin, T. R. 5: v E 1894 (1) 1897 (2); *v E 1896 (2)*

McLaren, J. W. 1: v E 1911

Maclean, J. A. 4: v E 1978 (4)

McLeod, C. E. 17: v E 1894 (1) 1897 (5) 1901 (2) 1903 (3); *v E 1899 (1) 1905 (5)*

McLeod, R. W. 6: v E 1891 (3); *v E 1893 (3)*

McShane, P. G. 3: v E 1884 (1) 1886 (1) 1887 (1)

Maddocks, L. V. 7: v E 1954 (3); *v E 1956 (2); v WI 1954 (1); v In 1956 (1)*

Maguire, J. N. 3: v P 1983 (1); *v WI 1983 (2)*

Mailey, A. A. 21: v E 1920 (5) 1924 (5); *v E 1921 (3) 1926 (5); v SA 1921 (3)*

Mallett, A. A. 38: v E 1970 (2) 1974 (5) 1979 (1); v WI 1968 (1) 1975 (6) 1979 (1); v NZ 1973 (3); v P 1972 (2); *v E 1968 (1) 1972 (2) 1975 (4) 1980 (1); v SA 1969 (1); v NZ 1973 (3); v In 1969 (5)*

Malone, M. F. 1: *v E 1977*

Mann, A. L. 4: v In 1977 (4)

Marr, A. P. 1: v E 1884

Marsh, G. R. 50: v E 1986 (5) 1987 (1) 1990 (5); v WI 1988 (5); v NZ 1987 (3); v In 1985 (3) 1991 (4); v P 1989 (2); v SL 1987 (1); *v E 1989 (6); v WI 1990 (5); v NZ 1985 (3) 1989 (1); v In 1986 (3); v P 1988 (3)*

Marsh, R. W. 96: v E 1970 (6) 1974 (6) 1976 (1) 1979 (3) 1982 (5); v WI 1975 (6) 1979 (3) 1981 (3); v NZ 1973 (3) 1980 (3); v In 1980 (3); v P 1972 (3) 1976 (3) 1981 (3) 1983 (5); *v E 1972 (5) 1975 (4) 1977 (5) 1980 (1) 1981 (6); v WI 1972 (5); v NZ 1973 (3) 1976 (2) 1981 (3); v P 1979 (3) 1982 (3)*

Martin, J. W. 8: v SA 1963 (1); v WI 1960 (3); *v SA 1966 (1); v In 1964 (2); v P 1964 (1)*

Massie, H. H. 9: v E 1881 (4) 1882 (3) 1884 (1); *v E 1882 (3)*

Massie, R. A. L. 6: v P 1972 (2); *v E 1972 (4)*

Matthews, C. D. 3: v E 1986 (2); v WI 1988 (1)

Matthews, G. R. J. 28: v E 1986 (4) 1990 (5); v WI 1984 (1); v NZ 1985 (3); v In 1985 (3); v P 1983 (2); *v E 1985 (1); v WI 1983 (1) 1990 (2); v NZ 1985 (3); v In 1986 (3)*

Matthews, T. J. 8: v E 1911 (2); *v E 1912 (3); v SA 1912 (3)*

May, T. B. A. 7: v WI 1988 (3); v NZ 1987 (1); *v P 1988 (3)*

Mayne, E. R. 4: *v E 1912 (1); v SA 1912 (1) 1921 (2)*

Mayne, L. C. 6: *v SA 1969 (2); v WI 1964 (3); v In 1969 (1)*

Meckiff, I. 18: v E 1958 (4); v SA 1963 (1); v WI 1960 (2); *v SA 1957 (4); v In 1959 (5); v P 1959 (2)*

Meuleman, K. D. 1: *v NZ 1945*

Midwinter, W. E. 8: v E 1876 (2) 1882 (1) 1886 (2); *v E 1884 (3)*

Miller, K. R. 55: v E 1946 (5) 1950 (5) 1954 (4); v SA 1952 (4); v WI 1951 (5); v In 1947 (5); *v E 1948 (5) 1953 (5) 1956 (5); v SA 1949 (5); v WI 1954 (5); v NZ 1945 (1); v P 1956 (1)*

Minnett, R. B. 9: v E 1911 (5); *v E 1912 (1); v SA 1912 (3)*

Misson, F. M. 5: v WI 1960 (3); *v E 1961 (2)*

Moody, T. M. 5: v NZ 1989 (1); v I 1991 (1); v P 1989 (1); v SL 1989 (2)

Moroney, J. R. 7: v E 1950 (1); v WI 1951 (1); *v SA 1949 (5)*

Morris, A. R. 46: v E 1946 (5) 1950 (5) 1954 (4); v SA 1952 (5); v WI 1951 (4); v In 1947 (4); *v E 1948 (5) 1953 (5); v SA 1949 (5); v WI 1954 (4)*

Morris, S. 1: v E 1884

Moses, H. 6: v E 1886 (2) 1887 (1) 1891 (2) 1894 (1)

Moss, J. K. 1: v P 1978

Moule, W. H. 1: *v E 1880*

Murdoch, W. L. 18: v E 1876 (1) 1878 (1) 1881 (4) 1882 (4) 1884 (1); *v E 1880 (1) 1882 (1) 1884 (3) 1890 (2)*

Musgrove, H. 1: v E 1884

Nagel, L. E. 1: v E 1932 (1)

Nash, L. J. 2: v E 1936 (1); v SA 1931 (1)

Nitschke, H. C. 2: v SA 1931 (2)

Noble, M. A. 42: v E 1897 (4) 1901 (5) 1903 (5) 1907 (5); *v E 1899 (5) 1902 (5) 1905 (5) 1909 (5); v SA 1902 (3)*

Noblet, G. 3: v SA 1952 (1); v WI 1951 (1); *v SA 1949 (1)*

Nothling, O. E. 1: v E 1928

O'Brien, L. P. J. 5: v E 1932 (2) 1936 (1); *v SA 1935 (2)*

O'Connor, J. D. A. 4: v E 1907 (3); *v E 1909 (1)*

O'Donnell, S. P. 6: v NZ 1985 (1); *v E 1985 (5)*

Ogilvie, A. D. 5: v In 1977 (3); *v WI 1977 (2)*

O'Keeffe, K. J. 24: v E 1970 (2) 1976 (1); v NZ 1973 (3); v P 1972 (2) 1976 (3); *v E 1977 (3); v WI 1972 (5); v NZ 1973 (3) 1976 (2)*

Oldfield, W. A. 54: v E 1920 (3) 1924 (5) 1928 (5) 1932 (4) 1936 (5); v SA 1931 (5); v WI 1930 (5); *v E 1921 (1) 1926 (5) 1930 (5) 1934 (5); v SA 1921 (1) 1935 (5)*

O'Neill, N. C. 42: v E 1958 (5) 1962 (5); v SA 1963 (4); v WI 1960 (5); *v E 1961 (5) 1964 (4); v WI 1964 (4); v In 1959 (5) 1964 (2); v P 1959 (3)*

O'Reilly, W. J. 27: v E 1932 (1) 1936 (5); v SA 1931 (2); *v E 1934 (5) 1938 (4); v SA 1935 (5); v NZ 1945 (1)*

Oxenham, R. K. 7: v E 1928 (3); v SA 1931 (1); v WI 1930 (3)

Palmer, G. E. 17: v E 1881 (4) 1882 (4) 1884 (2); *v E 1880 (1) 1884 (3) 1886 (3)*

Park, R. L. 1: v E 1920

Pascoe, L. S. 14: v E 1979 (2); v WI 1979 (1) 1981 (1); v NZ 1980 (3); v In 1980 (3); *v E 1977 (3) 1980 (1)*

Pellew, C. E. 10: v E 1920 (4); *v E 1921 (5); v SA 1921 (1)*

Phillips, W. B. 27: v WI 1984 (2); v NZ 1985 (3); v In 1985 (3); v P 1983 (5); *v E 1985 (6); v WI 1983 (5); v NZ 1985 (3)*

Phillips, W. N. 1: v I 1991

Philpott, P. I. 8: v E 1965 (3); *v WI 1964 (5)*

Ponsford, W. H. 29: v E 1924 (5) 1928 (2) 1932 (3); v SA 1931 (4); v WI 1930 (5); *v E 1926 (2) 1930 (4) 1934 (4)*

Pope, R. J. 1: v E 1884

Rackemann, C. G. 12: v E 1982 (1) 1990 (1); v WI 1984 (1); v NZ 1989 (1); v P 1983 (2) 1989 (3); v SL 1989 (1); *v WI 1983 (1); v NZ 1989 (1)*

Ransford, V. S. 20: v E 1907 (5) 1911 (5); v SA 1910 (5); *v E 1909 (5)*

Redpath, I. R. 66: v E 1965 (1) 1970 (6) 1974 (6); v SA 1963 (1); v WI 1968 (5) 1975 (6); v In 1967 (3); v P 1972 (3); *v E 1964 (5) 1968 (5); v SA 1966 (5) 1969 (4); v WI 1972 (5); v NZ 1973 (3); v In 1964 (2) 1969 (5); v P 1964 (1)*

Reedman, J. C. 1: v E 1894

Reid, B. A. 26: v E 1986 (5) 1990 (4); v NZ 1987 (2); v In 1985 (3) 1991 (2); *v WI 1990 (2); v NZ 1985 (3); v In 1986 (2); v P 1988 (3)*

Reiffel, P. R. 1: v I 1991

Renneberg, D. A. 8: v In 1967 (3); *v SA 1966 (5)*

Richardson, A. J. 9: v E 1924 (4); *v E 1926 (5)*

Richardson, V. Y. 19: v E 1924 (3) 1928 (2) 1932 (5); *v E 1930 (4); v SA 1935 (5)*

Rigg, K. E. 8: v E 1936 (3); v SA 1931 (4); v WI 1930 (1)

Ring, D. T. 13: v SA 1952 (5); v WI 1951 (5); v In 1947 (1); *v E 1948 (1) 1953 (1)*

Ritchie, G. M. 30: v E 1986 (4); v WI 1984 (1); v NZ 1985 (3); v In 1985 (2); *v E 1985 (6); v WI 1983 (5); v NZ 1985 (3); v In 1986 (3); v P 1982 (3)*

Rixon, S. J. 13: v WI 1984 (3); v In 1977 (5); *v WI 1977 (5)*

Robertson, W. R. 1: v E 1884

Robinson, R. D. 3: *v E 1977 (3)*

Robinson, R. H. 1: v E 1936

Rorke, G. F. 4: v E 1958 (2); *v In 1959 (2)*

Rutherford, J. W. 1: *v In 1956*

Ryder, J. 20: v E 1920 (5) 1924 (3) 1928 (5); *v E 1926 (4); v SA 1921 (3)*

Saggers, R. A. 6: *v E 1948 (1); v SA 1949 (5)*

Saunders, J. V. 14: v E 1901 (1) 1903 (2) 1907 (5); *v E 1902 (4); v SA 1902 (2)*

Scott, H. J. H. 8: v E 1884 (2); *v E 1884 (3) 1886 (3)*

Sellers, R. H. D. 1: *v In 1964*

Serjeant, C. S. 12: v In 1977 (4); *v E 1977 (3); v WI 1977 (5)*

Sheahan, A. P. 31: v E 1970 (2); v WI 1968 (5); v NZ 1973 (2); v In 1967 (4); v P 1972 (2); *v E 1968 (5) 1972 (2); v SA 1969 (4); v In 1969 (5)*

Shepherd, B. K. 9: v E 1962 (2); v SA 1963 (4); v P 1964 (1); *v WI 1964 (2)*

Sievers, M. W. 3: v E 1936 (3)

Simpson, R. B. 62: v E 1958 (1) 1962 (5) 1965 (3); v SA 1963 (5); v WI 1960 (5); v In 1967 (3) 1977 (5); v P 1964 (1); *v E 1961 (5) 1964 (5); v SA 1957 (5) 1966 (5); v WI 1964 (5) 1977 (5); v In 1964 (3); v P 1964 (1)*

Sincock, D. J. 3: v E 1965 (1); v P 1964 (1); *v WI 1964 (1)*

Slater, K. N. 1: v E 1958

Sleep, P. R. 14: v E 1986 (3) 1987 (1); v NZ 1987 (3); v P 1978 (1) 1989 (1); v SL 1989 (1); *v In 1979 (2); v P 1982 (1) 1988 (1)*

Slight, J. 1: *v E 1880*

Smith, D. B. M. 2: *v E 1912 (2)*

Smith, S. B. 3: *v WI 1983 (3)*

Spofforth, F. R. 18: v E 1876 (1) 1878 (1) 1881 (1) 1882 (4) 1884 (3) 1886 (1); *v E 1882 (1) 1884 (3) 1886 (3)*

Stackpole, K. R. 43: v E 1965 (2) 1970 (6); v WI 1968 (5); v NZ 1973 (3); v P 1972 (3); *v E 1972 (5); v SA 1966 (5) 1969 (4); v WI 1972 (4); v NZ 1973 (3); v In 1969 (5)*

Stevens, G. B. 4: *v In 1959 (2); v P 1959 (2)*

Taber, H. B. 16: v WI 1968 (1); *v E 1968 (1); v SA 1966 (5); 1969 (4); v In 1969 (5)*

Tallon, D. 21: v E 1946 (5) 1950 (5); v In 1947 (5); *v E 1948 (4) 1953 (1); v NZ 1945 (1)*

Taylor, J. M. 20: v E 1920 (5) 1924 (5); *v E 1921 (5) 1926 (3); v SA 1921 (2)*

Taylor, M. A. 30: v E 1990 (5); v WI 1988 (2); v NZ 1989 (1); v I 1991 (5); v P 1989 (3); v SL 1989 (2); *v E 1989 (6); v WI 1990 (5); v NZ 1989 (1)*

Taylor, P. L. 13: v E 1986 (1) 1987 (1); v WI 1988 (2); v I 1991 (2); v P 1989 (2); v SL 1987 (1); *v WI 1990 (1); v NZ 1989 (1); v P 1988 (2)*

Thomas, G. 8: v E 1965 (3); *v WI 1964 (5)*

Thoms, G. R. 1: v WI 1951

Thomson, A. L. 4: v E 1970 (4)

Thomson, J. R. 51: v E 1974 (5) 1979 (1) 1982 (4); v WI 1975 (6) 1979 (1) 1981 (2); v In 1977 (5); v P 1972 (1) 1976 (1) 1981 (3); *v E 1975 (4) 1977 (5) 1985 (2); v WI 1977 (5); v NZ 1981 (3); v P 1982 (3)*

Thomson, N. F. D. 2: v E 1876 (2)

Thurlow, H. M. 1: v SA 1931

Toohey, P. M. 15: v E 1978 (5) 1979 (1); v WI 1979 (1); v In 1977 (5); *v WI 1977 (3)*

Toshack, E. R. H. 12: v E 1946 (5); v In 1947 (2); *v E 1948 (4); v NZ 1945 (1)*

Travers, J. P. F. 1: v E 1901

Tribe, G. E. 3: v E 1946 (3)

Trott, A. E. 3: v E 1894 (3)

Trott, G. H. S. 24: v E 1891 (3) 1894 (3) 1897 (5); *v E 1888 (3) 1890 (2) 1893 (3) 1896 (3)*

Trumble, H. 32: v E 1894 (1) 1897 (5) 1901 (5) 1903 (4); *v E 1890 (2) 1893 (3) 1896 (3) 1899 (5) 1902 (3); v SA 1902 (1)*

Trumble, J. W. 7: v E 1884 (1); *v E 1886 (3)*

Trumper, V. T. 48: v E 1901 (5) 1903 (5) 1907 (5) 1911 (5); v SA 1910 (5); *v E 1899 (5) 1902 (5) 1905 (5) 1909 (5); v SA 1902 (3)*

Turner, A. 14: v WI 1975 (6); v P 1976 (3); *v E 1975 (3); v NZ 1976 (2)*

Turner, C. T. B. 17: v E 1886 (2) 1887 (1) 1891 (3) 1894 (3); *v E 1888 (3) 1890 (2) 1893 (3)*

Veivers, T. R. 21: v E 1965 (4); v SA 1963 (3); v P 1964 (1); *v E 1964 (5); v SA 1966 (4); v In 1964 (3); v P 1964 (1)*

Veletta, M. R. J. 8: v E 1987 (1); v WI 1988 (2); v NZ 1987 (3); v P 1989 (1); v SL 1987 (1)

Waite, M. G. 2: *v E 1938 (2)*

Walker, M. H. N. 34: v E 1974 (6); 1976 (1); v WI 1975 (3); v NZ 1973 (1); v P 1972 (2) 1976 (2); *v E 1975 (4); 1977 (5); v WI 1972 (5); v NZ 1973 (3) 1976 (2)*

Wall, T. W. 18: v E 1928 (1) 1932 (4); v SA 1931 (3); v WI 1930 (1); *v E 1930 (5) 1934 (4)*

Walters, F. H. 1: v E 1884

Walters, K. D. 74: v E 1965 (5) 1970 (6) 1974 (6) 1976 (1); v WI 1968 (4); v NZ 1973 (3) 1980 (3); v In 1967 (2) 1980 (3); v P 1972 (1) 1976 (3); *v E 1968 (5) 1972 (4) 1975 (4) 1977 (5); v SA 1969 (4); v WI 1972 (5); v NZ 1973 (3) 1976 (2); v In 1969 (5)*

Ward, F. A. 4: v E 1936 (3); *v E 1938 (1)*

Warne, S. K. 2: v I 1991 (2)

Watkins, J. R. 1: v P 1972

Watson, G. D. 5: *v E 1972 (2); v SA 1966 (3)*

Watson, W. 4: v E 1954 (1); *v WI 1954 (3)*

Waugh, M. E. 11: v E 1990 (2); v I 1991 (4); *v WI 1990 (5)*

Waugh, S. R. 44: v E 1986 (5) 1987 (3) 1990 (3); v WI 1988 (5); v NZ 1987 (3) 1989 (1); v In 1985 (2); v P 1989 (3); v SL 1987 (1) 1989 (2); *v E 1989 (6); v WI 1990 (2); v NZ 1985 (3) 1989 (1); v In 1986 (3); v P 1988 (3)*

Wellham, D. M. 6: v E 1986 (1); v WI 1981 (1); v P 1981 (2); *v E 1981 (1) 1985 (1)*

Wessels, K. C. 24: v E 1982 (4); v WI 1984 (5); v NZ 1985 (1); v P 1983 (5); *v E 1985 (6); v WI 1983 (2); v SL 1982 (1)*

Whatmore, D. F. 7: v P 1978 (2); *v In 1979 (5)*

Whitney, M. R. 9: v WI 1988 (1); v NZ 1987 (1); v I 1991 (3); *v E 1981 (2); v WI 1990 (2)*

Whitty, W. J. 14: v E 1911 (2); v SA 1910 (5); *v E 1909 (1) 1912 (3); v SA 1912 (3)*

Wiener, J. M. 6: v E 1979 (2); v WI 1979 (2); *v P 1979 (2)*

Wilson, J. W. 1: *v In 1956*

Wood, G. M. 59: v E 1978 (6) 1982 (1); v WI 1981 (3) 1984 (5) 1988 (3); v NZ 1980 (3); v In 1977 (1) 1980 (3); v P 1978 (1) 1981 (3); *v E 1980 (1) 1981 (6) 1985 (5); v WI 1977 (5) 1983 (1); v NZ 1981 (3); v In 1979 (2); v P 1982 (3) 1988 (3); v SL 1982 (1)*

Woodcock, A. J. 1: v NZ 1973

Woodfull, W. M. 35: v E 1928 (5) 1932 (5); v SA 1931 (5); v WI 1930 (5); *v E 1926 (5) 1930 (5) 1934 (5)*

Woods, S. M. J. 3: *v E 1888 (3)*

Woolley, R. D. 2: v WI 1983 (1); v SL 1982 (1)
Worrall, J. 11: v E 1884 (1) 1887 (1) 1894 (1) 1897 (1); v E 1888 (3) 1899 (4)
Wright, K. J. 10: v E 1978 (2); v P 1978 (2); v In 1979 (6)

Yallop, G. N. 39: v E 1978 (6); v WI 1975 (3) 1984 (1); v In 1977 (1); v P 1978 (1) 1981 (1) 1983 (5); v E 1980 (1) 1981 (6); v WI 1977 (4); v In 1979 (6); v P 1979 (3); v SL 1982 (1)
Yardley, B. 33: v E 1978 (4) 1982 (5); v WI 1981 (3); v In 1977 (1) 1980 (2); v P 1978 (1) 1981 (3); v WI 1977 (5); v NZ 1981 (3); v In 1979 (3); v P 1982 (2); v SL 1982 (1)

Zoehrer, T. J. 10: v E 1986 (4); v NZ 1985 (3); v In 1986 (3)

SOUTH AFRICA

Number of Test cricketers: 246

Adcock, N. A. T. 26: v E 1956 (5); v A 1957 (5); v NZ 1953 (5) 1961 (2); v E 1955 (4) 1960 (5)
Anderson, J. H. 1: v A 1902
Ashley, W. H. 1: v E 1888

Bacher, A. 12: v A 1966 (5) 1969 (4); v E 1965 (3)
Balaskas, X. C. 9: v E 1930 (2) 1938 (1); v A 1935 (3); v E 1935 (1); v NZ 1931 (2)
Barlow, E. J. 30: v E 1964 (5); v A 1966 (5) 1969 (4); v NZ 1961 (5); v E 1965 (3); v A 1963 (5); v NZ 1963 (3)
Baumgartner, H. V. 1: v E 1913
Beaumont, R. 5: v E 1913 (2); v E 1912 (1); v A 1912 (2)
Begbie, D. W. 5: v E 1948 (3); v A 1949 (2)
Bell, A. J. 16: v E 1930 (3); v E 1929 (3) 1935 (3); v A 1931 (5); v NZ 1931 (2)
Bisset, M. 3: v E 1898 (2) 1909 (1)
Bissett, G. F. 4: v E 1927 (4)
Blanckenberg, J. M. 18: v E 1913 (5) 1922 (5); v A 1921 (3); v E 1924 (5)
Bland, K. C. 21: v E 1964 (5); v A 1966 (1); v NZ 1961 (5); v E 1965 (3); v A 1963 (4); v NZ 1963 (3)
Bock, E. G. 1: v A 1935
Bond, G. E. 1: v E 1938
Bosch, T. 1: v WI 1991
Botten, J. T. 3: v E 1965 (3)
Brann, W. H. 3: v E 1922 (3)
Briscoe, A. W. 2: v E 1938 (1); v A 1935 (1)
Bromfield, H. D. 9: v E 1964 (3); v NZ 1961 (5); v E 1965 (1)
Brown, L. S. 2: v A 1931 (1); v NZ 1931 (1)
Burger, C. G. de V. 2: v A 1957 (2)
Burke, S. F. 2: v E 1964 (1); v NZ 1961 (1)
Buys, I. D. 1: v E 1922

Cameron, H. B. 26: v E 1927 (5) 1930 (5); v E 1929 (4) 1935 (5); v A 1931 (5); v NZ 1931 (2)
Campbell, T. 5: v E 1909 (4); v E 1912 (1)
Carlstein, P. R. 8: v A 1957 (1); v E 1960 (5); v A 1963 (2)
Carter, C. P. 10: v E 1913 (2); v A 1921 (3); v E 1912 (2) 1924 (3)
Catterall, R. H. 24: v E 1922 (5) 1927 (5) 1930 (4); v E 1924 (5) 1929 (5)
Chapman, H. W. 2: v E 1913 (1); v A 1921 (1)
Cheetham, J. E. 24: v E 1948 (1); v A 1949 (3); v NZ 1953 (5); v E 1951 (5) 1955 (3); v A 1952 (5); v NZ 1952 (2)
Chevalier, G. A. 1: v A 1969
Christy, J. A. J. 10: v E 1930 (1); v E 1929 (2); v A 1931 (5); v NZ 1931 (2)
Chubb, G. W. A. 5: v E 1951 (5)
Cochran, J. A. K. 1: v E 1930
Coen, S. K. 2: v E 1927 (2)
Commaille, J. M. M. 12: v E 1909 (5) 1927 (2); v E 1924 (5)
Conyngham, D. P. 1: v E 1922
Cook, F. J. 1: v E 1895

Cooper, A. H. C. 1: v E 1913
Cox, J. L. 3: v E 1913 (3)
Cripps, G. 1: v E 1891
Crisp, R. J. 9: v A 1935 (4); *v E 1935* (5)
Cronje, W. J. 1: *v WI 1991*
Curnow, S. H. 7: v E 1930 (3); *v A 1931* (4)

Dalton, E. L. 15: v E 1930 (1) 1938 (4); v A 1935 (1); *v E 1929 (1) 1935* (4); *v A 1931* (2); *v NZ 1931* (2)
Davies, E. Q. 5: v E 1938 (3); v A 1935 (2)
Dawson, O. C. 9: v E 1948 (4); *v E 1947* (5)
Deane, H. G. 17: v E 1927 (5) 1930 (2); *v E 1924 (5) 1929* (5)
Dixon, C. D. 1: v E 1913
Donald, A. A. 1: *v WI 1991*
Dower, R. R. 1: v E 1898
Draper, R. G. 2: v A 1949 (2)
Duckworth, C. A. R. 2: v E 1956 (2)
Dumbrill, R. 5: v A 1966 (2); *v E 1965* (3)
Duminy, J. P. 3: v E 1927 (2); *v E 1929* (1)
Dunell, O. R. 2: v E 1888 (2)
Du Preez, J. H. 2: v A 1966 (2)
Du Toit, J. F. 1: v E 1891
Dyer, D. V. 3: *v E 1947* (3)

Elgie, M. K. 3: v NZ 1961 (3)
Endean, W. R. 28: v E 1956 (5); v A 1957 (5); v NZ 1953 (5); *v E 1951 (1) 1955* (5); *v A 1952* (5); *v NZ 1952* (2)

Farrer, W. S. 6: v NZ 1961 (3); *v NZ 1963* (3)
Faulkner, G. A. 25: v E 1905 (5) 1909 (5); *v E 1907 (3) 1912 (3) 1924 (1)*; *v A 1910 (5) 1912* (3)
Fellows-Smith, J. P. 4: *v E 1960* (4)
Fichardt, C. G. 2: v E 1891 (1) 1895 (1)
Finlason, C. E. 1: v E 1888
Floquet, C. E. 1: v E 1909
Francis, H. H. 2: v E 1898 (2)
Francois, C. M. 5: v E 1922 (5)
Frank, C. N. 3: v A 1921 (3)
Frank, W. H. B. 1: v E 1895
Fuller, E. R. H. 7: v E 1957 (1); *v E 1955 (2)*; *v A 1952 (2); v NZ 1952* (2)
Fullerton, G. M. 7: v A 1949 (2); *v E 1947 (2) 1951* (3)
Funston, K. J. 18: v E 1956 (3); v A 1957 (5); v NZ 1953 (3); *v A 1952 (5); v NZ 1952* (2)

Gamsy, D. 2: v A 1969 (2)
Gleeson, R. A. 1: v E 1895
Glover, G. K. 1: v E 1895
Goddard, T. L. 41: v E 1956 (5) 1964 (5); v A 1957 (5) 1966 (5) 1969 (3); *v E 1955 (5) 1960 (5); v A 1963 (5); v NZ 1963* (3)
Gordon, N. 5: v E 1938 (5)
Graham, R. 2: v E 1898 (2)
Grieveson, R. E. 2: v E 1938 (2)
Griffin, G. M. 2: *v E 1960* (2)

Hall, A. E. 7: v E 1922 (4) 1927 (2) 1930 (1)
Hall, G. G. 1: v E 1964
Halliwell, E. A. 8: v E 1891 (1) 1895 (3) 1898 (1); v A 1902 (3)
Halse, C. G. 3: *v A 1963* (3)
Hands, P. A. M. 7: v E 1913 (5); v A 1921 (1); *v E 1924* (1)
Hands, R. H. M. 1: v E 1913
Hanley, M. A. 1: v E 1948
Harris, T. A. 3: v E 1948 (1); *v E 1947* (2)
Hartigan, G. P. D. 5: v E 1913 (3); *v E 1912 (1); v A 1912* (1)
Harvey, R. L. 2: v A 1935 (2)

Hathorn, C. M. H. 12: v E 1905 (5); v A 1902 (3); *v E 1907 (3); v A 1910 (1)*
Hearne, F. 4: v E 1891 (1) 1895 (3)
Hearne, G. A. L. 3: v E 1922 (2); *v E 1924 (1)*
Heine, P. S. 14: v E 1956 (5); v A 1957 (4); v NZ 1961 (1); *v E 1955 (4)*
Hime, C. F. W. 1: v E 1895
Hudson, A. C. 1: *v WI 1991*
Hutchinson, P. 2: v E 1888 (2)

Ironside, D. E. J. 3: v NZ 1953 (3)
Irvine, B. L. 4: v A 1969 (4)

Johnson, C. L. 1: v E 1895

Keith, H. J. 8: v E 1956 (3); *v E 1955 (4); v A 1952 (1)*
Kempis, G. A. 1: v E 1888
Kirsten, P. N. 1: *v WI 1991*
Kotze, J. J. 3: v A 1902 (2); *v E 1907 (1)*
Kuiper, A. P. 1: *v WI 1991*
Kuys, F. 1: v E 1898

Lance, H. R. 13: v A 1966 (5) 1969 (3); v NZ 1961 (2); *v E 1965 (3)*
Langton, A. B. C. 15: v E 1938 (5); v A 1935 (5); *v E 1935 (5)*
Lawrence, G. B. 5: v NZ 1961 (5)
Le Roux, F. le S. 1: v E 1913
Lewis, P. T. 1: v E 1913
Lindsay, D. T. 19: v E 1964 (3); v A 1966 (5) 1969 (2); *v E 1965 (3); v A 1963 (3); v NZ 1963 (3)*
Lindsay, J. D. 3: *v E 1947 (3)*
Lindsay, N. V. 1: v A 1921
Ling, W. V. S. 6: v E 1922 (3); v A 1921 (3)
Llewellyn, C. B. 15: v E 1895 (1) 1898 (1); v A 1902 (3); *v E 1912 (3); v A 1910 (5) 1912 (2)*
Lundie, E. B. 1: v E 1913

Macaulay, M. J. 1: v E 1964
McCarthy, C. N. 15: v E 1948 (5); v A 1949 (5); *v E 1951 (5)*
McGlew, D. J. 34: v E 1956 (1); v A 1957 (5); v NZ 1953 (5) 1961 (5); *v E 1951 (2) 1955 (5) 1960 (5); v A 1952 (4); v NZ 1952 (2)*
McKinnon, A. H. 8: v E 1964 (2); v A 1966 (2); v NZ 1961 (1); *v E 1960 (1) 1965 (2)*
McLean, R. A. 40: v E 1956 (5) 1964 (2); v A 1957 (4); v NZ 1953 (4) 1961 (5); *v E 1951 (3) 1955 (5) 1960 (5); v A 1952 (5); v NZ 1952 (2)*
McMillan, Q. 13: v E 1930 (5); *v E 1929 (2); v A 1931 (4); v NZ 1931 (2)*
Mann, N. B. F. 19: v E 1948 (5); v A 1949 (5); *v E 1947 (5) 1951 (4)*
Mansell, P. N. F. 13: *v E 1951 (2) 1955 (4); v A 1952 (5); v NZ 1952 (2)*
Markham, L. A. 1: v E 1948
Marx, W. F. E. 3: v A 1921 (3)
Meintjes, D. J. 2: v E 1922 (2)
Melle, M. G. 7: v A 1949 (2); *v E 1951 (1); v A 1952 (4)*
Melville, A. 11: v E 1938 (5) 1948 (1); *v E 1947 (5)*
Middleton, J. 6: v E 1895 (2) 1898 (2); v A 1902 (2)
Mills, C. 1: v E 1891
Milton, W. H. 3: v E 1888 (2) 1891 (1)
Mitchell, B. 42: v E 1930 (5) 1938 (5) 1948 (5); v A 1935 (5); *v E 1929 (5) 1935 (5) 1947 (5); v A 1931 (5); v NZ 1931 (5)*
Mitchell, F. 3: *v E 1912 (1); v A 1912 (2)*
Morkel, D. P. B. 16: v E 1927 (5); *v E 1929 (5); v A 1931 (5); v NZ 1931 (1)*
Murray, A. R. A. 10: v NZ 1953 (4); *v A 1952 (4); v NZ 1952 (2)*

Nel, J. D. 6: v A 1949 (5) 1957 (1)
Newberry, C. 4: v E 1913 (4)
Newson, E. S. 3: v E 1930 (1) 1938 (2)
Nicholson, F. 4: v A 1935 (4)
Nicolson, J. F. W. 3: v E 1927 (3)
Norton, N. O. 1: v E 1909

Nourse, A. D. 34: v E 1938 (5) 1948 (5); v A 1935 (5) 1949 (5); *v E 1935 (4) 1947 (5) 1951 (5)*
Nourse, A. W. 45: v E 1905 (5) 1909 (5) 1913 (5) 1922 (5); v A 1902 (3) 1921 (3); *v E 1907 (3) 1912 (3) 1924 (5); v A 1910 (5) 1912 (3)*
Nupen, E. P. 17: v E 1922 (4) 1927 (5) 1930 (3); v A 1921 (2) 1935 (1); *v E 1924 (2)*

Ochse, A. E. 2: v E 1888 (2)
Ochse, A. L. 3: v E 1927 (1); *v E 1929 (2)*
O'Linn, S. 7: v NZ 1961 (2); *v E 1960 (5)*
Owen-Smith, H. G. 5: *v E 1929 (5)*

Palm, A. W. 1: v E 1927
Parker, G. M. 2: *v E 1924 (2)*
Parkin, D. C. 1: v E 1891
Partridge, J. T. 11: v E 1964 (3); *v A 1963 (5); v NZ 1963 (3)*
Pearse, O. C. 3: *v A 1910 (3)*
Pegler, S. J. 16: v E 1909 (1); *v E 1912 (3) 1924 (5); v A 1910 (4) 1912 (3)*
Pithey, A. J. 17: v E 1956 (3) 1964 (5); *v E 1960 (2); v A 1963 (4); v NZ 1963 (3)*
Pithey, D. B. 8: *v A 1966 (2); v A 1963 (3); v NZ 1963 (3)*
Plimsoll, J. B. 1: *v E 1947*
Pollock, P. M. 28: v E 1964 (5); v A 1966 (5) 1969 (4); v NZ 1961 (3); *v E 1965 (3); v A 1963 (5); v NZ 1963 (3)*
Pollock, R. G. 23: v E 1964 (5); v A 1966 (5) 1969 (4); *v E 1965 (3); v A 1963 (5); v NZ 1963 (1)*
Poore, R. M. 3: v E 1895 (3)
Pothecary, J. E. 3: *v E 1960 (3)*
Powell, A. W. 1: v E 1898
Prince, C. F. H. 1: v E 1898
Pringle, M. W. 1: *v WI 1991*
Procter, M. J. 7: v A 1966 (3) 1969 (4)
Promnitz, H. L. E. 2: v E 1927 (2)

Quinn, N. A. 12: v E 1930 (1); *v E 1929 (4); v A 1931 (5); v NZ 1931 (2)*

Reid, N. 1: v A 1921
Richards, A. R. 1: v E 1895
Richards, B. A. 4: v A 1969 (4)
Richards, W. H. 1: v E 1888
Richardson, D. J. 1: *v WI 1991*
Robertson, J. B. 3: v A 1935 (3)
Rose-Innes, A. 2: v E 1888 (2)
Routledge, T. W. 4: v E 1891 (1) 1895 (3)
Rowan, A. M. B. 15: v E 1948 (5); *v E 1947 (5) 1951 (5)*
Rowan, E. A. B. 26: v E 1938 (4) 1948 (4); v A 1935 (3); 1949 (5); *v E 1935 (5) 1951 (5)*
Rowe, G. A. 5: v E 1895 (2) 1898 (2); v A 1902 (1)
Rushmere, M. W. 1: *v WI 1991*

Samuelson, S. V. 1: v E 1909
Schwarz, R. O. 20: v E 1905 (5) 1909 (4); *v E 1907 (3) 1912 (1); v A 1910 (5) 1912 (2)*
Seccull, A. W. 1: v E 1895
Seymour, M. A. 7: v E 1964 (2); v A 1969 (1); *v A 1963 (4)*
Shalders, W. A. 12: v E 1898 (1) 1905 (5); v A 1902 (3); *v E 1907 (3)*
Shepstone, G. H. 2: v E 1895 (1) 1898 (1)
Sherwell, P. W. 13: v E 1905 (5); *v E 1907 (3); v A 1910 (5)*
Siedle, I. J. 18: v E 1927 (1) 1930 (5); v A 1935 (5); *v E 1929 (3) 1935 (4)*
Sinclair, J. H. 25: v E 1895 (3) 1898 (2) 1905 (5) 1909 (4); v A 1902 (3); *v E 1907 (3); v A 1910 (5)*
Smith, C. J. E. 3: v A 1902 (3)
Smith, F. W. 3: v E 1888 (2) 1895 (1)
Smith, V. I. 9: v A 1949 (1) 1957 (1); *v E 1947 (4) 1955 (1)*
Snell, R. P. 1: *v WI 1991*
Snooke, S. D. 1: *v E 1907*
Snooke, S. J. 26: v E 1905 (5) 1909 (5) 1922 (3); *v E 1907 (3) 1912 (3); v A 1910 (5) 1912 (2)*
Solomon, W. R. 1: v E 1898
Stewart, R. B. 1: v E 1888

Stricker, L. A. 13: v E 1909 (4); *v E 1912 (2); v A 1910 (5) 1912 (2)*
Susskind, M. J. 5: *v E 1924 (5)*

Taberer, H. M. 1: v A 1902
Tancred, A. B. 2: v E 1888 (2)
Tancred, L. J. 14: v E 1905 (5) 1913 (1); v A 1902 (3); *v E 1907 (1) 1912 (2); v A 1912 (2)*
Tancred, V. M. 1: v E 1898
Tapscott, G. L. 1: v E 1913
Tapscott, L. E. 2: v E 1922 (2)
Tayfield, H. J. 37: v E 1956 (5); v A 1949 (5) 1957 (5); v NZ 1953 (5); *v E 1955 (5) 1960 (5); v A 1952 (5); v NZ 1952 (2)*
Taylor, A. I. 1: v E 1956
Taylor, D. 2: v E 1913 (2)
Taylor, H. W. 42: v E 1913 (5) 1922 (5) 1927 (5) 1930 (4); v A 1921 (3); *v E 1912 (3) 1924 (5) 1929 (3); v A 1912 (3) 1931 (5); v NZ 1931 (1)*
Theunissen, N. H. G. de J. 1: v E 1888
Thornton, P. G. 1: v A 1902
Tomlinson, D. S. 1: *v E 1935*
Traicos, A. J. 3: v A 1969 (3)
Trimborn, P. H. J. 4: v A 1966 (3) 1969 (1)
Tuckett, L. 9: v E 1948 (4); *v E 1947 (5)*
Tuckett, L. R. 1: v E 1913
Twentyman-Jones, P. S. 1: v A 1902

van der Bijl, P. G. V. 5: v E 1938 (5)
Van der Merwe, E. A. 2: v A 1935 (1); *v E 1929 (1)*
Van der Merwe, P. L. 15: v E 1964 (2); v A 1966 (5); *v E 1965 (3); v A 1963 (3); v NZ 1963 (2)*
Van Ryneveld, C. B. 19: v E 1956 (5); v A 1957 (4); v NZ 1953 (5); *v E 1951 (5)*
Varnals, G. D. 3: v E 1964 (3)
Viljoen, K. G. 27: v E 1930 (3) 1938 (4) 1948 (2); v A 1935 (4); *v E 1935 (4) 1947 (5); v A 1931 (4); v NZ 1931 (1)*
Vincent, C. L. 25: v E 1927 (5) 1930 (5); *v E 1929 (4) 1935 (4); v A 1931 (5); v NZ 1931 (2)*
Vintcent, C. H. 3: v E 1888 (2) 1891 (1)
Vogler, A. E. E. 15: v E 1905 (5) 1909 (5); *v E 1907 (3); v A 1910 (2)*

Wade, H. F. 10: v A 1935 (5); *v E 1935 (5)*
Wade, W. W. 11: v E 1938 (3) 1948 (5); v A 1949 (3)
Waite, J. H. B. 50: v E 1956 (5); 1964 (2); v A 1957 (5); v NZ 1953 (5) 1961 (5); *v E 1951 (4) 1955 (5) 1960 (5); v A 1952 (5) 1963 (4); v NZ 1952 (2) 1963 (3)*
Walter, K. A. 2: v NZ 1961 (2)
Ward, T. A. 23: v E 1913 (5) 1922 (5); v A 1921 (3); *v E 1912 (2) 1924 (5); v A 1912 (3)*
Watkins, J. C. 15: v E 1956 (2); v A 1949 (3); v NZ 1953 (3); *v A 1952 (5); v NZ 1952 (2)*
Wesley, C. 3: *v E 1960 (3)*
Wessels, K. C. 1: *v WI 1991*
Westcott, R. J. 5: v A 1957 (2); v NZ 1953 (3)
White, G. C. 17: v E 1905 (5) 1909 (4); *v E 1907 (3) 1912 (2); v A 1912 (3)*
Willoughby, J. T. I. 2: v E 1895 (2)
Wimble, C. S. 1: v E 1891
Winslow, P. L. 5: v A 1949 (2); *v E 1955 (3)*
Wynne, O. E. 6: v E 1948 (3); v A 1949 (3)

Zulch, J. W. 16: v E 1909 (5) 1913 (3); v A 1921 (3); *v A 1910 (5)*

WEST INDIES

Number of Test cricketers: 201

Achong, E. 6: v E 1929 (1) 1934 (2); *v E 1933 (3)*
Adams, J. C. 1: v SA 1991
Alexander, F. C. M. 25: v E 1959 (5); v P 1957 (5); *v E 1957 (2); v A 1960 (5); v In 1958 (5); v P 1958 (3)*

Ali, Imtiaz 1: v In 1975
Ali, Inshan 12: v E 1973 (2); v A 1972 (3); v In 1970 (1); v P 1976 (1); v NZ 1971 (3); *v E 1973 (1); v A 1975 (1)*
Allan, D. W. 5: v A 1964 (1); v In 1961 (2); *v E 1966 (2)*
Allen, I. B. A. 2: *v E 1991 (2)*
Ambrose, C. E. L. 34: v E 1989 (3); v A 1990 (5); v SA 1991 (1); v In 1988 (4); v P 1987 (3); *v E 1988 (5) 1991 (5); v A 1988 (5); v P 1990 (3)*
Arthurton, K. L. T. 6: v SA 1991 (1); v In 1988 (4); *v E 1988 (1)*
Asgarali, N. 2: *v E 1957 (2)*
Atkinson, D. St E. 22: v E 1953 (4); v A 1954 (4); v P 1957 (1); *v E 1957 (2); v A 1951 (2); v NZ 1951 (1) 1955 (4); v In 1948 (4)*
Atkinson, E. St E. 8: v P 1957 (3); *v In 1958 (3); v P 1958 (2)*
Austin, R. A. 2: v A 1977 (2)

Bacchus, S. F. A. F. 19: v A 1977 (2); *v E 1980 (5); v A 1981 (2); v In 1978 (6); v P 1980 (4)*
Baichan, L. 3: *v A 1975 (1); v P 1974 (2)*
Baptiste, E. A. E. 10: v E 1989 (1); v A 1983 (3); *v E 1984 (5); v In 1983 (1)*
Barrett, A. G. 6: v E 1973 (2); v In 1970 (2); *v In 1974 (2)*
Barrow, I. 11: v E 1929 (1) 1934 (1); *v E 1933 (3) 1939 (1); v A 1930 (5)*
Bartlett, E. L. 5: *v E 1928 (1); v A 1930 (4)*
Benjamin, K. C. G. 1: v SA 1991
Benjamin, W. K. M. 8: v In 1988 (1); v P 1987 (3); *v E 1988 (3); v In 1987 (1)*
Best, C. A. 8: v E 1985 (3) 1989 (3); *v P 1990 (2)*
Betancourt, N. 1: v E 1929
Binns, A. P. 5: v A 1954 (1); v In 1952 (1); *v NZ 1955 (3)*
Birkett, L. S. 4: *v A 1930 (4)*
Bishop, I. R. 11: v E 1989 (4); v In 1988 (4); *v P 1990 (3)*
Boyce, K. D. 21: v E 1973 (4); v A 1972 (4); v In 1970 (1); *v E 1973 (3); v A 1975 (4); v In 1974 (3); v P 1974 (2)*
Browne, C. R. 4: v E 1929 (2); *v E 1928 (2)*
Butcher, B. F. 44: v E 1959 (2) 1967 (5); v A 1964 (5); *v E 1963 (5) 1966 (5) 1969 (3); v A 1968 (5); v NZ 1968 (3); v In 1958 (5) 1966 (3); v P 1958 (3)*
Butler, L. 1: v A 1954
Butts, C. G. 7: v NZ 1984 (1); *v NZ 1986 (1); v In 1987 (3); v P 1986 (3)*
Bynoe, M. R. 4: *v In 1966 (3); v P 1958 (1)*

Camacho, G. S. 11: v E 1967 (5); v In 1970 (2); *v E 1969 (2); v A 1968 (2)*
Cameron, F. J. 5: *v In 1948 (5)*
Cameron, J. H. 2: *v E 1939 (2)*
Carew, G. M. 4: v E 1934 (1) 1947 (2); *v In 1948 (1)*
Carew, M. C. 19: v E 1967 (1); v NZ 1971 (3); v In 1970 (3); *v E 1963 (2) 1966 (1) 1969 (1); v A 1968 (2); v NZ 1968 (3)*
Challenor, G. 3: *v E 1928 (3)*
Chang, H. S. 1: *v In 1978*
Christiani, C. M. 4: v E 1934 (4)
Christiani, R. J. 22: v E 1947 (4) 1953 (1); v In 1952 (2); *v E 1950 (4); v A 1951 (5); v NZ 1951 (1); v In 1948 (5)*
Clarke, C. B. 3: *v E 1939 (3)*
Clarke, S. T. 11: v A 1977 (1); *v A 1981 (1); v In 1978 (5); v P 1980 (4)*
Constantine, L. N. 18: v E 1929 (3) 1934 (3); *v E 1928 (3) 1933 (1) 1939 (3); v A 1930 (5)*
Croft, C. E. H. 27: v E 1980 (4); v A 1977 (2); v P 1976 (5); *v E 1980 (3); v A 1979 (3) 1981 (3); v NZ 1979 (3); v P 1980 (4)*

Da Costa, O. C. 5: v E 1929 (1) 1934 (1); *v E 1933 (3)*
Daniel, W. W. 10: v A 1983 (2); v In 1975 (1); *v E 1976 (4); v In 1983 (3)*
Davis, B. A. 4: v A 1964 (4)
Davis, C. A. 15: v A 1972 (2); v NZ 1971 (5); v In 1970 (4); *v E 1969 (3); v A 1968 (1)*
Davis, W. W. 15: v A 1983 (1); v NZ 1984 (2); v In 1982 (1); *v E 1984 (1); v In 1983 (6) 1987 (4)*
De Caires, F. I. 3: v E 1929 (3)
Depeiza, C. C. 5: v A 1954 (1); *v NZ 1955 (2)*
Dewdney, T. 9: v A 1954 (2); v P 1957 (3); *v E 1957 (1); v NZ 1955 (3)*
Dowe, U. G. 4: v A 1972 (1); v NZ 1971 (1); v In 1970 (2)

Dujon, P. J. L. 81: v E 1985 (4) 1989 (4); v A 1983 (5) 1990 (5); v NZ 1984 (4); v In 1982 (5) 1988 (4); v P 1987 (3); *v E 1984 (5) 1988 (5) 1991 (5); v A 1981 (3) 1984 (5) 1988 (5); v NZ 1986 (3); v In 1983 (6) 1987 (4); v P 1986 (3) 1990 (3)*

Edwards, R. M. 5: *v A 1968 (2); v NZ 1968 (3)*

Ferguson, W. 8: v E 1947 (4) 1953 (1); *v In 1948 (3)*
Fernandes, M. P. 2: v E 1929 (1); *v E 1928 (1)*
Findlay, T. M. 10: v A 1972 (1); v NZ 1971 (5); v In 1970 (2); *v E 1969 (2)*
Foster, M. L. C. 14: v E 1973 (1); v A 1972 (4) 1977 (1); v NZ 1971 (3); v In 1970 (2); v P 1976 (1); *v E 1969 (1) 1973 (1)*
Francis, G. N. 10: v E 1929 (1); *v E 1928 (3) 1933 (1); v A 1930 (5)*
Frederick, M. C. 1: v E 1953
Fredericks, R. C. 59: v E 1973 (5); v A 1972 (5); v NZ 1971 (5); v In 1970 (4) 1975 (4); v P 1976 (5); *v E 1969 (3) 1973 (3) 1976 (5); v A 1968 (4) 1975 (6); v NZ 1968 (3); v In 1974 (5); v P 1974 (2)*
Fuller, R. L. 1: v E 1934
Furlonge, H. A. 3: v A 1954 (1); *v NZ 1955 (2)*

Ganteaume, A. G. 1: v E 1947
Garner, J. 58: v E 1980 (4) 1985 (5); v A 1977 (2) 1983 (5); v NZ 1984 (4); v In 1982 (4); v P 1976 (5); *v E 1980 (5) 1984 (5); v A 1979 (3) 1981 (3) 1984 (5); v NZ 1979 (3) 1986 (2); v P 1980 (3)*
Gaskin, B. B. M. 2: v E 1947 (2)
Gibbs, G. L. R. 1: v A 1954
Gibbs, L. R. 79: v E 1967 (5) 1973 (5); v A 1964 (5) 1972 (5); v NZ 1971 (2); v In 1961 (5) 1970 (1); v P 1957 (4); *v E 1963 (5) 1966 (5) 1969 (3) 1973 (3); v A 1960 (3) 1968 (5) 1975 (6); v NZ 1968 (3); v In 1958 (1) 1966 (3) 1974 (5); v P 1958 (3) 1974 (2)*
Gilchrist, R. 13: v P 1957 (5); *v E 1957 (4); v In 1958 (4)*
Gladstone, G. 1: v E 1929
Goddard, J. D. C. 27: v E 1947 (4); *v E 1950 (4) 1957 (5); v A 1951 (4); v NZ 1951 (2) 1955 (3); v In 1948 (5)*
Gomes, H. A. 60: v E 1980 (4) 1985 (5); v A 1977 (3) 1983 (2); v NZ 1984 (4); v In 1982 (5); *v E 1976 (2) 1984 (5); v A 1981 (3) 1984 (5); v NZ 1986 (3); v In 1978 (6) 1983 (6); v P 1980 (4) 1986 (3)*
Gomez, G. E. 29: v E 1947 (4) 1953 (4); v In 1952 (4); *v E 1939 (2) 1950 (4); v A 1951 (5); v NZ 1951 (1); v In 1948 (5)*
Grant, G. C. 12: v E 1934 (4); *v E 1933 (3); v A 1930 (5)*
Grant, R. S. 7: v E 1934 (4); *v E 1939 (3)*
Gray, A. H. 5: *v NZ 1986 (2); v P 1986 (3)*
Greenidge, A. E. 6: v A 1977 (2); *v In 1978 (4)*
Greenidge, C. G. 108: v E 1980 (4) 1985 (5) 1989 (4); v A 1977 (2) 1983 (5) 1990 (5); v NZ 1984 (4); v In 1982 (5) 1988 (4); v P 1976 (5) 1987 (3); *v E 1976 (5) 1980 (5) 1984 (5) 1988 (4); v A 1975 (2) 1979 (3) 1981 (2) 1984 (5) 1988 (5); v NZ 1979 (3) 1986 (3); v In 1974 (5) 1983 (6) 1987 (3); v P 1986 (3) 1990 (3)*
Greenidge, G. A. 5: v A 1972 (3); v NZ 1971 (2)
Grell, M. G. 1: v E 1929
Griffith, C. C. 28: v E 1959 (1) 1967 (4); v A 1964 (5); *v E 1963 (5) 1966 (5); v A 1968 (3); v NZ 1968 (2); v In 1966 (3)*
Griffith, H. C. 13: v E 1929 (3); *v E 1928 (3) 1933 (2); v A 1930 (5)*
Guillen, S. C. 5: *v A 1951 (3); v NZ 1951 (2)*

Hall, W. W. 48: v E 1959 (5) 1967 (4); v A 1964 (5); v In 1961 (5); *v E 1963 (5) 1966 (5); v A 1960 (5) 1968 (2); v NZ 1968 (1); v In 1958 (5) 1966 (3); v P 1958 (3)*
Harper, R. A. 24: v E 1985 (2); v A 1983 (4); v NZ 1984 (1); *v E 1984 (5) 1988 (5); v A 1984 (2) 1988 (1); v In 1983 (2) 1987 (1); v P 1986 (3)*
Haynes, D. L. 103: v E 1980 (4) 1985 (5) 1989 (4); v A 1977 (2) 1983 (5) 1990 (5); v SA 1991 (1); v NZ 1984 (4); v In 1982 (5) 1988 (4); v P 1987 (3); *v E 1980 (5) 1984 (5) 1988 (5) 1991 (5); v A 1979 (3) 1981 (3) 1984 (5) 1988 (5); v NZ 1979 (3) 1986 (3); v In 1983 (6) 1987 (4); v P 1980 (4) 1986 (3) 1990 (3)*
Headley, G. A. 22: v E 1929 (4) 1934 (4) 1947 (1) 1953 (1); *v E 1933 (3) 1939 (3); v A 1930 (5); v In 1948 (1)*
Headley, R. G. A. 2: *v E 1973 (2)*

Hendriks, J. L. 20: v A 1964 (4); v In 1961 (1); *v E 1966 (3) 1969 (1); v A 1968 (5); v NZ 1968 (3); v In 1966 (3)*

Hoad, E. L. G. 4: v E 1929 (1); *v E 1928 (1) 1933 (2)*

Holder, V. A. 40: v E 1973 (1); v A 1972 (3) 1977 (3); v NZ 1971 (4); v In 1970 (3) 1975 (1); v P 1976 (1); *v E 1969 (3) 1973 (2) 1976 (4); v A 1975 (3); v In 1974 (4) 1978 (6); v P 1974 (2)*

Holding, M. A. 60: v E 1980 (4) 1985 (4); v A 1983 (3); v NZ 1984 (3); v In 1975 (4) 1982 (5); *v E 1976 (4) 1980 (5) 1984 (4); v A 1975 (5) 1979 (3) 1981 (3) 1984 (3); v NZ 1979 (3) 1986 (1); v In 1983 (6)*

Holford, D. A. J. 24: v E 1967 (4); v NZ 1971 (5); v In 1970 (1) 1975 (2); v P 1976 (1); *v E 1966 (5); v A 1968 (2); v NZ 1968 (3); v In 1966 (1)*

Holt, J. K. 17: v E 1953 (5); v A 1954 (5); v In 1958 (5); v P 1958 (2)

Hooper, C. L. 32: v E 1989 (3); v A 1990 (5); v P 1987 (5); *v E 1988 (5) 1991 (5); v A 1988 (5); v In 1987 (3); v P 1990 (5)*

Howard, A. B. 1: v NZ 1971

Hunte, C. C. 44: v E 1959 (5); v A 1964 (5); v In 1961 (5); v P 1957 (5); *v E 1963 (5) 1966 (5); v A 1960 (5); v In 1958 (5) 1966 (3); v P 1958 (1)*

Hunte, E. A. C. 3: v E 1929 (3)

Hylton, L. G. 6: v E 1934 (4); *v E 1939 (2)*

Johnson, H. H. H. 3: v E 1947 (1); *v E 1950 (2)*

Johnson, T. F. 1: *v E 1939*

Jones, C. M. 4: v E 1929 (1) 1934 (3)

Jones, P. E. 9: v E 1947 (1); *v E 1950 (2); v A 1951 (1); v In 1948 (5)*

Julien, B. D. 24: v E 1973 (5); v In 1975 (4); v P 1976 (1); *v E 1973 (3) 1976 (2); v A 1975 (3); v In 1974 (4); v P 1974 (2)*

Jumadeen, R. R. 12: v A 1972 (1) 1977 (2); v NZ 1971 (1); v In 1975 (4); v P 1976 (1); *v E 1976 (1); v In 1978 (2)*

Kallicharran, A. I. 66: v E 1973 (5); v A 1972 (5) 1977 (5); v NZ 1971 (2); v In 1975 (4); v P 1976 (5); *v E 1973 (3) 1976 (3) 1980 (5); v A 1975 (6) 1979 (3); v NZ 1979 (3); v In 1974 (5) 1978 (6); v P 1974 (2) 1980 (4)*

Kanhai, R. B. 79: v E 1959 (5) 1967 (5) 1973 (5); v A 1964 (5) 1972 (5); v In 1961 (5) 1970 (5); v P 1957 (5); *v E 1957 (5) 1963 (5) 1966 (5) 1973 (3); v A 1960 (5) 1968 (5); v In 1958 (5) 1966 (3); v P 1958 (3)*

Kentish, E. S. M. 2: v E 1947 (1) 1953 (1)

King, C. L. 9: v P 1976 (1); *v E 1976 (3) 1980 (1); v A 1979 (1); v NZ 1979 (1)*

King, F. M. 14: v E 1953 (3); v A 1954 (4); v In 1952 (5); *v NZ 1955 (2)*

King, L. A. 2: v E 1967 (1); v In 1961 (1)

Lambert, C. B. 1: *v E 1991*

Lara, B. C. 2: v SA 1991 (1); *v P 1990 (1)*

Lashley, P. D. 4: *v E 1966 (2); v A 1960 (2)*

Legall, R. 4: v In 1952 (4)

Lewis, D. M. 3: v In 1970 (3)

Lloyd, C. H. 110: v E 1967 (5) 1973 (5) 1980 (4); v A 1972 (3) 1977 (2) 1983 (4); v NZ 1971 (2); v In 1970 (5) 1975 (4) 1982 (5); v P 1976 (5); *v E 1969 (3) 1973 (5) 1976 (5) 1980 (4) 1984 (5); v A 1968 (4) 1975 (6) 1979 (2) 1981 (3) 1984 (5); v NZ 1968 (3) 1979 (3); v In 1966 (3) 1974 (5) 1983 (6); v P 1974 (2) 1980 (4)*

Logie, A. L. 52: v E 1989 (3); v A 1983 (1) 1990 (5); v NZ 1984 (4); v In 1982 (5) 1988 (4); v P 1987 (3); *v E 1988 (5) 1991 (4); v A 1988 (5); v NZ 1986 (3); v In 1983 (3) 1987 (4); v P 1990 (3)*

McMorris, E. D. A. St J. 13: v E 1959 (4); v In 1961 (4); v P 1957 (1); *v E 1963 (2) 1966 (2)*

McWatt, C. A. 6: v E 1953 (5); v A 1954 (1)

Madray, I. S. 2: v P 1957 (2)

Marshall, M. D. 81: v E 1980 (1) 1985 (5) 1989 (2); v A 1983 (4) 1990 (5); v NZ 1984 (4); v In 1982 (5) 1988 (3); v P 1987 (2); *v E 1980 (4) 1984 (4) 1988 (5) 1991 (5); v A 1984 (5) 1988 (5); v In 1978 (3) 1983 (6); v P 1980 (4) 1986 (3) 1990 (3)*

Marshall, N. E. 1: v A 1954

Marshall, R. E. 4: *v A 1951 (2); v NZ 1951 (2)*

Martin, F. R. 9: v E 1929 (1); *v E 1928 (3); v A 1930 (5)*

Martindale, E. A. 10: v E 1934 (4); *v E 1933 (3) 1939 (3)*

Mattis, E. H. 4: v E 1980 (4)

Mendonca, I. L. 2: v In 1961 (2)
Merry, C. A. 2: *v E 1933 (2)*
Miller, R. 1: v In 1952
Moodie, G. H. 1: v E 1934
Moseley, E. A. 2: v E 1989 (2)
Murray, D. A. 19: v E 1980 (4); v A 1977 (3); *v A 1981 (2); v In 1978 (6); v P 1980 (4)*
Murray, D. L. 62: v E 1967 (5) 1973 (5); v A 1972 (4) 1977 (2); v In 1975 (4); v P 1976 (5);
  *v E 1963 (5) 1973 (3) 1976 (5) 1980 (5); v A 1975 (6) 1979 (3); v NZ 1979 (3); v In 1974 (5);
  v P 1974 (2)*

Nanan, R. 1: *v P 1980*
Neblett, J. M. 1: v E 1934
Noreiga, J. M. 4: v In 1970 (4)
Nunes, R. K. 4: v E 1929 (1); *v E 1928 (3)*
Nurse, S. M. 29: v E 1959 (1) 1967 (5); v A 1964 (4); v In 1961 (1); *v E 1966 (5); v A 1960 (3) 1968
  (5); v NZ 1968 (3); v In 1966 (2)*

Padmore, A. L. 2: v In 1975 (1); *v E 1976 (1)*
Pairaudeau, B. H. 13: v E 1953 (2); v In 1952 (5): *v E 1957 (2); v NZ 1955 (4)*
Parry, D. R. 12: v A 1977 (5); *v NZ 1979 (1); v In 1978 (6)*
Passailaigue, C. C. 1: v E 1929
Patterson, B. P. 27: v E 1985 (5) 1989 (1); v A 1990 (5); v SA 1991 (1); v P 1987 (1); *v E 1988 (2)
  1991 (3); v A 1988 (4); v In 1987 (4); v P 1986 (1)*
Payne, T. R. O. 1: v E 1985
Phillip, N. 9: v A 1977 (3); *v In 1978 (6)*
Pierre, L. R. 1: v E 1947

Rae, A. F. 15: v In 1952 (2); *v E 1950 (4); v A 1951 (3); v NZ 1951 (1); v In 1948 (5)*
Ramadhin, S. 43: v E 1953 (5) 1959 (4); v A 1954 (4); v In 1952 (4); *v E 1950 (4) 1957 (5); v A
  1951 (5) 1960 (2); v NZ 1951 (2) 1955 (4); v In 1958 (2); v P 1958 (2)*
Richards, I. V. A. 121: v E 1980 (4) 1985 (5) 1989 (3); v A 1977 (2) 1983 (5) 1990 (5); v NZ 1984
  (4); v In 1975 (4) 1982 (5) 1988 (4); v P 1976 (5) 1987 (2); *v E 1976 (4) 1980 (5) 1984 (5) 1988 (5)
  1991 (5); v A 1975 (6) 1979 (3) 1981 (3) 1984 (5) 1988 (5); v NZ 1986 (3); v In 1974 (5) 1983 (6)
  1987 (4); v P 1974 (2) 1980 (4) 1986 (3)*
Richardson, R. B. 63: v E 1985 (5) 1989 (4); v A 1983 (5) 1990 (5); v SA 1991 (1); v NZ 1984 (4);
  v In 1988 (4); v P 1987 (3); *v E 1988 (3) 1991 (5); v A 1984 (5) 1988 (5); v NZ 1986 (3); v In 1983
  (1) 1987 (4); v P 1986 (3) 1990 (3)*
Rickards, K. R. 2: v E 1947 (1); *v A 1951 (1)*
Roach, C. A. 16: v E 1929 (4) 1934 (1); *v E 1928 (3) 1933 (3); v A 1930 (5)*
Roberts, A. M. E. 47: v E 1973 (1) 1980 (3); v A 1977 (2); v In 1975 (2) 1982 (5); v P 1976 (5); *v E
  1976 (5) 1980 (3); v A 1975 (5) 1979 (3) 1981 (2); v NZ 1979 (2); v In 1974 (5) 1983 (2); v P
  1974 (2)*
Roberts, A. T. 1: *v NZ 1955*
Rodriguez, W. V. 5: v E 1967 (1); v A 1964 (1); v In 1961 (2); *v E 1963 (1)*
Rowe, L. G. 30: v E 1973 (5); v A 1972 (3); v NZ 1971 (4); v In 1975 (4); *v E 1976 (2); v A 1975 (6)
  1979 (3); v NZ 1979 (3)*

St Hill, E. L. 2: v E 1929 (2)
St Hill, W. H. 3: v E 1929 (1); *v E 1928 (2)*
Scarlett, R. O. 3: v E 1959 (3)
Scott, A. P. H. 1: v In 1952
Scott, O. C. 8: v E 1929 (1); *v E 1928 (2); v A 1930 (5)*
Sealey, B. J. 1: *v E 1933*
Sealy, J. E. D. 11: v E 1929 (2) 1934 (4); *v E 1939 (3); v A 1930 (2)*
Shepherd, J. N. 5: v In 1970 (2); *v E 1969 (3)*
Shillingford, G. C. 7: v NZ 1971 (2); v In 1970 (3); *v E 1969 (2)*
Shillingford, I. T. 4: v A 1977 (1); *v P 1976 (3)*
Shivnarine, S. 8: v A 1977 (3); *v In 1978 (5)*
Simmons, P. V. 8: v SA 1991 (1); v P 1987 (1); *v E 1991 (5); v In 1987 (1)*
Singh, C. K. 2: v E 1959 (2)
Small, J. A. 3: v E 1929 (1); *v E 1928 (2)*
Small, M. A. 2: v A 1983 (1); *v E 1984 (1)*

Smith, C. W. 5: v In 1961 (1); *v A 1960 (4)*
Smith, O. G. 26: v A 1954 (4); v P 1957 (5); *v E 1957 (5); v NZ 1955 (4); v In 1958 (5); v P 1958 (3)*
Sobers, G. S. 93: v E 1953 (1) 1959 (5) 1967 (5) 1973 (4); v A 1954 (4) 1964 (5); v NZ 1971 (5); v In
    1961 (5); 1970 (5); v P 1957 (5); *v E 1957 (5) 1963 (5) 1966 (5) 1969 (3) 1973 (3); v A 1960 (5)
    1968 (5); v NZ 1955 (4) 1968 (3); v In 1958 (5) 1966 (3); v P 1958 (3)*
Solomon, J. S. 27: v E 1959 (2); v A 1964 (4); v In 1961 (4); *v E 1963 (5); v A 1960 (5); v In 1958
    (4); v P 1958 (3)*
Stayers, S. C. 4: v In 1961 (4)
Stollmeyer, J. B. 32: v E 1947 (2) 1953 (5); v A 1954 (2); v In 1952 (5); *v E 1939 (3) 1950 (4); v A
    1951 (5); v NZ 1951 (2); v In 1948 (4)*
Stollmeyer, V. H. 1: *v E 1939*

Taylor, J. 3: v P 1957 (1); *v In 1958 (1); v P 1958 (1)*
Trim, J. 4: v E 1947 (1); *v A 1951 (1); v In 1948 (2)*

Valentine, A. L. 36: v E 1953 (3); v A 1954 (3); v In 1952 (5) 1961 (2); v P 1957 (1); *v E 1950 (4)
    1957 (2); v A 1951 (5) 1960 (5); v NZ 1951 (2) 1955 (4)*
Valentine, V. A. 2: *v E 1933 (2)*

Walcott, C. L. 44: v E 1947 (4) 1953 (5) 1959 (2); v A 1954 (5); v In 1952 (5); v P 1957 (4); *v E
    1950 (4) 1957 (5); v A 1951 (3); v NZ 1951 (2); v In 1948 (5)*
Walcott, L. A. 1: v E 1929
Walsh, C. A. 51: v E 1985 (1) 1989 (3); v A 1990 (5); v SA 1991 (1); v NZ 1984 (1); v In 1988 (4);
    v P 1987 (3); *v E 1988 (5) 1991 (5); v A 1984 (5) 1988 (5); v NZ 1986 (3); v In 1987 (4); v P 1986
    (3) 1990 (3)*
Watson, C. 7: v E 1959 (5); v In 1961 (1); *v A 1960 (1)*
Weekes, E. D. 48: v E 1947 (4) 1953 (4); v A 1954 (5) v In 1952 (5); v P 1957 (5); *v E 1950 (4) 1957
    (5); v A 1951 (5); v NZ 1951 (2) 1955 (4); v In 1948 (5)*
Weekes, K. H. 2: *v E 1939 (2)*
White, W. A. 2: v A 1964 (2)
Wight, C. V. 2: v E 1929 (1); *v E 1928 (1)*
Wight, G. L. 1: v In 1952
Wiles, C. A. 1: *v E 1933*
Willett, E. T. 5: v A 1972 (3); *v In 1974 (2)*
Williams, A. B. 7: v A 1977 (3); *v In 1978 (4)*
Williams, D. 1: v SA 1991
Williams, E. A. V. 4: v E 1947 (3); *v E 1939 (1)*
Wishart, K. L. 1: v E 1934
Worrell, F. M. M. 51: v E 1947 (3) 1953 (4) 1959 (4); v A 1954 (4); v In 1952 (5) 1961 (5); *v E 1950
    (4) 1957 (5) 1963 (5); v A 1951 (5) 1960 (5); v NZ 1951 (2)*

NEW ZEALAND

Number of Test cricketers: 177

Alabaster, J. C. 21: v E 1962 (2); v WI 1955 (1); v In 1967 (4); *v E 1958 (2); v SA 1961 (5); v WI
    1971 (2); v In 1955 (4); v P 1955 (1)*
Allcott, C. F. W. 6: v E 1929 (2); v SA 1931 (1); *v E 1931 (3)*
Anderson, R. W. 9: v E 1977 (3); *v E 1978 (3); v P 1976 (3)*
Anderson, W. M. 1: v A 1945
Andrews, B. 2: *v A 1973 (2)*

Badcock, F. T. 7: v E 1929 (3) 1932 (2); v SA 1931 (2)
Barber, R. T. 1: v WI 1955
Bartlett, G. A. 10: v E 1965 (2); v In 1967 (2); v P 1964 (1); *v SA 1961 (5)*
Barton, P. T. 7: v E 1962 (3); *v SA 1961 (4)*
Beard, D. D. 4: v WI 1951 (2) 1955 (2)
Beck, J. E. F. 8: v WI 1955 (4); *v SA 1953 (4)*
Bell, W. 2: *v SA 1953 (2)*
Bilby, G. P. 2: v E 1965 (2)
Blain, T. E. 3: *v E 1986 (1); v In 1988 (2)*

Blair, R. W. 19: v E 1954 (1) 1958 (2) 1962 (2); v SA 1952 (2) 1963 (3); v WI 1955 (2); *v E 1958 (3); v SA 1953 (4)*

Blunt, R. C. 9: v E 1929 (4); v SA 1931 (2); *v E 1931 (3)*

Bolton, B. A. 2: v E 1958 (2)

Boock, S. L. 30: v E 1977 (3) 1983 (2) 1987 (1); v WI 1979 (3) 1986 (2); v P 1978 (3) 1984 (2) 1988 (1); *v E 1978 (3); v A 1985 (1); v WI 1984 (3); v SL 1983 (3)*

Bracewell, B. P. 6: v P 1978 (1) 1984 (1); *v E 1978 (3); v A 1980 (1)*

Bracewell, J. G. 41: v E 1987 (3); v A 1985 (2) 1989 (1); v WI 1986 (3); v In 1980 (1) 1989 (2); v P 1988 (2); *v E 1983 (4) 1986 (3) 1990 (3); v A 1980 (3) 1985 (2) 1987 (3); v WI 1984 (1); v In 1988 (3); v P 1984 (2); v SL 1983 (2) 1986 (3)*

Bradburn, G. E. 4: v SL 1990 (1); *v P 1990 (3)*

Bradburn, W. P. 2: v SA 1963 (2)

Brown, V. R. 2: *v A 1985 (2)*

Burgess, M. G. 50: v E 1970 (1) 1977 (3); v A 1973 (1) 1976 (2); v WI 1968 (2); v In 1967 (4) 1975 (3); v P 1972 (3) 1978 (3); *v E 1969 (2) 1973 (3) 1978 (3); v A 1980 (3); v WI 1971 (5); v In 1969 (3) 1976 (3); v P 1969 (3) 1976 (3)*

Burke, C. 1: v A 1945

Burtt, T. B. 10: v E 1946 (1) 1950 (2); v SA 1952 (1); v WI 1951 (2); *v E 1949 (4)*

Butterfield, L. A. 1: v A 1945

Cairns, B. L. 43: v E 1974 (1) 1977 (1) 1983 (3); v A 1976 (1) 1981 (3); v WI 1979 (3); v In 1975 (1) 1980 (3); v P 1978 (3) 1984 (3); v SL 1982 (2); *v E 1978 (2) 1983 (4); v A 1973 (1) 1980 (3) 1985 (1); v WI 1984 (2); v In 1976 (2); v P 1976 (2); v SL 1983 (2)*

Cairns, C. L. 5: v E 1991 (3); v SL 1990 (1); *v A 1989 (1)*

Cameron, F. J. 19: v E 1962 (3); v SA 1963 (3); v P 1964 (3); *v E 1965 (2); v SA 1961 (5); v In 1964 (1); v P 1964 (2)*

Cave, H. B. 19: v E 1954 (2); v WI 1955 (3); *v E 1949 (4) 1958 (2); v In 1955 (5); v P 1955 (3)*

Chapple, M. E. 14: v E 1954 (1) 1965 (1); v SA 1952 (1) 1963 (3); v WI 1955 (1); *v SA 1953 (5) 1961 (2)*

Chatfield, E. J. 43: v E 1974 (1) 1977 (1) 1983 (3) 1987 (3); v A 1976 (2) 1981 (1) 1985 (3); v WI 1986 (3); v P 1984 (3) 1988 (2); v SL 1982 (2); *v E 1983 (3) 1986 (1); v A 1985 (2) 1987 (2); v WI 1984 (4); v In 1988 (3); v P 1984 (3); v SL 1983 (2) 1986 (1)*

Cleverley, D. C. 2: v SA 1931 (1); v A 1945 (1)

Collinge, R. O. 35: v E 1970 (2) 1974 (2) 1977 (3); v A 1973 (3); v In 1967 (2) 1975 (3); v P 1964 (3) 1972 (2); *v E 1965 (3) 1969 (1) 1973 (3) 1978 (1); v In 1964 (2) 1976 (1); v P 1964 (2) 1976 (2)*

Colquhoun, I. A. 2: v E 1954 (2)

Coney, J. V. 52: v E 1983 (3); v A 1973 (3) 1981 (3) 1985 (3); v WI 1979 (3) 1986 (3); v In 1980 (3); v P 1978 (3) 1984 (3); v SL 1982 (2); *v E 1983 (4) 1986 (3); v A 1973 (3) 1980 (2) 1985 (3); v WI 1984 (4); v P 1984 (3); v SL 1983 (3)*

Congdon, B. E. 61: v E 1965 (3) 1970 (2) 1974 (2) 1977 (3); v A 1973 (3) 1976 (2); v WI 1968 (3); v In 1967 (4) 1975 (3); v P 1964 (3) 1972 (3); *v E 1965 (3) 1969 (3) 1973 (3) 1978 (3); v A 1973 (3); v WI 1971 (5); v In 1964 (3) 1969 (3); v P 1964 (1) 1969 (3)*

Cowie, J. 9: v E 1946 (1); v A 1945 (1); *v E 1937 (3) 1949 (4)*

Cresswell G. F. 3: v E 1950 (2); *v E 1949 (1)*

Cromb, I. B. 5: v SA 1931 (2); *v E 1931 (3)*

Crowe, J. J. 39: v E 1983 (3) 1987 (2); v A 1989 (1); v WI 1986 (3); v P 1984 (3) 1988 (2); v SL 1982 (2); *v E 1983 (3) 1986 (3); v A 1985 (3) 1987 (3) 1989 (1); v WI 1984 (4); v P 1984 (3); v SL 1983 (3) 1986 (1)*

Crowe, M. D. 59: v E 1983 (3) 1987 (3) 1991 (3); v A 1981 (3) 1985 (3); v WI 1986 (3); v In 1989 (3); v P 1984 (3) 1988 (2); v SL 1990 (2); *v E 1983 (4) 1986 (3) 1990 (3); v A 1985 (3) 1987 (3) 1989 (1); v WI 1984 (4); v P 1984 (3) 1990 (3); v SL 1983 (3) 1986 (1)*

Cunis, R. S. 20: v E 1965 (3) 1970 (2); v SA 1963 (1); v WI 1968 (3); *v E 1969 (1); v WI 1971 (5); v In 1969 (3); v P 1969 (2)*

D'Arcy, J. W. 5: *v E 1958 (5)*

Dempster, C. S. 10: v E 1929 (4) 1932 (2); v SA 1931 (2); *v E 1931 (2)*

Dempster, E. W. 5: v SA 1952 (1); *v SA 1953 (4)*

Dick, A. E. 17: v E 1962 (3); v SA 1963 (2); v P 1964 (2); *v E 1965 (2); v SA 1961 (5); v P 1964 (3)*

Dickinson, G. R. 3: v E 1929 (2); v SA 1931 (1)

Donnelly, M. P. 7: *v E 1937 (3) 1949 (4)*

Dowling, G. T. 39: v E 1962 (3) 1970 (2); v In 1967 (4); v SA 1963 (3); v WI 1968 (3); v P 1964 (2); *v E 1965 (3) 1969 (3); v SA 1961 (4); v WI 1971 (2); v In 1964 (4) 1969 (3); v P 1964 (2) 1969 (3)*

Dunning, J. A. 4: v E 1932 (1); *v E 1937 (3)*

Edgar, B. A. 39: v E 1983 (3); v A 1981 (3) 1985 (3); v WI 1979 (3); v In 1980 (3); v P 1978 (3); v SL 1982 (2); *v E 1978 (3) 1983 (4) 1985 (3); v A 1980 (3) 1985 (3); v P 1984 (3)*

Edwards, G. N. 8: v E 1977 (1); v A 1976 (2); v In 1980 (3); *v E 1978 (2)*

Emery, R. W. G. 2: v WI 1951 (2)

Fisher, F. E. 1: v SA 1952

Foley, H. 1: v E 1929

Franklin, T. J. 21: v E 1987 (3); v A 1985 (1) 1989 (1); v In 1989 (3); v SL 1990 (3); *v E 1983 (1) 1990 (3); v In 1988 (3); v P 1990 (3)*

Freeman, D. L. 2: v E 1932 (2)

Gallichan, N. 1: *v E 1937*

Gedye, S. G. 4: v SA 1963 (3); v P 1964 (1)

Gillespie, S. R. 1: v A 1985

Gray, E. J. 10: *v E 1983 (2) 1986 (3); v A 1987 (1); v In 1988 (1); v P 1984 (2); v SL 1986 (1)*

Greatbatch, M. J. 20: v E 1987 (2) 1991 (1); v A 1989 (1); v In 1989 (3); v P 1988 (1); v SL 1990 (2); *v A 1989 (1); v In 1988 (3); v P 1990 (3)*

Guillen, S. C. 3: v WI 1955 (3)

Guy, J. W. 12: v E 1958 (2); v WI 1955 (2); *v SA 1961 (2); v In 1955 (5); v P 1955 (1)*

Hadlee, D. R. 26: v E 1974 (2) 1977 (1); v A 1973 (3) 1976 (1); v In 1975 (3); v P 1972 (2); *v E 1969 (2) 1973 (3); v A 1973 (3); v In 1969 (3); v P 1969 (3)*

Hadlee, Sir R. J. 86: v E 1977 (3) 1983 (3) 1987 (1); v A 1973 (2) 1976 (2) 1981 (3) 1985 (3) 1989 (1); v WI 1979 (3) 1986 (3); v In 1975 (2) 1980 (3) 1989 (3); v P 1972 (1) 1978 (3) 1984 (3) 1988 (2); v SL 1982 (2); *v E 1973 (1) 1978 (3) 1983 (4) 1986 (3) 1990 (3); v A 1973 (3) 1980 (3) 1985 (3) 1987 (3); v WI 1984 (4); v In 1976 (3) 1988 (3); v P 1976 (3); v SL 1983 (3) 1986 (1)*

Hadlee, W. A. 11: v E 1946 (1) 1950 (2); v A 1945 (1); *v E 1937 (3) 1949 (4)*

Harford, N. S. 8: *v E 1958 (4); v In 1955 (1); v P 1955 (2)*

Harford, R. I. 3: v In 1967 (3)

Harris, P. G. Z. 9: v P 1964 (1); *v SA 1961 (5); v In 1955 (1); v P 1955 (2)*

Harris, R. M. 2: v E 1958 (2)

Hartland, B. R. 3: v E 1991 (3)

Hastings, B. F. 31: v E 1974 (2); v A 1973 (3); v WI 1968 (3); v In 1975 (1); v P 1972 (2); *v E 1969 (3) 1973 (3); v A 1973 (3); v WI 1971 (5); v In 1969 (2); v P 1969 (3)*

Hayes, J. A. 15: v E 1950 (2) 1954 (1); v WI 1951 (2); *v E 1958 (4); v In 1955 (5); v P 1955 (1)*

Henderson, M. 1: v E 1929

Horne, P. A. 4: v WI 1986 (1); *v A 1987 (1); v P 1990 (1); v SL 1986 (1)*

Hough, K. W. 2: v E 1958 (2)

Howarth, G. P. 47: v E 1974 (2) 1977 (3) 1983 (3); v A 1976 (2) 1981 (3); v WI 1979 (3); v In 1980 (3); v P 1978 (3) 1984 (3); v SL 1982 (2); *v E 1978 (3) 1983 (4); v A 1980 (2); v WI 1984 (4); v In 1976 (2); v P 1976 (2); v SL 1983 (3)*

Howarth, H. J. 30: v E 1970 (2) 1974 (2); v A 1973 (3) 1976 (2); v In 1975 (2); v P 1972 (3); *v E 1969 (3) 1973 (2); v WI 1971 (5); v In 1969 (3); v P 1969 (3)*

James, K. C. 11: v E 1929 (4) 1932 (2); v SA 1931 (2); *v E 1931 (3)*

Jarvis, T. W. 13: v E 1965 (1); v P 1972 (3); *v WI 1971 (4); v In 1964 (2); v P 1964 (3)*

Jones, A. H. 23: v E 1987 (1) 1991 (1); v A 1989 (1); v In 1989 (3); v P 1988 (2); v SL 1990 (3); *v E 1990 (3); v A 1987 (3); v In 1988 (3); v SL 1986 (1)*

Kerr, J. L. 7: v E 1932 (2); v SA 1931 (2); *v E 1931 (2) 1937 (2)*

Kuggeleijn, C. M. 2: *v In 1988 (2)*

Latham, R. T. 1: v E 1991

Lees, W. K. 21: v E 1977 (2); v A 1976 (1); v WI 1979 (3); v P 1978 (3); v SL 1982 (2); *v E 1983 (2); v A 1980 (2); v In 1976 (3); v P 1976 (3)*

Leggat, I. B. 1: *v SA 1953*

Leggat, J. G. 9: v E 1954 (1); v SA 1952 (1); v WI 1951 (1) 1955 (1); *v In 1955 (3); v P 1955 (2)*

Lissette, A. F. 2: v WI 1955 (2)
Lowry, T. C. 7: v E 1929 (4); *v E 1931 (3)*

MacGibbon, A. R. 26: v E 1950 (2) 1954 (2); v SA 1952 (1); v WI 1955 (3); *v E 1958 (5); v SA 1953 (5); v In 1955 (5); v P 1955 (3)*
McEwan, P. E. 4: v WI 1979 (1); *v A 1980 (2); v P 1984 (1)*
McGirr, H. M. 2: v E 1929 (2)
McGregor, S. N. 25: v E 1954 (2) 1958 (2); v SA 1963 (3); v WI 1955 (4); v P 1964 (2); *v SA 1961 (5); v In 1955 (4); v P 1955 (3)*
McLeod E. G. 1: v E 1929
McMahon T. G. 5: v WI 1955 (1); *v In 1955 (3); v P 1955 (1)*
McRae, D. A. N. 1: v A 1945
Matheson, A. M. 2: v E 1929 (1); *v E 1931 (1)*
Meale, T. 2: *v E 1958 (2)*
Merritt, W. E. 6: v E 1929 (4); *v E 1931 (2)*
Meuli, E. M. 1: v SA 1952
Milburn, B. D. 3: v WI 1968 (3)
Miller, L. S. M. 13: v SA 1952 (2); v WI 1955 (3); *v E 1958 (4); v SA 1953 (4)*
Mills, J. E. 7: v E 1929 (3) 1932 (1); *v E 1931 (3)*
Moir, A. M. 17: v E 1950 (2) 1954 (2) 1958 (2); v SA 1952 (1); v WI 1951 (2) 1955 (1); *v E 1958 (2); v In 1955 (2); v P 1955 (3)*
Moloney D. A. R. 3: *v E 1937 (3)*
Mooney, F. L. H. 14: v E 1950 (2); v SA 1952 (2); v WI 1951 (2); *v E 1949 (3); v SA 1953 (5)*
Morgan, R. W. 20: v E 1965 (2) 1970 (2); v WI 1968 (1); v P 1964 (2); *v E 1965 (3); v WI 1971 (3); v In 1964 (4); v P 1964 (3)*
Morrison, B. D. 1: v E 1962
Morrison, D. K. 25: v E 1987 (3) 1991 (3); v A 1989 (1); v In 1989 (3); v P 1988 (1); v SL 1990 (3); *v E 1990 (3); v A 1987 (3) 1989 (1); v In 1988 (1); v P 1990 (3)*
Morrison, J. F. M. 17: v E 1974 (2); v A 1973 (3) 1981 (3); v In 1975 (3); *v A 1973 (3); v In 1976 (1); v P 1976 (2)*
Motz, R. C. 32: v E 1962 (2) 1965 (3); v SA 1963 (2); v WI 1968 (3); v In 1967 (4); v P 1964 (3); *v E 1965 (3) 1969 (3); v SA 1961 (5); v In 1964 (3); v P 1964 (1)*
Murray, B. A. G. 13: v E 1970 (1); v In 1967 (4); *v E 1969 (2); v In 1969 (3); v P 1969 (3)*

Newman J. 3: v E 1932 (2); v SA 1931 (1)

O'Sullivan, D. R. 11: v In 1975 (1); v P 1972 (1); *v A 1973 (3); v In 1976 (3); v P 1976 (3)*
Overton, G. W. F. 3: *v SA 1953 (3)*

Page, M. L. 14: v E 1929 (4) 1932 (2); v SA 1931 (2); *v E 1931 (3) 1937 (3)*
Parker, J. M. 36: v E 1974 (2) 1977 (3); v A 1973 (3) 1976 (2); v WI 1979 (3); v In 1975 (3); v P 1972 (1) 1978 (2); *v E 1973 (3) 1978 (2); v A 1973 (3) 1980 (3); v In 1976 (3); v P 1976 (3)*
Parker, N. M. 3: *v In 1976 (2); v P 1976 (1)*
Parore, A. C. 2: v E 1991 (1); *v E 1990 (1)*
Patel, D. N. 16: v E 1991 (3); v WI 1986 (3); v P 1988 (1); v SL 1990 (2); *v A 1987 (3) 1989 (1); v P 1990 (3)*
Petherick, P. J. 6: v A 1976 (1); *v In 1976 (3); v P 1976 (2)*
Petrie, E. C. 14: v E 1958 (2) 1965 (3); *v E 1958 (5); v In 1955 (2); v P 1955 (2)*
Playle, W. R. 8: v E 1962 (3); *v E 1958 (5)*
Pollard, V. 32: v E 1965 (3) 1970 (1); v WI 1968 (3); v In 1967 (4); v P 1972 (1); *v E 1965 (3) 1969 (3) 1973 (3); v In 1964 (4) 1969 (1); v P 1964 (3) 1969 (3)*
Poore, M. B. 14: v E 1954 (1); v SA 1952 (1); *v SA 1953 (5); v In 1955 (4); v P 1955 (3)*
Priest, M. W. 1: *v E 1990*
Pringle, C. 6: v E 1991 (1); v SL 1990 (2); *v P 1990 (3)*
Puna, N. 3: v E 1965 (3)

Rabone, G. O. 12: v E 1954 (2); v SA 1952 (1); v WI 1951 (2); *v E 1949 (4); v SA 1953 (3)*
Redmond, R. E. 1: v P 1972
Reid, J. F. 19: v A 1985 (3); v In 1980 (3); v P 1978 (1) 1984 (3); *v A 1985 (3); v P 1984 (3); v SL 1983 (3)*

Reid, J. R. 58: v E 1950 (2) 1954 (2) 1958 (2) 1962 (3); v SA 1952 (2) 1963 (3); v WI 1951 (2) 1955 (4); v P 1964 (3); *v E 1949 (2) 1958 (5) 1965 (3); v SA 1953 (5) 1961 (5); v In 1955 (5) 1964 (4); v P 1955 (3) 1964 (3)*

Roberts, A. D. G. 7: v In 1975 (2); *v In 1976 (3); v P 1976 (2)*

Roberts, A. W. 5: v E 1929 (1); v SA 1931 (2); *v E 1937 (2)*

Robertson, G. K. 1: v A 1985

Rowe, C. G. 1: v A 1945

Rutherford, K. R. 30: v E 1987 (2) 1991 (2); v A 1985 (3) 1989 (1); v WI 1986 (2); v In 1989 (3); v SL 1990 (3); *v E 1986 (1) 1990 (2); v A 1987 (1); v WI 1984 (4); v In 1988 (2); v P 1990 (3); v SL 1986 (1)*

Scott, R. H. 1: v E 1946

Scott, V. J. 10: v E 1946 (1) 1950 (2); v A 1945 (1); v WI 1951 (2); *v E 1949 (4)*

Shrimpton, M. J. F. 10: v E 1962 (2) 1965 (3) 1970 (2); v SA 1963 (1); *v A 1973 (3)*

Sinclair, B. W. 21: v E 1962 (3) 1965 (3); v SA 1963 (3); v In 1967 (3); v P 1964 (2); *v E 1965 (3); v In 1964 (2); v P 1964 (3)*

Sinclair, I. M. 2: v WI 1955 (2)

Smith, F. B. 4: v E 1946 (1); v WI 1951 (1); *v E 1949 (2)*

Smith, H. D. 1: v E 1932

Smith, I. D. S. 63: v E 1983 (3) 1987 (3) 1991 (2); v A 1981 (3) 1985 (3) 1989 (1); v WI 1986 (3); v In 1980 (3) 1989 (3); v P 1984 (3) 1988 (3); v SL 1990 (3); *v E 1983 (2) 1986 (2) 1990 (2); v A 1980 (1) 1985 (3) 1987 (3) 1989 (1); v WI 1984 (4); v In 1988 (3); v P 1984 (3) 1990 (3); v SL 1983 (3) 1986 (1)*

Snedden, C. A. 1: v E 1946

Snedden, M. C. 25: v E 1983 (1) 1987 (2); v A 1981 (3) 1989 (1); v WI 1986 (1); v In 1980 (3) 1989 (3); v SL 1982 (2); *v E 1983 (1) 1990 (3); v A 1985 (1) 1987 (1) 1989 (1); v In 1988 (1); v SL 1986 (1)*

Sparling, J. T. 11: v E 1958 (2) 1962 (1); v SA 1963 (2); *v E 1958 (3); v SA 1961 (3)*

Stirling, D. A. 6: *v E 1986 (2); v WI 1984 (1); v P 1984 (3)*

Su'a, M. L. 2: v E 1991 (2)

Sutcliffe, B. 42: v E 1946 (1) 1950 (2) 1954 (2) 1958 (2); v SA 1952 (2); v WI 1951 (2) 1955 (2); *v E 1949 (4) 1958 (4) 1965 (1); v SA 1953 (5); v In 1955 (5) 1964 (4); v P 1955 (3) 1964 (3)*

Taylor, B. R. 30: v E 1965 (1); v WI 1968 (3); v In 1967 (3); v P 1972 (3); *v E 1965 (2) 1969 (2) 1973 (3); v WI 1971 (4); v In 1964 (3) 1969 (2); v P 1964 (3) 1969 (1)*

Taylor, D. D. 3: v E 1946 (1); v WI 1955 (2)

Thomson, K. 2: v In 1967 (2)

Thomson, S. A. 4: v E 1991 (1); v In 1989 (1); v SL 1990 (2)

Tindill, E. W. T. 5: v E 1946 (1); v A 1945 (1); *v E 1937 (3)*

Troup, G. B. 15: v A 1981 (2) 1985 (2); v WI 1979 (3); v In 1980 (2); v P 1978 (2); *v A 1980 (2); v WI 1984 (1); v In 1976 (1)*

Truscott, P. B. 1: v P 1964

Turner, G. M. 41: v E 1970 (2) 1974 (2); v A 1973 (3) 1976 (2); v WI 1968 (3); v In 1975 (3); v P 1972 (3); v SL 1982 (2); *v E 1969 (2) 1973 (3); v A 1973 (2); v WI 1971 (5); v In 1969 (3) 1976 (3); v P 1969 (1) 1976 (2)*

Vance, R. H. 4: v E 1987 (1); v P 1988 (2); *v A 1989 (1)*

Vivian, G. E. 5: *v WI 1971 (4); v In 1964 (1)*

Vivian, H. G. 7: v E 1932 (1); v SA 1931 (1); *v E 1931 (2) 1937 (3)*

Wadsworth, K. J. 33: v E 1970 (2) 1974 (2); v A 1973 (3); v In 1975 (3); v P 1972 (3); *v E 1969 (3) 1973 (3); v A 1973 (3); v WI 1971 (5); v In 1969 (3); v P 1969 (3)*

Wallace, W. M. 13: v E 1946 (1) 1950 (2); v A 1945 (1); v SA 1952 (2); *v E 1937 (3) 1949 (4)*

Ward, J. T. 8: v SA 1963 (1); v In 1967 (1); v P 1964 (1); *v E 1965 (1); v In 1964 (4)*

Watson, W. 10: v E 1991 (1); v SL 1990 (3); *v E 1986 (2); v A 1989 (1); v P 1990 (3)*

Watt, L. 1: v E 1954

Webb, M. G. 3: v E 1970 (1); v A 1973 (1); *v WI 1971 (1)*

Webb, P. N. 2: v WI 1979 (2)

Weir, G. L. 11: v E 1929 (3) 1932 (2); v SA 1931 (3); *v E 1931 (3) 1937 (1)*

White, D. J. 2: *v P 1990 (2)*

Whitelaw, P. E. 2: v E 1932 (2)

Wright, J. G. 77: v E 1977 (3) 1983 (3) 1987 (3) 1991 (3); v A 1981 (3) 1985 (2) 1989 (1); v WI 1979 (3) 1986 (3); v In 1980 (3) 1989 (3); v P 1978 (3) 1984 (3) 1988 (2); v SL 1982 (2) 1990 (3); *v E 1978 (2) 1983 (3) 1986 (3) 1990 (3); v A 1980 (3) 1985 (3) 1987 (3) 1989 (1); v WI 1984 (4); v In 1988 (3); v P 1984 (3); v SL 1983 (3)*

Yuile, B. W. 17: v E 1962 (2); v WI 1968 (1); v In 1967 (1); v P 1964 (3); *v E 1965 (1); v In 1964 (3) 1969 (1); v P 1964 (1) 1969 (2)*

INDIA

Number of Test cricketers: 194

Abid Ali, S. 29: v E 1972 (4); v A 1969 (1); v WI 1974 (2); v NZ 1969 (3); *v E 1971 (3) 1974 (3); v A 1967 (4); v WI 1970 (5); v NZ 1967 (4)*

Adhikari, H. R. 21: v E 1951 (3); v A 1956 (2); v WI 1948 (5) 1958 (1); v P 1952 (2); *v E 1952 (3); v A 1947 (5)*

Amarnath, L. 24: v E 1933 (3) 1951 (3); v WI 1948 (5); v P 1952 (5); *v E 1946 (3); v A 1947 (5)*

Amarnath, M. 69: v E 1976 (2) 1984 (5); v A 1969 (1) 1979 (1) 1986 (3); v WI 1978 (2) 1983 (3) 1987 (3); v NZ 1976 (3); v P 1983 (2) 1986 (5); v SL 1986 (2); *v E 1979 (2) 1986 (2); v A 1977 (5) 1985 (3); v WI 1975 (4) 1982 (5); v NZ 1975 (3); v P 1978 (3) 1982 (6) 1984 (2); v SL 1985 (2)*

Amarnath, S. 10: v E 1976 (2); *v WI 1975 (2); v NZ 1975 (3); v P 1978 (3)*

Amar Singh 7: v E 1933 (3); *v E 1932 (1) 1936 (3)*

Amir Elahi 1: *v A 1947*

Ankola, S. A. 1: *v P 1989*

Apte, A. L. 1: *v E 1959*

Apte, M. L. 7: v P 1952 (2); *v WI 1952 (5)*

Arshad Ayub 13: v WI 1987 (4); v NZ 1988 (3); *v WI 1988 (4); v P 1989 (2)*

Arun, B. 2: v SL 1986 (2)

Arun Lal 16: v WI 1987 (4); v NZ 1988 (3); v P 1986 (1); v SL 1982 (1); *v WI 1988 (4); v P 1982 (3)*

Azad, K. 7: v E 1981 (3); v WI 1983 (2); v P 1983 (1); *v NZ 1980 (1)*

Azharuddin, M. 46: v E 1984 (3); v A 1986 (3); v WI 1987 (3); v NZ 1988 (3); v P 1986 (5); v SL 1986 (1) 1990 (1); *v E 1986 (3) 1990 (3); v A 1985 (3) 1991 (5); v WI 1988 (3); v NZ 1989 (3); v P 1989 (4); v SL 1985 (3)*

Baig, A. A. 10: v A 1959 (3); v WI 1966 (2); v P 1960 (3); *v E 1959 (2)*

Banerjee, S. A. 1: v WI 1948

Banerjee, S. N. 1: v WI 1948

Banerjee, S. T. 1: *v A 1991*

Baqa Jilani, M. 1: *v E 1936*

Bedi, B. S. 67: v E 1972 (5) 1976 (5); v A 1969 (5); v WI 1966 (2) 1974 (4) 1978 (3); v NZ 1969 (3) 1976 (3); *v E 1967 (3) 1971 (3) 1974 (3) 1979 (3); v A 1967 (2) 1977 (5); v WI 1970 (5) 1975 (4); v NZ 1967 (4) 1975 (2); v P 1978 (3)*

Bhandari, P. 3: v A 1956 (1); v NZ 1955 (1); *v P 1954 (1)*

Bhat, A. R. 2: v WI 1983 (1); v P 1983 (1)

Binny, R. M. H. 27: v E 1979 (1); v WI 1983 (6); v P 1979 (6) 1983 (2) 1986 (3); *v E 1986 (3); v A 1980 (1) 1985 (2); v NZ 1980 (1); v P 1984 (1); v SL 1985 (1)*

Borde, C. G. 55: v E 1961 (5) 1963 (5); v A 1959 (5) 1964 (3) 1969 (1); v WI 1958 (4) 1966 (3); v NZ 1964 (4); *v E 1959 (4) 1967 (3); v A 1967 (4); v WI 1961 (5); v NZ 1967 (4)*

Chandrasekhar, B. S. 58: v E 1963 (4) 1972 (5) 1976 (5); v A 1964 (2); v WI 1966 (3) 1974 (4) 1978 (4); v NZ 1964 (2) 1976 (3); *v E 1967 (3) 1971 (3) 1974 (2) 1979 (1); v A 1967 (2) 1977 (5); v WI 1975 (4); v NZ 1975 (3); v P 1978 (3)*

Chauhan, C. P. S. 40: v E 1972 (2); v A 1969 (1) 1979 (6); v WI 1978 (6); v NZ 1969 (2); v P 1979 (6); *v E 1979 (4); v A 1977 (4) 1980 (3); v NZ 1980 (3); v P 1978 (3)*

Chowdhury, N. R. 2: v E 1951 (1); v WI 1948 (1)

Colah, S. H. M. 2: v E 1933 (1); *v E 1932 (1)*

Contractor, N. J. 31: v E 1961 (5); v A 1956 (1) 1959 (5); v WI 1958 (5); v NZ 1955 (4); v P 1960 (5); *v E 1959 (4); v WI 1961 (2)*

Dani, H. T. 1: v P 1952

Desai, R. B. 28: v E 1961 (4) 1963 (2); v A 1959 (3); v WI 1958 (1); v NZ 1964 (3); v P 1960 (5); *v E 1959 (5); v A 1967 (1); v WI 1961 (3); v NZ 1967 (1)*

Dilawar Hussain 3: v E 1933 (2); *v E 1936 (1)*

Divecha, R. V. 5: v E 1951 (2); v P 1952 (1); *v E 1952 (2)*

Doshi, D. R. 33: v E 1979 (1) 1981 (6); v A 1979 (6); v P 1979 (6) 1983 (1); v SL 1982 (1); *v E 1982 (3); v A 1980 (3); v NZ 1980 (2); v P 1982 (4)*

Durani, S. A. 29: v E 1961 (5) 1963 (5) 1972 (3); v A 1959 (1) 1964 (3); v WI 1966 (1); v NZ 1964 (3); *v WI 1961 (5) 1970 (3)*

Engineer, F. M. 46: v E 1961 (4) 1972 (5); v A 1969 (5); v WI 1966 (1) 1974 (5); v NZ 1964 (4) 1969 (2); *v E 1967 (3) 1971 (3) 1974 (3); v A 1967 (4); v WI 1961 (3); v NZ 1967 (4)*

Gadkari, C. V. 6: *v WI 1952 (3); v P 1954 (3)*

Gaekwad, A. D. 40: v E 1976 (4) 1984 (3); v WI 1974 (3) 1978 (5) 1983 (6); v NZ 1976 (3); v P 1983 (3); *v E 1979 (2); v A 1977 (1); v WI 1975 (3) 1982 (5); v P 1984 (2)*

Gaekwad, D. K. 11: v WI 1958 (1); v P 1952 (2) 1960 (1); *v E 1952 (1) 1959 (4); v WI 1952 (2)*

Gaekwad, H. G. 1: v P 1952

Gandotra, A. 2: v A 1969 (1); v NZ 1969 (1)

Gavaskar, S. M. 125: v E 1972 (5) 1976 (5) 1979 (1) 1981 (6) 1984 (5); v A 1979 (6) 1986 (3); v WI 1974 (2) 1978 (6) 1983 (6); v NZ 1976 (3); v P 1979 (6) 1983 (3) 1986 (4); v SL 1982 (1) 1986 (3); *v E 1971 (3) 1974 (3) 1979 (4) 1982 (3) 1986 (3); v A 1977 (5) 1980 (3) 1985 (3); v WI 1970 (4) 1975 (4) 1982 (5); v NZ 1975 (3) 1980 (3); v P 1978 (3) 1982 (6) 1984 (2); v SL 1985 (3)*

Ghavri, K. D. 39: v E 1976 (3) 1979 (1); v A 1979 (6); v WI 1974 (3) 1978 (6); v NZ 1976 (2); v P 1979 (6); *v E 1979 (2); v A 1977 (3) 1980 (3); v NZ 1980 (1); v P 1978 (1)*

Ghorpade, J. M. 8: v A 1956 (1); v WI 1958 (1); v NZ 1955 (1); *v E 1959 (3); v WI 1952 (2)*

Ghulam Ahmed 22: v E 1951 (2); v A 1956 (2); v WI 1948 (3) 1958 (2); v NZ 1955 (1); v P 1952 (4); *v E 1952 (4); v P 1954 (4)*

Gopalan, M. J. 1: v E 1933

Gopinath, C. D. 8: v E 1951 (3); v A 1959 (1); v P 1952 (1); *v E 1952 (1); v P 1954 (2)*

Guard, G. M. 2: v A 1959 (1); v WI 1958 (1)

Guha, S. 4: v A 1969 (3); *v E 1967 (1)*

Gul Mahomed 8: v P 1952 (2); *v E 1946 (1); v A 1947 (5)*

Gupte, B. P. 3: v E 1963 (1); v NZ 1964 (1); v P 1960 (1)

Gupte, S. P. 36: v E 1951 (1) 1961 (2); v A 1956 (3); v WI 1958 (5); v NZ 1955 (5); v P 1952 (2) 1960 (2); *v E 1959 (5); v WI 1952 (5); v P 1954 (5)*

Gursharan Singh 1: *v NZ 1989*

Hafeez, A. 3: *v E 1946 (3)*

Hanumant Singh 14: v E 1963 (2); v A 1964 (3); v WI 1966 (2); v NZ 1964 (4) 1969 (1); *v E 1967 (2)*

Hardikar, M. S. 2: v WI 1958 (2)

Hazare, V. S. 30: v E 1951 (5); v WI 1948 (5); v P 1952 (3); *v E 1946 (3) 1952 (4); v A 1947 (5); v WI 1952 (5)*

Hindlekar, D. D. 4: *v E 1936 (1) 1946 (3)*

Hirwani, N. D. 14: v WI 1987 (1); v NZ 1988 (3); v SL 1990 (1); *v E 1990 (3); v WI 1988 (3); v NZ 1989 (3)*

Ibrahim, K. C. 4: v WI 1948 (4)

Indrajitsinhji, K. S. 4: v A 1964 (3); v NZ 1969 (1)

Irani, J. K. 2: *v A 1947 (2)*

Jahangir Khan, M. 4: *v E 1932 (1) 1936 (3)*

Jai, L. P. 1: v E 1933

Jaisimha, M. L. 39: v E 1961 (5) 1963 (5); v A 1959 (1) 1964 (3); v WI 1966 (2); v NZ 1964 (4) 1969 (1); v P 1960 (4); *v E 1959 (1); v A 1967 (2); v WI 1961 (4) 1970 (3); v NZ 1967 (4)*

Jamshedji, R. J. 1: v E 1933

Jayantilal, K. 1: *v WI 1970*

Joshi, P. G. 12: v E 1951 (2); v A 1959 (1); v WI 1958 (1); v P 1952 (1) 1960 (1); *v E 1959 (3); v WI 1952 (3)*

Kanitkar, H. S. 2: v WI 1974 (2)

Kapil Dev 115: v E 1979 (1) 1981 (6) 1984 (4); v A 1979 (6) 1986 (3); v WI 1978 (6) 1983 (6) 1987 (4); v NZ 1988 (3); v P 1979 (6) 1983 (3) 1986 (5); v SL 1982 (1) 1986 (3) 1990 (1); *v E 1979 (4) 1982 (3) 1986 (3) 1990 (3); v A 1980 (3) 1985 (3) 1991 (5); v WI 1982 (5) 1988 (4); v NZ 1980 (3) 1989 (3); v P 1978 (3) 1982 (6) 1984 (2) 1989 (4); v SL 1985 (3)*

Kardar, A. H. (*see* Hafeez)

Kenny, R. B. 5: v A 1959 (4); v WI 1958 (1)

Kirmani, S. M. H. 88: v E 1976 (5) 1979 (1) 1981 (6) 1984 (5); v A 1979 (6); v WI 1978 (6) 1983 (6); v NZ 1976 (3); v P 1979 (6) 1983 (3); v SL 1982 (1); *v E 1982 (3); v A 1977 (5) 1980 (3) 1985 (3); v WI 1975 (4) 1982 (5); v NZ 1975 (3) 1980 (3); v P 1978 (3) 1982 (6) 1984 (2)*

Kischenchand, G. 5: v P 1952 (1); *v A 1947 (4)*

Kripal Singh, A. G. 14: v E 1961 (3) 1963 (2); v A 1956 (2) 1964 (1); v WI 1958 (1); v NZ 1955 (4); *v E 1959 (1)*

Krishnamurthy, P. 5: *v WI 1970 (5)*

Kulkarni, R. R. 3: v A 1986 (1); v P 1986 (2)

Kulkarni, U. N. 4: *v A 1967 (3); v NZ 1967 (1)*

Kumar, V. V. 2: v E 1961 (1); v P 1960 (1)

Kumble, A. 1: *v E 1990*

Kunderan, B. K. 18: v E 1961 (1) 1963 (5); v A 1959 (4); v WI 1966 (3); v NZ 1964 (1); v P 1960 (2); *v E 1967 (2); v WI 1961 (2)*

Lall Singh 1: *v E 1932*

Lamba, R. 4: v WI 1987 (1); v SL 1986 (3)

Madan Lal 39: v E 1976 (2) 1981 (6); v WI 1974 (2) 1983 (3); v NZ 1976 (1); v P 1983 (3); v SL 1982 (1); *v E 1974 (2) 1982 (3) 1986 (1); v A 1977 (2); v WI 1975 (4) 1982 (2); v NZ 1975 (3); v P 1982 (3) 1984 (1)*

Maka, E. S. 2: v P 1952 (1); *v WI 1952 (1)*

Malhotra, A. 7: v E 1981 (2) 1984 (1); v WI 1983 (3); *v E 1982 (1)*

Maninder Singh 34: v A 1986 (3); v WI 1983 (4) 1987 (3); v P 1986 (4); v SL 1986 (3); *v E 1986 (3); v WI 1982 (3); v P 1982 (5) 1984 (1) 1989 (3); v SL 1985 (2)*

Manjrekar, S. V. 21: v WI 1987 (1); v SL 1990 (1); *v E 1990 (3); v A 1991 (5); v WI 1988 (4); v NZ 1989 (3) v P 1989 (4)*

Manjrekar, V. L. 55: v E 1951 (2) 1961 (5) 1963 (4); v A 1956 (3) 1964 (3); v WI 1958 (4); v NZ 1955 (5) 1964 (1); v P 1952 (3) 1960 (5); *v E 1952 (4) 1959 (2); v WI 1952 (4) 1961 (5); v P 1954 (5)*

Mankad, A. V. 22: v E 1976 (1); v A 1969 (5); v WI 1974 (1); v NZ 1969 (2) 1976 (3); *v E 1971 (3) 1974 (1); v A 1977 (3); v WI 1970 (3)*

Mankad, V. 44: v E 1951 (5); v A 1956 (3); v WI 1948 (5) 1958 (2); v NZ 1955 (4); v P 1952 (4); *v E 1946 (3) 1952 (3); v A 1947 (3); v WI 1952 (5); v P 1954 (5)*

Mansur Ali Khan (*see* Pataudi)

Mantri, M. K. 4: v E 1951 (1); *v E 1952 (2); v P 1954 (1)*

Meherhomji, K. R. 1: *v E 1936*

Mehra, V. L. 8: v E 1961 (1) 1963 (2); v NZ 1955 (2); *v WI 1961 (3)*

Merchant, V. M. 10: v E 1933 (3) 1951 (1); *v E 1936 (3) 1946 (3)*

Milkha Singh, A. G. 4: v E 1961 (1); v A 1959 (1); v P 1960 (2)

Modi, R. S. 10: v E 1951 (1); v WI 1948 (5); v P 1952 (1); *v E 1946 (3)*

More, K. S. 38: v A 1986 (2); v WI 1987 (4); v NZ 1988 (3); v P 1986 (5); v SL 1986 (3) 1990 (1); *v E 1986 (3) 1990 (3); v A 1991 (3); v WI 1988 (4); v NZ 1989 (3); v P 1989 (4)*

Muddiah, V. M. 2: v A 1959 (1); v P 1960 (1)

Mushtaq Ali, S. 11: v E 1933 (2) 1951 (1); v WI 1948 (1); *v E 1936 (3) 1946 (2)*

Nadkarni, R. G. 41: v E 1961 (1) 1963 (5); v A 1959 (5) 1964 (3); v WI 1958 (1) 1966 (1); v NZ 1955 (1) 1964 (4); v P 1960 (4); *v E 1959 (4); v A 1967 (3); v WI 1961 (5); v NZ 1967 (4)*

Naik, S. S. 3: v WI 1974 (2); *v E 1974 (2)*

Naoomal Jeoomal 3: v E 1933 (2); *v E 1932 (1)*

Narasimha Rao, M. V. 4: v A 1979 (2); v WI 1978 (2)

Navle, J. G. 2: v E 1933 (1); *v E 1932 (1)*

Nayak, S. V. 2: *v E 1982 (2)*

Nayudu, C. K. 7: v E 1933 (3); *v E 1932 (1) 1936 (3)*

Nayudu, C. S. 11: v E 1933 (2) 1951 (1); *v E 1936 (2) 1946 (2); v A 1947 (4)*

Nazir Ali, S. 2: v E 1933 (1); *v E 1932 (1)*

Nissar, Mahomed 6: v E 1933 (2); *v E 1932 (1) 1936 (3)*
Nyalchand, S. 1: v P 1952

Pai, A. M. 1: v NZ 1969
Palia, P. E. 2: *v E 1932 (1) 1936 (1)*
Pandit, C. S. 5: v A 1986 (2); *v E 1986 (1); v A 1991 (2)*
Parkar, G. A. 1: *v E 1982*
Parkar, R. D. 2: v E 1972 (2)
Parsana, D. D. 2: v WI 1978 (2)
Patankar, C. T. 1: v NZ 1955
Pataudi sen., Nawab of, 3: *v E 1946 (3)*
Pataudi jun., Nawab of (now Mansur Ali Khan) 46: v E 1961 (3) 1963 (5) 1972 (3); v A 1964 (3) 1969 (5); v WI 1966 (3) 1974 (4); v NZ 1964 (4) 1969 (3); *v E 1967 (3); v A 1967 (3); v WI 1961 (3); v NZ 1967 (4)*
Patel, B. P. 21: v E 1976 (5); v WI 1974 (3); v NZ 1976 (3); *v E 1974 (2); v A 1977 (2); v WI 1975 (3); v NZ 1975 (3)*
Patel, J. M. 7: v A 1956 (2) 1959 (3); v NZ 1955 (1); *v P 1954 (1)*
Patel, R. 1: v NZ 1988
Patiala, Yuvraj of, 1: v E 1933
Patil, S. M. 29: v E 1979 (1) 1981 (4) 1984 (2); v WI 1983 (2); v P 1979 (2) 1983 (3); v SL 1982 (1); *v E 1982 (2); v A 1980 (3); v NZ 1980 (3); v P 1982 (4) 1984 (2)*
Patil, S. R. 1: v NZ 1955
Phadkar, D. G. 31: v E 1951 (4); v A 1956 (1); v WI 1948 (4) 1958 (1); v NZ 1955 (4); v P 1952 (2); *v E 1952 (4); v A 1947 (4); v WI 1952 (4); v P 1954 (3)*
Prabhakar, M. 18: v E 1984 (2); v SL 1990 (1); *v E 1990 (3); v A 1991 (5); v NZ 1989 (3); v P 1989 (4)*
Prasanna, E. A. S. 49: v E 1961 (1) 1972 (3) 1976 (4); v A 1969 (5); v WI 1966 (1) 1974 (5); v NZ 1969 (3); *v E 1967 (3) 1974 (2); v A 1967 (4) 1977 (4); v WI 1961 (1) 1970 (3) 1975 (1); v NZ 1967 (4) 1975 (3); v P 1978 (2)*
Punjabi, P. H. 5: *v P 1954 (5)*

Rai Singh, K. 1: *v A 1947*
Rajinder Pal 1: v E 1963
Rajindernath, V. 1: v P 1952
Rajput, L. S. 2: *v SL 1985 (2)*
Raju, S. L. V. 7: v SL 1990 (1); *v A 1991 (4); v NZ 1989 (2)*
Raman, W. V. 6: v WI 1987 (1); v NZ 1988 (1); *v WI 1988 (1); v NZ 1989 (3)*
Ramaswami, C. 2: *v E 1936 (2)*
Ramchand, G. S. 33: v A 1956 (3) 1959 (5); v WI 1958 (3); v NZ 1955 (5); v P 1952 (3); *v E 1952 (4); v WI 1952 (5); v P 1954 (5)*
Ramji, L. 1: v E 1933
Rangachary, C. R. 4: v WI 1948 (2); *v A 1947 (2)*
Rangnekar, K. M. 3: *v A 1947 (3)*
Ranjane, V. B. 7: v E 1961 (3) 1963 (1); v A 1964 (1); v WI 1958 (1); *v WI 1961 (1)*
Razdan, V. 2: *v P 1989 (2)*
Reddy, B. 4: *v E 1979 (4)*
Rege, M. R. 1: v WI 1948
Roy, A. 4: v A 1969 (2); v NZ 1969 (2)
Roy, Pankaj 43: v E 1951 (5); v A 1956 (3) 1959 (5); v WI 1958 (5); v NZ 1955 (3); v P 1952 (3) 1960 (1); *v E 1952 (4) 1959 (5); v WI 1952 (4); v P 1954 (5)*
Roy, Pranab 2: v E 1981 (2)

Sandhu, B. S. 8: v WI 1983 (1); *v WI 1982 (4); v P 1982 (3)*
Sardesai, D. N. 30: v E 1961 (1) 1963 (5) 1972 (1); v A 1964 (1) 1969 (1); v WI 1966 (3); v NZ 1964 (3); *v E 1967 (1) 1971 (3); v A 1967 (2); v WI 1961 (3) 1970 (5)*
Sarwate, C. T. 9: v E 1951 (1); v WI 1948 (2); *v E 1946 (1); v A 1947 (5)*
Saxena, R. C. 1: *v E 1967*
Sekar, T. A. P. 2: *v P 1982 (2)*
Sen, P. 14: v E 1951 (2); v WI 1948 (5); v P 1952 (2); *v E 1952 (2); v A 1947 (3)*
Sengupta, A. K. 1: v WI 1958
Sharma, Ajay 1: v WI 1987

Sharma, Chetan 23: v E 1984 (3); v A 1986 (2); v WI 1987 (3); v SL 1986 (2); *v E 1986 (2); v A 1985 (2); v WI 1988 (4); v P 1984 (2); v SL 1985 (3)*
Sharma, Gopal 5: v E 1984 (1); v P 1986 (2); v SL 1990 (1); *v SL 1985 (1)*
Sharma, P. 5: v E 1976 (2); v WI 1974 (2); *v WI 1975 (1)*
Sharma, Sanjeev 2: v NZ 1988 (1); *v E 1990 (1)*
Shastri, R. J. 76: v E 1981 (6) 1984 (5); v A 1986 (3); v WI 1983 (6) 1987 (4); v NZ 1988 (3); v P 1983 (2) 1986 (5); v SL 1986 (3) 1990 (1); *v E 1982 (3) 1986 (3) 1990 (3); v A 1985 (3) 1991 (3); v WI 1982 (5) 1988 (4); v NZ 1980 (3); v P 1982 (2) 1984 (2) 1989 (4); v SL 1985 (3)*
Shinde, S. G. 7: v E 1951 (3); v WI 1948 (1) 1952 (2)
Shodhan, R. H. 3: v P 1952 (1); *v WI 1952 (2)*
Shukla, R. C. 1: v SL 1982
Sidhu, N. S. 20: v WI 1983 (2); v NZ 1988 (3); *v E 1990 (3); v A 1991 (3); v WI 1988 (4); v NZ 1989 (1); v P 1989 (4)*
Sivaramakrishnan, L. 9: v E 1984 (5); *v A 1985 (2); v WI 1982 (1); v SL 1985 (1)*
Sohoni, S. W. 4: v E 1951 (1); *v E 1946 (2); v A 1947 (1)*
Solkar, E. D. 27: v E 1972 (5) 1976 (1); v A 1969 (4); v WI 1974 (4); v NZ 1969 (1); *v E 1971 (3) 1974 (3); v WI 1970 (5) 1975 (1)*
Sood, M. M. 1: v A 1959
Srikkanth, K. 43: v E 1981 (4) 1984 (2); v A 1986 (3); v WI 1987 (4); v NZ 1988 (3); v P 1986 (5); v SL 1986 (3); *v E 1986 (3); v A 1985 (3) 1991 (4); v P 1982 (2) 1989 (4); v SL 1985 (3)*
Srinath, J. 5: *v A 1991 (5)*
Srinivasan, T. E. 1: *v NZ 1980*
Subramanya, V. 9: v WI 1966 (2); v NZ 1964 (1); *v E 1967 (2); v A 1967 (2); v NZ 1967 (2)*
Sunderram, G. 2: v NZ 1955 (2)
Surendranath, R. 11: v A 1959 (2); v WI 1958 (2); v P 1960 (2); *v E 1959 (5)*
Surti, R. F. 26: v WI 1963 (1); v A 1964 (2) 1969 (1); v WI 1966 (2); v NZ 1964 (1) 1969 (2); v P 1960 (2); *v E 1967 (2); v A 1967 (4); v WI 1961 (5); v NZ 1967 (4)*
Swamy, V. N. 1: v NZ 1955

Tamhane, N. S. 21: v A 1956 (3) 1959 (1); v WI 1958 (4); v NZ 1955 (4); v P 1960 (2); *v E 1959 (2); v P 1954 (5)*
Tarapore, K. K. 1: v WI 1948
Tendulkar, S. R. 16: v SL 1990 (1); *v E 1990 (3); v A 1991 (5); v NZ 1989 (3); v P 1989 (4)*

Umrigar, P. R. 59: v E 1951 (5) 1961 (4); v A 1956 (3) 1959 (3); v WI 1948 (1) 1958 (5); v NZ 1955 (5); v P 1952 (5) 1960 (5); *v E 1952 (4) 1959 (4); v WI 1952 (5) 1961 (5); v P 1954 (5)*

Vengsarkar, D. B. 116: v E 1976 (1) 1979 (1) 1981 (6) 1984 (5); v A 1979 (6) 1986 (2); v WI 1978 (6) 1983 (5) 1987 (3); v NZ 1988 (3); v P 1979 (5) 1983 (1) 1986 (5); v SL 1982 (1) 1986 (3) 1990 (1); *v E 1979 (4) 1982 (3) 1986 (3) 1990 (3); v A 1977 (5) 1980 (3) 1985 (3) 1991 (5); v WI 1975 (2) 1982 (5) 1988 (4); v NZ 1975 (3) 1980 (3) 1989 (2); v P 1978 (3) 1982 (6) 1984 (2); v SL 1985 (3)*
Venkataraghavan, S. 57: v E 1972 (2) 1976 (1); v A 1969 (5) 1979 (3); v WI 1966 (2) 1974 (2) 1978 (6); v NZ 1964 (4) 1969 (2) 1976 (3); v P 1983 (2); *v E 1967 (1) 1971 (3) 1974 (2) 1979 (4); v A 1977 (1); v WI 1970 (5) 1975 (3) 1982 (5); v NZ 1975 (1)*
Venkataramana, M. 1: *v WI 1988*
Viswanath, G. R. 91: v E 1972 (5) 1976 (5) 1979 (1) 1981 (6); v A 1969 (4) 1979 (6); v WI 1974 (5) 1978 (6); v NZ 1976 (3); v P 1979 (6); v SL 1982 (1); *v E 1971 (3) 1974 (3) 1979 (4) 1982 (3); v A 1977 (5) 1980 (3); v WI 1970 (3) 1975 (4); v NZ 1975 (3) 1980 (3); v P 1978 (3) 1982 (6)*
Viswanath, S. 3: *v SL 1985 (3)*
Vizianagram, Maharaj Kumar of, Sir Vijay A. 3: *v E 1936 (3)*

Wadekar, A. L. 37: v E 1972 (5); v A 1969 (5); v WI 1966 (2); v NZ 1969 (3); *v E 1967 (3) 1971 (3) 1974 (3); v A 1967 (4); v WI 1970 (5); v NZ 1967 (4)*
Wassan, A. S. 4: *v E 1990 (1); v NZ 1989 (3)*
Wazir Ali, S. 7: v E 1933 (3); *v E 1932 (1) 1936 (3)*

Yadav, N. S. 35: v E 1979 (1) 1981 (1) 1984 (4); v A 1979 (5) 1986 (3); v WI 1983 (3); v P 1979 (5) 1986 (4); v SL 1986 (2); *v A 1980 (2) 1985 (3); v NZ 1980 (1); v P 1984 (1)*
Yajurvindra Singh 4: v E 1976 (2); v A 1979 (1); *v E 1979 (1)*
Yashpal Sharma 37: v E 1979 (1) 1981 (2); v A 1979 (6); v WI 1983 (1); v P 1979 (6) 1983 (3); v SL 1982 (1); *v E 1979 (3) 1982 (3); v A 1980 (3); v WI 1982 (5); v NZ 1980 (1); v P 1982 (2)*
Yograj Singh 1: *v NZ 1980*

Note: Hafeez, on going later to Oxford University, took his correct name, Kardar.

PAKISTAN

Number of Test cricketers: 125

Aamer Malik 13: v E 1987 (2); v A 1988 (1); v WI 1990 (1); v In 1989 (4); *v A 1989 (2); v WI 1987 (1); v NZ 1988 (2)*

Aamir Sohail 5: *v E 1992 (5)*

Abdul Kadir 4: v A 1964 (1); *v A 1964 (1); v NZ 1964 (2)*

Abdul Qadir 67: v E 1977 (3) 1983 (3) 1987 (3); v A 1982 (3) 1988 (3); v WI 1980 (2) 1986 (3) 1990 (2); v NZ 1984 (3) 1990 (2); v In 1982 (5) 1984 (1) 1989 (4); v SL 1985 (3); *v E 1982 (3) 1987 (4); v A 1983 (5); v WI 1987 (3); v NZ 1984 (2) 1988 (2); v In 1979 (3) 1986 (3); v SL 1985 (2)*

Afaq Hussain 2: v E 1961 (1); *v A 1964 (1)*

Aftab Baloch 2: v A 1974 (1); v NZ 1969 (1)

Aftab Gul 6: v E 1968 (2); v NZ 1969 (1); *v E 1971 (3)*

Agha Saadat Ali 1: v NZ 1955

Agha Zahid 1: v WI 1974

Akram Raza 3: v WI 1990 (1); v In 1989 (1); v SL 1991 (1)

Alim-ud-Din 25: v E 1961 (2); v A 1956 (1) 1959 (1); v WI 1958 (1); v NZ 1955 (3); v In 1954 (3); *v E 1954 (3) 1962 (3); v WI 1957 (5); v In 1960 (1)*

Amir Elahi 5: *v In 1952 (5)*

Anil Dalpat 9: v E 1983 (3); v NZ 1984 (3); *v NZ 1984 (3)*

Anwar Hussain 4: *v In 1952 (4)*

Anwar Khan 1: *v NZ 1978*

Aqib Javed 13: v NZ 1990 (3); v SL 1991 (3); *v E 1992 (5); v A 1989 (1); v NZ 1988 (1)*

Arif Butt 3: *v A 1964 (1); v NZ 1964 (2)*

Ashraf Ali 8: v E 1987 (3); v In 1984 (2); v SL 1981 (2) 1985 (1)

Asif Iqbal 58: v E 1968 (3) 1972 (3); v A 1964 (1); v WI 1974 (2); v NZ 1964 (3) 1969 (3) 1976 (3); v In 1978 (3); *v E 1967 (3) 1971 (3) 1974 (3); v A 1964 (1) 1972 (3) 1976 (3) 1978 (2); v WI 1976 (5); v NZ 1964 (3) 1972 (3) 1978 (2); v In 1979 (6)*

Asif Masood 16: v E 1968 (2) 1972 (1); v WI 1974 (2); v NZ 1969 (1); *v E 1971 (3) 1974 (3); v A 1972 (3) 1976 (1)*

Asif Mujtaba 8: v E 1987 (1); v WI 1986 (2); *v E 1992 (5)*

Ata-ur-Rehman 1: *v E 1992*

Azeem Hafeez 18: v E 1983 (2); v NZ 1984 (3); v In 1984 (2); *v A 1983 (5); v NZ 1984 (3); v In 1983 (3)*

Azhar Khan 1: v A 1979

Azmat Rana 1: v A 1979

Burki, J. 25: v E 1961 (3); v A 1964 (1); v NZ 1964 (3) 1969 (1); *v E 1962 (5) 1967 (3); v A 1964 (1); v NZ 1964 (3); v In 1960 (5)*

D'Souza, A. 6: v E 1961 (2); v WI 1958 (1); *v E 1962 (3)*

Ehtesham-ud-Din 5: v A 1979 (1); *v E 1982 (1); v In 1979 (3)*

Farooq Hamid 1: *v A 1964*

Farrukh Zaman 1: v NZ 1976

Fazal Mahmood 34: v E 1961 (1); v A 1956 (1) 1959 (2); v WI 1958 (3); v NZ 1955 (2); v In 1954 (4); *v E 1954 (4) 1962 (2); v WI 1957 (5); v In 1952 (5) 1960 (5)*

Ghazali, M. E. Z. 2: *v E 1954 (2)*

Ghulam Abbas 1: *v E 1967*

Gul Mahomed 1: v A 1956

Hanif Mohammad 55: v E 1961 (3) 1968 (3); v A 1956 (1) 1959 (3) 1964 (1); v WI 1958 (1); v NZ 1955 (3) 1964 (3) 1969 (1); v In 1954 (5); *v E 1954 (4) 1962 (5) 1967 (3); v A 1964 (1); v WI 1957 (5); v NZ 1964 (3); v In 1952 (5) 1960 (5)*

Haroon Rashid 23: v E 1977 (3); v A 1979 (2) 1982 (3); v In 1982 (1); v SL 1981 (2); *v E 1978 (3) 1982 (1); v A 1976 (1) 1978 (1); v WI 1976 (5); v NZ 1978 (1)*

Haseeb Ahsan 12: v E 1961 (2); v A 1959 (1); v WI 1958 (1); *v WI 1957 (3); v In 1960 (5)*

Ibadulla, K. 4: v A 1964 (1); *v E 1967 (2); v NZ 1964 (1)*

Ijaz Ahmed 19: v E 1987 (3); v A 1988 (3); v WI 1990 (3); *v E 1987 (4); v A 1989 (3); v WI 1987 (2); v In 1986 (1)*

Ijaz Butt 8: v A 1959 (2); v WI 1958 (3); *v E 1962 (3)*

Ijaz Faqih 5: v WI 1980 (1); *v A 1981 (1); v WI 1987 (2); v In 1986 (1)*

Imran Khan 88: v A 1979 (2) 1982 (3); v WI 1980 (4) 1986 (3) 1990 (3); v NZ 1976 (3); v In 1978 (3) 1982 (6) 1989 (4); v SL 1981 (1) 1985 (3) 1991 (3); *v E 1971 (1) 1974 (3) 1982 (3) 1987 (5); v A 1976 (3) 1978 (2) 1981 (3) 1983 (2) 1989 (3); v WI 1976 (5) 1987 (3); v NZ 1978 (2) 1988 (2); v In 1979 (5) 1986 (5); v SL 1985 (3)*

Imtiaz Ahmed 41: v E 1961 (3); v A 1956 (1) 1959 (3); v WI 1958 (3); v NZ 1955 (3); v In 1954 (5); *v E 1954 (4) 1962 (4); v WI 1957 (5); v In 1952 (5) 1960 (5)*

Intikhab Alam 47: v E 1961 (2) 1968 (3) 1972 (3); v A 1959 (1) 1964 (1); v WI 1974 (2); v NZ 1964 (3) 1969 (3) 1976 (3); *v E 1962 (3) 1967 (3) 1971 (3) 1974 (3); v A 1964 (1) 1972 (3); v WI 1976 (1); v NZ 1964 (3) 1972 (3); v In 1960 (3)*

Inzamam-ul-Haq 4: *v E 1992 (4)*

Iqbal Qasim 50: v E 1977 (3) 1987 (3); v A 1979 (3) 1982 (2) 1988 (3); v WI 1980 (4); v NZ 1984 (3); v In 1978 (3) 1982 (2); v SL 1981 (3); *v E 1978 (3); v A 1976 (3) 1981 (2); v WI 1976 (2); v NZ 1984 (1); v In 1979 (6) 1983 (1) 1986 (3)*

Israr Ali 4: v A 1959 (2); *v In 1952 (2)*

Jalal-ud-Din 6: v A 1982 (1); v In 1982 (2) 1984 (2); v SL 1985 (1)

Javed Akhtar 1: *v E 1962*

Javed Miandad 117: v E 1977 (3) 1987 (3); v A 1979 (3) 1982 (3) 1988 (3); v WI 1980 (4) 1986 (3) 1990 (2); v NZ 1976 (3) 1984 (3) 1990 (3); v In 1978 (3) 1982 (6) 1984 (2) 1989 (4); v SL 1981 (3) 1985 (3) 1991 (3); *v E 1978 (3) 1982 (3) 1987 (5) 1992 (5); v A 1976 (3) 1978 (2) 1981 (3) 1983 (5) 1989 (3); v WI 1976 (1) 1987 (3); v NZ 1978 (3) 1984 (3) 1988 (2); v In 1979 (6) 1983 (3) 1986 (4); v SL 1985 (3)*

Kardar, A. H. 23: v A 1956 (1); v NZ 1955 (3); v In 1954 (5); *v E 1954 (4); v WI 1957 (5); v In 1952 (5)*

Khalid Hassan 1: *v E 1954*

Khalid Wazir 2: *v E 1954 (2)*

Khan Mohammad 13: v A 1956 (1); v NZ 1955 (3); v In 1954 (4); *v E 1954 (2); v WI 1957 (2); v In 1952 (1)*

Liaqat Ali 5: v E 1977 (2); v WI 1974 (1); *v E 1978 (2)*

Mahmood Hussain 27: v E 1961 (1); v WI 1958 (3); v NZ 1955 (1); v In 1954 (5); *v E 1954 (2) 1962 (3); v WI 1957 (3); v In 1952 (4) 1960 (5)*

Majid Khan 63: v E 1968 (3) 1972 (3); v A 1964 (1) 1979 (3); v WI 1974 (2) 1980 (4); v NZ 1964 (3) 1976 (3); v In 1978 (3) 1982 (1); v SL 1981 (1); *v E 1967 (3) 1971 (2) 1974 (3) 1982 (1); v A 1972 (3) 1976 (3) 1978 (2) 1981 (3); v WI 1976 (5); v NZ 1972 (3) 1978 (2); v In 1979 (6)*

Mansoor Akhtar 19: v A 1982 (3); v WI 1980 (2); v In 1982 (3); v SL 1981 (1); *v E 1982 (3) 1987 (5); v A 1981 (1) 1989 (1)*

Manzoor Elahi 4: v NZ 1984 (1); v In 1984 (1); *v In 1986 (2)*

Maqsood Ahmed 16: v NZ 1955 (2); v In 1954 (5); *v E 1954 (4); v In 1952 (5)*

Masood Anwar 1: v WI 1990

Mathias, Wallis 21: v E 1961 (1); v A 1956 (1) 1959 (2); v WI 1958 (3); v NZ 1955 (1); *v E 1962 (3); v WI 1957 (5); v In 1960 (5)*

Miran Bux 2: v In 1954 (2)

Mohammad Aslam 1: *v E 1954*

Mohammad Farooq 7: v NZ 1964 (3); *v E 1962 (2); v In 1960 (2)*

Mohammad Ilyas 10: v E 1968 (2); v NZ 1964 (3); *v E 1967 (1); v A 1964 (1); v NZ 1964 (3)*

Mohammad Munaf 4: v E 1961 (2); v A 1959 (2)

Mohammad Nazir 14: v E 1972 (1); v WI 1980 (4); v NZ 1969 (3); *v A 1983 (3); v In 1983 (3)*

Mohsin Kamal 7: v E 1983 (1); v SL 1985 (1); *v E 1987 (4); v SL 1985 (1)*

Mohsin Khan 48: v E 1977 (1) 1983 (3); v A 1982 (3); v WI 1986 (3); v NZ 1984 (2); v In 1982 (6) 1984 (2); v SL 1981 (2) 1985 (2); *v E 1978 (3) 1982 (3); v A 1978 (1) 1981 (2) 1983 (5); v NZ 1978 (1) 1984 (3); v In 1983 (3); v SL 1985 (3)*

Moin Khan 9: v WI 1990 (2); v SL 1991 (3); *v E 1992 (4)*

Mudassar Nazar 76: v E 1977 (3) 1983 (1) 1987 (3); v A 1979 (3) 1982 (3) 1988 (3); v WI 1986 (2); v NZ 1984 (3); v In 1978 (2) 1982 (6) 1984 (2); v SL 1981 (1) 1985 (3); *v E 1978 (3) 1982 (3) 1987 (5); v A 1976 (1) 1978 (1) 1981 (3) 1983 (5); v WI 1987 (3); v NZ 1978 (1) 1984 (3) 1988 (2); v In 1979 (5) 1983 (3); v SL 1985 (3)*

Mufasir-ul-Haq 1: *v NZ 1964*

Munir Malik 3: v A 1959 (1); *v E 1962 (2)*

Mushtaq Ahmed 8: v WI 1990 (2); *v E 1992 (5); v A 1989 (1)*

Mushtaq Mohammad 57: v E 1961 (3) 1968 (3) 1972 (3); v WI 1958 (1) 1974 (2); v NZ 1969 (2) 1976 (3); v In 1978 (3); *v E 1962 (5) 1967 (3) 1971 (3) 1974 (3); v A 1972 (3) 1976 (3) 1978 (2); v WI 1976 (5); v NZ 1972 (2) 1978 (3); v In 1960 (5)*

Nadeem Abbasi 3: v In 1989 (3)

Nadeem Ghauri 1: *v A 1989*

Nasim-ul-Ghani 29: v E 1961 (2); v A 1959 (2) 1964 (1); v WI 1958 (3); *v E 1962 (5) 1967 (2); v A 1964 (1) 1972 (1); v WI 1957 (5); v NZ 1964 (3); v In 1960 (4)*

Naushad Ali 6: v NZ 1964 (3); *v NZ 1964 (3)*

Naved Anjum 2: v NZ 1990 (1); v In 1989 (1)

Nazar Mohammad 5: *v In 1952 (5)*

Nazir Junior (*see* Mohammad Nazir)

Niaz Ahmed 2: v E 1968 (1); *v E 1967 (1)*

Pervez Sajjad 19: v E 1968 (1) 1972 (2); v A 1964 (1); v NZ 1964 (3) 1969 (3); *v E 1971 (3); v NZ 1964 (3) 1972 (3)*

Qasim Omar 26: v E 1983 (3); v WI 1986 (3); v NZ 1984 (3); v In 1984 (2); v SL 1985 (3); *v A 1983 (5); v NZ 1984 (3); v In 1983 (1); v SL 1985 (3)*

Ramiz Raja 44: v E 1983 (2) 1987 (3); v A 1988 (3); v WI 1986 (3) 1990 (2); v NZ 1990 (3); v In 1989 (4); v SL 1985 (1) 1991 (3); *v E 1987 (2) 1992 (5); v A 1989 (2); v WI 1987 (3); v In 1986 (5); v SL 1985 (3)*

Rashid Khan 4: v SL 1981 (2); *v A 1983 (1); v NZ 1984 (1)*

Rashid Latif 1: *v E 1992*

Rehman, S. F. 1: *v WI 1957*

Rizwan-uz-Zaman 11: v WI 1986 (1); v SL 1981 (2); *v A 1981 (1); v NZ 1988 (2); v In 1986 (5)*

Sadiq Mohammad 41: v E 1972 (3) 1977 (2); v WI 1974 (1) 1980 (3); v NZ 1969 (3) 1976 (3); v In 1978 (1); *v E 1971 (3) 1974 (3) 1978 (3); v A 1972 (3) 1976 (2); v WI 1976 (5); v NZ 1972 (3); v In 1979 (3)*

Saeed Ahmed 41: v E 1961 (3) 1968 (3); v A 1959 (3) 1964 (1); v WI 1958 (3); v NZ 1964 (3); *v E 1962 (5) 1967 (3) 1971 (1); v A 1964 (1) 1972 (1); v WI 1957 (5); v NZ 1964 (3); v In 1960 (5)*

Saeed Anwar 1: v WI 1990

Salah-ud-Din 5: v E 1968 (1); v NZ 1964 (3) 1969 (1)

Saleem Jaffer 14: v E 1987 (1); v A 1988 (2); v WI 1986 (1); v NZ 1990 (2); v In 1989 (1); v SL 1991 (2); *v WI 1987 (1); v NZ 1988 (2); v In 1986 (2)*

Salim Altaf 21: v E 1972 (3); v NZ 1969 (2); v In 1978 (1); *v E 1967 (2) 1971 (2); v A 1972 (3) 1976 (2); v WI 1976 (3); v NZ 1972 (3)*

Salim Malik 71: v E 1983 (3) 1987 (3); v A 1988 (3); v WI 1986 (1) 1990 (3); v NZ 1984 (3) 1990 (3); v In 1982 (6) 1984 (2) 1989 (4); v SL 1981 (2) 1985 (3) 1991 (3); *v E 1987 (5) 1992 (5); v A 1983 (3) 1989 (1); v WI 1987 (3); v NZ 1984 (3) 1988 (2); v In 1983 (2) 1986 (5); v SL 1985 (3)*

Salim Yousuf 32: v A 1988 (3); v WI 1986 (3) 1990 (1); v NZ 1990 (3); v In 1989 (1); v SL 1981 (1) 1985 (2); *v E 1987 (5); v A 1989 (3); v WI 1987 (3); v NZ 1988 (2); v In 1986 (5)*

Sarfraz Nawaz 55: v E 1968 (1) 1972 (2) 1977 (2) 1983 (3); v A 1979 (3); v WI 1974 (2) 1980 (2); v NZ 1976 (3); v In 1978 (3) 1982 (6); *v E 1974 (3) 1978 (2) 1982 (1); v A 1972 (2) 1976 (2) 1978 (2) 1981 (3) 1983 (3); v WI 1976 (4); v NZ 1972 (3) 1978 (3)*

Shafiq Ahmed 6: v E 1977 (3); v WI 1980 (2); *v E 1974 (1)*

Shafqat Rana 5: v E 1968 (2); v A 1964 (1); v NZ 1969 (2)

Shahid Israr 1: v NZ 1976

Shahid Mahboob 1: v In 1989

Shahid Mahmood 1: *v E 1962*

Shahid Saeed 1: v In 1989

Sharpe, D. 3: v A 1959 (3)

Shoaib Mohammad 39: v E 1983 (1) 1987 (1); v A 1988 (3); v WI 1990 (3); v NZ 1984 (1) 1990 (3); v In 1989 (4); v SL 1985 (1) 1991 (3); *v E 1987 (4) 1992 (1); v A 1989 (3); v WI 1987 (3); v NZ 1984 (1) 1988 (2); v In 1983 (2) 1986 (3)*

Shuja-ud-Din 19: v E 1961 (2); v A 1959 (3); v WI 1958 (3); v NZ 1955 (3); v In 1954 (5); *v E 1954 (3)*

Sikander Bakht 26: v E 1977 (2); v WI 1980 (1); v NZ 1976 (1); v In 1978 (2) 1982 (1); *v E 1978 (3) 1982 (2); v A 1978 (2) 1981 (3); v WI 1976 (1); v NZ 1978 (3); v In 1979 (5)*

Tahir Naqqash 15: v A 1982 (3); v In 1982 (2); v SL 1981 (3); *v E 1982 (2); v A 1983 (1); v NZ 1984 (1); v In 1983 (3)*

Talat Ali 10: v E 1972 (3); *v E 1978 (2); v A 1972 (1); v NZ 1972 (1) 1978 (3)*

Taslim Arif 6: v A 1979 (3); v WI 1980 (2); *v In 1979 (1)*

Tauseef Ahmed 33: v E 1983 (2) 1987 (2); v A 1979 (3) 1988 (3); v WI 1986 (3); v NZ 1984 (1) 1990 (2); v In 1984 (1); v SL 1981 (3) 1985 (1); *v E 1987 (2); v A 1989 (3); v NZ 1988 (1); v In 1986 (4); v SL 1985 (2)*

Waqar Hassan 21: v A 1956 (1) 1959 (1); v WI 1958 (1); v NZ 1955 (3); v In 1954 (5); *v E 1954 (4); v WI 1957 (1); v In 1952 (5)*

Waqar Younis 19: v WI 1990 (3); v NZ 1990 (3); v In 1989 (2); v SL 1991 (3); *v E 1992 (5); v A 1989 (3)*

Wasim Akram 44: v E 1987 (2); v WI 1986 (2) 1990 (3); v NZ 1990 (2); v In 1989 (4); v SL 1985 (3) 1991 (3); *v E 1987 (5) 1992 (4); v A 1989 (3); v WI 1987 (3); v NZ 1984 (2); v In 1986 (5); v SL 1985 (3)*

Wasim Bari 81: v E 1968 (3) 1972 (3) 1977 (3); v A 1982 (3); v WI 1974 (2) 1980 (2); v NZ 1969 (3) 1976 (2); v In 1978 (3) 1982 (6); *v E 1967 (3) 1971 (3) 1974 (3) 1978 (3) 1982 (3); v A 1972 (3) 1976 (3) 1978 (2) 1981 (3) 1983 (5); v WI 1976 (5); v NZ 1972 (3) 1978 (3); v In 1979 (6) 1983 (3)*

Wasim Raja 57: v E 1972 (1) 1977 (3) 1983 (3); v A 1979 (3); v WI 1974 (2) 1980 (4); v NZ 1976 (1) 1984 (1); v In 1982 (1) 1984 (1); v SL 1981 (3); *v E 1974 (2) 1978 (3) 1982 (1); v A 1978 (1) 1981 (3) 1983 (2); v WI 1976 (5); v NZ 1972 (3) 1978 (3) 1984 (2); v In 1979 (6) 1983 (3)*

Wazir Mohammad 20: v A 1956 (1) 1959 (1); v WI 1958 (3); v NZ 1955 (3); v In 1954 (5); *v E 1954 (2); v WI 1957 (5); v In 1952 (1)*

Younis Ahmed 4: v NZ 1969 (2); *v In 1986 (2)*

Zaheer Abbas 78: v E 1972 (2) 1983 (3); v A 1979 (2) 1982 (3); v WI 1974 (2) 1980 (3); v NZ 1969 (1) 1976 (3) 1984 (3); v In 1978 (3) 1982 (6) 1984 (2); v SL 1981 (1) 1985 (2); *v E 1971 (3) 1974 (3) 1982 (3); v A 1972 (3) 1976 (3) 1978 (2) 1981 (2) 1983 (5); v WI 1976 (3); v NZ 1972 (3) 1978 (2) 1984 (2); v In 1979 (5) 1983 (3)*

Zahid Fazal 6: v WI 1990 (3); v SL 1991 (3)

Zakir Khan 2: v In 1989 (1); *v SL 1985 (1)*

Zulfiqar Ahmed 9: v A 1956 (1); v NZ 1955 (3); *v E 1954 (2); v In 1952 (3)*

Zulqarnain 3: *v SL 1985 (3)*

SRI LANKA

Number of Test cricketers: 51

Ahangama, F. S. 3: v In 1985 (3)

Amalean, K. N. 2: v P 1985 (1); *v A 1987 (1)*

Amerasinghe, A. M. J. G. 2: v NZ 1983 (2)

Anurasiri, S. D. 8: v NZ 1986 (1); v P 1985 (2); *v E 1991 (1); v In 1986 (1); v P 1991 (3)*

Atapattu, M. S. 1: *v In 1990*

de Alwis, R. G. 11: v A 1982 (1); v NZ 1983 (3); v P 1985 (2); *v A 1987 (1); v NZ 1982 (1); v In 1986 (3)*

de Mel, A. L. F. 17: v E 1981 (1); v A 1982 (1); v In 1985 (3); v P 1985 (3); *v E 1984 (1); v In 1982 (1) 1986 (1); v P 1981 (3) 1985 (3)*

de Silva, D. S. 12: v E 1981 (1); v A 1982 (1); v NZ 1983 (3); *v E 1984 (1); v NZ 1982 (2); v In 1982 (1); v P 1981 (3)*

de Silva, E. A. R. 10: v In 1985 (1); v P 1985 (1); *v A 1989 (2); v NZ 1990 (3); v NZ 1990 (3); v In 1986 (3)*

de Silva, G. R. A. 4: v E 1981 (1); *v In 1982 (1); v P 1981 (2)*
de Silva, P. A. 25: v In 1985 (3); v P 1985 (3); *v E 1984 (1) 1988 (1) 1991 (1); v A 1987 (1) 1989 (2); v NZ 1990 (3); v In 1986 (3) 1990 (1); v P 1985 (3) 1991 (3)*
Dias, R. L. 20: v E 1981 (1); v A 1982 (1); v NZ 1983 (2) 1986 (1); v In 1985 (3); v P 1985 (1); *v E 1984 (1); v In 1982 (1) 1986 (3); v P 1981 (3) 1985 (3)*

Fernando, E. R. N. S. 5: v A 1982 (1); v NZ 1983 (2); *v NZ 1982 (2)*

Goonatillake, H. M. 5: v E 1981 (1); *v In 1982 (1); v P 1981 (3)*
Gunasekera, Y. 2: *v NZ 1982 (2)*
Guneratne, R. P. W. 1: v A 1982
Gurusinha, A. P. 17: v NZ 1986 (1); v P 1985 (2); *v E 1991 (1); v A 1989 (2); v NZ 1990 (3); v In 1986 (3) 1990 (1); v P 1985 (1) 1991 (3)*

Hathurusinghe, U. C. 6: *v E 1991 (1); v NZ 1990 (2); v P 1991 (3)*

Jayasekera, R. S. A. 1: *v P 1981*
Jayasuriya, S. T. 6: *v E 1991 (1); v NZ 1990 (2); v P 1991 (3)*
Jeganathan, S. 2: *v NZ 1982 (2)*
John, V. B. 6: v NZ 1983 (3); *v E 1984 (1); v NZ 1982 (2)*
Jurangpathy, B. R. 2: v In 1985 (1); *v In 1986 (1)*

Kaluperuma, L. W. 2: v E 1981 (1); *v P 1981 (1)*
Kaluperuma, S. M. S. 4: v NZ 1983 (3); *v A 1987 (1)*
Kuruppu, D. S. B. P. 4: v NZ 1986 (1); *v E 1988 (1) 1991 (1); v A 1987 (1)*
Kuruppuarachchi, A. K. 2: v NZ 1986 (1); v P 1985 (1)

Labrooy, G. F. 9: *v E 1988 (1); v A 1987 (1) 1989 (2); v NZ 1990 (3); v In 1986 (1) 1990 (1)*

Madugalle, R. S. 21: v E 1981 (1); v A 1982 (1); v NZ 1983 (3) 1986 (1); v In 1985 (3); *v E 1984 (1) 1988 (1); v A 1987 (1); v NZ 1982 (2); v In 1982 (1); v P 1981 (3) 1985 (3)*
Madurasinghe, A. W. R. 2: *v E 1988 (1); v In 1990 (1)*
Mahanama, R. S. 11: v NZ 1986 (1); v P 1985 (2); *v E 1991 (1); v A 1987 (1) 1989 (2); v NZ 1990 (1); v In 1990 (1); v P 1991 (2)*
Mendis, L. R. D. 24: v E 1981 (1); v A 1982 (1); v NZ 1983 (3) 1986 (1); v P 1985 (3); *v E 1984 (1) 1988 (1); v In 1982 (1) 1986 (3); v P 1981 (3) 1985 (3)*

Ramanayake, C. P. H. 10: *v E 1988 (1) 1991 (1); v A 1987 (1) 1989 (2); v NZ 1990 (3); v P 1991 (2)*
Ranasinghe, A. N. 2: *v In 1982 (1); v P 1981 (1)*
Ranatunga, A. 33: v E 1981 (1); v A 1982 (1); v NZ 1983 (3) 1986 (1); v In 1985 (3); v P 1985 (3); *v E 1984 (1) 1988 (1); v A 1987 (1) 1989 (2); v NZ 1990 (3); v In 1982 (1) 1986 (3) 1990 (1); v P 1981 (2) 1985 (3) 1991 (3)*
Ranatunga, D. 2: *v A 1989 (2)*
Ratnayake, R. J. 23: v A 1982 (1); v NZ 1983 (1) 1986 (1); v In 1985 (3); v P 1985 (1); *v E 1991 (1); v A 1989 (1); v NZ 1982 (2) 1990 (3); v In 1986 (2) 1990 (1); v P 1985 (3) 1991 (3)*
Ratnayeke, J. R. 22: v NZ 1983 (2) 1986 (1); v P 1985 (3); *v E 1984 (1) 1988 (1); v A 1987 (1) 1989 (2); v NZ 1982 (2); v In 1982 (1) 1986 (3); v P 1981 (2) 1985 (3)*

Samarasekera, M. A. R. 4: *v E 1988 (1); v A 1989 (1); v In 1990 (1); v P 1991 (1)*
Senanayake, C. P. 3: *v NZ 1990 (3)*
Silva, S. A. R. 9: v In 1985 (3); v P 1985 (1); *v E 1984 (1) 1988 (1); v NZ 1982 (1); v P 1985 (2)*

Tillekeratne, H. P. 9: *v E 1991 (1); v A 1989 (1); v NZ 1990 (3); v In 1990 (1); v P 1991 (3)*

Warnapura, B. 4: v E 1981 (1); *v In 1982 (1); v P 1981 (2)*
Warnaweera, K. P. J. 3: v P 1985 (1); *v NZ 1990 (1); v In 1990 (1)*
Weerasinghe, C. D. U. S. 1: v In 1985
Wettimuny, M. D. 2: *v NZ 1982 (2)*
Wettimuny, S. 23: v E 1981 (1); v A 1982 (1); v NZ 1983 (3); v In 1985 (3); v P 1985 (3); *v E 1984 (1); v NZ 1982 (2); v In 1986 (3); v P 1981 (3) 1985 (3)*
Wickremasinghe, A. G. D. 1: *v A 1989*
Wickremasinghe, G. P. 3: *v P 1991 (3)*
Wijegunawardene, K. I. W. 2: *v E 1991 (1); v P 1991 (1)*
Wijesuriya, R. G. C. E. 4: *v P 1981 (1) 1985 (3)*

TWO COUNTRIES

Thirteen cricketers have appeared for two countries in Test matches, namely:

Amir Elahi, *India and Pakistan*.
J. J. Ferris, *Australia and England*.
S. C. Guillen, *West Indies and NZ*.
Gul Mahomed, *India and Pakistan*.
F. Hearne, *England and South Africa*.
A. H. Kardar, *India and Pakistan*.
W. E. Midwinter, *England and Australia*.

F. Mitchell, *England and South Africa*.
W. L. Murdoch, *Australia and England*.
Nawab of Pataudi, sen., *England and India*.
A. E. Trott, *Australia and England*.
K. C. Wessels, *Australia and South Africa*.
S. M. J. Woods, *Australia and England*.

MOST TEST APPEARANCES FOR EACH COUNTRY

England: D. I. Gower 117.
Australia: A. R. Border 130.
South Africa: J. H. B. Waite 50.
West Indies: I. V. A. Richards 121.

New Zealand: Sir R. J. Hadlee 86.
India: S. M. Gavaskar 125.
Pakistan: Javed Miandad 117.
Sri Lanka: A. Ranatunga 33.

MOST TEST APPEARANCES AS CAPTAIN
FOR EACH COUNTRY

England: P. B. H. May 41.
Australia: A. R. Border 67.
South Africa: H. W. Taylor 18.
West Indies: C. H. Lloyd 74.

New Zealand: J. R. Reid 34.
India: S. M. Gavaskar 47.
Pakistan: Imran Khan 48.
Sri Lanka: L. R. D. Mendis 19.

ENGLAND v REST OF THE WORLD

The following were awarded England caps for playing against the Rest of the World in England in 1970, although the five matches played are now generally considered not to have rated as full Tests: D. L. Amiss (1), G. Boycott (2), D. J. Brown (2), M. C. Cowdrey (4), M. H. Denness (1), B. L. D'Oliveira (4), J. H. Edrich (2), K. W. R. Fletcher (4), A. W. Greig (3), R. Illingworth (5), A. Jones (1), A. P. E. Knott (5), P. Lever (1), B. W. Luckhurst (5), C. M. Old (2), P. J. Sharpe (1), K. Shuttleworth (1), J. A. Snow (5), D. L. Underwood (3), A. Ward (1), D. Wilson (2).

CRICKET RECORDS

Amended by BILL FRINDALL to end of the 1992 season in England

Unless stated to be of a minor character, all records apply only to first-class cricket including some performances in the distant past which have always been recognised as of exceptional merit.

* Denotes not out or an unbroken partnership.

(A), (SA), (WI), (NZ), (I), (P) or (SL) indicates either the nationality of the player, or the country in which the record was made.

FIRST-CLASS RECORDS

BATTING RECORDS

BOWLING RECORDS

ALL-ROUND RECORDS

WICKET-KEEPING RECORDS

FIELDING RECORDS

TEAM RECORDS

TEST MATCH RECORDS

BATTING RECORDS

BOWLING RECORDS

ALL-ROUND RECORDS

WICKET-KEEPING RECORDS

FIELDING RECORDS

TEAM RECORDS

TEST SERIES

LIMITED-OVERS INTERNATIONAL RECORDS

MISCELLANEOUS

FIRST-CLASS RECORDS

BATTING RECORDS

HIGHEST INDIVIDUAL SCORES

499	Hanif Mohammad	Karachi v Bahawalpur at Karachi	1958-59
452*	D. G. Bradman	NSW v Queensland at Sydney	1929-30
443*	B. B. Nimbalkar	Maharashtra v Kathiawar at Poona	1948-49
437	W. H. Ponsford	Victoria v Queensland at Melbourne	1927-28
429	W. H. Ponsford	Victoria v Tasmania at Melbourne	1922-23
428	Aftab Baloch	Sind v Baluchistan at Karachi	1973-74
424	A. C. MacLaren	Lancashire v Somerset at Taunton	1895
405*	G. A. Hick	Worcestershire v Somerset at Taunton	1988
385	B. Sutcliffe	Otago v Canterbury at Christchurch	1952-53
383	C. W. Gregory	NSW v Queensland at Brisbane	1906-07
377	S. V. Manjrekar	Bombay v Hyderabad at Bombay	1990-91
369	D. G. Bradman	South Australia v Tasmania at Adelaide	1935-36
366	N. H. Fairbrother	Lancashire v Surrey at The Oval	1990
365*	C. Hill	South Australia v NSW at Adelaide	1900-01
365*	G. S. Sobers	West Indies v Pakistan at Kingston	1957-58
364	L. Hutton	England v Australia at The Oval	1938
359*	V. M. Merchant	Bombay v Maharashtra at Bombay	1943-44
359	R. B. Simpson	NSW v Queensland at Brisbane	1963-64
357*	R. Abel	Surrey v Somerset at The Oval	1899
357	D. G. Bradman	South Australia v Victoria at Melbourne	1935-36
356	B. A. Richards	South Australia v Western Australia at Perth	1970-71
355*	G. R. Marsh	Western Australia v South Australia at Perth	1989-90
355	B. Sutcliffe	Otago v Auckland at Dunedin	1949-50
352	W. H. Ponsford	Victoria v NSW at Melbourne	1926-27
350	Rashid Israr	Habib Bank v National Bank at Lahore	1976-77
345	C. G. Macartney	Australians v Nottinghamshire at Nottingham	1921
344*	G. A. Headley	Jamaica v Lord Tennyson's XI at Kingston	1931-32
344	W. G. Grace	MCC v Kent at Canterbury	1876
343*	P. A. Perrin	Essex v Derbyshire at Chesterfield	1904
341	G. H. Hirst	Yorkshire v Leicestershire at Leicester	1905
340*	D. G. Bradman	NSW v Victoria at Sydney	1928-29
340	S. M. Gavaskar	Bombay v Bengal at Bombay	1981-82
338*	R. C. Blunt	Otago v Canterbury at Christchurch	1931-32
338	W. W. Read	Surrey v Oxford University at The Oval	1888
337*	Pervez Akhtar	Railways v Dera Ismail Khan at Lahore	1964-65
337†	Hanif Mohammad	Pakistan v West Indies at Bridgetown	1957-58
336*	W. R. Hammond	England v New Zealand at Auckland	1932-33
336	W. H. Ponsford	Victoria v South Australia at Melbourne	1927-28
334	D. G. Bradman	Australia v England at Leeds	1930
333	K. S. Duleepsinhji	Sussex v Northamptonshire at Hove	1930
333	G. A. Gooch	England v India at Lord's	1990
332	W. H. Ashdown	Kent v Essex at Brentwood	1934
331*	J. D. Robertson	Middlesex v Worcestershire at Worcester	1949
325*	H. L. Hendry	Victoria v New Zealanders at Melbourne	1925-26
325	A. Sandham	England v West Indies at Kingston	1929-30
325	C. L. Badcock	South Australia v Victoria at Adelaide	1935-36
324	J. B. Stollmeyer	Trinidad v British Guiana at Port-of-Spain	1946-47
324	Waheed Mirza	Karachi Whites v Quetta at Karachi	1976-77
323	A. L. Wadekar	Bombay v Mysore at Bombay	1966-67
322	E. Paynter	Lancashire v Sussex at Hove	1937
322	I. V. A. Richards	Somerset v Warwickshire at Taunton	1985

321	W. L. Murdoch	NSW v Victoria at Sydney	1881-82
320	R. Lamba	North Zone v West Zone at Bhilai	1987-88
319	Gul Mahomed	Baroda v Holkar at Baroda.	1946-47
318*	W. G. Grace	Gloucestershire v Yorkshire at Cheltenham	1876
317	W. R. Hammond	Gloucestershire v Nottinghamshire at Gloucester . . .	1936
317	K. R. Rutherford	New Zealanders v D. B. Close's XI at Scarborough.	1986
316*	J. B. Hobbs	Surrey v Middlesex at Lord's	1926
316*	V. S. Hazare	Maharashtra v Baroda at Poona.	1939-40
316	R. H. Moore	Hampshire v Warwickshire at Bournemouth.	1937
315*	T. W. Hayward	Surrey v Lancashire at The Oval	1898
315*	P. Holmes	Yorkshire v Middlesex at Lord's.	1925
315*	A. F. Kippax	NSW v Queensland at Sydney	1927-28
314*	C. L. Walcott	Barbados v Trinidad at Port-of-Spain	1945-46
313*	S. J. Cook	Somerset v Glamorgan at Cardiff.	1990
313	H. Sutcliffe	Yorkshire v Essex at Leyton	1932
313	W. V. Raman	Tamil Nadu v Goa at Panjim.	1988-89
312*	W. W. Keeton	Nottinghamshire v Middlesex at The Oval‡	1939
312*	J. M. Brearley	MCC Under-25 v North Zone at Peshawar	1966-67
311*	G. M. Turner	Worcestershire v Warwickshire at Worcester	1982
311	J. T. Brown	Yorkshire v Sussex at Sheffield	1897
311	R. B. Simpson	Australia v England at Manchester	1964
311	Javed Miandad	Karachi Whites v National Bank at Karachi	1974-75
310*	J. H. Edrich	England v New Zealand at Leeds	1965
310	H. Gimblett	Somerset v Sussex at Eastbourne	1948
309	V. S. Hazare	The Rest v Hindus at Bombay	1943-44
308*	F. M. M. Worrell	Barbados v Trinidad at Bridgetown	1943-44
307	M. C. Cowdrey	MCC v South Australia at Adelaide	1962-63
307	R. M. Cowper	Australia v England at Melbourne	1965-66
306*	A. Ducat	Surrey v Oxford University at The Oval	1919
306*	E. A. B. Rowan	Transvaal v Natal at Johannesburg	1939-40
306*	D. W. Hookes	South Australia v Tasmania at Adelaide	1986-87
305*	F. E. Woolley	MCC v Tasmania at Hobart.	1911-12
305*	F. R. Foster	Warwickshire v Worcestershire at Dudley	1914
305*	W. H. Ashdown	Kent v Derbyshire at Dover	1935
304	A. W. Nourse	Natal v Transvaal at Johannesburg	1919-20
304*	P. H. Tarilton	Barbados v Trinidad at Bridgetown	1919-20
304*	E. D. Weekes	West Indians v Cambridge University at Cambridge	1950
304	R. M. Poore	Hampshire v Somerset at Taunton	1899
304	D. G. Bradman	Australia v England at Leeds	1934
303*	W. W. Armstrong	Australians v Somerset at Bath	1905
303*	Mushtaq Mohammad	Karachi Blues v Karachi University at Karachi	1967-68
303*	Abdul Azeem	Hyderabad v Tamil Nadu at Hyderabad	1986-87
302*	P. Holmes	Yorkshire v Hampshire at Portsmouth.	1920
302*	W. R. Hammond	Gloucestershire v Glamorgan at Bristol	1934
302*	Arjan Kripal Singh	Tamil Nadu v Goa at Panjim.	1988-89
302	W. R. Hammond	Gloucestershire v Glamorgan at Newport	1939
302	L. G. Rowe	West Indies v England at Bridgetown	1973-74
301*	E. H. Hendren	Middlesex v Worcestershire at Dudley	1933
301	W. G. Grace	Gloucestershire v Sussex at Bristol	1896
300*	V. T. Trumper	Australians v Sussex at Hove	1899
300*	F. B. Watson	Lancashire v Surrey at Manchester	1928
300*	Imtiaz Ahmed	PM's XI v Commonwealth XI at Bombay	1950-51
300	J. T. Brown	Yorkshire v Derbyshire at Chesterfield	1898
300	D. C. S. Compton	MCC v N. E. Transvaal at Benoni	1948-49
300	R. Subba Row	Northamptonshire v Surrey at The Oval	1958

† *Hanif Mohammad batted for 16 hours 10 minutes – the longest innings in first-class cricket.*
‡ *Played at The Oval because Lord's was required for Eton v Harrow.*
Note: W. V. Raman (313) and Arjan Kripal Singh (302*) provide the only instance of two triple-hundreds in the same innings.

HIGHEST SCORE FOR EACH FIRST-CLASS COUNTY

Derbyshire	274	G. Davidson v Lancashire at Manchester	1896
Durham	157	D. M. Jones v Northamptonshire at Stockton-on-Tees	1992
Essex	343*	P. A. Perrin v Derbyshire at Chesterfield	1904
Glamorgan	287*	D. E. Davies v Gloucestershire at Newport	1939
Gloucestershire	318*	W. G. Grace v Yorkshire at Cheltenham	1876
Hampshire	316	R. H. Moore v Warwickshire at Bournemouth	1937
Kent	332	W. H. Ashdown v Essex at Brentwood	1934
Lancashire	424	A. C. MacLaren v Somerset at Taunton	1895
Leicestershire	252*	S. Coe v Northamptonshire at Leicester	1914
Middlesex	331*	J. D. Robertson v Worcestershire at Worcester	1949
Northamptonshire	300	R. Subba Row v Surrey at The Oval	1958
Nottinghamshire	312*	W. W. Keeton v Middlesex at The Oval†	1939
Somerset	322	I. V. A. Richards v Warwickshire at Taunton	1985
Surrey	357*	R. Abel v Somerset at The Oval	1899
Sussex	333	K. S. Duleepsinhji v Northamptonshire at Hove	1930
Warwickshire	305*	F. R. Foster v Worcestershire at Dudley	1914
Worcestershire	405*	G. A. Hick v Somerset at Taunton	1988
Yorkshire	341	G. H. Hirst v Leicestershire at Leicester	1905

† *Played at The Oval because Lord's was required for Eton v Harrow.*

HIGHEST SCORE AGAINST EACH FIRST-CLASS COUNTY

Derbyshire	343*	P. A. Perrin (Essex) at Chesterfield	1904
Durham	199	M. A. Atherton (Lancashire) at Gateshead Fell	1992
Essex	332	W. H. Ashdown (Kent) at Brentwood	1934
Glamorgan	313*	S. J. Cook (Somerset) at Cardiff	1990
Gloucestershire	296	A. O. Jones (Nottinghamshire) at Nottingham	1903
Hampshire	302*	P. Holmes (Yorkshire) at Portsmouth	1920
Kent	344	W. G. Grace (MCC) at Canterbury	1876
Lancashire	315*	T. W. Hayward (Surrey) at The Oval	1898
Leicestershire	341	G. H. Hirst (Yorkshire) at Leicester	1905
Middlesex	316*	J. B. Hobbs (Surrey) at Lord's	1926
Northamptonshire	333	K. S. Duleepsinhji (Sussex) at Hove	1930
Nottinghamshire	345	C. G. Macartney (Australians) at Nottingham	1921
Somerset	424	A. C. MacLaren (Lancashire) at Taunton	1895
Surrey	366	N. H. Fairbrother (Lancashire) at The Oval	1990
Sussex	322	E. Paynter (Lancashire) at Hove	1937
Warwickshire	322	I. V. A. Richards (Somerset) at Taunton	1985
Worcestershire	331*	J. D. B. Robertson (Middlesex) at Worcester	1949
Yorkshire	318*	W. G. Grace (Gloucestershire) at Cheltenham	1876

DOUBLE-HUNDRED ON DEBUT

227	T. Marsden	Sheffield & Leicester v Nottingham at Sheffield	1826
207	N. F. Callaway	New South Wales v Queensland at Sydney	1914-15
240	W. F. E. Marx	Transvaal v Griqualand West at Johannesburg	1920-21
200*	A. Maynard	Trinidad v MCC at Port-of-Spain	1934-35
232*	S. J. E. Loxton	Victoria v Queensland at Melbourne	1946-47
215*	G. H. G. Doggart	Cambridge University v Lancashire at Cambridge	1948
202	J. Hallebone	Victoria v Tasmania at Melbourne	1951-52
230	G. R. Viswanath	Mysore v Andhra at Vijayawada	1967-68

HUNDRED ON DEBUT IN BRITAIN

(The following list does not include instances of players who have previously appeared in first-class cricket outside the British Isles or who performed the feat before 1965. Full lists of earlier instances are in *Wisdens* prior to 1984.)

108	D. R. Shepherd	Gloucestershire v Oxford University at Oxford.....	1965
110*	A. J. Harvey-Walker	Derbyshire v Oxford University at Burton upon Trent	†1971
173	J. Whitehouse	Warwickshire v Oxford University at Oxford	1971
106	J. B. Turner	Minor Counties v Pakistanis at Jesmond..........	1974
112	J. A. Claughton	Oxford University v Gloucestershire at Oxford.....	†1976
100*	A. W. Lilley	Essex v Nottinghamshire at Nottingham..........	†1978
146*	J. S. Johnson	Minor Counties v Indians at Wellington	1979
110	N. R. Taylor	Kent v Sri Lankans at Canterbury...............	1979
146*	D. G. Aslett	Kent v Hampshire at Bournemouth...............	1981
116	M. D. Moxon	Yorkshire v Essex at Leeds.....................	†1981
100	D. A. Banks	Worcestershire v Oxford University at Oxford	1983
122	A. A. Metcalfe	Yorkshire v Nottinghamshire at Bradford.........	1983
117*	K. T. Medlycott	Surrey v Cambridge University at Banstead	‡1984
101*	N. J. Falkner		
106	A. C. Storie	Northamptonshire v Hampshire at Northampton ...	†1985
102	M. P. Maynard	Glamorgan v Yorkshire at Swansea	1985
117*	R. J. Bartlett	Somerset v Oxford University at Oxford	1986
100*	P. D. Bowler	Leicestershire v Hampshire at Leicester	1986
145	I. L. Philip	Scotland v Ireland at Glasgow	1986
114*	P. D. Atkins	Surrey v Cambridge University at The Oval	1988
100	B. M. W. Patterson	Scotland v Ireland at Dumfries.................	1988
116*	J. J. B. Lewis	Essex v Surrey at The Oval....................	1990
117	J. D. Glendenen	Durham v Oxford University at Oxford	1992
109	J. R. Wileman	Nottinghamshire v Cambridge U. at Nottingham ..	1992

† *In his second innings.*
‡ *The only instance in England of two players performing the feat in the same match.*

Notes: A number of players abroad have also made a hundred on a first appearance.
There are three instances of a cricketer making two separate hundreds on début: A. R. Morris, New South Wales, 148 and 111 against Queensland in 1940-41, N. J. Contractor, Gujarat, 152 and 102* against Baroda in 1952-53, and Aamer Malik, Lahore "A", 132* and 110* against Railways in 1979-80.

J. S. Solomon, British Guiana, scored a hundred in each of his first three innings in first-class cricket: 114* v Jamaica; 108 v Barbados in 1956-57; 121 v Pakistanis in 1957-58.

R. Watson-Smith, Border, scored 310 runs before he was dismissed in first-class cricket, including not-out centuries in his first two innings: 183* v Orange Free State and 125* v Griqualand West in 1969-70.

G. R. Viswanath and D. M. Wellham alone have scored a hundred on their début in both first-class cricket and Test cricket. Viswanath scored 230 for Mysore v Andhra in 1967-68 and 137 for India v Australia in 1969-70. Wellham scored 100 for New South Wales v Victoria in 1980-81 and 103 for Australia v England in 1981.

TWO DOUBLE-HUNDREDS IN A MATCH

A. E. Fagg........	244	202*	Kent v Essex at Colchester		1938

TRIPLE-HUNDRED AND HUNDRED IN A MATCH

G. A. Gooch	333	123	England v India at Lord's		1990

DOUBLE-HUNDRED AND HUNDRED IN A MATCH

C. B. Fry	125	229	Sussex v Surrey at Hove	1900
W. W. Armstrong	157*	245	Victoria v South Australia at Melbourne.	1920-21
H. T. W. Hardinge	207	102*	Kent v Surrey at Blackheath	1921
C. P. Mead	113	224	Hampshire v Sussex at Horsham	1921
K. S. Duleepsinhji	115	246	Sussex v Kent at Hastings	1929
D. G. Bradman	124	225	Woodfull's XI v Ryder's XI at Sydney	1929-30
B. Sutcliffe	243	100*	New Zealanders v Essex at Southend	1949
M. R. Hallam	210*	157	Leicestershire v Glamorgan at Leicester	1959
M. R. Hallam	203*	143*	Leicestershire v Sussex at Worthing	1961
Hanumant Singh	109	213*	Rajasthan v Bombay at Bombay	1966-67
Salah-ud-Din	256	102*	Karachi v East Pakistan at Karachi	1968-69
K. D. Walters	242	103	Australia v West Indies at Sydney	1968-69
S. M. Gavaskar	124	220	India v West Indies at Port-of-Spain	1970-71
L. G. Rowe	214	100*	West Indies v New Zealand at Kingston	1971-72
G. S. Chappell	247*	133	Australia v New Zealand at Wellington	1973-74
L. Baichan	216*	102	Berbice v Demerara at Georgetown	1973-74
Zaheer Abbas	216*	156*	Gloucestershire v Surrey at The Oval	1976
Zaheer Abbas	230*	104*	Gloucestershire v Kent at Canterbury	1976
Zaheer Abbas	205*	108*	Gloucestershire v Sussex at Cheltenham	1977
Saadat Ali	141	222	Income Tax v Multan at Multan	1977-78
Talat Ali	214*	104	PIA v Punjab at Lahore	1978-79
Shafiq Ahmad	129	217*	National Bank v MCB at Karachi	1978-79
D. W. Randall	209	146	Nottinghamshire v Middlesex at Nottingham	• 1979
Zaheer Abbas	215*	150*	Gloucestershire v Somerset at Bath	1981
Qasim Omar	210*	110	MCB v Lahore at Lahore	1982-83
A. I. Kallicharran	200*	117*	Warwickshire v Northamptonshire at Birmingham	1984
Rizwan-uz-Zaman	139	217*	PIA v PACO at Lahore	1989-90
G. A. Hick	252*	100*	Worcestershire v Glamorgan at Abergavenny	1990
N. R. Taylor	204	142	Kent v Surrey at Canterbury	1990
N. R. Taylor	111	203*	Kent v Sussex at Hove	1991
W. V. Raman	226	120	Tamil Nadu v Haryana at Faridabad	1991-92
A. J. Lamb	209	107	Northamptonshire v Warwickshire at Northampton	1992

TWO SEPARATE HUNDREDS IN A MATCH

Eight times: Zaheer Abbas.

Seven times: W. R. Hammond.

Six times: J. B. Hobbs, G. M. Turner.

Five times: C. B. Fry.

Four times: D. G. Bradman, G. S. Chappell, J. H. Edrich, L. B. Fishlock, T. W. Graveney, C. G. Greenidge, H. T. W. Hardinge, E. H. Hendren, Javed Miandad, G. L. Jessop, P. A. Perrin, B. Sutcliffe, H. Sutcliffe.

Three times: Agha Zahid, L. E. G. Ames, G. Boycott, I. M. Chappell, D. C. S. Compton, S. J. Cook, M. C. Cowdrey, D. Denton, K. S. Duleepsinhji, R. E. Foster, R. C. Fredericks, S. M. Gavaskar, G. A. Gooch, W. G. Grace, G. Gunn, M. R. Hallam, Hanif Mohammad, M. J. Harris, T. W. Hayward, V. S. Hazare, D. W. Hookes, L. Hutton, A. Jones, P. N. Kirsten, R. B. McCosker, P. B. H. May, C. P. Mead, Rizwan-uz-Zaman, A. C. Russell, Sadiq Mohammad, J. T. Tyldesley, K. C. Wessels.

Twice: Ali Zia, D. L. Amiss, C. W. J. Athey, L. Baichan, Basit Ali, A. R. Border, B. J. T. Bosanquet, R. J. Boyd-Moss, A. R. Butcher, C. C. Dacre, G. M. Emmett, A. E. Fagg, L. E. Favell, H. Gimblett, C. Hallows, R. A. Hamence, A. L. Hassett, G. A. Headley, G. A. Hick, D. M. Jones, A. I. Kallicharran, J. H. King, A. F. Kippax, A. J. Lamb, J. G. Langridge, H. W. Lee, E. Lester, C. B. Llewellyn, C. G. Macartney, M. P. Maynard,

C. A. Milton, A. R. Morris, H. Morris, P. H. Parfitt, Nawab of Pataudi jun., E. Paynter, C. Pinch, R. G. Pollock, R. M. Prideaux, Qasim Omar, W. Rhodes, B. A. Richards, I. V. A. Richards, R. T. Robinson, Pankaj Roy, Salim Malik, James Seymour, Shafiq Ahmad, R. B. Simpson, C. L. Smith, G. S. Sobers, M. A. Taylor, N. R. Taylor, E. Tyldesley, C. L. Walcott, W. W. Whysall, G. N. Yallop.

Notes: W. Lambert scored 107 and 157 for Sussex v Epsom at Lord's in 1817 and it was not until W. G. Grace made 130 and 102* for South of the Thames v North of the Thames at Canterbury in 1868 that the feat was repeated.

T. W. Hayward (Surrey) set up a unique record in 1906 when in one week – six days – he hit four successive hundreds, 144 and 100 v Nottinghamshire at Nottingham and 143 and 125 v Leicestershire at Leicester.

L. G. Rowe is alone in scoring hundreds in each innings on his first appearance in Test cricket: 214 and 100* for West Indies v New Zealand at Kingston in 1971-72.

Zaheer Abbas (Gloucestershire) set a unique record in 1976 by twice scoring a double hundred and a hundred in the same match without being dismissed: 216* and 156* v Surrey at The Oval and 230* and 104* v Kent at Canterbury. In 1977 he achieved this feat for a third time, scoring 205* and 108* v Sussex at Cheltenham, and in 1981 for a fourth time, scoring 215* and 150* v Somerset at Bath.

M. R. Hallam (Leicestershire), opening the batting each time, achieved the following treble: 210* and 157 v Glamorgan at Leicester, 1959; 203* and 143* v Sussex at Worthing, 1961; 107* and 149* v Worcestershire at Leicester, 1965. In the last two matches he was on the field the whole time.

C. J. B. Wood, 107* and 117* for Leicestershire v Yorkshire at Bradford in 1911, and S. J. Cook, 120* and 131* for Somerset v Nottinghamshire at Nottingham in 1989, are alone in carrying their bats and scoring hundreds in each innings.

W. L. Foster, 140 and 172*, and R. E. Foster, 134 and 101*, for Worcestershire v Hampshire at Worcester in July 1899, were the first brothers each to score two separate hundreds in the same first-class match.

FOUR HUNDREDS OR MORE IN SUCCESSION

Six in succession: C. B. Fry 1901; D. G. Bradman 1938-39; M. J. Procter 1970-71.

Five in succession: E. D. Weekes 1955-56.

Four in succession: C. W. J. Athey 1987; M. Azharuddin 1984-85; M. G. Bevan 1990-91; A. R. Border 1985; D. G. Bradman 1931-32, 1948-49; D. C. S. Compton 1946-47; N. J. Contractor 1957-58; S. J. Cook 1989; K. S. Duleepsinhji 1931; C. B. Fry 1911; C. G. Greenidge 1986; W. R. Hammond 1936-37, 1945-46; H. T. W. Hardinge 1913; T. W. Hayward 1906; J. B. Hobbs 1920, 1925; D. W. Hookes 1976-77; P. N. Kirsten 1976-77; J. G. Langridge 1949; C. G. Macartney 1921; K. S. McEwan 1977; P. B. H. May 1956-57; V. M. Merchant 1941-42; A. Mitchell 1933; Nawab of Pataudi sen. 1931; L. G. Rowe 1971-72; Pankaj Roy 1962-63; Rizwan-uz-Zaman 1989-90; Sadiq Mohammad 1976; Saeed Ahmed 1961-62; M. V. Sridhar 1990-91, 1991-92; H. Sutcliffe 1931, 1939; E. Tyldesley 1926; W. W. Whysall 1930; F. E. Woolley 1929; Zaheer Abbas 1970-71, 1982-83.

Note: The most fifties in consecutive innings is ten – by E. Tyldesley in 1926 and by D. G. Bradman in the 1947-48 and 1948 seasons.

MOST HUNDREDS IN A SEASON

Eighteen: D. C. S. Compton in 1947. These included six hundreds against the South Africans in which matches his average was 84.78. His aggregate for the season was 3,816, also a record.

Sixteen: J. B. Hobbs in 1925, when aged 42, played 16 three-figure innings in first-class matches. It was during this season that he exceeded the number of hundreds obtained in first-class cricket by W. G. Grace.

Fifteen: W. R. Hammond 1938.

Fourteen: H. Sutcliffe 1932.

Thirteen: G. Boycott 1971, D. G. Bradman 1938, C. B. Fry 1901, W. R. Hammond 1933 and 1937, T. W. Hayward 1906, E. H. Hendren 1923, 1927 and 1928, C. P. Mead 1928, H. Sutcliffe 1928 and 1931.

Since 1969 (excluding G. Boycott – above)

Twelve: G. A. Gooch 1990.
Eleven: S. J. Cook 1991, Zaheer Abbas 1976.
Ten: G. A. Hick 1988, H. Morris 1990, G. M. Turner 1970, Zaheer Abbas 1981.

MOST HUNDREDS IN A CAREER

(35 or more)

	100s	Total Inns	100th 100 Season	Inns	400+	300+	200+
J. B. Hobbs	197	1,315	1923	821	0	1	16
E. H. Hendren	170	1,300	1928-29	740	0	1	22
W. R. Hammond	167	1,005	1935	679	0	4	36
C. P. Mead	153	1,340	1927	892	0	0	13
G. Boycott	151	1,014	1977	645	0	0	10
H. Sutcliffe	149	1,088	1932	700	0	1	17
F. E. Woolley	145	1,532	1929	1,031	0	1	9
L. Hutton	129	814	1951	619	0	1	11
W. G. Grace	126	1,493	1895	1,113	0	3	13
D. C. S. Compton	123	839	1952	552	0	1	9
T. W. Graveney	122	1,223	1964	940	0	0	7
D. G. Bradman	117	338	1947-48	295	1	6	37
I. V. A. Richards	**112**	**764**	**1988-89**	**658**	**0**	**1**	**9**
Zaheer Abbas	108	768	1982-83	658	0	0	10
A. Sandham	107	1,000	1935	871	0	1	3
M. C. Cowdrey	107	1,130	1973	1,035	0	1	11
T. W. Hayward	104	1,138	1913	1,076	0	1	8
J. H. Edrich	103	979	1977	945	0	1	4
G. M. Turner	103	792	1982	779	0	1	10
E. Tyldesley	102	961	1934	919	0	0	9
L. E. G. Ames	102	951	1950	915	0	0	3
D. L. Amiss	102	1,139	1986	1,081	0	0	7

E. H. Hendren, D. G. Bradman and I. V. A. Richards scored their 100th hundreds in Australia, Zaheer Abbas scored his in Pakistan. Zaheer Abbas and G. Boycott did so in Test matches.

Most double-hundreds scored by batsmen not included in the above list:
Sixteen: C. B. Fry.
Fourteen: C. G. Greenidge, K. S. Ranjitsinhji.
Thirteen: W. H. Ponsford (including two 400s and two 300s), J. T. Tyldesley.
Twelve: P. Holmes, Javed Miandad, R. B. Simpson.
Eleven: J. W. Hearne, V. M. Merchant.
Ten: S. M. Gavaskar, J. Hardstaff, jun., V. S. Hazare, A. Shrewsbury, R. T. Simpson.

G. A. Gooch **99**	J. Hardstaff, jun. 83	C. Washbrook 76
J. W. Hearne 96	R. B. Kanhai 83	H. T. W. Hardinge 75
C. B. Fry 94	S. M. Gavaskar 81	R. Abel 74
C. G. Greenidge **92**	**Javed Miandad** **80**	G. S. Chappell 74
A. I. Kallicharran 87	M. Leyland 80	D. Kenyon 74
W. J. Edrich 86	B. A. Richards 80	**K. S. McEwan** **74**
G. S. Sobers 86	**A. J. Lamb** **79**	Majid Khan 73
J. T. Tyldesley 86	C. H. Lloyd 79	**M. W. Gatting** **72**
P. B. H. May 85	K. F. Barrington 76	Mushtaq Mohammad . . 72
R. E. S. Wyatt 85	J. G. Langridge 76	J. O'Connor 72

W. G. Quaife	72	D. L. Haynes	50	D. C. Boon	41
K. S. Ranjitsinhji	72	W. M. Lawry	50	M. J. Harris	41
D. Brookes	71	Sadiq Mohammad	50	K. R. Miller	41
A. C. Russell	71	F. B. Watson	50	A. D. Nourse	41
D. Denton	69	D. I. Gower	49	J. H. Parks	41
M. J. K. Smith	69	C. G. Macartney	49	R. M. Prideaux	41
R. E. Marshall	68	M. J. Stewart	49	G. Pullar	41
R. N. Harvey	67	K. G. Suttle	49	W. E. Russell	41
G. A. Hick	67	P. R. Umrigar	49	R. C. Fredericks	40
P. Holmes	67	W. M. Woodfull	49	J. Gunn	40
J. D. Robertson	67	C. J. Barnett	48	G. D. Mendis	40
P. A. Perrin	66	W. Gunn	48	M. J. Smith	40
R. G. Pollock	64	E. G. Hayes	48	C. L. Walcott	40
R. T. Simpson	64	P. N. Kirsten	48	D. M. Young	40
K. W. R. Fletcher	63	B. W. Luckhurst	48	Arshad Pervez	39
A. R. Border	62	M. J. Procter	48	W. H. Ashdown	39
G. Gunn	62	C. E. B. Rice	48	J. B. Bolus	39
V. S. Hazare	60	B. C. Broad	47	W. A. Brown	39
G. H. Hirst	60	A. C. MacLaren	47	R. J. Gregory	39
R. B. Simpson	60	W. H. Ponsford	47	W. R. D. Payton	39
P. F. Warner	60	C. L. Smith	47	J. R. Reid	39
I. M. Chappell	59	C. J. Tavaré	47	F. M. M. Worrell	39
A. L. Hassett	59	A. R. Butcher	46	K. J. Barnett	38
A. Shrewsbury	59	J. Iddon	46	F. L. Bowley	38
M. D. Crowe	58	A. R. Morris	46	P. J. Burge	38
A. E. Fagg	58	C. T. Radley	46	J. F. Crapp	38
P. H. Parfitt	58	R. T. Robinson	46	D. Lloyd	38
W. Rhodes	58	Younis Ahmed	46	V. L. Manjrekar	38
J. G. Wright	58	W. W. Armstrong	45	A. W. Nourse	38
L. B. Fishlock	56	Asif Iqbal	45	N. Oldfield	38
A. Jones	56	L. G. Berry	45	Rev. J. H. Parsons	38
C. A. Milton	56	J. M. Brearley	45	W. W. Read	38
S. J. Cook	55	A. W. Carr	45	J. Sharp	38
C. Hallows	55	C. Hill	45	N. R. Taylor	38
Hanif Mohammad	55	N. C. O'Neill	45	L. J. Todd	38
D. B. Vengsarkar	55	E. Paynter	45	J. Arnold	37
W. Watson	55	Rev. D. S. Sheppard	45	I. T. Botham	37
D. J. Insole	54	K. D. Walters	45	G. Brown	37
W. W. Keeton	54	H. H. I. Gibbons	44	G. Cook	37
W. Bardsley	53	V. M. Merchant	44	G. M. Emmett	37
B. F. Davison	53	A. Mitchell	44	H. W. Lee	37
A. E. Dipper	53	P. W. G. Parker	44	M. A. Noble	37
G. L. Jessop	53	P. E. Richardson	44	B. P. Patel	37
W. Larkins	53	B. Sutcliffe	44	H. S. Squires	37
James Seymour	53	G. R. Viswanath	44	R. T. Virgin	37
Shafiq Ahmad	53	P. Willey	44	C. J. B. Wood	37
E. H. Bowley	52	E. J. Barlow	43	N. F. Armstrong	36
D. B. Close	52	B. L. D'Oliveira	43	E. Oldroyd	36
A. Ducat	52	J. H. Hampshire	43	W. Place	36
D. W. Randall	52	A. F. Kippax	43	A. L. Wadekar	36
K. C. Wessels	52	J. W. H. Makepeace	43	E. D. Weekes	36
E. R. Dexter	51	C. W. J. Athey	42	C. S. Dempster	35
J. M. Parks	51	M. R. Benson	42	G. Fowler	35
W. W. Whysall	51	James Langridge	42	D. R. Jardine	35
G. Cox, jun.	50	Mudassar Nazar	42	T. E. Jesty	35
H. E. Dollery	50	H. W. Parks	42	B. H. Valentine	35
K. S. Duleepsinhji	50	T. F. Shepherd	42	M. E. Waugh	35
H. Gimblett	50	V. T. Trumper	42	G. M. Wood	35

Bold type denotes those who played in 1991-92 and 1992 seasons.

3,000 RUNS IN A SEASON

	Season	I	NO	R	HS	100s	Avge
D. C. S. Compton	1947	50	8	3,816	246	18	90.85
W. J. Edrich	1947	52	8	3,539	267*	12	80.43
T. W. Hayward	1906	61	8	3,518	219	13	66.37
L. Hutton	1949	56	6	3,429	269*	12	68.58
F. E. Woolley........	1928	59	4	3,352	198	12	60.94
H. Sutcliffe	1932	52	7	3,336	313	14	74.13
W. R. Hammond	1933	54	5	3,323	264	13	67.81
E. H. Hendren	1928	54	7	3,311	209*	13	70.44
R. Abel..............	1901	68	5	3,309	247	7	55.15
W. R. Hammond	1937	55	5	3,252	217	13	65.04
M. J. K. Smith	1959	67	11	3,245	200*	8	57.94
E. H. Hendren	1933	65	9	3,186	301*	11	56.89
C. P. Mead	1921	52	6	3,179	280*	10	69.10
T. W. Hayward	1904	63	5	3,170	203	11	54.65
K. S. Ranjitsinhji.....	1899	58	8	3,159	197	8	63.18
C. B. Fry	1901	43	3	3,147	244	13	78.67
K. S. Ranjitsinhji.....	1900	40	5	3,065	275	11	87.57
L. E. G. Ames	1933	57	5	3,058	295	9	58.80
J. T. Tyldesley	1901	60	5	3,041	221	9	55.29
C. P. Mead	1928	50	10	3,027	180	13	75.67
J. B. Hobbs	1925	48	5	3,024	266*	16	70.32
E. Tyldesley	1928	48	10	3,024	242	10	79.57
W. E. Alley	1961	64	11	3,019	221*	11	56.96
W. R. Hammond	1938	42	2	3,011	271	15	75.27
E. H. Hendren	1923	51	12	3,010	200*	13	77.17
H. Sutcliffe	1931	42	11	3,006	230	13	96.96
J. H. Parks..........	1937	63	4	3,003	168	11	50.89
H. Sutcliffe	1928	44	5	3,002	228	13	76.97

Notes: W. G. Grace scored 2,739 runs in 1871 – the first batsman to reach 2,000 runs in a season. He made ten hundreds and twice exceeded 200, with an average of 78.25 in all first-class matches. At the time, the over consisted of four balls.

The highest aggregate in a season since the reduction of County Championship matches in 1969 is 2,755 by S. J. Cook (42 innings) in 1991.

2,000 RUNS IN A SEASON

Since Reduction of Championship Matches in 1969

Four times: G. A. Gooch 2,746 (1990), 2,559 (1984), 2,324 (1988), 2,208 (1985).

Three times: D. L. Amiss 2,239 (1984), 2,110 (1976), 2,030 (1978); S. J. Cook 2,755 (1991), 2,608 (1990), 2,241 (1989); M. W. Gatting 2,257 (1984), 2,057 (1991), 2,000 (1992); G. A. Hick 2,713 (1988), 2,347 (1990), 2,004 (1986); G. M. Turner 2,416 (1973), 2,379 (1970), 2,101 (1981).

Twice: G. Boycott 2,503 (1971), 2,051 (1970); J. H. Edrich 2,238 (1969), 2,031 (1971); A. I. Kallicharran 2,301 (1984), 2,120 (1982); Zaheer Abbas 2,554 (1976), 2,306 (1981).

Once: M. Azharuddin 2,016 (1991); J. B. Bolus 2,143 (1970); P. D. Bowler 2,044 (1992); B. C. Broad 2,226 (1990); A. R. Butcher 2,116 (1990); C. G. Greenidge 2,035 (1986); M. J. Harris 2,238 (1971); D. L. Haynes 2,346 (1990); Javed Miandad 2,083 (1981); A. J. Lamb 2,049 (1981); K. S. McEwan 2,176 (1983); Majid Khan 2,074 (1972); A. A. Metcalfe 2,047 (1990); H. Morris 2,276 (1990); D. W. Randall 2,151 (1985); I. V. A. Richards 2,161 (1977); R. T. Robinson 2,032 (1984); M. A. Roseberry 2,044 (1992); C. L. Smith 2,000 (1985); R. T. Virgin 2,223 (1970); D. M. Ward 2,072 (1990); M. E. Waugh 2,072 (1990).

1,000 RUNS IN A SEASON MOST TIMES

(Includes Overseas Tours and Seasons)

28 times: W. G. Grace 2,000 (6); F. E. Woolley 3,000 (1), 2,000 (12).
27 times: M. C. Cowdrey 2,000 (2); C. P. Mead 3,000 (2), 2,000 (9).
26 times: G. Boycott 2,000 (2); J. B. Hobbs 3,000 (1), 2,000 (16).
25 times: E. H. Hendren 3,000 (3), 2,000 (12).
24 times: D. L. Amiss 2,000 (3); W. G. Quaife 2,000 (1); H. Sutcliffe 3,000 (3), 2,000 (12).
23 times: A. Jones.
22 times: T. W. Graveney 2,000 (7); W. R. Hammond 3,000 (3), 2,000 (9).
21 times: D. Denton 2,000 (5); J. H. Edrich 2,000 (6); W. Rhodes 2,000 (2).
20 times: D. B. Close; K. W. R. Fletcher; G. Gunn; T. W. Hayward 3,000 (2), 2,000 (8); James Langridge 2,000 (1); J. M. Parks 2,000 (3); A. Sandham 2,000 (8); M. J. K. Smith 3,000 (1), 2,000 (5); C. Washbrook 2,000 (2).
19 times: J. W. Hearne 2,000 (4); G. H. Hirst 2,000 (3); D. Kenyon 2,000 (7); E. Tyldesley 3,000 (1), 2,000 (5); J. T. Tyldesley 3,000 (1), 2,000 (4).
18 times: L. G. Berry 2,000 (1); H. T. W. Hardinge 2,000 (5); R. E. Marshall 2,000 (6); P. A. Perrin; G. M. Turner 2,000 (3); R. E. S. Wyatt 2,000 (5).
17 times: L. E. G. Ames 3,000 (1), 2,000 (5); T. E. Bailey 2,000 (1); D. Brookes 2,000 (6); D. C. S. Compton 3,000 (1), 2,000 (5); G. A. Gooch 2,000 (4); C. G. Greenidge 2,000 (1); L. Hutton 3,000 (1), 2,000 (8); J. G. Langridge 2,000 (11); M. Leyland 2,000 (3); K. G. Suttle 2,000 (1), Zaheer Abbas 2,000 (2).
16 times: D. G. Bradman 2,000 (4); D. E. Davies 2,000 (1); E. G. Hayes 2,000 (2); C. A. Milton 2,000 (1); J. O'Connor 2,000 (4); C. T. Radley; I. V. A. Richards 2,000 (1); James Seymour 2,000 (1); C. J. Tavaré.
15 times: G. Barker; K. F. Barrington 2,000 (3); E. H. Bowley 2,000 (4); M. H. Denness; A. E. Dipper 2,000 (5); H. E. Dollery 2,000 (2); W. J. Edrich 3,000 (1), 2,000 (8); M. W. Gatting 2,000 (3); J. H. Hampshire; P. Holmes 2,000 (7); Mushtaq Mohammad; R. B. Nicholls 2,000 (1); P. H. Parfitt 2,000 (7); W. G. A. Parkhouse 2,000 (1); B. A. Richards 2,000 (1); J. D. Robertson 2,000 (9); G. S. Sobers; M. J. Stewart 2,000 (1).

Notes: F. E. Woolley reached 1,000 runs in 28 consecutive seasons (1907-1938). C. P. Mead did so 27 seasons in succession (1906-1936).

Outside England, 1,000 runs in a season has been reached most times by D. G. Bradman (in 12 seasons in Australia).

Three batsmen have scored 1,000 runs in a season in each of four different countries: G. S. Sobers in West Indies, England, India and Australia; M. C. Cowdrey and G. Boycott in England, South Africa, West Indies and Australia.

HIGHEST AGGREGATES OUTSIDE ENGLAND

	Season	I	NO	R	HS	100s	Avge
In Australia D. G. Bradman	1928-29	24	6	1,690	340*	7	93.88
In South Africa J. R. Reid	1961-62	30	2	1,915	203	7	68.39
In West Indies E. H. Hendren	1929-30	18	5	1,765	254*	6	135.76
In New Zealand M. D. Crowe	1986-87	21	3	1,676	175*	8	93.11
In India C. G. Borde	1964-65	28	3	1,604	168	6	64.16
In Pakistan Saadat Ali	1983-84	27	1	1,649	208	4	63.42
In Sri Lanka A. Ranatunga	1985-86	16	2	739	135*	3	52.78

Note: In more than one country, the following aggregates of over 2,000 runs have been recorded:

In Pakistan	Season	I	NO	R	HS	100s	Avge
M. Amarnath (P/I/WI)	1982-83	34	6	2,234	207	9	79.78
J. R. Reid (SA/A/NZ)	1961-62	40	2	2,188	203	7	57.57
S. M. Gavaskar (I/P)	1978-79	30	6	2,121	205	10	88.37
R. B. Simpson (I/P/A/WI)	1964-65	34	4	2,063	201	8	68.76

LEADING BATSMEN IN AN ENGLISH SEASON

(Qualification: 8 innings)

Season	Leading scorer	Runs	Avge	Top of averages	Runs	Avge
1946	D. C. S. Compton	2,403	61.61	W. R. Hammond	1,783	84.90
1947	D. C. S. Compton	3,816	90.85	D. C. S. Compton	3,816	90.85
1948	L. Hutton	2,654	64.73	D. G. Bradman	2,428	89.92
1949	L. Hutton	3,429	68.58	J. Hardstaff	2,251	72.61
1950	R. T. Simpson	2,576	62.82	E. Weekes	2,310	79.65
1951	J. D. Robertson	2,917	68.79	P. B. H. May	2,339	68.79
1952	L. Hutton	2,567	61.11	D. S. Sheppard	2,262	64.62
1953	W. J. Edrich	2,557	47.35	W. A. Johnston	102	102.00†
1954	D. Kenyon	2,636	51.68	D. C. S. Compton	1,524	58.61
1955	D. J. Insole	2,427	42.57	D. J. McGlew	1,871	58.46
1956	T. W. Graveney	2,397	49.93	K. Mackay	1,103	52.52
1957	T. W. Graveney	2,361	49.18	P. B. H. May	2,347	61.76
1958	P. B. H. May	2,231	63.74	P. B. H. May	2,231	63.74
1959	M. J. K. Smith	3,245	57.94	V. L. Manjrekar	755	68.63
1960	M. J. K. Smith	2,551	45.55	R. Subba Row	1,503	55.66
1961	W. E. Alley	3,019	56.96	W. M. Lawry	2,019	61.18
1962	J. H. Edrich	2,482	51.70	R. T. Simpson	867	54.18
1963	J. B. Bolus	2,190	41.32	G. S. Sobers	1,333	47.60
1964	T. W. Graveney	2,385	54.20	K. F. Barrington	1,872	62.40
1965	J. H. Edrich	2,319	62.67	M. C. Cowdrey	2,093	63.42
1966	A. R. Lewis	2,198	41.47	G. S. Sobers	1,349	61.31
1967	C. A. Milton	2,089	46.42	K. F. Barrington	2,059	68.63
1968	B. A. Richards	2,395	47.90	G. Boycott	1,487	64.65
1969	J. H. Edrich	2,238	69.93	J. H. Edrich	2,238	69.93
1970	G. M. Turner	2,379	61.00	G. S. Sobers	1,742	75.73
1971	G. Boycott	2,503	100.12	G. Boycott	2,503	100.12
1972	Majid Khan	2,074	61.00	G. Boycott	1,230	72.35
1973	G. M. Turner	2,416	67.11	G. M. Turner	2,416	67.11
1974	R. T. Virgin	1,936	56.94	C. H. Lloyd	1,458	63.39
1975	G. Boycott	1,915	73.65	R. B. Kanhai	1,073	82.53
1976	Zaheer Abbas	2,554	75.11	Zaheer Abbas	2,554	75.11
1977	I. V. A. Richards	2,161	65.48	R. P. Baker	215	71.66‡
1978	D. L. Amiss	2,030	53.42	C. E. B. Rice	1,871	66.82
1979	K. C. Wessels	1,800	52.94	G. Boycott	1,538	102.53
1980	P. N. Kirsten	1,895	63.16	A. J. Lamb	1,797	66.55
1981	Zaheer Abbas	2,306	88.69	Zaheer Abbas	2,306	88.69
1982	A. I. Kallicharran	2,120	66.25	G. M. Turner	1,171	90.07
1983	K. S. McEwan	2,176	64.00	I. V. A. Richards	1,204	75.25
1984	G. A. Gooch	2,559	67.34	C. G. Greenidge	1,069	82.23
1985	G. A. Gooch	2,208	71.22	I. V. A. Richards	1,836	76.50
1986	C. G. Greenidge	2,035	67.83	J. G. Bracewell	386	77.20§
1987	G. A. Hick	1,879	52.19	M. D. Crowe	1,627	67.79
1988	G. A. Hick	2,713	77.51	R. A. Harper	622	77.75
1989	S. J. Cook	2,241	60.56	D. M. Jones	1,510	88.82
1990	G. A. Gooch	2,746	101.70	G. A. Gooch	2,746	101.70
1991	S. J. Cook	2,755	81.02	C. L. Hooper	1,501	93.81
1992	P. D. Bowler	2,044	65.93	Salim Malik	1,184	78.93
	M. A. Roseberry	2,044	56.77			

† *Johnston had 17 innings with 16 not outs, highest score 28*.*
‡ *Baker had 12 innings with 9 not outs, highest score 77*.*
§ *Bracewell had 11 innings with 6 not outs, highest score 110.*

Note: The highest average recorded in an English season was 115.66 (2,429 runs, 26 innings) by D. G. Bradman in 1938.

25,000 RUNS IN A CAREER

Dates in italics denote the first half of an overseas season; i.e. *1945* denotes the 1945-46 season.

		Career	R	I	NO	HS	100s	Avge
1	J. B. Hobbs............	1905-34	61,237	1,315	106	316*	197	50.65
2	F. E. Woolley.........	1906-38	58,969	1,532	85	305*	145	40.75
3	E. H. Hendren	1907-38	57,611	1,300	166	301*	170	50.80
4	C. P. Mead	1905-36	55,061	1,340	185	280*	153	47.67
5	W. G. Grace..........	1865-1908	54,896	1,493	105	344	126	39.55
6	W. R. Hammond	1920-51	50,551	1,005	104	336*	167	56.10
7	H. Sutcliffe..........	1919-45	50,138	1,088	123	313	149	51.95
8	G. Boycott	1962-86	48,426	1,014	162	261*	151	56.83
9	T. W. Graveney	1948-71	47,793	1,223	159	258	122	44.91
10	T. W. Hayward	1893-1914	43,551	1,138	96	315*	104	41.79
11	D. L. Amiss	1960-87	43,423	1,139	126	262*	102	42.86
12	M. C. Cowdrey	1950-76	42,719	1,130	134	307	107	42.89
13	A. Sandham	1911-37	41,284	1,000	79	325	107	44.82
14	L. Hutton	1934-60	40,140	814	91	364	129	55.51
15	M. J. K. Smith	1951-75	39,832	1,091	139	204	69	41.84
16	W. Rhodes	1898-1930	39,802	1,528	237	267*	58	30.83
17	J. H. Edrich	1956-78	39,790	979	104	310*	103	45.47
18	R. E. S. Wyatt	1923-57	39,405	1,141	157	232	85	40.04
19	D. C. S. Compton	1936-64	38,942	839	88	300	123	51.85
20	E. Tyldesley	1909-36	38,874	961	106	256*	102	45.46
21	J. T. Tyldesley	1895-1923	37,897	994	62	295*	86	40.66
22	K. W. R. Fletcher	1962-88	37,665	1,167	170	228*	63	37.77
23	**C. G. Greenidge**	**1970-92**	**37,354**	**889**	**75**	**273***	**92**	**45.88**
24	J. W. Hearne	1909-36	37,252	1,025	116	285*	96	40.98
25	L. E. G. Ames	1926-51	37,248	951	95	295	102	43.51
26	D. Kenyon	1946-67	37,002	1,159	59	259	74	33.63
27	W. J. Edrich	1934-58	36,965	964	92	267*	86	42.39
28	J. M. Parks..........	1949-76	36,673	1,227	172	205*	51	34.76
29	D. Denton...........	1894-1920	36,479	1,163	70	221	69	33.37
30	G. H. Hirst	1891-1929	36,323	1,215	151	341	60	34.13
31	**G. A. Gooch**	**1973-92**	**36,126**	**816**	**66**	**333**	**99**	**48.16**
32	A. Jones	1957-83	36,049	1,168	72	204*	56	32.89
33	W. G. Quaife	1894-1928	36,012	1,203	185	255*	72	35.37
34	R. E. Marshall	*1945*-72	35,725	1,053	59	228*	68	35.94
35	G. Gunn	1902-32	35,208	1,061	82	220	62	35.96
36	D. B. Close..........	1949-86	34,994	1,225	173	198	52	33.26
37	**I. V. A. Richards**	*1971-92*	**34,977**	**764**	**56**	**322**	**112**	**49.40**
38	Zaheer Abbas	*1965*-86	34,843	768	92	274	108	51.54
39	J. G. Langridge	1928-55	34,380	984	66	250*	76	37.45
40	G. M. Turner	*1964*-82	34,346	792	101	311*	103	49.70
41	C. Washbrook	1933-64	34,101	906	107	251*	76	42.67
42	M. Leyland	1920-48	33,660	932	101	263	80	40.50
43	H. T. W. Hardinge ...	1902-33	33,519	1,021	103	263*	75	36.51
44	R. Abel	1881-1904	33,124	1,007	73	357*	74	35.46
45	A. I. Kallicharran	*1966*-90	32,650	834	86	243*	87	43.64
46	C. A. Milton.........	1948-74	32,150	1,078	125	170	56	33.73
47	J. D. Robertson	1937-59	31,914	897	46	331*	67	37.50
48	J. Hardstaff, jun.	1930-55	31,847	812	94	266	83	44.35
49	James Langridge	1924-53	31,716	1,058	157	167	42	35.20

		Career	R	I	NO	HS	100s	Avge
50	K. F. Barrington	1953-68	31,714	831	136	256	76	45.63
51	C. H. Lloyd	1963-86	31,232	730	96	242*	79	49.26
52	Mushtaq Mohammad	1956-85	31,091	843	104	303*	72	42.07
53	C. B. Fry	1892-1921	30,886	658	43	258*	94	50.22
54	D. Brookes	1934-59	30,874	925	70	257	71	36.10
55	P. Holmes	1913-35	30,573	810	84	315*	67	42.11
56	R. T. Simpson	1944-63	30,546	852	55	259	64	38.32
57	L. G. Berry	1924-51	30,225	1,056	57	232	45	30.25
58	K. G. Suttle	1949-71	30,225	1,064	92	204*	49	31.09
59	P. A. Perrin	1896-1928	29,709	918	91	343*	66	35.92
60	P. F. Warner	1894-1929	29,028	875	75	244	60	36.28
61	R. B. Kanhai	1954-81	28,774	669	82	256	83	49.01
62	J. O'Connor	1921-39	28,764	903	79	248	72	34.90
63	T. E. Bailey	1945-67	28,641	1,072	215	205	28	33.42
64	**M. W. Gatting**	**1975-92**	**28,512**	**676**	**107**	**258**	**72**	**50.10**
65	**A. J. Lamb**	**1972-92**	**28,495**	**684**	**101**	**294**	**79**	**48.87**
66	E. H. Bowley	1912-34	28,378	859	47	283	52	34.94
67	B. A. Richards	1964-82	28,358	576	58	356	80	54.74
68	G. S. Sobers	1952-74	28,315	609	93	365*	86	54.87
69	**Javed Miandad**	**1973-92**	**28,248**	**618**	**94**	**311**	**80**	**53.90**
70	**D. W. Randall**	**1972-92**	**28,176**	**817**	**81**	**237**	**52**	**38.28**
71	A. E. Dipper	1908-32	28,075	865	69	252*	53	35.27
72	D. G. Bradman	1927-48	28,067	338	43	452*	117	95.14
73	J. H. Hampshire	1961-84	28,059	924	112	183*	43	34.55
74	P. B. H. May	1948-63	27,592	618	77	285*	85	51.00
75	B. F. Davison	1967-87	27,453	766	79	189	53	39.96
76	Majid Khan	1961-84	27,444	700	62	241	73	43.01
77	A. C. Russell	1908-30	27,358	717	59	273	71	41.57
78	E. G. Hayes	1896-1926	27,318	896	48	276	48	32.21
79	A. E. Fagg	1932-57	27,291	803	46	269*	58	36.05
80	James Seymour	1900-26	27,237	911	62	218*	53	32.08
81	P. H. Parfitt	1956-73	26,924	845	104	200*	58	36.33
82	G. L. Jessop	1894-1914	26,698	855	37	286	53	32.63
83	**K. S. McEwan**	**1972-91**	**26,628**	**705**	**67**	**218**	**74**	**41.73**
84	D. E. Davies	1924-54	26,564	1,032	80	287*	32	27.90
85	A. Shrewsbury	1875-1902	26,505	813	90	267	59	36.65
86	M. J. Stewart	1954-72	26,492	898	93	227*	49	32.90
87	C. T. Radley	1964-87	26,441	880	134	200	46	35.44
88	Younis Ahmed	1961-86	26,073	762	118	221*	46	40.48
89	P. E. Richardson	1949-65	26,055	794	41	185	44	34.60
90	**C. E. B. Rice**	**1969-91**	**26,045**	**753**	**122**	**246**	**48**	**41.27**
91	M. H. Denness	1959-80	25,886	838	65	195	33	33.48
92	S. M. Gavaskar	1966-87	25,834	563	61	340	81	51.46
93	J. W. H. Makepeace	1906-30	25,799	778	66	203	43	36.23
94	W. Gunn	1880-1904	25,691	850	72	273	48	33.02
95	W. Watson	1939-64	25,670	753	109	257	55	39.86
96	G. Brown	1908-33	25,649	1,012	52	232*	37	26.71
97	G. M. Emmett	1936-59	25,602	865	50	188	37	31.41
98	J. B. Bolus	1956-75	25,598	833	81	202*	39	34.03
99	W. E. Russell	1956-72	25,525	796	64	193	41	34.87
100	C. J. Barnett	1927-53	25,389	821	45	259	48	32.71
101	L. B. Fishlock	1931-52	25,376	699	54	253	56	39.34
102	D. J. Insole	1947-63	25,241	743	72	219*	54	37.61
103	**D. I. Gower**	**1975-92**	**25,203**	**699**	**69**	**228**	**49**	**40.00**
104	J. M. Brearley	1961-83	25,185	768	102	312*	45	37.81
105	J. Vine	1896-1922	25,171	920	79	202	34	29.92
106	R. M. Prideaux	1958-74	25,136	808	75	202*	41	34.29
107	J. H. King	1895-1925	25,122	988	69	227*	34	27.33

Bold type denotes those who played in 1991-92 and 1992 seasons.

Note: Some works of reference provide career figures which differ from those in this list, owing to the exclusion or inclusion of matches recognised or not recognised as first-class by *Wisden*.

Current Players with 20,000 Runs

	Career	R	I	NO	HS	100s	Avge
W. Larkins	1972-92	24,384	762	48	252	53	34.15
J. G. Wright	1975-91	24,360	619	43	192	58	42.29
C. J. Tavaré	1974-92	24,278	692	74	219	47	39.28
A. R. Border	1976-91	22,818	519	85	205	62	52.57
A. R. Butcher	1972-92	22,633	682	60	216*	46	36.38
D. L. Haynes	1976-92	21,176	510	58	255*	50	46.84
G. D. Mendis	1974-92	20,337	609	61	209*	40	37.11
R. T. Robinson	1978-92	20,209	544	71	220*	46	42.72
B. C. Broad	1979-92	20,147	557	38	227*	47	38.81
C. W. J. Athey	1976-92	20,129	639	62	184	42	34.88

CAREER AVERAGE OVER 50

(Qualification: 10,000 runs)

Avge		Career	I	NO	R	HS	100s
95.14	D. G. Bradman	1927-48	338	43	28,067	452*	117
71.22	V. M. Merchant	1929-51	229	43	13,248	359*	44
65.18	W. H. Ponsford	1920-34	235	23	13,819	437	47
64.99	W. M. Woodfull	1921-34	245	39	13,388	284	49
59.08	**G. A. Hick**	1983-92	364	41	19,083	405*	67
58.24	A. L. Hassett	1932-53	322	32	16,890	232	59
58.19	V. S. Hazare	1934-66	365	45	18,621	316*	60
57.22	A. F. Kippax	1918-35	256	33	12,762	315*	43
57.05	**M. D. Crowe**	1979-91	345	54	16,602	299	58
56.83	G. Boycott	1962-86	1,014	162	48,426	261*	151
56.78	**M. E. Waugh**	1985-92	217	33	10,448	229*	35
56.55	C. L. Walcott	1941-63	238	29	11,820	314*	40
56.37	K. S. Ranjitsinhji	1893-1920	500	62	24,692	285*	72
56.22	R. B. Simpson	1952-77	436	62	21,029	359	60
56.10	W. R. Hammond	1920-51	1,005	104	50,551	336*	167
55.51	L. Hutton	1934-60	814	91	40,140	364	129
55.34	E. D. Weekes	1944-64	241	24	12,010	304*	36
54.87	G. S. Sobers	1952-74	609	93	28,315	365*	86
54.74	B. A. Richards	1964-82	576	58	28,358	356	80
54.67	R. G. Pollock	1960-86	437	54	20,940	274	64
54.24	F. M. M. Worrell	1941-64	326	49	15,025	308*	39
53.90	**Javed Miandad**	1973-92	618	94	28,248	311	80
53.78	R. M. Cowper	1959-69	228	31	10,595	307	26
53.67	A. R. Morris	1940-63	250	15	12,614	290	46
52.86	**D. B. Vengsarkar**	1975-91	390	52	17,868	284	55
52.57	**A. R. Border**	1976-91	519	85	22,818	205	62
52.32	Hanif Mohammad	1951-75	371	45	17,059	499	55
52.27	P. R. Umrigar	1944-67	350	41	16,154	252*	49
52.20	G. S. Chappell	1966-83	542	72	24,535	247*	74
51.95	H. Sutcliffe	1919-45	1,088	123	50,138	313	149
51.93	**D. M. Jones**	1981-92	255	28	11,790	248	34
51.85	D. C. S. Compton	1936-64	839	88	38,942	300	123
51.54	Zaheer Abbas	1965-86	768	92	34,843	274	108
51.53	A. D. Nourse	1931-52	269	27	12,472	260*	41
51.46	S. M. Gavaskar	1966-87	563	61	25,834	340	81
51.44	W. A. Brown	1932-49	284	15	13,838	265*	39
51.00	P. B. H. May	1948-63	618	77	27,592	285*	85

Avge		Career	I	NO	R	HS	100s
50.95	N. C. O'Neill	1955-67	306	34	13,859	284	45
50.93	R. N. Harvey	1946-62	461	35	21,699	231*	67
50.90	W. M. Lawry	1955-71	417	49	18,734	266	50
50.90	A. V. Mankad	1963-82	326	71	12,980	265	31
50.80	E. H. Hendren	1907-38	1,300	166	57,611	301*	170
50.77	**K. C. Wessels**	**1973-91**	**410**	**35**	**19,042**	**254**	**52**
50.65	J. B. Hobbs	1905-34	1,315	106	61,237	316*	197
50.22	C. B. Fry	1892-1921	658	43	30,886	258*	94
50.10	**M. W. Gatting**	**1975-92**	**676**	**107**	**28,512**	**258**	**72**
50.01	Shafiq Ahmad	1967-90	449	58	19,555	217*	53

Bold type denotes those who played in 1991-92 and 1992 seasons.

FASTEST FIFTIES

Minutes

11	C. I. J. Smith (66)	Middlesex v Gloucestershire at Bristol 1938
14	S. J. Pegler (50)	South Africans v Tasmania at Launceston 1910-11
14	F. T. Mann (53)	Middlesex v Nottinghamshire at Lord's 1921
14	H. B. Cameron (56)	Transvaal v Orange Free State at Johannesburg 1934-35
14	C. I. J. Smith (52)	Middlesex v Kent at Maidstone 1935

Note: The following fast fifties were scored in contrived circumstances when runs were given from full tosses and long hops to expedite a declaration: C. C. Inman (8 minutes), Leicestershire v Nottinghamshire at Nottingham, 1965; T. M. Moody (11 minutes), Warwickshire v Glamorgan at Swansea, 1990; A. J. Stewart (14 minutes), Surrey v Kent at Dartford, 1986; M. P. Maynard (14 minutes), Glamorgan v Yorkshire at Cardiff, 1987.

FASTEST HUNDREDS

Minutes

35	P. G. H. Fender (113*)	Surrey v Northamptonshire at Northampton . . . 1920
40	G. L. Jessop (101)	Gloucestershire v Yorkshire at Harrogate 1897
40	Ahsan-ul-Haq (100*)	Muslims v Sikhs at Lahore 1923-24
42	G. L. Jessop (191)	Gentlemen of South v Players of South at Hastings 1907
43	A. H. Hornby (106)	Lancashire v Somerset at Manchester 1905
43	D. W. Hookes (107)	South Australia v Victoria at Adelaide 1982-83
44	R. N. S. Hobbs (100)	Essex v Australians at Chelmsford 1975

Notes: The fastest recorded authentic hundred in terms of balls received was scored off 34 balls by D. W. Hookes (above).

Research of the scorebook has shown that P. G. H. Fender scored his hundred from between 40 and 46 balls. He contributed 113 to an unfinished sixth-wicket partnership of 171 in 42 minutes with H. A. Peach.

E. B. Alletson (Nottinghamshire) scored 189 out of 227 runs in 90 minutes against Sussex at Hove in 1911. It has been estimated that his last 139 runs took 37 minutes.

The following fast hundreds were scored in contrived circumstances when runs were given from full tosses and long hops to expedite a declaration: T. M. Moody (26 minutes), Warwickshire v Glamorgan at Swansea, 1990; S. J. O'Shaughnessy (35 minutes), Lancashire v Leicestershire at Manchester, 1983; C. M. Old (37 minutes), Yorkshire v Warwickshire at Birmingham, 1977; N. F. M. Popplewell (41 minutes), Somerset v Gloucestershire at Bath, 1983.

FASTEST DOUBLE-HUNDREDS

Minutes
113	R. J. Shastri (200*)	Bombay v Baroda at Bombay	1984-85
120	G. L. Jessop (286)	Gloucestershire v Sussex at Hove	1903
120	C. H. Lloyd (201*)	West Indians v Glamorgan at Swansea	1976
130	G. L. Jessop (234)	Gloucestershire v Somerset at Bristol	1905
131	V. T. Trumper (293)	Australians v Canterbury at Christchurch	1913-14

FASTEST TRIPLE-HUNDREDS

Minutes
181	D. C. S. Compton (300)	MCC v N. E. Transvaal at Benoni	1948-49
205	F. E. Woolley (305*)	MCC v Tasmania at Hobart	1911-12
205	C. G. Macartney (345)	Australians v Nottinghamshire at Nottingham	1921
213	D. G. Bradman (369)	South Australia v Tasmania at Adelaide	1935-36

300 RUNS IN ONE DAY

345	C. G. Macartney	Australians v Nottinghamshire at Nottingham	1921
334	W. H. Ponsford	Victoria v New South Wales at Melbourne	1926-27
333	K. S. Duleepsinhji	Sussex v Northamptonshire at Hove	1930
331*	J. D. Robertson	Middlesex v Worcestershire at Worcester	1949
325*	B. A. Richards	S. Australia v W. Australia at Perth	1970-71
322†	E. Paynter	Lancashire v Sussex at Hove	1937
322	I. V. A. Richards	Somerset v Warwickshire at Taunton	1985
318	C. W. Gregory	New South Wales v Queensland at Brisbane	1906-07
317	K. R. Rutherford	New Zealanders v D. B. Close's XI at Scarborough	1986
316†	R. H. Moore	Hampshire v Warwickshire at Bournemouth	1937
315*	R. C. Blunt	Otago v Canterbury at Christchurch	1931-32
312*	J. M. Brearley	MCC Under 25 v North Zone at Peshawar	1966-67
311*	G. M. Turner	Worcestershire v Warwickshire at Worcester	1982
311*	N. H. Fairbrother	Lancashire v Surrey at The Oval	1990
309*	D. G. Bradman	Australia v England at Leeds	1930
307*	W. H. Ashdown	Kent v Essex at Brentwood	1934
306*	A. Ducat	Surrey v Oxford University at The Oval	1919
305*	F. R. Foster	Warwickshire v Worcestershire at Dudley	1914

† *E. Paynter's 322 and R. H. Moore's 316 were scored on the same day: July 28, 1937.*

1,000 RUNS IN MAY

	Runs	*Avge*
W. G. Grace, May 9 to May 30, 1895 (22 days):		
13, 103, 18, 25, 288, 52, 257, 73*, 18, 169	1,016	112.88
Grace was within two months of completing his 47th year.		
W. R. Hammond, May 7 to May 31, 1927 (25 days):		
27, 135, 108, 128, 17, 11, 99, 187, 4, 30, 83, 7, 192, 14	1,042	74.42
Hammond scored his 1,000th run on May 28, thus equalling		
Grace's record of 22 days.		
C. Hallows, May 5 to May 31, 1928 (27 days):		
100, 101, 51*, 123, 101*, 22, 74, 104, 58, 34*, 232	1,000	125.00

1,000 RUNS IN APRIL AND MAY

T. W. Hayward, April 16 to May 31, 1900:		
120*, 55, 108, 131*, 55, 193, 120, 5, 6, 3, 40, 146, 92	1,074	97.63
D. G. Bradman, April 30 to May 31, 1930:		
236, 185*, 78, 9, 48*, 66, 4, 44, 252*, 32, 47*	1,001	143.00
On April 30 Bradman was 75 not out.		

D. G. Bradman, April 30 to May 31, 1938:
258, 58, 137, 278, 2, 143, 145*, 5, 30* 1,056   150.85
   Bradman scored 258 on April 30, and his 1,000th run on May 27.

W. J. Edrich, April 30 to May 31, 1938:
104, 37, 115, 63, 20*, 182, 71, 31, 53*, 45, 15, 245, 0, 9, 20* 1,010   84.16
   Edrich was 21 not out on April 30. All his runs were scored at
   Lord's.

G. M. Turner, April 24 to May 31, 1973:
41, 151*, 143, 85, 7, 8, 17*, 81, 13, 53, 44, 153*, 3, 2, 66*, 30, 10*,
111 1,018   78.30

G. A. Hick, April 17 to May 29, 1988:
61, 37, 212, 86, 14, 405*, 8, 11, 6, 7, 172. 1,019   101.90
   Hick scored a record 410 runs in April, and his 1,000th run on
   May 28.

1,000 RUNS IN TWO SEPARATE MONTHS

Only four batsmen, C. B. Fry, K. S. Ranjitsinhji, H. Sutcliffe and L. Hutton, have scored over 1,000 runs in each of two months in the same season. L. Hutton, by scoring 1,294 in June 1949, made more runs in a single month than anyone else. He also made 1,050 in August 1949.

MOST RUNS SCORED OFF ONE OVER

(All instances refer to six-ball overs)

36	G. S. Sobers	off M. A. Nash, Nottinghamshire v Glamorgan at Swansea (six sixes)	1968
36	R. J. Shastri	off Tilak Raj, Bombay v Baroda at Bombay (six sixes) . . .	1984-85
34	E. B. Alletson	off E. H. Killick, Nottinghamshire v Sussex at Hove (46604446; including two no-balls)	1911
34	F. C. Hayes	off M. A. Nash, Lancashire v Glamorgan at Swansea (646666).	1977
34	M. P. Maynard	off S. A. Marsh, Glamorgan v Kent at Swansea (666646; runs were offered to expedite a declaration)	1992
32	I. T. Botham	off I. R. Snook, England XI v Central Districts at Palmerston North (466466)	1983-84
32	C. C. Inman	off N. W. Hill, Leicestershire v Nottinghamshire at Nottingham (466664; full tosses were provided for him to hit).	1965
32	T. E. Jesty	off R. J. Boyd-Moss, Hampshire v Northamptonshire at Southampton (666662)	1984
32	P. W. G. Parker	off A. I. Kallicharran, Sussex v Warwickshire at Birmingham (666664).	1982
32	I. R. Redpath	off N. Rosendorff, Australians v Orange Free State at Bloemfontein (666644)	1969-70
32	C. C. Smart	off G. Hill, Glamorgan v Hampshire at Cardiff (664664) .	1935

Notes: The greatest number of runs scored off an eight-ball over is 34 (40446664) by R. M. Edwards off M. C. Carew, Governor-General's XI v West Indies at Auckland, 1968-69.

   In a Shell Trophy match against Canterbury at Christchurch in 1989-90, R. H. Vance (Wellington), acting on the instructions of his captain, deliberately conceded 77 runs in an over of full tosses which contained 17 no-balls and, owing to the umpire's miscalculation, only five legitimate deliveries.

MOST SIXES IN AN INNINGS

15	J. R. Reid (296)	Wellington v N. Districts at Wellington		1962-63
14	Shakti Singh (128)	Himachal Pradesh v Haryana at Dharmsala		1990-91
13	Majid Khan (147*)	Pakistanis v Glamorgan at Swansea		1967
13	C. G. Greenidge (273*)	D. H. Robins' XI v Pakistanis at Eastbourne		1974
13	C. G. Greenidge (259)	Hampshire v Sussex at Southampton		1975
13	G. W. Humpage (254)	Warwickshire v Lancashire at Southport		1982
13	R. J. Shastri (200*)	Bombay v Baroda at Bombay		1984-85
12	Gulfraz Khan (207)	Railways v Universities at Lahore		1976-77
12	I. T. Botham (138*)	Somerset v Warwickshire at Birmingham		1985
12	R. A. Harper (234)	Northamptonshire v Gloucestershire at Northampton		1986
12	D. M. Jones (248)	Australians v Warwickshire at Birmingham		1989
12	D. N. Patel (204)	Auckland v Northern Districts at Auckland		1991-92
12	W. V. Raman (206)	Tamil Nadu v Kerala at Madras		1991-92
11	C. K. Nayudu (153)	Hindus v MCC at Bombay		1926-27
11	C. J. Barnett (194)	Gloucestershire v Somerset at Bath		1934
11	R. Benaud (135)	Australians v T. N. Pearce's XI at Scarborough		1953
11	R. Bora (126)	Assam v Tripura at Gauhati		1987-88
11	G. A. Hick (405*)	Worcestershire v Somerset at Taunton		1988

Note: W. J. Stewart (Warwickshire) hit 17 sixes in the match v Lancashire, at Blackpool, 1959: ten in his first innings of 155 and seven in his second innings of 125.

MOST SIXES IN A SEASON

80	I. T. Botham	1985	57	A. W. Wellard	1938
66	A. W. Wellard	1935	51	A. W. Wellard	1933
57	A. W. Wellard	1936			

MOST BOUNDARIES IN AN INNINGS

	4s/6s			
68	68/–	P. A. Perrin (343*)	Essex v Derbyshire at Chesterfield	1904
64	64/–	Hanif Mohammad (499)	Karachi v Bahawalpur at Karachi	1958-59
63	62/1	A. C. MacLaren (424)	Lancashire v Somerset at Taunton	1895
57	52/5	J. H. Edrich (310*)	England v New Zealand at Leeds	1965
55	55/–	C. W. Gregory (383)	NSW v Queensland at Brisbane	1906-07
55	53/2	G. R. Marsh (355*)	W. Australia v S. Australia at Perth	1989-90
54	53/1	G. H. Hirst (341)	Yorkshire v Leicestershire at Leicester	1905
54	51/2†	S. V. Manjrekar (377)	Bombay v Hyderabad at Bombay	1990-91
53	53/–	A. W. Nourse (304*)	Natal v Transvaal at Johannesburg	1919-20
53	45/8	K. R. Rutherford (317)	New Zealanders v D. B. Close's XI at Scarborough	1986
52	47/5	N. H. Fairbrother (366)	Lancashire v Surrey at The Oval	1990
51	47/4	C. G. Macartney (345)	Australians v Notts. at Nottingham	1921
51	50/1	B. B. Nimbalkar (443*)	Maharashtra v Kathiawar at Poona	1948-49
50	46/4	D. G. Bradman (369)	S. Australia v Tasmania at Adelaide	1935-36
50	47/–‡	A. Ducat (306*)	Surrey v Oxford U. at The Oval	1919
50	35/15	J. R. Reid (296)	Wellington v N. Districts at Wellington	1962-63
50	42/8	I. V. A. Richards (322)	Somerset v Warwickshire at Taunton	1985

† Plus one five.
‡ Plus three fives.

HIGHEST PARTNERSHIPS

577	V. S. Hazare (288) and Gul Mahomed (319), fourth wicket, Baroda v Holkar at Baroda	1946-47
574*	F. M. M. Worrell (255*) and C. L. Walcott (314*), fourth wicket, Barbados v Trinidad at Port-of-Spain	1945-46
561	Waheed Mirza (324) and Mansoor Akhtar (224*), first wicket, Karachi Whites v Quetta at Karachi	1976-77
555	P. Holmes (224*) and H. Sutcliffe (313), first wicket, Yorkshire v Essex at Leyton	1932
554	J. T. Brown (300) and J. Tunnicliffe (243), first wicket, Yorkshire v Derbyshire at Chesterfield	1898
502*	F. M. M. Worrell (308*) and J. D. C. Goddard (218*), fourth wicket, Barbados v Trinidad at Bridgetown	1943-44
490	E. H. Bowley (283) and J. G. Langridge (195), first wicket, Sussex v Middlesex at Hove	1933
487*	G. A. Headley (344*) and C. C. Passailaigue (261*), sixth wicket, Jamaica v Lord Tennyson's XI at Kingston	1931-32
475	Zahir Alam (257) and L. S. Rajput (239), second wicket, Assam v Tripura at Gauhati	1991-92
470	A. I. Kallicharran (230*) and G. W. Humpage (254), fourth wicket, Warwickshire v Lancashire at Southport	1982
467	A. H. Jones (186) and M. D. Crowe (299), third wicket, New Zealand v Sri Lanka at Wellington	1990-91
465*	J. A. Jameson (240*) and R. B. Kanhai (213*), second wicket, Warwickshire v Gloucestershire at Birmingham	1974

HIGHEST PARTNERSHIPS FOR EACH WICKET

First Wicket

561	Waheed Mirza and Mansoor Akhtar, Karachi Whites v Quetta at Karachi	1976-77
555	P. Holmes and H. Sutcliffe, Yorkshire v Essex at Leyton	1932
554	J. T. Brown and J. Tunnicliffe, Yorkshire v Derbyshire at Chesterfield	1898
490	E. H. Bowley and J. G. Langridge, Sussex v Middlesex at Hove	1933
456	E. R. Mayne and W. H. Ponsford, Victoria v Queensland at Melbourne . . .	1923-24
451*	S. Desai and R. M. H. Binny, Karnataka v Kerala at Chikmagalur	1977-78
431	M. R. J. Veletta and G. R. Marsh, Western Australia v South Australia at Perth	1989-90
428	J. B Hobbs and A. Sandham, Surrey v Oxford University at The Oval	1926
424	I. J. Siedle and J. F. W. Nicolson, Natal v Orange Free State at Bloemfontein	1926-27
421	S. M. Gavaskar and G. A. Parkar, Bombay v Bengal at Bombay	1981-82

Second Wicket

475	Zahir Alam and L. S. Rajput, Assam v Tripura at Gauhati	1991-92
465*	J. A. Jameson and R. B. Kanhai, Warwicks. v Gloucestershire at Birmingham	1974
455	K. V. Bhandarkar and B. B. Nimbalkar, Maharashtra v Kathiawar at Poona	1948-49
451	W. H. Ponsford and D. G. Bradman, Australia v England at The Oval . . .	1934
446	C. C. Hunte and G. S. Sobers, West Indies v Pakistan at Kingston	1957-58
429*	J. G. Dewes and G. H. G. Doggart, Cambridge U. v Essex at Cambridge .	1949
426	Arshad Pervez and Mohsin Khan, Habib Bank v Income Tax at Lahore . .	1977-78
403	G. A. Gooch and P. J. Prichard, Essex v Leicestershire at Chelmsford	1990
398	A. Shrewsbury and W. Gunn, Nottinghamshire v Sussex at Nottingham . . .	1890
385	E. H. Bowley and M. W. Tate, Sussex v Northamptonshire at Hove	1921

Third Wicket

467	A. H. Jones and M. D. Crowe, New Zealand v Sri Lanka at Wellington ..	1990-91
456	Khalid Irtiza and Aslam Ali, United Bank v Multan at Karachi	1975-76
451	Mudassar Nazar and Javed Miandad, Pakistan v India at Hyderabad	1982-83
445	P. E. Whitelaw and W. N. Carson, Auckland v Otago at Dunedin	1936-37
434	J. B. Stollmeyer and G. E. Gomez, Trinidad v British Guiana at Port-of-Spain	1946-47
424*	W. J. Edrich and D. C. S. Compton, Middlesex v Somerset at Lord's	1948
413	D. J. Bicknell and D. M. Ward, Surrey v Kent at Canterbury	1990
410	R. S. Modi and L. Amarnath, India in England v The Rest at Calcutta ...	1946-47
405	A. D. Jadeja and A. S. Kaypee, Haryana v Services at Faridabad	1991-92
399	R. T. Simpson and D. C. S. Compton, MCC v N. E. Transvaal at Benoni .	1948-49

Fourth Wicket

577	V. S. Hazare and Gul Mahomed, Baroda v Holkar at Baroda............	1946-47
574*	C. L. Walcott and F. M. M. Worrell, Barbados v Trinidad at Port-of-Spain	1945-46
502*	F. M. M. Worrell and J. D. C. Goddard, Barbados v Trinidad at Bridgetown	1943-44
470	A. I. Kallicharran and G. W. Humpage, Warwicks. v Lancs. at Southport .	1982
462*	D. W. Hookes and W. B. Phillips, South Australia v Tasmania at Adelaide	1986-87
448	R. Abel and T. W. Hayward, Surrey v Yorkshire at The Oval	1899
424	I. S. Lee and S. O. Quin, Victoria v Tasmania at Melbourne	1933-34
411	P. B. H. May and M. C. Cowdrey, England v West Indies at Birmingham .	1957
410	G. Abraham and P. Balan Pandit, Kerala v Andhra at Palghat	1959-60
402	W. Watson and T. W. Graveney, MCC v British Guiana at Georgetown ..	1953-54
402	R. B. Kanhai and K. Ibadulla, Warwicks. v Notts. at Nottingham	1968

Fifth Wicket

464*	M. E. Waugh and S. R. Waugh, New South Wales v Western Australia at Perth	1990-91
405	S. G. Barnes and D. G. Bradman, Australia v England at Sydney	1946-47
397	W. Bardsley and C. Kelleway, New South Wales v South Australia at Sydney	1920-21
393	E. G. Arnold and W. B. Burns, Worcestershire v Warwickshire at Birmingham	1909
360	U. M. Merchant and M. N. Raiji, Bombay v Hyderabad at Bombay......	1947-48
355	Altaf Shah and Tariq Bashir, HBFC v Multan at Multan	1976-77
355	A. J. Lamb and J. J. Strydom, OFS v Eastern Province at Bloemfontein ..	1987-88
347	D. Brookes and D. W. Barrick, Northamptonshire v Essex at Northampton	1952
344	M. C. Cowdrey and T. W. Graveney, MCC v South Australia at Adelaide.	1962-63
343	R. I. Maddocks and J. Hallebone, Victoria v Tasmania at Melbourne	1951-52

Note: The Waugh twins achieved the first instance of brothers each scoring a double-hundred in the same first-class innings. Their partnership includes 20 runs for no-balls under ACB playing conditions. Under the Laws of Cricket, only seven runs would have resulted from ten no-balls bowled in this partnership.

Sixth Wicket

487*	G. A. Headley and C. C. Passailaigue, Jamaica v Lord Tennyson's XI at Kingston	1931-32
428	W. W. Armstrong and M. A. Noble, Australians v Sussex at Hove	1902
411	R. M. Poore and E. G. Wynyard, Hampshire v Somerset at Taunton	1899
376	R. Subba Row and A. Lightfoot, Northamptonshire v Surrey at The Oval .	1958
371	V. M. Merchant and R. S. Modi, Bombay v Maharashtra at Bombay	1943-44
356	W. V. Raman and A. Kripal Singh, Tamil Nadu v Goa at Panjim	1988-89
353	Salah-ud-Din and Zaheer Abbas, Karachi v East Pakistan at Karachi.....	1968-69
346	J. H. W. Fingleton and D. G. Bradman, Australia v England at Melbourne	1936-37
332	N. G. Marks and G. Thomas, New South Wales v South Australia at Sydney	1958-59
323	E. H. Hendren and J. W. H. T. Douglas, MCC v Victoria at Melbourne ..	1920-21

Seventh Wicket

347	D. St E. Atkinson and C. C. Depeiza, West Indies v Australia at Bridgetown	1954-55
344	K. S. Ranjitsinhji and W. Newham, Sussex v Essex at Leyton	1902
340	K. J. Key and H. Philipson, Oxford University v Middlesex at Chiswick Park	1887
336	F. C. W. Newman and C. R. N. Maxwell, Sir J. Cahn's XI v Leicestershire at Nottingham.	1935
335	C. W. Andrews and E. C. Bensted, Queensland v New South Wales at Sydney	1934-35
325	G. Brown and C. H. Abercrombie, Hampshire v Essex at Leyton	1913
323	E. H. Hendren and L. F. Townsend, MCC v Barbados at Bridgetown.	1929-30
308	Waqar Hassan and Imtiaz Ahmed, Pakistan v New Zealand at Lahore. . . .	1955-56
299	B. Mitchell and A. Melville, Transvaal v Griqualand West at Kimberley . . .	1946-47
289	G. Goonesena and G. W. Cook, Cambridge U. v Oxford U. at Lord's	1957

Eighth Wicket

433	V. T. Trumper and A. Sims, A. Sims' Aust. XI v Canterbury at Christchurch	1913-14
292	R. Peel and Lord Hawke, Yorkshire v Warwickshire at Birmingham	1896
270	V. T. Trumper and E. P. Barbour, New South Wales v Victoria at Sydney. .	1912-13
263	D. R. Wilcox and R. M. Taylor, Essex v Warwickshire at Southend	1946
255	E. A. V. Williams and E. A. Martindale, Barbados v Trinidad at Bridgetown	1935-36
246	L. E. G. Ames and G. O. B. Allen, England v New Zealand at Lord's	1931
243	R. J. Hartigan and C. Hill, Australia v England at Adelaide	1907-08
242*	T. J. Zoehrer and K. H. MacLeay, W. Australia v New South Wales at Perth	1990-91
240	Gulfraz Khan and Raja Sarfraz, Railways v Universities at Lahore	1976-77
239	W. R. Hammond and A. E. Wilson, Gloucestershire v Lancashire at Bristol	1938

Ninth Wicket

283	J. Chapman and A. Warren, Derbyshire v Warwickshire at Blackwell	1910
251	J. W. H. T. Douglas and S. N. Hare, Essex v Derbyshire at Leyton	1921
245	V. S. Hazare and N. D. Nagarwalla, Maharashtra v Baroda at Poona.	1939-40
244*	Arshad Ayub and M. V. Ramanamurthy, Hyderabad v Bihar at Hyderabad	1986-87
239	H. B. Cave and I. B. Leggat, Central Districts v Otago at Dunedin	1952-53
232	C. Hill and E. Walkley, South Australia v New South Wales at Adelaide . .	1900-01
231	P. Sen and J. Mitter, Bengal v Bihar at Jamshedpur	1950-51
230	D. A. Livingstone and A. T. Castell, Hampshire v Surrey at Southampton .	1962
226	C. Kelleway and W. A. Oldfield, New South Wales v Victoria at Melbourne	1925-26
225	W. W. Armstrong and E. A. Windsor, Australian XI v The Rest at Sydney	1907-08

Tenth Wicket

307	A. F. Kippax and J. E. H. Hooker, New South Wales v Victoria at Melbourne	1928-29
249	C. T. Sarwate and S. N. Banerjee, Indians v Surrey at The Oval	1946
235	F. E. Woolley and A. Fielder, Kent v Worcestershire at Stourbridge	1909
233	Ajay Sharma and Maninder Singh, Delhi v Bombay at Bombay.	1991-92
230	R. W. Nicholls and W. Roche, Middlesex v Kent at Lord's	1899
228	R. Illingworth and K. Higgs, Leicestershire v Northamptonshire at Leicester	1977
218	F. H. Vigar and T. P. B. Smith, Essex v Derbyshire at Chesterfield.	1947
211	M. Ellis and T. J. Hastings, Victoria v South Australia at Melbourne	1902-03
196*	Nadim Yousuf and Maqsood Kundi, MCB v National Bank at Lahore	1981-82
192	H. A. W. Bowell and W. H. Livsey, Hampshire v Worcs. at Bournemouth .	1921

UNUSUAL DISMISSALS

Handled the Ball

J. Grundy	MCC v Kent at Lord's	1857
G. Bennett	Kent v Sussex at Hove	1872
W. H. Scotton	Smokers v Non-Smokers at East Melbourne	1886-87
C. W. Wright	Nottinghamshire v Gloucestershire at Bristol	1893
E. Jones	South Australia v Victoria at Melbourne	1894-95
A. W. Nourse	South Africans v Sussex at Hove	1907
E. T. Benson	MCC v Auckland at Auckland	1929-30
A. W. Gilbertson	Otago v Auckland at Auckland	1952-53
W. R. Endean	South Africa v England at Cape Town	1956-57
P. J. Burge	Queensland v New South Wales at Sydney	1958-59
Dildar Awan	Services v Lahore at Lahore	1959-60
Mahmood-ul-Hasan	Karachi University v Railways-Quetta at Karachi	1960-61
Ali Raza	Karachi Greens v Hyderabad at Karachi	1961-62
Mohammad Yusuf	Rawalpindi v Peshawar at Peshawar	1962-63
A. Rees	Glamorgan v Middlesex at Lord's	1965
Pervez Akhtar	Multan v Karachi Greens at Sahiwal	1971-72
Javed Mirza	Railways v Punjab at Lahore	1972-73
R. G. Pollock	Eastern Province v Western Province at Cape Town	1973-74
C. I. Dey	Northern Transvaal v Orange Free State at Bloemfontein	1973-74
Nasir Valika	Karachi Whites v National Bank at Karachi	1974-75
Haji Yousuf	National Bank v Railways at Lahore	1974-75
Masood-ul-Hasan	PIA v National Bank B at Lyallpur	1975-76
D. K. Pearse	Natal v Western Province at Cape Town	1978-79
A. M. J. Hilditch	Australia v Pakistan at Perth	1978-79
Musleh-ud-Din	Railways v Lahore at Lahore	1979-80
Jalal-ud-Din	IDBP v Habib Bank at Bahawalpur	1981-82
Mohsin Khan	Pakistan v Australia at Karachi	1982-83
D. L. Haynes	West Indies v India at Bombay	1983-84
K. Azad	Delhi v Punjab at Amritsar	1983-84
Athar A. Khan	Allied Bank v HBFC at Sialkot	1983-84
A. N. Pandya	Saurashtra v Baroda at Baroda	1984-85
G. L. Linton	Barbados v Windward Islands at Bridgetown	1985-86
R. B. Gartrell	Tasmania v Victoria at Melbourne	1986-87
R. Nayyar	Himachal Pradesh v Punjab at Una	1988-89
R. Weerawardene	Moratuwa v Nomads SC at Colombo	1988-89
A. M. Kane	Vidarbha v Railways at Nagpur	1989-90
P. Bali	Jammu and Kashmir v Services at Delhi	1991-92
M. J. Davis	Northern Transvaal B v OFS B at Bloemfontein	1991-92
J. T. C. Vaughan	Emerging Players v England XI at Hamilton	1991-92

Obstructing the Field

C. A. Absolom	Cambridge University v Surrey at The Oval	1868
T. Straw	Worcestershire v Warwickshire at Worcester	1899
T. Straw	Worcestershire v Warwickshire at Birmingham	1901
J. P. Whiteside	Leicestershire v Lancashire at Leicester	1901
L. Hutton	England v South Africa at The Oval	1951
J. A. Hayes	Canterbury v Central Districts at Christchurch	1954-55
D. D. Deshpande	Madhya Pradesh v Uttar Pradesh at Benares	1956-57
M. Mehra	Railways v Delhi at Delhi	1959-60
K. Ibadulla	Warwickshire v Hampshire at Coventry	1963
Qaiser Khan	Dera Ismail Khan v Railways at Lahore	1964-65
Ijaz Ahmed	Lahore Greens v Lahore Blues at Lahore	1973-74
Qasim Feroze	Bahawalpur v Universities at Lahore	1974-75
T. Quirk	Northern Transvaal v Border at East London	1978-79
Mahmood Rashid	United Bank v Muslim Commercial Bank at Bahawalpur	1981-82
Arshad Ali	Sukkur v Quetta at Quetta	1983-84
H. R. Wasu	Vidarbha v Rajasthan at Akola	1984-85
Khalid Javed	Railways v Lahore at Lahore	1985-86
C. Bindುhewa	Singha SC v Sinhalese SC at Colombo	1990-91

Hit the Ball Twice

H. E. Bull	MCC v Oxford University at Lord's	1864
H. R. J. Charlwood	Sussex v Surrey at Hove	1872
R. G. Barlow	North v South at Lord's	1878
P. S. Wimble	Transvaal v Griqualand West at Kimberley	1892-93
G. B. Nicholls	Somerset v Gloucestershire at Bristol	1896
A. A. Lilley	Warwickshire v Yorkshire at Birmingham	1897
J. H. King	Leicestershire v Surrey at The Oval	1906
A. P. Binns	Jamaica v British Guiana at Georgetown	1956-57
K. Bhavanna	Andhra v Mysore at Guntur	1963-64
Zaheer Abbas	PIA v Karachi Blues at Karachi	1969-70
Anwar Miandad	IDBP v United Bank at Lahore	1979-80
Anwar Iqbal	Hyderabad v Sukkur at Hyderabad	1983-84
Iqtidar Ali	Allied Bank v Muslim Commercial Bank at Lahore	1983-84
Aziz Malik	Lahore Division v Faisalabad at Sialkot	1984-85
Javed Mohammad	Multan v Karachi Whites at Sahiwal	1986-87
Shahid Pervez	Jammu and Kashmir v Punjab at Srinigar	1986-87

BOWLING RECORDS

TEN WICKETS IN AN INNINGS

	O	M	R		
E. Hinkly (Kent)				v England at Lord's	1848
*J. Wisden (North)				v South at Lord's	1850
V. E. Walker (England)	43	17	74	v Surrey at The Oval	1859
V. E. Walker (Middlesex)	44.2	5	104	v Lancashire at Manchester	1865
G. Wootton (All England)	31.3	9	54	v Yorkshire at Sheffield	1865
W. Hickton (Lancashire)	36.2	19	46	v Hampshire at Manchester	1870
S. E. Butler (Oxford)	24.1	11	38	v Cambridge at Lord's	1871
James Lillywhite (South)	60.2	22	129	v North at Canterbury	1872
A. Shaw (MCC)	36.2	8	73	v North at Lord's	1874
E. Barratt (Players)	29	11	43	v Australians at The Oval	1878
G. Giffen (Australian XI)	26	10	66	v The Rest at Sydney	1883-84
W. G. Grace (MCC)	36.2	17	49	v Oxford University at Oxford	1886
G. Burton (Middlesex)	52.3	25	59	v Surrey at The Oval	1888
†A. E. Moss (Canterbury)	21.3	10	28	v Wellington at Christchurch	1889-90
S. M. J. Woods (Cambridge U.)	31	6	69	v Thornton's XI at Cambridge	1890
T. Richardson (Surrey)	15.3	3	45	v Essex at The Oval	1894
H. Pickett (Essex)	27	11	32	v Leicestershire at Leyton	1895
E. J. Tyler (Somerset)	34.3	15	49	v Surrey at Taunton	1895
W. P. Howell (Australians)	23.2	14	28	v Surrey at The Oval	1899
C. H. G. Bland (Sussex)	25.2	10	48	v Kent at Tonbridge	1899
J. Briggs (Lancashire)	28.5	7	55	v Worcestershire at Manchester	1900
A. E. Trott (Middlesex)	14.2	5	42	v Somerset at Taunton	1900
F. Hinds (A. B. St Hill's XI)	19.1	6	36	v Trinidad at Port-of-Spain	1900-01
A. Fielder (Players)	24.5	1	90	v Gentlemen at Lord's	1906
E. G. Dennett (Gloucestershire)	19.4	7	40	v Essex at Bristol	1906
A. E. E. Vogler (E. Province)	12	2	26	v Griqualand W. at Johannesburg	1906-07
C. Blythe (Kent)	16	7	30	v Northants at Northampton	1907
A. Drake (Yorkshire)	8.5	0	35	v Somerset at Weston-s-Mare	1914
W. Bestwick (Derbyshire)	19	2	40	v Glamorgan at Cardiff	1921
A. A. Mailey (Australians)	28.4	5	66	v Gloucestershire at Cheltenham	1921
C. W. L. Parker (Glos.)	40.3	13	79	v Somerset at Bristol	1921
T. Rushby (Surrey)	17.5	4	43	v Somerset at Taunton	1921
J. C. White (Somerset)	42.2	11	76	v Worcestershire at Worcester	1921
G. C. Collins (Kent)	19.3	4	65	v Nottinghamshire at Dover	1922
H. Howell (Warwickshire)	25.1	5	51	v Yorkshire at Birmingham	1923

	O	M	R		
A. S. Kennedy (Players)	22.4	10	37	v Gentlemen at The Oval	1927
G. O. B. Allen (Middlesex)	25.3	10	40	v Lancashire at Lord's	1929
A. P. Freeman (Kent)	42	9	131	v Lancashire at Maidstone	1929
G. Geary (Leicestershire)	16.2	8	18	v Glamorgan at Pontypridd	1929
C. V. Grimmett (Australians)	22.3	8	37	v Yorkshire at Sheffield	1930
A. P. Freeman (Kent)	30.4	8	53	v Essex at Southend	1930
H. Verity (Yorkshire)	18.4	6	36	v Warwickshire at Leeds	1931
A. P. Freeman (Kent)	36.1	9	79	v Lancashire at Manchester	1931
V. W. C. Jupp (Northants)	39	6	127	v Kent at Tunbridge Wells	1932
H. Verity (Yorkshire)	19.4	16	10	v Nottinghamshire at Leeds	1932
T. W. Wall (South Australia)	12.4	2	36	v New South Wales at Sydney	1932-33
T. B. Mitchell (Derbyshire)	19.1	4	64	v Leicestershire at Leicester	1935
J. Mercer (Glamorgan)	26	10	51	v Worcestershire at Worcester	1936
T. W. J. Goddard (Glos.)	28.4	4	113	v Worcestershire at Cheltenham	1937
T. F. Smailes (Yorkshire)	17.1	5	47	v Derbyshire at Sheffield	1939
E. A. Watts (Surrey)	24.1	8	67	v Warwickshire at Birmingham	1939
*W. E. Hollies (Warwickshire)	20.4	4	49	v Notts. at Birmingham	1946
J. M. Sims (East)	18.4	2	90	v West at Kingston	1948
T. E. Bailey (Essex)	39.4	9	90	v Lancashire at Clacton	1949
J. K. Graveney (Glos.)	18.4	2	66	v Derbyshire at Chesterfield	1949
R. Berry (Lancashire)	36.2	9	102	v Worcestershire at Blackpool	1953
S. P. Gupte (President's XI)	24.2	7	78	v Combined XI at Bombay	1954-55
J. C. Laker (Surrey)	46	18	88	v Australians at The Oval	1956
J. C. Laker (England)	51.2	23	53	v Australia at Manchester	1956
G. A. R. Lock (Surrey)	29.1	18	54	v Kent at Blackheath	1956
K. Smales (Nottinghamshire)	41.3	20	66	v Gloucestershire at Stroud	1956-57
P. M. Chatterjee (Bengal)	19	11	20	v Assam at Jorhat	1956-57
J. D. Bannister (Warwickshire)	23.3	11	41	v Comb. Services at Birmingham	1959
A. J. G. Pearson (Cambridge U.)	30.3	8	78	v Leics. at Loughborough	1961
N. I. Thomson (Sussex)	34.2	19	49	v Warwickshire at Worthing	1964
P. J. Allan (Queensland)	15.6	3	61	v Victoria at Melbourne	1965-66
I. J. Brayshaw (W. Australia)	17.6	4	44	v Victoria at Perth	1967-68
Shahid Mahmood (Karachi Whites)	25	5	58	v Khairpur at Karachi	1969-70
E. E. Hemmings (International XI)	49.3	14	175	v West Indies XI at Kingston	1982-83
P. Sunderam (Rajasthan)	22	5	78	v Vidarbha at Jodhpur	1985-86
S. T. Jefferies (W. Province)	22.5	7	59	v Orange Free State at Cape Town	1987-88
Imran Adil (Bahawalpur)	22.5	3	92	v Faisalabad at Faisalabad	1989-90
G. P. Wickremasinghe (Sinhalese SC)	19.2	5	41	v Kalutara at Colombo (SSC)	1991-92

* *J. Wisden and W. E. Hollies achieved the feat without the direct assistance of a fielder. Wisden's ten were all bowled; Hollies bowled seven and had three lbw.*
† *On début in first-class cricket.*

Note: The following instances were achieved in 12-a-side matches:

	O	M	R		
E. M. Grace (MCC)	32.2	7	69	v Gents of Kent at Canterbury	1862
W. G. Grace (MCC)	46.1	15	92	v Kent at Canterbury	1873

OUTSTANDING ANALYSES

	O	M	R	W		
H. Verity (Yorkshire)	19.4	16	10	10	v Nottinghamshire at Leeds	1932
G. Elliott (Victoria)	19	17	2	9	v Tasmania at Launceston	1857-58
Ahad Khan (Railways)	6.3	4	7	9	v Dera Ismail Khan at Lahore	1964-65
J. C. Laker (England)	14	12	2	8	v The Rest at Bradford	1950
D. Shackleton (Hampshire)	11.1	7	4	8	v Somerset at Weston-s-Mare	1955
E. Peate (Yorkshire)	16	11	5	8	v Surrey at Holbeck	1883

	O	M	R	W		
F. R. Spofforth (Australians) .	8.3	6	3	7	v England XI at Birmingham	1884
W. A. Henderson (N.E. Transvaal)	9.3	7	4	7	v Orange Free State at Bloemfontein	1937-38
Rajinder Goel (Haryana).....	7	4	4	7	v Jammu and Kashmir at Chandigarh	1977-78
V. I. Smith (South Africans) .	4.5	3	1	6	v Derbyshire at Derby	1947
S. Cosstick (Victoria)........	21.1	20	1	6	v Tasmania at Melbourne.......	1868-69
Israr Ali (Bahawalpur).......	11	10	1	6	v Dacca U. at Bahawalpur.....	1957-58
A. D. Pougher (MCC)	3	3	0	5	v Australians at Lord's	1896
G. R. Cox (Sussex)	6	6	0	5	v Somerset at Weston-s-Mare....	1921
R. K. Tyldesley (Lancashire) .	5	5	0	5	v Leicestershire at Manchester ...	1924
P. T. Mills (Gloucestershire) .	6.4	6	0	5	v Somerset at Bristol	1928

MOST WICKETS IN A MATCH

19-90	J. C. Laker	England v Australia at Manchester	1956
17-48	C. Blythe	Kent v Northamptonshire at Northampton.......	1907
17-50	C. T. B. Turner	Australians v England XI at Hastings	1888
17-54	W. P. Howell	Australians v Western Province at Cape Town ...	1902-03
17-56	C. W. L. Parker	Gloucestershire v Essex at Gloucester	1925
17-67	A. P. Freeman	Kent v Sussex at Hove	1922
17-89	W. G. Grace	Gloucestershire v Nottinghamshire at Cheltenham .	1877
17-89	F. C. L. Matthews	Nottinghamshire v Northants at Nottingham	1923
17-91	H. Dean	Lancashire v Yorkshire at Liverpool	1913
17-91	H. Verity	Yorkshire v Essex at Leyton	1933
17-92	A. P. Freeman	Kent v Warwickshire at Folkestone.............	1932
17-103	W. Mycroft	Derbyshire v Hampshire at Southampton	1876
17-106	G. R. Cox	Sussex v Warwickshire at Horsham	1926
17-106	T. W. J. Goddard	Gloucestershire v Kent at Bristol	1939
17-119	W. Mead	Essex v Hampshire at Southampton	1895
17-137	W. Brearley	Lancashire v Somerset at Manchester	1905
17-159	S. F. Barnes	England v South Africa at Johannesburg	1913-14
17-201	G. Giffen	South Australia v Victoria at Adelaide	1885-86
17-212	J. C. Clay	Glamorgan v Worcestershire at Swansea........	1937

Notes: H. A. Arkwright took 18 wickets for 96 runs in a 12-a-side match for Gentlemen of MCC v Gentlemen of Kent at Canterbury in 1861.

W. Mead took 17 wickets for 205 runs for Essex v Australians at Leyton in 1893, the year before Essex were raised to first-class status.

F. P. Fenner took 17 wickets for Cambridge Town Club v University of Cambridge at Cambridge in 1844.

SIXTEEN OR MORE WICKETS IN A DAY

17-48	C. Blythe	Kent v Northamptonshire at Northampton.......	1907
17-91	H. Verity	Yorkshire v Essex at Leyton	1933
17-106	T. W. J. Goddard	Gloucestershire v Kent at Bristol	1939
16-38	T. Emmett	Yorkshire v Cambridgeshire at Hunslet..........	1869
16-52	J. Southerton	South v North at Lord's	1875
16-69	T. G. Wass	Nottinghamshire v Lancashire at Liverpool	1906
16-38	A. E. E. Vogler	E. Province v Griqualand West at Johannesburg ..	1906-07
16-103	T. G. Wass	Nottinghamshire v Essex at Nottingham.........	1908
16-83	J. C. White	Somerset v Worcestershire at Bath..............	1919

FOUR WICKETS WITH CONSECUTIVE BALLS

J. Wells	Kent v Sussex at Brighton	1862
G. Ulyett	Lord Harris's XI v New South Wales at Sydney	1878-79
G. Nash	Lancashire v Somerset at Manchester	1882
J. B. Hide	Sussex v MCC and Ground at Lord's	1890
F. J. Shacklock	Nottinghamshire v Somerset at Nottingham	1893
A. D. Downes	Otago v Auckland at Dunedin	1893-94
F. Martin	MCC and Ground v Derbyshire at Lord's	1895
A. W. Mold	Lancashire v Nottinghamshire at Nottingham	1895
W. Brearley†	Lancashire v Somerset at Manchester	1905
S. Haigh	MCC v Army XI at Pretoria	1905-06
A. E. Trott‡	Middlesex v Somerset at Lord's	1907
F. A. Tarrant	Middlesex v Gloucestershire at Bristol	1907
A. Drake	Yorkshire v Derbyshire at Chesterfield	1914
S. G. Smith	Northamptonshire v Warwickshire at Birmingham	1914
H. A. Peach	Surrey v Sussex at The Oval	1924
A. F. Borland	Natal v Griqualand West at Kimberley	1926-27
J. E. H. Hooker†	New South Wales v Victoria at Sydney	1928-29
R. K. Tyldesley†	Lancashire v Derbyshire at Derby	1929
R. J. Crisp	Western Province v Griqualand West at Johannesburg ..	1931-32
R. J. Crisp	Western Province v Natal at Durban	1933-34
A. R. Gover	Surrey v Worcestershire at Worcester	1935
W. H. Copson	Derbyshire v Warwickshire at Derby	1937
W. A. Henderson	N.E. Transvaal v Orange Free State at Bloemfontein	1937-38
F. Ridgway	Kent v Derbyshire at Folkestone	1951
A. K. Walker§	Nottinghamshire v Leicestershire at Leicester	1956
S. N. Mohol	President's XI v Combined XI at Poona	1965-66
P. I. Pocock	Surrey v Sussex at Eastbourne	1972
S. S. Saini†	Delhi v Himachal Pradesh at Delhi	1988-89
D. Dias	W. Province (Suburbs) v Central Province at Colombo ..	1990-91

  † *Not all in the same innings.*
  ‡ *Trott achieved another hat-trick in the same innings of this, his benefit match.*
  § *Walker dismissed Firth with the last ball of the first innings and Lester, Tompkin and Smithson with the first three balls of the second innings, a feat without parallel.*

Notes: In their match with England at The Oval in 1863, Surrey lost four wickets in the course of a four-ball over from G. Bennett.

Sussex lost five wickets in the course of the final (six-ball) over of their match with Surrey at Eastbourne in 1972. P. I. Pocock, who had taken three wickets in his previous over, captured four more, taking in all seven wickets with 11 balls, a feat unique in first-class matches. (The eighth wicket fell to a run-out.)

HAT-TRICKS

Double Hat-Trick

Besides Trott's performance, which is given in the preceding section, the following instances are recorded of players having performed the hat-trick twice in the same match, Rao doing so in the same innings.

A. Shaw	Nottinghamshire v Gloucestershire at Nottingham	1884
T. J. Matthews	Australia v South Africa at Manchester	1912
C. W. L. Parker	Gloucestershire v Middlesex at Bristol	1924
R. O. Jenkins	Worcestershire v Surrey at Worcester	1949
J. S. Rao	Services v Northern Punjab at Amritsar	1963-64
Amin Lakhani	Combined XI v Indians at Multan	1978-79

Five Wickets with Six Consecutive Balls

J. H. Copson	Derbyshire v Warwickshire at Derby	1937
J. A. Henderson	N.E. Transvaal v Orange Free State at Bloemfontein....	1937-38
P. I. Pocock	Surrey v Sussex at Eastbourne	1972

Most Hat-Tricks

Seven times: D. V. P. Wright.

Six times: T. W. J. Goddard, C. W. L. Parker.

Five times: S. Haigh, V. W. C. Jupp, A. E. G. Rhodes, F. A. Tarrant.

Four times: R. G. Barlow, J. T. Hearne, J. C. Laker, G. A. R. Lock, G. G. Macaulay, T. J. Matthews, M. J. Procter, T. Richardson, F. R. Spofforth, F. S. Trueman.

Three times: W. M. Bradley, H. J. Butler, S. T. Clarke, W. H. Copson, R. J. Crisp, J. W. H. T. Douglas, J. A. Flavell, A. P. Freeman, G. Giffen, K. Higgs, A. Hill, W. A. Humphries, R. D. Jackman, R. O. Jenkins, A. S. Kennedy, W. H. Lockwood, E. A. McDonald, T. L. Pritchard, C. S. Rao, A. Shaw, J. B. Statham, M. W. Tate, H. Trumble, D. Wilson, G. A. Wilson.

Twice (current players only): G. R. Dilley, E. E. Hemmings, M. D. Marshall, P. A. Smith, P. J. van Heerden.

250 WICKETS IN A SEASON

	Season	O	M	R	W	Avge
A. P. Freeman	1928	1,976.1	423	5,489	304	18.05
A. P. Freeman	1933	2,039	651	4,549	298	15.26
T. Richardson	1895‡	1,690.1	463	4,170	290	14.37
C. T. B. Turner**	1888†	2,427.2	1,127	3,307	283	11.68
A. P. Freeman	1931	1,618	360	4,307	276	15.60
A. P. Freeman	1930	1,914.3	472	4,632	275	16.84
T. Richardson	1897‡	1,603.4	495	3,945	273	14.45
A. P. Freeman	1929	1,670.5	381	4,879	267	18.27
W. Rhodes............	1900	1,553	455	3,606	261	13.81
J. T. Hearne	1896	2,003.1	818	3,670	257	14.28
A. P. Freeman	1932	1,565.5	404	4,149	253	16.39
W. Rhodes............	1901	1,565	505	3,797	251	15.12

† *Indicates 4-ball overs;* ‡ *5-ball overs.*
** *Exclusive of matches not reckoned as first-class.*

Notes: In four consecutive seasons (1928-31), A. P. Freeman took 1,122 wickets, and in eight consecutive seasons (1928-35), 2,090 wickets. In each of these eight seasons he took over 200 wickets.

T. Richardson took 1,005 wickets in four consecutive seasons (1894-97).

In 1896, J. T. Hearne took his 100th wicket as early as June 12. In 1931, C. W. L. Parker did the same and A. P. Freeman obtained his 100th wicket a day later.

LEADING BOWLERS IN AN ENGLISH SEASON

(Qualification: 10 wickets in 10 innings)

Season	Leading wicket-taker	Wkts	Avge	Top of averages	Wkts	Avge
1946	W. E. Hollies..........	184	15.60	A. Booth	111	11.61
1947	T. W. J. Goddard	238	17.30	J. C. Clay..........	65	16.44
1948	J. E. Walsh	174	19.56	J. C. Clay..........	41	14.17
1949	R. O. Jenkins..........	183	21.19	T. W. J. Goddard ...	160	19.18
1950	R. Tattersall	193	13.59	R. Tattersall	193	13.59
1951	R. Appleyard	200	14.14	R. Appleyard	200	14.14

Season	Leading wicket-taker	Wkts	Avge	Top of averages	Wkts	Avge
1952	J. H. Wardle	177	19.54	F. S. Trueman	61	13.7
1953	B. Dooland	172	16.58	C. J. Knott	38	13.7
1954	B. Dooland	196	15.48	J. B. Statham	92	14.1
1955	G. A. R. Lock	216	14.49	R. Appleyard	85	13.0
1956	D. J. Shepherd	177	15.36	G. A. R. Lock	155	12.4
1957	G. A. R. Lock	212	12.02	G. A. R. Lock	212	12.0
1958	G. A. R. Lock	170	12.08	H. L. Jackson	143	10.9
1959	D. Shackleton	148	21.55	J. B. Statham	139	15.0
1960	F. S. Trueman	175	13.98	J. B. Statham	135	12.3
1961	J. A. Flavell	171	17.79	J. A. Flavell	171	17.7
1962	D. Shackleton	172	20.15	C. Cook	58	17.1
1963	D. Shackleton	146	16.75	C. C. Griffith	119	12.8
1964	D. Shackleton	142	20.40	J. A. Standen	64	13.0
1965	D. Shackleton	144	16.08	H. J. Rhodes	119	11.0
1966	D. L. Underwood	157	13.80	D. L. Underwood	157	13.8
1967	T. W. Cartwright	147	15.52	D. L. Underwood	136	12.3
1968	R. Illingworth	131	14.36	O. S. Wheatley	82	12.9
1969	R. M. H. Cottam	109	21.04	A. Ward	69	14.8
1970	D. J. Shepherd	106	19.16	Majid Khan	11	18.8
1971	L. R. Gibbs	131	18.89	G. G. Arnold	83	17.1
1972	T. W. Cartwright	98	18.64	I. M. Chappell	10	10.6
	B. Stead	98	20.38			
1973	B. S. Bedi	105	17.94	T. W. Cartwright	89	15.8
1974	A. M. E. Roberts	119	13.62	A. M. E. Roberts	119	13.6
1975	P. G. Lee	112	18.45	A. M. E. Roberts	57	15.8
1976	G. A. Cope	93	24.13	M. A. Holding	55	14.3
1977	M. J. Procter	109	18.04	R. A. Woolmer	19	15.2
1978	D. L. Underwood	110	14.49	D. L. Underwood	110	14.4
1979	D. L. Underwood	106	14.85	J. Garner	55	13.8
	J. K. Lever	106	17.30			
1980	R. D. Jackman	121	15.40	J. Garner	49	13.9
1981	R. J. Hadlee	105	14.89	R. J. Hadlee	105	14.8
1982	M. D. Marshall	134	15.73	R. J. Hadlee	61	14.5
1983	J. K. Lever	106	16.28	Imran Khan	12	7.1
	D. L. Underwood	106	19.28			
1984	R. J. Hadlee	117	14.05	R. J. Hadlee	117	14.0
1985	N. V. Radford	101	24.68	R. M. Ellison	65	17.2
1986	C. A. Walsh	118	18.17	M. D. Marshall	100	15.0
1987	N. V. Radford	109	20.81	R. J. Hadlee	97	12.6
1988	F. D. Stephenson	125	18.31	M. D. Marshall	42	13.1
1989	D. R. Pringle	94	18.64	T. M. Alderman	70	15.6
	S. L. Watkin	94	25.09			
1990	N. A. Foster	94	26.61	I. R. Bishop	59	19.0
1991	Waqar Younis	113	14.65	Waqar Younis	113	14.6
1992	C. A. Walsh	92	15.96	C. A. Walsh	92	15.9

100 WICKETS IN A SEASON

Since Reduction of Championship Matches in 1969

Five times: D. L. Underwood 110 (1978), 106 (1979), 106 (1983), 102 (1971), 101 (1969).
Four times: J. K. Lever 116 (1984), 106 (1978), 106 (1979), 106 (1983).
Twice: B. S. Bedi 112 (1974), 105 (1973); T. W. Cartwright 108 (1969), 104 (1971); N. A.
Foster 105 (1986), 102 (1991); N. Gifford 105 (1970), 104 (1971); R. J. Hadlee 117 (1984), 105
(1981); P. G. Lee 112 (1975), 101 (1973); M. D. Marshall 134 (1982), 100 (1986); M. J. Procter
109 (1977), 108 (1969); N. V. Radford 109 (1987), 101 (1985); F. J. Titmus 105 (1970),
104 (1971).

Once: J. P. Agnew 101 (1987); I. T. Botham 100 (1978); K. E. Cooper 101 (1988); R. M. H. Cottam 109 (1969); D. R. Doshi 101 (1980); J. E. Emburey 103 (1983); L. R. Gibbs 131 (1971); R. N. S. Hobbs 102 (1970); Intikhab Alam 104 (1971); R. D. Jackman 121 (1980); A. M. E. Roberts 119 (1974); P. J. Sainsbury 107 (1971); Sarfraz Nawaz 101 (1975); M. W. W. Selvey 101 (1978); D. J. Shepherd 106 (1970); F. D. Stephenson 125 (1988); C. A. Walsh 118 (1986); Vaqar Younis 113 (1991); D. Wilson 102 (1969).

100 WICKETS IN A SEASON MOST TIMES

(Includes Overseas Tours and Seasons)

23 times: W. Rhodes 200 wkts (3).

20 times: D. Shackleton (In successive seasons – 1949 to 1968 inclusive).

17 times: A. P. Freeman 300 wkts (1), 200 wkts (7).

16 times: T. W. J. Goddard 200 wkts (4), C. W. L. Parker 200 wkts (5), R. T. D. Perks, F. J. Titmus.

15 times: J. T. Hearne 200 wkts (3), G. H. Hirst 200 wkts (1), A. S. Kennedy 200 wkts (1).

14 times: C. Blythe 200 wkts (1), W. E. Hollies, G. A. R. Lock 200 wkts (2), M. W. Tate 200 wkts (3), J. C White.

13 times: J. B. Statham.

12 times: J. Briggs, E. G. Dennett 200 wkts (1), C. Gladwin, D. J. Shepherd, N. I. Thomson, F. S. Trueman.

11 times: A. V. Bedser, G. Geary, S. Haigh, J. C. Laker, M. S. Nichols, A. E. Relf.

10 times: W. Attewell, W. G. Grace, R. Illingworth, H. L. Jackson, V. W. C. Jupp, G. G. Macaulay 200 wkts (1), W. Mead, T. B. Mitchell, T. Richardson 200 wkts (3), J. Southerton 200 wkts (1), R. K. Tyldesley, D. L. Underwood, J. H. Wardle, T. G. Wass, D. V. P. Wright.

9 times: W. E. Astill, T. E. Bailey, W. E. Bowes, C. Cook, R. Howorth, J. Mercer, A. W. Mold 200 wkts (2), J. A. Newman, C. F. Root 200 wkts (1), A. Shaw 200 wkts (1), H. Verity 200 wkts (2).

8 times: T. W. Cartwright, H. Dean, J. A. Flavell, A. R. Gover 200 wkts (2), H. Larwood, G. A. Lohmann 200 wkts (3), R. Peel, J. M. Sims, F. A. Tarrant, R. Tattersall, G. J. Thompson, G. E. Tribe, A. W. Wellard, F. E. Woolley, J. A. Young.

100 WICKETS IN A SEASON OUTSIDE ENGLAND

W		Season	Country	R	Avge
16	M. W. Tate	1926-27	India/Ceylon	1,599	13.78
07	Ijaz Faqih	1985-86	Pakistan	1,719	16.06
06	C. T. B. Turner. . . .	1887-88	Australia	1,441	13.59
06	R. Benaud	1957-58	South Africa	2,056	19.39
04	S. F. Barnes	1913-14	South Africa	1,117	10.74
04	Sajjad Akbar	1989-90	Pakistan	2,328	22.38
03	Abdul Qadir	1982-83	Pakistan	2,367	22.98

1,500 WICKETS IN A CAREER

Dates in italics denote the first half of an overseas season; i.e. *1970* denotes the 1970-71 season.

	Career	W	R	Avge
W. Rhodes	1898-1930	4,187	69,993	16.71
A. P. Freeman.	1914-36	3,776	69,577	18.42
C. W. L. Parker	1903-35	3,278	63,817	19.46
J. T. Hearne	1888-1923	3,061	54,352	17.75
T. W. J. Goddard	1922-52	2,979	59,116	19.84
W. G. Grace	1865-1908	2,876	51,545	17.92
A. S. Kennedy.	1907-36	2,874	61,034	21.23
D. Shackleton	1948-69	2,857	53,303	18.65
G. A. R. Lock	1946-*70*	2,844	54,709	19.23

		Career	W	R	Avge
10	F. J. Titmus	1949-82	2,830	63,313	22.37
11	M. W. Tate	1912-37	2,784	50,571	18.16
12	G. H. Hirst	1891-1929	2,739	51,282	18.72
13	C. Blythe	1899-1914	2,506	42,136	16.81
14	D. L. Underwood	1963-87	2,465	49,993	20.28
15	W. E. Astill	1906-39	2,431	57,783	23.76
16	J. C. White	1909-37	2,356	43,759	18.57
17	W. E. Hollies	1932-57	2,323	48,656	20.94
18	F. S. Trueman	1949-69	2,304	42,154	18.29
19	J. B. Statham	1950-68	2,260	36,999	16.37
20	R. T. D. Perks	1930-55	2,233	53,770	24.07
21	J. Briggs	1879-1900	2,221	35,431	15.95
22	D. J. Shepherd	1950-72	2,218	47,302	21.32
23	E. G. Dennett	1903-26	2,147	42,571	19.82
24	T. Richardson	1892-1905	2,104	38,794	18.43
25	T. E. Bailey	1945-67	2,082	48,170	23.13
26	R. Illingworth	1951-83	2,072	42,023	20.28
27	N. Gifford	1960-88	2,068	48,731	23.56
	F. E. Woolley	1906-38	2,068	41,066	19.85
29	G. Geary	1912-38	2,063	41,339	20.03
30	D. V. P. Wright	1932-57	2,056	49,307	23.98
31	J. A. Newman	1906-30	2,032	51,111	25.15
32	†A. Shaw	1864-97	2,027	24,580	12.12
33	S. Haigh	1895-1913	2,012	32,091	15.94
34	H. Verity	1930-39	1,956	29,146	14.90
35	W. Attewell	1881-1900	1,951	29,896	15.32
36	J. C. Laker	1946-*64*	1,944	35,791	18.41
37	A. V. Bedser	1939-60	1,924	39,279	20.41
38	W. Mead	1892-1913	1,916	36,388	18.99
39	A. E. Relf	1900-21	1,897	39,724	20.94
40	P. G. H. Fender	1910-36	1,894	47,458	25.05
41	J. W. H. T. Douglas	1901-30	1,893	44,159	23.32
42	J. H. Wardle	1946-*67*	1,846	35,027	18.97
43	G. R. Cox	1895-1928	1,843	42,136	22.86
44	G. A. Lohmann	1884-97	1,841	25,295	13.73
45	J. W. Hearne	1909-36	1,839	44,926	24.42
46	G. G. Macaulay	1920-35	1,837	32,440	17.65
47	M. S. Nichols	1924-39	1,833	39,666	21.63
48	J. B. Mortimore	1950-75	1,807	41,904	23.18
49	C. Cook	1946-64	1,782	36,578	20.52
50	R. Peel	1882-99	1,752	28,442	16.23
51	H. L. Jackson	1947-63	1,733	30,101	17.36
52	J. K. Lever	1967-89	1,722	41,772	24.25
53	T. P. B. Smith	1929-52	1,697	45,059	26.55
54	J. Southerton	1854-79	1,681	24,290	14.44
55	A. E. Trott	*1892*-1911	1,674	35,317	21.09
56	A. W. Mold	1889-1901	1,673	26,010	15.54
57	T. G. Wass	1896-1920	1,666	34,092	20.46
58	V. W. C. Jupp	1909-38	1,658	38,166	23.01
59	C. Gladwin	1939-58	1,653	30,265	18.30
60	W. E. Bowes	1928-47	1,639	27,470	16.76
61	A. W. Wellard	1927-50	1,614	39,302	24.35
62	P. I. Pocock	1964-86	1,607	42,648	26.53
63	N. I. Thomson	1952-72	1,597	32,867	20.58
64	J. Mercer	1919-47	1,591	37,210	23.38
	G. J. Thompson	1897-1922	1,591	30,058	18.89
66	J. M. Sims	1929-53	1,581	39,401	24.92
67	T. Emmett	1866-88	1,571	21,314	13.56
	Intikhab Alam	*1957*-82	1,571	43,474	27.67
69	B. S. Bedi	*1961*-81	1,560	33,843	21.69

		Career	W	R	Avge
'0	W. Voce.............	1927-52	1,558	35,961	23.08
'1	A. R. Gover	1928-48	1,555	36,753	23.63
'2 {	T. W. Cartwright	1952-77	1,536	29,357	19.11
	K. Higgs	1958-86	1,536	36,267	23.61
'4	James Langridge	1924-53	1,530	34,524	22.56
'5	J. A. Flavell............	1949-67	1,529	32,847	21.48
'6	**M. D. Marshall**	**1977-92**	**1,524**	**28,511**	**18.70**
'7 {	C. F. Root	1910-33	1,512	31,933	21.11
	F. A. Tarrant..........	*1898-1936*	1,512	26,450	17.49
'9	R. K. Tyldesley	1919-35	1,509	25,980	17.21

Bold type denotes player who appeared in 1991-92 and 1992 seasons.

† *The figures for A. Shaw exclude one wicket for which no analysis is available.*

Note: Some works of reference provide career figures which differ from those in this list, owing to the exclusion or inclusion of matches recognised or not recognised as first-class by *Wisden*.

Current Players with 1,000 Wickets

E. E. Hemmings	1966-92	1,404	41,461	29.53
J. E. Emburey	1973-92	1,366	35,599	26.06
Imran Khan	*1969-91*	1,287	28,726	22.32
P. H. Edmonds	1971-92	1,246	31,981	25.66
I. T. Botham	1974-92	1,159	31,386	27.08
P. Carrick.............	1970-92	1,078	32,115	29.79

ALL-ROUND RECORDS

HUNDRED AND TEN WICKETS IN AN INNINGS

V. E. Walker, England v Surrey at The Oval; 20*, 108, ten for 74, and four for 17.	1859
W. G. Grace, MCC v Oxford University at Oxford; 104, two for 60, and ten for 49.	1886

Note: E. M. Grace, for MCC v Gentlemen of Kent in a 12-a-side match at Canterbury in 1862, scored 192* and took five for 77 and ten for 69.

TWO HUNDRED RUNS AND SIXTEEN WICKETS

G. Giffen, South Australia v Victoria at Adelaide; 271, nine for 96, and seven for 70.	1891-92

HUNDRED IN EACH INNINGS AND FIVE WICKETS TWICE

G. H. Hirst, Yorkshire v Somerset at Bath; 111, 117*, six for 70, and five for 45.	1906

HUNDRED IN EACH INNINGS AND TEN WICKETS

B. J. T. Bosanquet, Middlesex v Sussex at Lord's; 103, 100*, three for 75, and eight for 53	1905
F. D. Stephenson, Nottinghamshire v Yorkshire at Nottingham; 111, 117, four for 105, and seven for 117	1988

HUNDRED AND HAT-TRICK

G. Giffen, Australians v Lancashire at Manchester; 13, 113, and six for 55 including
hat-trick   1884

W. E. Roller, Surrey v Sussex at The Oval; 204, four for 28 including hat-trick, and
two for 16. (Unique instance of 200 and hat-trick.)   1885

W. B. Burns, Worcestershire v Gloucestershire at Worcester; 102*, three for 56
including hat-trick, and two for 21   1913

V. W. C. Jupp, Sussex v Essex at Colchester; 102, six for 61 including hat-trick, and
six for 78   1921

R. E. S. Wyatt, MCC v Ceylon at Colombo; 124 and five for 39 including hat-trick.   1926-27

L. N. Constantine, West Indians v Northamptonshire at Northampton; seven for 45
including hat-trick, 107 (five 6s), and six for 67   1928

D. E. Davies, Glamorgan v Leicestershire at Leicester; 139, four for 27, and three for
31 including hat-trick   1937

V. M. Merchant, Dr C. R. Pereira's XI v Sir Homi Mehta's XI at Bombay; 1, 142,
three for 31 including hat-trick, and no wicket for 17   1946-47

M. J. Procter, Gloucestershire v Essex at Westcliff-on-Sea; 51, 102, three for 43, and
five for 30 including hat-trick (all lbw)   1972

M. J. Procter, Gloucestershire v Leicestershire at Bristol; 122, no wkt for 32, and
seven for 26 including hat-trick   1979

Note: W. G. Grace, for MCC v Kent in a 12-a-side match at Canterbury in 1874, scored 123 and
took five for 82 and six for 47 including a hat-trick.

SEASON DOUBLES

2,000 Runs and 200 Wickets

1906   G. H. Hirst   2,385 runs and 208 wickets

3,000 Runs and 100 Wickets

1937   J. H. Parks   3,003 runs and 101 wickets

2,000 Runs and 100 Wickets

	Season	R	W		Season	R	W
W. G. Grace	1873	2,139	106	F. E. Woolley	1914	2,272	125
W. G. Grace	1876	2,622	129	J. W. Hearne	1920	2,148	142
C. L. Townsend	1899	2,440	101	V. W. C. Jupp	1921	2,169	121
G. L. Jessop	1900	2,210	104	F. E. Woolley	1921	2,101	167
G. H. Hirst	1904	2,501	132	F. E. Woolley	1922	2,022	163
G. H. Hirst	1905	2,266	110	F. E. Woolley	1923	2,091	101
W. Rhodes	1909	2,094	141	L. F. Townsend	1933	2,268	100
W. Rhodes	1911	2,261	117	D. E. Davies	1937	2,012	103
F. A. Tarrant	1911	2,030	111	James Langridge	1937	2,082	101
J. W. Hearne	1913	2,036	124	T. E Bailey	1959	2,011	100
J. W. Hearne	1914	2,116	123				

1,000 Runs and 200 Wickets

	Season	R	W		Season	R	W
A. E. Trott	1899	1,175	239	M. W. Tate	1923	1,168	219
A. E. Trott	1900	1,337	211	M. W. Tate	1924	1,419	205
A. S. Kennedy	1922	1,129	205	M. W. Tate	1925	1,290	228

,000 Runs and 100 Wickets

Sixteen times: W. Rhodes.
Fourteen times: G. H. Hirst.
Ten times: V. W. C. Jupp.
Nine times: W. E. Astill.
Eight times: T. E. Bailey, W. G. Grace, M. S. Nichols, A. E. Relf, F. A. Tarrant, 4. W. Tate†, F. J. Titmus, F. E. Woolley.
Seven times: G. E. Tribe.
Six times: P. G. H. Fender, R. Illingworth, James Langridge.
Five times: J. W. H. T. Douglas, J. W. Hearne, A. S. Kennedy, J. A. Newman.
Four times: E. G. Arnold, J. Gunn, R. Kilner, B. R. Knight.
Three times: W. W. Armstrong (Australians), L. C. Braund, G. Giffen (Australians), N. E. 4aig, R. Howorth, C. B. Llewellyn, J. B. Mortimore, Ray Smith, S. G. Smith, L. F. Townsend, 4. W. Wellard.

† *M. W. Tate also scored 1,193 runs and took 116 wickets for MCC in first-class matches on the 926-27 MCC tour of India and Ceylon.*

Jote: R. J. Hadlee (1984) and F. D. Stephenson (1988) are the only players to perform the feat ince the reduction of County Championship matches. A complete list of those performing the eat before then will be found on p. 202 of the 1982 Wisden.

Wicket-Keepers' Double

	Season	R	D
, E. G. Ames	1928	1,919	122
, E. G. Ames	1929	1,795	128
, E. G. Ames	1932	2,482	104
. T. Murray	1957	1,025	104

20,000 RUNS AND 2,000 WICKETS IN A CAREER

	Career	R	Avge	W	Avge	'Doubles'
N. E. Astill	1906-39	22,731	22.55	2,431	23.76	9
T. E. Bailey	1945-67	28,641	33.42	2,082	23.13	8
N. G. Grace	1865-1908	54,896	39.55	2,876	17.92	8
3. H. Hirst	1891-1929	36,323	34.13	2,739	18.72	14
R. Illingworth	1951-83	24,134	28.06	2,072	20.28	6
N. Rhodes	1898-1930	39,802	30.83	4,187	16.71	16
4. W. Tate	1912-37	21,717	25.01	2,784	18.16	8
. J. Titmus	1949-82	21,588	23.11	2,830	22.37	8
. E. Woolley	1906-38	58,969	40.75	2,068	19.85	8

WICKET-KEEPING RECORDS

MOST DISMISSALS IN AN INNINGS

, (all ct)	A. T. W. Grout	Queensland v Western Australia at Brisbane	1959-60
, (all ct)†	D. E. East	Essex v Somerset at Taunton	1985
, (all ct)	S. A. Marsh‡	Kent v Middlesex at Lord's	1991
(4ct, 3st)	E. J. Smith	Warwickshire v Derbyshire at Birmingham	1926
(6ct, 1st)	W. Farrimond	Lancashire v Kent at Manchester	1930
(all ct)	W. F. F. Price	Middlesex v Yorkshire at Lord's	1937
(3ct, 4st)	D. Tallon	Queensland v Victoria at Brisbane	1938-39
(all ct)	R. A. Saggers	New South Wales v Combined XI at Brisbane	1940-41
(1ct, 6st)	H. Yarnold	Worcestershire v Scotland at Dundee	1951
(4ct, 3st)	J. Brown	Scotland v Ireland at Dublin	1957
(6ct, 1st)	N. Kirsten	Border v Rhodesia at East London	1959-60
(all ct)	M. S. Smith	Natal v Border at East London	1959-60

7 (all ct)	K. V. Andrew	Northamptonshire v Lancashire at Manchester ...	1962
7 (all ct)	A. Long	Surrey v Sussex at Hove	1964
7 (all ct)	R. M. Schofield	Central Districts v Wellington at Wellington	1964-65
7 (all ct)	R. W. Taylor	Derbyshire v Glamorgan at Derby	1966
7 (6ct, 1st)	H. B. Taber	New South Wales v South Australia at Adelaide ..	1968-69
7 (6ct, 1st)	E. W. Jones	Glamorgan v Cambridge University at Cambridge.	1970
7 (6ct, 1st)	S. Benjamin	Central Zone v North Zone at Bombay	1973-74
7 (all ct)	R. W. Taylor	Derbyshire v Yorkshire at Chesterfield	1975
7 (6ct, 1st)	Shahid Israr	Karachi Whites v Quetta at Karachi	1976-77
7 (4ct, 3st)	Wasim Bari	PIA v Sind at Lahore	1977-78
7 (all ct)	J. A. Maclean	Queensland v Victoria at Melbourne	1977-78
7 (5ct, 2st)	Taslim Arif	National Bank v Punjab at Lahore	1978-79
7 (all ct)	Wasim Bari	Pakistan v New Zealand at Auckland	1978-79
7 (all ct)	R. W. Taylor	England v India at Bombay	1979-80
7 (all ct)	D. L. Bairstow	Yorkshire v Derbyshire at Scarborough	1982
7 (6ct, 1st)	R. B. Phillips	Queensland v New Zealanders at Bundaberg ..	1982-83
7 (3ct, 4st)	Masood Iqbal	Habib Bank v Lahore at Lahore	1982-83
7 (3ct, 4st)	Arif-ud-Din	United Bank v PACO at Sahiwal	1983-84
7 (6ct, 1st)	R. J. East	OFS v Western Province B at Cape Town	1984-85
7 (all ct)	B. A. Young	Northern Districts v Canterbury at Christchurch ..	1986-87
7 (all ct)	D. J. Richardson	Eastern Province v OFS at Bloemfontein	1988-89
7 (6ct, 1st)	Dildar Malik	Multan v Faisalabad at Sahiwal	1988-89
7 (all ct)	W. K. Hegg	Lancashire v Derbyshire at Chesterfield	1989
7 (all ct)	Imran Zia	Bahawalpur v Faisalabad at Faisalabad	1989-90
7 (all ct)	I. D. S. Smith	New Zealand v Sri Lanka at Hamilton	1990-91
7 (all ct)	J. F. Holyman	Tasmania v Western Australia at Hobart	1990-91
7 (all ct)	P. J. L. Radley	OFS v Western Province at Cape Town	1990-91
7 (all ct)	C. P. Metson	Glamorgan v Derbyshire at Chesterfield	1991

† *The first eight wickets to fall.*   ‡ *S. A. Marsh also scored 108*.*

WICKET-KEEPERS' HAT-TRICKS

W. H. Brain, Gloucestershire v Somerset at Cheltenham, 1893 – three stumpings off successive balls from C. L. Townsend.

G. O. Dawkes, Derbyshire v Worcestershire at Kidderminster, 1958 – three catches off successive balls from H. L. Jackson.

R. C. Russell, Gloucestershire v Surrey at The Oval, 1986 – three catches off successive balls from C. A. Walsh and D. V. Lawrence (2).

MOST DISMISSALS IN A MATCH

12 (8ct, 4st)	E. Pooley	Surrey v Sussex at The Oval	1868
12 (9ct, 3st)	D. Tallon	Queensland v New South Wales at Sydney	1938-39
12 (9ct, 3st)	H. B. Taber	New South Wales v South Australia at Adelaide.	1968-69
11 (all ct)	A. Long	Surrey v Sussex at Hove	1964
11 (all ct)	R. W. Marsh	Western Australia v Victoria at Perth	1975-76
11 (all ct)	D. L. Bairstow	Yorkshire v Derbyshire at Scarborough	1982
11 (all ct)	W. K. Hegg	Lancashire v Derbyshire at Chesterfield	1989
11 (all ct)	A. J. Stewart	Surrey v Leicestershire at Leicester	1989
11 (all ct)	T. J. Nielsen	South Australia v Western Australia at Perth	1990-91
10 (5ct, 5st)	H. Phillips	Sussex v Surrey at The Oval	1872
10 (2ct, 8st)	E. Pooley	Surrey v Kent at The Oval	1878
10 (9ct, 1st)	T. W. Oates	Nottinghamshire v Middlesex at Nottingham ..	1906
10 (1ct, 9st)	F. H. Huish	Kent v Surrey at The Oval	1911
10 (9ct, 1st)	J. C. Hubble	Kent v Gloucestershire at Cheltenham	1923
10 (8ct, 2st)	H. Elliott	Derbyshire v Lancashire at Manchester	1935
10 (7ct, 3st)	P. Corrall	Leicestershire v Sussex at Hove	1936

10 (9ct, 1st)	R. A. Saggers	New South Wales v Combined XI at Brisbane .	1940-41
10 (all ct)	A. E. Wilson	Gloucestershire v Hampshire at Portsmouth ...	1953
10 (7ct, 3st)	B. N. Jarman	South Australia v New South Wales at Adelaide.	1961-62
10 (all ct)	L. A. Johnson	Northamptonshire v Sussex at Worthing	1963
10 (all ct)	R. W. Taylor	Derbyshire v Hampshire at Chesterfield	1963
10 (8ct, 2st)	L. A. Johnson	Northamptonshire v Warwickshire at Birmingham	1965
10 (9ct, 1st)	R. C. Jordon	Victoria v South Australia at Melbourne	1970-71
10 (all ct)	R. W. Marsh†	Western Australia v South Australia at Perth ..	1976-77
10 (6ct, 4st)	Taslim Arif	National Bank v Punjab at Lahore	1978-79
10 (9ct, 1st)	Arif-ud-Din	United Bank v Karachi B at Karachi.........	1978-79
10 (all ct)	R. W. Taylor	England v India at Bombay	1979-80
10 (all ct)	R. J. Parks	Hampshire v Derbyshire at Portsmouth	1981
10 (9ct, 1st)	A. Ghosh	Bihar v Assam at Bhagalpur	1981-82
10 (8ct, 2st)	Z. Parkar	Bombay v Maharashtra at Bombay	1981-82
10 (all ct)	R. V. Jennings	Transvaal v Arosa Sri Lankans at Johannesburg	1982-83
10 (9ct, 1st)	Kamal Najamuddin	Karachi v Lahore at Multan	1982-83
10 (all ct)	D. A. Murray	West Indies XI v South Africa at Port Elizabeth.	1983-84
10 (7ct, 3st)	Azhar Abbas	Bahawalpur v Lahore City Greens at Bahawalpur	1983-84
10 (7ct, 3st)	B. N. French	Nottinghamshire v Oxford University at Oxford.	1984
10 (8ct, 2st)	R. J. Ryall	Western Province v Transvaal at Cape Town ..	1984-85
10 (all ct)	S. J. Rixon	Australian XI v South Africa at Johannesburg .	1985-86
10 (8ct, 2st)	Anil Dalpat	Karachi v United Bank at Lahore............	1985-86
10 (all ct)	R. V. Jennings	Transvaal v Northern Transvaal at Verwoerdburg	1986-87
10 (all ct)	S. J. Rixon	Australian XI v South Africa at Johannesburg	1986-87
10 (all ct)	R. V. Jennings	Transvaal v Orange Free State at Johannesburg	1986-87
10 (9ct, 1st)	C. J. Richards	Surrey v Sussex at Guildford	1987
10 (all ct)	C. W. Scott	Nottinghamshire v Derbyshire at Derby.......	1988
10 (all ct)	D. J. Richardson	Eastern Province v OFS at Bloemfontein	1988-89
10 (all ct)	A. N. Aymes	Hampshire v Oxford University at Oxford	1989
10 (all ct)	L. R. Fernando	Moratuwa v Panadura at Moratuwa	1989-90
10 (all ct)	Imran Zia	Bahawalpur v Faisalabad at Faisalabad	1989-90
10 (9ct, 1st)	D. J. Richardson	Eastern Province v N. Transvaal at Verwoerdburg	1989-90

† *R. W. Marsh also scored 104.*

MOST DISMISSALS IN A SEASON

128 (79ct, 49st)	L. E. G. Ames	Kent......................	1929
122 (70ct, 52st)	L. E. G. Ames	Kent......................	1928
110 (63ct, 47st)	H. Yarnold	Worcestershire.............	1949
107 (77ct, 30st)	G. Duckworth	Lancashire	1928
107 (96ct, 11st)	J. G. Binks	Yorkshire.................	1960
104 (40ct, 64st)	L. E. G. Ames	Kent......................	1932
104 (82ct, 22st)	J. T. Murray	Middlesex	1957
102 (69ct, 33st)	F. H. Huish	Kent......................	1913
102 (95ct, 7st)	J. T. Murray	Middlesex	1960
101 (62ct, 39st)	F. H. Huish	Kent......................	1911
101 (85ct, 16st)	R. Booth	Worcestershire.............	1960
100 (91ct, 9st)	R. Booth	Worcestershire.............	1964

MOST DISMISSALS IN A CAREER

Dates in italics denote the first half of an overseas season; i.e. *1914* denotes the 1914-15 season.

		Career	M	Ct	St	Total
1	R. W. Taylor..........	1960-88	639	1,473	176	1,649
2	J. T. Murray..........	1952-75	635	1,270	257	1,527
3	H. Strudwick..........	1902-27	675	1,242	255	1,497
4	A. P. E. Knott	1964-85	511	1,211	133	1,344

		Career	M	Ct	St	Total
5	F. H. Huish	1895-1914	497	933	377	1,310
6	B. Taylor	1949-73	572	1,083	211	1,294
7	D. Hunter	1889-1909	548	906	347	1,253
8	H. R. Butt	1890-1912	550	953	275	1,228
9	J. H. Board	1891-1914	525	852	355	1,207
10	H. Elliott	1920-47	532	904	302	1,206
11	J. M. Parks	1949-76	739	1,088	93	1,181
12	R. Booth	1951-70	468	948	178	1,126
13	L. E. G. Ames	1926-51	593	703	418	1,121
14	D. L. Bairstow	1970-90	459	961	138	1,099
15	G. Duckworth	1923-47	504	753	343	1,096
16	H. W. Stephenson	1948-64	462	748	334	1,082
17	J. G. Binks	1955-75	502	895	176	1,071
18	T. G. Evans	1939-69	465	816	250	1,066
19	A. Long	1960-80	452	922	124	1,046
20	G. O. Dawkes	1937-61	482	895	148	1,043
21	R. W. Tolchard	1965-83	483	912	125	1,037
22	W. L. Cornford	1921-47	496	675	342	1,017

Current Players with 500 Dismissals

	Career	M	Ct	St	Total
B. N. French	1976-92	340	772	95	867
R. J. Parks	1980-92	255	638	72	710
R. C. Russell	1981-92	251	567	84	651
R. V. Jennings	1973-91	152	547	51	598
S. J. Rhodes	1981-92	208	491	57	548

FIELDING RECORDS

(Excluding wicket-keepers)

MOST CATCHES IN AN INNINGS

7	M. J. Stewart	Surrey v Northamptonshire at Northampton	1957
7	A. S. Brown	Gloucestershire v Nottinghamshire at Nottingham	1966

MOST CATCHES IN A MATCH

10	W. R. Hammond†	Gloucestershire v Surrey at Cheltenham	1928
8	W. B. Burns	Worcestershire v Yorkshire at Bradford	1907
8	F. G. Travers	Europeans v Parsees at Bombay	1923-24
8	A. H. Bakewell	Northamptonshire v Essex at Leyton	1928
8	W. R. Hammond	Gloucestershire v Worcestershire at Cheltenham	1932
8	K. J. Grieves	Lancashire v Sussex at Manchester	1951
8	C. A. Milton	Gloucestershire v Sussex at Hove	1952
8	G. A. R. Lock	Surrey v Warwickshire at The Oval	1957
8	J. M. Prodger	Kent v Gloucestershire at Cheltenham	1961
8	P. M. Walker	Glamorgan v Derbyshire at Swansea	1970
8	Masood Anwar	Rawalpindi v Lahore Division at Rawalpindi	1983-84

† *Hammond also scored a hundred in each innings.*

MOST CATCHES IN A SEASON

78	W. R. Hammond	1928		65	D. W. Richardson	1961
77	M. J. Stewart	1957		64	K. F. Barrington	1957
73	P. M. Walker	1961		64	G. A. R. Lock	1957
71	P. J. Sharpe	1962		63	J. Tunnicliffe	1896
70	J. Tunnicliffe	1901		63	J. Tunnicliffe	1904
69	J. G. Langridge	1955		63	K. J. Grieves	1950
69	P. M. Walker	1960		63	C. A. Milton	1956
66	J. Tunnicliffe	1895		61	J. V. Wilson	1955
65	W. R. Hammond	1925		61	M. J. Stewart	1958
65	P. M. Walker	1959				

Note: The most catches by a fielder since the reduction of County Championship matches in 1969 is 49 by C. J. Tavaré in 1978.

MOST CATCHES IN A CAREER

Dates in italics denote the first half of an overseas season; i.e. *1970* denotes the 1970-71 season.

1,018	F. E. Woolley (1906-38)		784	J. G. Langridge (1928-55)
887	W. G. Grace (1865-1908)		764	W. Rhodes (1898-1930)
830	G. A. R. Lock (1946-*70*)		758	C. A. Milton (1948-74)
819	W. R. Hammond (1920-51)		754	E. H. Hendren (1907-38)
813	D. B. Close (1949-86)			

Leading Current Fielders

516	C. G. Greenidge (*1970*-92)		403	J. E. Emburey (1973-92)
478	G. A. Gooch (1973-92)		396	C. J. Tavaré (1974-92)
447	I. V. A. Richards (*1971*-92)		394	C. E. B. Rice (*1969-91*)

TEAM RECORDS

HIGHEST TOTALS

1,107	Victoria v New South Wales at Melbourne	1926-27
1,059	Victoria v Tasmania at Melbourne	1922-23
951-7 dec.	Sind v Baluchistan at Karachi	1973-74
918	New South Wales v South Australia at Sydney	1900-01
912-8 dec.	Holkar v Mysore at Indore	1945-46
912-6 dec.†	Tamil Nadu v Goa at Panjim	1988-89
910-6 dec.	Railways v Dera Ismail Khan at Lahore	1964-65
903-7 dec.	England v Australia at The Oval	1938
887	Yorkshire v Warwickshire at Birmingham	1896
868†	North Zone v West Zone at Bhilai	1987-88
863	Lancashire v Surrey at The Oval	1990
855-6 dec.†	Bombay v Hyderabad at Bombay	1990-91
849	England v West Indies at Kingston	1929-30
843	Australians v Oxford and Cambridge Universities Past and Present at Portsmouth	1893

† *Tamil Nadu's total of 912-6 dec. included 52 penalty runs from their opponents' failure to meet the required bowling rate by 13 overs. North Zone's total of 868 included 68 penalty runs (17 overs) and Bombay's total of 855-6 dec. included 48 penalty runs (four overs).*

HIGHEST FOR EACH FIRST-CLASS COUNTY

Derbyshire	645	v Hampshire at Derby	1898
Durham	521-9 dec.	v Glamorgan at Cardiff	1992
Essex	761-6 dec.	v Leicestershire at Chelmsford	1990
Glamorgan	587-8 dec.	v Derbyshire at Cardiff	1951
Gloucestershire	653-6 dec.	v Glamorgan at Bristol	1928
Hampshire	672-7 dec.	v Somerset at Taunton	1899
Kent	803-4 dec.	v Essex at Brentwood	1934
Lancashire	863	v Surrey at The Oval	1990
Leicestershire	701-4 dec.	v Worcestershire at Worcester	1906
Middlesex	642-3 dec.	v Hampshire at Southampton	1923
Northamptonshire	636-6 dec.	v Essex at Chelmsford	1990
Nottinghamshire	739-7 dec.	v Leicestershire at Nottingham	1903
Somerset	675-9 dec.	v Hampshire at Bath	1924
Surrey	811	v Somerset at The Oval	1899
Sussex	705-8 dec.	v Surrey at Hastings	1902
Warwickshire	657-6 dec.	v Hampshire at Birmingham	1899
Worcestershire	633	v Warwickshire at Worcester	1906
Yorkshire	887	v Warwickshire at Birmingham	1896

HIGHEST AGAINST EACH FIRST-CLASS COUNTY

Derbyshire	662	by Yorkshire at Chesterfield	1898
Durham	562	by Lancashire at Gateshead Fell	1992
Essex	803-4 dec.	by Kent at Brentwood	1934
Glamorgan	653-6 dec.	by Gloucestershire at Bristol	1928
Gloucestershire	774-7 dec.	by Australians at Bristol	1948
Hampshire	742	by Surrey at The Oval	1909
Kent	676	by Australians at Canterbury	1921
Lancashire	707-9 dec.	by Surrey at The Oval	1990
Leicestershire	761-6 dec.	by Essex at Chelmsford	1990
Middlesex	665	by West Indians at Lord's	1939
Northamptonshire	670-9 dec.	by Sussex at Hove	1921
Nottinghamshire	706-4 dec.	by Surrey at Nottingham	1947
Somerset	811	by Surrey at The Oval	1899
Surrey	863	by Lancashire at The Oval	1990
Sussex	726	by Nottinghamshire at Nottingham	1895
Warwickshire	887	by Yorkshire at Birmingham	1896
Worcestershire	701-4 dec.	by Leicestershire at Worcester	1906
Yorkshire	630	by Somerset at Leeds	1901

LOWEST TOTALS

12	Oxford University v MCC and Ground at Oxford	†1877
12	Northamptonshire v Gloucestershire at Gloucester	1907
13	Auckland v Canterbury at Auckland	1877-78
13	Nottinghamshire v Yorkshire at Nottingham	1901
14	Surrey v Essex at Chelmsford	1983
15	MCC v Surrey at Lord's	1839
15	Victoria v MCC at Melbourne	†1903-04
15	Northamptonshire v Yorkshire at Northampton	†1908
15	Hampshire v Warwickshire at Birmingham	1922
	(Following on, Hampshire scored 521 and won by 155 runs.)	
16	MCC and Ground v Surrey at Lord's	1872
16	Derbyshire v Nottinghamshire at Nottingham	1879
16	Surrey v Nottinghamshire at The Oval	1880
16	Warwickshire v Kent at Tonbridge	1913
16	Trinidad v Barbados at Bridgetown	1942-43
16	Border v Natal at East London (first innings)	1959-60
17	Gentlemen of Kent v Gentlemen of England at Lord's	1850
17	Gloucestershire v Australians at Cheltenham	1896

18	The Bs v England at Lord's	1831
18	Kent v Sussex at Gravesend	†1867
18	Tasmania v Victoria at Melbourne	1868-69
18	Australians v MCC and Ground at Lord's	†1896
18	Border v Natal at East London (second innings)	1959-60
19	Sussex v Surrey at Godalming	1830
19	Sussex v Nottinghamshire at Hove	†1873
19	MCC and Ground v Australians at Lord's	1878
19	Wellington v Nelson at Nelson	1885-86

† *Signifies that one man was absent.*

Note: At Lord's in 1810, The Bs, with one man absent, were dismissed by England for 6.

LOWEST TOTAL IN A MATCH

34	(16 and 18) Border v Natal at East London	1959-60
42	(27 and 15) Northamptonshire v Yorkshire at Northampton	1908

Note: Northamptonshire batted one man short in each innings.

LOWEST FOR EACH FIRST-CLASS COUNTY

Derbyshire	16	v Nottinghamshire at Nottingham	1879
Durham	116	v Leicestershire at Leicester	1992
Essex	30	v Yorkshire at Leyton	1901
Glamorgan	22	v Lancashire at Liverpool	1924
Gloucestershire	17	v Australians at Cheltenham	1896
Hampshire	15	v Warwickshire at Birmingham	1922
Kent	18	v Sussex at Gravesend	1867
Lancashire	25	v Derbyshire at Manchester	1871
Leicestershire	25	v Kent at Leicester	1912
Middlesex	20	v MCC at Lord's	1864
Northamptonshire	12	v Gloucestershire at Gloucester	1907
Nottinghamshire	13	v Yorkshire at Nottingham	1901
Somerset	25	v Gloucestershire at Bristol	1947
Surrey	14	v Essex at Chelmsford	1983
Sussex	19	v Nottinghamshire at Hove	1873
Warwickshire	16	v Kent at Tonbridge	1913
Worcestershire	24	v Yorkshire at Huddersfield	1903
Yorkshire	23	v Hampshire at Middlesbrough	1965

LOWEST AGAINST EACH FIRST-CLASS COUNTY

Derbyshire	23	by Hampshire at Burton upon Trent	1958
Durham	108	by Yorkshire at Durham University	1992
Essex	14	by Surrey at Chelmsford	1983
Glamorgan	33	by Leicestershire at Ebbw Vale	1965
Gloucestershire	12	by Northamptonshire at Gloucester	1907
Hampshire	23	by Yorkshire at Middlesbrough	1965
Kent	16	by Warwickshire at Tonbridge	1913
Lancashire	22	by Glamorgan at Liverpool	1924
Leicestershire	24	by Oxford University at Oxford	1985
Middlesex	31	by Gloucestershire at Bristol	1924
Northamptonshire	33	by Lancashire at Northampton	1977
Nottinghamshire	16	by Derbyshire at Nottingham	1879
	16	by Surrey at The Oval	1880
Somerset	22	by Gloucestershire at Bristol	1920
Surrey	16	by MCC at Lord's	1872
Sussex	18	by Kent at Gravesend	1867
Warwickshire	15	by Hampshire at Birmingham	1922
Worcestershire	30	by Hampshire at Worcester	1903
Yorkshire	13	by Nottinghamshire at Nottingham	1901

HIGHEST MATCH AGGREGATES

2,376 for 37 wickets	Maharashtra v Bombay at Poona......................	1948-49
2,078 for 40 wickets	Bombay v Holkar at Bombay........................	1944-45
1,981 for 35 wickets	England v South Africa at Durban....................	1938-39
1,929 for 39 wickets	New South Wales v South Australia at Sydney	1925-26
1,911 for 34 wickets	New South Wales v Victoria at Sydney................	1908-09
1,905 for 40 wickets	Otago v Wellington at Dunedin	1923-24

In Britain

1,723 for 31 wickets	England v Australia at Leeds	1948
1,650 for 19 wickets	Surrey v Lancashire at The Oval	1990
1,641 for 16 wickets	Glamorgan v Worcestershire at Abergavenny...........	1990
1,614 for 30 wickets	England v India at Manchester	1990
1,603 for 28 wickets	England v India at Lord's..........................	1990
1,601 for 29 wickets	England v Australia at Lord's	1930
1,578 for 37 wickets	Sussex v Kent at Hove	1991
1,570 for 29 wickets	Essex v Kent at Chelmsford........................	1988
1,530 for 19 wickets	Essex v Leicestershire at Chelmsford.................	1990
1,509 for 36 wickets	Somerset v Worcestershire at Taunton	1990
1,507 for 28 wickets	England v West Indies at The Oval	1976
1,502 for 28 wickets	MCC v New Zealanders at Lord's...................	1927

LOWEST AGGREGATE IN A COMPLETED MATCH

105 for 31 wickets   MCC v Australians at Lord's 1878

Note: The lowest aggregate since 1900 is 158 for 22 wickets, Surrey v Worcestershire at The Oval, 1954.

HIGHEST FOURTH-INNINGS TOTALS

(Unless otherwise stated, the side making the runs won the match.)

654-5	England v South Africa at Durban................................	1938-39
	(After being set 696 to win. The match was left drawn on the tenth day.)	
604	Maharashtra v Bombay at Poona	1948-49
	(After being set 959 to win.)	
576-8	Trinidad v Barbados at Port-of-Spain	1945-46
	(After being set 672 to win. Match drawn on fifth day.)	
572	New South Wales v South Australia at Sydney....................	1907-08
	(After being set 593 to win.)	
529-9	Combined XI v South Africans at Perth	1963-64
	(After being set 579 to win. Match drawn on fourth day.)	
518	Victoria v Queensland at Brisbane	1926-27
	(After being set 753 to win.)	
507-7	Cambridge University v MCC and Ground at Lord's	1896
506-6	South Australia v Queensland at Adelaide........................	1991-92
502-6	Middlesex v Nottinghamshire at Nottingham	1925
	(Game won by an unfinished stand of 271; a county record.)	
502-8	Players v Gentlemen at Lord's	1900
500-7	South African Universities v Western Province at Stellenbosch	1978-79

LARGEST VICTORIES

Largest Innings Victories

Inns and 851 runs:	Railways (910-6 dec.) v Dera Ismail Khan (Lahore)	1964-65
Inns and 666 runs:	Victoria (1,059) v Tasmania (Melbourne)	1922-23
Inns and 656 runs:	Victoria (1,107) v New South Wales (Melbourne)	1926-27
Inns and 605 runs:	New South Wales (918) v South Australia (Sydney)	1900-01
Inns and 579 runs:	England (903-7 dec.) v Australia (The Oval)	1938
Inns and 575 runs:	Sind (951-7 dec.) v Baluchistan (Karachi)	1973-74
Inns and 527 runs:	New South Wales (713) v South Australia (Adelaide)	1908-09
Inns and 517 runs:	Australians (675) v Nottinghamshire (Nottingham)	1921

Largest Victories by Runs Margin

685 runs:	New South Wales (235 and 761-8 dec.) v Queensland (Sydney)	1929-30
675 runs:	England (521 and 342-8 dec.) v Australia (Brisbane)	1928-29
638 runs:	New South Wales (304 and 770) v South Australia (Adelaide)	1920-21
625 runs:	Sargodha (376 and 416) v Lahore Municipal Corporation (Faisalabad)	1978-79
609 runs:	Muslim Commercial Bank (575 and 282-0 dec.) v WAPDA (Lahore)	1977-78
573 runs:	Sinhalese SC (395-7 dec. and 350-2 dec.) v Sebastianites C and AC (63 and 109) at Colombo	1990-91
571 runs:	Victoria (304 and 649) v South Australia (Adelaide)	1926-27
562 runs:	Australia (701 and 327) v England (The Oval)	1934

Victory Without Losing a Wicket

Lancashire (166-0 dec. and 66-0) beat Leicestershire by ten wickets (Manchester)	1956
Karachi A (277-0 dec.) beat Sind A by an innings and 77 runs (Karachi)	1957-58
Railways (236-0 dec. and 16-0) beat Jammu and Kashmir by ten wickets (Srinagar)	1960-61
Karnataka (451-0 dec.) beat Kerala by an innings and 186 runs (Chikmagalur)	1977-78

TIED MATCHES IN FIRST-CLASS CRICKET

Since 1948 a tie has been recognised only when the scores are level with all the wickets down in the fourth innings.

The following are the instances since then:

D. G. Bradman's XI v A. L. Hassett's XI at Melbourne	1948-49
Hampshire v Kent at Southampton	1950
Sussex v Warwickshire at Hove	1952
Essex v Lancashire at Brentwood	1952
Northamptonshire v Middlesex at Peterborough	1953
Yorkshire v Leicestershire at Huddersfield	1954
Sussex v Hampshire at Eastbourne	1955
Victoria v New South Wales at Melbourne	1956-57
T. N. Pearce's XI v New Zealanders at Scarborough	1958
Essex v Gloucestershire at Leyton	1959
Australia v West Indies (First Test) at Brisbane	1960-61
Bahawalpur v Lahore B at Bahawalpur	1961-62
Hampshire v Middlesex at Portsmouth	1967
England XI v England Under-25 XI at Scarborough	1968
Yorkshire v Middlesex at Bradford	1973
Sussex v Essex at Hove	1974
South Australia v Queensland at Adelaide	1976-77
Central Districts v England XI at New Plymouth	1977-78
Victoria v New Zealanders at Melbourne	1982-83
Muslim Commercial Bank v Railways at Sialkot	1983-84
Sussex v Kent at Hastings	1984
Northamptonshire v Kent at Northampton	1984

Eastern Province B v Boland at Albany SC, Port Elizabeth 1985-86
Natal B v Eastern Province B at Pietermaritzburg 1985-86
India v Australia (First Test) at Madras 1986-87
Gloucestershire v Derbyshire at Bristol 1987
Bahawalpur v Peshawar at Bahawalpur 1988-89
Wellington v Canterbury at Wellington 1988-89
Sussex v Kent at Hove 1991
   Sussex (436) scored the highest total to tie a first-class match.

MATCHES BEGUN AND FINISHED ON FIRST DAY

Since 1900. A fuller list may be found in the Wisden *of 1981 and preceding editions.*

Yorkshire v Worcestershire at Bradford, May 7 1900
MCC and Ground v London County at Lord's, May 20 1903
Transvaal v Orange Free State at Johannesburg, December 30 1906
Middlesex v Gentlemen of Philadelphia at Lord's, July 20 1908
Gloucestershire v Middlesex at Bristol, August 26 1909
Eastern Province v Orange Free State at Port Elizabeth, December 26 1912
Kent v Sussex at Tonbridge, June 21 1919
Lancashire v Somerset at Manchester, May 21 1925
Madras v Mysore at Madras, November 4 1934
Ireland v New Zealanders at Dublin, September 11 1937
Derbyshire v Somerset at Chesterfield, June 11 1947
Lancashire v Sussex at Manchester, July 12 1950
Surrey v Warwickshire at The Oval, May 16 1953
Somerset v Lancashire at Bath, June 6 (H. F. T. Buse's benefit) 1953
Kent v Worcestershire at Tunbridge Wells, June 15 1960

TEST MATCH RECORDS

Note: This section covers all Tests up to August 9, 1992.

BATTING RECORDS

HIGHEST INDIVIDUAL INNINGS

365*	G. S. Sobers	West Indies v Pakistan at Kingston	1957-58
364	L. Hutton	England v Australia at The Oval	1938
337	Hanif Mohammad	Pakistan v West Indies at Bridgetown	1957-58
336*	W. R. Hammond	England v New Zealand at Auckland	1932-33
334	D. G. Bradman	Australia v England at Leeds	1930
333	G. A. Gooch	England v India at Lord's	1990
325	A. Sandham	England v West Indies at Kingston	1929-30
311	R. B. Simpson	Australia v England at Manchester	1964
310*	J. H. Edrich	England v New Zealand at Leeds	1965
307	R. M. Cowper	Australia v England at Melbourne	1965-66
304	D. G. Bradman	Australia v England at Leeds	1934
302	L. G. Rowe	West Indies v England at Bridgetown	1973-74
299*	D. G. Bradman	Australia v South Africa at Adelaide	1931-32
299	M. D. Crowe	New Zealand v Sri Lanka at Wellington	1990-91
291	I. V. A. Richards	West Indies v England at The Oval	1976
287	R. E. Foster	England v Australia at Sydney	1903-04
285*	P. B. H. May	England v West Indies at Birmingham	1957
280*	Javed Miandad	Pakistan v India at Hyderabad	1982-83
278	D. C. S. Compton	England v Pakistan at Nottingham	1954
274	R. G. Pollock	South Africa v Australia at Durban	1969-70
274	Zaheer Abbas	Pakistan v England at Birmingham	1971
271	Javed Miandad	Pakistan v New Zealand at Auckland	1988-89
270*	G. A. Headley	West Indies v England at Kingston	1934-35
270	D. G. Bradman	Australia v England at Melbourne	1936-37
268	G. N. Yallop	Australia v Pakistan at Melbourne	1983-84
267	P. A. de Silva	Sri Lanka v New Zealand at Wellington	1990-91
266	W. H. Ponsford	Australia v England at The Oval	1934
262*	D. L. Amiss	England v West Indies at Kingston	1973-74
261	F. M. M. Worrell	West Indies v England at Nottingham	1950
260	C. C. Hunte	West Indies v Pakistan at Kingston	1957-58
260	Javed Miandad	Pakistan v England at The Oval	1987
259	G. M. Turner	New Zealand v West Indies at Georgetown	1971-72
258	T. W. Graveney	England v West Indies at Nottingham	1957
258	S. M. Nurse	West Indies v New Zealand at Christchurch	1968-69
256	R. B. Kanhai	West Indies v India at Calcutta	1958-59
256	K. F. Barrington	England v Australia at Manchester	1964
255*	D. J. McGlew	South Africa v New Zealand at Wellington	1952-53
254	D. G. Bradman	Australia v England at Lord's	1930
251	W. R. Hammond	England v Australia at Sydney	1928-29
250	K. D. Walters	Australia v New Zealand at Christchurch	1976-77
250	S. F. A. F. Bacchus	West Indies v India at Kanpur	1978-79

The highest individual innings for India is:

236*	S. M. Gavaskar	India v West Indies at Madras	1983-84

HUNDRED ON TEST DEBUT

C. Bannerman (165*)	Australia v England at Melbourne	1876-77
W. G. Grace (152)	England v Australia at The Oval	1880
H. Graham (107)	Australia v England at Lord's	1893
†K. S. Ranjitsinhji (154*)	England v Australia at Manchester	1896

†P. F. Warner (132*)	England v South Africa at Johannesburg	1898-99
†R. A. Duff (104)	Australia v England at Melbourne	1901-02
R. E. Foster (287)	England v Australia at Sydney.	1903-04
G. Gunn (119).	England v Australia at Sydney	1907-08
†R. J. Hartigan (116)	Australia v England at Adelaide	1907-08
†H. L. Collins (104)	Australia v England at Sydney.	1920-21
W. H. Ponsford (110)	Australia v England at Sydney	1924-25
A. A. Jackson (164)	Australia v England at Adelaide	1928-29
†G. A. Headley (176)	West Indies v England at Bridgetown	1929-30
J. E. Mills (117)	New Zealand v England at Wellington.	1929-30
Nawab of Pataudi sen. (102)	England v Australia at Sydney.	1932-33
B. H. Valentine (136)	England v India at Bombay.	1933-34
†L. Amarnath (118)	India v England at Bombay.	1933-34
†P. A. Gibb (106).	England v South Africa at Johannesburg	1938-39
S. C. Griffith (140)	England v West Indies at Port-of-Spain	1947-48
A. G. Ganteaume (112) . . .	West Indies v England at Port-of-Spain	1947-48
†J. W. Burke (101*)	Australia v England at Adelaide	1950-51
P. B. H. May (138)	England v South Africa at Leeds.	1951
R. H. Shodhan (110)	India v Pakistan at Calcutta	1952-53
B. H. Pairaudeau (115). . . .	West Indies v India at Port-of-Spain	1952-53
†O. G. Smith (104)	West Indies v Australia at Kingston	1954-55
A. G. Kripal Singh (100*) .	India v New Zealand at Hyderabad	1955-56
C. C. Hunte (142)	West Indies v Pakistan at Bridgetown	1957-58
C. A. Milton (104*)	England v New Zealand at Leeds	1958
†A. A. Baig (112)	India v England at Manchester	1959
Hanumant Singh (105)	India v England at Delhi	1963-64
Khalid Ibadulla (166)	Pakistan v Australia at Karachi	1964-65
B. R. Taylor (105).	New Zealand v India at Calcutta	1964-65
K. D. Walters (155)	Australia v England at Brisbane	1965-66
J. H. Hampshire (107)	England v West Indies at Lord's	1969
†G. R. Viswanath (137)	India v Australia at Kanpur	1969-70
G. S. Chappell (108)	Australia v England at Perth	1970-71
‡L. G. Rowe (214, 100*) . . .	West Indies v New Zealand at Kingston	1971-72
A. I. Kallicharran (100*) . .	West Indies v New Zealand at Georgetown. . . .	1971-72
R. E. Redmond (107)	New Zealand v Pakistan at Auckland	1972-73
†F. C. Hayes (106*)	England v West Indies at The Oval	1973
†C. G. Greenidge (107)	West Indies v India at Bangalore	1974-75
†L. Baichan (105*)	West Indies v Pakistan at Lahore	1974-75
G. J. Cosier (109)	Australia v West Indies at Melbourne	1975-76
S. Amarnath (124).	India v New Zealand at Auckland	1975-76
Javed Miandad (163)	Pakistan v New Zealand at Lahore.	1976-77
†A. B. Williams (100).	West Indies v Australia at Georgetown	1977-78
†D. M. Wellham (103)	Australia v England at The Oval.	1981
†Salim Malik (100*)	Pakistan v Sri Lanka at Karachi	1981-82
K. C. Wessels (162)	Australia v England at Brisbane	1982-83
W. B. Phillips (159)	Australia v Pakistan at Perth.	1983-84
§M. Azharuddin (110)	India v England at Calcutta	1984-85
D. S. B. P. Kuruppu (201*)	Sri Lanka v New Zealand at Colombo (CCC) . .	1986-87
†M. J. Greatbatch (107*) . .	New Zealand v England at Auckland.	1987-88
M. E. Waugh (138)	Australia v England at Adelaide	1990-91
A. C. Hudson (163)	South Africa v West Indies at Bridgetown	1991-92

† *In his second innings of the match.*

‡ *L. G. Rowe is the only batsman to score a hundred in each innings on début.*

§ *M. Azharuddin is the only batsman to score hundreds in each of his first three Tests.*

Note: L. Amarnath and S. Amarnath provide the only instance of a father and son scoring a hundred on début.

300 RUNS IN FIRST TEST

314	L. G. Rowe (214, 100*)	West Indies v New Zealand at Kingston	1971-72
306	R. E. Foster (287, 19)	England v Australia at Sydney	1903-04

TWO SEPARATE HUNDREDS IN A TEST

Three times: S. M. Gavaskar v West Indies (1970-71), v Pakistan (1978-79), v West Indies (1978-79).

Twice in one series: C. L. Walcott v Australia (1954-55).

Twice: H. Sutcliffe v Australia (1924-25), v South Africa (1929); G. A. Headley v England (1929-30 and 1939); G. S. Chappell v New Zealand (1973-74), v West Indies (1975-76); ‡A. R. Border v Pakistan (1979-80), v New Zealand (1985-86).

Once: W. Bardsley v England (1909); A. C. Russell v South Africa (1922-23); W. R. Hammond v Australia (1928-29); E. Paynter v South Africa (1938-39); D. C. S. Compton v Australia (1946-47); A. R. Morris v England (1946-47); A. Melville v England (1947); B. Mitchell v England (1947); D. G. Bradman v India (1947-48); V. S. Hazare v Australia (1947-48); E. D. Weekes v India (1948-49); J. Moroney v South Africa (1949-50); G. S. Sobers v Pakistan (1957-58); R. B. Kanhai v Australia (1960-61); Hanif Mohammad v England (1961-62); R. B. Simpson v Pakistan (1964-65); K. D. Walters v West Indies (1968-69); †L. G. Rowe v New Zealand (1971-72); I. M. Chappell v New Zealand (1973-74); G. M. Turner v Australia (1973-74); C. G. Greenidge v England (1976); G. P. Howarth v England (1977-78); L. R. D. Mendis v India (1982-83); Javed Miandad v New Zealand (1984-85); D. M. Jones v Pakistan (1989-90); G. A. Gooch v India (1990); A. H. Jones v Sri Lanka (1990-91); A. P. Gurusinha v New Zealand (1990-91).

† L. G. Rowe's two hundreds were on his Test début.

‡ A. R. Border scored 150* and 153 against Pakistan to become the first batsman to score 150 in each innings of a Test match.

TRIPLE-HUNDRED AND HUNDRED IN SAME TEST

†G. A. Gooch (England)   333 and 123 v India at Lord's   1990

† G. A. Gooch became the first to score a hundred and a triple-hundred in the same first-class match.

DOUBLE-HUNDRED AND HUNDRED IN SAME TEST

K. D. Walters (Australia)	242 and 103 v West Indies at Sydney	1968-69
S. M. Gavaskar (India)	124 and 220 v West Indies at Port-of-Spain	1970-71
†L. G. Rowe (West Indies)	214 and 100* v New Zealand at Kingston	1971-72
G. S. Chappell (Australia)	247* and 133 v New Zealand at Wellington	1973-74

† On Test début.

MOST RUNS IN A SERIES

	T	I	NO	R	HS	100s	Avge		
D. G. Bradman ...	5	7	0	974	334	4	139.14	A v E	1930
W. R. Hammond .	5	9	1	905	251	4	113.12	E v A	1928-29
M. A. Taylor	6	11	1	839	219	2	83.90	A v E	1989
R. N. Harvey	5	9	0	834	205	4	92.66	A v SA	1952-53
I. V. A. Richards .	4	7	0	829	291	3	118.42	WI v E	1976
C. L. Walcott	5	10	0	827	155	5	82.70	WI v A	1954-55

	T	I	NO	R	HS	100s	Avge		
G. S. Sobers......	5	8	2	824	365*	3	137.33	WI v P	1957-58
D. G. Bradman ...	5	9	0	810	270	3	90.00	A v E	1936-37
D. G. Bradman ..	5	5	1	806	299*	4	201.50	A v SA	1931-32
E. D. Weekes	5	7	0	779	194	4	111.28	WI v I	1948-49
†S. M. Gavaskar ..	4	8	3	774	220	4	154.80	I v WI	1970-71
Mudassar Nazar ..	6	8	2	761	231	4	126.83	P v I	1982-83
D. G. Bradman ...	5	8	0	758	304	2	94.75	A v E	1934
D. C. S. Compton .	5	8	0	753	208	4	94.12	E v SA	1947
‡G. A. Gooch	3	6	0	752	333	3	125.33	E v I	1990

† *Gavaskar's aggregate was achieved in his first Test series.*

‡ *G. A. Gooch is alone in scoring 1,000 runs in Test cricket during an English season with 1,058 runs in eleven innings against New Zealand and India in 1990.*

1,000 TEST RUNS IN A CALENDAR YEAR

	T	I	NO	R	HS	100s	Avge	Year
I. V. A. Richards (WI)......	11	19	0	1,710	291	7	90.00	1976
S. M. Gavaskar (I)	18	27	1	1,555	221	5	59.80	1979
G. R. Viswanath (I)	17	26	3	1,388	179	5	60.34	1979
R. B. Simpson (A)	14	26	3	1,381	311	3	60.04	1964
D. L. Amiss (E)	13	22	2	1,379	262*	5	68.95	1974
S. M. Gavaskar (I)	18	32	4	1,310	236*	5	46.78	1983
G. A. Gooch (E)	9	17	1	1,264	333	4	79.00	1990
M. A. Taylor (A)	11	20	1	1,219	219	4	64.15	1989†
G. S. Sobers (WI)	7	12	3	1,193	365*	5	132.55	1958
D. B. Vengsarkar (I)........	18	27	4	1,174	146*	5	51.04	1979
K. J. Hughes (A)...........	15	28	4	1,163	130*	2	48.45	1979
D. C. S. Compton (E)........	9	15	1	1,159	208	6	82.78	1947
C. G. Greenidge (WI)	14	22	4	1,149	223	4	63.83	1984
A. R. Border (A)	11	20	3	1,099	196	4	64.64	1985
D. M. Jones (A)	11	18	3	1,099	216	4	73.26	1989
I. T. Botham (E)	14	22	0	1,095	208	3	49.77	1982
K. W. R. Fletcher (E)	13	22	4	1,090	178	2	60.55	1973
M. Amarnath (I)	14	24	1	1,077	120	4	46.82	1983
A. R. Border (A)	14	27	3	1,073	162	3	44.70	1979
C. Hill (A)	12	21	2	1,061	142	2	55.84	1902
D. I. Gower (E)	14	25	2	1,061	114	1	46.13	1982
D. I. Gower (E)	14	25	1	1,059	136	2	44.12	1986
W. M. Lawry (A)	14	27	2	1,056	157	2	42.24	1964
S. M. Gavaskar (I)	9	15	2	1,044	205	4	80.30	1978
G. A. Gooch (E)	9	17	1	1,040	174	3	65.00	1991
K. F. Barrington (E)........	12	22	2	1,039	132*	3	51.95	1963
E. R. Dexter (E)	11	15	1	1,038	205	2	74.14	1962
K. F. Barrington (E)........	10	17	4	1,032	172	2	79.38	1961
Mohsin Khan (P)	10	17	3	1,029	200	4	73.50	1982
D. G. Bradman (A)	8	13	4	1,025	201	5	113.88	1948
S. M. Gavaskar (I)	11	20	1	1,024	156	5	53.89	1976
A. R. Border (A)...........	11	19	3	1,000	140	5	62.50	1986

† *The year of his début.*

Notes: The earliest date for completing 1,000 runs is May 3 by M. Amarnath in 1983.

D. G. Bradman (A) scored 1,005 runs in five consecutive Tests, all against England, in 1936-37 and 1938: 13, 270, 26, 212, 169, 51, 144*, 18, 102*.

MOST RUNS IN A CAREER

(Qualification: 2,000 runs)

ENGLAND

		T	I	NO	R	HS	100s	Avge
1	D. I. Gower	117	204	18	8,231	215	18	44.25
2	G. Boycott	108	193	23	8,114	246*	22	47.72
3	M. C. Cowdrey	114	188	15	7,624	182	22	44.06
4	G. A. Gooch	99	179	6	7,573	333	17	43.77
5	W. R. Hammond	85	140	16	7,249	336*	22	58.45
6	L. Hutton	79	138	15	6,971	364	19	56.67
7	K. F. Barrington	82	131	15	6,806	256	20	58.67
8	D. C. S. Compton	78	131	15	5,807	278	17	50.06
9	J. B. Hobbs	61	102	7	5,410	211	15	56.94
10	I. T. Botham	102	161	6	5,200	208	14	33.54
11	J. H. Edrich	77	127	9	5,138	310*	12	43.54
12	T. W. Graveney	79	123	13	4,882	258	11	44.38
13	A. J. Lamb	79	139	10	4,656	142	14	36.09
14	H. Sutcliffe	54	84	9	4,555	194	16	60.73
15	P. B. H. May	66	106	9	4,537	285*	13	46.77
16	E. R. Dexter	62	102	8	4,502	205	9	47.89
17	A. P. E. Knott	95	149	15	4,389	135	5	32.75
18	M. W. Gatting	68	117	14	3,870	207	9	37.57
19	D. L. Amiss	50	88	10	3,612	262*	11	46.30
20	A. W. Greig	58	93	4	3,599	148	8	40.43
21	E. H. Hendren	51	83	9	3,525	205*	7	47.63
22	F. E. Woolley	64	98	7	3,283	154	5	36.07
23	K. W. R. Fletcher	59	96	14	3,272	216	7	39.90
24	M. Leyland	41	65	5	2,764	187	9	46.06
25	R. A. Smith	36	66	14	2,645	148*	7	50.86
26	C. Washbrook	37	66	6	2,569	195	6	42.81
27	B. L. D'Oliveira	44	70	8	2,484	158	5	40.06
28	D. W. Randall	47	79	5	2,470	174	7	33.37
29	W. J. Edrich	39	63	2	2,440	219	6	40.00
30	T. G. Evans	91	133	14	2,439	104	2	20.49
31	L. E. G. Ames	47	72	12	2,434	149	8	40.56
32	W. Rhodes	58	98	21	2,325	179	2	30.19
33	T. E. Bailey	61	91	14	2,290	134*	1	29.74
34	M. J. K. Smith	50	78	6	2,278	121	3	31.63
35	P. E. Richardson	34	56	1	2,061	126	5	37.47

AUSTRALIA

		T	I	NO	R	HS	100s	Avge
1	A. R. Border	130	224	42	9,532	205	23	52.37
2	G. S. Chappell	87	151	19	7,110	247*	24	53.86
3	D. G. Bradman	52	80	10	6,996	334	29	99.94
4	R. N. Harvey	79	137	10	6,149	205	21	48.41
5	K. D. Walters	74	125	14	5,357	250	15	48.26
6	I. M. Chappell	75	136	10	5,345	196	14	42.42
7	W. M. Lawry	67	123	12	5,234	210	13	47.15
8	R. B. Simpson	62	111	7	4,869	311	10	46.81
9	I. R. Redpath	66	120	11	4,737	171	8	43.45
10	D. C. Boon	63	115	12	4,538	200	13	44.05
11	K. J. Hughes	70	124	6	4,415	213	9	37.41
12	R. W. Marsh	96	150	13	3,633	132	3	26.51
13	A. R. Morris	46	79	3	3,533	206	12	46.48
14	C. Hill	49	89	2	3,412	191	7	39.21
15	G. M. Wood	59	112	6	3,374	172	9	31.83

		T	I	NO	R	HS	100s	Avge
16	**D. M. Jones**	**49**	**83**	**10**	**3,355**	**216**	**10**	**45.95**
17	V. T. Trumper	48	89	8	3,163	214*	8	39.04
18	C. C. McDonald	47	83	4	3,107	170	5	39.32
19	A. L. Hassett	43	69	3	3,073	198*	10	46.56
20	K. R. Miller	55	87	7	2,958	147	7	36.97
21	W. W. Armstrong	50	84	10	2,863	159*	6	38.68
22	**G. R. Marsh**	**50**	**93**	**7**	**2,854**	**138**	**4**	**33.18**
23	K. R. Stackpole	43	80	5	2,807	207	7	37.42
24	N. C. O'Neill	42	69	8	2,779	181	6	45.55
25	G. N. Yallop	39	70	3	2,756	268	8	41.13
26	S. J. McCabe	39	62	5	2,748	232	6	48.21
27	**M. A. Taylor**	**30**	**56**	**4**	**2,694**	**219**	**8**	**51.80**
28	W. Bardsley	41	66	5	2,469	193*	6	40.47
29	W. M. Woodfull	35	54	4	2,300	161	7	46.00
30	P. J. Burge	42	68	8	2,290	181	4	38.16
31	S. E. Gregory	58	100	7	2,282	201	4	24.53
32	R. Benaud	63	97	7	2,201	122	3	24.45
33	C. G. Macartney	35	55	4	2,131	170	7	41.78
34	W. H. Ponsford	29	48	4	2,122	266	7	48.22
35	S. R. Waugh	44	67	11	2,097	177*	3	37.44
36	R. M. Cowper	27	46	2	2,061	307	5	46.84

SOUTH AFRICA

		T	I	NO	R	HS	100s	Avge
1	B. Mitchell	42	80	9	3,471	189*	8	48.88
2	A. D. Nourse	34	62	7	2,960	231	9	53.81
3	H. W. Taylor	42	76	4	2,936	176	7	40.77
4	E. J. Barlow	30	57	2	2,516	201	6	45.74
5	T. L. Goddard	41	78	5	2,516	112	1	34.46
6	D. J. McGlew	34	64	6	2,440	255*	7	42.06
7	J. H. B. Waite	50	86	7	2,405	134	4	30.44
8	R. G. Pollock	23	41	4	2,256	274	7	60.97
9	A. W. Nourse	45	83	8	2,234	111	1	29.78
10	R. A. McLean	40	73	3	2,120	142	5	30.28

WEST INDIES

		T	I	NO	R	HS	100s	Avge
1	I. V. A. Richards	121	182	12	8,540	291	24	50.23
2	G. S. Sobers	93	160	21	8,032	365*	26	57.78
3	C. G. Greenidge	108	185	16	7,558	226	19	44.72
4	C. H. Lloyd	110	175	14	7,515	242*	19	46.67
5	**D. L. Haynes**	**103**	**180**	**21**	**6,725**	**184**	**16**	**42.29**
6	R. B. Kanhai	79	137	6	6,227	256	15	47.53
7	**R. B. Richardson**	**63**	**109**	**10**	**4,693**	**194**	**14**	**47.40**
8	E. D. Weekes	48	81	5	4,455	207	15	58.61
9	A. I. Kallicharran	66	109	10	4,399	187	12	44.43
10	R. C. Fredericks	59	109	7	4,334	169	8	42.49
11	F. M. M. Worrell	51	87	9	3,860	261	9	49.48
12	C. L. Walcott	44	74	7	3,798	220	15	56.68
13	P. J. L. Dujon	81	115	11	3,322	139	5	31.94
14	C. C. Hunte	44	78	6	3,245	260	8	45.06
15	H. A. Gomes	60	91	11	3,171	143	9	39.63
16	B. F. Butcher	44	78	6	3,104	209*	7	43.11
17	S. M. Nurse	29	54	1	2,523	258	6	47.60
18	A. L. Logie	52	78	9	2,470	130	2	35.79
19	G. A. Headley	22	40	4	2,190	270*	10	60.83
20	J. B. Stollmeyer	32	56	5	2,159	160	4	42.33
21	L. G. Rowe	30	49	2	2,047	302	7	43.55

NEW ZEALAND

		T	I	NO	R	HS	100s	Avge
1	J. G. Wright	77	138	6	4,964	185	12	37.60
2	M. D. Crowe	59	98	10	4,205	299	13	47.78
3	B. E. Congdon	61	114	7	3,448	176	7	32.22
4	J. R. Reid	58	108	5	3,428	142	6	33.28
5	R. J. Hadlee	86	134	19	3,124	151*	2	27.16
6	G. M. Turner	41	73	6	2,991	259	7	44.64
7	B. Sutcliffe	42	76	8	2,727	230*	5	40.10
8	M. G. Burgess	50	92	6	2,684	119*	5	31.20
9	J. V. Coney	52	85	14	2,668	174*	3	37.57
10	G. P. Howarth	47	83	5	2,531	147	6	32.44
11	G. T. Dowling	39	77	3	2,306	239	3	31.16

INDIA

		T	I	NO	R	HS	100s	Avge
1	S. M. Gavaskar	125	214	16	10,122	236*	34	51.12
2	D. B. Vengsarkar	116	185	22	6,868	166	17	42.13
3	G. R. Viswanath	91	155	10	6,080	222	14	41.93
4	Kapil Dev	115	168	13	4,690	163	7	30.25
5	M. Amarnath	69	113	10	4,378	138	11	42.50
6	R. J. Shastri	76	115	14	3,760	206	11	37.22
7	P. R. Umrigar	59	94	8	3,631	223	12	42.22
8	V. L. Manjrekar	55	92	10	3,208	189*	7	39.12
9	M. Azharuddin	46	70	3	3,168	199	11	47.28
10	C. G. Borde	55	97	11	3,061	177*	5	35.59
11	Nawab of Pataudi jun.	46	83	3	2,793	203*	6	34.91
12	S. M. H. Kirmani	88	124	22	2,759	102	2	27.04
13	F. M. Engineer	46	87	3	2,611	121	2	31.08
14	Pankaj Roy	43	79	4	2,442	173	5	32.56
15	V. S. Hazare	30	52	6	2,192	164*	7	47.65
16	A. L. Wadekar	37	71	4	2,113	143	1	31.07
17	V. Mankad	44	72	5	2,109	231	5	31.47
18	C. P. S. Chauhan	40	68	2	2,084	97	0	31.57
19	K. Srikkanth	43	72	3	2,062	123	2	29.88
20	M. L. Jaisimha	39	71	4	2,056	129	3	30.68
21	D. N. Sardesai	30	55	4	2,001	212	5	39.23

PAKISTAN

		T	I	NO	R	HS	100s	Avge
1	Javed Miandad	117	177	21	8,465	280*	23	54.26
2	Zaheer Abbas	78	124	11	5,062	274	12	44.79
3	Mudassar Nazar	76	116	8	4,114	231	10	38.09
4	Majid Khan	63	106	5	3,931	167	8	38.92
5	Hanif Mohammad	55	97	8	3,915	337	12	43.98
6	Imran Khan	88	126	25	3,807	136	6	37.69
7	Salim Malik	71	101	18	3,743	165	10	45.09
8	Mushtaq Mohammad	57	100	7	3,643	201	10	39.17
9	Asif Iqbal	58	99	7	3,575	175	11	38.85
10	Saeed Ahmed	41	78	4	2,991	172	5	40.41
11	Wasim Raja	57	92	14	2,821	125	4	36.16
12	Mohsin Khan	48	79	6	2,709	200	7	37.10
13	Sadiq Mohammad	41	74	2	2,579	166	5	35.81
14	Shoaib Mohammad	39	58	6	2,443	203*	7	46.98
15	Ramiz Raja	44	71	5	2,149	122	2	32.56
16	Imtiaz Ahmed	41	72	1	2,079	209	3	29.28

SRI LANKA: The highest aggregate is 1,830, average 33.88, by A. Ranatunga in 33 Tests.

Bold type denotes those who played Test cricket in 1991-92 and 1992 seasons.

CAREER AVERAGES

(Qualification: 20 innings)

Avge		T	I	NO	R	HS	100s
99.94	D. G. Bradman (A)	52	80	10	6,996	334	29
60.97	R. G. Pollock (SA)	23	41	4	2,256	274	7
60.83	G. A. Headley (WI)	22	40	4	2,190	270*	10
60.73	H. Sutcliffe (E)	54	84	9	4,555	194	16
59.23	E. Paynter (E)............	20	31	5	1,540	243	4
58.67	K. F. Barrington (E)	82	131	15	6,806	256	20
58.61	E. D. Weekes (WI).......	48	81	5	4,455	207	15
58.45	W. R. Hammond (E)	85	140	16	7,249	336*	22
57.78	G. S. Sobers (WI)	93	160	21	8,032	365*	26
56.94	J. B. Hobbs (E)...........	61	102	7	5,410	211	15
56.68	C. L. Walcott (WI).......	44	74	7	3,798	220	15
56.67	L. Hutton (E)	79	138	15	6,971	364	19
55.00	E. Tyldesley (E)	14	20	2	990	122	3
54.26	**Javed Miandad (P) ....**	**117**	**177**	**21**	**8,465**	**280***	**23**
54.20	C. A. Davis (WI)	15	29	5	1,301	183	4
53.86	G. S. Chappell (A)	87	151	19	7,110	247*	24
53.81	A. D. Nourse (SA)	34	62	7	2,960	231	9
52.37	**A. R. Border (A) ....**	**130**	**224**	**42**	**9,532**	**205**	**23**
52.13	**A. H. Jones (NZ) ....**	**23**	**42**	**5**	**1,929**	**186**	**6**
51.62	J. Ryder (A)	20	32	5	1,394	201*	3
51.12	S. M. Gavaskar (I)	125	214	16	10,122	236*	34
51.80	**M. A. Taylor (A)..........**	**30**	**56**	**4**	**2,694**	**219**	**8**
50.86	**R. A. Smith (E)............**	**36**	**66**	**14**	**2,645**	**148***	**7**
50.23	I. V. A. Richards (WI).....	121	182	12	8,540	291	24
50.06	D. C. S. Compton (E)	78	131	15	5,807	278	17

Bold type denotes those who played Test cricket in 1991-92 and 1992 seasons.

MOST HUNDREDS

	Total	200+	Inns	E	A	SA	Opponents WI	NZ	I	P	SL
S. M. Gavaskar (I) ..	34	4	214	4	8	–	13	2	–	5	2
D. G. Bradman (A)..	29	12	80	19	–	4	2	–	4	–	–
G. S. Sobers (WI) ...	26	2	160	10	4	–	–	1	8	3	–
G. S. Chappell (A) ..	24	4	151	9	–	–	5	3	1	6	0
I. V. A. Richards (WI)	24	3	182	8	5	–	–	1	8	2	–
A. R. Border (A)	**23**	**1**	**224**	**7**	**–**	**–**	**2**	**4**	**4**	**6**	**0**
Javed Miandad (P)...	**23**	**6**	**177**	**2**	**6**	**–**	**2**	**7**	**5**	**–**	**1**
G. Boycott (E)	22	1	193	–	7	1	5	2	4	3	–
M. C. Cowdrey (E) ..	22	0	188	–	5	3	6	2	3	3	–
W. R. Hammond (E).	22	7	140	–	9	6	1	4	2	–	–
R. N. Harvey (A) ...	21	2	137	6	–	8	3	–	4	0	–
K. F. Barrington (E).	20	1	131	–	5	2	3	3	3	4	–
C. G. Greenidge (WI)	19	4	185	7	4	–	–	2	5	1	–
L. Hutton (E).......	19	4	138	–	5	4	5	3	2	0	–
C. H. Lloyd (WI).....	19	1	175	5	6	–	–	0	7	1	–
D. I. Gower (E)	**18**	**2**	**204**	**–**	**9**	**–**	**1**	**4**	**2**	**2**	**0**
D. C. S. Compton (E)	17	2	131	–	5	7	2	2	0	1	–
G. A. Gooch (E).....	**17**	**1**	**179**	**–**	**2**	**–**	**5**	**3**	**5**	**1**	**1**
D. B. Vengsarkar (I) .	**17**	**0**	**185**	**5**	**2**	**–**	**6**	**0**	**–**	**2**	**2**

	Total	200s	Inns	E	A	SA	Opponents WI	NZ	I	P	SL
D. L. Haynes (WI) ..	16	0	180	5	5	0	–	**3**	**2**	**1**	–
H. Sutcliffe (E)	16	0	84	–	8	6	0	2	0	–	–
J. B. Hobbs (E)	15	1	102	–	12	2	1	–	–	–	–
R. B. Kanhai (WI) ..	15	2	137	5	5	–	–	–	4	1	–
C. L. Walcott (WI) ..	15	1	74	4	5	–	–	1	4	1	–
K. D. Walters (A) ...	15	2	125	4	–	0	6	3	1	1	–
E. D. Weekes (WI) ...	15	2	81	3	1	–	–	3	7	1	–

The most double-hundreds by batsmen not qualifying for the above list is four by Zaheer Abbas (12 hundreds for Pakistan) and three by R. B. Simpson (10 hundreds for Australia).

Bold type denotes those who played Test cricket in 1991-92 and 1992 seasons. Dashes indicate that a player did not play against the country concerned.

CARRYING BAT THROUGH TEST INNINGS

(Figures in brackets show side's total)

A. B. Tancred	26*	(47)	South Africa v England at Cape Town ..	1888-89
J. E. Barrett	67*	(176)	Australia v England at Lord's	1890
R. Abel	132*	(307)	England v Australia at Sydney	1891-92
P. F. Warner	132*	(237)	England v South Africa at Johannesburg	1898-99
W. W. Armstrong ..	159*	(309)	Australia v South Africa at Johannesburg	1902-03
J. W. Zulch	43*	(103)	South Africa v England at Cape Town ..	1909-10
W. Bardsley	193*	(383)	Australia v England at Lord's	1926
W. M. Woodfull	30*	(66)‡	Australia v England at Brisbane	1928-29
W. M. Woodfull	73*	(193)†	Australia v England at Adelaide	1932-33
W. A. Brown	206*	(422)	Australia v England at Lord's	1938
L. Hutton	202*	(344)	England v West Indies at The Oval	1950
L. Hutton	156*	(272)	England v Australia at Adelaide	1950-51
Nazar Mohammad ..	124*	(331)	Pakistan v India at Lucknow	1952-53
F. M. M. Worrell ..	191*	(372)	West Indies v England at Nottingham ...	1957
T. L. Goddard	56*	(99)	South Africa v Australia at Cape Town .	1957-58
D. J. McGlew	127*	(292)	South Africa v New Zealand at Durban .	1961-62
C. C. Hunte	60*	(131)	West Indies v Australia at Port-of-Spain .	1964-65
G. M. Turner	43*	(131)	New Zealand v England at Lord's	1969
W. M. Lawry	49*	(107)	Australia v India at Delhi	1969-70
W. M. Lawry	60*	(116)†	Australia v England at Sydney	1970-71
G. M. Turner	223*	(386)	New Zealand v West Indies at Kingston .	1971-72
I. R. Redpath	159*	(346)	Australia v New Zealand at Auckland ...	1973-74
G. Boycott........	99*	(215)	England v Australia at Perth	1979-80
S. M. Gavaskar ...	127*	(286)	India v Pakistan at Faisalabad	1982-83
Mudassar Nazar ...	152*	(323)	Pakistan v India at Lahore	1982-83
S. Wettimuny	63*	(144)	Sri Lanka v New Zealand at Christchurch	1982-83
D. C. Boon	58*	(103)	Australia v New Zealand at Auckland ...	1985-86
D. L. Haynes	88*	(211)	West Indies v Pakistan at Karachi	1986-87
G. A. Gooch......	154*	(252)	England v West Indies at Leeds	1991
D. L. Haynes	75*	(176)	West Indies v England at The Oval	1991
A. J. Stewart......	69*	(175)	England v Pakistan at Lord's	1992

† *One man absent.* ‡ *Two men absent.*

Notes: G. M. Turner (223*) holds the record for the highest score by a player carrying his bat through a Test innings. He is also the youngest player to do so, being 22 years 63 days old when he first achieved the feat (1969).

G. A. Gooch (61.11%) holds the record for the highest percentage of a side's total by anyone carrying his bat throughout a Test innings.

Nazar Mohammad and Mudassar Nazar provide the only instance of a father and son carrying their bat through a Test innings.

D. L. Haynes (55 and 105) opened the batting and was last man out in each innings for West Indies v New Zealand at Dunedin, 1979-80.

FASTEST FIFTIES

Minutes

28	J. T. Brown	England v Australia at Melbourne	1894-95
29	S. A. Durani	India v England at Kanpur	1963-64
30	E. A. V. Williams	West Indies v England at Bridgetown	1947-48
30	B. R. Taylor	New Zealand v West Indies at Auckland	1968-69
33	C. A. Roach	West Indies v England at The Oval	1933
34	C. R. Browne	West Indies v England at Georgetown	1929-30

The fastest fifties in terms of balls received (where recorded) are:

Balls

30	Kapil Dev	India v Pakistan at Karachi (2nd Test)	1982-83
32	I. V. A. Richards	West Indies v England at Kingston	1982-83
32	I. T. Botham	England v New Zealand at The Oval	1986
33	R. C. Fredericks	West Indies v Australia at Perth	1975-76
33	Kapil Dev	India v Pakistan at Karachi	1978-79
33	Kapil Dev	India v England at Manchester	1982
33	A. J. Lamb	England v New Zealand at Auckland	1991-92

FASTEST HUNDREDS

Minutes

70	J. M. Gregory	Australia v South Africa at Johannesburg	1921-22
75	G. L. Jessop	England v Australia at The Oval	1902
78	R. Benaud	Australia v West Indies at Kingston	1954-55
80	J. H. Sinclair	South Africa v Australia at Cape Town	1902-03
81	I. V. A. Richards	West Indies v England at St John's	1985-86
86	B. R. Taylor	New Zealand v West Indies at Auckland	1968-69

The fastest hundreds in terms of balls received (where recorded) are:

Balls

56	I. V. A. Richards	West Indies v England at St John's	1985-86
67	J. M. Gregory	Australia v South Africa at Johannesburg	1921-22
71	R. C. Fredericks	West Indies v Australia at Perth	1975-76
74	Kapil Dev	India v Sri Lanka at Kanpur	1986-87
76	G. L. Jessop	England v Australia at The Oval	1902
77	Majid Khan	Pakistan v New Zealand at Karachi	1976-77

FASTEST DOUBLE-HUNDREDS

Minutes

214	D. G. Bradman	Australia v England at Leeds	1930
223	S. J. McCabe	Australia v England at Nottingham	1938
226	V. T. Trumper	Australia v South Africa at Adelaide	1910-11
234	D. G. Bradman	Australia v England at Lord's	1930
240	W. R. Hammond	England v New Zealand at Auckland	1932-33
241	S. E. Gregory	Australia v England at Sydney	1894-95
245	D. C. S. Compton	England v Pakistan at Nottingham	1954

The fastest double-hundreds in terms of balls received (where recorded) are:

Balls

220	I. T. Botham	England v India at The Oval	1982
232	C. G. Greenidge	West Indies v England at Lord's	1984
240	C. H. Lloyd	West Indies v India at Bombay	1974-75
241	Zaheer Abbas	Pakistan v India at Lahore	1982-83
242	D. G. Bradman	Australia v England at The Oval	1934
242	I. V. A. Richards	West Indies v Australia at Melbourne	1984-85

FASTEST TRIPLE-HUNDREDS

Minutes

288	W. R. Hammond ..	England v New Zealand at Auckland	1932-33
336	D. G. Bradman....	Australia v England at Leeds	1930

MOST RUNS IN A DAY BY A BATSMAN

309	D. G. Bradman ......,	Australia v England at Leeds	1930
295	W. R. Hammond......	England v New Zealand at Auckland	1932-33
273	D. C. S. Compton	England v Pakistan at Nottingham...........	1954
271	D. G. Bradman	Australia v England at Leeds	1934

SLOWEST INDIVIDUAL BATTING

2* in 80 minutes	C. E. H. Croft, West Indies v Australia at Brisbane......	1979-80
3* in 100 minutes	J. T. Murray, England v Australia at Sydney	1962-63
5 in 102 minutes	Nawab of Pataudi jun, India v England at Bombay......	1972-73
7 in 123 minutes	G. Miller, England v Australia at Melbourne	1978-79
9 in 125 minutes	T. W. Jarvis, New Zealand v India at Madras	1964-65
10* in 133 minutes	T. G. Evans, England v Australia at Adelaide	1946-47
16* in 147 minutes	D. B. Vengsarkar, India v Pakistan at Kanpur	1979-80
17* in 166 minutes	G. M. Ritchie, Australia v India at Sydney............	1985-86
18 in 194 minutes	W. R. Playle, New Zealand v England at Leeds........	1958
19 in 217 minutes	M. D. Crowe, New Zealand v Sri Lanka at Colombo (SSC)	1983-84
25 in 242 minutes	D. K. Morrison, New Zealand v Pakistan at Faisalabad ..	1990-91
28* in 250 minutes	J. W. Burke, Australia v England at Brisbane	1958-59
31 in 264 minutes	K. D. Mackay, Australia v England at Lord's	1956
34* in 271 minutes	Younis Ahmed, Pakistan v India at Ahmedabad	1986-87
35 in 332 minutes	C. J. Tavaré, England v India at Madras	1981-82
55 in 336 minutes	B. A. Edgar, New Zealand v Australia at Wellington ...	1981-82
57 in 346 minutes	G. S. Camacho, West Indies v England at Bridgetown ...	1967-68
58 in 367 minutes	Ijaz Butt, Pakistan v Australia at Karachi	1959-60
60 in 390 minutes	D. N. Sardesai, India v West Indies at Bridgetown	1961-62
62 in 408 minutes	Ramiz Raja, Pakistan v West Indies at Karachi	1986-87
68 in 458 minutes	T. E. Bailey, England v Australia at Brisbane..........	1958-59
99 in 505 minutes	M. L. Jaisimha, India v Pakistan at Kanpur	1960-61
105 in 575 minutes	D. J. McGlew, South Africa v Australia at Durban	1957-58
114 in 591 minutes	Mudassar Nazar, Pakistan v England at Lahore	1977-78
120* in 609 minutes	J. J. Crowe, New Zealand v Sri Lanka, Colombo (CCC) .	1986-87
146* in 655 minutes	M. J. Greatbatch, New Zealand v Australia at Perth.....	1989-90
163 in 720 minutes	Shoaib Mohammad, Pakistan v New Zealand at Wellington	1988-89
201* in 777 minutes	D. S. B. P. Kuruppu, Sri Lanka v New Zealand at Colombo (CCC)	1986-87
337 in 970 minutes	Hanif Mohammad, Pakistan v West Indies at Bridgetown.	1957-58

SLOWEST HUNDREDS

557 minutes	Mudassar Nazar, Pakistan v England at Lahore..............	1977-78
545 minutes	D. J. McGlew, South Africa v Australia at Durban	1957-58
516 minutes	J. J. Crowe, New Zealand v Sri Lanka, Colombo (CCC)	1986-87
488 minutes	P. E. Richardson, England v South Africa at Johannesburg	1956-57

Notes: The slowest hundred for any Test in England is 458 minutes (329 balls) by K. W. R. Fletcher, England v Pakistan, The Oval, 1974.

The slowest double-hundred in a Test was scored in 777 minutes (548 balls) by D. S. B. P. Kuruppu for Sri Lanka v New Zealand at Colombo (CCC), 1986-87, on his début. It is also the slowest-ever first-class double-hundred.

HIGHEST PARTNERSHIPS FOR EACH WICKET

413 for 1st	V. Mankad (231)/Pankaj Roy (173)........	I v NZ	Madras	1955-56
451 for 2nd	W. H. Ponsford (266)/D. G. Bradman (244).	A v E	The Oval	1934
467 for 3rd	A. H. Jones (186)/M. D. Crowe (299)......	NZ v SL	Wellington	1990-91
411 for 4th	P. B. H. May (285*)/M. C. Cowdrey (154)..	E v WI	Birmingham	1957
405 for 5th	S. G. Barnes (234)/D. G. Bradman (234) ...	A v E	Sydney	1946-47
346 for 6th	J. H. W. Fingleton (136)/D. G. Bradman (270)	A v E	Melbourne	1936-37
347 for 7th	D. St E. Atkinson (219)/C. C. Depeiza (122)	WI v A	Bridgetown	1954-55
246 for 8th	L. E. G. Ames (137)/G. O. B. Allen (122) ..	E v NZ	Lord's	1931
190 for 9th	Asif Iqbal (146)/Intikhab Alam (51)	P v E	The Oval	1967
151 for 10th	B. F. Hastings (110)/R. O. Collinge (68*)...	NZ v P	Auckland	1972-73

PARTNERSHIPS OF 300 AND OVER

467	for 3rd	A. H. Jones (186)/M. D. Crowe (299)	NZ v SL	Wellington	1990-91
451	for 2nd	W. H. Ponsford (266)/D. G. Bradman (244) ..	A v E	The Oval	1934
451	for 3rd	Mudassar Nazar (231)/Javed Miandad (280*) ..	P v I	Hyderabad	1982-83
446	for 2nd	C. C. Hunte (260)/G. S. Sobers (365*)	WI v P	Kingston	1957-58
413	for 1st	V. Mankad (231)/Pankaj Roy (173)	I v NZ	Madras	1955-56
411	for 4th	P. B. H. May (285*)/M. C. Cowdrey (154) ..	E v WI	Birmingham	1957
405	for 5th	S. G. Barnes (234)/D. G. Bradman (234) ...	A v E	Sydney	1946-47
399	for 4th	G. S. Sobers (226)/F. M. M. Worrell (197*) ..	WI v E	Bridgetown	1959-60
397	for 3rd	Qasim Omar (206)/Javed Miandad (203*)	P v SL	Faisalabad	1985-86
388	for 4th	W. H. Ponsford (181)/D. G. Bradman (304) ..	A v E	Leeds	1934
387	for 1st	G. M. Turner (259)/T. W. Jarvis (182)	NZ v WI	Georgetown	1971-72
382	for 2nd	L. Hutton (364)/M. Leyland (187)	E v A	The Oval	1938
382	for 1st	W. M. Lawry (210)/R. B. Simpson (201)	A v WI	Bridgetown	1964-65
370	for 3rd	W. J. Edrich (189)/D. C. S. Compton (208).	E v SA	Lord's	1947
369	for 2nd	J. H. Edrich (310*)/K. F. Barrington (163) ..	E v NZ	Leeds	1965
359	for 1st	L. Hutton (158)/C. Washbrook (195)	E v SA	Johannesburg	1948-49
351	for 2nd	G. A. Gooch (196)/D. I. Gower (157)	E v A	The Oval	1985
350	for 4th	Mushtaq Mohammad (201)/Asif Iqbal (175) ..	P v NZ	Dunedin	1972-73
347	for 7th	D. St E. Atkinson (219)/C. C. Depeiza (122)..	WI v A	Bridgetown	1954-55
346	for 6th	J. H. Fingleton (136)/D. G. Bradman (270) ...	A v E	Melbourne	1936-37
344*	for 2nd	S. M. Gavaskar (182*)/D. B. Vengsarkar (157*)	I v WI	Calcutta	1978-79
341	for 3rd	E. J. Barlow (201)/R. G. Pollock (175)	SA v A	Adelaide	1963-64
338	for 3rd	E. D. Weekes (206)/F. M. M. Worrell (167) ..	WI v E	Port-of-Spain	1953-54
336	for 4th	W. M. Lawry (151)/K. D. Walters (242)	A v WI	Sydney	1968-69
331	for 2nd	R. T. Robinson (148)/D. I. Gower (215)	E v A	Birmingham	1985
329	for 1st	G. R. Marsh (138)/M. A. Taylor (219)	A v E	Nottingham	1989
323	for 1st	J. B. Hobbs (178)/W. Rhodes (179)	E v A	Melbourne	1911-12
322	for 4th	Javed Miandad (153*)/Salim Malik (165).....	P v E	Birmingham	1992
319	for 3rd	A. Melville (189)/A. D. Nourse (149)	SA v E	Nottingham	1947
316†	for 3rd	G. R. Viswanath (222)/Yashpal Sharma (140)..	I v E	Madras	1981-82
308	for 7th	Waqar Hassan (189)/Imtiaz Ahmed (209)	P v NZ	Lahore	1955-56
308	for 3rd	R. B. Richardson (154)/I. V. A. Richards (178).	WI v A	St John's	1983-84
308	for 3rd	G. A. Gooch (333)/A. J. Lamb (139)	E v I	Lord's	1990
303	for 3rd	I. V. A. Richards (232)/A. I. Kallicharran (97).	WI v E	Nottingham	1976
301	for 2nd	A. R. Morris (182)/D. G. Bradman (173*).....	A v E	Leeds	1948

† *415 runs were scored for this wicket in two separate partnerships: D. B. Vengsarkar retired hurt when he and Viswanath had added 99 runs.*

BOWLING RECORDS

MOST WICKETS IN AN INNINGS

10-53	J. C. Laker	England v Australia at Manchester.	1956
9-28	G. A. Lohmann . . .	England v South Africa at Johannesburg	1895-96
9-37	J. C. Laker	England v Australia at Manchester.	1956
9-52	R. J. Hadlee	New Zealand v Australia at Brisbane	1985-86
9-56	Abdul Qadir	Pakistan v England at Lahore	1987-88
9-69	J. M. Patel	India v Australia at Kanpur	1959-60
9-83	Kapil Dev	India v West Indies at Ahmedabad	1983-84
9-86	Sarfraz Nawaz	Pakistan v Australia at Melbourne	1978-79
9-95	J. M. Noreiga	West Indies v India at Port-of-Spain	1970-71
9-102	S. P. Gupte	India v West Indies at Kanpur	1958-59
9-103	S. F. Barnes	England v South Africa at Johannesburg	1913-14
9-113	H. J. Tayfield	South Africa v England at Johannesburg	1956-57
9-121	A. A. Mailey	Australia v England at Melbourne	1920-21
8-7	G. A. Lohmann . . .	England v South Africa at Port Elizabeth	1895-96
8-11	J. Briggs.	England v South Africa at Cape Town	1888-89
8-29	S. F. Barnes	England v South Africa at The Oval	1912
8-29	C. E. H. Croft.	West Indies v Pakistan at Port-of-Spain	1976-77
8-31	F. Laver.	Australia v England at Manchester.	1909
8-31	F. S. Trueman	England v India at Manchester	1952
8-34	I. T. Botham	England v Pakistan at Lord's	1978
8-35	G. A. Lohmann . . .	England v Australia at Sydney	1886-87
8-38	L. R. Gibbs.	West Indies v India at Bridgetown	1961-62
8-43†	A. E. Trott	Australia v England at Adelaide	1894-95
8-43	H. Verity	England v Australia at Lord's	1934
8-43	R. G. D. Willis	England v Australia at Leeds	1981
8-45	C. E. L. Ambrose . .	West Indies v England at Bridgetown	1989-90
8-51	D. L. Underwood . .	England v Pakistan at Lord's	1974
8-52	V. Mankad	India v Pakistan at Delhi	1952-53
8-53	G. B. Lawrence . . .	South Africa v New Zealand at Johannesburg .	1961-62
8-53†	R. A. L. Massie . . .	Australia v England at Lord's	1972
8-55	V. Mankad	India v England at Madras	1951-52
8-56	S. F. Barnes	England v South Africa at Johannesburg	1913-14
8-58	G. A. Lohmann . . .	England v Australia at Sydney	1891-92
8-58	Imran Khan	Pakistan v Sri Lanka at Lahore	1981-82
8-59	C. Blythe	England v South Africa at Leeds	1907
8-59	A. A. Mallett.	Australia v Pakistan at Adelaide	1972-73
8-60	Imran Khan	Pakistan v India at Karachi	1982-83
8-61†	N. D. Hirwani	India v West Indies at Madras	1987-88
8-65	H. Trumble	Australia v England at The Oval	1902
8-68	W. Rhodes.	England v Australia at Melbourne	1903-04
8-69	H. J. Tayfield	South Africa v England at Durban	1956-57
8-69	Sikander Bakht	Pakistan v India at Delhi	1979-80
8-70	S. J. Snooke	South Africa v England at Johannesburg	1905-06
8-71	G. D. McKenzie . . .	Australia v West Indies at Melbourne	1968-69
8-72	S. Venkataraghavan	India v New Zealand at Delhi	1964-65
8-75†	N. D. Hirwani	India v West Indies at Madras	1987-88
8-76	E. A. S. Prasanna . .	India v New Zealand at Auckland	1975-76
8-79	B. S. Chandrasekhar	India v England at Delhi.	1972-73
8-81	L. C. Braund	England v Australia at Melbourne	1903-04
8-83	J. R. Ratnayeke . . .	Sri Lanka v Pakistan at Sialkot	1985-86
8-84†	R. A. L. Massie . . .	Australia v England at Lord's	1972
8-85	Kapil Dev	India v Pakistan at Lahore	1982-83
8-86	A. W. Greig	England v West Indies at Port-of-Spain	1973-74
8-87	M. G. Hughes	Australia v West Indies at Perth	1988-89
8-92	M. A. Holding	West Indies v England at The Oval	1976
8-94	T. Richardson	England v Australia at Sydney	1897-98
8-97	C. J. McDermott . .	Australia v England at Perth	1990-91

8-103	I. T. Botham	England v West Indies at Lord's	1984
8-104†	A. L. Valentine	West Indies v England at Manchester	1950
8-106	Kapil Dev	India v Australia at Adelaide	1985-86
8-107	B. J. T. Bosanquet .	England v Australia at Nottingham	1905
8-107	N. A. Foster	England v Pakistan at Leeds	1987
8-112	G. F. Lawson	Australia v West Indies at Adelaide	1984-85
8-126	J. C. White	England v Australia at Adelaide	1928-29
8-141	C. J. McDermott ..	Australia v England at Manchester	1985
8-143	M. H. N. Walker ..	Australia v England at Melbourne	1974-75

† *On Test début.*

OUTSTANDING ANALYSES

	O	M	R	W		
J. C. Laker (E)	51.2	23	53	10	v Australia at Manchester	1956
G. A. Lohmann (E)	14.2	6	28	9	v South Africa at Johannesburg	1895-96
J. C. Laker (E)	16.4	4	37	9	v Australia at Manchester	1956
G. A. Lohmann (E)	9.4	5	7	8	v South Africa at Port Elizabeth	1895-96
J. Briggs (E)	14.2	5	11	8	v South Africa at Cape Town ..	1888-89
J. Briggs (E)	19.1	11	17	7	v South Africa at Cape Town ..	1888-89
M. A. Noble (A)	7.4	2	17	7	v England at Melbourne........	1901-02
W. Rhodes (E)	11	3	17	7	v Australia at Birmingham.....	1902
A. E. R. Gilligan (E)	6.3	4	7	6	v South Africa at Birmingham .	1924
S. Haigh (E)	11.4	6	11	6	v South Africa at Cape Town ..	1898-99
D. L. Underwood (E)	11.6	7	12	6	v New Zealand at Christchurch	1970-71
S. L. V. Raju (I)	17.5	13	12	6	v Sri Lanka at Chandigarh	1990-91
H. J. Tayfield (SA)	14	7	13	6	v New Zealand at Johannesburg.	1953-54
C. T. B. Turner (A)	18	11	15	6	v England at Sydney...........	1886-87
M. H. N. Walker (A)	16	8	15	6	v Pakistan at Sydney	1972-73
E. R. H. Toshack (A)	2.3	1	2	5	v India at Brisbane	1947-48
H. Ironmonger (A)	7.2	5	6	5	v South Africa at Melbourne...	1931-32
Pervez Sajjad (P)	12	8	5	4	v New Zealand at Rawalpindi..	1964-65
K. Higgs (E)	9	7	5	4	v New Zealand at Christchurch.	1965-66
P. H. Edmonds (E)	8	6	6	4	v Pakistan at Lord's	1978
J. C. White (E)	6.3	2	7	4	v Australia at Brisbane	1928-29
J. H. Wardle (E)	5	2	7	4	v Australia at Manchester	1953
R. Appleyard (E)	6	3	7	4	v New Zealand at Auckland ...	1954-55
R. Benaud (A)	3.4	3	0	3	v India at Delhi	1959-60

MOST WICKETS IN A MATCH

19-90	J. C. Laker	England v Australia at Manchester	1956
17-159	S. F. Barnes......	England v South Africa at Johannesburg ..	1913-14
16-136†	N. D. Hirwani....	India v West Indies at Madras	1987-88
16-137†	R. A. L. Massie ...	Australia v England at Lord's	1972
15-28	J. Briggs.........	England v South Africa at Cape Town	1888-89
15-45	G. A. Lohmann...	England v South Africa at Port Elizabeth	1895-96
15-99	C. Blythe	England v South Africa at Leeds	1907
15-104	H. Verity	England v Australia at Lord's	1934
15-123	R. J. Hadlee	New Zealand v Australia at Brisbane	1985-86
15-124	W. Rhodes	England v Australia at Melbourne.......	1903-04
14-90	F. R. Spofforth ...	Australia v England at The Oval........	1882
14-99	A. V. Bedser	England v Australia at Nottingham	1953
14-102	W. Bates	England v Australia at Melbourne.......	1882-83
14-116	Imran Khan......	Pakistan v Sri Lanka at Lahore	1981-82
14-124	J. M. Patel......	India v Australia at Kanpur...........	1959-60
14-144	S. F. Barnes.....	England v South Africa at Durban	1913-14
14-149	M. A. Holding....	West Indies v England at The Oval	1976
14-199	C. V. Grimmett...	Australia v South Africa at Adelaide	1931-32

† *On Test début.*

Notes: The best for South Africa is 13-165 by H. J. Tayfield against Australia at Melbourne, 1952-53.
The best for Sri Lanka is 9-125 by R. J. Ratnayake against India at Colombo (PSS), 1985-86.

MOST WICKETS IN A SERIES

	T	R	W	Avge		
S. F. Barnes	4	536	49	10.93	England v South Africa.	1913-14
J. C. Laker	5	442	46	9.60	England v Australia....	1956
C. V. Grimmett	5	642	44	14.59	Australia v South Africa	1935-36
T. M. Alderman	6	893	42	21.26	Australia v England....	1981
R. M. Hogg	6	527	41	12.85	Australia v England....	1978-79
T. M. Alderman	6	712	41	17.36	Australia v England....	1989
Imran Khan	6	558	40	13.95	Pakistan v India	1982-83
A. V. Bedser	5	682	39	17.48	England v Australia....	1953
D. K. Lillee	6	870	39	22.30	Australia v England....	1981
M. W. Tate	5	881	38	23.18	England v Australia....	1924-25
W. J. Whitty	5	632	37	17.08	Australia v South Africa	1910-11
H. J. Tayfield	5	636	37	17.18	South Africa v England.	1956-57
A. E. E. Vogler	5	783	36	25.83	South Africa v England.	1909-10
A. A. Mailey	5	946	36	26.27	Australia v England....	1920-21
G. A. Lohmann	3	203	35	5.80	England v South Africa.	1895-96
B. S. Chandrasekhar	5	662	35	18.91	India v England	1972-73
M. D. Marshall	5	443	35	12.65	West Indies v England .	1988

MOST WICKETS IN A CAREER

(Qualification: 100 wickets)

ENGLAND

		T	Balls	R	W	Avge	5 W/i	10 W/m
1	I. T. Botham	102	21,815	10,878	383	28.40	27	4
2	R. G. D. Willis	90	17,357	8,190	325	25.20	16	—
3	F. S. Trueman	67	15,178	6,625	307	21.57	17	3
4	D. L. Underwood	86	21,862	7,674	297	25.83	17	6
5	J. B. Statham	70	16,056	6,261	252	24.84	9	1
6	A. V. Bedser	51	15,918	5,876	236	24.89	15	5
7	J. A. Snow	49	12,021	5,387	202	26.66	8	1
8	J. C. Laker	46	12,027	4,101	193	21.24	9	3
9	S. F. Barnes	27	7,873	3,106	189	16.43	24	7
10	G. A. R. Lock	49	13,147	4,451	174	25.58	9	3
11	M. W. Tate	39	12,523	4,055	155	26.16	7	1
12	F. J. Titmus	53	15,118	4,931	153	32.22	7	—
13	H. Verity	40	11,173	3,510	144	24.37	5	2
14	C. M. Old	46	8,858	4,020	143	28.11	4	—
15	A. W. Greig	58	9,802	4,541	141	32.20	6	2
16	G. R. Dilley	41	8,192	4,107	138	29.76	6	—
17	J. E. Emburey	60	14,227	5,105	138	36.99	6	—
18	T. E. Bailey	61	9,712	3,856	132	29.21	5	1
19	W. Rhodes	58	8,231	3,425	127	26.96	6	1
20	P. H. Edmonds	51	12,028	4,273	125	34.18	2	—
21	D. A. Allen	39	11,297	3,779	122	30.97	4	—
22	R. Illingworth	61	11,934	3,807	122	31.20	3	—
23	J. Briggs	33	5,332	2,095	118	17.75	9	4
24	G. G. Arnold	34	7,650	3,254	115	28.29	6	—
25	G. A. Lohmann	18	3,821	1,205	112	10.75	9	5
26	D. V. P. Wright	34	8,135	4,224	108	39.11	6	1
27	J. H. Wardle	28	6,597	2,080	102	20.39	5	1
28	R. Peel	20	5,216	1,715	101	16.98	6	1
29	C. Blythe	19	4,546	1,863	100	18.63	9	4

AUSTRALIA

		T	Balls	R	W	Avge	5 W/i	10 W/m
1	D. K. Lillee	70	18,467	8,493	355	23.92	23	7
2	R. Benaud	63	19,108	6,704	248	27.03	16	1
3	G. D. McKenzie	60	17,681	7,328	246	29.78	16	3
4	R. R. Lindwall.......	61	13,650	5,251	228	23.03	12	—
5	C. V. Grimmett	37	14,513	5,231	216	24.21	21	7
6	J. R. Thomson	51	10,535	5,601	200	28.00	8	—
7	A. K. Davidson	44	11,587	3,819	186	20.53	14	2
8	G. F. Lawson.......	46	11,118	5,501	180	30.56	11	2
9	K. R. Miller........	55	10,461	3,906	170	22.97	7	1
10	T. M. Alderman	41	10,181	4,616	170	27.15	14	1
11	W. A. Johnston	40	11,048	3,826	160	23.91	7	—
12	**C. J. McDermott .....**	**36**	**8,356**	**4,329**	**153**	**28.29**	**9**	**2**
13	W. J. O'Reilly	27	10,024	3,254	144	22.59	11	3
14	**M. G. Hughes ......**	**37**	**8,421**	**4,154**	**144**	**28.84**	**5**	**1**
15	H. Trumble	32	8,099	3,072	141	21.78	9	3
16	M. H. N. Walker	34	10,094	3,792	138	27.47	6	—
17	A. A. Mallett	38	9,990	3,940	132	29.84	6	1
18	B. Yardley	33	8,909	3,986	126	31.63	6	1
19	R. M. Hogg	38	7,633	3,503	123	28.47	6	2
20	M. A. Noble	42	7,159	3,025	121	25.00	9	2
21	I. W. Johnson	45	8,780	3,182	109	29.19	3	—
22	**B. A. Reid........**	**26**	**5,926**	**2,633**	**106**	**24.84**	**4**	**2**
23	G. Giffen	31	6,457	2,791	103	27.09	7	1
24	A. N. Connolly	29	7,818	2,981	102	29.22	4	—
25	C. T. B. Turner	17	5,179	1,670	101	16.53	11	2

SOUTH AFRICA

		T	Balls	R	W	Avge	5 W/i	10 W/m
1	H. J. Tayfield........	37	13,568	4,405	170	25.91	14	2
2	T. L. Goddard	41	11,736	3,226	123	26.22	5	—
3	P. M. Pollock........	28	6,522	2,806	116	24.18	9	1
4	N. A. T. Adcock.....	26	6,391	2,195	104	21.10	5	—

WEST INDIES

		T	Balls	R	W	Avge	5 W/i	10 W/m
1	M. D. Marshall	81	17,584	7,876	376	20.94	22	4
2	L. R. Gibbs	79	27,115	8,989	309	29.09	18	2
3	J. Garner	58	13,169	5,433	259	20.97	7	—
4	M. A. Holding	60	12,680	5,898	249	23.68	13	2
5	G. S. Sobers	93	21,599	7,999	235	34.03	6	—
6	A. M. E. Roberts.....	47	11,136	5,174	202	25.61	11	2
7	W. W. Hall	48	10,421	5,066	192	26.38	9	1
8	**C. A. Walsh ....**	**51**	**10,121**	**4,444**	**178**	**24.96**	**5**	**1**
9	S. Ramadhin	43	13,939	4,579	158	28.98	10	1
10	**C. E. L. Ambrose .....**	**34**	**8,220**	**3,320**	**148**	**22.43**	**6**	**1**
11	A. L. Valentine	36	12,953	4,215	139	30.32	8	2
12	C. E. H. Croft	27	6,165	2,913	125	23.30	3	—
13	V. A. Holder	40	9,095	3,627	109	33.27	3	—

NEW ZEALAND

		T	Balls	R	W	Avge	5 W/i	10 W/m
1	R. J. Hadlee	86	21,918	9,611	431	22.29	36	9
2	B. L. Cairns	43	10,628	4,280	130	32.92	6	1
3	E. J. Chatfield	43	10,360	3,958	123	32.17	3	1
4	R. O. Collinge	35	7,689	3,392	116	29.24	3	—
5	B. R. Taylor	30	6,334	2,953	111	26.60	4	—
6	J. G. Bracewell	41	8,403	3,653	102	35.81	4	1
7	R. C. Motz	32	7,034	3,148	100	31.48	5	—

INDIA

		T	Balls	R	W	Avge	5 W/i	10 W/m
1	**Kapil Dev**	**115**	**24,967**	**11,894**	**401**	**29.66**	**23**	**2**
2	B. S. Bedi	67	21,364	7,637	266	28.71	14	1
3	B. S. Chandrasekhar	58	15,963	7,199	242	29.74	16	2
4	E. A. S. Prasanna	49	14,353	5,742	189	30.38	10	2
5	V. Mankad	44	14,686	5,236	162	32.32	8	2
6	S. Venkataraghavan	57	14,877	5,634	156	36.11	3	1
7	S. P. Gupte	36	11,284	4,403	149	29.55	12	1
8	**R. J. Shastri**	**76**	**15,391**	**6,027**	**148**	**40.72**	**2**	**—**
9	D. R. Doshi	33	9,322	3,502	114	30.71	6	—
10	K. D. Ghavri	39	7,042	3,656	109	33.54	4	—
11	N. S. Yadav	35	8,349	3,580	102	35.09	3	—

PAKISTAN

		T	Balls	R	W	Avge	5 W/i	10 W/m
1	**Imran Khan**	**88**	**19,458**	**8,258**	**362**	**22.81**	**23**	**6**
2	Abdul Qadir	67	17,126	7,742	236	32.80	15	5
3	Sarfraz Nawaz	55	13,927	5,798	177	32.75	4	1
4	Iqbal Qasim	50	13,019	4,807	171	28.11	8	2
5	**Wasim Akram**	**44**	**9,649**	**4,100**	**169**	**24.26**	**11**	**2**
6	Fazal Mahmood	34	9,834	3,434	139	24.70	13	4
7	Intikhab Alam	47	10,474	4,494	125	35.95	5	2

SRI LANKA: The highest aggregate is 73 wickets, average 35.11, by R. J. Ratnayake in 23 Tests.

Bold type denotes those who played Test cricket in 1991-92 and 1992 seasons.

WICKET WITH FIRST BALL IN TEST CRICKET

	Batsman dismissed			
A. Coningham	A. C. MacLaren	A v E	Melbourne	1894-95
W. M. Bradley	F. Laver	E v A	Manchester	1899
E. G. Arnold	V. T. Trumper	E v A	Sydney	1903-04
G. Macaulay	G. A. L. Hearne	E v SA	Cape Town	1922-23
M. W. Tate	M. J. Susskind	E v SA	Birmingham	1924
M. Henderson	E. W. Dawson	NZ v E	Christchurch	1929-30
H. D. Smith	E. Paynter	NZ v E	Christchurch	1932-33
T. F. Johnson	W. W. Keeton	WI v E	The Oval	1939
R. Howorth	D. V. Dyer	E v SA	The Oval	1947
Intikhab Alam	C. C. McDonald	P v A	Karachi	1959-60
R. K. Illingworth	P. V. Simmons	E v WI	Nottingham	1991

HAT-TRICKS

F. R. Spofforth	Australia v England at Melbourne	1878-79
W. Bates	England v Australia at Melbourne	1882-83
J. Briggs.........	England v Australia at Sydney	1891-92
G. A. Lohmann ...	England v South Africa at Port Elizabeth	1895-96
J. T. Hearne	England v Australia at Leeds	1899
H. Trumble	Australia v England at Melbourne	1901-02
H. Trumble	Australia v England at Melbourne	1903-04
T. J. Matthews† ...	} Australia v South Africa at Manchester	1912
T. J. Matthews		
M. J. C. Allom‡	England v New Zealand at Christchurch.........	1929-30
T. W. Goddard	England v South Africa at Johannesburg	1938-39
P. J. Loader.......	England v West Indies at Leeds	1957
L. F. Kline	Australia v South Africa at Cape Town	1957-58
W. W. Hall	West Indies v Pakistan at Lahore	1958-59
G. M. Griffin	South Africa v England at Lord's	1960
L. R. Gibbs.......	West Indies v Australia at Adelaide	1960-61
P. J. Petherick‡ ...	New Zealand v Pakistan at Lahore	1976-77
C. A. Walsh§	West Indies v Australia at Brisbane	1988-89
M. G. Hughes§ ...	Australia v West Indies at Perth...............	1988-89

† *T. J. Matthews did the hat-trick in each innings of the same match.*
‡ *On Test début.*
§ *Not all in the same innings.*

FOUR WICKETS IN FIVE BALLS

M. J. C. Allom	England v New Zealand at Christchurch..........	1929-30
	On début, in his eighth over : W-WWW	
C. M. Old	England v Pakistan at Birmingham	1978
	Sequence interrupted by a no-ball : WW-WW	
Wasim Akram.....	Pakistan v West Indies at Lahore (*WW-WW*).........	1990-91

MOST BALLS BOWLED IN A TEST

S. Ramadhin (West Indies) sent down 774 balls in 129 overs against England at Birmingham, 1957. It was the most delivered by any bowler in a Test, beating H. Verity's 766 for England against South Africa at Durban, 1938-39. In this match Ramadhin also bowled the most balls (588) in any single first-class innings, including Tests.

It should be noted that six balls were bowled to the over in the Australia v England Test series of 1928-29 and 1932-33, when the eight-ball over was otherwise in force in Australia.

ALL-ROUND RECORDS

100 RUNS AND FIVE WICKETS IN AN INNINGS

England
A. W. Greig	148	6-164	v West Indies	Bridgetown	1973-74
I. T. Botham	103	5-73	v New Zealand	Christchurch	1977-78
I. T. Botham	108	8-34	v Pakistan	Lord's	1978
I. T. Botham	114	6-58 7-48 }	v India	Bombay	1979-80
I. T. Botham	149*	6-95	v Australia	Leeds	1981
I. T. Botham	138	5-59	v New Zealand	Wellington	1983-84

Australia
C. Kelleway	114	5-33	v South Africa	Manchester	1912
J. M. Gregory	100	7-69	v England	Melbourne	1920-21
K. R. Miller	109	6-107	v West Indies	Kingston	1954-55
R. Benaud	100	5-84	v South Africa	Johannesburg	1957-58

South Africa					
J. H. Sinclair	106	6-26	v England	Cape Town	1898-99
G. A. Faulkner	123	5-120	v England	Johannesburg	1909-10
West Indies					
D. St E. Atkinson	219	5-56	v Australia	Bridgetown	1954-55
O. G. Smith	100	5-90	v India	Delhi	1958-59
G. S. Sobers	104	5-63	v India	Kingston	1961-62
G. S. Sobers	174	5-41	v England	Leeds	1966
New Zealand					
B. R. Taylor†	105	5-86	v India	Calcutta	1964-65
India					
V. Mankad	184	5-196	v England	Lord's	1952
P. R. Umrigar	172*	5-107	v West Indies	Port-of-Spain	1961-62
Pakistan					
Mushtaq Mohammad	201	5-49	v New Zealand	Dunedin	1972-73
Mushtaq Mohammad	121	5-28	v West Indies	Port-of-Spain	1976-77
Imran Khan	117	6-98 } 5-82 }	v India	Faisalabad	1982-83
Wasim Akram	123	5-100	v Australia	Adelaide	1989-90

† *On début.*

100 RUNS AND FIVE DISMISSALS IN AN INNINGS

D. T. Lindsay	182	6ct	SA v A	Johannesburg	1966-67
I. D. S. Smith	113*	4ct, 1st	NZ v E	Auckland	1983-84
S. A. R. Silva	111	5ct	SL v I	Colombo (PSS)	1985-86

100 RUNS AND TEN WICKETS IN A TEST

A. K. Davidson	44 80	5-135 } 6-87 }	A v WI	Brisbane..........	1960-61
I. T. Botham	114	6-58 } 7-48 }	E v I	Bombay	1979-80
Imran Khan	117	6-98 } 5-82 }	P v I	Faisalabad	1982-83

1,000 RUNS AND 100 WICKETS IN A CAREER

	Tests	Runs	Wkts	Tests for Double
England				
T. E. Bailey	61	2,290	132	47
†I. T. Botham	**102**	**5,200**	**383**	**21**
J. E. Emburey	60	1,540	138	46
A. W. Greig	58	3,599	141	37
R. Illingworth	61	1,836	122	47
W. Rhodes	58	2,325	127	44
M. W. Tate	39	1,198	155	33
F. J. Titmus	53	1,449	153	40
Australia				
R. Benaud	63	2,201	248	32
A. K. Davidson	44	1,328	186	34
G. Giffen	31	1,238	103	30
I. W. Johnson	45	1,000	109	45
R. R. Lindwall	61	1,502	228	38
K. R. Miller	55	2,958	170	33
M. A. Noble	42	1,997	121	27

	Tests	Runs	Wkts	Tests for Double
South Africa				
T. L. Goddard..........	41	2,516	123	36
West Indies				
M. D. Marshall..........	81	1,810	376	49
†G. S. Sobers	93	8,032	235	48
New Zealand				
J. G. Bracewell	41	1,001	102	41
R. J. Hadlee	86	3,124	431	28
India				
Kapil Dev...............	**115**	**4,690**	**401**	**25**
V. Mankad	44	2,109	162	23
R. J. Shastri	**76**	**3,760**	**148**	**44**
Pakistan				
Abdul Qadir	67	1,029	236	62
Imran Khan.............	**88**	**3,807**	**362**	**30**
Intikhab Alam	47	1,493	125	41
Sarfraz Nawaz	55	1,045	177	55

Bold type denotes those who played Test cricket in 1991-92 and 1992 seasons.

† I. T. Botham (120 catches) and G. S. Sobers (109) are the only players to have achieved the treble of 1,000 runs, 100 wickets and 100 catches.

WICKET-KEEPING RECORDS

Most Dismissals in an Innings

7 (all ct)	Wasim Bari	Pakistan v New Zealand at Auckland ...	1978-79
7 (all ct)	R. W. Taylor......	England v India at Bombay............	1979-80
7 (all ct)	I. D. S. Smith	New Zealand v Sri Lanka at Hamilton ...	1990-91
6 (all ct)	A. T. W. Grout....	Australia v South Africa at Johannesburg	1957-58
6 (all ct)	D. T. Lindsay	South Africa v Australia at Johannesburg	1966-67
6 (all ct)	J. T. Murray	England v India at Lord's	1967
6 (5ct, 1st)	S. M. H. Kirmani..	India v New Zealand at Christchurch ...	1975-76
6 (all ct)	R. W. Marsh......	Australia v England at Brisbane	1982-83
6 (all ct)	S. A. R. Silva	Sri Lanka v India at Colombo (SSC)	1985-86
6 (all ct)	R. C. Russell	England v Australia at Melbourne	1990-91

Note: The most stumpings in an innings is 5 by K. S. More for India v West Indies at Madras in 1987-88.

Most Dismissals in a Test

10 (all ct)	R. W. Taylor	England v India at Bombay............	1979-80
9 (8ct, 1st)	G. R. A. Langley ..	Australia v England at Lord's	1956
9 (all ct)	D. A. Murray	West Indies v Australia at Melbourne ...	1981-82
9 (all ct)	R. W. Marsh......	Australia v England at Brisbane	1982-83
9 (all ct)	S. A. R. Silva	Sri Lanka v India at Colombo (SSC) ...	1985-86
9 (8ct, 1st)	S. A. R. Silva	Sri Lanka v India at Colombo (PSS) ...	1985-86
8 (all ct)	J. J. Kelly	Australia v England at Sydney	1901-02
8 (6ct, 2st)	L. E. G. Ames	England v West Indies at The Oval	1933
8 (all ct)	G. R. A. Langley ..	Australia v West Indies at Kingston.....	1954-55

8 (6ct, 2st)	A. T. W. Grout....	Australia v Pakistan at Lahore	1959-60
8 (all ct)	A. T. W. Grout....	Australia v England at Lord's	1961
8 (all ct)	J. M. Parks	England v New Zealand at Christchurch .	1965-66
8 (all ct)	D. T. Lindsay	South Africa v Australia at Johannesburg	1966-67
8 (7ct, 1st)	H. B. Taber......	Australia v South Africa at Johannesburg	1966-67
8 (all ct)	Wasim Bari	Pakistan v England at Leeds	1971
8 (all ct)	R. W. Marsh	Australia v West Indies at Melbourne ...	1975-76
8 (all ct)	R. W. Marsh	Australia v New Zealand at Christchurch	1976-77
8 (7ct, 1st)	R. W. Marsh	Australia v India at Sydney	1980-81
8 (all ct)	W. K. Lees	New Zealand v Sri Lanka at Wellington .	1982-83
8 (all ct)	R. W. Marsh	Australia v England at Adelaide	1982-83
8 (all ct)	I. D. S. Smith	New Zealand v Sri Lanka at Hamilton ..	1990-91

Notes: S. A. R. Silva made 18 dismissals in two successive Tests.

The most stumpings in a match is 6 by K. S. More for India v West Indies at Madras in 1987-88.

Most Dismissals in a Series

(Played in 5 Tests unless otherwise stated)

28 (all ct)	R. W. Marsh......	Australia v England	1982-83
26 (23ct, 3st)	J. H. B. Waite	South Africa v New Zealand...........	1961-62
26 (all ct)	R. W. Marsh......	Australia v West Indies (6 Tests)	1975-76
24 (22ct, 2st)	D. L. Murray	West Indies v England	1963
24 (all ct)	D. T. Lindsay	South Africa v Australia	1966-67
24 (21ct, 3st)	A. P. E. Knott	England v Australia (6 Tests)	1970-71
24 (all ct)	I. A. Healy	Australia v England	1990-91
23 (16ct, 7st)	J. H. B. Waite	South Africa v New Zealand...........	1953-54
23 (22ct, 1st)	F. C. M. Alexander.	West Indies v England	1959-60
23 (20ct, 3st)	A. T. W. Grout....	Australia v West Indies	1960-61
23 (21ct, 2st)	A. E. Dick.......	New Zealand v South Africa...........	1961-62
23 (21ct, 2st)	R. W. Marsh......	Australia v England	1972
23 (22ct, 1st)	A. P. E. Knott	England v Australia (6 Tests)	1974-75
23 (all ct)	R. W. Marsh......	Australia v England (6 Tests)	1981
23 (21ct, 2st)	P. J. L. Dujon	West Indies v Australia	1990-91
22 (all ct)	S. J. Rixon	Australia v India...................	1977-78
22 (21ct, 1st)	S. A. R. Silva	Sri Lanka v India (3 Tests)	1985-86
21 (15ct, 6st)	H. Strudwick	England v South Africa	1913-14
21 (13ct, 8st)	R. A. Saggers	Australia v South Africa	1949-50
21 (16ct, 5st)	G. R. A. Langley ..	Australia v West Indies	1951-52
21 (20ct, 1st)	A. T. W. Grout....	Australia v England	1961
21 (all ct)	R. W. Marsh......	Australia v Pakistan	1983-84
20 (16ct, 4st)	D. Tallon........	Australia v England	1946-47
20 (16ct, 4st)	G. R. A. Langley ..	Australia v West Indies (4 Tests)	1954-55
20 (18ct, 2st)	T. G. Evans	England v South Africa	1956-57
20 (17ct, 3st)	A. T. W. Grout....	Australia v England	1958-59
20 (19ct, 1st)	H. B. Taber......	Australia v South Africa	1966-67
20 (18ct, 2st)	R. W. Taylor.....	England v Australia (6 Tests)	1978-79
20 (19ct, 1st)	P. J. L. Dujon.....	West Indies v Australia	1983-84
20 (19ct, 1st)	P. R. Downton	England v Australia (6 Tests)	1985
20 (all ct)	P. J. L. Dujon	West Indies v England	1988

Most Dismissals in a Career

	T	Ct	St	Total
1 R. W. Marsh (Australia).................	96	343	12	355
2 P. J. L. Dujon (West Indies)..............	81	267	5	272
3 A. P. E. Knott (England)	95	250	19	269
4 Wasim Bari (Pakistan)..................	81	201	27	228
5 T. G. Evans (England)..................	91	173	46	219

		T	Ct	St	Total
6	S. M. H. Kirmani (India)	88	160	38	198
7	D. L. Murray (West Indies)	62	181	8	189
8	A. T. W. Grout (Australia)	51	163	24	187
9	I. D. S. Smith (New Zealand)	63	168	8	176
10	R. W. Taylor (England)	57	167	7	174
11	J. H. B. Waite (South Africa)	50	124	17	141
12	W. A. Oldfield (Australia)	54	78	52	130
13	J. M. Parks (England)	46	103	11	114
14	I. A. Healy (Australia)	36	108	2	110
15	Salim Yousuf (Pakistan)	32	91	13	104

Notes: The records for P. J. L. Dujon and J. M. Parks each include two catches taken when not keeping wicket in two and three Tests respectively.

S. A. R. Silva (33ct, 1st) has made most dismissals for Sri Lanka.

Bold type denotes those who played Test cricket in 1991-92 and 1992 seasons.

FIELDING RECORDS

(Excluding wicket-keepers)

Most Catches in an Innings

5	V. Y. Richardson	Australia v South Africa at Durban	1935-36
5	Yajurvindra Singh	India v England at Bangalore	1976-77
5	M. Azharuddin	India v Pakistan at Karachi	1989-90
5	K. Srikkanth	India v Australia at Perth	1991-92

Most Catches in a Test

7	G. S. Chappell	Australia v England at Perth	1974-75
7	Yajurvindra Singh	India v England at Bangalore	1976-77
6	A. Shrewsbury	England v Australia at Sydney	1887-88
6	A. E. E. Vogler	South Africa v England at Durban	1909-10
6	F. E. Woolley	England v Australia at Sydney	1911-12
6	J. M. Gregory	Australia v England at Sydney	1920-21
6	B. Mitchell	South Africa v Australia at Melbourne	1931-32
6	V. Y. Richardson	Australia v South Africa at Durban	1935-36
6	R. N. Harvey	Australia v England at Sydney	1962-63
6	M. C. Cowdrey	England v West Indies at Lord's	1963
6	E. D. Solkar	India v West Indies at Port-of-Spain	1970-71
6	G. S. Sobers	West Indies v England at Lord's	1973
6	I. M. Chappell	Australia v New Zealand at Adelaide	1973-74
6	A. W. Greig	England v Pakistan at Leeds	1974
6	D. F. Whatmore	Australia v India at Kanpur	1979-80
6	A. J. Lamb	England v New Zealand at Lord's	1983
6	R. B. Richardson	West Indies v South Africa at Bridgetown	1991-92
6	G. A. Hick	England v Pakistan at Leeds	1982

Most Catches in a Series

15	J. M. Gregory	Australia v England	1920-21
14	G. S. Chappell	Australia v England (6 Tests)	1974-75
13	R. B. Simpson	Australia v South Africa	1957-58
13	R. B. Simpson	Australia v West Indies	1960-61

Most Catches in a Career

A. R. Border (Australia)	**135 in 130 matches**
G. S. Chappell (Australia)	122 in 87 matches
I. V. A. Richards (West Indies)	122 in 121 matches
I. T. Botham (England)	**120 in 102 matches**
M. C. Cowdrey (England)	120 in 114 matches
R. B. Simpson (Australia)	110 in 62 matches
W. R. Hammond (England)	110 in 85 matches
G. S. Sobers (West Indies)	109 in 93 matches
S. M. Gavaskar (India)	108 in 125 matches
I. M. Chappell (Australia)	105 in 75 matches

Bold type denotes those who played Test cricket in 1991-92 and 1992 seasons.

TEAM RECORDS

HIGHEST INNINGS TOTALS

903-7 dec.	England v Australia at The Oval	1938
849	England v West Indies at Kingston	1929-30
790-3 dec.	West Indies v Pakistan at Kingston	1957-58
758-8 dec.	Australia v West Indies at Kingston	1954-55
729-6 dec.	Australia v England at Lord's	1930
708	Pakistan v England at The Oval	1987
701	Australia v England at The Oval	1934
699-5	Pakistan v India at Lahore	1989-90
695	Australia v England at The Oval	1930
687-8 dec.	West Indies v England at The Oval	1976
681-8 dec.	West Indies v England at Port-of-Spain	1953-54
676-7	India v Sri Lanka at Kanpur	1986-87
674-6	Pakistan v India at Faisalabad	1984-85
674	Australia v India at Adelaide	1947-48
671-4	New Zealand v Sri Lanka at Wellington	1990-91
668	Australia v West Indies at Bridgetown	1954-55
659-8 dec.	Australia v England at Sydney	1946-47
658-8 dec.	England v Australia at Nottingham	1938
657-8 dec.	Pakistan v West Indies at Bridgetown	1957-58
656-8 dec.	Australia v England at Manchester	1964
654-5	England v South Africa at Durban	1938-39
653-4 dec.	England v India at Lord's	1990
652-7 dec.	England v India at Madras	1984-85
652-8 dec.	West Indies v England at Lord's	1973
652	Pakistan v India at Faisalabad	1982-83
650-6 dec.	Australia v West Indies at Bridgetown	1964-65

The highest innings for the countries not mentioned above are:

522-9 dec.	South Africa v Australia at Durban	1969-70
497	Sri Lanka v New Zealand at Wellington	1990-91

HIGHEST FOURTH-INNINGS TOTALS

To win

406-4	India (needing 403) v West Indies at Port-of-Spain	1975-76
404-3	Australia (needing 404) v England at Leeds	1948
362-7	Australia (needing 359) v West Indies at Georgetown	1977-78
348-5	West Indies (needing 345) v New Zealand at Auckland	1968-69
344-1	West Indies (needing 342) v England at Lord's	1984

To tie

347   India v Australia at Madras.................................... 1986-87

To draw

654-5   England (needing 696 to win) v South Africa at Durban............. 1938-39
429-8   India (needing 438 to win) v England at The Oval.................. 1979
423-7   South Africa (needing 451 to win) v England at The Oval.......... 1947
408-5   West Indies (needing 836 to win) v England at Kingston 1929-30

To lose

445   India (lost by 47 runs) v Australia at Adelaide 1977-78
440   New Zealand (lost by 38 runs) v England at Nottingham............... 1973
417   England (lost by 45 runs) v Australia at Melbourne 1976-77
411   England (lost by 193 runs) v Australia at Sydney..................... 1924-25

MOST RUNS IN A DAY (BOTH SIDES)

588   England (398-6), India (190-0) at Manchester (2nd day) 1936
522   England (503-2), South Africa (19-0) at Lord's (2nd day) 1924
508   England (221-2), South Africa (287-6) at The Oval (3rd day) 1935

MOST RUNS IN A DAY (ONE SIDE)

503   England (503-2) v South Africa at Lord's (2nd day) 1924
494   Australia (494-6) v South Africa at Sydney (1st day)................. 1910-11
475   Australia (475-2) v England at The Oval (1st day).................... 1934
471   England (471-8) v India at The Oval (1st day)....................... 1936
458   Australia (458-3) v England at Leeds (1st day)...................... 1930
455   Australia (455-1) v England at Leeds (2nd day) 1934

MOST WICKETS IN A DAY

27   England (18-3 to 53 out and 62) v Australia (60) at Lord's (2nd day) 1888
25   Australia (112 and 48-5) v England (61) at Melbourne (1st day) 1901-02

HIGHEST MATCH AGGREGATES

Runs	Wkts			Days played
1,981	35	South Africa v England at Durban..................	1938-39	10†
1,815	34	West Indies v England at Kingston	1929-30	9‡
1,764	39	Australia v West Indies at Adelaide	1968-69	5
1,753	40	Australia v England at Adelaide	1920-21	6

Runs	Wkts			Days played
4,723	31	England v Australia at Leeds	1948	5
4,661	36	West Indies v Australia at Bridgetown..............	1954-55	6

† *No play on one day.*   ‡ *No play on two days.*

LOWEST INNINGS TOTALS

26	New Zealand v England at Auckland.............................	1954-55
30	South Africa v England at Port Elizabeth	1895-96
30	South Africa v England at Birmingham.........................	1924
35	South Africa v England at Cape Town..........................	1898-99
36	Australia v England at Birmingham............................	1902
36	South Africa v Australia at Melbourne.........................	1931-32
42	Australia v England at Sydney................................	1887-88
42	New Zealand v Australia at Wellington	1945-46
42†	India v England at Lord's	1974
43	South Africa v England at Cape Town..........................	1888-89
44	Australia v England at The Oval..............................	1896
45	England v Australia at Sydney................................	1886-87
45	South Africa v Australia at Melbourne.........................	1931-32
47	South Africa v England at Cape Town..........................	1888-89
47	New Zealand v England at Lord's	1958

The lowest innings for the countries not mentioned above are:

53	West Indies v Pakistan at Faisalabad	1986-87
62	Pakistan v Australia at Perth................................	1981-82
82	Sri Lanka v India at Chandigarh	1990-91

† *Batted one man short.*

FEWEST RUNS IN A FULL DAY'S PLAY

95 At Karachi, October 11, 1956. Australia 80 all out; Pakistan 15 for two (first day, $5\frac{1}{2}$ hours).

104 At Karachi, December 8, 1959. Pakistan 0 for no wicket to 104 for five v Australia (fourth day, $5\frac{1}{2}$ hours).

106 At Brisbane, December 9, 1958. England 92 for two to 198 all out v Australia (fourth day, 5 hours). *England were dismissed five minutes before the close of play, leaving no time for Australia to start their second innings.*

112 At Karachi, October 15, 1956. Australia 138 for six to 187 all out; Pakistan 63 for one (fourth day, $5\frac{1}{2}$ hours).

115 At Karachi, September 19, 1988. Australia 116 for seven to 165 all out and 66 for five following on v Pakistan (fourth day, $5\frac{1}{2}$ hours).

117 At Madras, October 19, 1956. India 117 for five v Australia (first day, $5\frac{1}{2}$ hours).

117 At Colombo (SSC), March 21, 1984. New Zealand 6 for no wicket to 123 for four (fifth day, 5 hours, 47 minutes).

In England

251 At Lord's, August 26, 1978. England 175 for two to 289 all out; New Zealand 37 for seven (third day, 6 hours).

259 At Leeds, July 10, 1971. Pakistan 208 for four to 350 all out; England 17 for one (third day, 6 hours).

LOWEST MATCH AGGREGATES

(For a completed match)

Runs	Wkts			Days played
234	29	Australia v South Africa at Melbourne...............	1931-32	3†
291	40	England v Australia at Lord's	1888	2
295	28	New Zealand v Australia at Wellington	1945-46	2

					Days played
Runs	Wkts				
309	29	West Indies v England at Bridgetown	1934-35	3
323	30	England v Australia at Manchester..................	1888	2

† *No play on one day.*

YOUNGEST TEST PLAYERS

Years	Days			
15	124	Mushtaq Mohammad	Pakistan v West Indies at Lahore	1958-59
16	189	Aqib Javed	Pakistan v New Zealand at Wellington	1988-89
16	205	S. R. Tendulkar	India v Pakistan at Karachi	1989-90
16	221	Aftab Baloch	Pakistan v New Zealand at Dacca ...	1969-70
16	248	Nasim-ul-Ghani	Pakistan v West Indies at Bridgetown .	1957-58
16	352	Khalid Hassan	Pakistan v England at Nottingham ...	1954
17	5	Zahid Fazal.............	Pakistan v West Indies at Karachi....	1990-91
17	69	Ata-ur-Rehman	Pakistan v England at Birmingham ...	1992
17	118	L. Sivaramakrishnan	India v West Indies at St John's......	1982-83
17	122	J. E. D. Sealy	West Indies v England at Bridgetown .	1929-30
17	189	C. D. U. S. Weerasinghe..	Sri Lanka v India at Colombo (PSS) ..	1985-86
17	193	Maninder Singh	India v Pakistan at Karachi	1982-83
17	239	I. D. Craig	Australia v South Africa at Melbourne.	1952-53
17	245	G. S. Sobers	West Indies v England at Kingston ...	1953-54
17	265	V. L. Mehra	India v New Zealand at Bombay	1955-56
17	300	Hanif Mohammad	Pakistan v India at Delhi	1952-53
17	341	Intikhab Alam	Pakistan v Australia at Karachi	1959-60
17	364	Waqar Younis...........	Pakistan v India at Karachi	1989-90

Note: The youngest Test players for countries not mentioned above are: England – D. B. Close, 18 years 149 days, v New Zealand at Manchester, 1949; New Zealand – D. L. Freeman, 18 years 197 days, v England at Christchurch, 1932-33; South Africa – A. E. Ochse, 19 years 1 day, v England at Port Elizabeth, 1888-89.

OLDEST PLAYERS ON TEST DEBUT

Years	Days			
49	119	J. Southerton......	England v Australia at Melbourne	1876-77
47	284	Miran Bux.......	Pakistan v India at Lahore	1954-55
46	253	D. D. Blackie	Australia v England at Sydney	1928-29
46	237	H. Ironmonger ...	Australia v England at Brisbane	1928-29
42	242	N. Betancourt	West Indies v England at Port-of-Spain .	1929-30
41	337	E. R. Wilson.....	England v Australia at Sydney	1920-21
41	27	R. J. D. Jamshedji	India v England at Bombay...........	1933-34
40	345	C. A. Wiles......	West Indies v England at Manchester ..	1933
40	216	S. P. Kinneir	England v Australia at Sydney	1911-12
40	110	H. W. Lee	England v South Africa at Johannesburg .	1930-31
40	56	G. W. A. Chubb .	South Africa v England at Nottingham .	1951
40	37	C. Ramaswami ...	India v England at Manchester........	1936

Note: The oldest Test player on début for New Zealand was H. M. McGirr, 38 years 101 days, v England at Auckland, 1929-30; for Sri Lanka, D. S. de Silva, 39 years 251 days, v England at Colombo (PSS), 1981-82.

OLDEST TEST PLAYERS

(Age on final day of their last Test match)

Years	Days			
52	165	W. Rhodes..........	England v West Indies at Kingston ...	1929-30
50	327	H. Ironmonger	Australia v England at Sydney	1932-33
50	320	W. G. Grace	England v Australia at Nottingham ...	1899
50	303	G. Gunn	England v West Indies at Kingston ...	1929-30
49	139	J. Southerton	England v Australia at Melbourne	1876-77
47	302	Miran Bux	Pakistan v India at Peshawar	1954-55
47	249	J. B. Hobbs	England v Australia at The Oval	1930
47	87	F. E. Woolley	England v Australia at The Oval	1934
46	309	D. D. Blackie	Australia v England at Adelaide	1928-29
46	206	A. W. Nourse	South Africa v England at The Oval ..	1924
46	202	H. Strudwick	England v Australia at The Oval	1926
46	41	E. H. Hendren	England v West Indies at Kingston ...	1934-35
45	245	G. O. B. Allen	England v West Indies at Kingston ...	1947-48
45	215	P. Holmes	England v India at Lord's	1932
45	140	D. B. Close	England v West Indies at Manchester .	1976

MOST APPEARANCES FOR EACH COUNTRY

For	Total		E	A	SA	WI	NZ	I	P	SL
England	117	D. I. Gower	—	42	0	19	13	24	17	2
Australia	130	A. R. Border	41	—	0	26	17	20	22	4
South Africa	50	J. H. B. Waite	21	14	—	0	15	0	0	0
West Indies	121	I. V. A. Richards	36	34	0	—	7	28	16	0
New Zealand	86	R. J. Hadlee	21	23	0	10	—	14	12	6
India	125	S. M. Gavaskar	38	20	0	27	9	—	24	7
Pakistan	117	Javed Miandad	22	25	0	13	17	28	—	12
Sri Lanka	33	A. Ranatunga	3	4	0	0	7	8	11	—

MOST CONSECUTIVE TEST APPEARANCES

127*	A. R. Border (Australia)	March 1979 to February 1992
106	S. M. Gavaskar (India)	January 1975 to February 1987
87	G. R. Viswanath (India)	March 1971 to February 1983
85	G. S. Sobers (West Indies)......	April 1955 to April 1972
72	D. L. Haynes (West Indies)	December 1979 to June 1988
71	I. M. Chappell (Australia)	January 1966 to February 1976
66	Kapil Dev (India)..............	October 1978 to December 1984
65	I. T. Botham (England)	February 1978 to March 1984
65	A. P. E. Knott (England).......	March 1971 to August 1977

* Sequence still in progress.

The most consecutive Test appearances for the countries not mentioned above are:

58†	J. R. Reid (New Zealand)	July 1949 to July 1965
53	Javed Miandad (Pakistan)	December 1977 to January 1984
45†	A. W. Nourse (South Africa)....	October 1902 to August 1924
22	A. Ranatunga (Sri Lanka)	April 1983 to December 1989

† *Indicates complete Test career.*

SUMMARY OF ALL TEST MATCHES

		Tests	E	A	SA	WI	NZ	I	P	SL	Tied	Drawn
						Won by						
England	v Australia	274	88	104	–	–	–	–	–	–	–	82
	v South Africa	102	46	–	18	–	–	–	–	–	–	38
	v West Indies	104	24	–	–	43	–	–	–	–	–	37
	v New Zealand	72	33	–	–	–	4	–	–	–	–	35
	v India	78	31	–	–	–	–	11	–	–	–	36
	v Pakistan	52	14	–	–	–	–	–	7	–	–	31
	v Sri Lanka	4	3	–	–	–	–	–	–	0	–	1
Australia	v South Africa	53	–	29	11	–	–	–	–	–	–	13
	v West Indies	72	–	29	–	24	–	–	–	–	1	18
	v New Zealand	26	–	10	–	–	6	–	–	–	–	10
	v India	50	–	24	–	–	–	8	–	–	1	17
	v Pakistan	34	–	12	–	–	–	–	9	–	–	13
	v Sri Lanka	4	–	3	–	–	–	–	–	0	–	1
South Africa	v West Indies	1	–	–	0	1	–	–	–	–	–	–
	v New Zealand	17	–	–	9	–	2	–	–	–	–	6
West Indies	v New Zealand	24	–	–	–	8	4	–	–	–	–	12
	v India	62	–	–	–	26	–	6	–	–	–	30
	v Pakistan	28	–	–	–	10	–	–	7	–	–	11
New Zealand	v India	31	–	–	–	–	6	12	–	–	–	13
	v Pakistan	32	–	–	–	–	3	–	13	–	–	16
	v Sri Lanka	9	–	–	–	–	4	–	–	0	–	5
India	v Pakistan	44	–	–	–	–	–	4	7	–	–	33
	v Sri Lanka	8	–	–	–	–	–	3	–	1	–	4
Pakistan	v Sri Lanka	12	–	–	–	–	–	–	6	1	–	5
		1,193	239	211	38	112	29	44	49	2	2	467

	Tests	Won	Lost	Drawn	Tied	Toss Won
England	686	239	187	260	–	339
Australia	513	211	146	154	2	259
South Africa	173	38	78	57	–	81
West Indies	291	112	70	108	1	151
New Zealand	211	29	85	97	–	105
India	273	44	95	133	1	136
Pakistan	202	49	44	109	–	103
Sri Lanka	37	2	19	16	–	19

ENGLAND v AUSTRALIA

Season	England	Captains	Australia	T	E	A	D	
1876-77	James Lillywhite		D. W. Gregory	2	1	1	0	
1878-79	Lord Harris		D. W. Gregory	1	0	1	0	
1880	Lord Harris		W. L. Murdoch	1	1	0	0	
1881-82	A. Shaw		W. L. Murdoch	4	0	2	2	
1882	A. N. Hornby		W. L. Murdoch	1	0	1	0	

THE ASHES

Season	England	Captains	Australia	T	E	A	D	Held by
1882-83	Hon. Ivo Bligh		W. L. Murdoch	4*	2	2	0	E
1884	Lord Harris[1]		W. L. Murdoch	3	1	0	2	E

Captains

Season	England	Australia	T	E	A	D	Held by
1884-85	A. Shrewsbury	T. P. Horan[2]	5	3	2	0	E
1886	A. G. Steel	H. J. H. Scott	3	3	0	0	E
1886-87	A. Shrewsbury	P. S. McDonnell	2	2	0	0	E
1887-88	W. W. Read	P. S. McDonnell	1	1	0	0	E
1888	W. G. Grace[3]	P. S. McDonnell	3	2	1	0	E
1890†	W. G. Grace	W. L. Murdoch	2	2	0	0	E
1891-92	W. G. Grace	J. McC. Blackham	3	1	2	0	A
1893	W. G. Grace[4]	J. McC. Blackham	3	1	0	2	E
1894-95	A. E. Stoddart	G. Giffen[5]	5	3	2	0	E
1896	W. G. Grace	G. H. S. Trott	3	2	1	0	E
1897-98	A. E. Stoddart[6]	G. H. S. Trott	5	1	4	0	A
1899	A. C. MacLaren[7]	J. Darling	5	0	1	4	A
1901-02	A. C. MacLaren	J. Darling[8]	5	1	4	0	A
1902	A. C. MacLaren	J. Darling	5	1	2	2	A
1903-04	P. F. Warner	M. A. Noble	5	3	2	0	E
1905	Hon. F. S. Jackson	J. Darling	5	2	0	3	E
1907-08	A. O. Jones[9]	M. A. Noble	5	1	4	0	A
1909	A. C. MacLaren	M. A. Noble	5	1	2	2	A
1911-12	J. W. H. T. Douglas	C. Hill	5	4	1	0	E
1912	C. B. Fry	S. E. Gregory	3	1	0	2	E
1920-21	J. W. H. T. Douglas	W. W. Armstrong	5	0	5	0	A
1921	Hon. L. H. Tennyson[10]	W. W. Armstrong	5	0	3	2	A
1924-25	A. E. R. Gilligan	H. L. Collins	5	1	4	0	A
1926	A. W. Carr[11]	H. L. Collins[12]	5	1	0	4	E
1928-29	A. P. F. Chapman[13]	J. Ryder	5	4	1	0	E
1930	A. P. F. Chapman[14]	W. M. Woodfull	5	1	2	2	A
1932-33	D. R. Jardine	W. M. Woodfull	5	4	1	0	E
1934	R. E. S. Wyatt[15]	W. M. Woodfull	5	1	2	2	A
1936-37	G. O. B. Allen	D. G. Bradman	5	2	3	0	A
1938†	W. R. Hammond	D. G. Bradman	4	1	1	2	A
1946-47	W. R. Hammond[16]	D. G. Bradman	5	0	3	2	A
1948	N. W. D. Yardley	D. G. Bradman	5	0	4	1	A
1950-51	F. R. Brown	A. L. Hassett	5	1	4	0	A
1953	L. Hutton	A. L. Hassett	5	1	0	4	E
1954-55	L. Hutton	I. W. Johnson[17]	5	3	1	1	E
1956	P. B. H. May	I. W. Johnson	5	2	1	2	E
1958-59	P. B. H. May	R. Benaud	5	0	4	1	A
1961	P. B. H. May[18]	R. Benaud[19]	5	1	2	2	A
1962-63	E. R. Dexter	R. Benaud	5	1	1	3	A
1964	E. R. Dexter	R. B. Simpson	5	0	1	4	A
1965-66	M. J. K. Smith	R. B. Simpson[20]	5	1	1	3	A
1968	M. C. Cowdrey[21]	W. M. Lawry[22]	5	1	1	3	A
1970-71†	R. Illingworth	W. M. Lawry[23]	6	2	0	4	E
1972	R. Illingworth	I. M. Chappell	5	2	2	1	E
1974-75	M. H. Denness[24]	I. M. Chappell	6	1	4	1	A
1975	A. W. Greig[25]	I. M. Chappell	4	0	1	3	A
1976-77‡	A. W. Greig	G. S. Chappell	1	0	1	0	—
1977	J. M. Brearley	G. S. Chappell	5	3	0	2	E
1978-79	J. M. Brearley	G. N. Yallop	6	5	1	0	E
1979-80‡	J. M. Brearley	G. S. Chappell	3	0	3	0	—
1980‡	I. T. Botham	G. S. Chappell	1	0	0	1	—
1981	J. M. Brearley[26]	K. J. Hughes	6	3	1	2	E
1982-83	R. G. D. Willis	G. S. Chappell	5	1	2	2	A
1985	D. I. Gower	A. R. Border	6	3	1	2	E
1986-87	M. W. Gatting	A. R. Border	5	2	1	2	E
1987-88‡	M. W. Gatting	A. R. Border	1	0	0	1	—
1989	D. I. Gower	A. R. Border	6	0	4	2	A
1990-91	G. A. Gooch[27]	A. R. Border	5	0	3	2	A
	In Australia		145	51	70	24	
	In England		129	37	34	58	
	Totals		274	88	104	82	

* *The Ashes were awarded in 1882-83 after a series of three matches which England won 2-1. A fourth unofficial match was played, each innings being played on a different pitch, and this was won by Australia.*

† *The matches at Manchester in 1890 and 1938 and at Melbourne (Third Test) in 1970-71 were abandoned without a ball being bowled and are excluded.*

‡ *The Ashes were not at stake in these series.*

Notes: The following deputised for the official touring captain or were appointed by the home authority for only a minor proportion of the series:

[1]A. N. Hornby (First). [2]W. L. Murdoch (First), H. H. Massie (Third), J. McC. Blackham (Fourth). [3]A. G. Steel (First). [4]A. E. Stoddart (First). [5]J. McC. Blackham (First). [6]A. C. MacLaren (First, Second and Fifth). [7]W. G. Grace (First). [8]H. Trumble (Fourth and Fifth). [9]F. L. Fane (First, Second and Third). [10]J. W. H. T. Douglas (First and Second). [11]A. P. F. Chapman (Fifth). [12]W. Bardsley (Third and Fourth). [13]J. C. White (Fifth). [14]R. E. S. Wyatt (Fifth). [15]C. F. Walters (First). [16]N. W. D. Yardley (Fifth). [17]A. R. Morris (Second). [18]M. C. Cowdrey (First and Second). [19]R. N. Harvey (Second). [20]B. C. Booth (First and Third). [21]T. W. Graveney (Fourth). [22]B. N. Jarman (Fourth). [23]I. M. Chappell (Seventh). [24]J. H. Edrich (Fourth). [25]M. H. Denness (First). [26]I. T. Botham (First and Second). [27]A. J. Lamb (First).

HIGHEST INNINGS TOTALS

For England in England: 903-7 dec. at The Oval	1938
in Australia: 636 at Sydney	1928-29
For Australia in England: 729-6 dec. at Lord's	1930
in Australia: 659-8 dec. at Sydney	1946-47

LOWEST INNINGS TOTALS

For England in England: 52 at The Oval	1948
in Australia: 45 at Sydney	1886-87
For Australia in England: 36 at Birmingham	1902
in Australia: 42 at Sydney	1887-88

INDIVIDUAL HUNDREDS

For England (196)

R. Abel (1)
132*‡ Sydney 1891-92

L. E. G. Ames (1)
120 Lord's 1934

M. A. Atherton (1)
105 Sydney 1990-91

R. W. Barber (1)
185 Sydney 1965-66

W. Barnes (1)
134 Adelaide 1884-85

C. J. Barnett (2)
129 Adelaide 1936-37
126 Nottingham . 1938

K. F. Barrington (5)
132* Adelaide 1962-63
101 Sydney 1962-63
256 Manchester.. 1964

102 Adelaide 1965-66
115 Melbourne .. 1965-66

I. T. Botham (4)
119* Melbourne .. 1979-80
149* Leeds 1981
118 Manchester.. 1981
138 Brisbane 1986-87

G. Boycott (7)
113 The Oval.... 1964
142* Sydney 1970-71
119* Adelaide 1970-71
107 Nottingham . 1977
191 Leeds 1977
128* Lord's 1980
137 The Oval.... 1981

L. C. Braund (2)
103* Adelaide 1901-02
102 Sydney 1903-04

J. Briggs (1)
121 Melbourne .. 1884-85

B. C. Broad (4)
162 Perth....... 1986-87
116 Adelaide 1986-87
112 Melbourne .. 1986-87
139 Sydney 1987-88

J. T. Brown (1)
140 Melbourne .. 1894-95

A. P. F. Chapman (1)
121 Lord's 1930

D. C. S. Compton (5)
102† Nottingham . 1938
147 ⎫
103* ⎬ Adelaide 1946-47
184 Nottingham . 1948
145* Manchester.. 1948

M. C. Cowdrey (5)
102	Melbourne	1954-55
100*	Sydney	1958-59
113	Melbourne	1962-63
104	Melbourne	1965-66
104	Birmingham	1968

M. H. Denness (1)
188	Melbourne	1974-75

E. R. Dexter (2)
180	Birmingham	1961
174	Manchester	1964

B. L. D'Oliveira (2)
158	The Oval	1968
117	Melbourne	1970-71

K. S. Duleepsinhji (1)
173†	Lord's	1930

J. H. Edrich (7)
120†	Lord's	1964
109	Melbourne	1965-66
103	Sydney	1965-66
164	The Oval	1968
115*	Perth	1970-71
130	Adelaide	1970-71
175	Lord's	1975

W. J. Edrich (2)
119	Sydney	1946-47
111	Leeds	1948

K. W. R. Fletcher (1)
146	Melbourne	1974-75

R. E. Foster (1)
287†	Sydney	1903-04

C. B. Fry (1)
144	The Oval	1905

M. W. Gatting (3)
160	Manchester	1985
100*	Birmingham	1985
100	Adelaide	1986-87

G. A. Gooch (2)
196	The Oval	1985
117	Adelaide	1990-91

D. I. Gower (9)
102	Perth	1978-79
114	Adelaide	1982-83
166	Nottingham	1985
215	Birmingham	1985
157	The Oval	1985
136	Perth	1986-87
106	Lord's	1989
100	Melbourne	1990-91
123	Sydney	1990-91

W. G. Grace (2)
152†	The Oval	1880
170	The Oval	1886

T. W. Graveney (1)
111	Sydney	1954-55

A. W. Greig (1)
110	Brisbane	1974-75

G. Gunn (2)
119†	Sydney	1907-08
122*	Sydney	1907-08

W. Gunn (1)
102*	Manchester	1893

W. R. Hammond (9)
251	Sydney	1928-29
200	Melbourne	1928-29
119* 177 }	Adelaide	1928-29
113	Leeds	1930
112	Sydney	1932-33
101	Sydney	1932-33
231*	Sydney	1936-37
240	Lord's	1938

J. Hardstaff jun. (1)
169*	The Oval	1938

T. W. Hayward (2)
130	Manchester	1899
137	The Oval	1899

J. W. Hearne (1)
114	Melbourne	1911-12

E. H. Hendren (3)
127*	Lord's	1926
169	Brisbane	1928-29
132	Manchester	1934

J. B. Hobbs (12)
126*	Melbourne	1911-12
187	Adelaide	1911-12
178	Melbourne	1911-12
107	Lord's	1912
122	Melbourne	1920-21
123	Adelaide	1920-21
115	Sydney	1924-25
154	Melbourne	1924-25
119	Adelaide	1924-25
119	Lord's	1926
100	The Oval	1926
142	Melbourne	1928-29

K. L. Hutchings (1)
126	Melbourne	1907-08

L. Hutton (5)
100†	Nottingham	1938
364	The Oval	1938
122*	Sydney	1946-47
156*‡	Adelaide	1950-51
145	Lord's	1953

Hon. F. S. Jackson (5)
103	The Oval	1893
118	The Oval	1899
128	Manchester	1902
144*	Leeds	1905
113	Manchester	1905

G. L. Jessop (1)
104	The Oval	1902

A. P. E. Knott (2)
106*	Adelaide	1974-75
135	Nottingham	1977

A. J. Lamb (1)
125	Leeds	1989

M. Leyland (7)
137†	Melbourne	1928-29
109	Lord's	1934
153	Manchester	1934
110	The Oval	1934
126	Brisbane	1936-37
111*	Melbourne	1936-37
187	The Oval	1938

B. W. Luckhurst (2)
131	Perth	1970-71
109	Melbourne	1970-71

A. C. MacLaren (5)
120	Melbourne	1894-95
109	Sydney	1897-98
124	Adelaide	1897-98
116	Sydney	1901-02
140	Nottingham	1905

J. W. H. Makepeace (1)
117	Melbourne	1920-21

P. B. H. May (3)
104	Sydney	1954-55
101	Leeds	1956
113	Melbourne	1958-59

C. P. Mead (1)
182*	The Oval	1921

Nawab of Pataudi sen. (1)
102†	Sydney	1932-33

E. Paynter (1)
216*	Nottingham	1938

D. W. Randall (3)
174†	Melbourne	1976-77
150	Sydney	1978-79
115	Perth	1982-83

K. S. Ranjitsinhji (2)
154*†	Manchester	1896
175	Sydney	1897-98

W. W. Read (1)
117	The Oval	1884

W. Rhodes (1)
179	Melbourne	1911-12

C. J. Richards (1)
133	Perth	1986-87

P. E. Richardson (1)
104	Manchester	1956

R. T. Robinson (2)
175†	Leeds	1985
148	Birmingham	1985

A. C. Russell (3)
135*	Adelaide	1920-21
101	Manchester	1921
102*	The Oval	1921

R. C. Russell (1)
128*	Manchester	1989

J. Sharp (1)
105	The Oval	1909

Rev. D. S. Sheppard (2)
113	Manchester	1956
113	Melbourne	1962-63

A. Shrewsbury (3)
105*	Melbourne	1884-85
164	Lord's	1886
106	Lord's	1893

R. T. Simpson (1)
156*	Melbourne	1950-51

R. A. Smith (2)
143	Manchester	1989
101	Nottingham	1989

A. G. Steel (2)
135*	Sydney	1882-83
148	Lord's	1884

A. E. Stoddart (2)
134 Adelaide 1891-92
173 Melbourne .. 1894-95
R. Subba Row (2)
112† Birmingham . 1961
137 The Oval.... 1961
H. Sutcliffe (8)
115† Sydney 1924-25
176 ⎫
127 ⎬ Melbourne .. 1924-25
143 Melbourne .. 1924-25
161 The Oval.... 1926

135 Melbourne .. 1928-29
161 The Oval 1930
194 Sydney 1932-33
J. T. Tyldesley (3)
138 Birmingham . 1902
100 Leeds 1905
112* The Oval.... 1905
G. Ulyett (1)
149 Melbourne .. 1881-82
A. Ward (1)
117 Sydney 1894-95

C. Washbrook (2)
112 Melbourne .. 1946-47
143 Leeds 1948
W. Watson (1)
109† Lord's 1953
F. E. Woolley (2)
133* Sydney 1911-12
123 Sydney 1924-25
R. A. Woolmer (3)
149 The Oval.... 1975
120 Lord's 1977
137 Manchester.. 1977

† *Signifies hundred on first appearance in England–Australia Tests.*
‡ *Carried his bat.*
Note: In consecutive innings in 1928-29, W. R. Hammond scored 251 at Sydney, 200 and 32 at Melbourne, and 119* and 177 at Adelaide.

For Australia (214)

W. W. Armstrong (4)
133* Melbourne .. 1907-08
158 Sydney 1920-21
121 Adelaide 1920-21
123* Melbourne .. 1920-21
C. L. Badcock (1)
118 Melbourne .. 1936-37
C. Bannerman (1)
165*† Melbourne .. 1876-77
W. Bardsley (3)
136 ⎫
130 ⎬ The Oval.... 1909
193*‡ Lord's 1926
S. G. Barnes (2)
234 Sydney 1946-47
141 Lord's 1948
G. J. Bonnor (1)
128 Sydney 1884-85
D. C. Boon (3)
103 Adelaide 1986-87
184* Sydney 1987-88
121 Adelaide 1990-91
B. C. Booth (2)
112 Brisbane 1962-63
103 Melbourne .. 1962-63
A. R. Border (7)
115 Perth 1979-80
123* Manchester.. 1981
106* The Oval.... 1981
196 Lord's 1985
146* Manchester.. 1985
125 Perth 1986-87
100* Adelaide 1986-87
D. G. Bradman (19)
112 Melbourne .. 1928-29
123 Melbourne .. 1928-29
131 Nottingham . 1930
254 Lord's 1930
334 Leeds 1930
232 The Oval.... 1930
103* Melbourne .. 1932-33
304 Leeds 1934
244 The Oval.... 1934

270 Melbourne .. 1936-37
212 Adelaide 1936-37
169 Melbourne .. 1936-37
144* Nottingham . 1938
102* Lord's 1938
103 Leeds 1938
187 Brisbane 1946-47
234 Sydney 1946-47
138 Nottingham . 1948
173* Leeds 1948
W. A. Brown (3)
105 Lord's 1934
133 Nottingham . 1938
206*‡ Lord's 1938
P. J. Burge (4)
181 The Oval.... 1961
103 Sydney 1962-63
160 Leeds 1964
120 Melbourne .. 1965-66
J. W. Burke (1)
101*† Adelaide 1950-51
G. S. Chappell (9)
108† Perth 1970-71
131 Lord's 1972
113 The Oval.... 1972
144 Sydney 1974-75
102 Melbourne .. 1974-75
112 Manchester.. 1977
114 Melbourne .. 1979-80
117 Perth 1982-83
115 Adelaide 1982-83
I. M. Chappell (4)
111 Melbourne .. 1970-71
104 Adelaide 1970-71
118 The Oval.... 1972
192 The Oval.... 1975
H. L. Collins (3)
104† Sydney 1920-21
162 Adelaide 1920-21
114 Sydney 1924-25
R. M. Cowper (1)
307 Melbourne .. 1965-66

J. Darling (3)
101 Sydney 1897-98
178 Adelaide 1897-98
160 Sydney 1897-98
R. A. Duff (2)
104† Melbourne .. 1901-02
146 The Oval.... 1905
J. Dyson (1)
102 Leeds 1981
R. Edwards (2)
170* Nottingham . 1972
115 Perth 1974-75
J. H. Fingleton (2)
100 Brisbane 1936-37
136 Melbourne .. 1936-37
G. Giffen (1)
161 Sydney 1894-95
H. Graham (2)
107† Lord's 1893
105 Sydney 1894-95
J. M. Gregory (1)
100 Melbourne .. 1920-21
S. E. Gregory (4)
201 Sydney 1894-95
103 Lord's 1896
117 The Oval.... 1899
112 Adelaide 1903-04
R. J. Hartigan (1)
116† Adelaide 1907-08
R. N. Harvey (6)
112† Leeds 1948
122 Manchester.. 1953
162 Brisbane 1954-55
167 Melbourne .. 1958-59
114 Birmingham . 1961
154 Adelaide 1962-63
A. L. Hassett (4)
128 Brisbane 1946-47
137 Nottingham . 1948
115 Nottingham . 1953
104 Lord's 1953

H. S. T. L. Hendry (1)

112	Sydney	1928-29

A. M. J. Hilditch (1)

119	Leeds	1985

C. Hill (4)

188	Melbourne	1897-98
135	Lord's	1899
119	Sheffield	1902
160	Adelaide	1907-08

T. P. Horan (1)

124	Melbourne	1881-82

K. J. Hughes (3)

129	Brisbane	1978-79
117	Lord's	1980
137	Sydney	1982-83

F. A. Iredale (2)

140	Adelaide	1894-95
108	Manchester	1896

A. A. Jackson (1)

164†	Adelaide	1928-29

D. M. Jones (3)

184*	Sydney	1986-87
157	Birmingham	1989
122	The Oval	1989

C. Kelleway (1)

147	Adelaide	1920-21

A. F. Kippax (1)

100	Melbourne	1928-29

W. M. Lawry (7)

130	Lord's	1961
102	Manchester	1961
106	Manchester	1964
166	Brisbane	1965-66
119	Adelaide	1965-66
108	Melbourne	1965-66
135	The Oval	1968

R. R. Lindwall (1)

100	Melbourne	1946-47

J. J. Lyons (1)

134	Sydney	1891-92

C. G. Macartney (5)

170	Sydney	1920-21
115	Leeds	1921
133*	Lord's	1926
151	Leeds	1926
109	Manchester	1926

S. J. McCabe (4)

187*	Sydney	1932-33
137	Manchester	1934
112	Melbourne	1936-37
232	Nottingham	1938

C. L. McCool (1)

104*	Melbourne	1946-47

R. B. McCosker (2)

127	The Oval	1975
107	Nottingham	1977

C. C. McDonald (2)

170	Adelaide	1958-59
133	Melbourne	1958-59

P. S. McDonnell (3)

147	Sydney	1881-82
103	The Oval	1884
124	Adelaide	1884-85

C. E. McLeod (1)

112	Melbourne	1897-98

G. R. Marsh (2)

110†	Brisbane	1986-87
138	Nottingham	1989

R. W. Marsh (1)

110*	Melbourne	1976-77

G. R. J. Matthews (1)

128	Sydney	1990-91

K. R. Miller (3)

141*	Adelaide	1946-47
145*	Sydney	1950-51
109	Lord's	1953

A. R. Morris (8)

155	Melbourne	1946-47
122	Adelaide	1946-47
124*	Adelaide	1946-47
105	Lord's	1948
182	Leeds	1948
196	The Oval	1948
206	Adelaide	1950-51
153	Brisbane	1954-55

W. L. Murdoch (2)

153*	The Oval	1880
211	The Oval	1884

M. A. Noble (1)

133	Sydney	1903-04

N. C. O'Neill (2)

117	The Oval	1961
100	Adelaide	1962-63

C. E. Pellew (2)

116	Melbourne	1920-21
104	Adelaide	1920-21

W. H. Ponsford (5)

110†	Sydney	1924-25
128	Melbourne	1924-25
110	The Oval	1930
181	Leeds	1934
266	The Oval	1934

V. S. Ransford (1)

143*	Lord's	1909

I. R. Redpath (2)

171	Perth	1970-71
105	Sydney	1974-75

A. J. Richardson (1)

100	Leeds	1926

V. Y. Richardson (1)

138	Melbourne	1924-25

G. M. Ritchie (1)

146	Nottingham	1985

J. Ryder (2)

201*	Adelaide	1924-25
112	Melbourne	1928-29

H. J. H. Scott (1)

102	The Oval	1884

R. B. Simpson (2)

311	Manchester	1964
225	Adelaide	1965-66

K. R. Stackpole (3)

207	Brisbane	1970-71
136	Adelaide	1970-71
114	Nottingham	1972

J. M. Taylor (1)

108	Sydney	1924-25

M. A. Taylor (2)

136†	Leeds	1989
219	Nottingham	1989

G. H. S. Trott (1)

143	Lord's	1896

V. T. Trumper (6)

135*	Lord's	1899
104	Manchester	1902
185*	Sydney	1903-04
113	Adelaide	1903-04
166	Sydney	1907-08
113	Sydney	1911-12

K. D. Walters (4)

155†	Brisbane	1965-66
115	Melbourne	1965-66
112	Brisbane	1970-71
103	Perth	1974-75

M. E. Waugh (1)

138†	Adelaide	1990-91

S. R. Waugh (2)

177*	Leeds	1989
152*	Lord's	1989

D. M. Wellham (1)

103†	The Oval	1981

K. C. Wessels (1)

162†	Brisbane	1982-83

G. M. Wood (3)

100	Melbourne	1978-79
112	Lord's	1980
172	Nottingham	1985

W. M. Woodfull (6)

141	Leeds	1926
117	Manchester	1926
111	Sydney	1928-29
107	Melbourne	1928-29
102	Melbourne	1928-29
155	Lord's	1930

G. N. Yallop (3)

102†	Brisbane	1978-79
121	Sydney	1978-79
114	Manchester	1981

† *Signifies hundred on first appearance in England–Australia Tests.*
‡ *Carried his bat.*

Notes: D. G. Bradman's scores in 1930 were 8 and 131 at Nottingham, 254 and 1 at Lord's, 334 at Leeds, 14 at Manchester, and 232 at The Oval.

D. G. Bradman scored a hundred in eight successive Tests against England in which he batted – three in 1936-37, three in 1938 and two in 1946-47. He was injured and unable to bat at The Oval in 1938.

W. H. Ponsford and K. D. Walters each hit hundreds in their first two Tests.

C. Bannerman and H. Graham each scored their maiden hundred in first-class cricket in their first Test.

No right-handed batsman has obtained two hundreds for Australia in a Test match against England, and no left-handed batsman for England against Australia.

H. Sutcliffe, in his first two games for England, scored 59 and 115 at Sydney and 176 and 127 at Melbourne in 1924-25. In the latter match, which lasted into the seventh day, he was on the field throughout except for 86 minutes, namely 27 hours and 52 minutes.

C. Hill made 98 and 97 at Adelaide in 1901-02, and F. E. Woolley 95 and 93 at Lord's in 1921.

H. Sutcliffe in 1924-25, C. G. Macartney in 1926 and A. R. Morris in 1946-47 made three hundreds in consecutive innings.

J. B. Hobbs and H. Sutcliffe shared 11 first-wicket three-figure partnerships.

L. Hutton and C. Washbrook twice made three-figure stands in each innings, at Adelaide in 1946-47 and at Leeds in 1948.

H. Sutcliffe, during his highest score of 194, v Australia in 1932-33, took part in three stands each exceeding 100, viz. 112 with R. E. S. Wyatt for the first wicket, 188 with W. R. Hammond for the second wicket, and 123 with the Nawab of Pataudi sen. for the third wicket. In 1903-04 R. E. Foster, in his historic innings of 287, added 192 for the fifth wicket with L. C. Braund, 115 for the ninth with A. E. Relf, and 130 for the tenth with W. Rhodes.

When L. Hutton scored 364 at The Oval in 1938 he added 382 for the second wicket with M. Leyland, 135 for the third wicket with W. R. Hammond and 215 for the sixth wicket with J. Hardstaff jun.

D. C. S. Compton and A. R. Morris at Adelaide in 1946-47 provided the first instance of a player on each side hitting two separate hundreds in a Test match.

G. S. and I. M. Chappell at The Oval in 1972 provide the first instance in Test matches of brothers each scoring hundreds in the same innings.

RECORD PARTNERSHIPS FOR EACH WICKET

For England

323 for 1st	J. B. Hobbs and W. Rhodes at Melbourne		1911-12
382 for 2nd†	L. Hutton and M. Leyland at The Oval		1938
262 for 3rd	W. R. Hammond and D. R. Jardine at Adelaide		1928-29
222 for 4th	W. R. Hammond and E. Paynter at Lord's		1938
206 for 5th	E. Paynter and D. C. S. Compton at Nottingham		1938
215 for 6th {	L. Hutton and J. Hardstaff jun. at The Oval		1938
	G. Boycott and A. P. E. Knott at Nottingham		1977
143 for 7th	F. E. Woolley and J. Vine at Sydney		1911-12
124 for 8th	E. H. Hendren and H. Larwood at Brisbane		1928-29
151 for 9th	W. H. Scotton and W. W. Read at The Oval		1884
130 for 10th†	R. E. Foster and W. Rhodes at Sydney		1903-04

For Australia

329 for 1st	G. R. Marsh and M. A. Taylor at Nottingham		1989
451 for 2nd†	W. H. Ponsford and D. G. Bradman at The Oval		1934
276 for 3rd	D. G. Bradman and A. L. Hassett at Brisbane		1946-47
388 for 4th†	W. H. Ponsford and D. G. Bradman at Leeds		1934
405 for 5th†‡	S. G. Barnes and D. G. Bradman at Sydney		1946-47
346 for 6th†	J. H. Fingleton and D. G. Bradman at Melbourne		1936-37
165 for 7th	C. Hill and H. Trumble at Melbourne		1897-98
243 for 8th†	R. J. Hartigan and C. Hill at Adelaide		1907-08
154 for 9th†	S. E. Gregory and J. McC. Blackham at Sydney		1894-95
127 for 10th†	J. M. Taylor and A. A. Mailey at Sydney		1924-25

† *Denotes record partnership against all countries.*
‡ *Record fifth-wicket partnership in first-class cricket.*

MOST RUNS IN A SERIES

England in England	732 (average 81.33)	D. I. Gower	1985
England in Australia	905 (average 113.12)	W. R. Hammond . .	1928-29
Australia in England	974 (average 139.14)	D. G. Bradman	1930
Australia in Australia	810 (average 90.00)	D. G. Bradman	1936-37

TEN WICKETS OR MORE IN A MATCH

For England (36)

13-163 (6-42, 7-121)	S. F. Barnes, Melbourne	1901-02
14-102 (7-28, 7-74)	W. Bates, Melbourne	1882-83
10-105 (5-46, 5-59)	A. V. Bedser, Melbourne	1950-51
14-99 (7-55, 7-44)	A. V. Bedser, Nottingham	1953
11-102 (6-44, 5-58)	C. Blythe, Birmingham	1909
11-176 (6-78, 5-98)	I. T. Botham, Perth	1979-80
10-253 (6-125, 4-128)	I. T. Botham, The Oval	1981
11-74 (5-29, 6-45)	J. Briggs, Lord's	1886
12-136 (6-49, 6-87)	J. Briggs, Adelaide	1891-92
10-148 (5-34, 5-114)	J. Briggs, The Oval	1893
10-104 (6-77, 4-27)†	R. M. Ellison, Birmingham	1985
10-179 (5-102, 5-77)†	K. Farnes, Nottingham	1934
10-60 (6-41, 4-19)	J. T. Hearne, The Oval	1896
11-113 (5-58, 6-55)	J. C. Laker, Leeds	1956
19-90 (9-37, 10-53)	J. C. Laker, Manchester	1956
10-124 (5-96, 5-28)	H. Larwood, Sydney	1932-33
11-76 (6-48, 5-28)	W. H. Lockwood, Manchester	1902
12-104 (7-36, 5-68)	G. A. Lohmann, The Oval	1886
10-87 (8-35, 2-52)	G. A. Lohmann, Sydney	1886-87
10-142 (8-58, 2-84)	G. A. Lohmann, Sydney	1891-92
12-102 (6-50, 6-52)†	F. Martin, The Oval	1890
11-68 (7-31, 4-37)	R. Peel, Manchester	1888
15-124 (7-56, 8-68)	W. Rhodes, Melbourne	1903-04
10-156 (5-49, 5-107)†	T. Richardson, Manchester	1893
11-173 (6-39, 5-134)	T. Richardson, Lord's	1896
13-244 (7-168, 6-76)	T. Richardson, Manchester	1896
10-204 (8-94, 2-110)	T. Richardson, Sydney	1897-98
11-228 (6-130, 5-98)†	M. W. Tate, Sydney	1924-25
11-88 (5-58, 6-30)	F. S. Trueman, Leeds	1961
10-130 (4-45, 6-85)	F. H. Tyson, Sydney	1954-55
10-82 (4-37, 6-45)	D. L. Underwood, Leeds	1972
11-215 (7-113, 4-102)	D. L. Underwood, Adelaide	1974-75
15-104 (7-61, 8-43)	H. Verity, Lord's	1934
10-57 (6-41, 4-16)	W. Voce, Brisbane	1936-37
13-256 (5-130, 8-126)	J. C. White, Adelaide	1928-29
10-49 (5-29, 5-20)	F. E. Woolley, The Oval	1912

For Australia (38)

10-151 (5-107, 5-44)	T. M. Alderman, Leeds	1989
10-239 (4-129, 6-110)	L. O'B. Fleetwood-Smith, Adelaide	1936-37
10-160 (4-88, 6-72)	G. Giffen, Sydney	1891-92
11-82 (5-45, 6-37)†	C. V. Grimmett, Sydney	1924-25
10-201 (5-107, 5-94)	C. V. Grimmett, Nottingham	1930
10-122 (5-65, 5-57)	R. M. Hogg, Perth	1978-79
10-66 (5-30, 5-36)	R. M. Hogg, Melbourne	1978-79
12-175 (5-85, 7-90)†	H. V. Hordern, Sydney	1911-12

10-161 (5-95, 5-66)	H. V. Hordern, Sydney	1911-12
10-164 (7-88, 3-76)	E. Jones, Lord's	1899
11-134 (6-47, 5-87)	G. F. Lawson, Brisbane	1982-83
10-181 (5-58, 5-123)	D. K. Lillee, The Oval	1972
11-165 (6-26, 5-139)	D. K. Lillee, Melbourne	1976-77
11-138 (6-60, 5-78)	D. K. Lillee, Melbourne	1979-80
11-159 (7-89, 4-70)	D. K. Lillee, The Oval	1981
11-85 (7-58, 4-27)	C. G. Macartney, Leeds	1909
11-157 (8-97, 3-60)	C. J. McDermott, Perth	1990-91
10-302 (5-160, 5-142)	A. A. Mailey, Adelaide	1920-21
13-236 (4-115, 9-121)†	A. A. Mailey, Melbourne	1920-21
16-137 (8-84, 8-53)†	R. A. L. Massie, Lord's	1972
10-152 (5-72, 5-80)	K. R. Miller, Lord's	1956
13-77 (7-17, 6-60)	M. A. Noble, Melbourne	1901-02
11-103 (5-51, 6-52)	M. A. Noble, Sheffield	1902
10-129 (5-63, 5-66)	W. J. O'Reilly, Melbourne	1932-33
11-129 (4-75, 7-54)	W. J. O'Reilly, Nottingham	1934
10-122 (5-66, 5-56)	W. J. O'Reilly, Leeds	1938
11-165 (7-68, 4-97)	G. E. Palmer, Sydney	1881-82
10-126 (7-65, 3-61)	G. E. Palmer, Melbourne	1882-83
13-148 (6-97, 7-51)	B. A. Reid, Melbourne	1990-91
13-110 (6-48, 7-62)	F. R. Spofforth, Melbourne	1878-79
14-90 (7-46, 7-44)	F. R. Spofforth, The Oval	1882
11-117 (4-73, 7-44)	F. R. Spofforth, Sydney	1882-83
10-144 (4-54, 6-90)	F. R. Spofforth, Sydney	1884-85
12-89 (6-59, 6-30)	H. Trumble, The Oval	1896
10-128 (4-75, 6-53)	H. Trumble, Manchester	1902
12-173 (8-65, 4-108)	H. Trumble, The Oval	1902
12-87 (5-44, 7-43)	C. T. B. Turner, Sydney	1887-88
10-63 (5-27, 5-36)	C. T. B. Turner, Lord's	1888

† *Signifies ten wickets or more on first appearance in England–Australia Tests.*

Note: J. Briggs, J. C. Laker, T. Richardson in 1896, R. M. Hogg, A. A. Mailey, H. Trumble and C. T. B. Turner took ten wickets or more in successive Tests. J. Briggs was omitted, however, from the England team for the first Test match in 1893.

MOST WICKETS IN A SERIES

England in England	46 (average 9.60)	J. C. Laker	1956
England in Australia........	38 (average 23.18)	M. W. Tate............	1924-25
Australia in England........	42 (average 21.26)	T. M. Alderman (6 Tests)	1981
Australia in Australia	41 (average 12.85)	R. M. Hogg (6 Tests)...	1978-79

WICKET-KEEPING – MOST DISMISSALS

	M	Ct	St	Total
†R. W. Marsh (Australia)	42	141	7	148
A. P. E. Knott (England).......	34	97	8	105
†W. A. Oldfield (Australia).......	38	59	31	90
A. A. Lilley (England)	32	65	19	84
A. T. W. Grout (Australia)	22	69	7	76
T. G. Evans (England)	31	63	12	75

† *The number of catches by R. W. Marsh (141) and stumpings by W. A. Oldfield (31) are respective records in England–Australia Tests.*

SCORERS OF OVER 2,000 RUNS

	T		I		NO		R		HS		Avge
D. G. Bradman	37	..	63	..	7	..	5,028	..	334	..	89.78
J. B. Hobbs	41	..	71	..	4	..	3,636	..	187	..	54.26
D. I. Gower	42	..	77	..	4	..	3,269	..	215	..	44.78
A. R. Border	41	..	73	..	18	..	3,115	..	196	..	56.63
G. Boycott	38	..	71	..	9	..	2,945	..	191	..	47.50
W. R. Hammond	33	..	58	..	3	..	2,852	..	251	..	51.85
H. Sutcliffe	27	..	46	..	5	..	2,741	..	194	..	66.85
C. Hill	41	..	76	..	1	..	2,660	..	188	..	35.46
J. H. Edrich	32	..	57	..	3	..	2,644	..	175	..	48.96
G. S. Chappell	35	..	65	..	8	..	2,619	..	144	..	45.94
M. C. Cowdrey	43	..	75	..	4	..	2,433	..	113	..	34.26
L. Hutton	27	..	49	..	6	..	2,428	..	364	..	56.46
R. N. Harvey	37	..	68	..	5	..	2,416	..	167	..	38.34
V. T. Trumper	40	..	74	..	5	..	2,263	..	185*	..	32.79
W. M. Lawry	29	..	51	..	5	..	2,233	..	166	..	48.54
S. E. Gregory	52	..	92	..	7	..	2,193	..	201	..	25.80
W. W. Armstrong	42	..	71	..	9	..	2,172	..	158	..	35.03
I. M. Chappell	30	..	56	..	4	..	2,138	..	192	..	41.11
K. F. Barrington	23	..	39	..	6	..	2,111	..	256	..	63.96
A. R. Morris	24	..	43	..	2	..	2,080	..	206	..	50.73

BOWLERS WITH 100 WICKETS

	T		Balls		R		W		5W/i		Avge
D. K. Lillee	29	..	8,516	..	3,507	..	167	..	11	..	21.00
I. T. Botham	36	..	8,479	..	4,093	..	148	..	9	..	27.65
H. Trumble	31	..	7,895	..	2,945	..	141	..	9	..	20.88
R. G. D. Willis	35	..	7,294	..	3,346	..	128	..	7	..	26.14
M. A. Noble	39	..	6,845	..	2,860	..	115	..	9	..	24.86
R. R. Lindwall	29	..	6,728	..	2,559	..	114	..	6	..	22.44
W. Rhodes	41	..	5,791	..	2,616	..	109	..	6	..	24.00
S. F. Barnes	20	..	5,749	..	2,288	..	106	..	12	..	21.58
C. V. Grimmett	22	..	9,224	..	3,439	..	106	..	11	..	32.44
D. L. Underwood	29	..	8,000	..	2,770	..	105	..	4	..	26.38
A. V. Bedser	21	..	7,065	..	2,859	..	104	..	7	..	27.49
G. Giffen	31	..	6,457	..	2,791	..	103	..	7	..	27.09
W. J. O'Reilly	19	..	7,864	..	2,587	..	102	..	8	..	25.36
R. Peel	20	..	5,216	..	1,715	..	101	..	5	..	16.98
C. T. B. Turner	17	..	5,195	..	1,670	..	101	..	11	..	16.53
T. M. Alderman	17	..	4,717	..	2,117	..	100	..	11	..	21.17
J. R. Thomson	21	..	4,951	..	2,418	..	100	..	5	..	24.18

RESULTS ON EACH GROUND

In England

THE OVAL (30)

England (13) 1880, 1886, 1888, 1890, 1893, 1896, 1902, 1912, 1926, 1938, 1953, 1968, 1985.

Australia (5) 1882, 1930, 1934, 1948, 1972.

Drawn (12) 1884, 1899, 1905, 1909, 1921, 1956, 1961, 1964, 1975, 1977, 1981, 1989.

MANCHESTER (25)

England (7) 1886, 1888, 1905, 1956, 1972, 1977, 1981.

Australia (5) 1896, 1902, 1961, 1968, 1989.

Drawn (13) 1884, 1893, 1899, 1909, 1912, 1921, 1926, 1930, 1934, 1948, 1953, 1964, 1985.

The scheduled matches in 1890 and 1938 were abandoned without a ball bowled and are excluded.

LORD'S (29)

England (5)	1884, 1886, 1890, 1896, 1934.
Australia (11)	1888, 1899, 1909, 1921, 1930, 1948, 1956, 1961, 1972, 1985, 1989.
Drawn (13)	1893, 1902, 1905, 1912, 1926, 1938, 1953, 1964, 1968, 1975, 1977, 1980, 1981.

NOTTINGHAM (16)

England (3)	1905, 1930, 1977.
Australia (5)	1921, 1934, 1948, 1981, 1989.
Drawn (8)	1899, 1926, 1938, 1953, 1956, 1964, 1972, 1985.

LEEDS (20)

England (6)	1956, 1961, 1972, 1977, 1981, 1985.
Australia (6)	1909, 1921, 1938, 1948, 1964, 1989.
Drawn (8)	1899, 1905, 1926, 1930, 1934, 1953, 1968, 1975.

BIRMINGHAM (8)

England (3)	1909, 1981, 1985.
Australia (1)	1975.
Drawn (4)	1902, 1961, 1968, 1989.

SHEFFIELD (1)

| Australia (1) | 1902. |

In Australia

MELBOURNE (49)

England (18)	*1876, 1882, 1884(2), 1894(2), 1903, 1907, 1911(2), 1924, 1928, 1950, 1954, 1962, 1974, 1982, 1986.*
Australia (24)	*1876, 1878, 1882, 1891, 1897(2), 1901(2), 1903, 1907, 1920(2), 1924, 1928, 1932, 1936(2), 1950, 1958(2), 1976, 1978, 1979, 1990.*
Drawn (7)	*1881(2), 1946, 1965(2), 1970, 1974.*

One scheduled match in 1970-71 was abandoned without a ball bowled and is excluded.

SYDNEY (49)

England (20)	*1882, 1886(2), 1887, 1894, 1897, 1901, 1903(2), 1911, 1928, 1932(2), 1936, 1954, 1965, 1970(2), 1978(2).*
Australia (23)	*1881(2), 1882, 1884(2), 1891, 1894, 1897, 1901, 1907(2), 1911, 1920(2), 1924(2), 1946(2), 1950, 1962, 1974, 1979, 1986.*
Drawn (6)	*1954, 1958, 1962, 1982, 1987, 1990.*

ADELAIDE (25)

England (7)	*1884, 1891, 1911, 1928, 1932, 1954, 1978.*
Australia (13)	*1894, 1897, 1901, 1903, 1907, 1920, 1924, 1936, 1950, 1958, 1965, 1974, 1982.*
Drawn (5)	*1946, 1962, 1970, 1986, 1990.*

BRISBANE Exhibition Ground (1)

| England (1) | *1928.* |

BRISBANE Woolloongabba (14)

England (4)	*1932, 1936, 1978, 1986.*
Australia (7)	*1946, 1950, 1954, 1958, 1974, 1982, 1990.*
Drawn (3)	*1962, 1965, 1970.*

PERTH (7)
England (1)   *1978.*
Australia (3)   *1974, 1979, 1990.*
Drawn (3)   *1970, 1982, 1986.*

For Tests in Australia the first year of the season is given in italics; i.e. *1876* denotes the 1876-77 season.

ENGLAND v SOUTH AFRICA

		Captains				
Season	*England*	*South Africa*	*T*	*E*	*SA*	*D*
1888-89	C. A. Smith[1]	O. R. Dunell[2]	2	2	0	0
1891-92	W. W. Read	W. H. Milton	1	1	0	0
1895-96	Lord Hawke[3]	E. A. Halliwell[4]	3	3	0	0
1898-99	Lord Hawke	M. Bisset	2	2	0	0
1905-06	P. F. Warner	P. W. Sherwell	5	1	4	0
1907	R. E. Foster	P. W. Sherwell	3	1	0	2
1909-10	H. D. G. Leveson Gower[5]	S. J. Snooke	5	2	3	0
1912	C. B. Fry	F. Mitchell[6]	3	3	0	0
1913-14	J. W. H. T. Douglas	H. W. Taylor	5	4	0	1
1922-23	F. T. Mann	H. W. Taylor	5	2	1	2
1924	A. E. R. Gilligan[7]	H. W. Taylor	5	3	0	2
1927-28	R. T. Stanyforth[8]	H. G. Deane	5	2	2	1
1929	J. C. White[9]	H. G. Deane	5	2	0	3
1930-31	A. P. F. Chapman	H. G. Deane[10]	5	0	1	4
1935	R. E. S. Wyatt	H. F. Wade	5	0	1	4
1938-39	W. R. Hammond	A. Melville	5	1	0	4
1947	N. W. D. Yardley	A. Melville	5	3	0	2
1948-49	F. G. Mann	A. D. Nourse	5	2	0	3
1951	F. R. Brown	A. D. Nourse	5	3	1	1
1955	P. B. H. May	J. E. Cheetham[11]	5	3	2	0
1956-57	P. B. H. May	C. B. van Ryneveld[12]	5	2	2	1
1960	M. C. Cowdrey	D. J. McGlew	5	3	0	2
1964-65	M. J. K. Smith	T. L. Goddard	5	1	0	4
1965	M. J. K. Smith	P. L. van der Merwe	3	0	1	2
	In South Africa.................		58	25	13	20
	In England		44	21	5	18
	Totals..........................		102	46	18	38

Notes: The following deputised for the official touring captain or were appointed by the home authority for only a minor proportion of the series:
[1]M. P. Bowden (Second). [2]W. H. Milton (Second). [3]Sir T. C. O'Brien (First). [4]A. R. Richards (Third). [5]F. L. Fane (Fourth and Fifth). [6]L. J. Tancred (Second and Third). [7]J. W. H. T. Douglas (Fourth). [8]G. T. S. Stevens (Fifth). [9]A. W. Carr (Fourth and Fifth). [10]E. P. Nupen (First), H. B. Cameron (Fourth and Fifth). [11]D. J. McGlew (Third and Fourth). [12]D. J. McGlew (Second).

HIGHEST INNINGS TOTALS

For England in England: 554-8 dec. at Lord's	1947
in South Africa: 654-5 at Durban	1938-39
For South Africa in England: 538 at Leeds	1951
in South Africa: 530 at Durban	1938-39

LOWEST INNINGS TOTALS

For England in England: 76 at Leeds 1907
        in South Africa: 92 at Cape Town 1898-99

For South Africa in England: 30 at Birmingham 1924
        in South Africa: 30 at Port Elizabeth 1895-96

INDIVIDUAL HUNDREDS

For England (87)

R. Abel (1)
120   Cape Town .. 1888-89
L. E. G. Ames (2)
148* The Oval.... 1935
115   Cape Town .. 1938-39
K. F. Barrington (2)
148* Durban 1964-65
121   Johannesburg 1964-65
G. Boycott (1)
117   Pt Elizabeth . 1964-65
L. C. Braund (1)
104† Lord's 1907
D. C. S. Compton (7)
163† Nottingham . 1947
208   Lord's 1947
115   Manchester.. 1947
113   The Oval.... 1947
114   Johannesburg 1948-49
112   Nottingham . 1951
158   Manchester.. 1955
M. C. Cowdrey (3)
101   Cape Town .. 1956-57
155   The Oval.... 1960
105   Nottingham . 1965
D. Denton (1)
104   Johannesburg 1909-10
E. R. Dexter (1)
172   Johannesburg 1964-65
J. W. H. T. Douglas (1)
119† Durban 1913-14
W. J. Edrich (3)
219   Durban 1938-39
189   Lord's 1947
191   Manchester.. 1947
F. L. Fane (1)
143   Johannesburg 1905-06
C. B. Fry (1)
129   The Oval.... 1907
P. A. Gibb (2)
106† Johannesburg 1938-39
120   Durban 1938-39
W. R. Hammond (6)
138* Birmingham . 1929
101* The Oval.... 1929
136* Durban 1930-31

181   Cape Town .. 1938-39
120   Durban 1938-39
140   Durban 1938-39
T. W. Hayward (1)
122   Johannesburg 1895-96
E. H. Hendren (2)
132   Leeds 1924
142   The Oval.... 1924
A. J. L. Hill (1)
124   Cape Town .. 1895-96
J. B. Hobbs (2)
187   Cape Town .. 1909-10
211   Lord's 1924
L. Hutton (4)
100   Leeds 1947
158   Johannesburg 1948-49
123   Johannesburg 1948-49
100   Leeds 1951
D. J. Insole (1)
110* Durban 1956-57
M. Leyland (2)
102   Lord's 1929
161   The Oval.... 1935
F. G. Mann (1)
136* Pt Elizabeth . 1948-49
P. B. H. May (3)
138† Leeds 1951
112   Lord's 1955
117   Manchester.. 1955
C. P. Mead (3)
102   Johannesburg 1913-14
117   Pt Elizabeth . 1913-14
181   Durban 1922-23
P. H. Parfitt (1)
122* Johannesburg 1964-65
J. M. Parks (1)
108* Durban 1964-65
E. Paynter (3)
117   ⎱†Johannesburg 1938-39
100   ⎰
243   Durban 1938-39
G. Pullar (1)
175   The Oval.... 1960
W. Rhodes (1)
152   Johannesburg 1913-14

P. E. Richardson (1)
117† Johannesburg 1956-57
R. W. V. Robins (1)
108   Manchester.. 1935
A. C. Russell (2)
140   ⎱
111   ⎰Durban 1922-23
R. T. Simpson (1)
137   Nottingham . 1951
M. J. K. Smith (1)
121   Cape Town .. 1964-65
R. H. Spooner (1)
119† Lord's 1912
H. Sutcliffe (6)
122   Lord's 1924
102   Johannesburg 1927-28
114   Birmingham . 1929
100   Lord's 1929
104   ⎱
109* ⎰The Oval.... 1929
M. W. Tate (1)
100* Lord's 1929
E. Tyldesley (2)
122   Johannesburg 1927-28
100   Durban 1927-28
J. T. Tyldesley (1)
112   Cape Town .. 1898-99
B. H. Valentine (1)
112   Cape Town .. 1938-39
P. F. Warner (1)
132*†‡Johannesburg 1898-99
C. Washbrook (1)
195   Johannesburg 1948-49
A. J. Watkins (1)
111   Johannesburg 1948-49
H. Wood (1)
134* Cape Town .. 1891-92
F. E. Woolley (3)
115* Johannesburg 1922-23
134* Lord's 1924
154   Manchester.. 1929
R. E. S. Wyatt (2)
113   Manchester.. 1929
149   Nottingham . 1935

For South Africa (58)

E. J. Barlow (1)
138 Cape Town .. 1964-65

K. C. Bland (2)
127 The Oval.... 1965

R. H. Catterall (3)
120 Birmingham . 1924
120 Lord's 1924
119 Durban 1927-28

E. L. Dalton (2)
117 The Oval.... 1935
102 Johannesburg 1938-39

W. R. Endean (1)
116* Leeds 1955

G. A. Faulkner (1)
123 Johannesburg 1909-10

T. L. Goddard (1)
112 Johannesburg 1964-65

C. M. H. Hathorn (1)
102 Johannesburg 1905-06

D. J. McGlew (2)
104* Manchester .. 1955
133 Leeds 1955

R. A. McLean (3)
142 Lord's 1955
100 Durban 1956-57
109 Manchester.. 1960

A. Melville (4)
103 Durban 1938-39

189 ⎫
104* ⎭ Nottingham . 1947
117 Lord's 1947

B. Mitchell (7)
123 Cape Town .. 1930-31
164* Lord's 1935
128 The Oval.... 1935
109 Durban 1938-39
120 ⎫
189* ⎭ The Oval.... 1947
120 Cape Town .. 1948-49

A. D. Nourse (7)
120 Cape Town .. 1938-39
103 Durban 1938-39
149 Nottingham . 1947
115 Manchester .. 1947
112 Cape Town .. 1948-49
129* Johannesburg 1948-49
208 Nottingham . 1951

H. G. Owen-Smith (1)
129 Leeds 1929

A. J. Pithey (1)
154 Cape Town .. 1964-65

R. G. Pollock (2)
137 Pt Elizabeth . 1964-65
125 Nottingham . 1965

E. A. B. Rowan (2)
156* Johannesburg 1948-49
236 Leeds 1951

P. W. Sherwell (1)
115 Lord's 1907

I. J. Siedle (1)
141 Cape Town .. 1930-31

J. H. Sinclair (1)
106 Cape Town .. 1898-99

H. W. Taylor (7)
109 Durban 1913-14
176 Johannesburg 1922-23
101 Johannesburg 1922-23
102 Durban 1922-23
101 Johannesburg 1927-28
121 The Oval.... 1929
117 Cape Town .. 1930-31

P. G. V. van der Bijl (1)
125 Durban 1938-39

K. G. Viljoen (1)
124 Manchester .. 1935

W. W. Wade (1)
125 Pt Elizabeth . 1948-49

J. H. B. Waite (1)
113 Manchester.. 1955

G. C. White (2)
147 Johannesburg 1905-06
118 Durban 1909-10

P. L. Winslow (1)
108 Manchester.. 1955

† Signifies hundred on first appearance in England–South Africa Tests. The highest scores on *début* in this series for South Africa are (in South Africa) 93* by A. W. Nourse at Johannesburg in 1905-06 and (in England) 90 by P. N. F. Mansell at Leeds in 1951.

‡ P. F. Warner carried his bat through the second innings.

A. Melville's four hundreds were made in successive Test innings.

H. Wood scored the only hundred of his career in a Test match.

RECORD PARTNERSHIP FOR EACH WICKET

For England

359	for 1st†	L. Hutton and C. Washbrook at Johannesburg	1948-49
280	for 2nd	P. A. Gibb and W. J. Edrich at Durban	1938-39
370	for 3rd†	W. J. Edrich and D. C. S. Compton at Lord's	1947
197	for 4th	W. R. Hammond and L. E. G. Ames at Cape Town	1938-39
237	for 5th	D. C. S. Compton and N. W. D. Yardley at Nottingham	1947
206*	for 6th	K. F. Barrington and J. M. Parks at Durban	1964-65
115	for 7th	M. C. Bird and J. W. H. T. Douglas at Durban	1913-14
154	for 8th	C. W. Wright and H. R. Bromley-Davenport at Johannesburg	1895-96
71	for 9th	H. Wood and J. T. Hearne at Cape Town	1891-92
92	for 10th	A. C. Russell and A. E. R. Gilligan at Durban	1922-23

For South Africa

260	for 1st†	I. J. Siedle and B. Mitchell at Cape Town	1930-31
198	for 2nd†	E. A. B. Rowan and C. B. van Ryneveld at Leeds	1951
319	for 3rd	A. Melville and A. D. Nourse at Nottingham	1947
214	for 4th†	H. W. Taylor and H. G. Deane at The Oval	1929
157	for 5th†	A. J. Pithey and J. H. B. Waite at Johannesburg	1964-65
171	for 6th	J. H. B. Waite and P. L. Winslow at Manchester	1955
123	for 7th	H. G. Deane and E. P. Nupen at Durban	1927-28

109* for 8th   B. Mitchell and L. Tuckett at The Oval...................   1947
137 for 9th†   E. L. Dalton and A. B. C. Langton at The Oval............   1935
103 for 10th† H. G. Owen-Smith and A. J. Bell at Leeds   1929

   † *Denotes record partnership against all countries.*

MOST RUNS IN A SERIES

England in England ....   753 (average 94.12)   D. C. S. Compton..   1947
England in South Africa .....   653 (average 81.62)   E. Paynter   1938-39
South Africa in England .....   621 (average 69.00)   A. D. Nourse   1947
South Africa in South Africa..   582 (average 64.66)   H. W. Taylor......   1922-23

TEN WICKETS OR MORE IN A MATCH

For England (23)

11-110 (5-25, 6-85)†   S. F. Barnes, Lord's   1912
10-115 (6-52, 4-63)   S. F. Barnes, Leeds................................   1912
13-57 (5-28, 8-29)   S. F. Barnes, The Oval.............................   1912
10-105 (5-57, 5-48)   S. F. Barnes, Durban..............................   1913-14
17-159 (8-56, 9-103)   S. F. Barnes, Johannesburg........................   1913-14
14-144 (7-56, 7-88)   S. F. Barnes, Durban..............................   1913-14
12-112 (7-58, 5-54)   A. V. Bedser, Manchester..........................   1951
11-118 (6-68, 5-50)   C. Blythe, Cape Town..............................   1905-06
15-99 (8-59, 7-40)   C. Blythe, Leeds..................................   1907
10-104 (7-46, 3-58)   C. Blythe, Cape Town..............................   1909-10
15-28 (7-17, 8-11)   J. Briggs, Cape Town..............................   1888-89
13-91 (6-54, 7-37)†   J. J. Ferris, Cape Town...........................   1891-92
10-207 (7-115, 3-92)   A. P. Freeman, Leeds..............................   1929
12-171 (7-71, 5-100)   A. P. Freeman, Manchester.........................   1929
12-130 (7-70, 5-60)   G. Geary, Johannesburg............................   1927-28
11-90 (6-7, 5-83)   A. E. R. Gilligan, Birmingham.....................   1924
10-119 (4-64, 6-55)   J. C. Laker, The Oval.............................   1951
15-45 (7-38, 8-7)†   G. A. Lohmann, Port Elizabeth   1895-96
12-71 (9-28, 3-43)   G. A. Lohmann, Johannesburg.......................   1895-96
11-97 (6-63, 5-34)   J. B. Statham, Lord's.............................   1960
12-101 (7-52, 5-49)   R. Tattersall, Lord's.............................   1951
12-89 (5-53, 7-36)   J. H. Wardle, Cape Town...........................   1956-57
10-175 (5-95, 5-80)   D. V. P. Wright, Lord's...........................   1947

For South Africa (6)

11-112 (4-49, 7-63)†   A. E. Hall, Cape Town.............................   1922-23
11-150 (5-63, 6-87)   E. P. Nupen, Johannesburg.........................   1930-31
10-87 (5-53, 5-34)   P. M. Pollock, Nottingham.........................   1965
12-127 (4-57, 8-70)   S. J. Snooke, Johannesburg........................   1905-06
13-192 (4-79, 9-113)   H. J. Tayfield, Johannesburg......................   1956-57
12-181 (5-87, 7-94)   A. E. E. Vogler, Johannesburg   1909-10

   † *Signifies ten wickets or more on first appearance in England–South Africa Tests.*

Note: S. F. Barnes took ten wickets or more in his first five Tests v South Africa and in six of his seven Tests v South Africa. A. P. Freeman and G. A. Lohmann took ten wickets or more in successive matches.

MOST WICKETS IN A SERIES

England in England ....   34 (average 8.29)   S. F. Barnes   1912
England in South Africa .....   49 (average 10.93)   S. F. Barnes   1913-14
South Africa in England .....   26 (average 21.84)   H. J. Tayfield   1955
South Africa in England .....   26 (average 22.57)   N. A. T. Adcock ...   1960
South Africa in South Africa..   37 (average 17.18)   H. J. Tayfield   1956-57

ENGLAND v WEST INDIES

	Captains					
Season	England	West Indies	T	E	WI	D
1928	A. P. F. Chapman	R. K. Nunes	3	3	0	0
1929-30	Hon. F. S. G. Calthorpe	E. L. G. Hoad[1]	4	1	1	2
1933	D. R. Jardine[2]	G. C. Grant	3	2	0	1
1934-35	R. E. S. Wyatt	G. C. Grant	4	1	2	1
1939	W. R. Hammond	R. S. Grant	3	1	0	2
1947-48	G. O. B. Allen[3]	J. D. C. Goddard[4]	4	0	2	2
1950	N. W. D. Yardley[5]	J. D. C. Goddard	4	1	3	0
1953-54	L. Hutton	J. B. Stollmeyer	5	2	2	1
1957	P. B. H. May	J. D. C. Goddard	5	3	0	2
1959-60	P. B. H. May[6]	F. C. M. Alexander	5	1	0	4

THE WISDEN TROPHY

	Captains						
Season	England	West Indies	T	E	WI	D	Held by
1963	E. R. Dexter	F. M. M. Worrell	5	1	3	1	WI
1966	M. C. Cowdrey[7]	G. S. Sobers	5	1	3	1	WI
1967-68	M. C. Cowdrey	G. S. Sobers	5	1	0	4	E
1969	R. Illingworth	G. S. Sobers	3	2	0	1	E
1973	R. Illingworth	R. B. Kanhai	3	0	2	1	WI
1973-74	M. H. Denness	R. B. Kanhai	5	1	1	3	WI
1976	A. W. Greig	C. H. Lloyd	5	0	3	2	WI
1980	I. T. Botham	C. H. Lloyd[8]	5	0	1	4	WI
1980-81†	I. T. Botham	C. H. Lloyd	4	0	2	2	WI
1984	D. I. Gower	C. H. Lloyd	5	0	5	0	WI
1985-86	D. I. Gower	I. V. A. Richards	5	0	5	0	WI
1988	J. E. Emburey[9]	I. V. A. Richards	5	0	4	1	WI
1989-90‡	G. A. Gooch[10]	I. V. A. Richards[11]	4	1	2	1	WI
1991	G. A. Gooch	I. V. A. Richards	5	2	2	1	WI
	In England		59	16	26	17	
	In West Indies		45	8	17	20	
	Totals		104	24	43	37	

† *The Second Test, at Georgetown, was cancelled owing to political pressure and is excluded.*
‡ *The Second Test, at Georgetown, was abandoned without a ball being bowled and is excluded.*

Notes: The following deputised for the official touring captain or were appointed by the home authority for only a minor proportion of the series:
[1]N. Betancourt (Second), M. P. Fernandes (Third), R. K. Nunes (Fourth). [2]R. E. S. Wyatt (Third). [3]K. Cranston (First). [4]G. A. Headley (First), G. E. Gomez (Second). [5]F. R. Brown (Fourth). [6]M. C. Cowdrey (Fourth and Fifth). [7]M. J. K. Smith (First), D. B. Close (Fifth). [8]I. V. A. Richards (Fifth). [9]M. W. Gatting (First), C. S. Cowdrey (Fourth), G. A. Gooch (Fifth). [10]A. J. Lamb (Fourth and Fifth). [11]D. L. Haynes (Third).

HIGHEST INNINGS TOTALS

For England	in England: 619-6 dec. at Nottingham	1957
	in West Indies: 849 at Kingston	1929-30
For West Indies	in England: 687-8 dec. at The Oval	1976
	in West Indies: 681-8 dec. at Port-of-Spain	1953-54

LOWEST INNINGS TOTALS

For England in England: 71 at Manchester 1976
in West Indies: 103 at Kingston 1934-35

For West Indies in England: 86 at The Oval 1957
in West Indies: 102 at Bridgetown 1934-35

INDIVIDUAL HUNDREDS

For England (88)

L. E. G. Ames (3)			153	Kingston....	1980-81	100*	Manchester..	1984
105	Port-of-Spain	1929-30	146	Nottingham .	1988	113	Lord's	1988
149	Kingston....	1929-30	154*‡	Leeds	1991	132	Kingston....	1989-90
126	Kingston....	1934-35	**D. I. Gower** (1)			119	Bridgetown..	1989-90
D. L. Amiss (4)			154*	Kingston....	1980-81	**P. B. H. May** (3)		
174	Port-of-Spain	1973-74	**T. W. Graveney** (5)			135	Port-of-Spain	1953-54
262*	Kingston....	1973-74	258	Nottingham .	1957	285*	Birmingham .	1957
118	Georgetown .	1973-74	164	The Oval....	1957	104	Nottingham .	1957
203	The Oval....	1976	109	Nottingham .	1966	**C. Milburn** (1)		
A. H. Bakewell (1)			165	The Oval....	1966	126*	Lord's	1966
107†	The Oval....	1933	118	Port-of-Spain	1967-68	**J. T. Murray** (1)		
K. F. Barrington (3)			**A. W. Greig** (3)			112†	The Oval....	1966
128†	Bridgetown .	1959-60	148	Bridgetown .	1973-74	**J. M. Parks** (1)		
121	Port-of-Spain	1959-60	121	Georgetown .	1973-74	101*†	Port-of-Spain	1959-60
143	Port-of-Spain	1967-68	116	Leeds	1976	**W. Place** (1)		
G. Boycott (5)			**S. C. Griffith** (1)			107	Kingston....	1947-48
116	Georgetown .	1967-68	140†	Port-of-Spain	1947-48	**P. E. Richardson** (2)		
128	Manchester..	1969	**W. R. Hammond** (1)			126	Nottingham .	1957
106	Lord's	1969	138	The Oval....	1939	107	The Oval....	1957
112	Port-of-Spain	1973-74	**J. H. Hampshire** (1)			**J. D. Robertson** (1)		
104*	St John's....	1980-81	107†	Lord's	1969	133	Port-of-Spain	1947-48
D. C. S. Compton (2)			**F. C. Hayes** (1)			**A. Sandham** (2)		
120†	Lord's	1939	106*†	The Oval....	1973	152†	Bridgetown .	1929-30
133	Port-of-Spain	1953-54	**E. H. Hendren** (2)			325	Kingston....	1929-30
M. C. Cowdrey (6)			205*	Port-of-Spain	1929-30	**M. J. K. Smith** (1)		
154†	Birmingham .	1957	123	Georgetown .	1929-30	108	Port-of-Spain	1959-60
152	Lord's	1957	**J. B. Hobbs** (1)			**R. A. Smith** (2)		
114	Kingston....	1959-60	159	The Oval....	1928	148*	Lord's	1991
119	Port-of-Spain	1959-60	**L. Hutton** (5)			109	The Oval ...	1991
101	Kingston....	1967-68	196†	Lord's	1939	**D. S. Steele** (1)		
148	Port-of-Spain	1967-68	165*	The Oval....	1939	106†	Nottingham .	1976
E. R. Dexter (2)			202*‡	The Oval....	1950	**R. Subba Row** (1)		
136*†	Bridgetown .	1959-60	169	Georgetown .	1953-54	100†	Georgetown .	1959-60
110	Georgetown .	1959-60	205	Kingston....	1953-54	**E. Tyldesley** (1)		
J. H. Edrich (1)			**R. Illingworth** (1)			122†	Lord's	1928
146	Bridgetown .	1967-68	113	Lord's	1969	**C. Washbrook** (2)		
T. G. Evans (1)			**D. R. Jardine** (1)			114†	Lord's	1950
104	Manchester..	1950	127	Manchester..	1933	102	Nottingham .	1950
K. W. R. Fletcher (1)			**A. P. E. Knott** (1)			**W. Watson** (1)		
129*	Bridgetown .	1973-74	116	Leeds	1976	116†	Kingston....	1953-54
G. Fowler (1)			**A. J. Lamb** (6)			**P. Willey** (2)		
106	Lord's	1984	110	Lord's	1984	100*	The Oval....	1980
G. A. Gooch (2)			100	Leeds	1984	102*	St John's....	1980-81
123	Lord's	1980						
116	Bridgetown..	1980-81						

For West Indies (99)

I. Barrow (1)			106	} Lord's	1939	**R. B. Richardson** (4)		
105	Manchester..	1933	107			102	Port-of-Spain	1985-86
C. A. Best (1)			**D. A. J. Holford** (1)			160	Bridgetown..	1985-86
164	Bridgetown..	1989-90	105*	Lord's	1966	104	Birmingham	1991
B. F. Butcher (2)			**J. K. Holt** (1)			121	The Oval ...	1991
133	Lord's	1963	166	Bridgetown..	1953-54	**C. A. Roach** (2)		
209*	Nottingham	1966	**C. L. Hooper** (1)			122	Bridgetown..	1929-30
G. M. Carew (1)			111	Lord's	1991	209	Georgetown .	1929-30
107	Port-of-Spain	1947-48	**C. C. Hunte** (3)			**L. G. Rowe** (3)		
C. A. Davis (1)			182	Manchester..	1963	120	Kingston....	1973-74
103	Lord's	1969	108*	The Oval....	1963	302	Bridgetown..	1973-74
P. J. L. Dujon (1)			135	Manchester..	1966	123	Port-of-Spain	1973-74
101	Manchester..	1984	**B. D. Julien** (1)			**O. G. Smith** (2)		
R. C. Fredericks (3)			121	Lord's	1973	161†	Birmingham	1957
150	Birmingham .	1973	**A. I. Kallicharran** (2)			168	Nottingham	1957
138	Lord's	1976	158	Port-of-Spain	1973-74	**G. S. Sobers** (10)		
109	Leeds	1976	119	Bridgetown..	1973-74	226	Bridgetown..	1959-60
A. G. Ganteaume (1)			**R. B. Kanhai** (5)			147	Kingston....	1959-60
112†	Port-of-Spain	1947-48	110	Port-of-Spain	1959-60	145	Georgetown .	1959-60
H. A. Gomes (2)			104	The Oval....	1966	102	Leeds	1963
143	Birmingham	1984	153	Port-of-Spain	1967-68	161	Manchester..	1966
104*	Leeds	1984	150	Georgetown .	1967-68	163*	Lord's	1966
C. G. Greenidge (7)			157	Lord's	1973	174	Leeds	1966
134	} Manchester..	1976	**C. H. Lloyd** (5)			113*	Kingston....	1967-68
101			118†	Port-of-Spain	1967-68	152	Georgetown .	1967-68
115	Leeds	1976	113*	Bridgetown..	1967-68	150*	Lord's	1973
214*	Lord's	1984	132	The Oval....	1973	**C. L. Walcott** (4)		
223	Manchester..	1984	101	Manchester..	1980	168*	Lord's	1950
103	Lord's	1988	100	Bridgetown..	1980-81	220	Bridgetown..	1953-54
149	St John's....	1989-90	**S. M. Nurse** (2)			124	Port-of-Spain	1953-54
D. L. Haynes (5)			137	Leeds	1966	116	Kingston....	1953-54
184	Lord's	1980	136	Port-of-Spain	1967-68	**E. D. Weekes** (3)		
125	The Oval....	1984	**A. F. Rae** (2)			141	Kingston....	1947-48
131	St John's....	1985-86	106	Lord's	1950	129	Nottingham	1950
109	Bridgetown..	1989-90	109	The Oval....	1950	206	Port-of-Spain	1953-54
167	St John's....	1989-90	**I. V. A. Richards** (8)			**K. H. Weekes** (1)		
G. A. Headley (8)			232†	Nottingham .	1976	137	The Oval....	1939
176†	Bridgetown..	1929-30	135	Manchester..	1976	**F. M. M. Worrell** (6)		
114	} Georgetown .	1929-30	291	The Oval....	1976	131*	Georgetown .	1947-48
112			145	Lord's	1980	261	Nottingham	1950
223	Kingston....	1929-30	182*	Bridgetown..	1980-81	138	The Oval....	1950
169*	Manchester..	1933	114	St John's....	1980-81	167	Port-of-Spain	1953-54
270*	Kingston....	1934-35	117	Birmingham	1984	191*‡	Nottingham .	1957
			110*	St John's....	1985-86	197*	Bridgetown..	1959-60

† *Signifies hundred on first appearance in England–West Indies Tests. S. C. Griffith provides the only instance for England of a player hitting his maiden century in first-class cricket in his first Test.*
‡ *Carried his bat.*

RECORD PARTNERSHIPS FOR EACH WICKET

For England

212	for 1st	C. Washbrook and R. T. Simpson at Nottingham	1950
266	for 2nd	P. E. Richardson and T. W. Graveney at Nottingham.........	1957
264	for 3rd	L. Hutton and W. R. Hammond at The Oval	1939
411	for 4th†	P. B. H. May and M. C. Cowdrey at Birmingham	1957

130* for 5th	C. Milburn and T. W. Graveney at Lord's	1966
163 for 6th	A. W. Greig and A. P. E. Knott at Bridgetown	1973-74
197 for 7th†	M. J. K. Smith and J. M. Parks at Port-of-Spain	1959-60
217 for 8th	T. W. Graveney and J. T. Murray at The Oval	1966
109 for 9th	G. A. R. Lock and P. I. Pocock at Georgetown	1967-68
128 for 10th	K. Higgs and J. A. Snow at The Oval	1966

For West Indies

298 for 1st†	C. G. Greenidge and D. L. Haynes at St John's	1989-90
287* for 2nd	C. G. Greenidge and H. A. Gomes at Lord's	1984
338 for 3rd†	E. D. Weekes and F. M. M. Worrell at Port-of-Spain	1953-54
399 for 4th†	G. S. Sobers and F. M. M. Worrell at Bridgetown	1959-60
265 for 5th†	S. M. Nurse and G. S. Sobers at Leeds	1966
274* for 6th†	G. S. Sobers and D. A. J. Holford at Lord's	1966
155* for 7th‡	G. S. Sobers and B. D. Julien at Lord's	1973
99 for 8th	C. A. McWatt and J. K. Holt at Georgetown	1953-54
150 for 9th	E. A. E. Baptiste and M. A. Holding at Birmingham	1984
67* for 10th	M. A. Holding and C. E. H. Croft at St John's	1980-81

† *Denotes record partnership against all countries.*
‡ *231 runs were added for this wicket in two separate partnerships: G. S. Sobers retired ill and was replaced by K. D. Boyce when 155 had been added.*

TEN WICKETS OR MORE IN A MATCH

For England (11)

11-98 (7-44, 4-54)	T. E. Bailey, Lord's	1957
10-93 (5-54, 5-39)	A. P. Freeman, Manchester	1928
13-156 (8-86, 5-70)	A. W. Greig, Port-of-Spain	1973-74
11-48 (5-28, 6-20)	G. A. R. Lock, The Oval	1957
10-137 (4-60, 6-77)	D. E. Malcolm, Port-of-Spain	1989-90
11-96 (5-37, 6-59)†	C. S. Marriott, The Oval	1933
10-142 (4-82, 6-60)	J. A. Snow, Georgetown	1967-68
10-195 (5-105, 5-90)†	G. T. S. Stevens, Bridgetown	1929-30
11-152 (6-100, 5-52)	F. S. Trueman, Lord's	1963
12-119 (5-75, 7-44)	F. S. Trueman, Birmingham	1963
11-149 (4-79, 7-70)	W. Voce, Port-of-Spain	1929-30

For West Indies (12)

10-127 (2-82, 8-45)	C. E. L. Ambrose, Bridgetown	1989-90
11-147 (5-70, 6-77)†	K. D. Boyce, The Oval	1973
11-229 (5-137, 6-92)	W. Ferguson, Port-of-Spain	1947-48
11-157 (5-59, 6-98)†	L. R. Gibbs, Manchester	1963
10-106 (5-37, 5-69)	L. R. Gibbs, Manchester	1966
14-149 (8-92, 6-57)	M. A. Holding, The Oval	1976
10-96 (5-41, 5-55)†	H. H. H. Johnson, Kingston	1947-48
10-92 (6-32, 4-60)	M. D. Marshall, Lord's	1988
11-152 (5-66, 6-86)	S. Ramadhin, Lord's	1950
10-123 (5-60, 5-63)	A. M. E. Roberts, Lord's	1976
11-204 (8-104, 3-100)†	A. L. Valentine, Manchester	1950
10-160 (4-121, 6-39)	A. L. Valentine, The Oval	1950

† *Signifies ten wickets or more on first appearance in England–West Indies Tests.*

Note: F. S. Trueman took ten wickets or more in successive matches.

ENGLAND v NEW ZEALAND

Captains

Season	England	New Zealand	T	E	NZ	D
1929-30	A. H. H. Gilligan	T. C. Lowry	4	1	0	3
1931	D. R. Jardine	T. C. Lowry	3	1	0	2
1932-33	D. R. Jardine[1]	M. L. Page	2	0	0	2
1937	R. W. V. Robins	M. L. Page	3	1	0	2
1946-47	W. R. Hammond	W. A. Hadlee	1	0	0	1
1949	F. G. Mann[2]	W. A. Hadlee	4	0	0	4
1950-51	F. R. Brown	W. A. Hadlee	2	1	0	1
1954-55	L. Hutton	G. O. Rabone	2	2	0	0
1958	P. B. H. May	J. R. Reid	5	4	0	1
1958-59	P. B. H. May	J. R. Reid	2	1	0	1
1962-63	E. R. Dexter	J. R. Reid	3	3	0	0
1965	M. J. K. Smith	J. R. Reid	3	3	0	0
1965-66	M. J. K. Smith	B. W. Sinclair[3]	3	0	0	3
1969	R. Illingworth	G. T. Dowling	3	2	0	1
1970-71	R. Illingworth	G. T. Dowling	2	1	0	1
1973	R. Illingworth	B. E. Congdon	3	2	0	1
1974-75	M. H. Denness	B. E. Congdon	2	1	0	1
1977-78	G. Boycott	M. G. Burgess	3	1	1	1
1978	J. M. Brearley	M. G. Burgess	3	3	0	0
1983	R. G. D. Willis	G. P. Howarth	4	3	1	0
1983-84	R. G. D. Willis	G. P. Howarth	3	0	1	2
1986	M. W. Gatting	J. V. Coney	3	0	1	2
1987-88	M. W. Gatting	J. J. Crowe[4]	3	0	0	3
1990	G. A. Gooch	J. G. Wright	3	1	0	2
1991-92	G. A. Gooch	M. D. Crowe	3	2	0	1
	In New Zealand		35	13	2	20
	In England		37	20	2	15
	Totals.........................		72	33	4	35

Notes: The following deputised for the official touring captain or were appointed by the home authority for only a minor proportion of the series:
[1]R. E. S. Wyatt (Second). [2]F. R. Brown (Third and Fourth). [3]M. E. Chapple (First). [4]J. G. Wright (Third).

HIGHEST INNINGS TOTALS

For England in England: 546-4 dec. at Leeds.............................	1965
in New Zealand: 593-6 dec. at Auckland	1974-75

For New Zealand in England: 551-9 dec. at Lord's.......................	1973
in New Zealand: 537 at Wellington	1983-84

LOWEST INNINGS TOTALS

For England in England: 158 at Birmingham	1990
in New Zealand: 64 at Wellington	1977-78

For New Zealand in England: 47 at Lord's..............................	1958
in New Zealand: 26 at Auckland	1954-55

INDIVIDUAL HUNDREDS

For England (75)

G. O. B. Allen (1)
122† Lord's 1931

L. E. G. Ames (2)
137† Lord's 1931
103 Christchurch. 1932-33

D. L. Amiss (2)
138*† Nottingham . 1973
164* Christchurch. 1974-75

M. A. Atherton (1)
151† Nottingham .. 1990

T. E. Bailey (1)
134* Christchurch. 1950-51

K. F. Barrington (3)
126† Auckland ... 1962-63
137 Birmingham . 1965
163 Leeds 1965

I. T. Botham (3)
103 Christchurch. 1977-78
103 Nottingham . 1983
138 Wellington .. 1983-84

E. H. Bowley (1)
109 Auckland ... 1929-30

G. Boycott (2)
115 Leeds 1973
131 Nottingham . 1978

B. C. Broad (1)
114† Christchurch. 1987-88

D. C. S. Compton (2)
114 Leeds 1949
116 Lord's 1949

M. C. Cowdrey (2)
128* Wellington .. 1962-63
119 Lord's 1965

M. H. Denness (1)
181 Auckland ... 1974-75

E. R. Dexter (1)
141 Christchurch. 1958-59

B. L. D'Oliveira (1)
100 Christchurch. 1970-71

K. S. Duleepsinhji (2)
117 Auckland ... 1929-30
109 The Oval.... 1931

J. H. Edrich (3)
310*† Leeds 1965
115 Lord's 1969
155 Nottingham . 1969

W. J. Edrich (1)
100 The Oval.... 1949

K. W. R. Fletcher (2)
178 Lord's 1973
216 Auckland ... 1974-75

G. Fowler (1)
105† The Oval.... 1983

M. W. Gatting (1)
121 The Oval.... 1986

G. A. Gooch (3)
183 Lord's 1986
154 Birmingham . 1990
114 Auckland ... 1991-92

D. I. Gower (4)
111† The Oval.... 1978
112* Leeds 1983
108 Lord's 1983
131 The Oval.... 1986

A. W. Greig (1)
139† Nottingham . 1973

W. R. Hammond (4)
100* The Oval.... 1931
227 Christchurch. 1932-33
336* Auckland ... 1932-33
140 Lord's 1937

J. Hardstaff jun. (2)
114† Lord's 1937
103 The Oval.... 1937

L. Hutton (3)
100 Manchester.. 1937
101 Leeds 1949
206 The Oval.... 1949

B. R. Knight (1)
125† Auckland ... 1962-63

A. P. E. Knott (1)
101 Auckland ... 1970-71

A. J. Lamb (3)
102*† The Oval.... 1983
137* Nottingham . 1983
142 Wellington .. 1991-92

G. B. Legge (1)
196 Auckland ... 1929-30

P. B. H. May (3)
113* Leeds 1958
101 Manchester.. 1958
124* Auckland ... 1958-59

C. A. Milton (1)
104*† Leeds 1958

P. H. Parfitt (1)
131*† Auckland ... 1962-63

C. T. Radley (1)
158 Auckland ... 1977-78

D. W. Randall (2)
164 Wellington .. 1983-84
104 Auckland ... 1983-84

P. E. Richardson (1)
100† Birmingham . 1958

J. D. Robertson (1)
121† Lord's 1949

P. J. Sharpe (1)
111 Nottingham . 1969

R. T. Simpson (1)
103† Manchester.. 1949

A. J. Stewart (2)
148 Christchurch. 1991-92
107 Wellington .. 1991-92

H. Sutcliffe (2)
117† The Oval.... 1931
109* Manchester.. 1931

C. J. Tavaré (1)
109† The Oval.... 1983

C. Washbrook (1)
103* Leeds 1949

For New Zealand (36)

J. G. Bracewell (1)
110 Nottingham . 1986

M. G. Burgess (2)
104 Auckland ... 1970-71
105 Lord's 1973

J. V. Coney (1)
174* Wellington .. 1983-84

B. E. Congdon (3)
104 Christchurch. 1965-66
176 Nottingham . 1973
175 Lord's 1973

J. J. Crowe (1)
128 Auckland ... 1983-84

M. D. Crowe (3)
100 Wellington .. 1983-84
106 Lord's 1986
143 Wellington .. 1987-88

C. S. Dempster (2)
136 Wellington .. 1929-30
120 Lord's 1931

M. P. Donnelly (1)
206 Lord's 1949

T. J. Franklin (1)
101 Lord's 1990

M. J. Greatbatch (1)
107*† Auckland ... 1987-88

W. A. Hadlee (1)
116 Christchurch. 1946-47

G. P. Howarth (3)
122 } Auckland ... 1977-78
102 }
123 Lord's 1978

A. H. Jones (1)
143 Wellington .. 1991-92

E. Mills (1)		J. R. Reid (1)		B. Sutcliffe (2)	
7†	Wellington ..	1929-30	100	Christchurch.	1962-63	101	Manchester..	1949
M. L. Page (1)		K. R. Rutherford (1)		116	Christchurch.	1950-51
104	Lord's	1931	107*	Wellington ..	1987-88	J. G. Wright (4)	
M. Parker (1)		B. W. Sinclair (1)		130	Auckland ...	1983-84
121	Auckland ...	1974-75	114	Auckland ...	1965-66	119	The Oval....	1986
V. Pollard (2)		I. D. S. Smith (1)		103	Auckland ...	1987-88
116	Nottingham .	1973	113*	Auckland ...	1983-84	116	Wellington ..	1991-92
105*	Lord's	1973						

† *Signifies hundred on first appearance in England–New Zealand Tests.*

RECORD PARTNERSHIPS FOR EACH WICKET

For England

223	for 1st	G. Fowler and C. J. Tavaré at The Oval	1983
369	for 2nd	J. H. Edrich and K. F. Barrington at Leeds	1965
245	for 3rd	W. R. Hammond and J. Hardstaff jun. at Lord's	1937
266	for 4th	M. H. Denness and K. W. R. Fletcher at Auckland	1974-75
242	for 5th	W. R. Hammond and L. E. G. Ames at Christchurch	1932-33
240	for 6th†	P. H. Parfitt and B. R. Knight at Auckland	1962-63
149	for 7th	A. P. E. Knott and P. Lever at Auckland	1970-71
246	for 8th	L. E. G. Ames and G. O. B. Allen at Lord's	1931
163*	for 9th†	M. C. Cowdrey and A. C. Smith at Wellington	1962-63
59	for 10th	A. P. E. Knott and N. Gifford at Nottingham	1973

For New Zealand

276	for 1st	C. S. Dempster and J. E. Mills at Wellington	1929-30
241	for 2nd†	J. G. Wright and A. H. Jones at Wellington	1991-92
210	for 3rd	B. A. Edgar and M. D. Crowe at Lord's................	1986
155	for 4th	M. D. Crowe and M. J. Greatbatch at Wellington	1987-88
177	for 5th	B. E. Congdon and V. Pollard at Nottingham	1973
134	for 6th	K. R. Rutherford and J. G. Bracewell at Wellington	1987-88
117	for 7th	D. N. Patel and C. L. Cairns at Christchurch	1991-92
104	for 8th	D. A. R. Moloney and A. W. Roberts at Lord's	1937
118	for 9th	J. V. Coney and B. L. Cairns at Wellington	1983-84
57	for 10th	F. L. H. Mooney and J. Cowie at Leeds................	1949

† *Denotes record partnership against all countries.*

TEN WICKETS OR MORE IN A MATCH

For England (8)

11-140 (6-101, 5-39)	I. T. Botham, Lord's.....................	1978
10-149 (5-98, 5-51)	A. W. Greig, Auckland	1974-75
11-65 (4-14, 7-51)	G. A. R. Lock, Leeds..................	1958
11-84 (5-31, 6-53)	G. A. R. Lock, Christchurch............	1958-59
11-147 (4-100, 7-47)†	P. C. R. Tufnell, Christchurch	1991-92
11-70 (4-38, 7-32)†	D. L. Underwood, Lord's..............	1969
12-101 (6-41, 6-60)	D. L. Underwood, The Oval	1969
12-97 (6-12, 6-85)	D. L. Underwood, Christchurch	1970-71

For New Zealand (4)

10-144 (7-74, 3-70)	B. L. Cairns, Leeds....................	1983
10-140 (4-73, 6-67)	J. Cowie, Manchester..................	1937
10-100 (4-74, 6-26)	R. J. Hadlee, Wellington	1977-78
10-140 (6-80, 4-60)	R. J. Hadlee, Nottingham	1986

† *Signifies ten wickets or more on first appearance in England–New Zealand Tests.*

Note: D. L. Underwood took 12 wickets in successive matches against New Zealand in 1969 and 1970-71.

HAT-TRICK AND FOUR WICKETS IN FIVE BALLS

M. J. C. Allom, in his first Test match, v New Zealand at Christchurch in 1929-30, dismisse
C. S. Dempster, T. C. Lowry, K. C. James, and F. T. Badcock to take four wickets in fiv
balls (w-www).

ENGLAND v INDIA

Season	England		India	T	E	I	
		Captains					
1932	D. R. Jardine		C. K. Nayudu	1	1	0	
1933-34	D. R. Jardine		C. K. Nayudu	3	2	0	
1936	G. O. B. Allen	Maharaj of Vizianagram		3	2	0	
1946	W. R. Hammond		Nawab of Pataudi sen.	3	1	0	
1951-52	N. D. Howard[1]		V. S. Hazare	5	1	1	
1952	L. Hutton		V. S. Hazare	4	3	0	
1959	P. B. H. May[2]		D. K. Gaekwad[3]	5	5	0	
1961-62	E. R. Dexter		N. J. Contractor	5	0	2	
1963-64	M. J. K. Smith	Nawab of Pataudi jun.		5	0	0	
1967	D. B. Close	Nawab of Pataudi jun.		3	3	0	
1971	R. Illingworth		A. L. Wadekar	3	0	1	
1972-73	A. R. Lewis		A. L. Wadekar	5	1	2	
1974	M. H. Denness		A. L. Wadekar	3	3	0	
1976-77	A. W. Greig		B. S. Bedi	5	3	1	
1979	J. M. Brearley	S. Venkataraghavan		4	1	0	
1979-80	J. M. Brearley		G. R. Viswanath	1	1	0	
1981-82	K. W. R. Fletcher		S. M. Gavaskar	6	0	1	
1982	R. G. D. Willis		S. M. Gavaskar	3	1	0	
1984-85	D. I. Gower		S. M. Gavaskar	5	2	1	
1986	M. W. Gatting[4]		Kapil Dev	3	0	2	
1990	G. A. Gooch		M. Azharuddin	3	1	0	
	In England			38	21	3	
	In India			40	10	8	
	Totals			78	31	11	

Notes: The 1932 Indian touring team was captained by the Maharaj of Porbandar but he did n
play in the Test match.

The following deputised for the official touring captain or were appointed by the hor
authority for only a minor proportion of the series:
[1]D. B. Carr (Fifth). [2]M. C. Cowdrey (Fourth and Fifth). [3]Pankaj Roy (Second). [4]D. I. Gow
(First).

HIGHEST INNINGS TOTALS

For England in England: 653-4 dec. at Lord's 199
in India: 652-7 dec. at Madras............................... 1984-8

For India in England: 606-9 dec. at The Oval 199
in India: 553-8 dec. at Kanpur 1984-8

LOWEST INNINGS TOTALS

For England in England: 101 at The Oval 197
in India: 102 at Bombay................................. 1981-8

For India in England: 42 at Lord's 197
in India: 83 at Madras 1976-7

INDIVIDUAL HUNDREDS

For England (70)

. L. Amiss (2)
38 Lord's 1974
79 Delhi....... 1976-77
. A. Atherton (1)
31 Manchester.. 1990
. F. Barrington (3)
51* Bombay 1961-62
72 Kanpur 1961-62
13* Delhi 1961-62
T. Botham (5)
37 Leeds 1979
14 Bombay 1979-80
42 Kanpur 1981-82
28 Manchester.. 1982
08 The Oval.... 1982
. Boycott (4)
46*† Leeds 1967
55 Birmingham . 1979
25 The Oval.... 1979
05 Delhi....... 1981-82
. C. Cowdrey (3)
60 Leeds 1959
07 Calcutta 1963-64
51 Delhi 1963-64
. H. Denness (2)
18 Lord's 1974
00 Birmingham . 1974
. R. Dexter (1)
26* Kanpur 1961-62
. L. D'Oliveira (1)
09† Leeds 1967
. H. Edrich (1)
00* Manchester.. 1974
. G. Evans (1)
04 Lord's 1952
. W. R. Fletcher (2)
13 Bombay 1972-73
23* Manchester.. 1974

G. Fowler (1)
201 Madras 1984-85
M. W. Gatting (3)
136 Bombay 1984-85
207 Madras 1984-85
183* Birmingham . 1986
G. A. Gooch (5)
127 Madras 1981-82
114 Lord's 1986
333 }
123 } Lord's 1990
116 Manchester.. 1990
D. I. Gower (2)
200*† Birmingham . 1979
157* The Oval ... 1990
T. W. Graveney (2)
175† Bombay 1951-52
151 Lord's 1967
A. W. Greig (3)
148 Bombay 1972-73
106 Lord's 1974
103 Calcutta 1976-77
W. R. Hammond (2)
167 Manchester.. 1936
217 The Oval.... 1936
J. Hardstaff jun. (1)
205* Lord's 1946
L. Hutton (2)
150 Lord's 1952
104 Manchester.. 1952
R. Illingworth (1)
107 Manchester.. 1971
B. R. Knight (1)
127 Kanpur 1963-64

A. J. Lamb (3)
107 The Oval.... 1982
139 Lord's 1990
109 Manchester.. 1990
A. R. Lewis (1)
125 Kanpur 1972-73
D. Lloyd (1)
214* Birmingham . 1974
B. W. Luckhurst (1)
101 Manchester.. 1971
P. B. H. May (1)
106 Nottingham . 1959
P. H. Parfitt (1)
121 Kanpur 1963-64
G. Pullar (2)
131 Manchester.. 1959
119 Kanpur 1961-62
D. W. Randall (1)
126 Lord's 1982
R. T. Robinson (1)
160 Delhi....... 1984-85
D. S. Sheppard (1)
119 The Oval.... 1952
M. J. K. Smith (1)
100† Manchester.. 1959
R. A. Smith (2)
100*† Lord's 1990
121* Manchester.. 1990
C. J. Tavaré (1)
149 Delhi....... 1981-82
B. H. Valentine (1)
136† Bombay 1933-34
C. F. Walters (1)
102 Madras 1933-34
A. J. Watkins (1)
137*† Delhi....... 1951-52
T. S. Worthington (1)
128 The Oval.... 1936

For India (56)

.. Amarnath (1)
18† Bombay 1933-34
. Azharuddin (5)
10† Calcutta 1984-85
05 Madras 1984-85
22 Kanpur 1984-85
07 Lord's 1990
79 Manchester.. 1990
. A. Baig (1)
12† Manchester.. 1959
. M. Engineer (1)
21 Bombay 1972-73
. M. Gavaskar (4)
01 Manchester.. 1974
08 Bombay 1976-77

221 The Oval.... 1979
172 Bangalore ... 1981-82
Hanumant Singh (1)
105† Delhi....... 1963-64
V. S. Hazare (2)
164* Delhi....... 1951-52
155 Bombay 1951-52
M. L. Jaisimha (2)
127 Delhi....... 1961-62
129 Calcutta 1963-64
Kapil Dev (2)
116 Kanpur 1981-82
110 The Oval ... 1990
S. M. H. Kirmani (1)
102 Bombay 1984-85

B. K. Kunderan (2)
192 Madras 1963-64
100 Delhi....... 1963-64
V. L. Manjrekar (3)
133 Leeds 1952
189* Delhi....... 1961-62
108 Calcutta 1963-64
V. Mankad (1)
184 Lord's 1952
V. M. Merchant (3)
114 Manchester.. 1936
128 The Oval.... 1946
154 Delhi....... 1951-52
Mushtaq Ali (1)
112 Manchester.. 1936

R. G. Nadkarni (1)		**R. J. Shastri** (4)		157	Lord's 198
122*	Kanpur 1963-64	142	Bombay 1984-85	137	Kanpur 1984-8
Nawab of Pataudi jun. (3)		111	Calcutta 1984-85	126*	Lord's 198
103	Madras 1961-62	100	Lord's 1990	102*	Leeds 198
203*	Delhi....... 1963-64	187	The Oval ... 1990	**G. R. Viswanath** (4)	
148	Leeds 1967	**S. R. Tendulkar** (1)		113	Bombay 1972-7
S. M. Patil (1)		119*	Manchester.. 1990	113	Lord's 197
129*	Manchester.. 1982	**P. R. Umrigar** (3)		107	Delhi...... 1981-8
D. G. Phadkar (1)		130*	Madras 1951-52	222	Madras 1981-8
115	Calcutta 1951-52	118	Manchester.. 1959	**Yashpal Sharma** (1)	
Pankaj Roy (2)		147*	Kanpur 1961-62	140	Madras 1981-8
140	Bombay 1951-52	**D. B. Vengsarkar** (5)			
111	Madras 1951-52	103	Lord's 1979		

† *Signifies hundred on first appearance in England–India Tests.*

Notes: G. A. Gooch's match aggregate of 456 (333 and 123) for England at Lord's in 1990 is the record in Test matches and provides the only instance of a batsman scoring a triple-hundred and a hundred in the same first-class match. His 333 is the highest innings in any match at Lord's.

M. Azharuddin scored hundreds in each of his first three Tests.

RECORD PARTNERSHIPS FOR EACH WICKET

For England

225 for 1st	G. A. Gooch and M. A. Atherton at Manchester	199
241 for 2nd	G. Fowler and M. W. Gatting at Madras	1984-8
308 for 3rd	G. A. Gooch and A. J. Lamb at Lord's	199
266 for 4th	W. R. Hammond and T. S. Worthington at The Oval..........	19
254 for 5th†	K. W. R. Fletcher and A. W. Greig at Bombay..............	1972-7
171 for 6th	I. T. Botham and R. W. Taylor at Bombay.................	1979-8
125 for 7th	D. W. Randall and P. H. Edmonds at Lord's................	198
168 for 8th	R. Illingworth and P, Lever at Manchester.................	197
83 for 9th	K. W. R. Fletcher and N. Gifford at Madras...............	1972-7
70 for 10th	P. J. W. Allott and R. G. D. Willis at Lord's..............	198

For India

213 for 1st	S. M. Gavaskar and C. P. S. Chauhan at The Oval	19
192 for 2nd	F. M. Engineer and A. L. Wadekar at Bombay	1972-7
316 for 3rd†‡	G. R. Viswanath and Yashpal Sharma at Madras	1981-8
222 for 4th†	V. S. Hazare and V. L. Manjrekar at Leeds	195
214 for 5th†	M. Azharuddin and R. J. Shastri at Calcutta...............	1984-8
130 for 6th	S. M. H. Kirmani and Kapil Dev at The Oval...............	198
235 for 7th†	R. J. Shastri and S. M. H. Kirmani at Bombay..............	1984-8
128 for 8th	R. J. Shastri and S. M. H. Kirmani at Delhi	1981-8
104 for 9th	R. J. Shastri and Madan Lal at Delhi	1981-8
51 for 10th {	R. G. Nadkarni and B. S. Chandrasekhar at Calcutta	1963-6
	S. M. H. Kirmani and Chetan Sharma at Madras............	1984-8

† *Denotes record partnership against all countries.*
‡ *415 runs were added between the fall of the 2nd and 3rd wickets: D. B. Vengsarkar retired hur when he and Viswanath had added 99 runs.*

TEN WICKETS OR MORE IN A MATCH

For England (7)

0-78 (5-35, 5-43)†	G. O. B. Allen, Lord's	1936
1-145 (7-49, 4-96)†	A. V. Bedser, Lord's	1946
1-93 (4-41, 7-52)	A. V. Bedser, Manchester	1946
3-106 (6-58, 7-48)	I. T. Botham, Bombay	1979-80
1-163 (6-104, 5-59)†	N. A. Foster, Madras	1984-85
0-70 (7-46, 3-24)†	J. K. Lever, Delhi	1976-77
1-153 (7-49, 4-104)	H. Verity, Madras	1933-34

For India (4)

0-177 (6-105, 4-72)	S. A. Durani, Madras	1961-62
2-108 (8-55, 4-53)	V. Mankad, Madras	1951-52
0-188 (4-130, 6-58)	Chetan Sharma, Birmingham	1986
2-181 (6-64, 6-117)†	L. Sivaramakrishnan, Bombay	1984-85

† *Signifies ten wickets or more on first appearance in England–India Tests.*

Note: A. V. Bedser took 11 wickets in a match in the first two Tests of his career.

ENGLAND v PAKISTAN

	Captains					
Season	*England*	*Pakistan*	*T*	*E*	*P*	*D*
1954	L. Hutton[1]	A. H. Kardar	4	1	1	2
1961-62	E. R. Dexter	Imtiaz Ahmed	3	1	0	2
1962	E. R. Dexter[2]	Javed Burki	5	4	0	1
1967	D. B. Close	Hanif Mohammad	3	2	0	1
1968-69	M. C. Cowdrey	Saeed Ahmed	3	0	0	3
1971	R. Illingworth	Intikhab Alam	3	1	0	2
1972-73	A. R. Lewis	Majid Khan	3	0	0	3
1974	M. H. Denness	Intikhab Alam	3	0	0	3
1977-78	J. M. Brearley[3]	Wasim Bari	3	0	0	3
1978	J. M. Brearley	Wasim Bari	3	2	0	1
1982	R. G. D. Willis[4]	Imran Khan	3	2	1	0
1983-84	R. G. D. Willis[5]	Zaheer Abbas	3	0	1	2
1987	M. W. Gatting	Imran Khan	5	0	1	4
1987-88	M. W. Gatting	Javed Miandad	3	0	1	2
1992	G. A. Gooch	Javed Miandad	5	1	2	2
	In England		34	13	5	16
	In Pakistan		18	1	2	15
	Totals		52	14	7	31

Notes: The following deputised for the official touring captain or were appointed by the home authority for only a minor proportion of the series:
[1]D. S. Sheppard (Second and Third). [2]M. C. Cowdrey (Third). [3]G. Boycott (Third). [4]D. I. Gower (Second). [5]D. I. Gower (Second and Third).

HIGHEST INNINGS TOTALS

For England in England: 558-6 dec. at Nottingham		1954
in Pakistan: 546-8 dec. at Faisalabad		1983-84
For Pakistan in England: 708 at The Oval		1987
in Pakistan: 569-9 dec. at Hyderabad		1972-73

LOWEST INNINGS TOTALS

For England in England: 130 at The Oval 195
         in Pakistan: 130 at Lahore 1987-8

For Pakistan in England: 87 at Lord's 195
         in Pakistan: 191 at Faisalabad 1987-8

INDIVIDUAL HUNDREDS

For England (44)

D. L. Amiss (3)
112   Lahore 1972-73
158   Hyderabad .. 1972-73
183   The Oval.... 1974
C. W. J. Athey (1)
123   Lord's 1987
K. F. Barrington (4)
139†   Lahore 1961-62
148   Lord's 1967
109*   Nottingham . 1967
142   The Oval.... 1967
I. T. Botham (2)
100†   Birmingham . 1978
108   Lord's 1978
G. Boycott (3)
121*   Lord's 1971
112   Leeds 1971
100*   Hyderabad .. 1977-78
B. C. Broad (1)
116   Faisalabad .. 1987-88
D. C. S. Compton (1)
278   Nottingham . 1954
M. C. Cowdrey (3)
159†   Birmingham . 1962

182   The Oval.... 1962
100   Lahore 1968-69
E. R. Dexter (2)
205   Karachi 1961-62
172   The Oval.... 1962
B. L. D'Oliveira (1)
114*   Dacca 1968-69
K. W. R. Fletcher (1)
122   The Oval.... 1974
M. W. Gatting (2)
124   Birmingham . 1987
150*   The Oval.... 1987
G. A. Gooch (1)
135   Leeds 1992
D. I. Gower (2)
152   Faisalabad .. 1983-84
173*   Lahore 1983-84
T. W. Graveney (3)
153   Lord's 1962
114   Nottingham . 1962
105   Karachi 1968-69
A. P. E. Knott (1)
116   Birmingham . 1971

B. W. Luckhurst (1)
108*†   Birmingham . 197
C. Milburn (1)
139   Karachi 1968-6
P. H. Parfitt (4)
111   Karachi 1961-6
101*   Birmingham . 196
111   Leeds 196
101*   Nottingham . 196
G. Pullar (1)
165   Dacca 1961-6
C. T. Radley (1)
106†   Birmingham . 197
D. W. Randall (1)
105   Birmingham . 198
R. T. Robinson (1)
166†   Manchester.. 198
R. T. Simpson (1)
101   Nottingham . 195
R. A. Smith (1)
127†   Birmingham . 199
A. J. Stewart (1)
190†   Birmingham . 199

For Pakistan (33)

Aamir Sohail (1)
205   Manchester.. 1992
Alim-ud-Din (1)
109   Karachi 1961-62
Asif Iqbal (3)
146   The Oval.... 1967
104*   Birmingham . 1971
102   Lahore 1972-73
Hanif Mohammad (3)
111 ⎱
104 ⎰ Dacca 1961-62
187*   Lord's 1967
Haroon Rashid (2)
122†   Lahore 1977-78
108   Hyderabad .. 1977-78
Imran Khan (1)
118   The Oval.... 1987

Intikhab Alam (1)
138   Hyderabad .. 1972-73
Javed Burki (3)
138†   Lahore 1961-62
140   Dacca 1961-62
101   Lord's 1962
Javed Miandad (2)
260   The Oval.... 1987
153*   Birmingham . 1992
Mohsin Khan (2)
200   Lord's 1982
104   Lahore 1983-84
Mudassar Nazar (3)
114†   Lahore 1977-88
124   Birmingham . 1987
120   Lahore 1987-88

Mushtaq Mohammad (3)
100*   Nottingham . 196
100   Birmingham . 197
157   Hyderabad .. 1972-7
Nasim-ul-Ghani (1)
101   Lord's 196
Sadiq Mohammad (1)
119   Lahore 1972-7
Salim Malik (3)
116   Faisalabad .. 1983-8
102   The Oval.... 198
165   Birmingham . 199
Wasim Raja (1)
112   Faisalabad .. 1983-8
Zaheer Abbas (2)
274†   Birmingham . 197
240   The Oval.... 197

† *Signifies hundred on first appearance in England–Pakistan Tests.*

Note: Three batsmen – Majid Khan, Mushtaq Mohammad and D. L. Amiss – were dismisse
for 99 at Karachi, 1972-73: the only instance in Test matches.

RECORD PARTNERSHIPS FOR EACH WICKET

For England

98	for 1st	G. Pullar and R. W. Barber at Dacca	1961-62
248	for 2nd	M. C. Cowdrey and E. R. Dexter at The Oval	1962
227	for 3rd	A. J. Stewart and R. A. Smith at Birmingham	1992
188	for 4th	E. R. Dexter and P. H. Parfitt at Karachi	1961-62
192	for 5th	D. C. S. Compton and T. E. Bailey at Nottingham	1954
153*	for 6th	P. H. Parfitt and D. A. Allen at Birmingham	1962
167	for 7th	D. I. Gower and V. J. Marks at Faisalabad	1983-84
99	for 8th	P. H. Parfitt and D. A. Allen at Leeds	1962
76	for 9th	T. W. Graveney and F. S. Trueman at Lord's	1962
79	for 10th	R. W. Taylor and R. G. D. Willis at Birmingham	1982

For Pakistan

173	for 1st	Mohsin Khan and Shoaib Mohammad at Lahore	1983-84
291	for 2nd†	Zaheer Abbas and Mushtaq Mohammad at Birmingham	1971
180	for 3rd	Mudassar Nazar and Haroon Rashid at Lahore	1977-78
322	for 4th	Javed Miandad and Salim Malik at Birmingham	1992
197	for 5th	Javed Burki and Nasim-ul-Ghani at Lord's	1962
145	for 6th	Mushtaq Mohammad and Intikhab Alam at Hyderabad	1972-73
89	for 7th	Ijaz Ahmed and Salim Yousuf at The Oval	1987
130	for 8th†	Hanif Mohammad and Asif Iqbal at Lord's	1967
190	for 9th†	Asif Iqbal and Intikhab Alam at The Oval	1967
62	for 10th	Sarfraz Nawaz and Asif Masood at Leeds	1974

† *Denotes record partnership against all countries.*

TEN WICKETS OR MORE IN A MATCH

For England (2)

11-83 (6-65, 5-18)†	N. G. B. Cook, Karachi	1983-84
13-71 (5-20, 8-51)	D. L. Underwood, Lord's	1974

For Pakistan (6)

10-194 (5-84, 5-110)	Abdul Qadir, Lahore	1983-84
13-101 (9-56, 4-45)	Abdul Qadir, Lahore	1987-88
10-186 (5-88, 5-98)	Abdul Qadir, Karachi	1987-88
10-211 (7-96, 3-115)	Abdul Qadir, The Oval	1987
12-99 (6-53, 6-46)	Fazal Mahmood, The Oval	1954
10-77 (3-37, 7-40)	Imran Khan, Leeds	1987

† *Signifies ten wickets or more on first appearance in England–Pakistan Tests.*

FOUR WICKETS IN FIVE BALLS

C. M. Old, v Pakistan at Birmingham in 1978, dismissed Wasim Raja, Wasim Bari, Iqbal Qasim and Sikander Bakht to take four wickets in five balls (ww-ww).

ENGLAND v SRI LANKA

	Captains					
Season	England	Sri Lanka	T	E	SL	D
1981-82	K. W. R. Fletcher	B. Warnapura	1	1	0	0
1984	D. I. Gower	L. R. D. Mendis	1	0	0	1
1988	G. A. Gooch	R. S. Madugalle	1	1	0	0
1991	G. A. Gooch	P. A. de Silva	1	1	0	0
	In England		3	2	0	1
	In Sri Lanka		1	1	0	0
	Totals........................		4	3	0	1

INNINGS TOTALS

Highest innings total for England: 429 at Lord's 1988
for Sri Lanka: 491-7 dec. at Lord's 1984

Lowest innings total for England: 223 at Colombo (PSS) 1981-82
for Sri Lanka: 175 at Colombo (PSS)................. 1981-82

INDIVIDUAL HUNDREDS

For England (3)

G. A. Gooch (1)	A. J. Lamb (1)	A. J. Stewart (1)
174 Lord's 1991	107† Lord's 1984	113*† Lord's 1991

For Sri Lanka (3)

L. R. D. Mendis (1)	S. A. R. Silva (1)	S. Wettimuny (1)
111 Lord's 1984	102*† Lord's 1984	190 Lord's 1984

† *Signifies hundred on first appearance in England–Sri Lanka Tests.*

BEST BOWLING

Best bowling in an innings for England: 7-70 by P. A. J. DeFreitas at Lord's ... 1991
for Sri Lanka: 5-69 by R. J. Ratnayake at Lord's.... 1991

RECORD PARTNERSHIPS FOR EACH WICKET

For England

78 for 1st	G. A. Gooch and H. Morris at Lord's	1991
139 for 2nd	G. A. Gooch and A. J. Stewart at Lord's	1991
105 for 3rd	G. A. Gooch and R. A. Smith at Lord's	1991
87 for 4th	K. J. Barnett and A. J. Lamb at Lord's....................	1988
40 for 5th	A. J. Stewart and I. T. Botham at Lord's	1991
87 for 6th	A. J. Lamb and R. M. Ellison at Lord's	1984
63 for 7th	A. J. Stewart and R. C. Russell at Lord's	1991
12 for 8th	A. J. Stewart and P. A. J. DeFreitas at Lord's	1991
37 for 9th	P. J. Newport and N. A. Foster at Lord's	1988
9 for 10th	N. A. Foster and D. V. Lawrence at Lord's	1988

For Sri Lanka

50 for 1st	D. S. B. P. Kuruppu and U. C. Hathurusinghe at Lord's	.....	1991
83 for 2nd	B. Warnapura and R. L. Dias at Colombo (PSS)	....	1981-82
101 for 3rd	S. Wettimuny and R. L. Dias at Lord's	....	1984
48 for 4th	S. Wettimuny and A. Ranatunga at Lord's	....	1984
150 for 5th†	S. Wettimuny and L. R. D. Mendis at Lord's	....	1984
138 for 6th†	S. A. R. Silva and L. R. D. Mendis at Lord's	....	1984
74 for 7th	U. C. Hathurusinghe and R. J. Ratnayake at Lord's	....	1991
29 for 8th	R. J. Ratnayake and C. P. H. Ramanayake at Lord's	....	1991
12 for 9th	⎰ J. R. Ratnayeke and G. F. Labrooy at Lord's	....	1988
	⎱ C. P. H. Ramanayake and K. I. W. Wijegunawardene at Lord's		1991
64 for 10th†	J. R. Ratnayeke and G. F. Labrooy at Lord's	....	1988

† *Denotes record partnership against all countries.*

ENGLAND v REST OF THE WORLD

In 1970, owing to the cancellation of the South African tour to England, a series of matches was arranged, with the trappings of a full Test series, between England and the Rest of the World. It was played for the Guinness Trophy.

The following players represented the Rest of the World: E. J. Barlow (5), F. M. Engineer (2), L. R. Gibbs (4), Intikhab Alam (5), R. B. Kanhai (5), C. H. Lloyd (5), G. D. McKenzie (3), D. L. Murray (3), Mushtaq Mohammad (2), P. M. Pollock (1), R. G. Pollock (5), M. J. Procter (5), B. A. Richards (5), G. S. Sobers (5).

A list of players who appeared for England in these matches may be found on page 90.

AUSTRALIA v SOUTH AFRICA

Captains

Season	Australia	South Africa	T	A	SA	D
1902-03S	J. Darling	H. M. Taberer[1]	3	2	0	1
1910-11A	C. Hill	P. W. Sherwell	5	4	1	0
1912E	S. E. Gregory	F. Mitchell[2]	3	2	0	1
1921-22S	H. L. Collins	H. W. Taylor	3	1	0	2
1931-32A	W. M. Woodfull	H. B. Cameron	5	5	0	0
1935-36S	V. Y. Richardson	H. F. Wade	5	4	0	1
1949-50S	A. L. Hassett	A. D. Nourse	5	4	0	1
1952-53A	A. L. Hassett	J. E. Cheetham	5	2	2	1
1957-58S	I. D. Craig	C. B. van Ryneveld[3]	5	3	0	2
1963-64A	R. B. Simpson[4]	T. L. Goddard	5	1	1	3
1966-67S	R. B. Simpson	P. L. van der Merwe	5	1	3	1
1969-70S	W. M. Lawry	A. Bacher	4	0	4	0
	In South Africa	....	30	15	7	8
	In Australia	....	20	12	4	4
	In England	....	3	2	0	1
	Totals	....	53	29	11	13

S Played in South Africa. A Played in Australia. E Played in England.

Notes: The following deputised for the official touring captain or were appointed by the home authority for only a minor proportion of the series:
[1]J. H. Anderson (Second), E. A. Halliwell (Third). [2]L. J. Tancred (Third). [3]D. J. McGlew (First). [4]R. Benaud (First).

HIGHEST INNINGS TOTALS

For Australia in Australia: 578 at Melbourne	....	1910-11
in South Africa: 549-7 dec. at Port Elizabeth	....	1949-50
For South Africa in Australia: 595 at Adelaide	....	1963-64
in South Africa: 622-9 dec. at Durban	....	1969-70

LOWEST INNINGS TOTALS

For Australia in Australia: 153 at Melbourne............................ 1931-32
             in South Africa: 75 at Durban 1949-50

For South Africa in Australia: 36† at Melbourne 1931-32
               in South Africa: 85 at Johannesburg 1902-03

† *Scored 45 in the second innings giving the smallest aggregate of 81 (12 extras) in Test cricket.*

INDIVIDUAL HUNDREDS

For Australia (55)

W. W. Armstrong (2)	108 Johannesburg 1935-36	**C. G. Macartney** (2)
159*‡ Johannesburg 1902-03	118 Durban 1935-36	137 Sydney 1910-11
132 Melbourne .. 1910-11	**J. M. Gregory** (1)	116 Durban 1921-22
W. Bardsley (3)	119 Johannesburg 1921-22	**S. J. McCabe** (2)
132† Sydney 1910-11	**R. N. Harvey** (8)	149 Durban 1935-36
121 Manchester.. 1912	178 Cape Town .. 1949-50	189* Johannesburg 1935-36
164 Lord's 1912	151* Durban 1949-50	**C. C. McDonald** (1)
R. Benaud (2)	100 Johannesburg 1949-50	154 Adelaide 1952-53
122 Johannesburg 1957-58	116 Pt Elizabeth . 1949-50	**J. Moroney** (2)
100 Johannesburg 1957-58	109 Brisbane 1952-53	118 ⎱ Johannesburg 1949-50
B. C. Booth (2)	190 Sydney 1952-53	101* ⎰
169† Brisbane 1963-64	116 Adelaide 1952-53	**A. R. Morris** (2)
102* Sydney 1963-64	205 Melbourne .. 1952-53	111 Johannesburg 1949-50
D. G. Bradman (4)	**A. L. Hassett** (3)	157 Pt Elizabeth . 1949-50
226† Brisbane 1931-32	112† Johannesburg 1949-50	**K. E. Rigg** (1)
112 Sydney 1931-32	167 Pt Elizabeth . 1949-50	127† Sydney 1931-32
167 Melbourne .. 1931-32	163 Adelaide 1952-53	**J. Ryder** (1)
299* Adelaide 1931-32	**C. Hill** (3)	142 Cape Town .. 1921-22
W. A. Brown (1)	142† Johannesburg 1902-03	**R. B. Simpson** (1)
121 Cape Town .. 1935-36	191 Sydney 1910-11	153 Cape Town .. 1966-67
J. W. Burke (1)	100 Melbourne .. 1910-11	**K. R. Stackpole** (1)
189 Cape Town .. 1957-58	**C. Kelleway** (2)	134 Cape Town .. 1966-67
A. G. Chipperfield (1)	114 Manchester.. 1912	**V. T. Trumper** (2)
109† Durban 1935-36	102 Lord's 1912	159 Melbourne .. 1910-11
H. L. Collins (1)	**W. M. Lawry** (1)	214* Adelaide 1910-11
203 Johannesburg 1921-22	157 Melbourne .. 1963-64	**W. M. Woodfull** (1)
J. H. Fingleton (3)	**S. J. E. Loxton** (1)	161 Melbourne .. 1931-32
112 Cape Town .. 1935-36	101† Johannesburg 1949-50	

For South Africa (36)

E. J. Barlow (5)	**D. T. Lindsay** (3)	**B. A. Richards** (2)
114† Brisbane 1963-64	182 Johannesburg 1966-67	140 Durban 1969-70
109 Melbourne .. 1963-64	137 Durban 1966-67	126 Pt Elizabeth . 1969-70
201 Adelaide 1963-64	131 Johannesburg 1966-67	**E. A. B. Rowan** (1)
127 Cape Town .. 1969-70	**D. J. McGlew** (2)	143 Durban 1949-50
110 Johannesburg 1969-70	108 Johannesburg 1957-58	**J. H. Sinclair** (2)
K. C. Bland (1)	105 Durban 1957-58	101 Johannesburg 1902-03
126 Sydney 1963-64	**A. D. Nourse** (2)	104 Cape Town .. 1902-03
W. R. Endean (1)	231 Johannesburg 1935-36	**S. J. Snooke** (1)
162* Melbourne .. 1952-53	114 Cape Town .. 1949-50	103 Adelaide 1910-11
G. A. Faulkner (3)	**A. W. Nourse** (1)	**K. G. Viljoen** (1)
204 Melbourne .. 1910-11	111 Johannesburg 1921-22	111 Melbourne .. 1931-32
115 Adelaide 1910-11	**R. G. Pollock** (5)	**J. H. B. Waite** (2)
122* Manchester.. 1912	122 Sydney 1963-64	115 Johannesburg 1957-58
C. N. Frank (1)	175 Adelaide 1963-64	134 Durban 1957-58
152 Johannesburg 1921-22	209 Cape Town .. 1966-67	**J. W. Zulch** (2)
B. L. Irvine (1)	105 Pt Elizabeth . 1966-67	105 Adelaide 1910-11
102 Pt Elizabeth . 1969-70	274 Durban 1969-70	150 Sydney 1910-11

† *Signifies hundred on first appearance in Australia–South Africa Tests.*
‡ *Carried his bat.*

RECORD PARTNERSHIPS FOR EACH WICKET

For Australia

233 for 1st	J. H. Fingleton and W. A. Brown at Cape Town	....	1935-36
275 for 2nd	C. C. McDonald and A. L. Hassett at Adelaide	....	1952-53
242 for 3rd	C. Kelleway and W. Bardsley at Lord's	....	1912
168 for 4th	R. N. Harvey and K. R. Miller at Sydney	....	1952-53
143 for 5th	W. W. Armstrong and V. T. Trumper at Melbourne	....	1910-11
107 for 6th	C. Kelleway and V. S. Ransford at Melbourne	....	1910-11
160 for 7th	R. Benaud and G. D. McKenzie at Sydney	....	1963-64
83 for 8th	A. G. Chipperfield and C. V. Grimmett at Durban	....	1935-36
78 for 9th	{ D. G. Bradman and W. J. O'Reilly at Adelaide	....	1931-32
	{ K. D. Mackay and I. Meckiff at Johannesburg	....	1957-58
82 for 10th	V. S. Ransford and W. J. Whitty at Melbourne	....	1910-11

For South Africa

176 for 1st	D. J. McGlew and T. L. Goddard at Johannesburg	....	1957-58
173 for 2nd	L. J. Tancred and C. B. Llewellyn at Johannesburg	....	1902-03
341 for 3rd†	E. J. Barlow and R. G. Pollock at Adelaide	....	1963-64
206 for 4th	C. N. Frank and A. W. Nourse at Johannesburg	....	1921-22
129 for 5th	J. H. B. Waite and W. R. Endean at Johannesburg	....	1957-58
200 for 6th†	R. G. Pollock and H. R. Lance at Durban	....	1969-70
221 for 7th	D. T. Lindsay and P. L. van der Merwe at Johannesburg	......	1966-67
124 for 8th†	A. W. Nourse and E. A. Halliwell at Johannesburg	....	1902-03
85 for 9th	R. G. Pollock and P. M. Pollock at Cape Town	....	1966-67
53 for 10th	L. A. Stricker and S. J. Pegler at Adelaide	....	1910-11

† *Denotes record partnership against all countries.*

TEN WICKETS OR MORE IN A MATCH

For Australia (5)

14-199 (7-116, 7-83)	C. V. Grimmett, Adelaide	....	1931-32
10-88 (5-32, 5-56)	C. V. Grimmett, Cape Town	....	1935-36
10-110 (3-70, 7-40)	C. V. Grimmett, Johannesburg	....	1935-36
13-173 (7-100, 6-73)	C. V. Grimmett, Durban	....	1935-36
11-24 (5-6, 6-18)	H. Ironmonger, Melbourne	....	1931-32

For South Africa (2)

10-116 (5-43, 5-73)	C. B. Llewellyn, Johannesburg	....	1902-03
13-165 (6-84, 7-81)	H. J. Tayfield, Melbourne	....	1952-53

Note: C. V. Grimmett took ten wickets or more in three consecutive matches in 1935-36.

AUSTRALIA v WEST INDIES

		Captains					
Season	*Australia*		*West Indies*	*T*	*A*	*WI*	*T*	*D*
1930-31*A*	W. M. Woodfull		G. C. Grant	5	4	1	0	0
1951-52*A*	A. L. Hassett[1]	J. D. C. Goddard[2]		5	4	1	0	0
1954-55*W*	I. W. Johnson	D. St E. Atkinson[3]		5	3	0	0	2
1960-61*A*	R. Benaud	F. M. M. Worrell		5	2	1	1	1

THE FRANK WORRELL TROPHY

Season	Australia	West Indies	T	A	WI	T	D	Held by
		Captains						
1964-65 *W*	R. B. Simpson	G. S. Sobers	5	1	2	0	2	WI
1968-69 *A*	W. M. Lawry	G. S. Sobers	5	3	1	0	1	A
1972-73 *W*	I. M. Chappell	R. B. Kanhai	5	2	0	0	3	A
1975-76 *A*	G. S. Chappell	C. H. Lloyd	6	5	1	0	0	A
1977-78 *W*	R. B. Simpson	A. I. Kallicharran[4]	5	1	3	0	1	WI
1979-80 *A*	G. S. Chappell	C. H. Lloyd[5]	3	0	2	0	1	WI
1981-82 *A*	G. S. Chappell	C. H. Lloyd	3	1	1	0	1	WI
1983-84 *W*	K. J. Hughes	C. H. Lloyd[6]	5	0	3	0	2	WI
1984-85 *A*	A. R. Border[7]	C. H. Lloyd	5	1	3	0	1	WI
1988-89 *A*	A. R. Border	I. V. A. Richards	5	1	3	0	1	WI
1990-91 *W*	A. R. Border	I. V. A. Richards	5	1	2	0	2	WI
	In Australia		42	21	14	1	6	
	In West Indies		30	8	10	0	12	
	Totals		72	29	24	1	18	

A Played in Australia. W Played in West Indies.

Notes: The following deputised for the official touring captain or were appointed by the home authority for only a minor proportion of the series:
[1]A. R. Morris (Third). [2]J. B. Stollmeyer (Fifth). [3]J. B. Stollmeyer (Second and Third). [4]C. H. Lloyd (First and Second). [5]D. L. Murray (First). [6]I. V. A. Richards (Second). [7]K. J. Hughes (First and Second).

HIGHEST INNINGS TOTALS

For Australia in Australia: 619 at Sydney	1968-69
in West Indies: 758-8 dec. at Kingston	1954-55
For West Indies in Australia: 616 at Adelaide	1968-69
in West Indies: 573 at Bridgetown	1964-65

LOWEST INNINGS TOTALS

For Australia in Australia: 76 at Perth	1984-85
in West Indies: 90 at Port-of-Spain	1977-78
For West Indies in Australia: 78 at Sydney	1951-52
in West Indies: 109 at Georgetown	1972-73

INDIVIDUAL HUNDREDS

For Australia (70)

R. G. Archer (1)
128 Kingston.... 1954-55
R. Benaud (1)
121 Kingston.... 1954-55
D. C. Boon (2)
149 Sydney 1988-89
109* Kingston.... 1990-91
B. C. Booth (1)
117 Port-of-Spain 1964-65
A. R. Border (2)
126 Adelaide.... 1981-82
100* Port-of-Spain 1983-84
D. G. Bradman (2)
223 Brisbane 1930-31
152 Melbourne .. 1930-31

G. S. Chappell (5)
106 Bridgetown .. 1972-73
123 }
109* } ‡Brisbane ... 1975-76
182* Sydney 1975-76
124 Brisbane 1979-80
I. M. Chappell (5)
117† Brisbane 1968-69
165 Melbourne .. 1968-69
106* Bridgetown .. 1972-73
109 Georgetown .. 1972-73
156 Perth....... 1975-76
G. J. Cosier (1)
109† Melbourne .. 1975-76

R. M. Cowper (2)
143 Port-of-Spain 1964-65
102 Bridgetown .. 1964-65
J. Dyson (1)
127*† Sydney 1981-82
R. N. Harvey (3)
133 Kingston.... 1954-55
133 Port-of-Spain 1954-55
204 Kingston.... 1954-55
A. L. Hassett (2)
132 Sydney 1951-52
102 Melbourne .. 1951-52
A. M. J. Hilditch (1)
113† Melbourne .. 1984-85

K. J. Hughes (2)

130*†	Brisbane	1979-80
100*	Melbourne ..	1981-82

D. M. Jones (1)

216	Adelaide	1988-89

A. F. Kippax (1)

146†	Adelaide	1930-31

W. M. Lawry (4)

210	Bridgetown ..	1964-65
105	Brisbane	1968-69
205	Melbourne ..	1968-69
151	Sydney	1968-69

R. R. Lindwall (1)

118	Melbourne ..	1954-55

R. B. McCosker (1)

109*	Melbourne ..	1975-76

C. C. McDonald (2)

110	Port-of-Spain	1954-55
127	Kingston....	1954-55

K. R. Miller (4)

129	Sydney	1951-52

147	Kingston....	1954-55
137	Bridgetown..	1954-55
109	Kingston....	1954-55

A. R. Morris (1)

111	Port-of-Spain	1954-55

N. C. O'Neill (1)

181†	Brisbane	1960-61

W. B. Phillips (1)

120	Bridgetown..	1983-84

W. H. Ponsford (2)

183	Sydney	1930-31
109	Brisbane	1930-31

I. R. Redpath (4)

132	Sydney	1968-69
102	Melbourne ..	1975-76
103	Adelaide	1975-76
101	Melbourne ..	1975-76

C. S. Serjeant (1)

124	Georgetown .	1977-78

R. B. Simpson (1)

201	Bridgetown..	1964-65

K. R. Stackpole (1)

142	Kingston....	1972-73

M. A. Taylor (1)

144	St John's....	1990-91

P. M. Toohey (1)

122	Kingston....	1977-78

A. Turner (1)

136	Adelaide	1975-76

K. D. Walters (6)

118	Sydney	1968-69
110	Adelaide	1968-69
242	} Sydney	1968-69
103		
102*	Bridgetown..	1972-73
112	Port-of-Spain	1972-73

M. E. Waugh (1)

139*	St John's....	1990-91

K. C. Wessels (1)

173	Sydney	1984-85

G. M. Wood (2)

126	Georgetown .	1977-78
111	Perth........	1988-89

For West Indies (73)

F. C. M. Alexander (1)

108	Sydney	1960-61

D. St E. Atkinson (1)

219	Bridgetown..	1954-55

B. F. Butcher (3)

117	Port-of-Spain	1964-65
101	Sydney	1968-69
118	Adelaide	1968-69

C. C. Depeiza (1)

122	Bridgetown..	1954-55

P. J. L. Dujon (2)

130	Port-of-Spain	1983-84
139	Perth........	1984-85

M. L. C. Foster (1)

125†	Kingston....	1972-73

R. C. Fredericks (2)

169	Perth........	1975-76

H. A. Gomes (6)

101†	Georgetown .	1977-78
115	Kingston....	1977-78
126	Sydney	1981-82
124*	Adelaide	1981-82
127	Perth........	1984-85
120*	Adelaide	1984-85

C. G. Greenidge (4)

120*	Georgetown .	1983-84
127	Kingston....	1983-84
104	Adelaide	1988-89
226	Bridgetown..	1990-91

D. L. Haynes (5)

103*	Georgetown .	1983-84
145	Bridgetown..	1983-84
100	Perth........	1988-89

143	Sydney	1988-89
111	Georgetown .	1990-91

G. A. Headley (2)

102*	Brisbane	1930-31
105	Sydney	1930-31

C. C. Hunte (1)

110	Melbourne ..	1960-61

A. I. Kallicharran (4)

101	Brisbane	1975-76
127	Port-of-Spain	1977-78
126	Kingston....	1977-78
106	Adelaide	1979-80

R. B. Kanhai (5)

117	} Adelaide	1960-61
115		
129	Bridgetown..	1964-65
121	Port-of-Spain	1964-65
105	Bridgetown..	1972-73

C. H. Lloyd (6)

129†	Brisbane	1968-69
178	Georgetown .	1972-73
149	Perth........	1975-76
102	Melbourne ..	1975-76
121	Adelaide	1979-80
114	Brisbane	1984-85

F. R. Martin (1)

123*	Sydney	1930-31

S. M. Nurse (2)

201	Bridgetown..	1964-65
137	Sydney	1968-69

I. V. A. Richards (5)

101	Adelaide	1975-76
140	Brisbane	1979-80

178	St John's....	1983-84
208	Melbourne ..	1984-85
146	Perth........	1988-89

R. B. Richardson (7)

131*	Bridgetown..	1983-84
154	St John's....	1983-84
138	Brisbane	1984-85
122	Melbourne ..	1988-89
106	Adelaide	1988-89
104*	Sydney	1990-91
182	Georgetown .	1990-91

L. G. Rowe (1)

107	Brisbane	1975-76

O. G. Smith (1)

104†	Kingston....	1954-55

G. S. Sobers (4)

132	Brisbane	1960-61
168	Sydney	1960-61
110	Adelaide	1968-69
113	Sydney	1968-69

J. B. Stollmeyer (1)

104	Sydney	1951-52

C. L. Walcott (5)

108	Kingston....	1954-55
126	} Port-of-Spain	1954-55
110		
155	} Kingston....	1954-55
110		

E. D. Weekes (1)

139	Port-of-Spain	1954-55

A. B. Williams (1)

100†	Georgetown .	1977-78

F. M. M. Worrell (1)

108	Melbourne ..	1951-52

† *Signifies hundred on first appearance in Australia–West Indies Tests.*

‡ *G. S. Chappell is the only player to score hundreds in both innings of his first Test as captain.*

Note: F. C. M. Alexander and C. C. Depeiza scored the only hundreds of their careers in a Test match.

RECORD PARTNERSHIPS FOR EACH WICKET

For Australia

382 for 1st†	W. M. Lawry and R. B. Simpson at Bridgetown..............	1964-65
298 for 2nd	W. M. Lawry and I. M. Chappell at Melbourne..............	1968-69
295 for 3rd†	C. C. McDonald and R. N. Harvey at Kingston	1954-55
336 for 4th	W. M. Lawry and K. D. Walters at Sydney	1968-69
220 for 5th	K. R. Miller and R. G. Archer at Kingston	1954-55
206 for 6th	K. R. Miller and R. G. Archer at Bridgetown	1954-55
134 for 7th	A. K. Davidson and R. Benaud at Brisbane	1960-61
137 for 8th	R. Benaud and I. W. Johnson at Kingston	1954-55
114 for 9th	D. M. Jones and M. G. Hughes at Adelaide	1988-89
97 for 10th	T. G. Hogan and R. M. Hogg at Georgetown...............	1983-84

For West Indies

250* for 1st	C. G. Greenidge and D. L. Haynes at Georgetown	1983-84
297 for 2nd	D. L. Haynes and R. B. Richardson at Georgetown..........	1990-91
308 for 3rd	R. B. Richardson and I. V. A. Richards at St John's	1983-84
198 for 4th	L. G. Rowe and A. I. Kallicharran at Brisbane	1975-76
210 for 5th	R. B. Kanhai and M. L. C. Foster at Kingston	1972-73
165 for 6th	R. B. Kanhai and D. L. Murray at Bridgetown	1972-73
347 for 7th†‡	D. St E. Atkinson and C. C. Depeiza at Bridgetown.........	1954-55
87 for 8th	P. J. L. Dujon and C. E. L. Ambrose at Port-of-Spain.......	1990-91
122 for 9th	D. A. J. Holford and J. L. Hendriks at Adelaide	1968-69
56 for 10th	J. Garner and C. E. H. Croft at Brisbane	1979-80

† *Denotes record partnership against all countries.*
‡ *Record seventh-wicket partnership in first-class cricket.*

TEN WICKETS OR MORE IN A MATCH

For Australia (11)

11-96 (7-46, 4-50)	A. R. Border, Sydney...........................	1988-89
11-222 (5-135, 6-87)†	A. K. Davidson, Brisbane	1960-61
11-183 (7-87, 4-96)†	C. V. Grimmett, Adelaide	1930-31
10-115 (6-72, 4-43)	N. J. N. Hawke, Georgetown	1964-65
10-144 (6-54, 4-90)	R. G. Holland, Sydney	1984-85
13-217 (5-130, 8-87)	M. G. Hughes, Perth	1988-89
11-79 (7-23, 4-56)	H. Ironmonger, Melbourne	1930-31
11-181 (8-112, 3-69)	G. F. Lawson, Adelaide.........................	1984-85
10-127 (7-83, 3-44)	D. K. Lillee, Melbourne........................	1981-82
10-159 (8-71, 2-88)	G. D. McKenzie, Melbourne	1968-69
10-185 (3-87, 7-98)	B. Yardley, Sydney............................	1981-82

For West Indies (3)

10-113 (7-55, 3-58)	G. E. Gomez, Sydney...........................	1951-52
11-107 (5-45, 6-62)	M. A. Holding, Melbourne	1981-82
10-107 (5-69, 5-38)	M. D. Marshall, Adelaide	1984-85

† *Signifies ten wickets or more on first appearance in Australia–West Indies Tests.*

AUSTRALIA v NEW ZEALAND

		Captains				
Season	Australia	New Zealand	T	A	NZ	D
1945-46N	W. A. Brown	W. A. Hadlee	1	1	0	0
1973-74A	I. M. Chappell	B. E. Congdon	3	2	0	1
1973-74N	I. M. Chappell	B. E. Congdon	3	1	1	1
1976-77N	G. S. Chappell	G. M. Turner	2	1	0	1
1980-81A	G. S. Chappell	G. P. Howarth[1]	3	2	0	1
1981-82N	G. S. Chappell	G. P. Howarth	3	1	1	1

TRANS-TASMAN TROPHY

		Captains					
Season	Australia	New Zealand	T	A	NZ	D	Held by
1985-86A	A. R. Border	J. V. Coney	3	1	2	0	NZ
1985-86N	A. R. Border	J. V. Coney	3	0	1	2	NZ
1987-88A	A. R. Border	J. J. Crowe	3	1	0	2	A
1989-90A	A. R. Border	J. G. Wright	1	0	0	1	A
1989-90N	A. R. Border	J. G. Wright	1	0	1	0	NZ
	In Australia..................		13	6	2	5	
	In New Zealand..............		13	4	4	5	
	Totals.......................		26	10	6	10	

A Played in Australia. N Played in New Zealand.

Note: The following deputised for the official touring captain: [1]M. G. Burgess (Second).

HIGHEST INNINGS TOTALS

For Australia in Australia: 521-9 dec. at Perth 1989-90
    in New Zealand: 552 at Christchurch 1976-77

For New Zealand in Australia: 553-7 dec. at Brisbane 1985-86
    in New Zealand: 484 at Wellington 1973-74

LOWEST INNINGS TOTALS

For Australia in Australia: 162 at Sydney................... 1973-74
    in New Zealand: 103 at Auckland.......................... 1985-86

For New Zealand in Australia: 121 at Perth 1980-81
    in New Zealand: 42 at Wellington 1945-46

INDIVIDUAL HUNDREDS

For Australia (23)

D. C. Boon (2)
143 Brisbane 1987-88
200 Perth....... 1989-90
A. R. Border (4)
152* Brisbane 1985-86
140 ⎱
114* ⎰ Christchurch. 1985-86
205 Adelaide 1987-88
G. S. Chappell (3)
247* ⎱
133 ⎰ Wellington .. 1973-74
176 Christchurch. 1981-82

I. M. Chappell (2)
145 ⎱
121 ⎰ Wellington .. 1973-74
G. J. Gilmour (1)
101 Christchurch. 1976-77
G. R. Marsh (1)
118 Auckland ... 1985-86
R. W. Marsh (1)
132 Adelaide 1973-74
G. R. J. Matthews (2)
115† Brisbane 1985-86
130 Wellington .. 1985-86

I. R. Redpath (1)
159*‡ Auckland ... 1973-74
K. R. Stackpole (1)
122† Melbourne .. 1973-74
K. D. Walters (3)
104* Auckland ... 1973-74
250 Christchurch. 1976-77
107 Melbourne .. 1980-81
G. M. Wood (2)
111† Brisbane 1980-81
100 Auckland ... 1981-82

For New Zealand (17)

J. V. Coney (1)	**B. A. Edgar** (1)	**J. M. Parker** (1)
101* Wellington .. 1985-86	161 Auckland ... 1981-82	108 Sydney 1973-74
B. E. Congdon (2)	**M. J. Greatbatch** (1)	**J. F. Reid** (1)
132 Wellington .. 1973-74	146*† Perth....... 1989-90	108† Brisbane 1985-86
107* Christchurch. 1976-77	**B. F. Hastings** (1)	**G. M. Turner** (2)
M. D. Crowe (3)	101 Wellington .. 1973-74	101
188 Brisbane 1985-86	**A. H. Jones** (1)	110* ⎬ Christchurch. 1973-74
137 Christchurch. 1985-86	150 Adelaide 1987-88	**J. G. Wright** (2)
137 Adelaide 1987-88	**J. F. M. Morrison** (1)	141 Christchurch. 1981-82
	117 Sydney 1973-74	117* Wellington .. 1989-90

† *Signifies hundred on first appearance in Australia–New Zealand Tests.*
‡ *Carried his bat.*

Notes: G. S. and I. M. Chappell at Wellington in 1973-74 provide the only instance in Test matches of brothers both scoring a hundred in each innings and in the same Test.

RECORD PARTNERSHIPS FOR EACH WICKET

For Australia

106 for 1st	B. M. Laird and G. M. Wood at Auckland	1981-82
168 for 2nd	G. R. Marsh and W. B. Phillips at Auckland.................	1985-86
264 for 3rd	I. M. Chappell and G. S. Chappell at Wellington	1973-74
116 for 4th	A. R. Border and S. R. Waugh at Adelaide	1987-88
213 for 5th	G. M. Ritchie and G. R. J. Matthews at Wellington	1985-86
197 for 6th	A. R. Border and G. R. J. Matthews at Brisbane	1985-86
217 for 7th†	K. D. Walters and G. J. Gilmour at Christchurch	1976-77
93 for 8th	G. J. Gilmour and K. J. O'Keeffe at Auckland	1976-77
61 for 9th	A. I. C. Dodemaide and C. J. McDermott at Melbourne	1987-88
60 for 10th	K. D. Walters and J. D. Higgs at Melbourne...............	1980-81

For New Zealand

107 for 1st	G. M. Turner and J. M. Parker at Auckland	1973-74
128* for 2nd	J. G. Wright and A. H. Jones at Wellington	1989-90
224 for 3rd	J. F. Reid and M. D. Crowe at Brisbane	1985-86
229 for 4th†	B. E. Congdon and B. F. Hastings at Wellington............	1973-74
88 for 5th	J. V. Coney and M. G. Burgess at Perth	1980-81
109 for 6th	K. R. Rutherford and J. V. Coney at Wellington	1985-86
132* for 7th	J. V. Coney and R. J. Hadlee at Wellington...............	1985-86
88* for 8th	M. J. Greatbatch and M. C. Snedden at Perth..............	1989-90
73 for 9th	H. J. Howarth and D. R. Hadlee at Christchurch	1976-77
124 for 10th	J. G. Bracewell and S. L. Boock at Sydney..................	1985-86

† *Denotes record partnership against all countries.*

TEN WICKETS OR MORE IN A MATCH

For Australia (2)

10-174 (6-106, 4-68)	R. G. Holland, Sydney	1985-86
11-123 (5-51, 6-72)	D. K. Lillee, Auckland	1976-77

For New Zealand (4)

10-106 (4-74, 6-32)	J. G. Bracewell, Auckland	1985-86
15-123 (9-52, 6-71)	R. J. Hadlee, Brisbane	1985-86
11-155 (5-65, 6-90)	R. J. Hadlee, Perth..............................	1985-86
10-176 (5-109, 5-67)	R. J. Hadlee, Melbourne	1987-88

AUSTRALIA v INDIA

	Captains						
Season	*Australia*	*India*	*T*	*A*	*I*	*T*	*D*
1947-48*A*	D. G. Bradman	L. Amarnath	5	4	0	0	1
1956-57*I*	I. W. Johnson[1]	P. R. Umrigar	3	2	0	0	1
1959-60*I*	R. Benaud	G. S. Ramchand	5	2	1	0	2
1964-65*I*	R. B. Simpson	Nawab of Pataudi jun.	3	1	1	0	1
1967-68*A*	R. B. Simpson[2]	Nawab of Pataudi jun.[3]	4	4	0	0	0
1969-70*I*	W. M. Lawry	Nawab of Pataudi jun.	5	3	1	0	1
1977-78*A*	R. B. Simpson	B. S. Bedi	5	3	2	0	0
1979-80*I*	K. J. Hughes	S. M. Gavaskar	6	0	2	0	4
1980-81*A*	G. S. Chappell	S. M. Gavaskar	3	1	1	0	1
1985-86*A*	A. R. Border	Kapil Dev	3	0	0	0	3
1986-87*I*	A. R. Border	Kapil Dev	3	0	0	1	2
1991-92*A*	A. R. Border	M. Azharuddin	5	4	0	0	1
	In Australia.....................		25	16	3	0	6
	In India........................		25	8	5	1	11
	Totals...........................		50	24	8	1	17

A Played in Australia.   I Played in India.

Notes: The following deputised for the official touring captain or were appointed by the home authority for only a minor proportion of the series:
[1]R. R. Lindwall (Second). [2]W. M. Lawry (Third and Fourth). [3]C. G. Borde (First).

HIGHEST INNINGS TOTALS

For Australia in Australia: 674 at Adelaide	1947-48
in India: 574-7 dec. at Madras	1986-87
For India in Australia: 600-4 dec. at Sydney	1985-86
in India: 517-5 dec. at Bombay	1986-87

LOWEST INNINGS TOTALS

For Australia in Australia: 83 at Melbourne	1980-81
in India: 105 at Kanpur	1959-60
For India in Australia: 58 at Brisbane	1947-48
in India: 135 at Delhi	1959-60

INDIVIDUAL HUNDREDS

For Australia (51)

S. G. Barnes (1)
112   Adelaide 1947-48
D. C. Boon (6)
123†   Adelaide 1985-86
131   Sydney 1985-86
122   Madras 1986-87
129*   Sydney 1991-92
135   Adelaide 1991-92
107   Perth....... 1991-92
A. R. Border (4)
162†   Madras 1979-80
124   Melbourne .. 1980-81
163   Melbourne .. 1985-86
106   Madras 1986-87

D. G. Bradman (4)
185†   Brisbane ... 1947-48
132 ⎫
127* ⎬ Melbourne .. 1947-48
201   Adelaide 1947-48
J. W. Burke (1)
161   Bombay 1956-57
G. S. Chappell (1)
204†   Sydney 1980-81
I. M. Chappell (2)
151   Melbourne .. 1967-68
138   Delhi....... 1969-70
R. M. Cowper (2)
108   Adelaide 1967-68
165   Sydney 1967-68

L. E. Favell (1)
101   Madras 1959-60
R. N. Harvey (4)
153   Melbourne .. 1947-48
140   Bombay 1956-57
114   Delhi....... 1959-60
102   Bombay 1959-60
A. L. Hassett (1)
198*   Adelaide 1947-48
K. J. Hughes (2)
100   Madras 1979-80
213   Adelaide 1980-81
D. M. Jones (2)
210†   Madras 1986-87
150*   Perth....... 1991-92

W. M. Lawry (1)			**N. C. O'Neill** (2)		**K. R. Stackpole** (1)	
100	Melbourne ..	1967-68	163	Bombay 1959-60	103†	Bombay 1969-70
A. L. Mann (1)			113	Calcutta 1959-60	**M. A. Taylor** (1)	
105	Perth.......	1977-78	**G. M. Ritchie** (1)		100	Adelaide.... 1991-92
G. R. Marsh (1)			128†	Adelaide 1985-86	**K. D. Walters** (1)	
101	Bombay	1986-87	**A. P. Sheahan** (1)		102	Madras 1969-70
G. R. J. Matthews (1)			114	Kanpur..... 1969-70	**G. M. Wood** (1)	
100*	Melbourne ..	1985-86	**R. B. Simpson** (4)		125	Adelaide 1980-81
T. M. Moody (1)			103	Adelaide 1967-68	**G. N. Yallop** (2)	
101†	Perth.......	1991-92	109	Melbourne .. 1967-68	121†	Adelaide 1977-78
A. R. Morris (1)			176	Perth....... 1977-78	167	Calcutta 1979-80
100*	Melbourne ..	1947-48	100	Adelaide 1977-78		

For India (35)

M. Amarnath (2)			**M. L. Jaisimha** (1)		**R. J. Shastri** (2)	
100	Perth.......	1977-78	101	Brisbane 1967-68	121*	Bombay 1986-87
138	Sydney	1985-86	**Kapil Dev** (1)		206	Sydney 1991-92
M. Azharuddin (1)			119	Madras 1986-87	**K. Srikkanth** (1)	
106	Adelaide	1991-92	**S. M. H. Kirmani** (1)		116	Sydney 1985-86
N. J. Contractor (1)			101*	Bombay 1979-80	**S. R. Tendulkar** (2)	
108	Bombay	1959-60	**V. Mankad** (2)		148*	Sydney 1991-92
S. M. Gavaskar (8)			116	Melbourne .. 1947-48	114	Perth....... 1991-92
113†	Brisbane	1977-78	111	Melbourne .. 1947-48	**D. B. Vengsarkar** (2)	
127	Perth.......	1977-78	**Nawab of Pataudi jun.** (1)		112	Bangalore ... 1979-80
118	Melbourne ..	1977-78	128*†	Madras 1964-65	164*	Bombay 1986-87
115	Delhi.......	1979-80	**S. M. Patil** (1)		**G. R. Viswanath** (4)	
123	Bombay	1979-80	174	Adelaide 1980-81	137†	Kanpur..... 1969-70
166*	Adelaide	1985-86	**D. G. Phadkar** (1)		161*	Bangalore ... 1979-80
172	Sydney	1985-86	123	Adelaide 1947-48	131	Delhi....... 1979-80
103	Bombay	1986-87	**G. S. Ramchand** (1)		114	Melbourne .. 1980-81
V. S. Hazare (2)			109	Bombay 1956-57	**Yashpal Sharma** (1)	
116	Adelaide	1947-48			100*	Delhi....... 1979-80
145						

† *Signifies hundred on first appearance in Australia–India Tests.*

RECORD PARTNERSHIPS FOR EACH WICKET

For Australia

217	for 1st	D. C. Boon and G. R. Marsh at Sydney	1985-86
236	for 2nd	S. G. Barnes and D. G. Bradman at Adelaide	1947-48
222	for 3rd	A. R. Border and K. J. Hughes at Madras	1979-80
178	for 4th	D. M. Jones and A. R. Border at Madras	1986-87
223*	for 5th	A. R. Morris and D. G. Bradman at Melbourne	1947-48
151	for 6th	T. R. Veivers and B. N. Jarman at Bombay	1964-65
66	for 7th	G. R. J. Matthews and R. J. Bright at Melbourne	1985-86
73	for 8th	T. R. Veivers and G. D. McKenzie at Madras	1964-65
87	for 9th	I. W. Johnson and W. P. A. Crawford at Madras	1956-57
77	for 10th	A. R. Border and D. R. Gilbert at Melbourne	1985-86

For India

192	for 1st	S. M. Gavaskar and C. P. S. Chauhan at Bombay............	1979-80
224	for 2nd	S. M. Gavaskar and M. Amarnath at Sydney	1985-86
159	for 3rd	S. M. Gavaskar and G. R. Viswanath at Delhi	1979-80
159	for 4th	D. B. Vengsarkar and G. R. Viswanath at Bangalore	1979-80
196	for 5th	R. J. Shastri and S. R. Tendulkar at Sydney	1991-92
298*	for 6th†	D. B. Vengsarkar and R. J. Shastri at Bombay..............	1986-87
132	for 7th	V. S. Hazare and H. R. Adhikari at Adelaide	1947-48
127	for 8th	S. M. H. Kirmani and K. D. Ghavri at Bombay	1979-80
81	for 9th	S. R. Tendulkar and K. S. More at Perth	1991-92
94	for 10th	S. M. Gavaskar and N. S. Yadav at Adelaide...............	1985-86

† *Denotes record partnership against all countries.*

TEN WICKETS OR MORE IN A MATCH

For Australia (11)

11-105 (6-52, 5-53)	R. Benaud, Calcutta	1956-57
12-124 (5-31, 7-93)	A. K. Davidson, Kanpur	1959-60
12-166 (5-99, 7-67)	G. Dymock, Kanpur	1979-80
10-168 (5-76, 5-92)	C. J. McDermott, Adelaide	1991-92
10-91 (6-58, 4-33)†	G. D. McKenzie, Madras	1964-65
10-151 (7-66, 3-85)	G. D. McKenzie, Melbourne	1967-68
10-144 (5-91, 5-53)	A. A. Mallett, Madras	1969-70
10-249 (5-103, 5-146)	G. R. J. Matthews, Madras	1986-87
12-126 (6-66, 6-60)	B. A. Reid, Melbourne	1991-92
11-31 (5-2, 6-29)†	E. R. H. Toshack, Brisbane	1947-48
11-95 (4-68, 7-27)	M. R. Whitney, Perth	1991-92

For India (6)

10-194 (5-89, 5-105)	B. S. Bedi, Perth	1977-78
12-104 (6-52, 6-52)	B. S. Chandrasekhar, Melbourne	1977-78
10-130 (7-49, 3-81)	Ghulam Ahmed, Calcutta	1956-57
11-122 (5-31, 6-91)	R. G. Nadkarni, Madras	1964-65
14-124 (9-69, 5-55)	J. M. Patel, Kanpur	1959-60
10-174 (4-100, 6-74)	E. A. S. Prasanna, Madras	1969-70

† *Signifies ten wickets or more on first appearance in Australia–India Tests.*

AUSTRALIA v PAKISTAN

		Captains				
Season	Australia	Pakistan	T	A	P	D
1956-57 *P*	I. W. Johnson	A. H. Kardar	1	0	1	0
1959-60 *P*	R. Benaud	Fazal Mahmood[1]	3	2	0	1
1964-65 *P*	R. B. Simpson	Hanif Mohammad	1	0	0	1
1964-65 *A*	R. B. Simpson	Hanif Mohammad	1	0	0	1
1972-73 *A*	I. M. Chappell	Intikhab Alam	3	3	0	0
1976-77 *A*	G. S. Chappell	Mushtaq Mohammad	3	1	1	1
1978-79 *A*	G. N. Yallop[2]	Mushtaq Mohammad	2	1	1	0
1979-80 *P*	G. S. Chappell	Javed Miandad	3	0	1	2
1981-82 *A*	G. S. Chappell	Javed Miandad	3	2	1	0
1982-83 *P*	K. J. Hughes	Imran Khan	3	0	3	0
1983-84 *A*	K. J. Hughes	Imran Khan[3]	5	2	0	3
1988-89 *P*	A. R. Border	Javed Miandad	3	0	1	2
1989-90 *A*	A. R. Border	Imran Khan	3	1	0	2
	In Pakistan		14	2	6	6
	In Australia		20	10	3	7
	Totals		34	12	9	13

A Played in Australia. P Played in Pakistan.

Notes: The following deputised for the official touring captain or were appointed by the home authority for only a minor proportion of the series:
[1]Imtiaz Ahmed (Second). [2]K. J. Hughes (Second). [3]Zaheer Abbas (First, Second and Third).

HIGHEST INNINGS TOTALS

For Australia in Australia: 585 at Adelaide	1972-73
in Pakistan: 617 at Faisalabad	1979-80
For Pakistan in Australia: 624 at Adelaide	1983-84
in Pakistan: 501-6 dec. at Faisalabad	1982-83

LOWEST INNINGS TOTALS

For Australia in Australia: 125 at Melbourne	....	1981-82
in Pakistan: 80 at Karachi	....	1956-57
For Pakistan in Australia: 62 at Perth	....	1981-82
in Pakistan: 134 at Dacca	....	1959-60

INDIVIDUAL HUNDREDS

For Australia (37)

J. Benaud (1)
142   Melbourne .. 1972-73
A. R. Border (6)
105† Melbourne .. 1978-79
150*⎫
153 ⎬Lahore 1979-80
118   Brisbane 1983-84
117* Adelaide 1983-84
113* Faisalabad .. 1988-89
G. S. Chappell (6)
116* Melbourne .. 1972-73
121   Melbourne .. 1976-77
235   Faisalabad .. 1979-80
201   Brisbane 1981-82
150* Brisbane 1983-84
182   Sydney 1983-84
I. M. Chappell (1)
196   Adelaide 1972-73
G. J. Cosier (1)
168   Melbourne .. 1976-77

I. C. Davis (1)
105† Adelaide 1976-77
K. J. Hughes (2)
106   Perth 1981-82
106   Adelaide 1983-84
D. M. Jones (2)
116 ⎫
121*⎬Adelaide 1989-90
R. B. McCosker (1)
105   Melbourne... 1976-77
R. W. Marsh (1)
118† Adelaide 1972-73
N. C. O'Neill (1)
134   Lahore 1959-60
W. B. Phillips (1)
159† Perth 1983-84
I. R. Redpath (1)
135   Melbourne... 1972-73

G. M. Ritchie (1)
106* Faisalabad .. 1982-83
A. P. Sheahan (1)
127   Melbourne .. 1972-73
R. B. Simpson (2)
153 ⎫
115 ⎬†Karachi 1964-65
M. A. Taylor (2)
101† Melbourne .. 1989-90
101* Sydney 1989-90
K. D. Walters (1)
107   Adelaide 1976-77
K. C. Wessels (1)
179   Adelaide 1983-84
G. M. Wood (1)
100   Melbourne .. 1981-82
G. N. Yallop (3)
172   Faisalabad .. 1979-80
141   Perth 1983-84
268   Melbourne .. 1983-84

For Pakistan (31)

Asif Iqbal (3)
152* Adelaide 1976-77
120   Sydney 1976-77
134* Perth 1978-79
Hanif Mohammad (2)
101* Karachi 1959-60
104   Melbourne .. 1964-65
Ijaz Ahmed (2)
122   Faisalabad .. 1988-89
121   Melbourne .. 1989-90
Imran Khan (1)
136   Adelaide ... 1989-90
Javed Miandad (6)
129* Perth 1978-79
106* Faisalabad .. 1979-80
138   Lahore 1982-83

131   Adelaide 1983-84
211   Karachi 1988-89
107   Faisalabad .. 1988-89
Khalid Ibadulla (1)
166† Karachi 1964-65
Majid Khan (3)
158   Melbourne .. 1972-73
108   Melbourne .. 1978-79
110* Lahore 1979-80
Mansoor Akhtar (1)
111   Faisalabad .. 1982-83
Mohsin Khan (3)
135   Lahore 1982-83
149   Adelaide 1983-84
152   Melbourne .. 1983-84

Mushtaq Mohammad (1)
121   Sydney 1972-73
Qasim Omar (1)
113   Adelaide 1983-84
Sadiq Mohammad (2)
137   Melbourne .. 1972-73
105   Melbourne .. 1976-77
Saeed Ahmed (1)
166   Lahore 1959-60
Taslim Arif (1)
210* Faisalabad .. 1979-80
Wasim Akram (1)
123   Adelaide 1989-90
Zaheer Abbas (2)
101   Adelaide 1976-77
126   Faisalabad .. 1982-83

† *Signifies hundred on first appearance in Australia–Pakistan Tests.*

RECORD PARTNERSHIPS FOR EACH WICKET

For Australia

134 for 1st	I. C. Davis and A. Turner at Melbourne	1976-77
259 for 2nd	W. B. Phillips and G. N. Yallop at Perth	1983-84
203 for 3rd	G. N. Yallop and K. J. Hughes at Melbourne	1983-84
217 for 4th	G. S. Chappell and G. N. Yallop at Faisalabad	1979-80
171 for 5th	{ G. S. Chappell and G. J. Cosier at Melbourne	1976-77
	{ A. R. Border and G. S. Chappell at Brisbane	1983-84
139 for 6th	R. M. Cowper and T. R. Veivers at Melbourne	1964-65
185 for 7th	G. N. Yallop and G. R. J. Matthews at Melbourne	1983-84
117 for 8th	G. J. Cosier and K. J. O'Keeffe at Melbourne	1976-77
83 for 9th	J. R. Watkins and R. A. L. Massie at Sydney	1972-73
52 for 10th	{ D. K. Lillee and M. H. N. Walker at Sydney	1976-77
	{ G. F. Lawson and T. M. Alderman at Lahore	1982-83

For Pakistan

249 for 1st†	Khalid Ibadulla and Abdul Kadir at Karachi	1964-65
233 for 2nd	Mohsin Khan and Qasim Omar at Adelaide	1983-84
223* for 3rd	Taslim Arif and Javed Miandad at Faisalabad	1979-80
155 for 4th	Mansoor Akhtar and Zaheer Abbas at Faisalabad	1982-83
186 for 5th	Javed Miandad and Salim Malik at Adelaide	1983-84
191 for 6th	Imran Khan and Wasim Akram at Adelaide	1989-90
104 for 7th	Intikhab Alam and Wasim Bari at Adelaide	1972-73
111 for 8th	Majid Khan and Imran Khan at Lahore	1979-80
56 for 9th	Intikhab Alam and Afaq Hussain at Melbourne	1964-65
87 for 10th	Asif Iqbal and Iqbal Qasim at Adelaide	1976-77

† *Denotes record partnership against all countries.*

TEN WICKETS OR MORE IN A MATCH

For Australia (3)

10-111 (7-87, 3-24)†	R. J. Bright, Karachi	1979-80
10-135 (6-82, 4-53)	D. K. Lillee, Melbourne	1976-77
11-118 (5-32, 6-86)†	C. G. Rackemann, Perth	1983-84

For Pakistan (6)

11-218 (4-76, 7-142)	Abdul Qadir, Faisalabad	1982-83
13-114 (6-34, 7-80)†	Fazal Mahmood, Karachi	1956-57
12-165 (6-102, 6-63)	Imran Khan, Sydney	1976-77
11-118 (4-69, 7-49)	Iqbal Qasim, Karachi	1979-80
11-125 (2-39, 9-86)	Sarfraz Nawaz, Melbourne	1978-79
11-160 (6-62, 5-98)†	Wasim Akram, Melbourne	1989-90

† *Signifies ten wickets or more on first appearance in Australia–Pakistan Tests.*

AUSTRALIA v SRI LANKA

		Captains				
Season	Australia	Sri Lanka	T	A	SL	D
1982-83*SL*	G. S. Chappell	L. R. D. Mendis	1	1	0	0
1987-88*A*	A. R. Border	R. S. Madugalle	1	1	0	0
1989-90*A*	A. R. Border	A. Ranatunga	2	1	0	1
	In Australia		3	2	0	1
	In Sri Lanka		1	1	0	0
	Totals		4	3	0	1

A Played in Australia. SL Played in Sri Lanka.

INNINGS TOTALS

Highest innings total for Australia: 514-4 dec. at Kandy 1982-83
           for Sri Lanka: 418 at Brisbane 1989-90

Lowest innings total for Australia: 224 at Hobart 1989-90
          for Sri Lanka: 153 at Perth 1987-88

INDIVIDUAL HUNDREDS

For Australia (8)

D. W. Hookes (1)	**T. M. Moody** (1)	**S. R. Waugh** (1)
143*† Kandy 1982-83	106† Brisbane 1989-90	134* Hobart 1989-90
D. M. Jones (2)	**M. A. Taylor** (2)	**K. C. Wessels** (1)
102† Perth 1987-88	164† Brisbane . . . 1989-90	141† Kandy 1982-83
118* Hobart 1989-90	108 Hobart 1989-90	

For Sri Lanka (1)

P. A. de Silva (1)
167   Brisbane 1989-90

† *Signifies hundred on first appearance in Australia–Sri Lanka Tests.*

BEST BOWLING

Best bowling in an innings for Australia: 5-66 by T. G. Hogan at Kandy 1982-83
               for Sri Lanka: 6-66 by R. J. Ratnayake at Hobart . . . 1989-90

RECORD PARTNERSHIPS FOR EACH WICKET

For Australia

120	for 1st	G. R. Marsh and D. C. Boon at Perth	1987-88
170	for 2nd	K. C. Wessels and G. N. Yallop at Kandy	1982-83
158	for 3rd	T. M. Moody and A. R. Border at Brisbane	1989-90
163	for 4th	M. A. Taylor and A. R. Border at Hobart	1989-90
155*	for 5th	D. W. Hookes and A. R. Border at Kandy	1982-83
260*	for 6th	D. M. Jones and S. R. Waugh at Hobart	1989-90
51*	for 7th	I. A. Healy and M. G. Hughes at Brisbane	1989-90
44	for 8th	M. G. Hughes and G. F. Lawson at Brisbane	1989-90
17	for 9th	P. R. Sleep and G. D. Campbell at Hobart	1989-90
28	for 10th	C. G. Rackemann and T. M. Alderman at Brisbane	1989-90

For Sri Lanka

51	for 1st	R. S. Mahanama and D. S. B. P. Kuruppu at Perth	1987-88
70	for 2nd	D. Ranatunga and A. P. Gurusinha at Brisbane	1989-90
61	for 3rd	S. Wettimuny and R. J. Ratnayake at Kandy	1982-83
128	for 4th	R. S. Mahanama and P. A. de Silva at Hobart	1989-90
96	for 5th	L. R. D. Mendis and A. Ranatunga at Kandy	1982-83
78	for 6th	A. Ranatunga and D. S. de Silva at Kandy	1982-83
144	for 7th†	P. A. de Silva and J. R. Ratnayeke at Brisbane	1989-90
33	for 8th	A. Ranatunga and C. P. H. Ramanayake at Perth	1987-88
27	for 9th	A. Ranatunga and R. G. de Alwis at Kandy	1982-83
27	for 10th	P. A. de Silva and C. P. H. Ramanayake at Brisbane	1989-90

† *D . . otes record partnership against all countries.*

SOUTH AFRICA v WEST INDIES

	Captains					
Season	South Africa	West Indies	T	SA	WI	D
1991-92 *W*	K. C. Wessels	R. B. Richardson	1	0	1	0

W Played in West Indies.

HIGHEST INNINGS TOTALS

For South Africa: 345 at Bridgetown 1991-92

For West Indies: 283 at Bridgetown 1991-92

INDIVIDUAL HUNDREDS

For South Africa (1)

A. C. Hudson (1)

163†   Bridgetown . . 1991-92

Highest score for West Indies: 79* by J. C. Adams.

† *Signifies hundred on first appearance in South Africa–West Indies Tests.*

HIGHEST PARTNERSHIPS

For South Africa

125 for 2nd   A. C. Hudson and K. C. Wessels at Bridgetown............. 1991-92

For West Indies

99 for 1st   D. L. Haynes and P. V. Simmons at Bridgetown 1991-92

BEST MATCH BOWLING ANALYSES

For South Africa

8-158 (4-84, 4-74)   R. P. Snell, Bridgetown 1991-92

For West Indies

8-81 (2-47, 6-34)   C. E. L. Ambrose, Bridgetown 1991-92

SOUTH AFRICA v NEW ZEALAND

	Captains					
Season	South Africa	New Zealand	T	SA	NZ	D
1931-32 *N*	H. B. Cameron	M. L. Page	2	2	0	0
1952-53 *N*	J. E. Cheetham	W. M. Wallace	2	1	0	1
1953-54 *S*	J. E. Cheetham	G. O. Rabone[1]	5	4	0	1
1961-62 *S*	D. J. McGlew	J. R. Reid	5	2	2	1
1963-64 *N*	T. L. Goddard	J. R. Reid	3	0	0	3
	In New Zealand		7	3	0	4
	In South Africa		10	6	2	2
	Totals...........................		17	9	2	6

N Played in New Zealand. S Played in South Africa.

Note: The following deputised for the official touring captain:
[1]B. Sutcliffe (Fourth and Fifth).

HIGHEST INNINGS TOTALS

For South Africa in South Africa: 464 at Johannesburg 1961-62
in New Zealand: 524-8 at Wellington 1952-53

For New Zealand in South Africa: 505 at Cape Town 1953-54
in New Zealand: 364 at Wellington 1931-32

LOWEST INNINGS TOTALS

For South Africa in South Africa: 148 at Johannesburg 1953-54
in New Zealand: 223 at Dunedin 1963-64

For New Zealand in South Africa: 79 at Johannesburg 1953-54
in New Zealand: 138 at Dunedin 1963-64

INDIVIDUAL HUNDREDS

For South Africa (11)

X. C. Balaskas (1)
122* Wellington .. 1931-32
J. A. J. Christy (1)
103† Christchurch. 1931-32
W. R. Endean (1)
116 Auckland ... 1952-53
D. J. McGlew (3)
255*† Wellington .. 1952-53

127*‡ Durban 1961-62
120 Johannesburg 1961-62
R. A. McLean (2)
101 Durban 1953-54
113 Cape Town . 1961-62
B. Mitchell (1)
113† Christchurch. 1931-32

A. R. A. Murray (1)
109† Wellington .. 1952-53
J. H. B. Waite (1)
101 Johannesburg 1961-62

For New Zealand (7)

P. T. Barton (1)
109 Pt Elizabeth . 1961-62
P. G. Z. Harris (1)
101 Cape Town . 1961-62
G. O. Rabone (1)
107 Durban 1953-54

J. R. Reid (2)
135 Cape Town . 1953-54
142 Johannesburg 1961-62
B. W. Sinclair (1)
138 Auckland ... 1963-64

H. G. Vivian (1)
100† Wellington .. 1931-32

† *Signifies hundred on first appearance in South Africa–New Zealand Tests.*
‡ *Carried his bat.*

RECORD PARTNERSHIPS FOR EACH WICKET

For South Africa

196 for 1st	J. A. J. Christy and B. Mitchell at Christchurch	1931-32
76 for 2nd	J. A. J. Christy and H. B. Cameron at Wellington	1931-32
112 for 3rd	D. J. McGlew and R. A. McLean at Johannesburg	1961-62
135 for 4th	K. J. Funston and R. A. McLean at Durban	1953-54
130 for 5th	W. R. Endean and J. E. Cheetham at Auckland	1952-53
83 for 6th	K. C. Bland and D. T. Lindsay at Auckland	1963-64
246 for 7th†	D. J. McGlew and A. R. A. Murray at Wellington	1952-53
95 for 8th	J. E. Cheetham and H. J. Tayfield at Cape Town	1953-54
60 for 9th	P. M. Pollock and N. A. T. Adcock at Port Elizabeth	1961-62
47 for 10th	D. J. McGlew and H. D. Bromfield at Port Elizabeth	1961-62

For New Zealand

126	for 1st	G. O. Rabone and M. E. Chapple at Cape Town	....	1953-54
51	for 2nd	W. P. Bradburn and B. W. Sinclair at Dunedin	....	1963-64
94	for 3rd	M. B. Poore and B. Sutcliffe at Cape Town	....	1953-54
171	for 4th	B. W. Sinclair and S. N. McGregor at Auckland	....	1963-64
174	for 5th	J. R. Reid and J. E. F. Beck at Cape Town	....	1953-54
100	for 6th	H. G. Vivian and F. T. Badcock at Wellington	....	1931-32
84	for 7th	J. R. Reid and G. A. Bartlett at Johannesburg	....	1961-62
73	for 8th	P. G. Z. Harris and G. A. Bartlett at Durban	....	1961-62
69	for 9th	C. F. W. Allcott and I. B. Cromb at Wellington	....	1931-32
49*	for 10th	A. E. Dick and F. J. Cameron at Cape Town	....	1961-62

† *Denotes record partnership against all countries.*

TEN WICKETS OR MORE IN A MATCH

For South Africa (1)

11-196 (6-128, 5-68)† S. F. Burke, Cape Town............................ 1961-62

† *Signifies ten wickets or more on first appearance in South Africa–New Zealand Tests.*

Note: The best match figures by a New Zealand bowler are 8-180 (4-61, 4-119), J. C. Alabaster at Cape Town, 1961-62.

WEST INDIES v NEW ZEALAND

	Captains					
Season	West Indies	New Zealand	T	WI	NZ	D
1951-52N	J. D. C. Goddard	B. Sutcliffe	2	1	0	1
1955-56N	D. St E. Atkinson	J. R. Reid[1]	4	3	1	0
1968-69N	G. S. Sobers	G. T. Dowling	3	1	1	1
1971-72W	G. S. Sobers	G. T. Dowling[2]	5	0	0	5
1979-80N	C. H. Lloyd	G. P. Howarth	3	0	1	2
1984-85W	I. V. A. Richards	G. P. Howarth	4	2	0	2
1986-87N	I. V. A. Richards	J. V. Coney	3	1	1	1
	In New Zealand		15	6	4	5
	In West Indies		9	2	0	7
	Totals........................		24	8	4	12

N Played in New Zealand.   W Played in West Indies.

Notes: The following deputised for the official touring captain or were appointed by the home authority for only a minor proportion of the series:
[1]H. B. Cave (First). [2]B. E. Congdon (Third, Fourth and Fifth).

HIGHEST INNINGS TOTALS

For West Indies in West Indies: 564-8 at Bridgetown...................... 1971-72
        in New Zealand: 546-6 dec. at Auckland 1951-52

For New Zealand in West Indies: 543-3 dec. at Georgetown 1971-72
        in New Zealand: 460 at Christchurch 1979-80

LOWEST INNINGS TOTALS

For West Indies in West Indies: 133 at Bridgetown 1971-72
             in New Zealand: 77 at Auckland 1955-56

For New Zealand in West Indies: 94 at Bridgetown 1984-85
             in New Zealand: 74 at Dunedin 1955-56

INDIVIDUAL HUNDREDS

By West Indies (25)

M. C. Carew (1)
109†   Auckland ... 1968-69
C. A. Davis (1)
183   Bridgetown .. 1971-72
R. C. Fredericks (1)
163   Kingston.... 1971-72
C. G. Greenidge (2)
100   Port-of-Spain 1984-85
213   Auckland ... 1986-87
D. L. Haynes (3)
105†   Dunedin 1979-80
122   Christchurch . 1979-80
121   Wellington .. 1986-87
A. I. Kallicharran (2)
100*† Georgetown . 1971-72

101   Port-of-Spain 1971-72
C. L. King (1)
100*   Christchurch . 1979-80
S. M. Nurse (2)
168†   Auckland ... 1968-69
258   Christchurch . 1968-69
I. V. A. Richards (1)
105   Bridgetown .. 1984-85
R. B. Richardson (1)
185   Georgetown . 1984-85
L. G. Rowe (3)
214 ⎫
100* ⎬ †Kingston.... 1971-72
100   Christchurch. 1979-80

G. S. Sobers (1)
142   Bridgetown .. 1971-72
J. B. Stollmeyer (1)
152   Auckland ... 1951-52
C. L. Walcott (1)
115   Auckland ... 1951-52
E. D. Weekes (3)
123   Dunedin 1955-56
103   Christchurch. 1955-56
156   Wellington .. 1955-56
F. M. M. Worrell (1)
100   Auckland ... 1951-52

By New Zealand (17)

M. G. Burgess (1)
101   Kingston.... 1971-72
B. E. Congdon (2)
166*   Port-of-Spain 1971-72
126   Bridgetown .. 1971-72
J. J. Crowe (1)
112   Kingston.... 1984-85
M. D. Crowe (3)
188   Georgetown . 1984-85
119   Wellington .. 1986-87

104   Auckland ... 1986-87
B. A. Edgar (1)
127   Auckland ... 1979-80
R. J. Hadlee (1)
103   Christchurch . 1979-80
B. F. Hastings (2)
117*   Christchurch . 1968-69
105   Bridgetown .. 1971-72
G. P. Howarth (1)
147   Christchurch . 1979-80

T. W. Jarvis (1)
182   Georgetown . 1971-72
B. R. Taylor (1)
124†   Auckland ... 1968-69
G. M. Turner (2)
223*‡ Kingston.... 1971-72
259   Georgetown . 1971-72
J. G. Wright (1)
138   Wellington .. 1986-87

† *Signifies hundred on first appearance in West Indies–New Zealand Tests.*
‡ *Carried his bat.*

Notes: E. D. Weekes in 1955-56 made three hundreds in consecutive innings.
     L. G. Rowe and A. I. Kallicharran each scored hundreds in their first two innings in Test cricket, Rowe being the only batsman to do so in his first match.

RECORD PARTNERSHIPS FOR EACH WICKET

For West Indies

225 for 1st	C. G. Greenidge and D. L. Haynes at Christchurch...........	1979-80
269 for 2nd	R. C. Fredericks and L. G. Rowe at Kingston	1971-72
185 for 3rd	C. G. Greenidge and R. B. Richardson at Port-of-Spain	1984-85
162 for 4th {	E. D. Weekes and O. G. Smith at Dunedin	1955-56
	C. G. Greenidge and A. I. Kallicharran at Christchurch	1979-80
189 for 5th	F. M. M. Worrell and C. L. Walcott at Auckland	1951-52
254 for 6th	C. A. Davis and G. S. Sobers at Bridgetown................	1971-72
143 for 7th	D. St E. Atkinson and J. D. C. Goddard at Christchurch	1955-56
83 for 8th	I. V. A. Richards and M. D. Marshall at Bridgetown	1984-85
70 for 9th	M. D. Marshall and J. Garner at Bridgetown	1984-85
31 for 10th	T. M. Findlay and G. C. Shillingford at Bridgetown	1971-72

For New Zealand

387 for 1st†	G. M. Turner and T. W. Jarvis at Georgetown	1971-72
210 for 2nd	G. P. Howarth and J. J. Crowe at Kingston	1984-85
241 for 3rd	J. G. Wright and M. D. Crowe at Wellington	1986-87
175 for 4th	B. E. Congdon and B. F. Hastings at Bridgetown	1971-72
142 for 5th	M. D. Crowe and J. V. Coney at Georgetown	1984-85
220 for 6th	G. M. Turner and K. J. Wadsworth at Kingston	1971-72
143 for 7th	M. D. Crowe and I. D. S. Smith at Georgetown	1984-85
136 for 8th†	B. E. Congdon and R. S. Cunis at Port-of-Spain	1971-72
62* for 9th	V. Pollard and R. S. Cunis at Auckland	1968-69
41 for 10th	B. E. Congdon and J. C. Alabaster at Port-of-Spain	1971-72

† *Denotes record partnership against all countries.*

TEN WICKETS OR MORE IN A MATCH

For West Indies (1)

11-120 (4-40, 7-80)	M. D. Marshall, Bridgetown	1984-85

For New Zealand (3)

10-124 (4-51, 6-73)†	E. J. Chatfield, Port-of-Spain	1984-85
11-102 (5-34, 6-68)†	R. J. Hadlee, Dunedin	1979-80
10-166 (4-71, 6-95)	G. B. Troup, Auckland	1979-80

† *Signifies ten wickets or more on first appearance in West Indies–New Zealand Tests.*

WEST INDIES v INDIA

	Captains					
Season	*West Indies*	*India*	*T*	*WI*	*I*	*D*
1948-49*I*	J. D. C. Goddard	L. Amarnath	5	1	0	4
1952-53*W*	J. B. Stollmeyer	V. S. Hazare	5	1	0	4
1958-59*I*	F. C. M. Alexander	Ghulam Ahmed[1]	5	3	0	2
1961-62*W*	F. M. M. Worrell	N. J. Contractor[2]	5	5	0	0
1966-67*I*	G. S. Sobers	Nawab of Pataudi jun.	3	2	0	1
1970-71*W*	G. S. Sobers	A. L. Wadekar	5	0	1	4
1974-75*I*	C. H. Lloyd	Nawab of Pataudi jun.[3]	5	3	2	0
1975-76*W*	C. H. Lloyd	B. S. Bedi	4	2	1	1
1978-79*I*	A. I. Kallicharran	S. M. Gavaskar	6	0	1	5
1982-83*I*	C. H. Lloyd	Kapil Dev	5	2	0	3
1983-84*I*	C. H. Lloyd	Kapil Dev	6	3	0	3
1987-88*I*	I. V. A. Richards	D. B. Vengsarkar[4]	4	1	1	2
1988-89*W*	I. V. A. Richards	D. B. Vengsarkar	4	3	0	1
	In India		34	13	4	17
	In West Indies		28	13	2	13
	Totals		62	26	6	30

I Played in India. W Played in West Indies.

Notes: The following deputised for the official touring captain or were appointed by the home authority for only a minor proportion of the series:
[1]P. R. Umrigar (First), V. Mankad (Fourth), H. R. Adhikari (Fifth). [2]Nawab of Pataudi jun. (Third, Fourth and Fifth). [3]S. Venkataraghavan (Second). [4]R. J. Shastri (Fourth).

HIGHEST INNINGS TOTALS

For West Indies in West Indies: 631-8 dec. at Kingston	....	1961-62
in India: 644-8 dec. at Delhi	....	1958-59
For India in West Indies: 469-7 at Port-of-Spain	....	1982-83
in India: 644-7 dec. at Kanpur	....	1978-79

LOWEST INNINGS TOTALS

For West Indies in West Indies: 214 at Port-of-Spain	....	1970-71
in India: 127 at Delhi	....	1987-88
For India in West Indies: 97† at Kingston	....	1975-76
in India: 75 at Delhi	....	1987-88

† *Five men absent hurt. The lowest with 11 men batting is 98 at Port-of-Spain, 1961-62.*

INDIVIDUAL HUNDREDS

For West Indies (76)

S. F. A. F. Bacchus (1)
250 Kanpur 1978-79

B. F. Butcher (2)
103 Calcutta 1958-59
142 Madras 1958-59

R. J. Christiani (1)
107† Delhi 1948-49

C. A. Davis (2)
125* Georgetown . 1970-71
105 Port-of-Spain 1970-71

P. J. L. Dujon (1)
110 St John's 1982-83

R. C. Fredericks (2)
100 Calcutta 1974-75
104 Bombay 1974-75

H. A. Gomes (1)
123 Port-of-Spain 1982-83

G. E. Gomez (1)
101† Delhi 1948-49

C. G. Greenidge (5)
107† Bangalore ... 1974-75
154* St John's 1982-83
194 Kanpur 1983-84
141 Calcutta 1987-88
117 Bridgetown . 1988-89

D. L. Haynes (2)
136 St John's 1982-83
112* Bridgetown . 1988-89

J. K. Holt (1)
123 Delhi 1958-59

C. L. Hooper (1)
100* Calcutta 1987-88

C. C. Hunte (1)
101 Bombay 1966-67

A. I. Kallicharran (3)
124† Bangalore ... 1974-75
103* Port-of-Spain 1975-76
187 Bombay 1978-79

R. B. Kanhai (4)
256 Calcutta 1958-59
138 Kingston ... 1961-62
139 Port-of-Spain 1961-62
158* Kingston ... 1970-71

C. H. Lloyd (7)
163 Bangalore ... 1974-75
242* Bombay 1974-75
102 Bridgetown . 1975-76
143 Port-of-Spain 1982-83
106 St John's 1982-83
103 Delhi 1983-84
161* Calcutta 1983-84

A. L. Logie (2)
130 Bridgetown . 1982-83
101 Calcutta 1987-88

E. D. A. McMorris (1)
125† Kingston ... 1961-62

B. H. Pairaudeau (1)
115† Port-of-Spain 1952-53

A. F. Rae (2)
104 Bombay 1948-49
109 Madras 1948-49

I. V. A. Richards (8)
192* Delhi 1974-75
142 Bridgetown . 1975-76
130 Port-of-Spain 1975-76
177 Port-of-Spain 1975-76
109 Georgetown . 1982-83
120 Bombay 1983-84
109* Delhi 1987-88
110 Kingston ... 1988-89

R. B. Richardson (2)
194 Georgetown . 1988-89
156 Kingston ... 1988-89

O. G. Smith (1)
100 Delhi 1958-59

G. S. Sobers (8)
142*† Bombay 1958-59
198 Kanpur 1958-59
106* Calcutta 1958-59
153 Kingston ... 1961-62
104 Kingston ... 1961-62
108* Georgetown . 1970-71
178* Bridgetown . 1970-71
132 Port-of-Spain 1970-71

J. S. Solomon (1)
100* Delhi 1958-59

J. B. Stollmeyer (2)
160 Madras 1948-49
104* Port-of-Spain 1952-53

C. L. Walcott (4)
152† Delhi 1948-49
108 Calcutta 1948-49
125 Georgetown . 1952-53
118 Kingston ... 1952-53

E. D. Weekes (7)
128† Delhi 1948-49
194 Bombay 1948-49
162 ⎫
101 ⎬ Calcutta 1948-49
207 Port-of-Spain 1952-53
161 Port-of-Spain 1952-53
109 Kingston ... 1952-53

A. B. Williams (1)
111 Calcutta 1978-79

F. M. M. Worrell (1)
237 Kingston ... 1952-53

For India (55)

H. R. Adhikari (1)			120	Delhi	1978-79	**R. J. Shastri (2)**		
147*†	Delhi	1948-49	147*	Georgetown	1982-83	102	St John's	1982-83
M. Amarnath (3)			121	Delhi	1983-84	107	Bridgetown .	1988-89
101*	Kanpur	1978-79	236*	Madras	1983-84	**N. S. Sidhu (1)**		
117	Port-of-Spain	1982-83	**V. S. Hazare (2)**			116	Kingston ...	1988-89
116	St John's	1982-83	134*	Bombay	1948-49	**E. D. Solkar (1)**		
M. L. Apte (1)			122	Bombay	1948-49	102	Bombay	1974-75
163*	Port-of-Spain	1952-53	**Kapil Dev (3)**			**P. R. Umrigar (3)**		
C. G. Borde (3)			126*	Delhi	1978-79	130	Port-of-Spain	1952-53
109	Delhi	1958-59	100*	Port-of-Spain	1982-83	117	Kingston ...	1952-53
121	Bombay	1966-67	109	Madras	1987-88	172*	Port-of-Spain	1961-62
125	Madras	1966-67	**S. V. Manjrekar (1)**			**D. B. Vengsarkar (6)**		
S. A. Durani (1)			108	Bridgetown .	1988-89	157*	Calcutta	1978-79
104	Port-of-Spain	1961-62	**V. L. Manjrekar (1)**			109	Delhi	1978-79
F. M. Engineer (1)			118	Kingston ...	1952-53	159	Delhi	1983-84
109	Madras	1966-67	**R. S. Modi (1)**			100	Bombay	1983-84
A. D. Gaekwad (1)			112	Bombay	1948-49	102	Delhi	1987-88
102	Kanpur	1978-79	**Mushtaq Ali (1)**			102*	Calcutta	1987-88
S. M. Gavaskar (13)			106†	Calcutta	1948-49	**G. R. Viswanath (4)**		
116	Georgetown .	1970-71	**B. P. Patel (1)**			139	Calcutta	1974-75
117*	Bridgetown .	1970-71	115*	Port-of-Spain	1975-76	112	Port-of-Spain	1975-76
124 }	Port-of-Spain	1970-71	**Pankaj Roy (1)**			124	Madras	1978-79
220 }			150	Kingston ...	1952-53	179	Kanpur	1978-79
156	Port-of-Spain	1975-76	**D. N. Sardesai (3)**					
102	Port-of-Spain	1975-76	212	Kingston ...	1970-71			
205	Bombay	1978-79	112	Port-of-Spain	1970-71			
107 }	Calcutta	1978-79	150	Bridgetown .	1970-71			
182* }								

† *Signifies hundred on first appearance in West Indies–India Tests.*

RECORD PARTNERSHIPS FOR EACH WICKET

For West Indies

296	for 1st	C. G. Greenidge and D. L. Haynes at St John's	1982-83
255	for 2nd	E. D. A. McMorris and R. B. Kanhai at Kingston	1961-62
220	for 3rd	I. V. A. Richards and A. I. Kallicharran at Bridgetown	1975-76
267	for 4th	C. L. Walcott and G. E. Gomez at Delhi	1948-49
219	for 5th	E. D. Weekes and B. H. Pairaudeau at Port-of-Spain	1952-53
250	for 6th	C. H. Lloyd and D. L. Murray at Bombay	1974-75
130	for 7th	C. G. Greenidge and M. D. Marshall at Kanpur	1983-84
124	for 8th†	I. V. A. Richards and K. D. Boyce at Delhi	1974-75
161	for 9th†	C. H. Lloyd and A. M. E. Roberts at Calcutta	1983-84
98*	for 10th†	F. M. M. Worrell and W. W. Hall at Port-of-Spain	1961-62

For India

153	for 1st	S. M. Gavaskar and C. P. S. Chauhan at Bombay	1978-79
344*	for 2nd†	S. M. Gavaskar and D. B. Vengsarkar at Calcutta	1978-79
159	for 3rd	M. Amarnath and G. R. Viswanath at Port-of-Spain	1975-76
172	for 4th	G. R. Viswanath and A. D. Gaekwad at Kanpur	1978-79
204	for 5th	S. M. Gavaskar and B. P. Patel at Port-of-Spain	1975-76
170	for 6th	S. M. Gavaskar and R. J. Shastri at Madras	1983-84
186	for 7th	D. N. Sardesai and E. D. Solkar at Bridgetown	1970-71
107	for 8th	Yashpal Sharma and B. S. Sandhu at Kingston	1982-83
143*	for 9th	S. M. Gavaskar and S. M. H. Kirmani at Madras	1983-84
62	for 10th	D. N. Sardesai and B. S. Bedi at Bridgetown	1970-71

† *Denotes record partnership against all countries.*

TEN WICKETS OR MORE IN A MATCH

For West Indies (4)

11-126 (6-50, 5-76)	W. W. Hall, Kanpur	1958-59
11-89 (5-34, 6-55)	M. D. Marshall, Port-of-Spain..................	1988-89
12-121 (7-64, 5-57)	A. M. E. Roberts, Madras	1974-75
10-101 (6-62, 4-39)	C. A. Walsh, Kingston..........................	1988-89

For India (4)

11-235 (7-157, 4-78)†	B. S. Chandrasekhar, Bombay..................	1966-67
10-223 (9-102, 1-121)	S. P. Gupte, Kanpur	1958-59
16-136 (8-61, 8-75)†	N. D. Hirwani, Madras	1987-88
10-135 (1-52, 9-83)	Kapil Dev, Ahmedabad	1983-84

† *Signifies ten wickets or more on first appearance in West Indies–India Tests.*

WEST INDIES v PAKISTAN

		Captains					
Season	West Indies	Pakistan	T	WI	P	D
1957-58W	F. C. M. Alexander	A. H. Kardar	5	3	1	1
1958-59P	F. C. M. Alexander	Fazal Mahmood	3	1	2	0
1974-75P	C. H. Lloyd	Intikhab Alam	2	0	0	2
1976-77W	C. H. Lloyd	Mushtaq Mohammad	5	2	1	2
1980-81P	C. H. Lloyd	Javed Miandad	4	1	0	3
1986-87P	I. V. A. Richards	Imran Khan	3	1	1	1
1987-88W	I. V. A. Richards[1]	Imran Khan	3	1	1	1
1990-91P	D. L. Haynes	Imran Khan	3	1	1	1
	In West Indies		13	6	3	4
	In Pakistan		15	4	4	7
	Totals...........................		28	10	7	11

P Played in Pakistan. W Played in West Indies.

Note: The following was appointed by the home authority for only a minor proportion of the series:

[1]C. G. Greenidge (First).

HIGHEST INNINGS TOTALS

For West Indies in West Indies: 790-3 dec. at Kingston.....................		1957-58
in Pakistan: 493 at Karachi.............................		1974-75
For Pakistan in West Indies: 657-8 dec. at Bridgetown....................		1957-58
in Pakistan: 406-8 dec. at Karachi		1974-75

LOWEST INNINGS TOTALS

For West Indies in West Indies: 154 at Port-of-Spain......................		1976-77
in Pakistan: 53 at Faisalabad		1986-87
For Pakistan in West Indies: 106 at Bridgetown		1957-58
in Pakistan: 77 at Lahore		1986-87

INDIVIDUAL HUNDREDS

For West Indies (21)

L. Baichan (1)	**C. C. Hunte (3)**	**I. V. A. Richards (2)**
105*† Lahore 1974-75	142† Bridgetown .. 1957-58	120* Multan 1980-81
P. J. L. Dujon (1)	260 Kingston.... 1957-58	123 Port-of-Spain 1987-88
106* Port-of-Spain 1987-88	114 Georgetown . 1957-58	**I. T. Shillingford (1)**
R. C. Fredericks (1)	**B. D. Julien (1)**	120 Georgetown . 1976-77
120 Port-of-Spain 1976-77	101 Karachi 1974-75	**G. S. Sobers (3)**
C. G. Greenidge (1)	**A. I. Kallicharran (1)**	365* Kingston 1957-58
100 Kingston..... 1976-77	115 Karachi 1974-75	125 ⎱Georgetown . 1957-58
D. L. Haynes (1)	**R. B. Kanhai (1)**	109* ⎰Georgetown . 1957-58
117 Karachi 1990-91	217 Lahore 1958-59	**C. L. Walcott (1)**
C. L. Hooper (1)	**C. H. Lloyd (1)**	145 Georgetown . 1957-58
134 Lahore 1990-91	157 Bridgetown .. 1976-77	**E. D. Weekes (1)**
		197† Bridgetown .. 1957-58

For Pakistan (17)

Asif Iqbal (1)	**Javed Miandad (2)**	**Saeed Ahmed (1)**
135 Kingston.... 1976-77	114 Georgetown . 1987-88	150 Georgetown . 1957-58
Hanif Mohammad (2)	102 Port-of-Spain 1987-88	**Salim Malik (1)**
337† Bridgetown .. 1957-58	**Majid Khan (2)**	102 Karachi 1990-91
103 Karachi 1958-59	100 Karachi 1974-75	**Wasim Raja (2)**
Imtiaz Ahmed (1)	167 Georgetown . 1976-77	107* Karachi 1974-75
122 Kingston.... 1957-58	**Mushtaq Mohammad (2)**	117* Bridgetown .. 1976-77
Imran Khan (1)	123 Lahore 1974-75	**Wazir Mohammad (2)**
123 Lahore 1980-81	121 Port-of-Spain 1976-77	106 Kingston 1957-58
		189 Port-of-Spain 1957-58

† *Signifies hundred on first appearance in West Indies–Pakistan Tests.*

RECORD PARTNERSHIPS FOR EACH WICKET

For West Indies

182 for 1st	R. C. Fredericks and C. G. Greenidge at Kingston	1976-77
446 for 2nd†	C. C. Hunte and G. S. Sobers at Kingston	1957-58
162 for 3rd	R. B. Kanhai and G. S. Sobers at Lahore	1958-59
188* for 4th	G. S. Sobers and C. L. Walcott at Kingston	1957-58
185 for 5th	E. D. Weekes and O. G. Smith at Bridgetown	1957-58
151 for 6th	C. H. Lloyd and D. L. Murray at Bridgetown	1976-77
70 for 7th	C. H. Lloyd and J. Garner at Bridgetown	1976-77
50 for 8th	B. D. Julien and V. A. Holder at Karachi	1974-75
61* for 9th	P. J. L. Dujon and W. K. M. Benjamin at Bridgetown	1987-88
44 for 10th	R. Nanan and S. T. Clarke at Faisalabad	1980-81

For Pakistan

159 for 1st[1]	Majid Khan and Zaheer Abbas at Georgetown..............	1976-77
178 for 2nd	Hanif Mohammad and Saeed Ahmed at Karachi	1958-59
169 for 3rd	Saeed Ahmed and Wazir Mohammad at Port-of-Spain	1957-58
174 for 4th	Shoaib Mohammad and Salim Malik at Karachi	1990-91
87 for 5th	Mushtaq Mohammad and Asif Iqbal at Kingston	1976-77
166 for 6th	Wazir Mohammad and A. H. Kardar at Kingston	1957-58
128 for 7th[2]	Wasim Raja and Wasim Bari at Karachi...................	1974-75

94 for 8th	Salim Malik and Salim Yousuf at Port-of-Spain	1987-88
73 for 9th	Wasim Raja and Sarfraz Nawaz at Bridgetown	1976-77
133 for 10th†	Wasim Raja and Wasim Bari at Bridgetown	1976-77

† *Denotes record partnership against all countries.*

[1] *219 runs were added for this wicket in two separate partnerships: Sadiq Mohammad retired hurt and was replaced by Zaheer Abbas when 60 had been added. The highest partnership by two opening batsmen is 152 by Hanif Mohammad and Imtiaz Ahmed at Bridgetown, 1957-58.*

[2] *Although the seventh wicket added 168 runs against West Indies at Lahore in 1980-81, this comprised two partnerships with Imran Khan adding 72* with Abdul Qadir (retired hurt) and a further 96 with Sarfraz Nawaz.*

TEN WICKETS OR MORE IN A MATCH

For Pakistan (2)

12-100 (6-34, 6-66)	Fazal Mahmood, Dacca	1958-59
11-121 (7-80, 4-41)	Imran Khan, Georgetown	1987-88

Note: The best match figures by a West Indian bowler are 9-95 (8-29, 1-66) by C. E. H. Croft at Port-of-Spain, 1976-77.

NEW ZEALAND v INDIA

Captains

Season	New Zealand	India	T	NZ	I	D
1955-56 *I*	H. B. Cave	P. R. Umrigar[1]	5	0	2	3
1964-65 *I*	J. R. Reid	Nawab of Pataudi jun.	4	0	1	3
1967-68 *N*	G. T. Dowling[2]	Nawab of Pataudi jun.	4	1	3	0
1969-70 *I*	G. T. Dowling	Nawab of Pataudi jun.	3	1	1	1
1975-76 *N*	G. M. Turner	B. S. Bedi[3]	3	1	1	1
1976-77 *I*	G. M. Turner	B. S. Bedi	3	0	2	1
1980-81 *N*	G. P. Howarth	S. M. Gavaskar	3	1	0	2
1988-89 *I*	J. G. Wright	D. B. Vengsarkar	3	1	2	0
1989-90 *N*	J. G. Wright	M. Azharuddin	3	1	0	2
	In India		18	2	8	8
	In New Zealand		13	4	4	5
	Totals		31	6	12	13

I Played in India.   N Played in New Zealand.

Notes: The following deputised for the official touring captain or were appointed by the home authority for a minor proportion of the series:

[1]Ghulam Ahmed (First). [2]B. W. Sinclair (First). [3]S. M. Gavaskar (First).

HIGHEST INNINGS TOTALS

For New Zealand in New Zealand: 502 at Christchurch	1967-68
in India: 462-9 dec. at Calcutta	1964-65
For India in New Zealand: 482 at Auckland	1989-90
in India: 537-3 dec. at Madras	1955-56

LOWEST INNINGS TOTALS

For New Zealand in New Zealand: 100 at Wellington	1980-81
in India: 124 at Hyderabad	1988-89
For India in New Zealand: 81 at Wellington	1975-76
in India: 88 at Bombay	1964-65

INDIVIDUAL HUNDREDS

For New Zealand (21)

1. D. Crowe (1)	**J. M. Parker** (1)	230* Delhi.......	1955-56
13 Auckland ... 1989-90	104 Bombay 1976-77	151* Calcutta	1964-65
5. T. Dowling (3)	**J. F. Reid** (1)	**B. R. Taylor** (1)	
20 Bombay 1964-65	123* Christchurch. 1980-81	105† Calcutta	1964-65
43 Dunedin 1967-68	**J. R. Reid** (2)	**G. M. Turner** (2)	
39 Christchurch. 1967-68	119* Delhi....... 1955-56	117 Christchurch.	1975-76
W. Guy (1)	120 Calcutta 1955-56	113 Kanpur	1976-77
02† Hyderabad .. 1955-56	**I. D. S. Smith** (1)	**J. G. Wright** (3)	
P. Howarth (1)	173 Auckland ... 1989-90	110 Auckland ...	1980-81
37* Wellington .. 1980-81	**B. Sutcliffe** (3)	185 Christchurch.	1989-90
. H. Jones (1)	137*† Hyderabad .. 1955-56	113* Napier	1989-90
70* Auckland ... 1989-90			

For India (22)

. Amarnath (1)	177 Delhi....... 1955-56	**D. N. Sardesai** (2)	
24† Auckland ... 1975-76	102* Madras 1964-65	200* Bombay	1964-65
1. Azharuddin (1)	**V. Mankad** (2)	106 Delhi.......	1964-65
92 Auckland ... 1989-90	223 Bombay 1955-56	**N. S. Sidhu** (1)	
. G. Borde (1)	231 Madras 1955-56	116† Bangalore ...	1988-89
09 Bombay 1964-65	**Nawab of Pataudi jun.** (2)	**P. R. Umrigar** (1)	
. M. Gavaskar (2)	153 Calcutta 1964-65	223† Hyderabad ..	1955-56
16† Auckland ... 1975-76	113 Delhi....... 1964-65	**G. R. Viswanath** (1)	
19 Bombay 1976-77	**G. S. Ramchand** (1)	103* Kanpur.....	1976-77
. G. Kripal Singh (1)	106* Calcutta 1955-56	**A. L. Wadekar** (1)	
00*† Hyderabad .. 1955-56	**Pankaj Roy** (2)	143 Wellington ..	1967-68
. L. Manjrekar (3)	100 Calcutta 1955-56		
18† Hyderabad .. 1955-56	173 Madras 1955-56		

† *Signifies hundred on first appearance in New Zealand–India Tests. B. R. Taylor provides the only instance for New Zealand of a player scoring his maiden hundred in first-class cricket in his first Test.*

RECORD PARTNERSHIPS FOR EACH WICKET

For New Zealand

49 for 1st	T. J. Franklin and J. G. Wright at Napier....................	1989-90
55 for 2nd	G. T. Dowling and B. E. Congdon at Dunedin	1967-68
22* for 3rd	B. Sutcliffe and J. R. Reid at Delhi.......................	1955-56
25 for 4th	J. G. Wright and M. J. Greatbatch at Christchurch	1989-90
19 for 5th	G. T. Dowling and K. Thomson at Christchurch.............	1967-68
87 for 6th	J. W. Guy and A. R. MacGibbon at Hyderabad.............	1955-56
63 for 7th	B. Sutcliffe and B. R. Taylor at Calcutta..................	1964-65
33 for 8th	R. J. Hadlee and I. D. S. Smith at Auckland	1989-90
36 for 9th†	I. D. S. Smith and M. C. Snedden at Auckland	1989-90
61 for 10th	J. T. Ward and R. O. Collinge at Madras..................	1964-65

For India

13 for 1st†	V. Mankad and Pankaj Roy at Madras....................	1955-56
04 for 2nd	S. M. Gavaskar and S. Amarnath at Auckland	1975-76
38 for 3rd	P. R. Umrigar and V. L. Manjrekar at Hyderabad	1955-56
71 for 4th	P. R. Umrigar and A. G. Kripal Singh at Hyderabad........	1955-56
27 for 5th	V. L. Manjrekar and G. S. Ramchand at Delhi	1955-56
93* for 6th	D. N. Sardesai and Hanumant Singh at Bombay	1964-65
28 for 7th	S. R. Tendulkar and K. S. More at Napier.................	1989-90
43 for 8th†	R. G. Nadkarni and F. M. Engineer at Madras.............	1964-65
05 for 9th	{ S. M. H. Kirmani and B. S. Bedi at Bombay...............	1976-77
	{ S. M. H. Kirmani and N. S. Yadav at Auckland............	1980-81
57 for 10th	R. B. Desai and B. S. Bedi at Dunedin	1967-68

† *Denotes record partnership against all countries.*

TEN WICKETS OR MORE IN A MATCH

For New Zealand (2)

11-58 (4-35, 7-23)	R. J. Hadlee, Wellington	1975-7
10-88 (6-49, 4-39)	R. J. Hadlee, Bombay	1988-8

For India (2)

11-140 (3-64, 8-76)	E. A. S. Prasanna, Auckland	1975-7
12-152 (8-72, 4-80)	S. Venkataraghavan, Delhi	1964-6

NEW ZEALAND v PAKISTAN

Captains

Season	New Zealand	Pakistan	T	NZ	P
1955-56P	H. B. Cave	A. H. Kardar	3	0	2
1964-65N	J. R. Reid	Hanif Mohammad	3	0	0
1964-65P	J. R. Reid	Hanif Mohammad	3	0	2
1969-70P	G. T. Dowling	Intikhab Alam	3	1	0
1972-73N	B. E. Congdon	Intikhab Alam	3	0	1
1976-77P	G. M. Turner[1]	Mushtaq Mohammad	3	0	2
1978-79N	M. G. Burgess	Mushtaq Mohammad	3	0	1
1984-85P	J. V. Coney	Zaheer Abbas	3	0	2
1984-85N	G. P. Howarth	Javed Miandad	3	2	0
1988-89N†	J. G. Wright	Imran Khan	2	0	0
1990-91P	M. D. Crowe	Javed Miandad	3	0	3
	In Pakistan		18	1	11
	In New Zealand		14	2	2
	Totals		32	3	13

N Played in New Zealand.   P Played in Pakistan.
  † *The First Test at Dunedin was abandoned without a ball being bowled and is excluded.*

Note: The following deputised for the official touring captain:
  [1]J. M. Parker (Third).

HIGHEST INNINGS TOTALS

For New Zealand in New Zealand 492 at Wellington		1984-8
in Pakistan: 482-6 dec. at Lahore		1964-6
For Pakistan in New Zealand: 616-5 dec. at Auckland		1988-8
in Pakistan: 565-9 dec. at Karachi		1976-7

LOWEST INNINGS TOTALS

For New Zealand in New Zealand: 156 at Dunedin		1972-7
in Pakistan: 70 at Dacca		1955-
For Pakistan in New Zealand: 169 at Auckland		1984-8
in Pakistan: 102 at Faisalabad		1990-9

INDIVIDUAL HUNDREDS

For New Zealand (18)

M. G. Burgess (2)
119* Dacca 1969-70
111 Lahore 1976-77

J. V. Coney (1)
111* Dunedin 1984-85

M. D. Crowe (2)
174 Wellington .. 1988-89
108* Lahore 1990-91

B. A. Edgar (1)
129† Christchurch. 1978-79

B. F. Hastings (1)
110 Auckland ... 1972-73

G. P. Howarth (1)
114 Napier 1978-79

W. K. Lees (1)
152 Karachi 1976-77

S. N. McGregor (1)
111 Lahore 1955-56

R. E. Redmond (1)
107† Auckland ... 1972-73

J. F. Reid (3)
106 Hyderabad .. 1984-85
148 Wellington .. 1984-85
158* Auckland ... 1984-85

J. R. Reid (1)
128 Karachi 1964-65

B. W. Sinclair (1)
130 Lahore 1964-65

G. M. Turner (1)
110† Dacca 1969-70

J. G. Wright (1)
107 Karachi 1984-85

For Pakistan (33)

Asif Iqbal (3)
175 Dunedin 1972-73
166 Lahore 1976-77
104 Napier 1978-79

Hanif Mohammad (3)
103 Dacca 1955-56
100* Christchurch. 1964-65
203* Lahore 1964-65

Imtiaz Ahmed (1)
209 Lahore 1955-56

Javed Miandad (7)
163† Lahore 1976-77
206 Karachi 1976-77
160* Christchurch. 1978-79
104
103* } Hyderabad .. 1984-85

118 Wellington .. 1988-89
271 Auckland ... 1988-89

Majid Khan (3)
110 Auckland ... 1972-73
112 Karachi 1976-77
119* Napier 1978-79

Mohammad Ilyas (1)
126 Karachi 1964-65

Mudassar Nazar (1)
106 Hyderabad .. 1984-85

Mushtaq Mohammad (3)
201 Dunedin 1972-73
101 Hyderabad .. 1976-77
107 Karachi 1976-77

Sadiq Mohammad (2)
166 Wellington .. 1972-73
103* Hyderabad .. 1976-77

Saeed Ahmed (1)
172 Karachi 1964-65

Salim Malik (1)
119* Karachi 1984-85

Shoaib Mohammad (5)
163 Wellington .. 1988-89
112 Auckland ... 1988-89
203* Karachi 1990-91
105 Lahore 1990-91
142 Faisalabad .. 1990-91

Waqar Hassan (1)
189 Lahore 1955-56

Zaheer Abbas (1)
135 Auckland ... 1978-79

† *Signifies hundred on first appearance in New Zealand–Pakistan Tests.*

Notes: Mushtaq and Sadiq Mohammad, at Hyderabad in 1976-77, provide the fourth instance in Test matches, after the Chappells (thrice), of brothers each scoring hundreds in the same innings.

Shoaib Mohammad scored his first four hundreds in this series in successive innings.

RECORD PARTNERSHIPS FOR EACH WICKET

For New Zealand

159 for 1st	R. E. Redmond and G. M. Turner at Auckland	1972-73
195 for 2nd	J. G. Wright and G. P. Howarth at Napier.................	1978-79
178 for 3rd	B. W. Sinclair and J. R. Reid at Lahore	1964-65
128 for 4th	B. F. Hastings and M. G. Burgess at Wellington	1972-73
183 for 5th†	M. G. Burgess and R. W. Anderson at Lahore	1976-77
145 for 6th	J. F. Reid and R. J. Hadlee at Wellington	1984-85
186 for 7th†	W. K. Lees and R. J. Hadlee at Karachi	1976-77
100 for 8th	B. W. Yuile and D. R. Hadlee at Karachi	1969-70
96 for 9th	M. G. Burgess and R. S. Cunis at Dacca	1969-70
151 for 10th†	B. F. Hastings and R. O. Collinge at Auckland	1972-73

For Pakistan

172 for 1st	Ramiz Raja and Shoaib Mohammad at Karachi	1990-91
114 for 2nd	Mohammad Ilyas and Saeed Ahmed at Rawalpindi	1964-65
248 for 3rd	Shoaib Mohammad and Javed Miandad at Auckland..........	1988-89
350 for 4th†	Mushtaq Mohammad and Asif Iqbal at Dunedin	1972-73

281 for 5th†	Javed Miandad and Asif Iqbal at Lahore	1976-7
217 for 6th†	Hanif Mohammad and Majid Khan at Lahore	1964-6
308 for 7th†	Waqar Hassan and Imtiaz Ahmed at Lahore	1955-5
89 for 8th	Anil Dalpat and Iqbal Qasim at Karachi	1984-8
52 for 9th	Intikhab Alam and Arif Butt at Auckland	1964-6
65 for 10th	Salah-ud-Din and Mohammad Farooq at Rawalpindi	1964-6

† *Denotes record partnership against all countries.*

TEN WICKETS OR MORE IN A MATCH

For New Zealand (1)

11-152 (7-52, 4-100)	C. Pringle, Faisalabad	1990-9

For Pakistan (6)

10-182 (5-91, 5-91)	Intikhab Alam, Dacca	1969-7
11-130 (7-52, 4-78)	Intikhab Alam, Dunedin	1972-7
10-106 (3-20, 7-86)	Waqar Younis, Lahore	1990-9
12-130 (7-76, 5-54)	Waqar Younis, Faisalabad	1990-9
10-128 (5-56, 5-72)	Wasim Akram, Dunedin	1984-8
11-79 (5-37, 6-42)†	Zulfiqar Ahmed, Karachi	1955-5

† *Signifies ten wickets or more on first appearance in New Zealand–Pakistan Tests.*

Note: Waqar Younis's performances were in successive matches.

NEW ZEALAND v SRI LANKA

Captains

Season	New Zealand	Sri Lanka	T	NZ	SL	
1982-83N	G. P. Howarth	D. S. de Silva	2	2	0	
1983-84S	G. P. Howarth	L. R. D. Mendis	3	2	0	
1986-87S†	J. J. Crowe	L. R. D. Mendis	1	0	0	
1990-91N	M. D. Crowe¹	A. Ranatunga	3	0	0	
	In New Zealand		5	2	0	
	In Sri Lanka		4	2	0	
	Totals...........................		9	4	0	

N Played in New Zealand. S Played in Sri Lanka.

† *The Second and Third Tests were cancelled owing to civil disturbances.*

Note: The following was appointed by the home authority for only a minor proportion of th series:
¹I. D. S. Smith (Third).

HIGHEST INNINGS TOTALS

For New Zealand in New Zealand: 671-4 at Wellington	1990-9
in Sri Lanka: 459 at Colombo (CCC)	1983-8
For Sri Lanka in New Zealand: 497 at Wellington	1990-9
in Sri Lanka: 397-9 dec. at Colombo (CCC)	1986-8

LOWEST INNINGS TOTALS

For New Zealand in New Zealand: 174 at Wellington	1990-9
in Sri Lanka: 198 at Colombo (SSC)	1983-8
For Sri Lanka in New Zealand: 93 at Wellington	1982-8
in Sri Lanka: 97 at Kandy	1983-8

INDIVIDUAL HUNDREDS

For New Zealand (8)

J. J. Crowe (1)
120* Colombo
(CCC)...... 1986-87

M. D. Crowe (1)
299 Wellington .. 1990-91

R. J. Hadlee (1)
151* Colombo
(CCC)...... 1986-87

A. H. Jones (3)
186 Wellington .. 1990-91
122 } Hamilton ... 1990-91
100* }

J. F. Reid (1)
180 Colombo
(CCC)...... 1983-84

J. G. Wright (1)
101 Hamilton ... 1990-91

For Sri Lanka (6)

P. A. de Silva (2)
267† Wellington .. 1990-91
123 Auckland ... 1990-91

R. L. Dias (1)
108† Colombo
(SSC) 1983-84

A. P. Gurusinha (2)
119 } Hamilton ... 1990-91
102 }

D. S. B. P. Kuruppu (1)
201*† Colombo
(CCC)...... 1986-87

† *Signifies hundred on first appearance in New Zealand–Sri Lanka Tests.*

Note: A. P. Gurusinha and A. H. Jones at Hamilton in 1990-91 provided the second instance of a player on each side hitting two separate hundreds in a Test match.

RECORD PARTNERSHIPS FOR EACH WICKET

For New Zealand

161 for 1st	T. J. Franklin and J. G. Wright at Hamilton		1990-91
76 for 2nd	J. G. Wright and A. H. Jones at Auckland		1990-91
467 for 3rd†‡	A. H. Jones and M. D. Crowe at Wellington		1990-91
82 for 4th	J. F. Reid and S. L. Boock at Colombo (CCC)		1983-84
13 for 5th	A. H. Jones and S. A. Thomson at Hamilton		1990-91
246* for 6th†	J. J. Crowe and R. J. Hadlee at Colombo (CCC)		1986-87
30 for 7th {	R. J. Hadlee and I. D. S. Smith at Kandy		1983-84
	R. J. Hadlee and J. J. Crowe at Kandy		1983-84
79 for 8th	J. V. Coney and W. K. Lees at Christchurch		1982-83
42 for 9th	W. K. Lees and M. C. Snedden at Christchurch		1982-83
52 for 10th	W. K. Lees and E. J. Chatfield at Christchurch		1982-83

For Sri Lanka

95 for 1st	C. P. Senanayake and U. C. Hathurusinghe at Hamilton		1990-91
57 for 2nd	S. M. S. Kaluperuma and R. S. Madugalle at Colombo (CCC)		1983-84
159* for 3rd¹	S. Wettimuny and R. L. Dias at Colombo (SSC)		1983-84
78 for 4th	P. A. de Silva and A. Ranatunga at Wellington		1990-91
130 for 5th	R. S. Madugalle and D. S. de Silva at Wellington		1982-83
109* for 6th²	R. S. Madugalle and A. Ranatunga at Colombo (CCC)		1983-84
55 for 7th	A. P. Gurusinha and A. Ranatunga at Hamilton		1990-91
52 for 8th	H. P. Tillekeratne and G. F. Labrooy at Auckland		1990-91
31 for 9th {	G. F. Labrooy and R. J. Ratnayake at Auckland		1990-91
	S. T. Jayasuriya and R. J. Ratnayake at Auckland		1990-91
60 for 10th	V. B. John and M. J. G. Amerasinghe at Kandy		1983-84

† *Denotes record partnership against all countries.*
‡ *Record third-wicket partnership in first-class cricket.*
¹ *163 runs were added for this wicket in two separate partnerships: S. Wettimuny retired hurt and was replaced by L. R. D. Mendis when 159 had been added.*
² *119 runs were added for this wicket in two separate partnerships: R. S. Madugalle retired hurt and was replaced by D. S. de Silva when 109 had been added.*

TEN WICKETS OR MORE IN A MATCH

For New Zealand (1)

10-102 (5-73, 5-29)   R. J. Hadlee, Colombo (CCC) 1983-8

Note: The best match figures by a Sri Lankan bowler are 8-159 (5-86, 3-73), V. B. John a Kandy, 1983-84.

INDIA v PAKISTAN

		Captains					
Season	India	Pakistan	T	I	P	D
1952-53*I*	L. Amarnath	A. H. Kardar	5	2	1	2
1954-55*P*	V. Mankad	A. H. Kardar	5	0	0	5
1960-61*I*	N. J. Contractor	Fazal Mahmood	5	0	0	5
1978-79*P*	B. S. Bedi	Mushtaq Mohammad	3	0	2	1
1979-80*I*	S. M. Gavaskar[1]	Asif Iqbal	6	2	0	4
1982-83*P*	S. M. Gavaskar	Imran Khan	6	0	3	3
1983-84*I*	Kapil Dev	Zaheer Abbas	3	0	0	3
1984-85*P*	S. M. Gavaskar	Zaheer Abbas	2	0	0	2
1986-87*I*	Kapil Dev	Imran Khan	5	0	1	4
1989-90*P*	K. Srikkanth	Imran Khan	4	0	0	4
	In India		24	4	2	18
	In Pakistan		20	0	5	15
	Totals		44	4	7	33

I Played in India. P Played in Pakistan.

Note: The following was appointed by the home authority for only a minor proportion of the series:
[1]G. R. Viswanath (Sixth).

HIGHEST INNINGS TOTALS

For India in India: 539-9 dec. at Madras 1960-61
       in Pakistan: 509 at Lahore 1989-90

For Pakistan in India: 487-9 dec. at Madras 1986-87
       in Pakistan: 699-5 at Lahore 1989-90

LOWEST INNINGS TOTALS

For India in India: 106 at Lucknow 1952-53
       in Pakistan: 145 at Karachi 1954-55

For Pakistan in India: 116 at Bangalore 1986-87
       in Pakistan: 158 at Dacca 1954-55

INDIVIDUAL HUNDREDS

For India (31)

M. Amarnath (4)			166	Madras	1979-80	**K. Srikkanth (1)**		
109*	Lahore	1982-83	127*‡	Faisalabad ..	1982-83	123	Madras	1986-87
120	Lahore	1982-83	103*	Bangalore ...	1983-84	**P. R. Umrigar (5)**		
103*	Karachi	1982-83	**V. S. Hazare (1)**			102	Bombay	1952-53
101*	Lahore	1984-85	146*	Bombay	1952-53	108	Peshawar	1954-55
M. Azharuddin (3)			**S. V. Manjrekar (2)**			115	Kanpur	1960-61
141	Calcutta	1984-85	113*†	Karachi	1989-90	117	Madras	1960-61
110	Jaipur	1986-87	218	Lahore	1989-90	112	Delhi	1960-61
109	Faisalabad ..	1989-90	**S. M. Patil (1)**			**D. B. Vengsarkar (2)**		
C. G. Borde (1)			127	Faisalabad ..	1984-85	146*	Delhi	1979-80
177*	Madras	1960-61	**R. J. Shastri (3)**			109	Ahmedabad .	1986-87
A. D. Gaekwad (1)			128	Karachi	1982-83	**G. R. Viswanath (1)**		
201	Jullundur ...	1983-84	139	Faisalabad ..	1984-85	145†	Faisalabad ..	1978-79
S. M. Gavaskar (5)			125	Jaipur	1986-87			
111	} Karachi	1978-79	**R. H. Shodhan (1)**					
137			110†	Calcutta	1952-53			

For Pakistan (41)

Aamer Malik (2)			126	Faisalabad ..	1982-83	**Saeed Ahmed (2)**		
117	Faisalabad ..	1989-90	280*	Hyderabad ..	1982-83	121†	Bombay	1960-61
113	Lahore	1989-90	145	Lahore	1989-90	103	Madras	1960-61
Alim-ud-Din (1)			**Mohsin Khan (1)**			**Salim Malik (3)**		
103*	Karachi	1954-55	101*†	Lahore	1982-83	107	Faisalabad ..	1982-83
Asif Iqbal (1)			**Mudassar Nazar (6)**			102*	Faisalabad ..	1984-85
104†	Faisalabad ..	1978-79	126	Bangalore ...	1979-80	102*	Karachi	1989-90
Hanif Mohammad (2)			119	Karachi	1982-83	**Shoaib Mohammad (2)**		
142	Bahawalpur .	1954-55	231	Hyderabad ..	1982-83	101	Madras	1986-87
160	Bombay	1960-61	152*‡	Lahore	1982-83	203*	Lahore	1989-90
Ijaz Faqih (1)			152	Karachi	1982-83	**Wasim Raja (1)**		
105†	Ahmedabad .	1986-87	199	Faisalabad ..	1984-85	125	Jullundur ...	1983-84
Imtiaz Ahmed (1)			**Mushtaq Mohammad (1)**			**Zaheer Abbas (6)**		
135	Madras	1960-61	101	Delhi	1960-61	176†	Faisalabad ..	1978-79
Imran Khan (3)			**Nazar Mohammad (1)**			235*	Lahore	1978-79
117	Faisalabad ..	1982-83	124*‡	Lucknow	1952-53	215	Lahore	1982-83
135*	Madras	1986-87	**Qasim Omar (1)**			186	Karachi	1982-83
109*	Karachi	1989-90	210	Faisalabad ..	1984-85	168	Faisalabad ..	1982-83
Javed Miandad (5)			**Ramiz Raja (1)**			168*	Lahore	1984-85
154*†	Faisalabad ..	1978-79	114	Jaipur	1986-87			
100	Karachi	1978-79						

† *Signifies hundred on first appearance in India–Pakistan Tests.*
‡ *Carried his bat.*

RECORD PARTNERSHIPS FOR EACH WICKET

For India

200 for 1st	S. M. Gavaskar and K. Srikkanth at Madras	1986-87
135 for 2nd	N. S. Sidhu and S. V. Manjrekar at Karachi................	1989-90
190 for 3rd	M. Amarnath and Yashpal Sharma at Lahore	1982-83
186 for 4th	S. V. Manjrekar and R. J. Shastri at Lahore	1989-90
200 for 5th	S. M. Patil and R. J. Shastri at Faisalabad	1984-85
143 for 6th	M. Azharuddin and Kapil Dev at Calcutta	1986-87
155 for 7th	R. M. H. Binny and Madan Lal at Bangalore	1983-84
122 for 8th	S. M. H. Kirmani and Madan Lal at Faisalabad	1982-83
149 for 9th†	P. G. Joshi and R. B. Desai at Bombay	1960-61
109 for 10th†	H. R. Adhikari and Ghulam Ahmed at Delhi..............	1952-53

For Pakistan

162 for 1st	Hanif Mohammad and Imtiaz Ahmed at Madras	1960-6
250 for 2nd	Mudassar Nazar and Qasim Omar at Faisalabad	1984-8:
451 for 3rd†	Mudassar Nazar and Javed Miandad at Hyderabad	1982-8:
287 for 4th	Javed Miandad and Zaheer Abbas at Faisalabad	1982-8:
213 for 5th	Zaheer Abbas and Mudassar Nazar at Karachi	1982-8:
207 for 6th	Salim Malik and Imran Khan at Faisalabad	1982-8:
154 for 7th	Imran Khan and Ijaz Faqih at Ahmedabad	1986-8:
112 for 8th	Imran Khan and Wasim Akram at Madras	1986-8:
60 for 9th	Wasim Bari and Iqbal Qasim at Bangalore	1979-8:
104 for 10th	Zulfiqar Ahmed and Amir Elahi at Madras	1952-5:

† *Denotes record partnership against all countries.*

TEN WICKETS OR MORE IN A MATCH

For India (3)

11-146 (4-90, 7-56)	Kapil Dev, Madras		1979-8(
10-126 (7-27, 3-99)	Maninder Singh, Bangalore		1986-87
13-131 (8-52, 5-79)†	V. Mankad, Delhi		1952-53

For Pakistan (5)

12-94 (5-52, 7-42)	Fazal Mahmood, Lucknow		1952-53
11-79 (3-19, 8-60)	Imran Khan, Karachi		1982-8:
11-180 (6-98, 5-82)	Imran Khan, Faisalabad		1982-8:
10-175 (4-135, 6-40)	Iqbal Qasim, Bombay		1979-8(
11-190 (8-69, 3-121)	Sikander Bakht, Delhi		1979-8(

† *Signifies ten wickets or more on first appearance in India–Pakistan Tests.*

INDIA v SRI LANKA

Season	India	*Captains* Sri Lanka	T	I	SL	D
1982-83*I*	S. M. Gavaskar	B. Warnapura	1	0	0	1
1985-86*S*	Kapil Dev	L. R. D. Mendis	3	0	1	2
1986-87*I*	Kapil Dev	L. R. D. Mendis	3	2	0	1
1990-91*I*	M. Azharuddin	A. Ranatunga	1	1	0	0
	In India		5	3	0	2
	In Sri Lanka		3	0	1	2
	Totals		8	3	1	4

I Played in India. S Played in Sri Lanka.

HIGHEST INNINGS TOTALS

For India in India: 676-7 at Kanpur	1986-87
in Sri Lanka: 325-5 dec. at Kandy	1985-86
For Sri Lanka in India: 420 at Kanpur	1986-87
in Sri Lanka: 385 at Colombo (PSS)	1985-86

LOWEST INNINGS TOTALS

For India in India: 288 at Chandigarh	1990-91
in Sri Lanka: 198 at Colombo (PSS)	1985-86
For Sri Lanka in India: 82 at Chandigarh	1990-91
in Sri Lanka: 198 at Kandy	1985-86

INDIVIDUAL HUNDREDS

For India (9)

M. Amarnath (2)	**S. M. Gavaskar** (2)	**S. M. Patil** (1)
116* Kandy...... 1985-86	155† Madras..... 1982-83	114*† Madras...... 1982-83
131 Nagpur..... 1986-87	176 Kanpur..... 1986-87	**D. B. Vengsarkar** (2)
M. Azharuddin (1)	**Kapil Dev** (1)	153 Nagpur..... 1986-87
199 Kanpur..... 1986-87	163 Kanpur..... 1986-87	166 Cuttack..... 1986-87

For Sri Lanka (7)

R. L. Dias (1)	**A. Ranatunga** (1)
106 Kandy...... 1985-86	111 Colombo
R. S. Madugalle (1)	(SSC) 1985-86
103 Colombo	**S. A. R. Silva** (1)
(SSC) 1985-86	111 Colombo
L. R. D. Mendis (3)	(PSS)....... 1985-86
105 }†Madras..... 1982-83	
105	
124 Kandy...... 1985-86	

† *Signifies hundred on first appearance in India–Sri Lanka Tests.*

RECORD PARTNERSHIPS FOR EACH WICKET

For India

156	for 1st	S. M. Gavaskar and Arun Lal at Madras	1982-83
173	for 2nd	S. M. Gavaskar and D. B. Vengsarkar at Madras	1982-83
173	for 3rd	M. Amarnath and D. B. Vengsarkar at Nagpur	1986-87
163	for 4th	S. M. Gavaskar and M. Azharuddin at Kanpur..............	1986-87
78	for 5th	M. Amarnath and M. Azharuddin at Kandy..................	1985-86
272	for 6th	M. Azharuddin and Kapil Dev at Kanpur...................	1986-87
78*	for 7th	S. M. Patil and Madan Lal at Madras	1982-83
70	for 8th	Kapil Dev and L. Sivaramakrishnan at Colombo (PSS)........	1985-86
16	for 9th	S. M. Gavaskar and Gopal Sharma at Colombo (SSC)	1985-86
29	for 10th	Kapil Dev and Chetan Sharma at Colombo (PSS)	1985-86

For Sri Lanka

159	for 1st†	S. Wettimuny and J. R. Ratnayeke at Kanpur	1986-87
95	for 2nd	S. A. R. Silva and R. S. Madugalle at Colombo (PSS)........	1985-86
153	for 3rd	R. L. Dias and L. R. D. Mendis at Madras	1982-83
216	for 4th	R. L. Dias and L. R. D. Mendis at Kandy	1985-86
144	for 5th	R. S. Madugalle and A. Ranatunga at Colombo (SSC).......	1985-86
89	for 6th	L. R. D. Mendis and A. N. Ranasinghe at Madras	1982-83
77	for 7th	R. S. Madugalle and D. S. de Silva at Madras	1982-83
40*	for 8th	P. A. de Silva and A. L. F. de Mel at Kandy	1985-86
60	for 9th†	H. P. Tillekeratne and A. W. R. Madurasinghe at Chandigarh .	1990-91
44	for 10th	R. J. Ratnayake and E. A. R. de Silva at Nagpur	1986-87

† *Denotes record partnership against all countries.*

TEN WICKETS OR MORE IN A MATCH

For India (1)

10-107 (3-56, 7-51)	Maninder Singh, Nagpur	1986-87

Note: The best match figures by a Sri Lankan bowler are 9-125 (4-76, 5-49) by R. J. Ratnayake against India at Colombo (PSS), 1985-86.

PAKISTAN v SRI LANKA

		Captains				
Season	Pakistan	Sri Lanka	T	P	SL	D
1981-82P	Javed Miandad	B. Warnapura[1]	3	2	0	1
1985-86P	Javed Miandad	L. R. D. Mendis	3	2	0	1
1985-86S	Imran Khan	L. R. D. Mendis	3	1	1	1
1991-92P	Imran Khan	P. A. de Silva	3	1	0	2
	In Pakistan		9	5	0	4
	In Sri Lanka		3	1	1	1
	Totals		12	6	1	5

P Played in Pakistan.   S Played in Sri Lanka.

Note: The following deputised for the official touring captain:
[1]L. R. D. Mendis (Second).

HIGHEST INNINGS TOTALS

For Pakistan in Pakistan: 555-3 at Faisalabad	1985-86
in Sri Lanka: 318 at Colombo (PSS)	1985-86
For Sri Lanka in Pakistan: 479 at Faisalabad	1985-86
in Sri Lanka: 323-3 at Colombo (PSS)	1985-86

LOWEST INNINGS TOTALS

For Pakistan in Pakistan: 221 at Faisalabad	1991-92
in Sri Lanka: 132 at Colombo (CCC)	1985-86
For Sri Lanka in Pakistan: 149 at Karachi	1981-82
in Sri Lanka: 101 at Kandy	1985-86

INDIVIDUAL HUNDREDS

For Pakistan (8)

Haroon Rashid (1)
153† Karachi 1981-82
Javed Miandad (1)
203* Faisalabad . . 1985-86
Mohsin Khan (1)
129 Lahore 1981-82
Qasim Omar (1)
206† Faisalabad . . 1985-86

Ramiz Raja (1)
122 Colombo
    (PSS) 1985-86
Salim Malik (2)
100*† Karachi 1981-82
101 Sialkot 1991-92
Zaheer Abbas (1)
134† Lahore 1981-82

For Sri Lanka (6)

P. A. de Silva (2)
122† Faisalabad . . 1985-86
105 Karachi 1985-86
R. L. Dias (1)
109 Lahore 1981-82
A. P. Gurusinha (1)
116* Colombo
    (PSS) 1985-86

A. Ranatunga (1)
135* Colombo
    (PSS) 1985-86
S. Wettimuny (1)
157 Faisalabad . . 1981-82

† *Signifies hundred on first appearance in Pakistan–Sri Lanka Tests.*

RECORD PARTNERSHIPS FOR EACH WICKET

For Pakistan

28 for 1st	Ramiz Raja and Shoaib Mohammad at Sialkot		1991-92
51 for 2nd	Mohsin Khan and Majid Khan at Lahore		1981-82
97 for 3rd	Qasim Omar and Javed Miandad at Faisalabad		1985-86
52 for 4th	Salim Malik and Javed Miandad at Karachi		1981-82
32 for 5th	Salim Malik and Imran Khan at Sialkot		1991-92
00 for 6th	Zaheer Abbas and Imran Khan at Lahore		1981-82
04 for 7th	Haroon Rashid and Tahir Naqqash at Karachi		1981-82
29 for 8th	Ashraf Ali and Iqbal Qasim at Faisalabad		1981-82
	Salim Yousuf and Abdul Qadir at Sialkot		1985-86
	Salim Yousuf and Abdul Qadir at Karachi		1985-86
27 for 9th	Haroon Rashid and Rashid Khan at Karachi		1981-82
48 for 10th	Rashid Khan and Tauseef Ahmed at Faisalabad		1981-82

For Sri Lanka

81 for 1st	R. S. Mahanama and U. C. Hathurusinghe at Faisalabad		1991-92
17 for 2nd†	S. Wettimuny and R. L. Dias at Faisalabad		1981-82
85 for 3rd	S. Wettimuny and R. L. Dias at Faisalabad		1985-86
40* for 4th†	A. P. Gurusinha and A. Ranatunga at Colombo (PSS)		1985-86
58 for 5th	R. L. Dias and L. R. D. Mendis at Lahore		1981-82
21 for 6th	A. Ranatunga and P. A. de Silva at Faisalabad		1985-86
66 for 7th	P. A. de Silva and J. R. Ratnayeke at Faisalabad		1985-86
61 for 8th†	R. S. Madugalle and D. S. de Silva at Faisalabad		1981-82
52 for 9th	P. A. de Silva and R. J. Ratnayake at Faisalabad		1985-86
36 for 10th	R. J. Ratnayake and R. G. C. E. Wijesuriya at Faisalabad		1985-86

† *Denotes record partnership against all countries.*

TEN WICKETS OR MORE IN A MATCH

For Pakistan (1)

14-116 (8-58, 6-58)   Imran Khan, Lahore 1981-82

Note: The best match figures by a Sri Lankan bowler are 9-162 (4-103, 5-59), D. S. de Silva at Faisalabad, 1981-82.

TEST MATCH GROUNDS

In Chronological Sequence

City and Ground	First Test Match		Tests
1. Melbourne, Melbourne Cricket Ground	1877 Australia v England		84
2. London, Kennington Oval	1880 England v Australia		75
3. Sydney, Sydney Cricket Ground (No. 1)	1882 Australia v England		78
4. Manchester, Old Trafford	1884 England v Australia		59
5. London, Lord's	1884 England v Australia		89
6. Adelaide, Adelaide Oval	1884 Australia v England		50
7. Port Elizabeth, St George's Park	1889 South Africa v England		12
8. Cape Town, Newlands	1889 South Africa v England		24
9. Johannesburg, Old Wanderers*	1896 South Africa v England		22
10. Nottingham, Trent Bridge	1899 England v Australia		40
11. Leeds, Headingley	1899 England v Australia		54
12. Birmingham, Edgbaston	1902 England v Australia		29

City and Ground	First Test Match	Tes
13. Sheffield, Bramall Lane*	1902 England v Australia	
14. Durban, Lord's*	1910 South Africa v England	
15. Durban, Kingsmead	1923 South Africa v England	19
16. Brisbane, Exhibition Ground*	1928 Australia v England	2
17. Christchurch, Lancaster Park	1930 New Zealand v England	30
18. Bridgetown, Kensington Oval	1930 West Indies v England	28
19. Wellington, Basin Reserve	1930 New Zealand v England	27
20. Port-of-Spain, Queen's Park Oval	1930 West Indies v England	41
21. Auckland, Eden Park	1930 New Zealand v England	34
22. Georgetown, Bourda	1930 West Indies v England	22
23. Kingston, Sabina Park	1930 West Indies v England	29
24. Brisbane, Woolloongabba	1931 Australia v South Africa	34
25. Bombay, Gymkhana Ground*	1933 India v England	1
26. Calcutta, Eden Gardens	1934 India v England	26
27. Madras, Chepauk (Chidambaram Stadium)	1934 India v England	20
28. Delhi, Feroz Shah Kotla	1948 India v West Indies	23
29. Bombay, Brabourne Stadium*	1948 India v West Indies	17
30. Johannesburg, Ellis Park*	1948 South Africa v England	
31. Kanpur, Green Park (Modi Stadium)	1952 India v England	16
32. Lucknow, University Ground*	1952 India v Pakistan	
33. Dacca, Dacca Stadium*	1955 Pakistan v India	
34. Bahawalpur, Dring Stadium	1955 Pakistan v India	
35. Lahore, Lawrence Gardens (Bagh-i-Jinnah)*	1955 Pakistan v India	
36. Peshawar, Services Club Ground	1955 Pakistan v India	
37. Karachi, National Stadium	1955 Pakistan v India	30
38. Dunedin, Carisbrook	1955 New Zealand v England	8
39. Hyderabad, Fateh Maidan (Lal Bahadur Stadium)	1955 India v New Zealand	
40. Madras, Corporation Stadium*	1956 India v New Zealand	
41. Johannesburg, New Wanderers	1956 South Africa v England	1
42. Lahore, Gaddafi Stadium	1959 Pakistan v Australia	2
43. Rawalpindi, Pindi Club Ground	1965 Pakistan v New Zealand	
44. Nagpur, Vidarbha C.A. Ground	1969 India v New Zealand	
45. Perth, Western Australian C.A. Ground	1970 Australia v England	1
46. Hyderabad, Niaz Stadium	1973 Pakistan v England	
47. Bangalore, Karnataka State C.A. Ground (Chinnaswamy Stadium)	1974 India v West Indies	
48. Bombay, Wankhede Stadium	1975 India v West Indies	1
49. Faisalabad, Iqbal Stadium	1978 Pakistan v India	1
50. Napier, McLean Park	1979 New Zealand v Pakistan	
51. Multan, Ibn-e-Qasim Bagh Stadium	1980 Pakistan v West Indies	
52. St John's (Antigua), Recreation Ground	1981 West Indies v England	
53. Colombo, P. Saravanamuttu Stadium	1982 Sri Lanka v England	
54. Kandy, Asgiriya Stadium	1983 Sri Lanka v Australia	
55. Jullundur, Burlton Park	1983 India v Pakistan	
56. Ahmedabad, Gujarat Stadium	1983 India v West Indies	
57. Colombo, Sinhalese Sports Club Ground	1984 Sri Lanka v New Zealand	
58. Colombo, Colombo Cricket Club Ground	1984 Sri Lanka v New Zealand	
59. Sialkot, Jinnah Stadium	1985 Pakistan v Sri Lanka	
60. Cuttack, Barabati Stadium	1987 India v Sri Lanka	
61. Jaipur, Sawai Mansingh Stadium	1987 India v Pakistan	
62. Hobart, Bellerive Oval	1989 Australia v Sri Lanka	
63. Chandigarh, Sector 16 Stadium	1990 India v Sri Lanka	
64. Hamilton, Trust Bank (Seddon) Park	1991 New Zealand v Sri Lanka	
65. Gujranwala, Municipal Stadium	1991 Pakistan v Sri Lanka	

* Denotes no longer used for Test matches. In some instances the ground is no longer in existenc

FAMILIES IN TEST CRICKET

FATHERS AND SONS

England
M. C. Cowdrey (114 Tests, 1954-55–1974-75) and C. S. Cowdrey (6 Tests, 1984-85–1988).
J. Hardstaff (5 Tests, 1907-08) and J. Hardstaff jun. (23 Tests, 1935–1948).
L. Hutton (79 Tests, 1937–1954-55) and R. A. Hutton (5 Tests, 1971).
F. T. Mann (5 Tests, 1922-23) and F. G. Mann (7 Tests, 1948-49–1949).
J. H. Parks (1 Test, 1937) and J. M. Parks (46 Tests, 1954–1967-68).
M. J. Stewart (8 Tests, 1962–1963-64) and A. J. Stewart (22 Tests, 1989-90–1992).
F. W. Tate (1 Test, 1902) and M. W. Tate (39 Tests, 1924–1935).
C. L. Townsend (2 Tests, 1899) and D. C. H. Townsend (3 Tests, 1934-35).

Australia
E. J. Gregory (1 Test, 1876-77) and S. E. Gregory (58 Tests, 1890–1912).

South Africa
F. Hearne (4 Tests, 1891-92–1895-96) and G. A. L. Hearne (3 Tests, 1922-23–1924).
F. Hearne also played 2 Tests for England in 1888-89.
J. D. Lindsay (3 Tests, 1947) and D. T. Lindsay (19 Tests, 1963-64–1969-70).
A. W. Nourse (45 Tests, 1902-03–1924) and A. D. Nourse (34 Tests, 1935–1951).
L. R. Tuckett (1 Test, 1913-14) and L. Tuckett (9 Tests, 1947–1948-49).

West Indies
G. A. Headley (22 Tests, 1929-30–1953-54) and R. G. A. Headley (2 Tests, 1973).
O. C. Scott (8 Tests, 1928–1930-31) and A. P. H. Scott (1 Test, 1952-53).

New Zealand
W. M. Anderson (1 Test, 1945-46) and R. W. Anderson (9 Tests, 1976-77–1978).
W. P. Bradburn (2 Tests, 1963-64) and G. E. Bradburn (4 Tests, 1990-91).
B. L. Cairns (43 Tests, 1973-74–1985-86) and C. L. Cairns (5 Tests, 1989-90–1991-92).
W. A. Hadlee (11 Tests, 1937–1950-51) and D. R. Hadlee (26 Tests, 1969–1977-78); Sir R. J. Hadlee (86 Tests, 1972-73–1990).
H. G. Vivian (7 Tests, 1931–1937) and G. E. Vivian (5 Tests, 1964-65–1971-72).

India
L. Amarnath (24 Tests, 1933-34–1952-53) and M. Amarnath (69 Tests, 1969-70–1987-88); S. Amarnath (10 Tests, 1975-76–1978-79).
D. K. Gaekwad (11 Tests, 1952–1960-61) and A. D. Gaekwad (40 Tests, 1974-75–1984-85).
Nawab of Pataudi (Iftikhar Ali Khan) (3 Tests, 1946) and Nawab of Pataudi (Mansur Ali Khan) (46 Tests, 1961-62–1974-75).
Nawab of Pataudi sen. also played 3 Tests for England, 1932-33–1934.
V. L. Manjrekar (55 Tests, 1951-52–1964-65) and S. V. Manjrekar (21 Tests, 1987-88–1991-92).
V. Mankad (44 Tests, 1946–1958-59) and A. V. Mankad (22 Tests, 1969-70–1977-78).
Pankaj Roy (43 Tests, 1951-52–1960-61) and Pranab Roy (2 Tests, 1981-82).

India and Pakistan
M. Jahangir Khan (4 Tests, 1932–1936) and Majid Khan (63 Tests, 1964-65–1982-83).
S. Wazir Ali (7 Tests, 1932–1936) and Khalid Wazir (2 Tests, 1954).

Pakistan
Hanif Mohammad (55 Tests, 1954–1969-70) and Shoaib Mohammad (39 Tests, 1983-84–1992).
Nazar Mohammad (5 Tests, 1952-53) and Mudassar Nazar (76 Tests, 1976-77–1988-89).

GRANDFATHERS AND GRANDSONS

Australia
V. Y. Richardson (19 Tests, 1924-25–1935-36) and G. S. Chappell (87 Tests, 1970-71–1983-84); I. M. Chappell (75 Tests, 1964-65–1979-80); T. M. Chappell (3 Tests, 1981).

GREAT-GRANDFATHER AND GREAT-GRANDSON

Australia

W. H. Cooper (2 Tests, 1881-82 and 1884-85) and A. P. Sheahan (31 Tests, 1967-68–1973-74

BROTHERS IN SAME TEST TEAM

England

E. M., G. F. and W. G. Grace: 1 Test, 1880.
C. T. and G. B. Studd: 4 Tests, 1882-83.
A. and G. G. Hearne: 1 Test, 1891-92.
  F. Hearne, their brother, played in this match for South Africa.
D. W. and P. E. Richardson: 1 Test, 1957.

Australia

E. J. and D. W. Gregory: 1 Test, 1876-77.
C. and A. C. Bannerman: 1 Test, 1878-79.
G. and W. F. Giffen: 2 Tests, 1891-92.
G. H. S. and A. E. Trott: 3 Tests, 1894-95.
I. M. and G. S. Chappell: 43 Tests, 1970-71–1979-80.
S. R. and M. E. Waugh: 2 Tests, 1990-91 – the first instance of twins appearing together.

South Africa

S. J. and S. D. Snooke: 1 Test, 1907.
D. and H. W. Taylor: 2 Tests, 1913-14.
R. H. M. and P. A. M. Hands: 1 Test, 1913-14.
E. A. B. and A. M. B. Rowan: 9 Tests, 1948-49–1951.
P. M. and R. G. Pollock: 23 Tests, 1963-64–1969-70.
A. J. and D. B. Pithey: 5 Tests, 1963-64.

West Indies

G. C. and R. S. Grant: 4 Tests, 1934-35.
J. B. and V. H. Stollmeyer: 1 Test, 1939.
D. St E. and E. St E. Atkinson: 1 Test, 1957-58.

New Zealand

J. J. and M. D. Crowe: 34 Tests, 1983–1989-90.
D. R. and R. J. Hadlee: 10 Tests, 1973–1977-78.
H. J. and G. P. Howarth: 4 Tests, 1974-75–1976-77.
J. M. and N. M. Parker: 3 Tests, 1976-77.
B. P. and J. G. Bracewell: 1 Test, 1980-81.

India

S. Wazir Ali and S. Nazir Ali: 2 Tests, 1932–1933-34.
L. Ramji and Amar Singh: 1 Test, 1933-34.
C. K. and C. S. Nayudu: 4 Tests, 1933-34–1936.
A. G. Kripal Singh and A. G. Milkha Singh: 1 Test, 1961-62.
S. and M. Amarnath: 8 Tests, 1975-76–1978-79.

Pakistan

Wazir and Hanif Mohammad: 18 Tests, 1952-53–1959-60.
Wazir and Mushtaq Mohammad: 1 Test, 1958-59.
Hanif and Mushtaq Mohammad: 19 Tests, 1960-61–1969-70.
Hanif, Mushtaq and Sadiq Mohammad: 1 Test, 1969-70.
Mushtaq and Sadiq Mohammad: 26 Tests, 1969-70–1978-79.
Wasim and Ramiz Raja: 2 Tests, 1983-84.

Sri Lanka

A. and D. Ranatunga: 2 Tests, 1989-90.
M. D. and S. Wettimuny: 2 Tests, 1982-83.

LIMITED-OVERS INTERNATIONAL RECORDS

Note: Limited-overs international matches do not have first-class status.

SUMMARY OF ALL LIMITED-OVERS INTERNATIONALS

To end of 1992 season in England
(Excluding Sri Lanka v Australia 1992-93)

Team	Opponents	Matches	Won by												Tied	NR
			E	A	I	NZ	P	SA	SL	WI	B	C	EA	Z		
England	Australia	52	25	25	–	–	–	–	–	–	–	–	–	–	1	1
	India	23	13	–	10	–	–	–	–	–	–	–	–	–	–	–
	New Zealand	40	20	–	–	17	–	–	–	–	–	–	–	–	–	3
	Pakistan	36	23	–	–	–	12	–	–	–	–	–	–	–	–	1
	South Africa	2	2	–	–	–	–	0	–	–	–	–	–	–	–	–
	Sri Lanka	9	8	–	–	–	–	–	1	–	–	–	–	–	–	–
	West Indies	43	18	–	–	–	–	–	–	23	–	–	–	–	–	2
	Canada	1	1	–	–	–	–	–	–	–	–	0	–	–	–	–
	East Africa	1	1	–	–	–	–	–	–	–	–	–	0	–	–	–
	Zimbabwe	1	0	–	–	–	–	–	–	–	–	–	–	1	–	–
Australia	India	40	–	24	13	–	–	–	–	–	–	–	–	–	–	3
	New Zealand	50	–	34	–	14	–	–	–	–	–	–	–	–	–	2
	Pakistan	34	–	15	–	–	17	–	–	–	–	–	–	–	–	2
	South Africa	1	–	0	–	–	–	1	–	–	–	–	–	–	–	–
	Sri Lanka	21	–	16	–	–	–	–	3	–	–	–	–	–	–	2
	West Indies	63	–	24	–	–	–	–	–	37	–	–	–	–	1	1
	Bangladesh	1	–	1	–	–	–	–	–	–	0	–	–	–	–	–
	Canada	1	–	1	–	–	–	–	–	–	–	0	–	–	–	–
	Zimbabwe	5	–	4	–	–	–	–	–	–	–	–	–	1	–	–
India	New Zealand	29	–	–	16	13	–	–	–	–	–	–	–	–	–	–
	Pakistan	38	–	–	12	–	24	–	–	–	–	–	–	–	–	2
	South Africa	4	–	–	2	–	–	2	–	–	–	–	–	–	–	–
	Sri Lanka	26	–	–	17	–	–	–	7	–	–	–	–	–	–	2
	West Indies	40	–	–	10	–	–	–	–	29	–	–	–	–	1	–
	Bangladesh	2	–	–	2	–	–	–	–	–	0	–	–	–	–	–
	East Africa	1	–	–	1	–	–	–	–	–	–	–	0	–	–	–
	Zimbabwe	5	–	–	5	–	–	–	–	–	–	–	–	0	–	–
New Zealand	Pakistan	25	–	–	–	11	13	–	–	–	–	–	–	–	–	1
	South Africa	1	–	–	–	1	–	0	–	–	–	–	–	–	–	–
	Sri Lanka	23	–	–	–	19	–	–	4	–	–	–	–	–	–	–
	West Indies	14	–	–	–	2	–	–	–	11	–	–	–	–	–	1
	Bangladesh	1	–	–	–	1	–	–	–	–	0	–	–	–	–	–
	East Africa	1	–	–	–	1	–	–	–	–	–	–	0	–	–	–
	Zimbabwe	3	–	–	–	3	–	–	–	–	–	–	–	0	–	–
Pakistan	South Africa	1	–	–	–	–	0	1	–	–	–	–	–	–	–	–
	Sri Lanka	36	–	–	–	–	28	–	7	–	–	–	–	–	–	1
	West Indies	57	–	–	–	–	17	–	–	39	–	–	–	–	1	–
	Bangladesh	2	–	–	–	–	2	–	–	–	0	–	–	–	–	–
	Canada	1	–	–	–	–	1	–	–	–	–	0	–	–	–	–
	Zimbabwe	1	–	–	–	–	1	–	–	–	–	–	–	0	–	–
South Africa	Sri Lanka	1	–	–	–	–	–	0	1	–	–	–	–	–	–	–
	West Indies	4	–	–	–	–	–	1	–	3	–	–	–	–	–	–
	Zimbabwe	1	–	–	–	–	–	1	–	–	–	–	–	0	–	–
Sri Lanka	West Indies	12	–	–	–	–	–	–	1	11	–	–	–	–	–	–
	Bangladesh	3	–	–	–	–	–	–	3	–	0	–	–	–	–	–
	Zimbabwe	1	–	–	–	–	–	–	1	–	–	–	–	0	–	–
West Indies	Zimbabwe	3	–	–	–	–	–	–	–	3	–	–	–	0	–	–
		760	111	144	88	82	115	6	28	156	0	0	0	2	4	24

	Matches	Won	Lost	Tied	No Result	% Won (excl. NR)
West Indies	236	156	73	3	4	67.24
Australia	268	144	111	2	11	56.03
England	208	111	89	1	7	55.22
Pakistan	231	115	108	1	7	51.33
New Zealand	187	82	98	0	7	45.55
India	208	88	112	1	7	43.78
South Africa	15	6	9	0	0	40.00
Sri Lanka	132	28	99	0	5	22.04
Zimbabwe	20	2	18	0	0	10.00
Bangladesh	9	0	9	0	0	0
Canada	3	0	3	0	0	0
East Africa	3	0	3	0	0	0

MOST RUNS

	M	I	NO	R	HS	100s	Avge
D. L. Haynes (West Indies)	203	202	25	7,513	152*	16	42.44
I. V. A. Richards (West Indies)	187	167	24	6,721	189*	11	47.00
Javed Miandad (Pakistan)	197	187	37	6,550	119*	7	43.66
A. R. Border (Australia)	241	223	42	5,900	127*	3	30.89
C. G. Greenidge (West Indies)	128	127	13	5,134	133*	11	45.03
D. M. Jones (Australia)	132	129	23	5,048	145	7	47.62
R. B. Richardson (West Indies)	163	159	20	4,883	122	5	35.12
G. R. Marsh (Australia)	117	115	6	4,357	126*	9	39.97
Ramiz Raja (Pakistan)	133	132	10	4,176	119*	7	34.22
K. Srikkanth (India)	146	145	4	4,092	123	4	29.02
G. A. Gooch (England)	111	109	6	4,071	142	8	39.52
Salim Malik (Pakistan)	152	142	19	4,038	102	5	32.82
A. J. Lamb (England)	122	118	16	4,010	118	4	39.31
D. C. Boon (Australia)	122	118	9	4,001	122	5	36.70

Leading aggregates for other countries are:

M. D. Crowe (New Zealand)	122	121	15	3,950	105*	5	37.26
A. Ranatunga (Sri Lanka)	107	103	20	2,856	88*	0	34.40
K. C. Wessels (South Africa)	15	15	2	578	90	0	44.46
D. L. Houghton (Zimbabwe)	20	19	0	567	142	1	29.84

Note: K. C. Wessels also scored 1,740 runs for Australia.

HIGHEST INDIVIDUAL SCORE FOR EACH COUNTRY

189*	I. V. A. Richards	West Indies v England at Manchester	1984
175*	Kapil Dev	India v Zimbabwe at Tunbridge Wells	1983
171*	G. M. Turner	New Zealand v East Africa at Birmingham	1975
158	D. I. Gower	England v New Zealand at Brisbane	1982-83
145	D. M. Jones	Australia v England at Brisbane	1990-91
142	D. L. Houghton	Zimbabwe v New Zealand at Hyderabad (India)	1987-88
126*	Shoaib Mohammad	Pakistan v New Zealand at Wellington	1988-89
121	R. L. Dias	Sri Lanka v India at Bangalore	1982-83
90	K. C. Wessels	South Africa v India at Delhi	1991-92
90	P. N. Kirsten	South Africa v New Zealand at Auckland	1991-92

MOST HUNDREDS

Total		E	A	SA	WI	NZ	I	P	SL	Z
16	D. L. Haynes (West Indies)	1	6	0	–	2	2	4	1	0
11	C. G. Greenidge (West Indies)	0	1	–	–	3	3	2	1	1
11	I. V. A. Richards (West Indies)	3	3	–	–	1	3	0	1	0
9	G. R. Marsh (Australia)	1	–	0	2	2	3	1	0	0
8	G. A. Gooch (England)	–	4	0	1	1	1	1	0	0
7	D. I. Gower (England)	–	2	–	0	3	0	1	1	–
7	Javed Miandad (Pakistan)	1	0	–	1	0	3	–	2	0
7	D. M. Jones (Australia)	3	–	0	0	2	0	1	1	0
7	Ramiz Raja (Pakistan)	1	0	–	1	3	0	–	2	0
7	Zaheer Abbas (Pakistan)	0	2	–	0	1	3	–	1	–

HIGHEST PARTNERSHIP FOR EACH WICKET

212 for 1st	G. R. Marsh and D. C. Boon	A v I	Jaipur	1986-87
221 for 2nd	C. G. Greenidge and I. V. A. Richards	WI v I	Jamshedpur	1983-84
224* for 3rd	D. M. Jones and A. R. Border	A v SL	Adelaide	1984-85
173 for 4th	D. M. Jones and S. R. Waugh	A v P	Perth	1986-87
152 for 5th	I. V. A. Richards and C. H. Lloyd	I v SL	Brisbane	1984-85
154 for 6th	R. B. Richardson and P. J. L. Dujon	WI v P	Sharjah	1991-92
115 for 7th	P. J. L. Dujon and M. D. Marshall	WI v P	Gujranwala	1986-87
117 for 8th	D. L. Houghton and I. P. Butchart	Z v NZ	Hyderabad (India)	1987-88
126* for 9th	Kapil Dev and S. M. H. Kirmani	I v Z	Tunbridge Wells	1983
106* for 10th	I. V. A. Richards and M. A. Holding	WI v E	Manchester	1984

MOST WICKETS

	M	Balls	R	W	BB	4W/i	Avge
Kapil Dev (India)	189	9,527	5,933	226	5-43	4	26.25
Imran Khan (Pakistan)	175	7,461	4,845	182	6-14	4	26.62
Wasim Akram (Pakistan)	126	6,369	4,097	171	5-21	6	23.95
R. J. Hadlee (New Zealand) . . .	115	6,182	3,407	158	5-25	6	21.56
M. D. Marshall (West Indies) . .	136	7,175	4,233	157	4-18	6	26.96
J. Garner (West Indies)	98	5,330	2,752	146	5-31	5	18.84
I. T. Botham (England)	116	6,271	4,139	145	4-31	3	28.54
M. A. Holding (West Indies) . .	102	5,473	3,034	142	5-26	6	21.36
E. J. Chatfield (New Zealand). .	114	6,065	3,618	140	5-34	4	25.84
C. J. McDermott (Australia) . . .	88	4,769	3,301	132	5-44	4	25.00
Abdul Qadir (Pakistan)	102	4,996	3,375	131	5-44	6	25.76
R. J. Shastri (India)	145	6,415	4,498	127	5-15	3	35.41
S. R. Waugh (Australia)	129	5,102	3,772	124	4-33	2	30.41
I. V. A. Richards (West Indies)	187	5,644	4,228	118	6-41	3	35.83
M. C. Snedden (New Zealand) .	93	4,525	3,237	114	4-34	1	28.39
C. E. L. Ambrose (West Indies)	71	3,847	2,263	111	5-17	7	20.38
Mudassar Nazar (Pakistan)	122	4,855	3,431	111	5-28	2	30.90
S. P. O'Donnell (Australia)	87	4,350	3,102	108	5-13	6	28.72
C. A. Walsh (West Indies)	97	5,175	3,374	108	5-1	5	31.24
D. K. Lillee (Australia)	63	3,593	2,145	103	5-34	6	20.82

Leading aggregates for other countries are:

J. R. Ratnayeke (Sri Lanka) . . .	78	3,573	2,866	85	4-23	1	33.71
A. A. Donald (South Africa). . .	14	742	545	24	5-29	1	22.70
E. A. Brandes (Zimbabwe)	12	619	509	16	4-21	1	31.81
A. J. Traicos (Zimbabwe)	20	1,128	673	16	3-35	0	42.06

BEST BOWLING FOR EACH COUNTRY

7-37	Aqib Javed	Pakistan v India at Sharjah	1991-92
7-51	W. W. Davis	West Indies v Australia at Leeds	1983
6-14	G. J. Gilmour	Australia v England at Leeds	1975
5-15	R. J. Shastri	India v Australia at Perth	1991-92
5-20	V. J. Marks	England v New Zealand at Wellington	1983-84
5-23	R. O. Collinge	New Zealand v India at Christchurch	1975-76
5-26	S. H. U. Karnain	Sri Lanka v New Zealand at Moratuwa.	1983-84
5-29	A. A. Donald	South Africa v India at Calcutta.	1991-92
4-21	E. A. Brandes	Zimbabwe v England at Albury	1991-92

HAT-TRICKS

Jalal-ud-Din	Pakistan v Australia at Hyderabad	1982-83
B. A. Reid	Australia v New Zealand at Sydney	1985-86
Chetan Sharma	India v New Zealand at Nagpur	1987-88
Wasim Akram	Pakistan v West Indies at Sharjah	1989-90
Wasim Akram	Pakistan v Australia at Sharjah	1989-90
Kapil Dev	India v Sri Lanka at Calcutta	1990-91
Aqib Javed	Pakistan v India at Sharjah	1991-92

MOST DISMISSALS IN AN INNINGS

5 (all ct)	R. W. Marsh	Australia v England at Leeds	1981
5 (all ct)	R. G. de Alwis	Sri Lanka v Australia at Colombo (PSS) .	1982-83
5 (all ct)	S. M. H. Kirmani ...	India v Zimbabwe at Leicester.........	1983
5 (3ct, 2st)	S. Viswanath	India v England at Sydney	1984-85
5 (3ct, 2st)	K. S. More	India v New Zealand at Sharjah	1987-88
5 (all ct)	H. P. Tillekeratne ...	Sri Lanka v Pakistan at Sharjah	1990-91

MOST DISMISSALS IN A CAREER

	M	Ct	St	Total
P. J. L. Dujon (West Indies)...........	169	183	21	204
R. W. Marsh (Australia)	92	120	4	124
Salim Yousuf (Pakistan)	86	81	22	103
I. A. Healy (Australia)...............	70	81	8	89
K. S. More (India)	85	59	27	86
I. D. S. Smith (New Zealand).........	98	81	5	86
Wasim Bari (Pakistan)...............	51	52	10	62

MOST CATCHES IN AN INNINGS

(Excluding wicket-keepers)

4	Salim Malik........	Pakistan v New Zealand at Sialkot	1984-85
4	S. M. Gavaskar.....	India v Pakistan at Sharjah	1984-85
4	R. B. Richardson ...	West Indies v England at Birmingham..........	1991
4	K. C. Wessels	South Africa v West Indies at Kingston..........	1991-92

Note: While fielding as substitute, J. G. Bracewell held 4 catches for New Zealand v Australia at Adelaide, 1980-81.

MOST CATCHES IN A CAREER

	M	Ct		M	Ct
A. R. Border (A)	241	111	Javed Miandad (P)	197	64
I. V. A. Richards (WI)	187	101	Kapil Dev (I)	189	62

ALL-ROUND

1,000 Runs and 100 Wickets

	M	R	W
I. T. Botham (England)...........	116	2,113	145
R. J. Hadlee (New Zealand).......	115	1,751	158
Imran Khan (Pakistan)...........	175	3,709	182
Kapil Dev (India)	189	3,486	226
Mudassar Nazar (Pakistan)	122	2,653	111
S. P. O'Donnell (Australia)........	87	1,242	108
I. V. A. Richards (West Indies)	187	6,721	118
R. J. Shastri (India)..............	145	3,037	127
Wasim Akram (Pakistan)	126	1,013	171
S. R. Waugh (Australia)	129	2,542	124

1,000 Runs and 100 Dismissals

	M	R	D
P. J. L. Dujon (West Indies)	169	1,945	204
R. W. Marsh (Australia)..........	92	1,225	124

TEAM RECORDS

HIGHEST INNINGS TOTALS

363-7	(55 overs)	England v Pakistan at Nottingham.................	1992
360-4	(50 overs)	West Indies v Sri Lanka at Karachi..............	1987-88
338-4	(50 overs)	New Zealand v Bangladesh at Sharjah..............	1989-90
338-5	(60 overs)	Pakistan v Sri Lanka at Swansea	1983
334-4	(60 overs)	England v India at Lord's	1975
333-8	(45 overs)	West Indies v India at Jamshedpur	1983-84
333-9	(60 overs)	England v Sri Lanka at Taunton..................	1983
332-3	(50 overs)	Australia v Sri Lanka at Sharjah................	1989-90
330-6	(60 overs)	Pakistan v Sri Lanka at Nottingham	1975

Highest totals by other countries are:

313-7	(49.2 overs)	Sri Lanka v Zimbabwe at New Plymouth	1991-92
312-4	(50 overs)	Zimbabwe v Sri Lanka at New Plymouth	1991-92
299-4	(40 overs)	India v Sri Lanka at Bombay	1986-87
288-2	(46.4 overs)	South Africa v India at Delhi	1991-92

HIGHEST TOTALS BATTING SECOND

Winning

313-7	(49.2 overs)	Sri Lanka v Zimbabwe at New Plymouth	1991-92
298-6	(54.5 overs)	New Zealand v England at Leeds................	1990
297-6	(48.5 overs)	New Zealand v England at Adelaide	1982-83

Losing

289-7	(40 overs)	Sri Lanka v India at Bombay	1986-87
288-9	(60 overs)	Sri Lanka v Pakistan at Swansea	1983
288-8	(50 overs)	Sri Lanka v Pakistan at Adelaide	1989-90

HIGHEST MATCH AGGREGATES

626-14	(120 overs)	Pakistan v Sri Lanka at Swansea	1983
625-11	(99.2 overs)	Sri Lanka v Zimbabwe at New Plymouth	1991-92
619-19	(118 overs)	England v Sri Lanka at Taunton..................	1983
604-9	(120 overs)	Australia v Sri Lanka at The Oval	1975
603-11	(100 overs)	Pakistan v Sri Lanka at Adelaide	1989-90

LOWEST INNINGS TOTALS

45	(40.3 overs)	Canada v England at Manchester..................	1979
55	(28.3 overs)	Sri Lanka v West Indies at Sharjah	1986-87
63	(25.5 overs)	India v Australia at Sydney......................	1980-81
64	(35.5 overs)	New Zealand v Pakistan at Sharjah	1985-86
70	(25.2 overs)	Australia v England at Birmingham.............	1977
70	(26.3 overs)	Australia v New Zealand at Adelaide	1985-86

Note: This section does not take into account those matches in which the number of overs was reduced.

Lowest totals by other countries are:

74	(40.2 overs)	Pakistan v England at Adelaide	1991-92
93	(36.2 overs)	England v Australia at Leeds	1975
111	(41.4 overs)	West Indies v Pakistan at Melbourne.............	1983-84
134	(46.1 overs)	Zimbabwe v England at Albury	1991-92
152	(43.4 overs)	South Africa v West Indies at Port-of-Spain	1991-92

LARGEST VICTORIES

232 runs	Australia (323-2 in 50 overs) v Sri Lanka (91 in 35.5 overs) at Adelaide.. 1984-85
206 runs	New Zealand (276-7 in 50 overs) v Australia (70 in 26.3 overs) at Adelaide.. 1985-86
202 runs	England (334-4 in 60 overs) v India (132-3 in 60 overs) at Lord's 1975

By ten wickets: There have been nine instances of victory by ten wickets.

TIED MATCHES

West Indies 222-5 (50 overs) v Australia 222-9 (50 overs) at Melbourne........	1983-84
England 226-5 (55 overs) v Australia 226-8 (55 overs) at Nottingham..........	1989
West Indies 186-5 (39 overs) v Pakistan 186-9 (39 overs) at Lahore	1991-92
India 126 (47.4 overs) v West Indies 126 (41 overs) at Perth	1991-92

MOST APPEARANCES

(150 or more)

	Total	E	A	SA	WI	NZ	I	P	SL	Z	C	B
A. R. Border (A).......	241	41	–	1	57	45	38	32	20	5	1	1
D. L. Haynes (WI)	203	31	58	4	–	13	36	50	9	2	–	
Javed Miandad (P).....	197	26	31	–	51	20	34	–	32	1	1	1
Kapil Dev (I).........	189	17	40	4	39	25	–	32	25	5	–	2
I. V. A. Richards (WI)..	187	36	54	–	–	12	31	41	11	2	–	
Imran Khan (P).......	175	20	29	1	49	12	29	–	32	1	1	1
P. J. L. Dujon (WI)	169	26	47	–	–	9	31	44	10	2	–	
R. B. Richardson (WI)..	163	27	39	4	–	11	29	43	9	1	–	
Salim Malik (P)	152	21	17	1	37	20	26	–	28	1	–	1

Most appearances for other countries:

	Total	E	A	SA	WI	NZ	I	P	SL	Z	C	B
J. G. Wright (NZ)	147	30	42	–	11	–	21	18	22	2	–	1
A. J. Lamb (E)	122	–	23	1	26	28	15	22	6	1	–	
A. Ranatunga (SL)	107	7	17	1	8	19	22	30	–	1	–	2
D. L. Houghton (Z)	20	1	5	1	3	3	5	1	1	–	–	
A. J. Pycroft (Z)	20	1	5	1	3	3	5	1	1	–	–	
A. J. Traicos (Z).......	20	1	5	1	3	3	5	1	1	–	–	
A. P. Kuiper (SA).....	15	2	1	–	4	1	4	1	1	1	–	
D. J. Richardson (SA) ..	15	2	1	–	4	1	4	1	1	1	–	
R. P. Snell (SA)	15	2	1	–	4	1	4	1	1	1	–	
K. C. Wessels (SA).....	15	2	1	–	4	1	4	1	1	1	–	

Note: K. C. Wessels also appeared 54 times for Australia.

WORLD CUP RECORDS 1975-1992

RESULTS SUMMARY

	Played	Won	Lost	No Result
England	34	23	10	1
West Indies	32	22	9	1
Australia.........	30	17	13	0
Pakistan	31	17	13	1
New Zealand	29	16	13	0
India............	29	14	14	1
South Africa	9	5	4	0
Sri Lanka	26	4	20	2
Zimbabwe	20	2	18	0
Canada..........	3	0	3	0
East Africa.......	3	0	3	0

WORLD CUP FINALS

1975	WEST INDIES (291-8) beat Australia (274) by 17 runs	Lord's
1979	WEST INDIES (286-9) beat England (194) by 92 runs	Lord's
1983	INDIA (183) beat West Indies (140) by 43 runs	Lord's
1987-88	AUSTRALIA (253-5) beat England (246-8) by seven runs	Calcutta
1991-92	PAKISTAN (249-6) beat England (227) by 22 runs	Melbourne

BATTING RECORDS

Most Runs

	M	I	NO	R	HS	100s	Avge
Javed Miandad (P)	28	27	4	1,029	103	1	44.73
I. V. A. Richards (WI)....	23	21	4	1,013	181	3	59.58
G. A. Gooch (E).........	21	21	1	897	115	1	44.85
M. D. Crowe (NZ).......	21	21	5	880	100*	1	55.00
D. L. Haynes (WI)	25	25	2	854	105	1	37.13
D. C. Boon (A)	16	16	1	815	100	2	54.33

Highest Score

181   I. V. A. Richards   WI v SL   Karachi   1987-88

Hundred Before Lunch

101   A. Turner   A v SL   The Oval   1975

Most Hundreds

3   I. V. A. Richards (WI), Ramiz Raja (P)

Highest Partnership for Each Wicket

182	for 1st	R. B. McCosker and A. Turner	A v SL	The Oval	1975
176	for 2nd	D. L. Amiss and K. W. R. Fletcher	E v I	Lord's	1975
195*	for 3rd	C. G. Greenidge and H. A. Gomes	WI v Z	Worcester	1983
149	for 4th	R. B. Kanhai and C. H. Lloyd	WI v A	Lord's	1975
145*	for 5th	A. Flower and A. C. Waller	Z v SL	New Plymouth	1991-92
144	for 6th	Imran Khan and Shahid Mahboob	P v SL	Leeds	1983
75*	for 7th	D. A. G. Fletcher and I. P. Butchart	Z v A	Nottingham	1983
117	for 8th	D. L. Houghton and I. P. Butchart	Z v NZ	Hyderabad (India)	1987-88
126*	for 9th	Kapil Dev and S. M. H. Kirmani	I v Z	Tunbridge Wells	1983
71	for 10th	A. M. E. Roberts and J. Garner	WI v I	Manchester	1983

BOWLING RECORDS

Most Wickets

	Balls	R	W	BB	4W/i	Avge
Imran Khan (P)	1,017	655	34	4-37	2	19.26
I. T. Botham (E)..........	1,332	862	30	4-31	1	28.73
Kapil Dev (I)	1,422	892	28	5-43	1	31.85
A. M. E. Roberts (WI)	1,021	552	26	3-32	0	21.23
C. J. McDermott (A)	876	587	26	5-44	2	22.57
Wasim Akram (P)	918	633	25	4-32	1	25.32

Best Bowling

7-51   W. W. Davis   WI v A   Leeds   1983

Hat-trick

Chetan Sharma   I v NZ   Nagpur   1987-88

Most Economical Bowling

12-8-6-1   B. S. Bedi   I v EA   Leeds   1975

Most Expensive Bowling

12-1-105-2   M. C. Snedden   NZ v E   The Oval   1983

WICKET-KEEPING RECORDS

Most Dismissals

Wasim Bari (P)	22	(18 ct, 4 st)
P. J. L. Dujon (WI)	20	(19 ct, 1 st)
R. W. Marsh (A)..........	18	(17 ct, 1 st)
K. S. More (I)	18	(12 ct, 6 st)
D. L. Murray (WI)	16	(16 ct)
D. J. Richardson (SA)	15	(14 ct, 1 st)

Most Dismissals in an Innings

5 (5 ct)   S. M. H. Kirmani   I v Z   Leicester   1983

FIELDING RECORDS

Most Catches

C. H. Lloyd (WI)	12	I. T. Botham (E)	10
Kapil Dev (I)	12	A. R. Border (A)	10
D. L. Haynes (WI)	12		

Most Catches in an Innings

3	C. H. Lloyd	WI v SL	Manchester	1975
3	D. A. Reeve	E v P	Adelaide	1991-92
3	Ijaz Ahmed	P v A	Perth	1991-92
3	A. R. Border	A v Z	Hobart	1991-92

MOST APPEARANCES

28 Imran Khan (P), Javed Miandad (P)
26 Kapil Dev (I)
25 A. R. Border (A), D. L. Haynes (WI)

TEAM RECORDS

Highest Total	360-4	West Indies v Sri Lanka	Karachi	1987-88
– Batting Second	313-7	Sri Lanka v Zimbabwe	New Plymouth	1991-92
Lowest Total	45	Canada v England	Manchester	1979
Highest Aggregate	626	Pakistan v Sri Lanka	Swansea	1983
Largest Victories	10 wkts	India beat East Africa	Leeds	1975
	10 wkts	West Indies beat Zimbabwe	Birmingham	1983
	10 wkts	West Indies beat Pakistan	Melbourne	1991-92
	202 runs	England beat India	Lord's	1975
Narrowest Victories	1 wkt	West Indies beat Pakistan	Birmingham	1975
	1 wkt	Pakistan beat West Indies	Lahore	1987-88
	1 run	Australia beat India	Madras	1987-88
	1 run	Australia beat India	Brisbane	1991-92

MISCELLANEOUS

LARGE ATTENDANCES

Test Series

943,000	Australia v England (5 Tests)	1936-37
In England		
549,650	England v Australia (5 Tests)	1953

Test Match

†350,534	Australia v England, Melbourne (Third Test)	1936-37
325,000+	India v England, Calcutta (Second Test)	1972-73
In England		
158,000+	England v Australia, Leeds (Fourth Test)	1948
137,915	England v Australia, Lord's (Second Test)	1953

Test Match Day

90,800	Australia v West Indies, Melbourne (Fifth Test, 2nd day)	1960-61

Other First-Class Matches in England

80,000+	Surrey v Yorkshire, The Oval (3 days)	1906
78,792	Yorkshire v Lancashire, Leeds (3 days)	1904
76,617	Lancashire v Yorkshire, Manchester (3 days)	1926

One-day International

‡90,000	India v Pakistan, Calcutta	1986-87
‡90,000	India v South Africa, Calcutta	1991-92
87,182	England v Pakistan, Melbourne (World Cup final)	1991-92
86,133	Australia v West Indies, Melbourne	1983-84

† *Although no official figures are available, the attendance at the Fourth Test between India and England at Calcutta, 1981-82, was thought to have exceeded this figure.*

‡ *No official attendance figures were issued for these games, but 90,000 seats were believed to be occupied. Press reports which gave much higher figures included security guards, food vendors etc., as well as paying spectators.*

LORD'S CRICKET GROUND

Lord's and the MCC were founded in 1787. The Club has enjoyed an uninterrupted career since that date, but there have been three grounds known as Lord's. The first (1787-1810) was situated where Dorset Square now is; the second (1809-13), at North Bank, had to be abandoned owing to the cutting of the Regent's Canal; and the third, opened in 1814, is the present one at St John's Wood. It was not until 1866 that the freehold of Lord's was secured by the MCC. The present pavilion was erected in 1890 at a cost of £21,000.

HIGHEST INDIVIDUAL SCORES MADE AT LORD'S

333	G. A. Gooch	England v India	1990
316*	J. B. Hobbs	Surrey v Middlesex	1926
315*	P. Holmes	Yorkshire v Middlesex	1925
281*	W. H. Ponsford	Australians v MCC	1934
278	W. Ward	MCC v Norfolk (with E. H. Budd, T. Vigne and F. Ladbroke)	1820
278	D. G. Bradman	Australians v MCC	1938
277*	E. H. Hendren	Middlesex v Kent	1922

Note: The longest innings in a first-class match at Lord's was played by S. Wettimuny (636 minutes, 190 runs) for Sri Lanka v England, 1984.

HIGHEST TOTALS OBTAINED AT LORD'S

First-Class Matches

729-6 dec.	Australia v England	1930
665	West Indians v Middlesex	1939
653-4 dec.	England v India	1990
652-8 dec.	West Indies v England	1973
629	England v India	1974
612-8 dec.	Middlesex v Nottinghamshire	1921
610-5 dec.	Australians v Gentlemen	1948
609-8 dec.	Cambridge University v MCC and Ground	1913
608-7 dec.	Middlesex v Hampshire	1919
607	MCC and Ground v Cambridge University	1902

Minor Match

735-9 dec.	MCC and Ground v Wiltshire	1888

BIGGEST HIT AT LORD'S

The only known instance of a batsman hitting a ball over the present pavilion at Lord's occurred when A. E. Trott, appearing for MCC against Australians on July 31, August 1, 2, 1899, drove M. A. Noble so far and high that the ball struck a chimney pot and fell behind the building.

HIGHEST SCORE IN A MINOR COUNTY MATCH

323*	F. E. Lacey	Hampshire v Norfolk at Southampton	1887

HIGHEST SCORE IN MINOR COUNTIES CHAMPIONSHIP

282	E. Garnett	Berkshire v Wiltshire at Reading	1908
254	H. E. Morgan	Glamorgan v Monmouthshire at Cardiff	1901
253*	G. J. Whittaker	Surrey II v Gloucestershire II at The Oval	1950
253	A. Booth	Lancashire II v Lincolnshire at Grimsby	1950
252	J. A. Deed	Kent II v Surrey II at The Oval (on début)	1924

HIGHEST SCORE FOR ENGLISH PUBLIC SCHOOL

278 J. L. Guise   Winchester v Eton at Eton 1921

HIGHEST SCORES IN OTHER MATCHES

628*	A. E. J. Collins, Clark's House v North Town at Clifton College. (A Junior House match. His innings of 6 hours 50 minutes was spread over four afternoons.)	1899
566	C. J. Eady, Break-o'-Day v Wellington at Hobart...........................	1901-02
515	D. R. Havewalla, B.B. and C.I. Rly v St Xavier's at Bombay.............	1933-34
506*	J. C. Sharp, Melbourne GS v Geelong College at Melbourne	1914-15
502*	Chaman Lal, Mehandra Coll., Patiala v Government Coll., Rupar at Patiala	1956-57
485	A. E. Stoddart, Hampstead v Stoics at Hampstead	1886
475*	Mohammad Iqbal, Muslim Model HS v Islamia HS, Sialkot at Lahore	1958-59
466*	G. T. S. Stevens, Beta v Lambda (University College School House match) at Neasden..	1919
459	J. A. Prout, Wesley College v Geelong College at Geelong	1908-09

HIGHEST PARTNERSHIP IN MINOR CRICKET

664* for 3rd V. G. Kambli and S. R. Tendulkar, Sharadashram Vidyamandir
School v St Xavier's High School at Bombay 1987-88

RECORD HIT

The Rev. W. Fellows, while at practice on the Christ Church ground at Oxford in 1856, drove a ball bowled by Charles Rogers 175 yards from hit to pitch.

THROWING THE CRICKET BALL

140 yards 2 feet, Robert Percival, on the Durham Sands, Co. Durham Racecourse c1882
140 yards 9 inches, Ross Mackenzie, at Toronto 1872

Notes: W. F. Forbes, on March 16, 1876, threw 132 yards at the Eton College sports. He was then 18 years of age.

Onochie Onuorah, on June 5, 1987, threw a 4½oz ball 100 yards 1 foot 8½ inches (91.94 metres) at The Abbey School, Westgate, sports. He was then 13 years of age.

William Yardley, while a boy at Rugby, threw 100 yards with his right hand and 78 yards with his left.

Charles Arnold, of Cambridge, once threw 112 yards with the wind and 108 against.

W. H. Game, at The Oval in 1875, threw the ball 111 yards and then back the same distance. W. G. Grace threw 109 yards one way and back 105, and George Millyard 108 with the wind and 103 against. At The Oval in 1868, W. G. Grace made three successive throws of 116, 117 and 118 yards, and then threw back over 100 yards. D. G. Foster (Warwickshire) threw 133 yards, and in 1930 he made a Danish record with 120.1 metres – about 130 yards.

DATES OF FORMATION OF COUNTY CLUBS NOW FIRST-CLASS

County	First known county organisation	Present Club Original date	Reorganisation, if substantial
Derbyshire	November 4, 1870	November 4, 1870	—
Durham	January 24, 1874	May 10, 1882	March, 1991
Essex	By May, 1790	January 14, 1876	—
Glamorgan	August 5, 1861	July 6, 1888	—
Gloucestershire	November 3, 1863	1871	—
Hampshire	April 3, 1849	August 12, 1863	July, 1879
Kent	August 6, 1842	March 1, 1859	December 6, 1870
Lancashire	January 12, 1864	January 12, 1864	—
Leicestershire	By August, 1820	March 25, 1879	—
Middlesex	December 15, 1863	February 2, 1864	—
Northamptonshire	1820†	July 31, 1878	—
Nottinghamshire	March/April, 1841	March/April, 1841	December 11, 1866
Somerset	October 15, 1864	August 18, 1875	—
Surrey	August 22, 1845	August 22, 1845	—
Sussex	June 16, 1836	March 1, 1839	August, 1857
Warwickshire	May, 1826	1882	—
Worcestershire	1844	March 5, 1865	—
Yorkshire	March 7, 1861	January 8, 1863	December 10, 1891

† *Town club.*

DATES OF FORMATION OF CLUBS IN THE CURRENT MINOR COUNTIES CHAMPIONSHIP

County	First known county organisation	Present Club
Bedfordshire	May, 1847	November 3, 1899
Berkshire	By May, 1841	March 17, 1895
Buckinghamshire	November, 1864	January 15, 1891
Cambridgeshire	March 13, 1844	June 6, 1891
Cheshire	1819	September 29, 1908
Cornwall	1813	November 12, 1894
Cumberland	January 2, 1884	April 10, 1948
Devon	1824	November 26, 1899
Dorset	1862 *or* 1871	February 5, 1896
Herefordshire	July 13, 1836	January 9, 1991
Hertfordshire	1838	March 8, 1876
Lincolnshire	1853	September 28, 1906
Norfolk	January 11, 1827	October 14, 1876
Northumberland	1834	December, 1895
Oxfordshire	1787	December 14, 1921
Shropshire	1819 or 1829	June 28, 1956
Staffordshire	November 24, 1871	November 24, 1871
Suffolk	July 27, 1864	August, 1932
Wiltshire	February 24, 1881	January, 1893

CONSTITUTION OF COUNTY CHAMPIONSHIP

There are references in the sporting press to a champion county as early as 1825, but the list is not continuous and in some years only two counties contested the title. The earliest reference in any cricket publication is from 1864, and at this time there were eight leading counties who have come to be regarded as first-class from that date – Cambridgeshire, Hampshire, Kent, Middlesex, Nottinghamshire, Surrey, Sussex and Yorkshire. The newly formed Lancashire club began playing inter-county matches in 1865, Gloucestershire in

70 and Derbyshire in 1871, and they are therefore regarded as first-class from these respective ـtes. Cambridgeshire dropped out after 1871, Hampshire, who had not played inter-county ـtches in certain seasons, after 1885, and Derbyshire after 1887. Somerset, who had played ـtches against the first-class counties since 1879, were regarded as first-class from 1882 to ـ85, and were admitted formally to the Championship in 1891. In 1894, Derbyshire, Essex, ـicestershire and Warwickshire were granted first-class status, but did not compete in the ـampionship until 1895 when Hampshire returned. Worcestershire, Northamptonshire and ـlamorgan were admitted to the Championship in 1899, 1905 and 1921 respectively and are ـgarded as first-class from these dates. An invitation in 1921 to Buckinghamshire to enter ـe Championship was declined, owing to the lack of necessary playing facilities, and an ـplication by Devon in 1948 was unsuccessful. Durham were admitted to the Championship in ـ92 and were granted first-class status prior to their pre-season tour of Zimbabwe.

MOST COUNTY CHAMPIONSHIP APPEARANCES

763	W. Rhodes	Yorkshire	1898-1930
707	F. E. Woolley	Kent	1906-38
665	C. P. Mead	Hampshire	1906-36

MOST CONSECUTIVE COUNTY CHAMPIONSHIP APPEARANCES

423	K. G. Suttle	Sussex	1954-69
412	J. G. Binks	Yorkshire	1955-69
399	J. Vine	Sussex	1899-1914
344	E. H. Killick	Sussex	1898-1912
326	C. N. Woolley	Northamptonshire	1913-31
305	A. H. Dyson	Glamorgan	1930-47
301	B. Taylor	Essex	1961-72

ـotes: J. Vine made 417 consecutive appearances for Sussex in all first-class matches between ـly 1900 and September 1914.

J. G. Binks did not miss a Championship match for Yorkshire between making his début in ـne 1955 and retiring at the end of the 1969 season.

THE ASHES

ـn affectionate remembrance of English cricket which died at The Oval, 29th August, 1882. ـeeply lamented by a large circle of sorrowing friends and acquaintances, R.I.P. N.B. The body ـill be cremated and the Ashes taken to Australia."

Australia's first victory on English soil over the full strength of England, on August 29, 1882, ـspired a young London journalist, Reginald Shirley Brooks, to write this mock "obituary". It ـppeared in the *Sporting Times*.

Before England's defeat at The Oval, by 7 runs, arrangements had already been made for the ـon. Ivo Bligh, afterwards Lord Darnley, to lead a team to Australia. Three weeks later they set ـut, now with the popular objective of recovering the Ashes. In the event, Australia won the ـirst Test by nine wickets, but with England winning the next two it became generally accepted ـaat they brought back the Ashes.

It was long accepted that the real Ashes – a small urn believed to contain the ashes of a bail ـsed in the third match – were presented to Bligh by a group of Melbourne women. At the time ـ the 1982 centenary of The Oval Test match, however, evidence was produced which ـaggested that these ashes were the remains of a ball and that they were given to the England ـaptain by Sir William Clarke, the presentation taking place before the Test matches in ـustralia in 1883. The certain origin of the Ashes, therefore, is the subject of some dispute.

After Lord Darnley's death in 1927, the urn was given to MCC by Lord Darnley's Australian-ـorn widow, Florence. It can be seen in the cricket museum at Lord's, together with a red and ـold velvet bag, made specially for it, and the scorecard of the 1882 match.

PART THREE: ENGLISH CRICKET IN 1992

FEATURES OF 1992

Double-Hundreds (14)

Aamir Sohail	205	Pakistan v England (Third Test) at Manchester.
P. D. Bowler	241*	Derbyshire v Hampshire at Portsmouth.
T. S. Curtis	228*	Worcestershire v Derbyshire at Derby.
G. A. Hick	213*	Worcestershire v Nottinghamshire at Nottingham.
Inzamam-ul-Haq	200*	Pakistanis v Oxford & Cambridge Universities at Cambridge.
A. J. Lamb	209	Northamptonshire v Warwickshire at Northampton.
N. J. Lenham	222*	Sussex v Kent at Hove.
T. C. Middleton	221	Hampshire v Surrey at Southampton.
M. R. Ramprakash	233	Middlesex v Surrey at Lord's.
D. M. Smith	213	Sussex v Essex at Southend.
N. J. Speak	232	Lancashire v Leicestershire at Leicester.
G. P. Thorpe	216	Surrey v Somerset at The Oval.
R. G. Twose	233	Warwickshire v Leicestershire at Birmingham.
M. E. Waugh	219*	Essex v Lancashire at Ilford.

Hundred on First-Class Début

J. D. Glendenen	117	Durham v Oxford University at Oxford.
J. R. Wileman	109	Nottinghamshire v Cambridge University at Nottingham.

Three Hundreds in Successive Innings

M. W. Gatting (Middlesex)	117, 163* and 126*.
G. A. Gooch (Essex)	102, 108* and 135.
M. A. Roseberry (Middlesex)	118, 100* and 173.
A. P. Wells (Sussex)	144, 165* and 115.

Six Fifties in Successive Innings

P. D. Bowler (Derbyshire)	91, 112, 53, 104*, 155, 90*.

Hundred in Each Innings of a Match

M. W. Gatting	117	163*	Middlesex v Warwickshire at Coventry.
G. A. Gooch	102	108*	Essex v Sussex at Southend.
D. M. Jones	134*	105	Durham v Pakistanis at Chester-le-Street.
A. J. Lamb	209	107	Northamptonshire v Warwickshire at Northampton.
J. P. Stephenson	113*	159*	Essex v Somerset at Taunton.

Fastest Hundred

(For the Walter Lawrence Trophy)

M. P. Speight	62 balls	Sussex v Lancashire at Hove.

In 56 minutes, including five sixes and 12 fours, in contrived circumstances.

Hundred Before Lunch

J. Adams	103*	Derbyshire v Middlesex at Derby (2nd day).
A. Atherton	111*	Lancashire v Derbyshire at Blackpool (3rd day).
A. Gooch	105*	Essex v Leicestershire at Chelmsford (2nd day).
J. Lenham	122*†	Sussex v Kent at Hove (3rd day).
M. Moody	100*	Worcestershire v Oxford University at Oxford (2nd day).
P. Speight	119*†	Sussex v Lancashire at Hove (3rd day).

† *In contrived circumstances.*

Hundred Entirely with the Aid of a Runner

Larkins	117	Durham v Somerset at Taunton.
J. Lenham	118	Sussex v Durham at Horsham.

First to 1,000 Runs

T. C. Middleton (Hampshire) on June 17.

First to 2,000 Runs

P. D. Bowler (Derbyshire) on September 3.

Carrying Bat Through Completed Innings

J. Barnett	156*	Derbyshire (330) v Nottinghamshire at Nottingham.
E. Briers	73*	Leicestershire (160) v Derbyshire at Ilkeston.
P. Stephenson	113*	Essex (259) v Somerset at Taunton.
J. Stewart	69*	England (175) v Pakistan (Second Test) at Lord's.

First-Wicket Partnership of 100 in Each Innings

22 156 T. S. Curtis/W. P. C. Weston, Worcestershire v Derbyshire at Worcester.

Other Notable Partnerships

irst Wicket

90	T. R. Ward/M. R. Benson, Kent v Warwickshire at Birmingham.
85	A. J. Moles/R. G. Twose, Warwickshire v Leicestershire at Birmingham.
67	V. P. Terry/T. C. Middleton, Hampshire v Surrey at Southampton.
66	D. L. Haynes/M. A. Roseberry, Middlesex v Nottinghamshire at Nottingham.
50	S. P. James/H. Morris, Glamorgan v Lancashire at Colwyn Bay.

econd Wicket

59	P. D. Bowler/J. E. Morris, Derbyshire v Somerset at Taunton.

hird Wicket

47*†	M. E. Waugh/N. Hussain, Essex v Lancashire at Ilford.
65	R. J. Harden/C. J. Tavaré, Somerset v Nottinghamshire at Taunton.
63	N. J. Lenham/A. P. Wells, Sussex v Lancashire at Manchester.
59	P. D. Bowler/T. J. G. O'Gorman, Derbyshire v Hampshire at Portsmouth.

Fourth Wicket
322   Javed Miandad/Salim Malik, Pakistan v England (First Test) at Birmingham.

Fifth Wicket
251   D. M. Smith/P. Moores, Sussex v Essex at Southend.

Sixth Wicket
235   G. R. Cowdrey/S. A. Marsh, Kent v Yorkshire at Canterbury.

Seventh Wicket
243   M. A. Atherton/P. J. Martin, Lancashire v Durham at Gateshead Fell.

Tenth Wicket
109   E. E. Hemmings/R. A. Pick, Nottinghamshire v Warwickshire at Nottingham.

   * *Unbroken partnership.*   † *County record.*

Twelve or More Wickets in a Match

R. D. B. Croft......	14-169	Glamorgan v Warwickshire at Swansea.
T. A. Munton	12-110	Warwickshire v Leicestershire at Birmingham.
I. D. K. Salisbury ...	12-138	Sussex v Yorkshire at Hove.
K. J. Shine	13-105	Hampshire v Lancashire at Manchester.
H. R. J. Trump.....	14-104	Somerset v Gloucestershire at Gloucester.
N. F. Williams	12-139	Middlesex v Gloucestershire at Lord's.

Eight Wickets in an Innings

A. M. Babington....	8-107	Gloucestershire v Kent at Bristol.
R. D. B. Croft......	8-66	Glamorgan v Warwickshire at Swansea.
P. J. Hartley	8-111	Yorkshire v Sussex at Hove.
M. J. McCague.....	8-26	Kent v Hampshire at Canterbury.
K. J. Shine	8-47	Hampshire v Lancashire at Manchester.
S. D. Udal.........	8-50	Hampshire v Sussex at Southampton.
N. F. Williams	8-75	Middlesex v Gloucestershire at Lord's.

Hat-Tricks

K. J. Shine†	Hampshire v Lancashire at Manchester.
H. R. J. Trump.....	Somerset v Gloucestershire at Gloucester.
M. Watkinson......	Lancashire v Warwickshire at Birmingham.

   † *Also four wickets in five balls and eight wickets in 38 balls.*

100 Wickets

No bowler took 100 wickets. The highest aggregate was 92 by C. A. Walsh (Gloucester-shire).

Nine Wicket-Keeping Dismissals in a Match

B. N. French (9 ct)	Nottinghamshire v Warwickshire at Birmingham.
P. A. Nixon (9 ct)	Leicestershire v Essex at Leicester.

Six Wicket-Keeping Dismissals in an Innings

R. J. Blakey (5 ct, 1 st)   Yorkshire v Gloucestershire at Cheltenham College.
B. N. French (6 ct) ....   Nottinghamshire v Warwickshire at Birmingham.

Match Double (100 Runs and 10 Wickets)

F. D. Stephenson . .   87*, 29; 4-78, 7-29   Sussex v Worcestershire at Worcester.

No Byes Conceded in Total of 500 or More

N. D. Burns ......   Somerset v Surrey (557) at The Oval.
C. W. Scott ....   Durham v Somerset (534) at Taunton.

Highest Innings Totals

616-7 dec. . . .   Somerset v Nottinghamshire at Taunton.
603-8 dec. . . .   Kent v Warwickshire at Birmingham.
563 . . . .   Sussex v Lancashire at Manchester.
562 . . . .   Lancashire v Durham at Gateshead Fell.
557 . . . .   Surrey v Somerset at The Oval.
552-9 dec. . .   Hampshire v Surrey at Southampton.
534 . . . .   Somerset v Durham at Taunton.
526 . . . .   Essex v Kent at Chelmsford.
521-9 dec. . . .   Durham v Glamorgan at Cardiff.
510-2 dec. . . .   Essex v Lancashire at Ilford.
508 . . . .   Yorkshire v Northamptonshire at Scarborough.
507 . . . .   Kent v Gloucestershire at Bristol.
505-9 dec. . .   Pakistan v England (Third Test) at Manchester.
502-4 dec. . .   Kent v Leicestershire at Leicester.
500-9 dec. . . .   Derbyshire v Nottinghamshire at Derby.

Highest Fourth-Innings Total

442-6 . . . .   Essex v Derbyshire at Derby (set 440).

Victory after Following On

Essex (149, 310) beat Hampshire (300-8 dec., 80) at Bournemouth.
Kent (117, 332) beat Surrey (301-8 dec., 76) at Guildford.

Lowest Innings Totals

70 . . . .   Hampshire v Kent at Canterbury.
74 . . . .   Derbyshire v Yorkshire at Harrogate.
75 . . . .   Cambridge University v Essex at Cambridge.
75 . . . .   Essex v Leicestershire at Leicester.
76 . . . .   Surrey v Kent at Guildford.
77 . . . .   Leicestershire v Northamptonshire at Northampton.
80 . . . .   Hampshire v Essex at Bournemouth.
83 . . . .   Essex v Yorkshire at Leeds.
85 . . . .   Derbyshire v Warwickshire at Birmingham.
93† . . . .   Pakistanis v Worcestershire at Worcester.
95 . . . .   Middlesex v Northamptonshire at Northampton.
96 . . . .   Essex v Derbyshire at Derby.

† *One man absent injured.*

Match Aggregates of 1,400 Runs

Runs-Wkts
1,409-24 .... Sussex v Kent at Hove.

50 Extras in an Innings

	b	l-b	w	n-b	
55	8	22	3	22	Warwickshire v Middlesex at Lord's.
53	8	8	2	35	England v Pakistan (Third Test) at Manchester.

Career Aggregate Milestones†

20,000 runs..........	C. W. J. Athey, B. C. Broad, D. L. Haynes, R. T. Robinson.
10,000 runs..........	T. J. Boon, D. J. Capel, P. Carrick, J. E. Emburey, D. M. Jones, M. P. Maynard, A. A. Metcalfe, A. J. Moles, M. E. Waugh.

† *Achieved since September 1991.*

FIELDING IN 1992

(Qualification: 20 dismissals)

71 D. Ripley (66 ct, 5 st)	29 C. W. Scott (27 ct, 2 st)
57 K. M. Krikken (52 ct, 5 st)	27 M. E. Waugh
54 C. P. Metson (49 ct, 5 st)	25 C. L. Hooper
52 S. A. Marsh (44 ct, 8 st)	25 T. R. Ward
52 S. J. Rhodes (47 ct, 5 st)	24 M. A. Atherton
51 A. N. Aymes (47 ct, 4 st)	24 N. Hussain
50 K. R. Brown (39 ct, 11 st)	24 M. A. Lynch
49 R. J. Blakey (44 ct, 5 st)	24 A. P. Wells
45 N. D. Burns (42 ct, 3 st)	23 M. W. Alleyne
45 B. N. French (41 ct, 4 st)	23 S. A. Kellett
45 P. A. Nixon (40 ct, 5 st)	23 R. J. Parks (21 ct, 2 st)
44 M. A. Garnham (41 ct, 3 st)	22 R. J. Bailey
43 *K. J. Piper (41 ct, 2 st)	22 †A. J. Stewart
43 R. C. Russell (40 ct, 3 st)	21 S. Bramhall (16 ct, 5 st)
41 J. D. Carr	21 M. A. Crawley
41 N. F. Sargeant (35 ct, 6 st)	21 J. E. Emburey
39 W. K. Hegg (33 ct, 6 st)	21 Inzamam-ul-Haq
39 P. Moores (32 ct, 7 st)	21 G. D. Lloyd
32 G. A. Hick	20 C. J. Adams
30 J. D. R. Benson	20 S. P. James
30 D. Byas	20 †D. P. Ostler
29 *Moin Khan (28 ct, 1 st)	20 P. R. Pollard
29 *Rashid Latif (27 ct, 2 st)	

* *K. J. Piper took two catches in the field. Moin Khan and Rashid Latif shared wicket-keeping duties against Oxford & Cambridge Universities (where Moin took two catches) and World XI (where Latif took three).*

† *A. J. Stewart took 16 catches and D. P. Ostler one as wicket-keeper.*

FIRST-CLASS AVERAGES, 1992

BATTING

(Qualification: 8 innings)

* Signifies not out.   *† Denotes a left-handed batsman.*

	M	I	NO	R	HS	100s	50s	Avge
Salim Malik (*Pakistanis*)	15	21	6	1,184	165	2	8	78.93
M. E. Waugh (*Essex*)	16	24	7	1,314	219*	4	6	77.29
D. M. Jones (*Durham*)	14	23	7	1,179	157	4	5	73.68
G. A. Gooch (*Essex*)	18	29	3	1,850	160	8	7	71.15
M. W. Gatting (*Middx*)	24	36	6	2,000	170	6	10	66.66
P. D. Bowler (*Derbys*)	24	38	7	2,044	241*	6	11	65.93
†N. H. Fairbrother (*Lancs.*)	12	18	7	689	166*	1	5	62.63
A. J. Lamb (*Northants*)	18	28	4	1,460	209	6	5	60.83
Javed Miandad (*Pakistanis*)	12	17	3	809	153*	2	4	57.78
N. J. Speak (*Lancs.*)	22	36	3	1,892	232	4	12	57.33
R. J. Turner (*Somerset*)	7	10	5	286	101*	1	1	57.20
M. A. Roseberry (*Middx*)	25	41	5	2,044	173	9	8	56.77
†Asif Mujtaba (*Pakistanis*)	16	25	6	1,074	154*	2	6	56.52
R. T. Robinson (*Notts.*)	19	33	5	1,547	189	4	8	55.25
N. R. Taylor (*Kent*)	21	35	7	1,508	144	1	11	53.85
G. A. Hick (*Worcs.*)	17	27	2	1,337	213*	4	5	53.48
M. D. Moxon (*Yorks.*)	19	28	2	1,385	183	5	5	53.26
T. L. Penney (*Warwicks.*)	16	24	7	904	151	3	4	53.17
K. J. Barnett (*Derbys.*)	19	29	5	1,270	160	4	4	52.91
Inzamam-ul-Haq (*Pakistanis*)	15	21	7	736	200*	1	5	52.57
G. R. Cowdrey (*Kent*)	21	31	6	1,291	147	3	7	51.64
M. A. Atherton (*Lancs.*)	21	37	6	1,598	199	5	7	51.54
G. D. Lloyd (*Lancs.*)	23	37	10	1,389	132	4	10	51.44
†G. P. Thorpe (*Surrey*)	24	41	4	1,895	216	3	13	51.21
V. P. Terry (*Hants*)	11	17	2	766	141	3	3	51.06
T. S. Curtis (*Worcs.*)	23	41	5	1,829	228*	4	7	50.80
R. J. Harden (*Somerset*)	20	33	5	1,387	187	3	6	49.53
T. C. Middleton (*Hants*)	24	40	4	1,780	221	6	7	49.44
A. D. Brown (*Surrey*)	11	16	1	740	175	3	2	49.33
R. J. Bailey (*Northants*)	23	39	7	1,572	167*	2	8	49.12
A. P. Wells (*Sussex*)	22	35	5	1,465	165*	5	4	48.83
T. R. Ward (*Kent*)	21	37	3	1,648	153	5	9	48.47
C. White (*Yorks.*)	19	26	8	859	79*	0	7	47.72
G. F. Archer (*Notts.*)	7	13	5	475	117	1	4	47.50
C. L. Hooper (*Kent*)	21	32	4	1,329	131	5	7	47.46
†D. I. Gower (*Hants*)	20	33	7	1,225	155	1	8	47.11
†H. Morris (*Glam.*)	23	37	3	1,597	146	6	6	46.97
P. A. Cottey (*Glam.*)	20	28	5	1,076	141	2	6	46.78
J. J. B. Lewis (*Essex*)	13	20	4	746	133	1	4	46.62
S. R. Tendulkar (*Yorks.*)	16	25	2	1,070	100	1	7	46.52
R. J. Blakey (*Yorks.*)	21	32	9	1,065	125*	2	5	46.30
P. Johnson (*Notts.*)	19	29	4	1,147	107*	2	10	45.88
D. L. Haynes (*Middx*)	20	35	2	1,513	177	3	10	45.84
J. P. Crawley (*CUCC & Lancs.*)	17	29	3	1,175	172	2	7	45.19
†M. R. Benson (*Kent*)	21	35	2	1,482	139	4	6	44.90
Shoaib Mohammad (*Pakistanis*)	12	21	4	761	105*	1	7	44.76
P. Bainbridge (*Durham*)	17	30	9	923	92*	0	8	43.95
A. Fordham (*Northants*)	23	41	2	1,710	192	4	7	43.84
J. P. Stephenson (*Essex*)	21	37	5	1,401	159*	3	8	43.78
P. J. Prichard (*Essex*)	23	38	4	1,485	136	4	9	43.67
†B. C. Broad (*Notts.*)	14	27	3	1,040	159*	5	0	43.33

		M	I	NO	R	HS	100s	50s	Avg
52	Ramiz Raja (*Pakistanis*)	16	26	2	1,036	172	2	6	43.
53	M. A. Lynch (*Surrey*)	23	40	6	1,465	107	3	8	43.0
54	†R. C. Russell (*Glos.*)	20	34	11	985	75	0	5	42.8
55	†Aamir Sohail (*Pakistanis*)	17	28	2	1,110	205	2	4	42.6
56	T. M. Moody (*Worcs.*)	11	19	2	724	178	4	1	42.5
57	A. J. Stewart (*Surrey*)	19	33	4	1,234	190	2	8	42.5
58	D. Ripley (*Northants*)	22	31	10	891	107*	2	4	42.4
59	D. R. Pringle (*Essex*)	16	17	5	509	112*	2	2	42.4
60	A. Dale (*Glam.*)	22	33	5	1,159	150*	2	7	41.3
61	J. E. Morris (*Derbys.*)	23	33	0	1,358	120	3	12	41.1
62	C. J. Adams (*Derbys.*)	23	33	4	1,109	140*	4	4	41.0
63	C. L. Cairns (*Notts.*)	21	30	6	984	107*	2	6	41.0
64	†R. G. Twose (*Warwicks.*)	23	38	3	1,412	233	1	10	40.3
65	P. W. G. Parker (*Durham*)	20	35	2	1,331	124	3	8	40.3
66	M. R. Ramprakash (*Middx*)....	20	33	3	1,199	233	3	5	39.9
67	R. R. Montgomerie (*OUCC*) ...	9	15	3	477	103*	1	1	39.7
68	S. P. James (*Glam.*)	24	39	4	1,376	152*	3	6	39.3
69	J. W. Hall (*Sussex*)	20	34	5	1,125	140*	1	8	38.7
70	C. J. Tavaré (*Somerset*)	21	32	2	1,157	125	3	6	38.5
71	†P. N. Weekes (*Middx*)	17	21	7	539	95	0	3	38.5
71	†M. Saxelby (*Notts.*)	8	13	1	462	73	0	5	38.5
73	J. D. Carr (*Middx*)	25	39	7	1,228	114	2	8	38.3
74	N. E. Briers (*Leics.*)	24	42	6	1,372	123	3	9	38.1
75	T. J. Boon (*Leics.*)	24	41	3	1,448	139	2	10	38.1
76	M. P. Maynard (*Glam.*)........	23	36	4	1,219	176	2	7	38.0
77	M. P. Speight (*Sussex*)	20	33	2	1,180	179	5	0	38.0
78	R. A. Smith (*Hants*)	17	28	3	950	127	2	5	38.0
78	C. C. Lewis (*Notts.*)	17	26	4	836	134*	2	5	38.0
80	S. A. Kellett (*Yorks.*)	22	36	1	1,326	96	0	9	37.8
81	N. Hussain (*Essex*)	20	26	3	866	172*	1	5	37.6
82	†W. P. C. Weston (*Worcs.*)	14	23	5	675	66*	0	5	37.5
83	W. Larkins (*Durham*)	22	41	0	1,536	143	4	8	37.4
84	P. W. Jarvis (*Yorks.*).........	15	14	4	374	80	0	3	37.4
85	M. C. J. Nicholas (*Hants*)	21	32	5	1,003	95*	0	6	37.1
86	M. A. Crawley (*Notts.*)	25	44	9	1,297	160*	4	5	37.0
87	†N. D. Burns (*Somerset*)	22	33	12	772	73*	0	4	36.7
88	M. N. Lathwell (*Somerset*)	19	33	1	1,176	114	1	11	36.7
89	N. J. Lenham (*Sussex*)	20	34	2	1,173	222*	4	3	36.6
90	D. M. Ward (*Surrey*)	18	30	6	879	138	3	1	36.6
91	W. K. Hegg (*Lancs.*)..........	18	24	7	618	80	0	5	36.3
92	†D. J. Bicknell (*Surrey*)	24	42	5	1,340	120*	2	7	36.2
93	A. J. Moles (*Warwicks.*)	23	41	3	1,359	122	1	12	35.7
94	T. J. G. O'Gorman (*Derbys.*) ...	24	37	8	1,031	95	0	8	35.5
95	S. J. Rhodes (*Worcs.*)	24	34	11	815	116*	2	2	35.4
96	F. A. Griffith (*Derbys.*)	7	10	3	248	81	0	1	35.4
97	G. B. T. Lovell (*OUCC*)	9	13	1	422	110*	1	2	35.1
98	D. P. Ostler (*Warwicks.*)	22	37	2	1,225	192	3	4	35.0
99	G. D. Hodgson (*Glos.*)	21	36	1	1,224	147	2	8	34.9
100	†D. M. Smith (*Sussex*)	19	33	2	1,076	213	2	5	34.7
100	D. A. Reeve (*Warwicks.*)	17	28	4	833	79	0	7	34.7
102	†G. Fowler (*Lancs.*)	11	20	2	623	106	1	4	34.6
103	S. A. Marsh (*Kent*)	22	30	4	896	125	1	6	34.4
104	S. C. Goldsmith (*Derbys.*)......	10	11	3	273	100*	1	1	34.1
105	P. Moores (*Sussex*)	21	30	5	851	109	1	3	34.0
106	D. W. Randall (*Notts.*)	19	29	3	882	133*	1	5	33.9
107	†J. T. C. Vaughan (*Glos.*).......	11	18	4	473	99	0	4	33.7
108	M. A. Feltham (*Surrey*)	13	19	6	437	50	0	1	33.6
109	A. N. Hayhurst (*Somerset*)	23	38	2	1,197	102	1	9	33.
110	†K. D. James (*Hants*)	23	37	2	1,149	116	1	8	32.8
111	F. D. Stephenson (*Sussex*)	18	25	4	680	133	2	2	32.
112	M. W. Alleyne (*Glos.*)	22	36	3	1,065	93	0	7	32.

	M	I	NO	R	HS	100s	50s	Avge
113 †N. V. Knight (*Essex*)	20	30	6	774	109	2	3	32.25
114 C. W. J. Athey (*Glos.*)	20	32	0	1,022	181	2	4	31.93
115 S. P. Titchard (*Lancs.*)	14	24	3	668	74	0	6	31.80
116 †N. A. Felton (*Northants*)	22	37	3	1,076	103	1	9	31.64
117 I. V. A. Richards (*Glam.*)	14	23	0	722	127	1	4	31.39
118 J. E. R. Gallian (*OUCC*)	9	15	0	468	112	1	3	31.20
119 { G. D. Rose (*Somerset*)	22	34	4	930	132	1	6	31.00
I. T. Botham (*Durham*)	17	25	2	713	105	1	3	31.00
J. P. Arscott (*CUCC*)	10	14	3	341	79	0	3	31.00
122 V. J. Wells (*Leics.*)	17	23	6	526	56	0	3	30.94
123 †S. G. Hinks (*Glos.*)	10	16	3	402	88*	0	3	30.92
124 D. G. Cork (*Derbys.*)	19	21	2	578	72*	0	3	30.42
125 †D. Byas (*Yorks.*)	20	30	4	784	100	1	6	30.15
126 †P. R. Pollard (*Notts.*)	19	33	3	900	75	0	5	30.00
127 D. J. Capel (*Northants*)	23	34	4	892	103	1	5	29.73
128 D. B. D'Oliveira (*Worcs.*)	13	19	1	535	100	1	2	29.72
129 †P. A. Nixon (*Leics.*)	16	25	7	529	107*	1	1	29.38
130 I. Smith (*Durham*)	12	16	1	435	110	1	2	29.00
131 †I. D. Austin (*Lancs.*)	8	10	2	230	115*	1	1	28.75
132 N. Shahid (*Essex*)	15	21	1	561	132	1	3	28.05
133 R. M. Wight (*CUCC*)	10	17	3	388	62*	0	2	27.71
134 P. J. Martin (*Lancs.*)	22	24	6	492	133	1	2	27.33
135 D. A. Leatherdale (*Worcs.*)	23	40	4	983	112	1	5	27.30
136 P. D. Atkins (*Surrey*)	7	14	0	382	99	0	2	27.28
137 { T. H. C. Hancock (*Glos.*)	10	17	1	436	102	1	2	27.25
R. P. Snell (*Somerset*)	16	20	4	436	81	0	3	27.25
139 R. D. B. Croft (*Glam.*)	24	34	10	650	60*	0	3	27.08
140 R. J. Bartlett (*Somerset*)	8	13	0	352	72	0	2	27.07
141 †S. Hutton (*Durham*)	8	15	0	406	78	0	2	27.06
142 †R. J. Scott (*Glos.*)	19	31	3	751	73	0	4	26.82
143 J. J. Whitaker (*Leics.*)	22	34	3	830	74	0	5	26.77
144 K. H. MacLeay (*Somerset*)	12	19	3	427	74	0	3	26.68
145 M. V. Fleming (*Kent*)	21	32	2	797	100*	1	4	26.56
146 †A. C. H. Seymour (*Worcs.*)	11	21	0	556	133	1	1	26.47
147 J. E. Emburey (*Middx*)	23	27	6	554	102	1	3	26.38
148 A. A. Metcalfe (*Yorks.*)	11	17	1	422	73	0	1	26.37
149 G. R. Haynes (*Worcs.*)	9	13	2	288	66	0	2	26.18
150 R. S. M. Morris (*Hants*)	5	9	1	209	74	0	2	26.12
151 L. Potter (*Leics.*)	23	36	4	834	96	0	4	26.06
152 B. F. Smith (*Leics.*)	15	20	3	441	100*	1	3	25.94
153 K. R. Brown (*Middx*)	25	37	7	776	106	1	3	25.86
154 A. J. Wright (*Glos.*)	19	33	3	772	128	1	3	25.73
155 C. L. Keey (*OUCC*)	8	13	1	308	64	0	3	25.66
156 M. D. Marshall (*Hants*)	19	25	5	513	70	0	3	25.65
157 K. Greenfield (*Sussex*)	6	10	2	205	48	0	0	25.62
158 †J. D. Robinson (*Surrey*)	9	17	5	307	65*	0	1	25.58
159 N. M. K. Smith (*Warwicks.*)	12	20	0	454	67	0	1	25.22
160 K. M. Curran (*Northants*)	21	30	1	730	82	0	5	25.17
161 P. A. J. DeFreitas (*Lancs.*)	13	14	1	325	72	0	1	25.00
162 { †T. A. Lloyd (*Warwicks.*)	23	39	2	919	84*	0	5	24.83
M. P. Bicknell (*Surrey*)	19	26	8	447	88	0	2	24.83
164 P. J. Newport (*Worcs.*)	22	25	6	467	75*	0	3	24.57
165 D. W. Headley (*Middx*)	17	14	3	270	91	0	1	24.54
166 †J. R. Wood (*Hants*)	10	13	1	294	57	0	1	24.50
167 R. J. Parks (*Hants*)	7	10	3	169	33	0	0	24.14
168 R. P. Davis (*Kent*)	18	24	11	312	54*	0	1	24.00
169 J. R. Ayling (*Hants*)	18	26	1	593	121	1	2	23.72
170 { M. A. Garnham (*Essex*)	24	28	4	569	82*	0	4	23.70
Moin Khan (*Pakistanis*)	13	14	4	237	53	0	1	23.70
172 N. G. B. Cook (*Northants*)	17	11	6	118	37	0	0	23.60
173 S. R. Lampitt (*Worcs.*)	19	29	5	565	71*	0	4	23.54

		M	I	NO	R	HS	100s	50s	Avge
174	R. E. Bryson (*Surrey*)	11	13	2	257	76	0	1	23.36
175	N. A. Foster (*Essex*)	11	14	0	326	54	0	2	23.28
176	J. D. R. Benson (*Leics.*)	18	28	1	623	122	1	1	23.07
	†R. M. Ellison (*Kent*)	19	22	8	323	64	0	1	23.07
178	Zahid Fazal (*Pakistanis*)	6	8	3	115	51	0	1	23.00
179	C. W. Scott (*Durham*)	18	24	5	433	57*	0	2	22.78
180	G. T. J. Townsend (*Somerset*)	7	13	1	272	49	0	0	22.66
	Rashid Latif (*Pakistanis*)	8	8	2	136	50	0	1	22.66
182	J. D. Glendenen (*Durham*)	17	28	1	607	117	1	3	22.48
183	B. T. P. Donelan (*Sussex*)	16	25	6	421	68*	0	2	22.15
184	E. E. Hemmings (*Notts.*)	7	11	5	132	52*	0	1	22.00
185	K. P. Evans (*Notts.*)	19	24	4	438	104	1	2	21.90
186	N. V. Radford (*Worcs.*)	22	19	7	261	73*	0	1	21.75
187	†D. L. Hemp (*Glam.*)	12	17	2	326	84*	0	2	21.73
188	C. C. Remy (*Sussex*)	7	9	0	192	47	0	0	21.33
189	S. D. Udal (*Hants*)	23	29	10	400	44	0	0	21.05
190	R. K. Illingworth (*Worcs.*)	20	20	6	294	43	0	0	21.00
191	G. W. Jones (*CUCC*)	6	12	0	249	44	0	0	20.75
192	G. D. Mendis (*Lancs.*)	5	8	1	145	45	0	0	20.71
193	W. K. M. Benjamin (*Leics.*)	20	25	3	453	72	0	4	20.59
194	M. A. Ealham (*Kent*)	17	27	5	452	67*	0	4	20.54
195	I. R. Bishop (*Derbys.*)	20	21	2	388	90	0	1	20.42
196	K. J. Piper (*Warwicks.*)	19	25	8	345	72	0	2	20.29
197	R. P. Gofton (*Leics.*)	5	8	1	142	75	0	1	20.28
198	M. Watkinson (*Lancs.*)	20	25	1	482	96	0	1	20.08
199	A. R. Caddick (*Somerset*)	20	19	6	261	54*	0	1	20.07
200	†C. E. L. Ambrose (*Northants*)	18	20	10	200	49*	0	0	20.00
201	A. N. Aymes (*Hants*)	18	23	5	359	65	0	2	19.94
202	†Wasim Akram (*Pakistanis*)	14	18	3	299	45*	0	0	19.93
203	C. P. Metson (*Glam.*)	23	28	6	437	46*	0	0	19.86
204	A. A. Donald (*Warwicks.*)	21	22	0	234	41	0	0	19.50
205	J. P. Carroll (*CUCC*)	5	9	0	175	92	0	1	19.44
206	J. D. Ratcliffe (*Warwicks.*)	7	14	0	272	50	0	1	19.42
	†J. D. Fitton (*Lancs.*)	8	9	2	136	48*	0	0	19.42
208	M. P. Briers (*Durham*)	16	28	4	460	62*	0	4	19.16
209	N. M. Kendrick (*Surrey*)	17	21	5	306	55	0	2	19.12
210	A. R. Roberts (*Northants*)	14	19	3	304	62	0	1	19.00
	J. Boiling (*Surrey*)	19	21	11	190	29	0	0	19.00
	Waqar Younis (*Pakistanis*)	10	9	4	95	23*	0	0	19.00
213	P. A. Smith (*Warwicks.*)	19	27	5	416	45	0	0	18.90
214	A. M. Smith (*Glos.*)	12	14	5	169	51*	0	1	18.77
215	S. W. Johnson (*CUCC*)	9	13	2	201	50	0	1	18.27
216	†R. A. Pick (*Notts.*)	10	12	4	145	52	0	1	18.12
217	†A. M. Brown (*Derbys.*)	7	8	0	144	43	0	0	18.00
218	S. J. E. Brown (*Durham*)	20	24	13	197	47*	0	0	17.90
219	†M. I. Gidley (*Leics.*)	5	10	2	143	39	0	0	17.87
220	P. J. Hartley (*Yorks.*)	20	23	3	353	69	0	2	17.65
221	†J. P. Taylor (*Northants*)	23	19	8	188	74*	0	1	17.09
222	P. J. Berry (*Durham*)	9	15	3	205	76	0	1	17.08
223	A. R. C. Fraser (*Middx*)	18	20	7	218	33	0	0	16.76
224	D. A. Graveney (*Durham*)	21	29	9	333	36	0	0	16.65
225	G. C. Small (*Warwicks.*)	17	17	6	181	31*	0	0	16.45
226	C. S. Pickles (*Yorks.*)	6	9	1	131	49	0	0	16.37
227	S. Bramhall (*Notts.*)	8	10	3	114	37*	0	0	16.28
228	B. N. French (*Notts.*)	17	20	4	260	55	0	1	16.25
229	A. E. Warner (*Derbys.*)	17	15	2	210	55	0	1	16.15
230	K. M. Krikken (*Derbys.*)	23	27	3	383	57*	0	2	15.95
231	A. C. S. Pigott (*Sussex*)	17	19	7	191	27*	0	0	15.91
232	C. A. Connor (*Hants*)	16	13	5	127	51	0	1	15.87
233	O. H. Mortensen (*Derbys.*)	15	13	10	47	13*	0	0	15.66
234	M. B. Loye (*Northants*)	10	14	1	195	46	0	0	15.00
235	A. M. Hooper (*CUCC*)	10	19	1	268	48	0	0	14.88

		M	I	NO	R	HS	100s	50s	Avge
236	R. J. Maru (*Hants*)	8	11	3	119	27	0	0	14.87
237	C. M. Tolley (*Worcs.*)	13	10	4	89	27	0	0	14.83
238	I. D. K. Salisbury (*Sussex*)	20	22	3	279	50	0	1	14.68
239	S. N. Warley (*OUCC*)	7	10	2	117	35	0	0	14.62
240	†D. J. Millns (*Leics.*)	19	19	9	144	33*	0	0	14.40
241	J. D. Batty (*Yorks.*)	18	15	4	155	49	0	0	14.09
242	H. R. J. Trump (*Somerset*)	18	18	7	154	28	0	0	14.00
243	M. C. J. Ball (*Glos.*)	12	21	6	201	54	0	2	13.40
244	N. F. Williams (*Middx*)	17	17	3	186	46*	0	0	13.28
245	P. Carrick (*Yorks.*)	19	25	5	261	46	0	0	13.05
246	†A. L. Penberthy (*Northants*)	10	14	1	164	33	0	0	12.61
247	A. C. Storie (*OUCC*)	7	10	1	113	29	0	0	12.55
248	C. M. Pitcher (*CUCC*)	6	8	3	62	32*	0	0	12.40
249	P. N. Hepworth (*Leics.*)	10	15	1	173	38	0	0	12.35
250	T. A. Munton (*Warwicks.*)	19	19	7	148	47	0	0	12.33
251	†J. H. Childs (*Essex*)	22	17	8	110	43	0	0	12.22
252	R. M. Pearson (*CUCC & Northants*)	11	13	5	96	33*	0	0	12.00
253	N. A. Mallender (*Somerset*)	17	21	5	190	29*	0	0	11.87
254	†G. J. Parsons (*Leics.*)	14	14	2	142	35	0	0	11.83
255	N. F. Sargeant (*Surrey*)	14	19	4	176	30	0	0	11.73
256	R. C. Williams (*Glos.*)	7	11	1	117	44	0	0	11.70
257	C. A. Walsh (*Glos.*)	18	27	3	280	51	0	1	11.66
258	J. E. Benjamin (*Surrey*)	18	18	8	116	42	0	0	11.60
259	S. P. Hughes (*Durham*)	20	25	5	229	42	0	0	11.45
260	M. Davies (*Glos.*)	19	23	10	148	32*	0	0	11.38
261	P. M. Such (*Essex*)	15	13	3	113	35*	0	0	11.30
262	†A. N. Jones (*Sussex*)	10	9	4	56	17	0	0	11.20
263	†P. A. Booth (*Warwicks.*)	8	11	4	78	22*	0	0	11.14
264	R. I. Dawson (*Glos.*)	6	8	0	88	29	0	0	11.00
265	†A. M. Babington (*Glos.*)	9	11	4	75	24	0	0	10.71
265	†C. W. Taylor (*Middx*)	18	14	7	75	14	0	0	10.71
267	A. P. van Troost (*Somerset*)	11	9	5	42	12	0	0	10.50
268	D. K. Morrison (*Lancs.*)	14	12	1	113	30	0	0	10.27
269	A. R. Fothergill (*Durham*)	6	8	1	71	23	0	0	10.14
270	D. E. Malcolm (*Derbys.*)	19	19	4	150	26	0	0	10.00
270	T. D. Topley (*Essex*)	11	12	2	100	29	0	0	10.00
270	A. A. Barnett (*Lancs.*)	22	17	10	70	17	0	0	10.00
273	K. J. Shine (*Hants*)	16	12	6	59	22*	0	0	9.83
274	M. E. D. Jarrett (*CUCC*)	9	13	2	106	27	0	0	9.63
275	R. W. Sladdin (*Derbys.*)	13	16	3	131	39	0	0	9.35
276	M. J. McCague (*Kent*)	16	18	5	120	25*	0	0	9.23
277	†M. C. Ilott (*Essex*)	23	22	4	164	28	0	0	9.11
278	M. P. W. Jeh (*OUCC*)	9	11	2	81	23	0	0	9.00
278	D. Gough (*Yorks.*)	11	12	4	72	22*	0	0	9.00
280	P. Whitticase (*Leics.*)	8	10	3	62	18*	0	0	8.85
281	A. P. Igglesden (*Kent*)	16	13	5	67	16	0	0	8.37
282	Mushtaq Ahmed (*Pakistanis*)	17	12	3	73	12	0	0	8.11
283	P. C. R. Tufnell (*Middx*)	16	15	8	55	12	0	0	7.85
284	S. L. Watkin (*Glam.*)	22	24	4	153	41	0	0	7.65
285	E. S. H. Giddins (*Sussex*)	11	8	6	15	10*	0	0	7.50
286	A. D. Mullally (*Leics.*)	19	23	6	118	21	0	0	6.94
287	D. B. Pennett (*Notts.*)	12	11	1	69	29	0	0	6.90
288	A. C. Cottam (*Somerset*)	6	8	1	43	31	0	0	6.14
289	S. M. McEwan (*Durham*)	10	13	1	59	22	0	0	4.91
290	S. J. W. Andrew (*Essex*)	10	12	4	38	14*	0	0	4.75
291	D. J. Anderson (*OUCC*)	8	8	4	18	9	0	0	4.50
292	M. A. Robinson (*Yorks.*)	17	12	5	31	12	0	0	4.42
293	J. A. Afford (*Notts.*)	18	17	6	42	12	0	0	3.81
294	S. Bastien (*Glam.*)	10	10	3	21	9*	0	0	3.00
295	S. R. Barwick (*Glam.*)	18	15	4	31	9*	0	0	2.81
296	Aqib Javed (*Pakistanis*)	14	8	3	10	5*	0	0	2.00

BOWLING

(Qualification: 10 wickets in 10 innings)

† *Denotes a left-arm bowler.*

		O	M	R	W	BB	5W/i	Avge
1	C. A. Walsh (*Glos.*)	587.2	138	1,469	92	7-27	8	15.96
2	†Wasim Akram (*Pakistanis*)	499.5	127	1,330	82	6-32	7	16.21
3	I. R. Bishop (*Derbys.*)	483	116	1,118	64	7-34	4	17.46
4	J. R. Ayling (*Hants*)	356.2	78	989	48	5-12	1	20.60
5	D. J. Millns (*Leics.*)	470.5	107	1,526	74	6-87	6	20.62
6	†R. P. Davis (*Kent*)	582	150	1,609	74	7-64	5	21.74
7	A. A. Donald (*Warwicks.*)	576.2	139	1,647	74	7-37	6	22.25
8	M. A. Robinson (*Yorks.*)	413.5	79	1,134	50	6-57	3	22.68
9	V. J. Wells (*Leics.*)	301	93	751	33	4-26	0	22.75
10	N. A. Mallender (*Somerset*)	436.3	94	1,282	55	5-29	4	23.30
11	G. J. Parsons (*Leics.*)	343.2	92	955	39	6-70	2	24.48
12	Mushtaq Ahmed (*Pakistanis*)	614.4	158	1,620	66	5-46	4	24.54
13	Waqar Younis (*Pakistanis*)	287.1	50	913	37	5-22	4	24.67
14	†N. G. B. Cook (*Northants*)	325.1	90	939	38	7-34	1	24.71
15	F. A. Griffith (*Derbys.*)	113	31	373	15	4-33	0	24.86
16	D. R. Pringle (*Essex*)	423.5	99	1,177	47	5-63	1	25.04
17	D. J. Capel (*Northants*)	446	92	1,214	48	5-61	1	25.29
18	P. M. Such (*Essex*)	409.5	126	1,015	40	6-17	3	25.37
19	J. E. Emburey (*Middx*)	854.5	249	2,069	81	5-23	3	25.54
20	M. P. Bicknell (*Surrey*)	628.5	116	1,823	71	6-107	4	25.67
21	P. J. Newport (*Worcs.*)	618.2	130	1,770	68	5-22	4	26.02
22	†R. J. Maru (*Hants*)	204.2	75	444	17	4-8	0	26.11
23	C. E. L. Ambrose (*Northants*)	543.4	151	1,307	50	4-53	0	26.14
24	J. D. Robinson (*Surrey*)	93.4	14	341	13	3-22	0	26.23
25	N. F. Williams (*Middx*)	437	85	1,283	48	8-75	2	26.72
26	Aqib Javed (*Pakistanis*)	292	58	966	36	5-34	1	26.83
27	M. J. McCague (*Kent*)	457.2	86	1,430	53	8-26	5	26.98
28	A. R. Caddick (*Somerset*)	587.4	98	1,918	71	6-52	3	27.01
29	†J. H. Childs (*Essex*)	678.2	205	1,822	67	6-82	3	27.19
30	†I. J. Turner (*Hants*)	182.4	51	519	19	5-81	1	27.31
31	M. D. Marshall (*Hants*)	529	134	1,348	49	6-58	1	27.51
32	K. M. Curran (*Northants*)	452.4	96	1,376	50	6-45	1	27.52
33	C. S. Pickles (*Yorks.*)	120.1	27	387	14	4-40	0	27.64
33	E. S. H. Giddins (*Sussex*)	247.5	52	857	31	5-32	2	27.64
35	N. V. Radford (*Worcs.*)	532.2	99	1,670	60	6-88	4	27.83
36	R. G. Twose (*Warwicks.*)	249.3	48	794	28	6-63	1	28.35
37	D. G. Cork (*Derbys.*)	450.4	74	1,366	48	5-36	2	28.45
38	I. D. K. Salisbury (*Sussex*)	772.4	176	2,520	87	7-54	6	28.96
39	M. V. Fleming (*Kent*)	245	46	696	24	4-63	0	29.00
40	P. W. Jarvis (*Yorks.*)	393.4	89	1,164	40	4-27	0	29.10
41	†P. Carrick (*Yorks.*)	630.1	202	1,375	47	6-58	1	29.25
42	†M. Davies (*Glos.*)	560.5	143	1,661	56	4-73	0	29.66
43	N. A. Foster (*Essex*)	256	63	724	24	4-47	0	30.16
44	P. J. Hartley (*Yorks.*)	549.5	101	1,690	56	8-111	3	30.17
45	†J. P. Taylor (*Northants*)	648.2	119	2,072	68	7-23	3	30.47
46	M. E. Waugh (*Essex*)	184.4	31	671	22	3-38	0	30.50
47	A. E. Warner (*Derbys.*)	367.5	87	888	29	4-52	0	30.62
48	A. P. Igglesden (*Kent*)	480.4	95	1,413	46	5-41	0	30.71
49	†N. M. Kendrick (*Surrey*)	595.1	171	1,567	51	6-61	3	30.72
50	C. C. Lewis (*Notts.*)	594.3	119	1,633	53	6-90	2	30.81
51	S. L. Watkin (*Glam.*)	689.3	148	2,126	68	6-97	1	31.26
52	†J. A. Afford (*Notts.*)	509.1	128	1,599	51	6-68	2	31.35

		O	M	R	W	BB	5W/i	Avge
53	J. Wood (*Durham*)	134.2	17	534	17	5-68	1	31.41
54	R. D. B. Croft (*Glam.*)	657.1	124	2,152	68	8-66	5	31.64
55	W. K. M. Benjamin (*Leics.*)	489	102	1,498	47	4-34	0	31.87
56	P. A. J. DeFreitas (*Lancs.*)	349.5	66	1,091	34	6-94	1	32.08
57	A. Dale (*Glam.*)	234	62	644	20	3-30	0	32.20
58	K. J. Shine (*Hants*)	333.5	49	1,290	40	8-47	3	32.25
59	H. R. J. Trump (*Somerset*)	558	134	1,584	49	7-52	2	32.32
60	P. A. Smith (*Warwicks.*)	373	57	1,362	42	6-91	4	32.42
61	T. D. Topley (*Essex*)	240.4	54	779	24	5-15	1	32.45
62	J. T. C. Vaughan (*Glos.*)	202.4	44	588	18	3-46	0	32.66
63	M. Watkinson (*Lancs.*)	660	140	2,178	66	6-62	4	33.00
64	G. C. Small (*Warwicks.*)	367.2	83	1,003	30	3-43	0	33.43
65	E. E. Hemmings (*Notts.*)	259.5	95	602	18	4-30	0	33.44
66	D. K. Morrison (*Lancs.*)	335.4	52	1,209	36	6-48	1	33.58
67	M. A. Ealham (*Kent*)	406.1	70	1,243	37	4-67	0	33.59
68	T. A. Munton (*Warwicks.*)	640.4	176	1,725	51	7-64	3	33.82
69	†S. J. E. Brown (*Durham*)	509.1	75	1,973	58	7-105	3	34.01
70	M. A. Crawley (*Notts.*)	221.4	56	647	19	3-18	0	34.05
71	F. D. Stephenson (*Sussex*)	467.2	93	1,375	40	7-29	1	34.37
72	Ata-ur-Rehman (*Pakistanis*)	159.1	29	621	18	3-69	0	34.50
73	O. H. Mortensen (*Derbys.*)	338.4	87	795	23	2-22	0	34.56
74	S. D. Udal (*Hants*)	692.2	177	2,012	58	8-50	2	34.68
75	†A. M. Smith (*Glos.*)	249.2	35	835	24	3-53	0	34.79
76	J. E. R. Gallian (*OUCC*)	208	41	628	18	4-29	0	34.88
77	J. Boiling (*Surrey*)	591.1	156	1,579	45	6-84	1	35.08
78	C. L. Cairns (*Notts.*)	592.3	110	1,974	56	6-70	2	35.25
79	†A. D. Mullally (*Leics.*)	518.2	125	1,485	42	5-119	1	35.35
80 {	†M. C. Ilott (*Essex*)	675.3	145	2,264	64	6-87	3	35.37
	S. J. W. Andrew (*Essex*)	265	45	849	24	4-54	0	35.37
82	J. D. Fitton (*Lancs.*)	171.1	38	465	13	4-81	0	35.76
83	†R. W. Sladdin (*Derbys.*)	499.3	138	1,396	39	6-58	1	35.79
84	M. W. Alleyne (*Glos.*)	138.1	31	502	14	3-25	0	35.85
85	K. P. Evans (*Notts.*)	595.4	133	1,723	48	5-27	1	35.89
86	S. R. Lampitt (*Worcs.*)	369.3	44	1,257	35	4-57	0	35.91
87	†P. C. R. Tufnell (*Middx*)	596.2	144	1,559	43	5-83	2	36.25
88	D. Gough (*Yorks.*)	255.1	53	910	25	4-43	0	36.40
89	A. P. van Troost (*Somerset*)	175.4	20	766	21	6-48	2	36.47
90	D. E. Malcolm (*Derbys.*)	451.1	64	1,648	45	5-45	2	36.62
91	D. J. Foster (*Glam.*)	191.3	27	820	22	5-87	1	37.27
92	C. L. Hooper (*Kent*)	500.5	114	1,307	35	4-57	0	37.34
93	†R. K. Illingworth (*Worcs.*)	635.3	185	1,580	42	4-43	0	37.61
94	†R. D. Stemp (*Worcs.*)	331.5	80	1,054	28	6-67	3	37.64
95	D. B. Pennett (*Notts.*)	296.2	52	981	26	4-58	0	37.73
96	P. J. Berry (*Durham*)	178.3	27	649	17	7-113	1	38.17
97	M. C. J. Ball (*Glos.*)	322	61	1,072	28	5-101	1	38.28
98	J. P. Stephenson (*Essex*)	251.5	51	854	22	6-54	1	38.81
99	R. M. Wight (*CUCC*)	231.3	39	748	19	3-65	0	39.36
00	A. C. S. Pigott (*Sussex*)	363	74	1,063	27	3-34	0	39.37
01	J. E. Benjamin (*Surrey*)	582.2	94	1,780	45	6-30	2	39.55
02	†L. Potter (*Leics.*)	360.1	80	1,075	27	4-73	0	39.81
03	P. J. Martin (*Lancs.*)	520.2	129	1,490	37	4-45	0	40.27
04	†C. M. Tolley (*Worcs.*)	239	56	726	18	3-38	0	40.33
05	D. W. Headley (*Middx*)	385	74	1,258	31	3-31	0	40.58
06	P. Bainbridge (*Durham*)	188.1	39	569	14	5-100	1	40.64
07	†C. W. Taylor (*Middx*)	409.2	82	1,425	35	4-50	0	40.71
08	R. M. Ellison (*Kent*)	401.5	80	1,204	29	6-95	2	41.51
09	J. D. Batty (*Yorks.*)	426	87	1,408	33	4-34	0	42.66
10	†P. A. Booth (*Warwicks.*)	279.4	74	814	19	4-29	0	42.84
11	†D. A. Graveney (*Durham*)	380.4	87	1,201	28	3-22	0	42.89
12	C. A. Connor (*Hants*)	417.2	69	1,386	32	5-58	1	43.31
13	I. D. Austin (*Lancs.*)	164.5	41	522	12	3-44	0	43.50

		O	M	R	W	BB	5W/i	Avg
114	I. T. Botham (*Durham*)	346	70	1,144	26	4-72	0	44.0
115	R. P. Snell (*Somerset*)	339.1	60	1,194	27	3-29	0	44.2
116	A. M. Babington (*Glos.*)	188	21	753	17	8-107	1	44.2
117	G. D. Rose (*Somerset*)	392.1	84	1,250	28	4-59	0	44.6
118	M. A. Feltham (*Surrey*)	326.1	61	1,125	25	4-75	0	45.0
119	S. R. Barwick (*Glam.*)	602	155	1,627	36	4-67	0	45.1
120	S. M. McEwan (*Durham*)	229	44	800	17	3-52	0	47.0
121	†A. A. Barnett (*Lancs.*)	595	84	2,165	46	5-78	2	47.0
122	B. T. P. Donelan (*Sussex*)	404	85	1,323	28	6-77	1	47.2
123	R. A. Pick (*Notts.*)	254.1	50	862	18	3-33	0	47.8
124	R. J. Scott (*Glos.*)	267.4	40	959	20	2-9	0	47.9
125	A. R. Roberts (*Northants*)	323.2	60	1,056	22	4-101	0	48.0
126	D. A. Reeve (*Warwicks.*)	267	80	632	13	2-4	0	48.6
127	N. M. K. Smith (*Warwicks.*)	332.3	63	1,178	24	5-61	1	49.0
128	S. P. Hughes (*Durham*)	548.3	98	1,672	34	5-25	1	49.1
129	P. N. Weekes (*Middx*)	222	51	595	12	3-61	0	49.5
130	M. P. W. Jeh (*OUCC*)	233.5	38	846	17	3-44	0	49.7
131	S. Bastien (*Glam.*)	305.3	73	954	19	5-95	1	50.2
132	M. P. Briers (*Durham*)	144.3	22	621	12	3-109	0	51.7
133	M. B. Abington (*CUCC*)	146.4	23	530	10	3-33	0	53.0
134	D. B. D'Oliveira (*Worcs.*)	153.4	29	536	10	2-44	0	53.6
135	M. G. Field-Buss (*Notts.*)	169	29	590	11	4-71	0	53.6
136	S. W. Johnson (*CUCC*)	164	27	541	10	3-62	0	54.1
137	R. E. Bryson (*Surrey*)	333.4	41	1,256	23	5-48	2	54.6
138	A. R. C. Fraser (*Middx*)	426.4	90	1,273	23	3-16	0	55.3
139	†K. D. James (*Hants*)	264.3	65	781	14	2-23	0	55.7
140	R. M. Pearson (*CUCC & Northants*)	402.3	64	1,271	20	5-108	1	63.5
141	M. Frost (*Glam.*)	198.1	29	833	13	3-100	0	64.0
142	A. N. Jones (*Sussex*)	161.5	17	745	11	3-76	0	67.7

The following bowlers took ten wickets but bowled in fewer than ten innings:

	O	M	R	W	BB	5W/i	Avg
S. D. Thomas (*Glam.*)	113.2	18	404	18	5-79	2	22.4
Tanvir Mehdi (*Pakistanis*)	94	21	307	12	3-24	0	25.5
J. A. North (*Sussex*)	96.3	14	331	11	3-51	0	30.0
G. W. Mike (*Notts.*)	90.2	17	314	10	3-48	0	31.4
C. M. Wells (*Sussex*)	119	26	323	10	3-26	0	32.3
Naved Anjum (*Pakistanis*)	107.1	24	379	10	3-73	0	37.9
P. J. Bakker (*Hants*)	162	48	441	11	4-38	0	40.0
P. W. Henderson (*Durham*)	96	14	405	10	3-59	0	40.5
A. J. Murphy (*Surrey*)	178.4	34	531	11	3-97	0	48.2

INDIVIDUAL SCORES OF 100 AND OVER

There were 305 three-figure innings in first-class cricket in 1992, 10 fewer than in 1991. Of these, 14 were double-hundreds, compared with 18 in 1991. The list includes 256 hundreds hit in the County Championship, 12 by the Pakistani touring team and 37 in other first-class games.

* *Signifies not out.*

M. A. Roseberry (9)
101	Middx v Cambridge U., Cambridge
108*	Middx v Oxford U., Oxford
111*	Middx v Pakistanis, Lord's
148	Middx v Notts., Nottingham
102	Middx v Leics., Lord's
118	Middx v Worcs., Uxbridge
100*	Middx v Derbys., Derby
173	Middx v Durham, Lord's
120	Middx v Surrey, The Oval

G. A. Gooch (8)
160	Essex v Leics., Chelmsford
113	Essex v Durham, Hartlepool
102	} Essex v Sussex, Southend
108*	
135	England v Pakistan, Leeds
141	Essex v Pakistanis, Chelmsford
123*	Essex v Derbys., Derby
101	Essex v Glos., Bristol

P. D. Bowler (6)
112	Derbys. v Worcs., Derby
104*	Derbys. v Lancs., Blackpool
155	Derbys. v Notts., Derby
147*	Derbys. v Somerset, Taunton
241	Derbys. v Hants, Portsmouth
100*	Derbys. v Worcs., Worcester

M. W. Gatting (6)
170	Middx v Glam., Lord's
103	Middx v Lancs., Lord's
117	} Middx v Warwicks., Coventry
163*	
126*	Middx v Lancs., Manchester
102*	Middx v Kent, Canterbury

A. J. Lamb (6)
101	Northants v Worcs., Worcester
109*	Northants v Glam., Luton
209	} Northants v Warwicks.,
107	} Northampton
160	Northants v Hants, Bournemouth
122*	Northants v Leics., Leicester

T. C. Middleton (6)
153	Hants v Sussex, Southampton
221	Hants v Oxford U., Oxford
221	Hants v Surrey, Southampton
138	Hants v Lancs., Manchester
124	Hants v Warwicks., Birmingham
127*	Hants v Durham, Darlington

H. Morris (6)
146	Glam. v Middx, Lord's
104	Glam. v Lancs., Colwyn Bay
123	Glam. v Worcs., Worcester
117	Glam. v Somerset, Abergavenny
104*	Glam. v Sussex, Eastbourne
126	Glam. v Durham, Hartlepool

M. A. Atherton (5)
140*	Lancs. v Derbys., Blackpool
135	Lancs. v Middx, Manchester
130	Lancs. v Warwicks., Birmingham
119	Lancs. v Yorks., Manchester
199	Lancs. v Durham, Gateshead Fell

B. C. Broad (5)
104	Notts. v Warwicks., Nottingham
117	Notts. v Derbys., Derby
159*	Notts. v Northants, Nottingham
120	Notts. v Yorks., Scarborough
122	Notts. v Leics., Leicester

C. L. Hooper (5)
115*	Kent v Durham, Canterbury
121	Kent v Sussex, Hove
131	Kent v Surrey, Guildford
100	Kent v Glam., Swansea
102	Kent v Warwicks., Birmingham

M. D. Moxon (5)
141	Yorks. v Surrey, The Oval
117	Yorks. v Somerset, Middlesbrough
183	Yorks. v Glos., Cheltenham College
103	Yorks. v Glam., Cardiff
101*	Yorks. v Northants, Scarborough

M. P. Speight (5)
166	Sussex v Notts., Nottingham
119*	Sussex v Lancs., Hove
122	Sussex v Somerset, Taunton
179	Sussex v Glam., Eastbourne
126	Sussex v Essex, Hove

T. R. Ward (5)
140*	Kent v Worcs., Tunbridge Wells
103	Kent v Surrey, Guildford
118	Kent v Glam., Swansea
150	Kent v Middx, Canterbury
153	Kent v Warwicks., Birmingham

A. P. Wells (5)
144 Sussex v Kent, Hove
165* Sussex v Surrey, The Oval
115 Sussex v Warwicks., Hove
103 Sussex v Somerset, Taunton
143 Sussex v Lancs., Manchester

C. J. Adams (4)
121 Derbys. v Worcs., Derby
112* Derbys. v Middx, Derby
140* Derbys. v Worcs., Worcester
135 Derbys. v Essex, Derby

K. J. Barnett (4)
140* Derbys. v Surrey, The Oval
117* Derbys. v Leics., Ilkeston
160 Derbys. v Kent, Chesterfield
156* Derbys. v Notts., Nottingham

M. R. Benson (4)
117 Kent v Sussex, Hove
131 Kent v Notts., Maidstone
139 Kent v Leics., Leicester
122 Kent v Warwicks., Birmingham

M. A. Crawley (4)
110* Notts. v Oxford U., Oxford
160* Notts. v Derbys., Derby
102* Notts. v Kent, Maidstone
115 Notts. v Worcs., Nottingham

T. S. Curtis (4)
228* Worcs. v Derbys., Derby
140* Worcs. v Kent, Tunbridge Wells
124 Worcs. v Glam., Worcester
197 Worcs. v Yorks., Worcester

A. Fordham (4)
192 Northants v Surrey, Northampton
119 Northants v Notts., Nottingham
137 Northants v Glam., Luton
122 Northants v Lancs., Northampton

G. A. Hick (4)
131 Worcs. v Sussex, Worcester
213* Worcs. v Notts., Nottingham
168 Worcs. v Middx, Uxbridge
146 Worcs. v Warwicks., Worcester

D. M. Jones (4)
157 Durham v Northants, Stockton-on-Tees
134* ⎱ Durham v Pakistanis, Chester-le-
105 ⎰ Street
154* Durham v Notts., Nottingham

W. Larkins (4)
143 Durham v Glam., Cardiff
118 Durham v Pakistanis, Chester-le-Street
140 Durham v Glam., Hartlepool
117 Durham v Somerset, Taunton

N. J. Lenham (4)
222* Sussex v Kent, Hove
118 Sussex v Durham, Horsham
136 Sussex v Lancs., Manchester
135 Sussex v Yorks., Hove

G. D. Lloyd (4)
132 Lancs. v Kent, Manchester
102* Lancs. v Hants, Manchester
103* Lancs. v Middx, Manchester
101 Lancs. v Worcs., Manchester

T. M. Moody (4)
100* Worcs. v Oxford U., Oxford
118 Worcs. v Glos., Gloucester
100 Worcs. v Kent, Tunbridge Wells
178 Worcs. v Essex, Kidderminster

P. J. Prichard (4)
102 Essex v Leics., Chelmsford
133 Essex v Kent, Tunbridge Wells
106 Essex v Leics., Leicester
136 Essex v Notts., Colchester

R. T. Robinson (4)
100 Notts. v Northants, Nottingham
164* Notts. v Durham, Nottingham
189 Notts. v Warwicks., Birmingham
129* Notts. v Surrey, Nottingham

N. J. Speak (4)
232 Lancs. v Leics., Leicester
102 Lancs. v Somerset, Manchester
144 Lancs. v Glos., Manchester
111 Lancs. v Middx, Manchester

M. E. Waugh (4)
120 Essex v Kent, Chelmsford
219* Essex v Lancs., Ilford
125* Essex v Glos., Southend
138* Essex v Worcs., Kidderminster

N. E. Briers (3)
120 Leics. v Cambridge U., Cambridge
123 Leics. v Pakistanis, Leicester
122* Leics. v Worcs., Leicester

A. D. Brown (3)
111 Surrey v Notts., The Oval
175 Surrey v Durham, Durham University
129 Surrey v Somerset, The Oval

G. R. Cowdrey (3)
127 Kent v Yorks., Canterbury
147 Kent v Glos., Bristol
115 Kent v Durham, Gateshead Fell

R. J. Harden (3)
166* Somerset v Derbys., Taunton
126 Somerset v Durham, Taunton
187 Somerset v Notts., Taunton

D. L. Haynes (3)
114   Middx v Notts., Nottingham
127*   Middx v Northants, Uxbridge
177   Middx v Sussex, Hove

S. P. James (3)
152*   Glam. v Lancs., Colwyn Bay
111   Glam. v Oxford U., Oxford
105   Glam. v Surrey, Neath

M. A. Lynch (3)
107   Surrey v Worcs., The Oval
106   Surrey v Leics., The Oval
102   Surrey v Essex, Colchester

J. E. Morris (3)
120   Derbys. v Notts., Derby
109   Derbys. v Somerset, Taunton
107   Derbys. v Leics., Ilkeston

D. P. Ostler (3)
102   Warwicks. v Notts., Nottingham
108   Warwicks. v Sussex, Hove
192   Warwicks. v Surrey, Guildford

P. W. G. Parker (3)
103   Durham v Oxford U., Oxford
117   Durham v Leics., Durham University
124   Durham v Glam., Cardiff

T. L. Penney (3)
102*   Warwicks. v Cambridge U., Cambridge
100*   Warwicks. v Northants, Northampton
151   Warwicks. v Middx, Lord's

M. R. Ramprakash (3)
108   Middx v Lancs., Lord's
233   Middx v Surrey, Lord's
117   Middx v Surrey, The Oval

J. P. Stephenson (3)
113*   }
159*   } Essex v Somerset, Taunton
123*   Essex v Sussex, Southend

C. J. Tavaré (3)
115   Somerset v Hants, Weston-super-Mare
124   Somerset v Durham, Taunton
125   Somerset v Notts., Taunton

V. P. Terry (3)
141   Hants v Sussex, Southampton
131   Hants v Surrey, Southampton
113   Hants v Worcs., Worcester

G. P. Thorpe (3)
114*   Surrey v Cambridge U., Cambridge
216   Surrey v Somerset, The Oval
100   Surrey v Notts., Nottingham

D. M. Ward (3)
112*   Surrey v Cambridge U., Cambridge
103*   Surrey v Northants, The Oval
138   Surrey v Glam., Neath

Aamir Sohail (2)
124   Pakistanis v Glam., Cardiff
205   Pakistan v England, Manchester

Asif Mujtaba (2)
123   Pakistanis v Middx, Lord's
154*   Pakistanis v Hants, Southampton

C. W. J. Athey (2)
181   Glos. v Sussex, Cheltenham College
133   Glos. v Notts., Worksop

R. J. Bailey (2)
165   Northants v Glam., Luton
167*   Northants v Leics., Leicester

D. J. Bicknell (2)
115   England A v Essex, Lord's
120*   Surrey v Lancs., Lytham

R. J. Blakey (2)
125*   Yorks. v Glam., Cardiff
112*   Yorks. v Notts., Scarborough

T. J. Boon (2)
110   Leics. v Durham, Durham University
139   Leics. v Lancs., Leicester

C. L. Cairns (2)
102*   Notts. v Lancs., Nottingham
107*   Notts. v Glos., Worksop

J. D. Carr (2)
102   Middx v Essex, Ilford
114   Middx v Surrey, The Oval

P. A. Cottey (2)
112*   Glam. v Durham, Cardiff
141   Glam. v Kent, Canterbury

J. P. Crawley (2)
106*   Cambridge U. v Oxford U., Lord's
172   Lancs. v Surrey, Lytham

A. Dale (2)
150*   Glam. v Notts., Nottingham
127   Glam. v Warwicks., Birmingham

G. D. Hodgson (2)
124   Glos. v Yorks., Leeds
147   Glos. v Essex, Southend

Javed Miandad (2)
153*   Pakistan v England, Birmingham
142*   Pakistanis v Hants, Southampton

P. Johnson (2)
107* Notts. v Surrey, The Oval
107* Notts. v Warwicks., Birmingham

N. V. Knight (2)
104* Essex v Cambridge U., Cambridge
109   Essex v Middx, Ilford

C. C. Lewis (2)
134* Notts. v Northants, Northampton
107   Notts. v Durham, Nottingham

M. P. Maynard (2)
113* Glam. v Kent, Swansea
176   Glam. v Derbys., Chesterfield

D. R. Pringle (2)
102* Essex v England A, Lord's
112* Essex v Sussex, Hove

Ramiz Raja (2)
172   Pakistanis v Worcs., Worcester
135   Pakistanis v Glos., Bristol

S. J. Rhodes (2)
116* Worcs. v Warwicks., Worcester
107   Worcs. v Hants, Southampton

D. Ripley (2)
104   Northants v Durham, Stockton-on-Tees
107* Northants v Somerset, Bath

Salim Malik (2)
165   Pakistan v England, Birmingham
153* Pakistanis v Essex, Chelmsford

D. M. Smith (2)
213   Sussex v Essex, Southend
105   Sussex v Lancs., Hove

R. A. Smith (2)
107* Hants v Sussex, Southampton
127   England v Pakistan, Birmingham

A. J. Stewart (2)
140   Surrey v Sussex, The Oval
190   England v Pakistan, Birmingham

The following each played one three-figure innings:
G. F. Archer, 117, Notts. v Derbys., Nottingham; I. D. Austin, 115*, Lancs. v Derbys., Blackpool; J. R. Ayling, 121, Hants v Oxford U., Oxford.
J. D. R. Benson, 122, Leics. v Middx, Leicester; I. T. Botham, 105, Durham v Leics., Durham University; K. R. Brown, 106, Middx v Warwicks., Lord's; D. Byas, 100, Yorks. v Northants, Scarborough.
D. J. Capel, 103, Northants v Surrey, The Oval.
W. A. Dessaur, 148, Notts. v Cambridge U., Nottingham; D. B. D'Oliveira, 100, Worcs. v Essex, Kidderminster.
J. E. Emburey, 102, Middx v Leics., Leicester; K. P. Evans, 104, Notts. v Surrey, Nottingham.
N. H. Fairbrother, 166*, Lancs. v Yorks., Leeds; N. A. Felton, 103, Northants v Yorks., Northampton; M. V. Fleming, 100*, Kent v Hants, Canterbury; G. Fowler, 106, Lancs. v Oxford U., Oxford.
J. E. R. Gallian, 112, Oxford U. v Worcs., Oxford; J. D. Glendenen, 117, Durham v Oxford U., Oxford; S. C. Goldsmith, 100*, Derbys. v Worcs., Derby; D. I. Gower, 155, Hants v Yorks., Basingstoke.
J. W. Hall, 140*, Sussex v Lancs., Hove; T. H. C. Hancock, 102, Glos. v Somerset, Taunton; A. N. Hayhurst, 102, Somerset v Durham, Taunton; P. C. L. Holloway, 102*, Warwicks. v Worcs., Birmingham; N. Hussain, 172*, Essex v Lancs., Ilford.
Inzamam-ul-Haq, 200*, Pakistanis v Oxford & Camb. Univs, Cambridge.
K. D. James, 116, Hants v Yorks., Leeds.
M. N. Lathwell, 114, Somerset v Surrey, Bath; D. A. Leatherdale, 112, Worcs. v Notts., Nottingham; D. A. Lewis, 122*, Ireland v Scotland, Dundee; J. J. B. Lewis, 133, Essex v Sussex, Hove; J. I. Longley, 110, Kent v Cambridge U., Cambridge; G. B. T. Lovell, 110*, Oxford U. v Glam., Oxford.
S. A. Marsh, 125, Kent v Yorks., Canterbury; P. J. Martin, 133, Lancs. v Durham, Gateshead Fell; A. J. Moles, 122, Warwicks. v Sussex, Hove; R. R. Montgomerie, 103*, Oxford U. v Middx, Oxford; P. Moores, 109, Sussex v Essex, Southend.
P. A. Nixon, 107*, Leics. v Hants, Leicester.
D. W. Randall, 133*, Notts. v Lancs., Nottingham; I. V. A. Richards, 127, Glam. v Warwicks., Swansea; G. D. Rose, 132, Somerset v Surrey, The Oval.
G. Salmond, 118, Scotland v Ireland, Dundee; A. C. H. Seymour, 133, Worcs. v Oxford U., Oxford; N. Shahid, 132, Essex v Kent, Chelmsford; Shoaib Mohammad, 105*, Pakistanis v World XI, Scarborough; P. R. Sleep, 182, World XI v Pakistanis, Scarborough; B. F. Smith, 100*, Leics. v Durham, Durham University; I. Smith, 110, Durham v Somerset, Taunton; F. D. Stephenson, 133, Sussex v Somerset, Hove.

N. R. Taylor, 144, Kent v Leics., Leicester; S. R. Tendulkar, 100, Yorks. v Durham, Durham University; R. J. Turner, 101*, Somerset v Notts., Taunton; R. G. Twose, 233, Warwicks. v Leics., Birmingham.
J. R. Wileman, 109, Notts. v Cambridge U., Nottingham; A. J. Wright, 128, Glos. v Kent, Bristol.

TEN WICKETS IN A MATCH

There were 25 instances of bowlers taking ten or more wickets in a match in first-class cricket in 1992, six more than in 1991. The list includes 23 in the County Championship and two by the Pakistani touring team. Two of the instances occurred in the same match, when C. A. Walsh took ten wickets for Gloucestershire and H. R. J. Trump 14 for Somerset at Gloucester.

I. D. K. Salisbury (2)
11-83, Sussex v Lancs., Manchester; 12-138, Sussex v Yorks., Hove.

C. A. Walsh (2)
11-104, Glos. v Yorks., Leeds; 10-85, Glos. v Somerset, Gloucester.

Wasim Akram (2)
10-117, Pakistanis v Northants, Northampton; 11-76, Pakistanis v Glos., Bristol.

The following each took ten wickets in a match on one occasion:

J. A. Afford, 10-185, Notts. v Sussex, Nottingham.
P. J. Berry, 10-191, Durham v Middx, Lord's.
J. Boiling, 10-203, Surrey v Glos., Bristol.
A. R. Caddick, 10-157, Somerset v Kent, Canterbury; N. G. B. Cook, 10-97, Northants v Essex, Chelmsford; R. D. B. Croft, 14-169, Glam v Warwicks., Swansea.
C. C. Lewis, 10-155, Notts. v Surrey, Nottingham.
M. J. McCague, 10-86, Kent v Glos., Canterbury; D. J. Millns, 10-87, Leics. v Durham, Leicester; T. A. Munton, 12-110, Warwicks. v Leics., Birmingham.
N. V. Radford, 11-155, Worcs., v Derbys., Derby; M. A. Robinson, 10-101, Yorks. v Durham, Durham University.
K. J. Shine, 13-105, Hants v Lancs., Manchester; R. D. Stemp, 11-146, Worcs. v Glos., Gloucester; F. D. Stephenson, 11-107, Sussex v Worcs., Worcester.
J. P. Taylor, 10-54, Northants v Middx, Northampton; H. R. J. Trump, 14-104, Somerset v Glos., Gloucester.
M. Watkinson, 10-103, Lancs. v Warwicks., Birmingham; N. F. Williams, 12-139, Middx v Glos., Lord's.

THE PAKISTANIS IN ENGLAND, 1992

The Pakistanis' tour in 1992 was as eventful as any tour of England there has been. Beyond dispute, it was the most lucrative England had staged. For the first time, the formula was five Tests and five one-day internationals and they generated more than the £7 million which the Test and County Cricket Board had budgeted. But there were disputes, a rumbling sequence of them, as allegations were made of ball-tampering by Pakistan's fast bowlers and of partiality by England's umpires. In between whiles, especially in the three Tests which ended in four days, there was some magnificent cricket between two sides who were almost opposites in their outlook and method. In winning 2-1, when England felt they had the batting strength to draw the series at least, the Pakistanis confirmed their status as a world power, alongside Australia and West Indies.

It was the first Test series between the two countries since 1987, when Pakistan had won 1-0 both at home and away, and the sores had clearly not healed. Although Mike Gatting was not eligible to represent England, as he was still serving a ban for touring South Africa, his feud with the umpire Shakoor Rana in Faisalabad was never far from mind. In addition to that incident were the many others – from the David Constant decision at Headingley in 1982 back to Donald Carr's A tour of 1955-56, when the umpire Idris Begh was doused in water – that have so coloured relations between England and Pakistan that slights are perceived where none is intended. And the series came a few weeks after the teams' bizarre encounters in the World Cup: in the first Pakistan were all out for 74 and only stayed in the tournament because it rained; the second was the final, which they won.

Given this background, the atmosphere was heightened from the start. If England's players nursed grievances about the umpiring after their 1987-88 tour, the World Cup winners arrived with similar suspicions. The Pakistanis' fear of retribution was not allayed when John Holder disappeared from the Test panel: an umpire who had stood in Pakistan as a neutral in their 1989-90 series against India, Holder was one of the few the tourists were prepared to trust. Again, they saw little of Dickie Bird and David Shepherd, because the TCCB unwisely preferred to use as many as eight umpires in the five Tests. While this may have been a sincere desire on the TCCB's part to "spread it around", the effect was an abdication of responsibility, just as there had been in 1987-88 when Pakistan refused to use their best umpires. There are probably not eight umpires of international standard in the world, let alone in one country.

After a bland and rain-spoiled prelude at Edgbaston, and the tensest of Tests at Lord's, the accumulating tensions boiled over at Old Trafford, where Roy Palmer was umpiring in his first Test match. By the fourth evening, the game was a certain draw. But so rife were the tourists' suspicions about the umpiring that tempers overflowed in the most inconsequential of situations, after England had saved the follow-on. It did not help that Palmer's first decision had been to give Ramiz Raja out following an appeal too lukewarm to be called half-hearted; or that he was the younger brother of Ken Palmer, to whom the Pakistanis had objected in 1987. Still, there was no excuse for the furore which followed the warning given by Palmer to Aqib Javed for intimidating Devon Malcolm. Aqib reacted with a show of petulance which earned him a fine of half of his match fee by the referee. It was an illustration of Aqib's state of mind that he should then have perceived an insult, when Palmer handed him his sweater, where clearly none was intended. The television replay showed that the sweater caught in the belt of Palmer's coat as he handed it to Aqib and was not thrown at the bowler.

An impartial judge would have to say that for most of the series the tourists' suspicions about the umpiring had no foundation whatsoever. But in the Fourth Test at Headingley there was an impression of bias towards the home team which strengthened the call for third-country umpires. Much was made in Pakistan of a decision by Ken Palmer in Graham Gooch's favour, when replays showed the England captain to have been run out by a yard or two, at a stage in England's second innings when they could still have lost. Blown-up photographs of the "run-out" were reported to have been displayed on buses in Pakistan. In making much out of split-second judgments such as this, the visiting media in 1992 probably generated as much ill-feeling back home as the English media had done in 1987-88.

On the England side meanwhile, there was increasing concern about what was happening to the ball in the hands of Pakistan's two brilliant fast bowlers, Waqar Younis and Wasim Akram. These concerns, however, did not come into the open until after the series, when Allan Lamb, in an article for the *Daily Mirror*, made detailed allegations of ball-tampering. For speaking out and breaking his contract, Lamb was immediately fined an estimated £2,000 and suspended for two matches by Northamptonshire; later, at a TCCB disciplinary hearing, he was fined £5,000, with costs of £1,000, the stiffest penalty of its kind in English cricket to date. This was reduced on appeal, but only to £4,000 (half of it suspended for two years) and £500 costs.

Popular opinion was largely in favour of Lamb, if only for finding an excuse for England staging four spectacular collapses and thereby losing the series: at Lord's they lost their last six wickets for 42 runs in the first innings and 38 in the second; at Headingley their last eight for 28, and at The Oval their last seven for 25. Critical reaction, however, from former players of various countries, was more in support of the Pakistanis. By making the ball swing so effectively, by whatever means, and bowling straight, the tourists returned the focus of the game to the batsman's stumps, not his head and body, which had been the aim of short-pitched bowling in the 1970s and 1980s. While law-suits and threats of legal action began to fly off the field, Waqar and Wasim made the old ball swing further than most people had ever seen. No longer was the ball an especial threat when new but, in defiance of previous theory, when it was 60 or 70 overs old.

The umpires made frequent inspections of the ball, according to their brief, while the ICC match referee was required to examine it at every interval. But only once did anything untoward result, during the fourth one-day international, at Lord's, after it had been carried over into a second day. At the lunch interval, during England's innings, the umpires and the match referee changed the ball for one of similar condition. There was no end to the confusion which followed. The referee, the former West Indian wicket-keeper Deryck Murray, would only say that the ball had been changed, leaving the reason for it open to speculation. One informed source stated that the original ball had been changed under Law 42.5 because it had been tampered with. But Intikhab Alam, the touring team manager, asserted that the ball had been changed under Law 5.5 – simply because it had gone out of shape. Then, while accusation bred counter-accusation, it emerged that the umpires, according to the regulations for the Texaco Trophy, should have changed the ball for one of inferior, not similar, condition if the original had been deliberately damaged: and in the end, perhaps because of this slip-up in procedure, perhaps because of terror of the lawyers, the ICC finally decided to provide no further elucidation of the matter. In the darkness, further seeds of mistrust and animosity were sown for the future.

If anything was conclusive, it was that the ICC's new system of match referees was inadequate. The Council had already declared itself to be in favour of neutral, or independent, umpires, but had done nothing to implement a new system on the grounds of excessive cost. Yet there was the money to pay the expenses and fees of four referees during the summer in Bob Cowper, Clyde Walcott, Conrad Hunte and Deryck Murray. This expense, borne by the TCCB as the host country, could just as easily have gone into paying one or two umpires from a third country. While neutral umpires might not be considered necessary in every series in England, they would surely have taken the heat out of the Tests with Pakistan.

One of the most vocal supporters of neutral umpires, Imran Khan, had initially declared himself available for the tour, but withdrew shortly after the World Cup final. He pleaded a shoulder injury, but it was suspected that another factor was his declining popularity within the Pakistan team. Immediately, the prophecy was made that the tourists would go to pieces without Imran as their captain, and that he would be recalled in mid-season. But neither of these expectations was fulfilled. The tourists maintained their unity, except for the two episodes of indiscipline at Old Trafford and Headingley, while Imran was left to play in charity matches which he organised to raise money for a cancer hospital in Lahore.

Had Imran been captain, the tourists would surely still have won the series, but it is doubtful whether they would have achieved such an astonishing record in their first-class county games. In 1987 Imran had shown little interest in them except as practice, but under Javed Miandad the Pakistanis set out to win every one, both as a preparation for the Tests and as an end in itself. They scored rapidly and, led by Wasim and the leg-spinner Mushtaq Ahmed, bowled with a rare aggression. The outcome, nine wins in 12 matches, was the best record against county teams since the 1948 Australians won 15 of their 20 games against first-class counties. There can be no doubt that Tetley Bitter's sponsorship – £2,000 for each victory, and a jackpot of £50,000 for winning a minimum of eight out of 12 – provided a vital incentive which enlivened these matches.

In contrast to his reputation for waywardness, Miandad displayed a high level of leadership. Given three bowlers of a quality beyond anything England could field, he was more flexible in his field-placings than his counterpart, Gooch, and had plenty of experience of English conditions after his seasons with Sussex and Glamorgan. The one lapse into the immaturity which had marked his first attempts at captaincy came at Old Trafford where he failed to work with Roy Palmer in interpreting the law, and was then ostentatiously rude as he made play of Aqib's sweater. Some commentators thought Miandad should have been fined, along with Aqib. Instead, the referee Conrad Hunte simply urged Miandad to uphold standards of behaviour; and this he did in the following Test, when the

Pakistanis were upset by a decision against them in England's second innings, and the substitute Rashid Latif threw his cap on the ground and was also fined.

The one three-day county match which the tourists lost was their first, against Worcestershire, who won £4,000 from the sponsors. As instrumental as any player in their defeat was Philip Weston, the England Under-19 captain, in his third first-class match. In Pakistan, if a player is chosen for Test cricket at all, he is generally chosen at Weston's age, rather than in his mid-20s according to the English custom. Although some of the tourists' ages appear to be under-estimated, notably that of Waqar "aged 20", Pakistan's strength lay in the enthusiasm of so many young players, blended with the maturity of a few. County after county was overwhelmed by cricket which was all aggression and excited appealing and vitality, not safety-conscious, fearful of failure, and content with a draw, in the English manner.

Yet the psychological advantage was with England when the series began, though they made no use of it at Edgbaston. Comprehensive victories by England in the first two one-day internationals had raised doubts about Pakistan's self-assurance after winning the World Cup; and the tourists, at the outset, were short of Test experience, especially when they left out Shoaib Mohammad. In the First Test Aamir Sohail, Inzamam-ul-Haq and Ata-ur-Rehman all made their débuts, while four other players had no Test record to speak of. Had England therefore caught Pakistan on a traditional Edgbaston seamer's pitch, they might still have won in the time available. But the game was played on a bland relaid wicket, and Pakistan's confidence grew during a stand of 322 between Miandad and his vice-captain Salim Malik, who began to play under pressure as he never had before. Whatever Gooch and Essex had learnt about Malik the summer before, he had learned more about England. Self-belief restored, Pakistan won by two wickets at Lord's, perhaps inspired by their passion at the finish while England remained unexcitable. It was an unusually dry pitch, which again suited Pakistan, since they had Wasim back to join Waqar. At Old Trafford England might have gone 2-0 down but for a courageous opening stand by Gooch and Alec Stewart on the third evening, when Waqar and Wasim hurled the kitchen sink at England on the fastest, hardest pitch of the series. Only at Headingley did England find something to suit their seamers, and levelled the score at one-all. At The Oval, as at Old Trafford, a hard pitch was just what the tourists wanted, and their fast bowlers tested to the limit the new ICC regulation of one bouncer per batsman per over.

The previous record number of wickets by a Pakistani in a series in England, the 21 taken by Imran in 1982 and 1987, was equalled by Wasim in four Tests and surpassed by Waqar in five. Together they made a pair to enter the hall of fame along with Larwood and Voce, Lindwall and Miller, Trueman and Statham, Lillee and Thomson, and numerous West Indian fast bowlers. It was crucial that after Edgbaston the one had the other to complement the arrangement, so that batsmen had no escape. Together they made as effective a pair as there can have ever been in wiping out tail-enders, by aiming at the stumps. Of their 43 wickets in the series, 17 were bowled and nine lbw.

Waqar arrived with the stress fracture of the spine which had kept him out of the World Cup and was still nothing like match-fit at Edgbaston.

Indeed, not until the final Test was he consistently quick, as he had been the summer before for Surrey. When he dropped short early in the series he was often expensive, not having the pace to get away with it. On the whole tour, owing to the lingering effects of his back injury, he had only 37 first-class wickets. For the same reason Waqar's arm seemed to be lower than previously, yet this only served to make his bowling more deadly when he found his rhythm. At his best, he delivered the ball slightly round-arm on the line of off-stump; the ball then curled up to a foot outside off-stump before the in-swing took effect and arrowed in at the batsman's toes or leg-stump. Until the final Test Waqar only swung the ball – a Reader in eight of the international matches, a Duke in the two others – when it was of full length, and then only into the right-hander. But at The Oval he swung the ball away from the England batsmen at the start of their second innings while they groped for his in-swinger. In Waqar's opinion this spell, of four wickets for nine runs at one stage, was his best of the summer – and like all his spells it was backed up with verbal aggression.

Wasim finished with 82 wickets, the most by any bowler on a tour of England since 1964, and he missed the First Test with a stress fracture of the shin. Often he bowled too well: that is, when bowling over the wicket, he made the ball seam away so sharply that right-handers could not get a touch. For Wasim to have taken only one wicket at Headingley was as absurd as Richard Hadlee taking none at all during New Zealand's victory on the ground in 1983. Yet it was only as an innings wore on that Wasim went round the wicket to make the batsman play. Like Waqar, Wasim swung the ageing ball violently and late, but seldom from over the wicket. Only at The Oval, when he dismissed Mark Ramprakash and Chris Lewis, did he swing the ball into the right-hander from over the wicket in the classic style of Alan Davidson or Garfield Sobers. Otherwise his repertoire was complete, from outright fast and short-pitched bowling at the openers to swinging yorkers for the tailenders. It would be surprising if there has been a better left-arm bowler of pace; and he was the coolest of match-winners with the bat at Lord's.

The one threat to the pair's continued dominance lay in the strenuous programme ahead of them; after a packed winter with Pakistan, Waqar and Wasim were committed to several long and lucrative seasons with Surrey and Lancashire, without any time to rest back and groin respectively. They needed another strike bowler to share their duties, and while Aqib was a useful support at fast-medium, and as good a pace bowler as any on England's side, he did not have their pace or ability to swing the ball prodigiously. If Pakistan missed a trick during the series – other than playing Inzamam ahead of Shoaib – it was in preferring the less-than-fit Aqib at Headingley to the medium pace of Naved Anjum. Aqib was also the one poor fielder in the party.

Mushtaq secured himself a contract with Somerset as a result of being as effective as any leg-spinner to have toured England since the war. His role was vital as the stock bowler who kept the runs down to 2.6 an over while Waqar and Wasim rested; yet he was also a strike bowler when he dismissed England's middle order in their second innings at Lord's. In trying to attack him England found that Mushtaq was a fraction slower in pace than Abdul Qadir. But this worked in Mushtaq's favour; batsmen sometimes charged him, as they would not have done Qadir, and found themselves stranded: Robin Smith was a particular victim until the Oval

Test, by when he had learned to bide his time in the crease. Mushtaq's one poor performance was at Old Trafford, when he was suffering a mid-tour lull. Otherwise, he was almost the equal of his predecessor, favouring the googly no less than Qadir, though as yet without his range of top-spinners and flippers.

For all the brilliance of their bowling, though, the Pakistanis might still have not taken the series if two unproven left-handed batsmen had not come good and occupied two of the first three places in contrasting styles. Aamir Sohail, who had played 15 one-day internationals but no Tests, curbed his dashing ways just enough to become a commanding opener. A measure of his ability to learn and adapt was that he quickly cut down on the shuffle across the crease he had when he started the tour, which made him liable to hit the leg-side ball in the air. By the end of the series he had become a second slip too, thus strengthening the one area in which Pakistan had been weak, and allowing Salim Malik to escape to gully. Sohail's partner, Ramiz Raja, was equally dashing but he might not have got away with whipping straight balls through mid-wicket if the series had been staged on seaming pitches. The second left-hander, Asif Mujtaba, left to languish for several seasons in Pakistan's domestic cricket, justified Miandad's faith in him by batting quietly and methodically. With the captain and vice-captain filling the No. 4 and No. 5 places so capably – Malik topped the national batting averages, and with 488 Test runs set a new record for series between England and Pakistan – it seldom mattered that Inzamam failed. The World Cup prodigy, an ingenuous and dreamy fellow who would not wear a helmet at first, averaged only 13 in the series.

The depth of talent in the party – not a common feature of Pakistan touring teams – was illustrated this time when Moin Khan was dropped for the final Test and Rashid Latif made a remarkably composed and stylish 50 on his début, besides keeping wicket as competently as Moin had done. Tanvir Mehdi, a useful fast-medium, was sent home, along with Saleem Jaffer who had a thigh strain, once Waqar had proved his fitness. Ata-ur-Rehman was flown in to cover for Wasim at Edgbaston and bowled briskly, while Ijaz Ahmed became the 19th player when he was flown in for the last three internationals.

At Trent Bridge, when sorely vexed by Pakistan's victory in the Test series, England vented their frustrations by running up the highest total ever made by any country in one-day internationals, 363 for seven from 55 overs. On the attack, then and in the Test series, England had a fine array of batsmen led by Gooch and Stewart. But in the deciding Test at The Oval they went on to the defensive in their first innings, long before the ball started swinging after tea on the first day. Mike Atherton, in positive mode, was well-suited to opening at Headingley, but at No. 3 he did not have the strokes to dictate and went through 60 overs for as many runs. By then it had been acknowledged that batting at the top of the order against Pakistan was far easier than later on when the ball was ageing; the need to cash in early was therefore imperative.

At Headingley Gooch followed his greatest innings, his century against West Indies there, with another of scarcely less importance and calibre. Stewart maintained his astonishing rate of improvement – by Lord's he was quite brilliant and carried his bat – until he was asked to keep wicket in the last two Tests in place of Jack Russell, and the runs immediately dried up. Graeme Hick, on the other hand, made no advance at all in the Tests and came to be selected virtually as a specialist second slip, where he missed nothing and took his rate to two catches per Test, a remarkable achievement. He was dropped for The Oval, just as he had been the year before. Yet in the one-day games – which England won 4-1 – he tore to shreds the same Pakistan bowling, using feet that were frozen in Test matches when he had too much time to worry.

England's bowling was so unexceptional that in a sense they did well to lose by only two Tests to one. In the absence, for varying reasons, of Angus Fraser, Neil Foster, David Lawrence and John Emburey, and of Phillip DeFreitas (groin strain) for three Tests and Philip Tufnell (appendicitis) for four, it was seldom more than straightforward at best. On hard pitches Malcolm was alone in providing any threat. For the only seamer's pitch of the series, at Headingley, Neil Mallender was called up and took eight wickets, bowling that line a fraction outside off-stump which England preferred, if they did not always achieve.

Relations between the teams were not cordial, but they were no worse than, say, in England's 1989 series against Australia. It is true there was a nationalistic element in some crowds, as the tourists attracted wide and partisan support from British Asians, whose chants in turn provoked a reaction from a few England supporters; but the rivalry was predominantly good-humoured. What heightened the atmosphere was principally the media coverage, and that of the British tabloids in particular. When Khalid Mahmood, the tourists' courteous but hard-pressed tour manager, said after the series: "There is no hostility between England and Pakistan, only in the tabloid newspapers", he was close to the heart of the matter. Relations between the two countries have lacked understanding at most levels, but if the media coverage had been more restrained there would not have been the amount of controversy there was. Still, the series will also be remembered for the brilliant cricket that was generated, especially by the tourists. – Scyld Berry.

PAKISTANI TOURING PARTY

Javed Miandad (Karachi/Habib Bank) (*captain*), Salim Malik (Lahore/Habib Bank) (*vice-captain*), Aamir Sohail (Sargodha/Habib Bank), Aqib Javed (PACO), Asif Mujtaba (Karachi/PIA), Inzamam-ul-Haq (Multan/United Bank), Moin Khan (Karachi/PIA), Mushtaq Ahmed (Multan/United Bank), Naved Anjum (Lahore/Habib Bank), Ramiz Raja (Lahore/PNSC), Rashid Latif (Karachi/United Bank), Saleem Jaffer (Karachi/United Bank), Shoaib Mohammad (Karachi/PIA), Tanvir Mehdi (Lahore/United Bank), Waqar Younis (Multan/United Bank), Wasim Akram (Lahore/PIA), Zahid Fazal (PIA).

Ata-ur-Rehman (Lahore/PACO) joined the party in May as cover for injured bowlers, and Ijaz Ahmed (Habib Bank) in August to take part in the later one-day internationals. Saleem Jaffer (injured) and Tanvir Mehdi were flown home at the end of June.

Tour manager: Khalid Mahmood. *Team manager:* Intikhab Alam.

PAKISTANI TOUR RESULTS

Test matches – Played 5: Won 2, Lost 1, Drawn 2.
First-class matches – Played 19: Won 12, Lost 2, Drawn 5.
Wins – England (2), Glamorgan, Somerset, Leicestershire, Nottinghamshire, Northampton-shire, Oxford & Cambridge Universities, Hampshire, Durham, Essex, Gloucestershire.
Losses – England, Worcestershire.
Draws – England (2), Middlesex, Derbyshire, World XI.
One-day internationals – Played 5: Won 1, Lost 4.
Other non first-class matches – Played 7: Won 5, Lost 2. Abandoned 4. *Wins* – Lavinia, Duchess of Norfolk's XI, Kent, Sussex, England Amateur XI, Scotland. *Losses* – Sussex, Minor Counties. *Abandoned* – League Cricket Conference, Scotland, Somerset (2).

TEST MATCH AVERAGES

ENGLAND – BATTING

	T	I	NO	R	HS	100s	Avge	Ct/St
A. J. Stewart	5	8	1	397	190	1	56.71	5
D. I. Gower	3	5	2	150	73	0	50.00	1
G. A. Gooch	5	8	0	384	135	1	48.00	2
R. A. Smith	5	8	1	314	127	1	44.85	7
M. A. Atherton	3	5	0	145	76	0	29.00	5
R. C. Russell	3	4	2	56	29*	0	28.00	6/1
G. A. Hick	4	5	0	98	51	0	19.60	10
C. C. Lewis	5	7	0	114	55	0	16.28	4
M. R. Ramprakash	3	5	1	31	17	0	7.75	1
D. E. Malcolm	3	5	0	6	4	0	1.20	1
D. R. Pringle	3	4	1	2	1	0	0.66	0

Played in two Tests: I. T. Botham 2, 6 (2 ct); P. A. J. DeFreitas 3, 0; A. J. Lamb 12, 30, 12; N. A. Mallender 1, 4, 3; T. A. Munton 25*, 0; I. D. K. Salisbury 4, 12, 50. Played in one Test: P. C. R. Tufnell 0*, 0 (1 ct).

* *Signifies not out.*

BOWLING

	O	M	R	W	BB	5W/i	Avge
G. A. Gooch	51	15	94	5	3-39	0	18.80
N. A. Mallender	74.5	20	215	10	5-50	1	21.50
P. A. J. DeFreitas	59	14	179	7	4-121	0	25.57
D. E. Malcolm	102.5	14	380	13	5-94	1	29.23
C. C. Lewis	188	40	544	12	3-43	0	45.33
D. R. Pringle	70	10	227	5	3-66	0	45.40
I. D. K. Salisbury	70.1	3	306	5	3-49	0	61.20

Also bowled: I. T. Botham 24-8-61-0; G. A. Hick 18-3-63-0; T. A. Munton 67.3-15-200-4; M. R. Ramprakash 1.1-0-8-0; P. C. R. Tufnell 34-9-87-1.

PAKISTAN – BATTING

	T	I	NO	R	HS	100s	Avge	Ct/St
Salim Malik	5	8	2	488	165	1	81.33	1
Javed Miandad	5	8	2	364	153*	1	60.66	5
Aamir Sohail	5	9	1	413	205	1	51.62	3
Ramiz Raja	5	9	1	312	88	0	39.00	5
Asif Mujtaba	5	8	0	253	59	0	31.62	4
Wasim Akram	4	7	1	118	45*	0	19.66	0
Inzamam-ul-Haq	4	6	1	66	26	0	13.20	4
Waqar Younis	5	6	2	51	20*	0	12.75	0
Moin Khan	4	6	1	46	15	0	9.20	7
Mushtaq Ahmed	5	6	0	35	11	0	5.83	1
Aqib Javed	5	4	2	5	5*	0	2.50	0

Played in one Test: Rashid Latif 50 (2 ct, 1 st); Shoaib Mohammad 55; Ata-ur-Rehman did not bat.

* *Signifies not out.*

BOWLING

	O	M	R	W	BB	5W/i	Avge
Wasim Akram	168.5	36	462	21	6-67	2	22.00
Waqar Younis.....	166	29	557	22	5-52	3	25.31
Mushtaq Ahmed....	178.4	37	475	15	3-32	0	31.66
Aqib Javed	104.4	21	366	9	4-100	0	40.66

Also bowled: Aamir Sohail 5-2-14-0; Asif Mujtaba 13-5-30-1; Ata-ur-Rehman 18-5-69-3; Salim Malik 1-0-5-0.

PAKISTANI TOUR AVERAGES – FIRST-CLASS MATCHES

BATTING

	M	I	NO	R	HS	100s	Avge
Salim Malik..........	15	21	6	1,184	165	2	78.93
Javed Miandad	12	17	3	809	153*	2	57.78
Asif Mujtaba	16	25	6	1,074	154*	2	56.52
Inzamam-ul-Haq	15	21	7	736	200*	1	52.57
Shoaib Mohammad....	12	21	4	761	105*	1	44.76
Ramiz Raja	16	26	2	1,036	172	2	43.16
Aamir Sohail	17	28	2	1,110	205	2	42.69
Moin Khan	13	14	4	237	53	0	23.70
Zahid Fazal	6	8	3	115	51	0	23.00
Rashid Latif	8	8	2	136	50	0	22.66
Wasim Akram........	14	18	3	299	45*	0	19.93
Naved Anjum	5	6	2	77	56	0	19.25
Waqar Younis	10	9	4	95	23*	0	19.00
Mushtaq Ahmed	17	12	3	73	12	0	8.11
Aqib Javed	14	8	3	10	5*	0	2.00

Played in nine matches: Ata-ur-Rehman 1*, 0. Played in five matches: Tanvir Mehdi 13*, 0, 8. Played in four matches: Saleem Jaffer 1*. Played in one match: Ijaz Ahmed 36, 31.

* Signifies not out.

BOWLING

	O	M	R	W	BB	5W/i	Avge
Wasim Akram	499.5	127	1,330	82	6-32	7	16.21
Mushtaq Ahmed....	614.4	158	1,620	66	5-46	4	24.54
Waqar Younis......	287.1	50	913	37	5-22	4	24.67
Tanvir Mehdi	94	21	307	12	3-24	0	25.58
Aqib Javed	292	58	966	36	5-34	1	26.83
Aamir Sohail	103	29	251	9	3-31	0	27.88
Ata-ur-Rehman	159.1	29	621	18	3-69	0	34.50
Asif Mujtaba.......	129.5	35	325	9	4-73	0	36.11
Naved Anjum	107.1	24	379	10	3-73	0	37.90
Saleem Jaffer......	65	9	247	5	2-53	0	49.40

Also bowled: Inzamam-ul-Haq 2-0-13-1; Moin Khan 1-0-3-0; Rashid Latif 8-2-17-2; Salim Malik 18.1-0-71-3; Shoaib Mohammad 27-5-82-0; Zahid Fazal 13-2-73-0.

FIELDING

29 – Moin Khan (28 ct, 1 st), Rashid Latif (27 ct, 2 st); 21 – Inzamam-ul Haq; 14 – Aamir Sohail; 10 – Substitutes; 8 – Javed Miandad; 7 – Zahid Fazal; 6 – Asif Mujtaba, Mushtaq Ahmed; 5 – Wasim Akram; 4 – Salim Malik; 3 – Ata-ur-Rehman, Ramiz Raja; 2 – Shoaib Mohammad, Tanvir Mehdi; 1 – Aqib Javed, Ijaz Ahmed, Naved Anjum, Saleem Jaffer, Waqar Younis.

Note: Matches in this section which were not first-class are signified by a dagger.

†LAVINIA, DUCHESS OF NORFOLK'S XI v PAKISTANIS

At Arundel, May 3. Pakistanis won by 13 runs. Toss: Pakistanis. The tourists were given a good run by the Duchess's men, drawn principally from Derbyshire and Sussex. Bowler and O'Gorman, in particular, never looked deterred by an asking-rate above five an over, and none of the Pakistani bowlers could take control. But their batsmen had put on a fine display for the crowd of 7,000. Aamir Sohail reached 100 in 108 balls before quitting the crease at 226, and Salim Malik enjoyed his return to form after an unhappy World Cup.

Pakistanis

Aamir Sohail retired	104	Asif Mujtaba not out	2
Ramiz Raja b Jean-Jacques	23	L-b 4, w 2, n-b 3	9
Salim Malik b Base	84		
*Javed Miandad not out	31	1/86 2/226 3/240 (3 wkts, 50 overs)	253

Zahid Fazal, Wasim Akram, †Moin Khan, Saleem Jaffer, Aqib Javed and Naved Anjum did not bat.

Bowling: Base 10–0–51–1; Robson 10–0–44–0; Jean-Jacques 10–0–60–1; Kendrick 10–0–44–0; Donelan 10–0–50–0.

Lavinia, Duchess of Norfolk's XI

P. D. Bowler b Asif Mujtaba	82	†P. Moores not out	1
N. J. Lenham b Asif Mujtaba	36	B 2, l-b 10, w 1, n-b 4	17
T. J. G. O'Gorman b Aqib Javed	69		
*A. P. Wells b Naved Anjum	30	1/89 2/164 (4 wkts, 50 overs)	240
R. O. Butcher not out	5	3/223 4/239	

A. G. Robson, B. T. P. Donelan, N. M. Kendrick, M. Jean-Jacques and S. J. Base did not bat.

Bowling: Wasim Akram 10–0–45–0; Aqib Javed 10–0–50–1; Saleem Jaffer 10–0–49–0; Naved Anjum 10–0–47–1; Asif Mujtaba 10-2–37–2.

Umpires: V. A. Holder and P. B. Wight.

†KENT v PAKISTANIS

At Canterbury, May 4. Pakistanis won by 40 runs. Toss: Pakistanis. Kent were 60 for four in the 21st over, chasing 282, when the match was almost transformed by the explosive intervention of Fleming. He hit 74 from only 44 balls, out of 94 in 12 overs for the fifth wicket. Fleming took three sixes off Mushtaq Ahmed and a fourth off Asif Mujtaba; he was stumped next ball attempting a fifth. Earlier, there were stylish innings from Aamir Sohail and Inzamam-ul-Haq, though the tourists' total was chiefly built around Salim Malik's 129-run stand with Mujtaba. In the field, the Pakistanis needed so many substitutes that at one time they were down to ten men.

Pakistanis

Aamir Sohail c Marsh b Penn	37	Wasim Akram c Longley b Ealham	5
Ramiz Raja c Ealham b McCague	17	Naved Anjum not out	7
Inzamam-ul-Haq c Cowdrey b Fleming	40	L-b 5, w 3, n-b 3	11
*Salim Malik c Davis b Ealham	95		
Zahid Fazal c Fleming b Davis	0	1/35 2/59 3/121 (6 wkts, 55 overs)	281
Asif Mujtaba not out	69	4/126 5/255 6/265	

†Rashid Latif, Mushtaq Ahmed and Aqib Javed did not bat.

Bowling: McCague 11–0–74–1; Ealham 11–0–48–2; Davis 11–1–41–1; Penn 11–0–67–1; Fleming 11–0–46–1.

Kent

T. R. Ward c Rashid Latif b Wasim Akram	1	J. I. Longley b Mushtaq Ahmed	11
*M. R. Benson c Rashid Latif b Naved Anjum	10	N. J. Llong c and b Wasim Akram	41
G. R. Cowdrey c Mushtaq Ahmed b Aqib Javed	15	R. P. Davis c Asif Mujtaba b Aqib Javed	7
M. A. Ealham c Rashid Latif b Asif Mujtaba	27	M. J. McCague c Aamir Sohail	16
†S. A. Marsh c Inzamam-ul-Haq b Asif Mujtaba	24	C. Penn not out	3
M. V. Fleming st Rashid Latif b Asif Mujtaba	74	L-b 5, w 3, n-b 4	12
		1/3 2/29 3/29 (48 overs)	241
		4/60 5/154 6/162	
		7/183 8/216 9/221	

Bowling: Wasim Akram 10–0–34–2; Aqib Javed 9–4–15–2; Naved Anjum 1.4–0–10–1; Zahid Fazal 1.2–0–6–0; Mushtaq Ahmed 11–0–73–1; Asif Mujtaba 11–0–61–3; Aamir Sohail 4–0–37–1.

Umpires: A. A. Jones and R. C. Tolchard.

WORCESTERSHIRE v PAKISTANIS

At Worcester, May 6, 7, 8. Worcestershire won by five wickets. Toss: Pakistanis. The tourists' opening first-class fixture ended in defeat following a dramatic second-innings collapse on the final morning. Resuming at 31 for two, with an overall lead of 102, but without the injured Asif Mujtaba, they lost their last seven wickets adding 62 runs. On a wearing pitch with the ball swinging considerably, Newport fashioned their downfall in a spell of five wickets for eight in six overs. Only Shoaib Mohammad, who batted throughout the innings, put up any resistance before being last out for 46. Worcestershire achieved a target of 165 with 9.5 overs to spare. It was in stark contrast to the way the Pakistani batsmen had plundered the county attack on the opening day, watched by Keith Fletcher, just named as England's next manager. Acting-captain Salim Malik declared at 374 for four off just 90 overs, after sharing 165 in 38 overs with Ramiz Raja, who collected 28 fours in nearly five hours. Hick's first encounter with the tourists lasted only nine balls, but Curtis anchored Worcestershire's reply with a four-hour captain's innings. The highlight of the second day, however, was a promising unbeaten 64 from 18-year-old Philip Weston, his maiden first-class fifty, which allowed the county to declare 71 behind. As it turned out, Worcestershire were to be the only county to beat the Pakistanis in a first-class game and claim the £4,000 prizemoney offered by sponsors Tetley Bitter.

Close of play: First day, Worcestershire 43-0 (T. S. Curtis 27*, A. C. H. Seymour 9*); Second day, Pakistanis 31-2 (Shoaib Mohammad 12*, Salim Malik 1*).

Pakistanis

Aamir Sohail c Curtis b Tolley	36	– c Newport b Radford	11
Ramiz Raja c and b Illingworth	172	– (3) run out	5
Shoaib Mohammad b Radford	17	– (2) c Rhodes b Newport	46
*Salim Malik lbw b Illingworth	91	– c Seymour b Weston	7
Inzamam-ul-Haq not out	33	– c Radford b Newport	7
Asif Mujtaba not out	19	– absent injured	
Wasim Akram (did not bat)	–	(6) c D'Oliveira b Newport	4
†Rashid Latif (did not bat)	–	(7) c D'Oliveira b Weston	2
Mushtaq Ahmed (did not bat)	–	(8) lbw b Newport	4
Aqib Javed (did not bat)	–	(9) c Hick b Newport	0
Saleem Jaffer (did not bat)	–	(10) not out	1
L-b 1, n-b 5	6	B 1, l-b 2, w 1, n-b 2	6

1/80 2/156 3/321 4/322   (4 wkts dec.) 374   1/16 2/30 3/41 4/64 5/72   93
6/75 7/82 8/82 9/93

Bowling: *First Innings*—Radford 13–2–59–1; Tolley 16–1–67–1; Newport 13–2–54–0; Weston 15–1–73–0; Illingworth 20–4–81–2; Hick 13–1–39–0. *Second Innings*—Radford 6–1–20–1; Tolley 6–3–9–0; Newport 13.1–4–22–5; Weston 13–2–39–2.

Worcestershire

*T. S. Curtis lbw b Mushtaq Ahmed	85	– lbw b Wasim Akram	45
A. C. H. Seymour c Inzamam-ul-Haq b Aqib Javed	37	– c Mushtaq Ahmed b Wasim Akram	11
G. A. Hick c Salim Malik b Aqib Javed	0	– c and b Saleem Jaffer	33
D. A. Leatherdale st Rashid Latif b Mushtaq Ahmed	10	– c Rashid Latif b Saleem Jaffer	0
D. B. D'Oliveira b Mushtaq Ahmed	31	– b Mushtaq Ahmed	2
W. P. C. Weston not out	64	– not out	32
†S. J. Rhodes not out	46	– not out	21
B 4, l-b 7, w 3, n-b 16	30	B 5, l-b 6, n-b 11	22

1/85 2/100 3/119 4/165 5/198   (5 wkts dec.) 303   1/32 2/91 3/91   (5 wkts) 166
4/100 5/125

C. M. Tolley, R. K. Illingworth, P. J. Newport and N. V. Radford did not bat.

Bowling: *First Innings*—Wasim Akram 18–2–75–0; Aqib Javed 14–2–30–2; Mushtaq Ahmed 28–5–71–3; Saleem Jaffer 21–2–71–0; Shoaib Mohammad 7–0–16–0; Aamir Sohail 4–0–29–0. *Second Innings*—Wasim Akram 14–3–27–2; Aqib Javed 17–4–47–0; Saleem Jaffer 14–2–53–2; Mushtaq Ahmed 11–3–24–1; Salim Malik 0.1–0–4–0.

Umpires: J. H. Hampshire and B. J. Meyer.

GLAMORGAN v PAKISTANIS

At Cardiff, May 9, 10, 11. Pakistanis won by 206 runs. Toss: Pakistanis. After the first four sessions had been lost to rain Glamorgan were outclassed by the tourists, who compensated for their defeat at Worcester by winning with 17 overs to spare. A rapid 124 from Aamir Sohail, who struck a six and 14 fours, laid the foundation for a substantial Pakistani total and, after both captains had forfeited an innings, Glamorgan were set 355 from 78 overs. With Morris and Richards unfit and Butcher, playing his first game of the season, unable to bat after aggravating a knee injury, Glamorgan faced an awesome task. Their batsmen could counter neither the pace of Wasim Akram nor the leg-spin of Mushtaq Ahmed, who took four wickets apiece. After Hemp and Metson had compiled 45 for the sixth wicket – the biggest stand of the innings – the last four wickets fell for only seven runs.

Close of play: First day, No play; Second day, Pakistanis 285-4 (Salim Malik 0*, Inzamam-ul-Haq 12*).

Pakistanis

Aamir Sohail c Metson b Frost	124	Wasim Akram not out	21
Ramiz Raja c Butcher b Watkin	41		
Shoaib Mohammad b Dale	58	B 1, l-b 12, n-b 5	18
*Javed Miandad c and b Dale	35		
Salim Malik not out	41	1/100 2/210 3/272 (5 wkts dec.) 354	
Inzamam-ul-Haq lbw b Watkin	16	4/273 5/298	

†Moin Khan, Tanvir Mehdi, Saleem Jaffer and Mushtaq Ahmed did not bat.

Bowling: Frost 17-1-75-1; Watkin 24-2-80-2; Barwick 24-3-82-0; Croft 16-0-90-0; Dale 7-4-14-2.

Pakistanis forfeited their second innings.

Glamorgan

Glamorgan forfeited their first innings.

S. P. James b Wasim Akram	27	S. L. Watkin b Wasim Akram	6
A. Dale c Moin Khan b Saleem Jaffer	9	S. R. Barwick c Tanvir Mehdi b Mushtaq Ahmed	0
R. D. B. Croft c Moin Khan b Wasim Akram	7	M. Frost not out	0
M. P. Maynard c Javed Miandad b Mushtaq Ahmed	28	*A. R. Butcher absent injured	
P. A. Cottey c Aamir Sohail b Mushtaq Ahmed	12		
D. L. Hemp b Wasim Akram	23	B 7, l-b 1, w 1, n-b 7	16
†C. P. Metson c Aamir Sohail b Mushtaq Ahmed	20	1/19 2/36 3/62 4/91 5/96	148
		6/141 7/143 8/145 9/148	

Bowling: Wasim Akram 17-4-46-4; Tanvir Mehdi 11-0-31-0; Saleem Jaffer 11-1-35-1; Mushtaq Ahmed 19-8-26-4; Aamir Sohail 3-1-2-0.

Umpires: D. J. Constant and M. J. Kitchen.

SOMERSET v PAKISTANIS

At Taunton, May 13, 14, 15. Pakistanis won by five wickets. Toss: Somerset. On a dry, slightly variable pitch, Somerset struggled throughout against the three seamers and the leg-spinner Mushtaq Ahmed, who took eight for 124 in the match. Acting-captain Harden held them at bay, with help from MacLeay and Burns in the first innings and Hayhurst in the second, but Somerset rarely threatened seriously. The Pakistanis were rescued from an uncertain start by fine strokeplay from Salim Malik, who hit a six and 16 fours. He dominated a partnership of 106 with Javed Miandad, which left them only ten runs behind with seven wickets standing by the end of the day. However, a fine burst of five for 28 in 10.2 overs by Caddick next morning restricted the lead to 77, and Caddick and van Troost posed more problems in the second innings. Nineteen wickets had fallen on the second day, and the dismissal of night-watchman Tanvir Mehdi at the start of the third reduced the tourists to 28 for three, chasing 93. But that brought in Miandad, who attacked fiercely, facing only 23 balls and hitting six fours in his 35. The issue was settled in 45 minutes.

Close of play: First day, Pakistanis 153-3 (Javed Miandad 21*, Salim Malik 69*); Second day, Pakistanis 28-2 (Shoaib Mohammad 4*, Tanvir Mehdi 0*).

Somerset

A. N. Hayhurst lbw b Tanvir Mehdi	0	– c Aamir Sohail b Mushtaq Ahmed . 30
G. T. J. Townsend c Wasim Akram b Aqib Javed	8	– lbw b Tanvir Mehdi ... 12
*R. J. Harden lbw b Tanvir Mehdi	40	– c Moin Khan b Tanvir Mehdi .. 26
K. H. MacLeay c Aamir Sohail b Tanvir Mehdi	32	– c Inzamam-ul-Haq b Mushtaq Ahmed . 9
R. J. Bartlett c Aamir Sohail b Mushtaq Ahmed	2	– c Moin Khan b Wasim Akram.. 23
G. D. Rose lbw b Aqib Javed	5	– lbw b Wasim Akram ... 0
†N. D. Burns not out	44	– c Ramiz Raja b Mushtaq Ahmed 19
K. A. Parsons c Inzamam-ul-Haq b Aqib Javed.	1	– lbw b Mushtaq Ahmed ... 0
A. R. Caddick c Moin Khan b Mushtaq Ahmed	9	– not out ... 6
H. R. J. Trump lbw b Mushtaq Ahmed	11	– b Wasim Akram ... 1
A. P. van Troost lbw b Wasim Akram	0	– st Moin Khan b Mushtaq Ahmed 12
L-b 5, n-b 6	11	B 8, l-b 10, n-b 13 ... 31

1/7 2/23 3/84 4/92 5/92   163   1/21 2/72 3/83 4/97 5/98   169
6/111 7/113 8/144 9/160   6/142 7/143 8/154 9/156

Bowling: *First Innings*—Wasim Akram 14.4-6-25-1; Aqib Javed 11-4-26-3; Tanvir Mehdi 12-5-29-3; Mushtaq Ahmed 24-6-78-3. *Second Innings*—Wasim Akram 15-4-43-3; Aqib Javed 7-1-27-0; Tanvir Mehdi 10-3-35-2; Mushtaq Ahmed 20-8-46-5.

Pakistanis

Aamir Sohail c Harden b Rose	37	– c MacLeay b Caddick ... 8
Ramiz Raja lbw b Rose	10	– c Hayhurst b van Troost ... 12
Shoaib Mohammad c Harden b Caddick	1	– c and b van Troost ... 14
*Javed Miandad c Burns b Caddick	30	– (5) c MacLeay b Rose ... 35
Salim Malik b Caddick	89	– (6) not out ... 18
Inzamam-ul-Haq c Trump b Caddick	6	– (7) not out ... 0
Wasim Akram c Hayhurst b Caddick	30	
†Moin Khan lbw b Rose	0	
Mushtaq Ahmed c Burns b Hayhurst	4	
Tanvir Mehdi not out	13	– (4) c Burns b van Troost ... 0
Aqib Javed c Burns b Caddick	0	
B 8, l-b 6, n-b 6	20	L-b 1, n-b 5 ... 6

1/37 2/38 3/56 4/162 5/188   240   1/20 2/24 3/28   (5 wkts) 93
6/189 7/190 8/212 9/238   4/61 5/87

Bowling: *First Innings*—Caddick 20.2-3-73-6; van Troost 12-3-40-0; Rose 18-7-58-3; MacLeay 8-1-25-0; Trump 5-1-26-0; Hayhurst 5-2-4-1. *Second Innings*—Caddick 9-1-48-1; van Troost 8-0-31-3; Rose 1.1-0-13-1.

Umpires: R. Palmer and D. R. Shepherd.

†SUSSEX v PAKISTANIS

At Hove, May 16. Sussex won by three wickets. Toss: Sussex. A large crowd enjoyed glorious weather and a thrilling match, which Sussex won with 21 balls to spare. They had been 81 for four until Stephenson joined Speight to add 123 in 22 overs. Mushtaq Ahmed bowled 11 overs of probing leg-spin on a pitch offering plenty of bounce, but the Pakistanis paid the price for some poor batting down the order. Aamir Sohail and Ramiz Raja had started off at six an over, both scoring fifties and sharing an opening stand of 94, and after Ramiz strained his side Javed Miandad hit a brisk 33 off his old county. But the tourists slid from 205 for four to 230 all out.

Pakistanis

Aamir Sohail b Salisbury	54	Mushtaq Ahmed lbw b Pigott	2
Ramiz Raja retired hurt	53	Tanvir Mehdi run out	1
Inzamam-ul-Haq st Moores b Salisbury	15	Saleem Jaffer not out	0
Salim Malik b Robson	27	L-b 6, w 4	10
*Javed Miandad b North	33		
Zahid Fazal b Robson	1	1/94 2/140 3/164 (54.4 overs) 230	
Naved Anjum b Stephenson	34	4/169 5/205 6/205	
†Moin Khan b North	0	7/224 8/230 9/230	

Ramiz Raja retired hurt at 119.

Bowling: Stephenson 10.4–1–48–1; Robson 11–1–43–2; North 7–0–39–2; Salisbury 11–0–39–2; Pigott 10–1–34–1; Lenham 5–0–21–0.

Sussex

J. W. Hall c sub b Naved Anjum	21	J. A. North c sub b Tanvir Mehdi	0
D. M. Smith lbw b Mushtaq Ahmed	34	A. C. S. Pigott not out	5
N. J. Lenham b Naved Anjum	4	L-b 16, w 6, n-b 10	32
*A. P. Wells b Mushtaq Ahmed	4		
M. P. Speight c sub b Saleem Jaffer	57	1/45 2/53 3/66 (7 wkts, 51.3 overs) 233	
F. D. Stephenson c sub b Tanvir Mehdi	71	4/81 5/204	
†P. Moores not out	5	6/222 7/222	

I. D. K. Salisbury and A. G. Robson did not bat.

Bowling: Saleem Jaffer 11–1–57–1; Tanvir Mehdi 9–0–48–2; Naved Anjum 11–1–31–2; Mushtaq Ahmed 11–1–35–2; Aamir Sohail 7–0–35–0; Salim Malik 2.3–0–11–0.

Umpires: J. H. Harris and G. Sharp.

†SUSSEX v PAKISTANIS

At Hove, May 17. Pakistanis won by 85 runs. Toss: Pakistanis. The tourists avenged the previous day's defeat, rattling up a formidable 321 for two. After Stephenson bowled Aamir Sohail with his fifth ball Shoaib Mohammad and Inzamam-ul-Haq added 135, but the real fireworks came when Zahid Fazal joined Inzamam in an unbroken stand of 186 in 28 overs. Inzamam smashed five sixes in his 148-ball 157, made in sweltering heat. None of the bowlers escaped punishment, though Pigott maintained a steady line and length. A target of nearly six an over was far too much for Sussex, though Lenham hit a pleasant fifty, while Speight and Stephenson played well again. An awesome spell of 11 consecutive overs from Mushtaq Ahmed, who returned four for 35, was the county's undoing.

Pakistanis

Aamir Sohail b Stephenson	0
Shoaib Mohammad c Salisbury b Pigott	68
Inzamam-ul-Haq not out	157
Zahid Fazal not out	83
L-b 7, w 5, n-b 1	13

1/0 2/135 (2 wkts, 55 overs) 321

*Javed Miandad, Rashid Latif, Saleem Jaffer, Tanvir Mehdi, Mushtaq Ahmed, †Moin Khan and Naved Anjum did not bat.

Bowling: Stephenson 11–1–73–1; North 11–0–55–0; Donelan 6–0–37–0; Pigott 11–0–42–1; Salisbury 11–0–75–0; Greenfield 3–0–23–0; Lenham 2–0–9–0.

Sussex

N. J. Lenham run out	......	50
K. Greenfield c Moin Khan		
b Tanvir Mehdi	.	0
M. P. Speight c Rashid Latif		
b Shoaib Mohammad	.	43
*A. P. Wells c Rashid Latif		
b Mushtaq Ahmed	.	16
†P. Moores lbw b Mushtaq Ahmed	....	1
D. M. Smith b Mushtaq Ahmed	......	18
J. A. North c and b Shoaib Mohammad		6
F. D. Stephenson st Moin Khan		
b Aamir Sohail	.	47

A. C. S. Pigott c Zahid Fazal
           b Mushtaq Ahmed . ▮
B. T. P. Donelan not out............ 14▮
I. D. K. Salisbury c Naved Anjum
           b Zahid Fazal . 2▮

B 5, l-b 8, w 5, n-b 1 19

1/3 2/81 3/110   (54.1 overs) 23▮
4/111 5/116 6/133
7/174 8/183 9/202

Bowling: Naved Anjum 8–1–27–0; Tanvir Mehdi 6–2–13–1; Saleem Jaffer 11–1–44–0; Shoaib Mohammad 11–0–65–2; Mushtaq Ahmed 11–0–35–4; Aamir Sohail 6–0–34–1; Zahid Fazal 1.1–0–5–1.

Umpires: J. C. Balderstone and N. T. Plews.

†ENGLAND v PAKISTAN

First Texaco Trophy Match

At Lord's, May 20. England won by 79 runs. Toss: Pakistan. Eight weeks to the day afte▮ losing the World Cup final, England gained a measure of revenge by producing the kind o▮ efficient performance they had hoped for against Pakistan in Melbourne. It was Smith bitterly disappointed to be left out then, who claimed the top score and the match awar▮ after an uncertain start. Put in on a slow but true pitch, England quickly lost Gooch, bu▮ first Stewart, reclaiming the opener's role from Botham, and then Smith and Lamb compiled half-centuries to guarantee a commanding total. Stewart, in particular, neve▮ allowed leg-spinner Mushtaq Ahmed to dominate – as he had in Melbourne – and it wa▮ left to Wasim Akram to peg back the scoring-rate a little towards the end. Pakistan'▮ fielding was surprisingly sloppy and their batting, too, lacked conviction, save for a brie▮ early flurry from Salim Malik, which was ended in Botham's first over. Botham also held a bat-pad return catch to remove Inzamam-ul-Haq – the last of three wickets in the space o▮ 14 deliveries just before tea which left Pakistan 78 for five. The sequence effectively decided a contest producing record gate receipts for a day's cricket in England.

Man of the Match: R. A. Smith.   *Attendance:* 26,654; *receipts* £707,584.

England

*G. A. Gooch c Moin Khan		
b Aqib Javed	.	9
†A. J. Stewart c Asif Mujtaba		
b Naved Anjum	.	50
R. A. Smith c Moin Khan		
b Aqib Javed	.	85
A. J. Lamb c Javed Miandad		
b Naved Anjum	.	60
N. H. Fairbrother c Asif Mujtaba		
b Aqib Javed	.	25

G. A. Hick b Wasim Akram .... ▮
I. T. Botham not out............... 1▮
C. C. Lewis not out................ ▮

L-b 14, w 9, n-b 7.......... 3▮

1/20 (1) 2/115 (2)   (6 wkts, 55 overs) 27▮
3/213 (3) 4/238 (4)
5/250 (6) 6/265 (5)

D. R. Pringle, P. A. J. DeFreitas and R. K. Illingworth did not bat.

Bowling: Wasim Akram 11–0–39–1; Aqib Javed 11–0–54–3; Naved Anjum 11–0–48–2; Mushtaq Ahmed 11–0–56–0; Asif Mujtaba 11–0–67–0.

Pakistan

Aamir Sohail run out		36
Ramiz Raja c and b Pringle		0
Salim Malik c Stewart b Botham		24
*Javed Miandad c Hick b Pringle		7
Inzamam-ul-Haq c and b Botham		2
Asif Mujtaba c Smith b Hick		52
Wasim Akram st Stewart b Illingworth		34
Naved Anjum c Hick b Pringle		3
†Moin Khan c Stewart b Pringle		11
Mushtaq Ahmed not out		7
Aqib Javed b Hick		8
L-b 8, w 5, n-b 2		15
	(54.2 overs)	199

1/0 (2) 2/49 (3) 3/74 (4) 4/78 (1) 5/78 (5) 6/161 (7) 7/164 (8) 8/181 (6) 9/184 (9) 10/199 (11)

Bowling: DeFreitas 9-2-17-0; Pringle 11-1-42-4; Lewis 8-1-35-0; Botham 11-0-45-2; Illingworth 11-0-36-1; Hick 3.2-0-7-2; Fairbrother 1-0-9-0.

Umpires: B. J. Meyer and D. R. Shepherd. Referee: R. M. Cowper (Australia).

†ENGLAND v PAKISTAN

Second Texaco Trophy Match

At The Oval, May 22. England won by 39 runs. Toss: England. England took full advantage of a perfect pitch and the absence of both Wasim Akram (with a stress-fracture of the left shin) and Waqar Younis (back trouble) to run up a total of 302. Stewart, on his home ground, again revelled in opening, scoring his first one-day international century, in 140 balls with ten fours, while Fairbrother and Hick added 93 in just 11 overs. Even against a severely weakened attack, Stewart's innings was of the highest quality, establishing a platform which the later batsmen eagerly clambered aboard – none with more glee than Hick, whose unbeaten 71 took only 51 balls. Fairbrother persisted in his run-a-ball 63 even after pulling a hamstring and needing a runner. Pakistan's response at Lord's had been disappointing, but here they showed the defiance of world champions. Needing a flying start, Ramiz Raja and Aamir Sohail opened with 81 in 14 overs, and the chase continued above the required rate. When three wickets fell inside six overs for 30 runs, however, England could breathe a little easier. Botham then won a crucial lbw decision against Javed Miandad, and a magnificent contest was all over – bar the after-match shouting, with Miandad alleging Botham had uttered a swear word in his moment of triumph. Receipts from the first two games of this series topped £1 million.

Man of the Match: A. J. Stewart.   *Attendance:* 15,031; *receipts* £348,114.

England

*G. A. Gooch run out		25
†A. J. Stewart b Aqib Javed		103
R. A. Smith b Mushtaq Ahmed		7
A. J. Lamb st Moin Khan b Aamir Sohail		11
N. H. Fairbrother b Tanvir Mehdi		63
G. A. Hick not out		71
I. T. Botham not out		2
L-b 8, w 9, n-b 3		20
	(5 wkts, 55 overs)	302

1/71 (1) 2/81 (3) 3/108 (4) 4/202 (2) 5/295 (5)

C. C. Lewis, D. R. Pringle, P. A. J. DeFreitas and R. K. Illingworth did not bat.

Bowling: Aqib Javed 10-0-70-1; Naved Anjum 9-0-37-0; Tanvir Mehdi 11-0-72-1; Mushtaq Ahmed 11-0-47-1; Aamir Sohail 11-0-52-1; Asif Mujtaba 3-0-16-0.

Pakistan

Aamir Sohail b Illingworth		32
Ramiz Raja c sub (M. R. Ramprakash) b DeFreitas		86
Salim Malik b Pringle		26
Inzamam-ul-Haq lbw b Pringle		15
*Javed Miandad lbw b Botham		38
Asif Mujtaba lbw b Illingworth		29
Naved Anjum run out		6
†Moin Khan c and b Lewis		15
Mushtaq Ahmed c Illingworth b Lewis		8
Tanvir Mehdi b DeFreitas		0
Aqib Javed not out		0
L-b 4, w 3, n-b 1		8
	(50.5 overs)	263

1/81 (1) 2/144 (3) 3/148 (2) 4/174 (4) 5/220 (5) 6/232 (7) 7/249 (6) 8/263 (9) 9/263 (8) 10/263 (10)

Bowling: DeFreitas 10.5-0-59-2; Lewis 8-0-47-2; Botham 11-0-52-1; Illingworth 11-0-58-2; Pringle 9-1-35-2; Hick 1-0-8-0.

Umpires: M. J. Kitchen and R. Palmer. Referee: R. M. Cowper (Australia).

LEICESTERSHIRE v PAKISTANIS

At Leicester, May 23, 24, 25. Pakistanis won by eight wickets. Toss: Leicestershire. Seven of the side beaten in the previous day's one-day international helped to earn the tourists a third successive first-class win with 20 balls to spare. Once again Mushtaq Ahmed dominated the action; he came on inside the first hour, and claimed five victims, starting with Whitaker, who had added a grille to his helmet after fracturing his cheekbone at Chelmsford a fortnight earlier. Wicket-keeper Nixon was stranded one short of a maiden fifty. On a sweltering second day the Pakistanis established a lead of 137 against a modest attack, weakened further when strike bowler Millns was barred by umpire Dudleston for running on the pitch. Left-hander Asif Mujtaba hit 15 fours in his 95. Four county wickets went down before nightfall, including débutant Roseberry first ball. But the last day was dominated by Briers's 25th first-class century and Aamir Sohail's left-arm spin, which finally dismissed him after five and a half hours' defiance when he needed only two runs for 1,000 in all cricket in 1992. Sohail picked up another two wickets, but a knee injury kept him out of the chase for 133 in 35 overs. Inzamam-ul-Haq's second rapid fifty of the match provided the impetus for victory.

Close of play: First day, Pakistanis 87-1 (Ramiz Raja 43*, Shoaib Mohammad 19*); Second day, Leicestershire 84-4 (N. E. Briers 47*, L. Potter 0*).

Leicestershire

T. J. Boon c Zahid Fazal b Naved Anjum	13	– lbw b Naved Anjum	1
*N. E. Briers lbw b Saleem Jaffer	37	– lbw b Aamir Sohail	123
J. J. Whitaker b Mushtaq Ahmed	35	– c Inzamam-ul-Haq b Naved Anjum	21
A. Roseberry c Rashid Latif b Aamir Sohail	14	– c Rashid Latif b Naved Anjum	0
J. D. R. Benson b Mushtaq Ahmed	45	– c Inzamam-ul-Haq b Asif Mujtaba	7
L. Potter c Zahid Fazal b Aamir Sohail	0	– lbw b Mushtaq Ahmed	11
P. N. Hepworth lbw b Mushtaq Ahmed	38	– run out	4
†P. A. Nixon not out	49	– lbw b Aamir Sohail	29
R. P. Gofton c Rashid Latif b Mushtaq Ahmed	0	– not out	42
D. J. Millns lbw b Tanvir Mehdi	0	– c Tanvir Mehdi b Aamir Sohail	1
A. D. Mullally c Zahid Fazal b Mushtaq Ahmed	5	– b Asif Mujtaba	1
B 11, l-b 3, w 4, n-b 2	20	B 9, l-b 17, n-b 3	29

1/24 2/79 3/87 4/155 5/159   256   1/8 2/46 3/46 4/68 5/113   269
6/159 7/226 8/239 9/243   6/130 7/173 8/259 9/261

Bowling: *First Innings*—Naved Anjum 15-4-33-1; Tanvir Mehdi 17-3-56-1; Mushtaq Ahmed 20.1-2-49-5; Saleem Jaffer 9-1-48-1; Aamir Sohail 12-2-26-2; Shoaib Mohammad 4-1-13-0; Zahid Fazal 2-0-17-0. *Second Innings*—Naved Anjum 17-3-73-3; Tanvir Mehdi 10-4-31-0; Mushtaq Ahmed 43-20-72-1; Asif Mujtaba 22.5-8-36-2; Aamir Sohail 19-6-31-3.

Pakistanis

Aamir Sohail c Benson b Millns	24		
*Ramiz Raja c Briers b Gofton	65	– (1) c Whitaker b Mullally	29
Shoaib Mohammad c Potter b Mullally	25	– (2) b Millns	13
Inzamam-ul-Haq c Boon b Hepworth	57	– (3) not out	61
Zahid Fazal c Boon b Millns	26		
Asif Mujtaba c Millns b Mullally	95	– (4) not out	27
Naved Anjum c and b Benson	56		
†Rashid Latif c Gofton b Benson	16		
Mushtaq Ahmed not out	8		
B 6, l-b 13, w 2	21	L-b 3	3

1/38 2/121 3/123 4/200 5/227   (8 wkts dec.) 393   1/25 2/53   (2 wkts) 133
6/317 7/372 8/393

Tanvir Mehdi and Saleem Jaffer did not bat.

Bowling: *First Innings*—Millns 17.2–0–66–2; Mullally 23.2–4–80–2; Gofton 27–4–107–1;
otter 9–1–33–0; Hepworth 17–2–55–1; Benson 8.4–2–33–2. *Second Innings*—Millns
–0–32–1; Mullally 11–3–29–1; Gofton 8.4–1–38–0; Hepworth 5–0–31–0.

Umpires: B. Dudleston and J. H. Hampshire.

†ENGLAND AMATEUR XI v PAKISTANIS

t Luton, May 27, 28. Pakistanis won by an innings and 16 runs. Toss: Pakistanis. Against
team organised by the National Cricket Association, Waqar Younis, who returned after
is stress fracture, and the newly arrived Ata-ur-Rehman both staked their claims to be
onsidered for the more serious business ahead. Waqar bowled 12 overs in three spells, and
ismissed Roshier with the first ball of the second day. However, the most successful bowler
as slow left-armer Asif Mujtaba, with ten wickets. The Amateurs' only significant batting
ame from Roberts and Dean in the first innings – Dean hit 80 from 59 balls – and Folland,
nbeaten after two and a half hours, in the second. All 18 of their wickets (a broken finger
revented wicket-keeper Plimmer batting) were caught. On the first day three Pakistanis
cored hundreds. Shoaib Mohammad batted for four hours, but Javed Miandad hit 17 fours
n 108 balls before retiring at lunch, and Inzamam-ul-Haq 11 fours and a six from 96
eliveries.

Close of play: First day, England Amateur XI 141-5 (M. Hussain 3*, P. G. Roshier 1*).

Pakistanis

Asif Mujtaba run out	0	Zahid Fazal not out	7
Shoaib Mohammad not out	107	B 1, l-b 2, n-b 5	8
Javed Miandad retired	105		
Salim Malik b Hussain	3	1/1 2/158	(4 wkts dec.) 332
Inzamam-ul-Haq c Plimmer b Roshier	102	3/165 4/324	

Naved Anjum, †Moin Khan, Waqar Younis, Ata-ur-Rehman and Tanvir Mehdi did
not bat.

Bowling: Roshier 12–0–53–1; Hackett 14–3–40–0; French 12–1–48–0; Arnold 15–1–70–0;
vans 8–0–66–0; Hussain 9–0–52–1.

England Amateur XI

S. J. Dean c Zahid Fazal b Asif Mujtaba	80	– c Moin Khan b Ata-ur-Rehman . 4
A. J. Roberts c Naved Anjum b Salim Malik	45	– c Moin Khan b Naved Anjum . . 6
N. A. Folland c Zahid Fazal b Asif Mujtaba	3	– not out . 76
M. V. Patel c Javed Miandad b Asif Mujtaba	1	– c Shoaib Mohammad
		b Asif Mujtaba . 6
M. Hussain c Naved Anjum b Ata-ur-Rehman	20	– c Moin Khan b Ata-ur-Rehman . 10
N. French c Asif Mujtaba b Salim Malik	0	– c Tanvir Mehdi b Asif Mujtaba . 11
P. G. Roshier c Moin Khan b Waqar Younis	1	– c Ata-ur-Rehman b Asif Mujtaba 5
R. A. Evans c Inzamam-ul-Haq b Asif Mujtaba	6	– c Zahid Fazal b Asif Mujtaba . . 0
K. A. Arnold c sub b Asif Mujtaba	8	– c Tanvir Mehdi b Salim Malik . . 0
N. P. Hackett not out	0	– c Moin Khan b Asif Mujtaba . . 0
·G. Plimmer absent injured		– absent injured
L-b 2, w 1, n-b 7	10	B 4, l-b 12, w 1, n-b 7 . . . 24

/118 2/124 3/127 4/139 5/139	174	1/13 2/17 3/33 4/69 5/97 142
/141 7/158 8/165 9/174		6/107 7/107 8/116 9/142

Bowling: *First Innings*—Waqar Younis 9–3–16–1; Ata-ur-Rehman 7–0–55–1; Naved Anjum 4–0–39–0; Tanvir Mehdi 1–0–20–0; Asif Mujtaba 14.5–10–22–5; Salim Malik 8–2–20–2. *Second Innings*—Ata-ur-Rehman 11–1–35–2; Naved Anjum 8–2–17–1; Asif Mujtaba 11.5–3–25–5; Salim Malik 5–1–30–1; Waqar Younis 3–1–6–0; Tanvir Mehdi 5–1–13–0.

Umpires: D. O. Oslear and G. A. Stickley.

MIDDLESEX v PAKISTANIS

At Lord's, May 30, 31, June 1. Drawn. Toss: Middlesex. Rain stopped the Pakistanis pressing for a fourth first-class win, preventing play before 2.15 on the first day and allowing only 38 balls on the last. In between, their batsmen found conditions very easy, Ramiz Raja and Shoaib Mohammad began by battering some wayward bowling with 60 in nine overs before Ramiz retired with a back strain. Asif Mujtaba went on to a hundred on the second morning. In all he faced 292 balls, and hit 15 fours and a six. Roseberry scored exactly half the Middlesex runs, striking 12 fours in his unbeaten 111, but the tourists' bowlers were generally in control. Mushtaq Ahmed spun industriously, and Waqar Younis, with two convincing spells, had his first serious bowl for nearly five months, to prove his fitness for the imminent First Test.

Close of play: First day, Pakistanis 234-2 (Asif Mujtaba 89*, Salim Malik 37*); Second day, Middlesex 222-8 (M. A. Roseberry 111*, C. W. Taylor 11*).

Pakistanis

Ramiz Raja retired hurt	37		
Shoaib Mohammad c Ramprakash b Taylor	43	– not out	
Asif Mujtaba lbw b Weekes	123		
*Javed Miandad c Roseberry b Carr	14		
Salim Malik c Carr b Fraser	68		
Zahid Fazal not out	21	– (1) not out	
†Moin Khan not out	2		
L-b 7, n-b 12	19	L-b 1	

1/125 2/167 3/292 4/317 (4 wkts dec.) 327 (no wkt)

Waqar Younis, Mushtaq Ahmed, Aqib Javed and Ata-ur-Rehman did not bat.

In the first innings Ramiz Raja retired hurt at 60.

Bowling: *First Innings*—Taylor 8–0–37–1; Headley 23–5–105–0; Fraser 23–7–39–1; Sylvester 15–4–45–0; Carr 6–3–15–1; Weekes 29–8–79–1; Roseberry 1–1–0–0. *Second Innings*—Fraser 3.2–0–4–0; Gatting 3–3–0–0.

Middlesex

J. D. Carr lbw b Aqib Javed	21	A. R. C. Fraser c Javed Miandad		
M. A. Roseberry not out	111		b Mushtaq Ahmed .	2
†K. R. Brown lbw b Aqib Javed	2	C. W. Taylor not out		1
M. R. Ramprakash lbw b Waqar Younis	17			
*M. W. Gatting lbw b Mushtaq Ahmed	20	B 2, n-b 7		
P. N. Weekes c Moin Khan				
b Mushtaq Ahmed .	1	1/62 2/66 3/110	(8 wkts dec.) 22	
R. J. Sims run out	3	4/159 5/164 6/171		
D. W. Headley b Mushtaq Ahmed	0	7/178 8/208		

S. A. Sylvester did not bat.

Bowling: Waqar Younis 11–3–27–1; Aqib Javed 14–0–62–2; Ata-ur-Rehman 9–2–14–0; Mushtaq Ahmed 22–1–73–4; Asif Mujtaba 12–2–44–0.

Umpires: B. Dudleston and G. Sharp.

ENGLAND v PAKISTAN

First Cornhill Test

At Birmingham, June 4, 5, 6, 7, 8. Drawn. Toss: England. The game was a disappointing start to a series which promised so much, but not one without its controversy, emotion and memorable moments of cricket. The opening two days were saturated by rain, and the last three drowned in runs as England and Pakistan warily squared up, threw a couple of jabs and then retreated with honours even.

The central story of the Edgbaston Test unfurled before a ball had been bowled. Of the successful England side which finished the series in New Zealand, Tufnell, Lawrence and Reeve were all recovering from injury or illness. Without the muscle of Lawrence or the guile of Tufnell, the bowling attack looked frighteningly bland, so England's squad included the uncapped pair, Munton and Salisbury, and Ramprakash, who was recalled to bolster the batting. Attention focused on Salisbury. The 22-year-old Sussex player was poised to become England's first specialist leg-spinner since Robin Hobbs in 1971. On the eve of the Test, Gooch inspected the newly laid, untried Edgbaston pitch and announced that Salisbury would play. On Thursday morning, less than half an hour before he would have handed in his team-sheet, the rain arrived. By the time play was possible mid-way through the second day, Gooch, wary of dampness in the pitch and the atmosphere, had to tell Salisbury the team had been revised; England were playing safe with the extra batsman, Ramprakash.

Salisbury's omission was a bad decision, as Gooch later conceded. When play did start on Friday the conditions counted for nothing. Gooch put Pakistan in, but only two deliveries were possible and three runs scored before the umpires offered the light. On Thursday, refunds were offered to 8,500 ticket-holders, but on Friday there was no compensation for 15,000, under the Test and County Cricket Board's rules, because there had been play – however brief. Angry supporters, who had paid up to £26, gathered outside the pavilion while officials were ushered out of a side door. The Board's offer to Friday's ticket-holders of free entry on the last day of a match already doomed did nothing to mollify the protesters. (Later in the year, a Small Claims Court said the Board had been unfair to people who could not have read the conditions on the tickets before they bought them.)

The remaining three days became little more than high-class batting practice on a soulless wicket; 902 runs were scored while 11 wickets fell, as frustrated bowlers ran in with no hope and little heart. In contrast to England, Pakistan introduced three new caps: fluent left-handed opener Aamir Sohail, Inzamam-ul-Haq, the powerfully built and exciting middle-order batsman, and Ata-ur-Rehman, a teenage pace bowler of much promise, who had been summoned from Pakistan as cover for the injured Wasim Akram. But it was the old firm of Javed Miandad and Salim Malik who dominated the innings and the English bowlers. Together they scored 322, a record for any wicket between the countries. DeFreitas had given England false hope by reducing Pakistan to 110 for three shortly after lunch, but Miandad and Malik soon brought home reality. Malik batted with his usual calm and grace for his highest score in Tests, while Miandad played the artful dodger and pocketed runs at will to reach his 23rd Test century. When 14 he overtook G. Boycott as Test cricket's fourth most prolific run-scorer. Gooch tried seven bowlers but his only alternative to seam was Hick's steady off-spin. The cause was not aided by a spate of dropped chances.

With the first day washed out, the follow-on margin was reduced from 200 runs to 150, and Miandad's declaration at 446 for four left England needing 297 to avoid any embarrassment. They achieved their target comfortably and in some style. Pakistan, also employing seven bowlers, had more variety, but no one could coax life from such a pitch. Stewart took greatest advantage. Having established himself as Gooch's new opening partner on the winter tour, he opened the series with his most convincing Test innings to date. With sublime timing he hit 31 boundaries in 190, his fourth century in his last five Tests, and by far his largest. When he was third out, after nine minutes under six hours, England were already safe. Smith, who had added 227 with Stewart, pushed on to his seventh Test century – all scored in England – but no other batsman really seized his chance. Hick played well for his maiden fifty in his eighth Test, but missed out on the big score which would have eased his nerves; Ramprakash, also in need of runs, fell second ball to Rehman, who had evidently not been told the game was dead and still tore in enthusiastically, as if it could somehow be transformed. He was rewarded with three wickets in five overs before a thunderstorm brought an end. The Test was the first in England to have a referee to support the umpires: happily, former Australian batsman Bob Cowper had little to do except stay awake. – Colin Bateman.

Man of the Match: A. J. Stewart.   *Attendance:* 51,377; *receipts* £766,668.

Close of play: First day, No play; Second day, Pakistan 3-0 (Aamir Sohail 3*, Rami Raja 0*); Third day, Pakistan 290-3 (Javed Miandad 99*, Salim Malik 80*); Fourth day England 170-2 (A. J. Stewart 94*, R. A. Smith 10*).

Pakistan

Aamir Sohail c Stewart b DeFreitas	... 18	Inzamam-ul-Haq not out	
Ramiz Raja lbw b DeFreitas	 47	B 2, l-b 5, n-b 19............	2
Asif Mujtaba c Russell b DeFreitas	 29		
*Javed Miandad not out	153	1/33 (1) 2/96 (3)	(4 wkts dec.) 44
Salim Malik lbw b DeFreitas	165	3/110 (2) 4/432 (5)	

†Moin Khan, Mushtaq Ahmed, Waqar Younis, Aqib Javed and Ata-ur-Rehman did no bat.

Bowling: DeFreitas 33–6–121–4; Lewis 33–3–116–0; Pringle 28–2–92–0; Botham 19–6–52–0; Hick 13–1–46–0; Gooch 10–5–9–0; Ramprakash 1–0–3–0.

England

*G. A. Gooch c Asif Mujtaba		C. C. Lewis b Mushtaq Ahmed	 2
	b Aqib Javed . 8	†R. C. Russell not out	 2
A. J. Stewart c Salim Malik		D. R. Pringle not out	....
	b Ata-ur-Rehman .190		
G. A. Hick c Javed Miandad			
	b Waqar Younis . 51	B 5, l-b 5, w 1, n-b 7	 1
R. A. Smith lbw b Mushtaq Ahmed	...127		
M. R. Ramprakash c Moin Khan		1/28 (1) 2/121 (3)	(7 wkts dec.) 45
	b Ata-ur-Rehman . 0	3/348 (2) 4/348 (5)	
A. J. Lamb c Javed Miandad		5/378 (6) 6/415 (7)	
	b Ata-ur-Rehman . 12	7/446 (4)	

I. T. Botham and P. A. J. DeFreitas did not bat.

Bowling: Waqar Younis 24–2–96–1; Aqib Javed 16–3–86–1; Mushtaq Ahmed 50–8–156–2; Ata-ur-Rehman 18–5–69–3; Asif Mujtaba 8–1–29–0; Aamir Sohail 2–0–8–0 Salim Malik 1–0–5–0.

Umpires: M. J. Kitchen and B. J. Meyer. Referee: R. M. Cowper (Australia).

NOTTINGHAMSHIRE v PAKISTANIS

At Nottingham, June 10, 11, 12. Pakistanis won by eight wickets. Toss: Pakistanis. Wasim Akram, who had missed the First Test with a stress fracture of the shin, underlined hi return to fitness by claiming four victims in 9.2 overs without conceding a single run. Thi devastating spell, achieved off a seven-pace run-up, followed the change of the ball, wit the batsmen's consent, after it went out of shape. Evans spearheaded Nottinghamshire fightback as they restricted the Pakistanis to a first-innings lead of 47, and that was largel due to a sparkling 53 from Inzamam-ul-Haq. As wickets continued to tumble and Rashi Latif advanced to eight catches in the match, Johnson launched a furious assault on th bowling; all but four of his 60 runs, made off just 50 deliveries, came in boundaries. Th same approach proved rewarding for Lewis, leaving the Pakistanis with a target of 166 an more than a day to achieve it. Half-centuries from Aamir Sohail and Shoaib Mohamma ensured that there was no upset, and victory before lunch sealed a happy match for Wasim who had captained the team for the first time.

Close of play: First day, Pakistanis 155-7 (Inzamam-ul-Haq 53*, Tanvir Mehdi 4*) Second day, Pakistanis 93-1 (Shoaib Mohammad 23*, Asif Mujtaba 3*).

Nottinghamshire

B. C. Broad lbw b Wasim Akram	21	– c Ata-ur-Rehman	
		b Tanvir Mehdi .	19
M. A. Crawley c Zahid Fazal b Ata-ur-Rehman	9	– c Rashid Latif b Aqib Javed ...	2
*R. T. Robinson c Inzamam-ul-Haq			
		b Naved Anjum .	22 – c Rashid Latif b Ata-ur-Rehman	15
P. Johnson c Rashid Latif b Naved Anjum	6	– lbw b Wasim Akram	60
D. W. Randall c Rashid Latif b Tanvir Mehdi	14	– c Rashid Latif b Tanvir Mehdi .	3
C. C. Lewis c Rashid Latif b Wasim Akram	12	– c Asif Mujtaba b Aqib Javed ..	47
K. P. Evans lbw b Wasim Akram	8	– lbw b Aqib Javed	11
†B. N. French not out	11	– c Inzamam-ul-Haq b Aqib Javed	3
R. A. Pick c Rashid Latif b Tanvir Mehdi	0	– c Rashid Latif b Wasim Akram .	28
K. E. Cooper b Tanvir Mehdi	0	– (11) b Naved Anjum	2
M. A. Afford c Aqib Javed b Wasim Akram	2	– (10) not out	7
W 1, n-b 10	11	B 1, l-b 3, w 3, n-b 8	15

1/30 2/52 3/60 4/76 5/84   116   1/2 2/38 3/69 4/93 5/117   212
6/96 7/104 8/105 9/105   6/147 7/152 8/177 9/209

Bowling: *First Innings*—Wasim Akram 13.2–9–9–4; Aqib Javed 9–2–25–0; Ata-ur-Rehman 7–0–33–1; Naved Anjum 6–0–25–2; Tanvir Mehdi 8–1–24–3. *Second Innings*—Wasim Akram 14–8–24–2; Aqib Javed 15–0–51–4; Ata-ur-Rehman 8–2–24–1; Naved Anjum 9.3–2–59–1; Tanvir Mehdi 11–3–50–2.

Pakistanis

Aamir Sohail c French b Cooper	47	– c French b Afford	58
Shoaib Mohammad c Broad b Pick	16	– not out	50
Asif Mujtaba c French b Evans	8	– c French b Evans	33
Inzamam-ul-Haq c Johnson b Pick	53		
Zahid Fazal lbw b Cooper	0	– (4) not out	9
*Wasim Akram run out	8		
Naved Anjum b Evans	4		
†Rashid Latif c Crawley b Pick	8		
Tanvir Mehdi c French b Evans	8		
Aqib Javed c Broad b Evans	3		
Ata-ur-Rehman not out	1		
W 2, n-b 5	7	B 4, l-b 5, w 2, n-b 6	17

1/35 2/72 3/74 4/78 5/87   163   1/90 2/144   (2 wkts) 167
6/91 7/142 8/159 9/162

Bowling: *First Innings*—Lewis 7–2–31–0; Pick 16–4–56–3; Evans 21.5–4–54–4; Cooper 12–6–22–2. *Second Innings*—Lewis 12–2–43–0; Pick 4–0–22–0; Evans 15–5–36–1; Afford 14–2–36–1; Crawley 6–1–21–0; Randall 0.2–0–0–0.

Umpires: G. I. Burgess and R. A. White.

NORTHAMPTONSHIRE v PAKISTANIS

At Northampton, June 13, 14, 15. Pakistanis won by seven wickets. Toss: Pakistanis. The Pakistanis completed another comfortable victory over county opposition shortly after lunch on the third day, beating Northamptonshire for the first time in seven attempts. Wasim Akram warmed up for the Second Test with a match return of ten for 117. When Northamptonshire's second innings stood at 90 for seven, still four runs behind, the tourists looked likely to earn themselves a day off; but Ripley and Roberts halted the slide with an eighth-wicket partnership of 80 in 18 overs. Otherwise, the Pakistanis were in charge throughout, overcoming resistance from Bailey and Lamb to dismiss the home side for an inadequate total on the first day, and batting with commendable urgency to secure a lead of 94. Ramiz Raja, Salim Malik and Inzamam-ul-Haq all struck the ball handsomely, Ramiz hitting eight fours in his 55, and Wasim's demolition of Northamptonshire's middle order made the result a formality.

Close of play: First day, Pakistanis 134-3 (Shoaib Mohammad 19*, Salim Malik 6*); Second day, Northamptonshire 213.

Northamptonshire

	First Innings		Second Innings	
A. Fordham	c Aamir Sohail b Wasim Akram ..	2	– lbw b Waqar Younis	15
N. A. Felton	c Moin Khan b Wasim Akram ...	0	– c Moin Khan b Waqar Younis..	1
R. J. Bailey	c Ramiz Raja b Aqib Javed	51	– lbw b Wasim Akram	7
*A. J. Lamb	b Aqib Javed	38	– lbw b Wasim Akram	18
D. J. Capel	c Moin Khan b Aqib Javed	4	– lbw b Wasim Akram	0
K. M. Curran	lbw b Wasim Akram	19	– b Ata-ur-Rehman	26
A. L. Penberthy	c Salim Malik b Wasim Akram	8	– b Wasim Akram	9
†D. Ripley	not out	45	– c sub b Ata-ur-Rehman	64
A. R. Roberts	b Waqar Younis	4	– c Shoaib Mohammad b Aqib Javed.	41
J. P. Taylor	b Wasim Akram	7	– c Moin Khan b Wasim Akram..	1
N. G. B. Cook	c Inzamam-ul-Haq b Ata-ur-Rehman.	4	– not out.	6
	W 1, n-b 10	11	B 5, l-b 1, w 6, n-b 13 ...	25

1/2 2/5 3/81 4/89 5/106 193 1/6 2/14 3/43 4/43 5/47 213
6/128 7/133 8/138 9/163   6/78 7/90 8/170 9/190

Bowling: *First Innings*—Wasim Akram 15–4–43–5; Waqar Younis 14–1–54–1; Ata-ur-Rehman 6.3–0–45–1; Aqib Javed 13–3–45–3; Asif Mujtaba 1–1–6–0. *Second Innings*—Wasim Akram 22–2–74–5; Waqar Younis 12–2–52–2; Ata-ur-Rehman 7.2–2–37–2; Aqib Javed 13–6–25–1; Aamir Sohail 6–1–9–0; Shoaib Mohammad 2–0–10–0.

Pakistanis

	First Innings		Second Innings	
Aamir Sohail	c Capel b Cook	34	– c Bailey b Roberts	33
Ramiz Raja	c Ripley b Cook	55	– c Bailey b Cook	26
Asif Mujtaba	c and b Penberthy	20	– not out	39
Shoaib Mohammad	c Curran b Roberts	59	– c Lamb b Cook	18
*Salim Malik	c Ripley b Penberthy	45		
Wasim Akram	c Fordham b Penberthy........	9		
Inzamam-ul-Haq	lbw b Curran.............	33	– (5) not out................	4
†Moin Khan	c Fordham b Curran.........	6		
Waqar Younis	not out	19		
Aqib Javed	not out	2		
	B 2, l-b 3	5	B 1, l-b 1	2

1/81 2/92 3/122 4/194 5/208 (8 wkts dec.) 287 1/49 2/73 3/118 (3 wkts) 122
6/260 7/262 8/275

Ata-ur-Rehman did not bat.

Bowling: *First Innings*—Taylor 11–1–70–0; Capel 6–1–33–0; Cook 22–4–68–2; Curran 11–1–41–2; Penberthy 14–6–34–3; Roberts 10–1–36–1. *Second Innings*—Curran 5–0–17–0; Taylor 7–1–25–0; Cook 18–7–40–2; Roberts 15–4–38–1.

Umpires: K. E. Palmer and P. B. Wight.

ENGLAND v PAKISTAN

Second Cornhill Test

At Lord's, June 18, 19, 20, 21. Pakistan won by two wickets. Toss: England. Wasim Akram drove Salisbury through the covers at 6.40 on Sunday evening to give Pakistan a one-match lead in the series and conclude an astonishing day of Test cricket. Seventeen wickets tumbled and the close-to-capacity crowd could be forgiven for thinking this was a one-day final. Pakistan saw near-certain victory evaporate into near-certain defeat before Wasim and Waqar Younis – as a batting partnership for once – defied England's depleted and tiring attack for the final nerve-racking hour. That last boundary ended England's brave fightback, and provoked some of the most emotional scenes ever seen at Lord's as the Pakistan touring party raced on to the playing surface in celebration.

Wasim's elegant drive also saved the Test and County Cricket Board from facing the wrath of a frustrated crowd for the second successive Test. Had Salisbury bowled a maiden, proceedings for the day would have been concluded. The battle would have resumed on Monday morning with England needing two wickets to tie the Test and Pakistan wanting one run to win. In fact, it would not have been the TCCB's fault: the Pakistanis had rejected the customary provision for an extra half-hour before the tour began. It was not a great Test match, but Sunday was a great Test day, and it would have been dreadful if this ding-dong battle had not been resolved there and then because of a technicality.

The influence of Pakistan's heroes, Wasim and Waqar – with ball and bat – was all the more remarkable because there were serious doubts over both a few weeks earlier. Wasim missed the First Test because of shin trouble, while Waqar used Edgbaston for little more than a trial run after the stress fracture which kept him out of the World Cup. Less than a fortnight later, they put Pakistan in command of this Test with 13 wickets, and then held their bats and their nerves for a famous victory. Wasim had proved his fitness by taking 16 wickets in the conclusive victories over Nottinghamshire and Northamptonshire between the Tests. His return in place of Ata-ur-Rehman was Pakistan's only change from Edgbaston. England's bowling had been much criticised for its lack of variety, but their only alteration to the 13-man squad was Malcolm for Ramprakash. Malcolm had been out of the side, after playing 17 consecutive Tests, since the Lord's Test a year before, and was selected after England team manager Micky Stewart spent two days watching him at Harrogate, where he failed to add to his season's tally of 12 first-class wickets. Stewart and Gooch were passed fit after minor worries, as was Botham who was troubled by a groin strain. England left out Munton, again, and Pringle, allowing Salisbury, England's first specialist leg-spinner for 21 years, to make his début a fortnight later than expected. Gooch won the toss, and with Stewart put on 123 for the first wicket at almost a run a minute as Pakistan failed to utilise the new ball, the overcast conditions and poor light. The England captain passed W. R. Hammond's Test aggregate of 7,249 runs when he reached 53, and looked in no trouble until he edged Wasim onto his stumps. But England lost their way from the moment Hick lobbed an ambitious pull to mid-on. Smith became Wasim's 150th Test victim and Stewart was removed in the last over before tea, after which Waqar cleaned up with a devastating spell of four for 17 in 40 deliveries. Waqar showed no signs of his recent back problem as he claimed his eighth five-wicket haul in his 16th Test, but England contributed to their own downfall. Several were guilty of loose shots and only Russell offered any sensible resistance at the end.

Pakistan's first innings stretched past tea on Saturday, mainly because the second and third sessions on Friday were wiped out by rain. They faced only five overs from Botham, all on Saturday, after he aggravated his groin by slipping over on Thursday night. It did not prevent him catching Javed Miandad at first slip, to give Salisbury his first Test wicket, and following up with a brilliant diving catch to remove Moin Khan and equal M. C. Cowdrey's England record of 120 Test catches. But England's hero on Saturday was Malcolm. Pakistan were well set at 228 for three when he halted their charge by removing Asif Mujtaba, Inzamam-ul-Haq and Salim Malik in 13 balls. England did well to restrict Pakistan to a lead of 38. They pulled in front in the 18 overs negotiated on Saturday night, though Gooch was a casualty. Night-watchman Salisbury proved a stubborn obstacle on Sunday morning for half an hour; but his fellow leg-spinner, Mushtaq Ahmed, instigated England's collapse, dismissing Hick, Smith and Lamb in 22 deliveries. Any hope of setting Pakistan a stiff target was destroyed by Wasim, who took the final three wickets in four deliveries. Stewart, alone, stood defiant. He became the sixth Englishman to carry his bat in a Test, and the first at Lord's. It was a responsible and mature innings, confirming his recent progress.

The day's events had already been dramatic, but the climactic act was about to unfold. Pakistan needed 138 for victory, with nine hours remaining. They were soon 18 for three, as Lewis found the edge of the bats of Ramiz Raja, Asif Mujtaba and Miandad, all for ducks, in a high-quality spell. And when Salisbury had Malik caught with his fifth delivery, England had the sniff of victory. Gooch had two problems however. Botham, still troubled by his groin, had been hit on the toe, and DeFreitas had strained his groin, too; neither could bowl. But Salisbury refused to be overawed by the occasion and, with the help of a foolish run-out and another neat catch by Hick at second slip off Malcolm, Pakistan were reduced to 95 for eight. But the injuries told against England. Gooch had no one to administer the *coup de grâce*; Lewis, who had bowled his best spell in Test cricket, was running on empty. What England's captain needed was an over from Wasim or Waqar. But they were batting for the other side and, slowly but surely, they took Pakistan to victory. Rarely can a Test crowd have been through so many emotions in a single day's play.

England's players were fined £330 each by referee Bob Cowper for their slow over-rate; it could have been £1,210, more than half their match fee, had he not allowed for interruptions and the long walk from the Lord's dressing-rooms to the pitch. During the match, Cornhill announced an extension to their sponsorship of English Test cricket paying £3.2 million for the privilege in 1993 and 1994. But, like the lucky 26,000 spectators, Cornhill will never get better value for their money than they did on this Sunday at Lord's. – David Norrie.

Man of the Match: Wasim Akram.   *Attendance:* 96,576; *receipts* £1,797,204.

Close of play: First day, Pakistan 31-0 (Aamir Sohail 10*, Ramiz Raja 20*); Second day Pakistan 123-1 (Aamir Sohail 73*, Asif Mujtaba 22*); Third day, England 52-1 (A. J. Stewart 21*, I. D. K. Salisbury 1*).

England

*G. A. Gooch b Wasim Akram	69	– lbw b Aqib Javed	13
A. J. Stewart c Javed Miandad b Asif Mujtaba	74	– not out	69
G. A. Hick c Javed Miandad b Waqar Younis	13	– (4) c Moin Khan b Mushtaq Ahmed	11
R. A. Smith c sub (Rashid Latif) b Wasim Akram	9	– (5) b Mushtaq Ahmed	8
A. J. Lamb b Waqar Younis	30	– (6) lbw b Mushtaq Ahmed	12
I. T. Botham b Waqar Younis	2	– (7) lbw b Waqar Younis	6
C. C. Lewis lbw b Waqar Younis	2	– (8) b Waqar Younis	15
†R. C. Russell not out	22	– (9) b Wasim Akram	1
P. A. J. DeFreitas c Inzamam-ul-Haq b Waqar Younis	3	– (10) c Inzamam-ul-Haq b Wasim Akram	0
I. D. K. Salisbury hit wkt b Mushtaq Ahmed	4	– (3) lbw b Wasim Akram	12
D. E. Malcolm lbw b Mushtaq Ahmed	0	– b Wasim Akram	0
B 6, l-b 12, n-b 9	27	B 5, l-b 8, n-b 15	28
	255		**175**

1/123 (1) 2/153 (3) 3/172 (4) 4/197 (2)   255
5/213 (6) 6/221 (7) 7/232 (5) 8/242 (9)
9/247 (10) 10/255 (11)

1/40 (1) 2/73 (3) 3/108 (4)   175
4/120 (5) 5/137 (6) 6/148 (7)
7/174 (8) 8/175 (9)
9/175 (10) 10/175 (11)

Bowling: *First Innings*—Wasim Akram 19.5-5-49-2; Aqib Javed 14-3-40-0; Waqar Younis 21-4-91-5; Mushtaq Ahmed 19.1-5-57-2; Asif Mujtaba 3-3-0-1. *Second Innings*—Wasim Akram 17.4-2-66-4; Aqib Javed 12-3-23-1; Waqar Younis 13-3-40-2; Mushtaq Ahmed 9-1-32-3; Asif Mujtaba 1-0-1-0.

Pakistan

Aamir Sohail c Russell b DeFreitas	73	– b Salisbury	39
Ramiz Raja b Lewis	24	– c Hick b Lewis	0
Asif Mujtaba c Smith b Malcolm	59	– c Russell b Lewis	0
*Javed Miandad c Botham b Salisbury	9	– c Russell b Lewis	0
Salim Malik c Smith b Malcolm	55	– c Lewis b Salisbury	12
Inzamam-ul-Haq c and b Malcolm	0	– run out	8
Wasim Akram b Salisbury	24	– not out	45
†Moin Khan c Botham b DeFreitas	12	– c Smith b Salisbury	3
Mushtaq Ahmed c Russell b DeFreitas	4	– c Hick b Malcolm	5
Waqar Younis b Malcolm	14	– not out	20
Aqib Javed not out	5		
B 4, l-b 3, n-b 7	14	B 2, l-b 5, w 1, n-b 1	9
	293		**141**

1/43 (2) 2/123 (1) 3/143 (4) 4/228 (3)   293
5/228 (6) 6/235 (5) 7/263 (7) 8/271 (8)
9/276 (9) 10/293 (10)

1/6 (2) 2/10 (3)   (8 wkts) 141
3/18 (4) 4/41 (5)
5/62 (6) 6/68 (1)
7/81 (8) 8/95 (9)

Bowling: *First Innings*—DeFreitas 26-8-58-3; Malcolm 15.5-1-70-4; Lewis 29-7-76-1; Salisbury 23-3-73-2; Botham 5-2-9-0. *Second Innings*—Malcolm 15-2-42-1; Lewis 16-3-43-3; Salisbury 14.1-0-49-3.

Umpires: B. Dudleston and J. H. Hampshire. Referee: R. M. Cowper (Australia).

OXFORD & CAMBRIDGE UNIVERSITIES v PAKISTANIS

At Cambridge, June 24, 25, 26. Pakistanis won by nine wickets. Toss: Oxford & Cambridge Universities. The opening day was dominated by the Pakistani batsmen, and most of all by Inzamam-ul-Haq. He scored his unbeaten 200 from only 188 balls in 203 minutes, hitting 21 fours and four sixes, and adding 160 in 28 overs with Zahid Fazal, to enable the tourists to declare at 446 for five after just 92.4 overs. Cambridge captain Crawley held the students' first innings together, scoring 70 out of 164. He was the only batsman to combat the leg-spinning skills of Mushtaq Ahmed, who took five for 56 to make the Universities follow on 282 behind. Their second innings was a far worthier effort, lasting nearly seven hours and 123 overs. Oxford's Australian pair, Gallian, on his 21st birthday, and Lovell, with an injured hand, batted with great determination. Both fell in sight of what would have been deserved centuries, but their efforts enabled the Universities to avoid an innings defeat.

Close of play: First day, Oxford & Cambridge Universities 28-3 (J. P. Crawley 12*, M. P. W. Jeh 0*); Second day, Oxford & Cambridge Universities 215-3 (G. B. T. Lovell 68*, A. M. Hooper 17*).

Pakistanis

Aamir Sohail run out	43	– c Arscott b Jeh	0
*Shoaib Mohammad c Crawley b Wight	56	– not out	22
Asif Mujtaba b Jeh	48	– not out	24
Inzamam-ul-Haq not out	200		
Zahid Fazal c and b Gallian	51		
Moin Khan c Lovell b Hooper	22		
†Rashid Latif not out	2		
B 8, l-b 2, w 6, n-b 8	24		

1/52 2/144 3/179 4/339 5/399   (5 wkts dec.) 446   1/0   (1 wkt) 46

Ata-ur-Rehman, Mushtaq Ahmed, Tanvir Mehdi and Saleem Jaffer did not bat.

Bowling: *First Innings*—Wood 10–0–72–0; Jeh 17–1–90–1; Pearson 29–5–120–0; Gallian 15–2–58–1; Wight 18–3–71–1; Hooper 3.4–0–25–1. *Second Innings*—Jeh 4–0–20–1; Wood 4–0–26–0.

Oxford & Cambridge Universities

R. R. Montgomerie lbw b Saleem Jaffer	8	– c Inzamam-ul-Haq b Asif Mujtaba	22
J. E. R. Gallian b Ata-ur-Rehman	5	– b Asif Mujtaba	89
*J. P. Crawley c Inzamam-ul-Haq b Aamir Sohail	70	– c Inzamam-ul-Haq b Ata-ur-Rehman	6
G. B. T. Lovell lbw b Mushtaq Ahmed	2	– c Moin Khan b Mushtaq Ahmed	96
M. P. W. Jeh c Shoaib Mohammad b Mushtaq Ahmed	23	– (9) lbw b Mushtaq Ahmed	7
A. M. Hooper run out	6	– (5) c Zahid Fazal b Mushtaq Ahmed	19
C. L. Keey b Mushtaq Ahmed	10	– (6) c Aamir Sohail b Tanvir Mehdi	27
R. M. Wight b Aamir Sohail	1	– (7) not out	21
†J. P. Arscott not out	14	– (8) b Mushtaq Ahmed	9
R. M. Pearson b Mushtaq Ahmed	0	– c Zahid Fazal b Asif Mujtaba	8
B. S. Wood c Ata-ur-Rehman b Mushtaq Ahmed	13	– c Moin Khan b Asif Mujtaba	0
B 5, l-b 2, w 1, n-b 4	12	B 4, l-b 10, n-b 9	23

1/14 2/14 3/26 4/88 5/95   164   1/52 2/89 3/164 4/220 5/264   327
6/128 7/132 8/133 9/140   6/282 7/292 8/310 9/327

Bowling: *First Innings*: Saleem Jaffer 10–3–40–1; Ata-ur-Rehman 10–2–30–1; Mushtaq Ahmed 19.5–4–56–5; Aamir Sohail 7–4–6–2; Asif Mujtaba 8–3–17–0; Shoaib Mohammad 2–1–8–0. *Second Innings*—Ata-ur-Rehman 17–4–47–1; Tanvir Mehdi 15–2–51–1; Inzamam-ul-Haq 1–0–8–0; Aamir Sohail 16–7–30–0; Mushtaq Ahmed 42–15–91–4; Asif Mujtaba 27–4–73–4; Shoaib Mohammad 5–2–13–0.

Umpires: H. D. Bird and N. T. Plews (G. J. Saville deputised for H. D. Bird on 2nd day).

HAMPSHIRE v PAKISTANIS

At Southampton, June 27, 28, 29. Pakistanis won by an innings and 14 runs. Toss: Pakistanis. A match otherwise memorable for the batting of Asif Mujtaba and Javed Miandad was soured by an ugly incident when Nicholas, the Hampshire captain, was given out to a short-leg catch off Mushtaq Ahmed for 18. Umpire Tolchard was unsighted and had asked for confirmation from his colleague Palmer at square leg. Nicholas took his time to leave, then stopped to discuss the matter with Palmer. He was then reinstated, to the fury of the Pakistanis. On the first day, Mujtaba and his captain had delighted the crowd with a magnificent 223-run partnership on a typically bland pitch. It was only Miandad's retirement at tea, variously attributed to a sore back, a strained hamstring and finally a headache, which ended it after 48 overs. Miandad had faced 149 balls for his 142 and hit two sixes and 19 fours, while Mujtaba was unbeaten at the declaration, with one six and 25 fours. Hampshire struggled against Pakistan's full Test attack, but Gower, recalled by England on the first morning, scored a delightful fifty next day. However, Hampshire lost their last eight wickets for 34 and followed on. A five-hour 69 from James delayed the Pakistanis' win, but only until after lunch on the third day.

Close of play: First day, Hampshire 19-0 (K. D. James 14*, T. C. Middleton 4*); Second day, Hampshire 104-2 (K. D. James 30*, R. A. Smith 28*).

Pakistanis

Aamir Sohail retired hurt	6	Salim Malik not out	50
Ramiz Raja c Parks b James	31	B 2, l-b 9, w 6, n-b 6	23
Asif Mujtaba not out	154		
*Javed Miandad retired hurt	142	1/72	(1 wkt dec.) 406

Inzamam-ul-Haq, Wasim Akram, †Moin Khan, Waqar Younis, Mushtaq Ahmed and Aqib Javed did not bat.

Aamir Sohail retired hurt at 15 and Javed Miandad at 295.

Bowling: Shine 17-2-80-0; Bakker 25-5-78-0; James 14-4-40-1; Udal 18-4-76-0; Maru 15-1-91-0; Nicholas 3-0-30-0.

Hampshire

K. D. James c sub b Mushtaq Ahmed	29	– c Inzamam-ul-Haq b Waqar Younis	69
T. C. Middleton c sub b Mushtaq Ahmed	8	– c sub b Asif Mujtaba	23
D. I. Gower c Inzamam-ul-Haq b Aqib Javed	55	– c sub b Mushtaq Ahmed	15
*M. C. J. Nicholas c sub b Mushtaq Ahmed	30	– (5) c Moin Khan b Mushtaq Ahmed	1
J. R. Wood c Inzamam-ul-Haq b Aqib Javed	6	– (6) c sub b Waqar Younis	11
R. A. Smith lbw b Mushtaq Ahmed	4	– (4) c Moin Khan b Wasim Akram	33
†R. J. Parks c Moin Khan b Aqib Javed	0	– c Moin Khan b Waqar Younis	13
R. J. Maru b Mushtaq Ahmed	10	– (9) c Mushtaq Ahmed b Wasim Akram	11
S. D. Udal not out	7	– (8) not out	31
K. J. Shine c Moin Khan b Wasim Akram	0	– b Wasim Akram	0
P. J. Bakker b Wasim Akram	0	– b Wasim Akram	6
L-b 3, n-b 10	13	B 1, l-b 3, n-b 13	17

1/38 2/47 3/128 4/135 5/139   162   1/39 2/61 3/118 4/132 5/152   230
6/139 7/152 8/161 9/162   6/178 7/183 8/200 9/200

Bowling: *First Innings*—Wasim Akram 6.3-1-15-2; Waqar Younis 13-4-26-0; Aqib Javed 14-2-47-3; Mushtaq Ahmed 21-6-64-5; Asif Mujtaba 1-0-7-0. *Second Innings*—Wasim Akram 14.5-2-38-4; Waqar Younis 16-2-53-3; Mushtaq Ahmed 34-7-103-2; Asif Mujtaba 7-3-8-1; Aqib Javed 4-0-24-0.

Umpires: K. E. Palmer and R. C. Tolchard.

ENGLAND v PAKISTAN

Third Cornhill Test

At Manchester, July 2, 3, 4, 6, 7. Drawn. Toss: Pakistan. This Test had moments of pure pleasure – Aamir Sohail's batting, Wasim Akram's bowling, David Gower's record aggregate – yet it will be remembered best for the incident between Aqib Javed, umpire Roy Palmer and Pakistan captain Javed Miandad that soiled the end of the England innings on the evening of the fourth day. Palmer warned Aqib for intimidatory bowling against Malcolm, and the situation became inflamed when Palmer returned Aqib's sweater with more emphasis than usual, probably because it was caught in his belt. That set off an exchange orchestrated by Miandad, as a Pakistan supporter ran on waving a rolled-up newspaper and chased by two security men. It was all too reminiscent of the confrontation between Mike Gatting and Shakoor Rana at Faisalabad in 1987-88, except that Shakoor shouted back, while Palmer retained the dignity of a patient policeman watching a family squabble.

Conrad Hunte, deputising for match referee Clyde Walcott who had left early for an ICC meeting in London, fined Aqib half his match fee, approximately £300. He also severely reprimanded team manager Intikhab Alam for telling the press, while Hunte was holding his inquiry, that Palmer had insulted his players by throwing the sweater at Aqib. Hunte urged Miandad and Gooch to tell their men to play according to the spirit of the game, which infuriated Gooch, who had not been involved. Intikhab was censured again – this time by ICC – when he repeated his remarks, and declined to apologise, after the match. The Pakistan players were also fined 40 per cent of their match fees for their slow over-rate.

England had dropped Botham and Lamb, and DeFreitas was declared unfit with a groin strain. Gower had been in such fine form with Hampshire that his much-criticised attitude, not to mention his unauthorised flight in Queensland 18 months earlier, was temporarily forgiven and he was recalled for his 115th Test, passing M. C. Cowdrey's England record. Atherton, batting fluently again after his back operation, also returned, and Warwickshire seamer Munton made his début at the third attempt. Pakistan were unchanged after their victory at Lord's, since when Ramiz Raja had made a trip home to have treatment for his back.

Once Miandad won the toss there was no question about who would bat on a fast and springy pitch built for the stroke-makers and an outfield quick enough to ensure they received full value for their shots. Sohail and Ramiz, two opening batsmen who had clearly attended the Gordon Greenidge school of controlled aggression, set off in a blaze of boundaries and by lunch 131 runs were on the board for the loss of Ramiz, given out off an inside edge discernible only to umpire Palmer – the starting point, so it was said, of the ill-feeling that grew afterwards. While Asif Mujtaba put down an anchor, Sohail assaulted any ball of less than perfect length and direction, so that he reached his first Test double-hundred from 127 balls in under three hours in only his fourth innings. He was 131 by tea and, after reaching his maiden double-hundred, went for 205, playing a tired shot to a searching ball from Lewis, 20 minutes before time. He hit 32 fours in 284 balls, most memorably through the covers. Mujtaba managed his second fifty of the series in less than two hours before he essayed his only rash stroke. Miandad was quiet save for an over from Salisbury in which he hit five boundaries, just to remind spectators who was the master batsman in Test cricket now Viv Richards had gone. Each of the first three wickets put on more than a hundred runs.

The second day was washed out and after Miandad became Munton's first Test wicket on the third morning, within 12 runs of his 24th Test century, Pakistan looked unlikely to produce the really intimidating score that might yet have won the match. Gooch, who must have despaired of the quality produced by his senior bowlers, sent down 18 overs himself and claimed three wickets, as he recorded his best Test figures. When Pakistan declared in mid-afternoon on the third day, they were too short of time and runs to push hard for victory unless they instigated a rapid collapse. More bad light and rain hindered England's start, and Wasim's determination to make a showing on the ground where he had just signed to play four more years for Lancashire was illustrated both by his fire and by 32 no-balls in the innings. Most dramatically, in his eighth over he toppled both Stewart, playing at a wide ball, and Atherton, unable to deal with one swinging across him in the Bruce Reid manner. But Pakistan probably wrote off their chances of victory by dropping three catches before the close.

Gooch and Smith saw England to Monday morning (to avoid a clash with the men's final at Wimbledon, this Test was the only one of the summer which had a rest day) and, when Smith was lbw to a ball from Aqib that cut in, the crowd rose expectantly for Gower, who needed only 34 runs to overtake G. Boycott's record England aggregate of 8,114 Test runs. What followed was Gower in spades: a squeeze through slips, a superb cover drive, a delightful push through mid-wicket, a head-high chance to first slip and finally, only 31 minutes after he arrived at the crease, a cover-drive to the boundary, a fitting shot to make him England's most prolific scorer in his 200th Test innings. Both Gooch, who had battled for his 78, and Gower, out to a flash outside the off stump, were gone with 106 needed to save the follow-on. But Lewis, with his own mix of heavyweight drive and deliberate care, and Salisbury, with commendable spirit, both hit half-centuries to ensure Pakistan could not win. Wasim finished with five wickets, for the tenth time in Tests, and Aqib with four for 100, his best Test figures, including a nicely judged slow yorker to bowl Malcolm in his first over after the contretemps with Palmer. For once both outshone Waqar Younis. Guided by Miandad, Pakistan batted with scrupulous caution, but without difficulty, throughout a final day made interesting by more overs from Gooch, who bowled Malik for the second time as he returned a match analysis of five for 69. England were without Russell, who had a stomach complaint, and Stewart kept wicket, a sign of things to come. – Ted Corbett.

Man of the Match: Aamir Sohail.   *Attendance*: 44,891; *receipts* £618,204.

Close of play: First day, Pakistan 388-3 (Javed Miandad 59*, Moin Khan 7*); Second day, No play; Third day, England 72-2 (G. A. Gooch 39*, R. A. Smith 5*); Fourth day, England 390.

Pakistan

Aamir Sohail b Lewis	205	– c Smith b Lewis	1
Ramiz Raja c Russell b Malcolm	54	– c Hick b Lewis	88
Asif Mujtaba c Atherton b Lewis	57	– c Atherton b Lewis	40
*Javed Miandad c Hick b Munton	88	– not out	45
†Moin Khan c Gower b Malcolm	15	– (7) not out	11
Salim Malik b Gooch	34	– (5) b Gooch	16
Inzamam-ul-Haq c Gooch b Malcolm	26		
Wasim Akram st Russell b Gooch	0	– (6) c Atherton b Gooch	13
Waqar Younis not out	2		
Mushtaq Ahmed c Lewis b Gooch	6		
B 9, l-b 4, w 2, n-b 3	18	B 8, l-b 5, w 5, n-b 7	25

1/115 (2) 2/241 (3) 3/378 (1)   (9 wkts dec.) 505   1/1 (1) 2/143 (2)   (5 wkts dec.) 239
4/428 (4) 5/432 (5) 6/492 (6)   3/148 (3) 4/195 (5)
7/497 (7) 8/497 (8) 9/505 (10)   5/217 (6)

Aqib Javed did not bat.

Bowling: *First Innings*—Malcolm 31-3-117-3; Lewis 24-5-90-2; Munton 30-6-112-1; Salisbury 20-0-117-0; Gooch 18-2-39-3; Hick 3-0-17-0. *Second Innings*—Malcolm 12-2-57-0; Lewis 17-5-46-3; Munton 17-6-26-0; Gooch 16-5-30-2; Salisbury 13-0-67-0; Hick 2-2-0-0.

England

*G. A. Gooch c Moin Khan b Waqar Younis	78	†R. C. Russell c Aamir Sohail b Aqib Javed	4
A. J. Stewart c Inzamam-ul-Haq b Wasim Akram	15	I. D. K. Salisbury c Aamir Sohail b Wasim Akram	50
M. A. Atherton c Moin Khan b Wasim Akram	0	T. A. Munton not out	25
R. A. Smith lbw b Aqib Javed	11	D. E. Malcolm b Aqib Javed	4
D. I. Gower c Moin Khan b Wasim Akram	73	B 8, l-b 8, w 2, n-b 35	53
G. A. Hick b Aqib Javed	22		390
C. C. Lewis c Moin Khan b Wasim Akram	55		

1/41 (2) 2/42 (3) 3/93 (4) 4/186 (1)   390
5/200 (5) 6/252 (6) 7/256 (8)
8/315 (7) 9/379 (9) 10/390 (11)

Bowling: Wasim Akram 36-4-128-5; Waqar Younis 32-6-96-1; Aqib Javed 21.4-1-100-4; Asif Mujtaba 1-1-0-0; Mushtaq Ahmed 10-1-50-0.

Umpires: R. Palmer and D. R. Shepherd. Referee: C. L. Walcott (West Indies). C. C. Hunte (West Indies) deputised for C. L. Walcott on the 4th and 5th days.

†LEAGUE CRICKET CONFERENCE v PAKISTANIS

At Haslingden, July 9. Abandoned. Rain prevented any play at Haslingden, which had been chosen to stage the game against the tourists, in celebration of the Lancashire League's centenary. Ten of the selected Conference XI were drawn from Lancashire clubs.

†SCOTLAND v PAKISTANIS

At Titwood, Glasgow, July 11. Abandoned.

†SCOTLAND v PAKISTANIS

At Titwood, Glasgow, July 12. Pakistanis won on scoring-rate, Scotland's target having been revised to 146 from 34 overs. Toss: Pakistanis. The second of the two scheduled fixtures in Glasgow was interrupted by rain after 15 overs of Scotland's innings, and 21 overs were lost. Though their target was reduced by 90 runs, Scotland were well short when leg-spinner Mushtaq Ahmed had Duthie, Bee and Stanger stumped to complete a haul of six for 43. They had to be content with having dismissed the Pakistanis inside 55 overs, only Aamir Sohail reaching 50.

Pakistanis

Aamir Sohail c Everett b Henry		70
Shoaib Mohammad c Patterson		
	b Thomson	24
Asif Mujtaba b Stanger		4
Zahid Fazal b Thomson		6
*Salim Malik c Philip b Duthie		46
Naved Anjum run out		45
†Rashid Latif c Stanger b Russell		26
Waqar Younis c Everett b Russell		6

Mushtaq Ahmed st Philip b Russell		0
Aqib Javed b Bee		0
Ata-ur-Rehman not out		0
B 4, l-b 1, w 1, n-b 2		8

1/72 2/87 3/104 (53.3 overs) 235
4/117 5/177 6/219
7/233 8/235 9/235

Bowling: Duthie 11–2–38–1; Bee 8.3–0–47–1; Stanger 11–1–53–1; Thomson 8–0–33–2; Henry 7–0–34–1; Russell 8–0–25–3.

Scotland

B. M. W. Patterson c Salim Malik		
	b Ata-ur-Rehman	17
†I. L. Philip lbw b Aqib Javed		7
G. N. Reifer c Rashid Latif		
	b Waqar Younis	34
J. Everett c sub b Mushtaq Ahmed		2
G. Salmond run out		14
O. Henry c Shoaib Mohammad		
	b Mushtaq Ahmed	3
*A. B. Russell c Naved Anjum		
	b Mushtaq Ahmed	10

I. M. Stanger st Rashid Latif		
	b Mushtaq Ahmed	7
P. G. Duthie st Rashid Latif		
	b Mushtaq Ahmed	5
A. Bee st Rashid Latif		
	b Mushtaq Ahmed	3
K. Thomson not out		0
L-b 4, w 2		6

1/22 2/28 3/35 4/74 (34 overs) 108
5/78 6/82 7/92 8/97 9/102

Bowling: Waqar Younis 10–3–15–1; Aqib Javed 7–2–16–1; Ata-ur-Rehman 4–0–16–1; Mushtaq Ahmed 10–1–43–6; Aamir Sohail 3–0–14–0.

Umpires: J. Breslin and P. Brown.

DURHAM v PAKISTANIS

At Chester-le-Street, July 14, 15, 16. Pakistanis won by 107 runs. Toss: Pakistanis. Despite the brilliance of Waqar Younis, who turned a well-balanced contest in the final session, Jones provided the abiding memory of his last home game before leaving for Australia's tour of Sri Lanka. An emotional wave of his bat acknowledged the rapturous ovation as he departed after his second century of the match. Most of the Pakistani bowlers merely went through the motions in the first innings, as Jones made an unbeaten 134 in 133 balls, with six sixes and 13 fours. Larkins contributed a splendid 118 as they shared 162 in 28 overs. A total of 341 for four declared was the biggest yet conceded by the tourists in their county programme. But they held nothing back on the final day, after their lunchtime declaration set Durham 306 in 64 overs. At 123 for one at tea the odds favoured Durham, especially with Jones still there. Ignoring a blow to his finger early on, he became the first Durham batsman to score 1,000 first-class runs at 95; five runs later he was the first to score twin hundreds. But soon after the interval Waqar broke his partnership of 128 – in 25 overs – with Glendenen, and quickly dismissed Parker and Briers. With Jones fifth out and Botham absent since chipping a thumb on the first day, Durham subsided for 198. Waqar finished with five for 22.

Close of play: First day, Durham 56-0 (W. Larkins 26*, J. D. Glendenen 18*); Second day, Pakistanis 186-2 (Asif Mujtaba 8*, Salim Malik 18*).

Pakistanis

Aamir Sohail c Parker b Botham	53	– lbw b Brown		90
Ramiz Raja c Hughes b Brown	14	– c Parker b Briers		59
Asif Mujtaba b Berry	79	– b McEwan		8
Salim Malik c Fothergill b McEwan	23	– c Glendenen b McEwan		40
*Javed Miandad c Fothergill b Botham	25	– (6) c Parker b Jones		67
Wasim Akram c Fothergill b McEwan	21	– (5) c Brown b Berry		27
†Moin Khan c Larkins b McEwan	53	– not out		29
Waqar Younis not out	23			
Mushtaq Ahmed not out	10			
L-b 2, w 1, n-b 4	7	L-b 13, w 2, n-b 3		18

1/58 2/78 3/135 4/198 5/204 (7 wkts dec.) 308   1/139 2/160 3/194 (6 wkts dec.) 338
6/273 7/278   4/214 5/247 6/338

Aqib Javed and Ata-ur-Rehman did not bat.

Bowling: *First Innings*—McEwan 23-8-52-3; Brown 17-2-67-1; Botham 19-2-73-2; Hughes 14-2-37-0; Berry 8-0-40-1; Briers 9-0-37-0. *Second Innings*—McEwan 15-2-65-2; Brown 16-3-59-1; Hughes 15-2-41-0; Briers 14-0-99-1; Berry 12-2-57-1; Jones 1.4-0-4-1.

Durham

W. Larkins c Ata-ur-Rehman b Salim Malik	118	– b Waqar Younis		1
J. D. Glendenen c Mushtaq Ahmed b Aqib Javed	33	– lbw b Waqar Younis		36
D. M. Jones not out	134	– b Wasim Akram		105
*P. W. G. Parker c Waqar Younis b Ata-ur-Rehman	0	– c Mushtaq Ahmed b Waqar Younis		10
M. P. Briers c sub b Wasim Akram	13	– lbw b Waqar Younis		0
P. J. Berry not out	13	– c Moin Khan b Ata-ur-Rehman		8
†A. R. Fothergill (did not bat)		– lbw b Wasim Akram		13
S. M. McEwan (did not bat)		– b Wasim Akram		1
S. P. Hughes (did not bat)		– not out		2
S. J. E. Brown (did not bat)		– b Waqar Younis		2
I. T. Botham (did not bat)		– absent injured		
B 6, l-b 11, w 1, n-b 12	30	B 1, l-b 8, n-b 11		20

1/96 2/258 3/260 4/304 (4 wkts dec.) 341   1/1 2/129 3/159 4/159 5/171 198
6/187 7/188 8/193 9/198

Bowling: *First Innings*—Waqar Younis 22-6-63-0; Wasim Akram 20-4-58-0; Ata-ur-Rehman 18-4-63-1; Aqib Javed 16-2-54-1; Mushtaq Ahmed 18-5-53-0; Salim Malik 6-1-26-1; Aamir Sohail 1-0-7-0. *Second Innings*—Waqar Younis 16-4-22-5; Wasim Akram 17-4-58-3; Ata-ur-Rehman 14-2-59-2; Aqib Javed 8-0-36-0; Mushtaq Ahmed 4-0-14-0.

Bowling: *First Innings*—Wasim Akram 17–4–67–1; Aqib Javed 6.1–0–35–1; Mushtaq Ahmed 8.5–1–59–0; Waqar Younis 14–2–48–0; Ata-ur-Rehman 15–2–65–1; Asif Mujtaba 4–0–28–0; Salim Malik 4–0–15–1; Aamir Sohail 1–0–7–0. *Second Innings*—Wasim Akram 17–2–65–3; Waqar Younis 17.1–5–22–5; Ata-ur-Rehman 8–2–39–1; Mushtaq Ahmed 6–1–35–0; Salim Malik 7–0–28–0.

Umpires: H. D. Bird and M. J. Harris.

DERBYSHIRE v PAKISTANIS

At Derby, July 18, 19, 20. Drawn. Toss: Derbyshire. The Pakistanis were forced to concede first-innings lead for the second successive match, even though Wasim Akram gave Derbyshire a taste of his quality by sweeping away their tail. The last seven wickets fell for 28, and Wasim took four for seven in 23 balls. But then Malcolm, omitted from England's squad for Headingley when it was announced on the second day, bowled as if he had a point to prove, and Derbyshire worked their way through a powerful batting order to dismiss the Pakistanis for only 197; Waqar Younis became Mortensen's 400th wicket for the county. Bowler, out to an uncharacteristic stroke in the first innings, settled down for four and a quarter hours in the second, but rain ruined the final day and the tourists' lingering hopes of an eighth win over a county. The Derbyshire authorities found it hard to contain all the Pakistani supporters on the first two days; in one incident, a steward was head-butted.

Close of play: First day, Pakistanis 98-3 (Asif Mujtaba 39*, Salim Malik 5*); Second day, Derbyshire 182-4 (C. J. Adams 4*, R. W. Sladdin 0*).

Derbyshire

P. D. Bowler b Mushtaq Ahmed	28	– b Aamir Sohail	79
A. M. Brown c Asif Mujtaba b Mushtaq Ahmed	27	– c Moin Khan b Ata-ur-Rehman	43
*J. E. Morris c Moin Khan b Wasim Akram	49	– c Aamir Sohail b Ata-ur-Rehman	0
T. J. G. O'Gorman c Javed Miandad b Wasim Akram	46	– b Wasim Akram	42
C. J. Adams c Salim Malik b Ata-ur-Rehman	51	– not out	29
F. A. Griffith not out	2	– (7) not out	4
†K. M. Krikken c Moin Khan b Waqar Younis	4		
R. W. Sladdin lbw b Waqar Younis	0	– (6) b Waqar Younis	0
A. E. Warner b Wasim Akram	4		
D. E. Malcolm b Wasim Akram	0		
O. H. Mortensen b Wasim Akram	0		
L-b 3, w 1, n-b 1	5	B 1, 1-b 8, w 1, n-b 5	15

1/34 2/90 3/127 4/188 5/206 6/211 7/211 8/216 9/216   216   1/67 2/69 3/161 4/181 5/187   (5 wkts dec.) 212

Bowling: *First Innings*—Wasim Akram 16.5–2–59–5; Ata-ur-Rehman 10–1–33–1; Mushtaq Ahmed 23–5–82–2; Waqar Younis 10–1–30–2; Aamir Sohail 5–3–9–0. *Second Innings*—Waqar Younis 14–1–44–1; Ata-ur-Rehman 17–4–50–2; Mushtaq Ahmed 15–3–58–0; Wasim Akram 11–1–32–1; Asif Mujtaba 15–5–18–0; Aamir Sohail 3–2–1–1.

Pakistanis

Aamir Sohail c Krikken b Malcolm	2	Waqar Younis lbw b Mortensen	2
Ramiz Raja lbw b Warner	7	Mushtaq Ahmed c Brown b Sladdin	12
Asif Mujtaba c Warner b Malcolm	40	Ata-ur-Rehman c O'Gorman b Sladdin	0
Inzamam-ul-Haq b Griffith	43		
Salim Malik c and b Sladdin	21	L-b 2, n-b 1	3
*Javed Miandad c and b Malcolm	6		
Wasim Akram b Mortensen	26		197
†Moin Khan not out	35	1/9 2/15 3/91 4/100 5/106	
		6/144 7/160 8/168 9/189	

Bowling: Malcolm 16–2–62–3; Warner 13–6–19–1; Mortensen 15–6–24–2; Griffith 11–6–23–1; Sladdin 18.5–3–67–3.

Umpires: J. D. Bond and D. O. Oslear.

ENGLAND v PAKISTAN

Fourth Cornhill Test

At Leeds, July 23, 24, 25, 26. England won by six wickets. Toss: Pakistan. England may look back on this victory, their first over Pakistan since 1982, as an even greater personal triumph for Graham Gooch than the win against West Indies on the same ground the previous year. Their captain's positive thinking tailored a deliberately misshapen team to suit a Headingley pitch which lived up to every word of its wicked reputation. His majestic 135 was the pivotal innings of another absorbing Test and his phlegmatic second-innings 37 provided England with an essential heat-shield in a feverish final session.

Given his constant involvement, it was almost inevitable that Gooch should also be the innocent central character in the most controversial of several incidents that led Pakistan into a second conflict with ICC's Code of Conduct. They believed he had been run out as he completed his 14th run and England were still a worrying distance away from the 99 needed to win. Slow-motion playbacks suggested they were right. But umpire Ken Palmer, elder brother of the official they had clashed with in the Third Test, turned down the appeal and, thereafter, the Pakistanis could not conceal their frustration. After a noisy, argumentative climax, match referee Clyde Walcott fined substitute Rashid Latif for the "serious and obvious dissent" of hurling his cap in anger and gave wicket-keeper Moin Khan a verbal warning.

Though Pakistan will never be totally convinced they were not the victims of injustice, they were, overall, simply waylaid by the Headingley pitch. Gooch saw it coming and planned accordingly. Wicket-keeper Russell was sacrificed to make room for an extra batsman. Malcolm and Salisbury were left out because history suggested sheer pace and wrist-spin would be useless. England made four changes from their Old Trafford squad and, after sniffing Headingley's overcast atmosphere, omitted Newport and Childs, re-introduced Pringle and Ramprakash and gave the Somerset seamer Mallender his Test début.

A calculated gamble was instantly justified when Javed Miandad, believing the wicket could only get worse and not last five days, chose to bat. Pakistan struggled as the ball came off sluggishly, occasionally keeping low and always seaming and swinging. Although Lewis did not adapt well, Mallender collected three wickets with intelligently-controlled pace and Pringle was his usual steady self. Only Salim Malik prospered, through a selective mix of caution and sudden bouts of aggression. Several Pakistanis were as much victims of their own recklessness as of alien conditions. Asif Mujtaba and Ramiz Raja both edged into their stumps, Wasim Akram was run out in a misunderstanding with Malik and five others virtually steered the ball towards the slips. Hick took four of those catches, and collected two more when Pakistan batted again, thus equalling England's record for an innings and a match. Twenty-two catches in 11 Tests confirmed his status as one of the world's finest slip fielders; England still awaited confirmation that he was a Test batsman.

The last hour of Pakistan's 197 – and the finale of Malik's superb, unbeaten 82 – was played on a second day which dawned bright and crystal-clear. The change transformed batting into a very different art: it was still not easy, but the ball swung far less. Atherton, promoted because Stewart was resting after keeping wicket, rejoined Gooch for the first time in more than a year. Their compatibility was obvious as they put on 168, their seventh century stand together, and Atherton was heading elegantly towards three figures when a high-velocity, low-flying leg-break from Wasim hit his off stump.

Gooch, thriving on the wildest then surviving the finest of Pakistan's bowling, took England into a cloudy third day with a first-innings lead. The value of his seven-hour 135 was put into perspective only after he was bowled by Mushtaq Ahmed's last delivery before lunch. He had struck 19 fours and a six in 301 balls, and his maiden century against Pakistan, and 17th in all Tests, completed his set against the six countries he had faced. But he was the third casualty of an avalanche in which nine men perished for 50. Waqar Younis, suddenly quicker and devastatingly accurate, took all five of his wickets for 13 in just 38 balls. Among the debris of England's 320 was a sound 42 by Smith, another leaden-footed failure by Hick and a third successive Test duck by Ramprakash.

A lead of only 123 was disappointing but, ultimately, more than adequate. Mallender, noticeably more confident, used the pitch with all the know-how acquired in 13 seasons foot-slogging around the county circuit. Again Pakistan found the wobbling ball an irresistible lure. Mallender, chosen as the horse for this unique course, finished with five for 50, and match figures of eight for 122. Ramiz kept his instincts in check for more than two hours making 63, and another masterpiece of bad-wicket batting by Malik – this time an unbeaten 84 – dragged his team into a fourth afternoon. But England's supposedly simple task of scoring 99 turned into a three-hour trial of skill, nerve and self-control. Reduced to three front-line bowlers by an injury to Aqib, the tourists remembered Imran Khan's famous entreaty to act like "cornered tigers". Waqar, Wasim and Mushtaq bowled with magnificent, legitimate hostility, backed by a fierce gale of appeals for this, that and the other. Rejection by umpires Palmer and Kitchen brought several displays of theatrical astonishment by fielders, as well as three invasions by Pakistani spectators. The pressure increased when Atherton and Smith both fell to Waqar at 27 but, thanks to Palmer's unwitting help, Gooch clung on for two hours before he was caught at silly point off Mushtaq, soon to be followed by Stewart. Gower also stayed two hours, making an equally ice-cool 31, after Latif's cap-throwing act failed to convince either umpire he had been caught behind. With some late assistance from Ramprakash, Gower finally inched his way to the target which squared the series. – Peter Johnson.

Man of the Match: G. A. Gooch. *Attendance:* 53,870; *receipts* £760,000.

Close of play: First day, Pakistan 165-8 (Salim Malik 57*, Mushtaq Ahmed 6*); Second day, England 216-1 (G. A. Gooch 93*, R. A. Smith 22*); Third day, Pakistan 98-4 (Salim Malik 13*, Inzamam-ul-Haq 2*).

Pakistan

Aamir Sohail c Atherton b Mallender	23	– c Stewart b Mallender	1
Ramiz Raja b Pringle	17	– c Atherton b Munton	63
Asif Mujtaba b Mallender	7	– c Hick b Mallender	11
*Javed Miandad c Smith b Pringle	6	– c Stewart b Mallender	4
Salim Malik not out	82	– not out	84
Inzamam-ul-Haq c Hick b Munton	5	– c Smith b Pringle	19
Wasim Akram run out	12	– c Ramprakash b Pringle	17
†Moin Khan c Hick b Lewis	2	– c Hick b Mallender	3
Waqar Younis c Hick b Mallender	6	– (10) b Mallender	3
Mushtaq Ahmed b Lewis	11	– (9) lbw b Pringle	0
Aqib Javed c Hick b Munton	0	– run out	0
B 1, l-b 2, w 7, n-b 16	26	B 4, l-b 1, w 2, n-b 9	16

1/34 (1) 2/54 (3) 3/60 (2) 4/68 (4) 197 1/11 (1) 2/53 (3) 3/64 (4) 221
5/80 (6) 6/111 (5) 7/117 (8) 8/128 (9) 4/96 (2) 5/147 (6) 6/177 (7)
9/192 (10) 10/197 (11) 7/205 (8) 8/206 (9)
9/213 (10) 10/221 (11)

Bowling: *First Innings*—Lewis 23-6-48-2; Mallender 23-7-72-3; Pringle 17-6-41-2; Munton 10.3-3-22-2; Gooch 6-3-11-0. *Second Innings*—Lewis 16-3-55-0; Mallender 23-7-50-5; Pringle 19-2-66-3; Gooch 1-0-5-0.

England

*G. A. Gooch b Mushtaq Ahmed	135	– c Asif Mujtaba b Mushtaq Ahmed	37
M. A. Atherton b Wasim Akram	76	– lbw b Waqar Younis	5
R. A. Smith c Javed Miandad b Aqib Javed	42	– c sub (Zahid Fazal) b Waqar Younis	0
†A. J. Stewart lbw b Waqar Younis	8	– (5) c Moin Khan b Mushtaq Ahmed	2
D. I. Gower not out	18	– (4) not out	31
M. R. Ramprakash lbw b Mushtaq Ahmed	0	– not out	12
G. A. Hick b Waqar Younis	1		
C. C. Lewis lbw b Waqar Younis	0		
D. R. Pringle b Waqar Younis	0		
N. A. Mallender b Waqar Younis	1		
T. A. Munton c Inzamam-ul-Haq b Mushtaq Ahmed	0		
B 1, l-b 14, w 1, n-b 23	39	B 5, l-b 3, n-b 4	12

1/168 (2) 2/270 (3) 3/292 (4) 4/298 (1) 320 1/27 (2) 2/27 (3) (4 wkts) 99
5/298 (6) 6/303 (7) 7/305 (8) 8/305 (9) 3/61 (1) 4/65 (5)
9/313 (10) 10/320 (11)

Bowling: *First Innings*—Wasim Akram 36–12–80–1; Aqib Javed 16–3–48–1; Waqar Younis 30–3–117–5; Mushtaq Ahmed 29.5–6–60–3; Aamir Sohail 2–2–0–0. *Second Innings*—Wasim Akram 17–4–36–0; Waqar Younis 12–2–28–2; Mushtaq Ahmed 13.4–3–27–2.

Umpires: M. J. Kitchen and K. E. Palmer. Referee: C. L. Walcott (West Indies).

†MINOR COUNTIES v PAKISTANIS

At Marlow, July 29, 30. Minor Counties won by one wicket. Toss: Pakistanis. Ian Cockbain of Cheshire hit the last ball of the match through extra cover for his ninth four to secure a remarkable victory. A late selection for the team, he had taken 87 runs off 61 balls, including four sixes, as Mushtaq Ahmed removed his partners. Two days of positive cricket began with the Pakistanis slumping to 37 for five. They had not reached Marlow until 3 a.m., after a floodlit charity match at Crystal Palace, and had scant time to recuperate before Calway claimed three wickets in his third over. Zahid Fazal and Waqar Younis recovered ground, but Folland boldly declared 51 behind after putting on 104 with Cockbain. Shoaib Mohammad left Minor Counties 46 overs to score 250. With three overs to go and eight wickets down, 38 were still needed, but Cockbain hit 16 from one Naved Anjum over to bring an unexpected win into sight.

Close of play: First day, Minor Counties 130-2 (N. A. Folland 56*, I. Cockbain 30*).

Pakistanis

Asif Mujtaba b Calway	12	– (3) b Lewis 6
*Shoaib Mohammad c Davies b Donohue	2	– not out 63
Inzamam-ul-Haq c Adams b Lewis	4	– (4) st Humphries b Smith .. 44
Zahid Fazal c Smith b Lewis	93	– (5) not out 34
Naved Anjum c Humphries b Calway	0	
Moin Khan b Calway	0	
Aamir Sohail c Humphries b Toogood	7	– (1) lbw b Toogood 46
†Rashid Latif c Cockbain b Smith	14	
Mushtaq Ahmed c Humphries b Calway	16	
Waqar Younis c and b Adams	57	
Ata-ur-Rehman not out	9	
B 1, l-b 4, w 4, n-b 3	12	L-b 4, w 1 5

1/7 2/18 3/37 4/37 5/37   226   1/60 2/67 3/137   (3 wkts dec.) 198
6/54 7/98 8/132 9/189

Bowling: *First Innings*—Donohue 16–5–35–1; Lewis 19–4–67–2; Calway 12–4–30–4; Toogood 8–2–17–1; Smith 13–1–71–1; Adams 0.5–0–1–1. *Second Innings*—Lewis 9–2–28–1; Calway 5–1–32–0; Toogood 13–3–58–1; Smith 14–4–59–1; Adams 5–1–17–0.

Minor Counties

G. S. Calway c Rashid Latif b Naved Anjum	9	– c Aamir Sohail b Naved Anjum . 57
P. Burn lbw b Waqar Younis	21	– c Inzamam-ul-Haq b Naved Anjum . 28
*N. A. Folland not out	84	– (4) b Mushtaq Ahmed 36
I. Cockbain not out	45	– (5) not out 87
N. J. Adams (did not bat)		– (3) c Moin Khan b Mushtaq Ahmed . 28
M. R. Davies (did not bat)		– c Shoaib Mohammad b Mushtaq Ahmed . 28
G. J. Toogood (did not bat)		– run out 3
†M. I. Humphries (did not bat)		– b Mushtaq Ahmed 0
J. C. M. Lewis (did not bat)		– st Moin Khan b Mushtaq Ahmed 0
K. Donohue (did not bat)		– b Mushtaq Ahmed 2
A. Smith (did not bat)		– not out 0
B 1, l-b 2, n-b 13	16	L-b 6, w 2, n-b 3 11

1/20 2/71   (2 wkts dec.) 175   1/88 2/90 3/132   (9 wkts) 252
                              4/173 5/187 6/191
                              7/196 8/212 9/238

Bowling: *First Innings*—Ata-ur-Rehman 7-1-25-0; Naved Anjum 13-2-55-1; Mushtaq Ahmed 13-3-49-0; Waqar Younis 11-1-32-1; Shoaib Mohammad 4-1-11-0. *Second Innings*—Waqar Younis 9-0-28-0; Ata-ur-Rehman 8-0-57-0; Naved Anjum 7-1-44-2; Mushtaq Ahmed 14-2-43-6; Asif Mujtaba 3-0-27-0; Shoaib Mohammad 3-0-19-0; Inzamam-ul-Haq 1-0-14-0; Aamir Sohail 1-0-14-0.

Umpires: R. K. Curtis and D. J. Halfyard.

ESSEX v PAKISTANIS

At Chelmsford, August 1, 2, 3. Pakistanis won by seven wickets. Toss: Essex. The Pakistanis achieved victory with 23 deliveries to spare, their eighth win in their first-class programme against the counties and one which enabled them to collect a £50,000 bonus from sponsors Tetley Bitter. It was inspired by Salim Malik, who had helped Essex to the County Championship the previous season. His masterful 153 not out from 138 balls included 21 fours and two sixes. He reached 100 between lunch and tea after adding 133 with Javed Miandad in 26 overs, and followed up with a swift half-century in the final run-chase. Gooch's fifth century in seven visits to the crease in all cricket had provided the backbone of Essex's first innings, the highest total conceded by the tourists to a county. His four-and-a-half-hour occupation brought him 21 fours. But his quick departure when the county batted again was a setback they never overcame, although Lewis resisted for over three hours to set the tourists 193 in 38 overs. Another young player, the 18-year-old wicket-keeper Rollins, took two catches on a promising first-class début.

Close of play: First day, Essex 357-9 (N. Shahid 86*, J. H. Childs 3*); Second day, Essex 58-2 (J. J. B. Lewis 9*, P. M. Such 4*).

Essex

*G. A. Gooch c Wasim Akram b Ata-ur-Rehman	.141	– b Wasim Akram	4
J. P. Stephenson b Mushtaq Ahmed	45	– lbw b Mushtaq Ahmed	27
J. J. B. Lewis b Wasim Akram	8	– c Wasim Akram b Mushtaq Ahmed	55
N. Hussain lbw b Naved Anjum	11	– (5) b Mushtaq Ahmed	5
N. Shahid not out	86	– (6) c Rashid Latif b Salim Malik	8
M. A. Garnham c Rashid Latif b Wasim Akram	18	– (7) b Wasim Akram	24
†R. J. Rollins lbw b Wasim Akram	6	– (8) c Wasim Akram b Salim Malik	13
M. C. Ilott c Rashid Latif b Asif Mujtaba	1	– (9) b Wasim Akram	8
S. J. W. Andrew b Wasim Akram	3	– (10) b Wasim Akram	6
P. M. Such lbw b Naved Anjum	7	– (4) lbw b Naved Anjum	6
J. H. Childs not out	3	– not out	2
L-b 16, n-b 12	28	B 10, l-b 8, n-b 12	30

1/99 2/138 3/185 4/253 5/296 (9 wkts dec.) 357
6/314 7/315 8/325 9/349

1/8 2/49 3/101 4/107 5/130 188
6/131 7/165 8/177 9/185

Bowling: *First Innings*—Wasim Akram 35-6-102-4; Ata-ur-Rehman 17.2-2-76-1; Naved Anjum 23.4-4-69-2; Zahid Fazal 2-1-8-0; Mushtaq Ahmed 13-0-32-1; Asif Mujtaba 13-2-45-1; Shoaib Mohammad 1-0-5-0; Salim Malik 2-0-4-0. *Second Innings*—Wasim Akram 23.5-8-48-4; Naved Anjum 14-4-37-1; Mushtaq Ahmed 33-15-57-3; Asif Mujtaba 4-2-13-0; Salim Malik 4-0-15-2.

Pakistanis

Ramiz Raja c Rollins b Andrew	4	– c Garnham b Childs	22
Shoaib Mohammad lbw b Andrew	50	– b Childs	32
Asif Mujtaba b Ilott	25	– (4) not out	62
*Javed Miandad c Hussain b Andrew	91		
Salim Malik not out	153	– (3) c Rollins b Stephenson	50
Zahid Fazal c Hussain b Shahid	5		
Wasim Akram c Stephenson b Shahid	10	– (5) not out	25
Naved Anjum not out	6		
B 5, l-b 2, w 1, n-b 1	9	B 4, l-b 1	5

1/12 2/75 3/120 4/253   (6 wkts dec.) 353   1/47 2/64 3/152   (3 wkts) 196
5/289 6/303

†Rashid Latif, Mushtaq Ahmed and Ata-ur-Rehman did not bat.

Bowling: *First Innings*—Ilott 17-3-67-1; Andrew 16-2-64-3; Stephenson 14-2-44-0; Childs 17-1-73-0; Such 9.4-0-74-0; Shahid 6-0-24-2. *Second Innings*—Ilott 11-0-56-0; Andrew 2-0-6-0; Childs 10-0-51-2; Such 7-0-44-0; Stephenson 4.1-0-34-1.

Umpires: P. Adams and J. C. Balderstone.

ENGLAND v PAKISTAN

Fifth Cornhill Test

At The Oval, August 6, 7, 8, 9. Pakistan won by ten wickets. Toss: England. A game billed as "The Showdown Test" became instead a perfect showcase for the awesome fast bowling talents of Wasim Akram and Waqar Younis. Pakistan won 15 minutes before lunch on the fourth day, a more comprehensive victory than even they could have dared hope for – and the crowning triumph of the summer for their captain Javed Miandad. At last, Miandad was captain in his own right – the unchallenged leader of a young, multi-talented team that no longer needed, or wanted, the paternal and patrician guidance of Imran Khan. Fittingly too, Imran's record of 21 wickets in a series for Pakistan in England was equalled by Wasim and broken by Waqar, who claimed one more. Their combined total of 43 wickets was the main reason why Pakistan won their fourth successive series against England; at The Oval their haul of 15 left the home nation shattered and outclassed.

England's selectors recalled Malcolm and Tufnell, who had recovered from his appendix operation, and, for the time being, abandoned the attempt to persevere with Hick. Pakistan dropped Inzamam-ul-Haq, another promising young batsman who had disappointed at Test level, to give Shoaib Mohammad his first Test of the series, and unexpectedly replaced wicket-keeper Moin Khan with Rashid Latif. Another man making his first appearance of the series was umpire Dickie Bird, believed to inspire more confidence than most among the tourists.

Gooch won an important toss in conditions near-perfect for batting and for much of the opening day England's battle-plan went smoothly, even though Gooch himself and Stewart fell in the first session, after a flying start against the new ball. Stewart had asked to combine the opener's job with keeping wicket again, although in the event a blow to his foot meant that Smith had to stand in for him behind the stumps on the first evening. England were 40 minutes into the final session, on 182 for three, when Aqib Javed knocked out the first brick and then left Wasim to push over the whole structure. Gower's innings ended with a bottom-edged square cut into his stumps; Wasim, with a little help from Waqar, then took just 45 minutes more to rout England's lower order with a thrilling spell of five for 18 in 7.1 overs. Ramprakash was lbw pushing forward to an in-swinging full toss while the tail was blown away by a succession of near-unplayable in-swinging yorkers. Atherton, after batting with great determination, was eighth out, edging Waqar to the keeper after nearly four and a half hours.

Pakistan's top order then set about the business of building a match-winning lead, with five of the first six threatening but ultimately failing to play a major innings. Aamir Sohail, the double-centurion of Old Trafford, struck 10 fours in his 49, while Salim Malik's 40 took his tally to 488 and made him the most prolific scorer for either side in an England-Pakistan series, surpassing D. C. S. Compton's 453 in 1954. He was bowled early on

Saturday morning by a beauty from Malcolm, who went on to take five for 94 in a big-hearted display which justified his latest recall to arms. But while Malcolm was putting in a determined bid for a place on the winter tour to India, Test cricket's latest newcomer was announcing himself with a rare flourish. Latif, until now most familiar as a substitute fielder, came in unhelmeted with Pakistan's lead only 85 and proceeded – in just his fifth first-class innings of the entire tour – to play with the uninhibited joy and the effortless timing of a natural batsman. His 87-ball 50 featured six fours before he was last out aiming another blow.

Latif's vital contribution left England 173 behind and facing a long struggle to save the match, but Waqar, bowling with great pace and spirit, hungrily lapped up the cream of their batting. By tea he had single-handedly reduced them to 55 for three, and it was 59 for four when Gower shouldered arms to one that came back off the seam and took his off stump. The contest was effectively over. Ramprakash, desperate to improve a depressing Test record, made 17 in promising style before he was unluckily adjudged to have touched with a glove a ball from Mushtaq Ahmed that ballooned to short leg off his pad. Smith and Lewis ensured the match lasted into the fourth day, but Sunday morning brought just a final exhibition of Wasim and Waqar's ability to brush aside a tail. Smith's brave unbeaten 84, in four hours and from 179 balls, took him out of a poor run and represented a personal triumph against the leg-spin and googlies of Mushtaq which had mystified him all summer. Thanks to Smith, Pakistan were at least required to bat again. But a wide from Ramprakash and a square-cut boundary next ball from Sohail were sufficient to send into raptures the hundreds of Pakistani fans who gathered in front of the pavilion to salute their heroes. The only sour note for Pakistan came after their triumph, when the media indulged in more speculation about ball-tampering. This time the reports were sparked off by England manager Micky Stewart, who said he knew how the Pakistani bowlers managed to swing an old ball more than the new one – but was not prepared to reveal the secret. – Mark Baldwin.

Man of the Match: Wasim Akram. *Attendance:* 59,947; *receipts* £1,010,526.

Men of the Series: England – G. A. Gooch; Pakistan – Wasim Akram and Waqar Younis.

Close of play: First day, Pakistan 16-0 (Aamir Sohail 9*, Ramiz Raja 7*); Second day, Pakistan 275-4 (Salim Malik 38*, Asif Mujtaba 31*); Third day, England 137-5 (R. A. Smith 59*, C. C. Lewis 8*).

England

*G. A. Gooch c Asif Mujtaba b Aqib Javed	20	– c Aamir Sohail b Waqar Younis	24
†A. J. Stewart c Ramiz Raja b Wasim Akram	31	– lbw b Waqar Younis	8
M. A. Atherton c Rashid Latif b Waqar Younis	60	– c Rashid Latif b Waqar Younis	4
R. A. Smith b Mushtaq Ahmed	33	– not out	84
D. I. Gower b Aqib Javed	27	– b Waqar Younis	1
M. R. Ramprakash lbw b Wasim Akram	2	– c Asif Mujtaba b Mushtaq Ahmed	17
C. C. Lewis lbw b Wasim Akram	4	– st Rashid Latif b Mushtaq Ahmed	14
D. R. Pringle b Wasim Akram	1	– b Wasim Akram	1
N. A. Mallender b Wasim Akram	4	– c Mushtaq Ahmed b Wasim Akram	3
P. C. R. Tufnell not out	0	– b Wasim Akram	0
D. E. Malcolm b Wasim Akram	2	– b Waqar Younis	0
B 4, l-b 8, w 1, n-b 10	23	B 1, l-b 8, n-b 9	18

1/39 (1) 2/57 (2) 3/138 (4) 4/182 (5)	207	1/29 (2) 2/47 (3) 3/55 (1)	174
5/190 (6) 6/196 (7) 7/199 (8) 8/203 (3)		4/59 (5) 5/92 (6) 6/153 (7)
9/205 (9) 10/207 (11)		7/159 (8) 8/173 (9)
		9/173 (10) 10/174 (11)

Bowling: *First Innings*—Wasim Akram 22.1–3–67–6; Waqar Younis 16–4–37–1; Aqib Javed 16–6–44–2; Mushtaq Ahmed 24–7–47–1. *Second Innings*—Wasim Akram 21–6–36–3; Aqib Javed 9–2–25–0; Waqar Younis 18–5–52–5; Mushtaq Ahmed 23–6–46–2; Aamir Sohail 1–0–6–0.

Pakistan

Aamir Sohail c Stewart b Malcolm	49	– not out	4
Ramiz Raja b Malcolm	19	– not out	0
Shoaib Mohammad c and b Tufnell	55		
*Javed Miandad c and b Lewis	59		
Salim Malik b Malcolm	40		
Asif Mujtaba run out	50		
Wasim Akram c Stewart b Malcolm	7		
†Rashid Latif c Smith b Mallender	50		
Waqar Younis c Gooch b Malcolm	6		
Mushtaq Ahmed c Lewis b Mallender	9		
Aqib Javed not out	0		
B 2, l-b 6, w 4, n-b 24	36	W 1	1

1/64 (2) 2/86 (1) 3/197 (4) 4/214 (3)   380   (no wkt) 5
5/278 (5) 6/292 (7) 7/332 (6)
8/342 (9) 9/359 (10) 10/380 (8)

Bowling: *First Innings*—Mallender 28.5–6–93–2; Malcolm 29–6–94–5; Lewis 30–8–70–1 Tufnell 34–9–87–1; Pringle 6–0–28–0. *Second Innings*—Ramprakash 0.1–0–5–0.

Umpires: H. D. Bird and D. R. Shepherd. Referee: C. L. Walcott (West Indies).

†SOMERSET v PAKISTANIS

At Taunton, August 12. Abandoned.

†SOMERSET v PAKISTANIS

At Taunton, August 13. Abandoned. The Pakistanis' second trip to Taunton was not wholly without purpose, as Somerset announced that leg-spinner Mushtaq Ahmed had agreed to join them as an overseas player in 1993.

GLOUCESTERSHIRE v PAKISTANIS

At Bristol, August 15, 16, 17. Pakistanis won by 292 runs. Toss: Gloucestershire. The touring side simply toyed with Gloucestershire and could have won within two days had they made the county follow on 234 behind. But they opted for batting practice before the final three one-day internationals, for which Ijaz Ahmed had just flown in. This decision apart, the Pakistanis played as purposefully as ever, even though their jackpot bonus had already been banked. Ramiz Raja, with his first century since the opening first-class game at Worcester, dominated the first day, batting just over four hours, although Inzamam-ul-Haq provided most entertainment. Gloucestershire, without Athey, and with Hodgson forced down the order by a severe cold, were swept aside in little more than three hours after a late start on the second day. Wasim Akram and Aqib Javed, bowling to a full length, shared the wickets. Only tailender Davies reached 20, and though three players achieved that mark in the second innings, all the batsmen seemed overawed by Wasim. Relying on skill and variety rather than pace, he was in no way flattered by match figures of 11 for 76, which lifted him above Walsh as the season's leading wicket-taker.

Close of play: First day, Gloucestershire 12-0 (M. W. Alleyne 8*, A. J. Wright 4*). Second day, Pakistanis 184-4 (Inzamam-ul-Haq 54*, Naved Anjum 6*).

Pakistanis

Aamir Sohail c Davies b Hancock	46	– c and b Smith	30
Ramiz Raja c and b Vaughan	135		
Shoaib Mohammad b Vaughan	66	– (2) c Alleyne b Babington	14
Inzamam-ul-Haq c Wright b Babington	65	– not out	54
Ijaz Ahmed c Russell b Babington	36	– (3) c Russell b Vaughan	31
Wasim Akram c Vaughan b Williams	0		
†Rashid Latif c Russell b Williams	2	– (5) c Alleyne b Davies	42
Naved Anjum c Russell b Williams	0	– (6) not out	6
Mushtaq Ahmed not out	0		
L-b 3, n-b 4	7	L-b 5, n-b 2	7

1/76 2/213 3/268 4/345 5/346   (8 wkts dec.) 357   1/31 2/77   (4 wkts dec.) 184
6/356 7/357 8/357   3/78 4/163

*Salim Malik and Aqib Javed did not bat.

Bowling: *First Innings*—Babington 16-3-61-2; Smith 10-0-39-0; Vaughan 18-3-63-2; Hancock 7-2-34-1; Williams 18.3-5-44-3; Davies 26-4-100-0; Alleyne 5-2-13-0. *Second Innings*—Babington 10-1-50-1; Williams 11-0-47-0; Smith 7-0-32-1; Vaughan 6-1-26-1; Davies 5-1-24-1.

Gloucestershire

M. W. Alleyne c Rashid Latif b Aqib Javed	8	– c Rashid Latif b Mushtaq Ahmed	27
*A. J. Wright c Aamir Sohail b Wasim Akram	5	– lbw b Aqib Javed	13
R. I. Dawson c and b Wasim Akram	19	– c Rashid Latif b Wasim Akram	11
J. T. C. Vaughan c Inzamam-ul-Haq b Aqib Javed	3	– c Inzamam-ul-Haq b Aqib Javed	20
†R. C. Russell c Mushtaq Ahmed b Aqib Javed	18	– b Wasim Akram	7
T. H. C. Hancock c Rashid Latif b Wasim Akram	11	– c Ijaz Ahmed b Wasim Akram	29
R. C. Williams c Naved Anjum b Aqib Javed	17	– c Rashid Latif b Wasim Akram	0
G. D. Hodgson b Wasim Akram	7	– lbw b Wasim Akram	3
A. M. Smith c Rashid Latif b Wasim Akram	0	– b Wasim Akram	4
M. Davies not out	22	– c Rashid Latif b Mushtaq Ahmed	3
A. M. Babington c Inzamam-ul-Haq b Aqib Javed	8	– not out	4
L-b 1, n-b 4	5	L-b 5	5

1/13 2/14 3/24 4/51 5/67   123   1/14 2/27 3/66 4/80 5/80   126
6/70 7/78 8/78 9/105   6/81 7/105 8/115 9/118

Bowling: *First Innings*—Wasim Akram 22-11-44-5; Aqib Javed 15.1-4-34-5; Mushtaq Ahmed 2-1-1-0; Naved Anjum 9-2-43-0. *Second Innings*—Wasim Akram 24-12-32-6; Aqib Javed 13-5-49-2; Naved Anjum 8-4-23-0; Mushtaq Ahmed 15.1-5-17-2; Shoaib Mohammad 1-1-0-0.

Umpires: R. Julian and G. A. Stickley.

†ENGLAND v PAKISTAN

Third Texaco Trophy Match

At Nottingham, August 20. England won by 198 runs. Toss: Pakistan. After losing the Test series, England reverted to their tried and trusted one-day side, and the policy could hardly have been more successful. Gooch's batsmen produced the highest ever total in limited-overs internationals before his bowlers snuffed out any lingering hopes Pakistan had of keeping the Texaco Trophy series alive. When West Indies amassed 360 for four against Sri Lanka, in a World Cup match at Karachi in 1987, only 50 overs were available. But while England had 55, the quality of the opposition's attack made their performance even more remarkable, though the absence of a fifth specialist bowler did give England a chance – three makeweights bowled 11 overs for 106. Invited to bat, Gooch and Stewart laid the foundations with an opening stand of 84, but it was Smith and Fairbrother who set up a total of skyscraper proportions by adding 129 in 18 overs. Hick topped it off with a 34-ball fifty. In all, his 63 required just 42 deliveries, and he hit two of England's seven sixes and seven of their 28 fours. With Javed Miandad missing because of an upset stomach, Pakistan's task looked hopeless. So it proved as DeFreitas and Lewis made early inroads, to leave the understandably shocked tourists down and out at 27 for three. When last man Aqib Javed fell in the 47th over, Pakistan's only consolation was that they had avoided the heaviest defeat by runs in one-day international cricket.

Man of the Match: R. A. Smith.   *Attendance:* 12,195; *receipts* £263,349.

England

*G. A. Gooch b Waqar Younis	42	C. C. Lewis not out	1
†A. J. Stewart c Wasim Akram		P. A. J. DeFreitas not out	5
b Waqar Younis	34		
R. A. Smith c Ramiz Raja b Aqib Javed	77	B 4, l-b 12, w 18, n-b 5	39
N. H. Fairbrother b Aqib Javed	62		
A. J. Lamb lbw b Waqar Younis	16	1/84 (1) 2/95 (2) (7 wkts, 55 overs)	363
G. A. Hick b Wasim Akram	63	3/224 (3) 4/250 (4)	
I. T. Botham c Ramiz Raja		5/269 (5) 6/353 (7)	
b Waqar Younis	24	7/357 (6)	

R. K. Illingworth and G. C. Small did not bat.

Bowling: Wasim Akram 11-0-55-1; Aqib Javed 11-0-55-2; Waqar Younis 11-0-73-4; Mushtaq Ahmed 11-1-58-0; Ijaz Ahmed 4-0-29-0; Aamir Sohail 3-0-34-0; Asif Mujtaba 4-0-43-0.

Pakistan

Aamir Sohail c Botham b Lewis	17	Mushtaq Ahmed not out	14
Ramiz Raja c Gooch b DeFreitas	0	Aqib Javed c Stewart b Small	2
*Salim Malik c Small b Illingworth	45		
Asif Mujtaba c Lewis b DeFreitas	1	L-b 5, w 5	10
Inzamam-ul-Haq run out	10		—
Ijaz Ahmed c Gooch b Botham	23	(46.1 overs)	165
Wasim Akram lbw b Illingworth	1	1/2 (2) 2/22 (1) 3/27 (4)	
†Rashid Latif st Stewart b Illingworth	29	4/60 (5) 5/87 (3) 6/98 (7)	
Waqar Younis c Hick b DeFreitas	13	7/103 (6) 8/129 (9)	
		9/153 (8) 10/165 (11)	

Bowling: DeFreitas 11-1-33-3; Lewis 8-2-24-1; Botham 11-1-41-1; Small 5.1-0-28-1; Illingworth 11-1-34-3.

Umpires: B. Dudleston and D. R. Shepherd. Referee: D. L. Murray (West Indies).

†ENGLAND v PAKISTAN

Fourth Texaco Trophy Match

At Lord's, August 22, 23. Pakistan won by three runs. Toss: Pakistan. An enthralling contest, spread across two days, was decided in Pakistan's favour when Waqar Younis bowled last man Illingworth with the second delivery of the final over. Unhappily, the match will be remembered primarily for what followed off the field. Within minutes of the close, it was revealed that umpires Palmer and Hampshire had found it necessary, during the second-day lunch interval, to change the ball being used by Pakistan's bowlers. They had consulted with match referee Deryck Murray, who refused to make public comment. The implication was "ball-tampering", though Pakistan argued the ball was merely out of shape. Five days later – with allegations, counter-claims and threats to sue for libel still coming thick and fast – the International Cricket Council ruled the matter closed without either clearing or convicting Pakistan. What was undeniable was that the tourists had bowled brilliantly to win a match against the odds and end England's hopes of a clean sweep. On Saturday Pakistan's innings, reduced to 50 overs after a delayed start, was frequently interrupted by rain, but they still managed enough momentum to total 204 for five. Captain Javed Miandad, troubled by a bad back and calling for a runner, master-minded affairs with an undefeated 50 off 60 balls, though he offered débutant wicket-keeper Blakey a stumping chance when 17. Botham, deputising as opener for the injured Gooch, launched England's pursuit by hitting Wasim Akram's first three deliveries to the boundary before a halt was called after just two overs. Conditions were far better for batting on Sunday, and England looked set for victory when they reached 172 for five shortly after lunch. Lamb, however, was caught behind, and Wasim and Waqar cleaned up the tail with some magnificent fast bowling – and the replacement ball.

Man of the Match: Javed Miandad.   *Attendance:* 25,169; *receipts* £663,384.

Close of play: First day, England 15-1 (2 overs) (I. T. Botham 14*, R. A. Smith 0*).

Pakistan

Aamir Sohail c Stewart b DeFreitas	... 20	Naved Anjum not out	 4
Ramiz Raja c Stewart b Botham	 23	B 2, l-b 7, w 11	 20
Salim Malik st Blakey b Illingworth	.. 48		
*Javed Miandad not out	 50	1/32 (1) 2/91 (2)	(5 wkts, 50 overs) 204
Inzamam-ul-Haq c Blakey b Reeve	 16	3/102 (3) 4/137 (5)	
Wasim Akram b DeFreitas	 23	5/189 (6)	

†Moin Khan, Waqar Younis, Mushtaq Ahmed and Aqib Javed did not bat.

Bowling: DeFreitas 10-2-39-2; Lewis 10-0-49-0; Botham 10-1-33-1; Reeve 10-1-31-1; Illingworth 10-0-43-1.

England

I. T. Botham st Moin Khan		P. A. J. DeFreitas c Mushtaq Ahmed	
b Aamir Sohail .	40	b Wasim Akram .	0
*A. J. Stewart lbw b Waqar Younis	... 0	R. K. Illingworth b Waqar Younis	 4
R. A. Smith c Moin Khan b Aqib Javed	4		
N. H. Fairbrother b Aqib Javed	 33		
A. J. Lamb c Moin Khan		L-b 8, w 11, n-b 6	 25
b Mushtaq Ahmed .	55		
G. A. Hick b Aamir Sohail	 8	1/15 (2) 2/30 (3) 3/72 (4)	(49.2 overs) 201
†R. J. Blakey b Waqar Younis	 25	4/111 (1) 5/139 (6)	
D. A. Reeve not out	 6	6/172 (5) 7/191 (7)	
C. C. Lewis c sub (Asif Mujtaba)		8/193 (9) 9/193 (10)	
b Wasim Akram .	1	10/201 (11)	

Bowling: Wasim Akram 10-2-41-2; Waqar Younis 9.2-0-36-3; Mushtaq Ahmed 10-1-34-1; Aqib Javed 9-0-39-2; Aamir Sohail 5-0-22-2; Naved Anjum 6-0-21-0.

Umpires: J. H. Hampshire and K. E. Palmer. Referee: D. L. Murray (West Indies).

†ENGLAND v PAKISTAN

Fifth Texaco Trophy Match

At Manchester, August 24. England won by six wickets. Toss: Pakistan. England gave retiring manager Micky Stewart a memorable send-off, with a crushing victory to take the series 4-1. When Hick stroked the winning single, 11.2 overs remained – and that despite Pakistan's seemingly challenging total of 254 for five. The tourists, despite losing Javed Miandad to back problems and Salim Malik to a thigh injury, had made steady progress on another excellent pitch. Opener Aamir Sohail, reprieved early on when Lamb dropped a slip catch off newcomer Cork, rounded off a fine season with 87, while Inzamam-ul-Haq, so disappointing during the Tests, at last showed his true potential. He punctuated an 86-ball stay with a six and half a dozen fours before departing for 75, giving Cork a well-deserved wicket. Gooch and Alec Stewart launched the reply with a spectacular opening stand of 98 in 15 overs, to leave little doubt about the result. Hick twice drove Mushtaq Ahmed for soaring sixes while Smith, with 85 off 91 balls, made sure of his third Man of the Match award of the series. The final, explosive touches had been put to Stewart senior's one-day management record. During his six years in charge, England played 91 internationals, won 52 and lost 35, with one tie and three no-results. However, the Test record had been less impressive: of 58 games, 12 were won, 20 lost and 26 drawn.

Man of the Match: R. A. Smith.   *Attendance:* 18,790; *receipts* £379,800.

Men of the Series: England – R. A. Smith; Pakistan – Wasim Akram.

Pakistan

Aamir Sohail run out	87	Naved Anjum not out	12
*Ramiz Raja run out	37	L-b 6, w 2, n-b 1	9
Shoaib Mohammad b Reeve	9		
Inzamam-ul-Haq lbw b Cork	75	1/69 (2) 2/90 (3) (5 wkts, 55 overs) 254	
Asif Mujtaba c Smith b DeFreitas	10	3/189 (1) 4/210 (5)	
Wasim Akram not out	15	5/240 (4)	

†Moin Khan, Mushtaq Ahmed, Waqar Younis and Aqib Javed did not bat.

Bowling: DeFreitas 11–1–52–1; Cork 11–1–37–1; Botham 11–0–43–0; Reeve 11–1–57–1; Illingworth 11–0–59–0.

England

*G. A. Gooch b Aamir Sohail	45	G. A. Hick not out	42
†A. J. Stewart st Moin Khan b Aamir Sohail	51		
R. A. Smith not out	85		
N. H. Fairbrother b Waqar Younis	15	L-b 7, w 3, n-b 5	15
A. J. Lamb c Moin Khan b Waqar Younis	2	1/98 (1) 2/101 (2) (4 wkts, 43.4 overs) 255	
		3/149 (4) 4/159 (5)	

I. T. Botham, D. A. Reeve, D. G. Cork, P. A. J. DeFreitas and R. K. Illingworth did not bat.

Bowling: Wasim Akram 9.4–1–45–0; Waqar Younis 8–0–58–2; Aqib Javed 6–0–42–0; Mushtaq Ahmed 9–0–48–0; Aamir Sohail 7–0–29–2; Naved Anjum 4–0–26–0.

Umpires: H. D. Bird and M. J. Kitchen. Referee: D. L. Murray (West Indies).

WORLD XI v PAKISTANIS

At Scarborough, August 26, 27, 28. Drawn. Toss: Pakistanis. The tourists left the controversy over possible ball-abuse to the newspapers as they relaxed at the seaside. While Allan Lamb expressed his opinions in full, ICC declined to express any at all, the Pakistanis were organising impromptu games with the crowd amid the showers. When play was possible, Shoaib Mohammad reached his first first-class hundred of the tour, striking three sixes and 11 fours in four hours, and declaring late on the second day. Rain prevented the World XI's reply that evening, but on the final day South Australian Peter Sleep scored a career-best 182, with four sixes and 20 fours from 214 balls. He added 190 for the sixth wicket with New Zealand's Dipak Patel in exactly two hours, before falling to the occasional medium pace of wicket-keeper Rashid Latif, one of ten Pakistani bowlers used; meanwhile Aqib Javed tried his hand at leg-spin and Mushtaq Ahmed did Malcolm Marshall impersonations.

Close of play: First day, Pakistanis 151-5 (Shoaib Mohammad 57*, Moin Khan 13*); Second day, Pakistanis 253-6 dec.

Pakistanis

Aamir Sohail c Mudassar Nazar b Benjamin	15	†Moin Khan st Parore b Patel	44
*Shoaib Mohammad not out	105	Rashid Latif not out	14
Asif Mujtaba c Greatbatch b Benjamin	17		
Zahid Fazal lbw b Benjamin	0	L-b 4, n-b 11	15
Inzamam-ul-Haq c Harper b Patel	38	1/15 2/47 3/47 (6 wkts dec.) 253	
Naved Anjum c Simmons b Sleep	5	4/116 5/128 6/225	

Mushtaq Ahmed, Aqib Javed and Ata-ur-Rehman did not bat.

Bowling: Pringle 18–5–56–0; Benjamin 12–0–55–3; Patel 20–3–72–2; Sleep 10–3–34–1; Harper 15–0–32–0.

World XI

M. J. Greatbatch c Rashid Latif b Ata-ur-Rehman .	45	D. N. Patel c Aamir Sohail b Aqib Javed .	72
P. V. Simmons c Rashid Latif b Ata-ur-Rehman .	23	†A. C. Parore not out .	2
		C. Pringle b Rashid Latif .	0
*R. B. Richardson c Aamir Sohail b Mushtaq Ahmed .	5	K. C. G. Benjamin not out .	0
P. R. Sleep lbw b Rashid Latif .	182		
C. G. Greenidge c Zahid Fazal b Aamir Sohail .	24	L-b 8, n-b 13 .	21
R. A. Harper c Rashid Latif b Inzamam-ul-Haq .	11	1/65 2/76 3/85 (8 wkts dec.)	385
		4/138 5/183 6/373	
		7/385 8/385	

Mudassar Nazar did not bat.

Bowling: Aqib Javed 22–4–73–1; Naved Anjum 5–1–17–0; Mushtaq Ahmed 16–5–51–1; Ata-ur-Rehman 9–1–59–2; Shoaib Mohammad 5–0–17–0; Rashid Latif 8–2–17–2; Aamir Sohail 22–1–87–1; Zahid Fazal 9–1–48–0; Inzamam-ul-Haq 1–0–5–1; Moin Khan 1–0–3–0.

Umpires: J. H. Hampshire and B. Leadbeater.

BRITANNIC ASSURANCE
COUNTY CHAMPIONSHIP, 1992

The last County Championship before the switch to a programme of purely four-day cricket, which is supposed to help the stronger counties, went to the team agreed by just about everyone to be the strongest of all. Despite the absence of their captain, Graham Gooch, for 11 of the 22 games and their leading fast bowler, Neil Foster, for 12 of them, Essex retained the title by 41 points. It was the largest winning margin since 1979 when Essex won the first of their six titles by 77 points. In that time, their record has been matchless; since 1983 they have been out of the top four only once and they would have been champions again in 1989 if the title had not been given to Worcestershire by the fiat of a 25-point deduction from the Test and County Cricket Board.

The season hinged largely on one dramatic match at Bournemouth in June when Hampshire, the then leaders, forced Essex to follow on but collapsed themselves for 80 in the final hour, to lose by 79 runs. Five days later, on June 27, Essex completed a two-day win over Lancashire, took over at the top and between then and September 3, when they became mathematical certainties (barring further TCCB deductions), only their more nervous supporters could even envisage them being overhauled.

As usual, Essex made the most of their opportunities on their out-grounds, Ilford, Southend and Colchester, winning five matches out of six. Festival cricket will be hard hit by the change to four-day cricket and a higher proportion of Essex matches will in future be at Chelmsford where

BRITANNIC ASSURANCE CHAMPIONSHIP

Win = 16 points	Played	Won	Lost	Drawn	Bonus points Batting	Bonus points Bowling	Points
1 – Essex (1)	22	11	6	5	60	64	300
2 – Kent (6)	22	9	3	10	60	55	259
3 – Northamptonshire (10)	22	8	4	10	62	58	248
4 – Nottinghamshire (4) ..	22	7	7	8	54	58	224
5 – Derbyshire (3)	22	7	6	9	47	63	222
6 – Warwickshire (2)	22	6	8	8	55	68	219
7 – Sussex (11)	22	6	7	9	60	61	217
8 – Leicestershire (16)....	22	7	7	8	39	60	211
9 – Somerset (17)........	22	5	4	13	64	62	206
10 – Gloucestershire (13) ..	21	6	6	9	48	58	202
11 – Middlesex (15).......	22	5	3	14	62	60	202
12 – Lancashire (8)	22	4	6	12	73	51	188
13 – Surrey (5)..........	22	5	7	10	56	50	186
14 – Glamorgan (12)......	22	5	4	13	53	49	182
15 – Hampshire (9).......	22	4	6	12	61	57	182
16 – Yorkshire (14).......	22	4	6	12	56	52	172
17 – Worcestershire (6)....	21	3	4	14	54	65	167
18 – Durham (–)	22	2	10	10	46	53	131

1991 positions are shown in brackets.

The following match was abandoned and is not included in the above table: May 29, 30, June 1 – Worcestershire v Gloucestershire at Worcester.

they have generally found it harder to force victories. Essex resisted the change louder and harder than anyone else. None the less, they did win four of their six four-day games as well.

Their nearest rivals were Kent, who were 13th at the start of Maidstone Week on June 30 but then rose steadily, largely due to the bowling form of their Australian-bred Ulsterman, Martin McCague. They never really got close to the champions. Northamptonshire, playing near to their ability for once, were third. Nottinghamshire had games in hand for much of the summer and might have had Essex worried; but they lost two consecutive home matches by tiny margins – ten runs and seven – at the start of August before Essex stamped all over them at Colchester and put them out of the race.

The only other team who might have momentarily worried Essex were Leicestershire, 66-1 outsiders at the start of the season, who moved into second place on July 23 and immediately bowled Essex out for 75 at Grace Road, beat them by 68 runs and cut the lead to 31 points. This was Leicestershire's fourth win in July, and the third on the sometimes sporty Leicester wickets. But the loss of their fast bowler David Millns to injury was a major blow and they lost three of the next four games very heavily. Leicestershire were in the shake-up for place money until the very end, when they suddenly fell back to finish eighth, behind Derbyshire and Warwickshire, Essex's main challengers in 1991, and Sussex, who won their last two matches with an astonishing burst of 23 wickets from their leg-spinner Ian Salisbury and finished in their highest position since 1985.

Somerset rose from bottom place to ninth, their highest since 1984, just ahead of Gloucestershire. Few pre-season predictions would have put either of these teams ahead of the next three, Middlesex, Lancashire and Surrey. However, Middlesex, with key bowlers injured or ill, never found their Sunday League form in the week; Lancashire became introspective again, dropped out of the top ten for the first time in six seasons and went without a Championship win between mid-May and early August; Surrey that was hampered by the absence of Waqar Younis and pitches at The Oval that gave lesser bowlers no encouragement.

Glamorgan, in the top ten just twice in 22 years, came 14th. But they finished in front of Hampshire, who lost their way completely in the second half of the season and, having been top on Midsummer's Day, fell to 15th. Yorkshire, having broken tradition and signed Sachin Tendulkar from India, had a brief burst of encouragement when they had two successive innings wins in June, over Derbyshire and Essex; they had two more successive wins in early August, against their neighbours Lancashire and Durham – to win both the home Roses match and the new Durham Light Infantry Cup. But they had no other wins all season and finished 16th, equal to their second-worst placing ever, in 1989.

The real under-achievers of the 1992 Championship, however, were Worcestershire, second favourites in the pre-season betting. They won only three games and drew their last ten to finish 17th for the first time since 1932. They were saved from the wooden spoon only by the cushioning presence of the newcomers Durham, who had early wins over Glamorgan and Somerset but failed to win any of their last 16 matches. Durham thus came bottom in their first season, just as the last newcomers, Glamorgan, had done 71 years before.

Pre-season betting (William Hill): 3-1 Essex; 9-2 Worcestershire; 7-1 Lancashire and Middlesex; 9-1 Warwickshire; 11-1 Derbyshire, Nottinghamshire and Surrey; 14-1 Hampshire; 16-1 Northamptonshire; 25-1 Kent; 33-1 Durham; 40-1 Yorkshire; 50-1 Sussex; 66-1 Gloucestershire, Leicestershire and Somerset; 100-1 Glamorgan.

Leaders: from May 18 Nottinghamshire; from May 26 Hampshire; June 27 onwards Essex. Essex became champions on September 3.

Bottom place: from May 18 Sussex; from May 22 Surrey; from June 29 Glamorgan; August 10 onwards Durham.

Prizemoney

First (Essex)	£46,000
Second (Kent)	£23,000
Third (Northamptonshire)	£13,250
Fourth (Nottinghamshire)	£6,750
Fifth (Derbyshire)	£3,375
Winner of each match	£250
Championship Player of the Year (P. J. Prichard)	£1,000
County of the Month	£1,000
Player of the Month	£300

Scoring of Points

(*a*) For a win, 16 points plus any points scored in the first innings.

(*b*) In a tie, each side scores eight points, plus any points scored in the first innings.

(*c*) If the scores are equal in a drawn match, the side batting in the fourth innings scores eight points, plus any points scored in the first innings.

(*d*) First-innings points (awarded only for performances in the first 100 overs of each first innings and retained whatever the result of the match).

(i) A maximum of four batting points to be available: 150 to 199 runs – 1 point; 200 to 249 runs – 2 points; 250 to 299 – 3 points; 300 runs or over – 4 points.

(ii) A maximum of four bowling points to be available: 3 or 4 wickets taken – 1 point; 5 or 6 wickets taken – 2 points; 7 or 8 wickets taken – 3 points; 9 or 10 wickets taken – 4 points.

In 1993, first-innings points will be awarded in the first 120 overs. Batting points will be gained as follows: 200 to 249 runs – 1 point; 250 to 299 runs – 2 points; 300 to 349 runs – 3 points; 350 runs or over – 4 points. Bowling points will be unchanged.

(*e*) If play starts when less than eight hours' playing time remains and a one-innings match is played, no first-innings points shall be scored. The side winning on the one innings scores 12 points.

(*f*) A county which is adjudged to have prepared a pitch unsuitable for first-class cricket shall be liable to have 25 points deducted.

(*g*) The side which has the highest aggregate of points shall be the Champion County. Should any sides in the Championship table be equal on points the side with most wins will have priority.

CHAMPION COUNTY SINCE 1864

Note: The earliest county champions were decided usually by the fewest matches lost, but in 1888 an unofficial points system was introduced. In 1890, the Championship was constituted officially. From 1977 to 1983 it was sponsored by Schweppes, and since 1984 by Britannic Assurance.

1864	Surrey	1901	Yorkshire	1952	Surrey
1865	Nottinghamshire	1902	Yorkshire	1953	Surrey
1866	Middlesex	1903	Middlesex	1954	Surrey
1867	Yorkshire	1904	Lancashire	1955	Surrey
1868	Nottinghamshire	1905	Yorkshire	1956	Surrey
1869 {	Nottinghamshire	1906	Kent	1957	Surrey
	Yorkshire	1907	Nottinghamshire	1958	Surrey
1870	Yorkshire	1908	Yorkshire	1959	Yorkshire
1871	Nottinghamshire	1909	Kent	1960	Yorkshire
1872	Nottinghamshire	1910	Kent	1961	Hampshire
1873 {	Gloucestershire	1911	Warwickshire	1962	Yorkshire
	Nottinghamshire	1912	Yorkshire	1963	Yorkshire
1874	Gloucestershire	1913	Kent	1964	Worcestershire
1875	Nottinghamshire	1914	Surrey	1965	Worcestershire
1876	Gloucestershire	1919	Yorkshire	1966	Yorkshire
1877	Gloucestershire	1920	Middlesex	1967	Yorkshire
1878	Undecided	1921	Middlesex	1968	Yorkshire
1879 {	Nottinghamshire	1922	Yorkshire	1969	Glamorgan
	Lancashire	1923	Yorkshire	1970	Kent
1880	Nottinghamshire	1924	Yorkshire	1971	Surrey
1881	Lancashire	1925	Yorkshire	1972	Warwickshire
1882 {	Nottinghamshire	1926	Lancashire	1973	Hampshire
	Lancashire	1927	Lancashire	1974	Worcestershire
1883	Nottinghamshire	1928	Lancashire	1975	Leicestershire
1884	Nottinghamshire	1929	Nottinghamshire	1976	Middlesex
1885	Nottinghamshire	1930	Lancashire	1977 {	Middlesex
1886	Nottinghamshire	1931	Yorkshire		Kent
1887	Surrey	1932	Yorkshire	1978	Kent
1888	Surrey	1933	Yorkshire	1979	Essex
1889 {	Surrey	1934	Lancashire	1980	Middlesex
	Lancashire	1935	Yorkshire	1981	Nottinghamshire
	Nottinghamshire	1936	Derbyshire	1982	Middlesex
1890	Surrey	1937	Yorkshire	1983	Essex
1891	Surrey	1938	Yorkshire	1984	Essex
1892	Surrey	1939	Yorkshire	1985	Middlesex
1893	Yorkshire	1946	Yorkshire	1986	Essex
1894	Surrey	1947	Middlesex	1987	Nottinghamshire
1895	Surrey	1948	Glamorgan	1988	Worcestershire
1896	Yorkshire	1949 {	Middlesex	1989	Worcestershire
1897	Lancashire		Yorkshire	1990	Middlesex
1898	Yorkshire	1950 {	Lancashire	1991	Essex
1899	Surrey		Surrey	1992	Essex
1900	Yorkshire	1951	Warwickshire		

Notes: The title has been won outright as follows: Yorkshire 31 times, Surrey 18, Nottinghamshire 14, Middlesex 10, Lancashire 8, Essex 6, Kent 6, Worcestershire 5, Gloucestershire 3, Warwickshire 3, Glamorgan 2, Hampshire 2, Derbyshire 1, Leicestershire 1.

Eight times the title has been shared as follows: Nottinghamshire 5, Lancashire 4, Middlesex 2, Surrey 2, Yorkshire 2, Gloucestershire 1, Kent 1.

The earliest date the Championship has been won in any season since it was expanded in 1895 was August 12, 1910, by Kent.

BRITANNIC ASSURANCE CHAMPIONSHIP
STATISTICS FOR 1992

County	Runs	For Wickets	Avge	Runs	Against Wickets	Avge
Derbyshire	9,015	249	36.20	8,309	257	32.33
Durham	9,545	320	29.82	9,481	235	40.34
Essex	9,806	253	38.75	9,833	324	30.34
Glamorgan	8,942	272	32.87	9,438	259	36.44
Gloucestershire	8,620	295	29.22	8,570	287	29.86
Hampshire	9,102	271	33.58	9,236	280	32.98
Kent	10,700	278	38.48	10,147	308	32.94
Lancashire	10,206	258	39.55	10,404	248	41.95
Leicestershire	7,800	298	26.17	8,548	273	31.31
Middlesex	10,421	260	40.08	9,418	276	34.12
Northamptonshire	9,753	262	37.22	9,254	307	30.14
Nottinghamshire	10,624	291	36.50	10,250	281	36.47
Somerset	9,591	274	35.00	9,262	269	34.43
Surrey	9,797	294	33.32	10,384	273	38.03
Sussex	9,551	285	33.51	9,912	268	36.98
Warwickshire	9,244	299	30.91	10,025	288	34.80
Worcestershire	9,144	261	35.03	9,408	265	35.50
Yorkshire	8,929	259	34.47	8,911	281	31.71
	170,790	4,979	34.30	170,790	4,979	34.30

COUNTY CHAMPIONSHIP – MATCH RESULTS, 1864-1992

County	Years of Play	Played	Won	Lost	Tied	Drawn
Derbyshire	1871-87; 1895-1992	2,156	533	780	1	842
Durham	1992	22	2	10	0	10
Essex	1895-1992	2,119	607	607	5	900
Glamorgan	1921-1992	1,653	356	563	0	734
Gloucestershire	1870-1992	2,393	705	883	2	803
Hampshire	1864-85; 1895-1992	2,228	581	765	4	878
Kent	1864-1992	2,516	910	757	5	844
Lancashire	1865-1992	2,594	961	532	3	1,098
Leicestershire	1895-1992	2,086	451	776	1	858
Middlesex	1864-1992	2,296	850	582	5	859
Northamptonshire	1905-1992	1,853	442	653	3	755
Nottinghamshire	1864-1992	2,425	737	636	0	1,052
Somerset	1882-85; 1891-1992	2,126	492	860	3	771
Surrey	1864-1992	2,673	1,055	587	4	1,027
Sussex	1864-1992	2,565	712	880	6	967
Warwickshire	1895-1992	2,100	552	615	1	932
Worcestershire	1899-1992	2,040	502	711	1	826
Yorkshire	1864-1992	2,694	1,202	453	2	1,037
Cambridgeshire	1864-69; 1871	19	8	8	0	3
		19,279	11,658	11,658	23	7,598

Notes: Matches abandoned without a ball bowled are wholly excluded.

Counties participated in the years shown, except that there were no matches in the years 1915-18 and 1940-45; Hampshire did not play inter-county matches in 1868-69, 1871-74 and 1879; Worcestershire did not take part in the Championship in 1919.

COUNTY CHAMPIONSHIP – FINAL POSITIONS, 1890-1992

	Derbyshire	Essex	Glamorgan	Gloucestershire	Hampshire	Kent	Lancashire	Leicestershire	Middlesex	Northamptonshire	Nottinghamshire	Somerset	Surrey	Sussex	Warwickshire	Worcestershire	Yorkshire
'90	—	—	—	6	—	3	2	—	7	—	5	—	1	8	—	—	3
'91	—	—	—	9	—	5	2	—	3	—	4	5	1	7	—	—	8
'92	—	—	—	7	—	7	4	—	5	—	2	3	1	9	—	—	6
'93	—	—	—	9	—	4	2	—	3	—	6	8	5	7	—	—	1
'94	—	—	—	9	—	4	4	—	3	—	7	6	1	8	—	—	2
'95	5	9	—	4	10	14	2	12	6	—	12	8	1	11	6	—	3
'96	7	5	—	10	8	9	2	13	3	—	6	11	4	14	12	—	1
'97	14	3	—	5	9	12	1	13	8	—	10	11	2	6	7	—	4
'98	9	5	—	3	12	7	6	13	2	—	8	13	4	9	9	—	1
'99	15	6	—	9	10	8	4	13	2	—	10	13	1	5	7	12	3
'00	10	13	—	7	15	3	2	14	7	—	5	11	7	3	6	12	1
'01	15	10	—	14	7	7	3	12	2	—	9	12	6	4	5	11	1
'02	10	13	—	14	15	7	5	11	12	—	3	7	4	2	6	9	1
'03	12	8	—	13	14	8	4	14	1	—	5	10	11	2	7	6	3
'04	10	14	—	9	15	3	1	7	4	—	5	12	11	6	7	13	2
'05	14	12	—	8	16	6	2	5	11	13	10	15	4	3	7	8	1
'06	16	7	—	9	8	1	4	15	11	11	5	11	3	10	6	14	2
'07	16	7	—	10	12	8	6	11	5	15	1	14	4	13	9	2	2
'08	14	11	—	10	9	2	7	13	4	15	8	16	3	5	12	6	1
'09	15	14	—	16	8	1	2	13	6	7	10	11	5	4	12	8	3
'10	15	11	—	12	6	1	4	10	3	9	5	16	2	7	14	13	8
'11	14	6	—	12	11	2	4	15	3	10	8	16	5	13	1	9	7
'12	12	15	—	11	6	3	4	13	5	2	8	14	7	10	9	16	1
'13	13	15	—	9	10	1	8	14	6	4	5	16	3	7	11	12	2
'14	12	8	—	16	5	3	11	13	2	9	10	15	1	6	7	14	4
'19	9	14	—	8	7	2	5	9	13	12	3	5	4	11	15	—	1
'20	16	9	—	8	11	5	2	13	1	14	7	10	3	6	12	15	4
'21	12	15	17	7	6	4	5	11	1	13	8	10	2	9	16	14	3
'22	11	8	16	13	6	4	5	14	7	15	2	10	3	9	12	17	1
'23	10	13	16	11	7	5	3	14	8	17	2	9	4	6	12	15	1
'24	17	15	13	6	12	5	4	11	2	16	6	8	3	10	9	14	1
'25	14	7	17	10	9	5	3	12	6	11	4	15	2	13	8	16	1
'26	11	9	8	15	7	3	1	13	6	16	4	14	5	10	12	17	2
'27	5	8	15	12	13	4	1	7	9	16	2	14	6	10	11	17	3
'28	10	16	15	5	12	2	1	9	8	13	3	14	6	7	11	17	4
'29	7	12	17	4	11	8	2	9	6	13	1	15	10	4	14	16	2
'30	9	6	11	2	13	5	1	12	16	17	4	13	8	7	15	10	3
'31	7	10	15	2	12	3	6	16	11	17	5	13	8	4	9	14	1
'32	10	14	15	13	8	3	6	12	10	16	4	7	5	2	9	17	1
'33	6	4	16	10	14	3	5	17	12	13	8	11	9	2	7	15	1
'34	3	8	13	7	14	5	1	12	10	17	9	15	11	2	4	16	5
'35	2	9	13	15	16	10	4	6	3	17	5	14	11	7	8	12	1
'36	1	9	16	4	10	8	11	15	2	17	5	7	6	14	13	12	3
'37	3	6	7	4	14	12	9	16	2	17	10	13	8	5	11	15	1
'38	5	6	16	10	14	9	4	15	2	17	12	7	3	8	13	11	1
'39	9	4	13	3	15	5	6	17	2	16	12	14	8	10	11	7	1
'46	15	8	6	5	10	6	3	11	2	16	13	4	11	17	14	8	1
'47	5	11	9	2	16	4	3	14	1	17	11	11	6	9	15	7	7
'48	6	13	1	8	9	15	5	11	3	17	14	12	2	16	7	10	4
'49	15	9	8	7	16	13	11	17	1	6	11	9	5	13	4	3	1

	Derbyshire	Durham	Essex	Glamorgan	Gloucestershire	Hampshire	Kent	Lancashire	Leicestershire	Middlesex	Northamptonshire	Nottinghamshire	Somerset	Surrey	Sussex	Warwickshire	Worcestershire	Yorkshire
1950	5	—	17	11	7	12	9	1	16	14	10	15	7	1	13	4	6	
1951	11	—	8	5	12	9	16	3	15	7	13	17	14	6	10	1	4	
1952	4	—	10	7	9	12	15	3	6	5	8	16	17	1	13	10	14	
1953	6	—	12	10	6	14	16	3	3	5	11	8	17	1	2	9	15	1
1954	3	—	15	4	13	14	11	10	16	7	7	5	17	1	9	6	11	
1955	8	—	14	16	12	3	13	9	6	5	7	11	17	1	4	9	15	
1956	12	—	11	13	3	6	16	2	17	5	4	8	15	1	9	14	9	
1957	4	—	5	9	12	13	14	6	17	7	2	15	8	1	9	11	16	
1958	5	—	6	15	14	2	8	7	12	10	4	17	3	1	13	16	9	1
1959	7	—	9	6	2	8	13	5	16	10	11	17	12	3	15	4	14	
1960	5	—	6	11	8	12	10	2	17	3	9	16	14	7	4	15	13	
1961	7	—	6	14	5	1	11	13	9	3	16	17	10	15	8	12	4	
1962	7	—	9	14	4	10	11	16	17	13	8	15	6	5	12	3	2	
1963	17	—	12	2	8	10	13	15	16	6	7	9	3	11	4	4	14	
1964	12	—	10	11	17	12	7	14	16	6	3	15	8	4	9	2	1	
1965	9	—	15	3	10	12	5	13	14	6	2	17	7	8	16	11	1	
1966	9	—	16	14	15	11	4	12	8	12	5	17	3	7	10	6	2	
1967	6	—	15	14	17	12	2	11	2	7	9	15	8	4	13	10	5	
1968	8	—	14	3	16	5	2	6	9	10	13	4	12	15	17	11	7	
1969	16	—	6	1	2	5	10	15	14	11	9	8	17	3	7	4	12	1
1970	7	—	12	2	17	10	1	3	15	16	14	11	13	5	9	7	6	
1971	17	—	10	16	8	9	4	3	5	6	14	12	7	1	11	2	15	1
1972	17	—	5	13	3	9	2	15	6	8	4	14	11	12	16	1	7	1
1973	16	—	8	11	5	1	4	12	9	13	3	17	10	2	15	7	6	1
1974	17	—	12	16	14	2	10	8	4	6	3	15	5	7	13	9	1	1
1975	15	—	7	9	16	3	5	4	1	11	8	13	12	6	13	17	10	
1976	15	—	6	17	3	12	14	16	4	1	2	13	7	9	10	5	11	
1977	7	—	6	14	3	11	1	16	5	1	9	17	4	14	8	10	13	1
1978	14	—	2	13	10	8	1	12	6	3	17	7	5	16	9	11	15	
1979	16	—	1	17	10	12	5	13	6	14	11	9	8	3	4	15	2	
1980	9	—	8	13	7	17	16	15	10	1	12	3	5	2	4	14	11	
1981	12	—	5	14	13	7	9	16	8	4	15	1	3	6	2	17	11	1
1982	11	—	7	16	15	3	13	12	2	1	9	4	6	5	8	17	14	1
1983	9	—	1	15	12	3	7	12	4	2	6	14	10	8	11	5	16	1
1984	12	—	1	13	17	15	5	16	4	3	11	2	7	8	6	9	10	1
1985	13	—	4	12	3	2	9	14	16	1	10	8	17	6	7	15	5	1
1986	11	—	1	17	2	6	8	15	7	12	9	4	16	3	14	12	5	1
1987	6	—	12	13	10	5	14	2	3	16	7	1	11	4	17	15	9	
1988	14	—	3	17	10	15	2	9	8	7	12	5	11	4	16	6	1	1
1989	6	—	2	17	9	6	15	4	13	3	5	11	14	12	10	8	1	1
1990	12	—	2	8	13	3	16	6	7	1	11	13	15	9	17	5	4	1
1991	3	—	1	12	13	9	8	16	15	10	4	17	5	11	2	6	1	
1992	5	18	1	14	10	15	2	12	8	11	3	9	13	7	6	17	1	

Note: From 1969 onwards, positions have been given in accordance with the Championship regulations which state that "Should *any* sides in the table be equal on points the side with most wins will have priority".

DERBYSHIRE

President: C. S. Elliott
Chairman: C. N. Middleton
Chairman, Cricket Committee: B. Holling
Chief Executive: R. J. Lark
  County Ground, Nottingham Road, Derby
  DE21 6DA (Telephone: 0332-383211;
  fax 0332-290251)
Captain: K. J. Barnett
Coach: P. E. Russell

Derbyshire's emergence as a force in the County Championship was confirmed by fifth position, following third place in 1991. They always expect to do better in one-day competitions but they failed in those once again, as they have done since their Sunday title in 1990: Derbyshire were outwitted by Kent in the Benson and Hedges Cup quarter-finals, batted disastrously against Leicestershire in the NatWest Trophy and made no impression on the Sunday League. They were unable to handle critical, do-or-die situations.

With greater consistency, which they hope experience will bring, Derbyshire can become candidates for the Championship; the fact that they have been higher than fifth only once in 35 seasons gives perspective to what they have already achieved under Kim Barnett, the county's longest-serving captain. For the second successive season, Donald Carr's 1959 record of 2,165 runs was threatened. Mohammad Azharuddin became only the second batsman to score 2,000 for Derbyshire in 1991 and Peter Bowler ran Carr even closer with 2,044 at 65.93, the highest average for the county in a full season. It was disappointing that Bowler was not rewarded with a place in either touring team, especially as the runs were made in ways to suit occasions. Bowler has been reliable ever since Derbyshire engaged him from Leicestershire in 1988, and has extended his range. Unbeaten centuries against Lancashire at Blackpool and Somerset at Taunton set up two of Derbyshire's seven victories and his 241 not out in the innings win over Hampshire at Portsmouth was a magnificent effort.

Barnett completed 1,000 runs for the tenth consecutive season, equalling the Derbyshire record sequence set by Arnold Hamer (1950-59) but was forced to miss five matches with a knee injury. He had already hobbled through several games with hip trouble but was reluctant to acknowledge that anything was wrong until medical advice prevailed. In Barnett's absence, John Morris capably led the side to three victories. Although he averaged over 40, Morris did not make enough big scores to force himself back into Test contention and pre-season concern about replacing Azharuddin's runs was increased when Tim O'Gorman and Chris Adams started badly. O'Gorman reached 1,000 runs on the last day of the season, endorsing rather than enhancing his status, but Adams established himself as one of the best young strikers in the game.

Adams scored Derbyshire's fastest-ever century, in 57 minutes at Worcester to beat Stan Worthington's 1933 time by three minutes, and

made the county's highest-ever Sunday League score with 141 not out
against Kent at Chesterfield. He also showed that he is learning
patience to accompany his power and fine all-round fielding. Adam
O'Gorman and Karl Krikken were awarded county caps, but although
Krikken kept wicket expertly in his unconventional way, his batting
was disappointing. Dominic Cork, selected for the last one-day international against Pakistan and his second England A tour, improved his
batting enough to suggest that he will become a genuine all-rounder.
Ian Bishop, always blessed with time to play his shots, is capable of
more in this area and Frank Griffith, in his fifth season, began to
repay faith in his all-round potential.

After Azharuddin's success, Derbyshire faced a difficult decision
about Bishop. He had been released from his five-year contract for
1991, in the expectation that he would tour with West Indies, but was
ruled out of that by a back injury and, after returning home early from
Australia, missed the World Cup. He had played no first-class cricket
since January 1991 but assured Derbyshire's chief executive Bob Larkins
who flew out specially to Trinidad, that he was fit. With a remodelled
action but no loss of pace, Bishop was as good as his word and,
although he bowled through a persistent Achilles tendon injury, had no
problem with his back. Barnett described some of his spells as
awesome, including seven for 34 against Hampshire, six for 18 in the
epic match against Essex and five for 37 at Harrogate, where Derbyshire were outplayed by Yorkshire on a turning pitch.

Bishop took 64 wickets at 17.46 and his most reliable support came
from Cork, who had to regain his most effective rhythm after the A
tour to West Indies. Devon Malcolm's county returns were modest but
he won back his Test place and, for the fourth time, was England's
leading wicket-taker in a Test series, earning selection for the tour
of India. Simon Base bowled splendidly in the innings defeat of
Warwickshire but played in only one other first-class match because
he underwent a back operation. Derbyshire need him because Ole
Mortensen, at 34, found wickets more elusive. In his secondary role,
Allan Warner continued to chip away and Derbyshire will surely
make greater use of Richard Sladdin's left-arm spin in a four-day
Championship.

Martin Jean-Jacques has joined Hampshire and Derbyshire released
Steve Goldsmith and Andrew Brown, who were justifiably upset to
hear the news on local radio before the club informed them. There was
disquiet about a loss of £71,309, declared in December 1991, which was
alarming for a club with ambitious plans to develop the Derby ground.
But despite losing more than a hundred hours of cricket to the weather,
the club announced a profit of £20,046 for 1992; and an unexpected
benefactor, Frank Stretton, who was not even a member, left the club a
sum believed to be at least £100,000 in his will. In the final match, at
Cardiff, Alastair Richardson created history as the third generation to
represent Derbyshire. His grandfather, Arthur, led them to the 1936
Championship and his father, William, played from 1959 to 1965.
Gerald Mortimer.

DERBYSHIRE 1994

OS ACETATE • **Principal Sponsors — Derbyshire 'TEST CRIC**

[Bill Smith]

Back row: R. W. Sladdin, F. A. Griffith, T. J. G. O'Gorman, T. A. Tweats, A. W. Richardson, D. G. Cork, A. M. Brown, P. R. Whitaker. Middle row: S. W. Tacey (scorer), S. C. Goldsmith, A. E. Warner, P. D. Bowler, S. J. Base, M. Jean-Jacques, K. M. Krikken, C. J. Adams, R. J. Lark (chief executive). Front row: I. R. Bishop, B. J. M. Maher, J. E. Morris, K. J. Barnett (captain), P. E. Russell (coach), O. H. Mortensen, D. E. Malcolm.

DERBYSHIRE RESULTS

All first-class matches – Played 24: Won 7, Lost 6, Drawn 11.

County Championship matches – Played 22: Won 7, Lost 6, Drawn 9.

Bonus points – Batting 47, Bowling 63.

Competition placings – Britannic Assurance County Championship, 5th;
NatWest Bank Trophy, 2nd round; Benson and Hedges Cup, q-f;
Sunday League, 13th equal.

BRITANNIC ASSURANCE CHAMPIONSHIP AVERAGES

BATTING

	Birthplace	M	I	NO	R	HS	Avge
‡P. D. Bowler	Plymouth	22	35	7	1,862	241*	66.5
‡K. J. Barnett	Stoke-on-Trent	18	29	5	1,270	160	52.9
‡J. E. Morris	Crewe	21	30	0	1,236	120	41.2
S. C. Goldsmith	Ashford, Kent	9	10	3	270	100*	38.5
‡C. J. Adams	Whitwell	21	29	4	924	140*	36.9
F. A. Griffith	London	6	8	1	242	81	34.5
‡T. J. G. O'Gorman	Woking	22	33	6	880	95	32.5
D. G. Cork	Newcastle-under-Lyme	17	19	2	504	72*	29.6
‡O. H. Mortensen	Vejle, Denmark	13	12	10	47	13*	23.5
‡I. R. Bishop§	Port-of-Spain, Trinidad	20	21	2	388	90	20.4
‡D. E. Malcolm	Kingston, Jamaica	14	13	4	144	26	16.0
‡K. M. Krikken	Bolton	21	24	3	323	57*	15.3
‡A. E. Warner	Birmingham	15	13	2	151	29	13.7
A. M. Brown	Heanor	6	6	0	74	36	12.3
R. W. Sladdin	Halifax	11	13	2	126	39	11.4

Also batted: ‡S. J. Base (*Maidstone*) (2 matches) 3, 0*; M. Jean-Jacques (*Soufrière Dominica*) (2 matches) 0, 6; A. W. Richardson (*Derby*) (1 match) 5; T. A. Tweats (*Stoke-on-Trent*) (1 match) 24.

* Signifies not out.   ‡ Denotes county cap.   § Overseas player.

The following played a total of 18 three-figure innings for Derbyshire in County Championship matches – P. D. Bowler 6, C. J. Adams 4, K. J. Barnett 4, J. E. Morris 2, S. C. Goldsmith 1.

BOWLING

	O	M	R	W	BB	5W/i	Avge
I. R. Bishop	483	116	1,118	64	7-34	4	17.4
F. A. Griffith	102	25	350	14	4-33	0	25.0
D. G. Cork	406.2	67	1,237	44	5-36	2	28.1
A. E. Warner	335.5	79	817	27	4-52	0	30.2
O. H. Mortensen	307	76	736	19	2-22	0	38.7
D. E. Malcolm	318.2	48	1,130	29	5-45	1	38.
R. W. Sladdin	420.2	110	1,212	30	4-102	0	40.4

Also bowled: C. J. Adams 56-3-229-2; K. J. Barnett 77.4-11-250-4; S. J. Base 35-8-100-7; P. D. Bowler 17-3-69-0; A. M. Brown 3-0-9-0; S. C. Goldsmith 113-21-391-3; M. Jean-Jacques 35.4-5-135-5; T. J. G. O'Gorman 27-0-141-1; A. W. Richardson 13-2-38-2.

Wicket-keeper: K. M. Krikken 49 ct, 5 st.

Leading Fielder: C. J. Adams 20.

t Birmingham, May 7, 8, 9, 11. DERBYSHIRE lost to WARWICKSHIRE by nine wickets.

DERBYSHIRE v WORCESTERSHIRE

t Derby, May 14, 15, 16, 18. Drawn. Derbyshire 4 pts, Worcestershire 6 pts. Toss: erbyshire. Radford was the one bowler to achieve any success on a stiflingly slow pitch, king 11 for 155 in the match and bowling particularly well in the first innings when he nited Derbyshire to a completely inadequate total. Worcestershire's reply was dominated y Curtis, who batted for nine and a half hours, faced 477 balls and hit 23 fours. His nbeaten 228 was the highest innings for Worcestershire against Derbyshire, passing G. M. urner's 182 not out in 1980. Derbyshire were left with a day and a half to save the game nd after an uneasy start made it thanks to centuries by Bowler, Adams, who hit three sixes i his best Championship score, and Goldsmith, who completed his first Championship undred to take Derbyshire past one last difficult period when Radford took three wickets a three overs.

Close of play: First day, Worcestershire 8-0 (T. S. Curtis 3*, A. C. H. Seymour 5*); econd day, Worcestershire 283-7 (T. S. Curtis 137*, R. K. Illingworth 9*); Third day, erbyshire 153-3 (P. D. Bowler 65*, C. J. Adams 46*).

Derbyshire

K. J. Barnett c Rhodes b Newport	16	– c D'Oliveira b Radford	18
. D. Bowler c Rhodes b Lampitt	91	– lbw b Radford	112
E. Morris c Rhodes b Radford	55	– c Curtis b Radford	12
. J. G. O'Gorman b Radford	0	– c Rhodes b Newport	9
. J. Adams c D'Oliveira b Radford	6	– lbw b Radford	121
. C. Goldsmith c Seymour b Illingworth	17	– not out	100
K. M. Krikken c Illingworth b Lampitt	7	– b Radford	0
). G. Cork c Seymour b Radford	25		
R. Bishop c D'Oliveira b Radford	18	– (8) c Hick b Radford	17
. W. Sladdin run out	1	– (9) not out	27
). E. Malcolm not out	8		
L-b 4, w 2, n-b 1	7	L-b 12, w 2, n-b 3	17

/22 2/117 3/126 4/134 5/186   251   1/24 2/39 3/65   (7 wkts dec.) 433
/194 7/211 8/233 9/239   4/283 5/290
                           6/290 7/342

Bonus points – Derbyshire 2, Worcestershire 4 (Score at 100 overs: 240-9).

Bowling: *First Innings*—Radford 22.4–4–67–5; Newport 16–4–43–1; Lampitt 21–5–60–2; Weston 10–4–28–0; Illingworth 33–18–48–1; D'Oliveira 1–0–1–0. *Second Innings*—Radford 8–6–88–6; Newport 26–7–68–1; Lampitt 22–3–66–0; Weston 8–0–24–0; Illingworth 3–14–87–0; Leatherdale 3–0–10–0; Curtis 3.2–0–17–0; D'Oliveira 12–4–36–0; Hick 0–4–25–0.

Worcestershire

T. S. Curtis not out	228	R. K. Illingworth c sub b Malcolm	25
. C. H. Seymour c Krikken b Bishop	27	P. J. Newport c Adams b Goldsmith	42
. A. Hick c Bowler b Bishop	0	N. V. Radford not out	25
). A. Leatherdale lbw b Cork	15	B 4, l-b 29, n-b 3	36
). B. D'Oliveira c Krikken b Sladdin	37		
W. P. C. Weston b Sladdin	0	1/53 2/53 3/87 (9 wkts dec.) 470
S. J. Rhodes c sub b Sladdin	21	4/145 5/145 6/211
. R. Lampitt b Cork	14	7/250 8/333 9/426

Bonus points – Worcestershire 2, Derbyshire 2 (Score at 100 overs: 235-6).

Bowling: Bishop 28–3–61–2; Cork 21–4–51–2; Malcolm 28–3–98–1; Goldsmith 29–7–79–1; Sladdin 62–15–148–3.

Umpires: R. Julian and B. J. Meyer.

At Blackpool, May 20, 21, 22. DERBYSHIRE beat LANCASHIRE by five wickets.

DERBYSHIRE v NOTTINGHAMSHIRE

At Derby, May 23, 25, 26. Drawn. Derbyshire 8 pts, Nottinghamshire 5 pts. Toss: Derbyshire. On another bland Derby wicket, Bowler and Barnett began the match with their 15th three-figure opening partnership and spectacular batting by Morris too Derbyshire to a huge score. Bowler hit a six and 19 fours and completed 500 Championshi runs in ten days and four innings when he reached 140. But he was outshone by Morris who needed only 112 balls for his century, hit 103 between lunch and tea and struck tw sixes and 22 fours. Nottinghamshire failed by four to avoid the follow-on when Warner too two wickets in two balls. Derbyshire enforced it but appeared to regret it almost at once Their main bowlers shared only 14 overs before Broad and Crawley took charge agains the second-line attack; Crawley's century was his first in the Championship. Lewis wa 50 minutes late for the start of the match because of bad traffic and was reprimande by Nottinghamshire; umpire Kitchen, who had been involved in the same one-da international as Lewis, was on time.

Close of play: First day, Derbyshire 417-5 (A. E. Warner 1*, C. J. Adams 4*); Secon day, Nottinghamshire 312-7 (K. P. Evans 13*, B. N. French 15*).

Derbyshire

*K. J. Barnett c Evans b Crawley	71	†K. M. Krikken b Lewis	2	
P. D. Bowler c French b Cairns	155	I. R. Bishop not out	2	
J. E. Morris c Randall b Afford	120	D. E. Malcolm not out		
T. J. G. O'Gorman c French b Cairns	29	B 1, l-b 15, w 1, n-b 24	4	
M. Jean-Jacques run out	6			
A. E. Warner lbw b Lewis	8	1/126 2/320 3/391 (9 wkts dec.) 50		
C. J. Adams c French b Lewis	4	4/412 5/413 6/426		
S. C. Goldsmith b Lewis	9	7/427 8/456 9/491		

Bonus points – Derbyshire 4, Nottinghamshire 1 (Score at 100 overs: 391-3).

Bowling: Cairns 27-4-109-2; Pick 15-3-57-0; Evans 23-4-90-0; Afford 25-7-81-1 Lewis 26.3-3-88-4; Crawley 14-2-59-1.

Nottinghamshire

B. C. Broad c Goldsmith b Malcolm	29	– b O'Gorman	117
M. A. Crawley lbw b Malcolm	7	– not out	160
*R. T. Robinson c and b Malcolm	97		
P. Johnson lbw b Bishop	75		
D. W. Randall b Malcolm	23		
C. C. Lewis b Bishop	14		
C. L. Cairns c Krikken b Bishop	15	– (3) not out	52
K. P. Evans c Krikken b Bishop	14		
†B. N. French b Warner	29		
R. A. Pick not out	15		
J. A. Afford b Warner	0		
B 1, l-b 18, w 3, n-b 7	29	B 3, l-b 6, n-b 4	13

1/36 2/39 3/200 4/246 5/259   347   1/230   (1 wkt) 342
6/278 7/282 8/321 9/347

Bonus points – Nottinghamshire 4, Derbyshire 4.

Bowling: *First Innings*—Bishop 21-3-70-4; Malcolm 22-4-71-4; Warner 16-4-46-2 Jean-Jacques 7-0-43-0; Goldsmith 6-0-36-0; Barnett 24-5-62-0. *Second Innings*—Bishop 4-2-3-0; Malcolm 6-0-25-0; Jean-Jacques 1-0-6-0; Warner 3-0-11-0; Bowler 14-3-48-0 Goldsmith 15-4-51-0; Adams 13-0-39-0; Barnett 21-0-67-0; O'Gorman 17-0-83-1.

Umpires: J. D. Bond and M. J. Kitchen.

At Northampton, May 29, 30, June 1. DERBYSHIRE lost to NORTHAMPTONSHIRE by eight wickets.

At The Oval, June 2, 3, 4. DERBYSHIRE drew with SURREY.

DERBYSHIRE v DURHAM

At Chesterfield, June 5, 6, 8. Drawn. Toss: Derbyshire. Rain ruled out play on the first day and although the second was sunny, sodden areas on the outfield made a start impossible. Finally the teams began a one-innings match, played for 12 points with no bonuses. Graveney declared when Jones was close to his second century for Durham, setting a target of 242 in a minimum of 50 overs. But after 11 had been bowled, rain forced an early tea and, within half an hour, flooded the ground.

Close of play: First day, No play; Second day, No play.

Durham

W. Larkins c O'Gorman b Mortensen ..	5	P. Bainbridge not out 48
J. D. Glendenen c Krikken b Malcolm .	5	L-b 13, n-b 2 15
O. M. Jones not out	93	
P. W. G. Parker c Mortensen b Adams	75	1/6 2/22 3/159 (3 wkts dec.) 241

M. P. Briers, I. Smith, †C. W. Scott, S. P. Hughes, *D. A. Graveney and J. Wood did not bat.

Bowling: Bishop 6–1–17–0; Malcolm 6–1–29–1; Warner 4–1–11–0; Mortensen 8–0–29–1; Goldsmith 13–1–82–0; Adams 8–0–60–1.

Derbyshire

*K. J. Barnett not out	16
P. D. Bowler not out	15

(no wkt) 31

A. M. Brown, T. J. G. O'Gorman, C. J. Adams, †K. M. Krikken, S. C. Goldsmith, I. R. Bishop, A. E. Warner, D. E. Malcolm and O. H. Mortensen did not bat.

Bowling: Hughes 6–0–8–0; Wood 5–0–23–0.

Umpires: J. W. Holder and B. Leadbeater.

At Harrogate, June 12, 13, 15. DERBYSHIRE lost to YORKSHIRE by an innings and four runs.

At Cambridge, June 16, 17, 18. DERBYSHIRE drew with CAMBRIDGE UNIVERSITY.

DERBYSHIRE v WARWICKSHIRE

At Derby, June 26, 27. Derbyshire won by an innings and 48 runs. Derbyshire 24 pts, Warwickshire 3 pts. Toss: Derbyshire. Thanks to their seamers, who made the most of a helpful pitch, Derbyshire outplayed Warwickshire to win in two days. Bishop was magnificent on the first day, dismissing Lloyd and Ostler with perfect yorkers, and Warwickshire never recovered from 34 for five. They were all out in the 47th over and Morris, acting captain for the injured Barnett, never had to look beyond his three front-line bowlers. Conditions should have suited Warwickshire's own seam attack equally well, but they tended to bowl too short. That suited Morris, who scored 74 from 66 balls, with three sixes and ten fours. Base, in his first Championship match of the season after recovering from a back injury, had been done little justice by his first-innings figures, but he made up for it as Warwickshire collapsed again. Before he tired, his controlled hostility had brought him five for 15 and, despite Reeve's determination, Derbyshire chipped away the remaining wickets.

Close of play: First day, Derbyshire 249-4 (T. J. G. O'Gorman 58*, S. C. Goldsmith 18*)

Warwickshire

A. J. Moles b Base	1	– c Krikken b Base	1
R. G. Twose c Cork b Bishop	9	– c Brown b Base	1
*T. A. Lloyd b Bishop	1	– c Adams b Bishop	4
D. P. Ostler b Bishop	0	– b Base	0
D. A. Reeve c Brown b Base	10	– c Krikken b Bishop	60
T. L. Penney c Krikken b Cork	7	– c Krikken b Sladdin	9
P. A. Smith c Base b Cork	24	– c Krikken b Base	23
†K. J. Piper c Krikken b Cork	8	– b Base	6
G. C. Small not out	22	– b Cork	22
A. A. Donald c Adams b Cork	9	– not out	16
T. A. Munton c Adams b Bishop	3	– c Cork b Bishop	15
L-b 11, n-b 16	27	L-b 2, n-b 15	17

1/9 2/11 3/12 4/18 5/34   121   1/1 2/7 3/7 4/11 5/28   174
6/52 7/77 8/94 9/114   6/69 7/93 8/140 9/144

Bonus points – Derbyshire 4.

Bowling: *First Innings*—Bishop 18.2-7-32-4; Base 15-2-37-2; Cork 13-2-41-4. *Second Innings*—Bishop 12.2-2-29-3; Base 13-6-35-5; Cork 13-0-63-1; Sladdin 14-6-45-1.

Derbyshire

P. D. Bowler b Small	7	I. R. Bishop c and b Smith	29
A. M. Brown c Donald b Smith	17	S. J. Base b Small	2
*J. E. Morris c Donald b Smith	74	R. W. Sladdin not out	1
T. J. G. O'Gorman c Piper b Donald	75		
C. J. Adams c Piper b Munton	39	B 20, l-b 12, w 2, n-b 14	48
S. C. Goldsmith c Twose b Smith	40		
D. G. Cork b Donald	0	1/9 2/86 3/122 4/194 5/279	343
†K. M. Krikken lbw b Reeve	10	6/279 7/297 8/311 9/330	

Bonus points – Derbyshire 4, Warwickshire 3 (Score at 100 overs: 324-8).

Bowling: Donald 22-4-64-2; Small 25-9-47-2; Munton 20-3-76-1; Smith 14-3-67-4; Twose 8-1-26-0; Reeve 20-8-31-1.

Umpires: G. I. Burgess and A. A. Jones.

DERBYSHIRE v GLOUCESTERSHIRE

At Derby, June 30, July 1, 2. Drawn. Derbyshire 4 pts, Gloucestershire 3 pts. Toss: Derbyshire. Most of the first morning and the whole of the second day were lost to rain, so Gloucestershire, restrained by Warner on the first day, batted into the third morning. Alleyne took his score to a fine unbeaten 78 to back up an earlier half-century from Hodgson. After a forfeiture and an agreed declaration, Derbyshire were set 311 in a minimum of 72 overs; some obvious time-wasting, when Gloucestershire bowled only 14 overs in the 60 minutes between tea and the last hour, made sure they had no more than their ration. Smith's ability to swing the ball pegged back the home team and it was left to O'Gorman to organise the last phase. Though the visitors, lacking their strike bowler Walsh, showed no inclination to attack even when they needed only three wickets from 12 overs, O'Gorman and Bishop could not produce a telling burst of runs, and Derbyshire finished eight short.

Close of play: First day, Gloucestershire 202-7 (M. W. Alleyne 49*, R. C. J. Williams 5*). Second day, No play.

Gloucestershire

G. D. Hodgson c Base b Cork	50		
C. W. J. Athey b Warner	39		
S. G. Hinks c Adams b Cork	7		
*A. J. Wright lbw b Warner	4		
M. W. Alleyne not out	78		
R. J. Scott c Krikken b Warner	8		
R. I. Dawson c Brown b Warner	1		
R. C. Williams c Bishop b Cork	10	– (2) not out	10
†R. C. J. Williams run out	5	– (1) not out	18
A. M. Smith c Goldsmith b Cork	40		
A. M. Babington c Bishop b Cork	2		
B 1, l-b 22, w 4, n-b 10	37	W 1	1

1/81 2/93 3/107 4/136 5/157   281   (no wkt dec.) 29
6/159 7/191 8/217 9/273

Bonus points – Gloucestershire 3, Derbyshire 4.

Bowling: *First Innings*—Bishop 23–10–54–0; Base 7–0–28–0; Warner 23–4–52–4; Cork 30.5–4–103–5; Goldsmith 8–1–21–0. *Second Innings*—Brown 3–0–9–0; O'Gorman 3–0–20–0.

Derbyshire

Derbyshire forfeited their first innings.

P. D. Bowler c Athey b R. C. Williams	77		D. G. Cork b Smith	1
A. M. Brown c R. C. J. Williams b Babington	10		I. R. Bishop b Scott	31
*J. E. Morris c and b Athey	50		†K. M. Krikken run out	6
T. J. G. O'Gorman not out	70		S. J. Base not out	0
C. J. Adams b Smith	29		L-b 17, n-b 10	27
S. C. Goldsmith c R. C. J. Williams b Smith	0		1/27 2/118 3/186	(9 wkts) 303
A. E. Warner lbw b Scott	2		4/223 5/223 6/226	
			7/229 8/293 9/301	

Bowling: Babington 16–3–50–1; Smith 20–1–81–3; Scott 17–0–71–2; R. C. Williams 8–0–46–1; Athey 8–0–24–1; Alleyne 3–0–14–0.

Umpires: G. I. Burgess and A. A. Jones.

At Taunton, July 3, 4, 6. DERBYSHIRE beat SOMERSET by six wickets.

At Portsmouth, July 14, 15, 16. DERBYSHIRE beat HAMPSHIRE by an innings and 135 runs.

At Derby, July 18, 19, 20. DERBYSHIRE drew with PAKISTANIS (See Pakistani tour section).

DERBYSHIRE v MIDDLESEX

At Derby, July 21, 22, 23. Drawn. Derbyshire 4 pts, Middlesex 3 pts. Toss: Middlesex. Only seven wickets fell in the match, the result of a dull pitch as well as rain which cost more than a day's play. The match began at 2.30 on the first afternoon, when Morris batted enterprisingly before Adams and O'Gorman embarked on an unbroken partnership of 192 after which both were awarded county caps: O'Gorman's father witnessed the presentation on his 56th birthday. On the second morning Adams added 103 to his score, completing his century from 171 balls, with a six and 11 fours. Roseberry scored his seventh century of the season before Middlesex declared behind. Hopes of a finish were ruined when the weather allowed only two overs on the third morning. Derbyshire had little option but to bat on until, to general relief, it rained again at tea.

Close of play: First day, Derbyshire 175-3 (T. J. G. O'Gorman 21*, C. J. Adams 9*); Second day, Derbyshire 6-0 (P. D. Bowler 2*, A. M. Brown 1*).

Derbyshire

P. D. Bowler lbw b Williams	9	– b Haynes	46
A. M. Brown c Taylor b Emburey	36	– lbw b Fraser	11
J. E. Morris b Williams	82		
T. J. G. O'Gorman not out	68	– (3) not out	4
C. J. Adams not out	112		
B 1, l-b 10, n-b 16	27	L-b 3, n-b 2	5

1/17 2/141 3/142   (3 wkts dec.) 334   1/52 2/66   (2 wkts) 66

*K. J. Barnett, †K. M. Krikken, D. G. Cork, I. R. Bishop, A. E. Warner and D. E Malcolm did not bat.

Bonus points – Derbyshire 4, Middlesex 1.

Bowling: *First Innings*—Taylor 11–1–72–0; Williams 19–1–71–2; Fraser 19–4–68–0; Emburey 21–5–53–1; Tufnell 15–4–39–0; Gatting 3–0–12–0; Carr 4–3–4–0; Weekes 2–1–4–0. *Second Innings*—Fraser 11–4–13–1; Taylor 12–4–23–0; Weekes 7–2–14–0; Williams 7–5–9–0; Roseberry 2–2–0–0; Haynes 1.4–0–4–1.

Middlesex

D. L. Haynes c Krikken b Adams	70
M. A. Roseberry not out	100
J. D. Carr c Krikken b Malcolm	9
P. N. Weekes not out	22
B 4, l-b 4, n-b 7	15

1/147 2/179   (2 wkts dec.) 216

*M. W. Gatting, †K. R. Brown, J. E. Emburey, P. C. R. Tufnell, A. R. C. Fraser N. F. Williams and C. W. Taylor did not bat.

Bonus points – Middlesex 2.

Bowling: Bishop 12–2–25–0; Cork 11–0–35–0; Malcolm 13–0–56–1; Warner 13–4–28–0; Barnett 3–0–17–0; Adams 11–0–47–1.

Umpires: D. J. Constant and P. B. Wight.

At Worcester, July 24, 25, 27. DERBYSHIRE drew with WORCESTERSHIRE.

DERBYSHIRE v LEICESTERSHIRE

At Ilkeston, August 4, 5, 6. Derbyshire won by 139 runs. Derbyshire 23 pts, Leicestershire 5 pts. Toss: Leicestershire. At the Rutland Ground, which was staging its first Championship match since 1980, second-placed Leicestershire went down to their second heavy defeat of the week. A sightscreen, which looked of pre-1980 vintage, blew down to end the opening session early. The first day's hero was Gofton, on his third first-class appearance. His medium pace dismissed four of Derbyshire's top five batsmen, and the home team owed much to an 88-run stand between Griffith and Cork. It was Griffith who turned the game, his first Championship match of the season, next day, as Leicestershire lost their last eight wickets for 60 to concede a lead of 108. The captain, Briers, survived three chances and carried his bat, and was unimpressed by the efforts at the other end. Barnett and Morris exploited Derbyshire's advantage and put on 180 in 33 overs. Morris hit four sixes, two in succession off Mullally to bring up an 80-minute century. Leicestershire were set 363 in what would have been 98 overs, but Bishop's extra pace and Sladdin's control brought Derbyshire victory with 18 to spare.

Close of play: First day, Leicestershire 29-1 (N. E. Briers 11*, J. J. Whitaker 10*); Second day, Derbyshire 226-2 (K. J. Barnett 101*, T. J. G. O'Gorman 0*).

Derbyshire

*K. J. Barnett c Nixon b Gofton	47	– not out	117
P. D. Bowler lbw b Gofton	20	– b Gofton	13
J. E. Morris b Gofton	50	– c Benson b Mullally	107
T. J. G. O'Gorman c Nixon b Benjamin	16	– c Benson b Parsons	0
C. J. Adams c Potter b Gofton	14	– not out	12
F. A. Griffith b Potter	48		
†K. M. Krikken c Benson b Potter	8		
D. G. Cork c Whitaker b Benjamin	56		
I. R. Bishop c Nixon b Benjamin	1		
R. W. Sladdin c Benson b Benjamin	0		
O. H. Mortensen not out	0		
B 1, l-b 2, w 1, n-b 4	8	B 1, l-b 4	5

1/66 2/88 3/121 4/149 5/164   268 1/45 2/225 3/228 (3 wkts dec.) 254
6/177 7/265 8/268 9/268

Bonus points – Derbyshire 3, Leicestershire 4.

Bowling: *First Innings*—Benjamin 22.3-5-55-4; Mullally 17-3-50-0; Parsons 16-2-47-0; Gofton 22-5-81-4; Potter 18-6-32-2. *Second Innings*—Benjamin 11-1-60-0; Mullally 15-3-54-1; Gofton 13-3-63-1; Parsons 13-2-41-1; Potter 4-0-31-0.

Leicestershire

P. N. Hepworth c O'Gorman b Cork	1	– (3) lbw b Bishop	20
*N. E. Briers not out	73	– c Adams b Mortensen	27
J. J. Whitaker b Bishop	26	– (4) c Sladdin b Griffith	6
T. J. Boon c Adams b Griffith	18	– (1) c Adams b Griffith	45
J. D. R. Benson c Sladdin b Griffith	1	– c Mortensen b Sladdin	42
L. Potter c Cork b Griffith	0	– c Cork b Bishop	15
†P. A. Nixon c Morris b Griffith	5	– (8) lbw b Mortensen	28
W. K. M. Benjamin c Krikken b Mortensen	4	– (7) st Krikken b Sladdin	6
G. J. Parsons run out	5	– c Krikken b Bishop	12
R. P. Gofton c Adams b Cork	7	– lbw b Sladdin	11
A. D. Mullally lbw b Cork	2	– not out	0
L-b 10, w 2, n-b 6	18	L-b 8, w 1, n-b 2	11

1/1 2/56 3/100 4/102 5/103   160 1/59 2/85 3/96 4/147 5/147 223
6/118 7/126 8/140 9/152   6/172 7/178 8/194 9/217

Bonus points – Leicestershire 1, Derbyshire 4.

Bowling: *First Innings*—Bishop 18-1-52-1; Cork 18.1-2-48-3; Mortensen 12-5-17-1; Griffith 11-2-33-4. *Second Innings*—Bishop 20-5-51-3; Cork 12-3-41-0; Mortensen 10.3-4-22-2; Sladdin 25-10-57-3; Griffith 12-2-44-2.

Umpires: J. W. Holder and G. Sharp.

At Eastbourne, August 7, 8, 10. DERBYSHIRE lost to SUSSEX by four wickets.

DERBYSHIRE v KENT

At Chesterfield, August 14, 15, 17. Drawn. Derbyshire 6 pts, Kent 7 pts. Toss: Kent. Not for the first time in Derbyshire's season, rain sharply reduced the options on the third day. They were 125 runs ahead with nine second-innings wickets standing at the start but the loss of 50 overs limited their room for manoeuvre. As the captains could not agree on a target Barnett decided to bat through, to protests from Kent supporters; it was his only viable option. It did give Barnett the chance to make his highest score of an injury-troubled season, with 22 fours, as the match drifted away. Derbyshire's batting was more slapdash on the first day, justifying Benson's decision to field first, although Igglesden's figures did not reflect his merit. Only Bishop, who took three wickets in four overs when Kent replied, kept Derbyshire in the game. He went on to take five and with Malcolm, who snapped Taylor's leg stump, restricted the visitors' lead to 88.

Close of play: First day, Kent 190-4 (N. R. Taylor 60*, R. M. Ellison 0*); Second day, Derbyshire 213-1 (K. J. Barnett 116*, J. E. Morris 54*).

Derbyshire

*K. J. Barnett c McCague b Ellison	42	– c Marsh b Fleming	160
P. D. Bowler c McCague b Igglesden	8	– c Hooper b Ealham	38
J. E. Morris c Fleming b Ealham	17	– c Ellison b Ealham	55
T. J. G. O'Gorman b McCague	32	– not out	62
C. J. Adams c Ward b Ellison	8	– c Ward b Fleming	0
†K. M. Krikken c Marsh b Ellison	39	– not out	9
D. G. Cork b McCague	2		
I. R. Bishop c McCague b Igglesden	6		
A. E. Warner c Cowdrey b Ealham	26		
D. E. Malcolm c Fleming b McCague	7		
O. H. Mortensen not out	0		
B 4, l-b 14, n-b 2	20	L-b 2, w 1, n-b 7	10

1/24 2/49 3/93 4/103 5/117   207   1/86 2/221   (4 wkts dec.) 334
6/123 7/133 8/192 9/202   3/311 4/311

Bonus points – Derbyshire 2, Kent 4.

Bowling: *First Innings*—Igglesden 17–4–56–2; McCague 16.2–2–57–3; Ealham 11–1–47–2; Ellison 11–2–29–3. *Second Innings*—Igglesden 13–0–48–0; McCague 10–1–38–0; Ellison 24–3–85–0; Ealham 20–3–68–2; Hooper 17–6–35–0; Fleming 18–3–39–2; Cowdrey 4–1–12–0; Ward 3–0–7–0.

Kent

T. R. Ward c Krikken b Bishop	87	M. A. Ealham c Krikken b Bishop	10
*M. R. Benson b Mortensen	39	M. J. McCague not out	11
N. R. Taylor b Malcolm	71	A. P. Igglesden run out	3
C. L. Hooper c Krikken b Bishop	1		
G. R. Cowdrey c and b Bishop	2	W 3, n-b 5	8
R. M. Ellison c Krikken b Warner	19		
M. V. Fleming c O'Gorman b Bishop	15	1/80 2/174 3/176 4/188 5/215	295
†S. A. Marsh c Cork b Malcolm	29	6/238 7/238 8/264 9/291	

Bonus points – Kent 3, Derbyshire 4.

Bowling: Cork 10.4–2–46–0; Bishop 19–2–60–5; Malcolm 20–2–68–2; Mortensen 22–8–49–1; Warner 19–4–72–1.

Umpires: J. C. Balderstone and H. D. Bird.

DERBYSHIRE v GLAMORGAN

At Chesterfield, August 18, 19, 20. Drawn. Derbyshire 6 pts, Glamorgan 3 pts. Toss: Derbyshire. Malcolm, his confidence still high after The Oval Test, produced his best bowling figures of the season on the opening day and Glamorgan had to be saved from complete collapse by Cottey, who had been advised not to play after breaking a thumb against Durham. When Derbyshire replied, Darren Thomas, a 17-year-old student from Llanelli, took five wickets on his début, the youngest player ever to do so in the Championship apart from P. F. Judge of Middlesex in 1933. He bowled accurately, was slightly quicker than batsmen expected and had some distinguished victims but could not prevent Griffith, with his highest score, and Bishop adding 142, enabling Derbyshire to take a lead of 164. Glamorgan needed a major innings and Maynard played it. Despite a blow on the helmet from Bishop early on, he scored 103 between lunch and tea; his 176 in 214 minutes, including a six and 28 fours, passed the county's previous highest against Derbyshire, 170 by N. V. H. Riches, at Swansea in 1924. Derbyshire's seamers were at a loss, and though Barnett's leg-breaks wrapped up the innings, any thoughts of a chase for 203 in 20 overs vanished when Watkin took two wickets in his first five balls.

Close of play: First day, Derbyshire 93-2 (P. D. Bowler 40*, T. J. G. O'Gorman 20*); Second day, Glamorgan 46-1 (H. Morris 28*, A. Dale 12*).

Glamorgan

S. P. James c Adams b Warner	13	– c Krikken b Mortensen	2
H. Morris b Malcolm	12	– c Krikken b Bishop	52
A. Dale b Malcolm	16	– c Malcolm b Warner	82
*M. P. Maynard c Bowler b Malcolm	13	– b Griffith	176
I. V. A. Richards c Warner	14	– c and b Warner	15
P. A. Cottey c Krikken b Malcolm	62	– c Barnett b Griffith	5
R. D. B. Croft b Bishop	3	– c Griffith	7
†C. P. Metson c O'Gorman b Griffith	14	– c Griffith b Barnett	4
S. Bastien c O'Gorman b Mortensen	1	– c sub b Barnett	0
S. L. Watkin c and b Malcolm	4	– lbw b Barnett	1
S. D. Thomas not out	4	– not out	1
L-b 5, w 3, n-b 6	14	L-b 9, w 8, n-b 4	21

1/27 2/29 3/58 4/59 5/74   170   1/11 2/97 3/229 4/302 5/311   366
6/82 7/110 8/126 9/147   6/355 7/362 8/362 9/362

Bonus points – Glamorgan 1, Derbyshire 4.

Bowling: *First Innings*—Bishop 14–4–22–1; Mortensen 20–2–47–1; Malcolm 18.2–6–45–5; Warner 18–5–29–2; Griffith 6–2–22–1. *Second Innings*—Bishop 17–3–38–1; Mortensen 19–0–102–1; Malcolm 14–3–49–0; Warner 18–4–56–2; Griffith 19–4–88–3; Barnett 7.3–3–24–3.

Derbyshire

*K. J. Barnett c Metson b Watkin	29	– b Watkin	0
P. D. Bowler c Dale b Thomas	67	– not out	19
J. E. Morris c Morris b Thomas	1	– c Morris b Watkin	0
T. J. G. O'Gorman c Morris b Thomas	42	– not out	2
F. A. Griffith c Metson b Dale	81		
†K. M. Krikken c Maynard b Watkin	1		
I. R. Bishop b Thomas	90		
A. E. Warner not out	7		
D. E. Malcolm b Thomas	5		
B 1, l-b 5, w 2, n-b 3	11	L-b 1	1

1/49 2/58 3/135 4/156 5/167   (8 wkts dec.) 334   1/0 2/0   (2 wkts) 22
6/309 7/324 8/334

C. J. Adams and O. H. Mortensen did not bat.

Bonus points – Derbyshire 2, Glamorgan 2 (Score at 100 overs: 244-5).

Bowling: *First Innings*—Watkin 35–7–89–2; Bastien 33–9–82–0; Thomas 29.2–7–80–5; Dale 13–3–40–1; Croft 14–1–37–0. *Second Innings*—Watkin 3–1–9–2; Thomas 2–0–12–0; Metson 1–1–0–0.

Umpires: J. C. Balderstone and H. D. Bird.

DERBYSHIRE v SOMERSET

At Derby, August 26, 27, 28, 29. Derbyshire won by 121 runs. Derbyshire 20 pts, Somerset 4 pts. Toss: Somerset. Although the captains tossed on the first morning, there was no play until 2 p.m. on the third day. Barnett began as if determined to compensate for lost time and, when 47, completed 1,000 runs for the tenth consecutive season, equalling A. Hamer's Derbyshire record sequence. Caddick was severely treated early on but returned to take three wickets in four balls, bowling with speed and hostility. After two forfeitures, Somerset were set 321 to win in a minimum of 96 overs. They began badly, as Bishop and Cork reduced them to 20 for four, and could not recover, although Turner, the former Cambridge captain, scored his first Championship half-century and added 120 with MacLeay before he retired hurt.

Close of play: First day, No play; Second day, No play; Third day, Derbyshire 296-9 (K. M. Krikken 34*, D. E. Malcolm 15*).

Derbyshire

*K. J. Barnett c van Troost b Caddick .	68	I. R. Bishop lbw b Snell	1
P. D. Bowler lbw b Caddick..........	66	A. E. Warner b van Troost..........	8
J. E. Morris b Caddick	0	D. E. Malcolm not out	16
T. J. G. O'Gorman b Caddick	0	B 1, l-b 2, n-b 17.............	20
C. J. Adams c Lathwell b van Troost ..	24		
F. A. Griffith lbw b Caddick	33	1/93 2/93 3/93	(9 wkts dec.) 320
D. G. Cork c Turner b Rose	27	4/152 5/201 6/210	
†K. M. Krikken not out	57	7/253 8/254 9/276	

Bonus points – Derbyshire 4, Somerset 4.

Bowling: Mallender 10-0-44-0; Caddick 16-0-77-5; Snell 9-1-44-1; Rose 12-0-55-1; van Troost 11-1-46-2; MacLeay 12-3-27-0; Tavaré 1.2-0-9-0; Turner 1-0-15-0.

Derbyshire forfeited their second innings.

Somerset

Somerset forfeited their first innings.

A. N. Hayhurst lbw b Bishop.........	0	N. A. Mallender lbw b Cork	0
M. N. Lathwell b Bishop	11	A. R. Caddick b Cork..............	3
*C. J. Tavaré lbw b Cork	2	A. P. van Troost not out	0
R. J. Turner retired hurt	55		
†N. D. Burns c Krikken b Cork	1	B 4, l-b 8, w 4, n-b 7	23
G. D. Rose b Malcolm	20		
K. H. MacLeay b Warner............	73	1/0 2/16 3/18 4/20 5/59	199
R. P. Snell c Adams b Warner........	11	6/192 7/193 8/198 9/199	

R. J. Turner retired hurt at 179.

Bowling: Bishop 15-6-31-2; Cork 15-1-61-4; Malcolm 9-0-25-1; Warner 15-4-45-2; Griffith 5-1-25-0.

Umpires: V. A. Holder and M. J. Kitchen.

At Nottingham, August 31, September 1, 2, 3. DERBYSHIRE beat NOTTINGHAM-SHIRE by two wickets.

DERBYSHIRE v ESSEX

At Derby, September 7, 8, 9, 10. Essex won by four wickets. Essex 20 pts, Derbyshire 6 pts. Toss: Essex. Essex, already champions, showed all their professional quality as they recovered to score the third-highest fourth-innings total to win a County Championship match; Gooch described it as the most satisfying victory of his county career. Few other teams would have attempted, let alone achieved, a target of 440. On a green but not unduly lively pitch, 20 wickets had fallen on the first day. Conditions suited Pringle, who collected his only five-wicket haul of the season, and Bishop, just as accurate but considerably faster, made even more spectacular use of them. His opening spell of six for 18 in 11 overs had Essex in danger of following on until Gooch, who had passed the captaincy to Prichard, took batting on to a higher plane. Adams responded with a powerful 135, including two sixes and 20 fours, and when 42 he reached 1,000 runs in a season for the first time. After three hours he become one of six victims for Ilott, who returned his best-ever bowling figures. Essex faced a monumental task but they had time, a minimum of 230 overs, and Bishop was suffering from tendon and shin injuries; by the fourth morning Cork had a back spasm. Stephenson set the tone, with 97 over six hours, but the innings depended on Gooch, who batted for six hours and 13 minutes, facing 298 balls and hitting 17 fours in his 98th century. He scarcely erred, and had invaluable support from Garnham, whose contribution lasted 52 overs.

Close of play: First day, Derbyshire 4-0 (K. J. Barnett 1*, P. D. Bowler 2*); Second day, Essex 46-0 (N. V. Knight 17*, J. P. Stephenson 27*); Third day, Essex 283-5 (G. A. Gooch 43*, M. A. Garnham 27*).

Derbyshire

K. J. Barnett c Shahid b Topley	25	– c Knight b Pringle	12
*D. Bowler c Garnham b Ilott	4	– lbw b Ilott	4
E. Morris c Shahid b Topley	6	– b Ilott	55
†J. G. O'Gorman c Knight b Pringle	64	– c Pringle b Ilott	7
C. J. Adams c Knight b Pringle	60	– c Garnham b Ilott	135
D. G. Cork lbw b Pringle	0	– c Pringle b Ilott	21
†K. M. Krikken lbw b Pringle	3	– c Garnham b Ilott	5
R. Bishop not out	26	– c Gooch b Topley	25
A. E. Warner c Garnham b Pringle	11	– b Such	19
D. E. Malcolm run out	12	– c Lewis b Such	11
O. H. Mortensen lbw b Ilott	2	– not out	0
B 1, l-b 5, n-b 7	13	L-b 6, w 1, n-b 8	15

1/5 2/23 3/77 4/152 5/164 **226** 1/9 2/23 3/38 4/201 5/238 **309**
6/171 7/178 8/193 9/207 6/244 7/251 8/286 9/298

Bonus points – Derbyshire 2, Essex 4.

Bowling: *First Innings*—Ilott 16–2–54–2; Pringle 19–2–63–5; Topley 12–3–31–2; Stephenson 7–0–35–0; Gooch 12–4–32–0; Such 2–1–5–0. *Second Innings*—Ilott 26–3–87–6; Pringle 14–0–55–1; Topley 16–2–59–1; Such 28–10–69–2; Stephenson 2–0–17–0; Gooch 5–2–15–0; Shahid 1–0–1–0.

Essex

*P. Stephenson lbw b Bishop	0	– (2) b Malcolm	97
N. V. Knight b Bishop	10	– (1) lbw b Bishop	18
J. B. Lewis c Krikken b Cork	4	– b Warner	5
*P. J. Prichard lbw b Bishop	1	– lbw b Cork	12
N. Shahid b Bishop	1	– c Krikken b Cork	51
G. A. Gooch c Adams b Malcolm	53	– not out	123
†M. A. Garnham c Adams b Bishop	3	– lbw b Warner	66
D. R. Pringle c Krikken b Bishop	1	– not out	28
T. D. Topley c Krikken b Warner	1		
M. C. Ilott not out	6		
P. M. Such b Warner	1		
B 4, l-b 5, w 5, n-b 1	15	B 14, l-b 14, w 3, n-b 11	42

1/7 2/18 3/18 4/21 5/28 **96** 1/53 2/66 3/85 (6 wkts) **442**
6/40 7/46 8/59 9/89 4/173 5/229 6/358

Bonus points – Derbyshire 4.

Bowling: *First Innings*—Bishop 11–4–18–6; Cork 8–1–29–1; Warner 9.4–4–15–2; Malcolm 7–1–25–1. *Second Innings*—Malcolm 35–8–90–1; Mortensen 40–12–68–0; Cork 28–8–60–2; Warner 40.4–8–101–2; Bishop 19–4–39–1; Adams 15–1–40–0; Barnett 6–1–16–0.

Umpires: V. A. Holder and R. Palmer.

At Cardiff, September 12, 13, 14, 15. DERBYSHIRE lost to GLAMORGAN by 63 runs.

DURHAM

Patrons: Sir Donald Bradman and A. W. Austin
President: I. D. Caller
Chairman: J. D. Robson
Director of Cricket: G. Cook
Chief Executive: M. E. Gear
County Ground, Riverside, Chester-le-Street,
County Durham DH3 3QR
(Telephone: 091-387 1717)
Captain: D. A. Graveney

It was the best of times and the worst of times for Durham in their first season in the County Championship. First-class cricket was rapturously received by a membership of over 6,000, and the team made a highly encouraging start. But once the impetus provided by the successful launch was lost they began to struggle, and the early loss of Australian Test batsman Dean Jones plunged them into a depressing slide which left them 36 points adrift at the foot of the table. They finished joint eighth in the Sunday League, while after beating holders Worcestershire in the Benson and Hedges Cup they failed to reach the quarter-finals because of a disappointing home defeat by Derbyshire. It was a similar story in the NatWest Trophy, in which they surprised Middlesex at Uxbridge in the second round, then lost at Leicester in the quarter-finals.

The staff comprised an improbable blend of seasoned campaigners, who had been released by other counties to take up a new challenge in the twilight of their careers, and youngsters feeling their way into a brave new world. The senior members were chosen by Geoff Cook, the Director of Cricket, as much for their enthusiasm for the Durham concept as for their cricketing ability, and for a while it worked extremely well. The players were unanimous that the team spirit was excellent, and the juniors were full of admiration for the help they received. Every time a youngster came into the side he seemed to perform wonders. Paul Henderson, making his début at 17, removed three Test batsmen and made 46 runs in the innings victory against Glamorgan; paceman John Wood removed Hampshire opener Tony Middleton with his first ball in Championship cricket and David Gower with the sixth; and Stewart Hutton totalled 242 runs in his first five Championship innings.

All subsequently suffered what Cook called "mental relapses" when they realised how tough the first-class game was, and with Henderson and Wood also having injury problems their development was curtailed. Cook said lessons had been learned about the dangers of exposing youngsters too soon to the demands of the game, and the end-of-season battle to avoid the wooden spoon was left largely in the hands of the seniors, many of whom had their own problems with injuries and fatigue. However, in the last two games 18-year-old Jimmy Daley was pitched into the fray, and he responded with 88 against Somerset and 80 not out against Lancashire.

John Glendenen provided perhaps the best example of a player suffering from the lack of a Second Eleven apprenticeship. On his début against Oxford University he became the first player to score a century in first-class cricket for Durham, but his gradual decline culminated in four ducks in five innings before he was dropped. He returned for the last match and scored 76 and 43 against Lancashire.

The best of Ian Botham was seen early in the season under the dual incentive of helping his new county off to a good start and trying to impress the England selectors. Vice-captain Paul Parker also made a good start, with three centuries by mid-May. But the real revelation in the early stages was the bowling of left-arm paceman Simon Brown. He was the country's leading wicket-taker with 35 when he was injured in mid-June, but on his return the heavy responsibility he had to bear gradually wore him down. It had always been feared that bowling would be Durham's weakness and after Brown, with 58, the next-highest wicket-taker was Simon Hughes with 34 at an average of 49.17.

While there was never any doubt that David Graveney was the right man to lead the side, his left-arm spin produced only 28 wickets. The pre-season notion that Durham would rely heavily on spin in home matches quickly disappeared, partly through Graveney's worries about the dangers of slow bowlers being hit on the county's small grounds (a point illustrated at Jesmond when Graveney's own bowling was chipped effortlessly into the cemetery next door by John Morris of Derbyshire), but largely because the wickets were better than expected. Off-spinner Phil Berry suffered as a result, playing in only nine matches. He took ten of his 17 wickets in the match at Lord's, when Graveney was injured. Leg-spinner Mark Briers also had little opportunity, and although he made four half-centuries, he was another whose performances declined after a promising start.

After ten years as Bruce French's understudy at Nottinghamshire, Chris Scott proved himself a capable wicket-keeper and also contributed useful runs, particularly in some of the crises which followed Jones's departure. Jones was in peak form when his season was ended by a broken finger a week before he had to leave anyway to join the Australian squad in Sri Lanka at the end of July. He finished third in the national batting averages with 1,179 runs at 73.68 and was top of the Sunday averages with 656 runs at 82.00. His sheer professionalism and his dedication to the cause also made him a massive hit with his team-mates and the Durham public.

After his departure it was often left to the experienced men like Wayne Larkins and Phil Bainbridge to stave off innings defeats, and Larkins finished the season as leading scorer with 1,536 runs. Two of his three Championship centuries were against Glamorgan, but while the first helped to set up Durham's first Championship win, by an innings and 104 runs, the second came after they had followed on. This more than anything underlined Durham's slump in fortunes. After their second win, against Somerset on June 4, Durham stood fourth in the table. But there were no more victories and they lost eight of the remaining 16 Championship games to finish with ten defeats. The final two were by heavy margins, but they at least featured the remarkably composed batting of Daley, which provided a bright ray of hope for the future. – Tim Wellock.

DURHAM 1992

[Bill Smith]

Back row: S. Job (physiotherapist), S. M. McEwan, P. W. Henderson, J. D. Glendenen, S. J. E. Brown, S. Hutton, P. J. Berry, M. P. Briers, B. Hunt (scorer).
Front row: C. W. Scott, S. P. Hughes, I. T. Botham, D. A. Graveney (captain), P. W. G. Parker, D. M. Jones, W. Larkins.

DURHAM RESULTS

All first-class matches – Played 24: Won 2, Lost 11, Drawn 11.

County Championship matches – Played 22: Won 2, Lost 10, Drawn 10.

Bonus points – Batting 46, Bowling 53.

*Competition placings – Britannic Assurance County Championship, 18th;
NatWest Bank Trophy, q-f; Benson and Hedges Cup, 3rd in Group D;
Sunday League, 8th equal.*

BRITANNIC ASSURANCE CHAMPIONSHIP AVERAGES

BATTING

	Birthplace	M	I	NO	R	HS	Avge
J. A. Daley	Sunderland	2	4	1	190	88	63.33
D. M. Jones§	Coburg, Australia	12	20	5	904	157	60.26
P. Bainbridge	Stoke-on-Trent	16	29	8	899	92*	42.80
P. W. G. Parker	Bulawayo, S. Rhodesia	18	32	2	1,218	124	40.60
W. Larkins	Roxton	21	39	0	1,417	143	36.33
I. T. Botham	Heswall	14	23	2	705	105	33.57
I. Smith	Shotley Bridge	11	16	1	435	110	29.00
S. Hutton..........	Stockton-on-Tees	8	15	0	406	78	27.06
C. W. Scott	Thorpe-on-the-Hill	17	24	5	433	57*	22.78
G. K. Brown	Welling	3	6	0	136	48	22.66
M. P. Briers	Loughborough	15	26	4	447	62*	20.31
S. J. E. Brown	South Shields	19	23	13	195	47*	19.50
J. D. Glendenen ...	Middlesbrough	15	25	1	421	76	17.54
P. W. Henderson ...	Stockton-on-Tees	5	7	0	119	46	17.00
P. J. Berry........	Saltburn	7	13	2	184	76	16.72
D. A. Graveney	Bristol	20	29	9	333	36	16.65
J. Wood	Wakefield	7	6	1	80	28	16.00
S. P. Hughes	Kingston-upon-Thames	19	24	4	227	42	11.35
A. R. Fothergill	Newcastle-upon-Tyne	5	7	1	58	23	9.66
S. M. McEwan	Worcester	8	12	1	58	22	5.27

* Signifies not out.   § Overseas player.   Durham have awarded all their players county caps.

The following played a total of nine three-figure innings for Durham in County Championship matches – W. Larkins 3, D. M. Jones 2, P. W. G. Parker 2, I. T. Botham 1, I. Smith 1.

BOWLING

	O	M	R	W	BB	5W/i	Avge
J. Wood	120.2	12	510	16	5-68	1	31.87
S. J. E. Brown	476.1	70	1,847	56	7-105	3	32.98
P. J. Berry	141.3	20	527	15	7-113	1	35.13
P. W. Henderson......	96	14	405	10	3-59	0	40.50
I. T. Botham	303	60	1,010	24	4-72	0	42.08
P. Bainbridge.........	177.1	36	555	13	5-100	1	42.69
D. A. Graveney	376.4	86	1,196	28	3-22	0	42.71
M. P. Briers..........	121.3	22	485	11	3-109	0	44.09
S. P. Hughes..........	519.3	94	1,594	34	5-25	1	46.88
S. M. McEwan	180	30	657	12	3-107	0	54.75

Also bowled: G. K. Brown 9–1–64–0; S. Hutton 0.1–0–4–0; D. M. Jones 16.3–1–67–0; W. Larkins 2–1–4–0; P. W. G. Parker 3.2–0–31–0; I. Smith 82–17–231–8.

Wicket-keepers: C. W. Scott 26 ct, 2 st; A. R. Fothergill 7 ct, 1 st..

Leading Fielder: W. Larkins 15.

At Oxford, April 14, 15, 16. DURHAM drew with OXFORD UNIVERSITY.

DURHAM v LEICESTERSHIRE

At Durham University, April 25, 27, 28, 29. Leicestershire won by seven wickets. Leicestershire 23 pts, Durham 3 pts. Toss: Durham. Despite Botham's best efforts, Durham were unable to avoid defeat in their first County Championship match, after being dismissed for 164 when Leicestershire exploited a helpful wicket on the first day. Boon then went to his 11th first-class century, and Smith patiently compiled his first, despite twisting his ankle overnight, off 235 balls with 12 fours. He reached his target two balls before the last man was out, as Leicestershire forged a lead of 178. Durham were 112 for four in their second innings when Botham strode to the crease. In a glorious display of controlled aggression he almost saved the game, hitting five sixes and seven fours in running up Durham's first Championship hundred in 98 balls. Parker, with whom he put on 178, soon added the second, to follow his first-innings 77 – he batted in total for nine and a half hours. But Botham's exit began a spell of five for 12 for Millns, and the last six wickets went down for 28 runs. Leicestershire had a minimum of 51 overs to make 141 and got home with 4.4 overs to spare.

Close of play: First day, Leicestershire 66-2 (T. J. Boon 36*, L. Potter 14*); Second day, Leicestershire 310-7 (B. F. Smith 82*, G. J. Parsons 4*); Third day, Durham 183-4 (P. W. G. Parker 79*, I. T. Botham 26*).

Durham

W. Larkins c Hepworth b Mullally	5	– lbw b Mullally	9
J. D. Glendenen c Mullally b Wells	16	– lbw b Wells	18
D. M. Jones c Briers b Millns	2	– c Whitticase b Potter	32
P. W. G. Parker lbw b Wells	77	– c and b Millns	117
P. Bainbridge lbw b Millns	19	– c Briers b Wells	9
I. T. Botham c Whitticase b Wells	12	– c sub b Millns	105
P. J. Berry c Briers b Potter	9	– c Whitticase b Millns	2
†C. W. Scott c Whitticase b Potter	0	– lbw b Millns	1
*D. A. Graveney c Whitaker b Mullally	12	– b Wells	5
S. P. Hughes not out	3	– c sub b Millns	1
S. J. E. Brown c Whitticase b Mullally	0	– not out	2
L-b 6, w 1, n-b 2	9	B 2, l-b 14, n-b 1	17

1/12 2/18 3/33 4/82 5/96   164   1/24 2/30 3/91 4/112 5/290   318
6/132 7/134 8/156 9/164   6/292 7/304 8/315 9/315

Bonus points – Durham 1, Leicestershire 4.

Bowling: *First Innings*—Mullally 21.1–10–29–3; Millns 17–8–33–2; Wells 17–5–42–3; Parsons 14–1–31–0; Potter 13–3–23–2. *Second Innings*—Millns 21.3–4–69–5; Mullally 24–9–53–1; Wells 29–13–57–3; Parsons 12–3–28–0; Potter 26–10–50–1; Hepworth 8–0–45–0.

Leicestershire

T. J. Boon c Glendenen b Berry	110	– c Jones b Botham	6
*N. E. Briers c and b Botham	10	– c Parker b Graveney	43
J. J. Whitaker b Botham	2	– c Hughes b Berry	35
L. Potter c Jones b Graveney	31	– not out	38
B. F. Smith not out	100		
P. N. Hepworth lbw b Berry	8		
V. J. Wells lbw b Brown	42	– (5) not out	9
†P. Whitticase b Hughes	11		
G. J. Parsons c Scott b Brown	10		
D. J. Millns b Brown	6		
A. D. Mullally b Hughes	1		
L-b 8, n-b 3	11	B 2, l-b 5, w 4	11

1/22 2/28 3/101 4/197 5/215   342   1/6 2/63 3/114   (3 wkts) 142
6/287 7/304 8/327 9/335

Bonus points – Leicestershire 3, Durham 2 (Score at 100 overs: 268-5).

Bowling: *First Innings*—Botham 25-10-51-2; Brown 26-2-80-3; Hughes 25-9-63-2; Graveney 28-6-80-1; Berry 26-7-60-2. *Second Innings*—Botham 5-2-7-1; Hughes 9-3-17-0; Berry 12-4-44-1; Jones 7-0-20-0; Brown 3-0-10-0; Graveney 12.2-2-37-1.

Umpires: B. Dudleston and J. H. Harris.

At Canterbury, May 7, 8, 9, 11. DURHAM drew with KENT.

At Cardiff, May 14, 15, 16. DURHAM beat GLAMORGAN by an innings and 104 runs.

DURHAM v NORTHAMPTONSHIRE

At Stockton-on-Tees, May 23, 25, 26. Northamptonshire won by eight wickets. Northamptonshire 24 pts, Durham 5 pts. Toss: Northamptonshire. Northamptonshire won an excellent game of cricket off the last available ball when Bailey, needing to score a single, hit Botham over mid-off for four. But for most of the last day they had expected to win far more comfortably. Lamb had been able to force Durham to follow on even after being held up by a last-wicket stand of 61 between Bainbridge and the former Northamptonshire player, Brown. Durham staved off an innings defeat only after Jones broke out of a lean spell to score almost two-thirds of the second-innings total, reaching his maiden Championship century. Once again, an improbable batsman had to play a part, this time Hughes. After 338 minutes, Jones was out attempting to hit the boundary that would almost certainly have made the game safe. Northamptonshire were set to make 92 in nine overs. Lamb, promoting himself to open, and Fordham did the bulk of the work, leaving Bailey and Capel to get eight off the last over.

Close of play: First day, Northamptonshire 342-6 (K. M. Curran 53*, D. Ripley 74*); Second day, Durham 6-1 (W. Larkins 1*, D. M. Jones 3*).

Northamptonshire

A. Fordham c Jones b Brown	18	– c Jones b Botham	39
N. A. Felton c Hughes b Brown	20		
R. J. Bailey lbw b Botham	34	– not out	8
*A. J. Lamb c Jones b Hughes	58	– (2) c Bainbridge b Brown	30
D. J. Capel c Parker b Brown	36	– (4) not out	7
M. B. Loye lbw b Graveney	46		
K. M. Curran c Bainbridge b Hughes	82		
†D. Ripley lbw b Brown	104		
A. R. Roberts c Graveney b Brown	0		
C. E. L. Ambrose not out	16		
L-b 4, w 2	6	B 5, l-b 6	11

1/30 2/45 3/118 4/140 5/214   (9 wkts dec.) 420   1/78 2/79   (2 wkts) 95
6/218 7/379 8/379 9/420

J. P. Taylor did not bat.

Bonus points – Northamptonshire 4, Durham 2 (Score at 100 overs: 353-6).

Bowling: *First Innings*—Brown 27-3-124-5; Hughes 25-4-93-2; McEwan 16-2-65-0; Botham 18-2-59-1; Bainbridge 16-3-54-0; Graveney 8-2-21-1. *Second Innings*—Botham 5-0-41-1; Hughes 3-0-38-0; Brown 1-0-5-1.

Durham

W. Larkins lbw b Capel	46	– b Taylor	14
J. D. Glendenen c Ripley b Taylor	5	– c Loye b Ambrose	0
D. M. Jones lbw b Taylor	2	– c Bailey b Capel	.157
P. W. G. Parker c Taylor b Ambrose	35	– c Ripley b Taylor	5
P. Bainbridge not out	92	– c Ripley b Curran	5
I. T. Botham run out	18	– c Ripley b Curran	3
†A. R. Fothergill c Ripley b Taylor	1	– lbw b Capel	15
S. M. McEwan c Fordham b Roberts	22	– c Lamb b Ambrose	0
*D. A. Graveney c Lamb b Ambrose	5	– c Ripley b Curran	5
S. P. Hughes c Ripley b Ambrose	0	– b Capel	20
S. J. E. Brown c Ripley b Curran	19	– not out	5
B 4, l-b 6, w 2, n-b 1	13	B 4, l-b 11, w 4, n-b 5	24

1/10 2/20 3/80 4/112 5/143   258   1/2 2/37 3/47 4/57 5/75   253
6/144 7/185 8/197 9/197   6/111 7/112 8/153 9/240

Bonus points – Durham 3, Northamptonshire 4.

Bowling: *First Innings*—Ambrose 24–7–59–3; Taylor 17–2–48–3; Curran 12.3–2–58–1; Capel 16–0–44–1; Roberts 16–2–39–1. *Second Innings*—Ambrose 28–13–44–2; Taylor 24–4–90–2; Curran 17–4–41–3; Capel 17–3–45–3; Bailey 3–0–6–0; Roberts 7–1–12–0.

Umpires: B. J. Meyer and D. R. Shepherd.

At Southampton, May 29, 30, June 1. DURHAM drew with HAMPSHIRE.

DURHAM v SOMERSET

At Darlington, June 2, 3, 4. Durham won by eight wickets. Durham 23 pts, Somerset 6 pts. Toss: Somerset. Durham raced to their first home win in the Championship after Tavaré declared Somerset's second innings at 192 for six and set a target of 213 to win in 42 overs. Because Glendenen was absent, after suffering from breathing difficulties, Jones opened for the first time, so effectively that he shared a stand of 175 in 33 overs with Larkins, who was at his destructive best in making 92 off 101 balls. Both batsmen fell to Caddick, but Durham were home with eight wickets and three overs to spare. They had scored more than five an over on a slow wicket on which the scoring rate had until then lagged behind three. The visitors' first innings tailed off disappointingly, as the teenager Henderson continued to show his promise with three wickets in the top five, and Graveney declared behind as soon as Scott, with his maiden fifty for Durham, had secured the third batting point. Although opener Lathwell scored his second impressive fifty of the match, Somerset laboured for 70 overs in their second innings – newcomer Mark Briers claimed two wickets with leg-spin – and their lack of urgency even in the closing stages made the declaration something of a surprise.

Close of play: First day, Durham 53-1 (P. W. G. Parker 17*, D. M. Jones 9*); Second day, Somerset 15-0 (A. N. Hayhurst 6*, M. N. Lathwell 8*).

Somerset

A. N. Hayhurst b Henderson	76	– c Graveney b Hughes	7
M. N. Lathwell lbw b Bainbridge	53	– b Henderson	50
R. J. Harden b Brown	24	– lbw b Brown	35
*C. J. Tavaré c Hughes b Henderson	2	– b Briers	10
R. J. Bartlett c Scott b Henderson	21	– lbw b Briers	4
G. D. Rose c Briers b Brown	47	– lbw b Hughes	36
†N. D. Burns c Scott b Bainbridge	9	– not out	26
R. P. Snell lbw b Brown	5	– not out	10
N. A. Mallender lbw b Brown	7		
A. R. Caddick not out	1		
H. R. J. Trump c Scott b Hughes	4		
L-b 15, w 4, n-b 2	21	B 1, l-b 1, w 1, n-b 11	14

1/96 2/150 3/153 4/177 5/198   270   1/25 2/74 3/94   (6 wkts dec.) 192
6/221 7/236 8/254 9/265   4/108 5/125 6/175

Bonus points – Somerset 3, Durham 4.

Bowling: *First Innings*—Brown 19–3–71–4; Hughes 20.5–2–50–1; Henderson 19–1–59–3; Graveney 15–4–30–0; Bainbridge 20–4–45–2. *Second Innings*—Brown 15–3–45–1; Hughes 13.3–4–27–2; Bainbridge 9–3–15–0; Henderson 8–1–39–1; Briers 10–2–43–2; Graveney 15–7–21–0.

Durham

W. Larkins c Trump b Caddick	21	– c Bartlett b Caddick	92
P. W. G. Parker b Hayhurst	42	– (3) not out	16
D. M. Jones c Harden b Mallender	21	– (2) lbw b Caddick	78
P. Bainbridge c Burns b Mallender	45	– not out	14
M. P. Briers lbw b Mallender	12		
P. W. Henderson c Tavaré b Caddick	8		
†C. W. Scott not out	57		
*D. A. Graveney c Rose b Snell	13		
S. P. Hughes c Snell b Trump	6		
S. J. E. Brown not out	5		
B 4, l-b 6, n-b 10	20	B 1, l-b 11, w 1	13

1/27 2/73 3/123 4/146 5/159　　(8 wkts dec.) 250　1/175 2/182　　(2 wkts) 213
6/160 7/206 8/230

J. D. Glendenen did not bat.

Bonus points – Durham 3, Somerset 3.

Bowling: *First Innings*—Snell 17–3–61–1; Caddick 24–6–52–2; Trump 9.2–1–34–1; Mallender 15–3–42–3; Rose 12–4–25–0; Hayhurst 7–0–26–1. *Second Innings*—Mallender 5–0–27–0; Caddick 10–0–54–2; Snell 8–1–51–0; Rose 5–0–19–0; Hayhurst 5–0–24–0; Trump 6–0–26–0.

Umpires: H. D. Bird and N. T. Plews.

At Chesterfield, June 5, 6, 8. DURHAM drew with DERBYSHIRE.

DURHAM v ESSEX

At Hartlepool, June 12, 13, 15. Essex won by 190 runs. Essex 23 pts, Durham 8 pts. Toss: Essex. An excellent wicket greeted Essex at the compact Hartlepool ground, and Gooch made the most of it with a majestic 113, including 21 fours in 162 balls. He and Waugh added 157 in 41 overs. Next day Botham, whose OBE had just been announced, was one of four Durham players to pass 50, while débutant opener Stewart Hutton made 43, before Graveney declared 60 behind. But the match was effectively settled by a spate of Durham injuries. Strike bowler Brown had broken down with back trouble in the first innings, Wood was sidelined by a shin injury and Botham had damaged his groin. Mark Briers, one of three substitutes, held three catches in Essex's second innings, in which they plundered 309 off 52 overs, setting Durham 370 in 87. Jones had also been off the field after a blow to the groin, and Durham were further hampered because the regulations prevented him from batting before No. 6. Their final disaster occurred when Bainbridge's arm was broken by a ball from Ilott, and they capitulated by the 51st over.

Close of play: First day, Durham 63–1 (S. Hutton 24*, D. M. Jones 37*); Second day, Essex 245–4 (P. J. Prichard 62*, N. V. Knight 3*).

Essex

*G. A. Gooch c Scott b Wood	113	– c Scott b Berry	86
J. P. Stephenson c Glendenen b Brown	23	– c sub b Bainbridge	81
P. J. Prichard c Jones b Brown	19	– c sub b Graveney	66
M. E. Waugh c and b Graveney	75	– c sub b Graveney	7
N. V. Knight c Jones b Wood	21	– (6) not out	32
†M. A. Garnham c and b Bainbridge	17	– (7) c Scott b Graveney	16
D. R. Pringle run out	18	– (8) not out	14
N. A. Foster c Scott b Graveney	54	– (5) lbw b Bainbridge	0
M. C. Ilott run out	7		
P. M. Such not out	2		
J. H. Childs c Jones b Berry	4		
L-b 6, n-b 1	7	B 4, l-b 3	7

1/55 2/79 3/236 4/236 5/267			360	1/152 2/210 3/229	(6 wkts dec.) 309
6/280 7/307 8/325 9/355						4/235 5/251 6/277

Bonus points – Essex 4, Durham 4.

Bowling: *First Innings*—Wood 22–2–86–2; Brown 9–0–51–2; Botham 14–2–67–0; Bainbridge 24–7–46–1; Berry 5–0–39–1; Graveney 19–3–65–2. *Second Innings*—Wood 5–0–28–0; Bainbridge 22–0–87–2; Berry 12–0–99–1; Graveney 13–0–88–3.

Durham

J. D. Glendenen lbw b Ilott	1	– c Gooch b Foster	10
S. Hutton c Waugh b Ilott	43	– c Such b Foster	40
D. M. Jones c Stephenson b Childs	57	– (6) c Foster b Waugh	22
P. W. G. Parker c Knight b Childs	53	– (3) c Gooch b Ilott	22
P. Bainbridge c Foster b Childs	60	– (4) retired hurt	6
I. T. Botham not out	55	– (5) c Garnham b Foster	22
†C. W. Scott b Childs	0	– c Stephenson b Foster	2
P. J. Berry b Stephenson	6	– c Garnham b Pringle	30
*D. A. Graveney not out	5	– not out	25
J. Wood (did not bat)		– c Prichard b Pringle	8
S. J. E. Brown (did not bat)		– c Childs b Pringle	10
B 1, l-b 8, w 1, n-b 8	18	L-b 1, n-b 3	4

1/2 2/107 3/108 4/226 5/231	(7 wkts dec.) 300	1/14 2/15 3/82 4/83 5/98	179
6/231 7/277						6/106 7/143 8/151 9/179

Bonus points – Durham 4, Essex 3.

In the second innings P. Bainbridge retired hurt at 30.

Bowling: *First Innings*—Foster 20–4–52–0; Ilott 17–3–72–2; Childs 20–6–85–4; Pringle 15–5–31–0; Stephenson 5.4–0–35–1; Such 6–2–16–0. *Second Innings*—Foster 20–8–49–4; Ilott 11–2–43–1; Childs 3–0–9–0; Pringle 10.2–1–50–3; Waugh 6–0–27–1.

Umpires: J. H. Hampshire and M. J. Kitchen.

At Horsham, June 19, 20, 22. DURHAM lost to SUSSEX by four wickets.

DURHAM v KENT

At Gateshead Fell, June 27, 28, 29. Drawn. Durham 8 pts, Kent 6 pts. Toss: Durham. Durham's request for more grass to be left on their wickets, to produce more pace and bounce for the benefit of their strokeplayers, backfired when Jones was hit in the face by a steeply rising delivery from McCague. His abrupt exit from the match, which already lacked the injured Botham, seriously impaired Durham's chances of chasing 299 in 56 overs the next day. While the hostile McCague softened Durham up, left-arm spinner Davis relied on the subtleties of flight to improve his career-best figures for the second time in 11 days, finishing with seven for 64 to follow his seven for 99 against Gloucestershire. In Kent's first innings Cowdrey had made his third century of the season, hitting 15 fours in scoring 115 off 213 balls, but his team-mate Llong fell eight short of his maiden first-class hundred on the final day, which was remarkable for consisting of two 150-minute sessions, instead of three of two hours each, so that Kent could begin their southbound journey sooner.

Close of play: First day, Durham 20-0 (W. Larkins 4*, S. Hutton 12*); Second day, Kent 61-3 (N. J. Llong 35*, G. R. Cowdrey 6*).

Kent

M. A. Ealham b S. J. E. Brown	0	– c Larkins b S. J. E. Brown	2
*M. R. Benson c Scott b Hughes	46	– c Scott b S. J. E. Brown	5
N. J. Llong c Scott b Wood	2	– c Wood b Hughes	92
C. L. Hooper st Scott b Graveney	87	– c Larkins b Briers	8
G. R. Cowdrey c G. K. Brown b Graveney	115	– run out	46
N. R. Taylor b Wood	29	– not out	50
M. V. Fleming c Briers b Hughes	49	– c Briers b S. J. E. Brown	24
†S. A. Marsh c S. J. E. Brown b Graveney	24	– not out	0
R. M. Ellison not out	4		
R. P. Davis c Parker b Wood	1		
M. J. McCague c G. K. Brown b Wood	9		
B 2, l-b 15, w 2, n-b 7	26	L-b 6, w 1, n-b 1	8

1/2 2/15 3/78 4/186 5/237   **392**   1/3 2/8 3/52   (6 wkts dec.) **235**
6/323 7/359 8/374 9/382   4/144 5/205 6/234

Bonus points – Kent 4, Durham 4.

Bowling: *First Innings*—Wood 24.4-3-92-4; S. J. E. Brown 23-4-76-1; Hughes 30-6-114-2; Graveney 22-2-93-3. *Second Innings*—Wood 9-1-46-0; S. J. E. Brown 14-4-59-3; Hughes 5-2-13-1; Briers 3-1-5-50-1; G. K. Brown 4-0-25-0; Graveney 3.3-0-36-0.

Durham

W. Larkins c Cowdrey b Davis	90	– lbw b Ellison	41
S. Hutton c McCague b Davis	76	– c Marsh b Ellison	37
D. M. Jones retired hurt	6		
P. W. G. Parker not out	72	– (3) c Ellison b Davis	22
M. P. Briers c Llong b Hooper	16	– (4) not out	56
G. K. Brown lbw b Davis	16	– (5) c Ellison b Hooper	48
J. Wood c and b Davis	15	– (6) b McCague	3
†C. W. Scott c Benson b Davis	0	– (7) not out	3
*D. A. Graveney c Fleming b Davis	11		
S. P. Hughes lbw b Davis	1		
B 7, l-b 10, w 2, n-b 7	26	L-b 6	6

1/169 2/197 3/217 4/281 5/302   (8 wkts dec.) **329**   1/70 2/99 3/107   (5 wkts) **216**
6/304 7/320 8/329   4/197 5/205

S. J. E. Brown did not bat.

Bonus points – Durham 4, Kent 2 (Score at 100 overs: 304-5).

In the first innings D. M. Jones retired hurt at 176.

Bowling: *First Innings*—McCague 22-8-50-0; Ealham 17-4-58-0; Davis 24.1-7-64-7; Ellison 14-3-47-0; Hooper 20-4-53-1; Fleming 9-0-40-0. *Second Innings*—McCague 13.4-0-46-1; Ealham 4-0-13-0; Davis 13-0-62-1; Ellison 9-2-27-2; Hooper 11-2-49-1; Fleming 2-0-13-0.

Umpires: B. J. Meyer and G. A. Stickley.

DURHAM v GLOUCESTERSHIRE

At Stockton-on-Tees, July 3, 4, 6. Drawn. Toss: Durham. After rain washed out the first two days, the teams played a one-innings match without bonus points on the third. Durham captain Graveney missed the encounter with his former county because of a knee injury, but his deputy, Parker, put Gloucestershire in. The visitors spent 22 overs compiling their first 50 runs, and then leg-spinner Briers took three wickets to reduce them to 132 for four. However, Wright, who hit three sixes and ten fours, and Scott put on 127 in 49 minutes, before asking Durham to score 260 in what turned out to be 46 overs. Larkins led the chase with 74 as the target came down to 136 off 20 overs and 89 off ten. The left-arm spinner Davies was twice hit out of the ground by the tailender Wood, but when Williams took the third stumping off his bowling, Durham called off the chase, with 50 needed off five overs.

Close of play: First day, No play; Second day, No play.

Gloucestershire

G. D. Hodgson c Fothergill b Briers ... 35	R. J. Scott not out 51
C. W. J. Athey c Jones b Briers....... 56	B 4, l-b 6, n-b 3 13
S. G. Hinks b Smith 10	
*A. J. Wright not out 83	1/95 2/96 (4 wkts dec.) 259
M. W. Alleyne b Briers............. 11	3/109 4/132

R. C. Williams, †R. C. J. Williams, M. Davies, A. M. Babington and A. M. Smith did not bat.

Bowling: Wood 5–0–21–0; Brown 7–0–14–0; Hughes 6–3–8–0; Botham 7–3–28–0; Briers 23–3–109–3; Smith 10–2–35–1; Jones 6.3–1–34–0.

Durham

W. Larkins c Scott b Alleyne 74	I. Smith st R. C. J. Williams b Davies . 12
J. D. Glendenen lbw b Smith......... 4	J. Wood not out................... 25
D. M. Jones c R. C. J. Williams	†A. R. Fothergill not out............ 11
b Davies . 18	
*P. W. G. Parker lbw b Alleyne 43	B 1, l-b 6, w 1, n-b 6 14
I. T. Botham st R. C. J. Williams	
b Davies . 11	1/11 2/59 3/131 (7 wkts) 227
M. P. Briers st R. C. J. Williams	4/157 5/163
b Davies . 15	6/185 7/210

S. P. Hughes and S. J. E. Brown did not bat.

Bowling: Smith 9–0–43–1; Babington 13–0–64–0; R. C. Williams 3–1–4–0; Davies 14–0–73–4; Alleyne 5–0–28–2; Athey 2–0–8–0.

Umpires: A. A. Jones and G. A. Stickley.

At Chester-le-Street, July 14, 15, 16. DURHAM lost to PAKISTANIS by 107 runs (See Pakistani tour section).

At Nottingham, July 17, 18, 20. DURHAM drew with NOTTINGHAMSHIRE.

At Leicester, July 21, 22, 23. DURHAM lost to LEICESTERSHIRE by ten wickets.

At Lord's, July 24, 25, 27. DURHAM lost to MIDDLESEX by 175 runs.

DURHAM v SURREY

At Durham University, July 31, August 1, 3. Surrey won by seven wickets. Surrey 24 pts, Durham 4 pts. Toss: Surrey. Durham returned to base after an unhappy southern tour in which they lost two Championship matches and the NatWest quarter-final, bid an early farewell to Jones, with a broken finger, and lost Parker to a hamstring strain. But their fortunes did not improve. Put in by Surrey, who were probably planning a last-day run-chase on a pitch offering more pace and bounce than earlier in the season, they opted for all-out attack. They scored at five an over in a crazy morning session, reaching 167 for six. Benjamin polished them off for 189, taking the last six wickets for seven runs either side of lunch for a career-best six for 30. With Atkins providing the anchor Durham had so conspicuously lacked, Brown hammered a 71-ball century for Surrey and went on to 175 in 164 balls, with 25 fours and a six. It was his second consecutive hundred in only his fourth first-class match. Durham were in danger of an innings defeat but the last two wickets put on 115 and a tenth-wicket stand of 70 between Graveney and Brown gave them some hope. It was not enough to stop Surrey winning with nine overs to spare.

Close of play: First day, Surrey 269-5 (A. D. Brown 120*, M. P. Bicknell 19*); Second day, Durham 201-4 (I. Smith 72*, I. T. Botham 38*).

Durham

W. Larkins c Stewart b M. P. Bicknell	15	– lbw b Benjamin 9
S. Hutton b Bryson	0	– lbw b M. P. Bicknell 42
I. T. Botham c Benjamin b Boiling	36	– (6) c Lynch b M. P. Bicknell ... 48
P. Bainbridge b Lynch b Benjamin	39	– (3) c Sargeant b M. P. Bicknell . 9
M. P. Briers c Sargeant b Bryson	29	– (4) c sub b Boiling 4
I. Smith b Benjamin	29	– c Sargeant b M. P. Bicknell .. 74
†C. W. Scott c Sargeant b Benjamin	0	– (8) c D. J. Bicknell b M. P. Bicknell. 35
P. J. Berry b Benjamin	9	– (7) c Sargeant b Benjamin 0
S. M. McEwan c Thorpe b Benjamin	0	– c Stewart b Boiling 8
*D. A. Graveney c Brown b Benjamin ...	0	– c Boiling b Benjamin 36
S. J. E. Brown not out	4	– not out 47
L-b 16, n-b 12	28	B 5, l-b 11, w 4, n-b 25 .. 45
	189	**357**

1/2 2/42 3/80 4/125 5/141 6/155 7/177 8/178 9/182

1/26 2/49 3/58 4/127 5/216 6/217 7/224 8/242 9/287

Bonus points – Durham 1, Surrey 4.

Bowling: *First Innings*—M. P. Bicknell 15–4–39–1; Bryson 11–0–80–2; Boiling 5–0–24–1; Benjamin 15.3–9–30–6. *Second Innings*—M. P. Bicknell 34–3–120–5; Benjamin 32.1–3–98–3; Bryson 6–1–17–0; Boiling 36–9–72–2; Thorpe 8–3–32–0; Stewart 2–1–1–0; Brown 1–0–1–0.

Surrey

D. J. Bicknell c Larkins b Brown	8	– run out 49
P. D. Atkins b McEwan	60	– b McEwan 2
*A. J. Stewart lbw b McEwan	42	– c Scott b McEwan 1
G. P. Thorpe lbw b Botham	4	– not out 60
M. A. Lynch c Scott b McEwan	11	– not out 1
A. D. Brown lbw b Botham	175	
M. P. Bicknell c Larkins b Botham	21	
R. E. Bryson b Graveney	48	
†N. F. Sargeant c Scott b Graveney	30	
J. Boiling run out	18	
J. E. Benjamin not out	6	
B 1, l-b 5, w 2	8	B 1, l-b 2 3
	431	**(3 wkts) 116**

1/14 2/82 3/87 4/104 5/223 6/293 7/376 8/376 9/416

1/9 2/11 3/110

Bonus points – Surrey 4, Durham 3 (Score at 100 overs: 416-8).

Bowling: *First Innings*—Brown 16–3–77–1; Botham 40–6–135–3; McEwan 20–3–107–3; Bainbridge 6–0–41–0; Graveney 21.2–5–57–2; Briers 1–0–8–0. *Second Innings*—McEwan 9–1–40–2; Brown 7–0–31–0; Berry 9–1–15–0; Graveney 4–0–20–0; Briers 1–0–3–0; Hutton 0.1–0–4–0.

Umpires: M. J. Kitchen and D. O. Oslear.

DURHAM v YORKSHIRE

At Durham University, August 4, 5, 6. Yorkshire won by five wickets. Yorkshire 20 pts, Durham 6 pts. Toss: Durham. Yorkshire became the first winners of the Durham Light Infantry Cup, presented by the regiment to go to the winners of Championship matches between these two counties. The Racecourse ground, which had earned a reputation as a bowler's graveyard, suddenly yielded 16 wickets for 90 runs during the second day. But the pitch held no terrors for Tendulkar, whose maiden Championship century secured Yorkshire's win. Durham collapsed from 114 for one to 214 on the first day, with Robinson taking three wickets in 16 balls after lunch and three more in 13 after tea. Yorkshire, 56 for two overnight, added 30 in the first 20 minutes before their inability to cope with the seaming ball saw the last eight wickets go down for 22 runs. Botham took four for seven in 22 balls. The mayhem continued as Durham collapsed to 68 for eight, before conditions eased as the temperature dropped and Scott scored a classy half-century, adding 86 for the ninth wicket with Graveney. Needing 262 to win, Yorkshire were 87 for three before Tendulkar took regal command, reaching 100 off 96 balls with 16 fours.

Close of play: First day, Yorkshire 56-2 (D. Byas 18*, S. R. Tendulkar 7*); Second day, Yorkshire 85-2 (D. Byas 9*, P. Carrick 2*).

Durham

W. Larkins c Tendulkar b Robinson	67	– b Jarvis 0
S. Hutton c Byas b Carrick	31	– c Blakey b Jarvis 0
P. Bainbridge c Blakey b Robinson	14	– run out 21
M. P. Briers b Jarvis	15	– lbw b Hartley 7
I. Smith b Robinson	6	– b Robinson 8
I. T. Botham b Jarvis	29	– c Kellett b Jarvis 13
P. J. Berry lbw b Jarvis	1	– lbw b Robinson 10
†C. W. Scott not out	25	– c Kellett b Jarvis 54
S. M. McEwan c Batty b Robinson	12	– c Batty b Robinson 0
*D. A. Graveney c Blakey b Robinson	0	– not out 32
S. P. Hughes c Blakey b Robinson	1	– b Robinson 1
L-b 4, n-b 9	13	L-b 2, n-b 7 9

1/72 2/114 3/121 4/130 5/163   214   1/1 2/3 3/22 4/41 5/42   155
6/173 7/174 8/199 9/199   6/60 7/68 8/68 9/154

Bonus points – Durham 2, Yorkshire 4.

Bowling: *First Innings*—Jarvis 19–3–49–3; Hartley 13–3–62–0; Robinson 21.1–4–57–6; Carrick 12–5–26–1; Batty 12–5–16–0. *Second Innings*—Jarvis 15–4–43–4; Robinson 20.1–5–44–4; Hartley 11–0–51–1; Tendulkar 3–0–6–0; Moxon 3–0–7–0; Carrick 1–0–2–0.

Yorkshire

*M. D. Moxon c Bainbridge b McEwan	25	– c and b Graveney 44
S. A. Kellett b Hughes	6	– c Scott b McEwan 30
D. Byas lbw b Botham	37	– c sub b Botham 11
S. R. Tendulkar c Scott b Hughes	21	– (5) c Hutton b Botham 100
†R. J. Blakey c Smith b Botham	0	– (6) not out 26
C. White lbw b Botham	5	– (7) not out 5
P. W. Jarvis c Bainbridge b Hughes	0	
P. Carrick c McEwan b Hughes	3	– (4) lbw b Botham 46
P. J. Hartley c Scott b Botham	0	
J. D. Batty b Hughes	5	
M. A. Robinson not out	4	
L-b 1, w 1	2	B 1 1

1/16 2/45 3/86 4/87 5/94   108   1/70 2/79 3/87   (5 wkts) 263
6/95 7/95 8/96 9/101   4/217 5/242

Bonus points – Durham 4.

Bowling: *First Innings*—Botham 21–2–72–4; Hughes 15.4–8–25–5; McEwan 5–2–10–1. *Second Innings*—Botham 26–5–92–3; Hughes 23.1–6–77–0; McEwan 16–2–60–1; Graveney 9–3–33–1.

Umpires: M. J. Kitchen and D. O. Oslear.

At Birmingham, August 7, 8, 10. DURHAM drew with WARWICKSHIRE.

DURHAM v GLAMORGAN

At Hartlepool, August 14, 15, 17. Drawn. Durham 4 pts, Glamorgan 8 pts. Toss: Glamorgan. Glamorgan, who had just relinquished bottom place in the Championship table to Durham, came to Hartlepool in search of revenge for their defeat in May. They might have been successful had rain not wiped out most of the final session on the second day. Morris made 126, his sixth century of the season, enabling Maynard to declare at 396 for six. Glamorgan's bowlers, especially Foster, extracted unexpected life from the pitch to dismiss Durham for 201 and enforce the follow-on. Glendenen, the first player to score a first-class century for Durham, became the first to bag a pair, caught at short leg first ball. But rain intervened and when Foster retired with back trouble, Glamorgan's attack posed much less of a threat. Larkins led Durham to safety with 140 off 197 balls, to follow up his 143 in the May fixture. He hit five sixes and 19 fours.

Close of play: First day, Durham 5–1 (W. Larkins 3*, P. J. Berry 2*); Second day, Durham 59–1 (W. Larkins 42*, P. Bainbridge 16*).

Glamorgan

S. P. James b Brown	10	R. D. B. Croft not out	29
H. Morris c Briers b Graveney	126		
A. Dale c Scott b Hughes	68	B 10, l-b 8, w 1	19
*M. P. Maynard c Scott b Hughes	22		
I. V. A. Richards lbw b Brown	31	1/10 2/156 3/190	(6 wkts dec.) 396
P. A. Cottey c Hughes b Brown	91	4/232 5/315 6/396	

†C. P. Metson, S. L. Watkin, D. J. Foster and S. R. Barwick did not bat.

Bonus points – Glamorgan 4, Durham 2 (Score at 100 overs: 381–5).

Bowling: Brown 17.1–2–54–3; Hughes 26–2–84–2; Botham 16–1–66–0; Graveney 27–2–99–1; Berry 17–2–75–0.

Durham

W. Larkins c James b Watkin	9	– c Metson b Barwick	140
J. D. Glendenen c Maynard b Foster	0	– c James b Watkin	0
P. J. Berry b Barwick	26	– (8) not out	1
P. Bainbridge c Metson b Watkin	3	– (3) lbw b Dale	56
M. P. Briers lbw b Dale	25	– (4) b Maynard	52
I. Smith b Dale	23	– (5) c Metson b Croft	0
I. T. Botham c Richards b Foster	54	– (6) lbw b Croft	7
†C. W. Scott c Richards b Foster	16	– (7) c Dale b Croft	33
*D. A. Graveney c Maynard b Foster	6	– not out	1
S. P. Hughes not out	4		
S. J. E. Brown c Richards b Foster	16		
B 4, l-b 7, w 1, n-b 7	19	B 7, l-b 11, w 1, n-b 4	23

1/0 2/22 3/30 4/48 5/86 201   1/1 2/166 3/230 4/231   (7 wkts) 313
6/120 7/171 8/173 9/179   5/241 6/302 7/309

Bonus points – Durham 2, Glamorgan 4.

Bowling: *First Innings*—Watkin 13–4–35–2; Foster 22.4–2–87–5; Barwick 19–5–46–1; Dale 6–2–22–2. *Second Innings*—Watkin 27–8–75–1; Dale 22–5–56–1; Barwick 24–4–91–1; Croft 23–6–37–3; Foster 6–1–33–0; Maynard 2–0–3–1.

Umpires: D. J. Constant and R. C. Tolchard.

At Worcester, August 21, 22, 24. DURHAM drew with WORCESTERSHIRE.

DURHAM v HAMPSHIRE

At Darlington, August 26, 27, 28, 29. Drawn. Durham 5 pts, Hampshire 5 pts. Toss: Hampshire. Rain dominated the match at both ends. After Durham reduced Hampshire to 87 for four at lunch on the first day the next three sessions were lost. Then Middleton and Ayling survived the 52 overs possible on the second day, taking their stand to 195, with Ayling reaching his highest Championship score of 90. But he fell without addition to the fourth ball of the third morning. Middleton continued in stoical fashion, remaining unbeaten on 127. Durham declared 53 behind then fed Nicholas some easy runs to encourage him to declare, setting a target of 283 off 59 overs. Shine quickly reduced the home team to 36 for three, but Bainbridge tilted the balance back until Shine returned to take three more wickets. After another interruption, Hampshire had 9.1 overs to take the last two wickets, and failed.

Close of play: First day, Hampshire 87-4 (T. C. Middleton 35*, J. R. Ayling 2*); Second day, Hampshire 266-4 (T. C. Middleton 117*, J. R. Ayling 90*); Third day, Hampshire 47-1 (K. D. James 17*, D. I. Gower 14*).

Hampshire

T. C. Middleton not out	127	– c McEwan b S. J. E. Brown	12
K. D. James c Larkins b S. J. E. Brown	3	– c Larkins b Briers	57
D. I. Gower b Bainbridge	38	– c Bainbridge b Hughes	39
R. A. Smith b McEwan	1	– c G. K. Brown b Hughes	3
*M. C. J. Nicholas lbw b McEwan	0	– not out	95
J. R. Ayling c Graveney b Hughes	90	– lbw b Briers	0
†A. N. Aymes lbw b S. J. E. Brown	0	– not out	4
R. J. Maru not out	23		
B 1, l-b 7, w 11, n-b 2	21	B 9, l-b 8, w 2	19

1/7 2/70 3/71 4/71 (6 wkts dec.) 303   1/20 2/87 3/97 (5 wkts dec.) 229
5/266 6/268   4/198 5/210

I. J. Turner, C. A. Connor and K. J. Shine did not bat.

Bonus points – Hampshire 4, Durham 2.

Bowling: *First Innings*—Hughes 28.3–7–80–1; S. J. E. Brown 20–4–72–2; Bainbridge 14–4–46–1; McEwan 27–6–75–2; Graveney 5–1–13–0; Smith 3–0–9–0. *Second Innings*—S. J. E. Brown 12–1–40–1; Hughes 16–1–45–2; Bainbridge 2–1–3–0; McEwan 8–1–30–0; Briers 8–0–30–2; G. K. Brown 5–1–39–0; Parker 2–0–25–0.

Durham

W. Larkins b Connor	0	– b Shine	11
G. K. Brown b Ayling	10	– lbw b Ayling	39
P. W. G. Parker c Smith b James	68	– lbw b Shine	6
M. P. Briers c Turner b Ayling	5	– c Aymes b Shine	2
P. Bainbridge not out	84	– c Aymes b Shine	83
I. Smith not out	68	– lbw b Shine	18
†C. W. Scott (did not bat)		– b Maru	4
S. M. McEwan (did not bat)		– b Shine	0
S. J. E. Brown (did not bat)		– not out	3
*D. A. Graveney (did not bat)		– not out	9
L-b 6, w 3, n-b 6	15	L-b 10, w 1, n-b 8	19

1/0 2/38 3/44 4/136 (4 wkts dec.) 250   1/21 2/34 3/36 (8 wkts) 194
                                         4/102 5/169 6/178
                                         7/178 8/178

S. P. Hughes did not bat.

Bonus points – Durham 3, Hampshire 1.

Bowling: *First Innings*—Connor 16.2–2–55–1; Shine 12–3–48–0; Ayling 10–3–24–2; ␣rner 13–2–46–0; James 8–3–29–1; Maru 20–4–42–0. *Second Innings*—Connor 12–1–55–0; ␣ine 17–2–68–6; Turner 6–2–17–0; Ayling 11–3–35–1; Maru 5–2–9–1.

Umpires: G. I. Burgess and R. A. White.

␣t Taunton, September 7, 8, 9. DURHAM lost to SOMERSET by eight wickets.

DURHAM v LANCASHIRE

␣t Gateshead Fell, September 12, 13, 14, 15. Lancashire won by ten wickets. Lancashire ␣ pts, Durham 6 pts. Toss: Durham. What threatened to be an even contest was effectively ␣ecided by a seventh-wicket stand of 243 for Lancashire between Atherton, whose ␣ethodical 500-minute innings ended only one short of a maiden double-century, and ␣artin, who reached three figures for the first time. They came together at 220 for six, in ␣ply to 312, but with Durham relying heavily on medium-pacers Bainbridge and Smith, ␣ancashire eventually led by 250. Their total of 562 was the largest conceded by Durham. ␣he visitors would have won by an innings but for a remarkably composed unbeaten 80 ␣om the 18-year-old Jimmy Daley, playing only his second first-class match. He provided ␣me cheer for the 300 die-hards who stuck out Durham's inaugural season to the bitter end. ␣eFreitas's best figures of the season, six for 94, left Lancashire needing only 22 to win. ␣arker, who had started the season by facing Durham's first ball in first-class cricket, ended ␣by bowling the final delivery.

Close of play: First day, Durham 215-7 (J. D. Glendenen 36*, D. A. Graveney 0*); ␣econd day, Lancashire 224-6 (M. A. Atherton 85*, P. J. Martin 0*); Third day, Durham ␣-0 (W. Larkins 24*, P. W. G. Parker 25*).

␣urham

␣. Larkins c Fairbrother b DeFreitas	53	– lbw b Martin	24
W. G. Parker lbw b Watkinson	70	– b DeFreitas	52
␣ Smith lbw b DeFreitas	0	– lbw b DeF␣eitas	15
␣ Bainbridge c Watkinson b DeFreitas	18	– c Hegg b DeFreitas	18
␣ A. Daley run out	17	– not out	80
␣ D. Glendenen c Speak b Watkinson	76	– lbw b Austin	43
␣. P. Briers lbw b Watkinson	15	– b Austin	7
␣. R. Fothergill lbw b Watkinson	0	– c Hegg b DeFreitas	0
␣D. A. Graveney b Austin	0	– (10) c Hegg b Austin	0
␣ P. Hughes c Hegg b Watkinson	42	– (9) b DeFreitas	0
␣ J. E. Brown not out	6	– c Hegg b DeFreitas	18
B 1, l-b 10, n-b 4	15	B 7, l-b 3, n-b 4	14

␣104 2/104 3/146 4/148   312   1/57 2/88 3/102   271
␣172 6/206 7/210 8/217 9/293   4/121 5/222 6/238
                                                               7/239 8/243 9/244

Bonus points – Durham 4, Lancashire 4 (Score at 100 overs: 300-9).

Bowling: *First Innings*—DeFreitas 26–7–94–3; Martin 19–5–62–0; Watkinson ␣.1–7–63–5; Austin 22–11–52–1; Barnett 11–1–30–0. *Second Innings*—DeFreitas ␣.3–6–94–6; Martin 16–4–49–1; Watkinson 14–3–56–0; Austin 15–4–44–3; Barnett ␣–3–18–0.

Lancashire

G. D. Mendis st Fothergill b Bainbridge	45 – not out	
M. A. Atherton c Fothergill b Bainbridge	199 – not out	2
N. J. Speak b Smith	20	
*N. H. Fairbrother lbw b Hughes	0	
M. Watkinson c Larkins b Bainbridge	46	
G. D. Lloyd lbw b Smith	2	
†W. K. Hegg b Smith	16	
P. J. Martin c Smith b Brown	133	
P. A. J. DeFreitas c Brown b Bainbridge	22	
I. D. Austin c Larkins b Bainbridge	58	
A. A. Barnett not out	7	
B 2, l-b 9, w 2, n-b 1	14	

1/71 2/108 3/113 4/175   562   (no wkt) 2
5/188 6/220 7/463 8/483 9/546

Bonus points – Lancashire 4, Durham 2 (Score at 100 overs: 353-6).

Bowling: *First Innings*—Brown 28–4–137–1; Hughes 36–2–136–1; Bainbridge 27.1–4–100–5; Briers 12–2–31–0; Smith 38–7–85–3; Graveney 20–3–62–0. *Second Innings*—Hughes 3–1–14–0; Smith 2–0–6–0; Parker 0.1–0–4–0.

Umpires: H. D. Bird and J. H. Hampshire.

THE NEWCOMERS

Eight teams competed in the 1890 County Championship. The record of the remaining counties in their first year in the competition is as follows:

		M	W	L	D	Position	Teams competing
1891	Somerset	12	5	6	1	5=	9
1895	Derbyshire	16	5	4	7	5	14
	Warwickshire	18	6	6	6	6=	
	Essex	16	5	7	4	9	
	Hampshire	16	6	9	1	10	
	Leicestershire	16	3	10	3	12=	
1899	Worcestershire	12	2	5	5	12	15
1905	Northamptonshire	12	2	8	2	13	16
1921	Glamorgan	18	2	14	2	17	17
1992	Durham	22	2	10	10	18	18

Note: Hampshire had previously taken part in the Championship from 1864 to 1885, Derbyshire from 1871 to 1887 and Somerset from 1882 to 1885.

ESSEX

President: T. N. Pearce
Chairman: D. J. Insole
Chairman, Cricket Committee: G. J. Saville
Secretary/General Manager: P. J. Edwards
County Ground, New Writtle Street,
Chelmsford CM2 0PG
(Telephone: 0245-252420)
Captain: G. A. Gooch

Another chapter in the Essex success story was written in 1992 when they won the County Championship for the second year running and the sixth time since they broke their duck in 1979. The title was settled at Chelmsford on September 3, with two matches to spare, when John Stephenson scored a single off the bowling of Robin Smith of Hampshire.

It had been a victory against Hampshire at Bournemouth in June that had given the Essex season lift-off. They had looked doomed to a resounding defeat when they followed on and then left Hampshire only 60 to win. But with the tenacity and self-belief that has characterised their play in recent years, Essex fought back to win by 79 runs. They won their next match against Lancashire in two days and thus, on June 7, went top of the table; and there they remained, despite having to overcome a succession of injuries and Test calls.

Not once were the county able to field their full-strength side. And in one-day cricket Essex had their disappointments: finishing second in the Sunday League behind Middlesex and failing, in the last over of their semi-final against Leicestershire, to reach the final of the NatWest Trophy. But the overall quality of the staff ensured that the County Championship was never in serious doubt. In many ways, they reached their summit of achievement in the games in which they produced their worst performances. It happened first at Bournemouth and then again, in the match immediately after sealing the Championship, when they had been bowled out for 96 on a green pitch at Derby in a manner that suggested the players had been overdoing the celebrations. Set 440 to win, Essex got there, with Graham Gooch scoring an unbeaten century coming in at No. 6. It underlined the determination, as well as the talent, that has characterised Essex cricket in their years of success.

Predictably, the team were inspired throughout by Gooch and Mark Waugh, who had the highest Championship batting averages in the country. Whenever Gooch played, his very presence bred a confidence that enabled the others to play their natural game. The remarkable feature of the Essex season, however, was that even when Gooch was with England and in the final six weeks of the season when Waugh had to go on Australia's tour of Sri Lanka, other players bridged the gap.

The county's spirit was typified by Paul Prichard, who had his most prolific season, reached fifty 13 times and won the Britannic Assurance

Player of the Season award, partly for the positive way he led the team in Gooch's absence. Two youngsters did well: Jonathan Lewis won a regular place late in the summer and averaged over 46, showing a sound defence and unruffled temperament; and Nick Knight, a left hander with more attacking flair, started to confirm his promise before losing form. Nasser Hussain shared a county record third-wicket stand of 347 with Waugh against Lancashire at Ilford, scoring 172. But this was one of his few rewarding moments in a summer when he did not advance his claims for a resumption of his Test career. He was disciplined and dropped for one match following a dressing-room incident at Tunbridge Wells and missed the final games with a broken finger. He could learn something from Prichard's consistency.

Neil Foster missed more than half the season because of his trouble some knee, which eventually needed an operation. Since he was regarded as Essex's most potent weapon, his absence magnifies the team's achievement. Luckily, Mark Ilott recovered from the back injury that kept him out in 1991 and emerged with 64 wickets. Both in appearance and action, Ilott reminded one increasingly of John Lever the left-arm seamer he succeeded. Though he was yet to show the same consistency in his performances and variation in his methods, at 22 time was very much on his side.

Ilott, Prichard and the off-spinner Peter Such were all chosen for the England A tour. Such gained his selection after a splendid run in late summer that included match-winning performances at Southend and Colchester. Before then, on the dry pitches that marked the early part of the season, John Childs, rising 41, had bowled tellingly to reach 50 wickets by July 17. Don Topley, John Stephenson (an increasingly trustworthy opening bat), Steve Andrew and Waugh all finished with more than 20 wickets, which emphasised the way people chipped in when necessary. And Derek Pringle played a decisive role as an all rounder while still leaving the impression that he did not play to his full potential, particularly with the bat.

With the Australians touring in 1993, the gifted Pakistani Salim Malik was expected to return instead of Waugh. For the first time in more than 30 years it will be a season when the name Keith Fletcher does not appear on the county payroll. He captained Essex to every major honour in the game after years when they habitually tottered and fell on the very edge of success. For the last four seasons he had devoted himself to bringing players through the Second Eleven but despite his devotion to the county, he found the invitation to succeed Micky Stewart as England team manager too much of a temptation to resist. Essex owe Fletcher a debt they can never repay, a fact readily acknowledged by Gooch. The standards now set at Essex, which others strive to emulate, stem from his leadership, and England could not have chosen a wiser or more respected character for one of cricket's most arduous jobs. – Nigel Fuller.

ESSEX 1992

[*Bill Smith*]

Back row: R. J. Rollins, J. J. B. Lewis, J. P. Stephenson, A. C. Richards, M. C. Ilott, D. D. J. Robinson, D. M. Cousins, K. A. Butler, L. Tennant. *Middle row*: M. A. Garnham, J. W. S. Davis (*physiotherapist*), N. Hussain, M. E. Waugh, P. M. Such. S. J. W. Andrew, D. J. P. Boden, A. G. J. Fraser, N. Shahid, W. G. Lovell, N. V. Knight. *Front row*: J. H. Childs, P. J. Prichard, N. A. Foster, G. A. Gooch (*captain*), D. R. Pringle, T. D. Topley, K. W. R. Fletcher.

ESSEX RESULTS

All first-class matches – Played 25: Won 11, Lost 7, Drawn 7.

County Championship matches – Played 22: Won 11, Lost 6, Drawn 5.

Bonus points – Batting 60, Bowling 64.

*Competition placings – Britannic Assurance County Championship, winners;
NatWest Bank Trophy, s-f; Benson and Hedges Cup, 3rd in Group B;
Sunday League, 2nd.*

BRITANNIC ASSURANCE CHAMPIONSHIP AVERAGES

BATTING

	Birthplace	M	I	NO	R	HS	Avg
‡G. A. Gooch	Leytonstone	11	18	3	1,246	160	83.0
‡M. E. Waugh§	Sydney, Australia	15	23	7	1,253	219*	78.3
‡J. P. Stephenson	Stebbing	19	33	5	1,309	159*	46.7
‡N. Hussain	Madras, India	17	21	3	833	172*	46.2
J. J. B. Lewis	Isleworth	11	16	4	555	133	46.2
‡D. R. Pringle	Nairobi, Kenya	12	12	3	405	112*	45.0
‡P. J. Prichard	Billericay	21	36	4	1,399	136	43.7
N. V. Knight	Watford	18	27	5	603	109	27.4
N. Shahid	Karachi, Pakistan	13	18	0	467	132	25.9
‡N. A. Foster	Colchester	10	13	0	290	54	22.3
‡M. A. Garnham	Johannesburg, SA	21	24	3	445	66	21.1
‡P. M. Such	Helensburgh	13	11	3	100	35*	12.5
‡J. H. Childs	Plymouth	19	15	6	105	43	11.6
‡T. D. Topley	Canterbury	10	11	2	99	29	11.0
M. C. Ilott	Watford	21	19	3	143	28	8.9
S. J. W. Andrew	London	9	10	4	29	14*	4.8

Also batted: A. G. J. Fraser (*Edgware*) (1 match) 2. A. D. Brown (*Clacton-on-Sea*)
(1 match) did not bat.

* *Signifies not out.* ‡ *Denotes county cap.* § *Overseas player.*

The following played a total of 22 three-figure innings for Essex in County Championship
matches – G. A. Gooch 6, P. J. Prichard 4, M. E. Waugh 4, J. P. Stephenson 3, N. Hussain
1, N. V. Knight 1, J. J. B. Lewis 1, D. R. Pringle 1, N. Shahid 1.

BOWLING

	O	M	R	W	BB	5W/i	Avg
D. R. Pringle	324.5	83	870	39	5-63	1	22.3
P. M. Such	391.1	125	895	39	6-17	3	22.9
J. H. Childs	624.5	197	1,598	64	6-82	3	24.9
N. A. Foster	226	56	634	23	4-47	0	27.5
M. E. Waugh	173.4	31	614	21	3-38	0	29.2
M. C. Ilott	625.3	137	2,077	62	6-87	3	33.5
S. J. W. Andrew	247	43	779	21	4-54	0	37.0
T. D. Topley	223.4	47	753	18	4-67	0	41.8
J. P. Stephenson	226.4	45	773	18	6-54	1	42.9

Also bowled: A. G. J. Fraser 11-3-58-1; G. A. Gooch 69-21-149-3; N. Hussain
4-0-38-1; P. J. Prichard 8-0-100-0; N. Shahid 34-4-143-7.

Wicket-keepers: M. A. Garnham 35 ct, 3 st; A. D. Brown 4 ct, 1 st.

Leading Fielders: M. E. Waugh 25, N. Hussain 19, P. J. Prichard 18, G. A. Gooch 1
N. V. Knight 17.

At Lord's, April 13, 14, 15, 16. ESSEX drew with ENGLAND A (See Other First-class Matches).

At Cambridge, April 25, 27, 28. ESSEX drew with CAMBRIDGE UNIVERSITY.

ESSEX v LEICESTERSHIRE

At Chelmsford, May 7, 8, 9, 11. Drawn. Essex 7 pts, Leicestershire 3 pts. Toss: Leicestershire. A combination of Briers, Boon and rain, which restricted the third day to 21 overs while the rest of the country was washed out, frustrated Essex. Briers followed up his fifty in the first innings with 99 in the second, an effort spanning nearly four hours. The more enterprising Boon kept him company for most of that time as they put on 147. On the opening day Leicestershire had depended on Briers and Potter, after Whitaker, batting without a helmet, was forced to retire with a fractured cheekbone, sustained when he tried to hook Pringle. Gooch collected the 92nd century of his career when Essex replied. Scoreless overnight, he reached 100 before lunch, and went on to amass 106 of his 160 runs in boundaries, adding 238 with Stephenson. But it was Prichard, all elegance and exquisite timing, who provided the real gem in Essex's 424 for four as he reached three figures from 110 deliveries.

Close of play: First day, Essex 0-0 (G. A. Gooch 0*, J. P. Stephenson 0*); Second day, Essex 424-4 (M. E. Waugh 14*, N. V. Knight 6*); Third day, Leicestershire 55-0 (T. J. Boon 25*, N. E. Briers 26*).

Leicestershire

T. J. Boon run out	26	– c Childs b Ilott	82
N. E. Briers c Knight b Childs	51	– c Gooch b Waugh	99
J. J. Whitaker retired hurt	33		
L. Potter c and b Stephenson	70	– c Gooch b Waugh	27
P. D. R. Benson c Pringle b Such	1	– lbw b Childs	21
P. N. Hepworth c Hussain b Pringle	4	– (3) c Gooch b Waugh	13
V. J. Wells c Knight b Childs	0	– (6) c Knight b Childs	15
P. Whitticase lbw b Such	0	– (7) not out	14
W. K. M. Benjamin b Childs	0	– (8) c Hussain b Childs	9
D. J. Millns not out	22	– (9) not out	17
A. D. Mullally b Waugh	0		
B 4, l-b 8, n-b 4	16	B 2, l-b 13	15
	223	(7 wkts)	**312**

1/65 2/99 3/138 4/143 5/157 6/160 7/163 8/222 9/223

1/147 2/187 3/208 4/241 5/269 6/272 7/284

Bonus points – Leicestershire 2, Essex 3 (Score at 100 overs: 201-7).

In the first innings J. J. Whitaker retired hurt at 135.

Bowling: *First Innings*—Pringle 19-6-32-1; Ilott 11-4-26-0; Stephenson 21-8-48-1; Childs 33-12-55-3; Such 25-8-43-2; Waugh 2.4-0-7-1. *Second Innings*—Pringle 7-2-25-0; Ilott 17-1-69-1; Childs 39-17-69-3; Such 34-11-59-0; Stephenson 9-0-37-0; Waugh 6-4-38-3.

Essex

G. A. Gooch c Whitticase b Mullally	.160	N. V. Knight not out	6
J. P. Stephenson c Benson b Millns	91	L-b 14, n-b 4	18
P. J. Prichard c Briers b Benson	.102		
N. Hussain lbw b Wells	33	1/238 2/313	(4 wkts dec.) 424
M. E. Waugh not out	14	3/391 4/409	

D. R. Pringle, †M. A. Garnham, M. C. Ilott, J. H. Childs and P. M. Such did not bat.

Bonus points – Essex 4, Leicestershire 1 (Score at 100 overs: 400-3).

Bowling: Benjamin 17-1-66-0; Millns 13-2-61-1; Mullally 13-2-54-1; Wells 27-7-72-1; Potter 19-3-70-0; Hepworth 13-3-66-0; Benson 9-1-21-1.

Umpires: A. A. Jones and D. R. Shepherd.

ESSEX v KENT

At Chelmsford, May 14, 15, 16. Essex won by an innings and 86 runs. Essex 24 pts, Kent 3 pts. Toss: Essex. Childs spun Essex to victory with more than a day to spare. Hooper, who had gathered all but 12 of his runs in boundaries, was the first of his five second-innings victims, and the only other serious resistance came from Benson and Cowdrey, although Taylor batted fluently before Ilott struck his left thumb and forced him to retire. It was Ilott who had led the destruction of Kent's first innings, with four for 56. Pringle also collected three – his first, Taylor, being his 500th wicket for the county. Essex demonstrated that there was nothing wrong with the pitch by building a lead of 360. Waugh's elegant 120, with 14 fours, and Shahid's career-best 132, with 17 fours and a six, were the basis of their formidable total of 526, despite the valiant efforts of Ellison, who took six wickets. Waugh enjoyed Hussain's support in a stand of 142, while Shahid and Pringle, who were both warned for running down the pitch, added 152 for the seventh wicket.

Close of play: First day, Essex 227-2 (M. E. Waugh 108*, N. Hussain 61*); Second day, Kent 37-1 (M. R. Benson 16*, N. R. Taylor 20*).

Kent

T. R. Ward c Gooch b Ilott	7	– b Pringle	0
*M. R. Benson run out	37	– c Gooch b Waugh	53
N. R. Taylor lbw b Pringle	4	– retired hurt	42
C. L. Hooper c Garnham b Waugh	46	– c Waugh b Childs	74
G. R. Cowdrey c Garnham b Ilott	3	– not out	82
M. V. Fleming c Gooch b Childs	39	– c Garnham b Ilott	0
†S. A. Marsh c Waugh b Pringle	0	– c Waugh b Childs	1
R. M. Ellison b Ilott	3	– lbw b Topley	4
R. P. Davis lbw b Pringle	5	– lbw b Childs	3
C. Penn lbw b Ilott	9	– c Knight b Childs	0
M. J. McCague not out	8	– c Gooch b Childs	0
L-b 2, n-b 3	5	B 4, l-b 6, n-b 1	11

1/13 2/27 3/81 4/98 5/124   166   1/0 2/141 3/186 4/193 5/198   274
6/125 7/144 8/149 9/149   6/247 7/260 8/268 9/274

Bonus points – Kent 1, Essex 4.

In the second innings N. R. Taylor retired hurt at 63.

Bowling: *First Innings*—Pringle 17-7-33-3; Ilott 17.2-2-56-4; Topley 7-4-25-0; Stephenson 5-1-27-0; Waugh 5-1-21-1; Childs 2-1-2-1. *Second Innings*—Pringle 19-5-52-1; Ilott 23-8-41-1; Childs 35.2-17-69-5; Topley 15-3-41-1; Waugh 12-3-61-1; Shahid 1-1-0-0.

Essex

*G. A. Gooch c and b Hooper	43	T. D. Topley c Cowdrey b Ellison	10
J. P. Stephenson c Taylor b Ellison	6	M. C. Ilott not out	6
M. E. Waugh c Fleming b Ellison	120	J. H. Childs c Benson b Ellison	0
N. Hussain c Taylor b Ellison	77		
N. V. Knight c McCague b Ellison	0	B 4, l-b 3, w 4, n-b 4	15
N. Shahid c Taylor b Davis	132		
†M. A. Garnham c Marsh b Davis	43		526
D. R. Pringle b Davis	80	1/14 2/102 3/244 4/252 5/255	52
		6/352 7/504 8/525 9/526	

Bonus points – Essex 4, Kent 2 (Score at 100 overs: 383-6).

Bowling: McCague 29-4-117-0; Ellison 28-7-95-6; Penn 22-1-97-0; Fleming 10-2-34-0; Hooper 28-4-92-1; Davis 24-1-84-3.

Umpires: H. D. Bird and D. O. Oslear.

At Taunton, May 20, 21, 22. ESSEX lost to SOMERSET by four wickets.

ESSEX v GLAMORGAN

At Chelmsford, June 2, 3, 4. Drawn. Essex 8 pts, Glamorgan 6 pts. Toss: Glamorgan. Both counties arrived at the final day nursing hopes of victory, only for them to be completely washed out by rain. Waugh celebrated his 27th birthday with a highly entertaining fifty before Knight and Shahid, narrowly missing a second Chelmsford century, gathered 147 during a partnership spanning 53 overs. Maynard, whose 82 took 92 balls and contained 54 in boundaries, and Richards led Glamorgan's spirited response until they fell to the nagging left-arm spin of Childs. Stephenson batted attractively for 60 as Essex built upon their slender first-innings advantage, but the weather defeated both counties.

Close of play: First day, Glamorgan 11-0 (S. P. James 6*, H. Morris 5*); Second day, Essex 102-4 (N. V. Knight 11*, T. D. Topley 0*).

Essex

P. J. Prichard b Watkin	10	– c Richards b Barwick	22
J. P. Stephenson c James b Watkin	3	– c Cottey b Bastien	60
M. E. Waugh b Barwick	52	– c Morris b Watkin	1
N. Hussain c Cottey b Bastien	25	– c Barwick b Watkin	7
N. V. Knight c Richards b Croft	70	– not out	11
N. Shahid c Barwick b Watkin	96		
†M. A. Garnham not out	30		
*N. A. Foster c Richards b Watkin	0		
T. D. Topley not out	10	– (6) not out	0
B 5, l-b 3, w 1, n-b 8	17	N-b 1	1

1/11 2/42 3/82 4/104 5/251   (7 wkts dec.) 313   1/62 2/67 3/79 4/102   (4 wkts) 102
6/283 7/283

M. C. Ilott and J. H. Childs did not bat.

Bonus points – Essex 4, Glamorgan 3.

Bowling: *First Innings*—Watkin 21-4-80-4; Bastien 25-6-61-1; Barwick 26-5-108-1; Croft 16-3-41-1; Dale 10-3-15-0. *Second Innings*—Watkin 12-3-43-2; Bastien 9-4-32-1; Barwick 10-4-19-1; Croft 5-2-8-0.

Glamorgan

S. P. James c Hussain b Childs	45	S. L. Watkin c Hussain b Childs	10
H. Morris c Hussain b Foster	5	S. R. Barwick c Foster b Childs	8
A. Dale c Knight b Foster	7	S. Bastien not out	9
*M. P. Maynard c Garnham b Childs	82		
I. V. A. Richards c Waugh b Childs	51	B 1, l-b 3, w 2, n-b 1	7
P. A. Cottey c Knight b Topley	28		
R. D. B. Croft lbw b Childs	22	1/11 2/19 3/133 4/148 5/221	289
†C. P. Metson c Waugh b Ilott	15	6/223 7/255 8/265 9/272	

Bonus points – Glamorgan 3, Essex 4.

Bowling: Foster 18-5-57-2; Ilott 20-6-59-1; Topley 13-4-57-1; Waugh 5-0-30-0; Childs 27.4-8-82-6.

Umpires: J. C. Balderstone and R. C. Tolchard.

At Tunbridge Wells, June 5, 6, 8. ESSEX lost to KENT by four wickets.

At Hartlepool, June 12, 13, 15. ESSEX beat DURHAM by 190 runs.

At Leeds, June 16, 17, 18. ESSEX lost to YORKSHIRE by an innings and 55 runs.

At Bournemouth, June 19, 20, 22. ESSEX beat HAMPSHIRE by 79 runs.

ESSEX v LANCASHIRE

At Ilford, June 26, 27. Essex won by an innings and 37 runs. Essex 24 pts, Lancashire 2 pts. Toss: Essex. Waugh and Hussain established a county record partnership of 347 unbroken for the third wicket in only 64 overs, beating the previous best of 343 set by P. A. Gibb and R. Horsfall against Kent at Blackheath 41 years earlier. Waugh's demonstration of power and authority brought him his highest score for Essex, an unbeaten 219 off 243 balls including 34 fours and a six, while Hussain, who figures in Essex's records for the third, fourth and fifth wicket, hit 172 not out from 193 deliveries with 24 fours. Lloyd proved an enterprising figure in both Lancashire innings and found resolute support from Titchard when they followed on. Even so, the visitors were unable to stave off a two-day defeat, Essex claiming the extra half-hour and capturing the final wicket with three balls remaining to go top of the table.

Close of play: First day, Lancashire 33-1 (G. Fowler 21*, S. D. Fletcher 2*).

Essex

*G. A. Gooch c Fowler b Martin	46
P. J. Prichard c Hegg b Watkinson	50
M. E. Waugh not out	219
N. Hussain not out	172
B 14, l-b 8, n-b 1	23

1/76 2/163   (2 wkts dec.) 510

N. V. Knight, D. R. Pringle, †M. A. Garnham, N. A. Foster, M. C. Ilott, J. H. Childs and P. M. Such did not bat.

Bonus points – Essex 4.

Bowling: Morrison 10-0-83-0; Martin 17-3-61-1; Fletcher 13-3-66-0; Watkinson 21.1-2-114-1; Barnett 26-2-111-0; Atherton 10-0-53-0.

Lancashire

G. Fowler c Prichard b Childs	45	– (2) c Hussain b Such	5
*M. A. Atherton c Garnham b Ilott	9	– (1) lbw b Foster	8
S. D. Fletcher c Pringle b Childs	22	– (10) not out	15
N. J. Speak lbw b Ilott	1	– (3) c Waugh b Childs	35
G. D. Lloyd c Waugh b Such	61	– (4) c Garnham b Pringle	76
S. P. Titchard lbw b Childs	11	– (5) b Foster	74
M. Watkinson c Knight b Such	28	– (6) c Gooch b Pringle	8
†W. K. Hegg lbw b Such	9	– (7) c Waugh b Pringle	3
P. J. Martin not out	9	– (8) lbw b Such	1
D. K. Morrison c Prichard b Childs	1	– (9) lbw b Foster	12
A. A. Barnett c Waugh b Childs	6	– c Foster b Childs	1
L-b 9, w 1	10	B 8, l-b 14, n-b 1	23

1/26 2/85 3/86 4/86 5/103   212   1/10 2/48 3/48 4/180 5/188   261
6/171 7/194 8/199 9/204   6/192 7/201 8/231 9/250

Bonus points – Lancashire 2, Essex 4.

Bowling: *First Innings*—Foster 12-3-28-0; Ilott 18-4-75-2; Childs 17.2-6-50-5; Such 11-1-50-3. *Second Innings*—Foster 14-4-46-3; Ilott 9-2-30-0; Such 19-3-69-2; Childs 19.3-5-63-2; Pringle 10-3-31-3.

Umpires: D. J. Constant and B. Dudleston.

ESSEX v MIDDLESEX

At Ilford, June 30, July 1, 2. Essex won by eight wickets. Essex 22 pts, Middlesex 6 pts. Toss: Middlesex. Essex achieved victory with six balls to spare after reaching 255 in 42 overs. Knight, with a career-best 109 from 124 balls, and Waugh, whose unbeaten 94 included two sixes and nine fours in just 75 deliveries, were always in command as they added 152 for the second wicket. Carr's first century of the summer, containing 16 fours, held Middlesex together in the first innings, while Roseberry and Gatting prospered in the second against an attack that missed Foster, who was injured, and Pringle, who was with England. A considerable slice of the action was lost to rain during the first two days, but the final day's play produced 470 runs as Essex consolidated their position at the top of the table.

Close of play: First day, Middlesex 229-6 (J. D. Carr 77*, D. W. Headley 10*); Second day, Essex 174-6 (J. J. B. Lewis 16*, T. D. Topley 15*).

Middlesex

D. L. Haynes b Ilott	16	– run out	34	
M. A. Roseberry c Shahid b Andrew	12	– not out	70	
*M. W. Gatting lbw b Topley	31	– b Shahid	69	
M. R. Ramprakash c Prichard b Ilott	33	– c Prichard b Andrew	4	
†K. R. Brown c Waugh b Andrew	21	– not out	5	
J. D. Carr c Garnham b Waugh	102			
J. E. Emburey lbw b Topley	15			
D. W. Headley c Garnham b Topley	10			
A. R. C. Fraser c Knight b Childs	1			
C. W. Taylor c Waugh b Topley	6			
P. C. R. Tufnell not out	3			
B 6, l-b 6, n-b 11	23	L-b 2, n-b 1	3	

1/30 2/36 3/95 4/99 5/173   273   1/57 2/167 3/175   (3 wkts dec.) 185
6/206 7/232 8/240 9/252

Bonus points – Middlesex 3, Essex 4.

Bowling: *First Innings*—Ilott 17–3–75–2; Andrew 15–3–49–2; Topley 32–10–67–4; Waugh 10.4–1–44–1; Childs 16–2–26–1. *Second Innings*—Andrew 11–2–34–1; Topley 8–0–34–0; Waugh 9–0–31–0; Childs 14–1–56–0; Shahid 4–0–28–1.

Essex

*P. J. Prichard c Brown b Fraser	53	– c Emburey b Taylor	29	
N. V. Knight b Taylor	20	– b Tufnell	109	
M. E. Waugh c Gatting b Fraser	38	– not out	94	
N. Hussain c and b Emburey	9	– not out	16	
N. Shahid c Emburey b Tufnell	9			
J. J. B. Lewis not out	31			
†M. A. Garnham c Roseberry b Tufnell	8			
T. D. Topley b Emburey	17			
M. C. Ilott run out	3			
S. J. W. Andrew not out	10			
L-b 4, n-b 2	6	B 4, l-b 3	7	

1/62 2/100 3/122 4/135 5/135   (8 wkts dec.) 204   1/71 2/223   (2 wkts) 255
6/145 7/182 8/186

J. H. Childs did not bat.

Bonus points – Essex 2, Middlesex 3.

Bowling: *First Innings*—Fraser 13–1–46–2; Taylor 7–1–31–1; Headley 7–1–33–0; Tufnell 31.4–13–59–2; Emburey 24–13–31–2. *Second Innings*—Fraser 5–0–34–0; Taylor 12–0–54–1; Emburey 10–0–68–0; Tufnell 15–0–92–1.

Umpires: D. J. Constant and B. Dudleston.

At Birmingham, July 3, 4, 6. ESSEX drew with WARWICKSHIRE.

ESSEX v GLOUCESTERSHIRE

At Southend, July 14, 15, 16. Essex won by four wickets. Essex 20 pts, Gloucestershire 8 pts. Toss: Essex. Waugh, reaching three figures from 93 balls, sped Essex to victory with 13 deliveries to spare, steering them to a target of 335 in only 58.5 overs. Foster, who had been unable to bowl since the first day, made up for it with the bat, as they put on 116 in 16. Hodgson batted throughout the opening day, mostly with Wright, after Hinks's knee gave way completing a second run, and fell early next morning for a career-best 147; he struck 19 fours. With Walsh maintaining his form, Waugh was the only player to take full advantage of a docile pitch in Essex's first innings, in an entertaining 74. Gloucestershire then stretched their advantage against friendly bowling to prompt the declaration, after which Gooch and Prichard scored freely to pave the way for Waugh's later assault.

Close of play: First day, Gloucestershire 311-3 (G. D. Hodgson 145*, R. J. Scott 37*). Second day, Gloucestershire 43-0 (G. D. Hodgson 29*, C. W. J. Athey 12*).

Gloucestershire

G. D. Hodgson b Ilott	147	– lbw b Andrew	46
C. W. J. Athey c Garnham b Andrew	10	– c Ilott b Shahid	94
S. G. Hinks retired hurt	10		
*A. J. Wright c Waugh b Childs	69	– (3) c Waugh b Childs	27
M. W. Alleyne lbw b Ilott	23	– (4) c Waugh b Shahid	21
R. J. Scott c Gooch b Ilott	44	– (5) not out	9
†R. C. Russell b Ilott	6	– (6) not out	25
C. A. Walsh c Prichard b Andrew	4		
A. M. Smith b Ilott	18		
A. M. Babington not out	6		
B 1, l-b 5, w 3, n-b 10	19	L-b 4, w 2, n-b 2	8

1/30 2/171 3/220 4/313 5/326   (8 wkts dec.) 356   1/82 2/131   (4 wkts dec.) 230
6/332 7/339 8/356   3/176 4/201

M. Davies did not bat.

Bonus points – Gloucestershire 4, Essex 1 (Score at 100 overs: 303-3).

In the first innings S. G. Hinks retired hurt at 62.

Bowling: *First Innings*—Foster 18-4-62-0; Ilott 27.5-10-79-5; Andrew 25-1-80-2; Childs 25-9-36-1; Gooch 8-2-28-0; Stephenson 3-0-21-0; Waugh 5-1-25-0; Shahid 7-1-19-0. *Second Innings*—Andrew 15-1-40-1; Ilott 9-0-45-0; Childs 19-3-60-1; Shahid 6-0-31-2; Prichard 3-0-46-0; Waugh 1-0-4-0.

Essex

*G. A. Gooch c and b Babington	36	– b Scott	55
J. P. Stephenson lbw b Smith	5	– run out	22
P. J. Prichard c Russell b Walsh	8	– c Davies b Alleyne	47
M. E. Waugh c Russell b Walsh	74	– not out	125
N. Shahid c Russell b Walsh	17	– (6) run out	10
J. J. B. Lewis b Athey	34	– (8) not out	21
†M. A. Garnham run out	32	– (5) run out	3
N. A. Foster c Smith b Davies	26	– (7) c Scott b Smith	40
M. C. Ilott c Russell b Davies	5		
S. J. W. Andrew b Walsh	0		
J. H. Childs not out	2		
B 1, l-b 2, w 1, n-b 9	13	B 3, l-b 4, n-b 5	12

1/11 2/22 3/96 4/137 5/160   252   1/81 2/81 3/158   (6 wkts) 335
6/218 7/224 8/243 9/244   4/166 5/181 6/297

Bonus points – Essex 3, Gloucestershire 4.

Bowling: *First Innings*—Walsh 16–2–46–4; Smith 13–2–42–1; Babington 12–1–48–1; Davies 14.1–3–52–2; Scott 9–2–36–0; Alleyne 3–1–9–0; Athey 6–1–16–1. *Second Innings*—Walsh 15–0–75–0; Smith 10–0–49–1; Babington 3–0–30–0; Scott 6–0–31–1; Davies 9.5–2–61–0; Alleyne 11–1–53–1; Athey 4–0–29–0.

Umpires: V. A. Holder and N. T. Plews.

ESSEX v SUSSEX

At Southend, July 17, 18, 20. Essex won by eight wickets. Essex 22 pts, Sussex 4 pts. Toss: Sussex. Essex stretched their lead in the Championship to 51 points, despite their visitors' first-innings 429. Gooch scored a century in each innings, for the third time, and off-spinner Such returned a career-best six for 17. Smith's maiden double-century, containing 33 fours and lasting 426 minutes, saw Sussex to their formidable total, with solid support from Moores in a stand of 251. Gooch and Stephenson enabled Essex to extract maximum batting points with minimum fuss before declaring 126 behind. Sussex were 63 for two at the close but collapsed dramatically on the final morning when Such claimed his six wickets in an hour and a half. Sussex's only excuse was the absence of Moores who had injured his toe during the Sunday League match. Gooch's second century arrived from the 124th ball he faced, and he hit 15 fours; Waugh's unbeaten 85 came in 79 balls.

Close of play: First day, Sussex 341-5 (D. M. Smith 176*, B. T. P. Donelan 2*); Second day, Sussex 63-2 (N. J. Lenham 19*, A. P. Wells 13*).

Sussex

D. M. Smith run out	213	– run out	10
J. W. Hall lbw b Pringle	9	– b Ilott	19
N. J. Lenham b Childs	15	– c Hussain b Such	24
*A. P. Wells c Hussain b Childs	10	– lbw b Such	17
M. P. Speight c Waugh b Childs	2	– c Prichard b Such	7
†P. Moores c Stephenson b Childs	109	– absent injured	
B. T. P. Donelan c Gooch b Waugh	34	– (6) c Hussain b Such	6
A. C. S. Pigott b Ilott	4	– (7) not out	5
I. D. K. Salisbury c Such b Waugh	4	– (8) c Prichard b Such	0
A. N. Jones not out	6	– b Childs	8
E. S. H. Giddins (did not bat)	–	(9) c Waugh b Such	0
B 1, l-b 14, w 2, n-b 6	23	L-b 5, n-b 3	8

1/32 2/55 3/71 4/73 5/324   (9 wkts dec.) 429   1/23 2/38 3/76 4/79 5/88   104
6/414 7/415 8/419 9/429   6/91 7/91 8/95 9/104

Bonus points – Sussex 4, Essex 2 (Score at 100 overs: 334-5).

Bowling: *First Innings*—Ilott 20.5–3–92–1; Andrew 8–1–38–0; Pringle 7–2–75–1; Childs 32–8–101–4; Such 27–10–55–0; Waugh 4–0–21–2; Gooch 7–1–14–0; Stephenson 5–1–18–0. *Second Innings*—Ilott 9–2–37–1; Andrew 8–2–20–0; Such 16–7–17–6; Childs 12.3–5–20–1; Pringle 3–1–5–0.

Essex

*G. A. Gooch b Salisbury	102	– not out	108
J. P. Stephenson not out	123	– c Smith b Salisbury	12
P. J. Prichard not out	68	– c Lenham b Donelan	11
M. E. Waugh (did not bat)	–	not out	85
B 1, l-b 4, n-b 5	10	B 8, l-b 1, n-b 6	15

1/179   (1 wkt dec.) 303   1/42 2/72   (2 wkts) 231

N. Hussain, D. R. Pringle, †M. A. Garnham, M. C. Ilott, S. J. W. Andrew, J. H. Childs and P. M. Such did not bat.

Bonus points – Essex 4.

Bowling: *First Innings*—Jones 5–0–29–0; Pigott 10–3–48–0; Giddins 9–1–42–0; Salisbury 15–3–71–1; Donelan 10–1–60–0; Lenham 17–1–48–0. *Second Innings*—Pigott 6–0–27–0; Donelan 13–0–90–1; Lenham 3–0–16–0; Salisbury 17.3–1–89–1.

Umpires: V. A. Holder and N. T. Plews.

At Kidderminster, July 21, 22, 23. ESSEX drew with WORCESTERSHIRE.

At Leicester, July 24, 25, 27. ESSEX lost to LEICESTERSHIRE by 68 runs.

At Chelmsford, August 1, 2, 3. ESSEX lost to PAKISTANIS by seven wickets (See Pakistani tour section).

ESSEX v NORTHAMPTONSHIRE

At Chelmsford, August 4, 5, 6. Northamptonshire won by an innings and 13 runs. Northamptonshire 23 pts, Essex 5 pts. Toss: Northamptonshire. Essex lost their last seven wickets for ten runs in just under 14 overs, after reaching 148 for three in the over before tea. Six of the wickets fell in 41 balls from left-arm spinner Cook while he conceded only two runs. Essex's downfall sprang from tentative batting rather than any venom in the pitch. Ambrose had wound up their first innings in a 14-ball burst, forcing them to follow on 171 behind. Though the pitch, chosen after Lamb rejected the one just used by the Pakistani tourists, was so dry that the spinners dominated from the start, claiming 23 of the 29 wickets, Cook did not turn the ball very much. Nevertheless, his seven for 34 represented a career-best and helped him to ten wickets in a match for only the fourth time. Lamb led a consistent Northamptonshire batting performance against an attack lacking Pringle, away on Test duty, and the injured Foster.

Close of play: First day, Northamptonshire 366-7 (A. R. Roberts 10*, C. E. L. Ambrose 5*); Second day, Essex 266-6 (N. V. Knight 69*, M. C. Ilott 10*).

Northamptonshire

A. Fordham b Such	65	C. E. L. Ambrose not out	49
N. A. Felton b Childs	51	J. P. Taylor st Garnham b Such	9
R. J. Bailey lbw b Such	25	N. G. B. Cook not out	11
*A. J. Lamb c Hussain b Shahid	83	B 9, l-b 28, n-b 1	38
D. J. Capel b Such	61		
A. L. Penberthy b Shahid	33	1/116 2/140 3/172 (9 wkts dec.) 444
†D. Ripley b Childs	3	4/293 5/324 6/331
A. R. Roberts c Childs b Such	16	7/359 8/390 9/416

Bonus points – Northamptonshire 4, Essex 2 (Score at 100 overs: 336-6).

Bowling: Ilott 12–3–61–0; Andrew 17–1–59–0; Stephenson 7–1–21–0; Childs 49–13–121–2; Such 36–7–114–5; Shahid 7–0–31–2.

Essex

*P. J. Prichard c Penberthy b Bailey	46	c Ripley b Cook	23
J. P. Stephenson run out	64	st Ripley b Bailey	37
J. J. B. Lewis c Felton b Roberts	1	lbw b Cook	29
N. Hussain c Lamb b Penberthy	52	b Ambrose	33
N. V. Knight b Ambrose	69	c Felton b Cook	26
N. Shahid st Ripley b Cook	10	c Lamb b Cook	4
†M. A. Garnham c Ripley b Cook	2	c Lamb b Roberts	0
M. C. Ilott b Ambrose	13	not out	6
P. M. Such lbw b Ambrose	0	c Bailey b Cook	0
S. J. W. Andrew lbw b Cook	0	b Cook	0
J. H. Childs not out	1	c Felton b Cook	0
B 11, l-b 4	15		

1/113 2/114 3/117 4/205 5/222	273	1/43 2/63 3/113 4/148 5/149	158
6/230 7/266 8/270 9/271		6/150 7/158 8/158 9/158

Bonus points – Essex 3, Northamptonshire 3 (Score at 100 overs: 271-8).

Bowling: *First Innings*—Ambrose 16–4–27–3; Taylor 9–2–45–0; Cook 30.4–6–63–3; Capel 3–0–12–0; Roberts 18–6–59–1; Bailey 16–4–34–1; Penberthy 9–2–18–1. *Second Innings*—Ambrose 11–5–25–1; Taylor 6–2–16–0; Penberthy 5–2–7–0; Cook 18.4–8–34–7; Roberts 20–5–35–1; Bailey 17–5–41–1.

Umpires: B. Dudleston and B. Leadbeater.

ESSEX v NOTTINGHAMSHIRE

At Colchester, August 14, 15, 17. Essex won by an innings and 37 runs. Essex 24 pts, Nottinghamshire 3 pts. Toss: Nottinghamshire. Essex's win was their first in the Championship for four weeks, though they had never lost their grip at the top of the table. Nottinghamshire capitulated to spinners Such and Childs, who shared ten wickets on the final day to earn victory with 8.1 overs to spare. Nottinghamshire were undone in the first innings by the medium-paced Stephenson, who discovered just enough movement to return career-best figures of six for 54. Only Cairns faced him with any confidence. Then, along with Prichard, who hit 21 fours, Stephenson extended Essex's control with the bat, allowing Gooch to declare 167 ahead. The third-choice Essex wicket-keeper, Brown, enjoyed his first first-class game since 1988, making four catches and a leg-side stumping; he was called up after Garnham's eye injury in the NatWest defeat at Leicester, because the deputy, Rollins, was playing for England Under-19 against Sri Lanka.

Close of play: First day, Nottinghamshire 247-8 (C. L. Cairns 80*, E. E. Hemmings 5*); Second day, Essex 302-4 (N. V. Knight 13*, J. J. B. Lewis 1*).

Nottinghamshire

B. C. Broad c Gooch b Pringle	18	– c Lewis b Such	15
P. R. Pollard lbw b Stephenson	65	– c Brown b Such	11
*R. T. Robinson c Gooch b Pringle	37	– b Such	2
M. A. Crawley b Pringle	0	– c Knight b Such	15
D. W. Randall st Brown b Stephenson	1	– c Knight b Childs	1
C. C. Lewis c Brown b Stephenson	0	– c Knight b Childs	35
C. L. Cairns not out	82	– c Prichard b Such	26
K. P. Evans lbw b Stephenson	3	– b Such	13
†B. N. French c Brown b Stephenson	13	– lbw b Childs	6
E. E. Hemmings c Gooch b Stephenson	5	– not out	0
J. A. Afford c Brown b Pringle	0	– c Hussain b Childs	0
B 5, l-b 9, w 3, n-b 6	23	B 4, l-b 2	6

1/30 2/93 3/93 4/100 5/108   249   1/25 2/27 3/32 4/33 5/55   130
6/181 7/186 8/225 9/248   6/89 7/120 8/130 9/130

Bonus points – Nottinghamshire 2, Essex 4.

Bowling: *First Innings*—Ilott 21–4–65–0; Pringle 28–9–55–4; Gooch 8–3–15–0; Such 9–4–12–0; Childs 8–1–34–0; Stephenson 23–3–54–6. *Second Innings*—Pringle 3–1–5–0; Ilott 5–1–15–0; Such 30–15–39–6; Childs 27.5–10–59–4; Stephenson 2–1–6–0.

Essex

*G. A. Gooch c Robinson b Hemmings	28	D. R. Pringle c Broad b Lewis	48
J. P. Stephenson c Robinson b Crawley	74		
P. J. Prichard c Evans b Afford	136	B 3, l-b 13, w 4, n-b 5	25
N. Hussain c Pollard b Afford	31		
N. V. Knight lbw b Lewis	21	1/45 2/175 3/267 (6 wkts dec.)	416
J. J. B. Lewis not out	53	4/296 5/320 6/416	

M. C. Ilott, †A. D. Brown, P. M. Such and J. H. Childs did not bat.

Bonus points – Essex 4, Nottinghamshire 1 (Score at 100 overs: 301-4).

Bowling: Lewis 35.5–8–97–2; Evans 16–3–51–0; Cairns 14–2–53–0; Hemmings 41–14–122–1; Afford 16–3–51–2; Crawley 8–2–26–1.

Umpires: D. O. Oslear and R. A. White.

ESSEX v SURREY

At Colchester, August 18, 19, 20. Drawn. Essex 6 pts, Surrey 7 pts. Toss: Essex. Rain washed out the entire final day after Surrey had been frustrated for most of the second by Lewis and Garnham. They used up 61 overs while adding 118, coming together after a lively opening spell by Martin Bicknell sent back Stephenson, Hussain and Knight at a personal cost of 15 in ten overs. Lewis resisted for 281 minutes and Garnham for 225. The innings of the match had come from Lynch, leading the side while Stewart played in the one-day internationals. Superb driving and cutting brought him the majority of his 18 fours. Off-spinner Such was not introduced until the 73rd over, despite his recent form, but he removed Lynch with his second delivery before finishing off the tail. This was the only home Championship match of the six which Essex played away from Chelmsford that they failed to win.

Close of play: First day, Essex 25-0 (P. J. Prichard 15*, J. P. Stephenson 9*); Second day, Surrey 10-0 (D. J. Bicknell 4*, N. F. Sargeant 6*).

Surrey

D. J. Bicknell c Garnham b Pringle	53	– not out		4
†N. F. Sargeant lbw b Pringle	4	– not out		6
G. P. Thorpe c Garnham b Pringle	13			
*M. A. Lynch c Topley b Such	102			
D. M. Ward st Garnham b Stephenson	29			
A. D. Brown lbw b Pringle	32			
M. A. Feltham run out	24			
M. P. Bicknell b Such	6			
N. M. Kendrick c and b Such	2			
J. Boiling not out	1			
J. E. Benjamin c Knight b Such	5			
L-b 6, n-b 15	21			

1/11 2/40 3/113 4/203 5/252   292   (no wkt) 10
6/253 7/280 8/285 9/286

Bonus points – Surrey 3, Essex 4.

Bowling: *First Innings*—Pringle 21–1–63–4; Ilott 16–3–49–0; Topley 13–2–45–0; Stephenson 14–2–54–1; Childs 18–7–53–0; Such 10.1–3–22–4. *Second Innings*—Pringle 2–1–3–0; Such 2–0–7–0.

Essex

*P. J. Prichard c M. P. Bicknell b Benjamin	26	
J. P. Stephenson c Sargeant b M. P. Bicknell	9	
J. J. B. Lewis c Brown b Boiling	66	
N. Hussain c Lynch b M. P. Bicknell	13	
N. V. Knight c Ward b M. P. Bicknell	0	
†M. A. Garnham c Lynch b Kendrick	59	
D. R. Pringle c Thorpe b Boiling	12	
T. D. Topley c Lynch b Boiling	7	
M. C. Ilott b Kendrick	4	
P. M. Such not out	12	
J. H. Childs c Lynch b M. P. Bicknell	7	
B 1, l-b 2, w 1, n-b 10	14	

1/27 2/40 3/63 4/63 5/181   229
6/187 7/198 8/209 9/209

Bonus points – Essex 2, Surrey 4 (Score at 100 overs: 209-9).

Bowling: M. P. Bicknell 25–7–53–4; Benjamin 18–4–58–1; Feltham 14–2–39–0; Kendrick 26–10–43–2; Boiling 23–9–33–3; Lynch 1–1–0–0.

Umpires: D. O. Oslear and R. A. White.

At Hove, August 26, 27, 28, 29. ESSEX beat SUSSEX by nine wickets.

ESSEX v HAMPSHIRE

At Chelmsford, August 31, September 1, 2, 3. Essex won by eight wickets. Essex 22 pts, Hampshire 6 pts. Toss: Hampshire. An unbroken partnership of 133 in 31 overs from Stephenson and Prichard carried Essex to their sixth Championship title in 14 seasons at 3.35 p.m. on the final day. Appropriately, their opponents were Hampshire, whom they had beaten after being made to follow on in June, a result widely seen as the turning point of their season. Batting was never easy on a pitch offering some turn, but lack of application and rash strokes combined to bring about the downfall of several visiting players. Turner, their slow left-armer, had claimed five wickets for the first time in Essex's first innings, including Prichard, who had resisted for nearly three hours. A comical last-wicket partnership of 79 in 17 overs, during which Childs and Such both registered career-bests, carried the home team to a useful lead of 65, and Hampshire lost six wickets in clearing the arrears. The tail, led by Aymes, offered stubborn resistance, and with some help from the weather took the match into the fourth day. Then, despite the early loss of Gooch and Lewis, Essex reached the winning post with ease.

Close of play: First day, Hampshire 233; Second day, Hampshire 5-0 (T. C. Middleton 1*, K. D. James 0*); Third day, Hampshire 181-8 (A. N. Aymes 47*, I. J. Turner 0*).

Hampshire

K. D. James b Topley	20	– (2) lbw b Pringle	15
T. C. Middleton c Garnham b Ilott	17	– (1) c Stephenson b Pringle	2
D. I. Gower c Prichard b Gooch	30	– c Prichard b Ilott	4
R. A. Smith c Ilott b Childs	23	– b Such	23
*M. C. J. Nicholas c Ilott b Childs	19	– b Childs	0
M. D. Marshall lbw b Such	39	– c Prichard b Childs	12
J. R. Ayling c Gooch b Such	5	– c Ilott b Childs	31
†A. N. Aymes b Such	13	– c Childs b Pringle	65
S. D. Udal c Such b Pringle	44	– st Garnham b Stephenson	32
I. J. Turner c Topley b Such	8	– c Garnham b Ilott	16
K. J. Shine not out	4	– not out	5
B 4, l-b 4, w 3	11	B 8, l-b 10, n-b 6	24
	233		**229**

1/35 2/72 3/72 4/108 5/117
6/146 7/168 8/184 9/209

1/15 2/22 3/35 4/37 5/55
6/63 7/119 8/172 9/217

Bonus points – Hampshire 2, Essex 4 (Score at 100 overs: 214-9).

Bowling: *First Innings*—Pringle 18.3–7–32–1; Ilott 27–13–60–1; Topley 11–2–34–1; Gooch 3–1–5–1; Childs 30–11–71–2; Such 20–9–23–4. *Second Innings*—Ilott 16–4–44–2; Pringle 20.3–8–42–3; Such 29–13–46–1; Childs 35–17–67–3; Topley 2–0–7–0; Stephenson 3–2–5–1.

Essex

*G. A. Gooch c Smith b Ayling	22	– c Middleton b Turner	19
J. P. Stephenson c Aymes b Marshall	6	– not out	83
J. J. B. Lewis c Aymes b Ayling	43	– b Turner	4
P. J. Prichard b Turner	82	– not out	55
N. V. Knight b Turner	5		
†M. A. Garnham b Turner	14		
D. R. Pringle lbw b Turner	14		
T. D. Topley b Turner	16		
M. C. Ilott c Middleton b Udal	2		
P. M. Such not out	35		
J. H. Childs b Ayling	43		
B 2, l-b 5, w 1, n-b 8	16	L-b 3, n-b 1	4
	298		**(2 wkts) 165**

1/12 2/50 3/142 4/159 5/185
6/188 7/216 8/219 9/219

1/24 2/32

Bonus points – Essex 2, Hampshire 4 (Score at 100 overs: 243-9).

Bowling: *First Innings*—Marshall 24–7–40–1; Shine 5–0–25–0; Ayling 15.2–0–44–3; Turner 38–12–81–5; Udal 24–2–91–1; Nicholas 1–0–3–0; James 3–0–7–0. *Second Innings*—Marshall 11–3–33–0; Ayling 9–3–34–0; Turner 14–5–54–2; Udal 10–0–40–0; Smith 0.2–0–1–0.

Umpires: G. Sharp and A. G. T. Whitehead.

At Derby, September 7, 8, 9, 10. ESSEX beat DERBYSHIRE by four wickets.

At Bristol, September 12, 13, 14, 15. ESSEX lost to GLOUCESTERSHIRE by seven wickets.

THE CHAMPIONS

The dates on which the County Championship has been settled since 1979 are as follows:

			Final margin
1979	Essex	August 21	77 pts
1980	Middlesex	September 2	13 pts
1981	Nottinghamshire	September 14	2 pts
1982	Middlesex	September 11	39 pts
1983	Essex	September 13	16 pts
1984	Essex	September 11	14 pts
1985	Middlesex	September 17	18 pts
1986	Essex	September 10	28 pts
1987	Nottinghamshire	September 14	4 pts
1988	Worcestershire	September 16	1 pt
1989	Worcestershire	August 31	6 pts
1990	Middlesex	September 20	31 pts
1991	Essex	September 19	13 pts
1992	Essex	September 3	41 pts

GLAMORGAN

Patron: HRH The Prince of Wales
President: W. Wooller
Chairman: F. D. Morgan
Chairman, Cricket Committee: H. D. Davies
Secretary: G. R. Stone
  Sophia Gardens, Cardiff CF1 9XR
  (Telephone: 0222-343478)
Cricket secretary: M. Fatkin
Captain: 1992 – A. R. Butcher
  1993 – H. Morris
Senior Coach: A. Jones

Abysmal Welsh weather and failure to gain enough bonus points thwarted Glamorgan's hopes of finishing near halfway in the County Championship. They won five games – for the third successive season – but only three counties finished with fewer batting points and their 49 bowling points were the lowest in the Championship. Significantly, Glamorgan finished 24 points behind Somerset, who ended with the same number of wins, and two places behind Lancashire who won one game fewer. The weather denied them victory against Hampshire where a thunderstorm washed out the final five overs with Glamorgan needing only 14 runs with four wickets in hand, while 70 hours' playing time was lost during the final five games of the season.

Apart from qualifying for the quarter-finals of the NatWest Trophy, Glamorgan's one-day form was again particularly disappointing. They finished 16th in the Sunday League, winning only four games, and failed to qualify for the later stages of the Benson and Hedges Cup after beating Durham and the Combined Universities. They gave their supporters some hope of appearing in a one-day final by defeating Surrey and Nottinghamshire in the first two rounds of the NatWest Trophy, but then failed against Northamptonshire for the second successive year, in front of an 11,000 capacity crowd at Swansea. The bowlers contained the opposition to a modest total of 224 but the batsmen failed to make any impression against an accurate attack and Northamptonshire won easily by 83 runs.

The loss of Alan Butcher through injury for nearly all the season deprived Glamorgan of an astute captain and one of their most prolific batsmen. He played in only two Championship games and because of his fitness problems he was subsequently offered only a year's contract, with Hugh Morris succeeding him as captain. Butcher eventually accepted a coaching job at Essex, replacing Keith Fletcher – a measure of his standing in the game. Morris previously captained the club for three years but resigned in 1989 when the pressures of leadership affected his batting. At the start of 1992 Morris was left upset and disillusioned when he was superseded as vice-captain by Matthew Maynard, who did an effective job much more often than expected before the committee decided by a small majority to reinstate the former England A captain.

Morris, with 1,597 first-class runs in all, led the five Glamorgan players who passed 1,000 in the Championship. The others were

Maynard plus three rising talents who were all awarded their county caps: Stephen James who, in Butcher's absence, took the opportunity to establish himself as Morris's opening partner; Adrian Dale, whose skill was most evident in his career-best 150 not out on a turning pitch in Glamorgan's win at Trent Bridge; and Tony Cottey, whose Championship-best 141 set up the victory over Kent at Canterbury. The development of the younger batsmen compensated for Viv Richards's loss of form. The former West Indies captain, after striking seven hundreds in 1990, scored only 722 runs at 31.39 with one century. He was troubled by a back injury throughout the season but returned to contribute significantly to Glamorgan's successive wins in their last two games. Richards is due to return in 1993 to fulfil the final year of his contract, determined to end his first-class career in style.

Steve Watkin and Robert Croft were Glamorgan's leading bowlers with 68 wickets apiece. Watkin, who bowled 689 overs, was again a willing workhorse, hampered throughout by the absence of a strike bowler at the other end. Mark Frost, who took 65 wickets the previous season, struggled for form with only 13 first-class victims, Steve Bastien lacked consistency, while Daren Foster only occasionally threatened and eventually left the county by mutual consent. Croft's off-spin guided his side to three Championship wins and his non-selection for the England A tour to Australia was as surprising as his inclusion had been the previous year. He exploited a slow turner at Swansea, taking 14 for 169 against Warwickshire, and his 650 runs in the middle order underlined his value to the side as an all-rounder. He was also given his county cap, deservedly so. Steve Barwick was more successful in one-day cricket than the County Championship where his 36 wickets were taken at a high cost, though he was often required to alternate between seam and off-cutters. The bowling averages were headed by Darren Thomas, the 17-year-old Llanelli schoolboy who had a memorable start to his career. He took five wickets against Derbyshire in his first Championship match and followed up with another five-wicket haul in Kent's defeat at the end of the season. His success and potential were immediately recognised by the Young England's selectors who included him in their Under-18 team to tour South Africa. Colin Metson was again rated by many as the best wicket-keeper in the country, maintaining his high standard, yet his skills and expertise were ignored by the England selectors.

The development and emergence of Glamorgan's younger players reflected the success of the club's coaching policy backed by ASW Holdings, the county's main sponsors. Welsh identity within the side has also been maintained: ten of the team who played against Sussex near the end of the season were past members of Welsh Schools sides. Glamorgan's priorities for 1993 will be to consolidate in the County Championship and improve their dismal Sunday League record – targets which can be achieved if the young team, supplemented by a fit Richards, can maintain their development. – Edward Bevan.

GLAMORGAN 1992

[*Bill Smith*]

Back row: P. A. Cottey, A. J. Jones, A. D. Shaw, S. Bastien, E. P. M. Holland, J. R. A. Williams, G. H. J. Rees, S. Kirnon, J. Bishop, D. J. Foster. *Middle row*: B. T. Denning (*First Eleven scorer*), G. R. Stone (*secretary*), A. Jones (*senior coach*), R. D. B. Croft, S. P. James, D. L. Hemp, A. Dale, J. F. Steele (*assistant coach*), D. Conway (*physiotherapist*), G. N. Lewis (*Second Eleven scorer*). *Front row*: M. Frost, S. L. Watkin, M. P. Maynard, I. V. A. Richards, A. R. Butcher (*captain*), S. R. Barwick, C. P. Metson, C. S. Cowdrey. *Inset*: H. Morris.

GLAMORGAN RESULTS

All first-class matches – Played 24: Won 5, Lost 5, Drawn 14.

County Championship matches – Played 22: Won 5, Lost 4, Drawn 13.

Bonus points – Batting 53, Bowling 49.

*Competition placings – Britannic Assurance County Championship, 14th;
NatWest Bank Trophy, q-f; Benson and Hedges Cup, 4th in Group D;
Sunday League, 16th.*

BRITANNIC ASSURANCE CHAMPIONSHIP AVERAGES

BATTING

	Birthplace	M	I	NO	R	HS	Avge
‡P. A. Cottey	Swansea	18	25	5	1,008	141	50.40
‡H. Morris	Cardiff	22	36	3	1,546	146	46.84
‡A. Dale	Germiston, SA	20	30	4	1,056	150*	40.61
‡M. P. Maynard	Oldham	22	35	4	1,191	176	38.41
‡S. P. James	Lydney	22	37	4	1,238	152*	37.51
‡I. V. A. Richards§ . . .	St John's, Antigua	14	23	0	722	127	31.39
‡R. D. B. Croft	Morriston	22	32	9	592	60*	25.73
D. L. Hemp	Bermuda	10	15	2	276	84*	21.23
‡C. P. Metson	Goff's Oak	22	27	6	417	46*	19.85
D. J. Foster	Tottenham	7	4	1	40	17*	13.33
‡S. L. Watkin	Maesteg	21	23	4	147	41	7.73
S. D. Thomas	Morriston	6	7	2	25	10	5.00
‡S. R. Barwick	Neath	17	14	4	31	9*	3.10
S. Bastien	Stepney	10	10	3	21	9*	3.00
‡M. Frost	Barking	6	4	1	4	4	1.33

Also batted: ‡A. R. Butcher (*Croydon*) (2 matches) 23, 8, 59*. C. S. Cowdrey
(*Farnborough, Kent*) (1 match) did not bat.

* *Signifies not out.* ‡ *Denotes county cap.* § *Overseas player.*

The following played a total of 15 three-figure innings for Glamorgan in County Championship matches – H. Morris 6, P. A. Cottey 2, A. Dale 2, S. P. James 2, M. P. Maynard 2, I. V. A. Richards 1.

BOWLING

	O	M	R	W	BB	5W/i	Avge
S. D. Thomas	113.2	18	404	18	5-79	2	22.44
R. D. B. Croft	610.4	114	2,010	65	8-66	5	30.92
S. L. Watkin	665.3	146	2,046	66	6-97	1	31.00
A. Dale	211	53	594	15	3-30	0	39.60
S. R. Barwick	578	152	1,545	36	4-67	0	42.91
D. J. Foster	171.3	25	737	17	5-87	1	43.35
S. Bastien	305.3	73	954	19	5-95	1	50.21

Also bowled: P. A. Cottey 6–2–25–0; M. Frost 155.1–24–664–9; M. P. Maynard 7–0–72–1; C. P. Metson 1–1–0–0; H. Morris 4.5–0–57–0; I. V. A. Richards 12–2–34–0.

Wicket-keeper: C. P. Metson 48 ct, 5 st.

Leading Fielders: S. P. James 20, M. P. Maynard 19, I. V. A. Richards 18, H. Morris 15.

At Lord's, April 25, 27, 28, 29. GLAMORGAN drew with MIDDLESEX.

At Cardiff, May 9, 10, 11. GLAMORGAN lost to PAKISTANIS by 206 runs (See Pakistani tour section).

GLAMORGAN v DURHAM

At Cardiff, May 14, 15, 16. Durham won by an innings and 104 runs. Durham 24 pts, Glamorgan 3 pts. Toss: Glamorgan. Glamorgan were completely outplayed by Durham, their successors as junior first-class county, who recorded their first Championship win with a day to spare. The home team surrendered the initiative on the first day when, after Morris and Maynard had taken them to 121 for two, they were all out for 224. The 17-year-old seamer Paul Henderson, on his first-class début, began the collapse in his first over after lunch, claiming Morris and Richards in four balls and later dismissing Maynard. Then Durham ran up their highest total in history – first-class or minor county – as Larkins made his 50th first-class century, Jones narrowly missed his first for Durham, and Parker registered his third in six innings. Resuming 297 behind, Glamorgan's batsmen were immediately in trouble. They took lunch on the third day at 24 for three, after Botham collected two wickets and a catch. Cottey battled for four and a half hours and an unbeaten 112, with support from Metson and Watkin, which kept Durham waiting until the pen-ultimate over of the day. The country's leading wicket-taker, Brown, sealed the win with his 20th victim. Durham's historic victory was also Glamorgan's seventh defeat in their ten opening fixtures of 1992.

Close of play: First day, Durham 94-1 (W. Larkins 49*, D. M. Jones 17*); Second day, Durham 467-6 (P. W. G. Parker 119*, P. W. Henderson 9*).

Glamorgan

S. P. James c Fothergill b Brown	2	– c Parker b Botham	5
H. Morris c Jones b Henderson	46	– lbw b Brown	0
A. Dale c Jones b Brown	29	– c Botham b Brown	3
*M. P. Maynard c Larkins b Henderson	88	– c Larkins b Brown	15
I. V. A. Richards c Jones b Henderson	1	– c Botham b Brown	7
P. A. Cottey lbw b Brown	24	– not out	112
R. D. B. Croft lbw b Hughes	14	– b Brown	3
†C. P. Metson run out	1	– c Fothergill b Hughes	30
S. L. Watkin c Fothergill b Hughes	1	– c Fothergill b Botham	12
S. R. Barwick b Hughes	7	– c Brown b Graveney	0
S. Bastien not out	1	– b Brown	0
B 3, l-b 4, n-b 3	10	B 1, l-b 5	6

1/3 2/58 3/121 4/125 5/184   **224**   1/1 2/8 3/14 4/29 5/32   **193**
6/208 7/210 8/214 9/221   6/40 7/117 8/170 9/189

Bonus points – Glamorgan 2, Durham 4.

Bowling: *First Innings*—Botham 8–0–35–0; Brown 22–6–70–3; Hughes 22.5–5–51–3; Henderson 17–4–61–3; Graveney 2–2–0–0. *Second Innings*—Botham 22–7–47–3; Brown 26.1–8–66–5; Hughes 18–4–41–1; Graveney 16–5–20–1; Jones 3–0–13–0.

Durham

W. Larkins c Maynard b Croft	143	S. P. Hughes c Dale b Croft	1
J. D. Glendenen c Metson b Watkin	15	*D. A. Graveney not out	8
D. M. Jones c Barwick b Croft	94		
P. W. G. Parker c Metson b Watkin	124		
P. Bainbridge c James b Bastien	11	B 13, l-b 9, w 3, n-b 6	31
I. T. Botham c James b Bastien	40		
†A. R. Fothergill b Croft	8	(9 wkts. dec.)	521
P. W. Henderson c Metson b Croft	46		

1/44 2/250 3/301
4/317 5/371 6/416
7/481 8/484 9/521

S. J. E. Brown did not bat.

Bonus points – Durham 4, Glamorgan 1 (Score at 100 overs: 308-3).

Bowling: Watkin 42–11–115–2; Bastien 30–5–113–2; Barwick 30–7–86–0; Dale 23–8–54–0; Croft 32.5–8–105–5; Richards 9–1–26–0.

Umpires: B. Dudleston and A. A. Jones.

GLAMORGAN v WARWICKSHIRE

At Swansea, May 20, 21, 22. Glamorgan won by 93 runs. Glamorgan 24 pts, Warwickshire 4 pts. Toss: Glamorgan. The 21-year-old off-spinner Croft, with career-best figures of 14 for 169, enabled Glamorgan to achieve their first Championship victory of the season with only one ball remaining. When he began the final over Warwickshire were 171 for eight, but his fourth ball had Paul Smith caught at short leg and the next trapped Munton leg before. In the first innings Richards struck 127 from 129 balls, his 112th first-class century, and shared partnerships of 111 with Maynard and 108 with Cottey. Then Croft, whose previous best figures were five for 62 in the same fixture a year before, exploited a slow, turning pitch to capture six Warwickshire wickets for 103. Only Moles and Neil Smith batted with any confidence. Though they had lost Richards to a pulled hamstring, Glamorgan were able to set the visitors 266 from 72 overs. Warwickshire were soon in trouble at 34 for four, which became 92 for six. But Reeve and Paul Smith, adding 69 in 30 overs, appeared to have saved the game, until Croft dismissed Reeve with seven overs left to set up the exciting finish.

Close of play: First day, Warwickshire 36-0 (A. J. Moles 26*, J. D. Ratcliffe 6*); Second day, Glamorgan 78-2 (A. Dale 9*, S. L. Watkin 0*).

Glamorgan

S. P. James c Burns b Booth	26	– c Munton b N. M. K. Smith	...	35
H. Morris lbw b P. A. Smith	36	– c Reeve b Booth		28
A. Dale c Reeve b Twose	32	– not out		67
*M. P. Maynard c N. M. K. Smith b Booth	62	– (5) c Burns b Donald		0
I. V. A. Richards c Burns b Twose	127			
P. A. Cottey not out	42	– c Burns b Munton		9
R. D. B. Croft not out	2	– c Burns b Munton		8
†C. P. Metson (did not bat)		– not out		5
S. L. Watkin (did not bat)		– (4) lbw b Donald		1
B 4, l-b 8, n-b 7	19	B 9, l-b 3, n-b 2		14

1/54 2/80 3/115 4/226 5/334   (5 wkts dec.) 346   1/68 2/74 3/92   (6 wkts dec.) 167
4/92 5/126 6/146

S. R. Barwick and S. Bastien did not bat.

Bonus points – Glamorgan 4, Warwickshire 2.

Bowling: *First Innings*—Donald 12–3–51–0; Munton 24–8–44–0; Booth 32–4–129–2; P. A. Smith 19–5–52–1; Twose 6–0–22–2; N. M. K. Smith 5–1–28–0; Reeve 2–0–8–0. *Second Innings*—Donald 15–4–24–2; Munton 14–3–43–2; N. M. K. Smith 26–5–61–1; Booth 8–3–27–1.

Warwickshire

A. J. Moles c James b Croft	66	– b Croft		13
J. D. Ratcliffe c Metson b Watkin	9	– b Watkin		1
*T. A. Lloyd c James b Croft	13	– b Bastien		4
R. G. Twose c and b Croft	26	– (6) c Maynard b Croft		31
D. A. Reeve c James b Barwick	22	– (4) c Watkin b Croft		79
P. A. Smith c Metson b Barwick	25	– (8) c James b Croft		26
N. M. K. Smith b Croft	67	– (5) b Croft		1
†M. Burns c Richards b Croft	3	– (7) st Metson b Croft		4
P. A. Booth lbw b Watkin	1	– c Maynard b Croft		0
A. A. Donald not out	4	– not out		1
T. A. Munton c sub b Croft	0	– lbw b Croft		0
B 1, l-b 8, n-b 3	12	L-b 11, n-b 1		12

1/50 2/74 3/119 4/134 5/154   248   1/5 2/12 3/30 4/34 5/88   172
6/201 7/216 8/230 9/248   6/92 7/161 8/169 9/172

Bonus points – Warwickshire 2, Glamorgan 4.

Bowling: *First Innings*—Bastien 15–5–44–0; Watkin 16–5–38–2; Croft 37.4–5–103–6; Barwick 18–5–54–2. *Second Innings*—Watkin 16–3–34–1; Bastien 9–3–17–1; Croft 24.5–6–66–8; Barwick 19–6–42–0; Cottey 3–2–2–0.

Umpires: G. I. Burgess and D. J. Constant.

GLAMORGAN v LEICESTERSHIRE

At Swansea, May 29, 30, June 1. Drawn. Glamorgan 2 pts, Leicestershire 2 pts. Toss: Leicestershire. For the second successive year Leicestershire fell foul of the Welsh weather, which allowed only 79 overs on the first day, eight balls on the second, and no play on the third. Choosing to bat on a seaming pitch, they soon lost Briers and Whitaker in successive deliveries to Bastien, and Potter was perilously close to touching the hat-trick ball. But he remained to support the well-organised Boon in a productive partnership of 73, and then put on 83 with Benson for the fourth wicket. Glamorgan's quicker bowlers failed to exploit the pitch, concentrating on speed rather than line and length, and Leicestershire were deprived of a third and a possible fourth batting point by the rain which arrived ten minutes into the second morning.

Close of play: First day, Leicestershire 244-6 (V. J. Wells 32*, P. Whitticase 9*); Second day, Leicestershire 246-6 (V. J. Wells 34*, P. Whitticase 9*).

Leicestershire

T. J. Boon c Metson b Dale	69	V. J. Wells not out	34
*N. E. Briers c Metson b Bastien	7	†P. Whitticase not out	9
J. J. Whitaker c Croft b Bastien	0	L-b 8, w 3	11
L. Potter c Bastien b Watkin	65		
J. D. R. Benson c Cowdrey b Dale	49	1/23 2/23 3/96 (6 wkts) 246	
P. N. Hepworth c Metson b Dale	2	4/179 5/181 6/222	

W. K. M. Benjamin, R. P. Gofton and D. J. Millns did not bat.

Bonus points – Leicestershire 2, Glamorgan 2.

Bowling: Watkin 25.2–8–86–1; Bastien 22–9–53–2; Barwick 17–2–54–0; Dale 13–5–30–3; Croft 3–0–15–0.

Glamorgan

S. P. James, H. Morris, A. Dale, *M. P. Maynard, C. S. Cowdrey, P. A. Cottey, R. D. B. Croft, S. Bastien, †C. P. Metson, S. L. Watkin and S. R. Barwick.

Umpires: A. A. Jones and R. Palmer.

At Chelmsford, June 2, 3, 4. GLAMORGAN drew with ESSEX.

GLAMORGAN v LANCASHIRE

At Colwyn Bay, June 12, 13, 15. Drawn. Glamorgan 7 pts, Lancashire 7 pts. Toss: Glamorgan. A first-innings lead of only one run made it harder than usual to contrive a result. Though 300 from 58 overs was a fair challenge from Butcher – making his first Championship appearance of the season – Lancashire lost wickets at regular intervals in their chase, until Martin and the injured Hegg were left to block out 13 overs. A good crowd had seen a total of 22 sixes as both counties hit out. Richards took two off DeFreitas in Glamorgan's first innings, during which Hegg claimed five dismissals. But DeFreitas had his revenge, hitting six fours and six sixes, three in succession off Watkin, in a furious assault which looted 72 from 53 balls. Morris and James, with his maiden Championship century, also cleared the boundary a couple of times each, as they set up Glamorgan's declaration with an opening stand of 250. But DeFreitas, promoted to slog, went for nought second time round, and after Watkinson, who struck the game's last two sixes, was caught on the boundary Lancashire were forced onto the defensive.

Close of play: First day, Lancashire 15-0 (G. Fowler 3*, M. A. Atherton 12*); Second day, Glamorgan 69-0 (S. P. James 37*, H. Morris 25*).

Glamorgan

S. P. James c Hegg b DeFreitas	8	– not out	152
H. Morris c Hegg b Watkinson	33	– c Morrison b Atherton	104
A. Dale c Lloyd b Martin	28	– c Titchard b Atherton	8
M. P. Maynard c Hegg b DeFreitas	35	– not out	15
I. V. A. Richards lbw b DeFreitas	68		
*A. R. Butcher st Hegg b Barnett	23		
R. D. B. Croft c Speak b Morrison	34		
†C. P. Metson not out	46		
S. L. Watkin c Hegg b Morrison	0		
S. R. Barwick b Morrison	0		
S. Bastien b Morrison	4		
B 3, l-b 8, n-b 6	17	B 7, l-b 8, n-b 4	19

1/22 2/62 3/87 4/117 5/201   296   1/250 2/264   (2 wkts dec.) 298
6/209 7/265 8/265 9/267

Bonus points – Glamorgan 3, Lancashire 4.

Bowling: *First Innings*—DeFreitas 19–2–59–3; Morrison 17.2–5–55–4; Martin 15–3–45–1; Watkinson 17–3–42–1; Barnett 22–1–80–1; Atherton 4–3–4–0. *Second Innings*—DeFreitas 11–4–31–0; Morrison 10–1–32–0; Barnett 20–1–90–0; Martin 4.3–1–16–0; Watkinson 2–1–5–0; Atherton 16–0–109–2.

Lancashire

G. Fowler c Metson b Watkin	14	– c Butcher b Watkin	25
*M. A. Atherton c Metson b Bastien	48	– st Metson b Croft	69
N. J. Speak c Richards b Croft	71	– c Metson b Barwick	17
G. D. Lloyd b Bastien	1	– (5) c Barwick b Croft	52
S. P. Titchard b Bastien	17	– (6) c Croft b Barwick	7
M. Watkinson lbw b Barwick	32	– (7) c Richards b Barwick	20
P. A. J. DeFreitas c Richards b Barwick	72	– (4) c James b Watkin	0
†W. K. Hegg c James b Watkin	1	– not out	22
P. J. Martin c Croft b Watkin	9	– not out	24
D. K. Morrison not out	6		
A. A. Barnett c Metson b Barwick	4		
B 2, l-b 15, n-b 3	20	B 4, l-b 1, w 1	6

1/35 2/94 3/99 4/148 5/188   295   1/35 2/80 3/83 4/159   (7 wkts) 242
6/214 7/271 8/277 9/287   5/166 6/188 7/193

Bonus points – Lancashire 3, Glamorgan 4.

Bowling: *First Innings*—Watkin 26–4–83–3; Bastien 27–8–45–3; Croft 18–3–67–1; Barwick 23.4–7–71–3; Dale 5–1–12–0. *Second Innings*—Watkin 13–4–39–2; Bastien 6.4–0–33–0; Barwick 23–0–102–3; Croft 15–3–63–2.

Umpires: H. D. Bird and B. Leadbeater.

At Worcester, June 16, 17, 18. GLAMORGAN lost to WORCESTERSHIRE by eight wickets.

At Oxford, June 19, 20, 22. GLAMORGAN drew with OXFORD UNIVERSITY.

At Luton, June 26, 27, 29. GLAMORGAN lost to NORTHAMPTONSHIRE by an innings and 184 runs.

GLAMORGAN v SURREY

At Neath, July 3, 4, 6. Surrey won by 50 runs. Surrey 22 pts, Glamorgan 5 pts. Toss: Glamorgan. Glamorgan lost an opportunity of winning their second Championship game of the season when they succumbed to Martin Bicknell, who took the last four wickets in 11 deliveries without conceding a run. Lynch had set Glamorgan the reasonable target of 299 in 68 overs and at tea they were well placed on 96 for two with 37 overs remaining. Morris was dismissed just after the interval; much then depended on Maynard and Richards, but having threatened briefly they departed in quick succession. Despite 45 from Cottey the tail surrendered to Bicknell to give Surrey victory with nine balls left. In the first innings James had struck his second Championship century, sharing an opening partnership of 147 with Morris, after Ward had hit 138 for Surrey, one day after his 70-ball hundred against Northamptonshire, and added 211 with Thorpe for the fourth wicket.

Close of play: First day, Surrey 275-6 (J. D. Robinson 1*); Second day, Surrey 44-1 (P. D. Atkins 17*, J. Boiling 3*).

Surrey

D. J. Bicknell c Morris b Frost	15	– c Metson b Watkin	22
P. D. Atkins c Metson b Frost	11	– run out	49
G. P. Thorpe c Morris b Watkin	93	– (4) not out	69
*M. A. Lynch lbw b Bastien	13	– (5) c Cottey b Croft	32
D. M. Ward c Morris b Frost	138	– (6) c James b Croft	18
J. D. Robinson not out	10	– (7) not out	5
†N. F. Sargeant c Bastien b Watkin	1		
M. P. Bicknell not out	28		
J. Boiling (did not bat)		– (3) c Cottey b Watkin	29
B 2, l-b 1, w 2, n-b 2	7	L-b 3, w 3, n-b 2	8

1/18 2/33 3/59 4/270	(6 wkts. dec.) 316	1/32 2/87 3/135 (5 wkts. dec.) 232
5/273 6/275		4/194 5/222

A. J. Murphy and J. E. Benjamin did not bat.

Bonus points – Surrey 4, Glamorgan 2.

Bowling: *First Innings*—Watkin 25–6–76–2; Frost 24.2–100–3; Bastien 14.4–4–55–1; Croft 19–4–64–0; Dale 3–0–18–0. *Second Innings*—Watkin 16–3–49–2; Frost 7–0–48–0; Bastien 16–2–63–0; Croft 10–0–69–2.

Glamorgan

S. P. James lbw b Benjamin	105	– c Thorpe b Murphy	19
H. Morris c Lynch b Boiling	58	– c Thorpe b M. P. Bicknell	59
A. Dale c Sargeant b Murphy	8	– c Boiling b Benjamin	1
*M. P. Maynard c M. P. Bicknell b Robinson		– lbw b Robinson	66
I. V. A. Richards b Robinson	0	– c Sargeant b Murphy	27
P. A. Cottey c Sargeant b M. P. Bicknell	24	– c Boiling b M. P. Bicknell	45
R. D. B. Croft not out	16	– c Sargeant b Boiling	15
†C. P. Metson not out	14	– c Robinson b M. P. Bicknell	0
S. L. Watkin (did not bat)		– c Sargeant b M. P. Bicknell	0
S. Bastien (did not bat)		– not out	0
M. Frost (did not bat)		– lbw b M. P. Bicknell	0
L-b 7, w 2, n-b 10	19	L-b 1, w 1, n-b 14	16

1/147 2/188 3/188 4/188	(6 wkts. dec.) 250	1/43 2/47 3/123 4/178 5/201 248
5/195 6/231		6/228 7/247 8/247 9/248

Bonus points – Glamorgan 3, Surrey 2.

Bowling: *First Innings*—M. P. Bicknell 23–4–90–1; Benjamin 20–3–54–1; Murphy 12.3–3–33–1; Robinson 11.3–1–36–2; Boiling 11–3–30–1. *Second Innings*—M. P. Bicknell 15.3–2–43–5; Benjamin 17–1–75–1; Murphy 17–3–54–2; Robinson 7–1–43–1; Boiling 10–3–32–1.

Umpires: A. G. T. Whitehead and P. B. Wight.

At Portsmouth, July 17, 18, 20. GLAMORGAN drew with HAMPSHIRE.

GLAMORGAN v YORKSHIRE

At Cardiff, July 21, 22, 23. Drawn. Glamorgan 4 pts, Yorkshire 4 pts. Toss: Yorkshire. Glamorgan avoided defeat as their No. 11, Frost, played out the final over from Jarvis. He and Dale had survived the last four overs after Jarvis had taken two wickets in successive overs to reduce the home team to 217 for nine. Yorkshire had set Glamorgan 251 from 65 overs, which was reduced by 12 overs because of rain. Morris and James gave them a positive start, sharing 57 at five an over, but they then collapsed to 134 for five, and their last outside chance of victory ended when Dale lost his sixth-wicket partner, Croft. The final day's entertainment compensated for the slow progress made by both teams on the opening two days. Yorkshire averaged only 2.6 per over, while Blakey completed a five-hour century, the first of the season for Yorkshire not scored by Moxon, who had earlier completed his fourth. Glamorgan were even slower, at 2.2, on a slow low pitch which benefited no-one.

Close of play: First day, Yorkshire 286-6 (R. J. Blakey 100*, P. W. Jarvis 15*); Second day, Glamorgan 200-6 (R. D. B. Croft 11*, C. P. Metson 0*).

Yorkshire

*M. D. Moxon b Barwick	103		
S. A. Kellett c Metson b Watkin	1	– (1) b Watkin	1
D. Byas c Metson b Watkin	10	– (2) not out	68
S. R. Tendulkar lbw b Frost	18	– (3) c and b Croft	7
†R. J. Blakey not out	125	– (4) not out	21
C. White c James b Croft	35		
P. Carrick c Richards b Watkin	0		
P. W. Jarvis c Dale b Croft	45		
P. J. Hartley c James b Croft	6		
L-b 4, n-b 1	5	B 4, w 1	5

1/5 2/23 3/55 4/172 5/231   (8 wkts dec.) 348   1/10 2/29   (2 wkts dec.) 102
6/232 7/340 8/348

M. A. Robinson and J. D. Batty did not bat.

Bonus points – Yorkshire 2, Glamorgan 2 (Score at 100 overs: 236-6).

Bowling: *First Innings*—Watkin 30–6–81–3; Frost 25–4–103–1; Barwick 35–10–79–1; Dale 9–3–18–0; Croft 31–7–63–3. *Second Innings*—Watkin 5–2–20–1; Barwick 13–3–32–0; Croft 10–2–46–1.

Glamorgan

S. P. James b Hartley	80	– lbw b Hartley	26
H. Morris c sub b Carrick	5	– c Tendulkar b Robinson	39
D. L. Hemp lbw b Batty	22	– run out	6
*M. P. Maynard run out	30	– b Batty	36
I. V. A. Richards lbw b Hartley	12	– c Tendulkar b Batty	11
A. Dale c Byas b Carrick	21	– not out	59
R. D. B. Croft not out	11	– st Blakey b Batty	25
†C. P. Metson not out	0	– run out	0
S. L. Watkin (did not bat)		– lbw b Jarvis	0
S. R. Barwick (did not bat)		– b Jarvis	0
M. Frost (did not bat)		– not out	0
B 4, l-b 11, n-b 4	19	B 6, l-b 8, n-b 3	17

1/73 2/142 3/155 4/164   (6 wkts dec.) 200   1/57 2/74 3/88   (9 wkts) 219
5/189 6/197   4/109 5/134 6/196
                                                     7/217 8/217 9/217

Bonus points – Glamorgan 2, Yorkshire 2.

In the first innings H. Morris, when 2, retired hurt at 9 and resumed at 189.

Bowling: *First Innings*—Jarvis 15–5–48–0; Hartley 17–6–27–2; Carrick 32–16–51–2; Robinson 12–3–29–0; Batty 14–4–30–1. *Second Innings*—Jarvis 10–1–42–2; Hartley 7–2–30–1; Carrick 12–2–49–0; Robinson 7–1–25–1; Batty 17–3–59–3.

Umpires: B. Dudleston and G. Sharp.

GLAMORGAN v SOMERSET

At Abergavenny, July 24, 25, 27. Drawn. Glamorgan 5 pts, Somerset 7 pts. Toss: Glamorgan. The placid Abergavenny pitch and short boundaries did not produce the run feast of previous years, although Morris, with a match aggregate of 188, including his fourth century of the season, completed 1,000 runs for the sixth time in seven years. Glamorgan came within two wickets of their elusive second win after two declarations, the first by Tavaré 26 runs behind on first innings, and the second by Maynard, ten minutes after lunch on the third day, which left Somerset to chase 335 from 67 overs. They were always behind the required run-rate, but Maynard kept them interested by using Morris's rarely seen off-spin, which yielded 55 runs from four overs. After Rose had struck a rapid half-century Burns and Lefebvre put on 59 in just seven overs, until Lefebvre was run out, when Somerset settled for a draw and played out the remaining four overs.

Close of play: First day, Somerset 24–0 (A. N. Hayhurst 2*, G. T. J. Townsend 20*); Second day, Glamorgan 113–2 (H. Morris 58*, M. P. Maynard 18*).

Glamorgan

S. P. James c Trump b Rose	29	– c Burns b Caddick	8
H. Morris lbw b Rose	71	– c Lefebvre b Hayhurst	117
D. L. Hemp lbw b Lefebvre	0	– lbw b Caddick	16
*M. P. Maynard b Lefebvre	0	– c Turner b Trump	57
I. V. A. Richards c Rose b van Troost	27	– c Harden b Trump	13
A. Dale c Harden b Caddick	67	– not out	45
R. D. B. Croft b Trump	19	– not out	37
†C. P. Metson c Tavaré b van Troost	26		
S. L. Watkin c Burns b Rose	0		
D. J. Foster c Burns b Rose	2		
S. R. Barwick not out	9		
L-b 8, w 1, n-b 17	26	B 4, l-b 6, n-b 5	15

1/55 2/56 3/58 4/103 5/162	276	1/20 2/71 3/186 (5 wkts dec.)	308
6/235 7/245 8/246 9/248		4/206 5/248	

Bonus points – Glamorgan 3, Somerset 4 (Score at 100 overs: 266-9).

Bowling: *First Innings*—Caddick 24–5–60–1; van Troost 14–2–57–2; Rose 21–5–59–4; Lefebvre 14–3–33–2; Hayhurst 7–2–13–0; Trump 24–8–46–1. *Second Innings*—Caddick 10–3–40–2; van Troost 11–1–70–0; Trump 21–4–59–2; Rose 13–2–56–0; Lefebvre 7–2–15–0; Hayhurst 4–1–17–1; Harden 3–0–31–0; Tavaré 1–0–10–0.

Somerset

A. N. Hayhurst c Richards b Barwick	70	– lbw b Watkin	24
G. T. J. Townsend c Metson b Foster	46	– b Barwick	35
R. J. Harden c Maynard b Croft	27	– c Dale b Croft	48
*C. J. Tavaré b Croft	23	– run out	14
R. J. Turner not out	24	– (7) lbw b Dale	0
G. D. Rose c Richards b Croft	13	– c Metson b Barwick	50
†N. D. Burns not out	36	– (5) not out	71
R. P. Lefebvre (did not bat)		– run out	36
A. R. Caddick (did not bat)		– c Metson b Watkin	0
H. R. J. Trump (did not bat)		– not out	8
L-b 4, n-b 7	11	B 2, l-b 3, n-b 2	7

1/79 2/148 3/151 4/179 5/199	(5 wkts dec.) 250	1/50 2/77 3/107 4/134 (8 wkts)	293
		5/218 6/220 7/279 8/282	

A. P. van Troost did not bat.

Bonus points – Somerset 3, Glamorgan 2.

Bowling: *First Innings*—Watkin 10–4–12–0; Foster 22–5–92–1; Croft 29.2–4–94–3; Barwick 21–10–23–1; Dale 8–2–25–0. *Second Innings*—Watkin 10.5–3–32–2; Foster 4–0–16–0; Dale 11–1–35–1; Barwick 20.2–2–61–2; Croft 17–0–89–1; Morris 4–0–55–0.

Umpires: B. Dudleston and G. Sharp.

GLAMORGAN v KENT

At Swansea, July 31, August 1, 3. Glamorgan won by 36 runs. Glamorgan 21 pts, Kent 6 pts. Toss: Kent. Glamorgan gained their second Championship win of the season – both had come at St Helen's – with Croft and Barwick taking nine wickets with off-spin on the last afternoon. Kent were set 310 from 64 overs after a farcical quarter of an hour in which Maynard and Cottey were given 112 runs from five overs bowled by Marsh and Cowdrey. Maynard struck 34 runs – five sixes and a four – in one over from Marsh, which broke the county record of 32 set by C. C. Smart in 1935. Ward led Kent's assault with an attacking innings including four sixes and 14 fours. Although the middle order failed to contribute, the tail revived Kent's hopes by adding 93 for the last two wickets before Glamorgan ended the resistance with 6.1 overs to spare. In Kent's first innings Hooper struck a century from only 75 deliveries, and with Ward also in punishing form Kent raced to maximum batting points in only 56.1 overs. Glamorgan made more stately progress, with James taking five and a quarter hours to score 91.
Close of play: First day, Glamorgan 276-5 (P. A. Cottey 37*, R. D. B. Croft 14*); Second day, Glamorgan 45-0 (S. P. James 28*, H. Morris 17*).

Glamorgan

S. P. James st Marsh b Davis	91	– b Hooper	29
H. Morris c Hooper b Davis	31	– c Igglesden b Hooper	33
D. L. Hemp c Hooper b Igglesden	39	– c Marsh b Hooper	9
*M. P. Maynard b Davis	36	– not out	113
A. Dale c Marsh b Igglesden	10	– st Marsh b Davis	1
P. A. Cottey lbw b Ealham	37	– not out	65
R. D. B. Croft not out	60		
†C. P. Metson c Ward b Ealham	26		
B 8, l-b 13, w 2, n-b 1	24	B 4, l-b 1	5

1/59 2/119 3/185 4/216 5/216   (7 wkts dec.) 354   1/52 2/71   (4 wkts dec.) 255
6/276 7/354   3/72 4/77

S. L. Watkin, S. R. Barwick and D. J. Foster did not bat.

Bonus points – Glamorgan 3, Kent 2 (Score at 100 overs: 257-5).

Bowling: *First Innings*—Igglesden 28–4–96–2; Ellison 9–1–31–0; Ealham 19.2–4–76–2; Davis 39–10–69–3; Hooper 23–6–46–0; Fleming 5–1–15–0. *Second Innings*—Igglesden 8–1–31–0; Davis 27–9–54–1; Hooper 22–5–51–3; Ward 1–0–2–0; Marsh 3–0–73–0; Cowdrey 2–0–39–0.

Kent

T. R. Ward c Metson b Croft	85	– st Metson b Barwick	118
*M. R. Benson c James b Foster	4	– b Croft	9
N. R. Taylor c Maynard b Croft	42	– c Maynard b Croft	7
C. L. Hooper c Barwick b Watkin	100	– lbw b Croft	11
G. R. Cowdrey not out	27	– c Morris b Croft	14
M. V. Fleming c Barwick b Watkin	28	– c Metson b Barwick	12
†S. A. Marsh run out	1	– c Dale b Croft	0
M. A. Ealham not out	2	– c Croft b Barwick	4
R. M. Ellison (did not bat)		– run out	41
R. P. Davis (did not bat)		– not out	34
A. P. Igglesden (did not bat)		– lbw b Croft	16
B 4, l-b 4, n-b 3	11	B 1, l-b 5, n-b 1	7

1/10 2/128 3/185 4/262   (6 wkts dec.) 300   1/45 2/63 3/115 4/153 5/167   273
5/295 6/297   6/172 7/172 8/180 9/241

Bonus points – Kent 4, Glamorgan 2.

Bowling: *First Innings*—Watkin 14.1–1–78–2; Foster 11–1–79–1; Barwick 14–1–37–0; Dale 5–1–20–0; Croft 12–1–78–2. *Second Innings*—Watkin 8–0–27–0; Foster 3–0–27–0; Croft 25.5–4–112–6; Barwick 21–4–101–3.

Umpires: J. H. Hampshire and V. A. Holder.

At Eastbourne, August 4, 5, 6. GLAMORGAN drew with SUSSEX.

At Nottingham, August 7, 8, 10. GLAMORGAN beat NOTTINGHAMSHIRE by seven runs.

At Hartlepool, August 14, 15, 17. GLAMORGAN drew with DURHAM.

At Chesterfield, August 18, 19, 20. GLAMORGAN drew with DERBYSHIRE.

GLAMORGAN v GLOUCESTERSHIRE

At Swansea, August 21, 22, 24. Drawn. Glamorgan 2 pts, Gloucestershire 2 pts. Toss: Glamorgan. In a rain-ruined match of three declarations there was never any chance of a positive outcome once the weather intervened at 12.05 p.m. on the final day. On a pitch offering slow turn Gloucestershire crept along at two runs an over with the second bonus point not achieved until the 97th over. Their batsmen, apart from Russell, were tied down by Barwick and Croft, who bowled 80 overs between them and captured six of the eight wickets to fall. Hodgson spent 52 overs scoring 33 while Athey stayed three and a half hours for his 49, passing 1,000 runs in a season for the tenth time. But Russell enlivened proceedings, reaching his half-century from 70 deliveries. Only two overs were bowled in Glamorgan's first innings on Saturday, and although the captains adopted a positive approach on the final day, when Glamorgan were set 301 from a minimum of 90 overs, their good intentions were thwarted by rain.

Close of play: First day, Gloucestershire 272-8 (R. C. Russell 66*, M. C. J. Ball 0*); Second day, Glamorgan 3-0 (S. P. James 1*, H. Morris 2*).

Gloucestershire

G. D. Hodgson c Croft b Barwick	33		
R. J. Scott c Cottey b Croft	45		
M. W. Alleyne b Barwick	0		
C. W. J. Athey c Morris b Croft	49		
*A. J. Wright c Hemp b Barwick	30		
T. H. C. Hancock c Hemp b Croft	9		
†R. C. Russell not out	66		
R. C. Williams lbw b Thomas	14		
C. A. Walsh c Maynard b Frost	0		
M. C. J. Ball not out	0	– (1) not out	14
M. Davies (did not bat)		– (2) not out	17
B 7, l-b 11, n-b 8	26		

1/77 2/78 3/101 4/159 5/170   (8 wkts. dec.) 272   (no wkt dec.) 31
6/205 7/271 8/272

Bonus points – Gloucestershire 2, Glamorgan 2 (Score at 100 overs: 206-6).

Bowling: *First Innings*—Frost 16–2–68–1; Thomas 14–2–38–1; Barwick 38–13–59–3; Dale 3–0–10–0; Croft 42–11–79–3. *Second Innings*—Frost 4.1–0–21–0; Thomas 4–1–10–0.

Glamorgan

S. P. James not out	1 – not out......................	14
H. Morris not out........................	2 – not out.....................	12
	N-b 6	6
(no wkt dec.) 3		(no wkt) 32

A. Dale, *M. P. Maynard, D. L. Hemp, P. A. Cottey, R. D. B. Croft, †C. P. Metson, S. R. Barwick, S. D. Thomas and M. Frost did not bat.

Bowling: *First Innings*—Walsh 1–0–3–0; Williams 1–1–0–0. *Second Innings*—Walsh 4–1–15–0; Williams 3–0–16–0; Davies 1–0–1–0.

Umpires: A. G. T. Whitehead and P. B. Wight.

At Birmingham, August 26, 27, 28, 29. GLAMORGAN drew with WARWICKSHIRE.

GLAMORGAN v SUSSEX

At Cardiff, August 31, September 1, 2, 3. Drawn. Glamorgan 6 pts, Sussex 3 pts. Toss: Glamorgan. This was yet another game spoiled by the weather, with only 153.1 overs bowled in four days. It brought Glamorgan's tally of time lost in three Championship matches to more than 52 hours. On the first day, Morris passed 1,500 runs for the season for the third year running before Cottey and Croft, who was awarded his county cap before the start, added 70. Sussex then ran into trouble against Thomas, who produced an inspired spell of three for eight in 21 deliveries, while Barwick was a model of accuracy with his off-cutters. Stephenson staged a partial recovery and carried Sussex to within four runs of a batting point, but once rain stopped play at 5.15 p.m. on the third day nothing more could be done.

Close of play: First day, Glamorgan 170-5 (P. A. Cottey 21*, R. D. B. Croft 5*); Second day, Glamorgan 177-5 (P. A. Cottey 23*, R. D. B. Croft 8*); Third day, Sussex 146-7 (F. D. Stephenson 32*, B. T. P. Donelan 6*).

Glamorgan

S. P. James lbw b C. M. Wells	32	S. L. Watkin not out	18
H. Morris b Donelan................	80	S. D. Thomas st Moores b Salisbury ...	8
A. Dale c Moores b Donelan	18	S. R. Barwick lbw b Salisbury	0
*M. P. Maynard lbw b Salisbury	7		
P. A. Cottey lbw b C. M. Wells.......	58	L-b 3, w 2, n-b 5............	10
D. L. Hemp b Salisbury	2		
R. D. B. Croft c Giddins b C. M. Wells	33	1/91 2/126 3/142 4/160 5/162	268
†C. P. Metson run out	2	6/232 7/235 8/244 9/266	

Bonus points – Glamorgan 3, Sussex 3 (Score at 100 overs: 265-8).

Bowling: Stephenson 17–2–43–0; Giddins 8–2–26–0; Remy 20–1–70–0; C. M. Wells 24–12–26–3; Salisbury 26.1–5–79–4; Donelan 8–3–21–2.

Sussex

N. J. Lenham lbw b Watkin	30	F. D. Stephenson not out	32
J. W. Hall c Cottey b Thomas	13	B. T. P. Donelan not out............	6
C. C. Remy c Cottey b Thomas.......	18	L-b 5	5
*A. P. Wells lbw b Watkin..........	36		
M. P. Speight c Metson b Thomas....	0	1/34 2/64 3/71	(7 wkts) 146
C. M. Wells c Hemp b Barwick.......	0	4/71 5/80	
†P. Moores c Metson b Dale	6	6/103 7/108	

I. D. K. Salisbury and E. S. H. Giddins did not bat.

Bonus points – Glamorgan 3.

Bowling: Watkin 16–0–59–2; Thomas 13–3–46–3; Barwick 17–9–29–1; Croft 3–0–6–0; Dale 1–0–1–1.

Umpires: A. A. Jones and D. R. Shepherd.

t Canterbury, September 7, 8, 9, 10. GLAMORGAN beat KENT by 86 runs.

GLAMORGAN v DERBYSHIRE

t Cardiff, September 12, 13, 14, 15. Glamorgan won by 63 runs. Glamorgan 20 pts, erbyshire 4 pts. Toss: Glamorgan. Glamorgan gained their fifth Championship win in eir last game of the season, which was again affected by the weather. Play was washed t on the first two days. On the third day Glamorgan secured maximum batting points th Maynard and Richards sharing an entertaining partnership of 107 in 16 overs. After e captains had forfeited an innings each and rain had restricted play to only 17.4 overs by id-afternoon on the fourth day, Derbyshire required 198 from 29 overs with eight wickets t. Needing a win to finish in the top four of the County Championship, they attacked all e way, but Croft's off-spin thwarted their efforts. He took a wicket in his first, third and urth overs, a further two in his fifth, and his sixth wicket three overs later enabled amorgan to win with 7.3 overs to spare. It was their 200th home Championship win.

Close of play: First day, No play; Second day, No play; Third day, Glamorgan 307.

lamorgan

P. James lbw b Griffith	52		S. L. Watkin b Warner	4
Morris c O'Gorman b Mortensen	16		S. D. Thomas c Griffith b Sladdin	10
Dale c Mortensen b Sladdin	26		S. R. Barwick not out	0
A. P. Maynard c sub b Richardson	57			
V. A. Richards c Morris b Sladdin	85		B 1, l-b 6, n-b 2	9
A. Cottey c Griffith b Richardson	0			—
D. B. Croft lbw b Sladdin	17		1/23 2/94 3/98 4/205 5/215	307
C. P. Metson c Tweats b Barnett	31		6/253 7/258 8/267 9/307	

Bonus points – Glamorgan 4, Derbyshire 4.

Bowling: Mortensen 18–4–58–1; Warner 19–1–52–1; Richardson 13–2–38–2; Griffith –0–43–1; Sladdin 22–1–102–4; Barnett 1.1–0–7–1.

amorgan forfeited their second innings.

erbyshire

erbyshire forfeited their first innings.

. D. Bowler c Metson b Thomas	5		A. W. Richardson c Watkin b Croft	5
E. Morris b Dale	46		R. W. Sladdin b Croft	39
J. G. O'Gorman c Metson b Dale	41		O. H. Mortensen not out	6
K. J. Barnett run out	19			
E. Warner b Croft	29		L-b 8, w 1	9
A. Griffith b Croft	5			—
A. Tweats c Watkin b Croft	24		1/13 2/74 3/112 4/138 5/151	244
J. Adams c Richards b Croft	16		6/156 7/176 8/195 9/199	

Bowling: Watkin 13–0–48–0; Thomas 4–0–21–1; Barwick 3–0–16–0; Dale 9–1–29–2; ottey 2–0–17–0; Maynard 4–0–56–0; Croft 7.3–0–49–6.

Umpires: J. H. Harris and B. J. Meyer.

GLOUCESTERSHIRE

Patron: HRH The Princess of Wales
President: D. N. Perry
Chairman: R. W. Rossiter
Secretary: P. G. M. August
 Phoenix County Ground, Nevil Road,
 Bristol BS7 9EJ (Telephone: 0272-245216)
Captain: A. J. Wright
Coach: A. W. Stovold
Assistant Coach: P. W. Romaines
Youth Coach: G. G. M. Wiltshire

What Gloucestershire might have achieved in 1992 had Davi
Lawrence been available to partner Courtney Walsh can only b
imagined. Even with Lawrence injured, the county advanced thre
places up the Championship table to tenth, despite losing nine full day
to rain. Most of the credit for this respectable performance must go t
Walsh who finished at the head of the first-class bowling averages wit
92 wickets and was a deserving winner of the Cricketers' Associatio
award as player of the year.

Gloucestershire leaned on him almost as much as they did on Mik
Procter in his heyday. On eight occasions Walsh, who was in h
benefit season, took five or more wickets in an innings while his pac
bowling partners struggled to make an impact. He even took ove
the captaincy for the last two matches, setting up a win over th
champions, Essex, which sent everyone away for the winter in goo
heart.

Walsh assumed the leadership because Tony Wright was out o
action with a broken hand while Bill Athey, Wright's usual deputy, lo
the job after he had announced that he would be refusing a ne
contract. Athey had been the mainstay of the batting for nine season
and officials were left wondering how they might replace a player wh
had scored 11,383 runs for the county at an average of 42.79. Th
answer was simple and even symmetrical: the man whom Athey ha
effectively replaced on his arrival from Yorkshire in 1984, Chris Broa
was released by Nottinghamshire, and agreed to rejoin his hom
county, which he had accused of lacking ambition when he departe
nine years ago, saying he wanted to improve his chances of playin
Test cricket. Broad, who had rejected seven other approaches, said h
believed Gloucestershire to be a much more forward-looking club tha
when he had left and was impressed by the expensive improvement
made to the pavilion and ground at Bristol. "There is a new face t
Gloucestershire cricket", he said.

Dean Hodgson should certainly benefit from Broad's return. Despit
the lack of a regular opening partner he made a further advance
scoring two of the county's six hundreds, hitting his first one-da
century and generally playing with much more freedom. He and Simo
Hinks looked as if they might settle into a useful pairing but the forme
Kent player managed only half a season before being forced out by

g injury. First Athey, then Richard Scott stepped into the breach, although Scott was of more value further down the order. Mark Alleyne, who opened on Sundays, passed 1,000 runs and improved his Championship average; on the evidence of two fine innings against Essex, he looked ready to assume the responsibilities of a senior batsman. The leading player in the national averages, however, was Jack Russell. Having been rejected by England because he was considered an inadequate batsman, he played a succession of doughty innings for the county, employing a stance so open that he appeared to expect the ball to arrive from the direction of mid-wicket.

What was greatly encouraging for supporters was the promise shown by some of the younger players. One gem to emerge was Mark Davies, a left-arm spinner from Glamorgan whose previous first-class bowling experience had been limited to eight overs against Oxford University. Although at 5ft 6in he did not fit the traditional ideal for a member of his craft, he nagged and teased to such good effect that he ended the season with 55 Championship wickets. Only when he and Walsh were employed in tandem could Gloucestershire truly claim that pressure was being applied at both ends. It was a heartening sight when Davies and the off-spinner Martyn Ball were in action together, but Ball could not match his partner for accuracy.

Another new face was that of Justin Vaughan, a New Zealand doctor who qualified for Championship cricket by virtue of being born in Hereford. This assured left-hand batsman and improving seam bowler was restricted by a knee injury and did not become a regular member of the side until mid-July. Thereafter, he made some valuable contributions and missed a deserved maiden hundred for the county by a single run against Northamptonshire. Unfortunately for Gloucestershire, his qualification lapsed when he played for New Zealand in Sri Lanka. Tim Hancock, who revealed a welcome aggressive streak, scored his first century, against Somerset, and also gained a regular place towards the end of the season while Robert Dawson, from Devon, showed promise on his limited appearances. Matthew Windows, son of Tony, the Gloucestershire all-rounder of the 1960s, followed success with the England Under-19 side by playing an innings of notable coolness and maturity on his début against Essex. The young team's ground-fielding was one of its strengths and Davies, in particular, produced flashes of brilliance.

Until the win over Essex, the NatWest Trophy quarter-final against the same opponents on a Cheltenham College ground full to overflowing had been the season's highlight. Gloucestershire lost, but the scene was truly memorable. The other games at the Cheltenham festival were also well attended and its future is secure. But despite a council subsidy, the best weather of the summer and two closely-fought matches, the Gloucester week resulted in a loss. The new-look Championship programme may well suit a team which won three over the four-day course in 1992. But it makes fixture allocation difficult, especially with the need to make full use of Bristol's greatly-enhanced facilities. – Geoffrey Wheeler.

GLOUCESTERSHIRE 1992

[*Bill Smith*

Back row: M. G. N. Windows, R. C. Williams, T. H. C. Hancock, R. I. Dawson, A. M. Smith, M. Davies, R. C. J. Williams. *Middle row*: M. J. Gerrard, R. J. Scott, A. M. Babington, J. T. C. Vaughan, J. M. de la Pena, S. G. Hinks, R. M. Horrell, A. J. Hunt. *Front row*: M. C. J. Ball, M. W. Alleyne, R. C. Russell, C. W. J. Athey, A. J. Wright (*captain*) R. W. Rossiter (*chairman*), D. V. Lawrence,

GLOUCESTERSHIRE RESULTS

All first-class matches – Played 22: Won 6, Lost 7, Drawn 9. Abandoned 1.

County Championship matches – Played 21: Won 6, Lost 6, Drawn 9. Abandoned 1.

Bonus points – Batting 48, Bowling 58.

*Competition placings – Britannic Assurance County Championship, 10th;
NatWest Bank Trophy, q-f; Benson and Hedges Cup, 6th in Group A;
Sunday League, 8th equal.*

BRITANNIC ASSURANCE CHAMPIONSHIP AVERAGES

BATTING

	Birthplace	M	I	NO	R	HS	Avge
R. C. Russell......	Stroud	16	28	9	904	75	47.57
J. T. C. Vaughan ...	Hereford	10	16	4	450	99	37.50
G. D. Hodgson	Carlisle	20	34	1	1,214	147	36.78
M. W. Alleyne	Tottenham	21	34	3	1,030	93	33.22
C. W. J. Athey.....	Middlesbrough	20	32	0	1,022	181	31.93
S. G. Hinks	Northfleet	10	16	3	402	88*	30.92
T. H. C. Hancock ..	Reading	9	15	1	396	102	28.28
‡A. J. Wright	Stevenage	18	31	3	754	128	26.92
R. J. Scott	Bournemouth	19	31	3	751	73	26.82
A. M. Smith	Dewsbury	11	12	5	165	51*	23.57
R. C. J. Williams	Bristol	5	5	2	51	18*	17.00
M. C. J. Ball.......	Bristol	12	21	6	201	54	13.40
R. C. Williams	Camberwell	6	9	1	100	44	12.50
‡C. A. Walsh§	Kingston, Jamaica	18	27	3	280	51	11.66
A. M. Babington ...	London	8	9	3	63	24	10.50
M. Davies	Neath	18	21	9	123	32*	10.25
R. I. Dawson	Exmouth	5	6	0	58	29	9.66
M. J. Gerrard	Bristol	4	4	1	6	4	2.00

Also batted: M. G. N. Windows (*Bristol*) (1 match) 71.

* Signifies not out.   ‡ Denotes county cap.   § Overseas player.

The following played a total of six three-figure innings for Gloucestershire in County Championship matches – C. W. J. Athey 2, G. D. Hodgson 2, T. H. C. Hancock 1, A. J. Wright 1.

BOWLING

	O	M	R	W	BB	5W/i	Avge
C. A. Walsh..........	587.2	138	1,469	92	7-27	8	15.96
M. Davies	529.5	138	1,537	55	4-73	0	27.94
A. M. Smith	232.2	35	764	23	3-53	0	33.21
J. T. C. Vaughan	178.4	40	499	15	3-46	0	33.26
M. W. Alleyne........	133.1	29	489	14	3-25	0	34.92
M. C. J. Ball	322	61	1,072	28	5-101	1	38.28
A. M. Babington	162	17	642	14	8-107	1	45.85
R. J. Scott	267.4	40	959	20	2-9	0	47.95

Also bowled: C. W. J. Athey 58-7-184-2; M. J. Gerrard 93-20-297-7; T. H. C. Hancock 26.4-2-102-3; S. G. Hinks 2.5-1-14-0; G. D. Hodgson 4-0-65-0; R. C. Williams 48-5-209-2; A. J. Wright 2-0-27-0.

Wicket-keepers: R. C. Russell 30 ct, 2 st; R. C. J. Williams 9 ct, 4 st.

Leading Fielders: M. W. Alleyne 21, C. W. J. Athey 19.

At Taunton, April 25, 26, 27, 28. GLOUCESTERSHIRE drew with SOMERSET.

At Leeds, May 14, 15, 16, 17. GLOUCESTERSHIRE beat YORKSHIRE by 147 runs.

GLOUCESTERSHIRE v WORCESTERSHIRE

At Gloucester, May 19, 20, 21. Gloucestershire won by three wickets. Gloucestershire 22 pts, Worcestershire 7 pts. Toss: Worcestershire. The fourth day was not required for a hard-fought match on a slow pitch encouraging the spin bowlers. The bat was temporarily on top during a 181-run partnership between Moody and Leatherdale on the opening day when the powerful Australian pulled off-spinner Ball for three sixes and hit 15 fours. The slow left-armer Stemp, Illingworth's deputy, then bowled cleverly and with fine control to undermine Gloucestershire, finishing with career-best figures and taking the last five wickets for 16. Ball swept aside the later batsmen when Worcestershire went in again, but when Stemp resumed his mastery and took his match return to 11 for 146, a target of 210 seemed beyond the home side. However, Russell, showing admirable concentration, nudged and pushed his team towards victory, and some big hitting from Walsh completed it. The West Indian thus had the last word in a game which began two minutes late when he had the ball changed because it was not the one previously selected; he then dismissed Curtis with his first delivery.

Close of play: First day, Gloucestershire 27-3 (A. J. Wright 0*); Second day, Worcestershire 102-5 (D. B. D'Oliveira 19*, S. J. Rhodes 6*).

Worcestershire

*T. S. Curtis lbw b Walsh	0	– lbw b Smith	32
A. C. H. Seymour lbw b Smith	8	– lbw b Walsh	14
T. M. Moody c and b Scott	118	– lbw b Davies	18
D. A. Leatherdale c Davies b Scott	56	– lbw b Smith	3
D. B. D'Oliveira b Davies	17	– c Athey b Ball	36
W. P. C. Weston b Smith	5	– c Alleyne b Davies	2
†S. J. Rhodes c Walsh b Davies	8	– c Alleyne b Walsh	9
S. R. Lampitt not out	26	– c Hodgson b Ball	4
P. J. Newport c Alleyne b Davies	0	– b Ball	4
N. V. Radford c and b Davies	0	– b Ball	12
R. D. Stemp b Walsh	16	– not out	0
L-b 5, n-b 11	16	B 3, l-b 6, n-b 5	14

1/0 2/8 3/189 4/194 5/206   270   1/24 2/66 3/68 4/75 5/86   145
6/220 7/233 8/233 9/239   6/124 7/126 8/132 9/144

Bonus points – Worcestershire 3, Gloucestershire 4.

Bowling: *First Innings*—Walsh 16.3-4-30-2; Smith 16-2-55-2; Scott 14-4-33-2; Davies 30-8-75-4; Ball 17-3-52-0; Athey 6-0-20-0. *Second Innings*—Walsh 20-9-34-2; Smith 16-5-36-2; Ball 15.5-2-47-4; Davies 16-10-19-2.

Gloucestershire

G. D. Hodgson c Curtis b Radford	3	– c Rhodes b Stemp	17
S. G. Hinks b Stemp	17	– b Stemp	26
M. C. J. Ball lbw b Radford	4	– (8) c Curtis b D'Oliveira	2
*A. J. Wright lbw b Stemp	39	– (3) c and b Stemp	22
C. W. J. Athey lbw b Lampitt	42	– (4) b Stemp	3
M. W. Alleyne c Leatherdale b D'Oliveira	36	– c Leatherdale b Stemp	4
R. J. Scott c Newport b Stemp	13	– b D'Oliveira	16
†R. C. Russell c Seymour b Stemp	28	– not out	72
C. A. Walsh st Rhodes b Stemp	0	– not out	30
M. Davies b Stemp	0		
A. M. Smith not out	5		
L-b 14, w 1, n-b 4	19	B 8, l-b 4, n-b 5	17

1/23 2/27 3/27 4/83 5/140   206   1/44 2/48 3/68 4/85   (7 wkts) 210
6/162 7/180 8/180 9/184   5/91 6/157 7/169

Bonus points – Gloucestershire 2, Worcestershire 4.

Bowling: *First Innings*—Radford 12–3–23–2; Newport 13–5–34–0; Stemp 25.5–9–67–6; ~~ampitt 7–1–15–1; D'Oliveira 11–2–29–1; Moody 11–3–24–0. *Second Innings*—Radford ~~2–22–32–0; Newport 6–2–19–0; Stemp 28–3–79–5; Lampitt 11–2–14–0; D'Oliveira ~~–1–54–2.

Umpires: J. H. Harris and R. A. White.

GLOUCESTERSHIRE v SOMERSET

~~t Gloucester, May 23, 25, 26. Somerset won by 17 runs. Somerset 23 pts, Gloucestershire ~~pts. Toss: Somerset. This match ran a course very similar to the first game of the ~~loucester Week, with the visitors providing the only major partnership and a young slow ~~owler, in this case the off-spinner Trump, contributing the best performance of his career. ~~he difference was that Trump won the match for his county, taking 14 wickets for 104, ~~uriously returning the same figures in each innings. On the first day, Hayhurst was in for ~~4 overs and his partnership with Tavaré was crucial. With Trump enjoying himself against ~~me sketchy batting, Gloucestershire saved the follow-on only through the efforts of their ~~st pair, Russell and Smith. After Walsh had taken five wickets for the second time in the ~~ame, Gloucestershire were left to make 221. For a time, Russell, continuing his excellent ~~atting form, looked as if he might secure victory, and at 187 for five Gloucestershire were ~~ inning. But Trump would not be denied: Russell was the first man in his hat-trick, ~~ollowed by Ball and Walsh, and his figures after tea were five wickets for four in 18 balls.
Close of play: First day, Gloucestershire 22-0 (G. D. Hodgson 14*, S. G. Hinks 5*); ~~econd day, Somerset 127-8 (H. R. J. Trump 0*, A. C. Cottam 1*).

~~omerset

~~. N. Hayhurst lbw b Walsh	97	– c Russell b Walsh	15
~~. N. Lathwell lbw b Walsh	0	– lbw b Walsh	0
~~. J. Harden c Alleyne b Smith	0	– st Russell b Davies	56
C. J. Tavaré lbw b Walsh	74	– b Smith	12
~~. J. Bartlett c Alleyne b Walsh	0	– c Athey b Scott	13
~~. D. Rose c Russell b Smith	3	– lbw b Walsh	6
N. D. Burns c Athey b Smith	4	– b Walsh	8
~~. A. Mallender lbw b Bawley	24	– c Alleyne b Davies	6
~~. R. J. Trump c Russell b Walsh	3	– not out	3
~~. C. Cottam lbw b Ball	31	– b Smith	3
~~. P. van Troost not out	3	– c Hodgson b Walsh	8
L-b 7, w 2, n-b 9	18	L-b 6, w 1, n-b 3	10

~~/10 2/16 3/147 4/147 5/164   257   1/1 2/32 3/72 4/105 5/105   140
~~/172 7/210 8/214 9/249   6/113 7/126 8/126 9/129

Bonus points – Somerset 3, Gloucestershire 4 (Score at 100 overs: 253-9).

Bowling: *First Innings*—Walsh 22–6–55–5; Smith 18–1–53–3; Scott 13–3–45–0; Ball ~~1–5–29–1; Davies 39.4–17–68–1. *Second Innings*—Walsh 12.4–2–30–5; Smith 12–2–25–2; ~~cott 7–0–31–1; Davies 16–4–31–2; Ball 5–0–17–0.

~~loucestershire

~~. D. Hodgson b Trump	14	– lbw b Mallender	14
~~. G. Hinks st Burns b Trump	18	– lbw b Lathwell	60
A. J. Wright c Tavaré b Mallender	12	– run out	8
~~. W. J. Athey c and b Trump	5	– b Trump	4
~~. W. Alleyne b Trump	0	– c and b Trump	5
~~R. C. Russell not out	58	– c Burns b Trump	41
~~. J. Scott c Burns b Trump	5	– not out	33
~~. C. J. Ball lbw b Trump	2	– c Lathwell b Trump	0
~~. A. Walsh c Rose b Trump	4	– lbw b Trump	0
~~. Davies lbw b van Troost	0	– c and b Trump	0
~~. M. Smith c Bartlett b Cottam	34	– lbw b Trump	6
L-b 13, n-b 12	25	B 12, l-b 18, n-b 2	32

~~/22 2/46 3/53 4/53 5/68   177   1/34 2/44 3/63 4/69 5/129   203
~~/81 7/83 8/87 9/88   6/187 7/187 8/191 9/191

Bonus points – Gloucestershire 1, Somerset 4.

Bowling: *First Innings*—Mallender 15–2–47–1; van Troost 16–2–50–1; Trump 25–6–52–7; Rose 7–0–14–0; Cottam 1.5–0–1–1. *Second Innings*—Mallender 12–4–29–1; van Troos 1–0–10–0; Trump 33.4–16–52–7; Rose 5–1–7–0; Cottam 29–5–66–0; Lathwell 6–3–9–1.

Umpires: J. H. Harris and R. A. White.

At Worcester, May 29, 30, June 1. WORCESTERSHIRE v GLOUCESTERSHIRE Abandoned.

At Manchester, June 5, 6, 8. GLOUCESTERSHIRE drew with LANCASHIRE.

GLOUCESTERSHIRE v KENT

At Bristol, June 16, 17, 18. Drawn. Gloucestershire 5 pts, Kent 6 pts. Toss: Gloucestershire Gloucestershire's last pair, Williams and Smith, survived 38 deliveries to save the gam after Kent had made nearly all the running. A green pitch had encouraged Wright to go i without a slow bowler and ask Kent to bat. Three wickets went cheaply, but Hoope steadied things and the recovery was completed by Cowdrey in a career-best five-hou innings in which he hit two sixes and 16 fours. With Walsh nursing a knee strain, the Ken middle order took heavy toll of some nondescript seam bowling, the tireless Babingto being an honourable exception: his return of eight for 107 was easily his best. Despit Wright's first century of the season, Gloucestershire looked likely to follow on until Benson with two bowlers injured, opted to open up the game instead. The visitors were allowed t declare 244 behind, and Kent were presented with 96 runs in eight overs, before Gloucester shire set off in pursuit of 341 in what turned out to be 102 overs. Alleyne alone could fin the right tempo as slow left-armer Davis, with little help from the conditions, worked hi way through, for another career-best performance.

Close of play: First day, Kent 456-8 (M. A. Ealham 50*, R. P. Davis 7*); Second day Gloucestershire 263-6 (T. H. C. Hancock 23*).

Kent

T. R. Ward b Walsh	12		
*M. R. Benson c Babington	10		
N. R. Taylor lbw b Babington	0		
C. L. Hooper c Williams b Babington	52		
G. R. Cowdrey c Hodgson b Babington	147		
M. V. Fleming c Williams b Babington	65		
†S. A. Marsh c Athey b Babington	86		
M. A. Ealham c sub b Babington	58	– (2) not out	6
R. M. Ellison c and b Babington	12	– (1) not out	2
R. P. Davis not out	32		
M. J. McCague c Hancock b Smith	13		
B 4, l-b 10, n-b 6	20		

1/18 2/23 3/23 4/122 5/226　　　　　507　　　　(no wkt dec.) 9
6/363 7/402 8/422 9/473

Bonus points – Kent 4, Gloucestershire 2 (Score at 100 overs: 386-6).

Bowling: *First Innings*—Walsh 20–5–55–1; Smith 26–4–128–1; Babington 30–4–107–8 Scott 16–3–68–0; Alleyne 9–1–67–0; Athey 9–0–45–0; Hancock 6–0–23–0. *Second Innings*—Walsh 2–0–4–0; Hodgson 4–0–65–0; Wright 2–0–27–0.

Gloucestershire

G. D. Hodgson c Hooper b Ealham	32	– b Hooper	75
S. G. Hinks c Hooper b McCague	50	– (8) c Benson b Davis	6
*A. J. Wright c Marsh b Hooper	128	– c sub b Davis	5
C. W. J. Athey c Marsh b Ealham	11	– (2) st Marsh b Davis	33
M. W. Alleyne lbw b Ealham	2	– (4) c Fleming b Davis	69
R. J. Scott c Benson b Hooper	1	– (5) b Davis	27
†H. C. Hancock not out	23	– (6) lbw b Davis	22
C. A. Walsh (did not bat)		– (7) c Hooper b Davis	0
†R. C. J. Williams (did not bat)		– not out	11
A. M. Babington (did not bat)		– b Hooper	4
A. M. Smith (did not bat)		– not out	4
B 3, l-b 7, n-b 6	16	B 5, l-b 6, w 1, n-b 4	16

1/44 2/166 3/194 4/208 5/213 (6 wkts dec.) 263 1/103 2/113 3/149 (9 wkts) 272
6/263 4/199 5/246 6/246
7/251 8/256 9/265

Bonus points – Gloucestershire 3, Kent 2 (Score at 100 overs: 252-5).

Bowling: *First Innings*—McCague 21–4–44–1; Ealham 18–5–45–3; Ellison 15–5–44–0; Hooper 33.3–5–73–2; Davis 16–6–47–0. *Second Innings*—Ellison 16–2–50–0; Ealham 12–2–38–0; Hooper 38–13–74–2; Davis 36–11–99–7.

Umpires: B. Leadbeater and G. Sharp.

GLOUCESTERSHIRE v WARWICKSHIRE

At Bristol, June 19, 20, 22. Warwickshire won by 75 runs. Warwickshire 23 pts, Gloucestershire 5 pts. Toss: Warwickshire. Donald and Walsh were the dominant personalities of a game won by Warwickshire mainly because they provided superior support for their main strike bowler. Ostler's 83, packed with attractive strokes, and a stubborn half-century from Rhodesian-born Penney, on his Championship début, enabled the visitors to recover from a poor start. With Alleyne going well, Gloucestershire looked like challenging for the lead until Donald's impressively fast spell after lunch on the second day. Walsh hit back with some equally demanding fast bowling, but Reeve stood firm, enabling Lloyd to set 260 in 72 overs. Hodgson and Athey provided a platform before the innings disintegrated against the quick bowlers, although the end was delayed by Smith's chirpy maiden fifty from 44 balls.

Close of play: First day, Gloucestershire 66-2 (C. W. J. Athey 32*, M. W. Alleyne 12*); Second day, Warwickshire 119-5 (D. A. Reeve 46*, P. A. Smith 4*).

Warwickshire

A. J. Moles b Walsh	5	– lbw b Walsh	4
R. G. Twose c Alleyne b Babington	21	– c Williams b Walsh	5
*T. A. Lloyd c Alleyne b Walsh	23	– c Wright b Walsh	22
D. P. Ostler c Williams b Davies	83	– lbw b Walsh	19
D. A. Reeve lbw b Hancock	27	– st Williams b Davies	72
T. L. Penney c Athey b Scott	55	– b Scott	9
P. A. Smith c Walsh b Davies	9	– c Alleyne b Scott	20
†K. J. Piper c Wright b Davies	0	– not out	26
G. C. Small c Alleyne b Walsh	7	– c Athey b Davies	5
A. A. Donald not out	10	– c Williams b Davies	2
T. A. Munton lbw b Scott	0	– not out	5
B 1, l-b 4, n-b 8	13	L-b 12, n-b 4	16

1/8 2/48 3/54 4/130 5/188 253 1/8 2/9 3/51 (9 wkts dec.) 205
6/212 7/212 8/228 9/253 4/62 5/104 6/163
7/171 8/176 9/184

Bonus points – Warwickshire 3, Gloucestershire 4.

Bowling: *First Innings*—Walsh 19.4–4–52–3; Babington 14–2–45–1; Smith 6–1–36–0; Davies 37–6–102–3; Hancock 2–0–4–1; Scott 6.3–1–9–2. *Second Innings*—Walsh 23–7–60–4; Babington 9–0–31–0; Davies 31–7–72–3; Smith 4–2–3–0; Scott 13–4–27–2.

Gloucestershire

G. D. Hodgson c Piper b Donald	4	– lbw b Munton	32
C. W. J. Athey c Piper b Reeve	43	– c Twose b Smith	19
*A. J. Wright b Donald	10	– c Reeve b Donald	15
M. W. Alleyne b Small	55	– c and b Small	22
R. J. Scott c Penney b Munton	50	– lbw b Donald	0
T. H. C. Hancock b Twose	0	– b Munton	11
†R. C. J. Williams c Piper b Donald	11	– c Piper b Munton	6
C. A. Walsh c Moles b Donald	13	– c Moles b Small	2
M. Davies b Munton	1	– c Donald b Munton	0
A. M. Babington b Donald	0	– (11) b Donald	9
A. M. Smith not out	0	– (10) not out	51
B 5, l-b 6, n-b 1	12	B 5, l-b 11, n-b 1	17

1/18 2/38 3/91 4/137 5/140   199   1/51 2/61 3/77 4/77 5/96   184
6/169 7/191 8/195 9/199   6/115 7/115 8/117 9/123

Bonus points – Gloucestershire 1, Warwickshire 4.

Bowling: *First Innings*—Donald 21–8–44–5; Small 16–4–43–1; Smith 2–0–13–0; Munton 23–5–53–2; Reeve 12–4–28–1; Twose 5–1–7–1. *Second Innings*—Donald 19–4–47–3; Small 13–4–34–2; Smith 6–1–27–1; Munton 24–10–60–4; Reeve 1–1–0–0.

Umpires: B. Leadbeater and G. Sharp.

GLOUCESTERSHIRE v SURREY

At Bristol, June 26, 27, 29. Surrey won by four wickets. Surrey 22 pts, Gloucestershire 5 pts. Toss: Surrey. Despite lacking four leading bowlers Surrey gained their first Championship victory of the season, in a match which came to life on the final afternoon after some desultory sparring over the first two days. Wright was denied the luxury of a declaration when Gloucestershire got themselves into a tangle against the persistent off-breaks of Boiling, who became the fourth young spinner to improve his career-best figures on a visit to Gloucestershire during the first half of the season. A target of 231 in 46 overs on such a sluggish pitch was by no means an easy one, and Surrey still needed 128 from the final 20 overs. Ten of them were bowled by Walsh, who allowed only 26 runs, a sterling effort. Runs were cheap at the other end, however, and Ward, missed at long-off when 21, swung the game as he suddenly rediscovered form, hitting three sixes and eight fours. Surrey got home with five balls to spare.

Close of play: First day, Gloucestershire 305-6 (R. C. Russell 42*, M. C. J. Ball 21*). Second day, Gloucestershire 13-1 (G. D. Hodgson 13*, S. G. Hinks 0*).

Gloucestershire

G. D. Hodgson c and b Boiling	68	– c Robinson b Murphy	37
C. W. J. Athey lbw b Boiling	57	– lbw b Murphy	0
S. G. Hinks c Boiling b Murphy	8	– c Robinson b Boiling	6
*A. J. Wright c Thorpe b Robinson	47	– b Boiling	31
M. W. Alleyne lbw b Feltham	46	– b Boiling	49
R. J. Scott c Lynch b Murphy	5	– (7) st Sargeant b Boiling	1
†R. C. Russell c Sargeant b Murphy	47	– (6) c Sargeant b Boiling	32
M. C. J. Ball not out	53	– c Lynch b Boiling	12
C. A. Walsh c Stewart b Boiling	4	– b Robinson	7
M. Davies b Boiling	1	– lbw b Robinson	0
A. M. Babington not out	3	– not out	0
B 4, l-b 5, w 1, n-b 3	13	L-b 1, w 1, n-b 1	3

1/104 2/115 3/163 4/211 5/216   (9 wkts dec.) 352   1/11 2/38 3/44 4/118 5/135   178
6/257 7/318 8/325 9/352   6/154 7/163 8/174 9/174

Bonus points – Gloucestershire 3, Surrey 2 (Score at 100 overs: 269-6).

Bowling: *First Innings*—Murphy 35–8–97–3; Butcher 10–3–20–0; Feltham 22–2–74–1; Robinson 9–0–33–1; Boiling 44–11–119–4. *Second Innings*—Murphy 18–5–41–2; Boiling 24.2–4–84–6; Feltham 10–2–38–0; Robinson 7–4–14–2.

Surrey

D. J. Bicknell run out	81	– lbw b Ball	13
*A. J. Stewart lbw b Walsh	6	– lbw b Davies	41
G. P. Thorpe lbw b Ball	75	– lbw b Scott	29
M. A. Lynch c Wright b Davies	24	– b Babington	33
D. M. Ward b Scott	0	– c Wright b Scott	82
†D. Robinson not out	65	– b Walsh	6
M. A. Feltham not out	38	– not out	11
M. A. Butcher (did not bat)	–	– not out	5
B 2, l-b 8, n-b 1	11	B 1, l-b 5, w 1, n-b 5	12

1/27 2/147 3/187 4/187 5/205 (5 wkts dec.) 300   1/31 2/83 3/91 (6 wkts) 232
4/166 5/179 6/219

†N. F. Sargeant, J. Boiling and A. J. Murphy did not bat.

Bonus points – Surrey 4, Gloucestershire 2.

Bowling: *First Innings*—Walsh 11–2–33–1; Babington 14–5–47–0; Davies 24–9–51–1; Ball 30.3–3–126–1; Scott 12–3–33–1. *Second Innings*—Walsh 14–1–38–1; Babington 9–0–62–1; Davies 12–1–76–1; Ball 15–1–25–1; Scott 5.1–0–25–2.

Umpires: V. A. Holder and M. J. Kitchen.

At Derby, June 30, July 1, 2. GLOUCESTERSHIRE drew with DERBYSHIRE.

At Stockton-on-Tees, July 3, 4, 6. GLOUCESTERSHIRE drew with DURHAM.

At Southend, July 14, 15, 16. GLOUCESTERSHIRE lost to ESSEX by four wickets.

GLOUCESTERSHIRE v YORKSHIRE

At Cheltenham College, July 17, 18, 20. Drawn. Gloucestershire 6 pts, Yorkshire 8 pts. Toss: Gloucestershire. Yorkshire still held a slight advantage when rain washed out the third day, but on the second afternoon they must have harboured hopes of victory by an innings. Moxon, in his most assured and punishing form, had put his side in the driving seat by batting for nearly seven hours to achieve the highest score for Yorkshire on the ground. He hit two sixes and 23 fours before he was eighth out. When the visiting seamers and Carrick reduced Gloucestershire to 103 for eight the follow-on seemed a certainty. But Yorkshire's attack grew more and more frustrated as Walsh thrashed 44 and Vaughan, in his second Championship game, found a surprisingly competent partner in Davies, who helped him put on 90 for the last wicket. When Moxon and Kellett fell cheaply in their second innings Gloucestershire were back in the match.

Close of play: First day, Yorkshire 339-7 (M. D. Moxon 171*, P. W. Jarvis 26*); Second day, Yorkshire 30-2 (J. D. Batty 4*, D. Byas 1*).

Yorkshire

*M. D. Moxon c Russell b Smith	183	– b Walsh	14
S. A. Kellett lbw b Walsh	50	– c Russell b Alleyne	7
D. Byas c Hodgson b Walsh	0	– (4) not out	1
S. R. Tendulkar c Russell b Scott	45		
†R. J. Blakey c Davies b Alleyne	1		
C. White c Russell b Alleyne	0		
P. J. Hartley c and b Alleyne	9		
P. Carrick b Smith	20		
P. W. Jarvis not out	30		
J. D. Batty c Vaughan b Walsh	0	– (3) not out	4
M. A. Robinson c Alleyne b Smith	4		
L-b 9, n-b 13	22	B 1, n-b 3	4

1/103 2/103 3/227 4/236 5/236 364   1/23 2/24 (2 wkts) 30
6/246 7/296 8/356 9/358

Bonus points – Yorkshire 4, Gloucestershire 3 (Score at 100 overs: 310-7).

Bowling: *First Innings*—Walsh 28-4-80-3; Smith 21.4-5-68-3; Vaughan 13-1-43-0; Davies 21-4-65-0; Scott 24-4-70-1; Alleyne 12-3-29-3. *Second Innings*—Walsh 5-0-21-1; Smith 3-0-4-0; Alleyne 3-2-4-1.

Gloucestershire

G. D. Hodgson c Blakey b Hartley	2	A. M. Smith c White b Jarvis	7
C. W. J. Athey c Byas b Jarvis	2	C. A. Walsh c Blakey b Hartley	44
R. I. Dawson c Blakey b Robinson	5	M. Davies not out	32
*A. J. Wright c Kellett b Hartley	24		
M. W. Alleyne c Blakey b Hartley	5	L-b 7, n-b 10	17
R. J. Scott st Blakey b Carrick	27		
†R. C. Russell c White b Carrick	12	1/4 2/4 3/36 4/42 5/45	257
J. T. C. Vaughan c Blakey b Hartley	80	6/84 7/93 8/103 9/167	

Bonus points – Gloucestershire 3, Yorkshire 4.

Bowling: Hartley 23.1-4-66-5; Jarvis 18-4-65-2; Robinson 19-3-59-1; Carrick 18-6-50-2; Batty 5-1-10-0.

Umpires: J. W. Holder and R. C. Tolchard.

GLOUCESTERSHIRE v HAMPSHIRE

At Cheltenham College, July 21, 22, 23. Drawn. Gloucestershire 7 pts, Hampshire 2 pts. Toss: Hampshire. When almost everyone had given the game up for dead, Nicholas suddenly declared, setting Gloucestershire 103 in nine overs. Scott hit five sixes as he led the scramble for runs, and Marshall had to return for the final over to ensure that Nicholas's quixotic gesture did not rebound. Gloucestershire finished eight runs short with three wickets standing. Without four leading batsmen, Hampshire found Walsh too much of a handful on the opening day. But the home team batted drearily until Alleyne and Russell changed the tempo in a partnership worth 158. Middleton and Morris, on his Championship début, launched Hampshire's second innings with a century stand, before two brilliant run-outs by Davies helped send the visitors to 137 for five, still 35 behind Marshall and Ayling, who was dropped three times, combined to thwart Gloucestershire who were then held up by the tail, until Nicholas decided on his gamble to revive his side's Championship hopes. But the draw cost Hampshire their second place, which they never regained.

Close of play: First day, Gloucestershire 26-0 (G. D. Hodgson 13*, R. J. Scott 11*); Second day, Gloucestershire 339-8 (J. T. C. Vaughan 13*, A. M. Smith 0*).

Hampshire

T. C. Middleton lbw b Walsh	64	– c and b Ball	47
R. S. M. Morris c Vaughan b Smith	4	– run out	64
R. M. F. Cox lbw b Ball	1	– run out	13
*M. C. J. Nicholas c Vaughan b Walsh	42	– c Russell b Walsh	1
M. D. Marshall c Alleyne b Walsh	5	– c Scott b Walsh	39
†A. N. Aymes b Walsh	9	– c Alleyne b Ball	1
J. R. Ayling c sub b Walsh	0	– c Ball b Walsh	48
S. D. Udal c Smith b Ball	4		
R. J. Maru c Russell b Walsh	15	– (8) not out	12
P. J. Bakker run out	8	– (9) c Wright b Scott	17
K. J. Shine not out	7	– (10) not out	22
L-b 3, n-b 5	8	B 7, l-b 3	10
1/15 2/28 3/108 4/120 5/129	167	1/102 2/127 3/129 (8 wkts dec.)	274
6/131 7/137 8/149 9/164		4/136 5/137 6/219	
		7/219 8/246	

Bonus points – Hampshire 1, Gloucestershire 4.

In the first innings S. D. Udal, when 4, retired hurt at 138 and resumed at 164.

Bowling: *First Innings*—Walsh 22-8-33-6; Smith 7-1-16-1; Ball 20.3-3-79-2; Vaughan 4-1-6-0; Scott 6-1-17-0; Alleyne 4-2-13-0. *Second Innings*—Walsh 27-10-57-3; Smith 8-2-24-0; Scott 9-2-42-1; Davies 9-1-30-0; Ball 26-6-93-2; Vaughan 6-2-18-0.

Gloucestershire

G. D. Hodgson c Ayling b Marshall	56	– c Aymes b Udal	4
R. J. Scott c Maru b Shine	41	– c Nicholas b Maru	42
C. W. J. Athey c Aymes b Ayling	25	– (4) c Aymes b Udal	4
*A. J. Wright c Aymes b Shine	8	– (6) run out	17
M. W. Alleyne b Ayling	86	– (3) c Cox b Udal	0
†R. C. Russell c Marshall b Maru	75	– (7) not out	20
T. C. Vaughan not out	13	– (8) run out	1
C. A. Walsh b Ayling	0	– (5) c Morris b Udal	5
M. C. J. Ball c Aymes b Ayling	2	– not out	0
A. M. Smith not out	0		
B 10, l-b 8, n-b 15	33	L-b 1, n-b 1	2

1/101 2/125 3/148 4/157 5/315 (8 wkts dec.) 339   1/6 2/6 3/21 4/49 (7 wkts) 95
6/321 7/321 8/339   5/70 6/89 7/93

M. Davies did not bat.

Bonus points – Gloucestershire 3, Hampshire 1 (Score at 100 overs: 250-4).

Bowling: *First Innings*—Marshall 26–11–47–1; Bakker 28–7–84–0; Shine 24–4–79–2; Ayling 18–3–49–4; Maru 26–6–62–1. *Second Innings*—Marshall 2.5–0–20–0; Udal 4–0–36–4; Maru 2–0–38–1.

Umpires: J. W. Holder and R. C. Tolchard.

GLOUCESTERSHIRE v SUSSEX

At Cheltenham College, July 24, 25, 27. Gloucestershire won by four wickets. Gloucestershire 22 pts, Sussex 8 pts. Toss: Sussex. The Gloucestershire batsmen had made such a poor fist of handling the spin of Donelan and Salisbury first time round that a Sussex victory looked all but inevitable when Wells declared and left the home side to make 346 in what proved to be 92 overs. When Hodgson, who had held the first innings together, retired before scoring, the outcome seemed pre-ordained. But Athey produced his highest, and one of his best, innings for Gloucestershire. He was well supported, first by Alleyne, who showed the slow bowlers could be hit, and then by the dogged Russell. Batting for just under five hours and hitting 25 fours, Athey gained complete mastery over the spinners, who were disappointing after their performance on the second day. When Athey holed out at long leg, Gloucestershire needed only 32, and Vaughan shepherded them home with five balls to spare. Sussex, for whom Lenham played two breezy innings, were left regretting a careless first-day collapse in which their last five wickets went for 23. The young Gloucestershire spinners, Ball and Davies, shared 12 wickets in the match.

Close of play: First day, Gloucestershire 43-0 (G. D. Hodgson 25*, C. W. J. Athey 12*); Second day, Sussex 169-6 (C. C. Remy 1*, B. T. P. Donelan 0*).

Sussex

D. M. Smith b Ball	61	– c Davies b Ball	23
J. W. Hall c Russell b Walsh	8	– c Athey b Davies	34
N. J. Lenham c Wright b Alleyne	83	– b Scott	52
*A. P. Wells st Russell b Davies	63	– c Hodgson b Davies	20
M. P. Speight c and b Babington	5	– lbw b Ball	7
†P. Moores c Russell b Walsh	48	– c Russell b Ball	29
C. C. Remy b Walsh	42	– c Walsh b Ball	16
B. T. P. Donelan lbw b Walsh	0	– not out	28
A. C. S. Pigott c Athey b Davies	0	– c Walsh b Ball	2
I. D. K. Salisbury c Athey b Davies	2	– lbw b Davies	24
E. S. H. Giddins not out	1		
B 5, l-b 4, n-b 2	11	B 4, l-b 1, w 1, n-b 1	7

1/13 2/109 3/202 4/209 5/243 324   1/56 2/68 3/102 (9 wkts dec.) 242
6/301 7/301 8/302 9/316   4/111 5/168 6/168
                                   7/191 8/201 9/242

Bonus points – Sussex 4, Gloucestershire 4.

Bowling: *First Innings*—Walsh 17.2–6–39–4; Babington 15–0–55–1; Vaughan 6–1–25–0; Scott 12–3–38–0; Ball 17–1–86–1; Davies 16–3–47–3; Alleyne 5–2–25–1. *Second Innings*—Walsh 6.5–2–19–0; Babington 1–0–14–0; Ball 25–2–101–5; Davies 20.3–1–84–3; Scott 5–0–19–1.

Gloucestershire

G. D. Hodgson c Wells b Salisbury	82 – retired hurt		0
C. W. J. Athey c Salisbury b Giddins	22 – c sub b Pigott		181
*A. J. Wright c Smith b Giddins	0 – c Moores b Giddins		21
M. W. Alleyne b Donelan	21 – c Moores b Salisbury		46
R. J. Scott c Wells b Donelan	1 – c Wells b Giddins		5
†R. C. Russell c Moores b Donelan	41 – c sub b Giddins		57
J. T. C. Vaughan c Wells b Donelan	8 – (8) not out		19
M. C. J. Ball c Moores b Donelan	4 – (9) not out		6
C. A. Walsh b Salisbury	2 – (7) b Pigott		0
M. Davies not out	2		
A. M. Babington c Salisbury b Donelan	15		
B 7, l-b 10, w 1, n-b 5	23	B 1, l-b 3, w 4, n-b 3	11

1/62 2/66 3/108 4/112 5/174	221	1/38 2/125 3/134 (6 wkts) 346
6/197 7/201 8/204 9/206		4/314 5/315 6/321

Bonus points – Gloucestershire 2, Sussex 4.

In the second innings G. D. Hodgson retired hurt at 0.

Bowling: *First Innings*—Pigott 3–1–5–0; Giddins 12–4–35–2; Remy 9–2–23–0; Donelan 36.2–13–77–6; Salisbury 30–9–64–2; Lenham 1–1–0–0. *Second Innings*—Pigott 13–0–48–2; Giddins 19.1–5–60–3; Donelan 29–4–102–0; Salisbury 27–4–120–1; Remy 3–0–12–0.

Umpires: R. Julian and B. J. Meyer.

At Worksop, August 4, 5, 6. GLOUCESTERSHIRE beat NOTTINGHAMSHIRE by ten runs.

At Lord's, August 7, 8, 10. GLOUCESTERSHIRE lost to MIDDLESEX by five wickets.

At Bristol, August 15, 16, 17. GLOUCESTERSHIRE lost to PAKISTANIS by 292 runs (See Pakistani tour section).

GLOUCESTERSHIRE v NORTHAMPTONSHIRE

At Bristol, August 18, 19, 20. Gloucestershire won by 39 runs. Gloucestershire 22 pts, Northamptonshire 7 pts. Toss: Northamptonshire. A stand of 141 between Hancock and Vaughan, who came together with Gloucestershire in crisis at 113 for six, prepared the way for a fifth victory and dealt Northamptonshire's Championship ambitions a severe blow. Hancock, especially, pushed on the scoring-rate so effectively that Gloucestershire gained maximum batting points before the steady Vaughan, who was in for four hours, was caught at slip on the brink of a maiden Championship hundred. Bailey, missed twice during his assertive 91, declared 95 behind and made every attempt to bowl out the opposition again; despite the loss of an hour to rain on the last morning no easy runs were on offer. Wright's declaration, setting 272 in 54 overs, was stiff but fair. While Bailey was in, Northamptonshire had hope, but no-one could provide productive support. After sustaining the challenge for close to 200 minutes he played on, another wicket for Walsh, and there were nine balls remaining when Davies claimed his 50th victim of the season.

Close of play: First day, Gloucestershire 346; Second day, Gloucestershire 70-2 (C. W. J. Athey 40*, M. W. Alleyne 6*).

Gloucestershire

C. W. J. Athey lbw b Taylor	4	– b Taylor	42
R. J. Scott c Ripley b Capel	41	– c Felton b Ambrose	2
*A. J. Wright b Penberthy	30	– c Felton b Capel	21
M. W. Alleyne c Fordham b Penberthy	0	– c Felton b Curran	48
R. I. Dawson c Felton b Ambrose	7	– c Cook b Curran	16
†R. C. Russell lbw b Capel	27	– b Taylor	1
T. H. C. Hancock c Curran b Capel	82	– b Curran	9
J. T. C. Vaughan c Capel b Cook	99	– not out	13
R. C. Williams lbw b Capel	0	– b Cook	6
C. A. Walsh c Taylor b Cook	27	– not out	10
M. Davies not out	9		
B 4, l-b 11, w 2, n-b 3	20	B 5, l-b 3	8

1/7 2/78 3/78 4/78 5/113   346   1/19 2/44 3/73   (8 wkts dec.) 176
6/113 7/254 8/254 9/312   4/110 5/133 6/137
                              7/145 8/158

Bonus points – Gloucestershire 4, Northamptonshire 4 (Score at 100 overs: 312-9).

Bowling: *First Innings*—Ambrose 13-6-26-1; Taylor 19-3-60-1; Curran 21-4-59-0; Capel 26-6-65-4; Penberthy 15-1-58-2; Cook 12-3-51-2; Bailey 3-0-12-0. *Second Innings*—Ambrose 5-2-4-1; Taylor 16-2-75-2; Curran 18-1-56-3; Capel 7-2-12-1; Cook 5-2-14-1; Bailey 1-0-7-0.

Northamptonshire

A. Fordham c and b Davies	16	– c Russell b Walsh	25
N. A. Felton c Scott b Hancock	43	– run out	0
*R. J. Bailey c Athey b Williams	91	– b Walsh	96
R. J. Warren lbw b Hancock	19	– (6) lbw b Davies	5
D. J. Capel c Dawson b Vaughan	36	– (4) run out	11
K. M. Curran c Athey b Vaughan	16	– (5) c and b Scott	23
†D. Ripley not out	9	– (8) b Vaughan	25
C. E. L. Ambrose not out	9	– (9) c Hancock b Vaughan	5
A. L. Penberthy (did not bat)	–	(7) c Hancock b Davies	23
J. P. Taylor (did not bat)	–	c Alleyne b Davies	5
N. G. B. Cook (did not bat)	–	not out	2
L-b 2, n-b 10	12	B 1, l-b 3, n-b 8	12

1/25 2/106 3/155 4/191   (6 wkts dec.) 251   1/8 2/49 3/70 4/108 5/125   232
5/223 6/238   6/170 7/211 8/223 9/226

Bonus points – Northamptonshire 3, Gloucestershire 2.

Bowling: *First Innings*—Walsh 22-8-38-0; Vaughan 14.4-5-38-2; Davies 12-3-34-1; Williams 14-2-56-1; Scott 6-0-32-0; Alleyne 4-0-8-0; Hancock 9-0-43-2. *Second Innings*—Walsh 17-4-50-2; Vaughan 8-1-25-2; Williams 10-0-48-0; Davies 9.3-0-51-3; Scott 8-0-54-1.

Umpires: J. W. Holder and K. E. Palmer.

At Swansea, August 21, 22, 24. GLOUCESTERSHIRE drew with GLAMORGAN.

At Canterbury, August 26, 27, 28, 29. GLOUCESTERSHIRE lost to KENT by 233 runs.

GLOUCESTERSHIRE v LEICESTERSHIRE

At Bristol, August 31, September 1, 2, 3. Drawn. Gloucestershire 4 pts, Leicestershire 3 pts. Toss: Leicestershire. The weather was so dismal that Gloucestershire's first innings was not concluded until after lunch on the fourth day. Then, after two forfeitures and the loss of eight more overs to rain, Leicestershire had barely begun their pursuit of 303 when the ground was flooded. Millns, trying to prove his fitness for the NatWest Trophy final, struggled to discover line or length in the stop-and-go proceedings, and Parsons was easily the most impressive bowler, with three for 13 in 11 overs. Hodgson and Hancock improved their averages while Vaughan and Russell ensured the fourth batting point. In the absence of Wright, injured in the nets, Athey was originally named captain by Gloucestershire. But when he announced that he was leaving the county, Walsh took over.

Close of play: First day, No play; Second day, Gloucestershire 63-0 (G. D. Hodgson 40*, R. J. Scott 18*); Third day, Gloucestershire 157-3 (G. D. Hodgson 76*, T. H. C. Hancock 45*).

Gloucestershire

G. D. Hodgson c Nixon b Millns	81	M. C. J. Ball not out	9
R. J. Scott c Benson b Benjamin	24	M. Davies not out	4
M. W. Alleyne c Benjamin b Parsons	1	B 3, l-b 9, w 3, n-b 2	17
C. W. J. Athey lbw b Benjamin	1		
T. H. C. Hancock c Mullally b Potter	74	1/73 2/80 3/85	(7 wkts dec.) 302
J. T. C. Vaughan c Millns b Parsons	51	4/188 5/194	
†R. C. Russell lbw b Parsons	40	6/288 7/289	

*C. A. Walsh and M. J. Gerrard did not bat.

Bonus points – Gloucestershire 4, Leicestershire 3.

Bowling: Millns 20-5-80-1; Mullally 12-2-37-0; Benjamin 12-2-35-2; Wells 15-3-45-0; Parsons 11-6-13-3; Potter 12-3-28-1; Benson 10-2-27-0; Boon 4-0-21-0; Whitaker 0.1-0-4-0.

Gloucestershire forfeited their second innings.

Leicestershire

Leicestershire forfeited their first innings.

T. J. Boon not out	14
*N. E. Briers not out	10

(no wkt) 24

J. J. Whitaker, V. J. Wells, J. D. R. Benson, L. Potter, †P. A. Nixon, A. D. Mullally, W. K. M. Benjamin, G. J. Parsons and D. J. Millns did not bat.

Bowling: Walsh 4.1-1-13-0; Gerrard 4-1-11-0.

Umpires: J. W. Holder and P. B. Wight.

GLOUCESTERSHIRE v ESSEX

At Bristol, September 12, 13, 14, 15. Gloucestershire won by seven wickets. Gloucestershire 23 pts, Essex 2 pts. Toss: Gloucestershire. Gloucestershire's season ended in triumph as one of the youngest teams the county can have fielded for years got the better of the champions. It was, however, the old hand Walsh who laid the foundations of victory with another incisive and superbly varied display of fast bowling, after he had put Essex in. Alleyne, who had a splendid all-round game, set up Gloucestershire's lead of 198, but Windows also contributed handsomely. His crisp strokes showed remarkable assurance for a 19-year-old on his first-class début. Essex fought with great determination to escape from yet another tight corner. Stephenson batted nearly five hours and although three wickets fell at 227, Essex rallied again when Gooch and Topley added 107. Gooch, who had handed the

aptaincy to Prichard again, took more than four hours over his 99th hundred, which
included only five fours. After he holed out the last three wickets fell quickly. Sensibly,
Gloucestershire decided on a bold approach in pursuing 185 from 46 overs. Scott led the
charge, hitting three sixes, before Alleyne took control with an unbeaten 73 at a run a ball.
Gloucestershire won with nearly seven overs to spare.

Close of play: First day, Gloucestershire 175-3 (M. W. Alleyne 93*, M. G. N. Windows
8*); Second day, Essex 24-0 (N. V. Knight 13*, J. P. Stephenson 10*); Third day, Essex
65-5 (G. A. Gooch 26*, M. A. Garnham 11*).

Essex

N. V. Knight c Russell b Walsh	4	– c and b Ball	46
J. P. Stephenson c Russell b Gerrard	1	– b Gerrard	93
J. B. Lewis c Alleyne b Walsh	2	– b Ball	53
P. J. Prichard lbw b Walsh	30	– b Davies	22
N. Shahid lbw b Gerrard	0	– c Vaughan b Davies	0
G. A. Gooch b Walsh	28	– c Windows b Alleyne	101
M. A. Garnham b Walsh	17	– c Vaughan b Gerrard	11
T. D. Topley b Walsh	5	– c Russell b Walsh	29
M. C. Ilott c Vaughan b Davies	28	– c Hodgson b Alleyne	2
P. M. Such c Russell b Walsh	9	– c Hodgson b Alleyne	4
S. J. W. Andrew not out	0	– not out	0
L-b 4	4	B 1, l-b 15, w 1, n-b 4	21

1/4 2/6 3/20 4/20 5/63   128   1/113 2/188 3/227 4/227 5/227   382
6/74 7/89 8/94 9/118   6/266 7/373 8/377 9/377

Bonus points – Gloucestershire 4.

Bowling: *First Innings*—Walsh 18-5-38-7; Gerrard 16-6-51-2; Vaughan 6-2-15-0; Scott
4-1-13-0; Davies 2.3-0-7-1. *Second Innings*—Walsh 32-5-69-1; Gerrard 25-4-71-2;
Davies 37-21-30-2; Ball 33-7-81-2; Scott 15-0-49-0; Vaughan 15-2-41-0; Alleyne
6.1-6-25-3.

Gloucestershire

G. D. Hodgson b Ilott	7	– c Garnham b Andrew	27
R. J. Scott b Ilott	6	– c Topley b Shahid	73
M. W. Alleyne c Topley b Gooch	93	– not out	73
T. H. C. Hancock c Topley b Andrew	25	– c Ilott b Shahid	0
M. G. N. Windows c Shahid b Topley	71		
J. T. C. Vaughan b Andrew	29		
†R. C. Russell b Ilott	16	– (5) not out	7
M. C. J. Ball c Garnham b Andrew	7		
M. Davies c Topley b Andrew	22		
C. A. Walsh not out	26		
M. J. Gerrard c Garnham b Topley	4		
B 1, l-b 8, w 6, n-b 5	20	L-b 6, n-b 1	7

1/8 2/26 3/105 4/178 5/240   326   1/67 2/170 3/180   (3 wkts) 187
6/255 7/274 8/274 9/304

Bonus points – Gloucestershire 3, Essex 2 (Score at 100 overs: 255-5).

Bowling: *First Innings*—Ilott 33-5-111-3; Andrew 32-7-58-4; Topley 20.2-3-75-2;
Stephenson 7-2-19-0; Such 16-6-27-0; Gooch 20-8-27-1. *Second Innings*—Ilott 10-2-43-0;
Andrew 8-1-39-1; Such 14-1-55-0; Shahid 5-1-22-2; Topley 2.2-0-22-0.

Umpires: G. I. Burgess and R. Julian.

HAMPSHIRE

President: W. J. Weld
Chairman: D. Rich
Chairman, Cricket Committee: J. R. Gray
Chief Executive: A. F. Baker
  Northlands Road, Southampton SO9 2TY
  (Telephone: 0703-333788)
Captain: M. C. J. Nicholas
Coach: T. M. Tremlett

Hampshire won the Benson and Hedges Cup and finished third in the
Sunday League, a record that would have provided enough of a glow to
keep the members of most counties warm all winter. Most Hampshire
members felt a chill instead. Unfortunately, the Cup Final came in
mid-July when Hampshire were lying second in the Championship
table. It is the two months after that which will linger in the memory.
Hampshire failed to win another Championship match and collapsed to
15th in the final table.

Even the triumph at Lord's itself – convincing and well-executed
though it was – was something of an anticlimax. The weather forced
the match into a second day and by the time Mark Nicholas received
the trophy (Hampshire's second Lord's win in a row following the
NatWest win in 1991) the ground was half-empty. By then, it was
already possible to discern the signs of a collapse in the form of what
Nicholas regarded as the strongest and best-balanced squad he had led
in his eight years as captain.

There is no problem pinpointing the moment of truth: June 22, the
final day of the game against Essex at Bournemouth. Hampshire had
easily won three of their opening four Championship matches, against
Sussex, Surrey and Lancashire, generating a belief that Nicholas had
been right to suggest that Hampshire could realistically hope to be
champions. They were still leaders when they came to Bournemouth
and, on the third morning, appeared on the edge of a fourth victory
with Essex 46 adrift and six second-innings wickets standing. One lost
chance was disastrous: Tony Middleton missed Mike Garnham at
fourth slip – not his regular position – and Garnham went on to add 82
more for the eighth wicket with Derek Pringle. Hampshire still needed
only 160 and began the last 20 overs with 125 needed and eight wickets
left. Next ball, David Gower was brilliantly caught at deep cover by
Paul Prichard and Hampshire collapsed spectacularly to 80 all out.

They actually won the next Championship match, a rain-affected
game against Sussex at Arundel in which Malcolm Marshall claimed
his 1,500th first-class wicket. But of the remaining 12 games, they lost
five, drew seven and collected just 58 points, compared to 124 in the
first half of the season. During that period there were stark examples of
batting fragility from a line-up that, in theory, was one of the strongest
in the country: in successive matches in August Kent bowled them out
for 70, the lowest first-class score of the entire season, and Northamptonshire for 100. It was small consolation that, in the same period,

Hampshire were quietly coming through on the rails to get third place in the Sunday League: their successes included wins over both the winners Middlesex and runners-up Essex.

The major bonus of the season was the emergence of Middleton as a dependable opening batsman. He was the first player in the country to reach 1,000 runs and, though his method was thoroughly unexciting, he regularly laid foundations on which the more daring strokeplayers might have built large totals. Unfortunately, they rarely did so. Robin Smith's appearances were inevitably restricted by Test matches but when he did play he had his least successful season in county cricket. After a century in the opening first-class match, he passed fifty only four times in 19 innings. Gower's early-season form ensured that he won back his England place; after that, he seemed to lose his appetite for humdrum occasions and he failed to score a fifty in his last 12 Championship innings. The unluckiest player was Paul Terry, who looked in his best form since he was picked for England in 1984 but suffered a dislocated thumb against Surrey and then had his season prematurely terminated by an attack of sciatica.

Hampshire's attack was also inconsistent. Marshall bowled as enthusiastically as ever but, at 34, his figures became a little more mundane: only 49 Championship wickets from 529 overs at 27.51. As usual, he was short of a consistent opening partner. In May, Kevin Shine made his long-awaited breakthrough by taking eight for 47 on an Old Trafford wicket which had defeated every other bowler in the match; yet all too often he looked like a raw novice. The most encouraging progress was made by the off-spinner Shaun Udal, who won the opening match against Sussex by taking eight for 50 and passed a hundred wickets in all competitions; he was especially effective in one-day cricket. Late in the season, the seamer Jon Ayling and left-arm spinner Ian Turner also offered hope for the future.

In September, Hampshire announced that Bobby Parks, the most successful wicket-keeper in the county's history, had no further part in their plans. He had already lost his first-team place in 1990. However, a knee injury to his successor Adrian Aymes in June enabled him to return to the team for five games when he took the opportunity, which he feared he would miss, to beat Neil McCorkell's Hampshire record of 688 dismissals. Parks finished with exactly 700. Another, even longer-lasting era, also came to an end in August after the Middlesex match, when Hampshire left Dean Park, Bournemouth for economic reasons. Barring a new accommodation between the club and the ground's owner, which seemed improbable, first-class cricket has now ceased on one of the best-loved grounds on the circuit and one deeply embedded in the soul of Hampshire cricket. – Mike Neasom.

HAMPSHIRE 1992

[*Bill Smith*]

Back row: J. S. Laney, J. N. B. Bovill, T. C. Middleton, R. S. M. Morris, I. J. Turner, D. P. J. Flint, R. M. F. Cox. *Middle row*: R. E. Hayward (*assistant coach*), N. R. Taylor, A. N. Aymes, J. R. Ayling, S. D. Udal, K. J. Shine, M. J. Thursfield, J. R. Wood, T. M. Tremlett (*coach*). *Front row*: C. A. Connor, R. J. Maru, R. A. Smith, V. P. Terry, M. C. J. Nicholas (*captain*), D. I. Gower, R. J. Parks, P. J. Bakker, K. D. James. *Inset*: M. D. Marshall.

HAMPSHIRE RESULTS

All first-class matches – Played 24: Won 5, Lost 7, Drawn 12.

County Championship matches – Played 22: Won 4, Lost 6, Drawn 12.

Bonus points – Batting 61, Bowling 57.

Competition placings – Britannic Assurance County Championship, 15th; NatWest Bank Trophy, 2nd round; Benson and Hedges Cup, winners; Sunday League, 3rd.

BRITANNIC ASSURANCE CHAMPIONSHIP AVERAGES

BATTING

	Birthplace	M	I	NO	R	HS	Avge
‡V. P. Terry	Osnabruck, WG	11	17	2	766	141	51.06
‡T. C. Middleton	Winchester	22	37	4	1,628	221	49.33
‡D. I. Gower	Tunbridge Wells	16	26	5	1,005	155	47.85
‡M. C. J. Nicholas. . .	London	20	30	5	972	95*	38.88
‡R. A. Smith	Durban, SA	11	18	2	599	107*	37.43
‡K. D. James	Lambeth	21	33	2	1,006	116	32.45
J. R. Wood	Winchester	8	9	1	244	57	30.50
‡M. D. Marshall§	St Michael, Barbados	19	25	5	513	70	25.65
‡R. J. Parks	Cuckfield	5	7	2	125	33	25.00
R. S. M. Morris	Great Horwood	4	8	0	198	74	24.75
‡A. N. Aymes	Southampton	17	21	4	336	65	19.76
‡J. R. Ayling	Portsmouth	17	25	1	472	90	19.66
‡S. D. Udal	Farnborough, Hants	21	26	8	346	44	19.22
‡C. A. Connor	The Valley, Anguilla	16	13	5	127	51	15.87
‡P. J. Bakker	Vlaardingen, Netherlands	5	5	1	63	22	15.75
K. J. Shine	Bracknell	14	10	6	59	22*	14.75
‡R. J. Maru	Nairobi, Kenya	6	8	3	71	23*	14.20
I. J. Turner	Denmead	6	7	1	31	16	5.16

Also batted: R. M. F. Cox (*Guildford*) (3 matches) 1, 13, 12.

* *Signifies not out.*   ‡ *Denotes county cap.*   § *Overseas player.*

The following played a total of 11 three-figure innings for Hampshire in County Championship matches – T. C. Middleton 5, V. P. Terry 3, D. I. Gower 1, K. D. James 1, R. A. Smith 1.

BOWLING

	O	M	R	W	BB	5W/i	Avge
J. R. Ayling	326.2	69	939	43	5-12	1	21.83
R. J. Maru	157.2	54	331	15	4-8	0	22.06
I. J. Turner	182.4	51	519	19	5-81	1	27.31
M. D. Marshall	529	134	1,348	49	6-58	1	27.51
K. J. Shine	289.5	40	1,161	38	8-47	3	30.55
P. J. Bakker	137	43	363	11	4-38	0	33.00
S. D. Udal	637.2	156	1,867	50	8-50	1	37.34
C. A. Connor	417.2	69	1,386	32	5-58	1	43.31
K. D. James	230.3	52	705	12	2-23	0	58.75

Also bowled: A. N. Aymes 7–0–75–1; T. C. Middleton 10–0–57–0; M. C. J. Nicholas 22.3–2–71–2; R. A. Smith 8.1–0–41–0.

Wicket-keepers: A. N. Aymes 46 ct, 4 st; R. J. Parks 15 ct, 1 st; R. A. Smith 1 ct.

Leading Fielder: T. C. Middleton 15.

HAMPSHIRE v SUSSEX

At Southampton, April 25, 27, 28, 29. Hampshire won by 150 runs. Hampshire 20 pts, Sussex 1 pt. Toss: Sussex. A remarkable display of flight and control from off-spinner Udal, who did not appear in the Championship in 1991, bowled Hampshire to victory, after a weakened Sussex agreed a formula to revive a match nearly killed by rain. Wells had every reason to regret his decision to field, as he watched Hampshire's first three score centuries, emulating the county's feat against the 1901 South Africans. Terry reached his 25th first-class hundred in an opening stand of 246 with Middleton, who piled up a career-best 153; Smith was unbeaten on 107 with Gower looking good to make it four when the weather intervened and Nicholas finally declared. More rain washed out the third day. On the final morning Hampshire offered Sussex cheap runs – their wicket-keeper gave away 75 in seven overs – and then forfeited their second innings, leaving Sussex to chase 300 in 69 overs. Udal ensured they never had a chance, bowling Remy with his first ball after lunch and finishing with eight for 50 in 23 overs – his first haul of more than four – as Hampshire cruised home with 21 overs to spare.

Close of play: First day, Hampshire 334-1 (T. C. Middleton 145*, R. A. Smith 39*); Second day, Sussex 50-1 (D. M. Smith 17*, B. T. P. Donelan 3*); Third day, No play.

Hampshire

V. P. Terry c Jones b Robson	141
T. C. Middleton b Jones	153
R. A. Smith not out	107
D. I. Gower not out	55
B 1, l-b 3, w 6, n-b 2	12

1/246 2/373   (2 wkts dec.) 468

*M. C. J. Nicholas, K. D. James, M. D. Marshall, †A. N. Aymes, S. D. Udal, K. J. Shine and C. A. Connor did not bat.

Bonus points – Hampshire 4 (Score at 100 overs: 308-1).

Bowling: Stephenson 23–8–53–0; Robson 33–8–94–1; Jones 25–3–96–1; Pigott 22.2–1–95–0; Donelan 31–5–90–0; Greenfield 11–0–36–0.

Hampshire forfeited their second innings.

Sussex

D. M. Smith c and b Aymes	61 – b Udal	8
C. C. Remy c James b Connor	26 – b Udal	13
B. T. P. Donelan not out	68 – (8) lbw b Udal	14
K. Greenfield not out	10 – (3) b Udal	0
*A. P. Wells (did not bat)	– (4) c Marshall b Udal	25
R. Hanley (did not bat)	– (5) st Aymes b Udal	1
†P. Moores (did not bat)	– (6) c Nicholas b Marshall	29
F. D. Stephenson (did not bat)	– (7) b Udal	29
A. C. S. Pigott (did not bat)	– c Marshall b Udal	12
A. N. Jones (did not bat)	– c Nicholas b Connor	1
A. G. Robson (did not bat)	– not out	0
N-b 4	4 B 1, l-b 9, w 1, n-b 6	17

1/46 2/148   (2 wkts dec.) 169   1/27 2/27 3/56 4/59 5/66   149
                                         6/119 7/120 8/144 9/149

Bonus point – Sussex 1.

Bowling: *First Innings*—Marshall 5–0–16–0; Connor 6–3–4–1; Shine 5–2–6–0; Udal 8–1–8–0; James 3–0–16–0; Aymes 7–0–75–1; Middleton 6–0–44–0. *Second Innings*—Marshall 10–1–44–1; Connor 9–2–25–1; Udal 23–12–50–8; Shine 6–1–20–0.

Umpires: M. J. Kitchen and R. Palmer.

At Leeds, May 7, 8, 9, 10. HAMPSHIRE drew with YORKSHIRE.

At Oxford, May 15, 16, 18. HAMPSHIRE beat OXFORD UNIVERSITY by 161 runs.

HAMPSHIRE v SURREY

At Southampton, May 19, 20, 21, 22. Hampshire won by ten wickets. Hampshire 24 pts, Surrey 1 pt. Toss: Hampshire. Middleton's patient application and Marshall's cutting edge combined to sweep Hampshire to victory with almost a day to spare. Middleton eased to his third hundred of the season, and then expanded it to a maiden double-century as Hampshire built an impregnable first-innings total. In all he batted nine hours, hitting one six and 19 fours. He shared an opening partnership of 267 with Terry, their second over 200 in three innings. Kendrick's career-best six wickets cost him 164 runs. Surrey were then swept away by Marshall's controlled swing, which brought him six for 58, and followed on 368 behind. The brothers Bicknell and Thorpe restored some pride to Surrey's second innings. Hampshire claimed the extra half-hour on the third day but failed to finish Surrey off then. However, on the final morning Surrey lost their remaining three wickets after Martin Bicknell, with his highest score of 88, and Kendrick had extended their eighth-wicket stand to 103. Hampshire required only two runs to win; James shared them with Middleton, as Terry had dislocated his thumb in catching Robinson.

Close of play: First day, Hampshire 351-2 (T. C. Middleton 162*, K. D. James 21*); Second day, Surrey 163-6 (G. P. Thorpe 15*, J. D. Robinson 33*); Third day, Surrey 295-7 (M. P. Bicknell 43*, N. M. Kendrick 16*).

Hampshire

V. P. Terry c and b Kendrick	131		
T. C. Middleton c Kendrick b Bryson	221	– (1) not out	1
D. I. Gower c and b Kendrick	3		
K. D. James c Lynch b Bryson	35	– (2) not out	1
R. Wood st Sargeant b Kendrick	38		
*M. D. Marshall c and b Kendrick	10		
J. R. Ayling c M. P. Bicknell b Kendrick	14		
†A. N. Aymes not out	22		
R. J. Maru c Lynch b Kendrick	2		
C. A. Connor c Sargeant b Bryson	8		
S. D. Udal not out	24		
B 4, l-b 16, w 1, n-b 23	44		

1/267 2/273 3/384 4/452 5/479 (9 wkts dec.) 552   (no wkt) 2
6/495 7/496 8/499 9/511

Bonus points – Hampshire 4 (Score at 100 overs: 322-2).

Bowling: *First Innings*—Bryson 35-4-119-3; M. P. Bicknell 38-9-109-0; Benjamin 34-1-104-0; Robinson 9-2-27-0; Kendrick 45.5-9-164-6; Lynch 3-1-9-0. *Second Innings*—Lynch 0.4-0-2-0.

Surrey

D. J. Bicknell c Aymes b Marshall	23	– b Udal	71
P. D. Atkins c Middleton b Maru	7	– c Aymes b Ayling	1
G. P. Thorpe c Aymes b Marshall	16	– c Maru b Marshall	50
*M. A. Lynch c Terry b Ayling	21	– lbw b Udal	32
D. M. Ward c Wood b Marshall	45	– lbw b Connor	30
J. D. Robinson c Terry b Marshall	34	– c Terry b Connor	21
†N. F. Sargeant b Marshall	0	– b Marshall	9
M. P. Bicknell lbw b Marshall	4	– c Gower b Maru	88
N. M. Kendrick c Aymes b Connor	6	– lbw b Maru	26
R. E. Bryson not out	4	– c Gower b Maru	9
J. E. Benjamin run out	5	– not out	1
L-b 2, n-b 17	19	L-b 13, w 2, n-b 16	31

1/32 2/38 3/81 4/118 5/136 184   1/15 2/98 3/145 4/183 5/203 369
6/141 7/164 8/175 9/175   6/228 7/233 8/336 9/358

Bonus points – Surrey 1, Hampshire 4.

In the first innings G. P. Thorpe, when 4, retired hurt at 38 and resumed at 141.

Bowling: *First Innings*—Marshall 19.3–6–58–6; Connor 13–3–38–1; Maru 13–5–31–1; Ayling 5–1–15–1; Udal 10–3–40–0. *Second Innings*—Connor 30–7–77–2; Marshall 26–9–72–2; Ayling 16–3–58–1; Udal 30–8–73–2; James 6–0–20–0; Maru 26.4–9–56–3.

Umpires: N. T. Plews and P. B. Wight.

At Manchester, May 23, 25, 26. HAMPSHIRE beat LANCASHIRE by 172 runs.

HAMPSHIRE v DURHAM

At Southampton, May 29, 30, June 1. Drawn. Hampshire 6 pts, Durham 8 pts. Toss: Hampshire. Torrential rain on the final day, which left the ground submerged, wrecked an intriguing match when Durham were 183 runs ahead with eight second-innings wickets standing. John Wood made a sensational Championship début, removing Middleton and Gower with the first and sixth balls of his opening over, and adding Smith 28 runs later. James, aided by Julian Wood, averted total disaster, with a fifth-wicket partnership of 83, but Durham's first-innings lead was 96, and they built on that steadily before the weather intervened. Durham's own first innings was one of fluctuating fortunes. They seemed to be squandering an explosive start by Larkins and Parker, which brought 81 in only 18 overs, when they slumped to 107 for four after a short break for rain. But Glendenen, batting at No. 5 because of a scratched retina, and Botham pulled them round, sharing 99 runs in 23 overs, and a ninth-wicket stand of 63 between Graveney and Hughes made maximum bonus points possible.

Close of play: First day, Durham 265-8 (D. A. Graveney 18*, S. P. Hughes 15*); Second day, Durham 87-2 (D. M. Jones 20*, S. P. Hughes 0*).

Durham

W. Larkins c Nicholas b Shine	45	– lbw b Ayling	26
P. W. G. Parker lbw b Connor	41		
D. M. Jones b Connor	4	– not out	20
P. Bainbridge c Smith b James	6		
J. D. Glendenen c Gower b Connor	64	– (2) c and b Connor	38
I. T. Botham c Aymes b Connor	51		
†C. W. Scott b Ayling	3		
J. Wood c Connor b James	1		
*D. A. Graveney lbw b Connor	33		
S. P. Hughes b Shine	40	– (4) not out	0
S. J. E. Brown not out	0		
L-b 16, w 1, n-b 1	18	N-b 3	3

1/84 2/94 3/94 4/107 5/206   306   1/50 2/82   (2 wkts) 87
6/226 7/230 8/236 9/299

Bonus points – Durham 4, Hampshire 4.

Bowling: *First Innings*—Connor 27–10–58–5; Shine 24.4–3–99–2; Udal 12–2–38–0; Ayling 13–2–50–1; James 18–7–45–2. *Second Innings*—Connor 12–1–34–1; Shine 5–1–18–0; Ayling 2–0–17–1; Udal 4–0–18–0.

Hampshire

T. C. Middleton c Scott b Wood	0	S. D. Udal not out	14
K. D. James c Botham b Graveney	62	C. A. Connor b Graveney	0
D. I. Gower c Larkins b Wood	0	K. J. Shine b Wood	5
R. A. Smith c Bainbridge b Wood	25		
*M. C. J. Nicholas lbw b Botham	27	L-b 6, w 1	7
J. R. Wood lbw b Brown	57		
J. R. Ayling c Scott b Brown	6	1/0 2/0 3/28 4/62 5/145 210
†A. N. Aymes c Bainbridge b Wood	7	6/165 7/189 8/203 9/203

Bonus points – Hampshire 2, Durham 4.

Bowling: Wood 15.4–2–68–5; Brown 13–2–59–2; Hughes 13–2–25–0; Botham 8–2–14–1; Graveney 17–3–38–2.

Umpires: D. J. Constant and R. Julian.

HAMPSHIRE v YORKSHIRE

At Basingstoke, June 2, 3, 4. Drawn. Hampshire 7 pts, Yorkshire 3 pts. Toss: Yorkshire. A match neutered by a slow, low pitch was memorable merely for Gower's elegant century – his 49th, but only his second in the Championship for Hampshire. It was an impressive demonstration of the former England captain's determination to answer criticism by his deeds. After Yorkshire had been dismissed for 210, with Dutchman Bakker claiming four for 38 as he deputised for the injured Marshall and Shine, Gower alone truly mastered a grudging surface. Only one other player, James, reached 50. Gower's first 50 took just over an hour, but he then curbed his instincts and it took another two and a half hours to chisel out the second. He was finally dismissed for 155, having batted 289 minutes, faced 247 deliveries and hit 18 boundaries. Hampshire took a lead of 141, with a shade over a day to seek victory; Yorkshire were determined they would fail and suffocated the match, scoring 211 in the 104 overs possible on the final day before light rain brought a merciful release.

Close of play: First day, Hampshire 30-0 (T. C. Middleton 15*, K. D. James 15*); Second day, Yorkshire 11-0 (S. A. Kellett 5*, A. A. Metcalfe 5*).

Yorkshire

S. A. Kellett run out	29	– c Aymes b Ayling	37
*A. A. Metcalfe lbw b Bakker	39	– c Maru b Connor	38
D. Byas b Bakker	24	– c Udal b Bakker	4
S. R. Tendulkar b Bakker	0	– b James	34
†R. J. Blakey c Aymes b Ayling	20	– lbw b James	38
C. White c Middleton b Bakker	10	– not out	35
P. Carrick lbw b Maru	18	– c Wood b Udal	4
P. J. Hartley b Udal	46	– c Maru b Udal	0
D. Gough b Ayling	8	– not out	9
P. W. Jarvis not out	9		
J. D. Batty c Aymes b Ayling	1		
L-b 6	6	B 12, l-b 8, n-b 3	23
	210	(7 wkts)	222

1/44 2/95 3/95 4/96 5/116 6/130 7/171 8/199 9/199

1/79 2/86 3/95 4/133 5/187 6/194 7/194

Bonus points – Yorkshire 2, Hampshire 4 (Score at 100 overs: 210-9).

Bowling: *First Innings*—Connor 17–5–52–0; Bakker 22–8–38–4; James 14–6–35–0; Maru 13–5–17–1; Udal 15–8–21–1; Ayling 19.3–5–41–3. *Second Innings*—Connor 21–5–45–1; Bakker 21–9–34–1; Maru 13–5–22–0; Udal 32–15–49–2; Ayling 12–4–28–1; James 11–2–23–2; Nicholas 1–0–1–0.

Hampshire

T. C. Middleton lbw b Hartley	21	S. D. Udal lbw b Batty	12
K. D. James c Byas b Batty	59	C. A. Connor b Batty	0
D. I. Gower c Blakey b Batty	155		
*M. C. J. Nicholas b Carrick	27	L-b 8	8
J. R. Wood c Blakey b Gough	32		
J. R. Ayling lbw b Gough	0	1/50 2/150 3/196 (9 wkts dec.)	351
†A. N. Aymes not out	37	4/268 5/268 6/321	
R. J. Maru c Blakey b Tendulkar	0	7/322 8/351 9/351	

P. J. Bakker did not bat.

Bonus points – Hampshire 3, Yorkshire 1 (Score at 100 overs: 258-3).

Bowling: Hartley 28–6–70–1; Gough 24–8–79–2; Jarvis 17–3–52–0; Carrick 15–4–34–1; Batty 27.4–7–75–4; Tendulkar 8–0–33–1.

Umpires: D. J. Constant and R. Julian.

At Birmingham, June 12, 13, 15. HAMPSHIRE drew with WARWICKSHIRE.

At Leicester, June 16, 17, 18. HAMPSHIRE drew with LEICESTERSHIRE.

HAMPSHIRE v ESSEX

At Bournemouth, June 19, 20, 22. Essex won by 79 runs. Essex 19 pts, Hampshire 8 pts. Toss: Essex. Essex snatched an improbable victory by claiming the last eight wickets for 45 runs in 17 overs in the last hour. Hampshire, top of the table, had dominated the first two days after being put in; they claimed maximum batting points, thanks largely to a fine 81 by captain Nicholas, and later enforced the follow-on. When the final day started Essex were still 46 behind with six wickets standing, and a second consecutive innings defeat was not out of the question. But a spirited 48 by Shahid revived their ambitions and a 106-run eighth-wicket partnership between Garnham and Pringle made Hampshire's task harder than seemed likely: 160 in 31 overs. But they were still favourites when Pringle removed Gower with the first ball of the last 20 overs. From that point the left-arm spin of Childs and seam of Ilott, backed by sharp, close-to-the-wicket catching, sped Essex to victory, and Hampshire to their first Championship defeat of the season. On the second day Parks had caught Stephenson as his 689th dismissal for Hampshire, passing N. T. McCorkell's county record.

Close of play: First day, Hampshire 283-8 (R. J. Parks 10*, S. D. Udal 2*); Second day, Essex 105-4 (M. C. Ilott 4*, N. V. Knight 0*).

Hampshire

V. P. Terry lbw b Ilott	9	– (2) c and b Foster	12
T. C. Middleton c Garnham b Childs	29	– (1) c Garnham b Foster	0
K. D. James c Shahid b Childs	32	– (5) c Hussain b Ilott	12
D. I. Gower b Childs	41	– (3) c Prichard b Pringle	21
*M. C. J. Nicholas b Stephenson	81	– (4) b Childs	12
M. D. Marshall b Stephenson	36	– c Garnham b Ilott	2
J. R. Ayling c Waugh b Pringle	28	– c Foster b Ilott	5
†R. J. Parks not out	20	– c Foster b Childs	4
R. J. Maru lbw b Pringle	2	– c Waugh b Childs	4
S. D. Udal not out	8	– b Ilott	3
C. A. Connor (did not bat)		– not out	4
W 2, n-b 12	14	L-b 1	1

1/15 2/70 3/88 4/140 5/220　(8 wkts. dec.) 300　　1/0 2/31 3/35 4/54 5/59　　80
6/253 7/272 8/276　　　　　　　　　　　　　　6/60 7/67 8/69 9/76

Bonus points – Hampshire 4, Essex 3.

Bowling: *First Innings*—Foster 13–5–32–0; Ilott 22–4–63–1; Pringle 18.3–2–57–2; Stephenson 16–2–49–2; Childs 26–4–87–3; Waugh 3–0–12–0. *Second Innings*—Foster 7–0–23–2; Pringle 6–1–21–1; Ilott 7.5–1–19–4; Childs 7–1–16–3.

Essex

P. J. Prichard lbw b Marshall	0	– c Parks b Marshall	1
J. P. Stephenson c Parks b Connor	18	– c Gower b Maru	20
M. E. Waugh c Marshall b Connor	0	– run out	37
N. Hussain c Middleton b Marshall	63	– c Middleton b Maru	30
N. V. Knight c Nicholas b Maru	12	– (6) c Parks b Udal	0
N. Shahid b Ayling	16	– (7) b Connor	48
†M. A. Garnham c Parks b Connor	4	– (8) not out	60
D. R. Pringle b Udal	0	– (9) st Parks b Udal	51
*N. A. Foster c James b Udal	1	– (10) lbw b Ayling	13
M. C. Ilott c James b Udal	11	– (5) c Gower b Connor	7
J. H. Childs not out	0	– c Maru b Udal	12
L-b 3, n-b 11	14	B 4, l-b 9, w 1, n-b 17	31

1/20 2/20 3/30 4/55 5/73　　　　149　　1/4 2/61 3/99 4/102 5/107　　310
6/86 7/127 8/129 9/149　　　　　　　　6/152 7/165 8/271 9/294

Bonus points – Hampshire 4.

Bowling: *First Innings*—Marshall 14.1–6–32–2; Connor 15–2–48–3; Ayling 9–1–22–1; Maru 5–2–15–1; Udal 8–1–19–3; James 5–1–10–0. *Second Innings*—Marshall 32–7–68–1; Connor 19–3–61–2; Ayling 18–7–27–1; Udal 25.4–8–75–3; James 8–2–35–0; Maru 18–6–31–2.

Umpires: J. D. Bond and A. A. Jones.

At Southampton, June 27, 28, 29. HAMPSHIRE lost to PAKISTANIS by an innings and 14 runs (See Pakistani tour section).

At Arundel, June 30, July 1, 2. HAMPSHIRE beat SUSSEX by 130 runs.

HAMPSHIRE v NOTTINGHAMSHIRE

At Southampton, July 3, 4, 6. Nottinghamshire won by five wickets. Nottinghamshire 18 pts, Hampshire 3 pts. Toss: Nottinghamshire. Positive captaincy produced a positive result with 14 balls to spare, despite the weather which claimed the first five sessions. When play finally began after tea on the second day, on a wicket offering a shade more life and bounce than usual, Terry batted fluently and Middleton adhesively in an opening partnership of 89 in 31 overs. On the final morning, Middleton shared a stand of 77 with Nicholas before he was caught behind at 191, having completed his Championship 1,000 when 62. But at lunch the match seemed doomed with Hampshire 198 for six. After the interval nine overs of occasional bowling produced 63 runs, to allow Nicholas to declare and challenge Nottinghamshire to score 262 in a minimum of 54 overs after a double forfeiture. Robinson and the irrepressible Randall made it comparatively easy with a fourth-wicket partnership of 153 in only 25 overs. When Randall dragged a ball onto his stumps seven short of his second Championship century of the season, he had faced only 92 deliveries.

Close of play: First day, No play; Second day, Hampshire 100-2 (T. C. Middleton 34*, S. D. Udal 0*).

Hampshire

V. P. Terry c Randall b Cairns	52	J. R. Ayling b Crawley	0
T. C. Middleton c French b Afford	71	†R. J. Parks not out	32
K. D. James st French b Afford	8		
S. D. Udal retired ill	0	L-b 2, n-b 6	8
*M. C. J. Nicholas b Cairns	46		
J. R. Wood b Cairns	7	1/89 2/100 3/177	(6 wkts dec.) 261
M. D. Marshall not out	37	4/185 5/191 6/197	

C. A. Connor and K. J. Shine did not bat.

Bonus points – Hampshire 3, Nottinghamshire 2.

S. D. Udal retired ill at 100-2.

Bowling: Cairns 23–1–65–3; Pick 16–1–60–0; Evans 19–8–35–0; Afford 13–5–34–2; Crawley 2–0–2–1; Johnson 5–0–30–0; Pollard 4–0–33–0.

Hampshire forfeited their second innings.

Nottinghamshire

Nottinghamshire forfeited their first innings.

B. C. Broad c Parks b Marshall	8	M. A. Crawley not out	4
P. R. Pollard c sub b James	26		
*R. T. Robinson c Parks b Marshall	95	L-b 8, n-b 8	16
P. Johnson c Connor b Ayling	5		
D. W. Randall b Connor	93	1/21 2/65 3/83	(5 wkts) 262
C. L. Cairns not out	15	4/236 5/252	

†B. N. French, K. P. Evans, R. A. Pick and J. A. Afford did not bat.

Bowling: Connor 12–0–56–1; Marshall 13–1–55–2; Udal 7–0–42–0; Shine 8.4–1–41–0; James 7–1–24–1; Ayling 7–0–36–1.

Umpires: V. A. Holder and R. Julian.

HAMPSHIRE v DERBYSHIRE

At Portsmouth, July 14, 15, 16. Derbyshire won by an innings and 135 runs. Derbyshire 24 pts, Hampshire 2 pts. Toss: Derbyshire. Perhaps distracted by their weekend victory in the Benson and Hedges Cup final, Hampshire were overwhelmed by Bishop, falling shortly after lunch on the last day. Although the Burnaby Road pitch was less lively than usual, Derbyshire's seam attack, aided by some palsied batting, swept aside their hosts' first innings. Only Gower's eloquent fifty averted a rout, and when he was out nine wickets went for 60. Hampshire's hopes revived when Derbyshire were 13 for two, Marshall claiming his 1,000th wicket for the county in all cricket. But Bowler and O'Gorman added 259, a record for any Derbyshire wicket against Hampshire, and Bowler went on to the season's highest individual score, 241 not out, in nearly eight hours and 387 balls, hitting 26 fours, before Morris declared 317 ahead. Another cavalier innings saw Gower unbeaten on 47, with seven boundaries, by the close, but he fell to Bishop's second ball next morning. Within an hour Hampshire had collapsed to 103 for six, and a stubborn partnership between Nicholas and Parks only delayed the inevitable as Bishop returned career-best figures of seven for 34.

Close of play: First day, Derbyshire 174-2 (P. D. Bowler 102*, T. J. G. O'Gorman 54*); Second day, Hampshire 81-1 (T. C. Middleton 24*, D. I. Gower 47*).

Hampshire

T. C. Middleton c Krikken b Warner	35	– lbw b Bishop			30
V. P. Terry c Cork b Bishop	10	– lbw b Bishop			3
D. I. Gower lbw b Mortensen	54	– c Krikken b Bishop			48
R. A. Smith c Adams b Warner	8	– c Krikken b Mortensen			11
*M. C. J. Nicholas c Brown b Malcolm	8	– lbw b Warner			41
K. D. James c Brown b Malcolm	17	– lbw b Bishop			0
M. D. Marshall c Bowler b Mortensen	1	– c Adams b Bishop			0
†R. J. Parks b Malcolm	0	– c Adams b Bishop			26
S. D. Udal not out	10	– c Krikken b Bishop			7
C. A. Connor lbw b Cork	0	– not out			4
K. J. Shine b Cork	1	– b Warner			2
L-b 4, n-b 10	14	L-b 6, n-b 4			10
	158				182

1/19 2/98 3/115 4/117 5/143
6/144 7/144 8/152 9/156

1/3 2/82 3/99 4/103 5/103
6/103 7/167 8/176 9/176

Bonus points – Hampshire 1, Derbyshire 4.

Bowling: *First Innings*—Bishop 12–0–26–1; Malcolm 17–3–51–3; Mortensen 14–3–31–2; Cork 7.1–0–25–2; Warner 14–3–21–2. *Second Innings*—Bishop 16–7–34–7; Malcolm 17–2–80–0; Cork 8–1–28–0; Mortensen 10–3–24–1; Warner 8.3–3–10–2.

Derbyshire

P. D. Bowler not out	241	D. G. Cork not out		65
A. M. Brown c Terry b Connor	0	B 10, l-b 8, w 1, n-b 13		32
*J. E. Morris c Terry b Marshall	7			
T. J. G. O'Gorman c Parks b Nicholas	95	1/3 2/13	(4 wkts dec.)	475
C. J. Adams c Parks b Connor	35	3/272 4/365		

†K. M. Krikken, I. R. Bishop, A. E. Warner, D. E. Malcolm and O. H. Mortensen did not bat.

Bonus points – Derbyshire 4, Hampshire 1 (Score at 100 overs: 345-3).

Bowling: Marshall 21–1–77–1; Connor 22–5–80–2; Shine 22–3–108–0; Udal 34–5–91–0; James 14–2–50–0; Nicholas 10–1–26–1; Smith 6–0–25–0.

Umpires: R. Palmer and R. A. White.

HAMPSHIRE v GLAMORGAN

At Portsmouth, July 17, 18, 20. Drawn. Hampshire 8 pts, Glamorgan 5 pts. Toss: Glamorgan. Glamorgan were within 14 runs of their second Championship win with 4.5 overs remaining when rain claimed the match. A fascinating contest had developed from unpromising beginnings. For 30 minutes Glamorgan's seventh-wicket pair, Hemp and Metson, had defied Hampshire's attack, spearheaded by Marshall, in deteriorating light, and declined the umpires' offer to abandon the chase until the thunderstorm finally broke and submerged the ground. Thanks to Smith and Marshall, Hampshire claimed maximum batting points after being put in, despite losing Terry to a back injury for most of the innings. Maynard's dismissal at 152 heralded the loss of seven Glamorgan wickets for 56, and another belligerent fifty from Smith allowed Nicholas to set a target of 298 in 72 overs. Glamorgan were on course at 184 for one after 47, but when they slumped to 237 for six, Hampshire sensed an improbable victory. Then Hemp and Metson, batting through the gloom, almost saw Glamorgan home.

Close of play: First day, Glamorgan 13-1 (S. P. James 5*, C. P. Metson 8*); Second day, Hampshire 80-3 (R. A. Smith 15*).

Hampshire

T. C. Middleton c Morris b Bastien	17	–	run out	28
V. P. Terry not out	28	– (10)	not out	0
D. I. Gower lbw b Watkin	11	–	run out	9
R. A. Smith c Metson b Watkin	79	–	c Cottey b Croft	56
*M. C. J. Nicholas run out	7	–	c Metson b Frost	8
K. D. James lbw b Watkin	39	– (2)	c Richards b Croft	26
M. D. Marshall c Richards b Frost	70	– (6)	lbw b Watkin	1
†A. N. Aymes b Watkin	31	– (7)	c Metson b Bastien	18
S. D. Udal c Frost b Watkin	13	– (8)	run out	0
P. J. Bakker b Watkin	22	– (9)	c James b Croft	15
B 2, l-b 10, w 1, n-b 8	21		B 1, l-b 1, w 1, n-b 3	6

1/19 2/45 3/79 4/142 5/229   (9 wkts dec.) 338   1/50 2/56 3/80   (9 wkts dec.) 167
6/254 7/300 8/314 9/338   4/110 5/115 6/138
                                      7/138 8/160 9/167

K. J. Shine did not bat.

Bonus points – Hampshire 4, Glamorgan 3 (Score at 100 overs: 327-8).

In the first innings V. P. Terry, when 2, retired hurt at 3 and resumed at 254.

Bowling: *First Innings*—Watkin 29.5–8–97–6; Frost 22–5–79–1; Bastien 26–6–89–1; Croft 23–7–61–0. *Second Innings*—Watkin 23–8–45–1; Frost 17–4–64–1; Bastien 8.1–2–24–1; Croft 14–2–32–3.

Glamorgan

S. P. James lbw b Bakker	30	–	c James b Shine	73
H. Morris c Aymes b Bakker	0	–	lbw b Marshall	48
†C. P. Metson c Marshall b Shine	25	– (8)	not out	31
D. L. Hemp c Aymes b James	30	– (3)	not out	84
*M. P. Maynard c Marshall b James	73	– (4)	c James b Udal	0
I. V. A. Richards c Gower b Marshall	21	– (5)	c Marshall b Udal	19
P. A. Cottey c Aymes b Shine	3	– (6)	c Nicholas b Udal	5
R. D. B. Croft c Aymes b Shine	2	– (7)	c Nicholas b Udal	1
S. Bastien c Aymes b Shine	4			
S. L. Watkin not out	7			
M. Frost b Udal	4			
B 1, l-b 6, n-b 2	9		B 3, l-b 16, n-b 4	23

1/0 2/55 3/55 4/152 5/179   208   1/93 2/184 3/186   (6 wkts) 284
6/188 7/192 8/194 9/198   4/219 5/230 6/237

Bonus points – Glamorgan 2, Hampshire 4.

Bowling: *First Innings*—Marshall 19–6–37–1; Bakker 19–5–64–2; Shine 16–3–36–4; Udal 12.1–4–35–1; James 13–3–29–2. *Second Innings*—Marshall 18–5–54–1; Bakker 9–1–38–0; Shine 11–0–60–1; Udal 25.1–5–89–4; James 4–0–24–0.

Umpires: R. Palmer and R. A. White.

At Cheltenham College, July 21, 22, 23. HAMPSHIRE drew with GLOUCESTERSHIRE.

At Worcester, August 4, 5, 6. HAMPSHIRE drew with WORCESTERSHIRE.

At Canterbury, August 7, 8, 10. HAMPSHIRE lost to KENT by nine wickets.

HAMPSHIRE v NORTHAMPTONSHIRE

At Bournemouth, August 14, 15, 17. Northamptonshire won by ten wickets. Northamptonshire 22 pts, Hampshire 5 pts. Toss: Hampshire. The penultimate first-class match at Dean Park before the ground was mothballed did nothing to make Hampshire's players regret the county's decision to sacrifice the ground to financial necessity; they produced another numbing demonstration of their batting fragility. Left-arm Taylor, bowling well-controlled in-swing, took four wickets in an over, as six fell in 18 balls, to reduce the home side from 79 for three to 80 for nine in their second innings. Taylor claimed a career-best seven for 23. The pitch offered batsmen a limited excuse, but Lamb made a nonsense of its slowness with a masterly display, striking a six and 25 fours from 211 balls, while Ripley lent valuable support. Hampshire were obliged to work hard for their runs on the first day; only Smith batted with much freedom, and Curran's first spell consisted of eight maiden overs, plus the wicket of Middleton.

Close of play: First day, Hampshire 260; Second day, Hampshire 18-1 (T. C. Middleton 11*, A. N. Aymes 2*).

Hampshire

T. C. Middleton c Fordham b Curran	11	– c Lamb b Ambrose	23
K. D. James c Ripley b Capel	74	– lbw b Taylor	2
D. I. Gower c Ripley b Ambrose	24	– (4) c Ripley b Capel	13
R. A. Smith c Roberts b Cook	62	– (5) c Ripley b Taylor	12
*M. C. J. Nicholas c Capel b Curran	33	– (6) c Bailey b Ambrose	0
M. D. Marshall c Bailey b Curran	30	– (7) c Ripley b Taylor	3
J. R. Ayling c Bailey b Curran	9	– (8) lbw b Taylor	0
†A. N. Aymes c Lamb b Ambrose	0	– (3) c Felton b Taylor	24
S. D. Udal c Fordham b Curran	2	– c Ripley b Taylor	0
I. J. Turner not out	2	– lbw b Taylor	0
K. J. Shine c Ripley b Curran	0	– not out	12
B 1, l-b 8, w 4	13	L-b 5, n-b 6	11

1/28 2/67 3/167 4/179 5/238   260   1/14 2/33 3/58 4/79 5/80   100
6/254 7/255 8/257 9/257   6/80 7/80 8/80 9/80

Bonus points – Hampshire 2, Northamptonshire 2 (Score at 100 overs: 241-5).

Bowling: *First Innings*—Ambrose 26–7–52–2; Taylor 17–3–53–0; Curran 21.3–11–45–6; Capel 19–5–43–1; Bailey 9–3–15–0; Cook 15.4–4–43–1. *Second Innings*—Ambrose 17–9–35–2; Taylor 14–6–23–7; Cook 1–1–0–0; Curran 7–1–32–0; Capel 4–1–5–1.

Northamptonshire

A. Fordham c Turner b Shine	22	– not out	14
N. A. Felton c Aymes b Marshall	1	– not out	9
R. J. Bailey c Gower b Marshall	5		
*A. J. Lamb c Turner b Shine	160		
D. J. Capel c Aymes b Marshall	33		
K. M. Curran c Udal b Turner	12		
†D. Ripley c James b Udal	57		
A. R. Roberts c Udal b Marshall	20		
C. E. L. Ambrose not out	9		
L-b 12, w 1, n-b 6	19		

1/8 2/33 3/64 4/169 5/228   (8 wkts dec.) 338   (no wkt) 23
6/275 7/325 8/338

J. P. Taylor and N. G. B. Cook did not bat.

Bonus points – Northamptonshire 4, Hampshire 3.

Bowling: *First Innings*—Marshall 23.3–8–49–4; Shine 13–2–75–2; Ayling 20–6–65–0; James 8–1–43–0; Turner 14–4–34–1; Udal 20–3–60–1. *Second Innings*—Shine 4–0–17–0; Udal 3.4–1–6–0.

Umpires: M. J. Kitchen and P. B. Wight.

HAMPSHIRE v MIDDLESEX

At Bournemouth, August 18, 19, 20. Drawn. Hampshire 8 pts, Middlesex 2 pts. Toss: Hampshire. Hampshire's hopes of marking their final first-class match at Dean Park with a win were dashed by some obdurate Middlesex batting. The visitors still trailed by 118 with eight second-innings wickets in hand at the start of the last day and were without Ramprakash, dropped for disciplinary reasons. But the loss of 22 overs to rain eased their quest for survival, and Carr's 284-minute vigil saw his side safely to the close; Nicholas abandoned his push for victory with ten overs remaining. Earlier, Nicholas had under-pinned Hampshire's innings with a fine 95, including a six and 11 fours, and a seventh-wicket stand of 111 between Ayling and Aymes ensured maximum batting points. Ayling then produced a career-best bowling performance to force Middlesex to follow on 271 behind, but Carr – who added only 66 runs to his score as he batted throughout the final day – and Gatting prevented a second collapse. After the game, a spectator placed a solitary rose on the wicket with a card marked, "Fondest Memories of Hampshire cricket at Bournemouth – Will Ye No Come Back Again?"

Close of play: First day, Hampshire 341-8 (S. D. Udal 1*); Second day, Middlesex 153-2 (M. W. Gatting 35*, J. D. Carr 11*).

Hampshire

K. D. James c Gatting b Embury	33	S. D. Udal c Haynes b Williams	16	
T. C. Middleton c Brown b Williams	14	C. A. Connor not out	24	
D. I. Gower c Gatting b Embury	17			
*M. C. J. Nicholas b Embury	95	L-b 6, w 3, n-b 19	28	
R. M. F. Cox lbw b Fraser	12			
M. D. Marshall lbw b Taylor	37	1/16 2/40 3/110	(9 wkts dec.) 386	
J. R. Ayling c Weekes b Embury	57	4/168 5/218 6/228		
†A. N. Aymes c Carr b Embury	53	7/339 8/341 9/386		

K. J. Shine did not bat.

Bonus points – Hampshire 4, Middlesex 2 (Score at 100 overs: 315-6).

Bowling: Williams 20.2–3–85–2; Taylor 12–2–47–1; Embury 40–11–105–5; Tufnell 23–4–59–0; Fraser 20–3–76–1; Weekes 2–0–8–0.

Middlesex

D. L. Haynes c James b Shine	12	– c Aymes b Udal	44
M. A. Roseberry c and b Marshall	26	– c Middleton b Connor	52
*M. W. Gatting b Shine	2	– c Aymes b Shine	93
J. D. Carr c Aymes b Ayling	23	– not out	77
P. N. Weekes c Aymes b Marshall	9	– c Middleton b Udal	26
†K. R. Brown c Aymes b Marshall	6	– c Marshall b Connor	14
J. E. Emburey lbw b Ayling	1	– c Gower b Ayling	14
N. F. Williams c James b Ayling	0	– c and b Ayling	2
A. R. C. Fraser lbw b Ayling	5	– c Middleton b Udal	1
C. W. Taylor not out	4	– b Udal	0
P. C. R. Tufnell c Middleton b Ayling	12	– not out	0
L-b 4, w 6, n-b 5	15	B 3, l-b 3, w 5, n-b 12	23
	115	**(9 wkts)**	**346**

1/31 2/35 3/56 4/77 5/91
6/91 7/91 8/93 9/98

1/76 2/129 3/231
4/279 5/307 6/327
7/337 8/341 9/346

Bonus points – Hampshire 4.

Bowling: *First Innings*—Marshall 20–6–45–3; Connor 13–2–30–0; Shine 6–2–13–2; Udal 4–0–11–0; Ayling 8.4–3–12–5. *Second Innings*—Connor 21–2–78–2; Shine 14.3–2–66–1; Ayling 17–7–37–2; Udal 35.3–6–101–4; James 10–4–8–0; Marshall 21–5–50–0.

Umpires: M. J. Kitchen and P. B. Wight.

At Weston-super-Mare, August 21, 22, 24. HAMPSHIRE drew with SOMERSET.

At Darlington, August 26, 27, 28, 29. HAMPSHIRE drew with DURHAM.

At Chelmsford, August 31, September 1, 2, 3. HAMPSHIRE lost to ESSEX by eight wickets.

HAMPSHIRE v WORCESTERSHIRE

At Southampton, September 12, 13, 14, 15. Drawn. Hampshire 5 pts, Worcestershire 6 pts. Toss: Hampshire. Despite the disruption of rain, Worcestershire almost snatched an improbable fourth win of the season, but finished with their tenth successive draw. Hampshire's first innings was illuminated by one of Smith's most positive Championship contributions of the summer, a forthright 87. Worcestershire's batsmen, without Hick, on paternity leave, lurched along between the showers and Curtis declared, giving Hampshire a three-run lead in the hope of salvaging a positive finish. With Morris showing a sound technique and temperament, and Nicholas easing himself as he scored an unbeaten 88, Hampshire challenged Worcestershire to score 265 in a minimum of 57 overs, which would have raised them from 17th to 14th in the table. When the visitors were 70 for four, Hampshire looked favourites, until Rhodes and Lampitt added 166 and Worcestershire seemed to be cantering home. But Lampitt was stumped with only 29 required, and when Rhodes followed four runs later, the draw became inevitable.

Close of play: First day, Worcestershire 32-1 (W. P. C. Weston 16*, R. K. Illingworth 0*); Second day, Worcestershire 112-4 (D. B. D'Oliveira 5*, S. J. Rhodes 9*); Third day, Hampshire 112-2 (R. S. M. Morris 49*, R. A. Smith 2*).

Hampshire

C. Middleton c Radford b Newport	9	– c and b Tolley	50
S. M. Morris c D'Oliveira b Newport	0	– c M. J. Weston b Tolley	74
D. James b Illingworth	15	– (6) c W. P. C. Weston b D'Oliveira	21
A. Smith c Rhodes b Newport	87	– lbw b Newport	4
M. C. J. Nicholas c Rhodes b M. J. Weston	22	– not out	88
M. D. Marshall retired hurt	27		
R. Ayling lbw b Radford	29	– not out	8
A. N. Aymes b Radford	0		
S. D. Udal not out	11	– (3) lbw b Tolley	1
J. Turner lbw b Illingworth	0		
C. A. Connor c Lampitt b Illingworth	8		
L-b 14, w 1, n-b 8	23	B 4, l-b 3, n-b 8	15
	231	(5 wkts dec.)	261

1/2 2/21 3/50 4/93 5/190
6/193 7/218 8/219 9/231

1/108 2/110 3/114 (5 wkts dec.) 261
4/161 5/215

Bonus points – Hampshire 2, Worcestershire 4.

In the first innings M. D. Marshall retired hurt at 151.

Bowling: *First Innings*—Radford 18–4–39–2; Newport 19–5–51–3; Illingworth 12.3–9–39–3; Lampitt 3–0–23–0; M. J. Weston 12–3–34–1; Tolley 7–1–30–0; W. P. C. Weston 1–0–1–0. *Second Innings*—Radford 8–0–32–0; Newport 12–3–22–1; Illingworth 18–6–40–0; D'Oliveira 22.1–2–84–1; Tolley 15–3–38–3; Leatherdale 1–0–5–0; Lampitt 7–0–23–0; Curtis 2–0–10–0.

Worcestershire

T. S. Curtis c Middleton b Udal	11	– lbw b Marshall	3
W. P. C. Weston c Aymes b Marshall	36	– b Connor	36
R. K. Illingworth b Marshall	43		
D. A. Leatherdale lbw b Marshall	1	– (3) c sub b Turner	11
D. B. D'Oliveira b Turner	43	– (4) c Connor b Turner	2
S. J. Rhodes c Smith b Turner	45	– (5) c James b Marshall	107
S. R. Lampitt b Udal	22	– (6) st Aymes b Udal	69
P. J. Newport b Turner	5	– run out	0
M. J. Weston not out	8	– not out	1
N. V. Radford (did not bat)		– (7) not out	15
L-b 6, w 2, n-b 6	14	B 1, l-b 7, n-b 2	10
	228	(7 wkts)	254

1/28 2/91 3/95 4/98 5/183 (8 wkts dec.) 228
6/196 7/206 8/228

1/4 2/31 3/37 (7 wkts) 254
4/70 5/236
6/240 7/244

C. M. Tolley did not bat.

Bonus points – Worcestershire 2, Hampshire 3.

Bowling: *First Innings*—Connor 17–2–46–0; Ayling 12–0–34–0; Udal 40–13–76–2; James 1–1–0–0; Turner 13–1–33–3; Marshall 15–3–33–3. *Second Innings*—Connor 14–1–39–1; Marshall 13–1–51–2; Udal 22–3–94–1; Turner 18–3–62–2.

Umpires: B. Dudleston and R. C. Tolchard.

KENT

Patron: HRH The Duke of Kent
President: D. S. Kemp
Chairman: P. H. Edgley
Chairman, Cricket Committee: D. G. Ufton
Secretary: S. T. W. Anderson
  St Lawrence Ground, Old Dover Road,
  Canterbury CT1 3NZ
  (Telephone: 0227-456886)
Captain: M. R. Benson
Cricket Administrator: Ms D. F. Potter
Coach: D. H. Foster

For the 14th consecutive season Kent failed to win a trophy but they improved their all-round performance to an extent that suggested thi era might almost be over. They reached the final of the Benson an Hedges Cup, only to fail at Lord's against Hampshire, a side they hac beaten three days earlier in the NatWest Trophy. Then they began to move through the field in the second half of the summer to finish runners-up in the County Championship. When the Maidstone Festiva week started on June 30, Kent were 13th in the table and only the mos determined optimists were recalling that in 1970, when Kent won th title, they were bottom at the same stage.

But, sure enough, Kent beat Nottinghamshire in the first game a Maidstone. The second, against Lancashire, was ruined by rain. Bu there followed an amazing win after following on against Surrey a Guildford and a victory over Somerset, which took Kent dangerousl close to a 25-point penalty. The pitch at Canterbury was ruled unfi but Kent were excused because the local water shortage had made pre paration so difficult. That left Kent in third place and, though the failed to mount a sustained challenge to Essex, they won four mor matches, all of them by wide margins, and finished clear of everyon else. After losing to Essex in May, their only two defeats were both improbably, against lowly Glamorgan.

When the season began, the Championship was felt to be a mor remote possibility than a one-day competition, mainly because o doubts about Kent's ability to bowl anyone out. What changed was th emergence of the fast bowler Martin McCague – bred in Wester Australia but born in Northern Ireland and so not regarded as a overseas player. At the end of June McCague had taken six first-clas wickets for 576. By the end of the summer he had 53 wickets. He wa also, by some distance, Kent's leading one-day bowler, with 49 wickets He bowled with real pace and great accuracy and enjoyed an extra ordinary nine-day period in August when he recorded a Sunday Leagu hat-trick, was awarded his county cap and destroyed Hampshire wit figures of eight for 26, the best in the country all season. Ten days late he took seven more wickets against Leicestershire. McCague subse quently confirmed that he wanted to play international cricket fo England rather than Australia, giving Kent hope that his new-bal partnership with Alan Igglesden could develop into something very potent indeed.

Kent's new overseas player, Carl Hooper, also settled in well. He scored 1,329 runs at 47.46 and took 35 wickets with his off-spin, adding a valuable extra dimension to the Kent attack. He also took 25 catches and his ability in the slips added welcome strength there. The batting was always expected to be strong and the first five in the order all fulfilled expectations and comfortably exceeded 1,000 runs. Neil Taylor, in his benefit year, headed the averages and Trevor Ward had the highest aggregate. Graham Cowdrey and the captain Mark Benson also maintained good form and Benson's captaincy was quiet but astute and effective.

Mark Ealham also maintained his improvement but Matthew Fleming was easily the most successful of the all-rounders, especially early in the season when he led Kent's charge to the Lord's final. In their seven Benson and Hedges matches, he won three Gold Awards – in the zonal matches against Somerset and Yorkshire and the tightly-contested semi-final against Surrey. He mixed tight spells of bowling and tremendously powerful hitting. He launched a particularly ferocious attack on the Pakistani leg-spinner Mushtaq Ahmed, who tied down far better-known batsmen elsewhere, in the one-day game at Canterbury which left Mushtaq wondering how he could possibly avoid being hit.

Overall, though, Kent's one-day season was not as memorable as many expected. The Sunday League, in which they appeared a good bet at least to win place money, was the most disappointing aspect of the summer despite some explosive innings from Ward. They lost three of their first four matches at Canterbury and the other was rained off, as was the Maidstone match against Lancashire, and though they then won four matches in succession, the format of the competition is much harsher on slow starters than the Championship.

Ward, McCague and Richard Davis, the left-arm spinner who came top of the county's first-class bowling averages, can all have felt justifiably disappointed that they failed to find favour with the selectors even for the England A tour. Steve Marsh can also go into the same category. He maintained the tradition of Kent keepers by playing vital innings at the right time and scored 896 runs at 34.46. He was always a keen competitor with the bat and behind the stumps and did a good job as vice-captain.

The form of all these players helped breed confidence for 1993, along with the news that Daryl Foster, the former Western Australian coach who has contributed so markedly to Kent's cricket in the last two seasons, had accepted a long-term contract to continue the good work.
– Dudley Moore.

KENT 1992

[Bill Smith]

Back row: J. I. Longley, G. J. Kersey, N. W. Preston, D. P. Fulton, M. M. Patel, A. G. E. Ealham (director of youth coaching). Middle row: F. Errington (physiotherapist), M. A. Ealham, N. J. Llong, T. N. Wren, M. J. McCague, R. P. Davis, M. V. Fleming, D. H. Foster (coach), J. Foley (scorer). Front row: G. R. Cowdrey, C. Penn, N. R. Taylor, M. R. Benson (captain), S. A. Marsh, R. M. Ellison, A. P. Igglesden, T. R. Ward. Inset: C. L. Hooper.

KENT RESULTS

All first-class matches – Played 23: Won 9, Lost 4, Drawn 10.

County Championship matches – Played 22: Won 9, Lost 3, Drawn 10.

Bonus points – Batting 60, Bowling 55.

Competition placings – Britannic Assurance County Championship, 2nd; NatWest Bank Trophy, q-f; Benson and Hedges Cup, finalists; Sunday League, 5th equal.

BRITANNIC ASSURANCE CHAMPIONSHIP AVERAGES

BATTING

	Birthplace	M	I	NO	R	HS	Avge
‡N. R. Taylor	Orpington	21	35	7	1,508	144	53.85
‡G. R. Cowdrey	Farnborough, Kent	21	31	6	1,291	147	51.64
‡T. R. Ward	Farningham	21	37	3	1,648	153	48.47
‡C. L. Hooper§	Georgetown, Guyana	21	32	4	1,329	131	47.46
‡M. R. Benson	Shoreham, Sussex	21	35	2	1,482	139	44.90
‡S. A. Marsh	London	21	28	3	816	125	32.64
‡M. V. Fleming	Macclesfield	21	32	2	797	100*	26.56
‡R. P. Davis	Margate	17	23	11	297	54*	24.75
‡M. A. Ealham.....	Willesborough	16	25	5	426	67*	21.30
‡R. M. Ellison	Ashford, Kent	18	20	7	258	41	19.84
‡M. J. McCague....	Larne, N. Ireland	16	18	5	120	25*	9.23
‡A. P. Igglesden	Farnborough, Kent	16	13	5	67	16	8.37
‡C. Penn	Dover	6	4	1	12	9	4.00

Also batted: N. J. Llong (*Ashford, Kent*), (3 matches) 0, 2, 92; J. I. Longley (*New Brunswick, USA*) (2 matches) 5, 35, 19. G. J. Kersey (*Plumstead*) (1 match) did not bat.

* Signifies not out. ‡ Denotes county cap. § Overseas player.

The following played a total of 20 three-figure innings for Kent in County Championship matches – C. L. Hooper 5, T. R. Ward 5, M. R. Benson 4, G. R. Cowdrey 3, M. V. Fleming 1, S. A. Marsh 1, N. R. Taylor 1.

BOWLING

	O	M	R	W	BB	5W/i	Avge
R. P. Davis	536	141	1,469	67	7-64	5	21.92
M. J. McCague	457.2	86	1,430	53	8-26	5	26.98
M. V. Fleming........	245	46	696	24	4-63	0	29.00
A. P. Igglesden	480.4	95	1,413	46	5-41	3	30.71
M. A. Ealham	392.3	69	1,193	36	4-67	0	33.13
C. L. Hooper	500.5	114	1,307	35	4-57	0	37.34
R. M. Ellison........	401.5	80	1,204	29	6-95	2	41.51

Also bowled: M. R. Benson 3-0-25-1; G. R. Cowdrey 48-9-213-2; N. J. Llong 28-4-109-3; S. A. Marsh 8-0-126-0; C. Penn 141-22-460-5; T. R. Ward 39.5-4-109-0.

Wicket-keepers: S. A. Marsh 43 ct, 8 st; G. J. Kersey 5 ct, 1 st.

Leading Fielders: C. L. Hooper 25, T. R. Ward 25, M. R. Benson 15.

At Manchester, April 25, 26, 27, 28. KENT drew with LANCASHIRE.

At Canterbury, May 4. KENT lost to PAKISTANIS by 40 runs (See Pakistani tour section).

KENT v DURHAM

At Canterbury, May 7, 8, 9, 11. Drawn. Kent 5 pts, Durham 6 pts. Toss: Kent. Hooper's first century for Kent – the fastest of the season to date – was the highlight of the match He needed only 82 balls and struck 13 fours and five sixes, one clearing the famous lime tree. With Taylor he added 197 for the fourth wicket at seven an over, before Benson declared Kent's second innings, setting Durham 259 from 50 overs. They lost three early wickets but Bainbridge, completing his first fifty for Durham, and Glendenen, with his first in the Championship, secured the draw with a stand of 108. In the first innings Kent had looked set for a big score, but lost their last nine wickets for 78 runs in 22 overs. Brown's left-arm pace earned him career-best figures of seven for 105, including five for 61 bowling unchanged between lunch and tea. Next day Ellison's seam and swing troubled all the Durham batsmen, but Graveney and Hughes produced a valuable ninth-wicket stand of 49 Rain washed out the third day before Hooper's pyrotechnics revived the game.

Close of play: First day, Durham 80-1 (W. Larkins 38*, D. M. Jones 4*); Second day, Kent 38-1 (M. R. Benson 22*, R. P. Davis 0*); Third day, No play.

Kent

T. R. Ward c Fothergill b Botham	32	– lbw b Botham	9
*M. R. Benson c Parker b Brown	75	– b Brown	27
N. R. Taylor lbw b Brown	57	– (4) not out	78
C. L. Hooper lbw b Brown	1	– (5) not out	115
J. I. Longley c Botham b Brown	5		
M. V. Fleming c Glendenen b Brown	14		
†S. A. Marsh c Parker b Graveney	20		
M. A. Ealham c Parker b Brown	32		
R. M. Ellison c and b Graveney	0		
R. P. Davis not out	0	– (3) c Graveney b Brown	9
M. J. McCague b Brown	0		
B 4, l-b 4	8	B 4, l-b 9, w 1, n-b 1	15

1/57 2/166 3/168 4/174 5/185   244   1/32 2/47 3/56   (3 wkts dec.) 253
6/196 7/240 8/240 9/244

Bonus points – Kent 2, Durham 4.

Bowling: *First Innings*—Botham 12-3-40-1; Brown 27-4-105-7; Hughes 19-4-39-0; Bainbridge 13-3-40-0; Graveney 7-2-8-2; Berry 2-0-4-0. *Second Innings*—Hughes 14-0-63-0; Brown 19.2-2-94-2; Botham 7-3-5-1; Graveney 16-6-43-0; Bainbridge 3-0-35-0.

Durham

W. Larkins lbw b McCague	40	– c Longley b Ellison	4
J. D. Glendenen lbw b Ellison	28	– not out	57
D. M. Jones lbw b McCague	34	– c Ward b Ellison	1
P. W. G. Parker b Ealham	17	– b Hooper	14
P. Bainbridge lbw b McCague	11	– not out	61
I. T. Botham c Benson b Ellison	8		
†A. R. Fothergill c Hooper b Ellison	23		
P. J. Berry lbw b Ellison	0		
*D. A. Graveney c Marsh b Ealham	28		
S. P. Hughes b Ellison	18		
S. J. E. Brown not out	5		
B 1, l-b 22, n-b 4	27	B 4, l-b 3, n-b 1	8

1/68 2/84 3/118 4/137 5/152   239   1/5 2/7 3/37   (3 wkts) 145
6/158 7/159 8/184 9/233

Bonus points – Durham 2, Kent 3 (Score at 100 overs: 218-8).

Bowling: *First Innings*—McCague 26–8–75–3; Ealham 26–16–28–2; Ellison 34.4–6–77–5; Hooper 10–5–15–0; Fleming 13–6–21–0. *Second Innings*—McCague 10–2–35–0; Ellison ?–2–7–2; Hooper 20–2–59–1; Davis 14–6–33–0; Fleming 1–0–4–0.

Umpires: G. I. Burgess and B. Leadbeater.

At Chelmsford, May 14, 15, 16. KENT lost to ESSEX by an innings and 86 runs.

KENT v YORKSHIRE

At Canterbury, May 20, 21, 22. Drawn. Kent 7 pts, Yorkshire 6 pts. Toss: Kent. Yorkshire almost clinched an exciting win after Benson's sporting declaration left them to score 294 in 62 overs. First Byas, leading his county because of Moxon's injury and Metcalfe's loss of form, then Blakey took up the challenge; Blakey was still there at the close, needing three runs off the final ball. He managed only a single, as Hartley's desperate dive failed to beat an accurate throw from Davis, depriving Yorkshire of eight extra points for levelling the scores with wickets in hand. Kent's first-innings total was only 13 short of the county record against Yorkshire – 493 at Tonbridge in 1914. It was built round a sixth-wicket stand of 235 by Cowdrey and Marsh after four wickets fell in ten overs after lunch. Marsh's career-best 125 featured 17 fours, while Cowdrey hit 15 fours and five sixes, including 24 off five balls (466444) as he raced from 85 to 109. When Yorkshire were 244 for seven they needed 87 to save the follow-on, but White and Hartley passed that target without being parted.
Close of play: First day, Kent 480-7 (M. A. Ealham 6*, R. M. Ellison 29*); Second day, Yorkshire 340-7 (C. White 63*, P. J. Hartley 61*).

Kent

T. R. Ward c Byas b Hartley	53	– b Hartley	53
†M. R. Benson c Blakey b Hartley	78	– c Blakey b Hartley	0
N. R. Taylor c Pickles b Hartley	32	– not out	83
C. L. Hooper b Gough	4	– not out	8
G. R. Cowdrey c Parker b Gough	127		
M. V. Fleming c White b Gough	6		
*S. A. Marsh c Byas b Batty	125		
M. A. Ealham not out	6		
R. M. Ellison not out	29		
B 4, l-b 2, w 3, n-b 11	20	B 2, l-b 6, n-b 1	9

1/97 2/162 3/167 4/185 5/192 (7 wkts dec.) 480   1/1 2/131   (2 wkts dec.) 153
5/427 7/447

C. Penn and R. P. Davis did not bat.

Bonus points – Kent 4, Yorkshire 2 (Score at 100 overs: 429-6).

Bowling: *First Innings*—Hartley 27–3–117–3; Gough 25–7–97–3; Pickles 18–3–93–0; Tendulkar 6–1–17–0; Carrick 23–4–76–0; Batty 11–0–74–1. *Second Innings*—Hartley 10.1–1–44–2; Gough 8–0–51–0; Pickles 3–0–23–0; Tendulkar 5–0–27–0.

Yorkshire

S. A. Kellett lbw b Fleming	90	– c Marsh b Penn	0
B. Parker c Hooper b Penn	7	– c Hooper b Davis	30
*D. Byas c Marsh b Fleming	51	– c Hooper b Davis	82
S. R. Tendulkar c Davis b Penn	15	– c Taylor b Davis	8
†R. J. Blakey c Hooper b Ealham	28	– not out	95
C. White not out	63	– c Ellison b Hooper	38
C. S. Pickles c Hooper b Ellison	3	– c Ellison b Hooper	17
P. Carrick c Davis b Ellison	0	– c Penn b Hooper	3
P. J. Hartley not out	61	– run out	4
B 5, l-b 4, w 4, n-b 9	22	B 6, l-b 4, n-b 5	15

1/10 2/100 3/159 4/191 5/233 (7 wkts dec.) 340   1/1 2/68 3/104 4/163 (8 wkts) 292
6/244 7/244   5/236 6/265 7/278 8/292

D. Gough and J. D. Batty did not bat.

Bonus points – Yorkshire 4, Kent 3 (Score at 100 overs: 307-7).

Bowling: *First Innings*—Penn 29-6-69-2; Ellison 25-9-92-2; Davis 5-0-17-0; Hooper 9-3-25-0; Ealham 23-5-74-1; Fleming 19-5-54-2. *Second Innings*—Penn 7-0-24-1; Ellison 7-1-19-0; Ealham 8-1-27-0; Davis 26-4-101-3; Hooper 21-0-97-3; Fleming 3-0-14-0.

Umpires: V. A. Holder and K. E. Palmer.

At Hove, May 23, 25, 26. KENT beat SUSSEX by four wickets.

KENT v WORCESTERSHIRE

At Tunbridge Wells, June 2, 3, 4. Drawn. Kent 4 pts, Worcestershire 3 pts. Toss: Kent Though Curtis and Ward both scored 140 not out during the first two days, their inning had little else in common. The Worcestershire opener toiled nearly six hours to bring up hi hundred, which contained only five fours, and added 164 in 63 overs with Leatherdale. Hi Kent counterpart scored quickly; his century arrived in three and a half hours and included 12 fours. Ward put on an unbeaten 171 in 48 overs with Taylor, who meted out heavy punishment to Illingworth, hitting three sixes in rapid succession. Curtis departed withou scoring second time round, but Moody and Seymour took the second-wicket stand to 155 or the final morning. The Australian registered his third hundred of the summer, the fastest o the match in two and a half hours, with 11 fours, before becoming off-spinner Llong's firs first-class victim, one of three in the innings. Curtis set Kent 288 to win in a minimum o 72 overs, and Ward and Benson had put them well on course when rain intervened to ruin an interesting finish.

Close of play: First day, Worcestershire 291-5 (T. S. Curtis 124*, S. J. Rhodes 6*); Second day, Worcestershire 75-1 (A. C. H. Seymour 33*, T. M. Moody 39*).

Worcestershire

*T. S. Curtis not out	140	– c Marsh b Igglesden	0
A. C. H. Seymour c Igglesden b Penn	18	– st Marsh b Hooper	62
T. M. Moody c Marsh b Ealham	13	– c Benson b Llong	100
G. R. Haynes c Marsh b Hooper	12	– c and b Llong	7
D. A. Leatherdale lbw b Ealham	91	– b Llong	2
S. R. Lampitt lbw b Ealham	3	– lbw b Hooper	16
†S. J. Rhodes c Llong b Ealham	25	– not out	11
C. M. Tolley (did not bat)		– not out	2
L-b 14, w 6, n-b 5	25	B 5, l-b 4, n-b 1	10

1/33 2/67 3/89 4/253 5/273   (6 wkts dec.) 327   1/0 2/155 3/177   (6 wkts dec.) 210
6/327   4/180 5/181 6/207

P. J. Newport, R. K. Illingworth and R. D. Stemp did not bat.

Bonus points – Worcestershire 3, Kent 1 (Score at 100 overs: 261-4).

Bowling: *First Innings*—Igglesden 28-5-77-0; Penn 17-3-49-1; Ellison 18-1-57-0; Ealham 25.4-2-78-4; Hooper 28-11-52-1; Llong 1-1-0-0. *Second Innings*—Igglesden 10-1-31-1; Penn 5-0-27-0; Hooper 18-1-42-2; Llong 22-2-70-3; Ellison 8-1-31-0.

Kent

T. R. Ward not out	140	– c Haynes b Stemp	59
*M. R. Benson c Newport b Stemp	36	– not out	84
N. R. Taylor not out	67	– c Stemp b Illingworth	24
C. L. Hooper (did not bat)		– c Tolley b Illingworth	10
G. R. Cowdrey (did not bat)		– not out	6
L-b 1, n-b 6	7	L-b 4, w 1, n-b 2	7

1/79   (1 wkt dec.) 250   1/114 2/156 3/178   (3 wkts) 190

N. J. Llong, †S. A. Marsh, M. A. Ealham, R. M. Ellison, C. Penn and A. P. Igglesden did not bat.

Bonus points – Kent 3.

Bowling: *First Innings*—Newport 13–2–41–0; Tolley 14–4–48–0; Lampitt 6–0–19–0; Illingworth 13–5–40–0; Stemp 20.4–4–53–1; Haynes 7–3–14–0; Moody 8–0–34–0. *Second Innings*—Newport 7–0–33–0; Tolley 6–3–12–0; Illingworth 16–0–53–2; Lampitt 4–0–28–0; Stemp 12–1–49–1; Moody 1–0–11–0.

Umpires: J. H. Harris and P. B. Wight.

KENT v ESSEX

At Tunbridge Wells, June 5, 6, 8. Kent won by four wickets. Kent 17 pts, Essex 4 pts. Toss: Kent. The rain that allowed just 26 deliveries on the opening day – the only play in the Championship – also cut 90 minutes off the second morning. However a double innings forfeiture set up Kent's successful run-chase on the final afternoon. Prichard had dominated the Essex batting, scoring 133 with 12 fours and a six, and adding 145 with Hussain in 40 entertaining overs. Kent lost their wicket-keeper, Marsh, after lunch to a leg injury, and Benson stepped in before Cowdrey took over the gloves in the evening. Essex declared after half an hour of the final morning, and with both sides forfeiting an innings, Kent were asked to score 343 from 92 overs. Ward went early, but that was left-arm spinner Childs's only success as he suffered from Taylor's onslaught, conceding five fours in one over. Taylor had solid support from Benson and Hooper, and after his dismissal ten short of a century, Hooper shared 125 with Cowdrey for the fourth wicket. Then Cowdrey guided Kent home with 20 balls to spare, to register their second Championship win of the season.

Close of play: First day, Essex 12-0 (P. J. Prichard 3*, J. P. Stephenson 8*); Second day, Essex 305-4 (N. Hussain 66*, N. V. Knight 2*).

Essex

P. J. Prichard b Fleming	.133	N. V. Knight not out............... 28
J. P. Stephenson c Fleming b Ealham	.. 18	B 8, l-b 14, w 2, n-b 5 29
M. E. Waugh c Ward b Fleming	 24	
N. Hussain not out	... 75	1/39 2/90 (4 wkts dec.) 342
*N. A. Foster c Benson b Fleming	 35	3/235 4/297

N. Shahid, †M. A. Garnham, S. J. W. Andrew, M. C. Ilott and J. H. Childs did not bat.

Bonus points – Essex 4, Kent 1.

Bowling: Igglesden 4–0–13–0; Ellison 27–4–93–0; Ealham 27–4–76–1; Fleming 24–3–67–3; Hooper 9–0–32–0; Llong 5–1–39–0.

Essex forfeited their second innings.

Kent

Kent forfeited their first innings.

T. R. Ward c Hussain b Childs	 11	M. V. Fleming c and b Stephenson 19
*M. R. Benson c Waugh b Foster	 67	M. A. Ealham not out............... 5
N. R. Taylor b Ilott	 90	B 1, l-b 4, w 1, n-b 2 8
C. L. Hooper c Foster b Andrew	 86	
G. R. Cowdrey not out	 57	1/37 2/117 3/180 (6 wkts) 343
N. J. Llong c Garnham b Ilott	 0	4/305 5/305 6/334

†S. A. Marsh, R. M. Ellison and A. P. Igglesden did not bat.

Bowling: Andrew 20–1–73–1; Ilott 18.4–3–82–2; Childs 13–3–73–1; Foster 16–4–49–1; Stephenson 10–2–32–1; Waugh 11–1–29–0.

Umpires: J. H. Harris and P. B. Wight.

At Bristol, June 16, 17, 18. KENT drew with GLOUCESTERSHIRE.

At Cambridge, June 19, 20, 21. KENT lost to CAMBRIDGE UNIVERSITY by two wickets.

At Gateshead Fell, June 27, 28, 29. KENT drew with DURHAM.

KENT v NOTTINGHAMSHIRE

At Maidstone, June 30, July 1, 2. Kent won by 35 runs. Kent 21 pts, Nottinghamshire 4 pts. Toss: Nottinghamshire. Though only 68 overs were possible on the first day, Kent raced to their fourth batting point two overs before the close. Benson went from 82 to his second century of the season with three fours and a six, in all hitting three sixes and 16 fours. Fleming, using borrowed gear after leaving his own at Gateshead the previous day, helped him add 105 in 16 overs. But next morning, re-united with his usual bat, he went first ball, one of three wickets for Cairns for 17 runs in ten overs. Further rain forced the captains to contrive a finish; Robinson declared overnight, and after a quick slog, Kent set Nottinghamshire 302 from 70 overs. Igglesden's burst of three wickets for two runs in 11 balls left the visitors struggling, until Randall and Crawley added 94. Then Cairns helped Crawley step up the pace with 63 in 12 overs. But after his dismissal wickets fell at regular intervals, with Hooper mopping up the tail. Kent secured victory by dismissing débutant Pennett with eight balls to spare, leaving Crawley stranded on 102.

Close of play: First day, Kent 311-5 (M. V. Fleming 63*, S. A. Marsh 16*); Second day, Nottinghamshire 113-3 (R. T. Robinson 42*, D. W. Randall 3*).

Kent

T. R. Ward b Cairns	3	– c Robinson b Evans	26
*M. R. Benson c Crawley b Field-Buss	131		
N. R. Taylor c French b Pennett	40		
C. L. Hooper c Pollard b Field-Buss	36		
G. R. Cowdrey c Pennett b Cairns	12		
M. V. Fleming c Crawley b Cairns	63		
†S. A. Marsh lbw b Evans	17		
R. M. Ellison not out	27		
R. P. Davis c Robinson b Cairns	7	– (2) not out	18
M. J. McCague c Pollard b Cairns	3	– (3) not out	10
A. P. Igglesden c French b Evans	5		
B 1, l-b 7, n-b 7	15	L-b 1	1
	359	1/38 (1 wkt dec.)	55

1/6 2/71 3/132 4/170 5/275
6/311 7/317 8/332 9/342

Bonus points – Kent 4, Nottinghamshire 4.

Bowling: *First Innings*—Cairns 28-7-75-5; Evans 33-5-117-2; Pennett 13-2-65-1; Crawley 5-0-29-0; Field-Buss 9-0-65-2. *Second Innings*—Evans 6.3-0-33-1; Pennett 6-0-21-0.

Nottinghamshire

B. C. Broad c McCague b Igglesden	4	– b Igglesden	3
P. R. Pollard c Benson b Ellison	26	– lbw b Igglesden	9
*R. T. Robinson not out	42	– b Igglesden	1
P. Johnson c Marsh b Davis	30	– c Benson b Davis	14
D. W. Randall not out	3	– c Taylor b Igglesden	66
M. A. Crawley (did not bat)		– not out	102
C. L. Cairns (did not bat)		– c Davis b McCague	32
†B. N. French (did not bat)		– c Ellison b Hooper	14
K. P. Evans (did not bat)		– c Ellison b Hooper	8
M. G. Field-Buss (did not bat)		– lbw b McCague	1
D. B. Pennett (did not bat)		– lbw b Hooper	3
L-b 4, n-b 4	8	L-b 10, n-b 3	13
1/4 2/44 3/104 (3 wkts dec.)	113	1/8 2/10 3/19	266

4/46 5/140 6/203
7/228 8/245 9/251

Bonus point – Kent 1.

Bowling: *First Innings*—Igglesden 6–1–22–1; Ellison 12–4–35–1; McCague 4–1–11–0; Fleming 8–1–37–0; Davis 6–2–4–1. *Second Innings*—Igglesden 15–6–32–4; Ellison 1–1–37–0; McCague 11–2–53–2; Davis 16–6–66–1; Hooper 15.4–0–68–3.

Umpires: J. H. Hampshire and N. T. Plews.

KENT v LANCASHIRE

At Maidstone, July 3, 4, 6. Drawn. Kent 1 pt, Lancashire 4 pts. Toss: Lancashire. Kent's innings started disastrously, losing three wickets in eight balls. Taylor and Cowdrey launched a rescue mission, but they were 84 for four when play halted after 32 overs. Next day Morrison, with six for 48, his best return for Lancashire to date, and Martin continued to cause problems, though Cowdrey batted three and a half hours and Marsh hit 42 off 43 balls. Lancashire's reply was soon curtailed by rain, but an overnight declaration and the feeding of quick runs to Kent enabled the game to be contested seriously on the final day. Pursuing 296 in 90 overs, Fowler and Titchard opened with 112, a sound basis for victory, until Igglesden inspired a Kent revival, and four wickets fell for 19 runs in ten overs. Lancashire needed more than six an over from the last 20, and acting captain Watkinson took up the challenge with 32 off 29 balls. But after his dismissal the accent was on denying Kent victory, which Hegg and Martin achieved comfortably.

Close of play: First day, Kent 84-4 (G. R. Cowdrey 30*, M. V. Fleming 15*); Second day, Lancashire 11-0 (G. Fowler 7*, S. P. Titchard 2*).

Kent

T. R. Ward c Titchard b Martin	4	– not out	55
*M. R. Benson c Lloyd b Morrison	1		
N. R. Taylor c Lloyd b Martin	34		
C. L. Hooper c Titchard b Morrison	0		
G. R. Cowdrey c and b Martin	77		
M. V. Fleming c Lloyd b Martin	18	– (3) not out	4
†S. A. Marsh c Titchard b Morrison	42		
M. A. Ealham c Fowler b Morrison	1	– (2) c Lloyd b Fowler	54
R. M. Ellison b Morrison	0		
R. P. Davis c Hegg b Morrison	10		
A. P. Igglesden not out	2		
B 1, l-b 2, w 1	4		

1/5 2/5 3/5 4/62 5/96   **193**   1/109   (1 wkt dec.) **113**
6/156 7/163 8/163 9/191

Bonus points – Kent 1, Lancashire 4.

Bowling: *First Innings*—Morrison 18–4–48–6; Martin 21.3–9–67–4; Watkinson 14–2–52–0; Fletcher 8–1–23–0. *Second Innings*—Fowler 5–0–60–1; Speak 2–0–30–0; Lloyd 2–0–23–0.

Lancashire

G. Fowler not out	7	– c Benson b Fleming	52
S. P. Titchard not out	2	– c Fleming b Igglesden	71
N. J. Speak (did not bat)		– lbw b Igglesden	16
G. D. Lloyd (did not bat)		– c Taylor b Davis	7
R. C. Irani (did not bat)		– c Benson b Igglesden	9
*M. Watkinson (did not bat)		– c and b Hooper	32
†W. K. Hegg (did not bat)		– not out	29
P. J. Martin (did not bat)		– not out	11
L-b 1, n-b 1	2	B 4, l-b 2, w 1, n-b 8	15

(no wkt dec.) **11**   1/112 2/147 3/150   (6 wkts) **242**
          4/166 5/166 6/205

D. K. Morrison, A. A. Barnett and S. D. Fletcher did not bat.

Bowling: *First Innings*—Igglesden 3–1–4–0; Ellison 2.1–0–6–0. *Second Innings*—Igglesden 21–5–62–3; Ealham 19–3–42–0; Davis 27–3–70–1; Hooper 9–1–31–1; Fleming 10–2–24–1; Benson 1–0–7–0.

Umpires: J. H. Hampshire and N. T. Plews.

At Guildford, July 14, 15, 16. KENT beat SURREY by 72 runs.

KENT v SOMERSET

At Canterbury, July 21, 22, 23. Kent won by 82 runs. Kent 23 pts, Somerset 4 pts. Toss Kent. A TCCB panel spent three hours discussing the state of the pitch following Kent's victory, and although they ruled that it was not suitable for first-class cricket they refrained from imposing the 25-point penalty in view of the problems in preparation caused by the county's severe water shortage. Needing 303 in a minimum of 90 overs on the last day Somerset were given a marvellous start by Lathwell, who hit 72 off 69 balls with 12 fours. Then, on a turning pitch, the spinners took command, with Davis causing most problems for the visitors. Burns and Snell threatened late resistance but both were dismissed by McCague in successive overs as Kent finished the job. The home side's first innings recovered from a poor start with Fleming hitting 47 out of 50 for the fifth wicket, from 37 deliveries, including two sixes and seven fours, and Ealham contributing a valuable half century. Nineteen wickets fell on the second day; McCague, who claimed five for one in 17 balls, and Davis undermined Somerset, before Caddick hit back with career-best figures to finish with ten for 157 in the match.

Close of play: First day, Kent 195-7 (M. A. Ealham 4*, R. P. Davis 3*); Second day, Kent 129-6 (G. R. Cowdrey 22*, M. A. Ealham 0*).

Kent

T. R. Ward c Lathwell b Caddick	15	– b Rose	2
R. M. Ellison run out	0	– b Caddick	21
J. I. Longley b Lefebvre	35	– c Tavaré b Lefebvre	19
C. L. Hooper c Tavaré b Caddick	10	– c Lathwell b Caddick	48
G. R. Cowdrey b Snell	36	– c Townsend b Caddick	44
M. V. Fleming b Trump	47	– c Caddick	4
*†S. A. Marsh lbw b Caddick	35	– c Lefebvre b Caddick	8
M. A. Ealham b Lefebvre	50	– b Caddick	9
R. P. Davis run out	24	– not out	0
M. J. McCague b Caddick	0		
A. P. Igglesden not out	11		
L-b 4, n-b 8	12	L-b 5	5

1/13 2/33 3/51 4/82 5/132   275   1/5 2/33 3/58   (8 wkts dec.) 160
6/187 7/188 8/239 9/243   4/109 5/115 6/129
                                                 7/149 8/160

Bonus points – Kent 3, Somerset 4.

Bowling: *First Innings*—Caddick 24–5–105–4; Snell 19–3–61–1; Trump 19–5–53–1; Rose 7–3–14–0; Lefebvre 13–5–33–2; Hayhurst 4–1–5–0. *Second Innings*—Caddick 16.3–1–52–6; Rose 10–2–30–1; Trump 10–1–53–0; Lefebvre 7–1–15–1; Hayhurst 3–0–5–0.

Somerset

A. N. Hayhurst lbw b McCague	14	– c Marsh b Davis	11
M. N. Lathwell b Igglesden	4	– c Ward b Hooper	72
R. J. Harden c McCague b McCague	30	– c Ward b Davis	4
*C. J. Tavaré c Longley b McCague	0	– c Ward b Hooper	14
G. T. J. Townsend lbw b McCague	0	– b Davis	16
G. D. Rose c Longley b McCague	0	– b Davis	0
†N. D. Burns c Igglesden b Davis	42	– b McCague	33
R. P. Snell b Davis	20	– c Cowdrey b McCague	23
R. P. Lefebvre st Marsh b Davis	0	– c and b Davis	6
A. R. Caddick not out	5	– c and b Davis	0
H. R. J. Trump c Ward b Hooper	1	– not out	8
B 4, l-b 7, w 1, n-b 5	17	B 8, l-b 5, n-b 2	15

1/7 2/49 3/53 4/53 5/54   133   1/81 2/85 3/89 4/111 5/112   220
6/62 7/127 8/127 9/128   6/135 7/181 8/187 9/205

Bonus points – Kent 4.

Bowling: *First Innings*—Igglesden 13–3–30–1; McCague 14–4–23–5; Hooper 9.4–3–20–1; Ealham 7–0–18–0; Ellison 3–0–22–0; Davis 4–0–9–3. *Second Innings*—Igglesden 5–1–13–0; Ealham 2–0–15–0; Davis 31.2–10–75–6; McCague 9–2–47–2; Hooper 23–6–56–2; Fleming 1–0–1–0.

Umpires: R. Palmer and N. T. Plews.

At Swansea, July 31, August 1, 3. KENT lost to GLAMORGAN by 36 runs.

KENT v MIDDLESEX

At Canterbury, August 4, 5, 6. Drawn. Kent 7 pts, Middlesex 8 pts. Toss: Middlesex. Put in to bat, Kent made a stuttering start which turned to fluency with a stand of 160 off 32 overs between Ward, who made his second century in two days, and Hooper. In dominating form, Ward scored his runs off 196 balls in 249 minutes with one six and 28 fours, and Cowdrey kept Kent going when Emburey and Fraser subsequently caused problems. Middlesex then lost half their side for 158 before Pooley and Weekes added 80 off 31 overs to avert the follow-on. On the last day enterprising batting allowed Kent to set a target of 281 off a minimum of 49 overs. Haynes and Gatting put on 91 in a purposeful second-wicket stand, and Gatting then dominated a brisk partnership of 61 with Carr. The challenge petered out as wickets fell, but Gatting was compensated by a century off 92 balls in 129 minutes.

Close of play: First day, Middlesex 28-0 (D. L. Haynes 16*, M. A. Roseberry 11*); Second day, Kent 23-0 (T. R. Ward 4*, M. R. Benson 18*).

Kent

T. R. Ward c Carr b Headley	150	– c Carr b Emburey	4
*M. R. Benson c Taylor b Headley	21	– c Carr b Weekes	45
N. R. Taylor c Emburey b Taylor	3	– c Weekes b Headley	30
C. L. Hooper c Haynes b Carr	65	– c Carr b Emburey	0
G. R. Cowdrey not out	76	– c Brown b Fraser	60
M. V. Fleming c Brown b Fraser	21	– c Brown b Headley	35
†S. A. Marsh lbw b Fraser	6	– not out	52
M. A. Ealham c Gatting b Emburey	4	– c Headley b Emburey	1
R. P. Davis lbw b Headley	2	– not out	4
M. J. McCague c Gatting b Emburey	5		
A. P. Igglesden c Carr b Emburey	6		
L-b 2, n-b 8	10	B 3, l-b 2, w 2, n-b 4	11

1/55 2/68 3/228 4/253 5/295   369   1/31 2/51 3/52   (7 wkts dec.) 242
6/301 7/312 8/316 9/335   4/91 5/146
                                6/219 7/222

Bonus points – Kent 4, Middlesex 4.

Bowling: *First Innings*—Fraser 24–3–89–2; Taylor 22–1–91–1; Headley 26–8–82–3; Emburey 16–1–68–3; Carr 11–3–37–1. *Second Innings*—Taylor 7–1–26–0; Fraser 13–1–54–1; Emburey 23–2–87–3; Weekes 8–0–33–1; Headley 9–1–37–2.

Middlesex

D. L. Haynes run out	32	– c Ward b Davis	68
M. A. Roseberry c Marsh b McCague	27	– lbw b Fleming	17
*M. W. Gatting b Fleming	26	– not out	102
J. D. Carr run out	42	– run out	15
†K. R. Brown st Marsh b Davis	1	– (6) b Fleming	6
J. C. Pooley lbw b Ealham	69	– (7) c Marsh b McCague	3
P. N. Weekes c Fleming b Ealham	46	– (5) c Marsh b Fleming	3
J. E. Emburey c Ward b Davis	41	– not out	2
D. W. Headley c Ward b Davis	31		
A. R. C. Fraser not out	1		
L-b 8, w 1, n-b 6	15	L-b 11, w 1, n-b 1	13

1/47 2/80 3/100 4/107 5/158   (9 wkts dec.) 331   1/40 2/131 3/192   (6 wkts) 229
6/238 7/268 8/324 9/331   4/198 5/210 6/217

C. W. Taylor did not bat.

Bonus points – Middlesex 4, Kent 3 (Score at 100 overs: 304-7).

Bowling: *First Innings*—Igglesden 16–1–54–0; McCague 22–4–49–1; Fleming 13–3–34–1; Ealham 15–3–47–2; Davis 29.3–8–105–3; Hooper 9–3–34–0. *Second Innings*—Igglesden 11–2–44–0; McCague 16–2–59–1; Hooper 1–0–8–0; Ealham 7–0–36–0; Fleming 7–0–35–3; Davis 4–0–36–1.

Umpires: B. J. Meyer and A. G. T. Whitehead.

KENT v HAMPSHIRE

At Canterbury, August 7, 8, 10. Kent won by nine wickets. Kent 22 pts, Hampshire 5 pts. Toss: Hampshire. Hampshire's second innings was destroyed by McCague, whose eight for 26 – the best first-class analysis all summer – included the first three wickets for four runs in 16 deliveries, and they were dismissed for the lowest first-class total of the season to present Kent with a straightforward victory. McCague had been awarded his county cap on the first day. Hampshire struggled early on the first morning before Middleton and Wood led the revival with 75 in 25 overs, and Nicholas followed up by completing a 99-ball half-century. Kent's reply began badly, but the visitors were foiled by Fleming who reached 100 out of 149 added while he was at the crease. Hampshire's collapse then left Kent needing only 107 to win, and Ward drove the home side towards their target with 63 from 71 deliveries, including ten fours.

Close of play: First day, Hampshire 288; Second day, Hampshire 7-0 (T. C. Middleton 7*, R. S. M. Morris 0*).

Hampshire

T. C. Middleton c Kersey b Ealham	52	– lbw b McCague	17
R. S. M. Morris c Kersey b Igglesden	4	– b McCague	0
K. D. James c Ealham b Davis	4	– c Ward b McCague	0
J. R. Wood b Igglesden	44	– b McCague	4
*M. C. J. Nicholas c Fleming b Hooper	59	– c Ward b Davis	5
M. D. Marshall c Kersey b Ealham	17	– c and b McCague	6
J. R. Ayling c Hooper b Igglesden	26	– c Kersey b McCague	20
†A. N. Aymes c Hooper b McCague	15	– not out	12
S. D. Udal st Kersey b Hooper	38	– lbw b McCague	0
I. J. Turner c Taylor b Davis	5	– c Kersey b McCague	0
C. A. Connor not out	8	– run out	2
L-b 6, n-b 10	16	L-b 2, n-b 2	4

1/24 2/29 3/104 4/123 5/166   288   1/9 2/11 3/15 4/29 5/29   70
6/219 7/221 8/259 9/274   6/51 7/60 8/60 9/60

Bonus points – Hampshire 3, Kent 3 (Score at 100 overs: 261-8).

Bowling: *First Innings*—Igglesden 26–9–55–3; McCague 12–1–37–1; Ealham 22–3–49–2; Davis 28–5–75–2; Fleming 8–1–27–0; Hooper 13–1–39–2. *Second Innings*—Igglesden 6–2–13–0; Davis 12–6–29–1; McCague 12.2–5–26–8.

Kent

T. R. Ward lbw b Marshall	0	– c Morris b James	63
*M. R. Benson b Ayling	44	– not out	40
N. R. Taylor c Aymes b Ayling	39	– not out	2
C. L. Hooper lbw b Ayling	1		
G. R. Cowdrey lbw b Connor	10		
M. V. Fleming not out	100		
M. A. Ealham c Morris b Turner	9		
R. P. Davis not out	23		
B 5, l-b 6, n-b 15	26	B 3, n-b 1	4

1/0 2/79 3/98 4/103   (6 wkts dec.) 252   1/95   (1 wkt) 109
5/125 6/173

M. J. McCague, †G. J. Kersey and A. P. Igglesden did not bat.

Bonus points – Kent 3, Hampshire 2.

Bowling: *First Innings*—Marshall 19–4–47–1; Connor 14–2–63–1; James 12–4–41–0; Ayling 10–1–30–3; Turner 12–3–51–1; Udal 1.1–0–9–0. *Second Innings*—Marshall 4–1–18–0; Connor 4–0–20–0; Ayling 5–0–26–0; Udal 7–0–23–0; James 2.3–1–19–1.

Umpires: B. J. Meyer and A. G. T. Whitehead.

At Chesterfield, August 14, 15, 17. KENT drew with DERBYSHIRE.

At Leicester, August 18, 19, 20. KENT beat LEICESTERSHIRE by an innings and 138 runs.

At Northampton, August 21, 22, 24. KENT drew with NORTHAMPTONSHIRE.

KENT v GLOUCESTERSHIRE

At Canterbury, August 26, 27, 28, 29. Kent won by 233 runs. Kent 21 pts, Gloucestershire 5 pts. Toss: Kent. Excellent bowling by McCague and Davis enabled Kent to complete an emphatic win before lunch on the fourth day, although the early honours had belonged to Gloucestershire. Walsh's pace triggered a first-innings collapse, and he claimed four for seven in 33 balls as Kent lost their last seven wickets for 39. But McCague proved equally devastating and Gloucestershire in turn staged a spectacular slump which saw their last five wickets go down in as many overs. Eventually, the batsmen came into their own, with Taylor leading the way, and Kent's advantage was pressed home by Hooper, Fleming and Marsh. Left facing a formidable target of 398 in eight and a half hours Gloucestershire once again ran into trouble against McCague, well supported by Davis; a spell of five for seven in 23 balls gave McCague ten for 86 in the match.

Close of play: First day, Gloucestershire 64-1 (G. D. Hodgson 21*, M. W. Alleyne 31*); Second day, Kent 164-3 (C. L. Hooper 12*, R. P. Davis 1*); Third day, Gloucestershire 94-1 (R. J. Scott 36*, M. W. Alleyne 22*).

Kent

T. R. Ward b Vaughan	42	– c Gerrard b Vaughan	41
*M. R. Benson b Gerrard	6	– lbw b Davies	10
N. R. Taylor b Scott	39	– c Walsh b Vaughan	96
C. L. Hooper c Walsh b Alleyne	41	– lbw b Scott	56
G. R. Cowdrey c Vaughan b Walsh	22	– (6) lbw b Walsh	4
M. V. Fleming c Wright b Walsh	5	– (7) c Athey b Walsh	67
†S. A. Marsh c Hancock b Walsh	5	– (8) c Vaughan b Davies	70
R. M. Ellison c Hancock b Walsh	12	– (9) b Walsh	15
R. P. Davis c Hancock b Walsh	0	– (5) c Russell b Walsh	8
M. J. McCague c Wright b Vaughan	11	– c Hodgson b Davies	2
A. P. Igglesden not out	5	– not out	3
L-b 1	1	B 5, l-b 3, w 1, n-b 2	11
	189		**383**

1/6 2/83 3/87 4/150 5/152 6/159 7/160 8/164 9/183   **189**

1/22 2/142 3/155 4/182 5/196 6/235 7/307 8/375 9/379   **383**

Bonus points – Kent 1, Gloucestershire 4.

Bowling: *First Innings*—Walsh 23–6–50–5; Gerrard 9–2–39–1; Vaughan 14.3–3–35–2; Scott 7–0–30–1; Davies 2–0–8–0; Alleyne 12–4–26–1. *Second Innings*—Walsh 25–5–69–4; Gerrard 14–2–47–0; Davies 34.4–6–119–3; Vaughan 25–5–75–2; Alleyne 2–0–23–0; Hancock 6–2–21–0; Scott 5–1–21–1.

Gloucestershire

G. D. Hodgson lbw b Ellison	37	– c McCague b Davis	31
R. J. Scott b McCague	15	– c Benson b Davis	41
M. W. Alleyne c Ward b McCague	33	– c Marsh b McCague	27
C. W. J. Athey b McCague	12	– c Ellison b McCague	0
T. H. C. Hancock b Ellison	14	– (6) lbw b McCague	1
J. T. C. Vaughan c Hooper b Davis	19	– (8) c Marsh b McCague	0
†R. C. Russell c Davis b Igglesden	31	– not out	44
*A. J. Wright b McCague	4	– (5) lbw b McCague	4
C. A. Walsh lbw b Igglesden	1	– c Cowdrey b Davis	9
M. Davies not out	2	– c Ward b Davis	0
M. J. Gerrard b McCague	0	– c Ward b Davis	2
L-b 9, n-b 3	12	B 2, l-b 3	5

1/13 2/76 3/92 4/96 5/116   175   1/56 2/104 3/104 4/108 5/109   164
6/163 7/163 8/168 9/169   6/118 7/122 8/137 9/146

Bonus points – Gloucestershire 1, Kent 4.

Bowling: First Innings—McCague 20.5–3–42–5; Igglesden 22–6–45–2; Ellison 21–4–55–2; Fleming 2–0–9–0; Davis 9–3–15–1. *Second Innings*—McCague 21–4–44–5; Igglesden 14–1–51–0; Davis 27.4–9–61–5; Ellison 1–0–3–0.

Umpires: B. Dudleston and G. A. Stickley.

KENT v GLAMORGAN

At Canterbury, September 7, 8, 9, 10. Glamorgan won by 86 runs. Glamorgan 21 pts, Kent 6 pts. Toss: Glamorgan. Batting was never easy on a pitch being used for the first time since it was relaid in 1989, and after lunch on the first day Igglesden's pace produced four wickets for 27 runs in 8.2 overs. Kent fared no better until Taylor and Marsh shared a sixth-wicket stand of 113 in 53 overs which helped secure a lead of 61. Dale held up the Kent bowlers with a patient second-innings fifty before Richards and Cottey added 142 off 46 overs. Cottey's 141, his highest Championship score, featured two sixes, one five and 15 fours. Kent made a good enough start when they set off in pursuit of 329 to win, with more than a day available, but on the final day they fared badly against the pace of 17-year-old Thomas. He had three wickets for 22 runs in eight overs and finished with five for 79, as Glamorgan completed a Championship double over Kent.

Close of play: First day, Kent 134-5 (N. R. Taylor 60*, S. A. Marsh 27*); Second day, Glamorgan 176-4 (I. V. A. Richards 25*, P. A. Cottey 14*); Third day, Kent 119-2 (M. R. Benson 41*, R. P. Davis 2*).

Glamorgan

S. P. James c Marsh b McCague	2	– lbw b Igglesden	37
H. Morris b Igglesden	2	– c Ward b Igglesden	17
A. Dale c Marsh b Igglesden	48	– c Hooper b Fleming	50
*M. P. Maynard c Fleming b Ealham	16	– c Ward b Ealham	21
I. V. A. Richards b Fleming	4	– c Marsh b Davis	76
P. A. Cottey lbw b Igglesden	29	– c Hooper b Davis	141
R. D. B. Croft c Hooper b Fleming	7	– c Marsh b Davis	17
†C. P. Metson lbw b Igglesden	35	– c Marsh b Fleming	1
S. L. Watkin lbw b Fleming	1	– c Marsh b Fleming	1
S. D. Thomas lbw b Igglesden	2	– c Marsh b Fleming	0
S. R. Barwick not out	2	– not out	1
L-b 2, w 1, n-b 7	10	B 4, l-b 13, w 2, n-b 8	27

1/5 2/7 3/51 4/62 5/111   158   1/34 2/94 3/125 4/139 5/281   389
6/118 7/120 8/122 9/125   6/354 7/369 8/383 9/387

Bonus points – Glamorgan 1, Kent 4.

Bowling: First Innings—McCague 11–1–46–1; Igglesden 16.2–2–45–5; Ealham 9–1–27–1; Fleming 12–2–31–3; Davis 1–0–7–0. *Second Innings*—McCague 24–2–88–0; Igglesden 31–7–78–2; Fleming 29–6–63–4; Ealham 20–1–58–1; Hooper 10–2–39–0; Davis 15.1–4–46–3.

Kent

T. R. Ward lbw b Thomas	15	– c Watkin b Dale	53
M. R. Benson c Metson b Watkin	22	– b Thomas	41
N. R. Taylor c Richards b Thomas	74	– b Croft	16
C. L. Hooper lbw b Watkin	0	– (5) c Morris b Watkin	3
G. R. Cowdrey c James b Barwick	0	– (6) b Barwick	35
M. V. Fleming c James b Barwick	0	– (7) c Watkin b Thomas	0
S. A. Marsh c Richards b Dale	60	– (8) c Maynard b Barwick	6
M. A. Ealham c and b Thomas	1	– (9) c Maynard b Thomas	30
R. P. Davis not out	18	– (4) c Morris b Thomas	18
M. J. McCague lbw b Dale	0	– not out	25
A. P. Igglesden c Metson b Watkin	10	– c Metson b Thomas	2
B 9, l-b 7, w 1, n-b 2	19	B 5, l-b 6, n-b 2	13

1/27 2/37 3/39 4/55 5/55 219   1/93 2/112 3/126 4/136 5/144 242
6/168 7/182 8/193 9/193   6/144 7/165 8/189 9/235

Bonus points – Kent 2, Glamorgan 4.

Bowling: *First Innings*—Watkin 22.1–7–64–3; Thomas 19–4–52–3; Barwick 30–15–37–2; Dale 14–4–27–2; Croft 13–6–23–0. *Second Innings*—Watkin 20–4–60–1; Thomas 19–1–79–5; Barwick 15–4–29–2; Croft 14–6–28–1; Dale 13–5–35–1.

Umpires: J. C. Balderstone and R. C. Tolchard.

At Birmingham, September 12, 13, 14, 15. KENT beat WARWICKSHIRE by an innings and 143 runs.

YOUNG CRICKETER OF THE YEAR

(*Elected by the Cricket Writers Club*)

1950	R. Tattersall	1972	D. R. Owen-Thomas
1951	P. B. H. May	1973	M. Hendrick
1952	F. S. Trueman	1974	P. H. Edmonds
1953	M. C. Cowdrey	1975	A. Kennedy
1954	P. J. Loader	1976	G. Miller
1955	K. F. Barrington	1977	I. T. Botham
1956	B. Taylor	1978	D. I. Gower
1957	M. J. Stewart	1979	P. W. G. Parker
1958	A. C. D. Ingleby-Mackenzie	1980	G. R. Dilley
1959	G. Pullar	1981	M. W. Gatting
1960	D. A. Allen	1982	N. G. Cowans
1961	P. H. Parfitt	1983	N. A. Foster
1962	P. J. Sharpe	1984	R. J. Bailey
1963	G. Boycott	1985	D. V. Lawrence
1964	J. M. Brearley	1986	{ A. A. Metcalfe
1965	A. P. E. Knott		J. J. Whitaker
1966	D. L. Underwood	1987	R. J. Blakey
1967	A. W. Greig	1988	M. P. Maynard
1968	R. M. H. Cottam	1989	N. Hussain
1969	A. Ward	1990	M. A. Atherton
1970	C. M. Old	1991	M. R. Ramprakash
1971	J. Whitehouse	1992	I. D. K. Salisbury

An additional award, in memory of Norman Preston, Editor of *Wisden* from 1951 to 1980, was made to C. W. J. Athey in 1980.

LANCASHIRE

Patron: HM The Queen
President: K. Cranston
Chairman: R. Bennett
Chief Executive: J. M. Bower
Cricket Secretary: Miss R. B. FitzGibbon
  County Cricket Ground, Old Trafford,
  Manchester M16 0PX
  (Telephone: 061-848 7021)
Captain: N. H. Fairbrother
Manager/Coach 1992: J. A. Ormrod
Manager 1993: D. P. Hughes
Coach 1993: D. Lloyd

Lancashire had a miserable year. They finished 12th in the County Championship and joint 11th in the Sunday League, were knocked out of the NatWest Bank Trophy in the second round, and the Benson and Hedges Cup in the quarter-final. It all culminated in the manager, Alan Ormrod, being sacked and former England players Paul Allott and Graeme Fowler being released by the committee at a meeting held on August 10, five weeks before the end of the season.

Yet this was Ormrod's first poor season since taking over as manager in 1987 when he and the new captain, David Hughes, worked together in such harmony that Lancashire finished runners-up in the Championship after 11 years in the bottom six. In their five seasons together Lancashire finished second, ninth, fourth, sixth and eighth. After finishing ninth in the Sunday League in 1987 they were never out of the top three in the next four seasons, being champions in 1989 and runners-up twice. But their most triumphant season was in 1990 when they won both Lord's finals to take the NatWest Bank Trophy and the Benson and Hedges Cup. It looked as though Ormrod was made the scapegoat for a disappointing summer in which the rumbles of discontent both on and off the field became louder as time wore on. In October, Hughes, who had been Ormrod's assistant, was appointed manager and David Lloyd, captain from 1973 to 1977, became coach.

Just a glance at Lancashire's record in the Championship and their final averages tells the story of the season. Only one bowler, the big hearted Mike Watkinson, took more than 50 wickets, none of the regular bowlers averaged better than 33 runs per wicket, and only two teams had fewer than Lancashire's total of 51 bowling bonus points. Wasim Akram, of course, was absent, performing mighty deeds for Pakistan. But Lancashire still had an opening pair of Test bowlers in Phillip DeFreitas and New Zealander Danny Morrison, neither of whom measured up to their international status. Morrison was a whole hearted worker, but in 14 matches took only 36 wickets before injury ruled him out of the final eight weeks. DeFreitas was even more disappointing, carrying a groin injury through a season in which he bowled well below full pace for much of his 290.5 overs in the Championship. And it was that injury that probably cost Lancashire a place in the quarter-finals of the NatWest Trophy with DeFreitas breaking down after bowling only three balls in the second-round tie against Essex at Chelmsford. That finished Lancashire's season. With only one win out of 12 in the Championship and three out of ten in the Sunday League at that stage of the summer, the NatWest Bank Trophy had been their last hope of salvaging something.

Watkinson again bowled more overs than anybody else for Lancashire and the county relied heavily on this work-horse, who willingly turned from his usual medium pace to off-spin as the occasion demanded. He took most of his wickets with his spinners and was often bowled ahead of the specialists, Dexter Fitton and Alex Barnett. Barnett, a slow left-armer formerly with Middlesex, played in all but one of the Championship matches but took only 43 wickets at more than 48 runs each. Pace bowler Peter Martin also played in 21 Championship games, and had a similarly unrewarding season – but the promise was still there. The batting, as usual, took care of itself, and Lancashire achieved more batting bonus points that anyone, which they converted into only three victories, none of them on the excellent and often quick Old Trafford wickets. The formidable and long-established opening partnership of Fowler and Gehan Mendis was broken up, initially by injury and then by selection; between them they played 15 matches and totalled 647 runs without a century. But Nick Speak and Graham Lloyd, both of whom had disappointed in 1991, grasped opportunity with both hands this time. Speak was particularly impressive with 1,892 runs, the highest total for Lancashire since Geoff Pullar scored 1,974 in 1964. Lloyd, too, had his finest season and also excelled in the field, a quality that just might have given him the edge over Speak when he was chosen for England's A tour of Australia in the winter. Mike Atherton cast off the cares of the back injury which had necessitated an operation, scored five centuries and regained his place in the England team.

Neil Fairbrother, in his first season as official captain, was also severely restricted by injury and played in only 12 first-class matches. He finished seventh in the national averages, although he failed to reach 1,000 runs for the first time in nine years. But it was good to see him back in the England selectors' thoughts. He played in all the one-day internationals against Pakistan and was chosen for the England tour of India, along with DeFreitas and Atherton. But it was a dispiriting season for him as far as Lancashire were concerned, as they slipped back amongst county cricket's also-rans. It was true the team were affected by injuries, so badly at Hove that they included only two capped players, the senior of whom was Warren Hegg who became – after Fairbrother, Atherton and Watkinson – Lancashire's fourth captain of the summer. But there was also some inept cricket, particularly from the attack, too much disgruntlement throughout the club, too much unease that undermined players' confidence. – Brian Bearshaw.

428

LANCASHIRE 1992

[*Manchester Evening News*

Back row: J. D. Fitton, G. D. Lloyd, N. J. Speak, N. A. Derbyshire, A. A. Barnett. *Middle row*: L. Brown (*physiotherapist*), I. D. Austin, S. D. Fletcher, R. C. Irani, P. J. Martin, M. A. Sharp, S. P. Titchard, G. Yates, J. Stanworth, J. S. Savage (*coach*). *Front row*: D. P. Hughes (*assistant manager*), D. K. Morrison, P. A. J. DeFreitas, G. Fowler, M. A. Atherton, N. H. Fairbrother (*captain*), P. J. W. Allott, M. Watkinson, G. D. Mendis, W. K. Hegg, J. A. Ormrod (*manager*).

LANCASHIRE RESULTS

All first-class matches – Played 23: Won 4, Lost 6, Drawn 13.

County Championship matches – Played 22: Won 4, Lost 6, Drawn 12.

Bonus points – Batting 73, Bowling 51.

Competition placings – Britannic Assurance County Championship, 12th;
NatWest Bank Trophy, 2nd round; Benson and Hedges Cup, q-f;
Sunday League, 11th equal.

BRITANNIC ASSURANCE CHAMPIONSHIP AVERAGES

BATTING

	Birthplace	M	I	NO	R	HS	Avge
‡N. H. Fairbrother ..	*Warrington*	11	16	5	644	166*	58.54
‡N. J. Speak........	*Manchester*	22	36	3	1,892	232	57.33
J. P. Crawley	*Maldon*	7	10	0	558	172	55.80
‡M. A. Atherton	*Manchester*	17	30	5	1,351	199	54.04
‡G. D. Lloyd	*Accrington*	22	35	9	1,310	132	50.38
‡W. K. Hegg	*Whitefield*	18	24	7	618	80	36.35
S. P. Titchard......	*Warrington*	13	22	3	647	74	34.05
‡G. Fowler	*Accrington*	10	18	2	502	66	31.37
‡P. A. J. DeFreitas ..	*Scotts Head, Dominica*	11	12	1	322	72	29.27
‡I. D. Austin	*Haslingden*	8	10	2	230	115*	28.75
P. J. Martin	*Accrington*	21	24	6	492	133	27.33
J. D. Fitton........	*Littleborough*	7	8	2	135	48*	22.50
‡G. D. Mendis	*Colombo, Ceylon*	5	8	1	145	45	20.71
S. D. Fletcher	*Keighley*	5	4	1	62	23	20.66
‡M. Watkinson.....	*Westhoughton*	19	24	1	466	96	20.26
R. C. Irani	*Leigh*	5	6	0	68	22	11.33
D. K. Morrison§....	*Auckland, New Zealand*	14	12	1	113	30	10.27
A. A. Barnett	*Malaga, Spain*	21	16	10	61	17	10.16

Also batted: G. Chapple (*Skipton*) (2 matches) 1*, 18; ‡J. Stanworth (*Oldham*)
(4 matches) 21.

* *Signifies not out.* ‡ *Denotes county cap.* § *Overseas player.*

The following played a total of 17 three-figure innings for Lancashire in County
Championship matches – M. A. Atherton 5, G. D. Lloyd 4, N. J. Speak 4, I. D. Austin 1,
J. P. Crawley 1, N. H. Fairbrother 1, P. J. Martin 1.

BOWLING

	O	M	R	W	BB	5W/i	Avge
D. K. Morrison	335.4	52	1,209	36	6-48	1	33.58
P. A. J. DeFreitas	290.5	52	912	27	6-94	1	33.77
J. D. Fitton	166.1	37	453	13	4-81	0	34.84
M. Watkinson	629.2	128	2,118	59	6-62	3	35.89
P. J. Martin	512.3	128	1,476	36	4-45	0	41.00
I. D. Austin	164.5	41	522	12	3-44	0	43.50
A. A. Barnett.........	571.5	79	2,092	43	5-78	2	48.65

Also bowled: M. A. Atherton 66.1–4–337–3; G. Chapple 48–17–128–5; J. P. Crawley
10–0–90–1; S. D. Fletcher 83–16–363–4; G. Fowler 5–0–60–1; R. C. Irani 33–5–137–3;
G. D. Lloyd 7–0–45–0; N. J. Speak 6–0–66–0.

Wicket-keepers: W. K. Hegg 33 ct, 6 st; J. Stanworth 7 ct, 1 st.

Leading Fielders: G. D. Lloyd 21, N. J. Speak 18, M. A. Atherton 16.

LANCASHIRE v KENT

At Manchester, April 25, 26, 27, 28. Drawn. Lancashire 7 pts, Kent 7 pts. Toss: Lancashire. Lloyd's fourth first-class century, and his first since August 1989, revived Lancashire from 105 for four. It took him 211 minutes and 174 balls, including 14 fours, and developed into his highest score. Lancashire's new spinner, Barnett, had Ward "caught" off his first delivery – a no-ball. Kent looked likely to follow on at 167 for six on the third day, by which time nearly 72 overs had been lost to rain, but Marsh and Davis, with a partnership of 115, enabled them to acquire full batting points before declaring 97 behind. Fowler ended a run of 12 Championship matches without a fifty, before Lancashire set a sporting target of 311 in 75 overs. Kent's chances soon became theoretical, when they were four down for 58. But Benson played solidly for 41 overs to lead a rearguard action, which was completed by the ninth-wicket pair holding out for 13 balls.

Close of play: First day, Lancashire 328-7 (P. A. J. DeFreitas 17*, P. J. Martin 9*); Second day, Kent 130-1 (M. R. Benson 52*, N. R. Taylor 29*); Third day, Lancashire 112-2 (G. Fowler 57*, P. J. Martin 0*).

Lancashire

G. D. Mendis c McCague b Igglesden	12	– lbw b Igglesden		8
G. Fowler c Penn b Igglesden	0	– b Ealham		66
N. J. Speak c Taylor b Igglesden	47	– c and b Cowdrey		36
*N. H. Fairbrother b Ealham	24	– (5) not out		30
G. D. Lloyd c Marsh b Fleming	132	– (6) c Marsh b Benson		20
M. Watkinson b Davis	34	– (7) not out		7
†W. K. Hegg c Davis b Ealham	38			
P. A. J. DeFreitas not out	55			
P. J. Martin c McCague b Ealham	18	– (4) c Ealham b Fleming		30
D. K. Morrison c Marsh b Igglesden	0			
A. A. Barnett c Penn b Ealham	17			
B 1, l-b 11, w 1, n-b 7	20	L-b 6, w 2, n-b 8		16

1/3 2/27 3/72 4/105 5/168   **397**   1/21 2/112 3/124   (5 wkts dec.) **213**
6/285 7/316 8/365 9/366   4/170 5/201

Bonus points – Lancashire 4, Kent 3 (Score at 100 overs: 328-7).

Bowling: *First Innings*—Igglesden 34–5–85–4; McCague 24–4–82–0; Ealham 24.3–4–81–4; Penn 18–4–72–0; Davis 19–5–58–1; Fleming 4–1–7–1. *Second Innings*—Igglesden 7–2–20–1; McCague 5–0–20–0; Fleming 7–1–35–1; Penn 10–2–23–0; Cowdrey 6–2–15–1; Davis 8–2–33–0; Ealham 6–0–33–1; Benson 2–0–18–1; Ward 1.5–0–10–0.

Kent

T. R. Ward b Watkinson	40	– c Morrison b DeFreitas		6
*M. R. Benson c Hegg b Martin	53	– b Morrison		38
N. R. Taylor c Barnett b Watkinson	40	– c Lloyd b Martin		1
G. R. Cowdrey lbw b Watkinson	1	– c Hegg b Martin		27
M. V. Fleming lbw b Watkinson	6	– b Morrison		1
†S. A. Marsh c Fowler b Martin	78	– lbw b Morrison		37
M. A. Ealham c Hegg b DeFreitas	0	– b Watkinson		33
R. P. Davis not out	54	– not out		24
C. Penn not out	3	– c Lloyd b Watkinson		0
M. J. McCague (did not bat)		– not out		1
B 5, l-b 13, n-b 7	25	B 9, l-b 6, w 1, n-b 8		24

1/85 2/142 3/142 4/144 5/156   (7 wkts dec.) **300**   1/8 2/11 3/49 4/58   (8 wkts) **192**
6/167 7/282   5/117 6/133 7/191 8/191

A. P. Igglesden did not bat.

Bonus points – Kent 4, Lancashire 3.

Bowling: *First Innings*—DeFreitas 18–3–47–1; Martin 24–6–54–2; Morrison 14–1–63–0; Barnett 20–3–58–0; Watkinson 21–6–60–4. *Second Innings*—DeFreitas 13–2–34–1; Martin 11–1–26–2; Morrison 13–3–41–3; Watkinson 18.5–5–47–2; Barnett 12–4–29–0.

Umpires: B. Leadbeater and A. G. T. Whitehead.

At Lord's, May 7, 8, 9, 10. LANCASHIRE drew with MIDDLESEX.

At Leicester, May 14, 15, 16. LANCASHIRE beat LEICESTERSHIRE by an innings and 45 runs.

LANCASHIRE v DERBYSHIRE

At Blackpool, May 20, 21, 22. Derbyshire won by five wickets. Derbyshire 23 pts, Lancashire 8 pts. Toss: Lancashire. Austin scored the second Championship century of his career and shared with Hegg in a sixth-wicket stand of 178 to secure Lancashire's fourth batting point. Derbyshire also needed a middle-order revival, centred on Adams, to achieve full points. Atherton, captaining Lancashire for the first time, batted 69 overs for a flawless second-innings century, adding 111 to his overnight score before his lunchtime declaration gave Derbyshire 69 overs to score 301. Bowler, with his second hundred of the week, steered Derbyshire home with 11 balls to spare. He received considerable support from Morris, who hit a spectacular 98 off 94 balls, with four sixes and 11 fours, as they added 149 in 31 overs for the second wicket.

Close of play: First day, Derbyshire 27-2 (P. D. Bowler 15*); Second day, Lancashire 79-0 (M. A. Atherton 29*, S. P. Titchard 47*).

Lancashire

*M. A. Atherton c Bowler b Mortensen	18	– not out	140
S. P. Titchard c Bowler b Goldsmith	29	– lbw b Jean-Jacques	54
N. J. Speak c and b Jean-Jacques	61	– c Bowler b Sladdin	64
G. D. Lloyd b Mortensen	5	– not out	4
M. Watkinson c and b Jean-Jacques	15		
†W. K. Hegg lbw b Jean-Jacques	59		
I. D. Austin not out	115		
R. C. Irani c Morris b Jean-Jacques	5		
B 4, l-b 11, w 1, n-b 4	20	B 1, l-b 5, w 2, n-b 3	11

1/35 2/53 3/70 4/133 5/139 (7 wkts dec.) 327   1/103 2/241 (2 wkts dec.) 273
6/317 7/327

P. J. Martin, D. K. Morrison and A. A. Barnett did not bat.

Bonus points – Lancashire 4, Derbyshire 3.

Bowling: *First Innings*—Malcolm 16–1–64–0; Mortensen 21–6–46–2; Goldsmith 18–2–64–1; Jean-Jacques 17.4–5–46–4; Sladdin 27–4–92–0. *Second Innings*—Malcolm 6–2–22–0; Goldsmith 9–2–24–0; Mortensen 4–1–12–0; Sladdin 24.2–4–89–1; Jean-Jacques 10–0–40–1; Adams 8–2–36–0; O'Gorman 7–0–38–0; Bowler 1–0–6–0.

Derbyshire

*K. J. Barnett b Morrison	10	– b Barnett	44
P. D. Bowler st Hegg b Barnett	53	– not out	104
R. W. Sladdin c Lloyd b Martin	0		
J. E. Morris lbw b Martin	0	– (3) c Lloyd b Morrison	98
T. J. G. O'Gorman lbw b Watkinson	27	– (4) c Speak b Watkinson	42
C. J. Adams lbw b Watkinson	72	– (5) c Hegg b Barnett	0
S. C. Goldsmith not out	60	– (6) st Hegg b Barnett	6
†K. M. Krikken c Atherton b Austin	44	– (7) not out	0
M. Jean-Jacques b Austin	0		
O. E. Malcolm c Irani b Watkinson	5		
O. H. Mortensen not out	13		
B 8, l-b 5, n-b 3	16	B 1, l-b 3, w 1, n-b 2	7

1/25 2/27 3/27 4/79 5/127 (9 wkts dec.) 300   1/68 2/217 3/293 (5 wkts) 301
6/183 7/249 8/249 9/258   4/293 5/300

Bonus points – Derbyshire 4, Lancashire 4.

Bowling: *First Innings*—Morrison 21–2–59–1; Martin 20–5–40–2; Watkinson 19–1–75–3; Austin 10–3–30–2; Barnett 21.3–6–83–1. *Second Innings*—Morrison 11–1–53–1; Martin 10–2–32–0; Watkinson 17.1–2–70–1; Barnett 19–1–93–3; Austin 10–2–49–0.

Umpires: A. A. Jones and G. Sharp.

LANCASHIRE v HAMPSHIRE

At Manchester, May 23, 25, 26. Hampshire won by 172 runs. Hampshire 22 pts, Lancashire 6 pts. Toss: Hampshire. A remarkable final session in which Lancashire lost all ten wickets for 39 runs, eight of them to the fast-medium Shine, gave Hampshire an unexpected victory which made them Championship leaders. Lancashire had been given two sessions to score 344, on a strip so perfect that the TCCB pitches inspector Harry Brind had come to pay an admiring visit. In the third over after tea – taken with Lancashire 123 for no wicket – Shine made Titchard play on for the first of eight wickets for 13 runs in 38 balls. He moved the ball both ways off the seam for easily his best figures, whch included the hat-trick, with Lloyd, Hegg and Austin his victims, and he made it four in five balls by dismissing Martin before Marshall was recalled to take the last wicket with 8.5 overs remaining. Shine also took the first five wickets in Lancashire's previous innings, including Atherton, who had resumed after being struck on the wrist by his first ball. But Lloyd's unbeaten 102, off 124 balls, averted the possibility of the follow-on. Middleton's 211 runs in the match included his fourth hundred of the summer and made him the country's leading run-scorer with 762.

Close of play: First day, Lancashire 39-1 (S. P. Titchard 14*, N. J. Speak 15*); Second day, Hampshire 156-1 (T. C. Middleton 57*, D. I. Gower 60*).

Hampshire

K. D. James c Hegg b Martin	98	– (2) c Lloyd b Watkinson	24
T. C. Middleton c Speak b Watkinson	73	– (1) not out	138
D. I. Gower c Speak b Austin	74	– c Lloyd b Atherton	71
R. A. Smith c Atherton b Martin	34		
J. R. Wood b Barnett	14	– (6) not out	13
*M. C. J. Nicholas not out	26	– (4) b Barnett	45
M. D. Marshall not out	13		
†A. N. Aymes (did not bat)		– (5) c Lloyd b Barnett	6
B 4, l-b 6, n-b 7	17	B 11, l-b 7, n-b 1	19

1/164 2/215 3/296 4/296 5/325 (5 wkts dec.) 349 1/60 2/174 (4 wkts dec.) 316
3/264 4/294

S. D. Udal, C. A. Connor and K. J. Shine did not bat.

Bonus points – Hampshire 4, Lancashire 2 (Score at 100 overs: 336-5).

Bowling: *First Innings*—Morrison 17-2-63-0; Martin 23-6-40-2; Irani 6-0-21-0; Barnett 25-2-108-1; Watkinson 19-3-66-1; Austin 11-3-41-1. *Second Innings*—Morrison 7-1-30-0; Martin 8-5-8-0; Barnett 26-4-96-2; Watkinson 24-1-90-1; Atherton 17-0-74-1.

Lancashire

*M. A. Atherton c sub b Shine	13	– b Shine	52
S. P. Titchard c Aymes b Shine	47	– b Shine	73
P. J. Martin b Shine	4	– (9) c Aymes b Shine	2
N. J. Speak c Wood b Shine	58	– (3) c Gower b Connor	11
G. D. Lloyd not out	102	– (4) c Middleton b Shine	13
M. Watkinson c Aymes b Shine	0	– (5) c Gower b Shine	0
†W. K. Hegg lbw b Udal	80	– (6) b Shine	1
I. D. Austin not out	2	– (7) c Aymes b Shine	1
R. C. Irani (did not bat)		– (8) c Aymes b Marshall	8
D. K. Morrison (did not bat)		– b Shine	1
A. A. Barnett (did not bat)		– not out	0
B 5, l-b 2, n-b 9	16	L-b 3, n-b 6	9

1/4 2/111 3/118 4/135 5/135 (6 wkts dec.) 322 1/132 2/135 3/156 171
6/304   4/158 5/159 6/159
                                               7/160 8/162 9/164

Bonus points – Lancashire 4, Hampshire 2.

In the first innings M. A. Atherton retired hurt at 0 and resumed at 111.

Bowling: *First Innings*—Shine 16–3–58–5; Connor 15–1–91–0; Udal 18–5–61–1; Marshall 10–1–48–0; James 13–2–42–0; Smith 1.5–0–15–0. *Second Innings*—Marshall 5.1–2–8–1; Connor 11–0–44–1; Shine 16–3–47–8; Udal 17–5–41–0; James 7–0–28–0.

Umpires: A. A. Jones and G. Sharp.

LANCASHIRE v SOMERSET

At Manchester, May 29, 30, June 1. Drawn. Lancashire 8 pts, Somerset 7 pts. Toss: Lancashire. The feature of a game restricted by rain to 172.5 overs was the batting of two emerging talents in Lathwell and Speak. Lathwell scored 74 off 77 balls with high-quality strokes, while Speak further cemented his place in Lancashire's middle order with his second century of the summer in 114 balls. Somerset, fancying their chances of bowling out Lancashire twice, batted until after lunch on the second day and then took three quick wickets before rain ended play for the day at tea. Atherton and Tavaré were unable to agree on a contrived target on the final day, when Speak, forced to bat at No. 7 after being absent from the field with a hand injury throughout the second day, shared in a sixth-wicket stand of 163 in 34 overs with Watkinson to see Lancashire to safety.

Close of play: First day, Somerset 221–5 (R. J. Bartlett 43*, N. D. Burns 16*); Second day, Lancashire 81–3 (G. Fowler 43*, M. Watkinson 7*).

Somerset

A. N. Hayhurst c Watkinson b Morrison	6	N. A. Mallender c Barnett b Morrison	7
M. N. Lathwell c Fowler b Watkinson	74	A. R. Caddick c sub b Barnett	22
R. J. Harden lbw b DeFreitas	9		
*C. J. Tavaré c Hegg b Martin	49	B 3, l-b 16, w 4, n-b 6	29
R. J. Bartlett c Hegg b DeFreitas	43		
G. D. Rose c Hegg b Martin	9	1/17 2/86 3/92	(9 wkts dec.) 376
†N. D. Burns not out	73	4/169 5/191 6/221	
R. P. Snell c Watkinson b Barnett	55	7/309 8/330 9/376	

A. P. van Troost did not bat.

Bonus points – Somerset 4, Lancashire 4.

Bowling: DeFreitas 25.2–6–70–2; Morrison 25–2–111–2; Martin 12.4–1–45–2; Watkinson 17–3–69–1; Barnett 17.5–6–62–2.

Lancashire

G. Fowler c Lathwell b Caddick	56	†W. K. Hegg not out	6
S. P. Titchard b Mallender	7	P. J. Martin not out	14
*M. A. Atherton c Burns b Mallender	2	B 5, l-b 1, w 1, n-b 7	14
G. D. Lloyd c Caddick b Snell	16		
M. Watkinson c Bartlett b Hayhurst	96	1/20 2/22 3/72	(7 wkts) 313
P. A. J. DeFreitas c Snell b Rose	0	4/114 5/115	
N. J. Speak c Bartlett b Hayhurst	102	6/278 7/293	

D. K. Morrison and A. A. Barnett did not bat.

Bonus points – Lancashire 4, Somerset 3.

Bowling: Mallender 11–3–39–2; Caddick 13–2–34–1; Snell 15–1–86–1; van Troost 11–0–53–0; Rose 15–1–50–1; Hayhurst 8–1–36–2; Lathwell 2–0–9–0.

Umpires: J. D. Bond and D. R. Shepherd.

At Oxford, June 2, 3, 4. LANCASHIRE drew with OXFORD UNIVERSITY.

LANCASHIRE v GLOUCESTERSHIRE

At Manchester, June 5, 6, 8. Drawn. Lancashire 3 pts, Gloucestershire 4 pts. Toss: Gloucestershire. After the first day had been washed out, Speak scored his third Championship century of the season, batting in total for 344 minutes, facing 291 balls and hitting 15 fours and a five. He was last out trying to secure a fourth batting point from the last ball of the 100th over. The innings made him the country's leading run-scorer, and he was awarded his county cap before the Sunday League match the following day. Two declarations on the final day left Gloucestershire to chase 340 in a minimum of 79 overs, but with 192 more needed rain ended play at tea. Hinks was only 12 away from his first hundred since leaving Kent at the end of 1991. Fairbrother pulled a hamstring chasing the ball, a recurrence of his injury in the one-day international at The Oval on May 22, which had kept him out of the game for 11 days. This time he was to be absent for a month.

Close of play: First day, No play; Second day, Gloucestershire 29-1 (S. G. Hinks 16*, A. J. Wright 9*).

Lancashire

G. Fowler b Davies	28	– not out	39
M. A. Atherton c Athey b Walsh	4	– not out	25
N. J. Speak c Hinks b Davies	144		
*N. H. Fairbrother hit wkt b Walsh	21		
G. D. Lloyd c Athey b Walsh	6		
S. P. Titchard c Williams b Walsh	6		
M. Watkinson c Hinks b Davies	42		
†W. K. Hegg b Walsh	41		
I. D. Austin c Hinks b Walsh	1		
D. K. Morrison run out	0		
A. A. Barnett not out	0		
L-b 2, n-b 3	5	L-b 4, n-b 2	6

1/5 2/87 3/116 4/126 5/132   298   (no wkt dec.) 70
6/192 7/281 8/285 9/294

Bonus points – Lancashire 3, Gloucestershire 4.

Bowling: *First Innings*—Walsh 20–6–42–6; Smith 11–1–24–0; Scott 15–1–47–0; Davies 38–10–123–3; Alleyne 10–2–38–0; Athey 6–0–22–0. *Second Innings*—Alleyne 6–0–23–0; Scott 7–1–21–0; Athey 4–0–8–0; Hinks 2.5–1–14–0.

Gloucestershire

G. D. Hodgson c Hegg b Watkinson	0	– lbw b Watkinson	50
S. G. Hinks not out	16	– not out	88
*A. J. Wright not out	9	– not out	5
L-b 2, n-b 2	4	B 1, l-b 2, n-b 2	5

1/1   (1 wkt dec.) 29   1/132   (1 wkt) 148

C. W. J. Athey, M. W. Alleyne, R. J. Scott, R. I. Dawson, A. M. Smith, †R. C. J. Williams, C. A. Walsh and M. Davies did not bat.

Bowling: *First Innings*—Morrison 0.3–0–1–0; Watkinson 3.3–0–18–1; Austin 3–1–8–0. *Second Innings*—Morrison 6–2–7–0; Watkinson 17–1–57–1; Austin 11–1–28–0; Barnett 6–0–27–0; Atherton 6–0–26–0.

Umpires: R. Palmer and N. T. Plews.

At Colwyn Bay, June 12, 13, 15. LANCASHIRE drew with GLAMORGAN.

At Nottingham, June 16, 17, 18. LANCASHIRE drew with NOTTINGHAMSHIRE.

LANCASHIRE v MIDDLESEX

At Manchester, June 19, 20, 22. Drawn. Lancashire 5 pts, Middlesex 5 pts. Toss: Middlesex. After Lancashire were put in, Atherton scored his second century of the summer, Speak his fourth – which made him the first to reach 1,000 Championship runs for the season – and Lloyd his third on another Old Trafford pitch of pace and true bounce. Gatting replied with his third successive hundred in five days before he mistimed a hook off Fletcher and retired for stitches in his forehead; he missed the following day's Sunday League game at Derby. Middlesex, chasing a steep 341 in 66 overs, were put on course by Carr, who hit 80 off 114 balls and shared a third-wicket stand of 133 with Ramprakash, and a 38-ball fifty from Brown. Lancashire's hopes rose when Martin took two wickets, including that of Gatting, who had come in at No. 7, in the penultimate over, leaving Middlesex at 309 for nine. But Fraser survived an over of off-breaks from Watkinson to force a draw.

Close of play: First day, Lancashire 346-3 (G. D. Lloyd 43*, S. P. Titchard 24*); Second day, Middlesex 306-3 (K. R. Brown 38*, J. D. Carr 7*).

Lancashire

G. Fowler c Carr b Headley	19	– c and b Embs	28
*M. A. Atherton c Fraser b Taylor	135	– b Weekes	43
N. J. Speak c Carr b Weekes	111	– not out	74
G. D. Lloyd not out	103	– not out	34
S. P. Titchard not out	68		
B 5, l-b 10, w 1, n-b 4	20	B 4, l-b 4, w 1, n-b 2	11

1/32 2/265 3/287   (3 wkts dec.) 456   1/76 2/78   (2 wkts dec.) 190

M. Watkinson, S. D. Fletcher, D. K. Morrison, P. J. Martin, †J. Stanworth and A. A. Barnett did not bat.

Bonus points – Lancashire 4, Middlesex 1 (Score at 100 overs: 309-3).

Bowling: *First Innings*—Taylor 25-3-98-1; Fraser 28-4-73-0; Headley 19-1-72-1; Emburey 29-4-77-0; Weekes 29-2-95-1; Gatting 3-0-26-0. *Second Innings*—Fraser 5-1-14-0; Taylor 7-0-23-0; Emburey 7-2-25-1; Weekes 5-0-16-1; Ramprakash 7-0-34-0; Roseberry 7-0-70-0; Headley 1-1-0-0.

Middlesex

D. L. Haynes b Martin	17	– b Morrison	16
M. A. Roseberry c Atherton b Martin	32	– c Fletcher b Martin	23
*M. W. Gatting retired hurt	126	– (7) b Martin	27
M. R. Ramprakash c and b Martin	69	– (3) c Stanworth b Morrison	63
†K. R. Brown not out	38	– b Martin	56
J. D. Carr not out	7	– (4) c Fletcher b Watkinson	80
P. N. Weekes (did not bat)		– (6) st Stanworth b Watkinson	3
J. E. Emburey (did not bat)		– c sub b Fletcher	26
A. R. C. Fraser (did not bat)		– not out	2
D. W. Headley (did not bat)		– c Titchard b Martin	0
C. W. Taylor (did not bat)		– not out	0
L-b 6, w 1, n-b 10	17	B 5, l-b 8	13

1/53 2/57 3/195   (3 wkts dec.) 306   1/36 2/40 3/173   (9 wkts) 309
                                     4/215 5/242 6/264
                                     7/305 8/309 9/309

Bonus points – Middlesex 4, Lancashire 1.

In the first innings M. W. Gatting retired hurt at 294.

Bowling: *First Innings*—Morrison 15-2-43-0; Martin 20-7-67-3; Watkinson 26-5-85-0; Fletcher 8-0-33-0; Barnett 12-1-58-0; Atherton 3-0-14-0. *Second Innings*—Morrison 14-1-65-2; Martin 18-7-45-4; Watkinson 25-2-135-2; Barnett 7-0-38-0; Fletcher 2-0-13-1.

Umpires: J. H. Harris and V. A. Holder.

At Ilford, June 26, 27. LANCASHIRE lost to ESSEX by an innings and 37 runs.

At Maidstone, July 3, 4, 6. LANCASHIRE drew with KENT.

LANCASHIRE v LEICESTERSHIRE

At Southport, July 14, 15, 16. Leicestershire won by eight runs. Leicestershire 23 pts, Lancashire 7 pts. Toss: Leicestershire. Leicestershire's exciting victory brought revenge for their innings defeat two months earlier. After taking his first wicket during seven overs of seam bowling, Watkinson switched to off-spin to claim another five, his best return in three years, as Leicestershire were bowled out by tea. Fifteen wickets fell on the second day, on a pitch taking more and more spin, although Leicestershire relied on pace to restrict Lancashire's first-innings lead to 23. When Lancashire were 99 soon after lunch on the final day, needing 60 more for victory with eight wickets in hand, Briers made a double bowling change. Left-arm spinner Chris Hawkes, 20, in only his second first-class match, and seamer Parsons took those eight wickets in 19.5 overs.

Close of play: First day, Lancashire 125-2 (P. J. Martin 0*, N. J. Speak 8*); Second day, Leicestershire 141-7 (L. Potter 10*, G. J. Parsons 0*).

Leicestershire

T. J. Boon c Atherton b Watkinson	76	– c Atherton b Martin	24
*N. E. Briers b Morrison	8	– b Fitton	46
J. J. Whitaker c Atherton b Morrison	5	– c Speak b Morrison	25
B. F. Smith c and b Watkinson	20	– b Barnett	1
L. Potter c Speak b Watkinson	21	– b Barnett	24
V. J. Wells c Hegg b Morrison	51	– c Lloyd b Fitton	5
†P. A. Nixon c Speak b Watkinson	12	– c Speak b Barnett	3
W. K. M. Benjamin b Morrison	11	– c Lloyd b Watkinson	14
G. J. Parsons c and b Watkinson	19	– c Hegg b Watkinson	5
C. J. Hawkes not out	17	– c Fairbrother b Watkinson	12
D. J. Millns c Atherton b Watkinson	0	– not out	9
B 4, l-b 8, w 2, n-b 3	17	L-b 11, w 2	13

1/9 2/18 3/52 4/126 5/143   257   1/56 2/92 3/107 4/109 5/119   181
6/171 7/206 8/221 9/257   6/122 7/141 8/160 9/160

Bonus points – Leicestershire 3, Lancashire 4.

Bowling: *First Innings*—Morrison 12–0–70–4; Martin 18–9–43–0; Watkinson 26–7–82–6; Barnett 7–0–38–0; Fitton 4–1–12–0. *Second Innings*—Morrison 11–6–20–1; Martin 9–2–22–1; Watkinson 17.1–4–55–3; Barnett 21–4–57–3; Fitton 9–2–16–2.

Lancashire

G. Fowler c Smith b Millns	62	– c Benjamin b Millns	12
M. A. Atherton c Benjamin b Potter	36	– c Smith b Millns	11
P. J. Martin c Briers b Millns	18	– (9) b Hawkes	6
N. J. Speak c Nixon b Potter	13	– (3) c Boon b Hawkes	39
G. D. Lloyd c Whitaker b Millns	28	– (4) c Nixon b Parsons	30
*N. H. Fairbrother c Whitaker b Parsons	51	– (5) c Boon b Parsons	7
M. Watkinson c Briers b Millns	0	– (6) c Millns b Parsons	18
†W. K. Hegg c Smith b Parsons	21	– (7) c Benjamin b Hawkes	3
J. D. Fitton lbw b Parsons	0	– (8) c Parsons b Hawkes	6
D. K. Morrison c Boon b Parsons	14	– c Potter b Parsons	2
A. A. Barnett not out	5	– not out	0
B 15, l-b 7, w 1, n-b 9	32	B 8, l-b 6, n-b 2	16

1/114 2/114 3/130 4/173 5/180   280   1/26 2/33 3/100 4/100 5/131   150
6/185 7/246 8/246 9/267   6/136 7/142 8/148 9/148

Bonus points – Lancashire 3, Leicestershire 4.

Bowling: *First Innings*—Benjamin 21–3–67–0; Millns 18–6–65–4; Wells 14–2–41–0; Parsons 21–8–34–4; Hawkes 10–3–24–0; Potter 12–4–27–2. *Second Innings*—Benjamin 5–0–29–0; Millns 9–0–46–2; Potter 7–2–18–0; Hawkes 10–3–18–4; Parsons 9.5–4–25–4.

Umpires: K. E. Palmer and G. Sharp.

At Northampton, July 17, 18, 20. LANCASHIRE drew with NORTHAMPTONSHIRE.

At Hove, July 21, 22, 23. LANCASHIRE drew with SUSSEX.

At Leeds, July 31, August 1, 3. LANCASHIRE lost to YORKSHIRE by four wickets.

LANCASHIRE v SURREY

At Lytham, August 4, 5, 6. Lancashire won by 86 runs. Lancashire 20 pts, Surrey 3 pts. Toss: Lancashire. Lancashire's first Championship win for nearly 12 weeks, and only their second of the season, was achieved with 13 balls remaining after Surrey's last pair had hung on for 10.5 overs. Crawley, restored to the team after being dropped at Headingley, batted for almost the whole of the first day, a cultured innings and his second century of 1992. Speak, however, threw away the chance of his fifth hundred when he was stumped trying to get there with a six. Darren Bicknell's first century since April 13 came on a day reduced to two sessions, and he lost only two partners in making it. Reciprocal declarations left Surrey 66 overs in which to score 291, a target that soon became unrealistic.

Close of play: First day, Lancashire 376-3 (N. H. Fairbrother 66*, G. D. Lloyd 2*); Second day, Surrey 253-2 (D. J. Bicknell 120*, M. A. Lynch 20*).

Lancashire

S. P. Titchard c Sargeant b M. P. Bicknell	23	
J. P. Crawley lbw b Kendrick	172	– lbw b Kendrick 16
N. J. Speak st Sargeant b Kendrick	95	– c Brown b Kendrick 20
*N. H. Fairbrother not out	66	– (5) not out 16
G. D. Lloyd not out	2	– (4) lbw b Boiling 59
M. Watkinson (did not bat)		– c Sargeant b Kendrick 14
†W. K. Hegg (did not bat)		– not out 20
P. A. J. DeFreitas (did not bat)		– (1) c Boiling b Kendrick 17
B 4, l-b 8, n-b 6	18	L-b 2, n-b 3 5

1/55 2/216 3/368   (3 wkts. dec.) 376   1/35 2/43 3/117   (5 wkts dec.) 167
                                                4/117 5/139

J. D. Fitton, P. J. Martin and A. A. Barnett did not bat.

Bonus points – Lancashire 4 (Score at 100 overs: 323-2).

Bowling: *First Innings*—M. P. Bicknell 17–1–55–1; Benjamin 12–1–33–0; Boiling 37–6–109–0; Kendrick 41–6–143–2; Lynch 3–0–24–0. *Second Innings*—M. P. Bicknell 3–0–17–0; Benjamin 5–0–19–0; Kendrick 16–6–46–4; Boiling 14–3–55–1; Lynch 1.5–0–20–0; Brown 1–0–8–0.

Surrey

D. J. Bicknell not out	120	– lbw b DeFreitas	4
P. D. Atkins c Crawley b Barnett	33	– lbw b Martin	10
G. P. Thorpe c Watkinson b Fitton	66	– c Lloyd b Watkinson	28
*M. A. Lynch not out	20	– c Crawley b Watkinson	17
D. M. Ward (did not bat)		– c Crawley b Watkinson	11
A. D. Brown (did not bat)		– c Speak b Fitton	62
M. P. Bicknell (did not bat)		– not out	58
†N. F. Sargeant (did not bat)		– c Fairbrother b Fitton	2
J. E. Benjamin (did not bat)		– c Fairbrother b Barnett	2
N. M. Kendrick (did not bat)		– c Speak b Barnett	0
J. Boiling (did not bat)		– c Hegg b Watkinson	5
B 4, l-b 9, w 1	14	B 1, l-b 3, n-b 1	5

1/99 2/213   (2 wkts dec.) 253   1/14 2/14 3/57 4/64 5/85   204
                                                     6/172 7/183 8/190 9/190

Bonus points – Surrey 3.

Bowling: *First Innings*—DeFreitas 8–1–20–0; Martin 7–1–27–0; Watkinson 17–5–40–0; Barnett 22–1–86–1; Fitton 27–5–67–1. *Second Innings*—DeFreitas 10–2–33–1; Martin 9–3–13–1; Barnett 22–4–67–2; Watkinson 13.5–2–60–4; Fitton 9–0–27–2.

Umpires: J. D. Bond and G. I. Burgess.

LANCASHIRE v WORCESTERSHIRE

At Manchester, August 7, 8, 10. Drawn. Lancashire 4 pts, Worcestershire 2 pts. Toss: Lancashire. A double forfeiture after the second day had been lost to rain gave Worcestershire 83 overs in which to score 350, a target that was never in sight. Lloyd's best season continued with his fourth century, before Lancashire's bowlers took control on the final day. Sending down 54.5 overs of spin on a pitch that was responding only slowly, they were finally denied by Worcestershire's ninth-wicket pair, who held out for eight overs. The day was more memorable for the Lancashire committee meeting in the evening, at which it was decided to sack manager Alan Ormrod and release two distinguished players, Paul Allott and Graeme Fowler.

Close of play: First day, Lancashire 321-5 (N. H. Fairbrother 61*, W. K. Hegg 12*); Second day, No play.

Lancashire

G. Fowler lbw b Radford	16	†W. K. Hegg not out	31
J. P. Crawley lbw b Illingworth	29		
N. J. Speak c Rhodes b Radford	71	B 1, l-b 7, n-b 8	16
G. D. Lloyd c Rhodes b Illingworth	101		
*N. H. Fairbrother not out	70	1/23 2/67 3/202 (5 wkts dec.) 349	
M. Watkinson lbw b Illingworth	15	4/252 5/302	

P. A. J. DeFreitas, P. J. Martin, J. D. Fitton and A. A. Barnett did not bat.

Bonus points – Lancashire 4, Worcestershire 2 (Score at 100 overs: 326-5).

Bowling: Radford 19–5–61–2; Newport 18–2–64–0; Tolley 10–1–37–0; Illingworth 27–7–74–3; Haynes 11.2–2–32–0; Hick 6–1–23–0; Weston 3–0–13–0; D'Oliveira 17–6–37–0.

Lancashire forfeited their second innings.

Worcestershire

Worcestershire forfeited their first innings.

*T. S. Curtis c Lloyd b Watkinson	24	P. J. Newport c Fairbrother b Barnett . 5
W. P. C. Weston c Crawley b DeFreitas	9	R. K. Illingworth not out 16
G. A. Hick b Barnett	35	C. M. Tolley not out 4
D. A. Leatherdale c Lloyd b Fitton	40	B 4, l-b 6, w 3 13
D. B. D'Oliveira b Fitton	31	
G. R. Haynes c Fairbrother		1/23 2/50 3/87 (8 wkts) 197
b Watkinson .	4	4/122 5/136 6/166
†S. J. Rhodes b DeFreitas	16	7/173 8/182

N. V. Radford did not bat.

Bowling: DeFreitas 17–6–40–2; Martin 11–4–23–0; Watkinson 28–11–54–2; Barnett 14.5–3–40–2; Fitton 12–2–30–2.

Umpires: J. D. Bond and G. I. Burgess.

At Birmingham, August 18, 19, 20. LANCASHIRE beat WARWICKSHIRE by an innings and 25 runs.

LANCASHIRE v YORKSHIRE

At Manchester, August 26, 27, 28, 29. Drawn. Lancashire 4 pts, Yorkshire 2 pts. Toss: Yorkshire. This game was ruined by rain. After the first two days had been washed out, only 65 overs were possible on the third day, but that was enough to enable Atherton to score his fourth Roses century in consecutive years, all at Old Trafford. Lancashire batted on until lunchtime on the final day, when DeFreitas hit Batty for five sixes and two fours, before a declaration and double forfeiture left Yorkshire with a stiff target of 385 in at least 71 overs. A heavy shower cut out 16 overs and more rain ended the game at 5.15 p.m.

Close of play: First day, No play; Second day, No play; Third day, Lancashire 233-3 (M. A. Atherton 103*, G. D. Lloyd 15*).

Lancashire

M. A. Atherton b Batty...............	119	P. A. J. DeFreitas c Kellett b Robinson 44
J. P. Crawley c Byas b Jarvis........	1	J. D. Fitton not out 22
N. J. Speak c Robinson b Batty.......	42	B 6, l-b 3, n-b 3 12
*N. H. Fairbrother c Byas b Hartley...	67	
G. D. Lloyd not out...............	77	1/6 2/71 3/174 (6 wkts dec.) 384
M. Watkinson lbw b Jarvis	0	4/274 5/287 6/344

P. J. Martin, †J. Stanworth and A. A. Barnett did not bat.

Bonus points – Lancashire 4, Yorkshire 2.

Bowling: Jarvis 23–5–55–2; Hartley 18–0–72–1; Robinson 22–2–66–1; Batty 21–3–122–2; Grayson 12–1–60–0.

Lancashire forfeited their second innings.

Yorkshire

Yorkshire forfeited their first innings.

*M. D. Moxon lbw b Martin	21	†R. J. Blakey not out............... 0
S. A. Kellett b Watkinson...........	39	L-b 3 3
A. A. Metcalfe c Watkinson b Barnett .	34	
C. White not out	24	1/52 2/64 3/121 (3 wkts) 121

D. Byas, A. P. Grayson, P. W. Jarvis, P. J. Hartley, M. A. Robinson and J. D. Batty did not bat.

Bowling: DeFreitas 5–0–26–0; Martin 9–2–26–1; Watkinson 13–4–29–1; Fitton 11–4–31–0; Barnett 4–3–6–1.

Umpires: J. W. Holder and B. J. Meyer.

LANCASHIRE v SUSSEX

At Manchester, September 7, 8, 9. Sussex won by an innings and 182 runs. Sussex 24 pts, Lancashire 2 pts. Toss: Sussex. Salisbury, who was not in England's squad for the winter tour of India announced on the opening day, found some consolation by taking six for 29 in the first innings and 11 wickets for 83 in the match. These were the best figures of his career, yet he was to improve on both sets in his next match, against Yorkshire. Wells, whose century was his fifth of the summer, hit 19 fours and shared in a third-wicket stand of 263 with Lenham against an ineffective Lancashire attack; Martin's wicket was only his fourth in two months. Lancashire's miserable season was reflected in their batting with only Crawley showing sustained resistance in both innings; neither he nor Lloyd, who scored a rapid fifty on the second day, could avert the follow-on, or the defeat which arrived with more than four sessions left.

Close of play: First day, Sussex 331-3 (A. P. Wells 135*, B. T. P. Donelan 1*); Second day, Lancashire 170-9 (G. D. Lloyd 53*, A. A. Barnett 0*).

Sussex

D. M. Smith lbw b Watkinson	39	F. D. Stephenson c Atherton b Barnett . 17
J. W. Hall c Hegg b Martin	14	I. D. K. Salisbury b Barnett 10
N. J. Lenham c Barnett b Fitton	136	E. S. H. Giddins not out 3
*A. P. Wells c Lloyd b DeFreitas	143	
B. T. P. Donelan run out	68	B 3, l-b 13, n-b 1 17
M. P. Speight c Atherton b DeFreitas. .	3	
C. M. Wells c and b Barnett	39	1/49 2/55 3/318 4/349 5/365 563
†P. Moores c DeFreitas b Barnett	74	6/436 7/503 8/544 9/551

Bonus points – Sussex 4, Lancashire 1 (Score at 100 overs: 329-3).

Bowling: DeFreitas 24-8-73-2; Martin 22-2-80-1; Watkinson 47-12-154-1; Fitton 25-4-92-1; Barnett 43.5-7-148-4.

Lancashire

M. A. Atherton c Lenham b C. M. Wells	25	– c Moores b Stephenson	6
J. P. Crawley b Salisbury	43	– b C. M. Wells	93
N. J. Speak b Giddins	18	– b Stephenson	21
*N. H. Fairbrother c Speight b C. M. Wells	11	– b Donelan	20
G. D. Lloyd st Moores b Salisbury	56	– c A. P. Wells b Salisbury	2
M. Watkinson c Moores b Salisbury	2	– c Stephenson b Salisbury	1
†W. K. Hegg c Donelan b Salisbury	0	– not out	27
P. A. J. DeFreitas lbw b Salisbury	0	– c Giddins b C. M. Wells	14
J. D. Fitton b Stephenson	5	– c Smith b Salisbury	4
P. J. Martin c Donelan b Stephenson	0	– c Giddins b Salisbury	4
A. A. Barnett not out	1	– b Salisbury	0
B 1, l-b 3, n-b 9	13	B 5, l-b 5, n-b 5	15

1/49 2/75 3/99 4/109 5/117   174   1/10 2/46 3/81 4/84 5/90   207
6/127 7/127 8/144 9/146   6/171 7/195 8/200 9/206

Bonus points – Lancashire 1, Sussex 4.

Bowling: *First Innings*—Stephenson 14-3-50-1; Giddins 9-0-44-1; C. M. Wells 12-1-47-2; Salisbury 14.5-5-29-6. *Second Innings*—Stephenson 9-0-51-2; Giddins 5-0-34-0; C. M. Wells 11-1-43-2; Salisbury 18.5-5-54-5; Donelan 8-3-15-1.

Umpires: R. A. White and A. G. T. Whitehead.

At Gateshead Fell, September 12, 13, 14, 15. LANCASHIRE beat DURHAM by ten wickets.

LEICESTERSHIRE

President: C. H. Palmer
Chairman: J. M. Josephs
Chairman, Cricket Committee: P. R. Haywood
Chief Executive: F. M. Turner
   County Cricket Ground, Grace Road,
   Leicester LE2 8AD
   (Telephone: 0533-831880/832128)
Captain: N. E. Briers
Cricket Manager: J. Birkenshaw

After several summers of failing fortunes, it was difficult to find an assessment of Leicestershire's prospects in 1992 that did not indicate continuing gloom. The two-year tenure of Bobby Simpson as cricket manager had failed to arrest the county's decline and now the list of best players for whom the Running Fox had come to symbolise a quest for escape had acquired another name in Chris Lewis. Furthermore, membership had slipped to a miserable 3,500 and any prospect of recruiting a like replacement for Lewis had been knocked on the head by a record deficit of almost £70,000.

To finish eighth in the Championship (compared with 16th in 1991) and reach the final of the NatWest Trophy can be regarded therefore as a performance of considerable merit. In July, Leicestershire won four games out of six (the other two were rain-affected). On July 23, after the second win over Durham, they went second in the table and then they bowled out Essex for 75 at Grace Road in the next match and beat them, there was actually a moment when it appeared possible that Leicestershire might be in with a real chance of the Championship. However, their challenge never appeared particularly robust and its fragility was exposed at the beginning of August when David Millns and Vince Wells, the team's most successful bowlers, were simultaneously lost through injury. In their absence, the momentum quickly disappeared, though the improbability of the season was summed up when Jonathan Agnew, three years after his retirement, was tempted out of the BBC box to perform as an emergency stand-in in the NatWest semi-final. He bowled beautifully. Every effort was made to restore the pair to fitness in time for the final against Northamptonshire but Millns was short of match practice and below par. Wells was desperately unlucky: he recovered from the injury that originally put him out but was then rendered so weak by a virus that he collapsed the night before the final and spent the following few days in hospital.

Millns had become the country's leading wicket-taker just before his setback and there was talk that his genuinely fast pace might be unleashed against Pakistan in the final Test at The Oval. The injury made this impossible, but his achivement in taking 74 first-class wickets at 20.62 placed him fifth in the national averages and was recognised in selection for the England A tour to Australia. It was also rewarded by Leicestershire, who decided in mid-season to upgrade his

existing one-year contract to five years. The move was a clear sign
both to members and potential predators that Millns would not follo
the path away from Grace Road recently trodden by Phillip DeFreita
David Gower, Lewis, Peter Bowler of Derbyshire, who was the join
leading run-scorer in 1992, and the maturing off-spinner Peter Suc
now with Essex.

Simpson was believed to be no fan of Millns, which adds weight
the feeling that the Australian's credentials as an international coa
did not equip him to run a county side. His successor as Leicestershi
manager, Jack Birkenshaw, was able to draw on a deeper knowledge
the English game, illustrated, for example, by his recruitment of Well
from Kent. Wells scored 526 runs at 30.94 and his hitherto unde
employed medium pace brought him 33 wickets at 22.75 and nin
place in the national averages. Leicestershire had another seame
Gordon Parsons, only two places below Wells, which is an indication
where the team's strengths lay. With Winston Benjamin back
overseas player, in place of John Maguire, and left-armer Alan Mulla
recovered from a back injury, the seam attack was potentially one
the strongest in the country and Grace Road wickets were prepare
with this in mind.

The nature of home pitches explains in part why several recognise
batsmen achieved relatively modest aggregates compared with previo
seasons. Tim Boon bucked the trend, arguably batting as well as he h
during 13 seasons as a first-team player. In contrast, James Whitak
and Laurie Potter fell below their usual standard. Ben Smith, wh
had promised much as a 19-year-old in 1991, struggled to maintain h
progress but worked hard on his technique; Justin Benson had an i
consistent year and it was as well that he enhanced his reputation as
slip fielder; Paul Nixon took advantage of an injury to Phil Whittica
to claim the wicket-keeper's gloves as his own and demonstrated h
ability as a batsman with a maiden century against Hampshire.

The side had to manage without a quality spinner, although Pott
manfully carried the burden with his slow left-arm and did make son
progress. Martyn Gidley and Chris Hawkes, two specialist spinne
have both been released but the former Warwickshire off-spinn
Adrian Pierson has been recruited for 1993 and will provide Nig
Briers, who displayed a bolder approach in his third year as captai
with an option one hopes he will not employ too sparingly. Ph
Robinson, the former Yorkshire batsman, will be available full tin
after making several valuable contributions in one-day matches la
season, when he had commitments in Minor Counties and club cricke

Leicestershire were awarded a £100,000 grant from the Foundatio
for Recreation and the Arts, which matched a personal donation
£100,000 from the club's honorary life-president, Trevor Bennett. The
were thus able to relaunch a previously shelved scheme to build a
indoor cricket school which, with other improvements, will co
£750,000. – Jon Culley.

LEICESTERSHIRE 1992

[Neville Chadwick Photography

Back row: B. F. Smith, I. J. Sutcliffe, I. F. Plender, P. A. Nixon, M. I. Gidley, M. T. Brimson, D. G. White, D. L. Maddy.
Middle row: R. Stenner *(physiotherapist)*, R. P. Gofton, A. Roseberry, V. J. Wells, D. J. Millns, C. J. Hawkes, A. D. Mullally, J. D. R.
Benson, L. Potter, A. F. Haye, P. N. Hepworth, P. Whitticase, G. R. Blackburn *(scorer)*. *Front row:* G. J. Parsons, J. J. Whitaker, J. M.
Josephs *(chairman)*, N. E. Briers *(captain)*, C. H. Palmer *(president)*, J. Birkenshaw *(cricket manager)*, F. M. Turner *(chief executive)*, R. A. Cobb,
T. J. Boon. *Inset:* W. K. M. Benjamin.

LEICESTERSHIRE RESULTS

All first-class matches – Played 24: Won 8, Lost 8, Drawn 8.

County Championship matches – Played 22: Won 7, Lost 7, Drawn 8.

Bonus points – Batting 39, Bowling 60.

*Competition placings – Britannic Assurance County Championship, 8th;
NatWest Bank Trophy, finalists; Benson and Hedges Cup, 3rd in Group A;
Sunday League, 18th.*

BRITANNIC ASSURANCE CHAMPIONSHIP AVERAGES

BATTING

	Birthplace	M	I	NO	R	HS	Avge
‡T. J. Boon	Doncaster	22	38	3	1,383	139	39.51
‡N. E. Briers	Leicester	22	39	6	1,092	122*	33.09
V. J. Wells	Dartford	16	23	6	526	56	30.94
‡L. Potter	Bexleyheath	21	33	3	797	96	26.56
P. A. Nixon	Carlisle	15	23	6	451	107*	26.52
B. F. Smith	Corby	14	20	3	441	100*	25.94
‡J. J. Whitaker	Skipton	20	31	2	701	74	24.17
J. D. R. Benson	Dublin, Ireland	17	26	1	571	122	22.84
‡W. K. M. Benjamin§	St John's, Antigua	20	25	3	453	72	20.59
C. J. Hawkes	Loughborough	3	4	1	60	18	20.00
M. I. Gidley	Leicester	5	10	2	143	39	17.87
‡D. J. Millns	Clipstone	17	17	9	143	33*	17.87
R. P. Gofton	Scarborough	4	6	0	100	75	16.66
‡G. J. Parsons	Slough	13	14	2	142	35	11.83
P. N. Hepworth	Ackworth	8	13	1	131	29	10.91
‡P. Whitticase	Solihull	7	10	3	62	18*	8.85
A. D. Mullally	Southend-on-Sea	17	21	6	112	21	7.46

Also batted: P. E. Robinson (*Keighley*) (1 match) 0, 19.

* Signifies not out.   ‡ Denotes county cap.   § Overseas player.

The following played a total of six three-figure innings for Leicestershire in County
Championship matches – T. J. Boon 2, J. D. R. Benson 1, N. E. Briers 1, P. A. Nixon 1,
B. F. Smith 1.

BOWLING

	O	M	R	W	BB	5W/i	Avge
D. J. Millns	436.3	103	1,401	68	6-87	6	20.60
V. J. Wells	293	90	738	33	4-26	0	22.36
G. J. Parsons	335.2	88	943	36	6-70	2	26.19
W. K. M. Benjamin ...	489	102	1,498	47	4-34	0	31.87
A. D. Mullally	476	115	1,365	38	5-119	1	35.92
L. Potter.............	344.1	78	1,021	25	4-73	0	40.84

Also bowled: J. D. R. Benson 35-4-109-3; T. J. Boon 29-4-175-4; M. I. Gidley
80-20-248-2; R. P. Gofton 46-10-203-5; C. J. Hawkes 42-11-122-5; P. N. Hepworth
68.4-9-301-3; J. J. Whitaker 8-0-86-1.

Wicket-keepers: P. A. Nixon 40 ct, 5 st; P. Whitticase 18 ct.

Leading Fielders: J. D. R. Benson 28, W. K. M. Benjamin 15.

At Cambridge, April 14, 15, 16. LEICESTERSHIRE beat CAMBRIDGE UNIVERSITY by 133 runs.

At Durham University, April 25, 27, 28, 29. LEICESTERSHIRE beat DURHAM by seven wickets.

At Chelmsford, May 7, 8, 9, 11. LEICESTERSHIRE drew with ESSEX.

LEICESTERSHIRE v LANCASHIRE

At Leicester, May 14, 15, 16. Lancashire won by an innings and 45 runs. Lancashire 24 pts, Leicestershire 4 pts. Toss: Lancashire. On an easy-paced pitch, Lancashire were on top almost throughout and won with more than four sessions to spare, after Speak had dominated the first day with a career-best 232, the first double-century of the season. The 25-year-old right-hander faced 251 balls in a four-and-a-half-hour innings of masterful timing featuring 38 fours and two sixes. He scored 115 between lunch and tea, and shared partnerships of 160 with Fairbrother and 139 with Lloyd. Benjamin believed he had Speak caught behind off the glove on 37, but umpire Stickley's rejection of the claim seemed vindicated by bruising to the batsman's lower arm. For Leicestershire, Boon was dropped in the slips when one and survived to make 139, but the home side lost their last seven wickets for 62 as Barnett, the former Middlesex left-arm spinner, returned career-best figures. Following on 227 behind, Leicestershire showed little backbone, and were 84 for eight before Benjamin delayed the inevitable with a remarkable 52-ball 72, striking five fours and five sixes; he slowed down after reaching 50 off just 23 deliveries. Lancashire's satisfaction was tempered by injury to Mendis, whose finger was broken by Millns on the first day.

Close of play: First day, Lancashire 432-5 (G. D. Lloyd 52*, P. A. J. DeFreitas 14*); Second day, Leicestershire 258.

Lancashire

G. D. Mendis c Whitticase b Wells....	31	P. J. Martin c Benson b Benjamin..... 3
M. A. Atherton c Whitticase b Millns..	17	D. K. Morrison lbw b Millns......... 0
N. J. Speak c Boon b Hepworth 232		A. A. Barnett not out 2
*N. H. Fairbrother c Benson b Mullally	65	
G. D. Lloyd c and b Millns	56	L-b 6, w 2, n-b 7............ 15
M. Watkinson c Potter b Hepworth.....	7	
P. A. J. DeFreitas c Benjamin b Millns.	29	1/39 2/90 3/250 4/389 5/408 485
†W. K. Hegg c Hepworth b Benjamin .	28	6/440 7/457 8/464 9/465

Bonus points – Lancashire 4, Leicestershire 1 (Score at 100 overs: 403-4).

Bowling: Benjamin 23.3–4–76–2; Mullally 26–3–86–1; Millns 28–7–123–4; Wells 10–4–34–1; Gidley 19–6–70–0; Benson 4–0–14–0; Potter 11–1–47–0; Hepworth 8–0–29–2.

Leicestershire

T. J. Boon c Speak b Barnett 139	– c Lloyd b DeFreitas...........	5
*N. E. Briers c Hegg b Morrison.............	9	– c Fairbrother b Morrison.....	11
P. N. Hepworth c Watkinson b Martin........	28	– c Speak b Morrison	2
L. Potter c and b Barnett	10	– c Hegg b DeFreitas.........	2
J. D. R. Benson b Barnett	22	– lbw b Martin	22
V. J. Wells b Morrison	6	– c sub b Barnett.............	15
M. I. Gidley lbw b Morrison	0	– c Atherton b Barnett.........	6
†P. Whitticase not out.....................	18	– c Speak b Barnett...........	2
W. K. M. Benjamin b Watkinson	11	– c Hegg b Watkinson.........	72
D. J. Millns b Barnett.....................	0	– c Hegg b Morrison.........	21
A. D. Mullally c sub b Barnett.............	8	– not out.................	10
B 1, l-b 4, n-b 2..............	7	B 8, l-b 1, w 1, n-b 4	14

1/17 2/86 3/129 4/196 5/209	258	1/17 2/18 3/21 4/23 5/56	182
6/211 7/232 8/243 9/244		6/71 7/73 8/84 9/162	

Bonus points – Leicestershire 3, Lancashire 4.

Bowling: *First Innings*—DeFreitas 15–1–39–0; Morrison 15–2–52–3; Martin 8–1–23–1; Barnett 28.1–6–78–5; Watkinson 20–3–61–1. *Second Innings*—DeFreitas 13–1–32–2; Morrison 10–1–39–3; Barnett 11–1–74–3; Martin 7–2–23–1; Watkinson 1.4–0–5–1.

Umpires: J. D. Bond and G. A. Stickley.

LEICESTERSHIRE v MIDDLESEX

At Leicester, May 19, 20, 21, 22. Middlesex won by ten wickets. Middlesex 23 pts, Leicestershire 5 pts. Toss: Middlesex. Embury scored his first century in two years and took four wickets in each innings to give Middlesex their first Championship victory of the season, half an hour before lunch on the fourth day. Middlesex had been in some trouble on the first day after Gatting got out to a loose stroke on 86, leaving Leicestershire as the only county (apart from Middlesex and newcomers Durham) not to suffer a century from him. The eighth-wicket partnership of Embury and Headley, who made a career-best 91, began as a rearguard action but prospered unexpectedly to reach 160. Embury's catching was less reliable: he dropped two catches at second slip off Taylor on the third morning. Both were offered by Benson during a flamboyant period in which he scored 80 of the 118 Leicestershire added to their overnight total. Benson batted 273 minutes in all and hit 15 fours. It was not enough to prevent the follow-on, and the equally bright second-innings fifties from him and Wells, the new recruit from Kent, only just averted an innings defeat. Fraser, on his first Championship appearance for nearly 12 months, bowled with understandable caution.

Close of play: First day, Middlesex 288-7 (J. E. Embury 39*, D. W. Headley 15*); Second day, Leicestershire 130-5 (J. D. R. Benson 42*, M. I. Gidley 9*); Third day, Leicestershire 161-5 (V. J. Wells 23*, M. I. Gidley 6*).

Middlesex

D. L. Haynes c Whitticase b Benjamin	2	– not out	2
M. A. Roseberry lbw b Hepworth	51		
*M. W. Gatting c Benson b Wells	86		
J. D. Carr c Whitticase b Millns	12		
†K. R. Brown c Benjamin b Wells	21		
P. N. Weekes lbw b Millns	24		
J. E. Embury b Potter	102		
N. F. Williams c Briers b Benjamin	14		
D. W. Headley b Potter	91		
A. R. C. Fraser c Mullally b Potter	23		
C. W. Taylor not out	8	– (2) not out	4
B 8, l-b 19, w 1, n-b 5	33		

1/24 2/99 3/132 4/171 5/198   467   (no wkt) 6
6/213 7/249 8/409 9/456

Bonus points – Middlesex 3, Leicestershire 3 (Score at 100 overs: 263-7).

Bowling: *First Innings*—Benjamin 30–5–74–2; Millns 35–5–123–2; Mullally 25–3–55–0; Wells 24–10–38–2; Potter 19.5–4–52–3; Hepworth 24–5–85–1; Gidley 1–0–3–0; Benson 1–0–10–0. *Second Innings*—Hepworth 1.4–1–2–0; Boon 1–0–4–0.

Leicestershire

T. J. Boon c Brown b Taylor	0	– c Embury b Taylor	0
*N. E. Briers c Carr b Embury	21	– c Carr b Embury	53
P. N. Hepworth lbw b Williams	29	– b Headley	5
L. Potter c Brown b Embury	4	– c Carr b Headley	8
J. D. R. Benson c Carr b Embury	122	– c Brown b Headley	58
V. J. Wells c Williams b Taylor	11	– not out	50
M. I. Gidley lbw b Headley	16	– lbw b Embury	6
†P. Whitticase c Brown b Embury	6	– c Gatting b Williams	0
W. K. M. Benjamin c Roseberry b Embury	2	– c Brown b Taylor	16
D. J. Millns c Embury b Williams	1	– lbw b Embury	8
A. D. Mullally not out	13	– c and b Embury	4
B 4, l-b 7, w 2, n-b 10	23	B 1, l-b 3, w 1, n-b 11	16

1/0 2/54 3/59 4/67 5/108   248   1/0 2/17 3/35 4/122 5/148   224
6/194 7/216 8/222 9/225   6/161 7/165 8/195 9/214

Bonus points – Leicestershire 2, Middlesex 4 (Score at 100 overs: 248-9).

Bowling: *First Innings*—Taylor 16–2–60–2; Fraser 5–2–17–0; Williams 22–3–53–3; mburey 32.3–11–44–4; Headley 15–4–41–1; Weekes 10–4–22–0. *Second Innings*—Taylor 4–37–2; Fraser 14–6–20–0; Headley 9–0–31–3; Emburey 32.3–17–45–4; Williams –2–60–1; Weekes 3–0–26–0; Haynes 1–0–1–0.

Umpires: J. D. Bond and G. A. Stickley.

Leicester, May 23, 24, 25. LEICESTERSHIRE lost to PAKISTANIS by eight wickets (See Pakistani tour section).

Swansea, May 29, 30, June 1. LEICESTERSHIRE drew with GLAMORGAN.

Northampton, June 2, 3. LEICESTERSHIRE lost to NORTHAMPTONSHIRE by 166 runs.

Lord's, June 5, 6, 8. LEICESTERSHIRE drew with MIDDLESEX.

LEICESTERSHIRE v SUSSEX

Leicester, June 12, 13. Leicestershire won by ten wickets. Leicestershire 23 pts, Sussex pts. Toss: Leicestershire. An uncharacteristically green pitch could not be held responsible r the brevity of the contest. On the first morning Sussex batted so poorly that they were duced to 65 for six, despite the handicap to Leicestershire's attack when Benjamin ccumbed to a stomach disorder after bowling eight overs. The recovery, led by Moores, uld have been over sooner had the home team's catching been better. Only when hitaker and Smith were together for Leicestershire did the batting acquire any quality. ining forces when Boon retired, struck in the abdomen, they added 108 to reach 165 for e overnight. But they were parted eight runs into the second morning, as Leicestershire llapsed to 251 all out in an hour and 50 minutes. Showing as little resolve as they had in eir first innings, Sussex then lost six wickets before ensuring that their hosts would have bat again, and the eventual target was only 24. Millns, Leicestershire's decidedly sharp ght-arm fast-medium bowler, had match figures of seven for 54.

Close of play: First day, Leicestershire 165-1 (J. J. Whitaker 65*, B. F. Smith 52*).

ussex

. M. Smith c Wells b Millns	7	– lbw b Benjamin	0
W. Hall c Nixon b Benjamin	18	– c sub b Benjamin	0
. J. Lenham b Millns	1	– c Nixon b Benjamin	11
A. P. Wells c Benson b Mullally	32	– c Benjamin b Mullally	36
. P. Speight c Benson b Wells	2	– c Benson b Millns	0
. Moores b Millns	46	– c Benson b Potter	35
D. Stephenson b Mullally	0	– lbw b Potter	0
T. P. Donelan c Nixon b Wells	20	– run out	4
. C. S. Pigott not out	24	– c and b Millns	11
D. K. Salisbury b Millns	0	– not out	2
. N. Jones c Nixon b Mullally	17	– b Millns	0
B 1, l-b 2, w 1	4	L-b 3, n-b 1	4

25 2/25 3/30 4/49 5/65	171	1/0 2/1 3/29 4/30 5/77	103
65 7/129 8/129 9/129		6/78 7/85 8/95 9/101

Bonus points – Sussex 1, Leicestershire 4.

Bowling: *First Innings*—Benjamin 8–1–30–1; Millns 18–8–35–4; Wells 18–7–53–2; ullally 18–6–50–3. *Second Innings*—Benjamin 16–3–50–3; Millns 13.4–7–19–3; Mullally –4–22–1; Potter 5–0–9–2.

Leicestershire

T. J. Boon retired hurt	24	
*N. E. Briers lbw b Jones	18 – not out	▶
J. J. Whitaker hit wkt b Donelan	74	
B. F. Smith c Salisbury b Stephenson	56	
J. D. R. Benson b Donelan	17	
L. Potter c Smith b Donelan	0	
†P. A. Nixon c Salisbury b Pigott	20 – (1) not out	
V. J. Wells run out	28	
W. K. M. Benjamin not out	4	
D. J. Millns lbw b Pigott	1	
A. D. Mullally b Pigott	0	
L-b 4, n-b 5	9	L-b 1

1/31 2/173 3/189 4/189 5/198   251   (no wkt) 2
6/246 7/246 8/251 9/251

Bonus points – Leicestershire 3, Sussex 4.

In the first innings T. J. Boon retired hurt at 57.

Bowling: *First Innings*—Stephenson 17–6–46–1; Jones 7–0–56–1; Pigott 16.5–4–45–; Donelan 22–2–68–3; Salisbury 12–3–32–0. *Second Innings*—Stephenson 3–2–4–0; Pigo 2–0–5–0; Donelan 2.1–1–6–0; Wells 2–1–8–0.

Umpires: J. D. Bond and B. J. Meyer.

LEICESTERSHIRE v HAMPSHIRE

At Leicester, June 16, 17, 18. Drawn. Leicestershire 5 pts, Hampshire 5 pts. Toss: Leiceste shire. A dreadfully slow pitch produced largely dreary cricket, but there were some brig spells. Briers's 63 in 67 overs was not among these; Potter's 96, a hard-hitting 71 off 61 ba by Benjamin and a maiden century by the left-handed reserve wicket-keeper Nixon all wer and they put Leicestershire in a strong position. Hampshire's early progress was ve painful. Since Middleton needed 79 deliveries to make 16, the realisation that he had th scored 1,000 first-class runs sooner than any other batsman in the country, in a mere f visits to the crease, was difficult to digest; the innings was 61 overs old before the run-ra touched two an over. After this, the absorbing finish came as a surprise. Leicestershire declaration on the final morning left Hampshire to score 309 in 68 overs, a target mad possible by Gower's 80 in 82 balls. Parsons then hit back with five wickets for Leiceste shire and when time expired Hampshire were 15 short with one wicket left. With his fift catch, wicket-keeper Parks, in his first Championship match for nearly two years, equalle N. T. McCorkell's Hampshire record of 688 dismissals.

Close of play: First day, Leicestershire 422-7 (P. A. Nixon 94*, G. J. Parsons 9*); Secon day, Hampshire 282-3 (D. I. Gower 44*, M. C. J. Nicholas 37*).

Leicestershire

T. J. Boon c Parks b Shine	3 – c Parks b Connor	
*N. E. Briers b Marshall	63 – c Parks b Shine	1
J. J. Whitaker b Ayling	21 – c sub b Connor	2
B. F. Smith lbw b Marshall	16 – lbw b Connor	2
J. D. R. Benson c Parks b Shine	12 – not out	4
L. Potter c Connor b Shine	96 – c Parks b Nicholas	2
†P. A. Nixon not out	107 – not out	
W. K. M. Benjamin c James b Ayling	71	
G. J. Parsons not out	20	
B 5, l-b 27, n-b 9	41	B 4, l-b 11, n-b 3	1

1/20 2/50 3/74 4/101 5/199   (7 wkts dec.) 450   1/7 2/19 3/28   (5 wkts dec.) 14
6/271 7/390   4/66 5/120

A. D. Mullally and D. J. Millns did not bat.

Bonus points – Leicestershire 4, Hampshire 2 (Score at 100 overs: 383-6).

Bowling: First Innings—Marshall 23–9–48–2; Connor 28–4–89–0; Shine 16–0–74–3; Udal 35–8–137–0; Ayling 13–1–57–2; James 2–0–13–0. Second Innings—Shine 8–1–28–1; Connor 9–1–51–3; Ayling 5–0–17–0; Nicholas 4.3–1–16–1; Middleton 4–0–13–0.

Hampshire

V. P. Terry st Nixon b Potter	99	– c Potter b Parsons	69
T. C. Middleton c Nixon b Benjamin	18	– c Nixon b Mullally	1
K. D. James b Mullally	67	– c Benson b Parsons	34
D. I. Gower not out	44	– b Benjamin	80
*M. C. J. Nicholas not out	37	– not out	46
M. D. Marshall (did not bat)		– lbw b Parsons	8
J. R. Ayling (did not bat)		– c Whitaker b Parsons	1
†R. J. Parks (did not bat)		– c Benson b Parsons	10
S. D. Udal (did not bat)		– c Whitaker b Benjamin	29
C. A. Connor (did not bat)		– run out	0
K. J. Shine (did not bat)		– not out	1
B 11, l-b 3, w 1, n-b 2	17	B 5, l-b 10	15

1/57 2/187 3/195   (3 wkts dec.) 282   1/6 2/52 3/180   (9 wkts) 294
4/194 5/211 6/215
7/233 8/282 9/288

Bonus points – Hampshire 3, Leicestershire 1 (Score at 100 overs: 262-3).

Bowling: First Innings—Benjamin 20–6–47–1; Millns 14–4–38–0; Mullally 19–3–59–1; Potter 35–11–85–1; Parsons 14–4–39–0. Second Innings—Benjamin 16–2–63–2; Mullally 15–4–49–1; Millns 8–1–32–0; Parsons 18–3–79–5; Potter 11–1–56–0.

Umpires: J. D. Bond and B. J. Meyer (N. Dearman deputised for B. J. Meyer on 3rd day).

LEICESTERSHIRE v WORCESTERSHIRE

At Leicester, June 30, July 1, 2. Leicestershire won by nine wickets. Leicestershire 20 pts, Worcestershire 2 pts. Toss: Leicestershire. On the final day, Leicestershire won with ease after a double forfeiture. But they also had the best of the first day, when Millns enhanced his growing reputation by removing five Worcestershire batsmen, before a thunderstorm interrupted the innings at 141 for six. In the afternoon, with an old ball and in intense heat, he took three wickets for two runs in ten deliveries. The storm swamped the covers, and after the second day was lost the captains agreed a target for Leicestershire. So precise was the contract that Benjamin appeared to decline a straightforward catch as Worcestershire put on 91 in 33 overs. Thus the home side required 233 in what became 77 overs. The drying pitch did not give nearly as much help as expected to the spinners, Illingworth and Stemp, who bowled at least one bad ball per over and were ruthlessly punished by Briers and Boon. The Leicestershire openers displayed admirable concentration and technique and were parted only 20 runs from victory, although Briers was dropped three times.

Close of play: First day, Worcestershire 141-6 (P. J. Newport 15*, R. K. Illingworth 3*); Second day, No play.

Worcestershire

*T. S. Curtis c Benjamin b Millns	7	N. V. Radford c Parsons b Potter	5
W. P. C. Weston c Smith b Millns	27	R. D. Stemp not out	16
P. A. Neale c Nixon b Benjamin	38		
G. R. Haynes c Benson b Millns	24		
D. A. Leatherdale c Nixon b Millns	14	L-b 9, n-b 8	17
S. R. Lampitt c Briers b Millns	2		
†S. J. Rhodes lbw b Millns	0	1/17 2/83 3/114 (9 wkts dec.) 232
P. J. Newport not out	75	4/121 5/122 6/125
R. K. Illingworth c Benjamin b Potter	7	7/159 8/165 9/178

Bonus points – Worcestershire 2, Leicestershire 4.

W. P. C. Weston, when 27, retired hurt at 52 and resumed at 159.

Bowling: Benjamin 20–5–50–1; Millns 30–6–87–6; Parsons 17–6–15–0; Potter 9–4–17–2; Wells 10–6–14–0; Boon 4–0–17–0; Whitaker 3–0–23–0.

Worcestershire forfeited their second innings.

Leicestershire

Leicestershire forfeited their first innings.

T. J. Boon c and b Lampitt	....	97
*N. E. Briers not out	....	122
J. J. Whitaker not out	....	8
L-b 3, n-b 4	....	7

1/213   (1 wkt) 234

B. F. Smith, J. D. R. Benson, L. Potter, V. J. Wells, †P. A. Nixon, W. K. M. Benjamin, G. J. Parsons and D. J. Millns did not bat.

Bowling: Newport 10–1–43–0; Radford 3–0–13–0; Illingworth 25–8–58–0; Stemp 25.2–6–81–0; Lampitt 6–0–36–1.

Umpires: M. J. Kitchen and D. O. Oslear.

At Sheffield, July 3, 4, 6. LEICESTERSHIRE drew with YORKSHIRE.

At Southport, July 14, 15, 16. LEICESTERSHIRE beat LANCASHIRE by eight runs.

LEICESTERSHIRE v SOMERSET

At Leicester, July 17, 18, 20. Drawn. Leicestershire 6 pts, Somerset 7 pts. Toss: Leicestershire. Even on a sluggish pitch, Millns confirmed his genuine pace; his five first-innings wickets raised his first-class tally to 50. However, Somerset recovered from a traumatic start. Coming together at 16 for three, Tavaré and Townsend added 100. They were backed up by Rose and Snell, who survived a chance at mid-off second ball before striking 81 off 72 deliveries, the second half-century of his first-class career; 46 of his first 50 runs came in boundaries. Leicestershire had lost their captain and night-watchman in 12 overs overnight, and met more trouble on the second day. At 89 for six they needed to double their total to avoid the follow-on. But Nixon and Wells carefully launched a recovery, and a flourish of 53 from Benjamin left Somerset only 57 runs to the good. They lost both openers in adding 17 to that lead but rain restricted play to just 50 minutes on the last day.

Close of play: First day, Leicestershire 9-2 (T. J. Boon 4*, J. J. Whitaker 0*); Second day, Somerset 21-2 (R. J. Harden 13*, N. A. Mallender 2*).

Somerset

A. N. Hayhurst c and b Millns	5	– lbw b Parsons	....	5
M. N. Lathwell c Hawkes b Benjamin	3	– c sub b Millns	....	0
R. J. Harden lbw b Benjamin	6	– retired hurt	....	47
*C. J. Tavaré b Wells	69	– (5) c Millns b Boon	....	8
G. T. J. Townsend c Boon b Millns	49	– (8) not out	....	0
G. D. Rose c Benjamin b Millns	59	– c Millns b Boon	....	19
†N. D. Burns b Wells	23	– (9) not out	....	0
R. P. Snell c Nixon b Millns	81	– (7) c Wells b Whitaker	....	18
R. P. Lefebvre b Potter	28			
N. A. Mallender not out	0	– (4) c Potter b Benjamin	....	10
H. R. J. Trump c Benjamin b Millns	0			
L-b 4	4	B 1	....	1

1/8 2/14 3/16 4/116 5/136   327   1/1 2/17 3/29   (6 wkts) 108
6/184 7/254 8/323 9/327   4/47 5/103 6/108

Bonus points – Somerset 4, Leicestershire 4.

In the second innings R. J. Harden retired hurt at 81.

Bowling: *First Innings*—Millns 17.3-2-64-5; Benjamin 22-3-83-2; Parsons 18-7-46-0; Hawkes 8-2-28-0; Wells 22-6-71-2; Potter 7-2-31-1. *Second Innings*—Millns 9-3-15-1; Benjamin 9-1-22-1; Parsons 4-0-8-1; Hawkes 1-0-1-0; Boon 3-0-32-2; Whitaker 2-0-29-1.

Leicestershire

J. Boon c Lefebvre b Rose	24	W. K. M. Benjamin c Hayhurst b Rose	53
N. E. Briers c Lathwell b Mallender	1	C. J. Hawkes hit wkt b Snell	18
J. J. Parsons b Trump	1	D. J. Millns not out	0
J. Whitaker c Hayhurst b Trump	36		
B. F. Smith lbw b Snell	0	B 1, l-b 5, n-b 4	10
L. Potter c Burns b Mallender	17		
J. Wells b Rose	42	1/3 2/9 3/49 4/52 5/77	270
P. A. Nixon c Burns b Mallender	68	6/89 7/178 8/201 9/267	

Bonus points – Leicestershire 2, Somerset 3 (Score at 100 overs: 236-8).

Bowling: Mallender 24-8-55-3; Snell 23-6-61-2; Trump 34-13-73-2; Rose 16.4-5-45-3; Hayhurst 8-1-30-0.

Umpires: J. C. Balderstone and J. H. Hampshire.

LEICESTERSHIRE v DURHAM

At Leicester, July 21, 22, 23. Leicestershire won by ten wickets. Leicestershire 23 pts, Durham 4 pts. Toss: Leicestershire. Rain delayed the start until 4 p.m. on the first day, then Millns continued his impressive form on a green pitch. He took the first four wickets inside 19 deliveries; Durham were without Jones for the first time, because of his broken finger, and Botham, in London to receive his OBE. Leicestershire's first-innings lead of 111 owed much to Briers, who occupied the crease for nearly four and a half hours before the last six wickets fell for 36. Millns ran through the visitors' top order again in the second innings. Five more wickets gave him ten in a match for the second time in his career, and made him the country's leading wicket-taker with 61. Another wet start held up the last day, but in the 30 minutes possible before lunch Durham collapsed to 27 for five. An eventual total of 116 all out was their lowest of the season in any competition. It made Leicestershire bat again, but their victory was a formality, and took them to second in the Championship table.

Close of play: First day, Durham 130-8 (C. W. Scott 25*, D. A. Graveney 15*); Second day, Durham 14-1 (W. Larkins 8*, S. P. Hughes 0*).

Durham

W. Larkins c Nixon b Millns	8	– c Benson b Millns	8
Hutton c Nixon b Millns	13	– c Benson b Millns	5
M. P. Briers lbw b Millns	0	– (4) c Nixon b Benjamin	1
J. W. G. Parker c Boon b Benjamin	22	– (5) b Millns	10
D. Glendenen c Nixon b Millns	6	– (6) lbw b Benjamin	5
S. W. Henderson c Benson b Mullally	31	– (7) c Whitaker b Benjamin	27
C. W. Scott not out	35	– (8) c Nixon b Millns	33
I. M. McEwan c Benson b Mullally	4	– (9) c Potter b Benjamin	2
P. Hughes b Mullally	3	– (3) lbw b Millns	0
D. A. Graveney c Whitaker b Mullally	16	– retired hurt	8
J. E. Brown c Benson b Millns	0	– not out	4
L-b 5, n-b 2	7	L-b 10, n-b 3	13
1/16 2/16 3/31 4/39 5/82	145	1/13 2/14 3/15 4/25 5/27	116
6/82 7/86 8/100 9/134		6/49 7/74 8/78 9/116	

Bonus points – Leicestershire 4.

In the second innings D. A. Graveney retired hurt at 107.

Bowling: *First Innings*—Millns 16.1-2-41-5; Benjamin 13-5-50-1; Wells 5-1-10-0; Mullally 14-3-39-4. *Second Innings*—Millns 18.1-5-46-5; Benjamin 18-5-34-4; Mullally 8-2-11-0; Wells 5-1-15-0.

Leicestershire

T. J. Boon c Parker b Brown	33	– not out	5
*N. E. Briers lbw b Graveney	93	– not out	1
J. J. Whitaker c Scott b McEwan	40		
B. F. Smith lbw b Hughes	3		
J. D. R. Benson c Glendenen b Brown	33		
L. Potter c Graveney b Henderson	8		
V. J. Wells c Graveney b Henderson	3		
†P. A. Nixon c Larkins b Graveney	0		
W. K. M. Benjamin b Hughes	22		
D. J. Millns not out	8		
A. D. Mullally b Graveney	2		
L-b 9, w 2	11		

1/55 2/114 3/119 4/196 5/220   256   (no wkt) 6
6/222 7/222 8/236 9/249

Bonus points – Leicestershire 3, Durham 4.

Bowling: *First Innings*—Brown 20–2–84–2; Hughes 20–5–41–2; Henderson 13–1–56–2; McEwan 17–4–44–1; Graveney 15.2–6–22–3. *Second Innings*—Larkins 2–1–4–0; Parke 1.1–0–2–0.

Umpires: J. C. Balderstone and B. J. Meyer.

LEICESTERSHIRE v ESSEX

At Leicester, July 24, 25, 27. Leicestershire won by 68 runs. Leicestershire 21 pts, Essex 4 pts. Toss: Leicestershire. The Championship's two leading teams made a sensational start when 20 wickets fell on the first day, and Essex succumbed inside 24 overs. The pitch was not the one originally cut, and it later emerged that the balls used in both first innings had the higher seam no longer used in the Championship. But Essex's total of 75, the second lowest of the season to date, owed more to the pace barrage of Millns and Benjamin than such vagaries. At first it seemed that Briers had misused the toss, which he won for the 11th time in successive Championship matches. Foster reduced Leicestershire to 19 for five, but his failure to hold a return catch from Boon proved costly, and a total of 193 looked handsome as Essex crashed. Leicestershire took lunch on the second day at 152 for two but they collapsed again as the ball swung around. Stephenson and Prichard then reduced a target of 349 in four sessions to 246 by the close. With all their wickets standing this looked within Essex's scope, until the medium-pacer Wells broke through. Defeat cut their lead in the table to 31 points. But Leicestershire's triumph was diluted when Millns twisted his foot; England manager Micky Stewart had come to watch him with a view to selection for the Oval Test.

Close of play: First day, Leicestershire 35-0 (T. J. Boon 24*, N. E. Briers 11*); Second day, Essex 103-0 (P. J. Prichard 58*, J. P. Stephenson 38*).

Leicestershire

T. J. Boon c Hussain b Foster	58	– c Garnham b Stephenson	52
*N. E. Briers c Garnham b Ilott	0	– c Foster b Waugh	61
J. J. Whitaker b Stephenson b Foster	6	– b Ilott	40
B. F. Smith c Stephenson b Foster	2	– c Foster b Ilott	10
J. D. R. Benson c Waugh b Foster	0	– lbw b Waugh	2
L. Potter c Hussain b Ilott	0	– not out	27
V. J. Wells c Garnham b Ilott	38	– c Hussain b Andrew	13
†P. A. Nixon c Garnham b Waugh	28	– b Andrew	5
W. K. M. Benjamin lbw b Ilott	0	– c Stephenson b Andrew	3
D. J. Millns not out	33	– lbw b Andrew	1
A. D. Mullally c Prichard b Waugh	14	– lbw b Waugh	2
L-b 5, w 7, n-b 2	14	L-b 11, n-b 3	14

1/0 2/7 3/18 4/18 5/19   193   1/82 2/142 3/170 4/172 5/174   230
6/110 7/125 8/129 9/173   6/199 7/211 8/215 9/219

Bonus points – Leicestershire 1, Essex 4.

Bowling: *First Innings*—Foster 19–4–47–4; Ilott 23–3–73–4; Andrew 15–6–28–0; Waugh 13.1–5–40–2. *Second Innings*—Foster 4–1–13–0; Andrew 24–8–54–4; Childs 2–0–6–0; Stephenson 18–4–68–1; Ilott 17–5–34–2; Waugh 17.4–4–44–3.

Essex

P. J. Prichard c Nixon b Millns	2	– c Boon b Millns	106
J. P. Stephenson lbw b Millns	0	– c Nixon b Millns	42
M. E. Waugh b Benjamin	8	– c Nixon b Wells	36
N. Hussain b Benjamin	9	– c Benson b Wells	5
N. V. Knight b Millns	8	– (8) not out	11
N. Shahid c Nixon b Benjamin	9	– (5) c Nixon b Wells	4
†M. A. Garnham c Millns b Wells	21	– (6) lbw b Benjamin	24
*N. A. Foster c Smith b Mullally	13	– (7) c and b Millns	28
M. C. Ilott c Nixon b Wells	1	– c Nixon b Millns	0
S. J. W. Andrew c Nixon b Mullally	0	– b Millns	0
J. H. Childs not out	1	– c Nixon b Mullally	11
L-b 2, n-b 1	3	B 4, l-b 2, w 2, n-b 5	13
	75		**280**

1/1 2/11 3/19 4/28 5/32   1/121 2/184 3/199 4/199 5/212
6/38 7/73 8/73 9/73   6/249 7/258 8/260 9/260

Bonus points – Leicestershire 4.

Bowling: *First Innings*—Millns 7–1–23–3; Benjamin 6–2–32–3; Wells 5.4–2–16–2; Mullally 5–3–2–2. *Second Innings*—Millns 26–6–67–5; Mullally 21.1–3–59–1; Benjamin 23–6–60–1; Wells 21–4–55–3; Potter 10–4–33–0.

Umpires: D. J. Constant and R. A. White.

At Birmingham, July 31, August 1, 3. LEICESTERSHIRE lost to WARWICKSHIRE by an innings and 124 runs.

At Ilkeston, August 4, 5, 6. LEICESTERSHIRE lost to DERBYSHIRE by 139 runs.

At The Oval, August 14, 15, 17. LEICESTERSHIRE beat SURREY by 72 runs.

LEICESTERSHIRE v KENT

At Leicester, August 18, 19, 20. Kent won by an innings and 138 runs. Kent 24 pts, Leicestershire 1 pt. Toss: Leicestershire. With Millns still injured and Wells ill, Leicestershire lacked a cutting edge and Kent jumped above them into second place in the table. Kent built a commanding position around a 235-run stand between Taylor and the more painstaking Benson. Taylor survived a chance at 29 to reach the only century of his benefit season, striking 23 fours in four hours, while his captain hit 16 in just over six hours. Fleming dashed to 50 in 37 balls, and after Hooper and Cowdrey had turned the screw McCague bowled with pace and hostility. On a pitch that had looked bland before he bowled, he finished with seven for 52, including the wicket of Robinson, imported from Yorkshire via Cumberland, who marked his Championship début for his new county with a duck. Following on, Leicestershire collapsed embarrassingly before lunch on the third day: five wickets fell in eight balls from Davis and Igglesden, who took three in an over.

Close of play: First day, Kent 414-3 (C. L. Hooper 25*, M. V. Fleming 46*); Second day Leicestershire 114-2 (T. J. Boon 58*, R. P. Gofton 0*).

Kent

T. R. Ward c Nixon b Parsons	41	G. R. Cowdrey not out	3?
*M. R. Benson st Nixon b Gidley	139	B 7, l-b 5, w 5, n-b 4	2?
N. R. Taylor b Benjamin	144		—
C. L. Hooper not out	62	1/58 2/293 (4 wkts dec.)	50?
M. V. Fleming b Benjamin	58	3/355 4/434	

†S. A. Marsh, R. M. Ellison, R. P. Davis, M. J. McCague and A. P. Igglesden did not bat

Bonus points – Kent 4 (Score at 100 overs: 353-2).

Bowling: Mullally 33-6-121-0; Benjamin 27-2-125-2; Parsons 23-4-84-1; Goftor 7-1-40-0; Gidley 18-2-68-1; Potter 10-1-39-0; Boon 2-0-13-0.

Leicestershire

T. J. Boon c Marsh b McCague	25	– c Marsh b McCague	72
*N. E. Briers c Ward b McCague	2	– c Marsh b Igglesden	19
J. J. Whitaker c Hooper b Davis	27	– b Hooper	3?
P. E. Robinson c Ward b McCague	0	– (5) c McCague b Igglesden	19
L. Potter c Hooper b McCague	0	– (6) lbw b Davis	15
M. I. Gidley st Marsh b Davis	25	– (7) c Hooper b Igglesden	4
†P. A. Nixon b Davis	21	– (8) c Ellison b Davis	0
W. K. M. Benjamin not out	39	– (9) b Igglesden	0
R. P. Gofton c Benson b McCague	1	– (4) c Hooper b McCague	5
G. J. Parsons c Ellison b McCague	9	– lbw b Igglesden	4
A. D. Mullally c Taylor b McCague	4	– not out	0
B 5, l-b 14, n-b 9	28	B 4, l-b 6, n-b 5	15

1/27 2/40 3/44 4/55 5/88	181	1/55 2/114 3/134 4/146 5/171	183?
6/114 7/156 8/157 9/171		6/179 7/179 8/179 9/183	

Bonus points – Leicestershire 1, Kent 4.

Bowling: *First Innings*—McCague 14-1-52-7; Igglesden 8-1-27-0; Davis 20-7-40-3 Hooper 17-6-43-0. *Second Innings*—McCague 14-1-63-2; Igglesden 16-4-41-5; Elliso? 5-0-19-0; Davis 14.1-3-25-2; Hooper 21-9-24-1; Fleming 1-0-1-0.

Umpires: G. I. Burgess and R. Palmer.

LEICESTERSHIRE v NOTTINGHAMSHIRE

At Leicester, August 21, 22, 24. Drawn. Leicestershire 7 pts, Nottinghamshire 5 pts. Toss Nottinghamshire. On an unevenly grassed pitch Nottinghamshire were soon struggling against Leicestershire's seam attack. But Pennett regained some ground for the visitors and the home side were indebted to four lower-order left-handers, Gidley, Nixon, Hawkes and Parsons, for three batting points and a lead of 84. Broad's serene progress to a fifth Championship century on the last day guided his side away from danger to a declaration Leicestershire suffered for their lack of a decent spinner, highlighted when their attempts to chase 178 in 28 overs were thwarted by Hemmings and Afford, whom Nottinghamshire's acting-captain Crawley introduced as early as he dared.

Close of play: First day, Leicestershire 121-4 (N. E. Briers 65*, M. I. Gidley 5*); Second day, Nottinghamshire 31-0 (B. C. Broad 10*, D. W. Randall 20*).

Nottinghamshire

B. C. Broad c Nixon b Mullally	11	– st Nixon b Gidley	122
D. W. Randall c Briers b Parsons	21	– lbw b Benjamin	20
*R. T. Robinson c Nixon b Parsons	16	– c Mullally b Hawkes	24
M. A. Crawley c Nixon b Parsons	4	– c Benson b Benjamin	8
G. F. Archer c Gidley b Benjamin	21	– not out	52
M. Saxelby b Benjamin	26	– not out	22
C. L. Cairns c Potter b Benjamin	17		
D. B. Pennett c Nixon b Benjamin	0		
E. E. Hemmings c Gidley b Parsons	16		
†S. Bramhall not out	12		
J. A. Afford c Nixon b Mullally	9		
L-b 10, n-b 5	15	B 4, l-b 7, w 2	13

1/22 2/46 3/53 4/68 5/86   168   1/31 2/98   (4 wkts dec.) 261
6/118 7/118 8/133 9/145   3/113 4/219

Bonus points – Nottinghamshire 1, Leicestershire 4.

Bowling: *First Innings*—Benjamin 25–5–66–4; Mullally 14.2–2–42–2; Parsons 22–7–50–4. *Second Innings*—Benjamin 20–3–54–2; Mullally 14–2–51–0; Parsons 11–5–20–0; Gidley 25–9–51–1; Hawkes 13–3–51–1; Potter 9–0–23–0.

Leicestershire

T. J. Boon c Hemmings b Pennett	13	– (7) c Bramhall b Afford	7
*N. E. Briers run out	70	– not out	66
J. J. Whitaker b Pennett	17	– (1) b Hemmings	11
J. D. R. Benson lbw b Pennett	9	– (3) st Bramhall b Afford	9
L. Potter c Crawley b Afford	7	– c sub b Afford	30
M. I. Gidley b Afford	39	– (8) not out	2
†P. A. Nixon c Saxelby b Crawley	28	– (6) b Hemmings	0
W. K. M. Benjamin c Cairns b Crawley	6	– (4) c Randall b Afford	7
C. J. Hawkes st Bramhall b Hemmings	13		
G. J. Parsons st Bramhall b Afford	35		
A. D. Mullally not out	1		
L-b 10, n-b 4	14	L-b 1, w 1	2

1/21 2/45 3/66 4/94 5/128   252   1/23 2/38 3/46   (6 wkts) 134
6/174 7/182 8/201 9/247   4/103 5/105 6/112

Bonus points – Leicestershire 3, Nottinghamshire 4.

Bowling: *First Innings*—Cairns 19–5–56–0; Pennett 24–6–60–3; Crawley 15–3–45–2; Afford 21–8–51–3; Hemmings 21–10–30–1. *Second Innings*—Cairns 2–0–11–0; Pennett 3–0–17–0; Hemmings 12–0–70–2; Afford 10.3–1–35–4.

Umpires: G. I. Burgess and R. Palmer.

At Bristol, August 31, September 1, 2, 3. LEICESTERSHIRE drew with GLOUCESTER-SHIRE.

LEICESTERSHIRE v NORTHAMPTONSHIRE

At Leicester, September 12, 13, 14, 15. Northamptonshire won by six wickets. Northamptonshire 23 pts, Leicestershire 6 pts. Toss: Leicestershire. A contest that had Championship place money as well as the usual local rivalry at stake ended in a win for Northamptonshire with 19 balls to spare after a devastating century from Lamb, who made nonsense of Briers's declaration. Northamptonshire thus finished third in the table with Leicestershire well out of the frame. Briers had set a target of 290 in what proved to be 73 overs. Lamb hit an unbeaten 122 off 167 balls, with 16 fours and a six. Nine dropped catches on the first two days did not bode well for Northamptonshire and at 52 for four in their first innings, 300 behind, they were in danger of the follow-on. But Bailey made the most of some good fortune in a determined five-hour innings. That, combined with some bad weather, forced the captains to depend on mutual declarations to get a result.

Close of play: First day, Leicestershire 297-7 (W. K. M. Benjamin 51*, G. J. Parsons 3*); Second day, Northamptonshire 75-4 (R. J. Bailey 25*, K. M. Curran 6*); Third day, Leicestershire 123-3 (T. J. Boon 70*, L. Potter 7*).

Leicestershire

T. J. Boon c Ripley b Curran	81	– c Ripley b Curran	97
*N. E. Briers lbw b Curran	12	– c Loye b Curran	0
J. J. Whitaker b Capel	13	– lbw b Capel	29
J. D. R. Benson c Loye b Capel	0	– b Capel	7
L. Potter c Taylor b Capel	14	– c Snape b Cook	46
B. F. Smith c Fordham b Taylor	86	– not out	30
†P. A. Nixon b Snape	30	– not out	18
W. K. M. Benjamin c Bailey b Curran	71		
G. J. Parsons c Capel b Taylor	13		
D. J. Millns not out	9		
A. D. Mullally b Taylor	14		
L-b 3, n-b 6	9	B 2, l-b 9, w 1, n-b 1	13

1/30 2/64 3/64 4/100 5/146   352   1/6 2/71 3/92   (5 wkts dec.) 240
6/198 7/282 8/324 9/330   4/168 5/202

Bonus points – Leicestershire 3, Northamptonshire 3 (Score at 100 overs: 283-7).

Bowling: *First Innings*—Taylor 36.2-4-127-3; Curran 29-6-82-3; Capel 27-6-71-3; Penberthy 14-4-33-0; Cook 5-1-16-0; Snape 9-3-20-1. *Second Innings*—Taylor 12-1-50-0; Curran 21-6-58-2; Penberthy 11-1-38-0; Capel 6-2-19-2; Snape 17-5-42-0; Cook 8-1-22-1.

Northamptonshire

A. Fordham c Benjamin b Millns	34	– b Millns	9
M. B. Loye b Millns	1	– st Nixon b Potter	40
R. J. Bailey not out	167	– c sub b Parsons	27
*A. J. Lamb c Briers b Millns	0	– not out	122
D. J. Capel c Benson b Benjamin	1		
K. M. Curran lbw b Parsons	47	– (5) c Parsons b Potter	52
A. L. Penberthy c Smith b Potter	10	– (6) not out	17
†D. Ripley b Potter	24		
B 6, l-b 9, w 3, n-b 1	19	B 10, l-b 10, w 1, n-b 2	23

1/11 2/44 3/44 4/52 5/214   (7 wkts dec.) 303   1/18 2/67 3/114 4/249   (4 wkts) 290
6/241 7/303

J. P. Taylor, N. G. B. Cook and J. N. Snape did not bat.

Bonus points – Northamptonshire 4, Leicestershire 3.

Bowling: *First Innings*—Millns 21-2-90-3; Mullally 24-5-75-0; Benjamin 8-4-19-1; Parsons 21-10-54-1; Potter 22-5-50-2. *Second Innings*—Millns 13-1-52-1; Mullally 12-6-46-0; Benjamin 13-0-41-0; Parsons 11-1-46-1; Potter 20.5-3-85-2.

Umpires: B. Leadbeater and D. O. Oslear.

MIDDLESEX

Patron: HRH The Duke of Edinburgh
President: D. C. S. Compton
Chairman: M. P. Murray
Chairman, Cricket Committee: R. A. Gale
Secretary: J. Hardstaff
 Lord's Cricket Ground, St John's Wood,
 London NW8 8QN (Telephone: 071-289 1300)
Captain: M. W. Gatting
Coach: D. Bennett

Mike Gatting's tenth season as captain gave him yet another chance to flourish a trophy before Middlesex supporters. But unexpectedly, this one was for winning the Sunday League, the competition which had eluded the club for 23 years. The 40-overs title completed a Grand Slam for Gatting, who has led the team to two Championships, two NatWest Trophies and two Benson and Hedges Cups. Only Keith Fletcher of Essex had previously captained a team to all four competitions. When Gatting succeeded the honours-laden Brearley, he naturally wanted to maintain his predecessor's achievements, which comprised three Championships (and one shared) and two Gillette Cups in the period 1976-82. Gatting will not regard the books as quite balanced until another Championship is achieved.

Middlesex's storming Sunday form was one of the most remarkable features of the season. They won their first 12 matches and on July 5 went clear at the top, where they stayed. It was a triumphal progress. Their previous Sunday habits were either to flounder about at the back of the field or hint at a challenge, only to collapse in August. The previous best performance was second in 1982. This time they had the prize as good as banked before their first defeat, on August 2, and equalled Sussex's record – set in a 16-match League – of 14 wins. Desmond Haynes scored 839 runs but Gatting ascribed the success largely to the side's all-round skills, particularly those of Paul Weekes and John Carr, and sharp fielding.

Still, the League success was relatively meagre compensation for mediocrity in the other competitions, though 11th place in the Championship might have been four positions higher if either of the very last two balls of the first-class season had brought the tenth Surrey wicket for Phil Tufnell. The winning touch vanished in mid-August after consecutive victories over Gloucestershire and Yorkshire had hoisted Middlesex from 14th to fifth. The last five games were an anticlimax of three draws and two defeats. The longer limited-overs competitions brought severe disappointments. Second-round defeat in the NatWest by Durham was inexcusable, if only because the bowlers gave Durham 26 extra balls, through 17 wides and nine no-balls. In the Benson and Hedges quarter-final Middlesex ran into a Hampshire side operating in peak form.

Even in the opening weeks of the season Middlesex sensed 1992 would not be their year in the Championship. Ricky Ellock had finally retired after yielding to his back affliction; Norman Cowans could do no more than trundle up and bowl seven overs at Fenner's and seven more in the Sunday League before his season ended abruptly with a groin operation; and it rapidly became clear that Angus Fraser's recuperation from his side and hip problem was going to be tentative and prolonged. Fraser was in his sixth Championship game before he managed a wicket. It was a discouraging start, but he showed great fortitude in his efforts to become the best bowler in England again, as he had been in 1990, and he did appear to regain some of his nip in the closing weeks of the season. With two bowlers of England status absent and another semi-functional, life for opposing batsmen was always going to be far smoother than in recent years. Dean Headley, Chas Taylor and Neil Williams were, of necessity, the primary pace bowlers; they found it a demanding summer and at some time each one lost his rhythm. Williams had one match-winning effort with a career-best eight for 75 against Gloucestershire and Taylor sometimes produced spells of real speed.

What Middlesex needed above all, however, was a long, dry summer during which the spinners stayed fit and available. The weather declined to oblige and Tufnell fell victim to appendicitis. He missed six matches before recovering to bowl influentially in two of the later wins. During all his anxieties about the other bowlers Gatting could always turn to Emburey, who wheeled down far more overs than anyone else in the country in 1992 and prised out 80 batsmen in the Championship – his most successful year since 1983.

The top three batsmen were magnificent. Haynes transferred his most prolific form to Sundays, but still provided the exquisitely crafted 1,500 runs that were taken for granted. His effect on his opening partner was nearly as important as his runs. Roseberry missed his inspiration in 1991 and thrived when Haynes returned after his year away with the West Indies. In theory, Haynes was still the senior partner, but Roseberry out-batted one of the world's best players in match after match. Middlesex knew that Roseberry had the strokes, and the audacity to use them. What was unproven was his defensive technique and his maturity. He made his point gloriously and entertainingly. He began with centuries against Cambridge, Oxford and the Pakistanis before scoring five hundreds – with other big scores in between – in ten Championship matches. His selection for the England A tour was thoroughly deserved. Gatting was promptly restored to the England squad, after his Test-match suspension. But in or out of the England set-up, he has always given maximum commitment to Middlesex, and he had another wonderful season with big runs from the start. Statistically, Ramprakash also had a satisfactory season, but he was disciplined by the club twice, for getting into arguments on the field at Fenner's and off it at Uxbridge; the club had hoped he had put his teenage tantrums behind him. Carr's return added real substance to the middle order, but Keith Brown lost confidence in both batting and his new job as wicket-keeper. Brown, Carr and all the others will need to be extra-productive in 1993 if Gatting makes his expected return to the Test team. – Terry Cooper.

459

MIDDLESEX 1992

[Bill Smith]

Back row: P. Farbrace, R. J. Sims, A. Habib, S. A. Sylvester, T. A. Radford, D. A. Walker, P. N. Weekes, M. Keech. Middle row: D. Bennett (coach), H. P. H. Sharp (First Eleven scorer), I. J. F. Hutchinson, R. L. Johnson, J. C. Harrison, C. W. Taylor. R. M. Ellcock, J. C. Pooley, J. D. Carr, M. R. Ramprakash, D. W. Headley, A. Jones (Second Eleven scorer). S. Shephard (physiotherapist). Front row: P. C. R. Tufnell. K. R. Brown, N. F. Williams, J. E. Emburey, M. W. Gatting (captain), N. G. Cowans, A. R. C. Fraser, M. A. Roseberry, I. J. Gould (assistant coach). Inset: D. L. Haynes.

MIDDLESEX RESULTS

All first-class matches – Played 25: Won 5, Lost 4, Drawn 16.

County Championship matches – Played 22: Won 5, Lost 3, Drawn 14.

Bonus points – Batting 62, Bowling 60.

*Competition placings – Britannic Assurance County Championship, 11th;
NatWest Bank Trophy, 2nd round; Benson and Hedges Cup, q-f;
Sunday League, winners.*

BRITANNIC ASSURANCE CHAMPIONSHIP AVERAGES

BATTING

	Birthplace	M	I	NO	R	HS	Avge
‡M. W. Gatting	Kingsbury	22	35	6	1,980	170	68.27
J. C. Pooley	Hammersmith	2	4	1	149	69	49.66
‡M. A. Roseberry....	Houghton-le-Spring	22	38	3	1,724	173	49.25
‡M. R. Ramprakash .	Bushey	14	24	2	1,042	233	47.36
‡D. L. Haynes§	Holders Hill, Barbados	20	35	2	1,513	177	45.84
‡J. D. Carr	St John's Wood	22	34	6	1,068	114	38.14
P. N. Weekes	Hackney	14	17	5	431	89*	35.91
D. W. Headley	Stourbridge	14	12	3	268	91	29.77
‡J. E. Emburey......	Peckham	22	27	6	554	102	26.38
‡K. R. Brown	Edmonton	22	33	5	651	106	23.25
‡A. R. C. Fraser	Billinge	16	18	7	188	33	17.09
‡N. F. Williams	Hope Well, St Vincent	17	17	3	186	46*	13.28
‡P. C. R. Tufnell ...	Barnet	14	13	7	55	12	9.16
C. W. Taylor	Banbury	16	13	6	64	14	9.14

Also batted: A. Habib (*Reading*) (1 match) 12, 7*; R. L. Johnson (*Chertsey*) (1 match) 1;
S. A. Sylvester (*Chalfont St Giles*) (2 matches) 0*. ‡P. H. Edmonds (*Lusaka, N. Rhodesia*)
(1 match) did not bat.

* *Signifies not out.*   ‡ *Denotes county cap.*   § *Overseas player.*

The following played a total of 22 three-figure innings for Middlesex in County
Championship matches – M. W. Gatting 6, M. A. Roseberry 6, D. L. Haynes 3, M. R.
Ramprakash 3, J. D. Carr 2, K. R. Brown 1, J. E. Emburey 1.

BOWLING

	O	M	R	W	BB	5W/i	Avge
J. E. Emburey	848.5	245	2,064	80	5-23	3	25.80
N. F. Williams	437	86	1,283	48	8-75	2	26.72
P. C. R. Tufnell	517.2	122	1,366	41	5-83	2	33.31
D. W. Headley	304.3	62	968	26	3-31	0	37.23
C. W. Taylor	379.2	74	1,337	32	4-50	0	41.78
P. N. Weekes	155	36	428	10	3-61	0	42.80
A. R. C. Fraser	366.2	69	1,158	18	3-59	0	64.33

Also bowled: J. D. Carr 41–14–100–3; P. H. Edmonds 28–10–48–4; M. W. Gatting
6–0–38–0; D. L. Haynes 2.4–0–5–1; R. L. Johnson 14–2–71–1; M. R. Ramprakash
10–1–41–0; M. A. Roseberry 10–2–71–0; S. A. Sylvester 42–9–123–2.

Wicket-keeper: K. R. Brown 36 ct, 11 st.

Leading Fielders: J. D. Carr 39, J. E. Emburey 21, M. W. Gatting 15.

At Cambridge, April 17, 18, 20. MIDDLESEX drew with CAMBRIDGE UNIVERSITY.

MIDDLESEX v GLAMORGAN

At Lord's, April 25, 27, 28, 29. Drawn. Middlesex 5 pts, Glamorgan 6 pts. Toss: Middlesex. Gatting was instantly at his dominating best, playing as though the match was being staged in mid-July, and leagues removed from his faltering colleagues. He faced 297 balls, hit 27 fours to all parts of the ground and, after Bastien had taken three wickets in a six-ball spell, Emburey joined him in a partnership which added 148 at a run a minute. However, his batting was countered by Morris, who won his extended duel with the Middlesex spinners in an innings of wonderful judgment. He was run out by Ramprakash after batting five hours and striking 19 fours. Rain cut two hours from the second day, there was no play on the third and after mutual declarations Glamorgan were left to score 266 in 65 overs. James gave his team every chance, missing a maiden Championship hundred by six runs, but when Maynard was bowled with 34 runs needed off 26 balls neither side was in a position to win.

Close of play: First day, Glamorgan 21-0 (S. P. James 10*, H. Morris 10*); Second day, Glamorgan 255-3 (M. P. Maynard 12*, D. L. Hemp 0*); Third day, No play.

Middlesex

J. D. Carr c Metson b Watkin	10	– c Metson b Bastien	31
M. A. Roseberry c Hemp b Frost	6	– c Frost b Foster	86
*M. W. Gatting c James b Watkin	170	– not out	48
M. R. Ramprakash c Croft b Foster	30	– not out	6
†K. R. Brown c Metson b Bastien	17		
P. N. Weekes lbw b Bastien	2		
N. F. Williams b Bastien	0		
J. E. Emburey c Hemp b Foster	57		
D. W. Headley c Metson b Bastien	17		
P. C. R. Tufnell b Bastien	9		
S. A. Sylvester not out	0		
L-b 13, w 1, n-b 9	23	L-b 2, n-b 6	8

1/12 2/30 3/80 4/127 5/129   341   1/45 2/160   (2 wkts dec.) 179
6/129 7/277 8/317 9/337

Bonus points – Middlesex 4, Glamorgan 4.

Bowling: *First Innings*—Watkin 22.4–8–64–2; Frost 19–6–61–1; Bastien 26–6–95–5; Foster 17–2–73–2; Croft 11–1–35–0. *Second Innings*—Watkin 8–0–28–0; Frost 11–1–63–0; Bastien 10–1–30–1; Croft 5–0–23–0; Foster 7–0–33–1.

Glamorgan

S. P. James c Weekes b Headley	22	– c Williams b Emburey	94
H. Morris run out	146	– c Williams b Emburey	40
R. D. B. Croft b Emburey	51	– run out	18
*M. P. Maynard not out	12	– b Emburey	40
D. L. Hemp not out	0	– b Tufnell	3
P. A. Cottey (did not bat)		– not out	28
†C. P. Metson (did not bat)		– c Weekes b Emburey	1
S. L. Watkin (did not bat)		– not out	0
B 11, l-b 8, n-b 5	24	B 1, l-b 8, n-b 4	13

1/69 2/242 3/242   (3 wkts dec.) 255   1/69 2/157 3/160   (6 wkts) 237
                                           4/174 5/232 6/236

S. Bastien, D. J. Foster and M. Frost did not bat.

Bonus points – Glamorgan 2, Middlesex 1 (Score at 100 overs: 244-3).

Bowling: *First Innings*—Williams 15.4–6–40–0; Sylvester 12–1–45–0; Emburey 28–11–55–1; Headley 7–1–30–1; Tufnell 33–15–47–0; Weekes 8–3–19–0. *Second Innings*—Headley 9–1–32–0; Sylvester 4–0–13–0; Williams 9–0–36–0; Emburey 23.3–5–77–4; Tufnell 19–2–70–1.

Umpires: J. D. Bond and J. W. Holder.

MIDDLESEX v LANCASHIRE

At Lord's, May 7, 8, 9, 10. Drawn. Middlesex 7 pts, Lancashire 5 pts. Toss: Lancashire. Despite a blank third day, Middlesex rejected the idea of trying for a contrived victory and attempted to beat Lancashire by an innings. Lancashire had only to survive three and a quarter hours and they did this comfortably, after an assured stand between Speak and Atherton and then the loss of the last 16 overs. The first-innings batting from both sides was notably enterprising. Lancashire smote their way out of early trouble, with Speak only seven short of his hundred when run out, and both DeFreitas and Hegg striking 11 fours. But Middlesex were equally aggressive; Gatting, in his most combative form, took just over three hours for his century, with 16 fours, before handing over to Ramprakash.

Close of play: First day, Lancashire 316-8 (W. K. Hegg 45*, D. K. Morrison 18*); Second day, Middlesex 312-5 (M. R. Ramprakash 90*, J. E. Emburey 4*); Third day, No play.

Lancashire

G. D. Mendis c Gatting b Headley	17	– c Brown b Headley 1
M. A. Atherton c Carr b Williams	16	– not out.................... 51
N. J. Speak run out	93	– lbw b Sylvester 33
*N. H. Fairbrother c Ramprakash b Emburey	27	– c Gatting b Sylvester 3
G. D. Lloyd c Emburey b Williams	2	– not out.................... 17
P. A. J. DeFreitas c Ramprakash b Williams	69	
†W. K. Hegg lbw b Headley	63	
I. D. Austin c Sylvester b Tufnell	16	
P. J. Martin c Carr b Tufnell	0	
D. K. Morrison c Brown b Headley	20	
A. A. Barnett not out	6	
B 2, l-b 1, n-b 11	14	L-b 2, n-b 6 8

1/35 2/40 3/81 4/94 5/231   343   1/3 2/81 3/85   (3 wkts) 113
6/238 7/268 8/268 9/330

Bonus points – Lancashire 3, Middlesex 3 (Score at 100 overs: 271-8).

Bowling: *First Innings*—Headley 29.3–6–84–3; Sylvester 15–5–30–0; Williams 31–5–100–3; Emburey 29–10–69–1; Tufnell 23–7–57–2. *Second Innings*—Headley 8–0–21–1; Sylvester 11–3–35–2; Williams 5.1–1–12–0; Emburey 8–1–21–0; Tufnell 13–7–22–0.

Middlesex

D. L. Haynes c Hegg b Austin	62	D. W. Headley not out 40
M. A. Roseberry c Atherton b DeFreitas	4	P. C. R. Tufnell not out 9
*M. W. Gatting run out	103	
M. R. Ramprakash c Hegg b DeFreitas	108	B 4, l-b 10, n-b 3 17
†K. R. Brown c Barnett b Morrison	37	
J. D. Carr c Morrison b Martin	3	1/11 2/143 3/194 (8 wkts dec.) 493
J. E. Emburey lbw b Barnett	78	4/287 5/300 6/361
N. F. Williams c Atherton b Barnett	32	7/430 8/455

S. A. Sylvester did not bat.

Bonus points – Middlesex 4, Lancashire 2 (Score at 100 overs: 324-5).

Bowling: DeFreitas 35–1–125–2; Martin 29–3–92–1; Austin 22–6–59–1; Morrison 19–3–70–1; Barnett 29.5–2–111–2; Atherton 5–1–22–0.

Umpires: R. Palmer and G. Sharp.

At Oxford, May 12, 13, 14. MIDDLESEX lost to OXFORD UNIVERSITY by five wickets.

At Leicester, May 19, 20, 21, 22. MIDDLESEX beat LEICESTERSHIRE by ten wickets.

MIDDLESEX v SURREY

At Lord's, May 23, 25, 26. Drawn. Middlesex 8 pts, Surrey 3 pts. Toss: Middlesex. Surrey's last pair of Bryson and Benjamin fended off the last 13 balls to get a draw after their team had been comprehensively outplayed. Benjamin had given the match a dramatic start when he claimed two of the most sought-after wickets on the county circuit – Haynes and Gatting – in his third over, Gatting ending his prolific run by chopping a ball into his stumps. Ramprakash, especially, and Roseberry wiped out the damage with a flourish of boundaries, putting on 128. Carr and Weekes then helped Ramprakash to amass a maiden double-century, only the third for Middlesex against Surrey (after H. W. Lee in 1929 and D. C. S. Compton in 1946). He hit 31 fours and two sixes, faced 319 balls and added 206 in 46 overs with Weekes, whose 89 was also his highest score. Middlesex bowled and caught most efficiently to force Surrey to follow on 298 behind, but Surrey substantially increased their resolution and skill on the final day, when Middlesex wanted nine wickets and took only eight. Overnight opener Kendrick set the tone with a career-best 55 in 68 overs, and Lynch defied a strained hamstring to bat for 43 overs. Emburey was especially tireless, but his hard work was ultimately futile.

Close of play: First day, Middlesex 407-5 (M. R. Ramprakash 193*, P. N. Weekes 72*); Second day, Surrey 2-1 (N. M. Kendrick 0*, M. P. Bicknell 0*).

Middlesex

D. L. Haynes lbw b Benjamin	4	P. N. Weekes not out		89
M. A. Roseberry lbw b Kendrick	63	J. E. Emburey c Sargeant b Feltham		16
*M. W. Gatting b Benjamin	0	B 1, l-b 6, w 1, n-b 21		29
M. R. Ramprakash c Sargeant b Kendrick	.233			
†K. R. Brown c Lynch b Kendrick	0	1/12 2/12 3/140	(7 wkts dec.)	486
J. D. Carr c Ward b Lynch	52	4/140 5/251		
		6/457 7/486		

D. W. Headley, C. W. Taylor and N. F. Williams did not bat.

Bonus points – Middlesex 4, Surrey 2 (Score at 100 overs: 361-5).

Bowling: Bryson 28-2-125-0; Benjamin 16-1-55-2; Feltham 18.1-2-78-1; M. P. Bicknell 20-3-82-0; Kendrick 34-6-123-3; Lynch 6-2-16-1.

Surrey

D. J. Bicknell c Brown b Headley	28	– (2) c Weekes b Headley	2
*A. J. Stewart lbw b Emburey	6	– (4) lbw b Taylor	36
G. P. Thorpe b Headley	28	– (5) b Brown b Taylor	0
M. A. Lynch lbw b Headley	51	– (6) c Weekes b Emburey	42
D. M. Ward c Gatting b Williams	3	– (7) c sub b Taylor	21
M. A. Feltham c Carr b Emburey	13	– (8) c Gatting b Williams	21
M. P. Bicknell c Gatting b Weekes	17	– (3) c Brown b Taylor	3
N. M. Kendrick c Haynes b Williams	8	– (1) lbw b Headley	55
†N. F. Sargeant b Carr b Williams	2	– lbw b Williams	17
R. E. Bryson c Weekes b Williams	14	– not out	11
J. E. Benjamin not out	3	– not out	8
B 2, l-b 5, n-b 8	15	B 3, l-b 1, n-b 7	11
1/18 2/68 3/72 4/86 5/103	188	1/2 2/9 3/78	(9 wkts) 227
6/141 7/169 8/169 9/184		4/78 5/120 6/158	
		7/174 8/197 9/219	

Bonus points – Surrey 1, Middlesex 4.

Bowling: *First Innings*—Taylor 12-7-19-0; Headley 15-4-46-3; Emburey 28-11-50-2; Williams 14.3-4-31-4; Weekes 16-3-35-1. *Second Innings*—Taylor 18-5-50-4; Headley 22-12-34-2; Emburey 42-21-47-1; Williams 20-2-72-2; Weekes 14-7-23-0.

Umpires: K. E. Palmer and N. T. Plews.

At Lord's, May 30, 31, June 1. MIDDLESEX drew with PAKISTANIS (See Pakistani tour section).

At Nottingham, June 2, 3, 4. MIDDLESEX drew with NOTTINGHAMSHIRE.

MIDDLESEX v LEICESTERSHIRE

At Lord's, June 5, 6, 8. Drawn. Middlesex 2 pts, Leicestershire 4 pts. Toss: Leicestershire. Leicestershire's decision to bowl after a first-day wash-out was handsomely vindicated when Middlesex collapsed from 67 for two to 67 for six in 16 balls and then to 102 all out. Gatting had marked his 35th birthday with eight fours, and passed 20,000 runs for Middlesex, but his dismissal began the slump. Leicestershire's batting was only a little more comfortable and after Briers declared, 26 ahead, Middlesex compensated for their earlier shortcomings with Roseberry making his third century in successive first-class matches, and sharing 195 with Haynes for the first wicket. Set 240 in 44 overs, Leicestershire were again in early trouble against Williams and Taylor and, though Smith and Benson put aside thoughts of defeat, they made only a fleeting attempt to get the runs. Benson took his total against Middlesex in the home and away Championship matches to 265.

Close of play: First day, No play; Second day, Middlesex 10-0 (D. L. Haynes 0*, M. A. Roseberry 8*).

Middlesex

D. L. Haynes b Benjamin	7	– c Whitticase b Wells	94
M. A. Roseberry c Whitticase b Mullally	0	– c Whitaker b Millns	102
*M. W. Gatting c Smith b Millns	45		
J. D. Carr lbw b Wells	14	– not out	28
†K. R. Brown lbw b Millns	0	– (3) not out	34
P. N. Weekes c Whitticase b Wells	0		
J. E. Emburey c Smith b Benjamin	7		
D. W. Headley c Benjamin b Wells	15		
N. F. Williams b Benjamin	1		
A. R. C. Fraser not out	9		
C. W. Taylor c Benjamin b Wells	3		
L-b 1	1	B 3, l-b 3, w 1	7

1/0 2/16 3/67 4/67 5/67   102   1/195 2/201   (2 wkts dec.) 265
6/67 7/85 8/86 9/91

Bonus points – Leicestershire 4.

Bowling: *First Innings*—Benjamin 12-5-29-3; Mullally 9-4-25-1; Millns 9-3-20-2; Wells 11.1-3-27-4. *Second Innings*—Benjamin 8-3-23-0; Mullally 14-3-46-0; Millns 13.3-2-77-1; Wells 12-4-33-1; Hepworth 12-0-62-0; Boon 2-0-18-0.

Leicestershire

T. J. Boon c Brown b Williams	14	– c Brown b Williams	12
*N. E. Briers c Emburey b Williams	8	– c Carr b Taylor	11
J. J. Whitaker lbw b Taylor	1	– lbw b Williams	0
B. F. Smith lbw b Williams	24	– not out	67
J. D. R. Benson c Headley b Williams	46	– st Brown b Emburey	39
P. N. Hepworth not out	17	– c Fraser b Emburey	0
V. J. Wells not out	9	– not out	6
L-b 1, n-b 8	9	W 1, n-b 5	6

1/22 2/23 3/34 4/70 5/111   (5 wkts dec.) 128   1/19 2/19 3/46   (5 wkts) 141
                                                          4/114 5/114

†P. Whitticase, W. K. M. Benjamin, D. J. Millns and A. D. Mullally did not bat.

Bonus points – Middlesex 2.

Bowling: *First Innings*—Williams 17-4-45-4; Fraser 9-1-37-0; Taylor 7-1-33-1; Headley 5-1-11-0; Emburey 1-0-1-0. *Second Innings*—Williams 12-1-29-2; Fraser 4-0-20-0; Taylor 9-3-37-1; Headley 6-1-28-0; Emburey 10-3-27-2.

Umpires: G. I. Burgess and J. H. Hampshire.

At Coventry, June 16, 17, 18. MIDDLESEX beat WARWICKSHIRE by 226 runs.

At Manchester, June 19, 20, 22. MIDDLESEX drew with LANCASHIRE.

MIDDLESEX v SOMERSET

At Lord's, June 26, 27, 29. Drawn. Middlesex 7 pts, Somerset 4 pts. Toss: Middlesex. The phenomenal Gatting again dominated a solid Middlesex innings, dismissing the bowlers, especially Snell, with a showcase of powerful shots. Impatience cost him his hundred after he had faced 138 balls and hit 14 fours. It was one of three prize wickets for Trump, who kept his control during the battering. Somerset also enjoyed the easy nature of the pitch, with Hayhurst capably locking up one end, until he too fell within sight of a century after facing 263 balls. Tufnell, returning after an appendix operation, shared six wickets in a welcome reunion with Emburey, who became the ninth bowler to take 1,000 wickets for Middlesex. Haynes and Roseberry raced to 120 from 18 overs on the second evening, but the Middlesex batsmen were made to work far harder next morning before the declaration, which set Somerset 320 in 75 overs. Two early wickets from Taylor ensured that there would be no run-chase, but Harden and MacLeay saved the match with a 38-over alliance.

Close of play: First day, Middlesex 355-5 (J. D. Carr 33*, J. E. Emburey 7*); Second day, Middlesex 120-0 (D. L. Haynes 60*, M. A. Roseberry 60*).

Middlesex

D. L. Haynes lbw b MacLeay	54	– c Burns b Snell	84
M. A. Roseberry c Harden b Trump	85	– c Caddick b Snell	67
*M. W. Gatting c Caddick b Trump	90		
M. R. Ramprakash c and b Trump	68	– b MacLeay	18
†K. R. Brown c Burns b Snell	13	– (3) c MacLeay b Snell	2
J. D. Carr not out	33	– (5) c Snell b Mallender	13
J. E. Emburey not out	7	– not out	4
N. F. Williams (did not bat)		– (6) c Trump b Rose	17
D. W. Headley (did not bat)		– (8) not out	28
L-b 4, n-b 1	5	N-b 1	1

1/94 2/218 3/242 4/268 5/342   (5 wkts dec.) 355   1/135 2/143 3/158 (6 wkts dec.) 234
                                                       4/185 5/187 6/205

P. C. R. Tufnell and C. W. Taylor did not bat.

Bonus points – Middlesex 4, Somerset 1 (Score at 100 overs: 306-4).

Bowling: *First Innings*—Caddick 23-2-64-0; Snell 19-3-71-1; Mallender 17-3-47-0; Rose 11-2-44-0; Trump 34-4-103-3; MacLeay 9-4-22-1. *Second Innings*—Mallender 8-0-47-1; Caddick 12-0-54-0; Rose 4-0-37-1; Snell 14-3-29-3; Trump 4-0-26-0; MacLeay 6-1-28-1; Lathwell 1-0-13-0.

Somerset

A. N. Hayhurst c Brown b Tufnell	97	– c sub b Taylor	0
M. N. Lathwell b Taylor	22	– c Brown b Williams	1
R. J. Harden c Gatting b Emburey	30	– c Brown b Taylor	58
*C. J. Tavaré b Emburey	53	– c Brown b Taylor	2
K. H. MacLeay c Roseberry b Tufnell	0	– c Roseberry b Emburey	50
G. D. Rose b Emburey	0	– not out	27
†N. D. Burns c Gatting b Tufnell	7	– not out	5
R. P. Snell not out	35		
N. A. Mallender not out	13		
L-b 7, w 1, n-b 5	13	N-b 1	1

1/38 2/88 3/207 4/212 5/213   (7 wkts dec.) 270   1/0 2/6 3/17   (5 wkts) 144
6/213 7/239   4/105 5/126

A. R. Caddick and H. R. J. Trump did not bat.

Bonus points – Somerset 3, Middlesex 3.

Bowling: *First Innings*—Williams 13–3–34–0; Headley 14–3–63–0; Taylor 11–5–27–1; Emburey 36–14–76–3; Tufnell 24.4–3–63–3. *Second Innings*—Taylor 16–5–42–3; Williams 7–3–11–1; Tufnell 24–9–37–0; Emburey 20–9–35–1; Headley 3–0–18–0; Roseberry 1–0–1–0.

Umpires: J. H. Harris and B. Leadbeater.

At Ilford, June 30, July 1, 2. MIDDLESEX lost to ESSEX by eight wickets.

MIDDLESEX v NORTHAMPTONSHIRE

At Uxbridge, July 14, 15, 16. Drawn. Middlesex 6 pts, Northamptonshire 6 pts. Toss: Northamptonshire. A rain-interrupted match finished with Middlesex chasing a target of 313 in 65 overs only half-heartedly. They lost three of their top four early on and in the end firm defence from Emburey was needed to make sure they saved the game. Northamptonshire had achieved full batting points after a performance of relentless power from Lamb who hit 14 fours in his 65. Middlesex declared their first innings behind after a masterful innings from Haynes, who faced 187 balls and hit 17 fours, a five and a six for his fourth century at Uxbridge in eight innings.

Close of play: First day, Northamptonshire 316-7 (K. M. Curran 57*, C. E. L. Ambrose 0*); Second day, Middlesex 220-5 dec.

Northamptonshire

A. Fordham c Brown b Fraser	28	– c Haynes b Fraser	14
N. A. Felton c Emburey b Taylor	52	– run out	57
R. J. Bailey run out	39	– c Brown b Emburey	18
*A. J. Lamb c Emburey b Tufnell	65	– c and b Emburey	13
D. J. Capel c Roseberry b Emburey	14	– c Roseberry b Emburey	0
K. M. Curran c Fraser b Tufnell	82	– not out	47
†D. Ripley c Roseberry b Emburey	16	– not out	3
A. R. Roberts run out	31		
C. E. L. Ambrose c Brown b Tufnell	13		
J. P. Taylor st Brown b Emburey	1		
N. G. B. Cook not out	11		
L-b 6, n-b 11	17	B 4, l-b 2, n-b 5	11

1/65 2/102 3/170 4/207 5/215   369   1/21 2/59 3/73   (5 wkts dec.) 163
6/249 7/305 8/337 9/344   4/81 5/144

Bonus points – Northamptonshire 4, Middlesex 4 (Score at 100 overs: 369-9).

Bowling: *First Innings*—Taylor 12–0–69–1; Headley 20–4–70–0; Fraser 18–1–72–1; Tufnell 25.1–4–82–3; Emburey 25–5–70–3. *Second Innings*—Fraser 10–0–52–1; Taylor 8–4–15–0; Emburey 9.3–1–48–3; Tufnell 8–1–42–0.

Middlesex

D. L. Haynes not out	127	– lbw b Taylor	61
M. A. Roseberry c Bailey b Taylor	4	– c Felton b Taylor	0
*M. W. Gatting lbw b Taylor	24	– c Capel b Curran	18
M. R. Ramprakash c Bailey b Curran	54	– lbw b Ambrose	4
J. D. Carr lbw b Curran	0	– c Lamb b Cook	72
†K. R. Brown b Curran	0	– c and b Roberts	39
J. E. Emburey not out	5	– not out	50
D. W. Headley (did not bat)		– c Taylor b Roberts	2
A. R. C. Fraser (did not bat)		– not out	1
L-b 4, n-b 2	6	B 4, l-b 2	6

1/18 2/81 3/213 4/213 5/215   (5 wkts dec.) 220   1/0 2/44 3/51 4/151   (7 wkts) 253
                                          5/171 6/231 7/245

P. C. R. Tufnell and C. W. Taylor did not bat.

Bonus points – Middlesex 2, Northamptonshire 2.

Bowling: *First Innings*—Ambrose 16.2–6–51–0; Taylor 18–3–75–2; Curran 8–1–20–3; Cook 5–1–23–0; Capel 11–0–47–0. *Second Innings*—Ambrose 19.4–3–50–1; Taylor 9–1–31–2; Curran 7–0–42–1; Bailey 3–0–16–0; Roberts 13–1–65–2; Cook 10–0–32–1; Capel 3–0–11–0.

Umpires: R. Julian and A. G. T. Whitehead.

MIDDLESEX v WORCESTERSHIRE

At Uxbridge, July 17, 18, 20. Drawn. Middlesex 6 pts, Worcestershire 7 pts. Toss: Middlesex. Middlesex yielded the initiative in the first ten balls when Haynes and Gatting – pulling casually to square leg – were out without scoring. Despite the worthy efforts of Carr and Williams to excavate points from a position of 78 for six, the day belonged to Worcestershire's varied pace attack. Hick dedicated himself to a big score, which fell into two halves; on the first evening he advanced cautiously to 58, attacking only the bad ball. He expanded his repertoire after Worcestershire had slipped to 197 for seven, but his full range of strokeplay only appeared when he was joined by last man Stemp, who contributed 16 to a stand of 83; Hick finished with five sixes and 15 fours. Roseberry and Gatting seemed to be making light of a 144-run deficit, but the last morning developed into a fight for a defensible lead. Middlesex managed to get 177 ahead, which gave the visitors 38 overs to make the runs. It looked comfortable with 74 wanted from 13 and eight wickets in hand, but spinners Tufnell and Embury, aided by stunning catching, almost turned the match. Worcestershire's ninth-wicket pair saw out 32 balls.

Close of play: First day, Worcestershire 132-3 (G. A. Hick 58*, D. A. Leatherdale 5*); Second day, Middlesex 180-1 (M. A. Roseberry 113*, M. W. Gatting 57*).

Middlesex

D. L. Haynes lbw b Radford	0	– c Rhodes b Tolley	1
M. A. Roseberry b Lampitt	43	– lbw b Radford	118
*M. W. Gatting c Curtis b Tolley	0	– lbw b Radford	66
M. R. Ramprakash c Newport b Tolley	17	– b Radford	8
J. D. Carr c Leatherdale b Newport	64	– b Radford	9
†K. R. Brown b Newport	3	– c Rhodes b Hick	50
J. E. Emburey c Rhodes b Lampitt	3	– c Curtis b Stemp	20
N. F. Williams not out	46	– c Moody b Stemp	3
A. R. C. Fraser lbw b Newport	3	– not out	19
C. W. Taylor c Lampitt b Tolley	13	– c Hick b Newport	8
P. C. R. Tufnell c Lampitt b Newport	1	– b Radford	2
B 1, l-b 2, w 1, n-b 5	9	B 4, l-b 9, n-b 4	17
	202		**321**

1/2 2/3 3/39 4/70 5/73   1/3 2/187 3/204 4/205 5/230   321
6/78 7/175 8/179 9/200   6/284 7/290 8/291 9/316

Bonus points – Middlesex 2, Worcestershire 4.

Bowling: *First Innings*—Radford 12–1–56–1; Tolley 19–3–51–3; Newport 18.4–2–59–4; Lampitt 11–2–33–2. *Second Innings*—Radford 20–3–48–5; Tolley 6–2–10–1; Newport 10–1–26–1; Illingworth 27–7–66–0; Stemp 29–6–95–2; Hick 24–9–50–1; Lampitt 3–0–13–0.

Worcestershire

*T. S. Curtis c Emburey b Tufnell	40	– c Ramprakash b Emburey	60
C. M. Tolley c Carr b Taylor	4	– (9) b Tufnell	1
G. A. Hick run out	168	– c Tufnell b Fraser	7
T. M. Moody c Carr b Emburey	9	– (2) lbw b Taylor	9
D. A. Leatherdale c Carr b Emburey	26	– (4) c Taylor b Tufnell	12
S. R. Lampitt c Emburey b Tufnell	4	– (8) not out	6
†S. J. Rhodes b Emburey	2	– (6) c and b Tufnell	2
P. J. Newport c Williams b Tufnell	10	– (10) not out	2
R. K. Illingworth c Carr b Taylor	30	– (7) c Roseberry b Emburey	1
N. V. Radford lbw b Williams	0	– (5) c Carr b Tufnell	1
R. D. Stemp not out	16		
L-b 18, n-b 19	37	B 4, l-b 10, n-b 3	17
	346	(8 wkts)	**118**

1/5 2/94 3/106 4/165 5/174   346   1/27 2/71 3/104 4/105   (8 wkts) 118
6/179 7/197 8/262 9/263   5/107 6/113 7/115 8/116

Bonus points – Worcestershire 3, Middlesex 4 (Score at 100 overs: 276-9).

Bowling: *First Innings*—Fraser 12–4–35–0; Taylor 15–2–75–2; Williams 14–2–43–1; Tufnell 33–11–70–3; Emburey 34.3–5–98–3; Ramprakash 3–1–7–0. *Second Innings*—Taylor 7–2–25–1; Williams 2–0–10–0; Emburey 11.5–4–17–2; Fraser 6–0–28–1; Tufnell 11–4–24–4.

Umpires: R. Julian and A. G. T. Whitehead.

At Derby, July 21, 22, 23. MIDDLESEX drew with DERBYSHIRE.

MIDDLESEX v DURHAM

At Lord's, July 24, 25, 27. Middlesex won by 175 runs. Middlesex 23 pts, Durham 3 pts. Toss: Middlesex. Durham's first appearance at Lord's as a first-class county was a disappointment, ending in heavy defeat as they were dismissed inside 43 overs. But it was a personal triumph for off-spinner Berry, who claimed ten wickets and scored 90 runs in the match. The most dominant figure, however, was Middlesex's Durham-born opener Roseberry, who continued his marvellous mid-season form with his third century in consecutive games, and the highest score of his career. It was a mature display in great heat. He lasted into the second day, facing 313 balls while hitting one six and 17 fours. Meanwhile, Berry was on his way to seven wickets, improving his career total by 50 per cent, and he followed this up with a career-best 76 which made Middlesex bat again. Roseberry – whose father is on the Durham board of directors – added 81 more runs to his first-innings century before Durham were set 294 in 69 overs. Taylor opened the way for Middlesex, and Tufnell and Emburey spun briskly through the rest of the batsmen in familiar fashion.

Close of play: First day, Middlesex 344-8 (M. A. Roseberry 172*, C. W. Taylor 5*); Second day, Middlesex 12-0 (D. L. Haynes 10*, M. A. Roseberry 2*).

Middlesex

D. L. Haynes st Scott b Berry	26	– c Larkins b Berry	18
M. A. Roseberry b Berry	173	– b Berry	81
*M. W. Gatting c Botham b Berry	90	– c Hutton b Berry	37
J. D. Carr c Briers b Berry	1		
†K. R. Brown c Hutton b Berry	17	– (4) not out	18
P. N. Weekes c Briers b Berry	5		
J. E. Emburey run out	3		
N. F. Williams b Berry	0		
A. R. C. Fraser b Briers	4		
C. W. Taylor c Parker b Briers	14		
P. C. R. Tufnell not out	11		
B 7, l-b 15	22	L-b 5	5

1/72 2/239 3/247 4/285 5/299　　　366　　1/25 2/97 3/159　(3 wkts dec.) 159
6/312 7/325 8/330 9/346

Bonus points – Middlesex 3, Durham 1 (Score at 100 overs: 298-4).

Bowling: *First Innings*—Brown 17-3-48-0; Botham 16-4-41-0; Berry 40-5-113-7; Hughes 23-6-64-0; Briers 18-2-78-2. *Second Innings*—Brown 13-2-44-0; Berry 18.3-1-78-3; Briers 1-0-2-0; Hughes 5-0-30-0.

Durham

W. Larkins c Weekes b Tufnell	30	– c Williams b Taylor	11
S. Hutton c Brown b Tufnell	33	– c Brown b Taylor	1
I. T. Botham c Roseberry b Embury	16	– st Brown b Tufnell	20
P. W. G. Parker c Carr b Embury	4	– c Embury b Tufnell	42
M. P. Briers c Brown b Tufnell	0	– c Carr b Embury	4
I. D. Glendenen c Weekes b Embury	9	– c Carr b Embury	0
†C. W. Scott c Roseberry b Tufnell	3	– lbw b Embury	2
P. J. Berry c Carr b Embury	76	– not out	14
S. P. Hughes lbw b Fraser	33	– c Williams b Embury	2
S. J. E. Brown lbw b Tufnell	7	– c Gatting b Tufnell	4
*D. A. Graveney not out	4	– c Carr b Embury	1
B 2, l-b 9, w 1, n-b 5	17	B 2, l-b 6, n-b 9	17

1/61 2/72 3/79 4/82 5/88   232   1/3 2/40 3/50 4/57 5/59   118
5/101 7/101 8/190 9/217   6/61 7/101 8/106 9/114

Bonus points – Durham 2, Middlesex 4 (Score at 100 overs: 223-9).

Bowling: *First Innings*—Taylor 6–4–3–0; Williams 8–1–16–0; Embury 44.2–12–94–4; Tufnell 34–5–83–5; Weekes 2–0–5–0; Fraser 10–1–20–1. *Second Innings*—Taylor 7–2–16–2; Williams 5–0–20–0; Fraser 4–3–5–0; Tufnell 14–1–26–3; Embury 12.3–2–43–5.

Umpires: R. Palmer and G. A. Stickley.

At Canterbury, August 4, 5, 6. MIDDLESEX drew with KENT.

MIDDLESEX v GLOUCESTERSHIRE

At Lord's, August 7, 8, 10. Middlesex won by five wickets. Middlesex 21 pts, Gloucestershire 6 pts. Toss: Middlesex. All the Gloucestershire batsmen got started, but none could achieve the necessary degree of acceleration on a prosaic first day. For Middlesex, only Gatting could master the attack, playing with cavalier freedom and striking four boundaries in one over from Walsh. His declaration, 71 behind, paid off handsomely as Williams and Taylor picked up four cheap wickets before the close. Williams collected another five on the third day, seaming the ball about at a sharp pace for career-best figures of eight for 75. Needing 213 in 68 overs, Middlesex were in deep trouble when their three top batsmen fell quickly. But Carr worked long and diligently before an adventurous 56 in 59 balls from Pooley sent them galloping to the win with six overs left.

Close of play: First day, Gloucestershire 279-6 (J. T. C. Vaughan 14*, R. C. Williams 9*); Second day, Gloucestershire 39-4 (R. J. Scott 2*, M. C. J. Ball 0*).

Gloucestershire

G. D. Hodgson lbw b Headley	64	– c Headley b Williams	14
*C. W. J. Athey c Carr b Weekes	41	– b Williams	9
M. W. Alleyne c Brown b Williams	25	– c Headley b Taylor	7
R. J. Scott b Headley	44	– (5) c Haynes b Williams	21
R. I. Dawson c Weekes b Williams	29	– (7) c Carr b Taylor	0
†R. C. Russell lbw b Weekes	25	– (8) not out	43
J. T. C. Vaughan not out	33	– (9) b Williams	0
R. C. Williams lbw b Williams	9	– (10) c Brown b Williams	0
C. A. Walsh c and b Weekes	4	– (11) c Embury b Williams	22
M. C. J. Ball c Brown b Williams	0	– (6) c Embury b Williams	8
M. Davies not out	8	– (4) c Brown b Williams	5
B 7, l-b 22, w 5, n-b 6	40	L-b 1, w 2, n-b 9	12

1/101 2/140 3/140 4/204 5/248   (9 wkts dec.) 322   1/22 2/29 3/34 4/39 5/52   141
6/254 7/289 8/294 9/294   6/53 7/94 8/94 9/94

Bonus points – Gloucestershire 3, Middlesex 2 (Score at 100 overs: 254-5).

Bowling: *First Innings*—Taylor 14–3–46–0; Williams 26–6–64–4; Headley 22–5–58–2; Emburey 28–9–53–0; Carr 7–1–11–0; Weekes 25–8–61–3. *Second Innings*—Williams 22.5–7–75–8; Taylor 11–2–40–2; Emburey 7–6–1–0; Headley 4–0–24–0.

Middlesex

D. L. Haynes lbw b Vaughan	18	– c Dawson b Davies	22
M. A. Roseberry c Russell b Walsh	1	– lbw b Walsh	1
*M. W. Gatting b Davies	86	– b Scott	22
J. D. Carr lbw b Vaughan	15	– b Walsh	66
†K. R. Brown lbw b Walsh	8	– c Russell b Alleyne	28
J. C. Pooley c Ball b Davies	21	– not out	56
P. N. Weekes c Alleyne b Vaughan	36	– not out	4
J. E. Emburey b Walsh	29		
D. W. Headley not out	13		
N. F. Williams not out	11		
B 3, l-b 4, w 2, n-b 4	13	L-b 13, w 1	14

1/9 2/23 3/46 4/95 5/157   (8 wkts dec.) 251   1/11 2/40 3/56   (5 wkts) 213
6/164 7/219 8/233   4/129 5/197

C. W. Taylor did not bat.

Bonus points – Middlesex 3, Gloucestershire 3.

Bowling: *First Innings*—Walsh 22–2–97–3; Vaughan 18.3–7–46–3; Scott 9–2–24–0; Ball 11–3–41–0; Alleyne 4–0–11–0; Williams 5–0–17–0; Davies 8–5–8–2. *Second Innings*—Walsh 21–5–44–2; Vaughan 5–1–15–0; Scott 13–4–44–1; Davies 16–2–58–1; Alleyne 7–1–39–1.

Umpires: B. Leadbeater and R. C. Tolchard.

MIDDLESEX v YORKSHIRE

At Uxbridge, August 14, 15, 17. Middlesex won by six wickets. Middlesex 23 pts, Yorkshire 5 pts. Toss: Yorkshire. Ramprakash, playing his first Championship game for four weeks, returned to guide Middlesex to their third victory in four games, which carried them to fifth place in the table. He fell on 94 when his county were only three runs short of victory, which came with five balls to spare. On the first day Headley opened with three wickets, but the pitch provided greater encouragement for spinners as the game developed. Tendulkar organised a repair job on the Yorkshire innings, but Tufnell swept away the later batting. The visiting seamers made Middlesex struggle for runs and Haynes had to graft for four hours before Weekes achieved brisker progress. Rain extracted 23 overs from the final day, when Tendulkar combated spin in masterly fashion. Middlesex were set 231 in 46 overs, and after the early loss of both openers Gatting and Ramprakash took control.

Close of play: First day, Middlesex 33-0 (D. L. Haynes 20*, M. A. Roseberry 9*); Second day, Yorkshire 36-2 (P. Carrick 1*, A. A. Metcalfe 0*).

Yorkshire

*M. D. Moxon c Brown b Headley	5	– b Tufnell	18
S. A. Kellett c Haynes b Headley	25	– b Emburey	16
A. A. Metcalfe c Carr b Headley	21	– (4) c Carr b Emburey	3
S. R. Tendulkar c Williams b Weekes	82	– (5) not out	77
†R. J. Blakey c Carr b Emburey	46	– (6) not out	43
C. White b Tufnell	27		
P. W. Jarvis c Haynes b Tufnell	11		
P. Carrick c Ramprakash b Tufnell	11	– (3) st Brown b Tufnell	16
P. J. Hartley c Carr b Tufnell	1		
J. D. Batty not out	37		
M. A. Robinson b Emburey	2		
L-b 2, n-b 16	18	B 8, l-b 8, n-b 5	21

1/21 2/38 3/71 4/147 5/214   286   1/29 2/36   (4 wkts dec.) 194
6/233 7/234 8/239 9/261   3/47 4/75

Bonus points – Yorkshire 3, Middlesex 4 (Score at 100 overs: 270-9).

Bowling: *First Innings*—Williams 17–6–46–0; Headley 18–3–52–3; Tufnell 37–8–92–4; Emburey 27–5–83–2; Weekes 4–1–11–1. *Second Innings*—Williams 6–1–10–0; Headley 5–1–14–0; Tufnell 24.5–6–71–2; Emburey 19–6–63–2; Weekes 5–0–20–0.

Middlesex

D. L. Haynes lbw b Robinson	83	– run out	6
M. A. Roseberry c Kellett b Hartley	11	– c Blakey b Carrick	18
*M. W. Gatting lbw b Robinson	15	– b Jarvis	48
M. R. Ramprakash c Kellett b Hartley	16	– c Metcalfe b Carrick	94
J. D. Carr c Moxon b Carrick	36	– (6) not out	1
†K. R. Brown c Tendulkar b Robinson	6		
P. N. Weekes not out	64	– (5) not out	48
J. E. Emburey not out	9		
B 4, l-b 1, w 1, n-b 4	10	B 10, l-b 8, n-b 1	19

1/39 2/56 3/133 4/137 (6 wkts dec.) 250   1/10 2/38 (4 wkts) 234
5/147 6/226   3/135 4/228

D. W. Headley, N. F. Williams and P. C. R. Tufnell did not bat.

Bonus points – Middlesex 3, Yorkshire 2.

Bowling: *First Innings*—Jarvis 18–4–42–0; Hartley 23–6–64–2; Carrick 25.3–9–59–1; Batty 16–2–49–0; Robinson 16–2–31–3. *Second Innings*—Jarvis 11–2–49–1; Hartley 7–0–33–0; Carrick 12–0–59–2; Robinson 6–0–31–0; Batty 9.1–0–44–0.

Umpires: G. I. Burgess and D. R. Shepherd.

At Bournemouth, August 18, 19, 20. MIDDLESEX drew with HAMPSHIRE.

At Hove, August 21, 22, 24. MIDDLESEX drew with SUSSEX.

At Northampton, August 26, 27, 28. MIDDLESEX lost to NORTHAMPTONSHIRE by an innings and three runs.

MIDDLESEX v WARWICKSHIRE

At Lord's, September 8, 9, 10, 11. Warwickshire won by eight wickets. Warwickshire 24 pts, Middlesex 5 pts. Toss: Warwickshire. Warwickshire maintained sway for four days, despite low scores from three of their leading batsmen. The heroes of the first day were Twose, who was awarded his county cap as he left the field, and Penney, who went on next day to a six-hour 151, including 15 fours and a six. It was the highest of three centuries in his début season. He also extended his stand with Piper to 192 in 45 overs, and both showed particular assurance against spin. Middlesex's fast start was illusory. The change bowlers were soon among the wickets as the deteriorating pitch assisted the spinners: Smith earned career-best figures and even Lloyd, a very occasional off-spinner, weighed in with three wickets. Following on, Middlesex showed more defiance. They reached 94 with only one mishap, when Haynes retired with a neck injury, but then Small dismissed Roseberry and Ramprakash with consecutive balls, and Warwickshire's quick bowlers established control. Brown took the match into a fourth day, completing his first hundred of 1992, but the last four wickets fell in half an hour against the new ball.

Close of play: First day, Warwickshire 319-7 (T. L. Penney 88*, K. J. Piper 7*); Second day, Middlesex 161-7 (K. R. Brown 20*, A. R. C. Fraser 0*); Third day, Middlesex 305-6 (K. R. Brown 95*, N. F. Williams 2*).

Warwickshire

A. J. Moles c Carr b Williams	3	– b Tufnell 1
R. G. Twose st Brown b Emburey	84	– not out 36
*T. A. Lloyd st Brown b Tufnell	40	– b Tufnell 4
D. P. Ostler c Roseberry b Emburey	0	– not out 13
D. A. Reeve c Ramprakash b Williams	7	
T. L. Penney c Carr b Fraser	151	
N. M. K. Smith lbw b Fraser	39	
A. A. Donald c and b Emburey	15	
†K. J. Piper b Carr	72	
G. C. Small b Fraser	10	
T. A. Munton not out	0	
B 8, l-b 22, w 3, n-b 22	55	L-b 1, w 1, n-b 1 3

1/13 2/89 3/102 4/124 5/165   476   1/18 2/24   (2 wkts) 57
6/235 7/265 8/457 9/472

Bonus points – Warwickshire 4, Middlesex 3 (Score at 100 overs: 305-7).

Bowling: *First Innings*—Williams 14–3–47–2; Taylor 22–4–64–0; Fraser 32.2–5–96–3; Tufnell 38–7–130–1; Emburey 28–4–78–3; Carr 7–0–31–1. *Second Innings*—Taylor 3–0–18–0; Fraser 2–2–0–0; Tufnell 6–0–16–2; Emburey 6–1–22–0.

Middlesex

D. L. Haynes c Piper b Reeve	40	– c Munton b Small 28
M. A. Roseberry c Reeve b Smith	30	– lbw b Small 36
*M. W. Gatting c Reeve b Smith	19	– c and b Donald 71
M. R. Ramprakash c Twose b Smith	19	– c Piper b Small 0
J. D. Carr c Twose b Munton	0	– c Moles b Donald 32
†K. R. Brown c Moles b Smith	25	– c Piper b Donald 106
J. E. Emburey c Moles b Lloyd	21	– c Penney b Donald 24
N. F. Williams c and b Lloyd	1	– c Piper b Donald 11
A. R. C. Fraser c Reeve b Lloyd	28	– b Munton 2
C. W. Taylor b Smith	3	– not out 1
P. C. R. Tufnell not out	0	– b Munton 0
B 3, l-b 9, w 1, n-b 2	15	B 4, l-b 9, w 1, n-b 3 17

1/78 2/80 3/118 4/119 5/119   201   1/94 2/94 3/152 4/169 5/219   328
6/151 7/157 8/171 9/201   6/299 7/320 8/327 9/327

Bonus points – Middlesex 2, Warwickshire 4.

In the second innings D. L. Haynes, when 13, retired hurt at 16 and resumed at 169.

Bowling: *First Innings*—Donald 9–0–53–0; Small 6–1–20–0; Smith 21–8–61–5; Reeve 14–8–12–1; Munton 15–3–36–1; Lloyd 7.2–1–7–3. *Second Innings*—Donald 18–5–36–5; Small 22–3–74–3; Munton 22.4–3–71–2; Reeve 10–4–20–0; Lloyd 7–2–19–0; Smith 21–4–84–0; Twose 3–0–11–0.

Umpires: M. J. Kitchen and K. E. Palmer.

At The Oval, September 12, 13, 14, 15. MIDDLESEX drew with SURREY.

NORTHAMPTONSHIRE

Patron: The Earl of Dalkeith
President: W. R. F. Chamberlain
Chairman: L. A. Wilson
Chairman, Cricket Committee: A. P. Arnold
Chief Executive: S. P. Coverdale
   County Ground, Wantage Road,
   Northampton NN1 4TJ
   (Telephone: 0604-32917)
Captain: A. J. Lamb
Director of Cricket: 1992 – M. J. Procter
                   1993 – P. A. Neale
Coach: R. M. Carter
Cricket Development Officer: B. L. Reynolds

Two victories over Leicestershire in September ensured that 1992 would be remembered as a season of outstanding achievement for Northamptonshire. The first, at Lord's, earned Allan Lamb's side the NatWest Trophy, and brought to an end the club's frustrating and sometimes fractious 12-year wait for a major title. Then, in beating their old rivals again at Grace Road ten days later, Northamptonshire secured third place in the County Championship, their highest finish since 1976. The good news did not end there. The Second Eleven, supervised by chief coach Bob Carter, were runners-up to Surrey in both their competitions, emphasising the strength in depth of the current staff and raising hopes of more success in the years to come.

However, only the most optimistic of Northamptonshire's supporters – and there were few of those left – would have predicted the triumphs in store, during a barren spell from April 22 to May 23 when the first team failed to win a match in any competition. A spate of dropped catches ruled out progress beyond the zonal stage of the Benson and Hedges Cup, and four consecutive Sunday League defeats reversed the trend of improvement in the 40-overs game so apparent in 1991 when Northamptonshire jumped from bottom to third in the table. After these setbacks, Sundays were regularly and sensibly used to give valuable experience to younger players, and in the circumstances joint 13th place was not unduly disappointing. The turning point in the Championship campaign came at Stockton-on-Tees where Durham were overcome by eight wickets in a remarkable run-chase. The next two games, against Derbyshire and Leicestershire, were also won to establish Northamptonshire as serious challengers, and although the following eight matches yielded only one victory, some excellent cricket over the last six weeks boosted the final tally of wins to eight, and maintained an interest in the Championship race almost to the end.

Lamb himself was, in every sense, the central figure throughout the summer. He comfortably topped Northamptonshire's first-class averages with 1,406 runs at 66.95, including six centuries, while in his fourth year as captain he displayed a greater tactical awareness, particularly in the NatWest Trophy run, and was duly re-appointed for

1993. His allegations of ball-tampering against the Pakistani tourists which led to him being fined and suspended for two matches by the county, threatened to distract his Northamptonshire colleagues at a critical point in the season, although Director of Cricket Mike Procter subsequently said that the effect of the whole affair on dressing-room morale had been, if anything, a positive one.

The bulk of the first-class runs came from Lamb, Alan Fordham (1,710) and vice-captain Rob Bailey (1,572), with Fordham once more unfortunate to miss out on an England tour overseas. His opening partnership with Nigel Felton was again a key element in the overall strategy, both in one-day cricket and the Championship. The pair always strove to inject a sense of urgency right from the first over, and in that respect Felton's value to the side was greater than his final modest figures might suggest. Bailey's batting was rarely at its most fluent, but he contributed solidly and, when the opportunity arose, led the team with the same vigour and determination not to let the game drift that was shown by Lamb.

As batsmen, neither David Capel nor Kevin Curran consistently did themselves justice, but David Ripley played many vital innings in the early part of the summer and kept wicket outstandingly well, heading the national list with 71 dismissals. It was unfortunate that his reliability was not always matched by the other close fielders, Curtly Ambrose suffering more than most from missed chances. Ambrose was undoubtedly at his best in the NatWest Trophy, taking eight wickets for 82 runs in 50.5 overs spread over the county's five games – a scoring-rate against him of just 1.6 runs per over. His 50 first-class wickets came at an average of one every 11 overs, and that compared unfavourably with the other front-line seamers – Curran, Capel and Paul Taylor – and with left-arm spinner Nick Cook, who produced a match-winning effort against the champions Essex at Chelmsford in August. In mitigation, Ambrose was troubled for much of the season by a knee injury that required surgery after the NatWest final.

There were, though, relatively few fitness problems affecting key players, in welcome contrast to the unhappy experiences of the previous four years, and most of the time the full squad was available for selection. The left-armer Taylor, for example, played in all 23 first-class matches, as opposed to 13 in 1991, took 68 wickets and was chosen for England's tour of India. The team's late surge coincided with Taylor's most spectacular returns, notably against Hampshire and Middlesex when few batsmen could come to terms with his newly acquired late in-swinger to the right-hander. This brought Taylor a career-best seven for 23 at Bournemouth, including four wickets in an over, and he was the choice of both club and supporters as player of the year.

At the end of a satisfying season, Procter was released from his contract a year early to enable him to accept the job of coaching the South African Test team. In December, the former Worcestershire captain Phil Neale was named as his successor. This was also the year which saw Richard Williams's retirement. Williams's cleverly flighted bowling and pugnacious batting were part of the Northamptonshire scene for nearly 20 years, and his well-crafted skills will be missed in the county and beyond. – *Andrew Radd.*

NORTHAMPTONSHIRE 1992

[Bill Smith]

Back row: A. R. Roberts, J. G. Hughes, M. N. Bowen, R. J. Warren, M. B. Loye, T. C. Walton. *Middle row*: R. Norman (*physiotherapist*), J. N. Snape, N. A. Felton, A. Fordham, J. P. Taylor, N. A. Stanley, K. M. Curran, A. L. Penberthy, W. M. Noon, R. M. Carter (*coach*). *Front row*: D. Ripley, R. G. Williams, R. J. Bailey, A. J. Lamb (*captain*), N. G. B. Cook, D. J. Capel, A. Walker. *Insets*: R. R. Montgomerie, C. E. L. Ambrose.

NORTHAMPTONSHIRE RESULTS

All first-class matches – Played 23: Won 8, Lost 5, Drawn 10.

County Championship matches – Played 22: Won 8, Lost 4, Drawn 10.

Bonus points: Batting 62, Bowling 58.

*Competition placings – Britannic Assurance County Championship, 3rd;
NatWest Bank Trophy, winners; Benson and Hedges Cup, 4th in Group B;
Sunday League, 13th equal.*

BRITANNIC ASSURANCE CHAMPIONSHIP AVERAGES

BATTING

	Birthplace	M	I	NO	R	HS	Avge
‡A. J. Lamb	Langebaanweg, SA	15	23	4	1,350	209	71.05
‡R. J. Bailey	Biddulph	22	37	7	1,514	167*	50.46
‡A. Fordham	Bedford	22	39	2	1,693	192	45.75
‡D. Ripley	Leeds	21	29	9	782	107*	39.10
‡N. A. Felton	Guildford	21	35	3	1,075	103	33.59
‡D. J. Capel	Northampton	22	32	4	888	103	31.71
‡N. G. B. Cook	Leicester	16	9	5	108	37	27.00
K. M. Curran	Rusape, S. Rhodesia	20	28	1	685	82	25.37
‡C. E. L. Ambrose§	Swetes Village, Antigua	18	20	10	200	49*	20.00
J. P. Taylor	Ashby-de-la-Zouch	22	17	8	180	74*	20.00
A. R. Roberts	Kettering	13	17	3	259	62	18.50
M. B. Loye	Northampton	10	14	1	195	46	15.00
A. L. Penberthy	Troon	9	12	1	147	33	13.36

Also batted: M. N. Bowen (*Redcar*) (2 matches) 5; N. A. Stanley (*Bedford*) (1 match) 16, 7*; ‡A. Walker (*Emley*) (1 match) 39; R. J. Warren (*Northampton*) (2 matches) 19, 5, 3*; ‡R. G. Williams (*Bangor*) (2 matches) 12, 3, 14. W. M. Noon (*Grimsby*) (1 match), R. M. Pearson (*Batley*) (1 match) and J. N. Snape (*Stoke-on-Trent*) (1 match) did not bat.

* *Signifies not out.* ‡ *Denotes county cap.* § *Overseas player.*

The following played a total of 16 three-figure innings for Northamptonshire in County Championship matches – A. J. Lamb 6, A. Fordham 4, R. J. Bailey 2, D. Ripley 2, D. J. Capel 1, N. A. Felton 1.

BOWLING

	O	M	R	W	BB	5W/i	Avge
N. G. B. Cook	285.1	79	831	34	7-34	1	24.44
D. J. Capel	440	91	1,181	48	5-61	1	24.60
C. E. L. Ambrose	543.4	151	1,307	50	4-53	0	26.14
K. M. Curran	436.4	95	1,318	48	6-45	1	27.45
J. P. Taylor	630.2	117	1,977	68	7-23	3	29.07
A. R. Roberts	298.2	55	982	20	4-101	0	49.10

Also bowled: R. J. Bailey 120.1–31–291–9; M. N. Bowen 43–6–159–1; N. A. Felton 14–2–93–0; A. Fordham 12.2–0–72–0; R. M. Pearson 35.4–2–130–2; A. L. Penberthy 94–18–279–5; D. Ripley 1–0–14–0; J. N. Snape 26–8–62–1; A. Walker 45–14–90–2; R. G. Williams 31–5–83–4.

Wicket-keepers: D. Ripley 64 ct, 5 st; W. M. Noon 2 ct; A. Fordham 1 ct.

Leading Fielders: R. J. Bailey 20, N. A. Felton 18, D. J. Capel 15.

At Worcester, April 25, 27, 28, 29. NORTHAMPTONSHIRE drew with WORCESTER-SHIRE.

NORTHAMPTONSHIRE v SURREY

At Northampton, May 7, 8, 9, 11. Drawn. Northamptonshire 6 pts, Surrey 6 pts. Toss: Northamptonshire. The batting of Fordham overshadowed everything else in the match, which ended with Surrey, needing 244 to win in 57 overs, content to play out time after losing their first four wickets for 51. Fordham, sixth out at 318 in Northamptonshire's first innings, collected 124 of his 192 runs in boundaries – two sixes and 28 fours – and faced 272 balls in a magnificent innings which occupied 311 minutes. It was made all the more remarkable by the absence of any significant support from his team-mates. Darren Bicknell led Surrey's reply before playing on to the leg-spinner Roberts one short of his hundred, but the loss of the third day to rain obliged the visitors to declare 96 behind. Positive batting from Fordham and Capel enabled Bailey to set a challenging target, but Surrey were never on course, and it was left to Feltham and Sargeant to survive the last 13 overs.

Close of play: First day, Northamptonshire 375; Second day, Surrey 279-6 (D. M. Ward 38*, M. P. Bicknell 0*); Third day, No play.

Northamptonshire

A. Fordham lbw b Benjamin	192	– c M. P. Bicknell b Bryson	38
N. A. Felton b Feltham	22	– c Lynch b Benjamin	23
*R. J. Bailey c Kendrick b M. P. Bicknell	30	– c Benjamin b Bryson	28
D. J. Capel b Benjamin	6	– not out	41
N. A. Stanley lbw b Kendrick	16	– not out	7
R. G. Williams run out	14		
†D. Ripley c Sargeant b M. P. Bicknell	49		
A. R. Roberts lbw b M. P. Bicknell	6		
M. N. Bowen c Lynch b Feltham	5		
C. E. L. Ambrose not out	1		
J. P. Taylor run out	4		
B 2, l-b 13, n-b 15	30	L-b 3, n-b 7	10

1/84 2/169 3/182 4/231 5/275   375   1/46 2/83 3/131   (3 wkts dec.) 147
6/318 7/356 8/370 9/370

Bonus points – Northamptonshire 4, Surrey 3 (Score at 100 overs: 363-7).

Bowling: *First Innings*—Bryson 20-0-98-0; M. P. Bicknell 29.2-3-92-3; Benjamin 24-5-72-2; Feltham 13-4-50-2; Kendrick 21-7-48-1. *Second Innings*—Bryson 12-0-56-2; M. P. Bicknell 10-2-31-0; Benjamin 11-1-37-1; Feltham 3-0-20-0.

Surrey

D. J. Bicknell b Roberts	99	– c Fordham b Roberts	20
M. A. Lynch lbw b Capel	20	– c Ripley b Ambrose	1
*A. J. Stewart lbw b Ambrose	10	– b Taylor	1
G. P. Thorpe b Ambrose	64	– b Taylor	42
D. M. Ward not out	38	– lbw b Ambrose	4
M. A. Feltham lbw b Capel	33	– not out	42
†N. F. Sargeant c Ripley b Ambrose	5	– not out	14
M. P. Bicknell not out	0		
L-b 6, n-b 4	10	B 7, l-b 5, w 5, n-b 1	18

1/68 2/89 3/183 4/213   (6 wkts dec.) 279   1/5 2/16 3/46   (5 wkts) 142
5/272 6/278   4/51 5/109

R. E. Bryson, J. E. Benjamin and N. M. Kendrick did not bat.

Bonus points – Surrey 3, Northamptonshire 2 (Score at 100 overs: 273-5).

Bowling: *First Innings*—Ambrose 27-9-38-3; Taylor 18-1-65-0; Bowen 19-1-70-0; Capel 24-7-57-2; Roberts 22-7-43-1. *Second Innings*—Ambrose 17-4-32-2; Taylor 15-3-44-2; Capel 6-1-16-0; Roberts 16-2-34-1; Bailey 2-1-4-0.

Umpires: H. D. Bird and J. W. Holder.

NORTHAMPTONSHIRE v NOTTINGHAMSHIRE

At Northampton, May 14, 15, 16, 18. Nottinghamshire won by three wickets. Nottinghamshire 24 pts, Northamptonshire 6 pts. Toss: Nottinghamshire. Nottinghamshire achieved their first Championship victory at Northampton since 1966 but in the end had to work hard after a spirited fight-back led by Taylor with both bat and ball. Since Pollard had suffered a broken finger against Ambrose and was only available in emergency, the margin was even tighter than it looked. Few expected the match even to go into a fourth day when the home side were only 92 ahead with two wickets standing before lunch on the third, but Taylor, who in all his 21 previous first-class innings had scored just 61 runs, batted sensibly for three and a quarter hours, first in support of Capel and then supervising a last-wicket stand of 70 with Cook. Nevertheless, Nottinghamshire were still well placed on Saturday evening, requiring a further 91 to win. But on the last morning they lost their way against Taylor and Ambrose once Johnson had gone, and it took some brave blows from Hemmings to settle his side's nerves, and the result. Earlier, Northamptonshire's first innings had collapsed after an assured start, the last eight wickets falling for 75 in 26 overs, and Lewis's first century for Nottinghamshire ensured a useful lead.

Close of play: First day, Nottinghamshire 54-0 (B. C. Broad 34*, M. A. Crawley 4*); Second day, Northamptonshire 112-3 (A. J. Lamb 34*, D. Ripley 10*); Third day, Nottinghamshire 146-2 (P. Johnson 77*, D. W. Randall 18*).

Northamptonshire

A. Fordham c French b Lewis	88	– c Randall b Pick	16
N. A. Felton c Lewis b Evans	64	– c Johnson b Pick	1
R. J. Bailey c French b Lewis	5	– lbw b Lewis	40
*A. J. Lamb c Broad b Crawley	44	– b Lewis	46
D. J. Capel c French b Evans	31	– (6) c French b Evans	52
M. B. Loye c Pollard b Crawley	0	– (7) lbw b Lewis	0
K. M. Curran c Pollard b Pick	14	– (8) c Randall b Evans	0
†D. Ripley not out	22	– (5) b Lewis	12
C. E. L. Ambrose lbw b Evans	1	– b Lewis	9
N. G. B. Cook c French b Evans	0	– (11) run out	16
J. P. Taylor lbw b Evans	0	– (10) not out	74
L-b 2, n-b 11	13	B 3, l-b 7, n-b 20	30

1/133 2/141 3/207 4/211 5/211   282   1/12 2/37 3/96 4/117 5/129   296
6/241 7/269 8/273 9/277   6/130 7/132 8/152 9/226

Bonus points – Northamptonshire 3, Nottinghamshire 4.

Bowling: *First Innings*—Lewis 22–3–59–2; Pick 15–2–76–1; Evans 16.2–6–27–5; Cairns 19–2–87–0; Hemmings 3–1–11–0; Crawley 7–3–20–2. *Second Innings*—Cairns 13.5–3–57–0; Pick 19–4–71–2; Lewis 24–2–74–5; Evans 21–4–66–2; Hemmings 16–7–18–0.

Nottinghamshire

B. C. Broad c Loye b Curran	38	– b Bailey	40
P. R. Pollard retired hurt	13		
M. A. Crawley c Ripley b Taylor	15	– (2) b Ambrose	0
*P. Johnson c Ripley b Curran	3	– (3) c Ripley b Taylor	95
D. W. Randall lbw b Cook	49	– (4) c Loye b Taylor	28
C. C. Lewis not out	134	– (5) c sub b Ambrose	22
C. L. Cairns run out	35	– (6) c Ripley b Taylor	15
K. P. Evans b Ambrose	6	– (7) c Ripley b Taylor	5
†B. N. French b Ambrose	3	– (8) not out	4
E. E. Hemmings lbw b Curran	23	– (9) not out	12
R. A. Pick c Ripley b Taylor	0		
B 2, l-b 18, w 1, n-b 2	23	B 4, l-b 7, w 1, n-b 4	16

1/66 2/76 3/104 4/172 5/249   342   1/3 2/99 3/168 4/191   (7 wkts) 237
6/274 7/284 8/341 9/342   5/211 6/219 7/219

Bonus points – Nottinghamshire 4, Northamptonshire 3 (Score at 100 overs: 341-8).

In the first innings P. R. Pollard retired hurt at 35.

Bowling: *First Innings*—Ambrose 28–9–80–2; Taylor 23.2–1–94–2; Curran 21–3–64–3;
apel 18–4–63–0; Cook 9–4–17–1; Bailey 1–0–4–0. *Second Innings*—Ambrose 24–3–78–2;
aylor 17.2–1–76–4; Curran 10–2–28–0; Capel 11–0–36–0; Bailey 4–0–8–1.

Umpires: D. J. Constant and V. A. Holder.

.t Stockton-on-Tees, May 23, 25, 26. NORTHAMPTONSHIRE beat DURHAM by eight
wickets.

NORTHAMPTONSHIRE v DERBYSHIRE

.t Northampton, May 29, 30, June 1. Northamptonshire won by eight wickets. Northamp-
onshire 16 pts, Derbyshire 1 pt. Toss: Northamptonshire. Northamptonshire coasted to
ictory with 13.3 overs in hand after Barnett, choosing to back his seam attack on a
berally grassed pitch, had set an astonishingly generous target of 181 in 100 minutes plus
ne last 20 overs. Less than an hour's play had been possible on the first two days, and the
rospects were not encouraging on the third until the two captains agreed to make a start
fter lunch. Bowler, whose sixth consecutive half-century equalled T. S. Worthington's 57-
ear-old Derbyshire record, and Barnett were then fed runs for 50 minutes before the
eclaration came, and although Fordham departed early to Malcolm there only ever looked
ke being one result. Barnett was not particularly well-served by his bowlers, Mortensen
xcepted, and neither Felton nor Bailey, who added 137, were required to take any
nnecessary risks. Lamb finished the game with a flourish, hitting 23 off 12 balls, including
our fours.

Close of play: First day, No play; Second day, Derbyshire 32-0 (K. J. Barnett 20*, P. D.
Sowler 4*).

Derbyshire

K. J. Barnett not out	82
. D. Bowler not out	90
L-b 5, n-b 3	8

(no wkt dec.) 180

. E. Morris, S. C. Goldsmith, T. J. G. O'Gorman, †K. M. Krikken, D. G. Cork,
A. E. Warner, I. R. Bishop, O. H. Mortensen and D. E. Malcolm did not bat.

Bonus point – Derbyshire 1.

Bowling: Ambrose 5–1–16–0; Taylor 4–2–11–0; Capel 1–1–0–0; Curran 1–1–0–0; Felton
2–1–84–0; Fordham 11.2–0–64–0.

Derbyshire forfeited their second innings.

Northamptonshire

Northamptonshire forfeited their first innings.

A. Fordham c Bishop b Malcolm	15
J. A. Felton not out	58
R. J. Bailey c Cork b Bishop	72
A. J. Lamb not out	23
L-b 3, n-b 10	13

/18 2/155 (2 wkts) 181

D. J. Capel, M. B. Loye, K. M. Curran, †D. Ripley, A. L. Penberthy, C. E. L. Ambrose
and J. P. Taylor did not bat.

Bowling: Bishop 8.3–0–34–1; Malcolm 7–1–48–1; Cork 6–0–50–0; Warner 7–2–27–0;
Mortensen 8–0–19–0.

Umpires: G. A. Stickley and A. G. T. Whitehead.

NORTHAMPTONSHIRE v LEICESTERSHIRE

At Northampton, June 2, 3. Northamptonshire won by 166 runs. Northamptonshire 20 pts
Leicestershire 4 pts. Toss: Leicestershire. The condition of the pitch, relaid during the
autumn of 1990 in line with instructions from the TCCB's inspector of pitches Harry Brind
caused much discussion during the game, but there was no question of it being deemed unfi
by the umpires. It offered pace and bounce unusual at Northampton in recent seasons, an
the home attack exploited the conditions more effectively; Leicestershire's second-inning
batting performance, which lasted only 24 overs, lacked both conviction and application
Twenty-two wickets fell on the first day with Wells, Benjamin, Curran and Capel doing th
damage. Next morning, however, Northamptonshire's night-watchman Roberts stayed fo
just over an hour without apparent discomfort, and the middle order then demonstrated i
contrasting styles – Bailey and Loye cautious, Curran forthright – that scoring runs was no
impossible. Leicestershire were left to make 279 in four sessions, but once Briers had falle
to the second ball of the innings a two-day finish soon became inevitable.

Close of play: First day, Northamptonshire 56-2 (R. J. Bailey 12*, A. R. Roberts 2*).

Northamptonshire

A. Fordham c Whitticase b Benjamin	14	– c Boon b Wells 3
N. A. Felton c Whitticase b Wells	28	– c Whitaker b Benjamin ....
*R. J. Bailey c Benson b Benjamin	2	– lbw b Wells 4
D. J. Capel c Millns b Wells	7	– (5) b Benjamin 2
M. B. Loye c Benson b Benjamin	0	– (6) c Whitticase b Mullally 3
K. M. Curran c Boon b Wells	0	– (7) b Mullally 3
†D. Ripley c Benjamin b Mullally	18	– (8) b Wells ....
A. L. Penberthy c Whitticase b Millns	5	– (9) c Boon b Wells ....
A. R. Roberts lbw b Wells	16	– (4) c Whitticase b Millns .. 2
C. E. L. Ambrose b Mullally	5	– c Boon b Mullally 1
J. P. Taylor not out	11	– not out ....
B 4, l-b 5, w 2	11	B 4, l-b 13, n-b 1 1

1/24 2/34 3/49 4/49 5/50   117   1/31 2/45 3/96 4/140 5/140   23
6/69 7/83 8/83 9/90   6/187 7/197 8/199 9/227

Bonus points – Leicestershire 4.

Bowling: *First Innings*—Benjamin 20-8-33-3; Millns 13-4-25-1; Wells 13.1-3-26-4
Mullally 7-1-24-2. *Second Innings*—Benjamin 21-4-73-2; Millns 22-8-47-1; Well
22-5-68-4; Mullally 21.2-6-33-3.

Leicestershire

T. J. Boon c Ripley b Ambrose	4	– c Felton b Taylor 1
*N. E. Briers b Taylor	0	– b Ambrose ....
J. J. Whitaker c Felton b Ambrose	18	– b Curran 2
L. Potter lbw b Curran	19	– c Ripley b Curran 2
J. D. R. Benson c Penberthy b Curran	7	– c Curran b Taylor ....
B. F. Smith c Ripley b Capel	0	– b Curran ....
V. J. Wells run out	14	– b Curran ....
†P. Whitticase c Ripley b Capel	2	– c Ripley b Taylor ....
W. K. M. Benjamin c Ripley b Curran	3	– c Ripley b Ambrose 1
D. J. Millns not out	2	– not out ....
A. D. Mullally c Felton b Capel	3	– b Ambrose 1
L-b 2, n-b 3	5	B 9, l-b 3, n-b 1 1

1/4 2/4 3/42 4/51 5/52   77   1/1 2/36 3/56 4/62 5/62   11
6/54 7/60 8/72 9/74   6/63 7/85 8/88 9/102

Bonus points – Northamptonshire 4.

In the second innings L. Potter, when 7, retired hurt at 52 and resumed at 63.

Bowling: *First Innings*—Ambrose 13-2-34-2; Taylor 8-3-12-1; Curran 8-2-17-3; Cape
3.3-0-12-3. *Second Innings*—Ambrose 7-2-27-3; Taylor 11-2-53-3; Curran 6-2-20-4.

Umpires: G. A. Stickley and A. G. T. Whitehead.

At Northampton, June 13, 14, 15. NORTHAMPTONSHIRE lost to PAKISTANIS by seven wickets (See Pakistani tour section).

At Bath, June 16, 17, 18. NORTHAMPTONSHIRE drew with SOMERSET.

At Nottingham, June 19, 20, 22. NORTHAMPTONSHIRE lost to NOTTINGHAM-SHIRE by two wickets.

NORTHAMPTONSHIRE v GLAMORGAN

At Luton, June 26, 27, 29. Northamptonshire won by an innings and 184 runs. Northamptonshire 24 pts, Glamorgan 1 pt. Toss: Northamptonshire. Outplaying Glamorgan throughout, Northamptonshire recorded their fifth-largest Championship victory 40 minutes into the third day. Fordham, who struck 19 fours in just over four hours, and Bailey, with one six and 15 fours, laid the foundation for their county's second-highest total against Glamorgan. They added 206 in 65 overs, before Lamb pressed home the advantage with a brilliant display. He faced only 122 deliveries for his 109, hitting a six and 14 fours, but hay ever prevented him resuming on the second morning, when his omission from the England squad for the Third Test was announced. Northamptonshire piled on a further 83 in 35 minutes, and thereafter Glamorgan subsided to Ambrose in their first innings and Capel, who dismissed Maynard, Richards and Croft in the space of 19 balls, in their second. Northamptonshire claimed the extra ten overs on Saturday evening with Glamorgan 78 for six, but Butcher's brave effort, defying a calf injury, carried the match on into Monday.

Close of play: First day, Northamptonshire 416-2 (R. J. Bailey 148*, A. J. Lamb 109*); Second day, Glamorgan 98-7 (A. R. Butcher 27*).

Northamptonshire

A. Fordham c Maynard b Croft	137	†D. Ripley not out 24
N. A. Felton c Metson b Watkin	6	
R. J. Bailey c Metson b Watkin	165	B 1, l-b 21, n-b 6 28
*A. J. Lamb retired ill	109	
D. J. Capel c Maynard b Foster	30	1/23 2/229 3/449 (5 wkts dec.) 499
K. M. Curran c sub b Foster	0	4/450 5/499

A. R. Roberts, C. E. L. Ambrose, J. P. Taylor and N. G. B. Cook did not bat.

Bonus points – Northamptonshire 4 (Score at 100 overs: 346-2).

A. J. Lamb retired ill at 416.

Bowling: Watkin 28–2–121–2; Foster 22.5–1–123–2; Dale 15–3–58–0; Barwick 22–4–72–0; Croft 32–7–103–1.

Glamorgan

S. P. James c Capel b Taylor	0	– c Ripley b Ambrose 0
H. Morris c Ripley b Ambrose	12	– c Bailey b Taylor 19
A. Dale c Curran b Capel	18	– c Fordham b Curran 29
M. P. Maynard c Capel b Curran	8	– c Bailey b Capel 0
I. V. A. Richards c Taylor b Roberts	49	– c Roberts b Capel 13
R. D. B. Croft c Ripley b Taylor	7	– c Curran b Capel 2
*A. R. Butcher b Ambrose	8	– not out 59
†C. P. Metson not out	39	– c Ripley b Ambrose 6
S. L. Watkin b Ambrose	16	– c Capel b Ambrose 3
S. R. Barwick b Ambrose	0	– run out 0
D. J. Foster c Ripley b Roberts	15	– c Felton b Capel 6
B 1, l-b 3	4	L-b 2 2

1/1 2/19 3/34 4/48 5/73	176	1/0 2/36 3/37 4/63 5/65	139
6/105 7/107 8/135 9/135		6/71 7/98 8/130 9/130	

Bonus points – Glamorgan 1, Northamptonshire 4.

Bowling: *First Innings*—Ambrose 23–7–53–4; Taylor 14–4–27–2; Curran 10–3–20–1; Capel 8–0–21–1; Roberts 15.2–3–51–2. *Second Innings*—Ambrose 13–4–32–3; Taylor 8.2–3–21–1; Curran 6.4–1–37–1; Capel 13–4–41–4; Roberts 2–0–6–0.

Umpires: J. D. Bond and J. H. Hampshire.

At The Oval, June 30, July 1, 2. NORTHAMPTONSHIRE lost to SURREY by five wickets.

NORTHAMPTONSHIRE v SUSSEX

At Northampton, July 3, 4, 6. Drawn. Northamptonshire 3 pts, Sussex 3 pts. Toss Northamptonshire. With only 25 minutes' play possible on the first two days, the sides opted to play for bonus points on the third rather than contrive a run-chase. Speight and Greenfield added 86 in 29 overs to rescue Sussex from early trouble, and they were guided to a third batting point by Moores and Pigott. Northamptonshire faced just one delivery before declaring to end the match at 5.20 p.m.

Close of play: First day, No play; Second day, Sussex 18-0 (D. M. Smith 7*, J. W. Hall 9*).

Sussex

D. M. Smith b Capel	7		J. A. North st Ripley b Cook		3
J. W. Hall b Ambrose	18		A. C. S. Pigott not out		27
N. J. Lenham c Taylor b Curran	9				
*A. P. Wells c Ripley b Curran	12		B 3, l-b 13, w 6, n-b 5		27
M. P. Speight c Bailey b Taylor	42				
K. Greenfield c Fordham b Cook	48		1/35 2/35 3/53	(8 wkts dec.)	255
†P. Moores not out	39		4/64 5/150 6/167		
F. D. Stephenson c Ripley b Cook	19		7/197 8/205		

A. N. Jones did not bat.

Bonus points – Sussex 3, Northamptonshire 3.

Bowling: Ambrose 22.2–5–62–1; Taylor 17–4–36–1; Capel 16–5–41–1; Curran 10–3–37–2; Cook 20–10–38–3; Bailey 7–3–21–0.

Northamptonshire

A. Fordham not out	0
M. B. Loye not out	0

(no wkt dec.) 0

N. A. Felton, R. J. Bailey, *A. J. Lamb, D. J. Capel, K. M. Curran, †D. Ripley, C. E. L. Ambrose, J. P. Taylor and N. G. B. Cook did not bat.

Bowling: Lenham 0.1–0–0–0.

Umpires: G. I. Burgess and B. Dudleston.

At Uxbridge, July 14, 15, 16. NORTHAMPTONSHIRE drew with MIDDLESEX.

NORTHAMPTONSHIRE v LANCASHIRE

At Northampton, July 17, 18, 20. Drawn. Northamptonshire 8 pts, Lancashire 6 pts. Toss Lancashire. Rain ruled out any play after 2.20 p.m. on the third afternoon with Northamptonshire, who had set Lancashire 271 to win in 71 overs, in a strong position. Barnett bowled his left-arm spin intelligently in the home side's first innings, but Fordham, who batted for 286 minutes, and Felton laid the foundation for a solid total. Lancashire were still

2 short of avoiding the follow-on when their seventh wicket fell. They fought back ~~te~~naciously, principally through Hegg, although Northamptonshire contributed to their own ~~fr~~ustration by dropping five catches. With the last three wickets adding 124, Lancashire ~~w~~ere dismissed only 47 behind, and it was left to Fordham and Bailey to lead the push for ~~q~~uick runs on the final morning. Ambrose looked likely to pose a major threat on a wearing ~~pi~~tch, but the weather came to Lancashire's aid.

Close of play: First day, Lancashire 32-0 (M. A. Atherton 6*, S. P. Titchard 19*); Second ~~d~~ay, Northamptonshire 68-1 (A. Fordham 26*, R. J. Bailey 0*).

Northamptonshire

. Fordham st Hegg b Barnett	122	– c and b Watkinson	81
~~W~~. A. Felton c Hegg b Morrison	26	– c Atherton b Barnett	38
. J. Bailey c Hegg b Watkinson	25	– not out	76
A. J. Lamb c Barnett b Watkinson	10	– not out	24
~~D~~. J. Capel st Hegg b Barnett	59		
. M. Curran c Atherton b Barnett	5		
. L. Penberthy c Martin b Barnett	13		
D. Ripley b Barnett	21		
. E. L. Ambrose not out	7		
B 2, l-b 7, w 2, n-b 6	17	L-b 4	4

1/155 2/214 3/228 4/248 5/260	(8 wkts dec.) 345	1/67 2/172	(2 wkts dec.) 223
6/288 7/328 8/345			

P. Taylor and N. G. B. Cook did not bat.

Bonus points – Northamptonshire 4, Lancashire 3.

Bowling: *First Innings*—Morrison 12-1-44-1; Martin 16-3-38-0; Watkinson 36-6-136-2; ~~A~~ustin 10-1-36-0; Barnett 24.5-2-82-5. *Second Innings*—Morrison 5-0-11-0; Martin ~~1~~5-1-78-0; Watkinson 12-1-40-1; Barnett 10-0-66-1; Austin 6-0-24-0.

Lancashire

M. A. Atherton c Curran b Capel	15	– c Ripley b Taylor	12
P. Titchard b Fordham b Taylor	27	– c Capel b Ambrose	5
. J. Speak c and b Cook	49	– not out	5
. D. Lloyd lbw b Curran	24	– not out	0
P. Crawley c Felton b Taylor	16		
M. Watkinson c Taylor b Capel	17		
W. K. Hegg not out	76		
D. Austin c Capel b Taylor	3		
J. Martin c Bailey b Ambrose	10		
. K. Morrison run out	27		
A. Barnett b Penberthy	11		
B 13, l-b 7, w 2, n-b 1	23	W 1	1

1/48 2/56 3/123 4/133 5/163	298	1/17 2/19	(2 wkts) 23
6/163 7/174 8/210 9/272			

Bonus points – Lancashire 3, Northamptonshire 4.

Bowling: *First Innings*—Ambrose 21-6-56-1; Taylor 29-8-79-3; Capel 14-4-29-2; ~~C~~urran 11-5-29-1; Penberthy 10-3-32-1; Cook 10-2-53-1. *Second Innings*—Ambrose 1-1-5-1; Taylor 5-0-18-1.

Umpires: B. Leadbeater and D. R. Shepherd.

NORTHAMPTONSHIRE v WARWICKSHIRE

~~At~~ Northampton, July 21, 22, 23. Drawn. Northamptonshire 7 pts, Warwickshire 8 pts. ~~To~~ss: Northamptonshire. Lamb became the first batsman to score a double-century and a ~~ce~~ntury in the same match for Northamptonshire, but Warwickshire were better placed at ~~th~~e end after being asked to score 237 in 47 overs. Their openers, Moles and Twose,

provided the ideal start, reducing the requirement to 96 in 14 overs, only for the innings t
lose momentum against Capel and Ambrose. Lamb, who batted for 337 minutes and 29
balls and struck a six and 20 fours, dominated the first day with the highest innings eve
played for Northamptonshire against Warwickshire. It began in the second over, after tw
wickets had gone in seven balls, and his best support came from Roberts, who helped ad
106 in 29 overs. Warwickshire, in turn, were boosted by a maiden Championship centur
from Penney, with 11 fours in 222 minutes. Denied a substantial first-innings lea
Northamptonshire were obliged to set a generous target to keep the game alive, after Lam
had plundered another hundred against a hotchpotch attack.

Close of play: First day, Northamptonshire 307-7 (A. J. Lamb 188*, C. E. L. Ambros
1*); Second day, Warwickshire 316-7 dec.

Northamptonshire

A. Fordham c Twose b Donald	1	– c Moles b P. A. Smith	7
N. A. Felton run out	3	– c Moles b N. M. K. Smith	
R. J. Bailey c Moles b Small	21	– c Moles b Twose	1
*A. J. Lamb c P. A. Smith b N. M. K. Smith	.209	– run out	.10
D. J. Capel c Piper b P. A. Smith	12	– not out	
K. M. Curran c Small b Reeve	9		
†D. Ripley c Ostler b Small	18	– (6) not out	
A. R. Roberts c Piper b Reeve	39		
C. E. L. Ambrose b Donald	5		
J. P. Taylor not out	2		
B 3, l-b 8, n-b 4	15	B 4, l-b 1, w 1	

1/4 2/4 3/50 4/71 5/102 (9 wkts dec.) 334   1/11 2/45 (4 wkts dec.) 21
6/195 7/301 8/324 9/334   3/209 4/210

R. M. Pearson did not bat.

Bonus points – Northamptonshire 4, Warwickshire 4.

Bowling: *First Innings*—Donald 19-4-63-2; Small 16-0-50-2; P. A. Smith 19-4-67-
Reeve 18-3-55-2; N. M. K. Smith 26.2-3-88-1. *Second Innings*—Donald 3-0-4-0; Sma
2-0-6-0; N. M. K. Smith 16-2-72-1; Twose 7-2-33-1; Lloyd 3-0-18-0; Ostler 3-0-22-
Reeve 7-0-38-0; P. A. Smith 5-0-20-1.

Warwickshire

A. J. Moles lbw b Ambrose	12	– c Ripley b Ambrose	6
R. G. Twose c and b Pearson	49	– c Roberts b Capel	7
*T. A. Lloyd c Curran b Taylor	5	– c Roberts b Ambrose	
D. P. Ostler c Taylor b Pearson	29	– c Lamb b Capel	1
D. A. Reeve c Ripley b Taylor	48	– b Ambrose	1
T. L. Penney not out	.100	– not out	1
N. M. K. Smith b Capel	41	– not out	1
P. A. Smith b Roberts	3		
†K. J. Piper not out	11		
B 11, l-b 5, w 1, n-b 1	18	B 8, l-b 1, w 5, n-b 1	1

1/22 2/27 3/86 4/105 5/197 (7 wkts dec.) 316   1/141 2/146 3/175 (5 wkts) 20
6/272 7/285   4/175 5/204

G. C. Small and A. A. Donald did not bat.

Bonus points – Warwickshire 4, Northamptonshire 3.

Bowling: *First Innings*—Ambrose 17-6-37-1; Taylor 14-3-42-2; Pearson 27.4-2-90-
Curran 4-1-11-0; Roberts 25-4-91-1; Bailey 4-0-8-0; Capel 7-2-21-1. *Second Innings*
Taylor 4-0-18-0; Ambrose 13-2-38-3; Pearson 8-0-40-0; Curran 5-0-26-0; Rober
5-0-33-0; Capel 11-0-42-2.

Umpires: B. Leadbeater and D. R. Shepherd.

At Chelmsford, August 4, 5, 6. NORTHAMPTONSHIRE beat ESSEX by an innings and 13 runs.

NORTHAMPTONSHIRE v YORKSHIRE

At Northampton, August 7, 8, 10. Drawn. Northamptonshire 6 pts, Yorkshire 5 pts. Toss: Yorkshire. Yorkshire's seamers claimed the early honours on a thickly grassed pitch, but they met with determined resistance from Felton, who compiled his first Championship century for two years in four and a half hours, and was eighth man out at 220. Yorkshire found batting no easier despite the temporary absence of Ambrose, resting a sore knee, and they were particularly troubled by Capel. He had a hand in the first six wickets to fall on a rain-shortened second day, claiming four as a bowler and holding two slip catches. Northamptonshire struggled again in their second innings against Robinson and Pickles, but they were able to set Yorkshire 241 to win in 65 overs, and quickly removed Moxon. The visitors rallied through Kellett and Byas before the latter had his nose broken by an Ambrose bouncer at 101 for four, and from then on Yorkshire were content to survive. White and Pickles stayed together for 24 overs, and a further seven were lost to rain and bad light in the final session.

Close of play: First day, Yorkshire 47-3 (S. R. Tendulkar 19*, P. Carrick 1*); Second day, Northamptonshire 47-1 (A. Fordham 31*).

Northamptonshire

A. Fordham lbw b Gough	1	– b Jarvis	40
N. A. Felton c Carrick b Jarvis	103	– c Blakey b Robinson	15
R. J. Bailey c Blakey b Robinson	37	– c Blakey b Pickles	31
A. J. Lamb c Tendulkar b Pickles	6	– b Pickles	5
D. J. Capel c White b Pickles	1	– lbw b Robinson	6
K. M. Curran c Blakey b Gough	8	– c Kellett b Pickles	14
A. L. Penberthy lbw b Pickles	16	– c Tendulkar b Gough	22
*D. Ripley c Byas b Gough	18	– not out	24
C. E. L. Ambrose c Byas b Jarvis	15	– not out	5
J. P. Taylor not out	2		
N. G. B. Cook c Kellett b Pickles	0		
B 4, l-b 6, n-b 7	17	B 4, l-b 5, n-b 3	12

1/5 2/80 3/87 4/89 5/100   224   1/47 2/67 3/73   (7 wkts dec.) 174
6/144 7/199 8/220 9/223   4/84 5/117
                               6/122 7/167

Bonus points – Northamptonshire 2, Yorkshire 4.

Bowling: *First Innings*—Jarvis 17-7-45-2; Gough 15-0-81-3; Robinson 17-9-24-1; Pickles 17.3-3-40-4; Carrick 13-4-24-0. *Second Innings*—Jarvis 12-1-54-1; Gough 10-0-32-1; Robinson 16-2-38-2; Pickles 11-3-41-3.

Yorkshire

*M. D. Moxon c Ripley b Taylor	8	– b Taylor	1
A. A. Kellett run out	9	– c Ripley b Curran	41
D. Byas c Ripley b Bailey	8	– retired hurt	37
S. R. Tendulkar c Capel b Taylor	24	– b Curran	6
P. Carrick c Ripley b Capel	1		
†R. J. Blakey c Penberthy b Capel	11	– (5) run out	6
C. White c Fordham b Capel	35	– (6) c Bailey b Ambrose	40
C. S. Pickles c Capel b Curran	20	– (7) not out	19
P. W. Jarvis c Penberthy b Capel	16	– (8) not out	12
D. Gough not out	17		
M. A. Robinson b Curran	0		
B 5, l-b 2, n-b 2	9	B 3, l-b 8, n-b 1	12

1/17 2/20 3/46 4/47 5/67   158   1/9 2/62 3/74   (5 wkts) 174
6/67 7/104 8/129 9/155   4/89 5/155

Bonus points – Yorkshire 1, Northamptonshire 4.

In the second innings D. Byas retired hurt at 101.

Bowling: *First Innings*—Ambrose 2.3–1–1–0; Taylor 16–1–53–2; Curran 12.2–0–32–2; Capel 22–4–61–4; Penberthy 3–2–3–0; Cook 2–2–0–0; Bailey 1–0–1–1. *Second Innings*— Ambrose 16–2–48–1; Taylor 13–3–33–1; Capel 9–0–36–0; Curran 10–2–37–2; Cook 5–3–5–0; Bailey 4–1–4–0.

Umpires: B. Dudleston and D. O. Oslear.

At Bournemouth, August 14, 15, 17. NORTHAMPTONSHIRE beat HAMPSHIRE by te wickets.

At Bristol, August 18, 19, 20. NORTHAMPTONSHIRE lost to GLOUCESTERSHIRE by 39 runs.

NORTHAMPTONSHIRE v KENT

At Northampton, August 21, 22, 24. Drawn. Northamptonshire 4 pts, Kent 1 pt. Toss Northamptonshire. Kent, who went into the match occupying second place in th Championship table, and Northamptonshire, one place below, saw their efforts to contriv a result negated by the weather. Kent lost half their side for 75 after being put in, an despite a brief revival led by Cowdrey and Marsh, Northamptonshire hit back again b taking the last four wickets for eight runs in five overs. Rain intervened on the second day allowing only 22 overs, and on the final morning the onus was on the captains to agree target. Ward, whose unbeaten 95 came from only 89 deliveries, struck the bal magnificently, facing only Northamptonshire's regular bowlers. But he was denied a well deserved century as Benson kept his side of the bargain, setting 253 to win in 69 overs Fordham and Felton provided a solid platform, and the home side were preparing for th final assault, with a further 145 required from 28 overs, when more rain washed out potentially interesting finish.

Close of play: First day, Northamptonshire 22–0 (A. Fordham 7*, N. A. Felton 14*) Second day, Northamptonshire 85–2 (R. J. Bailey 18*, R. J. Warren 3*).

Kent

T. R. Ward c Loye b Curran	3	– not out	9!
*M. R. Benson c Noon b Capel	23	– c Noon b Taylor	(
N. R. Taylor c Bailey b Capel	33	– not out	4
C. L. Hooper c Bailey b Bowen	3		
G. R. Cowdrey run out	30		
M. V. Fleming lbw b Capel	4		
†S. A. Marsh lbw b Cook	65		
R. M. Ellison not out	21		
R. P. Davis lbw b Cook	0		
M. J. McCague lbw b Taylor	0		
A. P. Igglesden run out	3		
B 5, l-b 2, w 2, n-b 2	11	L-b 2	—

1/18 2/45 3/54 4/71 5/75   196   1/3   (1 wkt dec.) 14
6/143 7/188 8/188 9/193

Bonus points – Kent 1, Northamptonshire 4.

Bowling: *First Innings*—Taylor 19–4–43–1; Curran 17–5–39–1; Bowen 15–5–35–1; Cape 23–6–48–3; Cook 16–9–18–2; Bailey 7–4–6–0. *Second Innings*—Taylor 8–0–36–1; Curra 6–2–17–0; Cook 10–0–32–0; Bowen 9–0–54–0.

Northamptonshire

A. Fordham b Ellison	21	– c Fleming b Hooper	37
N. A. Felton b Igglesden	40	– not out	50
*R. J. Bailey not out	18	– not out	13
R. J. Warren not out	3		
L-b 2, n-b 1	3	B 3, l-b 3, n-b 2	8

1/61 2/73   (2 wkts dec.) 85   1/80   (1 wkt) 108

D. J. Capel, K. M. Curran, M. B. Loye, †W. M. Noon, M. N. Bowen, J. P. Taylor and N. G. B. Cook did not bat.

Bowling: *First Innings*—McCague 10–2–20–0; Igglesden 16–3–39–1; Ellison 6–0–24–1. *Second Innings*—McCague 9–1–27–0; Igglesden 12–2–38–0; Ellison 7–1–14–0; Fleming 1–1–0–0; Hooper 9–2–17–1; Davis 3–1–6–0.

Umpires: B. J. Meyer and R. A. White.

NORTHAMPTONSHIRE v MIDDLESEX

At Northampton, August 26, 27, 28. Northamptonshire won by an innings and three runs. Northamptonshire 22 pts, Middlesex 4 pts. Toss: Northamptonshire. Although the cricket was overshadowed by the controversy over Allan Lamb's newspaper allegations against the Pakistani tourists, which appeared on the first morning, Northamptonshire were not distracted. They needed the equivalent of only a day and a half to overcome Middlesex, whose batsmen twice failed to counter some impressive swing bowling from Taylor. The left-armer returned ten wickets in a match for the first time in his career, for only 54 runs, and victory was secured with three overs remaining on the third day, after 43 overs had been lost to rain on the first and nothing at all could be done on the second. Having dismissed Middlesex cheaply, Northamptonshire also struggled, against Fraser and Williams, who claimed five for eight in 29 balls to restrict the home side's lead to 108, despite a century stand between Fordham and night-watchman Cook. Middlesex began their second effort solidly enough before losing seven wickets for 12 runs in 14 overs. Late resistance from the tail could not avert an innings defeat.

Close of play: First day, Northamptonshire 38-1 (A. Fordham 9*, N. G. B. Cook 2*); Second day, No play.

Middlesex

D. L. Haynes lbw b Taylor	19	– lbw b Taylor	16
M. A. Roseberry c Cook b Taylor	11	– c Ripley b Taylor	9
*M. W. Gatting b Taylor	0	– lbw b Capel	1
M. R. Ramprakash c Ripley b Taylor	20	– b Capel	1
J. D. Carr lbw b Taylor	2	– lbw b Taylor	0
†K. R. Brown c Ripley b Curran	17	– c Ripley b Taylor	2
J. E. Emburey c Ripley b Ambrose	3	– b Taylor	5
D. W. Headley c Ripley b Ambrose	1	– c Lamb b Bailey	20
N. F. Williams lbw b Curran	10	– b Ambrose	19
A. R. C. Fraser not out	1	– c Lamb b Cook	30
P. C. R. Tufnell run out	1	– not out	0
B 4, l-b 3, n-b 3	10	L-b 2	2

1/18 2/18 3/37 4/55 5/62   95   1/24 2/27 3/27 4/27 5/29   105
6/68 7/76 8/87 9/94   6/35 7/36 8/60 9/105

Bonus points – Northamptonshire 4.

Bowling: *First Innings*—Ambrose 13–5–24–2; Taylor 16–9–24–5; Capel 11–1–25–0; Curran 8.4–4–15–2. *Second Innings*—Ambrose 11–6–12–1; Taylor 16–5–30–5; Capel 9–5–20–2; Curran 5–0–26–0; Cook 4–2–5–1; Penberthy 2–0–10–0; Bailey 0.1–0–0–1.

Northamptonshire

A. Fordham c Carr b Williams	91	†D. Ripley b Williams	6
N. A. Felton b Emburey	19	C. E. L. Ambrose b Williams	7
N. G. B. Cook c Carr b Fraser	37	J. P. Taylor not out	0
R. J. Bailey c Brown b Headley	0		
*A. J. Lamb lbw b Fraser	13	L-b 6, w 1, n-b 16	23
D. J. Capel c Brown b Fraser	3		
K. M. Curran c and b Williams	4	1/36 2/137 3/138 4/176 5/184	203
A. L. Penberthy b Williams	0	6/184 7/190 8/191 9/198	

Bonus points – Northamptonshire 2, Middlesex 4.

Bowling: Williams 18.1–2–49–5; Fraser 26–4–59–3; Headley 20–2–63–1; Emburey 10–2–26–1.

Umpires: J. C. Balderstone and N. T. Plews.

At Scarborough, August 31, September 1, 2, 3. NORTHAMPTONSHIRE drew with YORKSHIRE.

At Leicester, September 12, 13, 14, 15. NORTHAMPTONSHIRE beat LEICESTER-SHIRE by six wickets.

COUNTY CAPS AWARDED IN 1992

Derbyshire	C. J. Adams, K. M. Krikken, T. J. G. O'Gorman.
Glamorgan	P. A. Cottey, R. D. B. Croft, A. Dale, S. P. James.
Gloucestershire	G. D. Hodgson.
Hampshire	S. D. Udal.
Kent	M. A. Ealham, C. L. Hooper, M. J. McCague.
Lancashire	G. D. Lloyd, N. J. Speak.
Northamptonshire	K. M. Curran, J. P. Taylor.
Nottinghamshire	P. R. Pollard.
Somerset	A. R. Caddick, M. N. Lathwell.
Sussex	J. W. Hall, F. D. Stephenson.
Warwickshire	K. J. Piper, R. G. Twose.
Yorkshire	S. A. Kellett, M. A. Robinson, S. R. Tendulkar.

No caps were awarded by Essex, Leicestershire, Middlesex, Surrey or Worcestershire. Durham gave caps to all their playing staff and announced that they would not use the system to differentiate between players.

NOTTINGHAMSHIRE

President: R. T. Simpson
Chairman: C. W. Gillott
Chairman, Cricket Committee: A. Wheelhouse
General Manager/Secretary: B. Robson
   County Cricket Ground, Trent Bridge,
   Nottingham NG2 6AG
   (Telephone: 0602-821525)
Captain: R. T. Robinson
Cricket Manager: M. Hendrick

Nottinghamshire had expected an eventful season in 1992 and they got one, though not of the sort they had anticipated. They were second from bottom in the Sunday League, which they had won 12 months earlier, and their dismal one-day form also led to early exits from the other two one-day competitions.

The consolation was fourth place in the County Championship, but even that represented a major disappointment. In late July Nottinghamshire were closing on the leaders Essex, and with games in hand looked like their most serious rivals. But two slender defeats against Gloucestershire and Glamorgan did great damage and Nottinghamshire did not win again until the penultimate match.

In the circumstances, however, it was an achievement to mount any sort of challenge for the title. Events on the field were constantly overshadowed at Trent Bridge by comings and, to a much larger extent, goings, which began with the departure of John Birch. In his 18-month reign as team manager, Birch's vigorous style of leadership had given the club fresh impetus and his success in bringing together two of the most exciting all-rounders in the world in Chris Lewis and Chris Cairns had been a prime source of all the pre-season optimism. That made it all the more of a shock and a mystery when he resigned "to pursue business interests" in early May, just weeks after he had signed a three-year contract. There was no further explanation, which only fuelled rumours that there were other reasons for his sudden exit.

Tim Robinson was then placed in overall charge on a temporary basis. After six weeks in which Nottinghamshire won only one game out of 12, it was clear that Robinson was overburdened with the roles of manager, captain, batsman and beneficiary all at once. So Nottinghamshire appointed Mike Hendrick as manager. He immediately saw the side clinch victory over Northamptonshire and began to plan the next surprise.

This was the decision to release three of the club's stalwarts: Chris Broad, Eddie Hemmings and Kevin Cooper, leaving all three bewildered and bitter. Broad was sacked only 24 hours after his fifth century of the season had staved off the threat of defeat against Leicestershire. Although Hemmings and Cooper took more than 1,500 first-class wickets between them for the county, Nottinghamshire had to manage without the pair for a large part of 1992, due to long-standing injury problems. Broad's departure, like Birch's, suggested reasons which the club were not prepared to admit. Hendrick insisted the club were "investing in the future" by emphasising young players. Certainly, the way Graeme Archer finished the season with a flourish, hitting a maiden century against Derbyshire and three Championship fifties, justified that philosophy. Others, like Mark Saxelby and David Pennett, also showed promise. Saxelby is, like Broad, a tall left-hander and also possesses a sound technique which enabled him to adjust to the role of opener. Pennett, who began the season on trial after being released by the Yorkshire cricket academy, thrived at once and his lively seam bowling benefited from Hendrick's advice.

Robinson emerged as the leading run-maker, after missing the first month with a broken thumb, and three of his four Championship centuries set up victories; the other would surely have done the same had bad weather not helped Durham hold out. Mark Crawley seized the chance to make impressive progress in the first half of the season, hitting four centuries, but he suffered a loss of confidence late on, at a time when his credentials as a future captain passed a stern test in the absence of both Robinson and Paul Johnson. Both Pauls, Johnson and Pollard, were injured: Johnson broke a bone in his left hand in early August when he was in top form, which wrecked his hopes of another England A tour. Derek Randall's fluctuating fortunes made it likely that he would spend 1993, when he has been granted a testimonial, playing as a one-day specialist, with Archer filling his Championship place.

The most significant batting progress came from the New Zealander Cairns, prompting Robinson to say that he would be employed as a front line batsman in future. Cairns's confidence in his bowling suffered after a disappointing World Cup, but he too was helped by Hendrick's support. He might have made more impact had he not been hampered by a kidney ailment late on. As for Lewis, in between frequent absences for international duty, his Championship form, especially as a batsman, was of a high standard and in two cases, against Northamptonshire and Surrey, his all-round contribution was the catalyst for Nottinghamshire victories. While the blaze of publicity which surrounded the arrival of Lewis and Cairns fizzled out, there was still sufficient evidence in 1992 to support the belief that in the 1990s they might fulfil the roles performed so famously in the 1980s by Richard Hadlee and Clive Rice.

In a season fragmented by injuries on all fronts, the long-term absence of Andy Pick was by far the biggest blow. Hampered by shoulder trouble, he figured in only nine Championship matches and his absence prevented a potentially menacing pace attack from taking shape. As a result, the quietly efficient Kevin Evans often carried an under-strength attack, while Andy Afford overcame a bad run in mid-season to emerge, with Cairns, as one of only two bowlers to top 50 first-class wickets.

There will be a good deal more caution and considerably less expectancy in Nottinghamshire's outlook for 1993, although Hendrick insisted that "things aren't about to fall apart". Certainly, Nottinghamshire still possess a squad capable of doing well in the Championship, but the loss of experienced campaigners may well count against them in the one-day game. – Nick Lucy.

491

NOTTINGHAMSHIRE 1992

[*Bill Smith*]

Back row: M. G. Field-Buss, G. F. Archer, S. Bramhall, M. A. Crawley, M. Saxelby, R. T. Bates, G. W. Mike, W. A. Dessaur.
Middle row: G. Stringfellow (*Second Eleven scorer*), S. Ball (*physiotherapist*), R. J. Chapman, K. P. Evans, C. C. Lewis, C. L. Cairns, J. A. Afford, P. R. Pollard, L. Beaumont (*First Eleven scorer*). *Front row:* R. A. Pick, K. E. Cooper, D. W. Randall, E. E. Hemmings, J. D. Birch, P. Johnson, B. C. Broad, B. N. French, K. Saxelby, M. Newell. *Insets:* M. Hendrick (*cricket manager*), R. T. Robinson (*captain*).

NOTTINGHAMSHIRE RESULTS

All first-class matches – Played 25: Won 8, Lost 8, Drawn 9.

County Championship matches – Played 22: Won 7, Lost 7, Drawn 8.

Bonus points – Batting 54, Bowling 58.

Competition placings – Britannic Assurance County Championship, 4th;
NatWest Bank Trophy, 2nd round; Benson and Hedges Cup, 3rd in Group C;
Sunday League, 17th.

BRITANNIC ASSURANCE CHAMPIONSHIP AVERAGES

BATTING

	Birthplace	M	I	NO	R	HS	Avge
‡R. T. Robinson.....	Sutton-in-Ashfield	18	31	5	1,510	189	58.07
‡C. C. Lewis........	Georgetown, Guyana	10	15	3	591	134*	49.25
G. F. Archer.......	Carlisle	6	11	2	424	117	47.11
‡P. Johnson	Newark	15	24	3	963	107*	45.85
‡B. C. Broad........	Bristol	13	25	3	1,000	159*	45.45
‡C. L. Cairns§	Picton, New Zealand	20	29	6	983	107*	42.73
‡D. W. Randall.....	Retford	18	27	3	865	133*	36.04
M. Saxelby	Worksop	7	12	1	389	66	35.36
M. A. Crawley	Newton-le-Willows	22	39	7	1,115	160*	34.84
‡P. R. Pollard......	Nottingham	18	32	3	828	75	28.55
G. W. Mike	Nottingham	4	5	1	102	61*	25.50
‡K. P. Evans	Calverton	18	22	4	419	104	23.27
‡E. E. Hemmings....	Leamington Spa	7	11	5	132	52*	22.00
‡R. A. Pick........	Nottingham	9	10	4	117	52	19.50
S. Bramhall.......	Warrington	6	9	3	113	37*	18.83
‡B. N. French	Warsop	16	18	3	246	55	16.40
D. B. Pennett	Leeds	11	11	1	69	29	6.90
M. G. Field-Buss ..	Mtarfa, Malta	7	7	2	27	13	5.40
‡J. A. Afford	Crowland	15	15	5	33	12	3.30

Also batted: W. A. Dessaur (*Nottingham*) (1 match) 1, 15. R. J. Chapman (*Nottingham*)
(1 match) did not bat.

* *Signifies not out.*   ‡ *Denotes county cap.*   § *Overseas player.*

The following played a total of 21 three-figure innings for Nottinghamshire in County
Championship matches – B. C. Broad 5, R. T. Robinson 4, M. A. Crawley 3, C. L. Cairns
2, P. Johnson 2, C. C. Lewis 2, G. F. Archer 1, K. P. Evans 1, D. W. Randall 1.

BOWLING

	O	M	R	W	BB	5W/i	Avge
C. C. Lewis	370.3	67	991	40	6-90	2	24.77
J. A. Afford	445.1	111	1,434	43	6-68	1	33.34
E. E. Hemmings	259.5	95	602	18	4-30	0	33.44
C. L. Cairns	576.3	104	1,945	54	6-70	2	36.01
D. B. Pennett	272.2	49	924	25	4-58	0	36.96
M. A. Crawley........	206	52	601	16	3-38	0	37.56
K. P. Evans...........	558.5	124	1,633	43	5-27	1	37.97
R. A. Pick	234.1	46	784	15	3-33	0	52.26
M. G. Field-Buss......	159	24	571	10	4-71	0	57.10

Also bowled: R. J. Chapman 13–1–77–2; P. Johnson 5–0–30–0; G. W. Mike
68.2–9–276–8; P. R. Pollard 4–0–33–0; D. W. Randall 1–0–8–0; R. T. Robinson 1–0–4–0.

Wicket-keepers: B. N. French 36 ct, 4 st; S. Bramhall 13 ct, 5 st.

Leading Fielders: P. R. Pollard 19, M. A. Crawley 18.

NOTTINGHAMSHIRE v WARWICKSHIRE

At Nottingham, April 25, 26, 27, 28. Nottinghamshire won by eight wickets. Nottinghamshire 23 pts, Warwickshire 6 pts. Toss: Warwickshire. An unfortunate injury sustained by Munton changed the course of this match, when Nottinghamshire's first innings was in considerable trouble at 123 for six replying to Warwickshire's 249. The seam bowler broke the middle finger of his left hand in dropping a catch offered by Evans, who celebrated that let-off by playing his part in a tail-end fightback against an attack further depleted by Small's damaged hamstring. Hemmings and Pick rounded it off with a rousing last-wicket stand of 109 – the highest for the county since B. Dooland and A. K. Walker compiled 123 against Somerset in 1956. Their efforts earned Nottinghamshire maximum batting points and a lead of 62. Despite a fine hundred from Ostler, who hit 13 boundaries, and Munton's defiant gesture in batting with one hand behind his back, the home side were left to make 202 in 73 overs. With no Munton, nor Small once he broke down in his second over, Broad made light work of that, hitting 17 boundaries in his two-and-a-half-hour century.

Close of play: First day, Warwickshire 230-9 (K. J. Piper 10*, T. A. Munton 0*); Second day, Nottinghamshire 236-9 (E. E. Hemmings 13*, R. A. Pick 21*); Third day, Warwickshire 190-3 (D. P. Ostler 83*, Asif Din 35*).

Warwickshire

A. J. Moles c French b Hemmings	51	– c French b Pick	7
J. D. Ratcliffe c Johnson b Lewis	34	– b Pick	4
*T. A. Lloyd b Lewis	10	– c French b Cairns	41
D. P. Ostler b Pick	0	– b Evans	102
Asif Din b Cairns	40	– c Lewis b Cairns	35
R. G. Twose lbw b Hemmings	55	– c French b Hemmings	17
P. A. Smith c Pollard b Hemmings	3	– lbw b Lewis	5
†K. J. Piper not out	18	– c French b Pick	12
P. A. Booth lbw b Evans	8	– run out	10
G. C. Small b Evans	1	– c French b Lewis	7
T. A. Munton c Evans b Pick	9	– not out	0
B 3, l-b 4, w 1, n-b 12	20	B 2, l-b 5, n-b 16	23
	249		**263**

1/87 2/104 3/106 4/123 5/180   1/6 2/36 3/104 4/190 5/223
6/199 7/212 8/221 9/223   6/229 7/245 8/245 9/253

Bonus points – Warwickshire 2, Nottinghamshire 3 (Score at 100 overs: 222-8).

Bowling: *First Innings*—Lewis 16–4–35–2; Pick 19.1–8–46–2; Evans 24–7–45–2; Cairns 23–6–59–1; Hemmings 28–14–48–3; Crawley 4–1–9–0. *Second Innings*—Lewis 26.1–9–54–2; Pick 15–5–33–3; Cairns 17–5–53–2; Hemmings 34–12–65–1; Evans 17–5–40–1; Crawley 4–0–11–0.

Nottinghamshire

B. C. Broad c Moles b Munton	27	– c Piper b Twose	104
P. R. Pollard lbw b Smith	25	– b Smith	9
M. A. Crawley c Ostler b Munton	0	– not out	64
*P. Johnson lbw b Smith	12		
D. W. Randall c Ostler b Smith	9	– (4) not out	17
C. C. Lewis c Ostler b Smith	15		
C. L. Cairns c Twose b Moles	48		
K. P. Evans b Twose	28		
†B. N. French c Moles b Twose	24		
E. E. Hemmings not out	52		
R. A. Pick b Smith	52		
B 4, l-b 12, w 2, n-b 1	19	B 3, l-b 5	8
	311	(2 wkts)	**202**

1/50 2/52 3/52 4/66 5/75   1/31 2/158
6/123 7/152 8/193 9/202

Bonus points – Nottinghamshire 4, Warwickshire 4 (Score at 100 overs: 300-9).

Bowling: *First Innings*—Small 14–3–48–0; Munton 17–4–39–2; Smith 29.2–5–79–5; Moles 9–3–16–1; Booth 21–3–70–0; Twose 12–3–43–2. *Second Innings*—Small 1.2–0–9–0; Smith 10–1–44–1; Twose 16.4–2–41–1; Booth 27.5–3–81–0; Lloyd 2–1–8–0; Moles 2–0–11–0.

Umpires: G. A. Stickley and P. B. Wight.

At Oxford, May 7, 8, 9. NOTTINGHAMSHIRE drew with OXFORD UNIVERSITY.

At Northampton, May 14, 15, 16, 18. NOTTINGHAMSHIRE beat NORTHAMPTON-SHIRE by three wickets.

NOTTINGHAMSHIRE v SUSSEX

At Nottingham, May 20, 21, 22. Drawn. Nottinghamshire 5 pts, Sussex 8 pts. Toss: Sussex. Speight produced a dazzling century on the opening day to build a commanding position for Sussex. He hit 23 fours and two sixes in a career-best 166 in 230 balls; Donelan contributed 33 to their seventh-wicket stand of 145. Salisbury, enhancing his England claims, took four wickets to reduce Championship leaders Nottinghamshire to 138 for six, before French and Evans averted the follow-on. Although Afford claimed career-best figures of six for 68 in Sussex's second innings, the visitors left Nottinghamshire to chase a daunting 325 runs in 80 overs. For a time, it looked as though they would succeed, as Crawley gave them a good start, with 13 boundaries; but the innings lost its way after Randall and Cairns were run out in quick succession.

Close of play: First day, Nottinghamshire 1-0 (R. T. Robinson 1*, M. A. Crawley 0*); Second day, Sussex 112-4 (B. T. P. Donelan 0*, A. P. Wells 0*).

Sussex

D. M. Smith lbw b Cairns	1	– (2) c Evans b Afford	20
J. W. Hall c Randall b Evans	8	– (1) c Randall b Evans	24
N. J. Lenham b Pick	60	– st French b Afford	21
*A. P. Wells c Crawley b Afford	38	– (6) c Afford b Evans	31
M. P. Speight c Field-Buss b Evans	166	– (4) b Afford	41
†P. Moores c Crawley b Field-Buss	15	– (7) c Crawley b Afford	29
F. D. Stephenson run out	8	– (8) st French b Afford	15
B. T. P. Donelan b Afford	33	– (5) b Afford	5
I. D. K. Salisbury c Robinson b Afford	17	– not out	2
A. N. Jones not out	0	– not out	9
A. G. Robson st French b Afford	0		
L-b 4, n-b 15	19	L-b 2, n-b 9	11

1/3 2/25 3/87 4/134 5/172   **365**   1/29 2/57 3/111   (8 wkts dec.) **208**
6/186 7/331 8/365 9/365   4/112 5/129 6/168
                                           7/196 8/199

Bonus points – Sussex 4, Nottinghamshire 3 (Score at 100 overs: 344-7).

Bowling: *First Innings*—Pick 16–3–56–1; Cairns 16–0–47–1; Evans 25–6–84–2; Field-Buss 12–1–51–1; Afford 34.2–6–117–4; Crawley 4–1–6–0. *Second Innings*—Cairns 12–1–55–0; Evans 12–3–40–2; Pick 6–0–28–0; Afford 18–6–68–6; Field-Buss 3–0–15–0.

Nottinghamshire

R. T. Robinson c Wells b Stephenson	26 – lbw b Salisbury	11
M. A. Crawley c Lenham b Salisbury	43 – c Wells b Salisbury	76
P. Johnson c Stephenson b Donelan	26 – (4) c Hall b Stephenson	42
D. W. Randall c Moores b Salisbury	1 – (5) run out	34
M. Saxelby c Wells b Salisbury	4 – (3) c Speight b Stephenson	54
C. L. Cairns lbw b Salisbury	19 – run out	22
B. N. French b Stephenson	46 – not out	15
K. P. Evans run out	50 – b Salisbury	4
M. G. Field-Buss c Moores b Stephenson	2 – (10) not out	0
R. A. Pick not out	12 – (9) c Wells b Salisbury	0
J. A. Afford lbw b Salisbury	2	
L-b 7, w 4, n-b 7	18	B 15, l-b 12, n-b 9 36

1/56 2/92 3/104 4/108 5/108   249   1/43 2/121 3/194 4/232   (8 wkts) 294
6/138 7/222 8/225 9/236   5/264 6/269 7/279 8/279

Bonus points – Nottinghamshire 2, Sussex 4.

Bowling: *First Innings*—Donelan 17–5–35–1; Stephenson 20–1–64–3; Jones 6–1–34–0; Robson 5–0–31–0; Salisbury 24.4–7–69–5; Lenham 6–3–9–0. *Second Innings*—Stephenson 18.5–6–32–2; Robson 11–3–37–0; Salisbury 27–1–122–4; Jones 8–0–30–0; Donelan 15–4–46–0.

Umpires: B. Leadbeater and D. O. Oslear.

At Derby, May 23, 25, 26. NOTTINGHAMSHIRE drew with DERBYSHIRE.

NOTTINGHAMSHIRE v MIDDLESEX

At Nottingham, June 2, 3, 4. Drawn. Nottinghamshire 2 pts, Middlesex 8 pts. Toss: Middlesex. The game's principal excitement was the dramatic return to first-class cricket of 41-year-old left-arm spinner Phil Edmonds, who arrived by Rolls-Royce to come out of retirement after five years for this one game, while Tufnell recovered from an operation on his appendix. But before he stepped on to the field centuries from Haynes and Roseberry laid the foundations for a commanding Middlesex total. They put on 266 in 70 overs, with 22 fours and a six for Haynes while Roseberry hammered 15 fours and two sixes in his highest score of 148. Carr and Gatting added another 120 before the overnight declaration. Edmonds then bowled as if he had never been away, splitting eight wickets with his old partner Emburey on a helpful pitch as a bamboozled Nottinghamshire conceded a lead of 190 runs, and followed on for the second time in consecutive Championship matches. But rain washed out the final day's play and the game ended in anticlimax.

Close of play: First day, Middlesex 401-2 (J. D. Carr 47*, M. W. Gatting 65*); Second day, Nottinghamshire 53-0 (B. C. Broad 31*, M. A. Crawley 17*).

Middlesex

D. L. Haynes b Pick	114
M. A. Roseberry b Cairns	148
J. D. Carr not out	47
*M. W. Gatting not out	65
B 4, l-b 15, w 1, n-b 7	27

1/266 2/281   (2 wkts dec.) 401

*K. R. Brown, P. N. Weekes, J. E. Emburey, D. W. Headley, N. F. Williams, P. H. Edmonds and A. R. C. Fraser did not bat.

Bonus points – Middlesex 4 (Score at 100 overs: 353-2).

Bowling: Pick 22–4–78–1; Cairns 23–3–59–1; Evans 20–2–77–0; Afford 13–2–67–0; Field-Buss 24–1–82–0; Crawley 8–3–19–0.

Nottinghamshire

B. C. Broad c Williams b Edmonds	28	– not out	31
M. A. Crawley c Brown b Williams	0	– not out	17
*R. T. Robinson b Embury	33		
P. Johnson c Roseberry b Edmonds	4		
D. W. Randall b Embury	63		
C. L. Cairns c Weekes b Edmonds	14		
K. P. Evans b Embury	13		
†B. N. French b Embury	6		
M. G. Field-Buss c Headley b Edmonds	9		
R. A. Pick not out	20		
J. A. Afford b Williams	12		
L-b 1, n-b 8	9	L-b 2, n-b 3	5

1/15 2/41 3/57 4/106 5/143   211   (no wkt) 53
6/147 7/164 8/174 9/180

Bonus points – Nottinghamshire 2, Middlesex 4.

Bowling: *First Innings*—Williams 17.2–3–59–2; Fraser 10–3–29–0; Edmonds 28–10–48–4; Embury 25–4–55–4; Headley 6–0–19–0. *Second Innings*—Williams 4–0–11–0; Fraser 6–2–15–0; Embury 8–3–12–0; Headley 5–2–8–0; Weekes 4–2–5–0.

Umpires: K. E. Palmer and D. R. Shepherd.

At Nottingham, June 10, 11, 12. NOTTINGHAMSHIRE lost to PAKISTANIS by eight wickets (See Pakistani tour section).

NOTTINGHAMSHIRE v LANCASHIRE

At Nottingham, June 16, 17, 18. Drawn. Nottinghamshire 4 pts, Lancashire 7 pts. Toss: Lancashire. Cairns produced a fine all-round performance to remove the threat of defeat, returning his best bowling figures for the county and then hitting a maiden Championship century. Nottinghamshire were indebted to Cairns and Evans in the first innings for some late resistance after the top order had collapsed in face of the Lancashire seamers on a responsive wicket. The visitors also encountered early trouble against Cairns; Speak was particularly disappointed to be dismissed for 23, eight runs short of becoming the first player to 1,000 runs in 1992. But Martin made 80, his highest first-class score, to give Lancashire a lead of 93. The final day was dominated by an unbroken partnership of 203 between Randall and Cairns. Randall struck 18 fours and a six in his 133, while Cairns's 102 featured ten fours and five sixes in 119 balls. Though Cairns seemed anxious to be bowling again, Robinson was reluctant to press for victory, especially with Evans and French unfit. Assured that Nottinghamshire were safe, he set Lancashire an unlikely 300 in 44 overs.

Close of play: First day, Lancashire 90-4 (J. Stanworth 3*, S. P. Titchard 9*); Second day, Nottinghamshire 155-3 (P. Johnson 51*, D. W. Randall 32*).

Nottinghamshire

B. C. Broad c Stanworth b Morrison	16	– c and b Martin	1
P. R. Pollard c Fowler b Fletcher	22	– run out	36
*R. T. Robinson c Stanworth b Martin	4	– c Fowler b Martin	24
P. Johnson c and b Morrison	19	– lbw b Morrison	62
D. W. Randall b Martin	27	– not out	133
M. A. Crawley c Irani b Martin	13	– run out	4
C. L. Cairns c Speak b Fletcher	25	– not out	102
K. P. Evans b Morrison	43		
†B. N. French lbw b Irani	11		
R. A. Pick c Atherton b Irani	2		
J. A. Afford not out	1		
L-b 13, w 3	16	B 14, l-b 6, w 1, n-b 9	30

1/26 2/46 3/65 4/75 5/95   199   1/5 2/46 3/101   (5 wkts dec.) 392
6/125 7/139 8/181 9/189   4/175 5/189

Bonus points – Nottinghamshire 1, Lancashire 4.

Bowling: *First Innings*—Martin 22–6–43–3; Morrison 23.5–6–65–3; Fletcher 17–6–53–2; Barnett 2–1–4–0; Irani 7–1–21–2. *Second Innings*—Morrison 29–5–84–1; Martin 24–6–72–2; Fletcher 13–2–69–0; Barnett 17–1–81–0; Atherton 5.1–0–35–0; Irani 9–4–31–0.

Lancashire

G. Fowler c sub b Cairns	6	– c Johnson b Pick	22
*M. A. Atherton c Randall b Pick	34	– c sub b Afford	25
N. J. Speak c Pollard b Afford	23	– lbw b Pick	0
G. D. Lloyd c Crawley b Cairns	2	– not out	37
†J. Stanworth c French b Cairns	21		
S. P. Titchard c Crawley b Cairns	25	– (5) not out	15
R. C. Irani c sub b Pick	7		
P. J. Martin c French b Cairns	80		
D. K. Morrison lbw b Afford	30		
S. D. Fletcher c Afford b Cairns	23		
A. A. Barnett not out	1		
B 9, l-b 20, w 2, n-b 9	40	B 2, l-b 2	4

1/26 2/75 3/75 4/78 5/117   292   1/42 2/42 3/66   (3 wkts) 103
6/129 7/172 8/243 9/291

Bonus points – Lancashire 3, Nottinghamshire 3 (Score at 100 overs: 263-8).

Bowling: *First Innings*—Cairns 31.4–11–70–6; Pick 28–8–64–2; Crawley 24–5–84–0; Afford 24–9–45–2. *Second Innings*—Pick 10–1–39–2; Evans 9–1–27–0; Afford 7–0–8–1; Cairns 7–1–25–0.

Umpires: J. W. Holder and R. Palmer.

NOTTINGHAMSHIRE v NORTHAMPTONSHIRE

At Nottingham, June 19, 20, 22. Nottinghamshire won by two wickets. Nottinghamshire 23 pts, Northamptonshire 4 pts. Toss: Nottinghamshire. Nottinghamshire marked the appointment of Mike Hendrick as their manager on the final day by snatching victory off the penultimate ball – their first win of any sort since beating the same opponents at Northampton on May 18. The batsmen had been on top for most of the game after Northamptonshire recovered from 189 for six; Ripley sustained his fine batting form in leading the fightback to 326. The Nottinghamshire reply was dominated by Broad who overcame one or two painful blows from Ambrose to compile an unbeaten 159 in a little over five hours. Fordham led Northamptonshire's pursuit of quick runs by hammering 21 fours in 159 minutes, and that enabled Bailey to set a target of 297 in 68 overs. Robinson, relieved of the acting manager's role, batted as if a weight had been lifted from his shoulders, reaching his first hundred of the season in two hours. But he fell with the asking-rate climbing, and it was left to Crawley to see Nottinghamshire home in a thrilling finish.

Close of play: First day, Northamptonshire 326-9 (C. E. L. Ambrose 5*, N. G. B. Cook 21*); Second day, Northamptonshire 87-0 (A. Fordham 51*, N. A. Felton 36*).

Northamptonshire

A. Fordham c Pollard b Cairns	8	– c Evans b Crawley	119
N. A. Felton b Cairns	64	– b Cairns	41
*R. J. Bailey c French b Evans	54	– c Dessaur b Afford	46
D. J. Capel c Cairns b Pick	4	– not out	35
M. B. Loye c French b Evans	13	– b Crawley	14
K. M. Curran c Pick b Afford	10	– b Crawley	10
†D. Ripley b Cairns	54		
A. R. Roberts c Robinson b Crawley	62		
J. P. Taylor c Crawley b Afford	21		
C. E. L. Ambrose not out	5		
N. G. B. Cook not out	21		
L-b 10	10	L-b 6, n-b 1	7

1/14 2/127 3/133 4/133 5/149   (9 wkts dec.) 326   1/102 2/180 3/218   (5 wkts dec.) 272
6/189 7/250 8/292 9/304   4/238 5/272

Bonus points – Northamptonshire 3, Nottinghamshire 3 (Score at 100 overs: 279-7).

Bowling: *First Innings*—Cairns 25–9–68–3; Pick 20–4–49–1; Evans 26–5–67–2; Afford 18–1–76–2; Crawley 21–3–56–1. *Second Innings*—Pick 12–1–38–0; Cairns 9–0–51–1; Evans 12–0–45–0; Afford 15–1–94–1; Crawley 5.5–0–38–3.

Nottinghamshire

B. C. Broad not out	.159 – c Taylor b Bailey	31
P. R. Pollard c Ripley b Taylor	5 – c Ambrose b Curran	69
*R. T. Robinson lbw b Taylor	52 – st Ripley b Cook	100
P. Johnson c Ambrose b Bailey	44 – c Ripley b Roberts	11
W. A. Dessaur c Ripley b Ambrose	1 – (6) b Cook	15
M. A. Crawley not out	22 – (7) not out	26
C. L. Cairns (did not bat)	– (5) lbw b Roberts	3
†B. N. French (did not bat)	– lbw b Cook	7
K. P. Evans (did not bat)	– run out	4
R. A. Pick (did not bat)	– not out	3
B 9, l-b 8, w 2	19	B 13, l-b 12, n-b 3 ... 28

1/11 2/127 3/218 4/233   (4 wkts dec.) 302   1/76 2/155 3/202 4/208 (8 wkts) 297
                                                 5/245 6/256 7/268 8/291

J. A. Afford did not bat.

Bonus points – Nottinghamshire 4, Northamptonshire 1.

Bowling: *First Innings*—Ambrose 21–2–69–1; Taylor 15–3–39–2; Curran 11–2–29–0; Capel 7–0–29–0; Roberts 12–2–53–0; Cook 9–2–27–0; Bailey 12–3–39–1. *Second Innings*—Ambrose 13.5–2–38–0; Taylor 7–1–20–0; Capel 6–2–20–0; Roberts 16–3–79–2; Cook 10–1–43–3; Bailey 8–0–40–1; Curran 7–0–32–1.

Umpires: J. W. Holder and R. Palmer.

NOTTINGHAMSHIRE v CAMBRIDGE UNIVERSITY

At Nottingham, June 27, 28, 29. Nottinghamshire won by 162 runs. Toss: Cambridge University. In their final game before the University match, Cambridge were put to the sword by some county novices no older than themselves. Jonathan Wileman became only the second player in the county's history to score a century on his début – F. W. Stocks having made 114 against Kent in 1946. He hit 11 fours and a six in 255 minutes, sharing an opening stand of 234 with Dessaur, who struck his own maiden hundred in his second first-class match and cracked 14 boundaries in just over five hours. Another newcomer, Hindson, an 18-year-old left-arm spinner with an outstanding reputation in schools cricket, then dismissed five of the students for 42. Cambridge just managed to avoid the follow-on. After Paul Johnson and Lewis had boosted Nottinghamshire's lead to 326, their other left-armer, Afford, took the honours in the University's second innings, although Hindson mopped up the tail to finish with eight for 74 on début. Arscott and Simon Johnson arrived late on the first day because they had been in Cambridge receiving their degrees. The umpires deemed these "exceptional circumstances" and allowed Johnson to bowl at once.

Close of play: First day, Cambridge University 14-0 (A. M. Hooper 2*, G. W. Jones 11*); Second day, Nottinghamshire 179-3 (M. A. Crawley 51*, P. Johnson 60*).

Nottinghamshire

W. A. Dessaur st Arscott b Pearson	.148	
J. R. Wileman c Arscott b Pitcher	.109	
*P. Johnson c Abington b Pearson	5 – (5) not out	60
M. A. Crawley st Arscott b Wight	10 – (3) not out	51
M. Newell not out	5	
C. C. Lewis not out	10 – (1) c Johnson b Pearson	62
C. L. Cairns (did not bat)	– (2) c Wight b Pitcher	1
†S. Bramhall (did not bat)	– (4) c Crawley b Pearson	1
L-b 11, n-b 2	13	L-b 2, w 1, n-b 1 ... 4

1/234 2/243 3/282 4/288   (4 wkts dec.) 300   1/2 2/91 3/99   (3 wkts dec.) 179

J. E. Hindson, D. B. Pennett and J. A. Afford did not bat.

Bowling: *First Innings*—Pitcher 20–5–45–1; Hooper 7–4–19–0; Abington 16–2–49–0; Pearson 32.3–5–93–2; Wight 18–4–63–1; Johnson 3–0–20–0. *Second Innings*—Johnson 5–0–34–0; Pitcher 10.2–2–35–1; Hooper 3–1–11–0; Pearson 10–1–41–2; Wight 7–0–48–0; Abington 2–0–8–0.

Cambridge University

A. M. Hooper c Bramhall b Hindson	40	– c Crawley b Lewis	4
G. W. Jones c and b Cairns	19	– c Newell b Afford	21
*J. P. Crawley b Afford	20	– c Wileman b Cairns	4
R. M. Wight c Bramhall b Pennett	26	– c Lewis b Afford	26
J. P. Carroll lbw b Hindson	6	– b Afford	29
†J. P. Arscott lbw b Hindson	3	– b Hindson	28
M. E. D. Jarrett run out	0	– c Johnson b Afford	0
S. W. Johnson c Bramhall b Hindson	0	– c Newell b Afford	20
C. M. Pitcher not out	12	– not out	15
R. M. Pearson c Lewis b Afford	4	– c Wileman b Hindson	4
M. B. Abington c Cairns b Hindson	2	– c Crawley b Hindson	6
B 8, l-b 7, w 3, n-b 3	21	L-b 2, n-b 5	7

1/52 2/93 3/100 4/120 5/134   153   1/15 2/26 3/46 4/77 5/100   164
6/135 7/135 8/135 9/140   6/106 7/135 8/154 9/158

Bowling: *First Innings*—Lewis 9–5–10–0; Cairns 10–4–14–1; Hindson 20.5–9–42–5; Pennett 16–2–38–1; Afford 13–3–34–2. *Second Innings*—Cairns 6–2–15–1; Lewis 8–3–14–1; Pennett 8–1–19–0; Afford 24–8–75–5; Crawley 5–2–7–0; Hindson 12.5–2–32–3.

Umpires: Dr D. Fawkner-Corbett and A. G. T. Whitehead.

At Maidstone, June 30, July 1, 2. NOTTINGHAMSHIRE lost to KENT by 35 runs.

At Southampton, July 3, 4, 6. NOTTINGHAMSHIRE beat HAMPSHIRE by five wickets.

NOTTINGHAMSHIRE v WORCESTERSHIRE

At Nottingham, July 14, 15, 16. Worcestershire won by five wickets. Worcestershire 22 pts, Nottinghamshire 6 pts. Toss: Nottinghamshire. A game of fluctuating fortunes eventually swung Worcestershire's way thanks to a fine century by Leatherdale and explosive hitting by Radford. Crawley's fourth hundred of the season had laid the platform for a commanding Nottinghamshire total; he hit 14 boundaries in a patient five-hour innings, backed up by half-centuries from Johnson, Randall, Cairns and Evans. Worcestershire ran into early trouble at 52 for four in reply, but then Hick produced a masterful display, with four sixes and 24 fours in an unbeaten five-hour double-hundred. He dominated stands of 79 with Lampitt, who scored 16, and 148 with Rhodes (36). Robinson and Johnson boosted Nottinghamshire's second innings with an unbroken stand of 111 and Worcestershire were set a target of 259 in a minimum 58 overs. They made a disastrous start, losing Curtis, Hick and Moody for one run – Hick was brought down to earth with a bump, dismissed first ball. Leatherdale's three-hour innings subsequently repaired the damage, before Radford blasted 73 from 60 deliveries – his best batting display for the county – to see Worcestershire home with 13 balls to spare.

Close of play: First day, Nottinghamshire 350-6 (C. L. Cairns 38*, K. P. Evans 32*); Second day, Worcestershire 318-6 dec.

Nottinghamshire

M. A. Crawley st Rhodes b Illingworth	115	– c Hick b Newport	23
P. R. Pollard lbw b Newport	27	– c Rhodes b Stemp	32
*R. T. Robinson lbw b Lampitt	8	– not out	64
P. Johnson c Hick b Stemp	58	– not out	51
D. W. Randall b Illingworth	51		
C. C. Lewis lbw b Lampitt	8		
C. L. Cairns c Illingworth b Newport	62		
K. P. Evans not out	55		
†B. N. French lbw b Illingworth	0		
M. G. Field-Buss not out	0		
L-b 8, w 2, n-b 6	16	L-b 3, n-b 3	6

1/55 2/87 3/187 4/250 5/268 (8 wkts dec.) 400 1/53 2/65 (2 wkts dec.) 176
6/288 7/393 8/394

J. A. Afford did not bat.

Bonus points – Nottinghamshire 4, Worcestershire 2 (Score at 100 overs: 300-6).

Bowling: *First Innings*—Radford 15-2-45-0; Lampitt 21-3-70-2; Newport 22.4-4-67-2; Illingworth 35-6-103-3; Stemp 19-5-70-1; Hick 9-3-37-0. *Second Innings*—Radford 6-1-17-0; Lampitt 3-0-17-0; Illingworth 14-3-47-0; Newport 4-1-15-1; Stemp 9-1-35-1; Moody 3-0-25-0; Curtis 2-0-17-0.

Worcestershire

*T. S. Curtis b Lewis	0	– b Cairns	0
W. P. C. Weston c French b Cairns	7	– c Crawley b Afford	43
G. A. Hick not out	213	– lbw b Cairns	0
T. M. Moody lbw b Cairns	5	– c French b Lewis	0
D. A. Leatherdale c Field-Buss b Cairns	9	– lbw b Lewis	112
S. R. Lampitt lbw b Lewis	16	– (7) not out	14
†S. J. Rhodes lbw b Afford	36		
P. J. Newport not out	15		
N. V. Radford (did not bat)		– (6) not out	73
B 4, l-b 5, w 1, n-b 7	17	B 5, l-b 9, w 2, n-b 4	20

1/0 2/22 3/30 4/52 (6 wkts dec.) 318 1/0 2/0 3/1 (5 wkts) 262
5/131 6/279 4/117 5/227

R. K. Illingworth and R. D. Stemp did not bat.

Bonus points – Worcestershire 4, Nottinghamshire 2.

Bowling: *First Innings*—Lewis 14-0-44-2; Cairns 19-3-59-3; Evans 20-2-75-0; Afford 16-0-82-1; Field-Buss 18-4-42-0; Crawley 5.1-2-7-0. *Second Innings*—Cairns 13-1-52-2; Lewis 15.5-2-51-2; Field-Buss 12-2-50-0; Afford 13-0-64-1; Crawley 1-1-0-0; Evans 7-2-31-0.

Umpires: B. J. Meyer and P. B. Wight.

NOTTINGHAMSHIRE v DURHAM

At Nottingham, July 17, 18, 20. Drawn. Nottinghamshire 8 pts, Durham 2 pts. Toss: Durham. Robinson marked the occasion of his grand benefit dinner with a magnificent innings, taking many runs off Botham, his guest speaker at the dinner. The Nottinghamshire captain batted for five and a half hours in all, hitting 21 fours, and shared a fifth-wicket partnership of 185 with Lewis, who struck 15 fours and a six in his own century. Durham, having seen their bowlers suffer their heaviest punishment since joining the Championship, then slumped to what was at the time their lowest total as the Nottinghamshire seamers carved through their batting. Durham followed on 284 runs behind but Jones, with one finger bruised by Waqar Younis and another broken by Cairns, led spirited resistance, with some savage strokeplay, in what was to be his last innings for Durham. His unbeaten 154, in 204 minutes with three sixes and 19 fours, assisted by heavy showers on the final day, robbed Nottinghamshire of victory.

Close of play: First day, Nottinghamshire 431-6 (R. T. Robinson 164*, K. P. Evans 0*); Second day, Durham 167-1 (W. Larkins 47*, D. M. Jones 114*).

Nottinghamshire

M. A. Crawley lbw b Botham	21		C. L. Cairns c McEwan b Botham		42
P. R. Pollard lbw b Botham	23		K. P. Evans not out		0
*R. T. Robinson not out	164		B 6, l-b 14, w 12		32
P. Johnson c Briers b Brown	20				
D. W. Randall c Scott b McEwan	22		1/49 2/52 3/92	(6 wkts dec.)	431
C. C. Lewis c Scott b Briers	107		4/140 5/325 6/427		

†B. N. French, D. B. Pennett and M. G. Field-Buss did not bat.

Bonus points – Nottinghamshire 4, Durham 2 (Score at 100 overs: 365-5).

Bowling: McEwan 19-4-60-1; Brown 18-3-57-1; Henderson 14-2-68-0; Botham 27-4-104-3; Hughes 16-0-61-0; Briers 16-2-61-1.

Durham

W. Larkins c Robinson b Cairns	5	– c Robinson b Cairns	57
*P. W. G. Parker b Cairns	6	– (4) b Cairns	7
D. M. Jones b Pennett	15	– not out	154
M. P. Briers c Crawley b Cairns	53	– (5) not out	30
I. T. Botham b Evans	7		
P. W. Henderson c and b Lewis	7		
J. D. Glendenen c Evans b Cairns	13	– (2) b Cairns	0
†C. W. Scott c Evans b Pennett	10		
S. P. Hughes lbw b Evans	2		
S. M. McEwan c Evans b Lewis	3		
S. J. E. Brown not out	6		
L-b 7, n-b 13	20	B 1, l-b 11, n-b 5	17

1/11 2/18 3/60 4/69 5/90   147   1/9 2/178 3/194   (3 wkts) 265
6/111 7/132 8/132 9/139

Bonus points – Nottinghamshire 4.

Bowling: *First Innings*—Lewis 14-4-27-2; Cairns 14-2-41-4; Evans 15.5-4-31-2; Pennett 16-5-41-2. *Second Innings*—Cairns 20-4-93-3; Lewis 15-2-40-0; Pennett 5-1-21-0; Evans 15-2-63-0; Field-Buss 11-0-34-0; Crawley 4-2-2-0.

Umpires: B. J. Meyer and P. B. Wight.

At The Oval, July 21, 22, 23. NOTTINGHAMSHIRE beat SURREY by three wickets.

At Birmingham, July 24, 25, 27. NOTTINGHAMSHIRE beat WARWICKSHIRE by 117 runs.

NOTTINGHAMSHIRE v GLOUCESTERSHIRE

At Worksop, August 4, 5, 6. Gloucestershire won by ten runs. Gloucestershire 21 pts, Nottinghamshire 6 pts. Toss: Nottinghamshire. Both teams collapsed on a worn pitch on the third day when Gloucestershire crumpled before Hemmings and Evans, and Nottinghamshire were left with an excellent chance to close the gap on the leaders, Essex, by scoring 146 in 65 overs. Intelligent bowling by Walsh and indifferent strokes led to Nottinghamshire's downfall: they slumped to eight for three and never recovered. Their challenge for the Championship also faded from this point. Athey had batted for 288 minutes on the first day, for his second century in successive innings, to help Gloucestershire build a respectable total, before Hemmings, on his return from injury, polished off the tail. Nottinghamshire plunged into trouble at 107 for five, but then recovered through a rousing stand of 147 in 27 overs between Johnson and Cairns. Johnson struck 15 fours and two sixes in two hours, while Cairns, watched by his father Lance, reached his second Championship century with 17 fours and three sixes.

Close of play: First day, Gloucestershire 295-6 (J. T. C. Vaughan 32*, R. C. Williams 26*); Second day, Gloucestershire 24-0 (G. D. Hodgson 7*, C. W. J. Athey 9*).

Gloucestershire

G. D. Hodgson c Evans b Cairns	6	– c French b Cairns 14
C. W. J. Athey c Crawley b Evans	133	– c Evans b Pennett 13
*A. J. Wright lbw b Pennett	3	– b Broad b Hemmings 20
M. W. Alleyne c Pollard b Crawley	16	– c and b Hemmings 22
R. J. Scott b Evans	65	– lbw b Evans 0
†R. C. Russell c Pollard b Evans	0	– b Evans 0
J. T. C. Vaughan c Crawley b Hemmings	50	– b Evans 1
R. C. Williams b Hemmings	44	– run out 7
M. C. J. Ball c Broad b Hemmings	4	– c Broad b Hemmings 8
C. A. Walsh c Crawley b Hemmings	0	– c Crawley b Hemmings 9
M. Davies not out	0	– not out 1
L-b 10, n-b 4	14	B 4, l-b 6, n-b 7 17

1/9 2/18 3/57 4/224 5/224		335	1/31 2/45 3/67 4/67 5/67	112
6/239 7/331 8/331 9/331			6/79 7/79 8/98 9/108

Bonus points – Gloucestershire 2, Nottinghamshire 2 (Score at 100 overs: 239-6).

Bowling: *First Innings*—Cairns 29-9-86-1; Pennett 24-4-74-1; Evans 31-14-66-3; Hemmings 39.3-15-78-4; Crawley 13-6-21-1. *Second Innings*—Cairns 9-1-38-1; Pennett 7-3-21-1; Hemmings 13.2-5-30-4; Evans 12-4-13-3.

Nottinghamshire

B. C. Broad c Hodgson b Ball	41	– c Scott b Walsh 1
P. R. Pollard b Davies	32	– c Wright b Vaughan 1
*R. T. Robinson c Athey b Davies	1	– c Ball b Davies 34
P. Johnson c Russell b Vaughan	98	– c Vaughan b Walsh 2
D. W. Randall c Alleyne b Davies	0	– c Walsh b Ball 30
M. A. Crawley c Alleyne b Ball	1	– c and b Davies 44
C. L. Cairns not out	107	– c Athey b Davies 6
K. P. Evans c and b Ball	7	– b Walsh 2
†B. N. French c Alleyne b Walsh	4	– lbw b Walsh 2
E. E. Hemmings not out	0	– not out 4
D. B. Pennett (did not bat)		– c Alleyne b Walsh 1
L-b 8, n-b 3	11	L-b 7, w 1 8

1/65 2/67 3/83 4/88 5/107	(8 wkts dec.) 302	1/2 2/6 3/8 4/46 5/98	135
6/254 7/293 8/298			6/108 7/112 8/130 9/130

Bonus points – Nottinghamshire 4, Gloucestershire 3.

Bowling: *First Innings*—Walsh 17-2-43-1; Vaughan 12-1-48-1; Ball 24.1-4-89-3; Williams 4-1-22-0; Davies 15-2-63-3; Scott 3-0-29-0. *Second Innings*—Walsh 17.5-5-33-5; Vaughan 5-1-20-1; Ball 8-0-34-1; Davies 16-6-36-3; Alleyne 4-1-5-0.

Umpires: R. Julian and K. E. Palmer.

NOTTINGHAMSHIRE v GLAMORGAN

At Nottingham, August 7, 8, 10. Glamorgan won by seven runs. Glamorgan 20 pts, Nottinghamshire 3 pts. Toss: Glamorgan. Glamorgan clinched an exciting victory with the fourth delivery of the final over, when Barwick dismissed Johnson, who had broken a knuckle in his left hand during the previous day's Sunday League game. Set 330 to win in 100 overs, Nottinghamshire adopted a cautious approach. Although Crawley gave them hope with a stylish 88, their fortunes nosedived when Cairns was run out cheaply. However, French produced a sparkling half-century to keep his side in the hunt, hitting nine fours off 39 balls faced, before Barwick had the final say. Glamorgan's first innings was built around Dale's career-best performance, in 231 minutes and 233 balls, with 21 fours, after Nottinghamshire had made early inroads. Good support from Watkin and Foster enabled him to rescue the visitors from a precarious 214 from seven. Torrential rain then washed out the second day, forcing the two captains to contrive a finish.

Close of play: First day, Nottinghamshire 17-0 (B. C. Broad 7*, P. R. Pollard 10*); Second day, No play.

Glamorgan

S. P. James c French b Evans	45	– not out	8
H. Morris b Cairns	17		
D. L. Hemp c Robinson b Afford	51		
*M. P. Maynard c Crawley b Afford	11	– (2) not out	4
A. Dale not out	150		
P. A. Cottey c French b Evans	32		
R. D. B. Croft c Robinson b Evans	0		
†C. P. Metson c and b Cairns	1		
S. L. Watkin c Robinson b Hemmings	2		
D. J. Foster not out	17		
B 2, l-b 1, n-b 5	8		

1/31 2/88 3/110 4/147 5/206   (8 wkts. dec.) 334   (no wkt dec.) 12
6/206 7/214 8/271

S. R. Barwick did not bat.

Bonus points – Glamorgan 4, Nottinghamshire 3 (Score at 100 overs: 301-8).

Bowling: *First Innings*—Cairns 19–1–82–2; Evans 22–7–48–3; Crawley 5–1–17–0; Hemmings 29–8–79–1; Afford 31.3–6–105–2. *Second Innings*—Randall 1–0–8–0; Robinson 1–0–4–0.

Nottinghamshire

B. C. Broad not out	7	– b Croft	20
P. R. Pollard not out	10	– c James b Barwick	75
*R. T. Robinson (did not bat)		– c Morris b Watkin	13
M. A. Crawley (did not bat)		– c and b Croft	88
D. W. Randall (did not bat)		– c Hemp b Watkin	43
C. L. Cairns (did not bat)		– run out	3
K. P. Evans (did not bat)		– c Maynard b Watkin	5
†B. N. French (did not bat)		– st Metson b Barwick	55
E. E. Hemmings (did not bat)		– b Barwick	13
J. A. Afford (did not bat)		– not out	1
P. Johnson (did not bat)		– lbw b Barwick	0
		L-b 6	6

(no wkt dec.) 17   1/45 2/78 3/123 4/209 5/214   322
6/225 7/257 8/305 9/322

Bowling: *First Innings*—Watkin 3–1–14–0; Barwick 1–0–1–0; Croft 1–0–2–0. *Second Innings*—Watkin 23–5–85–3; Foster 18–2–52–0; Barwick 23.4–4–67–4; Croft 27–6–86–2; Dale 8–1–26–0.

Umpires: R. Julian and K. E. Palmer.

At Colchester, August 14, 15, 17. NOTTINGHAMSHIRE lost to ESSEX by an innings and 37 runs.

At Scarborough, August 18, 19, 20. NOTTINGHAMSHIRE drew with YORKSHIRE.

At Leicester, August 21, 22, 24. NOTTINGHAMSHIRE drew with LEICESTERSHIRE.

At Worcester, August 26, 27, 28, 29. NOTTINGHAMSHIRE drew with WORCESTER-SHIRE.

NOTTINGHAMSHIRE v DERBYSHIRE

At Nottingham, August 31, September 1, 2, 3. Derbyshire won by two wickets. Derbyshire 23 pts, Nottinghamshire 4 pts. Toss: Nottinghamshire. Fresh from his one-day international début for England, Cork tormented Nottinghamshire on the first day with a spell of five for ten in 10.3 overs as the home side squandered a good start. Derbyshire consolidated their strong position thanks to Barnett, who carried his bat for the first time in his career, surviving 439 minutes and 384 balls, and striking 21 fours. Nottinghamshire appeared to be sliding to a heavy defeat at 144 for six in their second innings, still 20 runs behind. Then Archer and Lewis loosened Derbyshire's grip on the game with a stand of 168, Archer completing a maiden first-class century, with three sixes and 11 fours. Lewis's three-hour innings ended in gloomy light on the third evening, but the tail offered further resistance, and when a shower interrupted play on the last day Derbyshire's apparently smooth progress towards their target of 222 in what was now 62 overs became a frantic dash. They eventually made it with 17 balls to spare, after Bowler had completed 2,000 first-class runs for the season, the first man to do so in 1992 and the third ever (after D. B. Carr and Mohammad Azharuddin) for the county.

Close of play: First day, Derbyshire 77-2 (K. J. Barnett 39*, R. W. Sladdin 2*); Second day, Nottinghamshire 5-1 (P. R. Pollard 3*, S. Bramhall 2*); Third day, Nottinghamshire 312-7 (G. F. Archer 100*, D. B. Pennett 0*).

Nottinghamshire

P. R. Pollard b Bishop	44	– b Warner	28
M. Saxelby run out	57	– lbw b Cork	0
*M. A. Crawley lbw b Cork	14	– (4) lbw b Sladdin	39
D. W. Randall c Bishop b Sladdin	6	– (5) c Cork b Bishop	24
G. F. Archer b Cork	3	– (6) c Griffith b Bishop	117
C. L. Cairns lbw b Cork	9	– (7) c Griffith b Warner	13
C. C. Lewis c Adams b Cork	8	– (8) b Griffith	82
D. B. Pennett c Krikken b Bishop	2	– (9) c O'Gorman b Bishop	29
M. G. Field-Buss c Krikken b Cork	2	– (10) c Bowler b Warner	13
†S. Bramhall not out	0	– (3) c Sladdin b Griffith	16
J. A. Afford b Bishop	0	– not out	5
B 4, l-b 15, n-b 2	21	B 1, l-b 13, w 3, n-b 2	19
	166		**385**

1/107 2/122 3/131 4/133 5/140   166   1/1 2/38 3/54 4/91 5/123   385
6/147 7/156 8/166 9/166   6/144 7/312 8/330 9/357

Bonus points – Nottinghamshire 1, Derbyshire 4.

Bowling: *First Innings*—Bishop 15.2–6–24–3; Warner 14–6–24–0; Cork 18–6–36–5; Sladdin 30–14–55–1; Griffith 7–6–8–0. *Second Innings*—Cork 26–4–70–1; Bishop 34–8–88–3; Warner 33–7–89–3; Griffith 16–4–47–2; Sladdin 33–13–77–1.

Derbyshire

K. J. Barnett not out	156	– b Cairns	37
*B. D. Bowler b Pennett	28	– c Bramhall b Afford	61
J. E. Morris lbw b Pennett	0	– c Pollard b Field-Buss	43
R. W. Sladdin c Pollard b Lewis	8		
T. J. G. O'Gorman c Field-Buss b Afford	5	– (4) c Bramhall b Cairns	27
C. J. Adams c Randall b Field-Buss	23	– (5) st Bramhall b Afford	3
P. A. Griffith run out	11	– (6) not out	18
†K. M. Krikken c Field-Buss b Lewis	22	– (7) c Cairns b Afford	0
D. G. Cork c Pollard b Cairns	27	– (8) c Lewis b Cairns	18
I. R. Bishop b Afford	24	– (9) c Crawley b Afford	4
A. E. Warner c Field-Buss b Afford	2	– (10) not out	4
B 7, l-b 12, n-b 5	24	B 2, l-b 4, n-b 1	7
	330	(8 wkts)	**222**

1/65 2/65 3/104 4/109 5/151   1/49 2/109 3/172

6/169 7/220 8/260 9/320   4/175 5/178 6/178

       7/213 8/218

Bonus points – Derbyshire 3, Nottinghamshire 3 (Score at 100 overs: 250-7).

Bowling: *First Innings*—Lewis 21-2-64-1; Cairns 19-2-77-1; Afford 37.4-15-70-3; Pennett 18-5-35-2; Field-Buss 29-13-60-2; Crawley 2-0-5-0. *Second Innings*—Lewis 13-1-32-0; Cairns 10-1-61-3; Afford 25.1-5-91-4; Field-Buss 11-1-32-1.

Umpires: J. C. Balderstone and J. H. Hampshire.

NOTTINGHAMSHIRE v SURREY

At Nottingham, September 7, 8, 9, 10. Nottinghamshire won by five wickets. Nottinghamshire 23 pts, Surrey 5 pts. Toss: Surrey. Lewis turned in a fine all-round performance, and it was appropriate that he made the winning hit with 15 deliveries to spare. He joined forces with Evans and Pennett to leave Surrey in deep trouble early on the first day, then Bryson hit vigorously to ensure respectability, and a Championship-best 76. Nottinghamshire made heavy weather of their reply until Lewis paved the way for a substantial lead with a robust 56-ball 52, and Evans, hitting nine fours in four and a quarter hours, capitalised, moving steadily to the second hundred of his career. Surrey wiped off a deficit of 150 for the loss of only one wicket as Bicknell and Thorpe shared a stand of 174, and with Stewart and Lynch then adding a further 138 a draw looked the most likely result. However, Lewis mopped up the tail efficiently, to return ten for 155 in the match. Nottinghamshire, needing 262 from 84 overs, were able to overcome an uneasy start thanks to a captain's innings from Robinson, who hit 16 fours in a 272-minute stay and received mature support from Archer.

Close of play: First day, Nottinghamshire 102-3 (M. A. Crawley 12*, G. F. Archer 10*); Second day, Surrey 34-1 (D. J. Bicknell 15*, G. P. Thorpe 15*); Third day, Surrey 377-5 (A. D. Brown 20*, M. A. Feltham 0*).

Surrey

D. J. Bicknell c Bramhall b Evans	2	– c and b Cairns	77
D. M. Ward c Archer b Evans	18	– c Bramhall b Lewis	1
G. P. Thorpe lbw b Lewis	6	– lbw b Evans	100
*†A. J. Stewart b Lewis	5	– b Crawley	85
M. A. Lynch c Bramhall b Pennett	29	– b Lewis	70
A. D. Brown c Pollard b Pennett	7	– not out	50
M. A. Feltham b Lewis	22	– c Bramhall b Lewis	0
M. P. Bicknell c and b Pennett	0	– c Bramhall b Lewis	1
N. M. Kendrick c Pollard b Lewis	10	– b Lewis	0
R. E. Bryson c Bramhall b Evans	76	– c Archer b Cairns	2
J. Boiling not out	14	– lbw b Lewis	0
L-b 5, w 5, n-b 8	18	B 7, l-b 10, n-b 8	25
	207		**411**

1/13 2/22 3/29 4/41 5/70   1/3 2/177 3/199 4/337 5/376

6/71 7/71 8/104 9/123   6/388 7/398 8/400 9/409

Bonus points – Surrey 2, Nottinghamshire 4.

Bowling: *First Innings*—Lewis 21–4–65–4; Evans 16.2–8–37–3; Cairns 9–1–41–0; Pennett 17–4–38–3; Afford 6–0–21–0. *Second Innings*—Lewis 32.4–4–90–6; Pennett 14–2–50–0; Cairns 31–4–110–2; Evans 25–3–79–1; Afford 31–15–54–0; Crawley 9–4–11–1.

Nottinghamshire

P. R. Pollard c Stewart b M. P. Bicknell	0	– c Stewart b M. P. Bicknell	0
M. Saxelby lbw b M. P. Bicknell	43	– b M. P. Bicknell	10
*R. T. Robinson b Bryson	21	– not out	129
M. A. Crawley lbw b M. P. Bicknell	22	– lbw b Feltham	5
G. F. Archer b Feltham	22	– b Bryson	66
C. L. Cairns b Feltham	5	– b Kendrick	9
C. C. Lewis c Stewart b M. P. Bicknell	52	– not out	26
K. P. Evans c Stewart b Bryson	104		
D. B. Pennett b M. P. Bicknell	12		
†S. Bramhall not out	37		
J. A. Afford lbw b Bryson	0		
B 3, l-b 16, n-b 20	39	B 1, l-b 8, n-b 8	17

1/0 2/66 3/89 4/124 5/124	**357**	1/1 2/30 3/39 (5 wkts) 262
6/159 7/201 8/233 9/357		4/171 5/211

Bonus points – Nottinghamshire 3, Surrey 3 (Score at 100 overs: 275-8).

Bowling: *First Innings*—M. P. Bicknell 36–12–89–5; Bryson 30–5–87–3; Feltham 28–5–88–2; Kendrick 22–7–45–0; Boiling 11–0–23–0; Brown 2–0–6–0. *Second Innings*—M. P. Bicknell 14–5–24–2; Bryson 21–2–82–1; Feltham 15–2–47–1; Kendrick 21.3–7–64–1; Boiling 10–1–36–0.

Umpires: A. A. Jones and B. Leadbeater.

At Taunton, September 12, 13, 14, 15. NOTTINGHAMSHIRE lost to SOMERSET by an innings and 163 runs.

COUNTY BENEFITS AWARDED FOR 1993

Essex . . . . N. A. Foster.	Nottinghamshire . . D. W. Randall.
Gloucestershire . . . D. V. Lawrence.	Surrey . . . . H. T. Brind
Hampshire . . . . . . T. M. Tremlett (coach).	(head groundsman)
Kent . . . . R. M. Ellison.	Sussex . . . . C. M. Wells.
Lancashire . . . . G. D. Mendis.	Worcestershire . . . D. B. D'Oliveira and
Leicestershire . . . . J. J. Whitaker.	M. J. Weston.
Middlesex . . . . N. G. Cowans.	Yorkshire . . . . M. D. Moxon.
Northamptonshire . R. J. Bailey.	

No benefit was awarded by Derbyshire, Durham, Glamorgan, Somerset or Warwickshire.

SOMERSET

President: J. Luff
Chairman: R. Parsons
Chairman, Cricket Committee: B. C. Rose
Chief Executive: P. W. Anderson
  The County Ground, St James's Street,
  Taunton TA1 1JT
  (Telephone: 0823-272946)
Captain: C. J. Tavaré
Director of Cricket: R. M. H. Cottam
Coach: P. J. Robinson

Somerset introduced two bright new talents to county cricket, and enjoyed a more successful and much more interesting year. Five Championship victories, including one, for the first time since 1975, over Essex, and two in September after a long barren spell, brought a rise from bottom to ninth position, the best since 1984. Nine Sunday League wins brought them near the prizemoney, and an appearance in the Benson and Hedges semi-final (after two superb recoveries over Yorkshire and Worcestershire) was encouraging. The big disappointment, however, was removal from the NatWest Trophy by Gloucestershire, despite great efforts by the newcomers, Andrew Caddick taking six for 30 and Mark Lathwell making 85.

The 23-year-old New Zealand-born Caddick, with his height, pace, and fitness, brought 71 first-class wickets at 27.01 each and a new bite to the attack. Lathwell, a 20-year-old opening bat, educated in Devon and under Somerset eyes for a long time, delighted watchers all over the country with his busy, forceful batting. Besides 1,176 Championship runs at 36.75, he often excelled in one-day games. (It is interesting to recall that in his first year, 1974, Viv Richards had very similar figures: 1,223 at 33.05.) Both thoroughly deserved their county caps and places with the England A team for the winter tour. It was a major achievement to replace an opening pair of the calibre of Jimmy Cook and Peter Roebuck. Lathwell and the steady, cricket-wise Hayhurst, with nearly 1,200 runs, did it splendidly.

Indeed, the batting rarely failed. Despite losing a month through injury, Richard Harden made a fine job of filling the vital No. 3 position; while the captain, Chris Tavaré, after a difficult start (which coincided with problems his wife had with the arrival of their first baby), recovered in fine style, and played very freely. Curiously, there was only one Somerset hundred before late August. Thereafter, the batsmen made up for lost time. Not since 1901 had Somerset produced three hundreds in an innings. In the final two matches Tavaré (two), Harden (two), Hayhurst and Rob Turner (a maiden century) did it twice. Only once was the side bowled out twice – at Canterbury in a match where Kent only narrowly escaped a 25-point penalty because of the pitch. Turner, a former Cambridge captain, demonstrated plenty of gritty batting, besides being a capable deputy keeper, while Neil Burns also made many useful runs and had perhaps his best year for the side behind the stumps.

Graham Rose, normally a fine attacking player, neared 1,000 runs, which included a marathon fighting century to ensure safety at The Oval, and he took important wickets too. His bowling is likely to be of more significance next year in view of the release of three other all-rounders: the South African Richard Snell, Ken MacLeay and Roland Lefebvre. Snell, who replaced his compatriot Cook as the overseas player, strove cheerfully but had a disappointing time with his bowling, though he did shine on occasion with the bat. Much the same might be said of MacLeay who, however, managed to put in several telling one-day spells. After a serious off-the-field accident, Lefebvre could not command a regular place and, surprisingly, was allowed to end his contract a year early, whereupon he was signed by Glamorgan.

Despite some successes, Ricky Bartlett and Gareth Townsend were also released, and the club's Director of Cricket, Bob Cottam, further put his stamp on his first year with a very bold, imaginative move: the Pakistani leg-spinner Mushtaq Ahmed was given a three-year contract, which, if he approaches his form for the touring team last summer, must greatly enhance the value of all the other bowlers. He will need suitable pitches, which Taunton provided in 1992, reliable wicket-keeping, and understanding captaincy. In this context, Tavaré's captaincy sometimes invited criticism for its reluctance to attack hard in the field, while two of the four Championship defeats resulted from declarations which looked too generous at the outset, and proved to be so.

The reliable Neil Mallender, often capable of match-winning bursts, was picked for England and performed superbly, while the other leading bowler was off-spinner Harvey Trump. His 49 wickets at 32.32 included a match-winning 14 for 104 to beat Gloucestershire, and this included a hat-trick. Of the other bowlers tried, Andre van Troost produced some telling but also some expensive spells with his undoubted pace, which clearly needs harnessing, and slow left-armer Andrew Cottam, Bob's son, entered the first-class game with strong credentials from Under-19 cricket. Nick Folland, the 28-year-old Devon captain, showed his batting pedigree in his single match, and will be a useful left-handed addition, while the Second Eleven reached the semi-final of the Bain Clarkson Trophy and should provide further support in the coming years. It was a better financial year, with membership increased, a splendid Bath Festival, and an entertaining, well-attended Weston-super-Mare Festival until it was ruined by rain. Somerset were against the switch to four-day matches and cricket at Weston looked like being doomed by the new format, but was reprieved for at least one year by local fund-raising. – Eric Hill.

SOMERSET 1992

[*Bill Smith*]

Back row: M. N. Lathwell, I. Fletcher, R. J. Turner, A. R. Caddick, K. H. MacLeay, K. A. Parsons, M. F. Robinson, T. Edwards.
Middle row: A. Payne, K. J. Parsons, J. I. D. Kerr, J. C. Hallett, A. P. van Troost, H. R. J. Trump, A. C. Cottam, G. T. J. Townsend, R. J. Bartlett.
Front row: P. J. Robinson (*coach*), N. D. Burns, R. J. Harden, C. J. Tavaré (*captain*), R. Parsons (*chairman*), R. M. H. Cottam (*director of cricket*), A. N. Hayhurst, G. D. Rose, N. A. Mallender, R. P. Lefebvre. *Inset:* R. P. Snell.

SOMERSET RESULTS

All first-class matches – Played 23: Won 5, Lost 5, Drawn 13.

County Championship matches – Played 22: Won 5, Lost 4, Drawn 13.

Bonus points – Batting 64, Bowling 62.

*Competition placings – Britannic Assurance County Championship, 9th;
NatWest Bank Trophy, 2nd round; Benson and Hedges Cup, s-f;
Sunday League, 5th equal.*

BRITANNIC ASSURANCE CHAMPIONSHIP AVERAGES

BATTING

	Birthplace	M	I	NO	R	HS	Avge
R. J. Turner	Malvern	7	10	5	286	101*	57.20
‡R. J. Harden	Bridgwater	19	31	5	1,321	187	50.80
‡C. J. Tavaré	Orpington	21	32	2	1,157	125	38.56
‡M. N. Lathwell	Bletchley	19	33	1	1,176	114	36.75
‡N. D. Burns	Chelmsford	21	31	11	709	73*	35.45
‡A. N. Hayhurst	Manchester	22	36	2	1,167	102	34.32
‡G. D. Rose	Tottenham	21	32	4	925	132	33.03
R. J. Bartlett.......	Ash Priors	7	11	0	327	72	29.72
K. H. MacLeay	Bradford-on-Avon	11	17	3	386	74	27.57
R. P. Snell§........	Durban, SA	16	20	4	436	81	27.25
G. T. J. Townsend ..	Tiverton	6	11	1	252	49	25.20
‡A. R. Caddick	Christchurch, New Zealand	19	17	5	246	54*	20.50
‡R. P. Lefebvre	Rotterdam, Netherlands	3	4	0	70	36	17.50
H. R. J. Trump	Taunton	17	16	7	142	28	15.77
A. P. van Troost ...	Schiedam, Netherlands	10	7	5	30	12	15.00
‡N. A. Mallender ...	Kirk Sandall	15	18	5	182	29*	14.00
A. C. Cottam	Northampton	6	8	1	43	31	6.14

Also batted: N. A. Folland (*Bristol*) (1 match) 22, 82*; A. Payne (*Rossendale*) (1 match) 51*.

* Signifies not out.   ‡ Denotes county cap.   § Overseas player.

The following played a total of ten three-figure innings for Somerset in County Championship matches – R. J. Harden 3, C. J. Tavaré 3, A. N. Hayhurst 1, M. N. Lathwell 1, G. D. Rose 1, R. J. Turner 1.

BOWLING

	O	M	R	W	BB	5W/i	Avge
N. A. Mallender	361.4	74	1,067	45	5-29	3	23.71
A. R. Caddick	558.2	94	1,797	64	6-52	2	28.07
H. R. J. Trump	553	133	1,558	49	7-52	2	31.79
A. P. van Troost	155.4	17	695	18	6-48	2	38.61
R. P. Snell	339.1	60	1,194	27	3-29	0	44.22
G. D. Rose	373	77	1,179	24	4-59	0	49.12

Also bowled: A. C. Cottam 116.1–24–280–6; R. J. Harden 3–0–31–0; A. N. Hayhurst 137–28–403–8; M. N. Lathwell 64–14–224–4; R. P. Lefebvre 41–11–96–5; K. H. MacLeay 107–27–286–9; A. Payne 27–8–71–1; C. J. Tavaré 3.2–0–33–0; R. J. Turner 2.1–0–26–0.

Wicket-keepers: N. D. Burns 38 ct, 3 st; R. J. Turner 2 ct.

Leading Fielder: C. J. Tavaré 15.

SOMERSET v GLOUCESTERSHIRE

At Taunton, April 25, 26, 27, 28. Drawn. Somerset 5 pts, Gloucestershire 4 pts. Toss: Somerset. Rain on all four days cost 148 overs and removed any possibility of a result. However, Caddick made full use of a green pitch and made an immediate impact on his Championship début. Had Athey been caught off him on 30 Gloucestershire might have collapsed. But Athey's vigilance, over four and a half hours, stabilised the innings and as the pitch eased Hancock completed a maiden century in only 144 balls. Any possibility of Somerset following on was removed by the batting of Rose and, with the match long since dead, 18-year-old Payne marked his first-class début with an unbeaten fifty.

Close of play: First day, Gloucestershire 168-6 (R. C. Russell 8*, T. H. C. Hancock 11*); Second day, Somerset 51-0 (A. N. Hayhurst 24*, G. T. J. Townsend 24*); Third day, Somerset 251-7 (G. D. Rose 68*, A. Payne 1*).

Gloucestershire

G. D. Hodgson c Tavaré b Caddick ...	1	M. C. J. Ball c Harden b Rose........	54
S. G. Hinks c Rose b Caddick	34	A. M. Babington c Rose b Trump	24
*A. J. Wright c Burns b Caddick......	0	M. J. Gerrard not out	0
C. W. J. Athey b MacLeay..........	65		
M. W. Alleyne c Tavaré b MacLeay ...	15	L-b 2, w 1, n-b 9...........	12
J. T. C. Vaughan b Payne	34		
†R. C. Russell lbw b Rose	13	1/2 2/2 3/67 4/74 5/149	344
T. H. C. Hancock c Rose b Caddick...102		6/149 7/201 8/296 9/340	

Bonus points – Gloucestershire 1, Somerset 2 (Score at 100 overs: 189-6).

Bowling: Caddick 38–9–96–4; Rose 28.2–9–60–2; Payne 27–8–71–1; Hayhurst 21–3–40–0; Trump 16–1–42–1; MacLeay 15–5–33–2.

Somerset

A. N. Hayhurst lbw b Babington	54	A. Payne not out	51
G. T. J. Townsend lbw b Ball	40	A. R. Caddick c Hodgson b Gerrard ...	2
R. J. Harden b Ball	13	H. R. J. Trump not out..............	24
*C. J. Tavaré b Ball	33	L-b 7, n-b 14	21
R. J. Bartlett c Russell b Vaughan	4		
K. H. MacLeay c Russell b Vaughan ..	1	1/97 2/114 3/140	(9 wkts dec.) 348
G. D. Rose b Ball	85	4/147 5/151 6/167	
†N. D. Burns c Russell b Gerrard	20	7/234 8/286 9/291	

Bonus points – Somerset 3, Gloucestershire 3 (Score at 100 overs: 264-7).

Bowling: Babington 26–2–89–1; Gerrard 25–5–78–2; Vaughan 26–7–49–2; Athey 4–3–1–0; Ball 47–14–103–4; Hancock 3.4–0–11–0; Alleyne 5–1–10–0.

Umpires: D. J. Constant and D. R. Shepherd.

At Hove, May 7, 8, 9, 11. SOMERSET drew with SUSSEX.

At Taunton, May 13, 14, 15. SOMERSET lost to PAKISTANIS by five wickets (See Pakistani tour section).

SOMERSET v ESSEX

At Taunton, May 20, 21, 22. Somerset won by four wickets. Somerset 23 pts, Essex 7 pts. Toss: Somerset. Somerset, bottom of the table in 1991, beat the reigning champions to record their first victory over Essex in the Championship since they won at Leyton in August 1975. On a hard, grassy pitch which gradually became easier under a hot sun, three batsmen dominated the match. Stephenson was on the field throughout, with two unbeaten centuries and carrying his bat through the first innings. However, the middle order collapsed to van Troost, who had a burst of five for 17 in 39 balls, and in the end it was the Somerset pair of Lathwell and Harden whose contributions proved decisive. Of Lathwell's 155 in the match, 128 came in boundaries. In the second innings, as Somerset chased four an over, he raced well ahead of the rate, hitting Topley and Fraser out of a firing line depleted by a muscle strain to Ilott. Harden was steady enough to keep Somerset in the game through long, telling spells from Childs and Stephenson, and the winning runs came with 26 balls remaining.

Close of play: First day, Somerset 139-1 (M. N. Lathwell 72*, R. J. Harden 60*); Second day, Essex 202-1 (J. P. Stephenson 103*, N. V. Knight 34*).

Essex

*P. J. Prichard c Rose b Snell	28	– c Bartlett b Mallender	55
J. P. Stephenson not out	113	– not out	159
N. V. Knight c Burns b van Troost	1	– c van Troost b Rose	47
N. Hussain c Harden b Mallender	43		
M. E. Waugh c Mallender b van Troost	19	– (4) not out	33
N. Shahid c Burns b van Troost	5		
†M. A. Garnham c Hayhurst b van Troost	0		
A. G. J. Fraser c Tavaré b van Troost	2		
T. D. Topley c Burns b van Troost	0		
M. C. Ilott c Burns b Mallender	13		
J. H. Childs c Burns b Snell	8		
L-b 7, w 2, n-b 18	27	B 4, w 4, n-b 12	20

1/35 2/52 3/119 4/148 5/167   259   1/81 2/239   (2 wkts dec.) 314
6/167 7/182 8/186 9/232

Bonus points – Essex 3, Somerset 4.

Bowling: *First Innings*—Mallender 16–2–63–2; Snell 14.1–3–53–2; van Troost 13–4–48–6; Caddick 16–1–45–0; Rose 10–0–43–0; Lathwell 1–1–0–0. *Second Innings*—Mallender 14–2–41–1; Snell 2–0–16–0; van Troost 13–0–64–0; Caddick 11–2–57–0; Rose 16–1–61–1; Lathwell 9–2–33–0; Hayhurst 9–1–38–0.

Somerset

A. N. Hayhurst b Ilott	0	– c Hussain b Childs	43
M. N. Lathwell c Garnham b Topley	76	– c Waugh b Stephenson	79
R. J. Harden c Shahid b Ilott	72	– b Childs	68
*C. J. Tavaré c Hussain b Topley	0	– c Childs b Stephenson	22
R. J. Bartlett b Childs	46	– b Childs	27
G. D. Rose lbw b Ilott	1	– b Childs	18
†N. D. Burns c Prichard b Fraser	2	– not out	10
R. P. Snell c Prichard b Ilott	20	– not out	16
N. A. Mallender b Waugh	7		
A. R. Caddick not out	9		
A. P. van Troost c and b Waugh	12		
B 5, l-b 7, n-b 18	30	B 6, l-b 8, n-b 5	19

1/0 2/145 3/146 4/170 5/181   275   1/125 2/129 3/187   (6 wkts) 302
6/200 7/236 8/246 9/253   4/217 5/273 6/274

Bonus points – Somerset 3, Essex 4.

Bowling: *First Innings*—Ilott 30–12–76–4; Topley 23–5–73–2; Stephenson 11–2–32–0; Waugh 12.2–3–46–2; Childs 11–5–13–1; Fraser 8–3–23–1. *Second Innings*—Ilott 2.5–0–12–0; Topley 8–0–46–0; Waugh 2.1–0–19–0; Childs 33.4–11–91–4; Fraser 3–0–35–0; Stephenson 23–6–85–2.

Umpires: H. D. Bird and A. G. T. Whitehead.

At Gloucester, May 23, 25, 26. SOMERSET beat GLOUCESTERSHIRE by 17 runs.

At Manchester, May 29, 30, June 1. SOMERSET drew with LANCASHIRE.

At Darlington, June 2, 3, 4. SOMERSET lost to DURHAM by eight wickets.

At Middlesbrough, June 5, 6, 8. SOMERSET drew with YORKSHIRE.

SOMERSET v NORTHAMPTONSHIRE

At Bath, June 16, 17, 18. Drawn. Somerset 6 pts, Northamptonshire 5 pts. Toss: Somerset. Northamptonshire recovered well from the early loss of four wickets on a grassy pitch as Loye and Curran put on 70 in 14 overs, and wicket-keeper Ripley scored a composed 107 not out, his second century of the season. When Somerset replied, Lathwell improved on his highest score again, hitting 13 fours and sharing a 133-run opening stand with Hayhurst. Later Rose and Harden added a brisk 83 to claim a third batting point before Tavaré declared 57 behind. Fordham and Felton also made the most of the pitch, now playing easily, with a century opening partnership, but on the final morning wickets fell quickly, leaving Somerset to chase 324 in 69 overs. Hayhurst and Harden put on 78 in 25, but when they departed in quick succession – Harden to a superb boundary catch by Ambrose – Tavaré and MacLeay turned down the challenge of attacking 236 in 38 overs, and settled for the draw.

Close of play: First day, Somerset 40-0 (A. N. Hayhurst 17*, M. N. Lathwell 19*); Second day, Northamptonshire 152-2 (N. A. Felton 54*, D. J. Capel 6*).

Northamptonshire

A. Fordham c MacLeay b Caddick	3 – lbw b Caddick	71
N. A. Felton b Mallender	4 – c Caddick b Trump	86
*R. J. Bailey lbw b Rose	14 – lbw b Caddick	14
D. J. Capel c Tavaré b MacLeay	17 – run out	18
M. B. Loye run out	34 – lbw b Mallender	10
K. M. Curran c Caddick	61 – b Mallender	2
†D. Ripley not out	107 – c Harden b Caddick	14
A. R. Roberts c Trump b Rose	15 – b Trump	6
J. P. Taylor b Trump	21 – c MacLeay b Trump	9
C. E. L. Ambrose not out	20 – c Rose b Caddick	7
N. G. B. Cook (did not bat)	– not out	10
L-b 9, w 1, n-b 1	11 B 10, l-b 6, n-b 3	19

1/3 2/18 3/26 4/51 5/121   (8 wkts dec.) 307   1/125 2/145 3/199 4/210 5/212   266
5/148 7/178 8/255   6/216 7/228 8/244 9/248

Bonus points – Northamptonshire 4, Somerset 3.

Bowling: *First Innings*—Mallender 17-2-48-1; Caddick 24-5-78-2; Rose 11-4-22-2; Snell 19-3-70-0; MacLeay 9-0-48-1; Trump 14-6-31-1; Hayhurst 2-1-1-0. *Second Innings*—Snell 14-1-53-0; Caddick 15.4-1-56-4; Rose 5-2-15-0; Mallender 13-1-43-2; Trump 27-7-75-3; Lathwell 1-0-8-0.

Somerset

A. N. Hayhurst c Fordham b Cook	53 – c Bailey b Roberts	38
M. N. Lathwell lbw b Roberts	86 – c Curran b Taylor	0
R. J. Harden not out	33 – c Ambrose b Roberts	39
K. H. MacLeay c Curran b Ambrose	5 – (5) not out	19
G. D. Rose not out	55	
*C. J. Tavaré (did not bat)	– (4) not out	35
B 1, l-b 9, n-b 8	18 B 4, l-b 4, n-b 8	16

1/133 2/160 3/167   (3 wkts dec.) 250   1/1 2/79 3/88   (3 wkts) 147

†N. D. Burns, R. P. Snell, A. R. Caddick, N. A. Mallender and H. R. J. Trump did not bat.

Bonus points – Somerset 3, Northamptonshire 1.

Bowling: *First Innings*—Ambrose 18–5–54–1; Taylor 17–0–59–0; Cook 14–5–43–1; Capel 10.2–2–28–0; Curran 7–2–16–0; Roberts 13–1–40–1. *Second Innings*—Ambrose 13–2–34–0; Taylor 6–1–22–1; Curran 7–1–20–0; Roberts 14–2–30–2; Cook 3–2–5–0; Capel 8–3–6–0; Bailey 11–6–5–0; Felton 2–1–9–0; Fordham 1–0–8–0.

Umpires: R. C. Tolchard and R. A. White.

SOMERSET v SURREY

At Bath, June 19, 20, 22. Somerset won by nine wickets. Somerset 24 pts, Surrey 3 pts. Toss: Somerset. Somerset owed a convincing win, which lifted them to second in the table, to a maiden century from 20-year-old Lathwell and destructive seam bowling from Mallender, who took eight for 80 in the match. Lathwell survived chances when 39 and 43 to become the first Somerset player to reach 100 in 1992. With solid assistance from Hayhurst and Harden he laid the foundations for a total of 376. On the second day Mallender undermined Surrey, removing Ligertwood, Thorpe and Ward in 29 balls and forcing them to follow on 260 behind. This time the visitors showed more defiance. Though Thorpe's determined 48 was ended by the second ball of the last morning, the night-watchman Boiling obstructed for an hour and a half, and even at 160 for seven Robinson and Martin Bicknell added 87 in 30 overs. Bicknell called on his brother as a runner after suffering a groin strain at 19 but reached 49 before Mallender removed his last two partners with successive balls. Somerset hit the winning runs with 22 overs to spare.

Close of play: First day, Surrey 4-0 (D. J. Bicknell 3*, D. G. C. Ligertwood 0*); Second day, Surrey 109-3 (G. P. Thorpe 48*, J. Boiling 1*).

Somerset

A. N. Hayhurst c Ligertwood b M. P. Bicknell	41		
M. N. Lathwell b Boiling	114	– lbw b Robinson	1
R. J. Harden c Ligertwood b Benjamin	73	– not out	6
*C. J. Tavaré c and b Kendrick	14		
K. H. MacLeay c and b M. P. Bicknell	12	– (1) not out	13
G. D. Rose c and b Kendrick	41		
†N. D. Burns b Robinson	27		
R. P. Snell c sub b Robinson	0		
N. A. Mallender c Boiling b Robinson	14		
H. R. J. Trump not out	18		
A. C. Cottam not out	1		
B 4, l-b 6, n-b 11	21		

1/139 2/192 3/229 4/256 5/276   (9 wkts dec.) 376   1/4   (1 wkt) 20
6/343 7/343 8/344 9/374

Bonus points – Somerset 4, Surrey 3 (Score at 100 overs: 357-8).

Bowling: *First Innings*—Bryson 14–2–63–0; M. P. Bicknell 22–2–58–2; Benjamin 20–2–82–1; Kendrick 21–7–80–2; Boiling 20–9–61–1; Robinson 6–1–22–3. *Second Innings*—Benjamin 3–0–7–0; Robinson 4–1–8–1; Lynch 1.3–0–5–0.

Surrey

D. J. Bicknell c Tavaré b Rose	12	– c Burns b Hayhurst	26
†D. G. C. Ligertwood b Mallender	11	– c Tavaré b MacLeay	4
G. P. Thorpe c Lathwell b Mallender	10	– c Burns b Rose	48
*M. A. Lynch b Trump	30	– lbw b Mallender	22
D. M. Ward c Burns b Mallender	5	– (6) lbw b Snell	24
J. D. Robinson c Hayhurst b Snell	1	– (7) b Cottam	53
N. M. Kendrick b Mallender	3	– (8) lbw b Rose	2
M. P. Bicknell lbw b Mallender	1	– (9) not out	49
R. E. Bryson c Burns b Cottam	28	– (10) b Mallender	15
J. Boiling c Burns b Snell	2	– (5) b Snell	0
J. E. Benjamin not out	0	– b Mallender	0
B 3, l-b 3, n-b 7	13	B 6, l-b 11, n-b 3	20

1/23 2/40 3/46 4/60 5/73   116   1/25 2/58 3/103 4/109 5/147   276
6/83 7/83 8/84 9/116   6/154 7/160 8/247 9/276

Bonus points – Somerset 4.

Bowling: *First Innings*—Mallender 14–4–29–5; Trump 15–4–35–1; Snell 14–6–17–2; Rose 7–2–21–1; Cottam 5.2–1–8–1. *Second Innings*—Snell 32–8–73–2; Rose 21–9–34–2; Mallender 22.2–7–51–3; Cottam 12–5–32–1; Trump 25–9–52–0; MacLeay 7–3–8–1; Hayhurst 5–2–9–1.

Umpires: R. C. Tolchard and R. A. White.

At Lord's, June 26, 27, 29. SOMERSET drew with MIDDLESEX.

SOMERSET v DERBYSHIRE

At Taunton, July 3, 4, 6. Derbyshire won by six wickets. Derbyshire 18 pts, Somerset 3 pts. Toss: Somerset. Derbyshire's batsmen responded with relish to the challenge of scoring 300 in 85 overs after a first-day wash-out and two forfeitures. They won with more than 32 overs to spare after Morris scored his fourth hundred in consecutive first-class innings at Taunton. His second-wicket stand of 259 in 43 overs with Bowler, who remained unbeaten after striking a six and 23 fours, virtually decided the issue; despite a late ripple when Snell and Caddick took three quick wickets. Tavaré had chosen to bat first, but Somerset found it a testing business against Derbyshire's seam trio, led by Bishop, on a fast, bouncy pitch. But with fortitude and some luck – both were put down – Harden and Tavaré put on a fighting 114 in 40 overs. On the final day Harden reached a career-best 166 not out, with one six and 20 fours.

Close of play: First day, No play; Second day, Somerset 236-5 (R. J. Harden 123*, N. D. Burns 10*).

Somerset

A. N. Hayhurst c Krikken b Bishop ...	13	†N. D. Burns not out...............	28	
M. N. Lathwell c Brown b Warner	2			
R. J. Harden not out................	166	L-b 2, w 2, n-b 9...........	13	
*C. J. Tavaré c and b Sladdin	59		—	
K. H. MacLeay lbw b Warner	2	1/6 2/43 3/157 (5 wkts dec.)	299	
G. D. Rose c Bowler b Cork	16	4/167 5/211		

R. P. Snell, H. R. J. Trump, A. P. van Troost and A. R. Caddick did not bat.

Bonus points – Somerset 3, Derbyshire 2 (Score at 100 overs: 264-5).

Bowling: Bishop 17–3–50–1; Warner 22–7–29–2; Cork 22–5–82–1; Sladdin 35–6–111–1; Goldsmith 10–3–25–0.

Somerset forfeited their second innings.

Derbyshire

Derbyshire forfeited their first innings.

P. D. Bowler not out................	147	S. C. Goldsmith not out	15	
A. M. Brown c Trump b Caddick	0			
*J. E. Morris c Rose b Snell..........	109	L-b 12, w 4, n-b 13..........	29	
T. J. G. O'Gorman c Burns b Snell	1		—	
C. J. Adams b Caddick..............	0	1/4 2/263 3/265 4/266 (4 wkts)	301	

†K. M. Krikken, D. G. Cork, I. R. Bishop, R. W. Sladdin and A. E. Warner did not bat.

Bowling: Caddick 13.5–0–55–2; Snell 12–0–66–2; van Troost 9–0–77–0; Rose 6–1–28–0; Trump 6–1–36–0; MacLeay 6–0–27–0.

Umpires: D. O. Oslear and K. E. Palmer.

At Taunton, July 13 (not first-class). No result. Toss: Transvaal. Somerset 260 for seven (55 overs) (M. N. Lathwell 60, G. T. J. Townsend 59, R. J. Harden 64 not out; B. M. White four for 43); Transvaal 60 for no wkt (14 overs) (S. J. Cook 43 not out).

At Leicester, July 17, 18, 20. SOMERSET drew with LEICESTERSHIRE.

At Canterbury, July 21, 22, 23. SOMERSET lost to KENT by 82 runs.

At Abergavenny, July 24, 25, 27. SOMERSET drew with GLAMORGAN.

SOMERSET v SUSSEX

At Taunton, July 31, August 1, 2. Drawn. Somerset 7 pts, Sussex 8 pts. Toss: Sussex. After some early fortune against Stephenson, Lathwell gave the match a delightful start by striking 11 fours in a 59-ball innings when a grassy pitch was at its most difficult. Hayhurst and Harden also prospered while Tavaré, hitting 19 fours from 104 balls, was one short of his hundred when he fell to Salisbury, who wound the innings up with five for eight in 34 balls. Wells and Speight prevented any Somerset thoughts of a significant advantage by putting on a rapid 161 in 37 overs, as the pitch became easier before the declaration 46 behind. Salisbury, conceding just 68 in one spell of 34 overs broken only by the Saturday close, hindered Somerset from setting a large target, but Rose and Turner ensured it would not be a simple one. The final equation was 279 in 52 overs. Sussex set off well, scoring at four an over, but when they lost their fourth wicket with 138 needed from 17 the attempt was abandoned.

Close of play: First day, Sussex 18-1 (J. W. Hall 11*, N. J. Lenham 5*); Second day, Somerset 103-2 (R. J. Harden 29*, C. J. Tavaré 11*).

Somerset

A. N. Hayhurst lbw b Stephenson	86	– c and b Pigott	15
M. N. Lathwell c Moores b Giddins	55	– st Moores b Salisbury	45
R. J. Harden c Speight b Pigott	52	– b Salisbury	30
*C. J. Tavaré c Wells b Salisbury	99	– c Speight b Giddins	55
G. T. J. Townsend b Stephenson	1	– c Remy b Giddins	12
G. D. Rose c Wells b Salisbury	25	– c Giddins b Salisbury	32
†R. J. Turner c Wells b Salisbury	0	– lbw b Stephenson	11
R. P. Snell c Hall b Salisbury	2	– not out	11
N. A. Mallender c Hall b Salisbury	9	– not out	9
A. R. Caddick c and b Stephenson	0		
H. R. J. Trump not out	12		
B 5, l-b 5, n-b 5	15	B 4, n-b 8	12

1/74 2/171 3/222 4/250 5/296   356   1/19 2/84 3/122   (7 wkts dec.) 232
6/322 7/330 8/339 9/340   4/153 5/167
                                        6/211 7/212

Bonus points – Somerset 4, Sussex 4.

Bowling: *First Innings*—Stephenson 22-4-92-3; Giddins 15-2-63-1; Pigott 13-2-52-1; Remy 14-1-60-0; Lenham 7-3-18-0; Salisbury 24.2-9-61-5. *Second Innings*—Stephenson 19-1-76-1; Pigott 14-5-29-1; Giddins 15-2-46-2; Salisbury 34-17-68-3; Remy 5-1-9-0.

Sussex

D. M. Smith lbw b Mallender	1	– c Trump b Mallender	21
J. W. Hall b Mallender	24	– not out	73
N. J. Lenham c Caddick b Snell	37		
*A. P. Wells c Turner b Rose	103	– run out	24
M. P. Speight c Turner b Caddick	122	– lbw b Caddick	3
†P. Moores not out	14	– not out	10
F. D. Stephenson b Caddick	0		
C. C. Remy b Caddick	1	– (3) c Lathwell b Snell	21
A. C. S. Pigott not out	4		
B 1, l-b 1, w 1, n-b 1	4	B 5, l-b 1, n-b 1	7

1/7 2/56 3/79 4/240 5/304   (7 wkts dec.) 310   1/41 2/85 3/127 4/141   (4 wkts) 159
6/304 7/306

I. D. K. Salisbury and E. S. H. Giddins did not bat.

Bonus points – Sussex 4, Somerset 3.

Bowling: *First Innings*—Mallender 17–6–45–2; Caddick 22–3–73–3; Snell 12–2–52–1; Rose 13–1–56–1; Trump 14–0–67–0; Hayhurst 7–2–15–0. *Second Innings*—Mallender 7–0–22–1; Caddick 10–0–36–1; Snell 9–0–35–1; Trump 8–2–32–0; Hayhurst 6–0–24–0; Lathwell 3–1–4–0.

Umpires: J. D. Bond and A. A. Jones.

SOMERSET v WARWICKSHIRE

At Taunton, August 4, 5, 6. Drawn. Somerset 7 pts, Warwickshire 6 pts. Toss: Somerset. A nicely balanced match went to the final over, when Caddick took one of Warwickshire's remaining two wickets and the tail managed four of the required 11 runs. The first day started unhappily for Somerset, when Donald dislocated Hayhurst's finger with his fourth ball, and then broke Harden's knuckle. On a bare pitch taking early spin, Tavaré and Townsend put on 73, and MacLeay played an attacking 74 in 76 balls. Lloyd countered Warwickshire's slide to 64 for three, with steady support from Penney, until Trump and Snell mopped up the tail. Lathwell, with 12 fours, led the way in Somerset's second innings, despite an escape in Donald's third over, which contained three bouncers. Trying to avoid the second, he disturbed a bail, but umpire Holder no-balled Donald for exceeding his limit to one batsman, and gave him a final warning when he added a third. Burns and MacLeay extended the lead on the third morning before four for five in 21 balls from Booth brought a rapid end, leaving the visitors to chase 267 in 60 overs. Paul Smith arrived with 115 needed from 21 overs, and Warwickshire were within 16 of victory when he was eighth out with two overs to go. But neither side could reach their final goal.

Close of play: First day, Warwickshire 60-1 (A. J. Moles 29*, D. P. Ostler 20*); Second day, Somerset 144-3 (N. D. Burns 19*, K. H. MacLeay 13*).

Somerset

A. N. Hayhurst retired hurt	0	– (10) not out	1
M. N. Lathwell c Moles b P. A. Smith	45	– (1) c Piper b Bell	71
R. J. Harden retired hurt	29	– absent injured	
*C. J. Tavaré b N. M. K. Smith	44	– (3) lbw b Bell	0
G. T. J. Townsend c Ostler b N. M. K. Smith	38	– (2) lbw b Bell	15
†N. D. Burns b Twose	13	– (4) lbw b Donald	68
K. H. MacLeay c N. M. K. Smith b Booth	74	– (5) b Donald	29
R. P. Snell b Donald	5	– (6) lbw b Booth	25
A. R. Caddick b Donald	7	– (7) c Ostler b Booth	14
H. R. J. Trump not out	8	– (8) c Ostler b Booth	5
A. C. Cottam st Piper b Booth	5	– (9) c Donald b Booth	0
B 4, l-b 1, w 1, n-b 4	10	B 17, l-b 5, n-b 14	36

1/71 2/153 3/166 4/213 5/220   278   1/69 2/69 3/118 4/205 5/220   264
6/230 7/272 8/278   6/251 7/262 8/263 9/264

Bonus points – Somerset 3, Warwickshire 3.

In the first innings A. N. Hayhurst retired hurt at 0 and R. J. Harden at 80.

Bowling: *First Innings*—Donald 22–7–41–2; P. A. Smith 13–2–53–1; Bell 5–0–20–0; Booth 24.4–6–85–2; N. M. K. Smith 15–3–51–2; Twose 6–1–23–1. *Second Innings*—Donald 21–3–68–2; P. A. Smith 8–0–26–0; Booth 14–4–29–4; Bell 25–2–84–3; N. M. K. Smith 9–3–35–0.

Warwickshire

A. J. Moles c Townsend b Trump	29	– c Burns b Snell	27
R. G. Twose c Burns b Caddick	7	– c Townsend b Trump	45
D. P. Ostler c MacLeay b Caddick	22	– c Townsend b MacLeay	25
*T. A. Lloyd c Burns b Lathwell	50	– b Trump	4
T. L. Penney c Burns b Snell	80	– b Cottam	38
N. M. K. Smith b Caddick	28	– c Burns b Trump	9
P. A. Smith st Burns b MacLeay	40	– b Caddick	45
†K. J. Piper b Trump	0	– run out	15
P. A. Booth b Trump	3	– not out	22
A. A. Donald not out	0	– b Caddick	3
M. A. V. Bell b Snell	0	– not out	2
B 8, l-b 7, n-b 2	17	B 17, l-b 8	25

1/19 2/60 3/64 4/127 5/168   276   1/51 2/85 3/101   (9 wkts) 260
6/262 7/264 8/276 9/276   4/127 5/152 6/174
                                       7/216 8/251 9/257

Bonus points – Warwickshire 3, Somerset 4.

Bowling: *First Innings*—Caddick 19–5–49–3; Snell 14–4–37–2; Trump 31–7–89–3; Cottam 14–3–33–0; Lathwell 9–1–35–1; MacLeay 7–0–18–1. *Second Innings*—Caddick 11–1–50–2; Snell 10–1–39–1; Trump 25–3–91–3; MacLeay 7–0–18–1; Cottam 7–0–37–1.

Umpires: V. A. Holder and A. A. Jones.

At Taunton, August 12. SOMERSET v PAKISTANIS. Abandoned.

At Taunton, August 13. SOMERSET v PAKISTANIS. Abandoned (See Pakistani tour section).

SOMERSET v WORCESTERSHIRE

At Weston-super-Mare, August 18, 19, 20. Drawn. Somerset 5 pts, Worcestershire 7 pts. Toss: Somerset. The home team struggled to 81 for five on a slow, slightly variable pitch which gave some early turn, but Rose launched a recovery carried on by Snell and Caddick, with a maiden fifty. Worcestershire's innings also needed early repairs, supplied by the steady D'Oliveira and Haynes, who enabled Curtis to declare 78 behind. After a crisp start, Folland marked his Championship début with an unbeaten 82, hitting 12 fours, mainly against the spinners. Tavaré set Worcestershire 254 in 62 overs, but when the first 20 overs of seam produced a score of 36 for one, a draw seemed inevitable. The visitors gave up the chase, though Phil Weston played steadily for a career-best unbeaten 66.

Close of play: First day, Somerset 293-9 (A. R. Caddick 33*, H. R. J. Trump 15*); Second day, Worcestershire 250-5 dec.

Somerset

A. N. Hayhurst lbw b Stemp	23	– c D'Oliveira b Stemp	36
M. N. Lathwell hit wkt b Radford	8	– lbw b Newport	20
N. A. Folland c Rhodes b Tolley	22	– not out	82
*C. J. Tavaré c Haynes b Stemp	3	– c Leatherdale b D'Oliveira	18
†N. D. Burns lbw b Newport	5	– c Curtis b Stemp	6
G. D. Rose c Rhodes b Stemp	51	– not out	11
K. H. MacLeay lbw b Stemp	19		
R. P. Snell b Newport	75		
N. A. Mallender c Radford b Stemp	7		
A. R. Caddick not out	54		
H. R. J. Trump c Tolley b Radford	28		
B 6, l-b 19, w 1, n-b 7	33	L-b 2	2

1/19 2/41 3/63 4/63 5/81   328   1/40 2/91   (4 wkts dec.) 175
6/127 7/183 8/202 9/248   3/122 4/135

Bonus points – Somerset 3, Worcestershire 4 (Score at 100 overs: 260-9).

Bowling: *First Innings*—Radford 26.2–8–48–2; Newport 26–7–70–2; Stemp 40–14–112–5; Tolley 10–4–25–1; D'Oliveira 14.4–4–24–0; M. J. Weston 7–0–24–0. *Second Innings*—Radford 4–0–30–0; Newport 6–1–16–1; Tolley 5–1–17–0; Stemp 15–1–60–2; D'Oliveira 12.2–1–50–1.

Worcestershire

*T. S. Curtis lbw b Caddick	11	– b Rose	18
W. P. C. Weston c Snell b Mallender	12	– not out	66
D. A. Leatherdale c Lathwell b Trump	35	– c Folland b Mallender	27
D. B. D'Oliveira b Lathwell	65	– not out	13
G. R. Haynes lbw b Trump	64		
†S. J. Rhodes not out	18		
M. J. Weston not out	17		
B 5, l-b 11, n-b 12	28	L-b 4, w 1, n-b 1	6

1/33 2/33 3/89 4/171 5/228   (5 wkts dec.) 250   1/28 2/105   (2 wkts) 130

C. M. Tolley, P. J. Newport, N. V. Radford and R. D. Stemp did not bat.

Bonus points – Worcestershire 3, Somerset 2.

Bowling: *First Innings*—Mallender 18–4–35–1; Caddick 13–1–32–1; Snell 15–3–49–0; Trump 26–8–62–2; Rose 7–2–18–0; Lathwell 10–2–32–1; MacLeay 7–3–6–0. *Second Innings*—Mallender 9–2–17–1; Caddick 13–4–25–0; Snell 4–0–13–0; Rose 6–2–4–1; Trump 12–2–44–0; Lathwell 8–2–23–0.

Umpires: B. Leadbeater and G. A. Stickley.

SOMERSET v HAMPSHIRE

At Weston-super-Mare, August 21, 22, 24. Drawn. Somerset 4 pts, Hampshire 3 pts. Toss: Hampshire. Rain wiped out all but 9.3 overs of the second day and, after the usual arrangements left Hampshire a target of 324 in 97 overs, intervened again when only 19 had been bowled, ending the game and a promising-looking innings by Gower. The first day saw some fine batting. Lathwell reached 50 for the 11th time in 1992, and Tavaré hit his first century of the season, with 20 fours from 138 balls in all; he scored 106 between lunch and tea. Somerset earned their fourth batting point with only two wickets down. Hampshire's bowlers then struck back.

Close of play: First day, Hampshire 6-0 (T. C. Middleton 4*, K. D. James 2*); Second day, Hampshire 22-1 (T. C. Middleton 6*, D. I. Gower 10*).

Somerset

A. N. Hayhurst run out	82	N. A. Mallender lbw b Udal	7
M. N. Lathwell b Marshall	73	A. R. Caddick not out	0
*C. J. Tavaré c Aymes b Udal	115		
R. J. Turner not out	41	B 8, l-b 18, n-b 1	27
†N. D. Burns c Aymes b Marshall	0		
G. D. Rose lbw b Marshall	1	1/116 2/238 3/302	(8 wkts dec.) 370
K. H. MacLeay lbw b Udal	23	4/303 5/311 6/344	
R. P. Snell b Bakker	1	7/349 8/368	

A. P. van Troost did not bat.

Bonus points – Somerset 4, Hampshire 3.

Bowling: Marshall 22–6–47–3; Bakker 15–6–51–1; Connor 12–0–61–0; Udal 29–1–90–3; James 16–1–70–0; Nicholas 6–0–25–0.

Somerset forfeited their second innings.

Hampshire

T. C. Middleton not out	27	– lbw b Caddick	5
K. D. James c Turner b Mallender	2	– not out	12
D. I. Gower not out	14	– not out	42
L-b 1, n-b 3	4	L-b 2, n-b 1	3

1/9	(1 wkt dec.) 47	1/9	(1 wkt) 62

R. M. F. Cox, *M. C. J. Nicholas, M. D. Marshall, J. R. Wood, †A. N. Aymes, S. D. Udal, C. A. Connor and P. J. Bakker did not bat.

Bowling: *First Innings*—Mallender 8.3–2–17–1; Caddick 8–4–4–0; Turner 1.1–0–11–0; Tavaré 1–0–14–0. *Second Innings*—Mallender 6–1–21–0; Caddick 8–3–19–1; Snell 4–0–19–0; van Troost 1–0–1–0.

Umpires: B. Leadbeater and G. A. Stickley.

At Derby, August 26, 27, 28, 29. SOMERSET lost to DERBYSHIRE by 121 runs.

At The Oval, August 31, September 1, 2, 3. SOMERSET drew with SURREY.

SOMERSET v DURHAM

At Taunton, September 7, 8, 9. Somerset won by eight wickets. Somerset 24 pts, Durham 3 pts. Toss: Durham. Durham's defeat with more than a day to spare was the price they paid for failing to exploit a well-grassed pitch. Somerset amassed 534, with centuries from Hayhurst, Harden and, most rapidly, Tavaré, who faced only 160 balls. Mallender and Caddick made no mistake, reducing the visitors to 69 for six, with Scott retired because of a broken finger. Only Smith, with a forthright 110, his first hundred for Durham, from 109 balls, responded in kind, though there were spirited contributions from Graveney and Hughes late on. By the close of the second day Durham had followed on and lost another three wickets. But a brave innings from Championship newcomer Daley provided welcome support for Larkins, who reached his 53rd century, despite needing a runner after a knee strain. Together they added 201 in 65 overs. Once they went only Botham's 71-ball 74, with 14 fours, made Somerset bat again. Their victory exactly reversed the result of the previous encounter in Darlington.

Close of play: First day, Somerset 398-5 (C. J. Tavaré 46*, G. D. Rose 11*); Second day, Durham 98-3 (W. Larkins 48*, J. A. Daley 25*).

Somerset

A. N. Hayhurst c Scott b Hughes	102	– c Graveney b Brown	8
M. N. Lathwell c Daley b Henderson	50	– c Parker b Brown	8
R. J. Harden c Henderson b Smith	126		
*C. J. Tavaré c Parker b Brown	124		
R. J. Turner c Parker b Hughes	0		
†N. D. Burns c Graveney b Bainbridge	54	– (3) not out	8
G. D. Rose c Daley b Smith	33	– (4) not out	1
R. P. Snell c Smith b Hughes	0		
N. A. Mallender b Hughes	1		
A. R. Caddick c sub b Brown	35		
A. P. van Troost not out	0		
L-b 5, w 4	9		

1/96 2/285 3/285 4/287 5/375   **534**   1/16 2/17   (2 wkts) 25
6/450 7/450 8/454 9/514

Bonus points – Somerset 4, Durham 1 (Score at 100 overs: 362-4).

Bowling: *First Innings*—Botham 11–2–45–0; Brown 22.1–3–115–2; Henderson 23–5–110–1; Hughes 32–5–112–4; Graveney 12–1–46–0; Bainbridge 14–5–31–1; Smith 21–6–70–2. *Second Innings*—Brown 3–0–13–2; Henderson 2–0–12–0.

Durham

W. Larkins c Burns b Mallender	0	– lbw b Lathwell	117
P. W. G. Parker c Snell b Caddick	16	– c Mallender b Caddick	10
I. Smith c Rose b Snell	110	– c Burns b Snell	7
P. Bainbridge c Burns b Caddick	0	– c Tavaré b Snell	0
J. A. Daley lbw b Mallender	5	– c Harden b Caddick	88
†C. W. Scott not out	10	– absent injured	
P. W. Henderson c and b Mallender	0	– c Burns b Caddick	0
I. T. Botham b Mallender	4	– (6) c Lathwell b Mallender	74
*D. A. Graveney c Burns b Caddick	29	– (8) c Tavaré b Caddick	3
S. P. Hughes c Snell b Mallender	24	– (9) hit wkt b Snell	4
S. J. E. Brown b Caddick	8	– (10) not out	19
B 4, l-b 2, n-b 7	13	L-b 10, n-b 7	17

1/0 2/23 3/23 4/44 5/61   **219**   1/12 2/29 3/29 4/230 5/234   **339**
6/69 7/175 8/185 9/197   6/255 7/279 8/309 9/339

Bonus points – Durham 2, Somerset 4.

In the first innings C. W. Scott, when 4, retired hurt at 50 and resumed at 197.

Bowling: *First Innings*—Mallender 13.4–2–65–5; Caddick 14–1–62–4; Snell 9–2–39–1; van Troost 4–0–31–0; Rose 4–1–16–0. *Second Innings*—Caddick 24–9–53–4; Snell 22–3–81–3; Rose 19–2–75–0; van Troost 4–0–22–0; Lathwell 12–2–41–1; Mallender 13.1–3–26–1; Hayhurst 8–0–31–0.

Umpires: R. Julian and G. Sharp.

SOMERSET v NOTTINGHAMSHIRE

At Taunton, September 12, 13, 14, 15. Somerset won by an innings and 163 runs. Somerset 24 pts, Nottinghamshire 4 pts. Toss: Somerset. Somerset's batsmen continued their phenomenal late-season form. Up to September 7 they had four first-class centuries between them; in their last two matches the tally rose to ten. Harden and Tavaré each scored a second hundred in consecutive innings, as they shared 265 in 71 overs against a damp ball on a wintry second day; Harden's 187 was a career-best and included 25 fours. Then Turner's maiden century took Somerset to 616, their highest first score at Taunton. It made Nottinghamshire's 265 on the first day look very skimpy, and that total was only made possible by Robinson, who was dropped when eight, and Archer, unbeaten on 83. Needing 351 to avoid an innings defeat, Nottinghamshire began promisingly. But when Pollard was run out by substitute Kerr's direct throw, Robinson and Crawley were swiftly removed. Caddick made two early breakthroughs next morning and Trump concluded with a spell of four for seven in 14 balls, including the wicket of Saxelby, who had resisted for nearly four hours. Nottinghamshire were beaten before lunch, but as Leicestershire and Derbyshire also lost, they claimed fourth place in the Championship.

Close of play: First day, Somerset 27-0 (A. N. Hayhurst 12*, M. N. Lathwell 12*); Second day, Somerset 342-3 (R. J. Harden 150*, R. J. Turner 12*); Third day, Nottinghamshire 100-3 (M. Saxelby 36*, S. Bramhall 3*).

Nottinghamshire

P. R. Pollard c Trump b Mallender	5	– run out	42
M. Saxelby c Burns b Rose	26	– c Rose b Trump	64
*R. T. Robinson c Tavaré b Trump	74	– b Rose	0
M. A. Crawley c Trump b Caddick	0	– b Caddick	9
G. F. Archer not out	83	– (6) c Lathwell b Caddick	0
C. C. Lewis c Harden b Caddick	1	– (7) lbw b Caddick	15
K. P. Evans c sub b Trump	27	– (8) not out	23
†S. Bramhall c Burns b Mallender	22	– (5) b Mallender	6
D. B. Pennett run out	4	– lbw b Trump	6
R. A. Pick c Turner b Trump	7	– c and b Trump	6
J. A. Afford c Burns b Caddick	0	– b Trump	0
B 2, l-b 8, n-b 6	16	B 4, l-b 7, n-b 6	17
	265		**188**

1/10 2/54 3/64 4/156 5/157
6/196 7/239 8/253 9/261

1/76 2/76 3/96 4/104 5/105
6/130 7/170 8/178 9/188

Bonus points – Nottinghamshire 3, Somerset 4.

Bowling: *First Innings*—Mallender 16-4-50-2; Caddick 20.5-4-69-3; Snell 9-3-18-0; Rose 15-3-48-1; Hayhurst 8-4-23-0; Trump 24-7-47-3. *Second Innings*—Caddick 22-4-61-3; Mallender 13-3-31-1; Trump 22-5-53-4; Rose 13-4-32-1.

Somerset

A. N. Hayhurst c Lewis b Evans	13	R. P. Snell c Robinson b Lewis ... 23
M. N. Lathwell c Bramhall b Evans	27	N. A. Mallender not out ... 29
R. J. Harden c Pollard b Evans	187	B 17, l-b 15, w 3, n-b 5 ... 40
*C. J. Tavaré c Afford b Lewis	125	
R. J. Turner not out	101	1/29 2/44 3/309 (7 wkts dec.) **616**
†N. D. Burns c Bramhall b Evans	31	4/411 5/454
G. D. Rose c Afford b Crawley	40	6/530 7/558

A. R. Caddick and H. R. J. Trump did not bat.

Bonus points – Somerset 4, Nottinghamshire 1 (Score at 100 overs: 342-3).

Bowling: Pick 21-2-89-0; Lewis 41-8-103-2; Evans 30-6-96-4; Afford 39-8-151-0; Pennett 15-0-85-0; Crawley 16-5-60-1.

Umpires: D. J. Constant and G. Sharp.

SURREY

Patron: HM The Queen
President: 1992 – D. F. Cox
            1993 – Sir John Stocker
Chairman: D. H. Newton
Chairman, Cricket Committee: A. Long
Chief Executive:
    The Oval, London SE11 5SS
    (Telephone: 071-582 6660)
Captain: A. J. Stewart
Coach: G. G. Arnold
Assistant Coach: G. S. Clinton

Surrey had a disappointing season, which was overshadowed at the end when they were punished by the Test and County Cricket Board for ball-tampering. The county launched their own enquiry and admitted not merely the three offences which had been reported – one in each of the past three seasons – but a fourth as well.

The club were fined £1,000, which was suspended for two years, by the TCCB. They had been reported for breaking both Law 42.5 (changing the condition of the ball) and 42.4 (lifting the seam) against Gloucestershire at Cheltenham in 1990, Yorkshire at Guildford in 1991 and Leicestershire at The Oval in 1992. The fourth occasion was the preceding game at Guildford, against Gloucestershire, in 1991. The upshot was that Surrey undertook that in future the ball would be returned to the umpire at the end of every over and the fall of a wicket, and they recommended that all other counties adopt a similar procedure. Derek Newton, the Surrey chairman, said the captain would be held responsible for any contravention by his players.

So it was not an entirely happy first season in charge for Alec Stewart, Ian Greig's successor as captain, despite all his successes with England. Thirteenth place in the County Championship was thoroughly unsatisfactory, especially after a mid-season spurt had taken them from bottom in late June into sixth place in early August. Successive defeats by Lancashire and Leicestershire then dragged them back down and they only won one more match. Of the nine Championship matches on the bland pitches at The Oval, only three produced a definite result and each of these had to be contrived. Surrey also lost in the first round of the NatWest Trophy against Glamorgan, although a century by David Ward took them tantalisingly close. But they had their moments in the other one-day competitions, losing narrowly to Kent in the Benson and Hedges semi-final and finishing fourth in the Sunday League, their highest position ever.

And there were compensations elsewhere. Out of the shadows stepped Alistair Brown, precocious, prolific and as yet thoroughly unspoiled by the grind of the county circuit. He immediately established himself as a favourite of the crowd. His three centuries took 79, 71 and 78 balls and Surrey hope they have unearthed not merely a major talent but a genuine entertainer. Graham Thorpe was a master of consistency with 13 half-centuries but it was the end of August before he reached his first Championship century, against Somerset, which he then made into his first-ever double-century. Monte Lynch was a reliable captain when Stewart was away on Test duty and he returned to his fluent and elegant best as a batsman with three hundreds.

Inevitably, the bowling suffered from Waqar Younis's absence with the Pakistanis. His replacement, the South African Rudi Bryson, had a disastrous year with only 17 Championship wickets, which cost 69 each. His batting was slightly more helpful. Joey Benjamin, the West Indian-born, England-qualified paceman signed from Warwickshire in the winter, made much more impact, taking 45 wickets and bowling more overs in the Championship than anyone except Martin Bicknell. After a faltering start, Bicknell himself surged to 71 wickets, while the slow left-arm bowler Neil Kendrick took 51, including a career-best six for 61 against Leicestershire. Kendrick was well supported by the off-spinner James Boiling who, apart from picking up 45 wickets, repeatedly demonstrated why he is regarded as one of the country's finest gully fielders. In January Boiling was called up for the England A tour, when Ian Salisbury joined the senior team in India.

The failures of the first team disguised the way in which Surrey's youth policy was starting to pay dividends. The Second Eleven, crammed with talent, won both their competitions. Mark Butcher looked an all-rounder of great promise and good things are also expected of Adam Hollioake. The problem area is that of wicket-keeper. David Ligertwood played four games as an opener and keeper but made few runs and was subsequently released. Neil Sargeant also failed to claim a regular place; though he is a doughty batsman who helped Mark Feltham save the game after Allan Donald had reduced Surrey to 45 for six at Guildford, the club did not think he was doughty enough. Stewart himself took over at the end of the season. Like England, Surrey seem to want someone to make a major contribution with the bat before going out to give a virtuoso performance behind the stumps. That is unrealistic and many good cricketers are going to be lost to the game if the trend continues.

In the winter, Feltham decided to join Middlesex. Jonathan Robinson, an all-rounder who had been promising much for too long, also went, as did the secretary David Seward. The timing of Seward's resignation was unfortunate, coming as it did just before the start of the internal inquiry. However, he insisted that his departure had nothing to do with the ball-tampering affair: he had simply found another job at a golf club. The saddest departure was that of Keith Medlycott, who was turned out little more than two years after he toured the West Indies with England without making a first-team appearance all season. He went out with a brief, bright blaze when he picked up four wickets in the second team's triumph in the Bain Clarkson final. – David Llewellyn.

SURREY 1992

[Bill Smith]

Back row: A. W. Smith, D. G. C. Ligertwood, M. A. Butcher, J. Boiling, A. J. Hollioake, M. R. Bainbridge, N. F. Sargeant. Middle row: M. R. L. W. Ayers (scorer), G. S. Clinton (assistant coach), J. D. Robinson, A. D. Brown, A. J. Murphy, R. I. Alikhan, P. D. Atkins, J. E. Benjamin, N. M. Kendrick, G. G. Arnold (county coach), J. Deary (physiotherapist). Front row: G. P. Thorpe, M. A. Feltham, D. J. Bicknell, D. M. Ward, A. J. Stewart (captain), M. A. Lynch, I. A. Greig, K. T. Medlycott, M. P. Bicknell. Inset: R. E. Bryson.

SURREY RESULTS

All first-class matches – Played 23: Won 6, Lost 7, Drawn 10.

County Championship matches – Played 22: Won 5, Lost 7, Drawn 10.

Bonus points – Batting 56, Bowling 50.

Competition placings – Britannic Assurance County Championship, 13th;
NatWest Bank Trophy, 1st round; Benson and Hedges Cup, s-f;
Sunday League, 4th.

BRITANNIC ASSURANCE CHAMPIONSHIP AVERAGES

BATTING

	Birthplace	M	I	NO	R	HS	Avge
A. D. Brown	*Beckenham*	11	16	1	740	175	49.33
‡G. P. Thorpe	*Farnham*	22	39	3	1,749	216	48.58
‡M. A. Lynch	*Georgetown, BG*	22	39	6	1,404	107	42.54
‡A. J. Stewart	*Merton*	13	24	3	766	140	36.47
‡D. J. Bicknell	*Guildford*	22	40	5	1,176	120*	33.60
‡D. M. Ward	*Croydon*	17	28	5	756	138	32.86
‡M. A. Feltham........	*St John's Wood*	12	17	5	392	50	32.66
P. D. Atkins	*Aylesbury*	7	14	0	382	99	27.28
J. D. Robinson	*Epsom*	9	17	5	307	65*	25.58
‡M. P. Bicknell	*Guildford*	18	25	8	426	88	25.05
R. E. Bryson§	*Springs, SA*	10	13	2	257	76	23.36
J. Boiling	*New Delhi, India*	18	21	11	190	29	19.00
N. M. Kendrick	*Bromley*	16	20	4	300	55	18.75
A. J. Murphy........	*Manchester*	5	5	2	45	32	15.00
N. F. Sargeant	*Hammersmith*	14	19	4	176	30	11.73
J. E. Benjamin.......	*Christ Church, St Kitts*	18	18	8	116	42	11.60
D. G. C. Ligertwood ..	*Oxford*	4	7	0	63	28	9.00

Also batted: R. I. Alikhan (*Westminster*) (1 match) 1, 10; M. A. Butcher (*Croydon*) (2 matches) 5*, 47; I. J. Ward (*Plymouth*) (1 match) 0.

* *Signifies not out.*   ‡ *Denotes county cap.*   § *Overseas player.*

The following played a total of 12 three-figure innings for Surrey in County Championship matches – A. D. Brown 3, M. A. Lynch 3, G. P. Thorpe 2, D. M. Ward 2, D. J. Bicknell 1, A. J. Stewart 1.

BOWLING

	O	M	R	W	BB	5W/i	Avge
M. P. Bicknell	597.5	107	1,734	67	6-107	4	25.88
J. D. Robinson	93.4	14	341	13	3-22	0	26.23
N. M. Kendrick	557.1	161	1,464	48	6-61	3	30.50
J. Boiling	557.2	143	1,506	41	6-84	1	36.73
J. E. Benjamin	582.2	94	1,780	45	6-30	2	39.55
M. A. Feltham	310.1	57	1,071	23	4-75	0	46.56
A. J. Murphy	178.4	34	531	11	3-97	0	48.27
R. E. Bryson	305.4	36	1,165	17	5-117	1	68.52

Also bowled: D. J. Bicknell 9.2-0-90-0; A. D. Brown 16-1-78-0; M. A. Butcher 44-10-115-1; M. A. Lynch 21-4-85-1; A. J. Stewart 7-1-14-0; G. P. Thorpe 17.4-5-79-0; D. M. Ward 4-0-16-0; I. J. Ward 8-0-35-0.

Wicket-keepers: N. F. Sargeant 35 ct, 6 st; D. G. C. Ligertwood 7 ct, 1 st; A. J. Stewart 8 ct.

Leading Fielders: M. A. Lynch 23, J. Boiling 18, G. P. Thorpe 17.

SURREY v YORKSHIRE

At The Oval, April 25, 27, 28, 29. Drawn. Surrey 2 pts, Yorkshire 8 pts. Toss: Yorkshire. On the washed-out third day Yorkshire's first imported star, the Indian Sachin Tendulkar, flew in and gave a series of press conferences. However, his new colleagues dominated the other days so thoroughly that at first Yorkshire seemed to have little urgent need of him. Moxon and Metcalfe began the game by putting together their 20th century opening partnership, and their third over 200. But on the way Moxon broke his right index finger, and Jarvis later strained a hamstring. This – along with the weather and some determined batting by Stewart – impeded Yorkshire's hopes of forcing a victory after Gough and Carrick had bowled Surrey out for 164, their lowest total at home since 1990, and enforced the follow-on. This would have come much earlier but for a last-wicket stand of 60, which included three sixes from the No. 11, Murphy. Yorkshire had declared their own innings as soon as Carrick had scored his 10,000th first-class run, having taken his 1,000th wicket in 1991. The only other current player to have achieved this double was Ian Botham.

Close of play: First day, Yorkshire 273-3 (S. A. Kellett 15*, P. W. Jarvis 19*); Second day, Surrey 6-2 (A. J. Stewart 5*, G. P. Thorpe 0*); Third day, No play.

Yorkshire

*M. D. Moxon c Lynch b Benjamin	141	P. Carrick not out	6
A. A. Metcalfe lbw b Murphy	73	D. Gough b Kendrick	6
S. A. Kellett c Sargeant b Benjamin	49	J. D. Batty not out	0
D. Byas c Thorpe b Kendrick	1	B 3, l-b 11, n-b 25	39
P. W. Jarvis c Sargeant b Benjamin	62		
†R. J. Blakey lbw b Kendrick	12	1/221 2/242 3/253	(9 wkts dec.) 495
A. P. Grayson c Thorpe b Kendrick	57	4/347 5/359 6/378	
C. S. Pickles run out	49	7/482 8/482 9/494	

Bonus points – Yorkshire 4, Surrey 1 (Score at 100 overs: 311-3).

Bowling: Bryson 38-9-120-0; Benjamin 44-13-107-3; Murphy 41.4-9-121-1; Kendrick 35-10-89-4; Thorpe 9-2-44-0.

Surrey

D. J. Bicknell b Jarvis	0	– b Pickles	10
R. I. Alikhan lbw b Gough	1	– lbw b Batty	10
*A. J. Stewart c Blakey b Gough	15	– not out	29
G. P. Thorpe b Pickles	21		
M. A. Lynch lbw b Gough	24	– (4) not out	5
D. M. Ward c Byas b Carrick	6		
†N. F. Sargeant c Byas b Gough	3		
N. M. Kendrick not out	31		
R. E. Bryson c Batty b Carrick	4		
J. E. Benjamin c Blakey b Carrick	19		
A. J. Murphy lbw b Carrick	32		
B 3, l-b 5	8	B 7, l-b 1, w 1, n-b 1	10

1/0 2/6 3/33 4/43 5/58	164	1/12 2/42 (2 wkts) 64
6/70 7/71 8/78 9/104		

Bonus points – Surrey 1, Yorkshire 4.

Bowling: *First Innings*—Jarvis 3.1-0-14-1; Gough 18-6-43-4; Pickles 15.5-5-28-1; Carrick 26.5-7-60-4; Batty 4-0-11-0. *Second Innings*—Gough 4-0-16-0; Pickles 8-2-16-1; Batty 12-5-18-1; Carrick 6-2-6-0.

Umpires: J. H. Hampshire and K. E. Palmer.

At Northampton, May 7, 8, 9, 11. SURREY drew with NORTHAMPTONSHIRE.

At Cambridge, May 15, 16, 18. SURREY beat CAMBRIDGE UNIVERSITY by 140 runs.

At Southampton, May 19, 20, 21, 22. SURREY lost to HAMPSHIRE by ten wickets.

At Lord's, May 23, 25, 26. SURREY drew with MIDDLESEX.

SURREY v SUSSEX

At The Oval, May 29, 30, June 1. Drawn. Surrey 6 pts, Sussex 7 pts. Toss: Surrey. The weather ensured another disappointing draw for Surrey, by now bottom of the table. Their attack was flogged round the field by the Sussex captain Wells, who took his total in successive innings to 309 for once out. Wells batted more than five hours, with two sixes and 17 fours. Before he had reached his hundred, Martin Bicknell was ordered out of the attack in mid-over by umpire Oslear for running on the pitch too often; his brother Darren completed the over. Stewart responded for Surrey by launching a high-class assault on the leg-spin of Salisbury, who had just been named, along with Stewart, in the England squad for the First Test. Stewart hit 24 fours, seven of them off Salisbury, in a stay of only 125 balls and two and a quarter hours. With the game dead on the last day, Lynch and Thorpe took the opportunity to bat themselves into form.

Close of play: First day, Sussex 99-3 (A. P. Wells 48*, M. P. Speight 9*); Second day, Surrey 203-4 (G. P. Thorpe 7*, M. A. Feltham 12*).

Sussex

D. M. Smith c Thorpe b M. P. Bicknell	4
J. W. Hall c Kendrick b M. P. Bicknell	32
N. J. Lenham b M. P. Bicknell	0
*A. P. Wells not out	165
M. P. Speight c Boiling b M. P. Bicknell	12
†P. Moores run out	20
F. D. Stephenson c Stewart b Kendrick	1
J. A. North not out	53
L-b 3, w 1, n-b 9	13

1/4 2/4 3/66   (6 wkts dec.) 300
4/105 5/164 6/166

A. C. S. Pigott, I. D. K. Salisbury and A. N. Jones did not bat.

Bonus points – Sussex 4, Surrey 2.

Bowling: M. P. Bicknell 15.4–0–47–4; Benjamin 24–4–69–0; Feltham 18–2–71–0; Kendrick 18.2–6–56–1; Boiling 11–3–50–0; D. J. Bicknell 0.2–0–4–0.

Surrey

D. J. Bicknell c Wells b Jones	3
†D. G. C. Ligertwood b Salisbury	28
*A. J. Stewart lbw b Salisbury	140
D. M. Ward c Smith b Lenham	5
G. P. Thorpe b Lenham	53
M. A. Feltham b Pigott	24
M. A. Lynch c Moores b North	71
M. P. Bicknell c Wells b Salisbury	6
N. M. Kendrick not out	24
J. Boiling not out	16
B 1, l-b 14, w 1, n-b 10	26

1/9 2/162 3/183   (8 wkts dec.) 396
4/185 5/226 6/290
7/329 8/359

J. E. Benjamin did not bat.

Bonus points – Surrey 4, Sussex 3 (Score at 100 overs: 388-8).

Bowling: Stephenson 12–6–19–0; Jones 14–0–69–1; Pigott 14–4–41–1; Salisbury 17–5–87–3; North 13.3–1–59–1; Lenham 16–3–61–2; Wells 15–4–45–0.

Umpires: G. I. Burgess and D. O. Oslear.

SURREY v DERBYSHIRE

At The Oval, June 2, 3, 4. Drawn. Surrey 6 pts, Derbyshire 6 pts. Toss: Derbyshire. Rain came at the start of the final 20 overs to thwart a slim chance of a Derbyshire win. By then, Surrey, chasing 241 off 47 overs, were already struggling. Martin Bicknell had given Surrey an early advantage, despite having to bowl from the Vauxhall End past umpire Oslear, who had removed him from the attack for running on in the previous game. Oslear again issued a warning, but this time Bicknell adjusted his follow-through before anything more dramatic happened. Cork enhanced his credentials as an all-rounder with a disciplined 44 that lasted three and a quarter hours. The most dominant innings of the match came from Barnett, but only 65 of his unbeaten 140 came off front-line bowlers. The rest came, as both sides tried to set up the declaration, off the occasionals Darren Bicknell and Brown. It was a peculiarly cruel punishment for Brown to endure on his first-class début.

Close of play: First day, Derbyshire 248-9 (R. W. Sladdin 4*, O. H. Mortensen 4*); Second day, Derbyshire 9-0 (K. J. Barnett 6*, P. D. Bowler 3*).

Derbyshire

*K. J. Barnett c Thorpe b Benjamin	10	– not out	140
P. D. Bowler c Ligertwood b Benjamin	40	– c Lynch b Boiling	31
J. E. Morris c and b Boiling	36		
T. J. G. O'Gorman c Ligertwood b M. P. Bicknell	14	– (3) not out	63
C. J. Adams c Brown b M. P. Bicknell	9		
D. G. Cork lbw b M. P. Bicknell	44		
†K. M. Krikken c Kendrick b Feltham	8		
I. R. Bishop lbw b Boiling	32		
A. E. Warner c Thorpe b M. P. Bicknell	21		
R. W. Sladdin c Ligertwood b Benjamin	4		
O. H. Mortensen not out	4		
B 5, l-b 12, n-b 10	27	B 5, l-b 3, w 1, n-b 1	10

1/27 2/87 3/101 4/116 5/129   249   1/91   (1 wkt dec.) 244
6/140 7/193 8/231 9/244

Bonus points – Derbyshire 2, Surrey 3 (Score at 100 overs: 205-7).

Bowling: *First Innings*—M. P. Bicknell 24-4-56-4; Benjamin 29-3-80-3; Feltham 18-4-47-1; Kendrick 25-7-41-0; Boiling 15-11-8-2. *Second Innings*—M. P. Bicknell 7-0-31-0; Benjamin 9-0-33-0; Boiling 12-4-16-1; Kendrick 8-3-18-0; D. J. Bicknell 9-0-86-0; Brown 8.3-0-52-0.

Surrey

D. J. Bicknell c Krikken b Bishop	4	– retired hurt	14
†D. G. C. Ligertwood c Krikken b Mortensen	0	– lbw b Cork	19
G. P. Thorpe c Krikken b Sladdin	70	– b Cork	14
*M. A. Lynch lbw b Cork	8		
D. M. Ward c O'Gorman b Sladdin	37	– (4) not out	12
A. D. Brown c and b Sladdin	6	– (5) c Krikken b Cork	0
M. A. Feltham not out	43		
M. P. Bicknell c sub b Cork	37	– (6) not out	1
N. M. Kendrick b Cork	15		
J. Boiling run out	12		
J. E. Benjamin not out	4		
B 2, l-b 4, w 3, n-b 8	17	L-b 8, n-b 1	9

1/0 2/6 3/40 4/123 5/130   (9 wkts dec.) 253   1/48 2/57 3/59   (3 wkts) 69
6/134 7/219 8/237 9/249

Bonus points – Surrey 3, Derbyshire 4.

In the first innings M. A. Feltham, when 39, retired hurt at 211 and resumed at 249; in the second innings D. J. Bicknell retired hurt at 24.

Bowling: *First Innings*—Bishop 15–7–17–1; Mortensen 17–5–39–1; Cork 23.1–4–66–3; Warner 11–2–36–0; Sladdin 28–6–71–3; Barnett 5–0–18–0. *Second Innings*—Bishop 5–3–13–0; Mortensen 8–1–10–0; Warner 4–0–11–0; Cork 5.2–1–9–3; Sladdin 5–1–18–0.

Umpires: G. I. Burgess and D. O. Oslear.

SURREY v WORCESTERSHIRE

At The Oval, June 12, 13, 15. Drawn. Surrey 7 pts, Worcestershire 5 pts. Toss: Surrey. Worcestershire came close to marking this match with the outstanding negative achievement of batting through 100 overs without a batting bonus point. They passed 150 just in time. The excuse, on a benign pitch, was that Lampitt and Illingworth were fighting hard to save their team from following on after Lynch had compiled a century for Surrey and the early Worcestershire batting had crumpled to 95 for seven. Their more celebrated colleagues had been just as slow, Hick spending 51 balls over nine. Surrey adjusted the tempo before declaring and setting a target of 276 in 68 overs. This time Hick and Curtis showed some urgency. But when they went soon after tea Worcestershire went back to blocking.

Close of play: First day, Worcestershire 20-0 (T. S. Curtis 10*, A. C. H. Seymour 9*); Second day, Surrey 11-1 (D. J. Bicknell 9*, N. M. Kendrick 0*).

Surrey

D. J. Bicknell b Lampitt	36	– b Stemp	19
†D. G. C. Ligertwood c Rhodes b Newport	0	– lbw b Radford	1
*A. J. Stewart c Rhodes b Lampitt	42	– (7) not out	23
G. P. Thorpe c Leatherdale b Radford	28	– not out	69
M. A. Lynch b Newport	107	– c Seymour b Illingworth	9
J. D. Robinson c Hick b Moody	1	– c Moody b Illingworth	7
M. A. Feltham lbw b Moody	0		
N. M. Kendrick c Leatherdale b Newport	51	– (3) b Newport	38
M. P. Bicknell not out	19		
J. Boiling b Illingworth	0		
J. E. Benjamin not out	9		
B 2, l-b 4, n-b 2	8	L-b 2, n-b 1	3

1/2 2/65 3/94 4/120 5/135   (9 wkts dec.) 301   1/11 2/26 3/84   (5 wkts dec.) 169
6/135 7/266 8/277 9/278   4/101 5/119

Bonus points – Surrey 4, Worcestershire 4.

Bowling: *First Innings*—Radford 22–5–74–1; Newport 24.1–10–56–3; Illingworth 16–2–58–1; Lampitt 17–2–54–2; Moody 12–2–32–2; Stemp 8–0–21–0. *Second Innings*—Radford 11–3–25–1; Newport 9–2–23–1; Stemp 14–1–61–1; Illingworth 8–2–58–2.

Worcestershire

*T. S. Curtis c Ligertwood b Benjamin	27	– st Ligertwood b Kendrick	48
A. C. H. Seymour lbw b M. P. Bicknell	9	– lbw b Benjamin	8
G. A. Hick lbw b Feltham	9	– b M. P. Bicknell	73
T. M. Moody c Benjamin b Feltham	1	– b Kendrick	22
D. A. Leatherdale c Stewart b Boiling	10	– not out	37
S. R. Lampitt not out	71	– c Benjamin b Boiling	19
†S. J. Rhodes c Ligertwood b Benjamin	0	– c Feltham b Kendrick	0
P. J. Newport b M. P. Bicknell	15	– c and b Kendrick	0
R. K. Illingworth not out	39	– not out	5
L-b 7, n-b 7	14	B 4, n-b 3	7

1/20 2/41 3/45 4/63 5/64   (7 wkts dec.) 195   1/16 2/126 3/132 4/158   (7 wkts) 219
6/64 7/95   5/201 6/201 7/201

R. D. Stemp and N. V. Radford did not bat.

Bonus points – Worcestershire 1, Surrey 3 (Score at 100 overs: 157-7).

Bowling: *First Innings*—Benjamin 30–10–59–2; M. P. Bicknell 20–5–44–2; Kendrick 26–12–31–0; Feltham 13–7–15–2; Boiling 19–6–39–1. *Second Innings*—M. P. Bicknell 10–1–42–1; Benjamin 15–5–40–1; Feltham 8–0–39–0; Kendrick 24.4–8–60–4; Boiling 10–1–34–1.

Umpires: G. Sharp and D. R. Shepherd.

At Bath, June 19, 20, 22. SURREY lost to SOMERSET by nine wickets.

At Bristol, June 26, 27, 29. SURREY beat GLOUCESTERSHIRE by four wickets.

SURREY v NORTHAMPTONSHIRE

At The Oval, June 30, July 1, 2. Surrey won by five wickets. Surrey 20 pts, Northamptonshire 4 pts. Toss: Northamptonshire. Surrey achieved their second Championship victory of the summer hard on the heels of their first; as at Bristol, it came courtesy of Ward. After Northamptonshire set a tempting target of 251 in 48 overs on the third day of another rain-hit match, Ward raced to the fastest hundred of the season to date, from 70 balls in as many minutes. He smashed two sixes and his 14th boundary simultaneously brought up his first Championship hundred of the season and won the game with seven balls to spare. But Surrey owed something to Lamb, not only for the generous declaration but also for persisting with his spinners just when their innings looking like drifting into the doldrums. Ward's high-speed chase to 103 was in sharp contrast to Capel's first Championship century for nearly two years. Though the two men both reached 103, with 14 fours each, Capel needed a more sedate 222 minutes and 204 balls – three times as long.

Close of play: First day, Northamptonshire 229-4 (D. J. Capel 51*, K. M. Curran 22*); Second day, Surrey 62-0 (P. D. Atkins 25*, G. P. Thorpe 20*).

Northamptonshire

A. Fordham c Thorpe b M. P. Bicknell	39	– c Lynch b M. P. Bicknell	10
N. A. Felton c Robinson b M. P. Bicknell	5	– b M. P. Bicknell	8
R. J. Bailey c Robinson b Kendrick	40	– not out	45
*A. J. Lamb st Sargeant b Boiling	56	– b M. P. Bicknell	0
D. J. Capel c D. J. Bicknell b M. P. Bicknell	103	– c Sargeant b Benjamin	30
K. M. Curran c Lynch b M. P. Bicknell	31	– c Atkins b Boiling	3
†D. Ripley c Lynch b M. P. Bicknell	16	– b Boiling	0
A. R. Roberts c Sargeant b M. P. Bicknell	0	– not out	0
C. E. L. Ambrose not out	2		
L-b 9, n-b 11	20	L-b 1, n-b 5	6

1/18 2/88 3/94 4/180 5/282   (8 wkts dec.) 312   1/18 2/19 3/19   (6 wkts dec.) 102
6/305 7/305 8/312   4/68 5/84 6/85

J. P. Taylor and N. G. B. Cook did not bat.

Bonus points – Northamptonshire 4, Surrey 3.

Bowling: *First Innings*—M. P. Bicknell 30–5–107–6; Benjamin 22–3–83–0; Robinson 6–0–20–0; Kendrick 16–6–44–1; Boiling 21–4–49–1. *Second Innings*—Benjamin 8.4–0–59–1; M. P. Bicknell 7–3–11–3; Boiling 4–0–31–2.

Surrey

D. J. Bicknell retired hurt	14		
P. D. Atkins c Ripley b Taylor	27	– (1) lbw b Cook	48
G. P. Thorpe c Curran b Taylor	21	– b Cook	20
*M. A. Lynch not out	69	– c Ambrose b Cook	13
D. M. Ward not out	30	– not out	103
†N. F. Sargeant (did not bat)		– (2) c Ambrose b Taylor	16
J. D. Robinson (did not bat)		– (6) c and b Bailey	16
M. P. Bicknell (did not bat)		– (7) not out	30
L-b 2, n-b 1	3	B 1, l-b 5	6

1/64 2/65   (2 wkts dec.) 164   1/45 2/72 3/94   (5 wkts) 252
                                                    4/126 5/171

N. M. Kendrick, J. E. Benjamin and J. Boiling did not bat.

Bonus point – Surrey 1.

In the first innings D. J. Bicknell retired hurt at 29.

Bowling: *First Innings*—Ambrose 11–1–21–0; Taylor 14–2–52–2; Curran 10–1–41–0; Roberts 5–0–20–0; Capel 5–0–16–0; Cook 4–1–12–0. *Second Innings*—Ambrose 12.5–2–45–0; Taylor 10–1–42–1; Cook 15–0–83–3; Roberts 6–0–63–0; Bailey 2–1–5–1; Curran 1–0–8–0.

Umpires: J. H. Harris and R. Julian.

At Neath, July 3, 4, 6. SURREY beat GLAMORGAN by 50 runs.

SURREY v KENT

At Guildford, July 14, 15, 16. Kent won by 72 runs. Kent 19 pts, Surrey 8 pts. Toss: Kent. The 50th Championship match at Guildford deserved better than Surrey's lowest score on the Woodbridge Road ground, which ended a run of three consecutive wins. Defeat was all the more humiliating because Kent had followed on and Surrey began their fateful second innings needing a modest 149 off 43 overs. This was the second Championship match of the season in which a team had won after following on, Essex having done so against Hampshire a month earlier. In the first innings Surrey lost the services of the in-form David Ward for a couple of weeks after a delivery from Igglesden broke his right thumb. Benjamin achieved an admirable double, following his highest score, 42 in 42 balls, by taking five for 29 to equal his career-best bowling. Kent began to turn the match round on the second evening, when Trevor Ward hit an astonishing 95-ball hundred, with four sixes and ten fours, during an opening stand of 116 with Benson. Next day Hooper contributed a masterful century, his highest for Kent, with three sixes and ten fours. The only blemish was a chance on 31. But Kent could hardly have dared hope for victory until Surrey's batting fell into disrepute, throwing away nine wickets for 23 to lose with 6.4 overs to spare.

Close of play: First day, Surrey 236-5 (J. D. Robinson 24*, M. P. Bicknell 4*); Second day, Kent 145-2 (N. R. Taylor 4*, C. L. Hooper 23*).

Surrey

D. J. Bicknell c Marsh b Ealham	44	– lbw b Ealham	29
*A. J. Stewart c Marsh b Ellison	3	– c Igglesden b McCague	10
G. P. Thorpe lbw b Ealham	52	– c Ward b Ealham	14
M. A. Lynch c Ward b Igglesden	48	– run out	10
D. M. Ward retired hurt	12	– (7) c Ward b McCague	2
J. D. Robinson c McCague b Igglesden	30	– (5) c Fleming b Ellison	4
†N. F. Sargeant lbw b Hooper	29	– (6) lbw b Ellison	0
M. P. Bicknell c Marsh b McCague	4	– (9) b McCague	0
J. Boiling not out	11	– (10) not out	0
J. E. Benjamin b Ellison	42	– (8) b Igglesden	6
A. J. Murphy not out	5	– b Igglesden	0
L-b 9, w 3, n-b 9	21	L-b 1	1

1/19 2/106 3/122 4/177 5/232   (8 wkts dec.) 301   1/28 2/53 3/54 4/63 5/65   76
6/242 7/242 8/296   6/68 7/72 8/72 9/76

Bonus points – Surrey 4, Kent 3.

In the first innings D. M. Ward retired hurt at 178.

Bowling: *First Innings*—Igglesden 33–8–122–2; Ellison 19–3–47–2; Ealham 16–1–65–2; Hooper 5–2–7–1; McCague 23.1–7–51–1. *Second Innings*—Igglesden 11.2–2–34–2; McCague 12–4–21–3; Ealham 6–0–11–2; Ellison 7–2–9–2.

Kent

T. R. Ward c Thorpe b Benjamin	12	– c Sargeant b Boiling	103
*M. R. Benson lbw b M. P. Bicknell	0	– c Lynch b Boiling	14
N. R. Taylor c Sargeant b Benjamin	7	– lbw b Benjamin	4
C. L. Hooper b Benjamin	4	– c Boiling b M. P. Bicknell	131
G. R. Cowdrey c Sargeant b Benjamin	29	– c Boiling b Benjamin	3
M. V. Fleming lbw b Murphy	23	– c M. P. Bicknell b Murphy	5
†S. A. Marsh c Sargeant b M. P. Bicknell	3	– c Sargeant b M. P. Bicknell	17
M. A. Ealham c Boiling b M. P. Bicknell	22	– b Boiling	23
R. M. Ellison lbw b Benjamin	0	– not out	11
M. J. McCague c D. J. Bicknell b M. P. Bicknell	5	– c Sargeant b M. P. Bicknell	13
A. P. Igglesden not out	1	– lbw b M. P. Bicknell	0
L-b 4, n-b 7	11	L-b 2, n-b 6	8

1/2 2/22 3/24 4/36 5/62   117   1/116 2/121 3/166 4/188 5/193   332
6/67 7/97 8/97 9/114   6/244 7/302 8/308 9/332

Bonus points – Surrey 4.

Bowling: *First Innings*—M. P. Bicknell 16.2–3–47–4; Benjamin 15–3–29–5; Murphy 11–0–37–1. *Second Innings*—M. P. Bicknell 25.5–5–62–4; Benjamin 26–4–69–2; Murphy 20–4–71–1; Robinson 8–1–45–0; Boiling 25–5–83–3.

Umpires: J. H. Harris and G. A. Stickley.

SURREY v WARWICKSHIRE

At Guildford, July 17, 18, 20. Drawn. Surrey 6 pts, Warwickshire 6 pts. Toss: Warwickshire. Feltham's first fifty of the summer saved Surrey from a second consecutive defeat at Guildford after they were 45 for the loss of six wickets – all to the pace of Donald – and wicket-keeper Sargeant was struck on the jaw by a bouncer when the South African was looking for a seventh. X-rays revealed no fracture but he took no further part. Meanwhile some gritty tail-end batting had steered Surrey to within 99 of their target of 230 in 54 overs when bad light, followed by a torrential thunderstorm, ended play with just under seven overs to go. On the first day Ostler revealed his class with a career-best 192. His only weak shot was the attempted hook which ended his stay after nearly five hours, and he ran up 32 fours and one six with immaculate driving, cutting and pulling, before falling short of a double-hundred, and C. G. Greenidge's ground record, by eight runs.

Close of play: First day, Surrey 8-1 (A. J. Stewart 4*, J. Boiling 1*); Second day, Warwickshire 64-2 (D. P. Ostler 27*, K. J. Piper 0*).

Warwickshire

A. J. Moles c Sargeant b Feltham	15	– c Thorpe b Feltham	22
R. G. Twose c Robinson b Benjamin	55	– c Feltham b Benjamin	14
*T. A. Lloyd c Robinson b M. P. Bicknell	4	– (5) c D. J. Bicknell b Robinson	31
D. P. Ostler c Sargeant b Benjamin	192	– (3) c Sargeant b Benjamin	31
D. A. Reeve c Sargeant b M. P. Bicknell	6	– (6) c Boiling b Robinson	1
T. L. Penney not out	70	– (7) run out	5
N. M. K. Smith c D. J. Bicknell b Robinson	7	– (8) c Sargeant b Benjamin	30
†K. J. Piper not out	2	– (4) lbw b M. P. Bicknell	3
G. C. Small (did not bat)		– b Benjamin	3
A. A. Donald (did not bat)		– not out	32
T. A. Munton (did not bat)		– not out	7
B 4, l-b 4, n-b 13	21	B 5, l-b 3, n-b 11	19

1/35 2/44 3/92 4/128   (6 wkts dec.) 372   1/26 2/57 3/69   (9 wkts dec.) 198
5/342 6/363   4/83 5/93 6/109
                                        7/116 8/150 9/151

Bonus points – Warwickshire 4, Surrey 2.

Bowling: *First Innings*—M. P. Bicknell 25–5–79–2; Benjamin 23–1–95–2; Feltham 25–6–74–1; Boiling 14–2–77–0; Robinson 7–0–39–1. *Second Innings*—M. P. Bicknell 14–0–39–1; Benjamin 21–5–81–4; Feltham 15–4–48–1; Boiling 4–1–4–0; Robinson 8–2–18–2.

Surrey

D. J. Bicknell c Piper b Small	1	– c Moles b Donald	4
*A. J. Stewart run out	67	– lbw b Donald	4
J. Boiling lbw b Smith	17	– (10) not out	3
G. P. Thorpe lbw b Lloyd	86	– (3) c and b Donald	19
M. A. Lynch c Reeve b Smith	63	– (4) c Munton b Donald	13
A. D. Brown c Donald b Lloyd	56	– (5) lbw b Donald	0
J. D. Robinson not out	14	– (6) b Donald	4
M. A. Feltham not out	22	– (7) c Lloyd b Munton	50
†N. F. Sargeant (did not bat)		– (8) retired hurt	18
M. P. Bicknell (did not bat)		– (9) not out	11
B 2, l-b 11, n-b 2	15	L-b 5	5

1/7 2/53 3/120 4/228   (6 wkts dec.) 341   1/5 2/16 3/40 4/40   (7 wkts) 131
5/296 6/309   5/44 6/45 7/123

J. E. Benjamin did not bat.

Bonus points – Surrey 4, Warwickshire 2 (Score at 100 overs: 320-6).

In the second innings N. F. Sargeant retired hurt at 95.

Bowling: *First Innings*—Donald 12–4–34–0; Small 9–3–23–1; Munton 17–7–33–0; Smith 29–4–128–2; Lloyd 23.3–3–90–2; Reeve 13–5–20–0. *Second Innings*—Donald 15–3–49–6; Small 10–3–24–0; Munton 13.1–3–42–1; Smith 9–3–11–0.

Umpires: J. H. Harris and G. A. Stickley.

SURREY v NOTTINGHAMSHIRE

At The Oval, July 21, 22, 23. Nottinghamshire won by three wickets. Nottinghamshire 19 pts, Surrey 4 pts. Toss: Nottinghamshire. Greg Mike's first Championship innings of the season lasted just four balls, but it turned the match. He arrived at the crease with 11 deliveries remaining, and Nottinghamshire on 327 for five, chasing 352 off 68 overs. Mike hit three successive sixes and then holed out going for a fourth to win. Bryson dismissed French at the start of his last over, but Cairns and Evans scrambled home off the last ball. There was another fine example of hitting when Brown reached his maiden Championship hundred off 79 balls, striking 11 fours and one six, after his colleague Atkins had fallen one short of his in the first innings. Atkins was doubly frustrated, having been dismissed on 99 four years before, against Lancashire. He spent almost an hour on an agonising crawl from 90 to 99, while his acting-captain, Lynch, scored 62; later Lynch put team interests before his own century, declaring three runs short. Johnson soon showed the Surrey opener how to overcome the nervous 90s, when a crunching four took him to his first hundred of the season.

Close of play: First day, Surrey 150-1 (P. D. Atkins 72*, G. P. Thorpe 9*); Second day, Surrey 60-0 (P. D. Atkins 15*, A. D. Brown 45*).

Surrey

D. J. Bicknell c Johnson b Mike	60	– (1) b Mike	18
P. D. Atkins c Randall b Pennett	99	– c Pollard b Field-Buss	19
G. P. Thorpe c Pennett b Mike	35	– c Mike b Field-Buss	1
*M. A. Lynch not out	97	– (2) c Evans b Pennett	111
A. D. Brown c French b Crawley	22	– (5) c Mike b Field-Buss	27
J. D. Robinson not out	9	– (6) c and b Field-Buss	2
M. A. Feltham (did not bat)	–	(7) b Pennett	14
R. E. Bryson (did not bat)	–	(8) not out	20
†N. F. Sargeant (did not bat)	–	(9) not out	5
J. E. Benjamin (did not bat)	–		
L-b 5, w 1, n-b 5	11	L-b 2	2

1/118 2/191 3/267 4/323   (4 wkts dec.) 333   1/78 2/122 3/124   (7 wkts dec.) 219
                                                     4/169 5/178
                                                     6/184 7/194

J. Boiling did not bat.

Bonus points – Surrey 4, Nottinghamshire 1.

Bowling: *First Innings*—Cairns 9–0–25–0; Evans 23–4–61–0; Pennett 21–5–81–1; Mike 16–3–70–2; Field-Buss 15–2–69–0; Crawley 5–1–22–1. *Second Innings*—Mike 7–1–52–1; Evans 14–1–49–0; Field-Buss 15–0–71–4; Pennett 8–0–45–2.

Nottinghamshire

P. R. Pollard run out	10	– st Sargeant b Boiling	74
M. A. Crawley b Benjamin	0	– c Thorpe b Boiling	95
*R. T. Robinson not out	73	– (4) b Feltham	28
P. Johnson not out	107	– (3) lbw b Feltham	78
D. W. Randall (did not bat)	–	c Robinson b Feltham	25
C. L. Cairns (did not bat)	–	not out	17
G. W. Mike (did not bat)	–	c Brown b Feltham	18
†B. N. French (did not bat)	–	b Bryson	0
K. P. Evans (did not bat)	–	not out	5
L-b 1, n-b 10	11	L-b 4, n-b 8	12

1/3 2/16   (2 wkts dec.) 201   1/159 2/216 3/255   (7 wkts) 352
                                                    4/310 5/327
                                                    6/346 7/346

M. G. Field-Buss and D. B. Pennett did not bat.

Bonus points – Nottinghamshire 2.

Bowling: *First Innings*—Bryson 12–0–43–0; Benjamin 14–2–39–1; Feltham 12–1–63–0; Boiling 6–2–18–0; Robinson 11.1–1–36–0; Lynch 1–0–1–0. *Second Innings*—Bryson 17–1–80–1; Benjamin 10–1–40–0; Feltham 17–0–118–4; Boiling 24–3–110–2.

Umpires: V. A. Holder and R. A. White.

At Durham University, July 31, August 1, 3. SURREY beat DURHAM by seven wickets.

At Lytham, August 4, 5, 6. SURREY lost to LANCASHIRE by 86 runs.

SURREY v LEICESTERSHIRE

At The Oval, August 14, 15, 17. Leicestershire won by 72 runs. Leicestershire 22 pts, Surrey 6 pts. Toss: Leicestershire. Leicestershire regained second place in the Championship with three balls remaining. Victory came from two unlikely bowling heroes – Boon and Potter. Briers evidently felt that the 266 runs in 51 overs asked of Surrey was a stiff enough target to permit experiments with his attack. Slow left-armer Potter claimed four surprising second-innings wickets, but the most remarkable piece of bowling came from Boon. He had nine first-class wickets to his name when Briers threw the ball to him with ten overs left and Surrey 182 for six. Three overs later, Boon had taken two wickets, including the vital one of Lynch, who had reached 50 in 39 balls, without conceding a run. Parsons had helped to restrict Surrey's first-innings lead to two runs, after Kendrick had dominated the first day with a career-best six for 61. The home team owed almost half their total to Lynch's second hundred of the season; he hit two sixes and 16 fours.

Close of play: First day, Surrey 7-1 (P. D. Atkins 0*, J. Boiling 0*); Second day, Leicestershire 104-3 (V. J. Wells 16*, R. P. Gofton 0*).

Leicestershire

T. J. Boon lbw b Kendrick	48	– lbw b Kendrick	32
*N. E. Briers b M. P. Bicknell	6	– c Stewart b Benjamin	5
J. J. Whitaker c Boiling b Benjamin	46	– b M. P. Bicknell	48
V. J. Wells c Benjamin b Kendrick	56	– c Boiling b Kendrick	44
L. Potter b Stewart b M. P. Bicknell	24	– (6) not out	46
B. F. Smith c and b Kendrick	16		
P. N. Hepworth b Benjamin	2		
†P. A. Nixon b Kendrick	5	– (7) not out	3
G. J. Parsons b Kendrick	1		
R. P. Gofton c Atkins b Kendrick	1	– (5) b M. P. Bicknell	75
A. D. Mullally not out	3		
L-b 2, n-b 6	8	B 1, l-b 6, n-b 7	14
	216	(5 wkts dec.)	**267**

1/14 2/93 3/123 4/185 5/189
6/204 7/210 8/211 9/213

1/14 2/72 3/98 (5 wkts dec.) 267
4/158 5/263

Bonus points – Leicestershire 2, Surrey 4.

Bowling: *First Innings*—M. P. Bicknell 21-2-53-2; Benjamin 24-4-52-2; Murphy 11-2-33-0; Kendrick 28.5-10-61-6; Boiling 7-2-15-0. *Second Innings*—M. P. Bicknell 18-2-48-2; Benjamin 17-0-67-1; Kendrick 25-5-60-2; Murphy 12.3-0-44-0; Boiling 8-2-41-0.

Surrey

D. J. Bicknell lbw b Parsons	6	– c Gofton b Parsons	37
P. D. Atkins c Potter b Mullally	13	– c Hepworth b Mullally	4
J. Boiling c Hepworth b Parsons	13	– (10) not out	0
*†A. J. Stewart c Nixon b Mullally	1	– (3) lbw b Parsons	20
G. P. Thorpe c Parsons b Mullally	30	– (4) lbw b Parsons	44
M. A. Lynch st Nixon b Parsons	106	– (5) c Nixon b Boon	58
A. D. Brown c Nixon b Mullally	19	– (6) c and b Potter	1
M. P. Bicknell c Hepworth b Parsons	5	– (7) c sub b Potter	11
N. M. Kendrick lbw b Parsons	11	– c Nixon b Potter	0
J. E. Benjamin b Parsons	0	– (8) c and b Boon	1
A. J. Murphy not out	0	– c sub b Potter	8
B 2, l-b 7, w 1, n-b 4	14	L-b 9	9
	218		**193**

1/7 2/23 3/30 4/44 5/99
6/140 7/145 8/179 9/195

1/19 2/50 3/79 4/144 5/145
6/181 7/182 8/185 9/185

Bonus points – Surrey 2, Leicestershire 4.

Bowling: *First Innings*—Mullally 22-5-56-4; Parsons 26.3-5-70-6; Wells 6-1-14-0; Potter 13-3-38-0; Gofton 4-1-19-0; Hepworth 2-0-12-0. *Second Innings*—Mullally 8-4-18-1; Parsons 21-4-93-3; Potter 18.3-2-73-4; Boon 3-3-0-2.

Umpires: B. Dudleston and J. W. Holder.

At Colchester, August 18, 29, 20. SURREY drew with ESSEX.

At Bradford, August 21, 22, 24. SURREY beat YORKSHIRE by one wicket.

SURREY v SOMERSET

At The Oval, August 31, September 1, 2, 3. Drawn. Surrey 6 pts, Somerset 3 pts. Toss: Surrey. Thorpe's delighted jig down the wicket, arms raised, celebrated not just the first double-hundred of his career, but the end of a frustrating run. He had reached fifty 13 times in 34 Championship innings in 1992. His seven-and-a-half-hour 216 included surprisingly few fours – 16 – and came from 388 balls. Thorpe shared a breathtaking stand of 211 in 34 overs with the gifted Brown, who scored his third Championship hundred in his 13th innings. All three had been exceptionally fast; this time he took 78 balls to reach three figures, compared to 79 and 71 on the previous occasions. His 129 contained three sixes and 14 fours, and helped Surrey to a mountainous first-innings total. Dutchman van Troost was the only bowler to find any life in a stubbornly unyielding wicket, and was rewarded when he wrapped up the innings with four for one in 15 balls. Rose made a patient, career-best 132, which took nearly seven hours. It could not save Somerset from following on, but it helped stave off defeat. Lathwell, who had earlier passed 1,000 runs in his first full season, Tavaré and Turner, with nine runs over 101 minutes, kept Surrey out until bad weather ended play early.

Close of play: First day, Surrey 397-4 (G. P. Thorpe 151*, A. D. Brown 44*); Second day, Somerset 159-5 (R. J. Turner 20*, G. D. Rose 38*); Third day, Somerset 330-7 (G. D. Rose 126*, H. R. J. Trump 10*).

Surrey

D. J. Bicknell c Lathwell b Cottam	45	N. M. Kendrick lbw b van Troost		0
M. A. Lynch...				

D. J. Bicknell c Lathwell b Cottam 45
M. A. Ward c Rose b van Troost 25
G. P. Thorpe b van Troost 216
†A. J. Stewart b van Troost 76
M. A. Lynch c Lathwell b Trump 39
A. D. Brown c Caddick b Trump 129
M. A. Feltham c Lathwell b van Troost   6
M. P. Bicknell b Trump 2

N. M. Kendrick lbw b van Troost..... 0
J. Boiling not out................... 0
J. E. Benjamin b van Troost.......... 0

L-b 12, w 5, n-b 2............ 19

557

1/34 2/118 3/264 4/327 5/538
6/554 7/557 8/557 9/557

Bonus points – Surrey 4, Somerset 1 (Score at 100 overs: 317-3).

Bowling: Caddick 31-4-134-0; van Troost 28.4-2-104-6; Rose 25-5-93-0; Hayhurst 7-2-19-0; Trump 40-6-143-3; Cottam 14-2-35-1; Lathwell 2-0-17-0.

Somerset

A. N. Hayhurst lbw b M. P. Bicknell .... 5 – c Thorpe b Kendrick 14
M. N. Lathwell b Feltham .... 44 – c Thorpe b Kendrick 49
R. J. Harden lbw b M. P. Bicknell .... 0 – b Kendrick 4
C. J. Tavaré c Ward b Feltham .... 24 – not out.................... 43
†R. J. Turner c Lynch b Kendrick .... 45 – not out.................... 9
N. D. Burns lbw b Boiling 27
G. D. Rose c and b Feltham 132
A. R. Caddick c Thorpe b Boiling............ 37
H. R. J. Trump c and b M. P. Bicknell 18
P. C. Cottam c Stewart b Feltham 0
A. P. van Troost not out 6

B 2, l-b 4, n-b 8 14

L-b 2, n-b 3........ 5

352 (3 wkts) 124

1/14 2/14 3/68 4/73 5/104
6/232 7/288 8/342 9/342

1/56 2/69 3/70

Bonus points – Somerset 2, Surrey 2 (Score at 100 overs: 207-5).

Bowling: *First Innings*—M. P. Bicknell 31.1-11-68-3; Kendrick 43-13-90-1; Benjamin 23-5-54-0; Feltham 24-5-75-4; Boiling 30-9-55-2; Lynch 2-0-4-0. *Second Innings*—M. P. Bicknell 10-1-23-0; Feltham 6-1-20-0; Kendrick 22-11-38-3; Boiling 21-5-26-0; Brown 3.3-1-11-0; Lynch 1-0-4-0.

Umpires: J. D. Bond and R. Palmer.

At Nottingham, September 7, 8, 9, 10. SURREY lost to NOTTINGHAMSHIRE by five wickets.

SURREY v MIDDLESEX

At The Oval, September 12, 13, 14, 15. Drawn. Middlesex 4 pts. Toss: Middlesex. Tufne
began the final over of the season with Middlesex needing three wickets and Surrey 15 run.
Seven runs were scored from his first two balls, followed by two wickets, but Boilin
survived the last two deliveries for the draw. Surrey had been set 333 from 92 overs, afte
they declared their first innings on the final morning, and sent down 9.4 overs of occasion.
bowling while Gatting ran the 25 he needed for 2,000 runs in the season, without
boundary. Roseberry had reached the landmark on the first day, during his ninth century c
1992, but his first for seven weeks. Middlesex's first innings, which spread into the thir
day when most of the second was lost to rain, also featured hundreds from Carr an
Ramprakash, his third of the season. Surrey's South African bowler, Bryson, took fiv
wickets in a Championship innings for the first time, and later endeared himself to hom
fans with a lively 24 that took Surrey within eight runs of victory.
Close of play: First day, Middlesex 304-3 (M. R. Ramprakash 37*, M. W. Gatting 9*
Second day, Middlesex 344-4 (M. R. Ramprakash 57*, A. Habib 3*); Third day, Surre
141-3 (A. J. Stewart 51*, M. A. Lynch 24*).

Middlesex

M. A. Roseberry c I. J. Ward b Boiling	120		
J. D. Carr c Brown b Boiling	114		
M. R. Ramprakash lbw b Bryson	117		
†K. R. Brown c Kendrick b Boiling	8		
*M. W. Gatting c Lynch b Butcher	22	– (1) not out	2!
A. Habib c Stewart b Bryson	12	– (2) not out	:
P. N. Weekes b Bryson	11		
R. L. Johnson c Kendrick b Boiling	1		
J. E. Emburey b Bryson	2		
A. R. C. Fraser b Bryson	4		
P. C. R. Tufnell not out	7		
L-b 8, n-b 15	23		

1/209 2/276 3/293 4/325 5/368   441   (no wkt dec.) 3
6/426 7/427 8/429 9/433

Bonus points – Middlesex 3 (Score at 100 overs: 276-2).

Bowling: *First Innings*—Bryson 45.4–10–117–5; Butcher 34–7–95–1; I. J. Ward 8–0–35–0
Boiling 59–15–126–4; Kendrick 18–3–60–0. *Second Innings*—Stewart 5–0–13–0; D. M. War
4–0–16–0; Thorpe 0.4–0–3–0.

Surrey

D. M. Ward c Brown b Fraser	9	– (2) c Emburey b Weekes	34
D. J. Bicknell lbw b Johnson	5	– (1) st Brown b Emburey	8?
G. P. Thorpe c Brown b Weekes	45	– st Brown b Tufnell	1:
*†A. J. Stewart not out	51	– st Brown b Tufnell	5:
M. A. Lynch not out	24	– c Johnson b Tufnell	2!
A. D. Brown (did not bat)		– c Ramprakash b Tufnell	34
M. A. Butcher (did not bat)		– st Brown b Emburey	47
R. E. Bryson (did not bat)		– c Roseberry b Tufnell	24
I. J. Ward (did not bat)		– run out	(
N. M. Kendrick (did not bat)		– not out	(
J. Boiling (did not bat)		– not out	(
B 2, l-b 2, n-b 3	7	B 1, l-b 4, w 1, n-b 3	9

1/9 2/15 3/109   (3 wkts dec.) 141   1/58 2/83 3/153   (9 wkts) 32!
    4/200 5/229 6/269
    7/318 8/325 9/325

Bonus point – Middlesex 1.

Bowling: *First Innings*—Johnson 6–2–25–1; Fraser 10–1–40–1; Emburey 14–3–25–0
Tufnell 14–4–21–0; Weekes 6–0–26–1. *Second Innings*—Fraser 15–3–35–0; Johnso
8–0–46–0; Emburey 30–6–104–2; Tufnell 34–4–130–5; Weekes 5–3–5–1.

Umpires: J. C. Balderstone and M. J. Kitchen.

SUSSEX

President: The Duke of Richmond and Gordon
Chairman: A. M. Caffyn
Secretary: N. Bett
    County Ground, Eaton Road,
    Hove BN3 3AN
    (Telephone: 0273-732161)
Captain: A. P. Wells
Manager: N. Gifford
Coach: C. E. Waller

Sussex ended their first season under the captaincy of Alan Wells in seventh position in the County Championship, their best placing for seven years. Having won the wooden spoon twice in the previous five years, Sussex could be encouraged by that, but Wells was disappointed that the club failed to make more impact – "a season of could have beens", he called it. The team never had a hope of a Lord's final, failing to get past the zonal stages of the Benson and Hedges and going out to Warwickshire in the NatWest. The one competition in which they did make an impression was the Sunday League, where Sussex began with six successive wins out of seven, the other game being rained off. But then they fell apart, losing the next seven, and their spirit never recovered from a dramatic collapse at Worcester with the game apparently in their grasp.

Overall, Sussex were left to regret a barren spell in mid-season when they went from June 29 to August 10, playing 13 matches in all competitions and failing to win any of them. But the victory over Derbyshire, their first at Eastbourne for six years, helped lift the gloom and Sussex perked up in the last few weeks. Wells remains enthusiastic about the prospects for the future: "I want people to look back on the Alan Wells era of captaincy and say that was when things started to happen at the club. I am very ambitious that should be the case."

The most satisfying feature of the season was the outstanding form of the leg-spinner Ian Salisbury, who was chosen for two Test matches – the first Sussex player to play a Test for England since Tony Pigott more than eight years earlier. Though he was originally named only for the England A tour, Salisbury was later called up to join the main tour of India. His form got better and better. He took 87 first-class wickets in all, 49 of them in a glorious patch starting at the end of July and 23 in the final two games, when Sussex convincingly beat both Lancashire and Yorkshire, who both found him almost unplayable. With the new four-day programme starting in 1993, Sussex decided to emphasise spin further by offering a two-year contract to the off-spinner Eddie Hemmings, 44 this year and the oldest player on the county circuit. The Sussex cricket manager, Norman Gifford, who played himself until he was 48, has a high regard for Hemmings, who was sacked by Nottinghamshire and jumped at the opportunity of playing for a team which is taking his craft seriously. Sussex hope his experience will help the development of their young off-spinner Bradleigh Donelan.

The new overseas player was the West Indian Franklyn Stephenson who settled in quickly but was handicapped by a knee injury and did not quite reproduce the figures that made him the last player to do the 1,000 runs-100 wickets double when he was with Nottinghamshire four years earlier. Most of the other seam bowlers were plagued by injury or loss of form: Pigott, in his 15th year, took only 27 wickets, his lowest return in a full season; Adrian Jones was completely out of sorts most of the time and finished with only 11 wickets at a cost of almost 63 each while Colin Wells was plagued by injury and played only six matches. The most encouraging performances came from 21-year-old Ed Giddins, a tall bowler from Eastbourne with genuine pace and good action, who turned in a match-winning performance against Derbyshire on his home-town ground. Sussex are also looking for further development from the young all-rounders, Carlos Remy and John North, who both had back injuries and limited opportunities in 1992.

Five batsmen reached 1,000 runs in 1992 compared to three the previous year and Alan Wells led the way with 1,465, at an average just below 49, including five Championship centuries, three of them in succession in a ten-day period in late May and early June. His own form slumped when the team's did, which may not have been a coincidence. Opener Jamie Hall, who was rewarded with his county cap, and Martin Speight both made plenty of runs in contrasting styles, Speight dashing and adventurous, Hall more diligent. Neil Lenham made four figures for the third successive season, and David Smith got there for the third time in four years since joining Sussex.

On the financial side, Sussex's income exceeded £1 million for the first time and the club reported a pre-tax profit of £64,814, the seventh surplus in the last eight years. Attendances at Eastbourne again fell away, with takings down nearly £2,500 on the disappointing 1991 figures; with the reduced programme in 1993, the Saffrons will lose one fixture. Rain badly disrupted the game at Arundel Castle but the weather was kinder at Horsham, where Sussex beat Durham in a thrilling finish. In the absence of a beneficiary, Sussex set up a fund to develop youth cricket in the county and this was expected to realise about £90,000. – Jack Arlidge.

541

SUSSEX 1992

Back row: C. C. Remy, J. A. North, R. Hanley, A. R. Hansford, J. W. Dean. *Middle row:* N. Gifford (*coach*), B. Turner (*physiotherapist*), A. G. Robson, B. T. P. Donelan, E. S. H. Giddins, F. D. Stephenson, J. W. Hall, K. Greenfield, I. C. Waring (*youth development officer*), C. P. Cale (*assistant coach*), C. E. Waller (*Second Eleven coach*). *Front row:* I. D. K. Salisbury, M. P. Speight, A. C. S. Pigott, C. M. Wells, A. P. Wells (*captain*), D. M. Smith, A. N. Jones, P. Moores, N. J. Lenham.

[*Bill Smith*]

SUSSEX RESULTS

All first-class matches – Played 22: Won 6, Lost 7, Drawn 9.

County Championship matches – Played 22: Won 6, Lost 7, Drawn 9.

Bonus points – Batting 60, Bowling 61.

*Competition placings – Britannic Assurance County Championship, 7th;
NatWest Bank Trophy, 2nd round; Benson and Hedges Cup, 4th in Group A;
Sunday League, 11th equal.*

BRITANNIC ASSURANCE CHAMPIONSHIP AVERAGES

BATTING

	Birthplace	M	I	NO	R	HS	Avge
‡A. P. Wells	Newhaven	22	35	5	1,465	165*	48.83
‡J. W. Hall	Chichester	20	34	5	1,125	140*	38.79
‡M. P. Speight	Walsall	20	33	2	1,180	179	38.06
‡N. J. Lenham	Worthing	20	34	2	1,173	222*	36.65
‡D. M. Smith	Balham	19	33	2	1,076	213	34.70
‡P. Moores	Macclesfield	21	30	5	851	109	34.04
‡F. D. Stephenson§ . .	St James, Barbados	18	25	4	680	133	32.38
K. Greenfield	Brighton	6	10	2	205	48	25.62
‡C. M. Wells	Newhaven	6	7	1	133	39	22.16
B. T. P. Donelan . . .	Park Royal	16	25	6	421	68*	22.15
C. C. Remy	Castries, St Lucia	7	9	0	192	47	21.33
‡A. C. S. Pigott	London	17	19	7	191	27*	15.91
J. A. North	Slindon	5	7	1	81	53*	13.50
‡A. N. Jones	Woking	10	9	4	56	17	11.20
‡I. D. K. Salisbury . . .	Northampton	17	18	2	177	42	11.06
E. S. H. Giddins . . .	Eastbourne	11	8	6	15	10*	7.50
A. G. Robson	East Boldon	5	4	3	0	0*	0.00

Also batted: R. Hanley (*Tonbridge*) (1 match) 1; A. R. Hansford (*Burgess Hill*) (1 match) 1.

* Signifies not out.   ‡ Denotes county cap.   § Overseas player.

The following played a total of 19 three-figure innings for Sussex in County Championship
matches – M. P. Speight 5, A. P. Wells 5, N. J. Lenham 4, D. M. Smith 2, J. W. Hall 1,
P. Moores 1, F. D. Stephenson 1.

BOWLING

	O	M	R	W	BB	5W/i	Avge
I. D. K. Salisbury	678.3	169	2,135	79	7-54	6	27.02
E. S. H. Giddins	247.5	52	857	31	5-32	2	27.64
J. A. North	96.3	14	331	11	3-51	0	30.09
C. M. Wells	119	26	323	10	3-26	0	32.30
F. D. Stephenson	467.2	93	1,375	40	7-29	1	34.37
A. C. S. Pigott	363	74	1,063	27	3-34	0	39.37
B. T. P. Donelan	404	85	1,323	28	6-77	1	47.25
A. N. Jones	161.5	17	745	11	3-76	0	67.72

Also bowled: K. Greenfield 17-0-84-0; J. W. Hall 2-1-14-0; A. R. Hansford 29-5-81-3;
N. J. Lenham 120.1-28-362-6; C. C. Remy 96.2-12-336-6; A. G. Robson 119-24-405-8;
D. M. Smith 4-1-18-0; M. P. Speight 3-0-30-1; A. P. Wells 29-7-94-0.

Wicket-keepers: P. Moores 32 ct, 7 st; M. P. Speight 3 ct.

Leading Fielders: A. P. Wells 24, I. D. K. Salisbury 15.

At Southampton, April 25, 27, 28, 29. SUSSEX lost to HAMPSHIRE by 150 runs.

SUSSEX v SOMERSET

At Hove, May 7, 8, 9, 11. Drawn. Sussex 6 pts, Somerset 6 pts. Toss: Somerset. Somerset batted out the game to get a draw after an uneasy moment on the final morning when they were still 57 behind and effectively three wickets down: their captain Tavaré had returned to Taunton to be with his pregnant wife. However, a gritty stand of 114 between Hayhurst and Bartlett put Somerset ahead, and Burns and Mallender completed Sussex's frustration. No play had been possible on the third day. Somerset had suffered their own irritations earlier when Sussex had been rescued from 128 for seven by their new overseas player, Stephenson – formerly with Nottinghamshire – who hit 17 fours and made his highest score in England. Stands of 105 with Pigott and 102 with Salisbury turned a potential first-innings deficit into a lead of 82.

Close of play: First day, Somerset 264; Second day, Sussex 320-8 (F. D. Stephenson 128*, I. D. K. Salisbury 25*); Third day, No play.

Somerset

A. N. Hayhurst c and b Salisbury	20	– b Salisbury	55
K. H. MacLeay c Salisbury b Pigott	25	– b Robson	2
R. J. Harden c Moores b Robson	36	– c Moores b Salisbury	6
*C. J. Tavaré lbw b Stephenson	12		
R. J. Bartlett c and b Salisbury	41	– (4) lbw b Pigott	72
G. D. Rose c Robson b Donelan	65	– (5) c Pigott b Salisbury	27
†N. D. Burns not out	35	– (6) not out	35
N. A. Mallender lbw b Robson	6	– (7) not out	26
A. R. Caddick b Robson	3		
H. R. J. Trump lbw b Robson	2		
A. C. Cottam c Moores b Salisbury	3		
B 2, l-b 11, w 1, n-b 2	16	B 6, l-b 10, w 14	30
	264	(5 wkts dec.)	253

1/48 2/50 3/73 4/122 5/160
6/240 7/250 8/254 9/258

1/8 2/25 3/139
4/151 5/200

Bonus points – Somerset 3, Sussex 3 (Score at 100 overs: 251-7).

Bowling: *First Innings*—Stephenson 20–6–30–1; Robson 18–7–37–4; Salisbury 29.1–10–73–3; Pigott 17–3–39–1; C. M. Wells 16–2–29–0; Donelan 13–1–43–1. *Second Innings*—Stephenson 8–1–18–0; Robson 9–3–26–1; Pigott 13–3–28–1; Salisbury 34–6–106–3; Donelan 19–7–55–0; A. P. Wells 2–1–4–0; Hall 1–1–0–0; Smith 1–1–0–0.

Sussex

D. M. Smith lbw b Trump	47	A. C. S. Pigott lbw b Mallender	27
J. W. Hall b Caddick	3	I. D. K. Salisbury c Cottam b Caddick	42
M. P. Speight c Tavaré b Mallender	0	A. G. Robson not out	0
*A. P. Wells st Burns b Cottam	61		
C. M. Wells b Mallender	9	B 1, l-b 9, n-b 14	24
†P. Moores b Mallender	0		
F. D. Stephenson b Caddick	133		346
B. T. P. Donelan lbw b Mallender	0		

1/14 2/16 3/90 4/126 5/126
6/126 7/128 8/233 9/335

Bonus points – Sussex 3, Somerset 3 (Score at 100 overs: 287-8).

Bowling: Caddick 26.3–3–94–3; Mallender 27–6–86–5; Hayhurst 6–1–20–0; Rose 14–1–55–0; Trump 20–6–46–1; Cottam 23–7–35–1.

Umpires: R. C. Tolchard and P. B. Wight.

At Hove, May 16. SUSSEX beat PAKISTANIS by three wickets (See Pakistani tour section).

At Hove, May 17. SUSSEX lost to PAKISTANIS by 85 runs (See Pakistani tour section).

At Nottingham, May 20, 21, 22. SUSSEX drew with NOTTINGHAMSHIRE.

SUSSEX v KENT

At Hove, May 23, 25, 26. Kent won by four wickets. Kent 22 pts, Sussex 7 pts. Toss: Kent. Kent, set 336 to win in 54 overs, won with four balls to spare. But the finish was made possible only because Kent resolved the problem of playing a three-day match on a perfect pitch by sending down 75 ludicrous overs to set up the declaration; these included five overs for 53 by the wicket-keeper Marsh while Fleming kept wicket. The chief beneficiary was Lenham, who scored 222 not out with 26 fours and four sixes, his career-best. There were far worthier centuries earlier. Wells hit 144, an innings notable mainly for its concentration – rock music was blaring from a nearby park. Hooper's 121 was more carefree, took Kent to a first-innings lead and ended only when he hit his own wicket. Hooper was just as effective in the closing stages but the win was primarily set up by Benson, who reached 100 in only 82 balls in all. He faced 102 balls in all.

Close of play: First day, Sussex 335; Second day, Sussex 88-0 (J. W. Hall 40*, N. J. Lenham 25*).

Sussex

J. W. Hall c Marsh b Ellison	14	– c Marsh b Cowdrey	99
D. M. Smith c Ward b McCague	9	– not out	35
N. J. Lenham b Ealham	36	– not out	222
*A. P. Wells c Hooper b Fleming	144		
M. P. Speight c Ellison b Ealham	27		
†P. Moores lbw b Fleming	47		
F. D. Stephenson c Taylor b Ealham	17		
B. T. P. Donelan lbw b Ealham	15		
I. D. K. Salisbury b Fleming	11		
A. N. Jones c Marsh b Hooper	1		
A. G. Robson not out	0		
L-b 10, w 2, n-b 2	14	L-b 6, w 2, n-b 4	12

1/9 2/39 3/73 4/141 5/241   **335**   1/265   **(1 wkt dec.) 368**
6/275 7/305 8/330 9/335

Bonus points – Sussex 4, Kent 2 (Score at 100 overs: 305-6).

In the second innings D. M. Smith, when 16, retired hurt at 22 and resumed at 265.

Bowling: *First Innings*—McCague 14-3-85-1; Ellison 26-7-65-1; Ealham 24-5-67-4; Penn 7-1-23-0; Fleming 22.5-5-50-3; Hooper 16.4-4-35-1. *Second Innings*—McCague 7-3-22-0; Ellison 9-3-25-0; Ealham 4-1-16-0; Hooper 4-3-9-0; Ward 34-4-90-0; Cowdrey 36-6-147-1; Marsh 5-0-53-0.

Kent

T. R. Ward c Wells b Jones	12	– c Salisbury b Jones	44
*M. R. Benson st Moores b Donelan	45	– b Stephenson	117
N. R. Taylor c Wells b Jones	47	– b Stephenson	61
C. L. Hooper hit wkt b Donelan	121	– not out	43
G. R. Cowdrey c Speight b Robson	62	– c Moores b Stephenson	12
M. V. Fleming b Robson	23	– b Salisbury	31
†S. A. Marsh not out	17	– st Moores b Salisbury	5
M. A. Ealham lbw b Jones	1	– not out	2
R. M. Ellison not out	6		
B 13, l-b 2, n-b 19	34	B 1, l-b 16, n-b 6	23

1/19 2/89 3/153 4/273 5/336   **(7 wkts dec.) 368**   1/133 2/225 3/234   **(6 wkts) 338**
6/351 7/353   4/248 5/297 6/321

M. J. McCague and C. Penn did not bat.

Bonus points – Kent 4, Sussex 3.

Bowling: *First Innings*—Stephenson 12-3-40-0; Jones 16-1-76-3; Robson 17-2-76-2; Donelan 12-2-58-2; Salisbury 22-2-102-0; Lenham 1-0-1-0. *Second Innings*—Stephenson 19-1-91-3; Jones 7-0-64-1; Robson 10-0-55-0; Donelan 7-0-40-0; Salisbury 10.2-0-71-2.

Umpires: J. W. Holder and V. A. Holder.

At The Oval, May 29, 30, June 1. SUSSEX drew with SURREY.

SUSSEX v WARWICKSHIRE

At Hove, June 2, 3, 4. Sussex won by two wickets. Sussex 22 pts, Warwickshire 8 pts. Toss: Warwickshire. Sussex won off the penultimate ball in terrible light but Warwickshire did exceptionally well to limp so close to victory. Their two main bowlers, Donald and Small, plus the spinner Booth were all out of the attack through injury. This made a keen declaration by Lloyd – setting Sussex 250 off a minimum of 47 overs – look extremely kind. The wicket-keeper Piper should have been off with a damaged hand, but had to field in the absence of a substitute while Ostler deputised behind the stumps. Twose needed stitches after being hit in the mouth while facing Stephenson. All this took place on another superb Hove batting pitch on which Warwickshire had gained the early initiative after a stand of 193 between the centurions Moles and Ostler. Donald's bowling was fearsomely fast in the Sussex first innings but Smith and Wells kept their team in the game. Wells struck his third consecutive first-class hundred.

Close of play: First day, Sussex 17-1 (D. M. Smith 8*, B. T. P. Donelan 8*); Second day, Warwickshire 24-1 (A. J. Moles 16*, T. A. Lloyd 4*).

Warwickshire

A. J. Moles c Pigott b Donelan	122	– c Stephenson b North	28
R. G. Twose retired hurt	7	– b Pigott	3
*T. A. Lloyd b Pigott	10	– c Stephenson b Jones	31
D. P. Ostler b North	108	– b Donelan	20
D. A. Reeve lbw b Donelan	57	– b Speight	46
N. M. K. Smith c Moores b Jones	18	– c Stephenson b Donelan	29
P. A. Smith not out	4	– not out	32
P. A. Booth not out	10		
G. C. Small (did not bat)		– (8) not out	31
L-b 4	4	B 1, l-b 1, w 1, n-b 1	4

1/30 2/223 3/259 4/324 5/328 (5 wkts dec.) 340 1/16 2/63 3/65 (6 wkts dec.) 224
4/90 5/157 6/166

†K. J. Piper and A. A. Donald did not bat.

Bonus points – Warwickshire 4, Sussex 2.

In the first innings R. G. Twose retired hurt at 15.

Bowling: *First Innings*—Stephenson 13.3-3-41-0; Pigott 17.3-5-52-1; Jones 15-3-54-1; North 20-3-78-1; Lenham 3-1-8-0; Donelan 23-3-91-2; Wells 4-1-12-0. *Second Innings*—Jones 16-6-35-1; Pigott 12-6-17-1; North 13-3-47-1; Donelan 20-6-60-2; Lenham 2-1-5-0; Smith 2-0-14-0; Speight 3-0-30-1; Hall 1-0-14-0.

Sussex

D. M. Smith c Ostler b Donald	77	– b N. M. K. Smith	82
J. W. Hall b Small	1	– c Twose b P. A. Smith	54
B. T. P. Donelan c Piper b Donald	25	– (9) not out	3
N. J. Lenham c Twose b N. M. K. Smith	12	– (8) b N. M. K. Smith	2
*A. P. Wells c Twose b Booth	115	– (7) run out	23
M. P. Speight c Reeve b Booth	5	– (3) lbw b N. M. K. Smith	38
†P. Moores c Ostler b Donald	0	– (5) c and b P. A. Smith	4
F. D. Stephenson c Ostler b Donald	14	– (4) b N. M. K. Smith	6
J. A. North b Small	9	– (6) c Piper b Donald	9
A. C. S. Pigott lbw b Donald	3	– not out	1
A. N. Jones not out	14		
B 23, l-b 13, w 4	40	B 2, l-b 22, w 4	28

1/6 2/61 3/77 4/163 5/176 315 1/88 2/171 3/183 4/198 (8 wkts) 250
6/177 7/191 8/237 9/259 5/218 6/232 7/234 8/248

Bonus points – Sussex 4, Warwickshire 4 (Score at 100 overs: 310-9).

Bowling: *First Innings*—Donald 27–6–82–5; Small 19–4–47–2; N. M. K. Smith 15–0–50–1; Booth 27.1–11–59–2; P. A. Smith 9–0–28–0; Lloyd 4–0–13–0. *Second Innings*—Donald 5–0–32–1; Small 4.3–2–5–0; P. A. Smith 18.3–1–88–2; N. M. K. Smith 20.5–2–101–4.

Umpires: J. H. Hampshire and G. Sharp.

At Leicester, June 12, 13. SUSSEX lost to LEICESTERSHIRE by ten wickets.

SUSSEX v DURHAM

At Horsham, June 19, 20, 22. Sussex won by four wickets. Sussex 20 pts, Durham 5 pts. Toss: Durham. The Championship's newest county had a memorable first encounter with one of the oldest, decided by the final ball. Sussex needed 12 off the last over, and though Stephenson hit a towering six off Hughes's third delivery, the fifth removed Moores. Finally Stephenson scampered through for the winning two. Smith and Lenham, who hit 118 with the aid of a runner, put on 157 in 40 overs, then Wells, smashing 65 off 37 balls, Speight and Stephenson stepped up the pace to give Sussex their second Championship victory of the season. Three declarations had been necessary to make a match of it after two sessions were lost to rain on the first day when Parker, returning to the county where he had spent the previous 16 summers, made 44. Durham opener Hutton, struck a painful blow in the groin by Stephenson, was probably glad of the rest; next day he advanced to a determined 78 in his second first-class match. Sussex declared behind before Jones, with a sparkling 89 full of fluent drives, and Briers added 139 for the fourth wicket to set the home team a target of 340 from 65 overs.

Close of play: First day, Durham 122-3 (S. Hutton 16*, M. P. Briers 1*); Second day, Durham 1-0 (W. Larkins 0*, S. Hutton 0*).

Durham

W. Larkins lbw b Pigott	53	– c Wells b Jones	15
S. Hutton c Pigott b Stephenson	78	– c Moores b Pigott	5
D. M. Jones c Moores b Stephenson	5	– not out	89
P. W. G. Parker b Pigott	44	– b Pigott	11
M. P. Briers lbw b Stephenson	2	– not out	62
I. Smith c Speight b Stephenson	17		
†C. W. Scott c Moores b Pigott	48		
*D. A. Graveney not out	27		
S. P. Hughes c Stephenson b Donelan	9		
S. M. McEwan not out	0		
L-b 16, n-b 1	17	B 1, l-b 3, n-b 4	8

1/20 2/108 3/119 4/125 5/149   (8 wkts dec.) 300   1/13 2/32 3/51   (3 wkts dec.) 190
6/247 7/272 8/299

J. Wood did not bat.

Bonus points – Durham 4, Sussex 3.
In the first innings S. Hutton, when 9, retired hurt at 10 and resumed at 108.

Bowling: *First Innings*—Stephenson 25–8–65–4; Robson 10–1–20–0; Pigott 15–3–34–3; Jones 13–0–63–0; Donelan 32.4–4–102–1. *Second Innings*—Stephenson 1–1–0–0; Jones 9–0–72–1; Pigott 11–2–38–2; Robson 6–0–29–0; Donelan 8–0–47–0.

Sussex

D. M. Smith c McEwan b Wood	3	– b Graveney	67
W. Hall not out	82	– b Hughes	0
N. J. Lenham c McEwan b Wood	1	– c Hughes b McEwan	118
A. P. Wells c McEwan b Wood	1	– (5) c Larkins b Wood	65
M. P. Speight run out	28	– (4) c Larkins b Wood	49
P. Moores not out	26	– (7) c McEwan b Hughes	1
F. D. Stephenson (did not bat)		– (6) not out	30
B. T. P. Donelan (did not bat)		– not out	0
L-b 6, w 1, n-b 3	10	B 2, l-b 8	10

1/7 2/9 3/32 4/85   (4 wkts dec.) 151   1/2 2/159 3/231   (6 wkts) 340
                                                                     4/247 5/322 6/338

A. C. S. Pigott, A. N. Jones and A. G. Robson did not bat.

Bonus points – Sussex 1, Durham 1.

Bowling: *First Innings*—Wood 11–0–47–3; McEwan 10–3–24–0; Hughes 8–0–30–0; Briers 7–2–29–0; Graveney 3.1–0–15–0. *Second Innings*—Wood 9–1–46–2; Hughes 15–3–57–2; McEwan 12–1–72–1; Briers 11–4–34–0; Graveney 18–2–121–1.

Umpires: J. C. Balderstone and D. R. Shepherd.

At Worcester, June 26, 27, 29. SUSSEX beat WORCESTERSHIRE by 80 runs.

SUSSEX v HAMPSHIRE

At Arundel, June 30, July 1, 2. Hampshire won by 130 runs. Hampshire 18 pts, Sussex 4 pts. Toss: Hampshire. At 34 years old, the West Indian pace bowler Marshall claimed his 1,500th first-class wicket on the final day, after a couple of forfeitures revived the rain-disrupted match at the picturesque Castle ground. Sussex were asked to score 272 from a minimum of 76 overs, but were never in the hunt as Hampshire's bowlers took full advantage of a damp pitch. Slow left-armer Maru finished with figures of four for eight from his 15.4 overs. He turned the match when he bowled Wells just before tea, caught Greenfield just after, and removed Stephenson and Moores seven overs later. Then Marshall returned to take three wickets, becoming the first man since J. K. Lever in 1985 to reach 1,500 when he had Smith caught behind, before Maru dismissed last man Hansford. In Hampshire's innings, spread over two days, James hit an impressive 59.

Close of play: First day, Hampshire 152-4 (K. D. James 48*, M. D. Marshall 0*); Second day, Hampshire 271-9 (R. J. Maru 13*, C. A. Connor 18*).

Hampshire

T. C. Middleton c Moores b North	27	S. D. Udal c Stephenson b North	9
V. P. Terry c Smith b Hansford	13	R. J. Maru not out	13
K. D. James c Greenfield b Hansford	59	C. A. Connor not out	18
M. C. J. Nicholas c Smith b Stephenson	17		
J. R. Wood c Smith b Hansford	35	B 4, l-b 9, w 1, n-b 6	20
M. D. Marshall c Moores b Pigott	12	1/46 2/46 3/84	(9 wkts dec.) 271
K. R. Ayling lbw b North	15	4/145 5/177 6/177	
R. J. Parks b Donelan	33	7/216 8/230 9/246	

Bonus points – Hampshire 2, Sussex 4 (Score at 100 overs: 248-9).

Bowling: Stephenson 21–5–41–1; Pigott 18–8–25–1; Hansford 29–5–81–3; North 13–1–51–3; Lenham 5–0–20–0; Donelan 9–2–27–1; Greenfield 2–0–13–0.

Hampshire forfeited their second innings.

Sussex

Sussex forfeited their first innings.

N. J. Lenham c Parks b James	12	B. T. P. Donelan c Middleton
J. W. Hall lbw b Ayling	27	b Marshall . 8
K. Greenfield c Maru b Udal	29	A. C. S. Pigott not out . 1
*A. P. Wells b Maru	7	A. R. Hansford c Nicholas b Maru . 1
F. D. Stephenson b Maru	4	B 4, l-b 8, n-b 2 . 14
D. M. Smith c Parks b Marshall	32	
†P. Moores c Wood b Maru	0	1/29 2/68 3/84 4/86 5/96 141
J. A. North lbw b Marshall	6	6/96 7/127 8/135 9/140

Bowling: Marshall 16–3–44–3; Connor 9–2–22–0; James 10–4–14–1; Ayling 6–2–8–1
Udal 19–8–33–1; Maru 15.4–10–8–4.

Umpires: J. C. Balderstone and G. Sharp.

At Northampton, July 3, 4, 6. SUSSEX drew with NORTHAMPTONSHIRE.

At Southend, July 17, 18, 20. SUSSEX lost to ESSEX by eight wickets.

SUSSEX v LANCASHIRE

At Hove, July 21, 22, 23. Drawn. Sussex 7 pts, Lancashire 6 pts. Toss: Lancashire. Martin
and Barnett, Lancashire's last-wicket pair, survived a tense last two overs to deny Sussex
The visitors had slumped to 233 for nine in pursuit of 296 off 71 overs as medium-pace
Giddins took five wickets in an innings for the first time, but Martin survived unbeaten on
52. Earlier in the day Sussex's Speight had bludgeoned the fastest century of the season
off declaration bowling. He reached three figures in 62 balls, and in all hit an undefeated
119 off 82 balls in 71 minutes, with five sixes and 15 fours, while adding 149 in 18 over
with Greenfield. Speight looked a shade embarrassed – and so did the members – as he
acknowledged their applause. Far more worthy were the centuries of Sussex's opening pair
Smith and Hall, in the first innings, when they shared a stand of 172. Hall, with 12 fours
drove and cut superbly to reach his highest score. Hegg, the novice captain of an under
strength Lancashire, declared with a lead of seven runs, after Lloyd had displayed his talen
in a pleasant 96, which took him past 1,000 runs in a season for the first time.

Close of play: First day, Lancashire 23-0 (J. P. Crawley 16*, S. P. Titchard 7*); Secon
day, Sussex 64-0 (D. M. Smith 32*, J. W. Hall 31*).

Sussex

D. M. Smith c Speak b Fitton	105 – retired hurt	32
J. W. Hall not out	140 – c Titchard b Irani	7
N. J. Lenham b Fitton	7 – c Hegg b Barnett	2
*A. P. Wells c Irani b Fletcher	19 – c Titchard b Crawley	3
†M. P. Speight lbw b Fitton	39 – not out	11
K. Greenfield c Lloyd b Fitton	14 – not out	3
B 9, l-b 7, n-b 2	18	L-b 7, n-b 2 .

1/172 2/180 3/229 4/304 5/342   (5 wkts dec.) 342   1/80 2/118 3/153   (3 wkts dec.) 30:

C. C. Remy, A. C. S. Pigott, I. D. K. Salisbury, A. N. Jones and E. S. H. Giddir
did not bat.

Bonus points – Sussex 4, Lancashire 2.

In the second innings D. M. Smith retired hurt at 64.

Bowling: *First Innings*—Martin 20–8–63–0; Fletcher 13–3–57–1; Chapple 12–1–55–0
Fitton 28.1–6–81–4; Barnett 11–2–31–0; Irani 6–0–39–0. *Second Innings*—Martin 5–0–15–0
Fletcher 9–1–49–0; Chapple 4–1–7–0; Fitton 7–1–18–0; Barnett 12–2–33–1; Irani 5–0–25–
Crawley 10–0–90–1; Speak 4–0–36–0; Lloyd 5–0–22–0.

Lancashire

J. P. Crawley c Wells b Salisbury	49	– c Speight b Giddins	65
S. P. Titchard c Speight b Remy	54	– c Greenfield b Jones	0
N. J. Speak c Lenham b Pigott	59	– b Giddins	62
G. D. Lloyd lbw b Pigott	96	– lbw b Giddins	0
*†W. K. Hegg b Giddins	5	– c Greenfield b Giddins	6
R. C. Irani lbw b Lenham	22	– (7) c Pigott b Salisbury	17
J. D. Fitton c Salisbury b Remy	45	– (6) b Salisbury	5
P. J. Martin c Speight b Remy	6	– not out	52
G. Chapple not out	1	– c Lenham b Salisbury	18
S. D. Fletcher (did not bat)		– b Giddins	2
A. A. Barnett (did not bat)		– not out	0
B 9, l-b 2, n-b 1	12	B 4, w 1, n-b 6	11

1/85 2/141 3/179 4/191 5/237   (8 wkts dec.) 349   1/1 2/119 3/119   (9 wkts) 238
6/329 7/339 8/349   4/141 5/143 6/159
7/166 8/228 9/233

Bonus points – Lancashire 4, Sussex 3.

Bowling: *First Innings*—Jones 14–2–51–0; Pigott 19.2–0–70–2; Salisbury 21–4–71–1; Giddins 10–1–43–1; Lenham 13–5–41–1; Remy 9–2–27–3; Greenfield 4–0–35–0. *Second Innings*—Jones 6.5–1–16–1; Pigott 16–3–54–0; Remy 4–0–23–0; Salisbury 25–8–54–3; Lenham 6–0–33–0; Giddins 13.1–2–54–5.

Umpires: G. A. Stickley and A. G. T. Whitehead.

At Cheltenham College, July 24, 25, 27. SUSSEX lost to GLOUCESTERSHIRE by four wickets.

At Taunton, July 31, August 1, 2. SUSSEX drew with SOMERSET.

SUSSEX v GLAMORGAN

At Eastbourne, August 4, 5, 6. Drawn. Sussex 7 pts, Glamorgan 7 pts. Toss: Sussex. Glamorgan's visit to the Saffrons will be remembered mainly by umpire John Harris and a 74-year-old spectator, both of whom were hit on the head by the ball. Harris was struck by a throw from Maynard on the first day and took no further part in the match; Sussex's assistant secretary, Michael Charman, stood in until Roy Palmer arrived from a Second Eleven game at Hove. Then, on the final day, Moores crashed a six over long-on so hard that Tony Hone of Farnborough required stitches. The rest of the day's play was routinely painful: bottom-of-the-table Glamorgan found 272 in what became 54 overs too stiff, even on a placid pitch. When the game ended three overs early they were 73 runs short, although Morris, with 17 fours in his unbeaten 104, provided some entertainment. Sussex's first-innings total of 360 was dominated by an aggressive 179 from Speight, his highest score, including 25 fours in just over four hours. Glamorgan plodded to 281 in reply, and the economical Foster and Barwick restricted Sussex in their second innings.

Close of play: First day, Glamorgan 20-0 (S. P. James 10*, H. Morris 8*); Second day, Sussex 33-3 (B. T. P. Donelan 8*, A. C. S. Pigott 1*).

Sussex

D. M. Smith c Metson b Foster	3	– (2) lbw b Watkin	0
J. W. Hall c Metson b Foster	16	– (10) not out	1
N. J. Lenham c Morris b Watkin	4	– (1) lbw b Foster	9
*A. P. Wells c Maynard b Foster	2	– (6) not out	74
M. P. Speight run out	179	– (3) b Watkin	6
†P. Moores lbw b Barwick	43	– (7) c Morris b Barwick	34
F. D. Stephenson b Watkin	80	– (8) c Maynard b Croft	30
B. T. P. Donelan run out	14	– (4) c Dale b Foster	13
I. D. K. Salisbury b Watkin	9	– st Metson b Barwick	0
A. C. S. Pigott b Watkin	3	– (5) lbw b Watkin	15
E. S. H. Giddins not out	0		
L-b 3, n-b 4	7	L-b 10	10

1/12 2/25 3/30 4/31 5/168   360   1/1 2/17 3/23 4/50 (8 wkts dec.) 192
6/305 7/337 8/349 9/355   5/52 6/140 7/187 8/187

Bonus points – Sussex 4, Glamorgan 4.

Bowling: *First Innings*—Watkin 28.2–4–92–4; Foster 23–2–106–3; Barwick 29–6–80–1; Croft 9–1–49–0; Dale 6–1–17–0; Maynard 1–0–13–0. *Second Innings*—Watkin 16–3–45–3; Foster 15–9–16–2; Croft 17–2–71–1; Barwick 17.4–5–44–2; Cottey 1–0–6–0.

Glamorgan

S. P. James lbw b Giddins	42	– c Speight b Giddins	20
H. Morris run out	32	– not out	104
D. L. Hemp c sub b Salisbury	7	– lbw b Pigott	0
*M. P. Maynard c Stephenson b Salisbury	49	– lbw b Donelan	9
A. Dale c Wells b Salisbury	26	– c Smith b Salisbury	5
P. A. Cottey c Salisbury b Donelan	37	– c and b Salisbury	45
R. D. B. Croft lbw b Salisbury	49	– not out	6
†C. P. Metson b Donelan	12		
S. L. Watkin not out	6		
B 5, l-b 7, n-b 9	21	B 4, l-b 3, w 1, n-b 2	10

1/64 2/86 3/86 4/141 5/170   (8 wkts dec.) 281   1/37 2/39 3/66   (5 wkts) 199
6/236 7/267 8/281   4/75 5/179

S. R. Barwick and D. J. Foster did not bat.

Bonus points – Glamorgan 3, Sussex 3 (Score at 100 overs: 267-7).

Bowling: *First Innings*—Stephenson 21–7–46–0; Giddins 16–4–44–1; Pigott 11–4–30–0; Salisbury 28.4–9–75–4; Donelan 23–7–61–2; Lenham 3–1–13–0. *Second Innings*—Stephenson 9–0–41–0; Giddins 5–2–17–1; Pigott 6–1–22–1; Donelan 16–1–49–1; Salisbury 15–1–63–2.

Umpires: D. J. Constant and J. H. Harris (M. Charman deputised for J. H. Harris on 1st day; R. Palmer on 2nd and 3rd days).

SUSSEX v DERBYSHIRE

At Eastbourne, August 7, 8, 10. Sussex won by four wickets. Sussex 22 pts, Derbyshire 6 pts. Toss: Derbyshire. Sussex won at the Saffrons for the first time since they beat Derbyshire in the Championship in 1986, after 13 winless matches on the ground in all competitions. Their hero was an Eastbourne man: seamer Giddins, who returned five for 32 after dismissing the first four Derbyshire batsmen in ten balls without conceding a run on the final morning. Salisbury, extracting plenty of turn from a wearing pitch, supported him well with three for 26, leaving Sussex an apparently easy target of 161 in 54 overs; they made heavy work of it and there were plenty of anxious moments before they got home with 21 balls to spare. In a low-scoring game on a pitch that assisted all the bowlers, a determined 68 from Morris in Derbyshire's first innings was the highest individual contribution to the match. Sussex's batsmen lacked application but makeshift opener Remy, who spent 59 overs compiling his highest score, and Speight ensured Sussex were only 16 runs in arrears.

Close of play: First day, Sussex 27-0 (N. J. Lenham 7*, C. C. Remy 16*); Second day, Derbyshire 28-0 (K. J. Barnett 19*, P. D. Bowler 9*).

Derbyshire

*K. J. Barnett b Giddins	11	– lbw b Stephenson	29
P. D. Bowler b Remy	30	– lbw b Giddins	26
J. E. Morris c Speight b Salisbury	68	– c Speight b Giddins	0
T. J. G. O'Gorman c Speight b Stephenson	10	– lbw b Giddins	0
C. J. Adams c Speight b Stephenson	3	– c Moores b Giddins	1
F. A. Griffith lbw b Giddins	23	– c Moores b Donelan	23
†K. M. Krikken c Salisbury b Pigott	24	– c Wells b Salisbury	20
D. G. Cork c Wells b Pigott	13	– c Moores b Giddins	32
I. R. Bishop c Wells b Salisbury	17	– c and b Salisbury	3
R. W. Sladdin c Wells b Donelan	21	– c Greenfield b Salisbury	0
O. H. Mortensen not out	12	– not out	1
B 4, l-b 7, w 1, n-b 4	16	B 4, l-b 2, n-b 1	7

1/19 2/88 3/117 4/130 5/133   248   1/53 2/53 3/53 4/56 5/58   142
6/170 7/186 8/207 9/217   6/104 7/105 8/118 9/118

Bonus points – Derbyshire 2, Sussex 4.

Bowling: *First Innings*—Stephenson 19-2-49-2; Giddins 13-4-33-2; Pigott 12-2-46-2; Remy 8-2-19-1; Donelan 8.5-2-23-1; Salisbury 30-11-67-2. *Second Innings*—Stephenson 13-3-36-1; Giddins 13.5-5-32-5; Pigott 3-0-4-0; Donelan 7-2-27-1; Salisbury 12-1-26-3; Remy 4-0-11-0.

Sussex

N. J. Lenham c Barnett b Griffith	39	– lbw b Cork	0
C. C. Remy c Krikken b Bishop	47	– lbw b Mortensen	8
K. Greenfield c Adams b Mortensen	5	– c Krikken b Bishop	43
*A. P. Wells lbw b Bishop	20	– (8) not out	7
M. P. Speight c Barnett b Sladdin	42	– (4) c Cork b Sladdin	30
†P. Moores c sub b Cork	15	– (5) b Bishop	5
F. D. Stephenson c Bowler b Sladdin	8	– (6) not out	44
B. T. P. Donelan c Krikken b Cork	11	– (7) lbw b Mortensen	11
I. D. K. Salisbury c Morris b Mortensen	20		
A. C. S. Pigott not out	11		
E. S. H. Giddins c Griffith b Sladdin	1		
B 2, l-b 1, w 1, n-b 7	11	B 3, l-b 6, n-b 4	13

1/82 2/89 3/110 4/127 5/176   230   1/0 2/35 3/67   (6 wkts) 161
6/177 7/198 8/198 9/225   4/75 5/112 6/132

Bonus points – Sussex 2, Derbyshire 4.

Bowling: *First Innings*—Bishop 19-7-35-2; Cork 26-3-52-2; Griffith 15-4-40-1; Mortensen 16-4-34-2; Sladdin 19.2-3-66-3. *Second Innings*—Cork 14-3-26-1; Bishop 10-1-29-2; Mortensen 14.3-4-32-2; Sladdin 12-0-65-1.

Umpires: D. J. Constant and R. Palmer.

SUSSEX v MIDDLESEX

At Hove, August 21, 22, 24. Drawn. Sussex 2 pts, Middlesex 5 pts. Toss: Sussex. Sussex opener Hall scored a fine 81 on the day he received his county cap, but that and a magnificent 177 from Haynes were the only highlights of a rain-affected game. The home side were set 322 to win in 80 overs but the heavens opened on the final afternoon with 243 required. The players passed the time with an impromptu game of American football in front of the pavilion. Haynes's century was his 50th in first-class cricket and put Middlesex in a strong position after Alan Wells asked them to bat. He hit 21 boundaries, adding 178 for the second wicket with Gatting as Middlesex piled up 445 from 123 overs. Hall's typically correct 81 ended when he was trapped by Emburey, whose probing spell made sure that Sussex's progress was never more than sedate. Alan Wells and Lenham tossed up some easy runs on the final morning in cheerless conditions, before the weather finally closed in.

Close of play: First day, Middlesex 407-7 (N. F. Williams 0*, A. R. C. Fraser 1*); Second day, Sussex 187-3 (A. P. Wells 18*, M. P. Speight 21*).

Middlesex

D. L. Haynes b Remy	177		
M. A. Roseberry c Hall b Remy	32	– (1) not out	32
*M. W. Gatting c A. P. Wells b Salisbury	73		
M. R. Ramprakash b Pigott	27		
J. D. Carr b C. M. Wells	51		
†K. R. Brown lbw b Salisbury	28	– (2) not out	25
J. E. Emburey b Lenham	8		
N. F. Williams not out	17		
A. R. C. Fraser not out	21		
B 1, l-b 10	11	B 5, l-b 1	6

1/51 2/229 3/311 4/327 5/396   (7 wkts dec.) 445   (no wkt dec.) 63
6/406 7/406

C. W. Taylor and P. C. R. Tufnell did not bat.

Bonus points – Middlesex 4, Sussex 1 (Score at 100 overs: 332-4).

Bowling: *First Innings*—Giddins 24–2–95–0; Pigott 20–3–52–1; Remy 17–3–72–2; Salisbury 34–6–124–2; C. M. Wells 18–2–64–1; Lenham 10–2–27–1. *Second Innings*—A. P. Wells 6–0–25–0; Lenham 8–2–18–0; Remy 3.2–0–10–0; Smith 1–0–4–0.

Sussex

D. M. Smith lbw b Emburey	36	– b Williams	10
J. W. Hall b Emburey	81	– not out	41
N. J. Lenham c Carr b Williams	19	– not out	17
*A. P. Wells not out	18		
M. P. Speight not out	21		
L-b 6, w 1, n-b 5	12	L-b 3, n-b 8	11

1/92 2/142 3/155   (3 wkts dec.) 187   1/32   (1 wkt) 79

C. M. Wells, †P. Moores, C. C. Remy, I. D. K. Salisbury, A. C. S. Pigott and E. S. H. Giddins did not bat.

Bonus points – Sussex 1, Middlesex 1.

Bowling: *First Innings*—Williams 16–6–31–1; Taylor 12–2–46–0; Emburey 20.4–4–57–2; Fraser 6–0–17–0; Tufnell 16–3–30–0. *Second Innings*—Taylor 6–0–28–0; Williams 13–4–25–1; Emburey 4–3–2–0; Tufnell 1–0–4–0; Fraser 6–3–17–0.

Umpires: R. Julian and G. Sharp.

SUSSEX v ESSEX

At Hove, August 26, 27, 28, 29. Essex won by nine wickets. Essex 24 pts, Sussex 3 pts. Toss: Essex. Another haul of maximum points virtually secured the title for Essex but they had to contend with some stubborn Sussex resistance on the final day. Sussex, 201 behind on first innings, slumped to 58 for five, and then 113 for seven, with Pringle and Ilott inflicting the worst blows, before Speight and Stephenson hit 136 in 32 overs. Speight bludgeoned 20 boundaries in nearly four hours while Stephenson offered more restrained backing. But Sussex were all out for 279 and Essex got the 79 runs they needed inside 17 overs. On the first day hostile bowling by Ilott, with five for 60, dismissed Sussex for a meagre 204. Only Moores provided much comfort. He was last out, for 73, the eighth lbw of the innings – a figure equalling that set by Warwickshire in dismissing Oxford University in 1980. Umpire Wight stood in both matches. Essex ground out 405, thanks to Lewis's marathon 133. He added 131 with Gooch, and then Pringle supported him with an entertaining 112.

Close of play: First day, Essex 1-0 (G. A. Gooch 1*, J. P. Stephenson 0*); Second day, Essex 195-2 (J. J. B. Lewis 81*, P. J. Prichard 14*); Third day, Sussex 37-1 (D. M. Smith *, I. D. K. Salisbury 9*).

Sussex

D. M. Smith lbw b Such	29	– lbw b Topley	19
W. Hall lbw b Ilott	15	– lbw b Childs	17
J. J. Lenham c Lewis b Topley	12	– (4) b Pringle	4
A. P. Wells lbw b Topley	3	– (5) c Topley b Pringle	3
M. P. Speight lbw b Topley	18	– (6) b Ilott	126
C. M. Wells lbw b Ilott	28	– (7) c Garnham b Ilott	13
†P. Moores lbw b Ilott	73	– (8) c Such b Ilott	2
F. D. Stephenson c Garnham b Ilott	4	– (9) c sub b Such	49
I. D. K. Salisbury lbw b Ilott	0	– (3) lbw b Pringle	9
C. S. Pigott lbw b Gooch	11	– c Garnham b Pringle	10
S. H. Giddins not out	0	– not out	0
B 1, l-b 2, n-b 8	11	B 8, l-b 4, n-b 15	27
	204		**279**

1/31 2/62 3/62 4/72 5/87 6/126 7/130 8/130 9/172   204

1/27 2/39 3/55 4/55 5/58 6/101 7/113 8/249 9/275   279

Bonus points – Sussex 2, Essex 4.

Bowling: *First Innings*—Pringle 20–5–70–0; Ilott 21–5–60–5; Topley 17–4–46–3; Such 11–1–12–1; Stephenson 3–1–9–0; Gooch 2–0–4–1. *Second Innings*—Ilott 20.3–1–77–3; Pringle 9–9–47–4; Such 14–3–37–1; Childs 9–1–31–1; Topley 16–4–53–1; Stephenson 4–1–13–0; Gooch 4–0–9–0.

Essex

G. A. Gooch c Moores b Pigott	77	– not out	46
J. P. Stephenson c Stephenson b Giddins	15	– c Lenham b C. M. Wells	3
J. J. B. Lewis run out	133		
P. J. Prichard c Speight b Stephenson	18	– (3) not out	24
M. A. Garnham lbw b Stephenson	0		
D. R. Pringle not out	112		
T. D. Topley c Lenham b Giddins	4		
M. C. Ilott lbw b Lenham	8		
P. M. Such st Moores b Salisbury	20		
J. H. Childs not out	0		
B 5, l-b 5, n-b 8	18	L-b 5, w 2	7
	405		**80**

1/30 2/161 3/205 4/209 5/314   (8 wkts dec.) 405   1/20   (1 wkt) 80

6/327 7/338 8/384

N. Hussain did not bat.

Bonus points – Essex 4, Sussex 1 (Score at 100 overs: 302-4).

Bowling: *First Innings*—Stephenson 28–3–88–2; Giddins 24–3–79–2; Pigott 22–1–87–1; C. M. Wells 11–1–33–0; Salisbury 45–15–106–1; Lenham 2–1–2–1. *Second Innings*—Stephenson 7–1–33–0; C. M. Wells 5–1–22–1; Salisbury 3–0–13–0; Giddins 1.4–0–7–0.

Umpires: R. C. Tolchard and P. B. Wight.

At Cardiff, August 31, September 1, 2, 3. SUSSEX drew with GLAMORGAN.

At Manchester, September 7, 8, 9. SUSSEX beat LANCASHIRE by an innings and 182 runs.

SUSSEX v YORKSHIRE

At Hove, September 12, 13, 14, 15. Sussex won by six wickets. Sussex 23 pts, Yorkshir
2 pts. Toss: Yorkshire. Sussex ended their season on a high, as their second successiv
victory ensured them seventh place in the Championship, their best for seven years. Leg
spinner Salisbury followed up his 11 for 83 in the win over Lancashire with a career-best 1
for 138, taking his final tally to 87. He took Yorkshire's last seven wickets, including fou
for no runs in 13 balls, on the first day, when Yorkshire struggled to 232. Only White mad
headway on a blameless Hove pitch. Hall and Lenham raised a century partnership by th
close, and had extended it to 224 when Hall was bowled in the 82nd over. Lenham hit 1
fours in his second hundred in successive innings, but Sussex were too leisurely to gain mor
than three batting points, and Hartley collected eight wickets as the innings fade
Yorkshire did little better at their second attempt, when Salisbury claimed another fiv
victims. Openers Moxon and Kellett batted defiantly, but no-one else reached 30 and Susse
were left needing 60 to win. Jarvis celebrated his England recall the week before with fou
wickets, but Colin Wells ended the game in style, hitting Batty for six over square leg.

Close of play: First day, Sussex 100-0 (N. J. Lenham 58*, J. W. Hall 40*); Second da
Sussex 282-2 (K. Greenfield 13*, A. P. Wells 25*); Third day, Yorkshire 145-4 (R. J. Blake
13*, D. Byas 23*).

Yorkshire

*M. D. Moxon lbw b Stephenson	14	– b Giddins	5
S. A. Kellett b C. M. Wells	53	– b Salisbury	3
A. A. Metcalfe c Speight b Giddins	43	– b Salisbury	1
C. White not out	71	– c Greenfield b Giddins	
†R. J. Blakey c Moores b Salisbury	23	– b Stephenson	2
D. Byas b Salisbury	10	– b Stephenson	2
P. W. Jarvis lbw b Salisbury	0	– lbw b Giddins	1
P. Carrick c C. M. Wells b Salisbury	0	– lbw b Salisbury	2
P. J. Hartley lbw b Salisbury	0	– st Moores b Salisbury	2
J. D. Batty lbw b Salisbury	5	– c Moores b Giddins	
M. A. Robinson b Salisbury	1	– not out	
B 4, l-b 2, n-b 6	12	B 4, l-b 11, w 1, n-b 8	2

1/20 2/100 3/127 4/180 5/192   232   1/86 2/90 3/90 4/106 5/152   25
6/192 7/196 8/196 9/213   6/170 7/195 8/236 9/237

Bonus points – Yorkshire 2, Sussex 4.

Bowling: *First Innings*—Stephenson 15-0-62-1; Giddins 12-4-38-1; Salisbury 19-7-54-7
C. M. Wells 14-4-42-1; Lenham 7-2-14-0; Donelan 7-3-16-0. *Second Innings*—Stephenso
19-1-57-1; Giddins 23-9-65-4; C. M. Wells 8-2-17-0; Lenham 6-1-21-0; Donela
4-4-0-0; Salisbury 30-9-84-5.

Sussex

N. J. Lenham c Blakey b Batty	135	– c Kellett b Jarvis	2
J. W. Hall b Hartley	90	– c Byas b Jarvis	
K. Greenfield c Metcalfe b Hartley	16	– lbw b Jarvis	
*A. P. Wells c Kellett b Hartley	27	– not out	1
M. P. Speight hit wkt b Hartley	18	– c Metcalfe b Jarvis	
C. M. Wells c Byas b Hartley	33	– not out	1
†P. Moores b Carrick	20		
F. D. Stephenson lbw b Hartley	24		
B. T. P. Donelan c White b Hartley	4		
I. D. K. Salisbury c and b Hartley	25		
E. S. H. Giddins not out	10		
B 4, l-b 9, n-b 17	30	N-b 1	

1/224 2/245 3/287 4/297 5/316   432   1/24 2/31 3/36 4/42   (4 wkts) 6
6/338 7/389 8/395 9/401

Bonus points – Sussex 3 (Score at 100 overs: 276-2).

Bowling: *First Innings*—Jarvis 27-6-79-0; Hartley 37.2-7-111-8; Carrick 52-21-93-
Robinson 18-2-72-0; Batty 17-2-64-1. *Second Innings*—Jarvis 10-3-27-4; Hartley 2-0-8-
Batty 8.5-2-25-0; Carrick 1-0-1-0.

Umpires: N. T. Plews and G. A. Stickley.

WARWICKSHIRE

President: The Earl of Aylesford
Chairman: M. J. K. Smith
Chairman, Cricket Committee: D. L. Amiss
Secretary: D. M. W. Heath
  County Ground, Edgbaston,
  Birmingham B5 7QU
  (Telephone: 021-446 4422)
Captain: 1992 – T. A. Lloyd
  1993 – D. A. Reeve
Director of Coaching: R. A. Woolmer

Warwickshire's perennial problems of batting and spin bowling were exposed too frequently for the side to mount a serious challenge in the County Championship, in contrast to the previous season when the strongest pace attack in county cricket swept the county to second place in the final table.

Their 1992 season was badly affected by the lack of full fitness for most of the summer of Dermot Reeve. Only in the last month did he shake off the effects of the pelvic stress fracture he sustained earlier in the year during England's World Cup campaign, and his drop in wickets from 45 at 21.26 to 13 at 48.61 left the attack woefully short of variety. Spinners Neil Smith and Paul Booth aggregated only 40 wickets between them in 19 Championship matches and, with county cricket due to be played exclusively over four days for three years, the club must resolve this long-standing problem if the side is to challenge for honours.

Donald spearheaded the attack in superb fashion and was, at times, quite magnificent – notably at Guildford on a slow pitch when he blasted out the first six Surrey batsmen on the final day with bowling as fast as many onlookers had ever seen. Compared to 1991, his strike-rate was not quite as good – a wicket every 46 balls compared with one every 38 – but his 74 wickets earned him seventh place in the national averages, and his haul of five wickets or more in an innings six times was bettered only by Courtney Walsh and Wasim Akram. Without him, Warwickshire would have finished much lower than their final position of sixth, and it must be a source of worry to the club that Donald has such a heavy workload all the year round, particularly now that South Africa are back in international cricket.

Tim Munton's dependable qualities earned him two England caps, but not a place on either of the winter tours, while Gladstone Small's benefit season was a patchy one. The biggest advance in the pace department was made by Paul Smith, whose 42 wickets were a personal best, including four performances of five or more wickets in an innings. His ability to generate hostility, even with an old ball on a flat pitch, made him a dangerous bowler, but he was dropped for the Championship run-in, and he initially refused a two-year contract to remain with Warwickshire.

The season at Edgbaston ended less than smoothly, with a precipitate announcement, made with two Championship matches still to be played, that Lloyd would be replaced as captain for 1993 by Reeve. The club said they had made the statement to prevent the news leaking. But that hardly justified the unsettling effect in the dressing-room for the games against Middlesex and Kent, nor does it explain why the decision had to be taken at that time at all. Lloyd's lack of runs made his position in the team uncertain and forced the change, although the marginal shortfall of an aggregate of 919 at 24.83 needs to be balanced against the undeniably positive approach he brought to captaincy, his totally unselfish approach to batting, and his contribution to the progress made by several of the young players. The left-handed Roger Twose responded well to his promotion to open the innings in place of the unlucky Jason Ratcliffe who, like Paul Smith, suffered because of the need to improve the balance of a side. Twose's 1,412 runs at 40.34 were invariably scored at a good rate, with an uncomplicated technique which enabled him to punish anything off line or length. He turned his maiden Championship hundred into a double, and also scored almost 900 one-day runs. With 28 first-class wickets, including a career-best six for 63 against Middlesex, his medium-pace swing bowling made him an invaluable member of the side, and his season was capped in the literal sense, when he became one of the few cricketers to receive their county cap on the players' balcony at Lord's.

Trevor Penney had an outstanding first season with 904 runs at 53.17, including three hundreds. His season ended in switchback fashion, with a career-best 151 at Lord's followed swiftly by a pair against Kent, inflicted in three balls. He is a brilliant fielder, as is Dominic Ostler, who had a good second full season. Ostler also scored three hundreds, including a career-best 192 at Guildford where he showed an ability to strike the ball cleanly and powerfully without ever slogging. If they had a dominating Test-class batsman alongside them he, Penney and Twose would benefit enormously, as would Andy Moles whose 1,359 runs at 35.76 reflected the burden he shouldered again as anchor man. It was a solid season, but 300 runs short of what a team with a substandard batting line-up really needed.

For the second successive year, Warwickshire fell at the penultimate hurdle in the NatWest Trophy, and again a home semi-final proved too much for their batsmen. A score of 149 against Northamptonshire was totally inadequate, even though good bowling by Reeve, Small and Munton and an inspired spell from Donald reduced the victory margin for the eventual trophy winners to three wickets. The side failed to qualify for the knockout stages of the Benson and Hedges Cup, and a possible high finish in the Sunday League was ruined by their failure to win any of the last four games.

Since the start of Sunday League cricket in 1969, only Northamptonshire, Gloucestershire and Glamorgan have won fewer games than Warwickshire's total of 147. The Director of Coaching, Bob Woolmer has helped bring about some improvement, but 1993 will be a difficult year for everyone at Edgbaston, with a newly appointed captain having to bed down in the first season of four-day cricket. – Jack Bannister.

WARWICKSHIRE 1992

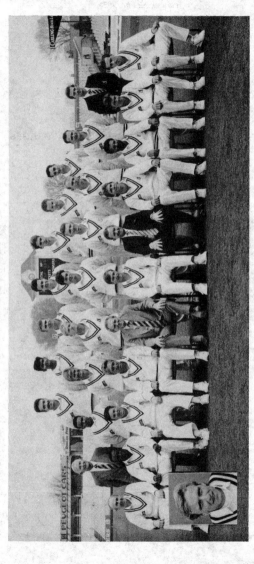

[Bill Smith]

Back row: R. G. Twose, Wasim Khan, M. Burns, A. F. Giles, B. C. Usher, G. Welch, P. C. L. Holloway. *Middle row*: D. M. W. Heath (*secretary*), K. J. Piper, T. L. Penney, D. P. Ostler, J. D. Ratcliffe, D. R. Brown, N. M. K. Smith, P. A. Booth, S. J. Nottingham (*physiotherapist*). *Front row*: R. N. Abberley (*coach*), G. C. Small, A. J. Moles, R. A. Woolmer (*director of cricket*), M. J. K. Smith (*chairman*), T. A. Lloyd (*captain*), D. L. Amiss (*chairman of cricket*), D. A. Reeve, Asif Din, P. A. Smith, T. A. Munton. *Inset*: A. A. Donald.

WARWICKSHIRE RESULTS

All first-class matches – Played 23: Won 6, Lost 8, Drawn 9.

County Championship matches – Played 22: Won 6, Lost 8, Drawn 8.

Bonus points – Batting 55, Bowling 68.

Competition placings – Britannic Assurance County Championship, 6th;
NatWest Bank Trophy, s-f; Benson and Hedges Cup, 4th in Group C;
Sunday League, 8th equal.

BRITANNIC ASSURANCE CHAMPIONSHIP AVERAGES

BATTING

	Birthplace	M	I	NO	R	HS	Avge
T. L. Penney	Salisbury, Rhodesia	15	23	6	802	151	47.17
‡R. G. Twose	Torquay	22	37	3	1,368	233	40.23
‡A. J. Moles	Solihull	22	39	3	1,292	122	35.88
‡D. A. Reeve	Kowloon, Hong Kong	17	28	4	833	79	34.70
‡D. P. Ostler	Solihull	21	35	1	1,172	192	34.47
‡T. A. Lloyd	Oswestry	22	38	2	914	84*	25.38
N. M. K. Smith	Birmingham	12	20	2	454	67	25.22
‡K. J. Piper	Leicester	19	25	8	345	72	20.29
‡A. A. Donald§	Bloemfontein, SA	21	22	10	234	41	19.50
‡P. A. Smith	Jesmond	18	25	4	394	45	18.76
J. D. Ratcliffe	Solihull	6	12	0	219	50	18.25
‡G. C. Small	St George, Barbados	17	17	6	181	31*	16.45
‡T. A. Munton	Melton Mowbray	15	17	6	123	47	11.18
P. A. Booth	Huddersfield	7	10	4	64	22*	10.66
M. A. V. Bell	Birmingham	3	5	2	10	5	3.33

Also batted: ‡Asif Din (*Kampala, Uganda*) (2 matches) 40, 35, 28; M. Burns (*Barrow-in-Furness*) (1 match) 3, 4; P. C. L. Holloway (*Helston*) (2 matches) 16, 102*, 15.

* *Signifies not out.* ‡ *Denotes county cap.* § *Overseas player.*

The following played a total of eight three-figure innings for Warwickshire in County Championship matches – D. P. Ostler 3, T. L. Penney 2, P. C. L. Holloway 1, A. J. Moles 1, R. G. Twose 1.

BOWLING

	O	M	R	W	BB	5W/i	Avge
A. A. Donald	576.2	139	1,647	74	7-37	6	22.25
P. A. Smith	364	55	1,334	42	6-91	4	31.76
R. G. Twose	221.3	37	735	23	6-63	1	31.95
T. A. Munton	520.2	145	1,389	42	7-64	3	33.07
G. C. Small	367.2	83	1,003	30	3-43	0	33.43
P. A. Booth	231.4	60	723	16	4-29	0	45.18
D. A. Reeve	267	80	632	13	2-4	0	48.61
N. M. K. Smith	332.3	63	1,178	24	5-61	1	49.08

Also bowled: M. A. V. Bell 79.2–17–247–8; T. A. Lloyd 68.5–8–295–6; A. J. Moles 42–8–167–2; D. P. Ostler 9–0–54–0; T. L. Penney 5–0–35–0; K. J. Piper 4.4–0–57–1.

Wicket-keepers: K. J. Piper 39 ct, 2 st, P. C. L. Holloway 8 ct; M. Burns 5 ct; D. P. Ostler 1 ct (K. J. Piper also took two catches in the field).

Leading Fielders: D. P. Ostler 19, A. J. Moles 18, R. G. Twose 16, D. A. Reeve 15.

At Nottingham, April 25, 26, 27, 28. WARWICKSHIRE lost to NOTTINGHAMSHIRE by eight wickets.

WARWICKSHIRE v DERBYSHIRE

At Birmingham, May 7, 8, 9, 11. Warwickshire won by nine wickets. Warwickshire 22 pts, Derbyshire 4 pts. Toss: Warwickshire. Warwickshire outplayed Derbyshire so completely that, despite losing nearly seven hours' play to rain, they still won by nine wickets with time to spare. On a pitch which afforded lateral seam movement throughout, Moles and Ratcliffe batted resolutely against Bishop and Malcolm. Their opening partnership of 82 underpinned a total of 235, which was exactly enough to enforce the follow-on. Donald ripped through the Derbyshire top order with Munton his ideal foil – at one stage the score was nine runs for five wickets. Malcolm was the unexpected and stylistically eccentric top-scorer on 26 but, with a single needed to avoid the follow-on and probably save the match, he was bowled swinging at Munton. Solid innings from Barnett, Morris and Cork, with a maiden fifty, and the loss of the entire third day, meant the home attack had to work hard, and they were indebted to Smith's career-best six for 91. But Derbyshire were all out after lunch and Moles, Ratcliffe and Lloyd punished Malcolm heavily, to register victory.

Close of play: First day, Derbyshire 21-5 (P. D. Bowler 8*, D. G. Cork 5*); Second day, Derbyshire 186-5 (K. M. Krikken 12*, D. G. Cork 4*); Third day, No play.

Warwickshire

A. J. Moles c Krikken b Bishop	50	– not out	86
J. D. Ratcliffe c Bowler b Cork	50	– c Warner b Malcolm	45
T. A. Lloyd c Morris b Cork	10	– not out	34
D. P. Ostler c Adams b Malcolm	0		
R. G. Twose c Bowler b Mortensen	37		
Asif Din c Krikken b Malcolm	28		
P. A. Smith c Adams b Malcolm	7		
*P. C. L. Holloway c Morris b Malcolm	16		
G. A. Booth not out	10		
A. A. Donald c and b Bishop	0		
T. A. Munton b Bishop	6		
B 4, l-b 9, w 1, n-b 7	21	B 5, l-b 1, w 7	13

1/82 2/100 3/104 4/151 5/169   235   1/120   (1 wkt) 178
6/187 7/215 8/224 9/225

Bonus points – Warwickshire 2, Derbyshire 4.

Bowling: *First Innings*—Bishop 17.2–7–32–3; Malcolm 21–1–83–4; Mortensen 21–6–39–1; Cork 19–5–45–2; Warner 14–5–23–0. *Second Innings*—Bishop 5–0–21–0; Mortensen 1–1–13–0; Warner 10–1–29–0; Malcolm 11–0–74–1; Cork 8–1–28–0; Adams 1–0–7–0.

Derbyshire

K. J. Barnett b Donald	0	– c Holloway b Booth	57
P. D. Bowler c Ostler b Donald	14	– b Smith	30
J. E. Morris c Ostler b Donald	1	– c Twose b Smith	69
J. G. O'Gorman b Donald	0	– b Donald	0
D. J. Adams c Holloway b Munton	5	– b Booth	4
K. M. Krikken c Holloway b Munton	0	– c and b Smith	28
D. G. Cork b Munton	13	– not out	72
R. Bishop c Ratcliffe b Munton	7	– c Holloway b Smith	6
A. E. Warner b Smith	1	– b Smith	13
D. E. Malcolm b Munton	26	– b Smith	16
O. H. Mortensen not out	9	– run out	0
B 1, l-b 7, n-b 1	9	B 13, l-b 7, w 10, n-b 2	32

1/0 2/4 3/4 4/9 5/9   85   1/85 2/99 3/105 4/111 5/182   327
6/35 7/47 8/48 9/63   6/237 7/255 8/275 9/319

Bonus points – Warwickshire 4.

Bowling: *First Innings*—Donald 14–5–22–4; Munton 15.2–2–44–5; Smith 2–0–11–1. *Second Innings*—Donald 26–5–74–1; Munton 39–14–87–0; Smith 27.1–5–91–6; Booth 24–13–39–2; Twose 3–0–16–0.

Umpires: B. Dudleston and A. G. T. Whitehead.

At Cambridge, May 12, 13, 14. WARWICKSHIRE drew with CAMBRIDGE UNIVERSITY.

At Swansea, May 20, 21, 22. WARWICKSHIRE lost to GLAMORGAN by 93 runs.

WARWICKSHIRE v WORCESTERSHIRE

At Birmingham, May 23, 25, 26. Warwickshire won by 52 runs. Warwickshire 24 pts, Worcestershire 5 pts. Toss: Worcestershire. Thanks to a maiden hundred from Holloway and a pace attack brilliantly spearheaded by Donald, Warwickshire beat their neighbours by 52 runs with 11 overs to spare. Put in to bat, the home side were reeling at 119 for six, with half the wickets gone to Moody. Holloway, playing as wicket-keeper because of Piper's injury, steered them to safety, hitting 13 fours and sharing an unbroken stand of 98 for the ninth wicket with Donald. Worcestershire then suffered an all too familiar collapse, losing their last eight wickets for 90, to hand Warwickshire a lead of 105. England team manager Micky Stewart saw some fine bowling from Munton, which was to prompt his call-up to the Test squad. But then Newport put Worcestershire back in the game, claiming four for 14 in nine overs of sustained fast-medium bowling, and a target of 295 off 80 overs was possible while Hick was there. His 70 included 13 fours in 95 balls, but when the hostile Donald dismissed him, Worcestershire lost their last six wickets for 40.

Close of play: First day, Worcestershire 14-0 (T. S. Curtis 8*, A. C. H. Seymour 6*). Second day, Warwickshire 142-4 (D. A. Reeve 38*, R. G. Twose 11*).

Warwickshire

A. J. Moles b Newport	4	– c Moody b Lampitt	10	
J. D. Ratcliffe c Hick b Newport	11	– c Moody b Newport	22	
*T. A. Lloyd c Seymour b Moody	38	– c D'Oliveira b Moody	20	
D. P. Ostler lbw b Lampitt	14	– c Seymour b Moody	30	
D. A. Reeve c Hick b Moody	1	– c Rhodes b Newport	49	
R. G. Twose c Rhodes b Moody	43	– c Rhodes b Lampitt	13	
P. A. Smith c Rhodes b Lampitt	30	– c Lampitt b Newport	5	
†P. C. L. Holloway not out	102	– c Curtis b Newport	15	
G. C. Small c Leatherdale b Moody	19	– b Newport	13	
A. A. Donald not out	33	– c Hick b Lampitt	5	
T. A. Munton (did not bat).		– not out	0	
L-b 7, w 1, n-b 10	18	B 1, l-b 4, n-b 3	8	

1/9 2/18 3/53 4/54 5/102   (8 wkts dec.) 313   1/38 2/38 3/68 4/109 5/149   180
6/119 7/166 8/215   6/150 7/158 8/173 9/175

Bonus points – Warwickshire 4, Worcestershire 3 (Score at 100 overs: 302-8).

Bowling: *First Innings*—Radford 17–0–71–0; Newport 25–8–69–2; Lampitt 23–3–80–2; Moody 21–5–50–4; Illingworth 12–3–21–0; Hick 4–1–15–0. *Second Innings*—Radford 4–1–26–0; Newport 22–3–45–5; Lampitt 17–2–51–3; Moody 9–2–24–2; Hick 7–3–18–0; Illingworth 5–0–20–0.

Worcestershire

*T. S. Curtis b Donald	40	– c Small b Donald	54
A. C. H. Seymour c Ratcliffe b Smith	31	– lbw b Donald	38
G. A. Hick c Holloway b Munton	17	– c Holloway b Donald	70
T. M. Moody lbw b Donald	54	– b Donald	1
D. A. Leatherdale lbw b Munton	2	– b Smith	21
D. B. D'Oliveira c Holloway b Munton	14	– c Moles b Munton	14
S. R. Lampitt lbw b Smith	24	– (8) c and b Small	9
R. K. Illingworth c Lloyd b Smith	9	– (9) c Ostler b Small	1
P. J. Newport c Reeve b Small	2	– (10) not out	1
†S. J. Rhodes not out	1	– (7) c Ostler b Munton	9
N. V. Radford c Donald b Small	0	– c Holloway b Donald	0
B 7, l-b 3, n-b 4	14	B 5, l-b 14, n-b 5	24

1/78 2/80 3/118 4/120 5/155   **208**   1/89 2/110 3/128 4/171 5/202   **242**
6/189 7/203 8/204 9/208   6/223 7/236 8/238 9/241

Bonus points – Worcestershire 2, Warwickshire 4.

Bowling: *First Innings*—Donald 17–2–60–2; Small 15–6–35–2; Smith 15–3–55–3; Munton 18–4–40–3; Moles 5–2–8–0. *Second Innings*—Donald 17.4–2–69–5; Small 19–6–46–2; Smith 9–2–51–1; Munton 23–9–57–2.

Umpires: H. D. Bird and R. C. Tolchard.

At Hove, June 2, 3, 4. WARWICKSHIRE lost to SUSSEX by two wickets.

WARWICKSHIRE v HAMPSHIRE

At Birmingham, June 12, 13, 15. Drawn. Warwickshire 5 pts, Hampshire 7 pts. Toss: Hampshire. A hard-fought game on a slow pitch ended in a draw, although Hampshire were close to a victory which would have doubled their lead in the Championship table to 32 points. They had reduced Warwickshire to 167 for seven, with 15 overs remaining, but determined resistance from Paul Smith, rounding off a good all-round match, and Small saved the game. Middleton scored 201 runs over nine hours, including his fifth century of the season, and came within 16 of winning the race to 1,000 runs, in just 11 innings. On the first day his team were 240 for three wickets, including that of Gower, whose OBE had just been announced, before losing their last seven for 50. Paul Smith, the seventh bowler tried, was chiefly responsible, with a devastating spell of five for 63 in 18 overs. Moles held Warwickshire's first innings together, but arrears of 74 enabled Nicholas to declare after lunch on the final day, leaving a target of 257 from 62 overs. Warwickshire gave up the challenge once Ostler and Twose were out.

Close of play: First day, Warwickshire 0-0 (A. J. Moles 0*, J. D. Ratcliffe 0*); Second day, Hampshire 39-1 (T. C. Middleton 14*, S. D. Udal 2*).

Hampshire

T. C. Middleton b Smith	124	– (2) c Ostler b Reeve	77
V. P. Terry lbw b Donald	38	– (1) c Piper b Donald	22
D. I. Gower lbw b Munton	22	– (4) not out	28
R. A. Smith c Piper b Smith	49	– (5) not out	15
K. D. James c Ostler b Smith	13		
*M. C. J. Nicholas b Smith	9		
M. D. Marshall c Small b Smith	0		
J. R. Ayling run out	4		
†A. N. Aymes c Twose b Donald	8		
S. D. Udal b Donald	10	– (3) b Twose	38
P. J. Bakker not out	1		
L-b 9, n-b 3	12	L-b 2	2

1/79 2/122 3/193 4/240 5/261   **290**   1/34 2/121 3/145   (3 wkts dec.) **182**
6/265 7/271 8/271 9/283

Bonus points – Hampshire 3, Warwickshire 3 (Score at 100 overs: 273-8).

Bowling: *First Innings*—Donald 17.4–5–46–3; Small 18–1–56–0; Munton 27–8–55–1; Reeve 10–2–28–0; Moles 4–0–12–0; Twose 10–4–21–0; Smith 18–2–63–5. *Second Innings*—Donald 11–4–24–1; Small 12–1–45–0; Twose 7–1–43–1; Munton 12–2–36–0; Reeve 7–0–32–1.

Warwickshire

A. J. Moles lbw b Ayling	95	– c Ayling b Bakker 2
J. D. Ratcliffe c Middleton b Udal	8	– c Nicholas b Bakker 0
*T. A. Lloyd lbw b Udal	14	– c Terry b Ayling............. 30
D. P. Ostler b Marshall.............	28	– c Marshall b Udal........... 65
D. A. Reeve c Aymes b Marshall	1	– lbw b Bakker 1
R. G. Twose c Gower b Marshall	2	– c Gower b Udal 51
P. A. Smith b Ayling..................	33	– lbw b Marshall 23
†K. J. Piper c Aymes b James	0	– c Smith b Udal.............. 0
G. C. Small not out	10	– not out................... 10
A. A. Donald c sub b Ayling	4	– not out................... 1
T. A. Munton not out	4	
B 5, l-b 6, n-b 6	17	B 11, l-b 3, w 1 15

1/19 2/46 3/93 4/120 5/122   (9 wkts dec.) 216   1/0 2/4 3/52 4/53   (8 wkts) 198
6/192 7/193 8/193 9/202   5/141 6/163 7/167 8/196

Bonus points – Warwickshire 2, Hampshire 4.

Bowling: *First Innings*—Marshall 23–4–59–3; Bakker 15–6–30–0; Udal 25–11–56–2; Ayling 20–6–37–3; James 14–4–23–1. *Second Innings*—Marshall 17–3–42–1; Bakker 8–1–24–3; Ayling 10.5–2–28–1; Udal 20–5–78–3; James 6–2–12–0.

Umpires: J. C. Balderstone and V. A. Holder.

WARWICKSHIRE v MIDDLESEX

At Coventry, June 16, 17, 18. Middlesex won by 226 runs. Middlesex 21 pts, Warwickshire 7 pts. Toss: Warwickshire. As well as supervising a convincing victory, Gatting enjoyed a personal triumph, with a match aggregate of 280 for once out, including two separate centuries for the first time in his career. His first-innings 117 was his 50th Championship hundred. But after his second-wicket partnership of 161 with Haynes, seven wickets fell for 48 as career-best bowling from Twose threatened to put Warwickshire in charge. His medium-pace swing and seam collected six wickets in 64 deliveries. Warwickshire's reply was led by Lloyd, whose unbeaten 84 was his first fifty of the season. If his declaration, 53 behind, suggested a captains' agreement, it was nearly spoiled by another ferocious exhibition of driving, cutting and pulling from Gatting. He hit an undefeated 163 in 169 balls, with six sixes and 18 fours, and shared 155 with Ramprakash, who managed only 33 of them. The eventual equation was 353 for Warwickshire to win in 74 overs. But Middlesex off-spinner Emburey and seamer Taylor quickly engineered a complete collapse. The last six wickets went in 19 balls, only one of which was faced by Smith, stranded on seven not out.

Close of play: First day, Warwickshire 20-0 (A. J. Moles 10*, J. D. Ratcliffe 10*); Second day, Middlesex 177-2 (M. W. Gatting 72*, M. R. Ramprakash 3*).

Middlesex

D. L. Haynes c Piper b Twose	67	– c Ratcliffe b Booth	72
M. A. Roseberry c Piper b Small	7	– lbw b Smith	26
*M. W. Gatting c Reeve b Moles	117	– not out	163
M. R. Ramprakash c Donald b Twose	0	– not out	33
†K. R. Brown c Piper b Twose	0		
J. D. Carr b Twose	7		
P. N. Weekes c Ostler b Small	39		
J. E. Emburey lbw b Twose	2		
N. F. Williams lbw b Twose	2		
A. R. C. Fraser b Small	33		
C. W. Taylor not out	0		
B 5, l-b 11, w 10, n-b 4	30	L-b 4, n-b 1	5

1/16 2/177 3/199 4/199 5/211   **304**   1/47 2/144   (2 wkts dec.) **299**
6/219 7/223 8/225 9/297

Bonus points – Middlesex 4, Warwickshire 4.

Bowling: *First Innings*—Donald 14–2–60–0; Small 15.3–3–43–3; Smith 17–3–60–0; Reeve 7–2–26–0; Booth 5–1–16–0; Twose 27–10–63–6; Moles 9–2–20–1. *Second Innings*—Donald 5–2–14–0; Small 5–1–19–0; Smith 8–0–34–1; Twose 11–1–37–0; Moles 5–1–25–0; Reeve 12–0–45–0; Booth 13–1–95–1; Lloyd 7–1–26–0.

Warwickshire

A. J. Moles lbw b Taylor	55	– c Weekes b Taylor	18
J. D. Ratcliffe lbw b Carr	35	– (7) c Gatting b Emburey	0
*T. A. Lloyd not out	84	– c Haynes b Emburey	43
D. P. Ostler st Brown b Emburey	49	– c Carr b Emburey	5
D. A. Reeve not out	8	– lbw b Taylor	10
R. G. Twose (did not bat)		– (2) b Emburey	28
P. A. Smith (did not bat)		– (6) not out	7
†K. J. Piper (did not bat)		– c Weekes b Emburey	8
P. A. Booth (did not bat)		– run out	0
G. C. Small (did not bat)		– b Taylor	0
A. A. Donald (did not bat)		– b Taylor	0
B 4, l-b 12, n-b 4	20	L-b 4, w 2, n-b 1	7

1/95 2/103 3/238   (3 wkts dec.) **251**   1/38 2/60 3/72 4/102 5/118   **126**
6/118 7/126 8/126 9/126

Bonus points – Warwickshire 3, Middlesex 1.

Bowling: *First Innings*—Williams 16–1–65–0; Taylor 20.5–3–72–1; Emburey 13–6–29–1; Fraser 16–7–52–0; Carr 12–7–17–1. *Second Innings*—Taylor 12.3–1–50–4; Williams 6–1–24–0; Emburey 11–3–23–5; Fraser 7–0–25–0.

Umpires: J. C. Balderstone and V. A. Holder.

At Bristol, June 19, 20, 22. WARWICKSHIRE beat GLOUCESTERSHIRE by 75 runs.

At Derby, June 26, 27. WARWICKSHIRE lost to DERBYSHIRE by an innings and 48 runs.

WARWICKSHIRE v ESSEX

At Birmingham, July 3, 4, 6. Drawn. Warwickshire 3 pts, Essex 3 pts. Toss: Warwickshire. Rain allowed only two and a half hours' play in the first two days, which made a double forfeiture inevitable. Beginning with bad luck when his first ball rolled on to Prichard's stumps without dislodging the bails, Donald bowled well for only three wickets, and later

Lloyd switched to sacrificing himself, giving away 54 in four overs to contrive a target of 276 off 66 overs. Essex's acting-captain, Foster, benefited with a 23-ball 53, and then dismissed both Warwickshire openers. Once Lloyd and Ostler had also gone cheaply, the home side settled for what was only their second draw in ten Championship matches. Reeve continued to rehabilitate himself after his World Cup injury with an unbeaten 54, and Penney underlined his rapid development with 41.

Close of play: First day, No play; Second day, Essex 123-3 (P. J. Prichard 62*, N. Shahid 28*).

Essex

P. J. Prichard c Piper b Donald	74		*N. A. Foster b Lloyd	53
N. V. Knight c Moles b Small	3			
M. E. Waugh c Twose b Donald	8		B 10, l-b 4, n-b 3	17
N. Hussain lbw b Twose	15			—
N. Shahid b Donald	28		1/12 2/25 3/46	(7 wkts dec.) 275
J. J. B. Lewis not out	60		4/127 5/138	
D. R. Pringle st Piper b N. M. K. Smith	17		6/192 7/275	

†M. A. Garnham, T. D. Topley and J. H. Childs did not bat.

Bonus points – Essex 3, Warwickshire 3.

Bowling: Donald 21–2–40–3; Small 9–1–18–1; P. A. Smith 10–1–42–0; Twose 11–1–43–1; N. M. K. Smith 11–2–47–1; Reeve 13–8–17–0; Lloyd 4–0–54–1.

Essex forfeited their second innings.

Warwickshire

Warwickshire forfeited their first innings.

A. J. Moles lbw b Foster	14		†K. J. Piper c Foster b Childs	15
R. G. Twose lbw b Foster	4		P. A. Smith not out	0
*T. A. Lloyd b Waugh	26			
D. P. Ostler c Waugh b Pringle	10		B 5, l-b 11, n-b 6	22
D. A. Reeve not out	54			—
T. L. Penney c Topley b Foster	41		1/7 2/26 3/51 4/73	(7 wkts) 204
N. M. K. Smith c Foster b Pringle	18		5/137 6/169 7/200	

G. C. Small and A. A. Donald did not bat.

Bowling: Foster 21–6–56–3; Pringle 13–5–23–2; Topley 8–1–38–0; Childs 14–2–40–1; Shahid 1–0–4–0; Waugh 9–2–27–1.

Umpires: J. D. Bond and J. H. Harris.

At Birmingham, July 12 (not first-class). Transvaal won by eight wickets. Toss: Transvaal. Warwickshire 197 for eight (50 overs) (J. D. Ratcliffe 72, D. P. Ostler 48, D. A. Reeve 37 not out; B. M. White three for 33); Transvaal 198 for two (44.2 overs) (S. J. Cook 101 not out, D. J. Cullinan 54 not out).

At Sheffield, July 14, 15, 16. WARWICKSHIRE beat YORKSHIRE by three wickets.

At Guildford, July 17, 18, 20. WARWICKSHIRE drew with SURREY.

At Northampton, July 21, 22, 23. WARWICKSHIRE drew with NORTHAMPTON-SHIRE.

WARWICKSHIRE v NOTTINGHAMSHIRE

At Birmingham, July 24, 25, 27. Nottinghamshire won by 117 runs. Nottinghamshire 23 pts, Warwickshire 5 pts. Toss: Warwickshire. Neither team could field a full-strength attack, because of Test calls and injuries, but the second-string bowlers seized their chance. At the finish Pennett and Mike won the game for Nottinghamshire, but on the first day it was the Warwickshire débutant, left-arm seamer Bell, who took the honours, reducing the visitors to 102 for four by dismissing Pollard, Johnson and Randall. Robinson inspired the recovery, stroking 23 fours in his 189 and drawing Championship-best performances from Saxelby and Mike, to steer Nottinghamshire to 415. None of the Warwickshire top order could build on a fair start, and Lloyd declared as soon as the ninth-wicket stand of Piper and Donald had averted the follow-on. Then demeaningly unsubtle bowling from Piper, discarding his pads to claim his first first-class wicket, and Moles enabled Robinson to set a target of 347 in 56 overs. Seamers Pennett and Mike plunged Warwickshire to 77 for seven, and although the tail showed their colleagues what might have been done, the visitors won with time to spare. Nottinghamshire keeper French made nine catches in the match.

Close of play: First day, Nottinghamshire 347-6 (R. T. Robinson 156*, G. W. Mike 35*); Second day, Warwickshire 232-8 (K. J. Piper 5*, A. A. Donald 2*).

Nottinghamshire

P. R. Pollard c Piper b Bell	37	– lbw b Reeve	0
M. A. Crawley lbw b Donald	15	– lbw b Reeve	2
*R. T. Robinson c Reeve b P. A. Smith	189	– b Piper	84
P. Johnson lbw b Bell	0	– not out	107
D. W. Randall c N. M. K. Smith b Bell	9		
M. Saxelby c Piper b Donald	66		
K. P. Evans c Ostler b Donald	0		
G. W. Mike not out	61		
†B. N. French not out	7		
B 8, l-b 15, w 4, n-b 4	31	L-b 1, w 2, n-b 1	4

1/42 2/74 3/74 4/102 5/254   (7 wkts. dec.) 415   1/0 2/14 3/197   (3 wkts. dec.) 197
6/256 7/390

D. B. Pennett and R. J. Chapman did not bat.

Bonus points – Nottinghamshire 4, Warwickshire 2 (Score at 100 overs: 312-6).

Bowling: *First Innings*—Donald 27-8-82-3; Bell 26-8-78-3; P. A. Smith 22-2-101-1; Twose 12-1-33-0; Reeve 17-5-35-0; N. M. K. Smith 20-5-63-0. *Second Innings*—Reeve 4-1-4-2; Twose 3-0-20-0; Ostler 6-0-32-0; Penney 5-0-35-0; Piper 4.4-0-57-1; Moles 4-0-48-0.

Warwickshire

A. J. Moles c Pollard b Pennett	35	– c Johnson b Mike	18
R. G. Twose c French b Chapman	30	– c French b Pennett	32
*T. A. Lloyd c French b Crawley	47	– c Evans b Pennett	13
D. P. Ostler c Pollard b Evans	21	– c Crawley b Pennett	2
D. A. Reeve c French b Evans	4	– c Johnson b Mike	6
T. L. Penney c French b Evans	40	– lbw b Pennett	1
N. M. K. Smith c French b Mike	19	– c French b Chapman	39
P. A. Smith c French b Pennett	16	– c French b Mike	1
†K. J. Piper not out	16	– not out	62
A. A. Donald not out	25	– lbw b Evans	41
M. A. V. Bell (did not bat)		– b Evans	5
L-b 2, w 4, n-b 7	13	L-b 4, w 1, n-b 4	9

1/46 2/110 3/138 4/146 5/147   (8 wkts. dec.) 266   1/46 2/60 3/64 4/73 5/73   229
6/173 7/209 8/228   6/74 7/77 8/126 9/213

Bonus points – Warwickshire 3, Nottinghamshire 3 (Score at 100 overs: 254-8).

Bowling: *First Innings*—Evans 32-5-74-3; Pennett 25.2-3-70-2; Chapman 8-1-39-1; Mike 15-3-44-1; Crawley 22-7-37-1. *Second Innings*—Evans 15.5-3-66-2; Pennett 19-4-58-4; Mike 13-1-48-3; Chapman 5-0-38-1; Crawley 2-0-15-0.

Umpires: G. I. Burgess and D. R. Shepherd.

WARWICKSHIRE v LEICESTERSHIRE

At Birmingham, July 31, August 1, 3. Warwickshire won by an innings and 124 runs. Warwickshire 24 pts, Leicestershire 1 pt. Toss: Warwickshire. Warwickshire moved up to third in the Championship when they dismissed second-placed Leicestershire 85 minutes into the third day. Munton claimed four wickets in his first four overs of the morning, and his match return of 12 for 110 was the best of his career. But Warwickshire's most emphatic victory of the season was set up by the much-improved Twose, with 233. It was his first double-hundred, and his maiden century in England. By the close he had struck 29 fours and two sixes in 320 balls, though he was caught first ball next morning. Moles contributed a more lethargic 91 in 92 overs to their five-and-a-half-hour stand of 285, Warwickshire's fourth-highest opening partnership. Mullally achieved career-best figures on the second morning, as five wickets fell for 48. But the home team's quicker bowlers then took control. Only Potter offered much resistance before Leicestershire followed on, and lost another four wickets by nightfall. Their excuses were a deteriorating pitch and the absence of their injured strike bowler Millns, who might have provided Warwickshire's batsmen with a greater challenge on the first day.

Close of play: First day, Warwickshire 385-2 (R. G. Twose 233*, T. L. Penney 23*); Second day, Leicestershire 60-4 (N. E. Briers 32*, L. Potter 16*).

Warwickshire

A. J. Moles b Mullally	91	†K. J. Piper c Briers b Mullally	6
R. G. Twose c Smith b Mullally	233	G. C. Small not out	12
D. P. Ostler lbw b Parsons	29	B 6, l-b 5	11
T. L. Penney not out	50		
N. M. K. Smith b Mullally	0	1/285 2/339 3/385 (7 wkts. dec.) 433	
P. A. Smith c Nixon b Mullally	0	4/395 5/395	
*T. A. Lloyd c Benson b Parsons	1	6/400 7/412	

T. A. Munton and A. A. Donald did not bat.

Bonus points – Warwickshire 4 (Score at 100 overs: 323-1).

Bowling: Benjamin 15-5-39-0; Mullally 34-8-119-5; Parsons 27-5-110-2; Gidley 17-3-56-0; Potter 24-3-85-0; Benson 3-0-13-0.

Leicestershire

T. J. Boon lbw b Donald	13	– b Munton	8
*N. E. Briers b Small	0	– b Munton	36
J. J. Whitaker c Piper b Small	36	– c Twose b Munton	0
J. D. R. Benson b Munton	4	– c Donald b Small	1
B. F. Smith b Munton	0	– lbw b Small	1
L. Potter c Donald b Munton	56	– lbw b Munton	21
M. I. Gidley c Piper b Donald	13	– not out	32
†P. A. Nixon b Munton	22	– c Moles b Munton	0
G. J. Parsons not out	1	– (10) c Donald b Munton	7
W. K. M. Benjamin retired ill	11	– (9) b Munton	8
A. D. Mullally lbw b Munton	0	– b Donald	21
B 5, l-b 7, w 1	13	L-b 4, n-b 1	5

1/1 2/25 3/40 4/52 5/72   169   1/17 2/17 3/30 4/32 5/68   140
6/114 7/150 8/157 9/169   6/71 7/71 8/81 9/105

Bonus points – Leicestershire 1, Warwickshire 4.

In the first innings W. K. M. Benjamin retired ill at 169.

Bowling: *First Innings*—Donald 16-7-27-2; Small 13-5-37-2; P. A. Smith 13-3-43-0; Munton 24.1-14-46-5; N. M. K. Smith 5-3-4-0. *Second Innings*—Donald 12.5-1-43-1; Munton 20-3-64-7; Small 8-2-29-2.

Umpires: R. Julian and N. T. Plews.

At Taunton, August 4, 5, 6. WARWICKSHIRE drew with SOMERSET.

WARWICKSHIRE v DURHAM

At Birmingham, August 7, 8, 10. Drawn. Warwickshire 8 pts, Durham 1 pt. Toss: Warwickshire. The loss of over half the second day, coupled with bad luck for their bowlers at the end, denied Warwickshire a win which seemed sure after magnificent bowling by Donald in the first innings. His seven for 37 was his best return for the county in six seasons, with four batsmen clean bowled. Only Botham resisted, with a belligerent 44 off 59 deliveries. Warwickshire batted in funereal light on the shortened second day to make up for lost time, and Moles, Twose and Lloyd made rapid fifties. The visitors needed 180 to avoid an innings defeat, but Larkins, with support from Bainbridge, ensured Donald would not repeat his first-innings destruction. When 67, Larkins became the first Durham batsman to reach 1,000 runs in the Championship. Durham lost only four wickets in 87 overs – two of them to Reeve, returning to form and fitness after his pelvic injury in the World Cup.

Close of play: First day, Warwickshire 89-1 (A. J. Moles 20*, T. A. Lloyd 3*); Second day, Warwickshire 316-4 (D. A. Reeve 44*, T. L. Penney 37*).

Durham

W. Larkins c Reeve b Donald	0	– c Smith b Twose	77
J. D. Glendenen b Donald	0	– c Piper b Donald	8
G. K. Brown b Donald	7	– lbw b Reeve	16
M. P. Briers c Piper b Donald	13	– c sub b Reeve	11
P. Bainbridge c Munton b Small	11	– not out	71
I. T. Botham c Penney b Donald	44	– not out	28
I. Smith c Munton b Small	4		
†C. W. Scott b Donald	29		
*D. A. Graveney c Lloyd b Munton	2		
S. J. E. Brown b Donald	7		
S. P. Hughes not out	12		
L-b 7	7	B 14, l-b 8, w 2, n-b 3	27

1/0 2/5 3/21 4/28 5/49   136   1/11 2/65 3/81 4/170   (4 wkts) 238
6/59 7/98 8/109 9/121

Bonus points – Warwickshire 4.

Bowling: *First Innings*—Donald 16.1-6-37-7; Small 13-3-41-2; Munton 22-7-45-1; Smith 3-1-6-0. *Second Innings*—Donald 18-6-59-1; Small 16-4-25-0; Smith 10-2-38-0; Munton 19-6-43-0; Reeve 16-7-30-2; Twose 8-2-21-1.

Warwickshire

A. J. Moles b Graveney	51	T. L. Penney not out	37
R. G. Twose b Hughes	65	B 2, l-b 9, w 2, n-b 1	14
*T. A. Lloyd c Botham b S. J. E. Brown	60		
D. P. Ostler c and b Graveney	45	1/85 2/175	(4 wkts dec.) 316
D. A. Reeve not out	44	3/200 4/256	

P. A. Smith, †K. J. Piper, G. C. Small, A. A. Donald and T. A. Munton did not bat.

Bonus points – Warwickshire 4, Durham 1.

Bowling: Botham 15-2-61-0; S. J. E. Brown 16-1-77-1; Hughes 22-0-88-1; Graveney 18-3-79-2.

Umpires: N. T. Plews and P. B. Wight.

WARWICKSHIRE v LANCASHIRE

At Birmingham, August 18, 19, 20. Lancashire won by an innings and 25 runs. Lancashire 24 pts, Warwickshire 3 pts. Toss: Lancashire. Lancashire's third win in 19 Championship games was a triumph for Watkinson, whose match figures of ten for 103 were a career-best. They included his first hat-trick when he claimed the first three wickets of the match at 111 – the "Nelson" score dreaded by superstitious batsmen – while bowling seamers rather than his more recently acquired off-breaks. Despite the century partnership from openers Moles and Twose, the home side were bowled out for 203, following a second collapse in which their last five wickets fell for 34. Atherton helped to ensure Lancashire's first Championship win under his command, with 130 including 21 fours; he scored off only 54 of the 268 balls he received. Speak and Crawley supported him with half-centuries and, with arrears of 212, Warwickshire's highest ambition was to survive the third day. But Watkinson was again too much for them, taking three wickets with seam and three with off-spin. Only Ostler and Penney offered worthwhile resistance, while Lloyd concentrated so entirely on defence that he faced 73 balls for a single. With the promising young seamer Chapple earning three wickets, Lancashire won with time to spare.

Close of play: First day, Lancashire 70-0 (G. D. Mendis 22*, M. A. Atherton 42*); Second day, Warwickshire 11-0 (K. J. Piper 9*, A. J. Moles 2*).

Warwickshire

A. J. Moles c Atherton b Chapple	86	– (2) c Speak b Watkinson	4
R. G. Twose lbw b Watkinson	53	– (3) lbw b Watkinson	0
D. P. Ostler lbw b Watkinson	0	– (4) c Watkinson b Chapple	56
T. L. Penney b Watkinson	0	– (5) lbw b Chapple	40
*T. A. Lloyd c Crawley b Watkinson	16	– (6) b Austin	1
N. M. K. Smith c Stanworth b Chapple	15	– (7) b Watkinson	20
†K. J. Piper b Fitton	0	– (1) c Stanworth b Watkinson	18
A. A. Donald not out	13	– (9) b Chapple	22
T. A. Munton c Stanworth b Austin	6	– (10) c Fitton b Watkinson	11
M. A. V. Bell c Stanworth b Austin	3	– (11) not out	0
P. A. Smith absent ill		– (8) c Speak b Watkinson	13
B 5, l-b 6	11	B 1, n-b 1	2

1/111 2/111 3/111 4/133 5/169   203   1/19 2/19 3/24 4/116 5/119   187
6/170 7/186 8/199 9/203   6/140 7/145 8/171 9/177

Bonus points – Warwickshire 2, Lancashire 4.

Bowling: *First Innings*—Martin 13–2–51–0; Chapple 14–7–26–2; Austin 10.1–4–33–2; Watkinson 19–6–41–4; Fitton 23–9–41–1. *Second Innings*—Chapple 18–8–40–3; Martin 5–2–16–0; Watkinson 34.5–13–62–6; Austin 16–5–30–1; Fitton 11–3–38–0.

Lancashire

G. D. Mendis c Piper b Donald	29	J. D. Fitton not out	48
*M. A. Atherton c Piper b N. M. K. Smith	130	P. J. Martin c Ostler b Bell	8
N. J. Speak lbw b Twose	52		
J. P. Crawley c Donald b Bell	74	B 16, l-b 8, w 4, n-b 1	29
G. D. Lloyd c Piper b P. A. Smith	31		
M. Watkinson b Twose	14	1/82 2/188 3/243 (8 wkts dec.) 415	
I. D. Austin lbw b Twose	0	4/302 5/329 6/329	
		7/395 8/415	

†J. Stanworth and G. Chapple did not bat.

Bonus points – Lancashire 4, Warwickshire 1 (Score at 100 overs: 300-3).

Bowling: Donald 17–6–42–1; Munton 29–7–113–0; Bell 23.2–7–65–2; N. M. K. Smith 38–10–99–1; Twose 10–1–28–3; P. A. Smith 11–0–44–1.

Umpires: J. H. Hampshire and B. J. Meyer.

WARWICKSHIRE v GLAMORGAN

At Birmingham, August 26, 27, 28, 29. Drawn. Warwickshire 4 pts, Glamorgan 4 pts. Toss: Warwickshire. With five and a quarter hours lost to rain on the first day, no play on the second, and nothing possible until 3 p.m. on the third, a double forfeiture was necessary before Warwickshire were set 317 in a minimum of 78 overs. The highlight of Glamorgan's innings was Dale's third Championship hundred, an attacking display with one six and 18 fours. He shared 163 with James after Morris was caught behind in the second over. Spirited bowling from Paul Smith earned him his fourth five-wicket return of the season. His hostility, even with an old ball, claimed the last three wickets in one over. Fearing rain, Warwickshire attacked so successfully that 100 came up in the 18th over, thanks to brilliant half-centuries from Twose and Lloyd, while Ostler hit a dazzling 60 off 42 balls. In sight of the win they needed to sustain their bid for Championship prizemoney, they were again frustrated. Rain removed 95 minutes before ending play when they were 60 behind with 9.2 overs and six wickets in hand.

Close of play: First day, Glamorgan 49-1 (S. P. James 18*, A. Dale 31*); Second day, No play; Third day, Glamorgan 225-5 (P. A. Cottey 7*, R. D. B. Croft 6*).

Glamorgan

S. P. James lbw b Reeve	64	S. L. Watkin c Piper b Smith	11
A. Morris c Piper b Small	0	M. Frost c Twose b Smith	0
A. Dale c Donald b Twose	127	S. D. Thomas c Piper b Smith	0
M. P. Maynard c and b Smith	6		
P. A. Cottey not out	67	B 5, l-b 2, n-b 1	14
D. L. Hemp c Small b Donald	7		—
R. D. B. Croft b Twose	18	1/0 2/163 3/202 4/202 5/213	316
†C. P. Metson c Piper b Smith	2	6/267 7/278 8/316 9/316	

Bonus points – Glamorgan 4, Warwickshire 4.

Bowling: Donald 23-8-64-1; Small 12-4-30-1; Munton 17-7-51-0; Twose 11-3-44-2; Reeve 10-2-41-1; Smith 22-4-73-5.

Glamorgan forfeited their second innings.

Warwickshire

Warwickshire forfeited their first innings.

A. J. Moles c Metson b Dale	30	T. L. Penney not out	13
R. G. Twose c Metson b Watkin	51	B 1, l-b 5, w 1, n-b 2	9
*T. A. Lloyd c Maynard b Frost	53		—
D. P. Ostler b Croft	60	1/71 2/125 (4 wkts) 256	
D. A. Reeve not out	40	3/146 4/238	

P. A. Smith, †K. J. Piper, A. A. Donald, G. C. Small and T. A. Munton did not bat.

Bowling: Watkin 13-0-47-1; Frost 10-0-57-1; Croft 7.4-1-50-1; Thomas 9-0-66-0; Dale 8-1-30-1.

Umpires: J. H. Harris and R. Julian.

At Worcester, August 31, September 1, 2, 3. WARWICKSHIRE drew with WORCESTERSHIRE.

At Lord's, September 8, 9, 10, 11. WARWICKSHIRE beat MIDDLESEX by eight wickets.

WARWICKSHIRE v KENT

At Birmingham, September 12, 13, 14, 15. Kent won by an innings and 143 runs. Kent 24 pts, Warwickshire 4 pts. Toss: Kent. Kent's ninth win of the season secured them second place in the final Championship table. Warwickshire, who started the game with an outside chance of overtaking them, finished sixth after being outplayed throughout. It was a good example of the four-day format allowing a side to extend a first-day advantage. Warwickshire's attack was heavily punished on the first day as the visitors reached 487 for three b the close, with Ward and Benson sharing an opening partnership of 290. Ward was i devastating form, hitting a six and 27 fours. Benson eventually declared at 603 for eight, th seventh-highest score for Kent, and the highest by any team against Warwickshire sinc 1928. Hooper's fifth hundred of the season underlined Kent's determination to bat the hom side out of the match. His first fifty took only 47 balls, but as he settled down to occupy th crease, the second used up 111. Igglesden swung the ball at good pace to take five wickets and despite a valiant 76 from Lloyd, who needed a runner, in his last match as captain Warwickshire followed on 314 behind. Spin was their downfall in the second innings, with Davis and Hooper sharing nine wickets to secure victory within an hour on the fourth day Slow left-arm Davis took his tally for the season to 74, and became the only spinner in th top six of the national averages.

Close of play: First day, Kent 487-3 (C. L. Hooper 95*, G. R. Cowdrey 8*); Second day Warwickshire 121-5 (T. A. Munton 10*, N. M. K. Smith 6*); Third day, Warwickshir 120-5 (D. P. Ostler 19*, T. A. Lloyd 6*).

Kent

T. R. Ward c and b Smith	153	R. M. Ellison c Reeve b Smith	
*M. R. Benson c Penney b Smith	122	R. P. Davis not out	
C. L. Hooper c Ostler b Munton	102	B 16, l-b 16, n-b 3	3
N. R. Taylor c Moles b Reeve	78		
G. R. Cowdrey c Piper b Smith	88	1/290 2/319 3/460 (8 wkts dec.) 60	
M. V. Fleming c Piper b Twose	11	4/511 5/535 6/559	
†S. A. Marsh c Smith b Reeve	7	7/576 8/603	

C. Penn and A. P. Igglesden did not bat.

Bonus points – Kent 4, Warwickshire 1 (Score at 100 overs: 468-3).

Bowling: Donald 14-3-50-0; Small 13-2-49-0; Reeve 26-3-65-2; Munton 28-1-131-1 Twose 27-2-91-1; Smith 30.2-3-160-4; Lloyd 5-0-25-0.

Warwickshire

A. J. Moles lbw b Igglesden	0	– c Marsh b Hooper	38
R. G. Twose b Igglesden	4	– c Benson b Davis	52
D. P. Ostler b Igglesden	40	– st Marsh b Davis	25
T. L. Penney lbw b Igglesden	0	– c Marsh b Hooper	0
D. A. Reeve b Igglesden	51	– run out	0
T. A. Munton b Davis	47	– (9) c Igglesden b Davis	6
N. M. K. Smith c Davis b Penn	39	– (6) c Fleming b Davis	3
*T. A. Lloyd b Davis	76	– (7) c Davis b Hooper	8
A. A. Donald b Davis	2	– (8) c Benson b Davis	1
†K. J. Piper c Davis b Hooper	8	– not out	24
G. C. Small not out	0	– c Ellison b Hooper	10
B 5, l-b 8, w 1, n-b 8	22	B 1, l-b 2, n-b 1	4

1/0 2/5 3/5 4/101 5/102   289   1/82 2/96 3/96 4/98 5/102   171
6/182 7/246 8/264 9/289   6/123 7/124 8/129 9/153

Bonus points – Warwickshire 3, Kent 4.

Bowling: *First Innings*—Igglesden 25-6-91-5; Ellison 15-4-38-0; Penn 21-4-55-1; Fleming 12-3-29-0; Davis 15-5-38-3; Hooper 6.2-0-25-1. *Second Innings*—Igglesden 5-0-16-0; Ellison 7-2-21-0; Penn 5-1-21-0; Fleming 4-0-12-0; Hooper 24-5-57-4; Davis 22-8-41-5.

Umpires: K. E. Palmer and D. R. Shepherd.

WORCESTERSHIRE

Patron: The Duke of Westminster
President: G. H. Chesterton
Chairman: C. D. Fearnley
Chairman, Cricket Committee: M. G. Jones
Secretary: The Rev. Michael Vockins
    County Ground, New Road, Worcester
    WR2 4QQ (Telephone: 0905-748474)
Captain: T. S. Curtis
Coach: K. J. Lyons

For a county widely tipped at the start of the season as having the pedigree and potential to win the Championship for the third time in five years, Worcestershire's decline in 1992 could hardly have been more dramatic or unexpected. They finished 17th for the first time since 1932, and it was only the presence of the newcomers Durham that ensured they were not actually bottom.

They did little better in the one-day game either, getting knocked out in the first round of the NatWest Trophy, going down to a particularly dire defeat against Somerset in the quarter-finals of the Benson and Hedges Cup and finishing seventh in the Sunday League. It was very different to the run of success of the previous five years when Phil Neale led Worcestershire to two Championships, two Sunday Leagues and their first-ever win in a Lord's final, in the 1991 Benson and Hedges Cup. In their wisdom, the cricket committee chose to relieve Neale of the captaincy only a month after that last triumph. He was then left out of the team as well throughout most of 1992.

With Ian Botham gone to Durham, it seemed folly to lose another experienced batsman from the middle order. But Neale's successor, Tim Curtis, put his faith in younger players. It was never rewarded. A series of middle-order collapses in the early part of the season left the team short of confidence, and there were several self-inflicted defeats. Long before the season was over, officials were saying the club was in "a transitional period". Certainly, a glorious chapter in the county's history had come to an end.

There were plenty of extenuating circumstances, not least the enforced retirement of the former England fast bowler Graham Dilley, who in six injury-plagued seasons at New Road had bowled only 1,213 Championship overs but still took 169 wickets at 22.17 each, getting five or more in an innings 13 times. The free-scoring Tom Moody also missed out on half the season, initially through injury, then because the Australians were touring Sri Lanka. He still made four first-class centuries, including 178 against the champions Essex, and completed 1,000 runs in the Sunday League in only 18 innings, the fastest ever. With Australia touring England in 1993, Moody is due to be replaced as Worcestershire's overseas player by the West Indian fast bowler Kenny Benjamin.

Most of all in 1992, Worcestershire lost out to the weather. The home match with Gloucestershire was abandoned without a ball being bowled and every one of the last 13 days play at Worcester was interrupted. The county drew their last ten games.

In his first year of captaincy, Curtis was chosen as the Supporters' Association Player of the Year, having been the second batsman in the country to score 1,000 runs, the day after Tony Middleton of Hampshire. His aggregate of 1,829 was a career-best and included the first double-century for Worcestershire against Derbyshire, 228 not out. He has now scored centuries against every first-class county except Durham. Graeme Hick was top of the batting averages and his four first-class centuries, including 213 not out at Trent Bridge, took his career total to 67, of which 47 have been for Worcestershire. Unfortunately, he left for England's winter tour still to register one in a Test match, having been dropped from the team again before the final Test against Pakistan.

Adam Seymour, signed from Essex to open with Curtis, became only the fifth Worcestershire player to score a century on his début in making 133 against Oxford. But he managed only one half-century in 17 Championship innings before being dropped. This had the beneficial effect of bringing in Philip Weston, the England Under-19 captain who underlined his immense promise with 675 runs at an average of 37.50 and was chosen as the county's Uncapped Player of the Year. Steve Rhodes backed up his wicket-keeping with centuries in the last two Championship matches but the middle order was too brittle too often, with Neale being obliged to switch his attentions to the club's commercial and marketing activities. In December, he was appointed Northamptonshire's Director of Cricket.

Phil Newport, with 68 wickets and 467 runs, was a popular winner of the Dick Lygon award for the player deemed to have done most for the club on and off the field. Neal Radford took 60 wickets, bringing his total for the county above 500 in only eight seasons. The left-arm spinner Richard Illingworth, who was picked for the five one-day internationals, shared 70 wickets with his understudy Richard Stemp, who then left the county to make the formerly impossible career move, for a Birmingham boy, of joining Yorkshire. But without Dilley's strike-power Worcestershire were always struggling to bowl sides out. – Chris Moore.

574

WORCESTERSHIRE 1992

[Bill Smith]

Back row: K. J. Lyons (county coach), S. R. Bevins, D. A. Leatherdale, R. D. Stemp, J. E. Brinkley, W. P. C. Weston, A. C. H. Seymour, A. Wylie,
C. M. Tolley, G. R. Haynes, M. J. Dallaway, M. S. Scott (assistant coach). Front row: S. R. Lampitt, G. R. Dilley, P. J. Newport, N. V. Radford,
P. A. Neale, T. S. Curtis (captain), D. B. D'Oliveira, G. A. Hick, R. K. Illingworth, M. J. Weston, T. M. Moody. Inset: S. J. Rhodes.

WORCESTERSHIRE RESULTS

All first-class matches – Played 23: Won 4, Lost 4, Drawn 15. Abandoned 1.

County Championship matches – Played 21: Won 3, Lost 4, Drawn 14. Abandoned 1.

Bonus points – Batting 54, Bowling 65.

Competition placings – Britannic Assurance County Championship, 17th;
NatWest Bank Trophy, 1st round; Benson and Hedges Cup, q-f;
Sunday League, 7th.

BRITANNIC ASSURANCE CHAMPIONSHIP AVERAGES

BATTING

	Birthplace	M	I	NO	R	HS	Avge
‡G. A. Hick	Salisbury, Rhodesia	11	19	2	1,179	213*	69.35
‡T. S. Curtis	Chislehurst	21	37	4	1,622	228*	49.15
‡T. M. Moody§	Adelaide, Australia	10	18	1	624	178	36.70
R. D. Stemp	Erdington	11	6	4	70	16*	35.00
W. P. C. Weston	Durham	13	21	3	579	66*	32.16
‡S. J. Rhodes	Bradford	21	29	7	703	116*	31.95
‡D. B. D'Oliveira	Cape Town, SA	12	17	1	502	100	31.37
D. A. Leatherdale	Bradford	21	36	3	882	112	26.72
G. R. Haynes	Stourbridge	9	13	2	288	66	26.18
‡P. J. Newport	High Wycombe	20	24	6	463	75*	25.72
‡S. R. Lampitt	Wolverhampton	18	28	5	562	71*	24.43
A. C. H. Seymour	Royston	9	17	0	373	62	21.94
‡R. K. Illingworth	Bradford	18	19	6	282	43	21.69
‡N. V. Radford	Luanshya, N. Rhodesia	20	18	7	195	73*	17.72
C. M. Tolley	Kidderminster	12	10	4	89	27	14.83

Also batted: ‡G. R. Dilley (*Dartford*) (1 match) 18, 4*; ‡P. A. Neale (*Scunthorpe*) (2 matches) 24, 17, 38; ‡M. J. Weston (*Worcester*) (2 matches) 17*, 8*, 1*.

* Signifies not out.   ‡ Denotes county cap.   § Overseas player.

The following played a total of 15 three-figure innings for Worcestershire in County Championship matches – T. S. Curtis 4, G. A. Hick 4, T. M. Moody 3, S. J. Rhodes 2, D. B. D'Oliveira 1, D. A. Leatherdale 1.

BOWLING

	O	M	R	W	BB	5W/i	Avge
P. J. Newport	576.1	121	1,655	61	5-45	3	27.13
N. V. Radford	497.2	91	1,553	57	6-88	4	27.24
S. R. Lampitt	356	39	1,239	33	4-57	0	37.54
R. D. Stemp	331.5	80	1,054	28	6-67	3	37.64
C. M. Tolley	217	52	650	17	3-38	0	38.23
R. K. Illingworth	570.3	170	1,420	36	4-43	0	39.44
D. B. D'Oliveira	153.4	29	536	10	2-44	0	53.60

Also bowled: T. S. Curtis 24–2–116–2; G. R. Dilley 11–3–34–0; G. R. Haynes 45.2–13–128–0; G. A. Hick 104.3–33–304–7; D. A. Leatherdale 10-2–33–0; T. M. Moody 67–12–235–8; M. J. Weston 19-3–58–1; W. P. C. Weston 46–6–125–0.

Wicket-keeper: S. J. Rhodes 41 ct, 5 st.

Leading Fielders: G. A. Hick 20, D. A. Leatherdale 15.

At Oxford, April 17, 18, 20. WORCESTERSHIRE drew with OXFORD UNIVERSITY.

WORCESTERSHIRE v NORTHAMPTONSHIRE

At Worcester, April 25, 27, 28, 29. Drawn. Worcestershire 6 pts, Northamptonshire 5 pts. Toss: Worcestershire. Curtis and his new opening partner, Seymour, set the tone for the first three days by dawdling 36 overs as they put on 79, and play only moved out of its measured mode on the fourth and final day. Even Lamb spent three and a half hours compiling his 44th century for Northamptonshire, delaying his declaration until the third afternoon. With Moody prevented from bowling by sore shins, Dilley removed by a strained Achilles' tendon and Illingworth nursing a trapped nerve in the neck, Worcestershire briefly had to borrow their visitors' 12th man, Tony Penberthy. But when the teams finally got down to business it became a fight almost to the finish. Set to score 274 in 53 overs, Northamptonshire took up the challenge and, while Lamb was racing to 66 off 67 balls, were well on course. But Illingworth took four middle-order wickets and was on a hat-trick until Bailey, batting with a runner at No. 9 after pulling a hamstring, joined Ripley to see out the last 18 overs.

Close of play: First day, Worcestershire 277-7 (P. J. Newport 10*, N. V. Radford 2*); Second day, Northamptonshire 204-4 (A. J. Lamb 86*, K. M. Curran 24*); Third day, Worcestershire 124-3 (T. M. Moody 33*, D. A. Leatherdale 19*).

Worcestershire

*T. S. Curtis c Bailey b Capel	43	– st Ripley b Roberts	38
A. C. H. Seymour lbw b Williams	37	– c Ripley b Walker	7
G. A. Hick b Taylor	92	– lbw b Roberts	23
T. M. Moody c Ripley b Taylor	21	– lbw b Roberts	33
D. A. Leatherdale c Capel b Curran	34	– c Ripley b Taylor	60
†S. J. Rhodes lbw b Capel	18	– lbw b Williams	45
R. K. Illingworth c Ripley b Capel	10	– lbw b Williams	12
P. J. Newport c Felton b Walker	30	– c Felton b Williams	10
N. V. Radford b Capel	23	– not out	17
G. R. Dilley c Bailey b Capel	18	– (11) not out	4
R. D. Stemp not out	7	– (10) c Felton b Roberts	15
B 4, l-b 7, n-b 1	12	B 4, l-b 12, n-b 2	18

1/79 2/89 3/125 4/192 5/250   345   1/19 2/59 3/77   (9 wkts dec.) 282
6/264 7/265 8/306 9/326   4/126 5/182 6/225
                                                 7/240 8/249 9/266

Bonus points – Worcestershire 3, Northamptonshire 2 (Score at 100 overs: 263-5).

Bowling: *First Innings*—Taylor 35–11–80–2; Curran 33–10–82–1; Walker 29–8–66–1; Williams 12–1–41–1; Capel 26.1–8–61–5; Roberts 1–0–4–0. *Second Innings*—Taylor 17–2–54–1; Curran 15–4–33–0; Walker 16–6–24–1; Capel 9–4–12–0; Roberts 35–8–101–4; Williams 19–4–42–3.

Northamptonshire

A. Fordham c Rhodes b Newport	32	– lbw b Newport	16
N. A. Felton c Hick b Newport	21	– c Hick b Radford	0
R. J. Bailey c Seymour b Newport	10	– (9) not out	14
*A. J. Lamb run out	101	– lbw b Stemp	66
D. J. Capel c Moody b Newport	22	– (3) c Moody b Illingworth	26
K. M. Curran c Moody b Radford	33	– (5) c Rhodes b Illingworth	34
R. G. Williams b Newport	12	– (6) c Hick b Illingworth	3
A. R. Roberts c Moody b Stemp	5	– c Moody b Illingworth	0
†D. Ripley not out	60	– (7) not out	14
A. Walker b Illingworth	39		
J. P. Taylor c Moody b Illingworth	6		
B 5, l-b 3, n-b 5	13	L-b 4, n-b 3	7

1/45 2/56 3/97 4/155 5/226   354   1/1 2/26 3/63 4/127   (7 wkts) 180
6/235 7/244 8/252 9/334   5/152 6/155 7/155

Bonus points – Northamptonshire 3, Worcestershire 3 (Score at 100 overs: 263-8).

Bowling: *First Innings*—Dilley 11–3–34–0; Radford 33–9–82–1; Newport 37–9–102–5; Illingworth 25.1–5–66–2; Leatherdale 5–2–13–0; Stemp 12–3–37–1; Hick 4–2–12–0. *Second Innings*—Newport 9–0–39–1; Radford 6–1–28–1; Illingworth 19.4–7–43–4; Stemp 15–2–66–1; Hick 3–3–0–0.

Umpires: J. C. Balderstone and R. A. White.

At Worcester, May 6, 7, 8. WORCESTERSHIRE beat PAKISTANIS by five wickets (See Pakistani tour section).

At Derby, May 14, 15, 16, 18. WORCESTERSHIRE drew with DERBYSHIRE.

At Gloucester, May 19, 20, 21. WORCESTERSHIRE lost to GLOUCESTERSHIRE by three wickets.

At Birmingham, May 23, 25, 26. WORCESTERSHIRE lost to WARWICKSHIRE by 52 runs.

WORCESTERSHIRE v GLOUCESTERSHIRE

At Worcester, May 29, 30, June 1. Abandoned. This was Worcestershire's first home Championship washout for 23 years.

At Tunbridge Wells, June 2, 3, 4. WORCESTERSHIRE drew with KENT.

At The Oval, June 12, 13, 15. WORCESTERSHIRE drew with SURREY.

WORCESTERSHIRE v GLAMORGAN

At Worcester, June 16, 17, 18. Worcestershire won by eight wickets. Worcestershire 24 pts, Glamorgan 2 pts. Toss: Worcestershire. At their eighth attempt, Worcestershire posted their first Championship win of the season, on the back of a six-hour century from Curtis on the first day. He was only 19 runs short of winning the race to 1,000 runs when Croft dismissed him for 124. With Hick on Test duty and Moody retiring with a twisted ankle, it was left to Haynes, with a maiden fifty, and Leatherdale to secure maximum batting points for the first time in 1992. Newport, swinging the ball both ways, pressed home Worcestershire's advantage. Taking three top-order wickets for three runs in 15 balls, he instigated Glamorgan's collapse in just 45 overs. Following on 257 in arrears, the Welsh county needed a fifth-wicket stand of 87 between Morris, reaching his third Championship century in seven matches, and Watkin, with a career-best 41, to avert an innings defeat. Newport's match figures of nine for 135 took his season's tally to 35, before Curtis completed his 1,000 runs, a day after Tony Middleton of Hampshire, as Worcestershire strolled to victory.

Close of play: First day, Worcestershire 329-4 (S. R. Lampitt 30*, S. J. Rhodes 5*); Second day, Glamorgan 159-4 (H. Morris 77*, S. L. Watkin 0*).

Worcestershire

*T. S. Curtis c Cottey b Croft	124	– not out	43
A. C. H. Seymour c Croft b Watkin	16	– b Barwick	29
T. M. Moody retired hurt	12		
G. R. Haynes c Metson b Croft	66	– (3) b Barwick	1
D. A. Leatherdale c Maynard b Croft	66	– (4) not out	4
S. R. Lampitt c Metson b Watkin	66		
†S. J. Rhodes not out	46		
B 1, l-b 4, w 1, n-b 5	11	B 3, l-b 1, w 1, n-b 1	6

1/25 2/157 3/278 4/317 5/407   (5 wkts dec.) 407   1/46 2/66   (2 wkts) 83

P. J. Newport, R. K. Illingworth, N. V. Radford and R. D. Stemp did not bat.

Bonus points – Worcestershire 4, Glamorgan 1 (Score at 100 overs: 306-3).

In the first innings T. M. Moody retired hurt at 46.

Bowling: *First Innings*—Watkin 21.1–5–58–2; Bastien 20–2–92–0; Barwick 35–9–91–0; Croft 37–5–137–3; Richards 3–1–8–0; Dale 6–3–16–0. *Second Innings*—Watkin 10–4–18–0; Bastien 8–1–26–0; Barwick 13–8–14–2; Croft 4–0–19–0; Morris 0.5–0–2–0.

Glamorgan

S. P. James c Rhodes b Newport	6	– b Radford	11
H. Morris b Newport	21	– c Rhodes b Lampitt	123
A. Dale b Newport	0	– c Stemp b Radford	7
*M. P. Maynard b Lampitt	12	– lbw b Newport	14
I. V. A. Richards c Curtis b Lampitt	18	– c Rhodes b Stemp	33
P. A. Cottey lbw b Lampitt	13	– (7) c Rhodes b Newport	6
R. D. B. Croft not out	19	– (8) not out	40
†C. P. Metson b Radford	27	– (9) c Rhodes b Newport	23
S. Bastien b Newport	1	– (10) b Lampitt	1
S. L. Watkin c Haynes b Radford	8	– (6) c Leatherdale b Newport	41
S. R. Barwick b Radford	0	– lbw b Newport	4
L-b 7, w 2, n-b 16	25	B 4, l-b 9, w 1, n-b 22	36

1/24 2/24 3/36 4/61 5/71   150   1/36 2/52 3/92 4/159 5/246   339
6/89 7/130 8/135 9/150   6/262 7/263 8/314 9/322

Bonus points – Glamorgan 1, Worcestershire 4.

Bowling: *First Innings*—Radford 15–1–52–3; Newport 13–4–34–4; Lampitt 10–1–36–3; Haynes 7–3–21–0. *Second Innings*—Radford 21–4–86–2; Newport 29.4–5–101–5; Haynes 9–3–18–0; Lampitt 21–1–85–2; Illingworth 5–2–12–0; Stemp 11–6–24–1.

Umpires: K. E. Palmer and A. G. T. Whitehead.

WORCESTERSHIRE v YORKSHIRE

At Worcester, June 19, 20, 22. Worcestershire won by 89 runs. Worcestershire 23 pts, Yorkshire 5 pts. Toss: Worcestershire. High-class seam bowling from Radford and Newport clinched Worcestershire's second successive Championship triumph after the captains had conspired to fashion a finish. Yorkshire, still 152 behind at the start of the final day with one wicket in hand, declared on the understanding that the follow-on would not be enforced, before being set 297 off a minimum of 71 overs. After the demise of the top order White held up the slide, with a career-best unbeaten 79, until Radford took a stunning slip catch off Newport to dismiss débutant Milburn. That brought in last man Robinson to survive 22 balls. He was leg before to a full toss in the same over. Curtis had crawled to his fourth Championship century of the season in two minutes under five hours on the first day, and next morning took his partnership with Newport to 136, a county record for the eighth wicket against Yorkshire. In the process he passed 2,000 runs in 20 first-class games since taking over the captaincy the previous July; one of his partners was his predecessor, Neale, in his first appearance since then.

Close of play: First day, Worcestershire 297-7 (T. S. Curtis 151*, P. J. Newport 24*); Second day, Yorkshire 234-9 (S. M. Milburn 2*, M. A. Robinson 0*).

Worcestershire

*T. S. Curtis c White b Carrick	197	– b Carrick	31
A. C. H. Seymour c Blakey b Hartley	22	– b Milburn	25
P. A. Neale b Gough	24	– lbw b Robinson	17
G. R. Haynes lbw b Gough	0	– not out	23
D. A. Leatherdale lbw b Robinson	17	– b Carrick	14
S. R. Lampitt c Carrick b Hartley	8	– not out	4
†S. J. Rhodes c Kellett b Gough	14		
C. M. Tolley lbw b Robinson	11		
P. J. Newport c and b Robinson	61		
R. K. Illingworth not out	5		
B 1, l-b 13, n-b 13	27	B 16, l-b 12, n-b 2	30

1/48 2/98 3/98 4/136 5/165   (9 wkts dec.) 386   1/40 2/83   (4 wkts dec.) 144
5/196 7/238 8/374 9/386   3/83 4/131

N. V. Radford did not bat.

Bonus points – Worcestershire 3, Yorkshire 3 (Score at 100 overs: 261-7).

Bowling: *First Innings*—Hartley 25-9-82-2; Gough 23-1-99-3; Robinson 27-5-70-3; Milburn 17-2-61-0; Carrick 29.1-11-52-1; Tendulkar 4-1-8-0. *Second Innings*—Gough 5-0-32-0; Milburn 11-0-54-1; Robinson 6-1-14-1; Carrick 9-2-16-2.

Yorkshire

*M. D. Moxon c Curtis b Tolley	47	– b Newport	17
S. A. Kellett b Radford	0	– c Rhodes b Lampitt	29
D. Byas c Illingworth b Radford	16	– lbw b Newport	7
S. R. Tendulkar c Illingworth b Lampitt	42	– lbw b Illingworth	46
†R. J. Blakey c Leatherdale b Radford	57	– lbw b Lampitt	5
C. White b Newport	31	– not out	79
P. Carrick lbw b Radford	3	– lbw b Radford	0
P. J. Hartley c Leatherdale b Illingworth	7	– b Radford	1
D. Gough c Leatherdale b Illingworth	1	– c Illingworth b Radford	3
S. M. Milburn not out	2	– c Radford b Newport	5
M. A. Robinson not out	0	– lbw b Newport	0
B 5, l-b 5, n-b 18	28	L-b 5, w 2, n-b 8	15

1/17 2/40 3/92 4/139 5/209   (9 wkts dec.) 234   1/39 2/49 3/75 4/88 5/158   207
5/220 7/227 8/227 9/234   6/159 7/163 8/176 9/207

Bonus points – Yorkshire 2, Worcestershire 4.

Bowling: *First Innings*—Radford 19-4-41-4; Newport 18-4-44-1; Lampitt 12-1-34-1; Tolley 17-4-52-1; Haynes 6-0-30-0; Illingworth 19-12-23-2. *Second Innings*—Radford 22-2-86-3; Newport 23-5-69-4; Lampitt 9-0-35-2; Tolley 5-3-2-0; Illingworth 9-2-10-1.

Umpires: K. E. Palmer and A. G. T. Whitehead.

WORCESTERSHIRE v SUSSEX

At Worcester, June 26, 27, 29. Sussex won by 80 runs. Sussex 23 pts, Worcestershire 6 pts. Toss: Sussex. Not even Hick's emergence from the most barren spell of his career, with his first century in any competition of the season, after 31 innings, could save Worcestershire from a comprehensive beating. Sussex owed much to their West Indian all-rounder, Stephenson. His unbeaten three-and-a-half-hour 87 on the first day pulled them round from 131 for five; the last three wickets added 109. Next he was instrumental in securing a lead of 81 as Worcestershire, despite a maiden Championship fifty from Weston, lost their last nine wickets for 110. The final day was a showdown between Stephenson and Hick, after the home team had been set 276 to win in 72 overs. Stephenson swept away three of the top order in five balls, but Hick countered with a century off 106 deliveries. He struck 13 fours and five sixes, including three off Salisbury, and without him Worcestershire totalled a measly 64. He fell at last to North, but Stephenson had the final word, finishing with seven for 29, his best figures for his new county, and a match return of 11 for 107 to go with his 116 runs.

Close of play: First day, Worcestershire 29-0 (T. S. Curtis 15*, W. P. C. Weston 11*);
Second day, Sussex 90-4 (A. P. Wells 30*, P. Moores 14*).

Sussex

D. M. Smith lbw b Radford	4	– (3) c Leatherdale b Tolley	10
J. W. Hall lbw b Radford	59	– b Radford	13
N. J. Lenham c Hick b Lampitt	9	– (1) c Illingworth b Newport	14
*A. P. Wells b Newport	26	– c Hick b Newport	46
M. P. Speight c Hick b Radford	17	– c Curtis b Tolley	4
†P. Moores c Rhodes b Newport	17	– not out	61
F. D. Stephenson not out	87	– st Rhodes b Illingworth	29
J. A. North b Newport	0	– run out	1
B. T. P. Donelan c Hick b Radford	31	– not out	0
A. C. S. Pigott c Leatherdale b Lampitt	20		
I. D. K. Salisbury c Hick b Lampitt	0		
L-b 4, n-b 15	19	L-b 10, w 1, n-b 5	16

1/19 2/47 3/101 4/130 5/131   289   1/23 2/38 3/51   (7 wkts dec.) 194
6/180 7/180 8/220 9/285   4/64 5/131
                                               6/186 7/190

Bonus points – Sussex 3, Worcestershire 4.

Bowling: *First Innings*—Radford 27-5-77-4; Newport 25-4-78-3; Lampitt 21-1-76-3;
Tolley 17-4-47-0; Illingworth 5-1-7-0. *Second Innings*—Radford 6-1-24-1; Newport
23-5-53-2; Lampitt 17-2-52-0; Tolley 13-2-38-2; Haynes 5-2-13-0; Illingworth 2-0-4-1.

Worcestershire

*T. S. Curtis c Hall b Stephenson	15	– c Moores b Stephenson	1
W. P. C. Weston c and b Salisbury	56	– c Moores b Stephenson	4
G. A. Hick b Pigott	40	– c Lenham b North	131
G. R. Haynes c Lenham b North	6	– c Smith b Stephenson	0
D. A. Leatherdale c Moores b Stephenson	5	– b North	6
S. R. Lampitt c Salisbury b Pigott	3	– lbw b Stephenson	9
†S. J. Rhodes c Hall b Stephenson	51	– b Stephenson	2
C. M. Tolley b North	7	– c Moores b North	16
P. J. Newport lbw b Lenham	11	– not out	16
R. K. Illingworth c Moores b Stephenson	2	– c Smith b Stephenson	4
N. V. Radford not out	2	– c Smith b Stephenson	0
B 4, l-b 1, n-b 5	10	L-b 3, n-b 3	6

1/34 2/98 3/118 4/124 5/126   208   1/4 2/5 3/5 4/27 5/62   195
6/136 7/150 8/185 9/198   6/105 7/170 8/177 9/195

Bonus points – Worcestershire 2, Sussex 4.

Bowling: *First Innings*—Stephenson 24.4-4-78-4; Pigott 18-5-28-2; Salisbury 21-5-45-1;
North 18-3-45-2; Lenham 4-1-7-1. *Second Innings*—Stephenson 17.2-5-29-7; Pigott
18-5-42-0; North 11-1-51-3; Salisbury 11-1-56-0; Donelan 3-0-14-0.

Umpires: J. W. Holder and D. O. Oslear.

At Leicester, June 30, July 1, 2. WORCESTERSHIRE lost to LEICESTERSHIRE by nine
wickets.

At Nottingham, July 14, 15, 16. WORCESTERSHIRE beat NOTTINGHAMSHIRE by
five wickets.

At Uxbridge, July 17, 18, 20. WORCESTERSHIRE drew with MIDDLESEX.

WORCESTERSHIRE v ESSEX

At Kidderminster, July 21, 22, 23. Drawn. Worcestershire 6 pts, Essex 5 pts. Toss: Essex. Rain denied Essex the chance to pursue 335 in a minimum of 54 overs. But a sixth win in seven games was never really on the cards after Moody bludgeoned their attack for 178, with 25 fours, out of Worcestershire's 364 for four on the opening day. He shared stands of 113 with Leatherdale and 153 with D'Oliveira, who went on from his first first-class fifty of the summer to his first Championship century for two years and a day. Waugh, like Moody about to leave his county to join Australia's tour of Sri Lanka, led Essex to maximum batting points with his fourth Championship hundred of the season, an unusually cautious 138, whereupon Foster declared 148 in arrears. Prichard and Hussain tossed up 92 runs in nine overs to prompt Curtis's second declaration but the rain had the final say. The Essex openers, Stephenson and Prichard, had their averages credited with an extra not out under Law 2.10, because they stepped on to the field (three times) before play was abandoned.

Close of play: First day, Worcestershire 364-4 (D. B. D'Oliveira 87*, G. R. Haynes 2*); Second day, Worcestershire 15-0 (T. S. Curtis 13*, W. P. C. Weston 1*).

Worcestershire

*T. S. Curtis c Ilott b Andrew	12	– lbw b Foster	20
W. P. C. Weston c Shahid b Waugh	22	– c Shahid b Waugh	26
T. M. Moody c Ilott b Andrew	178		
D. A. Leatherdale c Waugh b Such	36	– (3) c Garnham b Foster	0
D. B. D'Oliveira lbw b Such	100	– (4) b Andrew	8
G. R. Haynes not out	40		
S. R. Lampitt c Prichard b Andrew	26	– (5) c sub b Hussain	63
†S. J. Rhodes (did not bat)		– (6) not out	62
C. M. Tolley (did not bat)		– (7) not out	1
B 6, l-b 15, w 2, n-b 11	34	L-b 3, w 1, n-b 2	6

1/23 2/69 3/182 4/335　　(6 wkts dec.) 448　　1/28 2/32 3/56　　(5 wkts dec.) 186
5/397 6/448　　　　　　　　　　　　　　　　　4/67 5/173

R. K. Illingworth and N. V. Radford did not bat.

Bonus points – Worcestershire 4, Essex 1 (Score at 100 overs: 340-4).

Bowling: *First Innings*—Ilott 27-4-98-0; Andrew 20-2-86-3; Waugh 19-5-46-1; Foster 22-3-67-0; Stephenson 9-1-47-0; Such 24-5-83-2. *Second Innings*—Ilott 7-2-23-0; Such 4-3-4-0; Foster 9-1-19-2; Andrew 7-2-24-1; Waugh 4-0-14-1; Shahid 2-1-7-0; Prichard 5-0-54-0; Hussain 4-0-38-1.

Essex

P. J. Prichard b Radford	10	– not out	0
J. P. Stephenson c Rhodes b Radford	22	– not out	0
M. E. Waugh not out	138		
N. Hussain run out	78		
N. Shahid c Rhodes b D'Oliveira	27		
J. J. B. Lewis lbw b D'Oliveira	16		
†M. A. Garnham not out	0		
B 2, l-b 1, n-b 6	9		

1/26 2/33 3/186 4/247 5/297　　(5 wkts dec.) 300　　　　　　　(no wkt) 0

*N. A. Foster, S. J. W. Andrew, M. C. Ilott and P. M. Such did not bat.

Bonus points – Essex 4, Worcestershire 2.

Bowling: *First Innings*—Radford 11-1-50-2; Tolley 16-2-62-0; Lampitt 13-1-42-0; Illingworth 17-3-66-0; Weston 11-0-29-0; D'Oliveira 14.1-1-48-2. *Second Innings*—.

Umpires: H. D. Bird and A. A. Jones.

WORCESTERSHIRE v DERBYSHIRE

At Worcester, July 24, 25, 27. Drawn. Worcestershire 7 pts, Derbyshire 5 pts. Toss: Derbyshire. The final day produced pure farce in a vain attempt to fashion a finish. Adams was spoon-fed a career-best 140, with six sixes and 20 fours, having reached the fastest ever century by a Derbyshire batsman in 57 minutes off 65 balls. Bowler, who added 186 with Adams, was more cautious, labouring two hours over fifty. When he finally moved into three figures, Barnett declared, leaving Worcestershire a target of 266 in what became 51 overs. Curtis and Weston compiled their second century stand of the match, with the captain passing 15,000 career runs when 25. But after Krikken completed his fourth stumping off Sladdin in the match, the chase was abandoned, with 11 overs left. Worcestershire had been handicapped by the loss of Newport, who bowled only two overs before succumbing to a groin injury. Lampitt shouldered the added responsibility, with his best return of the season.

Close of play: First day, Worcestershire 29-0 (T. S. Curtis 17*, W. P. C. Weston 7*); Second day, Derbyshire 52-0 (K. J. Barnett 25*, P. D. Bowler 22*).

Derbyshire

*K. J. Barnett c Moody b Lampitt	1	– b Curtis	36
P. D. Bowler st Rhodes b D'Oliveira	50	– not out	100
J. E. Morris c D'Oliveira b Illingworth	67		
T. J. G. O'Gorman c Stemp b Illingworth	33	– (3) c Moody b Curtis	4
C. J. Adams c Leatherdale b D'Oliveira	18	– (4) not out	140
†K. M. Krikken c Rhodes b Illingworth	3		
D. G. Cork c D'Oliveira b Lampitt	34		
I. R. Bishop b Lampitt	12		
R. W. Sladdin lbw b Lampitt	7		
D. E. Malcolm c and b Illingworth	10		
O. H. Mortensen not out	0		
B 1, l-b 2, n-b 8	11	L-b 1, n-b 4	5

1/2 2/103 3/129 4/149 5/154   246   1/91 2/99   (2 wkts dec.) 285
6/211 7/215 8/233 9/246

Bonus points – Derbyshire 2, Worcestershire 4.

Bowling: *First Innings*—Radford 6-1-18-0; Lampitt 18-1-57-4; Newport 2-0-10-0; Stemp 16-4-49-0; Weston 5-0-9-0; Illingworth 32.1-13-56-4; D'Oliveira 12-3-44-2. *Second Innings*—Radford 6-1-18-0; Lampitt 6-1-21-0; Illingworth 7-3-10-0; Stemp 19-7-45-0; D'Oliveira 15-3-78-0; Curtis 16.4-2-72-2; Moody 2-0-35-0; Leatherdale 1-0-5-0.

Worcestershire

*T. S. Curtis c Krikken b Bishop	86	– st Krikken b Sladdin	96
W. P. C. Weston st Krikken b Sladdin	35	– not out	50
D. A. Leatherdale c O'Gorman b Malcolm	25	– (5) not out	1
D. B. D'Oliveira c Bowler b Sladdin	16		
S. R. Lampitt b Malcolm	2		
†S. J. Rhodes c and b Malcolm	1		
T. M. Moody b Sladdin	26	– (3) st Krikken b Sladdin	4
R. K. Illingworth c Bowler b Cork	19		
P. J. Newport b Bishop	15		
N. V. Radford not out	14	– (4) st Krikken b Sladdin	0
B 5, l-b 8, n-b 14	27	B 1, l-b 8, w 1, n-b 1	11

1/122 2/154 3/178 4/184 5/186   (9 wkts dec.) 266   1/156 2/160 3/160   (3 wkts) 162
6/199 7/219 8/245 9/266

R. D. Stemp did not bat.

Bonus points – Worcestershire 3, Derbyshire 3 (Score at 100 overs: 264-8).

Bowling: *First Innings*—Bishop 19.2-1-39-2; Malcolm 18-3-51-3; Sladdin 33-15-62-3; Cork 17-1-59-1; Mortensen 12-4-31-0; Barnett 2-0-11-0. *Second Innings*—Bishop 13-1-37-0; Mortensen 8-3-14-0; Malcolm 6-0-32-0; Cork 5-0-20-0; Sladdin 6-1-35-3; Bowler 2-0-15-0.

Umpires: H. D. Bird and A. A. Jones.

WORCESTERSHIRE v HAMPSHIRE

At Worcester, August 4, 5, 6. Drawn. Worcestershire 6 pts, Hampshire 6 pts. Toss: Worcestershire. A generous declaration, leaving Hampshire to score 254 from 61 overs, set up a thrilling finish as Terry and Nicholas, whose 71 came off 73 balls, added 126 in 20 overs to reduce the target to 12 off the final over. Terry pulled the penultimate delivery from Newport for six, leaving three wanted off the final ball, only to be bowled by the perfect yorker. Turner, in his first Championship game of the season, tied a knot in Worcestershire's opening innings, taking three wickets in five overs after lunch, as the home team struggled to reach batting points inside 100 overs. But Hampshire were in danger of following on at 140 for five after Hick, dropped from the final Test against Pakistan, held three smart catches, taking him to 31 in the season. Marshall, with two sixes and eight fours, and Ayling turned the tide by adding 84 in 16 overs.

Close of play: First day, Worcestershire 305-8 (R. K. Illingworth 24*, C. M. Tolley 7*); Second day, Worcestershire 10-0 (T. S. Curtis 5*, W. P. C. Weston 5*).

Worcestershire

*T. S. Curtis c Morris b Ayling	49	– lbw b Shine	30
W. P. C. Weston c Ayling b Turner	47	– not out	57
G. A. Hick c Aymes b Turner	34	– c Morris b Udal	63
D. A. Leatherdale c Aymes b Ayling	31	– c Udal b Turner	26
D. B. D'Oliveira c Morris b Turner	0		
S. R. Lampitt st Aymes b Turner	42		
†S. J. Rhodes c Turner b Ayling	4		
P. J. Newport c Aymes b James	60		
R. K. Illingworth not out	31		
C. M. Tolley c Aymes b Marshall	27		
N. V. Radford not out	3		
L-b 6, w 1	7	N-b 3	3

1/83 2/124 3/142 4/142 5/194   (9 wkts dec.) 335   1/50 2/137 3/179   (3 wkts dec.) 179
6/204 7/232 8/286 9/330

Bonus points – Worcestershire 3, Hampshire 3 (Score at 100 overs: 252-7).

Bowling: *First Innings*—Marshall 25-6-51-1; Shine 17-3-73-0; Turner 45-17-103-4; Udal 17-4-45-0; James 8-0-14-1; Ayling 15-1-43-3. *Second Innings*—Marshall 6-2-18-0; Udal 12-2-66-1; Shine 10-0-46-1; Ayling 6-1-11-0; Turner 9.4-2-38-1.

Hampshire

T. C. Middleton c Rhodes b Radford	12	– c Curtis b Newport	20
R. S. M. Morris c Hick b Lampitt	49	– b Radford	3
K. D. James c Hick b Newport	17	– lbw b Tolley	29
V. P. Terry c Rhodes b Hick	26	– b Newport	113
*M. C. J. Nicholas c Hick b Radford	5	– (6) c Leatherdale b Tolley	71
M. D. Marshall c and b Tolley	58	– (7) not out	4
J. R. Ayling c and b Tolley	48	– (5) c Tolley b Illingworth	4
†A. N. Aymes b Hick	7		
S. D. Udal not out	21		
B 2, l-b 6, w 1, n-b 9	18	B 1, l-b 4, n-b 2	7

1/20 2/53 3/102 4/117 5/140   (8 wkts dec.) 261   1/21 2/30 3/101   (6 wkts) 251
6/224 7/231 8/261   4/112 5/238 6/251

I. J. Turner and K. J. Shine did not bat.

Bonus points – Hampshire 3, Worcestershire 3.

Bowling: *First Innings*—Radford 16–6–35–2; Newport 16–1–46–1; Lampitt 14–3–61–1; Illingworth 18–8–63–0; Tolley 12–2–28–2; Hick 6.3–1–20–2. *Second Innings*—Radford 7–1–16–1; Newport 11–0–48–2; Illingworth 24–5–81–1; Hick 11–1–48–0; Tolley 5–1–32–2; D'Oliveira 3–0–21–0.

Umpires: J. H. Hampshire and G. A. Stickley.

At Manchester, August 7, 8, 10. WORCESTERSHIRE drew with LANCASHIRE.

At Weston-super-Mare, August 18, 19, 20. WORCESTERSHIRE drew with SOMERSET.

WORCESTERSHIRE v DURHAM

At Worcester, August 21, 22, 24. Drawn. Worcestershire 7 pts, Durham 3 pts. Toss: Durham. Bad weather scuppered Worcestershire's chances of a first win in seven games. Durham, already firmly anchored to the bottom of the table, soon regretted their decision to bat first as Radford reduced them to 29 for three, going on to collect his 50th Championship wicket of the season. When Worcestershire batted Brown reached 50 first-class wickets, the first Durham bowler to do so. Curtis, for once, shook off the shackles with 50 off only 48 balls to surpass his previous highest aggregate for a season, 1,731 in 1990. Graveney applied the brake with a remarkable spell of 15–12–5–2. But D'Oliveira, with 13 fours in his 81, eased Worcestershire into a commanding lead before rain washed out half the second day. On the third morning Parker and Bainbridge wiped out the deficit of 95 in a solid second-wicket stand of 145. Parker had hit 20 fours when he was trapped by D'Oliveira, but Durham were safe by the time rain cut the final 55 overs.

Close of play: First day, Worcestershire 117-2 (D. A. Leatherdale 10*, D. B. D'Oliveira 16*); Second day, Worcestershire 294-6 (S. J. Rhodes 24*, P. J. Newport 25*).

Durham

W. Larkins b Lampitt	40	lbw b Radford	13
P. W. G. Parker c Tolley b Radford	1	lbw b D'Oliveira	94
P. Bainbridge c Rhodes b Radford	20	not out	65
M. P. Briers c Rhodes b Radford	0	not out	11
S. Hutton c Weston b Tolley	2		
I. Smith b Lampitt	44		
†C. W. Scott c Curtis b Radford	30		
*D. A. Graveney c D'Oliveira b Radford	9		
J. Wood run out	28		
S. M. McEwan c Rhodes b Newport	7		
S. J. E. Brown not out	0		
L-b 2, n-b 16	18	B 8, l-b 3, n-b 5	16

1/2 2/29 3/29 4/32 5/104   199   1/15 2/160   (2 wkts) 199
6/126 7/152 8/169 9/198

Bonus points – Durham 1, Worcestershire 4.

Bowling: *First Innings*—Radford 21–3–60–5; Tolley 12–4–26–1; Newport 15–1–62–1; Lampitt 9.3–2–35–2; Stemp 9–6–14–0. *Second Innings*—Radford 7–0–21–1; Newport 12–4–41–0; Tolley 4–1–16–0; Lampitt 6.3–0–38–0; Stemp 4–1–36–0; Weston 6–1–17–0; D'Oliveira 7–2–19–1.

Worcestershire

T. S. Curtis b Graveney	50	S. R. Lampitt c Smith b Bainbridge	4
J. P. C. Weston b Graveney	34	P. J. Newport not out	25
D. A. Leatherdale c Graveney b Brown	20	B 1, l-b 7, w 2, n-b 5	15
D. B. D'Oliveira b Smith	81		
R. Haynes c Scott b Smith	41	1/82 2/87 3/147 (6 wkts dec.) 294	
S. J. Rhodes not out	24	4/236 5/237 6/246	

C. M. Tolley, N. V. Radford and R. D. Stemp did not bat.

Bonus points – Worcestershire 3, Durham 2.

Bowling: Wood 14–3–53–0; Brown 15.2–1–69–1; McEwan 21–1–70–0; Graveney 30–16–49–2; Briers 1–0–7–0; Smith 8–2–26–2; Bainbridge 7–2–12–1.

Umpires: J. H. Harris and J. W. Holder.

WORCESTERSHIRE v NOTTINGHAMSHIRE

At Worcester, August 26, 27, 28, 29. Drawn. Worcestershire 5 pts, Nottinghamshire 8 pts. Toss: Nottinghamshire. Rain on all four days, causing the loss of 240 overs including the entire second day, proved more of a frustration to the visitors, who dominated what play was possible. Lewis and Cairns, with four wickets each, dismissed Worcestershire for 162, then both all-rounders weighed in with half-centuries. Nottinghamshire established a commanding lead of 159 before Crawley, acting-captain since Robinson's injury in the previous match, declared. Worcestershire still trailed by 127, with 60 overs to survive, when play was abandoned.

Close of play: First day, Worcestershire 116-6 (S. R. Lampitt 5*, P. J. Newport 3*); second day, No play; Third day, Nottinghamshire 219-5 (C. L. Cairns 41*, C. C. Lewis 8*).

Worcestershire

T. S. Curtis c Archer b Lewis	27	– not out	10
A. C. H. Seymour c Lewis b Cairns	22	– b Cairns	0
G. A. Hick c Bramhall b Afford	41	– not out	17
D. A. Leatherdale lbw b Lewis	0		
D. B. D'Oliveira b Lewis	0		
S. J. Rhodes st Bramhall b Afford	6		
R. Lampitt c Lewis b Cairns	9		
P. J. Newport c Archer b Cairns	20		
R. K. Illingworth c Randall b Cairns	1		
C. M. Tolley not out	16		
N. V. Radford lbw b Lewis	5		
B 4, l-b 4, w 1, n-b 6	15	L-b 4, n-b 1	5

1/48 2/72 3/72 4/76 5/108	162	1/9	(1 wkt) 32
6/109 7/120 8/124 9/146			

Bonus points – Worcestershire 1, Nottinghamshire 4.

Bowling: *First Innings*—Lewis 26.3–6–64–4; Cairns 26–9–50–4; Mike 2–0–2–0; Pennett 10–0–25–0; Afford 15–8–13–2. *Second Innings*—Cairns 6–1–24–1; Lewis 6–5–4–0; Afford 6–1–0–0.

Nottinghamshire

P. R. Pollard c D'Oliveira b Tolley	41	D. B. Pennett b Illingworth	5
M. Saxelby c D'Oliveira b Newport	17	†S. Bramhall c Seymour b Hick	7
M. A. Crawley c Rhodes b Illingworth	35	J. A. Afford not out	0
D. W. Randall c Hick b Illingworth	66	B 2, l-b 11, n-b 5	18
G. F. Archer b Newport	4		
C. L. Lewis c Newport b Illingworth	58	1/29 2/85 3/116 (9 wkts dec.) 321	
C. C. Lewis not out	70	4/121 5/198 6/251	
G. W. Mike b Newport	0	7/251 8/266 9/307	

Bonus points – Nottinghamshire 4, Worcestershire 4.

Bowling: Radford 4–0–17–0; Tolley 18–5–65–1; Newport 22–4–42–3; Illingworth 34–7–111–4; Lampitt 12–2–47–0; D'Oliveira 1–0–2–0; Hick 8–0–24–1.

Umpires: D. J. Constant and D. O. Oslear.

WORCESTERSHIRE v WARWICKSHIRE

At Worcester, August 31, September 1, 2, 3. Drawn. Worcestershire 5 pts, Warwickshire 4 pts. Toss: Worcestershire. Another 202 overs were lost to the weather, and the final day of the season at New Road was washed out altogether. With the original pitch still soaked by weekend storms, the match was played on the strip used for the previous game with Nottinghamshire. Hick lit up the surrounding gloom with his 67th first-class century, striking 22 fours, before he was run out in a mix-up with Rhodes. The wicket-keeper remained at the crease for almost all of a shortened second day, compiling a career-best unbeaten 116 by the close. Moles advanced to within 15 runs of a century before the end came.

Close of play: First day, Worcestershire 90-3 (G. A. Hick 45*, D. B. D'Oliveira 19*). Second day, Worcestershire 409-7 (S. J. Rhodes 116*, R. K. Illingworth 22*); Third day, Warwickshire 210-6 (A. J. Moles 85*, P. A. Booth 0*).

Worcestershire

*T. S. Curtis c Lloyd b Small	7	P. J. Newport c Piper b Booth		39
W. P. C. Weston c Twose b Munton	5	R. K. Illingworth not out		22
G. A. Hick run out	146	B 7, l-b 11, w 2, n-b 2		22
D. A. Leatherdale c Munton b Donald	13			
D. B. D'Oliveira c Moles b Munton	25	1/11 2/13 3/43	(7 wkts dec.)	401
†S. J. Rhodes not out	116	4/128 5/244		
S. R. Lampitt c Reeve b Booth	14	6/271 7/361		

C. M. Tolley and N. V. Radford did not bat.

Bonus points – Worcestershire 3, Warwickshire 2 (Score at 100 overs: 272-6).

Bowling: Donald 20–2–81–1; Small 18–3–51–1; Munton 37–12–80–2; Booth 35–11–93–2; Reeve 24–10–53–0; Twose 8–0–33–0.

Warwickshire

A. J. Moles not out	85	†K. J. Piper c Curtis b Hick		8
R. G. Twose c Rhodes b Newport	20	P. A. Booth not out		0
*T. A. Lloyd c Curtis b Illingworth	21	B 1, l-b 7, w 1, n-b 4		13
D. P. Ostler b Illingworth	20			
D. A. Reeve st Rhodes b Hick	38	1/37 2/60 3/110	(6 wkts)	210
T. L. Penney lbw b Hick	7	4/186 5/200 6/210		

G. C. Small, T. A. Munton and A. A. Donald did not bat.

Bonus points – Warwickshire 2, Worcestershire 2.

Bowling: Radford 14–3–47–0; Newport 13–5–22–1; Illingworth 39–12–56–2; Tolley 6–2–14–0; Lampitt 6–0–18–0; D'Oliveira 2–0–9–0; Weston 2–1–4–0; Hick 12–5–32–3.

Umpires: D. J. Constant and D. O. Oslear.

At Southampton, September 12, 13, 14, 15. WORCESTERSHIRE drew with HAMPSHIRE.

YORKSHIRE

Patron: HRH The Duchess of Kent
President: Sir Lawrence Byford
Chairman: Sir Lawrence Byford
Chairman, Cricket Committee: D. B. Close
Chief Executive: C. D. Hassell
  Headingley Cricket Ground, Leeds LS6 3BU
  (Telephone: 0532-787394)
Captain: M. D. Moxon
Director of Cricket: S. Oldham

Yorkshire's decision to break with cherished tradition and sign an overseas player brought some commercial success, checking the worrying decline in membership. However, the county endured a disastrous season on the field, emphasising that there are no easy or short-term answers to long-standing problems. They slipped from 14th to 16th in the Championship and from seventh to 15th in the Sunday League, suffering seven successive defeats in the process. They lost interest in the Benson and Hedges Cup at the qualifying stage, while Northamptonshire humiliated them in the second round of the NatWest Trophy.

Australian fast bowler Craig McDermott, the original choice as Yorkshire's first officially recognised "outsider", broke down during the winter and required an operation for groin trouble, so, with little room for manoeuvre, the club turned their attentions at the last minute to Sachin Tendulkar. The 19-year-old Indian's appearance on the scene at least silenced all those who, from a distance, accused Yorkshire of being racist, and he proved extremely popular with the public and fellow-players. Tendulkar collected his runs with a good deal of style, scoring quickly in the limited-overs competitions and being prepared to apply himself diligently in the Championship, but he lacked the experience to dominate. Additionally, Martyn Moxon made a mistake in not moving him up the order from No. 4 to open the innings in the Sunday League. Tendulkar topped 50 in eight of his 25 Championship innings, yet he managed only one century, which won the match against Durham.

He also completed a Sunday League century, but, having arrived too late to influence Yorkshire's Benson and Hedges Cup prospects seriously, he departed unexpectedly early, missing the last four Championship fixtures to play in domestic cricket in India. Failing to appreciate the lessons of the situation, several influential figures, including cricket committee chairman Brian Close, were ready to gamble again by recruiting an emerging player as Tendulkar's replacement, with West Indian bowlers Kenny Benjamin and Anderson Cummins the popular choices. Instead, the majority opted for an experienced batsman, West Indies captain Richie Richardson. A 12-6 vote in the general committee provoked a heated public debate which generated more passion than common sense.

Moxon shouldered a heavy responsibility as the captain and leading batsman, particularly as an opener. Despite a lean spell in August, he remained the most reliable run-maker, while Simon Kellett became established as his opening partner. Although failing to reach three figures in the Championship, Kellett scored consistently and fully earned his cap. Kellett's advance came at the expense of vice-captain Ashley Metcalfe, who was dropped even when Moxon was injured, David Byas taking over the captaincy. Metcalfe appeared to lose confidence, batting hesitantly when recalled and moved down the order, and generally found himself on the fringe of things.

Richard Blakey, who kept wicket tidily enough to catch the eye of the England selectors, had a good season with the bat, again proving splendidly resourceful in the Sunday League. Further encouragement could be drawn from the form of Morley-born Craig White, who fulfilled much of the potential which marked him out as above average when he came back from Australia in 1990.

Overall, however, Yorkshire batted without much conviction. There were a number of spectacular collapses and, even when the side compiled a substantial total, the runs came too slowly. On very few occasions did they overwhelm the opposition bowling, being more often prepared to sacrifice batting points in pursuit of supposed tactical advantage. This approach, unfortunately, usually restricted the time available to their own limited attack. Phil Carrick and Peter Hartley did not make sufficient runs in the bottom half of the order, but Paul Jarvis gave glimpses of genuine all-round skills. Recovering from a long and frustrating period in which he nursed a persistent hamstring strain, Jarvis operated with a great deal of hostility at the brisk side of medium pace and hit the ball hard, stroking his way to a stylish career best 80 against Northamptonshire at Scarborough. His bowling figures would have been far better but for the poor fielding.

A host of chances went begging in the slips, despite a number of permutations, and catches were fluffed in virtually every part of the field. Until Yorkshire sort things out in this area, they cannot hope to challenge for honours. Among the seamers, Mark Robinson suddenly found his most effective rhythm and, like Kellett, deserved his cap while Hartley accepted a heavy workload without complaint and kept going extremely well. Darren Gough, on the other hand, could not exert the necessary control. His ability to produce superb deliveries hardly compensated for expensive inaccuracies and he surrendered his rating as one of the brightest prospects, at least for the time being. Chris Pickles could not command a regular place and was released, along with second-team captain Kevin Sharp, at the end of the season.

Carrick claimed his 1,000th first-class wicket for the county before standing down to give his understudy, Paul Grayson, a run in the first team. The signing of Worcestershire's Birmingham-born left-arm spinner, Richard Stemp, in the winter was expected to mark the end of Carrick's first-team career. It also emphasised that Yorkshire were now willing to sign anyone they can, regardless of birthplace. This will provide a new look to Yorkshire's slow bowling resources as they tackle the new-look programme under the shadow of a dreadful record in four-day cricket. Collectively, they continue to make too many unforced errors, which is why they let themselves down and under-achieve. Basically Yorkshire allowed too many games to drift along in 1992 and lost concentration along the way. – John Callaghan.

YORKSHIRE 1994

[Bill Smith.

589

Back row: C. A. Chapman, S. Bethel, W. P. Morton (physiotherapist), M. Broadhurst, D. Gough, B. Parker, I. J. Houseman, M. J. Doidge.
Middle row: C. White, P. J. Hartley, J. D. Batty, M. A. Robinson, S. Bartle, D. Byas, S. A. Kellett, C. S. Pickles, A. P. Grayson.
Front row: D. E. V. Padgett (coach), R. J. Blakey, P. W. Jarvis, A. A. Metcalfe, M. D. Moxon (captain), S. Oldham (director of cricket),
P. Carrick, K. Sharp, M. K. Bore (academy coach). Inset: S. R. Tendulkar.

YORKSHIRE RESULTS

All first-class matches – Played 22; Won 4, Lost 6, Drawn 12. Abandoned 1.

County Championship matches – Played 22; Won 4, Lost 6, Drawn 12.

Bonus points – Batting 56, Bowling 52.

*Competition placings – Britannic Assurance County Championship, 16th;
NatWest Bank Trophy, 2nd round; Benson and Hedges Cup, 5th in Group C;
Sunday League, 15th.*

BRITANNIC ASSURANCE CHAMPIONSHIP AVERAGES

BATTING

	Birthplace	M	I	NO	R	HS	Avge
‡M. D. Moxon	*Barnsley*	18	27	2	1,314	183	52.56
C. White	*Morley*	19	26	8	859	79*	47.77
‡S. R. Tendulkar§ . . .	*Bombay, India*	16	25	2	1,070	100	46.52
‡R. J. Blakey	*Huddersfield*	21	32	9	1,065	125*	46.30
‡S. A. Kellett	*Mirfield*	22	36	1	1,326	96	37.88
‡P. W. Jarvis	*Redcar*	15	14	4	374	80	37.40
‡D. Byas	*Kilham*	20	30	4	784	100	30.1
‡A. A. Metcalfe	*Horsforth*	11	17	1	422	73	26.3
A. P. Grayson	*Ripon*	6	6	0	116	57	19.33
‡P. J. Hartley	*Keighley*	20	23	3	353	69	17.65
C. S. Pickles	*Mirfield*	6	9	1	131	49	16.3
J. D. Batty	*Bradford*	18	15	4	155	49	14.09
‡P. Carrick	*Armley*	19	25	5	261	46	13.0
D. Gough	*Barnsley*	11	12	4	72	22*	9.00
‡M. A. Robinson	*Hull*	17	12	5	31	12	4.4

Also batted: C. A. Chapman (*Bradford*) (1 match) 8*; S. M. Milburn (*Harrogate*) (1 match) 2*, 5; B. Parker (*Mirfield*) (1 match) 7, 30.

* Signifies not out.   ‡ Denotes county cap.   § Overseas player.

The following played a total of nine three-figure innings for Yorkshire in County Championship matches – M. D. Moxon 5, R. J. Blakey 2, D. Byas 1, S. R. Tendulkar 1.

BOWLING

	O	M	R	W	BB	5W/i	Avge
M. A. Robinson	413.5	79	1,134	50	6-57	3	22.6
C. S. Pickles	120.1	27	387	14	4-40	0	27.6
P. W. Jarvis	393.4	89	1,164	40	4-27	0	29.1
P. Carrick	630.1	202	1,375	47	6-58	1	29.2
P. J. Hartley	549.5	101	1,690	56	8-111	3	30.1
D. Gough	255.1	53	910	25	4-43	0	36.4
J. D. Batty	426	87	1,408	33	4-34	0	42.6

Also bowled: A. P. Grayson 50-5-186-1; S. M. Milburn 28-2-115-1; M. D. Moxon 3-0-7-0; S. R. Tendulkar 62.3-10-195-4; C. White 3-0-22-0.

Wicket-keepers: R. J. Blakey 44 ct, 5 st; C. A. Chapman 1 ct.

Leading Fielders: D. Byas 30, S. A. Kellett 23.

t The Oval, April 25, 27, 28, 29. YORKSHIRE drew with SURREY.

YORKSHIRE v HAMPSHIRE

t Leeds, May 7, 8, 9, 10. Drawn. Yorkshire 5 pts, Hampshire 7 pts. Toss: Hampshire.
orkshire were rescued after a poor start on a good batting pitch by Tendulkar, on his
hampionship début. Though he was missed by Gower at slip when four, he went on to 86,
nd added 139 in 36 overs with Blakey. But there were no other significant contributions,
nd Yorkshire's last five wickets fell for 32. Gower, who benefited himself from a dropped
ip catch by Kellett, on 11, gave Hampshire's reply impetus with 68 from 77 balls. The
elders' generosity continued when James had an escape on 40, with Pickles at mid-on
uffing a chance. Rain washed out the third day, and Hampshire showed no sense of
rgency on the fourth. Acting-captain Marshall allowed the innings to drift along, as James
dvanced to 116, including 16 fours, over five and a half hours. In consequence, Yorkshire
ad no trouble in securing a draw.

Close of play: First day, Hampshire 7-1 (T. C. Middleton 3*, D. I. Gower 1*); Second
ay, Hampshire 230-5 (K. D. James 51*, C. A. Connor 8*); Third day, No play.

'orkshire

. A. Kellett c Aymes b Connor	19	– b Udal	37
A. A. Metcalfe c Middleton b Connor	1	– not out	27
). Byas c Aymes b Connor	0	– not out	9
R. Tendulkar lbw b Ayling	86		
R. J. Blakey c Aymes b Ayling	72		
. P. Grayson c Terry b Marshall	10		
'. S. Pickles c Aymes b Marshall	21		
. Carrick not out	6		
. J. Hartley run out	0		
). Gough c Gower b Udal	2		
1. A. Robinson b Marshall	12		
B 4, l-b 13, n-b 4	21	N-b 1	1

'7 2/15 3/27 4/166 5/193	250
'218 7/223 8/223 9/225	

1/59 (1 wkt) 74

Bonus points – Yorkshire 3, Hampshire 4.

Bowling: *First Innings*—Marshall 22.5-7-29-3; Connor 15-3-52-3; Ayling 8-1-41-2;
hine 8-0-34-0; Udal 23-6-52-1; James 5-0-25-0. *Second Innings*—Marshall 2-0-8-0;
onnor 4-0-12-0; Shine 5-1-22-0; Ayling 5-3-13-0; Udal 5-1-13-1; James 2-1-6-0.

lampshire

. P. Terry lbw b Hartley	0	†A. N. Aymes b Carrick	4
. C. Middleton c Blakey b Pickles	55	S. D. Udal not out	0
). I. Gower c Byas b Hartley	68		
.. A. Smith lbw b Hartley	0	B 1, l-b 13, w 1, n-b 18	33
. D. James c Grayson b Carrick	116		
R. Ayling c Robinson b Carrick	24	1/4 2/103 3/103	(8 wkts dec.) 397
. A. Connor b Robinson	51	4/169 5/221 6/292	
M. D. Marshall not out	46	7/385 8/397	

. J. Shine did not bat.

Bonus points – Hampshire 3, Yorkshire 2 (Score at 100 overs: 287-5).

Bowling: Hartley 33-12-85-3; Gough 25-4-90-0; Robinson 16-0-56-1; Pickles
)-4-66-1; Carrick 29.1-6-75-3; Tendulkar 7-1-11-0.

Umpires: V. A. Holder and D. O. Oslear.

YORKSHIRE v GLOUCESTERSHIRE

At Leeds, May 14, 15, 16, 17. Gloucestershire won by 147 runs. Gloucestershire 23 pts,
Yorkshire 5 pts. Toss: Gloucestershire. The toss proved important on a dry pitch which
deteriorated and was marked unfit by the umpires. Hodgson underpinned a total of 411 with
a patient 124, his highest Championship score, hitting 17 fours and sharing century
partnerships with Hinks and Wright. Then four wickets fell for 30 runs in 17 overs, but
Alleyne survived some edgy moments to prevent a collapse, and Walsh hit out. Tendulkar
held Yorkshire together, working his way to 92, and Blakey hung on to be ninth out, giving
Davies a third wicket on his Gloucestershire début. Yorkshire were still 27 short of saving
the follow-on, but crept past that target by the close. Given the conditions, Gloucestershire
might have baulked at batting fourth anyway. On the third day Hartley exploited some
uneven bounce, claiming four for six in 26 balls, and the visitors collapsed to 90 for eight.
Russell's application lifted them to 142, but Yorkshire's batsmen could not cope with
Walsh. Keeping the ball low, the West Indian allowed just 13 scoring strokes and virtually
bowled out Yorkshire single-handed. His match figures were 11 for 104.

Close of play: First day, Gloucestershire 319-7 (M. W. Alleyne 49*, C. A. Walsh 6*).
Second day, Yorkshire 264-9 (D. Gough 17*, J. D. Batty 16*); Third day, Yorkshire 105-4
(R. J. Blakey 12*, D. Gough 0*).

Gloucestershire

G. D. Hodgson c Hartley b Tendulkar	124	– c Byas b Hartley	7
S. G. Hinks c Byas b Carrick	31	– lbw b Hartley	15
*A. J. Wright lbw b Carrick	51	– b Hartley	7
C. W. J. Athey c Carrick b Tendulkar	3	– lbw b Hartley	0
M. W. Alleyne not out	88	– c Kellett b Gough	16
T. H. C. Hancock run out	7	– c Hartley b Carrick	4
†R. C. Russell c Byas b Pickles	29	– not out	48
M. C. J. Ball c Kellett b Pickles	1	– lbw b Carrick	7
C. A. Walsh b Carrick	51	– c and b Hartley	0
M. Davies lbw b Hartley	4	– lbw b Pickles	15
A. M. Smith lbw b Hartley	0	– lbw b Pickles	0
B 4, l-b 5, w 1, n-b 12	22	L-b 4	4
	411		**142**

1/104 2/217 3/221 4/221 5/247
6/297 7/311 8/390 9/411

1/20 2/31 3/31 4/32 5/65
6/65 7/83 8/90 9/140

Bonus points – Gloucestershire 3, Yorkshire 2 (Score at 100 overs: 259-5).

Bowling: *First Innings*—Hartley 24.2–3–65–2; Gough 21–5–76–0; Pickles 12–4–36–2;
Carrick 51–19–88–3; Batty 26–5–102–0; Tendulkar 15–4–35–2. *Second Innings*—Hartley
19–3–48–5; Gough 15–5–35–1; Carrick 21–5–44–2; Batty 4–1–9–0; Pickles 1.5–0–2–2.

Yorkshire

S. A. Kellett c Hancock b Walsh	15	– lbw b Alleyne	38
*A. A. Metcalfe lbw b Walsh	4	– lbw b Walsh	10
D. Byas c and b Davies	29	– b Davies	11
S. R. Tendulkar b Ball	92	– b Walsh	23
†R. J. Blakey c Athey b Davies	66	– c Russell b Walsh	26
A. P. Grayson b Walsh	0	– (7) lbw b Walsh	0
C. S. Pickles c Russell b Walsh	0	– (8) b Walsh	2
P. Carrick b Smith	7	– (9) lbw b Walsh	0
P. J. Hartley c Wright b Davies	3	– (10) b Smith	6
D. Gough not out	22	– (6) c Hancock b Walsh	0
J. D. Batty c Davies b Smith	19	– not out	0
B 4, l-b 3, n-b 8	15	L-b 6, n-b 11	17
	272		**134**

1/13 2/20 3/116 4/180 5/182
6/184 7/198 8/208 9/235

1/14 2/64 3/78 4/105 5/105
6/126 7/130 8/133 9/134

Bonus points – Yorkshire 3, Gloucestershire 4.

Bowling: *First Innings*—Walsh 26–4–77–4; Smith 16.3–3–40–2; Ball 18–4–58–1; Athey 9–3–11–0; Alleyne 3–1–21–0; Davies 17–4–58–3. *Second Innings*—Walsh 20–7–27–7; Smith 15.1–3–37–1; Ball 8–3–11–0; Davies 11–3–35–1; Alleyne 5–1–18–1.

Umpires: G. I. Burgess and J. H. Hampshire.

At Canterbury, May 20, 21, 22. YORKSHIRE drew with KENT.

At Oxford, May 29, 30, June 1. OXFORD UNIVERSITY v YORKSHIRE. Abandoned.

At Basingstoke, June 2, 3, 4. YORKSHIRE drew with HAMPSHIRE.

YORKSHIRE v SOMERSET

At Middlesbrough, June 5, 6, 8. Drawn. Yorkshire 7 pts, Somerset 3 pts. Toss: Somerset. The first day was washed out and Somerset, fielding a weakened batting line-up, evidently preferred to chase runs and put Yorkshire in. An excellent cricket wicket gave encouragement to both batsmen and bowlers, but Moxon dominated. His 117 was his second hundred in consecutive Championship innings, separated by 38 days as his broken finger mended. None of his colleagues had yet reached three figures. He and Kellett made their 203 from 66 overs. An accurate spell from Hayhurst, however, deprived Yorkshire of maximum bonus points. Moxon declared on the last morning, but Somerset could not agree on a target and declined to set up a positive finish. Events explained their caution. Carrick made the most of some slow turn, earning six wickets, three of them through excellent catches from Tendulkar at silly mid-off. Bartlett resisted for over two hours, and Caddick used his reach to good effect, but Somerset had to follow on. Time was too short for them to be in danger.

Close of play: First day, No play; Second day, Yorkshire 317-7 (P. Carrick 26*, D. Gough 4*).

Yorkshire

*M. D. Moxon c Burns b van Troost	..117	P. J. Hartley c MacLeay b Rose	 15
S. A. Kellett c Burns b Hayhurst	 87	D. Gough not out	 4
D. Byas lbw b Hayhurst	 0	L-b 8, n-b 4	 12
S. R. Tendulkar b Caddick	 13		
†R. J. Blakey c Harden b Hayhurst	 5	1/203 2/203 3/217	(7 wkts dec.) 317
C. White c Harden b MacLeay	 38	4/224 5/239	
P. Carrick not out	 26	6/284 7/311	

J. D. Batty and M. A. Robinson did not bat.

Bonus points – Yorkshire 3, Somerset 2 (Score at 100 overs: 293-6).

Bowling: Caddick 25–6–57–1; van Troost 19–5–62–1; Rose 14–3–43–1; MacLeay 22–8–51–1; Trump 8–1–36–0; Cottam 10–1–33–0; Hayhurst 13–6–27–3.

Somerset

A. N. Hayhurst c Blakey b Robinson	38	
M. N. Lathwell c Byas b Carrick	17 – not out	16
*R. J. Harden c Byas b Robinson	7	
R. J. Bartlett c Tendulkar b Carrick	56	
†N. D. Burns c Byas b Hartley	2	
G. D. Rose c Tendulkar b Carrick	1	
K. H. MacLeay c Tendulkar b Carrick	0 – (1) not out	39
A. R. Caddick c White b Carrick	37	
H. R. J. Trump c Byas b Carrick	0	
A. C. Cottam c Blakey b Robinson	0	
A. P. van Troost not out	1	
L-b 2, n-b 6	8	N-b 2 2

1/43 2/58 3/80 4/96 5/99   167   (no wkt) 57
6/111 7/154 8/154 9/157

Bonus points – Somerset 1, Yorkshire 4.

Bowling: *First Innings*—Hartley 16–2–52–1; Gough 5–0–17–0; Robinson 16–3–34–3; Carrick 23–6–58–6; Batty 4–2–4–0. *Second Innings*—Robinson 1–0–17–0; Batty 4–0–18–0; Gough 3–0–22–0.

Umpires: H. D. Bird and K. E. Palmer.

YORKSHIRE v DERBYSHIRE

At Harrogate, June 12, 13, 15. Yorkshire won by an innings and four runs. Yorkshire 22 pts, Derbyshire 3 pts. Toss: Derbyshire. Yorkshire's first Championship win of the season was the work of their spinners, who shared 15 wickets, and off-spinner Batty's match figures of eight for 118 were the best of his career. He and Carrick made the most of a pitch that provided a little turn and bounce, while Derbyshire failed to exploit winning the toss, despite a solid innings from Bowler. Yorkshire were ready to sacrifice bonus points in their steady building of a significant lead. Moxon used up 167 deliveries for his 64, waiting for the bad ball to hit 11 fours. Tendulkar also applied himself cautiously, scoring 89 from 212 balls while collecting 11 fours and one six, but Bishop cut through the tail with four wickets in 11 balls. Derbyshire batted without any conviction in their second innings, especially once the in-form Bowler went cheaply, having dropped down the order after being off the field because of illness.

Close of play: First day, Yorkshire 38-0 (M. D. Moxon 19*, S. A. Kellett 10*); Second day, Derbyshire 9-2 (R. W. Sladdin 2*, P. D. Bowler 0*).

Derbyshire

*K. J. Barnett b Hartley	16 – lbw b Gough	1
P. D. Bowler c Byas b Carrick	60 – (4) c Byas b Hartley	1
J. E. Morris c Moxon b Gough	8 – (2) c and b Gough	0
T. J. G. O'Gorman c Blakey b Batty	23 – (5) lbw b Batty	15
C. J. Adams c Gough b Carrick	25 – (10) not out	6
S. C. Goldsmith lbw b Carrick	10 – c Kellett b Batty	13
D. G. Cork b Batty	47 – (8) c Blakey b Carrick	7
†K. M. Krikken c Byas b Batty	0 – (7) c Hartley b Carrick	0
I. R. Bishop c Kellett b Batty	6 – c Blakey b Batty	11
R. W. Sladdin st Blakey b Carrick	14 – (3) c and b Carrick	4
D. E. Malcolm not out	14 – lbw b Batty	8
L-b 1, w 1, n-b 2	4	B 4, l-b 3, n-b 1 8

1/24 2/40 3/100 4/124 5/137   227   1/2 2/3 3/11 4/19 5/33   74
6/150 7/155 8/161 9/213   6/34 7/40 8/58 9/58

Bonus points – Derbyshire 2, Yorkshire 4.

Bowling: *First Innings*—Hartley 16–3–43–1; Gough 9–2–29–1; Robinson 9–4–12–0; Carrick 37.3–15–58–4; Batty 23–2–84–4. *Second Innings*—Hartley 8–2–17–1; Gough 3–2–1–2; Carrick 18–13–15–3; Batty 13.2–4–34–4.

Yorkshire

*M. D. Moxon run out	64	D. Gough c Krikken b Bishop	0
S. A. Kellett c Krikken b Bishop	15	J. D. Batty c Barnett b Bishop	0
D. Byas lbw b Sladdin	12	M. A. Robinson b Bishop	0
S. R. Tendulkar c Krikken b Cork	89		
†R. J. Blakey c O'Gorman b Sladdin	24	L-b 5, w 1, n-b 19	25
C. White b Goldsmith	53		
P. Carrick not out	13	1/44 2/79 3/111 4/155 5/275	305
P. J. Hartley c Krikken b Bishop	10	6/287 7/303 8/303 9/303	

Bonus points – Yorkshire 2, Derbyshire 1 (Score at 100 overs: 241-4).

Bowling: Bishop 18.5–6–37–5; Malcolm 21–7–44–0; Cork 21–6–63–1; Sladdin 45–13–119–2; Barnett 8–2–28–0; Goldsmith 5–1–9–1.

Umpires: R. Julian and N. T. Plews.

YORKSHIRE v ESSEX

At Leeds, June 16, 17, 18. Yorkshire won by an innings and 55 runs. Yorkshire 23 pts, Essex 5 pts. Toss: Essex. Outstanding bowling by Robinson, with five wickets in an innings for the first time, and match figures of nine for 68, gave Yorkshire two successive innings victories, for the first time since 1974. On an excellent pitch, he forced several errors and might also have had Hussain, caught off a no-ball when five. Yorkshire's reply was far from assured until Tendulkar, arriving at 35 for three, took charge with a determined 93. The Essex seamers lacked accuracy and were further handicapped when Foster left the field injured. Then White and Batty shared a ninth-wicket stand of 92 from 18 overs, which effectively took the game out of Essex's reach. But nothing could explain the champions' feeble batting second time around. Stephenson set the unhappy tone with a wild hook, caught on the fine-leg boundary. Knight ran out Such in a remarkable misunderstanding, but resisted for 26 overs before Ilott and Andrew, who came together at 40 for eight, put on 41 in nine overs.

Close of play: First day, Yorkshire 44-3 (D. Byas 9*, S. R. Tendulkar 4*); Second day, Essex 11-3 (N. V. Knight 6*, P. M. Such 1*).

Essex

P. J. Prichard b Robinson	29	– c Byas b Robinson	1
J. P. Stephenson c Byas b Robinson	9	– c Robinson b Gough	0
M. E. Waugh lbw b Robinson	46	– (6) c Kellett b Gough	0
N. Hussain lbw b Hartley	47	– c Blakey b Robinson	0
N. V. Knight c Kellett b Robinson	0	– (3) c Byas b Robinson	25
†M. A. Garnham run out	13	– (7) c Kellett b Gough	2
*N. A. Foster c Gough b Carrick	24	– (8) c Blakey b Robinson	3
M. C. Ilott b Hartley	5	– (9) c and b Carrick	22
S. J. W. Andrew b Hartley	5	– (10) not out	14
P. M. Such c White b Robinson	15	– (5) run out	2
J. H. Childs not out	16	– c White b Hartley	0
L-b 6, w 1, n-b 7	14	B 2, l-b 2, w 2, n-b 8	14
1/37 2/56 3/113 4/116 5/139	223	1/3 2/3 3/4 4/25 5/32	83
6/173 7/175 8/180 9/186		6/36 7/39 8/40 9/81	

Bonus points – Essex 2, Yorkshire 4.

Bowling: *First Innings*—Hartley 23.5–4–66–3; Gough 19.1–4–57–0; Robinson 23.3–3–48–5; Carrick 15–4–39–1; Batty 4–2–7–0. *Second Innings*—Gough 14–7–12–3; Robinson 12–6–20–4; Carrick 5–2–15–1; Hartley 11–1–32–1.

Yorkshire

*M. D. Moxon c Knight b Foster	7	P. J. Hartley c Such b Waugh	8
S. A. Kellett c Prichard b Andrew	22	J. D. Batty lbw b Ilott	49
D. Byas lbw b Childs	55	M. A. Robinson not out	1
D. Gough lbw b Foster	0		
S. R. Tendulkar lbw b Stephenson	93	L-b 5, n-b 1	6
†R. J. Blakey c Hussain b Stephenson	32		
C. White b Ilott	69	1/16 2/34 3/35 4/134 5/206	361
P. Carrick lbw b Childs	19	6/216 7/251 8/262 9/354	

Bonus points – Yorkshire 3, Essex 3 (Score at 100 overs: 269-8).

Bowling: Foster 13–4–34–2; Ilott 19.4–7–72–2; Andrew 22–5–97–1; Childs 26–11–53–2; Such 9–2–31–0; Stephenson 19–5–41–2; Waugh 6–1–28–1.

Umpires: J. H. Harris and M. J. Kitchen.

At Worcester, June 19, 20, 22. YORKSHIRE lost to WORCESTERSHIRE by 89 runs.

YORKSHIRE v LEICESTERSHIRE

At Sheffield, July 3, 4, 6. Drawn. Toss: Leicestershire. The game became a one-innings affair, played for 12 points with no bonuses, after rain washed out the first two days. Having been put in, Yorkshire scored at less than three an over until Leicestershire fed them runs to prompt the declaration, when White plundered his unbeaten 74 from 66 balls. Moxon's calculations left Leicestershire to score 208 from 47 overs, which was reasonable enough in favourable batting conditions, although the pitch was slow. Jarvis, in his first Championship match for a month and only his third of the season, claimed four wickets for seven runs in nine overs, but Yorkshire's hopes of an unexpected victory were undermined as Wells and Nixon, missed by Byas at slip to deprive Jarvis of a fifth victim, stood firm for an hour.

Close of play: First day, No play; Second day, No play.

Yorkshire

*M. D. Moxon lbw b Millns	7	P. J. Hartley not out	17
S. A. Kellett c Parsons b Benson	41		
D. Byas c Benson b Wells	22	B 5, l-b 6, w 1, n-b 4	16
S. R. Tendulkar run out	23		
†R. J. Blakey c Parsons b Benson	7	1/14 2/78 3/80	(5 wkts dec.) 207
C. White not out	74	4/88 5/153	

P. Carrick, D. Gough, P. W. Jarvis and M. A. Robinson did not bat.

Bowling: Benjamin 6–3–13–0; Millns 6–1–23–1; Wells 6–3–7–1; Potter 8–3–19–0; Parsons 5–1–10–0; Benson 8–1–24–2; Boon 10–1–70–0; Whitaker 2.3–0–30–0.

Leicestershire

T. J. Boon b Gough	28	V. J. Wells not out	29
*N. E. Briers c Blakey b Jarvis	6	†P. A. Nixon not out	31
J. J. Whitaker b Gough	14	L-b 6, n-b 5	11
B. F. Smith lbw b Jarvis	8		
J. D. R. Benson b Jarvis	0	1/7 2/35 3/56	(6 wkts) 132
L. Potter lbw b Jarvis	5	4/57 5/67 6/68	

W. K. M. Benjamin, G. J. Parsons and D. J. Millns did not bat.

Bowling: Jarvis 15–8–32–4; Hartley 9–0–29–0; Gough 12–2–41–2; Carrick 8–2–11–0; Robinson 2–0–5–0; Tendulkar 1–0–8–0.

Umpires: H. D. Bird and M. J. Kitchen.

YORKSHIRE v WARWICKSHIRE

At Sheffield, July 14, 15, 16. Warwickshire won by three wickets. Warwickshire 18 pts, Yorkshire 2 pts. Toss: Yorkshire. Warwickshire achieved a contrived target of 276 in 91 overs with three balls to spare. A captains' agreement was necessary after much of the second day was lost to rain, while on the first Yorkshire batted so slowly that Kellett did not score a boundary until the 37th over, when he pulled Neil Smith for six. On an easy-paced pitch, Kellett required three and a half hours to make his 59, and Donald beat the bat frequently without reward. When the run-chase began first Twose then Reeve survived missed chances and held the chase together; Twose eventually fell to Carrick, who thus took his 1,000th wicket for Yorkshire on his 40th birthday. Reeve provided the decisive acceleration, adding 37 in eight overs with Neil Smith and demonstrating a wide range of strokes. Although Robinson caused some late problems, the batsmen always held sway.

Close of play: First day, Yorkshire 247-5 (C. White 25*, P. Carrick 8*); Second day, Warwickshire 88-0 (A. J. Moles 34*, R. G. Twose 41*).

Yorkshire

*M. D. Moxon c Twose b N. M. K. Smith	34	– not out	28
S. A. Kellett c Reeve b Donald	59	– not out	32
D. Byas lbw b Donald	52		
A. A. Metcalfe c Piper b Donald	26		
†R. J. Blakey c Piper b P. A. Smith	10		
C. White not out	54		
P. Carrick lbw b Small	13		
P. J. Hartley not out	20		
B 5, l-b 12, w 4, n-b 12	33	L-b 1, w 1	2

1/48 2/137 3/187 4/203   (6 wkts dec.) 301   (no wkt dec.) 62
5/225 6/264

P. W. Jarvis, J. D. Batty and M. A. Robinson did not bat.

Bonus points – Yorkshire 2, Warwickshire 2 (Score at 100 overs: 232-5).

Bowling: *First Innings*—Donald 29-8-61-3; Small 23-5-49-1; Reeve 24-7-44-0; N. M. K. Smith 15-2-35-1; P. A. Smith 24-5-58-1; Twose 9.5-1-36-0; Lloyd 1-0-1-0. *Second Innings*—Lloyd 5-0-34-0; Moles 4-0-27-0.

Warwickshire

A. J. Moles not out	34	– b Jarvis	7
R. G. Twose not out	41	– c Blakey b Carrick	66
*T. A. Lloyd (did not bat)		– c White b Hartley	19
D. P. Ostler (did not bat)		– lbw b Jarvis	15
D. A. Reeve (did not bat)		– lbw b Robinson	74
T. L. Penney (did not bat)		– c Blakey b Robinson	37
N. M. K. Smith (did not bat)		– not out	31
P. A. Smith (did not bat)		– c Jarvis b Robinson	5
†K. J. Piper (did not bat)		– not out	9
L-b 7, n-b 6	13	B 4, l-b 6, n-b 3	13

                    (no wkt dec.) 88   1/10 2/76 3/102   (7 wkts) 276
                                        4/139 5/212
                                        6/249 7/257

G. C. Small and A. A. Donald did not bat.

Bowling: *First Innings*—Jarvis 7-3-16-0; Hartley 8-3-9-0; Robinson 8-1-27-0; Carrick 11-2-20-0; Batty 5-2-9-0. *Second Innings*—Jarvis 16-1-50-2; Hartley 16-3-47-1; Robinson 16.3-1-55-3; Batty 14-2-45-0; Carrick 28-6-69-1.

Umpires: J. D. Bond and B. Leadbeater.

At Cheltenham College, July 17, 18, 20. YORKSHIRE drew with GLOUCESTERSHIRE.

At Cardiff, July 21, 22, 23. YORKSHIRE drew with GLAMORGAN.

YORKSHIRE v LANCASHIRE

At Leeds, July 31, August 1, 3. Yorkshire won by four wickets. Yorkshire 23 pts, Lancashire 5 pts. Toss: Lancashire. This match followed the pattern of so many played on pitches offering no assistance to the bowlers. Fairbrother held the stage on the first day, reaching his fifth Roses hundred, with 18 fours and five sixes, although he was missed by Batty at mid-off when he mistimed against Robinson, with 80 to his credit. Carrick, bowling defensively, picked up wickets as a reward for accuracy. When Yorkshire replied, Martin bowled a good spell with the new ball, but both sides were obviously working their way towards a run-chase on the last afternoon. Martin underlined the lack of balance in the pitch by scoring 46 as night-watchman before Fairbrother set Yorkshire 282 in a minimum of 55 overs. Kellett settled into a supporting role as Tendulkar maintained the necessary tempo. Blakey also scored briskly as Lancashire employed slow left-armer Barnett and Watkinson, in his off-spin mode, in an attempt to buy wickets. Their options were limited by some poor bowling from DeFreitas, who appeared to lack match fitness on his return after injury.

Close of play: First day, Lancashire 399-8 (N. H. Fairbrother 166*, P. J. Martin 4*); Second day, Lancashire 27-1 (S. P. Titchard 17*, P. J. Martin 2*).

Lancashire

M. A. Atherton c Kellett b Jarvis	14	– (4) not out	53
S. P. Titchard lbw b Jarvis	0	– (1) lbw b Hartley	32
N. J. Speak c White b Robinson	59	– (5) not out	38
G. D. Lloyd b Jarvis	56		
*N. H. Fairbrother not out	166		
M. Watkinson c Moxon b Carrick	18		
†W. K. Hegg st Blakey b Carrick	33		
P. A. J. DeFreitas c Byas b Carrick	0		
I. D. Austin c and b Carrick	30	– (2) c Blakey b Hartley	4
P. J. Martin not out	4	– (3) c Kellett b Robinson	46
L-b 12, w 1, n-b 6	19	L-b 4, n-b 5	9

1/5 2/23 3/108 4/182 5/243   (8 wkts dec.) 399   1/19 2/65 3/100   (3 wkts dec.) 182
6/324 7/326 8/394

A. A. Barnett did not bat.

Bonus points – Lancashire 4, Yorkshire 3 (Score at 100 overs: 337-7).

Bowling: *First Innings*—Jarvis 20–4–77–3; Hartley 18–2–58–0; Robinson 19–4–71–1; Carrick 44–11–129–4; Batty 9–0–52–0. *Second Innings*—Jarvis 10–4–12–0; Hartley 14–1–38–2; Carrick 6–3–8–0; Batty 11–3–29–0; Robinson 9–0–41–1; White 3–0–22–0; Tendulkar 2.3–0–28–0.

Yorkshire

*M. D. Moxon b Watkinson	90	– lbw b Watkinson	25
S. A. Kellett b Barnett	91	– c Lloyd b DeFreitas	89
D. Byas lbw b Barnett	27	– lbw b Watkinson	6
S. R. Tendulkar not out	56	– st Hegg b Barnett	48
†R. J. Blakey not out	22	– c Titchard b DeFreitas	63
C. White (did not bat)		– b Austin	12
P. W. Jarvis (did not bat)		– not out	21
P. Carrick (did not bat)		– not out	1
L-b 11, w 1, n-b 2	14	B 4, l-b 10, w 2, n-b 2	18

1/169 2/215 3/228   (3 wkts dec.) 300   1/42 2/54 3/125   (6 wkts) 283
                                                     4/246 5/252 6/272

P. J. Hartley, J. D. Batty and M. A. Robinson did not bat.

Bonus points – Yorkshire 4, Lancashire 1.

Bowling: *First Innings*—Martin 13.5–3–41–0; DeFreitas 14–2–47–0; Austin 9–0–34–0; Watkinson 31–7–116–1; Barnett 25–5–51–2. *Second Innings*—DeFreitas 11–0–48–2; Martin 10–3–30–0; Watkinson 13–0–79–2; Barnett 14–0–58–1; Austin 9.4–0–54–1.

Umpires: J. W. Holder and R. A. White.

At Durham University, August 4, 5, 6. YORKSHIRE beat DURHAM by five wickets.

At Northampton, August 7, 8, 10. YORKSHIRE drew with NORTHAMPTONSHIRE.

At Uxbridge, August 14, 15, 17. YORKSHIRE lost to MIDDLESEX by six wickets.

YORKSHIRE v NOTTINGHAMSHIRE

At Scarborough, August 18, 19, 20. Drawn. Yorkshire 8 pts, Nottinghamshire 4 pts. Toss: Nottinghamshire. Pollard, coming in at No. 7 with Nottinghamshire only 49 ahead, because an injured hand had prevented him from fielding, batted bravely for 36 overs to keep Yorkshire out. He had begun the match with one fractured finger on his left hand, and Jarvis broke another before he fell to Tendulkar, who was playing his last game before returning to India. Hartley unsettled Nottinghamshire on a pacy pitch, taking three for five in 16 balls. Only Cairns, with a robust 69 including three sixes and eight fours, and the Championship débutant Archer responded positively, and the last six wickets fell for 15 in eight overs. Yorkshire struggled in turn until Blakey was joined by Jarvis, who helped him to add 88 for the sixth wicket, and then Hartley, who thrashed some dispirited bowling as Yorkshire plundered 135 from 29 overs. Blakey hit 15 fours in his unbeaten 112, and established a lead of 252. Broad led Nottinghamshire's rearguard action, resisting five and three quarter hours; Robinson gave staunch support, and Cairns hit out again. But Pollard might have had a stiffer task if Yorkshire had not missed five catches, including one offered by Broad and two by Cairns.

Close of play: First day, Yorkshire 144-5 (R. J. Blakey 8*, P. W. Jarvis 18*); Second day, Nottinghamshire 133-1 (B. C. Broad 69*, R. T. Robinson 57*).

Nottinghamshire

B. C. Broad c White b Hartley	9 – b Carrick	120
P. R. Pollard c Blakey b Tendulkar	10 – (7) not out	21
*R. T. Robinson c Jarvis b Hartley	1 – c Tendulkar b Jarvis	63
M. A. Crawley c Moxon b Hartley	6 – (2) c Blakey b Jarvis	1
G. F. Archer c Moxon b Robinson	27 – (4) c Kellett b Hartley	29
C. L. Cairns c Blakey b Batty	69 – (5) c Hartley b Batty	61
G. W. Mike c Moxon b Batty	0 – (6) lbw b Carrick	23
E. E. Hemmings c Moxon b Batty	6 – c Blakey b Batty	1
†S. Bramhall b Robinson	4 – c Blakey b Hartley	9
D. B. Pennett c Carrick b Robinson	0 – not out	7
J. A. Afford not out	3	
L-b 2, w 1, n-b 14	17	B 1, l-b 11, n-b 6	18

1/16 2/18 3/30 4/34 5/137   152   1/5 2/142 3/188   (8 wkts) 353
6/137 7/137 8/148 9/148   4/279 5/301 6/316
                                   7/317 8/336

Bonus points – Nottinghamshire 1, Yorkshire 4.

Bowling: First Innings—Jarvis 10–2–21–0; Hartley 15–3–40–3; Robinson 12.1–2–36–3; Tendulkar 6–1–13–1; Carrick 8–1–28–0; Batty 5–1–12–3. *Second Innings*—Jarvis 28–4–91–2; Hartley 19–4–62–2; Carrick 38–14–60–2; Robinson 18–5–44–0; Batty 32–10–75–2; Tendulkar 5–2–9–0.

Yorkshire

*M. D. Moxon b Pennett	25	P. J. Hartley c Robinson b Afford	69
S. A. Kellett b Pennett	30	J. D. Batty b Mike	16
A. A. Metcalfe lbw b Hemmings	22		
S. R. Tendulkar c Archer b Cairns	22	B 1, l-b 13, w 1, n-b 17	32
†R. J. Blakey not out	112		
C. White c Bramhall b Cairns	2	1/49 2/77 3/115	(9 wkts dec.) 404
P. W. Jarvis b Afford	55	4/115 5/125 6/213	
P. Carrick b Pennett	19	7/246 8/381 9/404	

M. A. Robinson did not bat.

Bonus points – Yorkshire 4, Nottinghamshire 3 (Score at 100 overs: 303-7).

Bowling: Cairns 34–5–106–2; Pennett 30–5–117–3; Mike 15.2–1–60–1; Hemmings 23–9–51–1; Afford 15–4–56–2.

Umpires: A. A. Jones and R. C. Tolchard.

YORKSHIRE v SURREY

At Bradford, August 21, 22, 24. Surrey won by one wicket. Surrey 19 pts, Yorkshire 4 pts. Toss: Yorkshire. Enterprising batting and a finish in doubt until the final over marked Bradford's first first-class match since 1985. The pitch was not without pace, but also yielded a little slow turn to assist spinners Kendrick and Boiling. Kellett hit 12 fours and Byas, returning after injury, 11 in a 97-ball 70. Most of the second day was lost to rain, and after Surrey had declared behind, Yorkshire forfeited an innings, to leave a target of 303 in what became 93 overs. Thorpe gave substance to the run-chase, but when he and Brown fell to careless strokes in one over from Hartley, Surrey were vulnerable at 199 for six. Feltham and Martin Bicknell revived their fortunes with 69 in 23 overs, until two wickets from Jarvis and a run-out put Yorkshire back on top. Last man Boiling joined Kendrick with 21 still needed, but they got home with two balls to spare, to ensure that Surrey were the only winners in the final round of three-day Championship matches.

Close of play: First day, Surrey 9-1 (D. J. Bicknell 8*, J. Boiling 0*); Second day, Surrey 39-1 (D. J. Bicknell 16*, J. Boiling 22*).

Yorkshire

*M. D. Moxon c Sargeant b Kendrick	48	P. J. Hartley st Sargeant b Kendrick	19
S. A. Kellett b Boiling	78	†C. A. Chapman not out	8
A. A. Metcalfe c Boiling b Feltham	35	J. D. Batty lbw b Kendrick	0
C. White c and b Boiling	3		
D. Byas lbw b Feltham	70	B 1, l-b 14, n-b 10	25
A. P. Grayson c Lynch b Kendrick	40		
P. W. Jarvis b Feltham	15	1/120 2/160 3/175 4/183 5/280	341
C. S. Pickles c and b Kendrick	0	6/296 7/313 8/313 9/341	

Bonus points – Yorkshire 4, Surrey 3 (Score at 100 overs: 331-8).

Bowling: M. P. Bicknell 21–3–75–0; Bryson 16–0–78–0; Feltham 24–5–67–3; Kendrick 19–2–60–5; Boiling 22–10–46–2.

Yorkshire forfeited their second innings.

Surrey

D. J. Bicknell not out	16	– lbw b Hartley	13
*N. F. Sargeant c Chapman b Jarvis	0	– b Jarvis	0
I. Boiling not out	22	– (11) not out	10
G. P. Thorpe (did not bat)		– (3) c Moxon b Hartley	79
*M. A. Lynch (did not bat)		– (4) c Pickles b Batty	43
D. M. Ward (did not bat)		– (5) c Grayson b Batty	18
A. D. Brown (did not bat)		– (6) c Kellett b Hartley	36
M. A. Feltham (did not bat)		– (7) lbw b Jarvis	41
M. P. Bicknell (did not bat)		– (8) run out	24
N. M. Kendrick (did not bat)		– (9) not out	18
R. E. Bryson (did not bat)		– (10) b Jarvis	8
N-b 1	1	L-b 10, n-b 6	16

1/3   (1 wkt dec.) 39   1/3 2/24 3/97   (9 wkts) 306
4/127 5/196 6/199
7/268 8/268 9/282

Bowling: *First Innings*—Jarvis 9–2–18–1; Hartley 7–1–19–0; Pickles 2–1–2–0. *Second Innings*—Jarvis 19.4–2–65–3; Hartley 17–4–51–0; Pickles 11–2–40–0; Batty 35–7–114–2; Grayson 10–2–26–0.

Umpires: A. A. Jones and R. C. Tolchard.

At Manchester, August 26, 27, 28, 29. YORKSHIRE drew with LANCASHIRE.

YORKSHIRE v NORTHAMPTONSHIRE

At Scarborough, August 31, September 1, 2, 3. Drawn. Yorkshire 5 pts, Northamptonshire 3 pts. Toss: Yorkshire. Yorkshire made painfully slow progress on a low, easy-paced pitch eventually reaching their highest Championship total since 1953. Byas needed almost four hours to complete his first century of the season, but Jarvis reached a career-best 80 from only 105 deliveries before being unluckily run out when sent back by Byas. Northampton-shire were equally circumspect and, with their captain Lamb suspended for making allegations about Pakistani bowling methods, failed to earn a third batting point. Capel's top score of 89 used up 341 minutes and only Curran showed any real enterprise. Robinson was the one bowler to draw any encouragement from the conditions, becoming the first to reach 50 Championship wickets for Yorkshire in 1992. Moxon completed his fifth Cham-pionship century of the season – in the first innings he had passed 15,000 career runs – before setting Northamptonshire to make 321 in 60 overs. They appeared well on course at 242 for two in the 49th; Capel changed gear to dramatic effect, hammering 66 from 52 balls with four sixes. Jarvis and Batty bowled tightly to put pressure on the batsmen, however, and Kellett reacted quickly to run out Capel. Northamptonshire then settled for the draw, and Yorkshire could not take the last two wickets in the final over.

Close of play: First day, Yorkshire 324-6 (D. Byas 47*, P. W. Jarvis 0*); Second day, Northamptonshire 147-3 (R. J. Bailey 82*, D. J. Capel 17*); Third day, Yorkshire 17-0 (M. D. Moxon 10*, S. A. Kellett 6*).

Yorkshire

*M. D. Moxon c Bailey b Penberthy	77	– not out	101
S. A. Kellett c Ripley b Curran	96	– c Felton b Roberts	29
A. A. Metcalfe c Capel b Curran	36	– c Penberthy b Cook	0
C. White run out	43	– c Capel b Cook	13
†R. J. Blakey run out	17	– not out	26
D. Byas c and b Capel	100		
A. P. Grayson lbw b Bailey	3		
P. W. Jarvis run out	80		
P. J. Hartley c Fordham b Cook	34		
J. D. Batty c Loye b Capel	1		
M. A. Robinson not out	2		
B 6, l-b 10, w 2, n-b 1	19	L-b 2	2

1/140 2/209 3/224 4/247 5/317   508   1/66 2/91 3/116   (3 wkts dec.) 171
6/324 7/457 8/482 9/488

Bonus points – Yorkshire 4, Northamptonshire 1 (Score at 100 overs: 300-4).

Bowling: *First Innings*—Taylor 29–6–79–0; Capel 23–3–66–2; Penberthy 19–3–64–1; Curran 23–3–79–2; Cook 35.5–9–117–1; Roberts 25–6–73–0; Bailey 4–0–14–1. *Second Innings*—Taylor 7–0–22–0; Curran 9–0–30–0; Bailey 1–0–1–0; Penberthy 6–0–16–0; Roberts 12–2–51–1; Cook 8–0–35–2; Ripley 1–0–14–0.

Northamptonshire

A. Fordham c Kellett b Robinson	18	– c Metcalfe b Jarvis	93
N. A. Felton c White b Robinson	19	– c White b Batty	49
*R. J. Bailey b Robinson	85	– b Batty	58
M. B. Loye c Blakey b Robinson	4	– (6) c Byas b Jarvis	2
D. J. Capel b Grayson	89	– (4) run out	66
K. M. Curran c Blakey b Robinson	50	– (5) b Batty	0
A. L. Penberthy c Grayson b Robinson	0	– c Blakey b Jarvis	8
†D. Ripley c Blakey b Batty	49	– st Blakey b Batty	5
A. R. Roberts not out	17	– not out	2
J. P. Taylor not out	8	– not out	0
B 5, l-b 5, n-b 10	20	B 7, l-b 5, n-b 3	15

1/38 2/39 3/60 4/150 5/251   (8 wkts dec.) 359   1/96 2/189 3/242   (8 wkts) 298
6/251 7/310 8/349   4/242 5/257 6/283
                                                      7/293 8/298

N. G. B. Cook did not bat.

Bonus points – Northamptonshire 2, Yorkshire 1 (Score at 100 overs: 249-4).

Bowling: *First Innings*—Jarvis 25–10–38–0; Hartley 18–3–48–0; Robinson 35.2–11–62–6; Batty 44–11–122–1; Grayson 23–2–79–1. *Second Innings*—Jarvis 18.5–1–80–3; Hartley 9–0–44–0; Robinson 9–0–46–0; Batty 18–1–95–4; Grayson 5–0–21–0.

Umpires: H. D. Bird and V. A. Holder.

At Hove, September 12, 13, 14, 15. YORKSHIRE lost to SUSSEX by six wickets.

NATWEST BANK TROPHY, 1992

Northamptonshire won a major cricketing prize for the third time when they took the NatWest Bank Trophy by beating Leicestershire, without much fuss or excitement, by eight wickets. It was their third NatWest final in six years; it was Leicestershire's first September Cup final, at the 30th attempt. They were the last first-class county (excluding the newcomers Durham) to get there.

The winners received £27,500 and the runners-up £13,500 out of a prize fund of £73,350. However, Northamptonshire were fined £2,640 for bowling their overs too slowly in the semi-final against Warwickshire. The beaten semi-finalists Warwickshire (fined £1,320 in the same game) and Essex received £6,750 and the beaten quarter-finalists, Durham, Glamorgan, Gloucestershire and Kent, £3,375. The prize money for Man of the Match awards was unchanged from 1991: first round, £125; second round, £150; quarter-finals, £250; semi-finals, £300; final, £550. The sponsors announced before the final that they would continue their involvement for another three years.

FIRST ROUND

BUCKINGHAMSHIRE v SUSSEX

At Beaconsfield, June 24. Sussex won by 201 runs. Toss: Sussex. Wells made his first hundred in any of the three limited-overs competitions, and Sussex's 327 was also their highest one-day score. The captain hit seven fours and seven sixes in his 70-ball innings, and his last 78 runs came from 31 deliveries. In the afternoon a 71-year-old male streaker ventured on to the field, wearing only socks.

Man of the Match: A. P. Wells.

Sussex

D. M. Smith b Scriven	62	A. C. S. Pigott not out		3
J. W. Hall c Roshier b Black	47			
M. P. Speight run out	28	B 5, l-b 8, w 9, n-b 1		23
*A. P. Wells c Sherman b Black	119			
K. Greenfield c Scriven b Black	19	1/112 2/132	(6 wkts, 60 overs)	327
F. D. Stephenson b Barry	12	3/160 4/205		
†P. Moores not out	14	5/268 6/318		

N. J. Lenham, I. D. K. Salisbury and A. G. Robson did not bat.

Bowling: Roshier 12–0–72–0; Edwards 12–0–38–0; Barry 12–0–73–1; Scriven 12–1–48–1; Black 12–0–83–3.

Buckinghamshire

A. R. Harwood c Salisbury b Stephenson	5	T. J. Barry c Moores b Stephenson		39
R. R. Baigent b Salisbury	44	†T. P. Russell lbw b Stephenson		8
T. J. A. Scriven lbw b Pigott	5	S. J. Edwards not out		1
N. W. Farrow b Robson	1	B 4, l-b 6, w 1, n-b 2		13
B. S. Percy c Salisbury b Pigott	2			
S. M. Shearman c Wells b Greenfield	8	1/15 2/37 3/38	(51 overs)	126
P. G. Roshier c Wells b Salisbury	0	4/41 5/59 6/60		
*G. R. Black c Moores b Salisbury	0	7/66 8/95 9/124		

Bowling: Stephenson 9–4–8–3; Pigott 8–0–18–2; Robson 10–1–29–1; Salisbury 12–4–28–3; Greenfield 12–5–33–1.

Umpires: D. J. Constant and D. B. Harrison.

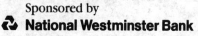

DERBYSHIRE v BERKSHIRE

At Derby, June 24. Derbyshire won by 141 runs. Toss: Derbyshire. Cork collected five wickets and the match award on his first appearance in the competition. Earlier Bowler and Adams both made their maiden hundreds in the Trophy.

Man of the Match: D. G. Cork.

Derbyshire

P. D. Bowler b Jones	111	I. R. Bishop b Stear	6
J. E. Morris c Mercer b Hartley	31	A. E. Warner not out	0
C. J. Adams not out	106	B 3, l-b 8, w 6, n-b 4	21
T. J. G. O'Gorman b Jones	1		—
S. C. Goldsmith c Cartmell b Jones	0	1/65 2/257 3/266 (6 wkts, 60 overs) 280
D. G. Cork c Cartmell b Jones	4	4/266 5/270 6/280

*K. M. Krikken, D. E. Malcolm and O. H. Mortensen did not bat.

Bowling: Jones 12–1–54–4; Oxley 12–0–67–0; Stear 12–1–54–1; Hartley 12–2–34–1; Fusedale 12–2–60–0.

Berkshire

G. E. Loveday lbw b Malcolm	2	N. A. Fusedale lbw b Cork	0
M. G. Lickley lbw b Cork	18	D. J. B. Hartley b Cork	0
D. J. M. Mercer c Krikken b Malcolm	0	J. H. Jones c Adams b Cork	0
*M. L. Simmons b Cork	2	B 3, l-b 7, w 9, n-b 6	25
K. S. Murray c Krikken b Mortensen	0		—
P. J. Oxley b sub b Adams	49	1/15 2/15 3/27 (51.5 overs) 139
†N. D. J. Cartmell run out	27	4/28 5/28 6/76
M. G. Stear not out	16	7/134 8/137 9/139

Bowling: Malcolm 9–1–29–2; Bishop 10–2–24–0; Cork 9.5–4–18–5; Mortensen 3–2–1–1; Warner 11–2–25–0; Goldsmith 3–0–5–0; Bowler 3–0–12–0; Adams 3–1–15–1.

Umpires: J. D. Bond and R. C. Tolchard.

ESSEX v CUMBERLAND

At Chelmsford, June 24. Essex won by 161 runs. Toss: Essex. Hussain struck 108, his first century in the competition, from 92 balls, and took four fours and a six off one over from Woods. He shared 124 in 21 overs with Knight, whose NatWest début brought him an unbeaten 81.

Man of the Match: N. Hussain.

Essex

*G. A. Gooch c Woods b Ellwood	77	T. D. Topley lbw b Sample	1
P. J. Prichard c Dutton b Scothern	23	M. C. Ilott not out	9
M. E. Waugh c Scothern b Ellwood	24	L-b 3, w 2	5
N. Hussain c Makinson b Woods	108		—
N. V. Knight not out	81	1/52 2/109 3/143 (8 wkts, 60 overs) 361
N. Shahid c and b Woods	18	4/267 5/304 6/324
D. R. Pringle c Scothern b Sample	10	7/334 8/344
†M. A. Garnham lbw b Sample	5	

P. M. Such did not bat.

Bowling: Makinson 12–0–82–0; Scothern 12–0–69–1; Sample 12–0–64–3; Ellwood 12–0–49–2; Woods 12–0–94–2.

Cumberland

C. J. Stockdale c Hussain b Ilott	0
S. Sharp c Ilott b Such	75
T. Hunte retired hurt	5
C. R. Knight lbw b Topley	21
G. J. Clarke b Waugh	0
*†S. M. Dutton c Prichard b Ilott	61
D. J. Makinson lbw b Shahid	9
K. Sample b Topley	1

R. Ellwood not out 5
M. G. Scothern b Topley 10

B 1, l-b 6, w 2, n-b 4 13

1/2 2/70 3/71 (8 wkts, 60 overs) 200
4/164 5/179 6/180
7/183 8/200

M. D. Woods did not bat.

T. Hunte retired hurt at 17.

Bowling: Ilott 11–2–23–2; Pringle 6–1–18–0; Such 12–3–37–1; Topley 11–1–47–3; Waugh 12–1–51–1; Gooch 5–0–17–0; Shahid 3–3–0–1.

Umpires: K. E. Palmer and C. T. Spencer.

GLAMORGAN v SURREY

At Swansea, June 24. Glamorgan won by four wickets. Toss: Glamorgan. Surrey, beaten finalists in 1991, unexpectedly went out to a team who had won only two one-day games out of 11 against other counties all season. The visitors were given a respectable score by Ward, whose hundred came at a run a ball and who hit 24 from Dale's 11th over. Barwick returned his best figures in the competition, bowling off-cutters. Glamorgan's innings got its impetus from Maynard, who controlled the situation until he was out with the scores level.

Man of the Match: M. P. Maynard.

Surrey

D. J. Bicknell c Metson b Barwick	21
M. A. Lynch c Metson b Barwick	27
*A. J. Stewart b Barwick	60
G. P. Thorpe c Metson b Dale	3
†D. M. Ward not out	101
J. D. Robinson b Barwick	4

M. A. Feltham st Metson b Barwick ... 4
M. A. Butcher not out 4
L-b 8, w 7 15

1/42 2/58 3/63 (6 wkts, 60 overs) 239
4/210 5/223 6/227

N. M. Kendrick, J. Boiling and J. E. Benjamin did not bat.

Bowling: Watkin 11–2–38–0; Bastien 7–0–56–0; Dale 11–1–50–1; Barwick 12–3–26–5; Croft 12–2–33–0; Richards 7–0–28–0.

Glamorgan

S. P. James c and b Boiling	19
H. Morris run out	55
A. Dale c Robinson b Boiling	16
*M. P. Maynard c Benjamin b Lynch	87
I. V. A. Richards b Kendrick	16
P. A. Cottey c and b Lynch	24
R. D. B. Croft not out	17

†C. P. Metson not out 0
L-b 5, w 4 9

1/44 2/82 (6 wkts, 59.1 overs) 243
3/135 4/162
5/212 6/239

S. Bastien, S. L. Watkin and S. R. Barwick did not bat.

Bowling: Benjamin 12–2–39–0; Butcher 12–3–36–0; Boiling 12–2–37–2; Kendrick 12–1–51–1; Feltham 5.1–0–39–0; Robinson 1–0–8–0; Lynch 5–0–28–2.

Umpires: B. J. Meyer and G. Sharp.

GLOUCESTERSHIRE v CHESHIRE

At Bristol, June 24. Gloucestershire won by 204 runs. Toss: Cheshire. After Wright made his maiden hundred in the competition, Walsh equalled his, and Gloucestershire's, best NatWest figures – six for 21 against Kent in Bristol two years earlier. Standing and O'Brien became the only Cheshire players to reach double figures after their team had collapsed to 24 for seven and 37 for eight.

Man of the Match: C. A. Walsh.

Gloucestershire

G. D. Hodgson b Peel	29	†R. C. Russell not out	13
C. W. J. Athey c Bean b Crawley	57	B 1, l-b 6, w 9	16
*A. J. Wright not out	107		
M. W. Alleyne run out	25	1/35 2/119 (4 wkts, 60 overs)	272
R. J. Scott c Hitchmough b Crawley	25	3/173 4/236	

R. I. Dawson, C. A. Walsh, M. C. J. Ball, A. M. Babington and A. M. Smith did not bat.

Bowling: Peel 12–1–57–1; Potts 12–0–47–0; Miller 12–1–33–0; Bostock 5–0–19–0; O'Brien 7–0–43–0; Crawley 12–0–66–2.

Cheshire

T. J. Bostock c Ball b Babington	7	†T. C. M. Standing c Alleyne b Walsh	14
S. T. Crawley c Russell b Babington	6	J. F. M. O'Brien not out	14
*I. Cockbain c Alleyne b Walsh	8	N. D. Peel b Walsh	0
D. W. Varey c Russell b Babington	0	L-b 4, w 4, n-b 2	10
J. J. Hitchmough lbw b Walsh	0		
J. D. Bean b Walsh	0	1/11 2/16 3/16 (34.4 overs)	68
G. Miller b Scott	9	4/17 5/17 6/24	
J. Potts b Walsh	0	7/24 8/37 9/68	

Bowling: Walsh 10.4–3–21–6; Babington 8–3–8–3; Scott 5–3–4–1; Smith 7–0–22–0; Ball 4–2–9–0.

Umpires: D. Dennis and D. O. Oslear.

HAMPSHIRE v DORSET

At Southampton, June 24. Hampshire won by nine wickets. Toss: Hampshire. Calway hit 11 fours and a six and Richings seven fours and a six as they added 180 for Dorset's second wicket. But Terry and Smith put on 120 without being parted after the Rev. Wingfield Digby, chaplain to the England team, dismissed Middleton.

Man of the Match: G. S. Calway.

Dorset

D. J. Pepperell c Parks b Connor	6	†G. D. Reynolds not out	5
G. S. Calway c Marshall b Connor	105	B 2, l-b 8, w 7, n-b 2	19
T. Richings not out	74		
J. J. E. Hardy b Connor	9	1/13 2/193 3/211 (3 wkts, 60 overs)	218

*V. B. Lewis, A. Willows, O. Parkin, Rev. A. R. Wingfield Digby, S. R. Walbridge and J. H. Shackleton did not bat.

Bowling: Connor 12–3–29–3; Marshall 12–3–26–0; Maru 12–1–39–0; Ayling 12–0–70–0; Udal 12–2–44–0.

Hampshire

V. P. Terry not out 108
T. C. Middleton c Reynolds
            b Wingfield Digby . 38
R. A. Smith not out.................. 59
      L-b 8, w 4, n-b 2............ 14

1/99   (1 wkt, 50.4 overs) 219

D. I. Gower, *M. C. J. Nicholas, J. R. Ayling, M. D. Marshall, †R. J. Parks, R. J. Maru, S. D. Udal and C. A. Connor did not bat.

Bowling: Parkin 6–0–31–0; Shackleton 12–4–34–0; Wingfield Digby 12–2–37–1; Walbridge 4–0–28–0; Calway 8.4–0–45–0; Willows 8–0–36–0.

Umpires: D. J. Halfyard and R. Palmer.

IRELAND v DURHAM

At Castle Avenue, Dublin, June 24. Durham won by 189 runs. Toss: Durham. Larkins was dropped twice as he advanced to 50 in 15 overs, but then took only 43 balls to reach Durham's second hundred in the NatWest Bank Trophy. The first had been scored by Glendenen against Glamorgan in 1991, and Durham's 305 matched their record in the competition set in the same match. McEwan's best performances with bat and ball in the Trophy earned him the award nomination.
Man of the Match: S. M. McEwan.

Durham

W. Larkins c Warke b Dunlop.......113		†A. R. Fothergill b Dunlop...........	4
J. D. Glendenen c Warke b P. McCrum 18		S. M. McEwan not out	34
D. M. Jones b Hoey	46	L-b 9, w 14	23
P. W. G. Parker c P. McCrum b Dunlop 10			
M. P. Briers not out	54	1/24 2/186 3/203 (6 wkts, 60 overs) 305	
I. Smith b McBrine	3	4/210 5/217 6/230	

*D. A. Graveney, S. P. Hughes and J. Wood did not bat.

Bowling: P. McCrum 10–2–47–1; Nelson 10–0–45–0; Lewis 8–0–44–0; Hoey 12–1–52–1; McBrine 12–0–63–1; Dunlop 8–0–45–3.

Ireland

*S. J. S. Warke c Fothergill b Wood . . .	10	C. J. Hoey c sub b Briers	12
M. P. Rea b Hughes	20	P. McCrum c Fothergill b Wood	5
S. Graham lbw b McEwan	7	A. N. Nelson not out...............	0
D. A. Lewis lbw b Smith	2	L-b 4, w 11, n-b 1..........	16
A. R. Dunlop lbw b Smith	8		
C. McCrum c Jones b McEwan	6	1/24 2/32 3/44 (37.2 overs) 116	
A. McBrine b McEwan..............	30	4/44 5/59 6/62	
†P. B. Jackson c Fothergill b McEwan .	0	7/63 8/105 9/115	

Bowling: Wood 7–1–22–2; Hughes 6–0–9–1; Smith 12–1–40–2; McEwan 12–1–41–4; Briers 0.2–0–0–1.

Umpires: J. C. Balderstone and D. R. Shepherd.

KENT v DEVON

At Canterbury, June 24. Kent won by 100 runs. Toss: Kent. Fleming took only 23 balls to reach his fifty after a solid 103-run second-wicket stand from Benson and Taylor.
Man of the Match: M. V. Fleming.

Kent

M. A. Ealham c Willis b Woodman	...	6	N. J. Llong not out	13
*M. R. Benson c Ward b White	...	58	M. J. McCague not out	4
N. R. Taylor c Pritchard b Butcher	...	43	L-b 15, w 9	24
C. L. Hooper c White b Butcher	...	22		
G. R. Cowdrey c Folland b Ward	...	33	1/11 2/114 3/138 (7 wkts, 60 overs) 266	
M. V. Fleming c Folland b Ward	...	53	4/159 5/216	
†S. A. Marsh c Butcher b Ward	...	10	6/241 7/253	

R. M. Ellison and R. P. Davis did not bat.

Bowling: Donohue 12–0–70–0; Woodman 12–3–16–1; Ward 9–0–60–3; White 12–1–45–1; Tall 3–0–12–0; Butcher 12–0–48–2.

Devon

S. M. Willis c Davis b Hooper	...	42	M. C. Woodman c sub b Cowdrey	0
G. W. White c Marsh b Davis	...	11	D. N. Butcher not out	1
*N. A. Folland c Cowdrey b Davis	...	20		
A. J. Pugh b McCague	...	20	B 1, l-b 12, w 5, n-b 4	22
D. A. Tall st Marsh b Llong	...	23		
G. R. Hill b McCague	...	14	1/32 2/69 3/92 (8 wkts, 60 overs) 166	
K. Donohue not out	...	7	4/128 5/150 6/151	
T. W. Ward c Benson b Cowdrey	...	6	7/163 8/163	

†C. S. Pritchard did not bat.

Bowling: Ealham 7–0–28–0; Ellison 7–1–21–0; Davis 12–0–40–2; Hooper 12–6–19–1; Fleming 7–3–14–0; McCague 8–0–16–2; Llong 4–0–11–1; Cowdrey 3–1–4–2.

Umpires: M. A. Johnson and B. Leadbeater.

LEICESTERSHIRE v NORFOLK

At Leicester, June 24. Leicestershire won by 132 runs. Toss: Norfolk. In his second match for Leicestershire, Robinson bettered his highest score in the competition for Yorkshire by seven runs.

Man of the Match: P. E. Robinson.

Leicestershire

*N. E. Briers run out	...	21	†P. A. Nixon not out	17
J. J. Whitaker c Lewis b Kingshott	...	42	V. J. Wells not out	6
B. F. Smith c Plumb b Thomas	...	49	B 8, l-b 10, w 14	32
P. E. Robinson c Bunting b Plumb	...	73		
J. D. R. Benson c and b Thomas	...	11	1/67 2/85 3/176 (7 wkts, 60 overs) 293	
L. Potter c Kingshott b Lewis	...	41	4/197 5/250	
W. K. M. Benjamin c Kingshott b Lewis	...	14	6/252 7/280	

D. J. Millns and A. D. Mullally did not bat.

Bowling: Lewis 12–1–66–2; Bunting 12–0–73–0; Plumb 12–2–39–1; Kingshott 12–2–29–1; Thomas 12–0–68–2.

Norfolk

C. J. Rogers c Smith b Potter	...	51	J. C. M. Lewis c Nixon b Mullally	1
S. G. Plumb c Nixon b Millns	...	1	R. Kingshott not out	5
S. K. Taylor b Millns	...	0	†D. M. Morrell c Millns b Benson	6
R. J. Finney b Wells	...	34	B 1, l-b 5, w 18, n-b 1	25
R. D. E. Farrow c Nixon b Millns	...	5		
S. J. B. Livermore lbw b Wells	...	0	1/2 2/2 3/78 (53.1 overs) 161	
*D. R. Thomas b Mullally	...	18	4/103 5/103 6/104	
R. A. Bunting c and b Benson	...	15	7/140 8/141 9/148	

Bowling: Benjamin 7–1–19–0; Millns 10–3–22–3; Mullally 11–1–49–2; Potter 12–1–32–1; Wells 9–0–15–2; Benson 4.1–0–18–2.

Umpires: A. Clarkson and R. A. White.

NORTHAMPTONSHIRE v CAMBRIDGESHIRE

At Northampton, June 24. Northamptonshire won by 68 runs. Toss: Cambridgeshire. The minor county pegged their hosts back to 96 for four until Curran joined Capel to share an unbroken 138 for the fifth wicket. Cambridgeshire's reply was dominated by Adams, so much so that he scored over two-thirds of the runs added after he came to the wicket.

Man of the Match: N. J. Adams.

Northamptonshire

A. Fordham b Ajaz Akhtar	15	K. M. Curran not out			78
N. A. Felton c Stephenson b Roberts	14	L-b 3, w 6, n-b 2			11
R. J. Bailey c Roberts b Adams	18				
*A. J. Lamb c and b Stephenson	26	1/19 2/52		(4 wkts, 60 overs)	234
D. J. Capel not out	72	3/52 4/96			

†D. Ripley, C. E. L. Ambrose, A. R. Roberts, J. P. Taylor and A. Walker did not bat.

Bowling: Ajaz Akhtar 12–1–60–1; S. C. Ecclestone 3–0–22–0; Roberts 12–5–32–1; Adams 10–3–52–1; Pierson 12–4–23–0; Stephenson 11–0–42–1.

Cambridgeshire

*N. T. Gadsby c Ripley b Taylor	3	A. R. K. Pierson run out			1
G. W. Ecclestone c Roberts b Taylor	6	A. M. Cade not out			18
B. Roberts c Felton b Curran	9	L-b 5, w 4, n-b 2			11
N. J. Adams not out	104				
S. C. Ecclestone c Ripley b Curran	1	1/8 2/14 3/32		(6 wkts, 60 overs)	166
D. P. Norman c Ripley b Roberts	13	4/37 5/77 6/80			

Ajaz Akhtar, †M. W. C. Olley and M. G. Stephenson did not bat.

Bowling: Ambrose 10–5–5–0; Taylor 6–3–8–2; Curran 9–0–32–2; Walker 10–1–46–0; Roberts 12–0–23–1; Bailey 12–3–27–0; Felton 1–0–20–0.

Umpires: P. Adams and J. W. Holder.

NOTTINGHAMSHIRE v WORCESTERSHIRE

At Nottingham, June 24. Nottinghamshire won by 57 runs. Toss: Worcestershire. Nottinghamshire secured their first one-day win at Trent Bridge in 1992 at the eighth attempt after Johnson and Randall added 97 in 14 overs and then Lewis scored 32 from 15 balls. He went on to take four catches, which equalled the tournament record for a fielder, as well as bowling Leatherdale.

Man of the Match: C. C. Lewis.

Nottinghamshire

B. C. Broad c Curtis b Newport	72	†B. N. French not out			8
P. R. Pollard b Lampitt	28	K. P. Evans not out			6
*R. T. Robinson c Neale b Illingworth	5	L-b 3, w 3, n-b 3			9
P. Johnson b Lampitt	78				
D. W. Randall run out	55	1/69 2/82 3/148		(7 wkts, 60 overs)	307
C. C. Lewis c Curtis b Radford	32	4/245 5/247			
C. L. Cairns c Rhodes b Radford	14	6/292 7/292			

R. A. Pick and M. G. Field-Buss did not bat.

Bowling: Newport 12–1–32–1; Radford 10–1–81–2; Haynes 10–0–80–0; Lampitt 12–0–64–2; Illingworth 12–2–25–1; Hick 4–0–22–0.

Worcestershire

*T. S. Curtis b Evans 12	P. J. Newport c Randall b Evans 9
*S. J. Rhodes b Field-Buss 54	N. V. Radford b Evans............. 32
G. A. Hick c Lewis b Field-Buss 14	R. K. Illingworth not out 12
P. A. Neale c Lewis b Evans 1	B 5, l-b 6, w 16, n-b 1 28
D. A. Leatherdale b Lewis 32	—
D. B. D'Oliveira c Cairns b Field-Buss 37	1/49 2/81 3/89 (56.4 overs) 250
S. R. Lampitt c Lewis b Cairns 14	4/89 5/163 6/166
G. R. Haynes c Lewis b Field-Buss 5	7/174 8/196 9/206

Bowling: Pick 12–1–53–0; Lewis 10–0–53–1; Cairns 12–0–28–1; Evans 10.4–1–43–4; Field-Buss 12–1–62–4.

Umpires: G. I. Burgess and J. H. Harris.

OXFORDSHIRE v LANCASHIRE

At Christ Church, Oxford, June 24. Lancashire won by 195 runs. Toss: Oxfordshire. Atherton's maiden NatWest hundred took nearly four hours, but he added 128 in 15 overs for the fifth wicket with Watkinson, whose 82 took 51 balls and included seven fours and four sixes. Half the Oxfordshire batsmen were out inside 20 overs and then Watkinson removed Garner with his first ball.
  Man of the Match: M. Watkinson.

Lancashire

G. Fowler run out 3	I. D. Austin not out................ 3
*M. A. Atherton not out 109	
N. J. Speak c Hughes b Laudat 35	L-b 3, w 21 24
G. D. Lloyd b Savin 7	—
S. P. Titchard c Hughes b Hartley..... 20	1/8 2/88 3/108 (5 wkts, 60 overs) 283
M. Watkinson run out............... 82	4/149 5/277

†W. K. Hegg, J. D. Fitton, D. K. Morrison and P. J. Martin did not bat.

Bowling: Arnold 12–3–56–0; Joyner 10–0–64–0; Laudat 12–2–44–1; Savin 12–0–39–1; Hartley 4–0–23–1; Curtis 10–0–54–0.

Oxfordshire

D. A. J. Wise c Martin b Morrison 6	†K. J. Hughes c Hegg b Watkinson ... 4
G. P. Savin lbw b Morrison 0	K. A. Arnold b Morrison 4
S. V. Laudat lbw b Austin 31	I. J. Curtis not out................. 0
P. M. Jobson lbw b Martin 5	L-b 1, w 5, n-b 1........... 7
T. A. Lester c Hegg b Martin 0	—
*P. J. Garner lbw b Watkinson 11	1/2 2/15 3/22 (34.1 overs) 88
J. S. Hartley c Hegg b Austin......... 20	4/24 5/50 6/64
S. G. Joyner c Speak b Watkinson 0	7/69 8/83 9/83

Bowling: Morrison 8.1–3–17–3; Martin 9–1–26–2; Austin 9–2–27–2; Watkinson 7–2–17–3; Fitton 1–1–0–0.

Umpires: B. Dudleston and H. Rhodes.

SHROPSHIRE v MIDDLESEX

At St George's, Telford, June 24. Middlesex won by 145 runs. Toss: Middlesex. Giles Toogood, a 30-year-old surgeon who was an Oxford Blue in 1982-85, stole the limelight – though not the match – with his second spell of medium-pace bowling, when he took six for 27 in seven overs. However, before that, Roseberry and Haynes had put on 199 for the first wicket and put Middlesex, who were without the injured Gatting, beyond danger of defeat. The only other wicket to fall went to the 50-year-old off-spinner Cronin.
  Man of the Match: G. J. Toogood.

Middlesex

D. L. Haynes c Cronin b Toogood 101	*J. E. Emburey lbw b Toogood 0
M. A. Roseberry c Barnard b Toogood .112	N. F. Williams not out 7
M. R. Ramprakash c Davidson	
b Toogood . 29	L-b 6, w 6, n-b 1 13
J. D. Carr b Cronin 15	
†K. R. Brown c sub b Toogood 2	1/199 2/222 3/252 (7 wkts, 60 overs) 294
P. N. Weekes c Byram b Toogood 2	4/264 5/264
R. J. Sims not out 13	6/282 7/283

D. W. Headley and A. R. C. Fraser did not bat.

Bowling: Thomas 8-0-54-0; Toogood 12-1-47-6; Edmunds 4-1-11-0; Cronin 12-1-84-1; Byram 12-0-52-0; Barnard 12-0-40-0.

Shropshire

A. R. Williams c Brown b Headley 6	P. A. Thomas not out 12
J. B. R. Jones c Emburey	G. Edmunds c and b Roseberry 0
b Ramprakash . 24	M. R. Cronin b Headley 1
T. Parton b Headley 0	
*M. R. Davies b Headley 0	L-b 1, w 9, n-b 6 16
G. J. Toogood c Brown b Fraser 1	
A. B. Byram c Williams b Ramprakash 19	1/11 2/11 3/11 (58.1 overs) 149
†M. J. Davidson c and b Emburey 42	4/19 5/46 6/60
A. S. Barnard b Headley 28	7/115 8/139 9/144

Bowling: Fraser 7-3-10-1; Headley 8.1-4-20-5; Weekes 12-6-23-0; Emburey 11-3-26-1; Ramprakash 12-2-38-2; Carr 2-1-2-0; Haynes 2-0-7-0; Roseberry 4-0-22-1.

Umpires: Dr D. Fawkner-Corbett and P. B. Wight.

SOMERSET v SCOTLAND

At Taunton, June 24. Somerset won by eight wickets. Toss: Scotland. Despite Somerset's margin of victory, Scotland broke new ground in this match. Philip scored their first ever century in either of the two major one-day tournaments in their 62nd match and he shared in two hundred partnerships, the first for Scotland in this competition.

Man of the Match: R. J. Harden.

Scotland

B. M. W. Patterson lbw b Mallender . . . 61	
†I. L. Philip not out 102	
G. N. Reifer c Burns b Caddick 55	
O. Henry not out 13	
L-b 8, w 5, n-b 1 14	

1/111 2/220   (2 wkts, 60 overs) 245

G. Salmond, J. Everett, *A. B. Russell, J. W. Govan, A. Bee, P. G. Duthie and I. M. Stanger did not bat.

Bowling: Mallender 12-2-47-1; Caddick 12-2-58-1; Snell 12-0-48-0; Trump 9-0-26-0; MacLeay 10-2-30-0; Rose 3-0-13-0; Hayhurst 2-0-15-0.

Somerset

A. N. Hayhurst st Philip b Russell 47	
M. N. Lathwell c Salmond b Duthie . . . 12	
R. J. Harden not out 108	
*C. J. Tavaré not out 60	
B 4, l-b 5, w 10 19	

1/25 2/99   (2 wkts, 56.5 overs) 246

G. D. Rose, †N. D. Burns, K. H. MacLeay, N. A. Mallender, A. R. Caddick, H. R. J. Trump and R. P. Snell did not bat.

Bowling: Duthie 9–1–32–1; Bee 10–0–41–0; Stanger 9–0–42–0; Reifer 5–2–17–0; Govan 8.5–0–46–0; Henry 7–0–23–0; Russell 8–0–36–1.

Umpires: V. A. Holder and R. Julian.

WARWICKSHIRE v STAFFORDSHIRE

At Birmingham, June 24. Warwickshire won by eight wickets. Toss: Staffordshire. Simon Myles, who briefly played for Warwickshire, had the satisfaction of sharing a stand of 102 in 32 overs with Dutton. But it was sandwiched between two devastating spells from Donald, who took five wickets, just as he did against Staffordshire when the teams met in the NatWest in 1987.

Man of the Match: A. A. Donald.

Staffordshire

S. J. Dean c Ostler b Donald	11	D. K. Page not out	6
R. Salmon b Donald	0	R. J. Dyer run out	0
A. D. Hobson b Donald	0	N. P. Hackett not out	2
S. D. Myles lbw b Donald	60		
A. J. Dutton c P. A. Smith	34	B 1, l-b 7, w 8, n-b 1	17
b N. M. K. Smith			
*N. J. Archer c Lloyd b Twose	27	1/1 2/11 3/12 (9 wkts, 60 overs) 172	
P. G. Newman c Reeve b Donald	0	4/114 5/120 6/120	
†M. I. Humphries c Lloyd b Twose	15	7/161 8/166 9/166	

Bowling: Donald 12–3–28–5; Small 12–3–34–0; Munton 12–3–27–0; Reeve 4–0–9–0; N. M. K. Smith 10–1–21–1; Twose 8–0–30–2; P. A. Smith 2–0–15–0.

Warwickshire

A. J. Moles c Salmon b Page	21
R. G. Twose not out	107
*T. A. Lloyd c Salmon b Myles	37
D. P. Ostler not out	0
L-b 2, w 5, n-b 1	8

1/63 2/172   (2 wkts, 39.4 overs) 173

D. A. Reeve, P. A. Smith, N. M. K. Smith, †P. C. L. Holloway, G. C. Small, T. A. Munton and A. A. Donald did not bat.

Bowling: Newman 8–3–13–0; Hackett 9–0–61–0; Dyer 7–0–29–0; Page 9–0–46–1; Myles 3.4–0–15–1; Dutton 3–0–7–0.

Umpires: M. J. Kitchen and G. A. Stickley.

YORKSHIRE v NORTHUMBERLAND

At Leeds, June 24. Yorkshire won by eight wickets. Toss: Yorkshire. Despite losing Benn and Burn in Gough's second over, Northumberland plodded on gamely and Morris batted for 41 overs in all. They then bowled tightly enough to force Yorkshire to work very hard for victory: 48-year-old Greensword was especially economical.

Man of the Match: G. R. Morris.

Northumberland

J. A. Benn c Moxon b Gough	1	W. Falla c Blakey b Robinson	6
*G. R. Morris run out	47	I. E. Conn c Kellett b Robinson	0
P. Burn c Kellett b Gough	0	P. C. Graham not out	4
P. Willey c Blakey b Pickles	10	L-b 8, w 4, n-b 13	25
P. N. S. Dutton c Blakey b Hartley	5		
K. Williams c Kellett b Pickles	20	1/4 2/4 3/53 (56.4 overs) 137	
†M. S. Tiffin c Byas b Carrick	2	4/76 5/96 6/105	
S. Greensword c Tendulkar b Robinson	17	7/111 8/126 9/126	

Bowling: Hartley 10–2–33–1; Gough 11–3–18–2; Robinson 11.4–4–18–3; Pickles 12–2–40–2; Carrick 12–4–20–1.

Yorkshire

*M. D. Moxon c Tiffin b Greensword	34
S. A. Kellett b Greensword	38
D. Byas not out	24
S. R. Tendulkar not out	32
L-b 2, w 7, n-b 1	10

1/67 2/80   (2 wkts, 51.3 overs) 138

†R. J. Blakey, C. White, C. S. Pickles, P. Carrick, D. Gough, P. J. Hartley and M. A. Robinson did not bat.

Bowling: Williams 12–2–28–0; Graham 12–3–25–0; Conn 10–1–34–0; Willey 3–0–19–0; Greensword 12–5–22–2; Dutton 2–0–4–0; Falla 0.3–0–4–0.

Umpires: A. G. T. Whitehead and T. G. Wilson.

SECOND ROUND

DERBYSHIRE v LEICESTERSHIRE

At Derby, July 9, 10. Leicestershire won by 98 runs. Toss: Derbyshire. Leicestershire recovered from an unpromising position to win with surprising ease on the second morning. They were 153 for eight when rain cut three and a half hours from a gloomy first day. But Nixon and Mills batted intelligently and put on 54, enabling Leicestershire to reach 200. Derbyshire's innings began at 7 p.m. and they immediately lost Morris and Bowler. With their captain Barnett out through injury, and the leading batsmen gone, Derbyshire had no fibre, nor any answer to Benjamin and Mills. Their last wicket fell only three balls into the second half of their innings, giving Benjamin five for 32. Even David Steele, a member of Derbyshire's successful 1981 team, felt obliged to comment on the lack of application as he made the match award. He advised them to spend the afternoon in the nets. Unfortunately, they were already committed to appear in a benefit golf tournament. Close of play: Derbyshire 9-2 (3.3 overs) (C. J. Adams 4*, T. J. G. O'Gorman 0*).

Man of the Match: D. J. Mills.

Leicestershire

T. J. Boon c Adams b Cork	17	G. J. Parsons lbw b Cork	5
*N. E. Briers c Adams b Malcolm	28	D. J. Mills not out	29
J. J. Whitaker run out	0	A. D. Mullally not out	1
B. F. Smith lbw b Cork	10		
P. E. Robinson c Bowler b Warner	40	L-b 6, w 9, n-b 1	16
V. J. Wells lbw b Warner	21		
†P. A. Nixon run out	32	1/32 2/35 3/52 (9 wkts, 60 overs) 201
W. K. M. Benjamin c Bowler		4/56 5/123 6/125
b Malcolm	2	7/130 8/146 9/200

Bowling: Bishop 12–1–37–0; Mortensen 12–2–43–0; Cork 12–1–36–3; Malcolm 12–0–39–2; Warner 12–2–40–2.

Derbyshire

P. D. Bowler c Nixon b Benjamin	4	A. E. Warner c Parsons b Mills	21
*J. E. Morris c and b Mills	0	D. E. Malcolm not out	10
C. J. Adams b Mullally	30	O. H. Mortensen lbw b Benjamin	0
T. J. G. O'Gorman c Nixon b Benjamin	0	L-b 1, w 3, n-b 5	9
S. C. Goldsmith b Mills	0		
D. G. Cork b Benjamin	11	1/5 2/7 3/10 (30.3 overs) 103
†K. M. Krikken c Boon b Benjamin	18	4/23 5/38 6/51
I. R. Bishop lbw b Mullally	0	7/51 8/89 9/94

Bowling: Benjamin 10.3–0–32–5; Mills 8–0–29–3; Mullally 7–1–22–2; Wells 5–0–19–0.

Umpires: N. T. Plews and G. Sharp.

ESSEX v LANCASHIRE

At Chelmsford, July 9. Essex won by one wicket. Toss: Essex. Essex pulled off an amazing victory at 8 p.m. with one delivery to spare, after Garnham and Childs came to the final over with 14 required. Garnham's drive wide of long-off against Atherton signalled victory and a half-century from just 37 deliveries. The last man Childs had joined him with 37 needed in a little more than three overs, after he had put on 54 in six overs with Topley. Fairbrother, in his first appearance for a month, was forced to use Atherton's leg-spin for nearly 12 overs when DeFreitas withdrew from the attack after only three deliveries with a recurring groin injury. Nevertheless, Essex had faltered following an opening stand of 123 in 26 overs from Gooch and Stephenson, and lost five wickets for 45 after a break for bad light. Fowler and Speak had laid the foundation for Lancashire's impressive total, taken to 318 by Watkinson and the tail. No team batting first in this competition had ever scored so many and lost: the previous record, 307, was held by Essex themselves.

Man of the Match: M. A. Garnham.

Lancashire

G. Fowler c Prichard b Topley	66	†W. K. Hegg st Garnham b Stephenson		7
M. A. Atherton c Shahid b Pringle	8	J. D. Fitton not out		17
N. J. Speak c Garnham b Pringle	60			
*N. H. Fairbrother run out	28	L-b 19, w 6, n-b 10		35
G. D. Lloyd lbw b Stephenson	24			
M. Watkinson c Stephenson b Topley	40	1/36 2/137 3/186	(8 wkts, 60 overs)	318
P. A. J. DeFreitas b Stephenson	0	4/192 5/249 6/249		
I. D. Austin not out	33	7/261 8/278		

D. K. Morrison did not bat.

Bowling: Foster 12-1-47-0; Topley 8-0-51-2; Pringle 12-3-50-2; Stephenson 12-0-78-3; Gooch 4-0-22-0; Childs 12-1-51-0.

Essex

*G. A. Gooch c Hegg b Atherton	49	†M. A. Garnham not out		53
J. P. Stephenson c DeFreitas b Morrison	75	T. D. Topley run out		15
M. E. Waugh b Watkinson	25	J. H. Childs not out		13
P. J. Prichard b Fitton	28	L-b 13, w 5, n-b 3		21
N. V. Knight run out	1			
N. Shahid b Atherton	12	1/123 2/133 3/179	(9 wkts, 59.5 overs)	319
D. R. Pringle c Hegg b Morrison	16	4/183 5/194 6/208		
N. A. Foster b Watkinson	11	7/228 8/228 9/282		

Bowling: DeFreitas 0.3-0-5-0; Atherton 11.2-0-83-2; Watkinson 12-2-39-2; Morrison 12-0-72-2; Austin 12-1-58-0; Fitton 12-0-49-1.

Umpires: R. A. White and P. B. Wight (G. Clark deputised for P. B. Wight).

HAMPSHIRE v KENT

At Southampton, July 9. Kent won by two wickets. Toss: Kent. Hampshire surrendered their title in disappointing fashion on a grey, overcast day in a match seen as a dress rehearsal for the Benson and Hedges Cup final two days later. Two of their prime batsmen were needlessly run out, and slack bowling (three wides and 15 no-balls in all) gave Kent three extra overs. Hampshire's innings owed everything to Terry, whose chanceless century was his second in successive NatWest matches. He shared 108 for the first wicket with Middleton, and though Hampshire kept impetus as Smith ran himself out and Gower chipped to mid-wicket, Nicholas joined Terry to add 61 in ten overs. The captain's run-out sparked a collapse, and six wickets fell for 31. Kent's reply was equally inconsistent; Benson went early, but Ward batted soundly, and his stand of 92 in 20 overs with Hooper suggested a comfortable victory. Then Hooper's dismissal started a slump to 211 for seven, in the 55th over, Ward falling eight short of a hundred. It was Ealham, playing with maturity beyond his years, who saw Kent home with five balls to spare.

Man of the Match: M. A. Ealham.

Hampshire

T. C. Middleton c Davis b Igglesden	43	S. D. Udal b Fleming	2
V. P. Terry c Benson b McCague	109	R. J. Maru b McCague	4
R. A. Smith run out	14		
D. I. Gower c Hooper b Davis	6	B 1, l-b 7, w 11	19
*M. C. J. Nicholas run out	25		
K. D. James c Davis b Fleming	4	1/108 2/135 3/151 (9 wkts, 60 overs) 243	
M. D. Marshall c Davis b Fleming	7	4/212 5/215 6/225	
†R. J. Parks not out	10	7/227 8/234 9/243	

C. A. Connor did not bat.

Bowling: Igglesden 12–0–33–1; Ealham 12–1–34–0; McCague 7–0–44–2; Hooper 12–1–43–0; Davis 8–0–47–1; Fleming 9–0–34–3.

Kent

T. R. Ward lbw b Udal	92	R. P. Davis c Maru b Connor	9
*M. R. Benson c Maru b Connor	11	M. J. McCague not out	3
N. R. Taylor c Connor b Udal	15		
C. L. Hooper c James b Udal	40	L-b 8, w 3, n-b 10	21
G. R. Cowdrey c Parks b Connor	6		
M. V. Fleming c Parks b Marshall	1	1/28 2/74 3/166 (8 wkts, 59.1 overs) 244	
†S. A. Marsh b Marshall	13	4/173 5/174 6/180	
M. A. Ealham not out	33	7/211 8/231	

A. P. Igglesden did not bat.

Bowling: Marshall 12–0–43–2; Connor 11.1–2–37–3; James 12–3–56–0; Maru 12–0–61–0; Udal 12–0–39–3.

Umpires: G. I. Burgess and M. J. Kitchen.

MIDDLESEX v DURHAM

At Uxbridge, July 9. Durham won by six wickets. Toss: Durham. Durham's day ended in delight as they reached the NatWest quarter-finals for the first time, one of the highlights of their opening season on the first-class circuit. But it had begun in dejection when Wood, attempting to deliver the first ball, slipped on the grass and twisted his knee so badly he was forced out of the match. After the umpires had sent for the mower, Durham's rearranged bowling line-up coped well enough. Against his former colleagues, Hughes's nip and pace earned four wickets. Still, Middlesex's shortfall was partly self-inflicted. Gatting had made a forceful fifty when he over-estimated his speed in taking a run to Larkins. Larkins himself went before Durham had a run on the board, but Glendenen batted for 31 overs, and his dismissal brought Botham in to join acting-captain Parker. The two 36-year-old campaigners simply stayed in and scored steadily: Botham's first 17 runs came in singles. When they had added 123 in 26 overs the match was effectively won.

Man of the Match: P. W. G. Parker.

Middlesex

D. L. Haynes c Fothergill b Hughes	20	N. F. Williams b Hughes	4
M. A. Roseberry c Parker b Brown	14	A. R. C. Fraser not out	1
*M. W. Gatting run out	57		
M. R. Ramprakash c Parker b McEwan	46	B 5, l-b 6, w 13	24
J. D. Carr c Parker b Hughes	45		
†K. R. Brown not out	44	1/39 2/51 3/137 (8 wkts, 60 overs) 259	
P. N. Weekes c Fothergill b Botham	0	4/184 5/212 6/213	
J. E. Emburey c Fothergill b Hughes	4	7/240 8/258	

C. W. Taylor did not bat.

Bowling: McEwan 12–1–45–1; Brown 12–2–43–1; Hughes 12–3–41–4; Botham 12–0–53–1; Smith 10–0–50–0; Jones 2–0–16–0.

Durham

W. Larkins c Carr b Taylor	0	I. Smith not out	12
D. Glendenen b Weekes	57	L-b 12, w 17, n-b 5	34
G. M. Jones lbw b Fraser	25		
P. W. G. Parker lbw b Williams	69	1/0 2/52 (4 wkts, 58.3 overs) 260	
T. Botham not out	63	3/116 4/239	

A. R. Fothergill, S. M. McEwan, J. Wood, S. J. E. Brown and S. P. Hughes did not bat.

Bowling: Taylor 11-1-54-1; Williams 10-0-55-1; Fraser 12-1-45-1; Carr 5-1-11-0; Amburey 10.3-1-36-0; Weekes 10-0-47-1.

Umpires: H. D. Bird and B. Dudleston.

NORTHAMPTONSHIRE v YORKSHIRE

At Northampton, July 9. Northamptonshire won by 133 runs. Toss: Yorkshire. Yorkshire's hopes of early wickets after putting Northamptonshire in were dashed by Fordham and Felton, who posted 129 in 31 overs, and from then on the home side were never under serious pressure. Lamb capitalised ruthlessly, scoring 69 in 58 balls, while Penberthy provided late impetus with his 21-ball 36, and twice pulled Gough over mid-wicket on to the sponsors' marquee. A total of 325 was Northamptonshire's highest in one-day competitions against a first-class county. Once Yorkshire had lost Kellett and Moxon in their first two overs, the rest was a formality. Blakey, whose fifty included only two fours and a six, ensured respectability with White, adding 97 in 23 overs for the fifth wicket, but Ambrose and Curran broke through again and tidied up efficiently. Ambrose's remarkable figures of four for seven in 8.3 overs earned him the match award.

Man of the Match: C. E. L. Ambrose.

Northamptonshire

A. Fordham run out	78	†D. Ripley not out	3
N. A. Felton c Blakey b Gough	48	C. E. L. Ambrose not out	4
R. J. Bailey run out	24	L-b 10, w 4, n-b 3	17
*A. J. Lamb lbw b Jarvis	69		
D. J. Capel run out	18	1/129 2/145 3/170 (7 wkts, 60 overs) 325	
K. M. Curran c Moxon b Jarvis	28	4/237 5/260	
A. L. Penberthy c Byas b Gough	36	6/304 7/319	

J. P. Taylor and N. G. B. Cook did not bat.

Bowling: Jarvis 12-0-53-2; Hartley 12-0-71-0; Robinson 12-1-73-0; Gough 12-1-73-2; Carrick 12-1-45-0.

Yorkshire

*M. D. Moxon c Ripley b Taylor	2	P. W. Jarvis c Taylor b Curran	11
S. A. Kellett c Ripley b Ambrose	0	D. Gough b Ambrose	4
D. Byas lbw b Cook	32	M. A. Robinson not out	1
S. R. Tendulkar c Ripley b Capel	21	L-b 12, w 4	16
†R. J. Blakey c and b Curran	64		
C. White b Ambrose	41	1/3 2/3 3/51 (50.3 overs) 192	
P. Carrick b Ambrose	0	4/70 5/167 6/167	
P. J. Hartley b Curran	0	7/168 8/182 9/186	

Bowling: Ambrose 8.3-4-7-4; Taylor 7-1-29-1; Capel 12-1-54-1; Curran 8-0-33-3; Cook 12-0-45-1; Bailey 3-0-12-0.

Umpires: J. D. Bond and V. A. Holder.

NOTTINGHAMSHIRE v GLAMORGAN

At Nottingham, July 9, 10. Glamorgan won by two wickets. Toss: Glamorgan. The toss proved decisive, enabling Watkin to exploit the helpful conditions. His fine opening burst in which he accounted for Randall, Broad and Johnson, left Nottinghamshire reeling at 26 for three. They had staggered on to 43 for five before Cairns came in to repair the damage, hitting eight fours and a six in his two-hour 77. Glamorgan's reply spilled over into the second day because of rain, and at lunch they were 127 for three, thanks to Maynard, who struck eight fours. Victory looked a formality, but fine bowling from Cairns and Field-Buss set up a tense finish, and Glamorgan required nine off the final over, from Lewis, or eight if they kept wickets in hand. Seven came off the first five balls. The field closed in for the last delivery but Bastien nervelessly hammered it to the long-off boundary. Close of play Glamorgan 10-0 (2.1 overs) (H. Morris 7*, A. Dale 3*).

Man of the Match: S. L. Watkin.

Nottinghamshire

B. C. Broad lbw b Watkin	8	†B. N. French lbw b Richards	12	
D. W. Randall b Watkin	5	R. A. Pick not out	24	
*R. T. Robinson b Dale	30	M. G. Field-Buss c Metson b Richards	1	
P. Johnson lbw b Watkin	6	B 2, l-b 4, w 7	13	
M. A. Crawley c Metson b Bastien	4			
C. C. Lewis c Maynard b Barwick	4	1/14 2/16 3/26 (59.3 overs) 194		
C. L. Cairns c Dale b Barwick	77	4/38 5/43 6/91		
K. P. Evans lbw b Dale	10	7/117 8/151 9/181		

Bowling: Watkin 12–3–21–3; Bastien 12–1–42–1; Barwick 12–3–48–2; Dale 12–0–46–2; Richards 11.3–1–31–2.

Glamorgan

H. Morris c Crawley b Lewis	26	†C. P. Metson b Pick	21	
A. Dale c and b Field-Buss	20	S. L. Watkin not out	4	
*M. P. Maynard c Robinson b Field-Buss	60	S. Bastien not out	7	
I. V. A. Richards c Robinson b Field-Buss	25	L-b 1, w 8	9	
C. S. Cowdrey b Cairns	6	1/32 2/77 3/117 (8 wkts, 60 overs) 197		
P. A. Cottey c Crawley b Pick	17	4/138 5/144 6/147		
R. D. B. Croft lbw b Cairns	2	7/184 8/186		

S. R. Barwick did not bat.

Bowling: Lewis 12–0–44–1; Pick 12–0–66–2; Cairns 12–2–38–2; Evans 12–3–25–0; Field-Buss 12–4–23–3.

Umpires: J. H. Hampshire and R. C. Tolchard.

SOMERSET v GLOUCESTERSHIRE

At Taunton, July 9. Gloucestershire won by 22 runs. Toss: Gloucestershire. Gloucestershire reached the quarter-finals despite excellent performances from two young Somerset players, Caddick and Lathwell. In cloudy weather Caddick's early fire reduced the visitors to 12 for two, but they recovered well thanks to Hinks and Wright, who put on 140. In his second, somewhat belated, spell Caddick removed both in three overs, and when he added Russell and Vaughan with consecutive balls he had six for 30. But Gloucestershire's last six wickets added 67 in 12 overs. Lathwell's excellent 85 from 105 deliveries, well supported by Hayhurst and Harden, took Somerset to 147 for one in 39 overs, but an athletic catch by Babington started a run of four wickets in four overs, from Scott and Walsh, which swung the match. In poor light Burns and Snell struck out boldly but Walsh, again, and Smith had the final word. They were backed up by Russell, who took five catches behind the stumps.

Man of the Match: A. R. Caddick.

Gloucestershire

G. D. Hodgson lbw b Caddick	0	C. A. Walsh c MacLeay b Hayhurst	10
C. W. J. Athey c Lathwell b Caddick	8	A. M. Smith c Tavaré b Hayhurst	6
S. G. Hinks b Caddick	67	A. M. Babington not out	1
*A. J. Wright c Trump b Caddick	71	L-b 6, w 14	20
M. W. Alleyne c and b MacLeay	17		
R. J. Scott c Caddick b Rose	4	1/5 2/12 3/152	(59.4 overs) 235
†R. C. Russell c Burns b Caddick	20	4/168 5/179 6/185	
M. T. C. Vaughan b Caddick	11	7/217 8/217 9/233	

Bowling: Mallender 12-2-32-0; Caddick 12-2-30-6; Snell 10-0-51-0; Rose 8-2-24-1; MacLeay 9-0-49-1; Trump 4-0-21-0; Hayhurst 4.4-0-22-2.

Somerset

A. N. Hayhurst c Russell b Smith	21	N. A. Mallender c Russell b Smith	1
M. N. Lathwell c Babington b Scott	85	A. R. Caddick b Walsh	0
R. J. Harden c Russell b Scott	39	H. R. J. Trump not out	1
*C. J. Tavaré c Russell b Walsh	2	L-b 7, w 3, n-b 1	11
G. D. Rose lbw b Walsh	2		
†N. D. Burns c Athey b Smith	24	1/55 2/147 3/150	(55.4 overs) 213
K. H. MacLeay c Russell b Babington	8	4/152 5/156 6/189	
R. P. Snell c sub b Walsh	19	7/205 8/211 9/211	

Bowling: Walsh 11.4-2-34-4; Babington 11-1-46-1; Vaughan 7-0-16-0; Smith 12-1-45-3; Athey 2-0-11-0; Alleyne 5-0-22-0; Scott 7-0-32-2.

Umpires: J. C. Balderstone and G. A. Stickley.

WARWICKSHIRE v SUSSEX

At Birmingham, July 9, 10. Warwickshire won by three wickets. Toss: Warwickshire. Hostile bowling by Donald, coupled with poor running by their batsmen, cost Sussex five wickets as they reached 55, and Warwickshire held their advantage for the rest of the rain-interrupted match. Sussex captain Wells batted for 39 overs, but found little support, except from Stephenson, who hit 40 out of a sixth-wicket partnership of 68. The visitors were bowled out with six overs to spare early on the second morning by a keen seam attack in which Twose underlined his all-round development with three wickets. Twose then put on 62 with Lloyd, which left Warwickshire only 73 to make, with eight wickets in hand. Though Stephenson and Pigott claimed two each, to give Sussex a slim chance of an improbable win, an unbeaten 21 from Smith brought Warwickshire victory with 6.3 overs left. Close of play: Sussex 149-9 (53 overs) (A. P. Wells 47*, A. N. Jones 4*).

Man of the Match: R. G. Twose.

Sussex

D. M. Smith run out	22	A. C. S. Pigott c Piper b Twose	0
J. W. Hall b Donald	0	I. D. K. Salisbury lbw b Twose	4
N. J. Lenham run out	14	A. N. Jones run out	5
*A. P. Wells not out	47	B 4, l-b 4, w 1, n-b 8	17
M. P. Speight c Ostler b Donald	1		
K. Greenfield run out	0	1/1 2/35 3/45	(54 overs) 150
F. D. Stephenson b Twose	40	4/55 5/55 6/123	
†P. Moores b Munton	0	7/124 8/125 9/135	

Bowling: Donald 11-4-17-2; Small 11-3-29-0; Munton 10-1-23-1; Reeve 8-3-21-0; Twose 12-0-39-3; Smith 2-0-13-0.

Warwickshire

A. J. Moles c Moores b Pigott	11	†K. J. Piper c Stephenson b Lenham	7
R. G. Twose b Salisbury	38	G. C. Small not out	6
*T. A. Lloyd c Moores b Pigott	40	B 1, l-b 8, w 4, n-b 1	14
D. P. Ostler b Stephenson	0		
D. A. Reeve c Greenfield b Pigott	8	1/16 2/78 3/80　　(7 wkts, 53.3 overs) 151	
T. L. Penney lbw b Stephenson	6	4/105 5/108	
N. M. K. Smith not out	21	6/125 7/144	

T. A. Munton and A. A. Donald did not bat.

Bowling: Stephenson 12–2–35–2; Pigott 12–1–31–3; Jones 9–0–31–0; Salisbury 9–1–21–1; Lenham 11.3–3–24–1.

Umpires: J. W. Holder and R. Julian.

QUARTER-FINALS

GLAMORGAN v NORTHAMPTONSHIRE

At Swansea, July 29. Northamptonshire won by 83 runs. Toss: Northamptonshire. For the third year running, Glamorgan failed at the quarter-final stage while Northamptonshire, their conquerors in 1991, went through. But the home team's hopes were raised when accurate bowling restricted Northamptonshire to 118 for four from 41 overs by lunch. Afterwards Bailey accelerated, with useful support from the tail, and his disciplined unbeaten 98, with six fours and a six, held the innings together. Still, a total of 224 was modest. James and Morris made a steady if unspectacular start to Glamorgan's reply, but then departed in the space of seven runs. Much depended on Maynard and Richards, but the West Indian disappointed a near-capacity 10,000 crowd when he was caught behind off Capel for two. Maynard stayed for 26 overs, and added 35 for the sixth wicket with Croft, but the innings quickly folded once he had gone.

Man of the Match: R. J. Bailey.

Northamptonshire

A. Fordham lbw b Foster	33	†D. Ripley run out	6
N. A. Felton b Watkin	2	C. E. L. Ambrose b Barwick	8
R. J. Bailey not out	98	L-b 7, w 5, n-b 4	16
*A. J. Lamb b Dale	8		
D. J. Capel c Richards b Croft	21	1/15 2/47 3/60　　(8 wkts, 60 overs) 224	
K. M. Curran c and b Watkin	19	4/97 5/148 6/166	
A. L. Penberthy b Barwick	13	7/175 8/224	

J. P. Taylor and N. G. B. Cook did not bat.

Bowling: Watkin 12–1–43–2; Foster 12–3–40–1; Barwick 12–3–36–2; Dale 6–1–14–1; Richards 8–0–39–0; Croft 10–0–45–1.

Glamorgan

S. P. James c Ripley b Curran	11	S. L. Watkin c Taylor b Penberthy	9
H. Morris c Felton b Curran	29	D. J. Foster c Ripley b Taylor	2
A. Dale c Penberthy b Capel	5	S. R. Barwick not out	0
*M. P. Maynard c Cook b Taylor	41	L-b 7, w 9	16
I. V. A. Richards c Ripley b Capel	2		
P. A. Cottey b Penberthy	9	1/38 2/45 3/49　　(51.1 overs) 141	
R. D. B. Croft c Curran b Taylor	16	4/59 5/86 6/121	
†C. P. Metson c Bailey b Capel	1	7/122 8/126 9/141	

Bowling: Ambrose 9–3–14–0; Taylor 12–1–41–3; Curran 7–1–19–2; Capel 12–1–21–3; Cook 4–0–10–0; Penberthy 7.1–0–29–2.

Umpires: B. Dudleston and A. A. Jones.

GLOUCESTERSHIRE v ESSEX

At Cheltenham College, July 29. Essex won by six wickets. Toss: Gloucestershire. With Bristol unavailable because of construction work, a large crowd packed into the college ground. Most of them were disappointed. Once Gooch had survived Walsh's opening salvo, Essex encountered few problems. Gloucestershire's total was well short of being challenging enough. Only 76 runs came from their first 30 overs, and when three wickets fell in 12 balls soon after lunch, including that of Athey, who batted 44 overs for his 59, the visitors had a firm grip. It was loosened somewhat by a composed fifty in 49 deliveries from Vaughan, who added 53 with Ball in the last five overs. But the spectators sensed that the duel between Gooch and Walsh could be decisive. The England captain was nearly caught off Walsh's first delivery, ran out Stephenson and might have lost Prichard, missed at short leg before scoring. Prichard then relieved the pressure by scoring 58 out of 96 before leaving the stage to Gooch, who relaxed sufficiently to complete his sixth century in the competition by on-driving the luckless Walsh for six. The unbeaten innings earned him a record ninth match award.

Man of the Match: G. A. Gooch.

Gloucestershire

G. D. Hodgson lbw b Foster	25	C. A. Walsh c Topley b Ilott		17
C. W. J. Athey c Garnham b Stephenson	59	M. C. J. Ball not out		16
*A. J. Wright b Topley	10	L-b 9, w 6, n-b 2		17
M. W. Alleyne c and b Stephenson	26			—
R. J. Scott run out	1	1/51 2/80 3/124	(7 wkts, 60 overs)	236
†R. C. Russell c Garnham b Ilott	11	4/126 5/128		
J. T. C. Vaughan not out	54	6/158 7/183		

A. M. Smith and A. M. Babington did not bat.

Bowling: Foster 12–3–25–1; Pringle 12–0–50–0; Topley 12–0–30–1; Ilott 12–0–67–2; Stephenson 10–1–42–2; Waugh 2–0–13–0.

Essex

*G. A. Gooch not out	105	D. R. Pringle not out		14
J. P. Stephenson run out	11	B 3, l-b 5, w 3, n-b 2		13
P. J. Prichard c Russell b Scott	58			—
M. E. Waugh b Alleyne	9	1/22 2/118	(4 wkts, 57.1 overs)	240
N. Hussain c Smith b Ball	30	3/129 4/195		

†M. A. Garnham, N. A. Foster, T. D. Topley, M. C. Ilott and P. M. Such did not bat.

Bowling: Walsh 12–2–43–0; Babington 8–1–36–0; Smith 3.1–1–23–0; Vaughan 9–0–41–0; Scott 12–0–43–1; Ball 4–0–24–1; Alleyne 9–0–22–1.

Umpires: J. H. Hampshire and J. H. Harris.

LEICESTERSHIRE v DURHAM

At Leicester, July 29. Leicestershire won by 45 runs. Toss: Durham. Durham's hopes of reaching the semi-finals in their début first-class season were high after Leicestershire's innings ended in farce: five wickets fell in 18 balls, four of them run-outs. A target of 250 appeared modest on a good pitch, despite the loss of Jones, whose absence with a broken finger prompted a rare appearance by Geoff Cook, Durham's 40-year-old director of cricket. But when they had reached 99 for one Benson removed Larkins and Cook in successive overs. Then Botham was run out cheaply by acting-captain Parker, and although Parker remained to make 54, batting with a runner later on, he received no worthwhile support. Benson, who had been recalled from a Second Eleven match in Cardiff when a suspected stress fracture ruled out Millns, earlier hit 42 in 59 balls for Leicestershire, bettered only by Whitaker's 63; his achievements earned him the match award.

Man of the Match: J. D. R. Benson.

Leicestershire

T. J. Boon st Fothergill b Bainbridge ..	25	V. J. Wells run out	0
*N. E. Briers c Fothergill b Botham ...	7	G. J. Parsons run out	3
J. J. Whitaker b Hughes	63	A. D. Mullally run out..............	0
P. E. Robinson lbw b Hughes	31	L-b 7, w 6	13
J. D. R. Benson c Cook b Brown......	42		
L. Potter run out	31	1/15 2/57 3/131 (59.3 overs) 249	
W. K. M. Benjamin not out	24	4/142 5/204 6/222	
†P. A. Nixon b Hughes..............	10	7/239 8/239 9/249	

Bowling: Botham 12–2–54–1; Brown 11.3–1–53–1; Bainbridge 8–0–29–1; Hughes 12–2–34–3; Smith 5–0–24–0; Berry 11–0–48–0.

Durham

W. Larkins c Boon b Benson	41	†A. R. Fothergill c Benjamin b Wells ..	7
J. D. Glendenen c Benson b Wells	39	S. P. Hughes c Mullally b Wells.......	2
G. Cook st Nixon b Benson	16	S. J. E. Brown not out..............	3
*P. W. G. Parker run out	54	B 1, l-b 9, w 10	20
I. T. Botham run out...............	5		
P. Bainbridge c and b Mullally........	6	1/66 2/99 3/106 (55.5 overs) 204	
I. Smith c Potter b Mullally	2	4/130 5/147 6/153	
P. J. Berry b Benjamin	9	7/175 8/198 9/198	

Bowling: Benjamin 10–3–18–1; Mullally 10–2–33–2; Wells 8.5–2–38–3; Parsons 3–0–24–0; Potter 12–0–37–0; Benson 12–1–44–2.

Umpires: H. D. Bird and B. Leadbeater.

WARWICKSHIRE v KENT

At Birmingham, July 29. Warwickshire won by 63 runs. Toss: Kent. Warwickshire's score of 224 proved to be a good one on a pitch which offered something to every bowler. The Kent seamers and two spinners made the most of it. But a typically solid 76 from Moles, who faced 138 balls and hit five fours, rescued the home team. He was fourth out at 150 after putting on 86 for the third wicket with the promising Ostler. When Warwickshire took the field, Small struck his best form of the season, picking up the early wickets of Taylor, Hooper and Cowdrey to reduce Kent to 35 for four. Donald and Munton, well supported by Reeve and Twose, maintained their control. Only Benson, with an obdurate 57 off 93 balls, held firm, and when he was eighth out the tail hung on for another 12 overs, but to no effect. Piper took the last catch and was then given his county cap.

Man of the Match: G. C. Small.

Warwickshire

A. J. Moles run out	76	G. C. Small b Fleming	10
R. G. Twose c Ward b Ealham	10	A. A. Donald not out	9
*T. A. Lloyd lbw b Ealham	12	T. A. Munton run out	0
D. P. Ostler b Hooper..............	30	B 2, l-b 15, w 8, n-b 1	26
D. A. Reeve b McCague.............	22		
T. L. Penney c and b Davis	6	1/12 2/31 3/117 (60 overs) 224	
N. M. K. Smith b McCague..........	12	4/150 5/164 6/183	
†K. J. Piper b Fleming	11	7/195 8/212 9/224	

Bowling: Igglesden 12–3–30–0; Ealham 12–0–33–2; McCague 11–0–44–2; Hooper 11–0–48–1; Davis 12–0–42–1; Fleming 2–0–10–2.

Kent

T. R. Ward c Piper b Donald	4	R. P. Davis c Piper b Donald	22
M. R. Benson c Piper b Twose	57	M. J. McCague c Penney b Twose	14
N. R. Taylor b Small	3	A. P. Igglesden not out	7
C. L. Hooper lbw b Small	5	L-b 6, w 3	9
G. R. Cowdrey c Reeve b Small	3		
M. V. Fleming run out	11	1/12 2/17 3/27	(52.5 overs) 161
†S. A. Marsh c Small b Twose	7	4/35 5/55 6/72	
M. A. Ealham c Twose b Munton	19	7/102 8/115 9/136	

Bowling: Donald 10.5–4–22–2; Small 12–1–28–3; Munton 10–0–26–1; Reeve 10–1–33–0; Twose 9–2–41–3; Smith 1–0–5–0.

Umpires: R. Palmer and A. G. T. Whitehead.

SEMI-FINALS

LEICESTERSHIRE v ESSEX

At Leicester, August 12, 13. Leicestershire won by five wickets. Toss: Leicestershire. Hit by injuries to Millns and Wells, Leicestershire recalled Jonathan Agnew, the 32-year-old former England fast bowler, who retired in 1990 and was now BBC cricket correspondent. He performed admirably, gaining one wicket for just 31 runs, with no boundaries, in an unbroken spell. He confessed later that he felt "absolutely exhausted". His return led to the entry c Nixon b Agnew in the scorebook, for the benefit of students of American history. Rain had prevented play until 4.30 p.m. and on a moist pitch Essex had similar difficulties against the other seamers, struggling to 66 in their first 30 overs. Hussain and Prichard put on 112 in 27 for the fourth wicket, but on the second morning Essex added only 38 in eight overs. In the field their bowlers were hampered by a wet ball, and there was drizzle for the final two hours. To add to the visitors' problems, wicket-keeper Garnham left the field for stitches after Benson deflected the ball on to his right eye. Briers played patiently, helped by two dropped catches by Gooch, but despite the low target Leicestershire still needed three from the last over. Potter tested his team-mates' nerves by failing to score from Stephenson's first four deliveries; he then ran on a wide, and Benson edged past the substitute wicket-keeper, Prichard, to take Leicestershire to their first 60-overs final with a ball to spare. Close of play: Essex 188-6 (52 overs) (N. V. Knight 8*, M. A. Garnham 1*).

Man of the Match: N. E. Briers.

Essex

*G. A. Gooch c Benson b Benjamin	8	T. D. Topley not out	19
J. P. Stephenson c Benson b Mullally	0	M. C. Ilott not out	10
J. J. B. Lewis c Nixon b Agnew	21		
P. J. Prichard b Potter	87	L-b 9, w 10, n-b 3	22
N. Hussain b Parsons	40		
D. R. Pringle c Potter b Parsons	3	1/1 2/17 3/50	(8 wkts, 60 overs) 226
N. V. Knight c Nixon b Benjamin	8	4/162 5/174 6/184	
†M. A. Garnham b Benjamin	8	7/188 8/208	

P. M. Such did not bat.

Bowling: Benjamin 12–1–40–3; Mullally 12–0–41–1; Parsons 12–3–29–2; Agnew 12–2–31–1; Potter 9–0–50–1; Benson 3–0–26–0.

Leicestershire

T. J. Boon c Prichard b Topley	31	J. D. R. Benson not out	25
*N. E. Briers c Hussain b Ilott	88	L. Potter not out	7
J. J. Whitaker c Stephenson b Ilott	46	L-b 7, w 5, n-b 4	16
W. K. M. Benjamin c Stephenson			
b Pringle	1	1/52 2/138 3/145	(5 wkts, 59.5 overs) 229
P. E. Robinson c Gooch b Topley	15	4/176 5/213	

†P. A. Nixon, G. J. Parsons, J. P. Agnew and A. D. Mullally did not bat.

Bowling: Ilott 12–2–36–2; Topley 12–1–58–2; Stephenson 11.5–1–56–0; Pringle 12–2–35–1; Such 12–0–37–0.

Umpires: D. O. Oslear and N. T. Plews.

WARWICKSHIRE v NORTHAMPTONSHIRE

At Birmingham, August 12, 13. Northamptonshire won by three wickets. Toss: Northamptonshire. Warwickshire lost their second successive home semi-final because their batsmen were never able to cope with a pitch inhibiting attacking strokeplay, or to break the grip of a tight, accurate attack, superbly spearheaded by Ambrose. Heavy overnight rain delayed the start until 1.25 p.m., and then the first seven wickets went for 99. Only Small's 23 enabled the home side to reach 149 – a total at least 30 short of par. Donald and Munton reduced the visitors to 47 for two overnight. Clearly taking wickets was Warwickshire's priority, but curiously Donald was not given a bowl until the target was down to 60 from 20 overs. He then produced a blistering six-over spell in which he was unlucky to take only one wicket. Reeve bounced out Capel and Curran, and Smith and Munton pressed hard, but Northamptonshire scraped home with three wickets in hand. Felton won the match award for his careful 58. An untidy corollary was that both sides were four overs short of their 60 after the prescribed 225 minutes, though Warwickshire were excused two overs for time taken to dry the ball. The Test and County Cricket Board's increased scale of fines – £660 per over in the semi-final – still appeared to be an insufficient deterrent, possibly because the players paid only half the fines themselves, the county clubs having agreed to pay the balance. Close of play: Northamptonshire 47-2 (23 overs) (N. A. Felton 24*, A. J. Lamb 8*).

Man of the Match: N. A. Felton.

Warwickshire

A. J. Moles lbw b Curran	19	G. C. Small c Capel b Taylor	23
R. G. Twose c Bailey b Capel	15	A. A. Donald not out	14
*T. A. Lloyd c and b Taylor	10	T. A. Munton run out	0
D. P. Ostler c Lamb b Ambrose	6	B 1, l-b 3, w 10, n-b 3	17
D. A. Reeve lbw b Ambrose	18		
T. L. Penney lbw b Capel	7	1/20 2/35 3/45 (59.2 overs) 149	
N. M. K. Smith c Fordham b Penberthy	8	4/56 5/82 6/87	
†K. J. Piper b Curran	12	7/99 8/121 9/143	

Bowling: Ambrose 11.2–3–21–2; Taylor 12–2–34–2; Capel 12–1–34–2; Penberthy 12–4–28–1; Curran 12–1–28–2.

Northamptonshire

A. Fordham c Piper b Donald	6	†D. Ripley not out	3
N. A. Felton c Lloyd b Smith	58	J. N. Snape not out	5
R. J. Bailey c Piper b Munton	7	L-b 2, w 3, n-b 2	7
*A. J. Lamb c Piper b Small	26		
D. J. Capel c and b Reeve	24	1/7 2/27 3/87 (7 wkts, 55.5 overs) 152	
K. M. Curran c Lloyd b Reeve	14	4/108 5/123	
A. L. Penberthy lbw b Donald	2	6/140 7/143	

C. E. L. Ambrose and J. P. Taylor did not bat.

Bowling: Donald 12–0–41–2; Small 12–3–30–1; Munton 11–3–17–1; Reeve 12–4–29–2; Twose 5–0–16–0; Smith 3.5–0–17–1.

Umpires: B. J. Meyer and K. E. Palmer.

FINAL

LEICESTERSHIRE v NORTHAMPTONSHIRE

At Lord's, September 5. Northamptonshire won by eight wickets. Toss: Northamptonshire. The county used to being criticised for fouling up promising situations won this match with such uncompromising efficiency that it could be remembered as the most boring of all the Lord's finals, if anyone outside Northamptonshire bothers to remember it. If so, that was entirely to the winners' credit. They did just about everything right on the day and Leicestershire, who played far above themselves simply to get this far, were in the end simply overmatched. What chance they might have had was probably wrecked the previous night when the all-rounder Wells collapsed in the team hotel and was taken to hospital. Leicestershire again approached Agnew, the improbable hero of the semi-final, and obtained an emergency registration for another former player, Peter Willey, who was working alongside Agnew in the BBC commentary box. In the end, they opted to play their fast bowler Millns but he was barely even quarter-fit.

Leicestershire also lost the toss and were forced to bat first, which proved to be the route to defeat for the seventh consecutive NatWest final. For once, though, this was nothing to do with the murk or dew of a September morn – batting conditions were easy all day. The decisive factor may well have been the speed at which Northamptonshire, having been fined for their slow over-rate in the semi-final, ran through their overs. While Whitaker and Robinson were putting on 130 for the third wicket, Leicestershire were, on the face of it, going very well indeed. But the overs were disappearing faster than the batsmen seemed to imagine and the solid platform they should have been building turned out to be structurally unsound when Ambrose and Curran returned to the attack.

The score of 208 for seven was nowhere near enough to withstand the assault it received from Fordham and Bailey, who put on 144 and gave no worries even to Northamptonshire supporters whose optimism had been poisoned by watching their team lose four successive Lord's finals. Fordham hit 13 fours in his 91 and struck the ball as sweetly as was possible on a slow surface. Ray Illingworth rightly made him Man of the Match.

The inevitability of the result made the closing stages very routine. From the start, the atmosphere had been lifeless: for the first time in many years the final was not a sell-out. Most people put this down to the presence of two of the smaller counties. More relevant were the weeks of bad weather before the event, the high prices (£35 for a half-decent view) at a time of recession and a certain loss of novelty value: for Northamptonshire this was their eighth Lord's final in 17 years. Those who did pay were able to watch skydivers in the lunch interval; they might have been more entertained had they been privy to events behind the scenes, especially when Lamb, the Northamptonshire captain, received a writ for libel from his former team-mate Sarfraz Nawaz because of allegations about ball-tampering. When he went out to bat, Lamb was accompanied through the Long Room by two county officials to prevent anyone choosing that moment to hand over another writ. – Matthew Engel.

Man of the Match: A. Fordham.   *Attendance*: 20,999; *receipts* £590,000.

Leicestershire

T. J. Boon run out	3	G. J. Parsons not out	1
*N. E. Briers run out	25		
J. J. Whitaker c Taylor b Curran	84	B 1, l-b 8, w 3, n-b 2	14
P. E. Robinson c Felton b Ambrose	62		
J. D. R. Benson b Ambrose	0	1/3 (1) 2/45 (2)	(7 wkts, 60 overs) 208
L. Potter c Capel b Curran	12	3/175 (3) 4/178 (5)	
W. K. M. Benjamin b Curran	0	5/197 (6) 6/198 (7)	
†P. A. Nixon not out	7	7/200 (4)	

A. D. Mullally and D. J. Millns did not bat.

Bowling: Ambrose 12–0–35–2; Taylor 7–1–19–0; Capel 11–3–39–0; Curran 12–1–41–3; Cook 12–0–43–0; Penberthy 6–0–22–0.

Northamptonshire

A. Fordham c Potter b Mullally	91
N. A. Felton b Mullally	6
R. J. Bailey not out	72
*A. J. Lamb not out	24
L-b 9, w 9	18

1/29 (2) 2/173 (1)   (2 wkts, 49.4 overs) 211

D. J. Capel, K. M. Curran, A. L. Penberthy, †D. Ripley, C. E. L. Ambrose, J. P. Taylor and N. G. B. Cook did not bat.

Bowling: Benjamin 12–0–65–0; Mullally 10–2–22–2; Millns 10–0–43–0; Parsons 9–1–31–0; Potter 4–0–18–0; Benson 4.4–1–23–0.

Umpires: D. J. Constant and D. R. Shepherd.

NATWEST BANK TROPHY RECORDS

(Including Gillette Cup, 1963-80)

Batting

Highest individual scores: 206, A. I. Kallicharran, Warwickshire v Oxfordshire, Birmingham, 1984; 177, C. G. Greenidge, Hampshire v Glamorgan, Southampton, 1975; 172*, G. A. Hick, Worcestershire v Devon, Worcester, 1987; 165*, V. P. Terry, Hampshire v Berkshire, Southampton, 1985; 162*, C. J. Tavaré, Somerset v Devon, Torquay, 1990; 159, C. L. Smith, Hampshire v Cheshire, Chester, 1989; 158, G. D. Barlow, Middlesex v Lancashire, Lord's, 1984; 158, Zaheer Abbas, Gloucestershire v Leicestershire, Leicester, 1983; 156, D. I. Gower, Leicestershire v Derbyshire, Leicester, 1984; 155, J. J. Whitaker, Leicestershire v Wiltshire, Swindon, 1984; 154*, H. Morris, Glamorgan v Staffordshire, Cardiff, 1989; 154, P. Willey, Leicestershire v Hampshire, Leicester, 1987; 153, A. Hill, Derbyshire v Cornwall, Derby, 1986; 151*, M. P. Maynard, Glamorgan v Durham, Darlington, 1991. (93 hundreds were scored in the Gillette Cup; 123 hundreds have been scored in the NatWest Bank Trophy.)

Most runs: 2,261, G. A. Gooch; 1,951, M. W. Gatting; 1,950, D. L. Amiss.

Fastest hundred: G. D. Rose off 36 balls, Somerset v Devon, Torquay, 1990.

Most hundreds: 7, C. L. Smith; 6, G. A. Gooch; 5, D. I. Gower and G. M. Turner.

Highest innings totals (off 60 overs): 413 for four, Somerset v Devon, Torquay, 1990; 404 for three, Worcestershire v Devon, Worcester, 1987; 392 for five, Warwickshire v Oxfordshire, Birmingham, 1984; 386 for five, Essex v Wiltshire, Chelmsford, 1988; 372 for five, Lancashire v Gloucestershire, Manchester, 1990; 371 for four, Hampshire v Glamorgan, Southampton, 1975; 365 for three, Derbyshire v Cornwall, Derby, 1986; 361 for eight, Essex v Cumberland, Chelmsford, 1992; 360 for two, Northamptonshire v Staffordshire, Northampton, 1990; 359 for four, Kent v Dorset, Canterbury, 1989; 354 for seven, Leicestershire v Wiltshire, Swindon, 1984; 349 for six, Lancashire v Gloucestershire, Bristol, 1984; 345 for two, Glamorgan v Durham, Darlington, 1991; 341 for six, Leicestershire v Hampshire, Leicester, 1987; 339 for four, Hampshire v Berkshire, Southampton, 1985; 336 for five, Worcestershire v Cumberland, Worcester, 1988; 336 for seven, Warwickshire v Hertfordshire, St Albans, 1990; 330 for four, Somerset v Glamorgan, Cardiff, 1978. *In the final:* 317 for four, Yorkshire v Surrey, 1965.

Highest innings total by a minor county: 305 for nine, Durham v Glamorgan, Darlington, 1991.

Highest innings by a side batting first and losing: 318 for eight (60 overs), Lancashire v Essex, Chelmsford, 1992. *In the final:* 242 for eight (60 overs), Lancashire v Sussex, 1986.

Highest totals by a side batting second: 326 for nine (60 overs), Hampshire v Leicestershire, Leicester, 1987; 319 for nine (59.5 overs), Essex v Lancashire, Chelmsford, 1992; 307 for five (60 overs), Hampshire v Essex, Chelmsford, 1990; 306 for six (59.3 overs), Gloucestershire v Leicestershire, Leicester, 1983; 305 for nine (60 overs), Durham v Glamorgan, Darlington, 1991; 298 (59 overs), Lancashire v Worcestershire, Manchester, 1985; 297 for four (57.1 overs), Somerset v Warwickshire, Taunton, 1978; 296 for four (58 overs), Kent v Surrey, Canterbury, 1985; 290 for seven (59.3 overs), Yorkshire v Worcestershire, Leeds, 1982; 287 for six (59 overs), Warwickshire v Glamorgan, Birmingham, 1976; 287 (60 overs), Essex v Somerset, Taunton, 1978; 282 for nine (60 overs), Leicestershire v Gloucestershire, Leicester, 1975. *In the final:* 279 for five (60 overs), Nottinghamshire v Essex, 1985.

Highest total by a side batting second and winning: 319 for nine (59.5 overs), Essex v Lancashire, Chelmsford, 1992. *In the final:* 243 for three (58.2 overs), Sussex v Lancashire, 1986; 243 for six (59.4 overs), Hampshire v Surrey, 1991.

Highest total by a side batting second and losing: 326 for nine (60 overs), Hampshire v Leicestershire, Leicester, 1987.

Lowest innings in the final: 118 (60 overs), Lancashire v Kent, 1974.

Lowest completed innings totals: 39 (26.4 overs), Ireland v Sussex, Hove, 1985; 41 (20 overs), Cambridgeshire v Buckinghamshire, Cambridge, 1972; 41 (19.4 overs), Middlesex v Essex, Westcliff, 1972; 41 (36.1 overs), Shropshire v Essex, Wellington, 1974.

Lowest total by a side batting first and winning: 98 (56.2 overs), Worcestershire v Durham, Chester-le-Street, 1968.

Shortest innings: 10.1 overs (60 for one), Worcestershire v Lancashire, Worcester, 1963.

Matches re-arranged on a reduced number of overs are excluded from the above.

Record partnerships for each wicket

242*	for 1st	M. D. Moxon and A. A. Metcalfe, Yorkshire v Warwickshire at Leeds	1990
286	for 2nd	I. S. Anderson and A. Hill, Derbyshire v Cornwall at Derby	1986
259*	for 3rd	H. Morris and M. P. Maynard, Glamorgan v Durham at Darlington	1991
234*	for 4th	D. Lloyd and C. H. Lloyd, Lancashire v Gloucestershire at Manchester	1978
166	for 5th	M. A. Lynch and G. R. J. Roope, Surrey v Durham at The Oval ..	1982
105	for 6th	G. S. Sobers and R. A. White, Nottinghamshire v Worcestershire at Worcester	1974
160*	for 7th	C. J. Richards and I. R. Payne, Surrey v Lincolnshire at Sleaford ..	1983
83	for 8th	S. N. V. Waterton and D. A. Hale, Oxfordshire v Gloucestershire at Oxford	1989
87	for 9th	M. A. Nash and A. E. Cordle, Glamorgan v Lincolnshire at Swansea	1974
81	for 10th	S. Turner and R. E. East, Essex v Yorkshire at Leeds	1982

Bowling

Most wickets: 81, G. G. Arnold; 79, J. Simmons.

Hat-tricks (7): J. D. F. Larter, Northamptonshire v Sussex, Northampton, 1963; D. A. D. Sydenham, Surrey v Cheshire, Hoylake, 1964; R. N. S. Hobbs, Essex v Middlesex, Lord's, 1968; N. M. McVicker, Warwickshire v Lincolnshire, Birmingham, 1971; G. S. le Roux, Sussex v Ireland, Hove, 1985; M. Jean-Jacques, Derbyshire v Nottinghamshire, Derby, 1987; J. F. M. O'Brien, Cheshire v Derbyshire, Chester, 1988.

Four wickets in five balls: D. A. D. Sydenham, Surrey v Cheshire, Hoylake, 1964.

Best bowling (12 overs unless stated): eight for 21 (10.1 overs), M. A. Holding, Derbyshire v Sussex, Hove, 1988; eight for 31 (11.1 overs), D. L. Underwood, Kent v Scotland, Edinburgh, 1987; seven for 15, A. L. Dixon, Kent v Surrey, The Oval, 1967; seven for 15 (9.3 overs), R. P. Lefebvre, Somerset v Devon, Torquay, 1990; seven for 19, N. V. Radford, Worcestershire v Bedfordshire, Bedford, 1991; seven for 30, P. J. Sainsbury, Hampshire v Norfolk, Southampton, 1965; seven for 32, S. P. Davis, Durham v Lancashire, Chester-le-Street, 1983; seven for 33, R. D. Jackman, Surrey v Yorkshire, Harrogate, 1970; seven for 37, N. A. Mallender, Northamptonshire v Worcestershire, Northampton, 1984.

Most economical analysis: 12–9–3–1, J. Simmons, Lancashire v Suffolk, Bury St Edmunds, 1985.

Most expensive analysis: 12–0–106–2, D. A. Gallop, Oxfordshire v Warwickshire, Birmingham, 1984.

Wicket-keeping and Fielding

Most dismissals: 66 (58 ct, 8 st), R. W. Taylor; 65 (59 ct, 6 st), A. P. E. Knott.

Most dismissals in an innings: 6 (5 ct, 1 st), R. W. Taylor, Derbyshire v Essex, Derby, 1981; 6 (4 ct, 2 st), T. Davies, Glamorgan v Staffordshire, Stone, 1986.

Most catches by a fielder: 26, J. Simmons; 25, G. Cook; 24, P. J. Sharpe.

Most catches by a fielder in an innings: 4 – A. S. Brown, Gloucestershire v Middlesex, Bristol, 1963; G. Cook, Northamptonshire v Glamorgan, Northampton, 1972; C. G. Greenidge, Hampshire v Cheshire, Southampton, 1981; D. C. Jackson, Durham v Northamptonshire, Darlington, 1984; T. S. Smith, Hertfordshire v Somerset, St Albans, 1984; H. Morris, Glamorgan v Scotland, Edinburgh, 1988; C. C. Lewis, Nottinghamshire v Worcestershire, Nottingham, 1992.

Results

Largest victories in runs: Somerset by 346 runs v Devon, Torquay, 1990; Worcestershire by 299 runs v Devon, Worcester, 1987; Essex by 291 runs v Wiltshire, Chelmsford, 1988; Sussex by 244 runs v Ireland, Hove, 1985; Lancashire by 241 runs v Gloucestershire, Manchester, 1990; Warwickshire by 227 runs v Oxfordshire, Birmingham, 1984; Essex by 226 runs v Oxfordshire, Chelmsford, 1985; Northamptonshire by 216 runs v Staffordshire, Northampton, 1990; Leicestershire by 214 runs v Staffordshire, Longton, 1975; Hampshire by 209 runs v Dorset, Southampton, 1987; Derbyshire by 204 runs v Cornwall, Derby, 1986; Gloucestershire by 204 runs v Cheshire, Bristol, 1992; Warwickshire by 201 runs v Buckinghamshire, Birmingham, 1987; Sussex by 201 runs v Buckinghamshire, Beaconsfield, 1992; Sussex by 200 runs v Durham, Hove, 1964. *In the final*: 175 runs, Yorkshire v Surrey, Lord's, 1965.

Victories by ten wickets (11): Northamptonshire v Leicestershire, Leicester, 1964; Warwickshire v Cambridgeshire, Birmingham, 1965; Sussex v Derbyshire, Hove, 1968; Hampshire v Nottinghamshire, Southampton, 1977; Middlesex v Worcestershire, Worcester, 1980; Yorkshire v Cheshire, Birkenhead, 1985; Yorkshire v Berkshire, Finchampstead, 1988; Yorkshire v Norfolk, Leeds, 1990; Yorkshire v Warwickshire, Leeds, 1990; Hampshire v Berkshire, Reading, 1991; Warwickshire v Hertfordshire, Birmingham, 1991.

Earliest finishes: both at 2.20 p.m. Worcestershire beat Lancashire by nine wickets at Worcester, 1963; Essex beat Middlesex by eight wickets at Westcliff, 1972.

Scores level (9): Nottinghamshire 215, Somerset 215 for nine at Taunton, 1964; Surrey 196, Sussex 196 for eight at The Oval, 1970; Somerset 287 for six, Essex 287 at Taunton, 1978; Surrey 195 for seven, Essex 195 at Chelmsford, 1980; Essex 149, Derbyshire 149 for eight at Derby, 1981; Northamptonshire 235 for nine, Derbyshire 235 for six in the final at Lord's, 1981; Middlesex 222 for nine, Somerset 222 for eight at Lord's, 1983; Hampshire 224 for eight, Essex 224 for seven at Southampton, 1985; Essex 307 for six, Hampshire 307 for five at Chelmsford, 1990. Under the rules the side which lost fewer wickets won.

Wins by a minor county over a first-class county (8): Durham v Yorkshire (by five wickets), Harrogate, 1973; Lincolnshire v Glamorgan (by six wickets), Swansea, 1974; Hertfordshire v Essex (by 33 runs), 2nd round, Hitchin, 1976; Shropshire v Yorkshire (by 37 runs), Telford, 1984; Durham v Derbyshire (by seven wickets), Derby, 1985; Buckinghamshire v Somerset (by 7 runs), High Wycombe, 1987; Cheshire v Northamptonshire (by one wicket), Chester, 1988; Hertfordshire v Derbyshire (2-1 in a bowling contest after the match was abandoned), Bishop's Stortford, 1991.

WINNERS

Gillette Cup

1963 SUSSEX beat Worcestershire by 14 runs.
1964 SUSSEX beat Warwickshire by eight wickets.
1965 YORKSHIRE beat Surrey by 175 runs.
1966 WARWICKSHIRE beat Worcestershire by five wickets.
1967 KENT beat Somerset by 32 runs.
1968 WARWICKSHIRE beat Sussex by four wickets.
1969 YORKSHIRE beat Derbyshire by 69 runs.
1970 LANCASHIRE beat Sussex by six wickets.
1971 LANCASHIRE beat Kent by 24 runs.
1972 LANCASHIRE beat Warwickshire by four wickets.
1973 GLOUCESTERSHIRE beat Sussex by 40 runs.
1974 KENT beat Lancashire by four wickets.
1975 LANCASHIRE beat Middlesex by seven wickets.
1976 NORTHAMPTONSHIRE beat Lancashire by four wickets.
1977 MIDDLESEX beat Glamorgan by five wickets.
1978 SUSSEX beat Somerset by five wickets.
1979 SOMERSET beat Northamptonshire by 45 runs.
1980 MIDDLESEX beat Surrey by seven wickets.

NatWest Bank Trophy

1981 DERBYSHIRE beat Northamptonshire by losing fewer wickets with the scores level.
1982 SURREY beat Warwickshire by nine wickets.
1983 SOMERSET beat Kent by 24 runs.
1984 MIDDLESEX beat Kent by four wickets.
1985 ESSEX beat Nottinghamshire by one run.
1986 SUSSEX beat Lancashire by seven wickets.
1987 NOTTINGHAMSHIRE beat Northamptonshire by three wickets.
1988 MIDDLESEX beat Worcestershire by three wickets.
1989 WARWICKSHIRE beat Middlesex by four wickets.
1990 LANCASHIRE beat Northamptonshire by seven wickets.
1991 HAMPSHIRE beat Surrey by four wickets.
1992 NORTHAMPTONSHIRE beat Leicestershire by eight wickets.

TEAM RECORDS 1963-92

| | Rounds reached | | | | Matches | | |
	W	F	SF	QF	P	W	L
Derbyshire	1	2	3	8	56*	27	29
Durham	0	0	0	1	30	8	22
Essex	1	1	4	13	63	34	29
Glamorgan	0	1	1	10	58	28	30
Gloucestershire	1	1	5	13	62	33	29
Hampshire	1	1	8	19	78	49	29
Kent	2	5	6	13	69	41	28
Lancashire	5	8	13	17	85	60	25
Leicestershire	0	1	3	14	61	31	30
Middlesex	4	6	13	17	84	58	26
Northamptonshire	2	6	9	16	75	47	28
Nottinghamshire	1	2	3	11	63	34	29
Somerset	2	4	8	14	71	43	28
Surrey	1	4	8	17	73*	44	29
Sussex	4	7	11	16	77	51	26
Warwickshire	3	6	12	16	79	52	27
Worcestershire	0	3	9	12	66	36	30
Yorkshire	2	2	4	12	59	31	28

* Derbyshire and Surrey totals each include a bowling contest after their first-round matches were abandoned in 1991; Derbyshire lost to Hertfordshire and Surrey beat Oxfordshire.

MINOR COUNTY RECORDS

From 1964 to 1979 the previous season's top five Minor Counties were invited to take part in the competition. In 1980 these were joined by Ireland, and in 1983 the competition was expanded to embrace 13 Minor Counties, Ireland and Scotland. The number of Minor Counties dropped to 12 in 1992 when Durham attained first-class status.

Between 1964 and 1991 Durham qualified 21 times, including 15 years in succession from 1977-1991. They reached the second round a record six times.

Of the other Minor Counties, Hertfordshire have qualified 18 times, Oxfordshire 16, Buckinghamshire and Staffordshire 15, Devon and Suffolk 14, Berkshire, Cambridgeshire and Cheshire 13, Norfolk, Shropshire and Wiltshire 12, Dorset 10, Bedfordshire and Lincolnshire 9, Cumberland and Northumberland 7, Cornwall 5 and Wales Minor Counties once. These figures include the 1993 NatWest Trophy, for which Wales Minor Counties have qualified, at the fifth attempt.

Only Hertfordshire have reached the quarter-finals, beating Berkshire and then Essex in 1976.

BENSON AND HEDGES CUP, 1992

Hampshire, who up to 1988 were the only first-class county never to have appeared in a Lord's final, won their second in barely ten months when they took the 1992 Benson and Hedges Cup, beating Kent in the final at Lord's by 41 runs. This followed their triumph in the 1991 NatWest Trophy. For the second year running (but only the third time in 21 years), the final was left unfinished on the Saturday and Hampshire had to return the following day to finish the job. A substantial crowd returned with them but they saw one of the less classic finishes, with Hampshire winning comfortably.

Both counties were deserving finalists: they were the only unbeaten teams in the zonal competition. For Kent, this was a record sixth final and their semi-final appearance was their 11th in the competition's 21 years. Essex, the perennial favourites, failed to qualify for the quarter-finals after being bowled out for 61 by Lancashire on the first morning of their first match. Gooch, their captain, finished the tournament with two noughts and two centuries.

Benson and Hedges provided £596,148 sponsorship of which £115,150 went in prize money. Hampshire won £27,500 and Kent £13,500. The losing semi-finalists, Somerset and Surrey, received £6,750 and the losing quarter-finalists, Derbyshire, Lancashire, Middlesex and Worcestershire £3,375. The winners of each group match received £850. Gold Award winners, in addition to a medallion, received £150 in the group matches, £250 in the quarter-finals, £300 in the semi-finals and £550 in the final.

To mark the 21st year of their sponsorship the company provided a special award (a mounted gold replica of a village cricketing scene) to the Player of the Tournament. This was worked out by a system of giving points for runs, wickets, catches and stumpings and dividing the total by the number of games played. It resulted in a win for Curtly Ambrose of Northamptonshire, who failed to reach the quarter-finals.

The tournament was the last, for the time being anyway, played under the system of zonal qualification groups which has remained fundamentally unchanged since 1972. The 1993 tournament is to be played as a straight knockout.

FINAL GROUP TABLE

	Played	Won	Lost	No Result	Pts	Run-rate
Group A						
SURREY	5	4	1	0	8	82.55
MIDDLESEX	5	4	1	0	8	74.48
Leicestershire	5	3	2	0	6	63.45
Sussex	5	2	3	0	4	63.82
Minor Counties	5	1	4	0	2	59.45
Gloucestershire	5	1	4	0	2	58.74
Group B						
HAMPSHIRE	4	3	0	1	7	70.58
LANCASHIRE	4	3	1	0	6	64.86
Essex	4	2	2	0	4	64.31
Northamptonshire	4	1	3	0	2	73.48
Scotland	4	0	3	1	1	51.21

	Played	Won	Lost	No Result	Pts	Run-rate
Group C						
KENT	4	4	0	0	8	65.98
SOMERSET	4	2	2	0	4	62.11
Nottinghamshire	4	2	2	0	4	61.38
Warwickshire	4	1	3	0	2	61.51
Yorkshire	4	1	3	0	2	48.03
Group D						
WORCESTERSHIRE	4	3	1	0	6	63.45
DERBYSHIRE	4	3	1	0	6	62.02
Durham	4	2	2	0	4	64.95
Glamorgan	4	2	2	0	4	58.96
Combined Universities	4	0	4	0	0	54.01

The top two teams in each group qualified for the quarter-finals.
Where two or more teams finished with the same number of points, the position in the group was based on run-rate per 100 balls.

GROUP A

GLOUCESTERSHIRE v LEICESTERSHIRE

At Cheltenham (Dowty Arle Court), April 21. Leicestershire won by ten wickets. Toss: Leicestershire. Gloucestershire's first competitive match on the picturesque Arle Court ground was not auspicious. Tight Leicestershire bowling set up the 15th ten-wicket victory in the history of the competition.

Gold Award: V. J. Wells.

Gloucestershire

S. G. Hinks st Whitticase b Benson.... 20	A. M. Smith c Whitticase b Parsons ... 7
M. W. Alleyne c Whitticase b Millns .. 1	A. M. Babington c Benson b Potter.... 27
*A. J. Wright b Millns 0	M. J. Gerrard not out 1
C. W. J. Athey b Wells.............. 9	L-b 2, w 3 5
J. T. C. Vaughan c and b Benson 12	
†R. C. Russell c Whitticase b Mullally .. 15	1/6 2/6 3/30 (47.5 overs) 110
T. H. C. Hancock c Whitaker b Wells .. 12	4/34 5/45 6/70
M. C. J. Ball c Boon b Wells 1	7/70 8/72 9/109

Bowling: Mullally 8–4–8–1; Millns 11–3–36–2; Parsons 3.5–0–13–1; Wells 11–5–13–3; Benson 6–0–27–2; Potter 8–2–11–1.

Leicestershire

T. J. Boon not out 54	
*N. E. Briers not out................ 51	
L-b 1, w 4, n-b 1............ 6	
(no wkt, 34.5 overs) 111	

J. J. Whitaker, L. Potter, B. F. Smith, J. D. R. Benson, V. J. Wells, G. J. Parsons, †P. Whitticase, D. J. Millns and A. D. Mullally did not bat.

Bowling: Babington 5–0–21–0; Smith 3–0–10–0; Ball 9–2–24–0; Gerrard 5.5–1–21–0; Vaughan 7–0–16–0; Alleyne 5–0–18–0.

Umpires: H. D. Bird and G. Sharp.

MIDDLESEX v MINOR COUNTIES

At Lord's, April 21. Middlesex won by seven wickets. Toss: Middlesex. Roberts of Buckinghamshire struck six fours in 63 balls, but Minor Counties were easily overtaken by Middlesex, for whom Roseberry hit his highest score in the Benson and Hedges Cup, with eight fours and two sixes.

Gold Award: M. A. Roseberry.

Minor Counties

M. J. Roberts b Weekes 44	R. A. Evans st Brown b Emburey 5
†S. N. V. Waterton c Brown b Williams 8	K. A. Arnold run out 1
S. J. Dean c Fraser b Williams 33	
N. A. Folland c Fraser b Emburey 8	B 2, l-b 9, w 4, n-b 3 18
J. D. Love c Carr b Sylvester 10	
S. G. Plumb c Brown b Williams 0	1/25 2/79 3/102 (9 wkts, 55 overs) 165
*S. Greensword st Brown b Emburey .. 25	4/102 5/103 6/134
P. G. Newman not out 13	7/144 8/152 9/165

N. R. Taylor did not bat.

Bowling: Williams 11–2–25–3; Sylvester 11–1–31–1; Carr 5–0–21–0; Fraser 11–2–50–0; Weekes 6–2–13–1; Emburey 11–5–14–3.

Middlesex

J. D. Carr lbw b Arnold 16	†K. R. Brown not out 9
M. A. Roseberry lbw b Newman 84	N-b 1 1
*M. W. Gatting c Waterton b Taylor .. 38	
M. R. Ramprakash not out 19	1/41 2/105 3/155 (3 wkts, 42 overs) 167

P. N. Weekes, J. E. Emburey, N. F. Williams, R. J. Sims, A. R. C. Fraser and S. A. Sylvester did not bat.

Bowling: Newman 11–3–36–1; Arnold 10–1–49–1; Evans 6–0–26–0; Taylor 10–1–43–1; Greensword 5–2–13–0.

Umpires: B. J. Meyer and R. C. Tolchard.

SUSSEX v SURREY

At Hove, April 21. Sussex won by eight runs. Toss: Surrey. Greenfield and Hall both reached their highest scores in the competition as they gave Sussex a strong opening. Surrey were on course at 146 for one in the 38th over, but lost their next six wickets in nine overs.

Gold Award: J. W. Hall.

Sussex

K. Greenfield c Stewart b Feltham 47	J. A. North not out 11
J. W. Hall c Feltham b M. P. Bicknell . 81	B. T. P. Donelan not out............ 9
M. P. Speight c Brown b Boiling 14	
*A. P. Wells c D. J. Bicknell b Feltham 61	L-b 4, w 1, n-b 2 7
F. D. Stephenson c M. P. Bicknell b Feltham 3	
A. C. S. Pigott c Stewart b Benjamin .. 13	1/89 2/112 3/191 (7 wkts, 55 overs) 246
†P. Moores run out 0	4/197 5/211
	6/212 7/225

A. N. Jones and A. R. Hansford did not bat.

Bowling: Bryson 11–0–62–0; M. P. Bicknell 11–0–55–1; Benjamin 11–0–59–1; Boiling 11–0–38–1; Feltham 11–1–28–3.

Surrey

D. J. Bicknell c Donelan b Stephenson .	71	M. P. Bicknell c Moores b Stephenson . 19
A. A. Lynch c Speight b Pigott	23	J. Boiling not out 7
†A. J. Stewart c Speight b Jones	41	
G. P. Thorpe c Greenfield b Donelan . .	3	B 2, l-b 9, w 4, n-b 4 19
D. M. Ward c Speight b Pigott	9	
A. D. Brown c Hall b Pigott	26	1/73 2/146 3/152 (8 wkts, 55 overs) 238
M. A. Feltham not out	20	4/153 5/188 6/189
R. E. Bryson lbw b Hansford	0	7/189 8/224
. E. Benjamin did not bat.		

Bowling: Stephenson 11-0-54-2; Jones 9-1-43-1; Donelan 11-1-41-1; Pigott 11-0-39-3; North 5-0-20-0; Hansford 8-0-30-1.

Umpires: G. A. Stickley and R. A. White.

GLOUCESTERSHIRE v MINOR COUNTIES

At Cheltenham (Dowty Arle Court), April 23. Gloucestershire won by seven wickets. Toss: Gloucestershire. Hodgson's century, in 172 minutes, was his first for the county in limited-overs competitions.

Gold Award: G. D. Hodgson.

Minor Counties

M. J. Roberts c Russell b Babington . . .	17	*S. Greensword not out 3
†S. N. V. Waterton lbw b Babington . . .	11	I. E. Conn not out 0
N. A. Folland lbw b Athey	63	L-b 3, w 3 6
. D. Love lbw b Athey	57	
G. J. Dean c Alleyne b Athey	40	1/23 2/30 3/142 (7 wkts, 55 overs) 212
*. G. Newman c Gerrard b Athey	3	4/169 5/180
S. G. Plumb c Ball b Vaughan	12	6/202 7/211
R. A. Evans and N. R. Taylor did not bat.		

Bowling: Gerrard 8-1-32-0; Babington 11-4-32-2; Vaughan 10-1-36-1; Alleyne 1-3-34-0; Ball 4-1-18-0; Athey 11-1-57-4.

Gloucestershire

G. D. Hodgson not out	103	†R. C. Russell not out 18
S. G. Hinks b Conn	28	L-b 8, w 8, n-b 2 18
*A. J. Wright c Roberts b Greensword .	33	
C. W. J. Athey c Roberts b Conn	13	1/48 2/126 3/175 (3 wkts, 52.4 overs) 213
M. W. Alleyne, J. T. C. Vaughan, T. H. C. Hancock, A. M. Babington, M. C. J. Ball and M. J. Gerrard did not bat.		

Bowling: Newman 9.4-2-29-0; Taylor 6-1-37-0; Conn 11-0-47-2; Evans 11-0-28-0; Greensword 10-0-43-1; Plumb 5-0-21-0.

Umpires: G. I. Burgess and K. E. Palmer.

LEICESTERSHIRE v SUSSEX

At Leicester, April 23. Leicestershire won by five wickets. Toss: Leicestershire. Briers, who hit 14 fours, narrowly missed his maiden Benson and Hedges hundred. Leicestershire benefited from 19 Sussex wides, including five in one over from North, and three in Jones's only over, the second of the innings. Earlier Greenfield made his first fifty in the competition.

Gold Award: N. E. Briers.

Sussex

J. W. Hall lbw b Wells	10	A. C. S. Pigott run out
K. Greenfield c Smith b Benson	62	B. T. P. Donelan not out
M. P. Speight c Wells b Parsons	39	L-b 10, w 8
*A. P. Wells not out	55	
F. D. Stephenson c Parsons b Millns	21	1/32 2/102 3/136 (7 wkts, 55 overs) 23
†P. Moores st Whitticase b Benson	10	4/161 5/183
J. A. North b Potter	9	6/199 7/205

A. N. Jones and A. R. Hansford did not bat.

Bowling: Mullally 8–0–37–0; Millns 7–1–34–1; Wells 7–0–42–1; Potter 11–1–44–1; Parsons 11–3–31–1; Benson 11–0–39–2.

Leicestershire

T. J. Boon c and b Stephenson	59	V. J. Wells not out	1
*N. E. Briers c Speight b North	98	
J. J. Whitaker b North	7	B 1, l-b 9, w 19, n-b 3	3
L. Potter c Pigott b North	1	
B. F. Smith c Speight b Pigott	2	1/135 2/156 3/169 (5 wkts, 52.5 overs) 24
J. D. R. Benson not out	23	4/187 5/199

†P. Whitticase, G. J. Parsons, A. D. Mullally and D. J. Millns did not bat.

Bowling: Stephenson 11–1–32–1; Jones 1–0–8–0; Hansford 11–0–48–0; Pigott 9.5–0–49–1; Donelan 7–0–32–0; Greenfield 9–0–37–0; North 4–0–24–3.

Umpires: H. D. Bird and G. A. Stickley.

SURREY v MIDDLESEX

At The Oval, April 23. Surrey won by 69 runs. Toss: Middlesex. Surrey openers Darre Bicknell and Lynch took only 24 overs to put on 140, Thorpe hit 11 fours in his highes Benson and Hedges score, and Brown hit 29 from 18 balls, to run up a total well out c Middlesex's reach. Ward kept wicket for Surrey when a calf strain prevented Stewart fror taking the field.

Gold Award: D. J. Bicknell.

Surrey

D. J. Bicknell c Carr b Fraser	70	D. M. Ward not out
M. A. Lynch run out	65	B 1, l-b 13, w 6, n-b 1	2
*†A. J. Stewart b Emburey	40	
G. P. Thorpe c Williams b Fraser	78	1/140 2/149 (4 wkts, 55 overs) 30
A. D. Brown not out	29	3/234 4/302

M. A. Feltham, R. E. Bryson, M. P. Bicknell, J. Boiling and J. E. Benjamin did not bat.

Bowling: Williams 11–2–40–0; Sylvester 6–0–52–0; Tufnell 10–0–65–0; Emburey 10–1–45–1; Fraser 11–1–52–2; Carr 5–0–29–0; Weekes 2–0–10–0.

Middlesex

J. D. Carr c Thorpe b Feltham	48	A. R. C. Fraser b Feltham
M. A. Roseberry c Ward b Bryson	5	P. C. R. Tufnell not out	1
*M. W. Gatting c Boiling b Bryson	16	S. A. Sylvester c Lynch b Bryson
M. R. Ramprakash b Feltham	39	L-b 7, w 14	2
†K. R. Brown c Lynch b M. P. Bicknell	31	
P. N. Weekes c Ward b Benjamin	20	1/11 2/39 3/101 (55 overs) 23
J. E. Emburey b Benjamin	19	4/112 5/155 6/177
N. F. Williams b Bryson	22	7/205 8/219 9/225

Bowling: Bryson 11–0–56–4; M. P. Bicknell 11–0–50–1; Benjamin 11–1–46–2; Boilin 11–0–35–0; Feltham 11–0–44–3.

Umpires: J. C. Balderstone and R. Julian.

LEICESTERSHIRE v SURREY

At Leicester, April 30, May 1. Surrey won by six wickets. Toss: Surrey. Rain delayed the start of play until 3.30 p.m. but in the 27.5 overs possible before the close Leicestershire were all out for 96. They lost three wickets in ten balls with the score on 53, two of them to the impressive Bryson and one to Feltham.

Gold Award: M. A. Feltham.

Leicestershire

T. J. Boon c Boiling b Bryson	0	G. J. Parsons lbw b Benjamin		1
*N. E. Briers c Stewart b Bryson	19	D. J. Millns not out		3
J. J. Whitaker b Feltham	26	A. D. Mullally c Stewart b Feltham		11
L. Potter b Bryson	4	B 4, w 5		9
V. J. Wells lbw b Bryson	0			
J. D. R. Benson c Stewart b Feltham	1	1/10 2/39 3/53	(27.5 overs)	96
P. A. Nixon b Feltham	5	4/53 5/53 6/58		
†P. Whitticase c and b Feltham	17	7/63 8/68 9/84		

Bowling: Bryson 8–1–31–4; M. P. Bicknell 4–1–16–0; Feltham 9.5–1–30–5; Benjamin 6–0–15–1.

Surrey

D. J. Bicknell not out	37	A. D. Brown not out		6
M. A. Lynch lbw b Millns	5	B 4, l-b 4, w 4		12
*†A. J. Stewart b Millns	0			
G. P. Thorpe c Boon b Parsons	28	1/15 2/15	(4 wkts, 22 overs)	100
D. M. Ward lbw b Parsons	12	3/60 4/94		

M. A. Feltham, R. E. Bryson, M. P. Bicknell, J. E. Benjamin and J. Boiling did not bat.

Bowling: Millns 6–0–31–2; Wells 4–0–27–0; Mullally 6–2–18–0; Parsons 6–2–16–2.

Umpires: V. A. Holder and R. Julian.

MIDDLESEX v GLOUCESTERSHIRE

At Lord's, April 30. Middlesex won by 87 runs. Toss: Gloucestershire. Roseberry went from 28 to 51 in singles, whereas Weekes hit his unbeaten 44 from 40 balls. Fraser took three for five in 21 balls to earn his best figures in the competition.

Gold Award: P. N. Weekes.

Middlesex

D. L. Haynes c and b Ball	28	J. E. Emburey run out		6
M. A. Roseberry run out	74	N. F. Williams not out		2
*M. W. Gatting c Russell b Vaughan	4	B 1, l-b 7, w 2, n-b 1		11
M. R. Ramprakash lbw b Babington	41			
†K. R. Brown b Walsh	33	1/69 2/78 3/148	(7 wkts, 55 overs)	249
J. D. Carr lbw b Babington	6	4/159 5/171		
P. N. Weekes not out	44	6/218 7/245		

D. W. Headley and A. R. C. Fraser did not bat.

Bowling: Babington 11–2–27–2; Walsh 11–1–58–1; Vaughan 11–0–64–1; Ball 9–0–39–1; Alleyne 10–1–38–0; Athey 3–0–15–0.

Gloucestershire

G. D. Hodgson c Embury b Fraser ...	26
S. G. Hinks c Ramprakash b Williams .	26
*A. J. Wright lbw b Weekes	13
C. W. J. Athey c Brown b Fraser	17
†R. C. Russell c Carr b Emburey......	7
M. W. Alleyne b Fraser	4
J. T. C. Vaughan st Brown b Emburey .	8
T. H. C. Hancock st Brown b Emburey	12

C. A. Walsh b Weekes	1
M. C. J. Ball c Carr b Williams......	1
A. M. Babington not out............	8
L-b 5, w 8, n-b 2.............	15
1/41 2/69 3/85 (43.2 overs) 162	
4/98 5/106 6/106	
7/127 8/128 9/140	

Bowling: Fraser 11–3–30–3; Headley 4–0–17–0; Williams 5.2–2–11–2; Emburey 8–1–25–3; Weekes 11–0–64–2; Carr 4–1–10–0.

Umpires: D. R. Shepherd and R. A. White.

MINOR COUNTIES v SUSSEX

At Marlow, April 30, May 1. Minor Counties won by 19 runs. Toss: Sussex. Minor Counties recorded their fifth win in the competition, and their first since 1987 when they beat Glamorgan at Oxford. They scored 68 from their last ten overs and then had Sussex struggling on a pitch which was drenched when an overnight downpour seeped through the tarpaulins covering the pitch. Sussex, 75 for two overnight (D. M. Smith 6*, A. P. Wells 9*), found themselves playing on an old-fashioned sticky wicket and only Smith – the one batsman with significant experience of uncovered pitches – showed any skill at it. Sussex assisted their own downfall by bringing their "whale" up from Hove to dry the outfield.

Gold Award: K. A. Arnold.

Minor Counties

M. J. Roberts c Hansford b Pigott.....	34
†S. N. V. Waterton c Moores b Pigott .	25
N. A. Folland lbw b C. M. Wells	0
S. J. Dean c Lenham b Stephenson	35
S. G. Plumb c Jones b Hansford	38
G. S. Calway c Greenfield b Stephenson	0
*S. Greensword c Smith b Stephenson .	36

P. G. Newman run out	33
I. E. Conn not out	3
L-b 6, w 7, n-b 3............	16
1/63 2/63 3/74 (8 wkts, 55 overs) 220	
4/134 5/141 6/143	
7/196 8/220	

K. A. Arnold and N. P. Hackett did not bat.

Bowling: Stephenson 11–1–28–3; Pigott 11–0–59–2; Hansford 11–1–44–1; C. M. Wells 11–3–32–1; Jones 11–0–51–0.

Sussex

K. Greenfield c Waterton b Arnold	31
J. W. Hall c Folland b Conn	20
D. M. Smith b Calway	61
*A. P. Wells c Hackett b Arnold......	15
C. M. Wells c Calway b Arnold.......	6
N. J. Lenham c Folland b Hackett	2
F. D. Stephenson lbw b Conn	4
†P. Moores c Arnold b Greensword....	5

A. C. S. Pigott c Folland b Greensword	6
A. N. Jones c Plumb b Newman	24
A. R. Hansford not out..............	4
B 1, l-b 9, w 13.............	23
1/60 2/60 3/88 (54.3 overs) 201	
4/98 5/104 6/109	
7/119 8/135 9/187	

Bowling: Newman 10.3–0–50–1; Hackett 11–1–40–1; Arnold 11–1–25–3; Conn 11–2–33–2; Greensword 8–1–33–2; Calway 3–0–10–1.

Umpires: J. H. Hampshire and A. G. T. Whitehead.

LEICESTERSHIRE v MIDDLESEX

At Leicester, May 2. Middlesex won by 99 runs. Toss: Leicestershire. Middlesex reached their highest total in any limited-overs competition, despite having to survive a remarkable opening spell from Benjamin who, apart from a no-ball, did not concede a run until the penultimate ball of his sixth over. The game was transformed by Ramprakash, who faced only 61 balls, hitting five sixes and eight fours. He shared a stand of 147 in 15 overs with Carr.

Gold Award: M. R. Ramprakash.

Middlesex

D. L. Haynes c Whitticase b Millns	67	P. N. Weekes not out	1
M. A. Roseberry c Whitaker b Millns	29		
*M. W. Gatting c Briers b Mullally	37	L-b 9, n-b 3	12
M. R. Ramprakash not out	108		
†K. R. Brown lbw b Millns	1	1/48 2/131 3/170 (5 wkts, 55 overs) 325	
J. D. Carr c Briers b Benjamin	70	4/172 5/319	

J. E. Emburey, N. F. Williams, D. W. Headley and A. R. C. Fraser did not bat.

Bowling: Benjamin 11–5–37–1; Mullally 11–0–64–1; Millns 10–0–55–3; Wells 7–0–44–0; Parsons 10–0–62–0; Potter 4–0–37–0; Benson 2–0–17–0.

Leicestershire

T. J. Boon b Williams	48	G. J. Parsons not out	2
*N. E. Briers c Brown b Williams	30	D. J. Millns not out	0
J. J. Whitaker run out	40		
L. Potter c Gatting b Williams	0	B 2, l-b 8, w 4, n-b 2	16
J. D. R. Benson st Brown b Emburey	14		
J. Wells c Headley b Fraser	19	1/63 2/111 (8 wkts, 55 overs) 226	
†P. Whitticase b Fraser	12	3/111 4/135	
W. K. M. Benjamin c Ramprakash b Haynes	45	5/153 6/175	
		7/180 8/226	

A. D. Mullally did not bat.

Bowling: Headley 9–1–47–0; Fraser 10–2–37–2; Emburey 11–0–35–1; Williams 11–0–36–3; Weekes 11–1–38–0; Haynes 2–0–21–1; Roseberry 1–0–2–0.

Umpires: D. J. Constant and A. G. T. Whitehead.

SURREY v MINOR COUNTIES

At The Oval, May 2. Surrey won by 168 runs. Toss: Minor Counties. The day after their triumph at Marlow, Minor Counties were put in their place by Lynch, who hit 13 fours in 133 balls.

Gold Award: M. A. Lynch.

Surrey

D. J. Bicknell c Folland b Greensword	55	G. P. Thorpe not out	14
M. A. Lynch c Folland b Greensword	105	L-b 16, w 7, n-b 1	24
*†A. J. Stewart not out	71		
A. D. Brown b Arnold	30	1/154 2/199 3/252 (3 wkts, 55 overs) 299	

D. M. Ward, M. A. Feltham, R. E. Bryson, M. P. Bicknell, J. E. Benjamin and J. Boiling did not bat.

Bowling: Newman 11–1–47–0; Arnold 11–3–57–1; Conn 11–0–58–0; Calway 11–1–50–0; Evans 4–0–37–0; Greensword 7–0–34–2.

Minor Counties

M. J. Roberts c Boiling b Feltham 15	*S. Greensword not out 1
†S. N. V. Waterton c Lynch b Benjamin 7	P. G. Newman not out ....
N. A. Folland c Feltham b Boiling 32	L-b 10, w 5, n-b 9 2
S. J. Dean b Feltham 8	
S. G. Plumb st Stewart b Boiling 27	1/24 2/26 3/55　　(6 wkts, 55 overs) 13
G. S. Calway lbw b Bryson 3	4/91 5/104 6/121

I. E. Conn, R. A. Evans and K. A. Arnold did not bat.

Bowling: Bryson 11–2–25–1; M. P. Bicknell 11–1–30–0; Benjamin 11–2–19–1; Feltham 7–2–14–2; Boiling 11–1–20–2; Lynch 4–1–13–0.

Umpires: A. A. Jones and B. Leadbeater.

SUSSEX v GLOUCESTERSHIRE

At Hove, May 2. Sussex won by four wickets. Toss: Sussex. Stephenson earned his award with a 19-ball 34 and three wickets.
Gold Award: F. D. Stephenson.

Gloucestershire

G. D. Hodgson c Smith b Salisbury.... 54	†R. C. Russell c Moores b Stephenson . 3
S. G. Hinks lbw b Robson 11	C. A. Walsh not out ....
*A. J. Wright lbw b Salisbury 36	
C. W. J. Athey not out 56	L-b 3, w 5 8
M. W. Alleyne c Moores b Stephenson . 24	
T. H. C. Hancock lbw b C. M. Wells . 1	1/22 2/96 3/107　　(7 wkts, 55 overs) 224
J. T. C. Vaughan c Salisbury	4/150 5/162
b Stephenson . 4	6/176 7/221

M. C. J. Ball and A. M. Babington did not bat.

Bowling: Stephenson 11–0–41–3; Robson 11–1–32–1; C. M. Wells 8–1–41–1; Salisbury 11–2–43–2; Pigott 11–1–49–0; Greenfield 3–0–15–0.

Sussex

K. Greenfield st Russell b Babington... 53	N. J. Lenham not out 15
J. W. Hall c Babington b Vaughan 70	†P. Moores not out ....
D. M. Smith c Ball b Vaughan........ 21	L-b 5, w 2, n-b 6............ 13
*A. P. Wells c Russell b Vaughan 2	
C. M. Wells run out 16	1/113 2/155 3/155　(6 wkts, 54.1 overs) 225
F. D. Stephenson lbw b Walsh........ 34	4/167 5/175 6/223

A. C. S. Pigott, I. D. K. Salisbury and A. G. Robson did not bat.

Bowling: Babington 11–0–32–1; Walsh 11–1–34–1; Alleyne 8.1–0–34–0; Vaughan 10–0–61–3; Ball 10–0–41–0; Athey 4–0–18–0.

Umpires: J. D. Bond and R. Palmer.

MINOR COUNTIES v LEICESTERSHIRE

At Stone, May 5. Leicestershire won by 36 runs. Toss: Leicestershire. Briers reached his maiden century in the competition before lunch, adding 186 in 38 overs with Whitaker. In a gallant chase, former Yorkshire batsman Love scored 48 from 49 balls, but he fell to Millns, who earned his best Cup figures.
Gold Award: N. E. Briers.

Leicestershire

T. J. Boon lbw b Newman	3	P. N. Hepworth not out	11
N. E. Briers c Hackett b Greensword	102	D. J. Millns not out	6
J. J. Whitaker lbw b Greensword	73		
L. Potter c Conn b Newman	9	B 2, l-b 8, w 5, n-b 2	17
B. D. R. Benson run out	10		
W. K. M. Benjamin b Hackett	39	1/5 2/191 3/193 (8 wkts, 55 overs) 289	
V. J. Wells c and b Hackett	19	4/210 5/213 6/255	
P. A. Nixon lbw b Hackett	0	7/255 8/276	

A. D. Mullally did not bat.

Bowling: Newman 11–2–49–2; Hackett 11–0–55–3; Conn 11–0–48–0; Calway 7–0–45–0; Plumb 9–1–48–0; Greensword 6–0–34–2.

Minor Counties

J. J. Dean b Hepworth	46	*S. Greensword lbw b Wells	2
M. J. Roberts b Millns	16	I. E. Conn b Benjamin	5
N. A. Folland c and b Hepworth	52	N. P. Hackett not out	3
K. D. Love c Briers b Millns	48	L-b 10, w 8, n-b 6	24
S. G. Plumb c Whitaker b Millns	24		
P. G. Newman c Briers b Millns	5	1/39 2/123 3/138 (54.3 overs) 253	
G. S. Calway b Mullally	2	4/202 5/204 6/209	
*M. I. Humphries c Potter b Wells	26	7/217 8/220 9/247	

Bowling: Mullally 11–1–47–1; Millns 11–0–51–4; Wells 9–0–44–2; Benjamin 10.3–0–48–1; Hepworth 11–2–44–2; Benson 2–0–9–0.

Umpires: D. R. Shepherd and G. A. Stickley.

SURREY v GLOUCESTERSHIRE

At The Oval, May 5, 6. Surrey won by two wickets. Toss: Surrey. After a first day disrupted by rain and bad light, Surrey were 178 for three from 41 overs (G. P. Thorpe 12*, D. M. Ward 9*). Next day, despite the loss of five wickets in seven overs, Bryson and Boiling hit 21 from the last two to win. Victory ensured Surrey top place in their group, and thus a home quarter-final, on run-rate.

Gold Award: G. D. Hodgson.

Gloucestershire

G. D. Hodgson c Benjamin b M. P. Bicknell	80	†R. C. Russell not out	8
S. G. Hinks c Benjamin b Feltham	42	B 1, l-b 6, w 2, n-b 4	13
*A. J. Wright c Stewart b Benjamin	62		
C. W. J. Athey b Benjamin	27	1/82 2/179 3/202 (5 wkts, 55 overs) 252	
M. W. Alleyne b Bryson	20	4/240 5/252	

A. M. Smith, T. H. C. Hancock, C. A. Walsh, M. C. J. Ball and A. M. Babington did not bat.

Bowling: Bryson 11–0–58–1; M. P. Bicknell 11–2–45–1; Benjamin 11–1–57–2; Feltham 11–3–36–1; Boiling 11–1–49–0.

Surrey

D. J. Bicknell c Wright b Babington	78	M. P. Bicknell run out	5
M. A. Lynch c Russell b Alleyne	21	J. Boiling not out	8
*†A. J. Stewart c Hancock b Walsh	46		
G. P. Thorpe run out	14	L-b 10, w 5, n-b 4	19
D. M. Ward run out	18		
A. D. Brown c Smith b Walsh	22	1/62 2/149 3/153 (8 wkts, 54.4 overs) 253	
M. A. Feltham c Hancock b Ball	4	4/189 5/196 6/209	
R. E. Bryson not out	18	7/218 8/226	

J. E. Benjamin did not bat.

Bowling: Babington 11–1–48–1; Walsh 10.4–0–46–2; Ball 9–0–53–1; Smith 11–0–39–0 Alleyne 8–0–25–1; Athey 5–0–32–0.

Umpires: D. J. Constant and B. Leadbeater.

SUSSEX v MIDDLESEX

At Hove, May 5. Middlesex won by ten wickets. Toss: Middlesex. Headley dismissed Greenfield with his first ball, to set up Middlesex's first ten-wicket victory in the Benson and Hedges Cup, and the 16th in all.

Gold Award: D. W. Headley.

Sussex

K. Greenfield c Gatting b Headley	0	A. C. S. Pigott lbw b Headley	17
J. W. Hall c Brown b Fraser	8	I. D. K. Salisbury not out	2
M. P. Speight c Weekes b Headley	14	A. G. Robson b Embury	0
*A. P. Wells c Williams b Carr	35	L-b 12, w 5, n-b 4	21
C. M. Wells c Roseberry b Carr	4		
F. D. Stephenson b Carr	16	1/0 2/16 3/45 (48.5 overs)	141
N. J. Lenham c Brown b Williams	9	4/56 5/68 6/88	
†P. Moores c Embury b Headley	15	7/94 8/132 9/140	

Bowling: Headley 10–4–19–4; Fraser 8–2–23–1; Williams 11–1–39–1; Carr 11–1–25–3; Embury 8.5–1–23–1.

Middlesex

D. L. Haynes not out	66
M. A. Roseberry not out	70
L-b 1, w 3, n-b 5	9

(no wkt, 44.3 overs) 145

*M. W. Gatting, M. R. Ramprakash, †K. R. Brown, J. D. Carr, P. N. Weekes, J. E. Embury, N. F. Williams, D. W. Headley and A. R. C. Fraser did not bat.

Bowling: Stephenson 9–2–27–0; Robson 11–3–29–0; C. M. Wells 8–0–31–0; Pigott 8–1–25–0; Salisbury 5.3–0–26–0; Lenham 3–0–6–0.

Umpires: H. D. Bird and G. I. Burgess.

GROUP B

ESSEX v LANCASHIRE

At Chelmsford, April 21. Lancashire won by eight wickets. Toss: Lancashire. Lancashire, aiming for their third successive final, made a sensational start when DeFreitas dismissed Gooch and Waugh in the opening over. Essex never recovered. They were bowled out for their lowest score in any limited-overs competition, eight lower than their total in the John Player League at Chesterfield in 1974. DeFreitas finished with five for 16 and ran out Essex's last man, Such.

Gold Award: P. A. J. DeFreitas.

Essex

*G. A. Gooch lbw b DeFreitas	0	T. D. Topley c Hegg b Morrison	4
J. P. Stephenson lbw b DeFreitas	8	M. C. Ilott c Hegg b Morrison	0
M. E. Waugh c Fairbrother b DeFreitas	0	P. M. Such run out	0
N. Hussain c Hegg b Watkinson	15	L-b 2, w 1	3
P. J. Prichard b DeFreitas	6		
D. R. Pringle c Hegg b DeFreitas	6	1/0 2/0 3/17 (25.3 overs)	61
†M. A. Garnham not out	17	4/25 5/34 6/37	
N. A. Foster c and b Watkinson	2	7/40 8/60 9/60	

Bowling: DeFreitas 8–2–16–5; Morrison 7–1–17–2; Watkinson 7–0–19–2; Austin 3.3–1–7–0.

Lancashire

G. D. Mendis b Foster		21
G. Fowler b Topley		22
N. J. Speak not out		9
*N. H. Fairbrother not out		6
L-b 1, w 5, n-b 1		7

1/36 2/50   (2 wkts, 28.5 overs) 65

G. D. Lloyd, M. Watkinson, †W. K. Hegg, P. A. J. DeFreitas, I. D. Austin, A. A. Barnett and D. K. Morrison did not bat.

Bowling: Foster 11–1–36–1; Ilott 5.5–0–13–0; Pringle 8–5–7–0; Topley 4–0–8–1.

Umpires: J. C. Balderstone and R. Julian.

SCOTLAND v NORTHAMPTONSHIRE

At Forfar, April 21. Northamptonshire won by 45 runs. Toss: Northamptonshire. Fordham's century ensured that there was no repeat of the embarrassment Northamptonshire suffered on the teams' previous meeting, in 1990. However, Scotland's off-spinner Govan took four wickets against his former county team-mates and Patterson, with 11 fours and a six, made the highest score for Scotland in either of the main one-day cups.

Gold Award: A. Fordham.

Northamptonshire

A. Fordham c Duthie b Reifer	103		R. G. Williams not out		18
N. A. Felton b Govan	31		A. L. Penberthy not out		7
R. J. Bailey c Swan b Govan	4		L-b 2, w 7		9
*A. J. Lamb b Govan	44				
D. J. Capel c Russell b Govan	7		1/73 2/80 3/167	(6 wkts, 55 overs) 235
K. M. Curran b Duthie	12		4/183 5/206 6/212	

†D. Ripley, J. P. Taylor and A. Walker did not bat.

Bowling: Bee 7–0–22–0; Duthie 10–1–38–1; Sheridan 10–1–40–0; Russell 7–0–30–0; Reifer 10–0–48–1; Govan 11–1–55–4.

Scotland

B. M. W. Patterson c Penberthy b Williams	96		A. Bee run out		8
			P. G. Duthie not out		14
R. G. Swan run out	9		K. L. P. Sheridan not out		3
G. N. Reifer c and b Capel	0				
†I. L. Philip b Penberthy	0		B 2, l-b 2, w 4		8
J. Everett lbw b Curran	16				
*A. B. Russell lbw b Curran	7		1/26 2/27 3/30	(9 wkts, 55 overs) 190
G. Salmond run out	6		4/66 5/74 6/103	
J. W. Govan run out	23		7/160 8/171 9/173	

Bowling: Taylor 10–2–25–0; Walker 9–0–25–0; Penberthy 8–1–36–1; Capel 8–1–33–1; Curran 9–0–32–2; Williams 11–1–35–1.

Umpires: N. T. Plews and A. G. T. Whitehead.

HAMPSHIRE v ESSEX

At Southampton, April 23. Hampshire won by 41 runs. Toss: Essex. Hampshire failed to build on a steady start, but were able to defend a modest 177 thanks to superb bowling by Marshall. His opening spell – Gooch, Stephenson and Waugh all lbw for one run in 17 balls – paved the way for his best figures and first match award in the Cup. There were eight lbw victims in the match, six given by umpire Holder.

Gold Award: M. D. Marshall.

Hampshire

V. P. Terry lbw b Ilott	14	R. J. Maru c Knight b Pringle	4	
T. C. Middleton lbw b Stephenson	41	S. D. Udal not out	3	
R. A. Smith c Garnham b Stephenson	42	C. A. Connor b Pringle	0	
D. I. Gower lbw b Foster	6	L-b 6, w 14, n-b 2	22	
*M. C. J. Nicholas lbw b Ilott	19			
J. R. Ayling c Foster b Such	14	1/25 2/108 3/111	(54.4 overs) 177	
M. D. Marshall c Garnham b Ilott	1	4/124 5/143 6/145		
†A. N. Aymes b Such	11	7/165 8/168 9/175		

Bowling: Foster 11–1–25–1; Ilott 11–1–27–3; Stephenson 11–0–47–2; Pringle 10.4–0–40–2; Such 11–2–32–2.

Essex

*G. A. Gooch lbw b Marshall	0	N. A. Foster b Udal	0	
J. P. Stephenson lbw b Marshall	1	M. C. Ilott not out	5	
M. E. Waugh lbw b Marshall	2	P. M. Such b Maru	3	
N. Hussain c Terry b Marshall	55	B 1, l-b 9, w 7, n-b 2	19	
P. J. Prichard c Aymes b Ayling	18			
N. V. Knight c Terry b Ayling	2	1/0 2/1 3/5	(49.3 overs) 136	
D. R. Pringle c Aymes b Udal	23	4/33 5/51 6/110		
†M. A. Garnham lbw b Udal	8	7/127 8/127 9/128		

Bowling: Marshall 11–3–20–4; Connor 9–1–23–0; Udal 11–1–27–3; Ayling 9–2–25–2; Maru 9.3–1–31–1.

Umpires: J. H. Hampshire and J. W. Holder.

LANCASHIRE v SCOTLAND

At Manchester, April 23. Lancashire won by six wickets. Toss: Scotland. Patterson, who survived chances at 4, 31 and 32, and Philip shared Scotland's first century partnership for any wicket in Benson and Hedges or NatWest games. But Mendis, reaching 2,000 runs in the competition, and Speak set up another victory for Lancashire.

Gold Award: I. L. Philip.

Scotland

B. M. W. Patterson c Morrison		J. Everett b DeFreitas	8	
	b Watkinson . 63	G. Salmond not out	1	
†I. L. Philip c Hegg b DeFreitas	80	L-b 12, w 7	19	
G. N. Reifer c Watkinson b Morrison	7			
R. G. Swan run out	15	1/144 2/157 3/175	(5 wkts, 55 overs) 219	
*A. B. Russell not out	26	4/193 5/211		

J. W. Govan, A. Bee, P. G. Duthie and J. D. Moir did not bat.

Bowling: DeFreitas 11–1–33–2; Morrison 11–0–41–1; Watkinson 11–0–33–1; Austin 11–0–45–0; Barnett 11–1–53–0.

Lancashire

G. D. Mendis c Moir b Russell	51	M. Watkinson not out	10	
G. Fowler b Reifer	36	L-b 7, w 4	11	
N. J. Speak run out	64			
*N. H. Fairbrother b Govan	26	1/84 2/100	(4 wkts, 52.5 overs) 221	
G. D. Lloyd not out	23	3/153 4/196		

†W. K. Hegg, P. A. J. DeFreitas, I. D. Austin, A. A. Barnett and D. K. Morrison did not bat.

Bowling: Duthie 8.5–1–32–0; Moir 11–1–43–0; Govan 11–0–46–1; Bee 8–1–38–0; Reifer 10–0–40–1; Russell 4–0–15–1.

Umpires: B. Dudleston and G. Sharp.

ESSEX v SCOTLAND

At Chelmsford, April 30, May 1. Essex won by 272 runs. Toss: Scotland. After their disastrous start to the competition, Essex took out their frustrations on the unfortunate Scots. Their total of 388 for seven passed the previous record in the Benson and Hedges Cup, 366 for four by Derbyshire against Combined Universities at Oxford in 1991. The winning margin also broke Essex's own record for a team batting first in the competition, 214 runs against Oxford & Cambridge Universities at Chelmsford in 1979. Gooch won his 20th Gold Award for his tenth hundred in the Cup, which he reached before lunch; in all he faced 108 balls for his 127, with 15 fours and four sixes. But the most startling display came from Foster. Promoted to No. 5, he hit 62 from only 27 balls, including six sixes and two fours. His day was marred when he had to retire with a torn side muscle after bowling the first two balls of Scotland's innings. Overnight Scotland were 49 for five from 15 overs (I. L. Philip 13*, A. B. Russell 1*).

Gold Award: G. A. Gooch.

Essex

*G. A. Gooch run out	127	N. V. Knight not out		18
J. P. Stephenson st Haggo b Henry	66	†M. A. Garnham not out		12
M. E. Waugh b Govan	34	L-b 7, w 8		15
N. Hussain run out	20			—
N. A. Foster b Govan	62	1/193 2/202 3/251	(7 wkts, 55 overs)	388
P. J. Prichard b Govan	25	4/281 5/349		
D. R. Pringle c Philip b Govan	9	6/350 7/369		

T. D. Topley and M. C. Ilott did not bat.

Bowling: Moir 11–2–63–0; Duthie 9–0–66–0; Reifer 11–0–60–0; Henry 10–0–79–1; Russell 4–1–42–0; Govan 10–0–71–4.

Scotland

B. M. W. Patterson b Ilott	3	P. G. Duthie c Pringle b Waugh		5
I. L. Philip b Topley	18	†D. J. Haggo lbw b Waugh		1
G. N. Reifer lbw b Ilott	17	J. D. Moir not out		4
O. Henry st Garnham b Stephenson	6	L-b 7, w 11, n-b 3		21
R. G. Swan c Garnham b Ilott	0			—
G. Salmond c Prichard b Ilott	3	1/4 2/32 3/39	(35.5 overs)	116
*A. B. Russell c Hussain b Waugh	22	4/40 5/47 6/65		
J. W. Govan c Garnham b Pringle	16	7/102 8/105 9/109		

Bowling: Foster 0.2–0–0–0; Pringle 7.4–3–15–1; Ilott 10–1–31–4; Stephenson 5–0–17–1; Topley 5–2–15–1; Waugh 7.5–0–31–3.

Umpires: G. I. Burgess and P. B. Wight.

HAMPSHIRE v NORTHAMPTONSHIRE

At Southampton, April 30, May 1. Hampshire won by six runs. Toss: Northamptonshire. Rain washed out the first day and restricted the second, turning the contest into a 33-over match beginning at 2.30 p.m. Gower's unbeaten 118 from 95 balls, his highest score in the competition, with three sixes and seven fours, enabled Hampshire to reach 197 for six. It was just enough, despite Bailey's unbeaten 109 from 99 deliveries; Northamptonshire needed 13 from Connor's final over and it was too much.

Gold Award: D. I. Gower.

Hampshire

R. A. Smith b Ambrose	40	M. D. Marshall c Lamb b Ambrose	4
V. P. Terry b Ambrose	0		
D. I. Gower not out	118	L-b 3, w 7	10
J. R. Ayling b Walker	8		—
*M. C. J. Nicholas c Felton b Curran	4	1/1 2/115 3/140 (6 wkts, 33 overs) 197	
K. D. James c Taylor b Walker	13	4/162 5/191 6/197	

†A. N. Aymes, S. D. Udal, C. A. Connor and R. J. Maru did not bat.

Bowling: Ambrose 7–1–27–3; Taylor 6–0–29–0; Walker 7–0–50–2; Curran 6–0–44–1; Capel 3–0–21–0; Williams 4–0–23–0.

Northamptonshire

A. Fordham lbw b Connor	7	R. G. Williams not out	0
R. J. Bailey not out	109		
*A. J. Lamb c James b Ayling	9	B 1, l-b 6, w 2	9
D. J. Capel c Terry b Udal	25		—
K. M. Curran b Marshall	29	1/24 2/47 3/104 (5 wkts, 33 overs) 191	
N. A. Felton c Gower b Connor	3	4/184 5/187	

†D. Ripley, C. E. L. Ambrose, A. Walker and J. P. Taylor did not bat.

Bowling: Connor 7–0–34–2; Marshall 7–0–34–1; Ayling 6–0–40–1; Udal 7–0–42–1; Maru 3–0–16–0; James 3–0–18–0.

Umpires: J. D. Bond and R. C. Tolchard.

LANCASHIRE v HAMPSHIRE

At Manchester, May 2. Hampshire won by 38 runs. Toss: Lancashire. Smith faced 147 balls for his third century in the competition. Atherton began Lancashire's reply with 24 in 24 overs. Then Speak added 97 with Fairbrother, but when they were parted Lancashire's last eight wickets fell for 52.
Gold Award: R. A. Smith.

Hampshire

V. P. Terry lbw b Allott	0	J. R. Ayling not out	18
T. C. Middleton b DeFreitas	48	L-b 8, w 5, n-b 4	17
R. A. Smith c DeFreitas b Morrison	109		—
D. I. Gower not out	44	1/0 2/134 (4 wkts, 55 overs) 241	
*M. C. J. Nicholas c and b Watkinson	5	3/202 4/215	

M. D. Marshall, R. J. Maru, †A. N. Aymes, S. D. Udal and C. A. Connor did not bat.

Bowling: DeFreitas 11–2–39–1; Allott 11–3–39–1; Morrison 11–0–48–1; Watkinson 9–0–51–1; Austin 9–0–34–0; Atherton 4–0–22–0.

Lancashire

G. D. Mendis c Aymes b Marshall	3	I. D. Austin b Marshall	20
M. A. Atherton run out	24	P. J. W. Allott st Aymes b Connor	3
N. J. Speak b Udal	82	D. K. Morrison st Aymes b Connor	0
*N. H. Fairbrother b Maru	44	L-b 11, w 4, n-b 1	16
G. D. Lloyd c Smith b Marshall	1		—
M. Watkinson b Udal	2	1/6 2/54 3/151 (53.3 overs) 203	
P. A. J. DeFreitas not out	8	4/158 5/164 6/175	
†W. K. Hegg lbw b Udal	0	7/175 8/200 9/203	

Bowling: Marshall 10–3–28–3; Connor 10.3–2–35–2; Maru 11–3–35–1; Ayling 11–0–54–0; Udal 11–0–40–3.

Umpires: J. H. Harris and D. O. Oslear.

NORTHAMPTONSHIRE v ESSEX

At Northampton, May 2. Essex won by 66 runs. Toss: Northamptonshire. Gooch's second hundred in consecutive Benson and Hedges matches was his 11th in the competition, but he was narrowly beaten for the match award by Waugh, with whom he added 206 in 33 overs before Essex lost their last nine wickets in 39 balls. Northamptonshire collapsed even more traumatically and were all out at 8.25 p.m.

Gold Award: M. E. Waugh.

Essex

*G. A. Gooch b Taylor	119	A. G. J. Fraser b Ambrose		6
J. P. Stephenson c Taylor b Walker	10	T. D. Topley b Ambrose		5
M. E. Waugh c Ripley b Curran	100	P. M. Such not out		1
D. R. Pringle c Ambrose b Curran	1	L-b 8, w 3		11
N. Hussain c Felton b Ambrose	2			
P. J. Prichard c Bailey b Walker	5	1/31 2/237 3/238	(55 overs)	264
N. V. Knight b Ambrose	2	4/242 5/244 6/250		
†M. A. Garnham run out	2	7/252 8/253 9/261		

Bowling: Ambrose 11-2-31-4; Taylor 11-1-30-1; Curran 10-0-64-2; Walker 11-1-49-2; Capel 11-0-76-0; Williams 1-0-6-0.

Northamptonshire

A. Fordham c Pringle b Topley	69	C. E. L. Ambrose b Such		1
N. A. Felton c Hussain b Pringle	5	A. Walker not out		3
R. J. Bailey b Topley	4	J. P. Taylor c Garnham b Fraser		3
*A. J. Lamb c Topley b Such	53	L-b 5, w 5		10
D. J. Capel c Knight b Stephenson	44			
K. M. Curran lbw b Topley	1	1/13 2/22 3/97	(51.1 overs)	198
R. G. Williams st Garnham b Such	1	4/163 5/170 6/177		
†D. Ripley c Waugh b Such	2	7/187 8/189 9/192		

Bowling: Pringle 9-2-16-1; Topley 11-2-40-3; Fraser 5.1-0-31-1; Stephenson 8-0-35-1; Gooch 7-1-28-0; Such 11-0-43-4.

Umpires: H. D. Bird and R. Julian.

NORTHAMPTONSHIRE v LANCASHIRE

At Northampton, May 5, 6. Lancashire won by eight runs. Toss: Northamptonshire. As in the NatWest semi-final at The Oval the previous year, Lamb opted to leave the field because of bad light when Northamptonshire were in sight of their target with a handful of overs to go. They resumed at 223 for five from 50.5 overs (A. J. Lamb 88*, R. G. Williams 6*), and lost again, when the Lancashire captain Fairbrother chose to bowl the last over himself, despite a finger injury. His rarely seen left-arm medium pace restricted the home team to only 13 of the 22 required. The match was riddled by injury; Watkinson made his highest score in the competition, batting with a runner because of a pulled hamstring, while Lamb also needed a runner after damaging his groin. None the less he added 144 in 28 overs with Felton, who made a Cup-best 82.

Gold Award: A. J. Lamb.

Lancashire

G. D. Mendis c Lamb b Curran	31	†W. K. Hegg not out		10
M. A. Atherton c Ripley b Taylor	8	P. J. W. Allott not out		1
N. J. Speak c Ripley b Walker	1			
*N. H. Fairbrother c Bailey b Curran	79	B 1, l-b 9, w 10, n-b 2		22
G. D. Lloyd b Capel	4			
M. Watkinson c Curran b Taylor	76	1/18 2/23 3/73	(8 wkts, 55 overs)	257
P. A. J. DeFreitas b Walker	24	4/89 5/188 6/235		
I. D. Austin b Taylor	1	7/236 8/251		

D. K. Morrison did not bat.

Bowling: Taylor 11–0–38–3; Walker 11–1–56–2; Cook 11–0–49–0; Capel 11–1–52–1; Curran 11–0–52–2.

Northamptonshire

A. Fordham c Mendis b DeFreitas	3	†D. Ripley lbw b Austin	4
N. A. Felton c Lloyd b Allott	82	A. Walker not out	0
R. J. Bailey lbw b Allott	21	B 1, l-b 5, w 2	8
*A. J. Lamb not out	108		
D. J. Capel c Hegg b Morrison	14	1/4 2/37 3/181 (7 wkts, 55 overs) 249	
K. M. Curran c Hegg b DeFreitas	2	4/201 5/213	
R. G. Williams run out	7	6/224 7/236	

N. G. B. Cook and J. P. Taylor did not bat.

Bowling: DeFreitas 11–2–35–2; Allott 11–1–41–1; Morrison 11–1–35–1; Austin 11–1–44–2; Atherton 5–0–38–0; Fairbrother 6–0–50–0.

Umpires: A. A. Jones and P. B. Wight.

SCOTLAND v HAMPSHIRE

At Hamilton Crescent, Glasgow, May 5, 6. No result. Toss: Hampshire. The umpires called the game off at the overnight score on the second morning. Both innings were included in the run-rate calculations, although Hampshire were already assured of heading their group.

Scotland

B. M. W. Patterson c Connor b Ayling	8	*A. B. Russell not out	20
†I. L. Philip c James b Udal	37		
G. N. Reifer not out	63	L-b 4, w 2, n-b 2	8
J. Everett c and b Maru	0		
G. Salmond c and b Udal	13	1/26 2/60 3/60 (5 wkts, 55 overs) 151	
O. Henry b Connor	2	4/100 5/108	

J. W. Govan, P. G. Duthie, A. Bee and J. D. Moir did not bat.

Bowling: Marshall 7–3–17–0; Connor 11–4–26–1; Ayling 11–2–42–1; Maru 11–4–19–1; Udal 11–1–23–2; James 4–0–20–0.

Hampshire

V. P. Terry not out	11	
T. C. Middleton b Duthie	2	
D. I. Gower b Duthie	0	
J. R. Ayling not out	1	
L-b 1, w 1	2	

1/14 2/14	(2 wkts, 6 overs) 16

*M. C. J. Nicholas, K. D. James, M. D. Marshall, †A. N. Aymes, S. D. Udal, C. A. Connor and R. J. Maru did not bat.

Bowling: Moir 3–0–9–0; Duthie 3–1–6–2.

Umpires: K. E. Palmer and R. A. White.

GROUP C

KENT v SOMERSET

At Canterbury, April 21. Kent won by 37 runs. Toss: Somerset. Longley and Fleming rescued Kent from 87 for four with a stand of 109 in 15 overs. Kent's last 16 overs added 142. In contrast, Somerset's last eight wickets fell for 21.

Gold Award: M. V. Fleming.

Kent

T. R. Ward lbw b Mallender	6	M. A. Ealham lbw b Hayhurst	13
*M. R. Benson c Burns b Rose	7		
N. R. Taylor b Hayhurst	45	L-b 8, w 1, n-b 4	13
G. R. Cowdrey lbw b Caddick	7		
J. I. Longley b Rose	57	1/9 2/18 3/37	(7 wkts, 55 overs) 231
M. V. Fleming c MacLeay b Rose	69	4/87 5/196	
†S. A. Marsh not out	14	6/210 7/231	

R. P. Davis, M. J. McCague and A. P. Igglesden did not bat.

Bowling: Mallender 10–0–61–1; Rose 8–3–21–3; MacLeay 8–1–21–0; Caddick 8–2–33–1; Trump 11–1–36–0; Hayhurst 10–3–51–2.

Somerset

A. N. Hayhurst run out	37	M. N. Lathwell b McCague	4
K. H. MacLeay lbw b McCague	16	H. R. J. Trump c Ward b Ealham	1
R. J. Harden lbw b Ealham	76	A. R. Caddick not out	1
*C. J. Tavaré c Marsh b McCague	30	B 1, l-b 11, w 3, n-b 3	18
R. J. Bartlett c Marsh b McCague	3		
G. D. Rose b Ealham	4	1/29 2/104 3/173	(52.4 overs) 194
†N. D. Burns b McCague	2	4/177 5/179 6/183	
N. A. Mallender c Benson b Ealham	2	7/185 8/191 9/193	

Bowling: Igglesden 9–2–31–0; Ealham 10–1–29–4; Davis 11–1–31–0; McCague 10.4–0–43–5; Fleming 9–0–34–0; Cowdrey 3–0–14–0.

Umpires: J. W. Holder and M. J. Kitchen.

WARWICKSHIRE v YORKSHIRE

At Birmingham, April 21. Yorkshire won by three runs. Toss: Warwickshire. Having made the highest score of the match, Twose needed four from the last over of Warwickshire's innings for victory. Instead he pulled Hartley's first ball to Moxon at mid-wicket.

Gold Award: R. J. Blakey.

Yorkshire

*M. D. Moxon c Asif Din b Munton	0	C. S. Pickles not out	37
A. A. Metcalfe c Penney b P. A. Smith	25	P. Carrick not out	13
D. Byas b P. A. Smith	26	L-b 9, w 4	13
S. A. Kellett c Moles b Small	40		
†R. J. Blakey lbw b N. M. K. Smith	12	1/1 2/50 3/54	(6 wkts, 55 overs) 188
A. P. Grayson b Small	22	4/90 5/125 6/144	

P. J. Hartley, D. Gough and P. W. Jarvis did not bat.

Bowling: Small 11–4–31–2; Munton 11–2–34–1; Moles 4–0–18–0; P. A. Smith 9–1–43–2; N. M. K. Smith 11–4–21–1; Asif Din 9–0–32–0.

Warwickshire

A. J. Moles lbw b Jarvis	1	†K. J. Piper c Blakey b Jarvis	1
Asif Din c Blakey b Jarvis	42	G. C. Small lbw b Jarvis	1
*T. A. Lloyd c and b Hartley	21	T. A. Munton not out	3
D. P. Ostler c Blakey b Hartley	14	L-b 4, w 3	7
R. G. Twose c Moxon b Hartley	62		
T. L. Penney c Blakey b Gough	17	1/6 2/44 3/66	(54.1 overs) 185
P. A. Smith c Carrick b Gough	13	4/90 5/128 6/146	
N. M. K. Smith c Blakey b Carrick	3	7/156 8/159 9/164	

Bowling: Jarvis 11–1–34–4; Gough 11–3–31–2; Hartley 10.1–3–32–3; Pickles 11–0–55–0; Carrick 11–0–29–1.

Umpires: V. A. Holder and D. R. Shepherd.

NOTTINGHAMSHIRE v KENT

At Nottingham, April 23. Kent won by 61 runs. Toss: Nottinghamshire. Lewis took five wickets, a feat he had never achieved in limited-overs matches for Leicestershire or England.

Gold Award: M. R. Benson.

Kent

T. R. Ward c French b Evans	29	M. J. McCague b Lewis		10
*M. R. Benson c Randall b Lewis	66	R. P. Davis b Lewis		1
N. R. Taylor c French b Lewis	48			
G. R. Cowdrey lbw b Cairns	15	B 1, l-b 9, w 3, n-b 4		17
M. V. Fleming b Pick	0			—
†S. A. Marsh c French b Lewis	26	1/68 2/150 3/160	(9 wkts, 55 overs)	228
J. I. Longley b Evans	10	4/162 5/179 6/207		
M. A. Ealham not out	6	7/209 8/226 9/228		

A. P. Igglesden did not bat.

Bowling: Lewis 11-1-46-5; Pick 11-0-38-1; Evans 11-2-38-2; Cairns 8-0-38-1; Hemmings 9-1-38-0; Crawley 5-0-20-0.

Nottinghamshire

B. C. Broad c Cowdrey b Davis	64	†B. N. French lbw b Igglesden		10
D. W. Randall lbw b Igglesden	0	E. E. Hemmings lbw b Ealham		4
M. A. Crawley c Fleming b Ealham	4	R. A. Pick not out		3
*P. Johnson c Marsh b McCague	39	L-b 5, w 5, n-b 3		13
P. R. Pollard run out	3			—
C. C. Lewis c Ealham b Davis	5	1/4 2/18 3/90	(45 overs)	167
C. L. Cairns c and b Fleming	16	4/101 5/117 6/130		
K. P. Evans c Marsh b Igglesden	6	7/146 8/152 9/157		

Bowling: Igglesden 9-2-24-3; Ealham 11-0-38-2; Davis 11-2-40-2; Fleming 6-0-26-1; McCague 8-0-34-1.

Umpires: J. H. Harris and R. C. Tolchard.

SOMERSET v YORKSHIRE

At Taunton, April 23. Somerset won by 23 runs. Toss: Yorkshire.
Gold Award: G. D. Rose.

Somerset

A. N. Hayhurst lbw b Jarvis	6	N. A. Mallender not out		14
G. T. J. Townsend lbw b Jarvis	1	A. R. Caddick run out		6
R. J. Harden b Pickles	19	H. R. J. Trump c Moxon b Hartley		1
*C. J. Tavaré c Metcalfe b Hartley	17	L-b 6, w 3		9
R. J. Bartlett run out	3			—
G. D. Rose c Blakey b Gough	28	1/3 2/8 3/48	(55 overs)	143
K. H. MacLeay lbw b Jarvis	23	4/49 5/53 6/103		
†N. D. Burns b Gough	16	7/105 8/130 9/141		

Bowling: Jarvis 11-3-14-3; Gough 9-1-29-2; Hartley 11-2-28-2; Pickles 11-1-30-1; Carrick 11-2-23-0; Moxon 2-0-13-0.

Yorkshire

*M. D. Moxon c Tavaré b Caddick....	3	P. Carrick not out		3
A. A. Metcalfe c Trump b Hayhurst ...	14	D. Gough c Burns b Rose...........		6
D. Byas lbw b Trump	19	P. W. Jarvis c Caddick b Rose		3
S. A. Kellett b Rose	36	L-b 4, w 5, n-b 2...........		11
†R. J. Blakey lbw b Mallender........	5			
P. J. Hartley c Rose b Trump	1	1/6 2/22 3/61	(51.5 overs)	120
A. P. Grayson c Mallender b Caddick..	10	4/77 5/80 6/92		
C. S. Pickles c Caddick b Hayhurst....	9	7/102 8/107 9/116		

Bowling: Mallender 11–4–18–1; Caddick 11–4–20–2; Hayhurst 8–0–24–2; Rose 10.5–2–31–3; Trump 11–0–23–2.

Umpires: D. J. Constant and B. J. Meyer.

WARWICKSHIRE v NOTTINGHAMSHIRE

At Birmingham, April 30, May 1. Nottinghamshire won by seven wickets. Toss: Nottinghamshire. Overnight Warwickshire were 209 for seven from their full 55 overs. After lunch on the second day the Zimbabwean Penney took over as Warwickshire's wicket-keeper from the injured Piper.

Gold Award: P. Johnson.

Warwickshire

A. J. Moles c French b Pick.........	8	N. M. K. Smith b Lewis...........		11
*T. A. Lloyd b Pick................	11	†K. J. Piper not out...............		0
R. G. Twose c Randall b Cairns	28	L-b 16, w 1, n-b 5..........		22
D. P. Ostler c and b Hemmings.......	16			
Asif Din not out...................	71	1/25 2/28 3/79	(7 wkts, 55 overs)	209
T. L. Penney run out	5	4/81 5/107		
P. A. Smith c Johnson b Lewis	37	6/186 7/207		

G. C. Small and A. A. Donald did not bat.

Bowling: Lewis 11–0–50–2; Pick 11–3–29–2; Hemmings 11–2–21–1; Crawley 1–0–7–0; Evans 11–2–45–0; Cairns 10–1–41–1.

Nottinghamshire

B. C. Broad run out................	26	D. W. Randall not out		7
P. R. Pollard not out..............	76			
M. A. Crawley c Piper b P. A. Smith ..	0	B 7, l-b 10, w 5, n-b 3		25
*P. Johnson st Penney				
b N. M. K. Smith .	76	1/41 2/41 3/184	(3 wkts, 54.4 overs)	210

C. C. Lewis, C. L. Cairns, K. P. Evans, †B. N. French, E. E. Hemmings and R. A. Pick did not bat.

Bowling: Small 11–2–42–0; Donald 11–1–26–0; P. A. Smith 11–2–42–1; N. M. K. Smith 10.4–2–34–1; Twose 4–0–22–0; Moles 6–1–19–0; Asif Din 1–0–8–0.

Umpires: A. A. Jones and B. J. Meyer.

YORKSHIRE v KENT

At Leeds, April 30, May 1. Kent won by 70 runs. Toss: Yorkshire. Yorkshire's first overseas player, the Indian Test batsman Sachin Tendulkar, led his new team out on to the field, and collected two wickets in his eighth over. He also ran out Fleming, who had hit 66 from 62 balls, with three sixes and five fours. Later Tendulkar was unluckily run out when Ellison deflected the ball on to the stumps attempting a return catch off Byas. West Indian Carl Hooper made his début for Kent but was overshadowed, despite taking two wickets with successive balls. On the first day rain ended play at 4 p.m. when Yorkshire were 13 without loss from six overs (S. A. Kellett 6*, A. A. Metcalfe 6*).

Gold Award: M. V. Fleming.

Kent

T. R. Ward run out	21	R. M. Ellison b Hartley	3
*M. R. Benson c Blakey b Gough	7	M. J. McCague not out	11
N. R. Taylor b Robinson	15	A. P. Igglesden not out	4
C. L. Hooper c Hartley b Carrick	17	B 4, l-b 8, w 5	17
G. R. Cowdrey lbw b Tendulkar	16		
M. V. Fleming run out	66	1/30 2/45 3/57 (9 wkts, 55 overs) 203	
†S. A. Marsh c and b Tendulkar	0	4/81 5/94 6/94	
M. A. Ealham b Gough	26	7/182 8/184 9/188	

Bowling: Hartley 10–3–39–1; Gough 8–1–29–2; Pickles 7–2–28–0; Robinson 8–1–46–1; Carrick 11–1–28–1; Tendulkar 11–2–21–2.

Yorkshire

S. A. Kellett c Fleming b Igglesden	8	P. J. Hartley not out	6
*A. A. Metcalfe c and b Ellison	11	D. Gough b McCague	5
D. Byas b Ellison	16	M. A. Robinson lbw b McCague	0
S. R. Tendulkar run out	7	L-b 9, w 5, n-b 1	15
†R. J. Blakey c Marsh b McCague	39		
A. P. Grayson b Hooper	11	1/20 2/33 3/48 (48.5 overs) 133	
C. S. Pickles c Benson b Hooper	15	4/48 5/87 6/119	
P. Carrick b Hooper	0	7/119 8/121 9/133	

Bowling: Igglesden 7–2–13–1; Ealham 8–2–20–0; Fleming 5–0–10–0; Ellison 11–0–27–2; Hooper 11–2–28–3; McCague 6.5–0–26–3.

Umpires: J. H. Harris and D. O. Oslear.

SOMERSET v WARWICKSHIRE

At Taunton, May 2. Warwickshire won by virtue of losing fewer wickets. Toss: Warwickshire. To win, Somerset needed four runs from Neil Smith's final over. They took three from the first four balls, but Snell was run out on the fifth and Mallender bowled by the sixth. Neil Smith recorded career-bests in the competition with both bat and ball; Rose's 58 came from 55 balls.

Gold Award: N. M. K. Smith.

Warwickshire

A. J. Moles st Burns b Trump	15	N. M. K. Smith b Snell	32
*T. A. Lloyd run out	51	†P. C. L. Holloway not out	0
R. G. Twose c Tavaré b Trump	45	L-b 9, w 5	14
D. P. Ostler not out	65		
Asif Din c Burns b Caddick	5	1/38 2/85 3/140 (6 wkts, 55 overs) 236	
P. A. Smith b Hayhurst	9	4/155 5/177 6/231	

T. A. Munton, G. C. Small and A. A. Donald did not bat.

Bowling: Mallender 11–1–39–0; Caddick 11–1–29–1; Trump 11–0–40–2; Snell 11–2–40–1; Rose 7–0–50–0; Hayhurst 4–0–29–1.

Somerset

A. N. Hayhurst c Holloway b N. M. K. Smith	78	R. P. Snell run out	17
K. H. MacLeay c Holloway b Donald	5	N. A. Mallender b N. M. K. Smith	0
R. J. Harden c Holloway b Donald	10	B 1, l-b 4, w 5, n-b 1	11
*C. J. Tavaré c Moles b P. A. Smith	9		
R. J. Bartlett b N. M. K. Smith	22	1/16 2/32 3/52 (8 wkts, 55 overs) 236	
G. D. Rose c Twose b Munton	58	4/100 5/178 6/202	
†N. D. Burns not out	26	7/236 8/236	

A. R. Caddick and H. R. J. Trump did not bat.

Bowling: Donald 11–0–43–2; Small 11–2–38–0; P. A. Smith 11–0–59–1; Munton 11–2–46–1; N. M. K. Smith 11–0–45–3.

Umpires: J. H. Hampshire and G. Sharp.

YORKSHIRE v NOTTINGHAMSHIRE

At Leeds, May 2. Nottinghamshire won by seven wickets. Toss: Yorkshire. Kellett was out to the first ball of the match, after a delay while groundstaff checked the positioning of the discs governing field placings. Crawley and Johnson, who scored 79 from 59 balls with three sixes and five fours, added 101 for Nottinghamshire's third wicket in 16 overs.

Gold Award: P. Johnson.

Yorkshire

S. A. Kellett lbw b Pick	0	P. J. Hartley c Johnson b Hemmings		5
*A. A. Metcalfe c Randall b Pick	29	D. Gough not out		7
D. Byas run out	31	J. D. Batty not out		2
S. R. Tendulkar b Pick	16	B 2, l-b 8, w 7		17
†R. J. Blakey lbw b Hemmings	29			
C. White run out	26	1/0 2/49 3/77	(9 wkts, 55 overs)	193
C. S. Pickles b Hemmings	13	4/79 5/127 6/155		
P. Carrick b Evans	18	7/163 8/179 9/189		

Bowling: Pick 10–2–35–3; Lewis 11–2–27–0; Evans 10–0–32–1; Cairns 6–0–42–0; Crawley 7–0–15–0; Hemmings 11–1–32–3.

Nottinghamshire

B. C. Broad c Byas b Pickles	19	D. W. Randall not out		4
P. R. Pollard c Batty b Tendulkar	39	B 1, l-b 3, w 4, n-b 1		9
M. A. Crawley b Hartley	44			
*P. Johnson not out	79	1/43 2/77 3/178	(3 wkts, 51.1 overs)	194

C. C. Lewis, C. L. Cairns, K. P. Evans, †B. N. French, E. E. Hemmings and R. A. Pick did not bat.

Bowling: Gough 7–1–35–0; Hartley 9–3–29–1; Pickles 8.1–3–16–1; Carrick 11–0–32–0; Batty 7–0–34–0; Tendulkar 9–0–44–1.

Umpires: J. C. Balderstone and G. A. Stickley.

KENT v WARWICKSHIRE

At Canterbury, May 5, 6. Kent won by 27 runs. Toss: Kent. Warwickshire lost wickets trying to improve their run-rate and reach the last eight. But their sacrifices cost them the match. Four of the visitors were run out, three of them on the second day, after Warwickshire reached 102 for four from 40.2 overs (T. A. Lloyd 53*, P. A. Smith 3*) on the first, ended by bad light.

Gold Award: C. L. Hooper.

Kent

T. R. Ward hit wkt b Donald	12	M. A. Ealham not out		12
*M. R. Benson c Ostler b Moles	62	M. J. McCague not out		13
J. I. Longley b Munton	9	B 4, l-b 5, w 7, n-b 1		17
C. L. Hooper c Small b P. A. Smith	39			
G. R. Cowdrey b Donald	7	1/19 2/54 3/114	(7 wkts, 55 overs)	209
M. V. Fleming c Ostler b P. A. Smith	29	4/133 5/159		
†S. A. Marsh b N. M. K. Smith	9	6/175 7/190		

R. P. Davis and A. P. Igglesden did not bat.

Bowling: Donald 11–3–33–2; Small 8–1–27–0; Twose 9–1–27–0; Munton 11–1–33–1; Moles 5–0–17–1; N. M. K. Smith 3–0–22–1; P. A. Smith 8–0–41–2.

Warwickshire

A. J. Moles run out	13	G. C. Small not out		20
*T. A. Lloyd b Fleming	61	A. A. Donald c Marsh b McCague		10
R. G. Twose c Ealham b Hooper	5	T. A. Munton c Davis b Fleming		3
D. P. Ostler b Hooper	10	B 4, l-b 11, w 5		20
Asif Din lbw b Igglesden	10			
P. A. Smith run out	17	1/24 2/40 3/69	(54 overs)	182
N. M. K. Smith run out	5	4/93 5/111 6/126		
†P. C. L. Holloway run out	8	7/132 8/144 9/171		

Bowling: Igglesden 11–3–34–1; Ealham 8–1–26–0; Davis 11–3–22–0; Hooper 11–0–29–2; Fleming 8–0–37–2; McCague 5–0–19–1.

Umpires: R. Palmer and R. C. Tolchard.

NOTTINGHAMSHIRE v SOMERSET

At Nottingham, May 5. Somerset won by four wickets. Toss: Somerset. To have a chance of reaching the quarter-finals, Somerset had to attain their target of 225 in 51.3 overs or less, and they lost several wickets in frenzied pursuit as the deadline approached. They achieved their goal, thanks largely to Hayhurst.

Gold Award: A. N. Hayhurst.

Nottinghamshire

B. C. Broad b Mallender	83	†B. N. French b Snell		5
P. R. Pollard c Snell b Rose	5	E. E. Hemmings not out		5
M. A. Crawley c Harden b Mallender	57	R. A. Pick b Snell		5
*P. Johnson c Bartlett b Hayhurst	20	B 1, l-b 7, w 3, n-b 4		15
D. W. Randall b Mallender	0			
C. C. Lewis lbw b Mallender	26	1/18 2/150 3/157	(55 overs)	224
C. L. Cairns c MacLeay b Hayhurst	1	4/157 5/193 6/205		
K. P. Evans run out	2	7/207 8/208 9/218		

Bowling: Mallender 11–2–49–4; Rose 7–1–14–1; Snell 11–0–47–2; Trump 6–0–26–0; MacLeay 8–0–27–0; Cottam 7–0–34–0; Hayhurst 5–0–19–2.

Somerset

K. H. MacLeay c Cairns b Hemmings	43	R. P. Snell not out		10
A. N. Hayhurst b Lewis	95	†N. D. Burns not out		0
R. J. Harden lbw b Hemmings	12	L-b 5, w 3, n-b 6		14
*C. J. Tavaré b Cairns	31			
G. D. Rose run out	18	1/91 2/111 3/182	(6 wkts, 49.4 overs)	227
R. J. Bartlett b Lewis	4	4/210 5/214 6/217		

N. A. Mallender, A. C. Cottam and H. R. J. Trump did not bat.

Bowling: Lewis 8–1–46–2; Pick 8–0–25–0; Evans 9.4–0–61–0; Cairns 11–1–34–1; Hemmings 11–1–46–2; Crawley 2–0–10–0.

Umpires: B. Dudleston and J. W. Holder.

GROUP D

The Combined Universities' squad of 14 named for the competition was: J. P. Crawley (Cambridge) (*captain*), J. N. B. Bovill (Durham), I. Fletcher (Loughborough), J. E. R. Gallian (Oxford), J. C. Hallett (Durham), A. M. Hooper (Cambridge), M. P. W. Jeh (Oxford), G. I. Macmillan (Southampton), R. R. Montgomerie (Oxford), R. M. Pearson (Cambridge), S. F. Shephard (Loughborough), J. N. Snape (Durham), A. C. Storie (Oxford) and B. C. Usher (London). I. Fletcher later withdrew because of injury.

DURHAM v GLAMORGAN

At Durham University, April 21. Glamorgan won by four wickets. Toss: Glamorgan. After 12 overs of their tournament début Durham were 18 for three, which brought in Botham, who hit nine fours and a six. He then took two wickets in his first two overs, but Glamorgan's latest import, Chris Cowdrey, made the most of two lives at 27 and 72 to steer the visitors to victory.

Gold Award: I. T. Botham.

Durham

W. Larkins c Croft b Frost	0	S. P. Hughes b Frost	3
J. D. Glendenen c Richards b Watkin	7	S. M. McEwan not out	12
D. M. Jones lbw b Watkin	6	S. J. E. Brown not out	4
P. W. G. Parker c and b Croft	22	B 4, l-b 7, w 7	18
I. T. Botham c Richards b Frost	86		
P. Bainbridge lbw b Dale	22	1/1 2/17 3/18	(9 wkts, 55 overs) 196
†C. W. Scott lbw b Dale	3	4/80 5/124 6/154	
*D. A. Graveney b Frost	13	7/166 8/173 9/176	

Bowling: Watkin 11–6–20–2; Frost 11–4–26–4; Barwick 11–0–32–0; Croft 9–0–28–1; Dale 6–0–40–2; Cowdrey 7–0–39–0.

Glamorgan

H. Morris c Jones b Brown	0	R. D. B. Croft not out	30
A. Dale c Larkins b Hughes	30	†C. P. Metson not out	6
*M. P. Maynard lbw b Botham	1	L-b 5, w 5, n-b 3	13
I. V. A. Richards c and b Botham	1		
C. S. Cowdrey c Graveney b Hughes	78	1/1 2/3 3/8	(6 wkts, 54.2 overs) 197
P. A. Cottey c Larkins b Brown	38	4/52 5/137 6/183	

S. L. Watkin, S. R. Barwick and M. Frost did not bat.

Bowling: Brown 10–0–36–2; Botham 11–2–21–2; Hughes 10.2–2–32–2; Graveney 11–1–41–0; McEwan 7–0–32–0; Bainbridge 6–0–30–0.

Umpires: J. D. Bond and B. Leadbeater.

WORCESTERSHIRE v DERBYSHIRE

At Worcester, April 21. Worcestershire won by 68 runs. Toss: Worcestershire.

Gold Award: T. M. Moody.

Worcestershire

*T. S. Curtis c Krikken b Warner	62	S. R. Lampitt not out	23
A. C. H. Seymour c Cork b Mortensen	9		
G. A. Hick run out	44	L-b 10, w 11	21
T. M. Moody not out	70		
D. A. Leatherdale c Krikken b Warner	1	1/33 2/122 3/139	(5 wkts, 55 overs) 232
†S. J. Rhodes c Barnett b Mortensen	2	4/149 5/168	

R. K. Illingworth, P. J. Newport, N. V. Radford and G. R. Dilley did not bat.

Bowling: Bishop 11–0–26–0; Mortensen 11–0–44–2; Cork 11–0–47–0; Malcolm 11–0–76–0; Warner 11–3–29–2.

Derbyshire

*K. J. Barnett c and b Illingworth	31	D. G. Cork lbw b Newport	0
P. D. Bowler c Rhodes b Radford	10	D. E. Malcolm b Newport	8
J. E. Morris c Hick b Lampitt	17	O. H. Mortensen c Rhodes b Radford	4
T. J. G. O'Gorman lbw b Newport	21	B 1, l-b 12, w 9	22
C. J. Adams c Rhodes b Newport	10		
A. E. Warner c Moody b Newport	4	1/25 2/61 3/72	(49.4 overs) 164
I. R. Bishop b Illingworth	0	4/87 5/97 6/97	
†K. M. Krikken not out	37	7/126 8/126 9/147	

Bowling: Dilley 7–0–33–0; Newport 11–1–31–5; Moody 4–1–10–0; Radford 7.4–0–26–2; Illingworth 11–3–23–2; Lampitt 9–1–28–1.

Umpires: J. H. Hampshire and P. B. Wight.

COMBINED UNIVERSITIES v WORCESTERSHIRE

At Oxford, April 23. Worcestershire won by four wickets. Toss: Combined Universities. *Gold Award:* J. N. Snape.

Combined Universities

R. R. Montgomerie c Illingworth b Newport	75	†S. F. Shephard run out	1
J. E. R. Gallian c Lampitt b Moody	0	J. C. Hallett not out	5
*J. P. Crawley c Curtis b Illingworth	20	B 1, l-b 5, w 6	12
A. C. Storie not out	53		
J. N. Snape run out	0	1/8 2/52 3/141	(6 wkts, 55 overs) 173
G. I. Macmillan b Radford	7	4/145 5/159 6/164	

R. M. Pearson, B. C. Usher and J. N. B. Bovill did not bat.

Bowling: Radford 8–1–31–1; Moody 10–3–24–1; Newport 11–0–37–1; Stemp 11–2–29–0; Illingworth 11–3–29–1; Hick 4–0–17–0.

Worcestershire

*T. S. Curtis b Snape	48	R. K. Illingworth not out	14
A. C. H. Seymour c Crawley b Snape	23	N. V. Radford not out	12
G. A. Hick b Pearson	6	B 4, l-b 2, w 16, n-b 4	26
T. M. Moody c and b Snape	14		
D. A. Leatherdale b Pearson	14	1/71 2/84 3/102	(6 wkts, 51.1 overs) 174
†S. J. Rhodes c Crawley b Macmillan	17	4/102 5/132 6/157	

S. R. Lampitt, P. J. Newport and R. D. Stemp did not bat.

Bowling: Hallett 8–1–27–0; Bovill 7–0–21–0; Gallian 7–0–26–0; Usher 2–0–9–0; Pearson 11–2–32–2; Snape 11–1–35–3; Macmillan 5.1–1–18–1.

Umpires: R. A. White and P. B. Wight.

DERBYSHIRE v GLAMORGAN

At Derby, April 23. Derbyshire won by four wickets. Toss: Derbyshire. Bowler batted throughout Derbyshire's innings, though he was dropped in the 50th over by Glamorgan's stand-in captain, Maynard, whose subsequent shy at the stumps cost four overthrows. *Gold Award:* P. D. Bowler.

Glamorgan

S. P. James c Adams b Mortensen	0	S. L. Watkin lbw b Malcolm	0
H. Morris c Adams b Malcolm	32	S. R. Barwick run out	7
*M. P. Maynard lbw b Malcolm	0	M. Frost not out	1
I. V. A. Richards c Barnett b Mortensen	48	L-b 4, w 7	11
C. S. Cowdrey c Krikken b Warner	6		
P. A. Cottey c Bowler b Bishop	8	1/3 2/28 3/67 (9 wkts, 55 overs) 155
R. D. B. Croft not out	24	4/84 5/114 6/118	
†C. P. Metson c Krikken b Malcolm	7	7/136 8/136 9/154	

Bowling: Bishop 11–1–29–1; Mortensen 11–4–26–2; Malcolm 11–0–43–4; Cork 11–0–27–0; Warner 11–1–26–1.

Derbyshire

*K. J. Barnett c Maynard b Frost	36	†K. M. Krikken c Cowdrey b Richards	4
P. D. Bowler not out	66	D. G. Cork not out	8
J. E. Morris c Cottey b Watkin	20	L-b 3, w 7	10
T. J. G. O'Gorman c Cowdrey b Watkin	9		
C. J. Adams lbw b Watkin	0	1/59 2/83 3/99 (6 wkts, 52 overs) 159
I. R. Bishop c Croft b Barwick	6	4/99 5/120 6/136	

A. E. Warner, D. E. Malcolm and O. H. Mortensen did not bat.

Bowling: Watkin 10–4–49–3; Frost 9–0–41–1; Barwick 11–1–33–1; Richards 11–5–18–1; Croft 11–4–15–0.

Umpires: V. A. Holder and B. Leadbeater.

DERBYSHIRE v COMBINED UNIVERSITIES

At Derby, April 30. Derbyshire won by nine wickets. Toss: Combined Universities. Barnett, who won his tenth Gold Award, and Bowler shared their 12th century opening stand in limited-overs cricket. They put on 132 in 41 overs.

Gold Award: K. J. Barnett.

Combined Universities

R. R. Montgomerie lbw b Bishop	0	J. C. Hallett b Warner	1
J. E. R. Gallian c Krikken b Bishop	50	R. M. Pearson not out	2
*J. P. Crawley c Krikken b Malcolm	12	L-b 11, w 11, n-b 3	25
A. C. Storie b Barnett	30		
J. N. Snape not out	22	1/4 2/31 3/103 (7 wkts, 55 overs) 164
G. I. Macmillan lbw b Warner	2	4/115 5/147	
†S. F. Shephard c Bowler b Bishop	10	6/160 7/161	

B. C. Usher and J. N. B. Bovill did not bat.

Bowling: Bishop 11–3–18–3; Mortensen 11–3–20–0; Malcolm 6–1–27–1; Cork 11–0–28–0; Warner 9–1–34–2; Barnett 7–0–26–1.

Derbyshire

*K. J. Barnett not out	84
P. D. Bowler st Shephard b Snape	55
J. E. Morris not out	21
L-b 2, w 2, n-b 3	7

1/132 (1 wkt, 45.1 overs) 167

C. J. Adams, T. J. G. O'Gorman, †K. M. Krikken, D. G. Cork, A. E. Warner, I. R. Bishop, D. E. Malcolm and O. H. Mortensen did not bat.

Bowling: Hallett 6–0–19–0; Bovill 7–1–14–0; Usher 6–0–28–0; Pearson 11–0–46–0; Gallian 4–0–11–0; Snape 10–2–32–1; Storie 1.1–0–15–0.

Umpires: B. Dudleston and G. A. Stickley.

WORCESTERSHIRE v DURHAM

At Worcester, April 30. Durham won by three wickets. Toss: Durham. Durham completed their first Benson and Hedges win at 8.04 p.m. after a match disrupted by rain. Despite dreadful light, Smith and Fothergill refused the umpires' offer to leave the field, and McEwan, who hit the winning four, scored an unbeaten 29 from only 22 balls against his former county.

Gold Award: P. Bainbridge.

Worcestershire

*T. S. Curtis c and b Bainbridge	60	G. R. Haynes c Glendenen b McEwan	14
A. C. H. Seymour c Larkins b McEwan	17	P. J. Newport c Jones b Hughes	9
G. A. Hick c Botham b Bainbridge	26	R. K. Illingworth not out	5
T. M. Moody b Bainbridge	8	B 2, l-b 4, w 5	11
D. A. Leatherdale lbw b Botham	14		
†S. J. Rhodes lbw b Bainbridge	0	1/51 2/101 3/115 (52.4 overs)	173
S. R. Lampitt c Parker b Brown	4	4/128 5/128 6/138	
N. V. Radford c Hughes b McEwan	5	7/138 8/149 9/162	

Bowling: Botham 10–2–27–1; Brown 11–1–27–1; McEwan 11–2–45–3; Bainbridge 11–0–38–4; Hughes 9.4–1–30–1.

Durham

W. Larkins c Haynes b Illingworth	19	†A. R. Fothergill lbw b Haynes	17
J. D. Glendenen c Haynes b Lampitt	45	S. M. McEwan not out	29
D. M. Jones run out	13		
*P. W. G. Parker st Rhodes		L-b 4, w 2, n-b 3	9
b Illingworth	9		
I. T. Botham c Rhodes b Newport	2	1/31 2/56 3/85 (7 wkts, 51.5 overs)	177
P. Bainbridge c Rhodes b Newport	5	4/89 5/92	
I. Smith not out	29	6/108 7/142	

S. P. Hughes and S. J. E. Brown did not bat.

Bowling: Newport 10.5–0–45–2; Radford 10–0–37–0; Haynes 9–1–33–1; Illingworth 11–4–22–2; Lampitt 9–1–28–1; Hick 2–0–8–0.

Umpires: J. W. Holder and K. E. Palmer.

COMBINED UNIVERSITIES v DURHAM

At Cambridge, May 2. Durham won by 51 runs. Toss: Durham. Both teams enjoyed century opening partnerships: Larkins and Glendenen put on 125 in 24 overs, and Oxford students Montgomerie and Gallian 103 in 32. The Universities lost their opening bowler, Hallett, to a back injury after he had bowled five overs.

Gold Award: W. Larkins.

Durham

W. Larkins c Storie b Pearson	73	†A. R. Fothergill not out	12
J. D. Glendenen c sub b Pearson	60	S. M. McEwan not out	1
D. M. Jones b Snape	6	L-b 3, w 5, n-b 1	9
*P. W. G. Parker b Snape	22		
I. T. Botham c Snape b Gallian	72	1/125 2/140 3/143 (6 wkts, 55 overs)	271
P. Bainbridge c and b Bovill	16	4/196 5/226 6/268	

P. J. Berry, S. P. Hughes and S. J. E. Brown did not bat.

Bowling: Hallett 5–2–21–0; Bovill 10–0–67–1; Usher 11–1–66–0; Pearson 11–2–31–2; Snape 11–0–44–2; Gallian 7–0–39–1.

Combined Universities

R. R. Montgomerie c and b Hughes	... 45	†S. F. Shephard not out	....	11
J. E. R. Gallian c Fothergill b Hughes	. 50			
*J. P. Crawley st Fothergill b Jones	... 42	L-b 8, w 8	....	16
J. N. Snape run out	 26			—
A. C. Storie lbw b Jones	 5	1/103 2/114 3/165	(5 wkts, 55 overs)	220
A. M. Hooper not out	 25	4/178 5/183		

J. C. Hallett, R. M. Pearson, B. C. Usher and J. N. B. Bovill did not bat.

Bowling: Brown 5-2-14-0; Botham 7-2-20-0; Bainbridge 10-0-41-0; McEwan 7-0-23-0; Berry 11-0-49-0; Hughes 8-0-31-2; Jones 7-0-34-2.

Umpires: G. I. Burgess and B. J. Meyer.

GLAMORGAN v WORCESTERSHIRE

At Cardiff, May 2. Worcestershire won by 97 runs. Toss: Glamorgan.
Gold Award: S. R. Lampitt.

Worcestershire

*T. S. Curtis c Barwick b Richards	 26	N. V. Radford not out	....	4
T. M. Moody c Croft b Cowdrey	 80	G. R. Haynes not out	....	3
G. A. Hick run out	 39	B 1, l-b 6, w 16	....	23
D. A. Leatherdale c Metson b Barwick	. 14			—
D. B. D'Oliveira c Frost b Richards	... 8	1/56 2/140 3/160	(7 wkts, 55 overs)	244
†S. J. Rhodes b Barwick	 25	4/168 5/190		
S. R. Lampitt c Croft b Richards	 22	6/234 7/238		

R. K. Illingworth and P. J. Newport did not bat.

Bowling: Frost 10-1-42-0; Barwick 11-2-32-2; Bastien 11-2-44-0; Richards 11-0-45-3; Croft 6-0-39-0; Cowdrey 6-0-35-1.

Glamorgan

S. P. James lbw b Radford	 1	S. R. Barwick lbw b Newport	....	5
H. Morris c Newport b Haynes	 40	S. Bastien not out	....	3
*M. P. Maynard b Lampitt	 16	M. Frost c Rhodes b Radford	....	4
I. V. A. Richards b Lampitt	 1	L-b 6, w 3, n-b 7	....	16
C. S. Cowdrey b Lampitt	 44			—
P. A. Cottey c Moody b Haynes	 2	1/2 2/28 3/36	(50.5 overs)	147
R. D. B. Croft c Lampitt b Illingworth	. 1	4/78 5/85 6/86		
†C. P. Metson b Illingworth	 14	7/124 8/132 9/139		

Bowling: Radford 8.5-4-15-2; Haynes 11-2-22-2; Lampitt 8-1-30-3; Newport 11-1-38-1; Illingworth 11-2-34-2; D'Oliveira 1-0-2-0.

Umpires: M. J. Kitchen and N. T. Plews.

DURHAM v DERBYSHIRE

At Jesmond, May 5. Derbyshire won by 80 runs. Toss: Durham. Reprieved on six, when Durham wicket-keeper Fothergill dropped him off Botham's bowling, Morris went on to his second Benson and Hedges hundred. His 121 came from 118 balls, and he hit 11 fours and four sixes. Durham's reply lost its way when four wickets fell in 18 balls after tea.
Gold Award: J. E. Morris.

Derbyshire

*K. J. Barnett b Bainbridge	28	†K. M. Krikken run out	5
P. D. Bowler lbw b Botham	8	D. G. Cork not out	5
J. E. Morris c Larkins b Brown	121	D. E. Malcolm c Parker b Hughes	2
T. J. G. O'Gorman c Glendenen		B 4, l-b 9, w 5, n-b 1	19
b McEwan	37		
C. J. Adams c Fothergill b McEwan	1	1/13 2/57 3/145 (9 wkts, 55 overs) 281
I. R. Bishop c Parker b Hughes	42	4/156 5/249 6/261
A. E. Warner run out	13	7/272 8/279 9/281

O. H. Mortensen did not bat.

Bowling: Botham 11–1–46–1; Brown 11–1–52–1; McEwan 11–1–54–2; Bainbridge 10–1–51–1; Hughes 11–0–52–2; Graveney 1–0–13–0.

Durham

W. Larkins lbw b Cork	58	S. M. McEwan c Barnett b Cork	9
J. D. Glendenen lbw b Mortensen	20	S. P. Hughes run out	0
D. M. Jones c Krikken b Mortensen	0	S. J. E. Brown not out	2
P. W. G. Parker run out	22	L-b 12, w 14, n-b 7	33
I. T. Botham c Krikken b Warner	6		
P. Bainbridge c Krikken b Mortensen	27	1/44 2/44 3/116 (46.2 overs) 201
†A. R. Fothergill lbw b Cork	3	4/117 5/123 6/134
*D. A. Graveney c Krikken b Cork	21	7/182 8/195 9/195

Bowling: Bishop 9–1–44–0; Mortensen 10–1–39–3; Malcolm 9–0–46–0; Warner 9–0–34–1; Cork 9.2–0–26–4.

Umpires: V. A. Holder and D. O. Oslear.

GLAMORGAN v COMBINED UNIVERSITIES

At Cardiff, May 5. Glamorgan won by 121 runs. Toss: Combined Universities. James, who played for the Universities in 1989 and 1990, scored his maiden hundred in limited-overs competition, striking eight fours and three sixes. He shared 140 for the second wicket with Dale.

Gold Award: S. P. James.

Glamorgan

S. P. James b Bovill	135	R. D. B. Croft not out	3
H. Morris c Shephard b Jeh	14		
A. Dale st Shephard b Snape	53	L-b 9, w 8, n-b 4	21
*M. P. Maynard run out	32		
C. S. Cowdrey c Usher b Gallian	11	1/30 2/170 3/225 (5 wkts, 55 overs) 277
P. A. Cottey not out	8	4/262 5/268

†C. P. Metson, S. Bastien, S. R. Barwick and D. J. Foster did not bat.

Bowling: Bovill 11–0–39–1; Jeh 11–0–37–1; Usher 6–0–24–0; Pearson 11–0–68–0; Snape 11–0–74–1; Gallian 5–0–26–1.

Combined Universities

R. R. Montgomerie b Dale	37	R. M. Pearson c James b Barwick	8
J. E. R. Gallian c Metson b Bastien	14	B. C. Usher c Maynard b Foster	15
*J. P. Crawley b Croft	6	J. N. B. Bovill not out	14
A. C. Storie c Maynard b Foster	6	L-b 2, w 7, n-b 3	12
J. N. Snape c Cowdrey b Croft	0		
A. M. Hooper c Morris b Croft	1	1/29 2/49 3/66 (9 wkts, 55 overs) 156
†S. F. Shephard c Metson b Barwick	23	4/67 5/70 6/74
M. P. W. Jeh not out	20	7/102 8/112 9/136

Bowling: Bastien 11–2–29–1; Foster 11–0–42–2; Barwick 11–2–29–2; Dale 9–2–24–1; Croft 11–3–28–3; Morris 1–0–1–0; Cottey 1–0–1–0.

Umpires: N. T. Plews and G. Sharp.

QUARTER-FINALS

HAMPSHIRE v MIDDLESEX

At Southampton, May 27. Hampshire won by six wickets. Toss: Hampshire. Hampshire's progress into the semi-finals was a stroll rather than a dash. Tight bowling, particularly by the off-spinner Udal, and some brilliant catching offset the fact that Marshall was injured after bowling five miserly overs. Udal worked through the middle and later order and Middlesex were dismissed inside 53 overs. Only Haynes batted to match his reputation, scoring his sixth consecutive one-day 50. When he was superbly caught on the boundary by the substitute Julian Wood in the 41st over, followed next ball by Carr, Middlesex lost their last six wickets for 30 runs. Hampshire could afford to pace their reply, and their anchor was Middleton, who continued his early-season form. When he went at 136, Gower and Nicholas added 56 in 11 overs. In the end they had four overs to spare.

Gold Award: S. D. Udal.

Middlesex

D. L. Haynes c sub b Connor	89	N. F. Williams run out		8
M. A. Roseberry c Udal b James	25	D. W. Headley c Smith b Udal		11
*M. W. Gatting c Maru b James	11	A. R. C. Fraser not out		0
M. R. Ramprakash c and b Maru	4	L-b 1, n-b 3		4
†K. R. Brown lbw b Udal	10			
J. D. Carr c Ayling b Connor	34	1/41 2/62 3/73	(52.4 overs)	206
P. N. Weekes c James b Udal	0	4/98 5/176 6/176		
J. E. Emburey lbw b Udal	10	7/178 8/190 9/204		

Bowling: Marshall 5-2-11-0; Connor 9.4-1-38-2; James 7-1-25-2; Maru 10-0-54-1; Ayling 10-0-37-0; Udal 11-1-40-4.

Hampshire

T. C. Middleton c Carr b Weekes	65	J. R. Ayling not out		0
K. D. James c Haynes b Weekes	30	L-b 1, w 2		3
R. A. Smith c Emburey b Carr	23			
D. I. Gower run out	49	1/44 2/102	(4 wkts, 51 overs)	207
*M. C. J. Nicholas not out	37	3/136 4/192		

M. D. Marshall, †A. N. Aymes, R. J. Maru, C. A. Connor and S. D. Udal did not bat.

Bowling: Williams 8-1-28-0; Fraser 10-1-35-0; Weekes 11-2-29-2; Emburey 9-0-56-0; Headley 8-0-40-0; Carr 5-1-18-1.

Umpires: D. J. Constant and R. Julian.

KENT v DERBYSHIRE

At Canterbury, May 27. Kent won by 33 runs. Toss: Kent. Having looked probable winners when Kent were struggling at 149 for eight, Derbyshire fell victim to crucial runs from the tailenders and their own disastrous start: Bowler, Morris and O'Gorman were all out for nought inside eight overs. Determined batting by Barnett kept the innings alive but the Kent spinners, Davis and Hooper, proved impossible to hit on a slow pitch and they maintained control throughout. Barnett was finally eighth out, with only two overs left and 49 still wanted. Kent had also struggled, mainly against Bishop. Only his fellow West Indian, Hooper, looked like overshadowing him and was in ominously good form before he fell to an excellent one-handed catch by Krikken.

Gold Award: R. P. Davis.

Kent

T. R. Ward c Cork b Bishop	6	R. P. Davis b Bishop		12
*M. R. Benson c Barnett b Warner	36	M. J. McCague b Goldsmith		30
N. R. Taylor c Morris b Goldsmith	29	A. P. Igglesden not out		0
C. L. Hooper c Krikken b Bishop	39	L-b 7, w 7, n-b 1		15
G. R. Cowdrey c Cork b Warner	1			
M. V. Fleming c O'Gorman b Warner	22	1/7 2/60 3/98	(54.1 overs)	193
†S. A. Marsh b Mortensen	3	4/105 5/126 6/136		
M. A. Ealham c Bowler b Bishop	0	7/137 8/149 9/193		

Bowling: Mortensen 11–3–17–1; Bishop 11–2–30–4; Cork 11–1–42–0; Warner 11–1–39–3; Goldsmith 5.1–0–25–2; Barnett 5–0–33–0.

Derbyshire

*K. J. Barnett c and b McCague	73	A. E. Warner not out		22
P. D. Bowler b Igglesden	0	D. G. Cork c McCague		0
J. E. Morris c Davis b Ealham	0	O. H. Mortensen not out		5
T. J. G. O'Gorman c and b Ealham	0	L-b 4, w 2, n-b 1		7
C. J. Adams c Davis b Hooper	18			
S. C. Goldsmith lbw b Hooper	9	1/3 2/4 3/10	(9 wkts, 55 overs)	160
†K. M. Krikken c and b Davis	6	4/43 5/67 6/80		
I. R. Bishop b Fleming	20	7/119 8/145 9/145		

Bowling: Igglesden 11–1–35–1; Ealham 8–2–19–2; McCague 6–0–22–2; Fleming 8–0–43–1; Hooper 11–3–20–2; Davis 11–4–17–1.

Umpires: J. C. Balderstone and K. E. Palmer.

SURREY v LANCASHIRE

At The Oval, May 27. Surrey won by 75 runs. Toss: Surrey. On the same strip where England had scored 302 in a one-day international five days earlier, Surrey surpassed them with a strong team performance in which nearly all their main batsmen hit form. Both teams had expected the pitch to turn and included an unusual number of spinners. In the event the match was won by the Bicknell brothers. Darren's 86 was his fifth half-century in six innings in the 1992 tournament (his other score was 37 not out). Later Martin removed Atherton and Speak in his opening spell and wiped out Hegg's late resistance. The opener Titchard, making his début in the competition, provided Lancashire's only performance of note and he was not removed until the 40th over, by Feltham, who finished the match by dismissing Fitton and Allott with successive balls.

Gold Award: M. P. Bicknell.

Surrey

D. J. Bicknell c Titchard b Allott	86	M. P. Bicknell run out		7
M. A. Lynch lbw b Fitton	54	N. M. Kendrick not out		1
*†A. J. Stewart b Fitton	64	B 1, l-b 8, w 5		14
A. D. Brown b DeFreitas	41			
G. P. Thorpe b DeFreitas	11	1/89 2/205 3/225	(7 wkts, 55 overs)	305
D. M. Ward not out	27	4/267 5/276		
M. A. Feltham run out	0	6/277 7/296		

J. Boiling and J. E. Benjamin did not bat.

Bowling: DeFreitas 11–0–51–2; Allott 11–1–56–1; Morrison 6–0–44–0; Fitton 11–0–56–2; Austin 11–0–56–0; Watkinson 5–0–33–0.

Lancashire

*M. A. Atherton b M. P. Bicknell	9	P. J. W. Allott c D. J. Bicknell		
S. P. Titchard c Benjamin b Feltham	82		b Feltham	9
N. J. Speak lbw b M. P. Bicknell	2	D. K. Morrison not out		0
G. D. Lloyd c Thorpe b Boiling	26			
M. Watkinson c Stewart b Boiling	25		B 2, l-b 4, w 2	8
P. A. J. DeFreitas c Lynch b Kendrick	3			
I. D. Austin run out	33	1/37 2/42 3/79	(48 overs) 230
†W. K. Hegg c Boiling b M. P. Bicknell	19	4/123 5/134 6/178	
J. D. Fitton c Kendrick b Feltham	14	7/199 8/216 9/230	

Bowling: Benjamin 7-0-47-0; M. P. Bicknell 10-0-43-3; Feltham 9-0-35-3; Kendrick 11-0-51-1; Boiling 11-2-48-2.

Umpires: M. J. Kitchen and B. J. Meyer.

WORCESTERSHIRE v SOMERSET

At Worcester, May 27. Somerset won by ten runs. Toss: Somerset. Cup-holders Worcestershire surrendered their trophy with a suicidal performance which dismayed a large crowd. Moody and Curtis appeared to have built a winning platform with an opening stand of 140 and Hick and Curtis then took the score to 198 for one. However, by then there were only eight overs left and panic set in. Hick and Curtis were out in the same over and six wickets fell for 13, three of them in 11 balls from Mallender, who had also been responsible for running out Curtis off his own bowling. Despite Haynes's staunchness, Worcestershire were all out in the final over. In contrast, Somerset's tail had wagged enthusiastically, adding 88 off the last ten overs after Lathwell had scored 93, his best in any competition. Moody's four for 59 helped him win the match award.

Gold Award: T. M. Moody.

Somerset

A. N. Hayhurst c Rhodes b Newport	10	N. A. Mallender not out		6
M. N. Lathwell c Leatherdale b Lampitt	93	H. R. J. Trump lbw b Lampitt		1
R. J. Harden c Rhodes b Illingworth	15	A. R. Caddick not out		6
*C. J. Tavaré c D'Oliveira b Moody	31		L-b 8, w 10	18
K. H. MacLeay c Rhodes b Moody	0			
G. D. Rose c D'Oliveira b Newport	30	1/31 2/69 3/149	(9 wkts, 55 overs) 256
†N. D. Burns c Radford b Moody	15	4/149 5/168 6/199	
R. P. Snell c Curtis b Moody	31	7/233 8/243 9/245	

Bowling: Radford 3-0-18-0; Haynes 10-1-38-0; Newport 11-2-38-2; Illingworth 11-0-38-1; Moody 11-0-59-4; Lampitt 9-0-57-2.

Worcestershire

*T. S. Curtis run out	78	G. R. Haynes not out		19
T. M. Moody c Burns b Caddick	80	P. J. Newport c MacLeay b Hayhurst		2
G. A. Hick lbw b Mallender	29	R. K. Illingworth b Snell		1
D. A. Leatherdale b Mallender	4		B 2, l-b 6, w 1, n-b 2	11
D. B. D'Oliveira c MacLeay b Mallender	3			
†S. J. Rhodes c Burns b Hayhurst	1	1/140 2/198 3/199	(54.4 overs) 246
S. R. Lampitt lbw b Snell	5	4/205 5/206 6/209	
N. V. Radford c Rose b Snell	13	7/211 8/226 9/234	

Bowling: Mallender 11-1-48-3; Caddick 11-0-37-1; Snell 10.4-0-47-3; Rose 3-0-17-0; MacLeay 10-0-41-0; Trump 3-0-17-0; Hayhurst 6-0-31-2.

Umpires: J. D. Bond and D. R. Shepherd.

SEMI-FINALS

HAMPSHIRE v SOMERSET

At Southampton, June 10. Hampshire won by six wickets. Toss: Somerset. Hampshire reached their second successive Lord's final, and third in five seasons, with a comfortable win. A hostile opening spell from Marshall and solid support from Connor put Hampshire on the way, and before lunch they restricted Somerset to 96 for four from 37 overs, suggesting that the contest might be reduced to anticlimax. Instead Rose played a violent innings of 65 in 61 deliveries, including three sixes. With eager support from Burns, in a sixth-wicket stand that added 72 in nine overs, he gave Somerset's bowlers something to defend. They sensed a chance when Middleton was caught in Mallender's first over, but while Terry occupied one end, Smith and then Gower quickly crushed their optimism, and Hampshire knocked off the runs with 11 balls to spare.

Gold Award: V. P. Terry.

Somerset

A. N. Hayhurst c James b Connor	11	N. A. Mallender run out	11
M. N. Lathwell c Aymes b Marshall	1	A. R. Caddick not out	1
R. J. Harden b Maru	13		
*C. J. Tavaré c Maru b Connor	28	L-b 7, w 12, n-b 3	22
K. H. MacLeay c Smith b Udal	25		
G. D. Rose c Gower b Connor	65	1/3 2/29 3/75 (8 wkts, 55 overs) 218
†N. D. Burns not out	39	4/85 5/107 6/179
R. P. Snell c Gower b Connor	2	7/186 8/215

H. R. J. Trump did not bat.

A. N. Hayhurst, when 3, retired hurt at 10 and resumed at 85.

Bowling: Marshall 11–3–37–1; Connor 11–3–32–4; Maru 11–1–26–1; James 11–0–58–0; Udal 11–0–58–1.

Hampshire

T. C. Middleton c Tavaré b Mallender	1	K. D. James not out	13
V. P. Terry not out	89	L-b 12, w 2, n-b 9	23
R. A. Smith run out	44		
D. I. Gower c Hayhurst b Rose	42	1/6 2/86 (4 wkts, 53.1 overs) 219
*M. C. J. Nicholas b Rose	7	3/170 4/186

M. D. Marshall, †A. N. Aymes, S. D. Udal, R. J. Maru and C. A. Connor did not bat.

Bowling: Mallender 9–2–44–1; Caddick 11–0–45–0; Rose 10–1–23–2; Snell 10.1–0–42–0; MacLeay 8–0–27–0; Trump 5–0–26–0.

Umpires: H. D. Bird and J. W. Holder.

KENT v SURREY

At Canterbury, June 10. Kent won by two wickets. Toss: Surrey. A match of fluctuating fortunes was always tense and reached a thrilling conclusion. Surrey recovered from the shock of losing three wickets in 23 balls thanks to Thorpe, who hit only three fours and ran 49 singles in two and a half hours. But Kent looked to be cruising to victory as Taylor and Hooper, with 50 in 46 balls, added 57 in 12 overs. Then Surrey's bowlers struck back to have them 139 for six, and when Fleming, after a hard-hitting innings, was eighth out in the 53rd over they must have fancied their chances. Seven were required off the final over and McCague cracked the first ball from Martin Bicknell through the covers for four. A single off the penultimate delivery enabled Kent to scramble home. Fleming's cavalier batting earned him his third Gold Award of the summer.

Gold Award: M. V. Fleming.

Surrey

D. J. Bicknell c Davis b Igglesden	13	N. M. Kendrick b McCague	24
M. A. Lynch c Hooper b Igglesden	9	J. Boiling b McCague	1
*†A. J. Stewart c Taylor b Ealham	5	J. E. Benjamin not out	0
G. P. Thorpe c Ealham b Fleming	82	L-b 5, n-b 1	6
D. M. Ward c Marsh b Ealham	7		
A. D. Brown c Marsh b Davis	16	1/22 2/27 3/27	(54.5 overs) 198
M. A. Feltham b McCague	35	4/41 5/91 6/152	
M. P. Bicknell lbw b Fleming	0	7/153 8/182 9/197	

Bowling: Igglesden 11–2–24–2; Ealham 11–2–30–2; Hooper 11–1–39–0; Davis 11–0–45–1; McCague 5.5–0–23–3; Fleming 5–0–32–2.

Kent

T. R. Ward lbw b M. P. Bicknell	4	R. P. Davis not out	12
*M. R. Benson c Lynch b Kendrick	17	M. J. McCague not out	7
N. R. Taylor c Stewart b Kendrick	41		
C. L. Hooper c Benjamin b Boiling	50		
G. R. Cowdrey c Lynch b Boiling	2	B 3, l-b 7, w 8	18
M. V. Fleming c Feltham b M. P. Bicknell	40		
†S. A. Marsh lbw b Feltham	3	1/14 2/45	(8 wkts, 54.5 overs) 199
M. A. Ealham c D. J. Bicknell b Benjamin	5	3/102 4/115	
		5/130 6/139	
		7/163 8/183	

A. P. Igglesden did not bat.

Bowling: M. P. Bicknell 10.5–2–24–2; Benjamin 11–2–25–1; Feltham 11–0–47–1; Kendrick 11–0–47–2; Boiling 11–0–46–2.

Umpires: B. Dudleston and R. Palmer.

FINAL

HAMPSHIRE v KENT

At Lord's, July 11, 12. Hampshire won by 41 runs. Toss: Kent. Hampshire won comfortably in the mid-afternoon of the second day, a Sunday remarkably well attended by about 8,000 supporters, who had travelled to Lord's knowing they would see less than 54 overs as Kent completed their innings started in the gloom of Saturday evening. Kent had defeated Hampshire in the NatWest Trophy during the week, and had high expectations of a double victory. But once the contest was transferred to the metropolitan stage, before a capacity crowd, Hampshire's power, class and experience were evident and decisive.

The weather forecast was gloomy, and all too accurate. The conditions prompted Benson to send in Hampshire, hoping that their rhythm would be interrupted. Hampshire in fact seized control from the first ten overs, in which they scored 37, and never lost their grip. A clear indication of the game's direction came in Benson's frequent use of his most penetrative bowler, Igglesden, who had finished his 11 overs by the mid-point of the innings. Terry was driving powerfully while Middleton improvised, and this well-matched opening pair had raised 68 in 19 overs when Middleton was leg-before to an inquisitive delivery from Hooper. Terry was bowled off his pads five overs later, which left Kent to contemplate Smith and Gower. By lunch, when the deluge arrived, Smith had scored 50; Gower, not at his best but always elegant, was 24 and Hampshire were 147. After 130 minutes' delay, play resumed in poor light, but for only five balls. The crowd waited patiently and then watched Fleming beat Gower's defence, Ealham catch Nicholas in the deep, and Marshall fling the bat. Smith was run out in the penultimate over, a long accurate throw from Taylor ending an innings of 90 off 108 balls, which all but the most partisan of Canterbury's pilgrims thought conclusive.

Kent started just before six o'clock, in light borrowed from November, needing 254, more than any county had ever made to win the Benson and Hedges Cup. Reprieved after eight balls, they resumed on a brighter, breezier morning, against Marshall, who, having missed Hampshire's two previous Lord's finals, was particularly fired up to win this one. With excellent support from Connor and Ayling, he ensured Kent were unable to bring the target into range. Benson played a sound captain's innings of 59, but was bowled trying to force the pace. The off-spinner, Udal, showed control and composure by taking three wickets, including Hooper's, though he paid heavily in runs as Kent belatedly blazed away. Ealham lifted Marshall for one six to wide long-on of such magnificence he is likely to remember it forever. Marshall, rightly, took the last wicket and was understandably emotional as he collected a Cup-winner's medal at last. And Mark Nicholas, who had missed the 1991 NatWest final through injury, was this time able to collect the trophy himself. – Derek Hodgson.

Gold Award: R. A. Smith.   *Attendance:* 22,177 (excl. members); *receipts* £543,526.
Close of play: First day, Kent 4-0 (1.2 overs) (T. R. Ward 1*, M. R. Benson 2*).

Hampshire

V. P. Terry b Igglesden	41	K. D. James not out	2
T. C. Middleton lbw b Hooper	27	L-b 3, w 3, n-b 4	10
R. A. Smith run out	90		—
D. I. Gower lbw b Fleming	29	1/68 (2) 2/86 (1) (5 wkts, 55 overs) 253
*M. C. J. Nicholas c Ealham b Fleming	25	3/171 (4) 4/205 (5)
M. D. Marshall not out	29	5/234 (3)

J. R. Ayling, †R. J. Parks, S. D. Udal and C. A. Connor did not bat.

Bowling: Igglesden 11–1–39–1; Ealham 9–0–46–0; McCague 11–0–43–0; Hooper 11–1–41–1; Davis 5–0–18–0; Fleming 8–0–63–2.

Kent

T. R. Ward c Parks b Marshall	5	R. P. Davis c Gower b Marshall	1
*M. R. Benson b James	59	A. P. Igglesden not out	1
N. R. Taylor c Parks b Ayling	8	B 1, l-b 11, w 5, n-b 4	21
C. L. Hooper b Udal	28		—
G. R. Cowdrey c Gower b Marshall	27	1/17 (1) 2/38 (3) (52.3 overs) 212
M. V. Fleming c Nicholas b Ayling	32	3/116 (2) 4/116 (4)
†S. A. Marsh b Udal	7	5/171 (6) 6/182 (7)
M. A. Ealham b Connor	23	7/186 (5) 8/194 (9)
M. J. McCague b Udal	0	9/204 (10) 10/212 (8)

Bowling: Connor 9.3–2–27–1; Marshall 10–1–33–3; Ayling 11–0–38–2; James 11–1–35–1; Udal 11–0–67–3.

Umpires: J. H. Hampshire and M. J. Kitchen.

BENSON AND HEDGES CUP RECORDS

Batting

Highest individual scores: 198*, G. A. Gooch, Essex v Sussex, Hove, 1982; 177, S. J. Cook, Somerset v Sussex, Hove, 1990; 173*, C. G. Greenidge, Hampshire v Minor Counties (South), Amersham, 1973; 158*, B. F. Davison, Leicestershire v Warwickshire, Coventry, 1972; 155*, M. D. Crowe, Somerset v Hampshire, Southampton, 1987; 155*, R. A. Smith, Hampshire v Glamorgan, Southampton, 1989; 154*, M. J. Procter, Gloucestershire v Somerset, Taunton, 1972; 154*, C. L. Smith, Hampshire v Combined Universities, Southampton, 1990. *In the final:* 132*, I. V. A. Richards, Somerset v Surrey, 1981. (226 hundreds have been scored in the competition. The most hundreds in one season is 24 in 1991.)

Most runs: 4,402, G. A. Gooch; 2,742, C. J. Tavaré; 2,658, D. W. Randall; 2,550, M. W. Gatting.

Fastest hundred: M. A. Nash in 62 minutes, Glamorgan v Hampshire at Swansea, 1976.

Most hundreds: 11, G. A. Gooch; 5, C. G. Greenidge, A. J. Lamb, W. Larkins and N. R. Taylor.

Highest totals in 55 overs: 388 for seven, Essex v Scotland, Chelmsford, 1992; 366 for four, Derbyshire v Combined Universities, Oxford, 1991; 350 for three, Essex v Oxford & Cambridge Univs, Chelmsford, 1979; 333 for four, Essex v Oxford & Cambridge Univs, Chelmsford, 1985; 331 for five, Surrey v Hampshire, The Oval, 1990; 330 for four, Lancashire v Sussex, Manchester, 1991; 327 for four, Leicestershire v Warwickshire, Coventry, 1972; 327 for two, Essex v Sussex, Hove, 1982; 325 for five, Middlesex v Leicestershire, Leicester, 1992; 321 for one, Hampshire v Minor Counties (South), Amersham, 1973; 321 for five, Somerset v Sussex, Hove, 1990. *In the final:* 290 for six, Essex v Surrey, 1979.

Highest total by a side batting second and winning: 291 for five (53.5 overs), Warwickshire v Lancashire (288 for nine), Manchester, 1981. *In the final:* 244 for six (55 overs), Yorkshire v Northamptonshire (244 for seven), 1987; 244 for seven (55 overs), Nottinghamshire v Essex (243 for seven), 1989.

Highest total by a side batting second and losing: 303 for seven (55 overs), Derbyshire v Somerset (310 for three), Taunton, 1990. *In the final:* 255 (51.4 overs), Surrey v Essex (290 for six), 1979.

Highest match aggregates: 613 for ten wickets, Somerset (310-3) v Derbyshire (303-7), Taunton, 1990; 602 runs for fourteen wickets, Essex (307-4) v Warwickshire (295), Birmingham, 1991; 601 runs for thirteen wickets, Somerset (307-6) v Gloucestershire (294-7), Taunton, 1982; 600 runs for sixteen wickets, Derbyshire (300-6) v Northamptonshire (300), Derby, 1987.

Lowest totals: 50 in 27.2 overs, Hampshire v Yorkshire, Leeds, 1991; 56 in 26.2 overs, Leicestershire v Minor Counties, Wellington, 1982; 59 in 34 overs, Oxford & Cambridge Univs v Glamorgan, Cambridge, 1983; 61 in 26 overs, Sussex v Middlesex, Hove, 1978; 61 in 25.3 overs, Essex v Lancashire, Chelmsford, 1992; 62 in 26.5 overs, Gloucestershire v Hampshire, Bristol, 1975. *In the final:* 117 in 46.3 overs, Derbyshire v Hampshire, 1988.

Shortest completed innings: 21.4 overs (156), Surrey v Sussex, Hove, 1988.

Record partnership for each wicket

252 for 1st	V. P. Terry and C. L. Smith, Hampshire v Combined Universities at Southampton		1990
285* for 2nd	C. G. Greenidge and D. R. Turner, Hampshire v Minor Counties (South) at Amersham		1973
269* for 3rd	P. M. Roebuck and M. D. Crowe, Somerset v Hampshire at Southampton		1987
184* for 4th	D. Lloyd and B. W. Reidy, Lancashire v Derbyshire at Chesterfield.		1980
160 for 5th	A. J. Lamb and D. J. Capel, Northamptonshire v Leicestershire at Northampton		1986
121 for 6th	P. A. Neale and S. J. Rhodes, Worcestershire v Yorkshire at Worcester		1988
149* for 7th	J. D. Love and C. M. Old, Yorkshire v Scotland at Bradford		1981
109 for 8th	R. E. East and N. Smith, Essex v Northamptonshire at Chelmsford.		1977
83 for 9th	P. G. Newman and M. A. Holding, Derbyshire v Nottinghamshire at Nottingham		1985
80* for 10th	D. L. Bairstow and M. Johnson, Yorkshire v Derbyshire at Derby . .		1981

Bowling

Most wickets: 147, J. K. Lever; 131, I. T. Botham.

Best bowling: Seven for 12, W. W. Daniel, Middlesex v Minor Counties (East), Ipswich, 1978; seven for 22, J. R. Thomson, Middlesex v Hampshire, Lord's, 1981; seven for 32, R. G. D. Willis, Warwickshire v Yorkshire, Birmingham, 1981. *In the final:* Five for 13, S. T. Jefferies, Hampshire v Derbyshire, 1988.

Hat-tricks (10): G. D. McKenzie, Leicestershire v Worcestershire, Worcester, 1972; K. Higgs, Leicestershire v Surrey in the final, Lord's, 1974; A. A. Jones, Middlesex v Essex, Lord's, 1977; M. J. Procter, Gloucestershire v Hampshire, Southampton, 1977; W. Larkins, Northamptonshire v Oxford & Cambridge Univs, Northampton, 1980; E. A. Moseley, Glamorgan v Kent, Cardiff, 1981; G. C. Small, Warwickshire v Leicestershire, Leicester, 1984; N. A. Mallender, Somerset v Combined Universities, Taunton, 1987; W. K. M. Benjamin, Leicestershire v Nottinghamshire, Leicester, 1987; A. R. C. Fraser, Middlesex v Sussex, Lord's, 1988.

Wicket-keeping and Fielding

Most dismissals: 122 (117 ct, 5 st), D. L. Bairstow.

Most dismissals in an innings: 8 (all ct), D. J. S. Taylor, Somerset v Oxford & Cambridge Univs, Taunton, 1982.

Most catches by a fielder: 61, G. A. Gooch; 53, C. J. Tavaré; 52, I. T. Botham.

Most catches by a fielder in an innings: 5, V. J. Marks, Oxford & Cambridge Univs v Kent, Oxford, 1976.

Results

Largest victories in runs: Essex by 272 runs v Scotland, Chelmsford, 1992, and by 214 runs v Oxford & Cambridge Univs, Chelmsford, 1979; Derbyshire by 206 runs v Combined Universities, Oxford, 1991; Yorkshire by 189 runs v Hampshire, Leeds, 1991; Sussex by 18 runs v Cambridge University, Hove, 1974.

Victories by ten wickets (16): By Derbyshire, Essex (twice), Glamorgan, Hampshire, Kent, Lancashire, Leicestershire (twice), Middlesex, Northamptonshire, Somerset, Warwickshire, Worcestershire, Yorkshire (twice).

WINNERS 1972-92

1972 LEICESTERSHIRE beat Yorkshire by five wickets.
1973 KENT beat Worcestershire by 39 runs.
1974 SURREY beat Leicestershire by 27 runs.
1975 LEICESTERSHIRE beat Middlesex by five wickets.
1976 KENT beat Worcestershire by 43 runs.
1977 GLOUCESTERSHIRE beat Kent by 64 runs.
1978 KENT beat Derbyshire by six wickets.
1979 ESSEX beat Surrey by 35 runs.
1980 NORTHAMPTONSHIRE beat Essex by six runs.
1981 SOMERSET beat Surrey by seven wickets.
1982 SOMERSET beat Nottinghamshire by nine wickets.
1983 MIDDLESEX beat Essex by four wickets.
1984 LANCASHIRE beat Warwickshire by six wickets.
1985 LEICESTERSHIRE beat Essex by five wickets.
1986 MIDDLESEX beat Kent by two runs.
1987 YORKSHIRE beat Northamptonshire, having taken more wickets with the scores tied.
1988 HAMPSHIRE beat Derbyshire by seven wickets.
1989 NOTTINGHAMSHIRE beat Essex by three wickets.
1990 LANCASHIRE beat Worcestershire by 69 runs.
1991 WORCESTERSHIRE beat Lancashire by 65 runs.
1992 HAMPSHIRE beat Kent by 41 runs.

WINS BY UNIVERSITIES

1973   OXFORD beat Northamptonshire at Northampton by two wickets.
1975 { OXFORD & CAMBRIDGE beat Worcestershire at Cambridge by 66 runs.
        { OXFORD & CAMBRIDGE beat Northamptonshire at Oxford by three wickets.
1976   OXFORD & CAMBRIDGE beat Yorkshire at Barnsley by seven wickets.
1984   OXFORD & CAMBRIDGE beat Gloucestershire at Bristol by 27 runs.
1989 { COMBINED UNIVERSITIES beat Surrey at Cambridge by nine runs.
        { COMBINED UNIVERSITIES beat Worcestershire at Worcester by five wickets.
1990   COMBINED UNIVERSITIES beat Yorkshire at Leeds by two wickets.

WINS BY MINOR COUNTIES AND SCOTLAND

1980   MINOR COUNTIES beat Gloucestershire at Chippenham by three runs.
1981   MINOR COUNTIES beat Hampshire at Southampton by three runs.
1982   MINOR COUNTIES beat Leicestershire at Wellington by 131 runs.
1986   SCOTLAND beat Lancashire at Perth by three runs.
1987   MINOR COUNTIES beat Glamorgan at Oxford (Christ Church) by seven wickets.
1990   SCOTLAND beat Northamptonshire at Northampton by two runs.
1992   MINOR COUNTIES beat Sussex at Marlow by 19 runs.

TEAM RECORDS 1972-92

	Rounds reached				Matches			
	W	F	SF	QF	P	W	L	NR
Derbyshire	0	2	3	7	96	49	40	7
Durham	0	0	0	0	4	2	2	0
Essex	1	5	8	13	110	70	39	1
Glamorgan	0	0	1	7	92	39	49	4
Gloucestershire	1	1	2	5	93	44	46	3
Hampshire	2	2	4	10	100	53	43	4
Kent	3	6	11	14	115	73	40	2
Lancashire	2	3	7	13	107	64	37	6
Leicestershire	3	4	5	8	102	57	39	6
Middlesex	2	3	5	13	106	57	41	8
Northamptonshire	1	2	3	8	97	44	45	8
Nottinghamshire	1	2	5	11	102	61	36	5
Somerset	2	2	7	10	103	57	44	2
Surrey	1	3	6	9	103	55	44	4
Sussex	0	0	1	8	94	47	46	1
Warwickshire	0	1	5	11	101	55	41	5
Worcestershire	1	4	6	12	106	55	47	4
Yorkshire	1	2	5	8	99	52	41	6
Cambridge University	0	0	0	0	8	0	8	0
Oxford University	0	0	0	0	4	1	3	0
Oxford & Cambridge Universities	0	0	0	0	48	4	42	2
Combined Universities	0	0	0	1	25	3	21	1
Minor Counties	0	0	0	0	53	5	45	3
Minor Counties (North)	0	0	0	0	20	0	20	0
Minor Counties (South)	0	0	0	0	20	0	19	1
Minor Counties (East)	0	0	0	0	12	0	12	0
Minor Counties (West)	0	0	0	0	12	0	12	0
Scotland	0	0	0	0	52	2	47	3

SUNDAY LEAGUE, 1992

Middlesex, a power in the land in every other competition in the 23 years since Sunday League cricket began in 1969, had somehow contrived never to win this one. They put that right in storming fashion in 1992, beginning the season with an unprecedented sequence of 12 consecutive victories and making certain of the title by August 16.

They became the 13th team to win the title, leaving Glamorgan, Gloucestershire, Northamptonshire, Surrey and, understandably, Durham, as the only first-class counties never to do so. Theirs would have been the third new name on the trophy in three years, except that a new one-off trophy had to be specially commissioned for Middlesex's benefit. For the first time, the League had no sponsor, following the withdrawal of Refuge Assurance, and at first no new company could be found, in recessionary times, for a tournament in which crowds and interest were dwindling. This followed the switch of televised matches from the BBC to the minority satellite channel, BSkyB.

Middlesex raced past Warwickshire's record of eight consecutive wins at the start of the season, set in 1980, and went on to pass the 11 successive wins of Kent in 1973 and Leicestershire in 1974. The sequence was halted by Hampshire at Southampton on August 2 and their final two games of

SUNDAY LEAGUE

	P	W	L	T	NR	Pts	Run-Rate
1 – Middlesex (11)	17	14	2	0	1	58	93.91
2 – Essex (6)	17	11	5	0	1	46	83.33
3 – Hampshire (17)	17	10	6	0	1	42	76.71
4 – Surrey (8)	17	10	7	0	0	40	90.46
5 { Somerset (8)	17	9	6	0	2	40	81.23
{ Kent (10)	17	8	5	0	4	40	89.84
7 – Worcestershire (4)	17	7	6	1	3	36	74.48
8 { Gloucestershire (12)	17	8	8	0	1	34	76.04
{ Durham (–)	17	7	7	0	3	34	89.11
{ Warwickshire (5)	17	7	7	1	2	34	82.55
11 { Sussex (12)	17	7	8	0	2	32	82.54
{ Lancashire (2)	17	6	7	0	4	32	84.07
13 { Northamptonshire (3)	17	7	9	0	1	30	83.21
{ Derbyshire (15)	17	7	9	0	1	30	81.06
15 – Yorkshire (7)	17	6	9	0	2	28	79.53
16 – Glamorgan (15)	17	4	10	0	3	22	86.21
17 – Nottinghamshire (1)	17	3	11	0	3	18	81.17
18 – Leicestershire (14)	17	3	12	0	2	16	81.08

1991 positions are shown in brackets.

When two or more counties finish with an equal number of points for any of the first four places, the positions are decided by a) most wins, b) runs per 100 balls.

No play was possible in the following eight matches: April 26 – Sussex v Yorkshire at Hove; July 5 – Kent v Lancashire at Maidstone; August 9 – Lancashire v Worcestershire at Manchester; August 12 – Kent v Nottinghamshire at Canterbury; August 30 – Durham v Yorkshire at Darlington, Glamorgan v Somerset at Cardiff, Leicestershire v Hampshire at Leicester, Worcestershire v Nottinghamshire at Worcester.

the season were a wash-out at Hove and a defeat at The Oval. This meant that they finished with 58 points, only equalling the record total set by Sussex in 1982 despite playing one game more because of Durham's promotion.

Most of the Middlesex victories were comprehensive and based on exceptional consistency from their major run-scorers, especially the West Indian Desmond Haynes, who scored 839 runs in 15 innings. Haynes scored ten fifties but no hundreds. The team totals of 3,505 runs and 27 fifties were both records; at least one batsman reached fifty in every match. For the early part of the season, they were pressed by the favourites Essex, who also won their first five matches. But Essex could not keep up the pace, especially when their team was weakened by Test calls. And they were horribly frustrated on August 9 when Gooch and Pringle had to sit out the crucial match against Middlesex at Lord's, even though the Test at The Oval had finished in the morning. This was due to regulations brought in after 1988, when Gooch took part in what was regarded as an unseemly dash in the other direction for a County Championship game at The Oval after the end of the Sri Lanka Test at Lord's. Middlesex won by 94 runs.

A lot of the counties seemed to play in streaks. In mid-June, the young Sussex team were only just behind the leaders with six wins and a wash-out from seven games. Then they lost their next seven and finished below halfway. Surrey had a run of six wins in a row in June and early July. Their batsmen scored seven centuries, including three for Darren Bicknell and two each for the captain Alec Stewart (in his last two games of the season) and their extraordinary new smiter Alistair Brown, who played at Sunday League pace even in the Championship. Bicknell finished the season with 651 league runs while his brother Martin took 26 wickets. In the end, Surrey finished fourth just behind Hampshire, whose 23-year-old off-spinner Shaun Udal was the league's leading wicket-taker with 31, at an average of 18.58 each. Martin McCague of Kent was his nearest rival, with 27 (at 16.96 each), followed by Bicknell on 26 and Ken MacLeay of Somerset and Allan Warner of Derbyshire on 23. Courtney Walsh had a better average than any of these, with 15 wickets at 16.66 each.

The newcomers Durham delighted the crowds which packed their all-ticket games with exciting wins in their first two matches. But they won only one more home game and finished equal eighth. Their Australian, Dean Jones, was the league's most spectacular run-scorer, with 656 (average 82) in the ten innings that were possible before he was called away on Test duty. After their grand start, they lost four in a row and then won four in a row. There were even more dramatic sequences at the bottom of the table. The most unexpected came from Nottinghamshire, the 1991 champions, who won their second match then lost their next nine. Beset by internal difficulties, they showed not even a glimmer of the previous year's form except against Middlesex when they came within one run of matching a total of 257 for five at Trent Bridge. The only teams they did manage to beat were the other three bottom teams, Yorkshire, Glamorgan and Leicestershire. Yorkshire won five games in a row and on June 28 were third in the table; they lost their next seven. Glamorgan had the other two of the five batsmen to pass 600, Matthew Maynard (650) and Hugh Morris (612), but still won only four games. Leicestershire, who were last of all, had the excuse of being diverted by their unexpected tilts at the County Championship and NatWest Trophy.

This competition marked the end of the 40-over format. It acquired some unlikely friends among the players when they realised they would be expected to play 50 overs a side from 1993. Initial objections to the other innovation, coloured clothing, came primarily from the more traditionally-minded spectators and journalists.

DISTRIBUTION OF PRIZEMONEY

Team awards
£25,000: MIDDLESEX.
£12,500 to runners-up: ESSEX.
£6,250 for third place: HAMPSHIRE.
£3,125 for fourth place: SURREY.
£275 each match to the winner – shared if tied or no result.

Individual awards
£300 for highest innings: C. J. Adams (Derbyshire), 141 not out v Kent at Chesterfield.
£300 for best bowling: K. H. MacLeay (Somerset), five for 20 v Worcestershire at Taunton.

Fastest televised fifty
£250 to S. R. Tendulkar (Yorkshire) – 33 balls v Lancashire at Leeds.

DERBYSHIRE

DERBYSHIRE v ESSEX

At Derby, April 19. Essex won by eight wickets. Toss: Essex. Ilott returned his best figures in the Sunday League in his first match for 11 months, during which he underwent an operation to fuse his vertebrae. Derbyshire collapsed from 100 for two to 121 all out.

Derbyshire

*K. J. Barnett c Gooch b Stephenson	31	A. E. Warner b Ilott		3
P. D. Bowler c Garnham b Topley	13	D. E. Malcolm c Waugh b Pringle		0
J. E. Morris c Waugh b Ilott	30	O. H. Mortensen c Garnham b Ilott		0
T. J. G. O'Gorman b Ilott	11	L-b 11, w 8, n-b 5		24
C. J. Adams lbw b Pringle	0			
†K. M. Krikken b Topley	5	1/28 2/80 3/100	(38.1 overs)	121
D. G. Cork b Such	3	4/103 5/106 6/114		
I. R. Bishop not out	1	7/114 8/119 9/120		

Bowling: Ilott 7.1–1–15–4; Pringle 7–0–22–2; Topley 8–0–22–2; Stephenson 8–0–22–1; Gooch 4–0–16–0; Such 4–0–13–1.

Essex

*G. A. Gooch c Morris b Bishop	19
J. P. Stephenson c Bowler b Mortensen	49
M. E. Waugh not out	37
N. Hussain not out	13
W 4	4

1/30 2/95   (2 wkts, 34.5 overs) 122

P. J. Prichard, N. V. Knight, †M. A. Garnham, D. R. Pringle, T. D. Topley, M. C. Ilott and P. M. Such did not bat.

Bowling: Bishop 6–1–14–1; Mortensen 8–1–26–1; Warner 5–1–32–0; Malcolm 8–0–21–0; Cork 7.5–0–29–0.

Umpires: D. R. Shepherd and R. C. Tolchard.

DERBYSHIRE v GLOUCESTERSHIRE

At Derby, May 10. Derbyshire won by 50 runs. Toss: Derbyshire. Rain during the Derbyshire innings limited the match to 36 overs. When three, Athey completed 6,000 Sunday League runs, but he was run out for 11 and Gloucestershire lost their last seven wickets in six overs.

Derbyshire

*K. J. Barnett c Hodgson b Ball	40	†K. M. Krikken c Russell b Walsh	1
*P. D. Bowler c Athey b Alleyne	44	D. G. Cork not out	1
J. E. Morris c Russell b Alleyne	0	L-b 8, w 3, n-b 2	13
T. J. G. O'Gorman run out	12		
C. J. Adams run out	10	1/77 2/77 3/100 (7 wkts, 36 overs) 153	
A. E. Warner not out	20	4/114 5/118	
R. Bishop run out	12	6/144 7/149	

R. W. Sladdin and O. H. Mortensen did not bat.

Bowling: Scott 8–0–30–0; Walsh 8–0–33–1; Babington 6–0–18–0; Smith 7–0–34–0; Ball 2–0–11–1; Alleyne 5–0–19–2.

Gloucestershire

G. D. Hodgson lbw b Sladdin	38	M. C. J. Ball c Barnett b Cork	5
S. G. Hinks c Krikken b Bishop	8	A. M. Babington not out	2
C. W. J. Athey run out	11	A. M. Smith b Cork	0
*A. J. Wright c Barnett b Warner	12	B 1, l-b 5, w 4, n-b 3	13
M. W. Alleyne c Adams b Warner	10		
†R. C. Russell b Adams b Bishop	3	1/22 2/48 3/72 (30 overs) 103	
C. A. Walsh c sub b Cork	1	4/86 5/91 6/91	
R. J. Scott c Krikken b Bishop	0	7/92 8/97 9/102	

Bowling: Bishop 7–0–18–3; Mortensen 8–1–22–0; Cork 6–0–26–3; Sladdin 4–1–15–1; Warner 5–0–16–2.

Umpires: J. C. Balderstone and R. A. White.

DERBYSHIRE v WORCESTERSHIRE

At Derby, May 17. Worcestershire won by seven wickets. Toss: Worcestershire. Hick and D'Oliveira achieved victory with 14 balls to spare after putting on 88 in 21 overs.

Derbyshire

*K. J. Barnett lbw b Lampitt	33	A. E. Warner not out	18
P. D. Bowler lbw b Radford	0	S. C. Goldsmith not out	7
J. E. Morris c Leatherdale b Lampitt	42	L-b 4, w 1	5
T. J. G. O'Gorman c Radford b Illingworth	30	1/0 2/71 3/80 (5 wkts, 40 overs) 152	
C. J. Adams run out	17	4/118 5/143	

†K. M. Krikken, S. J. Base, I. R. Bishop and O. H. Mortensen did not bat.

Bowling: Weston 8–1–24–0; Radford 8–1–30–1; Newport 8–0–38–0; Lampitt 8–2–25–2; Moody 4–0–10–0; Illingworth 4–0–21–1.

Worcestershire

*T. S. Curtis c Krikken b Warner	19	D. B. D'Oliveira not out	34
T. M. Moody b Base	31	L-b 6, w 3, n-b 4	13
G. A. Hick not out	51		
D. A. Leatherdale c Krikken b Warner	5	1/49 2/60 3/65 (3 wkts, 37.4 overs) 153	

†S. J. Rhodes, M. J. Weston, S. R. Lampitt, R. K. Illingworth, P. J. Newport and N. V. Radford did not bat.

Bowling: Mortensen 7–0–32–0; Bishop 8–0–28–0; Warner 8–1–25–2; Base 8–0–31–1; Goldsmith 6.4–0–31–0.

Umpires: R. Julian and B. J. Meyer.

DERBYSHIRE v NOTTINGHAMSHIRE

At Derby, May 24. Derbyshire won by 16 runs. Toss: Nottinghamshire. The return of their captain, Robinson, making his first one-day appearance of the season after injury, failed to save Nottinghamshire. They were 122 for one when he was run out by Goldsmith; then the last nine wickets fell for 64. Earlier Bishop had finished Derbyshire's innings with 36 from 27 balls.

Derbyshire

*K. J. Barnett b Lewis	6	I. R. Bishop not out	3.
P. D. Bowler run out	63	A. E. Warner not out	
C. J. Adams b Lewis	1	L-b 6, w 7	1.
T. J. G. O'Gorman c French b Cairns	28		
D. G. Cork run out	0	1/11 2/19 3/79 (7 wkts, 40 overs) 20.	
S. C. Goldsmith c Cairns b Field-Buss	20	4/81 5/112	
†K. M. Krikken b Lewis	27	6/133 7/180	

M. Jean-Jacques and O. H. Mortensen did not bat.

Bowling: Cooper 7–0–36–0; Lewis 8–1–34–3; Saxelby 4–0–14–0; Cairns 8–0–29–1; Field-Buss 7–0–40–1; Evans 6–0–43–0.

Nottinghamshire

B. C. Broad c Barnett b Cork	18	K. P. Evans not out	1.
D. W. Randall b Bishop	48	K. E. Cooper b Bishop	
*R. T. Robinson run out	48	M. G. Field-Buss b Bishop	2
P. Johnson c Krikken b Goldsmith	1	L-b 6, w 4	1.
C. C. Lewis c Mortensen b Warner	21		
M. Saxelby c Goldsmith b Warner	12	1/41 2/122 3/122 (39.5 overs) 18.	
C. L. Cairns b Cork	8	4/124 5/155 6/164	
†B. N. French b Warner	7	7/166 8/183 9/184	

Bowling: Mortensen 8–0–22–0; Bishop 7.5–0–31–3; Cork 8–0–40–2; Jean-Jacques 4–0–20–0; Warner 8–0–44–3; Goldsmith 4–0–23–1.

Umpires: J. D. Bond and M. J. Kitchen.

At Northampton, May 31. DERBYSHIRE lost to NORTHAMPTONSHIRE by eight wickets.

DERBYSHIRE v DURHAM

At Chesterfield, June 7. Derbyshire won by seven wickets. Toss: Derbyshire. Durham put down five chances on a gloomy day. Their batsmen had begun well, reaching 132 with only two wickets down in 30 overs, but insufficient acceleration left a target well within Derbyshire's reach.

Durham

W. Larkins lbw b Mortensen	3	†A. R. Fothergill not out	1.
D. M. Jones c Adams b Bishop	67	P. W. Henderson not out	2
P. W. G. Parker b Malcolm	17	L-b 11, w 6	17
P. Bainbridge c Warner b Malcolm	57		
J. D. Glendenen b Bishop	14	1/6 2/60 3/150 (6 wkts, 40 overs) 197	
I. Smith c Goldsmith b Malcolm	8	4/165 5/176 6/182	

S. P. Hughes, *D. A. Graveney and S. J. E. Brown did not bat.

Bowling: Mortensen 8–2–37–1; Bishop 8–0–25–2; Warner 8–0–24–0; Malcolm 8–0–52–3; Goldsmith 8–0–48–0.

Derbyshire

*K. J. Barnett c Glendenen	C. J. Adams not out 20
b Bainbridge . 53	
P. D. Bowler not out 77	L-b 7, w 8, n-b 1........... 16
S. C. Goldsmith st Fothergill b Smith .. 20	
T. J. G. O'Gorman c and b Graveney.. 15	1/97 2/148 3/168 (3 wkts, 37.1 overs) 201

A. M. Brown, †K. M. Krikken, I. R. Bishop, A. E. Warner, D. E. Malcolm and O. H. Mortensen did not bat.

Bowling: Hughes 7–0–35–0; Brown 7–0–23–0; Henderson 5–0–30–0; Bainbridge 8–0–41–1; Graveney 8–0–44–1; Smith 2–0–17–1; Jones 0.1–0–4–0.

Umpires: J. W. Holder and B. Leadbeater.

At Leeds, June 14. DERBYSHIRE lost to YORKSHIRE by 71 runs.

DERBYSHIRE v MIDDLESEX

At Derby, June 21. Middlesex won by 22 runs. Toss: Derbyshire. Carr dominated Middlesex's seventh straight Sunday League win, reaching 53 at a run a ball, and putting on 52 with Sims in the last five overs, then taking the vital wickets of Bowler and Adams.

Middlesex

D. L. Haynes c Krikken b Goldsmith .. 38	R. J. Sims not out 27
M. A. Roseberry c Barnett b Warner .. 25	
M. R. Ramprakash lbw b Goldsmith .. 18	L-b 15, w 2, n-b 4........... 21
J. D. Carr not out 53	
†K. R. Brown lbw b Cork 7	1/69 2/81 3/107 (5 wkts, 40 overs) 212
P. N. Weekes c Morris b Mortensen ... 23	4/124 5/160

*J. E. Emburey, N. F. Williams, A. R. C. Fraser and D. W. Headley did not bat.

Bowling: Mortensen 8–0–27–1; Warner 8–2–22–1; Base 8–0–58–0; Goldsmith 8–0–42–2; Cork 8–0–48–1.

Derbyshire

J. E. Morris c Ramprakash b Williams . 6	†K. M. Krikken run out 19
P. D. Bowler c Williams b Carr....... 15	S. J. Base c Sims b Headley 13
C. J. Adams c Carr................. 61	O. H. Mortensen not out............. 2
T. J. G. O'Gorman c Emburey b Fraser 41	L-b 3, w 7, n-b 2........... 12
*K. J. Barnett c Ramprakash b Fraser . 6	
A. E. Warner b Headley 2	1/9 2/54 3/104 (39.4 overs) 190
S. C. Goldsmith c Carr b Headley 8	4/115 5/124 6/142
D. G. Cork b Emburey 5	7/151 8/163 9/182

Bowling: Williams 6–2–16–1; Fraser 8–0–33–2; Emburey 7.4–0–34–1; Carr 8–1–29–2; Weekes 2–0–25–0; Headley 8–0–50–3.

Umpires: G. I. Burgess and G. A. Stickley.

DERBYSHIRE v LEICESTERSHIRE

At Derby, June 28. Derbyshire won by five wickets. Toss: Leicestershire. Bowler and Adams, who added 114 in 18 overs, set up a comfortable win. Adams's 75 took only 65 balls and featured three sixes; it was his third consecutive Sunday fifty.

Leicestershire

J. J. Whitaker c Morris b Cork	55	V. J. Wells not out	10
*N. E. Briers c Base b Warner	20	G. J. Parsons not out	5
B. F. Smith c Krikken b Goldsmith	12		
P. E. Robinson b Malcolm	59	L-b 12, w 8, n-b 5	25
J. D. R. Benson lbw b Goldsmith	0		
L. Potter b Malcolm	37	1/62 2/94 3/111 (8 wkts, 40 overs)	232
W. K. M. Benjamin b Base	1	4/112 5/192 6/199	
†P. A. Nixon c Base b Warner	8	7/208 8/222	

A. D. Mullally did not bat.

Bowling: Base 8–0–56–1; Malcolm 8–0–47–2; Warner 8–0–31–2; Cork 8–0–45–1; Goldsmith 8–0–41–2.

Derbyshire

P. D. Bowler not out	87	A. E. Warner not out	0
*J. E. Morris run out	35		
C. J. Adams c Benjamin b Potter	75	B 1, l-b 13, w 3	17
T. J. G. O'Gorman run out	8		
S. C. Goldsmith c Potter b Benjamin	2	1/72 2/186 3/203 (5 wkts, 38.5 overs)	233
D. G. Cork b Benjamin	9	4/217 5/229	

†K. M. Krikken, D. E. Malcolm, A. M. Brown and S. J. Base did not bat.

Bowling: Benjamin 7.5–0–32–2; Mullally 7–0–42–0; Wells 7–0–29–0; Parsons 8–0–61–0; Potter 8–0–45–1; Benson 1–0–10–0.

Umpires: G. I. Burgess and A. A. Jones.

At Taunton, July 5. DERBYSHIRE lost to SOMERSET by five wickets.

At The Oval, July 12. DERBYSHIRE lost to SURREY by three wickets.

At Pontypridd, July 26. GLAMORGAN v DERBYSHIRE. No result.

DERBYSHIRE v WARWICKSHIRE

At Leek, August 2. Derbyshire won by eight wickets. Toss: Warwickshire. Lloyd reached 50 from 29 balls on the small Leek ground, but Warwickshire's last nine wickets fell for 96. Derbyshire coasted to victory as Adams and Morris shared an unbroken partnership of 128 in 12 overs. Adams's unbeaten 75 came from 38 balls, with six sixes.

Warwickshire

A. J. Moles c Krikken b Mortensen	14	G. C. Small c Brown b Barnett	1
R. G. Twose c Krikken b Cork	47	G. Welch not out	4
*T. A. Lloyd c Barnett b Cork	50	T. A. Munton c Adams b Bishop	0
D. P. Ostler c Bowler b Malcolm	16	B 1, l-b 4, w 12, n-b 2	19
T. L. Penney c Adams b Malcolm	10		
Asif Din lbw b Cork	4	1/23 2/108 3/129 (36 overs)	204
P. A. Smith c Adams b Barnett	21	4/148 5/151 6/165	
†P. C. L. Holloway c Cork b Bishop	18	7/187 8/190 9/204	

Bowling: Mortensen 8–0–30–1; Bishop 6–1–20–2; Malcolm 8–0–47–2; Adams 4–0–40–0; Cork 6–0–39–3; Barnett 4–0–23–2.

Derbyshire

*K. J. Barnett c Ostler b Smith	....	41
P. D. Bowler c Twose b Welch	....	15
J. E. Morris not out	....	68
C. J. Adams not out	....	75
L-b 6, w 2, n-b 1	....	9

1/48 2/80   (2 wkts, 31.5 overs) 208

T. J. G. O'Gorman, †K. M. Krikken, D. G. Cork, I. R. Bishop, A. M. Brown, O. H. Mortensen and D. E. Malcolm did not bat.

Bowling: Munton 6–0–28–0; Welch 7.5–0–48–1; Twose 7–0–34–0; Smith 6–0–52–1; Small 3–0–17–0; Asif Din 2–0–23–0.

Umpires: R. Palmer and P. B. Wight.

At Eastbourne, August 9. DERBYSHIRE beat SUSSEX by 59 runs.

DERBYSHIRE v KENT

At Chesterfield, August 16. Derbyshire won by 48 runs. Toss: Kent. An awesome display of clean hitting by Adams gave Derbyshire a winning position. His unbeaten 141 was the season's best, Derbyshire's highest-ever Sunday score and was compiled in 105 minutes from 102 balls. He hit ten sixes, one caught by Malcolm on the pavilion balcony, and seven fours.

Derbyshire

*K. J. Barnett c Marsh b McCague	....	1	D. G. Cork not out	0
P. D. Bowler c Marsh b Ealham	.....	56		
J. E. Morris c Benson b Davis	....	27	L-b 1, w 4	5
C. J. Adams not out	....	141		
T. J. G. O'Gorman lbw b McCague	...	11	1/2 2/45 3/119 (5 wkts, 40 overs) 257	
†K. M. Krikken run out	....	16	4/166 5/257	

I. R. Bishop, A. E. Warner, D. E. Malcolm and O. H. Mortensen did not bat.

Bowling: McCague 8–0–76–2; Ealham 8–0–54–1; Hooper 8–1–19–0; Davis 8–0–46–1; Fleming 8–0–61–0.

Kent

T. R. Ward c Krikken b Warner	......	65	M. A. Ealham not out	43
*M. R. Benson b Mortensen	....	10	R. P. Davis c Cork b Malcolm	 3
N. R. Taylor b Malcolm	....	11	M. J. McCague c Adams b Warner	 1
C. L. Hooper c Krikken b Bishop	.....	11	L-b 12, w 4, n-b 2	 18
G. R. Cowdrey run out	....	11		
M. V. Fleming c Krikken b Warner	...	10	1/26 2/55 3/101 (37.2 overs) 209	
†S. A. Marsh c Adams b Warner	......	11	4/105 5/119 6/134	
N. J. Llong b Cork	....	15	7/139 8/188 9/200	

Bowling: Cork 8–0–43–1; Mortensen 8–0–30–1; Malcolm 8–0–66–2; Bishop 7–0–35–1; Warner 6.2–0–23–4.

Umpires: J. C. Balderstone and H. D. Bird.

At Southampton, August 23. DERBYSHIRE lost to HAMPSHIRE by seven wickets.

At Manchester, August 30. DERBYSHIRE lost to LANCASHIRE by five wickets.

DURHAM

DURHAM v LANCASHIRE

At Durham University, April 19. Durham won by nine runs. Toss: Lancashire. Durham's first home match as a first-class county took place in front of an excited crowd of around 6,000, the Racecourse ground's capacity. It could not have been scripted better. The Australian Jones announced his own and his team's arrival with the highest score ever made on début in the competition, hitting eight fours and four sixes; the last ten overs of Durham's innings yielded 90 runs. At 52 for four, Lancashire looked out of it. But they recovered, with DeFreitas blasting 33 off 11 balls. Lancashire needed ten to win off seven balls. Then Allott was caught at long-on. Morrison pushed the first ball of the 40th over to mid-on and tried for a single; Botham charged in and jubilantly threw down the wicket with Hegg well short of his ground. It was Lancashire's first away defeat in the Sunday League since they lost at Leicester in June 1989.

Durham

I. T. Botham st Hegg b Allott	14
W. Larkins c Austin b Atherton	59
D. M. Jones c Morrison b DeFreitas	114
P. Bainbridge c Fairbrother b Morrison	35
P. W. G. Parker not out	11
L-b 10, w 1, n-b 2	13

1/33 2/120   (4 wkts, 40 overs) 246
3/192 4/246

J. D. Glendenen, †A. R. Fothergill, S. M. McEwan, S. P. Hughes, *D. A. Graveney and S. J. E. Brown did not bat.

Bowling: Allott 8-0-30-1; Morrison 8-0-43-1; DeFreitas 8-0-53-1; Austin 7-0-46-0; Watkinson 5-0-34-0; Atherton 4-0-30-1.

Lancashire

G. Fowler c and b Hughes	27	†W. K. Hegg run out	22
M. A. Atherton c Hughes b McEwan	11	P. J. W. Allott c Parker b Brown	2
G. D. Lloyd c Brown b McEwan	4	D. K. Morrison not out	0
*N. H. Fairbrother c Botham b McEwan	2	B 1, l-b 8, w 4, n-b 1	14
N. J. Speak b Hughes	58		
M. Watkinson b Botham	37	1/38 2/48 3/52 (39.1 overs) 237
I. D. Austin lbw b Brown	27	4/52 5/121 6/168
P. A. J. DeFreitas b Brown	33	7/200 8/213 9/237

Bowling: McEwan 8-0-35-3; Brown 8-0-32-3; Hughes 7.1-0-31-2; Botham 8-0-57-1; Bainbridge 6-0-60-0; Graveney 2-0-13-0.

Umpires: N. T. Plews and A. G. T. Whitehead.

DURHAM v LEICESTERSHIRE

At Gateshead Fell, April 26. Durham won by eight runs. Toss: Leicestershire. Durham took 96 from their last 11 overs, including a stand of 58 in seven from Glendenen and Fothergill.

Durham

I. T. Botham b Mullally	67	*D. A. Graveney c Briers b Mullally	11
W. Larkins b Wells	17	S. M. McEwan not out	7
D. M. Jones c Benson b Parsons	21	L-b 5, w 5	10
P. W. G. Parker lbw b Millns	16		
P. Bainbridge c Millns b Benson	3	1/44 2/75 3/122 (7 wkts, 40 overs) 232
J. D. Glendenen c Whitticase b Benson	38	4/129 5/135
†A. R. Fothergill not out	42	6/193 7/214

S. P. Hughes and S. J. E. Brown did not bat.

Bowling: Mullally 8–0–42–2; Millns 8–0–45–1; Wells 8–0–44–1; Parsons 8–1–32–1; Benson 8–0–64–2.

Leicestershire

J. D. R. Benson c Bainbridge b Hughes	45	G. J. Parsons c Botham b Hughes	11
*N. E. Briers c Hughes b Bainbridge	36	D. J. Millns not out	1
J. J. Whitaker c and b Botham	0	A. D. Mullally not out	10
L. Potter c Glendenen b Bainbridge	21	B 1, l-b 5, w 2, n-b 1	9
B. F. Smith lbw b Graveney	31		
T. J. Boon run out	49	1/61 2/61 3/101 (9 wkts, 40 overs) 224	
V. J. Wells c McEwan b Hughes	4	4/116 5/147 6/164	
†P. Whitticase b Botham	7	7/176 8/205 9/210	

Bowling: McEwan 4–0–31–0; Brown 4–0–29–0; Botham 8–0–30–2; Hughes 8–0–46–3; Bainbridge 8–0–41–2; Graveney 8–0–41–1.

Umpires: B. Dudleston and J. H. Harris.

At Canterbury, May 10. KENT v DURHAM. No result.

DURHAM v NORTHAMPTONSHIRE

At Stockton-on-Tees, May 24. Northamptonshire won by six wickets. Toss: Durham. Durham suffered their first defeat in the Sunday League while Northamptonshire ended a run of seven consecutive one-day defeats when Bailey hit a six from the 22nd ball he faced.

Durham

I. T. Botham b Walker	8	*D. A. Graveney not out	11
W. Larkins c Ripley b Taylor	4	S. P. Hughes b Capel	0
D. M. Jones b Curran	26	S. J. E. Brown c Fordham b Taylor	1
P. Bainbridge run out	2	L-b 12, w 1	13
P. W. G. Parker b Curran	2		
J. D. Glendenen c Ripley b Capel	35	1/10 2/14 3/18 (35.3 overs) 124	
†A. R. Fothergill c Ripley b Capel	4	4/37 5/70 6/75	
S. M. McEwan b Capel	18	7/105 8/114 9/116	

Bowling: Walker 6–0–17–1; Taylor 7.3–1–15–2; Ambrose 6–1–10–0; Curran 8–0–29–2; Capel 8–1–41–4.

Northamptonshire

A. Fordham lbw b Botham	5	K. M. Curran not out	0
N. A. Felton c Brown b Bainbridge	27	W 4	4
*A. J. Lamb c Bainbridge b Graveney	42		
D. J. Capel st Fothergill b Graveney	16	1/8 2/58 (4 wkts, 30.3 overs) 127	
R. J. Bailey not out	33	3/87 4/118	

†D. Ripley, C. E. L. Ambrose, A. R. Roberts, J. P. Taylor and A. Walker did not bat.

Bowling: Botham 5–0–19–1; Hughes 8–0–22–0; Brown 5–0–25–0; Bainbridge 7–1–32–1; Graveney 5.3–0–29–2.

Umpires: B. J. Meyer and D. R. Shepherd.

At Southampton, May 31. DURHAM lost to HAMPSHIRE by two wickets.

At Chesterfield, June 7. DURHAM lost to DERBYSHIRE by seven wickets.

DURHAM v ESSEX

At Hartlepool, June 14. Essex won by 15 runs. Toss: Durham. Jones's second Sunday League hundred was not enough to secure victory. He lost the strike for the 39th over with 26 needed. Pringle then removed McEwan and conceded only one run. In the final over Jones fell just after reaching 100 in 115 balls. Hughes had trapped Gooch lbw with the third ball of the match, but Prichard led the Essex recovery.

Essex

*G. A. Gooch lbw b Hughes	0	D. R. Pringle c Botham b McEwan	37
J. P. Stephenson c Fothergill b Wigham	23	T. D. Topley not out	6
M. E. Waugh run out	22	L-b 4, w 2, n-b 1	7
P. J. Prichard c Larkins b Hughes	83		
N. V. Knight run out	28	1/0 2/46 3/46 (8 wkts, 40 overs) 220
N. Shahid c Smith b Graveney	10	4/108 5/129 6/139
†M. A. Garnham c Larkins b McEwan	4	7/207 8/220

P. M. Such and M. C. Ilott did not bat.

Bowling: Hughes 8–1–34–2; Wigham 8–1–43–1; McEwan 7–0–44–2; Bainbridge 8–1–39–0; Smith 5–0–37–0; Graveney 4–0–19–1.

Durham

I. T. Botham b Stephenson	27	S. P. Hughes not out	5
W. Larkins lbw b Topley	3	*D. A. Graveney not out	2
D. M. Jones c Knight b Ilott	100		
P. W. G. Parker c Shahid b Waugh	10	L-b 4, w 5, n-b 1	10
P. Bainbridge c Gooch b Ilott	41		
I. Smith c Topley b Pringle	3	1/7 2/48 3/80 (8 wkts, 40 overs) 205
†A. R. Fothergill c Topley b Ilott	4	4/163 5/169 6/191
S. M. McEwan c Such b Pringle	0	7/195 8/198

G. Wigham did not bat.

Bowling: Topley 6–1–31–1; Ilott 8–0–40–3; Stephenson 6–0–23–1; Pringle 8–0–37–2; Such 6–0–30–0; Waugh 6–0–40–1.

Umpires: J. H. Hampshire and M. J. Kitchen.

At Horsham, June 21. DURHAM beat SUSSEX by five runs.

DURHAM v GLOUCESTERSHIRE

At Stockton-on-Tees, July 5. Durham won by six wickets. Toss: Durham. Jones survived a stumping chance when 41 to pass 50 for the fifth time in consecutive Sunday innings as he steered Durham to victory in the final over. Wright had hit four sixes against an attack which lost captain Graveney to a knee injury in the 15th over.

Gloucestershire

G. D. Hodgson run out	12	R. I. Dawson not out	0
M. W. Alleyne c Fothergill b Botham	32		
C. W. J. Athey lbw b Jones	38	L-b 6, w 1, n-b 1	8
*A. J. Wright c Jones b Hughes	93		
R. J. Scott not out	39	1/31 2/59 3/117 (5 wkts, 40 overs) 226
S. G. Hinks c Larkins b Botham	4	4/210 5/219

†R. C. J. Williams, R. C. Williams, A. M. Smith and A. M. Babington did not bat.

Bowling: Hughes 8–0–47–1; Brown 8–0–56–0; McEwan 5–2–13–0; Botham 8–1–34–2; Smith 5–0–33–0; Jones 6–0–37–1.

Durham

I. T. Botham c and b Smith	23	I. Smith not out	23
W. Larkins c R. C. J. Williams b Scott	20	B 1, l-b 6, w 1, n-b 2	10
D. M. Jones not out	81		
P. W. G. Parker c Hinks b Alleyne	19	1/41 2/46	(4 wkts, 39.1 overs) 228
J. D. Glendenen run out	52	3/85 4/182	

†A. R. Fothergill, *D. A. Graveney, S. P. Hughes, S. M. McEwan and S. J. E. Brown did not bat.

Bowling: Babington 6.1-0-40-0; Smith 8-0-42-1; Scott 7-0-44-1; R. C. Williams 6-0-32-0; Alleyne 8-0-40-1; Athey 4-0-23-0.

Umpires: A. A. Jones and G. A. Stickley.

At Taunton, July 12. DURHAM beat SOMERSET by 11 runs.

At Nottingham, July 19. DURHAM beat NOTTINGHAMSHIRE by 21 runs.

At Lord's, July 26. DURHAM lost to MIDDLESEX by seven wickets.

DURHAM v SURREY

At Durham University, August 2. Surrey won by 100 runs. Toss: Durham. Surrey's massive 330 for six – in 39 overs – was the second-highest total in the history of the Sunday League, behind only Somerset's 360 for three against Glamorgan at Neath in 1990. Darren Bicknell scored 125 from 116 balls, with 14 fours and a six, but in an opening stand of 117 in 16 overs he was completely overshadowed by Brown's 75 from 46 balls. Durham's attempt at a reply was wrecked when they fell from 78 for one to 89 for four.

Surrey

D. J. Bicknell c Briers b Hughes	125	G. P. Thorpe not out	3
A. D. Brown c Smith b Botham	75	J. D. Robinson not out	3
D. M. Ward b Graveney	45	B 4, l-b 16, w 11, n-b 1	32
*†A. J. Stewart c and b Graveney	9		
A. J. Hollioake b Hughes	22	1/117 2/210 3/251	(6 wkts, 39 overs) 330
M. A. Lynch c Smith b Briers	16	4/298 5/315 6/325	

M. A. Feltham, J. Boiling and M. P. Bicknell did not bat.

Bowling: McEwan 6-0-57-0; Wood 5-0-26-0; Graveney 8-0-51-2; Botham 5-0-39-1; Hughes 8-0-72-2; Smith 2-0-18-0; Briers 5-0-47-1.

Durham

I. T. Botham run out	52	J. Wood not out	4
W. Larkins c Stewart b M. P. Bicknell	9		
G. Cook c Stewart b Robinson	14	L-b 6, w 5, n-b 1	12
I. Smith c Thorpe b Hollioake	3		
J. D. Glendenen c Brown b Boiling	28	1/32 2/78 3/83	(7 wkts, 39 overs) 230
M. P. Briers c and b Boiling	69	4/89 5/146	
†A. R. Fothergill c Ward b Boiling	39	6/217 7/230	

S. M. McEwan, *D. A. Graveney and S. P. Hughes did not bat.

Bowling: M. P. Bicknell 8-0-48-1; Feltham 8-0-45-0; Hollioake 8-0-37-1; Robinson 7-0-46-1; Boiling 8-0-48-3.

Umpires: M. J. Kitchen and D. O. Oslear.

At Birmingham, August 9. DURHAM beat WARWICKSHIRE by 17 runs.

DURHAM v GLAMORGAN

At Hartlepool, August 16. Glamorgan won by 16 runs. Toss: Durham. Morris and Maynard both broke Morris's own Glamorgan record of 587 runs in a Sunday League season set in 1986: Morris reached 612 and Maynard 650.

Glamorgan

S. P. James st Fothergill b Graveney	63	†C. P. Metson c McEwan b Hughes	6
H. Morris c Botham b Wood	26	D. J. Foster not out	2
*M. P. Maynard c Smith b Graveney	65	B 1, l-b 9, w 5, n-b 1	16
I. V. A. Richards lbw b Smith	2		
A. Dale c and b Smith	6	1/39 2/153 3/156 (7 wkts, 40 overs) 216	
D. L. Hemp c and b Smith	4	4/168 5/170	
R. D. B. Croft not out	26	6/176 7/191	

S. D. Thomas and S. Bastien did not bat.

Bowling: Wood 6-0-33-1; Hughes 7-1-27-1; McEwan 5-0-38-0; Botham 6-0-36-0; Graveney 8-0-40-2; Smith 8-1-32-3.

Durham

I. T. Botham c Foster b Bastien	9	S. M. McEwan not out	13
W. Larkins c Metson b Thomas	9	*D. A. Graveney b Richards	2
J. D. Glendenen c Croft b Dale	15	S. P. Hughes not out	10
M. P. Briers run out	32	L-b 7, w 6, n-b 5	18
S. Hutton b Richards	70		
I. Smith c Morris b Foster	18	1/20 2/22 3/66 (9 wkts, 40 overs) 200	
†A. R. Fothergill b Foster	0	4/95 5/128 6/139	
J. Wood st Metson b Richards	4	7/159 8/178 9/186	

Bowling: Thomas 8-1-34-1; Bastien 8-0-24-1; Dale 8-0-55-1; Foster 8-1-37-2; Richards 8-0-43-3.

Umpires: D. J. Constant and R. C. Tolchard.

At Worcester, August 23. WORCESTERSHIRE v DURHAM. No result.

DURHAM v YORKSHIRE

At Darlington, August 30. No result.

ESSEX

At Derby, April 19. ESSEX beat DERBYSHIRE by eight wickets.

ESSEX v SURREY

At Chelmsford, April 26. Essex won by ten wickets. Toss: Essex. Essex became the first county to notch up 200 wins in the Sunday League, after a ten-overs match staged when an earlier 31-overs match was abandoned because of rain; Surrey were then ten for no wicket from 2.1 overs. Gooch hit six fours in 28 balls, and his partner Stephenson faced 26. When four, Greig reached 2,000 runs in the competition.

Surrey

D. J. Bicknell c Gooch b Foster	15	R. E. Bryson not out	3
A. D. Brown lbw b Stephenson	22	J. E. Benjamin c Gooch b Ilott	7
*†A. J. Stewart b Stephenson	1		
G. P. Thorpe lbw b Pringle	6	B 2, l-b 3, w 5	10
M. A. Lynch c Stephenson b Pringle	5		
D. M. Ward c Knight b Stephenson	1	1/26 2/39 3/46 (9 wkts, 10 overs) 84	
I. A. Greig c Stephenson b Pringle	7	4/55 5/56 6/62	
J. D. Robinson b Ilott	7	7/71 8/73 9/84	

J. Boiling did not bat.

Bowling: Foster 2–0–16–1; Topley 2–0–22–0; Stephenson 2–0–10–3; Pringle 2–0–16–3; Ilott 2–0–15–2.

Essex

*G. A. Gooch not out	48
J. P. Stephenson not out	38
W 1, n-b 1	2

(no wkt, 8.4 overs) 88

M. E. Waugh, N. Hussain, N. V. Knight, D. R. Pringle, J. J. B. Lewis, †M. A. Garnham, T. D. Topley, M. C. Ilott and N. A. Foster did not bat.

Bowling: Boiling 2–0–12–0; Greig 2–0–27–0; Benjamin 1.4–0–22–0; Robinson 2–0–14–0; Bryson 1–0–13–0.

Umpires: J. H. Hampshire and K. E. Palmer.

At Leicester, May 3. ESSEX beat LEICESTERSHIRE by three wickets.

ESSEX v NORTHAMPTONSHIRE

At Chelmsford, May 10. Essex won by four wickets. Toss: Essex. Essex became clear Sunday League leaders after Gooch and Waugh set up victory with an 82-run stand in only 13 overs for the second wicket. Their good work was continued by Prichard and Knight until Prichard's innings came to a painful end, lbw to a delivery from Taylor which broke his toe.

Northamptonshire

A. Fordham lbw b Pringle	26	†D. Ripley not out	11
N. A. Felton c Prichard b Stephenson	28		
*R. J. Bailey b Ilott	19	B 4, l-b 11, w 5, n-b 2	22
N. A. Stanley c Topley b Stephenson	9		
D. J. Capel b Ilott	38	1/56 2/86 3/87 (5 wkts, 33 overs) 180	
M. B. Loye not out	27	4/114 5/146	

N. G. B. Cook, J. P. Taylor, C. E. L. Ambrose and A. Walker did not bat.

Bowling: Topley 8–1–34–0; Ilott 8–1–38–2; Pringle 8–0–41–1; Stephenson 8–0–44–2; Gooch 1–0–8–0.

Essex

*G. A. Gooch c Loye b Capel	48	D. R. Pringle not out	1
J. P. Stephenson c Ripley b Taylor	6	†M. A. Garnham not out	8
M. E. Waugh c Bailey b Capel	45	L-b 5, n-b 2	7
N. Hussain run out	8		
P. J. Prichard lbw b Taylor	25	1/20 2/102 3/112 (6 wkts, 32.2 overs) 183	
N. V. Knight c Felton b Taylor	35	4/112 5/174 6/174	

T. D. Topley, M. C. Ilott and P. M. Such did not bat.

Bowling: Ambrose 8-0-31-0; Taylor 8-0-38-3; Capel 8-0-40-2; Walker 5.2-0-46-0; Cook 3-0-23-0.

Umpires: A. A. Jones and D. R. Shepherd.

ESSEX v GLAMORGAN

At Chelmsford, May 24. Essex won by eight wickets. Toss: Essex. Both captains, Maynard and Gooch, scored 75 from 69 balls; but Gooch, supported by Stephenson, took Essex to their fifth win in five Sunday League games, while Glamorgan sank to their fourth consecutive defeat.

Glamorgan

S. P. James c Garnham b Fraser	13	R. D. B. Croft not out	1
H. Morris c Hussain b Such	19		
A. Dale run out	48	B 1, l-b 5, w 10, n-b 3	19
*M. P. Maynard c Knight b Pringle	75		
C. S. Cowdrey c Knight b Pringle	17	1/23 2/53 3/150 (5 wkts, 40 overs)	194
P. A. Cottey not out	2	4/190 5/190	

S. Bastien, †C. P. Metson, S. L. Watkin and S. R. Barwick did not bat.

Bowling: Topley 8-1-25-0; Pringle 8-0-35-2; Fraser 6-0-24-1; Stephenson 7-0-40-0; Such 5-0-28-1; Waugh 6-0-36-0.

Essex

*G. A. Gooch c Maynard b Cowdrey	75		
J. P. Stephenson c Maynard b Bastien	59		
M. E. Waugh not out	29		
N. Hussain not out	27		
B 1, l-b 1, w 1, n-b 2	5		

1/128 2/150   (2 wkts, 35.4 overs) 195

P. J. Prichard, N. V. Knight, D. R. Pringle, †M. A. Garnham, T. D. Topley, A. G. J. Fraser and P. M. Such did not bat.

Bowling: Bastien 5-0-32-1; Watkin 8-0-40-0; Barwick 8-0-49-0; Dale 8-1-30-0; Croft 3-0-25-0; Cowdrey 3-0-15-1; Maynard 0.4-0-2-0.

Umpires: R. Palmer and G. A. Stickley.

At Worcester, May 31. ESSEX lost to WORCESTERSHIRE by two wickets.

ESSEX v KENT

At Chelmsford, June 7. Essex won by six runs. Toss: Kent. The match was dominated by Waugh, who hit eight fours and three sixes, two in one over from Ealham, and faced only 84 balls for his unbeaten 105. Later he dismissed the potential dangers of Hooper and Fleming, and to round off his day took a running catch.

Essex

P. J. Prichard c Cowdrey b Fleming	22	†M. A. Garnham b McCague	6
J. P. Stephenson c McCague	30	T. D. Topley not out	2
M. E. Waugh not out	105	B 6, l-b 3, w 6	15
N. Hussain b Hooper	1		
N. V. Knight st Kersey b Davis	27	1/45 2/71 3/75 (7 wkts, 40 overs)	229
*N. A. Foster c Hooper b Davis	11	4/146 5/158	
N. Shahid c Hooper b Ealham	10	6/183 7/227	

M. C. Ilott and P. M. Such did not bat.

Bowling: Ealham 8–0–57–1; McCague 8–0–33–2; Hooper 8–0–17–1; Fleming 8–0–49–1; Davis 8–0–64–2.

Kent

T. R. Ward c Hussain b Ilott	27	R. P. Davis run out	2
*M. R. Benson c Garnham b Stephenson	64	M. J. McCague c Such b Ilott	16
N. R. Taylor c Shahid b Topley	18	†G. J. Kersey not out	0
C. L. Hooper lbw b Waugh	6	B 6, l-b 8, w 8	22
G. R. Cowdrey run out	5		
M. V. Fleming c Knight b Waugh	19	1/38 2/86 3/130 (9 wkts, 40 overs) 223
N. J. Llong not out	44	4/132 5/137 6/169
M. A. Ealham c Waugh b Ilott	0	7/169 8/176 9/213

Bowling: Foster 6–0–35–0; Ilott 8–0–45–3; Stephenson 8–1–46–1; Topley 8–0–21–1; Such 4–0–24–0; Waugh 6–1–38–2.

Umpires: B. Dudleston and R. Julian.

At Hartlepool, June 14. ESSEX beat DURHAM by 15 runs.

At Bournemouth, June 21. ESSEX lost to HAMPSHIRE by eight wickets.

ESSEX v LANCASHIRE

At Ilford, June 28. Essex won by seven wickets. Toss: Lancashire. Essex followed up their two-day Championship victory over Lancashire by overhauling their visitors' 238 with two overs to spare. Speak had put on a fine show, hitting four sixes as he added 119 in 24 overs with Atherton. But Gooch and Prichard responded with 120 in 23. When 62, the Essex captain reached 7,000 runs in the league, a distinction shared only with D. L. Amiss.

Lancashire

G. Fowler lbw b Childs	16	S. P. Titchard c Gooch b Pringle	8
*M. A. Atherton c Topley b Waugh	57	†W. K. Hegg not out	15
N. J. Speak c and b Childs	68	L-b 11, w 2, n-b 2	15
G. D. Lloyd lbw b Topley	7		
M. Watkinson c Prichard b Such	21	1/30 2/149 3/156 (7 wkts, 40 overs) 238
P. A. J. DeFreitas c Knight b Pringle	4	4/172 5/184
I. D. Austin not out	27	6/194 7/223

J. D. Fitton and P. J. Martin did not bat.

Bowling: Pringle 8–0–58–2; Topley 8–0–34–1; Childs 8–1–30–2; Such 8–0–56–1; Waugh 8–0–49–1.

Essex

*G. A. Gooch b DeFreitas	79	N. V. Knight not out	19
P. J. Prichard c Titchard b Fitton	60	L-b 15, w 4, n-b 2	21
M. E. Waugh not out	61		
N. Hussain c Hegg b Austin	2	1/120 2/195 3/201 (3 wkts, 38 overs) 242

N. Shahid, D. R. Pringle, †M. A. Garnham, T. D. Topley, J. H. Childs and P. M. Such did not bat.

Bowling: DeFreitas 8–0–56–1; Martin 8–0–42–0; Austin 8–0–32–1; Watkinson 8–0–55–0; Fitton 6–0–42–1.

Umpires: D. J. Constant and B. Dudleston.

At Birmingham, July 5. ESSEX lost to WARWICKSHIRE by 24 runs.

At Scarborough, July 12. ESSEX beat YORKSHIRE by three wickets.

ESSEX v SUSSEX

At Southend, July 19. Essex won by eight wickets. Toss: Essex. On a batsman's pitch, Wells reached his maiden Sunday hundred in 92 balls; his second 50 took only 26, and he hit 13 fours and a six. Sussex's last ten overs yielded 108 runs. Undaunted, Gooch and Stephenson put on 110 in 18 overs, and then Waugh and Prichard raced on to win the game with more than three overs to spare.

Sussex

K. Greenfield lbw b Foster	1	†P. Moores c Pringle b Ilott 24
J. W. Hall c Garnham b Pringle	52	A. C. S. Pigott not out 7
M. P. Speight lbw b Such	23	L-b 5, w 13, n-b 2.......... 20
*A. P. Wells not out	110	
F. D. Stephenson run out	0	1/5 2/69 3/101　　(6 wkts, 40 overs) 239
N. J. Lenham c Stephenson b Such	2	4/110 5/115 6/192

B. T. P. Donelan, I. D. K. Salisbury and A. G. Robson did not bat.

Bowling: Ilott 7–0–55–1; Foster 8–0–44–1; Pringle 8–1–39–1; Such 8–0–29–2; Topley 7–0–53–0; Stephenson 2–0–14–0.

Essex

*G. A. Gooch b Salisbury	50
J. P. Stephenson b Salisbury	64
M. E. Waugh not out	69
P. J. Prichard not out	52
L-b 3, w 2	5

1/110 2/137　　(2 wkts, 36.5 overs) 240

N. Hussain, N. A. Foster, D. R. Pringle, †M. A. Garnham, T. D. Topley, M. C. Ilott and P. M. Such did not bat.

Bowling: Robson 6–0–31–0; Stephenson 6–0–39–0; Lenham 7–0–38–0; Pigott 5.5–0–57–0; Salisbury 8–0–32–2; Greenfield 2–0–17–0; Donelan 2–0–23–0.

Umpires: V. A. Holder and N. T. Plews.

At Lord's, August 9. ESSEX lost to MIDDLESEX by 94 runs.

ESSEX v NOTTINGHAMSHIRE

At Colchester, August 16. Essex won by 11 runs. Toss: Nottinghamshire. The champions Nottinghamshire sank to their 11th defeat of the season, as they found too little acceleration to chase a modest target.

Essex

*G. A. Gooch st Bramhall b Field-Buss	55	T. D. Topley not out 3
J. P. Stephenson lbw b Mike	24	M. C. Ilott not out 2
P. J. Prichard lbw b Lewis	47	B 4, l-b 4, w 8, n-b 4 20
N. Hussain st Bramhall b Field-Buss	6	
D. R. Pringle run out	3	1/73 2/127 3/137　　(7 wkts, 40 overs) 176
N. V. Knight c Randall b Cairns	13	4/146 5/167
J. J. B. Lewis run out	3	6/167 7/174

†A. D. Brown and P. M. Such did not bat.

Bowling: Mike 8–0–33–1; Lewis 8–1–34–1; Cairns 8–1–27–1; Crawley 8–0–33–0; Field-Buss 8–0–41–2.

Nottinghamshire

B. C. Broad b Ilott	63	P. R. Pollard not out		20
D. W. Randall b Stephenson	10	M. A. Crawley not out		8
C. C. Lewis c Brown b Such	16	B 1, l-b 3, w 4, n-b 2		10
*R. T. Robinson c Pringle b Topley	9			
C. L. Cairns c Ilott b Stephenson	28	1/33 2/51 3/66	(6 wkts, 40 overs)	165
G. W. Mike run out	1	4/118 5/124 6/144		

M. G. Field-Buss, †S. Bramhall and G. F. Archer did not bat.

Bowling: Ilott 7–1–44–1; Pringle 8–2–28–0; Topley 8–0–36–1; Stephenson 8–1–18–2; Such 8–0–28–1; Gooch 1–0–7–0.

Umpires: D. O. Oslear and R. A. White.

At Weston-super-Mare, August 23. SOMERSET v ESSEX. No result.

ESSEX v GLOUCESTERSHIRE

At Chelmsford, August 30. Gloucestershire won on scoring-rate. Toss: Essex. An inexperienced Essex team were well behind the required rate of six an over when rain ended play. Gloucestershire had opened with 137 in 23 overs from Hodgson and Alleyne.

Gloucestershire

G. D. Hodgson c Lewis b Stephenson	73	J. T. C. Vaughan lbw b Stephenson		5
M. W. Alleyne c Knight b Stephenson	68	M. C. J. Ball c Prichard b Stephenson		1
*C. W. J. Athey c Garnham b Stephenson	11	L-b 6, w 10, n-b 3		19
R. J. Scott not out	50			
†R. C. Russell b Fraser	1	1/137 2/165 3/170	(8 wkts, 40 overs)	239
T. H. C. Hancock run out	5	4/174 5/179 6/190		
R. I. Dawson c Lewis b Andrew	6	7/237 8/239		

A. M. Smith and A. M. Babington did not bat.

Bowling: Topley 8–0–40–0; Andrew 8–0–41–1; Fraser 8–0–44–1; Childs 8–0–50–0; Stephenson 8–0–58–5.

Essex

J. P. Stephenson c Russell b Scott	25	K. A. Butler not out		5
N. V. Knight run out	15	L-b 3, n-b 4		7
*P. J. Prichard lbw b Ball	34			
†M. A. Garnham not out	15	1/27 2/61	(4 wkts, 24 overs)	106
N. Shahid run out	5	3/88 4/95		

J. J. B. Lewis, A. G. J. Fraser, T. D. Topley, S. J. W. Andrew and J. H. Childs did not bat.

Bowling: Babington 6–1–25–0; Smith 4–0–21–0; Ball 8–0–37–1; Scott 6–0–20–1.

Umpires: G. Sharp and A. G. T. Whitehead.

GLAMORGAN

At Birmingham, April 19. GLAMORGAN lost to WARWICKSHIRE by six wickets.

At Lord's, April 26. GLAMORGAN lost to MIDDLESEX by eight wickets.

GLAMORGAN v WORCESTERSHIRE

At Cardiff, May 3. Worcestershire won by eight wickets. Toss: Glamorgan. Only Richards (75 in 80 balls) presented any challenge to Worcestershire. Moody and Hick shared a stand of 166 and Moody's 68th run was his 1,000th for Worcestershire in 18 league innings, a record for any county.

Glamorgan

*M. P. Maynard run out	22	S. R. Barwick run out		6
H. Morris run out	1	S. Bastien not out		0
A. Dale run out	18			
I. V. A. Richards c Rhodes b Lampitt	75	L-b 3, w 4		7
C. S. Cowdrey b Newport	0			
P. A. Cottey c Rhodes b Lampitt	1	1/5 2/40 3/51	(8 wkts, 40 overs)	169
R. D. B. Croft c and b Illingworth	24	4/51 5/56 6/129		
†C. P. Metson not out	15	7/154 8/168		

D. J. Foster did not bat.

Bowling: Weston 8-0-27-0; Radford 8-0-47-0; Newport 8-1-25-1; Lampitt 8-0-44-2; Illingworth 8-0-23-1.

Worcestershire

*T. S. Curtis lbw b Bastien	2			
T. M. Moody not out	80			
G. A. Hick c Metson b Barwick	80			
D. A. Leatherdale not out	0			
L-b 3, w 4, n-b 1	8			
1/2 2/168		(2 wkts, 34.2 overs)		170

D. B. D'Oliveira, M. J. Weston, †S. J. Rhodes, S. R. Lampitt, R. K. Illingworth, P. J. Newport and N. V. Radford did not bat.

Bowling: Bastien 8-0-25-1; Foster 6-0-40-0; Barwick 8-0-32-1; Dale 6-0-29-0; Croft 2-0-17-0; Richards 1-0-6-0; Cowdrey 3.2-0-18-0.

Umpires: M. J. Kitchen and N. T. Plews.

At Chelmsford, May 24. GLAMORGAN lost to ESSEX by eight wickets.

GLAMORGAN v LEICESTERSHIRE

At Swansea, May 31. Glamorgan won by 59 runs. Toss: Leicestershire. Both teams entered their fifth Sunday game of the season looking for their first win. Glamorgan triumphed, thanks to Maynard's unbeaten 122 in 92 balls and Dale's four wickets.

Glamorgan

S. P. James b Gofton	74	C. S. Cowdrey not out		27
H. Morris c Benjamin b Mullally	5	B 1, l-b 11, w 4, n-b 1		17
A. Dale run out	19			
*M. P. Maynard not out	122	1/13 2/50 3/198	(3 wkts, 40 overs)	264

P. A. Cottey, R. D. B. Croft, †C. P. Metson, D. J. Foster, S. R. Barwick and M. Frost did not bat.

Bowling: Benjamin 8-0-43-0; Mullally 8-1-18-1; Gofton 8-0-46-1; Wells 8-0-59-0; Benson 3-0-23-0; Hepworth 2-0-15-0; Boon 1-0-18-0; Potter 2-0-30-0.

Leicestershire

J. D. R. Benson run out	42	V. J. Wells c Dale b Cowdrey	21
*N. E. Briers st Metson b Dale	43	P. N. Hepworth not out	8
J. J. Whitaker c Cowdrey b Dale	5	L-b 11, w 5, n-b 1	17
T. J. Boon c Morris b Cowdrey	17		
L. Potter c Frost b Dale	7	1/65 2/98 3/105 (7 wkts, 40 overs) 205	
W. K. M. Benjamin st Metson b Dale	0	4/119 5/119	
†P. A. Nixon not out	45	6/130 7/160	

R. P. Gofton and A. D. Mullally did not bat.

Bowling: Frost 7–0–40–0; Barwick 6–0–36–0; Dale 8–1–27–4; Foster 8–0–45–0; Cowdrey 5–0–20–2; Croft 6–0–26–0.

Umpires: A. A. Jones and R. Palmer.

At Hove, June 7. GLAMORGAN lost to SUSSEX by four wickets.

GLAMORGAN v LANCASHIRE

At Colwyn Bay, June 14. Lancashire won by six wickets. Toss: Lancashire. Lancashire's first win in any competition for four weeks came as DeFreitas carried on hitting sixes where he had left off the day before in the Championship match. He hit three, two in succession off Cowdrey, in a 26-ball unbeaten 41.

Glamorgan

S. P. James c Hegg b DeFreitas	1	P. A. Cottey not out	51
H. Morris not out	96	L-b 4, w 3	7
*M. P. Maynard b Fitton	25		
I. V. A. Richards b Watkinson	2	1/7 2/62 (4 wkts, 40 overs) 196	
C. S. Cowdrey lbw b Watkinson	14	3/67 4/96	

R. D. B. Croft, †C. P. Metson, A. Dale, S. R. Barwick and D. J. Foster did not bat.

Bowling: Allott 8–1–36–0; DeFreitas 8–0–44–1; Austin 8–0–41–0; Watkinson 8–0–31–1; Fitton 8–1–40–2.

Lancashire

G. Fowler c Maynard b Barwick	51	S. P. Titchard not out	1
*M. A. Atherton c Metson b Foster	45	L-b 1, w 2, n-b 1	4
N. J. Speak c Barwick b Cowdrey	25		
G. D. Lloyd c Cowdrey b Barwick	30	1/90 2/104 (4 wkts, 38.4 overs) 197	
P. A. J. DeFreitas not out	41	3/135 4/196	

M. Watkinson, I. D. Austin, †W. K. Hegg, P. J. W. Allott and J. D. Fitton did not bat.

Bowling: Dale 8–0–34–0; Croft 8–0–30–0; Barwick 5.4–0–36–2; Foster 6–0–28–1; Cowdrey 6–0–42–1; Richards 5–0–26–0.

Umpires: H. D. Bird and B. Leadbeater.

GLAMORGAN v YORKSHIRE

At Ebbw Vale, June 21. Yorkshire won by four wickets. Toss: Glamorgan. A confident start was wasted when Glamorgan lost four wickets for 13 runs, with Hartley removing Richards, Cowdrey and Maynard in three overs. Moxon and Tendulkar steered Yorkshire towards victory.

Glamorgan

S. P. James c Carrick b Robinson	5	†C. P. Metson c Carrick b Robinson	15
H. Morris c Blakey b Pickles	38	S. L. Watkin not out	7
*M. P. Maynard c Carrick b Hartley	45	L-b 6, w 1, n-b 3	10
I. V. A. Richards c Moxon b Hartley	15		
C. S. Cowdrey c Blakey b Hartley	1	1/19 2/65 3/100 (7 wkts, 40 overs)	167
P. A. Cottey lbw b Carrick	0	4/102 5/109	
R. D. B. Croft not out	31	6/113 7/146	

D. J. Foster and S. R. Barwick did not bat.

Bowling: Hartley 8–1–22–3; Robinson 8–0–43–2; Gough 8–0–32–0; Carrick 8–1–30–1; Pickles 8–1–34–1.

Yorkshire

*M. D. Moxon b Barwick	53	C. S. Pickles not out	11
S. A. Kellett c Maynard b Watkin	2	P. Carrick not out	2
†R. J. Blakey b Cowdrey	29	B 4, l-b 1, w 3, n-b 3	11
S. R. Tendulkar st Metson b Cowdrey	34		
D. Byas run out	1	1/7 2/83 3/111 (6 wkts, 38.4 overs)	171
C. White lbw b Watkin	28	4/112 5/133 6/163	

P. J. Hartley, D. Gough and M. A. Robinson did not bat.

Bowling: Watkin 8–0–37–2; Croft 8–3–16–0; Foster 7–0–41–0; Barwick 7.4–0–32–1; Cowdrey 8–1–40–2.

Umpires: R. Julian and D. O. Oslear.

At Luton, June 28. GLAMORGAN beat NORTHAMPTONSHIRE by seven wickets.

GLAMORGAN v SURREY

At Llanelli, July 5. Surrey won by seven wickets. Toss: Surrey. Brown reached his maiden Sunday hundred in 82 balls; he hit four sixes and ten fours in barely 90 minutes and put on 104 in 13 overs with Thorpe. It was enough to give Surrey a comfortable win, despite 139 in 23 overs from Morris and Maynard, and three sixes from Richards in a 41-ball 45.

Glamorgan

S. P. James b Kendrick	7	P. A. Cottey c Ward b Benjamin	1
H. Morris c Kendrick b M. P. Bicknell	98	R. D. B. Croft not out	0
*M. P. Maynard c Feltham		B 2, l-b 3, w 4, n-b 2	11
b M. P. Bicknell	72		
I. V. A. Richards not out	45	1/9 2/148 3/223 (5 wkts, 40 overs)	234
A. Dale c Kendrick b M. P. Bicknell	0	4/223 5/225	

†C. P. Metson, S. L. Watkin, S. R. Barwick and M. Frost did not bat.

Bowling: M. P. Bicknell 8–2–33–3; Kendrick 8–0–45–1; Boiling 7–1–33–0; Feltham 5–0–35–0; Benjamin 7–0–48–1; Robinson 5–0–35–0.

Surrey

D. J. Bicknell c Cottey b Frost	30	†D. M. Ward not out	3
A. D. Brown lbw b Dale	113	B 1, l-b 9, w 1, n-b 2	13
G. P. Thorpe not out	56		
*M. A. Lynch c Metson b Barwick	20	1/84 2/188 3/229 (3 wkts, 37.4 overs)	235

J. D. Robinson, M. A. Feltham, M. P. Bicknell, J. Boiling, J. E. Benjamin and N. M. Kendrick did not bat.

Bowling: Croft 5–0–35–0; Watkin 8–0–48–0; Barwick 8–0–40–1; Frost 6.4–0–48–1; Dale 8–0–41–1; Cottey 2–0–13–0.

Umpires: A. G. T. Whitehead and P. B. Wight.

At Portsmouth, July 19. GLAMORGAN beat HAMPSHIRE by seven wickets.

GLAMORGAN v DERBYSHIRE

At Pontypridd, July 26. No result. Toss: Derbyshire. For the second year running the Sunday fixture at Pontypridd was washed out, but not before Glamorgan's batsmen had made their mark. An unbroken third-wicket stand of 194 between Morris and Richards was Glamorgan's highest for any wicket in the league, passing 154 by R. C. Ontong and Javed Miandad against Kent at Canterbury in 1982. Morris hit four sixes, while Richards struck five in his 88 balls.

Glamorgan

S. P. James lbw b Sladdin	20	
H. Morris not out	104	
*M. P. Maynard lbw b Warner	5	
I. V. A. Richards not out	109	
L-b 4, w 3, n-b 1	8	

1/45 2/52   (2 wkts, 40 overs) 246

A. Dale, P. A. Cottey, R. D. B. Croft, †A. D. Shaw, S. D. Thomas, S. R. Barwick and M. Frost did not bat.

Bowling: Bishop 8–2–34–0; Mortensen 8–0–65–0; Warner 8–0–28–1; Sladdin 8–0–59–1; Cork 8–0–56–0.

Derbyshire

*K. J. Barnett not out	6	
P. D. Bowler not out	20	
W 4	4	

(no wkt, 7.4 overs) 30

A. M. Brown, C. J. Adams, T. J. G. O'Gorman, R. W. Sladdin, †K. M. Krikken, I. R. Bishop, D. G. Cork, A. E. Warner and O. H. Mortensen did not bat.

Bowling: Frost 4–0–16–0; Thomas 3.4–0–14–0.

Umpires: B. Dudleston and G. Sharp.

GLAMORGAN v KENT

At Swansea, August 2. Kent won by 47 runs. Toss: Kent. Glamorgan's promising start evaporated when McCague took a hat-trick, removing Cottey, Metson and Barwick with the score on 200.

Kent

T. R. Ward run out	26	M. J. McCague not out		22
*M. R. Benson b Croft	64	R. P. Davis not out		1
N. R. Taylor c Metson b Frost	1			
C. L. Hooper c Metson b Barwick	7	L-b 8, w 11, n-b 4		23
G. R. Cowdrey c Metson b Dale	10			
M. V. Fleming c Barwick b Dale	36	1/41 2/46 3/58	(8 wkts, 40 overs) 263	
†S. A. Marsh c Maynard b Frost	32	4/106 5/144 6/161		
M. A. Ealham c Croft b Frost	41	7/232 8/253		

A. P. Igglesden did not bat.

Bowling: Foster 8–0–66–0; Frost 8–1–52–3; Barwick 8–0–53–1; Croft 8–1–50–1; Dale 8–0–34–2.

Glamorgan

S. P. James b Igglesden	69	S. R. Barwick b McCague	0
H. Morris b Igglesden	67	D. J. Foster not out	10
*M. P. Maynard lbw b Fleming	18	M. Frost not out	6
I. V. A. Richards c Cowdrey b McCague	10	L-b 5, w 11	16
A. Dale run out	2		
P. A. Cottey c Marsh b McCague	12	1/134 2/162 3/168 (9 wkts, 40 overs) 216	
R. D. B. Croft c Igglesden b Fleming	1	4/171 5/187 6/191	
†C. P. Metson b McCague	5	7/200 8/200 9/200	

Bowling: Igglesden 8–0–48–2; Ealham 6–0–25–0; Hooper 8–0–36–0; McCague 8–0–41–4; Fleming 8–0–45–2; Davis 2–0–16–0.

Umpires: J. H. Hampshire and V. A. Holder.

At Nottingham, August 9. GLAMORGAN lost to NOTTINGHAMSHIRE by ten runs.

At Hartlepool, August 16. GLAMORGAN beat DURHAM by 16 runs.

At Bristol, August 23. GLOUCESTERSHIRE v GLAMORGAN. No result.

GLAMORGAN v SOMERSET

At Cardiff, August 30. No result.

GLOUCESTERSHIRE

At Southampton, April 19. GLOUCESTERSHIRE lost to HAMPSHIRE by six wickets.

At Lord's, May 3. GLOUCESTERSHIRE lost to MIDDLESEX by nine wickets.

At Derby, May 10. GLOUCESTERSHIRE lost to DERBYSHIRE by 50 runs.

GLOUCESTERSHIRE v SOMERSET

At Gloucester, May 24. Gloucestershire won by six wickets, their target having been revised to 145 from 35 overs. Toss: Somerset. Gloucestershire achieved their first Sunday win of the season, though they had a shaky start as Mallender took three in 11 balls. Russell and Alleyne shared an unbroken stand of 116 to reach a target reduced by two stoppages for rain.

Somerset

M. N. Lathwell lbw b Babington	6	R. P. Lefebvre not out	1
R. J. Bartlett run out	24	N. A. Mallender not out	0
*C. J. Tavaré b Scott	18		
R. J. Harden b Walsh	50	B 1, l-b 4, w 5, n-b 2	12
G. D. Rose c Athey b Scott	5		
A. N. Hayhurst c Alleyne b Babington	24	1/12 2/48 3/55 (8 wkts, 40 overs) 165	
K. H. MacLeay b Smith	10	4/61 5/121 6/145	
†N. D. Burns b Walsh	15	7/153 8/164	

H. R. J. Trump did not bat.

Bowling: Smith 8–1–33–1; Babington 8–1–35–2; Walsh 8–0–32–2; Scott 8–0–27–2; Alleyne 8–0–33–0.

Gloucestershire

G. D. Hodgson lbw b Mallender	13	M. W. Alleyne not out	58
S. G. Hinks c and b Mallender	2	L-b 7, w 2, n-b 1	10
C. W. J. Athey c Harden b Mallender	4		
*A. J. Wright b Rose	2	1/10 2/22	(4 wkts, 32.3 overs) 145
†R. C. Russell not out	56	3/23 4/29	

R. J. Scott, M. Davies, C. A. Walsh, A. M. Babington and A. M. Smith did not bat.

Bowling: Mallender 7–1–27–3; Rose 6–1–15–1; MacLeay 8–1–22–0; Lefebvre 5.3–0–38–0; Hayhurst 6–0–36–0.

Umpires: J. H. Harris and R. A. White.

At Nottingham, May 31. GLOUCESTERSHIRE beat NOTTINGHAMSHIRE by nine wickets.

At Manchester, June 7. GLOUCESTERSHIRE beat LANCASHIRE by five wickets.

GLOUCESTERSHIRE v KENT

At Swindon, June 14. Kent won by 15 runs. Toss: Kent. Babington was told off by umpire Jones, and later received an official rebuke from his county, for throwing the ball at Fleming's legs. He had just taken a return catch off the Kent batsman, who had hit 40 from 29 deliveries and, immediately before his dismissal, lifted Babington for six.

Kent

T. R. Ward c and b Smith	0	M. A. Ealham not out	6
*M. R. Benson run out	12	R. P. Davis b Walsh	3
N. R. Taylor c Russell b Smith	10	M. J. McCague b Walsh	11
C. L. Hooper c Hinks b Babington	23	B 1, l-b 5, w 1, n-b 2	9
G. R. Cowdrey run out	3		
M. V. Fleming c and b Babington	40	1/0 2/20 3/28	(40 overs) 171
†S. A. Marsh b Alleyne	34	4/39 5/80 6/101	
N. J. Llong c Walsh b Alleyne	20	7/144 8/153 9/157	

Bowling: Smith 8–1–18–2; Babington 8–1–33–2; Walsh 8–0–35–2; Scott 8–0–48–0; Alleyne 8–0–31–2.

Gloucestershire

G. D. Hodgson run out	45	C. A. Walsh run out	9
S. G. Hinks st Marsh b Davis	7	A. M. Babington not out	2
C. W. J. Athey lbw b Fleming	4	A. M. Smith not out	1
†R. C. Russell c and b Hooper	15	B 1, l-b 3, w 4	8
*A. J. Wright c Benson b Fleming	20		
M. W. Alleyne b McCague	25	1/28 2/45 3/73	(9 wkts, 40 overs) 156
R. J. Scott b McCague	6	4/78 5/121 6/127	
R. I. Dawson run out	14	7/133 8/150 9/154	

Bowling: McCague 8–0–39–2; Ealham 8–0–27–0; Davis 8–0–21–1; Fleming 8–0–37–2; Hooper 8–0–28–1.

Umpires: A. A. Jones and R. A. White.

GLOUCESTERSHIRE v WARWICKSHIRE

At Bristol, June 21. Warwickshire won by two wickets. Toss: Gloucestershire. Pursuing a straightforward target of 172, Warwickshire almost lost their way – three overs from the end they had needed 28 with five wickets standing. Six were required from Walsh's last over, and though Smith took five off the first two balls Walsh removed Lloyd and Holloway with the third and fifth. Donald managed an inside edge from a yorker to win the match.

Gloucestershire

G. D. Hodgson c Holloway b Munton	9	C. A. Walsh c Moles b N. M. K. Smith	8
M. W. Alleyne c Moles b Munton	19	A. M. Babington run out	6
C. W. J. Athey b Munton	5	A. M. Smith not out	1
*A. J. Wright c Munton b P. A. Smith	51		
R. J. Scott c N. M. K. Smith b Twose	18	B 2, l-b 4, w 6	12
R. I. Dawson c Holloway b P. A. Smith	17		
T. H. C. Hancock c Donald		1/20 2/28 3/35　　　　(40 overs) 171	
b P. A. Smith	8	4/91 5/125 6/128	
†R. C. J. Williams run out	17	7/137 8/164 9/164	

Bowling: Munton 7–1–19–3; N. M. K. Smith 8–0–43–1; Twose 8–0–27–1; Reeve 4–0–19–0; Donald 8–0–32–0; P. A. Smith 5–1–25–3.

Warwickshire

A. J. Moles c Babington b Alleyne	38	†P. C. L. Holloway b Walsh	0
R. G. Twose run out	48	A. A. Donald not out	1
P. A. Smith lbw b Babington	8		
D. P. Ostler c Hodgson b Walsh	17	L-b 6, w 1	7
D. A. Reeve run out	39		
T. L. Penney c Williams b Smith	0	1/87 2/98 3/100　　(8 wkts, 40 overs) 172	
N. M. K. Smith not out	14	4/138 5/140 6/165	
*T. A. Lloyd c and b Walsh	0	7/171 8/171	

T. A. Munton did not bat.

Bowling: Smith 7–0–33–1; Babington 8–1–31–1; Scott 7–0–31–0; Walsh 8–0–23–3; Alleyne 8–0–39–1; Hancock 2–0–9–0.

Umpires: B. Leadbeater and G. Sharp.

GLOUCESTERSHIRE v SURREY

At Bristol, June 28. Surrey won by 17 runs. Toss: Gloucestershire. Gloucestershire's attempts to catch up with a target of 207, created largely through the efforts of Lynch, with 50 in 41 balls, faded after the loss of Athey and Wright.

Surrey

D. J. Bicknell c Alleyne b Scott	44	M. A. Feltham not out	14
A. D. Brown c Wright b Gerrard	2	M. P. Bicknell not out	5
*†A. J. Stewart c Russell b Gerrard	3	L-b 2, w 5	7
G. P. Thorpe run out	38		
M. A. Lynch c Dawson b Alleyne	58	1/17 2/22 3/75　　(6 wkts, 40 overs) 206	
D. M. Ward c Hodgson b Smith	35	4/136 5/173 6/200	

J. Boiling, A. J. Murphy and J. E. Benjamin did not bat.

Bowling: Babington 7–0–24–0; Gerrard 8–0–35–2; Scott 7–0–41–1; Smith 6–0–38–1; Ball 4–0–19–0; Alleyne 8–0–47–1.

Gloucestershire

G. D. Hodgson c Feltham b Murphy...	1	A. M. Smith run out	5
M. W. Alleyne c Thorpe b Boiling.....	31	A. M. Babington run out	0
C. W. J. Athey run out	49	M. J. Gerrard not out	0
*A. J. Wright c Stewart b Benjamin ...	24	B 2, l-b 5, w 9	16
R. J. Scott c Feltham b M. P. Bicknell..	16		
†R. C. Russell c Ward b Benjamin	4	1/3 2/51 3/108 (39.3 overs) 189	
R. I. Dawson b Murphy	24	4/128 5/140 6/141	
M. C. J. Ball b Feltham	19	7/175 8/185 9/189	

Bowling: M. P. Bicknell 8-0-36-1; Murphy 8-1-35-2; Boiling 8-0-40-1; Benjamin 8-0-34-2; Feltham 7.3-0-37-1.

Umpires: V. A. Holder and M. J. Kitchen.

At Stockton-on-Tees, July 5. GLOUCESTERSHIRE lost to DURHAM by six wickets.

GLOUCESTERSHIRE v NORTHAMPTONSHIRE

At Moreton-in-Marsh, July 12. Gloucestershire won by 78 runs. Toss: Northamptonshire. The visitors' strong batting line-up failed to make any use of a small ground. Babington removed Fordham and Lamb in his first over, and Capel in his third.

Gloucestershire

G. D. Hodgson b Penberthy	22	C. A. Walsh b Curran	10
M. W. Alleyne c Cook b Ambrose.....	58	A. M. Smith not out	13
C. W. J. Athey lbw b Capel	12	L-b 5, w 2	7
*A. J. Wright c Curran b Cook	17		
R. I. Dawson c and b Cook	4	1/34 2/83 3/103 (7 wkts, 40 overs) 176	
R. J. Scott c and b Penberthy	7	4/110 5/121	
†R. C. Russell not out	26	6/133 7/156	

A. M. Babington and M. Davies did not bat.

Bowling: Taylor 8-1-34-0; Curran 8-0-33-1; Penberthy 8-0-29-2; Ambrose 8-1-33-1; Capel 4-0-19-1; Cook 4-0-23-2.

Northamptonshire

A. Fordham c Russell b Babington	1	C. E. L. Ambrose not out	14
N. A. Felton c Dawson b Scott	39	J. P. Taylor run out	1
*A. J. Lamb b Babington	0	N. G. B. Cook b Alleyne	0
D. J. Capel lbw b Babington	1	L-b 4, w 9, n-b 2	15
R. J. Bailey c Russell b Walsh	10		
K. M. Curran c Hodgson b Scott......	6	1/7 2/7 3/15 (32.1 overs) 98	
A. L. Penberthy lbw b Scott	0	4/46 5/57 6/57	
†D. Ripley c Scott b Babington	11	7/63 8/88 9/98	

Bowling: Smith 5-0-18-0; Babington 8-1-21-4; Walsh 6-2-16-1; Scott 8-2-23-3; Alleyne 5.1-0-16-1.

Umpires: J. H. Harris and K. E. Palmer.

GLOUCESTERSHIRE v YORKSHIRE

At Cheltenham College, July 19. Gloucestershire won by three wickets. Toss: Gloucestershire. The home team needed 12 from Jarvis's last over, but Russell despatched the first three balls for a six and two fours to reach 41 in 21 balls.

Yorkshire

*M. D. Moxon c Wright b Scott	26	P. W. Jarvis b Walsh		17
S. A. Kellett lbw b Smith	13	D. Gough run out		0
†R. J. Blakey b Ball	19	J. D. Batty not out		1
S. R. Tendulkar c Alleyne b Babington	63	L-b 6, w 9		15
D. Byas c Russell b Babington	29			
C. White run out	0	1/25 2/63 3/70	(39.5 overs)	200
C. S. Pickles c Russell b Babington	0	4/149 5/150 6/161		
P. J. Hartley c Wright b Smith	17	7/162 8/197 9/197		

Bowling: Smith 6–1–20–2; Babington 7–0–39–3; Walsh 7.5–3–38–1; Alleyne 6–0–35–0; Ball 8–0–39–1; Scott 5–0–23–1.

Gloucestershire

G. D. Hodgson lbw b Gough	8	C. A. Walsh run out		2
M. W. Alleyne c Hartley b Batty	41	M. C. J. Ball not out		0
C. W. J. Athey c Gough b Moxon	51	B 1, l-b 3, w 2		6
*A. J. Wright c Jarvis b Batty	26			
R. J. Scott c Jarvis b Moxon	23	1/33 2/61 3/102	(7 wkts, 39.3 overs)	203
†R. C. Russell not out	41	4/149 5/157		
R. I. Dawson run out	5	6/184 7/188		

A. M. Smith and A. M. Babington did not bat.

Bowling: Hartley 8–0–40–0; Jarvis 7.3–0–36–0; Pickles 5–1–22–0; Gough 6–0–37–1; Batty 8–1–32–2; Moxon 5–0–32–2.

Umpires: J. W. Holder and R. C. Tolchard.

GLOUCESTERSHIRE v SUSSEX

At Cheltenham College, July 26. Gloucestershire won by 92 runs. Toss: Sussex. Athey, who arrived at the crease in the first over, reached 50 in 88 balls but needed only 29 more for his hundred, hitting ten fours and a six.

Gloucestershire

G. D. Hodgson b Giddins	13	†R. C. Russell c and b Pigott		21
M. W. Alleyne c Speight b Pigott	0	J. T. C. Vaughan not out		1
C. W. J. Athey c Robson b Giddins	105	L-b 7, w 7, n-b 2		16
*A. J. Wright c Pigott b Remy	16			
R. I. Dawson c Wells b Giddins	35	1/1 2/37 3/61	(6 wkts, 40 overs)	232
R. J. Scott not out	25	4/155 5/188 6/224		

M. C. J. Ball, A. M. Smith and A. M. Babington did not bat.

Bowling: Pigott 8–0–45–2; Robson 8–2–23–0; Giddins 8–0–37–3; Remy 4–0–18–1; Salisbury 6–0–47–0; Lenham 6–0–55–0.

Sussex

K. Greenfield c Athey b Babington	17	I. D. K. Salisbury not out		27
J. W. Hall run out	9	E. S. H. Giddins c Hodgson b Alleyne		1
M. P. Speight c Russell b Scott	26	A. G. Robson run out		3
*A. P. Wells lbw b Scott	3	L-b 10, w 7		17
N. J. Lenham c Alleyne b Vaughan	15			
†P. Moores c Wright b Vaughan	6	1/22 2/31 3/36	(36.4 overs)	140
C. C. Remy b Alleyne	14	4/74 5/83 6/87		
A. C. S. Pigott lbw b Vaughan	2	7/97 8/103 9/112		

Bowling: Babington 6–1–18–1; Smith 3–0–11–0; Scott 8–1–23–2; Vaughan 8–0–31–3; Ball 7–1–24–0; Alleyne 4.4–1–23–2.

Umpires: R. Julian and B. J. Meyer.

At Worcester, August 2. GLOUCESTERSHIRE lost to WORCESTERSHIRE by six wickets.

GLOUCESTERSHIRE v LEICESTERSHIRE

At Bristol, August 9. Gloucestershire won by nine wickets. Toss: Gloucestershire. Alleyne's maiden Sunday hundred was the highest score for Gloucestershire in the competition, beating the 131 made by Sadiq Mohammad against Somerset in 1975. He hit nearly two-thirds of his team's runs, striking 12 fours and a six in 121 balls, and shared 155 with Athey to bring up victory.

Leicestershire

J. J. Whitaker c Wright b Babington	3	W. K. M. Benjamin c Athey b Smith	3
*N. E. Briers c Russell b Babington	3	G. J. Parsons not out	0
T. J. Boon run out	46	A. D. Mullally run out	1
P. E. Robinson c Wright b Smith	88	L-b 3, w 7, n-b 3	13
J. D. R. Benson run out	19		
L. Potter run out	2	1/4 2/9 3/131	(40 overs) 205
M. I. Gidley b Smith	17	4/157 5/162 6/181	
†P. Whitticase c Dawson b Smith	10	7/195 8/202 9/204	

Bowling: Vaughan 8-3-25-0; Babington 8-0-40-2; Smith 8-0-38-4; Scott 4-0-23-0; Ball 4-0-29-0; Alleyne 8-0-47-0.

Gloucestershire

M. W. Alleyne not out	134
G. D. Hodgson c Whitaker b Parsons	22
C. W. J. Athey not out	39
L-b 10, w 4	14

1/54   (1 wkt, 38.3 overs) 209

*A. J. Wright, R. J. Scott, †R. C. Russell, J. T. C. Vaughan, R. I. Dawson, M. C. J. Ball, A. M. Smith and A. M. Babington did not bat.

Bowling: Benjamin 7.3-0-37-0; Mullally 8-0-39-0; Parsons 7-0-34-1; Potter 8-0-37-0; Benson 3-0-27-0; Gidley 5-0-25-0.

Umpires: V. A. Holder and M. J. Kitchen.

GLOUCESTERSHIRE v GLAMORGAN

At Bristol, August 23. No result. Toss: Glamorgan. Rain reduced the match to 38 overs a side, then ended it after 12.

Gloucestershire

M. W. Alleyne not out	17
G. D. Hodgson c Thomas b Dale	23
C. W. J. Athey not out	0
L-b 1, w 2	3

1/43   (1 wkt, 12 overs) 43

*A. J. Wright, R. J. Scott, R. I. Dawson, †R. C. Russell, A. M. Smith, C. A. Walsh, M. C. J. Ball and A. M. Babington did not bat.

Bowling: Frost 6-1-20-0; Bastien 5-1-18-0; Dale 1-0-4-1.

Glamorgan

S. P. James, H. Morris, *M. P. Maynard, D. L. Hemp, A. Dale, P. A. Cottey, R. D. B. Croft, †C. P. Metson, M. Frost, S. D. Thomas and S. Bastien.

Umpires: A. G. T. Whitehead and P. B. Wight.

At Chelmsford, August 30. GLOUCESTERSHIRE beat ESSEX on scoring-rate.

HAMPSHIRE

HAMPSHIRE v GLOUCESTERSHIRE

At Southampton, April 19. Hampshire won by six wickets. Toss: Hampshire. Smith hit seven fours and put on 105 for the first wicket with Terry.

Gloucestershire

M. W. Alleyne c Turner b Ayling	16	T. H. C. Hancock c Smith b Connor	5
S. G. Hinks c James b Turner	16	M. C. J. Ball not out	2
C. W. J. Athey b Marshall	41	L-b 6, w 2, n-b 2	10
*A. J. Wright b Udal	27		
J. T. C. Vaughan c Udal b Marshall	20	1/34 2/44 3/81 (6 wkts, 40 overs)	150
†R. C. Russell not out	13	4/118 5/134 6/141	

A. M. Smith, A. M. Babington and M. J. Gerrard did not bat.

Bowling: Marshall 8–0–34–2; Connor 8–1–26–1; Turner 8–2–20–1; Ayling 5–1–18–1; Udal 8–1–35–1; James 3–0–11–0.

Hampshire

V. P. Terry c Hancock b Ball	37	M. D. Marshall not out	0
R. A. Smith b Gerrard	61	L-b 10, n-b 5	15
D. I. Gower c Alleyne b Vaughan	13		
J. R. Ayling not out	20	1/105 2/119 (4 wkts, 38.3 overs)	151
*M. C. J. Nicholas c Athey b Babington	5	3/122 4/136	

K. D. James, †A. N. Aymes, S. D. Udal, I. J. Turner and C. A. Connor did not bat.

Bowling: Smith 6.3–0–32–0; Babington 8–0–25–1; Gerrard 8–0–24–1; Vaughan 7–1–22–1; Ball 8–0–32–1; Alleyne 1–0–6–0.

Umpires: B. Dudleston and J. H. Hampshire.

At Manchester, May 3. HAMPSHIRE lost to LANCASHIRE by four wickets.

At Taunton, May 17. HAMPSHIRE lost to SOMERSET by 97 runs.

At Leeds, May 24. HAMPSHIRE beat YORKSHIRE by 59 runs.

HAMPSHIRE v DURHAM

At Southampton, May 31. Hampshire won by two wickets. Toss: Hampshire. Maru hit four off Bainbridge's last ball to secure a victory that had suddenly seemed to be slipping out of reach. At 146 for one in the 27th over, Hampshire were coasting; Smith and Gower had added 135 in 22 overs. But Botham removed both of his sometime England colleagues in successive overs to revive Durham's hopes.

Durham

T. Botham c Middleton b Udal	64	†A. R. Fothergill b Gower b Udal	8
V. Larkins c Aymes b James	8	S. P. Hughes not out	1
D. M. Jones c Middleton b Bakker	55	L-b 3, w 2	5
. Bainbridge c and b Udal	5		
*. W. G. Parker not out	42	1/24 2/109 3/117 (7 wkts, 40 overs) 209
D. Glendenen b Udal	2	4/162 5/166
. Smith b Connor	19	6/193 7/205

D. A. Graveney and S. J. E. Brown did not bat.

Bowling: Connor 8–0–26–1; James 8–0–32–1; Maru 8–0–43–0; Bakker 8–0–41–1; Udal 8–0–64–4.

Hampshire

R. A. Smith lbw b Botham	78	C. A. Connor run out	2
. C. Middleton c Parker b Brown	7	R. J. Maru not out	8
D. I. Gower c Parker b Botham	56		
M. C. J. Nicholas c Jones b Hughes	20	L-b 6, w 5	11
. D. James c Jones b Graveney	6		
. R. Wood c Parker b Bainbridge	12	1/11 2/146 3/151 (8 wkts, 40 overs) 212
A. N. Aymes not out	3	4/166 5/187 6/190
. D. Udal run out	9	7/200 8/204

*. J. Bakker did not bat.

Bowling: Brown 7–0–36–1; Hughes 8–0–37–1; Bainbridge 7–0–53–1; Botham 8–0–30–2; Smith 2–0–17–0; Graveney 8–0–33–1.

Umpires: D. J. Constant and R. Julian.

HAMPSHIRE v SURREY

At Basingstoke, June 7. Surrey won by nine wickets. Toss: Surrey. Surrey's former captain, Greig, returned to lead them to their second Sunday win of the season in a rare first-team appearance. His chosen weapon was spin; slow left-armer Kendrick opened the bowling. But it was the young off-spinner, Boiling, who engineered Hampshire's collapse, taking five wickets in four overs. Then Darren Bicknell and Thorpe saw Surrey home.

Hampshire

*. C. Middleton b Boiling	42	S. D. Udal c and b M. P. Bicknell	17
T. D. James c Ward b Robinson	24	C. A. Connor c M. P. Bicknell b Murphy	7
D. I. Gower c D. J. Bicknell b Boiling	25	P. J. Bakker not out	0
M. D. Marshall c Robinson b M. P. Bicknell	5	L-b 5, w 2	7
M. C. J. Nicholas c and b Boiling	2		
. R. Wood st Ligertwood b Boiling	5	1/49 2/94 3/98 (39.5 overs) 153
. R. Ayling c Thorpe b Boiling	7	4/104 5/106 6/107
A. N. Aymes c Thorpe b Murphy	18	7/112 8/141 9/147

Bowling: M. P. Bicknell 8–0–22–2; Kendrick 8–0–35–0; Robinson 8–0–28–1; Boiling 8–0–24–5; Murphy 7.5–0–39–2.

Surrey

D. J. Bicknell not out	74
A. D. Brown c Aymes b Udal	18
G. P. Thorpe not out	53
L-b 7, w 2, n-b 3	12

/38 (1 wkt, 35.3 overs) 157

D. M. Ward, J. D. Robinson, †D. G. C. Ligertwood, *I. A. Greig, M. P. Bicknell, N. M. Kendrick, J. Boiling and A. J. Murphy did not bat.

Bowling: Bakker 4–0–25–0; Connor 7–0–33–0; Udal 8–1–28–1; Marshall 8–0–30–‌
Ayling 5.3–0–18–0; James 3–0–16–0.

Umpires: J. C. Balderstone and A. G. T. Whitehead.

At Birmingham, June 14. HAMPSHIRE lost to WARWICKSHIRE by 40 runs.

HAMPSHIRE v ESSEX

At Bournemouth, June 21. Hampshire won by eight wickets. Toss: Hampshire. Esse‌
succumbed to their second Sunday defeat of the season, though they remained at the hea‌
of the table. Hampshire easily passed an undemanding target of 176 after Middleton an‌
Terry opened with 138 in 27 overs; Terry reached 4,000 runs in his league career.

Essex

P. J. Prichard c Terry b Ayling	22	*N. A. Foster lbw b Marshall	
J. P. Stephenson lbw b Udal	54	†M. A. Garnham not out	
M. E. Waugh c Udal b Maru	28	L-b 3, w 9, n-b 1	
N. Hussain c Maru b Connor	4		
N. V. Knight not out	29	1/44 2/106 3/113	(6 wkts, 40 overs) 17
D. R. Pringle c Parks b Marshall	11	4/120 5/141 6/141	

T. D. Topley, M. C. Ilott and P. M. Such did not bat.

Bowling: Connor 8–1–30–1; James 5–0–22–0; Ayling 7–0–28–1; Udal 6–0–30–1; Marsha‌
8–1–34–2; Maru 6–0–28–1.

Hampshire

T. C. Middleton run out	72		
V. P. Terry c Foster b Ilott	62		
D. I. Gower not out	15		
*M. C. J. Nicholas not out	23		
L-b 3, w 3	6		
1/138 2/141	(2 wkts, 36 overs) 178		

K. D. James, J. R. Ayling, M. D. Marshall, †R. J. Parks, R. J. Maru, S. D. Udal an‌
C. A. Connor did not bat.

Bowling: Foster 5–0–23–0; Ilott 8–1–28–1; Pringle 4–0–10–0; Topley 8–0–40–0; Suc‌
6–0–41–0; Stephenson 3–0–19–0; Waugh 2–0–14–0.

Umpires: J. D. Bond and A. A. Jones.

HAMPSHIRE v NOTTINGHAMSHIRE

At Southampton, July 5. Hampshire won by 24 runs. Toss: Nottinghamshire. Faced with‌
moderate target, Nottinghamshire fell to their eighth defeat in nine matches.

Hampshire

V. P. Terry run out	69	†R. J. Parks c Robinson b Evans	
T. C. Middleton b Pick	34	S. D. Udal not out	
K. D. James c Robinson b Cairns	24	L-b 11, w 4, n-b 2	
*M. C. J. Nicholas c Cairns b Evans	1		
J. R. Wood c Evans b Pick	4	1/86 2/126 3/130	(7 wkts, 40 overs) 17
M. D. Marshall not out	13	4/148 5/149	
J. R. Ayling b Cairns	5	6/162 7/171	

R. J. Maru and C. A. Connor did not bat.

Bowling: Pennett 8–0–38–0; Pick 8–0–34–2; Evans 8–1–22–2; Cairns 8–1–24–2; Fiel‌
Buss 4–1–22–0; Crawley 4–0–21–0.

Nottinghamshire

D. W. Randall c Maru b James	5	R. A. Pick b Connor	24
M. A. Crawley c Terry b James	2	M. G. Field-Buss not out	10
R. T. Robinson c Ayling b James	14	D. B. Pennett not out	2
P. Johnson c Parks b Marshall	27	L-b 2, w 5, n-b 2	9
*. R. Pollard c and b Udal	22		
W. A. Dessaur c Parks b Marshall	3	1/5 2/12 3/39 (9 wkts, 40 overs) 148	
C. L. Cairns lbw b Maru	0	4/57 5/62 6/63	
K. P. Evans c Middleton b Connor	30	7/93 8/133 9/142	

Bowling: Connor 8–0–35–2; James 8–1–25–3; Ayling 6–0–18–0; Marshall 7–0–26–2; Maru 6–0–24–1; Udal 5–0–18–1.

Umpires: V. A. Holder and R. Julian.

HAMPSHIRE v GLAMORGAN

At Portsmouth, July 19. Glamorgan won by seven wickets. Toss: Glamorgan. Hampshire disintegrated inside 37 overs as Barwick and Richards shared six very cheap wickets. Morris saw Glamorgan home in comfort.

Hampshire

R. A. Smith c Metson b Barwick	38	S. D. Udal lbw b Richards	1
T. C. Middleton c and b Watkin	5	C. A. Connor b Richards	0
D. I. Gower lbw b Dale	10	P. J. Bakker c Barwick b Frost	14
M. C. J. Nicholas lbw b Dale	5	B 1, l-b 11, w 7	19
M. D. Marshall st Metson b Barwick	0		
K. D. James c Metson b Barwick	1	1/12 2/49 3/58 (36.5 overs) 129	
I. R. Ayling c and b Richards	16	4/59 5/69 6/82	
A. N. Aymes not out	20	7/104 8/106 9/110	

Bowling: Watkin 8–0–31–1; Frost 5.5–1–25–1; Barwick 8–3–16–3; Dale 6–0–27–2; Richards 7–1–12–3; Croft 2–0–6–0.

Glamorgan

S. P. James c Connor b Ayling	29	A. Dale not out	8
H. Morris not out	51	L-b 1, w 3, n-b 3	7
*M. P. Maynard lbw b James	15		
I. V. A. Richards c Marshall b Udal	23	1/53 2/83 3/112 (3 wkts, 37 overs) 133	

P. A. Cottey, R. D. B. Croft, †C. P. Metson, S. L. Watkin, S. R. Barwick and M. Frost did not bat.

Bowling: Connor 7–2–21–0; Bakker 6–0–28–0; Marshall 8–1–29–0; Ayling 8–0–26–1; James 4–0–13–1; Udal 4–1–15–1.

Umpires: R. Palmer and R. A. White.

At Worcester, July 26. HAMPSHIRE beat WORCESTERSHIRE by six wickets.

HAMPSHIRE v MIDDLESEX

At Southampton, August 2. Hampshire won by five wickets. Toss: Hampshire. Middlesex's sequence of 12 wins ended with a straightforward defeat. Haynes continued his formidable form with his ninth fifty in his 11th match, but had too little support. When Hampshire replied, Middleton accelerated gently to hit the winning runs with an over to spare.

Middlesex

D. L. Haynes c Smith b Udal	77	J. E. Emburey not out			1
M. A. Roseberry c Marshall b James	3	N. F. Williams not out			
*M. W. Gatting c Middleton b Connor	1	L-b 1, w 1, n-b 1			
M. R. Ramprakash run out	23				—
J. D. Carr c Smith b Ayling	6	1/18 2/25 3/82	(7 wkts, 40 overs)	18
†K. R. Brown c Ayling b Turner	47	4/95 5/122			
P. N. Weekes c Aymes b Marshall	0	6/124 7/176			

D. W. Headley and A. R. C. Fraser did not bat.

Bowling: Connor 8–0–29–1; James 5–0–32–1; Turner 3–0–15–1; Ayling 8–0–20–1; Marshall 8–0–44–1; Udal 8–0–40–1.

Hampshire

R. A. Smith c Ramprakash b Williams	34	K. D. James not out			
T. C. Middleton not out	64				
D. I. Gower b Weekes	13	B 4, l-b 13, w 1, n-b 1			1
J. R. Ayling lbw b Headley	23				—
*M. C. J. Nicholas b Emburey	2	1/46 2/79 3/121	(5 wkts, 39 overs)	18
M. D. Marshall b Emburey	18	4/124 5/167			

†A. N. Aymes, S. D. Udal, C. A. Connor and I. J. Turner did not bat.

Bowling: Fraser 6–1–21–0; Williams 8–0–26–1; Weekes 8–0–33–1; Carr 4–0–15–0; Emburey 7–0–38–2; Headley 6–0–32–1.

Umpires: D. J. Constant and B. J. Meyer.

At Hove, August 3. HAMPSHIRE beat SUSSEX by eight wickets.

At Canterbury, August 9. HAMPSHIRE lost to KENT by six wickets.

HAMPSHIRE v NORTHAMPTONSHIRE

At Bournemouth, August 16. Hampshire won by 81 runs. Toss: Northamptonshire. Middleton's opening partnership with Smith and a closing rush of 100 runs in the final ten overs built an unassailable position. Udal's four wickets took his total for the season to 29, a competition record for Hampshire.

Hampshire

R. A. Smith c Capel b Penberthy	61	*M. C. J. Nicholas not out			29
T. C. Middleton c Capel b Walker	98	B 1, l-b 5, w 6			12
D. I. Gower b Curran	27				—
J. R. Ayling not out	28	1/103 2/191 3/199	(3 wkts, 40 overs)	255

M. D. Marshall, K. D. James, †A. N. Aymes, S. D. Udal, I. J. Turner and C. A. Connor did not bat.

Bowling: Walker 6–0–56–1; Capel 6–0–29–0; Bowen 6–0–45–0; Curran 8–0–52–1; Cook 8–0–37–0; Penberthy 6–0–30–1.

Northamptonshire

A. Fordham c Smith b Turner	31	M. N. Bowen c Turner b Connor			9
N. A. Felton c Aymes b Connor	0	A. Walker c Nicholas b Turner			3
R. J. Bailey c Marshall b Udal	64	N. G. B. Cook not out			1
D. J. Capel c Marshall b Udal	17	B 1, l-b 4, w 7			12
K. M. Curran c Smith b Marshall	20				—
*A. J. Lamb b Udal	0	1/4 2/55 3/88	(38.2 overs)	174
A. L. Penberthy c Connor b Udal	4	4/127 5/131 6/140			
†W. M. Noon c James b Connor	13	7/146 8/168 9/171			

Bowling: James 6–0–27–0; Connor 7.2–0–30–3; Ayling 4–0–7–0; Turner 5–1–31–2; Marshall 8–0–23–1; Udal 8–0–51–4.

Umpires: M. J. Kitchen and P. B. Wight.

HAMPSHIRE v DERBYSHIRE

At Southampton, August 23. Hampshire won by seven wickets, their target having been revised to 120 from 20 overs. Toss: Hampshire. Four interruptions for rain reduced the match to 24 overs a side, and then cut Hampshire's innings to the minimum 20 needed for the match to stand. They had eight balls to spare when Malcolm bowled two consecutive wides.

Derbyshire

*K. J. Barnett b Udal	55
P. D. Bowler not out	70
J. E. Morris c Wood b Udal	13
A. E. Warner not out	0
L-b 3, w 1, n-b 1	5

1/94 2/139 (2 wkts, 24 overs) 143

T. G. S. Steer, T. J. G. O'Gorman, †K. M. Krikken, F. A. Griffith, I. R. Bishop, D. E. Malcolm and R. W. Sladdin did not bat.

Bowling: James 4–0–23–0; Connor 7–0–34–0; Turner 1–0–3–0; Marshall 5–0–29–0; Udal 7–0–51–2.

Hampshire

T. C. Middleton c and b Griffith	28	*M. C. J. Nicholas not out	14
D. I. Gower c Warner b Bishop	0	L-b 1, w 10, n-b 1	12
J. R. Wood c Sladdin b Griffith	34		
J. R. Ayling not out	32	1/5 2/60 3/67 (3 wkts, 18.4 overs) 120	

M. D. Marshall, K. D. James, †A. N. Aymes, S. D. Udal, C. A. Connor and I. J. Turner did not bat.

Bowling: Bishop 7–0–42–1; Warner 5–0–25–0; Griffith 3–0–20–2; Malcolm 3.4–0–32–0.

Umpires: D. J. Constant and D. R. Shepherd.

At Leicester, August 30. LEICESTERSHIRE v HAMPSHIRE. No result.

KENT

KENT v SOMERSET

At Canterbury, April 19. Somerset won by four wickets. Toss: Kent. Lathwell's fifty came from 81 balls.

Kent

T. R. Ward run out	45	M. A. Ealham c Rose b Caddick	4
*M. R. Benson c Harden b MacLeay	17	R. P. Davis c Burns b Mallender	1
N. R. Taylor c Tavaré b Hayhurst	51	A. P. Igglesden not out	3
G. R. Cowdrey c Lathwell b Trump	12	L-b 2, w 2, n-b 1	5
M. V. Fleming lbw b Hayhurst	0		
†S. A. Marsh c Harden b Mallender	22	1/50 2/82 3/123 (38.4 overs) 163	
J. I. Longley run out	1	4/128 5/131 6/132	
R. M. Ellison c Burns b Hayhurst	2	7/136 8/152 9/154	

Bowling: Mallender 6.4–0–22–2; Rose 4–0–21–0; Caddick 7–0–30–1; MacLeay 7–0–40–1; Trump 8–0–24–1; Hayhurst 6–0–24–3.

Somerset

M. N. Lathwell run out	55	K. H. MacLeay b Fleming	3
R. J. Bartlett c Marsh b Ellison	4	†N. D. Burns not out	16
*C. J. Tavaré c and b Ellison	0	B 4, l-b 5, w 1	10
R. J. Harden c Ealham b Igglesden	14		
A. N. Hayhurst c Marsh b Igglesden	28	1/23 2/33 3/59 (6 wkts, 39.2 overs) 164	
G. D. Rose not out	34	4/98 5/119 6/138	

N. A. Mallender, A. R. Caddick and H. R. J. Trump did not bat.

Bowling: Ellison 7.2–0–43–2; Ealham 8–0–27–0; Fleming 7–0–22–1; Igglesden 8–0–30–2; Davis 6–0–21–0; Cowdrey 3–0–12–0.

Umpires: D. J. Constant and G. A. Stickley.

At Northampton, May 3. KENT beat NORTHAMPTONSHIRE by 84 runs.

KENT v DURHAM

At Canterbury, May 10. No result. Toss: Durham. Rain stopped play after 20 overs.

Kent

T. R. Ward c Parker b Botham	45
*M. R. Benson c Fothergill b Brown	0
N. R. Taylor not out	30
C. L. Hooper not out	13
L-b 5, w 1	6
1/10 2/64 (2 wkts, 20 overs) 94	

G. R. Cowdrey, M. V. Fleming, †S. A. Marsh, M. A. Ealham, R. P. Davis, M. J. McCague and R. M. Ellison did not bat.

Bowling: McEwan 5–1–27–0; Brown 3–0–21–1; Botham 6–0–12–1; Graveney 5–0–19–0; Bainbridge 1–0–10–0.

Durham

I. T. Botham, W. Larkins, D. M. Jones, P. W. G. Parker, P. Bainbridge, J. D. Glendenen, †A. R. Fothergill, *D. A. Graveney, S. M. McEwan, S. P. Hughes and S. J. E. Brown.

Umpires: G. I. Burgess and B. Leadbeater.

At The Oval, May 17. KENT beat SURREY by three wickets.

KENT v MIDDLESEX

At Canterbury, May 24. Middlesex won by seven wickets. Toss: Kent. Middlesex's fifth straight win came courtesy of Haynes, who hit an unbeaten 95 in 100 balls.

Kent

T. R. Ward c Roseberry b Williams	55	R. M. Ellison not out	17
*M. R. Benson c Weekes b Emburey	29	R. P. Davis not out	4
N. R. Taylor b Weekes	11		
C. L. Hooper c Carr b Williams	5	B 1, l-b 4, w 1, n-b 1	7
G. R. Cowdrey c and b Carr	31		
M. V. Fleming c Ramprakash b Carr	37	1/77 2/96 3/105 (8 wkts, 40 overs) 219	
†S. A. Marsh c Haynes b Emburey	11	4/107 5/160 6/178	
M. A. Ealham run out	12	7/192 8/198	

M. J. McCague did not bat.

Bowling: Fraser 6–0–33–0; Headley 4–1–19–0; Emburey 8–1–39–2; Williams 8–0–28–2; Weekes 8–0–53–1; Carr 6–0–42–2.

Middlesex

D. L. Haynes not out	95	†K. R. Brown not out 13
M. A. Roseberry c Davis b Hooper	19	B 4, l-b 6, w 2 12
M. W. Gatting c Hooper b Fleming	25	
M. R. Ramprakash c Davis b McCague	57	1/34 2/75 3/176 (3 wkts, 38.4 overs) 221

J. D. Carr, P. N. Weekes, J. E. Emburey, N. F. Williams, A. R. C. Fraser and D. W. Headley did not bat.

Bowling: Ellison 1–0–12–0; Ealham 8–0–34–0; Hooper 8–0–34–1; Davis 7–0–41–0; Fleming 8–0–42–1; McCague 6.4–0–48–1.

Umpires: J. W. Holder and V. A. Holder.

KENT v YORKSHIRE

At Canterbury, May 31. Yorkshire won by four runs. Toss: Kent. Yorkshire's innings failed to fulfil its promise when Tendulkar's dismissal in the 35th over began a collapse of five wickets in 28 balls.

Yorkshire

S. A. Kellett run out	4	P. Carrick not out 4
A. A. Metcalfe lbw b Fleming	39	J. D. Batty not out 0
R. J. Blakey c Igglesden b Hooper	28	
S. R. Tendulkar c Ward b McCague	33	L-b 5, w 8 13
D. Byas run out	28	
C. White run out	11	1/9 2/64 3/99 (8 wkts, 40 overs) 161
P. J. Hartley b Fleming	1	4/138 5/153 6/155
D. Gough c Ealham b McCague	0	7/156 8/158

P. W. Jarvis did not bat.

Bowling: Igglesden 8–0–23–0; Ealham 5–0–17–0; Davis 8–0–22–0; Hooper 8–0–37–1; Fleming 7–0–40–2; McCague 4–0–17–2.

Kent

T. R. Ward lbw b Jarvis	13	R. P. Davis run out 26
*M. R. Benson c and b Hartley	6	M. J. McCague b Gough 2
N. R. Taylor lbw b Batty	34	A. P. Igglesden not out 12
G. R. Cowdrey b Carrick	3	B 3, l-b 7, w 3, n-b 2 15
C. L. Hooper c and b Carrick	3	
M. V. Fleming lbw b Batty	3	1/20 2/24 3/37 (40 overs) 157
†S. A. Marsh c and b Batty	6	4/41 5/48 6/64
M. A. Ealham b Hartley	34	7/95 8/113 9/128

Bowling: Jarvis 8–1–37–1; Hartley 8–0–39–2; Gough 8–0–33–1; Carrick 8–0–17–2; Batty 8–0–21–3.

Umpires: G. I. Burgess and D. O. Oslear.

At Chelmsford, June 7. KENT lost to ESSEX by six runs.

At Swindon, June 14. KENT beat GLOUCESTERSHIRE by 15 runs.

KENT v LANCASHIRE

At Maidstone, July 5. No result.

KENT v WORCESTERSHIRE

At Canterbury, July 19. Kent won by 36 runs. Toss: Kent. Ward reached 50 in 25 balls and had scored all but eight of Kent's runs when he was dismissed in the sixth over. Though his colleagues could not maintain his momentum, 235 proved adequate once Hooper had removed Hick and Curtis – one with a diving catch, the other stumped off his off-spin.

Kent

T. R. Ward c Radford b Tolley	51	R. P. Davis lbw b Hick		4
*M. R. Benson c Rhodes b Illingworth	36	M. J. McCague not out		1
N. R. Taylor c Moody b Newport	28	A. P. Igglesden not out		2
C. L. Hooper lbw b Radford	9	L-b 7, w 1		8
G. R. Cowdrey run out	33			
M. V. Fleming run out	38	1/59 2/97 3/113	(9 wkts, 39 overs)	235
†S. A. Marsh c Hick b Tolley	16	4/133 5/196 6/206		
M. A. Ealham c Hick b Tolley	9	7/224 8/228 9/233		

Bowling: Weston 3–0–34–0; Tolley 6–0–43–3; Newport 8–0–39–1; Hick 8–0–45–1; Radford 6–1–23–1; Illingworth 8–0–44–1.

Worcestershire

T. M. Moody b Ealham	15	P. J. Newport b McCague		1
*T. S. Curtis st Marsh b Hooper	42	R. K. Illingworth not out		8
G. A. Hick c Hooper b Davis	37	C. M. Tolley not out		0
D. A. Leatherdale c Fleming b Davis	7	B 2, l-b 12, w 6		20
D. B. D'Oliveira st Marsh b Davis	3			
N. V. Radford c Marsh b Ward	55	1/30 2/100 3/109	(9 wkts, 39 overs)	199
†S. J. Rhodes c Igglesden b McCague	4	4/115 5/123 6/152		
M. J. Weston lbw b Fleming	7	7/169 8/172 9/198		

Bowling: Igglesden 8–1–46–0; Hooper 8–0–30–1; Ealham 8–0–32–2; Davis 8–0–35–3; McCague 5–0–26–2; Cowdrey 1–0–5–0; Ward 1–0–11–1.

Umpires: R. Julian and A. G. T. Whitehead.

At Leicester, July 26. KENT beat LEICESTERSHIRE by 62 runs.

At Swansea, August 2. KENT beat GLAMORGAN by 47 runs.

KENT v HAMPSHIRE

At Canterbury, August 9. Kent won by six wickets. Toss: Kent. Kent extracted a little revenge for their Benson and Hedges Cup final defeat, despite slipping to 86 for four in their first 27 overs; Cowdrey and Fleming put on 90 to pass Hampshire with six balls to spare. Earlier, Middleton had achieved the unusual feat of a third Sunday League fifty in eight days.

Hampshire

T. C. Middleton b Ealham	71	C. A. Connor c Marsh b Fleming		1
J. R. Wood c Marsh b Ealham	4	R. S. M. Morris not out		4
*M. C. J. Nicholas c Benson b Ealham	8			
J. R. Ayling b Igglesden	26	L-b 3, n-b 2		5
M. D. Marshall lbw b McCague	19			
K. D. James c Benson b McCague	1	1/16 2/28 3/84	(9 wkts, 40 overs)	172
†A. N. Aymes b Fleming	23	4/111 5/115 6/153		
S. D. Udal run out	10	7/158 8/160 9/172		

I. J. Turner did not bat.

Bowling: McCague 8–0–36–2; Ealham 8–2–24–3; Igglesden 8–0–34–1; Fleming 8–0–25–2; Hooper 8–0–50–0.

Kent

T. R. Ward c Middleton b James	6	M. V. Fleming not out	45
*M. R. Benson lbw b James	8	L-b 5, w 1, n-b 3	9
N. R. Taylor lbw b Udal	35		
C. L. Hooper c Udal b Marshall	22	1/7 2/28 (4 wkts, 39 overs) 176	
G. R. Cowdrey not out	51	3/71 4/86	

†S. A. Marsh, M. A. Ealham, N. J. Llong, M. J. McCague and A. P. Igglesden did not bat.

Bowling: James 8-0-17-2; Connor 7-0-27-0; Ayling 8-0-44-0; Marshall 8-0-41-1; Turner 4-0-19-0; Udal 4-0-23-1.

Umpires: B. J. Meyer and A. G. T. Whitehead.

KENT v NOTTINGHAMSHIRE

At Canterbury, August 12. No result. Rain prevented any play in this fixture, transferred to a Wednesday because of Kent's involvement in the Benson and Hedges Cup final on the weekend of July 11-12.

At Chesterfield, August 16. KENT lost to DERBYSHIRE by 48 runs.

At Birmingham, August 23. WARWICKSHIRE v KENT. No result.

KENT v SUSSEX

At Canterbury, August 30. Kent won by 76 runs. Toss: Sussex. Ward played another lightning innings, hitting 73 from 47 balls. Chasing more than seven an over in a match reduced by rain to 33 overs a side, Sussex reached 127 for four but then lost three wickets for five runs, and were quickly all out.

Kent

T. R. Ward c Giddins b Lenham	73	M. A. Ealham c Moores b Stephenson	0
*M. R. Benson c and b Lenham	38	M. J. McCague not out	1
N. R. Taylor b Salisbury	20	L-b 3, w 6, n-b 1	10
C. L. Hooper c Giddins b Stephenson	46		
G. R. Cowdrey b Salisbury	2	1/113 2/122 3/150 (7 wkts, 33 overs) 235	
M. V. Fleming run out	9	4/160 5/186	
†S. A. Marsh not out	36	6/232 7/233	

A. P. Igglesden and R. P. Davis did not bat.

Bowling: Stephenson 7-0-54-2; Giddins 7-0-54-0; Pigott 3-0-21-0; Remy 2-0-22-0; Lenham 7-0-41-2; Salisbury 7-0-40-2.

Sussex

J. W. Hall run out	14	I. D. K. Salisbury c Marsh b Fleming	6
D. M. Smith run out	23	A. C. S. Pigott not out	4
M. P. Speight run out	26	E. S. H. Giddins c Cowdrey b Davis	1
*A. P. Wells c Ealham b McCague	52	L-b 4, w 1	5
F. D. Stephenson b McCague	6		
†P. Moores lbw b McCague	7	1/25 2/61 3/82 (30.4 overs) 159	
N. J. Lenham b McCague	0	4/103 5/127 6/127	
C. C. Remy c Hooper b Davis	15	7/132 8/153 9/154	

Bowling: Ealham 3-0-16-0; Igglesden 7-0-30-0; Hooper 3-0-20-0; Fleming 6-0-22-1; McCague 7-0-45-4; Davis 4.4-0-22-2.

Umpires: B. Dudleston and G. A. Stickley.

LANCASHIRE

At Durham University, April 19. LANCASHIRE lost to DURHAM by nine runs.

LANCASHIRE v HAMPSHIRE

At Manchester, May 3. Lancashire won by four wickets. Toss: Hampshire. Speak put on 87 in 16 overs with Atherton, and DeFreitas's unbeaten 49 in 38 balls gave Lancashire victory.

Hampshire

V. P. Terry c Atherton b Watkinson	66	†A. N. Aymes not out	5
R. A. Smith c Fairbrother b Morrison	40	R. J. Maru not out	0
D. I. Gower c Speak b Watkinson	37	L-b 6, w 3, n-b 1	10
J. R. Ayling c Hegg b Austin	39		
K. D. James c Fairbrother b DeFreitas	0	1/77 2/130 3/182 (7 wkts, 40 overs) 209
*M. C. J. Nicholas run out	5	4/184 5/194
M. D. Marshall b DeFreitas	7	6/201 7/206

S. D. Udal and C. A. Connor did not bat.

Bowling: Allott 8–0–23–0; DeFreitas 8–0–34–2; Morrison 8–0–46–1; Austin 8–0–42–1; Barnett 3–0–21–0; Watkinson 5–0–37–2.

Lancashire

G. D. Lloyd c Aymes b Udal	18	I. D. Austin b Maru	1
N. J. Speak c Marshall b Connor	65	†W. K. Hegg not out	8
M. A. Atherton run out	35	B 1, l-b 6, w 11	18
*N. H. Fairbrother c Maru b Udal	9		
M. Watkinson c Aymes b Ayling	7	1/39 2/126 3/127 (6 wkts, 38.5 overs) 210
P. A. J. DeFreitas not out	49	4/138 5/155 6/176

P. J. W. Allott, D. K. Morrison and A. A. Barnett did not bat.

Bowling: Connor 6.5–0–47–1; Marshall 8–0–31–0; Udal 8–0–32–2; Ayling 6–0–37–1; Maru 8–0–44–1; James 2–0–12–0.

Umpires: J. H. Harris and D. O. Oslear.

At Northampton, May 17. LANCASHIRE beat NORTHAMPTONSHIRE by four wickets.

At Birmingham, May 24. WARWICKSHIRE v LANCASHIRE. No result.

LANCASHIRE v SOMERSET

At Manchester, May 31. Somerset won by nine wickets. Toss: Somerset. Lancashire's last eight wickets went down for 22 runs. Caddick claimed the last three in five balls, with the help of wicket-keeper Burns, who took five catches in the innings. Lancashire's last hopes were dashed when they lost Allott to a calf muscle strain in his first over, and they were beaten by five o'clock.

Lancashire

P. Titchard c Trump b Caddick	20	†W. K. Hegg not out	0
G. Fowler c Trump b Mallender	5	J. D. Fitton c Burns b Caddick	0
M. A. Atherton c Lathwell b Snell	13	P. J. W. Allott c Burns b Caddick	0
G. D. Lloyd c Burns b MacLeay	14	L-b 2, w 6	8
N. J. Speak c Lathwell b Trump	6		
M. Watkinson b MacLeay	3	1/24 2/30 3/55 (27.3 overs) 77	
*A. J. DeFreitas c Burns b Caddick	5	4/55 5/65 6/70	
D. Austin c Burns b Trump	3	7/75 8/75 9/75	

Bowling: Mallender 4–0–19–1; Caddick 5.3–0–18–4; Snell 5–1–13–1; MacLeay 8–1–17–2; Trump 5–1–8–2.

Somerset

A. N. Hayhurst not out	27	
M. N. Lathwell c Hegg b DeFreitas	14	
C. J. Tavaré not out	36	
L-b 1, n-b 1	2	

1/34 (1 wkt, 19.1 overs) 79

R. P. Snell, R. J. Harden, G. D. Rose, K. H. MacLeay, †N. D. Burns, A. R. Caddick, N. A. Mallender and H. R. J. Trump did not bat.

Bowling: DeFreitas 8–0–40–1; Allott 0.4–0–1–0; Watkinson 6.2–2–19–0; Austin 4.1–0–18–0.

Umpires: J. D. Bond and D. R. Shepherd.

LANCASHIRE v GLOUCESTERSHIRE

At Manchester, June 7. Gloucestershire won by five wickets. Toss: Gloucestershire. The visitors needed 25 from their last 14 balls, but hit 27 from nine, with Wright completing his fifty in 43 deliveries. Speak had been awarded his Lancashire cap before the game, but became one of Alleyne's four prime victims.

Lancashire

G. Fowler b Scott	57	†W. K. Hegg not out	18
M. A. Atherton c Hancock b Alleyne	42	J. D. Fitton not out	9
N. H. Fairbrother b Alleyne	7	L-b 4, w 2, n-b 1	7
N. J. Speak c Babington b Alleyne	12		
G. D. Lloyd c Athey b Smith	30	1/93 2/108 3/110 (7 wkts, 40 overs) 199	
M. Watkinson c Williams b Alleyne	2	4/129 5/131	
D. Austin b Smith	15	6/167 7/188	

J. D. Fletcher and D. K. Morrison did not bat.

Bowling: Smith 8–0–51–2; Babington 8–1–37–0; Hancock 8–0–36–0; Scott 8–0–36–1; Alleyne 8–1–35–4.

Gloucestershire

G. D. Hodgson c Speak b Fitton	40	R. J. Scott not out	12
R. G. Hinks lbw b Fletcher	12		
C. W. J. Athey c Fowler b Austin	47	L-b 7, w 3, n-b 1	11
A. J. Wright not out	59		
M. W. Alleyne c Atherton b Austin	18	1/26 2/95 3/132 (5 wkts, 39.1 overs) 202	
T. H. C. Hancock b Fletcher	3	4/167 5/172	

R. I. Dawson, †R. C. J. Williams, A. M. Babington and A. M. Smith did not bat.

Bowling: Morrison 8–0–46–0; Fletcher 7.1–0–45–2; Austin 8–1–28–2; Fitton 8–0–34–1; Watkinson 8–0–42–0.

Umpires: R. Palmer and N. T. Plews.

At Colwyn Bay, June 14. LANCASHIRE beat GLAMORGAN by six wickets.

LANCASHIRE v LEICESTERSHIRE

At Manchester, June 21. Leicestershire won by 95 runs. Toss: Leicestershire. Leicestershire owed their first Sunday win of the season to their débutant Robinson, who had never scored a limited-overs hundred for his former county Yorkshire but reached one now in 91 balls, with three sixes and nine fours; his second fifty took only 29 balls. Feeble batting from Lancashire saw them dismissed with six overs to spare.

Leicestershire

J. J. Whitaker b Fitton	59	V. J. Wells not out		3
*N. E. Briers run out	7	G. J. Parsons run out		2
B. F. Smith c Allott b Martin	2	A. D. Mullally not out		1
P. E. Robinson c Austin b Atherton	104	L-b 3, w 3		6
J. D. R. Benson c and b Watkinson	51			
L. Potter b Austin	5	1/9 2/20 3/110	(9 wkts, 40 overs)	248
W. K. M. Benjamin c sub b Austin	3	4/225 5/231 6/235		
†P. A. Nixon b Austin	5	7/241 8/243 9/247		

Bowling: Allott 5–0–16–0; Martin 8–0–65–1; Watkinson 8–0–52–1; Austin 8–0–38–3; Fitton 8–0–46–1; Atherton 3–0–28–1.

Lancashire

G. Fowler run out	10	J. D. Fitton not out		19
S. P. Titchard c Nixon b Mullally	10	P. J. Martin c Nixon b Wells		6
*M. A. Atherton c Mullally b Potter	3	P. J. W. Allott b Benjamin		3
G. D. Lloyd b Wells	21	B 5, l-b 8, w 8		21
N. J. Speak c Briers b Mullally	28			
M. Watkinson c Robinson b Parsons	18	1/23 2/23 3/31	(34 overs)	153
I. D. Austin b Parsons	12	4/62 5/100 6/119		
†W. K. Hegg c Briers b Parsons	2	7/121 8/122 9/135		

Bowling: Benjamin 5–1–13–1; Mullally 8–0–31–2; Potter 8–0–33–1; Wells 8–0–34–2; Parsons 5–0–29–3.

Umpires: J. H. Harris and V. A. Holder.

At Ilford, June 28. LANCASHIRE lost to ESSEX by seven wickets.

At Maidstone, July 5. KENT v LANCASHIRE. No result.

LANCASHIRE v MIDDLESEX

At Manchester, July 12. Middlesex won by two runs. Toss: Lancashire. Middlesex narrowly secured their tenth straight win after Lancashire's middle order pulled their innings round. The match was reduced to 36 overs a side after overnight rain delayed the start and, as usual, Haynes took the limelight with 84 in 91 balls. But Middlesex were checked when off-spinner Fitton took a wicket in each of his first three overs, thus giving Lancashire their chance.

Middlesex

D. L. Haynes c Hegg b Irani	84	P. N. Weekes not out	27
M. A. Roseberry st Hegg b Fitton	27		
*M. W. Gatting b Fitton	9	L-b 5, w 3	8
M. R. Ramprakash c Martin b Fitton	3		—
J. D. Carr c and b Fitton	18	1/63 2/78 3/82 (5 wkts, 36 overs)	201
†K. R. Brown not out	25	4/120 5/165	

J. E. Emburey, D. W. Headley, N. F. Williams and A. R. C. Fraser did not bat.

Bowling: Martin 8–0–30–0; Fletcher 4–0–32–0; Austin 7–0–47–0; Fitton 7–0–26–4; Watkinson 7–0–40–0; Irani 3–0–21–1.

Lancashire

G. Fowler b Headley	11	J. D. Fitton b Williams	13
*M. A. Atherton b Fraser	27	P. J. Martin not out	10
N. J. Speak st Brown b Weekes	9	S. D. Fletcher not out	6
G. D. Lloyd c Carr b Headley	28	L-b 11, w 5, n-b 4	20
M. Watkinson c Roseberry b Emburey	7		—
I. D. Austin b Fraser	31	1/18 2/54 3/54 (9 wkts, 36 overs)	199
†W. K. Hegg run out	34	4/79 5/126 6/130	
R. C. Irani c Weekes b Fraser	3	7/139 8/159 9/190	

Bowling: Headley 7–0–35–2; Williams 6–0–33–1; Weekes 5–1–14–1; Fraser 8–0–40–3; Carr 3–0–19–0; Emburey 7–0–47–1.

Umpires: D. O. Oslear and R. C. Tolchard.

LANCASHIRE v SURREY

At Manchester, July 26. Lancashire won by eight wickets, their target having been revised to 97 from 23 overs. Toss: Lancashire. Rain interrupted Lancashire's innings at 56 without loss from 15 overs, and they reached their new target with four balls to spare, courtesy of a no-ball from Benjamin. Lloyd received his county cap before the game.

Surrey

M. A. Feltham c and b Martin	11	†N. F. Sargeant lbw b Austin	1
A. D. Brown c Hegg b Martin	14	J. Boiling b Austin	0
G. P. Thorpe c Watkinson b Fitton	34		
*M. A. Lynch b Watkinson	12	L-b 10, w 1	11
J. D. Robinson c Irani b Fitton	21		—
A. A. Greig c Speak b Watkinson	27	1/22 2/33 3/70 (9 wkts, 40 overs)	168
R. E. Bryson b Watkinson	19	4/80 5/117 6/129	
M. P. Bicknell not out	18	7/165 8/168 9/168	

J. E. Benjamin did not bat.

Bowling: Martin 8–0–33–2; Allott 8–1–24–0; Austin 8–1–37–2; Watkinson 8–0–42–3; Fitton 8–1–22–2.

Lancashire

G. Fowler not out	49
N. J. Speak b Bicknell	40
G. D. Lloyd c Robinson b Bryson	2
*N. H. Fairbrother not out	4
L-b 2, n-b 3	5

1/84 2/93 (2 wkts, 22.2 overs) 100

M. Watkinson, †W. K. Hegg, R. C. Irani, I. D. Austin, J. D. Fitton, P. J. Martin and P. J. W. Allott did not bat.

Bowling: Bicknell 8–0–29–1; Bryson 8–1–32–1; Benjamin 2.2–0–15–0; Boiling 3–0–9–0; Greig 1–0–13–0.

Umpires: J. H. Hampshire and A. G. T. Whitehead.

At Leeds, August 2. LANCASHIRE beat YORKSHIRE by four runs.

LANCASHIRE v WORCESTERSHIRE

At Manchester, August 9. No result.

At Hove, August 16. LANCASHIRE lost to SUSSEX by six wickets.

At Nottingham, August 23. NOTTINGHAMSHIRE v LANCASHIRE. No result.

LANCASHIRE v DERBYSHIRE

At Manchester, August 30. Lancashire won by five wickets. Toss: Lancashire. The rain which cut the match to 31 overs a side probably deprived Bowler of a maiden Sunday League hundred; he remained unbeaten on 91 from 102 balls. Lancashire wasted no time in their pursuit of 156; Atherton hit three sixes and Lloyd two as they got home with more than seven overs to spare.

Derbyshire

P. D. Bowler not out	91	A. E. Warner run out		2
C. J. Adams b Martin	8	F. A. Griffith not out		4
J. E. Morris b DeFreitas	0			
D. G. Cork c Hegg b Austin	4	L-b 3, w 4		7
T. J. G. O'Gorman				
c Fairbrother b Fitton	8	1/24 2/25 3/35	(6 wkts, 31 overs)	155
*K. J. Barnett c Fairbrother b Martin	31	4/53 5/130 6/140		

†K. M. Krikken, D. E. Malcolm and O. H. Mortensen did not bat.

Bowling: DeFreitas 7–1–31–1; Martin 6–0–17–2; Watkinson 6–0–32–0; Austin 6–0–31–1; Fitton 6–0–41–1.

Lancashire

M. A. Atherton c O'Gorman b Warner	34	I. D. Austin not out		6
N. J. Speak b Mortensen	13			
G. D. Lloyd c Bowler b Griffith	41	L-b 10, w 3		13
*N. H. Fairbrother not out	27			
M. Watkinson b Warner	23	1/26 2/65 3/108	(5 wkts, 23.3 overs)	157
P. A. J. DeFreitas b Warner	0	4/144 5/148		

R. C. Irani, †W. K. Hegg, J. D. Fitton and P. J. Martin did not bat.

Bowling: Malcolm 5–0–19–0; Mortensen 5–1–29–1; Cork 3–0–35–0; Warner 6.3–0–22–3; Griffith 3–0–41–1; Adams 1–0–1–0.

Umpires: J. W. Holder and B. J. Meyer.

LEICESTERSHIRE

LEICESTERSHIRE v MIDDLESEX

At Leicester, April 19. Middlesex won by ten runs. Toss: Leicestershire. When 11, Briers reached 5,000 runs in the competition, and in the same innings Embatey took his 300th Sunday League wicket. The match was Fraser's first for Middlesex since June 1991, since when he had been recovering from his hip injury.

Middlesex

J. D. Carr c Briers b Millns	29	J. E. Emburey not out	7
M. A. Roseberry c Wells b Parsons	59	N. F. Williams not out	5
*M. W. Gatting c Wells b Parsons	9		
M. R. Ramprakash c Whitaker b Parsons	11	L-b 3, w 2	5
†K. R. Brown c Wells b Mullally	40	1/83 2/97 3/99 (7 wkts, 40 overs)	207
P. N. Weekes c Mullally b Hepworth	17	4/124 5/154	
R. J. Sims run out	25	6/177 7/195	

A. R. C. Fraser and N. G. Cowans did not bat.

Bowling: Mullally 8–1–50–1; Parsons 8–0–35–3; Wells 7–0–36–0; Millns 6–0–30–1; Benson 8–0–29–0; Hepworth 3–0–24–1.

Leicestershire

J. D. R. Benson b Williams	22	G. J. Parsons c Brown b Cowans	19
*N. E. Briers b Williams	18	D. J. Millns not out	11
J. J. Whitaker c Weekes b Carr	42	A. D. Mullally not out	2
L. Potter c Ramprakash b Cowans	52	B 2, l-b 3, w 1, n-b 1	7
B. F. Smith run out	10		
V. J. Wells c Gatting b Emburey	10	1/39 2/42 3/110 (9 wkts, 40 overs)	197
†P. Whitticase c Cowans b Weekes	3	4/128 5/151 6/162	
P. N. Hepworth b Emburey	1	7/165 8/174 9/188	

Bowling: Cowans 7–1–44–2; Williams 8–1–32–2; Fraser 8–1–25–0; Emburey 8–0–34–2; Weekes 7–0–44–1; Carr 2–0–13–1.

Umpires: R. Julian and D. O. Oslear.

At Gateshead Fell, April 26. LEICESTERSHIRE lost to DURHAM by eight runs.

LEICESTERSHIRE v ESSEX

At Leicester, May 3. Essex won by three wickets. Toss: Leicestershire. Waugh hit six fours and a six as he added 109 in 21 overs with Gooch.

Leicestershire

J. D. R. Benson c Prichard b Pringle	1	P. N. Hepworth c Prichard b Stephenson	0
*N. E. Briers c Such b Fraser	38	G. J. Parsons not out	24
J. J. Whitaker c Gooch b Fraser	68		
L. Potter run out	0	L-b 9, w 6	15
T. J. Boon b Such	3		
W. K. M. Benjamin c Waugh b Stephenson	7	1/4 2/85 3/86 (8 wkts, 40 overs)	189
V. J. Wells not out	29	4/96 5/109 6/142	
†P. A. Nixon c Hussain b Topley	4	7/150 8/151	

A. D. Mullally did not bat.

Bowling: Topley 8–0–32–1; Pringle 8–0–34–1; Stephenson 8–0–29–2; Fraser 8–0–39–2; Such 8–0–46–1.

Essex

*G. A. Gooch c Parsons b Benson	49	†M. A. Garnham not out	13
J. P. Stephenson c Benson b Mullally	1	A. G. J. Fraser not out	9
M. E. Waugh st Nixon b Hepworth	86	L-b 8, w 4	12
N. Hussain c Nixon b Benjamin	11		
P. J. Prichard c Briers b Mullally	5	1/3 2/112 3/146 (7 wkts, 39.1 overs)	193
N. V. Knight c Wells b Benjamin	5	4/159 5/161	
D. R. Pringle c and b Benson	2	6/167 7/175	

T. D. Topley and P. M. Such did not bat.

Bowling: Benjamin 8–1–28–2; Mullally 7.1–1–20–2; Wells 4–0–28–0; Parsons 4–0–21–0; Potter 2–0–19–0; Hepworth 8–0–34–1; Benson 6–0–35–2.

Umpires: D. J. Constant and A. G. T. Whitehead.

At Birmingham, May 17. LEICESTERSHIRE lost to WARWICKSHIRE by 100 runs.

At Swansea, May 31. LEICESTERSHIRE lost to GLAMORGAN by 59 runs.

LEICESTERSHIRE v SUSSEX

At Leicester, June 14. Sussex won by 69 runs. Toss: Leicestershire. In the Championship, Leicestershire had just beaten Sussex in two days, but their first Sunday win still eluded them. Stephenson reached 50 for Sussex from 32 balls, with seven fours and a six. When Leicestershire replied, Salisbury's leg-spin claimed four wickets in his first six overs and five in all.

Sussex

K. Greenfield b Benjamin	4	†P. Moores run out	7
J. W. Hall run out	17	J. A. North not out	9
M. P. Speight c Gofton b Parsons	44	B 5, l-b 7, w 2	14
*A. P. Wells lbw b Gofton	62		
N. J. Lenham c Gofton b Mullally	23	1/4 2/39 3/79	(6 wkts, 40 overs) 235
F. D. Stephenson not out	55	4/137 5/196 6/218	

A. C. S. Pigott, I. D. K. Salisbury and A. G. Robson did not bat.

Bowling: Benjamin 8–1–30–1; Millns 8–0–66–0; Mullally 7–1–39–1; Parsons 8–0–25–1; Gofton 6–0–41–1; Gidley 3–0–22–0.

Leicestershire

J. D. R. Benson lbw b Stephenson	11	R. P. Gofton c Hall b Pigott	2
*N. E. Briers c Greenfield b Robson	20	D. J. Millns c Wells b Salisbury	3
J. J. Whitaker c Stephenson b Salisbury	20	A. D. Mullally not out	5
B. F. Smith b Salisbury	24		
†P. A. Nixon lbw b Salisbury	21	B 1, l-b 11, w 5	17
W. K. M. Benjamin c Moores b Salisbury	2	1/15 2/46 3/66	(9 wkts, 40 overs) 166
M. I. Gidley c Salisbury b Pigott	10	4/91 5/95 6/111	
G. J. Parsons not out	31	7/136 8/145 9/156	

Bowling: Robson 8–1–34–1; Stephenson 8–2–21–1; Pigott 8–1–29–2; Salisbury 8–0–30–5; Greenfield 5–0–35–0; North 3–0–5–0.

Umpires: J. D. Bond and B. J. Meyer.

At Manchester, June 21. LEICESTERSHIRE beat LANCASHIRE by 95 runs.

At Derby, June 28. LEICESTERSHIRE lost to DERBYSHIRE by five wickets.

At Sheffield, July 5. LEICESTERSHIRE beat YORKSHIRE by six wickets.

LEICESTERSHIRE v WORCESTERSHIRE

At Leicester, July 12. Worcestershire won by six runs. Toss: Leicestershire. Both teams made a good start and then fell away. Worcestershire's last eight wickets went for 54, with Potter removing four of the top order. Then Leicestershire, who had reached 92 for one before halfway, well ahead of the rate, lost nine for 73.

Worcestershire

*T. S. Curtis c Benson b Wells	14	P. J. Newport c Benson b Wells		7
T. M. Moody b Potter	66	R. K. Illingworth not out		1
G. A. Hick b Potter	17	C. M. Tolley run out		0
D. A. Leatherdale c Robinson b Potter	13	B 2, l-b 3, w 7		12
D. B. D'Oliveira st Nixon b Potter	12			
G. R. Haynes b Parsons	8	1/48 2/90 3/117	(38.3 overs)	171
S. R. Lampitt c Mullally b Wells	6	4/127 5/139 6/143		
†S. J. Rhodes b Benjamin	15	7/152 8/167 9/171		

Bowling: Benjamin 7–2–19–1; Mullally 8–1–33–0; Wells 7.3–0–35–3; Parsons 8–0–46–1; Potter 8–0–33–4.

Leicestershire

J. J. Whitaker c Newport b Illingworth	49	V. J. Wells c and b Tolley		10
*N. E. Briers c Hick b Newport	34	G. J. Parsons c Tolley b Newport		1
B. F. Smith st Rhodes b Illingworth	18	A. D. Mullally not out		0
P. E. Robinson c D'Oliveira b Hick	3			
J. D. R. Benson run out	6	L-b 8, n-b 1		9
L. Potter c Curtis b Tolley	8			
†P. A. Nixon c Leatherdale b Newport	19	1/79 2/92 3/105	(39.4 overs)	165
W. K. M. Benjamin c Leatherdale b Tolley	8	4/109 5/114 6/124		
		7/141 8/156 9/165		

Bowling: Tolley 8–1–28–3; Haynes 6–0–14–0; Newport 7.4–0–38–3; Lampitt 2–0–18–0; Illingworth 8–2–23–2; Hick 8–0–36–1.

Umpires: R. Julian and P. B. Wight.

LEICESTERSHIRE v SOMERSET

At Leicester, July 19. Somerset won by nine wickets. Toss: Somerset. Lathwell faced 98 balls, hitting nine fours and a six as he and Hayhurst put on 169 in 30 overs for Somerset's first wicket.

Leicestershire

J. J. Whitaker c Lathwell b MacLeay	46	R. P. Gofton lbw b Caddick		0
*N. E. Briers c Tavaré b MacLeay	18	D. J. Millns not out		2
B. F. Smith c MacLeay b Trump	17			
P. E. Robinson b Snell	24	L-b 6, w 2, n-b 3		11
J. D. R. Benson run out	39			
L. Potter run out	10	1/50 2/76 3/108	(8 wkts, 40 overs)	200
†P. A. Nixon run out	27	4/117 5/149 6/167		
G. J. Parsons c Tavaré b Rose	6	7/189 8/193		

A. D. Mullally did not bat.

Bowling: Mallender 8–0–36–0; Caddick 8–0–44–1; MacLeay 8–0–29–2; Snell 8–0–35–1; Trump 7–0–40–1; Rose 1–0–10–1.

Somerset

A. N. Hayhurst not out	....	67
M. N. Lathwell b Gofton	....	96
*C. J. Tavaré not out	....	12
L-b 18, w 9	....	27

1/169　　　　　　　(1 wkt, 35.4 overs) 202

R. J. Harden, G. D. Rose, †N. D. Burns, K. H. MacLeay, R. P. Snell, N. A. Mallender, A. R. Caddick and H. R. J. Trump did not bat.

Bowling: Mullally 6–0–23–0; Parsons 6–0–45–0; Millns 7–0–37–0; Gofton 6.4–0–33–1; Potter 8–1–32–0; Benson 2–0–14–0.

Umpires: J. C. Balderstone and J. H. Hampshire.

LEICESTERSHIRE v KENT

At Leicester, July 26. Kent won by 62 runs. Toss: Leicestershire. Kent made rapid progress: Ward opened with 37 in 36 balls, Taylor hit 71 from 79 and 99 runs came off their last ten overs. Leicestershire were never in the hunt and fell to their 11th successive Sunday League home defeat.

Kent

T. R. Ward c Boon b Wells	....	37
*M. R. Benson c Nixon b Wells	.....	15
N. R. Taylor c Boon b Mullally	....	71
C. L. Hooper c Whitaker b Parsons	...	5
G. R. Cowdrey b Potter	....	23
M. V. Fleming c Gidley b Mullally	....	9
†S. A. Marsh c Wells b Gidley	....	27

N. J. Llong not out	....	18
M. A. Ealham not out	....	22
B 5, l-b 6, w 7	....	18

1/45　2/56　3/66　　　(7 wkts, 40 overs) 245
4/113　5/134
6/199　7/203

R. P. Davis and M. J. McCague did not bat.

Bowling: Mullally 8–0–38–2; Gofton 5–0–56–0; Wells 8–1–37–2; Parsons 8–0–39–1; Potter 8–0–39–1; Gidley 3–0–25–1.

Leicestershire

J. J. Whitaker c Taylor b Hooper	.....	15
*N. E. Briers c Ward b Fleming	......	29
T. J. Boon run out	....	1
P. E. Robinson c Ealham b McCague	..	40
L. Potter not out	....	47
†P. A. Nixon b McCague	....	14
V. J. Wells c Ward b Ealham	....	7
M. I. Gidley b McCague	....	8

G. J. Parsons b McCague	....	3
R. P. Gofton not out	....	2
B 1, l-b 10, w 6	....	17

1/27　2/31　3/82　　　(8 wkts, 40 overs) 183
4/109　5/130　6/147
7/172　8/178

A. D. Mullally did not bat.

Bowling: McCague 8–0–35–4; Ealham 8–0–30–1; Hooper 8–0–39–1; Davis 8–0–28–0; Fleming 8–0–40–1.

Umpires: D. J. Constant and R. A. White.

At Nottingham, August 2. LEICESTERSHIRE lost to NOTTINGHAMSHIRE by seven wickets.

At Bristol, August 9. LEICESTERSHIRE lost to GLOUCESTERSHIRE by nine wickets.

At The Oval, August 16. LEICESTERSHIRE beat SURREY by five wickets.

LEICESTERSHIRE v NORTHAMPTONSHIRE

At Leicester, August 23. No result. Toss: Northamptonshire. Leicestershire picked up their first points at Grace Road since May 19, 1991, when rain prevented Northamptonshire from batting. They had been 78 for six until Nixon and Gidley mounted a rescue which took them to 171.

Leicestershire

*N. E. Briers c and b Cook	14	M. I. Gidley not out	55
J. J. Whitaker c Bailey b Cook	12	G. J. Parsons not out	9
V. J. Wells lbw b Bowen	25	B 1, l-b 5, w 4	10
P. E. Robinson c Noon b Walton	18		—
J. D. R. Benson c Snape b Walton	2	1/27 2/28 3/63 (7 wkts, 40 overs) 171	
L. Potter run out	1	4/73 5/78	
†P. A. Nixon b Bailey	25	6/78 7/139	

R. P. Gofton and A. D. Mullally did not bat.

Bowling: Walker 7–2–30–0; Cook 8–2–20–2; Bowen 7–0–33–1; Snape 8–0–43–0; Walton 8–0–27–2; Bailey 2–0–12–1.

Northamptonshire

A. Fordham, N. A. Felton, *R. J. Bailey, D. J. Capel, K. M. Curran, T. C. Walton, †W. M. Noon, J. N. Snape, N. G. B. Cook, A. Walker and M. N. Bowen.

Umpires: G. I. Burgess and R. Palmer.

LEICESTERSHIRE v HAMPSHIRE

At Leicester, August 30. No result. Leicestershire's sequence without a Sunday League home win moved to 13, when play was completely washed out.

MIDDLESEX

At Leicester, April 19. MIDDLESEX beat LEICESTERSHIRE by ten runs.

MIDDLESEX v GLAMORGAN

At Lord's, April 26. Middlesex won by eight wickets. Toss: Middlesex. The match was reduced to 33 overs a side by rain. An unbroken partnership of 150 from Roseberry and Ramprakash won the day.

Glamorgan

S. P. James c Gatting b Williams	48	D. L. Hemp not out	1
H. Morris c Weekes b Williams	67		
*M. P. Maynard run out	49	L-b 8, w 2, n-b 1	11
C. S. Cowdrey c Gatting b Williams	3		—
S. Kirnon b Headley	1	1/118 2/130 3/151 (5 wkts, 33 overs) 181	
R. D. B. Croft not out	1	4/179 5/179	

†C. P. Metson, S. L. Watkin, D. J. Foster and M. Frost did not bat.

Bowling: Williams 8–1–34–3; Fraser 8–1–25–0; Headley 7–0–34–1; Gatting 3–0–32–0; Emburey 7–0–48–0.

Middlesex

J. D. Carr c Maynard b Frost	7	
M. A. Roseberry not out	71	
*M. W. Gatting run out	6	
M. R. Ramprakash not out	88	
L-b 6, w 6	12	

1/21 2/34   (2 wkts, 31.3 overs) 184

†K. R. Brown, P. N. Weekes, R. J. Sims, J. E. Emburey, N. F. Williams, D. W. Headley and A. R. C. Fraser did not bat.

Bowling: Frost 5–0–21–1; Foster 5.3–0–42–0; Cowdrey 4–0–26–0; Croft 8–0–37–0; Watkin 7–0–32–0; Kirnon 2–0–20–0.

Umpires: J. D. Bond and J. W. Holder.

MIDDLESEX v GLOUCESTERSHIRE

At Lord's, May 3. Middlesex won by nine wickets. Toss: Gloucestershire. Haynes hit eight fours in 81 balls on his first appearance in the league in 1992, as Middlesex won with nearly 15 overs in hand.

Gloucestershire

G. D. Hodgson run out	25	M. C. J. Ball c Headley b Williams	0	
S. G. Hinks c Gatting b Fraser	2	A. M. Smith c Haynes b Emburey	3	
C. W. J. Athey c Gatting b Headley	3	A. M. Babington not out	0	
*A. J. Wright st Brown b Emburey	9	L-b 3, w 2, n-b 2	7	
M. W. Alleyne c Brown b Weekes	7			
†R. C. Russell c Haynes b Fraser	42	1/15 2/25 3/40	(36.2 overs) 108	
J. T. C. Vaughan run out	2	4/47 5/56 6/58		
C. A. Walsh c Gatting b Williams	8	7/72 8/76 9/99		

Bowling: Headley 8–0–29–1; Fraser 6.2–1–16–2; Emburey 6–1–15–2; Williams 8–1–19–2; Weekes 8–0–26–1.

Middlesex

D. L. Haynes not out	59	
M. A. Roseberry c Vaughan b Walsh	10	
*M. W. Gatting not out	34	
L-b 2, w 2, n-b 4	8	

1/12   (1 wkt, 25.3 overs) 111

M. R. Ramprakash, †K. R. Brown, J. D. Carr, P. N. Weekes, J. E. Emburey, N. F. Williams, D. W. Headley and A. R. C. Fraser did not bat.

Bowling: Walsh 6–0–15–1; Babington 4–0–24–0; Ball 6–0–31–0; Smith 7–0–28–0; Vaughan 2.3–0–11–0.

Umpires: J. D. Bond and R. Palmer.

At Nottingham, May 17. MIDDLESEX beat NOTTINGHAMSHIRE by one run.

At Canterbury, May 24. MIDDLESEX beat KENT by seven wickets.

MIDDLESEX v WARWICKSHIRE

At Lord's, June 7. Middlesex won by 56 runs. Toss: Warwickshire. Warwickshire were handicapped by injuries to two of their bowlers: Small lost a fingernail attempting a return catch off Carr, and Paul Smith dislocated his shoulder in a collision with Haynes (Holloway resisted the chance to run the batsman out). Carr hit eight fours and three sixes in 94 balls. Warwickshire had to bat two men short and Lloyd's three sixes were little help.

Middlesex

D. L. Haynes lbw b Twose	84	†K. R. Brown not out		28
M. A. Roseberry c Holloway b Munton	1	L-b 5, w 4		9
*M. W. Gatting c Twose b Munton	9			
J. D. Carr not out	104	1/2 2/26 3/161	(3 wkts, 39 overs)	235

P. N. Weekes, J. E. Emburey, D. W. Headley, N. F. Williams, A. R. C. Fraser and R. J. Sims did not bat.

Bowling: Brown 6–0–26–0; Munton 8–0–37–2; Small 5.3–0–32–0; N. M. K. Smith 8–0–52–0; Twose 7.3–0–55–1; P. A. Smith 2.4–0–20–0; Moles 1.2–0–8–0.

Warwickshire

A. J. Moles b Williams	18	T. A. Munton not out		9
R. G. Twose c Brown b Weekes	32	P. A. Smith absent injured		
*T. A. Lloyd c Carr b Weekes	71	G. C. Small absent injured		
D. P. Ostler c Fraser b Weekes	0	L-b 5, w 1, n-b 1		7
D. A. Reeve b Headley	20			
N. M. K. Smith c Headley b Emburey	8	1/29 2/106 3/106	(37 overs)	179
†P. C. L. Holloway lbw b Emburey	0	4/139 5/152 6/152		
D. R. Brown lbw b Headley	14	7/160 8/179		

Bowling: Williams 8–1–53–1; Fraser 7–1–21–0; Headley 6–0–35–2; Weekes 8–1–31–3; Emburey 8–0–34–2.

Umpires: G. I. Burgess and J. H. Hampshire.

At Derby, June 21. MIDDLESEX beat DERBYSHIRE by 22 runs.

MIDDLESEX v SOMERSET

At Lord's, June 28. Middlesex won by 42 runs. Toss: Somerset. Middlesex's eighth win in eight games equalled the record for the best start to a season, set by Warwickshire in 1980. Gatting's 68, scored from 57 balls with ten fours, took him past 5,000 runs in the competition.

Middlesex

D. L. Haynes c MacLeay b Trump	54	†K. R. Brown not out		15
M. A. Roseberry st Burns b MacLeay	35	L-b 4, w 4		8
*M. W. Gatting lbw b MacLeay	68			
M. R. Ramprakash lbw b Hayhurst	23	1/88 2/99	(4 wkts, 40 overs)	245
J. D. Carr not out	42	3/155 4/200		

P. N. Weekes, J. E. Emburey, D. W. Headley, N. F. Williams and A. R. C. Fraser did not bat.

Bowling: Mallender 5–1–19–0; Lefebvre 8–0–51–0; Snell 8–0–56–0; Trump 8–0–53–1; MacLeay 8–0–46–2; Hayhurst 3–0–16–1.

Somerset

A. N. Hayhurst c Roseberry b Headley	24	R. P. Lefebvre b Weekes	0
M. N. Lathwell c Roseberry b Weekes	33	N. A. Mallender c Headley b Emburey	7
*C. J. Tavaré st Brown b Emburey	21	H. R. J. Trump not out	14
R. J. Harden c Carr b Fraser	32		
G. D. Rose c Ramprakash b Emburey	14	L-b 4, w 7, n-b 1	12
†N. D. Burns b Weekes	13		
R. P. Snell c Gatting b Fraser	24	1/56 2/70 3/105 (37.4 overs)	203
K. H. MacLeay c Ramprakash b Weekes	9	4/121 5/135 6/167 7/181 8/181 9/181	

Bowling: Williams 7-0-38-0; Fraser 8-1-39-2; Emburey 6.4-0-39-3; Headley 8-0-46-1; Weekes 8-1-37-4.

Umpires: J. H. Harris and B. Leadbeater.

MIDDLESEX v WORCESTERSHIRE

At Lord's, July 5. Middlesex won by nine wickets. Toss: Middlesex. A ninth successive win gave Middlesex sole possession of the top of the table, as well as the new record for a start to the season. They outpaced Worcestershire completely; while Curtis batted throughout 40 overs, falling to the last ball, his 118th, and scoring only four fours against 40 singles, Gatting scored 19 more runs in just 61 deliveries, and his stand of 151 in 22 overs with Roseberry brought victory with 11 overs to spare.

Worcestershire

*T. S. Curtis c Fraser b Emburey	69
T. M. Moody c Brown b Fraser	15
D. A. Leatherdale c Weekes b Carr	11
D. B. D'Oliveira c Williams b Weekes	58
S. R. Lampitt not out	10
L-b 14, w 1, n-b 3	18

1/40 2/55   (4 wkts, 40 overs) 181
3/151 4/181

G. R. Haynes, C. M. Tolley, †S. J. Rhodes, P. J. Newport, R. K. Illingworth and R. D. Stemp did not bat.

Bowling: Fraser 8-2-22-1; Williams 8-0-25-0; Emburey 6-0-33-1; Carr 6-0-23-1; Headley 7-1-28-0; Weekes 5-0-36-1.

Middlesex

D. L. Haynes run out	16
M. A. Roseberry not out	76
*M. W. Gatting not out	88
L-b 1, w 2	3

1/32   (1 wkt, 29 overs) 183

M. R. Ramprakash, †K. R. Brown, J. D. Carr, P. N. Weekes, J. E. Emburey, D. W. Headley, N. F. Williams and A. R. C. Fraser did not bat.

Bowling: Haynes 4-0-22-0; Newport 7-0-32-0; Tolley 5-0-33-0; Lampitt 6-0-45-0; Illingworth 4-0-24-0; Stemp 2-0-23-0; Leatherdale 1-0-3-0.

Umpires: D. J. Constant and R. A. White.

At Manchester, July 12. MIDDLESEX beat LANCASHIRE by two runs.

At Northampton, July 19. MIDDLESEX beat NORTHAMPTONSHIRE by eight wickets.

MIDDLESEX v DURHAM

At Lord's, July 26. Middlesex won by seven wickets. Toss: Middlesex. Twelve wins in succession beat the previous best sequences in the Sunday League: 11 by Kent in 1973 and Leicestershire in 1974. Meanwhile, Haynes's innings took his total for the season to 647, breaking his own record for Middlesex of 632 in 1990. His stand of 102 in 20 overs with Roseberry provided the ideal platform for Gatting. Durham's director of cricket, Geoff Cook, appeared for the first team for the first time since their promotion, and narrowly missed a fifty; Botham's 48 came from 44 balls.

Durham

I. T. Botham b Headley	48	P. J. Berry b Headley		6
W. Larkins b Williams	9	S. M. McEwan not out		1
G. Cook run out	49	L-b 4, w 8, n-b 1		13
*P. W. G. Parker c Brown b Headley	1			
J. D. Glendenen c Williams b Weekes	28	1/27 2/74 3/78	(7 wkts, 40 overs)	198
I. Smith c Emburey b Fraser	23	4/132 5/155		
†A. R. Fothergill not out	20	6/176 7/197		

S. P. Hughes and S. J. E. Brown did not bat.

Bowling: Fraser 7–0–35–1; Williams 4–0–27–1; Carr 7–0–30–0; Headley 6–0–21–3; Emburey 8–0–44–0; Weekes 8–0–37–1.

Middlesex

D. L. Haynes c Parker b McEwan	70	†K. R. Brown not out		10
M. A. Roseberry st Fothergill b Berry	44	B 3, l-b 4, w 3		10
*M. W. Gatting c McEwan b Hughes	48			
J. D. Carr not out	20	1/102 2/154 3/174	(3 wkts, 38.5 overs)	202

P. N. Weekes, J. E. Emburey, D. W. Headley, R. J. Sims, A. R. C. Fraser and N. F. Williams did not bat.

Bowling: Brown 7–0–40–0; McEwan 8–0–40–1; Botham 7.5–0–49–0; Hughes 8–0–31–1; Berry 8–0–35–1.

Umpires: R. Palmer and G. A. Stickley.

At Bournemouth, August 2. MIDDLESEX lost to HAMPSHIRE by five wickets.

MIDDLESEX v ESSEX

At Lord's, August 9. Middlesex won by 94 runs. Toss: Essex. Middlesex comprehensively defeated their only challengers for the Sunday League title, who were barred, under TCCB regulations, from playing Gooch and Pringle although the Oval Test had finished before lunch. Spectators from south of the river swelled the crowd to 8,000, and saw Gatting score 89 in 83 balls, hitting a six and seven fours, and adding 151 for the second wicket in 25 overs with Roseberry. Essex's batting was as tame as their bowling and their last eight wickets went down for 43.

Middlesex

D. L. Haynes c Garnham b Topley	1	R. J. Sims not out		0
M. A. Roseberry c Topley b Stephenson	57	J. E. Emburey not out		0
*M. W. Gatting c Childs b Fraser	89	B 3, l-b 7, w 8, n-b 4		22
J. D. Carr c and b Topley	19			
†K. R. Brown c Topley b Ilott	19	1/5 2/156 3/157	(6 wkts, 39 overs)	236
P. N. Weekes run out	29	4/189 5/229 6/236		

D. W. Headley, N. F. Williams and A. R. C. Fraser did not bat.

Bowling: Ilott 8-0-33-1; Topley 7-1-35-2; Such 8-0-45-0; Fraser 6-0-37-1; Childs 3-0-32-0; Stephenson 7-0-44-1.

Essex

*P. J. Prichard st Brown b Weekes	40	M. C. Ilott st Brown b Emburey	7
J. P. Stephenson c Weekes b Fraser	5	P. M. Such not out	0
N. V. Knight c Brown b Headley	29	J. H. Childs c Brown b Headley	1
N. Hussain c Gatting b Weekes	12	B 3, l-b 7, w 7	17
N. Shahid c sub b Headley	11		
†M. A. Garnham run out	0	1/20 2/67 3/99	(33.1 overs) 142
A. G. J. Fraser c Williams b Weekes	12	4/101 5/101 6/124	
T. D. Topley b Headley	8	7/127 8/137 9/141	

Bowling: Williams 8-1-29-0; Fraser 6-0-17-1; Emburey 5-0-22-1; Weekes 8-0-41-3; Headley 6.1-0-23-4.

Umpires: B. Leadbeater and R. C. Tolchard.

MIDDLESEX v YORKSHIRE

At Uxbridge, August 16. Middlesex won by five wickets. Toss: Middlesex. Away from headquarters, Middlesex won their first Sunday League title in 24 attempts. Their 14th victory of the season equalled Sussex's 1982 record. Yorkshire faded after a start of 140 for two, though Middlesex's top three batsmen went cheaply for a change, a stand of 107 in 20 overs between Ramprakash and Carr ensured that the triumph could be completed before a home crowd: 3,500 had crammed into the ground. But Ramprakash marred his day with a sharp answer to a spectator on his dismissal, which was followed by a suspension from the first team.

Yorkshire

*M. D. Moxon c Brown b Williams	9	C. S. Pickles b Weekes	2
S. A. Kellett c Gatting b Carr	68	P. W. Jarvis not out	10
†R. J. Blakey c Brown b Emburey	22	L-b 8, w 6	14
S. R. Tendulkar c Williams b Weekes	47		
A. A. Metcalfe c Headley b Carr	6	1/33 2/91 3/140	(6 wkts, 40 overs) 194
C. White not out	16	4/160 5/167 6/178	

P. J. Hartley, J. D. Batty and M. A. Robinson did not bat.

Bowling: Fraser 6-0-29-0; Williams 5-0-18-1; Headley 6-0-26-0; Emburey 7-0-39-1; Carr 8-0-34-2; Weekes 8-0-40-2.

Middlesex

D. L. Haynes c Robinson b Hartley	21	P. N. Weekes c Blakey b Jarvis	20
M. A. Roseberry c Metcalfe b Hartley	21	†K. R. Brown not out	0
*M. W. Gatting c White b Pickles	2	L-b 9, w 4	13
M. R. Ramprakash st Blakey b Tendulkar	58	1/45 2/45 3/52	(5 wkts, 38.5 overs) 195
J. D. Carr not out	60	4/159 5/188	

J. E. Emburey, D. W. Headley, N. F. Williams and A. R. C. Fraser did not bat.

Bowling: Robinson 5-0-20-0; Jarvis 7-0-37-1; Hartley 8-1-40-2; Pickles 5-0-24-1; Batty 7-0-47-0; Tendulkar 6.5-0-18-1.

Umpires: G. I. Burgess and D. R. Shepherd.

At Hove, August 23. SUSSEX v MIDDLESEX. No result.

At The Oval, August 30. SURREY beat MIDDLESEX on scoring-rate.

NORTHAMPTONSHIRE

At The Oval, April 19. NORTHAMPTONSHIRE beat SURREY by five wickets.

At Worcester, April 26. NORTHAMPTONSHIRE lost to WORCESTERSHIRE by seven wickets.

NORTHAMPTONSHIRE v KENT

At Northampton, May 3. Kent won by 84 runs. Toss: Kent. Longley added 124 in 17 overs with Benson. A bruised hand prevented Lamb batting.

Kent

T. R. Ward c Ripley b Ambrose	8	M. J. McCague b Ambrose	1
*M. R. Benson b Cook	68	R. P. Davis not out	2
J. I. Longley c Lamb b Cook	71	A. P. Igglesden not out	1
C. L. Hooper run out	36	L-b 2, w 3	5
G. R. Cowdrey c Ambrose b Williams	5		
M. V. Fleming b Taylor	18	1/11 2/135 3/155 (9 wkts, 40 overs)	221
†S. A. Marsh b Ambrose	4	4/166 5/194 6/199	
M. A. Ealham run out	2	7/210 8/218 9/219	

Bowling: Taylor 8-0-39-1; Ambrose 8-2-29-3; Cook 8-0-43-2; Capel 8-0-44-0; Williams 7-0-54-1; Fordham 1-0-10-0.

Northamptonshire

A. Fordham c and b Hooper	36	J. P. Taylor b Fleming	8
N. A. Felton lbw b Igglesden	6	N. G. B. Cook c Marsh b McCague	11
R. J. Bailey st Marsh b Davis	18	*A. J. Lamb absent injured	
D. J. Capel c Ward b Ealham	6	L-b 7, w 3	10
N. A. Stanley c Marsh b Davis	1		
R. G. Williams c and b Hooper	5	1/19 2/60 3/70 (35.4 overs)	137
†D. Ripley not out	24	4/75 5/80 6/82	
C. E. L. Ambrose b Igglesden	12	7/101 8/119 9/137	

Bowling: Igglesden 8-0-32-2; Ealham 5-0-20-1; Davis 8-0-23-2; Hooper 8-0-23-2; McCague 4.4-0-21-1; Fleming 2-0-11-1.

Umpires: H. D. Bird and R. Julian.

At Chelmsford, May 10. NORTHAMPTONSHIRE lost to ESSEX by four wickets.

NORTHAMPTONSHIRE v LANCASHIRE

At Northampton, May 17. Lancashire won by four wickets. Toss: Northamptonshire. Northamptonshire recovered from 30 for three through a stand of 164 in 28 overs from Capel and Curran, a county record for the fourth wicket; they took 88 off the last ten overs. Lancashire also began badly, with Walker taking three wickets in the first ten overs, but Atherton steered them home.

Northamptonshire

A. Fordham lbw b DeFreitas	1	K. M. Curran not out	80
R. J. Bailey c Hegg b Allott	0	L-b 1, w 1	2
*A. J. Lamb b Morrison	14		
D. J. Capel not out	97	1/1 2/1 3/30 (3 wkts, 40 overs)	194

N. A. Felton, †D. Ripley, C. E. L. Ambrose, A. R. Roberts, J. P. Taylor and A. Walker did not bat.

Bowling: Allott 6-0-13-1; DeFreitas 8-0-39-1; Morrison 6-0-41-1; Austin 8-0-39-0; Watkinson 8-0-42-0; Barnett 4-0-19-0.

Lancashire

G. D. Lloyd c Ripley b Walker	1	I. D. Austin not out	14
N. J. Speak c Capel b Walker	9	†W. K. Hegg not out	10
M. A. Atherton b Taylor	76	B 3, l-b 6, w 5, n-b 1	15
*N. H. Fairbrother c Bailey b Walker	2		
M. Watkinson c Fordham b Roberts	30	1/3 2/16 3/22 (6 wkts, 39.3 overs) 198
P. A. J. DeFreitas run out	41	4/79 5/169 6/177

P. J. W. Allott, D. K. Morrison and A. A. Barnett did not bat.

Bowling: Taylor 8–1–31–1; Walker 8–1–26–3; Curran 8–0–47–0; Ambrose 7.3–0–37–0; Roberts 7–1–41–1; Capel 1–0–7–0.

Umpires: D. J. Constant and V. A. Holder.

At Stockton-on-Tees, May 24. NORTHAMPTONSHIRE beat DURHAM by six wickets.

NORTHAMPTONSHIRE v DERBYSHIRE

At Northampton, May 31. Northamptonshire won by eight wickets. Toss: Northamptonshire. Goldsmith provided the home team's winning run when he was no-balled for a second bouncer in his last over, but the bulk of their total was provided by Fordham and Felton in an opening stand of 133.

Derbyshire

*K. J. Barnett c Capel b Penberthy	50	S. C. Goldsmith not out	1
P. D. Bowler c Ripley b Taylor	11	†K. M. Krikken not out	0
J. E. Morris b Ambrose	9	B 2, l-b 2, w 2, n-b 1	7
T. J. G. O'Gorman c Ripley b Ambrose	69		
C. J. Adams c Capel b Curran	27	1/20 2/36 3/96 (7 wkts, 40 overs) 189
A. E. Warner c Taylor b Ambrose	14	4/157 5/178
I. R. Bishop c Ripley b Walker	1	6/181 7/187

D. G. Cork and O. H. Mortensen did not bat.

Bowling: Walker 8–1–26–1; Taylor 7–1–19–1; Curran 8–0–57–1; Ambrose 8–0–33–3; Capel 5–0–23–0; Penberthy 4–0–27–1.

Northamptonshire

A. Fordham b Warner	81
N. A. Felton b Cork	62
*A. J. Lamb not out	33
D. J. Capel not out	1
L-b 3, w 6, n-b 4	13

1/133 2/184 (2 wkts, 38.4 overs) 190

R. J. Bailey, K. M. Curran, †D. Ripley, C. E. L. Ambrose, A. L. Penberthy, A. Walker and J. P. Taylor did not bat.

Bowling: Mortensen 8–0–33–0; Bishop 8–1–18–0; Cork 8–0–48–1; Goldsmith 7.4–0–48–0; Warner 7–0–40–1.

Umpires: G. A. Stickley and A. G. T. Whitehead.

At Nottingham, June 21. NORTHAMPTONSHIRE beat NOTTINGHAMSHIRE by eight wickets.

NORTHAMPTONSHIRE v GLAMORGAN

At Luton, June 28. Glamorgan won by seven wickets. Toss: Glamorgan. Glamorgan owed their second win of the season to Richards and Dale, who set a county record for the fourth wicket with their unbroken stand of 152 in just 17 overs. Richards hit four sixes and six fours in 53 balls, conserving the energy of the runner he required after pulling a hamstring when 47.

Northamptonshire

A. Fordham c James b Foster	88	†D. Ripley not out	19
N. A. Felton run out	14		
*A. J. Lamb c Maynard b Dale	10	L-b 9, w 2, n-b 1	12
D. J. Capel b Foster	26		
R. J. Bailey not out	52	1/51 2/90 3/134 (5 wkts, 40 overs) 262	
K. M. Curran c Morris b Croft	41	4/153 5/224	

A. R. Roberts, C. E. L. Ambrose, J. P. Taylor and A. Walker did not bat.

Bowling: Watkin 8-0-45-0; Croft 8-0-71-1; Foster 8-0-45-2; Barwick 8-0-61-0; Dale 8-0-31-1.

Glamorgan

S. P. James c Roberts b Capel	38	A. Dale not out	55
H. Morris b Walker	5	L-b 11, w 6	17
*M. P. Maynard run out	61		
I. V. A. Richards not out	87	1/10 2/108 3/111 (3 wkts, 38 overs) 263	

P. A. Cottey, R. D. B. Croft, †C. P. Metson, S. L. Watkin, D. J. Foster and S. R. Barwick did not bat.

Bowling: Walker 7-0-57-1; Taylor 8-1-46-0; Curran 6-0-41-0; Ambrose 7-0-44-0; Capel 4-0-36-1; Roberts 6-0-28-0.

Umpires: J. D. Bond and J. H. Hampshire.

NORTHAMPTONSHIRE v SUSSEX

At Northampton, July 5. Northamptonshire won by 74 runs. Toss: Sussex. Rain delayed the start until 3.45 p.m. But in the 25 overs available to them Northamptonshire scored at nine an over with their captain, Lamb, thrashing 120 from 62 balls. His 48-ball 100 was only two deliveries outside the record of 46 balls set by G. D. Rose for Somerset against Glamorgan at Neath in 1990, and he hit seven sixes and ten fours. Despite giving chances at 30 and 49 he added 128 in 13 overs with Felton. The match had been switched from Tring due to lack of sponsorship.

Northamptonshire

A. Fordham c Moores b Stephenson	14	K. M. Curran not out	4
N. A. Felton c Wells b Greenfield	61	L-b 5, w 14, n-b 1	20
*A. J. Lamb c Speight b Stephenson	120		
D. J. Capel run out	6	1/25 2/153 3/200 (5 wkts, 25 overs) 226	
R. J. Bailey c Hall b Stephenson	1	4/204 5/226	

†D. Ripley, A. L. Penberthy, C. E. L. Ambrose, J. P. Taylor and N. G. B. Cook did not bat.

Bowling: Stephenson 5-0-22-3; Robson 5-0-31-0; Pigott 5-0-35-0; North 4-0-46-0; Hansford 4-0-46-0; Greenfield 2-0-41-1.

Sussex

K. Greenfield b Penberthy	26	A. C. S. Pigott b Bailey	1
J. W. Hall c Ripley b Taylor	14	A. R. Hansford lbw b Bailey	0
M. P. Speight c Taylor b Cook	18	A. G. Robson not out	1
*A. P. Wells c Ripley b Cook	31	L-b 9, w 2	11
F. D. Stephenson run out	34		
J. A. North c Capel b Curran	8	1/29 2/62 3/66 (9 wkts, 25 overs) 152	
†P. Moores run out	2	4/122 5/135 6/138	
N. J. Lenham not out	6	7/145 8/149 9/149	

Bowling: Capel 5-0-36-0; Taylor 5-0-25-1; Penberthy 5-0-32-1; Cook 5-0-34-2; Ambrose 1-0-4-0; Curran 2-0-8-1; Bailey 2-0-4-2.

Umpires: G. I. Burgess and B. Dudleston.

At Moreton-in-Marsh, July 12. NORTHAMPTONSHIRE lost to GLOUCESTERSHIRE by 78 runs.

NORTHAMPTONSHIRE v MIDDLESEX

At Northampton, July 19. Middlesex won by eight wickets. Toss: Middlesex. Haynes and Gatting, who struck 96 from 79 balls, added 166 in 26 overs to steer Middlesex to their 11th straight win.

Northamptonshire

A. Fordham c Carr b Fraser	54	A. L. Penberthy not out	19
N. A. Felton c Haynes b Weekes	26		
*A. J. Lamb c Brown b Fraser	41	B 3, l-b 9, w 6	18
D. J. Capel st Brown b Weekes	22		—
R. J. Bailey b Williams	22	1/54 2/129 3/130 (5 wkts, 40 overs) 221	
K. M. Curran not out	19	4/173 5/182	

†W. M. Noon, C. E. L. Ambrose, J. P. Taylor and R. M. Pearson did not bat.

Bowling: Fraser 8-1-34-2; Williams 8-0-46-1; Weekes 8-0-40-2; Emburey 8-1-37-0; Headley 5-0-37-0; Carr 3-0-15-0.

Middlesex

D. L. Haynes not out	84
M. A. Roseberry c Felton b Capel	11
*M. W. Gatting b Capel	96
M. R. Ramprakash not out	19
L-b 6, w 6	12

1/20 2/186 (2 wkts, 36.4 overs) 222

†K. R. Brown, J. D. Carr, P. N. Weekes, J. E. Emburey, D. W. Headley, N. F. Williams and A. R. C. Fraser did not bat.

Bowling: Taylor 7-0-34-0; Capel 8-1-30-2; Ambrose 7.4-0-51-0; Curran 7-0-48-0; Pearson 2-0-18-0; Penberthy 5-0-35-0.

Umpires: B. Leadbeater and D. R. Shepherd.

At Taunton, July 26. NORTHAMPTONSHIRE lost to SOMERSET by 60 runs.

NORTHAMPTONSHIRE v YORKSHIRE

At Northampton, August 9. Northamptonshire won by 65 runs. Toss: Yorkshire. Jarvis finished off the home team's innings with four wickets for seven in 11 balls. But when Capel removed Moxon, Yorkshire's prospects of catching up diminished, and they suffered their fifth consecutive defeat.

Northamptonshire

A. Fordham c Batty b Jarvis	6	J. N. Snape b Jarvis	6
N. A. Felton st Blakey b Batty	45	N. G. B. Cook b Jarvis	0
K. M. Curran lbw b Pickles	62		
D. J. Capel b Pickles	46	B 1, l-b 3, w 10	14
R. J. Bailey c Robinson b Moxon	7		
A. L. Penberthy c and b Jarvis	10	1/19 2/92 3/160 (9 wkts, 40 overs) 222	
*A. J. Lamb not out	26	4/177 5/180 6/202	
†W. M. Noon lbw b Jarvis	0	7/202 8/222 9/222	

A. Walker did not bat.

Bowling: Robinson 7-0-32-0; Jarvis 8-0-29-5; Pickles 8-0-62-2; Carrick 8-1-44-0; Batty 8-1-46-1; Moxon 1-0-5-1.

Yorkshire

*M. D. Moxon c Lamb b Capel	53	P. Carrick c Penberthy b Snape	2
S. A. Kellett b Walker	9	J. D. Batty run out	0
†R. J. Blakey b Snape	22	M. A. Robinson b Capel	1
S. R. Tendulkar b Cook	13	B 3, l-b 7, w 5, n-b 2	17
D. Byas run out	1		
C. White not out	32	1/15 2/65 3/86	(36.5 overs) 157
C. S. Pickles b Cook	0	4/90 5/117 6/121	
P. W. Jarvis b Penberthy	7	7/140 8/145 9/146	

Bowling: Walker 6–0–22–1; Capel 6.5–0–20–2; Penberthy 8–0–32–1; Cook 8–0–33–2; Snape 8–0–40–2.

Umpires: B. Dudleston and D. O. Oslear.

At Bournemouth, August 16. NORTHAMPTONSHIRE lost to HAMPSHIRE by 81 runs.

At Leicester, August 23. LEICESTERSHIRE v NORTHAMPTONSHIRE. No result.

NORTHAMPTONSHIRE v WARWICKSHIRE

At Northampton, August 30. Northamptonshire won by 40 runs. Toss: Northamptonshire. Bailey, acting-captain because the county had suspended Lamb for his comments on ball-tampering in the *Daily Mirror*, ensured a winning close to the season with his unbeaten 63 in 50 balls. He chose slow left-armer Cook to open the bowling and was rewarded when he dismissed both Warwickshire openers. The 19-year-old off-spinner Snape also claimed three wickets to curb the middle order.

Northamptonshire

D. J. Capel b P. A. Smith	39	K. M. Curran not out	27
N. A. Felton run out	48	L-b 7, w 7, n-b 1	15
A. L. Penberthy b Welch	43		
*R. J. Bailey not out	63	1/82 2/101 3/179	(3 wkts, 40 overs) 235

M. B. Loye, T. C. Walton, †W. M. Noon, J. N. Snape, M. N. Bowen and N. G. B. Cook did not bat.

Bowling: Munton 8–2–35–0; Welch 8–1–42–1; Reeve 4–0–24–0; Twose 4–0–31–0; P. A. Smith 8–0–48–1; N. M. K. Smith 8–0–48–0.

Warwickshire

A. J. Moles lbw b Cook	15	P. A. Smith not out	14
R. G. Twose c Noon b Cook	21	G. Welch not out	1
D. P. Ostler b Walton	14		
*D. A. Reeve c Noon b Penberthy	48	B 2, l-b 13, w 8	23
T. L. Penney st Noon b Snape	0		
Wasim Khan lbw b Snape	7	1/36 2/42 3/64	(8 wkts, 40 overs) 195
N. M. K. Smith b Snape	1	4/65 5/82 6/110	
†P. C. L. Holloway b Bailey	51	7/142 8/193	

T. A. Munton did not bat.

Bowling: Bowen 5–0–20–0; Cook 8–0–22–2; Walton 7–0–36–1; Snape 8–1–33–3; Penberthy 8–0–41–1; Bailey 4–0–28–1.

Umpires: J. C. Balderstone and N. T. Plews.

NOTTINGHAMSHIRE

NOTTINGHAMSHIRE v SUSSEX

At Nottingham, April 19. Sussex won by seven wickets. Toss: Sussex. The reigning Sunday League champions made a disappointing start. They had already lost their regular captain, Robinson, to a fractured thumb, and his deputy, Johnson, damaged his hand in this game. Pollard was awarded his county cap during the afternoon, but the day belonged to the young men of Sussex, Greenfield and Hall, who put on 144 in 28 overs.

Nottinghamshire

B. C. Broad run out	31	†B. N. French not out	22
D. W. Randall c Salisbury b Stephenson	0	E. E. Hemmings run out	3
*P. Johnson st Speight b C. M. Wells	0		
P. R. Pollard run out	41	L-b 6, w 6, n-b 1	13
C. C. Lewis c Salisbury b Hansford	38		
C. L. Cairns lbw b Pigott	14	1/8 2/25 3/36 (9 wkts, 40 overs)	187
M. Saxelby c Hanley b Pigott	25	4/102 5/128 6/132	
K. P. Evans lbw b Stephenson	0	7/133 8/174 9/187	

R. A. Pick did not bat.

Bowling: C. M. Wells 8-1-28-1; Stephenson 8-0-38-2; Salisbury 8-0-26-0; Pigott 8-0-45-2; North 2-0-14-0; Hansford 6-0-30-1.

Sussex

K. Greenfield c French b Evans	77	C. M. Wells not out	4
J. W. Hall c Johnson b Evans	77	L-b 9, w 3	12
†M. P. Speight b Pick	9		
*A. P. Wells not out	12	1/144 2/172 3/176 (3 wkts, 38.2 overs)	191

R. Hanley, F. D. Stephenson, J. A. North, A. C. S. Pigott, I. D. K. Salisbury and A. R. Hansford did not bat.

Bowling: Pick 7.2-0-27-1; Lewis 6-0-30-0; Evans 8-0-28-2; Cairns 5-0-40-0; Hemmings 8-0-32-0; Saxelby 4-0-25-0.

Umpires: V. A. Holder and B. Leadbeater.

At Leeds, May 3. NOTTINGHAMSHIRE beat YORKSHIRE by nine wickets.

NOTTINGHAMSHIRE v SURREY

At Nottingham, May 10. Surrey won by six wickets. Toss: Surrey. Nottinghamshire lost their way after Randall and Johnson had put on 103 in 22 overs. Though Pick kept Surrey's earlier batsmen in check, Ward and Lynch saw them home. Randall's fourth run had taken him past C. T. Radley's career total of 6,650 in the Sunday League and made him the third-highest scorer in the competition's history, behind D. L. Amiss and G. A. Gooch.

Nottinghamshire

B. C. Broad c Stewart b M. P. Bicknell	1	M. Saxelby not out	1
D. W. Randall c Stewart b Boiling	55	L-b 2, w 3	5
*P. Johnson c Brown b Feltham	48		
P. R. Pollard not out	47	1/2 2/105 (4 wkts, 36 overs)	174
C. C. Lewis c Feltham b Bryson	17	3/108 4/161	

C. L. Cairns, K. P. Evans, †B. N. French, E. E. Hemmings and R. A. Pick did not bat.

Bowling: M. P. Bicknell 6-1-12-1; Benjamin 6-0-31-0; Boiling 8-0-40-1; Feltham 7-0-30-1; Bryson 6-0-35-1; Thorpe 3-0-24-0.

Surrey

D. J. Bicknell b Pick	36	D. M. Ward not out	46
A. D. Brown lbw b Lewis	13	L-b 7, w 2, n-b 2	11
*†A. J. Stewart run out	4		
G. P. Thorpe lbw b Pick	26	1/26 2/34 (4 wkts, 35.2 overs) 177	
M. A. Lynch not out	41	3/85 4/88	

M. A. Feltham, R. E. Bryson, J. Boiling, M. P. Bicknell and J. E. Benjamin did not bat.

Bowling: Lewis 8–0–34–1; Pick 8–1–38–2; Cairns 8–0–23–0; Evans 7.2–0–49–0; Hemmings 4–0–26–0.

Umpires: H. D. Bird and J. W. Holder.

NOTTINGHAMSHIRE v MIDDLESEX

At Nottingham, May 17. Middlesex won by one run. Toss: Nottinghamshire. Johnson produced an astonishing assault on the Middlesex attack, taking 90 off just 50 deliveries with eight fours and six sixes while his partner Randall advanced from 26 to 43. But with Emburey and Carr taking control, Nottinghamshire came to the last over still needing six, and Cooper, who needed three off the final ball, could manage only a single.

Middlesex

D. L. Haynes c Cooper b Saxelby	63	P. N. Weekes not out	13
M. A. Roseberry run out	4		
*M. W. Gatting b Cairns	24	L-b 5, w 2, n-b 4	11
M. R. Ramprakash lbw b Cairns	1		
†K. R. Brown not out	73	1/10 2/60 3/62 (5 wkts, 39 overs) 257	
J. D. Carr b Afford	68	4/120 5/217	

J. E. Emburey, N. F. Williams, A. R. C. Fraser and D. W. Headley did not bat.

Bowling: Lewis 7–0–45–0; Cooper 7–0–38–0; Cairns 8–0–51–2; Evans 7–0–39–0; Afford 6–0–32–1; Saxelby 2–0–19–1; Crawley 2–0–28–0.

Nottinghamshire

B. C. Broad c Emburey b Headley	21	K. P. Evans not out	7
D. W. Randall c and b Carr	68	K. E. Cooper not out	1
*P. Johnson c Williams b Emburey	90		
C. C. Lewis b Weekes	14	L-b 5, w 1, n-b 4	10
M. Saxelby b Emburey	9		
C. L. Cairns c and b Carr	18	1/50 2/159 3/183 (8 wkts, 39 overs) 256	
M. A. Crawley b Carr	1	4/210 5/222 6/230	
†B. N. French run out	17	7/235 8/254	

J. A. Afford did not bat.

Bowling: Headley 6–0–42–1; Fraser 6–0–57–0; Williams 6–0–48–0; Emburey 8–0–44–2; Weekes 5–1–18–1; Carr 8–0–42–3.

Umpires: K. E. Palmer and G. A. Stickley.

At Derby, May 24. NOTTINGHAMSHIRE lost to DERBYSHIRE by 16 runs.

NOTTINGHAMSHIRE v GLOUCESTERSHIRE

At Nottingham, May 31. Gloucestershire won by nine wickets. Toss: Gloucestershire. Walsh removed Broad and Johnson in his second over, and Nottinghamshire were 70 for five before Lewis and Cairns restored some respectability. Hodgson quickly made the target of 178 look inadequate.

Nottinghamshire

B. C. Broad c Ball b Walsh	6	G. W. Mike lbw b Walsh	11
M. A. Crawley c Athey b Scott	24	†B. N. French not out	4
P. Johnson b Walsh	0	L-b 7, w 6	13
M. Saxelby lbw b Ball	10		
*R. T. Robinson run out	15	1/16 2/16 3/43 (7 wkts, 40 overs) 177	
C. C. Lewis b Scott	39	4/47 5/70	
C. L. Cairns not out	55	6/136 7/155	

M. G. Field-Buss and R. A. Pick did not bat.

Bowling: Walsh 8–2–28–3; Smith 8–0–42–0; Scott 8–0–36–2; Ball 7.1–0–21–1; Alleyne 8–0–35–0; Athey 0.5–0–8–0.

Gloucestershire

G. D. Hodgson not out	84
S. G. Hinks c Broad b Field-Buss	39
C. W. J. Athey not out	46
L-b 7, w 4, n-b 1	12

1/77   (1 wkt, 39.3 overs) 181

*A. J. Wright, M. W. Alleyne, R. J. Scott, †R. C. Russell, C. A. Walsh, M. C. J. Ball, A. M. Smith and R. I. Dawson did not bat.

Bowling: Lewis 8–0–33–0; Pick 6.3–0–29–0; Cairns 8–0–36–0; Saxelby 3–0–16–0; Field-Buss 8–0–33–1; Mike 6–0–27–0.

Umpires: J. H. Hampshire and N. T. Plews.

At Bath, June 14. NOTTINGHAMSHIRE lost to SOMERSET by seven wickets.

NOTTINGHAMSHIRE v NORTHAMPTONSHIRE

At Nottingham, June 21. Northamptonshire won by eight wickets. Toss: Northamptonshire. The home team went down to their seventh defeat in seven one-day matches played at Trent Bridge in 1992, despite their captain Robinson's 71 in 74 balls. Fordham and Felton got Northamptonshire off to a flying start with 149, though each was given two lives. Broad reached 5,000 runs in the competition.

Nottinghamshire

B. C. Broad c Ripley b Walker	29	†B. N. French not out	1
M. A. Crawley run out	39		
*R. T. Robinson b Taylor	71	B 1, w 1	2
P. Johnson c Fordham b Roberts	8		
P. R. Pollard c Fordham b Curran	24	1/49 2/80 3/106 (5 wkts, 40 overs) 204	
C. L. Cairns not out	30	4/155 5/191	

K. P. Evans, M. G. Field-Buss, R. A. Pick and D. B. Pennett did not bat.

Bowling: Taylor 8–0–39–1; Walker 8–0–41–1; Capel 5–0–27–0; Ambrose 8–0–44–0; Curran 7–0–31–1; Roberts 4–0–21–1.

Northamptonshire

A. Fordham lbw b Pick	89
N. A. Felton not out	77
*R. J. Bailey c Cairns b Crawley	18
D. J. Capel not out	13
L-b 3, w 7	10

1/149 2/185   (2 wkts, 38.5 overs) 207

K. M. Curran, A. L. Penberthy, †D. Ripley, C. E. L. Ambrose, J. P. Taylor, A. Walker and A. R. Roberts did not bat.

Bowling: Pick 8–0–28–1; Evans 7–0–33–0; Cairns 6–0–33–0; Pennett 5–0–37–0; Field-
ıss 8–0–45–0; Crawley 4.5–0–28–1.

Umpires: J. W. Holder and R. Palmer.

t Southampton, July 5. NOTTINGHAMSHIRE lost to HAMPSHIRE by 24 runs.

NOTTINGHAMSHIRE v DURHAM

t Nottingham, July 19. Durham won by 21 runs. Toss: Nottinghamshire. The 1991 League
ﾉhampions remained bottom of the table after their eighth consecutive defeat. Larkins and
ﾐotham had already run up 72 by the 12th over, when Pennett dismissed them in
ﾐnsecutive balls. But though Nottinghamshire's bowlers pegged the visitors back, their
ﾐatsmen were never in the hunt. Parker reached 5,000 runs in the Sunday League.

Durham

T. Botham c Pollard b Pennett	19	S. M. McEwan c Bramhall b Evans	0
ﾉ. Larkins c Crawley b Pennett	47	P. W. Henderson not out	10
ﾐ. M. Jones b Cairns	35	L-b 2, w 5, n-b 2	9
ﾐ. W. G. Parker b Cairns	23		
D. Glendenen not out	33	1/72 2/72 3/132 (7 wkts, 40 overs) 211	
ﾏ. P. Briers c Bramhall b Mike	8	4/135 5/155	
A. R. Fothergill b Evans	27	6/196 7/196	

ﾑ. Hughes and S. J. E. Brown did not bat.

Bowling: Cairns 8–0–53–2; Pennett 8–0–28–2; Evans 8–0–53–2; Mike 8–0–37–1; Field-
ﾑss 8–0–38–0.

Nottinghamshire

ﾏ. R. Pollard c and b McEwan	9	M. G. Field-Buss b Botham	7
ﾏ. A. Crawley c Fothergill b Brown	1	†S. Bramhall run out	1
ﾏR. T. Robinson c Glendenen b Henderson	51	D. B. Pennett not out	12
ﾏ. Johnson b Hughes	11	B 2, 1-b 10, w 7	19
ﾓ. F. Archer b Henderson	9		
ﾏ. L. Cairns b Hughes	26	1/6 2/23 3/37 (9 wkts, 40 overs) 190	
ﾌ. P. Evans b Henderson	18	4/71 5/96 6/140	
ﾓ. W. Mike not out	26	7/142 8/153 9/155	

Bowling: McEwan 8–1–26–1; Brown 8–0–27–1; Hughes 8–0–37–2; Botham 8–0–41–1;
ﾏenderson 8–0–47–3.

Umpires: B. J. Meyer and P. B. Wight.

At Birmingham, July 26. NOTTINGHAMSHIRE lost to WARWICKSHIRE on scoring-
rate.

NOTTINGHAMSHIRE v LEICESTERSHIRE

ﾑt Nottingham, August 2. Nottinghamshire won by seven wickets. Toss: Nottinghamshire.
ﾏﾐottinghamshire ended a run of nine defeats with their second win of the season in their
ﾐth game; it was their visitors' 11th defeat in 13. Randall and Crawley swept Nottingham-
ﾐire towards victory by opening with 170 in 29 overs.

Leicestershire

J. J. Whitaker c Bramhall b Cairns	22	M. I. Gidley c and b Cairns	14
*N. E. Briers lbw b Cairns	21	G. J. Parsons not out	0
T. J. Boon b Crawley	25	B 2, l-b 3, w 3, n-b 1	9
P. E. Robinson st Bramhall b Hemmings	5		
J. D. R. Benson c Hemmings b Crawley	48	1/44 2/45 3/59 (8 wkts, 40 overs) 244	
L. Potter c Cairns b Crawley	40	4/123 5/127 6/210	
†P. A. Nixon b Cairns	60	7/240 8/244	

A. D. Mullally and R. P. Gofton did not bat.

Bowling: Lewis 8–0–39–0; Pennett 4–0–36–0; Mike 5–0–43–0; Cairns 8–1–30–4; Hemmings 8–0–50–1; Crawley 7–0–41–3.

Nottinghamshire

D. W. Randall c Briers b Gidley	91	P. R. Pollard not out	9
M. A. Crawley not out	94	B 6, l-b 7, w 5	18
P. Johnson c Nixon b Parsons	34		
*R. T. Robinson b Parsons	2	1/170 2/220 3/230 (3 wkts, 39.3 overs) 248	

C. C. Lewis, C. L. Cairns, G. W. Mike, E. E. Hemmings, †S. Bramhall and D. B. Pennett did not bat.

Bowling: Mullally 8–0–49–0; Parsons 8–0–51–2; Potter 4–0–27–0; Gofton 8–0–44–0; Gidley 8–0–42–1; Benson 3.3–0–22–0.

Umpires: B. Leadbeater and R. C. Tolchard.

NOTTINGHAMSHIRE v GLAMORGAN

At Nottingham, August 9. Nottinghamshire won by ten runs. Toss: Glamorgan. Rain delayed the start and reduced the match to 31 overs a side. It was barely under way when a delivery from Foster fractured Johnson's knuckle, to mar Nottinghamshire's enjoyment of their second consecutive win.

Nottinghamshire

P. Johnson retired hurt	0	M. A. Crawley not out	9
D. W. Randall c Cottey b Barwick	23	K. P. Evans b Barwick	6
*R. T. Robinson b Foster	0	B 2, l-b 11, w 2	15
P. R. Pollard lbw b Frost	61		
C. L. Cairns c James b Croft	23	1/5 2/59 3/117 (6 wkts, 31 overs) 158	
G. W. Mike c Hemp b Frost	21	4/130 5/147 6/158	

M. G. Field-Buss, †S. Bramhall and D. B. Pennett did not bat.

P. Johnson retired hurt at 1.

Bowling: Foster 6–2–24–1; Frost 7–0–35–2; Dale 6–0–23–0; Barwick 6–0–28–2; Croft 4–0–26–1; Cottey 2–0–9–0.

Glamorgan

S. P. James c Bramhall b Cairns	20	†C. P. Metson not out	
H. Morris c Pollard b Mike	14	D. J. Foster not out	9
A. Dale c Cairns b Crawley	28	B 1, l-b 3, w 5	9
*M. P. Maynard c Crawley b Field-Buss	18		
P. A. Cottey c Crawley b Cairns	18	1/34 2/35 3/74 (7 wkts, 31 overs) 148	
D. L. Hemp c sub b Cairns	10	4/96 5/114	
R. D. B. Croft b Robinson b Cairns	16	6/122 7/136	

S. R. Barwick and M. Frost did not bat.

Bowling: Evans 5–0–28–0; Pennett 3–0–18–0; Mike 6–1–25–1; Cairns 7–0–26–4; Field-Buss 5–0–28–1; Crawley 5–0–19–1.

Umpires: R. Julian and K. E. Palmer.

At Canterbury, August 12. KENT v NOTTINGHAMSHIRE. No result.

At Colchester, August 16. NOTTINGHAMSHIRE lost to ESSEX by 11 runs.

NOTTINGHAMSHIRE v LANCASHIRE

At Nottingham, August 23. No result. Toss: Nottinghamshire. Rain reduced the match to 28 overs a side and then ended it before Nottinghamshire could bat; with their final match also washed out, Randall had no chance to score the 38 he needed to join G. A. Gooch and D. L. Amiss as the only batsmen to score 7,000 Sunday League runs.

Lancashire

J. P. Crawley b Pennett	8
*M. A. Atherton b Field-Buss	32
N. J. Speak lbw b Mike	60
G. D. Lloyd not out	42
L-b 4, w 5	9

1/19 2/64 3/151   (3 wkts, 25.2 overs) 151

M. Watkinson, R. C. Irani, I. D. Austin, J. D. Fitton, P. J. Martin, †J. Stanworth and G. Yates did not bat.

Bowling: Pennett 6–0–25–1; Crawley 6–0–36–0; Cairns 6–0–43–0; Field-Buss 4–0–25–1; Mike 3.2–0–18–1.

Nottinghamshire

B. C. Broad, D. W. Randall, *R. T. Robinson, M. A. Crawley, G. F. Archer, M. Saxelby, C. L. Cairns, G. W. Mike, M. G. Field-Buss, D. B. Pennett and †S. Bramhall.

Umpires: H. D. Bird and M. J. Kitchen.

At Worcester, August 30. WORCESTERSHIRE v NOTTINGHAMSHIRE. No result.

SOMERSET

At Canterbury, April 19. SOMERSET beat KENT by four wickets.

SOMERSET v WARWICKSHIRE

At Taunton, May 3. Somerset won by 22 runs. Toss: Warwickshire. On his first appearance in the Sunday League, the South African, Snell, hit 62 from 54 balls, rescuing Somerset, who had been 92 for six.

Somerset

A. N. Hayhurst c Holloway b Twose	4	R. P. Snell c Lloyd b P. A. Smith	62
R. J. Bartlett c Holloway b Twose	0	A. Payne not out	6
*C. J. Tavaré b Small	28	N. A. Mallender not out	2
R. J. Harden c Holloway b Munton	2	B 1, l-b 16, w 6	23
G. D. Rose c Asif Din b P. A. Smith	44		
†N. D. Burns c Holloway b Small	6	1/4 2/5 3/12 (8 wkts, 40 overs) 199
K. H. MacLeay c N. M. K. Smith		4/82 5/90 6/92
b P. A. Smith	22	7/170 8/193

H. R. J. Trump did not bat.

Bowling: Twose 8–1–27–2; Munton 8–0–31–1; N. M. K. Smith 8–0–49–0; Small 8–0–25–2; P. A. Smith 8–0–50–3.

Warwickshire

A. J. Moles run out	60	†P. C. L. Holloway b Hayhurst	3
Asif Din lbw b Mallender	9	G. C. Small lbw b Snell	6
*T. A. Lloyd b Rose	5	T. A. Munton run out	5
D. P. Ostler c and b MacLeay	31	B 1, l-b 9, w 6	16
N. M. K. Smith c Tavaré b MacLeay	14		
R. G. Twose b Trump	0	1/16 2/23 3/88 (39.1 overs) 177	
T. L. Penney b Hayhurst	13	4/109 5/110 6/146	
P. A. Smith not out	15	7/150 8/154 9/162	

Bowling: Mallender 8–1–14–1; Rose 5–0–22–1; Snell 8–0–28–1; Trump 8–0–54–1; MacLeay 4–0–20–2; Hayhurst 6.1–0–29–2.

Umpires: J. H. Hampshire and G. Sharp.

At Hove, May 10. SOMERSET lost to SUSSEX by eight wickets.

SOMERSET v HAMPSHIRE

At Taunton, May 17. Somerset won by 97 runs. Toss: Hampshire. Hampshire collapsed abruptly from 46 for one to 87 all out; Caddick despatched most of the top order and Mallender polished off the tail with more than 11 overs to spare.

Somerset

M. N. Lathwell b Maru	17	R. P. Snell not out	9
R. J. Bartlett c and b Maru	14	†N. D. Burns not out	14
R. J. Harden b Marshall	53	L-b 5, w 5, n-b 2	12
*C. J. Tavaré c Smith b Udal	11		
G. D. Rose c Smith b Udal	34	1/34 2/41 3/72 (7 wkts, 40 overs) 184	
A. N. Hayhurst c and b Connor	9	4/133 5/142	
K. H. MacLeay lbw b Udal	11	6/158 7/162	

N. A. Mallender and A. R. Caddick did not bat.

Bowling: Marshall 8–0–29–1; Connor 8–1–30–1; Ayling 8–0–47–0; Maru 8–0–30–2; Udal 8–0–43–3.

Hampshire

R. A. Smith b Caddick	17	R. J. Maru c Burns b Mallender	4
V. P. Terry c Snell b Rose	2	C. A. Connor b Mallender	0
D. I. Gower lbw b Caddick	27	S. D. Udal not out	1
J. R. Ayling c Lathwell b Mallender	13	L-b 6, w 2, n-b 3	11
J. R. Wood lbw b Caddick	2		
K. D. James c Burns b Caddick	4	1/5 2/46 3/59 (28.4 overs) 87	
*M. D. Marshall run out	2	4/65 5/73 6/75	
†A. N. Aymes lbw b MacLeay	4	7/76 8/85 9/85	

Bowling: Mallender 6.4–0–16–3; Rose 4–1–12–1; Caddick 8–1–20–4; Snell 4–0–23–0; MacLeay 6–0–10–1.

Umpires: D. R. Shepherd and P. B. Wight.

At Gloucester, May 24. SOMERSET lost to GLOUCESTERSHIRE by six wickets.

At Manchester, May 31. SOMERSET beat LANCASHIRE by nine wickets.

At Middlesbrough, June 7. SOMERSET lost to YORKSHIRE by five wickets.

SOMERSET v NOTTINGHAMSHIRE

At Bath, June 14. Somerset won by seven wickets. Toss: Somerset. On a slow wicket, Nottinghamshire had trouble raising their run-rate, Broad taking 22 overs to contribute 32.

Nottinghamshire

B. C. Broad c Hayhurst b Rose	32	W. A. Dessaur not out	13
D. W. Randall c Burns b Lefebvre	15	†B. N. French not out	1
*R. T. Robinson b MacLeay	25	B 1, l-b 14, w 3	18
C. C. Lewis c Burns b Snell	27		
C. L. Cairns c MacLeay b Rose	4	1/34 2/77 3/84 (6 wkts, 40 overs) 162	
M. A. Crawley c Lefebvre b Caddick	27	4/103 5/129 6/160	

K. P. Evans, R. A. Pick and M. G. Field-Buss did not bat.

Bowling: Caddick 4-0-15-1; Lefebvre 7-0-21-1; Mallender 7-0-32-0; Snell 8-0-30-1; MacLeay 8-0-24-1; Rose 6-0-25-2.

Somerset

M. N. Lathwell c Field-Buss b Pick	22	G. D. Rose not out	36
A. N. Hayhurst c Robinson b Cairns	56	B 1, l-b 6, w 7	14
*C. J. Tavaré c Pick b Field-Buss	10		
R. J. Harden not out	25	1/74 2/92 3/108 (3 wkts, 37.2 overs) 163	

K. H. MacLeay, †N. D. Burns, R. P. Snell, N. A. Mallender, A. R. Caddick and R. P. Lefebvre did not bat.

Bowling: Evans 6-0-25-0; Lewis 7.2-0-29-0; Cairns 8-0-23-1; Crawley 3-0-15-0; Pick 5-0-35-1; Field-Buss 8-0-29-1.

Umpires: D. J. Constant and A. G. T. Whitehead.

SOMERSET v SURREY

At Bath, June 21. Surrey won by four wickets. Toss: Surrey. Somerset were 67 for four after 20 overs, but added 150 in the remaining half of their innings, led by Harden, whose unbeaten 90 came from 86 balls. In pursuit, Surrey needed five runs from their last three balls. Bicknell hit his seventh four to level the scores; then Lefebvre bowled a wide.

Somerset

A. N. Hayhurst c Ward b Feltham	31	K. H. MacLeay not out	40
M. N. Lathwell c Robinson b Boiling	13		
*C. J. Tavaré c Thorpe b Boiling	2	L-b 2, w 6, n-b 2	10
R. J. Harden not out	90		
G. D. Rose c and b Feltham	1	1/31 2/38 3/65 (5 wkts, 40 overs) 217	
†N. D. Burns b Feltham	30	4/67 5/148	

R. P. Snell, A. R. Caddick, N. A. Mallender and R. P. Lefebvre did not bat.

Bowling: Murphy 5-0-35-0; Benjamin 8-0-47-0; Boiling 8-0-26-2; Feltham 8-1-24-3; Butcher 8-0-55-0; Robinson 3-0-28-0.

Surrey

D. J. Bicknell not out	107	M. A. Feltham b Hayhurst	4
A. D. Brown b Snell	23	M. A. Butcher not out	1
G. P. Thorpe c Burns b Snell	11	L-b 5, w 4, n-b 1	10
*M. A. Lynch c Lathwell b MacLeay	28		
†D. M. Ward b Lefebvre	26	1/45 2/72 3/123 (6 wkts, 39.4 overs) 218	
J. D. Robinson b Lefebvre	8	4/187 5/200 6/209	

A. J. Murphy, J. Boiling and J. E. Benjamin did not bat.

Bowling: Mallender 7-0-40-0; Lefebvre 6.4-0-31-2; Snell 8-0-27-2; Caddick 8-0-45-0; MacLeay 5-0-27-1; Rose 3-0-29-0; Hayhurst 2-0-14-1.

Umpires: R. C. Tolchard and R. A. White.

At Lord's, June 28. SOMERSET lost to MIDDLESEX by 42 runs.

SOMERSET v DERBYSHIRE

At Taunton, July 5. Somerset won by five wickets. Toss: Somerset. The home side should have won more easily than they did. But from 139 for two, they lost three wickets in two overs, and eventually scraped home with four balls to spare.

Derbyshire

P. D. Bowler b Rose	5	†K. M. Krikken c Harden b Lefebvre	24
*J. E. Morris c Burns b Snell	33	A. E. Warner not out	6
C. J. Adams c Lefebvre b Rose	3	R. W. Sladdin not out	3
T. J. G. O'Gorman b Snell	4	L-b 1, n-b 4	5
S. C. Goldsmith c Harden b MacLeay	33		
D. G. Cork c MacLeay b Caddick	20	1/11 2/18 3/41 (9 wkts, 40 overs)	160
F. A. Griffith b Caddick	1	4/54 5/92 6/97	
I. R. Bishop b Lefebvre	23	7/108 8/151 9/151	

Bowling: Caddick 8–0–26–2; Rose 5–0–16–2; MacLeay 8–0–31–1; Snell 8–0–40–2; Trump 7–0–28–0; Lefebvre 4–0–18–2.

Somerset

A. N. Hayhurst c Adams b Cork	54	K. H. MacLeay not out	6
M. N. Lathwell c Adams b Griffith	21		
*C. J. Tavaré c Krikken b Goldsmith	33	B 1, l-b 3, w 9	13
R. J. Harden c Bowler b Bishop	27		
G. D. Rose not out	8	1/45 2/104 3/139 (5 wkts, 39.2 overs)	162
†N. D. Burns b Bishop	0	4/149 5/150	

R. P. Snell, H. R. J. Trump, A. R. Caddick and R. P. Lefebvre did not bat.

Bowling: Bishop 8–0–38–2; Warner 7.2–1–23–0; Cork 8–0–34–1; Griffith 5–0–21–1; Sladdin 8–0–28–0; Goldsmith 3–0–14–1.

Umpires: D. O. Oslear and K. E. Palmer.

SOMERSET v DURHAM

At Taunton, July 12. Durham won by 11 runs. Toss: Durham. The visitors were able to set a strong challenge, firstly through the efforts of Botham and Larkins, and then through a 141-run stand in 18.3 overs between Jones and Parker. Jones reached 50 for the sixth time in consecutive Sunday League matches; in all he scored 83 in 70 balls, while Parker hit 82 from 67.

Durham

I. T. Botham b MacLeay	27	I. Smith not out	0
W. Larkins b Lefebvre	52	B 1, l-b 10, w 3, n-b 1	15
D. M. Jones c Mallender b Rose	83		
*P. W. G. Parker c Harden b Rose	82	1/67 2/98 (4 wkts, 40 overs)	263
J. D. Glendenen not out	4	3/239 4/262	

†A. R. Fothergill, M. P. Briers, S. P. Hughes, S. M. McEwan and S. J. E. Brown did not bat.

Bowling: Caddick 8–0–40–0; Rose 8–1–63–2; Mallender 8–0–33–0; Snell 2–0–17–0; MacLeay 6–0–44–1; Lefebvre 6–0–44–1; Hayhurst 2–0–11–0.

Somerset

A. N. Hayhurst c Larkins b Brown	73	R. P. Lefebvre lbw b Botham.........	0
M. N. Lathwell c Jones b Hughes	33	N. A. Mallender not out	12
*C. J. Tavaré b McEwan	41		
R. J. Harden c Larkins b Brown	28	B 1, l-b 9, w 6..............	16
G. D. Rose c and b Botham..........	26		
†N. D. Burns not out...............	14	1/58 2/130 3/180 (8 wkts, 40 overs) 252	
K. H. MacLeay c Fothergill b Botham .	3	4/193 5/219 6/226	
R. P. Snell run out.................	6	7/237 8/237	

A. R. Caddick did not bat.

Bowling: Brown 8-0-61-2; McEwan 8-0-47-1; Hughes 8-0-49-1; Briers 8-0-48-0; Botham 8-0-37-3.

Umpires: B. Dudleston and V. A. Holder.

At Leicester, July 19. SOMERSET beat LEICESTERSHIRE by nine wickets.

SOMERSET v NORTHAMPTONSHIRE

At Taunton, July 26. Somerset won by 60 runs. Toss: Northamptonshire. Somerset won through an all-round performance: most of their batsmen contributed, Rose taking 42 from 28 balls, and their bowlers shared the wickets for a comprehensive victory.

Somerset

A. N. Hayhurst c Roberts b Taylor	0	†N. D. Burns not out...............	19
G. T. J. Townsend b Penberthy	33	K. H. MacLeay not out.............	3
*C. J. Tavaré c Fordham b Cook	45	B 1, l-b 7, w 3, n-b 1	12
R. J. Harden c Cook b Penberthy	53		
R. P. Snell c Lamb b Taylor.........	29	1/0 2/58 3/98 (6 wkts, 40 overs) 236	
G. D. Rose run out	42	4/149 5/183 6/221	

R. P. Lefebvre, H. R. J. Trump and A. R. Caddick did not bat.

Bowling: Taylor 8-1-48-2; Capel 8-1-36-0; Penberthy 8-0-50-2; Cook 8-0-49-1; Ambrose 8-0-45-0.

Northamptonshire

A. Fordham c Caddick b Rose........	27	C. E. L. Ambrose c Burns b Snell	7
N. A. Felton run out	17	J. P. Taylor b Snell	8
*A. J. Lamb lbw b Rose.............	9	N. G. B. Cook not out	4
D. J. Capel c and b Lefebvre	26	L-b 3, w 1, n-b 1	5
R. J. Bailey b MacLeay..............	27		
A. L. Penberthy c Harden b MacLeay .	14	1/30 2/42 3/63 (39 overs) 176	
†D. Ripley run out.................	28	4/106 5/118 6/139	
A. R. Roberts b Caddick	4	7/149 8/162 9/171	

Bowling: Caddick 8-0-39-1; Trump 3-0-15-0; Rose 8-0-34-2; Snell 7-0-24-2; Lefebvre 7-0-32-1; MacLeay 6-0-29-2.

Umpires: J. H. Harris and N. T. Plews.

SOMERSET v WORCESTERSHIRE

At Taunton, August 16. Somerset won by two wickets. Toss: Somerset. MacLeay returned the best figures in the league throughout the summer to dismiss Worcestershire for a trifling 125, but Somerset themselves slipped to 49 for six until the tail rescued them.

Worcestershire

*T. S. Curtis run out	13	P. J. Newport not out	7
D. B. D'Oliveira c Folland b Trump	38	R. K. Illingworth b MacLeay	3
G. A. Hick b Caddick	1	C. M. Tolley lbw b MacLeay	0
D. A. Leatherdale b Mallender	1	L-b 8, w 2, n-b 1	11
N. V. Radford c Burns b Snell	14		
†S. J. Rhodes lbw b MacLeay	17	1/29 2/33 3/41 (38.3 overs)	125
M. J. Weston lbw b MacLeay	5	4/64 5/80 6/91	
G. R. Haynes c Folland b MacLeay	15	7/104 8/117 9/125	

Bowling: Mallender 8–0–20–1; Rose 4–0–13–0; Caddick 7–1–25–1; Snell 4–0–13–1; Trump 8–0–26–1; MacLeay 7.3–0–20–5.

Somerset

A. N. Hayhurst c Hick b Weston	6	N. A. Mallender not out	19
M. N. Lathwell c Rhodes b Weston	22	A. R. Caddick not out	4
*C. J. Tavaré b Newport	9		
N. A. Folland st Rhodes b Illingworth	3	L-b 4, w 5	9
R. P. Snell st Rhodes b Hick	27		
G. D. Rose c Rhodes b Newport	1	1/19 2/34 3/39 (8 wkts, 39.3 overs)	126
†N. D. Burns b Illingworth	0	4/46 5/48 6/49	
K. H. MacLeay c Leatherdale b Tolley	26	7/84 8/106	

H. R. J. Trump did not bat.

Bowling: Haynes 8–0–28–0; Weston 8–0–20–2; Tolley 6–0–30–1; Illingworth 8–1–16–2; Newport 6–1–15–2; Hick 3.3–0–13–1.

Umpires: B. J. Meyer and R. Palmer.

SOMERSET v ESSEX

At Weston-super-Mare, August 23. No result. Toss: Essex. Two points were enough to secure Essex second place in the Sunday League, when the rain which had reduced the match to 21 overs a side returned to end it.

Somerset

A. N. Hayhurst not out	24
M. N. Lathwell not out	25
W 2	2

(no wkt, 8.2 overs) 51

K. J. Parsons, *C. J. Tavaré, K. H. MacLeay, †N. D. Burns, R. P. Snell, G. D. Rose, A. R. Caddick, N. A. Mallender and H. R. J. Trump did not bat.

Bowling: Pringle 3–0–16–0; Ilott 2–0–12–0; Stephenson 2–0–17–0; Such 1.2–0–6–0.

Essex

*P. J. Prichard, J. P. Stephenson, N. V. Knight, N. Hussain, J. J. B. Lewis, N. Shahid, D. R. Pringle, †M. A. Garnham, T. D. Topley, M. C. Ilott and P. M. Such.

Umpires: B. Leadbeater and G. A. Stickley.

At Cardiff, August 30. GLAMORGAN v SOMERSET. No result.

SURREY

SURREY v NORTHAMPTONSHIRE

At The Oval, April 19. Northamptonshire won by five wickets. Toss: Northamptonshire. Feeble batting by Surrey, none of whose players reached 30, set all too low a target.

Surrey

D. J. Bicknell b Curran	21	M. P. Bicknell not out	14
A. D. Brown c Ripley b Taylor	0	J. Boiling run out	4
*†A. J. Stewart b Walker	28	J. E. Benjamin not out	6
G. P. Thorpe c Capel b Curran	5	L-b 7, w 5	12
D. M. Ward lbw b Capel	22		
M. A. Lynch c Penberthy b Curran	25	1/3 2/46 3/50 (9 wkts, 40 overs)	166
M. A. Feltham c and b Taylor	9	4/65 5/91 6/110	
R. E. Bryson b Curran	20	7/127 8/142 9/148	

Bowling: Taylor 8-0-45-2; Walker 8-0-37-1; Curran 8-2-21-4; Penberthy 8-1-28-0; Capel 8-0-28-1.

Northamptonshire

A. Fordham lbw b Bryson	11	R. G. Williams not out	9
N. A. Felton run out	30		
R. J. Bailey not out	46	L-b 8, w 2, n-b 1	11
*A. J. Lamb b Boiling	24		
D. J. Capel c Stewart b Feltham	8	1/26 2/61 3/95 (5 wkts, 39.4 overs)	168
K. M. Curran b Bryson	29	4/106 5/156	

†D. Ripley, A. L. Penberthy, J. P. Taylor and A. Walker did not bat.

Bowling: Bryson 8-0-30-2; M. P. Bicknell 8-0-28-0; Benjamin 7.4-0-47-0; Boiling 8-0-30-1; Feltham 8-1-25-1.

Umpires: J. C. Balderstone and G. I. Burgess.

At Chelmsford, April 26. SURREY lost to ESSEX by ten wickets.

At Nottingham, May 10. SURREY beat NOTTINGHAMSHIRE by six wickets.

SURREY v KENT

At The Oval, May 17. Kent won by three wickets. Toss: Surrey. Darren Bicknell's maiden hundred, in his fifth season in the Sunday League, took 113 balls and included two sixes and six fours. But it was to no avail: Ealham hit six from the only ball he faced to secure victory for Kent with an over to spare.

Surrey

D. J. Bicknell c and b McCague	102	M. A. Feltham not out	1
A. D. Brown c Marsh b Fleming	37		
*†A. J. Stewart c Cowdrey b Ealham	54	L-b 3, w 5	8
G. P. Thorpe c Cowdrey b Fleming	20		
M. A. Lynch run out	15	1/71 2/187 3/220 (5 wkts, 40 overs)	241
D. M. Ward not out	4	4/228 5/240	

R. E. Bryson, M. P. Bicknell, J. Boiling and J. E. Benjamin did not bat.

Bowling: Ealham 8-0-56-1; Hooper 8-0-32-0; Davis 8-0-68-0; Fleming 8-0-41-2; McCague 8-0-41-1.

Kent

T. R. Ward c and b Boiling	56	J. I. Longley not out	1
*M. R. Benson run out	4	M. A. Ealham not out	6
C. L. Hooper c Stewart b Benjamin	90		
N. J. Llong c Stewart b M. P. Bicknell	11	L-b 3, w 2, n-b 6	11
G. R. Cowdrey c Stewart b M. P. Bicknell	56		
		1/38 2/93 3/128 (7 wkts, 39 overs)	246
M. V. Fleming c Stewart b Benjamin	0	4/200 5/200	
†S. A. Marsh b Bryson	11	6/232 7/240	

R. P. Davis and M. J. McCague did not bat.

Bowling: M. P. Bicknell 8–0–68–2; Benjamin 8–0–34–2; Bryson 7–0–55–1; Feltham 8–0–39–0; Boiling 8–0–47–1.

Umpires: H. D. Bird and D. O. Oslear.

SURREY v SUSSEX

At The Oval, May 24. Sussex won by five wickets. Toss: Sussex. Greenfield and Hall shared 104 for the first wicket, and Sussex had advanced to 167 for two when Butcher dismissed Speight, Wells and Stephenson in seven balls. But Lenham saw them home with a four off the penultimate ball.

Surrey

*†A. J. Stewart c Speight b Donelan	32	M. P. Bicknell run out	6
A. D. Brown c Wells b Robson	14	J. Boiling not out	0
G. P. Thorpe run out	51	N. M. Kendrick b Stephenson	1
M. A. Lynch c Wells b Donelan	3	B 1, l-b 2, w 3, n-b 2	8
D. M. Ward c Moores b Stephenson	63		
J. D. Robinson b Salisbury	12	1/20 2/66 3/70 (40 overs)	196
M. A. Feltham lbw b Robson	0	4/133 5/161 6/164	
M. A. Butcher b Pigott	6	7/174 8/190 9/195	

Bowling: Stephenson 8–2–37–2; Robson 8–0–38–2; Pigott 8–0–39–1; Donelan 8–0–39–2; Salisbury 8–0–40–1.

Sussex

K. Greenfield b Feltham	50	†P. Moores not out	9
J. W. Hall c Thorpe b Robinson	61		
M. P. Speight c Stewart b Butcher	41	L-b 3, w 2	5
*A. P. Wells c Stewart b Butcher	14		
F. D. Stephenson b Butcher	4	1/104 2/129 3/167 (5 wkts, 39.5 overs)	200
N. J. Lenham not out	16	4/174 5/176	

B. T. P. Donelan, A. C. S. Pigott, I. D. K. Salisbury and A. G. Robson did not bat.

Bowling: Bicknell 8–0–39–0; Kendrick 8–0–29–0; Boiling 7–0–36–0; Feltham 7.5–0–40–1; Butcher 5–0–23–3; Lynch 2–0–16–0; Robinson 2–0–14–1.

Umpires: K. E. Palmer and N. T. Plews.

At Basingstoke, June 7. SURREY beat HAMPSHIRE by nine wickets.

SURREY v WORCESTERSHIRE

At The Oval, June 14. Surrey won by four wickets. Toss: Worcestershire. Surrey won in the final over, when Radford's throw in from the deep eluded Rhodes and Curtis and crossed the boundary to add four overthrows to the batsman's single.

Worcestershire

*T. S. Curtis c Ward b Feltham	30	N. V. Radford b M. P. Bicknell	0
T. M. Moody c D. J. Bicknell b Boiling	51	P. J. Newport c Greig b M. P. Bicknell	5
G. A. Hick c Feltham b Bryson	2	R. K. Illingworth run out	5
D. B. D'Oliveira b Benjamin	7	L-b 7, w 6, n-b 3	16
D. A. Leatherdale c Thorpe b Feltham	37		
G. R. Haynes b Bryson	26	1/70 2/73 3/99 (39.5 overs) 200
S. R. Lampitt not out	19	4/100 5/166 6/170
†S. J. Rhodes b M. P. Bicknell	2	7/180 8/180 9/194

Bowling: Benjamin 8-0-27-1; M. P. Bicknell 8-0-47-3; Feltham 8-0-34-2; Bryson 7.5-0-44-2; Boiling 8-0-41-1.

Surrey

D. J. Bicknell run out	6	M. A. Feltham not out	8
A. D. Brown c Rhodes b Lampitt	84	M. P. Bicknell not out	5
G. P. Thorpe run out	12	B 1, l-b 2	3
†D. M. Ward lbw b Moody	51		
J. D. Robinson lbw b Lampitt	26	1/12 2/82 3/131 (6 wkts, 39.2 overs) 201
*I. A. Greig c Leatherdale b Lampitt	6	4/157 5/178 6/189

R. E. Bryson, J. Boiling and J. E. Benjamin did not bat.

Bowling: Haynes 8-0-32-0; Radford 3-0-19-0; Newport 8-1-28-0; Hick 7-0-48-0; Illingworth 4-0-20-0; Lampitt 4.2-0-28-3; Moody 5-0-23-1.

Umpires: G. Sharp and D. R. Shepherd.

At Bath, June 21. SURREY beat SOMERSET by four wickets.

At Bristol, June 28. SURREY beat GLOUCESTERSHIRE by 17 runs.

At Llanelli, July 5. SURREY beat GLAMORGAN by seven wickets.

SURREY v DERBYSHIRE

At The Oval, July 12. Surrey won by three wickets. Toss: Surrey. A hat-trick by Martin Bicknell went almost unnoticed. Morris was caught behind by Stewart off the last ball of Bicknell's seventh over, immediately after hitting a six and two fours. When Bicknell resumed 45 minutes later he had Krikken and Bishop caught off the first two balls of his eighth over. Later, Stewart's 86 set up Surrey's sixth consecutive Sunday win.

Derbyshire

P. D. Bowler c Stewart b M. P. Bicknell	9	A. E. Warner run out	4
*J. E. Morris c Stewart b M. P. Bicknell	78	D. E. Malcolm not out	3
C. J. Adams c Murphy b Feltham	23	S. J. Base not out	6
T. J. G. O'Gorman c Ward b Murphy	44	L-b 3	3
S. C. Goldsmith c Stewart b Feltham	27		
I. R. Bishop c Boiling b M. P. Bicknell	10	1/38 2/107 3/111 (8 wkts, 40 overs) 208
†K. M. Krikken c Feltham		4/174 5/192 6/194
b M. P. Bicknell	1	7/194 8/202

O. H. Mortensen did not bat.

Bowling: M. P. Bicknell 8-0-48-4; Benjamin 8-0-32-0; Murphy 8-0-58-1; Boiling 8-0-40-0; Feltham 8-0-27-2.

Surrey

D. J. Bicknell c O'Gorman b Mortensen	1	M. P. Bicknell not out	9
A. D. Brown c Morris b Warner	33	J. Boiling not out	4
*†A. J. Stewart run out	86	B 2, l-b 5, w 5, n-b 2	14
M. A. Lynch c Krikken b Base	11		
D. M. Ward c Krikken b Bishop	15	1/11 2/43 3/86 (7 wkts, 39.3 overs) 212		
J. D. Robinson c Base b Warner	27	4/122 5/184		
M. A. Feltham run out	12	6/188 7/208		

J. E. Benjamin and A. J. Murphy did not bat.

Bowling: Bishop 7.3–0–57–1; Mortensen 8–2–16–1; Warner 8–2–46–2; Malcolm 8–0–55–0; Base 8–0–31–1.

Umpires: H. D. Bird and D. J. Constant.

SURREY v WARWICKSHIRE

At The Oval, July 19. Warwickshire won by six wickets. Toss: Warwickshire. In a match reduced to 34 overs a side only one batsman, Penney, reached 30; Donald returned his best bowling figures in the Sunday League.

Surrey

D. J. Bicknell c Penney b Reeve	14	J. E. Benjamin c N. M. K. Smith	
A. D. Brown b Reeve	11	b Munton	11
*†A. J. Stewart c Penney b Munton	5	A. J. Murphy not out	9
G. P. Thorpe c Holloway b Munton	26		
M. A. Lynch c Holloway b Donald	14	L-b 3, w 7	10
J. D. Robinson b P. A. Smith	10		
M. A. Feltham b Donald	14	1/19 2/36 3/38 (34 overs) 132		
M. P. Bicknell lbw b Donald	3	4/75 5/80 6/97		
J. Boiling c Holloway b Donald	5	7/105 8/105 9/120		

Bowling: Twose 4–0–18–0; Reeve 8–0–32–2; Munton 7–0–27–3; Donald 8–0–23–4; P. A. Smith 7–1–29–1.

Warwickshire

A. J. Moles c Lynch b Feltham	27	T. L. Penney not out	32
R. G. Twose lbw b M. P. Bicknell	11		
†P. C. L. Holloway c D. J. Bicknell		L-b 3, w 2, n-b 3	8
b Robinson	17		
D. P. Ostler c D. J. Bicknell b Murphy	17	1/38 2/40 (4 wkts, 33.5 overs) 135		
D. A. Reeve not out	23	3/63 4/83		

*T. A. Lloyd, N. M. K. Smith, P. A. Smith, T. A. Munton and A. A. Donald did not bat.

Bowling: M. P. Bicknell 8–2–25–1; Benjamin 8–2–31–0; Feltham 8–1–27–1; Murphy 6.5–0–30–1; Robinson 3–0–19–1.

Umpires: J. H. Harris and G. A. Stickley.

At Manchester, July 26. SURREY lost to LANCASHIRE by eight wickets.

At Durham University, August 2. SURREY beat DURHAM by 100 runs.

SURREY v LEICESTERSHIRE

At The Oval, August 16. Leicestershire won by five wickets. Toss: Leicestershire. Whitaker's first century in any competition in 1992 earned Leicestershire their third win of the season but could not lift them off the bottom of the table. He combined with Nixon with the score on 86 for five and, with an unbroken sixth-wicket stand of 124 – which was a record for the competition – took Leicestershire to an improbable win. Stewart's unbeaten 105 for Surrey was outshone.

Surrey

D. J. Bicknell b Gidley	33	M. A. Feltham not out	0
A. D. Brown c Smith b Mullally	8		
*†A. J. Stewart not out	105	L-b 6, w 4, n-b 2	12
G. P. Thorpe run out	13		
M. A. Lynch c Gidley b Mullally	29	1/11 2/99 3/133 (5 wkts, 40 overs) 207	
D. M. Ward run out	7	4/189 5/205	

M. P. Bicknell, J. Boiling, J. E. Benjamin and A. J. Murphy did not bat.

Bowling: Mullally 8–0–40–2; Parsons 8–0–38–0; Benson 8–0–48–0; Gofton 8–0–40–0; Gidley 8–0–35–1.

Leicestershire

J. J. Whitaker not out	118	†P. A. Nixon not out	42
*N. E. Briers lbw b M. P. Bicknell	0		
T. J. Boon c Benjamin b M. P. Bicknell	9	L-b 5, w 2, n-b 3	10
P. E. Robinson st Stewart b Boiling	14		
J. D. R. Benson b Boiling	13	1/1 2/22 3/55 (5 wkts, 39.4 overs) 210	
B. F. Smith lbw b Feltham	4	4/73 5/86	

M. I. Gidley, R. P. Gofton, G. J. Parsons and A. D. Mullally did not bat.

Bowling: M. P. Bicknell 8–1–35–2; Benjamin 8–1–37–0; Murphy 8–0–41–0; Boiling 8–0–37–2; Feltham 7.4–0–55–1.

Umpires: B. Dudleston and J. W. Holder.

At Scarborough, August 23. SURREY beat YORKSHIRE on scoring-rate.

SURREY v MIDDLESEX

At The Oval, August 30. Surrey won on scoring-rate, Middlesex's target having been revised to 207 from 30 overs. Toss: Middlesex. Middlesex suffered only their second defeat of the Sunday League season at the hands of their neighbours, and were unable to break Sussex's 1982 record of 14 wins. But they took their run aggregate for the season to 3,505, the highest ever. Haynes extended the record aggregate for a Middlesex batsman to 839. Stewart's unbeaten century was his second in successive Sunday League matches.

Surrey

D. J. Bicknell lbw b Emburey	30	D. M. Ward not out	23
A. D. Brown b Williams	13	B 1, l-b 8, w 4	13
*†A. J. Stewart not out	103		
G. P. Thorpe c and b Williams	84	1/28 2/77 (4 wkts, 39 overs) 268	
M. A. Lynch lbw b Emburey	2	3/225 4/243	

A. J. Hollioake, M. P. Bicknell, J. Boiling, J. E. Benjamin and A. J. Murphy did not bat.

Bowling: Fraser 8–0–32–0; Williams 8–0–55–2; Emburey 8–0–33–2; Taylor 7–0–46–0; Weekes 5–0–60–0; Carr 3–0–33–0.

Middlesex

D. L. Haynes c Lynch b Benjamin 28	J. E. Emburey not out 30
M. A. Roseberry lbw b M. P. Bicknell . 7	A. R. C. Fraser b Benjamin 0
*M. W. Gatting c Stewart b Murphy . . 8	C. W. Taylor not out 3
M. R. Ramprakash c Stewart b Murphy 21	
J. D. Carr c Stewart b Benjamin 56	L-b 5, w 1 6
P. N. Weekes c Ward b M. P. Bicknell 14	
†K. R. Brown c Thorpe b Benjamin . . . 20	1/35 2/35 3/52 (9 wkts, 30 overs) 193
N. F. Williams c Thorpe	4/78 5/136 6/141
b M. P. Bicknell . 0	7/141 8/174 9/174

Bowling: M. P. Bicknell 8–1–38–3; Benjamin 8–0–44–4; Hollioake 7–0–57–0; Murphy 7–0–49–2.

Umpires: J. D. Bond and R. Palmer.

SUSSEX

At Nottingham, April 19. SUSSEX beat NOTTINGHAMSHIRE by seven wickets.

SUSSEX v YORKSHIRE

At Hove, April 26. No result.

SUSSEX v SOMERSET

At Hove, May 10. Sussex won by eight wickets. Toss: Sussex. Somerset were beaten without much difficulty after losing their first four wickets for 28. Speight and Alan Wells shared an unbroken partnership of 102, to which Wells contributed 28, to win with 15 balls to spare in a match reduced to 35 overs a side. In a sporting act, Pigott recalled Burns in the last over of Somerset's innings; he had been run out after Lefebvre had fended off a high full toss, which Pigott said had slipped from his hand.

Somerset

A. N. Hayhurst lbw b C. M. Wells . . 15	N. A. Mallender run out 17
R. J. Bartlett c Moores b C. M. Wells. . 0	R. P. Lefebvre not out 2
*C. J. Tavaré c A. P. Wells b Robson . 5	L-b 4, w 3 7
R. J. Harden b C. M. Wells 4	
G. D. Rose b Stephenson 37	1/2 2/16 3/25 (7 wkts, 35 overs) 141
K. H. MacLeay c Hall b Robson 33	4/28 5/88
†N. D. Burns not out. 21	6/105 7/135

A. R. Caddick and H. R. J. Trump did not bat.

Bowling: Stephenson 7–2–31–1; C. M. Wells 7–1–16–3; Robson 7–1–23–2; Pigott 7–0–35–0; Salisbury 7–0–32–0.

Sussex

K. Greenfield c Burns b Caddick 20	
J. W. Hall c Burns b Lefebvre 4	
M. P. Speight not out 87	
*A. P. Wells not out 28	
L-b 4, w 1 5	

1/8 2/42   (2 wkts, 32.3 overs) 144

C. M. Wells, N. J. Lenham, F. D. Stephenson, †P. Moores, A. C. S. Pigott, I. D. K. Salisbury and A. G. Robson did not bat.

Bowling: Mallender 7–1–31–0; Lefebvre 6.3–0–27–1; Caddick 7–0–29–1; Hayhurst 2–0–17–0; MacLeay 7–0–20–0; Trump 3–0–16–0.

Umpires: R. C. Tolchard and P. B. Wight.

At The Oval, May 24. SUSSEX beat SURREY by five wickets.

SUSSEX v WARWICKSHIRE

At Hove, May 31. Sussex won by eight wickets. Toss: Sussex. Once more Sussex made early inroads, reducing Warwickshire to 34 for four. Robson had the remarkably economical figures of two for 14 in his eight overs, while off-spinner Neil Smith, who opened the bowling for Warwickshire, was also miserly; he and Donald conceded only 29 in 13 overs. But their colleagues were more expensive. Again, Wells and Speight shared a century partnership for the third wicket to win the match.

Warwickshire

A. J. Moles run out	1	†P. C. L. Holloway not out	36
R. G. Twose c Stephenson b Pigott	71	G. C. Small not out	8
*T. A. Lloyd c Robson b Salisbury	9		
D. P. Ostler b Robson	0	L-b 4, w 6, n-b 3	13
Asif Din c Speight b Robson	4		
N. M. K. Smith c Greenfield b Stephenson	30	1/12 2/25 3/26 (7 wkts, 40 overs) 175
P. A. Smith lbw b North	3	4/34 5/96
		6/101 7/159	

A. A. Donald and T. A. Munton did not bat.

Bowling: Stephenson 8-1-40-1; Robson 8-1-14-2; Salisbury 8-1-35-1; Pigott 8-0-41-1; North 8-0-41-1.

Sussex

K. Greenfield c Holloway b Donald	29	
J. W. Hall run out	23	
M. P. Speight not out	47	
*A. P. Wells not out	55	
B 2, l-b 18, w 2	22	

1/62 2/76 (2 wkts, 34.5 overs) 176

N. J. Lenham, F. D. Stephenson, A. C. S. Pigott, †P. Moores, J. A. North, I. D. K. Salisbury and A. G. Robson did not bat.

Bowling: Munton 7.5-0-47-0; N. M. K. Smith 6-0-13-0; Small 8-0-49-0; Donald 7-1-16-1; P. A. Smith 6-0-31-0.

Umpires: R. A. White and P. B. Wight.

SUSSEX v GLAMORGAN

At Hove, June 7. Sussex won by four wickets. Toss: Glamorgan. Glamorgan started well enough but their last 15 overs yielded only 48, as Stephenson returned his best bowling figures in the competition. Nevertheless, Sussex had just four balls to spare when they won.

Glamorgan

S. P. James c Greenfield b Salisbury	35	S. L. Watkin lbw b Stephenson	2
H. Morris lbw b Stephenson	1	S. R. Barwick b Stephenson	3
*M. P. Maynard b Greenfield	47	D. J. Foster run out	0
I. V. A. Richards b Pigott	40	B 4, l-b 3, w 1, n-b 4	12
A. Dale c Pigott b Greenfield	20		
C. S. Cowdrey c Moores b Stephenson	1	1/3 2/82 3/101 (39.4 overs) 188
P. A. Cottey lbw b Pigott	12	4/140 5/144 6/157
†C. P. Metson not out	15	7/177 8/180 9/188

Bowling: Stephenson 7.4-1-22-4; Robson 8-0-28-0; Pigott 8-0-46-2; Salisbury 8-0-33-1; Greenfield 6-0-36-2; North 2-0-16-0.

Sussex

K. Greenfield c Maynard b Cottey.....	79	†P. Moores not out	3
J. W. Hall lbw b Foster	7	J. A. North not out	7
M. P. Speight c Watkin b Cottey......	19	B 6, l-b 3, w 6, n-b 1	16
*A. P. Wells st Metson b Cowdrey	7		—
N. J. Lenham c Cottey b Foster.......	42	1/19 2/88 3/114 (6 wkts, 39.2 overs) 192	
F. D. Stephenson c sub b Foster	12	4/140 5/166 6/185	

A. C. S. Pigott, I. D. K. Salisbury and A. G. Robson did not bat.

Bowling: Watkin 8–1–32–0; Foster 6–0–32–3; Dale 4–0–26–0; Barwick 7.2–0–40–0; Cowdrey 6–0–23–1; Cottey 8–0–30–2.

Umpires: J. H. Harris and P. B. Wight.

At Leicester, June 14. SUSSEX beat LEICESTERSHIRE by 69 runs.

SUSSEX v DURHAM

At Horsham, June 21. Durham won by five runs. Toss: Sussex. The home team's successful early-season sequence ended, but only after an unexpectedly close finish. They had entered the last ten overs needing a daunting 111, but North rose to the occasion with 56 from 25 balls, hitting five fours and four sixes. He was dismissed in the final over, and nine runs from the last four balls proved beyond his colleagues. Durham's weighty 275 was built on an opening stand of 107 in 17 overs from Larkins and Glendenen, who hit 64 in 45 balls.

Durham

W. Larkins c Hall b Lenham	86	†A. R. Fothergill not out............	0
J. D. Glendenen lbw b Greenfield	64	L-b 10, w 6	16
D. M. Jones not out	74		—
P. W. G. Parker run out.............	19	1/107 2/185 (4 wkts, 40 overs) 275	
M. P. Briers c Wells b Pigott	16	3/246 4/271	

P. W. Henderson, S. M. McEwan, S. P. Hughes, *D. A. Graveney and J. Wood did not bat.

Bowling: Stephenson 8–0–43–0; Robson 6–0–34–0; Pigott 8–0–65–1; Greenfield 7–0–39–1; Hansford 6–0–50–0; North 1–0–13–0; Lenham 4–0–21–1.

Sussex

K. Greenfield b Wood...............	1	A. C. S. Pigott run out	6
J. W. Hall c Fothergill b Hughes......	19	A. R. Hansford not out.............	5
M. P. Speight run out	38	A. G. Robson not out	1
*A. P. Wells c Fothergill b Graveney ..	36		
F. D. Stephenson c Henderson		B 4, l-b 7, w 2..............	13
b Graveney .	10		—
N. J. Lenham c Graveney b Wood	43	1/10 2/26 3/100 (9 wkts, 40 overs) 270	
†P. Moores c Hughes b Graveney	42	4/100 5/111 6/180	
J. A. North c Fothergill b Hughes.....	56	7/222 8/257 9/267	

Bowling: Wood 8–0–58–2; Hughes 8–0–51–2; Henderson 8–0–60–0; McEwan 8–0–50–0; Graveney 8–1–40–3.

Umpires: J. C. Balderstone and D. R. Shepherd.

At Worcester, June 28. SUSSEX lost to WORCESTERSHIRE by eight runs.

At Northampton, July 5. SUSSEX lost to NORTHAMPTONSHIRE by 74 runs.

At Southend, July 19. SUSSEX lost to ESSEX by eight wickets.

At Cheltenham College, July 26. SUSSEX lost to GLOUCESTERSHIRE by 92 runs.

SUSSEX v HAMPSHIRE

At Hove, August 3. Hampshire won by eight wickets. Toss: Hampshire. The match was played on a Monday because Hampshire were taking part in the Benson and Hedges Cup final on the weekend of July 11-12. Moores and Hall opened with 111, but then Sussex lost three wickets in eight balls, two to Marshall. Smith and Middleton set up Hampshire's second league win in two days.

Sussex

†P. Moores c and b Udal	57	A. C. S. Pigott not out	17
J. W. Hall b Marshall	58	I. D. K. Salisbury not out	10
M. P. Speight c Middleton b Ayling	30	L-b 3, w 2	5
*A. P. Wells c Gower b Marshall	1		
K. Greenfield c Aymes b Udal	18	1/111 2/117 3/118 (7 wkts, 40 overs)	206
F. D. Stephenson run out	6	4/147 5/154	
C. C. Remy c Nicholas b Connor	4	6/174 7/181	

E. S. H. Giddins and A. G. Robson did not bat.

Bowling: James 6-0-26-0; Connor 8-0-39-1; Turner 6-0-28-0; Ayling 4-0-35-1; Marshall 8-0-33-2; Udal 8-0-42-2.

Hampshire

R. A. Smith b Salisbury	55
T. C. Middleton not out	78
D. I. Gower b Pigott	44
J. R. Ayling not out	15
B 8, l-b 6, w 4	18

1/111 2/182   (2 wkts, 37.4 overs) 210

*M. C. J. Nicholas, K. D. James, M. D. Marshall, †A. N. Aymes, S. D. Udal, C. A. Connor and I. J. Turner did not bat.

Bowling: Stephenson 6-0-30-0; Robson 5-0-14-0; Pigott 7.4-0-46-1; Salisbury 8-0-31-1; Giddins 5-0-37-0; Remy 4-0-25-0; Greenfield 2-0-13-0.

Umpires: D. J. Constant and J. H. Harris.

SUSSEX v DERBYSHIRE

At Eastbourne, August 9. Derbyshire won by 59 runs. Toss: Derbyshire. Sussex went down to their seventh consecutive league defeat – after seven games unbeaten at the start of the season – when they lost their last seven wickets for 33 in the face of Bishop's pace and Sladdin's left-arm spin.

Derbyshire

*K. J. Barnett c Speight b Stephenson	1	A. E. Warner run out	17
P. D. Bowler c Moores b Giddins	7	I. R. Bishop not out	1
J. E. Morris c Moores b Pigott	51	B 4, l-b 5, w 7, n-b 1	17
C. J. Adams b Stephenson	0		
T. J. G. O'Gorman c Wells b Remy	55	1/8 2/14 3/15 (7 wkts, 40 overs)	183
D. G. Cork c Moores b Pigott	6	4/93 5/106	
†K. M. Krikken not out	28	6/139 7/179	

R. W. Sladdin and O. H. Mortensen did not bat.

Bowling: Stephenson 8-1-41-2; Giddins 6-0-23-1; Remy 5-0-18-1; Salisbury 8-1-25-0; Donelan 5-0-33-0; Pigott 8-1-34-2.

Sussex

†P. Moores c Sladdin b Bishop	56	*A. P. Wells c Krikken b Sladdin		0
C. C. Remy run out	8	A. C. S. Pigott not out		17
M. P. Speight lbw b Mortensen	2	E. S. H. Giddins c Barnett b Warner		2
K. Greenfield run out	19	L-b 5, w 3		8
R. Hanley c Warner b Bishop	3			
F. D. Stephenson c Barnett b Sladdin	1	1/28 2/35 3/77	(35.2 overs)	124
B. T. P. Donelan c O'Gorman b Bishop	1	4/91 5/93 6/95		
I. D. K. Salisbury c Morris b Cork	7	7/97 8/99 9/112		

Bowling: Mortensen 8-1-9-1; Cork 7-0-27-1; Warner 6.2-0-26-1; Sladdin 8-1-35-2; Bishop 6-0-22-3.

Umpires: D. J. Constant and R. Palmer.

SUSSEX v LANCASHIRE

At Hove, August 16. Sussex won by six wickets. Toss: Sussex. Lancashire owed their eventual total of 173 to Fitton, who came in at 103 for eight and scored 36. Salisbury conceded only ten runs in eight overs. Then Sussex slipped to 16 for three before a stand of 127 between Alan Wells and Lenham set up victory.

Lancashire

G. Fowler run out	9	P. A. J. DeFreitas b Pigott		20
M. A. Atherton c C. M. Wells b Remy	24	J. D. Fitton b Pigott		36
N. J. Speak c Moores b C. M. Wells	4	P. J. Martin not out		18
*N. H. Fairbrother c Salisbury				
b Lenham	24	B 1, l-b 2, w 8, n-b 1		12
G. D. Lloyd c Hall b Remy	15			
†J. P. Crawley b Remy	6	1/12 2/29 3/59	(39.3 overs)	173
I. D. Austin b Salisbury	2	4/77 5/89 6/94		
M. Watkinson c C. M. Wells b Remy	3	7/94 8/103 9/144		

Bowling: Giddins 8-0-52-0; C. M. Wells 8-0-27-1; Pigott 5.3-0-34-2; Lenham 2-0-16-1; Salisbury 8-3-10-1; Remy 8-0-31-4.

Sussex

D. M. Smith b Martin	0	†P. Moores not out		21
J. W. Hall lbw b Martin	2	L-b 3, w 4		7
M. P. Speight run out	8			
*A. P. Wells c and b Watkinson	56	1/0 2/7	(4 wkts, 38.4 overs)	175
N. J. Lenham not out	81	3/16 4/143		

C. M. Wells, A. C. S. Pigott, I. D. K. Salisbury, C. C. Remy and E. S. H. Giddins did not bat.

Bowling: Martin 8-0-28-2; DeFreitas 8-0-38-0; Austin 7.4-0-32-0; Fitton 7-0-40-0; Watkinson 8-0-34-1.

Umpires: B. Leadbeater and K. E. Palmer.

SUSSEX v MIDDLESEX

At Hove, August 23. No result. Toss: Sussex. Rain ended the match before Sussex could bat. Haynes's tenth fifty of the season was a league record, but Middlesex lost six wickets for 42 after reaching 175 for three.

Middlesex

D. L. Haynes lbw b Salisbury	65	A. R. C. Fraser c A. P. Wells b Giddins	9
M. A. Roseberry c Salisbury b Remy	29	D. W. Headley not out	4
M. R. Ramprakash c Moores b Remy	41	P. C. R. Tufnell not out	1
P. N. Weekes b Pigott	6	L-b 10, w 4	14
*M. W. Gatting c Pigott b Remy	24		
J. D. Carr c C. M. Wells b Pigott	15	1/80 2/100 3/117 (9 wkts, 40 overs) 220
†K. R. Brown c Salisbury b Remy	11	4/175 5/183 6/200
N. F. Williams c Salisbury b Pigott	1	7/201 8/214 9/217

Bowling: Giddins 8-0-43-1; C. M. Wells 8-0-31-0; Remy 8-0-49-4; Salisbury 8-0-38-1; Pigott 8-0-49-3.

Sussex

D. M. Smith, J. W. Hall, M. P. Speight, *A. P. Wells, N. J. Lenham, C. M. Wells, †P. Moores, C. C. Remy, A. C. S. Pigott, I. D. K. Salisbury and E. S. H. Giddins.

Umpires: R. Julian and G. Sharp.

At Canterbury, August 30. SUSSEX lost to KENT by 76 runs.

WARWICKSHIRE

WARWICKSHIRE v GLAMORGAN

At Birmingham, April 19. Warwickshire won by six wickets. Toss: Warwickshire. Moles batted throughout Warwickshire's innings and added 80 in 11.2 overs with Zimbabwean newcomer Trevor Penney. Earlier, Richards and Dale shared 123 in 23 overs for Glamorgan's third wicket.

Glamorgan

*M. P. Maynard c Twose b P. A. Smith	11	R. D. B. Croft b Munton	0
H. Morris c Piper b Small	20	†C. P. Metson not out	1
I. V. A. Richards c Penney b Munton	68	B 2, l-b 8, w 3	13
A. Dale b Munton	51		
C. S. Cowdrey c Ostler b Munton	9	1/16 2/39 3/162 (6 wkts, 40 overs) 180
P. A. Cottey not out	7	4/165 5/176 6/178

S. L. Watkin, S. R. Barwick and M. Frost did not bat.

Bowling: Twose 5-0-30-0; Munton 8-2-16-4; P. A. Smith 7-0-47-1; Moles 4-0-13-0; Small 8-0-24-1; N. M. K. Smith 8-0-40-0.

Warwickshire

A. J. Moles not out	96	T. L. Penney not out	33
Asif Din c Metson b Watkin	6	B 1, l-b 7, w 7	15
*T. A. Lloyd run out	21		
D. P. Ostler st Metson b Croft	0	1/17 2/64 (4 wkts, 39.2 overs) 181
R. G. Twose c Metson b Watkin	10	3/72 4/101

P. A. Smith, N. M. K. Smith, †K. J. Piper, G. C. Small and T. A. Munton did not bat.

Bowling: Frost 8-0-33-0; Watkin 8-1-25-2; Cowdrey 5-0-24-0; Croft 8-0-27-1; Dale 3-0-17-0; Barwick 7.2-0-47-0.

Umpires: H. D. Bird and K. E. Palmer.

At Taunton, May 3. WARWICKSHIRE lost to SOMERSET by 22 runs.

At Worcester, May 10. WARWICKSHIRE tied with WORCESTERSHIRE.

WARWICKSHIRE v LEICESTERSHIRE

At Birmingham, May 17. Warwickshire won by 100 runs. Toss: Warwickshire. Twose dominated the match, with his maiden hundred in any competition for Warwickshire, and he later ran out Briers with a direct throw from mid-on as Leicestershire collapsed.

Warwickshire

A. J. Moles b Benjamin	21	P. A. Smith not out 7
R. G. Twose run out	100	
*T. A. Lloyd c Wells b Benson	16	L-b 11, w 5 16
†P. C. L. Holloway b Boon	19	—
D. P. Ostler c Mullally b Wells	28	1/65 2/86 3/132 (5 wkts, 40 overs) 217
T. L. Penney not out	10	4/196 5/196

N. M. K. Smith, G. C. Small, A. A. Donald and T. A. Munton did not bat.

Bowling: Mullally 4–0–14–0; Parsons 4–0–21–0; Benjamin 8–1–47–1; Wells 7–0–27–1; Benson 5–0–32–1; Hepworth 8–0–42–0; Boon 4–0–23–1.

Leicestershire

J. D. R. Benson lbw b Munton	0	P. N. Hepworth c Moles b Small	4
*N. E. Briers run out	29	G. J. Parsons not out	14
T. J. Boon b N. M. K. Smith	9	
L. Potter b Donald	9	L-b 6, w 3, n-b 1	10
P. A. Nixon c Holloway b Donald	17	—
W. K. M. Benjamin b Small	6	1/0 2/15 3/31 (8 wkts, 40 overs) 117
V. J. Wells b P. A. Smith	4	4/70 5/75 6/79
†P. Whitticase not out	15	7/81 8/88

A. D. Mullally did not bat.

Bowling: Munton 6–3–7–1; N. M. K. Smith 7–1–18–1; Small 8–0–25–2; Donald 6–0–21–2; P. A. Smith 8–0–24–1; Twose 3–0–10–0; Penney 1–0–2–0; Ostler 1–0–4–0.

Umpires: M. J. Kitchen and R. C. Tolchard.

WARWICKSHIRE v LANCASHIRE

At Birmingham, May 24. No result. Toss: Warwickshire. A thunderstorm interrupted Lancashire's innings and prevented any further play. Warwickshire had scored at more than six an over and the most spectacular performance came from Andy Lloyd, who hit 68 from 47 balls.

Warwickshire

A. J. Moles lbw b Watkinson	56	Asif Din not out	1
R. G. Twose c Watkinson b Austin	54	B 1, l-b 10, w 1, n-b 2	14
*T. A. Lloyd b DeFreitas	68	—
D. P. Ostler c and b Austin	47	1/111 2/145 (4 wkts, 40 overs) 251
N. M. K. Smith not out	11	3/237 4/249

P. A. Smith, †P. C. L. Holloway, G. C. Small, A. A. Donald and T. A. Munton did not bat.

Bowling: DeFreitas 8–0–52–1; Allott 8–0–33–0; Martin 6–0–28–0; Irani 2–0–15–0; Watkinson 8–0–67–1; Austin 8–0–45–2.

Lancashire

N. J. Speak not out	36	M. Watkinson not out	1
S. P. Titchard lbw b Munton	5		
*M. A. Atherton		B 2, l-b 5	7
c and b N. M. K. Smith	5		
G. D. Lloyd b N. M. K. Smith	7	1/17 2/48 3/60	(3 wkts, 14 overs) 61

P. A. J. DeFreitas, I. D. Austin, †W. K. Hegg, P. J. W. Allott, P. J. Martin and R. C. Irani did not bat.

Bowling: Munton 5-0-20-1; N. M. K. Smith 7-0-28-2; Small 2-0-6-0.

Umpires: H. D. Bird and R. C. Tolchard.

At Hove, May 31. WARWICKSHIRE lost to SUSSEX by eight wickets.

At Lord's, June 7. WARWICKSHIRE lost to MIDDLESEX by 56 runs.

WARWICKSHIRE v HAMPSHIRE

At Birmingham, June 14. Warwickshire won by 40 runs. Toss: Hampshire. Ostler scored 49 in 41 balls, with five fours and two sixes, adding 72 in nine overs with Reeve. When Hampshire replied, wicket-keeper Holloway made four catches and two stumpings. Three of the catches helped the Scottish-born seamer Dougie Brown dismiss Smith, Gower and Marshall on his third Sunday League appearance.

Warwickshire

A. J. Moles b Udal	26	N. M. K. Smith c Smith b Connor	1
R. G. Twose c Terry b Udal	66	P. A. Smith not out	3
*T. A. Lloyd c Ayling b Udal	2	B 1, l-b 10, w 10	21
D. P. Ostler c Maru b Marshall	49		
D. A. Reeve not out	50	1/83 2/85 3/122	(6 wkts, 40 overs) 226
T. L. Penney c Gower b Marshall	8	4/194 5/213 6/216	

†P. C. L. Holloway, D. R. Brown and T. A. Munton did not bat.

Bowling: Connor 7-0-44-1; James 5-1-15-0; Maru 8-0-43-0; Ayling 6-0-44-0; Marshall 8-0-36-2; Udal 6-0-33-3.

Hampshire

R. A. Smith c Holloway b Brown	11	†R. J. Parks not out	14
V. P. Terry c Holloway b Twose	29	R. J. Maru run out	0
D. I. Gower c Holloway b Brown	1	C. A. Connor st Holloway	
M. D. Marshall c Holloway b Brown	9	b N. M. K. Smith	6
K. D. James c Penney b P. A. Smith	38		
*M. C. J. Nicholas c Moles		L-b 9, w 6, n-b 2	17
b P. A. Smith	53		
J. R. Ayling st Holloway		1/19 2/21 3/37	(38.1 overs) 186
b N. M. K. Smith	8	4/68 5/137 6/157	
S. D. Udal lbw b N. M. K. Smith	0	7/157 8/172 9/172	

Bowling: N. M. K. Smith 7.1-0-30-3; Brown 8-2-21-3; Munton 6-0-22-0; Reeve 8-0-36-0; Twose 3-0-18-1; P. A. Smith 6-0-50-2.

Umpires: J. C. Balderstone and V. A. Holder.

At Bristol, June 21. WARWICKSHIRE beat GLOUCESTERSHIRE by two wickets.

At Scarborough, June 28. WARWICKSHIRE lost to YORKSHIRE by 21 runs.

WARWICKSHIRE v ESSEX

At Birmingham, July 5. Warwickshire won by 24 runs. Toss: Essex. Essex's third defeat of the season finally knocked them off the top of the table for the first time. Penney scored 40 in 28 balls for Warwickshire, but when Essex replied they could not generate sufficient speed until Pringle scored 52 at a run a ball, rather too late.

Warwickshire

A. J. Moles b Topley	63	N. M. K. Smith not out		4
R. G. Twose c Foster b Waugh	42			
*T. A. Lloyd c Shahid b Waugh	13	L-b 8, w 1, n-b 4		13
D. P. Ostler c Foster b Fraser	14			
D. A. Reeve b Pringle	25	1/79 2/103 3/129	(5 wkts, 40 overs)	214
T. L. Penney not out	40	4/148 5/205		

P. A. Smith, †P. C. L. Holloway, G. C. Small and A. A. Donald did not bat.

Bowling: Foster 8-0-35-0; Topley 8-1-36-1; Fraser 8-0-33-1; Pringle 8-0-53-1; Waugh 8-0-49-2.

Essex

P. J. Prichard c P. A. Smith b Reeve	7	J. J. B. Lewis st Holloway		
N. V. Knight c and b Reeve	6	b N. M. K. Smith		7
M. E. Waugh b P. A. Smith	43	A. G. J. Fraser run out		1
N. Hussain c Penney b N. M. K. Smith	16	T. D. Topley not out		0
N. Shahid run out	30	L-b 5, w 4		9
D. R. Pringle b N. M. K. Smith	52			
*N. A. Foster lbw b N. M. K. Smith	18	1/11 2/21 3/60	(37.5 overs)	190
†M. A. Garnham c N. M. K. Smith		4/100 5/113 6/146		
b Small	1	7/149 8/188 9/189		

Bowling: Reeve 7-0-32-2; N. M. K. Smith 6.5-0-25-4; Donald 8-0-40-0; Small 8-0-52-1; Twose 3-0-9-0; P. A. Smith 5-0-27-1.

Umpires: J. D. Bond and J. H. Harris.

At The Oval, July 19. WARWICKSHIRE beat SURREY by six wickets.

WARWICKSHIRE v NOTTINGHAMSHIRE

At Birmingham, July 26. Warwickshire won on scoring-rate. Toss: Nottinghamshire. Rain stopped play in the 36th over of the visitors' innings, when they were well behind the required rate of 6.57 an over. Moles and Twose had enjoyed another century opening partnership and when they had gone, Warwickshire added 125 in their last 12 overs; Ostler's unbeaten 60 came from only 36 balls. Nottinghamshire never had much chance of evading a ninth consecutive defeat.

Warwickshire

A. J. Moles run out	55	T. L. Penney not out		13
R. G. Twose c Robinson b Evans	54	B 1, l-b 11, w 6, n-b 1		19
*T. A. Lloyd lbw b Crawley	44			
D. P. Ostler not out	60	1/107 2/137	(4 wkts, 40 overs)	262
D. A. Reeve c Pennett b Mike	17	3/189 4/218		

†P. C. L. Holloway, N. M. K. Smith, P. A. Smith, G. C. Small and A. A. Donald did not bat.

Bowling: Pennett 8-1-55-0; Mike 8-0-46-1; Evans 8-0-58-1; Crawley 8-0-42-1; Afford 3-0-27-0; Saxelby 5-0-22-0.

Nottinghamshire

P. R. Pollard c Reeve b P. A. Smith	36	M. A. Crawley not out		8
P. Johnson c Penney b Small	23	L-b 8, w 12		20
*R. T. Robinson b Donald	54			
M. Saxelby not out	42	1/28 2/97	(4 wkts, 35.4 overs)	183
G. W. Mike c Holloway b Donald	0	3/160 4/160		

G. F. Archer, K. P. Evans, †S. Bramhall, J. A. Afford and D. B. Pennett did not bat.

Bowling: Reeve 6-0-18-0; N. M. K. Smith 6-0-35-0; Small 8-0-37-1; Twose 4-0-17-0; Donald 6-0-28-2; P. A. Smith 5.4-0-40-1.

Umpires: G. I. Burgess and D. R. Shepherd.

At Leek, August 2. WARWICKSHIRE lost to DERBYSHIRE by eight wickets.

WARWICKSHIRE v DURHAM

At Birmingham, August 9. Durham won by 17 runs. Toss: Warwickshire. Durham wicket-keeper Fothergill took four catches as Warwickshire slumped to 66 for six. He later added a stumping.

Durham

I. T. Botham run out	10	S. Hutton not out		8
W. Larkins c Holloway b P. A. Smith	29	S. M. McEwan not out		1
J. D. Glendenen b Reeve	78			
I. Smith c Ostler b Twose	26	B 1, l-b 7, w 3		11
†A. R. Fothergill c N. M. K. Smith b Reeve	5	1/13 2/89 3/130	(6 wkts, 39 overs)	190
M. P. Briers b Munton	22	4/151 5/160 6/188		

S. J. E. Brown, *D. A. Graveney and S. P. Hughes did not bat.

Bowling: Munton 8-0-26-1; Welch 8-0-22-0; Reeve 8-0-40-2; P. A. Smith 7-0-39-1; N. M. K. Smith 3-0-21-0; Twose 5-0-34-1.

Warwickshire

A. J. Moles c Fothergill b Hughes	4	†P. C. L. Holloway not out		20
R. G. Twose c Fothergill b Hughes	1	G. Welch c Hutton b Brown		23
D. P. Ostler c Fothergill b Brown	8	T. A. Munton b Hughes		1
*D. A. Reeve c Hutton b McEwan	25	L-b 7, w 5		12
T. L. Penney c Fothergill b Brown	14			
M. Burns c Larkins b McEwan	1	1/5 2/13 3/23	(38.1 overs)	173
N. M. K. Smith c Hughes b McEwan	44	4/39 5/46 6/66		
P. A. Smith st Fothergill b Graveney	20	7/126 8/126 9/170		

Bowling: Brown 8-0-43-3; Hughes 7.1-0-26-3; Botham 4-0-17-0; McEwan 8-0-27-3; Graveney 8-0-36-1; Smith 3-0-17-0.

Umpires: N. T. Plews and P. B. Wight.

WARWICKSHIRE v KENT

At Birmingham, August 23. No result. Toss: Kent. Only nine overs of the 27 a side scheduled after a late start were possible.

Warwickshire

A. J. Moles c Marsh b Igglesden	10
R. G. Twose c Marsh b Ellison	0
*T. A. Lloyd not out	14
D. P. Ostler not out	9
L-b 1, w 2	3

1/1 2/19   (2 wkts, 9 overs) 36

T. L. Penney, A. A. Donald, †P. C. L. Holloway, P. A. Smith, N. M. K. Smith, G. Welch and T. A. Munton did not bat.

Bowling: Ellison 5–0–22–1; Igglesden 4–1–13–1.

Kent

T. R. Ward, *M. R. Benson, N. R. Taylor, C. L. Hooper, G. R. Cowdrey, M. V. Fleming, †S. A. Marsh, R. M. Ellison, M. A. Ealham, A. P. Igglesden and M. J. McCague.

Umpires: J. D. Bond and B. Dudleston.

At Northampton, August 30. WARWICKSHIRE lost to NORTHAMPTONSHIRE by 40 runs.

WORCESTERSHIRE

WORCESTERSHIRE v YORKSHIRE

At Worcester, April 19. Yorkshire won by seven runs. Toss: Worcestershire. Yorkshire restricted the home team's batsmen to 46 from the last ten overs.

Yorkshire

*M. D. Moxon c Leatherdale b Newport	13	D. Gough c and b Moody	1
A. A. Metcalfe c Rhodes b Newport	17	P. W. Jarvis run out	2
†R. J. Blakey c Hick b Lampitt	9		
D. Byas c Curtis b Illingworth	43	L-b 8, w 2	10
S. A. Kellett st Rhodes b Stemp	31		
C. S. Pickles not out	26	1/32 2/35 3/56 (9 wkts, 40 overs) 160	
P. Carrick c Curtis b Moody	3	4/117 5/127 6/136	
P. J. Hartley c Rhodes b Lampitt	5	7/150 8/152 9/160	

A. P. Grayson did not bat.

Bowling: Newport 8–1–19–2; Moody 8–0–33–2; Lampitt 7–0–21–2; Radford 5–0–29–0; Illingworth 8–1–28–1; Stemp 4–0–22–1.

Worcestershire

*T. S. Curtis c Blakey b Hartley	50	S. R. Lampitt not out	12
T. M. Moody b Gough	7	R. K. Illingworth not out	2
G. A. Hick st Blakey b Carrick	44	B 2, l-b 3, w 4	9
D. A. Leatherdale c Carrick b Moxon	6		
D. B. D'Oliveira c Blakey b Jarvis	11	1/12 2/89 3/104 (7 wkts, 40 overs) 153	
†S. J. Rhodes c Kellett b Jarvis	0	4/115 5/116	
N. V. Radford b Gough	12	6/136 7/142	

P. J. Newport and R. D. Stemp did not bat.

Bowling: Jarvis 8–2–22–2; Gough 8–1–23–2; Hartley 8–0–31–1; Pickles 4–0–24–0; Carrick 8–0–34–1; Moxon 4–0–14–1.

Umpires: J. D. Bond and G. Sharp.

WORCESTERSHIRE v NORTHAMPTONSHIRE

At Worcester, April 26. Worcestershire won by seven wickets. Toss: Worcestershire. Worcestershire had needed 158 from 23 overs, but Hick added 101 in 17 overs with Leatherdale and an unbroken 74 in 11 overs with D'Oliveira.

Northamptonshire

A. Fordham c Weston b Illingworth	...	50
N. A. Felton run out		33
R. J. Bailey b Radford		69
*A. J. Lamb st Rhodes b Illingworth	...	28
D. J. Capel c Curtis b Newport	...	11
K. M. Curran not out		8
R. G. Williams b Radford		0

A. L. Penberthy run out		1
†D. Ripley not out		2
L-b 4, w 1		5

1/70 2/117 3/164   (7 wkts, 40 overs) 207
4/178 5/204
6/204 7/205

J. P. Taylor and A. Walker did not bat.

Bowling: Weston 8–0–30–0; Newport 8–0–49–1; Haynes 8–0–40–0; Radford 8–0–43–2; Illingworth 8–0–41–2.

Worcestershire

*T. S. Curtis c Lamb b Walker		16
T. M. Moody c Ripley b Taylor		8
G. A. Hick not out		83
D. A. Leatherdale b Curran		46

D. B. D'Oliveira not out		40
L-b 12, w 3		15

1/21 2/33 3/134   (3 wkts, 38.5 overs) 208

†S. J. Rhodes, M. J. Weston, N. V. Radford, G. R. Haynes, R. K. Illingworth and P. J. Newport did not bat.

Bowling: Taylor 7.5–1–30–1; Walker 7–0–24–1; Capel 8–0–44–0; Curran 8–0–42–1; Penberthy 4–0–32–0; Williams 4–0–24–0.

Umpires: J. C. Balderstone and R. A. White.

At Cardiff, May 3. WORCESTERSHIRE beat GLAMORGAN by eight wickets.

WORCESTERSHIRE v WARWICKSHIRE

At Worcester, May 10. Tied. Toss: Worcestershire. The neighbours produced their second Sunday League tie in two years, and their third in all. Moody and Hick had added 125 for the second wicket, and Worcestershire came to the last two overs needing only five; but Munton managed to bowl a maiden, and Neil Smith restricted them to four from the last, with Moody run out off the last ball.

Warwickshire

A. J. Moles b Radford		19
Asif Din b Lampitt		22
*T. A. Lloyd b Illingworth		62
D. P. Ostler c Moody b Lampitt		1
R. G. Twose run out		6
N. M. K. Smith run out		9
P. A. Smith c Hick b Lampitt		18
†P. C. L. Holloway b Radford		8

G. C. Small not out		10
A. A. Donald c Radford b Lampitt	...	0
T. A. Munton not out		0
B 1, l-b 8, w 5, n-b 2		16

1/24 2/79 3/83   (9 wkts, 40 overs) 171
4/93 5/121 6/141
7/154 8/167 9/170

Bowling: Weston 8–1–32–0; Radford 8–0–22–2; Illingworth 8–0–31–1; Newport 8–0–37–0; Lampitt 8–1–40–4.

Worcestershire

*T. S. Curtis b N. M. K. Smith	1
T. M. Moody run out	78
G. A. Hick c Asif Din b P. A. Smith	60
D. A. Leatherdale b N. M. K. Smith	21
D. B. D'Oliveira not out	1
L-b 6, w 4	10

1/2 2/127   (4 wkts, 40 overs) 171
3/168 4/171

†S. J. Rhodes, M. J. Weston, S. R. Lampitt, R. K. Illingworth, P. J. Newport and N. V. Radford did not bat.

Bowling: Munton 8–2–13–0; N. M. K. Smith 6–0–39–2; Small 8–0–26–0; Donald 8–0–25–0; P. A. Smith 8–0–50–1; Moles 2–0–12–0.

Umpires: B. Dudleston and A. G. T. Whitehead.

At Derby, May 17. WORCESTERSHIRE beat DERBYSHIRE by seven wickets.

WORCESTERSHIRE v ESSEX

At Worcester, May 31. Worcestershire won by two wickets. Toss: Worcestershire. Essex lost their first Sunday match of the season after five straight wins. Though a target of 173 did not seem too challenging, Worcestershire collapsed from 80 for nought and Rhodes, at No. 9, had to secure the victory.

Essex

*G. A. Gooch st Rhodes b Haynes	17	A. G. J. Fraser run out		3
J. P. Stephenson c Weston b Newport	15	T. D. Topley not out		4
M. E. Waugh c Leatherdale		P. M. Such not out		9
b Illingworth	47			
N. Hussain c Leatherdale b Moody	30	B 1, l-b 11, w 2, n-b 1		15
P. J. Prichard c Lampitt b Illingworth	17			
N. V. Knight b Newport	10	1/35 2/43 3/118	(9 wkts, 40 overs)	172
D. R. Pringle c Rhodes b Newport	0	4/126 5/144 6/144		
†M. A. Garnham c Haynes b Illingworth	5	7/154 8/157 9/159		

Bowling: Weston 8–0–28–0; Haynes 6–0–18–1; Newport 8–1–36–3; Lampitt 4–0–23–0; Moody 6–0–25–1; Illingworth 8–0–30–3.

Worcestershire

*T. S. Curtis b Pringle	67	†S. J. Rhodes not out		16
T. M. Moody c Stephenson b Waugh	65	P. J. Newport not out		1
G. A. Hick c Knight b Waugh	5			
D. B. D'Oliveira run out	9	B 1, l-b 3, w 1		5
G. R. Haynes c Hussain b Waugh	1			
D. A. Leatherdale c Garnham b Such	2	1/80 2/95 3/124	(8 wkts, 39.4 overs)	173
M. J. Weston b Topley	1	4/128 5/135 6/138		
S. R. Lampitt lbw b Topley	1	7/144 8/166		

R. K. Illingworth did not bat.

Bowling: Topley 8–0–32–2; Pringle 8–1–25–1; Such 8–1–48–1; Stephenson 8–0–38–0; Waugh 7.4–1–26–3.

Umpires: J. C. Balderstone and R. C. Tolchard.

At The Oval, June 14. WORCESTERSHIRE lost to SURREY by four wickets.

WORCESTERSHIRE v SUSSEX

At Worcester, June 28. Worcestershire won by eight runs. Toss: Worcestershire. Curtis batted throughout the 40 overs for 77. The total of 186 proved enough when Sussex lost their last five wickets for six runs in 17 balls, after they had needed only 15 from the last 20 deliveries.

Worcestershire

*T. S. Curtis not out	77	S. R. Lampitt run out	0
†S. J. Rhodes c North b Robson	0	M. J. Weston not out	6
G. A. Hick run out	55		
D. A. Leatherdale c Greenfield b Salisbury	29	L-b 6, w 4, n-b 1	11
D. B. D'Oliveira c Stephenson b North	2	1/0 2/97 3/143	(6 wkts, 40 overs) 186
G. R. Haynes run out	6	4/147 5/160 6/170	

R. K. Illingworth, P. J. Newport and C. M. Tolley did not bat.

Bowling: Stephenson 8–2–24–0; Robson 8–0–30–1; Pigott 8–0–39–0; Salisbury 5–0–33–1; North 7–0–34–1; Greenfield 4–0–20–0.

Sussex

K. Greenfield c Lampitt b Weston	6	A. C. S. Pigott c Rhodes b Newport	1
J. W. Hall b Lampitt	42	I. D. K. Salisbury run out	0
M. P. Speight c Lampitt b Newport	19	A. G. Robson not out	0
*A. P. Wells c Rhodes b Lampitt	64	L-b 6, w 1	7
N. J. Lenham c D'Oliveira b Tolley	8		
F. D. Stephenson c D'Oliveira b Tolley	4	1/10 2/46 3/88	(39.3 overs) 178
†P. Moores lbw b Newport	24	4/112 5/130 6/172	
J. A. North c Hick b Tolley	3	7/175 8/177 9/178	

Bowling: Weston 4–0–18–1; Haynes 6–2–18–0; Newport 6–1–27–3; Tolley 8–0–31–3; Lampitt 7.3–0–40–2; Illingworth 8–0–38–0.

Umpires: J. W. Holder and D. O. Oslear.

At Lord's, July 5. WORCESTERSHIRE lost to MIDDLESEX by nine wickets.

At Leicester, July 12. WORCESTERSHIRE beat LEICESTERSHIRE by six runs.

At Canterbury, July 19. WORCESTERSHIRE lost to KENT by 36 runs.

WORCESTERSHIRE v HAMPSHIRE

At Worcester, July 26. Hampshire won by six wickets. Toss: Worcestershire. Moody scored 53 in his last Sunday League innings before leaving to join the Australian touring party for Sri Lanka. Hampshire's scoring-rate seemed too slow until Nicholas was dropped by D'Oliveira when six; this inspired him to add 60 in 12 overs with Ayling.

Worcestershire

*T. S. Curtis c Aymes b Ayling	18	S. R. Lampitt not out	14
T. M. Moody c Connor b Udal	53		
D. A. Leatherdale c Connor b Ayling	3	L-b 6, w 3, n-b 1	10
D. B. D'Oliveira c Wood b Marshall	20		
N. V. Radford not out	49	1/39 2/60 3/90	(5 wkts, 40 overs) 176
A. C. H. Seymour c and b Marshall	9	4/125 5/157	

M. J. Weston, †S. J. Rhodes, R. K. Illingworth and C. M. Tolley did not bat.

Bowling: Connor 7–1–34–0; Bakker 6–0–28–0; Marshall 8–1–19–2; Ayling 6–0–24–2; Turner 5–0–24–0; Udal 8–0–41–1.

Hampshire

R. M. F. Cox run out	5	M. D. Marshall not out	23
T. C. Middleton b Illingworth	27	L-b 2, w 1, n-b 1	4
J. R. Wood b Radford	35		
J. R. Ayling c D'Oliveira b Tolley	45	1/11 2/56 (4 wkts, 39.2 overs)	177
*M. C. J. Nicholas not out	38	3/74 4/134	

I. J. Turner, †A. N. Aymes, S. D. Udal, C. A. Connor and P. J. Bakker did not bat.

Bowling: Weston 8–0–23–0; Tolley 6–0–27–1; Lampitt 5–0–36–0; Illingworth 8–0–27–1; Radford 6.2–1–26–1; Moody 6–0–36–0.

Umpires: H. D. Bird and A. A. Jones.

WORCESTERSHIRE v GLOUCESTERSHIRE

At Worcester, August 2. Worcestershire won by six wickets. Toss: Worcestershire. Curtis put on 108 with his new opening partner D'Oliveira, and was not dismissed until only six runs were required for victory.

Gloucestershire

M. W. Alleyne b Tolley	55	C. A. Walsh c Rhodes b Lampitt	1
G. D. Hodgson c Curtis b Weston	22	M. C. J. Ball not out	4
C. W. J. Athey c Rhodes b Weston	1		
*A. J. Wright run out	9		
R. I. Dawson st Rhodes b Illingworth	19	L-b 10, w 6, n-b 3	19
R. J. Scott not out	34		
†R. C. Russell c Leatherdale b Lampitt	4	1/41 2/48 3/75 (8 wkts, 40 overs)	174
J. T. C. Vaughan c D'Oliveira b Radford	6	4/110 5/132 6/144	
		7/158 8/162	

A. M. Smith did not bat.

Bowling: Weston 8–1–28–2; Haynes 6–0–22–0; Radford 6–0–32–1; Lampitt 8–0–33–2; Tolley 4–0–18–1; Illingworth 8–0–31–1.

Worcestershire

*T. S. Curtis c Walsh b Ball	70	S. R. Lampitt not out	0
D. B. D'Oliveira c Walsh b Smith	48	L-b 8, w 6	14
G. A. Hick c Dawson b Walsh	14		
D. A. Leatherdale st Russell b Ball	19	1/108 2/125 (4 wkts, 36.4 overs)	175
N. V. Radford not out	10	3/152 4/169	

†S. J. Rhodes, M. J. Weston, R. K. Illingworth, G. R. Haynes and C. M. Tolley did not bat.

Bowling: Vaughan 6–2–21–0; Walsh 7–1–30–1; Alleyne 8–0–41–0; Scott 5–0–23–0; Ball 7–1–33–2; Smith 3.4–0–19–1.

Umpires: G. I. Burgess and N. T. Plews.

At Manchester, August 9. LANCASHIRE v WORCESTERSHIRE. No result.

At Taunton, August 16. WORCESTERSHIRE lost to SOMERSET by two wickets.

WORCESTERSHIRE v DURHAM

At Worcester, August 23. No result. Toss: Worcestershire. Only 23 overs' play was possible before rain.

Durham

W. Larkins c Rhodes b Weston	2	†C. W. Scott not out	8
J. D. Glendenen lbw b Radford	33		
P. Bainbridge c Rhodes b Weston	5	L-b 5, w 9	14
S. Hutton not out	29		
M. P. Briers lbw b Radford	0	1/19 2/35 3/53 (5 wkts, 23 overs) 94	
I. Smith c Tolley b Radford	3	4/53 5/72	

J. Wood, S. M. McEwan, *D. A. Graveney and S. P. Hughes did not bat.

Bowling: Haynes 2–0–15–0; Weston 8–0–27–2; Radford 8–0–27–3; Stemp 3–0–13–0; Newport 2–0–7–0.

Worcestershire

*T. S. Curtis, D. B. D'Oliveira, D. A. Leatherdale, G. R. Haynes, M. J. Weston, S. R. Lampitt, †S. J. Rhodes, P. J. Newport, N. V. Radford, C. M. Tolley and R. D. Stemp.

Umpires: J. H. Harris and J. W. Holder.

WORCESTERSHIRE v NOTTINGHAMSHIRE

At Worcester, August 30. No result.

YORKSHIRE

At Worcester, April 19. YORKSHIRE beat WORCESTERSHIRE by seven runs.

At Hove, April 26. SUSSEX v YORKSHIRE. No result.

YORKSHIRE v NOTTINGHAMSHIRE

At Leeds, May 3. Nottinghamshire won by nine wickets. Toss: Nottinghamshire. Randall's unbeaten 91 from 104 balls took him past D. R. Turner (6,639 Sunday League runs) to become the fourth-highest scorer in the competition with 6,647. When Yorkshire batted, Tendulkar, the first non-Yorkshireman to play Sunday League cricket for the county, made 40 from 49 balls on his league début, but he could not save his new team.

Yorkshire

D. Byas c Lewis b Pick	1	P. J. Hartley c Randall b Evans	1
*A. A. Metcalfe c Broad b Pick	18	D. Gough not out	0
†R. J. Blakey b Evans	72	L-b 1, w 5, n-b 1	7
S. R. Tendulkar c Saxelby b Cairns	40		
C. White c Broad b Hemmings	6	1/7 2/30 3/84 (7 wkts, 40 overs) 167	
A. P. Grayson b Evans	8	4/102 5/118	
C. S. Pickles not out	14	6/164 7/166	

P. Carrick and M. A. Robinson did not bat.

Bowling: Lewis 8–0–36–0; Pick 7–0–39–2; Evans 8–0–31–3; Saxelby 3–0–12–0; Cairns 6–2–21–1; Hemmings 8–0–27–1.

Nottinghamshire

B. C. Broad lbw b Hartley	....	62
D. W. Randall not out	....	91
*P. Johnson not out	....	11
L-b 1, w 6	....	7

1/120   (1 wkt, 34.3 overs) 171

P. R. Pollard, C. C. Lewis, C. L. Cairns, M. Saxelby, K. P. Evans, †B. N. French, E. E. Hemmings and R. A. Pick did not bat.

Bowling: Gough 6–0–29–0; Hartley 8–0–33–1; Robinson 6–0–23–0; Pickles 6.3–0–48–0; Carrick 8–0–37–0.

Umpires: J. C. Balderstone and G. A. Stickley.

YORKSHIRE v HAMPSHIRE

At Leeds, May 24. Hampshire won by 59 runs. Toss: Yorkshire. Smith and Middleton opened with 126 in 25 overs for Hampshire, but when Yorkshire replied they lost their first three wickets in four overs. James conceded only 11 runs in his eight overs.

Hampshire

R. A. Smith run out	....	77	*M. C. J. Nicholas not out	....	1
T. C. Middleton c Pickles b Carrick	...	66			
D. I. Gower c Byas b Carrick	....	8	L-b 5, w 7, n-b 2	....	14
M. D. Marshall c White b Gough	....	19			
K. D. James c Tendulkar b Hartley	....	24	1/126 2/150 3/169 (5 wkts, 40 overs) 211		
J. R. Ayling not out	....	2	4/207 5/208		

†A. N. Aymes, R. J. Maru, C. A. Connor and S. D. Udal did not bat.

Bowling: Hartley 6–0–36–1; Gough 8–1–38–1; Robinson 8–0–39–0; Pickles 4–0–19–0; Carrick 8–0–42–2; Tendulkar 6–0–32–0.

Yorkshire

S. A. Kellett run out	....	10	P. J. Hartley c Middleton b Udal	....	1
*A. A. Metcalfe b James	....	0	D. Gough c and b Udal	....	2
†R. J. Blakey lbw b Connor	....	2	M. A. Robinson st Aymes b Smith	....	3
S. R. Tendulkar run out	....	16	L-b 3, w 3, n-b 1	....	7
D. Byas c Ayling b Marshall	....	45			
C. White not out	.....	40	1/6 2/11 3/13 (38.2 overs) 152		
C. S. Pickles b Maru	....	15	4/55 5/91 6/121		
P. Carrick b Udal	....	11	7/142 8/146 9/149		

Bowling: Connor 7–0–29–1; James 8–1–11–1; Ayling 4–0–23–0; Maru 8–0–41–1; Marshall 4–0–15–1; Udal 7–0–30–3; Smith 0.2–0–0–1.

Umpires: A. A. Jones and G. Sharp.

At Canterbury, May 31. YORKSHIRE beat KENT by four runs.

YORKSHIRE v SOMERSET

At Middlesbrough, June 7. Yorkshire won by five wickets. Toss: Somerset. Harden, captaining Somerset because Tavaré had become a father the previous day, put on 167 in 24 overs with Rose. But the decisive partnership of the day proved to be that of 119 in 15 overs between Byas, who made 80 in 55 balls, and White.

Somerset

M. N. Lathwell c Batty b Carrick 39
R. J. Bartlett lbw b Batty 37
*R. J. Harden not out 76
G. D. Rose lbw b Gough 88

R. P. Snell not out................. 1
L-b 7, w 2, n-b 2........... 11

1/82 2/82 3/249   (3 wkts, 40 overs) 252

A. N. Hayhurst, †N. D. Burns, K. H. MacLeay, A. R. Caddick, N. A. Mallender and
H. R. J. Trump did not bat.

Bowling: Hartley 8–0–43–0; Robinson 8–0–59–0; Gough 5–0–38–1; Carrick 8–0–32–1;
Batty 8–0–49–1; Tendulkar 3–0–24–0.

Yorkshire

*M. D. Moxon c MacLeay b Trump ... 57
S. A. Kellett c Rose b MacLeay....... 18
†R. J. Blakey c Trump b MacLeay ... 31
S. R. Tendulkar run out 10
D. Byas c Mallender b Snell.......... 80
C. White not out 52

P. J. Hartley not out 1
L-b 2, w 4, n-b 1 7

1/45 2/96 3/118   (5 wkts, 39 overs) 256
4/127 5/246

D. Gough, P. Carrick, J. D. Batty and M. A. Robinson did not bat.

Bowling: Mallender 8–0–43–0; Caddick 8–0–53–0; MacLeay 8–0–32–2; Snell 6–0–53–1;
Trump 4–0–30–1; Hayhurst 5–0–43–0.

Umpires: H. D. Bird and K. E. Palmer.

YORKSHIRE v DERBYSHIRE

At Leeds, June 14. Yorkshire won by 71 runs. Toss: Derbyshire. Half of Yorkshire's runs
came from Kellett's maiden one-day century; he hit 13 fours in 122 balls. In the last seven
overs of the innings he added 67 with Tendulkar. Despite Adams, who hit four sixes off
Batty, Yorkshire completed an easy win.

Yorkshire

*M. D. Moxon c Morris b Warner 30
S. A. Kellett not out 118
†R. J. Blakey c and b Goldsmith 49
S. R. Tendulkar not out 32
L-b 4, w 3 7

1/72 2/169   (2 wkts, 40 overs) 236

D. Byas, C. White, P. J. Hartley, D. Gough, C. S. Pickles, J. D. Batty and M. A. Robinson
did not bat.

Bowling: Mortensen 8–1–20–0; Bishop 8–0–47–0; Cork 8–0–48–0; Warner 8–0–57–1;
Goldsmith 5–0–39–1; Bowler 3–0–21–0.

Derbyshire

*K. J. Barnett c and b Batty 35
P. D. Bowler b Hartley 0
J. E. Morris lbw b Hartley 0
T. J. G. O'Gorman c Moxon b Gough . 14
C. J. Adams lbw b Gough 58
I. R. Bishop run out 19
A. E. Warner b Gough 0
S. C. Goldsmith b Hartley 16

D. G. Cork c Pickles b Tendulkar 8
†K. M. Krikken c White b Tendulkar.. 3
O. H. Mortensen not out............ 3
B 4, l-b 3, w 1, n-b 1 9

1/3 2/5 3/39   (37.3 overs) 165
4/61 5/130 6/130
7/146 8/154 9/157

Bowling: Hartley 7–0–19–3; Robinson 5–0–8–0; Gough 8–1–30–3; Pickles 7–0–34–0;
Batty 5–1–39–1; Tendulkar 5.3–0–28–2.

Umpires: R. Julian and N. T. Plews.

At Ebbw Vale, June 21. YORKSHIRE beat GLAMORGAN by four wickets.

YORKSHIRE v WARWICKSHIRE

At Scarborough, June 28. Yorkshire won by 21 runs. Toss: Yorkshire. The 20-year-old Warwickshire débutant Graeme Welch removed Moxon early, but Kellett and Blakey, who hit 12 fours in his 109-ball innings, added 116 for the second wicket. Three of the Yorkshire wickets to fall went to stumpings by Holloway. Warwickshire could not catch up after being reduced to 48 for three, despite Penney who hit an unbeaten 53 in 32 balls.

Yorkshire

*M. D. Moxon c Penney b Welch	10	P. J. Hartley not out 7
S. A. Kellett run out	77	
†R. J. Blakey not out	105	B 1, l-b 3, w 1, n-b 1 6
S. R. Tendulkar st Holloway b Lloyd	15	
D. Byas st Holloway b Lloyd	3	1/33 2/149 3/197 (5 wkts, 40 overs) 224
C. White st Holloway b N. M. K. Smith	1	4/210 5/213

P. Carrick, D. Gough, J. D. Batty and M. A. Robinson did not bat.

Bowling: Welch 6–1–24–1; N. M. K. Smith 8–0–33–1; Reeve 6–0–28–0; Twose 3–0–22–0; Small 6–0–31–0; P. A. Smith 6–0–45–0; Lloyd 5–0–37–2.

Warwickshire

A. J. Moles c and b Batty	11	†P. C. L. Holloway b Gough 3
R. G. Twose lbw b Batty	22	G. Welch not out 1
*T. A. Lloyd c Moxon b Batty	12	
D. P. Ostler c Batty b Carrick	54	L-b 1, w 1 2
D. A. Reeve c Blakey b Hartley	29	
T. L. Penney not out	53	1/29 2/43 3/48 (8 wkts, 40 overs) 203
N. M. K. Smith c Robinson b Carrick	2	4/129 5/130 6/138
P. A. Smith b Gough	14	7/178 8/201

G. C. Small did not bat.

Bowling: Robinson 8–0–32–0; Hartley 8–1–39–1; Gough 8–0–26–2; Batty 8–0–50–3; Carrick 8–0–55–2.

Umpires: J. C. Balderstone and R. A. White.

YORKSHIRE v LEICESTERSHIRE

At Sheffield, July 5. Leicestershire won by six wickets. Toss: Leicestershire. The visiting county's second league win of the season came with five balls to spare, thanks to an unbeaten 82 from Whitaker.

Yorkshire

*M. D. Moxon b Wells	13	P. J. Hartley not out 4
S. A. Kellett c Briers b Benjamin	38	D. Gough not out 5
†R. J. Blakey b Potter	9	B 1, l-b 9, w 3 13
S. R. Tendulkar c Wells b Benjamin	41	
D. Byas c Robinson b Wells	7	1/29 2/48 3/83 (7 wkts, 40 overs) 148
C. White b Parsons	14	4/98 5/130
P. Carrick c Robinson b Parsons	4	6/138 7/138

J. D. Batty and M. A. Robinson did not bat.

Bowling: Benjamin 8–0–20–2; Mullally 8–2–25–0; Wells 8–1–28–2; Potter 8–0–31–1; Parsons 8–1–34–2.

eicestershire

J. Whitaker not out	82	L. Potter not out	1
N. E. Briers lbw b Gough	0	L-b 8, w 2, n-b 1	11
F. Smith c Blakey b Hartley	37		
E. Robinson b Gough	19	1/10 2/73 (4 wkts, 39.1 overs)	152
D. R. Benson st Blakey b Carrick	2	3/134 4/139	

J. K. M. Benjamin, †P. A. Nixon, V. J. Wells, G. J. Parsons and A. D. Mullally did not bat.

Bowling: Hartley 8–1–31–1; Gough 8–2–13–2; Robinson 7–1–30–0; Batty 8–1–25–0; Carrick 8–0–41–1; Moxon 0.1–0–4–0.

Umpires: H. D. Bird and M. J. Kitchen.

YORKSHIRE v ESSEX

t Scarborough, July 12. Essex won by three wickets. Toss: Essex. Essex all-rounder Pringle ould not bowl, because his size 13 boots had been left behind and he was too uncomforable to move freely in a hastily acquired pair of size 12s. But Gooch found his own steady edium pace ideally suited to a slow pitch. Later the England captain took his Sunday eague aggregate to 7,060, 20 runs ahead of the previous record of 7,040 by D. L. Amiss. fter his dismissal Essex were in difficulties until Garnham hit an unbeaten 33 from 32 alls.

orkshire

M. D. Moxon c and b Gooch	41	P. J. Hartley not out	13
A. Kellett b Gooch	27		
R. J. Blakey c Shahid b Stephenson	3	L-b 9, w 2, n-b 2	13
R. Tendulkar c Garnham b Waugh	13		
Byas lbw b Ilott	28	1/72 2/79 3/79 (5 wkts, 40 overs)	162
White not out	24	4/109 5/129	

Carrick, P. W. Jarvis, D. Gough and J. D. Batty did not bat.

Bowling: Ilott 8–1–36–1; Topley 4–0–20–0; Stephenson 8–2–22–1; Childs 4–0–20–0; ooch 8–1–24–2; Waugh 8–0–31–1.

ssex

G. A. Gooch b Gough	43	N. Shahid run out	6
P. Stephenson c Blakey b Jarvis	3	T. D. Topley not out	4
E. Waugh b Hartley	0	L-b 8, w 1	9
J. Prichard c and b Batty	33		
R. Pringle c Blakey b Jarvis	21	1/17 2/18 3/73 (7 wkts, 38.4 overs)	163
V. Knight c White b Hartley	11	4/104 5/111	
M. A. Garnham not out	33	6/137 7/147	

C. Ilott and J. H. Childs did not bat.

Bowling: Hartley 7.4–0–27–2; Jarvis 7–0–33–2; Gough 6–1–20–1; Carrick 5–0–22–0; atty 7–0–33–1; Moxon 6–0–20–0.

Umpires: B. Leadbeater and B. J. Meyer.

t Cheltenham College, July 19. YORKSHIRE lost to GLOUCESTERSHIRE by three wickets.

YORKSHIRE v LANCASHIRE

At Leeds, August 2. Lancashire won by four runs. Toss: Yorkshire. Two young playe
struck Roses hundreds. Speak's 102 came from 79 balls with two sixes and ten fours, and
Lancashire's last 17 overs he and Fairbrother put on 154; while later Tendulkar made h
maiden century for Yorkshire, facing 73 deliveries and hitting ten fours and a six. He h
the fastest televised fifty of the season off 33 balls and added 176 in 24 overs with Blake
Jarvis needed a six off the final ball to tie the scores, but managed only two.

Lancashire

G. Fowler c Byas b Gough 28	*N. H. Fairbrother not out ....
M. A. Atherton c Gough b Carrick 46	L-b 11, w 7 ....
G. D. Lloyd lbw b Pickles 6	—
N. J. Speak not out 102	1/43 2/62 3/110 (3 wkts, 40 overs) 2

M. Watkinson, †W. K. Hegg, I. D. Austin, J. D. Fitton, P. A. J. DeFreitas and P. J. V
Allott did not bat.

Bowling: Hartley 8-0-43-0; Jarvis 8-0-59-0; Gough 8-0-53-1; Pickles 8-0-44-
Carrick 8-0-54-1.

Yorkshire

*M. D. Moxon b Watkinson 24	C. S. Pickles not out ....
S. A. Kellett c Hegg b DeFreitas 1	P. W. Jarvis not out ....
†R. J. Blakey c Hegg b Fitton 86	L-b 13, w 1 ....
S. R. Tendulkar run out 107	—
D. Byas c Fitton b DeFreitas 9	1/16 2/43 3/219 (6 wkts, 40 overs) 2
C. White b DeFreitas 2	4/231 5/238 6/240

P. J. Hartley, D. Gough and P. Carrick did not bat.

Bowling: Allott 8-1-32-0; DeFreitas 8-0-53-3; Watkinson 8-0-53-1; Austin 8-0-41-
Fitton 8-0-68-1.

Umpires: J. W. Holder and R. A. White.

At Northampton, August 9. YORKSHIRE lost to NORTHAMPTONSHIRE by 65 runs.

At Uxbridge, August 16. YORKSHIRE lost to MIDDLESEX by five wickets.

YORKSHIRE v SURREY

At Scarborough, August 23. Surrey won on scoring-rate. Toss: Yorkshire. Surrey earne
victory in the nick of time; torrential rain stopped play just after they had completed the
overs needed for the match to stand, and the home team lost their seventh consecuti
league match. The game was transformed by an astonishing 105 from Brown, hitting thr
sixes and 13 fours in 68 balls; Darren Bicknell scored only 13 as they put on 76 in the fi
14 overs, and Thorpe 15 during 65 from six.

Yorkshire

*M. D. Moxon c Sargeant	P. J. Hartley c Boiling b Bryson ......
b M. P. Bicknell . 4	D. Gough b Benjamin ....
S. A. Kellett c Benjamin b Boiling 24	J. D. Batty not out ....
D. Byas c Boiling b Benjamin 14	
C. White run out 63	B 1, l-b 10, w 4 ....
A. A. Metcalfe c Brown b Feltham 43	—
†C. A. Chapman run out 13	1/6 2/38 3/50 (39.2 overs) 2
P. W. Jarvis lbw b Benjamin 1	4/151 5/162 6/167
C. S. Pickles b M. P. Bicknell 6	7/178 8/191 9/200

Bowling: Bryson 7.2-0-58-1; M. P. Bicknell 8-1-36-2; Benjamin 8-0-32-3; Boili
8-0-32-1; Feltham 8-0-35-1.

urrey

J. Bicknell b Batty	13
D. Brown not out	105
P. Thorpe not out	15
B 2, l-b 4, w 2	8

76   (1 wkt, 20.1 overs) 141

M. A. Lynch, D. M. Ward, M. A. Feltham, †N. F. Sargeant, M. P. Bicknell, J. Boiling, J. E. Benjamin and R. E. Bryson did not bat.

Bowling: Jarvis 5–1–32–0; Hartley 5.1–0–14–0; Gough 3–0–27–0; Batty 3–0–30–1; Pickles -0–32–0.

Umpires: A. A. Jones and R. C. Tolchard.

t Darlington, August 30. DURHAM v YORKSHIRE. No result.

SUNDAY LEAGUE RECORDS

Batting

Highest score: 176 – G. A. Gooch, Essex v Glamorgan (Southend), 1983.

Most hundreds: 11 – C. G. Greenidge and G. A. Gooch; 10 – W. Larkins; 9 – K. S. McEwan and B. A. Richards. 420 hundreds have been scored in the League. The most in one season is 40 in 1990.

Most runs: G. A. Gooch 7,165; D. L. Amiss 7,040; D. W. Randall 6,962; C. T. Radley 6,650; D. R. Turner 6,639; P. Willey 6,506; W. Larkins 6,425; C. W. J. Athey 6,420; C. G. Greenidge 6,344; C. E. B. Rice 6,265; G. M. Turner 6,144.

Most runs in a season: 917 – T. M. Moody (Worcestershire), 1991.

Most sixes in an innings: 13 – I. T. Botham, Somerset v Northamptonshire (Wellingborough School), 1986.

Most sixes by a team in an innings: 18 – Derbyshire v Worcestershire (Knypersley), 1985.

Most sixes in a season: 26 – I. V. A. Richards (Somerset), 1977.

Highest total: 360 for three – Somerset v Glamorgan (Neath), 1990.

Highest total – batting second: 301 for six – Warwickshire v Essex (Colchester), 1982.

Highest match aggregate: 604 – Surrey (304) v Warwickshire (300 for nine) (The Oval), 1985.

Lowest total: 23 (19.4 overs) – Middlesex v Yorkshire (Leeds), 1974.

Shortest completed innings: 16 overs – Northamptonshire 59 v Middlesex (Tring), 1974.

Shortest match: 2 hr 13 min (40.3 overs) – Essex v Northamptonshire (Ilford), 1971.

Biggest victories: 220 runs, Somerset beat Glamorgan (Neath), 1990.
   There have been 23 instances of victory by ten wickets – by Derbyshire, Essex (three times), Glamorgan, Hampshire, Leicestershire (twice), Middlesex (twice), Northamptonshire, Nottinghamshire, Somerset (twice), Surrey (twice), Warwickshire, Worcestershire (three times) and Yorkshire (three times). This does not include those matches in which the side batting second was set a reduced target but does include matches where both sides faced a reduced number of overs.

Ties: There have been 33 tied matches.

Record partnerships for each wicket

239	for 1st	G. A. Gooch and B. R. Hardie, Essex v Nottinghamshire at Nottingham	198
273	for 2nd	G. A. Gooch and K. S. McEwan, Essex v Nottinghamshire at Nottingham	198
223	for 3rd	S. J. Cook and G. D. Rose, Somerset v Glamorgan at Neath	199
219	for 4th	C. G. Greenidge and C. L. Smith, Hampshire v Surrey at Southampton	198
185*	for 5th	B. M. McMillan and Asif Din, Warwickshire v Essex at Chelmsford.	198
124*	for 6th	J. J. Whitaker and P. A. Nixon, Leicestershire v Surrey at The Oval	199
132	for 7th	K. R. Brown and N. F. Williams, Middlesex v Somerset at Lord's	198
105	for 8th	W. K. Hegg and I. D. Austin, Lancashire v Middlesex at Lord's	199
105	for 9th	D. G. Moir and R. W. Taylor, Derbyshire v Kent at Derby	198
57	for 10th	D. A. Graveney and J. B. Mortimore, Gloucestershire v Lancashire at Tewkesbury	197

Bowling

Best analyses: eight for 26, K. D. Boyce, Essex v Lancashire (Manchester), 1971; seven fo 15, R. A. Hutton, Yorkshire v Worcestershire (Leeds), 1969; seven for 39, A. Hodgson Northamptonshire v Somerset (Northampton), 1976; seven for 41, A. N. Jones, Sussex Nottinghamshire (Nottingham), 1986; six for 6, R. W. Hooker, Middlesex v Surre (Lord's), 1969; six for 7, M. Hendrick, Derbyshire v Nottinghamshire (Nottingham 1972; six for 9, N. G. Cowans, Middlesex v Lancashire (Lord's), 1991.

Four wickets in four balls: A. Ward, Derbyshire v Sussex (Derby), 1970.

Hat-tricks (21): A. Ward, Derbyshire v Sussex (Derby), 1970; R. Palmer, Somerset Gloucestershire (Bristol), 1970; K. D. Boyce, Essex v Somerset (Westcliff), 1971; G. D McKenzie, Leicestershire v Essex (Leicester), 1972; R. G. D. Willis, Warwickshire Yorkshire (Birmingham), 1973; W. Blenkiron, Warwickshire v Derbyshire (Buxton 1974; A. Buss, Sussex v Worcestershire (Hastings), 1974; J. M. Rice, Hampshire Northamptonshire (Southampton), 1975; M. A. Nash, Glamorgan v Worcestershir (Worcester), 1975; A. Hodgson, Northamptonshire v Somerset (Northampton), 1976 A. E. Cordle, Glamorgan v Hampshire (Portsmouth), 1979; C. J. Tunnicliffe, Derbyshir v Worcestershire (Derby), 1979; M. D. Marshall, Hampshire v Surrey (Southampton 1981; I. V. A. Richards, Somerset v Essex (Chelmsford), 1982; P. W. Jarvis, Yorkshire Derbyshire (Derby), 1982; R. M. Ellison, Kent v Hampshire (Canterbury), 1983; G. C Holmes, Glamorgan v Nottinghamshire (Ebbw Vale), 1987; K. Saxelby, Nottinghamshi v Worcestershire (Nottingham), 1987; K. M. Curran, Gloucestershire v Warwickshi (Birmingham), 1989; M. P. Bicknell, Surrey v Derbyshire (The Oval), 1992; M. McCague, Kent v Glamorgan (Swansea), 1992.

Most economical analysis: 8–8–0–0, B. A. Langford, Somerset v Essex (Yeovil), 1969.

Most expensive analyses: 7.5–0–89–3, G. Miller, Derbyshire v Gloucestershire (Gloucester 1984; 8–0–88–1, E. E. Hemmings, Nottinghamshire v Somerset (Nottingham), 1983.

Most wickets in a season: 34 – R. J. Clapp (Somerset), 1974, and C. E. B. Rice (Nottin hamshire), 1986.

Most wickets: J. K. Lever 386; D. L. Underwood 346; J. E. Emburey 320; J. Simmons 30 S. Turner 303; N. Gifford 284; E. E. Hemmings 274; J. N. Shepherd 267; T. E. Jest 249; I. T. Botham 247; R. D. Jackman 234; P. Willey 234.

Wicket-keeping and Fielding

Most dismissals: D. L. Bairstow 255 (231 ct, 24 st); R. W. Taylor 236 (187 ct, 49 st E. W. Jones 223 (184 ct, 39 st).

Most dismissals in a season: 29 (26 ct, 3 st) – S. J. Rhodes (Worcestershire), 1988.

Most dismissals in an innings: 7 (6 ct, 1 st) – R. W. Taylor, Derbyshire v Lancashire (Manchester), 1975.

Most catches in an innings: 6 – K. Goodwin, Lancashire v Worcestershire (Worcester), 1969; R. W. Taylor, Derbyshire v Lancashire (Manchester), 1975.

Most stumpings in an innings: 4 – S. J. Rhodes, Worcestershire v Warwickshire (Birmingham), 1986; N. D. Burns, Somerset v Kent (Taunton), 1991.

Most catches by a fielder (not a wicket-keeper): J. F. Steele 101; D. P. Hughes 97; G. Cook 94; C. T. Radley 91.

Most catches in a season: 16 – J. M. Rice (Hampshire), 1978.

Most catches in an innings: 5 – J. M. Rice, Hampshire v Warwickshire (Southampton), 1978.

CHAMPIONS 1969-92

John Player League		1982	Sussex
1969	Lancashire	1983	Yorkshire
1970	Lancashire	1984	Essex
1971	Worcestershire	1985	Essex
1972	Kent	1986	Hampshire
1973	Kent		*Refuge Assurance League*
1974	Leicestershire	1987	Worcestershire
1975	Hampshire	1988	Worcestershire
1976	Kent	1989	Lancashire
1977	Leicestershire	1990	Derbyshire
1978	Hampshire	1991	Nottinghamshire
1979	Somerset		*Sunday League*
1980	Warwickshire	1992	Middlesex
1981	Essex		

MATCH RESULTS 1969-92

		Matches				*League positions*		
	P	W	L	T	NR	1st	2nd	3rd
Derbyshire	385	165	182	2	36	1	0	1
Durham	17	7	7	0	3	0	0	0
Essex	385	209	137	4	35	3	5*	3
Glamorgan	385	124	217	3	41	0	0	0
Gloucestershire	385	136	201	3	45	0	1	1
Hampshire	385	200	148	6	31	3	1	3
Kent	385	200	141	5	39	3	2	3
Lancashire	385	190	144	7	44	3	2	2
Leicestershire	385	166	168	2	49	2	2*	2
Middlesex	385	181	159	4	41	1	1	3
Northamptonshire	385	145	198	2	40	0	0	1
Nottinghamshire	385	163	185	3	34	1	2	1
Somerset	385	191	154	2	38	1	6*	0
Surrey	385	164	177	4	40	0	0	0
Sussex	385	168	171	4	42	1	2*	1
Warwickshire	385	147	188	6	44	1	0	1
Worcestershire	385	187	159	7	32	3	2	1
Yorkshire	385	166	173	2	44	1	1	0

* *Includes one shared 2nd place in 1976.*

OXFORD UNIVERSITY 1992

[Bill Smith]

Back row: L. J. Lenham (coach), D. J. Anderson, C. J. Townsend, M. P. W. Jeh, R. H. Macdonald, B. S. Wood, A. C. Storie, C. M. Gupte, G. S. Gordon

THE UNIVERSITIES IN 1992

OXFORD

President: M. J. K. Smith (St Edmund Hall)
Hon. Treasurer: Dr S. R. Porter (Nuffield College)
Captain: G. B. T. Lovell (Sydney C. of E. GS, University of Sydney and Exeter)
Secretary: R. R. Montgomerie (Rugby and Worcester)
Captain for 1993: J. E. R. Gallian (Pittwater House, Sydney and Keble)
Secretary: C. J. Townsend (Dean Close, Cheltenham and Brasenose)

Oxford University achieved a rare first-class victory, thanks to a sporting declaration from Mike Gatting, the Middlesex captain, but overall the side rarely played to its full potential. The highlight was that long-awaited win, the first over a county since Imran Khan's team beat Northamptonshire in 1974. A target of 212 was not daunting, but it required an innings of substance and opener Richard Montgomerie, on Northamptonshire's staff, rose to the occasion with a mature and unbeaten maiden century.

The Oxford captain, Geoff Lovell, was fortunate to have another promising opener in Jason Gallian, an Australian qualifying for Lancashire who scored 112 against Worcestershire in his second match. These two provided the backbone of the batting. South African-born Chris Keey, formerly of Durham University, showed much promise – two half-centuries against Middlesex, following a maiden fifty in the previous game with Nottinghamshire, gave rise to hopes that Oxford had found a reliable middle-order batsman. Unfortunately, he struggled for runs afterwards. The lack of a consistent scorer threw extra weight on the openers until Lovell, affected initially by the responsibility of captaincy, found his form in June. He denied Glamorgan a win in the last match at Oxford with an unbeaten 110. Not since 1985 had the University run to three century-makers in a season.

On the bowling side, Lovell had an array of medium-pacers but on well-prepared pitches favouring batsmen they had few successes. Injuries did not help – Ben Wood and Rob Macdonald were absent for much of the season, and it was only at Lord's that Lovell was able to select his strongest XI. The bulk of the bowling was undertaken by Sri Lankan-born Australian Michael Jeh, Desmond Anderson and Gallian, and they returned their best figures when county captains reversed the batting order in the second innings to give other players batting practice. Spin is a frequent weakness in Oxford sides; Lovell had no slow left-arm bowlers and Henry Davies was the only off-spinner. His general lack of line and length was ruthlessly punished at times and it may well have been his ability to score runs in the lower order that earned him a Blue at Lord's, where he did not bowl. Wicket-keeping was another problem. Ralph Oliphant-Callum, who started the season, was displaced by the more reliable Chris Townsend, but neither came up to first-class standard.

Oxford lost only one of seven first-class matches at The Parks – t‹ Hampshire by 161 runs – but several draws were attributable to rain an‹ the follow-on not being enforced. The record against lesser opponents wa better. Though they lost to Oxfordshire, when several players were o‹ Benson and Hedges duty, the University beat Wiltshire without losing ‹ wicket, thanks to their policy of fielding their strongest available side, anc not scouring the University for 11 players. After the defeat in the Varsit‹ Match Gallian was elected captain for 1993. Although many of the mor‹ experienced players are in residence, several will be preparing fo examinations. It could result in a difficult season for Gallian unless there i a strong intake of Freshmen. – Paton Fenton.

OXFORD UNIVERSITY RESULTS

First-class matches – Played 8: Won 1, Lost 2, Drawn 5. Abandoned 1.

FIRST-CLASS AVERAGES

BATTING AND FIELDING

	Birthplace	M	I	NO	R	HS	Avge	Ct
R. R. Montgomerie....	Rugby	8	13	3	447	103*	44.70	3
G. B. T. Lovell	Sydney, Australia	8	11	1	324	110*	32.40	7
J. E. R. Gallian.......	Sydney, Australia	8	13	0	374	112	28.76	5
C. L. Keey...........	Johannesburg, SA	7	11	1	271	64	27.10	1
S. N. Warley.........	Sittingbourne	7	10	2	117	35	14.62	2
A. C. Storie.........	Bishopbriggs, Glasgow	7	10	1	113	29	12.55	4
H. R. Davies.........	Camberwell	6	7	1	62	39	10.33	0
M. P. W. Jeh.........	Colombo, Sri Lanka	8	9	2	51	16	7.28	3
C. M. Gupte	Poona, India	5	6	1	36	11	7.20	3
D. J. Anderson	Johannesburg, SA	8	8	4	18	9	4.50	3
C. J. Townsend	Wokingham	5	4	1	8	8	2.66	8

Also batted: R. H. Macdonald (*Cape Town, SA*) (3 matches) 1, 4, 8*; H. S. Mali‹ (*Harrow*) (1 match) 4; R. D. Oliphant-Callum (*Twickenham*) (3 matches) 19, 9 (1 ct‹ D. C. Sandiford (*Bolton*) (1 match) 20, 1; B. S. Wood (*Dewsbury*) (3 matches) 3*, 13.

* *Signifies not out.*

The following played a total of three three-figure innings for Oxford University – J. E. R‹ Gallian 1, G. B. T. Lovell 1, R. R. Montgomerie 1.

BOWLING

	O	M	R	W	BB	5W/i	Avge
J. E. R. Gallian	193	39	570	17	4-29	0	33.5
R. H. Macdonald....	79.4	22	188	5	2-13	0	37.6‹
M. P. W. Jeh.......	212.5	37	736	15	3-44	0	49.0‹
D. J. Anderson......	164.5	38	511	9	2-68	0	56.7
H. R. Davies	146.3	18	640	6	3-118	0	106.6

Also bowled: C. M. Gupte 28-2-133-1; H. S. Malik 25-4-88-0; R. R. Montgomeri‹ 10-2-31-0; A. C. Storie 40-5-128-2; B. S. Wood 73.2-7-254-4.

Note: Matches in this section which were not first-class are signified by a dagger.

†At Oxford, April 13. Middlesex won by 114 runs. Toss: Middlesex. Middlesex 234 fo‹ four (50 overs) (M. W. Gatting 58, K. R. Brown 70, P. N. Weekes 52 not out); Oxfor‹ University 120 for two (50 overs) (R. R. Montgomerie 31, J. E. R. Gallian 40).

OXFORD UNIVERSITY v DURHAM

At Oxford, April 14, 15, 16. Drawn. Toss: Oxford University. Watched by the assembled press and several members of the public, Parker received Durham's first ball in first-class cricket at 11.30 a.m. In two hours he and Glendenen had put on 119, but rain prevented any play after lunch and washed out the second day. Resuming on a chilly third morning, Glendenen, a survivor from minor county days, reached his and Durham's maiden first-class century with his 16th four, shortly after midday; Parker's 42nd hundred followed five minutes later. Their opening stand of 222 in 55 overs was the county's best at any level. There was time for Durham's Australian star, Jones, to warm up with seven fours in a 42-ball 36 before Graveney declared at lunch. The Oxford batsmen were untroubled by a limited attack, which looked short of pace for the more testing County Championship games ahead. Bainbridge and homegrown John Wood took a wicket each, but Gallian completed a maiden fifty before the close.

Close of play: First day, Durham 119-0 (J. D. Glendenen 64*, P. W. G. Parker 50*);
Second day, No play.

Durham

P. W. G. Parker b Gallian	103
J. D. Glendenen b Gallian	117
D. M. Jones not out	36
P. Bainbridge not out	24
B 2, l-b 4	6

1/222 2/235   (2 wkts dec.) 286

I. Smith, †C. W. Scott, P. J. Berry, G. K. Brown, *D. A. Graveney, S. M. McEwan and J. Wood did not bat.

Bowling: Jeh 20–4–74–0; Wood 12.3–0–39–0; Anderson 5–0–25–0; Gallian 15–1–64–2; Davies 13.3–2–62–0; Gupte 2–0–16–0.

Oxford University

R. R. Montgomerie c Parker b Bainbridge	17	C. M. Gupte not out	8
J. E. R. Gallian c Scott b Wood	53	N-b 4	4
A. C. Storie not out	23	1/45 2/89 (2 wkts)	105

*G. B. T. Lovell, S. N. Warley, D. J. Anderson, †R. D. Oliphant-Callum, M. P. W. Jeh, H. R. Davies and B. S. Wood did not bat.

Bowling: Wood 14–5–24–1; McEwan 11–4–26–0; Bainbridge 11–3–14–1; Smith 8–3–11–0; Berry 17–5–25–0; Graveney 4–1–5–0.

Umpires: J. C. Balderstone and G. Sharp.

OXFORD UNIVERSITY v WORCESTERSHIRE

At Oxford, April 17, 18, 20. Drawn. Toss: Oxford University. Vandals had removed the covers, delaying the start, and Oxford agreed to field, because the county bowlers feared injury on slippery run-ups. Curtis and Seymour responded by punishing a weak attack. They shared 181, and the former Essex player Seymour went on to 133, including 19 fours, on his Worcestershire début. On the second morning Moody, dropped by Anderson on 17, and Leatherdale plundered 168 off 25 overs. Moody reached three figures before lunch, and Curtis declared at once. Oxford's reply began positively, with Montgomerie dominating an opening stand of 54. Gallian went on to his maiden hundred, batting for six hours, but he had no further support. Though Worcestershire led by 186, they declined the follow-on in favour of batting practice for the lower order. Three wickets from Jeh saw them 29 for four, but Radford and Dilley added 90 without difficulty.

Close of play: First day, Worcestershire 221-1 (A. C. H. Seymour 119*, G. A. Hick 21*);
Second day, Oxford University 151-4 (J. E. R. Gallian 84*).

Worcestershire

*T. S. Curtis b Anderson	76	– (9) not out	1
A. C. H. Seymour b Gallian	133	– (8) c Lovell b Storie	2
G. A. Hick c Gallian b Anderson	27		
T. M. Moody not out	100		
D. A. Leatherdale c Jeh b Storie	67	– (7) not out	24
†S. J. Rhodes not out	0	– (1) c Montgomerie b Jeh	6
S. R. Lampitt (did not bat)		– (2) c Oliphant-Callum b Anderson	3
R. K. Illingworth (did not bat)		– (3) c Gallian b Jeh	12
P. J. Newport (did not bat)		– (4) c Keey b Jeh	4
N. V. Radford (did not bat)		– (5) c Jeh b Davies	66
G. R. Dilley (did not bat)		– (6) b Davies	39
B 1, l-b 3, w 5, n-b 1	10	L-b 3, n-b 2	5

1/181 2/238 3/242 4/410   (4 wkts dec.) 413   1/9 2/23 3/27   (7 wkts dec.) 162
                                                      4/29 5/119
                                                      6/153 7/155

Bowling: *First Innings*—Jeh 22–1–111–0; Gallian 17–4–59–1; Davies 24–3–113–0; Storie 16–2–58–1; Anderson 17.5–1–68–2. *Second Innings*—Jeh 14–5–44–3; Gallian 4–1–4–0; Anderson 5–2–20–1; Davies 12–1–52–2; Gupte 3–0–22–0; Storie 6–1–17–1; Montgomerie 2–2–0–0.

Oxford University

R. R. Montgomerie b Newport	32	M. P. W. Jeh b Lampitt 3
J. E. R. Gallian c Rhodes b Illingworth	112	H. R. Davies c Hick b Radford 5
A. C. Storie c Moody b Illingworth	15	D. J. Anderson not out 0
C. M. Gupte c Rhodes b Hick	11	
*G. B. T. Lovell c Moody b Illingworth	7	L-b 7, n-b 1 8
S. N. Warley c Leatherdale b Illingworth	4	
C. L. Keey c Rhodes b Newport	11	1/54 2/97 3/142 4/151 5/167 227
†R. D. Oliphant-Callum c and b Lampitt	19	6/192 7/199 8/210 9/225

Bowling: Dilley 14–4–23–0; Radford 16–5–38–1; Moody 5–1–14–0; Newport 16–3–39–2; Illingworth 45–11–79–4; Lampitt 13.3–5–18–2; Hick 7–3–9–1.

Umpires: J. C. Balderstone and G. Sharp.

†At Oxford, April 28. Oxford University v Berkshire. Abandoned.

†At Oxford, April 29. Oxford University v Loughborough University. Abandoned.

†At Oxford, May 1. Oxfordshire won by six wickets. Toss: Oxford University. Oxford University 182 for six (50 overs) (C. L. Keey 34, C. M. Gupte 42, G. B. T. Lovell 54); Oxfordshire 184 for four (40.3 overs) (J. S. Hartley 55, S. V. Laudat, P. M. Jobson 44 not out).

†At Oxford, May 5. Club Cricket Conference Under-25 won by eight wickets. Toss: Oxford University. Oxford University 146 for eight (50 overs) (S. N. Warley 45; J. Thompson three for 27); Club Cricket Conference Under-25 147 for two (38 overs) (I. Maynard 58 not out, J. Chambers 56 not out).

OXFORD UNIVERSITY v NOTTINGHAMSHIRE

At Oxford, May 7, 8, 9. Drawn. Toss: Oxford University. For the second year running Oxford's former captain, Crawley, returned to The Parks and scored a century. He put on 151 with Saxelby and was unbeaten on 110 when Johnson declared. The University had advanced to 40 without loss next morning when Cooper and Mike swept away half the side for four runs; Montgomerie, Storie, Gupte and Lovell all departed at 44. A stand of 72 from Keey and Warley helped the students to 161, still 14 short of saving the follow-on, but Nottinghamshire chose to bat again. Archer and Newell extended their lead to 263 before rain prevented play on the third day.

Close of play: First day, Oxford University 30-0 (R. R. Montgomerie 18*, J. E. R. Gallian 11*); Second day, Nottinghamshire 100-0 (M. Newell 48*, G. F. Archer 50*).

Nottinghamshire

P. R. Pollard b Anderson	72		
M. Newell c Gallian b Davies	22	– (1) not out	48
M. A. Crawley not out	110		
M. Saxelby b Davies	73		
G. F. Archer c Storie b Davies	1	– (2) not out	50
G. W. Mike not out	28		
B 8, l-b 4, w 1, n-b 5	18	N-b 2	2

1/85 2/104 3/255 4/259   (4 wkts dec.) 324   (no wkt) 100

*P. Johnson, †S. Bramhall, M. G. Field-Buss, K. E. Cooper and J. A. Afford did not bat.

Bowling: *First Innings*—Jeh 19-0-68-0; Gallian 13-5-30-0; Davies 30-4-118-3; Anderson 21-3-68-1; Storie 10-1-28-0. *Second Innings*—Jeh 9-3-13-0; Gallian 7-0-27-0; Davies 11-0-38-0; Anderson 7-2-16-0; Gupte 3-1-6-0.

Oxford University

R. R. Montgomerie b Mike	25	M. P. W. Jeh b Cooper	2	
J. E. R. Gallian lbw b Cooper	18	H. R. Davies not out	5	
A. C. Storie lbw b Mike	0	D. J. Anderson c Pollard b Crawley	0	
C. M. Gupte c Archer b Mike	0			
*G. B. T. Lovell lbw b Cooper	0			
C. L. Keey c Johnson b Crawley	60	B 1, l-b 2, w 1, n-b 3	7	
S. N. Warley lbw b Field-Buss	35		—	
†R. D. Oliphant-Callum c Newell b Crawley	9	1/40 2/44 3/44 4/44 5/44 6/116 7/153 8/155 9/156	161	

Bowling: Cooper 26-9-41-4; Mike 22-8-38-2; Afford 13-4-20-0; Crawley 4.4-1-18-3; Saxelby 6-2-22-0; Field-Buss 10-5-19-1.

Umpires: N. T. Plews and P. Willey.

OXFORD UNIVERSITY v MIDDLESEX

At Oxford, May 12, 13, 14. Oxford University won by five wickets. Toss: Middlesex. Oxford's victory was their first over a county in a first-class match for 18 years. Set a kindly 212 in 60 overs, they reached the target with five wickets in hand and 15 balls to spare. At 52 for two at tea a draw looked likely, but Montgomerie and Keey, who had already hit half-centuries in the first innings, changed the course of the game with 131 off 35 overs. Montgomerie completed a maiden century, though it was Warley who hit the winning runs. When Middlesex elected to bat on the first morning Jeh and Gallian claimed two early wickets, but Roseberry and Weekes hit back with 202, before Weekes fell within five runs of a maiden hundred and Roseberry was forced off by a groin strain. Gatting called his men in at 290 for five, and Lovell responded by declaring 68 behind, after England bowler Angus Fraser had bowled his first first-class spell for nearly a year, taking three for 16. Oxford Blue Carr contributed 75 not out before Gatting's second declaration set up the University's historic win.

Close of play: First day, Middlesex 290-5 dec.; Second day, Oxford University 222-8 (C. L. Keey 57*, D. J. Anderson 0*).

Middlesex

J. D. Carr lbw b Jeh	12	– not out	75
M. A. Roseberry retired hurt	108		
J. C. Pooley c Townsend b Gallian	10	– not out	27
P. N. Weekes c Townsend b Anderson	95		
†P. Farbrace not out	51		
A. R. C. Fraser c Lovell b Jeh	3		
D. W. Headley b Jeh	2		
K. R. Brown (did not bat)	–	(2) c Lovell b Anderson	36
L-b 3, w 2, n-b 4	9	L-b 2, w 1, n-b 2	5

1/16 2/32 3/234 4/256 5/290   (5 wkts dec.) 290   1/65   (1 wkt dec.) 143

*M. W. Gatting, P. C. R. Tufnell and C. W. Taylor did not bat.

In the first innings M. A. Roseberry retired hurt at 234-3.

Bowling: *First Innings*—Jeh 17–2–70–3; Gallian 20–5–41–1; Anderson 24–8–77–1; Davies 15–1–74–0; Storie 8–1–25–0. *Second Innings*—Jeh 6–3–9–0; Gallian 6–0–27–0; Anderson 12–4–30–1; Davies 13–4–41–0; Gupte 7–1–34–0.

Oxford University

R. R. Montgomerie c Farbrace b Headley	51	– not out	103
J. E. R. Gallian lbw b Taylor	37	– lbw b Taylor	5
A. C. Storie c Farbrace b Fraser	15	– c Brown b Headley	5
C. M. Gupte c Carr b Fraser	7		
*G. B. T. Lovell c Farbrace b Fraser	6	– c Gatting b Headley	11
C. L. Keey not out	57	– (4) hit wkt b Fraser	64
S. N. Warley c Brown b Weekes	11	– not out	10
M. P. W. Jeh c Brown b Carr	6		
H. R. Davies c Weekes b Tufnell	7	– (6) b Headley	0
D. J. Anderson not out	0		
L-b 9, w 1, n-b 15	25	B 4, l-b 4, w 2, n-b 4	14

1/79 2/100 3/119 4/126 5/135   (8 wkts dec.) 222   1/7 2/24 3/155   (5 wkts) 212
6/160 7/183 8/204   4/178 5/178

†C. J. Townsend did not bat.

Bowling: *First Innings*—Taylor 15–6–29–1; Headley 18–1–65–1; Fraser 16–8–16–3; Tufnell 28–12–42–1; Weekes 24–4–52–1; Carr 6–1–9–1. *Second Innings*—Taylor 7–2–22–1; Headley 12.3–1–38–3; Fraser 18–6–56–1; Tufnell 17–1–64–0; Weekes 3–0–24–0.

Umpires: R. C. Tolchard and A. G. T. Whitehead.

OXFORD UNIVERSITY v HAMPSHIRE

At Oxford, May 15, 16, 18. Hampshire won by 161 runs. Toss: Hampshire. Oxford were brought down to earth by Hampshire, who inflicted the University's first defeat of the season straight after their win over Middlesex. Their principal stumbling block was Ayling, who scored a maiden century during a 202-run stand with Middleton, after Ben Wood had removed James in his second over. Both batsmen scored 121. Next day Ayling and Udal took three wickets each, as Oxford were shot out for 133, 198 in arrears. But Parks did not enforce the follow-on and a second declaration left the students needing 310 in even time. Any hopes they might have had were destroyed by Ayling and Shine, who took four of the first five wickets, which fell for 95. Maru conceded only five runs in 17 overs, and Udal mopped up for eight wickets in the match. Umpire Holder had to withdraw because of conjunctivitis; he was replaced by Hampshire's 12th man, resting captain Mark Nicholas, and then by Oxford coach Les Lenham.

Close of play: First day, Oxford University 21-1 (J. E. R. Gallian 6*, A. C. Storie 2*); Second day, Hampshire 78-4 (R. S. M. Morris 3*, R. J. Maru 3*).

Hampshire

T. C. Middleton c Townsend b Gallian	121		
K. D. James c Lovell b Wood	0	– (1) b Anderson	45
J. R. Ayling c Storie b Gupte	121		
J. R. Wood c Gupte b Gallian	33	– (3) b Wood	0
A. N. Aymes not out	19	– (2) lbw b Wood	4
*†R. J. Parks not out	31		
S. D. Udal (did not bat)		– (4) lbw b Gallian	16
R. S. M. Morris (did not bat)		– (5) not out	11
R. J. Maru (did not bat)		– (6) b Jeh	27
L-b 4, w 1, n-b 1	6	B 1, l-b 2, w 2, n-b 3	8

1/0 2/202 3/277 4/288   (4 wkts dec.) 331   1/21 2/22 3/72   (5 wkts dec.) 111
                                                  4/72 5/111

M. J. Thursfield and K. J. Shine did not bat.

Bowling: *First Innings*—Jeh 16–6–53–0; Wood 26–1–111–1; Gallian 20–5–56–2; Anderson 15–1–52–0; Gupte 13–0–55–1. *Second Innings*—Jeh 13.5–2–38–1; Wood 16–6–29–2; Gallian 10–3–22–1; Anderson 7–3–19–1.

Oxford University

R. R. Montgomerie c Maru b Thursfield	10	– c Wood b Ayling	31
J. E. R. Gallian lbw b Ayling	28	– c Middleton b Thursfield	3
A. C. Storie lbw b James	12	– lbw b Shine	29
C. L. Keey lbw b Ayling	0	– c Parks b Shine	15
C. M. Gupte c Parks b Ayling	4	– (6) c Maru b Udal	6
*G. B. T. Lovell st Parks b Maru	14	– (7) c Parks b Udal	20
M. P. W. Jeh lbw b Udal	16	– (8) not out	10
D. J. Anderson b Maru	9	– (9) c Aymes b Udal	1
S. N. Warley b Udal	21	– (5) c Parks b Ayling	2
†C. J. Townsend c Wood b Udal	8	– c Parks b Udal	0
B. S. Wood not out	3	– c Morris b Udal	13
L-b 5, n-b 3	8	B 7, l-b 8, w 1, n-b 2	18

1/10 2/49 3/49 4/59 5/59   133   1/16 2/66 3/87 4/94 5/95   148
6/74 7/95 8/109 9/120   6/109 7/126 8/132 9/132

Bowling: *First Innings*—Thursfield 9–2–24–1; Ayling 17–4–31–3; Maru 15–7–17–2; Shine 13–6–11–0; James 11–6–23–1; Udal 10.5–3–22–3. *Second Innings*—Shine 14–1–38–2; Thursfield 7–1–11–1; James 9–3–13–0; Udal 26.1–14–47–5; Ayling 13–5–19–2; Maru 17–13–5–0.

Umpires: Dr D. Fawkner-Corbett and J. W. Holder (M. C. J. Nicholas and L. J. Lenham deputised for J. W. Holder on 3rd day).

†At Oxford, May 20. Oxford University won by 25 runs. Toss: Oxford University. Oxford University 213 for six (55 overs) (A. C. Storie 84, J. E. R. Gallian 36, C. M. Gupte 54); Royal Navy 188 (54.1 overs) (Sub Lt A. Falconer 44; D. J. Anderson five for 56).

†At Oxford, May 22. Oxford University won by ten wickets. Toss: Wiltshire. Wiltshire 186 (52.1 overs) (J. J. Newman 63, M. Beale 31; D. J. Anderson three for 48); Oxford University 190 for no wkt (34.1 overs) (R. R. Montgomerie 64 not out, J. E. R. Gallian 115 not out).

†At Oxford, May 23. Oxford University won by five wickets. Toss: Free Foresters. Free Foresters 210 (C. Rowe 82, C. B. Hamblin 53; H. S. Malik three for 55, R. H. Macdonald five for 42); Oxford University 214 for five (A. C. Storie 57, C. L. Keey 45, G. B. T. Lovell 60 not out).

†At Oxford, May 26, 27, 28. Drawn. Toss: MCC. MCC 299 for nine dec. (S. G. Hookey 97, A. Needham 36, J. G. Franks 36 not out, P. J. Hacker 86; M. P. W. Jeh four for 79) and 290 for five dec. (S. G. Plumb 40, D. C. Briance 51, P. Willey 111, G. V. Palmer 40); Oxford University 260 for one dec. (R. R. Montgomerie 128 not out, J. E. R. Gallian 103) and 241 for seven (A. C. Storie 100, G. B. T. Lovell 62).

OXFORD UNIVERSITY v YORKSHIRE

At Oxford, May 29, 30, June 1. Abandoned.

OXFORD UNIVERSITY v LANCASHIRE

At Oxford, June 2, 3, 4. Drawn. Toss: Lancashire. The county's upper order batted freely on the first day, but Fairbrother's attempt to give his tail the same opportunity in the second innings backfired. Fowler gave Lancashire a good start, surviving two catches off no-balls and two dropped chances to score 106, adding 151 with Atherton. Then Fairbrother marked his return after injury by sharing an unbroken stand of 105 with Lloyd. When Oxford batted only Montgomerie, with a stylish 36, could find an answer to the spin of Watkinson and Barnett, and the University collapsed from 103 for five to be all out for 104. Jeh and Gallian had their revenge, quickly reducing Lancashire's tail-first line-up to 39 for six, until Atherton restored decorum. Though an overnight lead of 306 seemed ample, Fairbrother batted for another 25 minutes before setting Oxford 330 in four and a quarter hours. They were 116 for four when rain arrived an hour after lunch.

Close of play: First day, Oxford University 27-1 (R. R. Montgomerie 14*); Second day, Lancashire 96-7 (M. A. Atherton 20*, G. Fowler 15*).

Lancashire

G. Fowler c Warley b Jeh	106	– (9) c Storie b Macdonald	15
S. P. Titchard lbw b Gallian	21	– lbw b Jeh	0
M. A. Atherton c Townsend b Jeh	65	– (8) not out	37
*N. H. Fairbrother not out	39	– (10) not out	6
G. D. Lloyd not out	56	– (7) c Lovell b Anderson	23
J. D. Fitton (did not bat)	–	(1) c Warley b Gallian	1
M. Watkinson (did not bat)	–	(3) c Townsend b Gallian	16
A. A. Barnett (did not bat)	–	(4) c Lovell b Jeh	9
†J. Stanworth (did not bat)	–	(5) lbw b Gallian	9
S. D. Fletcher (did not bat)	–	(6) c Lovell b Gallian	0
L-b 9, w 7, n-b 11	27	B 1, l-b 1, n-b 1	3

1/50 2/201 3/209   (3 wkts dec.) 314   1/2 2/2 3/18   (8 wkts dec.) 119
4/36 5/36 6/39
7/63 8/99

P. J. Martin did not bat.

Bowling: *First Innings*—Jeh 22-1-102-2; Gallian 17-4-47-1; Anderson 16-7-29-0; Macdonald 20-5-66-0; Malik 14-2-61-0. *Second Innings*—Jeh 11-4-28-2; Gallian 16-3-29-4; Anderson 14-6-22-1; Malik 11-2-27-0; Macdonald 10-5-11-1.

Oxford University

R. R. Montgomerie c Atherton b Watkinson ...	36	– not out..........................	45
J. E. R. Gallian c Atherton b Barnett	13	– lbw b Fletcher	8
A. C. Storie lbw b Fletcher..................	5	– b Watkinson....................	4
C. L. Keey lbw b Martin	5	– b Watkinson	9
*G. B. T. Lovell lbw b Watkinson.............	19	– c Fowler b Atherton	41
S. N. Warley c Fairbrother b Watkinson	16	– not out	4
H. S. Malik b Barnett	4		
M. P. W. Jeh c Atherton b Barnett............	0		
R. H. Macdonald c sub b Watkinson	1		
D. J. Anderson not out	0		
†C. J. Townsend lbw b Watkinson	0		
L-b 4, w 1	5	L-b 5	5

1/27 2/40 3/62 4/62 5/88   104   1/11 2/22 3/47 4/106   (4 wkts) 116
6/103 7/103 8/104 9/104

Bowling: *First Innings*—Martin 7.5–1–14–1; Fletcher 11–3–32–1; Barnett 15.1–4–38–3; Watkinson 12–6–16–5. *Second Innings*—Fletcher 7–4–14–1; Watkinson 18.4–6–44–2; Fitton 5–1–12–0; Atherton 8–5–6–1; Barnett 8–1–35–0.

Umpires: B. Dudleston and Dr D. Fawkner-Corbett.

†At Oxford, June 8. Midlands Club Cricket Conference won by four wickets. Toss: Oxford University. Oxford University 205 (54.2 overs) (J. E. R. Gallian 57); Midlands Club Cricket Conference 206 for six (49.3 overs) (W. Martin 101, G. Charlesworth 30).

†At Oxford, June 11, 12. Oxford University won by four wickets. Toss: Harlequins. Harlequins 195 for eight dec. (D. C. Sandiford 64, M. Cullinan 56; R. H. Macdonald four for 46) and 195 for eight dec. (A. Tucker 73); Oxford University 140 for four dec. (R. R. Montgomerie 32, G. B. T. Lovell 34 not out) and 254 for six (M. J. Russell 66, C. L. Keey 61, S. N. Warley 47).

†At Oxford, June 13 (C. B. Fry Centenary Match). C. A. Fry's XI won by seven wickets. Toss: Oxford University. Oxford University 264 for six dec. (R. R. Montgomerie 64, J. E. R. Gallian 96, A. C. Storie 33, S. N. Warley 32 not out; V. J. Marks five for 50); C. A. Fry's XI 265 for three (D. W. Randall 115, B. C. Broad 44, R. T. Robinson 31, M. A. Crawley 31 not out, J. D. Carr 40 not out).

†At Oxford, June 16, 17, 18. Drawn. Toss: Combined Services. Combined Services 302 for eight dec. (Lt R. J. Greatorex 64, Capt. J. W. S. Cotterill 82, Cpl A. Jones 80; M. P. W. Jeh three for 52) and 344 for four dec. (Lt R. J. Greatorex 108, Capt. J. W. S. Cotterill 84, Cpl A. Jones 92 not out; H. R. Davies three for 139); Oxford University 367 for six dec. (R. R. Montgomerie 61, J. E. R. Gallian 41, H. R. Davies 54, S. N. Warley 88, D. C. Sandiford 61, D. J. Anderson 31 not out; SAC M. Turner three for 102) and 101 for two (M. P. W. Jeh 53 not out).

OXFORD UNIVERSITY v GLAMORGAN

At Oxford, June 19, 20, 22. Drawn. Toss: Glamorgan. An unbeaten maiden century by Lovell, with 13 fours and a six, saved the University from losing their last match of the season at The Parks. Cowdrey, who was leading Glamorgan in one of his only two first-class appearances for the county, set a target of 271 in four hours, and Oxford faced defeat at 107 for six. But Lovell found a useful partner in opening bowler Jeh, who batted with such assurance for an hour that Cowdrey settled for a draw with ten overs remaining. James gave Glamorgan a good start with 111 and on an easy pitch Cowdrey, Cottey and Croft all contributed fifties. Oxford failed to exploit a promising opening stand of 53 from Montgomerie and Gallian, and were all out for 183 despite 64 from Lovell, then his highest score. Dale found batting easy in Glamorgan's second innings and débutant Jamie Bishop also passed 50 before the second declaration.

Close of play: First day, Glamorgan 206-2 (S. P. James 111*, P. A. Cottey 25*); Second day, Oxford University 183.

Glamorgan

S. P. James c Montgomerie b Gallian	111		
A. Dale c Jeh b Gallian	18	– (1) not out	76
*C. S. Cowdrey b Anderson	50		
P. A. Cottey c Anderson b Davies	50	– (2) b Jeh	6
D. L. Hemp c Townsend b Macdonald	27		
R. D. B. Croft not out	51		
M. C. Dobson not out	5		
†J. Bishop (did not bat)		– (3) not out	51
L-b 5	5	B 1, l-b 1, n-b 1	3

1/41 2/146 3/206 4/234 5/299　　(5 wkts dec.) 317　　1/11　　(1 wkt dec.) 136

D. J. Foster, S. Kirnon and M. Frost did not bat.

Bowling: First Innings—Jeh 17-3-45-0; Gallian 19-3-48-2; Macdonald 24-4-53-1; Anderson 17-1-56-1; Davies 23-3-101-1; Montgomerie 5-0-9-0. *Second Innings*—Jeh 12-2-39-1; Macdonald 8-2-15-0; Gallian 5-0-17-0; Davies 5-0-41-0; Montgomerie 3-0-22-0.

Oxford University

R. R. Montgomerie c Cowdrey b Croft	32	– c Bishop b Frost	4
J. E. R. Gallian c Bishop b Kirnon	18	– c Bishop b Foster	12
*G. B. T. Lovell c Hemp b Foster	64	– not out	110
C. L. Keey lbw b Dale	11	– c Dobson b Croft	6
S. N. Warley lbw b Frost	4	– c Cowdrey b Dale	10
D. C. Sandiford b Frost	20	– c Cowdrey b Dobson	1
H. R. Davies c Hemp b Foster	6	– c Bishop b Dale	0
M. P. W. Jeh lbw b Foster	0	– not out	6
D. J. Anderson c and b Foster	0		
R. H. Macdonald c Cowdrey b Croft	4		
†C. J. Townsend not out	0		
L-b 3, w 1, n-b 20	24	L-b 1, w 1, n-b 2	4

1/53 2/55 3/88 4/98 5/148　　183　　1/13 2/40 3/62　　(6 wkts) 153
6/164 7/166 8/170 9/180　　　　　　4/99 5/106 6/107

Bowling: First Innings—Frost 15-3-51-2; Foster 15-0-73-4; Kirnon 8-3-14-1; Croft 11.3-3-24-2; Dale 7-3-15-1; Dobson 3-1-3-0. *Second Innings*—Frost 11-1-43-1; Kirnon 6-2-7-0; Croft 19-7-28-1; Foster 5-2-10-1; Dobson 15-6-42-1; Dale 9-2-21-2; Cottey 1-0-1-0.

Umpires: D. O. Oslear and G. A. Stickley.

†At Aldershot, June 28. Oxford University won by 110 runs. Toss: Oxford University. Oxford University 228 (48 overs) (J. E. R. Gallian 46, C. L. Keey 35, H. R. Davies 31, M. P. W. Jeh 65; 2nd Lt A. P. Houldsworth four for 39); Army 118 (32.2 overs) (B. S. Wood three for 30).

At Lord's, June 30, July 1, 2. **OXFORD UNIVERSITY** lost to **CAMBRIDGE UNIVERSITY** by seven wickets (See The University Match, 1992, on page 787).

CAMBRIDGE

President: Professor A. D. Buckingham (Pembroke)

Captain: J. P. Crawley (Manchester GS and Trinity)
Secretary: J. P. Arscott (Tonbridge and Magdalene)

Captain for 1993: J. P. Crawley (Manchester GS and Trinity)
Secretary: C. M. Pitcher (St Edward's, Oxford and Selwyn)

It was appropriate that an unbeaten century by their captain, John Crawley, should have enabled Cambridge to complete their season by beating Oxford at Lord's. They also achieved an exciting victory over Kent, the university's first win over a county at Fenner's since 1982, though they had beaten Sussex at Hove in 1990. At a time when the first-class status of Oxbridge cricket was subject to considerable debate it was a result of some significance.

As always the students, faced with ever-growing academic pressures, generally found the contest with county cricketers an unequal battle. But under Crawley's thoughtful leadership, Cambridge played their cricket with optimism and a good deal of skill. Crawley's influence was immense both on and off the field, and he conducted himself with considerable dignity in what, at times, was a trying season for the university.

He lost the services of his older brother Peter, a promising all-rounder, midway through the Fenner's season, and Rory Jenkins, his main strike bowler, played only two matches because of a shoulder injury. Fortunately the captain was able to call upon several experienced lieutenants – not least Richard Pearson, the Northamptonshire-registered off-spinner, who again played so dominant a role that he even opened the bowling in two matches.

Without Jenkins, the Cambridge bowling was heavily spin-orientated, with three slow bowlers included regularly and another – Trevor Kemp, an off-spinner registered with Essex – unable to command a place. Pearson, fellow off-spinner Marcus Wight and Mike Abington, the slow left-armer, between them bowled 698 of the 1,140.2 overs sent down by Cambridge in 1992, claiming 46 of the 68 wickets taken by bowlers. Pearson's five for 108 against Warwickshire, when he opened the attack and bowled right through until tea, was the best haul of the season. He and Wight took 18 wickets each, though Wight added another when the pair played for Oxford & Cambridge Universities against the tourists.

The batting was erratic: Crawley's match-winning 106 at Lord's – surprisingly his first for Cambridge – was the only first-class century. But Arscott, the wicket-keeper, scored 318 runs, often digging his side out of considerable trouble, and Wight, who shared an unbroken 166-run stand with his captain at Lord's, after joining him at 72 for three, totalled 366. Simon Johnson often reminded his colleagues that cricket is played for enjoyment and a smile was never far away whenever he was batting. He bore the brunt of the new-ball bowling willingly, and it was fitting that his skills as a free-hitting batsman should secure the victory over Kent, after late-emerging Freshman John Carroll had played a match-winning innings of 92. – David Hallett.

CAMBRIDGE UNIVERSITY 1992

[*Bill Smith*]

Back row: G. J. Saville (*coach*), M. E. D. Jarrett, J. P. Carroll, M. B. Abington, C. M. Pitcher, R. M. Wight, G. W. Jones, G. E. Thwaites, A. R. May (*scorer*). *Front row*: A. M. Hooper, J. P. Arscott, J. P. Crawley (*captain*), S. W. Johnson, R. M. Pearson.

CAMBRIDGE UNIVERSITY RESULTS

First-class matches – Played 9: Won 2, Lost 3, Drawn 4.

FIRST-CLASS AVERAGES

BATTING AND FIELDING

	Birthplace	M	I	NO	R	HS	Avge	Ct/St
J. P. Crawley	Maldon	9	17	3	541	106*	38.64	5
J. P. Arscott	Tooting	9	12	2	318	79	31.80	10/6
P. M. Crawley	Newton-le-Willows	4	6	2	118	45	29.50	0
R. M. Wight	London	9	15	2	366	62*	28.15	3
G. W. Jones	Birmingham	6	12	0	249	44	20.75	1
J. P. Carroll	Bebington	5	9	0	175	92	19.44	1
S. W. Johnson	Newcastle-upon-Tyne	9	13	2	201	50	18.27	4
A. M. Hooper	Perivale	9	17	1	243	48	15.18	1
R. M. Pearson	Batley	9	11	5	88	33*	14.66	3
C. M. Pitcher	Croydon	6	8	3	62	32*	12.40	0
M. E. D. Jarrett....	London	9	13	2	106	27	9.63	2
S. S. K. Das	Newcastle-upon-Tyne	3	5	1	38	24*	9.50	1
M. B. Abington	Lusaka, Zambia	7	7	0	20	6	2.85	4

Also batted: R. H. J. Jenkins (*Leicester*) (2 matches) 1 (1 ct); T. R. Kemp (*Colchester*) (2 matches) 0 (1 ct); G. E. Thwaites (*Brighton*) (1 match) 0.

*Signifies not out.

J. P. Crawley played the only three-figure innings for Cambridge University.

BOWLING

	O	M	R	W	BB	5W/i	Avge
R. M. Wight	213.3	36	677	18	3-65	0	37.61
M. B. Abington....	146.4	23	530	10	3-33	0	53.00
S. W. Johnson	164	27	541	10	3-62	0	54.10
R. M. Pearson.....	337.5	57	1,021	18	5-108	1	56.72

Also bowled: P. M. Crawley 66–13–236–3; A. M. Hooper 20.2–7–63–3; R. H. J. Jenkins 32–5–137–2; T. R. Kemp 29–2–128–1; C. M. Pitcher 131–20–453–3.

Note: Matches in this section which were not first-class are signified by a dagger.

†At Cambridge, April 8. Cambridge University won by 84 runs. Toss: Cambridge University. Cambridge University 177 for eight (55 overs) (A. M. Hooper 35, P. M. Crawley 35; P. J. Rendell three for 30); Loughborough University 93 (46.5 overs).

†At Cambridge, April 9. Cambridge University won by 20 runs. Toss: Cambridge University. Cambridge University 234 for six (55 overs) (A. M. Hooper 90, S. S. K. Das 47, J. P. Crawley 36); Loughborough University 214 for seven (55 overs) (S. F. Shephard 70, A. McConkey 38).

†At Cambridge, April 11. Durham University won by six wickets. Toss: Durham University. Cambridge University 162 for six (55 overs) (J. P. Crawley 64; C. J. Hawkes three for 38); Durham University 166 for four (52.3 overs) (S. C. Ecclestone 53, A. C. Richards 37 not out).

†At Cambridge, April 12. Durham University won by four wickets. Toss: Cambridge University. Cambridge University 166 (54.1 overs) (M. E. D. Jarrett 39, R. M. Wight 31, J. P. Arscott 46; J. N. B. Bovill four for 27); Durham University 170 for six (53.5 overs) (J. R. A. Williams 35, S. C. Ecclestone 38, C. J. Hawkes 49 not out; T. R. Kemp three for 20).

CAMBRIDGE UNIVERSITY v LEICESTERSHIRE

At Cambridge, April 14, 15, 16. Leicestershire won by 133 runs. Toss: Cambridge University. Leicestershire completed an easy victory after the captains forfeited an innings each to compensate for the loss of the first afternoon and the entire second day to rain. Briers began the summer with a century, hitting 15 fours in all and sharing a 102-run opening stand with Boon. After the double forfeiture Millns started his season by bowling Hooper in his first over; he and his fellow-seamers had the University at 52 for seven. But Briers chose to exercise his inexperienced spin attack after lunch and a ninth-wicket partnership of 65 in 38 minutes between Johnson, who hit nine fours and a six, and Pitcher, restored some respectability to Cambridge.

Close of play: First day, Leicestershire 279-2 (J. J. Whitaker 73*, L. Potter 26*); Second day, No play.

Leicestershire

T. J. Boon c and b Pearson		51
*N. E. Briers st Arscott b Abington		120
J. J. Whitaker not out		73
L. Potter not out		26
L-b 6, n-b 3		9

1/102 2/208　　　　　(2 wkts dec.) 279

B. F. Smith, P. N. Hepworth, V. J. Wells, †P. Whitticase, A. D. Mullally, G. J. Parsons and D. J. Millns did not bat.

Bowling: Johnson 11–2–30–0; Pitcher 8–0–53–0; Hooper 1–0–5–0; Abington 25–5–97–1; Pearson 18–5–69–1; Wight 7–1–19–0.

Leicestershire forfeited their second innings.

Cambridge University

Cambridge University forfeited their first innings.

A. M. Hooper b Millns	0	S. W. Johnson b Potter		50
S. S. K. Das c Whitaker b Parsons	9	C. M. Pitcher not out		32
*J. P. Crawley b Millns	19	M. B. Abington st Whitticase b Potter		5
R. M. Wight c Boon b Mullally	12			
G. E. Thwaites lbw b Millns	0	B 1, l-b 9, n-b 1		11
†J. P. Arscott c Whitaker b Parsons	0			
M. E. D. Jarrett lbw b Parsons	7	1/0 2/28 3/28 4/28 5/35		146
R. M. Pearson b Hepworth	1	6/49 7/52 8/57 9/122		

Bowling: Millns 10–4–27–3; Mullally 8–3–11–1; Parsons 8–4–12–3; Wells 8–3–13–0; Hepworth 12–5–52–1; Potter 7–1–21–2.

Umpires: P. Adams and R. A. White.

CAMBRIDGE UNIVERSITY v MIDDLESEX

At Cambridge, April 17, 18, 20. Drawn. Toss: Middlesex. After the first day was washed out Roseberry scored the first of his nine hundreds in 1992, hitting three sixes and ten fours. He put on 107 for the second wicket with Ramprakash, who continued his good form in the second innings when he struck three sixes and four fours in a 64-ball 48. But Ramprakash was later fined by his county for an outburst at the off-spinner Wight, who had dismissed him twice, and for arguing with his captain, Emburey, when Wight's arrival at the crease to bat revived Ramprakash's annoyance. It was also an unhappy match for Cowans, who tried to deliver the first ball of Cambridge's second innings – twice – before retiring with an injured groin that ended his season. But a target of 253 in four hours was too much for the University to attempt, even against an inexperienced attack.

Close of play: First day, No play; Second day, Cambridge University 109-1 (S. S. K. Das 24*, J. P. Crawley 24*).

Middlesex

J. D. Carr b P. M. Crawley	36	– c Das b Jenkins 16
M. A. Roseberry c Jenkins b P. M. Crawley	...101	
M. R. Ramprakash lbw b Wight	49	– c Jarrett b Wight 48
K. R. Brown not out	34	– (2) not out 53
P. N. Weekes not out	7	– (4) not out 5
B 1, l-b 9, w 1	11	W 1 1

1/71 2/178 3/208   (3 wkts dec.) 238   1/24 2/114   (2 wkts dec.) 123

D. W. Headley, †P. Farbrace, *J. E. Emburey, N. G. Cowans, J. M. S. Whittington and S. A. Sylvester did not bat.

Bowling: *First Innings*—Jenkins 8–1–24–0; Johnson 10–3–24–0; Pearson 21–4–67–0; P. M. Crawley 15–3–36–2; Kemp 11–1–51–0; Wight 11–3–26–1. *Second Innings*—Jenkins 8–1–43–1; Johnson 7–0–18–0; Wight 10–4–25–1; P. M. Crawley 1–0–14–0; Pearson 8–0–23–0.

Cambridge University

A. M. Hooper lbw b Emburey	48	– lbw b Headley 4
S. S. K. Das not out	24	– c Farbrace b Sylvester 2
*J. P. Crawley not out	24	– not out 46
R. M. Wight (did not bat)		– c Farbrace b Sylvester 27
P. M. Crawley (did not bat)		– not out 22
B 8, l-b 3, n-b 2	13	L-b 5, w 1, n-b 6 12

1/57   (1 wkt dec.) 109   1/5 2/10 3/78   (3 wkts) 113

†J. P. Arscott, M. E. D. Jarrett, R. M. Pearson, S. W. Johnson, R. H. J. Jenkins and T. R. Kemp did not bat.

Bowling: *First Innings*—Cowans 7–3–9–0; Headley 9–0–50–0; Emburey 4–2–5–1; Sylvester 8–4–20–0; Whittington 7–2–14–0. *Second Innings*—Sylvester 19–5–34–2; Headley 18–5–32–1; Whittington 12–0–30–0; Weekes 11–3–12–0; Emburey 2–2–0–0; Roseberry 2–2–0–0.

Umpires: P. Adams and R. A. White.

CAMBRIDGE UNIVERSITY v ESSEX

At Cambridge, April 25, 27, 28. Drawn. Toss: Cambridge University. Garnham played the most attractive of the four half-centuries in Essex's first innings, and wrecked Peter Crawley's tidy figures of 15–7–17–0 by taking 17 runs off his 16th over. Only Crawley, the captain's older brother, made any headway after Topley had single-handedly reduced the students to 39 for five. Stephenson cashed in with three for three, and Cambridge were dismissed for 75. But following the common trend Prichard did not enforce the follow-on and Knight took advantage with an unbeaten 104 in two and a half hours with 12 fours. The University were 41 for three at the close of the second day, chasing a theoretical 436, and no play was possible on the third.

Close of play: First day, Cambridge University 10-1 (A. M. Hooper 1*, S. W. Johnson 3*); Second day, Cambridge University 41-3 (A. M. Hooper 30*).

Essex

*P. J. Prichard b Johnson	71		
J. P. Stephenson c Arscott b Johnson	15	– (1) lbw b Jenkins	5
N. V. Knight c and b Kemp	62	– not out	104
N. Hussain lbw b Wight	7	– (2) c Arscott b Johnson	10
J. J. B. Lewis c Arscott b Pearson	58	– (4) lbw b Wight	70
†M. A. Garnham not out	82		
A. G. J. Fraser st Arscott b Pearson	5	– (5) not out	4
T. D. Topley run out	1		
D. J. P. Boden lbw b Pearson	5		
B 4, l-b 5	9	L-b 2	2

1/30 2/135 3/142 4/165 5/298 (8 wkts dec.) 315   1/7 2/23 3/180 (3 wkts dec.) 195
6/306 7/307 8/315

J. H. Childs and P. M. Such did not bat.

Bowling: *First Innings*—Jenkins 10–3–46–0; Johnson 17–2–56–2; P. M. Crawley 16–7–34–0; Pearson 26.2–4–73–3; Kemp 8–0–35–1; Wight 21–1–62–1. *Second Innings*—Johnson 10–1–27–1; Jenkins 6–0–24–1; P. M. Crawley 5–0–29–0; Pearson 17–4–49–0; Kemp 10–1–42–0; Wight 5–1–22–1.

Cambridge University

A. M. Hooper c Boden b Topley	5	– not out	30
S. S. K. Das c Garnham b Topley	3	– c Hussain b Topley	0
S. W. Johnson lbw b Topley	3	– (4) c Hussain b Childs	0
*J. P. Crawley lbw b Topley	3	– (3) lbw b Such	6
R. M. Wight lbw b Topley	13		
P. M. Crawley not out	39		
†J. P. Arscott lbw b Stephenson	3		
M. E. D. Jarrett lbw b Stephenson	0		
R. M. Pearson b Stephenson	0		
R. H. J. Jenkins c and b Fraser	1		
T. R. Kemp c Hussain b Fraser	0		
L-b 1, w 2, n-b 2	5	L-b 5	5

1/6 2/10 3/16 4/20 5/39   75   1/16 2/38 3/41 (3 wkts) 41
6/59 7/59 8/67 9/75

Bowling: *First Innings*—Topley 14–6–15–5; Boden 12–5–19–0; Fraser 9.3–2–37–2; Stephenson 7–4–3–3. *Second Innings*—Boden 4–1–23–0; Topley 3–1–11–1; Such 2–1–2–1; Childs 1.3–1–0–1.

Umpires: R. Julian and P. Willey.

†At Cambridge, May 7. Cambridge University won by 26 runs. Toss: Cambridgeshire. Cambridge University 175 (49 overs) (S. W. Johnson 46; S. Aldis three for 51, C. R. F. Green four for 30); Cambridgeshire 149 (51.3 overs) (D. P. Norman 35, D. W. S. Pimblett 41 not out; R. M. Pearson four for 43, R. M. Wight five for 38).

†At Cambridge, May 10. No result. Toss: Cryptics. Cambridge University 216 for six (50 overs) (M. E. D. Jarrett 90 not out; A. Owen-Browne three for 58); Cryptics 119 for one (34.4 overs) (M. Nolan 52 not out, P. Nolan 50 not out).

CAMBRIDGE UNIVERSITY v WARWICKSHIRE

At Cambridge, May 12, 13, 14. Drawn. Toss: Warwickshire. Off-spinner Pearson opened the bowling for Cambridge on a newly laid pitch. He claimed the first four wickets to fall as he delivered 43 overs unchanged until 5 p.m., later returning to add a fifth. He had almost bowled Penney first ball, but the young man from Zimbabwe survived to rescue Warwickshire, putting on 124 with newcomer Burns for the seventh wicket. The county showed their appreciation by batting into the second day to enable Penney to complete a maiden century on his first-class début in England. Cambridge subsided to 78 for five, but wicket-keeper Arscott made an unbeaten 65 and useful support from Jarrett and Johnson enabled Crawley to declare 111 behind. Warwickshire's second declaration set the University 262 in two sessions, enough time for a few scares before they reached safety at 154 for eight.

Close of play: First day, Warwickshire 314-8 (T. L. Penney 97*, D. R. Brown 5*); Second day, Warwickshire 34-0 (A. J. Moles 5*, J. D. Ratcliffe 26*).

Warwickshire

A. J. Moles b Pearson	17	– b Abington	50
J. D. Ratcliffe c Arscott b Pearson	7	– b Wight	46
R. G. Twose c J. P. Crawley b Pearson	44		
D. P. Ostler b Pearson	9	– (3) not out	44
P. A. Smith lbw b Wight	22	– (4) not out	0
T. L. Penney not out	102		
*T. A. Lloyd b Wight	5		
†M. Burns b Johnson	78		
P. A. Booth lbw b Pearson	14		
D. R. Brown not out	5		
B 9, l-b 6, w 1	16	B 4, l-b 5, w 1	10

1/16 2/36 3/72 4/95 5/125   (8 wkts dec.) 319   1/85 2/143   (2 wkts dec.) 150
6/137 7/261 8/294

T. A. Munton did not bat.

Bowling: *First Innings*—Johnson 15-3-35-1; Pearson 45.1-11-108-5; Pitcher 11-0-56-0; Abington 14-4-31-0; Wight 20-6-48-2; P. M. Crawley 6-0-26-0. *Second Innings*—Johnson 12-2-31-0; Pearson 9-0-28-0; Wight 15-0-40-1; Abington 12-0-42-1.

Cambridge University

A. M. Hooper lbw b Munton	3	– run out	6
G. W. Jones c Burns b Brown	15	– b Munton	32
*J. P. Crawley st Burns b Booth	25	– lbw b Brown	22
R. M. Wight c Twose b Booth	17	– lbw b Twose	48
P. M. Crawley lbw b Brown	0	– c Burns b Brown	11
†J. P. Arscott not out	65	– lbw b Twose	7
M. E. D. Jarrett b Booth	27	– (8) not out	8
S. W. Johnson c Penney b Twose	33	– (7) c Munton b Brown	4
C. M. Pitcher lbw b Twose	0	– lbw b Twose	0
R. M. Pearson not out	3	– not out	2
B 11, l-b 8, n-b 1	20	B 4, l-b 8, n-b 2	14

1/10 2/49 3/49 4/50 5/78   (8 wkts dec.) 208   1/6 2/51 3/98   (8 wkts) 154
6/152 7/197 8/197   4/126 5/135 6/144
                                      7/144 8/144

M. B. Abington did not bat.

Bowling: *First Innings*—Munton 13-5-12-1; Brown 19-7-43-2; Booth 30-9-64-3; Smith 9-2-28-0; Twose 10-5-13-2; Ostler 4-0-29-0. *Second Innings*—Munton 16.5-4-40-1; Brown 15-7-27-3; Twose 18-6-46-3; Booth 18-5-27-0; Moles 1-0-2-0.

Umpires: B. Leadbeater and P. Willey.

CAMBRIDGE UNIVERSITY v SURREY

At Cambridge, May 15, 16, 18. Surrey won by 140 runs. Toss: Surrey. For the second match running Arscott saved Cambridge from major embarrassment. Coming in at 12 for six, he added 81 with captain John Crawley, so that the University's eventual deficit was only 220. The initial collapse was caused by Surrey's South African, Bryson, and his figures contrasted dramatically with those of his next four months. Then, at 78 for five in the second innings, Arscott joined Peter Crawley to put on 71, and reached a career-best 79 as he shared 70 in 38 minutes with Pearson, before two balls from Martin Bicknell finished Cambridge off. Stewart had passed the captaincy to Lynch to concentrate on batting and keeping wicket before the one-day internationals. Both scored freely as Surrey's top order piled on the runs. Off-spinner Pearson could not repeat his previous success as an opening bowler, and Thorpe hit an unbeaten 114. In the second innings Ward's 112 not out, at a run a ball with three sixes and 16 fours, enabled the county to take an impregnable lead of 399.

Close of play: First day, Cambridge University 11-5 (P. M. Crawley 1*); Second day, Cambridge University 25-1 (G. W. Jones 7*, M. E. D. Jarrett 0*).

Surrey

D. J. Bicknell c J. P. Crawley b Wight	49		
R. I. Alikhan c Arscott b Wight	54		
†A. J. Stewart c Arscott b Abington	71		
G. P. Thorpe not out	114		
*M. A. Lynch run out	61		
D. M. Ward lbw b Wight	11	– (1) not out	112
M. A. Feltham not out	12	– (2) c Abington b P. M. Crawley	33
M. P. Bicknell (did not bat)		– (3) b Wight	21
N. M. Kendrick (did not bat)		– (4) not out	6
L-b 9	9	L-b 4, w 3	7
1/101 2/118 3/212 4/326 5/353	(5 wkts dec.) 381	1/72 2/163	(2 wkts dec.) 179

R. E. Bryson and J. Boiling did not bat.

Bowling: *First Innings*—Johnson 12-1-51-0; Pearson 33.2-3-113-0; P. M. Crawley 13-2-37-0; Wight 30-2-117-3; Abington 11-0-54-1. *Second Innings*—Johnson 5-1-17-0; Pearson 8-1-26-0; P. M. Crawley 10-1-60-1; Wight 10-1-40-1; Abington 2.4-0-32-0.

Cambridge University

A. M. Hooper b Bryson	0	– b Boiling	16
G. W. Jones b Bryson	0	– c Stewart b M. P. Bicknell	38
S. W. Johnson b Bryson	0	– (9) b Kendrick	8
M. E. D. Jarrett run out	5	– (3) c Alikhan b Feltham	1
R. M. Wight c Alikhan b Bryson	4	– b Boiling	3
P. M. Crawley c Kendrick b Bryson	1	– c Stewart b Kendrick	45
*J. P. Crawley c Lynch b M. P. Bicknell	62	– (4) lbw b Bryson	10
†J. P. Arscott c Kendrick b Feltham	47	– (7) c Stewart b M. P. Bicknell	79
J. P. Carroll c Thorpe b Kendrick	3	– (8) c and b Boiling	11
R. M. Pearson not out	20	– not out	33
M. B. Abington c Stewart b Boiling	6	– b M. P. Bicknell	0
L-b 5, w 1, n-b 7	13	B 3, l-b 2, n-b 10	15
1/1 2/1 3/2 4/7 5/11	161	1/23 2/35 3/48 4/54 5/78	259
6/12 7/93 8/114 9/144		6/149 7/176 8/189 9/259	

Bowling: *First Innings*—Bryson 14-2-48-5; M. P. Bicknell 16-6-47-1; Feltham 8-3-25-1; Kendrick 15-6-33-1; Boiling 2.5-0-3-1. *Second Innings*—Bryson 14-3-43-1; M. P. Bicknell 15-3-42-3; Boiling 31-13-70-3; Feltham 8-1-29-1; Kendrick 23-4-70-2.

Umpires: A. Clarkson and K. E. Palmer.

†At Cambridge, June 7. Cambridge University won by 73 runs. Toss: Cambridge University. Cambridge University 203 for seven dec. (A. M. Hooper 85, J. P. Arscott 54; Rev. A. R. Wingfield Digby three for 54); Free Foresters 130 (A. G. Davies 51 not out; A. M. Hooper three for 23).

†At Cambridge, June 8, 9, 10. Drawn. Toss: MCC. MCC 330 for seven dec. (A. Flower 120, Parvez Mir 116, D. L. Houghton 35; C. M. Pitcher five for 57) and 146 for one dec. (M. J. Slater 103 not out, R. A. Jones 36); Cambridge University 213 (J. P. Carroll 70, Extras 43; Parvez Mir three for 13, B. A. Gilbert three for 24) and 198 for nine (J. P. Carroll 37, S. W. Johnson 54; Parvez Mir four for 53).

†At Uxbridge, June 11, 12, 13. Drawn. Toss: Cambridge University. Cambridge University 295 for eight dec. (G. W. Jones 30, J. P. Crawley 137, J. P. Carroll 48, J. P. Arscott 32; Lt P. H. G. Moore three for 36, Flt Lt A. W. J. Spiller three for 68) and 235 for five dec. (G. W. Jones 93 not out, J. P. Carroll 58); Combined Services 251 for six dec. (Capt. J. W. S. Cotterill 37, LS R. Learmouth 99, Cpl A. Jones 59; S. W. Johnson three for 77, M. B. Abington three for 75) and 205 for nine (Capt. J. W. S. Cotterill 49, Lt R. J. Greatorex 54, Cpl A. Jones 31; R. M. Pearson four for 65, M. B. Abington five for 58).

†At Cambridge, June 14. Cambridge University won by 16 runs. Toss: Cambridge University. Cambridge University 191 for five dec. (M. E. D. Jarrett 46 not out, J. P. Crawley 60 not out); Quidnuncs 175 (P. A. C. Bail 43, M. J. Morris 41; M. B. Abington three for 59, R. M. Wight four for 55).

†At Cambridge, June 15. Cambridge University won by three wickets. Toss: Club Cricket Conference Under-25. Club Cricket Conference Under-25 178 (50 overs) (B. Debenham 46; R. M. Wight three for 55); Cambridge University 182 for seven (49 overs) (J. P. Carroll 32, R. M. Wight 46).

CAMBRIDGE UNIVERSITY v DERBYSHIRE

At Cambridge, June 16, 17, 18. Drawn. Toss: Derbyshire. Five county players batted, and all made half-centuries against an attack dominated by the three spinners, Pearson, Abington and Wight. Crawley, batting for more than three hours, provided a solid foundation for the University's reply, but slow left-armer Sladdin cut through the innings to claim six wickets for the first time; the follow-on was avoided only with the last pair together. The county reversed their order when they batted again, giving Warner the chance to score a rare half-century and setting a target of 307. That was always beyond the students, but with Crawley scoring 92, his highest innings for Cambridge to date, and sharing 135 with Jones for the second wicket, defeat was never likely either.

Close of play: First day, Derbyshire 348-4 dec.; Second day, Derbyshire 86-1 (D. G. Cork 40*, A. E. Warner 39*).

Derbyshire

P. D. Bowler c Crawley b Abington	75		
C. J. Adams lbw b Abington	80	– (7) not out	25
J. E. Morris b Wight	73		
T. J. G. O'Gorman not out	51	– (6) not out	12
†K. M. Krikken b Hooper	55	– b Pearson	1
D. G. Cork (did not bat)		– (1) c and b Abington	47
S. C. Goldsmith (did not bat)		– (2) c Arscott b Johnson	3
A. E. Warner (did not bat)		– (3) b Abington	55
R. W. Sladdin (did not bat)		– (4) c Wight b Abington	5
B 7, l-b 5, w 2	14	B 5, l-b 5	10

1/137 2/182 3/258 4/348   (4 wkts dec.) 348   1/9 2/103 3/113   (5 wkts dec.) 158
                                               4/116 5/120

*K. J. Barnett and O. H. Mortensen did not bat.

Bowling: *First Innings*—Pitcher 16–1–57–0; Johnson 15–5–40–0; Pearson 30–3–84–0; Abington 23–5–83–2; Wight 21–6–61–1; Hooper 1.2–0–11–1. *Second Innings*—Johnson 6–1–34–1; Pitcher 6–0–26–0; Pearson 20–6–43–1; Wight 5–0–12–0; Abington 14–4–33–3.

Cambridge University

A. M. Hooper b Warner	18	– c and b Cork	2
G. W. Jones lbw b Mortensen	4	– run out	44
*J. P. Crawley b Mortensen	65	– c Krikken b Morris	92
R. M. Wight b Sladdin	15	– not out	19
J. P. Carroll c Cork b Sladdin	9	– c Krikken b O'Gorman	18
†J. P. Arscott c Cork b Sladdin	18		
M. E. D. Jarrett c Goldsmith b Sladdin	16		
S. W. Johnson not out	14		
C. M. Pitcher b Cork	3		
R. M. Pearson b Sladdin	13		
M. B. Abington c Barnett b Sladdin	0		
L-b 14, n-b 11	25	B 3, l-b 2, w 2, n-b 1	8

1/9 2/23 3/76 4/112 5/146   200   1/8 2/143   (4 wkts) 183
6/153 7/167 8/171 9/194   3/148 4/183

Bowling: *First Innings*—Mortensen 16.4–5–35–2; Warner 19–2–52–1; Cork 16.2–3–41–1; Sladdin 29.2–15–58–6. *Second Innings*—Cork 8–2–17–1; Goldsmith 6–1–28–0; Sladdin 31–10–59–0; Bowler 6–0–23–0; Adams 10–2–31–0; Morris 8–3–13–1; O'Gorman 1.2–0–7–1.

Umpires: A. Clarkson and D. R. Shepherd.

CAMBRIDGE UNIVERSITY v KENT

At Cambridge, June 19, 20, 21. Cambridge University won by two wickets. Toss: Cambridge University. The University enjoyed their first victory over a first-class county on home ground for ten years. Set to score 281 in what became 72 overs, they achieved their target with eight balls to spare. Carroll, in only his third match, scored 92, adding 77 with Wight and 82 with Johnson, who hit the winning runs and reached 45 off his 39th ball. Almost three hours' play was lost on the first day, but Longley, whose previous five first-class matches had brought him an aggregate of 47 runs, put on 144 for the third wicket with Ellison, and next morning his maiden century enabled Kent to declare at 300 for five. An unbeaten fifty from Arscott was the high spot of Cambridge's reply. Kent extended their lead by 160 for the loss of six wickets before Marsh made his challenging lunch-time declaration.

Close of play: First day, Kent 192-3 (J. I. Longley 79*, N. J. Llong 5*); Second day, Kent 27-1 (D. P. Fulton 9*, R. P. Davis 0*).

Kent

M. A. Ealham c Jarrett b Johnson	25	– (5) c Carroll b Pearson	1
D. P. Fulton c Wight b Hooper	16	– (1) c Johnson b Pearson	42
J. I. Longley b Abington b Wight	110		
R. M. Ellison b Johnson b Wight	64	– (8) not out	1
N. J. Llong c Hooper b Wight	25	– (2) c Arscott b Johnson	18
*S. A. Marsh not out	37	– b Wight	43
†G. J. Kersey not out	20	– st Arscott b Abington	22
R. P. Davis (did not bat)	–	(3) c Arscott b Pearson	15
C. Penn (did not bat)	–	(4) retired hurt	14
L-b 3	3	L-b 4	4

1/42 2/42 3/186 4/243 5/243   (5 wkts dec.) 300   1/25 2/57 3/89   (6 wkts dec.) 160
                      4/94 5/151 6/160

T. N. Wren and A. Tutt did not bat.

In the second innings C. Penn retired hurt at 78.

Bowling: *First Innings*—Johnson 7–2–26–1; Pitcher 20–6–73–0; Hooper 3–0–12–1; Abington 14–1–52–0; Pearson 19.3–3–69–0; Wight 17–2–65–3. *Second Innings*—Johnson 4–0–14–1; Pitcher 12–1–33–0; Pearson 18–3–67–3; Abington 9–1–40–1; Wight 0.3–0–2–1.

Cambridge University

A. M. Hooper run out	40 – c Kersey b Wren	9
G. W. Jones c Longley b Wren	10 – c Ellison b Davis	36
*J. P. Crawley c Fulton b Wren	9 – lbw b Davis	27
R. M. Wight c Kersey b Davis	28 – c Ealham b Wren	61
J. P. Carroll c Marsh b Davis	0 – c Wren b Davis	92
†J. P. Arscott not out	58 – lbw b Wren	5
M. E. D. Jarrett b Llong	13 – lbw b Llong	0
C. M. Pitcher c Fulton b Llong	0 – (9) b Ealham	0
S. W. Johnson c Llong b Davis	10 – (8) not out	45
R. M. Pearson c Wren b Davis	7 – not out	1
M. B. Abington c Ealham b Llong	1	
B 2, l-b 1, n-b 1	4	B 1, l-b 5, n-b 2 8

1/42 2/53 3/79 4/86 5/91   180   1/18 2/65 3/96 4/173   (8 wkts) 284
6/128 7/138 8/153 9/165   5/189 6/195 7/277 8/279

Bowling: *First Innings*—Penn 10–4–17–0; Wren 13–3–38–2; Davis 21–6–49–4; Tutt 10–3–23–0; Llong 15–3–50–3. *Second Innings*—Ealham 13.4–1–50–1; Wren 11–1–54–3; Davis 25–3–91–3; Tutt 9–2–30–0; Llong 12–0–53–1.

Umpires: A. Clarkson and D. J. Constant.

At Nottingham, June 27, 28, 29. CAMBRIDGE UNIVERSITY lost to NOTTINGHAM-SHIRE by 162 runs.

THE UNIVERSITY MATCH, 1992

OXFORD UNIVERSITY v CAMBRIDGE UNIVERSITY

At Lord's, June 30, July 1, 2. Cambridge University won by seven wickets. Toss: Oxford University. John Crawley led Cambridge to an unexpected victory, the first decisive result in the fixture for six years, when he scored an unbeaten 106 on the final day. It was his maiden century for Cambridge, and the first in the University Match since his brother Mark's 140 for Oxford in 1987; by coincidence, Mark made 102 not out for Nottinghamshire at Maidstone the same day. Oxford might have had the upper hand if Crawley had not been dropped, twice, on 20 by substitute Chinmay Gupte off the bowling of Anderson. Twenty overs remained and the asking-rate was seven an over. But Crawley, striking 13 fours and a six, and Wight took their partnership to an unbroken 166 from 26 overs to win with seven balls to spare. For the fifth year running the match was seriously disrupted by rain, which permitted 60 overs on the first day and just 22.5 on the second. Oxford struggled at first; both their leading batsmen, Gallian and Montgomerie, were out trying to hook Johnson, and though Lovell regained some ground they were 66 for four after 36 overs. But Keey dug in, scoring 33 at a run an over, and had valuable support from Davies, with a career-best 39. Lovell declared after half an hour more next morning, and his opening bowlers immediately seized the initiative. Hooper was caught at second slip off Gallian's second ball, while Jeh had Crawley held at gully and Wight at third slip; then Gallian had Jones caught behind. Cambridge were 26 for four from 15.5 overs overnight, and Crawley bravely declared at 60 for seven next day. This time Montgomerie and Gallian did not waste their opportunities; they put on 115 in 107 minutes. Gallian had hit ten fours when his stumping prompted Lovell's final declaration, which set Cambridge 238 to win in 52 overs. Crawley won the day, but it took the good will and determination of both captains to make a match of it.

Close of play: First day, Oxford University 153-6 (M. P. W. Jeh 3*, R. H. Macdonald 0*); Second day, Cambridge University 26-4 (J. P. Carroll 1*, J. P. Arscott 0*).

Oxford University

R. R. Montgomerie (*Rugby and Worcester*)
c Pearson b Johnson .... 16 – not out...................... 45
J. E. R. Gallian (*Pittwater House, Sydney
and Keble*) c Jones b Johnson .... 1 – st Arscott b Wight 66
A. C. Storie (*St Stithian's, Univ. of South Africa
and Keble*) c Johnson b Hooper 5
*G. B. T. Lovell (*Sydney C. of E. GS, Sydney U.
and Exeter*) c Crawley b Pitcher 32
C. L. Keey (*Harrow, Durham U. and Keble*)
lbw b Pearson 33
H. R. Davies (*St Dunstan's and Christ Church*)
lbw b Abington 39
M. P. W. Jeh (*Brisbane State High, Griffith U.
and Keble*) c Pearson b Johnson 8
R. H. Macdonald (*Rondebosch Boys' HS, Cape
Town U., Durham U. and Keble*) not out...... 8
D. J. Anderson (*Repton, Reading U. and St
Edmund Hall*) not out 8
    B 15, l-b 11, w 6 32   L-b 3, w 1 4

1/14 2/21 3/35 4/66 5/130   (7 wkts dec.) 182   1/115   (1 wkt dec.) 115
6/149 7/166

†C. J. Townsend (*Dean Close, Cheltenham and Brasenose*) and B. S. Wood (*Batley GS and
Worcester*) did not bat.

Bowling: *First Innings*—Johnson 18–4–62–3; Pitcher 17–5–36–1; Pearson 14–4–37–1;
Hooper 5–2–5–1; Wight 11–5–14–0; Abington 2–1–2–1. *Second Innings*—Johnson 6–0–22–0;
Pitcher 11–0–39–0; Pearson 8–0–31–0; Wight 5–0–13–1; Abington 2–0–7–0.

Cambridge University

A. M. Hooper (*Latymer Upper and St John's*)
c Montgomerie b Gallian .... 1 – b Jeh 17
G. W. Jones (*King's, Chester and Gonville &
Caius*) c Townsend b Gallian .... 12 – lbw b Macdonald 18
*J. P. Crawley (*Manchester GS and Trinity*)
c Gallian b Jeh......................... 1 – (4) not out................106
R. M. Wight (*KCS, Wimbledon, Exeter U. and
Trinity Hall*) c Storie b Jeh .... 5 – (5) not out 62
J. P. Carroll (*Rendcomb and Homerton*)
c Townsend b Wood 7
†J. P. Arscott (*Tonbridge and Magdalene*)
c Gallian b Macdonald 5
M. E. D. Jarrett (*Harrow and Girton*) not out ... 7 – (3) c Anderson b Gallian....... 22
S. W. Johnson (*Royal GS, Newcastle and
Magdalene*) c Anderson b Macdonald 14
    L-b 3, n-b 5...................... 8   B 3, l-b 4, w 4, n-b 2 13

1/5 2/11 3/24 4/25 5/35   (7 wkts dec.) 60   1/25 2/56 3/72   (3 wkts) 238
6/37 7/60

C. M. Pitcher (*St Edward's, Oxford and Selwyn*), R. M. Pearson (*Batley GS and St John's*)
and M. B. Abington (*Bedford, Brighton Polytechnic and Homerton*) did not bat.

Bowling: *First Innings*—Jeh 8–1–15–2; Gallian 8–4–10–2; Wood 6–0–19–1; Macdonald
5.4–3–13–2. *Second Innings*—Jeh 6–0–27–1; Gallian 16–1–89–1; Macdonald 12–3–30–1;
Wood 12.5–0–56–0; Anderson 4–0–29–0.

Umpires: J. D. Bond and V. A. Holder.

OXFORD v CAMBRIDGE, RESULTS AND HUNDREDS

The University match dates back to 1827. Altogether there have been 147 official matches,
Cambridge winning 55 and Oxford 46, with 46 drawn. The 1988 match was abandoned
without a ball bowled. Results since 1950:

1950	Drawn
1951	Oxford won by 21 runs
1952	Drawn
1953	Cambridge won by two wickets
1954	Drawn
1955	Drawn
1956	Drawn
1957	Cambridge won by an innings and 186 runs
1958	Cambridge won by 99 runs
1959	Oxford won by 85 runs
1960	Drawn
1961	Drawn
1962	Drawn
1963	Drawn
1964	Drawn
1965	Drawn
1966	Oxford won by an innings and nine runs
1967	Drawn
1968	Drawn
1969	Drawn
1970	Drawn
1971	Drawn

1972	Cambridge won by an innings and 25 runs
1973	Drawn
1974	Drawn
1975	Drawn
1976	Oxford won by ten wickets
1977	Drawn
1978	Drawn
1979	Cambridge won by an innings and 52 runs
1980	Drawn
1981	Drawn
1982	Cambridge won by seven wickets
1983	Drawn
1984	Oxford won by five wickets
1985	Drawn
1986	Cambridge won by five wickets
1987	Drawn
1988	Abandoned
1989	Drawn
1990	Drawn
1991	Drawn
1992	Cambridge won by seven wickets

Ninety-four three-figure innings have been played in the University matches. For those scored before 1919 see 1940 *Wisden*. Those subsequent to 1919 include the seven highest:

238*	Nawab of Pataudi, sen.	1931 Oxford		119	J. M. Brearley	1964 Cam.
211	G. Goonesena	1957 Cam.		118	H. Ashton	1921 Cam.
201*	M. J. K. Smith	1954 Oxford		118	D. R. W. Silk	1954 Cam.
201	A. Ratcliffe	1931 Cam.		117	M. J. K. Smith	1956 Oxford
200	Majid Khan	1970 Oxford		116*	D. R. W. Silk	1953 Cam.
193	D. C. H. Townsend	1934 Oxford		116	M. C. Cowdrey	1953 Oxford
174	P. A. C. Bail	1986 Cam.		115	A. W. Allen	1934 Cam.
170	M. Howell	1919 Oxford		114*	D. R. Owen-Thomas	1972 Cam.
167	B. W. Hone	1932 Oxford		114	J. F. Pretlove	1955 Cam.
158	P. M. Roebuck	1975 Cam.		113*	J. M. Brearley	1962 Cam.
157	D. R. Wilcox	1932 Cam.		113	E. R. T. Holmes	1927 Oxford
155	F. S. Goldstein	1968 Oxford		112*	E. D. Fursdon	1975 Oxford
149	J. T. Morgan	1929 Cam.		111*	G. W. Cook	1957 Cam.
149	G. J. Toogood	1985 Oxford		109	C. H. Taylor	1923 Oxford
146	R. O'Brien	1956 Cam.		109	G. J. Toogood	1984 Oxford
146	D. R. Owen-Thomas	1971 Cam.		108	F. G. H. Chalk	1934 Oxford
145*	H. E. Webb	1948 Oxford		106*	J. P. Crawley	1992 Cam.
145	D. P. Toft	1967 Oxford		106	Nawab of Pataudi, sen.	1929 Oxford
142	M. P. Donnelly	1946 Oxford		105	E. J. Craig	1961 Cam.
140	M. A. Crawley	1987 Oxford		104*	D. A. Thorne	1986 Oxford
139	R. J. Boyd-Moss	1983 Cam.		104	H. J. Enthoven	1924 Cam.
136	E. T. Killick	1930 Cam.		104	M. J. K. Smith	1955 Oxford
135	H. A. Pawson	1947 Oxford		103*	A. R. Lewis	1962 Cam.
131	Nawab of Pataudi, jun.	1960 Oxford		103*	D. R. Pringle	1979 Cam.
129	H. J. Enthoven	1925 Cam.		102*	A. P. F. Chapman	1922 Cam.
128*	A. J. T. Miller	1984 Oxford		101*	R. W. V. Robins	1928 Cam.
127	D. S. Sheppard	1952 Cam.		101	N. W. D. Yardley	1937 Cam.
124	A. K. Judd	1927 Cam.		100*	M. Manasseh	1964 Oxford
124	A. Ratcliffe	1932 Cam.		100	P. J. Dickinson	1939 Cam.
124	R. J. Boyd-Moss	1983 Cam.		100	N. J. Cosh	1967 Cam.
122	P. A. Gibb	1938 Cam.		100	R. J. Boyd-Moss	1982 Cam.
121	J. N. Grover	1937 Oxford				

Signifies not out.

Highest Totals

503	Oxford	1900	432-9	Cambridge	1936
457	Oxford	1947	431	Cambridge	1932
453-8	Oxford	1931	425	Cambridge	1938

Lowest Totals

32	Oxford	1878	42	Oxford	1890
39	Cambridge	1858	47	Cambridge	1838

Notes: A. P. F. Chapman and M. P. Donnelly enjoy the following distinction: Chapman scored a century at Lord's in the University match (102*, 1922); for Gentlemen v Players (160, 1922), (108, 1926); and for England v Australia (121, 1930). Donnelly scored a century at Lord's in the University match (142, 1946); for Gentlemen v Players (162*, 1947); and for New Zealand v England (206, 1949).

A. Ratcliffe's 201 for Cambridge in 1931 remained a record for the match for only one day, being beaten by the Nawab of Pataudi's 238* for Oxford next day.

M. J. K. Smith (Oxford) and R. J. Boyd-Moss (Cambridge) are the only players who have scored three hundreds. Apart from Brearley, Enthoven, Owen-Thomas, Nawab of Pautaudi, sen., Ratcliffe, Silk and Toogood – all listed above – the only other player to score two hundreds is W. Yardley (Cambridge), 100 in 1870 and 130 in 1872.

F. C. Cobden, in the Oxford v Cambridge match in 1870, performed the hat-trick by taking the last three wickets and won an extraordinary game for Cambridge by two runs. The feat is without parallel in first-class cricket. Other hat-tricks, all for Cambridge, have been credited to A. G. Steel (1879), P. H. Morton (1880), J. F. Ireland (1911), and R. G. H. Lowe (1926).

S. E. Butler, in the 1871 match, took all the wickets in the Cambridge first innings. The feat is unique in University matches. He bowled 24.1 overs. In the follow-on he took five wickets for 57, giving him match figures of 15 for 95 runs.

The best all-round performances in the history of the match have come from P. R. Le Couteur, who scored 160 and took 11 Cambridge wickets for 66 runs in 1910, and G. J. Toogood, who in 1985 scored 149 and took ten Cambridge wickets for 93.

D. W. Jarrett (Oxford 1975, Cambridge 1976), S. M. Wookey (Cambridge 1975-76, Oxford 1978) and G. Pathmanathan (Oxford 1975-78, Cambridge 1983) are alone in gaining cricket Blues for both Universities.

COMMERCIAL UNION UAU CHAMPIONSHIP, 1992

By GRENVILLE HOLLAND

The UAU season is a short one. It begins at the end of April and ends in mid-June, and examinations effectively remove several weeks in late May. It is a minor miracle that, with so many universities jostling to compete in such a restricted timespan and despite the weather, a champion is crowned within two months.

In 1993 the number jostling will rise from 45 to 64, with many more expected to join in 1994, because of the large number of educational institutions recently granted university status. Each of the regional mini-leagues, seven English and one Welsh, which supply the contenders for the knockout stages of the Championship, will expand, and for the first time a Scottish league, containing eight universities, will join the fray. Sponsors Commercial Union have renewed their support for what promises to be an interesting season.

That interest is intensified by the changes to university fixtures outside the Championship. In the Benson and Hedges Cup the Combined Universities will no longer be granted four games in a qualifying group. They will be restricted to a single knockout encounter, against Hampshire – their only competitive game if they fail to survive – and the best players may now come under pressure not to play and to keep themselves available for their county teams in later rounds. In compensation, two one-day matches, against Middlesex and Northamptonshire, have been arranged in Oxford to assist preparation for the Cup tie. Another historic change sees the fixture with the tourists, formerly the preserve of Oxford and Cambridge, thrown open to students from all universities – a truly combined team as in the Benson and Hedges Cup. It will be the first time UAU students have been eligible for first-class cricket.

The final season of the old era produced few surprises. Durham won their 12th Championship, breaking the record of 11 which they shared with Manchester and Loughborough; it was their third consecutive trophy and their ninth successive final. Their opponents, Kent, had reached the semi-finals for the first time only in 1991. This year they won all four matches in their South East South group, possessing sufficient depth in batting to overcome their sometimes shaky starts. David Fulton, who made his first-class début for the county of Kent in June, scored a powerful 132 to overcome an imposing 235 for six from City, but was out first ball against Sussex; Ravi Shah carried the innings, as he did against the London School of Economics, scoring 85 both times. Both were on form in the challenge round when they steered Kent past Royal Holloway and Bedford New College's 228 with three balls to spare, and Shah made an unbeaten 123 in the quarter-final against Birmingham.

In the semi-final they met Exeter, who had carried all before them in the South West. Nick Preston had run through the batsmen of Bristol and Bath, taking six for 40 and five for 32; and last year's finalists, Southampton, missing their captain Greg Macmillan, were swiftly despatched for 73, with David Butcher taking five for 18. Slow left-armer Butcher also took the heart out of Loughborough, with six for 35 in the challenge round. Loughborough could count themselves unlucky to be

isiting Exeter at all; they had been placed second to Birmingham in the
Midlands group on wickets taken per balls bowled – largely because Aston
had presented them with an unwanted walkover.

Exeter met Southampton again in the quarter-final, and this time had a
harder fight. Macmillan had returned, and batted throughout the innings
for a stylish 85. By the halfway mark Exeter had struggled to 81 for six,
with John Lishman claiming four. But no more wickets fell as captain Paul
Miles saw them home with a scintillating 80 not out. Meanwhile Durham,
whose team was packed with players on the fringe of their county teams,
sailed through the North East league with their usual efficiency. They beat
Hull by seven wickets, Leeds by nine and York by ten; Newcastle succumbed by 61 runs, and Sheffield by 96 as left-hander Simon Ecclestone's
unbeaten 155 underpinned Durham's massive 324 for five in 55 overs. They
reached 324 again in the quarter-final, when Jeremy Snape of Northamptonshire made 141, and a battery of eight bowlers – four of them spinners –
wiped out Sussex for 90 in 42.4 overs.

In the semi-final Durham met Reading, South Central winners, who had
gone on to beat Essex and Liverpool; invited to bat, they ran up 294 for six
at a brisk pace, and only Vije Wijegunawardene, brother of the Sri Lankan
Test player Kapila, made much impact with 75 in Reading's muted reply.
The other semi-final was more tense. Exeter started steadily, but lacked
urgency; Ian Muir batted 55 overs for his 68 and hit only four fours. Kent
began by losing three wickets, including Fulton and Shah, for only ten runs
in the first eight overs. Rob Archer and John Owen revived them with 148,
but they needed three from the last over. Andy Rogers hit four from the
fourth ball to carry Kent into their first UAU final.

SEMI-FINALS

At St Albans, June 22. Durham won by 98 runs. Toss: Reading. Durham 294 for six (60
overs) (J. R. A. Williams 34, A. C. Richards 84, S. C. Ecclestone 47, J. N. Snape 54, Extras
50); Reading 196 (57.5 overs) (V. Wijegunawardene 75, Mohammed Saleem 46; J. N. Snape
five for 54).

At Southgate, June 22. Kent won by four wickets. Exeter 200 for five (60 overs) (I. Muir
68); Kent 203 for six (59.4 overs) (R. E. Archer 85, J. Owen 72; O. D. M. Bell four for 64).

FINAL

At Finchley, June 23. Durham won by 93 runs. Toss: Kent. Durham were invited to bat on
an easy-paced wicket in bright sunshine, and the first four overs yielded 27 runs. The
bowling became more controlled later but Durham's progress was always comfortable.
Ecclestone, who hit the ball with power and authority, and Snape, with well-judged
footwork and wristy strokes, maintained an impressive run-rate as they added 132. After
they were out Durham slipped to 246 for seven and Archer deserved his four wickets for
persisting with his off-breaks amid a bewildering number of bowling changes. But a final
outburst from Chris Hawkes and Andy Webster added 52 in four overs. As in previous
rounds, Kent made an uncomfortable start. Archer gloved the third ball of James Bovill's
opening over down the leg side; Fulton, who was looking assured, casually played a ball
from Durham captain and Somerset player Jeremy Hallett straight to square leg; and Jamie
Lovatt perished the same way. Shah and John Owen restored order, but the asking-rate
seemed too high and thunderstorms over central London were casting an eerie gloom across
Finchley. Yet Kent kept Durham in the field almost to the end, even after stumbling to 164
for eight. Duncan Berry, in mischievous mood, had the fielders running around in the dark.
But with Kent 93 runs adrift, their last man, captain Tony Murphy, gave Chris Hollins his
fourth catch of the innings. Durham could take the cup home for the third year running,
matching Southampton's feat in 1968-70.

Durham

J. R. A. Williams b Shah	36	A. G. Webster c Fulton b Rogers	2
A. C. Richards c and b Archer	31	M. T. Brimson run out	6
S. C. Ecclestone c McGougan b Rogers	93	J. N. B. Bovill not out	
J. N. Snape c Rogers b Archer	56	B 3, l-b 7	10
†W. M. I. Bailey b Archer	13		
C. J. Hollins b Archer	7	1/57 2/76 3/208	(59.4 overs) 30
C. J. Hawkes c Archer b Rogers	32	4/227 5/237 6/246	
*J. C. Hallett run out	0	7/246 8/298 9/298	

Bowling: McGougan 2–0–15–0; Shah 12.4–2–70–1; Archer 19–3–77–4; Murphy 5–0–25–0 Berry 8–1–39–0; Rogers 13–1–72–3.

Kent

J. M. N. Lovatt c Hollins b Hallett	18	D. A. Berry c Ecclestone b Hawkes	3
R. E. Archer c Bailey b Bovill	0	A. N. J. McGougan not out	1
D. P. Fulton c Hollins b Hallett	10	*A. J. Murphy c Hollins b Hawkes	
R. D. Shah c Ecclestone b Hawkes	40	L-b 4, n-b 6	1
J. Owen c Williams b Snape	32		
A. P. Hansford c Webster b Brimson	25	1/0 2/24 3/37	(58.5 overs) 21.
†C. E. Williams c Bailey b Hallett	29	4/106 5/106 6/144	
A. P. Rogers c Hollins b Brimson	2	7/164 8/164 9/211	

Bowling: Hallett 10–1–29–3; Bovill 3–0–24–1; Webster 4–1–19–0; Snape 16–3–52–1 Hawkes 13.5–2–42–3; Brimson 12–1–45–2.

Umpires: K. Hopley and M. K. Reed.

WINNERS 1927-92

1927	Manchester	1954	Manchester	1973	{ Leicester
1928	Manchester	1955	Birmingham		{ Loughborough Colls.
1929	Nottingham	1956	Null and void	1974	Durham
1930	Sheffield	1957	Loughborough Colls.	1975	Loughborough Colls.
1931	Liverpool	1958	Null and void	1976	Loughborough
1932	Manchester	1959	Liverpool	1977	Durham
1933	Manchester	1960	Loughborough Colls.	1978	Manchester
1934	Leeds	1961	Loughborough Colls.	1979	Manchester
1935	Sheffield	1962	Manchester	1980	Exeter
1936	Sheffield	1963	Loughborough Colls.	1981	Durham
1937	Nottingham	1964	Loughborough Colls.	1982	Exeter
1938	Durham	1965	Hull	1983	Exeter
1939	Durham	1966	{ Newcastle	1984	Bristol
1946	Not completed		{ Southampton	1985	Birmingham
1947	Sheffield	1967	Manchester	1986	Durham
1948	Leeds	1968	Southampton	1987	Durham
1949	Leeds	1969	Southampton	1988	Swansea
1950	Manchester	1970	Southampton	1989	Loughborough
1951	Manchester	1971	Loughborough Colls.	1990	Durham
1952	Loughborough Colls.	1972	Durham	1991	Durham
1953	Durham			1992	Durham

OTHER FIRST-CLASS MATCHES, 1992

ENGLAND A v ESSEX

At Lord's, April 13, 14, 15, 16. Drawn. Toss: England A. For the first time the team selected to start the season against the county champions was designated England A, rather than MCC, and included only players chosen for the A team tour of the West Indies. As an England trial, the fixture was to provide little guidance, although the bowling of Munton, who removed Prichard and Hussain with successive balls, and Salisbury, whose leg-spin dismissed Waugh and Gooch, may have been significant. On a bone-chilling first day England A exploited a short Tavern boundary and Bicknell, who hit 18 fours and a six, matched M. A. Atherton in 1991 by scoring a century on April 13, the earliest ever in England. After the third day was washed out, Waugh struck 61 in 69 balls, out of 76 added while he was in. Gooch, recovering from flu, averted the hat-trick, and went on to 75. He shared a stand of 113 with Pringle, who reached his first hundred for almost four years off the last ball of the game.

Close of play: First day, England A 329-4 (P. Johnson 43*, G. P. Thorpe 22*); Second day, Essex 8-1 (P. J. Prichard 8*, M. E. Waugh 0*); Third day, No play.

England A

D. J. Bicknell c Garnham b Waugh	..115	D. G. Cork c Garnham b Foster	......	27
H. Morris c Waugh b Pringle	 51	I. D. K. Salisbury not out	....	36
*M. D. Moxon c Waugh b Gooch	 71	B 1, l-b 2, w 7, n-b 10	....	20
M. R. Ramprakash lbw b Pringle	 12			
P. Johnson c Garnham b Pringle	 53	1/113 2/212 3/257	(7 wkts dec.)	456
G. P. Thorpe c Garnham b Ilott	 32	4/270 5/348		
†S. J. Rhodes not out	 39	6/353 7/390		

T. A. Munton and D. E. Malcolm did not bat.

Bowling: Foster 30-7-90-1; Pringle 29-6-80-3; Ilott 22-5-64-1; Childs 25-6-100-0; Waugh 11-0-57-1; Gooch 14-2-62-1.

Essex

P. J. Prichard c Rhodes b Munton	 15	N. A. Foster c Thorpe b Salisbury	.....	36
*M. A. Garnham c Moxon b Munton	.. 0	M. C. Ilott not out	....	12
M. E. Waugh c Bicknell b Salisbury	.. 61			
N. Hussain lbw b Munton	 0	L-b 7, n-b 4	....	11
*G. A. Gooch c Johnson b Salisbury	.. 75			
N. Shahid c Rhodes b Cork	 0	1/8 2/35 3/35	(8 wkts dec.)	317
N. V. Knight c Morris b Cork	 5	4/84 5/91 6/106		
D. R. Pringle not out	 102	7/219 8/287		

J. H. Childs did not bat.

Bowling: Malcolm 14-0-76-0; Munton 23-7-84-3; Cork 20-2-71-2; Salisbury 24-4-79-3.

Umpires: M. J. Kitchen and B. J. Meyer.

SCOTLAND v IRELAND

At Broughty Ferry, Dundee, June 20, 21, 22. Drawn. Toss: Scotland. Fine weather and a batsman's pitch produced two centuries in this match, the only first-class fixture for either team, for the third year running. George Salmond struck a six to reach three figures for the first time on the opening day, and Irishman Alan Lewis scored his own maiden hundred in the final day's run-chase. Iain Philip and Bruce Patterson had laid their usual solid foundations for Scotland's first innings with a partnership of 111 and Salmond and his captain, Bruce Russell, added 114 for the fourth wicket. Jimmy Govan, the off-spinner formerly with Northamptonshire, returned career-best figures of six for 70 next day, as

Ireland were bowled out 110 behind. Salmond reclaimed the limelight when Scotland batte
again. He was eventually dismissed for 95, looking for another six and his second hundre
Russell declared at once, setting Ireland 324 in what turned out to be 88 overs. Lewis mac
a determined effort and it was well into the final hour before the Irish began blocking.

Close of play: First day, Ireland 17-0 (S. J. S. Warke 7*, M. P. Rea 10*); Second day
Scotland 109-3 (G. Salmond 25*, A. B. Russell 1*).

Scotland

B. M. W. Patterson lbw b Hoey	55	– c Warke b Lewis	3
I. L. Philip b P. McCrum	79	– b Lewis	2
J. Everett c Moore b C. McCrum	33	– c Warke b Hoey	2
G. Salmond c Rea b C. McCrum	118	– c Patterson b Dunlop	9
*A. B. Russell b Dunlop	33	– not out	2
†D. A. Orr not out	23		
J. W. Govan c Moore b C. McCrum	6		
A. Bee not out	1		
B 11, l-b 17, w 2, n-b 12	42	L-b 5, n-b 2	

1/111 2/161 3/198 4/312   (6 wkts dec.) 390   1/57 2/62   (4 wkts dec.) 21
5/378 6/389   3/100 4/213

M. S. Richardson, K. L. P. Sheridan and K. Thomson did not bat.

Bowling: *First Innings*—P. McCrum 23-5-80-1; C. McCrum 18-1-57-3; Lewis 9-0-42-C
Hoey 14-4-44-1; Dunlop 29-8-98-1. *Second Innings*—P. McCrur
12-0-65-0; C. McCrum 10-0-40-0; McBrine 17-8-41-0; Lewis 10-3-39-2; Hoey 5-2-15-1
Dunlop 1-0-8-1.

Ireland

*S. J. S. Warke c Orr b Thomson	13	– c Everett b Thomson	
M. P. Rea c Salmond b Richardson	89	– run out	2
S. Graham c Russell b Govan	35	– c Richardson b Govan	2
D. A. Lewis c Philip b Govan	4	– not out	12
A. R. Dunlop c Philip b Sheridan	15	– lbw b Russell	3
T. J. T. Patterson c Russell b Govan	28	– c Govan b Russell	
C. McCrum c Russell b Richardson	70	– st Orr b Govan	3
A. McBrine c Everett b Govan	9	– c Everett b Bee	
C. J. Hoey c Russell b Govan	7	– c Russell b Govan	
P. McCrum b Govan	0	– not out	
†P. D. Moore not out	0		
B 2, l-b 3, w 2, n-b 3	10	B 4, l-b 8, n-b 1	1

1/25 2/103 3/108 4/127 5/164   280   1/4 2/41 3/81   (8 wkts) 27
6/215 7/247 8/267 9/280   4/158 5/168 6/248
     7/255 8/272

Bowling: *First Innings*—Bee 13-2-52-0; Richardson 17-3-49-2; Thomson 13-4-27-1
Sheridan 19-6-62-1; Govan 21.3-4-70-6; Russell 5-1-15-0. *Second Innings*—Thomso
13-1-55-1; Richardson 7-4-15-0; Govan 29-9-86-3; Sheridan 16-4-42-0; Bee 13-2-39-1
Russell 10-4-27-2.

Umpires: D. Walker and A. W. Wood.

MCC MATCHES IN 1992

Although MCC played no first-class cricket in 1992, the club played more than 300 out-matches for the first time, including almost 200 against schools. MCC also staged their first Festival of Cricket. This comprised matches against Germany, winners of the European Cricketer Cup, Transvaal, the first South African team to play at Lord's since the boycott, and Scotland.

The match against Germany was widely reported because the MCC team included the England footballer Gary Lineker, who was out for one and was thus able to say that he always scored one against Germany. More substantial – and very attractive – innings came from Ken Rutherford, Bob Cooke and Roland Butcher, which set too high a target, though Germany, with Jung and Bhatti excelling, made a sparkling reply.

Transvaal, facing an MCC team with nine Test cricketers under the captaincy of Ian Greig, were put in to bat, and dismissed for 115 after some excellent seam bowling from Joel Garner – whose figures of two for 17 in eight overs were reminiscent of his younger days – the West Indian Kenny Benjamin and Greig himself. Robust strokeplay from the New Zealander Mark Greatbatch gave MCC an easy seven-wicket win. What might have been an excellent finish to the two-day match against Scotland was unfortunately ruined by heavy overnight rain.

In all, MCC played 305 out-matches. They won 120, drew 95 and lost 47. There were 42 games abandoned and one tie – at King's College School, Wimbledon. Of five games at Lord's, one was won, two lost and two drawn. – John Jameson.

Note: Matches in this section were not first-class.

At Lord's, May 6. MCC Young Cricketers won by two wickets. Toss: MCC Young Cricketers. MCC 268 for three dec. (T. K. Chadwick 54, B. C. Broad 65, R. J. Robinson 75 not out, R. O. Butcher 68); MCC Young Cricketers 269 for eight (C. J. Rogers 84, N. Pratt 5, S. J. Cooper 43 not out; S. C. Wundke three for 71).

At Wormsley, May 24. MCC won by five wickets. Toss: J. Paul Getty's XI. J. Paul Getty's XI 174 (C. D. A. Martin-Jenkins 59; D. R. Doshi three for 61); MCC 177 for five (P. Willey 44, I. J. Gould 50; R. A. Hutton three for 62).

At Oxford, May 26, 27, 28. MCC drew with OXFORD UNIVERSITY (See The Universities in 1992).

At Cambridge, June 8, 9, 10. MCC drew with CAMBRIDGE UNIVERSITY (See The Universities in 1992).

At Durham University, June 11, 12, 13. Durham University won by five wickets. Toss: Durham University. MCC 223 for eight dec. (R. J. Robinson 57, J. D. Love 83, D. A. Banks 40; S. James four for 42) and 254 for three dec. (D. A. Banks 112 not out, K. C. Williams 58, G. J. Toogood 48 not out); Durham University 215 for nine dec. (A. C. Richards 76; C. D. Hodgkins four for 64, J. Paul three for 47) and 264 for five (J. N. Snape 21 not out, C. J. Hollins 60).

At Nelson, June 17. A Lancashire League XI won by eight wickets. Toss: MCC. MCC 233 for nine dec. (T. K. Chadwick 31, A. Flower 66, R. O. Butcher 39; M. Ingham three for 34); A Lancashire League XI 237 for two (P. Thompson 38, P. Wood 122 not out, J. C. Scuderi 65 not out).

At Downpatrick, July 3, 4, 5. Drawn. Toss: Ireland. MCC 178 for five dec. (H. Cartwright 80, K. G. Sedgbeer 30) and 242 for seven dec. (H. Cartwright 81, A. J. Goldsmith 55, K. G. Sedgbeer 33, D. M. Cox 46); Ireland 188 for four dec. (M. P. Rea 74, D. A. Lewis 53 not out) and 174 for eight (S. J. S. Warke 54, A. R. Dunlop 34, G. D. Harrison 4 not out; A. R. K. Pierson four for 77).

At Arundel, July 5. MCC won by ten wickets. Toss: Lavinia, Duchess of Norfolk's XI Lavinia, Duchess of Norfolk's XI 220 for five dec. (D. Herbert 40, G. A. Tedstone 106 no out, T. A. Lester 39); MCC 224 for no wkt (C. K. Bullen 132 not out, D. C. Elstone 8 not out).

At Finchampstead, July 8. Drawn. Toss: MCC. MCC 185 for one dec. (V. P. Terry 10 J. E. M. Nicholson 67 not out); National Association of Young Cricketers 99 for five.

At Lord's, July 14. MCC lost to MCC SCHOOLS by six wickets (See Schools Cricket i 1992).

At Lord's, July 17. Drawn. Toss: Germany (winners of European Cricketer Cup). MC 289 for six dec. (K. R. Rutherford 87, R. M. O. Cooke 63, R. O. Butcher 68, F. Brooker 3 S. Taneja four for 84); Germany 180 for nine (A. Jung 52, H. Bhatti 57; R. M. O. Cook three for 10).

At Lord's, July 19. MCC won by seven wickets. Toss: MCC. Transvaal 115 (41 overs (K. C. G. Benjamin three for 40, I. A. Greig three for 17); MCC 116 for three (23.2 over (M. J. Greatbatch 47, K. R. Rutherford 32 not out).

At Lord's, July 20, 21 (no play second day). Drawn. Toss: Scotland. MCC 251 for six de (K. R. Rutherford 57, P. Willey 43, S. C. Wundke 102 not out); Scotland 275 for fou (B. M. W. Patterson 98, I. L. Philip 110, G. N. Reifer 35).

At Finchampstead, July 30. MCC won by six wickets. Toss: Club Cricket Conference Club Cricket Conference 218 (T. Russell 42, C. Annand 35, I. Harris 39; S. D. Welch fou for 33); MCC 219 for four (D. L. Houghton 109, A. J. Goldsmith 86 not out).

At Solihull, August 6. MCC won by five wickets. Toss: Midlands Club Cricket Co ference. Midlands Club Cricket Conference 244 for eight (N. Martin 88, D. Marsh 4 N. Moore 42; S. Cooper five for 65); MCC 245 for five (T. A. Brown 77, H. Cartwright 4 N. J. C. Gandon 32, S. C. Wundke 46 not out; N. Moore three for 81).

At Swansea, August 25, 26, 27. Wales v MCC. Abandoned.

HONOURS' LIST, 1992-93

In 1992-93, the following were decorated for their services to cricket:

New Year's Honours, 1992: L. J. Cheeseman (services to umpiring) BEM, Sir Colin Cowdre (England – chairman of International Cricket Council) Kt, M. D. Crowe (New Zealand MBE.

Queen's Birthday Honours: I. T. Botham (England) OBE, D. I. Gower (England) OBE B. Jessop (services to cricket in Yorkshire) BEM, C. H. Lloyd (West Indies – services cricket and public service in Lancashire) CBE.

New Year's Honours, 1993: G. H. G. Doggart (former treasurer of MCC and president English Schools' Cricket Association) OBE, M. J. Stewart (England – recently Englan manager) OBE.

OTHER MATCHES, 1992

Note: Matches in this section were not first-class.

At Arundel, June 7. Drawn. Toss: Lavinia, Duchess of Norfolk's XI. Lavinia, Duchess of Norfolk's XI 207 for five dec. (C. L. Keey 38, R. MacLeay 34, E. Gordon Lennox 63, T. James 31); Combined Services 146 for seven (Capt. R. E. C. Hollington 30 not out; J. R. T. Barclay four for 34).

TILCON TROPHY

A 55-over competition played to Benson and Hedges Cup rules contested by four invited counties.

At Harrogate, June 9. Sussex won by 37 runs. Toss: Durham. Sussex 214 for eight (55 overs) (M. P. Speight 71, A. P. Wells 43; I. Smith three for 34); Durham 177 (48.3 overs) (S. Hutton 41, P. W. G. Parker 31, I. Smith 35 not out; F. D. Stephenson three for 20, N. J. Lenham four for 32).

At Harrogate, June 10. Glamorgan won by eight runs. Toss: Glamorgan. Glamorgan 175 (54.3 overs) (H. Morris 82, R. D. B. Croft 32; M. A. Robinson five for 27, C. S. Pickles three for 28); Yorkshire 167 (54.3 overs) (D. Byas 37, S. R. Tendulkar 40; S. Bastien four for 29, S. R. Barwick three for 31).

At Harrogate, June 11. **Final:** Glamorgan won by 122 runs. Toss: Glamorgan. Glamorgan 291 for five (55 overs) (S. P. James 49, H. Morris 31, P. A. Cottey 91, M. P. Maynard 35, S. Dhaniram 65 not out); Sussex 169 (43.5 overs) (A. P. Wells 36, P. Moores 37; S. Bastien four for 31).

EUROPEAN CRICKETER CUP

A 40-over competition contested by teams, mostly comprising expatriates, representing ten European countries.

At Worksop College, July 16. **Final:** Germany won by three wickets. France 174 for nine (S. Shahzada 38; S. Taneja four for 29); Germany 177 for seven (A. Jung 99).

YUILL HERITAGE HOMES FESTIVAL

At Jesmond, July 29. England XI won by four wickets. Rest of the World XI 319 for six (55 overs) (M. J. Greatbatch 43, M. D. Crowe 56, S. R. Tendulkar 100, D. N. Patel 58 not out); England XI 320 for six (51 overs) (B. C. Broad 37, M. A. Roseberry 47, J. E. Morris 72, C. C. Lewis 66, S. J. Rhodes 39 not out).

At Jesmond, July 30. England XI won by 40 runs. Toss: Rest of the World XI. England XI 272 for eight (55 overs) (A. J. Stewart 34, N. H. Fairbrother 84, S. J. Rhodes 49, D. G. Cork 35; D. N. Patel three for 66, C. Pringle three for 73); Rest of the World XI 232 (45.2 overs) (M. J. Greatbatch 41, D. L. Haynes 52, R. B. Richardson 38, S. R. Tendulkar 38; D. G. Cork three for 38).

SCARBOROUGH FESTIVAL

At Scarborough, August 29. Eastern Province won by six runs. Toss: World XI. Eastern Province 219 for six (50 overs) (M. W. Rushmere 47, L. J. Koen 87 not out, M. C. Venter 40; Tahir Naqqash three for 47); World XI 213 for eight (50 overs) (T. J. Boon 92).

At Scarborough, August 30. World XI v Eastern Province. Abandoned.

JOSHUA TETLEY SCARBOROUGH FESTIVAL TROPHY

A 50-over competition contested by Yorkshire and three other invited counties.

At Scarborough, September 4. Hampshire won by nine wickets. Toss: Hampshire. Nottinghamshire 238 for five (50 overs) (P. R. Pollard 68, M. Saxelby 54, M. A. Crawley 48 not out, G. F. Archer 34); Hampshire 242 for one (48.2 overs) (T. C. Middleton 109 not out, R. M. F. Cox 68, J. R. Ayling 55 not out).

At Scarborough, September 5. Yorkshire won by nine wickets. Toss: Durham. Durham 244 for six (50 overs) (W. Larkins 103, P. W. G. Parker 40, I. Smith 30; P. W. Jarvis three for 52); Yorkshire 248 for one (48.1 overs) (M. D. Moxon 108, S. A. Kellett 109 not out).

At Scarborough, September 6. **Final:** Yorkshire v Hampshire. Abandoned. Yorkshire and Hampshire shared the Tetley Festival Trophy.

SEEBOARD TROPHY

A 50-over competition contested by Sussex and three other invited counties.

At Hove, September 4. Kent won by four runs. Toss: Surrey. Kent 254 for nine (50 overs) (N. R. Taylor 51, G. R. Cowdrey 91; R. E. Bryson five for 39); Surrey 250 for seven (50 overs) (D. J. Bicknell 40, D. M. Ward 47, A. D. Brown 78, A. W. Smith 40 not out).

At Hove, September 5. Sussex won by 15 runs. Toss: Sussex. Sussex 237 (49.3 overs) (J. W. Hall 44, F. D. Stephenson 62, A. P. Wells 79; M. Davies three for 38); Gloucestershire 222 (49.1 overs) (G. D. Hodgson 69, R. I. Dawson 42, J. T. C. Vaughan 35; F. D. Stephenson five for 36).

At Hove, September 6. **Final:** Kent beat Sussex 7-4 in a bowling contest, after the match was abandoned; each player bowled two balls at the unguarded stumps.

THE MINOR COUNTIES IN 1992

By MICHAEL BERRY and ROBERT BROOKE

Staffordshire and Devon enjoyed a monopoly on the 1992 Minor Counties season. They contested both finals, with Devon lifting the Holt Cup at Lord's in late August, and Staffordshire taking the Championship for the second successive season with a revenge win at Worcester just over a fortnight later. In doing so, Staffordshire, the 1991 double winners, joined an élite band of counties who have retained the title, and furthered their growing reputation as the new giants of the Minor Counties game.

An unusual aspect of **Staffordshire's** success was that rain seriously disrupted their programme, with six of their first seven Championship matches affected in one way or another. But then crushing wins in their final two fixtures against Lincolnshire and Bedfordshire banked them 45 crucial points. Their batting, traditionally strong, collected 27 bonus points out of a possible 36, and four of the remaining nine were lost to the elements when the opening day of the Norfolk match was washed out by the weather. Simon Myles, once of Warwickshire and Sussex, was a notable acquisition, particularly in the Holt Cup. In that competition Staffordshire produced some thrilling cricket, especially when beating Northumberland by one run in the quarter-final, in which Northumberland had a short run called off the penultimate ball. Paul Shaw, a left-hander, and opening batsman Ross Salmon were also eye-catching newcomers, Salmon scoring two unbeaten centuries, 100 not out and 102 not out, in the victory over Bedfordshire. Steve Dean made 675 runs at an average of 96.42 but was denied the Wilfred Rhodes Trophy by a technicality. He failed to figure in the official batting averages under a new ruling that set the yardstick for qualification at eight completed innings. Dean was one short. Nigel Hackett contributed to Staffordshire's end-of-season flourish with match figures of 12 for 79 against Lincolnshire.

Continued over

MINOR COUNTIES CHAMPIONSHIP, 1992

Eastern Division	M	W	L	D	NR	Bonus Points Batting	Bonus Points Bowling	Total Points
Staffordshire^{NW}	9	3	0	4	2*	27	21	101
Hertfordshire^{NW}	9	3	0	6	0	13	25	86
Suffolk^{NW}	9	2	1	5	1	14	19	70
Norfolk^{NW}	9	2	1	5	1	9	21	67
Buckinghamshire^{NW}	9	2	2	5	0	15	17	64
Cumberland	9	1	2	6	0	20	28	64
Lincolnshire	9	1	2	6	0	18	27	61
Cambridgeshire	9	1	1	7	0	10	25	51
Northumberland	9	1	3	5	0	13	18	47
Bedfordshire	9	0	4	5	0	11	20	31

Western Division	M	W	L	D	NR	Bonus Points Batting	Bonus Points Bowling	Total Points
Devon^{NW}	9	3	1	3	2	24	15	97
Oxfordshire^{NW}	9	3	0	3	3	10	12	85
Cheshire^{NW}	9	2	4	2	1	18	25	80
Wiltshire^{NW}	9	2	1	6	0	20	25	77
Wales^{NW}	9	2	1	5	1	12	26	75
Dorset^{NW}	9	3	1	5	0	4	22	74
Shropshire^{NW}	9	2	2	4	1	12	25	74
Berkshire	9	2	2	5	0	12	19	63
Herefordshire	9	1	2	6	0	12	24	52
Cornwall	9	0	6	3	0	9	15	24

* *Signifies points for one No Result match included in bonus-point columns.*

Win = 16 pts. No result (including abandoned games) = 5 pts.

^{NW} *Denotes qualified for NatWest Bank Trophy in 1993.*

Hertfordshire finished second behind Staffordshire, and their success could again be attributed to their bowlers, whose value was best demonstrated in the last-over wins against Buckinghamshire and Northumberland. David Surridge, their captain, took 28 wickets, which included the season's solitary hat-trick in the fixture with Cumberland at Millom, and Andy Needham 25. Although the hard-hitting Martin James scored 576 runs, and Giles Buchanan made 454, Hertfordshire's batting was brittle and lacked depth.

Ray East, the former Essex spin bowler, took on the captaincy of **Suffolk** at the age of 44, and they emerged as dark horses for the title after early victories over Cumberland and Lincolnshire. Phil Caley, with 663 runs, was the major individual success, although Craig Miller, a pace bowler recruited from Essex, showed great promise in collecting 26 Championship wickets. Simon Clements (539 runs) and Andy Squire (412) performed with great credit, and Jon Zagni, recalled for the first time since 1989 in the final fixture of the season against Norfolk at Copdock, took seven for 108 in the first innings.

Norfolk mustered only nine batting bonus points, but still managed to qualify for the 1993 NatWest Trophy in fourth place in the table. Rodney Bunting, back with his native county after four years with Sussex, enjoyed a successful summer in taking 30 wickets, and the always-productive Ray Kingshott, a slow left-armer, picked up 28. Carl Rogers was leading run-scorer with 513 runs, with Richard Farrow (486) and Steve Plumb (468) not far behind.

Buckinghamshire's enforced switch to the Eastern Division, necessitated by the departure of Durham and the subsequent election of Herefordshire into the Western Division, looked like being an unqualified flop for most of the season. But 27 points from their final two fixtures lifted them from ninth place to fifth to win them a place in the 1993 NatWest Trophy. Buckinghamshire had a new skipper in Gary Black, but injury and availability problems hampered his team selection, with Buckinghamshire using 23 players during the season. No batsman passed 500 runs, but Simon Shearman (488) got close, and Jason Harrison made 310 in only four appearances. Tim Scriven scored 445 runs and also finished with 26 wickets.

Cumberland had a new captain in Simon Dutton, who had replaced the successful John Moyes. But despite a healthy haul of 48 bonus points, Cumberland managed just one win and missed out on NatWest Trophy qualification. Steve Sharp (533) and Chris Stockdale (526) were their most successful batsmen, and Phil Robinson, formerly of Yorkshire, made 361 runs in five matches before being tempted away by Leicestershire. Malcolm Woods was Cumberland's leading bowler with 23 victims.

Jim Love led by example in his final season as captain of **Lincolnshire**. Love, who has taken up the full-time position of coach to the Scottish Cricket Association, made 733 runs, and also returned career-best bowling of six for 18 against Norfolk. Mark Fell gave Love solid support with 567 runs, and James Robinson amassed 477 in his first season. But the Lincolnshire bowling was seldom at full strength, with Simon Dennis, the former Yorkshire and Glamorgan left-armer, failing to live up to expectations. David Christmas claimed 21 wickets, but missed three matches due to injury.

Cambridgeshire, despite the recruitment of Bruce Roberts from Derbyshire and Adrian Pierson, formerly of Warwickshire, chalked up only one Championship win. Nigel Gadsby, their captain, hit 758 runs and Pierson was leading wicket-taker with 29. The usually prolific Stuart Turner was hampered by injury and finished with only 14 wickets from five matches.

Northumberland began the season with high hopes. They had taken on Peter Willey as their professional, and also benefited from Durham's expansive recruitment drive to pick up both Paul Burn and Ian Conn, two proven Minor Counties players who had been released by their new first-class neighbours. But Burn played just three Championship matches, Willey struggled to come to terms with the two-day game and Northumberland languished in ninth place in the table. Graeme Morris dominated their batting with 818 runs, and Oliver Youll, son of former Northumberland player Mike, made an encouraging start to his county career with 191 runs in four matches. Peter Graham, their 37-year-old seam bowler, took 26 wickets.

Wooden spoonists for the second successive season were **Bedfordshire**, and another disappointing year ended with captain John Wake calling it a day. Bedfordshire signed up a handful of newcomers, the most notable of whom were Chris Bullen of Surrey and Gareth Smith, the former Northamptonshire and Warwickshire left-arm paceman. Yet they still had to call up both Brian Marvin, for the first time since 1986, and Trevor Thomas, 44, out of semi-retirement. Bullen took 25 wickets, but the Bedfordshire batting was diffident. Ray Swann (475), Neil Folland (401) and David Clarke, a newcomer who scored 304 runs in five matches, supplied most of their runs.

Devon won their opening three Championship fixtures to take firm control of the Western Division. Although they never managed to win again, they had established an unassailable platform. Nick Folland, who had replaced Hiley Edwards as captain, scored 734 to top the Championship batting averages on the eight completed innings ruling and collect the Wilfred Rhodes Trophy. His form for the England Amateur XI and the Minor Counties Representative side was also impressive, and he will take up a two-year contract with Somerset in 1993. Nick Gaywood, a 29-year-old teacher who commuted to Devon's games from Sheffield, also had a golden summer, scoring 933 runs in the Championship and 167 in the Holt Cup. A left-hander, like Folland, he became only the fourth player in 14 years to aggregate over 1,000 runs in a Minor Counties season. The forceful Andy Pugh also made 495 runs, while Peter Roebuck, the former Somerset captain, joined Devon in June, but after 205 runs and 15 wickets in four Championship matches, a freak fielding accident against Berkshire ended his involvement for the season with a broken ankle.

Oxfordshire, the 1991 Western Division winners, made a concerted effort to catch Devon at the top, but the weather became their biggest enemy, with almost 22 hours lost to rain in their final four fixtures. The Oxfordshire bowling was their trump card, with Keith Arnold (23), Ian Curtis (27) and Rupert Evans (22) sharing the workload to maximum effect. Arnold also won the Gold Award when the Minor Counties Representative side beat Sussex at Marlow in the Benson and Hedges Cup. Of the Oxfordshire batsmen, Stuart Waterton, with 756 runs, and David Wise, who made 636, both scored freely.

The first-class pedigree of Ian Cockbain and Geoff Miller was the combination that earned **Cheshire** a place in the NatWest Trophy again. Cockbain, their captain, piled up 755 runs, while Miller and John O'Brien took 91 wickets between them. Miller collected 49 of them to win the Frank Edwards Trophy, including nine in the victory over Cornwall, and a match analysis of ten for 77 in the defeat by Dorset. Steve Crawley made 530 runs and Paul Simmonite, an opening batsman, scored 93 and 108 in his first two innings for the county. But the Cheshire batting suffered a series of alarming collapses.

Wiltshire had a successful season under Kevin Foyle, who had taken over the captaincy following the retirement of the long-serving Brian White. Foyle (467) and Lawrence Smith (533) were the mainstays of a solid batting line-up, and Stephen Thorpe announced his return to Minor Counties cricket at the age of 41 with a return of seven for 47 against Shropshire. Thorpe, who had played for Devon between 1976 and 1978, finished with 19 wickets.

Wales finished among the NatWest Trophy qualifiers for the first time since entering the Championship in 1988. They signed John Derrick, the former Glamorgan all-rounder, and his presence with both bat and ball was the key factor behind a major improvement. Derrick scored 551 runs, and took 23 wickets. Tony Smith (26 wickets) and Aamir Ikram, a leg-spinner who collected 19 victims in five games, also played important roles. They combined to take all ten wickets when Wales dismissed Shropshire for 114 at Colwyn Bay to clinch a 166-run triumph. Andy Puddle, their captain and an ever-present for Wales since they joined Minor Counties cricket, passed 2,000 Championship runs in the final fixture against Devon, in what was his 44th consecutive appearance.

Sean Walbridge and Julian Shackleton bowled **Dorset** into the 1993 NatWest Trophy. Walbridge, a slow left-armer, collected 41 victims, and Shackleton, son of former England man Derek, removed 32 opposition batsmen. Dorset's three victories owed much to Walbridge and Shackleton, in particular a remarkable game against Cheshire at Dorchester that produced scores of 154, 116, 76 and 80. Dorset's meagre return of batting points, just

four, was in contrast to the record-breaking partnership between Graeme Calway and Tim
Richings against Hampshire in the NatWest Trophy. Their second-wicket stand of 180 was
a Minor Counties record in the competition. Richings, in his début season, led the Dorset
run-scoring with 489.

Shropshire turned to Alvin Kallicharran, the former West Indian Test player who is
now England-qualified, when Paul Pridgeon, their professional, departed part way into
his second season. Kallicharran played the final three matches, scored 193 runs and was
voted an instant success. Mark Davies, who replaces John Foster as captain for 1993,
accumulated 561 runs, but Tony Parton was top scorer with 571. However, Shropshire
scored their runs far too slowly to make any serious impact. Adam Byram, a slow left-
armer, continued his progress with 31 wickets, but Geoff Edmunds was hampered by injury
and managed only 16.

Berkshire finished in the bottom half of the Western Division table for the first time since
1986. David Mercer piled up 806 runs, but the usually prodigious Martin Lickley made only
three appearances. David Hartley, a leg-spinner, claimed 32 wickets and Peter Lewington,
the off-spinner, took 23.

Herefordshire's historic entry into Minor Counties cricket began like a dream. They
opened the season by beating Shropshire in the Holt Cup, and then completed a thrilling
last-ball victory over Wales in their first Championship fixture. But that proved the extent
of their success where results were concerned, although the learning curve continued to go
in an upwards direction. Richard Skyrme, their captain, was one of only two ever-presents
during an experimental season and he emerged as leading run-scorer with 466. Paul Bent,
formerly of Worcestershire, claimed 20 wickets.

Only **Cornwall** finished below Herefordshire, but they were 28 points adrift as they
became the unwilling recipients of the Western Division wooden spoon for the eighth time
in ten years. They suffered six defeats in nine matches, but Simon Wherry had a memorable
summer with the bat. His 751 runs included an unbeaten 172 not out, the highest of the
season, against Devon. David Toseland, the off-spinner, took 20 wickets in his 20th season
to pass the milestone of 400 Championship victims in his career.

CHAMPIONSHIP FINAL

DEVON v STAFFORDSHIRE

At Worcester, September 13, 14. Staffordshire won by 79 runs. Toss: Devon. Staffordshire
retained the Championship for a second season with an emphatic victory over Devon, their
conquerors in the final of the Holt Cup. Rain prevented any play on the Sunday, and
Staffordshire were easy winners on the reserve day. Their innings embraced three different
segments. Early ascendancy at 74 for one in the 20th over was briefly disturbed by the loss
of three wickets in four overs, the slow left-arm deliveries of Allin doing most to curb the
Midland county's solid start on a wicket of variable bounce. But Archer and Newman then
added 81 runs in 23 overs. Devon, reduced to ten batsmen after Donohue broke his arm
when fielding, slumped from 48 for two to 91 for six, and only Folland's defiant 73 provided
any sort of resistance.

Staffordshire

S. J. Dean c Donohue b Allin	30	†M. I. Humphries not out		17
D. Cartledge c Folland b White	36	R. A. Spiers run out		1
D. A. Banks c Donohue b Allin	11	L-b 11, w 3, n-b 1		15
S. D. Myles lbw b Dawson	14			
A. J. Dutton c Pritchard b Allin	2	1/58 2/74 3/91	(8 wkts, 55 overs)	201
*N. J. Archer c White b Woodman	34	4/97 5/97 6/178		
P. G. Newman b Donohue	41	7/200 8/201		

N. P. Hackett and I. S. Worthington did not bat.

Bowling: Donohue 10.1–2–47–1; Woodman 10.5–1–43–1; Le Fleming 8–0–22–0; Allin
11–4–15–3; White 4–0–16–1; Dawson 11–2–47–1.

Devon

N. R. Gaywood b Hackett	1	M. C. Woodman lbw b Newman	0
R. I. Dawson c Dean b Newman	0	†C. S. Pritchard not out	0
*N. A. Folland b Newman	73	K. Donohue absent injured	
A. J. Pugh c Humphries b Worthington	8		
S. M. Willis b Worthington	0	L-b 8, w 6, n-b 5	19
G. W. White lbw b Myles	10		
O. F. A. Le Fleming c Worthington b Myles	8	1/1 2/6 3/48 (42.2 overs) 122
A. W. Allin b Spiers	3	4/48 5/66 6/91
		7/106 8/113 9/122

Bowling: Newman 6.2–1–12–3; Hackett 8–3–20–1; Worthington 8–3–21–2; Spiers 7–2–17–1; Myles 6–0–20–2; Dutton 7–0–24–0.

Umpires: R. K. Curtis and D. J. Halfyard.

HOLT CUP FINAL

DEVON v STAFFORDSHIRE

At Lord's, August 26, 27. Devon won by four wickets. Toss: Devon. Giles White, a 20-year-old Loughborough University student on the Somerset staff, steered Devon to only their second major honour in 93 years in a Holt Cup final that spilt into a second day. Devon, chasing 218, were uneasily placed at 54 for two off 23.3 overs when rain and bad light intervened. They subsided to 94 for four in the 35th over the following morning, but then White and Folland pulled them back into the picture with a fifth-wicket partnership of 58. White finished with 79 not out off 65 balls, hitting the winning boundary with five balls to spare. Half-centuries from Dean and Humphries had accounted for just about half of the Staffordshire total after they had been put in to bat on a damp pitch, Humphries facing just 30 deliveries for his spectacular 50 not out.

Staffordshire

S. J. Dean b Donohue	58	†M. I. Humphries not out	50
D. Cartledge lbw b Dawson	20	R. A. Spiers not out	9
R. D. Salmon c Woodman b Tierney	15	B 1, l-b 6, w 11, n-b 1	19
S. D. Myles c Pritchard b Woodman	25		
A. J. Dutton not out	2	1/47 2/75 3/127 (7 wkts, 55 overs) 217
*N. J. Archer c Pritchard b Donohue	5	4/131 5/138
P. G. Newman c Folland b Donohue	14	6/140 7/192

R. J. Dyer and N. P. Hackett did not bat.

Bowling: Donohue 11–1–48–3; Woodman 11–1–51–1; Dawson 10–2–31–1; White 4–0–23–0; Tierney 8–0–29–1; Allin 11–1–28–0.

Devon

N. R. Gaywood c Dean b Hackett	18	J. K. Tierney b Hackett	25
S. M. Willis lbw b Hackett	8	K. Donohue not out	0
*N. A. Folland run out	47	L-b 11, w 8	19
A. J. Pugh st Humphries b Dyer	21		
R. I. Dawson b Dyer	4	1/24 2/38 3/88 (6 wkts, 54.1 overs) 221
G. W. White not out	79	4/94 5/152 6/213

A. W. Allin, M. C. Woodman and †C. S. Pritchard did not bat.

Bowling: Newman 10.1–0–62–0; Hackett 11–3–41–3; Dutton 11–2–24–0; Spiers 11–2–31–0; Dyer 11–1–52–2.

Umpires: P. Adams and K. Bray.

*In the averages that follow, * against a score signifies not out, * against a name signifies the captain and † signifies a wicket-keeper.*

BEDFORDSHIRE

Secretary – D. J. F. Hoare, 5 Brecon Way, Bedford MK41 8DF.
Telephone: 0234-266648

Matches 9: Lost – Buckinghamshire, Lincolnshire, Norfolk, Staffordshire. Drawn – Cambridge-shire, Cumberland, Hertfordshire, Northumberland, Suffolk.

Batting Averages

	M	I	NO	R	HS	100s	50s	Avge
D. R. Clarke	5	9	2	304	108*	1	1	43.42
R. Swann	8	15	0	475	107	2	1	31.66
N. G. Folland	8	15	1	401	62	0	2	28.64
C. J. Birt	6	11	1	275	58	0	1	27.50
P. D. B. Hoare.......	8	15	4	300	88	0	2	27.27
Z. A. Sher	3	6	1	128	55	0	1	25.60
C. K. Bullen.........	9	15	2	310	120	1	0	23.84
R. N. Dalton	4	7	0	150	70	0	1	21.42
†M. R. Gouldstone ...	7	13	0	241	72	0	1	18.53
†G. D. Sandford	7	8	4	60	23	0	0	15.00
*J. R. Wake.........	8	11	2	82	30	0	0	9.11
G. Smith	5	7	2	37	24	0	0	7.40
K. P. Sheeraz........	7	10	4	27	7*	0	0	4.50

Played in five matches: P. A. Owen 0*, 0, 0*. Played in two matches: K. A. Davis 12, 0, 2, 9; I. M. Henderson 15*, 5, 0; B. L. Marvin 5*, 8*. Played in one match: R. G. Blair 65, 8; C. J. Good 1; T. C. Thomas 10, 33.

Bowling Averages

	O	M	R	W	BB	5W/i	Avge
C. K. Bullen.........	236.2	80	675	25	6-22	2	27.00
P. A. Owen	136.2	32	472	12	3-46	0	39.33
J. R. Wake	154.5	39	482	12	3-18	0	40.16
K. P. Sheeraz........	169.5	41	549	12	3-55	0	45.75

Also bowled: D. R. Clarke 1-0-6-0; R. N. Dalton 35-2-167-2; K. A. Davis 10-1-55-0; N. G. Folland 0.4-0-10-0; M. R. Gouldstone 1-0-4-0; I. M. Henderson 35-8-109-3; P. D. B. Hoare 25-4-68-2; B. L. Marvin 40-10-100-4; Z. A. Sher 44-6-209-2; G. Smith 118.2-22-433-8; R. Swann 54.1-19-131-5.

BERKSHIRE

Secretary – C. M. S. Crombie, Orchard Cottage, Waltham St Lawrence, Reading, Berkshire RG10 OJH. Telephone 0734-343387 (home); 0491-578555 (business)

Matches 9: Won – Cheshire, Herefordshire. Lost – Oxfordshire, Wiltshire. Drawn – Cornwall, Devon, Dorset, Shropshire, Wales.

Batting Averages

	M	I	NO	R	HS	100s	50s	Avge
D. J. M. Mercer	9	18	1	806	105	2	6	47.41
G. E. Loveday	8	16	0	475	77	0	3	29.68
D. A. Shaw	8	16	1	416	73	0	4	27.73
P. J. Oxley	9	18	7	265	43	0	0	24.09
*M. L. Simmons	7	14	0	309	66	0	1	22.07
N. A. Fusedale	4	7	1	121	36*	0	0	20.16
†N. D. J. Cartmell ...	9	18	6	216	64	0	1	18.00
M. G. Lickley	3	6	0	93	39	0	0	15.50
J. K. Barrow	7	10	2	118	34	0	0	14.75
M. G. Stear	4	7	1	65	26	0	0	10.83
D. J. B. Hartley	8	11	2	91	17	0	0	10.11
K. S. Murray	4	8	0	75	33	0	0	9.37
J. H. Jones	9	7	4	14	4*	0	0	4.66

Played in eight matches: P. J. Lewington 0, 8*, 3*, 0. Played in two matches: T. P. J. Dodd 11, 4, 14, 8.

Bowling Averages

	O	M	R	W	BB	5W/i	Avge
N. A. Fusedale	87.5	21	296	13	5-84	1	22.76
D. J. B. Hartley	186.5	25	799	32	6-54	2	24.96
P. J. Lewington	254	73	661	23	4-39	0	28.73
J. H. Jones	121	30	362	12	2-12	0	30.16
J. K. Barrow	120	26	452	11	2-8	0	41.09
P. J. Oxley	75.2	9	278	6	2-37	0	46.33

Also bowled: T. P. J. Dodd 10–2–30–1; M. G. Lickley 7–1–26–0; D. J. M. Mercer 10–0–92–0; D. A. Shaw 6–0–27–0; M. L. Simmons 6–0–62–1; M. G. Stear 37–6–140–3.

BUCKINGHAMSHIRE

Secretary – S. J. Tomlin, Orchardleigh Cottage, Bigfrith Lane, Cookham Dean, Berkshire SL6 9PH. Telephone: 0628-482202 (home); 06285-24922 (business)

Matches 9: Won – Bedfordshire, Cumberland. Lost – Cambridgeshire, Hertfordshire. Drawn – Lincolnshire, Norfolk, Northumberland, Staffordshire, Suffolk.

Batting Averages

	M	I	NO	R	HS	100s	50s	Avge
J. C. Harrison	4	7	1	310	90*	0	1	51.66
S. M. Shearman	9	17	6	488	75*	0	3	44.36
M. J. Roberts	5	9	0	351	78	0	4	39.00
T. J. A. Scriven	9	15	1	445	71*	0	4	31.78
S. Burrow	6	11	1	208	51	0	1	20.80
B. S. Percy	5	9	1	156	50	0	1	19.50
*G. R. Black	9	15	1	256	64	0	1	18.28
†T. P. Russell........	9	10	5	86	16*	0	0	17.20
S. J. Noyes	3	6	0	68	28	0	0	11.33
C. D. Booden	9	7	5	22	10*	0	0	11.00
T. J. Barry	9	15	2	119	34	0	0	9.15

Played in three matches: P. G. Roshier 10, 6*, 4. Played in two matches: R. R. Baigent 65, 15, 20, 30; J. N. B. Bovill 12*, 3*; S. J. Edwards 2, 2; N. W. Farrow 12, 9, 0, 11; N. G. Hames 15, 0, 20, 13; A. R. Harwood 62, 36, 36, 1; R. B. Hurd 7*, 23, 1, 4; S. A. Sylvester 13, 4. Played in one match: N. Farnon 6, 23; S. G. Lynch 12, 1; D. J. Porter 2.

Bowling Averages

	O	M	R	W	BB	5W/i	Avge
T. J. A. Scriven	185.1	39	624	26	5-69	1	24.00
T. J. Barry	138.2	21	512	16	4-42	0	32.00

Also bowled: R. R. Baigent 0.2–0–2–0; G. R. Black 59–10–287–7; C. D. Booden 147.1–33–431–8; J. N. B. Bovill 28.4–5–80–9; S. Burrow 131.3–25–355–9; S. J. Edwards 34–8–101–3; N. Farnon 9–3–23–0; J. C. Harrison 31–4–114–5; S. G. Lynch 7–1–22–0; B. S. Percy 9–2–32–0; D. J. Porter 8–0–53–0; M. J. Roberts 5–1–21–2; P. G. Roshier 71–21–232–6; S. M. Shearman 4–0–38–0; S. A. Sylvester 33–4–158–7.

CAMBRIDGESHIRE

Secretary – P. W. Gooden, The Redlands, Oakington Road, Cottenham, Cambridge CB4 4TW.   Telephone: 0954-50429

Matches 9: Won – Buckinghamshire. Lost – Cumberland. Drawn – Bedfordshire, Hertfordshire, Lincolnshire, Norfolk, Northumberland, Staffordshire, Suffolk.

Batting Averages

	M	I	NO	R	HS	100s	50s	Avge
*N. T. Gadsby	9	16	1	758	118	3	4	50.53
R. P. Merriman	4	7	1	300	107	1	2	50.00
S. C. Ecclestone	3	6	2	194	96*	0	2	48.50
D. P. Norman	9	15	5	420	85*	0	3	42.00
A. R. K. Pierson	9	9	4	203	46*	0	0	40.60
G. W. Ecclestone	9	17	2	489	83*	0	4	32.60
N. J. Adams	6	10	1	275	62	0	2	30.55
B. Roberts	7	13	4	237	63*	0	1	26.33
†M. W. C. Olley	8	8	3	91	21	0	0	18.20

Played in seven matches: Ajaz Akhtar 0, 0, 16*, 5; M. G. Stephenson 20*, 13*, 2*. Played in five matches: S. Turner 12, 5*. Played in three matches: T. C. Williams 6, 17*, 15, 0, 24. Played in two matches: A. M. Cade 20*, 0, 0; D. C. Collard 6, 4*, 15; R. A. Milne 1, 8; D. F. Ralf 0. Played in one match: D. W. S. Pimblett 2; T. S. Smith 26*; S. L. Williams 2; N. Mohammed and K. O. Thomas did not bat.

Bowling Averages

	O	M	R	W	BB	5W/i	Avge
M. G. Stephenson	108.4	15	352	17	5-27	1	20.70
S. Turner	141.2	37	346	14	4-79	0	24.71
Ajaz Akhtar	168.1	38	507	20	5-61	1	25.35
B. Roberts	120	23	358	13	4-39	0	27.53
A. R. K. Pierson	263.4	54	837	29	7-51	2	28.86

Also bowled: N. J. Adams 18–1–103–0; D. C. Collard 28.3–3–101–2; G. W. Ecclestone 7–2–32–0; S. C. Ecclestone 15–3–49–1; N. T. Gadsby 3–2–1–1; R. P. Merriman 14–3–72–1; D. P. Norman 2–1–2–0; D. F. Ralf 33–4–93–4; T. S. Smith 41–14–109–5; K. O. Thomas 26–4–93–2; T. C. Williams 48–4–188–1.

CHESHIRE

Secretary – J. B. Pickup, 2 Castle Street, Northwich, Cheshire CW8 1AB. Telephone: 0606-74970 (home); 0606-74301 (business)

Matches 9: Won – Cornwall, Shropshire. Lost – Berkshire, Devon, Dorset, Wales. Drawn – Herefordshire, Wiltshire. No result – Oxfordshire.

Batting Averages

	M	I	NO	R	HS	100s	50s	Avge
I. Cockbain	9	15	1	755	100*	1	7	53.92
T. J. Bostock	3	6	0	214	67	0	3	35.66
T. Crawley	9	16	1	530	125	1	2	35.33
G. K. Garner	4	6	3	85	36*	0	0	28.33
D. Bean	9	15	2	256	48	0	0	19.69
P. Berry	5	7	1	87	24	0	0	14.50
D. Gray	6	10	1	127	55	0	1	14.11
J. Hitchmough	5	8	1	98	30	0	0	14.00
G. Miller	9	9	4	67	18*	0	0	13.40
F. M. O'Brien	9	8	3	61	19*	0	0	12.20
T. C. M. Standing	9	9	2	61	26*	0	0	8.71
N. D. Peel	9	6	2	25	21	0	0	6.25

Played in six matches: J. Potts 4, 9, 36*, 1, 0. Played in three matches: R. G. Hignett 1, 0, 19, 0. Played in two matches: P. C. P. Simmonite 93, 108. Played in one match: R. Middlehurst 20*, 0; D. W. Varey 13*, 0.

Bowling Averages

	O	M	R	W	BB	5W/i	Avge
G. Miller	291	84	636	49	6-25	4	12.97
F. M. O'Brien	242	47	700	42	5-32	3	16.66
N. D. Peel	229.5	44	721	23	3-38	0	31.34
J. Potts	108	13	437	11	3-56	0	39.72

Also bowled: T. J. Bostock 5-2-14-0; S. T. Crawley 23-3-82-1; G. K. Garner 1-0-2-0; R. G. Hignett 2-0-6-1.

CORNWALL

Secretary – The Rev. Canon Kenneth Rogers, The Rectory, Priory Road, Bodmin, Cornwall PL31 2AB.   Telephone: 0208-73867

Matches 9: Lost – Cheshire, Devon, Dorset, Oxfordshire, Shropshire, Wiltshire. Drawn – Berkshire, Herefordshire, Wales.

Batting Averages

	M	I	NO	R	HS	100s	50s	Avge
S. Wherry	9	18	1	751	172*	1	4	44.17
R. T. Walton	7	13	2	398	127*	1	1	36.18
S. M. Williams	9	18	1	423	93	0	1	24.88
E. Nicolson	8	14	0	340	57	0	1	24.28
R. G. Furse	9	14	5	211	54	0	1	23.44
†D. J. Hollyoak	4	8	3	98	27*	0	0	19.60
J. P. Kent	6	10	2	141	49	0	0	17.62
S. Hooper	5	8	0	134	44	0	0	16.75
*G. G. Watts	8	12	4	102	25*	0	0	12.75
C. D. Libby	4	8	1	54	15	0	0	7.71
C. C. Lovell	4	6	0	29	10	0	0	4.83
D. A. Toseland	9	8	3	14	9	0	0	2.80

Played in five matches: R. M. Bell 1, 0, 0, 1. Played in four matches: †D. J. Rowe 10, 1*, 4*, 6. Played in two matches: K. Blackburn 26, 7, 59, 22; D. Pascoe 8, 21, 33, 4; S. Turner 3, 14*. Played in one match: M. Roberts 10, 0; G. Thomas 4, 0.

Bowling Averages

	O	M	R	W	BB	5W/i	Avge
R. G. Furse	157.5	30	551	17	7-75	1	32.41
G. G. Watts	158.2	25	500	11	4-41	0	45.45
D. A. Toseland	274.4	56	919	20	3-34	0	45.95

Also bowled: R. M. Bell 137.4–24–485–6; S. Hooper 1–1–0–0; J. P. Kent 91–23–300–7;
C. D. Libby 38.2–7–132–2; C. C. Lovell 68–6–322–6; D. Pascoe 7–2–43–0; G. Thomas
6–0–21–0; S. Turner 36–5–134–3; S. Wherry 1–0–2–0; S. M. Williams 1–1–0–0.

CUMBERLAND

Secretary – D. Lamb, 42 Croft Road, Carlisle, Cumbria CA3 9AG.
Telephone: 0228-23017

*Matches 9: Won – Cambridgeshire. Lost – Buckinghamshire, Suffolk. Drawn – Bedfordshire,
Hertfordshire, Lincolnshire, Norfolk, Northumberland, Staffordshire.*

Batting Averages

	M	I	NO	R	HS	100s	50s	Avge
S. Sharp	6	12	1	533	113*	2	1	48.45
P. E. Robinson	5	10	1	361	75	0	3	40.11
D. Pearson	4	8	1	265	130*	1	0	37.85
C. J. Stockdale	9	17	2	526	132*	1	2	35.06
B. W. Reidy	7	13	0	418	100	1	1	32.15
M. D. Woods	8	10	6	122	34*	0	0	30.50
*†S. M. Dutton	9	17	3	419	63	0	3	29.92
G. J. Clarke	4	6	0	151	41	0	0	25.16
D. Smith	3	6	0	147	38	0	0	24.50
S. James	6	12	3	167	48*	0	0	18.55
K. Sample	6	9	4	73	22*	0	0	14.60
C. R. Knight	4	8	0	110	48	0	0	13.75
M. G. Scothern	8	8	3	54	20	0	0	10.80
P. Beech	4	6	1	9	4*	0	0	1.80

Played in seven matches: D. J. Makinson 2*, 0, 5*, 6, 0*. Played in five matches:
R. Ellwood 1, 8*, 0, 1. Played in one match: M. Burns 44, 9; G. Fisher 1, 11; S. Moncaster
0, 11; S. Wall 45.

Bowling Averages

	O	M	R	W	BB	5W/i	Avge
B. W. Reidy	136.2	37	357	16	4-47	0	22.31
M. W. Woods	210	49	700	23	5-55	1	30.43
M. G. Scothern	176.1	24	637	20	3-32	0	31.85
K. Sample	122.2	21	424	13	4-70	0	32.61
D. J. Makinson	152.2	28	568	17	5-30	1	33.41
R. Ellwood	116	24	447	13	4-93	0	34.38

Also bowled: P. Beech 73.5–7–277–5; S. James 16–3–74–3; D. Smith 18–0–69–1; S. Wall
10.2–3–42–0.

DEVON

Secretary – G. R. Evans, Blueberry Haven, 20 Boucher Road,
Budleigh Salterton, Devon EX9 6JF. Telephone 0395-445216 (home);
0392-58406 (business). Fax: 0392-411697

*Matches 9: Won – Cheshire, Cornwall, Herefordshire. Lost – Dorset. Drawn – Berkshire,
Shropshire, Wiltshire. No result – Oxfordshire, Wales.*

Batting Averages

	M	I	NO	R	HS	100s	50s	Avge
*N. A. Folland	8	13	4	734	118*	2	6	81.55
N. R. Gaywood	8	13	1	933	125	3	7	77.75
A. J. Pugh	9	16	7	495	95*	0	3	55.00
S. M. Willis	9	12	1	370	80	0	4	33.63
P. M. Roebuck	4	7	0	205	137	1	0	29.28
D. A. Tall	6	8	1	194	67	0	1	27.71
G. W. White	6	7	1	111	28	0	0	18.50
M. C. Woodman	9	6	3	54	37	0	0	18.00
K. Donohue	6	7	3	64	18*	0	0	16.00

Played in nine matches: †C. S. Pritchard 2*, 0, 3, 5. Played in six matches: D. N. Butcher 3*, 0*, 1*. Played in four matches: T. W. Ward 7, 17, 0, 11*, 27. Played in three matches: O. F. A. Le Fleming 10*, 0*. Played in two matches: A. W. Allin 4*, 10; V. Chouhan 16; P. Handford 5, 2; J. K. Tierney 8, 3; J. Rhodes did not bat. Played in one match: G. Hill 0, 8*; K. G. Rice 4.

Bowling Averages

	O	M	R	W	BB	5W/i	Avge
P. M. Roebuck	100.4	26	213	15	3-10	0	14.20
T. W. Ward	52.1	9	170	10	4-20	0	17.00
D. N. Butcher	126.2	29	419	16	3-44	0	26.18
G. W. White	97.3	16	381	11	3-34	0	34.63
M. C. Woodman	158	29	460	10	2-9	0	46.00

Also bowled: A. W. Allin 43.3–11–123–4; V. Chouhan 44.4–8–172–5; K. Donohue 105–18–286–6; N. A. Folland 5–1–7–1; N. R. Gaywood 10–1–49–0; P. Handford 24–7–77–0; O. F. A. Le Fleming 51–6–137–7; J. Rhodes 43–6–192–3; K. G. Rice 24–5–104–3; D. A. Tall 20.2–10.2–4; J. K. Tierney 19–7–42–6.

DORSET

Secretary – K. H. House, The Barn, Higher Farm, Bagber Common, Sturminster Newton, Dorset DT10 2HB.   Telephone: 0258-73394

Matches 9: Won – Cheshire, Cornwall, Devon. Lost – Shropshire. Drawn – Berkshire, Herefordshire, Oxfordshire, Wales, Wiltshire.

Batting Averages

	M	I	NO	R	HS	100s	50s	Avge
†G. D. Reynolds	7	12	3	477	156*	1	2	53.00
J. A. Claughton	6	12	2	295	81*	0	2	29.50
J. H. Shackleton	8	9	4	136	37*	0	0	27.20
T. W. Richings	9	18	0	489	99	0	3	27.16
J. J. E. Hardy	9	17	4	331	108*	1	0	25.46
N. R. Taylor	5	9	3	144	51*	0	1	24.00
S. W. D. Rintoul	3	6	1	106	37	0	0	21.20
A. Willows	8	12	2	152	47	0	0	15.20
G. S. Calway	6	12	1	164	61	0	1	14.90
*V. B. Lewis	9	14	2	165	35*	0	0	13.75
R. A. Pyman	6	8	1	81	21	0	0	11.57
O. T. Parkin	7	8	2	52	16	0	0	8.66
S. R. Walbridge	9	8	3	17	10	0	0	3.40

Played in two matches: †S. M. Fitzgerald 12, 7*. Played in one match: R. V. Morgan 16; P. A. Norris 8; D. J. Pepperell 5, 6; P. L. Garlick and F. L. Stewart did not bat.

Bowling Averages

	O	M	R	W	BB	5W/i	Avge
S. R. Walbridge......	251.4	72	658	41	5-34	2	16.04
J. H. Shackleton	250.2	61	653	32	7-57	3	20.40
A. Willows	99	19	339	16	4-59	0	21.18
N. R. Taylor	103.5	19	325	11	3-47	0	29.54
O. T. Parkin........	135.3	32	366	12	3-30	0	30.50

Also bowled: G. S. Calway 29–11–62–4; P. L. Garlick 24.2–6–58–6; P. A. Norris 4–0–20–0; R. A. Pyman 68.5–24–205–2.

HEREFORDSHIRE

Secretary – P. Sykes, The Mews House, Mordiford,
Herefordshire HR1 4LN.   Telephone: 0432-870491 (home);
0432-382684 (business)

*Matches 9: Won – Wales. Lost – Berkshire, Devon. Drawn – Cheshire, Cornwall, Dorset,
Oxfordshire, Shropshire, Wiltshire.*

Batting Averages

	M	I	NO	R	HS	100s	50s	Avge
D. J. M. Martindale ..	3	6	1	287	129*	1	1	57.40
*R. P. Skyrme	9	18	6	466	78*	0	4	38.83
J. W. D. Leighton	7	14	3	387	76	0	3	35.18
M. F. D. Robinson ...	6	10	3	228	73*	0	3	32.57
R. Cox	3	6	0	147	96	0	1	24.50
H. V. Patel..........	6	12	1	268	124*	1	1	24.36
S. G. Watkins	5	10	0	222	70	0	2	22.20
M. C. Abberley	6	11	0	184	54	0	1	16.72
P. Bent	6	11	0	170	50	0	1	15.45
S. D. Verry..........	7	9	4	51	27	0	0	10.20
M. G. Fowles........	9	12	4	76	21	0	0	9.50
D. C. M. Robinson ..	7	6	3	11	9	0	0	3.66

Played in three matches: †R. Hall 5, 28, 51, 16; †D. J. Mokler 10*, 0, 0, 0*, 0; †J. M. Robinson 33, 0, 16, 0. Played in two matches: M. J. Bailey 23, 4, 25; S. M. Brogan 16, 15, 39; O. Chagar 16*, 24, 0*; †D. J. Griffiths 5, 5; N. M. Husbands 0, 0, 0; P. L. J. Sparrow 32, 13, 45*, 8. Played in one match: E. P. M. Holland 10*, 0; P. J. B. Hunt 8, 10; G. J. Lord 45, 36; P. Mirza did not bat.

Bowling Averages

	O	M	R	W	BB	5W/i	Avge
P. Bent	112.4	20	391	20	4-13	0	19.55
M. G. Fowles........	145.5	29	431	17	4-34	0	25.35
M. F. D. Robinson ...	114.1	16	391	10	3-57	0	39.10
D. C. M. Robinson ...	204	38	762	17	4-74	0	44.82

Also bowled: M. C. Abberley 5–0–13–2; M. J. Bailey 70–19–159–8; O. Chagar 48–9–121–3; R. Cox 1–0–5–0; E. P. M. Holland 20–2–85–1; P. J. B. Hunt 14–4–22–1; N. M. Husbands 31–4–128–5; J. W. D. Leighton 4–0–26–0; P. Mirza 32–6–89–5; R. P. Skyrme 14.1–3–53–1; S. D. Verry 81–11–296–4; S. G. Watkins 20–4–77–1.

HERTFORDSHIRE

Secretary – D. S. Dredge, "Trevellis", 38 Santers Lane, Potters Bar, Hertfordshire EN6 2BX.   Telephone: 0707-58377 (home); 071-359 3579 (business)

Matches 9: Won – Buckinghamshire, Norfolk, Northumberland. Drawn – Bedfordshire, Cambridgeshire, Cumberland, Lincolnshire, Staffordshire, Suffolk.

Batting Averages

	M	I	NO	R	HS	100s	50s	Avge
M. James	8	15	0	576	116	2	4	38.40
G. A. Buchanan	8	15	3	454	88	0	3	37.83
A. Needham	7	11	2	322	64*	0	3	35.77
C. N. Cavener	9	14	5	249	46*	0	0	27.66
N. J. Ilott	3	6	0	146	95	0	1	24.33
M. A. Everett	8	15	2	291	62	0	2	22.38
†J. D. Harvey	4	8	3	101	35	0	0	20.20
M. D. Dale	4	7	0	106	83	0	1	15.14
D. M. Cox	6	6	1	62	26	0	0	12.40
B. G. Evans	4	8	0	99	35	0	0	12.37
N. R. C. MacLaurin . .	4	8	0	81	25	0	0	10.12

Played in eight matches: *D. Surridge 4*, 0*, 6*, 2*. Played in four matches: P. A. Waterman 4, 1, 12, 10*, 0. Played in three matches: †P. A. Bashford 3*, 2, 1, 0; D. B. M. Fox 5, 7*, 0*, 5, 12*; M. D. Saxby 29, 67, 27, 95*, 14; D. M. Smith 0, 82, 14, 29, 24. Played in two matches: †G. J. Franks 3, 2, 13; N. Gilbert 4, 34, 45, 65*; G. A. R. Harris 0. Played in one match: R. Austin 2; J. H. W. Burns 3*; †D. G. C. Ligertwood 10, 1; M. J. Walshe 4.

Bowling Averages

	O	M	R	W	BB	5W/i	Avge
A. Needham	219.3	82	448	25	4-42	0	17.92
D. Surridge	212.1	51	521	28	5-43	1	18.60
P. A. Waterman	76	18	261	13	3-41	0	20.07
D. M. Cox	134.5	40	368	18	6-65	1	20.44
C. N. Cavener	114.2	19	385	15	6-32	1	25.66

Also bowled: M. A. Everett 28-8-70-1; J. H. W. Burns 8-1-37-1; D. B. M. Fox 62-6-245-7; G. A. R. Harris 40-11-119-3; J. D. Harvey 7-4-14-0; M. James 2-0-15-0; M. D. Saxby 9.2-4-17-1; D. M. Smith 62-16-167-9; M. J. Walshe 14.2-2-73-0.

LINCOLNSHIRE

Secretary – C. White, "Lyndonholme", Castle Terrace Road, Sleaford, Lincolnshire NG34 7QF.   Telephone: 0529-302341 (home); 0529-302181 (business)

Matches 9: Won – Bedfordshire. Lost – Staffordshire, Suffolk. Drawn – Buckinghamshire, Cambridgeshire, Cumberland, Hertfordshire, Norfolk, Northumberland.

Batting Averages

	M	I	NO	R	HS	100s	50s	Avge
M. A. Fell	6	12	5	567	171*	1	3	81.00
*J. D. Love	8	15	4	733	114	1	6	66.63
D. B. Storer	7	14	2	482	119*	1	2	40.16
N. J. C. Gandon	6	11	2	300	101*	1	0	33.33
N. J. B. Illingworth...	8	9	5	129	33	0	0	32.25
J. R. Robinson.......	9	17	0	477	74	0	4	28.05
S. N. Warman	6	12	1	233	95	0	2	21.18
†N. P. Dobbs........	9	6	4	35	15	0	0	17.50
D. A. Christmas	6	8	3	87	36	0	0	17.40
P. R. Butler	5	10	2	86	22	0	0	10.75
P. Rawden	5	8	1	54	14	0	0	7.71
S. J. Dennis	5	6	1	37	18	0	0	7.40

Played in five matches: S. A. Bradford 2, 23*. Played in three matches: S. M. Brown 1, 2*; K. V. Tillison 0. Played in two matches: M. Irving 0; P. Metheringham 6, 15; P. D. McKeown did not bat. Played in one match: M. Blackburn 0, 7; I. Ward did not bat.

Bowling Averages

	O	M	R	W	BB	5W/i	Avge
D. A. Christmas	124.3	28	401	21	6-56	1	19.09
M. A. Fell	79.1	16	255	12	3-45	0	21.25
J. D. Love	117	28	340	15	6-18	1	22.66
S. A. Bradford	157.3	37	532	19	4-88	0	28.00
S. J. Dennis	137	27	436	15	4-50	0	29.06
N. J. B. Illingworth...	182.1	30	600	15	3-58	0	40.00

Also bowled: M. Blackburn 28-4-102-5; S. M. Brown 80.4-15-275-4; P. R. Butler 21-3-86-3; M. Irving 37-10-102-4; P. D. McKeown 53-15-130-6; P. Rawden 6-0-21-0; J. R. Robinson 8.2-0-26-1; K. V. Tillison 56.3-12-180-2; I. Ward 14-3-50-0.

NORFOLK

Secretary – S. J. Skinner, 27 Colkett Drive, Old Catton, Norwich NR6 7ND.   Telephone: 0603-485940 (home); 0603-660255 ext. 5542 (business)

Matches 9: Won – Bedfordshire, Northumberland. Lost – Hertfordshire. Drawn – Buckinghamshire, Cambridgeshire, Cumberland, Lincolnshire, Suffolk. No result – Staffordshire.

Batting Averages

	M	I	NO	R	HS	100s	50s	Avge
S. G. Plumb	7	12	0	468	78	0	4	39.00
R. D. E. Farrow	8	15	1	486	78	0	3	34.71
C. J. Rogers	9	16	0	513	89	0	2	32.06
N. Fox	7	12	4	216	35*	0	0	27.00
R. J. Finney	9	16	1	396	65	0	2	26.40
*D. R. Thomas	6	7	2	124	36	0	0	24.80
S. J. B. Livermore ...	6	9	3	147	34	0	0	24.50
R. A. Bunting	9	13	6	169	49*	0	0	24.14
S. B. Dixon	7	13	1	269	79	0	2	22.41

Played in nine matches: R. Kingshott 0, 1*, 0*, 12*, 12*. Played in four matches: J. C. M. Lewis 11, 16, 13*, 25; †D. M. Morrell 3; S. A. Rowe 6, 0, 22, 5. Played in three matches: †M. M. Jervis 7, 1, 14*, 14, 1*. Played in two matches: B. C. A. Ellison 0, 0, 2; †A. N. Payne 0*; C. C. Read 4, 0, 6. Played in one match: C. S. Carey 1*, 2.

Bowling Averages

	O	M	R	W	BB	5W/i	Avge
N. Fox	78.4	12	300	14	5-69	1	21.42
R. A. Bunting	213.1	39	658	30	5-34	2	21.93
S. G. Plumb	115	23	315	13	3-32	0	24.23
R. Kingshott	236.5	43	809	28	4-64	0	28.89

Also bowled: C. S. Carey 13–1–58–1; S. B. Dixon 6.1–0–84–2; B. C. A. Ellison 25–1–92–2; R. J. Finney 10–0–70–6; J. C. M. Lewis 72–16–236–7; C. C. Read 7–1–72–0; C. J. Rogers 9–1–35–0; S. A. Rowe 60–17–166–4; D. R. Thomas 31–5–112–0.

NORTHUMBERLAND

Secretary – A. B. Stephenson, Northumberland County Cricket Club, Osborne Avenue, Jesmond, Newcastle-upon-Tyne NE2 1JS.
Telephone: 091-281 2738

Matches 9: Won – Suffolk. Lost – Hertfordshire, Norfolk, Staffordshire. Drawn – Bedfordshire, Buckinghamshire, Cambridgeshire, Cumberland, Lincolnshire.

Batting Averages

	M	I	NO	R	HS	100s	50s	Avge
O. S. Youll	4	7	5	191	53*	0	1	95.50
G. R. Morris	8	16	0	818	106	1	7	51.12
P. Burn	3	6	0	196	95	0	2	32.66
J. A. Benn	7	14	0	363	71	0	3	25.92
M. J. Green	5	9	1	203	48	0	0	25.37
P. Willey	8	16	1	362	82	0	2	24.13
P. N. S. Dutton	8	16	3	306	80*	0	2	23.53
H. M. Sidney-Wilmot	4	8	1	155	40	0	0	22.14
S. Greensword	6	10	4	118	33*	0	0	19.66
I. E. Conn	8	7	3	77	25	0	0	19.25
*M. E. Younger	6	10	3	123	29	0	0	17.57
W. Falla	4	6	3	30	12	0	0	10.00
†M. S. Tiffin	4	8	1	45	14	0	0	6.42

Played in seven matches: P. C. Graham 2*, 6, 8*. Played in five matches: †P. J. Nicholson 2, 0, 6, 12, 4. Played in four matches: C. Stanley 1*, 0*. Played in three matches: G. Angus 1; R. A. Darling 19*, 16*. Played in one match: J. P. Barrett 72, 30; B. Storey 6.

Bowling Averages

	O	M	R	W	BB	5W/i	Avge
P. C. Graham	212.1	63	568	26	5-82	1	21.84
M. E. Younger	54	11	221	10	3-58	0	22.10
S. Greensword	107	29	291	10	4-21	0	29.10
I. E. Conn	177.3	44	508	16	6-39	1	31.75
P. Willey	186	39	590	17	3-53	0	34.70

Also bowled: G. Angus 48–1–212–7; J. P. Barrett 5–0–20–1; R. A. Darling 57–19–170–6; P. N. S. Dutton 35–4–155–5; W. Falla 59–6–244–4; C. Stanley 77.5–15–318–6; O. S. Youll 23–1–147–5.

OXFORDSHIRE

Secretary – J. E. O. Smith, 2 The Green, Horton-cum-Studley,
Oxford OX9 1AE.   Telephone: 086-735 687

Matches 9: Won – Berkshire, Cornwall, Wiltshire. Drawn – Dorset, Herefordshire, Wales.
No result – Cheshire, Devon, Shropshire.

Batting Averages

	M	I	NO	R	HS	100s	50s	Avge
†S. N. V. Waterton ...	9	15	3	756	110*	1	6	63.00
D. A. J. Wise.........	9	15	2	636	153*	2	2	48.92
J. S. Hartley.........	9	13	5	276	62	0	1	34.50
*P. J. Garner	9	10	3	239	66*	0	1	34.14
T. A. Lester	9	14	4	320	67*	0	3	32.00
S. V. Laudat.........	5	7	0	164	45	0	0	23.42
G. P. Savin	9	9	3	105	41	0	0	17.50

Played in nine matches: K. A. Arnold 20; I. J. Curtis 0*; R. A. Evans 11, 6*, 7*, 0, 25*.
Played in six matches: S. G. Joyner 5*, 25*. Played in three matches: P. M. Jobson 11,
4*, 11, 8. Played in two matches: M. C. Cannons 14*, 14*, 10; R. J. Cunliffe 36*, 33.

Bowling Averages

	O	M	R	W	BB	5W/i	Avge
K. A. Arnold	198.5	44	627	23	4-76	0	27.26
I. J. Curtis	208.5	29	756	27	5-45	2	28.00
S. G. Joyner.........	94	11	312	11	3-41	0	28.36
R. A. Evans	241.1	49	717	22	4-22	0	32.59

Also bowled: P. J. Garner 1–0–12–0; J. S. Hartley 8.3–1–31–0; S. V. Laudat
52.1–5–219–7; G. P. Savin 47–10–140–2.

SHROPSHIRE

Secretary – N. H. Birch, 8 Port Hill Close, Shrewsbury,
Shropshire SY3 8RR.   Telephone: 0743-233650

Matches 9: Won – Cornwall, Dorset. Lost – Cheshire, Wales. Drawn – Berkshire, Devon,
Herefordshire, Wiltshire. No result – Oxfordshire.

Batting Averages

	M	I	NO	R	HS	100s	50s	Avge
M. R. Davies	9	16	7	561	101*	1	3	62.33
T. Parton	9	17	3	571	101*	1	3	40.78
*J. Foster	7	13	2	369	71	0	3	33.54
G. J. Toogood	6	10	2	251	53	0	1	31.37
A. R. Williams.......	5	10	0	219	69	0	1	21.90
A. B. Byram.........	9	12	2	186	57*	0	1	18.60
†M. J. Davidson	9	11	2	111	49	0	0	12.33

Played in seven matches: A. S. Barnard 6, 12*, 5, 4*; P. A. Thomas 4, 17*, 4*. Played in
four matches: G. J. Byram 11*, 0, 2; G. Edmunds 0*, 0; J. B. R. Jones 38, 13, 44, 7, 17.
Played in three matches: C. P. Goodier 1*, 0, 2*, 2; G. L. Home 10, 0, 0, 8, 2; A. I.
Kallicharran 38, 35, 34*, 86. Played in two matches: J. V. Anders 4*; A. N. Johnson 1, 26,
4*; A. P. Pridgeon 16, 0; P. W. Trimby did not bat. Played in one match: A. D. L. Donald
2; J. S. Roberts 2*.

Bowling Averages

	O	M	R	W	BB	5W/i	Avge
G. Edmunds	130	39	353	16	6-59	1	22.06
G. J. Toogood	107.2	22	303	13	4-24	0	23.30
A. B. Byram	245.4	47	778	31	5-55	1	25.09
A. S. Barnard	138.5	33	357	12	3-24	0	29.75
P. A. Thomas	159.1	21	541	13	4-82	0	41.61

Also bowled: J. V. Anders 10-2-26-1; G. J. Byram 56-9-217-7; A. D. L. Donald 12-5-20-0; J. Foster 3-0-22-0; C. P. Goodier 69.4-14-237-7; A. I. Kallicharran 28-4-83-1; A. P. Pridgeon 52.1-9-141-5; J. S. Roberts 25.1-7-78-3; P. W. Trimby 2-0-13-0.

STAFFORDSHIRE

Secretary – W. S. Bourne, 10 The Pavement, Brewood, Staffordshire ST19 9BZ. Telephone: 0902-850325 (home); 0902-23038 (business)

Matches 9: Won – Bedfordshire, Lincolnshire, Northumberland. Drawn – Buckinghamshire, Cambridgeshire, Cumberland, Hertfordshire. No result – Norfolk, Suffolk.

Batting Averages

	M	I	NO	R	HS	100s	50s	Avge
S. J. Dean	6	9	2	675	124	4	2	96.42
J. A. Waterhouse	7	9	4	359	91*	0	2	71.80
D. Cartledge	6	9	1	336	120*	1	1	42.00
A. D. Hobson	5	6	2	154	47*	0	0	38.50
S. D. Myles	9	12	2	279	56	0	2	27.90
A. J. Dutton	7	6	1	51	21	0	0	10.20

Played in nine matches: †M. I. Humphries 8, 19*, 32*, 4. Played in eight matches: P. G. Newman 22*, 24*, 16. Played in seven matches: *N. J. Archer 0*, 31*, 21*, 75*, 3, 32*. Played in six matches: N. P. Hackett and D. K. Page did not bat. Played in five matches: R. A. Spiers 19*, 17*. Played in four matches: P. K. Shaw 64*, 7, 68*, 20, 8. Played in three matches: R. D. Salmon 70, 19, 47, 100*, 102*. Played in two matches: D. A. Banks 55*, 2, 5, 21; D. C. Blank and I. S. Worthington did not bat. Played in one match: J. P. Addison 17; A. P. Bryan, R. J. Dyer, T. Heap and T. S. Tweats did not bat.

Bowling Averages

	O	M	R	W	BB	5W/i	Avge
N. P. Hackett	128.4	33	351	24	7-50	2	14.62
A. J. Dutton	59	13	218	11	5-49	1	19.81
D. K. Page	118.4	21	374	12	4-64	0	31.16
P. G. Newman	213	55	520	16	4-57	0	32.50
R. A. Spiers	146	41	424	12	4-48	0	35.33

Also bowled: N. J. Archer 2-0-9-0; D. C. Blank 54-14-114-6; A. P. Bryan 19-1-62-2; D. Cartledge 47-11-135-5; S. J. Dean 1-1-0-0; R. J. Dyer 27.1-12-58-6; T. Heap 17-3-43-2; M. I. Humphries 2-0-18-0; S. D. Myles 48-9-168-4; J. A. Waterhouse 1-0-17-0; I. S. Worthington 29-7-77-2.

SUFFOLK

Secretary – Toby Pound, 94 Henley Road, Ipswich IP1 4NJ.
Telephone: 0473-213288 (home); 0473-232121 (business)

Matches 9: Won – Cumberland, Lincolnshire. Lost – Northumberland. Drawn – Bedfordshire, Buckinghamshire, Cambridgeshire, Hertfordshire, Norfolk. No result – Staffordshire.

Batting Averages

	M	I	NO	R	HS	100s	50s	Avge
P. J. Caley	9	16	2	663	100	1	3	47.35
A. J. Squire	6	12	1	412	139	1	2	37.45
S. M. Clements	9	16	1	539	84	0	4	35.93
M. S. A. McEvoy	4	7	3	121	41*	0	0	30.25
I. D. Graham........	7	10	5	141	52*	0	1	28.20
R. R. Gregg	9	15	1	346	90	0	2	24.71
*R. E. East	9	11	4	131	48	0	0	18.71
M. J. Peck	9	16	2	261	38*	0	0	18.64
†S. J. Halliday	8	15	1	233	64	0	1	16.64
C. A. Miller	9	11	5	87	37*	0	0	14.50

Played in six matches: †A. D. Brown 1*, 2*, 1*, 1. Played in four matches: A. K. Golding 1, 2, 51, 0, 3*. Played in two matches: R. Catley 12, 2. Played in one match: R. M. Campbell 0, 6; A. Donner 2*; J. W. Edrich 18, 1; N. J. Gregory 0, 4; S. Leggatt 0*; D. Shorten 18, 5; J. J. Zagni 5*, 3; M. D. Bailey did not bat.

Bowling Averages

	O	M	R	W	BB	5W/i	Avge
R. E. East	91.4	18	245	12	3-17	0	20.41
C. A. Miller	154.5	16	605	26	6-80	1	23.26
I. D. Graham........	126	20	491	14	4-67	0	35.07
A. K. Golding	144	26	473	11	3-71	0	43.00
R. R. Gregg	177.5	25	747	15	2-41	0	49.80

Also bowled: M. D. Bailey 9-4-19-1; P. J. Caley 45-7-216-2; A. Donner 6-0-25-0; S. Leggatt 17-4-44-0; J. J. Zagni 25.1-2-143-8.

WALES MINOR COUNTIES

Secretary – Bill Edwards, 59A King Edward Road, Swansea SA1 4LN.
Telephone: 0792-462233

Matches 9: Won – Cheshire, Shropshire. Lost – Herefordshire. Drawn – Berkshire, Cornwall, Dorset, Oxfordshire, Wiltshire. No result – Devon.

Batting Averages

	M	I	NO	R	HS	100s	50s	Avge
J. Derrick...........	8	12	2	551	123	2	2	55.10
A. J. Jones	4	7	1	207	100*	1	0	34.50
*A. C. Puddle	9	12	5	226	53*	0	2	32.28
†A. W. Harris	8	14	1	383	118	1	1	29.46
J. P. J. Sylvester	6	9	1	201	100*	1	0	25.12
R. N. Moore	3	5	0	79	36	0	0	15.80
A. D. Griffiths	7	7	0	83	31	0	0	11.85
B. J. Lloyd	9	10	2	57	18	0	0	7.12

Played in six matches: A. Smith 3, 19*, 13, 2. Played in five matches: R. Wiseman 64*, 25, 4, 4, 9; A. Ikram did not bat. Played in four matches: W. G. Edwards 19*, 3*, 0, 11. Played in three matches: A. Dalton 73, 21, 0, 14; B. Metcalf 76, 28, 20, 2*. Played in two matches: C. Bell 47*, 39, 51; J. Bishop 8, 63, 38, 4; J. L. Griffiths 101, 0, 4; D. L. Hemp 127*, 33, 56, 0; M. A. G. Jones 13, 4, 0, 2*; S. D. Pearce 31, 13*, 22; †A. D. Shaw 1. Played in one match: A. Francis 4, 0; S. Jones 19*; P. Richards 4*, 2*; G. T. Wood 25, 15; I. Poole did not bat.

Bowling Averages

	O	M	R	W	BB	5W/i	Avge
A. Ikram	105	41	215	19	5-29	1	11.31
A. Smith	203.4	76	459	26	6-22	3	17.65
J. Derrick	178.5	39	506	23	5-32	2	22.00
A. D. Griffiths	107.3	20	365	16	3-8	0	22.81
B. J. Lloyd	176.2	47	453	15	3-36	0	30.20

Also bowled: C. Bell 22-6-58-1; W. G. Edwards 88-28-225-7; D. L. Hemp 2.5-0-19-0; S. Jones 4-1-10-1; S. D. Pearce 22.3-9-72-1; A. C. Puddle 2-0-16-0; J. P. J. Sylvester 19.5-5-60-2; R. Wiseman 37-5-120-3.

WILTSHIRE

Secretary – C. R. Sheppard, 45 Ipswich Street, Swindon SN2 1DB.
Telephone: 0793-511811

Matches 9: Won – Berkshire, Cornwall. Lost – Oxfordshire. Drawn – Cheshire, Devon, Dorset, Herefordshire, Shropshire, Wales.

Batting Averages

	M	I	NO	R	HS	100s	50s	Avge
*K. N. Foyle	8	14	3	467	98*	0	4	42.45
R. R. Savage	8	14	3	403	120*	1	2	36.63
†S. M. Perrin	8	14	2	415	73*	0	1	34.58
L. K. Smith	9	17	1	533	83	0	3	33.31
†P. M. Marsh	6	11	0	365	87	0	2	33.18
D. P. Simpkins	9	15	7	261	57*	0	1	32.62
D. R. Turner	5	10	1	217	55	0	1	24.11
J. J. Newman	8	12	0	214	69	0	1	17.83
S. R. Priscott	7	6	3	32	17	0	0	10.66
G. Sheppard	7	7	3	16	7*	0	0	4.00

Played in seven matches: S. J. Malone 10, 0*, 1*, 1. Played in five matches: N. Prigent 44, 6, 14*, 25. Played in four matches: S. Thorpe 0, 2*, 7, 3*, 4*. Played in three matches: D. R. Pike 27, 2, 21. Played in two matches: D. R. Parry 25, 14, 5, 44. Played in one match: M. Beale 0; S. Benbough 1, 74; N. Wood did not bat.

Bowling Averages

	O	M	R	W	BB	5W/i	Avge
S. J. Thorpe	146	33	443	19	7-47	1	23.31
L. K. Smith	53	5	252	10	2-29	0	25.20
S. R. Priscott	93.5	11	351	13	5-56	1	27.00
N. Prigent	130.3	24	429	15	4-93	0	28.60
S. J. Malone	120.1	21	416	14	4-20	0	29.71

Also bowled: M. Beale 7-0-30-1; K. N. Foyle 1-0-2-0; P. M. Marsh 60.5-11-204-5; J. J. Newman 9-0-76-1; S. M. Perrin 12-0-111-1; D. R. Pike 67-25-218-5; R. R. Savage 2.4-0-32-2; G. Sheppard 135-13-585-9; D. P. Simpkins 76-15-265-3; N. Wood 20-3-77-1.

LEADING MINOR COUNTIES CHAMPIONSHIP AVERAGES, 1992

BATTING

(Qualification: 8 innings)

	M	I	NO	R	HS	100s	Avge
S. J. Dean (*Staffordshire*)	6	9	2	675	124	4	96.42
N. A. Folland (*Devon*)	8	13	4	734	118*	2	81.55
M. A. Fell (*Lincolnshire*)	6	12	5	567	171*	1	81.00
N. R. Gaywood (*Devon*)	8	13	1	933	125	3	77.75
J. A. Waterhouse (*Staffordshire*)	7	9	4	359	91*	0	71.80
J. D. Love (*Lincolnshire*)	8	15	4	733	114	1	66.63
S. N. V. Waterton (*Oxfordshire*)	9	15	3	756	110*	1	63.00
M. R. Davies (*Shropshire*)	9	16	7	561	101*	1	62.33
J. Derrick (*Wales*)	8	12	2	551	123	2	55.10
A. J. Pugh (*Devon*)	9	16	7	495	95*	0	55.00

BOWLING

(Qualification: 20 wickets)

	O	M	R	W	BB	Avge
G. Miller (*Cheshire*)	291	84	636	49	6-25	12.97
N. P. Hackett (*Staffordshire*)	128.4	33	351	24	7-50	14.62
S. R. Walbridge (*Dorset*)	251.4	72	658	41	5-34	16.04
J. F. M. O'Brien (*Cheshire*)	242	47	700	42	5-32	16.66
A. Smith (*Wales*)	203.4	76	459	26	6-22	17.65
A. Needham (*Hertfordshire*)	219.3	82	448	25	4-42	17.92
D. Surridge (*Hertfordshire*)	212.1	51	521	28	5-43	18.60
D. A. Christmas (*Lincolnshire*)	124.3	28	401	21	6-56	19.09
P. Bent (*Herefordshire*)	112.4	20	391	20	4-13	19.55
J. H. Shackleton (*Dorset*)	250.2	61	653	32	7-57	20.40

THE MINOR COUNTIES CHAMPIONS

1895 {	Norfolk Durham Worcestershire	1911 1912 1913	Staffordshire In abeyance Norfolk	1937 1938 1939	Lancashire II Buckinghamshire Surrey II
1896	Worcestershire	1914	Staffordshire	1946	Suffolk
1897	Worcestershire	1920	Staffordshire	1947	Yorkshire II
1898	Worcestershire	1921	Staffordshire	1948	Lancashire II
1899 {	Northamptonshire Buckinghamshire	1922 1923	Buckinghamshire Buckinghamshire	1949 1950	Lancashire II Surrey II
1900 {	Glamorgan Durham Northamptonshire	1924 1925 1926	Berkshire Buckinghamshire Durham	1951 1952 1953	Kent II Buckinghamshire Berkshire
1901	Durham	1927	Staffordshire	1954	Surrey II
1902	Wiltshire	1928	Berkshire	1955	Surrey II
1903	Northamptonshire	1929	Oxfordshire	1956	Kent II
1904	Northamptonshire	1930	Durham	1957	Yorkshire II
1905	Norfolk	1931	Leicestershire II	1958	Yorkshire II
1906	Staffordshire	1932	Buckinghamshire	1959	Warwickshire II
1907	Lancashire II	1933	Undecided	1960	Lancashire II
1908	Staffordshire	1934	Lancashire II	1961	Somerset II
1909	Wiltshire	1935	Middlesex II	1962	Warwickshire II
1910	Norfolk	1936	Hertfordshire	1963	Cambridgeshire

LORDS AND COMMONS RESULTS, 1992

Matches 11: Won 2, Lost 5, Drawn 4. Abandoned 1.

At St Paul's School, Barnes, April 29. St Paul's School won by nine wickets. Lords and Commons 100 (R. Kershaw 43); St Paul's School 101 for one.

At Vincent Square, May 5. Drawn. Westminster School 233 for five dec.; Lords and Commons 231 for nine (Hon. M. Rawlinson 107, C. F. Horne 37).

At Bank of England Ground, Roehampton, June 3. Lords and Commons won by ten wickets. Mandarins 62 (29.2 overs); Lords and Commons 66 for no wkt (11.1 overs) (Dr W. A. Hollingsworth 42 not out).

At Bank of England Ground, Roehampton, June 17. Conservative Agents won by eight runs. Conservative Agents 169 for seven (30 overs); Lords and Commons 161 for eight (30 overs) (Rt Hon. T. J. King 42, D. J. C. Faber 42, E. H. Garnier 30).

At Burton Court, July 1. Drawn. Lords and Commons 124 for eight (Hon. M. Rawlinson 53); Guards CC five for no wkt.

At St Paul's School, Barnes, July 2. MCC won by 57 runs. MCC 227 for two dec.; Lords and Commons 170 (C. F. Horne 53 not out, C. Macgregor 37). (Lords and Commons had lost nine wickets, but one batsman retired "due to an appointment with the Prime Minister".)

At Burton Court, July 7. Eton Ramblers won by 121 runs. Eton Ramblers 283 for nine dec.; Lords and Commons 162 (R. Lee 42, Viscount Ebrington 38 not out, D. J. C. Faber 37).

At Linden Park CC, Tunbridge Wells, July 10. Drawn. Lords and Commons 198 (C. Guyver 108); Fleet Street 63 for one.

At Vincent Square, July 16. Lords and Commons won by five wickets. Old Westminsters 213 for five dec.; Lords and Commons 214 for five (G. W. Allen 101 not out, C. Macgregor 41, Hon. M. Rawlinson 33).

At Old Emmanuel, New Malden, August 19. Drawn. Law Society 217 for four dec. (Cmdr J. Sayer three for 70); Lords and Commons 117 for nine (D. Brooke 32).

At Harrow School, September 4. Harrow Wanderers won by 210 runs. Harrow Wanderers 310 for seven dec.; Lords and Commons 100.

At Highclere, September 6. Earl of Carnarvon's XI v Lords and Commons. Abandoned.

RAPID CRICKETLINE SECOND ELEVEN CHAMPIONSHIP, 1992

Surrey did the double in 1992, winning both the Second Eleven Championship and the Bain Clarkson Trophy, as Middlesex had done in 1989. It was their fifth success in the Championship, which they last won in 1988, and their first in the Bain Clarkson, although they had come close in 1991 when they lost the final to Nottinghamshire. The runners-up in both competitions were Northamptonshire, who shot up from the bottom of the Championship table to finish six points behind the leaders, with more bonus points than any other county. The losing semi-finalists in the Bain Clarkson Trophy were Warwickshire and Somerset, who dropped in the Championship from second and third respectively to share 12th place, nearly 100 points behind Surrey.

Nine batsmen passed 1,000 runs – just one fewer than the record ten in the vintage batting summer of 1990. The highest aggregate was 1,362 at 61.90 in 24 innings by Darren Robinson of Essex. Yet it was Jason Gallian of Lancashire who was without doubt the outstanding batsman. He reached his 1,015 at an average of 145.00 in only 12 innings, seven of which yielded centuries. Robinson made five hundreds and four each were scored by five other batsmen. Of those who passed 500 runs, Gallian was alone in recording a three-figure average, although Warwickshire's Trevor Penney came close with 97.50 for his 585 runs. Eight double-centuries were struck, of which the highest was 224 by Nick Knight of Essex.

Only two bowlers took 50 wickets, and no one came near Andrew Caddick's record 96 of the previous season. Gary Yates, the Lancashire off-spinner, was the most successful with 62 at 20.40, followed by the medium-pacer from Kent, Tim Wren, whose 58 cost 28.03 apiece. They worked hard for their wickets, sending down 568.2 and 536.4 overs respectively, and Yates was one of 11 players to appear in all his county's Championship matches. Of those who took more than 25 wickets, Kevin Shine was the most economical, his 139.4 overs yielding 28 at 12.64 for Hampshire. Michael Bell, Warwickshire's young left-arm swing bowler, achieved the season's best innings return, with nine for 103, and hat-tricks were recorded by James Brinkley of Worcestershire and the Dutch-born Somerset teenager, Andre van Troost.

SECOND ELEVEN CHAMPIONSHIP, 1992

					Bonus points		
Win = 16 points	M	W	L	D	Batting	Bowling	Points
1 – Surrey (6)	17	8	2	7	47	45	220
2 – Northamptonshire (17)	17	7	1	9	52	50	214
3 – Gloucestershire (16) . .	17	6	2	9	38	52	186
4 – Hampshire (4)	17	6	3	8	48	36	180
5 – Yorkshire (1)	17	5	2	10	48	48	176
6 { Durham (—)	17	5	3	9	42	52	174
{ Middlesex (11)	17	5	2	10*	44	50	174
8 – Kent (14)	17	4	5	8	38	55	157
9 – Sussex (7)	17	3	4	10	47	52	147
10 – Lancashire (11)	17	3	1	13	47	48	143
11 – Derbyshire (8)	17	3	5	9	43	51	142
12 { Somerset (3)	17	3	5	9	40	40	128
{ Warwickshire (2)	17	3	4	10	33	47	128
14 – Nottinghamshire (5) . .	17	1	5	11	47	39	110
15 – Leicestershire (10)	17	1	4	12	37	46	99
16 – Worcestershire (9)	17	1	4	12	39	37	92
17 – Glamorgan (13)	17	1	4	12	21	44	81
18 – Essex (15)	17	0	9	8*	35	43	78

1991 positions are shown in brackets.

The total for Nottinghamshire includes 8 points for batting second in a match drawn with the scores level.

* Includes one match abandoned without a ball bowled.

Yates was the leading all-rounder, adding 847 runs at 49.82 to his 62 wickets, although it was Gloucestershire's Ricardo Williams, with 438 runs at 25.76 and 45 wickets at 24.17, who won the Rapid Cricketline Second Eleven Championship Player of the Year award. He received £550 and a trophy. Graham Kersey, the Kent wicket-keeper, led the dismissals with 54 and Richard Williams of Gloucestershire had 51. They were both useful batsmen, too, scoring 653 and 578 runs respectively.

The match between Essex and Hampshire, at Leigh-on-Sea on June 23, 24, 25, was abandoned after five overs when the pitch was deemed too dangerous for play to continue. The fixture was rescheduled and played at Southampton on August 8, 9, 10, when Hampshire won by eight wickets.

With a relatively small number of staff players available, the season was always likely to be difficult for **Derbyshire**, who called on 36 players, an encouraging proportion of whom were local-born. As the season progressed a regular squad was formed, and a place in the top half of the table was expected. However, hard-earned winning positions against Warwickshire and Surrey were thrown away when the batting folded and 11th was all they could manage. Gary Steer, formerly of Warwickshire, had an excellent season and with 1,057 runs became the first Derbyshire batsman to achieve a four-figure aggregate in the competition. David Lovell and Tim Tweats were also prolific, each recording a maiden century. The main strike bowler – Martin Jean-Jacques, with 39 wickets at 19.84 – was released at the end of the season and signed for Hampshire for 1993. Close behind him with 38 wickets at 33.78 was the ever-present Alastair Richardson, and they were backed up by the economical slow left-armer, Richard Sladdin, who returned ten for 83 in the match against Somerset at Glastonbury. The most overs were delivered by Paul Whitaker, whose off-breaks brought him 30 wickets but at high cost. With 407 runs as well, he was the leading all-rounder, with useful support in both departments from Steve Goldsmith, Frank Griffith and Stuart Stoneman.

Durham enjoyed an encouraging first season in the competition, featuring in the top three for much of the time, although they finally settled in sixth place. Many local youngsters were enlisted, and it was particularly pleasing to see two of them finish top of the run-scorers: 18-year-old Jimmy Daley, the England Under-19 representative, was the most prolific with 810, while 22-year-old Stewart Hutton, a left-hander, followed with 788. Hutton began the season in fine style with 168 not out as Durham beat Leicestershire at Grace Road in their first match, while Derbyshire were beaten by an innings at Felling. There was also enterprising batting from John Glendenen, Mark Briers and England Under-19 left-hander Darren Blenkiron, three players from Durham's final Minor Counties campaign. Although he played for much of the season in the first team, the former Worcestershire fast bowler Steve McEwan was the leading wicket-taker with 32. Despite being restricted by injury, the lively paceman John Wood took 24 wickets – including four for nine as Gloucestershire were dismissed for 148 at Cheltenham – and the 6ft 8in Gary Wigham collected 23. Significant contributions also came from 17-year-old Paul Henderson, slow left-armer David Cox and Quentin Hughes, one of seven schoolboys called upon by the county.

Essex had their worst season ever in the competition and finished firmly at the bottom of the table, recording nine defeats and not a single victory. The main problem was injuries to bowlers, with David Boden able to play in only five matches, Lloyd Tennant in ten and Darren Cousins ruled out all summer with a stress fracture of the back. Opening bowler Alastair Fraser and slow left-armer Guy Lovell carried the main burden and were the leading wicket-takers, although Lovell was expensive with an average over 50. Three batsmen stood out. Darren Robinson, who represented England Under-19 during the summer, scored more runs than anyone else in the competition in 1992 and established a county record. His 1,362 easily passed A. C. H. Seymour's 1,172 in 1989 and included two centuries in a match twice – 164 and 134 against Lancashire at Manchester, followed by 206 and 124 not out against Leicestershire at Leicester. Muneeb Diwan, a 20-year-old Canadian-born opening bat who joined the staff halfway through the season, scored 120 and 74 not out on his début against Kent at Chelmsford and in all contributed 725 runs from nine games. Nick Knight, who played only four matches, scored 224 and 102 against Durham at Boldon. But no-one else averaged more than 30 – although all too many of the bowlers did. Robert Rollins kept wicket well and continued to represent England Under-19 in that capacity.

It was another disappointing season for **Glamorgan**, who salvaged only one win – against Somerset at Ebbw Vale – and struggled to find consistency as rain affected all their matches in August and September. Thirty-five players were called upon, six captaining the side at different times, and with the full-time county staff limited to 16, there was always going to be a lack of continuity in selection. An advantage of this situation was that the county were able to look at more young players, of whom David Hemp and James Williams were the two most impressive batsmen, well supported at times by Andrew Jones, Jamie Bishop, Alistair Dalton and Gary Butcher. Hemp, who made fifty in every other innings, was named Glamorgan Second Eleven Player of the year, while Jones scored his maiden century (114) against Northamptonshire at Northampton. Yet the side recorded the lowest number of batting points, their 21 being 12 adrift of the next-lowest, Warwickshire, and their overall total of bonus points was also the lowest of all. The most successful bowlers were the pacemen Daren Foster and Mark Frost, backed up by the competent wicket-keeping of Adrian Shaw. Darren Thomas, who also made a useful contribution in the first team on occasion, was selected for the England Under-18 tour to South Africa.

In their best season since 1965, **Gloucestershire** climbed from 16th to third with six wins. At full strength the middle-order batting was very strong, with Robbie Dawson hitting three centuries as he became only the second Gloucestershire batsman after G. D. Hodgson in 1989 to reach 1,000 runs in a season. Hundreds also came from Matt Windows, Tim Hancock, Justin Vaughan, Richard Williams and the impressive all-rounder Ricardo Williams; all five played for the first team during the season. Windows and Ricardo Williams scored 118 and 134 respectively as they compiled a county record seventh-wicket partnership of 237 against Sussex at Cheltenham Town, and there were four other partnerships in excess of 150. The greatest improvement, though, was in the bowling; five players took more than 20 wickets and the side accumulated the second-most bowling points (52) after Kent (55). The most successful bowler was Ricardo Williams, the Rapid Cricketline Second Eleven Championship Player of the Year, whose 45 wickets included seven for 73 in an innings against Worcestershire at Worcester and 11 for 76 against Kent at Sittingbourne, both matches being won. Meanwhile, Andy Babington's experience was crucial in the wins over Essex and Leicestershire. The bowling was complemented by the excellent wicket-keeping of Richard Williams, whose 51 dismissals (46 ct, 5 st) – including 18 off the bowling of his namesake – were a club record. Windows represented England Under-19 against Sri Lanka and the promising Robert Cunliffe, who hit six fifties, was selected for the England Under-19 tour to India.

Restricted at the beginning of their campaign by first-team calls and poor form, **Hampshire** won only two of their first nine matches. However, in the second half of the season the team played impressively as a unit to win four of the last eight games and retain fourth place. The bulk of the runs were scored by the left-handed Rupert Cox – whose four centuries were against Glamorgan (100), Kent (100 not out), Surrey (143) and Durham (103 not out) – Sean Morris and Julian Wood, although Morris could not quite capture his exceptional form of the previous season. Nineteen-year-old Jason Laney blossomed towards the end of the season, following an indifferent start with two fine centuries (127 against Lancashire at Southampton and 124 against Surrey on a poor pitch at Guildford), and Jim Bovill was another to gain confidence. The attack was not their strength and the side recorded the fewest bowling bonus points. Of the seven bowlers to take 20 wickets, Rajesh Maru and Kevin Shine were particularly economical, but only Paul-Jan Bakker and Maru went on to take 30. A highlight for Maru was his return of ten for 105 in the match against Worcestershire at Old Hill. The professionalism of Bobby Parks behind the stumps was exemplary and the fielding was of a high standard, especially that of Maru at slip. Team spirit was always good, thanks largely to the enthusiastic captaincy of Cox, who engendered a unique brand of humour in the side.

In a year of rebuilding which saw them move up to eighth place, **Kent** were encouraged by the performance of the 25 young players from outside the county staff, of whom Matthew Walker, a left-handed batsman and off-spin bowler, was chosen to captain the England Under-19 team to India. The leading staff player with the bat was David Fulton, whose 1,022 runs at 63.87 included a double-century against Worcestershire at Flagge Meadow. Jonathan Longley was another to pass 1,000 runs, also with a double-century to his name – against Glamorgan at Maidstone. They were ably supported by the all-rounder gel Llong and Graham Kersey, the excellent wicket-keeper-batsman whose 54 victims ct, 4 st) were the most by a wicket-keeper in 1992. His tally of dismissals was the third st in the Championship behind J. W. Elliott's 58 for Worcestershire in 1963 and L. A. hnson's 57 for Northamptonshire in 1959; Kersey's 50 catches stand alone as a record. Baldock also passed 500 runs, his 158 contributing to a Championship record 580 for in the innings defeat of Essex at Chelmsford. Llong scored 119 in that match, 117 at unton, 157 against Hampshire at Folkestone and 150 against Durham at Maidstone, as ll as taking 33 wickets. The leading wicket-taker was again Tim Wren, who sent down re than 500 overs at medium pace for 58 wickets at 28.03. He finished one short of W. Baker's county record of 59 at 18.71 in 1963. With Andrew Tutt (39 wickets), Wren d Llong were the mainstay of the attack, which earned more bowling bonus points than y other county and was expected to be even stronger in future with a few young bowlers erging. In addition, Min Patel should have recovered from a serious knee injury stained shortly after he returned from polytechnic and which kept him out for most of the son.

Lancashire were another county for whom two players achieved four-figure aggregates. son Gallian, the 1993 Oxford University captain, continued his form of the previous son and was outstanding, with 1,015 at 145.00 from just seven matches. He scored 106 d 14 in his first match against Somerset at Crosby, followed by two hundreds in each of following three matches – 158 not out and 105 not out against Sussex at Liverpool, 160 t out and 104 not out against Essex at Manchester and 154 and 105 against Warwickshire Blackpool. Seven centuries in eight innings and six in succession set a new standard for competition, passing T. C. Middleton's five for Hampshire in 1990. Australian-born of tish parents, Gallian becomes qualified for England in 1994. Ronnie Irani was the other pass a thousand runs, with 118 of them coming against Durham at Chester-le-Street. hn Crawley, who appeared only twice, scored 217 not out and 117 in the Somerset game. aying in all the matches, Gary Yates accumulated 847 runs and 62 wickets – more than yone else in the Championship – and underlined his all-round excellence in the match ainst Middlesex at Manchester, where he scored a century and had innings figures of six · 16. No other bowler took 30 wickets and, despite the enormous batting strength, ncashire finished only tenth in the table. They were well represented in the England uth sides, with Glen Chapple and Peter Wilcock selected to tour India with the Under-19 le and Jonathan Henderson and Nathan Wood, son of the former Test player, B. Wood, med in the Under-18 side to South Africa.

Leicestershire, who used a total of 42 players, were unable to sustain their improvement of previous season and dropped to 15th place with only one win – an emphatic innings uncing of Glamorgan. Martyn Gidley and Andrew Roseberry were the only two batsmen pass 700 runs. Gidley scored centuries against Lancashire (110 not out at Grace Road) d Glamorgan (151 at Cardiff), Gordon Parsons made 114 not out in the Lancashire atch, and later in the season Paul Nixon hit 125 not out at Northampton, Russell Cobb ored 116 against Worcestershire at Leicester and Ben Smith was the centurion against rrey at The Oval with 135. No bowler reached the heights, with the largest haul of 29 ckets being earned by Robert Gofton's off-spin, followed by Gidley's 24. Slow left-armer ris Hawkes was again the most economical.

Benefiting from the opportunity to field a much more settled side than in 1991, **Middlesex** oved up five places to sixth. Aftab Habib made excellent progress. His 994 runs included 3 not out against Worcestershire at Harrow, when he and the improving Toby Radford, th 104 not out in his first match following the university term, put on 267 for the fourth cket by wholly classical methods. The rest of the batting was always prolific, seven tsmen made hundreds and Jason Pooley, Paul Farbrace and the promising Robin Sims ored consistently. Matthew Keech got himself out too often when apparently on the verge a large innings, but by way of compensation his medium-pace bowling was more nsistent and yielded 30 wickets. When everyone was available, the attack was well lanced. Richard Johnson and Richard Ballinger, selected for the England Under-18 and nder-19 winter tours respectively, looked a promising pace duo. Keith Dutch, whose best rformance brought him match figures of 12 for 163 against Gloucestershire at Gloucester, wled his off-spin consistently to head the averages, and the left-arm seam bowler, Steve lvester, took the most wickets, albeit expensively.

Thanks to a number of fine all-round performances, **Northamptonshire** enjoyed particularly successful season, which saw them rocket from the bottom of the table runners-up, with more bonus points (102) than any other side. Russell Warren joined small group of players who have scored a thousand Second Eleven Championship runs i season for the county, and he might well have been joined by Malachy Loye and To Penberthy had first-team calls not restricted their appearances. Penberthy's 811 runs fr nine matches were boosted by a magnificent 218 against Glamorgan at Northampton, wh Warren reached three figures against Somerset (140 at North Perrott), Middlesex (131 out at Oundle School) and Yorkshire (150 at Marske-by-Sea). Wayne Noon captained side with maturity and enjoyed a good season behind the stumps, while the all-rou strength was emphasised by seven bowlers taking 20 wickets.

In contrast, **Nottinghamshire**, who had looked to continue their winning ways of 19 found themselves sliding down to 14th. Injuries to many players left the side unsettl although there was consolation in the excellent response of those who were called up first-team duty. Mark Saxelby scored 848 runs in only nine Second Eleven matches, wh Graeme Archer's 929 runs included four centuries – 105 not out against Yorkshire Harrogate, 109 not out against Surrey at The Oval, 151 not out against Somerset Clevedon and 149 against Warwickshire at Nottingham. Mike Newell, the captain, play in all the matches and made 118 against Glamorgan at Worksop College and 120 agai Warwickshire at Nottingham. He was appointed Second Eleven manager/coach for 19 following the release of Kevin Saxelby. Andy Afford, who sent down more than 300 ov in his six matches, was again the top bowler with 41 wickets, including 11 for 156 agai Northamptonshire at Worksop College. Another success was David Pennett, who signed Nottinghamshire after being released from the Yorkshire Cricket Academy and finished season opening the bowling for the First Eleven. Michael Field-Buss was again admirable all-rounder, averaging 46.75 with the bat and bowling more than 300 overs of spin for 24 wickets.

Somerset saw many changes to their successful side of the previous season, with Andr Caddick and Mark Lathwell in particular distinguishing themselves in first-class games. the new brigade, Keith Parsons did especially well with centuries against Hampshire (1 not out at Portsmouth), Nottinghamshire (160 not out at Clevedon) and Middlesex (129 out at Southgate). His identical twin, Kevin, gave his best performances at Taunton w 134 against Kent and 104 against Surrey, while Rob Turner, the wicket-keeper, score century in each innings (109 and 100) without being dismissed against Nottinghamsh at Clevedon. Gareth Townsend was also amongst the runs with 167 not out agai Gloucestershire at Bristol, 116 against Leicestershire at Kibworth, 109 against Worcest shire at Taunton and 101 against Surrey at the same venue. Youngsters Andrew Payne Jason Kerr took time to settle, although Kerr played a fine innings of 107 against Middle at Southgate and both were selected for the England Under-19 tour to India. The 19-ye old pace bowler, Andre van Troost, twice took ten wickets in a match – for 73 runs agai Middlesex at Southgate and for 81 runs against Durham at Eppleton, where his six for 16 the second innings included a hat-trick. Roland Lefebvre headed the averages with wickets at 17.51. Much will be expected of the younger players in 1993 with the depart of Ricky Bartlett, who averaged nearly 50 in his seven innings, Townsend and Lefebvre

Surrey attributed their success in winning both the Championship and Bain Clarks Trophy to their strong team spirit, and although there were many notable performanc no one player walked off with the honours. Early victories helped to motivate the si which featured a satisfying blend of youth and experience under the leadership of Ke Medlycott and the former First Eleven captain, Ian Greig. Nine centuries were scored, t each coming from Paul Atkins (116 against both Middlesex at Uxbridge and Essex Southend), Alistair Brown (128 against Nottinghamshire at The Oval and 145 against Ess at Southend) and Mark Butcher (119 against Glamorgan and 106 against Lancashire at 1 Oval). While success in the Bain Clarkson Trophy revolved around the batsmen, it was bowlers who led the way in the Championship, most noticeably the spin attack Medlycott, England Under-19 left-armer Mark Bainbridge and Andrew Smith, who w invaluable on slow, unresponsive pitches. Eleven of James Boiling's 12 wickets were tak for 118 runs in the match against Durham at The Oval.

Thirty players were used by **Sussex**, who took the opportunity to search for young talent. As a result contracts for 1993 were awarded to Keith Newell, Sean Humphries, Toby Peirce and Danny Law, who was selected for the England Under-18 tour to South Africa. The most prolific batsmen, Keith Greenfield and Carlos Remy, also played their part in the first team. Greenfield's three hundreds came at the expense of Derbyshire at Horsham (101), Gloucestershire at Cheltenham Town (104) and Lancashire at Liverpool (142 not out), while Remy's maiden Championship century (109) against Hampshire at Bournemouth was followed by 124 against Middlesex at Horsham. John North and Bradleigh Donelan continued to develop as promising all-rounders, North emphasising his multiple talents with innings figures of seven for 39 and a century (131) against Hampshire. The leading wicket-taker, Alan Hansford, whose best innings return was six for 39 against Warwickshire at Stratford-upon-Avon, decided at the end of the season to pursue a career outside cricket.

A drop of ten places for **Warwickshire**, runners-up in 1991, characterised a disappointing season, which started full of promise but finished in frustration as rain interfered with half the matches and badly affected some of the pitches. This led to several contrived games and difficult conditions for batting. Wasim Khan, Michael Burns and Asif Din were the leading scorers. Wasim Khan's 943 runs included 123 not out against Essex at Nuneaton, while Asif Din's 778 featured 109 not out and 104 not out in the match against Leicestershire at Oakham and 194 against Nottinghamshire at Nottingham. The 789 accumulated by Michael Burns were boosted by his maiden century (126) against Middlesex at Uxbridge, and 165 against Lancashire at Blackpool. Trevor Penney collected 585 runs at 97.50 in his five matches, with 155 not out against Derbyshire at Knowle and Dorridge, 148 against Middlesex and 142 not out against Kent at Studley. Michael Bell had an excellent season with his left-arm swing bowling, his 44 wickets at 16.81 including nine for 103 in an innings against Somerset at Walmley. He was well supported by Ashley Giles, Graeme Welch and Paul Booth.

It was not a memorable season for **Worcestershire**, who dropped to 16th place with a single win and fewer bonus points than any side apart from Glamorgan. Chris Tolley scored the most runs with 613 in eight matches, closely followed by 606 from Adam Seymour, the left-hander signed from Essex. The only other batsman to pass 500 was Martin Weston, who played the side's highest innings of 173 not out against Leicestershire at Leicester. Other hundreds came from Greg Hill (104 against Somerset at Taunton), Phil Weston (123 against Middlesex at Harrow), Damian D'Oliveira (113 against Yorkshire at Worcester), as well as Gavin Haynes and Tolley, who scored 123 and 168 not out respectively against Surrey at Worcester. That match was memorable, too, for a hat-trick in a return of six for 60 by James Brinkley, bowling at medium pace. His other 12 wickets must have been remarkably expensive, though, for he averaged 52.22 overall. Indeed, the bowling was particularly disappointing and it was no surprise that only Hampshire (36) had fewer bowling points than Worcestershire's 37. The one bowler to pass 20 wickets was the consistent all-rounder, Chris Eyers (also medium pace) and apart from D'Oliveira's 15 at 19.46 in five matches, economy was not a feature. Of the younger players who were called upon, Vikram Solanki and William Hearsey (who also played for Middlesex) were selected for the England Under-18 tour to South Africa.

Fielding a rather younger side than in their previous Championship-winning year, **Yorkshire** dropped to fifth place, although they might have expected to take second or third place had not the weather deprived them of probable maximum points in their last game. Of the young players who gained valuable experience, Bradley Parker became more selective in his strokeplay and scored consistently to pass 1,000 runs, while the 17-year-old Michael Vaughan showed patience and concentration when opening the batting. Vaughan hit three hundreds – 107 against Surrey at Leeds, 130 against Lancashire at Manchester and 126 against Glamorgan at Bradford – while Parker's two were 102 not out against Lancashire and 121 not out against Northamptonshire at Marske-by-Sea. David Byas made the side's highest score with an unbeaten double-century against Worcestershire at Worcester. The leading all-rounder was again Adrian Grayson, batting either as an opener or in the middle order and bowling his left-arm spin to take the most wickets. Jeremy Batty, bowling off-breaks, Darren Gough and the England Under-19 representative Michael Foster (both fast-medium) all averaged under 20. Three young players gained representative honours, Vaughan and Mark Broadhurst being selected for the England Under-19 tour to India and Gary Keedy being picked for the Under-18 side to South Africa.

*In the averages that follow, * against a score signifies not out, * against a name signifies the captain and † signifies a wicket-keeper.*

DERBYSHIRE SECOND ELEVEN

Matches 17: Won – Essex, Kent, Worcestershire. Lost – Durham, Middlesex, Northamptonshire, Surrey, Sussex. Drawn – Glamorgan, Gloucestershire, Hampshire, Lancashire, Leicestershire, Nottinghamshire, Somerset, Warwickshire, Yorkshire.

Batting Averages

	M	I	NO	R	HS	100s	Avge
G. F. Shephard	3	3	2	78	50*	0	78.00
I. G. S. Steer	13	25	2	1,057	149*	3	45.95
S. A. Stoneman	7	12	6	266	73*	0	44.33
D. J. Lovell	14	25	4	878	163*	2	41.80
T. A. Tweats	8	14	1	501	142	1	38.53
A. M. Brown	7	11	2	338	80	0	37.55
S. C. Goldsmith	5	10	2	289	62	0	36.12
F. A. Griffith	8	15	2	395	92	0	30.38
C. J. Rogers	2	4	0	116	75	0	29.00
M. J. Crookson	2	3	2	28	18*	0	28.00
S. J. Base	5	9	1	221	56	0	27.62
A. S. Rollins	6	10	0	276	99	0	27.60
M. Jean-Jacques	11	19	2	402	91	0	23.64
P. R. Whitaker	16	24	4	407	92*	0	20.35
G. M. Pooley	5	9	0	167	51	0	18.55
K. Hunter	2	3	0	40	20	0	13.33
M. R. Spencer	6	11	1	110	25	0	11.00
*†B. J. M. Maher	17	23	8	139	19*	0	9.26
A. W. Richardson	17	25	3	173	25*	0	7.86
M. Diwan	2	3	0	23	19	0	7.66
R. W. Sladdin	5	8	1	49	19	0	7.00
C. G. Belgrave	2	3	0	19	15	0	6.33
A. Agrawalla	11	15	3	56	12	0	4.66
K. S. Newbold	2	3	0	5	4	0	1.66

Played in one match: J. N. Batty 5, 8; P. J. Bennett 72, 33; R. I. Biggin 8, 16; R. D. E. Farrow 55, 1; A. J. Harris 0, 31; S. J. Lacey 20, 17; M. R. May 5, 6; D. B. K. Page 19, 2*; B. M. W. Patterson 45, 1; S. A. Price 1, 5; M. A. Wintle 17, 0; B. B. Moore did not bat.

Note: During the second innings of the match v Sussex at Horsham S. C. Goldsmith, called up for a first-team match, was replaced by B. B. Moore.

Bowling Averages

	O	M	R	W	BB	Avge
R. W. Sladdin	156.4	65	290	20	6-62	14.50
C. G. Belgrave	38	15	71	4	4-22	17.75
M. Jean-Jacques	283.2	64	774	39	5-48	19.84
F. A. Griffith	75	18	213	9	4-61	23.66
S. J. Base	134	26	362	13	2-20	27.84
S. C. Goldsmith	127	33	355	11	4-67	32.27
A. W. Richardson	384.5	97	1,284	38	4-56	33.78
A. Agrawalla	254.5	49	863	24	5-34	35.95
G. F. Shephard	66	15	252	7	2-37	36.00
A. S. Rollins	42	5	243	6	3-18	40.50
P. R. Whitaker	413.5	104	1,239	30	3-47	41.30
S. A. Stoneman	123.4	26	374	9	3-40	41.55
M. R. Spencer	46.1	10	175	4	1-0	43.75

Also bowled: P. J. Bennett 1-0-9-0; M. J. Crookson 29-7-90-2; A. J. Harris 24-6-90-3; K. Hunter 22-5-76-1; D. J. Lovell 58-20-138-3; B. J. M. Maher 2.2-0-12-0; K. S. Newbold 26-6-82-0; D. B. K. Page 20-5-54-2; I. G. S. Steer 64-17-201-2; T. A. Tweats 3-0-14-0.

DURHAM SECOND ELEVEN

Matches 17: Won – Derbyshire, Hampshire, Leicestershire, Sussex, Warwickshire. Lost – Somerset, Surrey, Yorkshire. Drawn – Essex, Glamorgan, Gloucestershire, Kent, Lancashire, Middlesex, Northamptonshire, Nottinghamshire, Worcestershire.

Batting Averages

	M	I	NO	R	HS	100s	Avge
†C. W. Scott	5	6	2	214	68	0	53.50
J. D. Glendenen	6	12	2	528	108	1	52.80
S. Hutton	11	19	3	788	168*	2	49.25
M. P. Briers	8	13	1	502	112	1	41.83
J. A. Daley	15	24	4	810	124*	3	40.50
G. K. Brown	13	21	3	675	111*	2	37.50
I. Smith	7	11	0	367	100	1	33.36
Q. J. Hughes	3	3	2	33	19*	0	33.00
D. A. Blenkiron	15	23	6	547	106*	1	32.17
*G. Cook	11	14	4	307	73*	0	30.70
R. M. S. Weston	6	11	2	227	91*	0	25.22
N. J. Adams	3	6	0	147	66	0	24.50
P. J. Berry	8	10	2	134	62*	0	16.75
J. Wood	6	8	0	129	55	0	16.12
S. M. McEwan	8	8	0	125	62	0	15.62
G. Wigham	12	12	7	71	21	0	14.20
P. W. Henderson	7	8	1	87	32*	0	12.42
†A. R. Fothergill	12	14	1	159	37	0	12.23
D. M. Cox	10	12	1	93	26	0	8.45

Played in five matches: N. Killeen 10*, 0*. Played in three matches: A. Jones 1, 0*. Played in two matches: G. Sheppard 1. Played in one match: P. Bainbridge 36, 29; M. M. Betts 0; S. J. E. Brown 18; S. Fleming 0; †W. J. Luntley 1; G. R. Mason 4; N. Pratt 22, 4; N. J. Pringle 31, 0; J. P. Searle 3*; N. J. Trainor 14*, 11; E. C. Antoine did not bat.

Bowling Averages

	O	M	R	W	BB	Avge
Q. J. Hughes	74.1	29	178	11	7-68	16.18
J. Wood	159.5	33	429	24	5-26	17.87
A. Jones	45.5	10	132	7	3-13	18.85
G. R. Mason	29	4	77	4	3-49	19.25
M. P. Briers	128	37	358	18	4-17	19.88
S. M. McEwan	278	76	670	32	5-67	20.93
N. J. Adams	47	9	138	6	3-41	23.00
D. A. Blenkiron	125.1	23	418	16	3-20	26.12
G. K. Brown	90	31	237	9	5-43	26.33
P. W. Henderson	151.1	32	460	16	5-52	28.75
P. J. Berry	181.4	50	435	14	4-52	31.07
G. Wigham	253.1	55	828	23	4-27	36.00
N. Killeen	95	22	247	6	3-27	41.16
D. M. Cox	380	115	973	21	6-35	46.33
I. Smith	113	15	427	9	2-45	47.44

Also bowled: E. C. Antoine 29-2-85-1; P. Bainbridge 5-1-10-0; M. M. Betts 24-4-95-1; S. J. E. Brown 19.3-2-69-2; S. Fleming 13-2-41-0; S. Hutton 0.4-0-7-0; J. P. Searle 30-8-84-1; G. Sheppard 12-1-43-0.

ESSEX SECOND ELEVEN

Matches 17: Lost – Derbyshire, Gloucestershire, Hampshire, Kent, Lancashire, Northamptonshire, Nottinghamshire, Surrey, Yorkshire. Drawn – Durham, Glamorgan, Leicestershire, Somerset, Sussex, Warwickshire, Worcestershire. Abandoned – Middlesex.

Batting Averages

	M	I	NO	R	HS	100s	Avge
N. V. Knight	4	6	0	441	224	2	73.50
D. D. J. Robinson	12	24	2	1,362	206	5	61.90
M. Diwan	9	18	3	725	206	1	48.33
A. C. Richards	8	15	1	389	78	0	27.78
J. J. B. Lewis	6	12	0	331	68	0	27.58
K. A. Butler	15	29	4	677	71	0	27.08
A. G. J. Fraser	14	25	3	577	69	0	26.22
S. C. Ecclestone	7	13	1	306	76	0	25.50
N. Shahid	4	8	0	191	42	0	23.87
K. O. Thomas	2	4	1	67	58*	0	22.33
A. W. Lilley	3	4	2	44	40	0	22.00
D. J. P. Boden	5	10	1	178	79	0	19.77
T. D. Topley	2	4	0	71	49	0	17.75
†R. J. Rollins	13	25	2	408	69	0	17.73
*K. W. R. Fletcher	7	12	4	139	38	0	17.37
L. Tennant	10	16	2	238	67	0	17.00
S. J. W. Andrew	8	12	2	163	42	0	16.30
A. J. E. Hibbert	4	8	0	120	32	0	15.00
C. B. Gladwin............	2	4	0	52	35	0	13.00
R. P. Collard.............	2	4	0	36	25	0	9.00
C. P. Harvey.............	3	4	0	35	21	0	8.75
G. M. Roberts	2	4	1	25	25	0	8.33
B. J. Hyam	2	4	0	32	13	0	8.00
G. A. Khan	2	4	0	30	14	0	7.50
S. D. Welch..............	2	4	0	21	12	0	5.25
W. G. Lovell..............	15	22	6	60	16*	0	3.75
D. P. McAllister	3	6	1	17	8*	0	3.40

Played in three matches: P. M. Such 0, 4*, 0*. Played in two matches: B. R. Hardie 1*, 12. Played in one match: A. D. Brown 1*; J. R. Culley 9, 6*; R. Ellwood 2, 0; R. A. Jones 33, 43; M. Powell 0, 9; R. Turner 0, 1.

Note: In the match v Worcestershire at Colchester N. V. Knight, called up for a first-team match, was replaced by C. P. Harvey.

Bowling Averages

	O	M	R	W	BB	Avge
P. M. Such	99.5	31	169	11	4-35	15.36
K. O. Thomas..............	66	22	168	9	6-41	18.66
T. D. Topley	62	15	180	5	2-42	36.00
A. G. J. Fraser	350.5	48	1,255	33	5-43	38.03
S. J. W. Andrew	189.3	43	537	13	4-50	41.30
N. Shahid	70.1	16	169	4	2-15	42.25
G. M. Roberts	94	30	223	5	3-100	44.60
L. Tennant	244.3	19	1,129	25	6-92	45.16
W. G. Lovell..............	532.1	132	1,483	29	6-91	51.13
D. J. P. Boden	133	26	515	9	3-83	57.22

Also bowled: K. A. Butler 10.2–3–24–0; R. P. Collard 3–0–14–0; J. R. Culley 19–1–76–1; M. Diwan 3–0–9–0; S. C. Ecclestone 34–3–128–2; R. Ellwood 42–21–80–2; C. B. Gladwin 10–2–23–1; C. P. Harvey 3–0–10–0; N. V. Knight 1–0–4–0; J. J. B. Lewis 23–2–119–3; D. P. McAllister 54–6–205–2; M. Powell 9–6–10–1; A. C. Richards 10–1–37–2; D. D. J. Robinson 0.5–0–1–0; S. D. Welch 42.2–11–79–1.

GLAMORGAN SECOND ELEVEN

Matches 17: Won – Somerset. Lost – Gloucestershire, Leicestershire, Middlesex, Sussex. Drawn – Derbyshire, Durham, Essex, Hampshire, Kent, Lancashire, Northamptonshire, Nottinghamshire, Surrey, Warwickshire, Worcestershire, Yorkshire.

atting Averages

	M	I	NO	R	HS	100s	Avge
L. Hemp	9	16	2	758	82*	0	54.14
R. Butcher	3	5	1	201	95	0	50.25
R. A. Williams	9	14	2	522	126	1	43.50
P. J. Sylvester	5	9	3	203	92*	0	33.83
C. Dobson	7	12	1	338	94*	0	30.72
J. Jones	16	26	2	597	114	1	24.87
H. J. Rees	5	5	1	91	46	0	22.75
Bishop	12	18	0	397	62	0	22.05
P. Butcher	14	23	2	419	64	0	19.95
J. Dalton	9	12	0	216	61	0	18.00
Kirnon	4	6	1	89	43	0	17.80
J. Foster	7	10	3	120	37*	0	17.14
A. D. Shaw	15	18	3	203	41*	0	13.53
Frost	12	11	3	83	26	0	10.37
M. Taylor	10	11	1	67	16	0	6.70
Bastien	7	7	3	26	11*	0	6.50
P. M. Holland	6	5	0	30	14	0	6.00

Played in five matches: P. A. Clitheroe 1, 1, 0, 5*; J. F. Steele 2*, 5*, 19*, 26*. Played in ur matches: S. D. Thomas 8*, 0, 11. Played in three matches: G. S. Calway 16, 38, 8; D. Pearce 9, 48, 8; M. J. Tamplin 0, 53*, 3, 55. Played in two matches: V. C. Drakes 0, , 1*; S. Mohammad 74, 2, 0, 14; O. T. Parkin 0*, 18, 0*, 0*. Played in one match: P. A. ottey 51, 78; R. D. B. Croft 4, 43*; A. Dale 33, 83; J. D. Davies 6, 0; P. S. Jones 15; J. M. Kelleher 53, 1; †J. H. Langworth 0, 15; C. M. Patel 3, 10; G. T. Wood 0.

Note: In the match v Kent at Maidstone M. C. Dobson, called up for a first-team match, as replaced by S. D. Thomas.

owling Averages

	O	M	R	W	BB	Avge
D. B. Croft	33.3	10	87	7	5-65	12.42
D. Thomas	54.4	14	202	8	3-66	25.25
J. Foster	190.5	27	663	26	4-68	25.50
Frost	319.3	61	909	27	7-87	33.66
Bastien	134.3	22	405	12	3-76	33.75
D. Pearce	53	14	174	5	2-29	34.80
C. Dobson	146.1	22	501	13	4-64	38.53
M. Taylor	158	37	474	11	3-106	43.09
A. Clitheroe	74	5	279	6	2-81	46.50
P. J. Sylvester	89.3	25	259	5	2-38	51.80
Kirnon	79.4	20	261	5	3-67	52.20
P. M. Holland	84	14	317	6	3-80	52.83

Also bowled: A. R. Butcher 0.1–0–1–0; G. P. Butcher 30.3-3–133-2; G. S. Calway 5–8–125-3; P. A. Cottey 3-0–14-1; A. Dale 8-3–12-1; A. J. Dalton 34-5–92-3; D. J. M. elleher 15-0–60-1; V. C. Drakes 46-6–144-3; D. L. Hemp 9-0–86-2; A. J. Jones 0–43-0; P. S. Jones 24-5–99-2; O. T. Parkin 40.4-5–135-4; C. M. Patel 29.5-5–124-4.

GLOUCESTERSHIRE SECOND ELEVEN

Matches 17: Won – Essex, Glamorgan, Kent, Leicestershire, Somerset, Worcestershire. Lost – orthamptonshire, Surrey. Drawn – Derbyshire, Durham, Hampshire, Lancashire, Middlesex, ottinghamshire, Sussex, Warwickshire, Yorkshire.

Batting Averages

	M	I	NO	R	HS	100s	Avg
R. I. Dawson	11	21	3	1,035	113	3	57.5
R. J. Cunliffe	9	15	5	529	81*	0	52.9
*A. W. Stovold	5	7	6	50	21*	0	50.0
T. H. C. Hancock	11	21	5	744	128	1	46.5
M. G. N. Windows	13	23	2	764	123	2	36.
J. T. C. Vaughan	9	14	2	390	119*	1	32.
M. Davies	4	4	1	92	38	0	30.6
R. I. Trotman	3	6	0	176	69	0	29.3
R. C. Williams	14	20	3	438	134	1	25.7
†R. C. J. Williams	16	27	1	578	139	1	22.2
A. J. Hunt	15	26	1	536	77	0	21.4
H. J. Morgan	7	13	0	221	55	0	17.0
*M. C. J. Ball	5	7	2	79	29	0	15.8
A. M. Smith	4	4	2	23	17*	0	11.5
J. M. A. Averis	3	5	0	56	31	0	11.2
*A. M. Babington	8	8	0	85	36	0	10.6
J. M. de la Pena	8	11	3	69	24	0	8.6
M. J. Gerrard	13	12	5	52	20*	0	7.4
R. Horrell	15	16	1	109	28	0	7.2

Played in two matches: N. D. Cross 3, 53*, 6; D. R. Hewson 12, 18, 35; K. P. Sheeraz 3, 4*; Z. A. Sher 47, 0; R. M. Wight 0, 40. Played in one match: J. E. Boyce 10; M. Cawdron 1; J. G. Whitby-Coles 0, 3; A. C. Walker did not bat.

Bowling Averages

	O	M	R	W	BB	Avg
J. T. C. Vaughan	164.1	38	375	24	6-32	15.6
A. M. Babington	265.4	54	654	36	5-56	18.1
T. H. C. Hancock	125	26	343	17	3-18	20.1
M. C. J. Ball	124	34	275	12	3-51	22.9
A. M. Smith	101.5	21	279	12	5-42	23.2
R. C. Williams	416.4	95	1,088	45	7-73	24.1
M. J. Gerrard	355.5	79	1,025	31	4-21	33.0
R. Horrell	357.3	114	927	25	4-88	37.0
J. M. de la Pena	125.1	23	472	11	4-31	42.9

Also bowled: J. M. A. Averis 50.2–11–151–0; J. E. Boyce 16–4–55–2; M. J. Cawdron 38–17–61–5; M. Davies 81–27–204–1; R. I. Dawson 22–1–107–2; A. J. Hunt 6–0–36–1; H. Morgan 20–8–51–0; K. P. Sheeraz 30.4–2–104–1; Z. A. Sher 7–0–18–0; R. I. Trotman 39–9–123–3; J. G. Whitby-Coles 18–6–40–1; R. M. Wight 52–17–109–5.

HAMPSHIRE SECOND ELEVEN

Matches 17: Won – Essex, Kent, Lancashire, Surrey, Warwickshire, Worcestershire. Lost Durham, Middlesex, Northamptonshire. Drawn – Derbyshire, Glamorgan, Gloucestershire, Leicestershire, Nottinghamshire, Somerset, Sussex, Yorkshire.

Batting Averages

	M	I	NO	R	HS	100s	Avg
A. N. Aymes	2	4	1	285	133*	1	95.0
*R. M. F. Cox	13	20	3	934	143	4	54.9
R. S. M. Morris	14	23	4	835	166	2	43.9
D. N. Crookes	3	5	1	164	90	0	41.0
J. R. Wood	11	20	1	731	149	3	38.4
J. S. Laney	9	15	2	499	127	2	38.3
T. J. Carter	3	5	2	104	36	0	34.6

	M	I	NO	R	HS	100s	Avge
R. J. Maru	8	12	2	307	84	0	30.70
†R. J. Parks	11	14	2	332	71	0	27.66
I. K. Maynard	5	9	1	206	62	0	25.75
N. Davey	3	5	1	99	45	0	24.75
I. J. Turner	6	5	1	96	40	0	24.00
M. J. Thursfield	14	16	7	202	58*	0	22.44
J. N. Batty	4	8	4	87	24*	0	21.75
J. P. Kent	4	5	0	101	45	0	20.20
P. J. Bakker	12	10	2	135	46	0	16.87
R. T. P. Miller	4	6	0	98	50	0	16.33
J. N. B. Bovill	10	10	5	64	26	0	12.80
M. Garaway	4	7	2	55	23*	0	11.00
B. A. Hames	3	5	0	40	25	0	8.00
D. P. J. Flint	17	10	3	39	17	0	5.57

Played in five matches: K. J. Shine 1, 9, 7. Played in three matches: C. Sketchley 1. Played in two matches: D. G. J. Carson 35, 14; R. E. Hayward 20, 5; W. S. Kendall 9, 13, 9; B. B. Moore 30. Played in one match: K. Bird 1; J. P. Dickson 0; G. R. Hill 17, 8; G. I. Macmillan 14; G. R. Mason 16*; B. A. Mayers 46, 16*; J. Maynard 17, 12; M. C. J. Nicholas 35, 0; P. C. P. Simmonite 13, 6; J. D. Swann 19*; N. R. Taylor 1; A. M. Whyte did not bat.

Note: In the match v Essex at Portsmouth, R. M. F. Cox, called up for a first-team match, was replaced by G. I. Macmillan.

Bowling Averages

	O	M	R	W	BB	Avge
K. J. Shine	139.4	33	354	28	7-61	12.64
R. J. Maru	279	113	500	30	6-46	16.66
P. J. Bakker	311.5	85	846	37	6-54	22.86
I. J. Turner	203.2	55	533	22	6-72	24.22
M. J. Thursfield	233.4	52	749	25	5-59	29.96
J. N. B. Bovill	191.5	24	673	21	4-73	32.04
C. Sketchley	47	14	161	5	2-5	32.20
D. P. J. Flint	411.2	97	1,279	27	4-71	47.37

Also bowled: K. Bird 25-8-76-2; D. N. Crookes 43-7-145-1; J. P. Dickson 14-1-60-1; J. P. Kent 4-1-6-0; J. S. Laney 11-5-30-0; G. R. Mason 9-3-28-1; J. Maynard 22-1-115-1; R. T. P. Miller 20-3-66-1; R. S. M. Morris 13-5-38-1; J. D. Swann 9-0-36-0; N. R. Taylor 20-6-43-4; A. M. Whyte 18-3-63-0; J. R. Wood 7-2-22-0.

KENT SECOND ELEVEN

Matches 17: Won – *Essex, Northamptonshire, Somerset, Sussex.* Lost – *Derbyshire, Gloucestershire, Hampshire, Middlesex, Warwickshire.* Drawn – *Durham, Glamorgan, Lancashire, Leicestershire, Nottinghamshire, Surrey, Worcestershire, Yorkshire.*

Batting Averages

	M	I	NO	R	HS	100s	Avge
D. P. Fulton	11	20	4	1,022	200*	3	63.87
J. I. Longley	14	21	5	1,006	200*	3	62.87
N. J. Llong	13	17	1	888	157	4	55.50
M. M. Patel	4	4	2	92	45*	0	46.00
L. E. Robson	4	4	2	84	28*	0	42.00
†G. J. Kersey	16	24	6	653	115*	1	36.27
*A. G. E. Ealham	10	7	3	122	46	0	30.50
A. J. Planck	7	11	1	264	82	0	26.40
I. Baldock	13	21	1	511	158	1	25.55

	M	I	NO	R	HS	100s	Avge
G. D. Myers	5	9	1	189	61	0	23.62
M. J. Walker	3	5	0	112	64	0	22.40
S. G. Milroy	4	5	1	79	27	0	19.75
C. Penn	5	6	0	117	38	0	19.50
C. J. Hollins	5	8	2	106	26	0	17.66
N. W. Preston	7	9	4	88	32	0	17.60
A. Tutt	14	15	7	123	36	0	15.37
P. A. Westrop	3	3	1	27	16*	0	13.50
J. B. Thompson	4	4	1	39	29	0	13.00
T. N. Wren	16	18	1	214	56*	0	12.58
S. C. Willis	12	16	2	155	43	0	11.07
R. M. Ellison	3	4	0	30	15	0	7.50

Played in two matches: R. P. Davis 7, 0; M. A. Ealham 51, 91, 34; J. L. Langer 0, 10, 61, 5*; D. R. Penfold 38, 7, 8. Played in one match: G. R. Cowdrey 0, 37; M. V. Fleming 102; M. R. Fletcher 14, 0; O. Iqbal 33, 0; M. J. McCague 5; J. F. Barr did not bat.

Bowling Averages

	O	M	R	W	BB	Avge
J. B. Thompson	72.4	16	222	11	5-35	20.18
C. Penn	119	37	305	15	4-12	20.33
R. M. Ellison	80	29	167	8	4-30	20.87
M. A. Ealham	42	12	91	4	4-34	22.75
M. M. Patel	88.5	40	168	7	4-73	24.00
A. Tutt	368.5	84	959	39	7-42	24.58
T. N. Wren	536.4	129	1,626	58	5-25	28.03
N. W. Preston	152.1	38	406	13	4-63	31.23
R. P. Davis	61	12	163	5	3-91	32.60
N. J. Llong	407	99	1,085	33	5-89	32.87
L. E. Robson	68.5	12	236	6	3-20	39.33
C. J. Hollins	81.5	8	368	9	3-65	40.88
P. A. Westropp	54.4	7	217	5	4-72	43.40

Also bowled: J. F. Barr 5-3-9-0; G. R. Cowdrey 7-1-26-0; M. V. Fleming 13-2-36-1; M. R. Fletcher 7-0-17-0; D. P. Fulton 7-1-24-1; J. I. Longley 1-0-8-0; M. J. McCague 33-13-55-3; S. G. Milroy 18-4-72-3; A. J. Planck 22-4-86-2; M. J. Walker 23.3-1-82-2; S. C. Willis 31.1-3-171-3.

LANCASHIRE SECOND ELEVEN

Matches 17: Won – Essex, Middlesex, Surrey. Lost – Hampshire. Drawn – Derbyshire, Durham, Glamorgan, Gloucestershire, Kent, Leicestershire, Northamptonshire, Nottinghamshire, Somerset, Sussex, Warwickshire, Worcestershire, Yorkshire.

Batting Averages

	M	I	NO	R	HS	100s	Avge
J. E. R. Gallian	7	12	5	1,015	160*	7	145.00
J. P. Crawley	2	4	1	389	217*	2	129.66
M. J. Clinning	2	3	2	125	72	0	125.00
G. Fowler	3	6	0	401	112	1	66.83
R. C. Irani	15	22	3	1,012	118	1	53.26
S. P. Titchard	4	6	0	304	75	0	50.66
G. Yates	17	25	8	847	147	1	49.82
G. D. Mendis	3	6	0	280	114	1	46.66
D. J. Murray	6	10	1	416	153	1	46.22
I. D. Austin	4	7	1	252	65	0	42.00
†W. J. Luntley	3	4	2	76	35*	0	38.00

	M	I	NO	R	HS	100s	Avge
I. D. Fitton	10	13	0	438	93	0	33.69
P. J. Wilcock	8	15	3	374	122	1	31.16
*†J. Stanworth	11	7	2	136	58	0	27.20
G. J. Cordingley	8	9	0	166	46	0	18.44
N. T. Wood	4	7	2	90	46	0	18.00
M. E. Harvey	5	8	1	101	31	0	14.42
I. M. Fielding	14	17	3	183	29*	0	13.07
D. T. Foy	10	12	1	88	38	0	8.00
N. D. R. Bannister	2	4	0	32	21	0	8.00
P. J. W. Allott	2	3	0	22	16	0	7.33
N. A. Derbyshire	13	12	5	25	5*	0	3.57
S. D. Fletcher	11	8	1	22	9	0	3.14

Played in seven matches: M. A. Sharp 4*, 0*, 0*. Played in four matches: G. Chapple 18*. Played in one match: G. K. C. Barker 31*, 1; A. A. Barnett 18, 17*; D. J. Callaghan 84; P. A. J. DeFreitas 54; D. Eckersley 15, 9; J. D. Harvey 78; J. A. L. Henderson 17; P. J. Neville 10, 9; †T. P. A. Standing 1*, 0; M. Wakefield 9*, 6*; C. Brown, P. J. Deakin, P. J. Heyes and A. M. James did not bat.

Note: Owing to first-team calls, R. C. Irani was replaced by M. J. Clinning in the match v Leicestershire at Leicester and J. D. Fitton was replaced by R. C. Irani in the match v Nottinghamshire at Worthington Simpson.

Bowling Averages

	O	M	R	W	BB	Avge
P. J. Deakin	43.5	6	141	7	4-64	20.14
G. Yates	568.2	186	1,265	62	6-16	20.40
G. Chapple	122	33	347	14	3-40	24.78
I. D. Austin	70.5	21	159	6	2-30	26.50
I. M. Fielding	297.4	90	779	27	5-53	28.85
A. A. Barnett	38	8	123	4	4-64	30.75
D. T. Foy	136.1	37	372	11	2-23	33.81
S. D. Fletcher	297	74	977	25	4-68	39.08
N. A. Derbyshire	235.3	29	924	23	5-41	40.17
M. A. Sharp	151	42	405	9	2-32	45.00
R. C. Irani	180	39	591	13	5-39	45.46
J. D. Fitton	242.5	74	592	11	3-12	53.81

Also bowled: P. J. W. Allott 30–7–51–0; C. Brown 15.2–4–25–3; M. J. Clinning 8–0–57–0; G. J. Cordingley 8–4–16–1; P. A. J. DeFreitas 26–6–67–2; D. Eckersley 5–1–11–0; J. E. R. Gallian 37.4–10–125–0; J. A. L. Henderson 18.2–1–83–3; A. M. James 10–3–21–0; D. J. Murray 2–0–21–1; S. P. Titchard 9–2–39–0.

LEICESTERSHIRE SECOND ELEVEN

Matches 17: Won – Glamorgan. Lost – Durham, Gloucestershire, Warwickshire, Yorkshire. Drawn – Derbyshire, Essex, Hampshire, Kent, Lancashire, Middlesex, Northamptonshire, Nottinghamshire, Somerset, Surrey, Sussex, Worcestershire.

Batting Averages

	M	I	NO	R	HS	100s	Avge
G. J. Parsons	4	7	2	321	114*	2	64.20
M. I. Gidley	10	19	4	764	151	2	50.93
B. F. Smith	4	8	1	339	135	1	48.42
*R. A. Cobb	15	24	8	686	116	1	42.87
†P. A. Nixon	6	12	1	439	125*	1	39.90
A. Roseberry	15	28	3	786	92	0	31.44
R. P. Gofton	9	14	5	273	74	0	30.33
†P. N. Hepworth	11	21	2	536	86	0	28.21

	M	I	NO	R	HS	100s	Avge
†P. Whitticase	9	15	0	415	71	0	27.66
J. M. Dakin	10	15	2	283	93*	0	21.76
D. L. Maddy	13	24	0	496	73	0	20.66
A. F. Haye	13	16	3	248	52*	0	19.07
C. J. Hawkes	4	6	2	73	23	0	18.25
I. F. Plender	7	14	0	246	66	0	17.57
I. J. Sutcliffe	6	12	1	167	39	0	15.18
M. T. Brimson	8	6	1	44	19	0	8.80
D. G. White	6	9	0	67	27	0	7.44
N. S. De Silva	8	7	2	29	10*	0	5.80
B. Leech	4	5	3	4	3	0	2.00

Played in two matches: S. Atkinson 1, 43*, 11*; P. S. Widdowson 2, 13. Played in one match: M. A. V. Bell 0, 1; J. D. R. Benson 57; R. Blockley 17*; C. Bloor 2, 18; C. D Crowe 18, 2; A. C. Cummins 30, 34; S. Herzberg 13, 12; G. N. Jackson 24, 18; T. J. Mason 20, 3; J. C. Maynard 33*; N. R. Newman 17, 2; L. Potter 67, 32; M. Powell 5, 6; M. J Rutterford 0; I. M. Stanger 0, 10*; M. D. R. Sutliff 3, 18; S. A. Sylvester 2*, 17; M. J Walshe 12; S. D. Welch 0, 17; A. Cutts and K. Thomson did not bat.

Bowling Averages

	O	M	R	W	BB	Avge
C. J. Hawkes	142.2	53	279	16	4-61	17.43
G. J. Parsons	92.4	31	198	10	4-43	19.80
R. P. Gofton	244.3	61	681	29	5-71	23.48
B. Leech	101.4	23	283	11	3-68	25.72
D. G. White	105.5	21	320	12	3-35	26.66
M. I. Gidley	281.2	81	667	24	3-25	27.79
M. T. Brimson	232.5	51	655	23	4-89	28.47
J. M. Dakin	199.4	36	611	20	3-36	30.55
P. N. Hepworth	146	42	402	10	3-28	40.20
A. F. Haye	172.1	27	623	14	3-24	44.50

Also bowled: S. Atkinson 35.5-10-134-2; M. A. V. Bell 23.3-3-99-3; A. C. Cummins 32-14-61-2; A. Cutts 23.4-4-95-2; N. S. De Silva 161-36-572-2; S. Herzberg 32-5-88-4; D. L. Maddy 2-0-7-0; T. J. Mason 40-13-82-7; J. C. Maynard 33-5-95-1; N. R. Newman 23-3-71-0; I. F. Plender 23-5-89-3; L. Potter 41-10-88-0; M. Powell 19-3-52-0; A. Roseberry 1-0-10-0; M. J. Rutterford 30-9-68-0; B. F. Smith 7-1-35-0; I. M. Stanger 32-8-130-3; S. A. Sylvester 33-6-134-4; K. Thomson 15-4-84-1; M. J. Walshe 23-5-67-1; S. D. Welch 32-8-90-1; P. S. Widdowson 37-7-129-5.

MIDDLESEX SECOND ELEVEN

Matches 17: Won – Derbyshire, Glamorgan, Hampshire, Kent, Nottinghamshire. Lost – Lancashire, Somerset. Drawn – Durham, Gloucestershire, Leicestershire, Northamptonshire Surrey, Sussex, Warwickshire, Worcestershire, Yorkshire. Abandoned – Essex.

Batting Averages

	M	I	NO	R	HS	100s	Avge
T. A. Radford	7	9	5	332	119*	2	83.00
A. Habib	15	22	9	994	203*	2	76.46
P. N. Weekes	3	4	1	174	65	0	58.00
*J. C. Pooley	14	22	4	843	136	4	46.83
†R. J. Sims	14	19	3	665	115	1	41.56
*†P. Farbrace	15	18	3	582	123	1	38.80
M. Keech	16	22	2	767	102	1	38.35
D. A. Walker	6	5	1	111	43	0	27.75
*I. J. Gould	5	3	0	83	47	0	27.66

	M	I	NO	R	HS	100s	Avge
I. J. F. Hutchinson	5	6	0	161	65	0	26.83
J. C. Harrison	13	20	1	465	68	0	24.47
K. P. Dutch	9	7	1	138	37	0	23.00
R. J. Ballinger	9	5	2	58	38*	0	19.33
R. S. Yeabsley	4	4	2	32	18*	0	16.00
R. L. Johnson	11	6	3	28	12*	0	9.33
J. M. S. Whittington	6	5	2	16	9	0	5.33
S. A. Sylvester	14	6	3	13	4*	0	4.33

Played in two matches: R. Rao 12*, 10. Played in one match: D. W. Headley 52; M. R. Ramprakash 111*; D. P. Rogers 0, 0; C. W. Taylor 23, 1. N. G. Cowans, R. A. Davidson, A. S. Lewis, M. D. Robinson and P. C. R. Tufnell did not bat.

Note: In the match v Yorkshire at Uxbridge S. A. Sylvester, called up for a first-team match, was replaced by R. L. Johnson.

Bowling Averages

	O	M	R	W	BB	Avge
K. P. Dutch	302	86	728	33	6-77	22.06
R. J. Ballinger	170	33	511	23	5-30	22.21
R. L. Johnson	253.2	63	678	30	5-66	22.60
M. Keech	273.1	71	728	30	4-53	24.26
P. N. Weekes	136.5	42	321	11	3-31	29.18
J. M. S. Whittington	128.1	35	341	10	3-50	34.10
S. A. Sylvester	363.4	99	1,234	35	4-50	35.25

Also bowled: N. G. Cowans 4–3–2–0; R. A. Davidson 18–4–60–1; I. J. Gould 21–9–50–2; A. Habib 46–7–183–7; J. C. Harrison 134–30–449–7; D. W. Headley 36–11–105–0; T. A. Radford 8–2–13–0; R. Rao 27.1–10–94–3; M. D. Robinson 20–2–74–1; R. J. Sims 1–1–0–0; C. W. Taylor 27–4–56–3; P. C. R. Tufnell 52.2–19–120–3; D. A. Walker 83–12–318–5; R. S. Yeabsley 67.2–11–196–3.

NORTHAMPTONSHIRE SECOND ELEVEN

Matches 17: Won – Derbyshire, Essex, Gloucestershire, Hampshire, Nottinghamshire, Somerset, Sussex. Lost – Kent. Drawn – Durham, Glamorgan, Lancashire, Leicestershire, Middlesex, Surrey, Warwickshire, Worcestershire, Yorkshire.

Batting Averages

	M	I	NO	R	HS	100s	Avge
M. B. Loye	6	10	2	556	166*	2	69.50
M. N. Bowen	13	12	7	327	64*	0	65.40
A. L. Penberthy	9	16	2	811	218	2	57.92
R. R. Montgomerie	10	14	2	585	137*	1	48.75
R. J. Warren	16	26	3	1,084	150	3	47.13
R. N. Dalton	4	4	0	151	59	0	37.75
T. C. Walton	11	15	1	493	114	2	35.21
R. M. Carter	8	5	3	62	33	0	31.00
K. J. Innes	10	13	4	269	60	0	29.88
S. J. Green	14	21	1	521	74	0	26.05
J. N. Snape	5	6	2	101	40	0	25.25
A. R. Roberts	4	7	0	174	93	0	24.85
N. A. Stanley	17	27	2	584	89	0	23.36
*†W. M. Noon	17	24	4	436	49	0	21.80
H. Kember	11	8	3	83	34	0	16.60
J. G. Hughes	10	12	5	112	31*	0	16.00
A. Walker	7	8	3	72	16*	0	14.40
R. M. Pearson	8	5	2	34	12*	0	11.33

Played in two matches: R. G. Williams 54, 6. Played in one match: J. M. Attfield 31, 13; S. M. Brogan 25, 6*; J. R. Goode 6, 0; T. W. Harrison 5; S. V. Laudat 27.

Bowling Averages

	O	M	R	W	BB	Avge
R. N. Dalton..............	49.3	12	146	8	4-22	18.25
A. L. Penberthy	187.3	35	488	22	5-55	22.18
T. C. Walton...............	169	38	467	20	4-37	23.35
R. M. Pearson..............	224.3	71	622	26	5-26	23.92
J. G. Hughes...............	167.3	29	510	21	4-27	24.28
H. Kember	287.5	100	614	23	3-57	26.69
A. Walker	187.2	40	579	21	4-50	27.57
A. R. Roberts	137.3	23	502	17	6-63	29.52
M. N. Bowen	290	74	796	26	5-38	30.61
N. A. Stanley	132	41	330	10	3-56	33.00
K. J. Innes	92.3	26	307	9	5-18	34.11

Also bowled: J. R. Goode 8.2–0–45–3; S. V. Laudat 7–1–30–0; M. B. Loye 15–0–91–3; J. N. Snape 89.3–28–208–3; R. J. Warren 9–0–72–0; R. G. Williams 38–11–68–0.

NOTTINGHAMSHIRE SECOND ELEVEN

Matches 17: Won – Essex. Lost – Middlesex, Northamptonshire, Surrey, Sussex, Yorkshire. Drawn – Derbyshire, Durham, Glamorgan, Gloucestershire, Hampshire, Kent, Lancashire, Leicestershire, Somerset, Warwickshire, Worcestershire.

Batting Averages

	M	I	NO	R	HS	100s	Avge
M. Saxelby	9	15	3	848	94*	0	70.66
G. F. Archer	12	22	3	929	151*	4	48.89
M. G. Field-Buss	7	11	7	187	66*	0	46.75
*M. Newell................	17	28	8	773	120	2	38.65
J. R. Wileman	12	22	1	733	128	1	34.90
G. W. Mike	4	5	1	131	54	0	32.75
W. A. Dessaur	16	30	4	843	135	1	32.42
M. P. Dowman.............	13	22	0	709	95	0	32.22
L. N. Walker	6	9	1	249	84	0	31.12
D. R. Brewis..............	4	4	3	29	21*	0	29.00
K. P. Evans	2	3	0	72	34	0	24.00
J. E. Hindson	8	13	2	262	69	0	23.81
†S. Bramhall	14	16	3	256	33	0	19.69
R. J. Chapman	16	11	5	99	52	0	16.50
D. B. Pennett	10	12	1	163	47	0	14.81
S. J. Musgrove	4	6	0	81	33	0	13.50
K. Saxelby................	6	5	1	51	39	0	12.75
J. A. Turner	4	6	0	64	26	0	10.66
R. A. Pick	3	4	1	32	16*	0	10.66
S. M. Brown	6	3	1	13	12*	0	6.50
J. A. Afford..............	6	5	3	13	6*	0	6.50

Played in two matches: K. E. Cooper 42, 0. Played in one match: M. A. Beazeley 0; V. J. P. Broadley 14, 4; B. Helps 16*; E. E. Hemmings 4; R. I. Howarth 1; R. L. Perkins 3; P. R. Pollard 35, 25; T. N. Sawrey-Cookson 12, 0.

Note: In the match v Yorkshire at Harrogate M. G. Field-Buss and M. Saxelby, called up for a first-team match, were replaced by S. M. Brown and K. E. Cooper.

Bowling Averages

	O	M	R	W	BB	Avge
M. Saxelby	26	7	51	5	4-40	10.20
J. A. Afford	326.3	114	658	41	7-81	16.04
R. A. Pick	74.4	10	214	9	3-51	23.77
M. G. Field-Buss	301	103	655	24	6-55	27.29
D. B. Pennett	295.2	63	913	27	6-88	33.81
M. P. Dowman	154	37	520	14	3-49	37.14
S. M. Brown	155.5	34	517	13	4-74	39.76
R. J. Chapman	317.3	55	1,186	29	3-37	40.89
J. E. Hindson	292.3	59	928	22	4-115	42.18
D. R. Brewis	50	8	204	4	2-36	51.00
G. W. Mike	95	22	375	5	2-31	75.00

Also bowled: G. F. Archer 8-1-59-0; M. A. Beazeley 6.5-0-19-0; S. Bramhall 2-0-21-0; K. E. Cooper 40-17-94-3; W. A. Dessaur 62-9-262-1; K. P. Evans 23.5-1-117-2; E. E. Hemmings 14-6-28-0; R. I. Howarth 21.3-4-86-1; S. J. Musgrove 40-3-164-2; M. Newell 40.1-10-179-2; R. L. Perkins 19-6-52-2; K. Saxelby 51-8-218-2; J. R. Wileman 1-0-12-0.

SOMERSET SECOND ELEVEN

Matches 17: Won – Durham, Middlesex, Warwickshire. Lost – Glamorgan, Gloucestershire, Kent, Northamptonshire, Worcestershire. Drawn – Derbyshire, Essex, Hampshire, Lancashire, Leicestershire, Nottinghamshire, Surrey, Sussex, Yorkshire.

Batting Averages

	M	I	NO	R	HS	100s	Avge
R. J. Bartlett	5	7	2	247	66	0	49.40
I. Fletcher	8	14	1	606	194	1	46.61
†R. J. Turner	14	24	5	803	109*	3	42.26
G. T. J. Townsend	9	18	1	702	167*	3	41.29
K. A. Parsons	15	27	5	874	160*	3	39.72
P. Deaken	2	4	2	74	41	0	37.00
J. C. Hallett	10	12	6	205	41*	0	34.16
M. Trescothick	4	5	1	116	44	0	29.00
*P. J. Robinson	7	9	7	56	16	0	28.00
R. P. Lefebvre	8	13	0	332	80	0	25.53
K. J. Parsons	16	27	3	575	134	2	23.95
G. W. White	10	17	1	343	56	0	21.43
M. F. Robinson	13	17	1	327	149	1	20.43
A. Payne	13	17	3	265	57	0	18.92
J. I. D. Kerr	13	20	0	351	107	1	17.55
K. G. Sedgbeer	3	5	1	69	43*	0	17.25
N. Davey	3	5	0	71	34	0	14.20
T. Edwards	3	6	0	85	50	0	14.16
M. Liddle	2	4	1	27	13*	0	9.00
A. C. Cottam	5	7	2	37	19	0	7.40
A. P. van Troost	8	8	2	41	15	0	6.83

Played in two matches: T. Deacon 0; †S. Griffiths 5, 0; H. R. J. Trump 0, 39*; A. Winstone 3*; J. P. Searle did not bat. Played in one match: M. N. Lathwell 59, 11; K. H. MacLeay 70, 8; R. J. Pannell 0; B. M. Wellington 4; J. G. Wyatt 9*, 5*; P. B. Kelly and G. Swinney did not bat.

Note: In the match v Gloucestershire at Bristol A. P. van Troost, called up for a first-team match, was replaced by A. Payne.

Bowling Averages

	O	M	R	W	BB	Avge
P. J. Robinson	48	21	58	6	4-35	9.66
R. P. Lefebvre	271.4	84	578	33	5-30	17.51
A. P. van Troost	184.3	27	589	29	7-47	20.31
H. R. J. Trump	81.5	28	179	8	3-23	22.37
P. Deaken	65	22	144	5	3-73	28.80
K. A. Parsons	112	14	312	10	3-44	31.20
A. C. Cottam	165.4	47	526	15	7-56	35.06
A. Payne	303.3	47	1,056	26	4-35	40.61
J. C. Hallett	266.1	50	911	22	4-58	41.40
M. F. Robinson	234.2	51	891	17	4-44	52.41
J. I. D. Kerr	189	26	718	13	3-48	55.23
G. W. White	97.4	24	409	5	2-36	81.80

Also bowled: R. J. Bartlett 22–7–66–1; T. Deacon 23–0–106–1; T. Edwards 0.4–0–4–0;
P. B. Kelly 15–4–39–1; M. N. Lathwell 19–6–49–0; K. H. MacLeay 22–3–68–2; R. J.
Pannell 14–2–58–0; K. J. Parsons 0.1–0–4–0; J. P. Searle 38–12–107–1; K. G. Sedgbeer
29–5–94–1; G. Swinney 2–0–5–0; B. M. Wellington 6–1–39–0; A. Winstone 46–14–141–1.

SURREY SECOND ELEVEN

Matches 17: Won – Derbyshire, Durham, Essex, Gloucestershire, Nottinghamshire, Sussex, Warwickshire, Yorkshire. Lost – Hampshire, Lancashire. Drawn – Glamorgan, Kent, Leicestershire, Middlesex, Northamptonshire, Somerset, Worcestershire.

Batting Averages

	M	I	NO	R	HS	100s	Avge
P. D. Atkins	11	16	7	744	116	2	82.66
A. D. Brown	5	7	0	391	145	2	55.85
*I. A. Greig	8	9	3	287	107	1	47.83
A. J. Hollioake	15	18	6	520	89	0	43.33
†D. G. C. Ligertwood	12	15	2	539	76	0	41.46
*K. T. Medlycott	16	19	3	627	67	0	39.18
A. W. Smith	17	22	3	735	135	1	38.68
J. D. Robinson	12	16	2	541	136	1	38.64
R. I. Alikhan	11	13	2	406	94	0	36.90
I. J. Ward	7	6	1	161	70	0	32.20
M. A. Butcher	14	18	0	577	119	2	32.05
D. J. M. Kelleher	9	13	3	289	67*	0	28.90
A. J. Murphy	10	8	4	107	36*	0	26.75
†N. F. Sargeant	7	8	1	185	53	0	26.42
M. R. Bainbridge	11	9	3	69	25	0	11.50

Played in five matches: R. E. Bryson 6, 3, 1. Played in three matches: J. Boiling 5, 7, 17;
M. A. Feltham 70, 8; N. M. Kendrick 0. Played in two matches: D. M. Ward did not bat.
Played in one match: D. J. Bicknell 39, 71; C. K. Bullen 0, 10; G. S. Clinton 23, 6;
R. Dwarka 5*; N. Mugdal 0, 0*; I. D. Turner 2*.

Bowling Averages

	O	M	R	W	BB	Avge
J. Boiling	93.5	37	175	12	7-85	14.58
A. W. Smith	213.5	48	607	29	4-25	20.93
N. M. Kendrick	148	47	313	14	4-62	22.35
M. A. Feltham	72	16	202	9	3-57	22.44
I. A. Greig	135.2	29	365	16	4-39	22.81
M. R. Bainbridge	227.4	76	565	23	5-32	24.56

	O	M	R	W	BB	Avge
. T. Medlycott	413.4	104	1,134	39	6-102	29.07
. A. Butcher..............	172	46	415	13	3-14	31.92
. J. Hollioake	254.3	39	883	26	5-37	33.96
. J. Murphy	276.4	44	928	23	4-36	40.34
. E. Bryson	95	12	290	6	4-53	48.33
D. Robinson	80.4	23	207	4	3-50	51.75
. J. M. Kelleher...........	138.2	41	323	6	2-21	53.83

Also bowled: R. I. Alikhan 21–4–83–2; P. D. Atkins 1–0–8–0; R. Dwarka 3–2–1–0;
. Mugdal 10–0–34–2; D. M. Ward 4–0–17–0; I. J. Ward 32–5–122–3.

SUSSEX SECOND ELEVEN

*Matches 17: Won – Derbyshire, Glamorgan, Nottinghamshire. Lost – Durham, Kent,
Northamptonshire, Surrey. Drawn – Essex, Gloucestershire, Hampshire, Lancashire, Leicestershire, Middlesex, Somerset, Warwickshire, Worcestershire, Yorkshire.*

Batting Averages

	M	I	NO	R	HS	100s	Avge
. Law	4	5	3	155	57	0	77.50
. Greenfield	11	20	4	933	142*	1	58.31
. W. Hall	4	8	1	371	188*	1	53.00
. M. Wells..............	5	9	1	392	177	1	49.00
. Newell	7	12	2	472	135	1	47.20
. C. Remy.	13	25	2	900	124	2	39.13
. A. North	13	22	3	724	131	1	38.10
. T. P. Donelan	7	11	5	222	62*	0	37.00
. J. Lenham	3	6	0	181	61	0	30.16
. W. Dean	3	4	2	59	44	0	29.50
. Hanley	14	25	0	701	71	0	28.04
. Cooper.	2	4	1	77	30*	0	25.66
. T. E. Peirce	15	25	2	588	73*	0	25.56
. N. Jones.	6	7	0	143	47	0	20.42
. R. Cornford	9	16	2	254	69	0	18.14
. R. Hansford	13	19	4	261	39	0	17.40
. Pretorius	2	3	0	49	28	0	16.33
. Davis	9	9	3	71	33	0	11.83
. Edwards	2	3	0	34	20	0	11.33
. Marchant	3	6	0	51	23	0	8.50
. C. Phillips	3	3	1	17	16	0	8.50
. S. H. Giddins	10	12	4	65	23	0	8.12
S. Humphries	12	13	4	70	14*	0	7.77
. Stevens	3	6	0	23	13	0	3.83
. E. Waller	4	6	2	7	3*	0	1.75
. G. Robson	7	3	0	5	4	0	1.66

Played in one match: M. Garaway 0; D. M. Smith 15*, 2; G. Thomas 40*; P. Wicker
42*.

Bowling Averages

	O	M	R	W	BB	Avge
N. J. Lenham	26.5	6	72	4	3-33	18.00
. R. Hansford.............	232.3	51	677	32	6-39	21.15
. A. North	200.2	44	564	26	7-39	21.69
. W. Dean	105.4	32	239	10	4-122	23.90
. G. Robson	135	31	413	16	4-47	25.81
. S. H. Giddins............	191.5	45	510	19	5-17	26.84

	O	M	R	W	BB	Avge
B. T. P. Donelan	324.5	98	824	28	6-29	29.42
C. C. Remy	73	12	252	8	3-14	31.50
N. Pretorius	52	7	177	5	2-32	35.40
M. T. E. Peirce	232	49	773	21	4-49	36.80
K. Newell	40	12	125	3	3-45	41.66
K. Greenfield	118.1	25	318	7	3-16	45.42
H. Davis	122.5	24	447	8	3-43	55.87
A. R. Cornford	93.1	17	289	5	2-57	57.80
A. N. Jones	139	20	434	7	1-33	62.00

Also bowled: S. Cooper 5–1–12–1; A. Edwards 23–1–98–1; D. Law 28–1–98–0; N. C Phillips 21.2–4–56–1; C. E. Waller 21.1–12–32–1; C. M. Wells 35–7–107–1.

WARWICKSHIRE SECOND ELEVEN

Matches 17: Won – Kent, Leicestershire, Yorkshire. Lost – Durham, Hampshire, Somerset Surrey. Drawn – Derbyshire, Essex, Glamorgan, Gloucestershire, Lancashire, Middlesex Northamptonshire, Nottinghamshire, Sussex, Worcestershire.

Batting Averages

	M	I	NO	R	HS	100s	Avge
T. L. Penney	5	9	3	585	155*	3	97.50
C. Patel	2	3	2	48	20*	0	48.00
*Asif Din	15	23	4	778	194	3	40.94
Wasim Khan	17	29	3	943	123*	1	36.26
J. D. Ratcliffe	12	21	4	600	130	2	35.29
J. M. A. Inglis	6	7	2	163	50	0	32.60
B. C. Usher	13	12	6	195	31	0	32.50
†M. Burns	16	26	0	789	165	2	30.34
S. F. Shephard	3	3	0	88	65	0	29.33
D. R. Brown	6	10	3	188	62*	0	26.85
N. M. K. Smith	5	7	1	152	35	0	25.33
†P. C. L. Holloway	11	18	3	359	61	0	23.93
P. A. Booth	8	8	1	158	54	0	22.57
A. F. Giles	16	23	0	469	60	0	20.39
G. Welch	16	22	4	354	74	0	19.66
M. A. V. Bell	13	10	5	61	13*	0	12.20
C. E. Mulraine	3	6	1	61	23	0	12.20
†K. J. Piper	4	7	0	45	18	0	6.42

Played in two matches: K. G. Bray 7*, 1, 0; M. J. Powell 10*, 3. Played in one match R. N. Abberley 0; P. Aldred 0; E. D. P. Bourke 17, 4; A. C. Cummins 12*, 3; G. W Ecclestone 30, 1; R. D. Hughes 3, 1; M. I. Humphries 10, 0; S. McDonald 9*; P. Mirza 4*, 0; R. Muggeridge 28. G. F. Shephard and P. A. Thomas did not bat.

Bowling Averages

	O	M	R	W	BB	Avge
P. A. Thomas	25	2	81	6	3-30	13.50
M. A. V. Bell	279.3	68	740	44	9-103	16.81
D. R. Brown	151	39	374	21	6-61	17.80
P. A. Booth	300.1	98	612	26	4-35	23.53
A. F. Giles	356.2	78	1,042	36	6-110	28.94
G. Welch	327.3	86	844	29	4-25	29.10
Asif Din	125.1	30	324	11	3-40	29.45
K. G. Bray	47	13	124	4	2-10	31.00
N. M. K. Smith	141.3	43	366	8	3-44	45.75
B. C. Usher	187.4	36	605	9	3-43	67.22

Also bowled: P. Aldred 17–3–42–0; E. D. P. Bourke 10–4–29–1; M. Burns 43–14–99–3; A. C. Cummins 22–4–56–1; J. M. A. Inglis 11–1–43–1; Wasim Khan 3–0–16–0; S. McDonald 7–0–44–0; P. Mirza 12–1–43–0; R. Muggeridge 8.1–0–46–0; C. Patel 27–2–120–3; T. L. Penney 1.3–0–6–1; M. J. Powell 5–0–35–1; J. D. Ratcliffe 9–0–39–1; G. F. Shephard 29–7–97–3.

WORCESTERSHIRE SECOND ELEVEN

Matches 17: Won – Somerset. Lost – Derbyshire, Gloucestershire, Hampshire, Yorkshire. Drawn – Durham, Essex, Glamorgan, Kent, Lancashire, Leicestershire, Middlesex, Northamptonshire, Nottinghamshire, Surrey, Sussex, Warwickshire.

Batting Averages

	M	I	NO	R	HS	100s	Avge
C. M. Tolley	8	16	3	613	168*	1	47.15
W. P. C. Weston	4	8	1	317	123	1	45.28
G. R. Haynes	7	12	1	435	123	1	39.54
G. R. Hill	5	8	0	301	104	1	37.62
A. C. H. Seymour	11	19	1	606	62	0	33.66
M. J. Weston	11	20	3	551	173*	1	32.41
D. B. D'Oliveira	5	9	0	284	113	1	31.55
K. R. Spiring	9	15	0	448	87	0	29.86
C. J. Eyers	11	15	3	343	68	0	28.58
†S. R. Bevins	15	24	8	428	59*	0	26.75
P. A. Neale	4	6	0	147	54	0	24.50
M. J. Dallaway	11	18	1	368	80	0	21.64
*M. S. Scott	15	11	9	43	10*	0	21.50
V. S. Solanki	8	14	0	295	82	0	21.07
G. C. Abbott	6	12	1	213	43	0	19.36
R. D. Stemp	7	10	3	123	23*	0	17.57
J. E. Brinkley	13	18	7	191	32	0	17.36
A. Wylie	5	7	3	63	23*	0	15.75
S. Collins	2	3	0	40	26	0	13.33
C. W. Boroughs	3	5	0	33	27	0	6.60
M. P. Clewley	4	4	1	14	6	0	4.66
J. G. Slater	3	3	0	11	10	0	3.66

Played in three matches: †T. Edwards 4, 3*. Played in two matches: N. M. Davies 13*; J. Grant 6*, 0. Played in one match: S. V. Bahutule 41; A. J. L. Barr 17*, 0; K. C. G. Benjamin 96, 10*; A. B. Byram 8, 6; G. J. Byram 3*, 1; J. M. Connor 5; A. P. Cowan 0; W. J. Hearsey 20; S. R. Lampitt 34, 24; D. R. McDonnell 40, 22; P. A. Thomas 5; N. J. Workman 7, 0; A. C. Cummins did not bat.

Bowling Averages

	O	M	R	W	BB	Avge
D. B. D'Oliveira	81	15	292	15	5-54	19.46
K. C. G. Benjamin	46	11	124	6	4-75	20.66
M. P. Clewley	100.1	17	306	11	5-69	27.81
C. J. Eyers	212.2	46	623	22	5-68	28.31
A. J. L. Barr	44.2	10	118	4	2-58	29.50
A. C. H. Seymour	48	12	149	4	3-52	37.25
C. M. Tolley	180.3	39	464	12	4-50	38.66
V. S. Solanki	148.3	28	483	11	3-50	43.90
G. R. Haynes	172.2	38	496	11	3-39	45.09
M. J. Weston	208.3	39	593	13	3-35	45.61
J. Grant	43	6	197	4	2-76	49.25
J. E. Brinkley	243.2	31	940	18	6-60	52.22
R. D. Stemp	290	78	812	14	3-89	58.00
J. G. Slater	65.3	12	237	4	2-66	59.25
G. C. Abbott	107.2	22	344	5	1-11	68.80

Also bowled: S. V. Bahutule 12–5–15–2; S. R. Bevins 4–0–61–0; A. B. Byram 34–14–75–1; G. J. Byram 17–4–41–2; A. P. Cowan 28–8–74–4; A. C. Cummins 6.3–2–10–0; M. J. Dallaway 1–0–2–0; N. M. Davies 38–5–124–2; S. R. Lampitt 20–5–41–3; P. A. Thomas 7–0–40–0; W. P. C. Weston 39–7–132–3; A. Wylie 36–2–161–3.

YORKSHIRE SECOND ELEVEN

Matches 17: Won – Durham, Essex, Leicestershire, Nottinghamshire, Worcestershire. Lost – Surrey, Warwickshire. Drawn – Derbyshire, Glamorgan, Gloucestershire, Hampshire, Kent, Lancashire, Middlesex, Northamptonshire, Somerset, Sussex.

Batting Averages

	M	I	NO	R	HS	100s	Avge
D. Byas	2	4	2	275	200*	1	137.50
R. A. Kettleborough	3	4	2	153	70*	0	76.50
A. A. Metcalfe	7	10	0	548	163	1	54.80
S. J. Foster	5	7	1	312	151*	1	52.00
*K. Sharp	17	16	6	512	71*	0	51.20
B. Parker	16	24	2	1,072	121*	2	48.72
C. White	3	6	1	243	122	1	48.60
D. Gough	4	5	2	130	64	0	43.33
M. P. Vaughan	13	22	1	867	130	3	41.28
A. P. Grayson	11	16	0	534	96	0	33.37
†C. A. Chapman	14	21	4	557	91	0	32.76
C. S. Pickles	6	8	0	252	72	0	31.50
M. J. Foster	7	7	1	150	72*	0	25.00
S. Bethel	15	22	1	516	118	2	24.57
A. I. Ditta	6	8	2	124	34	0	20.66
S. Bartle	7	10	0	154	35	0	15.40
M. Broadhurst	9	10	5	64	13*	0	12.80
I. J. Houseman	11	8	3	50	15	0	10.00
G. Keedy	10	5	4	2	1*	0	2.00

Played in eight matches: S. M. Milburn 0, 38*, 1*. Played in four matches: C. E. W. Silverwood 7*, 4*, 5. Played in three matches: †G. Brook 15*, 42, 11*. Played in two matches: J. D. Batty 1, 42*; P. W. Jarvis 72, 11*. Played in one match: R. M. Atkinson 14; M. A. Robinson did not bat.

Bowling Averages

	O	M	R	W	BB	Avge
J. D. Batty	117.2	47	297	19	7-70	15.63
D. Gough	108.5	24	296	15	5-93	19.73
M. J. Foster	112	29	297	15	5-43	19.80
A. P. Grayson	333.2	105	785	33	4-23	23.78
C. E. W. Silverwood	98	16	323	11	3-34	29.36
C. S. Pickles	163.4	51	382	13	4-30	29.38
M. Broadhurst	221	46	747	23	5-45	32.47
I. J. Houseman	242.4	54	757	23	4-68	32.91
S. Bartle	135.4	25	459	13	3-23	35.30
A. I. Ditta	101	34	263	7	2-4	37.57
G. Keedy	329	74	946	24	5-91	39.41
S. M. Milburn	160.1	37	470	10	3-34	47.00
M. P. Vaughan	95	14	359	4	1-13	89.75

Also bowled: R. M. Atkinson 14–2–34–0; S. Bethel 3–0–19–0; D. Byas 2.2–0–15–0; S. J. Foster 9–3–20–0; P. W. Jarvis 46–13–107–3; B. Parker 6–0–33–1; M. A. Robinson 27–9–62–1; K. Sharp 8–7–1–2; C. White 7–1–19–0.

SECOND ELEVEN CHAMPIONS

1959	Gloucestershire	1971	Hampshire	1983	Leicestershire
1960	Northamptonshire	1972	Nottinghamshire	1984	Yorkshire
1961	Kent	1973	Essex	1985	Nottinghamshire
1962	Worcestershire	1974	Middlesex	1986	Lancashire
1963	Worcestershire	1975	Surrey	1987	{ Kent
1964	Lancashire	1976	Kent		{ Yorkshire
1965	Glamorgan	1977	Yorkshire	1988	Surrey
1966	Surrey	1978	Sussex	1989	Middlesex
1967	Hampshire	1979	Warwickshire	1990	Sussex
1968	Surrey	1980	Glamorgan	1991	Yorkshire
1969	Kent	1981	Hampshire	1992	Surrey
1970	Kent	1982	Worcestershire		

BAIN CLARKSON TROPHY, 1992

North Zone	*P*	*W*	*L*	*NR*	*Points*	*Runs/100b*
Northamptonshire	12	7	2	3	17	73.81
Lancashire	12	6	5	1	13	71.56
Leicestershire	12	5	5	2	12	62.53
Derbyshire	12	5	6	1	11	67.53
Yorkshire	12	5	5	2	12	71.27
Nottinghamshire	12	4	6	2	10	66.25
Durham	12	4	7	1	9	59.28

South-West Zone	*P*	*W*	*L*	*NR*	*Points*	*Runs/100b*
Somerset	10	6	1	3	15	73.03
Warwickshire	10	5	2	3	13	66.17
Gloucestershire	10	5	3	2	12	70.91
Glamorgan	10	2	4	4	8	62.13
Worcestershire	10	3	5	2	8	59.30
Hampshire	10	1	7	2	4	59.93

South-East Zone	*P*	*W*	*L*	*NR*	*Points*	*Runs/100b*
Surrey	10	7	1	2	16	80.50
MCC Young Cricketers	10	4	4	2	10	70.93
Sussex	10	4	4	2	10	62.35
Kent	10	4	5	1	9	67.20
Middlesex	10	3	4	3	9	63.67
Essex	10	3	7	0	6	62.28

Notes: Warwickshire qualified for the semi-finals as the best runners-up after the zone matches.

Counties are restricted to players qualified for England and for competitive county cricket, only two of whom may be capped players. The matches are of 55 overs per side.

SEMI-FINALS

At Taunton, August 10. Northamptonshire won by 20 runs. Toss: Northamptonshire. Northamptonshire 161 for nine (40 overs) (W. M. Noon 51; J. C. Hallett five for 37; A. C. Cottam three for 46); Somerset 141 (38.5 overs) (K. J. Parsons 40; A. R. Roberts five for 34).

At The Oval, August 11. Surrey won by six wickets. Toss: Surrey. Warwickshire 99 (42 overs) (A. J. Murphy three for 10); Surrey 100 for four (23.4 overs) (A. D. Brown 66 not out).

FINAL

SURREY v NORTHAMPTONSHIRE

At The Oval, September 7. Surrey won by eight wickets. Toss: Surrey.
Man of the Match: K. T. Medlycott.

Northamptonshire

R. R. Montgomerie c and b Butcher	24	J. G. Hughes c Ligertwood b Smith	16
R. J. Warren c Hollioake b Medlycott	51	R. M. Pearson c and b Smith	1
A. L. Penberthy not out	68	A. Walker not out	1
N. A. Stanley c Butcher b Smith	10	B 8, l-b 4, w 3	15
*. J. Green c Smith b Medlycott	8		
A. R. Roberts b Medlycott	2	1/52 2/111 3/132 (9 wkts, 55 overs)	199
†W. M. Noon lbw b Medlycott	1	4/148 5/156 6/160	
A. N. Bowen c Greig b Smith	2	7/163 8/196 9/198	

Bowling: Murphy 6–2–17–0; Hollioake 4–1–15–0; Butcher 11–2–33–1; Greig 8–0–21–0; Robinson 4–0–16–0; Medlycott 11–0–43–4; Smith 11–1–42–4.

Surrey

R. I. Alikhan not out	69
*. D. Atkins b Roberts	46
D. Robinson b Penberthy	76
M. A. Butcher not out	1
L-b 3, w 6, n-b 1	10

1/87 2/191 (2 wkts, 49.3 overs) 202

A. W. Smith, *I. A. Greig, K. T. Medlycott, A. J. Hollioake, I. J. Ward, †D. G. C. Ligertwood and A. J. Murphy did not bat.

Bowling: Walker 7–0–36–0; Penberthy 10.3–1–39–1; Pearson 11–0–31–0; Bowen 7–0–23–0; Roberts 9–2–36–1; Hughes 3–0–21–0; Stanley 2–0–13–0.

Umpires: N. T. Plews and P. B. Wight.

WINNERS 1986-92

1986 NORTHAMPTONSHIRE beat Essex by 14 runs at Chelmsford.
1987 DERBYSHIRE beat Hampshire by seven wickets at Southampton.
1988 YORKSHIRE beat Kent by seven wickets at Leeds.
1989 MIDDLESEX beat Kent by six wickets at Canterbury.
1990 LANCASHIRE beat Somerset by eight wickets at Manchester.
1991 NOTTINGHAMSHIRE beat Surrey by eight wickets at The Oval.
1992 SURREY beat Northamptonshire by eight wickets at The Oval.

THE LANCASHIRE LEAGUES, 1992

By CHRIS ASPIN

The old axiom that bowling professionals win championships was turned on its head in the centenary year of both the Lancashire and the Central Lancashire Leagues. Ramsbottom claimed the Lancashire League for the first time in 18 years, thanks largely to West Indian Test batsman Keith Arthurton, whose 1,185 at 69.70 set a club record. And in the Central Lancashire League, Littleborough's league and cup double owed much to a bowler, but he was an amateur – Australian Michael Warden, who returned 105 wickets at 13.17.

Arthurton's consistent form enabled a well-balanced Ramsbottom team to reach first place by mid-season, and they kept their hold throughout what became a two-horse race with Haslingden. He was the only batsman to reach four figures, and also picked up 57 wickets; his nearest rival was his Test colleague Phil Simmons, who made 975 at 51.31 for Haslingden and took 61 wickets. Against East Lancashire, Simmons took 14 wickets in a weekend: eight in a league match and six in the Worsley Cup final, which Haslingden won by 20 runs. Another West Indian, Clint Yorke, scored 921 runs for Todmorden. Roger Harper headed the bowling averages with 70 wickets for Bacup at 13.11, and also made 838 runs, and the leading wicket taker was Steven Elworthy, from Northern Transvaal, who claimed 86 at 15.33 in his first season with Rishton. The fastest bowler was Enfield's Guyanese professional, Linden Joseph, who took 61 wickets at 13.77 before returning home early because of an injury. Another early leaver, and a more controversial one, was Robin Singh, who missed Colne's last eight matches when he was summoned back to India, where the selectors wanted a full complement of players to consider for the tour of South Africa. Colne finished bottom, and would have had the sympathies of clubs in other leagues who suffered in the same way. Singh failed to make the tour.

The most prolific amateur batsman was Gary Barker of Enfield, with 823 runs at 45.72, followed by David Pearson, who made 759 at 31.62 for East Lancashire, Chris Hartley of Nelson with 697 at 34.85 and Michael Ingham of Haslingden with 681 at 35.84. The welcome return to spin continued and three slow left-armers produced the best figures among the amateurs. Michael Tracey took 66 at 14.72 and broke a Haslingden club record when he finished with nine for 28 at Burnley, Keith Roscoe took 54 wickets for Rawtenstall at 17.40 and Abram Ali 48 for Todmorden at 15.97.

In the Central Lancashire League, the rare feat of an amateur leading the bowling averages was achieved convincingly by the young pace bowler Michael Warden, expected to turn professional in 1993 with a new club Stand, based at Whitefield, north of Manchester. Stand will replace Hyde who are joining the Cheshire County League in the new season. Only Warden and West Indian Test player Ezra Moseley, of Radcliffe, took more than 100 wickets. Warden arrived at Littleborough with their professional, fellow Queenslander Stuart Law. This League, unlike in Lancashire League, allows each team to field one overseas amateur. Law himself made a great impression with the bat, scoring 1,241 runs, including 152 in 113 balls in the Lees Wood Cup final against Stockport. He passed Everton Weekes's 1954 record of 151 in that fixture, and contributed almost half Littleborough's total of 311 for four, another record, setting up a 133-run victory. Littleborough's team was packed with run-makers; Phil Deakin scored 1,040 and the consistent Chris Dearden 991. Runners-up Rochdale also had two players who reached four figures: their professional David Callaghan, from Eastern Province, amassed 1,511, easily the highest in either league, at 83.94 and Darren Murray 1,208 at 57.52.

Rohan Merry, an Australian amateur at Stockport, recorded one notable batting feat when he hit five consecutive sixes against Oldham. A fortnight later he went one better by hitting six sixes in an over from Alan Berry of Hyde.

MARSDEN BS LANCASHIRE LEAGUE

	P	W	L	NR	Bonus Pts	Pts	Professional	Runs	Avge	Wkts	Avge
Ramsbottom	26	19	4	3	11	90	K. L. T. Arthurton	1,185	69.70	57	15.00
Haslingden	26	19	3	4	6	86	P. V. Simmons	975	51.31	61	17.88
Enfield	26	15	7	4	9	73	L. A. Joseph	622	47.84	61	13.77
Nelson	26	14	8	4	8	68	J. C. Scuderi	882	40.09	70	14.12
Bacup	26	12	9	5	8	61	R. A. Harper	838	46.55	70	13.11
East Lancs	26	12	11	3	9	60	A. I. C. Dodemaide	285	21.92	48	13.33
Todmorden	26	12	8	6	4	58	C. G. Yorke	921	43.85	31	26.00
Rawtenstall	26	10	11	5	7	52	C. R. Miller	405	21.31	75	17.72
Church	26	9	13	4	3	43	M. W. Priest	805	36.59	74	15.22
Accrington	26	8	13	5	5	42	D. N. Patel	720	34.28	66	14.89
Lowerhouse	26	8	14	4	4	40	C. J. Williamson	649	28.21	59	19.11
Burnley	26	7	15	4	4	36	S. M. Skeete	317	13.78	63	21.47
Rishton	26	5	17	4	6	30	S. Elworthy	536	26.80	86	15.33
Colne	26	1	18	7	1	12	Robin Singh	594	39.60	40	22.07

Note: Four points awarded for a win; one point for a no-result; one point for dismissing the opposition.

BROTHER CENTRAL LANCASHIRE LEAGUE

	P	OW	LW	L	D	Pts	Professional	Runs	Avge	Wkts	Avge
Littleborough	30	13	7	4	6	105	S. G. Law	1,241	42.79	51	17.09
Rochdale	30	10	7	7	6	90	D. J. Callaghan	1,511	83.94	64	16.79
Milnrow	30	6	11	9	4	82	G. I. Foley	1,350	61.36	77	17.00
Ashton	30	9	6	10	5	79	B. Roberts	1,183	51.43	73	14.00
Middleton	30	4	11	11	4	72	P. R. Sleep	1,458	60.75	71	20.39
Crompton	30	8	5	12	5	70†	C. L. King	834	34.75	23	20.60
Norden	30	9	3	12	6	69	W. J. Cronje	788	35.81	68	20.08
Heywood	30	7	5	11	7	69	A. Flower	1,213	50.54	34	28.61
Oldham	30	8	4	12	6	68†	Sajjad Ahmed	971	46.23	28	28.14
Stockport	30	5	7	12	6	65	S. C. Wundke	850	30.35	85	19.57
Unsworth	30	8	3	14	5	62	M. A. R. Samarasekera	970	37.30	39	23.97
Werneth	30	4	5	14	7	55*	B. Player	892	37.16	74	21.54
Royton	30	3	7	15	5	53	A. G. Daley	658	25.30	75	21.08
Radcliffe	30	6	1	16	7	49*	E. A. Moseley	1,020	46.36	102	13.67
Walsden	30	3	3	15	9	45	P. Skuse	1,215	45.00	33	22.57
Hyde	30	4	1	20	5	34	C. Ingram	347	14.45	50	33.64

* Includes three points for a tie. † Crompton fielded an ineligible player against Oldham and Ashton. The first match, which Crompton won, was awarded to Oldham, and Crompton were also deprived of the two points they gained in their washed-out match with Ashton.

Notes: Five points awarded for an outright win; four points for a limited win, two points for a draw. An outright win is gained when a team bowls the opposition out. Averages include cup games.

LEAGUE CRICKET IN ENGLAND AND WALES, 1992

By GEOFFREY DEAN

Despite the fact that it was one of the wettest summers in recent years – Cardiff in the Western League had seven out of 19 games abandoned – the season was characterised by a host of new run records, especially in the north. Perhaps the most impressive feat was that of Clayton Lambert, the Guyana and West Indies left-hander, who set a new league record of 1,859 for Redcar in the North Yorkshire & South Durham League, beating his own previous best by 72. His nine centuries were another record. He also took 48 wickets and led the league's representative side to their fifth successive League Cricket Conference President's Trophy win.

Overseas players were not the only record-breakers. The 19-year-old Atherton batsman, Neil Bannister, became the first amateur since 1946 to reach 1,000 runs in the Bolton Association. In the Lancashire & Cheshire League, Paul Berry of Roe Green established a new run record, scoring 1,696 at an average of 130. His namesake, Darren, the Victorian wicket-keeper, likewise set a new league batting record for the Cheshire County League champions Macclesfield. In the Northern League, Robert Haynes, the Jamaican and West Indies all-rounder, beat Ravi Shastri's record of 840 in helping Morecambe to their first league title since 1968. The West Indies captain, Richie Richardson, passed 1,000 runs in Blackpool's final game of the season. For an all-round performance, however, Donald Brown's in the Tyneside Senior League would be hard to beat. Brown, professional with champions Shotley Bridge, scored 1,550 runs and took 186 wickets in league and cup games. Another exceptional performance with the ball came from the Barbadian fast bowler Victor Walcott, professional with the Durham Senior League winners, South Shields. Walcott became the first bowler in this league to take 100 wickets since 1976.

Further south, Justin Langer, the Western Australian playing for Dover, set a new Kent League run record of 1,012. Two of his four hundreds were scored while the rest of the Dover batting collapsed – the most remarkable being his 125 out of his side's 151 against Bromley, who retained the title. For the champions, Mark Alexander made 783 runs and Bert Roebuck was the most successful bowler with 35 victims at 17. The League's leading wicket-takers were Kieran Knight of Chestfield and David Joseph of The Mote, who both picked up 40. Dover and Gore Court were involved in one of the more remarkable games of the season. Having been dismissed for only 79, Dover then bowled out their opponents for 64.

In the Essex League, where Chelmsford won their first title since 1975, Mel Hussain, brother of England batsman Nasser, had an outstanding season, scoring 832 runs and taking 53 wickets for Fives & Heronians. Old Brentwoods' Ian Hoffman, a South African, amassed 821 runs as well as claiming 32 victims but the leading run-scorer was Ahmed Waqas of South Woodford who made 842. Chelmsford won thanks to a collective effort: no one averaged 40 or took more than 32 wickets.

In winning the Southern League, Hursley Park achieved a notable league and cup double, for they were victorious in the final of the National Village Championship at Lord's. Refreshingly, eight of the top 12 in the bowling averages of this league were spinners; Portsmouth's Barry Boorah and

Lymington's Chris Allen led the way with 36 wickets each. Trevor Jesty returned to his home-town club, Gosport Borough, and, aged 44, topped the League batting averages with 82, although Havant's Paul Gover scored the most runs, 588. For Hursley Park, Adrian Small, 19, made 527 to earn the league's young cricketer award.

Wimbledon clinched the Surrey Championship title thanks to bowling out the opposition for under 150 in their last five matches and winning them all, mainly through the work of spinners Simon Dyson, Anthony Wreford and Marcus Wight. Runners-up Esher led for most of the season but were ultimately let down by their batsmen. Barbadian Dexter Toppin took 45 wickets and scored 400 runs for them. Banstead's Nick Falkner, the former Surrey and Sussex player, was the league's leading run-scorer with 959. Former Cambridge Blue Paul Bail made 884 for Richmond in the Middlesex League. Finchley looked to be running away with this title by mid-August when they were still unbeaten. They then lost three games in succession, however, and had to win their last match against North Middlesex to become champions. Glucka Wijesuriya's first hundred of the season saw them to 229, whereupon they dismissed their opponents with 16 overs to spare. Teddington finished just one point behind.

In the West Midlands, there was an extraordinary finish in the Midland Combined Counties League. Leaders Bromsgrove met second-placed Pershore on the final Saturday of the season needing only a draw. When the last over began, Bromsgrove were 66 for nine, well short of Pershore's total. No. 11 Adrian Lawton, widely regarded as the worst batsman in the league, was facing the man reckoned to be the best bowler, Paul Humphries. Lawton never touched a ball but he survived, and Bromsgrove won the league by a point.

Walsall, winners of the Birmingham League, owed much to Steve Dean, the Staffordshire opener, who made 879 runs. Moseley's Ian Stokes topped the averages with 870 runs at 58, his team-mate Simon Wootton being the only other batsman to pass 700. The season also brought the retirement of one of the league's most remarkable players, 55-year-old Gordon Smith of Stourbridge, whose innocuous-looking but effective off-breaks have been a highlight of West Midlands cricket for four decades. Smith may be the third player in Birmingham League history, after Bert Latham and Roy Abell, both of Moseley, to take 1,000 wickets. However, he spent most of his time with the now-defunct Dudley club, whose scorebooks have gone missing, so it is impossible to prove.

In the Western League, Peter Hardwicke of St Fagans took 50 wickets for the fourth time, with Malmesbury's Steve Thorpe returning the best analysis with nine for 59 against Keynsham. Bradford & Bingley cantered to the Bradford League title thanks largely to their Victorian fast bowler, Richard McCarthy, who took 65 wickets, and former Yorkshire and Glamorgan left-arm seamer Simon Dennis, with 41. John Whittle of Hanging Heaton was the leading run-scorer with 972. Rotherham Town became Yorkshire League champions for the first time since 1963, and Wolverton won the Northamptonshire County League for the first time since 1972. Welbeck Colliery's charge to the Bassetlaw title was started by Mark Saxelby, who made 494 runs from only eight innings but was lost to the club when he gained a regular place in the Nottinghamshire side towards the end of the season.

Sir Garfield Sobers's feat of hitting six sixes in an over was emulated by 20-year-old David Conlon, of Huyton, in a Liverpool Competition match against Sefton. Having taken 20 balls to get off the mark, Conlon needed only another 40 to get to his hundred, which included 11 sixes in all. Two other remarkable displays of hitting during the season have come to light: Anton Joyce's 36-ball hundred for Woodhouse against East Leeds which was the quickest in the Leeds League for 20 years; and Australian Steve Russell's 200 off just 95 balls for Sacriston against Greenside in the Tyneside Senior League.

Off the field, the League Cricket Conference decided to take decisive action to try to counter the problem of overseas professionals returning home before the end of the season. About a dozen players have been banned by individual leagues for breaking contracts for what was considered insufficient reason. The Conference has now asked its 62 member leagues to support these bans and not employ such players. The issue came to a head when four players – Maninder Singh, Robin Singh, Atul Wassan and Vinod Kambli – were summoned home by the Indian Board. The Bolton League went furthest of all. It demanded £2,500 compensation from the Indian Board and banned all players under Indian jurisdiction until it was paid.

LEAGUE WINNERS, 1992

League	Winners	League	Winners
Airedale & Wharfedale	Otley	Midland Club Championship	Barnt Green
Bassetlaw	Welbeck Colliery	Midland Combined Counties	Bromsgrove
Birmingham	Walsall	Norfolk Alliance	Norwich Barleycorns
Bolton	Bradshaw	Northants County	Wolverton
Bolton Association	Daisy Hill	Northern	Morecambe
Bradford	Bradford & Bingley	North Lancashire	Millom
Central	Lutterworth	North Staffs. & South Cheshire	Ashcombe Park
Central Yorkshire	Liversedge	Northumberland County	Tynedale
Cherwell	North Oxford	North Wales	Marchwiel
Cheshire County	Macclesfield	North Yorks. & South Durham	Redcar
Cornwall	Falmouth	Notts. Alliance	Notts. Forest
Cumbrian	Edenhall	Notts. Amateur	Gedling
Derbyshire County	Heanor Town	Ribblesdale	Barnoldswick
Devon	Exmouth	Saddleworth	Flowery Field
Dorset Premier	Colehill	Somerset	Taunton
Durham Senior	South Shields	Southern	Hursley Park
Essex	Chelmsford	South Thames	Kenley
Hertfordshire	North Mymms	South Wales Association	Neath
Home Counties	Leighton Buzzard	Surrey Championship	Wimbledon
Huddersfield	Skelmanthorpe	Sussex	Chichester
Kent	Bromley	Thames Valley	Reading
Lancashire & Cheshire	Roe Green	Two Counties (Suffolk-Essex)	Clacton
Leeds	Woodhouse	Tyneside Senior	Shotley Bridge
Liverpool Competition	Neston	Western	Cheltenham
Manchester Association	Wigan	Yorkshire	Rotherham Town
Middlesex	Finchley		

Note: To avoid confusion traditional League names have been given in this list and sponsors' names omitted.

NATIONAL CLUB CHAMPIONSHIP, 1992

The Bristol-based club Optimists, of the Western League, became the first West country winners of the National Club Championship since 1978 when they beat Kendal of the Northern League by seven wickets in the final at Lord's. Kevin Emery, the former Hampshire fast bowler, took three for 24 and played a vital role in restricting Kendal to 165 for nine in their 45 overs. Optimists began well then wobbled when they lost opener Kevin Blackburn and Jeremy Tavaré, brother of the Somerset captain, in quick succession. However, Richard Trotman then joined his captain Huw Ellison and they put on 91 in 22 overs to settle the game.

Optimists, whose ground is south of the River Avon at Failand, reached the final after beating Richmond (Surrey) by five runs in the semi-final. Kendal had scored a surprise 26-run win over three-time champions Old Hill. The two 1991 finalists had both gone down to shock defeats: Teddington, the holders, lost in the sixth round to the Berkshire club Finchampstead; Walsall failed even to get past the first round – they lost to Stourbridge by seven wickets. – Russell Grant.

FINAL

KENDAL v OPTIMISTS

At Lord's, August 29. Optimists won by seven wickets. Toss: Kendal.

Kendal

S. M. Stuart c Hughes b Trotman	21
G. Edmondson b Neill	0
T. A. Hunte c Harding b Emery	23
*J. R. Moyes c Bird b Emery	27
P. Fearnyough st Hughes b Harding	20
P. Stewart c Hughes b Neill	19
A. Wilson c Tavaré b Neill	14
†J. Moyes lbw b Emery	7
A. Potts run out	17
M. Parkinson not out	3
K. Barnes not out	1
B 1, l-b 7, w 3, n-b 2	13

1/8 2/49 3/49   (9 wkts, 45 overs) 165
4/94 5/116 6/131
7/137 8/154 9/163

Bowling: Neill 9–1–27–3; Bird 9–3–25–0; Trotman 7–0–50–1; Emery 9–2–24–3; Harding 9–1–22–1; Baldwin 2–0–9–0.

Optimists

*H. G. Ellison not out	62
K. R. Blackburn c J. Moyes b Wilson	19
J. M. Tavaré lbw b Hunte	1
R. I. Trotman c J. Moyes b Barnes	48
N. A. Baldwin not out	15
L-b 9, w 7, n-b 7	23

1/41 2/43 3/134   (3 wkts, 42.3 overs) 168

P. J. Bird, P. A. Redwood, K. St J. D. Emery, P. C. Neill, R. J. Harding and †R. D. M. Hughes did not bat.

Bowling: Parkinson 8–0–33–0; Potts 8–2–23–0; Hunte 8.3–0–43–1; Wilson 9–3–31–1; Barnes 9–2–29–1.

Umpires: D. Bushell and T. Singleton.

WINNERS 1969-92

1969	Hampstead	1977	Southgate	1985	Old Hill
1970	Cheltenham	1978	Cheltenham	1986	Stourbridge
1971	Blackheath	1979	Scarborough	1987	Old Hill
1972	Scarborough	1980	Moseley	1988	Enfield
1973	Wolverhampton	1981	Scarborough	1989	Teddington
1974	Sunbury	1982	Scarborough	1990	Blackpool
1975	York	1983	Shrewsbury	1991	Teddington
1976	Scarborough	1984	Old Hill	1992	Optimists

NATIONAL VILLAGE CRICKET CHAMPIONSHIP, 1992

The Village Cricket Championship, organised by *The Cricketer* magazine and sponsored by Rothmans, enjoyed perhaps the most thrilling climax of its 21-year history when Southern League champions Hursley Park from Hampshire, beaten finalists in 1984, beat Methley, from the Central Yorkshire League, by six wickets in a riveting finish at Lord's.

Hursley Park made hard work of chasing Methley's total of 150 for six from 40 overs, which included 57 from Australian wicket-keeper David Jones. They needed 34 from the last three overs and 15 from the last one. Graham Boothroyd, the Methley captain, chose his 54-year-old off-spinning brother, Allan, to bowl the last over, which included a six and two fours, hit by Clive Surry to the short Tavern boundary. One of the fours came after Graham Boothroyd had dropped a hard catch and collided with Kevin Rich at square leg, who then knocked the ball over the rope.

A record entry of 639 clubs had contested the first five regional rounds, during which a number of records tumbled. In Cornwall, Alan Wade scored 239 not out in an opening stand of 373, to help Goldsithney reach 404 for one against Ruan and Philliegh. Derbyshire club Lullington Park added 304 for their second wicket against Clifton, with P. Gough 135 not out and J. Grievson 151 not out. Bolney were bowled out for 19 by their Sussex neighbours Hartfield, and in Essex Dennis Fenton took nine for 15 for South Weald against Hordon on the Hill.

Three former finalists won through to the semi-finals, in which the 1991 winners, St Fagans, lost by 13 runs to Hursley Park, thanks largely to Chris Westbrook's five for 24, and Freuchie could muster only 96 for nine on a damp Scottish pudding of a pitch, and lost to Methley by seven wickets. – Amanda Ripley.

FINAL

HURSLEY PARK v METHLEY

At Lord's, August 30. Hursley Park won by six wickets. Toss: Hursley Park.

Methley

S. Bourne c Thow b Westbrook	16	L. Smith not out	8
*G. Boothroyd c Kellaway b Fox	11	L. Mills not out	0
†D. Jones c Arnold b Westbrook	57	B 1, l-b 7, w 2	10
K. Rich b Fox	19		
A. Jarvis c Surry b Westbrook	28	1/17 2/45 3/95 (6 wkts, 40 overs)	150
N. Lockett st Kellaway b Westbrook	1	4/128 5/141 6/147	

A. Boothroyd, M. Waite and M. Smart did not bat.

Bowling: Oliver 9–1–24–0; Fox 9–2–23–2; Mitchell 9–1–24–0; Westbrook 9–0–40–4; Burns 4–0–31–0.

Hursley Park

A. M. Small b Mills	8	S. P. Arnold not out		10
M. N. Oliver c Jones b Waite	27			
C. R. Surry not out	76	B 1, l-b 14, w 3		18
†M. J. Kellaway b Waite	11			
*F. D. Thow c G. Boothroyd		1/19 2/68	(4 wkts, 40 overs)	154
b A. Boothroyd	4	3/98 4/109		

G. S. Oliver, C. N. Mitchell, D. J. Fox, T. P. Burns and C. S. Westbrook did not bat.

Bowling: Smart 9–2–21–0; Mills 9–3–10–1; Waite 9–0–30–2; Jarvis 4–0–25–0; A. Boothroyd 9–0–53–1.

Umpires: G. Bennion and A. Davies.

WINNERS 1972-92

1972 Troon (Cornwall)	1979 East Bierley (Yorks.)	1986 Forge Valley (Yorks.)
1973 Troon (Cornwall)	1980 Marchwiel (Clwyd)	1987 Longparish (Hants)
1974 Bomarsund (Northumb.)	1981 St Fagans (Glam.)	1988 Goatacre (Wilts.)
1975 Gowerton (Glam.)	1982 St Fagans (Glam.)	1989 Toft (Cheshire)
1976 Troon (Cornwall)	1983 Quarndon (Derbys.)	1990 Goatacre (Wilts.)
1977 Cookley (Worcs.)	1984 Marchwiel (Clwyd)	1991 St Fagans (Glam.)
1978 Linton Park (Kent)	1985 Freuchie (Fife)	1992 Hursley Park (Hants)

I ZINGARI RESULTS, 1992

Matches 20: Won 7, Lost 2, Drawn 11. Abandoned 6.

April 21	Eton College	Drawn
May 16	Royal Artillery	Won by eight wickets
May 17	Staff College	Drawn
May 23	Eton Ramblers	Drawn
May 28	Harrow School	Drawn
May 30	Royal Armoured Corps	Won by two wickets
June 6	Hurlingham CC	Abandoned
June 7	Earl of Carnarvon's XI	Abandoned
June 13	Charterhouse School	Drawn
June 14	Sandhurst Wanderers	Won by six wickets
June 20	Guards CC	Lost by one run
June 28	J. Paul Getty's XI	Drawn
June 30	Winchester College	Drawn
July 4	Bradfield Waifs	Abandoned
July 11	Green Jackets Club	Abandoned
July 12	Rickling Green CC	Won by two wickets
July 18	Leicester Gentlemen	Drawn
July 19	Sir John Starkey's XI	Drawn
July 26	Lavinia, Duchess of Norfolk's XI	Won by nine wickets
August 1	R. Leigh-Pemberton's XI	Won by five wickets
August 2	Band of Brothers	Lost by four wickets
August 8, 9	South Wales Hunts XI	Drawn
August 23	Royal Navy CC	Won by seven wickets
August 29	Hampshire Hogs	Drawn
September 6	J. H. Pawle's XI	Abandoned
September 13	Captain R. H. Hawkins's XI	Abandoned

IRISH CRICKET IN 1992

By DEREK SCOTT

Irish cricket's biggest news of 1992 came at Lord's in July. The Associate Members of the International Cricket Council recommended that Ireland should be allowed to join them. This will come to a vote at the 1993 ICC meeting. If it is accepted, Ireland's cricketers will have a goal to match that of most other Irish sportsmen: a World Cup. They hope to compete in the ICC Trophy in Kenya in 1994.

The Irish team had a programme of eight matches in 1992, which produced one win, three defeats and four draws. Two of the defeats were expected: in a two-day match against Middlesex at Malahide, Dublin and the NatWest Trophy tie against Durham at Castle Avenue, Dublin. This was Ireland's fifth home tie in their 13 years in the competition and produced the best crowd so far.

The only first-class, and only away, fixture, against Scotland, ended in a high-scoring draw. The game against Wales was played on the historic College Park ground at Trinity College in the centre of Dublin. It was first used by Ireland in 1868 but the team had not played there since 1963. The match began with a record partnership for any Irish wicket: captain Stephen Warke and Michael Rea put on 224 for the first wicket, with Warke scoring 113 and Rea 106. There was a collapse after that and eventually Wales were left to make 201 to win. They finished 12 runs short with four wickets in hand.

Ireland's one win came in a limited-overs match against the England Amateur XI. The visitors had won by 50 runs on a good pitch at Eglinton the previous day but on an inferior surface at Coleraine the pace bowler Paul McCrum took three for 17 and off-spinner Garfield Harrison four for 24 to restrict the visitors to 116 for nine in reply to Ireland's 188.

Rain affected the other two games, against MCC at Downpatrick, and the one-day match against Gloucestershire on the new, fast wicket at Ormeau in Belfast. There was only time for Ireland to make 86 for nine, of which Michael Rea made 34 to complete a marvellous season. He made 408 runs for Ireland (average 40.80), 248 at Inter-Provincial level (average 62) and 737 (average 73.70) for his club, Clontarf. Warke became the second batsman, after Ivan Anderson, to pass 3,000 runs for Ireland. Fourteen men bowled for Ireland and they all took at least one wicket; the leg-spinner Conor Hoey, with 15 at 27.06, led the way.

The North-West convincingly won the Senior Inter-Provincial tournament, with four wins and a draw in five games. At Club level there were League/Cup doubles in all four provincial unions: by Limerick in Munster, Donemana (League champions for the eighth year running) in the North-West, Waringstown, who also won the Schweppes All Ireland Cup, in the Northern Union, and Clontarf in Leinster. Clontarf retained the League and won the Cup for the first time since 1969.

IRELAND v WALES

At College Park, Dublin, July 26, 27, 28 (not first-class). Drawn. Ireland 266 for seven dec. (S. J. S. Warke 113, M. P. Rea 106; R. Wiseman five for 20) and 145 for six dec. (R. Wiseman three for 37); Wales 211 (J. L. Griffiths 81, J. Derrick 39; E. R. P. Moore three for 36, C. J. Hoey four for 57) and 189 for six (J. P. J. Sylvester 37, A. W. Harris 45, J. Derrick 46, A. C. Puddle 36).

SCOTTISH CRICKET IN 1992

By J. WATSON BLAIR

There were two major setbacks for Scottish cricket in 1992. The abolition of the zonal round of the Benson and Hedges Cup, which means only one guaranteed match in 1993 instead of four, was combined with the rejection, on constitutional grounds, of Scotland's application to participate in the ICC Trophy for non-Test playing countries. The Scottish Cricket Union was left disappointed but not dismayed.

The cricketing year had begun on a high note in March with a tour to South Africa. This comprised a hectic two-week programme against strong teams in the Transvaal; Scotland won two, lost three and drew two. The Scots' greatest successes in the northern hemisphere came much later in two one-day limited-overs matches against the England Amateur XI, chosen by the National Cricket Association, which Scotland won by five wickets and eight wickets. There was talk of creating a quadrangular tournament involving the two teams, Ireland and Wales.

Iain Philip of Stenhousemuir, who made 83 in the first game, scored 121 not out in the second. This was his eighth century for Scotland, beating the Rev. James Aitchison's record. Earlier in the season, Philip had scored hundreds at Lord's in the rain-ruined match against MCC and against Somerset at Taunton in the NatWest Trophy. This was the first time any batsman had scored a hundred in either a Benson and Hedges or NatWest game for Scotland.

On the domestic scene, an initial burst of activity was halted by atrocious weather in July and August. There were three attempts to stage the Scottish Cup final between the holders Grange and Strathmore County. In the end, the match was postponed until the 1993 season. The Coatbridge club, Drumpellier, won the D. M. Hall Western Union Championship for the first time in 11 years without finishing a game after July 18. But before that they had established enough of a lead to finish ahead of Ferguslie and Greenock, who could only come third even with Gordon Greenidge opening the innings. Greenidge made 672 runs at an average of 84.00 but he was outscored by Drumpellier's Pakistani, Sajid Ali, who made 729 runs at an average of 66.27, including three centuries. The D. M. Hall Awards for the leading amateurs in the League went to Gordon McGurk of Uddingston, who made 560 runs, and Garry McLaughlan of Kelburne, who took 34 wickets.

Forfarshire won both the Scottish Counties Championship, ahead of West Lothian County and Aberdeenshire, and the Scottish section of the NCA Cup. Grange won the Ryden East League for the third successive year. Other winners included Mannofield in the Strathmore Union, Huntly in the North of Scotland and Kelso in the Border League (for the ninth successive year). West of Scotland won the Rowan Charity Cup for the first time since 1943, and Central won the Area Championship.

Grange were voted Team of the Year in the Famous Grouse Awards and Philip was Batsman of the Year. Ian Beven of Grange was Bowler of the Year; Beven, an Australian now settled in Scotland, began his career in the national team by taking a wicket with his first ball against MCC. David Fleming of West Lothian County won the wicket-keepers' award and

Jimmy Govan of Carlton, who was formerly with Northamptonshire, won the all-rounders' award. Scott Campbell of Fochabers received a special award for concluding a 30-year career with 1,535 wickets; the Young Player of the Year was Ian Stanger of Clydesdale.

In October, the SCU announced the appointment of the former Yorkshire player, Jim Love, as Director of Cricket with special responsibilities for coaching the Scotland B and Under-19 teams and planning and implementing development schemes. With Alex Ritchie now well into his job as general manager of the Union, the outlook for Scottish cricket appears bright.

CAREER FIGURES OF PLAYERS RETIRING OR NOT RETAINED

BATTING

	M	I	NO	R	HS	100s	Avge	1,000r season
P. J. W. Allott	245	262	64	3,360	88	0	16.96	0
P. J. Bakker	69	54	19	333	22	0	9.51	0
R. J. Bartlett	51	82	6	1,856	117*	2	24.42	0
S. R. Bevins	6	6	2	34	10	0	8.50	0
A. M. Brown	22	31	3	815	139*	1	29.10	0
G. K. Brown	6	10	1	345	103	1	38.33	0
K. A. Butler	1	1	1	10	10*	0	—	0
K. E. Cooper	273	281	67	2,141	46	0	10.00	0
C. S. Cowdrey	299	452	68	12,252	159	21	31.90	4
G. R. Dilley	234	252	93	2,339	81	0	14.71	0
R. M. Ellcock	46	47	13	424	45*	0	12.47	0
D. J. Foster	45	39	15	201	20	0	8.37	0
S. C. Goldsmith	75	118	12	2,646	127	2	24.96	1
I. A. Greig	253	339	50	8,301	291	8	28.72	2
R. Hanley	5	7	0	52	28	0	7.42	0
A. R. Hansford	10	11	3	109	29	0	13.62	0
I. J. F. Hutchinson	27	46	4	1,435	201*	5	34.16	0
Imran Khan	382	582	99	17,771	170	30	36.79	4
S. Kirnon	1	—	—	—	—	—	—	0
D. G. C. Ligertwood	4	7	0	63	28	0	9.00	0
K. T. Medlycott	141	180	38	3,684	153	3	25.94	0
P. A. Neale	354	571	93	17,445	167	28	36.49	8
R. J. Parks	255	284	82	3,944	89	0	19.52	0
J. D. Robinson	31	49	10	898	79	0	23.02	0
G. T. J. Townsend	12	22	2	414	53	0	20.70	0
R. G. Williams	284	447	65	11,817	175*	18	30.93	6

* Signifies not out.

BOWLING AND FIELDING

	R	W	BB	Avge	5W/i	10W/m	Ct/St
P. J. W. Allott	16,665	652	8-48	25.55	30	0	136
P. J. Bakker	5,406	193	7-31	28.01	7	0	9
R. J. Bartlett	145	4	1-9	36.25	—	—	35
S. R. Bevins	—	—	—	—	—	—	18
A. M. Brown	9	0	—	—	—	—	19
G. K. Brown	103	1	1-39	103.00	—	—	4
K. A. Butler........	—	—	—	—	—	—	—
K. E. Cooper	19,332	711	8-44	27.18	25	1	85
C. S. Cowdrey	7,962	200	5-46	39.81	2	0	295
G. R. Dilley	17,395	648	7-63	26.84	34	3	75
R. M. Ellcock	3,395	117	5-35	29.01	1	0	9
D. J. Foster	3,844	96	6-84	40.04	2	0	8
S. C. Goldsmith	1,571	29	3-42	54.17	—	—	37
I. A. Greig	13,023	419	7-43	31.08	10	2	152
R. Hanley..........	—	—	—	—	—	—	—
A. R. Hansford	991	30	5-79	33.03	1	0	3
I. J. F. Hutchinson ..	29	1	1-18	29.00	—	—	29
Imran Khan........	28,726	1,287	8-34	22.32	70	13	117
S. Kirnon	21	1	1-14	21.00	—	—	—
D. G. C. Ligertwood .	—	—	—	—	—	—	7/1
K. T. Medlycott.....	11,517	357	8-52	32.26	18	6	90
P. A. Neale	369	2	1-15	184.50	—	—	134
R. J. Parks	166	0	—	—	—	—	638/72
J. D. Robinson......	1,152	28	3-22	41.14	—	—	12
G. T. J. Townsend ...	—	—	—	—	—	—	10
R. G. Williams	12,722	376	7-73	33.83	9	—	99

Note: K. E. Cooper, once, was the only bowler from this list to take 100 wickets in a season.

OVERS BOWLED AND RUNS SCORED IN THE BRITANNIC ASSURANCE CHAMPIONSHIP, 1992

	Over-rate per hour	Run-rate/ 100 balls
Derbyshire (5)	18.6870	54.3760
Durham (18)............	18.6777	54.4270
Essex (1)...............	18.6613	54.8077
Glamorgan (14)	18.9132	53.4969
Gloucestershire (10)	19.1000	48.6090
Hampshire (15)	18.7966	51.4295
Kent (2)	18.6436	61.9860
Lancashire (12)	18.5686	56.9214
Leicestershire (8)	18.6315	48.8202
Middlesex (11)	18.7791	56.1567
Northamptonshire (3)	18.8045	57.8401
Nottinghamshire (4)	18.5555	54.2320
Somerset (9)	18.6458	51.2943
Surrey (13)	18.5843	52.6126
Sussex (7)	18.7373	54.8619
Warwickshire (6)	18.1734*	52.8760
Worcestershire (17)	18.7571	48.6356
Yorkshire (16)	18.5304	50.1686
1992 average rate........	18.68	53.53

1992 Championship positions are shown in brackets.

* £4,000 fine.

SRI LANKAN UNDER-19 IN ENGLAND, 1992

By GERALD HOWAT

The Sri Lankan Under-19 side who toured England in 1992 hit one of the wettest patches of recent English summers. Of their 11 games, all except the first two and the last one were drawn. The final game was the third in the three-match "Test" series against England Under-19 when England won by an innings to prove their superiority. In contrast to the 1991 tour, when the Australians had far more experience than England, the Sri Lankans were up against a team that was obviously more mature than they were. Seven of the England squad (the captain Philip Weston of Worcestershire, Mal Loye and Jeremy Snape of Northamptonshire, Glen Chapple of Lancashire, Matthew Windows of Gloucestershire, Robert Rollins of Essex and Andrew Cottam of Somerset) had played some county first-team cricket and all the others were attached to a first-class county.

The Sri Lankan cricket manager was Bandula Warnapura, who had captained the national team in their first Test match ten years earlier. He said the team had come to learn, and he wryly wondered when, after the tour, they would next play an important match. Many of the party would be returning to school for another year. They were a side of all-rounders rather than specialists, so it was not surprising to find their most successful batsmen, openers Russel Arnold and Sajith Fernando, sometimes bowling in tandem as spinners. Both scored over 400 runs, Arnold averaging 30.06 and Fernando 28.33, while Fernando also took 34 wickets at 17.50. There were four other slow bowlers, but the Sri Lankans' main weakness was the lack of any pace attack. The opening seamers had a moment of glory at Headingley at the start of the First "Test" when they reduced England to one for three. Otherwise, they posed little threat and Pulasthi Gunaratne, though quicker, was too inaccurate. As a batting side, the Sri Lankans were attractive to watch. Many of them were natural, if sometimes impetuous, strokeplayers. Upul Fernando, Naveed Nawaz and the two Pereras, Asanga and Gamini, were all impressive. Nevertheless, the batting could be brittle and was seriously exposed at Worcester by England's spinners, Snape and Mark Bainbridge of Surrey. The ability to build an innings was often wanting.

The Sri Lankan side was well led by Suchitra Alexander, who commanded the respect of the players. Appeals, though noisy, were good natured. Umpires remarked that they looked forward to the intervals for some peace and quiet, but the team were good ambassadors for their country and won many friends through their courtesy. They had been chosen from an initial squad of 275 and should be part of the cadre of future Sri Lankan Test sides; they may well find themselves playing at full international level earlier than their English opponents.

The tour party was: H. L. B. Gomes (*manager*), B. Warnapura (*cricket manager*), S. Alexander (*captain*), R. P. Arnold, B. S. D. de Silva, L. R. P. de Silva, E. F. M. U. Fernando, S. I. Fernando, P. W. Gunaratne, M. I. Z. Hamid, R. V. Hewage, C. P. Mapatuna, M. N. Nawaz, G. G. N. Perera, W. D. A. S. Perera, K. J. Silva and W. P. U. J. C. Waas. The tour was sponsored by Bull Information Systems.

RESULTS

Matches 11: Won 1, Lost 2, Drawn 8.

Note: None of the matches played was first-class.

v England Under-17: at Wellington College, August 2. Sri Lanka Under-19 won by 15 runs. Sri Lanka Under-19 259 for seven (55 overs) (S. I. Fernando 95, M. N. Nawaz 71); England Under-17 244 for nine (55 overs) (M. P. Vaughan 51, V. S. Solanki 50).

v England Under-17: at Wellington College, August 3, 4, 5. England Under-17 won by ten wickets. England Under-17 384 for six (R. M. S. Weston 102, P. W. Henderson 94 not out, M. Trescothick 76, K. J. Innes 52) and 11 for no wkt; Sri Lanka Under-19 130 (K. J. Innes four for 38) and 261 (G. Keedy four for 43).

v Bull Development Squad: at Oundle School, August 6, 7, 8. Drawn. Bull Development Squad 196 (M. Forster 71, M. P. Dowman 53; K. J. Silva five for 50) and 214 for six (D. A. Blenkiron 80 not out; K. J. Silva four for 54); Sri Lanka Under-19 242 (E. F. M. U. Fernando 56, S. I. Fernando 52; R. J. Ballinger four for 47).

v Leicestershire Second Eleven: at Oundle School, August 10, 11, 12. Drawn. Leicestershire Second Eleven 157 (I. J. Sutcliffe 58; S. I. Fernando six for 46) and 87 for four; Sri Lanka Under-19 189 (S. I. Fernando 41; T. K. Marriott seven for 33).

ENGLAND UNDER-19 v SRI LANKA UNDER-19

First "Test" Match

At Leeds, August 14, 15, 16, 17. Drawn. Toss: England Under-19. England probably had the better chance of forcing victory on the last day, after Weston's overnight declaration set Sri Lanka a target of 389, but their hopes were dented by brief stoppages for rain. Sri Lanka had seized the initiative to devastating effect on the first morning, when the first three England batsmen were dismissed in nine balls; Robinson was bowled by the first delivery of the match. But Matthew Walker of Kent and Windows batted fluently while Rollins, at No. 9, made an unbeaten 86 in two hours. The last three wickets took England from 155 to 285. Chapple, faster by far than any Sri Lankan bowler, took two quick wickets by the close, but the efforts of left-hander Arnold and Upul Fernando left the tourists only 34 behind. With the match evenly poised, England's top order made amends in style on the third day, though the runs might have come more quickly in the morning. Loye contributed an attractive 93, Weston anchored the innings with a century in 316 minutes and Walker again showed his class and strength. Sri Lanka tried a variety of bowlers, with Waas switching from seam to spin, and fielded splendidly but, off-spinner Sajith Fernando apart, they made little impact.

England Under-19

D. D. J. Robinson b Alexander	0	– b S. I. Fernando	33
*W. P. C. Weston b Alexander	0	– b Waas	107
M. B. Loye b Waas	1	– c E. F. M. U. Fernando b S. I. Fernando	93
M. J. Walker c Gunaratne b S. I. Fernando	68	– not out	71
J. N. Snape b Silva	9	– c Nawaz b Waas	14
M. G. N. Windows b Gunaratne	68	– not out	18
T. C. Walton c Hamid b Waas	10		
G. Chapple b Alexander	7		
†R. J. Rollins not out	86		
M. Broadhurst st Hamid b Silva	9		
A. C. Cottam c E. F. M. U. Fernando b S. I. Fernando	11		
B 3, l-b 9, w 1, n-b 3	16	B 7, l-b 6, w 1, n-b 4	18
	285	(4 wkts dec.)	**354**

1/0 2/1 3/1 4/40 5/110   285   1/62 2/204   (4 wkts dec.) 354
6/139 7/155 8/206 9/243   3/282 4/320

Bowling: *First Innings*—Alexander 12–4–29–3; Waas 17–3–56–2; Silva 21–8–58–2; Gunaratne 11–2–54–1; S. I. Fernando 18.5–4–46–2; Mapatuna 6–0–25–0; Arnold 2–0–5–0. *Second Innings*—Alexander 11–0–37–0; Waas 23–1–79–2; Silva 4–2–16–0; Gunaratne 11–0–51–0; S. I. Fernando 31–8–74–2; Arnold 23–7–84–0.

Sri Lanka Under-19

R. P. Arnold c Loye b Cottam	72	– c Rollins b Cottam	22
S. I. Fernando b Chapple	1	– c Weston b Broadhurst	1
M. N. Nawaz c Weston b Chapple	10	– (4) c Robinson b Broadhurst	52
W. D. A. S. Perera c Rollins b Chapple	7	– (5) lbw b Broadhurst	14
C. P. Mapatuna lbw b Cottam	36	– (6) c Robinson b Snape	13
E. F. M. U. Fernando not out	67	– (3) c Windows b Weston	73
*S. Alexander c Robinson b Cottam	8	– not out	48
W. P. U. J. C. Waas c Loye b Cottam	0	– b Snape	2
†M. I. Z. Hamid c Robinson b Snape	0	– c Windows b Broadhurst	40
P. W. Gunaratne b Chapple	31		
K. J. Silva b Broadhurst	2		
B 3, l-b 10, w 2, n-b 2	17	B 8, l-b 9, w 6	23

1/3 2/35 3/61 4/129 5/162   251   1/12 2/43 3/152   (8 wkts) 288
6/174 7/174 8/175 9/234   4/177 5/188 6/202
                                   7/206 8/288

Bowling: *First Innings*—Chapple 24–4–62–4; Broadhurst 16.1–2–58–1; Walton 11–4–17–0; Weston 4–3–2–0; Cottam 25–9–69–4; Snape 19–8–30–1. *Second Innings*—Chapple 18–5–58–0; Broadhurst 16–3–54–4; Cottam 20–1–79–1; Snape 25–11–60–2; Weston 5–2–12–1; Walton 5–1–8–0.

Umpires: J. D. Bond and N. T. Plews.

v MCC Young Cricketers: at Uppingham School, August 19, 20. Drawn. MCC Young Cricketers 135 (S. I. Fernando five for 49) and 142 for six dec. (M. Church 53); Sri Lanka Under-19 82 (S. D. Welch five for 16, P. J. Heaton five for 25) and 184 for nine (G. G. N. Perera 50; K. Bird four for 46).

v Bull Development Squad: at Oundle School, August 21, 22, 23. Drawn. Sri Lanka Under-19 246 (E. F. M. U. Fernando 54, R. P. Arnold 51; K. Dutch five for 79) and 191 for eight dec. (R. P. Arnold 43; K. Dutch four for 78); Bull Development Squad 236 for seven dec. (G. J. Kennis 49; S. I. Fernando five for 78) and 32 for two.

ENGLAND UNDER-19 v SRI LANKA UNDER-19

Second "Test" Match

At Taunton, August 25, 26, 27, 28. Drawn. Toss: Sri Lanka Under-19. The match was doomed as 16 hours were lost to rain, including the whole of the second and third days. England, put in to bat, had little trouble with the opening attack, running up 44 in the first hour. Though the quicker Gunaratne and the off-spinner Sajith Fernando each claimed a wicket shortly after coming on, and Weston gave three chances in the slips, he survived to give the innings its foundation. England ended a shortened first day at 136 for four, and did not resume until the afternoon of the last day. Windows batted attractively as they added a further 52 before Weston declared. Sajith Fernando hit powerfully when Sri Lanka replied but there was little support for his forceful 80; Richard Ballinger of Middlesex removed his opening partner, Arnold, with his third ball.

England Under-19

D. J. Robinson lbw b Gunaratne ...	24		G. Chapple not out	0
W. P. C. Weston c Silva b Alexander .	77			
B. Loye c Hamid b S. I. Fernando .	1			
J. Walker c Waas b Silva	15		B 4, l-b 6, w 2, n-b 1	13
G. N. Windows c Arnold b Silva ...	37			—
N. Snape c Nawaz b Silva	20		1/49 2/50 3/119	(7 wkts dec.) 188
C. Walton c E. F. M. U. Fernando			4/128 5/187	
b S. I. Fernando .	1		6/188 7/188	

R. J. Rollins, M. Broadhurst and R. J. Ballinger did not bat.

Bowling: Alexander 22–5–69–1; Waas 7–1–22–0; Gunaratne 18–5–30–1; S. I. Fernando 9–10–38–2; Silva 15.2–8–19–3.

Sri Lanka Under-19

R. P. Arnold c Robinson b Ballinger ...	10		W. D. A. S. Perera not out	14
S. I. Fernando c Chapple b Walton	80			
E. F. M. U. Fernando c Robinson			L-b 10, w 4	14
b Chapple .	13			—
M. N. Nawaz not out	22		1/34 2/111 3/113	(3 wkts) 153

G. G. N. Perera, *S. Alexander, †M. I. Z. Hamid, W. P. U. J. C. Waas, P. W. Gunaratne and K. J. Silva did not bat.

Bowling: Chapple 12–4–24–1; Broadhurst 10–0–54–0; Ballinger 9–3–32–1; Snape 4–2–12–0; Walton 9–3–21–1.

Umpires: K. E. Palmer and D. R. Shepherd.

v **National Association of Young Cricketers:** at Millfield School, August 30, 31. Drawn. Sri Lanka Under-19 184 for seven dec. (W. D. A. S. Perera 54; T. J. Mason four for 58); National Association of Young Cricketers 68 for four.

v **Bull Development Squad/England Under-18:** at Winchester College, September 3, 4, 5. Drawn. Bull Development Squad/England Under-18 198 for eight dec. (P. J. Wilcock 40) and 138 for three (R. M. S. Weston 42); Sri Lanka Under-19 193 for nine dec. (P. W. Gunaratne 50 not out; J. E. Hindson four for 56).

ENGLAND UNDER-19 v SRI LANKA UNDER-19

Third "Test" Match

At Worcester, September 7, 8, 9. England Under-19 won by an innings and 101 runs. Toss: Sri Lanka Under-19. England demonstrated their all-round superiority by taking the series 1-0 with a day to spare, and received the Bull Trophy from Ted Dexter, chairman of the England Committee. On the first day Sri Lanka collapsed after a promising opening partnership. Six wickets fell for 20 runs, largely through the nagging accuracy of the slow left-armer, Bainbridge, to whom Snape was an effective foil. England, batting through five sessions over three days, achieved their highest score in Under-19 cricket, eclipsing their 451 for seven – also against Sri Lanka, at Kandy – in 1986-87. Robinson and Loye both reached three figures in setting up a second-wicket record of 200, and batted admirably, the one cutting and driving, the other persistently sweeping. Half-centuries from Walker and Windows and 29, with six fours, from Rollins completed Sri Lanka's desolation. Resuming with 333 needed to make England bat again, Arnold and Mapatuna batted well but England dismissed Sri Lanka in just under four hours. Once again, the spinners did the bulk of the bowling. In the evening sunshine of what had been one of the nicest days of a rain-dominated tour, the Sri Lankans went for their shots right up to the end before an appreciative crowd.

Sri Lanka Under-19

S. I. Fernando c Loye b Payne	32	– (2) c Walker b Broadhurst	8
R. P. Arnold c Robinson b Snape	63	– (1) c Rollins b Bainbridge	75
†E. F. M. U. Fernando lbw b Chapple	8	– c Chapple b Snape	26
M. N. Nawaz c Rollins b Bainbridge	38	– lbw b Bainbridge	0
W. D. A. S. Perera b Bainbridge	10	– c Snape b Bainbridge	7
C. P. Mapatuna b Bainbridge	15	– c Loye b Snape	62
G. G. N. Perera c Rollins b Bainbridge	2	– b Snape	21
*S. Alexander c Snape b Chapple	7	– b Snape	0
P. W. Gunaratne c Robinson b Bainbridge	8	– c Chapple b Snape	18
W. P. U. J. C. Waas not out	0	– c Rollins b Chapple	13
K. J. Silva c Rollins b Bainbridge	0	– not out	0
L-b 5, w 1, n-b 1	7	L-b 2	2

1/51 2/66 3/126 4/137 5/170   190   1/18 2/80 3/80 4/90 5/143   232
6/173 7/176 8/190 9/190   6/182 7/192 8/201 9/226

Bowling: *First Innings*—Chapple 11–1–45–2; Broadhurst 9–1–38–0; Payne 9–1–22–1; Weston 3–1–5–0; Snape 21–6–49–1; Bainbridge 19–8–26–6. *Second Innings*—Chapple 12.5–4–33–1; Broadhurst 5–1–18–1; Bainbridge 36–11–106–3; Snape 31–12–62–5; Payne 6–3–11–0.

England Under-19

D. D. J. Robinson b G. G. N. Perera	124	†R. J. Rollins lbw b Silva	29
*W. P. C. Weston b Silva	15	A. Payne not out	18
M. B. Loye c E. F. M. U. Fernando b Arnold	162		
M. J. Walker run out	87	B 1, l-b 10, w 4, n-b 2	17
M. G. N. Windows c Arnold b Waas	52		
J. N. Snape c E. F. M. U. Fernando b Alexander	19		

1/54 2/254 3/366   (7 wkts dec.) 523
4/441 5/468
6/476 7/523

G. Chapple, M. R. Bainbridge and M. Broadhurst did not bat.

Bowling: Alexander 10–0–52–1; Waas 9–3–36–1; S. I. Fernando 41–7–114–0; Silva 32.3–6–102–2; Gunaratne 4–1–23–0; G. G. N. Perera 23–3–73–1; Arnold 29–4–104–1; Mapatuna 3–1–8–0.

Umpires: J. H. Harris and B. J. Meyer.

ESSO/NAYC UNDER-19 COUNTY FESTIVALS, 1992

By PHILIP HOARE

Yorkshire won the seventh Under-19 County Festival final in the manner in which past Yorkshire generations won their matches. They bowled out their opponents, Worcestershire, for 87 with a left-arm spinner, Gary Keedy, taking five for nine in 14 overs. They knocked off the runs with nearly 37 overs of their allotted 60 to spare.

Thirty-four counties took part in the two festivals, held at Oxford and Cambridge and sponsored by Esso, but all found their programme badly disrupted by rain. The Oxford games were particularly hard hit, but at both centres matches were abandoned, or played with a reduced number of overs. Before Worcestershire beat Buckinghamshire in the Oxford final, a match dominated by all-rounder Nick Davies, they had started only two of their scheduled four group matches, beating Staffordshire by 60 runs but failing to achieve a result against Cornwall, despite making 152 for one. In Cambridge, Yorkshire were luckier. They began the week with a resounding victory over Nottinghamshire. David Bates made 120 of their 259 for four, and Keedy took seven for 62 as they restricted Nottinghamshire to 88 for eight. All their subsequent matches were rain-affected, though they beat Lincolnshire and Bedfordshire over reduced playing time and had the better of the group leaders' encounter with Leicestershire before beating Sussex in the area final.

Despite the wet weather, six players managed to score centuries. The biggest innings of the week came from Rupert Thacker, who was unbeaten on 165 in Middlesex's group match with Huntingdon and Peterborough at The Leys. Matthew Dowman, a Nottinghamshire Second Eleven player, made 105 for his native county, Lincolnshire, against Cheshire, and completed an all-round performance by taking five for 34. But the best bowling in either festival was Alan Richardson's eight for 60, which set up Staffordshire's five-wicket victory over Devon in Oxford.

Most of the competing counties also took part in the Hilda Overy Championship, a 60-overs competition including fixtures both at the festivals and elsewhere. Yorkshire very nearly scored a double triumph; they won all their nine matches in this tournament. But Somerset achieved a higher points average, as well as winning six games out of six, and took the title.

AREA FINALS

At Clare College, Cambridge, August 14. Yorkshire won by seven wickets. Toss: Yorkshire. Sussex 134 for eight (S. Humphries 40; M. Bradford three for 22); Yorkshire 135 for three (L. P. Kingsbury 70, R. A. Kettleborough 36 not out).

At Jesus College, Oxford, August 14. Worcestershire won by 53 runs. Toss: Buckinghamshire. Worcestershire 128 (N. M. Davies 36; R. Parker four for 28, D. Plumeridge three for 32); Buckinghamshire 75 (M. Smith three for 26, N. M. Davies four for 22, S. Collins three for 22).

FINAL

WORCESTERSHIRE v YORKSHIRE

At Fenner's, Cambridge, August 15. Yorkshire won by seven wickets. Toss: Worcestershire. Castleford left-arm spinner Gary Keedy swept Worcestershire's batting aside to set up an easy victory for Yorkshire. Keedy, like six of his team-mates a member of the Yorkshire Cricket Academy, had taken four wickets for one run in 21 balls to reduce Worcestershire to 74 for seven at lunch, and a fifth in the afternoon gave him the remarkable figures of 14-8-9-5. Despite choosing to bat, Worcestershire were all out within 52 overs. Only captain Steve Collins, who batted just over an hour for a fighting 32 before becoming the first of Keedy's victims, had enabled them to reach 87. Yorkshire's own efforts were not wholly untroubled, as they lost three wickets for 30. But Michael Foster, who toured Pakistan with England Under-19 earlier in the year, and Richard Kettleborough saw them home with an unbroken partnership of 58. For the second year running the final – easily won by Middlesex in 1991 – finished before tea.

Worcestershire

D. R. McDonnell c Foster b Bradford	15	†N. J. Workman b Roberts		4
C. W. Boroughs b Foster	3	N. P. Haddock not out		0
*S. Collins c and b Keedy	32	M. Smith b Roberts		1
G. Pilgrim run out	4	B 2, l-b 3, n-b 1		6
N. Hagan c Kingsbury b Keedy	7			—
I. Duggan c Kingsbury b Keedy	1	1/20 2/24 3/32	(51.2 overs)	87
N. M. Davies c Foster b Keedy	0	4/63 5/64 6/64		
I. Cutler b Keedy	14	7/67 8/86 9/86		

Bowling: Silverwood 5-0-15-0; Bradford 10-7-11-1; Foster 7-2-16-1; Roberts 15.2-4-31-2; Keedy 14-8-9-5.

Yorkshire

L. P. Kingsbury lbw b Smith	16	*M. J. Foster not out		40
D. Bates run out	3	L-b 1		1
R. A. Kettleborough not out	24			—
C. D. Watson c Workman b Cutler	4	1/17 2/21 3/30	(3 wkts, 23.1 overs)	88

M. Bradford, J. Booth, †M. R. Gill, G. M. Roberts, C. E. W. Silverwood and G. Keedy did not bat.

Bowling: Smith 6-2-22-1; Davies 5-1-10-0; Haddock 6-0-18-0; Cutler 6.1-0-37-1.

Umpires: G. Sharp and A. G. T. Whitehead.

SCHOOLS CRICKET IN 1992

Of the players capped by English Schools in 1991, M. E. Harvey, J. E. Hindson, M. J. Walker, R. M. S. Weston and R. S. Yeabsley were still at school and would have been eligible to play again in 1992. In the event, Yeabsley was injured and withdrew from the MCC Schools Festival and the others were not available owing to commitments to counties and – in the case of Walker – to England Under-19. In addition, G. Chapple, who would otherwise have been considered, was playing in the Youth "Tests" against Australia and Pakistan before joining Lancashire. It was therefore possible for other players to test their ability at a higher representative level, and 16 appeared in the senior Schools side: J. M. A. Averis, M. J. Brooke, J. A. L. Henderson, N. Humphrey, A. M. James, W. S. Kendall, G. J. Kennis, G. A. Khan, T. J. Mason, C. E. Mulraine, P. J. Nicholson, D. B. Ratcliffe, S. J. Renshaw, C. J. Rika, M. Trescothick and P. J. Wilcock. Their schools may be found in the scorecards of matches played at the MCC Schools Festival, Oxford.

The overall standard was reasonable, with no player consistently outstanding. After the promise shown by the bowlers in the preliminary games, their later performances were somewhat disappointing. Henderson, probably the pick of the quicker bowlers, could play in only one of the internationals, leaving Averis and the two all-rounders, Renshaw and Rika, to bear the brunt and, while consistent, they were never penetrative enough. The off-spinner, Mason, was the most successful, as well as scoring some useful runs. The most consistent of the batsmen was Kendall, who batted positively at all times. He had sound support from Brooke, Humphrey, Khan and Wilcock, and Rika produced an impressive century when it was needed against Welsh Schools. Mulraine led the side well, made telling contributions with the bat and was outstanding in the field. Nicholson performed admirably behind the stumps in all the matches, but otherwise the fielding always left something to be desired.

The regional matches played at Radley and Rochdale prior to the Oxford festival were keenly contested and evenly balanced between bat and ball, a particularly pleasing feature being the general quality of the bowlers. It was disappointing that the weather at Oxford was so wet, although there were plenty of encouraging performances. Foremost among the quicker bowlers were Averis, Henderson, Rika and Wellington, while Mason and a trio of left-arm spinners – J. R. Carpenter, James and Ratcliffe – made an impression.

The first of the international matches, against Irish Youth, took place in Dublin on July 21 and 22. English Schools reached 204 for nine in the allotted 60 overs (Kendall 42, Humphrey 39), and after almost two hours had been lost to rain, Ireland finished the day on 75 for three. Next morning saw a dramatic collapse in which seven wickets fell for 38 runs in 75 minutes, the spinners Ratcliffe (four for 39) and Mason (three for 36) doing most of the damage. England then extended their lead to 243, with Brooke (57) pushing the score along. Survival was Ireland's aim and despite Mulraine's attacking fields the game finished in a draw with Irish Youth on 54 for four.

It was Welsh Schools who had the best of a draw in the next game, on July 27 and 28 at Pontarddulais, where Wales won the toss and fielded. The pitch generally favoured the bowlers, and it needed a careful century from the usually fluent Wilcock to take English Schools to 175 for five. However, the English bowlers were less effective and the fielding was disappointing, so that Dalton (67) and Jones (68 not out) were able to take Wales to a first-innings lead of 80. Prospects looked poor just after lunch on the second day, when England were five wickets down with a lead still only in the twenties. However, a magnificent stand of 124 between Rika (106) and Mason (39) in 115 minutes saw them to 259 (S. Jones five for 76), leaving time only for Welsh Schools to progress to 22 for one in pursuit of 180.

The game against Scottish Young Cricketers at Steetley on August 6 and 7 produced the most exciting cricket. Rika was taken ill before the start and his absence seemed to affect the bowlers, so that the Scots had no difficulty in reaching 245 for nine in their 60 overs. Khan (83) and Kendall (80 not out) then batted attractively and positively to take English Schools to a declaration at 269 for six after 56 overs. Scotland did not show the same purpose on the second day and eventually declared at 226 for nine, leaving England the daunting target of 203 in 20 minutes plus 20 overs. Wilcock set the tone with 23 off 26 balls, Humphrey and Mulraine accelerated further with a stand of 74 in 34 minutes, and when Humphrey was out for 50 from 53 balls, Brooke joined Mulraine. With a barrage of fours and sixes they knocked off the last 84 runs in 36 minutes, Mulraine 73 not out (58 balls) and Brooke 44 not out (23 balls), to complete an outstanding victory.

Welsh Schools' creditable draw against English Schools was the climax of an international season that began badly, with the three-day game against Irish Schools at Pontypridd completely washed out. They met Scotland in Edinburgh, where the Scots scored 195 (N. Ball 76, G. Hamilton 72, D. Parsons 35; C. Wiseman four for 34), in reply to which the Welsh took a lead with 256 (S. Jenkins 42; R. Gilmour four for 53, C. Mears three for 48). The Scots fought back strongly, declaring at 264 for six (A. Heather 61, J. Clutterbuck 90, N. Ball 38; S. D. Thomas three for 57) and had reduced Welsh Schools to 145 for six (P. Richards 46; D. Wylie four for 37) when time ran out.

HMC SOUTHERN SCHOOLS v HMC NORTHERN SCHOOLS

At Wadham College, Oxford, July 10, 11. Drawn. A promising match was ended by rain after only 44 overs on the second day. On the first, Hames made a bright start for Southern Schools, although it needed Cawdron and Averis to give the innings respectability after a middle-order collapse. The left-arm spin of Carpenter and Ratcliffe tied down all the batsmen, who never found it easy to get the ball away against generally accurate bowling on a slow wicket and outfield. When Northern Schools replied, it was the lively seam bowling of Wellington that caused a slump to 46 for four, before Mulraine and Renshaw rescued the innings with an excellent century stand. The South's second innings was interrupted three times by rain before the final deluge, but there was time for Kendall to play some vigorous strokes in scoring 87 out of 130, and for Carpenter and Henderson to stand out as the pick of the bowlers. In the field the throwing was good, some smart catches were held and the wicket-keeping of Nicholson was above average.

HMC Southern Schools

B. A. Hames (*Lord Wandsworth*) c Henderson			
b Carpenter .	37	– (4) c Ratcliffe b Carpenter	7
F. L. Stewart (*King's, Bruton*) b Henderson	1	– (1) b Carpenter	22
D. R. Hewson (*Cheltenham*) b Carpenter	11	– c Colclough b Henderson	25
*W. S. Kendall (*Bradfield*) c Colclough			
b Ratcliffe .	5	– (2) c Brooke b Henderson	87
J. S. G. Hargrove (*Victoria, Jersey*)			
c Colclough b Ratcliffe .	1		
M. J. Cawdron (*Cheltenham*) c Mulraine			
b Ratcliffe .	36	– (5) c Ratcliffe b Carpenter	1
B. M. Wellington (*Taunton*) c Renshaw			
b Ratcliffe .	0	– (6) not out	10
†W. J. A. Freisenbruch (*Bryanston*)			
c and b Ratcliffe .	14	– (7) not out	4
J. M. A. Averis (*Bristol Cathedral*)			
st Nicholson b Carpenter .	31		
I. J. Harvey (*Chigwell*) lbw b Renshaw	1		
A. M. James (*King's, Macclesfield*) not out	7		
Extras	9	Extras	7

1/36 2/43 3/54 4/55 5/56   153   1/66 2/130 3/146   (5 wkts) 163
6/56 7/113 8/118 9/120   4/147 5/147

Bowling: *First Innings*—Henderson 9–0–36–1; Waters 9–2–31–0; Carpenter 17–7–30–3; Ratcliffe 17–7–38–5; Renshaw 6–0–15–1. *Second Innings*—Henderson 14–1–46–2; Waters 10–1–35–0; Renshaw 6–1–19–0; Carpenter 7–2–27–3; Ratcliffe 7–0–33–0.

HMC Northern Schools

*R. I. Biggin (*Repton*) c Cawdron	S. J. Renshaw (*Birkenhead*) not out 61
b Wellington . 18	R. W. D. Waters (*Wellington C.*) not out 13
N. T. Wood (*William Hulme's GS*)	
c Cawdron b Wellington . 14	
M. J. Brooke (*Batley GS*)	Extras 18
lbw b Wellington . 3	
C. E. Mulraine (*Warwick*) b Cawdron .. 71	1/36 2/44 (5 wkts dec.) 198
M. H. Colclough (*Newcastle-under-*	3/45 4/46
Lyme) c Hames b Wellington . 0	5/164

†P. J. Nicholson (*Dame Allan's*), J. R. Carpenter (*Birkenhead*), O. B. Ratcliffe (*Downside*) and J. A. L. Henderson (*Hulme GS*) did not bat.

Bowling: Averis 16–4–58–0; Harvey 8–0–43–0; Wellington 13–3–25–4; James 13–5–28–0; Cawdron 10–1–35–1.

ESCA NORTH v ESCA SOUTH

At St Edward's School, Oxford, July 10, 11. Drawn. The North were generally on top in wet conditions which made run-scoring difficult. A stand of 107 between Humphrey and Kennis was the cornerstone of the South's innings, with Mason's off-spin the pick of the bowling. Wilcock batted with authority for the North before retiring with a pulled muscle, and then a contribution from Bairstow and Treagus enabled Powell to declare 21 behind. Humphrey again batted solidly before rain ended play after only 34 overs on the second day.

ESCA South

†S. T. Platt (*Coundon Court; Warwicks.*)
          c and b Morris . 4 – b Hart 6
N. Humphrey (*Kineton HS; Warwicks.*)
          c and b Mason . 51 – not out 47
G. J. Kennis (*Tiffin; Surrey*) c Powell b Hughes 61
G. A. Khan (*Ipswich; Essex*) c Rika b Morris . . 32 – (6) not out 4
M. Trescothick (*Sir B. Lovell; Avon*) c Bairstow
          b Mason . 19 – c Lapsia b Mason 20
A. Planck (*West Kent; Kent*) lbw b Mason . . . . . 5 – (3) b Hart 0
N. Harvey (*Forest; Berks.*) not out . . . . 5 – (4) c Powell b Morris 3
Extras 20   Extras 12

1/12 2/119 3/137 4/167   (6 wkts dec.) 197   1/25 2/28 3/43 4/80   (4 wkts) 92
5/179 6/197

*G. Sheppard (*Bath CFE; Wilts.*), L. Clarke (*Chatham GS; Kent*), D. Fossey (*Sponne; Northants*), S. McDonald (*Rowley Regis; Warwicks.*) and R. Dibden (*Barton Peveril; Hants*) did not bat.

Bowling: *First Innings*—Hart 7-0-26-0; Morris 12-1-40-2; Lapsia 12-0-41-0; Rika 6-1-16-0; Hughes 12-0-44-1; Mason 11-1-20-3. *Second Innings*—Hart 11-3-24-2; Morris 13-2-33-1; Mason 6-0-21-1; Hughes 4-1-9-0.

ESCA North

P. J. Wilcock (*Hopwood Hall; Lancs.*)
          retired hurt . 52
*M. Powell (*L. Sheriff; Warwicks.*)
          c Harvey b Sheppard . 10
T. J. Mason (*Denstone; Leics.*)
          c Humphrey b Fossey . 9
A. D. Bairstow (*Woodhouse Grove;*
          Yorks.*) not out . 59

G. Treagus (*King Edward VI, Southampton; Hants*) not out . 32

Extras 14

1/27 2/43   (2 wkts dec.) 176

C. J. Rika (*Woodhouse Grove; Yorks.*), S. K. Lapsia (*Stockport GS; Cheshire*), Q. J. Hughes (*D. Johnstone; Durham*), K. Morris (*Ryton CS; Durham*), J. Hart (*Coventry S., Bablake; Warwicks.*) and †T. Gane (*Stockport College; Cheshire*) did not bat.

Bowling: Clarke 13-6-30-0; Sheppard 9-0-33-1; Fossey 11-1-40-1; Dibden 18-6-38-0; McDonald 9-3-27-0.

At Wadham College, Oxford, July 12. Drawn. G. Sheppard's XI 198 for nine dec. (P. J. Wilcock 80; Q. J. Hughes five for 78); R. I. Biggin's XI 147 for six (R. I. Biggin 35, L. Clarke 52 not out; R. W. D. Waters three for 31).

At St Edward's School, Oxford, July 12. M. Powell's XI won by three wickets. W. S. Kendall's XI 203 for four dec. (S. T. Platt 34, M. J. Brooke 83 not out); M. Powell's XI 205 for seven (N. T. Wood 74, B. A. Hames 69; A. M. James five for 36).

At Christ Church, Oxford, July 13. Drawn. MCC Schools West 160 for nine dec. (N. Humphrey 32; J. R. Carpenter three for 65, T. J. Mason three for 47); MCC Schools East 113 for two (M. J. Brooke 43 not out, G. A. Khan 50 not out).

MCC v MCC SCHOOLS

At Lord's, July 14. MCC Schools won by six wickets. Toss: MCC Schools. Light rain brought a two-hour stoppage when MCC were 57 for no loss, but when play resumed after an early lunch Dracup and McEvoy doubled the score in the next half hour. Once they had departed in close succession, runs were at a premium as two wickets fell to Mason, the Denstone off-spinner who flighted the ball well. The South African Gilbert chanced his luck while Radley gave a brief and undefeated demonstration of how to find the gaps before declaring at 195 for five at tea. MCC Schools struggled against the pace of Fox and Fay, the former claiming the first two wickets at 12 before Kennis, with some off-drives, showed why he had been such a prolific scorer for his school. An attacking partnership of 98 between Mulraine and Kendall maintained the run-rate and once Mulraine was run out, Kendall took command with some glorious strokes, hitting nine fours in his 69 not out.

MCC

M. S. A. McEvoy c Nicholson b Averis	64	M. P. Hickson not out	1
J. B. H. Dracup c Kendall b Renshaw .	62		
N. G. Folland c Kendall b Mason	2	L-b 8, n-b 3	11
D. J. Price lbw b Mason	4		
B. A. Gilbert c Nicholson b Henderson.	29	1/114 2/130 3/132 (5 wkts dec.)	195
*C. T. Radley not out	22	4/152 5/181	

†C. F. E. Goldie, A. T. Crouch, R. A. Fay and D. B. M. Fox did not bat.

Bowling: Henderson 9–2–30–1; Averis 12–4–37–1; Mason 17–5–65–2; Renshaw 9–1–55–1.

MCC Schools

P. J. Wilcock (*Hopwood Hall*) lbw b Fox	9	S. J. Renshaw (*Birkenhead*) not out	20
G. J. Kennis (*Tiffin*) lbw b Crouch	34		
M. J. Brooke (*Batley GS*) c McEvoy b Fox	0	B 3, l-b 5, w 2	10
*C. E. Mulraine (*Warwick*) run out	57	1/12 2/12 (4 wkts)	199
W. S. Kendall (*Bradfield*) not out	69	3/57 4/155	

J. M. A. Averis (*Bristol Cathedral S*), T. J. Mason (*Denstone*), †P. J. Nicholson (*Dame Allen's*), J. A. L. Henderson (*Hulme GS*) and O. B. Ratcliffe (*Downside*) did not bat.

Bowling: Fox 12–2–38–2; Fay 11–5–47–0; Hickson 6–1–32–0; Crouch 10–0–40–1; Price 5–0–34–0.

Umpires: K. Hopley and G. A. Plow.

MCC SCHOOLS v NATIONAL ASSOCIATION OF YOUNG CRICKETERS

At Lord's, July 15. Drawn. Toss: MCC Schools. The NAYC team featured four of the boys who had played in the Oxford Festival, including Kennis, who had represented MCC Schools the previous day, and with the Schools making two additional changes, 17 of the Oxford trialists appeared at Lord's. On a slow, low wicket Kennis looked in no difficulty until well caught by Brooke at square leg and NAYC reached 127 before lunch. Averis went off injured after four overs and with their 12th man, J. A. L. Henderson, also injured, the Schools fielded ten men for most of the morning. The spinners, Mason and James, showed good control, although it was Colclough who dominated the afternoon in a fifth-wicket partnership of 65 with Spencer. As soon as Colclough was out – well caught by Nicholson, whose wicket-keeping was impeccable – NAYC rather belatedly declared, whereupon both the Schools' openers were dismissed within four overs. Thereafter Mulraine attacked well in a brisk partnership with Brooke, but NAYC seemed in no hurry to get through their overs and what was probably a vain pursuit ended when the rain came with 14 overs remaining. There was just a hint that Harris might have spun the Schools out.

National Association of Young Cricketers

G. J. Kennis (*Surrey*) c Brooke b Mason 52	*M. R. Spencer (*Derbys.*) run out......	41
J. R. Cunliffe (*Oxon.*) c Mulraine	A. J. Harris (*Derbys.*) not out.........	2
b Mason . 32		
M. H. Colclough (*Staffs.*) c Nicholson	B 4, l-b 6, n-b 1	11
b Renshaw . 72		
S. Moffatt (*Herts.*) c Nicholson b Rika . 14	1/67 2/96 3/137	(6 wkts dec.) 247
B. A. Hames (*Bucks.*) run out......... 23	4/177 5/242 6/247	

N. Bratt (*Staffs.*), †N. Harvey (*Berks.*), B. Walters (*Surrey*) and A. Lang (*Hants*) did not bat.

Bowling: Averis 4-1-13-0; Rika 14-1-43-1; Renshaw 11.4-1-64-1; James 16-2-49-0; Mason 27-5-68-2.

MCC Schools

P. J. Wilcock (*Hopwood Hall*)	G. A. Khan (*Ipswich*) c Cunliffe b Harris 12	
lbw b Bratt . 0	S. J. Renshaw (*Birkenhead*) not out	0
W. S. Kendall (*Bradfield*) b Lang...... 4	B 1, l-b 1, n-b 2	4
M. J. Brooke (*Batley GS*) not out..... 39		
*C. E. Mulraine (*Warwick*) c Cunliffe	1/2 2/4	(4 wkts) 89
b Harris . 30	3/67 4/89	

C. J. Rika (*Woodhouse Grove*), J. M. A. Averis (*Bristol Cathedral S*), T. J. Mason (*Denstone*), †P. J. Nicholson (*Dame Allen's*) and A. M. James (*King's, Macclesfield*) did not bat.

Bowling: Bratt 6-1-27-1; Lang 5-0-26-1; Harris 6-2-12-2; Walters 5-0-22-0.

Umpires: T. A. Brown and H. Cohen.

The National Cricket Association selected the following to play for NCA Young Cricketers against Combined Services: G. J. Kennis (Surrey), J. R. Cunliffe (Oxon.), M. H. Colclough (Staffs.), C. E. Mulraine (Warwicks.), W. S. Kendall (Surrey), S. J. Renshaw (Cheshire), *M. R. Spencer (Derbys.), †P. J. Nicholson (Durham), T. J. Mason (Leics.), C. J. Rika (Yorks.), N. Bratt (Staffs.).

At Lord's, July 16. Drawn. Toss: NCA Young Cricketers. Combined Services 262 for nine (Lt R. J. Greatorex 72, Cpl A. Jones 51; T. J. Mason six for 112); NCA Young Cricketers 161 for three (J. R. Cunliffe 90 not out, M. H. Colclough 48).

ETON v HARROW

At Lord's, June 24. Drawn. Toss: Eton. The oldest surviving fixture in the Lord's calendar was threatened with extinction, because its traditional Saturday was unavailable. A compromise shifted it to Wednesday, coincidentally the 80th birthday of Etonian and broadcaster Brian Johnston, who made Lord's the venue of his celebrations. His old school put Harrow in and within nine overs had reduced them to 13 for three; Douglas's pace dismissed Harrap and Danby in successive overs. Foster and Renshaw batted cautiously, reaching 81 by lunch. But in the afternoon their partnership gathered momentum, swelling to 196 over nearly four hours, despite the tidy spin of Wemyss and Lightfoot. The chief honours went to Foster, who scored the first hundred since T. M. H. James's unbeaten 112, also for Harrow, in 1978. He hit 13 fours in 239 balls. A few minutes later Hill declared, setting a target of 210 in what became 44 overs. It was a tall order for an inexperienced Eton side, none of whom had appeared at Lord's before. Evidently Harrow were wary of a third consecutive defeat, and they briefly scented victory when Hawkins claimed five wickets, for the second year running. But too little time was left, and Walsh steered Eton to the close with three wickets in hand.

Harrow

N. G. Harrap b Douglas	0	J. A. J. Renshaw not out	80
*C. G. Hill c Walsh b Christopher	3	B 6, l-b 4, w 10, n-b 3	23
C. B. J. Danby c Walsh b Douglas	1		—
H. St J. R. Foster not out	102	1/4 2/7 3/13	(3 wkts dec.) 209

T. R. Fulton, †S. D. Henson, N. W. Blake, M. P. Barker, R. G. Holyoake and M. M. J. Hawkins did not bat.

Bowling: Christopher 13–4–28–1; Douglas 16–3–40–2; Trusted 10–2–34–0; Price 7–1–20–0; Wemyss 21–6–44–0; Lightfoot 20–9–33–0.

Eton

H. C. Steel c Hawkins b Barker	22	C. G. R. Lightfoot c Henson b Hawkins	4
T. A. Simpson c Fulton b Hawkins	13	T. M. A. Wemyss not out	0
M. J. E. Millar lbw b Hawkins	26	B 1, l-b 10, w 9, n-b 3	23
E. J. M. Christopher b Holyoake	5		—
*D. M. Trusted b Hawkins	22	1/40 2/58 3/68	(7 wkts) 137
†J. J. Walsh not out	21	4/105 5/108	
O. W. R. Clayton b Hawkins	1	6/111 7/127	

H. W. F. Price and A. F. Douglas did not bat.

Bowling: Hawkins 17–6–35–5; Blake 9–2–27–0; Barker 8–3–14–1; Hill 7–0–25–0; Holyoake 3–0–25–1.

Umpires: A. R. Smith and R. Wood.

ETON v HARROW, RESULTS AND HUNDREDS

Of the 157 matches played Eton have won 52, Harrow 44 and 61 have been drawn. This is the generally published record, but Harrow men object strongly to the first game in 1805 being treated as a regular contest between the two schools, contending that it is no more correct to count that one than the fixture of 1857 which has been rejected.

The matches played during the war years 1915-18 and 1940-45 are not reckoned as belonging to the regular series.

Results since 1950:

1950	Drawn	1972	Drawn
1951	Drawn	1973	Drawn
1952	Harrow won by seven wickets	1974	Harrow won by eight wickets
1953	Eton won by ten wickets	1975	Harrow won by an innings and 151 runs
1954	Harrow won by nine wickets		
1955	Eton won by 38 runs	1976	Drawn
1956	Drawn	1977	Eton won by six wickets
1957	Drawn	1978	Drawn
1958	Drawn	1979	Drawn
1959	Drawn	1980	Drawn
1960	Harrow won by 124 runs	1981	Drawn
1961	Harrow won by an innings and 12 runs	1982	Drawn
		1983	Drawn
1962	Drawn	1984	Drawn
1963	Drawn	1985	Eton won by three runs
1964	Eton won by eight wickets	1986	Drawn
1965	Harrow won by 48 runs	1987	Drawn
1966	Drawn	1988	Drawn
1967	Drawn	1989	Drawn
1968	Harrow won by seven wickets	1990	Eton won by seven wickets
1969	Drawn	1991	Eton won by three wickets
1970	Eton won by 97 runs	1992	Drawn
1971	Drawn		

Forty-six three-figure innings have been played in matches between these two schools. Those since 1918:

161*	M. K. Fosh	1975 Harrow	106	D. M. Smith	1966 Eton
159	E. W. Dawson	1923 Eton	104	R. Pulbrook	1932 Harrow
158	I. S. Akers-Douglas	1928 Eton	103	L. G. Crawley	1921 Harrow
153	N. S. Hotchkin	1931 Eton	103	T. Hare	1947 Eton
151	R. M. Tindall	1976 Harrow	102*	P. H. Stewart-Brown	1923 Harrow
135	J. C. Atkinson-Clark	1930 Eton	102*	H. St J. R. Foster	1992 Harrow
115	E. Crutchley	1939 Eton	102	R. V. C. Robins	1953 Eton
112*	T. M. H. James	1978 Harrow	100*	P. V. F. Cazalet	1926 Eton
112	A. W. Allen	1931 Eton	100*	P. M. Studd	1935 Harrow
111	R. A. A. Holt	1937 Eton	100	R. H. Cobbold	1923 Eton
109	K. F. H. Hale	1929 Eton	100	A. N. A. Boyd	1934 Eton
109	N. S. Hotchkin	1932 Eton	100	S. D. D. Sainsbury	1947 Eton
107	W. N. Coles	1946 Eton	100	M. J. J. Faber	1968 Eton

* Signifies not out.

In 1904, D. C. Boles of Eton, making 183, set a record for the match, beating the 152 obtained for Eton in 1841 by Emilius Bayley, afterwards the Rev. Sir John Robert Laurie Emilius Bayley Laurie. M. C. Bird, Harrow, in 1907, scored 100 not out and 131, the only batsman who has made two 100s in the match. N. S. Hotchkin, Eton, played the following innings: 1931, 153; 1932, 109 and 96; 1933, 88 and 12.

HIGHLIGHTS FROM THE SCHOOLS

Although some schools reported as many as five games completely abandoned owing to the weather, a fine May offered some compensation. Six batsmen profited to pass 1,000 runs: R. W. Nowell of Trinity (1,505 at 79.21), A. Singh of King Edward's, Birmingham (1,138 at 63.22), W. J. Earl of Framlingham (1,084 at 83.38), J. E. Phillips of Royal GS, Worcester (1,082 at 60.11), R. M. S. Weston of Durham (1,046 at 104.60) and J. S. G. Hargrove of Victoria College, Jersey (1,043 at 65.18). Earl played only 16 innings and Weston 18, while Nowell played the most with 25. Weston was one of three batsmen to record three-figure averages, the others being S. C. Janes of Hampton, with 995 runs at 124.37, and M. H. Colclough of Newcastle-under-Lyme, with 622 at 103.66.

Three double-hundreds were reported. The highest was 221, scored by S. J. Hygate of Reigate GS, while 200 not out was achieved by both A. M. Barr of Victoria College, Jersey, and K. R. Spiring of Monmouth. Nowell made an incredible seven centuries in his 25 innings, Weston and Ardingly's A. C. Slight (15 innings) both hit five, and four each came from G. P. Barrett of King's, Chester (15 innings), Earl, Janes (14 innings) and E. W. H. Wiseman of The Perse (15 innings).

It was a significantly better year for the bowlers, six of whom passed 60 wickets. A. Choudry of Latymer Upper collected 77 at 11.88, followed by N. C. F. Taylor of Durham (68 at 10.88), Nowell (64 at 14.92), M. G. Burle of Bishop's Stortford (62 at 11.61), S. Hunt of Plymouth College (61 at 15.52) and D. C. Sainsbury of Reigate GS (61 at 17.47). All except for Hunt and Burle sent down more than 300 overs, and Sainsbury conceded 1,066 runs. Of those who took more than 35 wickets, four recorded single-figure averages: N. J. Watson of Oratory (52 at 7.75), J. M. Gayfer of The Glasgow Academy (38 at 8.55), L. J. Crozier of Royal GS, Newcastle (44 at 9.02) and O. F. A. Le Fleming of Exeter (39 at 9.53). The best innings returns were recorded by R. Oram of Forest (nine for 40), D. Keep of Reed's (nine for 57) and N. J. Wood of Rugby (nine for 64). Oram's nine-wicket haul included a hat-trick, and others to perform the feat were T. P. Howland of KCS, Wimbledon, D. Lupton of Ashville College and J. C. Orr of Exeter. Of the nine bowlers to take eight in an innings, the most impressive return was eight for nought by N. A. Doggett of Merchant Taylors', Crosby.

The leading all-rounder was again the remarkably talented England Under-16 representative Nowell, with his 1,505 runs and 64 wickets. He was followed by D. O. Dyer, another Under-16 player also from Trinity (811 runs, 51 wickets), A. Moss of Royal GS, Guildford (744 runs, 52 wickets), N. M. Davies of Royal GS, Worcester (772 runs, 41 wickets) and T. W. Earl of Brighton (758 runs, 40 wickets). The Wetherell Award, presented by the Cricket Society to the leading schoolboy all-rounder, went jointly to Nowell and D. Spencer of Kingston GS, who collected 522 runs at 47.45 and 32 wickets at 8.93.

It was encouraging to note the expanding fixture lists of many sides, although less encouraging were the references to negative cricket played by some XIs. In many cases an unbeaten record seemed more important than positive results and Haberdashers' Aske's commented that men's sides played much more positively than many schools. Ten of the schools who appear in this *Wisden* were unbeaten. Of these Glasgow Academy won ten of their 12 matches, Trinity won 13 of 25, Durham nine of 21 and Forest eight of 16; the remaining unbeaten sides were Bedford, Eton (who drew 12 of their 14 matches), King's, Canterbury, Manchester GS, Merchant Taylors', Crosby and Repton. At the other end of the scale, no victories were recorded by Culford, Fettes, Marlborough and Christ College, Brecon.

The match between Malvern and Berkhamsted was interesting for a strong Tolchard family connection. J. G. Tolchard (Leicestershire and Devon) was master-in-charge at Berkhamsted, while his brother, R. W. (England and Leicestershire), was the cricket professional at Malvern. Two of J. G. Tolchard's sons were playing in the match, the elder, J., as captain of Malvern and the younger, E., in the Berkhamsted XI.

The Sir Garfield Sobers Schools Tournament, held in Barbados in July, was won for the second year by Grenada Schools, who beat Michaelhouse from South Africa by 27 runs in the final. English and Scottish schools participating were Merchiston Castle, who reached the semi-finals where Grenada Schools beat them by seven wickets, Radley, who won three of their four matches, and Bradford GS, who were fourth in their group.

Masters reported a number of other outstanding performances and records broken, and these may be found in the returns from the schools which follow. (*Note:* The qualifications for inclusion in the averages in this *Wisden* have been increased to 150 runs and 15 wickets.)

THE SCHOOLS

(Qualification: Batting 150 runs; Bowling 15 wickets)

* *On name indicates captain.*   * *On figures indicates not out.*

Note: The line for batting reads Innings–Not Outs–Runs–Highest Score–100s–Average; that for bowling reads Overs–Maidens–Runs–Wickets–Best Bowling–Average.

ABINGDON SCHOOL

Played 16: Won 7, Lost 2, Drawn 7. Abandoned 3

Master i/c: A. M. Broadbent

Wins v: Magdalen College S.; Oratory; Reading; Lord Williams's, Thame; RGS, High Wycombe; Old Abingdonians; South Oxfordshire Amateurs.

Batting—*J. M. Allen 15–1–442–107*–1–31.57; J. S. Tilley 15–0–424–70–0–28.26; L. R. J. List 13–2–260–114–1–23.63; A. P. Harding 14–3–249–84*–0–22.63; A. N. Janisch 14–1–284–88–0–21.84; J. M. Wilkinson 13–2–153–40–0–13.90.

Bowling—J. M. Wilkinson 159–43–415–29–6/23–14.31; B. W. Gannon 195.4–61–441–25–5/32–17.64; J. M. Allen 106–22–354–17–5/13–20.82.

ALDENHAM SCHOOL

Played 9: Won 3, Lost 3, Drawn 3. Abandoned 3

Master i/c: P. K. Smith

Wins v: Westminster; King William's, Isle of Man; Liverpool C.

Batting—R. Robertson 6–1–247–126–1–49.40; C. Molyneux 9–1–350–85*–0–43.75; A. Tenant 8–3–185–52*–0–37.00; J. Springer 9–0–271–60–0–30.11; *R. Ullman 9–0–260–68–0–28.88.

Bowling—No bowler took 15 wickets.

ALLEYN'S SCHOOL

Played 18: Won 2, Lost 4, Drawn 12

Master i/c: S. E. Smith   Cricket professional: P. Edwards

Wins v: XL Club; Rutlish.

Batting—R. M. Ellis 8–1–197–53–0–28.14; R. McGill 18–4–393–61–0–28.07; S. J. P. Collins 18–2–403–102*–1–25.18; G. W. Francis 18–1–358–91–0–21.05; *N. P. Wharton 16–0–288–72–0–18.00; M. H. Berglund 18–3–227–75–0–15.13; B. McGill 17–1–169–33*–0–10.56.

Bowling—A. C. G. Clarke 94.5–17–262–17–5/12–15.41; N. P. Wharton 142.5–30–355–23–6/17–15.43; B. M. Ranford 116–21–314–17–3/27–18.47.

AMPLEFORTH COLLEGE

Played 17: Won 4, Lost 5, Drawn 8

Master i/c: G. D. Thurman

Wins v: Worksop; Stonyhurst; MCC; Pocklington.

Batting—G. Finch 14–4–401–105*–1–40.10; O. Mathias 18–2–572–105*–1–35.75; J. J. Hobbs 17–2–391–87–0–26.06; *R. M. Wilson 18–1–389–132*–1–22.88.

Bowling—A. Freeland 207.1–43–789–38–5/12–20.76; C. Williams 183.4–39–566–26–6/54–21.76; D. Thompson 134–39–539–20–5/55–26.95.

ARDINGLY COLLEGE

Played 15: Won 4, Lost 7, Drawn 4. Abandoned 1

Master i/c: T. J. Brooker   Cricket professional: S. S. Sawant

A. C. Slight had scored three of his five hundreds – 101 not out against each of Sevenoaks, Seaford and Brighton – before the end of May, adding two more against MCC and the XL Club in the last week of June. His average of 94 was believed to be a record for the school, and his 940 runs were the second-best ever recorded.

Wins v: St George's, Weybridge; Worth; Hurstpierpoint; Headmaster's XI.

Batting—A. C. Slight 15–5–940–118–5–94.00; J. Hubbard 11–3–252–81–0–31.50; J. Zang 9–2–157–44–0–22.42; J. Hewitt 14–0–299–58–0–21.35; A. Sadri 14–1–275–53*–0–21.15; N. Bradley Hole 15–0–199–54–0–13.26.

Bowling—P. Munden 189.5–42–596–33–5/13–18.06; T. Elliott 181.2–30–573–26–5/50–22.03; *M. Baxter 106–18–422–18–6/94–23.44.

ARNOLD SCHOOL

Played 15: Won 1, Lost 5, Drawn 9. Abandoned 2

Master i/c: S. Burnage   Cricket professional: J. Simmons

Highlights were a first visit by MCC and a tour to Northern Ireland, as well as C. J. Outram's innings of 142 not out off 114 balls against Royal Belfast AI.

Win v: Royal Belfast AI.

Batting—*C. J. Outram 14–4–464–142*–2–46.40; N. Gourlay 14–5–259–68*–0–28.77; R. Parkin 12–2–241–66–0–24.10; S. Knapman 15–1–309–114–1–22.07; A. Stewart 12–0–179–43–0–14.91.

Bowling—D. J. J. Miller 159–20–683–23–4/44–29.69; N. Gourlay 146–26–497–15–3/52–33.13

ASHVILLE COLLEGE

Played 16: Won 6, Lost 5, Drawn 5. Abandoned 1

Master i/c: S. Herrington

D. Lupton's return of three for four against Scarborough College featured a hat-trick.

Wins v: XL Club; Yarm GS; Ermysteds GS; Scarborough C.; Bury GS; School Staff.

Batting—S. Alexander 15–1–584–100*–1–41.71; *K. Crack 15–2–440–70–0–33.84; D. Lupton 15–1–375–86–0–26.78; A. White 13–3–267–63–0–26.70; S. Creber 10–1–196–45–0–21.77; R. Smart 10–2–170–64–0–21.25.

Bowling—S. Alexander 172–40–492–27–6/61–18.22; K. Crack 180–33–582–29–6/7–20.06; D. Lupton 97–10–442–21–3/4–21.04.

BANCROFT'S SCHOOL

Played 20: Won 5, Lost 7, Drawn 8. Abandoned 2

Master i/c: J. G. Bromfield   Cricket professional: J. K. Lever

A young side was held together by the performances and captaincy of C. S. Greenhill, whose 705 runs were a school record.

Wins v: St Albans; Royal Anglian Regiment; Buckhurst Hill CC; XL Club; King Edward's, Birmingham.

Batting—*C. S. Greenhill 18–4–705–111–2–50.35; A. A. Khan 19–4–548–93–0–36.53; P. T. Vohmann 16–3–406–105–1–31.23; P. Eacott 9–2–207–51–0–29.57; S. Treloar 17–2–218–52–0–14.53; P. D. Baker 15–0–197–36–0–13.13.

Bowling—E. Mann 134.2–30–449–20–5/8–22.45; A. A. Khan 218.3–33–812–30–5/37–27.06; C. S. Greenhill 168–37–472–16–3/31–29.50; M. Tisi 178.2–28–717–15–3/53–47.80.

BARNARD CASTLE SCHOOL

Played 18: Won 10, Lost 2, Drawn 6. Abandoned 1

Master i/c: C. P. Johnson

The batting averages were headed by S. G. Riddell, son of the former Durham captain, N. A. Riddell.

Wins v: N. A. Riddell's XI; Edinburgh Acad.; St Bees; MCC; Durham Pilgrims; Barnard Castle CC; UCS (twice); King Edward VI, Lytham; Woodbridge.

Batting—S. G. Riddell 16–2–618–116–2–44.14; *A. W. Hutchinson 19–4–625–93–0–41.66; N. R. Walker 15–3–354–86–0–29.50; S. E. W. Taylor 14–6–210–37*–0–26.25; J. W. Foster 19–2–421–92*–0–24.76; T. Mardon 14–2–262–54–0–21.83; J. P. Ormandy 12–1–157–65–0–14.27.

Bowling—J. Benson 113.3–41–252–15–3/5–16.80; A. D. Ballantyne 155.3–43–461–26–5/40–17.73; A. W. Hutchinson 93–21–320–15–2/9–21.33; N. R. Walker 137.5–21–518–22–5/22–23.54; J. M. Watson 104.4–19–380–16–5/19–23.75.

BEDFORD SCHOOL

Played 12: Won 4, Lost 0, Drawn 8. Abandoned 5

Master i/c: D. W. Jarrett   Cricket professional: R. G. Caple

A highlight in an unbeaten season was the run-chase against Wellington College, in which the young side reached a target of 226 in 55 overs with three balls to spare.

Wins v: Oundle; Wellington C.; Uppingham; Stowe.

Batting—G. Dros 12–2–604–104*–1–60.40; A. C. T. Gomarsall 13–6–250–66–0–35.71; *M. R. Evans 14–1–445–94*–0–34.23; M. E. Snell 13–0–353–71–0–27.15; A. Shankar 11–2–236–61*–0–26.22; L. J. K. Wood 13–1–262–58–0–21.83.

Bowling—M. R. Evans 138–33–397–22–4/41–18.04; S. C. Laite 150–48–432–23–5/80–18.78; R. M. Pape 179–30–566–20–6/58–28.30.

BEDFORD MODERN SCHOOL

Played 17: Won 2, Lost 1, Drawn 14. Abandoned 5

Master i/c: N. J. Chinneck

Wins v: Kimbolton; St Albans.

Batting—*P. D. Brownridge 17–5–591–101*–1–49.25; B. J. Young 12–3–286–46–0–31.77; R. J. Whitbread 15–4–337–56–0–30.63; G. S. Pilgrim 15–3–327–50*–0–27.25; R. C. Shah 17–2–350–50–0–23.33.

Bowling—N. T. Wildman 141–24–443–21–6/65–21.09; P. D. Brownridge 169.3–29–541–20–4/51–27.05; M. J. Brownridge 165–36–473–15–3/29–31.53.

BEECHEN CLIFF SCHOOL

Played 11: Won 6, Lost 1, Drawn 4. Abandoned 3

Master i/c: K. J. L. Mabe   Cricket professional: P. J. Colbourne

The most exciting match ended in the side's only defeat – by three runs at the hands of MCC. In the victory over Wells Cathedral School, N. J. Bursell and B. R. F. Staunton opened with a stand of 179.

Wins v: Kingswood; Monkton Combe; King Edward's, Bath; Newton Park; Wells Cathedral S.; St Wilfred's.

Batting—*D. M. Barnes 6–3–182–81*–0–60.66; N. J. Welch 9–2–339–92–0–48.42; B. R. F. Staunton 5–0–229–75–0–45.80; T. E. Smith 11–3–249–66*–0–31.12; N. J. Bursell 11–2–216–61–0–24.00.

Bowling—J. A. Brigden 62.3–9–232–15–4/33–15.46; D. E. Jones 79–20–253–15–3/20–16.86.

BERKHAMSTED SCHOOL

Played 15: Won 2, Lost 5, Drawn 8

Master i/c: J. G. Tolchard   Cricket professional: M. J. Herring

Wins v: Merchant Taylors', Northwood; Hemel Hempstead Colts.

Batting—N. A. Wolstenholme 15–0–445–88–0–29.66; R. D. Mackintosh 15–0–364–73–0–24.26; J. A. Crowther 15–3–247–46–0–20.58; L. Jasuja 14–3–213–32–0–19.36; B. A. King 12–0–178–65–0–14.83; D. T. L. Pountney 15–1–205–41–0–14.64.

Bowling—L. Jasuja 128.3–31–365–20–4/41–18.25; *B. P. Howard 144.5–21–493–26–5/56–18.96; N. A. Reed 147–33–424–21–4/47–20.19.

BETHANY SCHOOL

Played 13: Won 10, Lost 2, Drawn 1. Abandoned 2

Master i/c: P. Norgrove   Cricket professional: R. Hills

Wins v: Ewell Castle; Duke of York's RMS; Oakwood Park GS; City of London Freeman's; Masters' XI; St Bede's; Bethany Old Boys; Rochester Maths; Pioneers XI; XL Club.

Batting—M. Katugaha 11–4–488–114*–1–69.71; M. G. S. de St Croix 10–2–467–151–1–58.37; *G. R. Newell 12–1–260–88–0–23.63; F. Sadiqeen 11–2–208–41*–0–23.11.

Bowling—G. R. Newell 127–30–383–36–4/2–10.63; F. Sadiqeen 90–16–311–21–6/22–14.80; J. G. White 154–35–486–26–3/11–18.69.

BIRKENHEAD SCHOOL

Played 18: Won 9, Lost 2, Drawn 7

Master i/c: P. A. Whittel

S. J. Renshaw played for MCC Schools, NCA Young Cricketers and English Schools.

Wins v: Rydal; Ellesmere; St David's, Llandudno; St Francis Xavier; King's, Macclesfield; Coleraine Acad.; King's, Chester; Cowley; Latymer Upper.

Batting—*S. J. Renshaw 13–4–603–123*–3–67.00; B. L. Cooper 15–2–640–139–1–49.23; J. R. Carpenter 16–2–521–74*–0–37.21; Z. Feather 12–5–183–40–0–26.14.

Bowling—A. G. Cook 85.3–25–230–26–6/21–8.84; J. R. Carpenter 200.2–75–446–33–4/14–13.51; S. J. Renshaw 161.2–39–420–29–6/40–14.48.

BISHOP'S STORTFORD COLLEGE

Played 19: Won 8, Lost 1, Drawn 10. Abandoned 2

Master i/c: D. A. Hopper   Cricket professional: R. J. Pithey

With 62 wickets, many of which fell to his in-swinging yorkers, the captain and left-arm opening bowler, M. G. Burle, passed by one wicket the school record set in 1972 by T. S. Smith. In the match against Chigwell, the opposition's No. 10 batsman was timed out, taking too long over an attempt to adjust a thigh pad on the boundary.

Wins v: Brentwood; Framlingham; Newport GS; Chigwell; Bromsgrove; Gresham's; Oakham; Stamford.

Batting—W. E. Ayres 19–4–636–86*–0–42.40; *M. G. Burle 16–3–369–88–0–28.38; R. M. Webb 14–7–170–44–0–24.28; J. D. Lamb 12–1–243–79*–0–22.09; I. M. Bateman 18–1–361–86–0–21.23; R. N. Myers 14–0–284–93–0–20.28; A. J. Hill 16–3–256–41–0–19.69.

Bowling—M. G. Burle 289.4–90–720–62–8/15–11.61; J. A. Floyd 154.4–46–451–25–5/52–18.04; R. J. Walters 200.3–54–625–24–5/56–26.04; T. E. Laverack 114.2–24–420–15–4/28–28.00.

BLOXHAM SCHOOL

Played 14: Won 5, Lost 3, Drawn 6. Abandoned 1

Masters i/c: J. P. Horton and C. N. Boyns

Wins v: Rendcomb; Dean Close; Worksop; Oratory (Reading); St Bartholomew's, Newbury.

Batting—R. A. F. Whitton 11–1–356–89–0–35.60; J. F. F. Diamond 13–6–230–51*–0–32.85; C. W. Huntingford 10–0–193–36–0–19.30; *M. G. Wood 13–1–217–60–0–18.08; A. M. Kenward 12–1–170–35*–0–15.45.

Bowling—I. A. R. Adams 88.5–28–236–18–4/18–13.11; A. J. R. Hicks 86.3–20–279–16–4/27–17.43; P. R. Arber 157.3–22–656–31–6/59–21.16.

BRADFIELD COLLEGE

Played 12: Won 2, Lost 4, Drawn 6. Abandoned 2

Master i/c: F. R. Dethridge					Cricket professional: J. F. Harvey

The leading batsman, W. S. Kendall, represented MCC Schools, English Schools and Hampshire Second XI.

Wins v: Winchester; St Edward's, Oxford.

Batting—W. S. Kendall 10–1–569–125–1–63.22; S. A. Seymour 12–1–306–64–0–27.81; A. J. Williams 11–1–233–68–0–23.30; C. D. Gent 12–2–155–66–0–15.50.

Bowling—A. J. Williams 144–49–326–16–5/37–20.37; M. Burns 160–27–527–19–5/55–27.73.

BRADFORD GRAMMAR SCHOOL

Played 26: Won 12, Lost 9, Drawn 5. Abandoned 2

Master i/c: A. G. Smith

Wins v: St Peter's, York; Ashville; Bolton; Hymers; QEGS, Wakefield; Pocklington; Halifax Nomads; Parents' XI; St James, Barbados; Harrison C., Barbados; Presentation C., Trinidad; Tobago CA.

Batting—S. A. W. Davies 26–4–624–109*–1–28.36; A. B. Wharton 25–0–625–70–0–25.00; D. C. Illingworth 15–6–221–35*–0–24.55; A. J. Brosnan 11–0–256–46–0–23.27; *J. S. Pearson 23–4–410–58*–0–21.57; C. W. A. McIntosh 24–4–424–52–0–21.20; S. A. Marshall 22–1–312–41–0–14.85; D. J. Groom 21–0–282–56–0–13.42.

Bowling—C. W. A. McIntosh 214.2–36–671–49–5/25–13.69; P. S. Bachra 203.1–35–652–36–5/21–18.11; D. C. Illingworth 101.2–14–449–22–5/36–20.40; D. J. Collinge 204.2–42–720–30–4/28–24.00; N. A. Joy 132.4–26–542–20–4/36–27.10; S. W. Elson 134.5–11–650–16–4/23–40.62.

BRENTWOOD SCHOOL

Played 15: Won 5, Lost 3, Drawn 7. Abandoned 1

Master i/c: B. R. Hardie

Wins v: Sevenoaks; Essex U-16; Headmaster's XI; Old Brentwoods; Old Brentwoods Society.

Batting—D. A. R. Gilbert 16–1–557–90–0–37.13; G. K. Fletcher 11–1–316–92–0–31.60; *D. P. McAllister 13–2–325–113*–1–29.54; J. E. B. Vereker 18–1–447–80–0–26.29; O. M. Watkins 18–2–369–60*–0–23.06; B. Weller 16–0–230–112–1–14.37.

Bowling—D. P. McAllister 163–32–426–30–6/27–14.20; B. J. Tappin 160–24–558–22–5/49–25.36; L. D. Waite 199–43–639–23–4/58–27.78; J. E. B. Vereker 181–34–615–18–4/27–34.16; P. R. Brooks 188–39–625–18–4/25–34.72.

BRIGHTON COLLEGE

Played 24: Won 15, Lost 2, Drawn 7

Master i/c: J. Spencer					Cricket professional: J. D. Morley

Benefiting from a tour to India the previous Christmas, the side equalled the college record of 15 victories and won the Langdale Cup for the third time in succession.

Wins v: Headmaster's XI; Seaford (twice); Hurstpierpoint; Portsmouth GS; MCC; Reigate GS; Sussex Martlets; Lancing; Eastbourne; Common Room; Epsom; King's, Macclesfield; Edinburgh Acad.; Academicals Invitation XI.

Batting—P. D. L. Rennie 24–3–922–118*–1–43.90; A. R. Bidwell 23–3–716–139–1–35.80; T. W. Earl 24–1–758–104*–1–32.95; A. D. King 10–0–317–96–0–31.70; E. S. Hart 18–9–236–35–0–26.22; M. N. Dovey 24–4–432–63–0–21.60; M. R. Strong 18–2–229–36–0–14.31.

Bowling—P. E. Fokes 212–44–601–35–3/14–17.17; M. R. Strong 352.1–71–974–51–7/52–19.09; T. W. Earl 247.3–48–938–40–5/18–23.45; E. S. Hart 115–14–401–17–4/25–23.58.

BRYANSTON SCHOOL

Played 20: Won 3, Lost 8, Drawn 9. Abandoned 3

Master i/c: T. J. Hill

R. S. Wagstaffe, son of the former Oxford Blue and Dorset captain, M. C. Wagstaffe, carried his bat for 133 not out in a total of 192 against Bryanston Butterflies. P. Thornton, the girls' captain, played in the XI against Winchester and Dorset Rangers, helping to save the latter match with resolute batting.

Wins v: Canford; Merchant Taylors', Northwood; Portsmouth GS.

Batting—G. A. Bucknell 18–3–669–123*–1–44.60; R. S. Wagstaffe 20–1–677–133*–1–35.63; *W. J. A. Freisenbruch 15–2–403–71–0–31.00; R. J. White 18–3–413–74*–0–27.53.

Bowling—C. F. Austin 192.1–36–635–32–6/42–19.84; R. J. White 165.3–41–570–19–4/69–30.00; S. N. E. Williams 124–11–569–17–4/7–33.47.

CAMPBELL COLLEGE

Played 17: Won 11, Lost 3, Drawn 3

Master i/c: E. T. Cooke

Wins v: Sullivan Upper; King William's C., IOM; Limavady GS; Limavady FEC; Foyle C. (twice); Regent House; Dungannon Royal; Coleraine AI; Royal Belfast AI; Wallace HS.

Batting—*S. A. I. Dyer 16–1–759–115–1–50.60; G. M. Egan 14–1–346–59–0–26.61; P. K. Bell 8–2–156–43*–0–26.00; A. E. Logan 16–2–280–75*–0–20.00; R. H. Lucas 16–0–244–66–0–15.25.

Bowling—S. A. I. Dyer 74–12–232–22–3/10–10.54; S. R. J. Flanagan 127–41–246–23–4/30–10.69; R. H. Lucas 115–26–262–24–5/19–10.91; N. J. Brown 81–14–264–16–2/11–16.50.

CANFORD SCHOOL

Played 15: Won 9, Lost 2, Drawn 4. Abandoned 3

Master i/c: S. J. Turrill   Cricket professional: J. J. E. Hardy

D. A. W. Young found form to score 410 runs for twice out in the last week of the season, and M. T. C. Allom, grandson of the former England Test bowler M. J. C. Allom, took 40 wickets to finish his four-year career in the XI with a tally of 119.

Wins v: Wimborne CC; King's, Taunton; XL Club; King Edward VI, Southampton; Dorset Rangers; Taunton; Old Canfordians; Ampleforth; Uppingham.

Batting—*D. A. W. Young 15–6–656–129*–1–72.88; S. J. Neal 14–3–389–65–0–35.36; M. T. C. Allom 14–3–379–89*–0–34.45; G. P. A. Herring 13–4–150–40*–0–16.66.

Bowling—M. T. C. Allom 219.3–57–556–40–6/19–13.90; W. R. S. White-Cooper 184–22–382–21–6/32–18.19; M. A. Corrigan 124.2–18–378–20–3/17–18.90.

CATERHAM SCHOOL

Played 15: Won 4, Lost 5, Drawn 6

Master i/c: A. G. Tapp   Cricket professional: Wasim Raja

Wins v: King's, Rochester; Tiffin; Christ's Hospital; Old Caterhamians.

Batting—G. E. Owen 11–3–325–74*–0–40.62; D. J. Sales 5–0–195–84–0–39.00; J. Coppin 11–0–291–81–0–26.45; A. Ross 14–6–197–44*–0–24.62; J. C. Winter 15–0–228–40–0–15.20.

Bowling—K. Barton 217.5–55–596–46–7/15–12.95; T. Wahio 111–22–361–22–6/21–16.40; S. C. Turner 167–24–582–24–5/37–24.25.

CHARTERHOUSE

Played 15: Won 4, Lost 3, Drawn 8. Abandoned 1

Master i/c: J. M. Knight   Cricket professional: R. V. Lewis

Wins v: Butterflies; Brooke Hall; Westminster; Rugby.

Batting—L. J. Webb 15–1–451–60–0–32.21; A. R. Younie 15–1–376–76–0–26.85; A. T. Roberts-Miller 15–0–355–74–0–23.66; E. K. Sutton 14–1–260–34–0–20.00; G. H. Tassell 13–1–221–91*–0–18.41; M. G. Bristowe 15–0–229–33–0–15.26.

Bowling—E. K. Sutton 164.2–41–474–33–7/31–14.36; S. D. Parrish 136–21–477–25–5/64–19.08; M. G. Bristowe 152.5–31–534–25–3/31–21.36; J. D. A. Willson 146.4–25–485–21–6/59–23.09.

CHELTENHAM COLLEGE

Played 14: Won 4, Lost 2, Drawn 8. Abandoned 5

Master i/c: W. J. Wesson   Cricket professional: M. W. Stovold

D. R. Hewson and M. J. Cawdron both played for Gloucestershire Second XI.

Wins v: MCC; Pate's GS; Free Foresters; W. J. Wesson's XI.

Batting—D. R. Hewson 13–3–651–131*–3–65.10; J. T. G. Westbrook 10–3–225–91*–0–32.14; T. E. Phillips 12–3–272–85–0–30.22; B. J. C. Lawrence 13–1–362–72–0–30.16; M. J. Cawdron 12–1–315–86–0–28.63; N. R. Houson 14–2–309–79–0–25.75.

Bowling—M. J. Cawdron 233–59–575–34–4/39–16.91.

CHIGWELL SCHOOL

Played 17: Won 4, Lost 3, Drawn 10. Abandoned 1

Master i/c: D. N. Morrison

Although I. Mufti developed into a useful all-rounder, the young side were hampered by the absence of I. Harvey, who missed much of the season through illness.

Wins v: Romford Police; Enfield GS; St Edmund's, Ware; Pocklington.

Batting—I. J. Harvey 6–1–216–88–0–43.20; I. Mufti 14–4–348–72*–0–34.80; S. Khan 15–6–297–73–0–33.00; *G. Offen 16–1–443–86–0–29.53; A. Adetda 13–2–193–42–0–17.54; A. Mandrekar 16–1–260–52–0–17.33; J. Anderton 15–1–192–41–0–13.71.

Bowling—I. J. Harvey 75–29–148–17–5/13–8.70; G. Offen 161–24–504–27–4/31–18.66; I. Mufti 176.3–33–586–24–6/27–24.41.

CHRIST COLLEGE, BRECON

Played 13: Won 0, Lost 6, Drawn 7. Abandoned 2

Master i/c: C. W. Kleiser

Batting—A. Marshman 9–1–235–57–0–29.37; *R. Strawbridge 12–1–253–85*–0–23.00; G. A. R. Davies 11–0–232–42–0–21.09; D. Lally 12–1–223–53–0–20.27; J. N. Davies 10–0–202–46–0–20.20.

Bowling—I. Dewhurst 123.5–26–403–15–4/23–26.86.

CHRIST'S HOSPITAL

Played 15: Won 3, Lost 6, Drawn 6. Abandoned 1

Master i/c: H. Holdsworth   Cricket professionals: K. G. Suttle and P. J. Graves

Wins v: Seaford; Sussex Martlets; J. A. Snow's Celebrity XI.

Batting—R. Howard 14–0–326–84–0–23.28; B. J. Lewis 11–0–215–48–0–19.54; N. J. Atkinson 13–0–237–52–0–18.23; *C. J. A. Somma 13–1–188–60–0–15.66.

Bowling—R. Howard 117.2–27–404–22–5/7–18.36; M. A. S. Lemon 132.4–25–384–16–4/43–24.00.

CLAYESMORE SCHOOL

Played 12: Won 5, Lost 2, Drawn 5. Abandoned 4

Master i/c: R. J. Hammond

Highlights were returns of eight for 26 against Canford by J. H. C. Latimer and L. Coley's seven for 12 against Ryde, which included four wickets (all bowled) in the final over.

Wins v: Dorset Rangers; Embley Park; Ryde; Old Clayesmorians; Milton Abbey.

Batting—N. H. Peek 12–2–308–98–0–30.80; O. P. Dobbs 13–0–337–82–0–25.92; B. W. Julyan 11–1–183–53–0–18.30.

Bowling—J. H. C. Latimer 116.4–25–353–35–8/26–10.08; L. Coley 52.5–8–210–19–7/12–11.05.

CLIFTON COLLEGE

Played 18: Won 1, Lost 5, Drawn 12. Abandoned 2

Master i/c: C. M. E. Colquhoun   Cricket professional: F. J. Andrew

The outstanding batsman was G. H. J. Rees, whose 974 runs included 186 against Haileybury, 168 against Downside and 114 not out against Tonbridge. He went on to play for Glamorgan Second XI and Welsh Schools.

Win v: Clifton/Flax Bourton CC.

Batting—G. H. J. Rees 18–2–974–186–3–60.87; P. J. Hosegood 17–3–590–71–0–42.14; D. J. R. England 6–1–180–83–0–36.00; A. N. Baker 15–3–397–71*–0–33.08; G. V. T. Bretten 15–0–362–52–0–24.13; B. R. Harris 11–1–209–73–0–20.90; M. W. Dawson 14–1–260–46*–0–20.00.

Bowling—J. Whitby-Coles 140–43–346–19–4/45–18.21; *R. J. Kirtley 219.3–36–499–27–4/61–18.48; G. H. J. Rees 77.3–9–316–16–6/41–19.75.

COLFE'S SCHOOL

Played 12: Won 4, Lost 1, Drawn 7. Abandoned 2

Master i/c: D. P. H. Meadows   Cricket professional: A. Reid-Smith

Wins v: Hampton; XL Club; MCC; Watson's XI

Batting—*M. Quilter 11-2-355-117*-1-39.44; J. Harman 9-2-240-104*-1-34.28; S. Groves 11-2-303-64-0-33.66; P. Scott 10-1-283-71-0-31.44.

Bowling—P. Scott 128-27-412-19-5/13-21.68; M. Quilter 107.1-18-404-16-4/50-25.25.

COLSTON'S COLLEGIATE SCHOOL

Played 17: Won 8, Lost 2, Drawn 7. Abandoned 2

Masters i/c: M. P. B. Tayler and A. J. Palmer

D. S. C. Bell scored his maiden century (109 not out) against King Edward's, Bath, and followed it with successive innings with 119 not out against Balliol College and 118 not out against the XL Club. On the first occasion he shared in a school record third-wicket partnership of 224 unbroken with I. J. Webb.

Wins v: Kingswood; Christ C., Brecon; King Edward's, Bath; Master of the Society of Merchant Venturers' XI; Balliol College; XL Club; Hutton GS; Old Colstonians.

Batting—*I. J. Webb 16-5-769-129*-2-69.90; D. S. C. Bell 15-3-593-119*-3-49.41; R. J. Pandya 15-1-466-77-0-33.28; A. R. Nicholls 16-0-331-50-0-20.68; S. W. Brown 12-4-150-31*-0-18.75.

Bowling—R. I. Phillipson-Masters 51-9-194-16-4/42-12.12; D. S. C. Bell 116.2-22-440-20-5/18-22.00; S. W. Brown 149-25-490-22-3/4-22.27; R. J. Pandya 171.3-24-649-21-6/52-30.90.

COVENTRY SCHOOL, BABLAKE

Played 14: Won 10, Lost 1, Drawn 3. Abandoned 2

Master i/c: B. J. Sutton

The XI retained the Birmingham and Warwickshire Cup, recording a tenth success in 14 years.

Wins v: Woodlands; Abbot Beyne; King Edward's, Nuneaton; Handsworth GS; King's, Worcester; Captain's XI; King Edward's, Camp Hill; King Henry VIII, Coventry; Bishop Vesey's GS; Laurence Sheriff GS.

Batting—A. Cronin 12-4-243-52*-0-30.37; R. M. Tewkesbury 13-3-297-62*-0-29.70; *M. A. Ward 13-2-290-63*-0-26.36; D. J. Wheatley 11-3-203-38*-0-25.37; J. Hart 12-2-208-54-0-20.80.

Bowling—A. Cronin 54-18-141-15-4/9-9.40; J. Hart 113.3-25-284-29-4/16-9.79; J. D. Myton 100.4-21-235-18-4/34-13.05; W. E. Wood 76-10-255-16-4/11-15.93; R. D. East 93-25-290-17-5/51-17.05.

CRANBROOK SCHOOL

Played 15: Won 3, Lost 6, Drawn 6. Abandoned 5

Master i/c: A. J. Presnell

Wins v: Judd; St Edmund's; Pioneers CC.

Batting—M. Taylor 13-0-336-62-0-25.84; J. Steed 15-3-302-102-1-25.16; H. Sharman 12-1-258-54*-0-23.45.

Bowling—S. Drake 180.4-56-388-27-6/34-14.37; *R. Stace 182.1-29-648-32-5/30-20.25; C. Peskett 133-20-428-18-3/27-23.77.

CRANLEIGH SCHOOL

Played 17: Won 3, Lost 5, Drawn 9. Abandoned 1

Master i/c: D. C. Williams

Wins v: Old Cranleighans; Caterham; Loretto.

Batting—*B. R. Seal 17–4–498–69–0–38.30; N. J. G. Read 17–5–398–103*–1–33.16; B. J. F. Mullins 17–0–502–85–0–29.52; S. Harvey 11–0–259–61–0–23.54; N. A. Porter 15–3–186–47–0–15.50.

Bowling—N. Sahai 153.2–47–376–16–5/36–23.50; D. Riva 133–26–477–19–4/26–25.10; B. R. Seal 147.4–35–462–15–3/65–30.80.

CULFORD SCHOOL

Played 12: Won 0, Lost 7, Drawn 5. Abandoned 2

Master i/c: J. A. Cooper

Batting—J. J. W. Sallis 12–1–464–83–0–42.18; R. W. Pineo 12–0–330–83–0–27.50.

Bowling—R. W. Pineo 138–20–483–21–5/32–23.00; F. J. Bishop 104–14–402–17–5/59–23.64.

DAME ALLAN'S SCHOOL

Played 16: Won 9, Lost 6, Drawn 1

Master i/c: J. A. Benn

P. J. Nicholson's 137 (against Barnard Castle), thought to be a school record, came off 107 balls, with 16 fours and four sixes. He kept wicket for English Schools, NCA Young Cricketers and Northumberland.

Wins v: St Cuthbert's HS; Morpeth HS; Northumberland CCC Club and Ground; King's, Tynemouth; Monkseaton HS; Long Benton HS; Hexham HS; Queen's C., Barbados; Alleyne S., Barbados.

Batting—*P. J. Nicholson 9–3–435–137–2–72.50; M. J. Thompson 7–4–203–62*–0–67.66; T. P. Ditchburn 12–3–240–83*–0–26.66.

Bowling—M. J. Thompson 63–9–195–19–6/32–10.26; R. Black 106.1–18–362–26–5/17–13.92.

DAUNTSEY'S SCHOOL

Played 13: Won 8, Lost 3, Drawn 2

Master i/c: D. C. R. Baker   Cricket professional: P. Knowles

Against Dean Close, J. B. M. Thornton, batting at No. 8, and C. Mills, the No. 11, saved the game with a school record unbroken partnership of 133, scoring 126 not out and 18 not out respectively. Another recovery came when an Invitation XI had the side 79 for nine in reply to 207. This time it was A. J. Darbyshire (91 not out) and R. Thwaites (22) who put on 111, although it was not enough to save the game. The XL Club bore the brunt of a run-feast, when the school made a record total of 300 for four declared; by lunch they had reached 200, of which I. D. Hardman had contributed 100 of his 157. The XL Club were then dismissed for 94, with Darbyshire taking seven for 32.

Wins v: Prior Park; Colston's; MCC; King Edward's, Bath; XL Club; D. C. R. Baker's XI; Old Dauntseians; British School, Holland.

Batting—A. J. Darbyshire 10–7–229–91*–0–76.33; I. D. Hardman 12–1–548–157–1–49.81; J. B. M. Thornton 9–3–282–126*–1–47.00; J. H. Gaiger 10–2–218–50*–0–27.25; M. G. S. Hanscombe 8–1–152–62–0–21.71; S. W. C. Gilmour 13–2–211–57–0–19.18.

Bowling—A. J. Darbyshire 112.5–25–315–27–7/32–11.66; R. Thwaites 90.3–28–276–16–4/2–17.25; S. W. C. Gilmour 76.3–9–283–15–6/13–18.86; A. N. Field 126–22–388–20–5/59–19.40; I. D. Hardman 76–9–312–15–3/40–20.80.

DEAN CLOSE SCHOOL

Played 13: Won 3, Lost 4, Drawn 6. Abandoned 2

Master i/c: C. M. Kenyon   Cricket professional: S. Hansford

Wins v: Malvern; Free Foresters; Masters' Common Room.

Batting—B. M. Hyde 12–1–358–97*–0–32.54; *M. Butler 11–0–309–59–0–28.09; M. R. James 12–0–269–54–0–22.41; A. H. Odell 12–0–261–58–0–21.75.

Bowling—No bowler took 15 wickets.

DENSTONE COLLEGE (BOYS)

Played 16: Won 3, Lost 2, Drawn 11. Abandoned 3

Master i/c: A. N. James

T. J. Mason, the leading batsman and an effective off-spinner, shared with R. W. J. Howitt in a stand of 163 for the second wicket against the Old Boys. Mason went on to play for MCC Schools, NCA Young Cricketers and English Schools.

Wins v: Queen Mary's GS, Walsall; Abbot Beyne; Newton Lindford.

Batting—T. O. Kemp 14–3–559–92*–0–50.81; *T. J. Mason 14–1–578–133–1–44.46; C. E. Snow 12–2–240–62–0–24.00; R. W. J. Howitt 14–2–257–53–0–21.41; P. A. Handford 9–0–169–46–0–18.77.

Bowling—C. E. Snow 95–15–344–22–5/32–15.63; R. E. Wheatman 120–22–400–23–4/35–17.39; T. J. Mason 193–48–445–18–3/42–24.72.

DENSTONE COLLEGE (GIRLS)

Played 10: Won 8, Lost 2, Drawn 0. Abandoned 1

Mistress i/c: Miss J. R. Morris

Wins v: Wrekin; Ellesmere; Repton; Bromsgrove; Charterhouse; Newcastle HS; Woodlands, Derby; Denstone Colts.

Batting—*A. L. Bennett 10–3–169–34*–0–24.14.

Bowling—A. L. Bennett 57–12–121–32–6/35–3.78; K. M. Grandfield 64–9–183–23–5/38–7.95.

DOUAI SCHOOL

Played 10: Won 1, Lost 5, Drawn 4

Master i/c: J. Shaw

Win v: Arborfield.

Batting—C. Nicoll 11–0–239–53–0–21.72; D. McClement 10–1–190–40*–0–21.11; R. Leach 10–1–187–45–0–20.77.

Bowling—N. Lumb 67–10–134–15–6/15–8.93.

DOVER COLLEGE

Played 15: Won 4, Lost 3, Drawn 8

Master i/c: D. C. Butler

Opening bowlers B. C. Amedee and M. G. Craig bowled out St Lawrence College for 38 in 15.3 overs before lunch, returning figures of five for five and five for 33 respectively.

Wins v: Dover CC; XL Club; St Lawrence, Ramsgate; Sir Roger Manwood's.

Batting—A. N. Sims 15–1–549–92–0–39.21; A. S. Burrell 14–3–406–86*–0–36.90; *M. D. Schilder 15–3–215–33–0–17.91.

Bowling—M. G. Craig 154.5–28–516–24–5/33–21.50; B. C. Amedee 177.4–34–541–20–5/5–27.05.

DOWNSIDE SCHOOL

Played 12: Won 2, Lost 5, Drawn 5. Abandoned 3

Master i/c: K. J. M. Burke   Cricket professional: B. Bing

In the match against Downside Wanderers, unbeaten centuries were scored by M. G. F. Walker and O. B. Ratcliffe, of whom the latter went on to play for MCC Schools and English Schools.

Wins v: Downside Wanderers; Free Foresters.

Batting—M. G. F. Walker 11–2–363–101*–1–40.33; *O. B. Ratcliffe 12–2–312–105*–1–31.20; B. M. Kennard 8–1–176–61*–0–25.14; J. P. Burke 12–0–221–76–0–18.41.

Bowling—B. M. Kennard 101.2–24–338–19–6/17–17.78; O. B. Ratcliffe 180.1–46–515–28–6/32–18.39.

DUKE OF YORK'S ROYAL MILITARY SCHOOL

Played 12: Won 3, Lost 4, Drawn 5. Abandoned 4

Master i/c: S. Salisbury   Cricket professional: I. J. Hansen

Wins v: Maidstone GS; St Lawrence, Ramsgate; Old Boys XI.

Batting—E. J. Budd 9–2–166–42*–0–23.71; M. J. Muir 11–0–209–55–0–19.00; J. C. Relph 11–2–163–41–0–18.11; M. Pollock 12–0–209–55–0–17.41; M. T. Goodinson 12–0–166–47–0–13.83.

Bowling—M. Pollock 60–20–157–20–5/23–7.85; J. Stones 115–20–347–17–5/36–20.41; J. C. Wilkinson 102–22–311–15–3/46–20.73.

DULWICH COLLEGE

Played 14: Won 4, Lost 1, Drawn 9. Abandoned 1

Master i/c: N. D. Cousins   Cricket professionals: W. A. Smith and A. R. Ranson

T. J. J. Owens's 137 not out against Merchant Taylors' was the highest by a Dulwich batsman for a decade.

Wins v: Epsom; St Paul's; Downside; Incogniti.

Batting—W. E. S. Warrell 14–3–251–54*–0–22.81; R. W. Scholar 14–3–251–45–0–22.81; T. J. J. Owens 12–1–248–137*–1–22.54; S. C. Teesdale 13–1–266–46–0–22.16; P. D. S. Battley 14–1–278–83–0–21.38; S. P. Chambers 11–3–150–39*–0–18.75; N. J. Rusling 13–0–150–48–0–11.53.

Bowling—S. C. Teesdale 192–63–423–30–6/40–14.10; P. J. Smith 196.3–56–515–32–6/32–16.09.

DURHAM SCHOOL

Played 21: Won 9, Lost 0, Drawn 12. Abandoned 3

Master i/c: N. J. Willings   Cricket professional: M. Hirsch

Records were shattered in an outstanding season in which the school were unbeaten. The opening partnership record went first when R. M. S. Weston (122 not out) and C. Clark (95) put on 223 against Pocklington, and again when they scored 160 not out and 114 not out respectively in compiling 298 unbroken against Eglingham CC. The prolific Weston, whose 1,046 runs at an average of 104.60 featured five hundreds, played for England Under-17, Durham Second XI and was selected for the England Under-18 tour to South Africa. N. C. F. Taylor, whose twin brother, J. M. W. Taylor, was also in the XI, took 68 wickets, easily passing the previous best, recorded in 1962 by I. Hind. His return of six for 16 was instrumental in the dismissal of Rossall for 41, in which match W. Ritzema, promoted to open from No. 7, made an unbeaten 133.

Wins v: Hild/Bede C.; Dame Allan's; Anglo-Australian XI; Eglingham CC; Giggleswick; RGS, Newcastle; King's, Tynemouth; Rossall; Millfield.

Batting—R. M. S. Weston 18-8-1,046-160*-5-104.60; D. Parkin 9-2-264-79-0-37.71; C. Clark 20-4-603-114*-1-37.68; J. M. W. Taylor 14-3-376-82-0-34.18; W. Ritzema 16-3-366-133*-1-28.15; J. B. Windows 12-2-196-39-0-19.60.

Bowling—N. C. F. Taylor 340-112-740-68-6/16-10.88; J. B. Windows 155-55-342-27-5/33-12.66; N. Shearing 135-34-350-22-4/28-15.90; J. H. C. Bailey 115-31-377-19-6/39-19.84.

EASTBOURNE COLLEGE

Played 15: Won 11, Lost 3, Drawn 1

Master i/c: N. L. Wheeler   Cricket professional: J. N. Shepherd

Inspired perhaps by the arrival of their new cricket professional, J. N. Shepherd, the college won 11 matches, losing to no school in term time. A. J. H. Bogdanovski, nephew of P. H. Edmonds, showed potential as a forceful bat and effective off-spinner, while plentiful runs came from the bats of D. C. Richards and England Under-18 prop forward W. R. Green.

Wins v: Lancing (twice); Ardingly; St John's, Leatherhead; Cranleigh; Worth; Brighton; Christ's Hospital; Cranbrook; Felsted; Old Eastbournians.

Batting—D. C. Richards 18-2-660-96*-0-41.25; W. R. Green 17-4-533-80*-0-41.00; A. J. H. Bogdanovski 15-3-469-79-0-39.08; *P. F. Divito 13-3-237-51-0-23.70; N. R. W. Upton 17-0-270-81-0-15.88; R. H. Miller 16-0-239-47-0-14.93.

Bowling—A. J. H. Bogdanovski 166-47-468-29-5/38-16.13; T. C. H. Greenaway 159-38-517-26-5/29-19.88; D. A. Brown 170-38-552-26-5/20-21.23; T. C. Russell 234-60-629-25-4/21-25.16.

THE EDINBURGH ACADEMY

Played 16: Won 4, Lost 9, Drawn 3.

Master i/c: G. R. Bowe   Cricket professional: P. Steindel

Wins v: George Watson's; King's, Macclesfield; Holy Cross; XL Club.

Batting—R. E. Boyd 17-1-383-51-0-23.93; J. A. K. Macleod 16-0-284-64-0-17.75; J. S. D. Moffat 16-2-185-28-0-13.21.

Bowling—L. L. Moodley 58-13-203-16-6/32-12.68; *N. C. A. Moule 233-58-660-46-6/68-14.34; J. A. K. Macleod 173-47-513-25-5/33-20.52.

ELIZABETH COLLEGE, GUERNSEY

Played 21: Won 8, Lost 2, Drawn 11. Abandoned 1

Master i/c: M. E. Kinder

A highlight in a mixed season was the college's first-ever two-day game – albeit a defeat – against King's, Bruton. M. A. Smith completed three seasons in the XI with a total of 92 wickets.

Wins v: Royal Corps of Transport CC; Exeter Geriatrics CC; 2nd XI; Occasionals CC (London); Shambling Derelicts CC; Police CC; Guernsey Island CC; Pessimists CC.

Batting—*A. Biggins 20–4–504–59–0–31.50; P. J. le Ray 19–5–388–75*–0–27.71; S. R. Pitt 12–2–252–49–0–25.20; T. M. Carey 11–2–225–49–0–25.00; S. A. Beck 20–1–457–65–0–24.05; R. J. Newbould 19–1–376–59*–0–20.88; A. J. C. Whalley 16–4–243–45–0–20.25; J. Sherbourne 17–4–261–55–0–20.07.

Bowling—R. J. Newbould 121.1–24–420–28–5/19–15.00; M. A. Smith 191.4–39–703–37–4/36–19.00; S. R. Pitt 92–11–367–18–5/34–20.38; A. M. Mitchell 179–35–585–20–5/62–29.25.

ELLESMERE COLLEGE

Played 16: Won 3, Lost 4, Drawn 9. Abandoned 1

Master i/c: E. Marsh   Cricket professional: R. G. Mapp

Wins v: Wrekin; Foyle and Londonderry C.; Bloxham.

Batting—M. E. Gillison 16–2–770–120*–1–55.00; R. Slater 16–3–379–66*–0–29.15; R. Bruce-Payne 15–1–388–86*–0–27.71; *S. Montgomery 14–1–301–65*–0–23.15; D. C. Gervis 13–4–174–65*–0–19.33.

Bowling—R. Slater 124–23–385–20–4/38–19.25; M. Noakes 183–48–441–21–5/44–21.00; D. C. Gervis 203–30–683–27–5/59–25.29; D. W. Gervis 149–26–454–17–5/54–26.70.

ELTHAM COLLEGE

Played 14: Won 4, Lost 4, Drawn 6. Abandoned 4

Masters i/c: P. C. McCartney and   Cricket professionals: R. W. Hills and
B. M. Withecombe   R. H. Winup

Wins v: Old Elthamians; Valley Wanderers; St Dunstan's; Wallington HS.

Batting—*J. M. Ramsey 14–2–571–102*–1–47.58; K. Shanmuganathan 14–1–285–54–0–21.92; J. M. Huckle 11–1–191–41–0–19.10; S. B. Dissanayake 14–3–186–50–0–16.90.

Bowling—J. M. Ramsey 166.3–42–434–31–6/21–14.00; N. R. Wellard 153.5–42–446–21–3/39–21.23.

EMANUEL SCHOOL

Played 11: Won 5, Lost 5, Drawn 1. Abandoned 4

Master i/c: J. R. Cremer

The side were runners-up to Wanstead in the London Cup.

Wins v: Alleyn's (twice); St Joseph's; Wallington; Glyn.

Batting—J. S. W. Young 9–0–333–51–0–37.00; D. J. Legg 10–0–365–148–1–36.50; D. J. Darriba 11–5–161–51–0–26.83; T. A. Harris 10–3–160–74–0–22.85; S. Smith 10–0–204–66–0–20.40.

Bowling—D. J. Darriba 116.3–34–378–23–5/17–16.43; T. A. Harris 93–17–348–21–6/26–16.57.

ENFIELD GRAMMAR SCHOOL

Played 19: Won 2, Lost 4, Drawn 13. Abandoned 3

Master i/c: J. J. Conroy

Wins v: Merchant Taylors', Northwood; Watford GS.

Batting—R. Hore 18–4–313–88–0–22.35; L. Beskeen 16–5–155–32–0–14.09; E. Morris 17–2–170–36–0–11.33; I. Cully 16–1–161–41–0–10.73.

Bowling—E. Morris 78–9–273–18–6/38–15.16; J. Mitchell 88–7–344–18–5/56–19.11; R. Bake 176–25–518–25–4/31–20.72; L. Beskeen 206–33–658–30–5/31–21.93.

EPSOM COLLEGE

Played 11: Won 2, Lost 5, Drawn 4. Abandoned 2

Master i/c: M. D. Hobbs

Wins v: Cranleigh; Christ's Hospital.

Batting—*M. D. G. Day 11–0–302–85–0–27.45; N. J. Caffarate 9–1–173–32–0–21.62; J. A. Shattock 10–1–185–53–0–20.55; S. J. Head 10–0–173–47–0–17.30; N. J. Saunders-Griffith 10–0–152–43–0–15.20.

Bowling—D. D. J. Edwards 125.2–38–351–21–5/18–16.71; M. D. G. Day 137–37–452–20–5/28–22.60.

ETON COLLEGE

Played 14: Won 2, Lost 0, Drawn 12. Abandoned 2

Master i/c: J. A. Claughton   Cricket professional: J. M. Rice

With no colours returning from the 1991 side and lacking penetrative bowlers, the college recorded 12 consecutive draws in term-time. However, they remained unbeaten and won the Silk Trophy for the first time, overcoming Shrewsbury and a strong St Peter's, Adelaide side.

Wins v: Shrewsbury; St Peter's, Adelaide.

Batting—T. A. Simpson 14–1–502–87–0–38.61; J. J. Walsh 12–6–226–68*–0–37.66; H. C. Steel 14–0–382–64–0–27.28; *D. M. Trusted 14–3–260–72*–0–23.63; M. J. E. Milla 14–0–326–62–0–23.28; E. J. M. Christopher 13–2–188–64–0–17.09.

Bowling—H. W. F. Price 129–28–412–20–4/21–20.60; C. G. R. Lightfoot 165–38–535–25–5/29–21.40.

EXETER SCHOOL

Played 19: Won 10, Lost 1, Drawn 8. Abandoned 2

Master i/c: M. C. Wilcock

An opening partnership of 250 between P. B. Hughes (144) and M. J. Perring (101 not out) against Shebbear College formed the basis of one of five totals in excess of 250 runs. J. C. Orr took a hat-trick against Grenville College and hit the stumps five times for one run against Kelly College, who were beaten by 229 runs. The all-rounder, O. F. A. Le Fleming made his début for Devon against Cheshire in the Minor Counties Championship four weeks before his 16th birthday, becoming the second-youngest after M. A. Garnham to play for the county.

Wins v: Exeter St James CC; Kelly C.; Allhallows; Exeter CC; Exeter C.; Grenville C. Wells Cathedral S.; Invitation XI (twice); Pate's GS.

Batting—J. D. Evennett 13–1–556–106–1–46.33; M. D. Keylock 8–1–321–84–0–45.85; *P. B. Hughes 17–3–587–144–2–41.92; O. F. A. Le Fleming 12–4–296–89–0–37.00; R. J. Moody 13–4–260–57–0–28.88; M. J. Perring 14–2–335–101*–1–27.91.

Bowling—M. H. Price 55–24–99–16–7/34–6.18; O. F. A. Le Fleming 188.1–61–372–39–6/39–9.53; J. C. Orr 113.3–26–310–28–6/23–11.07; S. M. Joyner 53.3–1–276–18–5/11–15.33; S. R. Irvin 108.1–18–389–22–4/18–17.68.

FELSTED SCHOOL

Played 15: Won 6, Lost 4, Drawn 5. Abandoned 3

Master i/c: A. N. Grierson Rickford   Cricket professional: G. Barker

Against Harrow M. J. S. Martin and W. C. C. Cooper both reached three figures as they shared in a second-wicket partnership of 239, Martin going on to take six for 43, bowling slow left-arm.

Wins v: Harrow; The Leys; Merchant Taylors', Northwood; Haileybury; Brentwood; Gentlemen of Essex.

Batting—W. C. C. Cooper 15–1–686–123–3–49.00; *M. J. S. Martin 15–3–522–117*–1–43.50; G. J. A. Goodwin 11–5–187–66*–0–31.16; J. C. Forrester 12–2–226–49*–0–22.60; S. Edwards 13–2–234–50–0–21.27; K. H. Butcher 15–0–205–35–0–13.66.

Bowling—G. J. A. Goodwin 288–105–688–40–6/10–17.20; J. S. P. Willington 195–38–621–31–6/34–20.03.

FETTES COLLEGE

Played 12: Won 0, Lost 7, Drawn 5. Abandoned 2

Master i/c: C. H. Carruthers   Cricket professional: J. van Geloven

Batting—R. A. N. R. Llewellyn 12–0–194–39–0–16.16.

Bowling—A. I. F. Nelson 118–25–354–15–4/56–23.60.

FOREST SCHOOL

Played 16: Won 8, Lost 0, Drawn 8. Abandoned 2

Master i/c: S. Turner

R. Oram, bowling medium pace, returned nine for 40, including a hat-trick, against the Old Foresters.

Wins v: Gentlemen of Essex; MCC; Old Foresters; Kimbolton; Bancroft's; XL Club; RGS, Colchester; Essex U-16.

Batting—R. Oram 9–4–207–55*–0–41.40; S. Moss 14–2–392–66*–0–32.66; *C. Macnamara 13–2–330–72*–0–30.00; K. Oram 14–2–325–72–0–27.08; D. Pratt 12–2–222–57–0–22.20; N. Sims 14–2–225–54*–0–18.75.

Bowling—R. Oram 166–44–456–34–9/40–13.41; D. Pratt 159–40–349–24–5/27–14.54; A. Lawlor 104–28–313–16–3/15–19.56.

FOYLE AND LONDONDERRY COLLEGE

Played 17: Won 7, Lost 8, Drawn 2

Masters i/c: G. R. McCarter and I. McCracken

Wins v: Leprechauns XI; Belfast Royal Acad.; Belfast HS; Coleraine AI; Bangor GS; Campbell C. 2nd XI; Dungannon RS.

Batting—*J. Torrens 13–2–473–103*–2–43.00; L. Lindsay 16–2–281–66–0–20.07; A. McClure 15–4–189–33–0–17.18; A. Henderson 14–0–240–54–0–17.14; A. Tosh 16–0–228–40–0–14.25.

Bowling—J. Torrens 100–15–286–20–5/40–14.30; A. Tosh 104–30–338–23–7/5–14.69; B. Galbraith 131–32–377–25–4/16–15.08; A. Manning 135–25–455–15–5/5–30.33.

FRAMLINGHAM COLLEGE

Played 16: Won 10, Lost 1, Drawn 5. Abandoned 1

Master i/c: P. J. Hayes   Cricket professional: C. Rutterford

Success came from a strong all-round performance, spearheaded by the captain, W. J. Earl, whose 1,084 runs at 83.38 surpassed the school record set in 1939 and won him the *Daily Telegraph* Under-19 South batting award. He hit four centuries, including 191 not out against Chigwell and 153 not out against Woodbridge in successive innings, during an eight-day spell which brought him 613 runs.

Wins v: Gresham's; St Joseph's; Brentwood; MCC; Colchester; Norwich; Gentlemen of Suffolk; Berkhamsted; Winchester; Monmouth.

Batting—*W. J. Earl 16–3–1,084–191*–4–83.38; J. A. Newton 14–5–646–144*–1–71.77; R. I. Roberts 16–2–563–115–1–40.21; P. R. Dening-Smitherman 10–3–150–35–0–21.42; A. P. Cowan 11–1–192–51–0–19.20; D. M. Vipond 13–2–201–85–0–18.27.

Bowling—S. J. Holt 99–22–305–18–6/38–16.94; A. P. Cowan 157.3–32–432–25–4/14–17.28; R. A. C. Wilson 93.4–17–285–15–5/18–19.00; B. A. Emblin 143.5–26–438–23–5/16–19.04; W. D. Buck 166.3–43–460–19–4/22–24.21.

THE GLASGOW ACADEMY

Played 12: Won 10, Lost 0, Drawn 2

Master i/c: D. N. Barrett   Cricket professional: V. Hariharan

Unbeaten and winning ten of their 12 matches, the Academy recorded their best season in living memory.

Wins v: Edinburgh Acad.; Dollar Acad.; Keil S.; Morrison's Acad.; XL Club; George Watson's; Stewart's Melville C.; Wallace HS; Belfast Royal Acad.; Hutcheson's GS.

Batting—*J. M. Gayfer 11–5–399–88*–0–66.50; D. R. Lockhart 11–3–384–84*–0–48.00; J. M. Graham 10–1–154–45–0–17.11.

Bowling—J. M. Gayfer 170.5–63–325–38–8/18–8.55; A. C. Lindsay 81.5–29–264–19–5/19–13.89; J. M. Graham 142.5–27–402–23–4/35–17.47.

GLENALMOND

Played 10: Won 5, Lost 3, Drawn 2

Master i/c: A. James

The side were unbeaten by Scottish schools for the second successive season.

Wins v: Loretto; Fettes; Kelvinside Acad.; George Watson's; Old Glenalmonds.

Batting—J. I. M. Gully 10–0–307–58–0–30.70; W. Brooks 10–2–192–48–0–24.00; C. J. Jack 10–0–222–82–0–22.20; *A. R. L. Wager 10–0–158–32–0–15.80.

Bowling—J. I. M. Gully 170–57–357–34–7/23–10.50; A. R. L. Wager 122.3–23–311–23–5/44–13.52.

GORDONSTOUN SCHOOL

Played 9: Won 2, Lost 4, Drawn 3

Master i/c: C. J. Barton

The leading batsman, S. A. B. MacDonald, played for Scotland Under-16.

Wins v: Edinburgh Occasionals; C. J. Barton's XI.

Batting—S. A. B. MacDonald 10–6–284–71*–0–71.00; *J. J. Cave 10–1–219–98–0–24.33; R. T. A. Collett 8–1–150–82*–0–21.42; S. A. Walton 10–0–168–74–0–16.80.

Bowling—B. G. Clarke 98–14–381–22–4/18–17.31; R. T. A. Collett 89–12–412–19–6/41–21.68.

GRENVILLE COLLEGE

Played 10: Won 3, Lost 5, Drawn 2. Abandoned 1

Master i/c: C. R. Beechey

Wins v: Kelly C.; Plymouth C.; Shebbear.

Batting—E. Johns 8–0–233–104–1–29.12; C. Rendall-Reynolds 9–2–187–64*–0–26.71.

Bowling—R. Hann 59–12–163–15–4/20–10.86.

GRESHAM'S SCHOOL

Played 16: Won 4, Lost 8, Drawn 4. Abandoned 2

Master i/c: A. M. Ponder

Wins v: Wymondham C.; Culford; MCC; Bromsgrove.

Batting—A. R. Ponder 16–1–545–107*–1–36.33; K. H. I. Crampsie 11–0–332–59–0–30.18; H. T. Semple 14–2–324–82–0–27.00; *S. E. Child 16–1–348–60*–0–23.20; A. J. Middleditch 11–2–162–44–0–18.00; D. A. Jackson 15–0–176–37–0–11.73.

Bowling—D. A. Jackson 209.2–38–742–39–6/64–19.02; B. J. Threlfall 91–18–314–15–4/17–20.93.

HABERDASHERS' ASKE'S SCHOOL, ELSTREE

Played 16: Won 7, Lost 2, Drawn 7. Abandoned 1

Master i/c: N. G. Folland

R. S. Yeabsley, son of the Minor Counties player, D. I. Yeabsley, was the leading all-rounder. He appeared in both averages for a fourth year and played for Middlesex Second XI before going up to Oxford.

Wins v: Bancroft's; XL Club; Gentlemen of Hertfordshire; St Albans; Old Haberdashers'; Exmouth CC; Sidmouth CC.

Batting—G. I. Smart 13–4–437–110*–1–48.55; *R. S. Yeabsley 12–3–397–79*–0–44.11; C. V. Harris 14–3–430–95–0–39.09; S. C. Liddle 13–0–185–42–0–14.23.

Bowling—R. S. Yeabsley 207.4–60–472–37–5/45–12.75; C. V. Harris 150.1–39–420–17–7/12–24.70.

HAILEYBURY

Played 14: Won 3, Lost 2, Drawn 9. Abandoned 4

Master i/c: M. S. Seymour   Cricket professional: P. M. Ellis

Wins v: MCC; XL Club; Gentlemen of Hertfordshire.

Batting—P. A. Bhatia 14–3–705–107–1–64.09; A. S. Lewis 14–1–470–86–0–36.15; M. D. Fettes 12–5–173–39*–0–24.71; G. B. J. Mitchell 14–0–275–53–0–19.64.

Bowling—G. Seth 252–70–470–22–5/63–21.36; R. E. Walker 140–42–468–15–4/42–31.20.

HAMPTON SCHOOL

Played 17: Won 9, Lost 3, Drawn 5. Abandoned 1

Master i/c: A. J. Cook   Cricket professional: P. Farbrace

A feature of the season was the batting of S. C. Janes, in his third season with the XI. His last seven innings yielded 699 runs, including four centuries, the highlight of which was his 73-ball 125 not out in the final game – a victory over St George's, Weybridge.

Wins v: John Lyon; RGS, High Wycombe; Enfield; St Benedict's; Reed's; King Edward VI, Southampton; Old Hamptonians; XL Club; St George's, Weybridge.

Batting—S. C. Janes 14–6–995–153*–4–124.37; M. E. Hurles 14–2–464–101*–1–38.66; J. Dave 16–6–260–38–0–26.00; E. D. Parker 13–5–186–76*–0–23.25; *J. W. J. Reid 11–1–215–57–0–21.50.

Bowling—J. A. Scowen 172.5–51–418–29–5/6–14.41; S. E. J. Weller 133–27–409–23–5/18–17.78; M. P. Hall 151.3–20–534–27–7/58–19.77; A. C. King 173.5–61–473–23–3/2–20.56.

HARROW SCHOOL

Played 14: Won 1, Lost 2, Drawn 10, Tied 1. Abandoned 1

Master i/c: W. Snowden   Cricket professional: R. K. Sethi

Win v: MCC.

Batting—*C. G. Hill 13–1–423–100–1–35.25; S. D. Henson 11–6–163–35–0–32.60; H. St J. R. Foster 12–2–325–102*–1–32.50; C. B. J. Danby 14–1–304–97–0–23.38; N. G. Harrap 9–0–208–56–0–23.11; J. A. J. Renshaw 10–2–164–80*–0–20.50.

Bowling—M. M. J. Hawkins 195.4–45–542–33–6/49–16.42; N. W. Blake 97.5–12–322–16–4/18–20.12; M. P. Barker 147.2–35–477–21–4/19–22.71.

THE HARVEY GRAMMAR SCHOOL

Played 21: Won 8, Lost 5, Drawn 8. Abandoned 2

Master i/c: P. J. Harding

Wins v: Simon Langton GS; Chatham House GS; Chatham GS; Kent C.; Norton Knatchbull; Bishop's Stortford; Morebath CC; Watchet CC.

Batting—*M. R. Fletcher 16–6–566–87–0–56.60; D. Fletcher 15–3–471–76*–0–39.25; L. Stone 10–4–218–55–0–36.33; D. E. Johnson 14–6–235–46–0–29.37; G. Thompson 17–2–423–57–0–28.20; D. Himsworth 10–3–167–38*–0–23.85; S. Norman 17–1–288–94–0–18.00.

Bowling—M. R. Fletcher 44–10–92–16–5/12–5.75; L. Stone 174–49–355–26–4/22–13.65; S. Norman 145.2–34–427–21–7/41–20.33; J. F. Griggs 68–9–366–18–5/39–20.33.

HEREFORD CATHEDRAL SCHOOL

Played 14: Won 5, Lost 3, Drawn 6. Abandoned 3

Master i/c: A. Connop

Wins v: Belmont Abbey; Christ C., Brecon; Bristol Cathedral S.; Herefordshire Gentlemen; Wellington S.

Batting—*E. Symonds 14–3–735–106*–1–66.81; J. Rees 10–1–215–68*–0–23.88; N. Priday 11–0–199–45–0–18.09.

Bowling—E. Symonds 84.2–19–222–19–5/26–11.68; D. Kings 137–25–437–21–4/5–20.80; S. Albright 147–29–525–19–3/28–27.63.

HIGHGATE SCHOOL

Played 10: Won 2, Lost 4, Drawn 4. Abandoned 3

Master i/c: C. J. Davies   Cricket professional: R. E. O. Jones

The captain, E. N. Gladwin, a fifth-former, led the side by example, hitting three unbeaten centuries. The highest of these, 154 not out against The Leys, contributed to an unbroken second-wicket partnership of 197 with M. J. Robinson (80 not out).

Wins v: St Paul's; XL Club.

Batting—*E. N. Gladwin 10–3–581–154*–3–83.00; R. Parbhoo 7–3–184–67*–0–46.00; M. J. Robinson 10–1–243–80*–0–27.00.

Bowling—No bowler took 15 wickets.

HURSTPIERPOINT COLLEGE

Played 17: Won 5, Lost 6, Drawn 6. Abandoned 1

Master i/c: M. E. Allbrook   Cricket professional: D. J. Semmence

Wins v: Ardingly; Reigate GS; Sussex Martlets; Bloxham; Ellesmere.

Batting—J. E. R. Paterson 16–2–457–88–0–32.64; S. J. Cross 17–3–436–83*–0–31.14; C. K. Bates 17–0–521–89–0–30.64; A. D. Earl 11–2–182–49–0–20.22; J. J. Bates 16–0–290–84–0–18.12; S. P. May 10–1–155–48–0–17.22; R. E. L. Willsdon 17–4–219–33–0–16.84; *P. P. M. Riddy 17–2–160–52*–0–10.66.

Bowling—S. M. Smith 123.1–19–419–24–4/19–17.45; C. K. Bates 198.3–49–562–26–4/46–21.61; J. J. Bates 183.4–36–605–25–5/17–24.20; J. E. R. Paterson 144–24–512–21–4/38–24.38.

IPSWICH SCHOOL

Played 15: Won 8, Lost 1, Drawn 6. Abandoned 1

Master i/c: A. K. Golding   Cricket professional: R. E. East

Off-spinner R. Robinson returned five for two off 8.3 overs against RGS, Colchester, and G. A. Khan, who was registered with Essex, played for their Second XI, English Schools and MCC Schools.

Wins v: Suffolk Club and Ground; RGS, Colchester; Norwich S.; Gresham's; Felsted; Brighton; Edinburgh Acad.; King's, Macclesfield.

Batting—G. Warrington 15–2–693–127*–2–53.30; G. A. Khan 12–2–470–104*–1–47.00; *M. Holland 14–3–452–81–0–41.09; R. Robinson 10–3–244–63–0–34.85; D. Douglas 10–4–183–83–0–30.50; J. Lear 15–1–407–76–0–29.07.

Bowling—E. Hughes 100–33–253–19–4/19–13.31; N. Maser 137–34–341–25–5/50–13.64; R. Robinson 198.2–67–473–29–5/2–16.31.

KELLY COLLEGE

Played 11: Won 3, Lost 2, Drawn 6. Abandoned 2

Master i/c: G. C. L. Cooper

Wins v: XL Club; Allhallows; Old Kelleians.

Batting—*A. M. Dakin 9–4–258–51*–0–51.60; D. S. Edwards 11–2–310–108–1–34.44; A. J. Reeve 8–2–176–74*–0–29.33; A. Chung 10–0–156–53–0–15.60.

Bowling—J. M. Rowan 151.2–35–395–24–6/11–16.45; J. L. Rove 82.3–7–334–16–3/18–20.87; P. W. H. Spry 89–14–358–17–4/31–21.05.

KIMBOLTON SCHOOL

Played 21: Won 2, Lost 11, Drawn 8

Master i/c: R. P. Merriman   Cricket professional: M. E. Latham

The side played positive cricket, always prepared to risk defeat rather than settle for a dull draw.

Wins v: Leicestershire Gentlemen; Berkhamsted.

Batting—G. Sowter 20–2–553–107–2–30.72; R. Kanani 12–3–244–50–0–27.11; R. J. E. Butler 19–2–424–54*–0–24.94; C. Mear 19–0–473–91–0–24.89; J. P. Latham 20–2–325–35–0–18.05; D. Ford 21–8–171–34–0–13.15; P. Wright 13–1–152–43*–0–12.66.

Bowling—J. P. Latham 238.3–34–787–31–4/15–25.38; R. J. E. Butler 179.2–31–768–21–7/61–36.57.

KING EDWARD VI COLLEGE, STOURBRIDGE

Played 16: Won 4, Lost 4, Drawn 8

Masters i/c: M. L. Ryan and D. E. D. Campbell

The side specialised in exciting finishes: in six of their 16 matches different results were still possible when the last ball was bowled. A highlight was an opening partnership of 146 against Queen Mary's, Walsall, between S. R. Lawson and I. A. Sommerville.

Wins v: Abbot Beyne; Hagley S.; King Henry VIII, Coventry; Worcestershire U-15.

Batting—I. A. Sommerville 10–1–321–78–0–35.66; S. R. Lawson 14–0–320–67–0–22.85; *C. G. Willets 12–1–201–40*–0–18.27; D. R. Vaux 16–1–184–41–0–12.26.

Bowling—J. Dunn 79.1–24–213–24–6/15–8.87; H. Williams 109–18–338–22–5/16–15.36; C. Jonkers 133.3–41–299–16–5/33–18.68.

KING EDWARD VI SCHOOL, SOUTHAMPTON

Played 20: Won 6, Lost 5, Drawn 9. Abandoned 3

Master i/c: R. J. Putt

In the match against Bryanston hundreds were scored by both G. Treagus and E. Taylor. For a time the side seemed better at running out their opponents than bowling them out, with seven of ten run-outs in two matches being the result of direct hits.

Wins v: Taunton's C.; Totton C.; Barton Peveril C.; Alton C.; Peter Symonds C.; Winchester.

Batting—G. Treagus 20–3–843–105*–1–49.58; D. Wickes 8–2–237–77–0–39.50; E. Taylor 19–2–616–108*–2–36.23; N. Osman 16–4–289–50*–0–24.08; H. Prince 15–4–243–48–0–22.09; D. Mansbridge 14–0–198–62–0–14.14.

Bowling—G. Treagus 168.4–41–476–28–5/16–17.00; H. Little 122.2–20–464–24–3/29–19.33; H. Abernethy 120.3–22–432–16–3/21–27.00.

KING EDWARD VII SCHOOL, LYTHAM

Played 15: Won 4, Lost 7, Drawn 4. Abandoned 3

Master i/c: A. Crowther

G. D. Maitland scored 181 from 123 balls, hitting 25 fours and five sixes, as he and R. Macauley put on 259 for the third wicket against Arnold.

Wins v: RGS, Lancaster; St Mary's, Crosby; Woodbridge; UCS.

Batting—R. Macauley 9-4-198-69*-0-39.60; *G. D. Maitland 11-0-421-181-1-38.27; R. J. Tufft 12-1-304-66-0-27.63; D. J. Tomlinson 14-0-314-68-0-22.42.

Bowling—D. J. Tomlinson 210.3-71-541-37-5/10-14.62.

KING EDWARD'S SCHOOL, BIRMINGHAM

Played 23: Won 7, Lost 6, Drawn 10. Abandoned 4

Master i/c: M. D. Stead   Cricket professional: R. J. Newman

With 1,138 runs A. Singh, a fifth-former, broke the school record of 1,104 set in 1987 by N. Martin. M. A. Wagh played for England Under-15.

Wins v: King Edward VI, Stourbridge; Warwickshire U-16; King Henry VIII, Coventry; St Peter's, Adelaide; Bablake; Old Edwardians; Common Room.

Batting—A. Singh 22-4-1,138-133-2-63.22; *D. A. Bhadri 18-6-442-80*-0-36.83; M. R. Dunbar 22-3-633-83-0-33.31; N. M. Linehan 19-1-581-101*-1-32.27; C. T. P. Woodman 12-3-155-45-0-17.22; M. A. Wagh 12-1-189-92-0-17.18.

Bowling—D. A. Bhadri 169.1-37-558-34-4/11-16.41; P. N. W. Button 155-40-432-22-4/8-19.63; M. A. Wagh 134-28-396-18-4/28-22.00; N. M. Linehan 234.3-48-754-34-5/30-22.17; C. T. P. Woodman 125-11-598-25-5/34-23.92.

KING HENRY VIII SCHOOL, COVENTRY

Played 15: Won 4, Lost 5, Drawn 6. Abandoned 1

Master i/c: G. P. C. Courtois

Wins v: Queen Mary's GS, Walsall; G. O. Thomas' XI; Old Coventrians' XI; Masters' XI.

Batting—J. D. Ham 13-1-422-93*-0-35.16; *C. H. Field 14-1-299-101*-1-23.00; J. A. Taplin 9-1-150-48-0-18.75; S. W. B. Clayton 10-0-175-42-0-17.50; D. W. Everitt 9-0-157-56-0-17.44; N. S. Lightowler 13-1-193-50-0-16.08.

Bowling—N. S. Lightowler 113.5-23-440-29-5/30-15.17.

KING WILLIAM'S COLLEGE, ISLE OF MAN

Played 16: Won 4, Lost 8, Drawn 4. Abandoned 1

Master i/c: T. M. Manning   Cricket professional: D. Mark

Wins v: St Bees; Clontarf CC U-18; Latymer Upper; Liverpool C.

Batting—U. A. Nwachuku 15-2-338-100*-1-26.00; G. M. Atchison 16-0-228-62-0-14.25; L. W. H. Moreton 16-0-214-49-0-13.37.

Bowling—L. W. H. Moreton 95-18-315-17-3/6-18.52; R. C. Norrington 211.3-48-710-36-7/48-19.72; R. C. Turner 170.5-34-552-15-2/29-36.80.

KING'S COLLEGE, TAUNTON

Played 17: Won 3, Lost 4, Drawn 10

Master i/c: R. J. R. Yeates   Cricket professional: D. Breakwell

A highlight was an innings of 165 not out against Wellington School by the captain and middle-order batsman, M. K. Coley. A school record, it featured 16 sixes and nine fours off 68 balls.

Wins v: Wellington S.; XL Club; Old Aluredians.

Batting—J. G. M. Ross 16–2–439–64–0–31.35; D. A. Wrout 12–4–243–101*–1–30.37; *M. K. Coley 15–1–414–165*–1–29.57; E. J. Diment 14–4–280–46–0–28.00.

Bowling—W. G. S. Midgley 143.2–39–361–29–6/69–12.44; J. G. M. Ross 128.1–38–438–22–5/46–19.90; M. K. Coley 196.2–44–561–25–5/38–22.44; J. D. Fewings 156.3–29–509–21–5/72–24.23.

KING'S COLLEGE SCHOOL, WIMBLEDON

Played 18: Won 9, Lost 4, Drawn 4, Tied 1

Master i/c: G. C. McGinn   Cricket professional: L. J. Moody

In the match against MCC – in which father and son, P. C. and T. P. Howland respectively, captained the two sides – the school lost their last wicket to a run-out, going for the winning run off the last ball. Howland, who was followed in the batting averages by his brother B. J. Howland, completed his excellent career in the XI by taking a hat-trick against Cranleigh as the school won the Surrey Under-19 Cup.

Wins v: Wimbledon XI; Emanuel; Caterham; UCS; Kingston GS (twice); Alleyne's; Teddington CC; Cranleigh.

Batting—*T. P. Howland 16–2–549–94–0–39.21; B. J. Howland 18–0–697–101–1–38.72; N. H. C. Kidd 15–4–391–62–0–35.54; P. J. D. Redwood 13–3–300–69–0–30.00; D. E. Gorrod 17–0–318–38–0–18.70; G. Khangura 13–4–151–25*–0–16.77; C. Strickland 13–1–185–37–0–15.41.

Bowling—T. W. Flower 96–18–320–25–4/24–12.80; T. P. Howland 153–35–428–32–6/5–13.37; N. H. C. Kidd 179–41–578–23–4/12–25.13; D. P. Frost 112–17–473–16–3/18–29.56; B. J. Howland 140–18–538–16–3/27–33.62.

KING'S SCHOOL, BRUTON

Played 16: Won 11, Lost 1, Drawn 4

Master i/c: P. Platts-Martin   Cricket professional: N. J. Lockhart

In the school's best season ever, F. L. Stewart broke the batting record with 880 runs.

Wins v: Dorset Rangers; Bryanston; Allhallows; Canford; Headmaster's XI; Milton Abbey; Prior Park; Monkton Combe; XL Club; Old Boys; Queen Elizabeth C.

Batting—*F. L. Stewart 17–4–880–145*–1–67.69; T. R. Fowlston 13–6–318–96–0–45.42; O. R. Fowlston 16–3–506–81–0–38.92; J. K. Fleming 13–3–332–90–0–33.20; C. J. S. Upton 17–2–302–48–0–20.13; R. J. Squire 10–0–180–74–0–18.00.

Bowling—F. L. Stewart 83.2–30–266–19–4/8–14.00; J. P. Thomas 161.1–45–391–26–4/18–15.03; M. D. Cooper 143–36–394–25–4/44–15.76; O. R. Fowlston 149–46–370–22–4/33–16.81; J. A. Weir 135.3–41–384–22–4/37–17.45; T. R. Fowlston 119.1–18–447–18–3/41–24.83.

THE KING'S SCHOOL, CANTERBURY

Played 13: Won 5, Lost 0, Drawn 8. Abandoned 1

Master i/c: A. W. Dyer

At their best when chasing a target, the side recorded their first unbeaten season since 1984.

Wins v: KCS, Wimbledon; Sutton Valence; St Lawrence C.; OKS; Stragglers of Asia.

Batting—*A. S. Davies 12–3–471–89–0–52.33; C. J. Ferla 13–1–393–108*–1–32.75; J. R. E. Parker 13–1–325–70*–0–27.08; B. W. M. Craddock 12–4–205–53*–0–25.62; A. F. G. Mumford 10–2–162–74–0–20.25; J. B. Rayner 14–1–242–68*–0–18.61.

Bowling—E. P. G. Sayer 148.2–30–311–22–5/50–14.13; M. I. Odgers 95–18–292–20–4/20–14.60; D. M. Hodgson 164.4–34–497–25–6/27–19.88.

THE KING'S SCHOOL, CHESTER

Played 16: Won 8, Lost 4, Drawn 4. Abandoned 2

Master i/c: K. H. Mellor

Wins v: Sandbach S.; Shropshire Gentlemen; XL Club; William Hulme GS; Coleraine Acad.; Aldenham; King William's C., IOM; Liverpool C.

Batting—*G. P. Barrett 15–5–827–127*–4–82.70; G. K. Sherratt 12–3–328–64–0–36.44; A. C. Richardson 15–2–427–112–1–32.84; E. A. Spencer 14–3–242–46–0–22.00; P. R. T. Brotherhood 10–1–157–44–0–17.44.

Bowling—M. J. Cox 96.4–24–260–16–4/20–16.25; C. B. Place 161–32–503–29–5/53–17.34; N. Prothero 114–18–350–18–5/24–19.44.

THE KING'S SCHOOL, ELY

Played 15: Won 4, Lost 3, Drawn 8

Masters i/c: C. J. Limb and W. J. Marshall   Cricket professional: T. G. A. Morley

M. C. Savage broke the individual batting record with an innings of 172 against Ackworth School during a successful tour of Yorkshire.

Wins v: Long Road SFC; Wymondham; Bootham; Ackworth.

Batting—*M. C. Savage 13–0–488–172–1–37.53; R. M. James 14–0–516–87–0–36.85; C. J. Kisby 13–3–233–52*–0–23.30; C. D. Marshall 14–3–232–60*–0–21.09.

Bowling—C. J. Kisby 122–25–401–29–7/18–13.82; R. M. James 79.3–12–270–19–3/17–14.21; D. J. Parker 110–14–440–22–3/19–20.00.

THE KING'S SCHOOL, MACCLESFIELD

Played 20: Won 5, Lost 6, Drawn 9. Abandoned 2

Master i/c: D. M. Harbord   Cricket professional: S. Moores

Left-arm spinner A. M. James, who played for MCC Schools, English Schools and Lancashire Second XI, returned seven for 11 as Newcastle HS were bowled out for 76.

Wins v: King's, Chester; Bolton; Hulme GS; King Edward VII, Lytham; Old Boys.

Batting—C. M. Watson 12–5–252–52–0–36.00; S. R. Mitchell 15–3–340–72*–0–28.33; N. E. Sentance 15–2–359–100*–1–27.61; A. M. James 13–6–167–49*–0–23.85; M. J. Simpson 19–1–354–63–0–19.66; *M. J. Hammond 17–2–248–51*–0–16.53; R. J. Bones 16–4–185–40*–0–15.41.

Bowling—A. M. James 278–69–766–45–7/11–17.02; K. B. S. Spreckley 118–16–435–22–5/34–19.77; P. C. J. Fielding 181–44–636–26–3/20–24.46.

KING'S SCHOOL, ROCHESTER

Played 13: Won 4, Lost 4, Drawn 5. Abandoned 2

Master i/c: J. Irvine

The averages were headed by M. J. Walker, a left-handed batsman and off-spin bowler, who in five full seasons (four as captain) plus two matches scored 4,110 runs at 68.50, with 14 hundreds. He toured Pakistan with England Under-19, as well as captaining England Under-18 and playing for England Under-19 against Sri Lanka in the summer, being selected to captain the Under-19 winter tour to India.

Wins v: Dover C.; St Lawrence C.; XL Club; Diocesan Clergy.

Batting—*M. J. Walker 12–3–734–108*–3–81.55; D. P. Johnson 10–4–263–103*–1–43.83; J. Mitchell 11–4–225–52–0–32.14; R. Greer 12–1–162–56–0–14.72.

Bowling—M. J. Walker 153–32–475–27–6/36–17.59; D. P. Johnson 88–12–282–15–5/18–18.80; J. Mitchell 153–36–448–17–3/61–26.35.

KING'S SCHOOL, WORCESTER

Played 19: Won 3, Lost 6, Drawn 10. Abandoned 5

Master i/c: D. P. Iddon

Wins v: Dean Close; Hereford Cathedral S.; Worcester SFC.

Batting—T. P. Booton 16–0–321–61–0–20.06; P. A. Judge 15–0–290–81–0–19.33; R. B. Cook 19–0–362–57–0–19.05; I. J. Savage 15–1–258–50–0–18.42; *D. J. L. Wheeler 16–1–207–46–0–13.80; T. P. Bawden 15–2–171–40–0–13.15.

Bowling—T. P. Bawden 156.1–21–613–22–4/35–27.86.

KINGSTON GRAMMAR SCHOOL

Played 15: Won 5, Lost 7, Drawn 3. Abandoned 3

Master i/c: J. A. Royce   Cricket professional: S. Singh

With D. Spencer, the Surrey Under-19 captain, often unable to bowl because of a back injury, the side struggled at times to dismiss the opposition.

Wins v: Caterham; John Fisher; Halliford; Isleworth & Syon; Richmond.

Batting—*D. Spencer 12–1–522–102–1–47.45; J. M. Wallis 13–1–420–87–0–35.00; A. O. Malpas-Sands 14–2–340–75–0–28.33; D. J. Lipscomb 14–0–364–78–0–26.00; J. N. Makepeace-Taylor 8–0–203–67–0–25.37; G. T. Fordham 13–2–198–65–0–18.00.

Bowling—D. Spencer 108–10–286–32–5/20–8.93; A. J. Thomas 97–3–301–23–5/36–13.08; S. Lyon 46–5–316–16–3/42–19.75.

KINGSWOOD SCHOOL

Played 9: Won 1, Lost 3, Drawn 5

Master i/c: R. J. Lewis

Win v: Rutlish.

Batting—J. D. Pillinger 9–3–316–90*–0–52.66; *N. P. Dowling 8–2–208–55–0–34.66.

Bowling—No bowler took 15 wickets.

LANCING COLLEGE

Played 16: Won 5, Lost 5, Drawn 6

Master i/c: M. Bentley

Cricket professional: R. Davis

Wins v: Free Foresters; Ardingly; Cranleigh; Malvern C.; Charterhouse.

Batting—A. Lutwyche 16–2–601–91–0–42.92; J. Southorn 15–1–463–80–0–33.07; *I. Meadows 13–3–213–72–0–21.30; A. Pierce 14–2–247–103–1–20.58.

Bowling—A. Lutwyche 163–33–519–26–3/25–19.96; A. Hinton 122.3–24–364–18–5/23–20.22; I. Meadows 145–25–506–23–7/22–22.00; B. Clark 137–31–491–20–5/7–24.55.

LATYMER UPPER SCHOOL

Played 28: Won 15, Lost 3, Drawn 10

Master i/c: A. M. Weston

Cricket professional: K. Mayers

The record of 15 wins beat by one the previous best, set in 1969. The fixture list had been boosted to 28 by participation in the Middlesex Cup, the final of which saw the side lose to Christ's College. The outstanding performer was leg-spinner A. Choudry, who was responsible for bowling out seven sides and whose 77 wickets were another school record.

Wins v: Mill Hill; John Lyon; Old Latymerians; Emanuel; XL Club; Enfield GS; RGS, High Wycombe; Richmond TC; Isleworth & Syon; Glyn; Magdalen College S.; Kingsbury; Tiffin; St Francis Xavier, Liverpool; Liverpool C.

Batting—M. Thein 26–4–735–94–0–33.40; L. Buchanan 22–5–550–74*–0–32.35; M. Smith 16–7–287–44*–0–31.88; B. Taylor 22–0–660–80–0–30.00; *S. Phillips 23–3–513–60–0–25.65; C. Cockerell 21–2–379–62–0–19.94; J. Brook-Partridge 21–4–292–40–0–17.17.

Bowling—A. Choudry 352.3–106–915–77–7/40–11.88; M. Pryor 216.5–46–518–36–5/24–14.38; S. Thavam 181.1–45–501–28–5/29–17.89; S. Phillips 180–41–585–28–4/59–20.89.

LEEDS GRAMMAR SCHOOL

Played 14: Won 7, Lost 2, Drawn 5. Abandoned 2

Master i/c: R. Hill

Against QEGS, Wakefield, R. M. Atkinson (109) and I. J. Sutcliffe (89) put on 212 for the first wicket before Atkinson completed an excellent all-round performance with six for 45 off 17 overs. In a short season six hundreds were scored by four different batsmen. Five of the nine positive results came off the last over, four off the last ball, and in the game against Bradford GS any one of four results was possible as the last ball was bowled.

Wins v: Pocklington; QEGS, Wakefield; Bradford GS; Batley GS; Belfast RAI; Ashville C.; Past XI.

Batting—I. J. Sutcliffe 14–2–699–110*–1–58.25; G. D. Simmonds 12–1–530–129–2–48.18; D. G. Gait 11–4–299–100*–1–42.71; R. M. Atkinson 14–0–465–125–2–33.21; D. G. Kershaw 11–3–212–65*–0–26.50; O. T. Robertson 8–1–171–50–0–24.42.

Bowling—R. M. Atkinson 206.2–44–734–46–6/45–15.95; G. D. Simmonds 66.1–7–296–16–4/45–18.50.

THE LEYS SCHOOL

Played 18: Won 8, Lost 1, Drawn 9. Abandoned 2

Master i/c: P. S. D. Carpenter

Cricket professional: D. Gibson

For the eighth time the side won the Cambridgeshire Under-19 (Solway) Cup, beating Hills Road by nine wickets in the final. M. C. Donnor passed 500 runs for the third season, totalling 1,777 in his career with the XI.

Wins v: St Paul's; King's, Ely; Gresham's; Stamford; XL Club; Wisbech GS; Hills Road; Old Leysians.

Batting—T. C. W. Keates 18–5–596–84–0–45.84; *M. C. Donnor 18–2–660–109*–1–41.25; J. Crilley 16–3–513–92*–0–39.46; R. Erlebach 14–0–310–65–0–22.14; J. R. Tilbrook 15–2–251–53–0–19.30; D. M. Wingfield 14–2–172–34–0–14.33.

Bowling—T. H. Fairey 108–24–383–17–5/16–22.52; J. Crilley 141.3–25–495–21–3/12–23.57; D. M. Wingfield 200–39–676–25–4/21–27.04.

LIVERPOOL COLLEGE

Played 16: Won 3, Lost 5, Drawn 8

Master i/c: Rev. J. R. Macaulay

Wins v: Wrekin; Liverpool Blue Coat; Coleraine Acad.

Batting—D. Hines 16–2–381–66–0–27.21; *D. Talisman 16–1–331–65–0–22.06; M. Chang 14–2–244–87–0–20.33; J. L. Perry 15–3–234–49*–0–19.50; S. Singh 14–1–222–63–0–17.07.

Bowling—D. Mesa-Ashort 157–20–620–32–6/27–19.37; J. L. Perry 109–18–385–17–6/24–22.64; J. Rylance 176–28–554–18–3/24–30.77.

LLANDOVERY COLLEGE

Played 12: Won 3, Lost 3, Drawn 6. Abandoned 4

Master i/c: T. G. Marks

Wins v: St Davids UC, Lampeter; B. T. Edwards's XI; Carmarthen Wanderers.

Batting—S. C. Howells 12–2–222–59*–0–22.20.

Bowling—R. Mably 108–18–317–23–4/21–13.78; S. C. Howells 153–24–510–33–6/32–15.45.

LORD WANDSWORTH COLLEGE

Played 14: Won 8, Lost 3, Drawn 3

Master i/c: G. R. Smith

B. A. Hames made three unbeaten centuries – 139 in 75 balls against Reading, 154 in 87 balls against Farnborough SFC and 105 in 59 balls against Acorns. The innings against Farnborough SFC passed his own record of 151, set the previous year, and dominated a record opening stand of 190 with T. A. Dyson (60). Hames played for Hampshire Second XI and NAYC, as well as winning the *Daily Telegraph* Under-19 West batting award. D. A. Thomas, who won the Under-15 West bowling award, played for England Under-15. The eight victories achieved were the most in living memory.

Wins v: Leighton Park; Reading; King Edward's, Witley; XL Club; Acorns; Old Steameans; Kampang; QuiVive.

Batting—*B. A. Hames 13–4–807–154*–3–89.66; D. A. Thomas 7–2–204–84–0–40.80; S. A. English 14–4–324–58–0–32.40; C. Fairley 12–4–227–65*–0–28.37; T. A. Dyson 14–1–357–77–0–27.46.

Bowling—B. A. Hames 80–14–327–23–5/16–14.21; N. A. Bellamy 119.3–25–366–17–4/24–21.52.

LORD WILLIAMS'S SCHOOL

Played 12: Won 4, Lost 3, Drawn 5

Master i/c: J. E. Fulkes

Wins v: Dr Challoner's GS; Thame Town CC; Desborough S.; Old Tamensians.

Batting—M. F. White 11–3–242–63*–0–30.25; G. B. G. Yates 10–3–196–72*–0–28.00; C. D. Pigden 12–1–233–65–0–21.18; J. R. Gibbs 11–0–190–55–0–17.27.

Bowling—G. B. G. Yates 99–30–263–26–5/31–10.11.

LORETTO SCHOOL

Played 19: Won 5, Lost 4, Drawn 10

Master i/c: R. G. Selley

Wins v: Dollar Acad.; Edinburgh Acad.; George Watson's; Kelvinside Acad.; Bryanston.

Batting—A. Saikia 16–5–593–114*–1–53.90; N. A. S. Smith 18–4–502–79–0–35.85; S. C. Fraser 17–2–431–106–1–28.73; M. R. Stewart 15–2–241–44–0–18.53; A. G. King 18–0–324–61–0–18.00; R. S. F. Steenberg 12–1–184–43–0–16.72.

Bowling—N. A. S. Smith 202–46–672–38–6/31–17.68; G. C. Harden 250–54–699–39–4/25–17.92; A. J. Jamieson 128–23–461–19–5/29–24.26; A. G. Shaw 178–47–439–16–5/28–27.43.

LOUGHBOROUGH GRAMMAR SCHOOL

Played 18: Won 2, Lost 6, Drawn 10. Abandoned 4

Master i/c: J. Weitzel

In the 58-run win over Nottingham HS, S. A. Bajwa returned eight for 28.

Wins v: Nottingham HS; XL Club.

Batting—A. E. D. Duncombe 14–2–461–81–0–38.41; R. A. J. Parkin 14–2–349–53–0–29.08; S. A. Bajwa 11–4–163–36*–0–23.28; P. J. Gidley 17–1–331–57–0–20.68; *P. J. Noon 15–0–246–94–0–16.40; P. J. C. Meakin 12–1–171–52–0–15.54.

Bowling—S. A. Bajwa 230–78–577–37–8/28–15.59; M. K. Davies 230.1–51–728–36–7/59–20.22; M. Cooper 135.4–40–375–15–4/22–25.00; P. J. Noon 142.1–36–440–17–3/38–25.88.

MAGDALEN COLLEGE SCHOOL

Played 15: Won 2, Lost 7, Drawn 6. Abandoned 5

Master i/c: P. Askew

Wins v: Lord Williams's, Thame; William Hulme GS.

Batting—C. G. Winson 13–2–300–75–0–27.27; *J. H. Rea 14–3–256–49*–0–23.27; D. R. Bixby 15–1–223–51–0–15.92; S. R. D. Hayes 14–0–219–53–0–15.64; A. I. Gill 13–1–180–38–0–15.00.

Bowling—J. L. D. Sherwood 90.4–23–288–18–4/17–16.00; J. H. Rea 185.2–45–521–31–6/20–16.80.

MALVERN COLLEGE

Played 15: Won 5, Lost 4, Drawn 6. Abandoned 2

Master i/c: A. J. Murtagh   Cricket professional: R. W. Tolchard

Wins v: Berkhamsted; Christ C., Brecon; MCC; Old Malvernians; Free Foresters.

Batting—A. Scammell 13–3–423–101*–1–42.30; P. Hardinges 8–0–225–85–0–28.12; *J. Tolchard 14–1–331–63*–0–25.46; J. Noon 13–1–240–58–0–20.00; O. Brough 11–1–193–41–0–19.30; J. Poulton 15–2–154–27–0–11.84.

Bowling—A. Scammell 239.4–67–575–38–6/49–15.13; T. Sheehan 94–22–253–15–5/32–16.86; F. Nyaseme 118.2–19–458–25–6/36–18.32; J. Smart 263–64–525–17–3/43–30.88.

MANCHESTER GRAMMAR SCHOOL

Played 17: Won 4, Lost 0, Drawn 13. Abandoned 1

Master i/c: D. Moss

In an unbeaten season, albeit with a high proportion of draws, the highlight was the victory over Leeds GS, where an innings of 110 in 78 balls with 11 sixes from R. C. Wilcock – promoted from the Second XI – took them to their target of 266. M. J. Chilton played for England Under-15.

Wins v: Bradford GS; Leeds GS; King Edward VII, Lytham; Arnold.

Batting—*L. J. Marland 17–4–783–146*–2–60.23; M. J. Chilton 13–6–372–100*–1–53.14; P. D. Knott 15–3–464–94–0–38.66; R. C. Wilcock 10–0–277–110–1–27.70; G. J. Wilkinson 18–3–370–52–0–24.66; C. F. Sinton 10–3–167–58*–0–23.85; D. S. Marks 15–3–239–41*–0–19.91.

Bowling—C. F. Sinton 262.3–75–747–40–6/37–18.67; L. J. Marland 108.1–17–344–16–3/0–21.50; S. R. Hall 193.3–44–634–24–3/22–26.41; J. R. Wickins 140.2–32–440–15–4/27–29.33; R. M. Bipul 146–32–484–15–4/60–32.26.

MARLBOROUGH COLLEGE

Played 11: Won 0, Lost 3, Drawn 8. Abandoned 3

Master i/c: R. B. Pick   Cricket professional: R. M. Ratcliffe

Batting—L. J. Ratcliffe 11–3–216–92–0–27.00; *T. C. Stewart-Liberty 12–1–271–59–0–24.63; C. A. Gough 11–1–171–72*–0–17.10.

Bowling—L. J. Ratcliffe 143.1–29–427–20–4/28–21.35; J. W. F. Marx 118–34–343–16–5/40–21.43.

MERCHANT TAYLORS' SCHOOL, CROSBY

Played 16: Won 4, Lost 0, Drawn 12. Abandoned 1

Master i/c: Rev. D. A. Smith

With N. A. Doggett (medium-fast) taking eight wickets at no cost, Bolton were dismissed for 22, the lowest score by an opposing side since 1920. Opening batsman P. C. McKeown recorded the highest average for the school since W. Snowden's 127.25 in 1971, which was the last year in which the side was unbeaten. It was the first time since 1935 that as many as five batsmen had passed 200 runs in the same season.

Wins v: Rydal; Bolton S.; Cardinal Heenan; Camels.

Batting—P. C. McKeown 13–5–462–102*–2–57.75; G. A. Edwards 8–1–231–69–0–33.00; A. Sharma 15–1–399–66–0–28.50; P. K. Delaney 13–4–253–66–0–28.11; *D. G. Garland 9–2–184–52*–0–26.28; N. D. Wells 14–2–298–126*–1–24.83.

Bowling—N. A. Doggett 138–42–320–29–8/0–11.03; M. D. Thomas 121–36–404–26–5/42–15.53; G. N. Hedger 129–34–387–20–4/16–19.35.

MERCHANT TAYLORS' SCHOOL, NORTHWOOD

Played 23: Won 6, Lost 6, Drawn 11. Abandoned 2

Master i/c: W. M. B. Ritchie   Cricket professional: H. C. Latchman

Wins v: St Albans S.; Highgate; Isleworth & Syon; UCS; RGS, Colchester; Westminster.

Batting—P. V. Harris 10-3-300-103*-1-42.85; S. I. Haider 15-3-469-77-0-39.08; P. C. Smith 18-1-530-100*-1-31.17; T. N. S. Hewage 18-6-313-49*-0-26.08; *N. J. Hutchinson 21-4-437-60*-0-25.70; A. J. M. Smee 20-1-399-80-0-21.00; N. P. Sapra 15-3-203-60-0-16.91; J. A. Roberts 16-5-154-29*-0-14.00.

Bowling—J. A. Roberts 146.3-41-329-19-4/23-17.31; T. N. S. Hewage 248.1-71-595-30-4/16-19.83; P. Parekh 261.2-65-734-36-4/9-20.38.

MERCHISTON CASTLE SCHOOL

Played 16: Won 8, Lost 1, Drawn 7. Abandoned 3

Master i/c: C. W. Swan   Cricket professional: J. W. Govan

D. W. Hodge led the batting with centuries against Stewart's Melville, Loretto and Edinburgh Academy, as well as 97 against Dollar Academy.

Wins v: Merchistonians; S. D. Stranock's XI; XL Club; Stewart's Melville; Loretto; Dundee HS; RGS, Newcastle; Edinburgh Acad.

Batting—D. W. Hodge 15-3-661-146*-3-55.08; J. M. Prescott 16-0-348-79-0-21.75; E. J. W. Weston 10-2-165-43*-0-20.62; J. D. Taylor 14-1-265-79-0-20.38; J. A. M. Kerr 15-4-199-55-0-18.09; K. C. M. Roger 16-1-247-53-0-16.46; A. C. Wearmouth 15-2-187-38-0-14.38.

Bowling—S. J. Harries 73-13-219-21-5/40-10.42; J. D. Taylor 162-28-459-30-3/23-15.30; R. A. F. Dobson 164-43-457-26-4/34-17.57; D. W. Hodge 97-22-282-16-5/21-17.62.

MILLFIELD SCHOOL

Played 19: Won 3, Lost 4, Drawn 11, Tied 1. Abandoned 1

Master i/c: A. D. Curtis   Cricket professional: G. C. Wilson

Wins v: Clifton; XL Club; Downside.

Batting—*R. O. Jones 20-1-546-111*-1-28.73; K. A. O. Barrett 19-2-462-89*-0-27.17; C. T. Thomas 19-4-339-66-0-22.60; J. P. Hart 14-1-285-63*-0-21.92; A. Birkett 10-1-179-61-0-19.88.

Bowling—P. T. Jacques 256-144-611-37-5/45-16.51; D. W. Ayres 152.4-34-402-20-3/24-20.10; R. O. Jones 303.1-160-866-37-5/67-23.40; C. J. Chandler 158.3-33-517-21-4/52-24.61; W. B. K. Wingfield Digby 159-41-546-15-3/30-36.40.

MILL HILL SCHOOL

Played 13: Won 3, Lost 4, Drawn 6. Abandoned 3

Master i/c: S. T. Plummer   Cricket professional: P. A. Robin

Wins v: Merchant Taylors', Northwood; Norwich S.; Plymouth C.

Batting—*N. Kamath 12-1-382-100*-1-34.72; S. V. Harvey 9-0-245-56-0-27.22; C. L. L. Mortali 11-1-226-78*-0-22.60; J. E. H. Smith 12-2-224-53-0-22.40; D. L. Goodwin 12-0-175-36-0-14.58.

Bowling—N. Kamath 104-19-297-21-5/36-14.14.

MILTON ABBEY SCHOOL

Played 12: Won 3, Lost 4, Drawn 5. Abandoned 3

Master i/c: P. W. Wood

Wins v: Bryanston; P. Salmon's XI; P. Jouning's XI.

Batting—A. W. Harvey 11–2–342–97–0–38.00; S. A. M. Burroughes 12–1–401–82–0–36.45; M. N. Amin 9–0–233–62–0–25.88; *N. J. D. Foster 12–0–220–52–0–18.33.

Bowling—O. H. W. Williams 126–32–414–32–5/27–12.93; W. J. Pontifex 118–34–331–15–6/32–22.06.

MONKTON COMBE SCHOOL

Played 15: Won 7, Lost 4, Drawn 4. Abandoned 1

Masters i/c: P. C. Sibley and N. D. Botton

Wins v: Wycliffe; Kingswood; XL Club; Prior Park; Claysmore; Fettes; St Paul's.

Batting—J. B. A. Smith 15–3–522–79*–0–43.50; J. R. C. Ward 14–1–423–107*–2–32.53; *S. J. Lockyer 15–2–387–100*–1–29.76; J. F. A. St John 12–5–169–41*–0–24.14; J. H. Dollery 14–3–221–53–0–20.09; J. E. Cary 11–0–214–44–0–19.45.

Bowling—J. R. C. Meredith 164.5–45–426–22–5/51–19.36; J. F. A. St John 208.5–57–647–30–5/17–21.56; C. E. Page 118–15–447–19–4/37–23.52.

MONMOUTH SCHOOL

Played 19: Won 4, Lost 5, Drawn 10. Abandoned 3

Master i/c: D. H. Messenger   Cricket professional: G. I. Burgess

Records tumbled during the season. Three fell in the match against Kimbolton during the Framlingham Festival when M. J. Tamplin and K. R. Spiring put on 263 for the first wicket, Spiring scored 200 not out and the side compiled a total of 302 for one. Against the hosts on the final day of the festival, Tamplin took his aggregate of runs after four years in the XI to a record 1,592 and Spiring reached 777 for the season, passing the 702 compiled by A. H. Jones in 1990. Earlier in the season against MCC, I. E. MacKinlay's maiden hundred – 110 not out – was the best by a No. 5 batsman, while his fifth-wicket partnership of 111 with fourth-former J. Hern was also a record. Tamplin and Spiring shared in three century opening partnerships, Tamplin going on to play for Glamorgan Second XI and Spiring being awarded a summer contract with Worcestershire.

Wins v: Cheltenham; Colston's; Old Monmothians; Kimbolton.

Batting—K. R. Spiring 16–3–777–200*–3–59.76; *M. J. Tamplin 16–3–548–81–0–42.15; I. E. MacKinlay 13–3–372–110*–1–37.20; A. Mohindru 15–2–403–83–0–31.00; R. J. Cotterell 12–4–157–50–0–19.62; D. J. R. Price 16–1–267–55–0–17.80.

Bowling—I. E. MacKinlay 173.3–37–584–30–4/35–19.46; D. J. R. Price 169.4–35–562–25–5/40–22.48; M. J. Tamplin 112–23–392–15–4/43–26.13; P. W. Davies 124–26–404–15–4/49–26.93.

NEWCASTLE-UNDER-LYME SCHOOL

Played 13: Won 4, Lost 1, Drawn 8

Master i/c: S. A. Robson   Cricket professional: C. Coutts

M. H. Colclough continued to excel, leaving a trail of broken records as he completed his final season in the XI. His aggregate of 622 runs and average of 103.66 were both the best for the school, as was his innings of 127 not out against King's, Tynemouth. R. J. Howell became the first to score two centuries in a season, with successive innings of 101 against

Solihull and 106 not out against Sandbach. In addition three new partnership records were established: Howell and R. G. Feltbower opened with 179 unbroken against Sandbach; S. S. Shah and A. J. G. Cheetham put on 101 for the fourth wicket against Bishop Vesey's GS; and Colclough and R. Singh added 124 for the fifth against Denstone. In sad contrast only Howell, bowling off-spin, took 15 wickets. Colclough played for NAYC and NCA Young Cricketers.

Wins v: Stoke-on-Trent SFC; Cheadle Hulme; Old Newcastilians; Sandbach.

Batting—*M. H. Colclough 11–5–622–127*–1–103.66; R. J. Howell 13–3–540–106*–2–54.00; A. J. G. Cheetham 10–3–181–47–0–25.85; R. G. Feltbower 10–2–197–67*–0–24.62.

*Bowling—*R. J. Howell 102–24–368–15–4/37–24.53.

NOTTINGHAM HIGH SCHOOL

Played 13: Won 6, Lost 1, Drawn 6. Abandoned 6

Master i/c: Dr D. A. Slack   Cricket professional: K. Poole

Wins v: Oakham; Welbeck; Stamford; MCC; King's, Macclesfield; Ratcliffe.

*Batting—*S. W. Holliday 12–4–686–117*–2–85.75; D. T. Wootton 12–3–341–100*–1–37.88; S. H. Ferguson 8–1–216–47–0–30.85; D. Smit 13–1–257–70–0–21.41; J. N. Mangham 11–2–188–54–0–20.88.

*Bowling—*J. P. J. Cuming 145.5–37–289–22–7/27–13.13; A. E. Brydon 107–17–342–18–4/39–19.00; S. W. Holliday 112.2–31–422–21–4/8–20.09; N. J. Huckle 112–19–357–16–4/43–22.31.

OAKHAM SCHOOL

Played 19: Won 3, Lost 5, Drawn 11

Master i/c: J. Wills   Cricket professional: D. S. Steele

A very young XI featured three Under-14s and three Under-15s.

Wins v: Old Oakhamians; Oakham Town CC; Gresham's.

*Batting—*A. J. Aldridge 16–1–438–91*–0–29.20; J. J. Bull 17–1–441–69*–0–27.56; W. A. Davis 13–6–176–47*–0–25.14; C. D. Durant 17–4–302–46–0–23.23; *M. J. Lavey 19–0–360–72–0–18.94; A. Sawyerr 17–2–268–79–0–17.86; J. G. Warburton 17–1–166–33–0–10.37.

*Bowling—*W. A. Davis 157.2–33–486–26–3/20–18.69; S. W. Colegate 170.2–34–545–23–6/46–23.69; A. M. James 155.2–31–465–17–3/41–27.35.

THE ORATORY SCHOOL

Played 20: Won 10, Lost 5, Drawn 5. Abandoned 3

Master i/c: P. L. Tomlinson   Cricket professional: J. B. K. Howell

Highlights for an exciting young side were J. P. S. Tomlinson's century against Berkshire Gentlemen and the curious swing bowling of N. J. Watson, whose 52 wickets were just four short of the record.

Wins v: Pangbourne C.; St Edmund's; Bearwood; Leighton Park; Carmel C.; Magdalen College S.; Berkshire Gentlemen; XL Club; Emeriti; St David's, Llandudno.

*Batting—*J. P. S. Tomlinson 19–3–792–104–1–49.50; R. W. Atkins 16–2–583–89*–0–41.64; C. C. Trickey 13–0–370–89–0–28.46; R. D. Louisson 18–1–470–82–0–27.64; *R. M. Holmes 13–0–292–46–0–22.46; J. S. Rouse 14–0–179–44–0–12.78.

*Bowling—*N. J. Watson 135–17–403–52–8/34–7.75; D. F. Cole 146–21–472–31–7/29–15.22; R. M. Holmes 97–13–385–25–4/8–15.40; J. S. Rouse 103–9–310–19–4/22–16.31.

OUNDLE SCHOOL

Played 15: Won 1, Lost 6, Drawn 8. Abandoned 2

Master i/c: J. R. Wake   Cricket professional: A. Howorth

A magnificent 191 by A. Plowright against Oundle Rovers in the last match of the season was the best ever by an Oundle batsman.

Win v: Gentlemen of Leicestershire.

Batting—A. Plowright 14−0−717−191−3−51.21; H. Russell 11−2−274−63*−0−30.44; C. McInnes 8−0−189−48−0−23.62; A. Steele 12−1−246−56*−0−22.36; *M. White 13−2−204−47−0−18.54.

Bowling—A. MacLeod-Smith 135.4−28−508−24−5/38−21.16; G. Gilroy 127−16−528−16−3/33−33.00.

THE PERSE SCHOOL

Played 17: Won 7, Lost 2, Drawn 8. Abandoned 1

Master i/c: A. C. Porter   Cricket professional: D. C. Collard

E. W. H. Wiseman's four centuries in the season set a new school record, as did his innings of 160 not out and his first-wicket stand of 280 with T. B. L. Sheppard against The Leys. The partnership had stood as a record for any wicket for less than a month when Sheppard and R. T. Ragnauth broke it again with 281 for the second wicket against Greenock, during an enjoyable tour of Scotland.

Wins v: Royal Hospital S.; Kimbolton; Norwich; Old Perseans; XL Club; Clydesdale; Greenock.

Batting—*E. W. H. Wiseman 15−3−810−160*−4−67.50; T. B. L. Sheppard 15−5−669−135*−1−66.90; R. T. Ragnauth 14−5−462−138−1−51.33; P. Horsley 14−4−287−64−0−28.70.

Bowling—P. R. Lipscombe 113.2−14−437−22−5/44−19.86; J. R. Thiagarajah 181−31−707−32−5/73−22.09; J. R. N. Jack 193.1−32−680−26−4/45−26.15.

PLYMOUTH COLLEGE

Played 20: Won 7, Lost 5, Drawn 8

Master i/c: T. J. Stevens

S. Hunt, with 61 wickets, won the *Daily Telegraph* bowling trophy for the West.

Wins v: Philanthropists CC; Plymouth Univ.; Shebbear; Plymouth Hospitals; Truro; Norwich; Guernsey Island CC.

Batting—*D. Roke 19−3−725−109*−1−45.31; J. Whittall 20−1−649−126*−2−34.15; C. Pope 17−4−440−121*−1−33.84; L. Morgan 10−5−162−42−0−32.40; M. Ross 17−2−374−73−0−24.93 S. Hunt 19−5−335−45−0−23.92.

Bowling—S. Hunt 247.4−47−947−61−6/18−15.52; E. James 179.2−43−651−34−4/16−19.14; P. Jefford 175−36−632−28−6/45−22.57.

POCKLINGTON SCHOOL

Played 21: Won 6, Lost 8, Drawn 7

Master i/c: D. Nuttall

Wins v: King Edward VII, Birmingham; William Hulme GS; Barnard Castle; Craven Gentlemen; Londesborough Park; Old Pocklingtonians.

Batting—C. R. Wood 7–3–160–60*–0–40.00; B. E. Masson 19–4–444–88*–0–29.60; M. T. Atkinson 19–3–445–57*–0–27.81; *A. H. Wood 21–0–524–68–0–24.95; J. A. Etty 21–2–352–70*–0–18.52; M. B. Stacey 15–3–185–46*–0–15.41; S. A. J. Boswell 15–1–205–50–0–14.64.

Bowling—S. A. J. Boswell 142.3–28–497–29–6/29–17.13; A. P. Ray 103.2–19–328–18–5/50–18.22; W. E. Ellse 191.1–31–650–34–5/51–19.11; A. H. Wood 178.5–27–636–20–3/33–31.80.

PORTSMOUTH GRAMMAR SCHOOL

Played 13: Won 2, Lost 6, Drawn 5. Abandoned 1

Master i/c: G. D. Payne

Wins v: Victoria C.; Old Boys.

Batting—P. Moradi 10–1–195–57–0–21.66; C. C. Greer 12–1–235–62*–0–21.36; *J. R. N. Brooke 13–0–226–51–0–17.38; N. D. J. Plummer 11–2–152–28*–0–16.88; E. J. Anderson 11–0–177–32–0–16.09.

Bowling—R. J. Bridger 116–17–548–26–4/23–21.07.

PRIOR PARK COLLEGE

Played 15: Won 3, Lost 5, Drawn 7. Abandoned 1

Master i/c: D. R. Holland

Wins v: King Edward's, Bath; Head Master's Invitation XI; XL Club.

Batting—C. Hathaway 14–2–349–101–1–29.08; *J. Smithers 15–0–401–85–0–26.73; P. Bennett 13–3–237–51*–0–23.70; D. Gibney 15–0–336–60–0–22.40.

Bowling—J. Smithers 137–33–487–34–5/27–14.32; D. Gibney 158–24–648–40–6/33–16.20.

QUEEN ELIZABETH GRAMMAR SCHOOL, WAKEFIELD

Played 14: Won 4, Lost 5, Drawn 5. Abandoned 3

Master i/c: T. Barker

Wins v: Past Captain's XI; Ermysteds GS; South Craven S.; King William's C., IOM.

Batting—S. P. Kaye 8–3–203–70*–0–40.60; G. R. J. Dawson 14–1–350–81–0–26.92; D. A. Woffinden 15–1–331–52*–0–23.64; K. Jayarajasingham 15–4–224–60*–0–20.36; A. M. R. Birkby 12–2–182–30–0–18.20; S. K. Mandal 14–1–231–79–0–17.76; G. A. Daniels 11–1–176–31–0–17.60.

Bowling—S. K. Mandal 130–25–366–21–6/15–17.42; K. Jayarajasingham 104–17–362–20–6/24–18.10; J. E. Mardling 117.2–22–340–15–3/25–22.66; D. A. Woffinden 149–22–535–16–4/39–33.43.

QUEEN'S COLLEGE, TAUNTON

Played 14: Won 3, Lost 2, Drawn 9

Master i/c: J. W. Davies

A strong batting line-up featured in some exciting run-chases, particularly in the victory over Wellington School, when W. Thresher raced to his hundred in 78 minutes.

Wins v: Wellington S.; Queen Elizabeth's Hospital; Hereford Cathedral S.

Batting:—*W. Thresher 12–1–541–124*–1–49.18; S. Holland 11–1–446–79–0–44.60; R. Jones 12–0–311–83–0–25.91; C. Ameer 10–0–248–88–0–24.80.

Bowling:—R. Jones 135.2–37–374–29–6/19–12.89; S. Holland 87–19–298–15–6/8–19.86; P. Spencer-Ward 125–23–442–19–7/69–23.26.

RADLEY COLLEGE

Played 25: Won 12, Lost 6, Drawn 7

Master i/c: G. de W. Waller   Cricket professionals: A. G. Robinson and A. R. Wagner

The young all-rounder, R. S. C. Martin-Jenkins, played for England Under-15.

Wins v: Marlborough; Malvern; Stowe; Winchester; Radley Rangers; St Lucy, Barbados; Combesmere, Barbados; Grantley Adams, Barbados; Coleridge and Parry, Barbados; Presentation C., Trinidad; Tobago CA U-19; Bradford GS.

Batting:—J. C. Barker 17–5–439–68*–0–36.58; M. E. B. Hutchinson 21–1–507–116–1–25.35; H. A. Shuttleworth 22–2–477–126–1–23.85; R. S. C. Martin-Jenkins 21–0–432–82–0–20.57; J. E. R. Matthews 18–7–224–35–0–20.36; J. M. M. Coutts 11–1–169–82–0–16.90; C. L. Busk 18–2–265–56–0–16.56; *E. R. Cropley 18–1–255–42–0–15.00; R. A. G. Sinclair 21–3–270–45–0–15.00; M. E. McCowen 17–3–162–32*–0–11.57.

Bowling:—J. E. M. Turner 214–49–631–35–5/35–18.02; R. S. C. Martin-Jenkins 277–67–726–40–6/45–18.15; R. A. G. Sinclair 266–45–874–48–5/33–18.20; J. E. R. Matthews 143–19–490–20–4/35–24.50.

RATCLIFFE COLLEGE

Played 15: Won 6, Lost 5, Drawn 4. Abandoned 1

Master i/c: R. Hughes   Cricket professional: S. Smith

Wins v: Welbeck C.; Leicestershire Gentlemen; Glenthorpe CC; Wellingborough; R. Hughes's XI; Mount St Mary's.

Batting:—*E. J. Meredith 12–3–302–60*–0–33.55; A. Fernando 11–2–222–44–0–24.66; G. R. Walrond 12–2–186–53*–0–18.60.

Bowling:—A. Hall 80–16–228–19–4/14–12.00; G. R. Walrond 123.2–23–365–28–4/24–13.03; J. Congdon 56–6–240–15–5/57–16.00; E. J. Meredith 111.5–20–313–15–4/15–20.86.

READING SCHOOL

Played 15: Won 3, Lost 5, Drawn 7. Abandoned 2

Master i/c: R. G. Owen

Wins v: Magdalen College S.; Douai; B. L. R. Dowse's XI.

Batting:—S. N. Weithers 8–5–151–50*–0–50.33; D. R. Airey 14–2–381–73–0–31.75; *M. P. Bold 11–3–207–42–0–25.87; B. T. Clacy 15–0–369–89–0–24.60; B. Mayhew 13–1–291–71–0–24.25; R. E. Boot 14–4–168–31–0–16.80; R. S. Sangha 15–0–221–38–0–14.73.

Bowling:—M. P. Bold 83–22–258–15–3/31–17.20; S. N. Weithers 149–31–497–15–3/23–33.13; R. F. Mascarenhas 122–18–610–17–5/88–35.88.

REED'S SCHOOL

Played 13: Won 2, Lost 1, Drawn 10. Abandoned 1

Master i/c: S. G. Wilson

D. Keep began the season in style with a return of nine for 57 off 20 overs against Caterham in April.

Wins v: Tiffin; Old Reedonians.

Batting—*M. R. Neal-Smith 13–1–716–133–2–59.66; B. B. Woolnough 12–0–225–59–0–18.75; D. Keep 12–3–155–25–0–17.22; T. Makhzangi 13–1–167–39–0–13.91.

Bowling—R. M. Coleman 146.5–49–373–21–4/32–17.76; D. Keep 171.1–28–711–33–9/57–21.54; N. P. Stanger 133.1–26–547–18–5/102–30.38.

REIGATE GRAMMAR SCHOOL

Played 26: Won 8, Lost 4, Drawn 14. Abandoned 2

Master i/c: D. C. R. Jones   Cricket professional: H. Newton

Although the experienced side might have expected more victories, there was a wealth of achievement. S. J. Hygate scored 938 runs to take his career aggregate in four seasons to 2,304, second only to N. J. Falkner's. Against Emanuel he compiled the school's first ever double-century; opening the batting he hit 39 fours in 175 minutes as he contributed 221 to the 270 scored while he was at the wicket, reaching 132 before lunch. Following a declaration at 278 for six, Reigate went on to win by 156 runs, the biggest margin in their history. Against a strong Staff XI he was joined by M. H. Hetherington in a record second-wicket partnership of 157. With the ball, the sixteen-year-old leg-spinner, D. C. Sainsbury, broke all known records with 61 wickets, while N. J. Chapman became the fourth to reach 100 wickets for the school. N. R. Cook equalled another school record with five catches in one match.

Wins v: Emanuel; Ardingly; John Fisher; Alleyn's; King Edward's, Louth; Staff XI; President's XI; R. E. S. Youngs' XI.

Batting—*S. J. Hygate 25–3–938–221–3–42.63; D. R. C. Holder 17–8–308–48*–0–34.22; J. B. Drewett 21–1–631–94–0–31.55; S. J. Martin 19–4–399–91–0–26.60; N. J. Chapman 17–4–226–57–0–17.38; M. E. Hickman 14–1–211–32–0–16.23; M. H. Hetherington 21–4–241–50–0–14.17; N. R. Cook 19–2–206–31–0–12.11.

Bowling—N. J. Chapman 176–54–469–29–5/14–16.17; D. C. Sainsbury 322.5–52–1,066–61–6/61–17.47; D. R. C. Holder 292.4–67–744–41–6/40–18.14.

RENDCOMB COLLEGE

Played 13: Won 1, Lost 5, Drawn 7. Abandoned 2

Master i/c: C. J. Burden   Cricket professional: D. E. Essenhigh

The attack was held together by the brothers C. and G. Lawton, while another pair of brothers, M. and G. Head, both appeared in the side.

Win v: Old Boys.

Batting—P. Irving 8–5–170–63*–0–56.66; H. Pugh 12–2–324–78*–0–32.40; C. Lawton 9–3–181–41*–0–30.16; *M. Head 13–1–336–101*–1–28.00; M. Valentine 12–0–292–56–0–24.33; M. Giggs 12–0–205–52–0–17.08.

Bowling—G. Lawton 89.5–23–282–17–5/15–16.58; C. Lawton 128–17–446–26–5/38–17.15.

REPTON SCHOOL

Played 13: Won 6, Lost 0, Drawn 7. Abandoned 1

Masters i/c: M. Stones and D. L. Murray   Cricket professional: M. K. Kettle

Wins v: Oundle; Rugby; Malvern; King Edward's, Birmingham; Free Foresters; Ashby CC.

Batting—J. N. Batty 11–4–509–83*–0–72.71; *R. I. Biggin 13–5–520–84*–0–65.00; A. R. Paulett 12–3–320–67*–0–35.55; M. Redfern 8–3–164–50*–0–32.80.

Bowling—W. D. Haxby 181.2–43–414–25–6/41–16.56; E. G. Prince 173–61–331–18–4/15–18.38; M. Redfern 142.5–34–384–17–5/45–22.58; J. W. S. Piper 134.4–33–396–15–5/48–26.40.

RICHARD HUISH COLLEGE

Played 13: Won 3, Lost 2, Drawn 8. Abandoned 1

Master i/c: W. J. Maidlow

B. C. Law's unbeaten 114 against Totnes was a school record for a No. 5 batsman.

Wins v: Huish Occasionals; Kelly College; King Edward VI, Southampton.

Batting—B. C. Law 11–1–361–114*–1–36.10; D. Pearcey 12–1–345–64–0–31.36; M. Saunders 11–2–154–49–0–17.11.

Bowling—D. J. Cross 90.1–31–236–19–5/24–12.42; *P. Dimond 103.4–19–397–23–6/41–17.26.

ROEDEAN SCHOOL

Played 13: Won 5, Lost 7, Drawn 1

Staff i/c: A. S. England and A. F. Romanov

Wins v: Old Roedeanians; St Bede's; Cottesmore; Sevenoaks; Tunbridge Wells Girls GS.

Batting—G. M. Baker 10–3–172–39*–0–24.57.

Bowling—G. M. Baker 66.3–15–166–20–4/8–8.30; N. J. Bowes 76.3–9–244–24–6/34–10.16.

ROSSALL SCHOOL

Played 22: Won 7, Lost 3, Drawn 12

Master i/c: A. T. Crouch

L. J. Botham, son of I. T. Botham, played for England Under-15.

Wins v: King Edward's, Lytham; Stonyhurst; Giggleswick; Bolton; Belfast Royal Acad.; XL Club; Bryanston.

Batting—*J. R. Newbold 21–5–587–69*–0–36.68; L. J. Botham 18–3–396–94–0–26.40; L. C. Powell 21–4–327–55–0–19.23; N. D. S. Perry 20–2–320–59*–0–17.77; A. B. Mathers 23–1–388–55*–0–17.63; M. Denley 16–1–170–66*–0–11.33.

Bowling—J. D. Mathers 223–46–490–32–7/32–15.31; C. L. Simpson 92–18–265–17–3/8–15.58; M. Booth 274.1–46–815–38–7/10–21.44; L. J. Botham 186.5–30–552–24–5/11–23.00.

ROYAL GRAMMAR SCHOOL, GUILDFORD

Played 18: Won 9, Lost 3, Drawn 6. Abandoned 4

Master i/c: S. B. R. Shore

A successful tour to Holland was a feature for the XI, whose leading all-rounder, A. Moss, broke the school batting and bowling records with 744 runs and 52 wickets.

Wins v: Portsmouth GS; Hampton; Wallington; Charterhouse; RGS, High Wycombe; RGS, Colchester; RGS, Newcastle; De Kievetin; Quick CC.

Batting—A. Moss 18–2–744–107–1–46.50; R. Gilbert 14–1–467–70–0–35.92; B. Fraser 11–1–265–62–0–26.50; T. Fraser 14–1–237–55–0–18.23.

Bowling—I. Nordon 166–36–518–38–6/40–13.63; A. Moss 238–43–760–52–7/27–14.61.

ROYAL GRAMMAR SCHOOL, NEWCASTLE

Played 16: Won 12, Lost 3, Drawn 1

Master i/c: D. W. Smith   Cricket professional: J. Hill

The economical off-break bowlers, L. J. Crozier and M. J. Smalley, dominated the attack with 44 and 22 wickets respectively; in fact 78 of the 129 wickets taken fell to spin and opponents were often dismissed cheaply.

Wins v: Barnard Castle; Cramlington; Austin Friars; QEGS, Penrith; Edinburgh Acad.; Alnwick; Whitley Bay HS; Dame Allan's; Old Boys; RGS, Worcester; RGS, Colchester; RGS, High Wycombe.

Batting—J. C. Hammill 16–3–520–85*–0–40.00; *L. J. Crozier 13–1–369–75–0–30.75; B. Jones-Lee 11–2–190–54*–0–21.11; N. R. Gandy 14–3–176–50*–0–16.00; J. D. V. Ryan 13–2–169–57–0–15.36.

Bowling—L. J. Crozier 174.2–52–397–44–6/9–9.02; M. J. Smalley 90–21–216–22–5/12–9.81; K. Walton 91.3–36–185–15–5/10–12.33; J. D. V. Ryan 100.5–21–265–16–4/10–16.56.

ROYAL GRAMMAR SCHOOL, WORCESTER

Played 26: Won 15, Lost 2, Drawn 9. Abandoned 4

Master i/c: B. M. Rees   Cricket professional: M. J. Horton

It was a notable season for the XI, who won the Chesterton Cup, beating King's, Worcester by nine wickets in the final, and equalled the school record of 15 wins. Despite a poor May, opening batsman J. E. Phillips recorded the highest aggregate for the school with 1,082 runs.

Wins v: Wolverhampton GS; Pate's GS; Christ C., Brecon; King Edward VII, Birmingham; XL Club; Monmouth (twice); Loughborough GS; MCC; Solihull; RGS, Colchester; RGS, High Wycombe; RGS, Guildford; Rendcomb; King's Worcester.

Batting—J. E. Phillips 25–7–1,082–112*–1–60.11; N. M. Davies 21–5–772–102*–1–48.25; J. M. Connor 22–3–708–87*–0–37.26; M. J. McNelis 14–3–284–58*–0–25.81; J. A. Davies 16–2–356–58–0–25.42; *C. M. B. Tetley 14–5–218–65–0–24.22; L. P. Wilks 19–1–302–55*–0–16.77.

Bowling—N. M. Davies 254.1–74–684–42–4/9–16.28; C. M. B. Tetley 293–64–920–43–7/41–21.39; P. M. Stephens 206–49–782–36–4/49–21.72; I. H. Duckhouse 148.4–36–423–19–5/21–22.26.

RUGBY SCHOOL

Played 15: Won 2, Lost 5, Drawn 8. Abandoned 1

Master i/c: K. Siviter   Cricket professional: W. J. Stewart

N. J. Wood's 54 wickets included returns of nine for 64 against Clifton, eight for 51 against Marlborough and seven for 76 as Free Foresters were beaten.

Wins v: Malvern; Free Foresters.

Batting—M. A. Goodhart 14–1–450–100–1–34.61; E. J. Lowe 14–3–309–68–0–28.09; C. J. C. Robards 15–0–400–61–0–26.66; *N. J. Wood 15–0–331–93–0–22.06; H. L. Green 14–7–151–34–0–21.57; J. N. Plews 13–1–250–58*–0–20.83; C. H. D. Boddington 13–2–176–51*–0–16.00.

Bowling—N. J. Wood 286.2–55–924–54–9/64–17.11.

RYDAL SCHOOL

Played 11: Won 1, Lost 6, Drawn 4. Abandoned 2

Master i/c: M. T. Leach   Cricket professional: R. W. C. Pitman

M. H. Bennett's unbeaten 122 against Northern CC was a high point in an otherwise disappointing season.

Win v: Oswestry S.

Batting—M. H. Bennett 11–1–271–122*–1–27.10; *S. M. Ashley 9–0–181–46–0–20.11.

Bowling—M. G. Macdonald 100–26–249–17–5/17–14.64; M. G. C. Watchorn 92–18–300–18–6/89–16.66.

ST ALBANS SCHOOL

Played 17: Won 5, Lost 7, Drawn 5. Abandoned 3

Master i/c: I. Jordan

Wins v: Roundwood S.; St Columba's C.; Hitchin; Gentlemen of Hertfordshire; John Lyon.

Batting—S. Chapman 16–3–453–93*–0–34.84; J. Newbery 13–2–343–65–0–31.18; S. Baines 15–0–333–61–0–22.20; *A. Harwood 15–4–197–31*–0–17.90; P. Summers 15–4–196–53*–0–17.81; M. Seller 14–0–243–51–0–17.35.

Bowling—M. Seller 158–21–610–24–6/49–25.41; T. Hunt 160–33–567–21–6/34–27.00.

ST DUNSTAN'S COLLEGE

Played 12: Won 3, Lost 3, Drawn 6. Abandoned 3

Masters i/c: C. Matten and O. T. Price

Wins v: RGS, Guildford; Masters; XL Club.

Batting—P. A. R. Hobson 12–3–445–98–0–49.44; N. J. Andrews 10–4–275–68*–0–45.83; C. J. Cowley 11–1–326–75–0–32.60.

Bowling—P. J. Gaskell 77.4–23–209–15–4/33–13.93; D. L. Kirby 159–24–506–15–3/46–33.73.

ST EDMUND'S SCHOOL, CANTERBURY

Played 8: Won 1, Lost 2, Drawn 5

Master i/c: R. M. Parsons   Cricket professional: R. M. Ellison

Win v: Dover C.

Batting—N. Whittington 8–0–310–75–0–38.75; P. Walker 8–2–201–76*–0–33.50.

Bowling—No bowler took 15 wickets.

ST EDWARD'S SCHOOL, OXFORD

Played 12: Won 3, Lost 3, Drawn 6. Abandoned 2

Master i/c: M. D. Peregrine   Cricket professional: G. V. Palmer

Against Stowe, O. M. Slipper, a Colt, scored 111, putting on 152 for the first wicket with A. J. R. Robinson.

Wins v: Abingdon; Oundle; Radley.

Batting—C. D. H. Jolly 5–1–175–73–0–43.75; O. M. Slipper 11–0–378–111–1–34.36; N. S. Platt 11–3–260–75*–0–32.50; J. G. Drake-Brockman 10–0–295–80–0–29.50; A. J. R. Robinson 12–0–212–64–0–17.66; *E. J. Montague 12–0–201–50–0–16.75.

Bowling—J. G. Drake-Brockman 80–23–198–16–5/16–12.37; E. C. Lonsdale 147–28–473–21–5/84–22.52; J. R. Summers 149–33–455–19–6/55–23.94.

ST GEORGE'S COLLEGE, WEYBRIDGE

Played 17: Won 2, Lost 7, Drawn 8

Master i/c: B. O'Gorman

Much promise was shown by N. Hoyle, an Under-15 bowler whose off-breaks brought him 42 wickets.

Wins v: Hurstpierpoint; Sussex Martlets.

Batting—*C. Segal 17–1–628–113–2–39.25; T. R. Carroll 7–0–258–109–1–36.85; G. Henderson 15–3–275–50–0–22.91; M. Nicholson 17–1–337–68*–0–21.06; J. Stephens 17–0–266–70–0–15.64; N. Hoyle 13–1–175–48–0–14.58.

Bowling—N. Hoyle 243.2–66–756–42–7/31–18.00; C. Segal 201.2–38–701–29–5/32–24.17.

ST JOHN'S SCHOOL, LEATHERHEAD

Played 12: Won 3, Lost 3, Drawn 6. Abandoned 3

Master i/c: A. B. Gale   Cricket professional: E. Shepperd

R. J. Vickery contributed a notable all-round performance against St George's, Weybridge, with a return of eight for 56 and an innings of 72.

Wins v: Grasshoppers CC; Hurstpierpoint; Old Johnians.

Batting—A. R. Wildey 12–2–304–59–0–30.40; M. I. Ridgway 11–2–215–55*–0–23.88; R. J. Vickery 12–0–271–72–0–22.58; W. Letts 12–0–233–55–0–19.41; I. A. D. Grove 10–2–154–40*–0–19.25; *C. A. Musson 12–2–191–51–0–19.10.

Bowling—R. J. Vickery 111–26–357–23–8/56–15.52.

ST JOSEPH'S COLLEGE, IPSWICH

Played 17: Won 8, Lost 4, Drawn 5. Abandoned 2

Master i/c: A. C. Rutherford					Cricket professional: J. Pugh

J. McLoughlin completed five seasons in the XI with 2,045 runs, 97 wickets, 27 catches and five stumpings.

Wins v: Culford; Colchester SFC; Woodbridge; Royal Hospital S.; J. Bidwell's XI; Old Oakhillians; St Ives CC; Headmaster's XI.

Batting—M. P. Noah 9–5–207–62*–0–51.75; J. McLoughlin 15–5–424–75*–0–42.40; D. White 8–1–249–102*–1–35.57; R. R. Farrow 13–4–293–97–0–32.55; N. K. Marshall 12–1–289–76–0–26.27; *A. M. P. Heyland 17–0–380–56–0–22.35; E. G. Manning 12–1–221–95*–0–20.09.

Bowling—M. A. M. McDonough 54.3–4–228–17–6/26–13.41; J. Aitken 114.4–14–401–22–6/41–18.22; D. S. J. Miller 151.3–26–522–27–5/41–19.33; R. R. Farrow 122.2–24–384–19–5/61–20.21; M. S. Blake 98.5–10–422–15–6/16–28.13.

ST LAWRENCE COLLEGE, RAMSGATE

Played 15: Won 3, Lost 9, Drawn 3. Abandoned 1

Master i/c: N. O. S. Jones

Wins v: Old Lawrentians; Common Room; St Edmund's.

Batting—G. Tait 15–1–370–80*–0–26.42; *A. G. Morris 15–0–298–60–0–19.86; N. D. Ash 13–0–250–80–0–19.23; S. L. Sirwani 13–1–151–49*–0–12.58; D. D. Zaher 12–0–150–63–0–12.50.

Bowling—J. A. S. Clifford 67–12–263–19–5/41–13.84; A. G. Morris 213–47–541–31–6/40–17.45; G. Tait 116–13–438–20–4/49–21.90.

ST PAUL'S SCHOOL

Played 16: Won 5, Lost 5, Drawn 6. Abandoned 1

Master i/c: G. Hughes					Cricket professional: M. Heath

Wins v: Felsted; Old Pauline CC; Incogniti; Lords and Commons; Fettes.

Batting—J. O. Morris 16–4–582–94*–0–48.50; R. S. Stanier 9–1–230–54–0–28.75; T. B. Peters 12–2–286–49*–0–28.60; A. D. Frewer 16–1–387–71–0–25.80; F. A. Badat 14–1–306–73–0–23.53.

Bowling—D. C. Hitchins 180.5–42–506–19–4/63–26.63; T. J. Gregory-Smith 185.5–31–644–19–3/43–33.89.

ST PETER'S SCHOOL, YORK

Played 21: Won 4, Lost 2, Drawn 15

Master i/c: D. Kirby					Cricket professional: K. F. Mohan

Wins v: Pocklington; King's, Tynemouth; York CC; Saints CC.

Batting—O. Gardner 20–4–508–79*–0–31.75; R. F. T. Musgrave 19–3–451–56–0–28.18; B. R. Neary 19–3–430–64–0–26.87; *M. J. Davies 20–1–460–54–0–24.21; F. J. Black 17–4–296–46–0–22.76; N. P. R. McBride 16–5–200–53*–0–18.18; T. W. F. Cockroft 20–2–303–66–0–16.83; C. D. H. Roberts 18–1–249–37–0–14.64.

Bowling—O. Gardner 70.5–13–263–16–3/12–16.43; N. P. R. McBride 76–13–314–18–5/19–17.44; J. Lovell 185.2–42–519–28–4/49–18.53; B. R. Neary 148–26–574–23–4/60–24.95; R. F. T. Musgrave 150–32–479–18–4/44–26.61; T. W. F. Cockroft 177–39–511–18–4/19–28.38.

SEDBERGH SCHOOL

Played 14: Won 5, Lost 1, Drawn 8. Abandoned 2

Master i/c: N. A. Rollings   Cricket professional: K. Benjamin

Wins v: QEGS, Penrith; Ampleforth; St Bees; Glenalmond; Llandovery.

Batting—J. Edington 14–2–463–100*–1–38.58; S. Lewis 13–3–359–51*–0–35.90; M. Parrish 13–2–338–63–0–30.72; J. Overend 9–2–204–62*–0–29.14; W. Browne 13–1–201–46–0–16.75.

Bowling—R. Theakston 125–24–322–28–6/35–11.50; A. Murray 131–23–444–20–4/72–22.20; J. Brown 157–46–447–20–4/34–22.35; S. Light 150–38–384–17–4/29–22.58.

SEVENOAKS SCHOOL

Played 16: Won 3, Lost 1, Drawn 12. Abandoned 2

Master i/c: I. J. B. Walker

The batting was headed by Hesham Iqbal, younger son of the Pakistan Test player, Asif Iqbal.

Wins v: MCC; St Peter's, Adelaide; Old Sennockians.

Batting—*Hesham Iqbal 16–3–492–81–0–37.84; W. House 15–2–420–65*–0–32.30; T. Briggs 14–2–343–63–0–28.58; N. Payton 15–2–266–58–0–20.46; D. Thomas 10–0–173–56–0–17.30.

Bowling—J. Smeeton 206.3–48–517–41–5/18–12.60; W. House 167.5–31–511–32–6/25–15.96.

SHERBORNE SCHOOL

Played 14: Won 7, Lost 1, Drawn 6. Abandoned 1

Master i/c: G. C. Allen   Cricket professional: A. Willows

Wins v: Free Foresters; Taunton; King's, Taunton; Dorset Rangers; Clifton; Downside; Sherborne Pilgrims.

Batting—C. J. Colby 5–2–187–80*–0–62.33; S. Gillett 12–2–522–106*–1–52.20; *J. D. Ricketts 12–2–399–84–0–39.90; G. W. Garrett 13–1–412–64*–0–34.33; A. S. Cossins 11–3–246–77*–0–30.75; T. G. Rankine 12–0–184–48–0–15.33.

Bowling—F. M. J. Costeloe 191.5–61–430–25–5/29–17.20; J. W. O. Freeth 193–46–558–27–4/34–20.66; J. D. Ricketts 184.5–52–487–21–5/26–23.19.

SHIPLAKE COLLEGE

Played 12: Won 3, Lost 5, Drawn 4

Master i/c: P. M. Davey   Cricket professional: M. C. Hobbs

Wins v: Oratory; Berkshire Gentlemen; Cokethorpe S.

Batting—A. S. Kidd 9–0–266–53–0–29.55; *T. P. J. Caston 12–1–294–67–0–26.72; T. P. Ratcliff 10–3–164–46*–0–23.42; D. Jacobs 10–1–208–66–0–23.11; J. C. S. Williams 10–1–169–39–0–18.77; M. J. Baker 12–0–180–47–0–15.00.

Bowling—D. Jacobs 101–20–347–17–3/32–20.41; T. P. Ratcliff 108.4–10–389–16–5/51–24.31.

SHREWSBURY SCHOOL

Played 16: Won 4, Lost 2, Drawn 10. Abandoned 1

Master i/c: S. M. Holroyd   Cricket professionals: A. P. Pridgeon and P. H. Bromley

A highlight for a young side, who played positive cricket, was the batting of A. F. Cutler, who played the side's only three-figure innings in the victory over MCC.

Wins v: Wrekin; MCC; Birkenhead; Radley.

Batting—A. F. Cutler 13–4–603–105*–1–67.00; M. R. H. Pike 15–3–329–76–0–27.41; B. E. Hughes 14–1–348–76*–0–26.76; S. W. K. Ellis 13–1–295–79*–0–24.58; S. C. Belfield 10–3–164–46*–0–23.42; B. R. Parfitt 12–1–202–87–0–18.36; C. J. Clarke 16–0–287–57–0–17.93.

Bowling—M. A. Randall 108–17–397–19–5/17–20.89; M. D. Tattersall 199–41–665–22–5/49–30.22; S. W. K. Ellis 180–24–653–20–3/39–32.65; *I. K. Mainwaring 196–38–673–17–4/76–39.58.

SIMON LANGTON GRAMMAR SCHOOL

Played 14: Won 6, Lost 2, Drawn 6

Master i/c: R. H. Green

Wins v: Chatham GS; St Edmund's; Rochester Maths; Bishop's Stortford HS; Chislehurst and Sidcup GS; Staff XI.

Batting—P. Gambrill 14–2–348–106*–1–29.00; N. Bielby 11–0–298–73–0–27.09; J. Chadwick 12–4–185–51*–0–23.12; S. Hart 13–1–269–74–0–22.41; *D. Isard 14–1–239–50*–0–18.38; P. Livesey 14–0–190–34–0–13.57.

Bowling—M. Relf 97–19–305–27–4/7–11.29; P. Livesey 61–14–241–18–5/19–13.38; N. Bielby 130–24–464–26–4/48–17.84.

SOLIHULL SCHOOL

Played 16: Won 4, Lost 3, Drawn 9. Abandoned 1

Master i/c: D. J. Dunn   Cricket professional: S. P. Perryman

Both batting and bowling averages were headed by R. A. Kallicharran, son of the West Indian Test batsman. Although he was the only bowler to qualify for the averages in *Wisden*, five others took more than ten wickets.

Wins v: King's, Worcester; Woodlands; MCC; Recent Old Silhillians.

Batting—R. A. Kallicharran 11–1–419–126*–1–41.90; S. J. Legg 14–2–471–115*–1–39.25; J. R. Vaughan 13–5–253–52*–0–31.62; N. M. Faber 9–3–167–59–0–27.83; *R. A. Chapman 11–0–226–60–0–20.54; C. R. Briggs 12–2–192–75*–0–19.20; M. J. Ketland-Jones 11–1–150–55–0–15.00.

Bowling—R. A. Kallicharran 145.4–26–492–17–5/39–28.94.

STAMFORD SCHOOL

Played 16: Won 5, Lost 5, Drawn 6. Abandoned 2

Master i/c: P. McKeown   Cricket professional: H. Trump

Wins v: Kimbolton; Staff XI; Old Stamfordians; Burghley Park CC; Oakham.

Batting—D. P. M. Herrick 15–1–525–76–0–37.50; G. S. Paulson 15–6–278–85*–0–30.88; J. P. Moore 16–0–344–63–0–21.50; B. T. Bonney-James 15–3–234–68–0–19.50; *R. E. Grundy 13–0–231–59–0–17.76.

Bowling—P. Holland 182–42–561–30–6/59–18.70; G. S. Paulson 147–16–651–24–6/75–27.12.

STOCKPORT GRAMMAR SCHOOL

Played 11: Won 2, Lost 3, Drawn 6

Master i/c: S. Teasdale   Cricket professional: D. Makinson

S. K. Lapsia, who headed the batting but did not take enough wickets for the school to qualify for inclusion here, none the less won the *Daily Telegraph* Under-19 North bowling award.

Wins v: King's, Chester; William Hulme GS.

Batting—*S. K. Lapsia 11–3–388–78*–0–48.50.

*Bowling—*N. S. Thompson 111–11–416–17–5/63–24.47.

STRATHALLAN SCHOOL

Played 15: Won 7, Lost 3, Drawn 4, Tied 1. Abandoned 1

Master i/c: R. J. W. Proctor

The season was memorable for a tie against the XL Club, as well as the innocuous-looking deliveries of N. R. L. Mackenzie, which deceived many batsmen.

Wins v: Loretto; Fettes; Stewart's Melville; Downside; Crieff; Old Strathallians; Occasionals.

*Batting—*M. A. Smith 14–2–505–85–0–42.08; N. A. Gray 14–2–329–116–1–27.41; N. R. L. Mackenzie 11–4–175–58–0–25.00; *K. L. Salters 12–2–227–102*–1–22.70; M. S. R. Tench 11–3–162–27–0–20.25.

*Bowling—*N. R. L. Mackenzie 212–63–408–35–5/21–11.65; E. D. Anderson 166.1–47–393–26–6/30–15.11; M. S. R. Tench 103.5–24–240–15–6/7–16.00; K. L. Salters 150–47–403–23–4/18–17.52.

SUTTON VALENCE SCHOOL

Played 14: Won 4, Lost 4, Drawn 6. Abandoned 2

Master i/c: D. Pickard

The innings of the season was W. G. Waters's unbeaten 132 to win the match against MCC.

Wins v: St Dunstan's; MCC; Headmaster's XI; Duke of York's.

*Batting—*W. G. Waters 8–3–471–132*–1–94.20; A. R. Barr 12–4–618–107–2–77.25; *A. P. Hudd 13–2–387–85*–0–35.18.

*Bowling—*B. Painter 108–29–351–19–4/20–18.47; A. P. Hudd 133–26–493–20–4/45–24.65.

TAUNTON SCHOOL

Played 14: Won 2, Lost 3, Drawn 9

Master i/c: D. Baty   Cricket professional: A. Kennedy

An invaluable all-round contribution was made by B. M. Wellington, a fast-medium bowler and No. 4 batsman, who also played for Somerset Second XI.

Wins v: MCC; Queen's, Taunton.

*Batting—*B. M. Wellington 14–3–575–108*–1–52.27; A. T. M. Snow 14–3–315–60*–0–28.63; G. A. White 10–2–175–62*–0–21.87; P. Nott 13–3–212–55*–0–21.20; E. S. Little 15–1–296–63–0–21.14; G. Crompton 13–2–219–63–0–19.90; G. D. Hector 12–1–206–64–0–18.72; J. P. Hunt 10–0–154–37–0–15.40.

*Bowling—*B. M. Wellington 282–93–648–45–6/48–14.40; J. Ord 137–33–451–19–4/52–23.73.

TIFFIN SCHOOL

Played 18: Won 4, Lost 5, Drawn 9. Abandoned 1

Master i/c: M. J. Williams

G. J. Kennis completed two and a half seasons in the XI with a total of 2,374 runs at 65.94, including nine centuries. Scoring 122 not out, he shared with N. Evans in a second-wicket stand of 207 against Elizabeth College, Guernsey; the previous record of 162 had been set in 1980 by A. J. Stewart and P. R. C. Robinson. Kennis went on to play for MCC Schools and English Schools.

Wins v: St Benedict's; Surrey YC; St George's, Weybridge; Emanuel.

Batting—G. J. Kennis 7–2–420–122*–2–84.00; N. G. Hodgson 9–2–332–102*–1–47.42; *I. P. Burrows 9–5–151–60*–0–37.75; N. Evans 16–2–493–106*–1–35.21; J. Watson 11–5–180–44–0–30.00; S. Schollar 8–1–179–99–0–25.57; S. Amfo-Okamphah 14–4–255–58*–0–25.50; A. Rafique 17–2–357–62–0–23.80; A. G. Douglas-Smith 11–1–209–46–0–20.90.

Bowling—D. Morrow 145.2–22–617–24–5/57–25.70; N. Evans 192–51–572–19–3/24–30.10; J. C. Gray 151.3–34–535–17–5/42–31.47.

TONBRIDGE SCHOOL

Played 17: Won 7, Lost 1, Drawn 9. Abandoned 2

Master i/c: I. S. MacEwen Cricket professional: C. Stone

The XI's only defeat came at the hands of the formidable touring side from St Peter's, Adelaide.

Wins v: Lancing; Charterhouse; Band of Brothers; MCC; Clifton; Brentwood; Hilton C., South Africa.

Batting—R. A. Arscott 18–7–604–81–0–54.90; W. R. C. Dawes 18–2–583–74*–0–36.43; *M. O. Church 14–0–422–77–0–30.14; C. D. Walsh 18–1–450–81–0–26.47; J. A. Ford 14–2–303–83*–0–25.25; J. D. Chaplin 18–0–453–70–0–25.16.

Bowling—J. D. Chaplin 137–30–390–23–6/35–16.95; M. J. H. Bryant 128–28–382–16–4/30–23.87; J. E. Baird 222.1–39–682–23–4/54–29.65.

TRENT COLLEGE

Played 22: Won 8, Lost 7, Drawn 7

Master i/c: Dr T. P. Woods Cricket professional: L. Spendlove

A highlight in an exciting season was a first tour to Denmark, which proved to be both interesting and enjoyable.

Wins v: Wellingborough; XL Club; Welbeck; Oakham; Bedford Modern; Copenhagen Youth XI; Holbaek CC; Silkeborg CC.

Batting—A. J. Vaughan 18–2–560–115–1–35.00; *N. D. Johnson 22–1–704–135*–2–33.52; G. M. Johnson 19–2–381–68–0–22.41; M. N. Diprose 21–6–277–34*–0–18.46; M. J. Goodley 17–1–278–57–0–17.37; G. C. Whitehead 17–5–152–48–0–12.66; B. G. Martin 20–0–246–47–0–12.30.

Bowling—M. N. Diprose 192–30–687–33–5/61–20.81; A. J. Vaughan 131.5–13–699–27–3/33–25.88; S. Yates 92–11–429–16–3/16–26.81; G. M. Johnson 208.4–35–733–26–5/27–28.19; J. M. Cottrill 165.3–26–560–18–4/23–31.11.

TRINITY SCHOOL

Played 25: Won 13, Lost 0, Drawn 12. Abandoned 2

Masters i/c: I. W. Cheyne and B. Widger

With 13 wins, the school were unbeaten for the third time in their history, 147 of the wickets taken falling to their left-arm spin bowlers, R. W. Nowell, D. O. Dyer and P. S. Kember, son of the Crystal Palace footballer, Steve Kember. The 16-year-old Nowell, who won the *Daily Telegraph* Under-18 batting award, was simply outstanding, and he broke many records. New landmarks for the school were his 1,505 runs in the season; 2,916 in a First XI career (to date – he is expected to return for another two seasons); seven centuries in a season and 11 in a First XI career. In addition, he scored 170 in establishing a first-wicket record of 240 with D. L. Fifield (62) against Guernsey CA. Nowell captained Surrey Under-16, played for Surrey Under-19 and was named as a reserve for the England Under-18 tour to South Africa. In admiring the achievements of Nowell, one should not overlook the all-round excellence of Dyer, another Surrey Under-16 representative, whose 811 runs and 51 wickets were similarly significant.

Wins v: King's, Rochester; Colfe's; Tiffin; Langley Park; John Fisher; Worth; Caterham; RGS, Guildford; MCC; Common Room; Guernsey Island CC; Guernsey Cricket Association; Plymouth College.

Batting—*R. W. Nowell 25–6–1,505–170–7–79.21; D. O. Dyer 23–5–811–102*–1–45.05; A. J. Codling 21–4–492–65–0–28.94; P. S. Kember 16–3–365–62*–0–28.07; S. Higgins 17–9–188–32–0–23.50; D. L. Fifield 20–0–339–81–0–16.95.

Bowling—D. O. Dyer 306.1–91–750–51–7/51–14.70; R. W. Nowell 321.3–80–955–64–5/11–14.92; P. S. Kember 179.4–57–505–32–4/85–15.78.

TRURO SCHOOL

Played 11: Won 6, Lost 3, Drawn 2

Master i/c: D. M. Phillips

Wins v: Penwith SFC; Cornish Choughs; St Austell SFC; Mr Hurrell's XI; Truro School Society; Old Boys.

Batting—R. A. Atkins 10–0–287–72–0–28.70; S. J. Perkins 10–0–170–41–0–17.00.

Bowling—S. J. Perkins 111.1–20–265–33–7/17–8.03; N. C. Worley 74–13–204–20–4/5–10.20.

UNIVERSITY COLLEGE SCHOOL

Played 16: Won 5, Lost 6, Drawn 5. Abandoned 1

Master i/c: S. M. Bloomfield   Cricket professional: W. G. Jones

The Quint brothers – D. S., the captain and off-break bowler, and the younger A. M., bowling at medium pace – were the leading all-rounders. A highlight was their third-wicket partnership of 210, when they scored 121 not out and 99 respectively, in pursuit of a target of 260 to beat Aldenham.

Wins v: Mill Hill; Aldenham; Highgate; Abingdon; Woodbridge.

Batting—*D. S. Quint 17–4–567–121*–1–43.61; A. R. Gishen 17–1–439–90–0–27.43; A. M. Quint 16–2–294–99–0–21.00; F. J. Revton 17–2–270–48–0–18.00.

Bowling—A. M. Quint 194.4–61–385–33–6/27–11.66; D. S. Quint 274.4–64–793–41–6/68–19.34; G. Taylor 110–20–404–15–3/87–26.93.

UPPINGHAM SCHOOL

Played 17: Won 6, Lost 5, Drawn 6, Abandoned 1

Master i/c: I. E. W. Sanders   Cricket professional: M. R. Hallam

Especially memorable in the side's best season for some time was the nine-wicket defeat of Rugby. Chasing 239 in 90 minutes plus 20 overs, they won with eight overs to spare thanks to innings of 101 not out from S. D. Smith and 105 not out by C. E. Ferry.

Wins v: Haileybury; Oakham; Oundle; Loughborough GS; Rugby; Shrewsbury.

Batting—C. E. Ferry 14–3–511–147–2–46.45; *S. D. Smith 15–2–490–101*–1–37.69; J. N. Beaumont 17–1–565–128*–2–35.31; C. J. Maitland 12–4–249–61–0–31.12; T. O. Hamilton 14–2–327–68–0–27.25; E. A. Stoddart 9–2–167–61–0–23.85; A. B. Greig 12–2–206–60–0–20.60.

Bowling—C. E. Ferry 248.2–45–808–36–6/35–22.44; A. B. Greig 194.3–43–540–23–6/22–23.47; I. D. Ambler 211–44–652–20–4/48–32.60; M. Bird 182–35–516–15–4/37–34.40.

VICTORIA COLLEGE, JERSEY

Played 23: Won 10, Lost 4, Drawn 9, Abandoned 1

Master i/c: D. A. R. Ferguson   Cricket professional: R. A. Pearce

J. S. G. Hargrove passed 1,000 runs for the second successive season, his 1,043 runs taking his aggregate to 3,414 – already 309 ahead of the previous best, and with another year to come. In the match against King Edward's, Louth, A. M. Barr scored the first double-century for the college as he established a record of 279 unbroken for the first wicket with C. Jones (54 not out). Leg-spinner S. A. Ramskill collected 53 wickets, while the side's best return of eight for 25 against MCC came from G. M. Carnegie.

Wins v: Yorkies; Old Victorians; President's XI; London Private Banks; Cornwall O-50s; King's, Worcester; Reed's Choughs; Abbotsholme; Bearwood; King Edward's, Louth.

Batting—J. S. G. Hargrove 21–5–1,043–102–3–65.18; A. M. Barr 18–3–847–200*–3–56.46; *D. T. McKeon 16–2–484–105–1–34.57; I. D. Rogers 13–5–249–72*–0–31.12; C. Jones 19–3–461–77–0–28.81; T. J. Colclough 14–3–236–53–0–21.45.

Bowling—G. M. Carnegie 183–47–458–34–8/25–13.47; S. A. Ramskill 311–70–750–53–7/22–14.15; J. S. G. Hargrove 75–11–259–16–7/70–16.18; C. Jones 210–56–535–31–4/24–17.25; R. Sahai 132–33–333–17–3/12–19.58; S. D. Billingham 116–25–346–15–3/16–23.06.

WARWICK SCHOOL

Played 11: Won 5, Lost 1, Drawn 5

Master i/c: D. C. Elstone

A powerful batting line-up was headed by C. E. Mulraine, who, although not the school captain, fulfilled that role for MCC Schools and English Schools. He also played for Warwickshire Second XI and was selected for the England Under-19 tour to India.

Wins v: Trent College; XL Club; Solihull S.; Loughborough GS; King Edward VII Birmingham.

Batting—C. E. Mulraine 8–3–339–91–0–67.80; S. Webb 6–2–152–70–0–38.00; D. Dalton 12–1–379–73–0–34.45; *T. McCann 9–1–272–72–0–34.00; L. Edwards 12–1–249–55–0–22.63.

Bowling—E. Butcher 145–54–329–27–6/3–12.18; A. Jordan 91–17–270–15–5/56–18.00; P. Smith 104.5–23–326–15–4/25–21.73.

WATFORD GRAMMAR SCHOOL

Played 12: Won 5, Lost 2, Drawn 5. Abandoned 4

Master i/c: W. E. Miller

The side's best win was over Haberdashers' Aske's, who were bowled out for 67.

Wins v: St George's, Weybridge; Gentlemen of Hertfordshire; Queen Elizabeth's, Barnet; Haberdashers' Aske's; Old Fullerian CC.

Batting—*D. H. T. Warren 12–3–347–115*–1–38.55; M. G. Wheeler 9–1–260–63*–0–32.50; G. McDonald 7–1–173–43*–0–28.83; P. J. Ambrose 10–0–277–77–0–27.70; D. J. Rylett 1–1–204–67–0–20.40.

Bowling—D. H. T. Warren 148.1–43–341–23–4/16–14.82; C. C. N. Freeman 48.5–40–391–22–5/48–17.77.

WELLINGBOROUGH SCHOOL

Played 20: Won 5, Lost 3, Drawn 12

Master i/c: M. H. Askham   Cricket professional: J. C. J. Dye

Fifteen-year-old M. V. Steele, son of D. S. Steele, showed promise opening both the batting and the bowling.

Wins v: Lord Williams's, Thame; King Henry VIII, Coventry; Pocklington; William Hulme's GS; Magdalen College S.

Batting—M. J. Haste 18–4–483–98*–0–34.50; M. V. Steele 20–4–547–92–0–34.18; *R. D. Mann 20–2–587–122*–2–32.61; M. A. R. Prabhu 14–4–215–63*–0–21.50; D. W. Hallworth 15–3–154–21*–0–12.83.

Bowling—D. W. Hallworth 204–48–620–37–5/37–16.75.

WELLINGTON COLLEGE

Played 15: Won 7, Lost 3, Drawn 5. Abandoned 2

Masters i/c: C. M. St G. Potter and   Cricket professional: P. J. Lewington
R. I. H. B. Dyer

The best XI for some time enjoyed their first victory over Harrow for 29 years. D. R. H. Churton played for Northumberland Under-19 and R. W. D. Waters for Buckinghamshire at that level.

Wins v: Royal Corps of Transport; Free Foresters; Winchester; Marlborough; Old Wellingtonians; Harrow; Mount St Mary's.

Batting—D. R. H. Churton 16–1–618–84–0–41.20; T. P. Newman 16–1–574–95–0–38.26; T. P. Hodgson 16–1–533–107*–1–35.53; A. M. Terris 11–4–234–84–0–33.42; A. J. Parker 3–3–300–51–0–30.00; R. W. D. Waters 15–2–339–81–0–26.07.

Bowling—A. J. Parker 236.4–38–703–42–6/48–16.73; R. W. D. Waters 132–23–386–23–4/14–16.78; A. M. Terris 119.5–31–321–19–4/20–16.89; D. M. Simpson 53.5–32–458–15–2/20–30.53.

WELLINGTON SCHOOL

Played 16: Won 4, Lost 5, Drawn 7

Master i/c: P. M. Pearce

D. Hine completed his three-and-a-half-year career in the XI with a total of 1,347 runs – more than any other batsman for the school – as well as completing a haul of 56 wickets with his leg-spin.

Wins v: Mallards CC; Queen Elizabeth's Hospital; Allhallows; Christ C., Brecon.

Batting—G. Scott 9–3–226–52–0–37.66; *D. Hine 16–1–492–97–0–32.80; D. Davidson 15–0–379–81–0–25.26; R. Cooper 15–1–309–91–0–22.07; C. Reah 14–0–169–37–0–12.07; L. Wardell 15–0–178–38–0–11.86.

Bowling—D. Hine 171–33–666–35–5/23–19.02; J. Clarke 179–38–533–27–4/26–19.74; D. Davidson 129–33–451–19–5/13–23.73.

WELLS CATHEDRAL SCHOOL

Played 11: Won 4, Lost 6, Drawn 1. Abandoned 6

Master i/c: M. C. H. Stringer

Wins v: XL Club; Old Boys; Rutlish; Allhallows.

Batting—A. Murphy 10–1–231–66–0–25.66; A. Frankpitt 10–1–163–47–0–18.11; B. Pinfield 11–1–170–82*–0–17.00; D. Tong 11–1–166–40*–0–16.60; C. Gould 11–0–164–45–0–14.90.

Bowling—J. Keen 69.2–12–306–17–4/15–18.00.

WHITGIFT SCHOOL

Played 17: Won 7, Lost 1, Drawn 9. Abandoned 1

Master i/c: P. C. Fladgate

Unbeaten by schools, the side owed much to the captain, R. Shah and J. D. G. Ufton, son of the Kent player, D. G. Ufton. Shah's 905 runs were a post-war record, which took his First XI aggregate to 2,181 runs, while Ufton, also prolific, increased his aggregate to 1,991. The two shared five century opening partnerships, the highest being 182 against St John's, Leatherhead on which occasion Shah made a hundred before lunch. The wicket-keeper, N. J. Edwards, effected his 74th dismissal in three years.

Wins v: Hurstpierpoint; KCS, Wimbledon; Reigate GS; St George's, Weybridge; MCC; Domini; Voorburg CC.

Batting—J. D. G. Ufton 14–7–610–113*–1–87.14; *R. Shah 17–3–905–120–3–64.64; B. Goward 15–3–321–63–0–26.75; R. S. Gibson 11–1–219–44–0–21.90; T. R. K. Hird 11–2–191–55–0–21.22; C. E. Catling 12–0–216–69–0–18.00.

Bowling—P. S. V. Middleton 109.4–18–389–22–5/42–17.68; G. K. Spring 141.5–39–411–22–3/12–18.68; S. N. Jackson 216–45–679–31–5/61–21.90; J. P. Blasco 128–20–404–16–3/26–25.25.

WILLIAM HULME'S GRAMMAR SCHOOL

Played 18: Won 2, Lost 10, Drawn 6. Abandoned 4

Master i/c: H. W. Timm   Cricket professional: R. Collins

N. T. Wood, son of the former England batsman, B. Wood, played for Lancashire Second XI and England Under-17 and was selected for the England Under-18 tour to South Africa.

Wins v: King Edward VII, Lytham; Rydal.

Batting—N. T. Wood 5–0–287–105–1–57.40; P. D. Warren 15–1–496–80–0–35.42; J. Hall 14–5–293–69*–0–32.55; T. Allen 16–3–212–28–0–16.30; Y. Sayyid 16–2–187–33–0–13.35; F. Baama 14–1–151–42–0–11.61; A. Kniveton 17–0–168–44–0–9.88.

Bowling—P. D. Warren 120.2–26–383–15–4/30–25.53.

WINCHESTER COLLEGE

Played 20: Won 9, Lost 6, Drawn 5

Master i/c: K. N. Foyle   Cricket professional: I. C. D. Stuart

Wins v: Stowe; Bryanston; Marlborough; Charterhouse; St George's, Weybridge; Old Wykehamists; Monmouth; Berkhamsted; Kimbolton.

Batting—N. D. Freebody 15-2-519-104-1-39.92; *N. R. Hall 18-2-608-87-0-38.00; S. H. R. Brooke 20-1-492-67-0-25.89; H. W. Foster 16-2-355-59*-0-25.35; E. J. Daniels 18-1-429-65-0-25.23.

Bowling—H. W. Foster 219.4-40-657-41-8/13-16.02; D. R. Minford 120-19-367-22-5/25-16.68; A. J. P. Thomas 129.4-25-339-18-4/29-18.83; G. W. Phillips 124-18-434-18-4/45-24.11; N. R. Hall 151-33-465-16-2/22-29.06.

WOODBRIDGE SCHOOL

Played 13: Won 3, Lost 4, Drawn 6

Master i/c: P. Kesterton

Wins v: Ipswich S. Second XI; Culford; Royal Hospital S.

Batting—J. Percival 12-5-256-52*-0-36.57; N. Pearson 13-3-178-34*-0-17.80.

Bowling—P. Birchley 148-30-507-28-5/28-18.10; J. Percival 145.2-26-522-25-5/23-20.88; A. Barham 99-11-402-18-5/62-22.33.

WOODHOUSE GROVE SCHOOL

Played 13: Won 3, Lost 2, Drawn 8. Abandoned 3

Master i/c: E. R. Howard   Cricket professional: A. Sidebottom

The English Schools all-rounder, C. J. Rika, headed the batting, although injury restricted his contribution with the ball to only 30 overs. The promising batting of A. D. Bairstow, son of D. L. Bairstow, earned him selection for English Schools North and the MCC Schools final trial.

Wins v: Stockport GS; South Craven S.; Craven Gentlemen.

Batting—*C. J. Rika 11-2-630-114*-1-70.00; N. J. Sheard 12-2-302-63-0-30.20; A. M. Cadman 11-3-222-84*-0-27.75; A. D. Bairstow 9-0-205-38-0-22.77; J. A. Lockwood 12-3-177-45*-0-19.66.

Bowling—D. J. Webster 161.4-46-490-25-5/20-19.60; N. J. Sheard 135-29-434-16-4/32-27.12.

WORKSOP COLLEGE

Played 18: Won 3, Lost 6, Drawn 9. Abandoned 1

Master i/c: B. Wilks   Cricket professional: A. Kettleborough

Wins v: Trent; Hurstpierpoint; Sheffield CA.

Batting—R. J. Fox-Andrews 17-3-331-47-0-23.64; *A. S. Hunter 13-1-278-49-0-23.16; M. A. Czernek 18-0-342-46-0-19.00; I. P. Jenkinson 14-0-241-51-0-17.21; J. S. Berry 18-1-280-63-0-16.47; J. M. Meir 18-1-242-42-0-14.23; D. J. Smith 17-0-175-37-0-10.29.

Bowling—A. S. Hunter 149-44-480-31-6/47-15.48; L. Mackay 78-13-303-18-5/31-16.83; M. A. Czernek 174-31-584-15-4/43-38.93.

WREKIN COLLEGE

Played 19: Won 6, Lost 4, Drawn 9. Abandoned 1

Master i/c: M. de Weymarn   Cricket professional: D. A. Banks

Wins v: Wellington CC; King's, Worcester; King Edward's, Birmingham; Hereford Cathedral S.; Denstone; King's, Peterborough.

Batting—C. Ingram 17–4–601–78*–0–46.23; R. Burton 19–2–477–81*–0–28.05; D. Tuckett-Good 17–2–395–61*–0–26.33; N. Harrison 18–0–420–107–1–23.33; *G. Howell 13–1–264–58*–0–22.00; R. Davies 13–1–208–42–0–17.33; B. Morley 15–3–190–58*–0–15.83.

Bowling—G. Howell 130–25–387–20–6/31–19.35; N. Edwards 231–44–699–36–5/49–19.41.

WYCLIFFE COLLEGE

Played 13: Won 2, Lost 3, Drawn 8. Abandoned 3

Master i/c: M. C. Russell   Cricket professional: K. D. Biddulph

While playing challenging and positive cricket themselves, the XI were frequently disappointed by the negative attitudes of opposing sides. Their batting was strong, built on the successful opening partnership of I. M. Collins and P. W. Lewis, son of the Glamorgan leg-spinner D. W. Lewis. Both scoring centuries, they put on an undefeated 219 in 34.4 overs against Kingswood, breaking the college record for any wicket – 210 in 1900 put on by C. S. and E. Barnett (father and uncle of C. J. Barnett of Gloucestershire and England).

Wins v: Bristol GS; Queen's, Taunton.

Batting—I. M. Collins 11–1–301–100*–1–30.10; P. W. Lewis 13–1–349–109*–1–29.08; M. A. House 11–1–271–64*–0–27.10; B. Harding 10–1–186–48–0–20.66; H. R. D. Aldridge 12–3–185–50–0–20.55.

Bowling—M. A. House 128.5–20–458–20–5/27–22.90; *W. R. Tovey 101–8–431–15–4/18–28.73.

WYGGESTON & QUEEN ELIZABETH I SIXTH FORM COLLEGE

Played 10: Won 5, Lost 2, Drawn 3

Master i/c: G. G. Wells

Six different players featured in three century partnerships: 202 for the first wicket between J. D. Hanger (115 not out) and J. D. Lawrence (82) against Queen Mary's GS, Walsall, which was a college record for any wicket; 155, a record for the sixth wicket between S. J Patel (103 not out) and B. Thaney (52) against Guthlaxton; and 143 for the fourth between R. J. H. Green (94) and J. E. Kent (72) against Abbot Beyne.

Wins v: King Edward VI, Stourbridge; Guthlaxton S.; High Pavement; Abbot Beyne Manager's XI.

Batting—J. D. Hanger 8–1–326–115*–1–46.57; R. J. H. Green 9–2–296–94–0–42.28; J. E. Kent 9–1–242–72–0–30.25; J. D. Lawrence 8–0–225–82–0–28.12.

Bowling—S. J. Patel 89.3–27–205–24–6/28–8.54.

WOMEN'S CRICKET, 1992

By CAROL SALMON

Financial problems surrounding the staging of the 1993 World Cup in England overshadowed much of the women's cricket season. Seemingly all avenues of sponsorship had been exhausted, and the Women's Cricket Association decided that if insufficient funds had been raised by October 11 the event would have to be cancelled. But just two days before the deadline, the Foundation for Sport and the Arts announced that it had approved a grant of £90,000. While this was only half the budgeted figure, it boosted the World Cup's credibility. With around £40,000 already in the WCA's coffers, officials redoubled their efforts to raise the rest of the money through sponsorship.

The 55-overs competition is scheduled to be contested in late July by eight teams: Australia, the holders, New Zealand, England, The Netherlands, Ireland, Denmark, Caribbean Federation – an unknown quantity – and India, who confirmed their participation just in time. Each team will play the others once. The bulk of the 28 qualifying games are to be played in the Home Counties, as the North and Midlands were unable to host many matches. The top two qualifiers will meet in the final at Lord's on August 1, with the next day available if necessary.

The 1993 World Cup returns to England exactly 20 years after the WCA, Rachael Heyhoe-Flint and Sir Jack Hayward combined to fund and run the first one. England won in 1973, under the captaincy of Heyhoe-Flint, but they have been runners-up to Australia in three finals since then, in India (1977-78), New Zealand (1981-82) and Australia (1988-89). Faced with the task of breaking Australian domination, England's selection panel chose a 19-strong squad to prepare throughout the winter. Of these, 13 toured New Zealand and Australia in 1991-92, and they have been strengthened by the return of seamers Clare Taylor, who missed the tour through football commitments, and Gill Smith, who was injured, as well as some up and coming youngsters. The final selection was due to be made after the 1993 county tournament in Wellingborough from May 29 to June 2.

In 1992 the county tournament was reduced to three days, and contested by teams qualifying from groups of four. Yorkshire took the championship when they beat East Midlands by 36 runs in the 55-overs final at Cambridge. Middlesex won the third-place play-off against West Midlands by 47 runs. The Mid West won the territorial tournament in Oxford, with two victories, after Sunday's play was washed out. They beat the South by ten runs and thrashed the East by 123. Both successes owed much to the form of Wendy Watson, who scored 37 and 47, and Karen Smithies, with three for 35 against the South and an unbeaten 45 against the East. The South had the consolation of a six-wicket victory over the North, who in turn had beaten the East by eight wickets. Wakefield won the National League, ahead of Vagabonds and Redoutables, with last year's winners, Wolverhampton, fourth. There was no club knockout competition in 1992.

COUNTY TOURNAMENT FINAL, 1992

At Cambridge, August 2. Yorkshire won by 36 runs. Yorkshire 214 for eight (55 overs) (M. P. Moore 50, S. Metcalfe 45); East Midlands 178 for eight (55 overs) (K. Smithies 49; K. Jobling three for 21).

PART FOUR: OVERSEAS CRICKET IN 1991-92

FEATURES OF 1991-92

Double-Hundreds (32)

Abdul Azeem	208	Hyderabad v Andhra at Secunderabad.
K. Bhaskar Pillai	221	Delhi v Bombay at Bombay.
S. S. Bhave (2)	229	Maharashtra v Bihar at Pune.
	231*	Maharashtra v Haryana at Pune.
R. Bora	235	Assam v Bihar at Ranchi.
G. P. Burnett	203*	Wellington v Northern Districts at Hamilton.
Abhijit P. Deshpande	217	Maharashtra v Gujarat at Valsad.
S. G. Gujar	221	Vidarbha v Madhya Pradesh at Nagpur.
D. L. Haynes	246	Barbados v Windward Islands at Bridgetown.
A. D. Jadeja (2)	256	Haryana v Services at Faridabad.
	228	Haryana v Punjab at Gurgaon.
D. M. Jones (3)	243*	Victoria v Tasmania at Melbourne.
	214	Victoria v South Australia at Melbourne.
	204	Victoria v Western Australia at Perth.
V. G. Kambli (2)	262	Bombay v Saurashtra at Bombay.
	208	West Zone v East Zone at Bombay.
A. S. Kaypee	200	Haryana v Services at Faridabad.
S. K. Kulkarni	200*	Assam v Bihar at Ranchi.
D. N. Patel	204	Auckland v Northern Districts at Auckland.
K. K. Patel	202	Madhya Pradesh v Railways at Gwalior.
L. S. Rajput	239	Assam v Tripura at Guwahati.
W. V. Raman (2)	206	Tamil Nadu v Kerala at Madras.
	226	Tamil Nadu v Haryana at Faridabad.
A. Ranatunga	200*	Sinhalese SC v Sebastianites C and AC at Colombo.
Ajay Sharma	259*	Delhi v Bombay at Bombay.
R. J. Shastri	206	India v Australia at Sydney.
P. V. Simmons	202	Trinidad & Tobago v Guyana at Pointe-à-Pierre.
S. S. Tanna	253*	Saurashtra v Baroda at Rajkot.
D. B. Vengsarkar	284	Bombay v Madhya Pradesh at Bombay.
K. C. Wessels	212	Eastern Province v Griqualand West at Cradock.
V. S. Yadav	201	North Zone v South Zone at Surat.
Zahir Alam	257	Assam v Tripura at Gauhati.

Hundred on First-Class Début

R. Bittu	131*	Himachal Pradesh v Services at Dharamsala.
M. L. Hayden	149	Queensland v South Australia at Brisbane.
G. G. Khoda	116	Rajasthan v Uttar Pradesh at Lucknow.
A. G. Lawson	117*	Border v Orange Free State at Bloemfontein.
J. P. B. Mulder	119	Western Transvaal v Griqualand West at Kimberley.
B. A. Nash	129*	Natal B v Orange Free State B at Durban.
J. V. Paranjpe	106	Bombay v Gujarat at Surat.
Rizwan Umar	151	Sargodha v Karachi Whites at Karachi.

Three or More Hundreds in Successive Innings

S. S. Bhave (Maharashtra) . . . . 117 v Bombay at Bombay, 229 v Bihar at Pune, 231* v Haryana at Pune.

R. S. Dravid (Karnataka) . . . . 134 v Bengal at Calcutta (1990-91), 126 v Goa at Kolar Gold Fields, 128 v Kerala at Bijapur.

M. P. Maynard (Northern Districts) 142 v Otago at Hamilton, 195 and 110 v Auckland at Auckland.

W. V. Raman (Tamil Nadu) . . . . . . 110 v Uttar Pradesh at Kanpur, 226 and 120 v Haryana at Faridabad.

Robin Singh (Tamil Nadu) .... 123* South Zone v West Zone at Rourkela (1990-91),
100* v Kerala at Madras, 121* v Goa at Madras.
M. V. Sridhar (Hyderabad) (4) ..... 112* v Bihar at Ranchi (1990-91), 184 v Bombay
at Bombay (1990-91), 140 v Goa at Panjim, 105 v
Andhra at Secunderabad.

Hundred in Each Innings of a Match

A. Malhotra	151	101*	Bengal v Orissa at Baripada.
M. P. Maynard	195	110	Northern Districts v Auckland at Auckland.
S. M. Patil	157	119	Madhya Pradesh v Uttar Pradesh at Indore.
W. V. Raman	226	120	Tamil Nadu v Haryana at Faridabad.
K. C. Wessels	115	147*	Eastern Province v OFS at Port Elizabeth.

Hundred Before Lunch

D. N. Patel .... 139* Auckland v Northern Districts at Auckland (3rd day).

Carrying Bat Through Completed Innings

S. S. Bhave	231*	Maharashtra (557) v Haryana at Pune.
R. Bittu	131*	Himachal Pradesh (222) v Services at Dharamsala.
A. G. Lawson	117*	Border (250) v Orange Free State at Bloemfontein.
T. N. Lazard	108*	W. Province (220) v N. Transvaal at Verwoerdburg.
W. E. Schonegevel	96*	Griqualand West (252) v E. Province at Cradock.
D. Sudhakar Reddy (2)†	91*	Andhra (251) v Kerala at Calicut.
	30*	Andhra (94) v Kerala at Calicut.
S. S. Tanna	253*	Saurashtra (499) v Baroda at Rajkot.
M. R. J. Veletta	101*	Western Australia (252) v New South Wales at Sydney.

† *In the same match.*

First-Wicket Partnership of 100 in Each Innings

129 127 Rizwan-uz-Zaman/Ameer-ud-Din, Karachi Blues v Multan at Sahiwal.
111 107 Ghulam Ali/Abdullah Khan, PACO v Combined Universities at Lahore.

Other Notable Partnerships

First Wicket
264 M. Yachad/P. H. Barnard, Northern Transvaal v Border at East London.

Second Wicket
475† Zahir Alam/L. S. Rajput, Assam v Tripura at Guwahati.
302 W. N. Phillips/D. M. Jones, Victoria v South Australia at Melbourne.
291 Shahid Saeed/Aamer Malik, Lahore City v Bahawalpur at Lahore.
287 Abhijit P. Deshpande/S. V. Jedhe, Maharashtra v Gujarat at Valsad.
284 Abdul Azeem/M. V. Sridhar, Hyderabad v Andhra at Secunderabad.
253 P. G. Amm/K. C. Wessels, Eastern Province v Boland at Worcester.

Third Wicket
405 A. D. Jadeja/A. S. Kaypee, Haryana v Services at Faridabad.
346 G. P. Burnett/R. A. Verry, Wellington v Northern Districts at Hamilton.

Fourth Wicket
327 V. G. Kambli/Iqbal Khan, Bombay v Saurashtra at Bombay.
287 A. Malhotra/R. Venkatraman, Bengal v Orissa at Baripada.
280 J. J. Crowe/D. N. Patel, Auckland v Northern Districts at Auckland.
280 S. S. Bhave/M. D. Gunjal, Maharashtra v Bihar at Pune.
259 R. Bora/S. K. Kulkarni, Assam v Bihar at Ranchi.
258 M. C. Venter/M. Michau, Eastern Province v Natal at Durban.

Fifth Wicket
263   Yashpal Sharma/Abhay Sharma, Railways v Vidarbha at Nagpur.
253   S. G. Gujar/ U. I. Gani, Vidarbha v Madhya Pradesh at Nagpur.

Sixth Wicket
242*   K. S. McEwan/D. H. Howell, Border v Transvaal at East London.

Seventh Wicket
205   L. K. Germon/M. W. Priest, Canterbury v Northern Districts at Christchurch.
200   Kapil Dev/C. S. Pandit, Indians v Queensland at Brisbane.

Eighth Wicket
206   Ajay Sharma/V. Razdan, Delhi v Tamil Nadu at Delhi.
154   G. E. Bradburn/S. B. Doull, Northern Districts v Canterbury at Christchurch.

Ninth Wicket
196   R. P. Singh/Gopal Sharma, Uttar Pradesh v Rajasthan at Lucknow.
185   M. P. Maynard/S. B. Doull, Northern Districts v Auckland at Auckland.

Tenth Wicket
233   Ajay Sharma/Maninder Singh, Delhi v Bombay at Bombay.
139   V. S. Yadav/Maninder Singh, North Zone v South Zone at Surat.

  * *Unbroken partnership.*   † *World record.*

Out Handled the Ball

M. J. Davis . . . .   Northern Transvaal B v Orange Free State B at Bloemfontein.
Pradeep Bali . . . .   Jammu and Kashmir v Services at Delhi.
J. T. C. Vaughan . . . .   New Zealand Emerging Players v England XI at Hamilton.

Twelve or More Wickets in a Match

P. L. A. W. N. Alwis.   12-146   Antonians SC v Sebastianites C and AC at Moratuwa.
Arshad Ayub.   12-141   Hyderabad v Andhra at Secunderabad.
G. Dutta   14-96   Assam v Tripura at Guwahati.
Iqbal Sikandar   14-94   Karachi Whites v Bahawalpur at Bahawalpur.
Kabir Khan.   12-132   Peshawar v Karachi Blues at Peshawar.
Masood Anwar   12-47   United Bank v Combined Universities at Lahore.
Mohammad Hasnain   12-116   Karachi Blues v Sargodha at Sargodha.
Mohsin Mirza   13-140   Karachi Whites v Karachi Blues at Karachi.
B. A. Reid.   12-126   Australia v India at Melbourne.
Tanvir Mehdi   12-162   Lahore v Bahawalpur at Lahore.
G. P. Wickremasinghe   13-87   Sinhalese SC v Kalutara PCC at Colombo.

Eight or More Wickets in an Innings

Ata-ur-Rehman   8-87   PACO v Combined Universities at Lahore.
G. Dutta   9-52   Assam v Tripura at Guwahati.
Mohammad Hasnain   8-61   Karachi Blues v Sargodha at Sargodha.
Mohsin Mirza   8-92   Karachi Whites v Karachi Blues at Karachi.
Naved Anjum   9-45   Habib Bank v National Bank at Lahore.
G. P. Wickremasinghe   10-41   Sinhalese SC v Kalutara PCC at Colombo.

Hat-Tricks

U. Chandana. . . . .   Tamil Union C and AC v Old Cambrians SC at Moratuwa.
A. Kumble. . . . .   Karnataka v Andhra at Vishakhapatnam.
Mohsin Kamal . . . .   PNSC v United Bank at Karachi.
R. P. Singh . . . .   Uttar Pradesh v Vidarbha at Kanpur.

Most Overs Bowled in a Match

110-26-265-6..... Arshad Ayub   Hyderabad v Madhya Pradesh at Secunderabad.

Most Overs Bowled in an Innings

98-24-203-5	Arshad Ayub	Hyderabad v Madhya Pradesh at Secunderabad.
92-18-210-6	R. K. Chauhan	Madhya Pradesh v Railways at Gwalior.
80.5-28-140-3	S. S. Lahore	Madhya Pradesh v Railways at Gwalior.
77-26-117-4	P. Sushil Kumar	Orissa v Bihar at Sambalpur.

Nine Wicket-Keeping Dismissals in a Match

R. V. Jennings (2)	(9 ct)	Northern Transvaal v Transvaal at Johannesburg.
	(9 ct)	Northern Transvaal v Western Province at Verwoerdburg.
R. J. Ryall	(9 ct)	Western Province v Northern Transvaal at Verwoerdburg.

Six Wicket-Keeping Dismissals in an Innings

D. S. Berry (2)	(6 ct)	Victoria v Queensland at Brisbane.
	(6 ct)	Victoria v Queensland at Melbourne.
I. A. Healy	(5 ct, 1 st)	Australian XI v West Indians at Hobart.
R. D. Jacobs	(6 ct)	Leeward Islands v Barbados at Bridgetown.
R. V. Jennings	(6 ct)	Northern Transvaal v Western Province at Verwoerdburg.
S. S. Karim	(5 ct, 1 st)	East Zone v West Zone at Bombay.
B. McBride	(6 ct)	Transvaal v Natal at Durban.
B. Randall	(4 ct, 2 st)	Eastern Transvaal v Griqualand West at Kimberley.
R. J. Ryall	(5 ct, 1 st)	Western Province v Eastern Province at Port Elizabeth.
Wasim Arif	(4 ct, 2 st)	National Bank v Habib Bank at Lahore.

Five Catches in an Innings in the Field

D. N. Crookes	Natal v Northamptonshire at Durban.
R. C. Haynes	Jamaica v Barbados at Bridgetown.
K. Srikkanth	India v Australia at Perth.

Match Double (100 Runs and 10 Wickets)

Asif Mujtaba	105, 22*; 5-76, 5-47	Karachi Whites v Rawalpindi at Karachi.
P. D. de Vaal	100*; 3-32, 7-94	Eastern Transvaal v Western Transvaal at Potchefstroom.
G. R. J. Matthews ...	85*, 67; 6-63, 5-70	New South Wales v Queensland at Sydney.
Naved Anjum	115; 9-45, 1-20	Habib Bank v National Bank at Lahore.
D. N. Patel	6, 204; 6-117, 4-116	Auckland v Northern Districts at Auckland.
J. C. Scuderi	110; 7-79, 3-86	South Australia v New South Wales at Adelaide.

No Byes Conceded in Total of 500 or More

T. J. Nielsen	South Australia v Queensland (588-5 dec.) at Brisbane.
R. Vivekanand	Andhra v Hyderabad (575-6 dec.) at Secunderabad.
S. S. Dighe	Bombay v Delhi (574) at Bombay.
S. M. H. Kirmani....	Karnataka v Hyderabad (563) at Secunderabad.
B. K. Patel	Gujarat v Bombay (554-4 dec.) at Surat.
T. J. Nielsen	South Australia v Victoria (514-8 dec.) at Melbourne.
I. A. Healy	Queensland v South Australia (506-6) at Adelaide.

Highest Innings Totals

757-7 dec. ... Maharashtra v Bihar at Pune.
721-8 dec. ... Bombay v Madhya Pradesh at Bombay.
684-7 dec. ... Assam v Tripura at Gauhati.
682-9 dec. ... West Zone v East Zone at Bombay.
673-9 dec. ... Haryana v Maharashtra at Pune.
649-9 dec. ... Assam v Bihar at Ranchi.
641-9 dec. ... Bombay v Maharashtra at Bombay.
633 .... Delhi v Bengal at Delhi.
628 .... Tamil Nadu v Uttar Pradesh at Kanpur.
604-7 dec. ... Tamil Nadu v Goa at Madras.
603-8 dec. ... Karnataka v Kerala at Bijapur.
600-6 dec. ... Tamil Nadu v Kerala at Madras.

Some Indian totals include penalty runs for slow over-rate.

Highest Fourth-Innings Total

506-6 .... South Australia v Queensland at Adelaide (the highest total to win a first-class match in Australia, and the second-highest to win in all first-class matches).

Lowest Innings Totals

54 .... Karachi Blues v Sargodha at Sargodha.
54 .... Combined Universities v United Bank at Lahore.
64 .... Orissa v Bihar at Sambalpur.
69 .... Jammu and Kashmir v Haryana at Bhiwani.
71 .... Western Australia v New South Wales at Sydney.
72 .... Auckland v Northern Districts at Rotorua.
74 .... Tripura v Bihar at Agartala.
74 .... Rawalpindi v Bahawalpur at Bahawalpur.

Highest Match Aggregate

Runs-Wkts
1,526-33 .. Bombay v Delhi at Bombay.

50 Extras in an Innings

	b	l-b	w	n-b	
78	1	16	1	60†	South Australia (554) v Queensland at Brisbane.
64	0	22	16	26	Eastern Province B (365) v Transvaal B at Johannesburg.
62	11	10	23	18	Delhi (569-6 dec.) v Jammu and Kashmir at Delhi.
55	6	15	2	32	Delhi (532) v Tamil Nadu at Delhi.
53	5	9	1	38†	Western Australia (509-8 dec.) v Queensland at Perth.
51	15	13	0	23	Uttar Pradesh (496-5 dec.) v Vidarbha at Kanpur.
50	11	11	13	15	Delhi (315) v Punjab at Amritsar.
50	26	12	2	10	West Indies A (241-9 dec.) v England A at Port-of-Spain.

† *Under Australian Cricket Board playing conditions, two extras were scored for every no-ball, excluding runs scored off the delivery. The total of 78 extras in South Australia's innings thus exceeded the world record of 74 for British Guiana v W. Shepherd's XI at Georgetown in 1909-10; under normal playing conditions, only 40 extras would have been recorded by South Australia.*

THE BENSON AND HEDGES WORLD CUP, 1991-92

After the manner of the Olympic Games, cricket's World Cup quadrennially grows larger and more spectacular. The event, staged in Australia (25 matches) and New Zealand (14 matches) in 1992, featured, for the first time, all eight Test-playing teams, with aspiring Zimbabwe taking the number of competing sides to an unprecedented nine. The final was the 39th match. The first two tournaments, in 1975 and 1979 in England, featured only 15 matches, while in 1983 (England) and 1987 (India and Pakistan) there were 27.

The fifth World Cup was the first to be played in coloured clothing, with a white ball and some games under floodlights. Although it was again 50 overs a side rather than the original 60, it was generally considered to have been the fairest: each side played all the others once before the top four in the qualifying table played off in the semi-finals. Lasting 33 days from first ball to last, it could be faulted seriously only in the matter of the rules governing rain-interrupted matches.

Recognising the imperfection of a straight run-rate calculation when a second innings has to be shortened after rain, and unable to schedule spare days within the time-frame of the tournament, the World Cup committee adopted a scheme whereby the reduction in the target would be commensurate with the lowest-scoring overs of the side which batted first. Against South Africa in Melbourne, England lost nine overs but their target of 237 was reduced by only 11 runs. When the teams next met, in the Sydney semi-final, another rain pause, this time at the climactic moment, led to an uproar which echoed for weeks afterwards.

Pakistan won the World Cup for the first time, beating England (twice previous finalists, never winners) by 22 runs on a memorably dramatic autumn night in Melbourne, before an Australian limited-overs record crowd of 87,182 who paid \$A2 million (£880,000). Almost half of them sat in the newly completed Great Southern Stand, which cost \$A140 million and is the largest construction ever conceived for Australian sport. It was further claimed that the global television audience exceeded one billion, in 29 countries. In Pakistan, where it was still early evening, jubilation verging on the hysterical splashed over into the streets, and upon their return the players were placed on the highest pedestals of heroism.

Imran Khan, the captain, in his 40th year and nursing a troublesome right shoulder, unsurprisingly declared this as his finest hour, a claim clearly supported by the pictures of him holding the £7,500 Waterford crystal trophy, eyes wide with exhilaration, after ICC chairman Sir Colin Cowdrey had presented it to him on the MCG dais. This accomplished all-rounder, top-scorer in the final with a measured 72, had urged his young team on through times when it seemed that qualification for the semi-finals was out of the question. They were, he said, to take on the stance and response of the cornered tiger. He dedicated the victory to the cause of a cancer hospital in Lahore for which he was fund-raising in memory of his mother. The World Cup organisers seemed content to overlook Imran's earlier remark that it was the worst-organised of all the World Cups. He and Javed Miandad (who became the highest overall run-scorer) alone have played in all five tournaments.

Excitement was high from the opening day, when New Zealand caused the first upset by beating Australia, the holders and favourites, by a comfortable margin at Auckland. Led by Martin Crowe, who made a century, New Zealand were initiating a remarkable run of victories on their slow pitches, Patel bowling off-spin at the start of the innings, followed by a bevy of harmless-looking medium-pacers challenging batsmen to come at them. Crowe's brilliant batsmanship and imaginative command in the field, augmented by the shameless six-hitting of opener Greatbatch, who earned a place only when Wright was injured, took New Zealand almost to the ultimate glory. The co-hosts won their first seven matches, and were not harmed by defeat (by Pakistan) in the eighth, for it assured them of a home semi-final. The sub-plots were multiple, for Pakistan, through this victory at Christchurch, managed to reach the semi-finals . . . so long as Australia (who had just lost their last chance) beat West Indies at Melbourne a few hours later. Boon's century, his second of the series, and Whitney's four wickets ensured this, putting West Indies out of the competition too.

Australia had started as favourites, but their approach was too inflexible and their form too fickle. New strategies had not so much passed them by as struck no receptive chords in captain Allan Border or coach Bob Simpson. There had been a reluctance to drop the faithful Marsh, who was taking far too much time over his runs, and Simon O'Donnell, voted top player the previous season, was not even chosen in the squad. The nation was mortified as the defeats piled up, the only victory in Australia's first four matches coming by a solitary run in the most thrilling of all the finishes: at Brisbane, when the last ball seemed successively to be a winning boundary for India, then a catch, then again a spillage into the boundary gutter, with Steve Waugh's long recovery throw perhaps too wide, but gathered by substitute wicket-keeper Boon, who made ground to beat the batsman by a few inches. Towards the end of the competition, Australians had been compelled to adopt other allegiances, with no small amount of sympathy being extended South Africa's way.

Readmitted to the international brotherhood after 21 years of political isolation, South Africa, led by Bloemfontein-born former Australian Test batsman Kepler Wessels, were an unpredictable commodity. They had won one of their three introductory limited-overs matches in India in some style three months previously. Now, overseen by coach Mike Procter, one of the world's greatest cricketers at the time of South Africa's expulsion, and spearheaded by the speedy Donald, they stepped coolly on to the stage and beat Australia by nine wickets before a clamorous crowd of almost 40,000 at Sydney, proportionate noise issuing from the throats of hundreds of South African supporters, some of them now resident in Australia. Wessels's partner at the end was Peter Kirsten, who was left out of the original tour squad but was to average 68.33 in the preliminary matches.

Setbacks against New Zealand and Sri Lanka were put behind them as South Africa won their historic encounter with West Indies in a cordially-conducted match at Christchurch, following this with a rain-assisted victory over Pakistan at Brisbane, where Jonty Rhodes, already having attracted notice by his electrifying fielding, immortalised himself with an airborne demolition of the stumps to run out Inzamam-ul-Haq. Their place in the semi-finals was secured with victory over India in a shortened match at Adelaide, only for their campaign to be ended cruelly by the sudden heavy shower which fell on the SCG just before 10 p.m., transforming a requirement of 22 off 13 balls to a mocking 21 off one. The crowd's frustration and hostility focused upon the England players in lieu of the

UP FOR THE CUP ...

"... and if you break next door's satellite dish again – you're out."

© Bryan McAllister

'I bought these South African oranges because I felt so guilty about the cricket'

[From The Best of Matt 1992, courtesy Telegraph Books]

Cartoonists' views of the World Cup and the controversial semi-final: Bryan McAllister of *The Guardian* (right) and Matt of the *Daily Telegraph* (far right).

rule-makers, while the South Africans absorbed their acute disappointment with a dignified and somehow joyous lap of honour. Beyond the bounds of cricket, it was believed that their success in the tournament had had an influence on the crucial referendum which decided whether President de Klerk's reforms were to be continued. Support for his progressive dismantling of apartheid was shown in a substantial majority of the white population's votes, some of it unquestionably swayed by live pictures from the far side of the Indian Ocean which showed the national team competing popularly and successfully after having been excommunicated for so long.

The odds after two weeks of competition were affected by the vacillating form most particularly of India and West Indies, both past winners. Reshaped after the jettisoning of several senior players, and led by an out-of-touch Richie Richardson, West Indies won their first match convincingly by making 221 without losing a wicket. This was not against the lesser Zimbabwe or Sri Lanka. It was against Pakistan, the eventual champions. Thereafter they seemed out of sorts, though Brian Lara, the flowery left-hander, finished with four half-centuries. India lost a tight opening match against England, beat Pakistan, who fell apart under the Sydney lights, but were themselves soon to fall by the wayside through poor fielding and an indecisiveness in all departments.

Sri Lanka managed two victories, scoring 313 at New Plymouth to deny Zimbabwe what had seemed a certain triumph given the weight of their own innings, centurion Andy Flower having had his effort capitalised by Andy Waller's 32-ball half-century. Sri Lanka's other success was against South Africa at Wellington, when Ranatunga steered them home by three wickets with only a ball to spare.

The most unexpected result came on the last day of the qualifying matches, when Zimbabwe, having made only 134 on a sporting pitch at Albury, overthrew England by nine runs, Eddo Brandes taking the bowling honours. England could afford to lose, as was the case in their previous match, against New Zealand, although the long run of success which began when they landed in New Zealand for their Test-match tour as the year opened was now broken and in urgent need of repair, particularly as several key players were carrying injuries. The somewhat fortuitous semi-final victory over South Africa restored their direction even if it could not dispel the accumulated weariness. In retrospect, they might have looked back upon their crushing defeat of Australia as their sweetest moment.

Graham Gooch's combination became favourites when Australia began to crack. The depth of batting and breadth of bowling alternatives made possible by so many all-rounders, together with the blend of experience and, in key positions, athleticism in the field, gave England the appearance of certain finalists and probable trophy-winners. Fatigue and Pakistan's inspired surge were to deny them on the night.

Not unexpectedly, the World Cup was given wide coverage in Australasia, though Channel 9's television cameras were installed only at venues where the organisers felt the interest would be greatest. Matches which they did cover were comprehensively treated, although this was of little comfort to the legions of cricket enthusiasts in Britain who had no access to the BSkyB satellite television reception which was beamed almost around the clock. Apart from two-minute news segments, only half an hour of highlights of the final was shown on BBC TV. Some of the lower-shelf fixtures were staged in rural areas, Albury's reward being the historic upset when Zimbabwe beat England, contrasting with Mackay's fate after all the months of preparation, which was a washout after two balls.

The emergence of new faces was refreshing. Hudson, Snell and Pringle from South Africa, Lara from West Indies, Inzamam-ul-Haq, Mushtaq Ahmed and Aamir Sohail from Pakistan all made a mark, five of them still not Test players. And electrifying incidents were captured not only in the television replays but subsequently in the proliferation of commemorative video-cassettes. Rhodes's flying run-out at Brisbane was memorable, but wicket-keeper More's back-flick to run out Crowe at Dunedin may well have been the most extraordinary dismissal of all. Not that Border's throwing accuracy, such as when he ran out Azharuddin at Brisbane, will soon be forgotten, or the stumping of Harris from a Mushtaq Ahmed wide, or the demolition of Botham's middle stump (which contained the miniature TV camera) by McMillan, or some of Healy's catches behind the wicket, or Mushtaq's googly to defeat Hick and Wasim Akram's wicked in-swinger to bowl Lewis in the final.

The pool of umpires from the competing nations brought an added flavour of internationalism without quite ensuring the exclusion of errors, some of them quite glaring. Messrs Bucknor and Shepherd were generally regarded as the most reliable. The no-ball penalty for shoulder-high bouncers was not always consistently interpreted, but ensured that the matches were safeguarded from the excesses so often witnessed in the recent past, especially at Test level.

Perversely, as in 1987, neither host nation won through to the final. Seriously stunned in 1987 by their loss to Australia in the semi-final at Lahore, Pakistan somehow lifted themselves in the 1992 tournament after having won only one of their first five matches. Handicapped by the absence through injury of their outstanding fast bowler, Waqar Younis, they were spurred on by their rarefied captain, Imran Khan. As far as bowling strategy went they played aggressively throughout – and with the bat too, once the disciplined foundation had been laid. There was satisfaction in seeing the best two teams in the final, and, for the rare objective onlooker, a slight sadness that only one of them could triumph. For a month, the World Cup not only generated large profits but stirred many hearts and touched countless nerve-ends around the cricket world. – David Frith.

Note: Matches in this section were not first-class.

NEW ZEALAND v AUSTRALIA

At Auckland, February 22. New Zealand won by 37 runs. Toss: New Zealand. An unexpected result thrilled the home crowd and threw the Cup favourites into consternation. The Australians had reckoned on a sluggish pitch favouring New Zealand, but not on Crowe's sharp thinking: he gave the new ball to Patel, an off-spinner, and then juggled his attack so frequently that the batsmen never settled. Yet the home team had struggled in the morning, when the pitch retained its bounce. After two wides, McDermott bowled Wright with his first legitimate ball; Reid had Latham dropped, then trapped Jones; and Healy took a low, one-handed catch. But Rutherford added 118 in 25 overs with Crowe, who ignored a knee injury to reach his century (11 fours) with one ball to spare. Next came his gambit with the ball. New Zealand's fastest bowler, Morrison, had been omitted, and the strategy soon seemed justified; while Cairns conceded 30 from four overs, at the other end Patel unnerved Boon and Marsh so much that they took only 19 from his first seven. Constant bowling changes maintained the Australians' uncertainty, and though Boon pushed doggedly on to his hundred, the asking rate crept towards double figures. Steve Waugh's attempts to hit out were cut short with 50 needed from less than five overs. When Boon was run out, the Australians disintegrated. Their last five wickets were captured for 12 runs in 17 balls.

Man of the Match: M. D. Crowe.   *Attendance:* 22,262.

New Zealand

J. G. Wright b McDermott	0	†I. D. S. Smith c Healy b McDermott		14
R. T. Latham c Healy b Moody	26	C. L. Cairns not out		16
A. H. Jones lbw b Reid	4	L-b 6, w 7, n-b 4		17
*M. D. Crowe not out	100			
K. R. Rutherford run out	57	1/2 2/13 3/53	(6 wkts, 50 overs)	248
C. Z. Harris run out	14	4/171 5/191 6/215		

D. N. Patel, G. R. Larsen and W. Watson did not bat.

Bowling: McDermott 10-1-43-2; Reid 10-0-39-1; Moody 9-1-37-1; S. R. Waugh 10-0-60-0; Taylor 7-0-36-0; M. E. Waugh 4-0-27-0.

Australia

D. C. Boon run out	100	C. J. McDermott run out		1
G. R. Marsh c Latham b Larsen	19	P. L. Taylor c Rutherford b Watson		1
D. M. Jones run out	21	B. A. Reid c Jones b Harris		3
*A. R. Border c Cairns b Patel	3	L-b 6, w 2, n-b 1		9
T. M. Moody c and b Latham	7			
M. E. Waugh lbw b Larsen	2	1/62 2/92 3/104	(48.1 overs)	211
S. R. Waugh c and b Larsen	38	4/120 5/125 6/199		
†I. A. Healy not out	7	7/200 8/205 9/206		

Bowling: Cairns 4-0-30-0; Patel 10-1-36-1; Watson 9-1-39-1; Larsen 10-1-30-3; Harris 7.1-0-35-1; Latham 8-0-35-1.

Umpires: Khizar Hayat and D. R. Shepherd.

ENGLAND v INDIA

At Perth, February 22 (day/night). England won by nine runs. Toss: England. Ian Botham, at his most irrepressible, won this game for England, though the margin was narrower than might have been expected for much of the game. With an over to go – after Banerjee had lifted Pringle's last ball for six – India needed 11 to win and appeared to have momentum on their side. However, the last of four run-outs, by Botham, settled the result two balls later. Most of the England players had trouble adjusting to the pace of Perth after playing in New Zealand, struggling with the bat or bowling too short. But Gooch, after a scratchy start, marked his 100th one-day international with 51, and Smith hit 91 in 108 balls, including two sixes pulled over the 90-yard mid-wicket boundary. After Fairbrother was out England lost six wickets in five overs. India's reply rested on contrasting innings from their openers: Srikkanth blazed briefly with seven fours in his 39; Shastri hit only two fours in two and a half hours. Finally, he offered a steepling return catch to DeFreitas, who dropped it but threw down the stumps, a manoeuvre that typified the resourcefulness of England's fielding.

Man of the Match: I. T. Botham.   *Attendance:* 12,902.

England

*G. A. Gooch c Tendulkar b Shastri	51	D. A. Reeve not out	8
I. T. Botham c More b Kapil Dev	9	P. A. J. DeFreitas run out	1
R. A. Smith c Azharuddin b Prabhakar	91	P. C. R. Tufnell not out	3
G. A. Hick c More b Banerjee	5	B 1, l-b 6, w 13	20
N. H. Fairbrother c Srikkanth b Srinath	24		
†A. J. Stewart b Prabhakar	13	1/21 2/131 3/137 (9 wkts, 50 overs)	236
C. C. Lewis c Banerjee b Kapil Dev	10	4/197 5/198 6/214	
D. R. Pringle c Srikkanth b Srinath	1	7/222 8/223 9/224	

Bowling: Kapil Dev 10–0–38–2; Prabhakar 10–3–34–2; Srinath 9–1–47–2; Banerjee 7–0–45–1; Tendulkar 10–0–37–0; Shastri 4–0–28–1.

India

R. J. Shastri run out	57	†K. S. More run out	1
K. Srikkanth c Botham b DeFreitas	39	M. Prabhakar b Reeve	0
*M. Azharuddin c Stewart b Reeve	0	J. Srinath run out	11
S. R. Tendulkar c Stewart b Botham	35	L-b 9, w 7, n-b 1	17
V. G. Kambli c Hick b Botham	3		
P. K. Amre run out	22	1/63 2/63 3/126 (49.2 overs)	227
Kapil Dev c DeFreitas b Reeve	17	4/140 5/149 6/187	
S. T. Banerjee not out	25	7/194 8/200 9/201	

Bowling: Pringle 10–0–53–0; Lewis 9.2–0–36–0; DeFreitas 10–0–39–1; Reeve 6–0–38–3; Botham 10–0–27–2; Tufnell 4–0–25–0.

Umpires: J. D. Buultjens and P. J. McConnell.

SRI LANKA v ZIMBABWE

At New Plymouth, February 23. Sri Lanka won by three wickets. Toss: Sri Lanka. Away from the limelight, the Cup's least-fancied teams staged a record-breaking encounter. The bare pitch and short boundaries of Pukekura Park helped them both to reach 300 for the first time in a limited-overs international, and no other team had passed that mark batting second. Their aggregate was one short of the 626 shared by Pakistan and Sri Lanka at Swansea in 1983. Of the 12 bowlers, only Traicos, the 44-year-old off-spinner, emerged with respectable figures. Zimbabwe's opener, Flower, scored an unbeaten 115 and earned the match award on his full international début. He was supported first by Arnott, and then Waller in an unbroken fifth-wicket stand of 145 – a World Cup record – in 13 overs. Waller's 83 took a mere 45 balls (three sixes, nine fours), and his 32-ball 50 was also a Cup record. Zimbabwe looked forward to the second win that had eluded them since 1983, but the Sri Lankans were undaunted. Mahanama and Samarasekera (50 in 33 balls) opened with 128, and though the middle order faltered, Ranatunga (61 balls) approached his task with relish, securing victory with his ninth four.

Man of the Match: A. Flower.   *Attendance:* 3,100.

Zimbabwe

†A. Flower not out	115	K. J. Arnott c Tillekeratne	
W. R. James c Tillekeratne		b Wickremasinghe	52
b Wickremasinghe	17	A. C. Waller not out	83
A. J. Pycroft c Ramanayake		B 2, l-b 6, w 13, n-b 9	30
b Gurusinha	5		
*D. L. Houghton c Tillekeratne		1/30 2/57 (4 wkts, 50 overs)	312
b Gurusinha	10	3/82 4/167	

K. G. Duers, I. P. Butchart, E. A. Brandes, M. P. Jarvis and A. J. Traicos did not bat.

Bowling: Ramanayake 10–0–59–0; Wijegunawardene 7–0–54–0; Wickremasinghe 10–1–50–2; Gurusinha 10–0–72–2; Kalpage 10–0–51–0; Jayasuriya 3–0–18–0.

Sri Lanka

R. S. Mahanama c Arnott b Brandes	.. 59		R. S. Kalpage c Duers b Brandes	11
M. A. R. Samarasekera c Duers			C. P. H. Ramanayake not out	1
	b Traicos . 75			
*P. A. de Silva c Houghton b Brandes	. 14		L-b 5, w 5	10
A. P. Gurusinha run out	5			—
A. Ranatunga not out	88		1/128 2/144 3/155 (7 wkts, 49.2 overs) 313	
S. T. Jayasuriya c Flower b Houghton	.. 32		4/167 5/212	
†H. P. Tillekeratne b Jarvis	18		6/273 7/309	

K. I. W. Wijegunawardene and G. P. Wickremasinghe did not bat.

Bowling: Jarvis 9.2–0–61–1; Brandes 10–0–70–3; Duers 10–0–72–0; Butchart 8–0–53–0; Traicos 10–1–33–1; Houghton 2–0–19–1.

Umpires: P. D. Reporter and S. J. Woodward.

PAKISTAN v WEST INDIES

At Melbourne, February 23. West Indies won by ten wickets. Toss: West Indies. The West Indians returned to form, overhauling Pakistan's 220 without losing a wicket. Their only disappointment was that Lara, who had responded to the opener's job with his highest score in limited-overs internationals, missed the chance of a hundred when Wasim Akram's yorker struck his right foot. He had struck 11 fours and faced 101 balls, whereas Haynes contributed a more stately 93 from 144 and offered three chances. The winning runs, however, were provided by Aqib Javed, whose two bouncers were called as no-balls. Pakistan were without their captain, Imran Khan, who was injured. His deputy, Javed Miandad, pleased the crowd with a lively 57 from 61 balls, and shared an unbroken stand of 123 with Ramiz Raja. They took 81 from their last ten overs, Ramiz finally cutting loose, but Pakistan paid for their slow scoring earlier. In keeping with the tournament's unexpected fashion, Richardson bowled his off-spinners, Hooper and Harper, in tandem for 13 overs, enabling West Indies to complete their 50 overs half an hour ahead of schedule.

Man of the Match: B. C. Lara.   *Attendance:* 14,162.

Pakistan

Ramiz Raja not out	102
Aamir Sohail c Logie b Benjamin	23
Inzamam-ul-Haq c Hooper b Harper	27
*Javed Miandad not out	57
B 1, l-b 3, w 5, n-b 2	11

1/45 2/97   (2 wkts, 50 overs) 220

Salim Malik, Ijaz Ahmed, †Moin Khan, Wasim Akram, Iqbal Sikandar, Wasim Haider and Aqib Javed did not bat.

Bowling: Marshall 10–1–53–0; Ambrose 10–0–40–0; Benjamin 10–0–49–1; Hooper 10–0–41–0; Harper 10–0–33–1.

West Indies

D. L. Haynes not out	93
B. C. Lara retired hurt	88
*R. B. Richardson not out	20
B 2, l-b 8, w 7, n-b 3	20

(no wkt, 46.5 overs) 221

C. L. Hooper, K. L. T. Arthurton, A. L. Logie, R. A. Harper, M. D. Marshall, †D. Williams, C. E. L. Ambrose and W. K. M. Benjamin did not bat.

B. C. Lara retired hurt at 175.

Bowling: Wasim Akram 10–0–37–0; Aqib Javed 8.5–0–42–0; Wasim Haider 8–0–42–0; Ijaz Ahmed 6–1–29–0; Iqbal Sikandar 8–1–26–0; Aamir Sohail 6–0–35–0.

Umpires: S. G. Randell and I. D. Robinson.

NEW ZEALAND v SRI LANKA

At Hamilton, February 25. New Zealand won by six wickets. Toss: New Zealand. New Zealand were guided home on a grassless pitch by Rutherford, who was missed by Ranatunga at slip before scoring, but went on to his second consecutive fifty. Mahanama also continued his good form, though he enjoyed less solid support. De Silva and Ranatunga helped him take the score to 172, but the lower order could add only 34 in the last ten overs. Wright started well, despite injuring his shoulder in the field, but the slow left-arm of Anurasiri and the off-spin of Kalpage put the brakes on and they restricted Crowe to five runs in ten overs. He was caught at long leg trying to force the pace when Wickremasinghe returned, but that brought in Rutherford, whose stand of 81 with Jones was the highest of the game. Afterwards Sri Lanka, who had already lost their strike bowler Ratnayake with a dislocated shoulder, were given permission to add Graeme Labrooy to their squad.

Man of the Match: K. R. Rutherford.   *Attendance*: 8,268.

Sri Lanka

R. S. Mahanama c and b Harris	80	C. P. H. Ramanayake run out	2
M. A. R. Samarasekera c Wright		S. D. Anurasiri not out	3
b Watson	9	G. P. Wickremasinghe not out	3
A. P. Gurusinha c Smith b Harris	9		
*P. A. de Silva run out	31	B 1, l-b 15, w 4, n-b 5	25
A. Ranatunga c Rutherford b Harris	20		
S. T. Jayasuriya run out	5	1/18 2/50 3/120 (9 wkts, 50 overs) 206	
†H. P. Tillekeratne c Crowe b Watson	8	4/172 5/172 6/181	
R. S. Kalpage c Larsen b Watson	11	7/195 8/199 9/202	

Bowling: Morrison 8-0-36-0; Watson 10-0-37-3; Larsen 10-1-29-0; Harris 10-0-43-3; Latham 3-0-13-0; Patel 9-0-32-0.

New Zealand

J. G. Wright c and b Kalpage	57	C. Z. Harris not out	5
R. T. Latham b Kalpage	20		
A. H. Jones c Jayasuriya b Gurusinha	49	L-b 3, w 3, n-b 3	9
*M. D. Crowe c Ramanayake			
b Wickremasinghe	5	1/77 2/91 (4 wkts, 48.2 overs) 210	
K. R. Rutherford not out	65	3/105 4/186	

D. N. Patel, †I. D. S. Smith, D. K. Morrison, G. R. Larsen and W. Watson did not bat.

Bowling: Ramanayake 9.2-0-46-0; Wickremasinghe 8-1-40-1; Anurasiri 10-1-27-0; Kalpage 10-0-33-2; Gurusinha 4-0-19-1; Ranatunga 4-0-22-0; Jayasuriya 2-0-14-0; de Silva 1-0-6-0.

Umpires: P. D. Reporter and D. R. Shepherd.

AUSTRALIA v SOUTH AFRICA

At Sydney, February 26 (day/night). South Africa won by nine wickets. Toss: Australia. South Africa returned to the ground where they played their first Test in Australia, in 1910-11, and their last, in 1963-64, and won their first World Cup match with ease. Their captain, Wessels, the former Australian player, was hugged by his opposite number and former team-mate Border after hitting the winning run. But the match had a disheartening start for the returning prodigals. Donald's first ball appeared to find the edge of Marsh's bat before reaching the wicket-keeper, but umpire Aldridge thought not. The visitors' calm in disappointment was rewarded when no Australian reached 30: only Boon looked comfortable. South Africa's medium-pacers took control, and Kuiper removed Marsh and Border with consecutive balls. The fielding, in particular that of Rhodes at cover, was universally praised. In contrast the Australians bowled and fielded untidily, and were quite unable to defend a mediocre total of 170. They were further hampered by the loss of Healy, who pulled a hamstring while batting; Boon took over behind the stumps. Victory secured, the South Africans returned to their dressing-room to receive messages of congratulation from President F. W. de Klerk and ANC leader Nelson Mandela, while Cup-holders Australia digested their second defeat in their opening two games.

Man of the Match: K. C. Wessels.   *Attendance*: 39,789.

Australia

G. R. Marsh c Richardson b Kuiper	25	C. J. McDermott run out	6
D. C. Boon run out	27	M. R. Whitney not out	9
D. M. Jones c Richardson b McMillan	24	B. A. Reid not out	5
*A. R. Border b Kuiper	0	L-b 2, w 11, n-b 4	17
T. M. Moody lbw b Donald	10		
S. R. Waugh c Cronje b McMillan	27	1/42 2/76 3/76 (9 wkts, 49 overs) 170	
†I. A. Healy c McMillan b Donald	16	4/97 5/108 6/143	
P. L. Taylor b Donald	4	7/146 8/156 9/161	

Bowling: Donald 10-0-34-3; Pringle 10-0-52-0; Snell 9-1-15-0; McMillan 10-0-35-2; Kuiper 5-0-15-2; Cronje 5-1-17-0.

South Africa

*K. C. Wessels not out	81
A. C. Hudson b Taylor	28
P. N. Kirsten not out	49
L-b 5, w 6, n-b 2	13

1/74   (1 wkt, 46.5 overs) 171

W. J. Cronje, A. P. Kuiper, J. N. Rhodes, B. M. McMillan, †D. J. Richardson, R. P. Snell, M. W. Pringle and A. A. Donald did not bat.

Bowling: McDermott 10-1-23-0; Reid 8.5-0-41-0; Whitney 6-0-26-0; Waugh 4-1-16-0; Taylor 10-1-32-1; Border 4-0-13-0; Moody 4-0-15-0.

Umpires: B. L. Aldridge and S. A. Bucknor.

PAKISTAN v ZIMBABWE

At Hobart, February 27. Pakistan won by 53 runs. Toss: Zimbabwe. Aamir Sohail reached his maiden hundred (136 balls, 12 fours) in one-day internationals, though four chances went down after he reached 50. The bowlers did well to restrict Pakistan to 96 from the first 30 overs, but the next 20 yielded nearly eight an over, with the veteran off-spinner Traicos uncharacteristically expensive. The charge was led by the inventive Javed Miandad, who took 89 from 94 balls and added 145 in 25 overs with Sohail. The Zimbabweans started shakily when Flower and Pycroft gave Wasim Akram his 150th and 151st wickets in limited-overs internationals. By the 20th over they were only 33 for three, but Shah and Houghton shared 70 before falling in quick succession to Sohail's left-arm spin. Far too late to matter, Waller and Butchart added 79 in nine overs. Imran Khan returned to lead Pakistan, but did not bat or bowl, and his right shoulder seemed to pain him in the field.
Man of the Match: Aamir Sohail.   *Attendance:* 1,107.

Pakistan

Ramiz Raja c Flower b Jarvis	9	Wasim Akram not out	1
Aamir Sohail c Pycroft b Butchart	114	L-b 9, n-b 4	13
Inzamam-ul-Haq c Brandes b Butchart	14		
Javed Miandad lbw b Butchart	89	1/29 2/63 (4 wkts, 50 overs) 254	
Salim Malik not out	14	3/208 4/253	

*Imran Khan, †Moin Khan, Aqib Javed, Mushtaq Ahmed and Iqbal Sikandar did not bat.

Bowling: Brandes 10-1-49-0; Jarvis 10-1-52-1; Shah 10-1-24-0; Butchart 10-0-57-3; Traicos 10-0-63-0.

Zimbabwe

K. J. Arnott c Wasim Akram	
b Iqbal Sikandar . 7	
†A. Flower b Inzamam-ul-Haq	
b Wasim Akram . 6	
A. J. Pycroft b Wasim Akram 0	
*D. L. Houghton c Ramiz Raja	
b Aamir Sohail . 44	
A. H. Shah b Aamir Sohail 33	
A. C. Waller b Wasim Akram 44	

I. P. Butchart c Javed Miandad
    b Aqib Javed . 33
E. A. Brandes not out 2
A. J. Traicos not out 8
    B 3, l-b 15, w 6 24

1/14 2/14 3/33   (7 wkts, 50 overs) 201
4/103 5/108
6/187 7/190

W. R. James and M. P. Jarvis did not bat.

Bowling: Wasim Akram 10-2-21-3; Aqib Javed 10-1-49-1; Iqbal Sikandar 10-1-35-1; Mushtaq Ahmed 10-1-34-0; Aamir Sohail 6-1-26-2; Salim Malik 4-0-18-0.

Umpires: J. D. Buultjens and S. G. Randell.

ENGLAND v WEST INDIES

At Melbourne, February 27 (day/night). England won by six wickets. Toss: England. A convincing victory, with more than ten overs to spare, was England's eighth in succession in one-day internationals, and their fourth in a row over West Indies. Four top-order batsmen went for 55 runs while the white ball was moving prodigiously for the seamers. Lara, his toe still swollen, was hit on the box by Lewis's first ball and edged the second to Stewart. When Haynes, who had held firm for 20 overs, pulled to square leg, everything depended on Arthurton and Logie. The former obliged by driving and cutting to a fifty, though he offered three chances before giving Fairbrother a second catch; the same fielder had run out Logie, looking for a leg-bye when DeFreitas appealed for lbw. West Indies' 157 was their second-lowest completed total in the World Cup. In reply, Gooch opened with complete confidence while Botham scored only eight out of 50 in the first 14 overs. Hick's 54 from 55 balls dominated the later innings, until he fell to a diving return catch by Harper, whom he had just driven for six through the covers.

Man of the Match: C. C. Lewis.   *Attendance:* 18,521.

West Indies

D. L. Haynes c Fairbrother b DeFreitas 38
B. C. Lara c Stewart b Lewis 0
*R. B. Richardson c Botham b Lewis .. 5
C. L. Hooper c Reeve b Botham 5
K. L. T. Arthurton c Fairbrother
    b DeFreitas . 54
A. L. Logie run out 20
R. A. Harper c Hick b Reeve 3
M. D. Marshall run out.............. 3

†D. Williams c Pringle b DeFreitas.... 6
C. E. L. Ambrose c DeFreitas b Lewis . 4
W. K. M. Benjamin not out 11

    L-b 4, w 3, n-b 1............ 8

1/0 2/22 3/36   (49.2 overs) 157
4/55 5/91 6/102
7/114 8/131 9/145

Bowling: Pringle 7-3-16-0; Lewis 8.2-1-30-3; DeFreitas 9-2-34-3; Botham 10-0-30-1; Reeve 10-1-23-1; Tufnell 5-0-20-0.

England

*G. A. Gooch st Williams b Hooper ... 65
I. T. Botham c Williams b Benjamin... 8
R. A. Smith c Logie b Benjamin 8
G. A. Hick c and b Harper 54
N. H. Fairbrother not out............ 13

†A. J. Stewart not out 0
    L-b 7, w 4, n-b 1............ 12

1/50 2/71   (4 wkts, 39.5 overs) 160
3/126 4/156

D. A. Reeve, C. C. Lewis, D. R. Pringle, P. A. J. DeFreitas and P. C. R. Tufnell did not bat.

Bowling: Ambrose 8-1-26-0; Marshall 8-0-37-0; Benjamin 9.5-2-22-2; Hooper 10-1-38-1; Harper 4-0-30-1.

Umpires: K. E. Liebenberg and S. J. Woodward.

INDIA v SRI LANKA

At Mackay, February 28. No result. Toss: Sri Lanka. Mackay's first international match was not worth the wait: play was delayed for five hours, and when the teams came out to face 20 overs each, torrential rain flooded the ground after two balls. Srikkanth had blocked one and then taken a single. The only entertainment was afforded by the "aerobic dancing" of the Indian players seeking exercise at the lunch interval.

Attendance: approx. 3,000.

India

K. Srikkanth not out	1
Kapil Dev not out	0

(no wkt, 0.2 overs) 1

*M. Azharuddin, A. D. Jadeja, V. G. Kambli, S. R. Tendulkar, M. Prabhakar, P. K. Amre, †K. S. More, J. Srinath and S. L. V. Raju did not bat.

Bowling: Ramanayake 0.2–0–1–0.

Sri Lanka

R. S. Mahanama, U. C. Hathurusinghe, A. P. Gurusinha, *P. A. de Silva, A. Ranatunga, S. T. Jayasuriya, †H. P. Tillekeratne, R. S. Kalpage, C. P. H. Ramanayake, K. I. W. Wijegunawardene and G. P. Wickremasinghe.

Umpires: I. D. Robinson and D. R. Shepherd.

NEW ZEALAND v SOUTH AFRICA

At Auckland, February 29. New Zealand won by seven wickets. Toss: South Africa. The South Africans' return to Auckland after nearly 28 years was a disappointment. Instead of the bounce they had exploited in Sydney, they were confronted with the same slow pitch on which Australia had succumbed a week before. The spectacle of an off-spinner with the new ball had lost little of its surprise value; Patel conceded 13 runs in his opening seven overs, and bowled Hudson in his third. The faster Watson was just as effective. When Cronje went to Harris's first ball, South Africa were 29 for three, and they needed the experience of Kirsten – originally excluded from the World Cup selection. Greatbatch, recalled to open for New Zealand after Wright's injury, ended his poor run with 68 in 60 balls, including three sixes. With Latham he put on 103 in the first 15 overs, while the number of players in the outfield was restricted. New Zealand swept back to the top of the table with 15.3 overs to spare.

Man of the Match: M. J. Greatbatch. | *Attendance:* 27,450.

South Africa

*K. C. Wessels c Smith b Watson	3	B. M. McMillan not out	33
A. C. Hudson b Patel	1	R. P. Snell not out	11
P. N. Kirsten c Cairns b Watson	90	L-b 8, n-b 1	9
W. J. Cronje c Smith b Harris	7		
†D. J. Richardson c Larsen b Cairns	28	1/8 2/10 3/29 (7 wkts, 50 overs) 190
A. P. Kuiper run out	2	4/108 5/111
J. N. Rhodes c Crowe b Cairns	6	6/121 7/162

T. Bosch and A. A. Donald did not bat.

Bowling: Watson 10–2–30–2; Patel 10–1–28–1; Larsen 10–1–29–0; Harris 10–2–33–1; Latham 2–0–19–0; Cairns 8–0–43–2.

New Zealand

M. J. Greatbatch b Kirsten	68	*M. D. Crowe not out	3
R. T. Latham c Wessels b Snell	60	B 1, w 5, n-b 1	7
A. H. Jones not out	34		
†I. D. S. Smith c Kirsten b Donald	19	1/114 2/155 3/179　(3 wkts, 34.3 overs) 191	

K. R. Rutherford, C. Z. Harris, D. N. Patel, C. L. Cairns, G. R. Larsen and W. Watson did not bat.

Bowling: Donald 10-0-38-1; McMillan 5-1-23-0; Snell 7-0-56-1; Bosch 2.3-0-19-0; Cronje 2-0-14-0; Kuiper 1-0-18-0; Kirsten 7-1-22-1.

Umpires: Khizar Hayat and P. D. Reporter.

WEST INDIES v ZIMBABWE

At Brisbane, February 29. West Indies won by 75 runs. Toss: Zimbabwe. There were no shocks in this encounter between world power and underdog. Lara recovered his match-award-winning form to hit 72, and his cover drives dominated a stand of 78 in 16 overs with his new opening partner, Simmons. Richardson and Hooper added 117 in 21 overs for the third wicket, but they both fell to outfield catches and only Arthurton offered much in the closing stages. Shah bowled tidily, and also hit an unbeaten 60 after joining Houghton at 63 for seven wickets were gone, as Arnott had retired with a broken finger. Zimbabwe's original opener, James, was out with a similar injury; in this match, too, Pycroft was struck on the cheek-bone, and Houghton needed pain-killers after his toe was broken. He and Shah added 69 together, but had little chance against a target of 265.

Man of the Match: B. C. Lara.　　　*Attendance*: 2,221.

West Indies

P. V. Simmons b Brandes	21	†D. Williams not out	8
B. C. Lara c Houghton b Shah	72	W. K. M. Benjamin b Brandes	1
*R. B. Richardson c Brandes b Jarvis	56	B 1, l-b 6, w 2, n-b 1	10
C. L. Hooper c Pycroft b Traicos	63		
K. L. T. Arthurton b Duers	26	1/78 2/103 3/220　(8 wkts, 50 overs) 264	
A. L. Logie run out	5	4/221 5/239 6/254	
M. D. Marshall c Houghton b Brandes	2	7/255 8/264	

A. C. Cummins and B. P. Patterson did not bat.

Bowling: Brandes 10-1-45-3; Jarvis 10-1-71-1; Duers 10-0-52-1; Shah 10-2-39-1; Traicos 10-0-50-1.

Zimbabwe

K. J. Arnott retired hurt	16	E. A. Brandes c and b Benjamin	6
†A. Flower b Patterson	6	A. J. Traicos run out	8
A. J. Pycroft c Williams b Benjamin	10	M. P. Jarvis not out	5
*D. L. Houghton c Patterson b Hooper	55	L-b 9, w 5, n-b 8	22
A. C. Waller c Simmons b Benjamin	0		
A. D. R. Campbell c Richardson		1/21 2/43 3/48　(7 wkts, 50 overs) 189	
b Hooper	1	4/63 5/132	
A. H. Shah not out	60	6/161 7/181	

K. G. Duers did not bat.

K. J. Arnott retired hurt at 43-2.

Bowling: Patterson 10-0-25-1; Marshall 6-0-23-0; Benjamin 10-2-27-3; Cummins 10-0-33-0; Hooper 10-0-47-2; Arthurton 4-0-25-0.

Umpires: K. E. Liebenberg and S. J. Woodward.

AUSTRALIA v INDIA

At Brisbane, March 1. Australia won by one run, India's target having been revised to 236 from 47 overs. Toss: Australia. The result turned on the rule that was to dog the competition. Rain cut 15 minutes and three overs when India were 45 from 16.2, but their target dropped by only two runs, because Australia's three least productive overs were removed. In fine weather earlier, Kapil Dev and Prabhakar had bowled well to restrict Australia, until Jones launched his 109-ball innings with a six and a four. India also began slowly, with Shastri impeded by a knee injury. But Azharuddin's wristy strokeplay collected 93 from 103 balls, and Manjrekar (42 balls) hit three fours and a six. The lower order approached the final assault gallantly; 13 runs were required from Moody's final over, and More struck the first two to the fine-leg boundary. The next hit his middle stump. Prabhakar took a single, but was run out on the fifth ball. Needing four from the last delivery, Srinath swung; Waugh dropped the ball just inside the boundary, but threw it in to Australia's acting wicket-keeper, Boon. Raju was beaten returning for the third run which would have levelled the scores.

Man of the Match: D. M. Jones.   *Attendance:* 11,734.

Australia

M. A. Taylor c More b Kapil Dev	13		P. L. Taylor run out		1
G. R. Marsh b Kapil Dev	8		M. G. Hughes not out		0
†D. C. Boon c Shastri b Raju	43				
D. M. Jones c and b Prabhakar	90		L-b 7, w 5, n-b 4		16
S. R. Waugh b Srinath	29				
T. M. Moody b Prabhakar	25		1/18 2/31 3/102 (9 wkts, 50 overs)		237
*A. R. Border c Jadeja b Kapil Dev	10		4/156 5/198 6/230		
C. J. McDermott c Jadeja b Prabhakar	2		7/235 8/236 9/237		

M. R. Whitney did not bat.

Bowling: Kapil Dev 10-2-41-3; Prabhakar 10-0-41-3; Srinath 8-0-48-1; Tendulkar 5-0-29-0; Raju 10-0-37-1; Jadeja 7-0-34-0.

India

R. J. Shastri c Waugh b Moody	25		J. Srinath not out		8
K. Srikkanth b McDermott	0		M. Prabhakar run out		1
*M. Azharuddin run out	93		S. L. V. Raju run out		0
S. R. Tendulkar c Waugh b Moody	11		L-b 8, w 5		13
Kapil Dev lbw b Waugh	21				
S. V. Manjrekar run out	47		1/6 2/53 3/86 (47 overs)		234
A. D. Jadeja b Hughes	1		4/128 5/194 6/199		
†K. S. More b Moody	14		7/216 8/231 9/232		

Bowling: McDermott 9-1-35-1; Whitney 10-2-36-0; Hughes 9-1-49-1; Moody 9-0-56-3; Waugh 10-0-50-1.

Umpires: B. L. Aldridge and I. D. Robinson.

ENGLAND v PAKISTAN

At Adelaide, March 1. No result. Toss: England. Rain deprived England of the emphatic victory expected when Pakistan were dismissed for their lowest total in limited-overs internationals, and the smallest by a Test country in the World Cup. The loss of three hours created a much stiffer target than the Pakistani batsmen had done. For the match to stand, a minimum of 15 overs had to be available to England; but as Pakistan's most successful 15 overs had yielded 62 of their 74 runs, under the "rain rule" the minimum target had to be 63. After a further shower it was set at 64 from 16, and England still needed 40 from eight when play was abandoned and the points shared. (They had already passed 23, the total which would have sufficed had they been asked to match the original 1.5 run-rate for 15 overs.) Five runs an over could have been a daunting task, with the evidence of Pakistan's precipitous collapse still on the scoreboard. The pitch, which had been covered during heavy rain the previous day, still encouraged swing and seam mightily, and Pringle captured three wickets for eight in 8.2 overs. Only Salim Malik, with three fours in 20 balls, seemed capable of handling the conditions, until the tail improved the score from 47 for eight. At 17 for one from six overs at lunch, when rain first intervened, England should have had few worries.

Attendance: 7,537.

Pakistan

Ramiz Raja c Reeve b DeFreitas	1	Wasim Haider c Stewart b Reeve	13	
Aamir Sohail c and b Pringle	9	Mushtaq Ahmed c Reeve b Pringle	17	
Inzamam-ul-Haq c Stewart b DeFreitas	0	Aqib Javed not out	1	
*Javed Miandad b Pringle	3	L-b 2, w 8, n-b 1	10	
Salim Malik c Reeve b Botham	17			
Ijaz Ahmed c Stewart b Small	0	1/5 2/5 3/14	(40.2 overs) 74	
Wasim Akram b Botham	1	4/20 5/32 6/35		
†Moin Khan c Hick b Small	2	7/42 8/47 9/62		

Bowling: Pringle 8.2–5–8–3; DeFreitas 7–1–22–2; Small 10–1–29–2; Botham 10–4–12–2; Reeve 5–3–2–1.

England

*G. A. Gooch c Moin Khan		
b Wasim Akram	3	
I. T. Botham not out	6	
R. A. Smith not out	5	
B 1, l-b 3, w 5, n-b 1	10	
1/14	(1 wkt, 8 overs) 24	

G. A. Hick, N. H. Fairbrother, †A. J. Stewart, D. A. Reeve, C. C. Lewis, D. R. Pringle, P. A. J. DeFreitas and G. C. Small did not bat.

Bowling: Wasim Akram 3–0–7–1; Aqib Javed 3–1–7–0; Wasim Haider 1–0–1–0; Ijaz Ahmed 1–0–5–0.

Umpires: S. A. Bucknor and P. J. McConnell.

SOUTH AFRICA v SRI LANKA

At Wellington, March 2. Sri Lanka won by three wickets. Toss: Sri Lanka. None the worse for a 15-hour journey from Queensland, the Sri Lankans won their first meeting with South Africa to occupy third place in the table. The South Africans included the slow left-armer Henry (their first non-white player), while Hudson lost the opener's job to Kuiper. They made slow progress; Wessels took 94 balls for his 40, and though Kirsten pushed the score on, the last nine wickets went for 81 in 15 overs. Ramanayake conceded only seven runs in his first seven-over spell. The fielding was also impressive, especially that of Jayasuriya in the covers, who dived to dismiss Rushmere and leapt high to catch Rhodes one-handed. Donald quickly reduced Sri Lanka to 35 for three, but he and his colleagues contributed 17 wides and no-balls. Meanwhile, Mahanama became the first player in the tournament to reach 200 runs. He fell at 154, but Ranatunga saw his team home, and danced off the field with Ramanayake when the tailender struck the winning runs.

Man of the Match: A. Ranatunga. *Attendance:* 3,815.

South Africa

*K. C. Wessels c and b Ranatunga	40	B. M. McMillan not out	18	
A. P. Kuiper b Anurasiri	18	†D. J. Richardson run out	0	
P. N. Kirsten c Hathurusinghe		O. Henry c Kalpage b Ramanayake	11	
b Kalpage	47	A. A. Donald run out	3	
J. N. Rhodes c Jayasuriya				
b Wickremasinghe	28	L-b 9, w 4, n-b 1	14	
M. W. Rushmere c Jayasuriya				
b Ranatunga	4	1/27 2/114 3/114	(50 overs) 195	
W. J. Cronje st Tillekeratne b Anurasiri	3	4/128 5/149 6/153		
R. P. Snell b Anurasiri	9	7/165 8/165 9/186		

Bowling: Ramanayake 9–2–19–1; Wickremasinghe 7–0–32–1; Anurasiri 10–1–41–3; Kalpage 10–0–38–1; Gurusinha 8–0–30–0; Ranatunga 6–0–26–2.

Sri Lanka

R. S. Mahanama c Richardson b McMillan .	68	S. T. Jayasuriya st Richardson b Kirsten	3
U. C. Hathurusinghe c Wessels b Donald .	5	R. S. Kalpage run out	5
A. P. Gurusinha lbw b Donald	0	C. P. H. Ramanayake not out	4
*P. A. de Silva b Donald	7	B 1, l-b 7, w 13, n-b 4	25
†H. P. Tillekeratne c Rushmere b Henry	17		
A. Ranatunga not out	64	1/11 2/12 3/35 (7 wkts, 49.5 overs) 198	
		4/87 5/154	
		6/168 7/189	

G. P. Wickremasinghe and S. D. Anurasiri did not bat.

Bowling: McMillan 10–2–34–1; Donald 9.5–0–42–3; Snell 10–1–33–0; Henry 10–0–31–1; Kuiper 5–0–25–0; Kirsten 5–0–25–1.

Umpires: Khizar Hayat and S. J. Woodward.

NEW ZEALAND v ZIMBABWE

At Napier, March 3. New Zealand won by 48 runs, Zimbabwe's target having been revised to 154 from 18 overs. Toss: Zimbabwe. After this severely curtailed match, Crowe admitted he had contemplated dropping a skied catch from Campbell, from the fifth ball of the 15th over. The sixth ball had to be bowled to produce a valid result; he feared the rain, already falling, would grow heavier and the two-minute gap between batsmen might have been crucial. The umpires conferred as Shah came out, but allowed play to continue. New Zealand's innings had been delayed and twice interrupted. At the second break, 52 for two from 11.2 overs was not a particularly strong showing. But in what proved to be their last session at the crease, 110 came from 9.3 overs. By now the Zimbabweans were handicapped by the slippery outfield; Butchart fell twice running in to bowl, and was hit for 53 in four overs. Crowe's 50 in 31 balls was a World Cup record, and he finished unbeaten on 74 from 44 balls (eight fours, two sixes). He shared 129 in 14 overs with Jones (58 balls, nine fours) before the latter fell to Waller's running catch, in drizzle, in front of the sightscreen.

Man of the Match: M. D. Crowe.   *Attendance:* 6,581.

New Zealand

M. J. Greatbatch b Duers	15	C. L. Cairns not out	1
R. T. Latham b Brandes	2	B 7, l-b 6	13
A. H. Jones c Waller b Butchart	57		
*M. D. Crowe not out	74	1/9 2/25 3/154 (3 wkts, 20.5 overs) 162	

K. R. Rutherford, C. Z. Harris, D. N. Patel, †I. D. S. Smith, G. R. Larsen and D. K. Morrison did not bat.

Bowling: Brandes 5–1–28–1; Duers 6–0–17–1; Shah 4–0–34–0; Butchart 4–0–53–1; Burmester 1.5–0–17–0.

Zimbabwe

†A. Flower b Larsen	30	A. H. Shah b Harris	7
A. C. Waller b Morrison	11	M. G. Burmester not out	4
*D. L. Houghton b Larsen	10	L-b 9, w 3, n-b 1	13
I. P. Butchart c Cairns b Larsen	3		
E. A. Brandes b Harris	6	1/22 2/41 3/63 (7 wkts, 18 overs) 105	
A. J. Pycroft not out	13	4/63 5/75	
A. D. R. Campbell c Crowe b Harris	8	6/86 7/97	

K. G. Duers and A. J. Traicos did not bat.

Bowling: Morrison 4–0–14–1; Cairns 2–0–27–0; Larsen 4–0–16–3; Harris 4–0–15–3; Latham 3–0–18–0; Crowe 1–0–6–0.

Umpires: J. D. Buultjens and K. E. Liebenberg.

INDIA v PAKISTAN

At Sydney, March 4 (day/night). India won by 43 runs. Toss: India. India won without much difficulty when Pakistan lost their last eight wickets for 68 runs, but the neighbours' first World Cup encounter was marred by a less palatable confrontation, between More and Javed Miandad. The wicket-keeper's over-optimistic appeal for a leg-side catch led to verbal exchanges, and later Miandad mockingly leapt up and down, in apparent imitation. After the umpires made their report (minus the dialogue, which they could not understand), match referee Ted Wykes asked the tour managers to sort matters out. More had the better of the cricketing contest, with two catches, a stumping and the run-out of Imran Khan, while Miandad took 34 overs to score 40, leaving his colleagues with a tall order. Though he added 88 for the third wicket with Aamir Sohail, it was Sohail who caught the eye. India had dropped Shastri and asked Jadeja, in his second international, to open. He acquitted himself well, but once again the finest innings came from Tendulkar, unbeaten on 54 from 62 deliveries. He put on 60 in eight overs with Kapil Dev.

Man of the Match: S. R. Tendulkar.   *Attendance:* 10,330.

India

A. D. Jadeja c Zahid Fazal b Wasim Haider	46	S. V. Manjrekar b Mushtaq Ahmed	0
K. Srikkanth c Moin Khan b Aqib Javed	5	Kapil Dev c Imran Khan b Aqib Javed	35
*M. Azharuddin c Moin Khan b Mushtaq Ahmed	32	†K. S. More run out	4
		M. Prabhakar not out	2
V. G. Kambli c Inzamam-ul-Haq b Mushtaq Ahmed	24	L-b 3, w 9, n-b 2	14
S. R. Tendulkar not out	54		

1/25 2/86 3/101 (7 wkts, 49 overs) 216
4/147 5/148
6/208 7/213

J. Srinath and S. L. V. Raju did not bat.

Bowling: Wasim Akram 10–0–45–0; Aqib Javed 8–2–28–2; Imran Khan 8–0–25–0; Wasim Haider 10–1–36–1; Mushtaq Ahmed 10–0–59–3; Aamir Sohail 3–0–20–0.

Pakistan

Aamir Sohail c Srikkanth b Tendulkar	62	†Moin Khan c Manjrekar b Kapil Dev	12
Inzamam-ul-Haq lbw b Kapil Dev	2	Mushtaq Ahmed run out	3
Zahid Fazal c More b Prabhakar	2	Aqib Javed not out	1
Javed Miandad b Srinath	40	L-b 6, w 15, n-b 1	22
Salim Malik c More b Prabhakar	12		
*Imran Khan run out	0	1/8 2/17 3/105 (48.1 overs) 173
Wasim Akram st More b Raju	4	4/127 5/130 6/141
Wasim Haider b Srinath	13	7/141 8/161 9/166

Bowling: Kapil Dev 10–0–30–2; Prabhakar 10–1–22–2; Srinath 8.1–0–37–3; Tendulkar 10–0–37–1; Raju 10–1–41–1.

Umpires: P. J. McConnell and D. R. Shepherd.

SOUTH AFRICA v WEST INDIES

At Christchurch, March 5. South Africa won by 64 runs. Toss: West Indies. The South African bowlers took full advantage of a quick pitch by New Zealand standards and, aided by some reckless shots from the West Indian top order, they ended this long-awaited first encounter level on points in the table. Their batting was disappointing, with Wessels going early and Kirsten again the only significant contributor. His 56 from 91 balls, with a runner, made him the leading run-scorer in the tournament, but even he scored only two fours and a five. Yet the unease caused by Ambrose and Marshall was nothing to the havoc unleashed by Pringle. He had Lara caught low at point, with the score on ten; when it reached 19, Pringle removed Richardson, Hooper and Arthurton. The four wickets took him only 11 balls. Logie attempted to regain the initiative – he struck four fours in an over off Kuiper – and Haynes gave him brave support after being hit twice on his right forefinger, which was already in a splint. He retired, intending to go to hospital, but when two more wickets fell he returned. Only when he and Logie fell in the same over could South Africa feel safe, but they dismissed West Indies for their lowest total in the World Cup.

Man of the Match: M. W. Pringle.   *Attendance*: 12,116.

South Africa

A. C. Hudson c Lara b Cummins	22	R. P. Snell c Haynes b Ambrose	3
*K. C. Wessels c Haynes b Marshall	1	M. W. Pringle not out	5
P. N. Kirsten c Williams b Marshall	56		
M. W. Rushmere b Williams b Hooper	10	L-b 8, w 3, n-b 7	18
A. P. Kuiper b Ambrose	23		
J. N. Rhodes c Williams b Cummins	22	1/8 2/52 3/73 (8 wkts, 50 overs)	200
B. M. McMillan c Lara b Benjamin	20	4/118 5/127 6/159	
†D. J. Richardson not out	20	7/181 8/187	

A. A. Donald did not bat.

Bowling: Ambrose 10-1-34-2; Marshall 10-1-26-2; Benjamin 10-0-47-1; Cummins 10-0-40-2; Hooper 10-0-45-1.

West Indies

D. L. Haynes c Richardson b Kuiper	30	C. E. L. Ambrose run out	12
B. C. Lara c Rhodes b Pringle	9	A. C. Cummins c McMillan b Donald	6
*R. B. Richardson lbw b Pringle	1	W. K. M. Benjamin not out	1
C. L. Hooper c Wessels b Pringle	0	L-b 9, w 1	10
K. L. T. Arthurton c Wessels b Pringle	0		
A. L. Logie c Pringle b Kuiper	61	1/10 2/19 3/19 (38.4 overs)	136
M. D. Marshall c Rhodes b Snell	6	4/19 5/70 6/70	
†D. Williams c Richardson b Snell	0	7/116 8/117 9/132	

D. L. Haynes, when 13, retired hurt at 50 and resumed at 70-6.

Bowling: Donald 6.4-2-13-1; Pringle 8-4-11-4; McMillan 8-2-36-0; Snell 7-2-16-2; Kuiper 9-0-51-2.

Umpires: B. L. Aldridge and S. G. Randell.

AUSTRALIA v ENGLAND

At Sydney, March 5 (day/night). England won by eight wickets. Toss: Australia. The combination of the old enemy, the bright lights and the noisily enthusiastic crowd demanded a show-stopper from Botham, and he provided it. His best bowling figures in limited-overs internationals stopped the Australian innings in its tracks, and he followed up with a confident fifty which made England's victory a formality. With Marsh omitted, Moody was promoted to open for Australia. He responded with 51, and with Jones took Australia to a promising 106 for two. Then DeFreitas had Jones well caught by the diving Lewis, and Tufnell bowled Moody off the glove. But the match turned in the 38th over, when Botham bowled Border with the fifth ball. In his next over, Healy drove to Fairbrother at mid-wicket, Taylor was trapped lbw, and McDermott fell to DeFreitas's running catch. Botham had claimed four wickets for no runs in seven balls, and Australia were 155 for eight. They took only 16 from their last nine overs. Their only hope was to capture some early wickets, and Gooch was repeatedly beaten in McDermott's fiery opening spell. Botham's self-confidence was now complete, however, and he led the way to the hundred partnership in the 23rd over, reaching his first World Cup fifty one ball later. He hit six fours before giving Healy a low leg-side catch.

Man of the Match: I. T. Botham.   *Attendance*: 38,951.

Australia

T. M. Moody b Tufnell	51	C. J. McDermott c DeFreitas b Botham	0
M. A. Taylor lbw b Pringle	0	M. R. Whitney not out	8
D. C. Boon run out	18	B. A. Reid b Reeve	1
D. M. Jones c Lewis b DeFreitas	22	B 2, l-b 8, w 5, n-b 4	19
S. R. Waugh run out	27		
*A. R. Border b Botham	16	1/5 2/35 3/106	(49 overs) 171
†I. A. Healy c Fairbrother b Botham	9	4/114 5/145 6/155	
P. L. Taylor lbw b Botham	0	7/155 8/155 9/164	

Bowling: Pringle 9-1-24-1; Lewis 10-2-28-0; DeFreitas 10-3-23-1; Botham 10-1-31-4; Tufnell 9-0-52-1; Reeve 1-0-3-1.

England

*G. A. Gooch b Waugh	58	
I. T. Botham c Healy b Whitney	53	
R. A. Smith not out	30	
G. A. Hick not out	7	
L-b 13, w 8, n-b 4	25	
1/107 2/153	(2 wkts, 40.5 overs) 173	

N. H. Fairbrother, †A. J. Stewart, D. A. Reeve, C. C. Lewis, D. R. Pringle, P. A. J. DeFreitas and P. C. R. Tufnell did not bat.

Bowling: McDermott 10-1-29-0; Reid 7.5-0-49-0; Whitney 10-2-28-1; Waugh 6-0-29-1; P. L. Taylor 3-0-7-0; Moody 4-0-18-0.

Umpires: S. A. Bucknor and Khizar Hayat.

INDIA v ZIMBABWE

At Hamilton, March 7. India won by 55 runs, India's total having been revised to 158 and Zimbabwe's to 103 from their highest-scoring 19 overs. Toss: India. Another rain-affected match was decided by the controversial rule on shortened innings. This time India, unlucky against Australia, were the beneficiaries. But there was widespread sympathy for Zimbabwe, who were making good progress in pursuit of 204 from 32 overs. Their 104 for one from 19.1 compared well with 106 for three at the same point of the Indian innings. With Flower, who had reached 200 runs in the tournament, still at the crease, another 100 from 13 was not impossible. In the morning, three hours had been lost to rain, and Tendulkar dominated the 32 overs allotted to India. He scored 81 from 77 balls (one six, eight fours), and with Manjrekar added 99 in 15 overs for the fourth wicket.

Man of the Match: S. R. Tendulkar. *Attendance*: 1,520.

India

K. Srikkanth b Burmester	32	†K. S. More not out	15
Kapil Dev lbw b Brandes	10	J. Srinath not out	6
*M. Azharuddin c Flower b Burmester	12	L-b 3, w 3	6
S. R. Tendulkar c Campbell b Burmester	81		
S. V. Manjrekar c Duers b Traicos	34	1/23 2/43 3/69	(7 wkts, 32 overs) 203
V. G. Kambli b Traicos	1	4/168 5/170	
A. D. Jadeja c Shah b Traicos	6	6/182 7/184	

M. Prabhakar and S. L. V. Raju did not bat.

Bowling: Brandes 7-0-43-1; Duers 7-0-48-0; Burmester 6-0-36-3; Shah 6-1-38-0; Traicos 6-0-35-3.

Zimbabwe

A. H. Shah b Tendulkar	31
†A. Flower not out	43
A. C. Waller not out	13
B 1, l-b 11, w 5	17

1/79   (1 wkt, 19.1 overs) 104

A. J. Pycroft, *D. L. Houghton, A. D. R. Campbell, E. A. Brandes, I. P. Butchart, M. G. Burmester, A. J. Traicos and K. G. Duers did not bat.

Bowling: Kapil Dev 4-0-6-0; Prabhakar 3-0-14-0; Srinath 4-0-20-0; Tendulkar 6-0-35-1; Raju 2.1-0-17-0.

Umpires: J. D. Buultjens and S. G. Randell.

AUSTRALIA v SRI LANKA

At Adelaide, March 7. Australia won by seven wickets. Toss: Australia. Australia were much relieved to record a second win. Their run chase was given a solid foundation by Marsh, recalled to open in place of Mark Taylor, and Moody, who survived an lbw appeal to share 120 for the first wicket. Mark Waugh, with two sixes, and Boon continued their good work. The Sri Lankan batsmen had contributed to their own downfall with four run-outs. The first, and most serious, was that of their leading scorer Mahanama, who responded too late to a call from Samarasekera. The burden of the innings then fell on de Silva, who eventually lost his wicket trying to force the pace as he ran out of partners. Sri Lanka were also restricted by tight bowling from McDermott and Whitney, on a pitch offering enough turn for Border to bowl ten overs of slow left-arm himself, supplementing Peter Taylor's off-breaks.

Man of the Match: T. M. Moody.   *Attendance:* 11,663.

Sri Lanka

R. S. Mahanama run out	7	C. P. H. Ramanayake run out	5
M. A. R. Samarasekera c Healy b Taylor	34	S. D. Anurasiri not out	4
A. P. Gurusinha lbw b Whitney	5		
*P. A. de Silva c Moody b McDermott	62	B 3, l-b 6, w 5, n-b 1	15
A. Ranatunga c Jones b Taylor	23		
S. T. Jayasuriya lbw b Border	15	1/8 2/28 3/72	(9 wkts, 50 overs) 189
†H. P. Tillekeratne run out	5	4/123 5/151 6/163	
R. S. Kalpage run out	14	7/166 8/182 9/189	

G. P. Wickremasinghe did not bat.

Bowling: McDermott 10-0-28-1; S. R. Waugh 7-0-34-0; Whitney 10-3-26-1; Moody 3-0-18-0; Taylor 10-0-34-2; Border 10-0-40-1.

Australia

T. M. Moody c Mahanama		D. C. Boon not out	27
b Wickremasinghe	57	D. M. Jones not out	12
G. R. Marsh c Anurasiri b Kalpage	60	L-b 2, w 3, n-b 3	8
M. E. Waugh c Mahanama			
b Wickremasinghe	26	1/120 2/130 3/165	(3 wkts, 44 overs) 190

*A. R. Border, S. R. Waugh, †I. A. Healy, P. L. Taylor, C. J. McDermott and M. R. Whitney did not bat.

Bowling: Wickremasinghe 10-3-29-2; Ramanayake 9-1-44-0; Anurasiri 10-0-43-0; Gurusinha 6-0-20-0; Ranatunga 1-0-11-0; Kalpage 8-0-41-1.

Umpires: P. D. Reporter and I. D. Robinson.

NEW ZEALAND v WEST INDIES

At Auckland, March 8. New Zealand won by five wickets. Toss: New Zealand. In 13 previous limited-overs encounters with West Indies, New Zealand had won only once; but they hardly surprised themselves when they inflicted the third defeat of the tournament on Richardson's men. The now-familiar ploy of opening with off-spin continued to be rewarded, with Patel conceding only seven runs in his first five overs. Haynes and Lara survived to put on 65 in 19 overs, but West Indies would not have reached 200 without Arthurton and Williams. The game was to be dominated by two New Zealand batsmen, however. First Greatbatch launched a ferocious assault on the West Indian bowlers, deprived of their bouncers. He hit Ambrose, Marshall and Cummins for sixes, and also struck seven fours. In an opening stand of 67 in 12 overs, Latham scored only 14. When Greatbatch gave Haynes a steepling catch with the score at 100, New Zealand faltered briefly; but Crowe restored their ascendancy, with a stylish 81 in as many balls. His 12th boundary won the match, and took him to 263 runs in the competition for only one dismissal. He collected his third award in five matches, and that was no surprise either.

Man of the Match: M. D. Crowe.   *Attendance*: 24,281.

West Indies

D. L. Haynes c and b Harris	22	†D. Williams not out	32
B. C. Lara c Rutherford b Larsen	52	W. K. M. Benjamin not out	2
R. B. Richardson c Smith b Watson	29	L-b 8, w 7, n-b 1	16
C. L. Hooper c Greatbatch b Patel	2		—
K. L. T. Arthurton b Morrison	40	1/65 2/95 3/100 (7 wkts, 50 overs)	203
A. L. Logie b Harris	3	4/136 5/142	
M. D. Marshall b Larsen	5	6/156 7/201	

C. E. L. Ambrose and A. C. Cummins did not bat.

Bowling: Morrison 9-1-33-1; Patel 10-2-19-1; Watson 10-2-56-1; Larsen 10-0-41-2; Harris 10-2-32-1; Latham 1-0-14-0.

New Zealand

M. J. Greatbatch c Haynes b Benjamin	63	D. N. Patel not out	10
R. T. Latham c Williams b Cummins	14		
A. H. Jones c Williams b Benjamin	10	L-b 7, w 5, n-b 1	13
M. D. Crowe not out	81		—
K. R. Rutherford c Williams b Ambrose	8	1/67 2/97 3/100 (5 wkts, 48.3 overs)	206
C. Z. Harris c Williams b Cummins	7	4/135 5/174	

I. D. S. Smith, G. R. Larsen, D. K. Morrison and W. Watson did not bat.

Bowling: Ambrose 10-1-41-1; Marshall 9-1-35-0; Cummins 10-0-53-2; Hooper 10-0-36-0; Benjamin 9.3-3-34-2.

Umpires: K. E. Liebenberg and P. J. McConnell.

PAKISTAN v SOUTH AFRICA

At Brisbane, March 8. South Africa won by 20 runs, Pakistan's target having been revised to 194 from 36 overs. Toss: Pakistan. A third win for South Africa placed them third in the table, though Pakistan's chances were undermined by rain. Imran Khan risked fielding first after a forecast of "light showers". Continuing problems controlling the white ball brought Wasim Akram's tally of wides to 27 in five matches, and the ball gave Aqib Javed another sort of headache when Moin Khan, lobbing it back to him, struck his forehead to remove him from the field. He joined Javed Miandad, Ramiz Raja and Wasim Haider on the casualty list. Hudson made his maiden international fifty, and Cronje and McMillan added 31 in 12 overs. In reply, Pakistan had reached 74 for two in the 22nd over when heavy rain stopped play. They now had to surpass 193, representing South Africa's most successful 3 overs. In the first nine after the halt, Inzamam-ul-Haq and Imran resumed confidently with 61 runs, but both fell within three balls. Inzamam, seeking a leg-bye, turned back to see th low-flying Rhodes crashing through the stumps, and Imran edged to the wicket-keeper Another 58 runs from five overs proved too much for those who followed, and three of ther perished in one eventful over from Kuiper.

Man of the Match: A. C. Hudson.   *Attendance:* 8,108.

South Africa

A. C. Hudson c Ijaz Ahmed b Imran Khan . 54	W. J. Cronje not out	4
*K. C. Wessels c Moin Khan b Aqib Javed . 7	B. M. McMillan b Wasim Akram	3
	†D. J. Richardson b Wasim Akram	
M. W. Rushmere c Aamir Sohail b Mushtaq Ahmed . 35	R. P. Snell not out	
	L-b 8, w 9, n-b 2	1
A. P. Kuiper c Moin Khan b Imran Khan . 5	1/31 2/98 3/110 (7 wkts, 50 overs) 21
J. N. Rhodes lbw b Iqbal Sikandar 5	4/111 5/127
	6/198 7/207

A. A. Donald and M. W. Pringle did not bat.

Bowling: Wasim Akram 10-0-42-2; Aqib Javed 7-1-36-1; Imran Khan 10-0-34-2 Iqbal Sikandar 8-0-30-1; Ijaz Ahmed 7-0-26-0; Mushtaq Ahmed 8-1-35-1.

Pakistan

Aamir Sohail b Snell	23	Mushtaq Ahmed run out
Zahid Fazal c Richardson b McMillan .	11	Iqbal Sikandar not out
Inzamam-ul-Haq run out	48	
*Imran Khan c Richardson b McMillan	34	L-b 2, w 17, n-b 1 2
Salim Malik c Donald b Kuiper	12	
Wasim Akram c Snell b Kuiper	9	1/50 2/50 3/135 (8 wkts, 36 overs) 17
Ijaz Ahmed c Rhodes b Kuiper	6	4/136 5/156 6/157
†Moin Khan not out	5	7/163 8/171

Aqib Javed did not bat.

Bowling: Donald 7-1-31-0; Pringle 7-0-31-0; Snell 8-2-26-1; McMillan 7-0-34-2 Kuiper 6-0-40-3; Cronje 1-0-9-0.

Umpires: B. L. Aldridge and S. A. Bucknor.

ENGLAND v SRI LANKA

At Ballarat, March 9. England won by 106 runs. Toss: England. Ballarat closed its gates o a crowd of over 13,000, including at least 5,000 Sri Lankans who had streamed out fro Melbourne. For England the satisfaction of a big victory was diminished by Gooch hamstring injury as he chased a ball through the covers. It had not been his day; afte making eight in 40 minutes, he was bowled by Labrooy's fourth ball. But his colleague especially those who had been waiting for time in the middle, launched a spectacula display of fireworks. At 40 overs England were 174 for four; their next five overs brough 33 runs, and the last five 73. Fairbrother added 80 in nine overs with Stewart, who hit dazzling 59 from 36 balls (one six, seven fours, 50 in 32). Finally Lewis smashed a unbeaten 20 from six balls, driving the second out of the ground. Faced with the bigge total of the tournament since their opening match, Mahanama and Samarasekera (with runner) wiped out 33 in five overs. But Lewis turned the game. In four overs he ha Mahanama edge to slip, Samarasekera drive to mid-on, de Silva caught by the divin Fairbrother, and Gurusinha present a simple return.

Man of the Match: C. C. Lewis.   *Attendance:* 13,037.

England

*G. A. Gooch b Labrooy	8	C. C. Lewis not out	20
I. T. Botham b Anurasiri	47	D. R. Pringle not out	0
R. A. Smith run out	19		
G. A. Hick b Ramanayake	41	B 1, l-b 9, w 9, n-b 4	23
N. H. Fairbrother c Ramanayake b Gurusinha	63		
†A. J. Stewart c Jayasuriya b Gurusinha	59	1/44 2/80 3/105 (6 wkts, 50 overs) 280
		4/164 5/244 6/268	

D. A. Reeve, P. A. J. DeFreitas and R. K. Illingworth did not bat.

Bowling: Wickremasinghe 9-0-54-0; Ramanayake 10-1-42-1; Labrooy 10-1-68-1; Anurasiri 10-1-27-1; Gurusinha 10-0-67-2; Jayasuriya 1-0-12-0.

Sri Lanka

R. S. Mahanama c Botham b Lewis	9	G. F. Labrooy c Smith b Illingworth	19
M. A. R. Samarasekera c Illingworth b Lewis	23	C. P. H. Ramanayake c and b Reeve	12
A. P. Gurusinha c and b Lewis	7	S. D. Anurasiri lbw b Reeve	11
*P. A. de Silva c Fairbrother b Lewis	7	G. P. Wickremasinghe not out	6
A. Ranatunga c Stewart b Botham	36	L-b 7, w 8, n-b 6	21
†H. P. Tillekeratne run out	4	1/33 2/46 3/56 (44 overs) 174
S. T. Jayasuriya c DeFreitas b Illingworth	19	4/60 5/91 6/119 7/123 8/156 9/158

Bowling: Pringle 7-1-27-0; Lewis 8-0-30-4; DeFreitas 5-1-31-0; Botham 10-0-33-1; Illingworth 10-0-32-2; Reeve 4-0-14-2.

Umpires: Khizar Hayat and P. D. Reporter.

INDIA v WEST INDIES

At Wellington, March 10. West Indies won by five wickets, their target having been revised to 195 from 46 overs. Toss: India. West Indies became the first team of the tournament to reach a rain-adjusted target, but there were alarms along the way. Pursuing 198, they had taken 50 from their first six overs, with Lara on 36, and were a comfortable 81 from 11 when rain forced them off for 20 minutes. But the break, which cut four overs and three runs from the equation, unsettled the batsmen: Lara went almost at once, swiftly followed by Simmons, to a falling catch by Tendulkar. Richardson and Logie also went quickly, but an unbroken stand of 83 from Arthurton and Hooper saw West Indies through. The Indian innings had shown promise, with Azharuddin in his best form, though Tendulkar found Ambrose's lifter a problem. India had reached 166 in the 43rd over when Azharuddin, caught at deep mid-off, gave Cummins the first of his four wickets, as seven fell for 31 runs. Ambrose conceded a mere 24 in ten overs.

Man of the Match: A. C. Cummins.   *Attendance:* 6,634.

India

A. D. Jadeja c Benjamin b Simmons	27	M. Prabhakar c Richardson b Cummins	8
K. Srikkanth c Logie b Hooper	40	J. Srinath not out	5
*M. Azharuddin c Ambrose b Cummins	61	S. L. V. Raju run out	1
S. R. Tendulkar c Williams b Ambrose	4	L-b 6, w 5, n-b 1	12
S. V. Manjrekar run out	27		
Kapil Dev c Haynes b Cummins	3	1/56 2/102 3/115 (49.4 overs) 197
P. K. Amre c Hooper b Ambrose	4	4/166 5/171 6/172
†K. S. More c Hooper b Cummins	5	7/180 8/186 9/193

Bowling: Ambrose 10-1-24-2; Benjamin 9.4-0-35-0; Cummins 10-0-33-4; Simmons 10-0-48-1; Hooper 10-0-46-1; Arthurton 1-0-5-0.

West Indies

D. L. Haynes c Manjrekar b Kapil Dev	16	C. L. Hooper not out	34
B. C. Lara c Manjrekar b Srinath	41		
P. V. Simmons c Tendulkar b Prabhakar	22	L-b 8, w 2, n-b 4	14
*R. B. Richardson c Srikkanth b Srinath	3		—
K. L. T. Arthurton not out	58	1/57 2/81 3/88 (5 wkts, 40.2 overs)	195
A. L. Logie c More b Raju	7	4/98 5/112	

†D. Williams, C. E. L. Ambrose, A. C. Cummins and W. K. M. Benjamin did not bat.

Bowling: Kapil Dev 8-0-45-1; Prabhakar 9-0-55-1; Raju 10-2-32-1; Srinath 9-2-23-2; Tendulkar 3-0-20-0; Srikkanth 1-0-7-0; Jadeja 0.2-0-5-0.

Umpires: S. G. Randell and S. J. Woodward.

SOUTH AFRICA v ZIMBABWE

At Canberra, March 10. South Africa won by seven wickets. Toss: South Africa. Zimbabwe were bowled out for the first time in the tournament. Already handicapped by an injury to the consistent Flower, who was struck on the fingers trying to cut Donald, they lost their middle order to the off-breaks of Kirsten. A calf strain had made him a doubtful starter, but nevertheless he removed Waller, Houghton and Shah within two overs. Later he added 112 for the second wicket with Wessels, who hit 70 despite a thumb injury. Zimbabwe's best hope was an early breakthrough, but after Hudson's departure Duers, at fine leg, dropped Wessels (then 16) off the bowling of Burmester. There were no more chances until South Africa, anxious to improve their run-rate, began to force the pace. In Flower's absence, Houghton resumed his old role as wicket-keeper.

Man of the Match: P. N. Kirsten. *Attendance:* 3,165.

Zimbabwe

W. R. James lbw b Pringle	5	A. J. Traicos not out	16
†A. Flower c Richardson b Cronje	19	M. P. Jarvis c and b McMillan	17
A. J. Pycroft c Wessels b McMillan	19	K. G. Duers b Donald	5
*D. L. Houghton c Cronje b Kirsten	15	L-b 11, w 13, n-b 4	28
A. C. Waller c Cronje b Kirsten	15		—
A. H. Shah c Wessels b Kirsten	3	1/7 2/51 3/72 (48.3 overs)	163
E. A. Brandes c Richardson b McMillan	20	4/80 5/80 6/115	
M. G. Burmester c Kuiper b Cronje	1	7/117 8/123 9/151	

A. Flower, when 6, retired hurt at 26 and resumed at 80-5.

Bowling: Donald 9.3-1-25-1; Pringle 9-0-25-1; Snell 10-3-24-0; McMillan 10-1-30-3; Cronje 5-0-17-2; Kirsten 5-0-31-3.

South Africa

*K. C. Wessels b Shah	70	J. N. Rhodes not out	3
A. C. Hudson b Jarvis	13	L-b 4, w 2, n-b 3	9
P. N. Kirsten not out	62		
A. P. Kuiper c Burmester b Brandes	7	1/27 2/139 3/151 (3 wkts, 45.1 overs)	164

W. J. Cronje, B. M. McMillan, M. W. Pringle, R. P. Snell, †D. J. Richardson and A. A. Donald did not bat.

Bowling: Brandes 9.1-0-39-1; Jarvis 9-2-23-1; Burmester 5-0-20-0; Shah 8-2-33-1; Duers 8-1-19-0; Traicos 6-0-26-0.

Umpires: S. A. Bucknor and D. R. Shepherd.

AUSTRALIA v PAKISTAN

At Perth, March 11 (day/night). Pakistan won by 48 runs. Toss: Pakistan. A despondent Border admitted afterwards that it would be a travesty if Australia reached the semi-finals. The loss of their last eight wickets for 56 (of which Mark Waugh scored 30) typified the World Cup holders' desperate campaign. Australia were disadvantaged by batting in the evening, when dew added to the swing of the ball. Earlier conditions were easier, though Aamir Sohail was caught behind off a Reid no-ball before scoring. He then took his personal aggregate to 307 in six innings, putting on 78 in 20 overs with Ramiz Raja and 77 in 16 with Javed Miandad. Steve Waugh's three wickets put a brake on the later innings. Pakistan's bowlers were rewarded for keeping a good length. Aqib Javed quickly removed Moody and Boon, but Marsh, batting 34 overs for 39, and the more forceful Jones added 85, before Jones was caught on the extra-cover boundary trying to hit the leg-spinner Mushtaq Ahmed. When Marsh fell, only Mark Waugh delayed Pakistan's victory. The tense struggle to reach the last four was reflected in disciplinary fines of $A250 each for Sohail, Moin Khan and Whitney.

Man of the Match: Aamir Sohail.   *Attendance:* 21,214.

Pakistan

Aamir Sohail c Healy b Moody	76	†Moin Khan c Healy b McDermott	5
Ramiz Raja c Border b Whitney	34	Mushtaq Ahmed not out	3
Salim Malik b Moody	0		
Javed Miandad c Healy b S. R. Waugh.	46		
*Imran Khan c Moody b S. R. Waugh.	13	L-b 9, w 16, n-b 2	27
Inzamam-ul-Haq run out	16		
Ijaz Ahmed run out	0	1/78 2/80 3/157 (9 wkts, 50 overs)	220
Wasim Akram c M. E. Waugh		4/193 5/194 6/205	
b S. R. Waugh.	0	7/205 8/214 9/220	

Aqib Javed did not bat.

Bowling: McDermott 10–0–33–1; Reid 9–0–37–0; S. R. Waugh 10–0–36–3; Whitney 10–1–50–1; Moody 10–0–42–2; M. E. Waugh 1–0–13–0.

Australia

T. M. Moody c Salim Malik b Aqib Javed.	4	S. R. Waugh c Moin Khan b Imran Khan.	5
G. R. Marsh c Moin Khan b Imran Khan.	39	†I. A. Healy c Ijaz Ahmed b Aqib Javed	8
D. C. Boon c Mushtaq Ahmed b Aqib Javed.	5	C. J. McDermott lbw b Wasim Akram.	0
		M. R. Whitney b Wasim Akram	5
D. M. Jones c Aqib Javed b Mushtaq Ahmed.	47	B. A. Reid not out	0
M. E. Waugh c Ijaz Ahmed b Mushtaq Ahmed.	30	L-b 7, w 14, n-b 7	28
*A. R. Border c Ijaz Ahmed b Mushtaq Ahmed.	1	1/13 2/31 3/116 (45.2 overs)	172
		4/122 5/123 6/130	
		7/156 8/162 9/167	

Bowling: Wasim Akram 7.2–0–28–2; Aqib Javed 8–1–21–3; Imran Khan 10–1–32–2; Ijaz Ahmed 10–0–43–0; Mushtaq Ahmed 10–0–41–3.

Umpires: K. E. Liebenberg and P. D. Reporter.

NEW ZEALAND v INDIA

At Dunedin, March 12. New Zealand won by four wickets. New Zealand's sixth win effectively ended India's ambitions, and equalled West Indies' record run of six World Cup victories in 1983. Fearing rain, Azharuddin chose to bat. Srikkanth was caught on the long-on boundary off Patel's third ball and Jadeja pulled a hamstring, but then the captain and Tendulkar added 127 in 30 overs. When Patel returned, Azharuddin hit him for six and then, seeking another, pulled him into the hands of the diving Greatbatch. Tendulkar and Kapil took India towards a total of 230, which might have been defended, but not against Greatbatch. Hitting out powerfully, he struck 73 in 77 deliveries, and New Zealand were ahead of the required rate when he was caught on the square-leg boundary midway through the innings. Jones remained to ensure victory, though he lost four more partners, notably Crowe. The New Zealand captain was run out when More dashed to gully and knocked the ball back at stumps he could not even see.

Man of the Match: M. J. Greatbatch.   *Attendance*: 9,134.

India

A. D. Jadeja retired hurt	13	†K. S. More not out	2
K. Srikkanth c Latham b Patel	0	J. Srinath not out	4
*M. Azharuddin c Greatbatch b Patel	55		
S. R. Tendulkar c Smith b Harris	84	B 1, l-b 4, w 4, n-b 1	10
S. V. Manjrekar c and b Harris	18		—
Kapil Dev c Larsen b Harris	33	1/4 2/149 3/167 (6 wkts, 50 overs)	230
S. T. Banerjee c Greatbatch b Watson	11	4/201 5/222 6/223	

S. L. V. Raju and M. Prabhakar did not bat.

A. D. Jadeja retired hurt at 22.

Bowling: Cairns 8-1-40-0; Patel 10-0-29-2; Watson 10-1-34-1; Larsen 9-0-43-0; Harris 9-0-55-3; Latham 4-0-24-0.

New Zealand

M. J. Greatbatch c Banerjee b Raju	73	C. Z. Harris b Prabhakar	4
R. T. Latham b Prabhakar	8	C. L. Cairns not out	4
A. H. Jones not out	67		
*M. D. Crowe run out	26	B 4, l-b 3, w 4, n-b 8	19
†I. D. S. Smith c sub (P. K. Amre) b Prabhakar	9		—
K. R. Rutherford lbw b Raju	21	1/36 2/118 3/162 (6 wkts, 47.1 overs)	231
		4/172 5/206 6/225	

D. N. Patel, G. R. Larsen and W. Watson did not bat.

Bowling: Kapil Dev 10-0-55-0; Prabhakar 10-0-46-3; Banerjee 6-1-40-0; Srinath 9-0-35-0; Raju 10-0-38-2; Tendulkar 1-0-2-0; Srikkanth 1.1-0-8-0.

Umpires: P. J. McConnell and I. D. Robinson.

ENGLAND v SOUTH AFRICA

At Melbourne, March 12 (day/night). England won by three wickets, their target having been revised to 226 from 41 overs. Toss: England. The first meeting of old adversaries since 1965 produced a thriller; England overcame a fine South African performance, assorted injuries, and the infamous "rain rule" to notch up their 12th limited-overs international without defeat. Deputising for the injured Gooch, Stewart trusted in the weather and chose to field. No wicket fell until the 36th over, when South Africa were 151. England's attack lacked Lewis, restricted by a side strain; DeFreitas bowled ten overs though he was limping so badly he left the field after each spell; Small proved too expensive to be risked; and Reeve fell, bruised his back and could not go on. His replacement, Hick, made the breakthrough, with a return catch from Hudson. Wessels batted on watchfully for 46 overs and South Africa reached 236. Stewart wasted no time: in 12 overs he was 40, and England 62 without loss. Rain transformed the target, and the match too. They were set to pass the 225 scored in South Africa's best 41 overs. Then Botham was bowled, and within seven balls Smith and Hick were caught behind. But Fairbrother, anxious to impress, added 68 in 13 overs with Stewart, 34 with Reeve and a glorious 50 in six overs with Lewis. Like Stewart, Lewis was run out by the athletic Rhodes. England then needed ten off two overs. Eight came from Meyrick Pringle's last over, but with the scores level Derek Pringle drove a full toss to short mid-wicket. DeFreitas emerged to hit the winning run with one ball to spare.

Man of the Match: A. J. Stewart.   *Attendance*: 25,248.

South Africa

K. C. Wessels c Smith b Hick	85	W. J. Cronje not out	13
A. C. Hudson c and b Hick	79	B 4, l-b 4, w 4, n-b 3	15
*P. N. Kirsten c Smith b DeFreitas	11		
J. N. Rhodes run out	18	1/151 2/170	(4 wkts, 50 overs) 236
A. P. Kuiper not out	15	3/201 4/205	

B. M. McMillan, †D. J. Richardson, R. P. Snell, M. W. Pringle and A. A. Donald did not bat.

Bowling: Pringle 9–2–34–0; DeFreitas 10–1–41–1; Botham 8–0–37–0; Small 2–0–14–0; Illingworth 10–0–43–0; Reeve 2.4–0–15–0; Hick 8.2–0–44–2.

England

*†A. J. Stewart run out	77	D. R. Pringle c Kuiper b Snell	1
I. T. Botham b McMillan	22	P. A. J. DeFreitas not out	1
R. A. Smith c Richardson b McMillan	0	L-b 3, w 1, n-b 2	6
G. A. Hick c Richardson b Snell	1		
N. H. Fairbrother not out	75	1/63 2/63 3/64	(7 wkts, 40.5 overs) 226
D. A. Reeve c McMillan b Snell	10	4/132 5/166	
C. C. Lewis run out	33	6/216 7/225	

R. K. Illingworth and G. C. Small did not bat.

Bowling: Donald 9–1–43–0; Pringle 8–0–44–0; Snell 7.5–0–42–3; McMillan 8–1–39–2; Kuiper 4–0–32–0; Cronje 3–0–14–0; Kirsten 1–0–9–0.

Umpires: B. L. Aldridge and J. D. Buultjens.

SRI LANKA v WEST INDIES

At Berri, March 13. West Indies won by 91 runs. Toss: Sri Lanka. The West Indians pressed on, their hopes of a semi-final place growing, while the exhausted Sri Lankans continued their slide down the table. Simmons reached his highest score in limited-overs internationals in 125 balls, with the help of two sixes and nine fours, and three dropped catches when he was six and 47 (twice). Receiving valuable support from Haynes and Arthurton, he took West Indies to 197 by the 40th over. Then five wickets went cheaply before the tail hit out; the No. 10, Benjamin, struck an unbeaten 24 from 20 deliveries. Samarasekera gave Sri Lanka another promising start, with 40 from 41 balls. But he fell to Hooper's off-spin, and 80 for one became 99 for four. Briefly, Ranatunga organised some resistance and the last man, Wickremasinghe, saved his team from the indignity of being bowled out for under 150.

Man of the Match: P. V. Simmons.   *Attendance:* 3,107.

West Indies

D. L. Haynes c Tillekeratne b Ranatunga	38	†D. Williams c Tillekeratne b Hathurusinghe	2
B. C. Lara c and b Ramanayake	1	C. E. L. Ambrose not out	15
P. V. Simmons c Wickremasinghe b Hathurusinghe	110	W. K. M. Benjamin not out	24
*R. B. Richardson run out	8		
K. L. T. Arthurton c Tillekeratne b Hathurusinghe	40	L-b 9, w 3, n-b 6	18
A. L. Logie b Anurasiri	0	1/6 2/72 3/103	(8 wkts, 50 overs) 268
C. L. Hooper c Gurusinha b Hathurusinghe	12	4/197 5/199 6/219 7/223 8/228	

A. C. Cummins did not bat.

Bowling: Wickremasinghe 7–0–30–0; Ramanayake 7–1–17–1; Anurasiri 10–0–46–1; Gurusinha 1–0–10–0; Ranatunga 7–0–35–1; Kalpage 10–0–64–0; Hathurusinghe 8–0–57–4.

Sri Lanka

R. S. Mahanama c Arthurton b Cummins	.	11
M. A. R. Samarasekera lbw b Hooper	.	40
U. C. Hathurusinghe run out		16
*P. A. de Silva c and b Hooper		11
A. Ranatunga c Benjamin b Arthurton	.	24
A. P. Gurusinha c Richardson b Ambrose	.	10
†H. P. Tillekeratne b Ambrose		3

R. S. Kalpage not out		13
C. P. H. Ramanayake b Arthurton		1
S. D. Anurasiri b Benjamin		3
G. P. Wickremasinghe not out		21
L-b 8, w 14, n-b 2		24

1/56 2/80 3/86 (9 wkts, 50 overs) 177
4/99 5/130 6/135
7/137 8/139 9/149

Bowling: Ambrose 10-2-24-2; Benjamin 10-0-34-1; Cummins 9-0-49-1; Hooper 10-1-19-2; Arthurton 10-0-40-2; Simmons 1-0-3-0.

Umpires: D. R. Shepherd and S. J. Woodward.

AUSTRALIA v ZIMBABWE

At Hobart, March 14. Australia won by 128 runs. Toss: Zimbabwe. A straightforward win over point-less Zimbabwe was a relief for the demoralised Australians and a showcase for the Waugh twins. It even gave Australia faint hopes of reaching the last four on run-rate. A shower after 15 overs, with Australia 72 for one, reduced the match to 46 overs a side. By the time Steve Waugh joined his brother Mark, Australia had reached 144 from 34 overs, but in 69 balls they added 113 (50 runs coming from a mere 17 deliveries). Though Steve went for 55, Mark remained undefeated on 66 from 39 balls. Later, Steve collected two top-order wickets and Mark two catches, propelling Zimbabwe from 47 for no wicket to 97 for seven.

Man of the Match: S. R. Waugh.   *Attendance*: 7,411.

Australia

T. M. Moody run out	6
D. C. Boon b Shah	48
D. M. Jones b Burmester	54
*A. R. Border st Flower b Traicos	22
M. E. Waugh not out	66
S. R. Waugh b Brandes	55

†I. A. Healy lbw b Duers	0
P. L. Taylor not out	1
B 2, l-b 8, w 2, n-b 1	13

1/8 2/102 3/134 (6 wkts, 46 overs) 265
4/144 5/257 6/258

C. J. McDermott, M. R. Whitney and B. A. Reid did not bat.

Bowling: Brandes 9-0-59-1; Duers 9-1-48-1; Burmester 9-0-65-1; Shah 9-0-53-1; Traicos 10-0-30-1.

Zimbabwe

A. H. Shah run out	23
†A. Flower c Border b S. R. Waugh	20
A. D. R. Campbell c M. E. Waugh b Whitney	4
A. J. Pycroft c M. E. Waugh b S. R. Waugh	0
*D. L. Houghton b McDermott	2
A. C. Waller c Taylor b Moody	18
K. J. Arnott b Whitney	8

E. A. Brandes c McDermott b Taylor	23
M. G. Burmester c Border b Reid	12
A. J. Traicos c Border b Taylor	3
K. G. Duers not out	2
L-b 12, w 8, n-b 2	22

1/47 2/51 3/51 (41.4 overs) 137
4/57 5/69 6/88
7/97 8/117 9/132

Bowling: McDermott 8-0-26-1; Reid 9-2-17-1; S. R. Waugh 7-0-28-2; Whitney 10-3-15-2; Moody 4-0-25-1; Taylor 3.4-0-14-2.

Umpires: B. L. Aldridge and S. A. Bucknor.

NEW ZEALAND v ENGLAND

At Wellington, March 15. New Zealand won by seven wickets. Toss: New Zealand. New Zealand avenged their recent Test defeats with a record seventh successive World Cup win, and ended England's run of 17 matches without defeat since leaving home. England were severely depleted, with Gooch and Fairbrother unfit, Lewis unable to bowl, and DeFreitas and Reeve carrying injuries. Lamb played his first game of the tournament, but Pringle became a new casualty, departing in mid-over with damaged ribs. Crowe, relieved by the omission of New Zealand's bogey-man Tufnell, gave Patel the new ball, and was rewarded with a five-over spell which conceded only seven runs and removed Botham; even Jones's rather occasional off-spin merited nine overs and picked up two wickets. England's best effort came from Stewart and Hick, who added 70 in 14 overs. But on Patel's return Stewart swept to square leg, and only 105 came from the last 30. Hick edged to Greatbatch, keeping wicket for Ian Smith, who had migraine. The remaining batsmen found the boundary only twice, and the hands of deep fielders all too often. Greatbatch had no such difficulties. He smashed 35 from 37 balls, and took New Zealand to 64 by the 13th over. Then Jones (13 fours) and Crowe, driving and cutting, put on 108 in 23 overs. Their victory confirmed that New Zealand would head the qualifying table, with England second.

Man of the Match: A. H. Jones.   *Attendance:* 13,612.

England

†A. J. Stewart c Harris b Patel	41	P. A. J. DeFreitas c Cairns b Harris	0
I. T. Botham b Patel	8	R. K. Illingworth not out	2
G. A. Hick c Greatbatch b Harris	56		
R. A. Smith c Patel b Jones	38		
A. J. Lamb c Cairns b Watson	12	B 1, l-b 7, w 4	12
J. C. Lewis c and b Watson	0		
D. A. Reeve not out	21	1/25 2/95 3/135 (8 wkts, 50 overs)	200
D. R. Pringle c sub (R. T. Latham)		4/162 5/162 6/169	
b Jones	10	7/189 8/195	

G. C. Small did not bat.

Bowling: Patel 10–1–26–2; Harris 8–0–39–2; Watson 10–0–40–2; Cairns 3–0–21–0; Larsen 10–3–24–0; Jones 9–0–42–2.

New Zealand

M. J. Greatbatch c DeFreitas b Botham	35	K. R. Rutherford not out	3
J. G. Wright b DeFreitas	1	B 1, l-b 8, w 1, n-b 1	11
A. H. Jones run out	78		
*M. D. Crowe not out	73	1/5 2/64 3/172 (3 wkts, 40.5 overs)	201

C. Z. Harris, †I. D. S. Smith, C. L. Cairns, D. N. Patel, G. R. Larsen and W. Watson did not bat.

Bowling: Pringle 6.2–1–34–0; DeFreitas 8.3–1–45–1; Botham 4–0–19–1; Illingworth 9–1–46–0; Hick 6–0–26–0; Reeve 3–0–9–0; Small 4–0–13–0.

Umpires: S. G. Randell and I. D. Robinson.

INDIA v SOUTH AFRICA

At Adelaide, March 15. South Africa won by six wickets. Toss: South Africa. Heavy rain reduced the match to 30 overs a side, and South Africa did well to surpass the Indians' six runs an over. After Srikkanth fell quickly to Kirsten's one-handed catch, Azharuddin (77 balls) stylishly added 78 with India's latest opener, Manjrekar, and then 71 in eight overs with Kapil Dev (a hectic 42 in 29 balls). Promoted to open for South Africa, Kirsten scored at almost a run a ball, and put on 128 with Hudson, who reached his third fifty in four innings. When Kirsten was yorked with 24 needed from three overs, Wessels supervised the final chase. Victory assured South Africa of a semi-final appearance, unless politics intervened; Geoff Dakin, president of the United Cricket Board of South Africa, said he would feel obliged to withdraw if the all-white referendum two days later rejected constitutional reform. Pakistan and West Indies, however, urged them to remain, and a decisive vote for reform made the matter academic.

Man of the Match: P. N. Kirsten. *Attendance:* 6,272.

India

K. Srikkanth c Kirsten b Donald	0	P. K. Amre not out		1
S. V. Manjrekar b Kuiper	28	J. Srinath not out		0
*M. Azharuddin c Kuiper b Pringle	79	L-b 7, w 6, n-b 2		15
S. R. Tendulkar c Wessels b Kuiper	14			
Kapil Dev b Donald	42	1/1 2/79 3/103	(6 wkts, 30 overs)	180
V. G. Kambli run out	1	4/174 5/177 6/179		

M. Prabhakar, †K. S. More and S. L. V. Raju did not bat.

Bowling: Donald 6-0-34-2; Pringle 6-0-37-1; Snell 6-1-46-0; McMillan 6-0-28-0; Kuiper 6-0-28-2.

South Africa

A. C. Hudson b Srinath	53	W. J. Cronje not out		8
P. N. Kirsten b Kapil Dev	84	L-b 10, n-b 3		13
A. P. Kuiper run out	7			
J. N. Rhodes c Raju b Prabhakar	7	1/128 2/149	(4 wkts, 29.1 overs)	181
*K. C. Wessels not out	9	3/157 4/163		

B. M. McMillan, †D. J. Richardson, R. P. Snell, A. A. Donald and M. W. Pringle did not bat.

Bowling: Kapil Dev 6-0-36-1; Prabhakar 5.1-1-33-1; Tendulkar 6-0-20-0; Srinath 6-0-39-1; Raju 6-0-43-0.

Umpires: J. D. Buultjens and Khizar Hayat.

PAKISTAN v SRI LANKA

At Perth, March 15. Pakistan won by four wickets. Toss: Sri Lanka. After their promising start, Sri Lanka ended the tournament as the lowest-placed of the Test nations, while Pakistan's regeneration continued. Once more, however, they were profligate with wides and no-balls, and de Silva added 51 in ten overs with Samarasekera. The innings lost momentum without them, and 213 seemed within Pakistan's reach. In a nervous start Aamir Sohail was caught in the second over, and Imran took nearly an hour over two runs. At the halfway mark they were 84 for three. But the chase was given momentum by Javed Miandad and Salim Malik, who added 101 in 21 overs for the fourth wicket. When Miandad left, the target was down to 28 from six overs, and in the end Pakistan had five balls to spare.

Man of the Match: Javed Miandad. *Attendance:* 3,071.

Sri Lanka

R. S. Mahanama b Wasim Akram	12	A. Ranatunga c sub (Zahid Fazal)		
M. A. R. Samarasekera st Moin Khan		b Aamir Sohail		7
b Mushtaq Ahmed	38	†H. P. Tillekeratne not out		25
U. C. Hathurusinghe		R. S. Kalpage not out		13
b Mushtaq Ahmed	5			
*P. A. de Silva c Aamir Sohail		L-b 15, w 11, n-b 6		32
b Ijaz Ahmed	43			
A. P. Gurusinha c Salim Malik		1/29 2/48 3/99	(6 wkts, 50 overs)	212
b Imran Khan	37	4/132 5/158 6/187		

C. P. H. Ramanayake, G. P. Wickremasinghe and K. I. W. Wijegunawardene did not bat.

Bowling: Wasim Akram 10-0-37-1; Aqib Javed 10-0-39-0; Imran Khan 8-1-36-1; Mushtaq Ahmed 10-0-43-2; Ijaz Ahmed 8-0-28-1; Aamir Sohail 4-0-14-1.

Pakistan

Aamir Sohail c Mahanama b Ramanayake .	1	Salim Malik c Kalpage b Ramanayake .	51
Ramiz Raja c Gurusinha b Wickremasinghe .	32	Inzamam-ul-Haq run out .	11
*Imran Khan c de Silva b Hathurusinghe .	22	Ijaz Ahmed not out .	8
		Wasim Akram not out .	5
Javed Miandad c Wickremasinghe b Gurusinha .	57	L-b 12, w 9, n-b 8 .	29

†Moin Khan, Mushtaq Ahmed and Aqib Javed did not bat.

1/7 2/68 3/84   (6 wkts, 49.1 overs) 216
4/185 5/201 6/205

Bowling: Wijegunawardene 10-1-34-0; Ramanayake 10-1-37-2; Wickremasinghe 1-0-41-1; Gurusinha 9-0-38-1; Hathurusinghe 9-0-40-1; Kalpage 2-0-14-0.

Umpires: K. E. Liebenberg and P. J. McConnell.

NEW ZEALAND v PAKISTAN

At Christchurch, March 18. Pakistan won by seven wickets. Toss: Pakistan. New Zealand dropped their first points, but as the result killed Australia's chances it guaranteed them a home semi-final. Pakistan had to wait until West Indies lost in the evening to know that they would meet their hosts again in Auckland. It was the leg-spinner, Mushtaq Ahmed, who claimed the bowling honours and the match award, but Ramiz Raja was a strong rival. His second unbeaten hundred of the World Cup, and its highest score (16 fours, 155 balls), sustained Pakistan after they were nine for two. Aamir Sohail was caught off Morrison's first ball, which bounced enough to be an arguable no-ball, and Inzamam was bowled in his next over. Patel then put down a return catch from Javed Miandad, on three; Miandad stayed to contribute 30 to a 115-run stand with Ramiz. The victory had been set up by the bowlers, however, especially Mushtaq, who came on in the eighth over. He conceded no boundaries and only 18 runs in all; he also removed Harris, stumped off a wide, and Greatbatch, the one batsman in the top eight to reach double figures (hitting two fours and a six in Aqib Javed's first over). Only a ninth-wicket partnership of 44 from Larsen and Morrison, both batting for the first time in the tournament, presented any challenge.

Man of the Match: Mushtaq Ahmed.   *Attendance*: 9,974.

New Zealand

M. J. Greatbatch c Salim Malik b Mushtaq Ahmed .	42	†I. D. S. Smith b Imran Khan .	1
R. T. Latham c Inzamam-ul-Haq b Aqib Javed .	6	G. R. Larsen b Wasim Akram .	37
A. H. Jones lbw b Wasim Akram .	2	D. K. Morrison c Inzamam-ul-Haq b Wasim Akram .	12
*M. D. Crowe c Aamir Sohail b Wasim Akram .	3	W. Watson not out .	5
K. R. Rutherford run out .	8	B 3, l-b 23, w 12, n-b 4 .	42
C. Z. Harris st Moin Khan b Mushtaq Ahmed .	1		
D. N. Patel c Mushtaq Ahmed b Aamir Sohail .	7	1/23 2/26 3/39 (48.2 overs) 166 4/85 5/88 6/93 7/96 8/106 9/150	

Bowling: Wasim Akram 9.2-0-32-4; Aqib Javed 10-1-34-1; Mushtaq Ahmed 10-0-18-2; Imran Khan 8-0-22-1; Aamir Sohail 10-1-29-1; Ijaz Ahmed 1-0-5-0.

Pakistan

Aamir Sohail c Patel b Morrison .	0	Salim Malik not out .	9
Ramiz Raja not out .	119	L-b 1, w 1, n-b 2 .	4
Inzamam-ul-Haq b Morrison .	5		
Javed Miandad lbw b Morrison .	30	1/0 2/9 3/124 (3 wkts, 44.4 overs) 167	

*Imran Khan, Ijaz Ahmed, Wasim Akram, †Moin Khan, Aqib Javed and Mushtaq Ahmed did not bat.

Bowling: Morrison 10–0–42–3; Patel 10–2–25–0; Watson 10–3–26–0; Harris 4–0–18–0; Larsen 3–0–16–0; Jones 3–0–10–0; Latham 2–0–13–0; Rutherford 1.4–0–11–0; Greatbatch 1–0–5–0.

Umpires: S. A. Bucknor and S. G. Randell.

ENGLAND v ZIMBABWE

At Albury, March 18. Zimbabwe won by nine runs. Toss: England. In the upset of the tournament, Cup favourites England were bowled out by Zimbabwe, ten runs short of a paltry target of 135. Zimbabwe earned their first points of the competition and their first win after 18 defeats since beating Australia on their World Cup début in 1983. On that day, Houghton was top-scored with 29, and the ducks were collected by Gooch and Hick, a very junior member of Zimbabwe's 1983 party. Ironically Zimbabwe owed victory to their much-derided bowling. A bowlers' pitch was no excuse for England, who had enjoyed the same advantage. Gooch departed first ball, a feather in the cap of Brandes, whose single spell plucked four prize wickets. Just as heroic were Shah and Traicos, whose 20 overs cost a mere 33 runs. At 43 for five Stewart joined Fairbrother for the biggest stand of the match, a painfully slow 52 in 24 overs. Fairbrother, still suffering from a stomach infection, batted over two hours without reaching the boundary. England narrowly ran out of wickets before overs.

Man of the Match: E. A. Brandes.　　　*Attendance:* 5,645.

Zimbabwe

W. R. James c and b Illingworth	13	E. A. Brandes st Stewart b Illingworth	14	
†A. Flower b DeFreitas	7	A. J. Traicos not out	0	
A. J. Pycroft c Gooch b Botham	3	M. P. Jarvis lbw b Illingworth	0	
K. J. Arnott lbw b Botham	11	L-b 8, w 8	16	
*D. L. Houghton c Fairbrother b Small	29			
A. C. Waller b Tufnell	8	1/12 2/19 3/30	(46.1 overs) 134	
A. H. Shah c Lamb b Tufnell	3	4/52 5/65 6/77		
I. P. Butchart c Fairbrother b Botham	24	7/96 8/127 9/127		

Bowling: DeFreitas 8–1–14–1; Small 9–1–20–1; Botham 10–3–23–3; Illingworth 9.1–0–33–3; Tufnell 10–2–36–2.

England

*G. A. Gooch lbw b Brandes	0	R. K. Illingworth run out	1	
I. T. Botham c Flower b Shah	18	G. C. Small c Pycroft b Jarvis	5	
A. J. Lamb c James b Brandes	17	P. C. R. Tufnell not out	0	
R. A. Smith b Brandes	2	B 4, l-b 3, w 11, n-b 1	19	
G. A. Hick b Brandes	0			
N. H. Fairbrother c Flower b Butchart	20	1/0 2/32 3/42	(49.1 overs) 125	
†A. J. Stewart c Waller b Shah	29	4/42 5/43 6/95		
P. A. J. DeFreitas c Flower b Butchart	4	7/101 8/108 9/124		

Bowling: Brandes 10–4–21–4; Jarvis 9.1–0–32–1; Shah 10–3–17–2; Traicos 10–4–16–0; Butchart 10–1–32–2.

Umpires: B. L. Aldridge and Khizar Hayat.

AUSTRALIA v WEST INDIES

At Melbourne, March 18 (day/night). Australia won by 57 runs. Toss: Australia. Forty-five minutes into their innings, Australia's semi-final aspirations were ended by news of Pakistan's victory. But their own win eliminated the West Indians, and earned themselves consolatory fifth place in the final table on run-rate. West Indies could blame themselves the Australians' total was well within reach after they failed to build on an opening stand of 107 in 27 overs. Boon scored his sixth international century of the season, duplicating his 100 in the opening World Cup match in Auckland. For a mere 4.34 an over, the West

Indians would have been in the last four. But only Lara met the challenge, batting 38 overs for 70. Haynes and Simmons went to consecutive balls in McDermott's fourth over, and Whitney bowled his ten straight through to remove Richardson, Arthurton, Logie and Hooper. Lara's off-drives and sweeps pushed the score on until, at 137, he called Benjamin for a run. When his colleague made no response, West Indies' last chance was shattered with Lara's stumps.

Man of the Match: D. C. Boon.   *Attendance*: 47,572.

Australia

T. M. Moody c Benjamin b Simmons .. 42	†I. A. Healy not out	11
D. C. Boon c Williams b Cummins 100	P. L. Taylor not out	10
D. M. Jones c Williams b Cummins ... 6	L-b 2, w 3, n-b 6...........	12
*A. R. Border lbw b Simmons 8		
M. E. Waugh st Williams b Hooper ... 21	1/107 2/128 3/141 (6 wkts, 50 overs) 216	
S. R. Waugh b Cummins 6	4/185 5/189 6/200	

C. J. McDermott, M. R. Whitney and B. A. Reid did not bat.

Bowling: Ambrose 10-0-46-0; Benjamin 10-1-49-0; Cummins 10-1-38-3; Hooper 10-0-40-1; Simmons 10-1-40-2.

West Indies

D. L. Haynes c Jones b McDermott ... 14	W. K. M. Benjamin lbw b S. R. Waugh	15
B. C. Lara run out	70	C. E. L. Ambrose run out 2
P. V. Simmons lbw b McDermott 0	A. C. Cummins not out 5
*R. B. Richardson c Healy b Whitney . 10		
K. L. T. Arthurton c McDermott	B 3, l-b 5, w 3, n-b 4	15
b Whitney . 15		
A. L. Logie c Healy b Whitney 5	1/27 2/27 3/59 (42.4 overs) 159	
C. L. Hooper c M. E. Waugh b Whitney 4	4/83 5/99 6/117	
†D. Williams c Border b Reid 4	7/128 8/137 9/150	

Bowling: McDermott 6-1-29-2; Reid 10-1-26-1; Whitney 10-1-34-4; S. R. Waugh 6.4-0-24-1; Taylor 4-0-24-0; Moody 6-1-14-0.

Umpires: P. D. Reporter and D. R. Shepherd.

QUALIFYING TABLE

	Played	Won	Lost	No result	Pts	Net run-rate
NEW ZEALAND......	8	7	1	0	14	0.59
ENGLAND..........	8	5	2	1	11	0.47
SOUTH AFRICA......	8	5	3	0	10	0.13
PAKISTAN..........	8	4	3	1	9	0.16
Australia............	8	4	4	0	8	0.20
West Indies	8	4	4	0	8	0.07
India...............	8	2	5	1	5	0.14
Sri Lanka	8	2	5	1	5	−0.68
Zimbabwe	8	1	7	0	2	−1.14

Net run-rate was calculated by subtracting runs conceded per over from runs scored per over, revising figures in shortened matches and discounting those not played to a result.

SEMI-FINALS

NEW ZEALAND v PAKISTAN

At Auckland, March 21. Pakistan won by four wickets. Toss: New Zealand. Pakistan reached their first World Cup final by defeating the previously invincible New Zealanders twice in four days. This win seemed unlikely when they needed 123 from 15 overs at 8.2. But the match was transformed by Inzamam-ul-Haq, whose aggressive hitting gave him 60 from 37 balls (one six, seven fours, 50 in 31) and a partnership of 87 in ten overs with Javed Miandad. When Inzamam was run out the target was 36 from five, which was passed with ease thanks to Wasim Akram, Moin Khan (20 not out in 11 balls) and Miandad, who chivvied his partners along for two hours and came in unbeaten on 57. Imran Khan ran out to welcome him as his opposite number, Crowe, limped on for New Zealand's lap of honour. He had sat out Pakistan's innings with a pulled hamstring, and Wright led in the field. Yet Crowe's day had begun happily enough: he was named Man of the Series for his batting and captaincy to date; he won the toss, and going in he re-emphasised his class with an accomplished 91 in 83 balls including three sixes. When he arrived New Zealand were tangled in Mushtaq Ahmed's leg-spin after Greatbatch's usual explosion (sixes off Wasim and Aqib Javed). Crowe accelerated smoothly, adding 107 in 113 balls with Rutherford. But when Rutherford skied the ball to Moin, the batsmen crossed and Crowe's hamstring went. He continued with Greatbatch as his runner, and this supposed aide ran him out. Still, Smith and the tail hurried on to 262. It was an imposing target, especially in mid-innings when Imran seemed bogged down. But against Inzamam's dynamism, New Zealand's successful stratagems of the past month had no power. Even their surprise weapon, Patel, whose opening eight overs of off-breaks garnered one for 28, yielded 22 when he returned for his last two.

Man of the Match: Inzamam-ul-Haq.   *Attendance:* 32,439.

New Zealand

M. J. Greatbatch b Aqib Javed	17	†I. D. S. Smith not out 18
J. G. Wright c Ramiz Raja b Mushtaq Ahmed	13	D. N. Patel lbw b Wasim Akram 8
A. H. Jones lbw b Mushtaq Ahmed	21	G. R. Larsen not out 8
*M. D. Crowe run out	91	
K. R. Rutherford c Moin Khan b Wasim Akram	50	B 4, l-b 7, w 8, n-b 4 23
C. Z. Harris st Moin Khan b Iqbal Sikandar	13	1/35 2/39 3/87 (7 wkts, 50 overs) 262
		4/194 5/214
		6/221 7/244

D. K. Morrison and W. Watson did not bat.

Bowling: Wasim Akram 10–0–40–2; Aqib Javed 10–2–45–1; Mushtaq Ahmed 10–0–40–2; Imran Khan 10–0–59–0; Iqbal Sikandar 9–0–56–1; Aamir Sohail 1–0–11–0.

Pakistan

Aamir Sohail c Jones b Patel	14	Wasim Akram b Watson 9
Ramiz Raja c Morrison b Watson	44	†Moin Khan not out 20
*Imran Khan c Larsen b Harris	44	
Javed Miandad not out	57	B 4, l-b 10, w 1 15
Salim Malik c sub (R. T. Latham) b Larsen	1	1/30 2/84 3/134 (6 wkts, 49 overs) 264
Inzamam-ul-Haq run out	60	4/140 5/227 6/238

Iqbal Sikandar, Mushtaq Ahmed and Aqib Javed did not bat.

Bowling: Patel 10–1–50–1; Morrison 9–0–55–0; Watson 10–2–39–2; Larsen 10–1–34–1; Harris 10–0–72–1.

Umpires: S. A. Bucknor and D. R. Shepherd.

ENGLAND v SOUTH AFRICA

At Sydney, March 22 (day/night). England won by 19 runs, South Africa's target having been revised to 252 from 43 overs. Toss: South Africa. This game's closing minutes buried South Africa's World Cup hopes, and whatever credibility the "rain rule" had retained. By putting pressure on the team batting second, the rule supposedly created exciting finishes; on this occasion 12 minutes' heavy rain, when South Africa needed 22 from 13 balls, adjusted their target first to 22 from seven, and then to 21 from one. McMillan could only take a single off Lewis. The losers were disconsolate, the winners embarrassed, and the crowd furious. Why, they asked, were the two overs not played out under the floodlights?

The majority blamed the World Cup's organising committee, and the inflexibility which prevented a second-day resumption. (The next day was set aside only for a completely new match, to be played if the second team had not faced 25 overs.) Justice was probably done; Wessels chose to field, knowing the rules and the forecast, and his bowlers were fined for going slow and depriving England of five overs' acceleration. But it was not seen to be done, and fine performances on both sides were overshadowed by indignation.

Most of England's batsmen scored fluently, but the *tour de force* came from Hick. He survived an lbw appeal first ball, and was caught off a no-ball before scoring, but went on to 83 in 90 balls, adding 71 in 14 overs with Stewart, and 73 with Fairbrother. Reeve raced out to score 25 from 14 balls, including 17 of the 18 plundered from Donald's final over. Pursuing 5.62 an over, South Africa made 58 from their first ten. For once they did not depend on Kirsten, hampered by an injury. Hudson narrowly missed a fourth fifty, Kuiper hit three consecutive fours off Small, and Rhodes proved his worth as a batsman, reducing the target to 47 from just over five overs; McMillan and Richardson knocked off 25 from three before the rain, and the rules, made their task impossible.

Man of the Match: G. A. Hick.   *Attendance*: 35,088.

England

*G. A. Gooch c Richardson b Donald .	2	C. C. Lewis not out 18
I. T. Botham b Pringle	21	D. A. Reeve not out 25
†A. J. Stewart c Richardson		
b McMillan .	33	B 1, l-b 7, w 9, n-b 6 23
G. A. Hick c Rhodes b Snell	83	—
N. H. Fairbrother b Pringle	28	1/20 2/39 3/110 (6 wkts, 45 overs) 252
A. J. Lamb c Richardson b Donald	19	4/183 5/187 6/221

P. A. J. DeFreitas, R. K. Illingworth and G. C. Small did not bat.

Bowling: Donald 10–0–69–2; Pringle 9–2–36–2; Snell 8–0–52–1; McMillan 9–0–47–1; Kuiper 5–0–26–0; Cronje 4–0–14–0.

South Africa

*K. C. Wessels c Lewis b Botham	17	B. M. McMillan not out 21
A. C. Hudson lbw b Illingworth	46	†D. J. Richardson not out........... 13
P. N. Kirsten b DeFreitas	11	L-b 17, w 4 21
A. P. Kuiper b Illingworth	36	—
W. J. Cronje c Hick b Small	24	1/26 2/61 3/90 (6 wkts, 43 overs) 232
J. N. Rhodes c Lewis b Small	43	4/131 5/176 6/206

R. P. Snell, M. W. Pringle and A. A. Donald did not bat.

Bowling: Botham 10–0–52–1; Lewis 5–0–38–0; DeFreitas 8–1–28–1; Illingworth 10–1–46–2; Small 10–1–51–2.

Umpires: B. L. Aldridge and S. G. Randell.

FINAL

ENGLAND v PAKISTAN

At Melbourne, March 25 (day/night). Pakistan won by 22 runs. Toss: Pakistan. Imran Khan's erratically brilliant Pakistanis won their first World Cup final while Gooch and England lost their third, on the broad field of Melbourne with nearly 90,000 in attendance. Afterwards Imran said it was "the most fulfilling and satisfying cricket moment of my life". He described the victory as a triumph for his young team's talent over England's experience; he also stressed the role of his aggressive specialist bowlers rather than the "stereotyped" attack of Gooch's all-rounders. But he enjoyed an all-round triumph himself with the match's highest score and the final wicket.

Imran's role went deeper, however. He had virtually hand-picked the team, and after the disappointment of losing a key player, the pace bowler Waqar Younis, to a stress fracture before leaving Pakistan, and a disastrous start when they won only one in five matches (two of which he missed), he urged them to imitate the action of a cornered tiger before they went on to five successive wins. They reached the giant stadium in peak form, while England looked exhausted. The players who had toured New Zealand unconquered had gradually weakened in the face of constant travel and frequent injury. As Pakistan had picked up, they had been losing, first to New Zealand and then, most embarrassingly, to Zimbabwe. "It's not the end of the world," said Gooch after the match, "but it is close to it. We got beaten fair and square." England were worn down by the century partnership of veterans Imran and Javed Miandad, which started slowly but gathered force, and the spirit of their batsmen was broken by successive balls from Man of the Match Wasim Akram which dismissed Lamb and Lewis, one swinging in and then straightening again, the next cutting in sharply.

Remembering the baleful potential of rain, and knowing that no one had won a World Cup final chasing runs, Imran had chosen to bat. At first England prospered. In nine overs Pringle reduced Pakistan to 24 for two. Then Imran and Miandad, the sole survivors in this World Cup of the 1975 tournament, settled down to see off the new ball. Progress was slow: Imran was nine from 16 overs when Gooch spilled a running catch. But although Pakistan were only 70 halfway through, and Miandad had summoned a runner, they accelerated to add 139 in 31 overs before Miandad attempted a reverse sweep. Soon Imran's strokeplaying protégés, Inzamam-ul-Haq (35 balls) and Wasim Akram (18 balls), took up the fight. Their 52 in six overs brought the runs from the last 20 overs to 153, though Pringle's final over cost just two and saw them both dismissed.

England's pursuit of five an over started badly when Botham was surprised to be given caught behind. The next time Moin Khan claimed a catch, Stewart escaped judgment, but not for long, and Mushtaq Ahmed's leg-spin accounted for Hick (baffled by the googly) and Gooch. With England requiring 181 from 29 overs, Lamb, preferred for his experience to Smith, whose fitness was in doubt, added 72 in 14 with Fairbrother. But Wasim returned to devastating effect. Deprived of heavyweight partners, and using a runner, Fairbrother top-edged to Moin after an hour and a half. The tail threw the bat to no avail. Imran dismissed Illingworth to complete his triumph, and pledged the proceeds of his success to the cancer hospital planned in his mother's memory.

Man of the Match: Wasim Akram.   *Attendance:* 87,182.

Pakistan

Aamir Sohail c Stewart b Pringle	4	Salim Malik not out	0
Ramiz Raja lbw b Pringle	8	L-b 19, w 6, n-b 7	32
*Imran Khan c Illingworth b Botham	72		—
Javed Miandad c Botham b Illingworth	58	1/20 (1) 2/24 (2) (6 wkts, 50 overs) 249
Inzamam-ul-Haq b Pringle	42	3/163 (4) 4/197 (3)
Wasim Akram run out	33	5/249 (5) 6/249 (6)

Ijaz Ahmed, †Moin Khan, Mushtaq Ahmed and Aqib Javed did not bat.

Bowling: Pringle 10-2-22-3; Lewis 10-2-52-0; Botham 7-0-42-1; DeFreitas 10-1-42-0; Illingworth 10-0-50-1; Reeve 3-0-22-0.

England

*G. A. Gooch c Aqib Javed		D. R. Pringle not out	18
b Mushtaq Ahmed	29	P. A. J. DeFreitas run out	10
I. T. Botham c Moin Khan		R. K. Illingworth c Ramiz Raja	
b Wasim Akram	0	b Imran Khan	14
†A. J. Stewart c Moin Khan			
b Aqib Javed	7		
G. A. Hick lbw b Mushtaq Ahmed	17	L-b 5, w 13, n-b 6	24
N. H. Fairbrother c Moin Khan			—
b Aqib Javed	62	1/6 (2) 2/21 (3) (49.2 overs) 227
A. J. Lamb b Wasim Akram	31	3/59 (4) 4/69 (1)
C. C. Lewis b Wasim Akram	0	5/141 (6) 6/141 (7)
D. A. Reeve c Ramiz Raja		7/180 (5) 8/183 (8)
b Mushtaq Ahmed	15	9/208 (10) 10/227 (11)

Bowling: Wasim Akram 10-0-49-3; Aqib Javed 10-2-27-2; Mushtaq Ahmed 10-1-41-3; Ijaz Ahmed 3-0-13-0; Imran Khan 6.2-0-43-1; Aamir Sohail 10-0-49-0.

Umpires: B. L. Aldridge and S. A. Bucknor.

ENGLAND IN NEW ZEALAND, 1991-92

By SCYLD BERRY

Few tours undertaken by England, or MCC before them, have been as successful as this one: their last full tour without a defeat was in the West Indies in 1967-68, when they won four and drew 12 of their various games. This time England won the majority of their matches: two out of three Tests, all three one-day internationals, another one-day game against Auckland (the closest they came to defeat), and two out of four practice matches, while in the two others they were on top. For seven weeks, in fine weather, England played to the peak of their form.

If there was a secret, it lay in what the England players did before landing in New Zealand. Firstly, they had six weeks of rest after the English season, some of them having played without respite since January 1990. Secondly, they prepared for their tour over the following six weeks, together at Lilleshall or at regional centres. Specialist coaches, all of them former England players, were called in to help develop individual techniques, thanks to the sponsorship of the City firm, Whittingdale. Before England's visit to the West Indies in 1989-90 a similar exercise had been tried, but this time the preparations were even more thorough, so that when England played their opening game against Auckland, their bowling and fielding were close to peak performance levels.

Whether England trained too hard in advance, so that they were too run-down by the time they reached the World Cup final three months after their tour began, can only be conjectured. What is undeniable is that by arriving "hot" in New Zealand, they caught their opponents cold, so that England were overtly superior from the start. A young side, missing not only Sir Richard Hadlee but John Bracewell and Martin Snedden, New Zealand were unable to bowl accurately, take their catches or put together partnerships in their first two Tests. But during the Second, they made a discovery in Murphy Su'a, a fast-medium left-armer born in New Zealand of Western Samoan parents, capable of spin as well during the Wellington Test and a useful tailender. Given his stock bowling to support the speed of Chris Cairns and Danny Morrison, New Zealand had the foundation of a new Test team. But it was a measure of England's power and purpose that not until the Third Test were New Zealand allowed to compete on equal terms.

The co-ordinated nature of England's effort was such that there could be no one outstanding player: throughout, a contribution was made by everyone who could get into the team, under the orchestration of Graham Gooch. But the greatest strides were made by Alec Stewart, the vice-captain and opening batsman, and the wicket-keeper in one-day internationals, who was finally made captain in the third of them, so that he would have some experience in the event of an accident to Gooch. England's selectors had been criticised for not choosing another opening batsman when Mike Atherton had to withdraw because of a back injury (along with Angus Fraser, who was replaced by Dermot Reeve); but there was no need for a specialist opener against inexperienced bowling on largely docile pitches. Aggressive strokeplay was required of England, to

give their bowlers time to winkle New Zealand out twice, and Stewart's 148 on the opening day of the series defined exactly the right tone.

Of England's other batsmen, Allan Lamb was less troubled than Robin Smith by the ball not coming on to the bat. Indeed, Lamb was at his best, until he pulled a hamstring in his right leg during the last international. There was no Test place for Mark Ramprakash or Neil Fairbrother – they might not have had a game at all if Atherton had been fit to take up his place – although Fairbrother was selected mainly with the World Cup in mind. If there was a disappointment, it was that Graeme Hick was still not able to make the transition to Test cricket. In two of his three first-class centuries he was dropped before scoring, and the same fallibility was evident at the start of his Test innings against pace, when the straight short ball sometimes found him transfixed with eyes averted. Of the 63 first-class centuries which Hick had made by the end of the tour, 13 had been made in only 35 non-Test innings in New Zealand, which suggested the milieu in which he was happiest.

England's medium-pacers had a mostly unrewarding time, except on the one pitch to suit them, in the Auckland Test; Phillip DeFreitas had to be re-classified into this category after straining his groin on the first day of practice in New Zealand. The extremes of their attack were therefore important, the pace of David Lawrence and Chris Lewis on the one hand, and the spin of Phil Tufnell on the other. Lawrence, however, strained his left side in Napier, and though desperately keen to play in the Second Test, had to wait until the Third, when he could not overcome the slowness of the Basin Reserve. In his absence Lewis stepped up a gear to become an outright fast bowler in the Auckland Test and Christchurch international. Add to that his fielding anywhere and his growing presence as a batsman – notably his back-foot driving through the off side and off the front foot through mid-wicket – and there seemed to be little that Lewis, at the age of 24, could not accomplish.

Tufnell's bowling was as excellent as Jack Russell's wicket-keeping. In the year since his unsatisfactory tour of Australia the left-arm spinner had worked on his fielding and his attitude to authority, to the point where Gooch said that Tufnell's approach was "first-class". In general, the pitches were too slow, too lacking in bounce, too reluctant to wear and tear, for Tufnell to gain much help there. What he did have, especially at Christchurch, was a strong wind to enable him to drift the ball into right-handers and make it dip.

On England's previous Test visit, in 1987-88, they had been tired, jaded, and content to play New Zealand at their own defensive game. England's strategy this time was precisely the opposite, although Gooch had not had the experience of playing a Test in New Zealand before. If it was not his most productive tour, he made a hundred of great sagacity in Auckland; and, like a true elder statesman, he was often happier in helping younger members of his team to fulfil themselves.

Under the new ICC regulations, bouncers were limited to one per over, but they would have been strictly rationed in any event, so slow were the pitches; and relations were so cordial that the match referee, Peter Burge, was not called upon to deal with any controversy between the teams. However, on the last day of the series, when Lawrence broke his left knee-cap, there was a scene as he was being carried from the field on a stretcher. Micky Stewart, England's team manager, was incensed by a cameraman whom he thought to be intrusive and became involved in a scuffle. As an attempt to intimidate, albeit an understandable one in an emotionally charged situation, it seemed a clear violation of the new Code of Conduct, but no action was taken. There was only a letter of regret to TVNZ from Bob Bennett, England's well-liked tour manager, in which Stewart was not even mentioned.

ENGLAND TOUR PARTY

G. A. Gooch (Essex) (*captain*), A. J. Stewart (Surrey) (*vice-captain*), P. A. J. DeFreitas (Lancs.), N. H. Fairbrother (Lancs.), G. A. Hick (Worcs.), A. J. Lamb (Northants), D. V. Lawrence (Glos.), C. C. Lewis (Leics.), D. R. Pringle (Essex), M. R. Ramprakash (Middx), D. A. Reeve (Warwicks.), R. C. Russell (Glos.), R. A. Smith (Hants) and P. C. R. Tufnell (Middx).

I. T. Botham and R. K. Illingworth (both Worcs.) joined the party during the tour. Botham had been allowed to start the tour late to fulfil television and pantomime commitments; Illingworth joined in preparation for the World Cup.

Tour manager: R. M. Bennett (Lancs.). *Team manager:* M. J. Stewart.

ENGLAND TOUR RESULTS

Test matches – Played 3: Won 2, Drawn 1.
First-class matches – Played 7: Won 4, Drawn 3.
Wins – New Zealand (2), New Zealand Emerging Players, New Zealand XI.
Draws – New Zealand, Minor Associations' XI, Central Districts.
One-day internationals – Played 3: Won 3.
Other non first-class match – Won against Auckland.

TEST MATCH AVERAGES

NEW ZEALAND – BATTING

	T	I	NO	R	HS	100s	Avge
M. L. Su'a	2	3	2	56	36	0	56.00
J. G. Wright	3	6	0	258	116	1	43.00
M. D. Crowe	3	6	1	212	56	0	42.40
A. H. Jones	3	6	0	226	143	1	37.66
D. N. Patel	3	5	0	155	99	0	31.00
C. L. Cairns	3	5	0	119	61	0	23.80
K. R. Rutherford ...	2	4	1	68	32	0	22.66
B. R. Hartland	3	6	0	88	45	0	14.66
I. D. S. Smith	2	3	0	42	21	0	14.00
D. K. Morrison	3	5	2	20	12	0	6.66

Played in one Test: M. J. Greatbatch 11, 0; R. T. Latham 25; A. C. Parore 0, 15; C. Pringle 6, 5*; S. A. Thomson 5, 0; W. Watson 2, 5*.

* Signifies not out.

BOWLING

	O	M	R	W	BB	5W/i	Avge
M. L. Su'a	100	31	236	8	3-87	0	29.50
W. Watson	50	23	100	3	2-41	0	33.33
D. N. Patel	143.3	34	374	10	4-87	0	37.40
C. L. Cairns	117	20	429	11	6-52	1	39.00
C. Pringle	36	4	127	3	3-127	0	42.33
D. K. Morrison ...	116.5	24	361	8	3-44	0	45.12

Also bowled: A. H. Jones 4-0-15-0; S. A. Thomson 15-3-47-0.

ENGLAND – BATTING

	T	I	NO	R	HS	100s	Avge
A. J. Lamb	3	5	0	338	142	1	67.60
A. J. Stewart	3	5	0	330	148	2	66.00
R. A. Smith	3	5	0	213	96	0	42.60
C. C. Lewis	2	3	0	126	70	0	42.00
R. C. Russell	3	5	1	135	36	0	33.75
G. A. Gooch	3	5	0	161	114	1	32.20
G. A. Hick	3	5	0	134	43	0	26.80
D. A. Reeve	3	5	0	124	59	0	24.80
D. R. Pringle	2	3	0	53	41	0	17.66
P. A. J. DeFreitas ...	3	4	1	11	7*	0	3.66
P. C. R. Tufnell	3	3	3	8	6*	0	–

Played in one Test: I. T. Botham 15, 1; D. V. Lawrence 6.

* Signifies not out.

BOWLING

	O	M	R	W	BB	5W/i	Avge
P. C. R. Tufnell	186.1	69	367	16	7-47	1	22.93
C. C. Lewis	100	23	249	10	5-31	1	24.90
I. T. Botham	22	5	76	3	2-23	0	25.33
P. A. J. DeFreitas ...	106.4	39	235	8	4-62	0	29.37
D. R. Pringle	58	16	162	5	2-21	0	32.40
G. A. Hick	87	36	148	4	4-126	0	37.00

Also bowled: D. V. Lawrence 29.1-8-71-1; D. A. Reeve 24.5-8-60-2; R. A. Smith 4-2-6-0.

ENGLAND AVERAGES – FIRST-CLASS MATCHES

BATTING

	M	I	NO	R	HS	100s	Avge
A. J. Lamb	5	8	2	563	142	1	93.83
A. J. Stewart	7	10	2	550	148	3	68.75
G. A. Hick	7	10	1	562	129*	3	62.44
C. C. Lewis	4	5	1	184	70	0	46.00
G. A. Gooch	7	10	1	379	114	2	42.11
D. A. Reeve	6	8	2	214	59	0	35.66
R. C. Russell	7	8	1	242	57	0	34.57

	M	I	NO	R	HS	100s	Avge
R. A. Smith	7	10	0	284	96	0	28.40
M. R. Ramprakash ..	4	5	2	47	19*	0	15.66
D. R. Pringle	5	6	1	63	41	0	12.60
P. C. R. Tufnell	5	4	3	10	6*	0	10.00
P. A. J. DeFreitas ...	5	4	1	11	7*	0	3.66

Played in three matches: D. V. Lawrence 4, 6. Played in two matches: I. T. Botham 15, 1; N. H. Fairbrother 9, 14*. R. K. Illingworth played in one match but did not bat.

* *Signifies not out.*

BOWLING

	O	M	R	W	BB	5W/i	Avge
D. V. Lawrence	93.1	28	200	10	5-52	1	20.00
P. C. R. Tufnell	290.3	100	590	28	7-47	2	21.07
I. T. Botham	38	9	116	5	2-23	0	23.20
C. C. Lewis	155.5	41	381	14	5-31	1	27.21
D. R. Pringle	149	42	361	12	2-21	0	30.08
D. A. Reeve	97	29	254	8	2-19	0	31.75
P. A. J. DeFreitas ...	160.4	57	372	11	4-62	0	33.81
G. A. Hick	157	60	312	5	4-126	0	62.40

Also bowled: G. A. Gooch 27–12–85–3; R. K. Illingworth 21–7–53–1; A. J. Lamb 1–0–6–0; M. R. Ramprakash 12–2–40–1; R. C. Russell 1–0–5–0; R. A. Smith 11–4–33–0; A. J. Stewart 2–0–9–0.

FIELDING

23 – R. C. Russell (22 ct, 1 st); 10 – G. A. Hick; 8 – A. J. Stewart; 7 – R. A. Smith; 3 – G. A. Gooch, A. J. Lamb, M. R. Ramprakash, D. A. Reeve, P. C. R. Tufnell; 2 – D. R. Pringle; 1 – I. T. Botham, C. C. Lewis.

Note: Matches in this section which were not first-class are signified by a dagger.

†At Auckland, January 2. England XI won by five wickets. Toss: England XI. Auckland 156 for nine (50 overs) (A. J. Hunt 38 not out; P. C. R. Tufnell four for 25); England XI 158 for five (49.5 overs) (N. H. Fairbrother 44, G. A. Hick 34 not out).

NEW ZEALAND EMERGING PLAYERS v ENGLAND XI

At Hamilton, January 3, 4, 5. England XI won by an innings and 105 runs. Toss: England XI. A side comprising youngsters, save for the captain Ian Smith, were overawed and far too cautious when batting against an England team under the captaincy of Stewart for the first time. Pocock blocked for 112 minutes in scoring eight to set the tone, and only Howell, the Young New Zealand captain of a year before, was confident enough to play strokes. In his first innings the left-handed Vaughan, a doctor born in Hereford, played forward to Hick, saw the ball trickling backwards towards his stumps, and used his left hand to sweep the ball away; it was only the third instance of a handled-ball dismissal in New Zealand. Gooch, ten not out at the end of the first day, went on to reach his 90th first-class century by lunch on the second, while Hick – 20 fours in 231 minutes – made a century to go with the one he had scored for Northern Districts against England four years before on the same ground. The tourists were sharp again in the field as the Emerging Players, lacking Pawson, whose hand had been broken by Lawrence, were defeated before tea on the last day.

Close of play: First day, England XI 15-1 (G. A. Gooch 10*, R. C. Russell 3*); Second day, England XI 434-4 (M. R. Ramprakash 10*, C. C. Lewis 22*).

New Zealand Emerging Players

B. R. Hartland c Russell b Lawrence	1	– c Russell b Lawrence	0
B. A. Pocock c Hick b Gooch	8	– c Russell b Lawrence	1
L. G. Howell c Tufnell b Gooch	28	– c Gooch b Lewis	28
J. T. C. Vaughan handled the ball	28	– c and b Tufnell	24
C. Z. Harris c Russell b Lawrence	60	– c Lewis b Tufnell	14
J. D. Wells c Hick b DeFreitas	13	– c Russell b Lewis	29
*†I. D. S. Smith c Hick b DeFreitas	10	– c Lamb b Tufnell	6
M. H. Richardson b Tufnell	5	– c Russell b Tufnell	16
M. J. Pawson not out	4	– absent injured	
C. Pringle not out	5	– (10) not out	8
M. L. Su'a (did not bat)		– (9) c Ramprakash b Tufnell	13
L-b 9, w 5	14	B 5, l-b 2, n-b 7	14

1/2 2/34 3/39 4/108 5/139	(8 wkts dec.) 176	1/4 2/13 3/42 4/63 5/84	153
6/154 7/161 8/167		6/90 7/114 8/141 9/153

Bowling: *First Innings*—Lawrence 18–7–28–2; DeFreitas 18–7–38–2; Lewis 16–5–35–0; Gooch 11–6–14–2; Tufnell 21–7–34–1; Hick 10–5–18–0. *Second Innings*—Lawrence 12–5–15–2; DeFreitas 10–3–24–0; Lewis 11.5–3–37–2; Tufnell 23–4–66–5; Hick 4–2–4–0.

England XI

G. A. Gooch retired hurt	101	M. R. Ramprakash not out		10
*A. J. Stewart c Smith b Pringle	0	C. C. Lewis not out		22
†R. C. Russell c sub b Vaughan	50	B 4, l-b 4, n-b 9		17
G. A. Hick retired hurt	129			
R. A. Smith b Pringle	17	1/7 2/143	(4 wkts dec.)	434
A. J. Lamb c Smith b Su'a	88	3/204 4/387		

P. A. J. DeFreitas, P. C. R. Tufnell and D. V. Lawrence did not bat.

G. A. Gooch retired hurt at 181. G. A. Hick retired hurt at 407.

Bowling: Su'a 24–2–96–1; Pringle 27–5–95–2; Vaughan 25–7–77–1; Richardson 15–0–88–0; Harris 15–3–70–0.

Umpires: B. L. Aldridge and S. J. Woodward.

MINOR ASSOCIATIONS' XI v ENGLAND XI

At Napier, January 7, 8, 9. Drawn. Toss: Minor Associations' XI. In an opening spell of nine overs for ten runs Lawrence took three wickets and broke the left forearm of Franklin, New Zealand's Test opener, with the second ball – and bouncer – of the match. After such a start England should have gone on to beat a team largely assembled from more rural cricket associations, but they were denied by some spirited tail-end batting, notably from Hayes, who had not scored a first-class run before. Hick, promoted to open when Stewart had a cold, reached his second consecutive century against a team deprived of a pace bowler, but England were restrained by some lively fast-medium bowling from Wilson. On the last day, on a pitch ever more lifeless, and without Lawrence to take the second new ball because of a strained side, England again found the tail just too stubborn and made only the briefest attempt to score 153 in the last 85 minutes. Russell took two catches in the field when Stewart kept wicket on the first afternoon.

Close of play: First day, England XI 85-1 (G. A. Hick 25*, R. A. Smith 14*); Second day, Minor Associations' XI 92-4 (B. A. Young 45*, G. E. Bradburn 0*).

Minor Associations' XI

T. J. Franklin c Stewart b Lawrence	0	– absent injured	
K. A. Wealleans c Gooch b Lawrence	3	– lbw b Reeve	12
B. A. Young b Lawrence	5	– c Hick b Tufnell	80
*K. R. Rutherford c Russell b Tufnell	64	– (5) b Tufnell	0
M. J. Lamont c Russell b Lawrence	29	– (1) c Ramprakash b Hick	30
G. E. Bradburn b Reeve	26	– c Reeve b Pringle	28
†A. C. Parore c Hick b Pringle	27	– run out	15
M. N. Hart c Stewart b Reeve	8	– (4) lbw b Tufnell	0
T. J. Wilson b Lawrence	0	– (8) c Smith b Tufnell	27
S. B. Doull not out	41	– (9) c Reeve b Pringle	15
R. L. Hayes c Ramprakash b Tufnell	22	– (10) not out	33
B 3, l-b 6, n-b 11	20	B 2, l-b 7, n-b 11	20
	245		260

1/0 2/11 3/22 4/117 5/117   1/22 2/89 3/89 4/89 5/138
6/163 7/180 8/180 9/180   6/164 7/184 8/210 9/260

Bowling: First Innings—Lawrence 22–5–52–5; Pringle 24–5–65–1; Reeve 23–6–61–2; Tufnell 22.2–6–58–2. *Second Innings*—Lawrence 12–3–34–0; Pringle 23–6–57–2; Reeve 10–2–45–1; Hick 30–14–39–1; Tufnell 38–14–65–4; Ramprakash 4–1–11–0.

England XI

*G. A. Gooch lbw b Wilson	42		
G. A. Hick c and b Hart	113		
R. A. Smith c sub b Hayes	15	– (1) b Rutherford	4
A. J. Stewart c Bradburn b Hayes	46		
M. R. Ramprakash c Young b Wilson	13	– (3) b Hayes	5
N. H. Fairbrother lbw b Bradburn	9	– (2) not out	14
D. A. Reeve not out	42	– (5) not out	6
D. R. Pringle c Bradburn b Wilson	0	– (4) c sub b Rutherford	9
†R. C. Russell c sub b Wilson	57		
D. V. Lawrence c sub b Hayes	4		
P. C. R. Tufnell c sub b Bradburn	2		
L-b 6, w 2, n-b 2	10		
	353		(3 wkts) 38

1/58 2/89 3/209 4/233 5/241   1/5 2/10 3/24
6/257 7/260 8/338 9/347

Bowling: First Innings—Hayes 21–0–91–3; Wilson 32–3–103–4; Doull 4–0–21–0; Bradburn 25.4–2–86–2; Hart 16–1–46–1. *Second Innings*—Hayes 5–0–16–1; Rutherford 6–3–9–2; Bradburn 4–0–13–0.

Umpires: D. B. Cowie and R. L. McHarg.

†NEW ZEALAND v ENGLAND

First One-day International

At Auckland, January 11. England won by seven wickets. Toss: New Zealand. Playing cricket of exceptional confidence and certainty, England stunned a young New Zealand team by winning with all of 16.1 overs to spare. In their first international match for more than ten months the home side could never break free from tight bowling and fielding and were 81 for five in the 31st over before Cairns gave the 15,000 crowd their only satisfaction with his 42 from 59 balls. Bowling far straighter than the New Zealanders did later, Reeve took three wickets in his second one-day international, varied his medium-pace with a slow leg-break and took the Man of the Match award, while Tufnell's analysis was the most economical recorded for England in one-day internationals against New Zealand. Whereas New Zealand's batsmen hit only three boundaries in the first 15 overs, when all bar two fielders had to be inside the semi-circles, England hit 13 fours and reached 97 for one. Robin Smith took 13 off his first four balls, then 18 out of 19 off one over from Larsen. In both countries' first experience of a match referee, Peter Burge was not required to act, although Tufnell was abused and pelted with fruit by a section of the crowd.

Man of the Match: D. A. Reeve.

New Zealand

J. G. Wright c Stewart b Lewis 6	C. Pringle not out 9
R. T. Latham lbw b Pringle 25	
*M. D. Crowe b Reeve 31	L-b 13, w 4, n-b 3. 20
A. H. Jones c Stewart b Reeve. 1	
M. J. Greatbatch c Hick b Reeve 4	1/21 (1) 2/45 (2) (7 wkts, 50 overs) 178
C. Z. Harris not out 38	3/51 (4) 4/61 (5)
C. L. Cairns c Hick b Pringle 42	5/81 (3) 6/165 (7)
†I. D. S. Smith c Gooch b Lewis 2	7/167 (8)

G. R. Larsen and D. K. Morrison did not bat.

Bowling: DeFreitas 10–1–34–0; Lewis 8–0–33–2; Pringle 6–1–32–2; Reeve 10–3–20–3; Tufnell 10–3–17–0; Hick 6–0–29–0.

England

*G. A. Gooch c Greatbatch b Harris . . 47	
G. A. Hick b Cairns 23	
R. A. Smith not out. 61	
A. J. Lamb c Crowe b Harris. 12	
N. H. Fairbrother not out. 23	
L-b 6, w 3, n-b 4. 13	

1/64 (2) 2/109 (1)   (3 wkts, 33.5 overs) 179
3/123 (4)

†A. J. Stewart, D. A. Reeve, C. C. Lewis, D. R. Pringle, P. A. J. DeFreitas and P. C. R. Tufnell did not bat.

Bowling: Morrison 5.5–0–35–0; Pringle 5–0–26–0; Cairns 5–0–32–1; Larsen 9–3–36–0; Harris 8–0–40–2; Latham 1–0–4–0.

Umpires: D. B. Cowie and S. J. Woodward.

NEW ZEALAND XI v ENGLAND XI

At Nelson, January 13, 14, 15. England XI won by two wickets. Toss: New Zealand XI. After heavy overnight rain had delayed the start till 3.30, both sides agreed to play until 7.30 to make up time on the opening day. England's attack lacked variety in the absence of Lawrence and Tufnell, so, following Greatbatch's declaration before lunch on the second day, Gooch reciprocated after Stewart and Lamb had hit 136 together in 27 overs. Runs were then fed to Auckland with all 11 players bowling – even Russell in his pads while Smith took his gloves – until Greatbatch set England 315 in four and a half hours on a slow pitch which was beginning to flake under the hot sun. Su'a was unable to find the in-swing which had made his new-ball spell in the first innings so formidable. Stead, a Young New Zealand leg-spinner on his first-class début, bowled some good deliveries but was otherwise punished so mercilessly that England needed no more than 100 in the last 80 minutes (there was no minimum number of overs in the last hour as the tourists had a plane to catch). Lamb and Lewis hit 70 from ten overs to steer England to their fourth victory in five games.

Close of play: First day, New Zealand XI 128-4 (S. A. Thomson 34*, J. T. C. Vaughan 18*); Second day, New Zealand XI 224-2 (B. A. Pocock 94*, S. A. Thomson 62*).

New Zealand XI

S. W. Brown lbw b Lewis	30	– c Stewart b Pringle	2
B. A. Pocock c Russell b Lewis	12	– not out	110
M. W. Douglas run out	0	– c Stewart b Ramprakash	59
S. A. Thomson c Hick b Pringle	75	– not out	88
*M. J. Greatbatch c Gooch b Reeve	25		
J. T. C. Vaughan c Russell b DeFreitas	26		
†T. E. Blain not out	27		
M. N. Hart lbw b Reeve	1		
L-b 10, n-b 1	11	B 5, l-b 1, w 1	7

1/42 2/44 3/47 4/94 5/143   (7 wkts dec.) 207   1/3 2/123   (2 wkts dec.) 266
6/202 7/207

G. A. Stead, M. L. Su'a and R. M. Ford did not bat.

Bowling: *First Innings*—DeFreitas 20–7–60–1; Lewis 20–7–48–2; Pringle 17–7–20–1; Reeve 13.1–7–19–2; Hick 15–0–50–0. *Second Innings*—Lewis 8–3–12–0; Pringle 7–2–20–1; Hick 11–3–53–0; DeFreitas 6–1–15–0; Ramprakash 8–1–29–1; Reeve 7–0–20–0; Smith 7–2–27–0; Gooch 8–2–64–0; Stewart 2–0–9–0; Lamb 1–0–6–0; Russell 1–0–5–0.

England XI

*G. A. Gooch c Blain b Su'a	3	– (6) c Blain b Vaughan	64
A. J. Stewart not out	71	– (1) lbw b Su'a	2
G. A. Hick c Brown b Su'a	0	– c and b Hart	71
R. A. Smith b Su'a	0	– b Stead	35
A. J. Lamb not out	76	– (7) not out	61
M. R. Ramprakash (did not bat)		– (2) b Ford	0
D. A. Reeve (did not bat)		– (5) c and b Hart	42
†R. C. Russell (did not bat)		– lbw b Vaughan	0
C. C. Lewis (did not bat)		– c sub b Su'a	36
D. R. Pringle (did not bat)		– not out	1
L-b 3, w 2, n-b 4	9	L-b 3, n-b 1	4

1/8 2/12 3/23   (3 wkts dec.) 159   1/2 2/6 3/104   (8 wkts) 316
    4/112 5/215 6/215
    7/221 8/291

P. A. J. DeFreitas did not bat.

Bowling: *First Innings*—Su'a 12–1–54–3; Ford 6–0–30–0; Brown 7–2–19–0; Thomson 6–0–27–0; Hart 4–0–26–0. *Second Innings*—Su'a 15–2–72–2; Ford 8–3–21–1; Brown 4–0–27–0; Stead 19–1–97–1; Vaughan 12.4–6–34–2; Hart 14–1–62–2.

Umpires: R. S. Dunne and C. E. King.

NEW ZEALAND v ENGLAND

First Test Match

At Christchurch, January 18, 19, 20, 21, 22. England won by an innings and four runs. Toss: New Zealand. A Test match that was otherwise as sedate as it was one-sided ended in the most thrilling fashion ten minutes from time when the New Zealand captain went to hit the boundary which would have levelled the scores. But having gone down the pitch to drive a flighted, dropping delivery from England's match-winner, Tufnell, Crowe could do no more than sky the ball to mid-off. The consequence was England's third Test victory in a row, something which they had not achieved since 1981. For New Zealand it was only their third Test defeat at home in 35 Tests since 1979-80.

Throughout the game the only question was whether England would have the time to win or not; they were on top from the first hour. Although the pitch was then damp enough to help the pace bowlers for the one time in the match, Morrison and Cairns were too wayward as they strained for an opening. Thereafter the pitch was plain slow, and being bound together by grass which was hardly scarred in the course of five days, encouraged spin only little, even Tufnell's. Plenty of rolling by the groundsman, Russell Wylie, and his removal of rubbishy top soil, had produced a benign clay-based strip far from the "result wicket" which England had seen on their two previous Test tours.

Stewart, in his highest and most controlled Test innings to that point, counteracted the early fall of Gooch and the uncertainty of Hick. The vice-captain reached 50 by lunch and 102 by tea, and it needed a ball which bounced abnormally to have him caught at first slip in the final over of the opening day. Stewart's cutting, cover-driving and pulling fully punished the regular bad balls; but it was his compactness, in not playing loose off-side shots early on, which was most impressive. So it was an expensive mistake when Crowe, the sole slip, dropped Smith on 44. England's third-wicket pair had added 179 in 50 overs and the bat was completely in command by the time Smith repeated his back-foot drive and edged to the new first slip, Greatbatch. Stewart hit 17 fours, Smith 16, Lamb and Lewis 13 each (with a six for Lamb), as New Zealand lacked not only Hadlee but a medium-pacer to keep one end tight.

If England's run-scoring was slightly more leisurely on the second day, as Lamb sought a century on his return to the side and Reeve played his début innings, it was still thoroughly efficient. Such was their confidence that DeFreitas, having blocked his first ball of the tour, drove the second over long-on for six. This was England's highest total at Christchurch, surpassing their 560 for eight in 1932-33. Poor weather limited New Zealand's reply to 2.2 overs on the second evening and allowed no play at all on the third morning. The prospect of a result receded further as Hartland defended calmly on his Test début. But then Tufnell had the first of his two inspired spells in the match, using the wind off Cashmere Hills to drift the ball into the right-hander and taking four top-order wickets for 20. Wright, lured at last into driving, edged to slip, Hartland gave Smith the first of four close-in catches off pad and bat, and Thomson completely misread a ball drifting into him. Yet the game changed abruptly again when Patel counter-attacked against Tufnell, who had been similarly hammered by the same player on his first-class début for Middlesex in 1986.

Patel and Cairns carried on aggressively on the fourth morning to a new seventh-wicket record for New Zealand against England, of 117 in 120 minutes. But just as the follow-on target of 381 was coming within range, Patel went for a third run to Pringle, running back towards long-on, and missed out on his maiden Test century by a yard. It was the ninth instance of a Test batsman run out for 99, all post-war. Reeve chipped in by taking a wicket with his eighth ball in Test cricket, and New Zealand were batting again before tea on the fourth day. Thereafter it was hard work for an increasingly footsore England. Only one wicket fell before the close, another – the nightwatchman – on the last morning, and a third in the afternoon session, as New Zealand defended with great defiance. After tea England still had to take more wickets – seven – than had fallen on any of the previous days. Reeve was off the field with a stomach upset by food poisoning, DeFreitas limped off before the close, and the pitch had barely worn at all. But Tufnell had rediscovered his length and flight.

Wright, tied down on 99 for 23 minutes either side of the tea interval, became ever more fretful at Tufnell's accuracy and for the first time in more than six hours went down the pitch to try and hit him over the top. The second time he charged, he was stranded by a wider ball bouncing out of the footmarks. In Tufnell's next over but one Greatbatch and Thomson were out. When Patel, torn between defending and attacking, skied to mid-off, 65 minutes remained. After Lewis had bounced out Ian Smith, the last pair were left with half an hour to survive and 18 runs to make. They knocked off 14 of them, until Crowe gambled all against a field brought in to save every run, and lost. It was the third consecutive Test in which Tufnell had taken five wickets in an innings, and his figures of 85.1 overs and 11 wickets for 147 runs were the fruit of flighted bowling of rare, old-fashioned craft.

Man of the Match: P. C. R. Tufnell.

Close of play: First day, England 310-4 (A. J. Lamb 17*, R. C. Russell 0*); Second day, New Zealand 3-0 (B. R. Hartland 0*, J. G. Wright 2*); Third day, New Zealand 169-6 (D. N. Patel 55*, C. L. Cairns 3*); Fourth day, New Zealand 81-1 (J. G. Wright 28*, D. K. Morrison 0*).

England

*G. A. Gooch c Smith b Morrison	2
A. J. Stewart c Crowe b Morrison	148
G. A. Hick lbw b Cairns	35
R. A. Smith c Greatbatch b Pringle ...	96
A. J. Lamb b Patel	93
†R. C. Russell run out	36
D. A. Reeve c Jones b Pringle	59
C. C. Lewis b Pringle	70

D. R. Pringle c Greatbatch b Patel	10
P. A. J. DeFreitas not out...........	7
B 5, l-b 10, w 1, n-b 8	24
(9 wkts dec.)	580

P. C. R. Tufnell did not bat.

1/6 (1) 2/95 (3) 3/274 (4)
4/310 (2) 5/390 (6)
6/466 (5) 7/544 (7)
8/571 (9) 9/580 (8)

Bowling: Morrison 33-5-133-2; Cairns 30-3-118-1; Pringle 36-4-127-3; Thomson 15-3-47-0; Patel 46-5-132-2; Jones 3-0-8-0.

New Zealand

B. R. Hartland c Smith b Tufnell..............	22	– c Smith b Tufnell	45
J. G. Wright c Lamb b Tufnell	28	– st Russell b Tufnell	99
A. H. Jones lbw b Lewis..............	16	– (4) c Russell b Pringle	39
M. J. Greatbatch c Stewart b Tufnell	11	– (6) c Smith b Tufnell	0
S. A. Thomson b Tufnell...................	5	– (7) lbw b Tufnell	0
D. N. Patel run out..............	99	– (8) c Pringle b Tufnell	6
*M. D. Crowe c Stewart b Pringle..............	20	– (5) c Pringle b Tufnell	48
C. L. Cairns c Hick b Reeve	61	– (9) c Smith b Tufnell	0
†I. D. S. Smith lbw b DeFreitas..............	20	– (10) c Russell b Lewis	1
D. K. Morrison not out..............	8	– (3) c Russell b Lewis	0
C. Pringle c Hick b DeFreitas	6	– not out..........	5
B 1, l-b 7, n-b 8	16	B 1, l-b 7, n-b 13	21

1/51 (2) 2/52 (1) 3/73 (3) 4/87 (4)	312
5/91 (5) 6/139 (7) 7/256 (6)	
8/279 (8) 9/306 (9) 10/312 (11)	

1/81 (1) 2/81 (3) 3/182 (4)	264
4/211 (2) 5/222 (6) 6/222 (7)	
7/236 (8) 8/241 (9)	
9/250 (10) 10/264 (5)	

Bowling: *First Innings*—DeFreitas 32.4-16-54-2; Lewis 30-9-69-1; Pringle 15-2-54-1; Tufnell 39-10-100-4; Hick 3-0-11-0; Reeve 8-4-16-1. *Second Innings*—DeFreitas 23-6-54-0; Pringle 21-5-64-1; Tufnell 46.1-25-47-7; Hick 14-8-11-0; Lewis 22-3-66-2; Reeve 2-0-8-0; Smith 4-2-6-0.

Umpires: B. L. Aldridge and R. S. Dunne.

CENTRAL DISTRICTS v ENGLAND XI

At New Plymouth, January 24, 25, 26. Drawn. Toss: England XI. Rain took large chunks out of the first two days and wiped out the third. In the time available Botham had his first spell of the tour after Central Districts had been sent in by Stewart, acting-captain for the second time. In the only aggressive innings played by a proper batsman against England in their four practice games, Blain hit three sixes off the other new arrival, Illingworth. The short boundaries at Pukekura Park – 60 yards or less on three sides – were then enjoyed by Stewart, who hit 14 fours and four sixes in under three hours, and by Hick, who hit 15 fours and seven sixes. In his third century of the tour, off 69 balls, Hick took three successive sixes off Duff's left-arm spin, and four fours in an over from Briasco. In all he faced 75 balls in his 100 minutes at the crease.

Close of play: First day, Central Districts 97-5 (P. S. Briasco 41*); Second day, England XI 246-2 (A. J. Stewart 101*, M. R. Ramprakash 19*).

Central Districts

C. D. Ingham c Russell b Botham	13	S. W. Duff not out	36
R. G. Twose lbw b Botham	13	D. J. Leonard not out	10
*P. S. Briasco c Russell b Pringle	41		
S. W. J. Wilson c Russell b Gooch	12	L-b 3, n-b 7	10
M. J. Greatbatch c Smith b Pringle	4		
M. W. Douglas c Stewart b Illingworth	5	1/23 2/45 3/71 4/84 (7 wkts dec.) 189	
†T. E. Blain c Russell b Reeve	45	5/97 6/97 7/161	

D. N. Askew and C. L. Auckram did not bat.

Bowling: Botham 16–4–40–2; Pringle 20–6–37–2; Reeve 19–6–49–1; Gooch 8–4–7–1; Illingworth 21–7–53–1.

England XI

G. A. Gooch c Blain b Leonard	8
*A. J. Stewart not out	101
G. A. Hick b Leonard	115
M. R. Ramprakash not out	19
L-b 3	3

1/12 2/192   (2 wkts) 246

R. A. Smith, I. T. Botham, N. H. Fairbrother, †R. C. Russell, D. A. Reeve, D. R. Pringle and R. K. Illingworth did not bat.

Bowling: Leonard 13–2–39–2; Auckram 10–1–45–0; Askew 4–0–37–0; Twose 5–1–21–0; Duff 10–0–77–0; Briasco 2–0–24–0

Umpires: R. W. Hutchison and D. M. Quested.

NEW ZEALAND v ENGLAND

Second Test Match

At Auckland, January 30, 31, February 1, 2, 3. England won by 168 runs. Toss: New Zealand. To their credit, New Zealand went all out for a series-levelling victory in Auckland, on a pitch which began very damp and remained difficult because of its uneven bounce when it dried. Dropping Thomson, Greatbatch and Pringle from their Christchurch side, and replacing Ian Smith, who had a little-finger injury, with Parore, New Zealand sent England in on winning the toss and soon had them two for three. Thereafter, however, New Zealand's bowling was so wayward, their fielding so fallible and the captaincy so uninspiring that England were able to escape, and the end result – on a bowlers' pitch – was as emphatic as at Christchurch.

Rain delayed the start until 2.15. Immediately England wickets tumbled, though not so many as should have. Morrison again landed an out-swinger in exactly the right place for Gooch to edge it, and Cairns followed by taking two wickets in his second over: Stewart cover-drove while Smith fell to an outstanding right-handed catch by Parore, who finished with six catches and one miss in his second Test. But Cairns, the most threatening bowler, was given no more than four overs before tea. Afterwards he returned to remove Hick, who had already been dropped twice, but it was too late for New Zealand to make full use of their advantage. When England took their overnight score past 200, thanks to a last-wicket stand orchestrated by Pringle, they had tenaciously clawed their way back on top.

For instead of flattening out as forecast, the pitch remained as favourable to seam bowlers as a traditional Headingley one. The new ball was particularly liable to shoot through or, more rarely, bounce abnormally from the cracks of the loosely compacted surface. Needing a first-innings lead, New Zealand conceded one of 61, following a tremendous duel between Crowe and Lewis. Encouraged by his captain after the First Test to bowl consistently fast, Lewis nevertheless maintained such accuracy that only 11 scoring strokes were made off him in 21 overs (and 13 of the runs he conceded were no-balls). Calling on the stamina which they had built up in pre-tour training, England took five wickets in the last eight overs of the second day and virtually sealed the result.

If the match went momentarily back into the balance on the third morning, when Su'a on his Test début had a promising spell, the afternoon of the third day saw "the killer session", as Crowe later described it. From 29 overs, while the ball still moved around, England scored 138 runs. Smith began the assault with square-cutting and off-driving of immense force, to be followed by Lamb – dropped before scoring by Patel at cover – hammering 60 off 47 balls. Of Test fifties recorded in terms of balls, only Kapil Dev (30 balls), Ian Botham and Viv Richards (32 balls), had made one faster than Lamb (33). So demoralising to the bowlers was Lamb's strokeplay and demeanour, and so heartening to his captain, that Gooch went on to his 16th Test hundred after the scratchiest start imaginable. It hardly mattered that Reeve ran out his captain by trying a single to Watson in his follow-through, or that he became immobile himself. England added only 11 runs in the final hour of the third day, when Wright took over from Crowe and brought a surer touch to New Zealand's out-cricket.

At the start of the fourth day, for the third time in the match, three wickets fell at the same score, but England's lead was already unassailable on a still-awkward pitch. Wright and Jones were undone by virtual shooters, Hartland bagged a pair in his second Test, and although the middle order resisted when the ball lost its hardness, England were left with only two wickets to take on the final morning. When Su'a was leg-before, ducking into a short ball which did not rise, it was the 13th lbw of the game, a number exceeded in Test cricket only by the 14 in Pakistan's match with Sri Lanka at Faisalabad a few weeks before.

Man of the Match: G. A. Gooch.

Close of play: First day, England 146-7 (R. C. Russell 23*, D. R. Pringle 8*); Second day, New Zealand 141-9 (M. L. Su'a 0*, W. Watson 1*); Third day, England 272-6 (C. C. Lewis 3*, R. C. Russell 0*); Fourth day, New Zealand 203-8 (M. L. Su'a 36*, D. K. Morrison 6*).

England

*G. A. Gooch c Parore b Morrison	4 – run out	114
A. J. Stewart c Parore b Cairns	4 – c Parore b Su'a	8
G. A. Hick lbw b Cairns	30 – lbw b Su'a	4
R. A. Smith c Parore b Cairns	0 – b Morrison	35
A. J. Lamb b Su'a	13 – c Watson b Patel	60
D. A. Reeve c Parore b Watson	22 – lbw b Watson	25
C. C. Lewis c Cairns b Watson	33 – run out	23
†R. C. Russell c Parore b Cairns	33 – c Hartland b Cairns	24
D. R. Pringle lbw b Cairns	41 – lbw b Cairns	2
P. A. J. DeFreitas c Crowe b Cairns	1 – c Wright b Morrison	0
P. C. R. Tufnell not out	6 – not out	0
L-b 11, n-b 5	16	B 8, l-b 16, n-b 2	26
	203		**321**

1/9 (1) 2/9 (2) 3/9 (4) 4/34 (5)   1/29 (2) 2/33 (3) 3/93 (4)   321
5/72 (3) 6/91 (6) 7/128 (7)   4/182 (5) 5/263 (1) 6/269 (6)
8/165 (8) 9/171 (10) 10/203 (9)   7/319 (8) 8/321 (7)
                                         9/321 (9) 10/321 (10)

Bowling: *First Innings*—Morrison 17-2-55-1; Cairns 21-4-52-6; Watson 24-13-41-2; Su'a 18-8-44-1. *Second Innings*—Morrison 21.4-6-66-2; Cairns 19-6-86-2; Watson 26-10-59-1; Su'a 10-3-43-2; Patel 22-7-43-1.

New Zealand

B. R. Hartland lbw b Lewis	0 – c Russell b DeFreitas	0
J. G. Wright b Pringle	15 – lbw b Lewis	0
A. H. Jones c Smith b DeFreitas	14 – lbw b DeFreitas	5
*M. D. Crowe c Hick b Lewis	45 – c Lamb b DeFreitas	56
K. R. Rutherford c Russell b DeFreitas	26 – c Stewart b Pringle	32
D. N. Patel lbw b Lewis	24 – c and b Tufnell	17
C. L. Cairns c Hick b Tufnell	1 – c Russell b Tufnell	24
†A. C. Parore b Pringle	0 – lbw b Lewis	15
M. L. Su'a not out	0 – lbw b DeFreitas	36
D. K. Morrison lbw b Lewis	0 – run out	12
W. Watson b Lewis	2 – not out	5
N-b 15	15	L-b 1, n-b 11	12
	142		**214**

1/2 (1) 2/35 (3) 3/91 (5) 4/102 (4)   1/0 (1) 2/0 (2) 3/7 (3) 4/77 (5)   214
5/123 (2) 6/124 (7) 7/139 (8)   5/109 (6) 6/118 (4) 7/153 (7)
8/139 (6) 9/139 (10) 10/142 (11)   8/173 (8) 9/203 (9) 10/214 (10)

In the first innings J. G. Wright, when 5, retired hurt at 13 and resumed at 91.

Bowling: *First Innings*—DeFreitas 16–2–53–2; Lewis 21–7–31–5; Pringle 15–7–21–2; Reeve 7–1–21–0; Tufnell 4–2–16–1. *Second Innings*—DeFreitas 27–11–62–4; Lewis 27–4–83–2; Pringle 7–2–23–1; Tufnell 17–5–45–2; Hick 1–1–0–0.

Umpires: B. L. Aldridge and R. S. Dunne.

NEW ZEALAND v ENGLAND

Third Test Match

At Wellington, February 6, 7, 8, 9, 10. Drawn. Toss: England. Given only two days of rest after the Second Test, England could not summon up the energy to make a clean sweep of the series, whereas New Zealand made their most co-ordinated effort. After dropping six more catches on the opening day, New Zealand's fielders improved considerably thereafter, Su'a supplied some fine stock bowling, and Wright and Jones shared a record second-wicket stand. But the match will be as much remembered for the cry of pain when Lawrence broke his left knee-cap in the final session, and the unseemly scuffle which followed when he was carried off on a stretcher. The match was also notable for being Botham's 100th Test. Not included in the original 12, he was brought in when Lewis and Pringle withdrew, the former having lost a fingernail, the latter with a back strain. Lawrence was therefore given his first Test abroad, and his misfortunes began when England chose to bat first, when the pitch was damp and as near as it ever came to being lively. By the second day it had became a slow, low turner, typical of the Basin Reserve, and both teams were content in the end to settle for a draw.

Yet by the 45th over of the opening day England had reached 159, and batting was almost too easy – too easy, at any rate, for England to maintain their concentration. Stewart put away the one bad ball an over, survived three pulled chances, and went on to his third century in five Tests since his recall the previous August; when 74 he reached 1,000 runs for England. Hick began a Test innings against spin for once, and looked the happier for it, driving Patel twice for six in his first five overs at the wicket. But the game suddenly shifted, and New Zealand at last came into their own. Su'a pegged England back by bowling 24 overs for 41 runs before the close, moving the ball around more than any other pace bowler in the match; Patel got the ball to turn, and pushed one through to bowl Hick when he stayed on his crease; even the catches started to stick. Reeve did little to prevent New Zealand regaining their confidence by taking 166 minutes over his runs. Botham, in his first innings of the tour, could not adjust to the slowness of the pitch, and England's last 90 runs took 51 overs.

The partnership of 241 between Wright and Jones broke the previous second-wicket record for New Zealand against all countries, the 210 made by Geoff Howarth and Jeff Crowe against West Indies at Kingston in 1984-85. But as it took six hours and 23 minutes, and 107 overs, it was more of a match-saving than match-winning stand. Wright, with his pulling, and Jones, with his cutting, did not allow Tufnell the stranglehold he had achieved at Christchurch, but Hick's occasional off-spin of full length was treated with immense respect. Only when 59 runs were scored off the first 12 overs of the second new ball were England pressed in the field. Wright's 12th Test century lasted 406 minutes in all, and Jones's sixth 465 minutes. Another record was that Tufnell's 71 overs surpassed Steve Boock's 70 against Pakistan in 1988-89 as the highest number of overs in a first-class innings in New Zealand. At one point Tufnell and Hick bowled together for 77 overs, or five hours.

Stewart was Man of the Match for adding 63 to his first-innings century. But when Botham mis-swept on the fifth morning, England were only 127 runs ahead with four wickets remaining. It was an irony that Russell should have helped Lamb to save the game with a century stand, hours before he was omitted from England's World Cup party for not being an adequate batsman. With nerveless certainty Lamb proceeded past 139 to his highest Test score, and the first of his 14 Test centuries to be made outside England or the West Indies. When he reverse-swept to backward point, England declared and left New Zealand 233 to win in a minimum 32 overs, and the target was never attempted.

It was in these closing stages, as Lawrence ran in to bowl the first ball of his third over, that the fast bowler's left knee buckled in delivery and he collapsed with an appalling scream. Still in pain, he was carried from the field on a stretcher and taken to Wellington Hospital, where the knee-cap – cleanly broken – was wired up the following morning. While he was being carried to the England dressing-room, there was a scene in front of the pavilion when the England team manager, Micky Stewart, thought a 41-year-old TVNZ cameraman, Vaughan Scott, to be intrusive. A scuffle followed as Stewart tried to pull the cameraman away from Lawrence.

Man of the Match: A. J. Stewart.

Close of play: First day, England, 239-5 (D. A. Reeve 9*, D. V. Lawrence 0*); Second day, New Zealand 104-1 (J. G. Wright 44*, A. H. Jones 51*); Third day, New Zealand 340-6 (R. T. Latham 12*, C. L. Cairns 0*); Fourth day, England 171-3 (R. A. Smith 41*, A. J. Lamb 24*).

England

*G. A. Gooch b Patel	30	– c Rutherford b Cairns	11
A. J. Stewart b Morrison	107	– c Smith b Patel	63
G. A. Hick b Patel	43	– c Smith b Su'a	22
R. A. Smith c Rutherford b Patel	6	– c and b Su'a	76
A. J. Lamb c Smith b Patel	30	– c Latham b Patel	142
D. A. Reeve c Latham b Su'a	18	– b Su'a	0
D. V. Lawrence c Rutherford b Cairns	6		
I. T. Botham c Cairns b Su'a	15	– (7) lbw b Patel	1
†R. C. Russell lbw b Morrison	18	– (8) not out	24
P. A. J. DeFreitas lbw b Morrison	3		
P. C. R. Tufnell not out	2		
B 4, l-b 12, n-b 11	27	L-b 13, n-b 7	20

1/83 (1) 2/159 (3) 3/169 (4) 4/215 (5) 305
5/235 (2) 6/248 (7) 7/277 (8)
8/286 (6) 9/298 (9) 10/305 (10)

1/17 (1) 2/52 (3)   (7 wkts dec.) 359
3/127 (2) 4/249 (4)
5/249 (6) 6/254 (7)
7/359 (5)

Bowling: First Innings—Morrison 22.1–6–44–3; Cairns 25–3–89–1; Su'a 36–10–62–2; Patel 34–10–87–4; Jones 1–0–7–0. *Second Innings*—Morrison 23–5–63–0; Cairns 22–4–84–1; Su'a 33–10–87–3; Patel 41.3–12–112–3.

New Zealand

B. R. Hartland c Botham b Lawrence	2	– lbw b Botham	19
J. G. Wright c Reeve b Tufnell	116	– c Russell b Botham	0
A. H. Jones b Hick	143	– (4) lbw b Reeve	9
*M. D. Crowe b Tufnell	30	– (3) not out	13
K. R. Rutherford run out	8	– not out	2
R. T. Latham b Hick	25		
D. N. Patel lbw b Hick	9		
C. L. Cairns c Russell b Botham	33		
†I. D. S. Smith b Hick	21		
M. L. Su'a not out	20		
D. K. Morrison not out	0		
B 1, l-b 15, w 1, n-b 8	25		

1/3 (1) 2/244 (2) 3/308 (3)   (9 wkts dec.) 432
4/312 (4) 5/327 (5) 6/340 (7)
7/369 (6) 8/404 (9) 9/430 (8)

1/4 (2) 2/24 (1)   (3 wkts) 43
3/41 (4)

Bowling: First Innings—DeFreitas 8–4–12–0; Lawrence 27–7–67–1; Tufnell 71–22–147–2; Hick 69–27–126–4; Botham 14–4–53–1; Reeve 3–1–11–0. *Second Innings*—Lawrence 2.1–1–4–0; Botham 8–1–23–2; Reeve 4.5–2–4–1; Tufnell 9–5–12–0.

Umpires: B. L. Aldridge and R. S. Dunne.

†NEW ZEALAND v ENGLAND

Second One-day International

At Dunedin, February 12. England won by three wickets. Toss: New Zealand. The second of the three one-day internationals was made the least one-sided by the slowest of all the pitches which England came across on their tour. The slower a seam bowler was, the harder he was to hit, and the slowest of all was Latham, who came on in the 31st over of England's innings and took two wickets with his first three balls. After he had later dismissed Lamb, England's last four wickets had to make 55 from ten overs, then 45 off seven. But at just the right time Reeve and Lewis used their feet, and in spite of all the previous evidence Crowe used his quickest bowlers at the end. With 22 wanted from three overs, deft improvisation by Pringle enabled England to win with five balls to spare. Earlier, Rutherford had made 52 off 86 balls, which was enough in the eyes of Steve Boock to win the Man of the Match award.

Man of the Match: K. R. Rutherford.

New Zealand

R. T. Latham run out	12	M. L. Su'a not out		4
A. H. Jones b Botham	20			
M. J. Greatbatch c Stewart b Reeve	10	B 1, l-b 12, w 3, n-b 3		19
*M. D. Crowe c sub b Illingworth	29			
K. R. Rutherford run out	52	1/14 (1) 2/35 (3)	(7 wkts, 50 overs)	186
C. Z. Harris b Pringle	32	3/54 (2) 4/89 (4)		
C. L. Cairns b Lewis	3	5/163 (6) 6/170 (7)		
†I. D. S. Smith not out	5	7/180 (5)		

G. R. Larsen and D. K. Morrison did not bat.

Bowling: Pringle 10-2-31-1; Lewis 9-0-32-1; Reeve 8-1-19-1; Botham 6-1-27-1; Illingworth 9-1-33-1; Tufnell 8-0-31-0.

England

*G. A. Gooch c Smith b Larsen	24	D. R. Pringle not out		14
G. A. Hick lbw b Morrison	7			
R. A. Smith b Larsen	17	L-b 2, w 7		9
A. J. Lamb lbw b Latham	40			
I. T. Botham c Rutherford b Latham	28	1/21 (2) 2/54 (1)	(7 wkts, 49.1 overs)	188
†A. J. Stewart b Latham	0	3/63 (3) 4/108 (5)		
D. A. Reeve not out	31	5/108 (6) 6/131 (4)		
C. C. Lewis c Greatbatch b Morrison	18	7/165 (8)		

R. K. Illingworth and P. C. R. Tufnell did not bat.

Bowling: Morrison 7-0-27-2; Su'a 8-1-35-0; Larsen 10-1-24-2; Cairns 6.1-0-36-0; Harris 10-1-39-0; Latham 8-1-25-3.

Umpires: B. L. Aldridge and R. S. Dunne.

†NEW ZEALAND v ENGLAND

Third One-day International

At Christchurch, February 15. England won by 71 runs. Toss: New Zealand. England's third victory in the one-day series was as complete as their first one. After overnight rain had been tipped from the covers on to one side of the square, the game had to be reduced to 40 overs a side, and England raced to 69 for one during the first 12 overs. New Zealand were limited to 32 for three in the same period, and also lost Wright temporarily when hit on the side of the helmet during a hostile spell from Lewis. The pace of the one quick pitch of the tour also suited Botham, who opened the batting and played some remarkable strokes, none more so than his flat-bat smash over mid-on when he moved out to Watson and the bowler dropped short. After Botham had reached his highest one-day score for England, off 73 balls, Smith hit 85 off 71 no less forcefully, and added 54 in five overs with Lamb. At such a scoring-rate something had to give, and it was the hamstring in Lamb's right leg, an injury which ruled him out of the first part of the World Cup. Stewart, in his first outing as captain in an international match, had a relaxed time as England coasted home.

Man of the Match: I. T. Botham.

England

I. T. Botham c Greatbatch b Latham . .	79		D. A. Reeve not out	2
G. A. Hick c Greatbatch b Larsen	18			
R. A. Smith c Smith b Cairns	85		L-b 2, w 4	6
*†A. J. Stewart c Crowe b Su'a	13			
A. J. Lamb c Harris b Watson	25		1/60 (2) 2/125 (1) (7 wkts, 40 overs) 255	
G. A. Gooch not out	22		3/166 (4) 4/220 (5)	
C. C. Lewis c Latham b Watson	0		5/228 (3) 6/231 (7)	
D. R. Pringle c Watson b Cairns	5		7/248 (8)	

R. K. Illingworth and G. C. Small did not bat.

Bowling: Cairns 6–0–37–2; Watson 8–1–64–2; Larsen 6–2–34–1; Su'a 5–0–35–1; Harris 8–0–35–0; Latham 7–0–48–1.

New Zealand

R. T. Latham c Reeve b Lewis	0		M. L. Su'a not out	12
J. G. Wright c Hick b Reeve	36		G. R. Larsen not out	3
M. J. Greatbatch b Pringle	5		L-b 6, w 6, n-b 3	15
*M. D. Crowe c Stewart b Pringle	6			
K. R. Rutherford c sub b Botham	37		1/4 (1) 2/20 (3) (8 wkts, 40 overs) 184	
C. Z. Harris run out	37		3/23 (4) 4/92 (5)	
C. L. Cairns c Smith b Illingworth	6		5/100 (7) 6/112 (6)	
†I. D. S. Smith c sub b Small	27		7/148 (8) 8/171 (2)	

W. Watson did not bat.

J. G. Wright, when 5, retired hurt at 10 and resumed at 100.

Bowling: Lewis 6–1–21–1; Pringle 6–2–11–2; Small 8–0–46–1; Reeve 5–0–26–1; Botham 7–1–36–1; Illingworth 8–0–38–1.

Umpires: R. L. McHarg and S. J. Woodward.

ENGLAND A IN BERMUDA AND THE WEST INDIES, 1991-92

By STEPHEN THORPE

Although they lost the three-match "Test" series 2-0, England's A team to the Eastern Caribbean were far from disgraced on a tour which the coach, Keith Fletcher, considered more beneficial than the two previous England A tours put together. Professional, determined West Indian opposition, underpinned by senior Test experience, provided the severest examination of a team considerably changed from the original selection and weakened throughout by injury. England's performance was meritorious in the circumstances, though they only spasmodically came to terms with the demands imposed by a quartet of fast bowlers, supplemented by the off-spin of Nehemiah Perry – a Test-class attack in its own right.

All the front-line batsmen made substantial scores at various stages, but without ever showing real consistency; and the young spinners, Ian Salisbury and Robert Croft, deserved great credit for their attacking outlook. Steve Rhodes's four leg-side stumpings epitomised England's depth of wicket-keeping talent, but the seam attack, with the improbable exception of John Stephenson, struggled after the injury early on to the strike bowler, Devon Malcolm.

The disparity in bowling strength was the essential difference between the sides. For the home team, Courtney Walsh and Tony Gray were already proven, and Kenneth Benjamin and Linden Joseph advanced their claims for Test cricket with a combined haul of 27 wickets at little cost. Joseph, from Guyana, had put an unhappy time at Hampshire behind him, and he bowled rhythmically fast from a smooth action, missing the final "Test" only because of a groin strain. Perry simply confirmed what Jamaican supporters had known for some time – that here was a first-rate bowler whose opportunities were restricted by West Indies' reliance on pace. Roland Holder, the Barbados batsman, raised his profile with a string of compact innings, but he was overlooked for the later games against South Africa, the selectors preferring the left-hander Jimmy Adams. Against England A, however, Adams failed to recapture the form which had seen him score heavily in the domestic Red Stripe Cup series. Junior Murray, too, a much-lauded wicket-keeper from Grenada, did little to enhance his reputation, although he made important contributions with the bat in the last two "Tests".

The England team was unlucky from the start. Mike Atherton withdrew before the tour began to aid his recuperation from a back operation and was replaced by Stephenson, something of a bonus as it transpired. When the Surrey fast bowler, Martin Bicknell, dislocated a shoulder in training, Steve Watkin, who played in two Tests against West Indies in 1991, was drafted in for his third A tour as, on the eve of departure, was Rhodes, the Worcestershire wicket-keeper, who received a hasty summons from club cricket in Western Australia after Warren Hegg developed glandular fever. But the biggest setback of all was the loss of Martyn Moxon, the captain, who broke his left thumb on the opening day of the tour in a match played only because the scheduled fixture had finished two hours early. Nasser Hussain and Malcolm both missed the first two "Tests", the former suffering from a cracked index finger and the other troubled by recurrent back muscle spasms, and their lack of match practice showed in desultory performances in the final game. Physiotherapist David Roberts claimed he had spent more time in hospitals than anywhere else.

Mark Ramprakash joined the team after his omission from England's World Cup squad, and as a final twist, Northamptonshire's Alan Fordham was summoned from MCC's tour of the Leeward Islands as cover for Hussain in St Vincent. However, he was not called to arms.

For all that, it was a happy tour, with cordial press relations developed by the manager, Steve Coverdale, on his first overseas assignment. The affable Hugh Morris, who won the Player of the Tour award, led the side well after Moxon's departure, putting to good effect the experience he had gained the previous winter as captain in Pakistan and Sri Lanka. Andrew Wingfield Digby, director of Christians in Sport, offered spiritual uplift in Trinidad, and Ossie Wheatley, chairman of the TCCB's cricket committee, also dropped in to provide guidance and monitor the progress of the tour. He saw it as "a useful exercise", but he would have done well to address at least one inconsistency in a tour costing about £300,000, almost four times the outlay of the visit to Zimbabwe in 1989-90. The programme gave the team an over-long acclimatisation period in Bermuda, which did little to prepare them for the cricket which lay ahead. None the less, after four one-day victories in Bermuda, and another in Barbados, the players soon came to terms with the sterner opposition in the three-day matches against the Windwards, in Grenada, and Trinidad & Tobago in the pungent atmosphere at Guaracara Park.

Once Malcolm had broken down after a gentle work-out half an hour before the start of the First "Test", England A lacked the firepower to compete on equal terms on a dreadful Queen's Park pitch, which forced the batsmen to concentrate on self-preservation. The second game of the series, at the idyllic, breeze-blown Arnos Vale ground in St Vincent, was an altogether different match. Although off-spinner Perry was its central figure, this game highlighted again the inability of the England batsmen to attempt to dictate terms to the West Indies fast bowlers. Paul Johnson, recipient of the Outstanding Newcomer tour award, for which only non-Test players were considered, briefly hinted at an attacking approach, but for the most part the accuracy and attritional qualities of the bowling prevailed.

Walsh, his maturity as a leader exemplified by Jamaica's Red Stripe Cup success, had the tactical wit to switch the opening attack to himself and Gray after Joseph and Benjamin had performed admirably at Queen's Park. But for the most part he allowed the young pretenders their heads, except in the final match when the West Indian selectors were assessing form with the South African series in mind. England, however, were perhaps guilty of misjudgment in playing a fourth seamer throughout, when a case existed for bowling the spinners in tandem at some stage.

ENGLAND A TOUR PARTY

M. D. Moxon (Yorks.) (*captain*), H. Morris (Glam.) (*vice-captain*), D. J. Bicknell (Surrey), D. G. Cork (Derbys.), R. D. B. Croft (Glam.), N. Hussain (Essex), P. Johnson (Notts.), D. E. Malcolm (Derbys.), T. A. Munton (Warwicks.), R. A. Pick (Notts.), M. R. Ramprakash (Middx), S. J. Rhodes (Worcs.), I. D. K. Salisbury (Sussex), J. P. Stephenson (Essex), G. P. Thorpe (Surrey) and S. L. Watkin (Glam.).

Ramprakash joined the party directly from England's tour of New Zealand. Rhodes, Stephenson and Watkin were called up to cover for M. A. Atherton and W. K. Hegg (both Lancs.) and M. P. Bicknell (Surrey), who withdrew because of injury or illness before the tour began.

Tour manager: S. P. Coverdale (Northants). *Team manager:* K. W. R. Fletcher (Essex).

ENGLAND A TOUR RESULTS

First-class matches – Played 5: Lost 2, Drawn 3.
Losses – West Indies A (2).
Draws – Windward Islands, Trinidad & Tobago, West Indies A.
Non first-class matches – Played 6: Won 5, No result 1. *Wins* – Bermuda Cricket Board of Control President's XI, Bermuda, Bermuda Select XI, Devonshire Recreation Club, Barbados. *No result* – Bermuda Cricket Board of Control President's XI.

ENGLAND A AVERAGES – FIRST-CLASS MATCHES

BATTING

	M	I	NO	R	HS	100s	Avge
H. Morris	5	9	0	443	135	1	49.22
M. R. Ramprakash	5	9	1	322	86	0	40.25
G. P. Thorpe	4	7	0	226	57	0	32.28
P. Johnson	4	7	0	221	71	0	31.57
I. D. K. Salisbury	4	7	3	95	39*	0	23.75
D. J. Bicknell	5	9	0	205	54	0	22.77
J. P. Stephenson	5	9	0	122	37	0	13.55
T. A. Munton	4	7	3	44	15	0	11.00
S. J. Rhodes	5	8	0	80	18	0	10.00
R. A. Pick	2	4	1	13	7	0	4.33
D. G. Cork	3	5	1	12	7	0	3.00

Played in three matches: D. E. Malcolm 1*, 0; S. L. Watkin 0, 0*, 0. Played in two matches: R. D. B. Croft 22, 17, 0. Played in one match: N. Hussain 5, 27.

* Signifies not out.

BOWLING

	O	M	R	W	BB	5W/i	Avge
J. P. Stephenson	114.4	32	260	20	5-53	1	13.00
D. G. Cork	66	19	186	8	3-14	0	23.25
R. A. Pick	37.5	4	147	6	3-62	0	24.50
R. D. B. Croft	51	15	128	5	4-90	0	25.60
I. D. K. Salisbury	119.3	26	384	14	4-21	0	27.42
D. E. Malcolm	74	8	279	8	4-68	0	34.87
S. L. Watkin	62	9	213	5	1-28	0	42.60
T. A. Munton	96	24	304	4	1-46	0	76.00

Also bowled: M. R. Ramprakash 9-1-28-0.

FIELDING

18 – S. J. Rhodes (13 ct, 5 st); 6 – H. Morris, J. P. Stephenson; 3 – P. Johnson, T. A. Munton, M. R. Ramprakash, I. D. K. Salisbury; 2 – D. G. Cork, N. Hussain, G. P. Thorpe; 1 – S. L. Watkin, Substitute (T. A. Munton).

Note: Matches in this section which were not first-class are signified by a dagger.

†At Somerset Field, Bermuda, February 22. England A won by six wickets. Toss: England A. Bermuda Cricket Board of Control President's XI 86 (36.4 overs) (J. P. Stephenson four for 31); England A 88 for four (25 overs).

†At Somerset Field, Bermuda, February 22. No result. Toss: England A. England A 138 for seven (20 overs) (D. J. Bicknell 40, M. D. Moxon 56 not out; K. H. Phillips three for 26); Bermuda Cricket Board of Control President's XI 80 for three (17 overs).
In the penultimate over before bad light ended play Moxon fractured his left thumb.

†At Somerset Field, Bermuda, February 23. England A won by nine wickets. Toss: England A. Bermuda 145 for eight (47 overs) (N. A. Gibbons 35; I. D. K. Salisbury three for 37); England A 147 for one (29.2 overs) (J. P. Stephenson 74 not out, G. P. Thorpe 59 not out).

†At Somerset Field, Bermuda, February 25. England A won by seven wickets. Toss: England A. Bermuda Select XI 184 for seven (42 overs) (N. A. Gibbons 84, C. P. Wade 34); England A 185 for three (37.4 overs) (D. J. Bicknell 51, H. Morris 89).

†At Somerset Field, Bermuda, February 27. England A won by 116 runs. Toss: Devonshire Recreation Club. England A 192 for five (31 overs) (M. R. Ramprakash 59, N. Hussain 61); Devonshire Recreation Club 76 (22.4 overs) (J. Pace 31; I. D. K. Salisbury three for 27, S. L. Watkin three for 16).

†At Bridgetown, Barbados, March 4. England A won by six wickets. Toss: Barbados. Barbados 171 for nine (50 overs) (P. A. Wallace 50, A. E. Proverbs 32, C. O. Browne 39 not out); England A 172 for four (48 overs) (D. J. Bicknell 44, P. Johnson 56).

WINDWARD ISLANDS v ENGLAND A

At St George's, Grenada, March 6, 7, 8. Drawn. Toss: Windward Islands. After the cosy introduction of one-day victories in Bermuda and against a poor Barbados side, England were made aware of the realities of West Indies cricket in their opening first-class fixture. In their first innings, Croft ducked into a bouncer from Davis, and Stephenson was struck on the shoulder by a beamer from Allen. No apology was forthcoming, and Fletcher, the England coach, expressed his distaste. However, all the top five batsmen enjoyed worthwhile innings after England had been put in on a pitch of moderate pace. The Windwards' reply featured a fine 68 by the precocious St Lucian, Eugene, an innings ended only by a surge of genuine speed from Malcolm. The declaration gave Ramprakash and, in particular, Thorpe the opportunity to adapt further their techniques to Caribbean conditions, helped by some friendly spin bowling. With Malcolm laid low by back trouble and the Windwards chasing a target of 208 in an hour and 20 overs, a definite result was never likely. However, Cork's three early wickets gave the tourists a boost before the match petered into a draw.

Close of play: First day, England A 262; Second day, England A 27-1 (H. Morris 10*, I. D. K. Salisbury 0*).

England A

D. J. Bicknell c Murray b Charles	47	– c Murray b Allen	15
*H. Morris c Joseph b Allen	54	– c Davis b Cuffy	38
M. R. Ramprakash c Murray b Davis	53	– (4) not out	75
G. P. Thorpe c Joseph b Cuffy	27	– (5) c Crafton b Allen	45
J. P. Stephenson c Charles b Allen	23	– (6) lbw b Allen	0
†S. J. Rhodes c Kentish b Davis	12		
R. D. B. Croft c and b Kentish	22		
D. G. Cork b Kentish	0		
I. D. K. Salisbury lbw b Allen	2	– (3) c and b Allen	2
S. L. Watkin b Allen	0		
D. E. Malcolm not out	1		
B 7, l-b 6, w 1, n-b 7	21	L-b 2, w 1	3

1/106 2/137 3/195 4/195 5/220   262   1/27 2/37 3/71   (5 wkts dec.) 178
6/238 7/238 8/258 9/258   4/178 5/178

Bowling: *First Innings*—Allen 20–4–58–4; Davis 18–1–47–2; Cuffy 15–4–42–1; Lewis 5–0–26–0; Kentish 18.3–5–47–2; Charles 6–0–29–1. *Second Innings*—Allen 19.3–2–56–4; Davis 11–3–28–0; Cuffy 10–3–17–1; Lewis 18–2–61–0; Joseph 5–1–14–0.

Windward Islands

D. A. Joseph b Malcolm	20	– c Cork b Watkin 24
A. Crafton c Rhodes b Salisbury	27	– b Cork 0
J. Eugene c Rhodes b Malcolm	68	– c sub b Cork 8
S. L. Mahon st Rhodes b Salisbury	1	– c and b Cork 0
†J. R. Murray st Rhodes b Cork	37	– not out 38
*J. D. Charles not out	34	– not out 17
I. B. A. Allen b Malcolm	1	
C. A. Davis b Watkin	21	
R. N. Lewis c Rhodes b Stephenson	18	
B 7, l-b 2, n-b 2	6	B 1, n-b 1 2

1/26 2/74 3/78 4/141 5/165   (8 wkts dec.) 233   1/2 2/25 3/25 4/40   (4 wkts) 89
6/167 7/203 8/233

T. Z. Kentish and C. E. Cuffy did not bat.

Bowling: *First Innings*—Malcolm 17–0–63–3; Watkin 16–4–42–1; Cork 17–7–35–1; Salisbury 21–5–62–2; Croft 5–0–16–0; Stephenson 2–0–10–1. *Second Innings*—Watkin 8–0–28–1; Cork 6–3–14–3; Croft 10–5–13–0; Stephenson 5–0–14–0; Ramprakash 4–0–19–0.

Umpires: G. T. Browne and G. T. Johnson.

TRINIDAD & TOBAGO v ENGLAND A

At Pointe-à-Pierre, Trinidad, March 10, 11, 12. Drawn. Toss: England A. The tourists came close to an innings victory before two late partnerships held them up on the last day, leaving a victory target of 40 runs in just one over. English disappointment was tempered, however, by the sight of Malcolm bowling with the speed and rhythm which earned him 17 consecutive Test caps. On the first day Williams struck three sixes which fell two runs short of his century when Rhodes took advantage of a misunderstanding between Williams and his partner, Bidhesi, and ran him out. There was valuable support from Carew, son of Joey, the former Test batsman and West Indies selector, before Stephenson wrapped up the innings with his deceptive seamers. Guaracara Park's fast outfield is one of its redeeming features and Morris hit 13 boundaries in his six-and-a-half-hour stay for 135. Johnson, with characteristic back-foot belligerence, had ten in his 71. These two added 130 for the fourth wicket to help England towards a lead of 149 by the time Morris declared. Fumes from the nearby oil refinery made the atmosphere unpleasant and affected the eyes of some of the players.

Close of play: First day, England A 51-1 (H. Morris 23*, S. J. Rhodes 7*); Second day, England A 321-6 (G. P. Thorpe 40*, I. D. K. Salisbury 0*).

Trinidad & Tobago

C. G. Yorke lbw b Munton	1	– (2) c Rhodes b Malcolm 26
*S. Ragoonath c Johnson b Watkin	51	– (1) c Thorpe b Munton 1
K. A. Williams run out	98	– c Rhodes b Malcolm 6
R. A. M. Smith lbw b Salisbury	5	– c Stephenson b Watkin 33
N. Bidhesi c Munton b Stephenson	10	– c Munton b Malcolm 44
M. P. Carew c Rhodes b Malcolm	61	– c Watkin b Salisbury 13
†R. Mahadeo st Rhodes b Stephenson	4	– c Stephenson b Malcolm 4
A. Jumadeen c Rhodes b Stephenson	3	– c and b Salisbury 31
R. E. Elvin run out	16	– b Salisbury 24
R. Dhanraj b Stephenson	0	– c Morris b Salisbury 0
E. C. Antoine not out	0	– not out 0
L-b 6, n-b 2	8	L-b 4, n-b 2 6

1/5 2/95 3/121 4/173 5/174   257   1/2 2/9 3/43 4/100 5/118   188
6/185 7/209 8/257 9/257   6/125 7/130 8/172 9/185

Bowling: *First Innings*—Malcolm 14–3–53–1; Munton 15–3–50–1; Watkin 10–1–56–1; Salisbury 14–3–66–1; Stephenson 12.3–3–26–4. *Second Innings*—Malcolm 16–1–68–4; Munton 16–6–49–1; Salisbury 8–2–21–4; Watkin 12–1–33–1; Stephenson 6–2–13–0.

England A

D. J. Bicknell lbw b Antoine	20	I. D. K. Salisbury not out	39
*H. Morris c Smith b Jumadeen	135	T. A. Munton not out	11
†S. J. Rhodes c Mahadeo b Antoine	7		
M. R. Ramprakash c Mahadeo b Dhanraj	33	B 13, l-b 13, n-b 5	31
P. Johnson c Carew b Antoine	71		
G. P. Thorpe b Antoine	57	1/41 2/53 3/121 (7 wkts dec.)	406
J. P. Stephenson c Ragoonath b Jumadeen	2	4/251 5/307 6/321 7/367	

S. L. Watkin and D. E. Malcolm did not bat.

Bowling: Antoine 31–3–112–4; Elvin 19–2–72–0; Dhanraj 37–5–110–1; Jumadeen 27–3–67–2; Carew 3–0–14–0; Bidhesi 1–0–5–0.

Umpires: C. E. Cumberbatch and Z. Maccum.

WEST INDIES A v ENGLAND A

First Unofficial "Test"

At Port-of-Spain, Trinidad, March 14, 15, 16, 17. West Indies A won by 130 runs. Toss: England A. The managements of both teams condemned an underprepared pitch which was patchily green at the outset and prompted lifters and shooters alike as the match progressed. Keith Fletcher, the England coach, said it might have been deemed unfit for first-class cricket in England while Jackie Hendriks, the West Indies manager, called it totally unsatisfactory and protested to the Queen's Park club.

But the England batting was also undermined by a consistently impressive West Indian pace quartet spearheaded by Joseph, who bowled fast with exceptional control. Benjamin did not have Joseph's fluid action but he also disturbed all the batsmen throughout the match. England's hopes of responding in kind were dashed when Malcolm, who had taken ten wickets on this ground in the Test match two years earlier, withdrew after suffering further back spasms during a gentle pre-match workout. His absence was immediately felt when England won the toss and put West Indies in on a pitch traditionally helpful to seamers at the start. Even so, they had West Indies 146 for seven, despite a half-century from Holder. The home side recovered to 249, by dint of an enterprising 50 from Gray and late-order hitting from Joseph and Walsh.

England's reply was laboured but brave. Despite feeling nauseous in the heat, Bicknell stayed almost four hours for 54 and Stephenson and Munton shared a partnership of 46 in nearly two hours. Munton later went to hospital for X-rays after being struck on the right shoulder by Joseph. The West Indies second innings was built on Best's 71 – the product of four and a half hours of concentration and mature discipline which effectively put the game beyond England's reach. And although Stephenson and Salisbury, who bowled round the wicket, worked their way through the order, Benjamin and Walsh had a final thrash which enabled West Indies to declare before the last day began, setting England 279. Johnson and Thorpe resisted admirably but the loss of four wickets in 34 balls sealed England's fate. *Man of the Match:* C. A. Best.

Close of play: First day, England A 7-0 (D. J. Bicknell 3*, H. Morris 2*); Second day, England A 196-8 (J. P. Stephenson 30*, T. A. Munton 7*); Third day, West Indies A 241-9 (K. C. G. Benjamin 24*, C. A. Walsh 16*).

West Indies A

C. B. Lambert c Rhodes b Pick	4	– c Morris b Pick	0
R. G. Samuels c Rhodes b Munton	0	– lbw b Cork	14
C. A. Best lbw b Stephenson	11	– st Rhodes b Stephenson	71
J. C. Adams c Rhodes b Pick	27	– c Morris b Salisbury	37
R. I. C. Holder c and b Salisbury	54	– b Salisbury	8
J. Eugene c Thorpe b Cork	12	– b Stephenson	1
†J. R. Murray run out	16	– c Ramprakash b Salisbury	10
A. H. Gray b Cork	50	– lbw b Stephenson	6
L. A. Joseph lbw b Pick	27	– c Morris b Stephenson	4
K. C. G. Benjamin c Johnson b Cork	5	– not out	24
*C. A. Walsh not out	20	– not out	16
B 2, l-b 1, w 4, n-b 16	23	B 26, l-b 12, w 2, n-b 10	50

1/4 2/13 3/34 4/66 5/101   249   1/12 2/30 3/119   (9 wkts dec.) 241
6/140 7/146 8/212 9/223   4/143 5/152 6/175
                                     7/189 8/193 9/211

Bowling: *First Innings*—Pick 13.5–0–62–3; Munton 17–3–46–1; Cork 16–4–61–3; Stephenson 18–7–39–1; Salisbury 10–2–38–1. *Second Innings*—Pick 10–3–25–1; Munton 9–4–23–0; Cork 12–3–19–1; Stephenson 22–6–57–4; Salisbury 28–9–79–3.

England A

D. J. Bicknell c Lambert b Gray	54	– b Joseph	10
*H. Morris c Adams b Gray	19	– lbw b Walsh	6
M. R. Ramprakash run out	22	– lbw b Benjamin	7
P. Johnson c Gray b Benjamin	4	– lbw b Walsh	35
G. P. Thorpe c Murray b Walsh	27	– lbw b Joseph	37
J. P. Stephenson c Holder b Benjamin	37	– c Murray b Joseph	0
†S. J. Rhodes c Lambert b Joseph	3	– b Best	9
D. G. Cork c Gray b Benjamin	2	– b Joseph	0
I. D. K. Salisbury lbw b Joseph	0	– b Benjamin	13
T. A. Munton b Joseph	15	– not out	9
R. A. Pick not out	0	– b Benjamin	0
B 7, l-b 6, n-b 16	29	B 12, l-b 7, n-b 3	22

1/43 2/87 3/96 4/123 5/148   212   1/14 2/29 3/29 4/106 5/106   148
6/158 7/166 8/166 9/212   6/106 7/110 8/130 9/148

Bowling: *First Innings*—Walsh 21–6–35–1; Joseph 22.2–4–61–3; Gray 18–2–36–2; Benjamin 24–8–49–3; Best 9–2–18–0. *Second Innings*—Joseph 16–6–30–4; Benjamin 13.5–6–26–3; Walsh 13–3–35–2; Gray 12–2–32–0; Adams 1–1–0–0; Best 5–2–6–1.

Umpires: C. E. Cumberbatch and Farouk Ali.

WEST INDIES A v ENGLAND A

Second Unofficial "Test"

At Arnos Vale, St Vincent, March 21, 22, 23, 24. West Indies A won by nine wickets. Toss: England A. England lost any chance of squaring the series after a batting collapse of dire proportions, in which they lost nine wickets for 62 runs on the final day when the surface was still reliable. They were beaten not by pace bowling but by a high-class exhibition of off-spin by a little-known Jamaican rejoicing in the name of Nehemiah Odolphus Perry. Having begun the day at 46 for one, England then crumbled in less than 30 overs.

Choosing to bat first on a pitch far more conducive to batting than the one at Queen's Park, England lost Bicknell in the first over, but a partnership of 88 between Morris, the captain, and Ramprakash saw them in a more comfortable position by lunch. A typically exuberant undefeated half-century from Johnson followed, before rain restricted play. Perry, meanwhile, had already bowled an encouraging spell which included the wicket of a non-plussed Stephenson, stunningly caught in Lambert's armpit at short leg off a full-blooded pull, and next day he ran through the lower order, taking three wickets in 31 balls without conceding a run. Johnson failed to add to his overnight 56, and only Rhodes and Croft briefly promised a lengthy stay.

This second day was extraordinary, in that six batsmen, in an international match in the Caribbean, fell to off-spin, including two Test players, Lambert and Best, both snared by Croft in his first two overs during the West Indian reply. Croft bowled Lambert round his legs with his first ball, then had Best superbly held at silly-point by Morris in his next over. Holder and Murray furthered West Indies' cause with a fifth-wicket partnership of 77, before Rhodes's fourth leg-side stumping of the tour removed Holder for 77. But Stephenson's four-wicket haul, incorporating a remarkable sequence of three caught-and-bowled dismissals, limited West Indies' lead to 61 after Joseph and Benjamin had added 42 in eight overs for the ninth wicket. Rain again interrupted England's innings, and then Perry's flight and turn, assisted by the strong cross-breeze and Lambert's adroitness at short leg, left West Indies a simple target of 48, which they accomplished in nine overs. Crowds of up to 4,000 watched the first two days, demonstrating the wisdom of taking the match to one of the smaller islands.

Man of the Match: N. O. Perry.

Close of play: First day, England A 190-5 (P. Johnson 56*, S. J. Rhodes 2*); Second day, West Indies A 142-4 (R. I. C. Holder 16*, J. R. Murray 17*); Third day, England A 46-1 (D. J. Bicknell 18*, M. R. Ramprakash 2*).

England A

D. J. Bicknell c Murray b Joseph	4	– b Benjamin	20
*H. Morris c Best b Gray	48	– c Murray b Perry	23
M. R. Ramprakash c Gray b Perry	41	– c Lambert b Benjamin	5
P. Johnson lbw b Gray	56	– c Murray b Joseph	3
G. P. Thorpe c Murray b Benjamin	19	– c Murray b Gray	14
J. P. Stephenson c Lambert b Perry	6	– c Lambert b Perry	25
†S. J. Rhodes c Lambert b Perry	18	– c Best b Perry	2
R. D. B. Croft c Murray b Joseph	17	– c Gray b Walsh	0
D. G. Cork b Perry	7	– not out	3
T. A. Munton c Best b Perry	4	– b Walsh	0
S. L. Watkin not out	0	– c Lambert b Perry	0
B 1, l-b 6, n-b 14	21	B 2, l-b 5, w 1, n-b 5	13

1/4 2/92 3/114 4/154 5/183   241   1/44 2/52 3/55 4/63 5/96   108
6/191 7/230 8/230 9/238   6/99 7/105 8/105 9/105

Bowling: *First Innings*—Joseph 22-5-58-2; Benjamin 20-4-28-1; Walsh 21-8-37-0; Gray 15-2-52-2; Perry 24.1-9-47-5; Best 1-0-12-0. *Second Innings*—Walsh 10-5-14-2; Gray 11-2-27-1; Perry 12-6-26-4; Benjamin 7-3-9-2.

West Indies A

C. B. Lambert b Croft	17	– c Ramprakash b Croft	21
R. G. Samuels c Ramprakash b Croft	54	– not out	15
C. A. Best c Morris b Croft	1	– not out	12
J. C. Adams c Rhodes b Watkin	23		
R. I. C. Holder st Rhodes b Croft	77		
†J. R. Murray lbw b Stephenson	44		
N. O. Perry c and b Stephenson	1		
A. H. Gray b Munton	16		
L. A. Joseph c and b Stephenson	22		
K. C. G. Benjamin not out	17		
*C. A. Walsh c and b Stephenson	4		
B 5, l-b 8, n-b 13	26		

1/36 2/83 3/102 4/108 5/185   302   1/32   (1 wkt) 48
6/187 7/250 8/254 9/296

Bowling: *First Innings*—Munton 21-4-69-1; Cork 13-2-45-0; Watkin 16-3-54-1; Croft 33-9-90-4; Ramprakash 5-1-9-0; Stephenson 11.1-4-22-4. *Second Innings*—Cork 2-0-12-0; Munton 4-0-27-0; Croft 3-1-9-1.

Umpires: D. M. Archer and G. T. Johnson.

WEST INDIES A v ENGLAND A

Third Unofficial "Test"

At Bridgetown, Barbados, March 28, 29, 30, 31. Drawn. Toss: West Indies A. England's most resilient batting performance of the tour was not enough to bring them a consolation victory. On the best surface of the series West Indies had no difficulty in playing out time on the final afternoon. England's cause was not helped on the opening day when Morris, the captain, was taken to hospital for precautionary X-rays on a hand damaged in fielding practice. Fortunately, only a burst blood vessel in his thumb was diagnosed, and he returned to bolster the middle order in a fifth-wicket stand of 145 with Ramprakash. Ramprakash's innings, an epic of six and a quarter hours which produced only 86 runs from 252 balls, confirmed that he had the temperament to combat an attritional four-man pace attack, while in contrast Johnson underlined his propensity for punishing strokeplay with 43 from 55 balls. Morris batted nearly five hours for his 73.

For the West Indians, Benjamin was again outstanding, and when their turn came to enjoy the benefits of a mellow pitch, they raced to 146 for one by the close on the second evening. This blistering response was fuelled mainly by Lambert's power play, which exposed an England attack handicapped by Malcolm's lack of match fitness. Lambert struck 14 fours in his 83, but England rallied well on the third morning to earn a lead of 36. Stephenson, who bowled unchanged through the morning session of the third day, was again England's most successful bowler, improving his best career figures for the third time on the tour. Accuracy, variations of pace, and a hint of out-swing, allied to an aggressive, competitive approach, were his strengths and marked him as a potential all-rounder.

Bicknell and Morris improved the lead to 83 by the close; but distrust of a pitch showing signs of wear heralded another England batting collapse, prompted this time by Walsh, who dismissed Bicknell and Ramprakash with successive balls. West Indies' target was 208 in 39 overs, and another fusillade from Lambert, including two sixes hoisted over mid-wicket off Salisbury, offered the promise of West Indies taking up the challenge. When Samuels was caught at backward square leg, however, the impetus was lost, and Best and Adams quietly played out time until the match was given up with nine overs unbowled.

Man of the Match: K. C. G. Benjamin and J. P. Stephenson (shared).

Close of play: First day, England A 260-4 (M. R. Ramprakash 82*, H. Morris 51*); Second day, West Indies A 146-1 (C. B. Lambert 80*, C. A. Best 30*); Third day, England A 47-0 (D. J. Bicknell 14*, H. Morris 28*).

England A

D. J. Bicknell b Benjamin	21	– c Murray b Walsh	14
J. P. Stephenson c Gray b Benjamin	26	– (6) c sub b Benjamin	3
M. R. Ramprakash b Walsh	86	– lbw b Walsh	0
P. Johnson b Benjamin	43	– lbw b Benjamin	9
N. Hussain lbw b Benjamin	5	– c Holder b Perry	27
*H. Morris c Murray b Gray	73	– (2) b Walsh	47
†S. J. Rhodes c Murray b Gray	12	– b Gray	17
I. D. K. Salisbury not out	21	– not out	18
T. A. Munton lbw b Walsh	2	– (10) not out	3
R. A. Pick c Best b Benjamin	7	– (9) run out	6
D. E. Malcolm b Benjamin	0		
L-b 14, w 2, n-b 30	46	B 3, l-b 7, n-b 17	27

1/51 2/62 3/135 4/145 5/290   342   1/54 2/54 3/70   (8 wkts dec.) 171
6/305 7/306 8/314 9/342   4/89 5/99 6/125
                                                7/143 8/160

Bowling: *First Innings*—Gray 26-4-74-2; Gibson 18-1-75-0; Walsh 28-8-45-2; Benjamin 26.5-10-72-6; Perry 19-7-38-0; Best 9-3-22-0; Adams 2-1-2-0. *Second Innings*—Benjamin 18-0-55-2; Gray 11-0-39-1; Walsh 21-4-41-3; Perry 6-1-26-1; Best 1-1-0-0.

West Indies A

C. B. Lambert lbw b Stephenson	83	– c Rhodes b Stephenson 32
R. G. Samuels c Hussain b Pick	19	– c Stephenson b Salisbury 32
C. A. Best c Munton b Salisbury	34	– not out 21
J. C. Adams c Johnson b Stephenson	1	– not out 6
R. I. C. Holder c Hussain b Stephenson	40	
†J. R. Murray not out	47	
A. H. Gray c Morris b Stephenson	11	
N. O. Perry c Rhodes b Pick	7	
K. C. G. Benjamin run out	25	
*C. A. Walsh b Stephenson	6	
O. D. Gibson c and b Salisbury	0	
B 4, l-b 4, n-b 25	33	B 3, l-b 1, n-b 2 6

1/66 2/151 3/154 4/179 5/203   306   1/58 2/81   (2 wkts) 97
6/220 7/257 8/295 9/304

Bowling: *First Innings*—Malcolm 22-4-78-0; Munton 14-4-40-0; Pick 10-1-46-2; Salisbury 28.3-5-81-2; Stephenson 27-9-53-5. *Second Innings*—Malcolm 5-0-17-0; Pick 4-0-14-0; Stephenson 11-1-26-1; Salisbury 10-0-36-1.

Umpires: D. M. Archer and L. H. Barker.

ERRATA

WISDEN, 1986

Page 1210   George Cox's unbroken partnership of 326 in 1949 was with James Langridge, not John.

WISDEN, 1988

Pages 264, 265 and 266   D. L. Houghton scored 142, not 141, for Zimbabwe against New Zealand in the World Cup.

WISDEN, 1991

Page 822   See also Errata in *Wisden*, 1992, page 1313: the correct bowling figures of A. J. Murphy were 7.3-0-26-1 and those of A. G. Robson were 7-0-37-1

WISDEN, 1992

Page 169   In the footnote to the list of most catches in a season, C. J. Tavaré took his 49 catches in 1978, not 1979.

Page 181   M. J. Greatbatch should be omitted from the list of highest averages in Tests; his average at the end of 1990-91 was 42.50 in 19 Tests.

Page 1184   After the 1992 *Wisden* went to press, and contrary to a previous announcement, the Board of Control for Cricket in Pakistan ruled that Pakistan B's match against Young Zimbabwe was first-class. The scores were as follows:

At Alexandra Sports Club, Harare, October 16, 17, 18, 1990. Drawn. Toss: Pakistan B. Pakistan B 469 (Mujahid Jamshed 46, Zahid Fazal 50, Asif Mujtaba 193 not out, Moin Khan 60, Shakil Khan 43, Extras 33; D. B. Gibbs four for 78) and 86 for three (Shakeel Ahmed 50 not out); Young Zimbabwe 187 (A. Flower 121 not out; Athar Laeeq seven for 55).

Page 1313   See *Wisden*, 1991, page 822 above.

THE SOUTH AFRICANS IN INDIA, 1991-92

By MATTHEW ENGEL

Twenty-one years and eight months after Ali Bacher took a catch at mid-off to dismiss Alan Connolly in a Test at Port Elizabeth, the cricketers of South Africa – isolated ever since because of global opposition to the apartheid policy – rejoined the world by playing three one-day internationals in India. In the intervening years people had often wondered how, when or even whether South Africa's isolation might end; no-one could have dared invent an ending quite so ironic and incongruous as this.

The South Africans arrived in Calcutta, four months after rejoining the International Cricket Council, at the insistence of the Board of Control for Cricket in India after Pakistan had called off a scheduled tour because of worsening Hindu-Moslem tensions. The visit was arranged almost as hurriedly as some of the rebel tours in which South Africa had lately specialised. But it was organised with the special blessing of the Marxist government of West Bengal. Thousands of people lined the route from the airport to the hotel to welcome the team, carrying banners with slogans that only a few months earlier would have been politically unthinkable: "South Africa–India friendship long live". The tourists' plane was said to be the first from South Africa ever to land in India.

Another banner at the hotel welcomed "the Springboks", but this was hurriedly torn down at the insistence of the United Cricket Board of South Africa, which was anxious not to use a nickname associated with the days of exclusively white sport. The 14-man squad – captained by Clive Rice and managed by Bacher, South Africa's last Test captain before isolation – was all white, but the party included four youngsters, two white and two black, brought along for the experience and to make a political and diplomatic point.

The whole South African team, except Kepler Wessels, who had played for Australia, were making their official international débuts and there were signs of naïveté in their tactics both on and off the field. Their self-belief was hit by defeats in the two opening matches and was only partially restored by victory in the third. And the Indians were surprised when, in South Africa's very first game back, Bacher made "an informal protest" about the state of the ball, which had apparently been gouged while the Indians were fielding to help it swing. World-weary observers thought it was a little too soon for South Africa to switch from being cricket's pariah to its preacher. The Indians denied any wrong-doing and the South African board president, Geoff Dakin, was obliged to apologise to his hosts.

However, the team itself was experienced, too experienced in the view of the selectors afterwards. They dropped the two most senior batsmen, 42-year-old Rice and 38-year-old Jimmy Cook, before the World Cup and were intent on doing the same to 36-year-old Peter Kirsten before relenting. South Africa's rheumaticky performance in the field, so alien to the country's cricketing traditions, was one of the most surprising features of the trip.

Note: Matches in this section were not first-class.

INDIA v SOUTH AFRICA

First One-Day International

At Calcutta, November 10. India won by three wickets. Toss: India. South Africa's first officially blessed representative match in almost 22 years, first one-day international and first-ever game against India attracted a crowd widely claimed as beating the world record for a day's cricket of 90,800. However, Jagmohan Dalmiya, president of the Cricket Association of Bengal, said Eden Gardens now contained 90,452 seats and estimates putting the attendance higher included all the various officials, pressmen, policemen and peanut vendors. The cricket was a disappointment and India's victory was easier than the margin suggested. South Africa were obliged to bat at 9 a.m. when the ball swung in the Calcutta smog and, understandably, the batting was nervy since 90,000 people, many of them throwing firecrackers, were able to create quite an atmosphere even if they did not break the record. Wessels's 50 was made too slowly. South Africa were given some hope when Donald took three wickets in his first four overs, but Tendulkar and the débutant Praveen Amre took India towards victory. Even in defeat, the South Africans were still overwhelmed by the occasion: "I know how Neil Armstrong felt when he stood on the moon," said their captain Rice.

Men of the Match: A. A. Donald and S. R. Tendulkar.

South Africa

S. J. Cook lbw b Srinath	17	†D. J. Richardson not out		4
A. C. Hudson c More b Kapil Dev	0	T. G. Shaw not out		0
K. C. Wessels b Tendulkar	50			
P. N. Kirsten b Raju	7	L-b 13, w 11		24
A. P. Kuiper c Amre b Prabhakar	43			
*C. E. B. Rice b Prabhakar	14	1/3 2/28 3/49	(8 wkts, 47 overs)	177
R. P. Snell c Amre b Kapil Dev	16	4/109 5/151 6/156		
B. M. McMillan run out	2	7/167 8/176		
A. A. Donald did not bat.				

Bowling: Kapil Dev 9-2-23-2; Prabhakar 10-1-26-2; Srinath 10-0-39-1; Raju 10-0-32-1; Shastri 3-0-17-0; Tendulkar 5-0-27-1.

India

R. J. Shastri c Richardson b Donald	0	M. Prabhakar not out		12
N. S. Sidhu c McMillan b Donald	6	†K. S. More not out		0
S. V. Manjrekar b Donald	1	L-b 2, w 11, n-b 2		15
S. R. Tendulkar c Snell b Donald	62			
*M. Azharuddin st Richardson b Shaw	16	1/1 2/3 3/20	(7 wkts, 40.4 overs)	178
P. K. Amre lbw b Donald	55	4/60 5/116		
Kapil Dev b Kuiper	11	6/148 7/177		

S. L. V. Raju and J. Srinath did not bat.

Bowling: Donald 8.4-0-29-5; Snell 6-0-35-0; McMillan 6-0-30-0; Shaw 10-0-46-1; Rice 5-0-14-0; Kuiper 5-0-22-1.

Umpires: V. K. Ramaswamy and R. S. Rathore.

INDIA v SOUTH AFRICA

Second One-Day International

At Gwalior, November 12. India won by 38 runs. Toss: South Africa. India ensured victory in the three-match series after another poor performance by South Africa, though the game was overshadowed by the revelation that the touring team had, in effect, accused the Indians of cheating by tampering with the ball during the opening match. Having been put in after fog delayed the start, India's openers, Sidhu and Srikkanth, put on 130 in 28 overs. The later batsmen failed to capitalise on this start and South Africa were going well at 144 for three. But the Indians held some good catches in the deep – Kapil Dev's to dismiss Richardson was superb – and the result was not in doubt for long. A crowd of 25,000 filled the Roop Singh stadium, chosen because Gwalior was the home town of the Indian Board president, Madhavrao Scindia. There was some rock-throwing but the crowd demonstrated their hospitality by aiming only at the Indians: two fielders, Raju and Sidhu, required treatment.

Men of the Match: S. V. Manjrekar and K. C. Wessels.

India

K. Srikkanth c Yachad b Snell	68	Kapil Dev b Donald	3
N. S. Sidhu c Eksteen b Rice	61	P. K. Amre b Donald	4
S. V. Manjrekar not out	52	B 1, w 10, n-b 1	12
S. R. Tendulkar c Richardson b Matthews	4	1/130 2/144 3/159 (6 wkts, 45 overs)	223
*M. Azharuddin c Kirsten b Donald	19	4/202 5/218 6/223	

†K. S. More, M. Prabhakar, S. L. V. Raju and J. Srinath did not bat.

Bowling: Donald 9-1-36-3; Snell 9-0-43-1; Matthews 9-0-41-1; Eksteen 2-0-18-0; Rice 9-0-46-1; Kuiper 7-0-38-0.

South Africa

S. J. Cook c More b Kapil Dev	0	R. P. Snell c Manjrekar b Srinath	2
M. Yachad lbw b Raju	31	C. R. Matthews not out	10
K. C. Wessels c More b Srinath	71	C. E. Eksteen not out	6
P. N. Kirsten lbw b Prabhakar	2	B 3, l-b 14, w 5, n-b 3	25
A. P. Kuiper c Azharuddin b Kapil Dev	21		
*C. E. B. Rice c sub (C. S. Pandit) b Raju	12	1/0 2/94 3/97 (8 wkts, 45 overs)	185
†D. J. Richardson c Kapil Dev b Raju	5	4/144 5/145 6/162 7/164 8/167	

A. A. Donald did not bat.

Bowling: Kapil Dev 9-3-27-2; Prabhakar 9-1-19-1; Tendulkar 7-0-31-0; Srinath 9-0-34-2; Raju 9-0-43-3; Srikkanth 2-0-14-0.

Umpires: S. K. Bansal and R. V. Ramani.

INDIA v SOUTH AFRICA

Third One-Day International

At Nehru Stadium, New Delhi, November 14 (day/night). South Africa won by eight wickets. Toss: India. South Africa's first win in a one-day international was professionally executed after India had scored an apparently invulnerable 287 for four. The cricketing validity of the game was somewhat reduced by the use of the city's athletics stadium where the outfield included four separate surfaces: grass, the Tartan of the running track, artificial grass over the long-jump pit and tarpaulins. However, 75,000 watched the run-feast with great enthusiasm even when India started losing. Shastri, having been dropped for the previous game, was brought back as captain and put on 175 for the second wicket with Manjrekar at seven an over. But South Africa made light work of the chase: Wessels's third consecutive half-century was much freer than his previous two and his 90 came off 105 balls; Kuiper's 63 not out took only 41 balls. Firecrackers and thunderflashes went off all round the stadium continually, regardless of the state of the game.

Man of the Match: P. N. Kirsten.

Men of the Series: S. V. Manjrekar and K. C. Wessels.

India

*R. J. Shastri run out	109
K. Srikkanth st Richardson b Kirsten	53
S. V. Manjrekar c McMillan b Rice	105
S. R. Tendulkar c Cook b Donald	1
Kapil Dev not out	3
B 4, l-b 5, w 6, n-b 1	16

1/86 2/261   (4 wkts, 50 overs) 287
3/264 4/287

D. B. Vengsarkar, P. K. Amre, M. Prabhakar, †C. S. Pandit, S. L. V. Raju and J. Srinath did not bat.

Bowling: Donald 10-0-55-1; Snell 10-1-56-0; Matthews 10-1-50-0; McMillan 8-0-40-0; Rice 9-0-54-1; Kirsten 3-0-23-1.

South Africa

S. J. Cook c Prabhakar b Srinath	35
K. C. Wessels lbw b Raju	90
P. N. Kirsten not out	86
A. P. Kuiper not out	63
B 2, l-b 4, w 4, n-b 3	14

1/72 2/183   (2 wkts, 46.4 overs) 288

A. C. Hudson, *C. E. B. Rice, C. R. Matthews, B. M. McMillan, †D. J. Richardson, R. P. Snell and A. A. Donald did not bat.

Bowling: Kapil Dev 8-0-37-0; Prabhakar 8.4-0-64-0; Srinath 10-0-69-1; Tendulkar 6-0-38-0; Raju 10-0-48-1; Srikkanth 4-0-25-0.

Umpires: S. Banerjee and P. D. Reporter.

FUTURE TOURS

1993 Australians to England Zimbabweans to England	1993-94 Pakistanis to New Zealand Australians to Pakistan*
	1994 New Zealanders to England South Africans to England
1993-94 Indians to Sri Lanka South Africans to Sri Lanka West Indians to Sri Lanka* New Zealanders to Australia South Africans to Australia Indians to Pakistan England to West Indies Australians to South Africa Indians to Sri Lanka	1994-95 Pakistanis to Sri Lanka England to Australia West Indians to India New Zealanders to South Africa South Africans to India* Pakistanis to India* West Indians to New Zealand

* Signifies unconfirmed.

Note: The following tours were scheduled for 1992-93: Australians to Sri Lanka, Indians and New Zealanders to Zimbabwe, Indians to South Africa, New Zealanders to Sri Lanka, West Indians and Pakistanis to Australia, Pakistanis to New Zealand, England to India and Sri Lanka, Australians to New Zealand, Pakistanis to India and Pakistanis to West Indies. In addition, Pakistanis and West Indians were to play a one-day tournament in South Africa.

THE INDIANS IN AUSTRALIA, 1991-92

By DICKY RUTNAGUR

India's 4-0 defeat in their first full series in Australia in 14 years betrayed serious shortcomings in the team, but it also highlighted the tourists' handicap of inadequate preparation for the Tests. On the insistence of their own Board, India were allowed only one first-class match before the opening Test. While Australia won the First, Second and Fifth Tests by crushing margins, India were deprived by the weather of almost certain victory in the Third. In addition, they salvaged much glory from the Fourth. Although the outcome of the series was no surprise, the Tests did not follow the predicted course. It was expected that India's batting would hold its own while the bowling would be annihilated. As it happened, India, except at Sydney, were always short of runs while the bowling had Australia in trouble at some stage of every Test. The major weakness of the Indians' batting was at the top of the order, where a more dependable opening pair would have helped the middle order yield better returns. This view was reinforced by the course India's innings took in the Third Test, in which Shastri scored a double-century.

The outstanding Indian batsman was Tendulkar, whose 148 not out in the Third Test was so largely responsible for giving India a glimpse of victory and whose 114 at Perth saved them from an even quicker rout in the Fifth. On the placid Adelaide pitch, Azharuddin scored a spectacular century but, at all other times, he gave the impression of lacking both the technique and the determination to cope with Australian conditions.

The pillar of India's attack was a rejuvenated Kapil Dev who, with 25 wickets, had his most successful series on foreign soil. In the final Test, he reached a career aggregate of 400 Test wickets, a mark hitherto passed only by Sir Richard Hadlee. Prabhakar, who shared the new ball with Kapil Dev, also bowled with great heart and India's new pace bowling discovery, Srinath, was often unlucky and looked an excellent prospect for the future. The spinners were allowed a minor role, although it was Shastri who bowled India within range of victory in Sydney, and it was unfortunate that a knee injury ended his tour not many days later. India's fielding was below acceptable standards, although it did improve as the series progressed.

While Mark Taylor was a heavy scorer, Marsh had a poor series and outside the First Test, Australia, like their opponents, invariably lost an early wicket. Nor was there much stability in the middle order. Jones was averaging below 23 until he scored a magnificent unbeaten 150 in the final innings of the series, leading to his omission from the Fifth Test. Mark Waugh looked in good touch and yet had a poor series, leading to his omission from the Fifth Test. For a batsman with an outstanding record against India, Border was also short of runs, but the three major innings he played were all in times of need. It was he who staved off defeat in the Third Test. Boon was the bulwark of the Australian batting, his batting as sturdy and robust as his build. He amassed 556 runs, including centuries in each of the last three Tests, while the lack of depth to India's bowling often helped the tailenders make telling contributions. Marsh, with Waugh, was dropped from the Fifth Test. It was a move which placed his captain, Border, at odds with the selectors and provoked from him an angry public outburst which, under a less indulgent administration, would have incurred disciplinary action.

Australia's main strength was their bowling, with McDermott consistently hostile. He took five wickets in an innings three times and collected 31 wickets, a record for Australia in a series against India. The Indians found Reid, who missed the First Test and broke down early in the Third, unplayable in the Second, in which he took six wickets in each innings. Hughes and Whitney also had their turns as match-winners. Hughes took 22 wickets in the series and was prominent in Australia's victories in the First and Fourth Tests. Whitney, filling Reid's role of left-arm pace bowler, wrecked India's second innings at Perth, bringing the Fifth Test to an abrupt end. Australia dropped catches, some of them proving expensive; but they also held many that were outstanding for speed of reflexes and athleticism. On the ground, they gave away nothing.

The series was historic in that it was the first to be played under the ICC's new code of conduct and the first in which the restriction on short-pitched bowling applied. It also marked the inception of the office of referee – shared by former England captains Mike Smith and Peter May. Played in amicable spirit, the series was free of altercations. However, when the Indian manager, Ranbir Singh Mahendra, stated publicly, halfway through the Second Test, that he had asked the Australian Board not to reappoint one of the umpires in subsequent Tests, Smith warned the Indian management of its responsibilities. There were other occasions when the Indians expressed dissatisfaction with the umpiring. As often as not, television showed their complaints to be justified. At one stage, India's cricket manager, Abbas Ali Baig, drew attention to the disparity in lbw decisions given against the two sides. "Perhaps", he noted drily, "there are changes in the lbw law of which we have not been made aware."

INDIAN TOUR RESULTS

Test matches – Played 5: Lost 4, Drawn 1.
First-class matches – Played 7: Won 1, Lost 5, Drawn 1.
Win – Queensland.
Losses – Australia (4), New South Wales.
Draw – Australia.
One-day internationals – Played 10: Won 3, Lost 6, Tied 1. *Wins* – Australia, West Indies (2). *Losses* – Australia (5), West Indies. *Tie* – West Indies.
Other non first-class matches – Played 4: Won 1, Lost 3. *Win* – New South Wales Country XI. *Losses* – ACB Chairman's XI, Western Australia, Prime Minister's XI.

TEST MATCH AVERAGES

AUSTRALIA – BATTING

	T	I	NO	R	HS	100s	Avge
D. C. Boon	5	9	2	556	135	3	79.42
A. R. Border	5	9	4	275	91*	0	55.00
M. A. Taylor	5	10	1	422	100	1	46.88
D. M. Jones	5	8	1	310	150*	1	44.28
G. R. Marsh	4	8	1	185	86	0	26.42

	T	I	NO	R	HS	100s	Avge
M. R. Whitney	3	4	3	20	12	0	20.00
I. A. Healy.........	5	8	0	157	60	0	19.62
M. G. Hughes	5	8	0	154	36	0	19.25
M. E. Waugh.......	4	6	0	83	34	0	13.83
C. J. McDermott....	5	7	1	77	31	0	12.83
S. K. Warne	2	4	1	28	20	0	9.33

Played in two Tests: B. A. Reid 3, 0; P. L. Taylor 31, 11. Played in one Test: T. M. Moody 50, 101; W. N. Phillips 8, 14; P. R. Reiffel 9.

* *Signifies not out.*

BOWLING

	O	M	R	W	BB	5W/i	Avge
B. A. Reid	59.2	16	136	12	6-60	2	11.33
M. R. Whitney	116.5	21	359	17	7-27	1	21.11
C. J. McDermott....	264.2	75	670	31	5-54	3	21.61
M. G. Hughes....	199.3	46	511	22	4-50	0	23.22

Also bowled: A. R. Border 16–3–47–0; T. M. Moody 2–0–15–0; P. R. Reiffel 28–7–80–2; P. L. Taylor 35–6–116–1; S. K. Warne 68–9–228–1; M. E. Waugh 37–9–89–1.

INDIA – BATTING

	T	I	NO	R	HS	100s	Avge
R. J. Shastri........	3	5	0	300	206	1	60.00
S. R. Tendulkar	5	9	1	368	148*	2	46.00
K. S. More	3	6	1	143	67*	0	28.60
M. Prabhakar.......	5	9	1	224	64	0	28.00
S. V. Manjrekar.....	5	9	0	197	45	0	21.88
M. Azharuddin	5	9	0	192	106	1	21.33
N. S. Sidhu.........	3	5	0	102	35	0	20.40
Kapil Dev..........	5	9	0	165	56	0	18.33
D. B. Vengsarkar....	5	9	0	158	54	0	17.55
K. Srikkanth	4	8	0	135	38	0	16.87
J. Srinath	5	9	4	78	21	0	15.60
S. L. V. Raju	4	8	2	82	31	0	13.66

Played in two Tests: C. S. Pandit 9, 15, 7. Played in one Test: S. T. Banerjee 3.

* *Signifies not out.*

BOWLING

	O	M	R	W	BB	5W/i	Avge
R. J. Shastri....	48	11	114	5	4-45	0	22.80
Kapil Dev	284	76	645	25	5-97	2	25.80
M. Prabhakar ..	251.5	61	680	19	5-101	1	35.78
S. L. V. Raju ...	171.4	42	438	9	3-11	0	48.66
J. Srinath	201.1	41	553	10	3-59	0	55.30

Also bowled: S. T. Banerjee 18–4–47–3; S. V. Manjrekar 0.5–0–4–0; K. Srikkanth 1–0–5–0; S. R. Tendulkar 36–10–94–3.

INDIAN AVERAGES – FIRST-CLASS MATCHES

BATTING

	M	I	NO	R	HS	100s	Avge
S. R. Tendulkar	6	11	1	509	148*	2	50.90
R. J. Shastri	4	7	0	336	206	1	48.00
C. S. Pandit	3	4	0	158	127	1	39.50
M. Azharuddin	7	13	1	340	106	1	28.33
M. Prabhakar.......	6	11	1	270	64	0	27.00
S. V. Manjrekar	7	12	0	312	110	1	26.00
Kapil Dev..........	6	10	0	245	80	0	24.50
D. B. Vengsarkar....	7	13	1	290	82*	0	24.16
K. S. More	4	8	1	155	67*	0	22.14
N. S. Sidhu.........	3	5	0	102	35	0	20.40
J. Srinath	6	11	4	107	24	0	15.28
K. Srikkanth	6	12	0	152	38	0	12.66
S. L. V. Raju	5	9	2	86	31	0	12.28
S. T. Banerjee	3	4	2	15	12	0	7.50

Played in two matches: S. C. Ganguly 20, 8, 29; N. D. Hirwani 6*, 0.

* Signifies not out.

BOWLING

	O	M	R	W	BB	5W/i	Avge
Kapil Dev.......	306	79	699	26	5-97	2	26.88
N. D. Hirwani ...	65	6	206	6	2-53	0	34.33
R. J. Shastri	68	12	175	5	4-45	0	35.00
S. T. Banerjee....	71	10	288	8	3-47	0	36.00
M. Prabhakar....	268.5	62	723	20	5-101	1	36.15
S. L. V. Raju	223.3	51	595	15	6-81	1	39.66
J. Srinath	221.1	44	605	11	3-59	0	55.00

Also bowled: S. C. Ganguly 10–0–48–0; S. V. Manjrekar 0.5–0–4–0; K. Srikkanth 19–3–57–2; S. R. Tendulkar 39–10–104–3.

FIELDING

13 – C. S. Pandit (12 ct, 1 st); 11 – K. S. More (10 ct, 1 st); 8 – K. Srikkanth; 6 – M. Azharuddin; 5 – S. R. Tendulkar; 4 – Kapil Dev, D. B. Vengsarkar, Substitutes (3 ct, 1 st); 3 – M. Prabhakar; 2 – S. T. Banerjee, N. D. Hirwani, S. L. V. Raju; 1 – S. C. Ganguly, S. V. Manjrekar, N. S. Sidhu, J. Srinath.

Note: Matches in this section which were not first-class are signified by a dagger.

†At Lilac Hill, November 17. ACB Chairman's XI won by 29 runs. Toss: Indians. ACB Chairman's XI 254 for six (50 overs) (G. R. Marsh 106, M. P. Lavender 54, T. M. Moody 35; J. Srinath three for 56); Indians 225 for seven (50 overs) (R. J. Shastri 40, D. B. Vengsarkar 58 not out; D. R. Martyn three for 26).

†At Perth, November 18 (day/night). Western Australia won by nine wickets. Toss: Western Australia. Indians 64 (31.5 overs) (T. M. Alderman three for 11, T. M. Moody three for eight); Western Australia 65 for one (13 overs) (M. R. J. Veletta 30 not out). *The match finished in daylight.*

†At Wagga Wagga, November 21. Indians won by eight wickets. Toss: New South Wales Country XI. New South Wales Country XI 220 for seven (50 overs) (G. G. Geise 102, M. S. Curry 40; M. Prabhakar five for 26); Indians 221 for two (47.2 overs) (R. J. Shastri 72, S. V. Manjrekar 116 not out).

NEW SOUTH WALES v INDIANS

At Lismore, November 23, 24, 25. New South Wales won by an innings and eight runs. Toss: New South Wales. The tourists derived little benefit from their only first-class fixture before the First Test. They lost with a day to spare, their batting undermined by a pitch which was damp at the start and remained inconsistent in bounce. On the first day Tendulkar made 82 runs of high quality, but no one else reached 30. New South Wales's reply was a showcase for the class of Mark Waugh and the promise of the 21-year-old left-hander, Bevan. Making the most of a dropped catch in the slips when he was three, Bevan went on to a belligerent 115 in 145 balls. Whitney's recall for the First Test was announced on the third morning. The news evidently inspired him: his six wickets destroyed the Indians' second innings. Only Prabhakar batted with any determination; Tendulkar was again top scorer, but was dropped four times in a cavalier innings.

Close of play: First day, New South Wales 22-0 (S. M. Small 11*, M. A. Taylor 8*); Second day, Indians 4-0 (K. Srikkanth 4*, M. Prabhakar 0*).

Indians

K. Srikkanth c Emery b Holdsworth	5	– c McNamara b Whitney	4
M. Prabhakar lbw b Whitney	5	– c Matthews b Whitney	41
S. V. Manjrekar c Taylor b Holdsworth	2	– lbw b Holdsworth	3
D. B. Vengsarkar c Taylor b S. R. Waugh	17	– c Matthews b Whitney	6
*M. Azharuddin b S. R. Waugh	23	– c Emery b Lawson	17
S. R. Tendulkar c Taylor b Holdsworth	82	– c McNamara b Matthews	59
S. C. Ganguly c Bevan b Holdsworth	20	– c Emery b Whitney	8
†K. S. More lbw b Matthews	9	– b Matthews	3
J. Srinath c Taylor b Whitney	24	– c S. R. Waugh b Whitney	5
S. T. Banerjee c Emery b Whitney	12	– not out	0
N. D. Hirwani not out	6	– c Taylor b Whitney	0
B 1, l-b 3	4	N-b 1	1

1/11 2/11 3/13 4/47 5/56   209   1/4 2/7 3/22 4/53 5/111   147
6/100 7/167 8/167 9/202   6/127 7/141 8/147 9/147

Bowling: *First Innings*—Whitney 19.3–4–45–3; Holdsworth 17–2–38–4; Lawson 14–3–23–0; S. R. Waugh 13–6–24–2; Matthews 18–4–56–1; M. E. Waugh 7–2–19–0. *Second Innings*—Whitney 19.4–7–37–6; McNamara 1–1–0–0; Holdsworth 6–2–23–1; Lawson 7–0–23–1; S. R. Waugh 6–1–20–0; Matthews 14–4–37–2; M. E. Waugh 3–1–7–0.

New South Wales

S. M. Small b Prabhakar	58	*G. F. Lawson c and b Hirwani	2
M. A. Taylor b Banerjee	15	M. R. Whitney not out	2
S. R. Waugh b Banerjee	13	W. J. Holdsworth c Hirwani b Srikkanth	4
M. E. Waugh b Srinath	79		
M. G. Bevan c Azharuddin b Banerjee	115	L-b 20, n-b 12	32
B. E. McNamara run out	18		
G. R. J. Matthews b Srikkanth	23	1/60 2/83 3/112 4/287 5/320	364
†P. A. Emery st sub b Hirwani	3	6/344 7/354 8/358 9/358	

Bowling: Prabhakar 17–1–43–1; Srinath 20–3–52–1; Banerjee 17–2–79–3; Tendulkar 3–0–10–0; Hirwani 20–1–82–2; Ganguly 6–0–26–0; Srikkanth 18–3–52–2.

Umpires: G. E. Reed and I. S. Thomas.

AUSTRALIA v INDIA

First Test Match

At Brisbane, November 29, 30, December 1, 2. Australia won by ten wickets. Toss: Australia. Australia's win was fashioned by superb bowling from McDermott, who captured nine wickets in all, and Hughes, whose opening spell on the third day wrecked India's second innings beyond repair. The failure of their batsmen in their only first-class match to date, against New South Wales, had done untold damage to the Indians' morale. Their fear of batting first was increased by an overcast sky on the eve of the match, and was not dispelled by bright sunshine as it began.

The pitch contained some moisture and provided movement. But its bounce, rather than any deviation of the ball, defeated technique moulded by flat Indian pitches. Srikkanth and Shastri soon fell once McDermott had found a good line, and by lunch Hughes had reduced India to 53 for four. Not long after this became 83 for six. Only a breezy 44 in 41 balls from Kapil Dev and a fighting 54 by Prabhakar, unbeaten at No. 8, prolonged the innings towards the end of the day.

At 235 for two by the end of the second day, Australia looked to be playing India out of the match. Marsh and Taylor built the foundations in workmanlike fashion before Marsh became Srinath's first Test victim; Taylor swept once too often and missed his century by six runs. But Boon was solidly established and Border, in his record 126th Test, was already rattling his sword. Next morning, however, the second new ball and a flash of brilliance from Kapil Dev produced a dramatic twist. With only nine runs added, he bowled what Boon, the non-striker, described as the best three consecutive balls he had seen in a Test. The first cut back at Border and bowled him through the gate; the next swung away late to beat Jones who, playing for out-swing at the third, left a fatal gap. Only resolute batting by Peter Taylor kept Australia on course for a lead of 101. India's relief that it was no larger soon turned to despair. Hughes pounded the ball in and obtained disconcerting bounce, to remove four men with 32 on the board; three were held at short leg. Although Shastri batted doggedly for over three hours, India were six down before they wiped out their deficit. Australia needed no more than 56 to complete a four-day victory.

Man of the Match: C. J. McDermott. *Attendance:* 22,009.

Close of play: First day, India 239; Second day, Australia 235-2 (D. C. Boon 59*, A. R. Border 24*); Third day, India 104-6 (R. J. Shastri 37*, M. Prabhakar 9*).

India

R. J. Shastri c Waugh b McDermott	8	– c Healy b McDermott 41
K. Srikkanth c Boon b McDermott	13	– c Boon b Hughes 0
S. V. Manjrekar c and b Hughes	17	– c Boon b Hughes 5
D. B. Vengsarkar c Waugh b Hughes	5	– lbw b Hughes 0
*M. Azharuddin c Hughes b Whitney	10	– c Boon b Hughes 12
S. R. Tendulkar b Whitney	16	– c Healy b McDermott 7
Kapil Dev b McDermott	44	– c Waugh b McDermott 25
M. Prabhakar not out	54	– c Healy b Whitney 39
†K. S. More c Whitney b Hughes	19	– lbw b McDermott 1
S. L. V. Raju c Healy b McDermott	12	– c Healy b Whitney 2
J. Srinath c Healy b McDermott	21	– not out 12
B 1, l-b 6, n-b 13	20	L-b 4, n-b 8 12

1/21 (2) 2/24 (1) 3/50 (4) 4/53 (3)   239   1/0 (2) 2/14 (3) 3/14 (4)   156
5/67 (5) 6/83 (6) 7/141 (7) 8/186 (9)   4/32 (5) 5/47 (6) 6/87 (7)
9/206 (10) 10/239 (11)   7/136 (1) 8/140 (9)
                                                   9/142 (8) 10/156 (10)

Bowling: *First Innings*—McDermott 28.1–11–54–5; Whitney 21–2–82–2; Hughes 20–5–34–3; Waugh 1–0–6–0; P. L. Taylor 18–3–56–0. *Second Innings*—McDermott 25–7–47–4; Hughes 16–4–50–4; Whitney 17.2–3–55–2.

Australia

G. R. Marsh b Srinath	47 – (2) not out	17
M. A. Taylor c Vengsarkar b Raju	94 – (1) not out	35
D. C. Boon c More b Prabhakar	66	
*A. R. Border b Kapil Dev	28	
D. M. Jones b Kapil Dev	0	
M. E. Waugh c More b Srinath	11	
†I. A. Healy lbw b Prabhakar	12	
P. L. Taylor c Raju b Srinath	31	
M. G. Hughes b Kapil Dev	11	
C. J. McDermott c Azharuddin b Kapil Dev	8	
M. R. Whitney not out	7	
L-b 15, w 1, n-b 9	25	L-b 4, n-b 2	6

1/95 (1) 2/178 (2) 3/244 (4) 4/244 (5)   340   (no wkt) 58
5/265 (3) 6/278 (6) 7/280 (7) 8/301 (9)
9/316 (10) 10/340 (8)

Bowling: *First Innings*—Kapil Dev 34–9–80–4; Prabhakar 37–10–88–2; Srinath 24.4–4–59–3; Raju 31–5–90–1; Tendulkar 1–0–8–0. *Second Innings*—Kapil Dev 9–0–23–0; Prabhakar 2–1–3–0; Srinath 9–5–6–0; Raju 3–1–13–0; Tendulkar 1–0–5–0; Manjrekar 0.5–0–4–0.

Umpires: P. J. McConnell and S. G. Randell. Referee: M. J. K. Smith (England).

India's matches v Australia and West Indies in the Benson and Hedges World Series Cup (December 6–December 15) may be found in that section.

†At Canberra, December 17. Prime Minister's XI won by 75 runs. Toss: Prime Minister's XI. Prime Minister's XI 244 for seven (50 overs) (G. S. Blewett 65, M. G. Bevan 60, D. R. Martyn 50 not out); Indians 169 (44 overs) (M. Prabhakar 34, D. B. Vengsarkar 44, S. R. Tendulkar 34; G. J. Rowell six for 27).

QUEENSLAND v INDIANS

At Brisbane, December 20, 21, 22, 23. Indians won by 39 runs. Toss: Indians. With an excellent batting pitch, bowling below strength on both sides, and time lost to rain and bad light, the match would have been drawn if it had run its full course. Instead reciprocal declarations set up a tight win for the tourists. Despite a splendid century with 20 fours from Manjrekar, the Indians scored very slowly on the first day. But the innings then received a 200-run boost from a seventh-wicket stand between Pandit, who hit 21 fours in his 127, and Kapil Dev. Queensland declared at tea on the third day, 135 behind, to keep the match alive and some friendly bowling enabled the Indians to set them 313 to win in a minimum 75 overs. Ritchie made a polished 107 and forceful batting from Barsby and Prestwidge kept the state in the hunt. They might well have won if Border had batted higher than No. 8. Raju's excellent control brought him six wickets to foil Queensland's final charge.

Close of play: First day, Indians 255-6 (Kapil Dev 11*, C. S. Pandit 8*); Second day, Queensland 118-1 (T. J. Barsby 66*, G. M. Ritchie 36*); Third day, Indians 91-2 (D. B. Vengsarkar 41*, M. Azharuddin 46*).

Indians

R. J. Shastri c Anderson b Prestwidge	35	– c Border b Prestwidge	1
K. Srikkanth c Taylor b Prestwidge	7	– lbw b Williams	1
S. V. Manjrekar st Anderson b Oxenford	110	
D. B. Vengsarkar c Anderson b Williams	27	– (3) not out	82
*M. Azharuddin run out	18	– (4) not out	90
S. C. Ganguly run out	29	
Kapil Dev b Williams	80	
†C. S. Pandit run out	127	
S. L. V. Raju c and b Rackemann	4	
S. T. Banerjee not out	0	
B 2, l-b 1, w 5, n-b 9	17	L-b 1, n-b 2	3

1/9 2/62 3/136 4/161 5/233   (9 wkts dec.) 454   1/1 2/5   (2 wkts dec.) 177
6/238 7/438 8/443 9/454

N. D. Hirwani did not bat.

Bowling: *First Innings*—Williams 29.3-4-114-2; Prestwidge 25-3-113-2; Rackemann 29-6-95-1; Taylor 21-1-97-0; Oxenford 12-2-32-1. *Second Innings*—Williams 11-2-39-1; Prestwidge 9-1-31-1; Taylor 11-0-46-0; Oxenford 8-0-29-0; Ritchie 3-0-21-0; Goggin 4-0-10-0.

Queensland

T. J. Barsby c Pandit b Banerjee	83	– c and b Banerjee	22
M. L. Hayden c Azharuddin b Kapil Dev	8	– c Srikkanth b Raju	38
G. M. Ritchie c Pandit b Hirwani	68	– c sub b Raju	107
A. R. Border b Hirwani	85	– (8) c Banerjee b Hirwani	33
P. J. T. Goggin b Hirwani	8	– (4) lbw b Raju	5
S. A. Prestwidge not out	48	– (5) c Ganguly b Raju	24
†P. W. Anderson (did not bat)		– (6) run out	1
P. L. Taylor (did not bat)		– (7) c sub b Raju	12
B. N. J. Oxenford (did not bat)		– not out	9
S. B. Williams (did not bat)		– c Azharuddin b Hirwani	14
*C. G. Rackemann (did not bat)		– b Raju	0
B 1, l-b 7, n-b 11	19	L-b 4, w 1, n-b 3	8

1/25 2/150 3/189 4/213   (4 wkts dec.) 319   1/34 2/122 3/128 4/166 5/167   273
6/198 7/246 8/255 9/272

Bowling: *First Innings*—Banerjee 22-3-106-1; Kapil Dev 16-2-32-1; Ganguly 4-0-22-0; Raju 27-6-76-0; Hirwani 25-2-53-2; Shastri 7-0-22-0. *Second Innings*—Banerjee 14-1-56-1; Kapil Dev 6-1-22-0; Raju 24.5-3-81-6; Hirwani 20-3-71-2; Shastri 13-1-39-0.

Umpires: M. D. Ralston and C. D. Timmins.

AUSTRALIA v INDIA

Second Test Match

At Melbourne, December 26, 27, 28, 29. Australia won by eight wickets. Toss: India. Australia brought in Reid for Whitney, and the tall left-arm pace bowler proved their trump card, much as he was a year earlier against England. With six wickets in each innings he propelled India to a second four-day defeat.

Azharuddin might have put Australia in. Almost halfway through the tour, his bowlers seemed to have found their land legs better than the batsmen, while there was damp under the pitch's surface and the sky was overcast. It was inept batting as much as the conditions that reduced India to 64 for four, however. They were still floundering at 151 for eight before a reviving ninth-wicket stand of 77. More batted over three hours for his unbeaten 67, with almost two hours of support from Raju. The Indian wicket-keeper was put down by Mark Taylor, clipping off his legs, and the same fielder had earlier missed an easy chance at slip off Hughes, when Manjrekar was two.

Australia's start was also unsound. Boon and Border went in one over from Kapil Dev after lunch. But Marsh and Jones initiated a revival with 108 for the fourth wicket, perhaps assisted by Azharuddin's reluctance to use his spinners. During this partnership the umpiring controversy reached its height when Jones trapped a ball from Raju between glove and thigh. As More swooped, hoping for a catch, the batsman swept the ball away with his palm. The Indians appealed, for either handling the ball or obstructing the field. But umpire King ruled against them on both counts, adding to their earlier disgruntlement, caused when he had declined an lbw appeal against Marsh. Jones did not add to his score, and on his dismissal Waugh sparkled for 55 minutes. Kapil Dev removed Marsh with the second new ball on the third morning, but the tail, led by Healy, wagged vigorously.

India lost half their wickets in wiping off the arrears of 86, with Reid and McDermott claiming three in ten balls. This time it was incisive bowling which caused the collapse; only Azharuddin played a bad shot. On the fourth day Vengsarkar and Tendulkar, showing courage and skill, held the Australians at bay until 20 minutes before lunch. Border, when running back from mid-on, took an astonishing catch from Tendulkar. Reid then mopped up three wickets in ten overs before Vengsarkar was last out, after a stoical 286 minutes. Australia were left to get 128. As they hurried to complete their win on the fourth evening, the competence of the umpiring was again questioned; a run-out appeal against Border was rejected, though television suggested he was short of the line.

Man of the Match: B. A. Reid.   *Attendance:* 89,169.

Close of play: First day, India 243-9 (K. S. More 50*, J. Srinath 12*); Second day, Australia 215-5 (G. R. Marsh 79*, I. A. Healy 4*); Third day, India 92-5 (D. B. Vengsarkar 14*, S. R. Tendulkar 8*).

India

R. J. Shastri c Healy b Reid	23	– c Healy b Reid	22
K. Srikkanth c Boon b Reid	5	– lbw b Reid	6
M. Prabhakar b Reid	0	– (9) c Healy b Reid	17
S. V. Manjrekar c Waugh b Reid	25	– (3) c M. A. Taylor b McDermott	30
D. B. Vengsarkar c Reid b Hughes	23	– (4) c sub (M. R. Whitney) b McDermott	54
*M. Azharuddin c Jones b McDermott	22	– (5) c M. A. Taylor b Reid	2
S. R. Tendulkar c Waugh b Reid	15	– b Border b P. L. Taylor	40
Kapil Dev c Hughes b McDermott	19	– c Healy b Reid	12
†K. S. More not out	67	– (10) lbw b Reid	12
S. L. V. Raju c Border b Hughes	31	– (6) c and b McDermott	1
J. Srinath c Border b Reid	14	– not out	0
B 1, l-b 8, w 6, n-b 4	19	B 1, l-b 6, n-b 10	17

1/11 (2) 2/11 (3) 3/61 (1) 4/64 (4)	**263**	1/13 (2) 2/48 (1) 3/75 (3)	**213**
5/109 (6) 6/109 (5) 7/128 (7) 8/151 (8)		4/78 (5) 5/79 (6) 6/141 (7)
9/228 (10) 10/263 (11)		7/155 (8) 8/173 (9)
		9/213 (10) 10/213 (4)

Bowling: *First Innings*—McDermott 30–6–100–2; Reid 26.2–7–66–6; Hughes 23–6–52–2; Waugh 8–1–16–0; P. L. Taylor 6–0–20–0. *Second Innings*—McDermott 29–8–63–3; Reid 29–9–60–6; Hughes 19–6–43–0; P. L. Taylor 11–3–40–1.

Australia

G. R. Marsh c Vengsarkar b Kapil Dev	86	– (2) lbw b Prabhakar	10
M. A. Taylor c Tendulkar b Prabhakar	13	– (1) st More b Raju	60
D. C. Boon c Srikkanth b Kapil Dev	11	– not out	44
*A. R. Border b Kapil Dev	0	– not out	5
D. M. Jones c More b Prabhakar	59		
M. E. Waugh c More b Shastri	34		
†I. A. Healy lbw b Kapil Dev	60		
P. L. Taylor c More b Prabhakar	11		
M. G. Hughes c Tendulkar b Kapil Dev	36		
C. J. McDermott not out	16		
B. A. Reid c Kapil Dev b Prabhakar	3		
L-b 9, n-b 11	20	L-b 3, n-b 6	9

1/24 (2) 2/55 (3) 3/55 (4) 4/163 (5)	**349**	1/16 (2) 2/122 (1)	**(2 wkts) 128**
5/211 (6) 6/229 (1) 7/262 (6) 8/326 (7)		
9/337 (9) 10/349 (11)		

Bowling: *First Innings*—Kapil Dev 35–9–97–5; Prabhakar 34–7–84–4; Srinath 25–3–71–0; Raju 17–3–52–0; Tendulkar 4–1–16–0; Shastri 7–1–20–1. *Second Innings*—Kapil Dev 12–1–30–0; Prabhakar 11–0–38–1; Srinath 8–0–28–0; Raju 6–0–17–1; Shastri 3–1–12–0.

Umpires: L. J. King and T. A. Prue. Referee: M. J. K. Smith (England).

AUSTRALIA v INDIA

Third Test Match

At Sydney, January 2, 3, 4, 5, 6. Drawn. Toss: India. Deferring to the Sydney pitch's reputation as a turner, Australia took aboard the uncapped leg-spinner Shane Warne, instead of off-spinner Peter Taylor. Adopting the opposite policy, India replaced slow left-armer Raju with a fourth seamer, the débutant Banerjee, and put Australia in, a hard pitch and a clear sky notwithstanding. Though Banerjee took three out of four wickets on the first day, India sorely missed a specialist spinner as they sought victory on the last afternoon, when the bounce was uneven and the ball was turning, albeit slowly.

The Indians not only batted and bowled better than Australia; their fielding and running between wickets were so vastly improved that they were unrecognisable. But for the loss of 94.1 overs to bad light and rain on the third and fourth days, they would have won. Australia's bowling was grievously weakened when Reid strained a side muscle after bowling four overs. But on the first day the Indians seemed to have shot themselves in the foot by fielding. It was only when they took the new ball next morning that, helped by cloud cover, India seized the initiative. Kapil Dev dismissed Border for the third time in the series, and three wickets from Prabhakar pinned back Australia to 269 for eight within an hour. Boon, who punished the bad ball unerringly, was to remain unbeaten on 129.

By the end of the day India had lost Sidhu, recently flown in as a replacement opener, and Manjrekar. Shastri and Vengsarkar batted stoically through the shortened third day, though Shastri offered Warne a difficult return chance. In the morning McDermott removed Vengsarkar and Azharuddin in one over with the new ball, but Australia did not claim another wicket until tea when Shastri, having reached his first double-century in a Test, fell to a tired shot at Warne after nine and a half hours, 17 fours and two sixes. He had shared India's highest ever fifth-wicket partnership (196) against Australia with Tendulkar, who later became the youngest man to score a Test century in Australia. His mature and fluent innings lasted 298 minutes.

India batted on into the fifth day – mistakenly, it seemed. But the decision looked far better when the pace bowlers reduced Australia to 55 for three, and then Shastri took three wickets to make the score 114 for six. The collapse was checked by Border, assisted first by Hughes and then by Warne, who helped block out the last seven minutes.

Man of the Match: R. J. Shastri.   *Attendance:* 54,263.

Close of play: First day, Australia 234-4 (D. C. Boon 89*, A. R. Border 14*); Second day, India 103-2 (R. J. Shastri 52*, D. B. Vengsarkar 13*); Third day, India 178-2 (R. J. Shastri 95*, D. B. Vengsarkar 43*); Fourth day, India 445-7 (S. R. Tendulkar 120*, C. S. Pandit 3*).

Australia

G. R. Marsh b Banerjee	8	– (2) c Pandit b Kapil Dev	4
M. A. Taylor c Pandit b Banerjee	56	– (1) c Kapil Dev b Shastri	35
D. C. Boon not out	129	– c Azharuddin b Srinath	7
M. E. Waugh c Prabhakar b Banerjee	5	– lbw b Prabhakar	18
D. M. Jones run out	35	– c Pandit b Shastri	18
*A. R. Border c Pandit b Kapil Dev	19	– not out	53
†I. A. Healy c sub (K. Srikkanth) b Prabhakar	1	– c Prabhakar b Shastri	7
M. G. Hughes c Pandit b Prabhakar	2	– c Prabhakar b Tendulkar	21
C. J. McDermott b Prabhakar	1	– c Vengsarkar b Shastri	0
S. K. Warne c Pandit b Kapil Dev	20	– not out	1
B. A. Reid c Tendulkar b Kapil Dev	0		
B 4, l-b 14, w 1, n-b 18	37	L-b 4, w 1, n-b 4	9

1/22 (1) 2/117 (2) 3/127 (4) 4/210 (5)   313   1/9 (2) 2/31 (3)   (8 wkts) 173
5/248 (6) 6/251 (7) 7/259 (8) 8/269 (9)   3/55 (4) 4/85 (5)
9/313 (10) 10/313 (11)   5/106 (1) 6/114 (7)
                                                        7/164 (8) 8/171 (9)

Bowling: *First Innings*—Kapil Dev 33-9-60-3; Prabhakar 39-12-82-3; Banerjee 18-4-47-3; Srinath 21-5-69-0; Shastri 13-1-37-0. *Second Innings*—Kapil Dev 19-5-41-1; Prabhakar 25-10-53-1; Srinath 12-0-28-1; Shastri 25-8-45-4; Tendulkar 1-0-2-1.

India

R. J. Shastri c Jones b Warne	206	†C. S. Pandit run out	9
N. S. Sidhu c Waugh b McDermott	0	S. T. Banerjee c Border b McDermott	3
S. V. Manjrekar c Waugh b Hughes	34	J. Srinath run out	1
D. B. Vengsarkar c Waugh b McDermott	54	B 1, l-b 4, n-b 5	10
*M. Azharuddin c Boon b McDermott	4		
S. R. Tendulkar not out	148	1/7 (2) 2/86 (3) 3/197 (4) 4/201 (5)	483
M. Prabhakar c Taylor b Hughes	14	5/397 (1) 6/434 (7) 7/434 (8)	
Kapil Dev c Marsh b Hughes	0	8/458 (9) 9/474 (10) 10/483 (11)	

Bowling: McDermott 51-12-147-4; Reid 4-0-10-0; Hughes 41.4-8-104-3; Waugh 14-5-28-0; Warne 45-7-150-1; Border 13-3-39-0.

Umpires: P. J. McConnell and S. G. Randell. Referee: P. B. H. May (England).

India's matches v Australia and West Indies in the Benson and Hedges World Series Cup (January 11–January 20) may be found in that section.

AUSTRALIA v INDIA

Fourth Test Match

At Adelaide, January 25, 26, 27, 28, 29. Australia won by 38 runs. Toss: India. Marred though it was by controversy over lbw decisions – eight times Indians were given out, while all but two of their own appeals were rejected – the match produced a thrilling finish, ending a sequence of six drawn Tests at the Adelaide Oval. An older Adelaide tradition, of captains electing to field and losing, was restored instead. Meanwhile, the pitch, relaid a year before to give it more bone, turned out slower than ever.

Australia's first-innings collapse in four and a half hours was the result of poor batting, though credit was also due to Kapil Dev and Prabhakar for moving the ball in the air on a fine, clear day. The spinner Raju's use of flight earned three victims, among them Jones, who was the one batsman who put down roots, batting two hours. The faster Australian bowlers obtained greater movement off the pitch, and McDermott undermined India's front-line batsmen, apart from Sidhu who stayed 136 minutes. He was caught when Hughes dug one in and made it lift to the shoulder of the bat. India recovered from 70 for six through a sterling partnership between Kapil Dev and Prabhakar, and the grit of the tail.

After 21 wickets had fallen in two days, India claimed only one on the third, and that 40 minutes before the close. Kapil Dev's first delivery with the new ball – taken 16 overs late – dismissed Taylor after a stand of 221 with Boon. Not long after, Border survived a confident lbw appeal; this refusal aggrieved the Indians as much as that of two against Boon the day before. Boon finally departed when he took too long over a single on the fourth morning. His run-out precipitated another collapse: Jones was caught behind, and Waugh taken at slip, from successive balls in Kapil's next over. But Border and Healy survived chances, and the Australian captain recovered his touch to build a formidable lead of 371, with almost seven hours to bowl India out.

Australia's uncharacteristic lapses in the field – Sidhu, Manjrekar and Azharuddin all had lives – almost gave the game to India, though when Azharuddin began to play shots with abandon he probably believed defeat was inevitable. By then India had been set back by the run-out of Manjrekar and two lbw decisions which looked harsh. But the captain's drives, effortlessly struck, wristy cuts and deflections off the legs blended into the elegant splendour of the Adelaide Oval. With Prabhakar, he added 101 in 26 overs, completing his century in 144 balls. Despite the surge, Border maintained attacking fields. India needed 89 when McDermott took the new ball, and at once had Azharuddin caught at slip. Even then, the gap shrank to 44 before the last threat, Prabhakar, was lbw; he was ninth out, in the final hour, before Srinath gave McDermott his 150th Test wicket and the victory.

Man of the Match: C. J. McDermott.   *Attendance:* 57,684.

Close of play: First day, India 45-2 (N. S. Sidhu 15*, D. B. Vengsarkar 8*); Second day, Australia 36-1 (M. A. Taylor 18*, D. C. Boon 11*); Third day, Australia 245-2 (D. C. Boon 121*, A. R. Border 6*); Fourth day, India 31-0 (K. Srikkanth 13*, N. S. Sidhu 13*).

Australia

G. R. Marsh b Prabhakar	8	– (2) b Kapil Dev	5
M. A. Taylor b Tendulkar	11	– (1) c Raju b Kapil Dev	100
D. C. Boon b Kapil Dev	19	– run out	135
*A. R. Border c Pandit b Prabhakar	0	– not out	91
D. M. Jones c Azharuddin b Raju	41	– c Pandit b Kapil Dev	0
M. E. Waugh lbw b Prabhakar	15	– c Tendulkar b Kapil Dev	0
†I. A. Healy c Pandit b Kapil Dev	1	– c Srikkanth b Kapil Dev	41
M. G. Hughes c Manjrekar b Kapil Dev	26	– lbw b Srinath	23
S. K. Warne st Pandit b Raju	7	– c Pandit b Srinath	0
C. J. McDermott b Raju	0	– b Raju	21
M. R. Whitney not out	0	– c Srinath b Raju	12
L-b 10, n-b 7	17	L-b 15, n-b 8	23
	145		**451**

1/13 (1) 2/36 (2) 3/39 (4) 4/50 (3)   145
5/77 (6) 6/81 (7) 7/117 (5) 8/141 (9)
9/145 (8) 10/145 (10)

1/10 (2) 2/231 (1) 3/277 (3)   451
4/277 (5) 5/277 (6) 6/348 (7)
7/383 (8) 8/383 (9)
9/409 (10) 10/451 (11)

Bowling: *First Innings*—Kapil Dev 23–11–33–3; Prabhakar 18–3–55–2; Srinath 10–2–26–0; Tendulkar 4–2–10–2; Raju 11.4–7–11–3. *Second Innings*—Kapil Dev 51–12–130–5; Prabhakar 21–5–60–0; Raju 56–15–121–2; Srinath 37–13–76–2; Srikkanth 1–0–5–0; Tendulkar 20–5–44–0.

India

K. Srikkanth c Healy b McDermott	17	– b McDermott	22
N. S. Sidhu c Healy b Hughes	27	– lbw b Hughes	35
S. V. Manjrekar lbw b Hughes	2	– run out	45
D. B. Vengsarkar c Waugh b McDermott	13	– (5) lbw b Hughes	4
*M. Azharuddin lbw b McDermott	1	– (6) c Taylor b McDermott	106
S. R. Tendulkar lbw b McDermott	6	– (4) lbw b Waugh	17
Kapil Dev c Border b Hughes	56	– c Marsh b Hughes	5
M. Prabhakar lbw b Whitney	33	– lbw b McDermott	64
†C. S. Pandit c Boon b McDermott	15	– c Waugh b McDermott	7
S. L. V. Raju not out	19	– not out	8
J. Srinath c Healy b Whitney	21	– c Warne b McDermott	3
L-b 5, n-b 10	15	B 3, l-b 9, n-b 5	17
	225		**333**

1/30 (1) 2/33 (3) 3/55 (4) 4/64 (5)   225
5/70 (2) 6/70 (6) 7/135 (8) 8/174 (7)
9/192 (9) 10/225 (11)

1/52 (1) 2/72 (2) 3/97 (4)   333
4/102 (5) 5/172 (3) 6/182 (7)
7/283 (6) 8/291 (9)
9/327 (8) 10/333 (11)

Bowling: *First Innings*—McDermott 31–9–76–5; Whitney 26.2–6–68–2; Hughes 18–5–55–3; Warne 7–1–18–0; Waugh 2–1–3–0. *Second Innings*—McDermott 29.1–8–92–5; Whitney 17–3–59–0; Hughes 23–5–66–3; Waugh 12–2–36–1; Warne 16–1–60–0; Border 3–0–8–0.

Umpires: D. B. Hair and P. J. McConnell. Referee: P. B. H. May (England).

AUSTRALIA v INDIA

Fifth Test Match

At Perth, February 1, 2, 3, 4, 5. Australia won by 300 runs. Toss: Australia. Tom Moody made a triumphant return as the final Test brought another resounding victory. The substitution of the uncapped opener Wayne Phillips (no relation to the former Test opener of the same name) for Marsh was less successful. But another newcomer, the fast-medium Paul Reiffel, was preferred to a spinner on the WACA pitch and he assisted in the demolition of India's second innings by Whitney, who returned match figures of 11 for 95.

Though India took only four wickets on the first day, they restricted Australia to 222 runs. Once again Boon, who completed his third hundred of the series early on the second day, shored up the innings. Prabhakar, who bowled with great heart, accounted for Boon and Moody in 40 minutes on the second morning. But as the ball lost its shine, the last four wickets added 87 and Healy collected his 1,000th Test run, to go with his 100th Test dismissal earlier in the series. Srikkanth's five catches in the innings, four in bat-pad positions, earned him a fourth share in the Test record for fielders.

India's bedrock was a captivating 114 from Tendulkar from 161 balls with 16 fours, the bulk of them from square cuts. He came in at 69 for two and was ninth out at 240, after 228 minutes, and a record ninth-wicket stand for India against Australia, of 81, with More. On the third morning, as he ran out of partners, he scored his second 50 from 55 balls. While Hughes and Whitney shared the bowling honours, McDermott's two wickets took him past the series record for an Australian against India, jointly held by Richie Benaud and Alan Davidson with 29. In his second spell of Australia's second innings, Kapil Dev claimed his 400th wicket when Taylor was lbw. With Australia's overall lead just 105, the match was still wide open, until Boon, Jones and Moody – who shared 173 for the fourth wicket – put it out of India's reach. Jones, who had disappointed hitherto, batted discreetly but positively for an unbeaten 150 in 265 balls while Moody, lethal off the front foot, took 101 from 149 balls.

India were left a minimum of 107 overs to chase 442. With McDermott enervated by a stiff neck, Srikkanth and Sidhu started briskly, and on the final morning took their stand to 82, India's highest opening partnership of the series. Yet less than two hours after Reiffel broke it with his maiden Test wicket, Australia were winners. Whitney, brought on 40 minutes before lunch, toppled seven batsmen in 8.5 overs, while conceding 26 runs. Five of his victims were caught in the arc between wicket-keeper and gully, as were both of Reiffel's, including the prize wicket of Tendulkar.

Man of the Match: M. R. Whitney.   *Attendance:* 30,908.

Man of the Series: C. J. McDermott.

Close of play: First day, Australia 222-4 (D. C. Boon 91*, T. M. Moody 42*); Second day, India 135-5 (S. R. Tendulkar 31*, S. L. V. Raju 1*); Third day, Australia 104-2 (D. C. Boon 35*, D. M. Jones 34*); Fourth day, India 55-0 (K. Srikkanth 26*, N. S. Sidhu 24*).

Australia

M. A. Taylor c Srikkanth b Kapil Dev	2	– (2) lbw b Kapil Dev	16
W. N. Phillips c More b Prabhakar	8	– (1) c Kapil Dev b Srinath	14
D. C. Boon c Sidhu b Prabhakar	107	– c Kapil Dev b Prabhakar	38
*A. R. Border c Srikkanth b Kapil Dev	59	– (8) not out	20
D. M. Jones c Srikkanth b Raju	7	– (4) not out	150
T. M. Moody c Vengsarkar b Prabhakar	50	– (5) c More b Kapil Dev	101
†I. A. Healy c More b Srinath	28	– (6) c More b Raju	7
M. G. Hughes c Srikkanth b Srinath	24	– (7) c Tendulkar b Srinath	11
P. R. Reiffel c More b Prabhakar	9		
C. J. McDermott c Srikkanth b Prabhakar	31		
M. R. Whitney not out	1		
B 1, l-b 7, n-b 12	20	L-b 4, n-b 6	10

1/10 (2) 2/21 (1) 3/138 (4) 4/145 (5)   346   1/27 (1) 2/31 (2)   (6 wkts dec.) 367
5/232 (6) 6/259 (3) 7/290 (7) 8/303 (8)   3/113 (3) 4/286 (5)
9/338 (9) 10/346 (10)   5/298 (6) 6/315 (7)

Bowling: *First Innings*—Kapil Dev 40-12-103-2; Prabhakar 32.5-9-101-5; Srinath 25-5-69-2; Tendulkar 5-2-9-0; Raju 23-6-56-1. *Second Innings*—Kapil Dev 28-8-48-2; Prabhakar 32-4-116-1; Srinath 29.3-4-121-2; Raju 24-5-78-1.

India

K. Srikkanth c Boon b McDermott	34	– c Jones b Whitney	38
N. S. Sidhu c Healy b Hughes	5	– c Jones b Reiffel	35
S. V. Manjrekar c Jones b Hughes	31	– c Healy b Whitney	8
S. R. Tendulkar c Moody b Whitney	114	– c Moody b Reiffel	5
D. B. Vengsarkar c Taylor b Hughes	1	– c Moody b Whitney	4
*M. Azharuddin c Healy b McDermott	11	– lbw b Whitney	24
S. L. V. Raju c Taylor b Whitney	1	– (10) c Healy b Whitney	8
Kapil Dev c Hughes b Whitney	4	– (7) lbw b Whitney	0
M. Prabhakar c Reiffel b Whitney	0	– (8) c Healy b McDermott	3
†K. S. More c Healy b Hughes	43	– (9) c Taylor b Whitney	1
J. Srinath not out	5	– not out	1
L-b 14, n-b 9	23	L-b 11, n-b 3	14

1/25 (2) 2/69 (1) 3/100 (3) 4/109 (5)   272   1/82 (2) 2/90 (1) 3/97 (4)   141
5/130 (6) 6/135 (7) 7/159 (8) 8/159 (9)   4/103 (5) 5/111 (3) 6/111 (5)
9/240 (4) 10/272 (10)   7/126 (8) 8/129 (9)
                                               9/134 (6) 10/141 (10)

Bowling: *First Innings*—McDermott 21-6-47-2; Hughes 26.5-5-82-4; Reiffel 17-5-46-0; Whitney 23-4-68-4; Moody 2-0-15-0. *Second Innings*—McDermott 20-8-44-1; Hughes 12-2-25-0; Reiffel 11-2-34-2; Whitney 12.1-1-3-27-7.

Umpires: A. R. Crafter and T. A. Prue. Referee: P. B. H. May (England).

THE CRICKETER CUP WINNERS, 1967-1992

1967	REPTON PILGRIMS	beat Radley Rangers by 96 runs.
1968	OLD MALVERNIANS	beat Harrow Wanderers by five wickets.
1969	OLD BRIGHTONIANS	beat Stowe Templars by 156 runs.
1970	OLD WYKEHAMISTS	beat Old Tonbridgians by 94 runs.
1971	OLD TONBRIDGIANS	beat Charterhouse Friars on faster scoring-rate.
1972	OLD TONBRIDGIANS	beat Old Malvernians by 114 runs.
1973	RUGBY METEORS	beat Old Tonbridgians by five wickets.
1974	OLD WYKEHAMISTS	beat Old Alleynians on faster scoring-rate.
1975	OLD MALVERNIANS	beat Harrow Wanderers by 97 runs.
1976	OLD TONBRIDGIANS	beat Old Blundellians by 170 runs.
1977	SHREWSBURY SARACENS	beat Oundle Rovers by nine wickets.
1978	CHARTERHOUSE FRIARS	beat Oundle Rovers by nine wickets.
1979	OLD TONBRIDGIANS	beat Uppingham Rovers by five runs.
1980	MARLBOROUGH BLUES	beat Old Wellingtonians by 31 runs.
1981	CHARTERHOUSE FRIARS	beat Old Wykehamists by nine wickets.
1982	OLD WYKEHAMISTS	beat Old Malvernians on faster scoring-rate.
1983	REPTON PILGRIMS	beat Haileybury Hermits by seven wickets.
1984	OLD TONBRIDGIANS	beat Old Malvernians by seven wickets.
1985	OUNDLE ROVERS	beat Repton Pilgrims by three wickets.
1986	OLD MALVERNIANS	beat Downside Wanderers by six wickets.
1987	SHREWSBURY SARACENS	beat Old Cliftonians by 58 runs.
1988	OUNDLE ROVERS	beat Shrewsbury Saracens by 19 runs.
1989	OUNDLE ROVERS	beat Shrewsbury Saracens by nine runs.
1990	OLD MALVERNIANS	beat Harrow Wanderers by four wickets.
1991	OLD TONBRIDGIANS	beat Charterhouse Friars by 27 runs.
1992	ETON RAMBLERS	beat Old Reptonians by 115 runs.

From 1967 to 1983 the final was played at Burton Court, Chelsea. Since then, it has been played at Vincent Square, Westminster.

THE WEST INDIANS IN PAKISTAN AND AUSTRALIA, 1991-92

By QAMAR AHMED

Before travelling to Australia to take part in the World Series Cup, West Indies played three one-day internationals in Pakistan. They emerged 2-0 winners of a closely contested series, and for a while it was assumed they had won the tied match in Lahore, where they lost fewer wickets. But the teams had agreed to play by World Cup regulations, which made no distinction between level scores. In the only departure from World Cup rules, the number of overs a side was limited to 40, because of the early sunsets; but even this proved too much for Pakistan, who bowled only 34 and 39 in the first two matches. No financial penalty was applied, however.

The pitches did not encourage the strokeplayers, but for West Indies Desmond Haynes, Brian Lara and Carl Hooper played some impressive innings. Barbadian opener Philo Wallace made an assured international début, but the performance of captain Richie Richardson, with only 21 runs in three innings, was a disappointment. Curtly Ambrose and Malcolm Marshall bowled consistently and another newcomer from Barbados, Anderson Cummins, showed promise.

Pakistan's batting lacked depth, especially when Javed Miandad, their highest scorer in the opening match, missed the rest with back trouble. But the series provided useful international experience for some of Pakistan's younger players before the World Cup in February. Inzamam-ul-Haq, who made his début at Lahore, and Zahid Fazal both recorded fine fifties at Faisalabad, where the crowd was thrilled by Inzamam's driving. As that match progressed, however, some spectators began to vent their disappointment at the prospect of losing to fruit and plastic bottles at the West Indian fielders; Keith Arthurton was forced to wear a helmet at deep mid-wicket in the last over. There was similar trouble at Karachi.

West Indies' subsequent visit to Australia was not a success. They failed to reach the finals of the World Series Cup, their primary object, after winning only two of their eight qualifying matches. Haynes was the most honourable exception to a series of poor performances by the batsmen. An Australian XI defeated them by an innings in the four-day game at Hobart. This was the only first-class match played by the West Indian team between the Oval Test in August 1991 and the inaugural Test with South Africa in April. In that time they played 26 one-day internationals.

WEST INDIAN TOUR RESULTS

First-class match – Lost to Australian XI.
One-day internationals – Played 11: Won 4, Lost 4, Tied 2, No result 1. *Wins* – Pakistan (2), India, Australia. *Losses* – Australia (2), India (2). *Ties* – Pakistan, India. *No result* – Australia.
Other non first-class matches – Played 8: Won 7, Lost 1. *Wins* – Western Australian Invitation XI, Victorian Country XI, Queensland XI (3), New South Wales Country XI, New South Wales. *Loss* – Western Australia.

Note: Matches in this section which were not first-class are signified by a dagger.

†PAKISTAN v WEST INDIES

First One-day International

At Karachi, November 20. West Indies won by 24 runs. Toss: West Indies. When West Indies chose to bat, Haynes and the 21-year-old débutant from Barbados, Wallace, opened with 55 in 13 overs. After Richardson went cheaply, Haynes added another 68 in 13 overs with Lara, whose first international fifty took 59 balls. Pakistan having failed to bowl the stipulated 40 overs by lunch, the game was curtailed to 34 a side, setting an asking rate of just over five an over. Opener Aamir Sohail was soon run out, as was Salim Malik. By the 27th over half the side had gone for 82. Only Javed Miandad and wicket-keeper Moin Khan offered any resistance and Pakistan were bowled out for 146 with one ball remaining. Disappointed by imminent defeat, some of the 50,000-strong crowd invaded the pitch, and Wallace went off with a bruised shoulder after being hit by a missile at long leg.

Man of the Match: B. C. Lara.

West Indies

D. L. Haynes lbw b Mushtaq Ahmed	45	K. L. T. Arthurton b Wasim Akram	4
P. A. Wallace b Mushtaq Ahmed	22	†D. Williams not out	5
*R. B. Richardson b Aqib Javed	2	I. R. Bishop not out	3
B. C. Lara c Javed Miandad b Wasim Akram	54	L-b 10, w 5, n-b 3	18
C. L. Hooper c Mushtaq Ahmed b Wasim Akram	17	1/55 2/58 3/126 (6 wkts, 34 overs) 170
		4/152 5/156 6/170

B. P. Patterson, C. E. L. Ambrose and A. C. Cummins did not bat.

Bowling: Imran Khan 8-1-30-0; Wasim Akram 6-0-27-3; Aqib Javed 7-0-38-1; Mushtaq Ahmed 8-0-43-2; Waqar Younis 5-0-22-0.

Pakistan

Aamir Sohail run out	1	Mushtaq Ahmed c Bishop b Hooper	6
Ramiz Raja c Williams b Patterson	11	Waqar Younis not out	11
Zahid Fazal c Lara b Patterson	17	Aqib Javed b Hooper	2
Salim Malik run out	16		
Javed Miandad c Richardson b Ambrose	31	L-b 5, w 8, n-b 5	18
*Imran Khan c Arthurton b Hooper	15	1/8 2/25 3/45 (33.5 overs) 146
Wasim Akram st Williams b Hooper	0	4/57 5/82 6/82
†Moin Khan c Richardson b Ambrose	18	7/119 8/129 9/134

Bowling: Bishop 6-2-23-0; Ambrose 7-0-28-2; Patterson 8-0-29-2; Cummins 5-0-27-0; Hooper 7.5-0-34-4.

Umpires: Khizar Hayat and Riazuddin.

†PAKISTAN v WEST INDIES

Second One-day International

At Lahore, November 22. Tied. Toss: Pakistan. Needing two runs from Ambrose's last ball, Mushtaq Ahmed was run out returning for the second, as Richardson's throw came straight into the wicket-keeper's gloves. Although West Indies had lost fewer wickets, the match was tied under playing conditions agreed before the series. Put in by Pakistan, West Indies responded with another brisk opening partnership, and the innings was dominated by Haynes, fifth out for 69. Pakistan were not far behind the asking-rate of 4.79 until Marshall's in-cutter bowled the 21-year-old newcomer Inzamam-ul-Haq in the 16th over. When Salim Malik was run out and Ramiz Raja caught one-handed by Williams, three wickets had fallen for one in ten balls. Imran Khan steadied the innings, but went for 51 with 16 required from nine balls. This was ten by the last over, whose first two balls yielded Waqar Younis three runs. On the third Moin Khan was caught and bowled by Ambrose, but Waqar, who had crossed, then hit a four to long-on. A single from the fifth left Mushtaq to face the last ball. He hit it into the covers, but could only level the scores.

Man of the Match: D. L. Haynes.

West Indies

D. L. Haynes b Aqib Javed	69	K. L. T. Arthurton not out 5
C. A. Wallace lbw b Imran Khan	32	M. D. Marshall not out 2
R. B. Richardson c Aamir Sohail		
b Aqib Javed	14	B 2, l-b 11, w 9, n-b 2 24
B. C. Lara b Wasim Akram	18	
C. L. Hooper c Inzamam-ul-Haq		1/53 2/85 3/134 (5 wkts, 39 overs) 186
b Wasim Akram	22	4/178 5/183

D. Williams, C. E. L. Ambrose, B. P. Patterson and I. R. Bishop did not bat.

Bowling: Imran Khan 8-0-19-1; Wasim Akram 7-0-36-2; Aqib Javed 8-0-49-2; Mushtaq Ahmed 8-0-22-0; Waqar Younis 8-0-47-0.

Pakistan

Aamir Sohail c and b Patterson	13	Waqar Younis not out 12
Ramiz Raja c Williams b Marshall	26	Mushtaq Ahmed run out 1
Inzamam-ul-Haq b Marshall	20	
Salim Malik run out	0	L-b 6, w 9, n-b 2 17
Imran Khan c Richardson b Patterson	51	
Ijaz Ahmed c Williams b Ambrose	27	1/27 2/69 3/69 (9 wkts, 39 overs) 186
Wasim Akram b Marshall	12	4/70 5/117 6/136
Moin Khan c and b Ambrose	7	7/171 8/180 9/186

Aqib Javed did not bat.

Bowling: Bishop 7-0-41-0; Ambrose 8-1-28-2; Patterson 8-0-44-2; Marshall 8-0-39-3; Hooper 8-1-28-0.

Umpires: Khizar Hayat and Riazuddin.

†PAKISTAN v WEST INDIES

Third One-day International

At Faisalabad, November 24. West Indies won by 17 runs. Toss: Pakistan. Pakistan lost the three-match series 2-0 when Ambrose and Marshall killed off their innings with four wickets in four balls. They had made a slow start, as Ramiz Raja and makeshift opener Inzamam-ul-Haq took half the overs available to put on 65. By the time Salim Malik was bowled by Hooper, only ten overs were left and 79 runs required. Pakistan were still just in the game with 30 wanted from 14 balls but then Zahid Fazal was fifth out, caught at long-off. Ijaz Ahmed was caught at mid-wicket next ball and when Marshall began the penultimate over he immediately dismissed Wasim Akram and Waqar Younis. West Indies' total of 204 owed much to a stylish 57 by Hooper, who came in with the innings in difficulties in the 13th over. Aqib Javed had accounted for Wallace and then had Richardson and Haynes caught off successive balls. But Hooper's 93 for the fourth wicket with Lara, followed by 41 in six overs with Arthurton, set a challenging target.

Man of the Match: C. L. Hooper.

West Indies

D. L. Haynes c Moin Khan		K. L. T. Arthurton not out 29
b Aqib Javed	8	M. D. Marshall not out 7
C. A. Wallace b Aqib Javed	36	
R. B. Richardson c Wasim Akram		
b Aqib Javed	5	L-b 7, w 10 17
B. C. Lara c Moin Khan		
b Inzamam-ul-Haq	45	1/43 2/52 (5 wkts, 40 overs) 204
C. L. Hooper c Zahid Fazal		3/52 4/145
b Aqib Javed	57	5/186

R. C. Haynes, †D. Williams, C. E. L. Ambrose and A. C. Cummins did not bat.

Bowling: Imran Khan 8–0–36–0; Wasim Akram 8–1–43–0; Mushtaq Ahmed 8–0–33–0;
Aqib Javed 8–1–31–4; Waqar Younis 5–0–30–0; Inzamam-ul-Haq 3–0–24–1.

Pakistan

Ramiz Raja c and b R. C. Haynes 29	Waqar Younis c and b Marshall	
Inzamam-ul-Haq c Lara b Cummins ... 60	Mushtaq Ahmed not out	
Zahid Fazal c Cummins b Ambrose ... 53		
Salim Malik b Hooper.............. 10	L-b 3, w 2	—
*Imran Khan c Lara b Cummins...... 14		
Ijaz Ahmed c Richardson b Ambrose .. 4	1/65 2/106 3/126 (8 wkts, 40 overs) 18	
Wasim Akram b Marshall........... 0	4/161 5/175 6/175	
†Moin Khan not out 7	7/175 8/175	

Aqib Javed did not bat.

Bowling: Ambrose 8–0–35–2; Cummins 8–1–27–2; Marshall 8–0–44–2; R. C. Haynes
8–0–34–1; Hooper 8–0–44–1.

Umpires: Athar Zaidi and Khizar Hayat.

†At Northam, December 1. West Indians won by 66 runs. Toss: West Indians. West
Indians 241 for seven (46 overs) (C. A. Best 43, B. C. Lara 54, K. L. T. Arthurton 5
not out; G. Ireland three for 18); Western Australian Invitation XI 175 for four (46 over
(J. L. Langer 41, J. B. Szeliga 37 not out).

†At Perth, December 4 (day/night). Western Australia won by seven wickets. Toss: West
Indians. West Indians 177 (46.1 overs) (D. L. Haynes 56, H. A. G. Anthony 38; B. A. Rei
three for 18, T. M. Moody three for 23); Western Australia 180 for three (40.5 overs)
(G. R. Marsh 55, M. R. J. Veletta 51, T. M. Moody 47 not out).

†At Leongatha, December 10. West Indians won by 45 runs. Toss: West Indians. West
Indians 143 for four (30 overs) (C. A. Best 32); Victorian Country XI 98 for five (30 overs).

West Indies' matches v Australia and India in the Benson and Hedges World Series Cu
(December 6–December 18) may be found in that section.

AUSTRALIAN XI v WEST INDIANS

At Hobart, December 20, 21, 22, 23. Australian XI won by an innings and 93 runs. Tos
West Indians. The visitors rested Richardson, Ambrose and Marshall for the only first-cla
game of the tour. Acting-captain Desmond Haynes chose to bat on a green pitch after rai
washed out the first day, and the Australian bowlers made the most of it. Only Lara reache
50, and he was dropped four times in his 222-minute innings. In contrast most of th
Australian batsmen scored heavily, from Phillips and Moody, who added 132 for the secon
wicket, down the order to Matthews and Reiffel, who put on 90 in just over an hour for th
eighth. Their progress was aided by several dropped catches and abetted by 30 no-balls. O
the final day the West Indians surrendered their last eight wickets for 83 runs. Lara playe
on in the first over of the morning, and Arthurton, already dropped, was caught behind o
Reiffel's first delivery. Hooper's 32-ball 33 was ended by the Victorian leg-spinner Warn
who shared eleven of the 29 wickets which fell with his Jamaican counterpart, Robe
Haynes.
Close of play: First day, No play; Second day, Australian XI 106-1 (W. N. Phillips 32
T. M. Moody 41*); Third day, West Indians 50-2 (B. C. Lara 10*, K. L. T. Arthurton 7*

West Indians

C. A. Best c Phillips b Matthews	37	– c Healy b Reiffel	12
P. A. Wallace c Healy b Reiffel	21	– c Healy b Reiffel	13
B. C. Lara c Phillips b Warne	83	– b Matthews	10
K. L. T. Arthurton b Reid	2	– c Healy b Reiffel	8
C. L. Hooper b Reid	4	– c Bevan b Warne	33
*D. L. Haynes c Healy b Waugh	20	– c Healy b Reid	6
†D. Williams not out	4	– (8) c Healy b Matthews	8
R. C. Haynes c Waugh b Reid	13	– (7) c Matthews b Warne	1
A. C. Cummins b Warne	23	– not out	15
H. A. G. Anthony c Moody b Reiffel	8	– c sub b Warne	15
B. P. Patterson c Reiffel b Warne	2	– st Healy b Warne	0
L-b 8, n-b 10	18	L-b 2, n-b 10	12

1/43 2/79 3/88 4/99 5/150   235   1/23 2/33 3/51 4/51 5/89   133
6/192 7/203 8/230 9/231   6/94 7/95 8/109 9/133

In the first innings D. Williams, when 2, retired hurt at 155 and resumed at 230.

Bowling: *First Innings*—Reid 19–4–73–3; Reiffel 17–2–63–2; Matthews 16–2–40–1; Waugh 12–3–37–1; Warne 5.1–1–14–3. *Second Innings*—Reid 13–3–38–1; Reiffel 10–2–32–3; Warne 15.2–6–42–4; Matthews 5–0–19–2; Moody 1–1–0–0.

Australian XI

D. C. Boon lbw b Patterson	10	
W. N. Phillips lbw b Cummins	51	
T. M. Moody c Williams b Anthony	70	
S. R. Waugh c Best b Patterson	11	
M. G. Bevan c Williams b Anthony	58	
S. G. Law c Hooper b R. C. Haynes	68	
*†I. A. Healy c Anthony b R. C. Haynes	44	
C. D. Matthews c Best b R. C. Haynes	63	

P. R. Reiffel c D. L. Haynes
  b R. C. Haynes . 44
S. K. Warne not out 1
  L-b 11, n-b 30 41

1/28 2/160 3/160   (9 wkts dec.) 461
4/193 5/254 6/348
7/358 8/448 9/461

B. A. Reid did not bat.

Bowling: Patterson 17–1–85–2; Cummins 26–1–80–1; Anthony 21–1–107–2; Hooper 27–1–72–0; R. C. Haynes 27.5–4–106–4.

Umpires: R. J. Evans and S. G. Randell.

†At Cairns, December 26. West Indians won by three wickets. Toss: Queensland XI. Queensland XI 258 for five (50 overs) (T. J. Barsby 56, E. J. Harris 39, P. J. T. Goggin 73, S. G. Law 78 not out); West Indians 260 for seven (49.4 overs) (C. L. Hooper 110, K. L. T. Arthurton 47; S. A. Prestwidge three for 38).

†At Bundaberg, December 29. West Indians won by 11 runs. Toss: West Indians. West Indians 225 for nine (50 overs) (D. L. Haynes 94, C. A. Best 30; S. B. Williams six for 54); Queensland XI 214 for eight (50 overs) (M. L. Hayden 49, D. M. Wellham 74 not out; B. P. Patterson four for 35).

†At Carrara, January 1 (day/night). West Indians won by seven wickets. Toss: Queensland XI. Queensland XI 79 (28.4 overs) (C. E. L. Ambrose three for 16); West Indians 80 for three (19.2 overs) (P. A. Wallace 40 not out). *The match was over before nightfall.*

†At Armidale, January 3. West Indians won by 46 runs. Toss: West Indians. West Indians 266 for five (50 overs) (P. A. Wallace 50, K. L. T. Arthurton 93 not out, C. L. Hooper 61); New South Wales Country XI 220 for eight (50 overs) (G. J. Arms 34, P. Dyson 70, R. Merlo 42 not out; R. B. Richardson three for 22).

†At Lismore, January 5. West Indians won by 21 runs. Toss: West Indians. West Indians 198 for seven (50 overs) (K. L. T. Arthurton 81 not out, C. E. L. Ambrose 38 not out; W. J. Holdsworth three for 46); New South Wales 177 for nine (50 overs) (P. A. Emery 33 not out; A. C. Cummins three for 35, M. D. Marshall three for 32).

West Indies' matches v Australia and India in the Benson and Hedges World Series Cup (January 9–January 16) may be found in that section.

THE SRI LANKANS IN PAKISTAN, 1991-92

By GUL HAMEED BHATTI

In a tense match at Faisalabad, the Sri Lankans came very close to winning their first-ever Test away from home. But a lack of killer instinct, little knowledge of local conditions and the dominance of the Pakistani pace attack meant that they just let the opportunity slip by. Pakistan scraped home to victory by three wickets and thus took the series 1-0, after two draws. Nevertheless, the Sri Lankans were a popular team and, playing most of their games in the smaller centres, attracted some good crowds. Their lack of experience under pressure at the highest level was evident in the one-day international rubber, where the Pakistanis dominated them, except at Multan, where Sri Lanka measured themselves against a run-rate above five an over to win with consummate ease. It was their only victory of the tour.

Sri Lanka badly missed the contributions that former captain Arjuna Ranatunga could have made in the middle order. He appeared drastically out of form, and failed to score in his first three Test innings, but it later transpired that he was not fully fit. Before the start of the limited-overs series, he was on his way home to recuperate. Similarly, the tourists' main strike bowler, Rumesh Ratnayake, failed to come up to expectations and left soon after the Tests because of complications resulting from injury. Two replacements were summoned, fast bowler Graeme Labrooy and off-spinner Ruwan Kalpage, but did nothing of note.

Aravinda de Silva, who had taken over as captain when Ranatunga fell from grace soon after the 1990-91 tour of New Zealand, tried to make the best of the situation. Unfortunately, his own dwindling form affected the team's confidence on several occasions. The batting heroes of the tour were two left-handers, Sanath Jayasuriya and the wicket-keeper, Hashan Tillekeratne. Jayasuriya again found the Pakistani pitches to his liking; in 1988-89, touring with Sri Lanka B, he hit three unbeaten hundreds, including two double-centuries.

The emergence and success of the two young pace bowlers, Kapila Wijegunawardene and Pramodya Wickremasinghe, who took 11 first-class wickets each, was encouraging. Unfortunately, Champaka Ramanayake failed to share the burden of the pace attack with these two and Ratnayake, claiming only one wicket in three matches. The Sri Lankans had dropped fast bowler Saliya Ahangama, wicket-keepers Romesh Kaluwitharana and Brendon Kuruppu and young off-spinner Muttiah Muralitharan from the party that toured England five months earlier. Their places were taken by the recalled Ranatunga, Wickremasinghe, opener Athula Samarasekera and wicket-keeper Ashley de Silva.

The chinks in the Pakistanis' armour were covered by the tremendous form of fast bowler Waqar Younis, ably supported by Wasim Akram and Aqib Javed. The batting was strengthened by Ramiz Raja, Imran Khan himself and the youngster Zahid Fazal, who played a match-winning 78 at Faisalabad. The poor form of Javed Miandad was thus less serious than it might have been. But the highlight of the limited-overs series was the emergence of the 21-year-old Inzamam-ul-Haq of Multan. His nonchalant batting brought him two consecutive one-day hundreds and made it all worthwhile for the host nation.

SRI LANKAN TOUR RESULTS

Test matches – Played 3: Lost 1, Drawn 2.
First-class matches – Played 5: Lost 1, Drawn 4.
Loss – Pakistan.
Draws – Pakistan (2), BCCP President's XI, Punjab Governor's XI.
One-day internationals – Played 5: Lost 4, Won 1.

TEST MATCH AVERAGES

PAKISTAN – BATTING

	T	I	NO	R	HS	100s	Avge
Ramiz Raja	3	4	1	220	98	0	73.33
Imran Khan.........	3	3	1	115	93*	0	57.50
Wasim Akram........	3	3	1	87	54	0	43.50
Zahid Fazal	3	4	0	148	78	0	37.00
Salim Malik	3	3	0	109	101	1	36.33
Shoaib Mohammad....	3	4	0	81	43	0	20.25
Javed Miandad	3	4	1	37	20*	0	12.33

Played in three Tests: Aqib Javed 10; Moin Khan 3, 22*; Waqar Younis 6, 1*. Played in two Tests: Saleem Jaffer 8*. Played in one Test: Akram Raza did not bat.

* *Signifies not out.*

BOWLING

	O	M	R	W	BB	5W/i	Avge
Waqar Younis ...	83.3	10	279	16	5-65	2	17.43
Saleem Jaffer	25	6	55	3	3-36	0	18.33
Akram Raza	35	13	71	3	2-37	0	23.66
Aqib Javed	50.1	14	145	6	3-70	0	24.16
Wasim Akram...	85	21	211	6	3-71	0	35.16

Also bowled: Imran Khan 9–1–16–0; Salim Malik 1–0–7–0.

SRI LANKA – BATTING

	T	I	NO	R	HS	100s	Avge
S. T. Jayasuriya	3	4	1	238	81	0	79.33
H. P. Tillekeratne........	3	4	1	116	49	0	38.66
P. A. de Silva	3	4	0	100	38	0	25.00
U. C. Hathurusinghe	3	4	0	93	49	0	23.25
A. P. Gurusinha	3	4	0	73	33	0	18.25
R. J. Ratnayake	3	3	1	22	13	0	11.00
A. Ranatunga	3	4	0	6	6	0	1.50
S. D. Anurasiri	3	3	1	3	3*	0	1.50
G. P. Wickremasinghe....	3	3	1	1	1*	0	0.50

Played in two Tests: R. S. Mahanama 58, 8; C. P. H. Ramanayake 0. Played in one Test: M. A. R. Samarasekera 19, 6; K. I. W. Wijegunawardene 2, 2.

* *Signifies not out.*

BOWLING

	O	M	R	W	BB	5W/i	Avge
K. I. W. Wijegunawardene....	48.4	15	98	7	4-51	0	14.00
A. P. Gurusinha	29	14	46	3	2-19	0	15.33
G. P. Wickremasinghe	92	20	273	8	5-73	1	34.12
S. D. Anurasiri.............	78	24	154	3	3-106	0	51.33
R. J. Ratnayake............	66.3	9	222	3	1-39	0	74.00

Also bowled: P. A. de Silva 4-0-13-0; U. C. Hathurusinghe 5-1-13-0; C. P. H. Ramanayake 43-11-91-0; A. Ranatunga 4-3-2-0.

SRI LANKAN TOUR AVERAGES – FIRST-CLASS MATCHES

BATTING

	M	I	NO	R	HS	100s	Avge
S. T. Jayasuriya	5	6	1	249	81	0	49.80
H. P. Tillekeratne	4	6	2	185	56*	0	46.25
P. A. de Silva...............	4	6	2	176	69*	0	44.00
R. S. Mahanama	4	5	0	187	58	0	37.40
A. P. Gurusinha	5	7	0	174	43	0	24.85
M. A. R. Samarasekera.......	2	3	0	70	45	0	23.33
U. C. Hathurusinghe.........	5	7	0	146	49	0	20.85
A. Ranatunga...............	5	7	0	87	50	0	12.42
R. J. Ratnayake.............	3	3	1	22	13	0	11.00
K. I. W. Wijegunawardene....	3	3	1	10	6*	0	5.00
S. D. Anurasiri.............	4	4	2	10	7*	0	5.00
G. P. Wickremasinghe	5	4	2	1	1*	0	0.50

Played in three matches: C. P. H. Ramanayake 0, 13. Played in one match: M. S. Atapattu 1; A. M. de Silva 13; A. W. R. Madurasinghe 0.

* Signifies not out.

BOWLING

	O	M	R	W	BB	5W/i	Avge
A. P. Gurusinha	29	14	46	3	2-19	0	15.33
U. C. Hathurusinghe.........	13.4	3	63	4	3-5	0	15.75
K. I. W. Wijegunawardene....	86.4	21	279	11	4-51	0	25.36
A. W. R Madurasinghe........	45	14	109	4	3-42	0	27.25
G. P. Wickremasinghe	126	22	415	11	5-73	1	37.72
S. D. Anurasiri.............	88	26	184	3	3-106	0	61.33
R. J. Ratnayake.............	66.3	9	222	3	1-39	0	74.00

Also bowled: M. S. Atapattu 1-0-4-0; P. A. de Silva 7-0-32-1; S. T. Jayasuriya 17-3-53-1; C. P. H. Ramanayake 57-11-151-1; A. Ranatunga 13-6-27-1.

FIELDING

7 – H. P. Tillekeratne; 6 – A. P. Gurusinha; 5 – A. M. de Silva; 2 – S. D. Anurasiri, R. S. Mahanama; 1 – P. A. de Silva, U. C. Hathurusinghe, S. T. Jayasuriya, R. J. Ratnayake, M. A. R. Samarasekera, G. P. Wickremasinghe, Substitute (M. S. Atapattu).

Note: Matches in this section which were not first-class are signified by a dagger.

BCCP PRESIDENT'S XI v SRI LANKANS

At Karachi, December 7, 8, 9. Drawn. Toss: Sri Lankans. The visitors gained some useful match practice in their only fixture before the First Test as their batsmen acclimatised to the windy but dry conditions in Karachi. Progress in the match was irritatingly slow, but the touring captain de Silva, his deputy Gurusinha, opener Mahanama and wicket-keeper Tillekeratne all found themselves among the runs. From the President's XI no Test hopefuls seized their chance to impress the selectors, and the best performances came from those out of the running for the national side.

Close of play: First day, BCCP President's XI 26-0 (Shahid Saeed 12*, Inzamam-ul-Haq 9*); Second day, Sri Lankans 45-1 (R. S. Mahanama 12*, A. P. Gurusinha 17*).

Sri Lankans

R. S. Mahanama c Bilal Ahmed b Nadeem Nazar .	37	– c Ijaz Ahmed b Athar Laeeq ... 40
J. C. Hathurusinghe b Ata-ur-Rehman........	29	– b Tanvir Mehdi 14
A. P. Gurusinha run out	33	– lbw b Athar Laeeq 43
*P. A. de Silva not out	69	– (6) not out 7
A. Ranatunga lbw b Tanvir Mehdi	1	– c Bilal Ahmed b Tanvir Mehdi . 30
S. T. Jayasuriya c Tanvir Mehdi b Ata-ur-Rehman .	11	
†H. P. Tillekeratne b Ata-ur-Rehman	13	– (4) not out.................. 56
C. P. H. Ramanayake c Inzamam-ul-Haq b Nadeem Nazar .	13	
S. D. Anurasiri not out	7	
L-b 7, w 1, n-b 1..................	9	L-b 5 5

1/36 2/101 3/104 4/107 5/122   (7 wkts dec.) 222   1/22 2/92 3/121 4/173   (4 wkts) 195
6/164 7/206

K. I. W. Wijegunawardene and G. P. Wickremasinghe did not bat.

Bowling: *First Innings*—Ata-ur-Rehman 18-4-53-3; Tanvir Mehdi 17-4-57-1; Athar Laeeq 9-1-35-0; Umar Rasheed 8-3-16-0; Nadeem Nazar 16-2-54-2. *Second Innings*—Ata-ur-Rehman 6-1-19-0; Tanvir Mehdi 13-4-57-2; Ijaz Ahmed 7-4-6-0; Athar Laeeq 9-4-52-2; Umar Rasheed 5-2-15-0; Nadeem Nazar 8-1-41-0.

BCCP President's XI

Shahid Saeed not out...............	67	†Bilal Ahmed b Ramanayake........	6
Inzamam-ul-Haq c Tillekeratne b Wickremasinghe .	17	Ata-ur-Rehman c Tillekeratne b Hathurusinghe .	6
*Ijaz Ahmed c Anurasiri b Wickremasinghe .	18	Athar Laeeq b Hathurusinghe	0
Shahid Anwar c Tillekeratne b Ranatunga .	5	L-b 12, w 1, n-b 16..........	29
Sagheer Abbas c Hathurusinghe b de Silva .	42	1/40 2/65 3/80 (8 wkts dec.) 221	
Umar Rasheed lbw b Hathurusinghe...	31	4/180 5/192 6/212	
		7/221 8/221	

Tanvir Mehdi and Nadeem Nazar did not bat.

Shahid Saeed, when 48, retired hurt at 126 and resumed at 192.

Bowling: Ramanayake 14-0-60-1; Wickremasinghe 14-2-46-2; Wijegunawardene 11-1-41-0; Ranatunga 6-3-8-1; Anurasiri 10-2-30-0; Hathurusinghe 2.4-1-5-3; de Silva 3-0-19-1.

Umpires: Mahboob Shah and Riazuddin.

PAKISTAN v SRI LANKA

First Test Match

At Sialkot, December 12, 13, 14, 16, 17. Drawn. Toss: Sri Lanka. Pakistan appeared well on the way to an innings victory before lunch on the final day, after three Sri Lankan wickets fell on 58 and half the side were back in the pavilion with 95 needed to make the hosts bat again. De Silva was caught by Ijaz Ahmed at short square leg off the off-spinner Akram Raza, attempting a big hit; and within eight balls Gurusinha was trapped lbw by Aqib Javed and Ranatunga edged one behind the stumps. He thus registered a pair in his first Test since losing the captaincy earlier in the year. But after the interval left-handers Jayasuriya and Tillekeratne took the fight to the bowlers. When bad light stopped play in the 47th over, they had added 79 for the sixth wicket. The captains agreed to call off the match with Sri Lanka still 16 runs behind.

On each of the five days the fading light of early winter put a dampener on Pakistan's ambitions, although none of the Sri Lankan batsmen except Jayasuriya and Tillekeratne came to terms with the swing and movement generated by the home team's pace quartet on a fast Sialkot wicket. Opting to bat first, Sri Lanka started well, but an 18-ball blitz from Aqib Javed helped to reduce them to 128 for five. Jayasuriya and Tillekeratne then added 101 before Jayasuriya fell for a 222-minute 77, his highest Test score. Waqar Younis's five-wicket haul was his sixth in his 12th Test.

In the 78.2 overs possible on the third day Pakistan could add only 171 runs to their overnight score, as left-arm spinner Anurasiri, with figures of 39.2–15–61–2, kept a tight length and gave absolutely nothing away. He dismissed Ramiz Raja two runs short of 100, after he had batted nearly four and a half hours, hitting 11 fours and dominating a 128-run opening partnership with Shoaib Mohammad. On the fourth day Salim Malik reached his ninth Test century, in 298 minutes and 212 balls, with a five and ten fours, and Imran Khan might have had his seventh. He had batted nearly four hours for 93 when he declared 20 minutes after tea, having set up a lead of 153.

Man of the Match: Salim Malik.

Close of play: First day, Sri Lanka 191-5 (S. T. Jayasuriya 60*, H. P. Tillekeratne 14*), Second day, Pakistan 72-0 (Ramiz Raja 43*, Shoaib Mohammad 19*); Third day, Pakistan 243-4 (Salim Malik 36*, Imran Khan 5*); Fourth day, Sri Lanka 13-1 (U. C. Hathurusinghe 2*, A. P. Gurusinha 2*).

Sri Lanka

M. A. R. Samarasekera c Moin Khan b Waqar Younis .	19	– b Waqar Younis 6
U. C. Hathurusinghe c Akram Raza b Aqib Javed .	17	– c Ramiz Raja b Wasim Akram . 7
A. P. Gurusinha b Aqib Javed	33	– lbw b Aqib Javed 23
*P. A. de Silva b Waqar Younis	31	– c sub (Ijaz Ahmed) b Akram Raza . 19
A. Ranatunga lbw b Aqib Javed	0	– c Moin Khan b Waqar Younis . . 0
S. T. Jayasuriya b Akram Raza	77	– not out 35
†H. P. Tillekeratne c Akram Raza b Waqar Younis .	49	– not out 42
R. J. Ratnayake b Waqar Younis	13	
C. P. H. Ramanayake b Akram Raza	0	
S. D. Anurasiri not out	3	
G. P. Wickremasinghe b Waqar Younis	0	
B 5, l-b 11, n-b 12	28	N-b 5 5

1/21 (1) 2/70 (2) 3/89 (3) 4/89 (5)   270   1/6 (1) 2/33 (2)   (5 wkts) 137
5/128 (4) 6/229 (6) 7/244 (8) 8/245 (9)   3/58 (4) 4/58 (3)
9/270 (10) 10/270 (11)   5/58 (5)

Bowling: *First Innings*—Wasim Akram 32–7–47–0; Waqar Younis 30.5–5–84–5; Akram Raza 24–10–37–2; Aqib Javed 23–4–70–3; Imran Khan 9–1–16–0. *Second Innings*—Waqar Younis 14.4–1–43–2; Wasim Akram 13–4–31–1; Aqib Javed 7–3–22–1; Akram Raza 11–3–34–1; Salim Malik 1–0–7–0.

Pakistan

Ramiz Raja c Tillekeratne b Anurasiri . 98	Wasim Akram not out..............	20
Shoaib Mohammad		
c and b Wickremasinghe . 43	L-b 6, n-b 25..............	31
Zahid Fazal c and b Ratnayake....... 36		—
Salim Malik c Gurusinha b Anurasiri . .101	1/128 (2) 2/169 (1)	(5 wkts dec.) 423
Javed Miandad c Jayasuriya b Anurasiri 1	3/232 (3) 4/233 (5)	
*Imran Khan not out.............. 93	5/365 (4)	

†Moin Khan, Akram Raza, Waqar Younis and Aqib Javed did not bat.

Bowling: Ratnayake 31–4–100–1; Ramanayake 33–9–75–0; Wickremasinghe 27–3–120–1; Hathurusinghe 1–0–3–0; Anurasiri 61–21–106–3; de Silva 4–0–13–0.

Umpires: Ikram Rabbani and Khizar Hayat. Referee: D. B. Carr (England).

PAKISTAN v SRI LANKA

Second Test Match

At Gujranwala, December 20, 21, 22, 24, 25. Drawn. Toss: Sri Lanka. Test cricket's 65th venue, an industrial town 40 miles north of Lahore, saw only 36 overs in two and a half hours' play on an interrupted first day. Over the next four not a single ball was sent down, because of bad light, persistent drizzle and the dreadful state of the pitch and square. Sri Lanka had brought in Mahanama for the unfit opener Samarasekera, while Pakistan, guessing correctly that the pitch would help seamers, brought in Saleem Jaffer instead of the off-spinner Akram Raza. But, as de Silva chose to field, it was the Sri Lankan front-line bowlers, especially Wickremasinghe, in his second Test, who had the chance to impress. Ramiz Raja reached his second fifty of the series, with six fours, while the 18-year-old Zahid Fazal enhanced his reputation through an obdurate 21 spread over an hour and a half. But with a second draw inevitable, the rubber was left to be decided in Faisalabad.

Close of play: First day, Pakistan 109-2 (Ramiz Raja 51*, Javed Miandad 20*); Second day, No play; Third day, No play; Fourth day, No play.

Pakistan

*Ramiz Raja not out............. 51	Javed Miandad not out..............	20
Shoaib Mohammad c Tillekeratne		
b Ratnayake . 1	L-b 10, n-b 6..............	16
Zahid Fazal c Tillekeratne		
b Wickremasinghe . 21	1/3 (2) 2/59 (3)	(2 wkts) 109

Salim Malik, *Imran Khan, †Moin Khan, Wasim Akram, Waqar Younis, Aqib Javed and Saleem Jaffer did not bat.

Bowling: Ratnayake 13–3–39–1; Ramanayake 10–2–16–0; Wickremasinghe 7–2–27–1; Hathurusinghe 2–1–6–0; Anurasiri 1–0–2–0; Gurusinha 2–0–9–0; Ranatunga 1–1–0–0.

Sri Lanka

R. S. Mahanama, U. C. Hathurusinghe, A. P. Gurusinha, *P. A. de Silva, A. Ranatunga, S. T. Jayasuriya, †H. P. Tillekeratne, R. J. Ratnayake, C. P. H. Ramanayake, S. D. Anurasiri and G. P. Wickremasinghe.

Umpires: Athar Zaidi and Khizar Hayat. Referee: D. B. Carr (England).

PUNJAB GOVERNOR'S XI v SRI LANKANS

At Lahore, December 27, 28, 29. Drawn. Toss: Punjab Governor's XI. Transferred from Peshawar, and with a combined team as late replacements for a Lahore CCA XI, the match was dominated by left-hander Aamir Sohail, who also captained the Governor's XI. On a final day consigned to batting practice by an appallingly slow over-rate, he scored a brilliant

102 in 106 balls, while Inzamam-ul-Haq contributed a more sedate 40 to their 136-run opening partnership. When they had gone Ijaz Ahmed, with nine fours, and Zahid Fazal put on 76 for the third wicket. None of the six bowlers employed by the Sri Lankan acting-captain, Gurusinha, made much headway. They had more success on the first day, when Wijegunawardene's disconcerting movement and pace reduced the Governor's XI to 147 for six. The tourists also batted erratically, their problems compounded by the home side's persistent line and length. But Ranatunga achieved a pleasant 50 which heralded a return to form.

Close of play: First day, Sri Lankans 5-0 (R. S. Mahanama 1*, U. C. Hathurusinghe 4*); Second day, Sri Lankans 219-9 dec.

Punjab Governor's XI

*Aamir Sohail c Gurusinha b Madurasinghe	... 71	– c Mahanama b Hathurusinghe ..102
Inzamam-ul-Haq c de Silva b Wijegunawardene.		– c de Silva b Madurasinghe 40
Ijaz Ahmed c de Silva b Wijegunawardene.....	4	– not out...................... 38
Zahid Fazal lbw b Wickremasinghe...........	11	– not out...................... 36
Tahir Shah c de Silva b Madurasinghe........	61	
Naved Anjum c de Silva b Wijegunawardene...	1	
†Rashid Latif c Gurusinha b Wijegunawardene .	0	
Wasim Haider not out......................	50	
Akram Raza c Mahanama b Jayasuriya	19	
Mushtaq Ahmed c Samarasekera		
b Madurasinghe .	4	
B 2, l-b 6, n-b 12...................	20	L-b 1, n-b 5............ 6

1/16 2/20 3/43 4/146 5/147 (9 wkts dec.) 251   1/136 2/146 (2 wkts) 222
6/147 7/207 8/244 9/251

Saleem Jaffer did not bat.

Bowling: *First Innings*—Wickremasinghe 12-0-70-1; Wijegunawardene 17-3-86-4; Hathurusinghe 2-0-16-0; Ranatunga 3-0-17-0; Madurasinghe 19-6-42-3; Jayasuriya 6-0-12-1. *Second Innings*—Wickremasinghe 8-0-26-0; Wijegunawardene 10-2-54-0; Madurasinghe 26-8-67-1; Jayasuriya 11-3-41-0; Hathurusinghe 4-1-29-1; Atapattu 1-0-4-0.

Sri Lankans

R. S. Mahanama lbw b Wasim Haider .	44	S. T. Jayasuriya lbw b Saleem Jaffer ... 0
U. C. Hathurusinghe c Rashid Latif		A. W. R. Madurasinghe
b Naved Anjum .	10	lbw b Wasim Haider . 0
M. A. R. Samarasekera		K. I. W. Wijegunawardene not out 6
b Mushtaq Ahmed .	45	G. P. Wickremasinghe not out 0
A. Ranatunga c Zahid Fazal		
b Saleem Jaffer .	50	L-b 14, n-b 11 25
*A. P. Gurusinha b Naved Anjum	25	
M. S. Atapattu c Rashid Latif		1/20 2/102 3/104 (9 wkts dec.) 219
b Saleem Jaffer .	1	4/166 5/182 6/196
†A. M. de Silva c Zahid Fazal		7/204 8/207 9/216
b Saleem Jaffer .	13	

Bowling: Saleem Jaffer 21-3-71-4; Naved Anjum 18-4-56-2; Wasim Haider 17-0-46-2; Mushtaq Ahmed 8-3-20-1; Akram Raza 5-2-12-0.

Umpires: Mian Aslam and Mohammad Iqbal.

PAKISTAN v SRI LANKA

Third Test Match

At Faisalabad, January 2, 3, 4, 6, 7. Pakistan won by three wickets. Toss: Pakistan. Sri Lanka gave Pakistan a big scare as they almost achieved their first victory on foreign soil and their first series-win over Pakistan in the decisive Test at Faisalabad. They had competed on equal terms right through the five days. Eventually they lost with just three

Pakistan wickets intact. The home team started the final day at 95 for four, requiring another 90 runs. Zahid Fazal provided much-needed solidity, adding 23 runs in 80 minutes to his overnight 55. When he was fifth out, at 149, the target looked attainable. Opening in place of Shoaib Mohammad, who was unwell, he batted in all more than four hours, reaching his first fifty in his sixth Test. Wasim Akram hit a worthy 54 and the winning runs were brought up by wicket-keeper Moin Khan.

After Imran Khan had invited Sri Lanka to bat, the visitors made a good start; the 81-run opening stand between Mahanama and Hathurusinghe broke the previous record for Sri Lanka against Pakistan, 77 by S. Wettimuny and H. M. Goonatillake, also at Faisalabad, in 1981-82. But the innings of the day was played by left-hander Jayasuriya, who reached an unbeaten 50 from 68 balls, with nine fours, by close of play, to lift his team to 205 for nine after Ranatunga had fallen for his third successive duck of the series. He went on to 81, his highest Test score.

On the second day, marred by a couple of stoppages for bad light, Pakistan started slowly, and consumed 54 overs on their way to an overnight score of 117 for two. Ramiz Raja made his third consecutive fifty in a 102-run first-wicket partnership with Shoaib. But the third day belonged to Sri Lanka, whose seamers, Wijegunawardene and Wickremasinghe, gained them a 19-run first-innings lead. The 20-year-old Wickremasinghe took five wickets in a Test innings for the first time. By the close, Sri Lanka had extended that lead to 87, but for the loss of three batsmen. Next day they crashed for 165. Once again Jayasuriya was left fighting for his team's cause, against the pace trio of Wasim Akram, Waqar Younis and Aqib Javed; Waqar finished with match figures of nine for 152 and his seventh five-wicket haul in his 14th Test. Judging by the low scores in the previous three innings, Pakistan's target of 185 was a tall order, and so it proved. But Zahid and Wasim put them on the road to victory.

The Faisalabad Test was also notable for a record 14 lbw decisions, given by two umpires making a comeback. Shakoor Rana had not stood in a Test since his confrontation with Mike Gatting, at the same venue in 1987-88, whereas Khalid Aziz last officiated at Test level in 1979-80.

Man of the Match: Wasim Akram.

Close of play: First day, Sri Lanka 205-9 (S. T. Jayasuriya 50*, G. P. Wickremasinghe 0*); Second day, Pakistan 117-2 (Zahid Fazal 6*, Javed Miandad 0*); Third day, Sri Lanka 68-3 (P. A. de Silva 18*, K. I. W. Wijegunawardene 1*); Fourth day, Pakistan 95-4 (Zahid Fazal 55*, Wasim Akram 19*).

Sri Lanka

R. S. Mahanama c Moin Khan b Saleem Jaffer .	58	– lbw b Waqar Younis 8
U. C. Hathurusinghe b Waqar Younis	49	– c Zahid Fazal b Waqar Younis . 20
A. P. Gurusinha c Zahid Fazal b Wasim Akram	3	– lbw b Aqib Javed 14
*P. A. de Silva c Moin Khan b Saleem Jaffer . .	12	– lbw b Waqar Younis 38
A. Ranatunga lbw b Saleem Jaffer.	0	– (8) c Javed Miandad
		b Wasim Akram . 6
S. T. Jayasuriya run out	81	– c Salim Malik b Waqar Younis . 45
†H. P. Tillekeratne c Shoaib Mohammad		
b Waqar Younis .	11	– c Moin Khan b Aqib Javed 14
R. J. Ratnayake lbw b Waqar Younis	4	– (9) not out 5
S. D. Anurasiri c Shoaib Mohammad		
b Waqar Younis .	0	– (10) b Wasim Akram 0
K. I. W. Wijegunawardene lbw b Wasim Akram	2	– (5) b Waqar Younis 2
G. P. Wickremasinghe not out	1	– b Wasim Akram 0
B 3, l-b 6, w 2, n-b 8	19	L-b 3, n-b 10 13

1/81 (2) 2/89 (3) 3/130 (4) 4/130 (5)   240   1/28 (1) 2/43 (2) 3/67 (3)   165
5/150 (1) 6/179 (7) 7/185 (8) 8/193 (9)   4/72 (5) 5/105 (4) 6/136 (7)
9/205 (10) 10/240 (6)   7/146 (8) 8/160 (6)
    9/165 (10) 10/165 (11)

Bowling: *First Innings*—Wasim Akram 22-8-62-2; Saleem Jaffer 17-4-36-3; Waqar Younis 21-1-87-4; Aqib Javed 12.1-3-46-0. *Second Innings*—Wasim Akram 18-2-71-3; Waqar Younis 17-3-65-5; Saleem Jaffer 8-2-19-0; Aqib Javed 8-4-7-2.

Pakistan

Ramiz Raja lbw b Wickremasinghe	63	– lbw b Wickremasinghe	8
Shoaib Mohammad lbw b Wickremasinghe	30	– (7) b Ratnayake	7
Zahid Fazal lbw b Wijegunawardene	13	– (2) c Anurasiri b Gurusinha	78
Javed Miandad c Gurusinha b Wickremasinghe	14	– (3) c Gurusinha	
		b Wijegunawardene .	2
Salim Malik c Tillekeratne b Gurusinha	4	– (4) c Gurusinha	
		b Wijegunawardene .	4
*Imran Khan b Wijegunawardene	22	– (5) lbw b Wijegunawardene	0
Wasim Akram lbw b Gurusinha	13	– (6) c de Silva b Wijegunawardene	54
†Moin Khan lbw b Wickremasinghe	3	– not out	22
Waqar Younis lbw b Wickremasinghe	6	– not out	1
Saleem Jaffer not out	8		
Aqib Javed c sub (M. S. Atapattu)			
b Wijegunawardene .	10		
L-b 8, w 1, n-b 26	35	B 2, l-b 3, n-b 7	12

1/102 (1) 2/110 (2) 3/141 (4) 4/146 (5)   221   1/31 (1) 2/52 (3)   (7 wkts) 188
5/162 (3) 6/186 (7) 7/196 (8) 8/197 (6)   3/60 (4) 4/60 (5)
9/205 (9) 10/221 (11)   5/149 (2) 6/156 (6)
                                                             7/179 (7)

Bowling: *First Innings*—Ratnayake 13-2-40-0; Wijegunawardene 31.2-13-47-3; Wickremasinghe 32-9-73-5; Anurasiri 10-2-28-0; Gurusinha 15-9-19-2; Ranatunga 3-2-2-0; Hathurusinghe 2-0-4-0. *Second Innings*—Ratnayake 9.3-0-43-1; Wickremasinghe 26-6-53-1; Wijegunawardene 17.2-2-51-4; Gurusinha 12-5-18-1; Anurasiri 6-1-18-0.

Umpires: Khalid Aziz and Shakoor Rana. Referee: D. B. Carr (England).

†PAKISTAN v SRI LANKA

First One-day International

At Sargodha, January 10. Pakistan won by eight wickets. Toss: Pakistan. Pakistan immediately took a 1-0 lead in the five-match rubber. Put in to bat, Sri Lanka found it hard to come to terms with accurate and effective bowling, in overcast conditions and on a pitch of uncertain bounce, and were restricted to a rate of under four runs in their allotted 40 overs. Ramiz Raja continued his fine form of the Test series, hitting a belligerent 74 with ten fours in 107 balls. His 112-run second-wicket partnership with Javed Miandad, who reached 50 in 96 deliveries, enabled Pakistan to complete their victory off the penultimate ball of the 37th over, with only two wickets down.

Man of the Match: Ramiz Raja.

Sri Lanka

R. S. Mahanama lbw b Waqar Younis	5	†H. P. Tillekeratne not out	37
U. C. Hathurusinghe c Moin Khan		M. S. Atapattu b Aqib Javed	4
b Imran Khan .	6	R. S. Kalpage not out	5
A. P. Gurusinha c Imran Khan			
b Akram Raza .	37	B 1, l-b 5, w 7, n-b 3	16
*P. A. de Silva c Wasim Akram			
b Waqar Younis .	19	1/11 2/27 3/69 (6 wkts, 40 overs) 155	
S. T. Jayasuriya run out	26	4/79 5/118 6/138	

K. I. W. Wijegunawardene, G. P. Wickremasinghe and C. P. H. Ramanayake did not bat.

Bowling: Wasim Akram 8-0-33-0; Waqar Younis 8-2-13-2; Aqib Javed 8-1-26-1; Imran Khan 8-0-35-1; Akram Raza 8-0-42-1.

Pakistan

Ramiz Raja c Mahanama			Salim Malik not out..............	9
b Wijegunawardene .	74		L-b 1, w 2, n-b 2...........	5
Zahid Fazal b Ramanayake	9			
Javed Miandad not out	60		1/19 2/131	(2 wkts, 36.5 overs) 157

*Imran Khan, Inzamam-ul-Haq, †Moin Khan, Wasim Akram, Waqar Younis, Akram Raza and Aqib Javed did not bat.

Bowling: Ramanayake 6–1–19–1; Wijegunawardene 8–0–41–1; Wickremasinghe 5–0–14–0; Gurusinha 4–0–21–0; Kalpage 7–1–32–0; Jayasuriya 6.5–0–29–0.

Umpires: Amanullah Khan and Khizar Hayat.

†PAKISTAN v SRI LANKA

Second One-day International

At Karachi, January 13. Pakistan won by 29 runs. Toss: Sri Lanka. Once again the Sri Lankans were overwhelmed, but they had the satisfaction of an exhilarating start to their chase of more than five runs an over. Led by Mahanama, they took 25 runs off the first three overs, and the 100 came up in the 20th. But their charge suffered a setback when Mahanama had to retire with cramp. The rest of the batting crumbled against the pace of Wasim Akram and Waqar Younis and the leg-spin of Mushtaq Ahmed. Earlier, Inzamam-ul-Haq opened with an innings of 48 which virtually booked his place in the World Cup squad. Imran Khan's unbeaten 44 off 27 balls, and the 39 runs that came off the last three overs, sealed Sri Lanka's fate.

Man of the Match: Imran Khan.

Pakistan

Ramiz Raja c Labrooy b Jayasuriya ...	35	Ijaz Ahmed not out	1
Inzamam-ul-Haq run out	48		
Javed Miandad b Wijegunawardene ..	29		
Salim Malik b Labrooy	36	L-b 4, w 1, n-b 5............	10
*Imran Khan not out................	44		
Wasim Akram c Kalpage		1/89 2/89 3/150	(5 wkts, 40 overs) 210
b Wijegunawardene .	7	4/160 5/194	

†Moin Khan, Waqar Younis, Aqib Javed and Mushtaq Ahmed did not bat.

Bowling: Ramanayake 6–2–17–0; Labrooy 8–0–56–1; Wickremasinghe 5–1–26–0; Wijegunawardene 8–0–43–2; Kalpage 8–0–37–0; Jayasuriya 5–0–27–1.

Sri Lanka

R. S. Mahanama retired hurt	60	G. F. Labrooy b Imran Khan.........	13
U. C. Hathurusingha b Wasim Akram .	14	C. P. H. Ramanayake b Wasim Akram	4
A. P. Gurusinha c Wasim Akram		K. I. W. Wijegunawardene run out	7
b Waqar Younis .	13	G. P. Wickremasinghe b Wasim Akram	0
*P. A. de Silva c Ramiz Raja		L-b 10, w 3, n-b 1..........	14
b Mushtaq Ahmed .	24		
S. T. Jayasuriya lbw b Waqar Younis .	0	1/46 2/66 3/109	(36.1 overs) 181
†H. P. Tillekeratne not out	29	4/111 5/134 6/155	
R. S. Kalpage b Mushtaq Ahmed	3	7/167 8/178 9/181	

R. S. Mahanama retired hurt at 128.

Bowling: Wasim Akram 6.1–0–31–3; Waqar Younis 8–1–38–2; Aqib Javed 6–0–19–0; Imran Khan 8–0–44–1; Mushtaq Ahmed 8–0–39–2.

Umpires: Mahboob Shah and Riazuddin.

†PAKISTAN v SRI LANKA

Third One-day International

At Hyderabad, January 15. Pakistan won by 59 runs. Toss: Sri Lanka. Pakistan's third win in a row, which settled the limited-overs rubber, was emphatic. Inzamam-ul-Haq set the tempo with a blistering 60 off 77 balls, featuring a five and four sixes, before Javed Miandad took over the reins with a masterly back-to-form display. After sharing 109 runs in 21 overs with Inzamam, he added 86 in just 68 deliveries with Salim Malik. Miandad struck two sixes and 12 fours in his unbeaten 115. Sri Lanka's first wicket produced 70 runs, but Aqib Javed and Imran Khan, who claimed three for 15 in eight overs, broke the back of their middle order. Although Tillekeratne and Atapattu added 40 for the seventh wicket, the visitors never really looked like matching an asking rate above six an over.

Man of the Match: Javed Miandad.

Pakistan

Ramiz Raja c Labrooy b Ramanayake	12	Wasim Akram not out	7
Inzamam-ul-Haq c Atapattu b Labrooy	60		
Javed Miandad not out	115	L-b 2, w 2, n-b 3	7
Salim Malik c de Silva			
b Wijegunawardene	40	1/25 2/134 3/220 (3 wkts, 40 overs)	241

*Imran Khan, †Moin Khan, Waqar Younis, Mushtaq Ahmed, Ijaz Ahmed and Aqib Javed did not bat.

Bowling: Ramanayake 8-2-26-1; Wijegunawardene 8-0-49-1; Labrooy 6-0-51-1; Madurasinghe 8-2-34-0; Gurusinha 2-0-13-0; Jayasuriya 8-0-66-0.

Sri Lanka

U. C. Hathurusinghe c Ijaz Ahmed		M. S. Atapattu not out	19
b Imran Khan	19	C. P. H. Ramanayake b Wasim Akram	1
M. A. R. Samarasekera c Moin Khan		K. I. W. Wijegunawardene	
b Aqib Javed	43	c Imran Khan b Aqib Javed	1
*P. A. de Silva c Moin Khan		A. W. R. Madurasinghe not out	3
b Aqib Javed	2		
†H. P. Tillekeratne b Wasim Akram	44	L-b 14, w 8, n-b 6	28
S. T. Jayasuriya lbw b Imran Khan	0		
A. P. Gurusinha c Salim Malik		1/70 2/72 3/80 (9 wkts, 40 overs)	182
b Mushtaq Ahmed	15	4/80 5/119 6/127	
G. F. Labrooy lbw b Imran Khan	7	7/167 8/174 9/177	

Bowling: Wasim Akram 8-0-34-2; Waqar Younis 8-0-42-0; Aqib Javed 8-0-30-3; Imran Khan 8-3-15-3; Mushtaq Ahmed 8-0-47-1.

Umpires: Shakil Khan and Taufiq Khan.

†PAKISTAN v SRI LANKA

Fourth One-day International

At Multan, January 17. Sri Lanka won by four wickets. Toss: Sri Lanka. The Sri Lankans' first win of the tour ended Pakistan's aspirations of a clean sweep of the series. They restricted their hosts to 205 after Ramiz Raja and Inzamam-ul-Haq opened with 149 runs. On his home ground, Inzamam scored a maiden one-day hundred, in his sixth international, off just 121 balls, to confirm his growing stature. Ijaz Ahmed continued the run-a-ball onslaught, but three wickets fell and the pace slackened. Sri Lanka's progress was well planned, and their second-wicket stand virtually won the match. Samarasekera hit 76 from 88 balls, with a six, a five and five fours, and Gurusinha 74 off 85 balls, (one six and seven fours) to add 157 in 27.4 overs. The rest was easy, despite generally tight Pakistani bowling.

Man of the Match: Inzamam-ul-Haq.

Pakistan

Ramiz Raja st Tillekeratne b Jayasuriya 52	†Moin Khan not out 2
Inzamam-ul-Haq c sub (R. S. Kalpage)	Mushtaq Ahmed b Ramanayake 1
b Jayasuriya .101	L-b 5, w 5, n-b 2. 12
Ijaz Ahmed c de Silva b Ramanayake . . 31	
Wasim Akram c Hathurusinghe	
b Wijegunawardene . 6	1/149 2/180 3/196 (5 wkts, 40 overs) 205
	4/201 5/205

*Imran Khan, Salim Malik, Javed Miandad, Waqar Younis and Aqib Javed did not bat.

Bowling: Ramanayake 8-1-30-2; Wijegunawardene 6-1-37-1; Gurusinha 2-0-14-0; Madurasinghe 8-1-36-0; Anurasiri 8-0-42-0; Jayasuriya 8-0-41-2.

Sri Lanka

M. A. R. Samarasekera	†H. P. Tillekeratne run out 10
c Inzamam-ul-Haq b Mushtaq Ahmed . 76	S. T. Jayasuriya lbw b Aqib Javed 5
U. C. Hathurusinghe c Moin Khan	M. S. Atapattu not out 5
b Waqar Younis . 2	C. P. H. Ramanayake not out 0
A. P. Gurusinha st Moin Khan	B 2, l-b 6, w 5, n-b 3 16
b Mushtaq Ahmed . 74	
*P. A. de Silva c Inzamam-ul-Haq	1/4 2/161 3/161 (6 wkts, 39.4 overs) 206
b Aqib Javed . 18	4/183 5/192 6/203

A. W. R. Madurasinghe, S. D. Anurasiri and K. I. W. Wijegunawardene did not bat.

Bowling: Wasim Akram 8-0-31-0; Waqar Younis 8-1-36-1; Aqib Javed 7.4-0-40-2; Imran Khan 6-0-41-0; Mushtaq Ahmed 8-0-36-2; Inzamam-ul-Haq 2-0-14-0.

Umpires: Mian Aslam and Shakoor Rana.

†PAKISTAN v SRI LANKA

Fifth One-day International

At Rawalpindi, January 19. Pakistan won by 117 runs. Toss: Sri Lanka. The Sri Lankans were pulverised at Rawalpindi's newly built stadium as the Pakistanis ran up a massive total of 271 for four at almost 6.8 runs an over and went on to take the series 4-1. After Ramiz Raja's cheap dismissal, the second-wicket stand realised 204 runs. Inzamam-ul-Haq hit his second consecutive hundred, his 117 coming off 104 deliveries, with 13 boundaries, while Salim Malik took 102 off 106 balls, with five fours. Javed Miandad's first run was his 6,000th in his 185th one-day international. Sri Lanka had little chance, and succumbed to the nagging Pakistan attack for 154 runs in the 39th over. The day was marred by crowd interruptions after the ground authorities failed to manage the entry gates properly. Play was held up for nearly 30 minutes as the police attempted to control spectators with baton charges and tear gas.

Man of the Match: Inzamam-ul-Haq.

Pakistan

Ramiz Raja b Wijegunawardene 5	Ijaz Ahmed not out 4
Inzamam-ul-Haq c Wickremasinghe	Wasim Akram not out. 16
b Ramanayake .117	B 1, l-b 2, w 5. 8
Salim Malik c Jayasuriya	
b Ramanayake .102	1/5 2/209 (4 wkts, 40 overs) 271
Javed Miandad run out 19	3/251 4/251

*Imran Khan, †Moin Khan, Waqar Younis, Aqib Javed and Mushtaq Ahmed did not bat.

Bowling: Ramanayake 8-1-48-2; Wijegunawardene 8-0-68-1; Wickremasinghe 6-0-32-0; Madurasinghe 8-0-54-0; Gurusinha 3-0-23-0; Jayasuriya 7-0-43-0.

Sri Lanka

R. S. Mahanama lbw b Aqib Javed.... 18	K. I. W. Wijegunawardene
M. A. R. Samarasekera b Waqar Younis 13	c Imran Khan b Wasim Akram . 0
A. P. Gurusinha c Ramiz Raja	A. W. R. Madurasinghe not out....... 6
b Aqib Javed . 16	G. P. Wickremasinghe st Moin Khan
*P. A. de Silva run out 17	b Inzamam-ul-Haq . 5
†H. P. Tillekeratne c Ramiz Raja	L-b 4, w 6, n-b 1............ 11
b Mushtaq Ahmed . 36	———
S. T. Jayasuriya run out 3	1/31 2/37 3/63 (38.4 overs) 154
M. S. Atapattu run out 3	4/75 5/84 6/91
C. P. H. Ramanayake b Waqar Younis. 26	7/117 8/130 9/149

Bowling: Wasim Akram 8–2–20–1; Waqar Younis 8–0–42–2; Aqib Javed 6–0–25–2; Mushtaq Ahmed 8–0–29–1; Imran Khan 8–0–30–0; Inzamam-ul-Haq 0.4–0–4–1.

Umpires: Javed Akhtar and Siddiq Khan.

ENGLAND UNDER-19 IN PAKISTAN, 1991-92

England Under-19 toured Pakistan in January and February 1992, playing ten games. They won one, lost four, and drew five. The three-match "Test" series was shared 1-1, with innings wins for Pakistan Under-19 at Karachi and England at Lahore; the second match at Gujranwala was all but washed out, with only 113 minutes' play possible on the third day. Pakistan Under-19 won the one-day series 3-0.

The squad of 15 originally named for the tour was: W. P. C. Weston (Worcs.) (*captain*), M. R. Bainbridge (Surrey), D. A. Blenkiron (Durham), M. Broadhurst (Yorks.), G. Chapple (Lancs.), A. C. Cottam (Somerset), J. M. de la Pena (Glos.), M. J. Foster (Yorks.), M. B. Loye (Northants), D. D. J. Robinson (Essex), R. J. Rollins (Essex), J. N. Snape (Northants), M. J. Walker (Kent), T. C. Walton (Northants) and M. G. N. Windows (Glos.). *Manager:* N. Gifford (Sussex). *Coach:* G. J. Saville (Essex). R. J. Ballinger (Middx) and A. Payne (Lancs./Somerset) joined the party as replacements for M. Broadhurst and J. M. de la Pena.

First Under-19 "Test": At Karachi, January 16, 17, 18. Pakistan Under-19 won by an innings and four runs. Toss: England Under-19. Pakistan Under-19 342 for nine dec. (Aslam Raza 62, Mohammad Shafiq 36, Aley Haider 103, Abdullah Khan 74, Mohammad Afzal 44; J. N. Snape four for 61); England Under-19 136 (J. N. Snape 33; Kazim Rizvi four for 38, Murtaza Hussain three for eight) and 202 (D. D. J. Robinson 31, M. J. Walker 63; Murtaza Hussain three for 48, Mohammad Afzal three for 39).

Second Under-19 "Test": At Gujranwala, January 26, 27, 28, 29. Drawn. Toss: Pakistan Under-19. Pakistan Under-19 53 for two v England Under-19.

Third Under-19 "Test": At Lahore, February 1, 2, 3, 4. England Under-19 won by an innings and 22 runs. Toss: Pakistan Under-19. England Under-19 310 (W. P. C. Weston 68, M. B. Loye 31, J. N. Snape 78, T. C. Walton 69, Extras 32; Ali Hussain Rizvi five for 121, Murtaza Hussain three for 55); Pakistan Under-19 122 (R. J. Ballinger five for 32) and 166 (Aslam Raza 95).

THE PAKISTANIS IN AUSTRALIA, 1991-92

As the nine teams taking part in the World Cup assembled in Australia and New Zealand during February, they played in a total of 23 practice matches. Most of these were limited-overs games against Australian state sides or other local teams. But the Pakistanis played two three-day matches, against Victoria and Tasmania, which were accorded first-class status, as well as 50-over matches against South Africa – the first meeting of the two countries – and Sri Lanka. The International Cricket Council later ruled that the two international matches, both of which Pakistan lost, should not have official status, as they were not included in any formal programme.

VICTORIA v PAKISTANIS

At Bendigo, February 4, 5, 6. Drawn. Toss: Pakistanis. As Victoria lacked Jones, Hughes and Reiffel, all playing against India in the Perth Test, the Pakistanis must have expected some gentle batting practice. Instead their top order's fallibility was exposed. Five wickets went down in 15 overs after O'Donnell's declaration on the first evening, with Dodemaide claiming three for 13 and newcomer Maxwell two wickets in consecutive balls. The visitors fared little better in the second innings, chasing 204 from 54 overs. The last pair, Moin Khan and Aqib Javed, had to survive 20 minutes after their colleagues had stumbled to 140 for nine. The match was also an unhappy one for the Victorian captain, O'Donnell, whose failure to cope with Wasim Akram's pace probably ended his chances of joining Australia's World Cup squad.

Close of play: First day, Pakistanis 45-5 (Imran Khan 4*, Ijaz Ahmed 0*); Second day, Victoria 89-3 (D. J. Ramshaw 20*, D. S. Berry 14*).

Victoria

D. J. Ramshaw c Salim Malik b Shahid Saeed .	39	– c Inzamam-ul-Haq b Wasim Akram .	35
P. C. Nobes c Zahid Fazal b Wasim Akram . . .	53	– b Wasim Akram	0
*S. P. O'Donnell b Mushtaq Ahmed	9	– c Moin Khan b Wasim Akram . .	13
D. S. Lehmann c Zahid Fazal b Mushtaq Ahmed	12	– lbw b Mushtaq Ahmed	30
W. G. Ayres c Ramiz Raja b Mushtaq Ahmed .	21		
G. R. Parker c Moin Khan b Aqib Javed	28	– c Inzamam-ul-Haq b Aqib Javed	2
A. I. C. Dodemaide not out	24	– (8) lbw b Wasim Akram	4
N. D. Maxwell not out	16	– (7) c Ramiz Raja b Shahid Saeed	12
†D. S. Berry (did not bat)		– (5) c Ijaz Ahmed b Shahid Saeed	49
D. W. Fleming (did not bat)		– (9) not out	14
P. W. Jackson (did not bat)		– (10) c Shahid Saeed b Wasim Akram .	2
B 6, l-b 4, n-b 5	15	B 6, l-b 5, n-b 8	19

1/88 2/105 3/125 4/125 (6 wkts dec.) 217
5/167 6/177

1/1 2/28 3/73 (9 wkts dec.) 180
4/112 5/122 6/156
7/157 8/173 9/180

Bowling: *First Innings*—Wasim Akram 14-6-14-1; Aqib Javed 16-2-49-1; Imran Khan 6-3-20-0; Shahid Saeed 9-0-22-1; Ijaz Ahmed 7-2-27-0; Mushtaq Ahmed 25-8-75-3. *Second Innings*—Wasim Akram 19.5-4-47-5; Aqib Javed 13.2-5-22-1; Mushtaq Ahmed 17-3-56-1; Shahid Saeed 12.4-1-39-2; Ijaz Ahmed 5-2-5-0.

Pakistanis

Ramiz Raja b Dodemaide	6	– c Berry b Maxwell	18
Inzamam-ul-Haq c Ramshaw b Dodemaide	2	– c Nobes b Dodemaide	9
Zahid Fazal c Berry b Maxwell	10	– c Fleming b Jackson	39
Salim Malik b Dodemaide	22	– (7) c Ramshaw b Dodemaide	26
†Moin Khan b Maxwell	0	– (9) not out	6
*Imran Khan b Jackson	29	– b Jackson	5
Ijaz Ahmed c Berry b Maxwell	67	– (5) c Berry b O'Donnell	0
Shahid Saeed not out	40	– (4) b Maxwell	5
Wasim Akram st Berry b Jackson	10	– (8) st Berry b Jackson	30
Mushtaq Ahmed c O'Donnell b Maxwell	0	– c Berry b Dodemaide	0
Aqib Javed not out	2	– not out	1
B 1, l-b 1, n-b 4	6	B 5, l-b 2, w 1, n-b 2	10

1/5 2/8 3/38 4/38 5/45   (9 wkts dec.) 194   1/28 2/32 3/45   (9 wkts) 149
6/114 7/156 8/167 9/168   4/46 5/69 6/88
7/136 8/139 9/140

Bowling: *First Innings*—Dodemaide 15-4-25-3; Fleming 11-3-28-0; Maxwell 18-4-50-4; O'Donnell 13-2-38-0; Jackson 15-4-51-2. *Second Innings*—Dodemaide 16-7-30-3; Fleming 6-1-12-0; Maxwell 9-2-35-2; O'Donnell 12-4-26-1; Jackson 11-1-39-3.

Umpires: D. W. Holt and Khizar Hayat.

TASMANIA v PAKISTANIS

At Devonport, February 9, 10, 11. Drawn. Toss: Pakistanis. The tourists were still struggling to find form against Tasmania, who had beaten them comfortably in a 50-over match in Launceston the previous day. But Ramiz Raja appeared to be adapting to Australian conditions when he reached his second fifty of the match, just before the end of the second day. Rain prevented him from adding to his score when the last day was washed out. Further encouragement for the Pakistanis came from Imran Khan, who bowled 15 overs in Tasmania's innings, his longest stint since suffering a groin injury in the series against Sri Lanka. For Tasmania, Atkinson made a promising début with an unbeaten 55, two catches and a stumping, while Young claimed five wickets in an innings for the first time.

Close of play: First day, Tasmania 25-1 (G. A. Hughes 15*, B. A. Cruse 6*); Second day, Pakistanis 93-1 (Ramiz Raja 50*, Aamir Sohail 27*).

Pakistanis

Ramiz Raja c Matthews b Young	50	– not out	50
Inzamam-ul-Haq c Gilbert b Matthews	16	– c Buckingham b Gilbert	13
Aamir Sohail c Atkinson b Young	20	– not out	27
Shahid Saeed c Atkinson b Young	5		
Zahid Fazal st Atkinson b Young	47		
Ijaz Ahmed c Matthews b Young	0		
Wasim Akram b Tucker	30		
*Imran Khan c Tucker b Matthews	8		
†Moin Khan not out	3		
Akram Raza not out	5		
L-b 4, w 1, n-b 9	14	B 2, n-b 1	3

1/36 2/76 3/98 4/105 5/105   (8 wkts dec.) 198   1/17   (1 wkt) 93
6/152 7/190 8/190

Saleem Jaffer did not bat.

Bowling: *First Innings*—Gilbert 12-2-39-0; McPhee 22-8-43-0; Matthews 16-4-49-2; Young 15-5-36-5; Tucker 7-1-27-1. *Second Innings*—Gilbert 7-0-32-1; McPhee 11-1-36-0; Matthews 4-0-8-0; Young 7-3-11-0; Hughes 1-0-4-0.

Tasmania

D. F. Hills c Akram Raza b Wasim Akram .	0	D. J. Buckingham run out	41	
G. A. Hughes c Inzamam-ul-Haq b Saleem Jaffer .	29	R. J. Tucker not out	3	
B. A. Cruse run out	31			
J. Cox c and b Akram Raza	11	L-b 3, w 3, n-b 7	13	
†M. N. Atkinson not out	55			

1/1 2/53 3/82   (5 wkts dec.) 183
4/84 5/176

S. Young, C. D. Matthews, *D. R. Gilbert and P. T. McPhee did not bat.

Bowling: Wasim Akram 10–5–12–1; Saleem Jaffer 13–2–36–1; Akram Raza 14–7–15–1; Ijaz Ahmed 15–3–33–0; Imran Khan 15–4–32–0; Shahid Saeed 8–3–27–0; Aamir Sohail 10–5–25–0.

Umpires: D. R. Close and S. G. Randell.

THE COOPERS & LYBRAND RATINGS

Introduced in 1987, the Coopers & Lybrand Ratings (formerly the Deloitte Ratings) rank Test cricketers on a scale from 0 to 1,000 according to their performances in Test matches since 1981. The ratings are calculated by computer and take into account playing conditions, the quality of the opposition and the result of the matches. The value of a player's performance is assessed in relation to the Coopers & Lybrand Ratings of the opposing players and it also reflects his ability to score match-winning runs or take match-winning wickets. Updated after every Test match, with a player's most recent performances carrying more weight than his earlier ones, the Coopers & Lybrand Ratings endeavour to provide a current assessment of a Test cricketer's form and his place among his peers. A player cannot get a full rating until he has played 20 innings or taken 50 wickets in Tests.

The leading 20 batsmen and bowlers in the Ratings after the 1992 series between England and Pakistan were:

	Batsmen	Rating		Bowler	Rating
1.	G. A. Gooch (*Eng.*)	866	1.	Waqar Younis (*Pak.*)	872
2.	R. B. Richardson (*WI*)	790	2.	C. E. L. Ambrose (*WI*)	843
3.	Salim Malik (*Pak.*)	768	3.	C. J. McDermott (*Aus.*)	777
4.	R. A. Smith (*Eng.*)	767	4.	B. A. Reid (*Aus.*)	772
5.	D. C. Boon (*Aus.*)	738	5.	Wasim Akram (*Pak.*)	742
6.	A. R. Border (*Aus.*)	732	6.	M. G. Hughes (*Aus.*)	732
6.	M. A. Taylor (*Aus.*)	732	7.	Imran Khan (*Pak.*)	707
8.	D. L. Haynes (*WI*)	718	8.	C. A. Walsh (*WI*)	645
9.	M. D. Crowe (*NZ*)	706	9.	Kapil Dev (*Ind.*)	640
10.	Shoaib Mohammad (*Pak.*)	673	10.	P. A. J. DeFreitas (*Eng.*)	620
11.	Imran Khan (*Pak.*)	670	11.	P. C. R. Tufnell (*Eng.*)	561*
12.	Javed Miandad (*Pak.*)	641	12.	M. R. Whitney (*Aus.*)	513*
13.	D. M. Jones (*Aus.*)	629	13.	B. P. Patterson (*WI*)	495
14.	A. J. Stewart (*Eng.*)	622	14.	D. E. Malcolm (*Eng.*)	450
15.	J. G. Wright (*NZ*)	611	15.	R. J. Ratnayake (*SL*)	434
16.	A. L. Logie (*WI*)	605	16.	D. K. Morrison (*NZ*)	413
16.	A. H. Jones (*NZ*)	605	16.	Saleem Jaffer (*Pak.*)	413*
18.	R. J. Shastri (*Ind.*)	592	18.	R. J. Shastri (*Ind.*)	406
19.	M. Azharuddin (*Ind.*)	589	19.	M. Prabhakar (*Ind.*)	399
20.	S. R. Tendulkar (*Ind.*)	577	20.	C. C. Lewis (*Eng.*)	388*

* *Signifies the bowler has taken fewer than 50 wickets.*

THE SOUTH AFRICANS IN THE WEST INDIES, 1991-92

By GEOFFREY DEAN

South Africa were beaten in every match on their first-ever tour of the West Indies but the results were in contrast to the overwhelming political success of the three-week tour. The whole affair would have been cancelled had not South African whites voted in favour of President de Klerk's programme of reform just three weeks earlier. But in the event there were hardly any demonstrations and a South African team with just one non-white player, Omar Henry, was received warmly throughout the Caribbean. In Trinidad, the centre of anti-apartheid demonstrations when England toured six years earlier, the players were given a standing ovation when they came out to jog round the boundary before the game.

There was one significant protest which led to a boycott of the Test match by Barbadian spectators: only a few hundred people watched each day of a momentous Test match. But in an extraordinary twist to history, this was nothing to do with South Africa or the apartheid policy. It was ostensibly caused by the omission of the Barbadian Anderson Cummins from the West Indian team. However, this was the culmination of various grievances against the selectors about the treatment of Barbadian heroes, including the exclusion of Carlisle Best from the previous Bridgetown Test, the passing over of Desmond Haynes for the captaincy and the exclusion of Malcolm Marshall from the World Cup party.

The protesters missed a remarkable game of cricket which looked certain to end in a triumph for South Africa until the final morning. They had looked far better geared up for Test cricket than the West Indians, several of whom still seemed to be in one-day mode. The boycott cost the West Indies Board an estimated £100,000 in gate receipts but the touring team's expenses were met by the South African arm of the oil company BP, thus ensuring that the West Indies were able to make a profit on a tour for the first time in 15 years. Back in South Africa, the tour was on national TV instead of the satellite channel which showed the World Cup to a predominantly white audience.

The one-day series had been both well-attended and completely uncompetitive. The South Africans went straight into the first game without a practice match 72 hours after their arrival. The nets in both Kingston and Port-of-Spain were unsatisfactory and the team were unable to get used to the perfect batting pitches and, after the white ball of the World Cup, a red ball which hardly swung.

Along with the senior side, the South Africans sent out a 15-strong under-19 squad, of whom 11 were non-white. Although they were not an officially representative side, they managed to beat their Barbadian counterparts after drawing in Trinidad and losing in Jamaica.

SOUTH AFRICAN TOUR RESULTS

Test match – Played 1: Lost 1.
One-day internationals – Played 3: Lost 3.

Note: Matches in this section which were not first-class were signified by a dagger.

†WEST INDIES v SOUTH AFRICA

First One-day International

At Kingston, Jamaica, April 7. West Indies won by 107 runs. Toss: South Africa. Destructive hitting by Simmons, whose 122 came off only 113 balls, propelled West Indies to their highest one-day total at Sabina Park. Simmons took advantage of a bare pitch and short straight boundaries to hit through the line, all his five sixes coming in an arc between long-on and deep extra cover. One, off Henry, led to a five-minute delay when the ball landed outside the ground and was stolen but then recovered by police. South Africa were briefly in contention after progressing to 79 for one by the 20th over, but the loss of Hudson and Kirsten in successive Patterson overs proved decisive. The West Indian bowling, mean and just short of a length, was in contrast to South Africa's, which was innocuous and ill-directed. The West Indian captain Richardson was booed throughout by the crowd protesting against the omission of the Jamaican Jeffrey Dujon from the World Cup squad.

Man of the Match: P. V. Simmons.

West Indies

D. L. Haynes c Henry b Donald	9	W. K. M. Benjamin c Wessels b Kuiper	8
B. C. Lara c Wessels b Henry	50	C. E. L. Ambrose not out	0
P. V. Simmons c Wessels b Kuiper	122	B 1, l-b 5, w 12, n-b 4	22
*R. B. Richardson lbw b Kuiper	30		
K. L. T. Arthurton c Wessels b Donald	27	1/32 2/104 3/209 (6 wkts, 50 overs) 287	
C. L. Hooper not out	19	4/238 5/277 6/286	

†D. Williams, A. C. Cummins and B. P. Patterson did not bat.

Bowling: Donald 10-1-47-2; Snell 10-1-56-0; van Zyl 8-2-53-0; Henry 10-0-53-1; Cronje 3-0-18-0; Kirsten 4-0-21-0; Kuiper 5-0-33-3.

South Africa

A. C. Hudson c and b Patterson	50	C. J. P. G. van Zyl c Ambrose b Benjamin	0
*K. C. Wessels run out	8	O. Henry b Benjamin	1
P. N. Kirsten c Lara b Patterson	15	A. A. Donald not out	5
A. P. Kuiper st Williams b Hooper	15	L-b 8, w 10, n-b 3	21
W. J. Cronje b Cummins	42		
J. N. Rhodes c Cummins	17	1/10 2/79 3/82 (42.2 overs) 180	
R. P. Snell run out	1	4/121 5/153 6/155	
†D. J. Richardson c Arthurton b Benjamin	5	7/161 8/168 9/174	

Bowling: Ambrose 7-0-20-0; Patterson 7-2-17-2; Benjamin 9.2-0-45-3; Cummins 9-0-34-2; Hooper 8-0-44-1; Simmons 2-0-12-0.

Umpires: S. A. Bucknor and G. T. Johnson.

†WEST INDIES v SOUTH AFRICA

Second One-day International

At Port-of-Spain, Trinidad, April 11. West Indies won by ten wickets. Toss: West Indies. Seldom can any one-day international have been won so comprehensively. South Africa's top six all contributed to their own downfall. Wessels and Kirsten chased wide deliveries before Hudson was beaten by Simmons's direct hit from backward point. Cronje took a suicidal single to Richardson at mid-wicket, and later Rhodes, who played the only innings of note, unwisely took on Arthurton at cover. The West Indian openers, Lara and Haynes, destroyed some indifferent bowling with wonderful strokeplay, needing only 25.5 overs to reach their modest target on a splendid pitch. Lara played some sublime shots, hitting 13 fours as well as two sixes off Henry.

Man of the Match: B. C. Lara.

South Africa

A. C. Hudson run out	6	O. Henry not out	8
*K. C. Wessels c Williams b Ambrose	1	M. W. Pringle b Ambrose	1
P. N. Kirsten c Benjamin b Cummins	9	A. A. Donald b Ambrose	0
A. P. Kuiper c Lara b Harper	19		
W. J. Cronje run out	22	L-b 10, w 15, n-b 2	27
J. N. Rhodes run out	45		
†D. J. Richardson c Arthurton		1/17 2/24 3/36	(43.4 overs) 152
b Cummins	6	4/68 5/98 6/118	
R. P. Snell c Arthurton b Cummins	8	7/138 8/146 9/152	

Bowling: Ambrose 7.4–0–24–3; Patterson 9–2–30–0; Cummins 9–0–40–3; Benjamin 8–0–21–0; Harper 10–0–27–1.

West Indies

D. L. Haynes not out	59
B. C. Lara not out	86
B 1, l-b 1, w 2, n-b 5	9

(no wkt, 25.5 overs) 154

P. V. Simmons, *R. B. Richardson, K. L. T. Arthurton, R. A. Harper, †D. Williams, C. E. L. Ambrose, W. K. M. Benjamin, A. C. Cummins and B. P. Patterson did not bat.

Bowling: Donald 8–1–49–0; Pringle 7–0–32–0; Henry 4.5–0–41–0; Snell 6–0–30–0.

Umpires: L. H. Barker and C. E. Cumberbatch.

†WEST INDIES v SOUTH AFRICA

Third One-day International

At Port-of-Spain, Trinidad, April 12. West Indies won by seven wickets. Toss: West Indies. Simmons's third hundred in four one-day international innings saw West Indies to their second victory of the weekend, but only after a very tentative start by their batsmen. Haynes was bowled by the first ball of the innings, from Pringle, whose superb opening spell of five overs cost only six runs before an injury prevented him from taking any further part in the match. There were no fewer than nine unsuccessful lbw appeals in the first eight overs. Simmons, missed when 23, needed 103 balls to reach fifty, but only 32 more for his hundred, delighting his home crowd. On a slow, low pitch, the South Africans had been unable to accelerate against accurate bowling after reaching 58 for one from 20 overs.

Man of the Match: P. V. Simmons.

South Africa

A. C. Hudson c Williams b Harper	30	†D. J. Richardson not out	17
M. W. Rushmere c and b Harper	29	C. J. P. G. van Zyl not out	3
*K. C. Wessels b Benjamin	45	L-b 8, w 3, n-b 1	12
P. N. Kirsten c Harper b Benjamin	28		
A. P. Kuiper c Richardson b Patterson	2	1/54 2/67 3/135	(6 wkts, 50 overs) 189
W. J. Cronje run out	23	4/139 5/142 6/185	

R. P. Snell, T. Bosch and M. W. Pringle did not bat.

Bowling: Ambrose 10–1–39–0; Patterson 10–2–35–1; Benjamin 10–1–37–2; Cummins 10–0–39–0; Harper 10–0–31–2.

West Indies

D. L. Haynes b Pringle	0	K. L. T. Arthurton not out	1
B. C. Lara c Pringle b Kuiper	35	L-b 7, w 4, n-b 2	13
P. V. Simmons c Cronje b Snell	104		—
*R. B. Richardson not out	37	1/0 2/78 3/182 (3 wkts, 43 overs) 190	

R. A. Harper, W. K. M. Benjamin, C. E. L. Ambrose, †D. Williams, A. C. Cummins and B. P. Patterson did not bat.

Bowling: Pringle 5–3–6–1; Bosch 6–0–47–0; Snell 10–2–45–1; van Zyl 10–0–40–0; Kuiper 7–0–28–1; Kirsten 5–0–17–0.

Umpires: L. H. Barker and C. E. Cumberbatch.

WEST INDIES v SOUTH AFRICA

Test Match

At Bridgetown, Barbados, April 18, 19, 20, 22, 23. West Indies won by 52 runs. Toss: South Africa. An epic inaugural Test between the two countries ended in West Indies' 11th consecutive victory at the Kensington Oval. But South Africa were on top for the first four days, until a dramatic collapse preserved their hosts' 57-year-old unbeaten record in Barbados. Needing only 201 to win, the South Africans were well placed at 122 for two at the start of the fifth day. Quality fast bowling from Ambrose and Walsh removed their last eight wickets while another 26 runs were scored, and they were bowled out for 148, 20 minutes before lunch. Attendances throughout the game were minimal because Barbadians stayed away in protest against West Indian selection policy. The total attendance was only 6,500 and there were fewer than 500 spectators on the ground to witness one of West Indies' finest fightbacks, but scores of them charged ecstatically after their team on its lap of honour. All 11 players linked hands "to show the people of the Caribbean how united we are", said a visibly relieved Richardson. It was his first Test as captain of a West Indian side in transition after the era of Richards, Greenidge, Marshall and Dujon, and missing Logie and Hooper through injury.

Wessels, who played 24 Tests for Australia between 1982-83 and 1985-86, became the 13th player to represent two countries at Test level. He won a good toss, and followed the example set in the previous ten Bridgetown Tests by electing to field first. Just before tea West Indies had reached 219 for three and a big score looked likely. Richardson, Arthurton and Williams all played loose shots, however, and the last seven wickets fell for 43. Arthurton drove gloriously for his first Test fifty, with ten fours, but he was caught slashing to point.

The South Africans took advantage of a true pitch at its best on the second day to gain a first-innings lead of 83. Nearly half their runs came from Hudson, the first man to score a hundred for South Africa on his Test début. Displaying unflagging concentration and a solid technique, he hit 20 fours and defied a lacklustre attack for eight hours and 40 minutes. The four West Indian fast bowlers, including newcomer Kenny Benjamin, seemed hamstrung by their first experience of the ICC restriction of one bouncer per over per batsman. Crucially, Hudson was dropped when 22 by Walsh at long leg, from the first ball Ambrose had banged in really short to him, and again on 66 by West Indies' new wicket-keeper, Williams, off Patterson.

The West Indians then succumbed to some incisive bowling. At the end of the third day, they were 184 for seven, and the tourists appeared to be on the brink of a famous victory. Even to get there, West Indies had had two pieces of extreme good fortune. Haynes played the second ball of the innings, from Donald, on to his off stump without dislodging a bail. Later Lara, who had just reached his maiden Test fifty, trod on his off stump going back to Bosch. The incident was clear in television replays, but neither umpire had seen it. This was the only moment of friction between the teams on the whole tour. Adams, the left-handed débutant, batted with composure and common sense for 221 minutes and his last-wicket partnership of 62 with Patterson, who was beaten umpteen times, proved a match-winner. Adams capitalised on Wessels's refusal to employ a sweeper on the cover boundary, which might have saved 50 runs.

On a pitch that was now uneven, the South Africans quickly lost both openers. But they were manoeuvred into a winning position by Wessels and Kirsten, the senior members of the side; Kirsten, at 36, was the second-oldest South African to make his Test début after 40-year-old G. W. A. Chubb in 1951. They had added 95 in 42 overs by the close, but were swept away next morning by Walsh, in an inspired spell of four for eight in 11 overs. Cutting the ball both ways, he finally found the form that eluded him earlier. Ambrose mopped up the tail to finish with match figures of 60.4–26–81–8.

Men of the Match: C. E. L. Ambrose and A. C. Hudson.

Close of play: First day, South Africa 13-0 (M. W. Rushmere 2*, A. C. Hudson 9*); Second day, South Africa 254-4 (A. C. Hudson 135*, A. P. Kuiper 19*); Third day, West Indies 184-7 (J. C. Adams 23*, K. C. G. Benjamin 6*); Fourth day, South Africa 122-2 (K. C. Wessels 74*, P. N. Kirsten 36*).

West Indies

D. L. Haynes c Wessels b Snell	58	– c Richardson b Snell	23
P. V. Simmons c Kirsten b Snell	35	– c Kirsten b Bosch	3
B. C. Lara c Richardson b Bosch	17	– c Richardson b Donald	64
*R. B. Richardson c Richardson b Snell	44	– lbw b Snell	2
K. L. T. Arthurton c Kuiper b Pringle	59	– b Donald	22
J. C. Adams b Donald	11	– not out	79
†D. Williams c Hudson b Donald	1	– lbw b Snell	5
C. E. L. Ambrose not out	6	– c Richardson b Donald	6
K. C. G. Benjamin b Snell	1	– lbw b Donald	7
C. A. Walsh b Pringle	6	– c Richardson b Snell	13
B. P. Patterson run out	0	– b Bosch	11
L-b 7, n-b 17	24	B 17, l-b 11, n-b 20	48
	262		**283**

1/99 (2) 2/106 (1) 3/137 (3) 4/219 (4)   262   1/10 (2) 2/66 (1) 3/68 (4)   283
5/240 (5) 6/241 (7) 7/250 (6) 8/255 (9)   4/120 (5) 5/139 (3) 6/164 (7)
9/262 (10) 10/262 (11)   7/174 (8) 8/196 (9)
                              9/221 (10) 10/283 (11)

Bowling: *First Innings*—Donald 20–1–67–2; Bosch 15–2–43–1; Pringle 18.4–2–62–2; Snell 18–3–83–4. *Second Innings*—Donald 25–3–77–4; Bosch 24.3–7–61–2; Snell 16–1–74–4; Pringle 16–0–43–0.

South Africa

M. W. Rushmere c Lara b Ambrose	3	– (2) b Ambrose	3
A. C. Hudson b Benjamin	163	– (1) c Lara b Ambrose	0
*K. C. Wessels c Adams b Ambrose	59	– c Lara b Walsh	74
P. N. Kirsten c Lara b Benjamin	11	– b Walsh	52
W. J. Cronje c Lara b Adams	5	– c Williams b Ambrose	2
A. P. Kuiper c Williams b Patterson	34	– c Williams b Walsh	0
†D. J. Richardson c Ambrose b Adams	8	– c Williams b Ambrose	2
R. P. Snell run out	6	– c Adams b Walsh	4
M. W. Pringle c Walsh b Adams	15	– b Ambrose	4
A. A. Donald st Williams b Adams	0	– (11) b Ambrose	0
T. Bosch not out	5	– (10) not out	0
B 4, l-b 6, w 1, n-b 25	36	B 4, l-b 3, n-b 4	11
	345		**148**

1/14 (1) 2/139 (3) 3/168 (4) 4/187 (5)   345   1/0 (1) 2/27 (2) 3/123 (3)   148
5/279 (6) 6/293 (7) 7/312 (2) 8/316 (8)   4/130 (5) 5/131 (6) 6/142 (4)
9/336 (10) 10/345 (9)   7/142 (8) 8/147 (9)
                             9/148 (7) 10/148 (11)

Bowling: *First Innings*—Ambrose 36–19–47–2; Patterson 23–4–79–1; Walsh 27–7–71–0; Benjamin 25–3–87–2; Arthurton 3–0–8–0; Adams 21.5–5–43–4. *Second Innings*—Ambrose 24.4–7–34–6; Patterson 7–1–26–0; Benjamin 9–2–21–0; Walsh 22–10–31–4; Adams 5–0–16–0; Simmons 5–1–13–0.

Umpires: D. M. Archer and S. A. Bucknor.

WILLS TROPHY, 1991-92

By QAMAR AHMED

Pakistan won their fifth competition in Sharjah in four seasons, to claim the new Wills Trophy and $US30,000. Though favourites, they had lost their first two matches, and their position seemed hopeless until West Indies failed to score two runs from the last three balls of the third. It was the fast bowlers who kept their hopes alive. Waqar Younis and Aqib Javed collected 11 wickets each, but Aqib was the pick of the attack. His sustained accuracy and late out-swing bewildered batsmen, and his seven for 37 bettered W. W. Davis's seven for 51 against Australia in the 1983 World Cup. It included an extraordinary hat-trick of three lbws, which the Indians found too extraordinary. They left furious at both the umpiring and what they claimed was bias against them by Moslem organisers. The Indians had started with three wins while the West Indians managed only one win, in their first match, and would have been humiliated without two fine centuries from their new captain, Richie Richardson.

The beneficiaries of the tournament were Wasim Raja and Mahmood Hussain of Pakistan, C. K. Nayudu and E. A. S. Prasanna of India and West Indies' C. G. Greenidge.

Note: Matches in this section were not first-class.

PAKISTAN v WEST INDIES

At Sharjah, October 17. West Indies won by one wicket. Toss: West Indies. Richardson overcame cramp to score an unbeaten hundred and secure victory in his first match as West Indies captain. His runner, Lambert, helped him to 106 from 142 balls, with ten fours. Richardson came in when Lambert was caught behind in the third over, and saw three more batsmen perish cheaply before Hooper offered him some support. But a second collapse left West Indies at 158 for eight, until Bishop joined his captain to add 45 for the ninth wicket. The target was reached with 15 balls to spare. Pakistan's total of 215, not a challenging one, had depended largely on Ramiz Raja and Javed Miandad, the only batsmen other than Richardson to approach 50.

Man of the Match: R. B. Richardson.

Pakistan

Ramiz Raja c Logie b Patterson	49	Mushtaq Ahmed lbw b Ambrose	4
Sajid Ali c Dujon b Ambrose	11	Waqar Younis b Bishop	9
Ijaz Ahmed lbw b Hooper	9	Aqib Javed not out	1
Salim Malik b Hooper	1	L-b 15, w 17, n-b 7	39
Javed Miandad b Simmons	47		
*Imran Khan c Logie b Patterson	11	1/25 2/54 3/59	(48.3 overs) 215
Wasim Akram run out	16	4/132 5/150 6/171	
†Moin Khan c Hooper b Bishop	18	7/185 8/199 9/212	

Bowling: Ambrose 9–1–33–2; Bishop 9.3–0–40–2; Patterson 10–0–48–2; Hooper 10–0–33–2; Benjamin 9–0–38–0; Simmons 1–0–8–1.

West Indies

P. V. Simmons run out	14	W. K. M. Benjamin	
C. B. Lambert c Moin Khan		lbw b Waqar Younis	1
b Wasim Akram	0	C. E. L. Ambrose lbw b Imran Khan	1
*R. B. Richardson not out	106	I. R. Bishop lbw b Waqar Younis	19
B. C. Lara c Moin Khan		B. P. Patterson not out	1
b Waqar Younis	5		
A. L. Logie c Moin Khan		B 4, l-b 4, w 8, n-b 5	21
b Waqar Younis	11		
C. L. Hooper run out	23	1/6 2/38 3/49 (9 wkts, 47.3 overs) 217	
†P. J. L. Dujon c Moin Khan		4/70 5/121 6/152	
b Imran Khan	15	7/157 8/158 9/203	

Bowling: Wasim Akram 8.3–1–37–1; Aqib Javed 10–2–32–0; Waqar Younis 9–0–48–4; Mushtaq Ahmed 10–0–54–0; Imran Khan 10–0–38–2.

Umpires: B. C. Cooray and P. W. Vidanagamage.

INDIA v PAKISTAN

At Sharjah, October 18. India won by 60 runs. Toss: India. Pakistan lost again, bowled out for a humiliating 178 in the 45th over when the last eight wickets fell for 54. Even Javed Miandad made heavy weather of his 61 as Prabhakar and Raju tied the Pakistanis down. India's batsmen had made smoother progress, especially after Tendulkar joined Manjrekar to increase the tempo. Tendulkar's unbeaten 52 came from 40 balls, and he was especially hard on Waqar Younis, whose last over he hit for 14.

Man of the Match: S. V. Manjrekar.

India

R. J. Shastri run out	22	Kapil Dev not out	10
N. S. Sidhu b Wasim Akram	38	L-b 4, w 3, n-b 5	12
S. V. Manjrekar lbw b Waqar Younis	72		
*M. Azharuddin b Waqar Younis	32	1/44 2/93 (4 wkts, 50 overs) 238	
S. R. Tendulkar not out	52	3/149 4/193	

†K. S. More, V. G. Kambli, M. Prabhakar, S. L. V. Raju and J. Srinath did not bat.

Bowling: Imran Khan 10–0–44–0; Aqib Javed 10–3–38–0; Waqar Younis 10–0–65–2; Wasim Akram 10–0–42–1; Akram Raza 10–0–45–0.

Pakistan

Ramiz Raja run out	35	Akram Raza c Azharuddin b Kapil Dev	0
Sajid Ali c More b Prabhakar	5	Waqar Younis b Prabhakar	6
Javed Miandad lbw b Raju	61	Aqib Javed b Prabhakar	4
Salim Malik lbw b Shastri	19	W 2, n-b 10	12
*Imran Khan b Prabhakar	1		
Ijaz Ahmed c and b Raju	4	1/8 2/84 3/124 (44.4 overs) 178	
Wasim Akram b Srinath	14	4/129 5/129 6/139	
†Moin Khan not out	17	7/155 8/156 9/166	

Bowling: Prabhakar 7.4–1–25–4; Srinath 9–1–31–1; Kapil Dev 8–0–30–1; Shastri 10–1–53–1; Raju 10–0–39–2.

Umpires: P. W. Vidanagamage and W. A. U. Wickremasinghe.

INDIA v WEST INDIES

At Sharjah, October 19. India won by 19 runs. Toss: West Indies. West Indies wasted a solid start to be all out with seven balls to spare. Lambert dominated their innings, but his dismissal at 123 started the slide. Earlier India reached a creditable 240, built around a second-wicket partnership of 128 in 24.5 overs from Sidhu (113 balls) and Manjrekar.

Man of the Match: M. Prabhakar.

India

R. J. Shastri st Dujon b Hooper	6	Kapil Dev c Simmons b Bishop	7
N. S. Sidhu st Dujon b Hooper	98	M. Prabhakar not out	2
S. V. Manjrekar c Hooper b Bishop	56	L-b 2, w 7, n-b 5	14
*M. Azharuddin c and b Simmons	12		
S. R. Tendulkar run out	22	1/33 2/161 3/181 (6 wkts, 50 overs) 240		
V. G. Kambli not out	23	4/184 5/216 6/232		

†K. S. More, S. L. V. Raju and A. Kumble did not bat.

Bowling: Ambrose 10-2-32-0; Bishop 10-0-49-2; Patterson 10-0-47-0; Hooper 10-0-46-2; Simmons 8-0-49-1; Arthurton 2-0-15-0.

West Indies

P. V. Simmons lbw b Shastri	20	C. E. L. Ambrose lbw b Prabhakar	0
C. B. Lambert c and b Kumble	66	I. R. Bishop c Shastri b Prabhakar	23
*R. B. Richardson c Azharuddin b Shastri	28	B. P. Patterson not out	3
B. C. Lara b Prabhakar	45	B 2, l-b 7, n-b 4	13
A. L. Logie lbw b Kumble	4		
C. L. Hooper lbw b Kumble	17	1/54 2/116 3/123 (48.5 overs) 221		
K. L. T. Arthurton st More b Kumble	2	4/132 5/171 6/185		
†P. J. L. Dujon lbw b Prabhakar	0	7/186 8/186 9/194		

Bowling: Kapil Dev 9-0-50-0; Prabhakar 9.5-0-30-4; Shastri 10-0-38-2; Kumble 10-0-50-4; Raju 10-0-44-0.

Umpires: B. C. Cooray and W. A. U. Wickremasinghe.

PAKISTAN v WEST INDIES

At Sharjah, October 21. Pakistan won by one run. Toss: Pakistan. Pakistan clinched a win with the last ball of the match. Needing ten from Waqar Younis's final over, West Indies' last-wicket pair managed eight from the first three balls, including a six to long-on from Bishop. But he could not score from the next two, and was bowled by the last. West Indies were put in sight of victory by Richardson's second hundred of the tournament. His 122 runs came from 121 balls, and he put on 154 with Dujon after five wickets had fallen for 57. Imran Khan also batted convincingly, adding 137 in 28 overs with Ramiz Raja.

Man of the Match: R. B. Richardson.

Pakistan

Ramiz Raja c Logie b Ambrose	90	†Moin Khan b Ambrose	0
Sajid Ali c Dujon b Ambrose	7	Akram Raza not out	1
Javed Miandad b Ambrose	2	L-b 8, w 7, n-b 1	16
Salim Malik c Logie b Hooper	10		
*Imran Khan c Hooper b Ambrose	77	1/17 2/63 3/200 (7 wkts, 50 overs) 236		
Ijaz Ahmed not out	14	4/202 5/229		
Wasim Akram c Patterson b Bishop	19	6/229 7/229		

Waqar Younis and Aqib Javed did not bat.

Javed Miandad, when 2, retired hurt at 38 and resumed at 229-6.

Bowling: Ambrose 10-1-53-5; Bishop 10-1-44-1; Walsh 10-0-48-0; Patterson 10-1-53-0; Hooper 10-0-30-1.

West Indies

P. V. Simmons b Aqib Javed	8	C. E. L. Ambrose lbw b Waqar Younis	0
C. B. Lambert b Aqib Javed	7	C. A. Walsh b Wasim Akram	0
*R. B. Richardson c Ijaz Ahmed b Waqar Younis	122	B. P. Patterson not out	1
B. C. Lara lbw b Aqib Javed	0	L-b 6, w 9	15
C. L. Hooper lbw b Waqar Younis	13		
A. L. Logie run out	0	1/16 2/32 3/32 (50 overs) 235	
†P. J. L. Dujon run out	53	4/56 5/57 6/211	
I. R. Bishop b Waqar Younis	16	7/217 8/220 9/227	

Bowling: Wasim Akram 10-0-59-1; Aqib Javed 10-2-54-3; Akram Raza 10-0-40-0; Waqar Younis 10-1-39-4; Ijaz Ahmed 7-0-24-0; Imran Khan 3-0-13-0.

Umpires: B. C. Cooray and P. W. Vidanagamage.

INDIA v WEST INDIES

At Sharjah, October 22. India won by seven wickets. Toss: India. India had never beaten West Indies batting second in a one-day international, but when Azharuddin asked his opponents to bat they stumbled to 145 all out, and a third successive win put India through to the final. The unlikely instrument of West Indies' downfall was Tendulkar's gentle medium pace. Kapil Dev became the first bowler to collect 200 wickets in limited-overs internationals when he had Benjamin lbw. Though India lost Raman with one run on the board, Sidhu and Manjrekar put them on the right track with 107 for the second wicket. When they were dismissed in quick succession, Tendulkar and Azharuddin raced to victory with more than 12 overs to spare.

Man of the Match: S. R. Tendulkar.

West Indies

P. V. Simmons c Prabhakar b Kapil Dev	14	I. R. Bishop c and b Prabhakar	14
C. B. Lambert lbw b Tendulkar	11	W. K. M. Benjamin lbw b Kapil Dev	9
*R. B. Richardson c Azharuddin b Tendulkar	16	C. E. L. Ambrose not out	4
C. L. Hooper run out	8	B. P. Patterson run out	1
A. L. Logie c More b Tendulkar	0	L-b 3, w 4, n-b 2	9
K. L. T. Arthurton c and b Prabhakar	59	1/24 2/39 3/47 (46.2 overs) 145	
†P. J. L. Dujon c More b Tendulkar	0	4/47 5/78 6/78	
		7/129 8/130 9/143	

Bowling: Kapil Dev 8-1-23-2; Prabhakar 8.2-0-32-2; Tendulkar 10-1-34-4; Kumble 10-2-24-0; Raju 10-1-29-0.

India

W. V. Raman lbw b Bishop	0	S. R. Tendulkar not out	11
N. S. Sidhu c Logie b Benjamin	44	B 8, l-b 4, w 18	30
S. V. Manjrekar lbw b Bishop	43		
*M. Azharuddin not out	19	1/1 2/108 3/108 (3 wkts, 37.3 overs) 147	

Kapil Dev, V. G. Kambli, M. Prabhakar, †K. S. More, S. L. V. Raju and A. Kumble did not bat.

Bowling: Bishop 7-2-28-2; Ambrose 8-1-22-0; Patterson 6.3-0-16-0; Hooper 6-0-24-0; Benjamin 9-0-34-1; Arthurton 1-0-11-0.

Umpires: P. W. Vidanagamage and W. A. U. Wickremasinghe.

INDIA v PAKISTAN

At Sharjah, October 23. Pakistan won by four runs. Toss: Pakistan. A growing injury list forced Pakistan to call for reinforcements. Their first three batsmen in this match had just flown in, and the left-hander Aamir Sohail played the decisive innings in a close encounter. His 91 came from 132 balls. Another of the newcomers, Zahid Fazal, gave worthwhile support. An opening stand of 124 from Shastri and Kambli put India in a good position, but a superb catch by substitute Mushtaq Ahmed to dismiss Tendulkar tipped the balance, and Kapil Dev was trapped first ball. In fading light, 12 from Waqar Younis's last over was too stiff a target.

Man of the Match: Aamir Sohail.

Pakistan

Aamir Sohail c Tendulkar b Kapil Dev.	91	†Moin Khan not out	1
Saeed Anwar run out	1	Akram Raza not out	0
Zahid Fazal b Raju	39	B 1, l-b 5, w 16, n-b 7	29
Salim Malik c Azharuddin b Srinath	42		
*Imran Khan b Prabhakar	43	1/4 2/90 3/181 (7 wkts, 50 overs)	257
Wasim Akram b Srinath	2	4/202 5/214	
Ijaz Ahmed run out	9	6/255 7/257	

Waqar Younis and Aqib Javed did not bat.

Bowling: Kapil Dev 9-2-31-1; Prabhakar 10-0-62-1; Srinath 8-0-55-2; Tendulkar 6-0-20-0; Kumble 7-0-35-0; Raju 10-0-48-1.

India

R. J. Shastri b Waqar Younis	77	Kapil Dev lbw b Wasim Akram	0
V. G. Kambli c Moin Khan		M. Prabhakar not out	19
b Aqib Javed .	40	†K. S. More run out	1
S. V. Manjrekar c Ijaz Ahmed		B 1, l-b 3, w 12, n-b 2	18
b Wasim Akram .	40		
*M. Azharuddin b Akram Raza	0	1/124 2/133 3/134 (7 wkts, 50 overs)	253
S. R. Tendulkar c sub (Mushtaq Ahmed)		4/219 5/219	
b Salim Malik .	49	6/240 7/253	

A. Kumble, S. L. V. Raju and J. Srinath did not bat.

Bowling: Wasim Akram 9-0-44-2; Aqib Javed 10-1-36-1; Imran Khan 2-0-17-0; Akram Raza 10-0-43-1; Waqar Younis 10-0-59-1; Aamir Sohail 6-0-34-0; Salim Malik 3-0-16-1.

Umpires: B. C. Cooray and W. A. U. Wickremasinghe.

QUALIFYING TABLE

	Played	Won	Lost	Points	Run-rate
India	4	3	1	6	4.68
Pakistan	4	2	2	4	4.43
West Indies	4	1	3	2	4.14

FINAL

INDIA v PAKISTAN

At Sharjah, October 25. Pakistan won by 72 runs. Toss: India. Pakistan set up victory with the highest score of the tournament, and made sure of it through Aqib Javed's hat-trick. It was the seventh in limited-overs internationals, and his figures of seven for 37 were the best in all such cricket. He initiated India's collapse in his first over, dismissing Sidhu, but the fatal blows were struck in his third, as Shastri, Azharuddin and Tendulkar were lbw to the third, fourth and fifth balls. Aqib's performance overshadowed his colleagues' earlier exploits: Zahid Fazal and Salim Malik added 171 for the third wicket; Zahid had hit eight fours and a six in 120 balls when he was carried off the field with cramp.

Man of the Match: Aqib Javed.   *Man of the Series:* S. V. Manjrekar.

Pakistan

Aamir Sohail c Kapil Dev b Prabhakar	1	Wasim Akram b Kapil Dev 3
Sajid Ali c More b Kapil Dev	10	†Moin Khan c More b Prabhakar 5
Zahid Fazal retired hurt	98	L-b 15, w 10, n-b 4 29
Salim Malik c Azharuddin b Prabhakar	87	
*Imran Khan c Manjrekar b Kapil Dev	13	1/6 2/23 3/223 (6 wkts, 50 overs) 262
Ijaz Ahmed not out	16	4/230 5/247 6/262

Akram Raza, Waqar Younis and Aqib Javed did not bat.

Zahid Fazal retired hurt at 194.

Bowling: Prabhakar 10-2-54-3; Kapil Dev 10-0-36-3; Tendulkar 5-0-24-0; Srinath 10-0-49-0; Shastri 8-0-39-0; Raju 7-0-45-0.

India

R. J. Shastri lbw b Aqib Javed	15	†K. S. More not out 26
N. S. Sidhu c Moin Khan b Aqib Javed	21	J. Srinath c Wasim Akram
S. V. Manjrekar c Waqar Younis		b Akram Raza . 14
b Aqib Javed .	52	S. L. V. Raju run out 2
*M. Azharuddin lbw b Aqib Javed	0	
S. R. Tendulkar lbw b Aqib Javed	0	L-b 5, w 8, n-b 2 15
V. G. Kambli run out	30	—
Kapil Dev b Aqib Javed	8	1/32 2/47 3/47 (46 overs) 190
M. Prabhakar c Aamir Sohail		4/47 5/100 6/129
b Aqib Javed .	7	7/132 8/143 9/177

Bowling: Wasim Akram 10-3-21-0; Imran Khan 4-0-24-0; Aqib Javed 10-1-37-7; Waqar Younis 9-2-28-0; Akram Raza 9-0-56-1; Ijaz Ahmed 2-0-11-0; Salim Malik 2-0-8-0.

Umpires: B. C. Cooray and W. A. U. Wickremasinghe.

BENSON AND HEDGES WORLD SERIES CUP, 1991-92

By DICKY RUTNAGUR

Note: Matches in this section were not first-class.

INDIA v WEST INDIES

At Perth, December 6 (day/night). Tied. Toss: West Indies. A spirited rearguard action by the West Indian tail created an exciting finish to a match made tedious by the bowlers' easy dominance. The ball deviated copiously, in the air and off the seam, giving them a simple task against batsmen on both sides lacking form and confidence. Although India survived all but 14 balls of their allotted 50 overs, their meagre 126 included only two fours, both from Shastri. West Indies lost Haynes to Kapil Dev's first delivery, and their innings followed the same dreary pattern. They were on the run until their eighth wicket fell, with 51 wanted. But Ambrose and Cummins showed more will than the recognised batsmen, and were 14 runs from victory when Ambrose was run out. A superb slip catch by Azharuddin, off Tendulkar's part-time medium pace, claimed the last wicket with the scores level.

Man of the Match: C. E. L. Ambrose.   *Attendance:* 5,494.

India

R. J. Shastri c Lara b Marshall	33		†K. S. More c Richardson b Ambrose	4
K. Srikkanth c Hooper b Patterson	3		S. T. Banerjee not out	2
S. V. Manjrekar c Williams b Cummins	15		J. Srinath run out	0
S. R. Tendulkar c Richardson b Cummins	1			
*M. Azharuddin c Lara b Ambrose	6		L-b 13, w 10, n-b 1	24
P. K. Amre run out	20		1/8 2/35 3/41	(47.4 overs) 126
Kapil Dev c Richardson b Marshall	5		4/58 5/74 6/88	
M. Prabhakar run out	13		7/111 8/122 9/125	

Bowling: Patterson 10–1–28–1; Ambrose 8.4–3–9–2; Marshall 10–2–23–2; Cummins 9–1–21–2; Hooper 10–1–32–0.

West Indies

D. L. Haynes c More b Kapil Dev	0		C. E. L. Ambrose run out	17
P. A. Wallace b Prabhakar	11		A. C. Cummins c Azharuddin b Tendulkar	24
*R. B. Richardson c More b Kapil Dev	12			
B. C. Lara c More b Banerjee	14		B. P. Patterson not out	8
C. L. Hooper b Srinath	12		L-b 4, w 9, n-b 3	16
K. L. T. Arthurton b Srinath	0			
M. D. Marshall c More b Banerjee	7		1/0 2/23 3/25 4/55 5/55	(41 overs) 126
†D. Williams c Srikkanth b Banerjee	5		6/61 7/69 8/76 9/113	

Bowling: Kapil Dev 10–3–30–2; Prabhakar 10–1–30–1; Srinath 10–2–27–2; Banerjee 10–2–30–3; Tendulkar 1–0–5–1.

Umpires: R. J. Evans and P. J. McConnell.

AUSTRALIA v INDIA

At Perth, December 8. India won by 107 runs. Toss: India. Conditions again favoured seam bowling, and India exploited them to keep Australia pinned to the ropes. The left-arm spinner Shastri seized the last five wickets in 32 balls, but the innings had already been reduced to fragments by the seamers when he came on at 69 for five. Boon and Jones went with just six scored, and Australia's only hint of recovery was the third-wicket stand of 46 between Marsh and Border. Earlier, the Indian batsmen had made uneven progress: Srikkanth's slogging brought him eight fours and 60 invaluable runs off as many balls, while Tendulkar and Amre grafted 46 for the fifth wicket. Kapil Dev batted with discretion to keep India afloat in the closing stages.

Man of the Match: K. Srikkanth.   *Attendance:* 12,444.

India

R. J. Shastri c Jones b Waugh 10	M. Prabhakar lbw b Waugh 2
K. Srikkanth c Moody b Waugh 60	S. T. Banerjee not out 6
S. V. Manjrekar run out 2	B 1, l-b 10, w 16, n-b 1 28
S. R. Tendulkar c Taylor b Moody . . 36	
*M. Azharuddin c Healy b Moody 6	1/49 2/64 3/95 (7 wkts, 50 overs) 208
P. K. Amre c Jones b McDermott 33	4/112 5/158
Kapil Dev not out 25	6/183 7/193

†K. S. More and J. Srinath did not bat.

Bowling: McDermott 10-1-40-1; Reid 10-2-16-0; O'Donnell 7-0-39-0; Waugh 10-1-46-3; Taylor 4-0-18-0; Moody 9-0-38-2.

Australia

G. R. Marsh c More b Banerjee 15	P. L. Taylor c Amre b Shastri 6
D. C. Boon c Kapil Dev b Prabhakar . . 1	C. J. McDermott c Tendulkar c Shastri . 5
D. M. Jones b Kapil Dev 1	B. A. Reid not out 1
*A. R. Border c More b Srinath 32	L-b 4, w 6, n-b 5 15
T. M. Moody c More b Srinath 7	
S. R. Waugh c and b Shastri 5	1/3 2/6 3/52 (37.5 overs) 101
S. P. O'Donnell c Kapil Dev b Shastri . 10	4/65 5/68 6/75
†I. A. Healy st More b Shastri 3	7/84 8/93 9/99

Bowling: Kapil Dev 6-2-5-1; Prabhakar 6-2-19-1; Srinath 7-0-24-2; Banerjee 8-1-26-1; Shastri 6.5-1-15-5; Tendulkar 4-0-8-0.

Umpires: R. J. Evans and T. A. Prue.

AUSTRALIA v INDIA

At Hobart, December 10. Australia won by eight wickets. Toss: India. McDermott's opening spell of seven overs, which removed both Indian openers, gave Australia a grip which never loosened. The innings was stabilised by Manjrekar and Tendulkar, who shared 102 runs for the third wicket. Each scored 57 but they could not raise the momentum to build a defensible total. On a slow pitch, not the truest in bounce, the Australians treated India's bowling with respect. They were not stretched, however, and Boon and Jones took them within two runs of their objective. As the target approached, Jones denied himself runs and the strike to allow his colleague to reach a century on his home ground. Boon's unbeaten 102 came from 163 balls, with eight fours.

Man of the Match: D. C. Boon.   *Attendance:* 9,218.

India

R. J. Shastri lbw b McDermott 0	M. Prabhakar run out 1
K. Srikkanth c Healy b McDermott . . . 7	J. Srinath not out 2
S. V. Manjrekar c Healy b Reid 57	
S. R. Tendulkar c Waugh b Taylor 57	B 1, l-b 7, w 4, n-b 2 14
Kapil Dev c and b Taylor 3	
P. K. Amre b O'Donnell 8	1/2 2/18 3/120 (8 wkts, 50 overs) 175
*M. Azharuddin not out 21	4/134 5/137 6/151
S. T. Banerjee c Jones b McDermott . . 5	7/163 8/168

†K. S. More did not bat.

Bowling: Reid 10-1-24-1; McDermott 10-3-19-3; O'Donnell 10-1-35-1; Waugh 7-0-31-0; Taylor 10-0-43-2; Moody 3-0-15-0.

Australia

D. C. Boon not out	102
G. R. Marsh b Srinath	8
D. M. Jones c Tendulkar b Manjrekar	48
A. R. Border not out	0
B 3, l-b 4, w 7, n-b 4	18

1-45 2/174 (2 wkts, 48.3 overs) 176

T. M. Moody, S. R. Waugh, S. P. O'Donnell, P. L. Taylor, †I. A. Healy, C. J. McDermott and B. A. Reid did not bat.

Bowling: Kapil Dev 10-3-21-0; Prabhakar 10-0-32-0; Srinath 10-1-37-1; Banerjee 10-0-41-0; Shastri 10-0-29-0; Srikkanth 2-0-7-0; Manjrekar 0.3-0-2-1.

Umpires: S. G. Randell and C. D. Timmins.

AUSTRALIA v WEST INDIES

At Melbourne, December 12 (day/night). Australia won by nine runs. Toss: Australia. Australia celebrated the opening of the Great Southern Stand at the MCG with a hard-earned win, thrillingly completed. Take away Moody's buccaneering 51, in 44 balls, featuring two driven sixes, and the drama at the end as Ambrose slogged a four and a six in the penultimate over, and it was a dull match, fashioned by a slow, uneven pitch. Marsh and Border batted with circumspection, adding 68 to erect the platform for Moody's spectacular assault. When West Indies replied, Haynes waged almost a lone battle to keep them in contention. Waugh had a hand in the capture of five of the first seven wickets. Besides dismissing the dangerous Lara and Hooper in successive overs, he caught Richardson and effected two run-outs with spectacular agility and lightning judgment.

Man of the Match: S. R. Waugh.   *Attendance*: 59,426.

Australia

G. R. Marsh c Richardson b Marshall	43	C. J. McDermott lbw b Marshall	0
D. C. Boon b Marshall	8	M. R. Whitney not out	2
D. M. Jones c Williams b Marshall	0	B. A. Reid not out	2
A. R. Border st Williams b Hooper	37	L-b 9, w 2, n-b 3	14
T. M. Moody run out	51		
S. R. Waugh c Williams b Cummins	8	1/21 2/29 3/97 (9 wkts, 50 overs) 173	
†I. A. Healy b Patterson	5	4/103 5/141 6/154	
P. L. Taylor c Lara b Ambrose	3	7/159 8/167 9/170	

Bowling: Ambrose 10-2-31-1; Patterson 10-0-49-1; Marshall 10-4-18-4; Cummins 10-1-35-1; Hooper 10-0-31-1.

West Indies

D. L. Haynes c and b Taylor	62	C. E. L. Ambrose b Taylor	18
C. A. Best c Border b McDermott	5	A. C. Cummins b McDermott	6
R. B. Richardson c Waugh b McDermott	10	B. P. Patterson not out	1
B. C. Lara c and b Waugh	11	B 1, l-b 5, w 2, n-b 2	10
C. L. Hooper lbw b Waugh	0		
K. L. T. Arthurton run out	28	1/9 2/34 3/64 (49.1 overs) 164	
M. D. Marshall run out	3	4/64 5/119 6/124	
D. Williams run out	10	7/129 8/145 9/162	

Bowling: Reid 9-1-33-0; McDermott 9.1-2-23-3; Whitney 10-3-29-0; Waugh 6-0-16-2; Moody 5-0-21-0; Taylor 10-1-36-2.

Umpires: A. R. Crafter and P. J. McConnell.

INDIA v WEST INDIES

At Adelaide, December 14. India won by ten runs. Toss: India. Given a good pitch, India batting came into its own. Srikkanth batted through half their innings for a typically volatile 82 (88 balls, ten fours, one six), with Patterson suffering hardest from h aggression. Although they could not impose the same authority, Manjrekar and Tendulka found the gaps with imaginative placements and ran enterprisingly to add 75 from 14 over Then Azharuddin and Kapil Dev levied 42 from the last six. India's prosperity wa enhanced by an early excess of wides and no-balls. West Indies had a magnificent sta when Haynes (seven fours, one six) and Wallace shared 124 in 28 overs, but their midd order again proved brittle. After Hooper, Haynes and Arthurton fell for seven runs i consecutive overs, they were effectively out of the game.

Man of the Match: K. Srikkanth.   *Attendance:* 5,673.

India

R. J. Shastri c Williams b Ambrose	4	Kapil Dev not out	2
K. Srikkanth st Williams b Hooper	82	L-b 5, w 11, n-b 5	2
S. V. Manjrekar c Wallace b Arthurton	55		
S. R. Tendulkar c and b Arthurton	48	1/27 2/123	(4 wkts, 50 overs) 26
*M. Azharuddin not out	31	3/198 4/220	

P. K. Amre, M. Prabhakar, †K. S. More, J. Srinath and N. D. Hirwani did not bat.

Bowling: Ambrose 10-1-35-1; Patterson 6-0-47-0; Marshall 10-0-59-0; Cummin 10-0-41-0; Hooper 10-0-52-1; Arthurton 4-0-23-2.

West Indies

D. L. Haynes c Shastri b Srinath	89	C. E. L. Ambrose b Kapil Dev	
P. A. Wallace c Srinath b Hirwani	52	A. C. Cummins b Kapil Dev	
*R. B. Richardson run out	2	B. P. Patterson not out	
B. C. Lara lbw b Shastri	29	B 1, l-b 11, w 9, n-b 4	2
C. L. Hooper c Manjrekar b Kapil Dev	12		
K. L. T. Arthurton c Amre b Kapil Dev	5	1/124 2/127 3/184	(50 overs) 25
M. D. Marshall lbw b Srinath	17	4/205 5/206 6/212	
†D. Williams c and b Prabhakar	3	7/220 8/243 9/251	

Bowling: Kapil Dev 10-1-54-4; Prabhakar 9-1-42-1; Srinath 10-0-35-2; Tendulka 2-0-10-0; Hirwani 9-0-54-1; Shastri 10-0-45-1.

Umpires: D. B. Hair and L. J. King.

AUSTRALIA v INDIA

At Adelaide, December 15. Australia won by six wickets. Toss: India. On the same blissfu pitch on which they had thrived the previous day, India collapsed to 69 for six; all-rounde Kapil Dev and Prabhakar could not revive their hopes. The misery was inflicted by kee bowling and high-class fielding, at its best in the run-out of Manjrekar: Moody skidded t stop the ball inches inside the long third man boundary, and returned it to Healy who, sti wearing his glove, relayed it accurately to the bowler's end before Manjrekar completed third run. Australia, too, lost early wickets, but a partnership of 137 from Jones and Borde took them to within four runs of their target. Border lost his wicket trying for a match winning six.

Man of the Match: A. R. Border.   *Attendance:* 18,335.

India

R. J. Shastri lbw b Reid	1	†K. S. More lbw b McDermott	2
K. Srikkanth c and b McDermott	3	J. Srinath run out	
S. V. Manjrekar run out	12	S. L. V. Raju not out	
S. R. Tendulkar c Jones b Waugh	21	L-b 6, w 4	1
*M. Azharuddin c Healy b Whitney	13		
P. K. Amre c Healy b Whitney	10	1/2 2/4 3/37	(48.4 overs) 15
Kapil Dev c Moody b Taylor	39	4/41 5/64 6/69	
M. Prabhakar run out	17	7/119 8/133 9/149	

Bowling: Reid 10–1–32–1; McDermott 8.4–0–29–2; Waugh 10–1–27–1; Whitney 0–3–22–2; Taylor 10–1–41–1.

Australia

D. C. Boon b Kapil Dev	6	S. R. Waugh not out		0
G. R. Marsh b Prabhakar	3	L-b 3, w 4, n-b 3		10
D. M. Jones not out	63			
A. R. Border c sub b Raju	76	1/10 2/17	(4 wkts, 40.5 overs)	158
T. M. Moody c Tendulkar b Raju	0	3/154 4/156		

I. A. Healy, P. L. Taylor, C. J. McDermott, M. R. Whitney and B. A. Reid did not bat.

Bowling: Kapil Dev 6–2–12–1; Prabhakar 6–0–20–1; Shastri 10–0–34–0; Srinath 9–0–30–0; Raju 9–1–32–2; Srikkanth 2–0–24–0; Tendulkar 1.5–0–3–0.

Umpires: A. R. Crafter and I. S. Thomas.

AUSTRALIA v WEST INDIES

At Sydney, December 18 (day/night). Australia won by 51 runs. Toss: Australia. A formidable 32-over stand between Marsh and Boon, their eighth of three figures in one-day internationals, was the cornerstone of Australia's victory. It was built in the face of splendid opening spells by Ambrose and Cummins and a testing first stint from Marshall; Cummins's figures suffered from umpire King's harsh judgment of width outside off stump. Boon dominated until, in the 24th over, Marsh hoisted two huge sixes to mid-wicket. He batted on for another 22 overs and faced 146 balls for his 82. West Indies' reply was crippled when Haynes was caught behind off an unplayable ball from McDermott. Richardson made little headway in 30 balls, and only Hooper's sparkling 77 (87 balls) prevented an embarrassing rout.

Man of the Match: G. R. Marsh. *Attendance:* 37,770.

Australia

G. R. Marsh c D. L. Haynes b Cummins	82	†I. A. Healy not out		17
D. C. Boon b Arthurton	61	P. L. Taylor not out		2
D. M. Jones b Ambrose	2	B 2, l-b 15, w 4, n-b 6		27
S. R. Waugh b Ambrose	34			
T. M. Moody run out	8	1/128 2/137 3/190	(6 wkts, 50 overs)	234
*A. R. Border b Hooper	1	4/204 5/211 6/214		

C. J. McDermott, M. R. Whitney and B. A. Reid did not bat.

Bowling: Ambrose 10–3–26–2; Cummins 10–0–53–1; Marshall 9–2–39–0; R. C. Haynes 5–0–35–0; Hooper 10–0–42–1; Arthurton 5–1–22–1.

West Indies

D. L. Haynes c Healy b McDermott	9	R. C. Haynes c Moody b McDermott		0
P. A. Wallace lbw b Reid	9	C. E. L. Ambrose b Waugh		2
*R. B. Richardson c Healy b Reid	6	A. C. Cummins not out		1
B. C. Lara c Waugh b Whitney	19	L-b 13, w 4, n-b 5		22
C. L. Hooper c Waugh b Moody	77			
K. L. T. Arthurton b Waugh	38	1/13 2/17 3/36	(46.5 overs)	183
M. D. Marshall b Whitney	7	4/70 5/146 6/177		
†D. Williams b Whitney	0	7/177 8/178 9/181		

Bowling: Reid 10–2–29–2; McDermott 8–1–29–2; Waugh 6.5–0–33–2; Whitney 10–1–25–3; Taylor 5–0–32–0; Moody 7–0–22–1.

Umpires: L. J. King and S. G. Randell.

AUSTRALIA v WEST INDIES

At Melbourne, January 9 (day/night). No result. Toss: West Indies. Though West Indies' score was by no means impressive, they could not have been written off when rain intervened. There was life and abundant movement in the pitch, and Australia would have had to bat well if their reply had been reduced to a slog over a curtailed quota of overs. The batsmen took several body blows, and West Indies owed much to Haynes in reaching 97 with only one wicket down. But once Lara was run out the innings went into a downward spiral, with the momentum dropping as wickets fell.

Attendance: 64,558.

West Indies

D. L. Haynes c S. R. Waugh b Taylor	56	C. E. L. Ambrose b McDermott	7
P. A. Wallace c S. R. Waugh		A. C. Cummins not out	1
b McDermott	22		
B. C. Lara run out	22	B 5, l-b 9, w 1, n-b 1	16
*R. B. Richardson run out	13		—
C. L. Hooper b Taylor	7	1/33 2/97 3/113 (7 wkts, 47 overs)	160
K. L. T. Arthurton not out	12	4/128 5/137	
M. D. Marshall c Healy b Whitney	4	6/144 7/159	

†D. Williams and B. P. Patterson did not bat.

Bowling: McDermott 9–0–25–2; Whitney 10–0–28–1; Moody 5–0–28–0; S. R. Waugh 8–0–19–0; Taylor 10–1–28–2; M. E. Waugh 5–0–18–0.

Australia

G. R. Marsh, D. C. Boon, D. M. Jones, M. E. Waugh, S. R. Waugh, T. M. Moody, *A. R. Border, †I. A. Healy, P. L. Taylor, C. J. McDermott and M. R. Whitney.

Umpires: A. R. Crafter and L. J. King.

INDIA v WEST INDIES

At Brisbane, January 11. West Indies won by six wickets. Toss: India. West Indies preyed voraciously on the weaknesses of their opponents, who missed the injured Shastri, to register their first win of the competition. Ignoring their experience of the Gabba and the help a fresh pitch there offers seam bowlers, India batted first and were dismissed cheaply. Outstanding West Indian bowling, bad shots from the openers and the early run-out of Manjrekar all undermined the innings. It was kept alive by Tendulkar's immaculate 77 and his seventh-wicket partnership of 76 with Kapil Dev. Extras also made a valuable contribution, thanks to umpire Hair's bizarre interpretation of wides. West Indies, too, started poorly. But they were assured of victory by Haynes, whose 52 stretched through 38 overs, and Richardson, who regained his touch after five failures.

Man of the Match: A. C. Cummins.   *Attendance:* 7,567.

India

K. Srikkanth c Marshall b Cummins	4	†K. S. More not out	11
N. S. Sidhu c Hooper b Marshall	1	S. L. V. Raju c Williams b Cummins	8
S. V. Manjrekar run out	1	J. Srinath c Williams b Cummins	0
S. R. Tendulkar c sub b Cummins	77	B 4, l-b 9, w 15, n-b 8	36
*M. Azharuddin lbw b Marshall	8		—
S. C. Ganguly lbw b Cummins	3	1/14 2/20 3/21 (48.3 overs)	191
M. Prabhakar c and b Patterson	14	4/35 5/62 6/85	
Kapil Dev c Marshall b Patterson	28	7/161 8/178 9/191	

Bowling: Ambrose 10–0–41–0; Marshall 10–0–30–2; Cummins 9.3–1–31–5; Patterson 9–0–52–2; Hooper 10–0–24–0.

West Indies

D. L. Haynes c sub b Raju	52	C. A. Best not out	9
P. A. Wallace c Srinath b Prabhakar	4	B 2, l-b 8, w 13, n-b 9	32
B. C. Lara c Manjrekar b Srinath	4		
R. B. Richardson lbw b Prabhakar	72	1/13 2/24 (4 wkts, 48.3 overs) 192	
C. L. Hooper not out	19	3/133 4/170	

†D. Williams, M. D. Marshall, C. E. L. Ambrose, A. C. Cummins and B. P. Patterson did not bat.

Bowling: Kapil Dev 10-3-33-0; Prabhakar 9-1-39-2; Srinath 9-3-27-1; Tendulkar 7-0-27-0; Raju 10-0-33-1; Srikkanth 3-0-21-0; Sidhu 0.3-0-2-0.

Umpires: D. B. Hair and S. G. Randell.

AUSTRALIA v WEST INDIES

At Brisbane, January 12. West Indies won by 12 runs. Toss: Australia. Bowling with discipline and verve, and fielding magnificently, Australia contained West Indies to a moderate 215. More than half came from a third-wicket partnership of 110 between the busy Richardson and Lara, who batted delightfully for 85 balls. When the innings began to taper away Best responded with a boisterous 30 in 21 balls. Initially the West Indian attack held little menace on a pitch much slower than it had been the previous day. A solid start from Marsh and Boon promised a comfortable win until Patterson, the fourth seamer, tried, dismissed Marsh and Jones. This triggered a collapse given momentum by three run-outs, effected by deadly throwing from substitute Hamesh Anthony and Hooper. At 164 for eight, Australia looked hopelessly outplayed. But a blustery 33 by Taylor took the fight to the last two overs, from which 16 runs were needed.

Man of the Match: B. C. Lara. *Attendance*: 19,273.

West Indies

D. L. Haynes c Marsh b Whitney	11	A. C. Cummins c Boon b S. R. Waugh	2
P. A. Wallace c Whitney b Moody	31	†D. Williams not out	0
B. C. Lara run out	69	B. P. Patterson lbw b McDermott	0
*R. B. Richardson c Moody b Taylor	50		
C. L. Hooper c and b S. R. Waugh	6	L-b 8, w 2	10
C. A. Best b McDermott	30		
M. D. Marshall c Border b S. R. Waugh	4	1/27 2/58 3/168 (49.3 overs) 215	
		4/173 5/185 6/193	
C. E. L. Ambrose b McDermott	2	7/210 8/215 9/215	

Bowling: McDermott 9.3-2-36-3; Whitney 10-2-39-1; S. R. Waugh 10-2-31-3; Moody 6-0-29-1; Taylor 10-0-44-1; M. E. Waugh 4-0-28-0.

Australia

D. C. Boon run out	77	P. L. Taylor b Hooper	33
G. R. Marsh lbw b Patterson	29	C. J. McDermott c Haynes b Hooper	10
D. M. Jones b Patterson	0	M. R. Whitney not out	1
*A. R. Border run out	8	B 1, l-b 4, w 2, n-b 4	11
M. E. Waugh c Cummins	17		
T. M. Moody b Ambrose	3	1/70 2/73 3/84 (49 overs) 203	
S. R. Waugh b Patterson	3	4/120 5/135 6/141	
†I. A. Healy run out	11	7/152 8/164 9/200	

Bowling: Marshall 9-1-39-0; Ambrose 10-1-37-1; Cummins 10-0-49-1; Patterson 10-1-37-3; Hooper 10-0-36-2.

Umpires: I. S. Thomas and C. D. Timmins.

AUSTRALIA v INDIA

At Sydney, January 14 (day/night). Australia won by nine wickets. Toss: India. Assured of a place in the final, Australia included the uncapped seamer, Reiffel, at the expense of a batsman of no less repute than Jones. As first change, Reiffel neutralised India's solid, if slow, start, removing Shastri and Srikkanth after the visitors' only half-century opening stand in the tournament. Within three overs India were 69 for three. Tendulkar and Azharuddin prevented total disintegration. But Australia were under no pressure and cantered home with more than ten overs to spare.

Man of the Match: C. J. McDermott.   *Attendance: 28,824.*

India

R. J. Shastri b Reiffel	22	†C. S. Pandit c Healy b McDermott ...	2
K. Srikkanth b Reiffel	42	S. L. V. Raju not out	6
N. S. Sidhu c Boon b S. R. Waugh	1	J. Srinath b S. R. Waugh	5
S. V. Manjrekar c Marsh b Moody	16	B 3, l-b 5, w 4, n-b 1	13
S. R. Tendulkar run out	31		
*M. Azharuddin c Border b McDermott	22	1/52 2/57 3/69 (49.4 overs)	175
Kapil Dev run out	7	4/111 5/129 6/150	
M. Prabhakar c and b Whitney	8	7/156 8/161 9/163	

Bowling: McDermott 10–2–17–2; Whitney 10–1–36–1; Reiffel 10–1–27–2; S. R. Waugh 5.4–0–29–2; Taylor 9–0–40–0; Moody 5–0–18–1.

Australia

G. R. Marsh b Prabhakar	3
D. C. Boon not out	79
T. M. Moody not out	87
L-b 5, w 2, n-b 1	8

1/10   (1 wkt, 39.2 overs) 177

S. R. Waugh, M. E. Waugh, *A. R. Border, †I. A. Healy, P. L. Taylor, P. R. Reiffel, C. J. McDermott and M. R. Whitney did not bat.

Bowling: Kapil Dev 6–0–11–0; Prabhakar 8–0–29–1; Tendulkar 2–0–14–0; Srinath 8–1–28–0; Shastri 8–0–40–0; Raju 7–0–46–0; Manjrekar 0.2–0–4–0.

Umpires: D. B. Hair and T. A. Prue.

INDIA v WEST INDIES

At Melbourne, January 16 (day/night). India won by five wickets. Toss: West Indies. The last round-robin match decided which of the two teams would make the final, and both opened nervously. West Indies slumped to 84 for four when Hirwani's leg-spin accounted for the fluent Lara and Richardson, who came into his own after a slow start. Hooper, at a run a ball, and Best began a revival. But there was another collapse before Ambrose striking the ball firmly off his legs, inspired a rally. India also seemed subdued, and were 38 for two after 19 overs. Then Srikkanth launched a flurry of adventurous shots, and subsequently Tendulkar took charge. Though less belligerent than Srikkanth, he pierced the gaps skilfully and ran sharply between the wickets for his unbeaten 57. India won with 20 balls to spare.

Man of the Match: S. R. Tendulkar.   *Attendance: 13,320.*

West Indies

?. L. Haynes c Pandit b Srinath	14	C. E. L. Ambrose not out	24
?. A. Wallace run out	2	A. C. Cummins not out	10
?. C. Lara st Pandit b Hirwani	11		
R. B. Richardson lbw b Hirwani	20	B 1, l-b 8, w 6, n-b 2	17
?. L. Hooper c Manjrekar b Prabhakar	45		
?. A. Best b Srinath	29	1/21 2/24 3/45 (8 wkts, 50 overs) 175	
?. D. Marshall run out	0	4/84 5/127 6/128	
?O. Williams run out	3	7/138 8/147	

?. P. Patterson did not bat.

Bowling: Prabhakar 9-1-20-1; Kapil Dev 10-2-27-0; Srinath 10-1-39-2; Hirwani ?0-0-34-2; Tendulkar 10-1-38-0; Shastri 1-0-8-0.

India

?. J. Shastri c Hooper b Ambrose	11	Kapil Dev not out	1
?. Srikkanth c Williams b Ambrose	60		
?. V. Manjrekar c Williams b Patterson	2	L-b 11, w 2, n-b 9	22
?. R. Tendulkar not out	57		
M. Azharuddin c Lara b Hooper	5	1/20 2/38 3/100 (5 wkts, 46.4 overs) 176	
?. K. Amre c sub b Hooper	18	4/115 5/169	

?C. S. Pandit, M. Prabhakar, J. Srinath and N. D. Hirwani did not bat.

Bowling: Marshall 10-1-33-0; Ambrose 10-4-17-2; Cummins 10-0-47-0; Patterson ?-1-31-1; Hooper 8-0-35-2; Richardson 0.4-0-2-0.

Umpires: P. J. McConnell and C. D. Timmins.

QUALIFYING TABLE

	Played	Won	Lost	Tied	No result	Points	Net run-rate
Australia	8	5	2	0	1	11	0.06
India	8	3	4	1	0	7	0.10
West Indies	8	2	4	1	1	6	−0.18

AUSTRALIA v INDIA

First Final Match

At Melbourne, January 18 (day/night). Australia won by 88 runs. Toss: Australia. Appropriately chastened by his brief omission, Jones joined Boon to lay the base of a solid total. He played a supporting role to Boon, and then moved into the firing line, without becoming extravagant. His runs came from 96 balls, yet contained only three fours. If India suffered from Kapil Dev bowling below his best, they were compensated when McDermott also had a poor day. On an easy pitch, India threatened to run Australia close as they reached 72 with only one wicket down. But Srikkanth, who had the measure of the bowling, fell to a magnificent catch by Taylor at mid-on. Thereafter, wickets fell at regular intervals, the last five going for only 15 runs.

Attendance: 48,010.

Australia

?. C. Boon c Pandit b Prabhakar	78	S. R. Waugh not out	5
?. R. Marsh c Azharuddin b Tendulkar	21		
?. M. Jones c sub b Kapil Dev	73	L-b 7, w 4, n-b 1	12
?. M. Moody c Amre b Shastri	13		
M. E. Waugh c Amre b Shastri	3	1/54 2/142 3/169 (5 wkts, 50 overs) 233	
*A. R. Border not out	28	4/176 5/216	

?I. A. Healy, P. L. Taylor, C. J. McDermott and M. R. Whitney did not bat.

Bowling: Kapil Dev 10-0-40-1; Prabhakar 10-2-53-1; Srinath 9-2-32-0; Tendulkar 6-0-29-1; Hirwani 5-0-34-0; Shastri 10-0-38-2.

India

R. J. Shastri run out	17	†C. S. Pandit c S. R. Waugh b Taylor .	
K. Srikkanth c Taylor b S. R. Waugh . .	41	J. Srinath run out.	
S. V. Manjrekar c Healy b S. R. Waugh	18	N. D. Hirwani c Marsh b McDermott .	
S. R. Tendulkar c Whitney b Moody. . .	4	L-b 6, w 1, n-b 1.	
*M. Azharuddin c Healy b Moody	13		
P. K. Amre c Border b Taylor	20	1/37 2/72 3/79	(42 overs) 14?
Kapil Dev not out	20	4/84 5/114 6/130	
M. Prabhakar run out	0	7/135 8/136 9/136	

Bowling: McDermott 8-0-27-1; Whitney 8-2-19-0; S. R. Waugh 7-0-32-2; Moody 10-0-34-2; Taylor 9-0-27-2.

Umpires: A. R. Crafter and T. A. Prue.

AUSTRALIA v INDIA

Second Final Match

At Sydney, January 20 (day/night). Australia won by six runs. Toss: Australia. Despite their heavy win two days before, Australia felt the tension no less than India. They fell below their high standards in all departments, but most conspicuously in their fielding. India's main contributors, Shastri and Tendulkar, were missed at 41 and 62 respectively, enabling them to take India to within 88 runs of their objective with 11.2 overs left. Shastri batted for much of his 116 balls with an injured leg, and Tendulkar, weighed down by responsibility, took 69 from 100 balls before he was out to an astonishing catch at extra cover by Whitney. The Indian middle order was unable to sustain the momentum. Their own fielding had also been untidy. Besides letting off Marsh on nine and 39, they presented Australia with a significant proportion of their runs. But Raju's left-arm spin prevented the middle order from building on Marsh's diligence.

Players of the Finals: D. C. Boon and G. R. Marsh. *Attendance:* 34,490.

Australia

G. R. Marsh c Amre b Srinath	78	P. L. Taylor not out.	8
D. C. Boon b Prabhakar	20	C. J. McDermott b Prabhakar	?
D. M. Jones st Pandit b Raju.	9	M. R. Whitney not out	0
T. M. Moody c Tendulkar b Raju	15	L-b 9, w 3, n-b 7.	19
M. E. Waugh st Pandit b Raju	0		
*A. R. Border run out	38	1/47 2/74 3/114	(9 wkts, 50 overs) 208
S. R. Waugh b Prabhakar.	5	4/117 5/168 6/175	
†I. A. Healy run out	11	7/192 8/200 9/208	

Bowling: Kapil Dev 10-1-42-0; Prabhakar 9-0-31-3; Srinath 7-1-30-1; Tendulkar 4-0-18-0; Shastri 10-1-46-0; Raju 10-1-32-3.

India

R. J. Shastri c Whitney b Moody.	61	†C. S. Pandit not out	3
K. Srikkanth c M. E. Waugh b Whitney	11	M. Prabhakar not out	4
S. V. Manjrekar run out	10		
S. R. Tendulkar c Whitney		L-b 3, w 1, n-b 3.	7
b S. R. Waugh .	69		
*M. Azharuddin c Whitney b Border . .	11	1/19 2/45 3/121	(7 wkts, 50 overs) 202
Kapil Dev lbw b McDermott	2	4/146 5/154	
P. K. Amre c Jones b McDermott	22	6/190 7/195	

J. Srinath and S. L. V. Raju did not bat.

Bowling: McDermott 9-1-37-2; Whitney 10-0-32-1; S. R. Waugh 10-1-40-1; Moody 10-1-31-1; Taylor 9-0-44-0; Border 2-0-15-1.

Umpires: P. J. McConnell and S. G. Randell.

ENGLAND WOMEN IN NEW ZEALAND AND AUSTRALIA, 1991-92

By CAROL SALMON

Like their male counterparts, England's women toured New Zealand in early 1992. They won the series of three Tests 1-0. Only wet weather prevented a more comfortable margin, by wiping out most of the last two days in Auckland and all of the third and fourth days in New Plymouth. England were on top in both matches, and achieved a well-deserved four-wicket victory in the Second Test at Wanganui. These were England's first Tests since 1987. A more experienced Australia disposed of the tourists without difficulty when England, by now lacking three key players, crossed the Tasman for the first-ever women's five-day Test. As ever, work commitments and financial considerations restricted the party, each of whom contributed upwards of £1,000 to the tour.

As well as playing in the Tests, England joined New Zealand and Australia in the annual Shell Rosebowl, giving the 60-over competition fresh impetus. This tournament also suffered from the weather. One of England's matches was washed out and the final, which they reached on run-rate, was called off before they could bat. World Cup holders Australia claimed the trophy, having lost only one of their four preliminary matches. It was a fair result, as Australia had amassed a formidable 282 for four in the aborted final, with Denise Annetts scoring an unbeaten 100.

There was only one century for England throughout the tour, Wendy Watson's 153 not out against the New Zealand Under-23 XI in Napier. The most successful batsmen were Carole Hodges, with 483 runs at 34.50, Watson (451 at 34.69) and Janette Brittin (303 at 30.30). Hodges scored 224 runs in the Tests, passing 1,000 in her career; she ended the tour with 1,164 Test runs, third only to Brittin, who reached 1,193 in New Zealand, and the leader Rachael Heyhoe-Flint on 1,814. No less valuable was Hodges's supremely economical off-spin, which brought her 26 wickets on the tour, and ten in the Tests at an average of 13.70. But at Wanganui, where she took no wickets, her 56 overs yielded only 27 runs. Seamer Jo Chamberlain was the chief wicket-taker, with 14 in Tests at 15.92, and 31 on the tour. Behind the stumps Lisa Nye, not always a unanimous selection for England, responded to the challenge from East Midlands keeper Jane Smit with a record-breaking eight dismissals in an innings in the New Plymouth Test.

ENGLAND WOMEN'S TOUR PARTY

Helen Plimmer (Yorks.) (*captain*), Janette Brittin (Surrey) (*vice-captain*), Jo Chamberlain (East Midlands), Janet Godman (Thames Valley), Carole Hodges (Lancs. and Cheshire), Suzie Kitson (East Anglia), Debra Maybury (Yorks.), Sue Metcalfe (Yorks.), Lisa Nye (Middx), Jane Smit (East Midlands), Karen Smithies (East Midlands), Debbie Stock (Thames Valley), Janet Tedstone (Yorks.) and Wendy Watson (East Midlands).

   Manager: Norma Izard (Kent).   *Coach:* Ruth Prideaux (Sussex).

ENGLAND WOMEN'S TOUR RESULTS

Test matches – Played 4: Won 1, Lost 1, Drawn 2.
All matches – Played 12: Won 5, Lost 3, Drawn 3, No result 1. Abandoned 1.
Wins – New Zealand (2), Northern Districts (2), New Zealand President's XI.
Losses – Australia (3).
Draws – New Zealand (2), New Zealand Under-23 XI.
No result – Australia.
Abandoned – New Zealand.

Note: Matches in this section were not first-class.

At Melville Park, Auckland, January 8. England won by 99 runs. England 184 for seven (60 overs) (S. Metcalfe 56 not out); Northern Districts 85 (40.3 overs) (J. M. Chamberlain three for 15).

At Devonport Domain, Auckland, January 9. England won by 51 runs. England 142 for nine (60 overs) (S. J. Kitson 31 not out; E. Drumm four for 27); Northern Districts 91 (46.1 overs) (J. M. Chamberlain five for 26, C. A. Hodges four for 21).

NEW ZEALAND v ENGLAND

First Test Match

At Cornwall Park, Auckland, January 11, 12, 13, 14. Drawn. Toss: England. Despite the loss of nearly two days' play, the First Test ended dramatically when the injured Nancy Williams returned to the wicket to save New Zealand from following on. When play resumed at 2 p.m. on the final day, they needed another 106 to make England bat again, but Williams and Karen Gunn had added 56 when a wild return to the wicket hit Williams on the head. On her return from hospital, she ignored medical advice, returned to the crease at 194 for nine, and was unbeaten on 35 when rain ensured the draw. England's innings of 356 for nine declared had been noteworthy for several landmarks. Brittin, who top scored with 68, became her country's second-highest run-maker in Tests when eight, passing Enid Bakewell's 1,078. With Hodges she added 129, a record for England's third wicket in four-day Tests. Kitson and Tedstone, with an undefeated 55, shared 99 for the ninth wicket, a record in all Tests.

England

*H. Plimmer run out	14	S. J. Kitson b Gunn		35
W. A. Watson b Kainuku	10	J. Tedstone not out		55
C. A. Hodges b Turner	57			
J. A. Brittin c Clark b Turner	68	B 6, l-b 15, w 2		23
S. Metcalfe c Plummer b Gunn	40			
K. Smithies st Fruin b Williams	30	1/18 2/25 3/154	(9 wkts dec.)	356
D. Maybury c Clark b Gunn	17	4/155 5/211 6/229		
J. M. Chamberlain c and b Turner	7	7/249 8/257 9/356		

†L. Nye did not bat.

Bowling: Turner 32–7–89–3; Gunn 44.5–20–68–3; Williams 39–13–66–1; Kainuku 15–3–50–1; Harris 22–9–46–0; Hockley 7–3–16–0.

New Zealand

D. Hockley c Kitson b Tedstone	29	†S. Fruin c Hodges b Smithies	0
J. Clark c Smithies b Hodges	41	J. Harris c Maybury b Hodges	9
*K. Plummer b Chamberlain	1	Y. Kainuku not out	23
K. McDonald c Smithies b Hodges	1	B 7, l-b 3, w 2	12
N. Williams not out	35		
M. Lewis b Kitson	11	1/80 2/80 3/81	(9 wkts) 214
K. Gunn c Maybury b Smithies	49	4/93 5/115 6/178	
J. Turner b Hodges	3	7/179 8/179 9/194	

N. Williams, when 33, retired hurt at 171 and resumed at 194.

Bowling: Chamberlain 26–9–71–1; Smithies 26–15–36–2; Tedstone 17–12–19–1; Hodges 38–30–21–4; Brittin 9–2–12–0; Maybury 5–2–15–0; Kitson 17–7–30–1.

Umpires: T. A. McCall and O. C. Paul.

Shell Rosebowl Tri-Series

At Wellington, January 17. New Zealand v England. Abandoned.

At Wellington, January 18. Australia won by 42 runs. Australia 192 for seven (60 overs) (B. J. Haggett 59, D. A. Annetts 40); England 150 for nine (60 overs) (J. A. Brittin 69; J. Broadbent three for 26).

At Wellington, January 19. Australia won by seven wickets. New Zealand 130 (57 overs) (K. Gunn 49; K. Fazackerley three for 18); Australia 131 for three (39.3 overs) (B. Clark 51 not out, L. Hunter 41).

At Wellington, January 20. England won by 42 runs. England 168 for nine (60 overs) (C. A. Hodges 49, K. Smithies 35; K. Gunn three for 11); New Zealand 126 (56.4 overs) (J. M. Chamberlain three for 20, J. Tedstone three for 27).

At Christchurch, January 22. Australia won by six wickets. England 178 for eight (60 overs) (W. A. Watson 31, J. A. Brittin 40); Australia 179 for four (49 overs) (B. J. Haggett 46, B. Clark 59).

At Christchurch, January 23. New Zealand won by three wickets. Australia 190 for seven (60 overs) (B. J. Haggett 31, B. Clark 36, L. Hunter 47); New Zealand 191 for seven (53.4 overs) (D. Hockley 57, K. Gunn 49, S. McLauchlan 34 not out).

England qualified for the final on run-rate.

Final

At Christchurch, January 25. No result. Australia 282 for four (60 overs) (B. J. Haggett 58, B. Clark 44, D. A. Annetts 100 not out, Z. J. Goss 33 not out) v England.

Australia won the trophy by winning three matches in the preliminary round to England's one.

At Christchurch, January 27, 28, 29. England won by 150 runs. England 244 for eight dec. (W. A. Watson 92, C. A. Hodges 32, J. Godman 33) and 198 for five dec. (S. Metcalfe 62 not out, J. M. Chamberlain 61); New Zealand President's XI 209 for five dec. (J. M. Chamberlain three for 71) and 83 (S. J. Kitson three for 11, D. Stock three for 17).

At Napier, February 1, 2, 3. Drawn. England 247 for six dec. (W. A. Watson 153 not out, K. Smithies 38; E. Drumm three for 58) and 238 for nine dec. (H. Plimmer 65, C. A. Hodges 83, D. Maybury 40); New Zealand Under-23 XI 248 for seven dec. (M. Lewis 67, L. Astle 57, E. Drumm 39) and 157 for eight.

NEW ZEALAND v ENGLAND

Second Test Match

At Cook's Gardens, Wanganui, February 6, 7, 8, 9. England won by four wickets. Toss: New Zealand. All-rounder Hodges was the key player in England's victory. Requiring 173 to win on an unpredictable pitch, they had been reduced to 57 for three, but her watchful 41 put them back on course, and with Metcalfe's 41 set up the win. Earlier, her wonderfully controlled off-spin had reduced New Zealand's batting, notoriously painstaking, to a crawl. Though she claimed no wickets, over two innings her 56 overs cost a mere 27 runs and included 39 maidens. Left-arm seamer Chamberlain reaped the benefit with a match return of eight for 126. The only significant contributions for New Zealand came from Debbie Hockley and Penny Kinsella, whose third-wicket stand of 101 was a record for their country and formed almost half of a first-innings total of 212. Even England's disappointing batting performance on the second day, when they made 137 for nine, offered a moment of triumph for Hodges: when three she became the fifth English woman to reach 1,000 runs in Test cricket.

New Zealand

J. Clark lbw b Kitson	36	– (2) run out	12
*K. Plummer b Chamberlain	1	– (6) run out	4
D. Hockley c Nye b Maybury	79	– (1) run out	22
P. Kinsella c Nye b Chamberlain	53	– (3) c Plummer b Maybury	12
M. Lewis c Hodges b Kitson	2	– (4) b Chamberlain	24
N. Williams b Maybury	5	– (11) c Nye b Chamberlain	1
K. Gunn b Chamberlain	23	– (5) c Metcalfe b Kitson	12
S. McLauchlan b Chamberlain	0	– c Nye b Kitson	0
†S. Fruin lbw b Maybury	2	– (7) c Brittin b Stock	4
J. Turner b Chamberlain	0	– (9) lbw b Chamberlain	4
T. Woodbury not out	0	– (10) not out	7
B 3, l-b 4, w 4	11	L-b 1, w 1	2
	212		**104**

1/7 2/57 3/158 4/168 5/184
6/200 7/205 8/210 9/210

1/35 2/35 3/67 4/78 5/88
6/88 7/88 8/94 9/96

Bowling: *First Innings*—Chamberlain 33–9–84–5; Maybury 21.4–8–37–3; Hodges 30–19–15–0; Kitson 20–8–25–2; Stock 17–7–20–0; Smithies 6–3–10–0; Brittin 4–1–14–0. *Second Innings*—Chamberlain 20.1–5–42–3; Kitson 10–5–16–2; Hodges 26–20–12–0; Smithies 10–5–6–0; Stock 14–5–21–1; Maybury 8–5–6–1.

England

*H. Plummer lbw b Gunn	46	– c Kinsella b Gunn	22
W. A. Watson lbw b McLauchlan	0	– lbw b Turner	4
C. A. Hodges c Lewis b Williams	13	– c Gunn b Woodbury	48
J. A. Brittin c and b Williams	21	– lbw b Hockley	17
S. Metcalfe c Lewis b Woodbury	3	– lbw b Turner	41
K. Smithies b Woodbury	0	– not out	23
J. M. Chamberlain c Lewis b Hockley	13	– c Lewis b Turner	4
D. Maybury lbw b Hockley	0	– not out	13
D. Stock b Turner	22		
S. J. Kitson c Fruin b Turner	4		
†L. Nye not out	11		
B 7, l-b 4	11	L-b 1	1
	144	(6 wkts)	**173**

1/0 2/32 3/60 4/67 5/67
6/87 7/87 8/114 9/118

1/13 2/33 3/57
4/115 5/140 6/144

Bowling: *First Innings*—Turner 26–11–42–2; McLauchlan 5.4–3–7–1; Gunn 27–12–27–1; Woodbury 16–7–29–2; Williams 11.2–7–19–2; Hockley 12–7–9–2. *Second Innings*—Turner 25–14–42–3; Woodbury 17–7–38–1; Gunn 50.2–30–51–1; Williams 24–11–23–0; Hockley 5–2–11–1; McLauchlan 3–1–7–0.

Umpires: R. W. Hutchison and D. Rice.

NEW ZEALAND v ENGLAND

Third Test Match

At Pukekura Park, New Plymouth, February 12, 13, 14, 15. Drawn. Toss: New Zealand. Middlesex wicket-keeper Nye established a Test record for dismissals in an innings with six catches and two stumpings as New Zealand were all out for 142 on the first day. Nye surpassed Beverley Bentall's six dismissals for New Zealand against South Africa in 1972 and established a better mark than the men's Test record of seven. Three of her catches came off the bowling of Chamberlain, who repeated her Second Test feat of five wickets in an innings. Though England captain Plimmer was dismissed in the one over before the close, her colleagues took control on the second day, when Hodges and Watson shared 126 for the second wicket. Only a superb catch by Mai Lewis at point deprived Hodges of her century. Rain throughout the last two days prevented England from exploiting their advantage.

New Zealand

D. Hockley c Nye b Hodges	65	†S. Fruin b Chamberlain	3
J. Clark c Nye b Chamberlain	13	J. Turner c Nye b Chamberlain	4
P. Kinsella c Nye b Hodges	17	T. Woodbury not out	0
M. Lewis c Nye b Chamberlain	14		
K. Gunn c Kitson b Chamberlain	0	L-b 5, w 5	10
E. Drumm c Nye b Kitson	12		
*K. Plummer st Nye b Hodges	0	1/25 2/61 3/86 4/86 5/114	142
S. McLauchlan st Nye b Hodges	4	6/117 7/121 8/136 9/141	

Bowling: Chamberlain 23–15–26–5; Tedstone 14–4–26–0; Maybury 6–3–4–0; Kitson 13–4–32–1; Hodges 28–14–24–4; Smithies 21–11–25–0.

England

*H. Plimmer c and b Turner	0	D. Maybury lbw b Turner	4
W. A. Watson c McLauchlan b Hockley	70	J. Tedstone not out	4
C. A. Hodges c Lewis b Gunn	96		
J. A. Brittin lbw b Woodbury	16	B 1, w 1	2
S. Metcalfe c Plummer b Turner	10		
K. Smithies b McLauchlan	8	1/0 2/126 3/150 4/172	(7 wkts) 228
J. M. Chamberlain not out	18	5/195 6/215 7/223	

S. J. Kitson and †L. Nye did not bat.

Bowling: Turner 20–8–49–3; Drumm 19–3–48–0; Woodbury 16–5–33–1; McLauchlan 18–6–41–1; Hockley 13–6–18–1; Gunn 27–10–38–1.

Umpires: B. Pitcairn and G. Webby.

AUSTRALIA v ENGLAND

Five-day Test Match

At North Sydney Oval, February 19, 20, 21, 22, 23. Australia won by an innings and 85 runs. Toss: England. Australia re-emphasised their superiority in women's cricket through an innings win in this, the first five-day Test played by women. Lacking three key players in Brittin, Chamberlain and Smithies, England were bowled out within a day for 146, with Hodges suffering a rare failure. When Australia batted she embarked on a lengthy spell of off-spin, which brought her two wickets, but the home nation amassed 346 from 150 overs before declaring. Denise Annetts, who scored an unbeaten hundred off England's bowling in the Shell Rosebowl final, plundered another and shared a fourth-wicket stand of 222 with her captain and New South Wales colleague, Lyn Larsen. The third day had been washed out, and England were almost saved by a three-hour interruption when they were 114 for nine on the last day, but the weather relented long enough for Smit to be dismissed, giving Australia the crushing victory they deserved.

England

*H. Plimmer b Mason	26	– c Matthews b Fazackerley	26
W. A. Watson b Brown	35	– c Larsen b Tsakiris	29
C. A. Hodges c Goss b Mason	10	– c Larsen b Tsakiris	0
S. Metcalfe b Tsakiris	25	– lbw b Hunter	0
J. Godman c Brown b Tsakiris	12	– lbw b Hunter	0
D. Maybury c Brown b Tsakiris	8	– c Annetts b Mason	4
D. Stock c Matthews b Tsakiris	4	– (8) c Matthews b Brown	18
†L. Nye st Matthews b Larsen	6	– (9) c Matthews b Mason	16
J. Tedstone c Matthews b Mason	11	– (7) b Tsakiris	14
S. J. Kitson c Brown b Mason	0	– not out	4
J. Smit not out	1	– c Brown b Mason	1
B 2, l-b 4, w 2	8	L-b 3	3

1/46 2/62 3/87 4/112 5/115　　　　　146　　1/51 2/56 3/57 4/57 5/57　　　　115
6/124 7/127 8/133 9/137　　　　　　　　　6/75 7/75 8/102 9/113

Bowling: *First Innings*—Goss 12–3–19–0; Mason 21.5–6–40–4; Brown 20–6–36–1; Fazackerley 11–6–6–0; Tsakiris 27–16–27–4; Larsen 11–6–12–1; Hunter 1–1–0–0. *Second Innings*—Goss 8–4–12–0; Mason 25.2–11–39–3; Brown 15–6–19–1; Fazackerley 14–10–5–1; Tsakiris 23–14–18–3; Larsen 3–0–6–0; Hunter 11–8–7–2; Annetts 3–1–6–0.

Australia

B. J. Haggett st Nye b Hodges	32	Z. J. Goss not out		4
B. Clark c Plimmer b Stock	28	B 2, l-b 13, w 2		17
D. A. Annetts not out	148			
L. Hunter lbw b Hodges	31	1/57 2/69	(4 wkts dec.)	346
*L. A. Larsen c Watson b Maybury	86	3/117 4/339		

†C. Matthews, K. M. Brown, K. Fazackerley, C. Mason and I. Tsakiris did not bat.

Bowling: Kitson 31–12–57–0; Tedstone 32–9–78–0; Maybury 35–7–86–1; Hodges 38–10–65–2; Stock 14–1–45–1.

Umpires: S. Harman and G. E. Reed.

ONE HUNDRED YEARS AGO

From JOHN WISDEN'S CRICKETERS' ALMANACK FOR 1893

LORD SHEFFIELD'S TEAM IN AUSTRALIA: "Beyond everything else the tour was remarkable for the reappearance in Australia, after an interval of eighteen years, of Mr W. G. Grace. When the most famous of all cricketers visited the Colonies in 1873 he was at the very height of his powers, and not a few of his warmest admirers regarded it as rather a hazardous venture on his part to go out again at so late a period in his career. Events proved, however, that Mr Grace's confidence in himself was not misplaced. Alike in the eleven-a-side matches and in all engagements he came out at the head of the batting averages. When we remember that he was in his forty-fourth year, and that his position as the finest batsman in the world had been established at a time when all the other members of the team were children, this feat must be pronounced nothing less than astonishing."

HINTS FROM THE PRESS BOX By C.S.C.: "Another help to reporters I should like to see extended to all grounds would be the erection of scoring boards, upon which each run is registered as it is made, such as are in use at Lord's, Kennington Oval, and Nottingham, and the practice at Lord's, the Oval, and Brighton of granting newspaper men unlimited printed slips of the score during the day is also a great convenience. A Press Box should be placed as nearly as possible in a line with the two wickets, so that an end-on view is obtained therefrom, and it should be raised a considerable height from the ground, with the scorers close at hand, and the telegraph clerks below. These requirements are absolutely necessary for the due fulfilment of a cricket reporter's duties . . ."

CRICKET IN AUSTRALIA, 1991-92

By JOHN MACKINNON

The Sheffield Shield season came to a marvellous climax in Perth where Western Australia fought off a sustained challenge from New South Wales to win the Shield for the 13th time. But it was not much of a climax for most of Australia, with the World Cup finishing three days before the game began and the Eastern seaboard already pre-occupied with its various forms of football. Television showed its traditional disregard for what was arguably the best match of the season.

It is a wonder that the Sheffield Shield competition survives, and the players must take credit for their ability to adapt from limited-overs games. Some pay a heavy price for the higgledy-piggledy schedule. Steve Waugh was Australia's champion in 1989. In 1992, at the ripe old age of 26, and battling to salvage his international career, he went into the Shield final with only nine first-class innings behind him. He took on the best pace bowling combination in the land and amassed scores of 113 and 68 batting at No. 3. It made no immediate impact on the national selectors.

At least there was no clash with a tour and the two teams contesting the final were at full strength. Western Australia, in keeping with their tradition, had depth in batting and pace bowling, a combination ideally suited to the Perth climate and wicket. In the final Justin Langer, in his first year, and Damien Martyn, with only a handful of games behind him, showed that they were ready to survive and even flourish at the top level. Langer, a 21-year-old left-hander whose uncle, Rob, played for the state in the 1970s, got his chance when Geoff Marsh was with Australia and might have missed the final but for an injury to Mark Lavender. Not only did he save his side from likely defeat, he went on to set up a platform for victory with some wonderfully mature batting. Martyn, Australia's Under-19 captain on the 1991 tour of England, made a telling contribution to the same rescue act and was selected for the senior touring team to Sri Lanka. He was comfortably Western Australia's most prolific run-scorer, a brilliant fieldsman, useful bowler and even shared the wicket-keeping with Tim Zoehrer and Mike Veletta against Victoria in December. But Zoehrer was versatility itself. Against South Australia, he surrendered his keeping gloves to Veletta, bowled 40 overs of leg-spin, took seven wickets and established a pattern. In all, he took 15 wickets, scored five fifties and took 38 catches, three of them off his own bowling.

The team had plenty more batting talent in Wayne Andrews, Lavender, Veletta and, when available, Marsh and Tom Moody. Moody's bowling, too, was invaluable, enabling Western Australia to call on six top-class pace bowlers, many of giant physique, including Jo Angel, who was the state's leading wicket-taker in his first season. Of the older players, Terry Alderman was steady, but never threatened to win back his international place, Bruce Reid waged his traditional battle with injury, while Ken MacLeay played only one first-class game. Brendan Julian showed promise in his first full season. Coach Daryl Foster, in mid-contract with Kent, decided to finish his distinguished career at Western Australia on a high note and handed over to Alderman.

New South Wales began their season with a flourish, annihilating all and sundry in the limited-overs FAI Cup. This included an unexpected demolition of Western Australia at Perth in the final, and they returned there a few days later to make first-innings points, courtesy of twin centuries from the Waughs. By Christmas, however, they languished at the bottom of the table with a miserable four points and outright losses to Queensland, Tasmania and South Australia. The New Year heralded a change in fortunes: Greg Matthews and the newcomer, David Freedman, spun them to three victories in Sydney and the fast bowlers despatched Tasmania in Hobart. Matthews had an outstanding season, becoming the first Australian this century to achieve the double of 500 runs and 50 wickets, and persuading the selectors to recall him yet again for the tour of Sri Lanka. His bowling benefited immeasurably from the unearthing of the left-arm wrist-spinner Freedman from the Sydney reserve grade. Significantly, Freedman obtained all but three of his 22 wickets in Sydney; his selection for the final in Perth was probably misguided, but his support for Matthews was instrumental in New South Wales's end-of-season charge. The pace bowling depended on the occasionally devastating but still erratic Wayne Holdsworth, the spasmodically fit 34-year-old Geoff Lawson and the ever-competitive left-armer Michael Whitney. Whitney's form got better and better, and he had acquired the ability to bring the ball in to the right-hander. His success at international level received widespread acclaim.

By its own high standards, the New South Wales batting was often brittle. The opening partnerships were inconsistent, with Mark Taylor's brilliant hundred at the MCG his only par performance. It was as well that Mark Waugh was dropped from the Test team, as he applied himself to making Shield hundreds instead. His brother's predicament has already been analysed, and the rest of the batting was mostly Matthews. Michael Bevan, in his third season, was the most conspicuous disappointment. At 21, he had a fine array of shots and a quick eye, yet he fell repeatedly to wild slashes or injudicious pulls. For Lawson, the Shield final was an emotional end to a distinguished career. His 367 Shield wickets (one more than Alderman's) put him second to Clarrie Grimmett, with 513, and his captaincy was a revelation, never lacking in courage or imagination, and never ignoring a chance of outright victory even at the risk of defeat. Some starchy critics saw it differently; other captains could do worse than emulate him.

Defending champions Victoria were the only undefeated state, but this was a very limited achievement since they failed to make the final. It was laudable that they took first-innings points from eight out of ten games, but they converted these to only two outright wins. In both victories Dean Jones's emphatic double centuries set up totals of 500, and the bowlers were able to do the rest. Otherwise, they eliminated all possibility of defeat before thinking of victory, even against non-contenders like Tasmania. Jones had made only modest contributions for Victoria in recent years. This time, he answered his critics with four hundreds – three of them double-hundreds – in five games, and gave the batting the sort of impetus that breeds confidence in colleagues. Darren Lehmann, the big left-hander, seemed to have settled in after huge expectations the previous year. Warren Ayres, initially dumped from the squad, justified his recall, and Wayne Phillips established himself as a gritty opening batsman. His exposure to the last Test against India, however, was a selectors' whim and unfair to the player, especially as he was replacing the apparently irreplaceable Marsh. Paul Nobes arrived from South Australia and, with the help of the Supreme Court, reversed the Australian Cricket Board's ban on players representing two states in one season; he had played for his native state in the FAI Cup. But Australia's Shield Player of the Year was Tony Dodemaide. Once again he took time to recover from a rigorous English county campaign, but in seven matches he took 37 wickets. His bowling form improved as his rhythm and confidence developed, and for good measure he scored his maiden Shield hundred. The selectors duly rewarded him with a trip to Sri Lanka. Merv Hughes appeared to combat the long season by carrying an inch or two extra round the waist; he was still combative, formidable and wholehearted. Paul Reiffel's improvement was a mixed blessing. He carried the drinks for Australia a couple of times before getting a belated chance in Perth. Shane Warne became the new leg-spinning hope, thanks to some promising returns in Zimbabwe, and dismissing mostly tailenders for the Australian XI against the West Indies. Again expectation exceeded fulfilment, but Warne demonstrated control if not variety; that may come with experience. The captain, Simon O'Donnell, was frustrated both in terms of personal and team achievement. His own battle for form may have contributed towards the caution of his leadership.

Queensland's campaign got off to a dynamic start, with 14 points from the first three games. Runs flowed from the bats of the newcomer Matthew Hayden, Dirk Wellham, now with his third State, and Allan Border. The fast bowlers, Craig McDermott, Carl Rackemann and Greg Rowell, were irresistible. Then, with the onset of the international season and the loss of McDermott, Border and Ian Healy, points became an elusive commodity. The team took only two from the last seven games. On the credit side was the form of Hayden, a 20-year-old left-hander, who not only scored 149 in his first match but went on to beat Mark Taylor's first-season aggregate record. He ultimately exceeded 1,000 runs, the only Australian other than Dean Jones to do so. Wellham had his best year since leaving New South Wales for Tasmania, while Trevor Barsby was a useful opening partner for Hayden. Much was expected of Stuart Law, but the Shield Player of the Year in 1990-91 scored only two fifties in 17 innings this time. Greg Ritchie returned after a year's retirement, and scored splendid hundreds against Western Australia and the Indians, but never achieved the desired level of fitness and retired again, in dispute over contract payments. Rowell's arrival from New South Wales was a great boost to the bowling but, with McDermott away so often, Rackemann had to carry the attack and the captaincy. Healy took over the leadership for 1992-93, but the team needed more depth in pace bowling plus a spinner.

South Australia were in difficulties from the start. The arrival of Jamie Siddons from Victoria created much excitement and anticipation and he was immediately put in charge, which left two former captains, David Hookes and Andrew Hilditch, licking their wounds; Hookes even considered playing in Victoria, but soon returned to play out his time in Adelaide. Nobes's departure after a dispute with the coach did nothing to ease Siddons's task, and the season was always destined to be a struggle. In their contrasting styles, Siddons and Hilditch led the batting, the one never quite able to repeat his feats on the Adelaide Oval when visiting with Victoria, the other plodding away with no lack of dedication but often with considerable lack of support. Hookes passed John Inverarity's Shield run-scoring record, reaching 9,364, but at 36 retired to concentrate on sports broadcasting. He may have left the game disillusioned, and wishing he had never hit five consecutive fours off Tony Greig on his début in the Centenary Test, but he was never dull. Like the late Les Favell, he could empty nearby offices and fill the Oval with his followers. The rest of the batting was workmanlike, with Greg Blewett, Jamie Brayshaw and Joe Scuderi making useful runs. Scuderi continued to improve as an all-rounder, bowling nearly 400 overs in a desperately undermanned attack. Tim May managed 17 wickets from more than 400 overs, and Denis Hickey was expensive. Shining through the gloom was the day in early February when Peter Sleep's involuntary edge off Carl Rackemann took South Australia's total to a match-winning 506 and an indelible entry in the history books.

Tasmania's prospects rested substantially on the broad shoulders of their left-arm fast bowling recruit from Western Australia, Chris Matthews. He did not let them down, taking 48 Shield wickets, a State record. There was little else to celebrate, however. Of the batsmen, only Danny Buckingham measured up consistently, and the bowling depended too heavily on Matthews, Rod Tucker and Dave Gilbert. Gilbert gave up his battle with injury and retired at the end of the season. International calls spared David Boon for only four Shield games, but he won the prestigious Lord's Taverners Cricketer of the Year award, voted on by players for performance in all the competitions of a congested season.

So the year of the World Cup ended with the strong Shield sides seeming stronger and the weak in dire straits. It was symptomatic of the age that, in reviewing Australia's failure in the Cup, the Board hierarchy regretted the involvement of squad members in first-class cricket the week before the competition began. Regret that batsmen should be allowed a decent bat and bowlers a decent bowl is an intriguing assessment, when limited-overs cricket denies most participants these opportunities. Pakistan included two three-day matches in their World Cup preparation, and in the long term that did them no harm at all.

FIRST-CLASS AVERAGES, 1991-92

BATTING

(Qualification: 500 runs)

	M	I	NO	R	HS	100s	Avge
D. M. Jones (*Vic.*)	10	15	2	1,248	243*	5	96.00
D. C. Boon (*Tas.*)	10	16	2	819	135	4	58.50
D. M. Wellham (*Qld*)	10	18	3	873	167	2	58.20
A. R. Border (*Qld*)	11	19	6	747	196	1	57.46
D. S. Lehmann (*Vic.*)	11	19	4	846	148	3	56.40
T. M. Moody (*WA*)	8	13	1	652	168	2	54.33
M. L. Hayden (*Qld*)	11	21	2	1,028	149	3	54.10
D. R. Martyn (*WA*)	11	19	3	822	110	2	51.37
M. E. Waugh (*NSW*)	12	18	0	924	163	3	51.33
G. M. Ritchie (*Qld*)	11	19	3	748	137	2	46.75
J. D. Siddons (*SA*)	9	14	0	650	149	2	46.42
A. M. J. Hilditch (*SA*)	10	17	1	721	137	2	45.06
W. S. Andrews (*WA*)	11	17	2	663	98	0	44.20

	M	I	NO	R	HS	100s	Avge
J. L. Langer (*WA*)	7	12	0	527	149	2	43.91
J. A. Brayshaw (*SA*)	7	12	0	516	101	1	43.00
T. J. Barsby (*Qld*)	11	21	1	848	165	1	42.40
D. J. Buckingham (*Tas.*)	11	17	1	662	110	1	41.37
T. J. Zoehrer (*WA*)	11	17	3	579	88	0	41.35
M. R. J. Veletta (*WA*)	11	19	2	684	121	2	40.23
M. A. Taylor (*NSW*)	14	24	1	925	158	2	40.21
G. R. J. Matthews (*NSW*) . .	12	17	2	603	139	1	40.20
G. R. Marsh (*WA*)	8	15	1	559	104	1	39.92
J. C. Scuderi (*SA*)	9	14	1	502	125*	2	38.61
W. N. Phillips (*Vic.*)	9	16	1	577	123	1	38.46
M. G. Bevan (*NSW*)	12	17	1	588	115	1	36.75
M. P. Lavender (*WA*)	10	17	1	580	172	1	36.25
G. S. Blewett (*SA*)	10	18	2	571	98	0	35.68
D. W. Hookes (*SA*)	10	17	0	530	156	1	31.17
S. M. Small (*NSW*)	12	18	1	511	98	0	30.05

* *Signifies not out.*

BOWLING

(Qualification: 20 wickets)

	O	M	R	W	BB	5W/i	Avge
D. A. Freedman (*NSW*)	147.2	35	409	22	4-17	0	18.59
A. I. C. Dodemaide (*Vic.*)	360	110	858	43	6-80	2	19.95
C. J. McDermott (*Qld*)	441.2	105	1,248	60	6-58	6	20.80
B. A. Reid (*WA*)	261.2	76	697	33	6-55	3	21.12
G. R. J. Matthews (*NSW*)	482.4	153	1,116	52	6-63	4	21.46
M. R. Whitney (*NSW*)	391.5	84	1,122	52	7-27	3	21.57
C. D. Matthews (*Tas.*)	418.5	89	1,182	53	6-89	6	22.30
M. G. Hughes (*Vic.*)	495.1	120	1,339	53	4-32	0	25.26
J. Angel (*WA*)	223.4	40	787	31	4-46	0	25.38
C. G. Rackemann (*Qld*)	395.2	101	1,043	34	5-89	1	30.67
G. J. Rowell (*Qld*)	372.5	77	1,099	35	7-46	2	31.40
P. R. Reiffel (*Vic.*)	304.1	67	915	29	4-44	0	31.55
W. J. Holdsworth (*NSW*)	341.2	67	1,201	38	6-33	1	31.60
T. M. Alderman (*WA*)	351.2	104	923	29	5-51	1	31.82
B. P. Julian (*WA*)	262.2	69	809	25	5-26	1	32.36
J. C. Scuderi (*SA*)	393.2	114	1,053	28	7-79	1	37.60
S. K. Warne (*Vic.*)	312	81	853	20	4-42	0	42.65
D. J. Hickey (*SA*)	305.4	41	1,234	22	4-96	0	56.09

SHEFFIELD SHIELD, 1991-92

	Played	Won	Lost	Drawn	1st-inns Points	Points	Quotient
Western Australia	10	4	2	4	4	28	1.197
New South Wales	10	4	3	3	4	28	1.143
Victoria	10	2	0	8	12	24	1.314
Queensland	10	2	3*	5	4	16	1.033
South Australia	10	2	4*	4	2	14	0.752
Tasmania	10	1	3	6	8	14	0.687

* *1 outright loss after leading on first innings.*
Outright win = 6 pts; lead on first innings in a drawn or lost game = 2 pts.
Quotient = runs per wkt scored divided by runs per wkt conceded.

Final: Western Australia beat New South Wales by 44 runs.

Under Australian Cricket Board playing conditions, two extras are scored for every no-ball bowled whether scored off or not. Any runs scored off the bat are credited to the batsman, while byes and leg-byes are counted as no-balls, in accordance with Law 24.9, in addition to the initial penalty.

QUEENSLAND v SOUTH AUSTRALIA

At Brisbane, November 1, 2, 3, 4. Drawn. Queensland 2 pts. Toss: South Australia. Batsmen thrived on a pitch which reduced pace and spin bowlers alike to bit players. It was an ideal initiation for 20-year-old Matthew Hayden, who dominated a 209-run partnership with the itinerant Wellham (now with his third state) and demonstrated power and timing with 23 fours in 251 minutes. Border also made the most of the conditions, taking only five hours over 196, hitting 24 fours and two sixes. It was his highest score for Queensland, and he shared stands of 157 and 156 with Law and Ritchie, until he was run out in a mix-up with Ritchie, at which point Rackemann declared. Siddons, captaining South Australia on his first-class début for the state, led the reply. He lasted until McDermott produced a fiery spell with the new ball. Nielsen and May then took their side to 533 for eight, with a real chance of first-innings points, until McDermott dismissed them both. But his 15 no-balls, each counting for two runs under ACB rules, contributed 30 to a world record of 78 extras. Normally, the total of extras would have been 40, with 22 no-balls. Under these rules, the eight that were scored off were added to the 22 and doubled to make 60.

Close of play: First day, Queensland 366-3 (A. R. Border 61*, S. G. Law 43*); Second day, South Australia 169-2 (M. P. Faull 50*, J. D. Siddons 69*); Third day, South Australia 495-7 (T. J. Nielsen 59*, T. B. A. May 15*).

Queensland

T. J. Barsby c Siddons b Hickey	4	– c Nielsen b Hickey	12
M. L. Hayden c Bishop b Faull	149	– lbw b Scuderi	5
D. M. Wellham c Nielsen b Scuderi	80	– (7) not out	63
A. R. Border run out	196	– (8) not out	39
S. G. Law c Blewett b Scuderi	64	– (6) c Hilditch b Hickey	22
G. M. Ritchie not out	53	– (4) c Faull b George	6
†I. A. Healy (did not bat)	–	(3) b George	48
P. L. Taylor (did not bat)	–	(5) run out	12
L-b 16, n-b 26	42	L-b 4, w 6, n-b 22	32

1/8 2/217 3/275 4/432 5/588   (5 wkts dec.) 588   1/14 2/38 3/47   (6 wkts) 239
                                                4/91 5/101 6/148

C. J. McDermott, G. J. Rowell and *C. G. Rackemann did not bat.

Bowling: *First Innings*—Hickey 28.3-1-129-1; Scuderi 33-6-143-2; George 20-3-72-0; May 43-5-151-0; Faull 4-1-22-1; Hookes 9-2-33-0; Blewett 2-0-22-0. *Second Innings*—Hickey 15-1-73-2; Scuderi 17-7-40-1; George 10-0-57-2; May 5-1-30-0; Blewett 7-2-23-0; Hilditch 1-0-12-0.

South Australia

G. S. Blewett c Border b Rowell	18	J. C. Scuderi c Law b McDermott	37
A. M. J. Hilditch lbw b McDermott	4	T. B. A. May lbw b McDermott	33
M. P. Faull run out	51	D. J. Hickey run out	6
*J. D. Siddons c Border b McDermott	149	S. P. George not out	0
G. A. Bishop c Rackemann		B 1, l-b 16, w 1, n-b 60	78
b McDermott	64		
D. W. Hookes c Wellham b Rackemann	26	1/9 2/29 3/178 4/311 5/361	554
†T. J. Nielsen c Healy b McDermott	88	6/367 7/441 8/533 9/554	

Bowling: McDermott 45-7-150-6; Rowell 31-8-89-1; Rackemann 34-5-124-1; Taylor 42.1-14-122-0; Border 19-6-52-0.

Umpires: M. D. Ralston and C. D. Timmins.

VICTORIA v TASMANIA

At Melbourne, November 1, 2, 3, 4. Drawn. Victoria 2 pts. Toss: Victoria. Both teams struggled to combat a slow pitch and an unyielding outfield and it took Jones to save the match from being totally forgettable. Restored to No. 3, he was virtually untroubled by Tasmania's pace-oriented attack. He was deferential at first, with 122 in five and a half hours on the first day. But he almost doubled his score in three and a half hours on the second, and looked good for quite a few more when O'Donnell declared. Tasmania's ambitions were inevitably limited to first-innings points. They demonstrated the ease of survival but the comparative difficulty of scoring as they ground out 240 runs on the third day while Victoria prised out just three batsmen. On the last morning, Hughes ended the stand of 152 between Cox and Buckingham before Warne was rewarded for a long and accurate spell of leg-spin with four for 75. In the last three hours the Victorian débutant Dowling and Ramshaw had some gentle batting practice.

Close of play: First day, Victoria 248-5 (D. M. Jones 122*, P. R. Reiffel 5*); Second day, Tasmania 68-2 (D. C. Boon 7*, C. D. Matthews 0*); Third day, Tasmania 308-5 (J. Cox 68*, D. J. Buckingham 70*).

Victoria

G. P. Dowling c Holyman b Tucker	41	– not out	43
D. J. Ramshaw c Cruse b Gilbert	14	– not out	58
D. M. Jones not out	243		
D. S. Lehmann c Holyman b Buckingham	30		
*S. P. O'Donnell b Matthews	0		
G. J. Allardice c Tucker b Gilbert	12		
P. R. Reiffel c Holyman b Gilbert	5		
M. G. Hughes b Buckingham	12		
†D. S. Berry b Campbell	33		
S. K. Warne not out	11		
B 2, l-b 9, n-b 22	33	B 1, l-b 3, n-b 4	8

1/27 2/106 3/175 4/178 5/214   (8 wkts dec.) 434   (no wkt) 109
6/248 7/282 8/400

D. W. Fleming did not bat.

Bowling: *First Innings*—Gilbert 33-8-81-3; Campbell 30-6-96-1; Matthews 34-8-81-1; Tucker 26-6-73-1; Buckingham 23-2-88-2; Hughes 2-0-4-0. *Second Innings*—Gilbert 6-1-19-0; Campbell 8-3-11-0; Matthews 5-3-11-0; Tucker 6-4-4-0; Buckingham 10-3-20-0; Hughes 13-3-28-0; Cruse 7-0-12-0.

Tasmania

R. J. Bennett run out	31	†J. F. Holyman lbw b Reiffel	2	
B. A. Cruse b Warne	25	D. R. Gilbert c O'Donnell b Warne	2	
*D. C. Boon c Ramshaw b O'Donnell	35	G. D. Campbell not out	2	
C. D. Matthews c Lehmann b O'Donnell	40			
R. J. Tucker c Berry b Warne	7	B 5, l-b 7, n-b 23	35	
J. Cox c Berry b Warne	82			
D. J. Buckingham c Berry b Hughes	73	1/53 2/59 3/125 4/144 5/162	372	
G. A. Hughes b Reiffel	38	6/314 7/340 8/347 9/358		

Bowling: Hughes 32-5-80-1; Fleming 32-7-82-0; Warne 47-14-75-4; Reiffel 28.1-8-61-2; O'Donnell 20-5-50-2; Jones 8-5-11-0; Lehmann 3-2-1-0.

Umpires: P. H. Jensen and L. J. King.

WESTERN AUSTRALIA v NEW SOUTH WALES

At Perth, November 1, 2, 3, 4. Drawn. New South Wales 2 pts. Toss: New South Wales. Buoyed up by their win at the WACA in the FAI Cup final a few days earlier, New South Wales had the better of this match until rain eliminated most of the fourth day. Outstanding batting by the Waugh twins secured first-innings points. The same fixture the previous season produced their record partnership of 464. This time they put on only 98 together but their centuries dominated the innings. No other batsman, apart from the watchful Taylor, was able to combat the wiles of Alderman and a late burst from Angel, a pacy stand-in for Reid. Earlier, the New South Wales bowlers were well in control after Lawson put Western Australia in: the first ball of the match was an in-swinger from Whitney which claimed Veletta. Matthews tied up one end so completely that he conceded only 26 in 29 overs, but he also earned a $A500 fine for disputing umpire McConnell's rejection of a bat/pad appeal against Lavender. Lavender remained to hold the fort for six hours as his team lurched towards a reasonable total of 294.

Close of play: First day, Western Australia 219-6 (T. J. Zoehrer 16*); Second day, New South Wales 252-5 (M. E. Waugh 76*, P. A. Emery 1*); Third day, Western Australia 208-4 (D. R. Martyn 13*, W. S. Andrews 9*).

Western Australia

M. R. J. Veletta c Small b Whitney	0	– (2) lbw b Whitney	14
*G. R. Marsh b Holdsworth	53	– (1) c Taylor b S. R. Waugh	98
M. P. Lavender b Lawson	71	– c S. R. Waugh b Holdsworth	34
T. M. Moody c Taylor b Holdsworth	5	– c and b Matthews	20
D. R. Martyn c S. R. Waugh b M. E. Waugh	57	– c M. E. Waugh b S. R. Waugh	22
W. S. Andrews c Emery b M. E. Waugh	0	– not out	25
†T. J. Zoehrer b Whitney	58	– not out	23
B. P. Julian c Emery b Lawson	3		
M. J. McCague c M. E. Waugh b Matthews	18		
J. Angel not out	7		
T. M. Alderman c Taylor b Whitney	5		
L-b 4, w 1, n-b 12	17	B 6, l-b 13, n-b 4	23

1/0 2/92 3/102 4/184 5/184   294   1/37 2/121 3/182   (5 wkts) 259
6/219 7/243 8/282 9/282   4/182 5/222

Bowling: *First Innings*—Whitney 20.2-4-54-3; Holdsworth 19-1-80-2; S. R. Waugh 12-5-33-0; Lawson 24-4-66-2; Matthews 29-16-26-1; Bevan 8-1-20-0; M. E. Waugh 6-3-11-2. *Second Innings*—Whitney 19-4-62-1; Holdsworth 17-5-65-1; S. R. Waugh 13-4-26-2; Lawson 12-3-25-0; Matthews 19-3-53-1; M. E. Waugh 2-0-9-0.

New South Wales

S. M. Small c Veletta b Alderman	0	*G. F. Lawson b Alderman	4
M. A. Taylor c Alderman b Julian	39	M. R. Whitney c Veletta b Angel	0
S. R. Waugh lbw b Alderman	115	W. J. Holdsworth not out	0
M. E. Waugh c Zoehrer b Angel	136		
M. G. Bevan c Zoehrer b Alderman	11	L-b 5, w 1, n-b 6	12
T. H. Bayliss c Zoehrer b Moody	3		
†P. A. Emery c Marsh b McCague	6	1/1 2/115 3/213 4/239 5/250	332
G. R. J. Matthews lbw b Angel	6	6/277 7/323 8/328 9/328	

Bowling: McCague 21-5-81-1; Alderman 33.2-9-101-4; Angel 11-1-54-3; Moody 13-1-39-1; Julian 13-3-52-1.

Umpires: P. J. McConnell and T. A. Prue.

NEW SOUTH WALES v VICTORIA

At Sydney, November 8, 9, 10, 11. Drawn. New South Wales 2 pts. Toss: New South Wales. Easily the best day of this match was the first, when control shifted between the two sides. Small got away to a spectacular start: swinging hard and often, he reached 50 in 37 balls and was unluckily run out, backing up, by a ricochet off Hughes. Steve Waugh batted beautifully for 225 minutes, but Hughes and Reiffel ran through the middle order. Then Matthews flung his bat at pace and spin alike. By the time he missed a slower ball from O'Donnell, New South Wales had set up the game perfectly, scoring at more than four an over, so that Victoria were batting by mid-morning on the second day. Their reply was painful to players and spectators; only Jones gave it any class or momentum. Ramshaw's

316-minute fifty was the slowest ever by an Australian, and Victoria eventually followed on, 199 behind. Second time around, Ramshaw managed to play some shots, but again it was Jones who held up New South Wales. He batted over six hours, hit 17 fours and when he finally missed a full toss from Whitney, Victoria were safe.

Close of play: First day, New South Wales 368-6 (G. R. J. Matthews 81*, P. A. Emery 27*); Second day, Victoria 164-4 (D. J. Ramshaw 38*, D. W. Fleming 4*); Third day, Victoria 153-2 (D. M. Jones 72*, D. S. Berry 7*).

New South Wales

S. M. Small run out	79	*G. F. Lawson b O'Donnell	27
M. A. Taylor c Berry b Hughes	2	M. R. Whitney run out	0
S. R. Waugh c Berry b Reiffel	88	W. J. Holdsworth not out	0
M. E. Waugh b Hughes	19		
M. G. Bevan b Reiffel	14	B 3, l-b 9, n-b 18	30
T. H. Bayliss c Jones b Reiffel	34		
G. R. J. Matthews b O'Donnell	139	1/27 2/147 3/182 4/200 5/247	459
†P. A. Emery c Berry b Hughes	27	6/274 7/368 8/449 9/459	

Bowling: Hughes 28–6–111–3; Fleming 19–4–82–0; Reiffel 25–3–112–3; O'Donnell 19.1–5–66–2; Warne 22–3–76–0.

Victoria

G. P. Dowling lbw b Holdsworth	5	– lbw b Whitney	10
D. J. Ramshaw c Matthews b Whitney	53	– c Small b Matthews	60
D. M. Jones lbw b S. R. Waugh	68	– lbw b Whitney	144
D. S. Lehmann c M. E. Waugh b Holdsworth	3	– (5) c Emery b Matthews	66
*S. P. O'Donnell c Matthews b M. E. Waugh	34	– (6) b M. E. Waugh	5
D. W. Fleming c S. R. Waugh b Matthews	7		
G. J. Allardice b Matthews	0	– not out	38
P. R. Reiffel not out	42	– not out	29
M. G. Hughes c M. E. Waugh b Whitney	8		
†D. S. Berry lbw b Matthews	3	– (4) c S. R. Waugh b Matthews	7
S. K. Warne c sub b M. E. Waugh	16		
B 1, l-b 10, n-b 10	21	B 5, l-b 3, w 1, n-b 26	35

1/8 2/89 3/97 4/156 5/168	260	1/25 2/135 3/153	(6 wkts) 394
6/172 7/186 8/194 9/203		4/291 5/300 6/328	

Bowling: First Innings—Holdsworth 18–3–49–2; Whitney 24–6–52–2; Lawson 24–9–47–0; Matthews 34–17–52–3; S. R. Waugh 7–2–15–1; Bevan 6–0–19–0; M. E. Waugh 4.5–1–15–2. *Second Innings*—Holdsworth 18–4–64–0; Whitney 22–1–67–2; Lawson 17–1–49–0; Matthews 40–13–90–3; S. R. Waugh 1–0–6–0; Bevan 18–2–85–0; M. E. Waugh 15–6–18–1; Bayliss 4–1–6–0; Taylor 2–1–1–0.

Umpires: D. B. Hair and I. S. Thomas.

SOUTH AUSTRALIA v TASMANIA

At Adelaide, November 8, 9, 10, 11. Drawn. Tasmania 2 pts. Toss: Tasmania. It took three and a half days to reach a first-innings result in a terrible game. Occasionally, the cricket rose above slow-motion mediocrity, specifically when Siddons was hitting 19 fours in yet another successful venture on to the Adelaide Oval. The first day was easily the most productive, with South Australia scoring 270; Tasmania made only 218, losing four wickets, off 103 overs on the third. Six-hour centuries by Cruse and Boon were just enough to get Tasmania two points, but South Australia dropped ten catches.

Close of play: First day, South Australia 270-4 (J. D. Siddons 123*, G. A. Bishop 25*); Second day, Tasmania 96-1 (B. A. Cruse 52*, D. C. Boon 11*); Third day, Tasmania 314-5 (D. J. Buckingham 28*, G. A. Hughes 7*).

South Australia

G. S. Blewett c Cruse b Gilbert	63	– not out	31
A. M. J. Hilditch c Holyman b Matthews	23		
†T. J. Nielsen c Holyman b Tucker	10	– not out	31
*J. D. Siddons c and b Gilbert	141		
D. W. Hookes c Buckingham b Tucker	16		
G. A. Bishop c Holyman b Matthews	34	– (2) c and b Hughes	31
J. C. Scuderi st Holyman b Buckingham	30		
T. B. A. May b Buckingham	43		
C. R. Miller b Gilbert	23		
D. J. Hickey not out	6		
M. J. Minagall b Gilbert	9		
L-b 10, n-b 6	16		

1/43 2/72 3/158 4/195 5/292   414   1/52   (1 wkt) 93
6/311 7/353 8/397 9/399

Bowling: *First Innings*—Gilbert 29.5–8–88–4; Campbell 35–11–108–0; Matthews 30–7–89–2; Tucker 23–7–34–2; Buckingham 23–3–81–2; Hughes 2–1–4–0. *Second Innings*—Campbell 7–1–19–0; Tucker 5–0–20–0; Buckingham 13–3–34–0; Hughes 11–4–14–1; Bennett 3–2–4–0; Cruse 4–2–2–0.

Tasmania

R. J. Bennett lbw b Miller	26	C. D. Matthews c Hickey b Minagall	18
B. A. Cruse c Nielsen b Scuderi	100	D. R. Gilbert c Miller b Scuderi	12
*D. C. Boon st Nielsen b May	130	G. D. Campbell not out	0
R. J. Tucker c Hilditch b Scuderi	0		
J. Cox lbw b May	6	B 1, l-b 20, n-b 8	29
D. J. Buckingham lbw b Hickey	60		
G. A. Hughes c Hookes b Hickey	7	1/56 2/212 3/212 4/244 5/295	426
†J. F. Holyman c Nielsen b Scuderi	38	6/320 7/382 8/396 9/426	

Bowling: Hickey 44–11–121–2; Miller 26–10–50–1; Scuderi 30–7–50–4; May 72–27–108–2; Minagall 29.3–9–76–1.

Umpires: A. R. Crafter and D. J. Harper.

QUEENSLAND v NEW SOUTH WALES

At Brisbane, November 15, 16, 17. Queensland won by ten wickets. Queensland 6 pts. Toss: Queensland. Two weeks earlier, the Gabba pitch had been a batsman's paradise, but now the bowlers, especially Queensland's, carried all before them. Rackemann's delight at winning the toss increased as he and McDermott had New South Wales floundering at 24 for five after only half an hour. And Hayden's aggressive batting wrapped up first-innings points shortly after tea. He pressed on to reach the highest score of the match. Whitney and his fellow pacemen revived New South Wales's hopes of recovering the situation, but their second innings looked doomed again when McDermott accounted for Small and Steve Waugh with only four on the board. Mark Taylor and Mark Waugh, in their contrasting styles, added 101 in even time, until both succumbed to their former colleague, Peter Taylor. Some defiance by Matthews prolonged the game into the third day, but a blazing stand of 84 in 50 minutes by Barsby and Hayden ended the match before lunch, with more than five sessions to spare. It was Queensland's sixth successive win against New South Wales at Brisbane.

Close of play: First day, Queensland 196-5 (G. M. Ritchie 12*, I. A. Healy 25*); Second day, New South Wales 185-7 (G. R. J. Matthews 22*, G. F. Lawson 10*).

New South Wales

S. M. Small c Hayden b McDermott	0	– c Healy b McDermott	1
M. A. Taylor c Border b Rackemann	4	– b Taylor	57
S. R. Waugh c Wellham b McDermott	10	– b McDermott	2
M. E. Waugh c Healy b McDermott	0	– c Rackemann b Taylor	60
M. G. Bevan c Barsby b McDermott	17	– c Healy b Rackemann	10
T. H. Bayliss c Rowell b Rackemann	8	– c Healy b Rackemann	13
G. R. J. Matthews c Healy b McDermott	17	– c Healy b Rowell	50
†P. A. Emery not out	37	– c Taylor b Rackemann	0
*G. F. Lawson c Barsby b Rowell	6	– lbw b McDermott	24
M. R. Whitney c Healy b Rackemann	0	– not out	1
W. J. Holdsworth b Rackemann	4	– b Rowell	0
N-b 16	16	B 1, l-b 3, n-b 8	12

1/0 2/10 3/10 4/14 5/24   119   1/2 2/4 3/105 4/130 5/142   230
6/62 7/80 8/105 9/105   6/163 7/163 8/222 9/230

Bowling: *First Innings*—McDermott 14-3-54-5; Rackemann 8-2-35-4; Rowell 8-0-30-1. *Second Innings*—McDermott 25-8-57-3; Rackemann 21-9-59-3; Rowell 11.5-2-58-2; Taylor 19-3-52-2.

Queensland

T. J. Barsby lbw b Holdsworth	45	– not out	27
M. L. Hayden c Small b Lawson	64	– not out	43
D. M. Wellham c Taylor b Whitney	37		
A. R. Border b Whitney	2		
S. G. Law c Emery b Whitney	3		
G. M. Ritchie c Matthews b S. R. Waugh	25		
†I. A. Healy lbw b Lawson	49		
P. L. Taylor lbw b Whitney	8		
C. J. McDermott c Lawson b Holdsworth	17		
G. J. Rowell not out	5		
*C. G. Rackemann c Emery b Holdsworth	0		
L-b 3, n-b 10	13	B 4, l-b 2, n-b 8	14

1/49 2/129 3/139 4/159 5/159   268   (no wkt) 84
6/225 7/240 8/250 9/268

Bowling: *First Innings*—Lawson 23-10-60-2; Whitney 28-6-91-4; S. R. Waugh 17-4-51-1; Holdsworth 14.5-1-52-3; M. E. Waugh 3-0-11-0. *Second Innings*—Whitney 5-1-25-0; Holdsworth 4-0-25-0; Matthews 3-0-19-0; Bevan 1.1-0-9-0.

Umpires: P. D. Parker and C. D. Timmins.

VICTORIA v SOUTH AUSTRALIA

At Melbourne, November 15, 16, 17, 18. Victoria won by an innings and 24 runs. Victoria 6 pts. Toss: South Australia. The South Australian captain, Jamie Siddons, had an unforgettable homecoming to Melbourne. He put his former team-mates in to bat, dropped Ramshaw off the first ball of the match, watched Victoria declare at 514 for eight, was stumped for two in his first innings and was out hit wicket for nought in the second, having collected a short ball from Hughes in the face; he had surgery a few days later. Jones dominated Victoria's innings, scoring 188 on the first day and adding 302 in 285 minutes with a very determined Phillips. The South Australian bowling looked undermanned without the injured Scuderi, but their batting benefited from a typically sturdy innings by Hilditch. Once he fell to the second new ball, Hughes and Reiffel made short work of a disheartened team, and the last seven wickets fell for 41. Following on 270 behind, only Hilditch and Brayshaw, on his début for his new state, held up Victoria. Hughes and Reiffel shared another eight wickets, and Siddons's painful demise sealed South Australia's fate.

Close of play: First day, Victoria 355-3 (D. M. Jones 188*, D. S. Lehmann 1*); Second day, South Australia 158-3 (A. M. J. Hilditch 76*, D. W. Hookes 10*); Third day, South Australia 110-2 (J. A. Brayshaw 39*, T. B. A. May 1*).

Victoria

D. J. Ramshaw c Minagall b Miller	... 18	M. G. Hughes c Bishop b May	0
W. N. Phillips c Bishop b Hickey	121	S. K. Warne not out	30
D. M. Jones b Miller	214		
†D. S. Berry c Nielsen b Hickey	3	L-b 10, w 1, n-b 22	33
D. S. Lehmann c Blewett b Hickey	1		
*S. P. O'Donnell b Miller	23	1/38 2/340 3/354	(8 wkts dec.) 514
G. J. Allardice not out	37	4/363 5/397 6/413	
P. R. Reiffel run out	34	7/473 8/473	

D. W. Fleming did not bat.

Bowling: Hickey 32–2–136–3; Miller 38–7–125–3; Siddons 1–0–3–0; May 31–3–131–1; Minagall 13–2–66–0; Brayshaw 8–0–27–0; Hookes 2–0–10–0; Blewett 2–0–6–0.

South Australia

G. S. Blewett b Reiffel	32	– c Hughes b Fleming	11
A. M. J. Hilditch lbw b Hughes	103	– c Reiffel b Hughes	50
J. A. Brayshaw b Warne	23	– c Berry b Reiffel	90
*J. D. Siddons st Berry b Warne	2	– (5) hit wkt b Warne	0
D. W. Hookes c Jones b Reiffel	26	– (6) c Ramshaw b Reiffel	9
G. A. Bishop b Hughes	12	– (7) c Jones b O'Donnell	41
†T. J. Nielsen c Berry b Reiffel	3	– (8) lbw b Hughes	1
T. B. A. May c Berry b Reiffel	0	– (4) b Reiffel	8
C. R. Miller c O'Donnell b Hughes	0	– c Ramshaw b Hughes	4
D. J. Hickey lbw b Warne	13	– b Reiffel	10
M. J. Minagall not out	11	– not out	3
L-b 11, n-b 8	19	B 3, l-b 6, n-b 10	19

1/64 2/105 3/113 4/203 5/207	244	1/27 2/106 3/117 4/118 5/139	246
6/216 7/220 8/220 9/225		6/218 7/229 8/229 9/240	

Bowling: *First Innings*—Hughes 33–8–73–3; Fleming 17–6–35–0; O'Donnell 5–0–14–0; Reiffel 28–9–44–4; Warne 25.3–3–67–3. *Second Innings*—Hughes 21.1–6–32–4; Fleming 14–3–35–1; O'Donnell 18–4–73–1; Reiffel 22–5–54–4; Warne 16–7–43–0.

Umpires: D. W. Holt and L. J. King.

SOUTH AUSTRALIA v WESTERN AUSTRALIA

At Adelaide, November 22, 23, 24, 25. Western Australia won by seven wickets. Western Australia 6 pts, South Australia 2 pts. Toss: South Australia. Generous declarations by both sides set up victory for the visitors. Marsh forfeited first-innings points by declaring 122 runs behind South Australia's 460 and then, almost unbelievably, Hilditch invited Western Australia to score 303 in a full day on a perfect pitch against some pretty friendly bowling. Marsh led the way with a four-hour century, and his colleagues had few problems in achieving the necessary run-rate. South Australia started well enough, with Hookes showing something like his old form in scoring 75 in 107 minutes. Scuderi hit his maiden hundred in a chanceless innings, well supported by the keeper, Nielsen. The Western Australian reply was dominated by Moody and Martyn, who put on 229 for the fourth wicket in 227 minutes. Western Australia had relegated Graeme Wood, the former Test opener, to twelfth man, to make room for four fast bowlers; in the event their most successful bowler was the keeper, Zoehrer. He periodically surrendered his gloves to Veletta and took seven wickets in the match from 40 overs of leg-spin.

Close of play: First day, South Australia 282-6 (T. J. Nielsen 30*, J. C. Scuderi 15*); Second day, Western Australia 151-3 (T. M. Moody 75*, D. R. Martyn 12*); Third day, South Australia 180-6 (T. J. Nielsen 35*, M. P. Faull 20*).

South Australia

G. S. Blewett c Veletta b Julian	78	– lbw b Alderman	0
*A. M. J. Hilditch c Zoehrer b Reid	43	– b Zoehrer	24
J. A. Brayshaw c Alderman b Zoehrer	16	– c Zoehrer b Andrews	40
M. P. Faull c Veletta b Reid	4	– (8) not out	20
D. W. Hookes c Martyn b Zoehrer	75	– (4) b Zoehrer	13
G. H. Armstrong lbw b Moody	2	– c Zoehrer b Andrews	5
†T. J. Nielsen b Andrews	81	– not out	35
J. C. Scuderi not out	125	– (5) c McCague b Andrews	36
T. B. A. May b Zoehrer	6		
D. J. Hickey b Zoehrer	1		
C. J. Owen c and b Zoehrer	0		
B 6, l-b 5, n-b 18	29	L-b 5, n-b 2	7

1/95 2/140 3/148 4/167 5/204   **460**   1/1 2/51 3/83   **(6 wkts dec.) 180**
6/253 7/373 8/422 9/444   4/93 5/100 6/133

Bowling: *First Innings*—Reid 34-8-112-2; Alderman 28-6-69-0; Julian 14-0-56-1; McCague 19-2-74-0; Andrews 12-1-32-1; Zoehrer 22-3-58-5; Moody 14-3-48-1. *Second Innings*—Reid 6-1-16-0; Alderman 6-3-12-1; Andrews 13-2-55-3; Zoehrer 18-3-79-2; Martyn 5-0-13-0.

Western Australia

M. R. J. Veletta c Nielsen b May	36	– (2) c Hilditch b May	39
*G. R. Marsh run out	1	– (1) c and b May	104
M. P. Lavender lbw b Hickey	2	– run out	58
T. M. Moody c Nielsen b Owen	168	– not out	54
D. R. Martyn c Nielsen b Owen	90	– not out	39
W. S. Andrews not out	6		
†T. J. Zoehrer not out	5		
L-b 4, n-b 26	30	B 4, l-b 8	12

1/10 2/21 3/92 4/321 5/328   **(5 wkts dec.) 338**   1/74 2/191 3/223   **(3 wkts) 306**

B. P. Julian, M. J. McCague, T. M. Alderman and B. A. Reid did not bat.

Bowling: *First Innings*—Hickey 22-3-94-1; Scuderi 22-4-54-0; May 28-5-110-1; Hookes 6-0-23-0; Owen 19-3-53-2. *Second Innings*—Hickey 12.1-1-62-0; Scuderi 20-6-50-0; May 34-7-106-2; Hookes 3-1-11-0; Owen 9-1-41-0; Faull 14-5-24-0.

Umpires: A. R. Crafter and S. J. Davis.

TASMANIA v QUEENSLAND

At Hobart, November 22, 23, 24. Queensland won by an innings and 129 runs. Queensland 6 pts. Toss: Tasmania. Queensland achieved their second three-day win in consecutive matches. The result reflected their depth in pace bowling. In the absence of the injured captain, Rackemann, the unlikely hero was their recruit from New South Wales, Rowell, who showed command of cut and swing and claimed seven wickets as Tasmania were dismissed on the first afternoon for 138. Then, to add insult to injury, Wellham scored a century, his first for five years, and something he had never achieved in three seasons captaining Tasmania. With the left-hander, Hayden, he defied a slow outfield to put on 167 for the second wicket in just over three hours, though they could manage only 12 boundaries between them. The burly Hayden continued his good form with a hundred in four and a half hours. Disheartened by Queensland's lead of 309, the Tasmanian batsmen were easy prey for McDermott and Rowell in the second innings. They succumbed soon after tea on the third day with Campbell absent, nursing a broken bone in his wrist.

Close of play: First day, Queensland 100-1 (M. L. Hayden 45*, D. M. Wellham 2*); Second day, Queensland 447.

Tasmania

R. J. Bennett b McDermott	0	lbw b Rowell 19
B. A. Cruse c Law b Rowell	3	c Healy b McDermott 1
*D. C. Boon c Healy b Williams	22	c Healy b McDermott 8
R. J. Tucker c Healy b Rowell	0	c and b Rowell 26
J. Cox lbw b Rowell	41	lbw b Williams 30
D. J. Buckingham lbw b Rowell	16	b McDermott 11
†J. F. Holyman lbw b Rowell	0	c Healy b Rowell 14
C. D. Matthews c Border b Rowell	10	c and b Taylor 29
D. R. Gilbert not out	20	c Rowell b McDermott 15
G. D. Campbell c Law b Rowell	2	absent injured
P. T. McPhee c Border b Williams	9	(10) not out 1
L-b 7, n-b 8	15	B 2, l-b 3, w 1, n-b 20 ... 26

138   180

1/0 2/4 3/4 4/56 5/87
6/87 7/96 8/99 9/109

1/7 2/25 3/60 4/61 5/73
6/107 7/134 8/160 9/180

Bowling: *First Innings*—McDermott 16–3–48–1; Rowell 20–6–46–7; Williams 11.4–3–37–2. *Second Innings*—McDermott 17–1–65–4; Rowell 17–4–50–3; Williams 12–1–41–1; Taylor 18.5–8–19–1.

Queensland

T. J. Barsby lbw b Campbell	46	C. J. McDermott lbw b Tucker 18
M. L. Hayden c Boon b Tucker	108	G. J. Rowell c sub b Matthews 7
D. M. Wellham c and b Gilbert	100	S. B. Williams c Boon b Gilbert 29
*A. R. Border c Bennett b Matthews	20	
S. G. Law c Gilbert b Matthews	5	B 4, l-b 9, w 3, n-b 18 34
G. M. Ritchie lbw b Tucker	18	
†I. A. Healy not out	55	1/84 2/251 3/293 4/299 5/300 447
P. L. Taylor lbw b Matthews	7	6/343 7/352 8/379 9/390

Bowling: Gilbert 30.4–5–81–2; Campbell 18–3–62–1; Matthews 39–7–118–4; McPhee 19–0–85–0; Buckingham 13–1–49–0; Tucker 13–1–39–3.

Umpires: B. T. Knight and S. G. Randell.

TASMANIA v WESTERN AUSTRALIA

At Hobart, November 29, 30, December 1, 2. Western Australia won by ten wickets. Western Australia 6 pts. Toss: Western Australia. Tasmania's batsmen surrendered twice to some fine left-arm pace bowling. In the first innings, Julian took four for one in 18 balls, reducing Tasmania to 37 for five. Young, on his début, and Buckingham put on 82 in two hours, but the home team could manage only 172. In spite of some mid-innings frailty, the Western Australian batsmen played steadily to set up a match-winning lead of 159. Veletta held the early order together, and Martyn scored his maiden Shield century in five hours, enjoying four lives. Alderman injured his back while batting, but his bowling was hardly missed. Reid showed a devastating return to form and fitness and collected six wickets. Buckingham was the only player to combat him, with a battling century, though it ended ingloriously on the final morning as he chased a wide ball from Moody. Once again, Zoehrer handed over the wicket-keeper's gloves to Veletta while he bowled his leg-breaks.

Close of play: First day, Western Australia 20-0 (M. P. Lavender 5*, M. R. J. Veletta 14*); Second day, Western Australia 276-5 (D. R. Martyn 80*, T. J. Zoehrer 31*); Third day, Tasmania 166-4 (D. J. Buckingham 99*, B. A. Cruse 23*).

Tasmania

D. F. Hills c Zoehrer b Julian	12	– (2) lbw b Reid	2
B. A. Cruse c Moody b Reid	9	– (6) c Lavender b Andrews	28
M. G. Farrell lbw b Julian	12	– (1) c Veletta b Reid	0
J. Cox lbw b Julian	0	– (3) c Zoehrer b Reid	4
R. J. Tucker b Julian	1	– c Zoehrer b Reid	24
D. J. Buckingham c Wood b McCague	37	– (4) c Veletta b Moody	110
S. Young c Alderman b Julian	55	– lbw b Andrews	0
†J. F. Holyman run out	6	– lbw b Reid	9
C. D. Matthews b McCague	24	– c Zoehrer b McCague	1
*D. R. Gilbert lbw b Moody	5	– not out	0
T. D. Bower not out	0	– lbw b Reid	0
B 1, l-b 8, w 2	11	L-b 3, n-b 12	15

1/19 2/32 3/32 4/35 5/37   172   1/0 2/3 3/16 4/92 5/172   193
6/119 7/142 8/143 9/148   6/178 7/182 8/192 9/192

Bowling: *First Innings*—Reid 15-6-22-1; Alderman 16-3-34-0; McCague 17.3-6-47-2; Julian 16-6-26-5; Moody 12-6-12-1; Andrews 1-1-0-0; Zoehrer 7-1-22-0. *Second Innings*—Reid 24-13-55-6; McCague 17.5-38-1; Julian 9-5-18-0; Moody 17-9-21-1; Andrews 17-3-37-2; Zoehrer 4-0-14-0; Martyn 3-1-7-0.

Western Australia

M. P. Lavender c Tucker b Bower	25	– (2) not out	5
*M. R. J. Veletta c sub b Matthews	84	– (1) not out	26
G. M. Wood lbw b Gilbert	1		
T. M. Moody run out	5		
D. R. Martyn c Holyman b Matthews	110		
W. S. Andrews b Farrell	35		
†T. J. Zoehrer b Matthews	36		
B. P. Julian lbw b Matthews	2		
M. J. McCague b Tucker	3		
T. M. Alderman c sub b Matthews	14		
B. A. Reid not out	1		
B 1, l-b 5, w 1, n-b 8	15	N-b 4	4

1/72 2/86 3/92 4/152 5/220   331   (no wkt) 35
6/288 7/290 8/303 9/330

Bowling: *First Innings*—Gilbert 26-8-60-1; Matthews 36-8-102-5; Bower 30-6-78-1; Young 16-5-31-0; Tucker 14-5-45-1; Farrell 4-2-9-1. *Second Innings*—Matthews 3-0-10-0; Bower 5-1-8-0; Young 2-0-8-0; Farrell 3-1-7-0; Buckingham 2.3-2-2-0.

Umpires: D. R. Close and B. T. Knight.

NEW SOUTH WALES v TASMANIA

At Sydney, December 12, 13, 14, 15. Tasmania won by 48 runs. Tasmania 6 pts. Toss: New South Wales. With only 79 minutes' play possible on the first two days, the captains resorted to contrivance to revive the contest for outright points. Lawson forfeited an innings, arousing howls of protest from other state associations. These were muted when New South Wales lost – for the first time in Sydney since 1983-84. The last defeat was also inflicted by Tasmania. Lawson's woes began when he pulled a hamstring on the first day, which prevented him bowling thereafter. Nevertheless, his bowlers dominated the Tasmanian batsmen in both innings, and batting held sway only when Small and Bevan took New South Wales to the threshold of victory. Chasing a target of 261 in 89 overs, they reached 132 for two. Bevan had hit his second ball for six and reached 50 in 48 minutes, then skied another big hit back to the bowler, Chris Matthews. This inspired Matthews and, aided by some superb slip catching by Buckingham and Farrell, he exposed the brittle New South Wales batting with five wickets.

Close of play: First day, Tasmania 34-2 (M. G. Farrell 3*, J. Cox 6*); Second day, No play; Third day, Tasmania 109-8 (J. F. Holyman 6*, D. R. Gilbert 3*).

Tasmania

B. A. Cruse b Holdsworth	17	– c Bayliss b Matthews 12
D. F. Hills c McNamara b Holdsworth	6	– c Matthews b Alley 21
M. G. Farrell c Emery b Holdsworth	16	– c Emery b Alley 4
J. Cox c Emery b Matthews	32	– c Bayliss b Alley 35
R. J. Tucker c Taylor b Freedman	14	– c Taylor b Alley 0
D. J. Buckingham c Matthews b Freedman	29	– b Matthews......... 1
S. Young c Small b Matthews	19	– b Holdsworth 4
C. D. Matthews not out	5	– c Taylor b Freedman 14
†J. F. Holyman (did not bat)		– c Taylor b Holdsworth......... 11
*D. R. Gilbert (did not bat)		– b McNamara 3
T. D. Bower (did not bat)		– not out. 0
B 1, l-b 3, w 2	6	L-b 2, w 1, n-b 8 11

1/21 2/24 3/68 4/91 5/91   (7 wkts dec.) 144   1/38 2/42 3/42 4/42 5/49   116
6/126 7/144   6/64 7/95 8/100 9/110

Bowling: *First Innings*—Holdsworth 16–5–35–3; Alley 9–5–14–0; Lawson 2.3–0–4–0; McNamara 8–2–22–0; Matthews 12.1–4–34–2; Freedman 10–4–31–2. *Second Innings*—Holdsworth 16.5–5–50–2; Alley 13–2–25–4; McNamara 7–1–18–1; Matthews 18–15–7–2; Freedman 6–1–14–1.

New South Wales

New South Wales forfeited their first innings.

S. M. Small c Buckingham b Matthews	51	*G. F. Lawson c Farrell b Matthews... 4
M. A. Taylor lbw b Gilbert	4	D. A. Freedman b Matthews 8
B. E. McNamara b Bower	13	P. J. S. Alley not out......... 21
M. G. Bevan c and b Matthews	52	W. J. Holdsworth c Cox b Young 1
T. H. Bayliss c Farrell b Young	7	B 6, l-b 10, w 1, n-b 2 19
G. R. J. Matthews c Buckingham		
b Bower	22	1/17 2/55 3/132 4/139 5/139 212
†P. A. Emery c Farrell b Matthews....	10	6/168 7/172 8/176 9/207

Bowling: Gilbert 15–2–44–1; Matthews 20–5–50–5; Bower 13–3–42–2; Tucker 6–0–29–0; Young 11.2–3–31–2.

Umpires: I. G. Jackson and G. E. Reed.

QUEENSLAND v VICTORIA

At Brisbane, December 13, 14, 15, 16. Drawn. Victoria 2 pts. Toss: Victoria. Queensland did well to recover from 71 for four in their first innings. Barsby and Goggin punished the Victorian bowlers in a brilliant partnership of 192, before Barsby fell to the chastened Hughes for his highest score, 165, which included 24 fours. Hughes continued to suffer from the flailing bat of Anderson, but Queensland's last four wickets went for 28 on the second morning. The wicket-keeper, Berry, finished with six catches. Victoria made a steady start, though they could not raise the momentum until the leg-spinner, Oxenford, began to drop short. Ayres went on to a grafting century but Rackemann's persistence kept Queensland in with a chance of first-innings points until Victoria overtook them at tea on the third day. Victoria used occasional bowlers in the second innings to expedite a declaration and Hayden and Wellham enjoyed some easy pickings. They even broke Queensland's record for the second wicket, with 248 in 220 minutes, but Rackemann declared only after Law had achieved his first "pair". A challenge of 324 in 49 overs was never realistic, and the umpires called a halt 30 minutes early.

Close of play: First day, Queensland 336-6 (P. W. Anderson 44*); Second day, Victoria 222-2 (W. G. Ayres 86*, D. S. Lehmann 31*); Third day, Queensland 114-1 (M. L. Hayden 48*, D. M. Wellham 54*).

Queensland

T. J. Barsby c Phillips b Hughes	165	– run out	5
M. L. Hayden c Berry b Reiffel	8	– c Fleming b Phillips	116
D. M. Wellham c Parker b Fleming	14	– c Fleming b Hughes	167
G. M. Ritchie c Lehmann b Dodemaide	8	– not out	26
S. G. Law c Berry b Dodemaide	0	– c Phillips b Hughes	0
P. J. T. Goggin c Berry b Hughes	91		
†P. W. Anderson c Berry b Reiffel	52		
B. N. J. Oxenford c Berry b Fleming	10		
G. J. Rowell c Berry b Hughes	2		
S. B. Williams c Dodemaide b Fleming	16		
*C. G. Rackemann not out	0		
L-b 6, n-b 2	8	B 1, l-b 7, n-b 2	10

1/34 2/60 3/71 4/71 5/263   374   1/10 2/258   (4 wkts dec.) 324
6/336 7/346 8/355 9/374   3/324 4/324

Bowling: *First Innings*—Hughes 31-4-139-3; Reiffel 27-8-51-2; Fleming 20.4-3-71-3; Dodemaide 19-5-60-2; Parker 7-1-41-0; Lehmann 5-1-6-0. *Second Innings*—Hughes 9.3-0-34-2; Reiffel 12-3-38-0; Fleming 10-2-43-0; Dodemaide 12-2-40-0; Lehmann 18-4-62-0; Phillips 11-1-59-1; Ayres 5-0-23-0; Allardice 3-0-17-0.

Victoria

W. N. Phillips c Anderson b Rackemann	38	– (2) c Anderson b Rackemann	2
D. J. Ramshaw c Rowell b Williams	52	– (1) st Anderson b Oxenford	14
W. G. Ayres c Ritchie b Rowell	115	– c Oxenford b Williams	28
D. S. Lehmann c Anderson b Rackemann	65	– not out	27
G. R. Parker c Oxenford b Rowell	1	– not out	10
G. J. Allardice lbw b Williams	17		
P. R. Reiffel c Anderson b Rackemann	1		
*A. I. C. Dodemaide c Oxenford b Rowell	23		
M. G. Hughes not out	27		
†D. S. Berry not out	9		
B 1, l-b 12, n-b 14	27	B 4, l-b 2, n-b 2	8

1/65 2/141 3/287 4/288 5/289   (8 wkts dec.) 375   1/4 2/33 3/60   (3 wkts) 89
6/290 7/331 8/345

D. W. Fleming did not bat.

Bowling: *First Innings*—Rackemann 35-9-59-3; Rowell 43-8-132-3; Williams 29.2-10-77-2; Oxenford 22-2-89-0; Law 3-2-5-0. *Second Innings*—Rackemann 12-5-12-1; Rowell 6-0-19-0; Williams 3-1-10-1; Oxenford 11-3-27-1; Barsby 5-1-13-0; Ritchie 1-0-2-0; Wellham 1-1-0-0.

Umpires: A. J. McQuillan and C. D. Timmins.

SOUTH AUSTRALIA v NEW SOUTH WALES

At Adelaide, December 20, 21, 22, 23. South Australia won by ten wickets. South Australia 6 pts. Toss: South Australia. The 22-year-old South Australia all-rounder Joe Scuderi became only the third player in Shield history to take ten wickets and score a century in the same match. He made the most of his captain's decision to bowl, producing his best figures on a wicket with enough grass to encourage movement off the seam. The only other players to match Scuderi's feat were P. H. Carlson of Queensland, in 1978-79, and G. Giffen, who did it for South Australia in 1892-93. The New South Wales batsmen offered little resistance, apart from Mark Waugh, who hit 15 fours before being run out by a direct hit from cover. After a hamstring injury forced Lawson from the field, the South Australians went on to plunder the bowling, scoring 398 on the second day. In the last session, Hookes and Scuderi shared 171 before Scuderi holed out to long-on shortly before stumps, having hit a six and 16 fours. Hookes went early next morning, after a vintage four-and-a-half-hour effort, but South Australia pressed on relentlessly. New South Wales were left 331 behind with virtually five sessions to see out. They managed four, thanks to a last-wicket stand of 58 between McNamara and Holdsworth, both of whom hit their highest first-class scores.

Close of play: First day, South Australia 31-1 (G. S. Blewett 11*, J. A. Brayshaw 12*); Second day, South Australia 429-5 (D. W. Hookes 151*, T. J. Nielsen 0*); Third day, New South Wales 151-4 (B. E. McNamara 4*, P. A. Emery 1*).

New South Wales

S. M. Small c Nielsen b Scuderi	42	– b Hickey	15
M. A. Taylor c Siddons b Scuderi	16	– c Nielsen b Scuderi	54
B. E. McNamara c Nielsen b Owen	6	– (5) b May	80
M. E. Waugh run out	94	– b Scuderi	24
T. H. Bayliss c Brayshaw b Scuderi	1	– (3) b May	37
G. R. J. Matthews c Sleep b Scuderi	11	– (7) c Owen b Sleep	40
†P. A. Emery c Nielsen b Scuderi	36	– (6) c Hilditch b Owen	8
*G. F. Lawson b Hickey	7	– (9) c Hilditch b Scuderi	28
D. A. Freedman c Siddons b Scuderi	2	– (8) c Hookes b May	1
M. R. Whitney lbw b Scuderi	0	– c Hilditch b Owen	0
W. J. Holdsworth not out	0	– not out	33
L-b 6, n-b 4	10	B 1, l-b 3, n-b 18	22
	225		342

1/30 2/53 3/81 4/91 5/123
6/199 7/214 8/224 9/224

1/16 2/101 3/129 4/148 5/170
6/222 7/223 8/283 9/284

Bowling: *First Innings*—Hickey 22–7–68–1; Scuderi 32.1–11–79–7; Owen 15–2–48–1; May 4–0–24–0. *Second Innings*—Hickey 8–1–31–1; Scuderi 32–10–86–3; Owen 26–9–68–2; May 45.3–9–135–3; Sleep 8–0–18–1.

South Australia

G. S. Blewett c Taylor b Matthews	56	– not out	13
A. M. J. Hilditch c Emery b Whitney	6	– not out	1
J. A. Brayshaw c Emery b Whitney	19		
*J. D. Siddons c Holdsworth b Matthews	68		
D. W. Hookes c Taylor b Holdsworth	156		
J. C. Scuderi c Holdsworth b Whitney	110		
†T. J. Nielsen b Freedman	32		
P. R. Sleep not out	70		
T. B. A. May run out	6		
D. J. Hickey b Freedman	1		
C. J. Owen c Emery b Freedman	0		
B 9, l-b 9, n-b 14	32	W 1	1
	556	(no wkt)	15

1/9 2/49 3/127 4/216 5/427
6/434 7/516 8/550 9/556

Bowling: *First Innings*—Whitney 41–11–105–3; Holdsworth 30–8–135–1; Matthews 43–6–145–2; Lawson 4.5–2–15–0; McNamara 12.1–1–54–0; Freedman 20–2–84–3. *Second Innings*—Whitney 2.5–0–14–0; Small 2–1–1–0.

Umpires: S. J. Davis and D. J. Harper.

WESTERN AUSTRALIA v VICTORIA

At Perth, December 20, 21, 22, 23. Victoria won by eight wickets. Victoria 6 pts. Toss: Victoria. Dean Jones's third double-century of the season carried Victoria to an impregnable position by tea on the second day. Revelling in perfect conditions, he made the most of a life to Alderman when 24, hitting 30 fours to all parts of the ground. He had fine support, including a fifty from Nobes on his début for the state. Jones was eventually caught down the leg-side by Western Australia's deputy wicket-keeper, Veletta. Western Australia used a third keeper, Martyn, in this match while their first choice, Zoehrer, returned the best figures of the innings with assorted wrist-spinners. The Victorian total of 500 was never under threat as the four-man pace attack kept the home batsmen on the lefensive. Martyn looked most at ease, until he fell to a wide half-volley from Jones, who was bowling a rare spell of innocent-looking off-breaks. At 329 for nine on the fourth morning, Western Australia looked set for a draw, but they lost 11 wickets to the seam bowlers in a little over four hours, leaving Victoria 20 overs to make 37.

Close of play: First day, Victoria 301-3 (D. M. Jones 170*, S. P. O'Donnell 13*); Second day, Western Australia 53-1 (J. L. Langer 22*, M. P. Lavender 19*); Third day, Western Australia 329-9 (B. P. Julian 38*, T. M. Alderman 0*).

Victoria

D. J. Ramshaw c Zoehrer b Julian	8	– (2) not out 19
P. C. Nobes c Lavender b Alderman	51	– (1) lbw b McCague 0
D. M. Jones c Veletta b Julian	204	– c Wood b Julian 11
D. S. Lehmann c and b Zoehrer	51	– not out 7
*S. P. O'Donnell c Zoehrer b Julian	31	
W. G. Ayres c Martyn b McCague	70	
A. I. C. Dodemaide b Zoehrer	16	
M. G. Hughes c McCague b Zoehrer	7	
†D. S. Berry st Martyn b Zoehrer	32	
D. W. Fleming c Martyn b McCague	14	
M. A. Sutherland not out	6	
B 1, l-b 3, w 2, n-b 4	10	L-b 1, w 2 3

1/15 2/134 3/258 4/341 5/362   500   1/0 2/27   (2 wkts) 40
6/409 7/421 8/472 9/488

Bowling: *First Innings*—Alderman 26-9-62-1; McCague 32.5-5-106-2; Julian 36-10-119-3; MacLeay 21-5-61-0; Andrews 12-3-49-0; Martyn 3-0-13-0; Zoehrer 32-10-86-4. *Second Innings*—Alderman 7-0-24-0; McCague 5-2-10-1; Julian 2.3-1-5-1.

Western Australia

*M. R. J. Veletta b Fleming	8	– b Hughes 7
J. L. Langer c Berry b Dodemaide	59	– c Berry b Sutherland 18
M. P. Lavender c Ramshaw b Dodemaide	33	– c Nobes b Dodemaide 13
G. M. Wood lbw b Sutherland	15	– c Jones b Hughes 32
D. R. Martyn c O'Donnell b Jones	60	– c Berry b Fleming 21
W. S. Andrews c Berry b Fleming	44	– c Ramshaw b Fleming 71
†T. J. Zoehrer c Lehmann b Hughes	5	– c Fleming b Dodemaide 13
K. H. MacLeay c O'Donnell b Hughes	19	– c Berry b Hughes 6
B. P. Julian not out	38	– lbw b Sutherland 4
M. J. McCague b Fleming	34	– lbw b Fleming 3
T. M. Alderman c Lehmann b Hughes	1	– not out 5
B 1, l-b 9, n-b 4	14	L-b 8, w 5 13

1/19 2/81 3/112 4/134 5/216   330   1/12 2/44 3/68 4/100 5/102   206
6/222 7/248 8/262 9/329   6/145 7/158 8/179 9/195

Bowling: *First Innings*—Hughes 33.3-14-67-3; Fleming 34-12-77-3; Sutherland 22-8-64-1; Dodemaide 27-6-74-2; Jones 7-1-29-1; Lehmann 5-1-9-0. *Second Innings*—Hughes 20-4-76-3; Fleming 19.3-5-55-3; Sutherland 12-2-39-2; Dodemaide 12-3-28-2.

Umpires: R. A. Emerson and P. J. McConnell.

NEW SOUTH WALES v QUEENSLAND

At Sydney, January 10, 11, 12, 13. New South Wales won by 133 runs. New South Wales 6 pts. Toss: Queensland. Aggressive batting by Matthews and his career-best match bowling figures of 11 for 133 secured New South Wales's first outright win of the season. Rackemann opted to bowl, but he and Rowell lacked adequate support to follow up two early wickets. First Taylor and Bayliss, then Matthews helped New South Wales along. Queensland's reply lasted a mere four and a half hours, and Matthews bowled his 26 overs unchanged. Despite his better figures, he acknowledged the superior form of his wrist-spinning partner, Freedman. Queensland fought back on the third day as the New South Wales second innings subsided to 76 for five, but Matthews and Bayliss added 132 in 146 minutes. Leg-spinner Oxenford paid heavily, until he had Matthews caught on the mid-wicket boundary and wrapped up the tail to leave Queensland chasing 346. The efforts of Barsby and Hayden against the pace attack were just a prelude to another unhappy confrontation with Matthews and Freedman. These two shared eight more wickets before Bayliss unexpectedly took the last two with consecutive balls. Ritchie earned a suspended $A500 fine for using language that breached the code of conduct.

Close of play: First day, New South Wales 298-8 (G. R. J. Matthews 71*, P. J. S. Alley 0*); Second day, New South Wales 12-0 (S. M. Small 4*, M. A. Taylor 6*); Third day, Queensland 50-0 (T. J. Barsby 25*, M. L. Hayden 13*).

New South Wales

S. M. Small b Rackemann	0	– c Anderson b Rowell	11
*M. A. Taylor c Goggin b Rowell	52	– c Anderson b Rackemann	24
G. S. Milliken c Wellham b Rackemann	7	– b Oxenford	7
T. H. Bayliss c Oxenford b Rackemann	80	– c Oxenford b Rowell	75
M. G. Bevan c Anderson b Rowell	9	– c Wellham b Prestwidge	10
B. E. McNamara c Prestwidge b Rowell	14	– c Rackemann b Oxenford	3
G. R. J. Matthews not out	85	– c Hayden b Oxenford	67
†P. A. Emery run out	20	– not out	21
D. A. Freedman c Goggin b Rowell	15	– (11) run out	0
P. J. S. Alley c Barsby b Rowell	1	– (9) b Oxenford	2
W. J. Holdsworth b Rackemann	12	– (10) c Hayden b Oxenford	0
L-b 12, n-b 24	36	B 1, l-b 3, n-b 20	24
	331		**244**

1/0 2/14 3/128 4/160 5/175   331   1/38 2/40 3/56 4/71 5/76   244
6/200 7/261 8/298 9/314   6/208 7/226 8/239 9/239

Bowling: *First Innings*—Rackemann 35-12-75-4; Rowell 37-9-92-5; Prestwidge 22-2-94-0; Oxenford 12-1-55-0; Law 1-0-3-0. *Second Innings*—Rackemann 21-3-58-1; Rowell 22-3-58-2; Prestwidge 12-2-26-1; Oxenford 22.4-6-91-5; Law 7-4-7-0.

Queensland

T. J. Barsby c Emery b Holdsworth	6	– c and b Matthews	49
M. L. Hayden c Taylor b McNamara	13	– c Taylor b Matthews	34
D. M. Wellham c Small b Matthews	53	– b Matthews	4
G. M. Ritchie c Holdsworth b Freedman	31	– b Freedman	47
S. G. Law c Bayliss b Matthews	2	– c Small b Matthews	22
P. J. T. Goggin b Matthews	55	– c Taylor b Freedman	14
†S. A. Prestwidge lbw b Freedman	18	– b Freedman	6
P. W. Anderson b Matthews	39	– c Holdsworth b Matthews	3
B. N. J. Oxenford c and b Matthews	0	– not out	6
G. J. Rowell not out	0	– lbw b Bayliss	5
*C. G. Rackemann c Small b Matthews	0	– b Bayliss	0
B 2, l-b 2, w 1, n-b 8	13	B 2, l-b 4, n-b 16	22
	230		**212**

1/8 2/46 3/107 4/109 5/125   230   1/90 2/98 3/113 4/163 5/189   212
6/177 7/211 8/217 9/230   6/194 7/197 8/202 9/212

Bowling: *First Innings*—Holdsworth 12-2-49-1; Alley 7-1-48-0; McNamara 8-0-21-1; Matthews 26-8-63-6; Freedman 18-2-45-2. *Second Innings*—Holdsworth 17-1-62-0; Alley 7-1-33-0; Matthews 34-13-70-5; Freedman 19-6-40-3; Bayliss 0.4-0-1-2.

Umpires: I. G. Jackson and G. E. Reed.

WESTERN AUSTRALIA v TASMANIA

At Perth, January 10, 11, 12, 13. Drawn. Tasmania 2 pts. Toss: Tasmania. Tasmania's captain, Gilbert, chose to field and was well pleased when his bowlers had Western Australia out on the first day for 200. Matthews, whose departure from Perth the previous year was not especially tranquil, enjoyed the conditions and inspired his colleagues to produce some tight and effective seam bowling. The Tasmanians also found run-scoring difficult, with Cruse spending three and a half hours over 39, before Tucker and Young broke the shackles to add 116 for the sixth wicket in 112 minutes. This gave Tasmania first-innings points, and the remaining batsmen built up a healthy lead. In the second innings, the Western Australians were in no mood for another capitulation. Matthews took all five wickets that fell to bowlers, but they were costly, as the batsmen hit out. Lavender escaped a chance to Young at second slip when 30, and went on to his highest score. Veletta declared soon after this splendid innings ended, but a target of 265 from 38 overs was of no consequence to either side.

Close of play: First day, Tasmania 28-1 (D. F. Hills 17*, B. A. Cruse 5*); Second day, Tasmania 302-6 (S. Young 69*, C. D. Matthews 16*); Third day, Western Australia 221-2 (M. P. Lavender 89*, M. R. J. Veletta 26*).

Western Australia

M. W. McPhee c Hills b Tucker	37	– run out	54
L. Langer lbw b Matthews	25	– c Holyman b Matthews	20
M. P. Lavender c Young b Matthews	41	– c Gilbert b Matthews	172
*M. R. J. Veletta b Bower	11	– c Holyman b Matthews	64
D. R. Martyn c Young b Matthews	13	– lbw b Matthews	24
W. S. Andrews c Cruse b Bower	23	– lbw b Matthews	9
†T. J. Zoehrer c Cruse b Young	19	– not out	36
B. P. Julian c Holyman b Bower	0	– not out	5
M. J. McCague not out	10		
P. A. Capes lbw b Young	8		
T. M. Alderman run out	1		
L-b 2, n-b 10	12	B 4, l-b 11, w 1, n-b 22	38
	200	(6 wkts dec.)	**422**

1/62 2/63 3/98 4/136 5/141   1/45 2/138 3/289
5/173 7/173 8/181 9/199   4/339 5/355 6/404

Bowling: *First Innings*—Gilbert 9-2-28-0; Bower 21-10-37-3; Matthews 17-1-72-3; Tucker 11-2-28-1; Young 19-8-27-2; Buckingham 1-0-6-0. *Second Innings*—Gilbert 23-8-53-0; Bower 24-5-81-0; Matthews 37-7-128-5; Tucker 11-2-30-0; Young 27-8-76-0; Buckingham 6-0-39-0.

Tasmania

R. J. Bennett c Zoehrer b Alderman	3	– c Zoehrer b Alderman	7
D. F. Hills c Zoehrer b Alderman	23	– c Lavender b McCague	27
B. A. Cruse c Veletta b McCague	39	– not out	51
J. Cox c Andrews b Capes	33		
R. J. Tucker lbw b Capes	72	– (4) not out	9
D. J. Buckingham c Lavender b Julian	20		
S. Young c McPhee b Julian	69		
C. D. Matthews c Veletta b Julian	32		
†J. F. Holyman b Zoehrer	20		
*D. R. Gilbert c Julian b Capes	10		
T. D. Bower not out	5		
B 6, l-b 12, w 6, n-b 8	32	L-b 3, n-b 2	5
	358	(2 wkts)	**99**

1/3 2/36 3/105 4/111 5/142   1/10 2/70
6/258 7/305 8/336 9/346

Bowling: *First Innings*—Capes 27.3-5-72-3; Alderman 25-12-52-2; Julian 28-8-73-3; McCague 27-5-94-1; Andrews 1-0-1-0; Zoehrer 15-4-37-1; Martyn 5-2-11-0. *Second Innings*—Alderman 10-5-12-1; McCague 12-3-35-1; Zoehrer 9-0-34-0; Martyn 7-2-15-0.

Umpires: G. J. Bibby and R. J. Evans.

QUEENSLAND v WESTERN AUSTRALIA

At Brisbane, January 17, 18, 19, 20. Drawn. Western Australia 2 pts. Toss: Western Australia. Western Australia's bowlers did well to restrict Queensland's first innings to 275. Alderman was at his best in taking the first three wickets, and Queensland were kept in the game only by Ritchie's defiant batting. This was his first Shield hundred since returning to the game after one season's retirement. He batted for over five hours, though he escaped a difficult chance to Zoehrer when only 11. Western Australia seemed interested only in first innings points and Langer, in his third match, made sure they succeeded. In scoring his maiden hundred, he batted for 442 minutes and hit 12 fours. His team prolonged their innings until after tea on the third day. Barsby and Hayden had no trouble in making up a deficit of 169, but fell frustratingly short of their hundreds, and one run short of a 200 partnership. The final day had little else to interest spectators, and only 380 of them even came along on the off-chance that it might have.

Close of play: First day, Queensland 261-8 (G. M. Ritchie 125*, G. J. Rowell 0*); Second day, Western Australia 196-3 (J. L. Langer 86*, D. R. Martyn 50*); Third day, Queensland 74-0 (T. J. Barsby 35*, M. L. Hayden 35*).

Queensland

T. J. Barsby c Angel b Alderman	14	– c Capes b Andrews	99
M. L. Hayden c Zoehrer b Alderman	10	– c Zoehrer b Alderman	93
D. M. Wellham c and b Alderman	33	– (4) not out	64
G. M. Ritchie c Zoehrer b Angel	137	– (6) c Langer b Julian	2
S. G. Law c Julian b Angel	23	– (3) b Angel	47
P. J. T. Goggin c Julian b Andrews	2	– (5) run out	16
†P. W. Anderson c Martyn b Andrews	7	– c Andrews b Julian	0
B. N. J. Oxenford lbw b Alderman	20	– c Andrews b Angel	16
S. B. Williams c Martyn b Alderman	4	– (10) not out	1
G. J. Rowell not out	2	– (9) c Andrews b Martyn	1
*C. G. Rackemann b Angel	0		
B 5, l-b 8, w 2, n-b 8	23	B 11, l-b 5, w 1	17

1/15 2/46 3/117 4/198 5/201   275   1/199 2/219 3/276 4/296 (8 wkts) 355
6/217 7/253 8/259 9/275   5/302 6/306 7/317 8/335

Bowling: *First Innings*—Capes 20–4–73–0; Alderman 23–9–51–5; Angel 24.4–6–60–3; Julian 20–6–41–0; Martyn 4–2–10–0; Andrews 11–2–27–2. *Second Innings*—Capes 22–4–61–0; Alderman 19–6–50–1; Angel 24–2–65–2; Julian 25–4–76–2; Martyn 3–0–10–1; Andrews 3–1–9–1; Zoehrer 15–1–56–0; McPhee 1–0–12–0.

Western Australia

M. W. McPhee c Ritchie b Rackemann	1	J. Angel c Hayden b Oxenford	0
J. L. Langer c Anderson b Rackemann	131	P. A. Capes not out	15
M. P. Lavender lbw b Williams	11	T. M. Alderman c Williams b Oxenford	9
*M. R. J. Veletta run out	27		
D. R. Martyn c Anderson b Rackemann	75	B 5, l-b 6, w 11, n-b 14	36
W. S. Andrews c sub b Oxenford	87		
†T. J. Zoehrer lbw b Rowell	45	1/2 2/50 3/105 4/241 5/310	444
B. P. Julian c Hayden b Oxenford	7	6/405 7/417 8/417 9/420	

Bowling: Rackemann 38–14–69–3; Williams 34–6–133–1; Rowell 40–9–97–1; Oxenford 41.1–7–126–4; Law 2–1–8–0.

Umpires: C. A. Bertwistle and A. J. McQuillan.

TASMANIA v VICTORIA

At Hobart, January 17, 18, 19, 20. Drawn. Victoria 2 pts. Toss: Victoria. Runs were at a premium on the first two days as batsmen strove to combat the slowest of outfields and persistent seam bowling. Phillips and Ramshaw had the Victorians away to a fine start, but when Phillips fell on his wicket, pulling a full toss from Tucker, the innings ground to a standstill. All ten wickets went for 107 in 51 overs, with Matthews taking five. Tasmania's

...atting was even duller. They only scavenged their way to 152 for nine on the second day, despite an opening stand of 76. Dodemaide's five for 34 from 35 overs was fair reward for a bowler wearing a brace to support a broken rib. It was also Dodemaide who, with Ayres, produced the most positive batting of the match. They allowed O'Donnell to declare the second innings by putting on 143 for the sixth wicket without being parted. The declaration, setting a target of 290 from a minimum of 78 overs, seemed conservative, and Tasmania never threatened to get close, but Merv Hughes's tireless efforts left Victoria just two wickets short of victory.

Close of play: First day, Victoria 200; Second day, Tasmania 152-9 (J. F. Holyman 18*, T. D. Bower 5*); Third day, Victoria 166-5 (W. G. Ayres 50*, A. I. C. Dodemaide 27*).

Victoria

W. N. Phillips hit wkt b Tucker	67	– (2) c Holyman b Matthews 18
D. J. Ramshaw lbw b Matthews	28	– (1) c sub b Young 19
P. C. Nobes c and b Tucker	9	– c Holyman b Young.......... 1
D. S. Lehmann c Cruse b Gilbert	18	– c Tucker b Matthews......... 34
*S. P. O'Donnell lbw b Matthews	0	– c Hills b Matthews........... 1
W. G. Ayres b Matthews	38	– not out....................100
A. I. C. Dodemaide lbw b Young	3	– not out................... 53
M. G. Hughes b Matthews	0	
S. K. Warne c Holyman b Tucker	10	
*D. S. Berry b Matthews	12	
D. W. Fleming not out	4	
L-b 5, n-b 6	11	B 1, l-b 5, w 2, n-b 12 ... 20
	200	**(5 wkts dec.) 246**

1/93 2/109 3/113 4/113 5/134   1/40 2/44 3/44   (5 wkts dec.)
5/170 7/173 8/174 9/195   4/46 5/103

Bowling: *First Innings*—Gilbert 13-5-24-1; Bower 13-3-31-0; Matthews 27-8-48-5; Young 23-8-49-1; Tucker 15-5-43-3. *Second Innings*—Gilbert 3-0-12-0; Bower 23-6-63-0; Matthews 27-10-72-3; Young 13-3-42-2; Tucker 10-0-39-0; Hughes 4-0-12-0.

Tasmania

D. F. Hills b Berry b Dodemaide	41	– lbw b Hughes 17
G. A. Hughes b Hughes	45	– c O'Donnell b Warne 18
B. A. Cruse c O'Donnell b Dodemaide	10	– c Ramshaw b Hughes 3
M. Cox c Ramshaw b Hughes	0	– lbw b Hughes 55
R. J. Tucker c Ramshaw b Dodemaide	3	– b Dodemaide 37
D. J. Buckingham c O'Donnell b Dodemaide	6	– c Berry b Fleming 24
S. Young c Lehmann b Dodemaide	0	– not out................... 38
C. D. Matthews c Berry b Warne	15	– c Warne b Hughes........... 4
*J. F. Holyman not out	19	– run out 1
*D. R. Gilbert c Lehmann b Warne	0	
T. D. Bower c Dodemaide b Hughes	5	– (10) not out 2
B 6, l-b 5, w 2	13	L-b 10, w 2 12
	157	**(8 wkts) 211**

1/76 2/100 3/101 4/104 5/114   1/40 2/44 3/52 4/107   (8 wkts)
5/114 7/114 8/136 9/140   5/158 6/178 7/202 8/206

Bowling: *First Innings*—Hughes 30-11-38-3; Fleming 20-6-48-0; Warne 14-7-26-2; Dodemaide 35-18-34-5. *Second Innings*—Hughes 26-9-71-4; Fleming 15-6-27-1; Warne 22-6-66-1; Dodemaide 15-6-37-1; O'Donnell 1-1-0-0.

Umpires: D. R. Close and B. T. Knight.

VICTORIA v WESTERN AUSTRALIA

At Melbourne, January 24, 25, 26, 27. Drawn. Western Australia 2 pts. Toss: Victoria. The grassy pitch persuaded O'Donnell to bowl first, but Western Australia batted stubbornly and reached 267 for four on the first day. Veletta and Andrews, who added 142 for the fifth wicket, both lost their nerve in the 90s, Veletta running himself out and Andrews losing patience against the slow left-armer Jackson. Victoria's bowlers took the last five wicket for 38, but their batting then struggled against the probing medium pace of Alderman McCague and Moody. Lehmann was the outstanding exception, hitting 23 fours all over th ground in a stay of 254 minutes, having been caught at slip by Moody off a no-ball befor scoring. Dodemaide also batted well, but when he was eighth out at 299, O'Donnell allowe the tail to meander on for another 30 minutes, when his bowlers could have bee undermining Western Australia's second innings. As it was they took five for 59 on th third evening. However, Martyn dug in and batted splendidly for over four hours, hitting 1 fours, until Veletta declared. Victoria faced an impossible 312 in 38 overs.

Close of play: First day, Western Australia 267-4 (M. R. J. Veletta 77*, W. S. Andrew 57*); Second day, Victoria 128-3 (D. S. Lehmann 54*, W. G. Ayres 22*); Third day Western Australia 59-5 (D. R. Martyn 12*, W. S. Andrews 1*).

Western Australia

M. P. Lavender lbw b Dodemaide	10	– b Dodemaide	(
J. L. Langer b Sutherland	33	– b Fleming	12
T. M. Moody c Lehmann b Fleming	56	– c Ramshaw b Dodemaide	23
*M. R. J. Veletta run out	99	– lbw b Fleming	(
D. R. Martyn c Sutherland b O'Donnell	20	– not out	10!
W. S. Andrews st Berry b Jackson	98	– (7) c Jackson b Fleming	7
†T. J. Zoehrer lbw b Sutherland	29	– (8) lbw b O'Donnell	19
B. P. Julian b Nobes b Jackson	1	– (9) c Jackson b O'Donnell	29
J. Angel not out	25	– (6) c Berry b Dodemaide	7
M. J. McCague c O'Donnell b Jackson	7	– st Berry b Jackson	11
T. M. Alderman c O'Donnell b Dodemaide	5		
B 2, l-b 6, n-b 6	14	B 3, l-b 5, n-b 2	10

1/18 2/55 3/133 4/161 5/303   397   1/18 2/30 3/30   (9 wkts dec.) 222
6/359 7/359 8/360 9/372   4/56 5/56 6/69
                         7/114 8/187 9/222

Bowling: *First Innings*—Dodemaide 37.1–12–81–2; Fleming 33–7–100–1; O'Donnel 25–7–68–1; Sutherland 26–5–71–2; Jackson 21–6–69–3. *Second Innings*—Dodemaid 24–6–63–3; Fleming 20–4–53–3; O'Donnell 13–3–38–2; Sutherland 10–3–35–0; Jackson 11–5–25–1.

Victoria

W. N. Phillips lbw b McCague	0	– (2) c and b Zoehrer	37
D. J. Ramshaw c Andrews b McCague	9	– (1) c McCague b Angel	19
P. C. Nobes b Alderman	17	– not out	9
D. S. Lehmann c Lavender b McCague	148	– not out	23
W. G. Ayres lbw b Alderman	22		
*S. P. O'Donnell c Moody b McCague	8		
A. I. C. Dodemaide c Andrews b Moody	46		
†D. S. Berry c Veletta b Moody	14		
J. A. Sutherland lbw b Moody	6		
D. W. Fleming c Langer b Alderman	0		
P. W. Jackson not out	4		
B 4, l-b 6, n-b 24	34	L-b 1, n-b 6	7

1/0 2/30 3/52 4/128 5/161   308   1/58 2/66   (2 wkts) 9!
6/252 7/290 8/299 9/302

Bowling: *First Innings*—McCague 22–9–44–4; Alderman 33–10–79–3; Angel 15–3–57–0 Moody 24.4–11–42–3; Julian 1–1–0–0; Zoehrer 22–6–69–0; Martyn 2–1–7–0. *Secon Innings*—McCague 3–0–16–0; Alderman 6–2–18–0; Angel 8–2–18–1; Moody 3–0–10–0 Zoehrer 9–3–26–1; Lavender 1–0–2–0; Langer 1–0–4–0.

Umpires: R. C. Bailhache and K. A. P. Knott.

NEW SOUTH WALES v SOUTH AUSTRALIA

At Sydney, January 31, February 1, 2, 3. New South Wales won by an innings and 30 runs. New South Wales 6 pts. Toss: South Australia. David Hookes dominated the first day with a typically carefree innings. He launched a tremendous onslaught on Holdsworth's bowling, scoring 20 off one over, but was then beaten by a slower ball from Steve Waugh and thus missed his first-ever hundred at Sydney. The reply was set up by a partnership of 93 from the Waugh brothers, and when Mark was joined by Bayliss, the runs came even faster as they shared 178 for the fourth wicket. After tea, they added 50 in six overs before Waugh charged at a ball from Sleep and missed. On the third day Bayliss completed a superb hundred and, when South Australia batted again, the spinners Freedman and Matthews had them in disarray. Although Sleep defended resolutely, he could only extend the game into the 48th minute of the fourth morning.

Close of play: First day, South Australia 282; Second day, New South Wales 373-5 (T. H. Bayliss 91*, P. A. Emery 4*); Third day, South Australia 152-7 (P. R. Sleep 16*, T. B. A. May 6*).

South Australia

G. S. Blewett c Small b Holdsworth	11	– c Emery b Lawson	11
A. M. J. Hilditch c Emery b Matthews	68	– b Holdsworth	9
G. A. Bishop lbw b Lawson	10	– b Matthews	22
*J. D. Siddons c Matthews b Lawson	38	– c and b Freedman	34
D. W. Hookes lbw b S. R. Waugh	87	– c M. E. Waugh b Matthews	26
J. C. Scuderi c Milliken b Freedman	40	– b Freedman	19
†T. J. Nielsen lbw b Lawson	1	– c S. R. Waugh b Freedman	0
P. R. Sleep c Holdsworth b Freedman	1	– not out	28
T. B. A. May c Emery b Holdsworth	7	– c S. R. Waugh b Matthews	6
D. J. Hickey not out	11	– b Matthews	11
C. J. Owen b Holdsworth	1	– c M. E. Waugh b Matthews	0
L-b 5, n-b 2	7	B 2, l-b 5, w 1, n-b 2	10

1/14 2/45 3/124 4/136 5/209   282   1/19 2/35 3/54 4/93 5/115   176
6/218 7/219 8/270 9/272   6/118 7/127 8/152 9/174

Bowling: *First Innings*—Holdsworth 23.2–2–104–3; Lawson 25–9–60–3; S. R. Waugh 9–1–29–1; Matthews 21–6–43–1; M. E. Waugh 1–0–4–0; Freedman 13–1–37–2. *Second Innings*—Holdsworth 9–2–37–1; Lawson 8–1–18–1; S. R. Waugh 4–1–16–0; Matthews 25.5–8–61–5; Freedman 21–9–37–3.

New South Wales

S. M. Small c Blewett b Hickey	19	*G. F. Lawson b May	0
G. S. Milliken c Nielsen b Hickey	16	D. A. Freedman not out	26
S. R. Waugh c Nielsen b Owen	41	W. J. Holdsworth c Nielsen b Owen	14
M. E. Waugh b Sleep	158		
T. H. Bayliss b May	133	B 5, l-b 8, n-b 8	21
M. G. Bevan lbw b Owen	29		
†P. A. Emery c Nielsen b Scuderi	12	1/33 2/38 3/131 4/309 5/353	488
G. R. J. Matthews c Siddons b May	19	6/414 7/432 8/438 9/461	

Bowling: Hickey 21–2–117–2; Scuderi 40–13–86–1; Owen 22–5–67–3; May 35–4–120–3; Sleep 19–2–85–1.

Umpires: P. E. Dodd and I. S. Thomas.

SOUTH AUSTRALIA v QUEENSLAND

At Adelaide, February 7, 8, 9, 10. South Australia won by four wickets. South Australia 6 pts, Queensland 2 pts. Toss: South Australia. South Australia became the first Australian team to score more than 500 in the fourth innings to win a first-class match. Their 506 has been exceeded only by Cambridge University's 507 for seven against MCC and Ground at

Lord's in 1896. Coming in when Queensland declared soon after lunch on the third day, Hilditch and Blewett put their heads down and scored 204 by stumps. Blewett was out early next morning, and when McDermott took three more quick wickets Queensland looked home and dry. However, Siddons and Sleep took advantage of the tired bowlers to add 152, and when the last over began, the scores were level. The first three balls evaded Sleep's bat, but the fourth took an inside edge and the batsmen scampered through. Queensland established a first-innings lead of 204 having been put in to bat, thanks to some inferior bowling and batting by South Australia. Rackemann did not enforce the follow-on, as he was nursing a leg injury and McDermott had put in 18 superlative overs unchanged. With the weather set fair, it seemed that only a miracle could thwart Queensland when they added another 301. But with hindsight, it can be seen that the match turned when Border missed a return catch off Hilditch, then 69. Hilditch went on to bat for nearly six hours, and Blewett, Siddons and Sleep all responded brilliantly to his example.

Close of play: First day, Queensland 313-9 (G. J. Rowell 30*, C. G. Rackemann 3*); Second day, Queensland 149-1 (M. L. Hayden 71*, D. M. Wellham 1*); Third day, South Australia 204-0 (G. S. Blewett 97*, A. M. J. Hilditch 93*).

Queensland

T. J. Barsby c Owen b Hickey	6	– lbw b Scuderi	67
M. L. Hayden run out	79	– c Owen b May	80
D. M. Wellham lbw b Hickey	34	– c Nielsen b Hickey	28
A. R. Border c Hookes b Hickey	0	– (5) c Nielsen b Scuderi	46
S. G. Law c Siddons b Hickey	12	– (4) not out	35
G. M. Ritchie run out	58	– not out	23
†I. A. Healy c Nielsen b Scuderi	31		
P. L. Taylor c Brayshaw b Sleep	29		
C. J. McDermott lbw b Scuderi	5		
G. J. Rowell not out	45		
*C. G. Rackemann run out	9		
L-b 7, w 3, n-b 16	26	B 5, l-b 3, n-b 14	22
	334	**(4 wkts dec.)**	**301**

1/13 2/80 3/80 4/92 5/208
6/212 7/264 8/277 9/282

1/143 2/184
3/194 4/271

Bowling: *First Innings*—Hickey 23-2-96-4; Scuderi 30.1-5-96-2; Owen 14-3-49-0; May 24-8-52-0; Blewett 5-1-10-0; Sleep 6-0-24-1. *Second Innings*—Hickey 14-1-81-1; Scuderi 17-5-62-2; Owen 11-5-40-0; May 14-3-45-1; Blewett 7-0-31-0; Sleep 12-6-34-0.

South Australia

G. S. Blewett c Barsby b McDermott	34	– c Healy b McDermott	98
A. M. J. Hilditch c Rowell b Rackemann	5	– c Healy b McDermott	137
J. A. Brayshaw c Rowell b McDermott	1	– b Rowell	39
*J. D. Siddons c Barsby b McDermott	4	– c Border b McDermott	87
D. W. Hookes c Taylor b McDermott	5	– c Border b McDermott	3
J. C. Scuderi c sub b Rowell	10	– lbw b McDermott	0
P. R. Sleep c Rackemann b McDermott	16	– not out	97
†T. J. Nielsen lbw b McDermott	1	– not out	14
T. B. A. May not out	20		
D. J. Hickey c Law b Rackemann	12		
C. J. Owen c Border b Rackemann	0		
L-b 6, n-b 20	26	L-b 11, n-b 20	31
	130	**(6 wkts)**	**506**

1/8 2/15 3/19 4/27 5/44
6/86 7/90 8/95 9/130

1/209 2/283 3/307
4/314 5/316 6/468

Bowling: *First Innings*—McDermott 18-2-58-6; Rackemann 10.4-3-22-3; Rowell 7-0-44-1. *Second Innings*—McDermott 37-6-124-4; Rackemann 32.4-6-117-1; Rowell 18-1-64-1; Taylor 42-6-126-0; Law 1-0-1-0; Border 23-4-63-0.

Umpires: S. J. Davis and D. J. Harper.

TASMANIA v SOUTH AUSTRALIA

At Hobart, February 13, 14, 15, 16. Drawn. Tasmania 2 pts. Toss: South Australia. Tasmania owed much of their solid position on the first day to Tucker, who was unluckily dismissed in fading light just before stumps. But next morning their innings faltered in the face of some good seam bowling by South Australia's newcomer, Hutchison. Then Hilditch and Blewett made the most of six lives to put up 168 for the visitors' first wicket. Brayshaw seemed to be steering them towards an inevitable first-innings lead, especially as Tasmania had lost Campbell to a strained back. But Matthews, as ever, refused to give in. As the fielding improved, South Australia folded ignominiously, losing their last seven wickets for 63 to trail by three runs. Tasmania immediately surrendered this tenuous advantage, with five batsmen going for 88 by the close. The last day was a battle of attrition. Buckingham, with help from Young, kept the South Australian bowlers at bay until only 24 overs remained, and stalemate was assured.

Close of play: First day, Tasmania 236-5 (D. J. Buckingham 20*, M. N. Atkinson 1*); Second day, South Australia 142-0 (G. S. Blewett 70*, A. M. J. Hilditch 63*); Third day, Tasmania 88-5 (R. J. Tucker 1*, D. J. Buckingham 0*).

Tasmania

D. F. Hills c Nielsen b Hutchison	44	– c May b Scuderi	33
G. A. Hughes lbw b Scuderi	19	– lbw b Scuderi	1
*D. C. Boon c Nielsen b Hutchison	34	– c Siddons b Williamson	24
J. Cox c Hookes b May	27	– b May	5
R. J. Tucker lbw b Hutchison	75	– (6) c Sleep b Hutchison	8
D. J. Buckingham not out	71	– (7) c Nielsen b Sleep	82
†M. N. Atkinson c Nielsen b Hutchison	7	– (5) b May	12
S. Young c Siddons b Williamson	7	– c Siddons b Hutchison	38
C. D. Matthews c Nielsen b Williamson	8	– c Sleep b May	9
G. D. Campbell c Williamson b Hutchison	15	– c Brayshaw b Sleep	8
D. R. Gilbert (did not bat)	–	– not out	3
L-b 13, w 2, n-b 6	21	L-b 8, w 1, n-b 8	17

1/37 2/104 3/109 4/169 5/235   (9 wkts dec.) 328
6/263 7/277 8/300 9/328

1/4 2/45 3/60 4/78 5/88   240
6/104 7/184 8/218 9/233

Bowling: *First Innings*—Scuderi 36-12-81-1; Hutchison 39.4-10-87-5; Williamson 23-4-71-2; Blewett 6-1-17-0; May 21-6-50-1; Sleep 4-1-9-0. *Second Innings*—Scuderi 23-9-57-2; Hutchison 22-4-68-2; Williamson 16-6-42-1; May 36-21-48-3; Sleep 9.5-3-17-2.

South Australia

G. S. Blewett lbw b Matthews	86		
A. M. J. Hilditch c Atkinson b Matthews	76		
J. A. Brayshaw c Gilbert b Young	75		
*J. D. Siddons run out	24		
D. W. Hookes c Boon b Matthews	14	– (2) lbw b Gilbert	5
J. C. Scuderi c Matthews b Young	2		
P. R. Sleep lbw b Matthews	0		
†T. J. Nielsen run out	17	– (1) not out	14
C. J. Williamson not out	8	– (3) not out	13
T. B. A. May c Atkinson b Tucker	0		
P. J. Hutchison run out	0		
B 2, l-b 9, w 2, n-b 10	23		

1/68 2/181 3/237 4/262 5/290   325
6/290 7/294 8/323 9/325

1/11   (1 wkt) 32

Bowling: *First Innings*—Gilbert 32-7-84-0; Campbell 6-0-18-0; Young 22-4-77-2; Matthews 37.2-9-89-4; Tucker 11-4-33-1; Buckingham 5-4-13-0; Hughes 1-1-0-0. *Second Innings*—Gilbert 7-2-13-1; Campbell 4-2-6-0; Young 3-2-4-0; Matthews 1-0-1-0; Hills 1-0-8-0.

Umpires: B. T. Knight and S. G. Randell.

VICTORIA v NEW SOUTH WALES

At Melbourne, February 13, 14, 15, 16. Drawn. Victoria 2 pts. Toss: Victoria. After the first day was lost to rain, O'Donnell put New South Wales in, and with his fellow pace bowlers had the batsmen struggling. Taylor scored his first hundred against Victoria, but the only worthwhile support came from Matthews, in a partnership of 92. After batting six hours, Taylor was last out, having a swing at Hughes. In reply Phillips and Nobes made a brisk start. The New South Wales bowlers became more and more frustrated as catches were dropped and the umpires steadfastly refused to give a single lbw. Victoria passed New South Wales's score on the third evening, and continued for half an hour the next day, effectively eliminating any ideas Lawson may have had of setting up a run-chase. But after Dodemaide had threatened to bowl New South Wales out cheaply, Mark Waugh and Bevan provided some entertainment with a terrific partnership of 123 in 87 minutes. Both hit sixes off the embattled leg-spinner Warne.

Close of play: First day, No play; Second day, New South Wales 280; Third day, Victoria 310-7 (A. I. C. Dodemaide 18*, M. G. Hughes 23*).

New South Wales

S. M. Small b Dodemaide	17	– c O'Donnell b Dodemaide	37
M. A. Taylor c Jones b Hughes	158	– b Dodemaide	53
S. R. Waugh c Berry b Reiffel	5	– c Ayres b Dodemaide	6
M. E. Waugh c Dodemaide b Reiffel	13	– b Dodemaide	76
T. H. Bayliss c Berry b Reiffel	0	– c Phillips b Warne	7
M. G. Bevan c Jones b O'Donnell	16	– c Phillips b Jones	70
G. R. J. Matthews c Berry b Dodemaide	33	– not out	4
†P. A. Emery c Berry b Reiffel	8	– not out	4
*G. F. Lawson c Lehmann b O'Donnell	12		
W. J. Holdsworth c Nobes b Hughes	2		
M. R. Whitney not out	0		
L-b 4, n-b 12	16	L-b 8, n-b 8	16

1/33 2/44 3/72 4/76 5/105   280   1/83 2/105 3/108   (6 wkts dec.) 273
6/197 7/269 8/269 9/277   4/121 5/244 6/266

Bowling: *First Innings*—Hughes 22.3–7–52–2; Dodemaide 23–3–58–2; Reiffel 19–5–59–4; O'Donnell 16–1–72–2; Warne 10–2–35–0. *Second Innings*—Hughes 9–0–55–0; Dodemaide 21.5–1–69–4; Reiffel 10–0–37–0; O'Donnell 2–0–19–0; Warne 20–8–78–1; Jones 2–0–7–1.

Victoria

W. N. Phillips b S. R. Waugh	34	– (2) not out	7
P. C. Nobes c Emery b Lawson	61	– (1) not out	3
D. M. Jones c M. E. Waugh b Whitney	54		
D. S. Lehmann b Matthews	32		
W. G. Ayres b Whitney	12		
*S. P. O'Donnell c Emery b Holdsworth	45		
P. R. Reiffel b Holdsworth	6		
A. I. C. Dodemaide not out	32		
M. G. Hughes c Bevan b S. R. Waugh	23		
†D. S. Berry c M. E. Waugh b S. R. Waugh	1		
S. K. Warne c S. R. Waugh b M. E. Waugh	10		
L-b 12, w 1, n-b 15	28	B 5, l-b 1, w 1	7

1/77 2/140 3/195 4/215 5/226   338   (no wkt) 10
6/259 7/272 8/310 9/317

Bowling: *First Innings*—Whitney 20–6–62–2; Holdsworth 20–2–67–2; Lawson 22–7–55–1; S. R. Waugh 11–2–23–3; Matthews 23–2–76–1; M. E. Waugh 12–5–29–1; Bayliss 1–0–14–0. *Second Innings*—Whitney 4–2–3–0; Holdsworth 4–2–8–0.

Umpires: D. W. Holt and P. H. Jensen.

WESTERN AUSTRALIA v QUEENSLAND

At Perth, February 13, 14, 15, 16. Western Australia won by an innings and 15 runs. Western Australia 6 pts. Toss: Western Australia. Western Australia were in complete control from the moment Marsh asked Queensland to bat. In spite of a fighting four-hour innings by Wellham, they were out soon after tea, with Angel, an eleventh-hour recruit to the team and the fifth seamer, collecting four wickets at a lively pace. By contrast, Queensland's fast bowling depended on just Rackemann and Rowell once McDermott succumbed to flu after five overs. The batsmen took full advantage; Marsh batted relentlessly for five and a half hours. His colleagues showed similar application, and even extras passed 50. Declaring 302 ahead, Western Australia had four sessions to bowl Queensland out, which they did comfortably. With Alderman incapacitated (hamstring trouble and stomach bug), Moody became the chief destroyer with the second new ball, ending three and a half hours' defiance by Border courtesy of a blinding catch by Martyn at square leg. He ended the match by bowling Rackemann after he had held out for 79 minutes with Healy, who curbed his aggressive instincts and was unlucky to miss a maiden hundred.

Close of play: First day, Western Australia 53-0 (G. R. Marsh 23*, M. R. J. Veletta 19*); Second day, Western Australia 298-3 (M. P. Lavender 69*, D. R. Martyn 38*); Third day, Queensland 103-3 (T. J. Barsby 39*, A. R. Border 2*).

Queensland

T. J. Barsby c Veletta b Reid	5	– c Moody b Reid 43
M. L. Hayden c Zoehrer b Alderman	5	– c Zoehrer b Julian 31
D. M. Wellham c Zoehrer b Angel	83	– c Zoehrer b Angel 6
A. R. Border c Zoehrer b Julian	8	– (5) c Martyn b Moody 43
S. G. Law c Alderman b Moody	15	– (6) c Zoehrer b Angel 4
G. M. Ritchie b Angel	30	– (7) b Reid 22
†I. A. Healy c Alderman b Moody	14	– (8) not out 87
P. L. Taylor lbw b Angel	22	– (9) c and b Moody 2
C. J. McDermott not out	19	– (10) c Zoehrer b Moody 0
G. J. Rowell c Zoehrer b Angel	2	– (4) lbw b Julian 2
C. G. Rackemann run out	0	– b Moody 10
L-b 2, n-b 2	4	L-b 8, w 1, n-b 28 37
	207	**287**

1/6 2/10 3/31 4/60 5/113   1/66 2/79 3/82 4/112 5/128
6/132 7/177 8/190 9/204   6/158 7/220 8/226 9/226

Bowling: First Innings—Reid 14-4-38-1; Alderman 13-1-35-1; Julian 11.5-2-45-1; Moody 17.4-4-41-2; Angel 17-5-46-4; Martyn 1-1-0-0. *Second Innings*—Reid 24-9-40-2; Alderman 7-2-26-0; Julian 21-9-40-2; Moody 30.4-13-61-4; Angel 23-4-78-2; Martyn 3-1-5-0; Andrews 3-0-22-0; Zoehrer 2-0-7-0.

Western Australia

*G. R. Marsh lbw b Rowell 88	J. Angel not out 13
*M. R. J. Veletta run out 46	B. A. Reid not out 14
M. P. Lavender c Hayden b Rackemann 83	
T. M. Moody c Healy b Rowell 21	B 5, l-b 9, w 1, n-b 38 53
D. R. Martyn c sub b Rackemann 64	
W. S. Andrews c sub b Taylor 67	1/111 2/200 3/248 (8 wkts dec.) 509
†T. J. Zoehrer b Taylor 57	4/334 5/354 6/473
B. P. Julian c Healy b Rowell 3	7/482 8/482

T. M. Alderman did not bat.

Bowling: McDermott 5-0-22-0; Rackemann 52-16-124-2; Rowell 45-12-121-3; Taylor 46-9-136-2; Law 21-2-73-0; Border 7-2-19-0.

Umpires: R. J. Evans and T. A. Prue.

SOUTH AUSTRALIA v VICTORIA

At Adelaide, February 21, 22, 23, 24. Drawn. Victoria 2 pts. Toss: Victoria. Although South Australia's last two batsmen denied Victoria outright victory by surviving the last ten balls, much of the interest focused on Hookes's efforts to surpass R. J. Inverarity's Sheffield Shield aggregate of 9,341 runs. The scene was set on the third day, with a good Sunday crowd, plenty of TV cameras and Hookes needing 47 for the record. When South Australia lost their third wicket at 198, the crowd rose in anticipation of Hookes's entry. Instead Nielsen emerged to protect him from the second new ball. There was another anticlimax: when Hookes did make his belated appearance, he was promptly caught for four. He was lucky to get a second chance. But Siddons fed Victoria runs, and O'Donnell responded by declaring overnight. South Australia made a good fist of a target of 321, although Hookes gave his fans palpitations by snicking a catch to Reiffel when ten. The chance went down, and he duly reached the record with consecutive fours off O'Donnell. Victoria established their dominance from the first day when Lehmann and O'Donnell put on 129 in 127 minutes for the fifth wicket. Next morning Dodemaide battered his way to a maiden century for the state, completed while he shared an undefeated partnership of 86 for the last wicket with Jackson. South Australia's reply was pedestrian, but Brayshaw reached his first century after agonising on 99 for 38 minutes.

Close of play: First day, Victoria 338-8 (A. I. C. Dodemaide 25*, S. K. Warne 4*); Second day, South Australia 173-2 (J. A. Brayshaw 77*, J. D. Siddons 11*); Third day, Victoria 175-4 (P. C. Nobes 76*).

Victoria

W. N. Phillips c Nielsen b Hickey	30	– c Scuderi b Blewett 23
P. C. Nobes c Blewett b Hutchison	0	– not out 76
W. G. Ayres c Hilditch b Scuderi	5	– b Brayshaw 1
D. S. Lehmann st Nielsen b Sleep	112	– c Scuderi b Brayshaw 48
D. A. Harris lbw b Hickey	11	
*S. P. O'Donnell c Siddons b Sleep	87	– (5) c Blewett b Hilditch 23
P. R. Reiffel c Hickey b Sleep	27	
A. I. C. Dodemaide not out	117	
†D. S. Berry b Hutchison	15	
S. K. Warne c Blewett b Sleep	14	
P. W. Jackson not out	20	
L-b 17, n-b 6	23	B 2, l-b 1, w 1 4

1/13 2/20 3/68 4/104 5/233   (9 wkts dec.) 461   1/44 2/50   (4 wkts dec.) 175
6/274 7/297 8/318 9/375   3/122 4/175

Bowling: First Innings—Hutchison 19-0-88-2; Scuderi 26-7-66-1; Hickey 25-3-95-2; May 32-5-112-0; Sleep 28-7-83-4. *Second Innings*—Hutchison 1-0-6-0; Scuderi 4-1-14-0; Blewett 10-0-50-1; Brayshaw 11-2-47-2; Siddons 6-0-40-0; Hilditch 1-0-15-1.

South Australia

G. S. Blewett c Nobes b Dodemaide	6	– c Berry b Dodemaide 0
A. M. J. Hilditch st Berry b Jackson	63	– c Phillips b Jackson 38
J. A. Brayshaw b Reiffel	101	– b Dodemaide 0
*J. D. Siddons c Dodemaide b Warne	21	– c Dodemaide b Jackson 65
†T. J. Nielsen run out	23	– (8) b Dodemaide 0
D. W. Hookes c Berry b Dodemaide	4	– (5) c Nobes b Jackson 49
J. C. Scuderi b Jackson	28	– (6) c Phillips b O'Donnell 5
P. R. Sleep not out	33	– (7) c Berry b O'Donnell 38
T. B. A. May not out	13	– b O'Donnell 12
P. J. Hutchison (did not bat)		– not out 0
D. J. Hickey (did not bat)		– not out 0
B 8, l-b 10, n-b 6	24	B 2, l-b 8, n-b 6 16

1/15 2/138 3/198 4/230 5/234   (7 wkts dec.) 316   1/13 2/13 3/112   (9 wkts) 296
6/242 7/279   4/125 5/211 6/243
                                                            7/268 8/288 9/299

Bowling: *First Innings*—Reiffel 28–5–92–1; Dodemaide 30–15–55–2; Warne 35–15–67–1; O'Donnell 13–7–23–0; Jackson 32–12–61–2. *Second Innings*—Reiffel 17–4–63–0; Dodemaide 23–6–66–3; Warne 11–1–36–0; O'Donnell 15–2–39–3; Jackson 30–9–85–3.

Umpires: A. R. Crafter and S. J. Davis.

WESTERN AUSTRALIA v SOUTH AUSTRALIA

At Perth, February 28, 29, March 1, 2. Western Australia won by ten wickets. Western Australia 6 pts. Toss: South Australia. South Australia were no match for a buoyant Western Australia, who ensured their place in the Shield final after a game lasting just over three days. The visitors failed to make the most of batting first on a flat pitch, and Angel recovered from an erratic opening to polish off the tail. He also contributed 23 as nightwatchman to set up the big Western Australian total. Veletta survived a couple of hefty blows from Hickey to anchor the innings: he spent six hours over his 121, while Langer and Andrews busied themselves at the other end. South Australia's batting failed again, apart from Brayshaw and Hilditch, in his last match, who defended solidly. Hookes's farewell was less successful. The first eight batsmen were all caught behind by Veletta or Zoehrer, who shared the wicket-keeping.

Close of play: First day, Western Australia 75-2 (M. R. J. Veletta 22*, J. Angel 2*); Second day, Western Australia 402-7 (T. J. Zoehrer 63*, B. P. Julian 1*); Third day, South Australia 231-8 (T. J. Nielsen 22*, P. J. Hutchison 4*).

South Australia

G. S. Blewett c Zoehrer b McCague	16	– c Zoehrer b Angel		0
A. M. J. Hilditch c Alderman b McCague	16	– c Veletta b Julian		55
J. A. Brayshaw c Langer b Alderman	52	– c Veletta b Julian		60
*J. D. Siddons c McPhee b Angel	5	– c Zoehrer b Angel		16
G. A. Bishop c Martyn b Julian	19	– c Veletta b Angel		37
D. W. Hookes c Zoehrer b Alderman	5	– c Veletta b McCague		11
J. C. Scuderi c Andrews b Julian	5	– c Veletta b Alderman		3
P. R. Sleep c Veletta b Angel	13	– c Veletta b McCague		4
†T. J. Nielsen not out	20	– c Langer b Andrews		40
P. J. Hutchison b Angel	11	– c McCague b Angel		14
D. J. Hickey c Alderman b Angel	1	– not out		9
L-b 4, n-b 34	38	B 2, l-b 3, n-b 16		21

1/39 2/64 3/71 4/124 5/142	201	1/0 2/124 3/131 4/172 5/179	270
5/153 7/153 8/181 9/195		6/193 7/197 8/197 9/255	

Bowling: *First Innings*—Angel 15.2–2–78–4; Alderman 14–4–38–2; McCague 13–7–24–2; Julian 11–4–33–2; Martyn 3–0–12–0; Andrews 1–1–0–0; Zoehrer 10–3–12–0. *Second Innings*—Angel 24–5–97–4; Alderman 15–7–37–1; McCague 23–5–65–2; Julian 15–3–50–2; Andrews 2–0–4–1; Zoehrer 9–6–12–0.

Western Australia

M. W. McPhee c Nielsen b Hickey	33		
*M. R. J. Veletta c Nielsen b Scuderi	121		
M. P. Lavender b Hickey	10		
J. Angel c Hilditch b Hutchison	23		
D. R. Martyn c Siddons b Sleep	0	– (2) not out	1
J. L. Langer b Sleep	70		
W. S. Andrews c Sleep b Scuderi	50		
†T. J. Zoehrer c Sleep b Hutchison	88		
B. P. Julian c Nielsen b Hutchison	23	– (1) not out	4
M. J. McCague c Hickey b Sleep	10		
T. M. Alderman not out	3		
B 7, l-b 13, w 1, n-b 16	37	W 1	1

1/53 2/73 3/127 4/130 5/240	468	(no wkt)	6
6/323 7/348 8/447 9/458			

Bowling: *First Innings*—Hutchison 24-4-97-3; Hickey 39-6-131-2; Scuderi 31-11-89-2; Sleep 36.4-10-101-3; Blewett 7-1-30-0. *Second Innings*—Hutchison 2-2-0-0; Blewett 1.3-0-6-0.

Umpires: R. J. Evans and T. A. Prue.

TASMANIA v NEW SOUTH WALES

At Hobart, February 29, March 1, 2. New South Wales won by an innings and four runs. New South Wales 6 pts. Toss: New South Wales. Lawson's decision to put Tasmania in reaped greater rewards than he could ever have hoped as the home team crumbled for 76, their lowest total in the Sheffield Shield. McNamara and Greg Matthews made the early breakthrough, then Holdsworth produced a devastating spell after lunch to claim six wickets for 18. Three times he took wickets with consecutive balls. Chris Matthews also took two consecutive wickets when he upset the early New South Wales batsmen, reducing them to 22 for three. But Bevan and McNamara put on 130 for the fourth wicket, the only time that bat established any sort of mastery over ball. Bevan looked quite perturbed when given out, caught down the leg side, five short of a hundred. His dismissal started another collapse, with Chris Matthews and Tucker removing the last six wickets for 29. Tasmania's second innings was little better than their first, and the New South Wales bowlers finished off the match early on the third day.

Close of play: First day, New South Wales 132-3 (M. G. Bevan 65*, B. E. McNamara 36*); Second day, Tasmania 114-7 (T. D. Bower 0*, M. N. Atkinson 3*).

Tasmania

D. F. Hills c Emery b McNamara	17	– c Small b Holdsworth	5
G. A. Hughes c McNamara b Holdsworth	16	– c Emery b Holdsworth	38
M. G. Farrell b McNamara	1	– b McNamara	7
J. Cox c Small b Matthews	4	– c Emery b Lawson	29
R. J. Tucker c McNamara b Matthews	0	– (7) c Bayliss b Matthews	6
D. J. Buckingham c Emery b Holdsworth	11	– c Emery b Matthews	10
†M. N. Atkinson c Small b Holdsworth	0	– (9) not out	15
S. Young not out	12	– (5) c Holdsworth b McNamara	16
C. D. Matthews c and b Holdsworth	0	– (10) c Small b Holdsworth	2
*D. R. Gilbert c Slater b Holdsworth	2	– (11) c Small b Lawson	4
T. D. Bower c Small b Holdsworth	0	– (8) lbw b Lawson	2
B 1, l-b 6, n-b 6	13	L-b 2	2
	76		137

1/26 2/40 3/47 4/47 5/49   6/49 7/66 8/66 9/76

1/18 2/34 3/59 4/82 5/101   6/111 7/111 8/119 9/130

Bowling: *First Innings*—Holdsworth 12.2-5-33-6; Lawson 15-4-20-0; McNamara 8-4-8-2; Matthews 5-2-8-2. *Second Innings*—Holdsworth 16-4-55-3; Lawson 21.5-8-33-3; McNamara 12-5-16-2; Matthews 21-7-31-2; Freedman 1-1-0-0.

New South Wales

S. M. Small c Buckingham b Matthews	10	D. A. Freedman c Young b Tucker	0
M. J. Slater c Young b Matthews	10	*G. F. Lawson not out	0
T. H. Bayliss c Atkinson b Matthews	0	W. J. Holdsworth b Matthews	0
M. G. Bevan c Atkinson b Matthews	95		
B. E. McNamara c Young b Gilbert	43	L-b 9, n-b 10	19
G. R. J. Matthews c Farrell b Tucker	27		
M. T. Haywood c Atkinson b Tucker	5	1/19 2/19 3/22 4/152 5/188	217
†P. A. Emery c Young b Matthews	7	6/203 7/208 8/214 9/214	

Bowling: Gilbert 18-5-46-1; Matthews 28.3-4-89-6; Bower 6-2-14-0; Young 7-2-18-0; Tucker 11-3-21-3; Hughes 1-0-5-0; Farrell 3-1-15-0.

Umpires: D. R. Close and B. T. Knight.

VICTORIA v QUEENSLAND

At Melbourne, February 29, March 1, 2, 3. Drawn. Victoria 2 pts. Toss: Queensland. Rackemann's decision to bowl looked ill-judged when the Victorian openers batted aggressively until just before tea. But then Nobes was dismissed after reaching a maiden century for his new state with his 12th four and Phillips became one of four wickets to fall for 14 in the last hour. Victoria's batsmen continued to struggle on the second day, which lost several hours to rain. But once O'Donnell declared before lunch, Queensland's batsmen were undone by the precision bowling of Dodemaide, who achieved his best Shield figures. All the accredited batsmen got a start, but no one reached 50. When Victoria batted again late on the third day, there was little chance of an outright result, and they seemed unhurried, until Lehmann inspired an assault of 74 in 30 minutes. A declaration set Queensland 286 in 53 overs but, even then, O'Donnell adopted defensive tactics as he sought to save the match rather than win it. To this end he succeeded; Queensland fell 58 short despite a spirited unbeaten 82 from Law. But first-innings points turned out to be insufficient for Victoria's pursuit of the final.

Close of play: First day, Victoria 299-5 (S. P. O'Donnell 6*, D. S. Berry 5*); Second day, Queensland 79-1 (T. J. Barsby 32*, D. M. Wellham 9*); Third day, Victoria 22-1 (P. C. Nobes 12*, W. G. Ayres 6*).

Victoria

W. N. Phillips c Anderson b Rackemann	123	– c Law b Rowell	4
P. C. Nobes c Rackemann b Polzin	103	– c Goggin b Rowell	21
W. G. Ayres lbw b Rackemann	28	– run out	15
D. S. Lehmann c Anderson b Rowell	2	– not out	137
D. A. Harris c Law b Rackemann	3	– b Oxenford	17
*S. P. O'Donnell not out	27	– c Anderson b Polzin	22
†D. S. Berry c Oxenford b Rowell	12		
P. R. Reiffel c Oxenford b Rackemann	1	– (7) not out	1
A. I. C. Dodemaide b Rackemann	0		
N. D. Maxwell not out	20		
B 5, l-b 10, n-b 16	31	B 8, l-b 4, w 1	13

1/194 2/271 3/276 4/282 5/285   (8 wkts. dec.) 350   1/4 2/33 3/62   (5 wkts. dec.) 230
6/306 7/307 8/307   4/102 5/188

P. W. Jackson did not bat.

Bowling: First Innings—Rackemann 27-4-89-5; Rowell 27-6-86-2; Polzin 17-3-52-1; Oxenford 23-3-81-0; Law 16-5-27-0. *Second Innings*—Rackemann 10-2-31-0; Rowell 10-1-39-2; Polzin 5-1-40-1; Oxenford 12-1-51-1; Law 1-0-9-0; Goggin 8-0-43-0; Ritchie 1-0-5-0.

Queensland

T. J. Barsby b Reiffel	32	– c Nobes b Dodemaide	19
M. L. Hayden c Berry b Dodemaide	24	– c Maxwell b O'Donnell	44
D. M. Wellham lbw b Reiffel	25	– (5) c Lehmann b Dodemaide	22
G. M. Ritchie c Berry b Jackson	40	– (3) b Jackson	41
S. G. Law c Berry b Dodemaide	42	– (4) not out	82
P. J. T. Goggin c Maxwell b Dodemaide	49	– c O'Donnell b Dodemaide	2
†P. W. Anderson c and b Dodemaide	34	– not out	13
B. N. J. Oxenford c Berry b Maxwell	3		
M. A. Polzin c Berry b Dodemaide	0		
G. J. Rowell c Berry b Dodemaide	0		
*C. G. Rackemann not out	4		
L-b 9, w 1, n-b 32	42	L-b 1, n-b 4	5

1/65 2/82 3/147 4/147 5/225   295   1/49 2/77 3/121   (5 wkts) 228
6/280 7/284 8/284 9/284   4/174 5/181

Bowling: *First Innings*—Reiffel 29–6–105–2; Dodemaide 37–14–80–6; Maxwell 22.1–6–42–1; Jackson 20–9–32–1; O'Donnell 7–1–27–0. *Second Innings*—Reiffel 4–0–24–0; Dodemaide 13–2–58–3; Maxwell 5–0–22–0; Jackson 16–2–62–1; O'Donnell 12–4–40–1; Nobes 2–0–18–0; Harris 1–0–3–0.

Umpires: L. J. King and W. P. Sheahan.

NEW SOUTH WALES v WESTERN AUSTRALIA

At Sydney, March 7, 8, 9. New South Wales won by 98 runs. New South Wales 6 pts. Toss: New South Wales. New South Wales needed at least first-innings points to join their visitors in the Shield final. After the first day their hopes were muted as only two novices, in their second match, handled the varied Western Australian attack successfully. Slater stood firm for 215 minutes as five wickets fell and put on 65 with Haywood, who struck 13 fours in three hours. But next day slow bowlers Matthews and Freedman had the table-topping Western Australians out for 71, the lowest completed total of the season, soon after lunch. Certainly the pitch allowed some spin, but Bevan and Small had few problems batting in the afternoon. Lawson's overnight declaration was prompted by the calculation that, by bowling out their opponents for 146 or less, New South Wales could head the table. A five-and-a-half-hour century from Veletta scotched that plan; indeed, while he and Andrews were adding 124, a Western Australian victory was just possible. However, McNamara broke the partnership, and Matthews disposed of the tail with another effective spell of off-breaks.

Close of play: First day, Western Australia 1-0 (M. W. McPhee 0*, M. R. J. Veletta 1*); Second day, New South Wales 176-2 (S. M. Small 62*, M. G. Bevan 62*).

New South Wales

S. M. Small c McPhee b Angel	1 – not out	62
M. J. Slater lbw b Alderman	62 – lbw b Zoehrer	26
T. H. Bayliss b Alderman	20 – c Lavender b Herzberg	11
M. G. Bevan lbw b Julian	0 – not out	62
B. E. McNamara c Zoehrer b Angel	15
G. R. J. Matthews c Martyn b Herzberg	5
M. T. Haywood b Herzberg	79
†P. A. Emery c Veletta b Julian	7
D. A. Freedman c Angel b Martyn	20
*G. F. Lawson not out	9
W. J. Holdsworth b Herzberg	7
L-b 12, n-b 8	20	B 2, l-b 8, w 1, n-b 4 ….	15

1/2 2/42 3/43 4/78 5/89   245   1/65 2/78   (2 wkts dec.) 176
6/154 7/172 8/218 9/231

Bowling: *First Innings*—Angel 16–5–41–2; Alderman 21–7–45–2; Julian 16–3–54–2; Herzberg 13.1–2–33–3; Andrews 5–2–15–0; Zoehrer 12–2–30–0; Martyn 3–0–15–1. *Second Innings*—Angel 8–1–38–0; Alderman 10–4–18–0; Julian 7–1–25–0; Herzberg 14–3–35–1; Zoehrer 16–3–50–1.

Western Australia

M. W. McPhee st Emery b Matthews	8 – c Haywood b Freedman	26
*M. R. J. Veletta c Bevan b Holdsworth	1 – not out	101
M. P. Lavender b Matthews	6 – lbw b Freedman	0
D. R. Martyn lbw b Matthews	2 – st Emery b Matthews	21
J. L. Langer c Emery b Lawson	6 – c Small b Matthews	0
W. S. Andrews lbw b Freedman	5 – c McNamara	59
†T. J. Zoehrer b Freedman	7 – lbw b McNamara	0
B. P. Julian lbw b Freedman	10 – c Small b Matthews	3
S. Herzberg c sub b Matthews	4 – c Freedman b Matthews	3
J. Angel not out	15 – c McNamara b Matthews	12
T. M. Alderman lbw b Freedman	0 – c Slater b Matthews	0
L-b 7	7	B 3, l-b 15, w 1, n-b 8 ….	27

1/1 2/14 3/16 4/23 5/27   71   1/53 2/57 3/90 4/90 5/214   252
6/38 7/51 8/56 9/60   6/214 7/227 8/233 9/252

Bowling: *First Innings*—Holdsworth 6–3–9–1; Matthews 16–5–30–4; Lawson 10–6–8–1; Freedman 9.2–5–17–4. *Second Innings*—Holdsworth 3–1–12–0; Matthews 42–9–99–6; Lawson 17–7–34–0; Freedman 18–4–60–2; Bayliss 5–2–3–0; Bevan 6–0–10–0; McNamara 10–2–16–2.

Umpires: D. B. Hair and I. G. Jackson.

QUEENSLAND v TASMANIA

At Brisbane, March 13, 14, 15, 16. Drawn. Tasmania 2 pts. Toss: Tasmania. Queensland's wretched season ended, appropriately, in the wash-out of most of the third day and all of the last. By that time, their bowlers had been hit around by an inexperienced Tasmanian side, and their batsmen humiliated by Matthews. Tasmania's total of 400 was due largely to the young left-hander, Hills, whose maiden hundred contained ten fours. Buckingham and Young also batted aggressively. Wellham apart, Queensland's batsmen showed neither the heart nor the inclination to resist Matthews's left-arm swing on the second day. Five wickets took his season's total to 48 in the Shield, comfortably a record for Tasmania. Following on, Barsby and Hayden showed better form before the rains came.

Close of play: First day, Tasmania 287-4 (S. Young 31*, J. Cox 10*); Second day, Queensland 23-0 (T. J. Barsby 5*, M. L. Hayden 18*); Third day, Queensland 145-1 (M. L. Hayden 57*, D. M. Wellham 0*).

Tasmania

D. F. Hills run out	106	M. J. Di Venuto not out 33
G. A. Hughes c and b Rackemann	45	*R. J. Tucker not out 35
N. C. P. Courtney c Anderson b Rowell	19	B 1, l-b 11, n-b 8 20
D. J. Buckingham c Ritchie b Oxenford	60	
S. Young lbw b Oxenford	63	1/106 2/151 3/199 (6 wkts dec.) 400
J. Cox c Anderson b Rackemann	19	4/261 5/301 6/338

†M. N. Atkinson, C. D. Matthews and P. T. McPhee did not bat.

Bowling: Rackemann 30–5–74–2; Rowell 30–8–74–1; Kasprowicz 9–3–35–0; Law 22–9–54–0; Oxenford 25–4–116–2; Hayden 8–1–35–0.

Queensland

T. J. Barsby c Courtney b Matthews	14	– c Di Venuto b Young	85
M. L. Hayden c Tucker b Matthews	19	– not out	57
D. M. Wellham c and b McPhee	60	– not out	0
G. M. Ritchie c Young b McPhee	6		
S. G. Law c Atkinson b Matthews	0		
P. J. T. Goggin b Tucker	5		
†P. W. Anderson b Matthews	11		
G. J. Rowell c Hills b Tucker	30		
B. N. J. Oxenford c Atkinson b Matthews	1		
M. S. Kasprowicz c Atkinson b Tucker	10		
*C. G. Rackemann not out	5		
L-b 3, n-b 18	21	B 1, l-b 2	3

1/33 2/46 3/53 4/58 5/99   182   1/143   (1 wkt) 145
6/129 7/133 8/139 9/151

Bowling: *First Innings*—Matthews 18–3–53–5; McPhee 16–2–71–2; Young 5–1–13–0; Tucker 9.2–2–42–3. *Second Innings*—Matthews 18–3–53–0; McPhee 13–4–52–0; Young 12.1–4–29–1; Tucker 8–4–8–0.

Umpires: A. J. McQuillan and C. D. Timmins.

FINAL

WESTERN AUSTRALIA v NEW SOUTH WALES

At Perth, March 28, 29, 30, 31, April 1. Western Australia won by 44 runs. Toss: Western Australia. A game of unrelenting tension demonstrated conventional cricket at its best, at least for those who do not mind the success of incessant seam bowling. On a dry, placid pitch and fast outfield, Western Australia played no recognised slow bowler, while New South Wales favoured the left-arm wrist-spinner, Freedman, to support Matthews, at the expense of the batsman Bayliss. The decision did not pay off: Freedman took no wickets and the New South Wales lower-order batting failed twice. Western Australia's batsmen were soon 58 for three against Lawson, playing his last match, and Whitney, but Moody responded positively, until he attempted a quick single and finished at the same end as Andrews, who unselfishly but unsuccessfully attempted to leave himself. Andrews and Zoehrer then prospered to share a stand of 115 and Julian contributed usefully before Matthews's off-breaks snatched the last three wickets in 23 balls. For the third time running in Perth, the Waugh twins dominated the New South Wales batting with individual centuries. They benefited from four dropped chances (Steve three, Mark one), but their 204-run stand was full of wonderful strokes. Steve hit 17 fours and a six, and Mark 24 fours before holing out to Zoehrer's leg-spin. The innings ended as ingloriously as Western Australia's second began: five New South Wales wickets fell for 15 and then the home team tottered to three for three. Two of their youngest players came to the rescue. Martyn struck 57 off 49 balls, with ten fours, while Langer played chancelessly for six hours. With Zoehrer, he built a lead of 301 before Whitney parted them. The left-armer claimed the last six wickets to complete his best Shield figures, leaving New South Wales a reasonable target of 326. Thanks to the enterprise of Small and Steve Waugh, they reached 202 for two. Then Small mistimed a pull, and Alderman and Reid took charge. A last-wicket flurry between Holdsworth and Whitney momentarily threatened a final twist until Whitney was caught behind by Veletta.

Close of play: First day, Western Australia 295-5 (W. S. Andrews 50*, T. J. Zoehrer 58*); Second day, New South Wales 208-2 (S. R. Waugh 97*, M. E. Waugh 71*); Third day, Western Australia 99-4 (J. L. Langer 33*, J. Angel 4*); Fourth day, New South Wales 71-1 (S. M. Small 42*, S. R. Waugh 15*).

Western Australia

*G. R. Marsh c Small b Lawson	30	– (2) c Emery b Lawson	0
M. R. J. Veletta c Matthews b Whitney	0	– (1) c Emery b Whitney	0
J. L. Langer c Matthews b Lawson	4	– c M. E. Waugh b Whitney	149
T. M. Moody run out	78	– c Small b Lawson	1
D. R. Martyn c Emery b S. R. Waugh	41	– c Bevan b Holdsworth	57
W. S. Andrews b Holdsworth	73	– (7) lbw b Whitney	4
†T. J. Zoehrer c Emery b Whitney	58	– (8) c Matthews b Whitney	81
B. P. Julian b Matthews	54	– (9) b Whitney	13
J. Angel not out	11	– (6) c Matthews b Whitney	4
T. M. Alderman b Matthews	6	– c Emery b Whitney	0
B. A. Reid c and b Matthews	0	– not out	1
B 4, l-b 13, w 2, n-b 22	41	B 4, l-b 6, n-b 24	34

1/11 2/36 3/58 4/160 5/180   396   1/0 2/2 3/3 4/94 5/105   344
6/295 7/360 8/382 9/388   6/129 7/320 8/331 9/331

Bowling: *First Innings*—Whitney 26-5-71-2; Holdsworth 25-4-96-1; Lawson 30-10-84-2; S. R. Waugh 16-6-36-1; Matthews 18.4-5-49-3; Freedman 5-0-19-0; M. E. Waugh 3-0-24-0. *Second Innings*—Whitney 23.4-6-75-7; Holdsworth 17-3-53-1; Lawson 16-3-66-2; S. R. Waugh 4-0-26-0; Matthews 20-3-67-0; Freedman 7-0-25-0; M. E. Waugh 4-1-22-0.

New South Wales

S. M. Small c Veletta b Angel	10	– c Zoehrer b Angel	98
M. A. Taylor c Zoehrer b Reid	16	– lbw b Alderman	9
S. R. Waugh c Andrews b Reid	113	– c Veletta b Reid	68
M. E. Waugh c Reid b Zoehrer	163	– c Andrews b Angel	19
M. G. Bevan c Zoehrer b Angel	0	– run out	20
G. R. J. Matthews c Zoehrer b Alderman	42	– c Veletta b Alderman	13
†P. A. Emery run out	30	– c Veletta b Alderman	0
D. A. Freedman not out	6	– c Moody b Reid	1
*G. F. Lawson c Langer b Alderman	1	– c Moody b Reid	4
W. J. Holdsworth b Angel	0	– not out	31
M. R. Whitney c Veletta b Angel	2	– c Veletta b Moody	8
B 4, l-b 4, n-b 24	32	L-b 4, n-b 6	10

1/16 2/56 3/260 4/271 5/350   **415**   1/39 2/157 3/202 4/210 5/225   **281**
6/400 7/404 8/410 9/413   6/225 7/226 8/236 9/244

Bowling: *First Innings*—Angel 24.4–4–82–4; Alderman 20–4–87–2; Reid 29–6–106–2; Moody 9–3–33–0; Julian 12–1–83–0; Andrews 2–1–5–0; Zoehrer 5–1–11–1. *Second Innings*—Angel 13–0–73–2; Alderman 19–1–73–3; Reid 24–6–61–3; Moody 5.2–1–19–1; Julian 4–2–13–0; Zoehrer 10–1–38–0.

Umpires: A. R. Crafter and T. A. Prue.

SHEFFIELD SHIELD WINNERS

1892-93	Victoria	1929-30	Victoria
1893-94	South Australia	1930-31	Victoria
1894-95	Victoria	1931-32	New South Wales
1895-96	New South Wales	1932-33	New South Wales
1896-97	New South Wales	1933-34	Victoria
1897-98	Victoria	1934-35	Victoria
1898-99	Victoria	1935-36	South Australia
1899-1900	New South Wales	1936-37	Victoria
1900-01	Victoria	1937-38	New South Wales
1901-02	New South Wales	1938-39	South Australia
1902-03	New South Wales	1939-40	New South Wales
1903-04	New South Wales	1940-46	No competition
1904-05	New South Wales	1946-47	Victoria
1905-06	New South Wales	1947-48	Western Australia
1906-07	New South Wales	1948-49	New South Wales
1907-08	Victoria	1949-50	New South Wales
1908-09	New South Wales	1950-51	Victoria
1909-10	South Australia	1951-52	New South Wales
1910-11	New South Wales	1952-53	South Australia
1911-12	New South Wales	1953-54	New South Wales
1912-13	South Australia	1954-55	New South Wales
1913-14	New South Wales	1955-56	New South Wales
1914-15	Victoria	1956-57	New South Wales
1915-19	No competition	1957-58	New South Wales
1919-20	New South Wales	1958-59	New South Wales
1920-21	New South Wales	1959-60	New South Wales
1921-22	Victoria	1960-61	New South Wales
1922-23	New South Wales	1961-62	New South Wales
1923-24	Victoria	1962-63	Victoria
1924-25	Victoria	1963-64	South Australia
1925-26	New South Wales	1964-65	New South Wales
1926-27	South Australia	1965-66	New South Wales
1927-28	Victoria	1966-67	Victoria
1928-29	New South Wales	1967-68	Western Australia

1968-69	South Australia	1980-81	Western Australia
1969-70	Victoria	1981-82	South Australia
1970-71	South Australia	1982-83	New South Wales
1971-72	Western Australia	1983-84	Western Australia
1972-73	Western Australia	1984-85	New South Wales
1973-74	Victoria	1985-86	New South Wales
1974-75	Western Australia	1986-87	Western Australia
1975-76	South Australia	1987-88	Western Australia
1976-77	Western Australia	1988-89	Western Australia
1977-78	Western Australia	1989-90	New South Wales
1978-79	Victoria	1990-91	Victoria
1979-80	Victoria	1991-92	Western Australia

New South Wales have won the Shield 40 times, Victoria 25, Western Australia 13, South Australia 12, Queensland 0, Tasmania 0.

FAI CUP

Note: Matches in this section were not first-class.

At Perth, October 11. Western Australia won by ten wickets. Toss: Western Australia. Tasmania 121 (40.5 overs) (M. J. McCague four for 34); Western Australia 125 for no wkt (25.5 overs) (G. R. Marsh 44 not out, T. M. Moody 69 not out).

At Brisbane, October 12. Queensland won by eight wickets. Toss: Queensland. Victoria 135 (50 overs) (Extras 31; G. J. Rowell three for 30); Queensland 137 for two (32.1 overs) (T. J. Barsby 65 not out, S. Monty 41).

At Brisbane, October 13. New South Wales won by six wickets. Toss: New South Wales. Queensland 190 for nine (50 overs) (A. R. Border 42, I. A. Healy 33; S. R. Waugh three for 25); New South Wales 191 for four (43.2 overs) (M. A. Taylor 39, S. R. Waugh 74, M. E. Waugh 40 not out).

At Adelaide, October 13. Western Australia won by six wickets. Toss: Western Australia. South Australia 167 (50 overs) (P. C. Nobes 77, G. A. Bishop 30; B. P. Julian three for 25); Western Australia 168 for four (45.1 overs) (G. R. Marsh 67, T. M. Moody 30).

At Adelaide, October 14. Tasmania won by two runs. Toss: Tasmania. Tasmania 161 for eight (50 overs) (D. C. Boon 57; S. P. George three for 29); South Australia 159 (49.2 overs) (T. J. Nielsen 43; D. R. Gilbert three for 34).

At North Sydney, October 15. New South Wales won by 100 runs. Toss: New South Wales. New South Wales 310 for five (50 overs) (S. R. Waugh 126, M. E. Waugh 112); Victoria 210 for eight (50 overs) (S. P. O'Donnell 56; G. R. J. Matthews three for 46).

Semi-finals

At Perth, October 19. No result. Western Australia qualified for the final by virtue of having won two matches to Queensland's one in the earlier rounds. Western Australia's innings had already been restricted by rain to 41 overs. Toss: Queensland. Western Australia 166 for nine (41 overs) (M. P. Lavender 61, D. R. Martyn 34 not out; C. J. McDermott four for 14) v Queensland.

At North Sydney, October 20. New South Wales won by 17 runs. Toss: New South Wales. New South Wales 250 for six (50 overs) (M. A. Taylor 79, M. G. Bevan 93; C. D. Matthews three for 52); Tasmania 233 for eight (50 overs) (B. A. Cruse 43, G. A. Hughes 31, D. C. Boon 37, J. Cox 55).

FINAL

WESTERN AUSTRALIA v NEW SOUTH WALES

At Perth, October 26. New South Wales won by 69 runs. Toss: New South Wales. Western Australia hosted the final owing to their superior net run-rate from the three preceding matches.

Man of the Match: M. A. Taylor.

New South Wales

S. M. Small lbw b Reid	11	*G. F. Lawson c Wood b Moody	6
M. A. Taylor c McCague b Reid	50	M. R. Whitney run out	7
S. R. Waugh c Zoehrer b MacLeay	17	W. J. Holdsworth not out	4
M. E. Waugh c Zoehrer b Julian	6	L-b 10, w 15, n-b 1	26
M. G. Bevan c Andrews b McCague	18		—
T. H. Bayliss c Marsh b Reid	28	1/12 2/39 3/67	(9 wkts, 50 overs) 199
G. R. J. Matthews not out	23	4/109 5/129 6/151	
†P. A. Emery c Zoehrer b Moody	3	7/156 8/169 9/190	

Bowling: Reid 10–0–35–3; MacLeay 10–1–39–1; Julian 10–0–50–1; McCague 10–0–32–1; Moody 10–0–33–2.

Western Australia

*G. R. Marsh lbw b Whitney	13	B. P. Julian run out	5
T. M. Moody c M. E. Waugh b Holdsworth	1	M. J. McCague c Holdsworth b Matthews	1
M. P. Lavender c Emery b Holdsworth	0	B. A. Reid not out	1
†T. J. Zoehrer c Emery b Whitney	16	L-b 2, w 3	5
W. S. Andrews c and b Lawson	7		—
G. M. Wood run out	24	1/16 2/16 3/21	(40.1 overs) 130
K. H. MacLeay run out	3	4/35 5/63 6/106	
D. R. Martyn b Lawson	54	7/116 8/121 9/126	

Bowling: Holdsworth 6–2–14–2; Whitney 10–4–19–2; M. E. Waugh 1–0–2–0; S. R. Waugh 4–0–25–0; Matthews 10–0–31–1; Lawson 9.1–0–37–2.

Umpires: A. R. Crafter and P. J. McConnell.

CRICKET IN SOUTH AFRICA, 1991-92

The 1991-92 season was regularly described as "historic", "epoch-making" and "a watershed" by ecstatic South African commentators. It was all of these, not just because the country returned to international cricket after 21 years, but because it joined the world game in the fullest sense for the first time. And the remarkable features were that a sport traditionally played by a small number of mostly wealthy people assumed the profile of a truly national game; the bitterness that surrounded the rebel tours matured into all-embracing popular support for the World Cup team; and the previously warring factions came to provide a model of conciliation.

World cricket itself proved to be a more hostile place than South African cricket followers had sometimes imagined in the years of exile. The team played 15 one-day internationals during the year, won six and lost nine and were beaten by West Indies in their only Test. But they proved themselves capable of beating anyone on their day and some of their performances gave people at home enormous pleasure: after the World Cup the team was welcomed back to Johannesburg with a ticker-tape parade and a crowd estimated at 100,000.

Ticket sales soared and the enthusiasm spread quickly on to the cricket fields themselves; at last all youngsters could feel there was no bar to their own development and at times the turn-outs at practice sessions overwhelmed the facilities. It was possible to feel the euphoria at every level from the street corner to the first-class game. This was matched by a new virility in playing standards with bright, young talent emerging everywhere. Only spin bowling seemed exempt from the general improvement. It was perhaps a sign of South African cricket's underlying good health that the papers soon began to be full of the kind of argument about selection policies which are normal in every other Test-playing country. However, the bitterness that surrounded the sacking of captain Clive Rice before the World Cup suggested differences that were deep and personal. Eventually, Peter Van der Merwe, the convenor of selectors, stepped down to be replaced by Peter Pollock, with Garth le Roux coming on to the panel.

The new order took hold in the major first-class competition: the Castle Cup (formerly the Currie Cup) which became a four-day competition. It was won for the third time (including a shared title) in four years by Eastern Province; their nearest rivals were Orange Free State, who were only promoted to the top division in 1985. The teams who completely dominated the Currie Cup from 1893 to 1988 – Western Province, Transvaal and Natal – all struggled.

The dominant figure was the national team captain, Kepler Wessels, whose Eastern Province team not only won the Castle Cup in the most professional fashion but reached the two major one-day finals, winning one and losing one. Wessels finished the domestic season with a first-class average of 132.50 – scoring 795 runs in six completed innings – and he had strong support from Mark Rushmere. Eastern Province's bowling was also consistent: the left-arm spinner Tim Shaw fell away badly, with only nine wickets in the Castle Cup, but the presence of Rudi Bryson, Brett Schultz, Eldine Baptiste and the improving Paul Rayment gave them unmatched depth in seam.

Meanwhile, in the traditional rugby territory of the Orange Free State, that formidable competitor Eddie Barlow bullied a young squad to a level of physical and mental fitness South Africa had not seen before. With Barlow as manager-coach, Free State evolved a theory based on time management: the faster they batted the more time they had to bowl out their opponents. Usually it worked and until the last week of the season it looked as though Free State might add the Castle Cup to their triumph in the 55-over Nissan Shield. Franklyn Stephenson's incisive bowling and thunderous hitting gave the team the balance they had lacked for so long. Allan Donald played close to his full potential while Hansie Cronje's batting and captaincy cemented the team. The fielding was superb.

Northern Transvaal started the Castle Cup with three wins out of three with their overseas players Ezra Moseley and Mike Haysman leading the way. But internal disputes marred their season and they finished in some disarray. Afterwards, they lost their captain Mandy Yachad, who rejoined Transvaal, and the Australian Haysman took over. Below them, the deposed champions Western Province fell apart through inconsistent batting with only Gary Kirsten (Peter's younger brother) and the opener Terence Lazard showing much resilience or application. The attack, headed by Meyrick Pringle, who led the national averages with 31 wickets at 13.61, and Craig Matthews was far more effective. Transvaal had a completely miserable season. There were only two survivors from the "mean machine" team of the 1980s, Rice and Jimmy Cook, who were meant to guide the new young team but instead became the focal points for controversy themselves during the row over their omission from the World Cup squad. Rice eventually dropped out of the side and Roy Pienaar became captain. The arrival of Barlow from Orange Free State to take charge off the field provides a fascinating new dimension for Transvaal's future.

Natal and Border both stumbled through the season. Natal's cricket was enlivened mainly by Jonty Rhodes's fielding. Border initiated a comeback by Ken McEwan, who had some brilliant innings but, as was always his wont in South Africa, a high percentage of failure as well. Their campaign to follow Orange Free State and fully justify their place in the Castle Cup should be enhanced by the arrival of some interesting cast-offs from elsewhere, notably Pieter Strydom of Eastern Province and Piet Botha of Transvaal.

The teams outside the Castle Cup, whose right to first-class status remains controversial, were split into two divisions. What was now called the United Cricket Board Bowl comprised four teams: Boland and Griqualand West plus two newcomers, Eastern and Western Transvaal. Eastern Transvaal did themselves especially proud by winning the Bowl under the inspirational leadership of 46-year-old Peter de Vaal, whose career dates back to 1965. Against Western Transvaal, he scored a century and took ten wickets. In the President's Cup for second teams, Western Province B were in a class of their own.

During this high summer for South African cricket, two of the men who had battled longest against racial divisions in cricket both died without seeing their aims wholly realised. Hassan Howa, the former head of the mainly non-white South African Cricket Board, who had battled long and hard against cricket's establishment, died still refusing to visit the ground at Newlands. He described the process of unification as "indecently hasty".

John Passmore, who dedicated his life to the development of cricket among the disadvantaged long before it became fashionable, died before he could witness the spectacular success of his black schoolboy protégés on their tour of the West Indies.

That tour symbolised South Africa's hopes for the future as did the arrival in first-class cricket of no fewer than three young members of the Pollock family, Anthony, Andrew and Shane. Another 17-year-old, Herschelle Gibbs, batted in the Western Province middle order and was named as the season's best fielder for catches that would have made even Jonty Rhodes proud. The big grounds were being upgraded and modernised. Everywhere, there were signs of the country's cricket emerging from its nightmares into the light.

FIRST-CLASS AVERAGES, 1991-92

BATTING

(Qualification: 8 innings, average 35.00)

	M	I	NO	R	HS	100s	Avge
K. C. Wessels (*E. Province*)	5	8	2	795	212	4	132.50
M. Erasmus (*Boland*)	8	14	6	547	103*	1	68.37
G. C. Abbott (*Griqualand West*)	7	13	1	754	127	3	62.83
M. Yachad (*N. Transvaal*)	6	11	1	553	169	2	55.30
M. W. Rushmere (*E. Province*)	6	11	2	490	177	2	54.44
G. C. Victor (*E. Province/E. Province B*)	8	15	3	635	127	2	52.91
T. N. Lazard (*W. Province*)	8	15	2	674	150*	4	51.84
P. J. Grobler (*E. Transvaal*)	6	8	2	310	81	0	51.66
N. M. Snyman (*Boland*)	7	13	0	656	137	3	50.46
L. J. Koen (*Boland/E. Province*)	7	11	2	448	121*	1	49.77
F. D. Stephenson (*OFS*)	6	9	0	430	100	1	47.77
D. Jordaan (*OFS B*)	5	9	1	379	118	2	47.37
J. N. Rhodes (*Natal*)	4	8	0	378	131	1	47.25
J. M. Arthur (*OFS*)	7	13	1	566	120	1	47.16
V. F. du Preez (*N. Transvaal/N. Transvaal B*)	7	14	1	588	132	2	45.23
G. F. J. Liebenberg (*OFS/OFS B*)	7	12	1	476	115	2	43.27
A. P. Kuiper (*W. Province*)	5	10	1	384	122	1	42.66
W. N. van As (*Boland*)	4	8	1	296	155	1	42.28
D. J. Cullinan (*Transvaal*)	7	13	1	472	79	0	39.33
T. J. Mitchell (*W. Province/W. Province B*)	6	11	5	231	61	0	38.50
A. J. van Deventer (*Transvaal*)	6	11	1	379	80	0	37.90
B. M. Osborne (*Border*)	6	12	1	414	92	0	37.63
G. Kirsten (*W. Province*)	8	16	2	525	91	0	37.50
M. C. Venter (*E. Province*)	8	13	1	450	119	1	37.50
C. S. N. Marais (*Griqualand West*)	7	13	0	483	106	1	37.15
E. L. R. Stewart (*Natal*)	5	10	0	371	121	1	37.10
R. F. Pienaar (*Transvaal*)	6	11	0	397	98	0	36.09
W. E. Schonegevel (*Griqualand West*)	7	12	2	359	153*	1	35.90
F. Davids (*W. Province/W. Province B*)	7	13	0	463	146	1	35.61
H. H. Gibbs (*W. Province/W. Province B*)	6	11	0	385	90	0	35.00
F. B. Touzel (*W. Province B*)	5	9	0	315	132	1	35.00
C. R. Norris (*E. Transvaal*)	6	8	1	245	69*	0	35.00

* *Signifies not out.*

BOWLING

(Qualification: 20 wickets)

	O	M	R	W	BB	5W/i	Avge
M. W. Pringle (*W. Province*)	179.1	42	422	31	6-37	3	13.61
E. A. Moseley (*N. Transvaal*)	244.2	56	608	36	6-66	2	16.88
C. R. Matthews (*W. Province*)	217.5	52	482	28	6-22	1	17.21
B. S. Forbes (*E. Province B*)	141.5	33	381	22	5-65	1	17.31
T. J. Packer (*Natal*)	165.3	43	458	25	5-67	2	18.32
R. E. Bryson (*E. Province*)	249.2	52	760	41	6-48	3	18.53
F. D. Stephenson (*OFS*)	219.3	60	488	25	5-39	2	19.52
P. D. de Vaal (*E. Transvaal*)	219.5	62	590	29	7-94	1	20.34
E. A. E. Baptiste (*E. Province*)	309.5	100	596	28	5-30	1	21.28
T. Bosch (*N. Transvaal*)	184.4	25	535	24	6-54	2	22.29
H. C. Bakkes (*OFS/OFS B*)	193	57	448	20	6-28	1	22.40
P. A. Rayment (*E. Province/E. Province B*)	201	54	503	22	6-25	2	22.86
C. E. Eksteen (*Transvaal*)	388	159	736	32	5-83	2	23.00
I. M. Kidson (*Griqualand West*)	202.4	49	510	21	5-70	1	24.28
A. J. McClement (*W. Province/W. Province B*)	198.5	46	530	21	5-65	2	25.23
B. N. Schultz (*E. Province*)	238	64	597	22	4-66	0	27.13
C. W. Henderson (*Boland*)	293	87	792	29	7-102	1	27.31
S. Elworthy (*N. Transvaal*)	223.4	38	741	27	6-85	2	27.44
T. G. Shaw (*E. Province*)	251.2	87	559	20	5-64	1	27.95
M. N. Angel (*Griqualand West*)	289	66	790	28	5-30	2	28.21
H. Barnard (*Boland*)	207	38	624	21	4-110	0	29.71
R. K. McGlashan (*Natal/Natal B*)	236.4	50	761	25	5-63	1	30.44
A. L. Hobson (*E. Province/E. Province B*)	315.5	69	982	31	5-59	2	31.67
D. G. Payne (*W. Province/W. Province B*)	243	48	762	24	3-33	0	31.75

CASTLE CUP, 1991-92

	Played	Won	Lost	Drawn	1st-inns Points	Points
Eastern Province	6	4	0	2	4	28
Orange Free State	6	3	2	1	6	24
Northern Transvaal	6	3	3	0	2	20
Western Province	6	3	1	2	1*	19
Transvaal	6	2	2	2	4	16
Border	6	1	4	1	0	6
Natal	6	1	5	0	0	6

Win = 6 pts; lead on first innings = 2 pts.
* First-innings scores level in lost match.

In the following scores, * by the name of a team indicates that they won the toss.

At Kingsmead, Durban, November 15, 16, 17, 18. Eastern Province won by nine wickets. Natal 238 (M. B. Logan 68, J. Payn 35, R. K. McGlashan 30; B. N. Schultz three for 39) and 193 (G. M. Walsh 42, A. R. Wormington 32; A. L. Hobson five for 84); Eastern Province* 398 (M. C. Venter 119, M. Michau 130, G. C. Victor 49, E. A. E. Baptiste 39; R. A. Lyle three for 82, R. K. McGlashan three for 140) and 34 for one. *Eastern Province 6 pts.*

At Springbok Park, Bloemfontein, November 15, 16, 17. Orange Free State won by ten wickets. Orange Free State* 464 for seven dec. (P. J. R. Steyn 109, C. J. van Heerden 38, F. D. Stephenson 49, C. J. P. G. van Zyl 119, G. F. J. Liebenberg 38, O. Henry 64 not out) and 17 for no wkt; Border 250 (A. G. Lawson 117 not out, B. M. Osborne 83; F. D. Stephenson five for 40) and 227 (E. A. N. Emslie 62 not out, I. L. Howell 45; O. Henry five for 56). *Orange Free State 6 pts.*

At Wanderers, Johannesburg, November 15, 16, 17. Northern Transvaal won by seven wickets. Transvaal* 143 (R. F. Pienaar 39; S. Elworthy five for 61, E. A. Moseley four for 24) and 193 (N. E. Wright 86; S. Elworthy four for 50, T. Bosch three for 70); Northern Transvaal 200 (M. D. Haysman 39, M. J. R. Rindel 36, S. Elworthy 30, G. Grobler 44; S. Jacobs four for 40, D. R. Laing three for 41, S. D. Jack three for 58) and 138 for three (P. H. Barnard 57 not out, L. P. Vorster 36). *Northern Transvaal 6 pts.*

At St George's Park, Port Elizabeth, November 28, 29, 30, December 1. Eastern Province won by nine wickets. Eastern Province* 307 (M. W. Rushmere 35, M. C. Venter 48, L. J. Koen 121 not out, Extras 33; W. K. Watson four for 36) and 189 for one (P. G. Amm 37, M. W. Rushmere 85 not out, K. C. Wessels 54 not out); Border 103 (R. E. Bryson six for 48, E. A. E. Baptiste three for 35) and 389 (L. M. Fuhri 50, P. N. Kirsten 32, D. H. Howell 41, D. O. Nosworthy 53, I. L. Howell 115 not out, Extras 30; R. E. Bryson five for 111). *Eastern Province 6 pts.*

At Centurion Park, Verwoerdburg, November 28, 29, 30, December 1. Northern Transvaal won by 21 runs. Northern Transvaal 220 (M. D. Haysman 93, M. J. R. Rindel 40; M. W. Pringle three for 51) and 210 (M. Yachad 66, L. P. Vorster 75; M. W. Pringle six for 37); Western Province* 220 (T. N. Lazard 108 not out; T. Bosch six for 54) and 189 (T. N. Lazard 56, G. Kirsten 39; T. Bosch five for 50, E. A. Moseley four for 43). *Northern Transvaal 6 pts, Western Province 1 pt.*

At Springbok Park, Bloemfontein, November 28, 29, 30. Orange Free State won by an innings and 34 runs. Natal 244 (G. M. Walsh 30, A. R. Wormington 63 not out, R. J. Varner 38; F. D. Stephenson four for 34, A. A. Donald four for 77) and 168 (R. M. Bentley 32 not out, J. N. Rhodes 56; O. Henry four for 60, A. A. Donald three for 27); Orange Free State* 446 (P. J. R. Steyn 45, J. M. Arthur 82, W. J. Cronje 76, L. J. Wilkinson 64, F. D. Stephenson 76, Extras 33; R. A. Lyle three for 94). *Orange Free State 6 pts.*

At Buffalo Park, East London, December 26, 27, 28, 29. Northern Transvaal won by nine wickets. Border* 245 (A. G. Lawson 34, P. N. Kirsten 107, S. J. Palframan 48; E. A. Moseley five for 50, T. Bosch four for 71) and 266 (B. M. Osborne 69, P. N. Kirsten 54, K. S. McEwan 54; E. A. Moseley six for 66, T. Bosch three for 69); Northern Transvaal 460 for six dec. (M. Yachad 169, P. H. Barnard 117, L. P. Vorster 61, M. J. R. Rindel 48) and 52 for one (M. Yachad 32 not out). *Northern Transvaal 6 pts.*

At Kingsmead, Durban, December 26, 27, 28, 29. Western Province won by three wickets. Natal 272 (A. C. Hudson 45, M. B. Logan 44, J. N. Rhodes 64, E. L. R. Stewart 57, Extras 38; B. M. McMillan five for 60, M. W. Pringle four for 60) and 206 (A. C. Hudson 52, P. W. E. Rawson 32, T. J. Packer 32; M. W. Pringle three for 59); Western Province* 320 (T. N. Lazard 130, K. C. Jackson 36, A. P. Kuiper 32; P. W. E. Rawson three for 52, R. J. McCurdy three for 67) and 162 for seven (M. F. Voss 30, G. Kirsten 56). *Western Province 6 pts.*

At Wanderers, Johannesburg, December 26, 27, 28, 29. Drawn. Transvaal 227 (N. E. Wright 60, R. F. Pienaar 36; R. E. Bryson four for 63, E. A. E. Baptiste three for 34, T. G. Shaw three for 40) and 260 for six (S. J. Cook 88, D. J. Cullinan 49, R. P. Snell 40 not out); Eastern Province* 451 (M. W. Rushmere 177, M. C. Venter 34, L. J. Koen 34, E. A. E. Baptiste 63, R. E. Bryson 61 not out; R. P. Snell four for 70). *Eastern Province 2 pts.*

At Buffalo Park, East London, January 1, 2, 3, 4. Border won by nine wickets. Natal* 159 (J. N. Rhodes 52; I. L. Howell six for 38, B. C. Fourie three for 47) and 214 (A. C. Hudson 65, E. L. R. Stewart 55; S. J. Base five for 38, B. C. Fourie three for 47); Border 257 (A. G. Lawson 30, B. M. Osborne 92, K. S. McEwan 37, S. J. Palframan 49 not out; R. K. McGlashan four for 72) and 118 for one (B. M. Osborne 54 not out, P. N. Kirsten 60 not out). *Border 6 pts.*

At St George's Park, Port Elizabeth, January 1, 2, 3, 4. Eastern Province won by five wickets. Orange Free State* 401 (J. M. Arthur 59, W. J. Cronje 112, L. J. Wilkinson 30, F. D. Stephenson 71, C. J. P. G. van Zyl 39, O. Henry 39; E. A. E. Baptiste three for 75, T. G. Shaw three for 112) and 213 for three dec. (P. J. R. Steyn 95, J. M. Arthur 51, O. Henry 49); Eastern Province 326 (M. W. Rushmere 48, K. C. Wessels 115, M. Michau 31, D. J. Richardson 72; C. J. P. G. van Zyl three for 67, O. Henry three for 78, A. A. Donald three for 102) and 291 for five (M. C. Venter 86, K. C. Wessels 147 not out). *Eastern Province 6 pts, Orange Free State 2 pts.*

At Newlands, Cape Town, January 1, 2, 3, 4. Western Province won by four wickets. Transvaal* 223 (D. J. Cullinan 73, C. E. B. Rice 35; M. W. Pringle five for 57) and 266 for eight dec. (N. E. Wright 49, R. F. Pienaar 46, D. J. Cullinan 32, C. E. B. Rice 80 not out; A. J. McClement five for 86, M. W. Pringle three for 69); Western Province 221 (B. M. McMillan 40, D. B. Rundle 35; D. R. Laing three for 34) and 272 for six (K. C. Jackson 61, A. P. Kuiper 89, B. M. McMillan 32; C. E. Eksteen four for 87). *Western Province 6 pts, Transvaal 2 pts.*

At Centurion Park, Verwoerdburg, January 24, 25, 26, 27. Natal won by 70 runs. Natal 143 (Extras 33; P. S. de Villiers four for 21, E. A. Moseley four for 41) and 272 (J. N. Rhodes 131; S. Elworthy six for 85, E. A. Moseley three for 79); Northern Transvaal* 207 (M. Yachad 95, P. S. de Villiers 31; T. J. Packer five for 67) and 138 (R. L. Malamba three for seven, R. A. Lyle three for 42). *Natal 6 pts, Northern Transvaal 2 pts.*

At Wanderers, Johannesburg, January 24, 25, 26, 27. Transvaal won by two wickets. Orange Free State* 329 (J. M. Arthur 120, W. J. Cronje 57, L. J. Wilkinson 63, F. D. Stephenson 31, G. F. J. Liebenberg 35 not out; C. E. Eksteen five for 83, R. P. Snell three for 80) and 136 (O. Henry 38; S. Jacobs five for 26, C. E. Eksteen four for 44); Transvaal 258 (S. J. Cook 42, L. Seeff 53, D. J. Cullinan 46, C. E. B. Rice 53; A. A. Donald four for 64, F. D. Stephenson three for 52) and 210 for eight (S. J. Cook 40, L. Seeff 33, R. F. Pienaar 36; B. T. Player six for 43). *Transvaal 6 pts, Orange Free State 2 pts.*

At Newlands, Cape Town, January 24, 25, 26. Western Province won by seven wickets. Western Province 335 (G. Kirsten 31, A. P. Kuiper 122, B. M. McMillan 88, M. W. Pringle 30; S. J. Base four for 80, W. K. Watson four for 83) and 32 for three (S. J. Base three for 11); Border* 155 (S. J. Palframan 36, I. L. Howell 36, W. K. Watson 37 not out; M. W. Pringle six for 42) and 209 (K. S. McEwan 54; C. R. Matthews three for 26, B. M. McMillan three for 35). *Western Province 6 pts.*

At Buffalo Park, East London, February 7, 8, 9, 10. Drawn. Transvaal* 405 for five dec. (N. E. Wright 42, R. F. Pienaar 98, D. J. Cullinan 79, C. E. B. Rice 33, D. R. Laing 71 not out, S. Jacobs 54 not out; S. J. Base three for 70); Border 199 (D. H. Howell 37, I. L. Howell 33; N. A. Foster three for 60) and 399 for five (A. G. Lawson 68, B. M. Osborne 41, K. S. McEwan 134 not out, D. H. Howell 100 not out). *Transvaal 2 pts.*

At St George's Park, Port Elizabeth, February 7, 8, 9, 10. Drawn. Western Province* 263 (G. Kirsten 91, E. O. Simons 50; E. A. E. Baptiste five for 30, B. N. Schultz four for 66) and 235 (H. H. Gibbs 41, G. Kirsten 52, E. O. Simons 51; P. A. Rayment five for 41); Eastern Province 328 (L. J. Koen 72, G. C. Victor 83, E. A. E. Baptiste 32; E. O. Simons five for 93, D. G. Payne three for 86) and 151 for eight (P. G. Amm 36). *Eastern Province 2 pts.*

At Springbok Park, Bloemfontein, February 7, 8, 9, 10. Orange Free State won by 144 runs. Orange Free State* 375 (J. M. Arthur 59, G. F. J. Liebenberg 115, F. D. Stephenson 100; G. Grobler three for 76, E. A. Moseley three for 96, S. Elworthy three for 97) and 243 for six dec. (J. M. Arthur 42, F. D. Stephenson 59, C. J. P. G. van Zyl 58 not out; S. Elworthy three for 88); Northern Transvaal 292 (V. F. du Preez 132, M. Yachad 38, M. D. Haysman 34; B. T. Player four for 67, F. D. Stephenson three for 43) and 182 (L. P. Vorster 54, L. J. Barnard 35, G. Grobler 31; J. F. Venter four for 41). *Orange Free State 6 pts.*

At Kingsmead, Durban, February 21, 22, 23, 24. Transvaal won by seven wickets. Transvaal* 355 (G. A. Pollock 49, D. R. Laing 97, B. McBride 84; T. J. Packer five for 69, R. A. Lyle three for 77) and 215 for three (N. E. Wright 90, R. F. Pienaar 57, D. J. Cullinan 41 not out); Natal 134 (M. B. Logan 53; G. C. Yates five for 46, C. E. Eksteen three for 29) and 433 (M. B. Logan 150, E. L. R. Stewart 121, B. A. Nash 30, D. N. Crookes 61, Extras 30; C. E. Eksteen five for 90). *Transvaal 6 pts.*

At Centurion Park, Verwoerdburg, February 21, 22, 23. Eastern Province won by seven wickets. Northern Transvaal 129 (P. A. Rayment six for 25) and 145 (V. F. du Preez 38; R. E. Bryson five for 48, P. A. Rayment three for 25); Eastern Province* 189 (L. J. Koen 37; E. A. Moseley four for 51, P. S. de Villiers four for 58) and 88 for three. *Eastern Province 6 pts.*

At Newlands, Cape Town, February 21, 22, 23, 24. Drawn. Orange Free State* 372 for seven dec. (P. J. R. Steyn 30, G. F. J. Liebenberg 104, L. J. Wilkinson 67, J. F. Venter 63 not out; C. R. Matthews three for 69, E. O. Simons three for 99) and 167 (C. J. van Heerden 40, J. F. Venter 82; E. O. Simons four for 41, E. O. Simons four for 45); Western Province 197 (M. F. Voss 36, H. H. Gibbs 44, E. O. Simons 40; F. D. Stephenson five for 39, B. T. Player three for 37) and 155 for four (M. F. Voss 56, G. Kirsten 43 not out). *Orange Free State 2 pts.*

CURRIE CUP AND CASTLE CUP WINNERS

The Currie Cup was replaced by the Castle Cup after the 1990-91 season.

1889-90	Transvaal	1959-60	Natal
1890-91	Kimberley	1960-61	Natal
1892-93	Western Province	1962-63	Natal
1893-94	Western Province	1963-64	Natal
1894-95	Transvaal	1965-66	Natal/Transvaal (Tied)
1896-97	Western Province	1966-67	Natal
1897-98	Western Province	1967-68	Natal
1902-03	Transvaal	1968-69	Transvaal
1903-04	Transvaal	1969-70	Transvaal/W. Province (Tied)
1904-05	Transvaal	1970-71	Transvaal
1906-07	Transvaal	1971-72	Transvaal
1908-09	Western Province	1972-73	Transvaal
1910-11	Natal	1973-74	Natal
1912-13	Natal	1974-75	Western Province
1920-21	Western Province	1975-76	Natal
1921-22	Transvaal/Natal/W. Prov. (Tied)	1976-77	Natal
1923-24	Transvaal	1977-78	Western Province
1925-26	Transvaal	1978-79	Transvaal
1926-27	Transvaal	1979-80	Transvaal
1929-30	Transvaal	1980-81	Natal
1931-32	Western Province	1981-82	Western Province
1933-34	Natal	1982-83	Transvaal
1934-35	Transvaal	1983-84	Transvaal
1936-37	Natal	1984-85	Transvaal
1937-38	Natal/Transvaal (Tied)	1985-86	Western Province
1946-47	Natal	1986-87	Transvaal
1947-48	Natal	1987-88	Transvaal
1950-51	Transvaal	1988-89	Eastern Province
1951-52	Natal	1989-90	E. Province/W. Province (Shared)
1952-53	Western Province		
1954-55	Natal	1990-91	Western Province
1955-56	Western Province	1991-92	Eastern Province
1958-59	Transvaal		

UCB BOWL, 1991-92

	Played	Won	Lost	Drawn	1st-inns Points	Points
Eastern Transvaal	6	3	0	3	0	18
Boland	6	1	1	4	10	16
Griqualand West	6	2	1	3	2	14
Western Transvaal......	6	0	4	2	2	2

Win = 6 pts; lead on first innings = 2 pts.

At Brackenfell, October 18, 19, 20. Drawn. Western Transvaal 205 (H. M. de Vos 35; C. W. Henderson seven for 102) and 52 for one; Boland* 326 for six dec. (W. S. Truter 57, N. M. Snyman 137, L. J. Koen 33, K. J. Bridgens 32; M. A. Liebenberg three for 88). *Boland 2 pts.*

At Kimberley, October 18, 19, 20. Drawn. Griqualand West* 296 (G. C. Abbott 127, H. F. Wilson 81; T. A. Marsh four for 22) and 159 for seven (M. J. Cann 60, G. C. Abbott 62; P. D. de Vaal four for 52); Eastern Transvaal 265 (B. Randall 33, P. J. Grobler 69, P. D. de Vaal 36 not out, Extras 33; M. J. Cann four for 74, M. N. Angel four for 75). *Griqualand West 2 pts.*

At Brackenfell, November 29, 30, December 1. Drawn. Boland* 402 for seven dec. (C. P. Dettmer 66, N. M. Snyman 134, J. G. de Villiers 59, M. Erasmus 98; S. E. Mitchley four for 51) and 176 for seven dec. (W. S. Truter 56, M. Erasmus 36 not out; T. A. Marsh three for 25, P. D. de Vaal four for 60); Eastern Transvaal 271 for eight dec. (K. A. Moxham 67, P. J. Grobler 34, C. R. Norris 68, S. E. Mitchley 45; C. W. Henderson three for 45) and 86 for four (P. J. Grobler 30 not out). *Boland 2 pts.*

At Potchefstroom, November 29, 30, December 1. Griqualand West won by an innings and 12 runs. Western Transvaal* 168 (S. Wessels 38, A. J. van Deventer 44 not out; M. N. Angel five for 30, I. M. Kidson three for 58) and 248 (J. J. Scholtz 38, H. M. de Vos 36, A. J. van Deventer 67, A. M. Hutton 49; I. M. Kidson four for 49, J. E. Johnson three for 34); Griqualand West 428 for three dec. (W. E. Schonegevel 153 not out, C. S. N. Marais 106, G. C. Abbott 115). *Griqualand West 6 pts.*

At Potchefstroom, January 3, 4, 5. Eastern Transvaal won by an innings and 37 runs. Eastern Transvaal* 440 for eight dec. (C. R. Norris 46, P. J. Grobler 60, S. E. Mitchley 33, P. D. de Vaal 100 not out, B. Randall 30, G. Radford 34, T. A. Marsh 51 not out, Extras 42; A. F. Zietsman three for 86, D. J. van Schalkwyk three for 119); Western Transvaal 146 (H. M. de Vos 41, A. J. van Deventer 41; P. D. de Vaal three for 32) and 257 (H. M. de Vos 74, A. J. van Deventer 34; P. D. de Vaal seven for 94). *Eastern Transvaal 6 pts.*

At Kimberley, January 10, 11, 12. Griqualand West won by seven wickets. Boland 349 (C. P. Dettmer 49, J. G. de Villiers 48, M. Erasmus 72, P. A. Koen 101; A. J. Swanepoel three for 67, M. N. Angel three for 127) and 182 for six dec. (N. M. Snyman 51, M. Erasmus 67 not out); Griqualand West* 264 (M. J. Cann 48, G. C. Abbott 42, M. A. Fletcher 30, H. F. Wilson 45, R. E. Hannie 45; C. W. Henderson four for 43, M. Erasmus three for 46) and 268 for three (W. E. Schonegevel 34, C. S. N. Marais 64, G. C. Abbott 112 not out). *Griqualand West 6 pts, Boland 2 pts.*

At Springs, January 24, 25, 26. Eastern Transvaal won by seven wickets. Griqualand West 182 (M. J. Cann 35, C. S. N. Marais 39, G. C. Abbott 33, M. A. Fletcher 39; P. D. de Vaal three for 20, L. C. R. Jordaan three for 36) and 139 (C. S. N. Marais 58; G. Radford four for 43, L. D. Botha three for 49); Eastern Transvaal* 226 (K. A. Moxham 101, C. R. Norris 40, S. E. Mitchley 31; P. McLaren six for 50) and 96 for three. *Eastern Transvaal 6 pts.*

At Potchefstroom, January 24, 25, 26. Boland won by nine wickets. Western Transvaal* 96 (H. Barnard three for 22) and 354 (J. J. Scholtz 56, H. G. Prinsloo 64, A. J. van Deventer 80, D. B. Blignaut 50; B. A. S. Chedburn three for 88); Boland 362 for eight dec. (J. S. Roos 81, K. J. Bridgens 130 not out; D. J. van Schalkwyk three for 102) and 92 for one (W. S. Truter 47 not out). *Boland 6 pts.*

At Springs, February 7, 8, 9. Drawn. Boland* 404 for nine dec. (N. M. Snyman 38, W. N. van As 155, J. S. Roos 39, K. J. Bridgens 64, P. A. Koen 37; T. A. Marsh three for 41) and 189 for five (N. M. Snyman 58, C. P. Dettmer 47, W. S. Truter 50); Eastern Transvaal 329 (K. A. Moxham 122, P. A. Cottey 76, Extras 37; B. A. S. Chedburn five for 64, H. Barnard three for 59). *Boland 2 pts.*

At Kimberley, February 7, 8, 9. Drawn. Griqualand West* 279 (M. A. Fletcher 32, C. S. N. Marais 60, G. C. Abbott 70, P. McLaren 42; J. P. B. Mulder four for 41, J. Peens three for 89) and 228 for seven dec. (C. S. N. Marais 31, G. C. Abbott 60, H. F. Wilson 55, G. F. Venter 31); Western Transvaal 335 (J. J. Scholtz 54, D. P. le Roux 65, A. J. van Deventer 42, J. P. B. Mulder 119; M. N. Angel five for 108, M. J. Cann three for 108) and 146 for six (G. P. Bouwer 42, D. P. le Roux 42, A. Viljoen 30; M. J. Cann four for 54). *Western Transvaal 2 pts.*

At Brackenfell, February 21, 22, 23. Drawn. Boland 289 (C. P. Dettmer 97, N. M. Snyman 45, J. S. Roos 52, M. Erasmus 37; I. M. Kidson five for 70, P. McLaren three for 57) and 193 (C. P. Dettmer 43, W. S. Truter 52, P. A. Koen 40; M. N. Angel four for 41, P. McLaren four for 82); Griqualand West* 166 (M. J. Cann 60, W. E. Schonegevel 32; C. W. Henderson three for 26) and 247 for seven (C. S. N. Marais 73, G. C. Abbott 76, H. F. Wilson 31; H. Barnard three for 77). *Boland 2 pts.*

At Springs, February 21, 22, 23. Eastern Transvaal won by 81 runs. Eastern Transvaal 268 (B. Randall 57, P. A. Cottey 55, P. J. Grobler 81; J. P. B. Mulder four for 78, A. F. Zietsman three for 54) and 228 for two dec. (B. Randall 45, C. R. Norris 69 not out, P. A. Cottey 52, J. E. Burger 52 not out); Western Transvaal* 174 (J. P. B. Mulder 59, D. J. van Schalkwyk 34; G. Radford four for 24, L. D. Botha three for 17, P. D. de Vaal three for 44) and 241 (D. P. le Roux 35, H. M. de Vos 54 not out, D. J. van Schalkwyk 35, Extras 37; L. C. R. Jordaan four for 50). *Eastern Transvaal 6 pts.*

PRESIDENT'S CUP, 1991-92

	Played	Won	Lost	Drawn	1st-inns Points	Points
Western Province B	5	3	0	2	2	20
Eastern Province B	5	1	0	4	4	10
Orange Free State B......	5	1	3	1	3*	9
Natal B	5	1	0	4	2	8
Transvaal B	5	0	1	4	4	4
Northern Transvaal B	5	0	2	3	4	4

Win = 6 pts; lead on first innings = 2 pts.
* *Includes first-innings scores level in lost match.*

At Port Elizabeth, October 18, 19, 20. Drawn. Natal B* 290 (J. M. Chellan 30, G. M. Walsh 117 not out, R. J. Varner 39; A. L. Hobson four for 81, B. S. Forbes three for 54) and 117 for five (K. A. Forde 34); Eastern Province B 292 for seven dec. (M. P. Stonier 54, A. Peters 62, P. A. Tullis 35 not out, R. E. Veenstra 41 not out, Extras 36). *Eastern Province B 2 pts.*

At Verwoerdburg, October 18, 19, 20. Drawn. Northern Transvaal B* 217 (B. J. Sommerville 39, A. M. Ferreira 93; L. C. R. Jordaan three for 25) and 275 for nine dec. (M. B. Mare 35, B. J. Sommerville 63, N. T. Day 59, Extras 37; G. D. Stevenson five for 76); Transvaal B 228 (J. J. Strydom 36, H. A. Manack 30, D. R. Laing 61; D. W. McCosh three for 69) and 246 for seven (P. J. Botha 55, M. J. Mitchley 47, J. J. Strydom 73 not out, H. A. Manack 31; D. W. McCosh four for 60, M. J. Davis three for 91). *Transvaal B 2 pts.*

At Constantia, October 18, 19, 20. Western Province B won by 42 runs. (First innings of both teams limited to ten overs after first day lost to rain.) Western Province B 82 for five dec. (M. J. Karsten three for 29) and 235 for seven dec. (K. C. Jackson 39, F. Davids 51, L. F. Bleekers 43, T. J. Mitchell 38; C. A. van Ee four for 66); Orange Free State B* 82 for one dec. (D. Jordaan 54 not out) and 193 (J. M. Truter 56, L. J. Wenzler 31, F. J. C. Cronje 33; A. J. McClement four for 72, D. G. Payne three for 33). *Western Province B 6 pts, Orange Free State B 1 pt.*

At Durban, November 29, 30, December 1. Natal B won by 73 runs. Natal B 300 for seven dec. (C. M. Casalis 31, J. Nel 52, B. A. Nash 129 not out; H. C. Bakkes four for 44) and 185 for five dec. (C. M. Casalis 32, J. Payn 53 not out); Orange Free State B* 245 (D. Jordaan 118, L. J. Wenzler 30 not out; R. K. McGlashan four for 84, B. A. Nash three for 38) and 167 (G. F. J. Liebenberg 84; R. K. McGlashan five for 63). *Natal B 6 pts.*

At Johannesburg, November 29, 30, December 1. Drawn. Eastern Province B 365 (B. E. van der Vyver 30, A. Peters 51, N. C. Johnson 39, P. C. Strydom 67, R. E. Veenstra 43, Extras 64; T. C. Webster six for 65, A. Manack three for 65) and 167 for four dec. (C. B. Rhodes 79 not out); Transvaal B* 256 for seven dec. (M. J. Mitchley 31, B. M. White 34, H. A. Manack 66, D. R. Laing 41; P. A. Rayment four for 72) and 34 for two. *Eastern Province B 2 pts.*

At Cape Town, November 29, 30, December 1. Western Province B won by an innings and 74 runs. Northern Transvaal B* 180 (M. B. Mare 38, J. D. du Toit 37; T. J. Mitchell three for 30, D. G. Payne three for 51) and 159 (I. A. Hoffmann 58; D. G. Payne three for 68); Western Province B 413 for eight dec. (F. B. Touzel 69, M. F. Voss 115, F. Davids 63, H. H. Gibbs 51, T. J. Mitchell 59 not out; C. van Noordwyk three for 89, D. W. McCosh three for 101). *Western Province B 6 pts.*

At Verwoerdburg, December 13, 14, 15. Drawn. Northern Transvaal B* 318 (V. F. du Preez 57, M. B. Mare 88, N. T. Day 30, A. M. Ferreira 32, J. R. Meyer 32; R. L. Malamba three for 64) and 131 (M. B. Mare 34; R. L. Malamba four for 21, S. J. S. Kimber four for 38); Natal B 194 (J. Payn 33, B. A. Nash 45, A. J. Forde 64; C. van Noordwyk four for 65, D. W. McCosh three for 41, J. R. Meyer three for 56) and 121 for seven (C. van Noordwyk four for 43). *Northern Transvaal B 2 pts.*

At Johannesburg, December 13, 14, 15. Western Province B won by three wickets. Transvaal B 209 (P. J. Botha 30, J. J. Strydom 59, J. P. van der Westhuizen 46, Extras 30; A. J. McClement five for 65) and 310 for six dec. (P. J. Botha 95, W. V. Rippon 65, J. J. Strydom 58; A. J. McClement three for 91); Western Province B* 279 for six dec. (M. F. Voss 37, H. H. Gibbs 81, F. Davids 68) and 242 for seven (F. B. Touzel 48, M. F. Voss 65, L. F. Bleekers 36 not out; A. Manack three for 59). *Western Province B 6 pts.*

At Bloemfontein, December 20, 21, 22. Eastern Province B won by 34 runs. Eastern Province B 240 (G. C. Victor 33, K. G. Bauermeister 64, A. L. Hobson 30 not out; H. C. Bakkes six for 28) and 287 for eight dec. (G. C. Victor 127, P. A. Tullis 37; F. J. C. Cronje three for 44, N. W. Pretorius three for 69); Orange Free State B* 232 (R. A. Brown 43, J. M. Truter 46, C. J. van Heerden 61, H. C. Bakkes 44; A. L. Hobson five for 86, B. S. Forbes four for 36) and 261 (D. Jordaan 48, R. A. Brown 47, L. J. Wenzler 31, F. J. C. Cronje 36 not out; B. S. Forbes five for 65). *Eastern Province B 6 pts.*

At Bloemfontein, January 9, 10, 11. Orange Free State B won by six wickets. Northern Transvaal B* 220 (M. B. Mare 87, N. T. Day 33, P. S. de Villiers 32; C. J. van Heerden three for 19) and 199 (V. F. du Preez 58, G. Grobler 31, P. S. de Villiers 50; H. C. Bakkes four for 58); Orange Free State B 325 for seven dec. (D. Jordaan 100, R. A. Brown 57, F. J. C. Cronje 42) and 96 for four (C. J. van Heerden 45 not out; I. A. Hoffmann three for 47). *Orange Free State 6 pts.*

At Johannesburg, January 10, 11, 12. Drawn. Transvaal B* 282 for nine dec. (G. A. Pollock 34, H. A. Manack 34, V. B. N. Vermeulen 78, J. P. van der Westhuizen 46; S. J. S. Kimber five for 63) and 219 for seven dec. (P. J. Botha 55, G. A. Pollock 31, H. A. Manack 33, A. J. Forde three for 28); Natal B 241 for eight dec. (J. Payn 47, B. A. Nash 47, G. W. Bashford 36 not out; A. G. Pollock three for 63) and 166 for five (J. Payn 67; A. G. Pollock three for 38). *Transvaal B 2 pts.*

At Plumstead, January 10, 11, 12. Drawn. Western Province B 338 for eight dec. (H. H. Gibbs 90, F. Davids 146, T. J. Mitchell 30; K. G. Bauermeister three for 33) and 281 for nine dec. (F. B. Touzel 132, H. Pangarker 36, F. Davids 66; B. S. Forbes four for 41, N. C. Johnson four for 86); Eastern Province B* 193 for nine dec. (C. B. Rhodes 30, G. C. Victor 30, P. C. Strydom 46, K. G. Bauermeister 39; D. G. Payne three for 56, V. A. Barnes three for 60) and 194 for two (M. P. Stonier 73 not out, G. C. Victor 79 not out). *Western Province B 2 pts.*

At Port Elizabeth, January 24, 25, 26. Drawn. Northern Transvaal B* 413 (B. J. Sommerville 41, J. D. du Toit 33, Q. Jacobs 89, G. Grobler 122, Extras 38; B. S. Forbes three for 33, K. G. Bauermeister three for 63) and 234 for nine dec. (V. F. du Preez 97, Q. Jacobs 41, C. van Noordwyk 33; A. L. Hobson five for 59); Eastern Province B 297 (C. B. Rhodes 46, G. C. Victor 112, P. C. Strydom 44, K. G. Bauermeister 33; J. R. Meyer three for 49) and 189 for eight (M. P. Stonier 48, P. C. Strydom 69; G. Grobler three for 19). *Northern Transvaal B 2 pts.*

At Pietermaritzburg, January 24, 25, 26. Drawn. Natal B* 256 (M. R. Woodburn 31, A. J. Forde 41, G. W. Bashford 79 not out; V. A. Barnes three for 44) and 210 for seven dec. (J. Payn 36, B. A. Nash 36, R. J. Varner 41; W. F. Stelling three for 52); Western Province B 204 (T. J. Mitchell 61, D. B. Rundle 31, W. F. Stelling 53; R. J. Varner four for 42) and 167 for five (M. F. Voss 64 not out, H. H. Gibbs 36; D. N. Crookes three for 69). *Natal B 2 pts.*

At Bloemfontein, January 24, 25, 26. Drawn. Orange Free State B* 421 for six dec. (D. Jordaan 30, J. M. Truter 46, N. R. Davis 83, F. J. C. Cronje 152 not out, A. Wessels 50 not out; A. G. Pollock three for 96); Transvaal B 183 (M. J. Mitchley 41, H. A. Manack 31, J. P. van der Westhuizen 46 not out; F. J. C. Cronje five for 29) and 414 for six (M. J. Mitchley 156, P. J. Botha 75, G. A. Pollock 115). *Orange Free State B 2 pts.*

WESTERN PROVINCE v YORKSHIRE

At Newlands, Cape Town, March 17, 18, 19. Western Province won by 126 runs. Toss: Western Province.

Western Province

T. N. Lazard st Blakey b Carrick	48	– c Blakey b Hartley	100
M. F. Voss c Kellett b Hartley	0	– (4) c Kellett b Carrick	2
G. Kirsten b Carrick	29	– c and b Batty	38
K. C. Jackson st Blakey b Carrick	15	– (2) c Blakey b Hartley	2
L. F. Bleekers c Kellett b Carrick	50	– b Robinson	6
D. B. Rundle c Hartley b Batty	4	– lbw b Hartley	42
†R. J. Ryall lbw b Carrick	0	– c Hartley b Gough	12
S. T. Jefferies c Grayson b Batty	0	– c Carrick b Batty	10
*C. R. Matthews b Carrick	0		
W. F. Stelling c Blakey b Gough	15	– (9) b Batty	5
V. A. Barnes not out	8	– (10) not out	1
B 2, l-b 7, n-b 10	19	B 4, l-b 5, w 1, n-b 15	25

1/2 2/75 3/105 4/114 5/125	188	1/8 2/92 3/107 (9 wkts dec.)	243
6/126 7/137 8/137 9/164		4/122 5/200 6/219	
		7/233 8/239 9/243	

Bowling: *First Innings*—Hartley 10-3-34-1; Robinson 12-2-29-0; Gough 9-3-20-1; Carrick 23.3-3-70-6; Batty 11-4-26-2. *Second Innings*—Hartley 14-1-56-3; Robinson 9-0-27-1; Gough 9-2-20-1; Carrick 26-7-44-1; Batty 24.1-3-76-3; Grayson 3-0-11-0.

Yorkshire

S. A. Kellett b Matthews	4	– c Ryall b Barnes............. 17
*A. A. Metcalfe lbw b Matthews	8	– c Kirsten b Rundle 50
D. Byas lbw b Matthews	7	– lbw b Barnes 0
†R. J. Blakey lbw b Matthews	3	– c Matthews b Jefferies 64
A. P. Grayson lbw b Matthews	0	– b Rundle 12
C. White c Ryall b Stelling	29	– st Ryall b Jackson 2
P. Carrick c Ryall b Stelling	3	– c Jackson b Rundle 4
D. Gough lbw b Matthews	15	– st Ryall b Rundle 4
P. J. Hartley b Barnes	28	– not out 4
J. D. Batty c Jackson b Jefferies	7	– c Ryall b Jefferies 5
M. A. Robinson not out	6	– c Voss b Rundle 0
B 2, l-b 3, w 1, n-b 7	13	B 5, l-b 7, w 1, n-b 7 20

1/7 2/14 3/25 4/25 5/31   123   1/35 2/35 3/118 4/154 5/159   182
6/49 7/70 8/86 9/109   6/164 7/172 8/173 9/182

Bowling: *First Innings*—Matthews 13-3-22-6; Jefferies 14-0-56-1; Barnes 7.3-2-12-1; Stelling 9-1-22-2; Rundle 5-2-6-0. *Second Innings*—Matthews 1-0-1-0; Jefferies 21-9-36-2; Barnes 16-2-47-2; Stelling 13-4-25-0; Rundle 31.1-6-56-5; Jackson 3-0-5-1.

Umpires: J. P. Lewis and H. Reid.

NATAL v NORTHAMPTONSHIRE

At Kingsmead, Durban, March 29, 30, 31. Drawn. Toss: Natal.

Natal

M. B. Logan c Hughes b Roberts	64	– c Noon b Hughes 4
I. B. Hobson c Felton b Fordham	92	– (5) run out 28
J. Payn run out	63	– (2) b Hughes 4
B. A. Nash c Noon b Roberts	1	– b Penberthy 19
A. J. Forde c and b Roberts	0	– (6) run out 23
†G. W. Bashford c Felton b Penberthy	16	– (3) b Bowen 21
D. N. Crookes c Penberthy b Walker	2	– b Hughes 19
*P. W. E. Rawson not out	31	– (9) not out 22
R. K. McGlashan c Ripley b Roberts	32	– (8) st Noon b Roberts 14
T. J. Packer not out	15	– not out 16
L-b 17, w 3, n-b 8	28	B 2, l-b 7, n-b 8 17

1/118 2/230 3/239 4/239 5/243   (8 wkts dec.) 344   1/5 2/19 3/53   (8 wkts dec.) 187
6/264 7/266 8/327   4/53 5/94 6/111
                                                        7/144 8/148

D. J. Pryke did not bat.

Bowling: *First Innings*—Walker 17-7-24-1; Penberthy 14-3-59-1; Bowen 13-0-65-0; Hughes 9-0-58-0; Roberts 27-9-63-4; Bailey 6-0-33-0; Fordham 15-6-25-1. *Second Innings*—Hughes 15-1-56-3; Penberthy 15-5-29-1; Roberts 21-5-56-1; Bowen 12-1-23-1; Fordham 9-3-14-0.

Northamptonshire

A. Fordham c Crookes b Packer	48	– c Bashford b Packer	84
N. A. Felton c Bashford b Packer	14	– b Crookes	80
*R. J. Bailey lbw b McGlashan	76	– b Packer	6
N. A. Stanley c Forde b McGlashan	22	– not out	54
A. L. Penberthy c and b Crookes	39	– (6) st Bashford b McGlashan	6
A. R. Roberts c and b Crookes	0	– (5) st Bashford b McGlashan	2
D. Ripley c Crookes b Packer	24	– c Pryke b Crookes	4
†W. M. Noon b Crookes	0	– run out	11
J. G. Hughes run out	6	– st Bashford b McGlashan	1
M. N. Bowen not out	13	– not out	8
A. Walker c Crookes b Packer	1		
B 1, l-b 1, n-b 3	5	B 1, l-b 8	9

1/49 2/70 3/112 4/201 5/203   248   1/148 2/160 3/179   (8 wkts) 265
6/204 7/208 8/218 9/237   4/186 5/206 6/219
                                   7/245 8/253

Bowling: *First Innings*—Packer 17.2–4–57–4; Rawson 2–1–3–0; McGlashan 32–12–79–2; Crookes 27–4–81–3; Pryke 4–0–14–0; Forde 2–0–12–0. *Second Innings*—Packer 8–1–29–2; Pryke 9–0–36–0; Crookes 15–0–88–2; McGlashan 19–2–86–3; Nash 5–1–17–0.

Umpires: W. Diedricks and D. L. Orchard.

BOLAND v WARWICKSHIRE

At Brackenfell, April 2, 3, 4. Drawn. Toss: Boland.

Boland

C. P. Dettmer b N. M. K. Smith	26	– c Ratcliffe b Booth	10
N. M. Snyman c Brown b Booth	103	– c Brown b Booth	44
J. G. de Villiers c Piper b P. A. Smith	0	– c N. M. K. Smith b Booth	2
W. N. van As c Twose b P. A. Smith	28	– lbw b Booth	42
M. S. van der Merwe c Twose b N. M. K. Smith	48	– b Brown	48
*†K. J. Bridgens c Moles b P. A. Smith	6	– c N. M. K. Smith b Asif Din	39
M. Erasmus not out	51	– not out	103
P. A. Koen c Piper b N. M. K. Smith	5	– st Piper b Asif Din	0
B. A. S. Chedburn c Asif Din b Booth	1	– st Piper b Asif Din	26
C. W. Henderson c Piper b Brown	1	– not out	11
D. Smith lbw b Brown	0		
B 4, l-b 3, w 1	8	B 15, l-b 4, n-b 3	22

1/76 2/81 3/163 4/164 5/176   277   1/39 2/57 3/57   (8 wkts dec.) 347
6/242 7/262 8/265 9/269   4/158 5/162 6/233
                                   7/233 8/273

Bowling: *First Innings*—P. A. Smith 15–4–54–3; Brown 10.1–3–31–2; N. M. K. Smith 17–5–55–3; Booth 23–6–65–2; Twose 13–2–53–0; Moles 4–0–12–0. *Second Innings*—P. A. Smith 6–1–16–0; Brown 15–3–57–1; Booth 37–14–82–4; N. M. K. Smith 27–6–75–0; Asif Din 20–3–94–3; Twose 3–2–1–0; Lloyd 2–0–3–0.

Warwickshire

A. J. Moles c sub b Chedburn	3	– not out	88
J. D. Ratcliffe b Chedburn	104	– (5) c sub b Chedburn	4
*T. A. Lloyd c van der Merwe b Koen	32	– (7) c van der Merwe b de Villiers	4
T. L. Penney b Henderson	45		
Asif Din c Snyman b Erasmus	76	– (8) not out	0
P. A. Smith c Chedburn b Smith	11	– (3) c sub b Dettmer	5
R. G. Twose b Smith	0	– (2) b Smith	16
N. M. K. Smith not out	56	– (6) run out	3
†K. J. Piper (did not bat)		– (4) lbw b Chedburn	25
B 11, l-b 6, w 2, n-b 1	20	B 5, l-b 9, w 2	16

1/8 2/111 3/194 4/211 5/240   (7 wkts dec.) 347   1/36 2/60 3/134   (6 wkts) 161
6/244 7/347   4/148 5/153 6/160

D. R. Brown and P. A. Booth did not bat.

Bowling: *First Innings*—Chedburn 16–4–42–2; Smith 13–2–58–2; Erasmus 17.1–2–57–1; Koen 13–5–32–1; de Villiers 20–5–62–0; Henderson 24–6–79–1; Snyman 1–1–0–0. *Second Innings*—Chedburn 14.1–0–48–2; Smith 5–0–14–1; Dettmer 7–2–20–1; Henderson 2–0–17–0; Snyman 4–0–18–0; de Villiers 8–0–30–1.

Umpires: W. Richard and B. van Wyk.

OTHER FIRST-CLASS MATCHES

At Verwoerdburg, September 12, 13, 14. Western Province won by six wickets. Northern Transvaal* 269 for two dec. (M. Yachad 102, V. F. du Preez 111 not out) and 272 for six dec. (M. J. R. Rindel 59, L. P. Vorster 83, A. M. Ferreira 63 not out); Western Province 261 for seven dec. (T. N. Lazard 150 not out, L. Seeff 54) and 284 for four (G. Kirsten 49, J. B. Commins 85, A. P. Kuiper 66, F. Davids 35).

At Virginia, September 21, 22, 23. Orange Free State won by 101 runs. Orange Free State* 222 for nine dec. (J. M. Arthur 76; C. E. Eksteen three for 26, P. J. Botha three for 54) and 200 for seven dec. (W. J. Cronje 41, L. J. Wenzler 32, B. T. Player 30 not out; P. E. Smith three for 36); Transvaal 123 (P. J. Botha 30; M. J. Karsten four for 19, N. W. Pretorius four for 24) and 198 (D. J. Cullinan 57, J. J. Strydom 30, H. A. Manack 33; N. W. Pretorius four for 51, W. J. Cronje three for 25).

At Worcester, September 27, 28, 29. Eastern Province won by 300 runs. Eastern Province* 392 (K. C. Wessels 79, T. G. Shaw 105, R. E. Bryson 100, B. N. Schultz 36 not out; H. Barnard four for 110, C. W. Henderson three for 99) and 328 for three dec. (P. G. Amm 124, K. C. Wessels 168); Boland 233 (L. J. Koen 90, J. S. Roos 43; T. G. Shaw five for 64, R. E. Bryson three for 52) and 187 (K. J. Bridgens 47, J. S. Roos 41; B. N. Schultz four for 59, A. L. Hobson three for 35, R. E. Bryson three for 69).

At Cradock, October 25, 26, 27. Eastern Province won by 155 runs. Eastern Province* 333 for five dec. (K. C. Wessels 212, D. J. Richardson 55 not out) and 221 for three dec. (M. W. Rushmere 100 not out, M. C. Venter 37, E. A. E. Baptiste 61); Griqualand West 252 (W. E. Schonegevel 96 not out, M. N. Angel 67, R. E. Hannie 34) and 147 (C. S. N. Marais 32, M. N. Angel 34 not out; T. G. Shaw four for 31, R. E. Bryson three for 29).

NISSAN SHIELD

(55 overs a side, not first-class.)

At Brackenfell, November 23. Border won by 47 runs. Border 247 for seven (P. N. Kirsten 30, K. S. McEwan 42, D. O. Nosworthy 69, I. L. Howell 50); Boland* 200 (W. S. Truter 42, T. L. Penney 39, K. J. Bridgens 38).

At King William's Town, November 23. Eastern Province won by 77 runs. Eastern Province 266 for seven (M. W. Rushmere 139, K. C. Wessels 33, T. G. Shaw 42; H. C. Lindenberg three for 28, R. E. Cullinan three for 61); Border Country Districts* 189 for nine (M. Dilley 50, D. H. Howell 60; B. N. Schultz four for 26).

At Graaff-Reinet, November 23. Northern Transvaal won by nine wickets. Eastern Province Country Districts 126 (P. A. Amm 42, G. D. Dixon 42; E. A. Moseley four for 12, S. Elworthy three for 28); Northern Transvaal* 127 for one (I. A. Hoffmann 33, P. J. Barnard 61 not out).

At Springs, November 23. Eastern Transvaal won by five wickets. Griqualand West 202 for seven (M. J. Cann 106 not out, G. C. Abbott 30); Eastern Transvaal* 203 for five (H. M. Human 30, P. A. Cottey 66, S. E. Mitchley 31).

At Witbank, November 23. Natal won by 180 runs. Natal* 364 for two (M. B. Logan 115 not out, A. C. Hudson 107, R. M. Bentley 46 not out, J. N. Rhodes 61); Eastern Transvaal Country Districts 184 for six (B. W. Marais 56, C. Gilbert 53 not out).

At Empangeni, November 23. Transvaal won by 148 runs. Transvaal 254 for seven (S. J. Cook 63, M. J. Mitchley 84, C. E. B. Rice 55); Natal Country Districts* 106 (B. Whiting 30, R. Gill 33; S. Jacobs four for six).

At Pietersburg, November 23. Orange Free State won by 186 runs. Orange Free State 282 for three (P. J. R. Steyn 127 not out, W. J. Cronje 83); Northern Transvaal Country Districts* 96 (A. A. Donald five for 25).

At Potchefstroom, November 23. Western Province won by eight wickets. Western Transvaal* 162 (J. J. Scholtz 48, H. G. Prinsloo 32, A. J. van Deventer 35; C. R. Matthews three for 29); Western Province 164 for two (T. N. Lazard 65, K. C. Jackson 51 not out).

Quarter-finals

First leg: At East London, December 14. Border won by 35 runs. Border* 227 for eight (A. G. Lawson 81, B. M. Osborne 62); Eastern Transvaal 192 for nine (K. A. Moxham 64, P. D. de Vaal 33 not out; W. K. Watson three for 26, M. K. van Vuuren three for 26).

First leg: At Bloemfontein, December 14. Orange Free State won by 49 runs. Orange Free State* 225 for eight (P. J. R. Steyn 52, W. J. Cronje 79; S. Jacobs three for 49); Transvaal 176 (D. J. Cullinan 61; F. D. Stephenson three for 28, C. J. P. G. van Zyl three for 37).

First leg: At Port Elizabeth, December 15. Eastern Province won by six wickets. Western Province* 261 for eight (T. N. Lazard 105, K. C. Jackson 58, A. P. Kuiper 42; E. A. E. Baptiste three for 52); Eastern Province 263 for four (K. C. Wessels 57, M. W. Rushmere 108 not out, M. C. Venter 47).

First leg: At Durban, December 15. Natal won by virtue of losing fewer wickets. Northern Transvaal 200 (M. J. R. Rindel 66, L. J. Barnard 70, Extras 31; D. Norman four for 23, D. J. Pryke three for 35); Natal* 200 for nine (A. C. Hudson 79, J. N. Rhodes 32).

Second leg: At Springs, December 21. Border won by 20 runs in a match reduced by rain to 26 overs a side. Border* 156 for three (B. M. Osborne 62 not out, P. N. Kirsten 43); Eastern Transvaal 136 (S. E. Mitchley 36; B. C. Fourie five for 16).

Second leg: At Verwoerdburg, December 21. Northern Transvaal won on run-rate after rain limited their innings to 40 overs and reduced Natal's target to 171 off 37 overs (only 33 were bowled). Northern Transvaal 171 for four (L. P. Vorster 93 not out); Natal* 106 for six (D. Norman 30 not out; E. A. Moseley three for 19, W. F. Morris three for 24).

Second leg: At Johannesburg, December 21. Orange Free State won by 56 runs. Orange Free State* 233 for five (P. J. R. Steyn 53, J. M. Arthur 39, W. J. Cronje 82 not out); Transvaal 177 (D. R. Laing 38).

Second leg: At Cape Town, December 21. Eastern Province won by 12 runs. Eastern Province 215 for five (M. Michau 94, D. J. Richardson 51 not out; C. R. Matthews three for 30); Western Province* 203 (K. C. Jackson 59, B. M. McMillan 44, F. Davids 30; P. A. Rayment three for 33, R. E. Bryson three for 35, B. N. Schultz three for 36).

Third leg: At Verwoerdburg, December 22. Northern Transvaal won by five wickets. Natal* 193 for seven (R. M. Bentley 43, D. Norman 41); Northern Transvaal 197 for five (M. D. Haysman 74, L. J. Barnard 44).

Semi-finals

First leg: At Bloemfontein, January 11. Orange Free State won by 22 runs. Orange Free State 212 for nine (W. J. Cronje 46, L. J. Wilkinson 91); Border* 190 for five (A. G. Lawson 40, B. M. Osborne 36, E. A. N. Emslie 36 not out; O. Henry three for 26).

First leg: At Verwoerdburg, January 12. Eastern Province won by 31 runs. Eastern Province 199 (L. J. Koen 63, E. A. E. Baptiste 36; T. Bosch three for 33, S. Elworthy three for 33); Northern Transvaal* 168 (P. H. Barnard 50; T. G. Shaw three for 28).

Second leg: At East London, January 18. Orange Free State won by 36 runs. Orange Free State* 232 for five (W. J. Cronje 40, L. J. Wilkinson 102, C. J. P. G. van Zyl 38 not out); Border 196 for seven (A. G. Lawson 99 not out, P. N. Kirsten 32).

Second leg: At Port Elizabeth, January 18. Eastern Province won on run-rate, after rain stopped play when Northern Transvaal had faced 43 overs. Eastern Province 240 for eight (M. C. Venter 68, L. J. Koen 86; T. Bosch five for 56); Northern Transvaal* 167 for seven (M. Yachad 56, P. H. Barnard 35, M. J. R. Rindel 41 not out).

Final

At Port Elizabeth, February 1. Orange Free State won by six wickets. Eastern Province* 120 (D. J. Richardson 36 not out; C. J. P. G. van Zyl four for 24); Orange Free State 124 for four (J. M. Arthur 45, W. J. Cronje 32 not out).

BENSON AND HEDGES NIGHT SERIES

(Day/night matches of 45 overs a side, not first-class.)

At Durban, October 16. Natal won by ten runs. Natal 208 for seven (R. M. Bentley 60, J. N. Rhodes 60); Border* 198 (B. M. Osborne 65, P. N. Kirsten 51; R. J. McCurdy three for 39).

At East London, October 18. Northern Transvaal won by five wickets in a match reduced by rain to 35 overs a side. Border 131 for one (A. G. Lawson 50 not out, P. N. Kirsten 71 not out); Northern Transvaal* 133 for five (L. P. Vorster 40 not out).

At Bloemfontein, October 18. Orange Free State won by five wickets. Eastern Province 162 for six (K. C. Wessels 49, P. G. Amm 36); Orange Free State* 163 for five (F. D. Stephenson 49, C. J. P. G. van Zyl 43 not out).

At Cape Town, October 23. Impalas won by eight wickets. Western Province* 203 for six (A. P. Kuiper 37, B. M. McMillan 44, J. B. Commins 43, D. B. Rundle 36 not out); Impalas 204 for two (M. J. Cann 60, N. M. Snyman 54, W. S. Truter 32 not out, L. J. Koen 45 not out).

At Verwoerdburg, October 25. No result, floodlight failure and rain having stopped play. Northern Transvaal* 129 (M. D. Haysman 33, R. V. Jennings 45; A. A. Donald three for 14, F. D. Stephenson three for 22); Orange Free State 40 for two.

At Bloemfontein, October 30. Border won by four runs. Border* 174 for four (A. G. Lawson 42, B. M. Osborne 41, B. Roberts 35); Orange Free State 170 for nine (F. D. Stephenson 53, P. J. R. Steyn 36; B. C. Fourie four for 28).

At East London, November 1. Western Province won by eight wickets. Border 47 (E. O. Simons four for three, including a hat-trick, B. M. McMillan three for eight); Western Province* 51 for two.

At Durban, November 1. Transvaal won by 26 runs. Transvaal 158 for eight (D. J. Cullinan 51; P. W. E. Rawson three for 11); Natal* 132 (C. E. Eksteen four for eight).

At Port Elizabeth, November 6. Eastern Province won by six wickets. Impalas* 150 (L. J. Koen 39; P. A. Rayment four for 29); Eastern Province 151 for four (K. C. Wessels 39, M. W. Rushmere 48 not out; P. E. Smith three for 32).

At Verwoerdburg, November 6. Western Province won by six wickets. Northern Transvaal* 187 for five (M. Yachad 42, M. D. Haysman 96); Western Province 190 for four (T. N. Lazard 77 not out, K. C. Jackson 31, J. B. Commins 50).

At Johannesburg, November 8. Transvaal won by six wickets. Border* 202 for eight (B. M. Osborne 69, B. W. Lones 40; H. A. Page four for 36); Transvaal 205 for four (R. F. Pienaar 87).

At Bloemfontein, December 9. Western Province won by 27 runs. Western Province* 209 for nine (K. C. Jackson 40, B. M. McMillan 57; A. A. Donald four for 32); Orange Free State 182 for eight (J. M. Arthur 126 not out; E. O. Simons three for 35).

At Verwoerdburg, December 10. Natal won by ten wickets. Northern Transvaal 157 for eight (M. Yachad 90; P. W. E. Rawson three for 20); Natal* 158 for no wkt (A. C. Hudson 87 not out, M. B. Logan 58 not out).

At East London, December 11. Border won on run-rate after rain had reduced Eastern Province's target to 134 off 37 overs. Border* 154 for nine (D. O. Nosworthy 57; B. N. Schultz three for 14, P. A. Rayment three for 44); Eastern Province 115 for three (M. C. Venter 30 not out).

At Johannesburg, December 12. Orange Free State won by 72 runs. Orange Free State* 217 for six (P. J. R. Steyn 31, W. J. Cronje 108, L. J. Wilkinson 31; R. P. Snell three for 40); Transvaal 145 (S. Jacobs 61; C. J. P. G. van Zyl three for 21).

At Port Elizabeth, December 17. Eastern Province won by 33 runs. Eastern Province* 221 for eight (K. C. Wessels 76 not out, M. W. Rushmere 57, P. A. Rayment 43 not out; W. F. Morris three for 34); Northern Transvaal 188 for nine (M. D. Haysman 59; B. N. Schultz four for 32).

At Cape Town, December 18. Western Province won by seven wickets. Transvaal* 178 (R. F. Pienaar 62, C. E. B. Rice 58; M. W. Pringle five for 36, E. O. Simons four for 54); Western Province 181 for three (T. N. Lazard 76 not out, B. M. McMillan 31 not out).

At Durban, December 19. Orange Free State won by 63 runs. Orange Free State* 214 for seven (J. M. Arthur 49, W. J. Cronje 97); Natal 151 (A. C. Hudson 61, J. N. Rhodes 37; B. T. Player four for 24, C. J. P. G. van Zyl three for 22).

At Durban, February 5. Impalas won by six wickets. Natal* 200 for eight (E. L. R. Stewart 53, B. A. Nash 60 not out; P. D. de Vaal three for 24); Impalas 201 for four (M. J. Cann 87 not out, W. S. Truter 50).

At Cape Town, February 12. Western Province won by five runs. Western Province 181 for seven (K. C. Jackson 45, E. O. Simons 38 not out, D. B. Rundle 75); Natal* 176 (I. B. Hobson 55; C. R. Matthews three for 41).

At Bloemfontein, February 13. Impalas won by five wickets. Orange Free State 200 for seven (P. J. R. Steyn 66, J. M. Arthur 65); Impalas* 201 for five (C. S. N. Marais 61, G. C. Abbott 34).

At Port Elizabeth, February 14. Eastern Province won by 91 runs. Eastern Province* 215 for five (P. G. Amm 35, M. C. Venter 33, D. J. Callaghan 61, G. C. Victor 30); Transvaal 124 (R. F. Pienaar 41).

At Port Elizabeth, February 26. Eastern Province won by three wickets. Natal* 202 for five (J. Payn 42, E. L. R. Stewart 86 not out); Eastern Province 204 for seven (L. J. Koen 35, D. J. Callaghan 78 not out; D. N. Crookes three for 40).

At East London, February 27. No result, rain having stopped play. Impalas 116 for three (N. M. Snyman 45, W. S. Truter 31 not out) v Border*.

At Johannesburg, February 28. Transvaal won by one wicket. Northern Transvaal 199 for six (M. Yachad 48, V. F. du Preez 36, M. J. R. Rindel 55 not out); Transvaal* 200 for nine (G. A. Pollock 94 not out; E. A. Moseley three for 40).

At Verwoerdburg, March 4. Impalas won by five wickets. Northern Transvaal* 209 for six (M. J. R. Rindel 50 not out, B. J. Sommerville 35, S. Elworthy 43 not out); Impalas 211 for five (W. S. Truter 64, G. C. Abbott 68 not out; C. van Noordwyk three for 42).

At Cape Town, March 5. Western Province won by 65 runs. Western Province* 213 for six (K. C. Jackson 37, G. Kirsten 56); Eastern Province 148 (G. C. Victor 56).

At Johannesburg, March 6. Transvaal won by eight wickets. Impalas 209 for four (M. J. Cann 46, N. M. Snyman 51, W. S. Truter 31, C. S. N. Marais 41, G. C. Abbott 35 not out); Transvaal* 213 for two (N. E. Wright 43, H. A. Page 57, R. F. Pienaar 72 not out).

Semi-finals

First leg: At Port Elizabeth, March 10. Eastern Province won by 171 runs. Eastern Province 257 (M. C. Venter 39, P. G. Amm 108, L. J. Koen 56); Impalas* 86 (T. G. Shaw three for eight, P. A. Rayment three for 17).

First leg: At Johannesburg, March 11. Western Province won by three wickets. Transvaal 198 for nine (D. J. Cullinan 104 not out; V. A. Barnes three for 39); Western Province* 201 for seven (T. N. Lazard 88, K. C. Jackson 47).

Second leg: At Port Elizabeth, March 13. Eastern Province won by 116 runs. Eastern Province 275 for three (P. G. Amm 69, M. C. Venter 49, L. J. Koen 74 not out, D. J. Callaghan 59); Impalas* 159 (C. S. N. Marais 48, K. J. Bridgens 40; R. E. Bryson three for 26).

Second leg: At Cape Town, March 13. Western Province won by four wickets. Transvaal* 140 (H. A. Page 44; V. A. Barnes three for 18); Western Province 141 for six (G. Kirsten 39, M. F. Voss 41; H. A. Page four for 25).

Final

At Johannesburg, April 1. Eastern Province won by six wickets. Western Province* 244 for two (T. N. Lazard 108 not out, A. P. Kuiper 107); Eastern Province 246 for four (K. C. Wessels 103, P. G. Amm 33, M. W. Rushmere 64).

CRICKET IN THE WEST INDIES, 1991-92

By TONY COZIER

Jamaica were indebted for their third Red Stripe Cup in the five seasons since it replaced the Shell Shield as the regional first-class tournament to the record-breaking performances of Courtney Walsh and Jimmy Adams. The experienced Walsh, in his second year as captain, was omitted from West Indies' World Cup squad, and thus was free to lead not only Jamaica, throughout the season, but also the West Indies A team during England A's subsequent tour. His 36 wickets at 11.30 each in the Cup surpassed Curtly Ambrose's record, set in 1988 for the Leeward Islands, by one. The left-handed Adams finally fulfilled the promise he had shown since his Jamaican début at the age of 17 in 1984-85, gathering three centuries and a 99 in nine Cup innings, for an aggregate of 586, 33 more than Easton McMorris in 1965-66.

Walsh gained his bowling support principally from an equally seasoned campaigner, the leg-spinner Robert Haynes, who bowled consistently well for his 17 wickets, while at No. 3, Adams's solidity was complemented by the dashing aggression of another left-hander, 20-year-old Robert Samuels. His return of 426 runs was bettered only by Adams, who made 586, and Guyanese opener Clayton Lambert who amassed 489 at 54.33. Walsh's captaincy had been widely criticised after Jamaica finished next to bottom the previous season, and he admitted to having made mistakes. This time, with former West Indies captain Rohan Kanhai back as coach, he engendered a keen team spirit among his young players. Jamaica won three of their five matches, including their first-ever (in 18 matches since 1896) at Kensington Oval over the 1990-91 champions, Barbados. It was a comfortable victory, too, and virtually settled the outcome of the tournament.

The World Cup, contracts in South Africa that attracted Ezra Moseley and Eldine Baptiste, the belated decision of Viv Richards not to participate and the retirements of other stalwarts meant that more than a hundred players turned out for the six teams. Some sides found their balance badly upset. Barbados, for instance, missed the influence of their former captain and West Indies opener, Desmond Haynes, who was limited to three innings in which he scored 246 against the Windwards (his highest score in the Caribbean), and 135 and 28 against the Leewards. They won both matches, but were immediately beaten by Jamaica on his departure. Trinidad & Tobago's opener, Philip Simmons, regained his West Indies place with successive scores of 50, 77, 202 (against Guyana) and 57, and the left-handed Brian Lara began the season with 135 against Barbados. After they left for Australia, Trinidad & Tobago lost by an innings to the Leewards. On the other hand, the many vacancies offered chances to less familiar players. The Leewards demonstrated their depth of talent when, without Richie Richardson, Keith Arthurton, Winston Benjamin and Ambrose, they beat Guyana and Trinidad & Tobago to steal second place from Barbados. Kenneth Benjamin, Hamesh Anthony, and Vaughn Walsh were more than adequate understudies as the pace attack.

Fast bowling again dominated the Caribbean. Linden Joseph of Guyana had recovered from the last season's back problems, and his speed and out-swing earned him 23 wickets at 17.61 each and a place with West Indies A. Victor Walcott, strong and untiring, captured 21 and Ottis Gibson 18 for Barbados. With Ian Bishop still incapacitated by a stress fracture, Eugene Antoine was a worthy stand-in as Tony Gray's new-ball partner for Trinidad & Tobago, the pair sharing 36 wickets. Casper Davis's 17 wickets in his début season offered some consolation to the disappointing Windwards, although their outstanding individual was Junior Murray.

Murray's wicket-keeping had earned high praise and, realising that the selectors would soon be seeking a replacement for Jeffrey Dujon, he set about improving his batting. His reward was a maiden first-class century, 102 against a Leewards attack spearheaded by Ambrose and Winston Benjamin, and an average of 47.87 from 383 runs. This placed him marginally above Barbados captain Roland Holder, whose best season (376 runs, average 41.77) was followed by convincing performances against England A. At 24, Holder looked ready for promotion to the Test team.

The final of the one-day Geddes Grant Shield was delayed to await the return of the World Cup players. Two contributed significantly to Trinidad & Tobago's eight-wicket victory over Barbados, at the Queen's Park Oval. Simmons was named Man of the Match for his one for 41 and unbeaten 60, sharing an unbroken 124 with Lara, who hit 77. Dissatisfied by the Shield's schedule of a mere six zonal matches before the final, the West Indies Cricket Board of Control decided in May to revert to the system tried in 1982, when each team played the others in a total of 15 round-robin matches, and the top two qualified.

With the Test team in transition, it was a contentious year for the Board. Richards retired as captain, but when he was not chosen to play in the World Cup, his comments were typically biting. Gordon Greenidge, Dujon and Malcolm Marshall, all record-setting members of the great West Indies teams of the 1970s and 1980s, also departed the international stage, though not without bitterness. Intending to build for the future, the Board appointed Richie Richardson to succeed Richards, in preference to the incumbent vice-captain, Desmond Haynes, nearly six years his senior. It was a widely expected and, at first, generally popular choice. But disappointing results in both the Australian World Series and the World Cup, along with Richardson's loss of form and the caustic remarks of Richards, Dujon and Marshall, incensed a passionate public. Richardson was booed in his first match as captain on Caribbean soil, a one-day international against South Africa at Sabina Park. When the Barbadian fast bowler, Anderson Cummins, was not selected for the Bridgetown Test, his compatriots boycotted the historic game.

These were unmistakable signs of difficult times and, at its annual general meeting in May, the Board established a specialist committee, headed by businessman and former Jamaican all-rounder, Teddy Griffith, "to devise a strategic plan covering the Board's operations over the next five years". It also gave the chairman of selectors the freedom to explain "matters of policy" to the media – although not to comment on individual selections. And, for the first time, it appointed a cricket manager. Rohan Kanhai was named for the planned tours of Australia and South Africa in 1992-93. The Board said this was for "an unspecified period", until it had the chance "to further assess and define the duties of the proposed appointee".

FIRST-CLASS AVERAGES, 1991-92

BATTING

(Qualification: 200 runs)

	M	I	NO	R	HS	100s	Avge
D. L. Haynes (*Barbados*)	3	5	0	490	246	2	98.00
P. V. Simmons (*T & T*)	4	6	0	424	202	1	70.66
J. C. Adams (*Jamaica*)	9	16	5	770	128*	3	70.00
K. L. T. Arthurton (*Leeward I.*)	3	6	1	335	117	1	67.00
R. A. Harper (*Guyana*)	3	5	1	203	74	0	50.75
J. R. Murray (*Windward I.*)	9	15	3	575	102	1	47.91
B. C. Lara (*T & T*)	4	6	0	282	135	1	47.00
C. B. Lambert (*Guyana*)	8	15	0	646	144	2	43.06
R. I. C. Holder (*Barbados*)	8	13	0	555	123	1	42.69
L. L. Harris (*Leeward I.*)	5	7	0	291	98	0	41.57
R. G. Samuels (*Jamaica*)	8	15	1	560	104	1	40.00
R. D. Jacobs (*Leeward I.*)	5	9	2	227	78	0	32.42
K. A. Williams (*T & T*)	5	8	1	220	98	0	31.42
C. A. Best (*Barbados*)	7	13	3	314	79	0	31.40
R. W. Staple (*Jamaica*)	4	7	0	219	79	0	31.28
L. D. John (*Windward I.*)	5	9	0	257	64	0	28.55
N. E. F. Barry (*Guyana*)	5	8	0	215	71	0	26.87
C. G. Yorke (*T & T*)	5	8	0	212	91	0	26.50
A. C. H. Walsh (*Leeward I.*)	5	9	1	211	77	0	26.37
D. A. Joseph (*Windward I.*)	6	11	0	256	61	0	23.27
P. A. Wallace (*Barbados*)	5	9	0	206	66	0	22.88
A. H. Gray (*T & T*)	8	10	0	210	55	0	21.00

* *Signifies not out.*

BOWLING

(Qualification: 15 wickets)

	O	M	R	W	BB	5W/i	Avge
C. A. Walsh (*Jamaica*)	349.1	101	716	50	6-62	3	14.32
C. E. L. Ambrose (*Leeward I.*)	141.1	47	241	16	6-34	1	15.06
L. A. Joseph (*Guyana*)	201.2	45	579	33	6-51	2	17.54
V. deC. Walcott (*Barbados*)	161.1	38	425	21	5-41	1	20.23
K. C. G. Benjamin (*Leeward I.*)	276	68	677	33	6-72	1	20.51
N. O. Perry (*Jamaica*)	168.1	52	364	17	5-47	1	21.41
V. A. Walsh (*Leeward I.*)	97	15	354	16	6-77	1	22.12
R. C. Haynes (*Jamaica*)	171.5	48	378	17	4-21	0	22.23
H. A. G. Anthony (*Leeward I.*)	126.1	12	464	20	4-23	0	23.20
C. G. Butts (*Guyana*)	163.3	35	405	17	7-29	1	23.82
E. C. Antoine (*T & T*)	197.4	41	566	23	6-49	2	24.60
C. A. Davis (*Windward I.*)	148.4	26	499	19	6-101	1	26.26
O. D. Gibson (*Barbados*)	144	15	496	18	7-78	1	27.55
A. H. Gray (*T & T*)	257.4	43	703	25	5-49	1	28.12
R. Dhanraj (*T & T*)	173.5	36	516	15	4-35	0	34.40

RED STRIPE CUP, 1991-92

	Played	Won	Lost	Drawn	1st-inns Points	Points
Jamaica	5	3	0	2	4	60
Leeward Islands	5	3	1	1	4	56
Barbados	5	2	1	2	4	44
Guyana	5	1	2	2	5	29
Trinidad & Tobago	5	0	1	4	8	24
Windward Islands	5	0	4	1	4	8

Win = 16 pts; draw = 4 pts; 1st-innings lead in drawn match = 4 pts; 1st-innings lead in lost match = 5 pts.

In the following scores, * by the name of a team indicates that they won the toss.

At Sabina Park, Kingston, Jamaica, January 24, 25, 26, 27. Jamaica won by six wickets. Guyana 173 (S. Dhaniram 81, N. E. F. Barry 32; R. C. Haynes four for 21) and 232 (C. B. Lambert 57, N. E. F. Barry 37, R. A. Harper 57; C. A. Walsh five for 51); Jamaica* 171 (J. C. Adams 57; L. A. Joseph six for 51, B. St A. Browne three for 57) and 235 for four (R. G. Samuels 33, J. C. Adams 102 not out, P. J. L. Dujon 66 not out, Extras 30). *Jamaica 16 pts, Guyana 5 pts.*

At Antigua Recreation Ground, St John's, Antigua, January 24, 25, 26, 27. Leeward Islands won by eight wickets. Windward Islands 193 (J. R. Murray 49, N. F. Williams 50; C. E. L. Ambrose three for 44, W. K. M. Benjamin four for 65) and 248 (J. R. Murray 102, T. Z. Kentish 33; C. E. L. Ambrose four for 70, H. A. G. Anthony four for 67); Leeward Islands* 242 (A. C. H. Walsh 34, R. B. Richardson 62, R. D. Jacobs 36; C. A. Davis three for 57, J. D. Charles three for 31) and 200 for two (S. C. Williams 40, K. L. T. Arthurton 97 not out, R. D. Jacobs 52 not out). *Leeward Islands 16 pts.*

At Queen's Park Oval, Port-of-Spain, Trinidad, January 24, 25, 26, 27. Drawn. Trinidad & Tobago 250 (P. V. Simmons 50, B. C. Lara 135; O. D. Gibson seven for 78) and 208 for four dec. (P. V. Simmons 77, C. G. Yorke 65, B. C. Lara 37); Barbados* 109 (F. L. Reifer 31, R. I. C. Holder 30; A. H. Gray four for 23, R. Dhanraj four for 35) and 309 for seven (P. A. Wallace 36, R. I. C. Holder 123, L. K. Puckerin 32, C. O. Browne 62 not out). *Trinidad & Tobago 8 pts, Barbados 4 pts.*

At Kensington Oval, Bridgetown, Barbados, January 31, February 1, 2, 3. Barbados won by seven wickets. Windward Islands 379 (L. D. John 38, D. A. Joseph 61, S. L. Mahon 31, J. R. Murray 36, J. D. Charles 54, T. Z. Kentish 37, I. B. A. Allen 36; V. deC. Walcott three for 65, W. N. Reid four for 112) and 201 (J. R. Murray 65; A. C. Cummins four for 56); Barbados* 499 (D. L. Haynes 246, P. A. Wallace 66, W. N. Reid 78; C. A. Davis six for 101) and 82 for three (C. A. Best 42). *Barbados 16 pts.*

At Sabina Park, Kingston, Jamaica, January 31, February 1, 2, 3. Drawn. Leeward Islands 389 (S. C. Williams 39, K. L. T. Arthurton 117, L. L. Harris 85, H. A. G. Anthony 30, W. K. M. Benjamin 45 not out; C. A. Walsh four for 51, R. C. Haynes four for 75) and 171 (A. C. H. Walsh 77; B. P. Patterson five for 44); Jamaica* 324 (R. G. Samuels 104, N. O. Perry 57, P. A. Gayle 33 not out, Extras 39; H. A. G. Anthony four for 71) and 79 for three. *Jamaica 4 pts, Leeward Islands 8 pts.*

At Guaracara Park, Pointe-à-Pierre, Trinidad, January 31, February 1, 2, 3. Drawn. Trinidad & Tobago 358 (P. V. Simmons 202, A. H. Gray 55; C. G. Butts three for 92, R. A. Harper six for 92); Guyana* 193 (C. B. Lambert 53, S. Dhaniram 42, R. Seeram 43; A. H. Gray five for 49, R. Dhanraj three for 58) and 387 for six (C. B. Lambert 144, N. E. F. Barry 35, R. Seeram 58, R. A. Harper 62 not out, L. A. Joseph 37 not out; P. V. Simmons four for 44). *Trinidad & Tobago 8 pts, Guyana 4 pts.*

At Kensington Oval, Bridgetown, Barbados, February 7, 8, 9, 10. Barbados won by three wickets. Leeward Islands 246 (S. C. Williams 66, R. D. Jacobs 78; V. deC. Walcott four for 49) and 175 (W. Davis 46; V. C. Drakes three for 17); Barbados* 315 (D. L. Haynes 135, P. A. Wallace 55, R. I. C. Holder 72; H. A. G. Anthony three for 67) and 110 for seven (A. C. Cummins 45 not out; V. A. Walsh three for 52). *Barbados 16 pts.*

At Mindoo Phillip Park, Castries, St Lucia, February 7, 8, 9, 10. Guyana won by an innings and 41 runs. Windward Islands 106 (N. F. Williams 30; L. A. Joseph three for 56, C. G. Butts seven for 29) and 207 (L. D. John 63, U. Pope 35; L. A. Joseph four for 52); Guyana* 354 (C. B. Lambert 125, R. A. Harper 74, C. G. Butts 41, Extras 34; I. B. A. Allen three for 70, C. A. Davis three for 94). *Guyana 16 pts.*

At Queen's Park Oval, Port-of-Spain, Trinidad, February 8, 9, 10, 11. Drawn. Jamaica 324 (R. G. Samuels 94, J. C. Adams 99, R. C. Haynes 51; E. C. Antoine three for 60, R. Dhanraj four for 92) and 175 (R. G. Samuels 45, F. R. Redwood 30; A. H. Gray three for 41, E. C. Antoine six for 49); Trinidad & Tobago* 186 (P. V. Simmons 57, K. A. Williams 33; C. A. Walsh six for 62, K. F. Ebanks three for 10). *Trinidad & Tobago 4 pts, Jamaica 8 pts.*

At Kensington Oval, Bridgetown, Barbados, February 14, 15, 16, 17. Jamaica won by 144 runs. Jamaica 296 (J. C. Adams 118, R. W. Staple 79; V. C. Drakes three for 60) and 183 (R. G. Samuels 43, J. C. Adams 30; V. deC. Walcott five for 43, O. D. Gibson three for 61); Barbados* 187 (S. L. Campbell 62; C. A. Walsh four for 48, N. O. Perry three for 39) and 148 (V. C. Drakes 34; C. A. Walsh four for 37). *Jamaica 16 pts.*

At Bourda, Georgetown, Guyana, February 14, 15, 16, 17. Leeward Islands won by eight wickets. Leeward Islands* 350 (L. L. Harris 98, M. V. Simon 43, H. A. G. Anthony 71, Extras 36; L. A. Joseph five for 80, C. G. Butts three for 75) and 55 for two; Guyana 161 (S. N. Mohammed 42, C. G. Butts 31; K. C. G. Benjamin four for 33) and 243 (P. D. Persaud 38, S. Chanderpaul 90, C. G. Butts 47; K. C. G. Benjamin three for 52, V. A. Walsh six for 77). *Leeward Islands 16 pts.*

At Queen's Park, St George's, Grenada, February 14, 15, 16, 17. Drawn. Trinidad & Tobago 131 (S. Ragoonath 67, M. P. Carew 30; N. F. Williams five for 33); Windward Islands* 135 for two (L. D. John 64, D. A. Joseph 48). *Windward Islands 8 pts, Trinidad & Tobago 4 pts.*

At Albion Sports Centre, Berbice, Guyana, February 21, 22, 23, 24. Drawn. Guyana* 256 (S. Chanderpaul 66, N. E. F. Barry 71; C. A. Best three for 29) and 183 for three (C. B. Lambert 68, N. A. McKenzie 67); Barbados 404 for nine dec. (F. L. Reifer 126, R. I. C. Holder 71, C. A. Best 79, Extras 30, C. G. Butts three for 81, A. Nandu four for 119). *Guyana 4 pts, Barbados 8 pts.*

At Sabina Park, Kingston, Jamaica, February 21, 22, 23. Jamaica won by an innings and 168 runs. Windward Islands 130 (J. R. Murray 60; C. A. Walsh four for 57, K. F. Ebanks three for 10) and 113 (L. D. John 38; C. A. Walsh five for 17); Jamaica* 411 for five dec. (D. S. Morgan 77, R. G. Samuels 74, J. C. Adams 128 not out, R. W. Staple 58, F. R. Redwood 38 not out; C. A. Davis three for 71). *Jamaica 16 pts.*

At Warner Park, Basseterre, St Kitts, February 22, 23, 24, 25. Leeward Islands won by an innings and 41 runs. Trinidad & Tobago 322 (C. G. Yorke 91, K. A. Williams 69, N. Bidhesi 37, A. H. Gray 33; J. Maynard four for 52) and 115 (M. P. Carew 37; V. A. Walsh three for 38, H. A. G. Anthony four for 23); Leeward Islands* 478 (A. C. H. Walsh 44, W. Davis 99, L. L. Harris 82, N. C. Guishard 79, K. C. G. Benjamin 52, Extras 45; E. C. Antoine six for 117, R. E. Elvin three for 94). *Leeward Islands 16 pts.*

SHELL SHIELD AND RED STRIPE CUP WINNERS

The Shell Shield was replaced by the Red Stripe Cup after the 1986-87 season.

1965-66	Barbados	1979-80	Barbados
1966-67	Barbados	1980-81	Combined Islands
1968-69	Jamaica	1981-82	Barbados
1969-70	Trinidad	1982-83	Guyana
1970-71	Trinidad	1983-84	Barbados
1971-72	Barbados	1984-85	Trinidad & Tobago
1972-73	Guyana	1985-86	Barbados
1973-74	Barbados	1986-87	Guyana
1974-75	Guyana	1987-88	Jamaica
1975-76 {	Trinidad / Barbados	1988-89	Jamaica
		1989-90	Leeward Islands
1976-77	Barbados	1990-91	Barbados
1977-78	Barbados	1991-92	Jamaica
1978-79	Barbados		

GEDDES GRANT SHIELD, 1991-92

Note: Matches in this section were not first-class.

Zone A

At Sabina Park, Kingston, Jamaica, January 29. Leeward Islands won by six runs. Leeward Islands 244 for seven (50 overs) (R. D. Jacobs 85, L. L. Harris 62; J. B. Grant three for 52); Jamaica* 238 for eight (50 overs) (J. C. Adams 112, M. C. Neita 50; W. K. M. Benjamin five for 26).

At Queen's Park Oval, Port-of-Spain, Trinidad, February 6. Trinidad & Tobago won by 22 runs. Trinidad & Tobago 221 for six (50 overs) (B. C. Lara 41, A. L. Logie 81, D. Williams 45 not out); Jamaica* 199 (46.3 overs) (F. R. Redwood 35, C. A. Walsh 32 not out; A. H. Gray four for 54, R. Dhanraj four for 27).

At Grove Park, Charlestown, Nevis, February 20. Trinidad & Tobago won by three runs in a match reduced by rain to 23 overs a side. Trinidad & Tobago 127 for seven (23 overs) (C. G. Yorke 37; J. Maynard three for 33, including a hat-trick); Leeward Islands* 124 (23 overs) (W. Davis 37; D. Sultan three for 19).

Zone B

At Kensington Oval, Bridgetown, Barbados, January 29. Barbados won by 145 runs. Barbados 261 for four (50 overs) (C. A. Best 88 not out, R. I. C. Holder 111, L. K. Puckerin 40); Windward Islands* 116 for six (50 overs) (D. A. Joseph 33; H. W. daC. Springer three for 34).

At Mindoo Phillip Park, Castries, St Lucia, February 5. Guyana won on scoring-rate after rain stopped play. Windward Islands 101 (38.1 overs) (C. B. Cort three for 15, C. G. Butts three for 15); Guyana* 94 for nine (35.4 overs) (I. B. A. Allen three for 25, T. Z. Kentish four for 12).

At Bourda, Georgetown, Guyana, February 19. No result, rain having stopped play. Barbados qualified for the final by virtue of a faster scoring-rate in zonal matches. Guyana 39 for two (12.3 overs) v Barbados*.

Final

At Queen's Park Oval, Port-of-Spain, Trinidad, April 4. Trinidad & Tobago won by eight wickets. Barbados* 163 (49.3 overs) (C. A. Best 57, C. O. Browne 52; E. C. Antoine three for 20); Trinidad & Tobago 167 for two (37.3 overs) (P. V. Simmons 60 not out, B. C. Lara 77 not out).

CRICKET IN NEW ZEALAND, 1991-92

By C. R. BUTTERY

The 1991-92 domestic season was overshadowed by the England tour and World Cup but both the main competitions produced exceptionally tense finales. The one-day Shell Cup ended amid high drama and the first-class competition, the Shell Trophy, was eventually won jointly by Northern Districts and Central Districts, with Canterbury just two points behind. This was the first time either this trophy or its predecessor, the Plunket Shield, had ever been shared.

Both teams had the advantage of fielding full-strength sides for nearly every game while both Canterbury and Auckland regularly lost players to Test teams. Northern Districts also owed much to their import from Glamorgan, Matthew Maynard, who scored four centuries and played a major role in two of their wins and their escape from defeat against Auckland. Batting support for Maynard was provided by wicket-keeper Bryan Young and – in the final, vital game against Wellington – Shane Thomson, who scored 57 and 126 without being dismissed, to set up victory.

Central Districts went tantalisingly close to becoming outright competition winners. Needing just first-innings lead points in their last match against Otago, they could manage only 269 in reply to Otago's 362 for nine declared. Nevertheless they could look back on the season with considerable satisfaction. They achieved their highest placing since 1986-87, the team responded well to all challenges, and with a nucleus of young, experienced players to draw on, the future looks promising. Fast-medium bowler David Leonard collected 33 wickets, while Mark Douglas batted solidly for 773 runs, average 42.94, while the all-round performances of Roger Twose and Stuart Duff were particularly useful.

Canterbury were arguably the strongest side in the competition. For most of the season they were lying either first or second and their only defeat was against Auckland in the final game. First-innings lead would have been enough for them too. Unfortunately for Canterbury, their batting inexplicably failed in the first innings, they were forced to follow on and went out of contention. On the bright side, Llorne Howell overcame three successive ducks to emerge as one of Canterbury's most promising young batsmen. Chris Cairns bowled at times with genuine pace and on his day could be a match-winner. He took 42 wickets during the season including match figures of 11 for 100 against Central Districts.

Auckland, as usual, lost more players to the national team than the others. Six Aucklanders were selected for the Second Test against England and five for each of the other two. This went some way to explaining why Auckland played five successive games without a win and finished fourth out of six. The most outstanding player was Jeff Crowe, who seemed unaffected by the burdens of captaincy and had an excellent season. He scored four centuries, 1,063 runs in all, averaging 62.53, and failed to reach double figures only once. Dipak Patel's all-round performances were also most impressive. Against Northern Districts he wrote himself into the record books by hitting 204 and taking six for 117 and four for 116. The feat of scoring a double-century and taking ten wickets in the same game puts him in a most select group: only E. G. Arnold, J. W. H. T. Douglas, G. Giffen and W. G. Grace (both twice) have achieved it before.

Otago won only two matches and finished fifth, despite the bowling of Neil Mallender, who collected 49 wickets at low cost and was easily the competition's most successful bowler. Young pace bowler Jeff Wilson also bowled well to take 30 wickets in his first season. But there was inadequate support for these two and the batting was weak. Ken Rutherford scored well throughout the season but the other recognised batsmen lacked consistency. One exception was Scott McHardy, another newcomer to the side, who was chosen only for the last three games, failed in his first match but then made successive scores of 100, 67, 53 and 85 not out.

Wellington had another dismal season, winning only once and finishing last for the second consecutive year. Andrew Jones and Martin Crowe were unavailable for much of the season because of Test match commitments and, in Crowe's case, injury. Without these two, the batting looked decidedly brittle although in the final game against Northern Districts Graham Burnett found form to score an unbeaten 203 in a third-wicket stand of 346 with Ross Verry. They still lost.

In the one-day Shell Cup tournament Wellington and Canterbury contested an unforgettable final which saw some of the best cricket of the entire season. In reply to Canterbury's seemingly unassailable total of 252, Wellington reached 247 before losing their ninth wicket in the penultimate over. This forced injured captain Gavin Larsen to the crease. Larsen had earlier suffered a severe fielding accident requiring eight stitches to his left hand. Batting one-handed, he managed to keep his wicket intact while two further runs were scored. However he was bowled by the third-last ball, leaving Wellington just four runs short of victory. Andrew Jones of Wellington made the day's top score of 67 and was also the tournament's leading batsman, scoring 11, 40, 44, 74 and 51 in the other matches. Steve Woodward, New Zealand's most experienced Test umpire, announced his retirement at the end of the season, 13 years after his first Test.

FIRST-CLASS AVERAGES, 1991-92

BATTING

(Qualification: 5 completed innings, average 35.00)

	M	I	NO	R	HS	100s	Avge
M. P. Maynard (*N. Districts*) ..	10	13	0	893	195	4	68.69
D. S. McHardy (*Otago*)	3	6	1	316	100	1	63.20
J. J. Crowe (*Auckland*)	10	19	2	1,063	142*	4	62.52
L. K. Germon (*Canterbury*)	10	10	4	335	91	0	55.83
A. C. Parore (*Auckland*)	9	12	4	420	155*	1	52.50
B. A. Young (*N. Districts*)	11	16	4	606	129	1	50.50
S. A. Thomson (*N. Districts*) ...	10	19	6	608	126*	1	46.76
S. W. Duff (*C. Districts*)	11	17	5	559	164*	1	46.58
L. G. Howell (*Canterbury*)	10	15	2	583	112	1	44.84
C. Z. Harris (*Canterbury*)	8	13	3	403	94*	0	44.77
D. N. Patel (*Auckland*)	8	14	1	574	204	1	44.15
K. R. Rutherford (*Otago*)	10	20	2	787	133	1	43.72
B. Z. Harris (*Canterbury*)	6	9	1	347	133	2	43.37
M. W. Douglas (*C. Districts*) ...	12	22	4	773	144	2	42.94

	M	I	NO	R	HS	100s	Avge
R. T. Latham (*Canterbury*)	7	11	0	470	87	0	42.72
G. P. Burnett (*Wellington*)	9	17	3	561	203*	1	40.07
A. P. O'Dowd (*Auckland*)	7	12	4	306	113	1	38.25
J. G. Wright (*Auckland*)	7	14	0	518	116	2	37.00
D. A. Stirling (*Wellington*)	4	7	1	222	70	0	37.00
R. G. Twose (*C. Districts*)	11	20	2	653	107*	2	36.27
A. H. Jones (*Wellington*)	7	13	0	457	143	2	35.15

* Signifies not out.

BOWLING

(Qualification: 20 wickets)

	O	M	R	W	BB	5W/i	Avge
N. A. Mallender (*Otago*)	284.4	74	603	49	7-39	5	12.30
G. R. Larsen (*Wellington*)	210.4	89	396	20	6-64	1	19.80
C. L. Cairns (*Canterbury*)	294	67	872	42	7-34	2	20.76
J. W. Wilson (*Otago*)	211.4	49	562	26	5-48	2	21.61
R. G. Twose (*C. Districts*)	188	57	455	20	3-22	0	22.75
D. N. Askew (*C. Districts*)	155.2	35	527	23	4-42	0	22.91
S. B. Doull (*N. Districts*)	204.2	50	551	24	5-35	1	22.95
D. J. Leonard (*C. Districts*)	285.5	78	857	33	6-67	1	25.96
R. P. de Groen (*N. Districts*)	281	85	664	25	5-18	1	26.56
D. N. Patel (*Auckland*)	316.4	75	857	32	7-72	2	26.78
S. W. Brown (*Auckland*)	216.3	53	677	25	5-39	2	27.08
S. W. Duff (*C. Districts*)	324.1	103	774	28	4-13	0	27.64
R. G. Petrie (*Canterbury*)	240.5	45	734	26	5-70	1	28.23
M. J. Sears (*Wellington*)	228.1	47	718	25	6-48	1	28.72
D. K. Morrison (*Auckland*)	209.4	41	596	20	3-38	0	29.80
M. N. Hart (*N. Districts*)	254.4	77	695	23	5-45	1	30.21
M. W. Priest (*Canterbury*)	359	120	855	28	6-59	1	30.53
C. Pringle (*Auckland*)	315.1	70	941	29	4-52	0	32.44
M. L. Su'a (*Auckland*)	238.4	55	738	21	3-54	0	35.14
R. L. Hayes (*N. Districts*)	236.5	53	711	20	4-55	0	35.55
G. E. Bradburn (*N. Districts*)	308	84	808	21	4-47	0	38.47

SHELL TROPHY, 1991-92

	Played	Won	Lost	Drawn	1st-inns Points	Points
Central Districts	10	3	2	5	24*	62
Northern Districts....	10	3	1	6	24*	62
Canterbury...........	10	3	1	6	24	60
Auckland	10	3	2	5	16	52
Otago	10	2	4	4	20	33
Wellington	10	1	5	4	8	14

Win = 12 pts; lead on first innings = 4 pts.

* *First-innings points shared in one match.*

Otago were penalised 11 points and Wellington 6 points for failing to achieve an average of 17 overs per hour.

In the following scores, * *by the name of a team indicates that they won the toss.*

At Eden Park, Auckland, November 29, 30, December 1. Auckland won by five wickets. Otago* 254 (M. H. Austen 73, K. R. Rutherford 79; D. K. Morrison three for 59, S. W. Brown five for 57) and 289 (K. R. Rutherford 32, I. S. Billcliff 34, R. N. Hoskin 61, E. J. Marshall 47; C. Pringle five for 89, J. T. C. Vaughan five for 72); Auckland 264 for five dec. (J. J. Crowe 36, D. N. Patel 56 not out, S. W. Brown 56, A. J. Hunt 50 not out; N. A. Mallender three for 53) and 283 for five (J. J. Crowe 102, D. N. Patel 51, S. W. Brown 62). *Auckland 16 pts.*

At Lancaster Park, Christchurch, November 29, 30, December 1. Drawn. Wellington 286 (G. P. Burnett 63, E. B. McSweeney 63, D. A. Stirling 56 not out; C. L. Cairns three for 79, R. G. Petrie three for 67) and 266 (E. B. McSweeney 119, D. A. Stirling 70; R. M. Ford six for 35); Canterbury* 304 for seven dec. (B. R. Hartland 127, L. G. Howell 44, R. T. Latham 50; G. R. Larsen six for 64) and 58 for one (L. G. Howell 37 not out). *Canterbury 4 pts.*

At Trustbank Park, Masterton, November 29, 30, December 1. Central Districts won by four wickets. Northern Districts* 172 (S. A. Thomson 51, B. A. Young 49 not out; S. W. Duff four for 13) and 238 for six dec. (K. A. Wealleans 58, B. A. Young 86 not out; S. W. Duff three for 59); Central Districts 173 for six dec. (M. J. Greatbatch 30, M. W. Douglas 31, P. S. Briasco 47; S. B. Doull three for 44) and 238 for six (R. G. Twose 79, M. J. Greatbatch 87; G. E. Bradburn three for 56). *Central Districts 16 pts.*

At Burnside Park, Christchurch, December 6, 7, 8. Canterbury won by three wickets. Central Districts* 134 (T. E. Blain 34; C. L. Cairns four for 28) and 178 (C. D. Ingham 31, T. E. Blain 63; C. L. Cairns four for 38, M. W. Priest three for 46); Canterbury 124 (L. K. Germon 36 not out; D. J. Leonard six for 67) and 189 for seven (B. R. Hartland 59, R. T. Latham 62; S. W. Duff four for 34). *Canterbury 12 pts, Central Districts 4 pts.*

At Trustbank Park, Hamilton, December 6, 7, 8. Northern Districts won by eight wickets. Otago 212 (I. S. Billcliff 44, D. J. Hunter 34; R. P. de Groen three for 72, R. L. Hayes four for 60) and 177 (M. H. Austen 56; R. P. de Groen four for 40, M. N. Hart three for 31); Northern Districts* 284 for four dec. (S. A. Thomson 79 not out, M. P. Maynard 142) and 106 for two (G. E. Bradburn 63 not out). *Northern Districts 16 pts.*

At Basin Reserve, Wellington, December 6, 7, 8. Wellington won by five wickets. Auckland 173 (J. G. Wright 48, I. D. S. Smith 33 not out; J. P. Millmow five for 49, G. R. Larsen three for 39) and 291 for seven dec. (T. J. Franklin 34, J. G. Wright 100, J. T. C. Vaughan 37; J. P. Millmow three for 44); Wellington* 125 (D. K. Morrison three for 38, C. Pringle three for 34) and 340 for five (R. B. Reid 56, A. H. Jones 103, J. D. Wells 102; D. K. Morrison four for 49). *Wellington 12 pts, Auckland 4 pts.*

At Eden Park, Auckland, December 12, 13, 14. Drawn. Auckland* 244 (A. J. Hunt 68; R. P. de Groen three for 56, S. B. Doull three for 49) and 424 for four dec. (J. J. Crowe 142 not out, D. N. Patel 204); Northern Districts 284 (M. P. Maynard 195, S. B. Doull 44; C. Pringle four for 83, D. N. Patel six for 117) and 335 for eight (D. J. White 39, G. E. Bradburn 37, M. P. Maynard 110, B. A. Young 82, M. N. Hart 46; D. N. Patel four for 116). *Northern Districts 4 pts.*

At Centennial Park, Oamaru, December 12, 13, 14. Canterbury won by five wickets. Otago* 350 for seven dec. (M. H. Austen 36, I. S. Billcliff 48, R. N. Hoskin 53, S. A. Robinson 49 not out, K. R. Rutherford 133) and 198 for seven dec. (M. J. Lamont 60, K. R. Rutherford 44; R. G. Petrie three for 38); Canterbury 295 for nine dec. (D. J. Boyle 84, R. T. Latham 68, C. Z. Harris 94 not out; N. A. Mallender three for 59, J. K. Lindsay five for 72) and 257 for five (L. G. Howell 34, R. T. Latham 87, C. Z. Harris 65, P. G. Kennedy 30 not out; N. A. Mallender four for 28). *Canterbury 12 pts, Otago 4 pts.*

At Basin Reserve, Wellington, December 12, 13, 14. Central Districts won by seven wickets. Wellington 88 (D. J. Leonard three for 26, R. G. Twose three for 22) and 256 (A. H. Jones 53, J. D. Wells 86, E. B. McSweeney 30 not out; C. L. Auckram three for 39, D. N. Askew three for 56); Central Districts* 136 (T. E. Blain 47, D. J. Leonard 46; M. J. Sears six for 48) and 212 for three (R. G. Twose 107 not out, M. J. Greatbatch 47). *Central Districts 16 pts.*

At Molyneux Park, Alexandra, January 2, 3, 5. Northern Districts won by 24 runs. Northern Districts 266 (D. J. White 30, K. A. Wealleans 56, B. A. Young 42, M. D. Bailey 60; N. A. Mallender six for 52) and 153 (G. E. Bradburn 33; J. W. Wilson five for 48); Otago* 203 (R. N. Hoskin 52, K. R. Rutherford 42, I. S. Billcliff 30; D. F. Potter five for 69, S. A. Thomson three for 31) and 192 (K. R. Rutherford 55; S. B. Doull three for 36, D. F. Potter three for 62). *Northern Districts 16 pts.*

At Eden Park, Auckland, January 3, 4, 5. Auckland won by five wickets. Wellington* 201 (A. H. Jones 48, J. R. Murtagh 41, E. J. Gray 51; W. Watson three for 51) and 199 (R. B. Reid 61, J. R. Murtagh 44; W. Watson three for 67, D. N. Patel seven for 72); Auckland 258 (J. J. Crowe 118, D. N. Patel 60; H. T. Davis five for 63) and 145 for five (T. J. Franklin 44; G. R. Larsen three for 14). *Auckland 16 pts.*

At Pukekura Park, New Plymouth, January 3, 4, 5. Canterbury won by six wickets. Central Districts* 269 (M. W. Douglas 144; C. L. Cairns four for 66, R. G. Petrie four for 91) and 171 (C. D. Ingham 50, S. W. J. Wilson 31, S. W. Duff 38; C. L. Cairns seven for 34, M. W. Priest three for 49); Canterbury 374 (R. G. Petrie 100, R. T. Latham 84, B. Z. Harris 33, Extras 42; D. J. Leonard three for 88, C. L. Auckram three for 73, D. N. Askew four for 70) and 68 for four (R. T. Latham 32). *Canterbury 16 pts.*

At Lancaster Park, Christchurch, January 10, 11, 12. Drawn. Auckland 428 for seven dec. (J. J. Crowe 128, A. P. O'Dowd 113, M. R. Pringle 35, A. C. Parore 54 not out; M. F. Sharpe three for 98, M. W. Priest three for 96); Canterbury* 431 for seven (B. R. Hartland 89, L. G. Howell 112, P. G. Kennedy 74, M. W. Priest 89; S. W. Brown three for 79, M. J. Haslam three for 72). *Canterbury 4 pts.*

At Carisbrook, Dunedin, January 10, 11, 12. Drawn. Otago 305 for eight dec. (R. N. Hoskin 80, M. J. Lamont 35, K. R. Rutherford 64, M. H. Austen 40 not out, S. A. Robinson 35; D. N. Askew four for 88) and 156 for six dec. (R. N. Hoskin 36, M. J. Lamont 34, K. R. Rutherford 49; S. W. Duff three for 34); Central Districts* 159 (R. K. Brown 38, S. W. Duff 32, D. N. Askew 31; N. A. Mallender seven for 39) and 212 for nine (R. G. Twose 43, S. W. J. Wilson 32, P. S. Briasco 56; N. A. Mallender four for 50, K. R. Rutherford three for 26). *Otago 4 pts.*

At Basin Reserve, Wellington, January 10, 11, 12. Drawn. Northern Districts 258 (K. A. Wealleans 108, B. A. Young 59; M. J. Sears four for 56) and 265 for five dec. (M. P. Maynard 53, M. D. Bailey 77 not out, M. N. Hart 65 not out; M. J. Sears three for 51); Wellington* 204 (R. B. Reid 38, E. B. McSweeney 31, D. A. Stirling 50; M. N. Hart five for 45, G. E. Bradburn three for 33) and 300 for eight (R. B. Reid 84, R. A. Verry 76; M. N. Hart three for 87). *Northern Districts 4 pts.*

At Trustbank Park, Hamilton, January 16, 17, 18. Drawn. Central Districts 288 for six (S. W. J. Wilson 81, T. E. Blain 59, R. K. Brown 60 not out, S. W. Duff 39 not out) v Northern Districts*. No play on last two days. *Central Districts 2 pts, Northern Districts 2 pts.*

At Carisbrook, Dunedin, January 16, 17, 18. Drawn. Auckland* 127 (A. C. Parore 57 not out; J. W. Wilson five for 50, P. J. Marshall three for 28) and 402 for five dec. (B. A. Pocock 71, A. P. O'Dowd 75 not out, A. C. Parore 155 not out; J. W. Wilson three for 108); Otago 301 (R. N. Hoskin 47, S. A. Robinson 41, K. R. Rutherford 41, I. S. Billcliff 45, J. W. Wilson 47 not out; M. L. Su'a three for 57, S. W. Brown three for 72) and 135 for seven (S. A. Robinson 53, M. H. Austen 56; R. J. Drown four for six). *Otago 4 pts.*

At Eden Park, Auckland, January 20, 21, 22. Drawn. Central Districts* 354 for five dec. (P. S. Briasco 104, S. W. J. Wilson 94, M. W. Douglas 76 not out, T. E. Blain 42) and 222 for one dec. (R. G. Twose 107 not out, M. W. Douglas 103 not out); Auckland 264 for three dec. (S. J. Peterson 77, B. A. Pocock 101, J. J. Crowe 50) and 233 for seven (S. J. Peterson 55, J. J. Crowe 77, J. T. C. Vaughan 36; D. J. Leonard three for 54). *Central Districts 4 pts.*

At Trustbank Park, Hamilton, January 20, 21, 22. Drawn. Northern Districts* 311 (B. A. Young 129, M. P. Maynard 31; R. M. Ford three for 85, R. T. Latham three for 20); Canterbury 235 (L. G. Howell 59, P. G. Kennedy 34, L. K. Germon 85 not out; R. P. de Groen three for 76, G. E. Bradburn four for 47). *Northern Districts 4 pts.*

At Petone Recreation Ground, Wellington, January 21, 22, 23. Otago won by eight wickets. Wellington* 142 (G. P. Burnett 33; N. A. Mallender five for 39, P. J. Marshall three for 40) and 205 (E. B. McSweeney 107; N. A. Mallender five for 37); Otago 300 for eight dec. (R. N. Hoskin 48, M. J. Lamont 49, K. R. Rutherford 87; B. R. Williams four for 60) and 51 for two. *Otago 16 pts.*

At Smallbone Park, Rotorua, January 25, 26, 27. Drawn. Northern Districts 231 (D. J. White 30, S. A. Thomson 32, M. P. Maynard 92; M. L. Su'a three for 88, W. Watson three for 53, D. N. Patel three for 32); Auckland* 72 (R. P. de Groen five for 18, S. B. Doull five for 35) and 92 for one (B. A. Pocock 32 not out, J. J. Crowe 37 not out). *Northern Districts 4 pts.*

At Basin Reserve, Wellington, January 25, 26, 27. Drawn. Wellington 134 (C. L. Cairns four for 61, M. B. Owens four for 18); Canterbury* 136 for four (L. G. Howell 62 not out). *Canterbury 4 pts.*

At Lancaster Park, Christchurch, February 1, 2, 3. Drawn. Northern Districts* 385 (K. A. Wealleans 62, M. N. Hart 38, M. P. Maynard 50, G. E. Bradburn 72, S. B. Doull 108; M. B. Owens four for 74, R. G. Petrie three for 100) and 51 for two; Canterbury 397 (B. Z. Harris 45, L. G. Howell 62, C. Z. Harris 37, L. K. Germon 91, M. W. Priest 103, Extras 30; R. L. Hayes four for 55). *Canterbury 4 pts.*

At Victoria Park, Wanganui, February 1, 2, 3. Central Districts won by 74 runs. Central Districts* 312 (M. W. Douglas 63, S. W. Duff 164 not out, C. Pringle three for 80, S. W. Brown three for 111) and 248 for eight dec. (M. W. Douglas 99, T. E. Blain 66; S. W. Brown four for 45); Auckland 261 for nine dec. (J. J. Crowe 68, J. T. C. Vaughan 40, A. J. Hunt 59; D. J. Leonard four for 84) and 225 (S. J. Peterson 41, J. J. Crowe 88; S. W. Duff four for 57). *Central Districts 16 pts.*

At Carisbrook, Dunedin, February 1, 2, 3. Otago won by one wicket. Wellington 214 (G. P. Burnett 45, J. D. Wells 40, B. R. Williams 33; N. A. Mallender five for 44, J. W. Wilson three for 52) and 227 for five dec. (S. P. Blackmore 107 not out, J. D. Wells 39); Otago* 200 (P. W. Dobbs 86, I. S. Billcliff 45; P. W. O'Rourke three for 42, M. J. Sears four for 65) and 245 for nine (M. J. Lamont 67, M. H. Austen 68; B. R. Williams three for 105). *Otago 12 pts, Wellington 4 pts.*

At Lancaster Park, Christchurch, February 5, 6, 7. Drawn. Canterbury* 247 for nine dec. (L. G. Howell 85, P. G. Kennedy 61; N. A. Mallender three for 42, J. W. Wilson three for 47) and 245 for one dec. (D. J. Boyle 74 not out, B. Z. Harris 133); Otago 236 (D. S. McHardy 100, N. A. Mallender 49; M. B. Owens four for 52, M. W. Priest three for 52) and 181 for nine (P. W. Dobbs 32, D. S. McHardy 67, I. S. Billcliff 35; M. W. Priest six for 59). *Canterbury 4 pts.*

At McLean Park, Napier, February 5, 6, 7. Drawn. Wellington* 220 (R. A. Verry 31, G. R. Larsen 70; D. J. Leonard three for 43, D. N. Askew four for 42) and 295 for four dec. (S. P. Blackmore 31, G. P. Burnett 83 retired hurt, G. R. Larsen 56, E. B. McSweeney 50, G. R. Baker 33 not out); Central Districts 222 for seven dec. (R. G. Twose 33, M. W. Douglas 86 not out, S. W. Duff 55; G. R. Larsen three for 36) and 232 for nine (R. G. Twose 83, M. J. Greatbatch 67, T. E. Blain 41; H. T. Davis three for 55, B. R. Williams three for 50). *Central Districts 4 pts.*

At Eden Park, Auckland, February 9, 10, 11. Auckland won by eight wickets. Auckland 304 (J. J. Crowe 55, J. T. C. Vaughan 81, A. C. Parore 41, Extras 32; R. G. Petrie five for 70) and 86 for two (J. J. Crowe 38); Canterbury* 131 (N. J. Astle 37; C. Pringle four for 52, S. W. Brown five for 39) and 257 (B. Z. Harris 122, L. K. Germon 35; C. Pringle three for 61, M. J. Haslam three for 29). *Auckland 16 pts.*

At Fitzherbert Park, Palmerston North, February 9, 10, 11. Drawn. Otago* 362 for nine dec. (D. S. McHardy 53, M. H. Austen 31, S. A. Robinson 35, N. A. Mallender 100 not out, J. W. Wilson 67; M. J. Pawson three for 55, R. G. Twose three for 23) and 194 for four dec. (D. S. McHardy 85 not out, S. A. Robinson 72 not out; S. W. Duff three for 19); Central Districts 269 for nine dec. (T. E. Blain 96, S. W. Duff 69; P. J. Marshall six for 59) and 198 for nine (R. G. Twose 37, D. J. Leonard 67; J. W. Wilson four for 49). *Otago 4 pts.*

At Trustbank Park, Hamilton, February 9, 10, 11. Northern Districts won by six wickets. Wellington 370 for three dec. (G. P. Burnett 203 not out, R. A. Verry 132) and 146 for five dec. (G. P. Burnett 47); Northern Districts* 146 for two dec. (D. J. White 68 not out, S. A. Thomson 57 not out) and 371 for four (S. A. Thomson 126 not out, M. P. Maynard 102, G. E. Bradburn 52 not out). *Northern Districts 12 pts, Wellington 4 pts.*

PLUNKET SHIELD AND SHELL TROPHY WINNERS

The Plunket Shield was replaced by the Shell Trophy after the 1974-75 season.

1921-22	Auckland	1959-60	Canterbury
1922-23	Canterbury	1960-61	Wellington
1923-24	Wellington	1961-62	Wellington
1924-25	Otago	1962-63	Northern Districts
1925-26	Wellington	1963-64	Auckland
1926-27	Auckland	1964-65	Canterbury
1927-28	Wellington	1965-66	Wellington
1928-29	Auckland	1966-67	Central Districts
1929-30	Wellington	1967-68	Central Districts
1930-31	Canterbury	1968-69	Auckland
1931-32	Wellington	1969-70	Otago
1932-33	Otago	1970-71	Central Districts
1933-34	Auckland	1971-72	Otago
1934-35	Canterbury	1972-73	Wellington
1935-36	Wellington	1973-74	Wellington
1936-37	Auckland	1974-75	Otago
1937-38	Auckland	1975-76	Canterbury
1938-39	Auckland	1976-77	Otago
1939-40	Auckland	1977-78	Auckland
1940-45	No competition	1978-79	Otago
1945-46	Canterbury	1979-80	Northern Districts
1946-47	Auckland	1980-81	Auckland
1947-48	Otago	1981-82	Wellington
1948-49	Canterbury	1982-83	Wellington
1949-50	Wellington	1983-84	Canterbury
1950-51	Otago	1984-85	Wellington
1951-52	Canterbury	1985-86	Otago
1952-53	Otago	1986-87	Central Districts
1953-54	Central Districts	1987-88	Otago
1954-55	Wellington	1988-89	Auckland
1955-56	Canterbury	1989-90	Wellington
1956-57	Wellington	1990-91	Auckland
1957-58	Otago	1991-92 {	Central Districts
1958-59	Auckland		Northern Districts

SHELL CUP, 1991-92

Note: Matches in this section were not first-class.

At Eden Park, Auckland, December 15. Auckland won by 103 runs. Auckland* 265 for three (50 overs) (J. G. Wright 45, J. J. Crowe 130 not out, S. W. Brown 63); Northern Districts 162 (46 overs) (M. N. Hart 52 not out; S. W. Brown five for 23).

At Carisbrook, Dunedin, December 15. Canterbury won by 63 runs. Canterbury 239 for five (44 overs) (R. T. Latham 46, P. G. Kennedy 57, C. Z. Harris 33, C. L. Cairns 62); Otago* 176 (38.2 overs) (M. H. Austen 65, M. J. Lamont 31). Match reduced to 44 overs because of rain.

At Basin Reserve, Wellington, December 15. Central Districts won by five wickets. Wellington* 204 for nine (50 overs) (M. D. Crowe 86, R. B. Reid 35; R. G. Twose three for 27, P. S. Briasco four for 31); Central Districts 208 for five (49.2 overs) (M. J. Greatbatch 78 not out, S. W. J. Wilson 31, T. E. Blain 52 not out).

At Eden Park, Auckland, December 22. Auckland won by 42 runs. Auckland* 164 (49.3 overs) (J. T. C. Vaughan 63; M. J. Sears three for 32); Wellington 122 (44.3 overs) (A. H. Jones 40; J. T. C. Vaughan three for 25).

At Blake Park, Mount Maunganui, December 27. Central Districts won by 73 runs. Central Districts* 193 for nine (50 overs) (R. G. Twose 72, M. W. Douglas 40); Northern Districts 120 (39.2 overs) (R. G. Twose four for 34, P. S. Briasco three for 5).

At Molyneux Park, Alexandra, December 27. Auckland won by 123 runs. Auckland 233 for four (50 overs) (J. J. Crowe 86 not out, J. T. C. Vaughan 72); Otago* 110 (41.3 overs) (R. N. Hoskin 40; J. T. C. Vaughan four for 27).

At Basin Reserve, Wellington, December 27. Wellington won by four wickets. Canterbury 219 for nine (50 overs) (R. T. Latham 31, C. Z. Harris 46, L. G. Howell 40 not out, R. G. Petrie 36); Wellington* 222 for six (49 overs) (G. P. Burnett 47, A. H. Jones 44, J. D. Wells 58 not out).

At Levin Domain, Levin, December 29. Otago won by three wickets. Central Districts* 156 (46.3 overs) (R. L. Glover 32; E. J. Marshall three for 28); Otago 157 for seven (48.1 overs) (K. R. Rutherford 48, M. J. Lamont 35; M. J. Pawson four for 21).

At Blake Park, Mount Maunganui, December 29. Wellington won by three wickets. Northern Districts* 202 for six (50 overs) (D. J. White 44, M. P. Maynard 32, M. D. Bailey 41 not out); Wellington 203 for seven (49.5 overs) (G. P. Burnett 67, A. H. Jones 74).

At Lancaster Park, Christchurch, December 30. Canterbury v Auckland. Abandoned without a ball bowled, owing to rain.

At Eden Park, Auckland, December 31. Auckland v Central Districts. Abandoned without a ball bowled, owing to rain.

At Lancaster Park, Christchurch, January 1. Canterbury won by seven wickets. Northern Districts* 178 (50 overs) (B. A. Young 49); Canterbury 181 for three (38.5 overs) (B. R. Hartland 103 not out, C. Z. Harris 34).

At Basin Reserve, Wellington, January 1. Wellington v Otago. Abandoned without a ball bowled, owing to rain.

At Pukekura Park, New Plymouth, January 2. Canterbury won by eight wickets. Central Districts 130 for eight (50 overs) (M. B. Owens three for 33); Canterbury* 134 for two (39.4 overs) (B. R. Hartland 65 not out, L. G. Howell 33).

At Molyneux Park, Alexandra, January 4. Otago won by seven wickets. Northern Districts* 212 (49.3 overs) (K. A. Wealleans 77 not out, M. D. Bailey 75; N. A. Mallender three for 39, A. J. Gale five for 43); Otago 216 for three (48.3 overs) (K. R. Rutherford 115 not out, M. J. Lamont 32 not out; R. L. Hayes three for 50).

Auckland 8 pts, Canterbury 7 pts, Wellington 5 pts, Central Districts 5 pts, Otago 5 pts, Northern Districts 0 pts. Wellington and Central Districts qualified for the semi-finals on net run-rate.

Semi-finals

At Eden Park, Auckland, January 8. Wellington won by five wickets. Auckland* 170 for eight (50 overs) (A. J. Hunt 30, C. Pringle 38 not out; D. A. Stirling three for 40, B. R. Williams three for 29); Wellington 171 for five (49.3 overs) (G. P. Burnett 78, A. H. Jones 51).

At Lancaster Park, Christchurch, January 8. Canterbury won by 131 runs. Canterbury 242 for seven (50 overs) (R. T. Latham 80, L. G. Howell 30, P. G. Kennedy 56 not out); Central Districts* 111 (35.1 overs) (P. S. Briasco 30 not out; M. W. Priest three for 30).

Final

At Lancaster Park, Christchurch, January 14. Canterbury won by three runs. Canterbury* 252 (49.4 overs) (B. R. Hartland 46, R. T. Latham 38, L. G. Howell 62, P. G. Kennedy 33; M. J. Sears three for 38); Wellington 249 (49.4 overs) (A. H. Jones 67).

CRICKET IN INDIA, 1991-92

By R. MOHAN and SUDHIR VAIDYA

The fortunes of the national team, absent for five months in Australia and New Zealand for six Tests followed by the World Cup, predictably distracted attention from the domestic season. But in India runs continued to be scored freely, with 149 centuries in 74 first-class matches, despite an experiment with uncovered wickets. There was no clear evidence of the benefit of this radical reform.

There was a marginal increase in the number of outright wins, with the Ranji Trophy's 60 league games yielding 39, up from 32 in 1990-91. But that season had also witnessed an increase, from 23 the previous year, after the introduction of a fourth day's play. The shift towards decisive results may have owed as much to this extra day as to the effect of the elements on pitches notorious for their lifelessness. The Ranji final and semi-finals, played over five days, were all decided on first-innings lead, and captains continued to air their routine complaints about the wickets. An argument against four-day matches and uncovered pitches was the risk of widening the gulf in standards between teams, exemplified by Assam's victory by an innings and 472 runs over Tripura, in which Zahir Alam and Lalchand Rajput set a new world record of 475 for the second wicket.

The case for uncovered pitches was seen to good effect only in the four inter-zonal Duleep Trophy games. Here all the matches ended in outright victories, and 129 wickets fell, 90 of them to seamers, as 4,032 runs were scored, a marked change of emphasis from the previous season, when the four matches featured 5,275 runs for 104 wickets. Captains may have been encouraged to use their pace bowlers by the deduction of four minutes for drinks breaks and two for the fall of each wicket, which lessened the threat of over-rate penalties. It was incisive bowling from the pace trio of Chetan Sharma, Atul Wassan and Vivek Razdan which won North Zone their ninth Duleep Trophy (including one shared title). Other pace bowlers able to make the most of some life in the wickets of western India were Prashant Vaidya of Central Zone, Abey Kuruvilla and Raju Kulkarni of West and Venkatesh Prasad and Divakar Vasu of South.

The Irani Cup, the regular pre-season trial game, was a personal triumph for Kapil Dev, who led 1991-92 Ranji champions Haryana to an improbable victory over Rest of India, before setting off for Australia to claim his 400th Test wicket. The Rest had piled up 518 for nine, and then contained a keen bid from Haryana for the first-innings lead. With a day to go, the match seemed headed for a dreary draw – until Kapil picked up four wickets in one burst to slice through the Rest's top order. Bowled out for 144, they could not keep Haryana short of a target of 204, which featured a battling 53 from Kapil, dismissed when his team were only one run from victory.

To make the final stages of the Ranji Trophy more competitive, it was agreed that a third team from each of the five zones should progress to the knockout stage in 1992-93. Under the old format, of ten teams qualifying for the knockout, Delhi won their sixth Ranji title since 1979. They reasserted themselves strongly after two disappointing years when they suffered more from a crisis of confidence than paucity of talent. Their defeat of Bombay in the semi-final, amassing two totals in excess of 500 runs, typified their vigour throughout the season. Delhi were expected to dominate the final, played at home against Tamil Nadu. India's failure to reach the last four in the World Cup meant they were reinforced by all-rounder Manoj Prabhakar, who formed a useful partnership with the season's leading wicket-taker, slow left-armer Maninder Singh. But there was a close contest for the first-innings lead, which was to prove decisive. Maninder claimed five wickets in Tamil Nadu's innings, his eighth haul of five or more in the season. Twice he had ten in a match and 26-year-old Maninder, ignored by the Test side since 1989-90, took 71 wickets at 17.33, an outstanding effort; his nearest rival was Kuruvilla of Bombay, on 51.

Maninder Singh also earned a place in the record books for his batting, contributing 78 to a 233-run stand for the tenth wicket with the prolific Ajay Sharma in Delhi's semi-final against Bombay. It was the first double-century last-wicket partnership on Indian soil. Ajay Sharma was one of four batsmen to reach 1,000 runs; the leading scorer was Vinod Kambli of Bombay, with 1,218 at an average of 110.72, followed by Woorkeri Raman of Tamil Nadu, with 1,137. Ajay Jadeja of Haryana scored 1,036. Raman, an elegant left-hander, scored six centuries, including three against defending champions Haryana. He launched his season with 149 against them in the Irani Cup match, and ran up 226 and 120 in the Ranji Trophy semi-final.

Compared to recent seasons, in which the game was dragged into the law courts and one player tried to assault another with a stump, there was less that was contentious. A notable aberration was in the Ranji final, but there the controversy centred on the umpires, one of whom challenged the other's explanation of an incident in which he rejected an appeal for lbw. Correspondents said R. S. Rathore, a former Test umpire, took more than a minute to react to the appeal. More happily, there was praise for the work of a few former first-class cricketers, including the former Test bowler Venkataraghavan, who took up umpiring under a scheme started two seasons earlier.

In limited-overs cricket, the Board President's XI won the Wills Trophy tournament that kicked off the season in September. Last year's winners, the Wills XI, defeated Habib Bank, Pakistan's Wills Cup-holders, in Delhi in October, to take the second Super Wills Cup for the two countries' limited-overs champions. South Zone won the inter-zonal tournament for the Deodhar Trophy, not long after Professor D. B. Deodhar, the world's oldest first-class cricketer after whom the competition was named, completed a grand century of his own on January 14, 1992, when he reached the ripe age of 100. But the Deodhar Trophy was also touched by tragedy: the promising 18-year-old batsman, Dhruv Pandove of Punjab, who made his first-class début at the age of 13, was killed in a car accident returning from North Zone's defeat by South. – R. M.

FIRST-CLASS AVERAGES, 1991-92

BATTING

(Qualification: 500 runs)

	M	I	NO	R	HS	100s	Avge
V. G. Kambli (*Bombay*)	7	12	1	1,218	262	5	110.72
Ajay Sharma (*Delhi*)	9	12	1	1,037	259*	4	94.27
A. D. Jadeja (*Haryana*)	8	12	1	1,036	256	4	94.18
S. S. Bhave (*Maharashtra*)	6	10	3	651	231*	3	93.00
W. V. Raman (*Tamil Nadu*)	9	13	0	1,137	226	6	87.46
V. S. Yadav (*Haryana*)	10	12	3	714	201	2	79.33
S. S. Sugwekar (*Maharashtra*)	8	11	1	753	180	2	75.30
S. M. Patil (*Madhya Pradesh*)	6	11	2	675	157	2	75.00
Abdul Azeem (*Hyderabad*)	6	9	0	650	208	3	72.22
A. S. Kaypee (*Haryana*)	10	15	2	938	200	3	72.15
S. S. Karim (*Bihar*)	6	9	1	529	176	2	66.12
Zakir Hussain (*Hyderabad*)	8	11	0	716	161	3	65.09
A. R. Khurasia (*Madhya Pradesh*)	6	11	2	584	132	2	64.88
K. Bhaskar Pillai (*Delhi*)	10	13	1	749	221	3	62.41
M. V. Sridhar (*Hyderabad*)	7	10	1	523	140	2	58.11
S. V. Jedhe (*Maharashtra*)	8	13	2	622	156	3	56.54
K. S. Chavan (*Baroda*)	6	11	0	619	129	3	56.27
V. B. Chandrasekhar (*Tamil Nadu*)	8	12	1	572	144	2	52.00
M. Senthilnathan (*Tamil Nadu*)	8	11	0	545	109	1	49.54
M. Nayyar (*Delhi*)	9	12	0	573	172	1	47.75
Robin Singh (*Tamil Nadu*)	10	14	2	573	121*	3	47.75
R. Puri (*Haryana*)	10	15	2	611	136	1	47.00
N. Gautam (*Tamil Nadu*)	8	12	0	543	190	2	45.25

* *Signifies not out.*

BOWLING

(Qualification: 20 wickets, average 30)

	O	M	R	W	BB	5W/i	Avge
M. I. Singh (*Punjab*)	94.1	17	248	23	7-33	2	10.78
G. Dutta (*Assam*)	87	17	264	20	9-52	3	13.20
Bhupinder Singh, sen. (*Punjab*)	118	16	345	20	7-38	1	17.25
Maninder Singh (*Delhi*)	588.4	204	1,231	71	7-43	8	17.33
K. V. P. Rao (*Bihar*)	164	34	449	24	5-25	2	18.70
A. Kumble (*Karnataka*)	294.4	84	661	33	6-41	1	20.03
D. Vasu (*Tamil Nadu*)	347.3	90	861	41	5-39	3	21.00
S. P. Mukherjee (*Bengal*)	197.3	63	467	22	6-85	1	21.22
Chetan Sharma (*Haryana*)	356.4	67	1,088	50	6-179	4	21.76
Deepak Sharma (*Haryana*)	201.5	43	503	23	4-12	0	21.86
S. Subramaniam (*Tamil Nadu*)	351.2	108	855	38	7-45	2	22.50
A. Kuruvilla (*Bombay*)	350.4	66	1,158	51	6-98	2	22.70
V. Razdan (*Delhi*)	239.5	52	731	30	5-67	1	24.36
S. J. Jadhav (*Maharashtra*)	289.3	73	641	26	6-179	1	24.65
S. Sensharma (*Bengal*)	209.3	45	577	23	5-63	2	25.08
Arshad Ayub (*Hyderabad*)	471.1	112	1,317	49	6-16	6	26.87
Avinash Kumar (*Bihar*)	312.3	71	834	31	6-198	3	26.90
A. S. Wassan (*Delhi*)	298.5	55	969	36	6-72	2	26.91
R. R. Kulkarni (*Bombay*)	181.3	30	597	22	4-47	0	27.13
Abdul Qayyum (*Jammu and Kashmir*)	180.1	24	612	22	6-122	3	27.81
P. Sushil Kumar (*Orissa*)	255.4	84	566	20	6-84	1	28.30
Sanjeeva Sharma (*Railways*)	211.1	34	667	23	5-70	1	29.00
B. Ramaprakash (*Kerala*)	233	33	614	21	6-30	2	29.23
A. R. Kapoor (*Tamil Nadu*)	285	63	826	28	4-41	0	29.50

In the following scores, * by the name of a team indicates that they won the toss. When the fielding side failed to meet the required rate of 15 overs an hour, 17 penalty runs were added to the innings total for every over short.

IRANI CUP, 1991-92

Ranji Trophy Champions (Haryana) v Rest of India

At Nahar Singh Stadium, Faridabad, October 2, 3, 4, 5, 6. Haryana won by four wickets. Rest of India* 518 for nine dec. (W. V. Raman 149, V. G. Kambli 116, P. K. Amre 120, S. M. H. Kirmani 30, Extras 37; Chetan Sharma four for 90) and 144 (P. K. Amre 40; P. Jain three for 47, Kapil Dev four for 26); Haryana 459 (N. R. Goel 54, Deepak Sharma 50, A. D. Jadeja 131, Kapil Dev 135, Extras 49; J. Srinath five for 120. S. T. Banerjee four for 70) and 207 for six (N. R. Goel 51, Deepak Sharma 31, Kapil Dev 53, R. Puri 36; Maninder Singh five for 79).

RANJI TROPHY, 1991-92

Central Zone

At Modi Stadium, Green Park, Kanpur, November 21, 22, 23, 24. Uttar Pradesh won by an innings and 46 runs. Vidarbha* 210 (P. B. Hingnikar 62, U. I. Ghani 35, M. Kaore 40; R. P. Singh five for 51, including a hat-trick, A. W. Zaidi three for 60) and 240 (A. M. Kane 39, M. Kaore 35; A. W. Zaidi four for 47, Gopal Sharma three for 88); Uttar Pradesh 496 for five dec. (S. S. Khandkar 92, V. S. Vats 35, S. Chaturvedi 97, A. Gautam 144 not out, V. S. Yadav 62, Extras 51). *Uttar Pradesh 22 pts, Vidarbha 1 pt.*

At VCA Ground, Nagpur, November 28, 29, 30, December 1. Madhya Pradesh won by seven wickets. Vidarbha 190 (P. B. Hingnikar 74, H. R. Wasu 31, P. S. Vaidya 35; D. K. Nilosey five for 68, S. S. Lahore four for 60) and 503 (S. G. Gujar 221, U. I. Ghani 140; D. K. Nilosey five for 152); Madhya Pradesh* 476 (A. V. Vijayvargiya 40, A. R. Khurasia 99, P. K. Dwevedi 114, R. K. Chauhan 40, A. Prabhakar 57 not out, Extras 35; P. S. Vaidya four for 130, P. V. Gandhe three for 140) and 218 for three (A. R. Khurasia 99 not out, D. K. Nilosey 32, S. M. Patil 40 not out). *Madhya Pradesh 20 pts, Vidarbha 6 pts.*

At Roop Singh Stadium, Gwalior, December 5, 6, 7, 8. Drawn. Madhya Pradesh* 427 (A. V. Vijayvargiya 42, K. K. Patel 202, S. M. Patil 55, M. S. Sahni 45, A. Prabhakar 39; Sanjeeva Sharma three for 93) and 47 for no wkt dec.; Railways 417 (Yusuf Ali Khan 125, S. M. Kharge 42, A. S. Negi 46, K. B. Kala 48, Abhay Sharma 85; R. K. Chauhan six for 210, S. S. Lahore three for 140) and 11 for no wkt. *Madhya Pradesh 7 pts. Railways 5 pts.*

At K. D. Singh "Babu" Stadium, Lucknow, December 5, 6, 7, 8. Drawn. Uttar Pradesh 532 for nine dec. (S. S. Khandkar 46, G. K. Pandey 178, A. Gautam 58, R. P. Singh 98, Gopal Sharma 100 not out; R. Rathore four for 103) and 250 for six dec. (S. S. Khandkar 32, V. S. Vats 55, R. V. Sapru 81, G. K. Pandey 35, A. Gautam 31); Rajasthan* 411 (G. G. Khoda 116, Aslam Beg 70, V. Joshi 89, H. Joshi 42, Y. M. Mathur 37 not out; Gopal Sharma five for 86) and 14 for one. *Uttar Pradesh 15 pts, Rajasthan 12 pts.*

At Karnail Singh Stadium, Delhi, December 12, 13, 14, 15. Drawn. Railways* 304 (Yashpal Sharma 52, Abhay Sharma 40, Sanjeeva Sharma 111 not out, Vijay Bahadur 48; A. W. Zaidi three for 76, Gopal Sharma four for 89) and 270 for five dec. (Yusuf Ali Khan 116 not out, K. B. Kala 42, Sanjeeva Sharma 57 not out; R. P. Singh three for 48); Uttar Pradesh 370 (S. Chaturvedi 57, R. V. Sapru 94, A. Gautam 50, G. K. Pandey 54 not out, A. W. Zaidi 31, Extras 34; Sanjeeva Sharma five for 70, R. Venkatesh three for 83) and 80 for two (S. Chaturvedi 30 not out). *Railways 9 pts, Uttar Pradesh 13 pts.*

At Northern Railway Ground, Bikaner, December 12, 13, 14, 15. Drawn. Vidarbha* 312 (P. B. Hingnikar 49, Y. T. Ghare 52, P. S. Rawat 79, U. I. Ghani 58) and 297 for four dec. (A. V. Sarwate 63, Y. T. Ghare 71, S. G. Gujar 98); Rajasthan 238 (Parminder Singh 34, D. Chawla 42, H. Joshi 37, R. Rathore 39; P. S. Vaidya three for 71, R. P. Gawande three for 38) and 210 for eight (A. Sinha 61, V. Joshi 77 not out; R. P. Gawande three for 66, P. V. Gandhe five for 53). *Rajasthan 9 pts, Vidarbha 14 pts.*

At Nehru Stadium, Indore, December 19, 20, 21, 22. Drawn. Madhya Pradesh* 546 (K. K. Patel 74, A. R. Khurasia 38, C. P. Singh 59, S. M. Patil 157, M. S. Sahni 90, Extras 45; Gopal Sharma three for 184, G. K. Pandey three for 43) and 251 for seven dec. (S. M. Patil 119, D. K. Nilosey 50; M. A. Ansari three for 92); Uttar Pradesh 554 for seven dec. (V. S. Vats 92, V. S. Yadav 97, S. S. Khandkar 66, G. K. Pandey 40, R. V. Sapru 139, S. Chaturvedi 30, A. Gautam 55 not out; R. K. Chauhan four for 187). *Madhya Pradesh 12 pts, Uttar Pradesh 15 pts.*

At VCA Ground, Nagpur, December 19, 20, 21, 22. Railways won by ten wickets. Vidarbha 104 (Sanjeeva Sharma four for 63, D. Mishra six for 34) and 382 (A. V. Sarwate 40, P. B. Hingnikar 115, S. G. Gujar 92, P. S. Rawat 67, M. Pande 33 not out; Sanjeeva Sharma four for 140, Ratan Singh three for 67); Railways* 426 (R. Chanda 33, Yashpal Sharma 144, Abhay Sharma 143, Penalty 51; P. S. Vaidya five for 93, R. B. Sangar three for 114) and 61 for no wkt (Yusuf Ali Khan 30 not out). *Railways 18 pts, Vidarbha 5 pts.*

At Mansarovar, Jaipur, December 26, 27, 28, 29. Drawn. Madhya Pradesh 397 (A. V. Vijayvargiya 68, P. K. Dwevedi 114, S. M. Patil 51, M. S. Sahni 45 not out, R. K. Chauhan 43; Parminder Singh four for 92) and 290 for three dec. (A. V. Vijayvargiya 41, A. R. Khurasia 59, P. K. Dwevedi 67 not out, S. M. Patil 77 not out, Penalty 34); Rajasthan* 213 (Mustan Amer 56, A. Sinha 55, H. Joshi 37; R. K. Chauhan four for 58) and 148 for five (V. Joshi 37, A. Sinha 36; S. S. Lahore four for 56). *Rajasthan 9 pts, Madhya Pradesh 19 pts.*

At Palam Ground, Delhi, January 1, 2, 3, 4. Railways won by an innings and 49 runs. Rajasthan* 274 (Parminder Singh 65, A. Sinha 57, C. Bodha 31, Extras 37; Sanjeeva Sharma three for 122, K. Bharatan four for 28) and 192 (A. Sinha 44, C. Bodha 46; Yashpal Sharma four for 4); Railways 515 (Yusuf Ali Khan 46, R. Chanda 48, K. Bharatan 99, Yashpal Sharma 100, S. Sawant 58, Sanjeeva Sharma 70, Extras 46; S. Sharma three for 78). *Railways 22 pts, Rajasthan 4 pts.*

Uttar Pradesh 65 pts, Madhya Pradesh 58 pts, Railways 54 pts, Rajasthan 34 pts, Vidarbha 26 pts. Uttar Pradesh and Madhya Pradesh qualified for the knockout stage.

East Zone

At Eden Gardens, Calcutta, November 21, 22, 23, 24. Bengal won by nine wickets. Assam 177 (Rajinder Singh 35, S. K. Kulkarni 31; S. Sensharma five for 63, J. G. Dastidar three for 34) and 225 (L. S. Rajput 70, D. Das 45, P. Dutta 30; S. P. Mukherjee six for 85); Bengal* 339 (M. Das 61, Arun Lal 48, Snehashish Ganguly 50, A. Malhotra 61, R. Venkatraman 69; S. Chakraborty five for 91) and 65 for one. *Bengal 17 pts, Assam 6 pts.*

At V. S. S. Stadium, Sambalpur, November 21, 22, 23, 24. Bihar won by an innings and 142 runs. Bihar* 384 (S. Chatterjee 142, K. V. P. Rao 72, D. K. Singh 39 not out, Extras 46; P. Sushil Kumar four for 117, R. B. Biswal five for 91); Orissa 64 (Avinash Kumar five for 19, V. Venkatram five for 32) and 178 (P. Mohapatra 60; V. Venkatram three for 39, K. V. P. Rao five for 40). *Bihar 17 pts, Orissa 3 pts.*

At Polytechnic Ground, Agartala, November 28, 29, 30. December 1. Bihar won by an innings and 234 runs. Tripura 104 (Avinash Kumar four for 35, K. V. P. Rao five for 25) and 74 (Avinash Kumar three for 21, K. V. P. Rao four for 17); Bihar* 412 for five dec. (H. Gidwani 160, Adil Hussain 125, S. S. Karim 62; C. Dey three for 107). *Bihar 24 pts, Tripura 2 pts.*

At BOS Engineering College Ground, Cuttack, November 29, 30, December 1, 2. Orissa won by ten wickets. Assam* 200 (R. Bora 34, P. Dutta 39, G. Dutta 43; Rajesh Singh four for 44, P. Sushil Kumar four for 69) and 246 (L. S. Rajput 60, Zahir Alam 69, S. K. Kulkarni 33; R. B. Biswal three for 78, P. Sushil Kumar six for 84); Orissa 411 (B. Mohanty 42, R. B. Biswal 47, A. Roy 125, Rajesh Singh 59, S. Mohapatra 40, Extras 37; R. Bora four for 110) and 36 for no wkt. *Orissa 17 pts, Assam 3 pts.*

At Eden Gardens, Calcutta, December 5, 6, 7, 8. Bengal won by an innings and 222 runs. Tripura 124 (Arup Deb-Burman 50, Pawan Kumar 32; S. Sensharma four for 17) and 89 (R. Seth three for 12, S. P. Mukherjee four for 12); Bengal* 435 for nine dec. (M. Das 51, Arun Lal 51, S. J. Kalyani 63, Snehashish Ganguly 136, R. Venkatraman 59; Pawan Kumar three for 61). *Bengal 25 pts, Tripura 4 pts.*

At Mecon, Ranchi, December 5, 6, 7, 8. Drawn. Assam* 649 for nine dec. (D. Das 49, L. S. Rajput 39, R. Bora 235, S. K. Kulkarni 200 not out, K. K. Barua 34, G. Dutta 55; Avinash Kumar six for 198) and 222 for seven (Zahir Alam 94, L. S. Rajput 50; K. V. P. Rao four for 64); Bihar 454 (P. Khanna 107, H. Gidwani 91, Adil Hussain 128, S. S. Karim 40; G. Dutta six for 92). *Bihar 13 pts, Assam 12 pts.*

At Keenan Stadium, Jamshedpur, December 12, 13, 14, 15. Drawn. Bihar* 310 (S. Das 52, P. Khanna 83, Adil Hussain 54, S. S. Karim 63; S. P. Mukherjee four for 65) and 246 for six dec. (H. Gidwani 34, S. S. Karim 102 not out; S. Sensharma three for 53); Bengal 234 (S. J. Kalyani 82, R. Venkatraman 33, S. P. Mukherjee 51 not out) and 53 for two. *Bihar 12 pts, Bengal 8 pts.*

At BOS Engineering College Ground, Cuttack, December 12, 13, 14, 15. Orissa won by an innings and 89 runs. Tripura 117 (P. Sushil Kumar four for 19) and 208 (Ankur Deb-Burman 34, J. K. Deb-Burman 44; R. B. Biswal four for 40); Orissa* 414 (M. Bhatt 51, S. Chowdhary 73, D. Lenka 55, R. B. Biswal 107, A. Khatua 35 not out, Extras 45; C. Dey three for 90, Arup Deb-Burman three for 65). *Orissa 23 pts, Tripura 4 pts.*

At Nehru Stadium, Guwahati, December 19, 20, 21, 22. Assam won by an innings and 472 runs. Assam 684 for seven dec. (Zahir Alam 257, L. S. Rajput 239, S. K. Kulkarni 44, Rajinder Singh 42, Extras 43); Tripura* 129 (R. Vats 33, J. K. Deb-Burman 48; G. Dutta nine for 52) and 83 (H. Barua five for 38, G. Dutta five for 44). *Assam 25 pts, Tripura 2 pts.*

At Baripada Stadium, Baripada, December 19, 20, 21, 22. Drawn. Bengal 514 for four dec. (Arun Lal 130, S. J. Kalyani 52, A. Malhotra 151, R. Venkatraman 140 not out) and 259 for three dec. (Arun Lal 99, A. Malhotra 101 not out, R. Venkatraman 34 not out; S. Mohapatra three for 76); Orissa* 225 (M. Bhatt 69, D. Lenka 37; S. Sensharma five for 65, S. Chatterjee four for 69) and 187 for four (P. Mohapatra 44, M. Bhatt 86, D. Lenka 43 not out). *Orissa 7 pts, Bengal 19 pts.*

Bengal 69 pts, Bihar 66 pts, Orissa 50 pts, Assam 46 pts, Tripura 12 pts. Bengal and Bihar qualified for the knockout stage.

North Zone

At Nahar Singh Stadium, Faridabad, October 28, 29, 30, 31. Haryana won by an innings and 212 runs. Haryana* 567 for nine dec. (A. D. Jadeja 256, A. S. Kaypee 200, V. S. Yadav 49); Services 161 (S. Bhatnagar 38, Chinmoy Sharma 63; Y. Bhandari four for 55, Deepak Sharma four for 25) and 194 (K. M. Roshan 61, Chinmoy Sharma 67 not out; Y. Bhandari three for 61, Deepak Sharma three for 46). *Haryana 24 pts, Services 1 pt.*

At Air Force Ground, Palam, Delhi. November 2, 3, 4, 5. Delhi won by an innings and 147 runs. Delhi 543 for six dec. (M. Prabhakar 134, Bantoo Singh 72, K. Bhaskar Pillai 52, K. Azad 67, Sanjay Sharma 65, V. Razdan 100 not out); Services* 180 (Arijit Ghosh 48, Chinmoy Sharma 36; Maninder Singh three for 20, Harpreet Singh four for 55) and 216 (K. M. Roshan 50, M. Subramaniam 31 not out, M. V. Rao 30; A. S. Wassan three for 43, V. Razdan three for 32). *Delhi 21 pts, Services 2 pts.*

At Kangda Police Stadium, Dharamsala, November 15, 16, 17, 18. Services won by 135 runs. Services* 258 (S. Bhatnagar 62, Chinmoy Sharma 64, G. S. Thapa 46; Brijinder Sharma three for 28, Jaswant Rai three for 43) and 339 (Arijit Ghosh 33, Chinmoy Sharma 133, V. Natke 32, M. Subramaniam 49 not out, Extras 31; A. Sen four for 98); Himachal Pradesh 222 (R. Bittu 131 not out, Brijinder Sharma 43; S. C. Sadangi three for 41, M. Subramaniam four for 48) and 240 (R. Nayyar 55, Shambu Sharma 51, D. Berki 36; M. V. Rao four for 46). *Services 16 pts, Himachal Pradesh 8 pts.*

At Government College for Boys Ground, Ludhiana, November 15, 16, 17, 18. Punjab won by an innings and 106 runs. Jammu and Kashmir* 203 (A. Gupta 40, V. Bhaskar 39; S. V. Mehra three for 62, M. I. Singh four for 38) and 84 (M. I. Singh seven for 33); Punjab 393 (V. Rathore 54, Gursharan Singh 191, K. Mohan 70, Extras 38; A. Gupta four for 93, Ranjit Bali three for 54). *Punjab 24 pts, Jammu and Kashmir 4 pts.*

At Maulana Azad Stadium, Jammu, November 20, 21, 22, 23. Jammu and Kashmir won by an innings and 64 runs. Himachal Pradesh 142 (R. Nayyar 59, V. Sen 32; Abdul Qayyum five for 45, Sanjay Sharma three for 30) and 267 (A. Vij 34 not out, R. Bittu 39, R. Nayyar 109, D. Berki 37; Abdul Qayyum six for 122, A. Gupta three for 78); Jammu and Kashmir* 473 (Ranjit Bali 34, A. Gupta 124, V. Bhaskar 130, Sanjay Sharma 41 not out, P. Bali 41; R. Nayyar five for 117). *Jammu and Kashmir 24 pts, Himachal Pradesh 6 pts.*

At Gandhi Ground, Amritsar, November 21, 22, 23, 24. Delhi won by an innings and 40 runs. Delhi* 315 (R. Vinayak 76, Ajay Sharma 51, Sanjay Sharma 57, Extras 50; Bhupinder Singh, jun. three for 80, S. V. Mehra three for 87, M. I. Singh three for 55); Punjab 100 (V. Rathore 40; Maninder Singh three for 21, Harpreet Singh four for 20) and 175 (S. Chopra 40, Gursharan Singh 37, M. Arora 40; Maninder Singh seven for 43). *Delhi 23 pts, Punjab 5 pts.*

At TIT Ground, Bhiwani, November 26, 27, 28, 29. Haryana won by an innings and 119 runs. Jammu and Kashmir* 189 (Kamaljit Singh 53, Ranjit Bali 49; Chetan Sharma three for 55, P. Jain three for 39) and 69 (Chetan Sharma five for 45, Deepak Sharma four for 12); Haryana 377 (A. D. Jadeja 65, V. S. Yadav 82, A. S. Kaypee 35, R. Puri 44, Extras 38; A. Gupta four for 134, Sanjay Sharma four for 65). *Haryana 24 pts, Jammu and Kashmir 4 pts.*

At Gandhi Ground, Amritsar, November 26, 27, 28, 29. Punjab won by an innings and 118 runs. Punjab* 396 (Ajay Mehra 42, R. Kalsi 40, Gursharan Singh 75, K. Mohan 75, M. Arora 72 not out, S. V. Mehra 31; A. Sen four for 117); Himachal Pradesh 128 (M. I. Singh three for 28) and 150 (Balsinder Singh 73; J. D. Singh five for 62). *Punjab 24 pts, Himachal Pradesh 4 pts.*

At Nehru Stadium, Gurgaon, December 1, 2, 3, 4. Drawn. Punjab* 240 (D. M. Pandove 51, S. Chopra 108; P. Jain five for 75, Deepak Sharma three for 26) and 304 for six dec. (S. Chopra 64, V. Rathore 54, Gursharan Singh 72, Bhupinder Singh, jun. 63 not out, K. Mohan 33); Haryana 506 (A. D. Jadeja 228, A. S. Kaypee 72, R. Puri 70, Chetan Sharma 52; J. D. Singh four for 120) and 15 for one. *Haryana 14 pts, Punjab 6 pts.*

At Indira Gandhi Stadium, Una, December 1, 2, 3, 4. Delhi won by an innings and 163 runs. Delhi* 475 for seven dec. (M. Nayyar 47, Ajay Sharma 159, K. Bhaskar Pillai 178, Sanjay Sharma 58 not out; Brijinder Sharma three for 96); Himachal Pradesh 86 (V. Razdan four for 55, Maninder Singh five for 14) and 226 (R. Bittu 76, A. Kanwar 35, Extras 31; Maninder Singh five for 73, Ajay Sharma three for 21). *Delhi 23 pts, Himachal Pradesh 3 pts.*

At Air Force Ground, Palam, Delhi, December 2, 3, 4, 5. Services won by 48 runs. Services* 283 (Chinmoy Sharma 50, K. M. Roshan 104 not out; M. Qaiser four for 56, Sanjay Sharma three for 70) and 363 (D. Ahuja 86, S. Bhatnagar 47, G. S. Thapa 50, K. D. Pandey 76, M. V. Rao 31; Abdul Qayyum five for 103); Jammu and Kashmir 369 (A. Gupta 183 not out, V. Bhaskar 51, Ranjit Bali 35; S. C. Sadangi four for 62, M. Subramaniam three for 87) and 229 (S. Chowdhary 36, A. Gupta 55, Kamaljit Singh 34, Sanjay Sharma 30; M. Subramaniam four for 74). *Services 16 pts, Jammu and Kashmir 9 pts.*

At Ferozshah Kotla Ground, Delhi, December 7, 8, 9, 10. Delhi won by an innings and 197 runs. Jammu and Kashmir* 161 (Kamaljit Singh 43, Ranjit Bali 56; V. Razdan five for 67, Maninder Singh three for 17) and 211 (Vikram Singh 32, Vivek Bahadur 34, Abdul Qayyum 45; Maninder Singh six for 93); Delhi 569 for six dec. (M. Nayyar 172, H. Sharma 36, Sanjay Sharma 80, Ajay Sharma 169, Extras 62). *Delhi 25 pts, Jammu and Kashmir 3 pts.*

At Nahar Singh Stadium, Faridabad, December 7, 8, 9, 10. Haryana won by an innings and 102 runs. Himachal Pradesh* 86 (Chetan Sharma four for 25) and 256 (R. Nayyar 91, A. Vij 30, Raj Kumar 44 not out, A. Sen 30 not out; Chetan Sharma four for 101); Haryana 444 (A. D. Jadeja 199, N. R. Goel 37, V. S. Yadav 82, Chetan Sharma 47; Brijinder Sharma three for 103, A. Sen three for 106, Jaswant Rai three for 111). *Haryana 24 pts, Himachal Pradesh 4 pts.*

At Ferozshah Kotla Ground, Delhi, December 12, 13, 14, 15. Drawn. Haryana* 336 (A. S. Kaypee 90, R. Puri 136, V. S. Yadav 33; A. S. Wassan six for 92) and 303 for four (Dhanraj Singh 34, A. S. Kaypee 118 not out, R. Puri 77); Delhi 322 (M. Nayyar 42, H. Sharma 41, Ajay Sharma 36, K. Bhaskar Pillai 85, A. S. Wassan 32; Chetan Sharma five for 118, Deepak Sharma three for 77). *Delhi 10 pts, Haryana 11 pts.*

At Gandhi Ground, Amritsar, December 15, 16, 17, 18. Punjab won by an innings and 285 runs. Services* 164 (K. M. Roshan 38; M. I. Singh five for 60, J. D. Singh three for 39) and 117 (M. Subramaniam 33; Bhupinder Singh, sen. seven for 38); Punjab 566 for nine dec. (D. M. Pandove 170, S. Chopra 32, N. S. Sidhu 77, V. Rathore 43, Bhupinder Singh, jun. 103, S. V. Mehra 45, Extras 35; Chinmoy Sharma four for 95). *Punjab 25 pts, Services 2 pts.*

Delhi 102 pts, Haryana 97 pts, Punjab 84 pts, Jammu and Kashmir 44 pts, Services 37 pts, Himachal Pradesh 25 pts. Delhi and Haryana qualified for the knockout stage.

South Zone

At Panji Gymkhana, Panjim, November 3, 4, 5, 6. Hyderabad won by an innings and 267 runs. Hyderabad* 535 for eight dec. (Abdul Azeem 158, M. V. Sridhar 140, V. Jaisimha 48, Ehtesham Ali Khan 67, Arshad Ayub 70; A. Shetty four for 184); Goa 103 (M. V. Ramanamurthy three for 35, Arshad Ayub six for 16) and 165 (R. M. H. Binny 102, A. Shetty 42; N. R. Yadav three for 18, S. L. V. Raju three for 43). *Hyderabad 25 pts, Goa 2 pts.*

At Arlem Ground, Margao, November 12, 13, 14, 15. Kerala won by six wickets. Goa* 154 (R. M. H. Binny 37, A. Shetty 39; K. G. Jayakumar three for 45, K. N. A. Padmanabhan three for 49) and 261 (N. P. Parikkar 53, A. Gaikwad 80, R. M. H. Binny 62 not out; K. N. A. Padmanabhan four for 96); Kerala 183 (P. V. Ranganathan 49, P. T. Subramaniam 35; H. B. P. Angle three for 72, A. Shetty six for 55) and 233 for four (V. Narayan Kutty 51, P. G. Sunder 47 not out, B. Ramaprakash 81 not out; H. B. P. Angle three for 79). *Kerala 14 pts, Goa 6 pts.*

At BGML Sports Complex, Kolar Gold Fields. November 22, 23, 24, 25. Karnataka won by ten wickets. Goa* 169 (A. Kumble three for 27) and 161 (R. M. H. Binny 63, A. Shetty 35 not out; A. Kumble four for 61); Karnataka 324 (P. V. Shashikanth 43, R. S. Dravid 126, A. R. Bhat 46; H. B. P. Angle three for 61, A. Shetty five for 78) and seven for no wkt. *Karnataka 15 pts, Goa 3 pts.*

At M. A. Chidambaram Stadium, Chepauk, Madras. November 22, 23, 24. Tamil Nadu won by an innings and 137 runs. Tamil Nadu* 600 for six dec. (W. V. Raman 206, N. Gautam 42, Arjan Kripal Singh 67, M. Senthilnathan 71, Robin Singh 100 not out, D. Vasu 41 not out; B. Ramaprakash three for 162) and Kerala 162 (B. Ramaprakash 41; S. Subramaniam four for 47) and 301 (P. T. Subramaniam 39, P. G. Sunder 32, B. Ramaprakash 152; D. Vasu four for 20, A. R. Kapoor four for 86). *Tamil Nadu 22 pts, Kerala 3 pts.*

At Gymkhana Ground, Secunderabad, November 29, 30, December 1, 2. Hyderabad won by an innings and 89 runs. Andhra* 322 (O. Vinod Kumar 75, V. Vijayasarathy 98, R. Vivekanand 40; Arshad Ayub six for 82) and 164 (A. Pathak 37, K. V. S. D. Kamaraju 32; Arshad Ayub six for 59); Hyderabad 575 for six dec. (Abdul Azeem 208, M. V. Sridhar 105, V. Jaisimha 57, Zakir Hussain 108, M. V. Ramanamurthy 41 not out; V. Vinay Kumar three for 128). *Hyderabad 24 pts, Andhra 3 pts.*

At District Stadium, Bijapur, November 29, 30, December 1, 2. Karnataka won by an innings and 242 runs. Karnataka* 603 for eight dec. (C. Saldanha 88, R. S. Dravid 128, S. M. H. Kirmani 150, A. Kumble 154 not out, K. G. Sekhar 39; K. G. Jayakumar three for 131, K. N. A. Padmanabhan three for 159), Kerala 189 (T. P. Ajit Kumar 30, P. T. Subramaniam 39; A. R. Bhat five for 67, R. Ananth three for 54) and 172 (P. T. Subramaniam 56 not out; A. Kumble three for 34, A. R. Bhat three for 49, R. Ananth three for 33). *Karnataka 25 pts, Kerala 2 pts.*

At M. A. Chidambaram Stadium, Chepauk, Madras. November 29, 30, December 1, 2. Tamil Nadu won by an innings and 280 runs. Tamil Nadu* 604 for seven dec. (V. B. Chandrasekhar 144, N. Gautam 129, Arjan Kripal Singh 52, Robin Singh 121 not out D. Vasu 43, A. R. Kapoor 30; R. Kambli three for 159); Goa 201 (U. R. Radhakrishnan 32, Ishan Bakhle 80, H. B. P. Angle 41; S. Subramaniam five for 69, A. R. Kapoor four for 60) and 123 (R. M. H. Binny 31; D. Vasu five for 39). *Tamil Nadu 25 pts, Goa 2 pts.*

At Municipal Ground, Thalassery, December 6, 7, 8, 9. Drawn. Hyderabad* 380 (Ehtesham Ali Khan 43, Abdul Azeem 40, M. V. Sridhar 75, V. Jaisimha 46, Zakir Hussain 86; K. N. A. Padmanabhan four for 112, Suresh Kumar three for 64) and 339 (Ehtesham Ali Khan 106, Abdul Azeem 34, Zakir Hussain 52, N. R. Yadav 48; Suresh Kumar six for 93, B. Ramaprakash three for 111); Kerala 461 (P. V. Ranganathan 60, B. Ramaprakash 81, P. G. Sunder 81, P. T. Subramaniam 89, F. V. Rasheed 59, K. N. A. Padmanabhan 33; N. R. Yadav three for 59, M. V. Ramanamurthy five for 60) and 182 for four (B. Ramaprakash 57, P. G. Sunder 58 not out). *Kerala 16 pts, Hyderabad 16 pts.*

At Vishakhapatnam Steel Plant Ground, Vishakhapatnam, December 13, 14, 15, 16. Karnataka won by an innings and 74 runs. Karnataka* 461 (C. Saldanha 71, S. M. H. Kirmani 35, K. A. Jeshwant 151, A. Kumble 64, K. G. Sekhar 37; G. V. V. Gopalraju three for 127, V. Vijayasarathy four for 98); Andhra 140 (O. Vinod Kumar 56, A. Pathak 37; A. Kumble six for 41, including a hat-trick, R. Ananth three for 38) and 247 (A. Pathak 101, M. F. Rehman 41, V. Vinay Kumar 41 not out; A. Kumble three for 78, R. Ananth three for 63). *Karnataka 22 pts, Andhra 3 pts.*

At M. A. Chidambaram Stadium, Chepauk, Madras, December 13, 14, 15, 16. Drawn. Hyderabad* 529 (R. A. Swarup 131, Zakir Hussain 161, Ehtesham Ali Khan 36, Arshad Ayub 81, N. R. Yadav 71; D. Vasu four for 141, S. Subramaniam three for 111, A. R. Kapoor three for 153) and 83 for one dec. (R. A. Swarup 31 not out, M. V. Sridhar 31 not out); Tamil Nadu 420 (V. B. Chandrasekhar 36, M. Mujib-ur-Rehman 61, N. Gautam 68, M. Senthilnathan 42, D. Vasu 53, A. R. Kapoor 48, S. Subramaniam 53; Arshad Ayub five for 172) and 47 for two. *Tamil Nadu 8 pts, Hyderabad 12 pts.*

At Municipal Stadium, Cuddapah, December 19, 20, 21, 22. Andhra won by eight wickets. Goa* 327 (U. R. Radhakrishnan 182; G. V. V. Gopalraju six for 122) and 243 (D. Avinash 71, S. Harmalkar 48; D. Sudhakar Reddy three for 35); Andhra 279 (A. Pathak 40, K. V. S. D. Kamaraju 36, V. Vijayasarathy 49, R. Vivekanand 34; A. Shetty six for 89) and 295 for two (A. Pathak 126, M. F. Rehman 136 not out). *Andhra 20 pts, Goa 7 pts.*

At Medical College Ground, Calicut, December 26, 27, 28, 29. Kerala won by six wickets. Andhra* 251 (O. Vinod Kumar 30, D. Sudhakar Reddy 91 not out, M. F. Rehman 40, K. V. S. D. Kamaraju 37; B. Ramaprakash five for 63, K. N. A. Padmanabhan four for 73) and 94 (D. Sudhakar Reddy 30 not out; B. Ramaprakash six for 30, K. N. A. Padmanabhan four for 38); Kerala 226 (K. N. A. Padmanabhan 59, P. G. Sunder 66; V. Vijayasarathy five for 68, G. V. V. Gopalraju four for 91) and 125 for four (V. Narayan Kutty 32, B. Ramaprakash 37). *Kerala 17 pts, Andhra 7 pts.*

At Gymkhana Ground, Secunderabad, December 27, 28, 29, 30. Drawn. Hyderabad* 563 (R. A. Swarup 32, M. V. Sridhar 83, V. Jaisimha 115, Zakir Hussain 139, N. R. Yadav 75 not out; A. Kumble three for 125); Karnataka 301 for eight dec. (C. Saldanha 84, V. A. Raja 56, K. Srinath 41 not out; Arshad Ayub three for 109) and 202 for eight (C. Saldanha 31, S. M. H. Kirmani 62; Arshad Ayub five for 76). *Hyderabad 15 pts, Karnataka 9 pts.*

At S. V. University Ground, Tirupathi, January 2, 3, 4, 5. Tamil Nadu won by an innings and 166 runs. Tamil Nadu 503 for nine dec. (W. V. Raman 122, N. Gautam 34, M. Sanjay 43, Arjan Kripal Singh 117, M. Senthilnathan 39, Robin Singh 41, D. Vasu 36; V. Vijayasarathy five for 142); Andhra* 204 (O. Vinod Kumar 41, M. F. Rehman 34, M. S. Kumar 32; M. Venkataramana four for 69) and 133 (S. Subramaniam seven for 45). *Tamil Nadu 25 pts, Andhra 2 pts.*

At Bhadravathi, February 6, 7, 8, 9. Karnataka won by one wicket. Tamil Nadu* 172 (M. Venkataramana 35 not out; S. Somasunder three for 15, A. Kumble three for 65, A. R. Bhat three for 28) and 139 (V. B. Chandrasekhar 32; A. Kumble four for 50, A. R. Bhat four for 39); Karnataka 209 for eight dec. (C. Saldanha 34, V. A. Raja 56, R. S. Dravid 61 not out; D. Vasu five for 45) and 106 for nine (D. Vasu five for 42, S. Subramaniam three for 32). *Karnataka 17 pts, Tamil Nadu 8 pts.*

Hyderabad 92 pts, Tamil Nadu 88 pts (quotient 3.40), Karnataka 88 pts (quotient 3.00), Kerala 52 pts, Andhra 35 pts, Goa 20 pts. Hyderabad and Tamil Nadu qualified for the knockout stage.

West Zone

At Baroda Rayon Ground, Udhna, Surat, December 6, 7, 8, 9. Drawn. Bombay* 554 for four dec. (J. B. Jadhav 139, J. V. Paranjpe 106, V. G. Kambli 179 not out, Iqbal Khan 64, S. S. Dighe 47 not out) and 272 for six dec. (J. B. Jadhav 63, V. G. Kambli 41, S. K. Talpade 50 not out; D. T. Patel three for 87); Gujarat 242 (M. H. Parmar 37, B. H. Mistry 38, N. Y. Laliwala 46, D. T. Patel 35 not out; A. Kuruvilla three for 88, S. V. Bahutule three for 53) and 121 for six (R. R. Kulkarni three for 24). *Gujarat 7 pts, Bombay 20 pts.*

At Corporation Stadium, Rajkot, December 6, 7, 8, 9. Drawn. Baroda* 290 (K. S. Chavan 84, N. R. Mongia 32, M. S. Narula 77 not out; B. M. Radia five for 104) and 252 for eight (K. S. Chavan 111, R. B. Parikh 40); Saurashtra 499 (S. S. Tanna 253 not out, B. Dutta 53, R. M. Mehta 41, C. C. Mankad 54; S. Patel six for 106) and nine for no wkt. *Saurashtra 15 pts, Baroda 9 pts.*

At Wankhede Stadium, Bombay, December 13, 14, 15, 16. Drawn. Bombay 511 for nine dec. (J. B. Jadhav 40, V. G. Kambli 262, Iqbal Khan 105, S. S. Patil 32 not out; B. M. Radia five for 136) and 227 for eight dec. (V. G. Kambli 55, Iqbal Khan 44, R. R. Kulkarni 36 not out; B. M. Radia three for 66); Saurashtra* 380 (B. M. Jadeja 129, A. N. Pandya 44, B. Dutta 110; A. Kuruvilla three for 78, S. S. Patil four for 86) and 62 for six (S. V. Bahutule three for 5). *Bombay 19 pts, Saurashtra 12 pts.*

At Sardar Patel Stadium, Valsad, December 13, 14, 15, 16. Maharashtra won by nine wickets. Gujarat* 361 for nine dec. (M. H. Parmar 147, B. H. Mistry 50, J. P. Saigal 30; S. V. Ranjane three for 74) and 157 (B. H. Mistry 50; R. T. Yerwadekar three for 57, S. V. Ranjane four for 67); Maharashtra 502 for eight dec. (Abhijit P. Deshpande 217, S. V. Jedhe 118, S. S. Sugwekar 63, Extras 33; D. T. Patel three for 116, T. N. Varsania three for 86) and 17 for one. *Maharashtra 21 pts, Gujarat 5 pts.*

At Poona Club, Pune, December 20, 21, 22, 23. Drawn. Saurashtra 345 (B. S. Pujara 71, A. N. Pandya 71, B. Dutta 76; R. T. Yerwadekar three for 70, S. J. Jadhav three for 42) and 264 for nine dec. (B. S. Pujara 55, B. Dutta 49, H. J. Parsana 39, B. M. Radia 71; S. V. Ranjane four for 54, R. T. Yerwadekar three for 77); Maharashtra* 498 (Abhijit P. Deshpande 57, S. V. Jedhe 123, S. S. Sugwekar 180, S. J. Jadhav 33, S. V. Ranjane 36) and 23 for one. *Maharashtra 16 pts, Saurashtra 9 pts.*

At Motibaug Palace Ground, Baroda, December 20, 21, 22, 23. Drawn. Bombay* 268 (V. G. Kambli 57, S. K. Talpade 79, R. R. Kulkarni 44; K. D. Amin three for 88, M. S. Narula four for 57) and 339 (S. S. Hattangadi 53, J. B. Jadhav 35, Iqbal Khan 30, S. S. Dighe 71 not out, S. K. Talpade 49; M. S. Narula five for 90); Baroda 404 (R. B. Parikh 76, K. S. Chavan 129, A. C. Bedade 102; A. Kuruvilla four for 96) and 187 for four (T. B. Arothe 70). *Baroda 16 pts, Bombay 11 pts.*

At Chhatrapati Shivaji Stadium, Kolhapur, December 27, 28, 29, 30. Maharashtra won by six wickets. Baroda 224 (R. B. Parikh 62, S. S. Hazare 30; S. V. Ranjane three for 52, S. J. Jadhav four for 38) and 312 (K. S. Chavan 88, T. B. Arothe 109, A. D. Gaekwad 40, S. S. Hazare 32; R. T. Yerwadekar three for 64, S. J. Jadhav three for 68, S. V. Jedhe three for 64); Maharashtra* 328 (Abhijit P. Deshpande 42, S. S. Sugwekar 90, S. J. Jadhav 45, S. C. Gudge 61, Y. S. Kadam 36; S. Patel three for 54, S. A. Doshi three for 51) and 209 for four (S. V. Jedhe 60, S. S. Sugwekar 65 not out, S. J. Jadhav 43 not out). *Maharashtra 17 pts, Baroda 7 pts.*

At Corporation Stadium, Rajkot, December 27, 28, 29, 30. Drawn. Saurashtra 422 for seven dec. (B. M. Jadeja 62, A. N. Pandya 32, B. Dutta 139, B. M. Radia 42, C. C. Mankad 65 not out; N. Y. Laliwala three for 28) and 237 (B. S. Pujara 73, B. Dutta 35, M. Parmar 53; Nilesh Patel three for 55); Gujarat* 358 (M. H. Parmar 152, N. Bakriwala 31, N. Y. Laliwala 60) and 81 for three. *Saurashtra 17 pts, Gujarat 13 pts.*

At Wankhede Stadium, Bombay, January 2, 3, 4, 5. Bombay won by an innings and 85 runs. Maharashtra* 237 (S. S. Sugwekar 33, M. D. Gunjal 61, S. J. Jadhav 48, S. C. Gudge 48; A. Kuruvilla three for 60, S. S. Patil three for 52, S. V. Bahutule three for 37) and 319 (S. S. Bhave 117, S. S. Sugwekar 39, S. J. Jadhav 64; A. Kuruvilla five for 60); Bombay 641 for nine dec. (S. S. Dighe 54, V. G. Kambli 182, Iqbal Khan 76, S. K. Talpade 66, S. V. Bahutule 111 not out, R. R. Kulkarni 69; S. J. Jadhav four for 138). *Bombay 22 pts, Maharashtra 5 pts.*

At Motibaug Palace Ground, Baroda, January 3, 4, 5, 6. Drawn. Baroda 383 (R. B. Parikh 37, T. B. Arothe 45, A. D. Gaekwad 143, M. S. Narula 57; B. H. Mistry five for 77) and 251 for five dec. (T. B. Arothe 35, A. C. Bedade 72, M. S. Narula 43 not out, J. J. Martin 50); Gujarat* 367 (Maqbul Malam 51, N. Bakriwala 68, B. H. Mistry 138 not out, N. Y. Laliwala 37; J. J. Martin five for 51) and 116 for four (M. H. Parmar 67 not out). *Baroda 14 pts, Gujarat 11 pts.*

Bombay 72 pts, Maharashtra 59 pts, Saurashtra 53 pts, Baroda 46 pts, Gujarat 36 pts. Bombay and Maharashtra qualified for the knockout stage.

Pre-quarter finals

At Nehru Stadium, Pune, February 13, 14, 15, 16, 17. Drawn. Maharashtra were declared winners by virtue of their first-innings lead. Maharashtra* 757 for seven dec. (S. S. Bhave 229, S. V. Jedhe 156, S. S. Sugwekar 32, M. D. Gunjal 162, S. J. Jadhav 77 not out, S. V. Ranjane 64 not out; K. V. P. Rao three for 130); Bihar 270 (P. Khanna 71, H. Gidwani 99; R. T. Yerwadekar three for 55) and 424 for seven (Sunil Kumar 90, S. S. Karim 176, S. Chatterjee 79; P. Kanade three for 85).

At Gymkhana Ground, Secunderabad, February 15, 16, 17, 18. Madhya Pradesh won by seven wickets. Hyderabad* 409 (Abdul Azeem 130, C. Jaikumar 66, V. Jaisimha 42, Arshad Ayub 45, M. V. Ramanamurthy 72; S. S. Lahore five for 116) and 249 (Abdul Azeem 34, C. Jaikumar 59, R. A. Swarup 34, Zakir Hussain 42; S. M. Patil five for 86); Madhya Pradesh 535 (A. V. Vijayvargiya 85, K. K. Patel 54, A. R. Khurasia 132, P. K. Dwevedi 67, S. M. Patil 47, D. K. Nilosey 47 not out; Arshad Ayub five for 203, Kanwaljit Singh three for 141) and 127 for three (S. M. Patil 65).

Quarter-finals

At Wankhede Stadium, Bombay, February 28, 29, March 1, 2, 3. Bombay won by an innings and 118 runs. Madhya Pradesh 230 (P. K. Dwevedi 41, R. K. Chauhan 55 not out, S. Lahore 37, N. D. Hirwani 33; R. R. Kulkarni three for 26, A. Kuruvilla three for 70, . Shahane three for 76) and 373 (A. V. Vijayvargiya 52, A. R. Khurasia 104, D. K. Nilosey 7, R. K. Chauhan 51, S. S. Lahore 46 not out; A. Kuruvilla four for 73, Iqbal Khan four or 107); Bombay* 721 for eight dec. (J. B. Jadhav 110, J. V. Paranjpe 118, D. B. engsarkar 284, Iqbal Khan 52, S. K. Talpade 38, S. V. Bahutule 32, R. R. Kulkarni 34 not ut; S. S. Lahore four for 169).

At Ferozshah Kotla Ground, Delhi, February 28, 29, March 1, 2, 3. Delhi won by an nnings and 168 runs. Bengal* 237 (Arun Lal 40, A. Malhotra 40, Saurav Ganguly 74 not ut; A. S. Wassan three for 71, V. Razdan four for 53) and 228 (Arun Lal 33, Saurav Ganguly 51, M. Das 39; Maninder Singh seven for 57); Delhi 633 (M. Nayyar 34, . Vinayak 67, Bantoo Singh 164, Ajay Sharma 64, V. Razdan 101, A. S. Wassan 110, Extras 37; S. Chatterjee five for 169, S. P. Mukherjee three for 161).

At Nehru Stadium, Pune, February 28, 29, March 1, 2, 3. Drawn. Haryana were declared winners by virtue of their first-innings lead. Haryana* 673 for nine dec. (Dhanraj Singh 32, N. R. Goel 45, P. Kaushik 41, A. S. Kaypee 131, R. Puri 63, A. Banerjee 83, V. S. Yadav 29, Y. Bhandari 34, Chetan Sharma 31, S. Dangi 44 not out, Extras 38; S. J. Jadhav six or 179) and 95 for no wkt (Dhanraj Singh 37 not out, N. R. Goel 40 not out); Maharashtra 57 (Abhijit P. Deshpande 86, S. S. Bhave 231 not out, S. S. Sugwekar 59, M. D. Gunjal 59, . J. Jadhav 49; Y. Bhandari four for 194).

At Modi Stadium, Green Park, Kanpur, February 28, 29, March 1, 2, 3. Drawn. Tamil Nadu were declared winners by virtue of their first-innings lead. Tamil Nadu* 349 M. Senthilnathan 109, Robin Singh 39, D. Vasu 84; R. P. Singh three for 79, A. W. Zaidi nree for 50) and 628 (V. B. Chandrasekhar 131, W. V. Raman 110, N. Gautam 190, Arjan Kripal Singh 40, M. Senthilnathan 59, Extras 33; G. K. Pandey seven for 167); Uttar radesh 203 (V. S. Vats 44, S. Chaturvedi 33, G. K. Pandey 55 not out; S. Subramaniam hree for 42, A. R. Kapoor four for 41) and 77 for no wkt (S. Chaturvedi 40 not out, R. P. ingh 35 not out).

Semi-finals

At Wankhede Stadium, Bombay, March 13, 14, 15, 16, 17. Drawn. Delhi were declared vinners by virtue of their first-innings lead. Delhi 516 (M. Nayyar 39, K. Bhaskar Pillai 21, K. Azad 66, Sanjay Sharma 44, Maninder Singh 56, Extras 41; A. Kuruvilla four for 24, V. Shahane three for 91) and 574 (M. Nayyar 61, Ajay Sharma 259 not out, K. Azad 0, Maninder Singh 78); Bombay* 254 (J. B. Jadhav 39, S. S. Dighe 61, S. V. Bahutule 45 ot out; Maninder Singh five for 63) and 182 for three (J. B. Jadhav 32, S. S. Dighe 100 ot out).

At Nahar Singh Stadium, Faridabad, March 13, 14, 15, 16, 17. Drawn. Tamil Nadu were eclared winners by virtue of their first-innings lead. Tamil Nadu* 507 (V. B. Chandrasekhar 39, W. V. Raman 226, Robin Singh 40, D. Vasu 58, Extras 35; Chetan harma three for 97, Deepak Sharma three for 132) and 340 (V. B. Chandrasekhar 43, W. V. Raman 120, M. Senthilnathan 68; Y. Bhandari four for 111, P. Jain three for 105); Haryana 375 (N. R. Goel 44, A. S. Kaypee 82, R. Puri 38, A. Banerjee 32, V. S. Yadav 59 ot out, Chetan Sharma 52, Extras 47; S. Subramaniam four for 71) and 233 for seven A. S. Kaypee 71, R. Puri 49, V. S. Yadav 30 not out; D. Vasu three for 66).

Final

At Ferozshah Kotla Ground, Delhi, March 27, 28, 29, 30, 31. Drawn. Delhi were declared hampions by virtue of their first-innings lead. Delhi* 532 (R. Lamba 80, M. Prabhakar 56, jay Sharma 175, V. Razdan 93, Extras 55; D. Vasu four for 106) and 273 for four M. Nayyar 85, K. Bhaskar Pillai 31 not out, Bantoo Singh 123); Tamil Nadu 449 (V. B. Chandrasekhar 59, W. V. Raman 82, M. Senthilnathan 54, D. Vasu 63, A. R. Kapoor 61 ot out; M. Prabhakar three for 108, Maninder Singh five for 130).

RANJI TROPHY WINNERS

1934-35	Bombay	1954-55	Madras	1974-75	Bombay
1935-36	Bombay	1955-56	Bombay	1975-76	Bombay
1936-37	Nawanagar	1956-57	Bombay	1976-77	Bombay
1937-38	Hyderabad	1957-58	Baroda	1977-78	Karnataka
1938-39	Bengal	1958-59	Bombay	1978-79	Delhi
1939-40	Maharashtra	1959-60	Bombay	1979-80	Delhi
1940-41	Maharashtra	1960-61	Bombay	1980-81	Bombay
1941-42	Bombay	1961-62	Bombay	1981-82	Delhi
1942-43	Baroda	1962-63	Bombay	1982-83	Karnataka
1943-44	Western India	1963-64	Bombay	1983-84	Bombay
1944-45	Bombay	1964-65	Bombay	1984-85	Bombay
1945-46	Holkar	1965-66	Bombay	1985-86	Delhi
1946-47	Baroda	1966-67	Bombay	1986-87	Hyderabad
1947-48	Holkar	1967-68	Bombay	1987-88	Tamil Nadu
1948-49	Bombay	1968-69	Bombay	1988-89	Delhi
1949-50	Baroda	1969-70	Bombay	1989-90	Bengal
1950-51	Holkar	1970-71	Bombay	1990-91	Haryana
1951-52	Bombay	1971-72	Bombay	1991-92	Delhi
1952-53	Holkar	1972-73	Bombay		
1953-54	Bombay	1973-74	Karnataka		

DULEEP TROPHY, 1991-92

At Wankhede Stadium, Bombay, January 8, 9, 10, 11. South Zone won by an innings and 50 runs. Central Zone* 173 (K. K. Patel 42, Sanjeeva Sharma 43; V. Prasad six for 40, Arshad Ayub three for 63) and 268 (S. S. Khandkar 46, Abhay Sharma 59, Sanjeeva Sharma 53, S. S. Lahore 53; D. Vasu three for 56); South Zone 491 (M. V. Sridhar 56, W V. Raman 45, Zakir Hussain 51, Robin Singh 108, A. Kumble 88 not out, Extras 42; P. S Vaidya five for 113).

Semi-finals

At Baroda Rayon Ground, Udhna, Surat, January 15, 16, 17, 18, 19. North Zone won by an innings and 83 runs. South Zone 220 (Robin Singh 34, A. Kumble 48, Arshad Ayub 47 not out; A. S. Wassan six for 72) and 230 (Zakir Hussain 32; Chetan Sharma five for 80) North Zone* 533 (Ajay Sharma 89, A. S. Kaypee 30, V. S. Yadav 201, Chetan Sharma 57 Maninder Singh 41; V. Prasad three for 117).

At Wankhede Stadium, Bombay, January 15, 16, 17, 18, 19. West Zone won by an innings and 355 runs. East Zone 185 (Snehashish Ganguly 49, S. S. Karim 43, R. B. Biswa 34; R. R. Kulkarni four for 27, A. Kuruvilla three for 62) and 142 (A. Kuruvilla four for 59 S. S. Patil five for 36); West Zone* 682 for nine dec. (K. S. Chavan 123, S. V. Jedhe 57, V G. Kambli 208, S. S. Sugwekar 158, N. R. Mongia 55, Extras 31; Avinash Kumar five fo 153).

Final

At Sardar Patel Stadium, Valsad, January 21, 22, 23, 24, 25. North Zone won by 236 runs North Zone* 279 (R. Puri 58, V. Razdan 33, Extras 30; A. Kuruvilla three for 60, M. S Narula five for 48) and 393 (A. D. Jadeja 66, K. Bhaskar Pillai 104, A. S. Kaypee 72 V. Razdan 50, Maninder Singh 44 not out; A. Kuruvilla six for 98); West Zone 21 (M. H. Parmar 31, N. R. Mongia 52, B. M. Radia 39; Chetan Sharma six for 65) and 22 (K. S. Chavan 37, S. V. Jedhe 44, V. G. Kambli 58; V. Razdan three for 46, Maninder Singl four for 55).

CRICKET IN PAKISTAN, 1991-92

By ABID ALI KAZI

The season of 1991-92 will long be remembered in Pakistan for the national team's triumph in the World Cup, at their fifth attempt. World Cup fever overshadowed the domestic season, and even the international cricket played earlier in the year.

The main domestic tournament, the Quaid-e-Azam Trophy, was contested by nine teams, instead of the usual eight, after the Board of Control for Cricket in Pakistan (BCCP) were unable to settle disputes concerning matches in 1990-91, which affected the question of relegation. Amid confusion, the BCCP decided no team should go down that season. Instead, they demoted two teams, Peshawar and Karachi Blues, rather than one at the end of 1991-92 – leaving Karachi with only one first-class side. Rawalpindi headed the points table, but lost their semi-final to Lahore City, while second-placed Karachi Whites beat Bahawalpur to join them in the final. In their group match a month earlier Lahore City had won, but they could not repeat the feat, and Karachi Whites retained the national crown on first-innings lead when the match was drawn. Islamabad were the surprise champions of Grade II, beating Karachi Greens, and earned the right to a first-class début in 1992-93.

The Wills Cup, the country's premier one-day competition, was contested by 14 teams, and the Pakistan selectors took it into account in picking their team for the international Wills Trophy in Sharjah. Opener Sajid Ali booked his place in Sharjah by scoring 171 on the first day of the tournament, breaking the tournament record set by Abdus Sami of Railways nearly ten years before. His first-wicket stand of 297 with Shahid Anwar was the highest for any wicket in the competition. Habib Bank claimed the trophy for the third year running, despite the protests of PIA, who scored 234 in the final to their 214. But Habib Bank's total was supplemented by 40 penalty runs, awarded when PIA fell four short of the 43 overs to be bowled in the allotted time. The umpires' decision, absolutely correct by tournament rules, enabled Habib Bank to equal PIA's five Wills Cups, the only other winner being United Bank.

The Patron's Trophy went to Habib Bank, who led by 133 in the first innings of their drawn final with National Bank. The two teams had not had to contest the usual semi-finals, which were scrapped by the Domestic Tournament Monitoring Committee in order to complete the competition before the holy month of Ramadan. The decision puzzled many, as two weeks were available before Ramadan began on March 5. Nor did the committee's chairman, Javed Zaman, convince the critics with his explanation that "there were a lot of protests and we thought if we sat down to decide them, it would have taken a long time". Grade II of the trophy also had its share of controversy. House Building Finance Corporation (HBFC) beat Pakistan Customs in the final, to gain promotion at the expense of Combined Universities, who had secured no points at all. But Pakistan Customs accused HBFC of unfair tactics, time-wasting and having the support of both umpires.

Mansoor Rana, of Lahore City and ADBP, headed the batting averages with 618 runs, at 68.66, while Aamer Malik had the leading aggregate with 1,269 at 63.45. He scored four centuries, as did Zahoor Elahi (Multan and ADBP), who reached 1,000 runs for the third successive year, with 1,103. Shahid Saeed (Lahore City and PACO) also achieved the feat, with 1,222. Masood Anwar of Multan and United Bank took most wickets, with 72 at 23.22, to follow up last season's success when he tied with Waqar Younis on 70. Only one other player, Nadeem Ghauri (Lahore City and Habib Bank) reached 50, claiming 54 at 25.24. The best return of the season came from Naved Anjum, who took nine for 45 in an innings for Habib Bank against National Bank, and also headed the bowling averages with 47 wickets at 15.91. Mohsin Kamal performed the only hat-trick, for PNSC against United Bank. The leading wicket-keeper was Ashraf Ali of Lahore City, with 26 catches and three stumpings in nine matches, and the top fielder was Asif Mujtaba of Karachi Whites and PIA with 19 catches. Asif was in fact the complete all-rounder, with 29 wickets from his slow left-arm spin and 735 runs from 14 matches, including a century and ten wickets in Karachi Whites' match against Rawalpindi.

Domestic cricket had begun with the National Under-19 Championship, sponsored this year by Pepsi-Cola. Ten teams took part in Grade I, divided into two groups. Karachi Whites and Multan headed Group A, and reached the final by defeating Lahore City and Karachi Blues of Group B. Despite spirited resistance, Multan surrendered the first-innings lead in the final, so Karachi Whites became champions when the match was drawn. Three Karachi teams will compete in next year's Under-19 Championship, as Grade II winners Karachi Greens replace Rawalpindi, who failed to gain any points.

FIRST-CLASS AVERAGES, 1991-92

BATTING

(Qualification: 500 runs, average 25.00)

	M	I	NO	R	HS	100s	Avge
Mansoor Rana (*Lahore City/ADBP*)	10	13	4	618	124*	2	68.66
Zahoor Elahi (*Multan/ADBP*)	14	21	4	1,103	148	4	64.88
Aamer Malik (*Lahore City/PIA*)	13	22	2	1,269	162	4	63.45
Shahid Saeed (*Lahore City/PACO*)	14	24	3	1,222	161	3	58.19
Ghulam Ali (*Karachi Whites/PACO*)	12	20	1	988	164	3	52.00
Basit Ali (*Karachi Whites/United Bank*)	7	12	0	594	134	2	49.50
Mujahid Jamshed (*Combined Universities*) . .	6	12	0	586	149	2	48.83
Mohammad Ramzan (*Faisalabad*)	8	16	0	721	144	2	45.06
Iqbal Saleem (*Karachi Blues*)	8	16	2	603	172*	1	43.07
Shahid Anwar (*Bahawalpur/National Bank*) .	16	25	2	971	161	1	42.21
Azam Khan (*Karachi Whites*)	9	18	3	627	135*	2	41.80
Asif Mujtaba (*Karachi Whites/PIA*)	14	25	7	735	105*	1	40.83
Sajid Ali (*Karachi Blues/National Bank*)	12	18	0	729	143	1	40.50
Umar Rasheed (*Bahawalpur/PACO*)	14	20	3	675	147*	1	39.70
Ameer-ud-Din (*Karachi Blues*)	8	16	0	640	122	2	40.00
Rizwan-uz-Zaman (*Karachi Blues/PIA*)	9	17	1	582	142	1	36.37
Aamer Hanif (*Karachi Whites/PACO*)	15	24	3	757	163*	3	36.04

	M	I	NO	R	HS	100s	Avge
Shahid Javed (*Rawalpindi/Habib Bank*).....	16	26	6	718	105*	1	35.90
Moin-ul-Atiq (*Karachi Whites/Habib Bank*) .	12	19	0	673	88	0	35.42
Manzoor Elahi (*Multan/ADBP*)...........	14	16	0	562	85	0	35.12
Shakeel Qasim (*Bahawalpur/Habib Bank*) ..	15	25	1	788	84	0	32.83
Shahid Nawaz (*Faisalabad/PACO*)	11	19	3	523	112	1	32.68
Aamer Bashir (*Multan/United Bank*).......	14	20	0	504	93	0	25.20

* *Signifies not out.*

BOWLING

(Qualification: 25 wickets)

	O	M	R	W	BB	5W/i	Avge
Naved Anjum (*Habib Bank*)..............	241.4	48	748	47	9-45	3	15.91
Bilal Rana (*Bahawalpur*)...............	162.3	33	485	29	7-57	2	16.72
Mohammad Hasnain (*Karachi Blues*).......	132.2	16	486	28	8-61	2	17.35
Iqbal Qasim (*National Bank*).............	229.4	55	515	28	6-78	2	18.39
Mohsin Mirza (*Karachi Whites*)	209.3	51	483	26	8-92	2	18.57
Naeem Khan (*Sargodha/Habib Bank*)	280	37	964	48	7-42	5	20.08
Iqbal Sikandar (*Karachi Whites/PIA*)	307.1	56	887	42	7-34	5	21.11
Mohammad Riaz (*Rawalpindi*)	204.1	45	587	26	6-63	3	22.57
Masood Anwar (*Multan/United Bank*)	684.4	176	1,672	72	6-23	4	23.22
Zakir Khan (*Peshawar/ADBP*)	203.2	47	583	25	6-36	3	23.32
Shahid Mahboob (*Karachi Whites/PACO*) ...	264	42	857	36	7-109	2	23.80
Mohammad Zahid (*Bahawalpur/PACO*)	279.3	55	837	35	4-20	0	23.91
Asif Mujtaba (*Karachi Whites/PIA*)	269	70	694	29	5-38	3	23.93
Raja Afaq (*Rawalpindi/ADBP*)	229.3	26	702	29	6-85	2	24.20
Tanvir Mehdi (*Lahore City/United Bank*)....	314.3	42	1,134	45	7-74	3	25.20
Nadeem Ghauri (*Lahore City/Habib Bank*) ..	516	143	1,363	54	5-24	4	25.24
Athar Laeeq (*Karachi Whites*)	248.5	44	760	30	5-60	3	25.33
Tauseef Ahmed (*United Bank*)	251	53	715	26	7-46	2	27.50
Haaris Khan (*Karachi Blues*)............	379	64	1,056	38	5-83	2	27.78
Nadeem Khan (*Karachi Blues/National Bank*)	451.1	70	1,493	49	5-56	4	30.46
Sajjad Akbar (*Sargodha/PNSC*)	444.3	56	1,301	36	6-118	2	36.13
Nadeem Nazar (*Multan*)	423.3	46	1,494	39	5-102	1	38.30

In the following scores, * by the name of a team indicates that they won the toss.

QUAID-E-AZAM TROPHY, 1991-92

	Played	Won	Lost	Drawn	1st-inns lead in drawn match	Points
Rawalpindi	8	4	2	2	2	50
Karachi Whites	8	4	2	2	0	40
Lahore City.........	8	2	1	5	3	40*
Bahawalpur.........	8	3	2	3	1	35
Faisalabad..........	8	2	2	4	1	35†
Multan.............	8	1	2	5	5	35
Sargodha	8	2	1	5	1	25
Peshawar............	8	2	3	3	1	15†
Karachi Blues	8	1	6	1	1	15

* *Lahore City awarded 10 points instead of 5 after their protest against Sargodha.*
† *Faisalabad awarded 10 points originally assigned to Peshawar after they protested over Peshawar's victory.*

Win = *10 pts; 1st-innings lead in drawn match* = *5 pts.*

***Semi-finals**: Lahore City beat Rawalpindi by virtue of their first-innings lead; Karachi Whites beat Bahawalpur by nine wickets.*
***Final**: Karachi Whites beat Lahore City by virtue of their first-innings lead.*

Note: First innings closed at 85 overs in the group matches and semi-finals.

At Iqbal Stadium, Faisalabad, October 19, 20, 21, 22. Peshawar won by four wickets. Faisalabad 297 for four (Mohammad Ramzan 144, Nadeem Arshad 71, Shahid Nawaz 54 not out) and 182 (Nadeem Arshad 38 not out, Mohammad Ashraf 36; Zakir Khan six for 67); Peshawar* 336 for eight (Jehangir Khan 30, Sagheer Abbas 156 not out, Wasim Yousufi 40, Extras 34; Saadat Gul three for 57) and 146 for six (Jehangir Khan 38, Sagheer Abbas 32 not out, Mohammad Saleem 41 not out). *Peshawar 10 pts (later reassigned to Faisalabad).*

At National Stadium, Karachi, October 19, 20, 21, 22. Karachi Whites won by 34 runs. Karachi Whites 339 for six (Azam Khan 53, Basit Ali 34, Asif Mujtaba 105 not out, Iqbal Sikandar 47, Jawwad Ali 39 not out) and 267 for two dec. (Azam Khan 135 not out, Basit Ali 64, Asif Mujtaba 35 not out); Karachi Blues* 288 for eight (Ameer-ud-Din 120, Munir-ul-Haq 77; Mohsin Mirza five for 48) and 284 (Iqbal Saleem 48, Ameer-ud-Din 66, Rashid Latif 31, Tahir Mahmood 51, Fareed Hasan 45; Mohsin Mirza eight for 92). *Karachi Whites 10 pts.*

At Montgomery Biscuit Factory Ground, Sahiwal, October 19, 20, 21, 22. Drawn. Bahawalpur* 302 for eight (Shakeel Ahmed 57, Umar Rasheed 87, Murtaza Hussain 67 not out; Nadeem Nazar five for 102) and 415 for eight dec. (Shakeel Ahmed 55, Shahid Anwar 161, Imran Zia 49, Bilal Rana 59 not out; Masood Anwar three for 155, Nadeem Nazar four for 178); Multan 305 for nine (Zahoor Elahi 76, Manzoor Elahi 85, Aamer Bashir 68; Mohammad Altaf five for 77, Bilal Rana three for 82) and 94 for three (Masroor Hussain 46 not out). *Multan 5 pts.*

At KRL Cricket Ground, Rawalpindi, October 19, 20, 21. Rawalpindi won by seven wickets. Lahore City* 199 (Aamer Malik 63, Kashif Khan 30, Mohammad Asif 43; Zahir Shah four for 59, Tauqeer Hussain four for 31) and 139 (Shahid Saeed 31; Mohammad Riaz six for 63); Rawalpindi 197 (Sabih Azhar 47; Mohammad Asif five for 66) and 144 for three (Saleem Taj 42, Naseer Ahmed 70). *Rawalpindi 10 pts.*

At Bahawal Stadium, Bahawalpur, October 26, 27, 28. Bahawalpur won by 116 runs. Bahawalpur 199 (Shakeel Ahmed 55, Shahid Anwar 54, Mohammad Tayyab 43; Raja Sarfraz seven for 64) and 133 (Murtaza Hussain 36; Naeem Akhtar three for 41); Rawalpindi* 74 (Nadeem Abbasi 32 not out; Shahzad Arshad six for 14) and 142 (Saleem Taj 41, Shakeel Ahmed 37; Umar Rasheed three for 34, Mohammad Altaf three for 29, Mohammad Zahid four for 20). *Bahawalpur 10 pts.*

At National Stadium, Karachi, October 26, 27, 28, 29. Karachi Whites won by four wickets. Sargodha 284 (Rizwan Umar 151; Mohsin Mirza three for 40) and 216 (Mohammad Hasnain 37, Azhar Sultan 49, Sajjad Akbar 33; Iqbal Sikandar six for 36, Aamer Hanif three for 27); Karachi Whites* 363 for six (Azam Khan 63, Aamer Hanif 163 not out, Salim Yousuf 52) and 138 for six (Aamer Khurshid 41 not out; Naeem Khan four for 73). *Karachi Whites 10 pts.*

At Montgomery Biscuit Factory Ground, Sahiwal, October 26, 27, 28, 29. Karachi Blues won by seven wickets. Multan* 337 (Zahoor Elahi 126, Manzoor Elahi 50, Tariq Mahboob 33, Aamer Bashir 37; Nadeem Khan four for 130, Haaris Khan three for 134) and 234 (Zahoor Elahi 38, Masroor Hussain 41, Aamer Bashir 34, Mohammad Shafiq 42; Haaris Khan five for 83); Karachi Blues 322 (Rizwan-uz-Zaman 74, Ameer-ud-Din 72, Rashid Latif 51, Iqbal Imam 36; Nadeem Nazar three for 102, Zahoor Elahi four for 64) and 252 for three (Rizwan-uz-Zaman 60, Ameer-ud-Din 122, Iqbal Saleem 59 not out; Masood Anwar three for 72). *Karachi Blues 10 pts.*

At Arbab Niaz Stadium, Peshawar, October 26, 27, 28, 29. Drawn. Peshawar* 204 (Jehangir Khan 51, Farrukh Zaman 51; Iqbal Zahoor three for 33) and 320 (Nasir Khan 59, Jehangir Khan 51, Sher Ali 93, Shahid Hussain 41; Mohammad Asif five for 65); Lahore City 287 (Tariq Baig 33, Shahid Saeed 67, Aamer Malik 30, Ali Zia 61, Iqbal Zahoor 42; Shahid Hussain three for 74, Farrukh Zaman five for 90) and 46 for no wkt. *Lahore City 5 pts.*

At Bahawal Stadium, Bahawalpur, November 2, 3, 4. Bahawalpur won by 157 runs. Bahawalpur* 151 (Imran Zia 30, Shahzad Arshad 50 not out; Haaris Khan three for 31, Nadeem Khan five for 56) and 286 (Shakeel Ahmed 42, Imran Zia 43, Umar Rasheed 36, Murtaza Hussain 51; Haaris Khan three for 98, Nadeem Khan five for 92); Karachi Blues 166 (Sajid Ali 30, Haaris Khan 35, Iqbal Saleem 33; Bilal Rana three for 55, Mohammad Zahid four for 27) and 114 (Sajid Ali 63; Bilal Rana six for 37, Mohammad Zahid three for 42). *Bahawalpur 10 pts.*

At LCCA Ground, Lahore, November 2, 3, 4, 5. Drawn. Sargodha* 343 (Rizwan Umar 58, Salim Malik 86, Maqsood Ahmed 61, Sajjad Akbar 50; Nadeem Ghauri four for 114, Sohail Khan three for 89) and 320 for nine dec. (Mohammad Hasnain 58, Rizwan Umar 64, Arshad Pervez 65, Maqsood Ahmed 31 not out; Sohail Khan six for 109); Lahore City 347 for eight (Mazhar Qayyum 30, Shahid Saeed 109, Aamer Malik 61, Mansoor Rana 79 not out; Mohammad Nawaz four for 65) and 266 for seven (Shahid Saeed 72, Aamer Malik 50, Kashif Khan 46, Ali Zia 58; Ashraf Bashir three for 80, Sajjad Akbar three for 67). *Lahore City 5 pts (later increased to 10 pts).*

At KRL Cricket Ground, Rawalpindi, November 2, 3, 4, 5. Rawalpindi won by six wickets. Multan 259 (Masroor Hussain 47, Tariq Mahboob 48, Raja Arshad 42; Mohammad Riaz five for 52) and 147 (Zahoor Elahi 35, Manzoor Elahi 34; Raja Afaq four for 48); Rawalpindi* 274 for nine (Masood Anwar 65, Ghaffar Kazmi 67, Nadeem Abbasi 72 not out; Masood Anwar four for 74) and 135 for four (Ghaffar Kazmi 50 not out; Masood Anwar three for 48). *Rawalpindi 10 pts.*

At National Stadium, Karachi, November 3, 4, 5, 6. Faisalabad won by five wickets. Karachi Whites 202 (Salim Yousuf 42, Asif Mujtaba 40, Iqbal Sikandar 52; Nadeem Afzal five for 77, Saadat Gul three for 43) and 159 (Azam Khan 48, Sajid Riaz 34; Naseer Shaukat seven for 62); Faisalabad* 156 (Shahid Nawaz 33 not out, Mohammad Ashraf 35; Shahid Mahboob five for 53, Aamer Hanif three for 29) and 208 for five (Mohammad Ramzan 68, Shahid Nawaz 46, Extras 38; Shahid Mahboob four for 78). *Faisalabad 10 pts.*

At National Stadium, Karachi, November 9, 10, 11, 12. Karachi Whites won by 69 runs. Karachi Whites 272 for eight (Azam Khan 30, Aamer Hanif 35, Mohsin Mirza 58 not out, Sohail Mehdi 50 not out; Mohammad Saleem three for 14) and 260 for eight dec. (Asif Mujtaba 69 not out, Aamer Khurshid 73, Extras 41; Mohammad Saleem three for 27, Farrukh Zaman three for 34); Peshawar* 195 (Javed Khan 68, Mohammad Saleem 38, Shahid Hussain 30; Athar Laeeq five for 60) and 268 (Sher Ali 45, Sagheer Abbas 103 not out; Mohammad Saleem 63; Shahid Mahboob four for 84, Athar Laeeq four for 56). *Karachi Whites 10 pts.*

At Montgomery Biscuit Factory Ground, Sahiwal, November 9, 10, 11, 12. Drawn. Faisalabad* 245 (Shahid Nawaz 32, Saadat Gul 44, Naseer Shaukat 75; Nadeem Iqbal three for 28, Masood Anwar four for 69) and 395 for six (Ijaz Ahmed 100, Mohammad Ramzan 72, Nadeem Arshad 52 not out, Shahid Nawaz 38, Mohammad Ashraf 44, Bilal Ahmed 45; Nadeem Nazar three for 138); Multan 251 (Masroor Hussain 80, Manzoor Elahi 43, Raja Arshad 55; Tanvir Afzal five for 90). *Multan 5 pts.*

At KRL Cricket Ground, Rawalpindi, November 9, 10, 11, 12. Rawalpindi won by 147 runs. Rawalpindi* 301 for seven (Shahid Javed 105 not out, Nadeem Abbasi 33; Haaris Khan five for 114) and 221 (Masood Anwar 49, Shahid Javed 60, Naseer Ahmed 50; Haaris Khan four for 69, Nadeem Khan five for 72); Karachi Blues 200 (Munir-ul-Haq 53, Tahir Mahmood 52; Mohammad Riaz five for 66) and 175 (Sajid Ali 68; Raja Afaq three for 42, Shakeel Ahmed six for 60). *Rawalpindi 10 pts.*

At Sargodha Stadium, Sargodha, November 9, 10, 11, 12. Drawn. Bahawalpur 256 (Shakeel Ahmed 47, Bilal Rana 77; Aziz-ur-Rehman five for 62, Sajjad Akbar three for 83) and 354 (Shakeel Ahmed 47, Shahid Anwar 39, Imran Zia 32, Umar Rasheed 147 not out; Sajjad Akbar five for 102); Sargodha* 265 (Mohammad Hasnain 31, Azhar Sultan 44, Arshad Pervez 44, Sajjad Akbar 37; Shahzad Arshad three for 53) and 28 for one. *Sargodha 5 pts.*

At LCCA Ground, Lahore, November 16, 17, 18, 19. Lahore City won by six wickets. Bahawalpur 292 (Nasir Jam 31, Umar Rasheed 49, Bilal Rana 92; Tanvir Mehdi five for 88) and 241 (Shahid Anwar 77, Umar Rasheed 60, Shahzad Arshad 35; Tanvir Mehdi seven for 74); Lahore City* 398 for four (Shahid Saeed 141, Aamer Malik 162) and 136 for four (Shahid Saeed 75, Tariq Javed 39 not out). *Lahore City 10 pts.*

At Montgomery Biscuit Factory Ground, Sahiwal, November 16, 17, 18, 19. Drawn. Sargodha 279 for nine (Mohammad Hasnain 53, Mohammad Nawaz 77, Azhar Sultan 71, Arshad Pervez 39 not out; Masood Anwar five for 78) and 345 (Rizwan Umar 60, Azhar Sultan 75, Pervez Shah 58, Arshad Pervez 37, Mohammad Nawaz 35; Masood Anwar three for 83, Nadeem Nazar four for 151); Multan* 353 for seven (Masroor Hussain 40, Zahoor Elahi 63, Mohammad Shafiq 68, Manzoor Elahi 30, Raja Arshad 56, Shahbaz Aslam 38 not out, Masood Anwar 30 not out; Sajjad Akbar four for 128) and 70 for two. *Multan 5 pts.*

At Arbab Niaz Stadium, Peshawar, November 16, 17, 18, 19. Peshawar won by 59 runs. Peshawar* 142 (Sher Ali 48; Mohammad Hasnain five for 36, Nadeem Khan four for 50) and 316 (Sher Ali 45, Mohammad Saleem 59, Sagheer Abbas 31, Javed Khan 70, Extras 32; Mohammad Hasnain three for 78, Nadeem Khan three for 101); Karachi Blues 154 (Sajid Ali 41; Kabir Khan seven for 69, Farrukh Zaman three for 32) and 245 (Sajid Ali 33, Iqbal Saleem 80, Munir-ul-Haq 54; Kabir Khan five for 63, Shahid Hussain five for 66). *Peshawar 10 pts.*

At Bagh-e-Jinnah Ground, Faisalabad, November 17, 18, 19, 20. Drawn. Faisalabad* 306 for five (Mohammad Ramzan 133, Shahid Nawaz 61) and 360 (Sami-ul-Haq 99, Bilal Ahmed 126, Saadat Gul 42, Extras 37; Zahir Shah five for 73); Rawalpindi 322 for six (Masood Anwar 80, Saleem Taj 34, Shahid Javed 38, Naseer Ahmed 101 not out, Nadeem Abbasi 30; Tanvir Afzal four for 138) and 63 for one (Saleem Taj 32 not out). *Rawalpindi 5 pts.*

At Bahawal Stadium, Bahawalpur, November 23, 24, 25. Bahawalpur won by eight wickets. Faisalabad* 225 (Mohammad Ramzan 74, Ijaz Ahmed 67; Bilal Rana three for 58, Murtaza Hussain six for 37) and 114 (Bilal Rana seven for 57, Mohammad Zahid three for 34); Bahawalpur 264 for seven (Shakeel Ahmed 51, Shahid Anwar 43, Bilal Rana 42, Shahzad Arshad 65 not out; Nadeem Afzal three for 37, Fazal Hussain three for 67) and 76 for two. *Bahawalpur 10 pts.*

At National Stadium, Karachi, November 23, 24, 25. Lahore City won by six wickets. Karachi Whites 194 (Moin-ul-Atiq 50, Asif Mujtaba 30; Tanvir Mehdi three for 17, Nadeem Ghauri three for 55, Sohail Khan three for 64) and 182 (Moin-ul-Atiq 79, Saeed Azad 32; Tanvir Mehdi four for 72, Nadeem Ghauri five for 50); Lahore City* 251 for nine (Aamer Majeed 35, Ashraf Ali 107 not out; Iqbal Sikandar three for 91) and 126 for four (Shahid Saeed 65). *Lahore City 10 pts.*

At Montgomery Biscuit Factory Ground, Sahiwal, November 23, 24, 25, 26. Multan won by eight wickets. Peshawar 182 (Mohammad Saleem 45, Zahid Ahmed 67, Wasim Yousufi 46; Nadeem Iqbal three for 43, Nadeem Nazar four for 39) and 237 (Sher Ali 76, Mohammad Saleem 45, Wasim Yousufi 38; Masood Anwar four for 53, Nadeem Nazar four for 69); Multan* 362 (Zahoor Elahi 138, Masroor Hussain 80, Manzoor Elahi 73; Zahid Ahmed four for 48) and 59 for two (Raja Arshad 35). *Multan 10 pts.*

At Sargodha Stadium, Sargodha, November 23, 24, 25. Sargodha won by 131 runs. Sargodha 190 (Pervez Shah 84, Sajjad Akbar 33, Extras 30; Baqar Rizvi six for 75, Mohammad Hasnain four for 55) and 132 (Arshad Pervez 33; Mohammad Hasnain eight for 61); Karachi Blues* 54 (Iqbal Saleem 32; Naeem Khan six for 19, Pervez Shah three for 33) and 137 (Naeem Khan five for 86, Pervez Shah three for 23). *Sargodha 10 pts.*

At Iqbal Stadium, Faisalabad, November 30, December 1, 2. Faisalabad won by 93 runs. Faisalabad 299 (Mohammad Ramzan 50, Nadeem Arshad 58, Mohammad Ashraf 67, Naseer Shaukat 68; Mohammad Hasnain three for 86) and 95 (Bilal Ahmed 34; Baqar Rizvi five for 50, Mohammad Hasnain four for 20); Karachi Blues* 153 (Ameer-ud-Din 72; Fazal Hussain seven for 41) and 148 (Tahir Mahmood 34, Rashid Latif 53; Nadeem Afzal three for 23, Saadat Gul four for 40). *Faisalabad 10 pts.*

At National Stadium, Karachi, November 30, December 1, 2, 3. Drawn. Rawalpindi* 320 for nine (Saleem Taj 31, Sabih Azhar 54, Ghaffar Kazmi 54, Shahid Javed 45, Naseer Ahmed 55; Asif Mujtaba five for 76) and 287 (Arif Butt 91, Ghaffar Kazmi 36, Naseer Ahmed 74, Extras 42; Asif Mujtaba five for 47, Sohail Mehdi four for 95); Karachi Whites 310 for nine (Aamer Hanif 65, Asif Mujtaba 105; Shakeel Ahmed four for 94) and 59 for three. *Rawalpindi 5 pts.*

At LCCA Ground, Lahore, November 30, December 1, 2, 3. Drawn. Lahore City 131 (Shahid Saeed 47, Ali Zia 45; Masood Anwar five for 12) and 374 for three (Shahid Saeed 161, Aamer Malik 87, Ali Zia 55 not out, Ashraf Ali 56 not out); Multan* 318 for eight (Mohammad Shafiq 37, Manzoor Elahi 77, Tariq Mahboob 80, Raja Arshad 47; Tanvir Mehdi four for 76). *Multan 5 pts.*

At Arbab Niaz Stadium, Peshawar, November 30, December 1, 2, 3. Drawn. Sargodha 122 (Mohammad Hasnain 30; Farrukh Zaman four for 59, Shahid Hussain six for 40) and 149 for seven (Mohammad Hasnain 35, Mohammad Nawaz 42; Kabir Khan three for 35); Peshawar* 176 (Zafar Sarfraz 35, Wasim Yousufi 64 not out; Naeem Khan five for 52). *Peshawar 5 pts.*

At Bahawal Stadium, Bahawalpur, December 7, 8. Karachi Whites won by eight wickets. Bahawalpur 102 (Iqbal Sikandar seven for 34) and 155 (Abdul Rahim 45; Iqbal Sikandar seven for 60); Karachi Whites* 227 (Ghulam Ali 48, Asif Mujtaba 72, Mansoor Akhtar 34; Mohammad Altaf three for 50, Abdul Rahim three for 30) and 31 for two. *Karachi Whites 10 pts.*

At Iqbal Stadium, Faisalabad, December 7, 8, 9, 10. Drawn. Sargodha 180 (Asad Malik 68, Naeem Khan 34; Saadat Gul five for 52, Naseer Shaukat three for 51) and 273 (Mohammad Nawaz 45, Sajjad Akbar 58 not out, Azhar Sultan 60; Saadat Gul three for 77, Naved Nazir five for 64); Faisalabad* 233 (Mohammad Ramzan 31, Shahid Nawaz 112; Pervez Shah three for 39) and 53 for two. *Faisalabad 5 pts.*

At LCCA Ground, Lahore, December 7, 8, 9, 10. Drawn. Lahore City* 334 for four (Ahmad Munir 42, Aamer Malik 132 not out, Mansoor Rana 85; Haaris Khan three for 91) and 319 (Ahmad Munir 36, Tariq Javed 37, Aamer Malik 42, Kashif Khan 47, Ashraf Ali 87; Nadeem Khan five for 128, Haaris Khan four for 86); Karachi Blues 338 for three (Iqbal Saleem 172 not out, Munir-ul-Haq 111; Nadeem Ghauri three for 105) and 188 for five (Ameer-ud-Din 54, Iqbal Saleem 75, Munir-ul-Haq 36; Nadeem Ghauri four for 57). *Karachi Blues 5 pts.*

At KRL Cricket Ground, Rawalpindi, December 7, 8, 9. Rawalpindi won by ten wickets. Peshawar* 165 (Zafar Sarfraz 37; Raja Afaq five for 59, Shakeel Ahmed four for 34) and 91 (Shakeel Ahmed six for 35); Rawalpindi 229 (Mujahid Hameed 30, Naseer Ahmed 77, Raja Afaq 31; Arshad Khan four for 63, Shahid Hussain four for 66) and 30 for no wkt. *Rawalpindi 10 pts.*

At National Stadium, Karachi, December 14, 15, 16, 17. Drawn. Karachi Whites 244 (Azam Khan 35, Aamer Hanif 30, Iqbal Sikandar 51, Mohsin Mirza 44 not out; Aamer Bashir three for 36, Masood Anwar three for 64, Nadeem Nazar three for 46) and 362 (Ghulam Ali 71, Mansoor Akhtar 182; Aamer Bashir three for 68); Multan* 360 for nine (Zahoor Elahi 148, Tariq Mahboob 80, Extras 32; Aamer Hanif six for 125) and 26 for no wkt. *Multan 5 pts.*

At LCCA Ground, Lahore, December 14, 15, 16, 17. Drawn. Lahore City* 246 (Fayyaz Shah 39, Shahid Saeed 35, Kashif Khan 92 not out; Tanvir Afzal three for 68, Naved Nazir four for 68) and 257 for seven dec. (Shahid Saeed 49, Tariq Javed 75, Ali Zia 55, Ashraf Ali 34; Tanvir Afzal three for 76); Faisalabad 210 (Mohammad Ashraf 36, Sami-ul-Haq 62 not out, Ijaz Ahmed 37; Tanvir Mehdi three for 63) and 87 for six (Mohammad Asif three for 18). *Lahore City 5 pts.*

At Arbab Niaz Stadium, Peshawar, December 14, 15, 16, 17. Drawn. Peshawar 186 (Nasir Khan 47; Imran Adil three for 41, Mohammad Altaf four for 45); Bahawalpur* 257 (Shakeel Ahmed 84, Shahid Anwar 48, Extras 41; Arshad Khan five for 98, Farrukh Zaman five for 94). *Bahawalpur 5 pts.*

At Sargodha Stadium, Sargodha, December 14, 15, 16, 17. Sargodha won by 54 runs. Sargodha 194 (Mohammad Nawaz 40; Sabih Azhar five for 69, Naeem Akhtar four for 64) and 84 (Sabih Azhar six for 40, Jamal Siddiqi three for 23; Rawalpindi* 103 (Naeem Khan seven for 42, Pervez Shah three for 42) and 121 (Arif Butt 30; Naeem Khan three for 43, Mohammad Hasnain five for 28). *Sargodha 10 pts.*

Semi-finals

At National Stadium, Karachi, December 21, 22, 23, 24. Karachi Whites won by nine wickets. Bahawalpur 161 (Murtaza Hussain 37 not out; Athar Laeeq five for 69, Humayun Hussain four for 51) and 291 (Shakeel Ahmed 36, Mohammad Tayyab 34, Imran Zia 55, Bilal Rana 42, Murtaza Hussain 34; Athar Laeeq three for 73, Humayun Hussain three for 81); Karachi Whites* 297 (Azam Khan 109, Asif Mujtaba 76; Mohammad Altaf three for 58) and 157 for one (Ghulam Ali 94, Azam Khan 47 not out).

At Gaddafi Stadium, Lahore, December 21, 22, 23, 24. Drawn. Lahore City were declared winners by virtue of their first-innings lead. Lahore City 371 for six (Shahid Saeed 64, Tariq Javed 80, Aamer Malik 84, Maqsood Rana 41, Ali Zia 61 not out; Sabih Azhar three for 165) and 254 for five (Tariq Javed 72, Aamer Malik 64, Mansoor Rana 70 not out); Rawalpindi* 201 (Naeem Akhtar 57, Sabih Azhar 47; Tanvir Mehdi three for 79, Ali Zia three for 46, Shahid Khan three for 5).

Final

At National Stadium, Karachi, December 27, 28, 29, 30, 31. Drawn. Karachi Whites were declared winners by virtue of their first-innings lead. Karachi Whites 364 (Ghulam Ali 164, Aamer Hanif 121; Shahid Khan three for 85, Mohammad Afzal four for 51) and 306 (Moin-ul-Atiq 88, Mansoor Akhtar 71, Amjad Butt 39; Tanvir Mehdi three for 62, Shahid Khan four for 54); Lahore City* 288 (Fayyaz Shah 79, Ali Zia 56, Ashraf Ali 61; Athar Laeeq five for 119, Humayun Hussain three for 92) and 43 for no wkt.

QUAID-E-AZAM TROPHY WINNERS

1953-54	Bahawalpur	1975-76	National Bank
1954-55	Karachi	1976-77	United Bank
1956-57	Punjab	1977-78	Habib Bank
1957-58	Bahawalpur	1978-79	National Bank
1958-59	Karachi	1979-80	PIA
1959-60	Karachi	1980-81	United Bank
1961-62	Karachi Blues	1981-82	National Bank
1962-63	Karachi A	1982-83	United Bank
1963-64	Karachi Blues	1983-84	National Bank
1964-65	Karachi Blues	1984-85	United Bank
1966-67	Karachi	1985-86	Karachi
1968-69	Lahore	1986-87	National Bank
1969-70	PIA	1987-88	PIA
1970-71	Karachi Blues	1988-89	ADBP
1972-73	Railways	1989-90	PIA
1973-74	Railways	1990-91	Karachi Whites
1974-75	Punjab A	1991-92	Karachi Whites

BCCP PATRON'S TROPHY, 1991-92

	Played	Won	Lost	Drawn	Abandoned	1st-inns lead in drawn match	Points
Habib Bank	7	2	0	5	0	3	35
National Bank	7	1	1	5	0	4	30
United Bank	6	2	2	2	1	2	30
PACO	7	2	1	4	0	1	25
PIA	5	1	1	3	2	2	25*
ADBP	6	1	0	5	1	2	20
PNSC	6	0	0	6	1	2	10
Combined Universities	6	0	4	2	1	0	0

* *PIA were awarded 10 points instead of 5 after their protest against Habib Bank.*

Win = 10 pts; 1st-innings lead in a drawn match = 5 pts.

Final: *Habib Bank beat National Bank by virtue of their first-innings lead.*

Note: First innings closed at 85 overs in all the matches except the final.

At National Stadium, Karachi, January 4, 5, 6. PACO won by eight wickets. United Bank 271 (Mansoor Akhtar 74, Pervez Shah 49, Rashid Latif 51, Tauseef Ahmed 38; Fakharuddin Baloch three for 81) and 147 (Aamer Bashir 45, Pervez Shah 47; Shahid Mahboob three for 39, Fakharuddin Baloch four for 45); PACO* 303 for three (Ghulam Ali 136, Aamer Hanif 104 not out) and 116 for two (Shahid Saeed 55 not out). *PACO 10 pts.*

At Aga Khan Gymkhana Ground, Karachi, January 4, 5, 6, 7. PIA v PNSC. Abandoned without a ball bowled, owing to rain.

At Gaddafi Stadium, Lahore, January 4, 5, 6. National Bank won by eight wickets. Combined Universities 102 (Idrees Baig 32; Barkatullah four for 52, Habib Baloch six for 48) and 336 (Ahmad Munir 36, Mujahid Jamshed 149, Idrees Baig 33, Asadullah Butt 30, Extras 34; Barkatullah three for 94); National Bank* 300 (Sajid Ali 39, Shahid Anwar 81, Ameer Akbar 56; Shahid Ali Khan three for 35) and 142 for two (Sajid Ali 68, Shahid Anwar 62 not out). *National Bank 10 pts.*

At Jinnah Stadium, Sialkot, January 4, 5, 6, 7. Drawn. ADBP 250 (Mansoor Rana 76, Saeed Anwar 44; Naved Anjum three for 59, Nadeem Ghauri five for 69) and 59 for two; Habib Bank* 267 (Shakeel Ahmed 64, Agha Zahid 46, Shahid Javed 37; Qasim Shera five for 52). *Habib Bank 5 pts.*

At Iqbal Stadium, Faisalabad, January 11, 12, 13, 14. PIA won by nine wickets. PACO 246 (Shahid Saeed 89, Shahid Nawaz 62; Asif Mujtaba five for 38, Zahid Ahmed three for 78) and 121 (Ghulam Ali 55; Iqbal Sikandar five for 29); PIA* 288 (Rizwan-uz-Zaman 52, Aamer Malik 104, Asif Mujtaba 35, Iqbal Sikandar 30; Shahid Mahboob seven for 109) and 82 for one (Rizwan-uz-Zaman 44 not out, Aamer Malik 33). *PIA 10 pts.*

At Bagh-e-Jinnah Ground, Lahore, January 11, 12, 13, 14. Drawn. Habib Bank 349 for seven (Aamir Sohail 44, Shakeel Ahmed 31, Moin-ul-Atiq 59, Shaukat Mirza 88, Naved Anjum 52; Asadullah Butt three for 77); Combined Universities* 149 (Idrees Baig 32; Naved Anjum four for 62, Nadeem Ghauri three for 24) and 218 for five (Mujahid Jamshed 85, Rizwan Umar 36, Ahmad Munir 50; Aamir Sohail three for 75). *Habib Bank 5 pts.*

At LCCA Ground, Lahore, January 11, 12, 13, 14. Drawn. ADBP 282 (Saeed Anwar 50, Zahoor Elahi 67, Atif Rauf 30, Manzoor Elahi 42, Javed Hayat 45; Iqbal Qasim six for 78); National Bank* 285 for five (Sajid Ali 64, Shahid Anwar 40, Saeed Azad 97, Ameer Akbar 31; Raja Afaq three for 73). *National Bank 5 pts.*

At Aga Khan Gymkhana Ground, Karachi, January 12, 13, 14, 15. Drawn. United Bank* 343 for five (Saifullah 40, Raees Ahmed 56, Basit Ali 74, Mansoor Akhtar 74, Aamer Bashir 71) and 296 (Saifullah 80, Aamer Bashir 93, Pervez Shah 72; Mohsin Kamal six for 60, including a hat-trick, Zafar Iqbal three for 84); PNSC 259 (Aamer Ishaq 67, Sohail Miandad 126; Masood Anwar three for 74, Raees Ahmed four for 26) and 303 for five (Aamer Ishaq 34, Sohail Miandad 99, Mohammad Javed 60 not out, Nasir Wasti 32). *United Bank 5 pts.*

At Montgomery Biscuit Factory Ground, Sahiwal, January 18, 19, 20, 21. Drawn. PNSC* 333 for eight (Aamer Ishaq 123, Nasir Wasti 71, Mahmood Hamid 63; Shahid Mahboob four for 111) and 409 for five (Aamer Ishaq 56, Nasir Wasti 67, Mahmood Hamid 115 not out, Sajjad Akbar 67 not out); PACO 296 (Ghulam Ali 83, Ayaz Jilani 53; Amin Lakhani seven for 119, Sajjad Akbar three for 106). *PNSC 5 pts.*

At Iqbal Stadium, Faisalabad, January 18, 19, 20, 21. United Bank won by three wickets. PIA 303 for nine (Sajid Khan 53, Aamer Malik 142, Zahid Ahmed 58) and 183 (Tanvir Mehdi five for 58); United Bank* 306 for five (Saifullah 45, Raees Ahmed 46, Basit Ali 107, Mansoor Akhtar 34, Pervez Shah 39 not out; Asif Mujtaba three for 87) and 183 for seven (Basit Ali 96; Zahid Ahmed three for 38, Asif Mujtaba three for 75). *United Bank 10 pts.*

At Gaddafi Stadium, Lahore, January 18, 19, 20. ADBP won by ten wickets. Combined Universities* 89 (Zakir Khan six for 36) and 169 (Aziz-ur-Rehman 39, Idrees Baig 38; Zakir Khan five for 64, Qasim Shera three for 19); ADBP 222 for nine dec. (Zahoor Elahi 42, Ghaffar Kazmi 79 not out, Qasim Shera 30; Asadullah Butt six for 91) and 38 for no wkt. *ADBP 10 pts.*

At LCCA Ground, Lahore, January 18, 19, 20. Habib Bank won by nine wickets. National Bank 151 (Saeed Azad 48, Nadeem Khan 45; Naved Anjum nine for 45) and 298 (Sajid Ali 143, Tahir Shah 54, Nadeem Khan 31; Nadeem Ghauri three for 120, Sarmad Khan six for 121); Habib Bank* 375 (Aamir Sohail 124, Naved Anjum 115, Shahid Javed 71 not out; Barkatullah four for 71, Iqbal Qasim four for 89) and 75 for one (Aamir Sohail 45). *Habib Bank 10 pts.*

At Model Town Ground, Lahore, January 25, 26, 27, 28. Combined Universities v PIA. Abandoned without a ball bowled, owing to rain.

At KRL Ground, Rawalpindi, January 25, 26, 27, 28. United Bank v ADBP. Abandoned without a ball bowled, owing to rain.

At LCCA Ground, Lahore, January 25, 26, 27, 28. Drawn. PACO 161 (Ghulam Ali 57, Kamran Khan 42; Iqbal Qasim four for 44, Hafeez-ur-Rehman three for 44); National Bank* 177 for four (Saeed Azad 32, Shahid Anwar 59, Sajid Ali 49). *National Bank 5 pts.*

At Iqbal Stadium, Faisalabad, January 26, 27, 28, 29. Drawn. PNSC 93 (Mohsin Kamal 35 not out; Naved Anjum five for 58, Naeem Khan five for 25); Habib Bank* 165 for eight (Shaukat Mirza 40 not out; Mohsin Kamal three for 59, Nadeem Afzal four for 81). *Habib Bank 5 pts.*

At Iqbal Stadium, Faisalabad, February 1, 2, 3, 4. Drawn. PNSC* 231 (Farrukh Bari 31, Mohsin Kamal 43, Extras 35; Barkatullah three for 35, Habib Baloch three for 70, Hafeez-ur-Rehman three for 53) and 271 for two (Aamer Ishaq 66, Sohail Miandad 33, Sohail Jaffer 84 not out, Farrukh Bari 45 not out, Extras 43); National Bank 298 (Tahir Shah 62, Shahid Anwar 68, Ameer Akbar 79, Mohammad Jamil 39; Sajjad Akbar six for 118). *National Bank 5 pts.*

At LCCA Ground, Lahore, February 1, 2, 3, 4. United Bank won by an innings and 132 runs. United Bank 279 for six (Raees Ahmed 59, Basit Ali 134); Combined Universities* 93 (Masood Anwar six for 23) and 54 (Tauseef Ahmed four for 24, Masood Anwar six for 24). *United Bank 10 pts.*

At KRL Ground, Rawalpindi, February 1, 2, 3, 4. Drawn. PIA 248 (Sajid Khan 65, Rizwan-uz-Zaman 95; Javed Hayat seven for 81) and 51 for two; ADBP* 248 for nine (Mansoor Rana 93, Ghaffar Kazmi 38, Atif Rauf 31; Iqbal Sikandar five for 85). *PIA 5 pts.* (PIA scored their runs in 82.4 overs to ADBP's 85.)

At Bagh-e-Jinnah Ground, Lahore, February 2, 3, 4, 5. Drawn. PACO 216 (Ghulam Ali 31, Kamran Khan 32, Umar Rasheed 71, Shahid Nawaz 39; Naved Anjum four for 59, Nadeem Ghauri three for 72); Habib Bank* 183 (Agha Zahid 39; Mohammad Zahid four for 47). *PACO 5 pts.*

At LCCA Ground, Lahore, February 8, 9, 10, 11. Drawn. ADBP 287 for seven (Saeed Anwar 46, Zahoor Elahi 90, Atif Rauf 33, Bilal Ahmed 30 not out; Yahya Toor four for 83); PACO* 270 (Kamran Khan 109, Aamer Hanif 52; Javed Hayat six for 104). *ADBP 5 pts.*

At Gaddafi Stadium, Lahore, February 8, 9, 10, 11. Drawn. PNSC 375 (Sohail Miandad 36, Nasir Wasti 134, Mahmood Hamid 84, Mohsin Kamal 35; Asadullah Butt four for 122) and 189 for five dec. (Sohail Miandad 30, Sohail Jaffer 51); Combined Universities* 259 for six (Shafqat Hussain 31, Mujahid Jamshed 79, Aziz-ur-Rehman 50 not out, Asadullah Butt 31 not out; Amin Lakhani three for 112) and 185 for seven (Mujahid Jamshed 46, Aziz-ur-Rehman 35, Asadullah Butt 45; Mohsin Kamal four for 72). *PNSC 5 pts.*

At KRL Ground, Rawalpindi, February 8, 9, 10, 11. Drawn. National Bank 337 for eight (Sajid Ali 53, Ameer Akbar 68, Tahir Shah 89, Shakil Sajjad 32; Zahid Ahmed three for 145); PIA* 240 (Aamer Malik 83, Asif Mohammad 34; Nadeem Khan three for 73, Iqbal Qasim five for 81). *National Bank 5 pts.*

At Iqbal Stadium, Faisalabad, February 8, 9, 10, 11. Habib Bank won by 162 runs. Habib Bank* 357 for seven (Moin-ul-Atiq 65, Shaukat Mirza 139, Shahid Javed 89; Masood Anwar three for 105) and 178 (Moin-ul-Atiq 33, Shahid Javed 32; Tauseef Ahmed seven for 46); United Bank 186 (Saifullah 59, Raees Ahmed 46; Nadeem Ghauri five for 71, Shakil Khan three for 40) and 187 (Raees Ahmed 44, Masood Anwar 56; Naved Anjum four for 68, Nadeem Ghauri four for 51). *Habib Bank 10 pts.*

At Gaddafi Stadium, Lahore, February 15, 16, 17, 18. PACO won by nine wickets. Combined Universities* 295 for six (Mujahid Jamshed 35, Idrees Baig 78, Aziz-ur-Rehman 84 not out, Ahmad Munir 36; Shahid Mahboob four for 94) and 289 (Mujahid Jamshed 117, Idrees Baig 71, Aziz-ur-Rehman, 30, Extras 30; Ata-ur-Rehman eight for 87); PACO 347 for seven (Ghulam Ali 46, Abdullah Khan 90, Umar Rasheed 56, Yahya Toor 51 not out, Sanaullah Khan 31 not out; Asadullah Butt four for 142, Aziz-ur-Rehman three for 55) and 239 for one (Ghulam Ali 102 not out, Abdullah Khan 45, Kamran Khan 56 not out, Extras 36). *PACO 10 pts.*

At LCCA Ground, Lahore, February 15, 16, 17, 18. Drawn. PNSC 282 for nine (Sohail Miandad 67, Farrukh Bari 42, Nasir Wasti 47; Raja Afaq six for 85); ADBP* 285 for three (Zahoor Elahi 121, Mansoor Rana 124 not out). *ADBP 5 pts.*

At National Stadium, Karachi, February 15, 16, 17, 18. Drawn. PIA 255 for nine (Rizwan-uz-Zaman 40, Asif Mujtaba 35, Wasim Haider 32, Asif Mohammad 44; Naved Anjum six for 84) and 294 for five dec. (Rizwan-uz-Zaman 142, Aamer Malik 52; Naved Anjum three for 73); Habib Bank* 191 (Moin-ul-Atiq 43; Ashfaq Ahmed three for 58, Wasim Haider five for 50) and 197 for eight (Shakeel Ahmed 35, Moin-ul-Atiq 50, Tahir Rasheed 31 not out; Ashfaq Ahmed six for 69). *PIA 5 pts (later increased to 10 pts).*

At KRL Ground, Rawalpindi, February 15, 16, 17, 18. Drawn. United Bank* 284 (Raees Ahmed 53, Basit Ali 72, Aamer Bashir 37, Iqbal Imam 50; Nadeem Khan three for 77, Hafeez-ur-Rehman four for 104, Iqbal Qasim three for 50); National Bank 218 (Shahid Anwar 60, Saeed Azad 61; Tauseef Ahmed six for 112, Masood Anwar three for 31). *United Bank 5 pts.*

Final

At Gaddafi Stadium, Lahore, February 23, 24, 25, 26, 27. Drawn. Habib Bank were declared winners by virtue of their first-innings lead. Habib Bank* 379 (Shakeel Ahmed 50, Moin-ul-Atiq 36, Agha Zahid 72, Anwar Miandad 67, Naved Anjum 43, Shahid Javed 30, Extras 33; Iqbal Qasim four for 48) and 390 (Moin-ul-Atiq 40, Shaukat Mirza 141, Naved Anjum 33, Shahid Javed 31, Akram Raza 34; Habib Baloch three for 78, Nadeem Khan three for 113); National Bank 246 (Saeed Azad 51, Tahir Shah 32, Shahid Tanvir 84; Naved Anjum three for 69, Shakil Khan four for 47) and 20 for one.

WILLS CUP, 1991-92

Note: Matches in this section were not first-class.

Semi-finals

At Gaddafi Stadium, Lahore, October 4. Habib Bank won by 132 runs. Habib Bank 323 for six (50 overs) (Ijaz Ahmed 69, Salim Malik 121 not out, Javed Miandad 45); PNSC* 191 for seven (50 overs) (Ramiz Raja 70, Nasir Wasti 34, Sajjad Akbar 35 not out; Naved Anjum three for 19).

At National Stadium, Karachi, October 4. PIA won by seven wickets. PACO 168 (49.2 overs) (Shahid Saeed 77 not out, Sanaullah Khan 35; Zahid Ahmed three for 38); PIA 169 for three (43.2 overs) (Rizwan-uz-Zaman 62, Sagheer Abbas 50 not out).

Final

At Arbab Niaz Stadium, Peshawar, October 11. Habib Bank won by five wickets. PIA 234 for eight (43 overs) (Shoaib Mohammad 74, Zahid Fazal 82; Akram Raza four for 60); Habib Bank* 254 for five (39 overs) (Aamir Sohail 53, Ijaz Ahmed 71, Salim Malik 44, penalty for PIA bowling four overs short 40).

FIFTY YEARS AGO

From WISDEN CRICKETERS' ALMANACK 1943

NOTES ON SEASON 1942 By R. C. Robertson-Glasgow: "Cricket in summer 1942. I have an almost irresistible urge to tax the benevolence of the editor and the patience of the proprietor with the cricket which is England – matches played often in the uniform of Service, at random, at the sudden idea of someone, somewhere, with no scoreboard, a tea-interval of an hour and a half, and umpires who bowled if they happened to feel that way. I had the fortune to take part in several such games, on Sunday afternoons, after we had all discarded those curious little gaiters which illumine the extremities of the Junior Service. In most of them there stood an umpire of long experience and of an integrity that surmounted the not infrequent appeals of his favourite son. His authority was unshakeable: he gave no answers to unofficial questions; and, at the end of a certain match in which he had sent back their best batsman on a somewhat delicate l.b.w. decision, he said to me: 'the secret of umpiring is never to bandy words. Bandy, and you're done.' Only once did this principle tremble. We were using the eight-ball over. Suddenly the scorer, if such he can be termed, shouted to him: 'Nine balls.' 'No,' shouted back the umpire, 'seven'. 'Nine,' resumed the scorer. 'Seven,' reiterated the umpire, 'and, whichever it is, it's a —— odd number, and we're not going to stop on *her*.'"

CRICKET IN SRI LANKA, 1991-92

By GERRY VAIDYASEKERA and IHITHISHAM KAMARDEEN

Sri Lanka's lengthy season was further prolonged by rain, which dominated the entire programme. The P. Saravanamuttu Trophy, the country's leading inter-club competition, sponsored by J & B, also suffered from the weather, but was able to proceed to its four-day final in December. That match, decided by a nine-run first-innings lead because of bad weather, saw Colts win the trophy for the first time in their history. Their beaten opponents, Sinhalese SC, had not finished empty-handed since the closing rounds of the competition became first-class in 1988-89, when they shared the title with Nondescripts.

Colts' success completed the rehabilitation of their captain, Hemantha Devapriya, after serving seven years of a ban for his role in the rebel tour of South Africa in 1982-83. Choosing to bat, he saw his team limp to 93 for five, but then his 64, scored over nearly three and a half hours, inspired their recovery to a respectable 261. Sinhalese SC's top order also struggled, though a brave ninth-wicket stand of 65 between R. S. Jayawardene and Manjula Munasinghe took them within 15 runs of Colts' total. Jayawardene fell after two hours to Duleep Liyanage, named man of the match for his five for 90.

Sinhalese SC undoubtedly suffered from the absence of four stalwarts touring Pakistan, the batsmen Arjuna Ranatunga, Asanka Gurusinha and Marvan Atapattu, who had scored four centuries between them in the first-class rounds, and pace bowler Pramodya Wickremasinghe, who had become the first Sri Lankan to take ten wickets in a first-class innings when he claimed ten for 41 against Kalutara Physical Culture Club in November. Ranatunga's unbeaten 200 against Sebastianites was the only first-class double-century of the competition, though he had also made 231 against Moratuwa and in his next match, against Antonians, reached 100 in 62 balls, during the preliminary rounds. Sinhalese swept through their seven qualifying matches unbeaten, and headed their first-class group of seven with three outright wins and three on first innings. In the same group two clubs making their first appearance in the final rounds, Kurunegala Youth, who had headed the Central League with six successive wins, and Wattala Antonians, performed creditably with two outright victories and a first-innings lead apiece. Colts did not lose a match throughout the competition; their two outright wins owed much to Chaminda Mendis, who scored 177 not out in their innings victory over Kandy Youth (followed by 119 when he next batted, against Nondescripts) and Liyanage, who took 11 for 85 in Colts' nine-wicket win over Moors, and earned a Test place against Australia at the start of the next season.

Those members of Division One who failed to qualify for the first-class rounds played out their own Section B Championship, won by Bloomfield with Nomads as runners-up. Division Two was won by Colombo, who beat Sinhalese SC in the final. The most remarkable performance in that division came from a schoolboy, Anjana Jayasuriya, who hit 339 from 240 balls, with 16 sixes and 27 fours, for Old Anandians against Ambalangoda Rio, adding 472 for the second wicket with Sanjaya Attanayaka. Panadura won Division Three and Nomads took the Hatna Trophy. A new floodlit competition, in which eight clubs were invited to play for the R. Premadasa Challenge Trophy, was won by Tamil Union when they defeated Colts by 37 runs in the Khettarama Stadium in January. Test opener Chandika Hathurusinghe made 88 to set up Tamil Union's 196 for seven in 45 overs, and off-spinner Muttiah Muralitharan took three wickets as Colts were dismissed for 159 with four overs to spare. Tamils added the trophy to the success of their Under-23 team at the very beginning of the season, in May, when Hathurusinghe led them to victory over Sinhalese SC in the final of the GTE Yellow Pages Under-23 Tournament.

In schools cricket Ananda Colombo won the Division One Coca-Cola Trophy, and also the schools' floodlit competition. Russel Arnold, St Peter's left-handed opener, won the batsmen's award, Punnayalantha Abeyguna-sekera of Nalanda the bowlers' and Sajith Fernando of St Anthony's was best all-rounder. At St Anne's College in Kurunegala three brothers, Zameen, Jehan and Roshan Jaymon, all captained various age-group teams, while triplets Dhamika, Danthila and Danthika Dayaratne played for Nalanda Under-13.

In July and August of 1991 the visiting tourists of Pakistan A were much afflicted by rain. All three of their one-day fixtures were washed out, and the three unofficial Tests were drawn. An innings win over Central North Western Provinces Combined XI was the only positive result from five matches played.

In the following scores, * by the name of a team indicates that they won the toss.

P. SARAVANAMUTTU TROPHY, 1991-92

At Panadura Esplanade, Panadura, October 25, 26, 27. Drawn. Kalutara Physical Culture Club 172 (P. Perera 61, L. Karunaratne 34; P. L. A. W. N. Alwis five for 55, K. Dharmasena four for 17) and 55 for one (P. Perera 36 not out); Antonians SC* 249 (N. Wijesuriya 36, G. H. Perera 37, T. P. Kodikara 41, K. Dharmasena 52, C. I. Dunusinghe 70; L. Karunaratne four for 59, K. J. Silva four for 90).

At Maitland Crescent, Colombo, October 25, 26, 27. Drawn. Colombo CC 133 (A. C. Seneviratne 33; A. P. Weerakkody three for 42, R. J. Ratnayake three for 27) and 22 for two; Nondescripts CC* 85 (H. P. Tillekeratne 30; K. I. W. Wijegunawardene seven for 28).

At Havelock Park, Colombo (Colts), October 25, 26, 27. Drawn. Colts CC 347 (C. Mendis 61, N. Ranatunga 81, S. de S. Wijesekera 85; S. D. Anurasiri three for 118, M. V. Deshapriya three for 50); Panadura SC* 219 (S. Jayawardene 35, S. Sooriyarachchi 88; D. K. Liyanage four for 54).

At Braybrook Place, Colombo, October 25, 26, 27. Drawn. Moors SC 90 (P. de Silva five for 32, K. P. J. Warnaweera three for 11) and 16 for no wkt; Galle CC* 72 (Mohamed Zanhar five for 14).

At Maitland Place, Colombo (SSC), October 25, 26, 27. Drawn. Sinhalese SC 354 for three dec. (A. Ranatunga 200 not out, M. S. Atapattu 110 not out) and 176 for six (A. Ranatunga 76, A. H. Wickremaratne 50; S. de Silva four for 54); Sebastianites C and AC* 255 (S. K. Silva 74, N. Abeyratne 48, K. Perera 37; M. B. Halangoda four for 20).

At Maitland Place, Colombo (NCC), October 25, 26, 27. Drawn. Tamil Union C and AC 129 (E. Upashantha four for 40, A. W. Ekanayake three for 29) and 57 for four (W. Kumara four for 14); Kurunegala Youth CC* 76 (C. P. H. Ramanayake five for 23, M. Muralitharan three for 13).

At Maitland Crescent, Colombo, November 1, 2, 3. Drawn. Moors SC 149 (G. F. Labrooy three for 35, C. D. C. Edirimanne three for 29) and 100 for four (B. R. Jurangpathy three for 11); Colombo CC* 245 (M. A. R. Samarasekera 68, B. R. Jurangpathy 38, S. T. Jayasuriya 46, A. M. de Silva 35; Riyaz Farook three for 63).

At Campus Grounds, Peradeniya, November 1, 2, 3. Drawn. Nondescripts CC 148 for six (P. A. de Silva 54) v Kandy Youth CC*.

At Tyronne Fernando Stadium, Moratuwa, November 1, 2, 3. Antonians SC won by eight wickets. Old Cambrians SC 180 (S. Priyantha 66; P. L. A. W. N. Alwis four for 40, T. J. Fernando three for 26) and 219 (S. Peiris 40, R. P. Shaman 35, N. Bopage 40; P. L. A. W. N. Alwis five for 74, Nalliah Devarajan three for 44); Antonians SC 346 (G. H. Perera 71, N. Wijesuriya 34, T. P. Kodikara 69, C. I. Dunusinghe 51, K. Dharmasena 57; L. J. Fernando three for 66, A. Bulankulame four for 72) and 57 for two (P. Fernando 31).

At Panadura Esplanade, Panadura, November 1, 2, 3. Drawn. Panadura SC 226 (S. Sooriyarachchi 49, M. Jayasena 41; K. P. J. Warnaweera three for 63) and 177 for five (S. Jayawardene 51, H. Jayasena 45; K. P. J. Warnaweera three for 23); Galle CC* 94 (S. Kodituwakku 35; S. D. Anurasiri four for 17, M. V. Deshapriya five for 22).

At Havelock Park, Colombo, November 1, 2, 3. Kurunegala Youth CC won by eight wickets. Sebastianites C and AC 103 (A. W. Ekanayake four for 29, A. W. R. Madurasinghe four for 30) and 87 (A. W. Ekanayake three for 20, A. W. R. Madurasinghe four for 33); Kurunegala Youth CC* 151 (A. W. R. Madurasinghe 47; A. D. B. Ranjith three for 52, Abdul Jabbar three for 35) and 43 for two.

At P. Saravanamuttu Stadium, Colombo, November 1, 2, 3. Drawn. Tamil Union C and AC 195 (S. Dharmasena 63, K. Baddegama 30, C. P. H. Ramanayake 32; P. Perera three for 44, L. Karunaratne four for 34) and 96 for one (T. M. Wijesinghe 44, U. C. Hathurusinghe 50 not out); Kalutara Physical Culture Club* 112 (P. Peiris 33; U. Chandana four for 11).

At Havelock Park, Colombo (Colts), November 8, 9, 10. Drawn. Galle CC* 189 (G. R. M. A. Perera four for 46, C. D. U. S. Weerasinghe four for 32); Colts CC 345 (C. Mendis 37, D. S. G. Bulankulame 37, S. Ranatunga 87, N. Ranatunga 89; M. Ekanayake three for 72).

At Campus Grounds, Peradeniya, November 8, 9, 10. Drawn. Moors SC 180 (W. Fernando 71; H. N. T. Gamage five for 60) and 91 for three (Mohamed Zanhar 43; S. Madanayake three for 18); Kandy Youth CC* 114 (U. H. Kodituwakku 48 not out; Ishak Shabdeen four for 34, Riyaz Farook three for 26).

At Tyronne Fernando Stadium, Moratuwa, November 8, 9, 10. Tamil Union C and AC won by an innings and 28 runs. Old Cambrians SC 138 (B. P. de Silva 42; C. P. H. Ramanayake four for 59) and 88 (C. P. H. Ramanayake four for 37, M. Muralitharan three for 20, U. Chandana three for eight, including a hat-trick); Tamil Union C and AC* 254 (U. C. Hathurusinghe 73, D. C. Wickremasinghe 39, S. Dharmasena 58, K. Baddegama 41).

At Panadura Esplanade, Panadura, November 8, 9, 10. Drawn. Panadura SC 274 (S. Jayawardene 46, S. Thenuwara 81, S. Sooriyarachchi 46, K. P. J. A. de Silva 30; C. D. C. Edirimanne four for 38, D. C. M. Perera three for 30); Colombo CC* 134 for six (A. M. de Silva 38, A. C. Seneviratne 54 not out; R. Wickremaratne three for 27).

At St Sebastian's College Grounds, Moratuwa, November 8, 9, 10. Sebastianites C and AC won by eight wickets. Kalutara Physical Culture Club 115 (T. Silva 66; A. D. B. Ranjith three for 44, Abdul Jabbar three for 27) and 89 (A. D. B. Ranjith seven for 25); Sebastianites C and AC* 128 (A. D. B. Ranjith 59; P. Perera three for 30, L. Karunaratne four for 41, K. J. Silva three for 37) and 79 for two (S. Fernando 47).

At Maitland Place, Colombo (SSC), November 8, 9, 10. Sinhalese SC won by six wickets. Kurunegala Youth CC* 143 (G. P. Wickremasinghe three for 54; M. B. Halangoda three for 20) and 106 (E. Upashantha 32; G. P. Wickremasinghe four for 37); Sinhalese SC 180 for one dec. (A. A. W. Gunawardene 100 not out, C. N. Fernando 31, A. P. Gurusinha 45 not out) and 73 for four.

At Maitland Crescent, Colombo, November 15, 16, 17. Drawn. Colts CC 294 for seven dec. (D. S. G. Bulankulame 75, S. Ranatunga 36, D. P. Samaraweera 35, H. H. Devapriya 56 not out) v Colombo CC.*

At Maitland Place, Colombo (NCC), November 15, 16, 17. Drawn. Moors SC 124 (M. R. D. Hameen 45; E. A. R. de Silva four for 10); Nondescripts CC* 167 (D. Morris 53; Mohamed Zanhar three for 63, S. Dharmasena three for 40).

At Tyronne Fernando Stadium, Moratuwa, November 15, 16, 17. Drawn. Old Cambrians SC 222 (S. Peiris 67, N. Bopage 73; D. Dias three for 42, A. D. B. Ranjith five for 55); Sebastianites C and AC* 109 for nine (P. Salgado 40 not out; B. P. de Silva three for 30).

At Panadura Esplanade, Panadura, November 15, 16, 17. Drawn. Panadura SC 143 for eight dec. (K. P. J. A. de Silva 34, S. D. Anurasiri 35 not out); Kandy Youth CC* eight for no wkt.

At Maitland Place, Colombo (SSC), November 15, 16, 17. Sinhalese SC won by five wickets. Kalutara Physical Culture Club 82 (S. Warusamana 36 not out; G. P. Wickremasinghe ten for 41) and 183 (T. Silva 57, L. Karunaratne 36; G. P. Wickremasinghe three for 46); Sinhalese SC* 108 for three dec. (A. P. Gurusinha 58 not out, M. S. Atapattu 32 not out; S. Devapriya three for 33) and 160 for five (A. Ranatunga 89 not out, U. N. K. Fernando 31).

At P. Saravanamuttu Stadium, Colombo, November 15, 16, 17. Drawn. Antonians SC 130 (C. P. H. Ramanayake six for 53); Tamil Union C and AC* 274 for three (U. C. Hathurusinghe 95, D. C. Wickremasinghe 35, S. Dharmasena 68 not out, D. N. Nadarajah 36 not out).

At Havelock Park, Colombo (Colts), November 22, 23, 24. Colts CC won by an innings and 100 runs. Colts CC 351 for four dec. (C. Mendis 177 not out, D. S. G. Bulankulame 42, D. P. Samaraweera 46, H. H. Devapriya 50 not out); Kandy Youth CC* 182 (N. Sawall 42, T. A. Miskin 42; D. K. Liyanage four for 21) and 69 (N. Ranatunga four for 29).

At Galle Esplanade, Galle, November 22, 23, 24. Colombo CC won by seven wickets. Galle CC 145 (D. D. Wickremasinghe 33) and 146 (S. Fonseka 92; D. C. M. Perera four for 37); Colombo CC* 182 (M. A. R. Samarasekera 31, B. R. Jurangpathy 47; K. P. J. Warnaweera four for 59) and 110 for three (M. A. R. Samarasekera 45).

At Braybrook Place, Colombo, November 22, 23, 24. Drawn. Kalutara Physical Culture Club 87 (E. Upashantha three for 37, A. W. R. Madurasinghe four for 21); Kurunegala Youth CC* 124 for seven (R. Jaymon 43, E. Upashantha 33; K. J. Silva five for 44).

At Panadura Esplanade, Panadura, November 22, 23, 24. Drawn. Nondescripts CC 143 (N. Kalpage 45; S. D. Anurasiri four for 33) and 57 for two; Panadura SC* 134 (R. Soysa 35, S. Kumara 32; A. P. Weerakkody three for 25, A. K. Kuruppuarachchi three for 30, R. S. Kalpage three for 49).

At St Sebastian's College Ground, Moratuwa, November 22, 23, 24. Sebastianites C and AC won by 190 runs. Sebastianites C and AC 178 (S. K. Silva 34; P. L. A. W. N. Alwis seven for 78) and 211 (S. K. Silva 52; P. L. A. W. N. Alwis five for 68); Antonians SC* 107 (T. P. Kodikara 33; A. D. B. Ranjith five for 32) and 92 (A. D. B. Ranjith five for 33).

At Maitland Place, Colombo (SSC), November 22, 23, 24. Drawn. Old Cambrians SC 193 (P. Bandara 60 not out; G. P. Wickremasinghe four for 76, C. Ranasinghe three for 34) and 191 (S. Peiris 50, C. Perera 33; C. Ranasinghe four for 40, R. S. Jayawardene five for 56); Sinhalese SC* 208 for one dec. (C. N. Fernando 131 not out, A. P. Gurusinha 54 not out) and 165 for no wkt (A. A. W. Gunawardene 55 not out, U. N. K. Fernando 95 not out).

At Campus Grounds, Peradeniya, November 29, 30, December 1. Galle CC won by an innings and three runs. Galle CC* 281 (D. D. Wickremasinghe 102, H. Rajapakse 60; T. N. Samath five for 83); Kandy Youth CC 110 (T. N. Samath 30; K. P. J. Warnaweera three for 20, H. Rajapakse three for 20) and 168 (U. H. Kodituwakku 65; K. P. J. Warnaweera five for 45).

At Braybrook Place, Colombo, November 29, 30, December 1. Panadura SC won by an innings and 34 runs. Moors SC* 89 (R. Wickremaratne three for 32) and 221 (D. Kumarasinghe 56, S. H. U. Karnain 69; M. V. Deshapriya five for 73); Panadura SC 344 for nine dec. (H. Jayasena 60, S. Thenuwara 65, S. Kumara 40, K. P. J. A. de Silva 33, R. Wickremaratne 53; S. H. U. Karnain three for 26).

At Maitland Place, Colombo (NCC), November 29, 30, December 1. Drawn. Colts CC* 259 (C. Mendis 119, M. V. Perera 57; A. P. Weerakkody three for 78, R. J. Ratnayake four for 50) and 176 for two (S. Ranatunga 57 not out, D. P. Samaraweera 54 not out); Nondescripts CC 157 (S. A. R. Silva 47, A. G. D. Wickremasinghe 30; D. K. Liyanage three for 49, N. Ranatunga five for 38).

At Tyronne Fernando Stadium, Moratuwa, November 29, 30, December 1. Kurunegala Youth CC won by an innings and 84 runs. Old Cambrians SC 102 (A. W. Ekanayake six for 38) and 167 (C. Perera 42, P. de Silva 56; A. W. Ekanayake three for 81, A. W. R. Madurasinghe four for 48); Kurunegala Youth CC* 353 (G. W. D. S. A. K. Gunaratne 47, R. Jaymon 55, J. Kulatunge 55, A. W. R. Madurasinghe 83 not out; P. Mendis three for 73).

At Maitland Place, Colombo (SSC), November 29, 30, December 1. Sinhalese SC won by an innings and 87 runs. Antonians SC 200 (P. Fernando 30, T. P. Kodikara 44; G. P. Wickremasinghe six for 71) and 100 (K. Dharmasena 32; G. P. Wickremasinghe five for 34); Sinhalese SC* 387 for six dec. (A. A. W. Gunawardene 80, A. P. Gurusinha 115, A. Ranatunga 101, M. S. Atapattu 54).

At P. Saravanamuttu Stadium, Colombo, November 29, 30, December 1. Drawn. Sebastianites C and AC* 219 (S. K. Silva 40, A. Nissanka 33 not out; C. P. H. Ramanayake three for 60, M. Muralitharan six for 62) and 171 (P. Salgado 40, K. Perera 33; M. Muralitharan three for 52, U. Chandana four for 68); Tamil Union C and AC 239 (T. de Silva 45, D. C. Wickremasinghe 39, U. Chandana 42; D. Dias three for 59, Abdul Jabbar four for 50) and 137 for eight (T. de Silva 32; A. D. B. Ranjith five for 53).

At Reid Avenue, Colombo, December 6, 7, 8. Antonians SC won by 88 runs. Antonians SC 292 (P. Fernando 43, T. P. Kodikara 87, K. Dharmasena 53, P. L. A. W. N. Alwis 35; E. Upashantha three for 92) and 279 for seven dec. (Nalliah Devarajan 101, G. H. Perera 60, C. I. Dunusinghe 57; A. W. Ekanayake three for 113); Kurunegala Youth CC* 193 (R. Jaymon 47; P. L. A. W. N. Alwis four for 32) and 290 (S. Gunawardene 32, D. Amarasena 61, G. W. D. S. A. K. Gunaratne 46, N. Munasinghe 32; T. P. Kodikara three for 75, P. L. A. W. N. Alwis five for 73).

At Havelock Park, Colombo (Colts), December 6, 7, 8. Colts CC won by nine wickets. Moors SC 134 (D. Kumarasinghe 42, M. I. I. Azeez 52; D. K. Liyanage six for 36, G. R. M. A. Perera three for 53) and 149 (S. M. Irfan 70; D. K. Liyanage five for 49, N. Ranatunga four for 39); Colts CC* 260 for eight dec. (C. Mendis 72, S. Ranatunga 40, D. P. Samaraweera 33, D. K. Liyanage 37; S. Dharmasena three for 64) and 25 for one.

At Asgiriya Stadium, Kandy, December 6, 7, 8. Colombo CC won by ten wickets. Kandy Youth CC 132 (M. Perera 33; U. Wijesena three for 43, B. R. Jurangpathy four for 42) and 246 (C. K. Rajapakse 45, T. N. Samath 98, T. A. Miskin 38; G. F. Labrooy three for 51, B. R. Jurangpathy five for 74); Colombo CC* 352 (Praveen Ramanathan 127, B. R. Jurangpathy 62, A. S. Hashim 67; T. N. Samath four for 155) and 28 for no wkt.

At Maitland Place, Colombo (NCC), December 6, 7, 8. Nondescripts CC won by three wickets. Galle CC* 133 (S. M. Faumi 32, G. Lanka 57; A. P. Weerakkody five for 62) and 274 (D. D. Wickremasinghe 61, H. Rajapakse 80; R. S. Kalpage five for 51); Nondescripts CC 222 for nine dec. (S. Weerasinghe 37, S. A. R. Silva 36; K. P. J. Warnaweera six for 65) and 188 for seven (S. Weerasinghe 58; K. P. J. Warnaweera four for 70).

At Tyronne Fernando Stadium, Moratuwa, December 6, 7, 8. Old Cambrians SC won by five wickets. Old Cambrians SC 447 (S. Peiris 68, R. P. Shaman 98, C. Perera 47, B. P. de Silva 46, L. J. Fernando 48, P. de Silva 32, G. Gunasena 39; P. Perera four for 99, K. J. Silva three for 149) and 110 for five (S. Peiris 32; K. J. Silva three for 38); Kalutara Physical Culture Club* 147 (B. P. de Silva five for 58) and 406 (K. Mendis 34, M. Hemantha 163, S. Warusamana 32, P. Perera 112 not out).

At Maitland Place, Colombo (SSC), December 6, 7, 8. Drawn. Sinhalese SC 531 (A. A. W. Gunawardene 56, S. L. Anthonisz 82, U. N. K. Fernando 41, A. H. Wickremaratne 61, C. N. Fernando 96, C. Ranasinghe 64, M. B. Halangoda 71; R. K. B. Amunugama three for 77) and 214 for five (A. A. W. Gunawardene 78, A. H. Wickremaratne 46); Tamil Union C and AC* 208 (D. N. Nadarajah 87 not out, U. Gunasena 30; F. S. Ahangama three for 40, P. K. Wijetunge three for 44).

Final

At P. Saravanamuttu Stadium, Colombo, December 12, 13, 14, 15. Drawn. Colts CC won by virtue of their first-innings lead. Colts CC* 261 (C. Mendis 35, D. P. Samaraweera 55, H. H. Devapriya 64; F. S. Ahangama five for 55, M. Munasinghe three for 78); Sinhalese SC 252 (U. N. K. Fernando 30, C. N. Fernando 47, R. S. Jayawardene 50; D. K. Liyanage five for 90, N. Ranatunga three for 88).

It has not been possible to obtain reliable scores of other first-class competitions in Sri Lanka. They have accordingly been held over.

PAKISTAN A IN SRI LANKA, 1991-92

At Matara, July 21, 22, 23. Drawn. Toss: Pakistan A. Pakistan A 136 (Aamir Sohail 56; R. Palliyaguru four for 37, J. A. Mahindaratne three for 17, K. Ratnaweera three for 10) and 135 for two (Aamir Sohail 50, Inzamam-ul-Haq 62 not out); Southern Province XI 156 for eight dec. (H. Premasiri 31, S. M. Faumi 30; Iqbal Sikandar four for 37).

At Maitland Place, Colombo (SSC), July 25, 26, 27, 28. Drawn. Toss: Pakistan A. Pakistan A 304 (Aamir Hanif 76, Saeed Anwar 61; G. P. Wickremasinghe three for 74, R. S. Kalpage three for 52) and 198 for seven dec. (Ghulam Ali 40, Aamir Hanif 44, Athar Laeeq 32 not out; R. S. Kalpage three for 36); Sri Lanka A 262 (R. S. Kalpage 113, C. D. C. Edirimanne 30; Aamir Sohail three for 34) and 23 for no wkt.

At Welagedera Stadium, Kurunegala, July 30, 31, August 1, 2. Drawn. Toss: Pakistan A. Pakistan A 172 for two dec. (Aamir Sohail 78, Ghulam Ali 69); Sri Lanka A 42 for one.

At Asgiriya Stadium, Kandy, August 5, 6, 7. Pakistan A won by an innings and 29 runs. Toss: Pakistan A. Central-North Western Provinces Combined XI 160 (R. Jaymon 67; Athar Laeeq three for 33, Tanvir Mehdi three for 13) and 168 (R. Jaymon 53, S. Senanayake 32; Athar Laeeq five for 23); Pakistan A 357 (Inzamam-ul-Haq 48, Aamer Hanif 33, Saeed Anwar 110, Moin Khan 66; A. W. Ekanayake five for 128).

At Maitland Place, Colombo (SSC), August 9, 10, 11, 12. Drawn. Toss: Sri Lanka A. Sri Lanka A 291 (T. M. Wijesinghe 43, D. Ranatunga 53, A. H. Wickremaratne 55, R. S. Kalpage 30, M. B. Halangoda 35; Iqbal Sikandar five for 48) and 92 for four (D. C. Wickremasinghe 34 not out); Pakistan A 227 (Aamir Sohail 100, Aamer Hanif 37, Saeed Anwar 37; G. P. Wickremasinghe four for 70, P. K. Wijetunge four for 26).

CRICKET IN ZIMBABWE, 1991-92

By MARK WILLIAMS

In their last season as an Associate Member of ICC before attaining Test status, Zimbabwe had a busy programme, culminating in the World Cup in Australia and New Zealand. If the tour by an Australian XI in September provided the most testing cricket, the highlight of the home season was the one-day international against South Africa at the Harare Sports Club in early February. Although Zimbabwe lost by six wickets the result seemed secondary to the occasion, which marked the restoration of cricketing relations between the countries and was attended by a packed crowd. The subsequent World Cup campaign was not as successful as the Zimbabweans had hoped – the batting falling short of expectations. But they came within a whisker of beating Sri Lanka, had victory over India in their sights when the rain came and lowered England's colours at Albury. Few would have predicted a better balance sheet.

Australia did Zimbabwe the honour of sending a strong side, including current Test players Mark Taylor, Steve Waugh and Tom Moody. The Australians won the two first-class matches in Bulawayo and Harare with some ease but the one-day series was decided, 2-1 in Australia's favour, in the last over of the final game. For the Australians, Steve Waugh was in his most felicitous touch, scoring two centuries in the one-day internationals and a third in the four-day match at Bulawayo, when a partnership of 240 with Tom Moody on the first day put Australia in an impregnable position and set a third-wicket record for first-class games in Zimbabwe. Australia's best bowling return came from leg-spinner Shane Warne, whose seven for 49 wrapped up Zimbabwe's second innings in the four-day match in Harare. For Zimbabwe, Grant Flower's two innings of 74 and 84 provided the only gleams of light in a lacklustre batting performance in Bulawayo. In Harare, David Houghton similarly held the batting together with undefeated scores of 105 and 57.

The second half of the season was dominated by the visit of Durham, on a tour designed to let their new staff get to know each other before their first season of first-class county cricket. Barely out of their aircraft, they were brushed aside twice in one-day games by the full Zimbabwe XI on the eve of their departure for the World Cup. But Durham's subsequent exposure to Zimbabwe's second echelon players benefited all parties. By the time they departed Durham were beginning to show that they would be no pushover in the English game. Of their remaining five one-day matches, they won three; and they performed particularly well in their longer games, beating Zimbabwe by an innings over four days and registering one win and almost completing a second in their two three-day matches.

Domestically, the season was a triumph for Old Georgians, who won all three major trophies – the Logan Cup and the Rothmans National League and Knockout. Their success owed much to the Flower brothers, Andy and Grant, to Mark Burmester, the season's leading wicket-taker, and to Gavin Briant, the leading run-scorer, who was unlucky not to join the others in the World Cup squad. Looking to the future, the Zimbabwe Schools side toured Australia and Hong Kong with great success under Jonathan Bourdillon's mature captaincy and the management of Clive Barnes, headmaster of

Prince Edward School. Encouraging performances came from batsman Stuart Carlisle and bowlers Sean Davies and George Thandi, the latter a product of the Zimbabwe Cricket Union's Development Programme. In addition, 15-year-old Gavin Rennie looked to be a cricketer of rare talent.

To round affairs off, Harare hosted a happy cricketing occasion during the Commonwealth Heads of Government Conference in October, which gave its seal of approval to South Africa's admission to the World Cup. Clive Lloyd, Graeme Hick and David Houghton joined the British Prime Minister John Major, Bob Hawke of Australia, Nawaz Sharif of Pakistan and other leaders in scoring runs for charity in front of a large and appreciative crowd at the Harare Sports Club.

FIRST-CLASS MATCHES, 1991-92

Australian XI in Zimbabwe

At Bulawayo, September 16, 17, 18, 19. Australian XI won by ten wickets. Toss: Zimbabwe. Australian XI 483 (M. A. Taylor 31, T. M. Moody 141, S. R. Waugh 119, M. G. Bevan 54, P. R. Reiffel 54 not out, D. J. Hickey 32; M. P. Jarvis three for 112, A. H. Shah four for 113) and 20 for no wkt; Zimbabwe 193 (G. W. Flower 74, A. D. R. Campbell 35; P. R. Reiffel four for 34, D. J. Hickey three for 46) and 309 (K. J. Arnott 60, G. W. Flower 84, A. J. Pycroft 30, S. G. Peall 41 not out; P. R. Reiffel five for 43, S. K. Warne three for 76).

At Harare, September 21, 23, 24, 25. Australian XI won by nine wickets. Toss: Zimbabwe. Zimbabwe 239 (K. J. Arnott 31, D. L. Houghton 105 not out, M. P. Jarvis 33; D. J. Hickey five for 72, P. E. McIntyre four for 42) and 179 (K. J. Arnott 47, D. L. Houghton 57 not out; S. K. Warne seven for 49); Australian XI 383 (M. A. Taylor 41, T. M. Moody 85, S. G. Law 94, R. J. Tucker 62, S. K. Warne 35 not out; E. A. Brandes six for 95) and 36 for one.

OTHER MATCHES, 1991-92

Durham in Zimbabwe

At Harare, February 3. Zimbabwe won by 123 runs. Toss: Durham. Zimbabwe 274 for four (50 overs) (W. R. James 37, A. Flower 90, A. J. Pycroft 83 not out); Durham 151 for eight (50 overs) (J. D. Glendenen 41; M. P. Jarvis four for 17).

At Harare, February 4. Zimbabwe won by two wickets. Toss: Durham. Durham 206 for four (50 overs) (J. D. Glendenen 49, P. Bainbridge 64, G. K. Brown 39 not out); Zimbabwe 207 for eight (49 overs) (A. C. Waller 47, D. L. Houghton 35, A. H. Shah 42 not out).

At Harare, February 6. Durham won by six wickets. Toss: Zimbabwe Under-19 XI. Zimbabwe Under-19 XI 152 (47.1 overs) (S. G. Davies 41; G. Wigham three for 10, G. K. Brown three for 26); Durham 155 for four (46 overs) (M. P. Briers 63 not out, P. W. Henderson 36 not out).

At Harare, February 8. Durham won by one run. Toss: Zimbabwe Country Districts. Durham 200 for seven (50 overs) (J. A. Daley 45, P. W. G. Parker 36 not out); Zimbabwe Country Districts 199 for seven (50 overs) (M. H. Dekker 67, G. A. Paterson 32, G. J. Crocker 31).

At Harare, February 9. Zimbabwe XI won by 13 runs. Toss: Zimbabwe XI. Zimbabwe XI 200 for six (50 overs) (E. A. Essop-Adam 34, G. J. Whittal 41, G. J. Crocker 31 not out, J. A. Rennie 34 not out); Durham 187 (48.5 overs) (G. K. Brown 51, I. Smith 41; J. A. Rennie three for 45).

At Mutare, February 11, 12, 13. Durham won by seven wickets. Toss: Manicaland Select XI. Manicaland Select XI 220 (M. H. Dekker 43, J. P. Brent 52; G. Wigham four for 36, D. A. Graveney four for 39) and 286 for two dec. (N. P. Hough 200 not out, M. H. Dekker 40 not out); Durham 300 for seven dec. (P. W. G. Parker 39, P. Bainbridge 52, M. P. Briers 74, I. Smith 69; S. G. Peall three for 76, P. A. Strang three for 40) and 209 for three (W. Larkins 119, I. Smith 55 not out).

At Harare, February 16. President's XI won by nine wickets. Toss: President's XI. Durham 120 (45 overs) (I. Smith 33; J. D. Gibson three for 32); President's XI 121 for one (39.5 overs) (S. Dudhia 65 not out, E. A. Essop-Adam 31 not out).

At Harare, February 18, 19, 20, 21. Durham won by an innings and 90 runs. Toss: Durham. Zimbabwe B 230 (N. P. Hough 31, G. J. Whittal 30, J. A. Rennie 84, S. G. Peall 46; P. W. Henderson five for 51, including a hat-trick, S. J. E. Brown four for 45) and 127 (P. J. Berry four for 47); Durham 447 for six dec. (J. D. Glendenen 51, S. Hutton 143, G. K. Brown 65, P. W. G. Parker 100 not out, P. J. Berry 51 not out).

At Bulawayo, February 23. Durham won by four wickets. Toss: Durham. Zimbabwe XI 144 (47.5 overs) (M. H. Dekker 42, G. J. Whittal 34; D. A. Graveney three for 22); Durham 147 for six (35.5 overs) (W. Larkins 69, J. D. Glendenen 37; H. Streak five for 19).

At Bulawayo, February 24, 25, 26. Drawn. Toss: Durham. Durham 316 for six dec. (M. P. Briers 132 not out, C. W. Scott 47, W. Larkins 71; D. H. Brain three for 73) and 202 for four dec. (S. Hutton 54, M. P. Briers 30 retired hurt, P. Bainbridge 79 not out); Zimbabwe XI 262 for six dec. (G. J. Crocker 63 not out, G. C. Martin 61, D. H. Brain 49 not out; D. A. Graveney three for 81) and 205 for nine (S. G. Peall 36, M. H. Dekker 66, S. V. Carlisle 34; D. A. Graveney three for 25, P. J. Berry four for 58).

ZIMBABWE v SOUTH AFRICA

Unofficial One-day International

At Harare, February 5. South Africa won by six wickets. Toss: South Africa.

Zimbabwe

W. R. James run out	27
†A. Flower b Donald	5
A. D. R. Campbell b Donald	0
A. J. Pycroft c Richardson b Bosch	21
*D. L. Houghton c Cronje b Henry	14
A. C. Waller c Richardson b Bosch	27
A. H. Shah c Richardson b Donald	11
I. P. Butchart lbw b Cronje	10
E. A. Brandes not out	14
A. J. Traicos c Richardson b Pringle	4
M. P. Jarvis run out	7
L-b 5, w 19, n-b 6	30
1/20 2/20 3/54 (49.3 overs)	170
4/81 5/83 6/107	
7/134 8/134 9/158	

Bowling: Donald 10-2-29-3; Pringle 10-0-35-1; Bosch 9.3-0-44-2; Kuiper 6-1-12-0; Henry 10-1-27-1; Cronje 4-0-18-1.

South Africa

*K. C. Wessels lbw b Brandes	19
A. C. Hudson c Flower b Brandes	8
P. N. Kirsten c Shah b Traicos	64
W. J. Cronje c Waller b Shah	47
A. P. Kuiper not out	23
J. N. Rhodes not out	1
L-b 4, w 4, n-b 1	9
1/21 2/30 (4 wkts, 49.2 overs)	171
3/129 4/166	

†D. J. Richardson, O. Henry, M. W. Pringle, T. Bosch and A. A. Donald did not bat.

Bowling: Brandes 10-3-26-2; Jarvis 10-1-29-0; Shah 10-1-32-1; Butchart 10-0-32-0; Traicos 9-0-43-1; Houghton 0.2-0-5-0.

Umpires: K. Kanjee and I. D. Robinson.

CRICKET IN DENMARK, 1992

By PETER S. HARGREAVES

Were it not for two decisive defeats against Holland at the end of July in Utrecht, the Danish national side would have had a satisfactory season. The Danes won the first of two matches against Wales in Copenhagen convincingly and only lost the second in a cliff-hanger. Three clear wins were then recorded against less testing opposition in North-East London – to raise the question of what had changed since the two close matches against Holland in 1991.

At least three factors contributed to the Dutch victories – the addition of yet another strong, imported professional batsman to the home side in the person of the Australian Peter Cantrell, the absence of the best Danish all-rounder Søren Henriksen and, in the second encounter, some badly planned tactical Danish batting. All this led to Denmark's worst performance against their chief rivals since 1969. On this evidence much thinking, as well as work, will be necessary for the Danish side before the 1994 ICC Trophy in Kenya.

There was better news from the Under-19 national team, which looked highly promising as it approached the International Youth Tournament to be held in 1993 in North Jutland. They easily beat the visiting team from Trent College, they pushed hard against a strong Under-23 combination from the Durham Coast League and only just failed to repeat their 1991 defeat of Sweden, whose national team is improving. The potential is definitely there.

In the domestic programme Svanholm did the double by winning the national knockout cup competition early in the season and then going through unbeaten, to claim the Danish championship ahead of Glostrup and Esbjerg. At the foot of the table AB – after finishing third in both 1990 and 1991 – had a luckless season and will change places with Skanderborg, from the second division, in 1993. Skanderborg finished behind Glostrup's second team, who could not be given promotion.

Steen Anker Nielsen had the highest batting aggregate, with 1,088 runs. Søren Westergaard headed the bowling with 51 wickets at 12 apiece; Westergaard is fast developing as an all-rounder and he finished just ahead of Henriksen in the averages. Svanholm and Glostrup bowlers filled the first six places.

The Under-18 final was won by Svanholm, the Under-15 by Ishøj, and the Lilleput Under-13 by Chang-Aalborg who beat Albertslund, like Ishøj a Copenhagen Pakistani club, which shows that their next generation have plenty of good material.

CRICKET IN THE NETHERLANDS, 1992

By DAVID HARDY

Dutch cricketers will remember 1992 not so much for any events on the field but for two decisions off it. Firstly, the award of Test status to Zimbabwe, to whom Holland had lost the two previous finals of the ICC Trophy, cleared a route for Holland to compete in the next World Cup, especially as it was decided to allow three non-Test countries to take part. Secondly, the Dutch Cricket Association began to look at the possibility of creating the country's first turf wickets by 1994. That would enhance Dutch chances of being allowed into one of the English one-day competitions.

The Dutch again had a visit from a Test nation that had just finished touring England. The Pakistanis played the national team (without any of its English professionals) at The Hague, failed to take the match very seriously – Waqar Younis opened and Aqib Javed batted at No. 5 – and were lucky to escape with a seven-run win.

At the start of the season the national team toured the English counties, losing by only nine runs to Sussex but more comprehensively in two games against Somerset: by 115 and 132 runs. The Hampshire match was rained off. In August, the old European enemy Denmark were thrashed twice in Utrecht, by eight wickets – with 97 not out from the Australian Peter Cantrell – and 181 runs, with 81 from Rob Vos and 80 from Clarke. Cantrell, at 29, has settled in Holland, given up all ambitions at home and committed himself to the Dutch team.

Kampong, the Utrecht club, won the Premier League championship for the third time in five years. Cantrell broke his own league record by scoring 1,197 runs, including five centuries, at an average of 85.50. The return to the team of Ron Elferink, probably Holland's best all-rounder, was also vital.

Two of Holland's best-known players, Nolan Clarke and Steven Lubbers, caused a surprise by exchanging clubs. Clarke, the 44-year-old Barbadian, returned to his old team Koninklijke UD. The move revived him: he scored 1,145 runs at 71.56 and six centuries. Lubbers took Clarke's place with Hermes DVS in Schiedam and continued to score runs, take wickets and captain the national team with aplomb – though he still bats too low in the order. Batsmen dominated the league with a record 28 centuries. There were only three hauls of five wickets in an innings – matches are in a 60-over format and bowlers are restricted to 15 overs, which may be hurting them. The leading wicket-takers were Tim Zoehrer of Excelsior, the former Australian Test wicket-keeper, and Kenny Jackson, Voorburg's South African, but they had only 40 each. Ewout de Man of VRA Amstelveen had the best average, with 16.11.

THE NETHERLANDS v PAKISTANIS

At The Hague CC, August 30 (not first-class). Pakistanis won by seven runs. Pakistanis 192 (32.2 overs) (Mushtaq Ahmed 36, Inzamam-ul-Haq 49, Wasim Akram 35; P. Groeneveld three for 52); The Netherlands 185 for five (35 overs) (P. E. Cantrell 34, R. Vos 52, N. E. Clarke 50 not out).

CRICKET ROUND THE WORLD

BELGIUM

Antwerp emerged as worthy winners of the nine-team Belgian League in 1992, although Royal Brussels and Belgian Pakistanis fought them all the way. The climax of the league came in early August when Royal Brussels met Antwerp needing only a draw to secure the title. However, after being put in to bat, they could only score 117 for nine off 50 overs and Antwerp cruised home by seven wickets. Derek Underwood, Antwerp's president, watched the match. An increasing number of born-and-bred Belgians are taking up the game – four of them have so far played for the national team – and the Belgian Cricket Federation's main problem is finding a qualified coach to help them. Mechelen and Mechelen Eagles consist mostly of Belgians and need to be encouraged. Unfortunately, the cost is a major drawback. Many touring clubs have visited Belgium; this has helped improve the standard and, of course, the bar takings. Any teams wishing to tour should contact the BCF secretary, Colin Wolfe, Rue de l'Eglise St Martin 12, B-1390 Biez. – Ken Farmiloe.

BERMUDA

Bermuda's cricket season, which normally runs from April to September, began early in 1992 because of the visit of the England A team *en route* to the West Indies. The touring professionals set welcome standards of well-disciplined tactical cricket for Bermuda's amateurs to follow. In June, the Bermuda national team toured England. This was regarded as a learning experience and the side lost to a strong Minor Counties team, MCC Young Cricketers and three county second elevens before defeating Leicestershire Second Eleven in the final game. A significant developmental step was the appointment, on a short-term contract, of the NCA coach Doug Ferguson, partly to conduct courses for club cricketers and primary school teachers. This initiative resulted in 12 new NCA coaches and 18 school staff qualified to teach cricket. Twenty Kwik Cricket sets were generously donated to the primary schools by Michael Collins, a Bermuda resident. Another innovation in 1992 was Bermuda's first day-night match, a very successful charity event. In the Open League championship, Western Stars Sports Club went through the season undefeated and won the title for the first time. This small community centre on the edge of Hamilton was further recognised when the Bermuda Umpires Association gave their annual Captain's Award to Western Stars skipper Gary Brangman. Their all-rounder Arnold Manders won the league's Most Valuable Player Award; he had a batting average of 88.75 and took 22 wickets at 12.05 each. The premier cricket event is the unique Cup Match, which has long been established as a public holiday; this two-innings, two-day match between Somerset and St George's was drawn in 1992, so St George's retained the 90-year-old trophy. – Maurice Hankey.

GERMANY

Pride of place in German cricket in 1992 must go to the German team which went undefeated through the European Cricketer Cup in England in June and went on to draw with MCC at Lord's, where the German flag flew proudly for the first time. For the DCB (German Cricket Association) this was another important step, following membership of ICC in 1991, towards recognition in the game. It brought in much-needed publicity and the DCB's first sponsors, British Airways and the *Financial Times*. The team at Lord's did not include a German native. However, in Berlin in July, a team composed of eight German nationals and two naturalised players beat an Italian team of similar composition by 91 runs; Italy were bowled out for 71. ASV Frankfurt were German champions in 1992, beating Hamburg in the final by 36 runs. In the Championship for teams of eight nationals and three ex-pats, Darmstadt CC were the winners. The coaching of young Germans has been laid down as a priority for 1993. – Brian Fell.

GIBRALTAR

The highlight of 1992 was the first visit of any national team to Gibraltar when Israel came in September. Gibraltar and Israel are great friends and rivals, having met in the 1986 and 1990 ICC Trophy competitions. Gibraltar had won those games and Israel came determined for revenge, which they achieved by passing Gibraltar's 226 for six with five wickets and three balls to spare. They lost to a Rock XI in another close game but beat a President's XI by six wickets. In the major senior competition, the BSG League, clubs from the Costa del Sol joined local teams, and the Gibraltar Cricket Club, the oldest club on the Rock, were the winners – their first major trophy since modern competitions began in 1960. GCC also won the annual Simon Allen six-a-side and the 20-overs Cup. The Murto Cup, which dates back to the 1920s, was won by Combined Services. – T. J. Finlayson.

HONG KONG

Cricket in Hong Kong remains active with wide participation. There are nine grounds (though three of these are military grounds, whose long-term future is far from assured) and two major clubs – the Hong Kong Cricket Club, which fields six teams, and the Kowloon Cricket Club with five – plus various other institutional and independent sides. Teams from HKCC won two of the main competitions in 1991-92: the all-day Connaught Sunday League, won by Scorpions, and the 35-overs-per-side Connaught Saturday League, won by Nomads. Tai Koo, who mainly draw their players from the Swire Group, won the 50-overs Rothmans Cup, and the Butani Cup, involving 24 teams, was again won by Hong Kong University. In June the Hong Kong team went to Singapore to play Bangladesh, Singapore, Malaysia and Thailand in a round-robin tournament. Hong

Kong won their games against the last three countries to retain the Tunku Ja'afar Cup. This did not involve Bangladesh, who won all their matches to take the South-East Asian Cup and qualify for the main Asia Cup. As part of a four-year development plan, the Hong Kong Cricket Association appointed David Wilson, former national coach for Scotland, as the first coaching/development officer for 1992-93. Hong Kong remain committed to participating as fully as possible in cricket internationally. Unfortunately, cricket is not widely played in local schools, largely because of lack of facilities in crowded Hong Kong. Most of the best players are from elsewhere and the association has drawn ICC's attention to the difficulties posed by the qualification rules for the ICC Trophy. There is a genuinely different situation here and Hong Kong hope this may be taken into account. – John Cribbin.

ISRAEL

All 13 clubs participated in the 1992 League and Knockout Competition. The League was won by the powerful Ashdod Cricket Club who regained the trophy after 15 years, beating Hapoel Netanya. Ashdod's outstanding player was St Ivel Neblett, a West Indian serving with the United Nations forces in Lebanon, who scored 60 out of the 111 required to win. In the knockout competition Ashdod surprisingly lost to Eleven Stars, for whom Bension Kehimkar took six for 26. – Noah Davidson.

ITALY

Italian cricket had an extremely contradictory season in 1992 with a sharp contrast between the positive growth of the structure and the negative results of the national team on the field. Italy's goal is to rise from affiliate to associate membership of the ICC by the end of the decade and Joe Buzaglo of Gibraltar, chairman of the ICC Associates, visited in August. This marked the beginning of a new era of development, demonstrated by the Italian Cricket Association's decision to make artificial wickets compulsory in the first division from 1994 onwards to raise the standard of play. Conversely, despite wonderful coaching by the New Zealand Test captain, Martin Crowe, the national team's performances were extremely disappointing. Only passport-holders represent Italy and, out of 16 players used, just one was not Italian-born. However, none of the players – except the all-rounders Massimo da Costa and Alessandro Braschi – performed to their own capabilities and there were heavy defeats against France, Greece and Germany. Cesena won the 1992 championship, followed by Capannelle, Lazio, Torino, Bergamo and Bologna, who were relegated to the second division, to be replaced by Pianoro. – Simone Gambino.

NEPAL

In Nepal cricket is second only to soccer in popularity. A festival of daily matches in Kathmandu in early 1992 was watched by crowds of up to 4,000, with 8,000 watching the final. In 1989 at least 15,000 people in Biratnagar, south of Everest in the Eastern Region, watched two teams from India, Patna and Benares, in the final of an invitation tournament. More than 25 teams are now competing in Kathmandu alone and eight of them competed for the Rameshwore Memorial Shield in April. This was won by Kathmandu Khel Mandal. Their player Sri Nivas Rana was named as Man of the Series and he was awarded a television set, courtesy of Khetri Sausages. The tenth national tournament for the JAI Trophy took place in Birgunj with teams from nine zones; Koshi Zone were the winners. All matches are played on matting. – Jai Kumar Shah.

UNITED STATES

As American cricket approaches the centenary of its greatest moment, it is enjoying a boom in popularity, caused by the large number of immigrants from the cricket-playing countries. In October 1893 the Philadelphians beat the Australian Test team by an innings. In 1993 Philadelphia's clubs, with their grand clubhouses, are enjoying a revival although the major centres of the sport are now in New York and New England. Once again teams of Test stars came to New York to play heavily sponsored, well-attended exhibition matches at Randall's Island. India beat West Indies while the Pakistanis, under Imran Khan, lost by four runs to a Rest of the World team containing Malcolm Marshall, Richie Richardson and Sachin Tendulkar. But the strength of the game lies in the leagues across the country. New York's oldest league, the Metropolitan, which flourished in the 1890s, was won by Westbury, ahead of the New York West Indians. Somerset A won the American League, with the help of 537 runs from Hubert Blackman, while the Brooklyn Championship went to Carricou and Cambridge. Emite Evertz, with a century against New England and six wickets for six against Mahasabha, contributed most to Norwalk's success in the Connecticut League. Hillside's two formidable batsmen, Amanath Ramcharitar, with three centuries, and Khamal Singh, ensured them the Eastern American President's Trophy. Eclipse won the New Jersey League in which Ram Budhu of Mirror took ten wickets for four, including a hat-trick, against General Electric. New York Eagles, for whom Amjad Khan scored over 600 runs, won the Commonwealth League. Representatives of all these leagues played in the Eastern Zone competition, which the Metropolitan League won, beating the Commonwealth League by 56 runs in the final. The season in Philadelphia included a completely rain-ruined visit from Bermuda while cricket in Southern California was beset by both floods and the Los Angeles riots. The interrupted League was eventually won by Corinthians. Stanford University won the North California League. Southern California beat the North to retain the Raisinland Trophy and also won the inaugural match at under-21 level. – Gerald Howat.

PART FIVE:
ADMINISTRATION AND LAWS

INTERNATIONAL CRICKET COUNCIL

On June 15, 1909, representatives of cricket in England, Australia and South Africa met at Lord's and founded the Imperial Cricket Conference. Membership was confined to the governing bodies of cricket in countries within the British Commonwealth where Test cricket was played. India, New Zealand and West Indies were elected as members on May 31, 1926, Pakistan on July 28, 1952, Sri Lanka on July 21, 1981, and Zimbabwe on July 8, 1992. South Africa ceased to be a member of ICC on leaving the British Commonwealth in May, 1961, but was elected as a Full Member on July 10, 1991.

On July 15, 1965, the Conference was renamed the International Cricket Conference and new rules were adopted to permit the election of countries from outside the British Commonwealth. This led to the growth of the Conference, with the admission of Associate Members, who were each entitled to one vote, while the Foundation and Full Members were each entitled to two votes, on ICC resolutions. On July 12, 13, 1989, the Conference was renamed the International Cricket Council and revised rules were adopted.

Officers

Chairman: Sir Colin Cowdrey.
Secretary: Lt-Col. J. R. Stephenson.
Administrator: Miss S. A. Lawrence.

Constitution

Chairman: The nominee of the President of MCC, with the confirmation of the members at the annual conference. Prior to making his nomination, the President of MCC shall have appropriate consultations, to include all Foundation and Full Members. The term of office is for one year, commencing October 1, but subject to the proviso that no Chairman shall remain continuously in office for more than four years, the Chairman may offer himself for re-nomination for a further year.

Secretary: To be appointed by members at the annual conference.

Administrator: Appointed for such periods as determined by members at the annual conference.

Membership

Foundation Members: Australia and United Kingdom.

Full Members: India, New Zealand, Pakistan, South Africa, Sri Lanka, West Indies and Zimbabwe.

Associate Members*: Argentina (1974), Bangladesh (1977), Bermuda (1966), Canada (1968), Denmark (1966), East and Central Africa (1966), Fiji (1965), Gibraltar (1969), Hong Kong (1969), Israel (1974), Kenya (1981), Malaysia (1967), Namibia (1966), Netherlands (1966), Papua New Guinea (1973), Singapore (1974), United Arab Emirates (1990), USA (1965) and West Africa (1976).

Affiliate Members*: Austria (1992), Bahamas (1987), Belgium (1991), Brunei (1992), France (1987), Germany (1991), Italy (1984), Japan (1989), Nepal (1988), Spain (1992) and Switzerland (1985).

* Year of election shown in parentheses.

The following governing bodies for cricket shall be eligible for election.

Foundation Members: The governing bodies for cricket in the United Kingdom and Australia are known as Foundation Members (while also being Full Members of ICC) and have certain additional rights as set out in the Rules of the Council.

Full Members: The governing body for cricket recognised by ICC of a country, or countries associated for cricket purposes, or a geographical area, from which representative teams are qualified to play official Test matches.

Associate Members: The governing body for cricket recognised by ICC of a country, or countries associated for cricket purposes, or a geographical area, which does not qualify as a Full Member but where cricket is firmly established and organised.

Affiliate Members: The governing body for cricket recognised by ICC of a country, or countries associated for cricket purposes, or a geographical area (which is not part of one of those already constituted as a Full or Associate Member) where ICC recognises that cricket is played in accordance with the Laws of Cricket. Affiliate Members have no right to vote or to propose or second resolutions at ICC meetings.

THE CRICKET COUNCIL

The Cricket Council, which was set up in 1968 and reconstituted in 1974 and 1983, acts as the governing body for cricket in the British Isles. It comprises the following.

Chairman: W. R. F. Chamberlain.
Vice-Chairman: J. D. Robson.
8 Representatives of the Test and County Cricket Board: 1991-92 – W. R. F. Chamberlain, D. J. Insole, M. P. Murray, D. H. Newton, D. N. Perry, H. J. Pocock, D. Rich, F. M. Turner. 1992-93 – J. R. T. Barclay, Sir Lawrence Byford, W. R. F. Chamberlain, D. J. Insole, M. P. Murray, H. J. Pocock, D. Rich, F. M. Turner.
5 Representatives of the National Cricket Association: M. J. K. Smith, J. D. Robson, F. H. Elliott, E. K. Ingman, J. G. Overy.
3 Representatives of the Marylebone Cricket Club: 1991-92 – M. E. L. Melluish, G. H. G. Doggart, R. H. Burton. 1992-93 – D. R. W. Silk, M. E. L. Melluish, Field Marshal The Rt Hon. The Lord Bramall.
1 Representative (non-voting) of the Minor Counties Cricket Association: J. E. O. Smith.
1 Representative (non-voting) of the Irish Cricket Union: D. Scott. (Ireland resigned from the Cricket Council in 1992 with a view to joining the International Cricket Council.)
1 Representative (non-voting) of the Scottish Cricket Union: R. W. Barclay.

Secretary: A. C. Smith.

THE TEST AND COUNTY CRICKET BOARD

The TCCB was set up in 1968 to be responsible for Test matches, official tours, and first-class and minor county competitions. It is composed of representatives of the 18 first-class counties, Marylebone Cricket Club and Minor Counties Cricket Association (voting members); as well as Oxford University Cricket Club, Cambridge University Cricket Club, the Irish Cricket Union and the Scottish Cricket Union (non-voting members).

Officers

Chairman: W. R. F. Chamberlain.

Chairmen of Committees: W. R. F. Chamberlain (Executive); D. B. Carr (Pitches); O. S. Wheatley (Cricket); D. J. Insole (International); P. R. Bromage (Discipline); M. P. Murray (Finance); B. G. K. Downing (Marketing); D. R. W. Silk (Registration); E. R. Dexter (England Committee); A. C. Smith (Appointment of Umpires); Rev. M. D. Vockins (Second XI Competitions).

Chief Executive: A. C. Smith. *Cricket Secretary:* T. M. Lamb. *Administration Secretary:* A. S. Brown. *Accountant:* C. A. Barker. *Marketing Manager:* T. D. M. Blake. *Media Relations Manager:* K. D. Lawrence. *England Team Manager:* 1991-92 – M. J. Stewart; 1992-93 – K. W. R. Fletcher.

THE NATIONAL CRICKET ASSOCIATION

With the setting up of the Cricket Council in 1968 it was necessary to form a separate organisation to represent the interests of all cricket below the first-class game, and it is the National Cricket Association that carries out this function. It comprises representatives from 51 county cricket associations and 17 national cricketing organisations. The following were in office in both 1991-92 and 1992-93:

Officers

President: M. J. K. Smith.
Chairman: J. D. Robson.
Vice-Chairman: F. H. Elliott.
Chief Executive: K. V. Andrew.

Cricket Development and Administration Manager: T. N. Bates.
Marketing Executive: D. A. Clarke.
Hon. Treasurer: D. W. Carter.

THE MARYLEBONE CRICKET CLUB

Patron: HER MAJESTY THE QUEEN

Officers

President: 1991-92 – M. E. L. Melluish.
1992-93 – D. R. W. Silk.

Treasurer: 1991-92 – G. H. G. Doggart.
1992-93 – M. E. L. Melluish.

Chairman of Finance: D. L. Hudd.

Trustees: J. J. Warr, D. J. Insole, Sir Oliver Popplewell.

Hon. Life Vice-Presidents: Sir Donald Bradman, D. G. Clark, G. H. G. Doggart, S. C. Griffith, F. G. Mann, C. H. Palmer, C. G. A. Paris, E. W. Swanton, R. E. S. Wyatt.

Secretary: Lt-Col. J. R. Stephenson (Lord's Cricket Ground, London NW8 8QN).

Assistant Secretaries: M. R. Blow (Finance), J. A. Jameson (Cricket), J. R. Smith (Administration).

Curator: S. E. A. Green.

Ground Administrator: A. W. P. Fleming.

MCC Committee, 1992-93: D. R. W. Silk (President), J. R. T. Barclay, Field Marshal The Rt Hon. The Lord Bramall, C. A. Fry, R. G. Gibbs, The Rt Hon. The Lord Griffiths, R. P. Hodson, D. L. Hudd, D. J. Insole, A. R. Lewis, Sir Ian MacLaurin, D. R. Male, P. B. H. May, M. E. L. Melluish, S. G. Metcalfe, Sir Oliver Popplewell, T. M. B. Rice, R. V. C. Robins, M. O. C. Sturt, J. A. F. Vallance, J. J. Warr, J. C. Woodcock. (Compared with the committee in 1991-92, C. A. Fry, The Rt Hon. The Lord Griffiths, R. P. Hodson and J. C. Woodcock were elected to replace R. H. Burton, R. A. Hutton, R. D. V. Knight and M. D. T. Loup. R. V. C. Robins became a member on replacing G. H. G. Doggart as chairman of the General Purposes sub-committee.)

Chairmen of main sub-committees: G. H. G. Doggart (General Purposes, 1991-92); P. B. H. May (Cricket); D. R. Male (Estates); D. L. Hudd (Finance); R. V. C. Robins (General Purposes, 1992-93).

Chairmen of specialist sub-committees: T. M. B. Sissons (Arts and Libraries); Sir Colin Cowdrey (Indoor School Management); A. J. B. Mason (Tennis and Squash).

THE LAWS OF CRICKET

(1980 CODE)

As updated in 1992. World copyright of MCC and reprinted by permission of MCC. Copies of the "Laws of Cricket" may be obtained from Lord's Cricket Ground.

INDEX TO THE LAWS

LAW 1. THE PLAYERS

1. Number of Players and Captain

A match is played between two sides each of 11 players, one of whom shall be captain. In the event of the captain not being available at any time, a deputy shall act for him.

2. Nomination of Players

Before the toss for innings, the captain shall nominate his players, who may not thereafter be changed without the consent of the opposing captain.

Note

(a) More or Less than 11 Players a Side
A match may be played by agreement between sides of more or less than 11 players, but not more than 11 players may field.

LAW 2. SUBSTITUTES AND RUNNERS: BATSMAN OR FIELDSMAN LEAVING THE FIELD: BATSMAN RETIRING: BATSMAN COMMENCING INNINGS

1. Substitutes

In normal circumstances, a substitute shall be allowed to field only for a player who satisfies the umpires that he has become injured or become ill during the match. However, in very exceptional circumstances, the umpires may use their discretion to allow a substitute for a player who has to leave the field for other wholly acceptable reasons, subject to consent being given by the opposing captain. If a player wishes to change his shirt, boots, etc., he may leave the field to do so (no changing on the field), but no substitute will be allowed.

2. Objection to Substitutes

The opposing captain shall have no right of objection to any player acting as substitute in the field, nor as to where he shall field; however, no substitute shall act as wicket-keeper.

3. Substitute not to Bat or Bowl

A substitute shall not be allowed to bat or bowl.

4. A Player for whom a Substitute has Acted

A player may bat, bowl or field even though a substitute has acted for him.

5. Runner

A runner shall be allowed for a batsman who, during the match, is incapacitated by illness or injury. The person acting as runner shall be a member of the batting side and shall, if possible, have already batted in that innings.

6. Runner's Equipment

The player acting as runner for an injured batsman shall wear the same external protective equipment as the injured batsman.

7. Transgression of the Laws by an Injured Batsman or Runner

An injured batsman may be out should his runner break any one of Laws 33 (Handled the Ball), 37 (Obstructing the Field) or 38 (Run Out). As striker he remains himself subject to the Laws. Furthermore, should he be out of his ground for any purpose and the wicket at the wicket-keeper's end be put down he shall be out under Law 38 (Run Out) or Law 39 (Stumped), irrespective of the position of the other batsman or the runner, and no runs shall be scored.

When not the striker, the injured batsman is out of the game and shall stand where he does not interfere with the play. Should he bring himself into the game in any way, then he shall suffer the penalties that any transgression of the Laws demands.

8. Fieldsman Leaving the Field

No fieldsman shall leave the field or return during a session of play without the consent of the umpire at the bowler's end. The umpire's consent is also necessary if a substitute is required for a fieldsman, when his side returns to the field after an interval. If a member of the fielding side leaves the field or fails to return after an interval and is absent from the field for longer than 15 minutes, he shall not be permitted to bowl after his return until he has been on the field for at least that length of playing time for which he was absent. This restriction shall not apply at the start of a new day's play.

9. Batsman Leaving the Field or Retiring

A batsman may leave the field or retire at any time owing to illness, injury or other unavoidable cause, having previously notified the umpire at the bowler's end. He may resume his innings at the fall of a wicket, which for the purposes of this Law shall include the retirement of another batsman.

If he leaves the field or retires for any other reason he may resume his innings only with the consent of the opposing captain.

When a batsman has left the field or retired and is unable to return owing to illness, injury or other unavoidable cause, his innings is to be recorded as "retired, not out". Otherwise it is to be recorded as "retired, out".

10. Commencement of a Batsman's Innings

A batsman shall be considered to have commenced his innings once he has stepped on to the field of play.

Note

(a) Substitutes and Runners

For the purpose of these Laws, allowable illnesses or injuries are those which occur at any time after the nomination by the captains of their teams.

LAW 3. THE UMPIRES

1. Appointment

Before the toss for innings, two umpires shall be appointed, one for each end, to control the game with absolute impartiality as required by the Laws.

2. Change of Umpires

No umpire shall be changed during a match without the consent of both captains.

3. Special Conditions

Before the toss for innings, the umpires shall agree with both captains on any special conditions affecting the conduct of the match.

4. The Wickets

The umpires shall satisfy themselves before the start of the match that the wickets are properly pitched.

5. Clock or Watch

The umpires shall agree between themselves and inform both captains before the start of the match on the watch or clock to be followed during the match.

6. Conduct and Implements

Before and during a match the umpires shall ensure that the conduct of the game and the implements used are strictly in accordance with the Laws.

7. Fair and Unfair Play

The umpires shall be the sole judges of fair and unfair play.

8. Fitness of Ground, Weather and Light

(a) The umpires shall be the sole judges of the fitness of the ground, weather and light for play.

   (i) However, before deciding to suspend play, or not to start play, or not to resume play after an interval or stoppage, the umpires shall establish whether both captains (the batsmen at the wicket may deputise for their captain) wish to commence or to continue in the prevailing conditions; if so, their wishes shall be met.

   (ii) In addition, if during play the umpires decide that the light is unfit, only the batting side shall have the option of continuing play. After agreeing to continue to play in unfit light conditions, the captain of the batting side (or a batsman at the wicket) may appeal against the light to the umpires, who shall uphold the appeal only if, in their opinion, the light has deteriorated since the agreement to continue was made.

(b) After any suspension of play, the umpires, unaccompanied by any of the players or officials, shall, on their own initiative, carry out an inspection immediately the conditions improve and shall continue to inspect at intervals. Immediately the umpires decide that play is possible they shall call upon the players to resume the game.

9. Exceptional Circumstances

In exceptional circumstances, other than those of weather, ground or light, the umpires may decide to suspend or abandon play. Before making such a decision the umpires shall establish, if the circumstances allow, whether both captains (the batsmen at the wicket may deputise for their captain) wish to continue in the prevailing conditions; if so, their wishes shall be met.

10. Position of Umpires

The umpires shall stand where they can best see any act upon which their decision may be required.

Subject to this over-riding consideration, the umpire at the bowler's end shall stand where he does not interfere with either the bowler's run-up or the striker's view.

The umpire at the striker's end may elect to stand on the off instead of the leg side of the pitch, provided he informs the captain of the fielding side and the striker of his intention to do so.

11. Umpires Changing Ends

The umpires shall change ends after each side has had one innings.

12. Disputes

All disputes shall be determined by the umpires, and if they disagree the actual state of things shall continue.

13. Signals

The following code of signals shall be used by umpires who will wait until a signal has been answered by a scorer before allowing the game to proceed.

Boundary	– by waving the arm from side to side.
Boundary 6	– by raising both arms above the head.
Bye	– by raising an open hand above the head.
Dead Ball	– by crossing and re-crossing the wrists below the waist.
Leg-bye	– by touching a raised knee with the hand.
No-ball	– by extending one arm horizontally.
Out	– by raising the index finger above the head. If not out, the umpire shall call "not out".
Short Run	– by bending the arm upwards and by touching the nearer shoulder with the tips of the fingers.
Wide	– by extending both arms horizontally.

14. Correctness of Scores

The umpires shall be responsible for satisfying themselves on the correctness of the scores throughout and at the conclusion of the match. See Law 21.6 (Correctness of Result).

Notes

(a) Attendance of Umpires

The umpires should be present on the ground and report to the ground executive or the equivalent at least 30 minutes before the start of a day's play.

(b) Consultation between Umpires and Scorers

Consultation between umpires and scorers over doubtful points is essential.

(c) Fitness of Ground

The umpires shall consider the ground as unfit for play when it is so wet or slippery as to deprive the bowlers of a reasonable foothold, the fieldsmen, other than the deep-fielders, of the power of free movement, or the batsmen of the ability to play their strokes or to run between the wickets. Play should not be suspended merely because the grass and the ball are wet and slippery.

(d) Fitness of Weather and Light

The umpires should suspend play only when they consider that the conditions are so bad that it is unreasonable or dangerous to continue.

LAW 4.   THE SCORERS

1. Recording Runs

All runs scored shall be recorded by scorers appointed for the purpose. Where there are two scorers they shall frequently check to ensure that the score-sheets agree.

2. Acknowledging Signals

The scorers shall accept and immediately acknowledge all instructions and signals given to them by the umpires.

LAW 5. THE BALL

1. Weight and Size

The ball, when new, shall weigh not less than $5\frac{1}{2}$ ounces/155.9g, nor more than $5\frac{3}{4}$ ounces/163g; and shall measure not less than $8\frac{13}{16}$ inches/22.4cm, nor more than 9 inches/22.9cm in circumference.

2. Approval of Balls

All balls used in matches shall be approved by the umpires and captains before the start of the match.

3. New Ball

Subject to agreement to the contrary, having been made before the toss, either captain may demand a new ball at the start of each innings.

4. New Ball in Match of Three or More Days' Duration

In a match of three or more days' duration, the captain of the fielding side may demand a new ball after the prescribed number of overs has been bowled with the old one. The governing body for cricket in the country concerned shall decide the number of overs applicable in that country, which shall be not less than 75 six-ball overs (55 eight-ball overs).

5. Ball Lost or Becoming Unfit for Play

In the event of a ball during play being lost or, in the opinion of the umpires, becoming unfit for play, the umpires shall allow it to be replaced by one that in their opinion has had a similar amount of wear. If a ball is to be replaced, the umpires shall inform the batsman.

Note

> **(a) Specifications**
> The specifications, as described in 1 above, shall apply to top-grade balls only. The following degrees of tolerance will be acceptable for other grades of ball.
>
> (i) *Men's Grades 2–4*
> Weight: $5\frac{5}{16}$ ounces/150g to $5\frac{13}{16}$ ounces/165g.
> Size: $8\frac{11}{16}$ inches/22.0cm to $9\frac{1}{16}$ inches/23.0cm.
>
> (ii) *Women's*
> Weight: $4\frac{15}{16}$ ounces/140g to $5\frac{5}{16}$ ounces/150g.
> Size: $8\frac{1}{4}$ inches/21.0cm to $8\frac{7}{8}$ inches/22.5cm.
>
> (iii) *Junior*
> Weight: $4\frac{11}{16}$ ounces/133g to $5\frac{1}{16}$ ounces/143g.
> Size: $8\frac{1}{16}$ inches/20.5cm to $8\frac{11}{16}$ inches/22.0cm.

LAW 6. THE BAT

1. Width and Length

The bat overall shall not be more than 38 inches/96.5cm in length; the blade of the bat shall be made of wood and shall not exceed $4\frac{1}{4}$ inches/10.8cm at the widest part.

Note

> (a) The blade of the bat may be covered with material for protection, strengthening or repair. Such material shall not exceed $\frac{1}{16}$ inch/1.56mm in thickness.

LAW 7. THE PITCH

1. Area of Pitch

The pitch is the area between the bowling creases – see Law 9 (The Bowling and Popping Creases). It shall measure 5 feet/1.52m in width on either side of a line joining the centre of the middle stumps of the wickets – see Law 8 (The Wickets).

2. Selection and Preparation

Before the toss for innings, the executive of the ground shall be responsible for the selection and preparation of the pitch; thereafter the umpires shall control its use and maintenance.

3. Changing Pitch

The pitch shall not be changed during a match unless it becomes unfit for play, and then only with the consent of both captains.

4. Non-Turf Pitches

In the event of a non-turf pitch being used, the following shall apply:

(a) Length: That of the playing surface to a minimum of 58 feet/17.68m.

(b) Width: That of the playing surface to a minimum of 6 feet/1.83m.

See Law 10 (Rolling, Sweeping, Mowing, Watering the Pitch and Re-marking of Creases) Note (a).

LAW 8. THE WICKETS

1. Width and Pitching

Two sets of wickets, each 9 inches/22.86cm wide, and consisting of three wooden stumps with two wooden bails upon the top, shall be pitched opposite and parallel to each other at a distance of 22 yards/20.12m between the centres of the two middle stumps.

2. Size of Stumps

The stumps shall be of equal and sufficient size to prevent the ball from passing between them. Their tops shall be 28 inches/71.1cm above the ground, and shall be dome-shaped except for the bail grooves.

3. Size of Bails

The bails shall be each 4⅜ inches/11.1cm in length and when in position on the top of the stumps shall not project more than ½ inch/1.3cm above them.

Notes

(a) **Dispensing with Bails**
In a high wind the umpires may decide to dispense with the use of bails.

(b) **Junior Cricket**
For junior cricket, as defined by the local governing body, the following measurements for the wickets shall apply:

Width – 8 inches/20.32cm.
Pitched – 21 yards/19.20m.
Height – 27 inches/68.58cm.
Bails – each 3⅞ inches/9.84cm in length and should not project more than ½ inch/1.3cm above the stumps.

LAW 9. THE BOWLING, POPPING AND RETURN CREASES

1. The Bowling Crease

The bowling crease shall be marked in line with the stumps at each end and shall be 8 feet 8 inches/2.64m in length, with the stumps in the centre.

2. The Popping Crease

The popping crease, which is the back edge of the crease marking, shall be in front of and parallel with the bowling crease. It shall have the back edge of the crease marking 4 feet/1.22m from the centre of the stumps and shall extend to a minimum of 6 feet/1.83m on either side of the line of the wicket.

The popping crease shall be considered to be unlimited in length.

3. The Return Crease

The return crease marking, of which the inside edge is the crease, shall be at each end of the bowling crease and at right angles to it. The return crease shall be marked to a minimum of 4 feet/1.22m behind the wicket and shall be considered to be unlimited in length. A forward extension shall be marked to the popping crease.

LAW 10.   ROLLING, SWEEPING, MOWING, WATERING THE PITCH AND RE-MARKING OF CREASES

1. Rolling

During the match the pitch may be rolled at the request of the captain of the batting side, for a period of not more than seven minutes before the start of each innings, other than the first innings of the match, and before the start of each day's play. In addition, if, after the toss and before the first innings of the match, the start is delayed, the captain of the batting side may request to have the pitch rolled for not more than seven minutes. However, if in the opinion of the umpires the delay has had no significant effect upon the state of the pitch, they shall refuse any request for the rolling of the pitch.

The pitch shall not otherwise be rolled during the match.

The seven minutes' rolling permitted before the start of a day's play shall take place not earlier than half an hour before the start of play and the captain of the batting side may delay such rolling until ten minutes before the start of play should he so desire.

If a captain declares an innings closed less than 15 minutes before the resumption of play, and the other captain is thereby prevented from exercising his option of seven minutes' rolling or if he is so prevented for any other reason, the time for rolling shall be taken out of the normal playing time.

2. Sweeping

Such sweeping of the pitch as is necessary during the match shall be done so that the seven minutes allowed for rolling the pitch, provided for in 1 above, is not affected.

3. Mowing

(a) Responsibilities of Ground Authority and of Umpires

All mowings which are carried out before the toss for innings shall be the responsibility of the ground authority; thereafter they shall be carried out under the supervision of the umpires. See Law 7.2 (Selection and Preparation).

(b) Initial Mowing

The pitch shall be mown before play begins on the day the match is scheduled to start, or in the case of a delayed start on the day the match is expected to start. See 3(a) above (Responsibilities of Ground Authority and of Umpires).

(c) Subsequent Mowings in a Match of Two or More Days' Duration

In a match of two or more days' duration, the pitch shall be mown daily before play begins. Should this mowing not take place because of weather conditions, rest days or other reasons, the pitch shall be mown on the first day on which the match is resumed.

(d) Mowing of the Outfield in a Match of Two or More Days' Duration

In order to ensure that conditions are as similar as possible for both sides, the outfield shall normally be mown before the commencement of play on each day of the match, if ground and weather conditions allow. See Note (b) to this Law.

4. Watering

The pitch shall not be watered during a match.

5. Re-marking Creases

Whenever possible the creases shall be re-marked.

6. Maintenance of Foot-holes

In wet weather, the umpires shall ensure that the holes made by the bowlers and batsmen are cleaned out and dried whenever necessary to facilitate play. In matches of two or more days' duration, the umpires shall allow, if necessary, the re-turfing of foot-holes made by the bowler in his delivery stride, or the use of quick-setting fillings for the same purpose, before the start of each day's play.

7. Securing of Footholds and Maintenance of Pitch

During play, the umpires shall allow either batsman to beat the pitch with his bat and players to secure their footholds by the use of sawdust, provided that no damage to the pitch is so caused, and Law 42 (Unfair Play) is not contravened.

Notes

(a) Non-turf Pitches

The above Law 10 applies to turf pitches.

The game is played on non-turf pitches in many countries at various levels. Whilst the conduct of the game on these surfaces should always be in accordance with the Laws of Cricket, it is recognised that it may sometimes be necessary for governing bodies to lay down special playing conditions to suit the type of non-turf pitch used in their country.

In matches played against touring teams, any special playing conditions should be agreed in advance by both parties.

(b) Mowing of the Outfield in a Match of Two or More Days' Duration

If, for reasons other than ground and weather conditions, daily and complete mowing is not possible, the ground authority shall notify the captains and umpires, before the toss for innings, of the procedure to be adopted for such mowing during the match.

(c) Choice of Roller

If there is more than one roller available, the captain of the batting side shall have a choice.

LAW 11. COVERING THE PITCH

1. Before the Start of a Match

Before the start of a match, complete covering of the pitch shall be allowed.

2. During a Match

The pitch shall not be completely covered during a match unless prior arrangement or regulations so provide.

3. Covering Bowlers' Run-up

Whenever possible, the bowlers' run-up shall be covered, but the covers so used shall not extend further than 4 feet/1.22m in front of the popping crease.

Note

(a) Removal of Covers

The covers should be removed as promptly as possible whenever the weather permits.

LAW 12. INNINGS

1. Number of Innings

A match shall be of one or two innings of each side according to agreement reached before the start of play.

2. Alternate Innings

In a two-innings match each side shall take their innings alternately except in the case provided for in Law 13 (The Follow-on).

3. The Toss

The captains shall toss for the choice of innings on the field of play not later than 15 minutes before the time scheduled for the match to start, or before the time agreed upon for play to start.

4. Choice of Innings

The winner of the toss shall notify his decision to bat or to field to the opposing captain not later than ten minutes before the time scheduled for the match to start, or before the time agreed upon for play to start. The decision shall not thereafter be altered.

5. Continuation after One Innings of Each Side

Despite the terms of 1 above, in a one-innings match, when a result has been reached on the first innings, the captains may agree to the continuation of play if, in their opinion, there is a prospect of carrying the game to a further issue in the time left. See Law 21 (Result).

Notes

    (a) Limited Innings – One-innings Match

    In a one-innings match, each innings may, by agreement, be limited by a number of overs or by a period of time.

    (b) Limited Innings – Two-innings Match

    In a two-innings match, the first innings of each side may, by agreement, be limited to a number of overs or by a period of time.

LAW 13.   THE FOLLOW-ON

1. Lead on First Innings

In a two-innings match the side which bats first and leads by 200 runs in a match of five days or more, by 150 runs in a three-day or four-day match, by 100 runs in a two-day match, or by 75 runs in a one-day match, shall have the option of requiring the other side to follow their innings.

2. Day's Play Lost

If no play takes place on the first day of a match of two or more days' duration, 1 above shall apply in accordance with the number of days' play remaining from the actual start of the match.

LAW 14.   DECLARATIONS

1. Time of Declaration

The captain of the batting side may declare an innings closed at any time during a match, irrespective of its duration.

2. Forfeiture of Second Innings

A captain may forfeit his second innings, provided his decision to do so is notified to the opposing captain and umpires in sufficient time to allow seven minutes' rolling of the pitch. See Law 10 (Rolling, Sweeping, Mowing, Watering the Pitch and Re-marking of Creases). The normal ten-minute interval between innings shall be applied.

LAW 15.   START OF PLAY

1. Call of Play

At the start of each innings and of each day's play, and on the resumption of play after any interval or interruption, the umpire at the bowler's end shall call "play".

2. Practice on the Field

At no time on any day of the match shall there be any bowling or batting practice on the pitch.

No practice may take place on the field if, in the opinion of the umpires, it could result in a waste of time.

3. Trial Run-up

No bowler shall have a trial run-up after "play" has been called in any session of play, except at the fall of a wicket when an umpire may allow such a trial run-up if he is satisfied that it will not cause any waste of time.

LAW 16. INTERVALS

1. Length

The umpire shall allow such intervals as have been agreed upon for meals, and ten minutes between each innings.

2. Luncheon Interval – Innings Ending or Stoppage within Ten Minutes of Interval

If an innings ends or there is a stoppage caused by weather or bad light within ten minutes of the agreed time for the luncheon interval, the interval shall be taken immediately.

The time remaining in the session of play shall be added to the agreed length of the interval but no extra allowance shall be made for the ten-minute interval between innings.

3. Tea Interval – Innings Ending or Stoppage within 30 Minutes of Interval

If an innings ends or there is a stoppage caused by weather or bad light within 30 minutes of the agreed time for the tea interval, the interval shall be taken immediately.

The interval shall be of the agreed length and, if applicable, shall include the ten-minute interval between innings.

4. Tea Interval – Continuation of Play

If, at the agreed time for the tea interval, nine wickets are down, play shall continue for a period not exceeding 30 minutes or until the innings is concluded.

5. Tea Interval – Agreement to Forgo

At any time during the match, the captains may agree to forgo a tea interval.

6. Intervals for Drinks

If both captains agree before the start of a match that intervals for drinks may be taken, the option to take such intervals shall be available to either side. These intervals shall be restricted to one per session, shall be kept as short as possible, shall not be taken in the last hour of the match, and in any case shall not exceed five minutes.

The agreed times for these intervals shall be strictly adhered to, except that if a wicket falls within five minutes of the agreed time then drinks shall be taken out immediately.

If an innings ends or there is a stoppage caused by weather or bad light within 30 minutes of the agreed time for a drinks interval, there will be no interval for drinks in that session.

At any time during the match the captains may agree to forgo any such drinks interval.

Notes

    (a) Tea Interval – One-day Match

    In a one-day match, a specific time for the tea interval need not necessarily be arranged, and it may be agreed to take this interval between the innings of a one-innings match.

    (b) Changing the Agreed Time of Intervals

    In the event of the ground, weather or light conditions causing a suspension of play, the umpires, after consultation with the captains, may decide in the interests of time-saving to bring forward the time of the luncheon or tea interval.

LAW 17. CESSATION OF PLAY

1. Call of Time

The umpire at the bowler's end shall call "time" on the cessation of play before any interval or interruption of play, at the end of each day's play, and at the conclusion of the match. See Law 27 (Appeals).

2. Removal of Bails

After the call of "time", the umpires shall remove the bails from both wickets.

3. Starting a Last Over

The last over before an interval or the close of play shall be started provided the umpire, after walking at his normal pace, has arrived at his position behind the stumps at the bowler's end before time has been reached.

4. Completion of the Last Over of a Session

The last over before an interval or the close of play shall be completed unless a batsman is out or retires during that over within two minutes of the interval or the close of play or unless the players have occasion to leave the field.

5. Completion of the Last Over of a Match

An over in progress at the close of play on the final day of a match shall be completed at the request of either captain, even if a wicket falls after time has been reached.

If, during the last over, the players have occasion to leave the field, the umpires shall call "time" and there shall be no resumption of play and the match shall be at an end.

6. Last Hour of Match – Number of Overs

The umpires shall indicate when one hour of playing time of the match remains according to the agreed hours of play. The next over after that moment shall be the first of a minimum of 20 six-ball overs (15 eight-ball overs), provided a result is not reached earlier or there is no interval or interruption of play.

7. Last Hour of Match – Intervals between Innings and Interruptions of Play

If, at the commencement of the last hour of the match, an interval or interruption of play is in progress or if, during the last hour, there is an interval between innings or an interruption of play, the minimum number of overs to be bowled on the resumption of play shall be reduced in proportion to the duration, within the last hour of the match, of any such interval or interruption.

The minimum number of overs to be bowled after the resumption of play shall be calculated as follows:

(a) In the case of an interval or interruption of play being in progress at the commencement of the last hour of play, or in the case of a first interval or interruption, a deduction shall be made from the minimum of 20 six-ball overs (or 15 eight-ball overs).

(b) If there is a later interval or interruption, a further deduction shall be made from the minimum number of overs which should have been bowled following the last resumption of play.

(c) These deductions shall be based on the following factors:

(i) The number of overs already bowled in the last hour of the match or, in the case of a later interval or interruption, in the last session of play.

(ii) The number of overs lost as a result of the interval or interruption allowing one six-ball over for every full three minutes (or one eight-ball over for every full four minutes) of interval or interruption.

(iii) Any over left uncompleted at the end of an innings to be excluded from these calculations.

(iv) Any over of the minimum number to be played which is left uncompleted at the start of an interruption of play to be completed when play is resumed and to count as one over bowled.

(v) An interval to start with the end of an innings and to end ten minutes later; an interruption to start on the call of "time" and to end on the call of "play".

(d) In the event of an innings being completed and a new innings commencing during the last hour of the match, the number of overs to be bowled in the new innings shall be calculated on the basis of one six-ball over for every three minutes or part thereof remaining for play (or one eight-ball over for every four minutes or part thereof remaining for play); or alternatively on the basis that sufficient overs be bowled to enable the full minimum quota of overs to be completed under circumstances governed by (a), (b) and (c) above. In all such cases the alternative which allows the greater number of overs shall be employed.

8. Bowler Unable to Complete an Over during Last Hour of the Match

If, for any reason, a bowler is unable to complete an over during the period of play referred to in 6 above, Law 22.7 (Bowler Incapacitated or Suspended during an Over) shall apply.

LAW 18. SCORING

1. A Run

The score shall be reckoned by runs. A run is scored:

(a) So often as the batsmen, after a hit or at any time while the ball is in play, shall have crossed and made good their ground from end to end.

(b) When a boundary is scored. See Law 19 (Boundaries).

(c) When penalty runs are awarded. See 6 below.

2. Short Runs

(a) If either batsman runs a short run, the umpire shall call and signal "one short" as soon as the ball becomes dead and that run shall not be scored. A run is short if a batsman fails to make good his ground on turning for a further run.

(b) Although a short run shortens the succeeding one, the latter, if completed, shall count.

(c) If either or both batsmen deliberately run short the umpire shall, as soon as he sees that the fielding side have no chance of dismissing either batsman, call and signal "dead ball" and disallow any runs attempted or previously scored. The batsmen shall return to their original ends.

(d) If both batsmen run short in one and the same run, only one run shall be deducted.

(e) Only if three or more runs are attempted can more than one be short and then, subject to (c) and (d) above, all runs so called shall be disallowed. If there has been more than one short run the umpires shall instruct the scorers as to the number of runs disallowed.

3. Striker Caught

If the striker is caught, no run shall be scored.

4. Batsman Run Out

If a batsman is run out, only that run which was being attempted shall not be scored. If, however, an injured striker himself is run out, no runs shall be scored. See Law 2.7 (Transgression of the Laws by an Injured Batsman or Runner).

5. Batsman Obstructing the Field

If a batsman is out Obstructing the Field, any runs completed before the obstruction occurs shall be scored unless such obstruction prevents a catch being made, in which case no runs shall be scored.

6. Runs Scored for Penalties

Runs shall be scored for penalties under Laws 20 (Lost Ball), 24 (No-ball), 25 (Wide-ball), 41.1 (Fielding the Ball) and for boundary allowances under Law 19 (Boundaries).

7. Batsman Returning to Wicket he has Left

If, while the ball is in play, the batsmen have crossed in running, neither shall return to the wicket he has left, even though a short run has been called or no run has been scored as in the case of a catch. Batsmen, however, shall return to the wickets they originally left in the cases of a boundary and of any disallowance of runs and of an injured batsman being, himself, run out. See Law 2.7 (Transgression by an Injured Batsman or Runner).

Note

(a) Short Run

A striker taking stance in front of his popping crease may run from that point without penalty.

LAW 19. BOUNDARIES

1. The Boundary of the Playing Area

Before the toss for innings, the umpires shall agree with both captains on the boundary of the playing area. The boundary shall, if possible, be marked by a white line, a rope laid on the ground, or a fence. If flags or posts only are used to mark a boundary, the imaginary line joining such points shall be regarded as the boundary. An obstacle, or person, within the playing area shall not be regarded as a boundary unless so decided by the umpires before the toss for innings. Sightscreens within, or partially within, the playing area shall be regarded as the boundary and when the ball strikes or passes within or under or directly over any part of the screen, a boundary shall be scored.

2. Runs Scored for Boundaries

Before the toss for innings, the umpires shall agree with both captains the runs to be allowed for boundaries, and in deciding the allowance for them, the umpires and captains shall be guided by the prevailing custom of the ground. The allowance for a boundary shall normally be four runs, and six runs for all hits pitching over and clear of the boundary line or fence, even though the ball has been previously touched by a fieldsman. Six runs shall also be scored if a fieldsman, after catching a ball, carries it over the boundary. See Law 32 (Caught) Note (a). Six runs shall not be scored when a ball struck by the striker hits a sightscreen full pitch if the screen is within, or partially within, the playing area, but if the ball is struck directly over a sightscreen so situated, six runs shall be scored.

3. A Boundary

A boundary shall be scored and signalled by the umpire at the bowler's end whenever, in his opinion:

(a) A ball in play touches or crosses the boundary, however marked.

(b) A fieldsman with ball in hand touches or grounds any part of his person on or over a boundary line.

(c) A fieldsman with ball in hand grounds any part of his person over a boundary fence or board. This allows the fieldsman to touch or lean on or over a boundary fence or board in preventing a boundary.

4. Runs Exceeding Boundary Allowance

The runs completed at the instant the ball reaches the boundary shall count if they exceed the boundary allowance.

5. Overthrows or Wilful Act of a Fieldsman

If the boundary results from an overthrow or from the wilful act of a fieldsman, any runs already completed and the allowance shall be added to the score. The run in progress shall count provided that the batsmen have crossed at the instant of the throw or act.

Note

(a) Position of Sightscreens
Sightscreens should, if possible, be positioned wholly outside the playing area, as near as possible to the boundary line.

LAW 20. LOST BALL

1. Runs Scored

If a ball in play cannot be found or recovered, any fieldsman may call "lost ball" when six runs shall be added to the score; but if more than six have been run before "lost ball" is called, as many runs as have been completed shall be scored. The run in progress shall count provided that the batsmen have crossed at the instant of the call of "lost ball".

2. How Scored

The runs shall be added to the score of the striker if the ball has been struck, but otherwise to the score of byes, leg-byes, no-balls or wides as the case may be.

LAW 21. THE RESULT

1. A Win – Two-innings Matches

The side which has scored a total of runs in excess of that scored by the opposing side in its two completed innings shall be the winner.

2. A Win – One-innings Matches

(a) One-innings matches, unless played out as in 1 above, shall be decided on the first innings, but see Law 12.5 (Continuation after One Innings of Each Side).

(b) If the captains agree to continue play after the completion of one innings of each side in accordance with Law 12.5 (Continuation after One Innings of Each Side) and a result is not achieved on the second innings, the first innings result shall stand.

3. Umpires Awarding a Match

(a) A match shall be lost by a side which, during the match, (i) refuses to play, or (ii) concedes defeat, and the umpires shall award the match to the other side.

(b) Should both batsmen at the wickets or the fielding side leave the field at any time without the agreement of the umpires, this shall constitute a refusal to play and, on appeal, the umpires shall award the match to the other side in accordance with (a) above.

4. A Tie

The result of a match shall be a tie when the scores are equal at the conclusion of play, but only if the side batting last has completed its innings.

If the scores of the completed first innings of a one-day match are equal, it shall be a tie but only if the match has not been played out to a further conclusion.

5. A Draw

A match not determined in any of the ways as in 1, 2, 3 and 4 above shall count as a draw.

6. Correctness of Result

Any decision as to the correctness of the scores shall be the responsibility of the umpires. See Law 3.14 (Correctness of Scores).

If, after the umpires and players have left the field in the belief that the match has been concluded, the umpires decide that a mistake in scoring has occurred, which affects the result, and provided time has not been reached, they shall order play to resume and to continue until the agreed finishing time unless a result is reached earlier.

If the umpires decide that a mistake has occurred and time has been reached, the umpires shall immediately inform both captains of the necessary corrections to the scores and, if applicable, to the result.

7. Acceptance of Result

In accepting the scores as notified by the scorers and agreed by the umpires, the captains of both sides thereby accept the result.

Notes

(a) **Statement of Results**
The result of a finished match is stated as a win by runs, except in the case of a win by the side batting last when it is by the number of wickets still then to fall.

(b) **Winning Hit or Extras**
As soon as the side has won, see 1 and 2 above, the umpire shall call "time", the match is finished, and nothing that happens thereafter other than as a result of a mistake in scoring (see 6 above) shall be regarded as part of the match.

However, if a boundary constitutes the winning hit – or extras – and the boundary allowance exceeds the number of runs required to win the match, such runs scored shall be credited to the side's total and, in the case of a hit, to the striker's score.

LAW 22.   THE OVER

1. Number of Balls

The ball shall be bowled from each wicket alternately in overs of either six or eight balls according to agreement before the match.

2. Call of "Over"

When the agreed number of balls has been bowled, and as the ball becomes dead or when it becomes clear to the umpire at the bowler's end that both the fielding side and the batsmen at the wicket have ceased to regard the ball as in play, the umpire shall call "over" before leaving the wicket.

3. No-ball or Wide-ball

Neither a no-ball nor a wide-ball shall be reckoned as one of the over.

4. Umpire Miscounting

If an umpire miscounts the number of balls, the over as counted by the umpire shall stand.

5. Bowler Changing Ends

A bowler shall be allowed to change ends as often as desired, provided only that he does not bowl two overs consecutively in an innings.

6. The Bowler Finishing an Over

A bowler shall finish an over in progress unless he be incapacitated or be suspended under Law 42.8 (The Bowling of Fast Short-pitched Balls), 9 (The Bowling of Fast High Full Pitches), 10 (Time Wasting) and 11 (Players Damaging the Pitch). If an over is left incomplete for any reason at the start of an interval or interruption of play, it shall be finished on the resumption of play.

7. Bowler Incapacitated or Suspended during an Over

If, for any reason, a bowler is incapacitated while running up to bowl the first ball of an over, or is incapacitated or suspended during an over, the umpire shall call and signal "dead ball" and another bowler shall be allowed to bowl or complete the over from the same end, provided only that he shall not bowl two overs, or part thereof, consecutively in one innings.

8. Position of Non-striker

The batsman at the bowler's end shall normally stand on the opposite side of the wicket to that from which the ball is being delivered, unless a request to do otherwise is granted by the umpire.

LAW 23. DEAD BALL

1. The Ball Becomes Dead

When:

   (a) It is finally settled in the hands of the wicket-keeper or the bowler.

   (b) It reaches or pitches over the boundary.

   (c) A batsman is out.

   (d) Whether played or not, it lodges in the clothing or equipment of a batsman or the clothing of an umpire.

   (e) A ball lodges in a protective helmet worn by a member of the fielding side.

   (f) A penalty is awarded under Law 20 (Lost Ball) or Law 41.1 (Fielding the Ball).

   (g) The umpire calls "over" or "time".

2. Either Umpire Shall Call and Signal "Dead Ball"

When:

   (a) He intervenes in a case of unfair play.

   (b) A serious injury to a player or umpire occurs.

   (c) He is satisfied that, for an adequate reason, the striker is not ready to receive the ball and makes no attempt to play it.

   (d) The bowler drops the ball accidentally before delivery, or the ball does not leave his hand for any reason other than in an attempt to run out the non-striker (See Law 24.5 – Bowler Attempting to Run Out Non-striker before Delivery).

   (e) One or both bails fall from the striker's wicket before he receives delivery.

   (f) He leaves his normal position for consultation.

   (g) He is required to do so under Law 26.3 (Disallowance of Leg-byes), etc.

3. The Ball Ceases to be Dead

When:

   (a) The bowler starts his run-up or bowling action.

4. The Ball is Not Dead

When:

   (a) It strikes an umpire (unless it lodges in his dress).

   (b) The wicket is broken or struck down (unless a batsman is out thereby).

   (c) An unsuccessful appeal is made.

   (d) The wicket is broken accidentally either by the bowler during his delivery or by a batsman in running.

   (e) The umpire has called "no-ball" or "wide".

Notes

(a) Ball Finally Settled

Whether the ball is finally settled or not – see 1(a) above – must be a question for the umpires alone to decide.

(b) Action on Call of "Dead Ball"

(i) If "dead ball" is called prior to the striker receiving a delivery, the bowler shall be allowed an additional ball.

(ii) If "dead ball" is called after the striker receives a delivery, the bowler shall not be allowed an additional ball, unless a "no-ball" or "wide" has been called.

LAW 24. NO-BALL

1. Mode of Delivery

The umpire shall indicate to the striker whether the bowler intends to bowl over or round the wicket, overarm or underarm, right or left-handed. Failure on the part of the bowler to indicate in advance a change in his mode of delivery is unfair and the umpire shall call and signal "no-ball".

2. Fair Delivery – The Arm

For a delivery to be fair the ball must be bowled, not thrown – see Note (a) below. If either umpire is not entirely satisfied with the absolute fairness of a delivery in this respect he shall call and signal "no-ball" instantly upon delivery.

3. Fair Delivery – The Feet

The umpire at the bowler's wicket shall call and signal "no-ball" if he is not satisfied that in the delivery stride:

(a) The bowler's back foot has landed within and not touching the return crease or its forward extension; or

(b) Some part of the front foot whether grounded or raised was behind the popping crease.

4. Bowler Throwing at Striker's Wicket before Delivery

If the bowler, before delivering the ball, throws it at the striker's wicket in an attempt to run him out, the umpire shall call and signal "no-ball". See Law 42.12 (Batsman Unfairly Stealing a Run) and Law 38 (Run Out).

5. Bowler Attempting to Run Out Non-striker before Delivery

If the bowler, before delivering the ball, attempts to run out the non-striker, any runs which result shall be allowed and shall be scored as no-balls. Such an attempt shall not count as a ball in the over. The umpire shall not call "no-ball". See Law 42.12 (Batsman Unfairly Stealing a Run).

6. Infringement of Laws by a Wicket-keeper or a Fieldsman

The umpire shall call and signal "no-ball" in the event of the wicket-keeper infringing Law 40.1 (Position of Wicket-keeper) or a fieldsman infringing Law 41.2 (Limitation of On-side Fieldsmen) or Law 41.3 (Position of Fieldsmen).

7. Revoking a Call

An umpire shall revoke the call "no-ball" if the ball does not leave the bowler's hand for any reason. See Law 23.2 (Either Umpire Shall Call and Signal "Dead Ball").

8. Penalty

A penalty of one run for a no-ball shall be scored if no runs are made otherwise.

9. Runs from a No-ball

The striker may hit a no-ball and whatever runs result shall be added to his score. Runs made otherwise from a no-ball shall be scored no-balls.

10. Out from a No-ball

The striker shall be out from a no-ball if he breaks Law 34 (Hit the Ball Twice) and either batsman may be run out or shall be given out if either breaks Law 33 (Handled the Ball) or Law 37 (Obstructing the Field).

11. Batsman Given Out off a No-ball

Should a batsman be given out off a no-ball the penalty for bowling it shall stand unless runs are otherwise scored.

Notes

(a) Definition of a Throw

A ball shall be deemed to have been thrown if, in the opinion of either umpire, the process of straightening the bowling arm, whether it be partial or complete, takes place during that part of the delivery swing which directly precedes the ball leaving the hand. This definition shall not debar a bowler from the use of the wrist in the delivery swing.

(b) No-ball Not Counting in Over

A no-ball shall not be reckoned as one of the over. See Law 22.3 (No-ball or Wide-ball).

LAW 25. WIDE-BALL

1. Judging a Wide

If the bowler bowls the ball so high over or so wide of the wicket that, in the opinion of the umpire, it passes out of reach of the striker, standing in a normal guard position, the umpire shall call and signal "wide-ball" as soon as it has passed the line of the striker's wicket.

The umpire shall not adjudge a ball as being wide if:

(a) The striker, by moving from his guard position, causes the ball to pass out of his reach.

(b) The striker moves and thus brings the ball within his reach.

2. Penalty

A penalty of one run for a wide shall be scored if no runs are made otherwise.

3. Ball Coming to Rest in Front of the Striker

If a ball which the umpire considers to have been delivered comes to rest in front of the line of the striker's wicket, "wide" shall not be called. The striker has a right, without interference from the fielding side, to make one attempt to hit the ball. If the fielding side interfere, the umpire shall replace the ball where it came to rest and shall order the fieldsmen to resume the places they occupied in the field before the ball was delivered.

The umpire shall call and signal "dead ball" as soon as it is clear that the striker does not intend to hit the ball, or after the striker has made an unsuccessful attempt to hit the ball.

4. Revoking a Call

The umpire shall revoke the call if the striker hits a ball which has been called "wide".

5. Ball Not Dead

The ball does not become dead on the call of "wide-ball" – see Law 23.4 (The Ball is Not Dead).

6. Runs Resulting from a Wide

All runs which are run or result from a wide-ball which is not a no-ball shall be scored wide-balls, or if no runs are made one shall be scored.

7. Out from a Wide

The striker shall be out from a wide-ball if he breaks Law 35 (Hit Wicket), or Law 39 (Stumped). Either batsman may be run out and shall be out if he breaks Law 33 (Handled the Ball), or Law 37 (Obstructing the Field).

8. Batsman Given Out off a Wide

Should a batsman be given out off a wide, the penalty for bowling it shall stand unless runs are otherwise made.

Note

(a) Wide-ball Not Counting in Over
A wide-ball shall not be reckoned as one of the over – see Law 22.3 (No-ball or Wide-ball).

LAW 26. BYE AND LEG-BYE

1. Byes

If the ball, not having been called "wide" or "no-ball", passes the striker without touching his bat or person, and any runs are obtained, the umpire shall signal "bye" and the run or runs shall be credited as such to the batting side.

2. Leg-byes

If the ball, not having been called "wide" or "no-ball", is unintentionally deflected by the striker's dress or person, except a hand holding the bat, and any runs are obtained the umpire shall signal "leg-bye" and the run or runs so scored shall be credited as such to the batting side.

Such leg-byes shall be scored only if, in the opinion of the umpire, the striker has:

(a) Attempted to play the ball with his bat; or

(b) Tried to avoid being hit by the ball.

3. Disallowance of Leg-byes

In the case of a deflection by the striker's person, other than in 2(a) and (b) above, the umpire shall call and signal "dead ball" as soon as one run has been completed or when it is clear that a run is not being attempted, or the ball has reached the boundary.

On the call and signal of "dead ball" the batsmen shall return to their original ends and no runs shall be allowed.

LAW 27. APPEALS

1. Time of Appeals

The umpires shall not give a batsman out unless appealed to by the other side which shall be done prior to the bowler beginning his run-up or bowling action to deliver the next ball. Under Law 23.1 (g) (The Ball Becomes Dead), the ball is dead on "over" being called; this does not, however, invalidate an appeal made prior to the first ball of the following over provided "time" has not been called – see Law 17.1 (Call of Time).

2. An Appeal "How's That?"

An appeal "How's That?" shall cover all ways of being out.

3. Answering Appeals

The umpire at the bowler's wicket shall answer appeals before the other umpire in all cases except those arising out of Law 35 (Hit Wicket) or Law 39 (Stumped) or Law 38 (Run Out) when this occurs at the striker's wicket.

When either umpire has given a batsman not out, the other umpire shall, within his jurisdiction, answer the appeal or a further appeal, provided it is made in time in accordance with 1 above (Time of Appeals).

4. Consultation by Umpires

An umpire may consult with the other umpire on a point of fact which the latter may have been in a better position to see and shall then give his decision. If, after consultation, there is still doubt remaining the decision shall be in favour of the batsman.

5. Batsman Leaving his Wicket under a Misapprehension

The umpires shall intervene if satisfied that a batsman, not having been given out, has left his wicket under a misapprehension that he has been dismissed.

6. Umpire's Decision

The umpire's decision is final. He may alter his decision, provided that such alteration is made promptly.

7. Withdrawal of an Appeal

In exceptional circumstances the captain of the fielding side may seek permission of the umpire to withdraw an appeal provided the outgoing batsman has not left the playing area. If this is allowed, the umpire shall cancel his decision.

LAW 28.   THE WICKET IS DOWN

1. Wicket Down

The wicket is down if:

    (a) Either the ball or the striker's bat or person completely removes either bail from the top of the stumps. A disturbance of a bail, whether temporary or not, shall not constitute a complete removal, but the wicket is down if a bail in falling lodges between two of the stumps.

    (b) Any player completely removes with his hand or arm a bail from the top of the stumps, provided that the ball is held in that hand or in the hand of the arm so used.

    (c) When both bails are off, a stump is struck out of the ground by the ball, or a player strikes or pulls a stump out of the ground, providing that the ball is held in the hand(s) or in the hand of the arm so used.

2. One Bail Off

If one bail is off, it shall be sufficient for the purpose of putting the wicket down to remove the remaining bail, or to strike or pull any of the three stumps out of the ground in any of the ways stated in 1 above.

3. All the Stumps Out of the Ground

If all the stumps are out of the ground, the fielding side shall be allowed to put back one or more stumps in order to have an opportunity of putting the wicket down.

4. Dispensing with Bails

If, owing to the strength of the wind, it has been agreed to dispense with the bails in accordance with Law 8, Note (a) (Dispensing with Bails), the decision as to when the wicket is down is one for the umpires to decide on the facts before them. In such circumstances and if the umpires so decide, the wicket shall be held to be down even though a stump has not been struck out of the ground.

Note

(a) **Remaking the Wicket**
If the wicket is broken while the ball is in play, it is not the umpire's duty to remake the wicket until the ball has become dead – see Law 23 (Dead Ball). A member of the fielding side, however, may remake the wicket in such circumstances.

LAW 29.   BATSMAN OUT OF HIS GROUND

1. When out of his Ground

A batsman shall be considered to be out of his ground unless some part of his bat in his hand or of his person is grounded behind the line of the popping crease.

LAW 30.   BOWLED

1. Out Bowled

The striker shall be out *Bowled* if:

(a) His wicket is bowled down, even if the ball first touches his bat or person.

(b) He breaks his wicket by hitting or kicking the ball on to it before the completion of a stroke, or as a result of attempting to guard his wicket. See Law 34.1 (Out Hit the Ball Twice).

Note

(a) **Out Bowled – Not lbw**
The striker is out bowled if the ball is deflected on to his wicket even though a decision against him would be justified under Law 36 (lbw).

LAW 31.   TIMED OUT

1. Out Timed Out

An incoming batsman shall be out *Timed Out* if he wilfully takes more than two minutes to come in – the two minutes being timed from the moment a wicket falls until the new batsman steps on to the field of play.

If this is not complied with and if the umpire is satisfied that the delay was wilful and if an appeal is made, the new batsman shall be given out by the umpire at the bowler's end.

2. Time to be Added

The time taken by the umpires to investigate the cause of the delay shall be added at the normal close of play.

Notes

(a) **Entry in Scorebook**
The correct entry in the scorebook when a batsman is given out under this Law is "timed out", and the bowler does not get credit for the wicket.

(b) **Batsmen Crossing on the Field of Play**
It is an essential duty of the captains to ensure that the in-going batsman passes the out-going one before the latter leaves the field of play.

LAW 32. CAUGHT

1. Out Caught

The striker shall be out *Caught* if the ball touches his bat or if it touches below the wrist his hand or glove, holding the bat, and is subsequently held by a fieldsman before it touches the ground.

2. A Fair Catch

A catch shall be considered to have been fairly made if:

    (a) The fieldsman is within the field of play throughout the act of making the catch.

        (i) The act of making the catch shall start from the time when the fieldsman first handles the ball and shall end when he both retains complete control over the further disposal of the ball and remains within the field of play.

        (ii) In order to be within the field of play, the fieldsman may not touch or ground any part of his person on or over a boundary line. When the boundary is marked by a fence or board the fieldsman may not ground any part of his person over the boundary fence or board, but may touch or lean over the boundary fence or board in completing the catch.

    (b) The ball is hugged to the body of the catcher or accidentally lodges in his dress or, in the case of the wicket-keeper, in his pads. However, a striker may not be caught if a ball lodges in a protective helmet worn by a fieldsman, in which case the umpire shall call and signal "dead ball". See Law 23 (Dead Ball).

    (c) The ball does not touch the ground even though a hand holding it does so in effecting the catch.

    (d) A fieldsman catches the ball, after it has been lawfully played a second time by the striker, but only if the ball has not touched the ground since being first struck.

    (e) A fieldsman catches the ball after it has touched an umpire, another fieldsman or the other batsman. However, a striker may not be caught if a ball has touched a protective helmet worn by a fieldsman.

    (f) The ball is caught off an obstruction within the boundary provided it has not previously been agreed to regard the obstruction as a boundary.

3. Scoring of Runs

If a striker is caught, no run shall be scored.

Notes

    (a) Scoring from an Attempted Catch
    When a fieldsman carrying the ball touches or grounds any part of his person on or over a boundary marked by a line, six runs shall be scored.

    (b) Ball Still in Play
    If a fieldsman releases the ball before he crosses the boundary, the ball will be considered to be still in play and it may be caught by another fieldsman. However, if the original fieldsman returns to the field of play and handles the ball, a catch may not be made.

LAW 33. HANDLED THE BALL

1. Out Handled the Ball

Either batsman on appeal shall be out *Handled the Ball* if he wilfully touches the ball while in play with the hand not holding the bat unless he does so with the consent of the opposite side.

Note

    (a) Entry in Scorebook
    The correct entry in the scorebook when a batsman is given out under this Law is "handled the ball", and the bowler does not get credit for the wicket.

LAW 34.   HIT THE BALL TWICE

1. Out Hit the Ball Twice

The striker, on appeal, shall be out *Hit the Ball Twice* if, after the ball is struck or is stopped by any part of his person, he wilfully strikes it again with his bat or person except for the sole purpose of guarding his wicket: this he may do with his bat or any part of his person other than his hands, but see Law 37.2 (Obstructing a Ball From Being Caught).

For the purpose of this Law, a hand holding the bat shall be regarded as part of the bat.

2. Returning the Ball to a Fieldsman

The striker, on appeal, shall be out under this Law if, without the consent of the opposite side, he uses his bat or person to return the ball to any of the fielding side.

3. Runs from Ball Lawfully Struck Twice

No runs except those which result from an overthrow or penalty – see Law 41 (The Fieldsman) – shall be scored from a ball lawfully struck twice.

Notes

(a) Entry in Scorebook
The correct entry in the scorebook when the striker is given out under this Law is "hit the ball twice", and the bowler does not get credit for the wicket.

(b) Runs Credited to the Batsman
Any runs awarded under 3 above as a result of an overthrow or penalty shall be credited to the striker, provided the ball in the first instance has touched the bat, or, if otherwise, as extras.

LAW 35.   HIT WICKET

1. Out Hit Wicket

The striker shall be out *Hit Wicket* if, while the ball is in play:

(a) His wicket is broken with any part of his person, dress, or equipment as a result of any action taken by him in preparing to receive or in receiving a delivery, or in setting off for his first run, immediately after playing, or playing at, the ball.

(b) He hits down his wicket whilst lawfully making a second stroke for the purpose of guarding his wicket within the provisions of Law 34.1 (Out Hit the Ball Twice).

Notes

(a) Not Out Hit Wicket
A batsman is not out under this Law should his wicket be broken in any of the ways referred to in 1(a) above if:

(i) It occurs while he is in the act of running, other than in setting off for his first run immediately after playing at the ball, or while he is avoiding being run out or stumped.

(ii) The bowler after starting his run-up or bowling action does not deliver the ball; in which case the umpire shall immediately call and signal "dead ball".

(iii) It occurs whilst he is avoiding a throw-in at any time.

LAW 36.   LEG BEFORE WICKET

1. Out lbw

The striker shall be out *lbw* in the circumstances set out below:

(a) Striker Attempting to Play the Ball
The striker shall be out lbw if he first intercepts with any part of his person, dress or equipment a fair ball which would have hit the wicket and which has not previously touched his bat or a hand holding the bat, provided that:

(i) The ball pitched in a straight line between wicket and wicket or on the off side of the striker's wicket, or was intercepted full pitch; and

(ii) The point of impact is in a straight line between wicket and wicket, even if above the level of the bails.

(b) Striker Making No Attempt to Play the Ball

The striker shall be out lbw even if the ball is intercepted outside the line of the off stump if, in the opinion of the umpire, he has made no genuine attempt to play the ball with his bat, but has intercepted the ball with some part of his person and if the other circumstances set out in (a) above apply.

LAW 37. OBSTRUCTING THE FIELD

1. Wilful Obstruction

Either batsman, on appeal, shall be out *Obstructing the Field* if he wilfully obstructs the opposite side by word or action.

2. Obstructing a Ball From Being Caught

The striker, on appeal, shall be out should wilful obstruction by either batsman prevent a catch being made.

This shall apply even though the striker causes the obstruction in lawfully guarding his wicket under the provisions of Law 34. See Law 34.1 (Out Hit the Ball Twice).

Notes

(a) Accidental Obstruction
The umpires must decide whether the obstruction was wilful or not. The accidental interception of a throw-in by a batsman while running does not break this Law.

(b) Entry in Scorebook
The correct entry in the scorebook when a batsman is given out under this Law is "obstructing the field", and the bowler does not get credit for the wicket.

LAW 38. RUN OUT

1. Out Run Out

Either batsman shall be out *Run Out* if in running or at any time while the ball is in play – except in the circumstances described in Law 39 (Stumped) – he is out of his ground and his wicket is put down by the opposite side. If, however, a batsman in running makes good his ground he shall not be out run out if he subsequently leaves his ground, in order to avoid injury, and the wicket is put down.

2. "No-ball" Called

If a no-ball has been called, the striker shall not be given run out unless he attempts to run.

3. Which Batsman Is Out

If the batsmen have crossed in running, he who runs for the wicket which is put down shall be out; if they have not crossed, he who has left the wicket which is put down shall be out. If a batsman remains in his ground or returns to his ground and the other batsman joins him there, the latter shall be out if his wicket is put down.

4. Scoring of Runs

If a batsman is run out, only that run which is being attempted shall not be scored. If, however, an injured striker himself is run out, no runs shall be scored. See Law 2.7 (Transgression of the Laws by an Injured Batsman or Runner).

Notes

(a) Ball Played on to Opposite Wicket
If the ball is played on to the opposite wicket, neither batsman is liable to be run out unless the ball has been touched by a fieldsman before the wicket is broken.

(b) Entry in Scorebook

The correct entry in the scorebook when a batsman is given out under this Law is "run out", and the bowler does not get credit for the wicket.

(c) Run Out off a Fieldsman's Helmet

If, having been played by a batsman, or having come off his person, the ball rebounds directly from a fieldsman's helmet on to the stumps, with either batsman out of his ground, the batsman shall be "not out".

LAW 39.   STUMPED

1. Out Stumped

The striker shall be out *Stumped* if, in receiving the ball, not being a no-ball, he is out of his ground otherwise than in attempting a run and the wicket is put down by the wicket-keeper without the intervention of another fieldsman.

2. Action by the Wicket-keeper

The wicket-keeper may take the ball in front of the wicket in an attempt to stump the striker only if the ball has touched the bat or person of the striker.

Note

(a) Ball Rebounding from Wicket-keeper's Person

The striker may be out stumped if, in the circumstances stated in 1 above, the wicket is broken by a ball rebounding from the wicket-keeper's person or equipment other than a protective helmet or is kicked or thrown by the wicket-keeper on to the wicket.

LAW 40.   THE WICKET-KEEPER

1. Position of Wicket-keeper

The wicket-keeper shall remain wholly behind the wicket until a ball delivered by the bowler touches the bat or person of the striker, or passes the wicket, or until the striker attempts a run.

In the event of the wicket-keeper contravening this Law, the umpire at the striker's end shall call and signal "no-ball" at the instant of delivery or as soon as possible thereafter.

2. Restriction on Actions of the Wicket-keeper

If the wicket-keeper interferes with the striker's right to play the ball and to guard his wicket, the striker shall not be out except under Laws 33 (Handled the Ball), 34 (Hit the Ball Twice), 37 (Obstructing the Field), and 38 (Run Out).

3. Interference with the Wicket-keeper by the Striker

If in the legitimate defence of his wicket, the striker interferes with the wicket-keeper, he shall not be out, except as provided for in Law 37.2 (Obstructing a Ball From Being Caught).

LAW 41.   THE FIELDSMAN

1. Fielding the Ball

The fieldsman may stop the ball with any part of his person, but if he wilfully stops it otherwise, five runs shall be added to the run or runs already scored; if no run has been scored five penalty runs shall be awarded. The run in progress shall count provided that the batsmen have crossed at the instant of the act. If the ball has been struck, the penalty shall be added to the score of the striker, but otherwise to the score of byes, leg-byes, no-balls or wides as the case may be.

2. Limitation of On-side Fieldsmen

The number of on-side fieldsmen behind the popping crease at the instant of the bowler's delivery shall not exceed two. In the event of infringement by the fielding side the umpire at the striker's end shall call and signal "no-ball" at the instant of delivery or as soon as possible thereafter.

3. Position of Fieldsmen

Whilst the ball is in play and until the ball has made contact with the bat or the striker's person or has passed his bat, no fieldsman, other than the bowler, may stand on or have any part of his person extended over the pitch (measuring 22 yards/20.12m × 10 feet/3.05m). In the event of a fieldsman contravening this Law, the umpire at the bowler's end shall call and signal "no-ball" at the instant of delivery or as soon as possible thereafter. See Law 40.1 (Position of Wicket-keeper).

4. Fieldsmen's Protective Helmets

Protective helmets, when not in use by members of the fielding side, shall be placed, if above the surface, only on the ground behind the wicket-keeper. In the event of the ball, when in play, striking a helmet whilst in this position, five penalty runs shall be awarded as laid down in Law 41.1 and Note (a).

Note

> **(a) Batsmen Changing Ends**
> The five runs referred to in 1 and 4 above are a penalty and the batsmen do not change ends solely by reason of this penalty.

LAW 42. UNFAIR PLAY

1. Responsibility of Captains

The captains are responsible at all times for ensuring that play is conducted within the spirit of the game as well as within the Laws.

2. Responsibility of Umpires

The umpires are the sole judges of fair and unfair play.

3. Intervention by the Umpire

The umpires shall intervene without appeal by calling and signalling "dead ball" in the case of unfair play, but should not otherwise interfere with the progress of the game except as required to do so by the Laws.

4. Lifting the Seam

A player shall not lift the seam of the ball for any reason. Should this be done, the umpires shall change the ball for one of similar condition to that in use prior to the contravention. See Note (a).

5. Changing the Condition of the Ball

Any member of the fielding side may polish the ball provided that such polishing wastes no time and that no artificial substance is used. No-one shall rub the ball on the ground or use any artificial substance or take any other action to alter the condition of the ball.

In the event of a contravention of this Law, the umpires, after consultation, shall change the ball for one of similar condition to that in use prior to the contravention.

This Law does not prevent a member of the fielding side from drying a wet ball, or removing mud from the ball. See Note (b).

6. Incommoding the Striker

An umpire is justified in intervening under this Law and shall call and signal "dead ball" if, in his opinion, any player of the fielding side incommodes the striker by any noise or action while he is receiving a ball.

7. Obstruction of a Batsman in Running

It shall be considered unfair if any fieldsman wilfully obstructs a batsman in running. In these circumstances the umpire shall call and signal "dead ball" and allow any completed runs and the run in progress, or alternatively any boundary scored.

8. The Bowling of Fast Short-pitched Balls

The bowling of fast short-pitched balls is unfair if, in the opinion of the umpire at the bowler's end, it constitutes an attempt to intimidate the striker. See Note (d).

Umpires shall consider intimidation to be the deliberate bowling of fast short-pitched balls which by their length, height and direction are intended or likely to inflict physical injury on the striker. The relative skill of the striker shall also be taken into consideration.

In the event of such unfair bowling, the umpire at the bowler's end shall adopt the following procedure:

(a) In the first instance the umpire shall call and signal "no-ball", caution the bowler and inform the other umpire, the captain of the fielding side and the batsmen of what has occurred.

(b) If this caution is ineffective, he shall repeat the above procedure and indicate to the bowler that this is a final warning.

(c) Both the above caution and final warning shall continue to apply even though the bowler may later change ends.

(d) Should the above warnings prove ineffective the umpire at the bowler's end shall:

(i) At the first repetition call and signal "no-ball" and when the ball is dead direct the captain to take the bowler off forthwith and to complete the over with another bowler, provided that the bowler does not bowl two overs or part thereof consecutively. See Law 22.7 (Bowler Incapacitated or Suspended during an Over).

(ii) Not allow the bowler, thus taken off, to bowl again in the same innings.

(iii) Report the occurrence to the captain of the batting side as soon as the players leave the field for an interval.

(iv) Report the occurrence to the executive of the fielding side and to any governing body responsible for the match, who shall take any further action which is considered to be appropriate against the bowler concerned.

9. The Bowling of Fast High Full Pitches

The bowling of fast high full pitches is unfair. See Note (e).

In the event of such unfair bowling the umpire at the bowler's end shall adopt the procedures of caution, final warning, action against the bowler and reporting as set out in 8 above.

10. Time Wasting

Any form of time wasting is unfair.

(a) In the event of the captain of the fielding side wasting time or allowing any member of his side to waste time, the umpire at the bowler's end shall adopt the following procedure:

(i) In the first instance he shall caution the captain of the fielding side and inform the other umpire of what has occurred.

(ii) If this caution is ineffective he shall repeat the above procedure and indicate to the captain that this is a final warning.

(iii) The umpire shall report the occurrence to the captain of the batting side as soon as the players leave the field for an interval.

(iv) Should the above procedure prove ineffective the umpire shall report the occurrence to the executive of the fielding side and to any governing body responsible for that match, who shall take appropriate action against the captain and the players concerned.

(b) In the event of a bowler taking unnecessarily long to bowl an over the umpire at the bowler's end shall adopt the procedures, other than the calling of "no-ball", of caution, final warning, action against the bowler and reporting as set out in 8 above.

(c) In the event of a batsman wasting time (See Note (f)) other than in the manner described in Law 31 (Timed Out), the umpire at the bowler's end shall adopt the following procedure:

    (i) In the first instance he shall caution the batsman and inform the other umpire at once, and the captain of the batting side, as soon as the players leave the field for an interval, of what has occurred.

    (ii) If this proves ineffective, he shall repeat the caution, indicate to the batsman that this is a final warning and inform the other umpire.

    (iii) The umpire shall report the occurrence to both captains as soon as the players leave the field for an interval.

    (iv) Should the above procedure prove ineffective, the umpire shall report the occurrence to the executive of the batting side and to any governing body responsible for that match, who shall take appropriate action against the player concerned.

11. Players Damaging the Pitch

The umpires shall intervene and prevent players from causing damage to the pitch which may assist the bowlers of either side. See Note (c).

(a) In the event of any member of the fielding side damaging the pitch, the umpire shall follow the procedure of caution, final warning, and reporting as set out in 10(a) above.

(b) In the event of a bowler contravening this Law by running down the pitch after delivering the ball, the umpire at the bowler's end shall first caution the bowler. If this caution is ineffective the umpire shall adopt the procedures, other than the calling of "no-ball", as set out in 8 above.

(c) In the event of a batsman damaging the pitch the umpire at the bowler's end shall follow the procedures of caution, final warning and reporting as set out in 10(c) above.

12. Batsman Unfairly Stealing a Run

Any attempt by the batsman to steal a run during the bowler's run-up is unfair. Unless the bowler attempts to run out either batsman – see Law 24.4 (Bowler Throwing at Striker's Wicket before Delivery) and Law 24.5 (Bowler Attempting to Run Out Non-striker before Delivery) – the umpire shall call and signal "dead ball" as soon as the batsmen cross in any such attempt to run. The batsmen shall then return to their original wickets.

13. Player's Conduct

In the event of a player failing to comply with the instructions of an umpire, criticising his decisions by word or action, or showing dissent, or generally behaving in a manner which might bring the game into disrepute, the umpire concerned shall, in the first place, report the matter to the other umpire and to the player's captain requesting the latter to take action. If this proves ineffective, the umpire shall report the incident as soon as possible to the executive of the player's team and to any governing body responsible for the match, who shall take any further action which is considered appropriate against the player or players concerned.

Notes

    (a) The Condition of the Ball
    Umpires shall make frequent and irregular inspections of the condition of the ball.

    (b) Drying of a Wet Ball
    A wet ball may be dried on a towel or with sawdust.

    (c) Danger Area
    The danger area on the pitch, which must be protected from damage by a bowler, shall be regarded by the umpires as the area contained by an imaginary line 4 feet/1.22m from the popping crease, and parallel to it, and within two imaginary and parallel lines drawn down the pitch from points on that line 1 foot/30.48cm on either side of the middle stump.

(d) Fast Short-pitched Balls

As a guide, a fast short-pitched ball is one which pitches short and passes, or would have passed, above the shoulder height of the striker standing in a normal batting stance at the crease.

(e) The Bowling of Fast Full Pitches

The bowling of one fast, high full pitch shall be considered to be unfair if, in the opinion of the umpire, it is deliberate, bowled at the striker, and if it passes or would have passed above the shoulder height of the striker when standing in a normal batting stance at the crease.

(f) Time Wasting by Batsmen

Other than in exceptional circumstances, the batsman should always be ready to take strike when the bowler is ready to start his run-up.

CHANGES IN THE LAWS

The following significant changes in the Laws of Cricket have been made since the publication of *Wisden*, 1992.

Law 2.1 (Substitutes) The phrase "or does not take the field" previously appeared after "who has to leave the field". This has been deleted.

Law 2.2 The law barring substitutes from acting as wicket-keeper was introduced experimentally in 1989. It has now been formally adopted.

Law 10.1 (Rolling the Pitch) The law previously gave the captain of the batting side the right to have the pitch rolled if the start was delayed. The umpires now have the right to refuse if the delay has had no significant effect.

Law 23.2 (Dead Ball) The phrase "other than in an attempt to run out the non-striker" has been added.

Law 36.1 (Leg Before Wicket) The phrase "or was intercepted full pitch" replaces "or in the case of a ball intercepted full pitch would have pitched in a straight line between wicket and wicket".

Law 38.4 (Run Out) Note (c) is new.

Law 39 (Stumped) – Note – The phrase "other than a protective helmet" has been added.

REGULATIONS OF THE INTERNATIONAL CRICKET COUNCIL, 1992

Extracts

1. Playing Conditions

The official Laws of Cricket shall be followed on all tours unless an agreement to meet special cases is arrived at between the Members concerned before the visiting team commences the first match of any tour.

2. Classification of First-class Matches

1. Definitions

A match of three or more days' duration between two sides of 11 players officially adjudged first-class shall be regarded as a first-class fixture.

2. Rules

    (a) Foundation and Full Members of ICC shall decide the status of matches of three or more days' duration played in their countries.

    (b) In matches of three or more days' duration played in countries which are not Foundation Members or Full Members of ICC:

        (i) If the visiting team comes from a country which is a Foundation or Full Member of ICC, that country shall decide the status of matches.

        (ii) If the visiting team does not come from a country which is a Foundation or Full Member of ICC, or is a Commonwealth team composed of players from different countries, ICC shall decide the status of matches.

Notes

    (a) Governing bodies agree that the interest of first-class cricket will be served by ensuring that first-class status is *not* accorded to any match in which one or other of the teams taking part cannot on a strict interpretation of the definition be adjudged first-class.

    (b) In case of any disputes arising from these Rules, the Secretary of ICC shall refer the matter for decision to the Council, failing unanimous agreement by postal communication being reached.

3. First-class Status

The following matches shall be regarded as first-class, subject to the provisions of 1(a) being completely complied with:

    (a) In the British Isles

    The following matches of three or more days' duration shall automatically be considered first-class:

        (i) County Championship matches.

        (ii) Official representative tourist matches from Full Member countries unless specifically excluded.

        (iii) MCC v any first-class county.

        (iv) Oxford v Cambridge and either University against first-class counties.

        (v) Scotland v Ireland.

    (b) In Australia

        (i) Sheffield Shield matches.

        (ii) Matches played by teams representing states of the Commonwealth of Australia between each other or against opponents adjudged first-class.

(c) In India

  (i) Ranji Trophy matches.

  (ii) Duleep Trophy matches.

  (iii) Irani Trophy matches.

  (iv) Matches played by teams representing state or regional associations affiliated to the Board of Control between each other or against opponents adjudged first-class.

  (v) All three-day matches played against representative visiting sides.

(d) In New Zealand

  (i) Shell Trophy matches.

  (ii) Matches played by teams representing major associations of the North and South Islands, between each other or against opponents adjudged first-class.

(e) In Pakistan

  (i) Matches played by teams representing divisional associations affiliated to the Board of Control, between each other or against teams adjudged first-class.

  (ii) Matches between the divisional associations and the Universities Past and Present XI.

  (iii) Quaid-e-Azam Trophy matches.

  (iv) BCCP Patron's Trophy matches.

(f) In South Africa

  (i) Castle Cup competition four-day matches between Transvaal, Northern Transvaal, OFS, Western Province, Eastern Province, Border and Natal.

  (ii) The President's Cup competition three-day matches between the 'B' teams of Transvaal, Northern Transvaal, Western Province, Eastern Province, OFS and Natal. This competition was discontinued in 1992-93.

  (iii) The United Cricket Board Bowl competition three-day cricket between Eastern Transvaal, Western Transvaal, Griqualand West and Boland.

(g) In Sri Lanka

  (i) Matches of three days or more against touring sides adjudged first-class.

  (ii) Singer Inter-Provincial Cricket tournament matches played over three days for the President's Trophy.

  (iii) Inter-Club Division I tournament matches played over three days for the P. Saravanamuttu Trophy.

  (iv) Super Tournament.

(h) In West Indies

  (i) Matches played by teams representing Barbados, Guyana, Jamaica, Trinidad & Tobago, the Windward Islands and the Leeward Islands, either for the Red Stripe Cup or against other opponents adjudged first-class.

  (ii) The final of the Inter-County tournament in Guyana between Berbice, Demerara and Essequibo.

(i) In all Foundation and Full Member countries represented on the Council

  (i) Test matches and matches against teams adjudged first-class played by official touring teams.

  (ii) Official Test Trial matches.

  (iii) Special matches between teams adjudged first-class by the governing body or bodies concerned.

Classification of Limited-over International Matches

The following should be classified as limited-over internationals:

(a) All matches played between the Full Member countries of ICC as part of an official tour itinerary.

(b) All matches played as part of an official tournament by Full Member countries. These need not necessarily be held in a Full Member country.

(c) All matches played in the official World Cup competition, including matches involving Associate Member countries.

(d) All matches played in the Asia Cup competition.

Qualification Rules for Test Matches and Limited-over International Matches

Qualification by Birth

A cricketer is qualified to play cricket for the country of his birth provided he has not played cricket for any other Member country during the two immediately preceding years.

Qualification by Residence

A cricketer is qualified to play cricket for any Full or Associate Member country in which he has resided for at least 183 days in each of the four immediately preceding years provided that in each such case he has not played cricket for any other Member country during that period of four years.

Member Countries May Impose More Stringent Rules

The governing body for cricket of any Member country may impose more stringent qualification rules for that country.

REGULATIONS OF ICC FULL MEMBERS, 1992

Extracts

Duration of Test Matches

Within a maximum of 30 hours' playing time, the duration of Test matches shall be a matter for negotiation and agreement between the two countries in any particular series of Test matches.

When agreeing the Playing Conditions prior to the commencement of a Test series, the participating countries may:

(a) Extend the playing hours of the last Test beyond the limit of 30 hours, in a series in which, at the conclusion of the penultimate match, one side does not hold a lead of more than one match.

(b) In the event of play being suspended for any reason other than normal intervals, extend the playing time on that day by the amount of time lost up to a maximum of one hour, except in the last hour of the match.

(c) Play on the rest day, conditions and circumstances permitting, should a full day's play be lost on either the second or third scheduled days of play.

(d) Make up time lost in excess of five minutes in each day's play owing to circumstances outside the game, other than acts of God.

Note: The umpires shall determine when such time shall be made up. This could, if conditions and circumstances permit, include the following day.

The Appointment of Umpires

The following rules for the selection and appointment of Test match umpires shall be followed as far as is practicable to do so:

(a) The home authority shall appoint a committee for the purpose of nominating umpires to officiate in all Test matches.

(b) Test match umpires will be nominated by this committee from those umpires officiating in first-class matches during the current season.

(c) Wherever possible, umpires likely to be nominated by this committee shall officiate in matches against the visiting team, thus giving the visiting captain an opportunity to judge the umpires to be nominated. As long as possible before each Test match, the manager of the touring team and the secretary of the home authority will be informed of the names of the umpires nominated for the particular Test match. Any objection against either umpire must be lodged within three days of the notice being received or at least seven days before the match, whichever is the later, and will be dealt with by the committee as set up in (a), or by a special committee appointed by the home authority whose decision shall be final. The names of the umpires shall not be given to the media until after this time has elapsed.

(d) While a captain is entitled to submit objections to a particular umpire nominated for a Test match, he may not ask for a particular umpire to be given precedence for appointment over any other. If either captain raises what is considered by the committee (or by the special committee appointed by the home authority) to be a definite and reasonable objection to any particular umpire, his wishes shall be met.

(e) The sole authority for handling media enquiries shall be the official representative appointed by the home authority for the purpose, and not the captains or any of the players.

(f) Provided the two countries involved in a tour agree, nothing shall prevent them from appointing independent umpires from another country or countries rather than using home authority umpires.

Minimum Overs in the Day in Test Matches

Regulation for Test matches only.

(a) Play shall continue on each day until the completion of a minimum number of overs or until the scheduled cessation time, whichever is the later. The minimum number of overs to be completed, unless an innings ends or an interruption occurs, shall be:

    (i) on days other than the last day – a minimum of 90 overs.

    (ii) on the last day – a minimum of 75 overs (or 15 overs per hour) for playing time other than the last hour when a minimum of 15 six-ball overs shall be bowled. All calculations with regard to suspensions of play or the start of a new innings shall be based on one over for each full four minutes. If, however, at any time after 30 minutes of the last hour have elapsed both captains (the batsmen at the wicket may act for their captain) accept that there is no prospect of a result to the match, they may agree to cease play at that time.

Penalties for Slow Over-rates

(i) **Test Matches**

Over-rates shall be assessed on 15 overs per hour, i.e. a minimum of 90 overs in a six-hour day, subject to the following deductions:

Two minutes per wicket taken;
Actual time where treatment by authorised medical personnel is required on the ground, and also for a player leaving the field owing to serious injury;
Four minutes for one drinks break per session, except in the West Indies, where it is accepted that an additional drinks break should be permitted.

Overs will be calculated at the end of the match. For each over short of the target number, five per cent of each player's match fee in the fielding side is to be deducted.

(ii) Limited-overs International Matches

The target over-rate is to be 15 overs per hour. In the event of the target over-rate not being reached, for each over short of the number required to be bowled in the scheduled time, the fielding side will be fined an amount equal to five per cent of each player's match fee for the match.

For touring teams where a tour fee is paid, the match fee will be taken to be the match fee paid by the touring team's country in its previous domestic season.

A penalty may be reviewed by the match referee if, after consultation with the umpires, he is of the opinion that events beyond the control of the fielding side, including time-wasting by the batting side, prevented that team from bowling the required number of overs. The batting side may be fined at the same rate as the fielding side if, in the opinion of the match referee, the batting side is guilty of slowing down the over-rate.

THE BOWLING OF FAST, SHORT-PITCHED BALLS: LAW 42.8

Experimental Regulation for Test matches only for three years with effect from October 1, 1991

A bowler shall be limited to one fast, short-pitched ball per over per batsman. If this limit is exceeded, the following procedure shall be applied:

(a) If a bowler delivers a second fast, short-pitched ball in an over to the same batsman, the umpire shall call and signal "no-ball" and indicate the reason to the bowler, to the captain of the fielding side and to the other umpire.

(b) If a bowler is no-balled a second time in the innings for the same offence, the umpire shall warn the bowler, indicate to him that this is a final warning, and inform the captain of the fielding side and the other umpire of what has occurred.

(c) If the bowler is no-balled a third time in the same innings for the same offence, the umpire shall:

    (i) As soon as the ball is dead, direct the captain of the fielding side to take the bowler off forthwith and to complete the over with another bowler, provided that the bowler does not bowl two overs, or part thereof, consecutively;

    (ii) Not allow the bowler, thus taken off, to bowl in the same innings;

    (iii) Report the occurrence to the captain of the batting side as soon as the players leave the field for an interval;

    (iv) Report the occurrence immediately after the day's play to the management of the fielding side and to the governing body responsible for the match, who shall take any further action which is considered to be appropriate against the bowler concerned.

Definition

A fast, short-pitched ball shall be defined as a ball which passes, or would have passed, above the shoulder of the batsman standing upright at the crease.

THE BOWLING OF FAST, HIGH FULL PITCHES: LAW 42.9

The bowling of fast, high full pitches is unfair.

In Test matches and limited-overs internationals played by Test match countries, Law 42.9 shall be replaced by the following:

A fast, high full-pitched ball shall be defined as a ball that passes, or would have passed, on the full above the shoulder height of a batsman standing upright at the crease. Should a bowler bowl a fast, high-pitched ball, either umpire shall call and signal "no-ball".

In the event of such unfair bowling, the umpire at the bowler's end shall adopt the procedures of caution, final warning, action against the bowler and reporting as set out in Law 42.8 of the Laws of Cricket.

ICC CODE OF CONDUCT

1. The captains are responsible at all times for ensuring that play is conducted within the spirit of the game as well as within the Laws.

2. Players and team officials shall not at any time engage in conduct unbecoming to an international player or team official which could bring them or the game into disrepute.

3. Players and team officials must at all times accept the umpire's decision. Players must no show dissent at the umpire's decision.

4. Players and team officials shall not intimidate, assault or attempt to intimidate or assault an umpire, another player or a spectator.

5. Players and team officials shall not use crude or abusive language (known as "sledging" nor make offensive gestures.

6. Players and team officials shall not use or in any way be concerned in the use on distribution of illegal drugs.

7. Players and team officials shall not disclose or comment upon any alleged breach of the Code or upon any hearing, report or decision arising from such breach.

8. Players and team officials shall not make any public pronouncement or media comment which is detrimental either to the game in general; or to a particular tour in which they are involved; or about any tour between other countries which is taking place; or to relations between the Boards of the competing teams.

Application, Interpretation and Enforcement of the Code

1. The Code shall apply:

   (a) To players and, where applicable, to team officials of both teams for all Test matches and limited-overs international matches;

   (b) To players and, where applicable, to team officials of official touring teams for all matches, other than Test matches and limited-overs internationals ("other matches" with such modifications as ICC shall consider necessary in the absence of a match referee for other matches.

2. Breaches of the Code shall be deemed also to include a breach of any ICC Regulation in force from time to time, including (without limitation) those relating to advertising on cricket clothing and equipment, and, in Test matches, those relating to minimum over-rates.

3. The Code, breach of which may render a player or team official liable to disciplinary action, shall be enforced:

   (a) In the case of Test matches and limited-overs internationals in accordance with procedures and guidelines laid down for the match referee; and

   (b) In the case of other matches, in such manner as ICC shall consider appropriate at the time when the incident occurs. This shall, so far as is practicable, follow the procedures and guidelines laid down for the match referee.

Note: In 1992 ICC decided that the Code should also apply to Associate and Affiliate members of ICC but ruled that "application, interpretation and enforcement shall be determined in the way deemed most suitable by those concerned with the running of the game at these levels".

   ICC also ruled that breaches of Clause 8 of the Code of Conduct (public pronouncements should be dealt with by match referees during a tour (except where related to a non international match) and the home board of the player or official concerned in other circumstances.

ICC MATCH REFEREE

Extracts

1. Objective

To act on behalf of ICC to:

(a) see that the full implications of Law 42.1 are properly understood and upheld; and

(b) to ensure that the spirit of the game is observed and the conduct of the game maintained during Test matches and limited-overs internationals by players, umpires and team officials, either on or off the field, his responsibility being confined to the precincts of the ground.

2. Terms of Reference

(a) To be the independent representative of ICC (appointed by the Chairman or, in his absence, the Secretary, after consultation with the Boards concerned), at all Test matches and limited-overs internationals, the latter being part of a Test match tour, respecting the authority of the host country which is promoting a series, or the ground authority which is administering a match or series of matches.

(b) To liaise with the appointed umpires, but not in any way to interfere with their traditional role.

(c) To carry out the following duties:

(i) Observe and adjudicate upon breaches of the Code of Conduct.

(ii) Impose penalties for failure to maintain the minimum over-rate as set by ICC (presently 15 overs per hour).

(iii) Impose penalties for deliberate acts of unfair play, e.g. the deliberate slowing-down of over-rates and the deliberate speeding-up of overs to make up for any shortfall during a day's play.

(iv) Impose penalties for infringements of the ICC Regulation relating to advertising on cricket clothing and equipment.

(v) Impose penalties incurred under any other ICC Regulation which may be passed from time to time and which falls within the Terms of Reference.

(vi) Ensure the conduct of the game is upheld by the umpires in accordance with the Laws of Cricket and the Playing Conditions as agreed by the two Boards concerned in a series, and to give support to the umpires in this regard if required.

3. Method of Operation

The match referee must be present on all days of the match or matches assigned to him from the time the players arrive within the precincts of the ground until a reasonable time after close of play, bearing in mind that reports can be submitted up to one hour after the end of the day's play. He must ensure, in conjunction with the ground authority, that he has a good view of the match and has access to a television monitor and video equipment.

The match referee must lay down the standards expected from the players, making it clear that the captains are responsible for their teams and for the good conduct of the game. The match referee must make it clear that *no* public criticism of the umpires will be tolerated.

The match referee must not interfere with the traditional role of umpires but should urge umpires to be decisive in upholding the Law.

4. Disciplinary Procedures

Should an umpire decide to report a player for an alleged breach of the Code of Conduct or other offence, he must inform the player's captain or manager and the match referee of his intention at the earliest opportunity and complete a report and hand it to the match referee not later than one hour after the close of the day's play . . . the match referee's decision is final.

5. Penalties

The referee may in his absolute discretion impose any penalty by way of reprimand and/or fine and/or suspension.

(a) Maximum fine to be imposed for breaches of the Code of Conduct and other ICC Regulations (excluding over-rates) – 75 per cent of a player's match fee.

When a player is on tour, the fine shall be calculated on the last match fee paid to that player in his previous domestic season. If a player did not participate in an international match during his previous domestic season, that player shall be fined on the basis which would have applied had he played in an international match in his previous domestic season.

(b) Maximum suspension to be imposed for breaches of the Code of Conduct and other ICC Regulations – three Test matches.

If any matches of international standard take place between Test matches, the ban will also include these. This ban may well carry over into a future series. In a series of one-day internationals, the maximum suspension will be three internationals but may not be carried over. A player's participation in his own domestic cricket during the period of any ban imposed by the ICC match referee will be up to his own Board to determine.

6. Payment of Fines

Fines must be paid within one calendar month by the player(s) to his (their) Board who will, in turn, forward such fine(s) to the Secretary of ICC. Any player(s) failing to meet this requirement will be rendered unavailable for selection in any fixture under the control of his (their) own Board.

REGULATIONS FOR FIRST-CLASS MATCHES IN BRITAIN, 1992

Hours of Play

1st, 2nd [3rd] days.... 11.00 a.m. to 6.30 p.m. or after 110 overs, whichever is the later. (For Sunday play, the home county may decide to play from 12 noon to 7.30 p.m.)

Final day .... 11.00 a.m. to 6.00 p.m. or after 102 overs, whichever is the later.

Non-Championship matches:

1st, 2nd days .... 11.30 a.m. to 6.30 p.m.
3rd day .... 11.00 a.m. to 6.00 p.m.

Note: The hours of play, including intervals, are brought forward by half an hour for matches in September.

(a) If play is suspended (including any interval between innings) the minimum number of overs to be bowled in a day to be reduced by one over for each $3\frac{1}{2}$ minutes or part thereof of such suspension or suspensions in aggregate (including the last hour).

(b) If at 5.00 p.m. on the final day, 19 overs or less remain to be bowled, the umpires shall indicate that play shall continue until a minimum of a further 20 overs has been bowled, or until 6.00 p.m., whichever is the later. Play may cease on the final day at any time between 5.30 p.m. and 6.00 p.m. by mutual agreement of the captains. Should an innings end between 4.50 p.m. and 5.00 p.m., the time at the end of the ten-minute interval to replace 5.00 p.m.

(c) The captains may agree or, in the event of disagreement, the umpires may decide to play 30 minutes (or minimum ten overs) extra time at the end of the first and/or second day's play (and/or the third day of four) if, in their opinion, it would bring about a definite result on that day. In the event of the possibility of a finish disappearing before the full period has expired, the whole period must be played out. Any time so claimed does not affect the timing for cessation of play on the final day.

(d) The minimum number of overs remaining to be bowled in the day shall be shown on the scoreboard.

(e) If an innings ends during the course of an over, that part shall count as a full over so far as the minimum number of overs per day is concerned.

(f) If play is suspended for the day in the middle of an over, that over must be completed next day in addition to the minimum overs required that day.

Intervals

Lunch: 1.15 p.m. to 1.55 p.m. (1st, 2nd [3rd] days), 2.15 p.m. to 2.55 p.m. on Sundays when play commences at 12 noon
1.00 p.m. to 1.40 p.m. (final day)
In the event of lunch being taken early because of a stoppage caused by weather or bad light (Law 16.2), the interval shall be limited to 40 minutes.

Tea: 4.10 p.m. to 4.30 p.m. (1st, 2nd [3rd] days), 5.10 p.m. to 5.30 p.m. on Sundays when play commences at 12 noon; or when 40 overs remain to be bowled, whichever is the later. 3.40 p.m. to 4.00 p.m. (final day), or when 40 overs remain to be bowled, whichever is the later.

Substitutes

(County Championship matches only) Law 2.1 will apply, but in addition:

No substitute may take the field until the player for whom he is to substitute has been absent from the field for five consecutive complete overs, with the exception that if a fieldsman sustains an obvious, serious injury or is taken ill, a substitute shall be allowed immediately. In the event of any disagreement between the two sides as to the seriousness of an injury or illness, the umpires shall adjudicate. If a player leaves the field during an over, the remainder of that over shall not count in the calculation of the five complete overs.

A substitute shall be allowed by right immediately in the event of a cricketer currently playing in a Championship match being required to join the England team for a Test match (or one-day international). Such a substitute may be permitted to bat or bowl in that match, subject to the approval of the TCCB. The player who is substituted may not take further part in the match, even though he might not be required by England. If batting at the time, the player substituted shall be retired "not out" and his substitute may be permitted to bat later in that innings subject to the approval of the TCCB.

Fieldsman Leaving the Field

No fieldsman shall leave the field or return during a session of play without the consent of the umpire at the bowler's end. The umpire's consent is also necessary if a substitute is required for a fieldsman at the start of play or when his side returns to the field after an interval.

If a member of the fielding side does not take the field at the start of play, leaves the field, or fails to return after an interval and is absent from the field longer than 15 minutes, he shall not bowl in that innings after his return until he has been on the field for at least the length of playing time for which he was absent; nor shall he be permitted to bat unless or until, in the aggregate, he has returned to the field and/or his side's innings has been in progress for at least the length of playing time for which he was absent or, if earlier, when his side has lost five wickets. The restrictions shall not apply if he has been absent for exceptional and acceptable reasons (other than injury or illness) and consent for a substitute has been granted by the opposing captain.

New ball

The captain of the fielding side shall have the choice of taking the new ball after 100 overs have been bowled with the old one.

Covering of Pitches and Bowler's Run-up

The whole pitch shall be covered:

    (a) The night before a match and, if necessary, until the first ball is bowled; and whenever necessary and possible at any time prior to that during the preparation of the pitch.

    (b) On each night of a match and, if necessary, throughout any rest days.

    (c) In the event of play being suspended because of bad light or rain, during the hours of play.

The bowler's run-up shall be covered to a distance of at least ten yards, with a width of four yards.

Declarations

Law 14 will apply, but, in addition, a captain may also forfeit his first innings, subject to the provisions set out in Law 14.2. If, owing to weather conditions, the match has not started when fewer than eight hours of playing time remain, the first innings of each side shall automatically be forfeited and a one-innings match played.

ADDRESSES OF REPRESENTATIVE BODIES

ICC MEMBERS

INTERNATIONAL CRICKET COUNCIL: Lt-Col. J. R. Stephenson, OBE, Lord's Ground, London NW8 8QN.

AUSTRALIA: Australian Cricket Board, D. L. Richards, 90 Jolimont Street, Jolimont, Victoria 3002.

ENGLAND: Cricket Council, A. C. Smith, Lord's Ground, London NW8 8QZ.

INDIA: Board of Control for Cricket in India, C. Nagaraj, Chinnaswamy Stadium, Mahatma Gandhi Road, Bangalore 560 001.

NEW ZEALAND: New Zealand Cricket Inc., G. T. Dowling, OBE, PO Box 958, 109 Cambridge Terrace, Christchurch.

PAKISTAN: Board of Control for Cricket in Pakistan, Shahid Rafi, Gaddafi Stadium, Lahore.

SOUTH AFRICA: United Cricket Board of South Africa, Dr A. Bacher, PO Box 55009, Northlands 2116, Transvaal.

SRI LANKA: Board of Control for Cricket in Sri Lanka, N. Perera, 35 Maitland Place, Colombo 7.

WEST INDIES: West Indies Cricket Board of Control, G. S. Camacho, Kensington Oval, Fontabelle, St Michael, Barbados.

ZIMBABWE: Zimbabwe Cricket Union, P. Chingoka, PO Box 2739, Harare.

ARGENTINA: Argentine Cricket Association, C. M. Gibson, c/o The English Club, 25 de Mayo 586, 1002 Buenos Aires.

AUSTRIA: Austrian Cricket Association, W. Tesar, Brunner Strasse 34-38/17/16, A-1210 Vienna.

BAHAMAS: Bahamas Cricket Association, Mrs J. M. Forbes, PO Box N-10101, Nassau.

BANGLADESH: Bangladesh Cricket Board of Control, M. Aminul Huq Moni, National Stadium, Dhaka 1000.

BELGIUM: Belgian Cricket Federation, C. Wolfe, Rue de l'Eglise St Martin 12, B-1390 BIEZ.

BERMUDA: Bermuda Cricket Board of Control, W. Smith, PO Box 992, Hamilton.

BRUNEI: Brunei National Cricket Association, D. L. Gardiner (FAC/51), c/o Brunei Shell Petroleum Sdn Bhd, Seria 7082, Brunei via Singapore.

CANADA: Canadian Cricket Association, K. R. Bullock, PO Box 1364, Brockville, Ontario, K6V 5Y6.

DENMARK: Danish Cricket Association, J. Holmen, Idraettens Hus, Brøndby, DK 2605.

EAST AND CENTRAL AFRICA: East and Central African Cricket Conference, R. Patel, PO Box 34321, Lusaka, Zambia.

FIJI: Fiji Cricket Association, P. I. Knight, PO Box 300, Suva.

FRANCE: Fédération Française du Cricket, O. Dubaut, 73 Rue Curial, 75019 Paris.

GERMANY: Deutscher Cricket Bund, R. Schwiete, Adalbert-Stifter-Strasse 6d, 6450 Hanau.

GIBRALTAR: Gibraltar Cricket Association, T. J. Finlayson, 21 Sandpits House, Withams Road.

HONG KONG: Hong Kong Cricket Association, J. A. Cribbin, University of Hong Kong, School of Professional and Continuing Education, Pokfulam Road.

ISRAEL: Israel Cricket Association, N. Davidson, PO Box 93, Ben-Gurion Airport 70100.

ITALY: Associazione Italiana Cricket, S. Gambino, Via S. Ignazio 9, 00186 Rome.

JAPAN: Japan Cricket Association, R. G. Martineau, Shizuoka City, Chiyoda 736, Yamadai Corp. 305, Japan 420.

KENYA: Kenya Cricket Association, B. Mauladad, PO Box 45870, Nairobi.

MALAYSIA: Malaysian Cricket Association, Lt-Cdr K. Selvaratnam (Retd), c/o Delcom Services Sdn Bhd, No. 42 Jalan 1/82B, Bangsar Utama, Bangsar, 59000 Kuala Lumpur.

NAMIBIA: Namibia Cricket Board, L. Pieters, PO Box 457, Windhoek 9000.

NEPAL: Cricket Association of Nepal, Jaikumar N. Shah, PO Box 925, Kathmandu.

NETHERLANDS: Royal Netherlands Cricket Board, A. de la Mar, Neuiwe Kalfjeslaan 21-B, 1182 AA Amstelveen.

PAPUA NEW GUINEA: Papua New Guinea Cricket Board of Control, W. Satchell, PO Box 1105, Boroko.

SINGAPORE: Singapore Cricket Association, H. Singh, No. 7 Jalan Mahir, Singapore 1953.

SPAIN: Asociacion Española de Cricket, C. E. Woodbridge, Villa Valor, A14 Hacienda Guadalupe, 29692 Sabinillas, Manilva (Malaga).

SWITZERLAND: Swiss Cricket Association, P. Nixon, Spitzackerstrasse 32, 4103 Bottmingen.

UNITED ARAB EMIRATES: Emirates Cricket Board, Abdul Rahman Bukhatir, Sharjah Cricket Stadium, PO Box 88, Sharjah.

USA: United States of America Cricket Association, Naseeruddin Khan, 2361 Hickory Road, Plymouth Meeting, Pennsylvania 19462.

WEST AFRICA: West Africa Cricket Conference, Mrs Tayo Oreweme, National Sports Commission, National Stadium, PO Box 145, Surulere, Lagos, Nigeria.

BRITISH REPRESENTATIVE BODIES

BRITISH UNIVERSITIES SPORTS FEDERATION: 28 Woburn Square, London WC1.

CLUB CRICKET CONFERENCE: A. E. F. Stevens, 353 West Barnes Lane, New Malden, Surrey, KT3 6JF.

ENGLAND SCHOOLS' CRICKET ASSOCIATION: C. J. Cooper, 68 Hatherley Road, Winchester, Hampshire SO22 6RR.

IRISH CRICKET UNION: D. Scott, 45 Foxrock Park, Foxrock, Dublin 18, Ireland.

MINOR COUNTIES CRICKET ASSOCIATION: D. J. M. Armstrong, Thorpe Cottage, Mill Common, Ridlington, North Walsham, NR28 9TY.

NATIONAL CRICKET ASSOCIATION: K. V. Andrew, Lord's Ground, London NW8 8QZ.

SCARBOROUGH CRICKET FESTIVAL: Colin T. Adamson, Cricket Ground, North Marine Road, Scarborough, North Yorkshire, YO12 7TJ.

SCOTTISH CRICKET UNION: R. W. Barclay, Caledonia House, South Gyle, Edinburgh, EH12 9DQ.

UNIVERSITIES ATHLETIC UNION: Suite 36, London Fruit Exchange, Brushfield Street, London E1 6EU.

COMBINED SERVICES: Lt-Col. K. Hitchcock, c/o Army Sport Control Board, Clayton Barracks, Aldershot, Hampshire GU11 2BG.

THE SPORTS COUNCIL: Director-General, 16 Upper Woburn Place, London WC1 0QP.

ASSOCIATION OF CRICKET UMPIRES: L. J. Cheeseman, 16 Ruden Way, Epsom Downs, Surrey, KT17 3LN.

WOMEN'S CRICKET ASSOCIATION: J. Featherstone, 41 St Michael's Lane, Headingley, Leeds LS6 3BR.

The addresses of the First-Class Counties and Minor Counties are given at the head of each separate section and that of MCC on page 1176.

MEETINGS IN 1992

TCCB SPRING MEETING

At its spring meeting on March 3, the Test and County Cricket Board appointed Dennis Amiss, the former Warwickshire and England player, to the panel of England Test selectors. Frank Chamberlain of Northamptonshire was appointed Chairman of the TCCB for a further one-year term from October. It was also decided that over-rate fines in limited-overs cricket should be split 50-50 between players and their counties.

MARYLEBONE CRICKET CLUB

The 205th annual general meeting of MCC, held at Lord's on May 6, accepted a proposal advanced by the immediate past president, Lord Griffiths, that future presidents should be entitled to serve for two years, if they wish, instead of one. The President, Michael Melluish, named Dennis Silk as his successor and thus the first incumbent entitled to the two-year term. Melluish was himself elected Treasurer to replace Hubert Doggart, who was retiring after five and a half years. In his statement to members, the President reported that the club was spending an increased portion of its budget on coaching and overseas development and was working on a new edition of the MCC coaching manual. He reiterated that the committee had "continued to resist all attempts to paint logos on the turf of Lord's". However, after negotiations with the TCCB a compromise had been agreed whereby a mat carrying the sponsors' logo may be placed at the Nursery End. "There will therefore be no advertising on the ground in front of the pavilion, and at the end of the match the mat will be removed, leaving no unsightly fading logo at the Nursery End," he said. He also reported that agreement had finally been reached with the contractors over the delays in completing the Compton and Edrich Stands.

The chairman of finance, David Hudd, reported a surplus after tax in 1991 of £167,000 compared to £369,000 the previous year, which included the premium paid for the assignment of the catering lease. Operating net income rose from £3.84 million to £4.75 million and operating expenditure from £4 million to £4.2 million.

Membership of the club on December 31, 1991 was 19,291, made up of 16,892 full members, 1,950 associate members and 449 honorary members. There were 9,352 candidates awaiting election. In 1991, 301 vacancies arose, 142 caused by death, 89 by resignation and 70 by lapsed memberships.

TCCB SPECIAL MEETING

At a special meeting on May 19, the Test and County Cricket Board voted by 11 to eight (with one abstention) to accept the recommendations of the Structure Working Party, chaired by Michael Murray. This recommended that from 1993 the County Championship should consist solely of four-day cricket, with each of the 18 first-class counties playing each other once and almost all games starting on Thursdays; that the zonal rounds of the Benson and Hedges Cup should be abolished and the competition should be played only on a knockout basis; and that the Sunday League should be a 50-over rather than 40-over competition with no restrictions on the bowlers' run-ups. Before the vote, it was agreed that the new system should last for a minimum of three years, rather than a minimum of five as originally recommended by the report.

INTERNATIONAL CRICKET COUNCIL

At its annual meeting on July 8, 9, the International Cricket Council reprieved all the players who had been banned from Test cricket for continuing sporting contacts with South Africa. These included the 16 English players who were banned for five years for going on tour under Mike Gatting's captaincy in early 1990. The ban was to be lifted on October 1, halfway through the scheduled period. Zimbabwe became the ninth Test-playing nation when they were elected to full membership of ICC. England opposed Zimbabwe's election but did not veto it. The future of the veto, held by England and Australia as ICC's foundation members, was to be considered by a special committee under the ICC Chairman Sir Colin Cowdrey. Namibia were elected associate members and Austria, Brunei and Spain affiliate members.

TCCB WINTER MEETING

At its winter meeting, held at Lord's on December 9, 10, the Test and County Cricket Board agreed that no-balls should count as two runs rather than one in 1993 in an attempt to encourage bowlers to adhere to the front-foot law. The new regulation, based on the system used by the Australian Cricket Board, imposes the penalty in addition to any other runs scored off the ball – thus a six hit off a no-ball would mean eight runs from the delivery. It was also decided that "beamers" should count as no-balls rather than wides. The Board agreed to change the bonus points system for the 1993 County Championship to fit four-day cricket, with 120 overs being available for first-innings points instead of 100. However, the first batting point will be for 200 rather than 150 with further points at 250, 300 and 350 instead of 200, 250 and 300. This system had remained unchanged since 1974. The Board also agreed to introduce an Australian-inspired rule in the Sunday League: in 1993 two fielders must be within 15 yards of the bat in the first 15 overs of each innings.

UMPIRES FOR 1993

FIRST-CLASS UMPIRES

J. C. Balderstone, H. D. Bird, J. D. Bond, G. I. Burgess, D. J. Constant, B. Dudleston, J. H. Hampshire, J. H. Harris, J. W. Holder, V. A. Holder, A. A. Jones, R. Julian, M. J. Kitchen, B. Leadbeater, B. J. Meyer, D. O. Oslear, K. E. Palmer, R. Palmer, N. T. Plews, G. Sharp, D. R. Shepherd, G. A. Stickley, R. A. White, A. G. T. Whitehead, P. B. Wight and P. Willey. *Reserves*: P. Adams, A. Clarkson, M. J. Harris, M. K. Reed.

Note: The panel of umpires for Test matches and one-day internationals was not available at the time *Wisden* went to press.

MINOR COUNTIES UMPIRES

P. Adams, N. P. Atkins, K. Bray, P. Brown, D. L. Burden, R. K. Curtis, J. B. Foulkes, P. Gray, D. J. Halfyard, R. F. Harriott, M. A. Johnson, B. Knight, S. W. Kuhlmann, G. I. McLean, T. G. A. Morley, D. Norton, M. K. Reed, K. S. Shenton, C. Smith, C. T. Spencer, D. S. Thompsett, J. M. Tythcott, J. Waite, R. Walker and T. G. Wilson. *Reserves*: K. Coburn, H. W. Cook, R. F. Elliott, A. G. Forster, K. Hopley, R. E. Lawson, G. Lowden, P. R. Mitchell, M. P. Moran, W. Morgan, C. T. Puckett, G. Randall-Johnson, J. Reed, G. B. Smith, C. Stone, T. J. White, B. H. Willey, G. Williams and R. Wood.

PART SIX: MISCELLANEOUS

BIRTHS AND DEATHS OF CRICKETERS

Editor's Note: The 1993 Births and Deaths section excludes J. H. Hodges, who was formerly believed to have played in the first two Test matches ever staged, at Melbourne in 1876-77. Recent researches by Ray Webster, Irving Rosenwater and Robert Brooke suggest that the Hodges supposed until now to have played in these games played for neither Australia nor even Victoria. The Test cricketer is now believed to be James Robart (sic) Hodges, born in England on August 11, 1855, who sailed from Liverpool to Australia with his parents and two elder brothers on the *Atalanta* in 1856 and settled in Melbourne. There is no record of his death; descendants of his brother Fred say he disappeared about 1890 and was never heard of again. Researches are continuing. However, there appears to be enough evidence to justify his inclusion in this section in place of J. H. Hodges. Webster's work has also led to a change in the details for N. F. D. Thomson (formerly listed as Thompson), who also played for Australia in these matches.

The qualifications for inclusion are as follows:

1. All players who have appeared in a Test match or a one-day international for a Test-match playing country.

2. English county players who have appeared in 50 or more first-class matches during their careers and, if dead, were still living ten years ago.

3. Players who appeared in 15 or more first-class matches in the 1992 English season.

4. English county captains, county caps and captains of Oxford and Cambridge Universities who, if dead, were still living ten years ago.

5. All players chosen as *Wisden* Cricketers of the Year, including the Public Schoolboys chosen for the 1918 and 1919 Almanacks. Cricketers of the Year are identified by the italic notation *CY* and year of appearance. A list of the Cricketers of the Year from 1889 to 1988 appeared in *Wisden* 1989.

6. Players or personalities not otherwise qualified who are thought to be of sufficient interest to merit inclusion.

Key to abbreviations and symbols

CUCC – Cambridge University, OUCC – Oxford University.

Australian states: NSW – New South Wales, Qld – Queensland, S. Aust. – South Australia, Tas. – Tasmania, Vic. – Victoria, W. Aust. – Western Australia.

Indian teams: Guj. – Gujarat, H'bad – Hyderabad, Ind. Rlwys – Indian Railways, Ind. Serv. – Indian Services, J/K – Jammu and Kashmir, Karn. – Karnataka (Mysore to 1972-73), M. Pradesh – Madhya Pradesh (Central India [C. Ind.] to 1939-40, Holkar to 1954-55, Madhya Bharat to 1956-57), M'tra – Maharashtra, Naw. – Nawanagar, Raja. – Rajasthan, S'tra – Saurashtra (West Ind. [W. Ind.] to 1945-46, Kathiawar to 1949-50), S. Punjab – Southern Punjab (Patiala to 1958-59, Punjab since 1968-69), TC – Travancore-Cochin (Kerala since 1956-57), TN – Tamil Nadu (Madras to 1959-60), U. Pradesh – Uttar Pradesh (United Provinces [U. Prov.] to 1948-49), Vidarbha (CP & Berar to 1949-50, Madhya Pradesh to 1956-57).

New Zealand provinces: Auck. – Auckland, Cant. – Canterbury, C. Dist. – Central Districts, N. Dist. – Northern Districts, Wgtn – Wellington.

Pakistani teams: ADBP – Agricultural Development Bank of Pakistan, B'pur – Bahawalpur, HBFC – House Building Finance Corporation, HBL – Habib Bank Ltd, IDBP – Industrial Development Bank of Pakistan, Kar. – Karachi, MCB – Muslim Commercial Bank, NBP – National Bank of Pakistan, NWFP – North-West Frontier Province, PACO – Pakistan Automobile Corporation, Pak. Rlwys – Pakistan Railways, Pak. Us – Pakistan Universities, PIA – Pakistan International Airlines, PNSC – Pakistan National Shipping Corporation, PWD – Public Works Department, R'pindi – Rawalpindi, UBL – United Bank Ltd, WAPDA – Water and Power Development Authority.

South African provinces: E. Prov. – Eastern Province, E. Tvl – Eastern Transvaal, Griq. W. – Griqualand West, N. Tvl – Northern Transvaal, NE Tvl – North-Eastern Transvaal, OFS – Orange Free State, Rhod. – Rhodesia, Tvl – Transvaal, W. Prov. – Western Province.

Sri Lankan teams: BRC – Burgher Recreation Club, CCC – Colombo Cricket Club, Mor. – Moratuwa Sports Club, NCC – Nondescripts Cricket Club, Pan. – Panadura Sports Club, SLAF – Air Force, SSC – Sinhalese Sports Club, TU – Tamil Union Cricket and Athletic Club.

West Indies islands: B'dos – Barbados, BG – British Guiana (Guyana since 1966), Comb. Is. – Combined Islands, Jam. – Jamaica, T/T – Trinidad & Tobago.

* *Denotes Test player.* ** *Denotes appeared for two countries. There is a list of Test players country by country from page 45.*
† *Denotes also played for team under its previous name.*

Aamer Hameed (Pak. Us, Lahore, Punjab & OUCC) b Oct. 18, 1954

*Aamer Malik (ADBP, PIA & Multan) b Jan. 3, 1963

*Aamir Sohail (HBL & Sargodha) b Sept. 14, 1966

Abberley, R. N. (Warwicks.) b April 22, 1944

*a'Beckett, E. L. (Vic.) b Aug. 11, 1907, d June 2, 1989

*Abdul Kadir (Kar. & NBP) b May 10, 1944

*Abdul Qadir (HBL, Lahore & Punjab) b Sept. 15, 1955

*Abel, R. (Surrey; *CY 1890*) b Nov. 30, 1857, d Dec. 10, 1936

Abell, Sir G. E. B. (OUCC, Worcs. & N. Ind.) b June 22, 1904, d Jan. 11, 1989

Aberdare, 3rd Lord (*see* Bruce, Hon. C. N.)

*Abid Ali, S. (H'bad) b Sept. 9, 1941

Abrahams, J. (Lancs.) b July 21, 1952

*Absolom, C. A. (CUCC & Kent) b June 7, 1846, d July 30, 1889

Acfield D. L. (CUCC & Essex) b July 24, 1947

*Achong, E. (T/T) b Feb. 16, 1904, d Aug. 29, 1986

Ackerman, H. M. (Border, NE Tvl, Northants, Natal & W. Prov.) b April 28, 1947

A'Court, D. G. (Glos.) b July 27, 1937

Adam, Sir Ronald, 2nd Bt (Pres. MCC 1946-47) b Oct. 30, 1885, d Dec. 26, 1982

Adams, C. J. (Derbys.) b May 6, 1970

*Adams, J. C. (Jam.) b Jan. 9, 1968

Adams, P. W. (Cheltenham & Sussex; *CY 1919*) b 1900, d Feb. 28, 1962

*Adcock, N. A. T. (Tvl & Natal; *CY 1961*) b March 8, 1931

*Adhikari, H. R. (Guj., Baroda & Ind. Serv.) b July 31, 1919

*Afaq Hussain (Kar., Pak. Us, PIA & PWD) b Dec. 31, 1939

Afford, J. A. (Notts.) b May 12, 1964

*Aftab Baloch (PWD, Kar., Sind, NBP & PIA) b April 1, 1953

*Aftab Gul (Punjab U., Pak. Us & Lahore) b March 31, 1946

*Agha Saadat Ali (Pak. Us, Punjab, B'pur & Lahore) b June 21, 1929

*Agha Zahid (Pak. Us, Punjab, Lahore & HBL) b Jan. 7, 1953

*Agnew, J. P. (Leics; *CY 1988*) b April 4, 1960

*Ahangama, F. S. (SSC) b Sept. 14, 1959

Aird, R. (CUCC & Hants; Sec. MCC 1953-62, Pres. MCC 1968-69) b May 4, 1902, d Aug. 16, 1986

Aitchison, Rev. J. K. (Scotland) b May 26, 1920

*Akram Raza (Sargodha & HBL) b Nov. 22, 1964

*Alabaster, J. C. (Otago) b July 11, 1930

Alcock, C. W. (Sec. Surrey CCC 1872-1907, Editor *Cricket* 1882-1907) b Dec. 2, 1842, d Feb. 26, 1907

Alderman, A. E. (Derbys.) b Oct. 30, 1907, d June 4, 1990

*Alderman, T. M. (W. Aust., Kent & Glos.; *CY 1982*) b June 12, 1956

Aldridge, K. J. (Worcs & Tas.) b March 13, 1935

Alexander of Tunis, 1st Lord (Pres. MCC 1955-56) b Dec. 10, 1891, d June 16, 1969

*Alexander, F. C. M. (CUCC & Jam.) b Nov. 2, 1928

*Alexander, G. (Vic.) b April 22, 1851, d Nov. 6, 1930

*Alexander, H. H. (Vic.) b June 9, 1905

Alikhan, R. I. (Sussex, PIA & Surrey) b Dec. 28, 1962

*Alim-ud-Din (Rajputana, Guj., Sind, B'pur, Kar. & PWD) b Dec. 15, 1930

*Allan, D. W. (B'dos) b Nov. 5, 1937

*Allan, F. E. (Vic.) b Dec. 2, 1849, d Feb. 9, 1917

Allan, J. M. (OUCC, Kent, Warwicks. & Scotland) b April 2, 1932

*Allan, P. J. (Qld) b Dec. 31, 1935

*Allcott, C. F. W. (Auck.) b Oct. 7, 1896, d Nov. 19, 1973

Allen, A. W. (CUCC & Northants) b Dec. 22, 1912

*Allen, D. A. (Glos.) b Oct. 29, 1935

*Allen, Sir G. O. B. (CUCC & Middx; Pres. MCC 1963-64; *special portrait 1987*) b July 31, 1902, d Nov. 29, 1989

*Allen, I. B. A. (Windwards) b Oct. 6, 1965

Allen, M. H. J. (Northants & Derbys.) b Jan. 7, 1933

*Allen, R. C. (NSW) b July 2, 1858, d May 2, 1952

Alletson, E. B. (Notts.) b March 6, 1884, d July 5, 1963

Alley, W. E. (NSW & Som.; *CY 1962*) b Feb. 3, 1919

Alleyne, H. L. (B'dos, Worcs., Natal & Kent) b Feb. 28, 1957

Alleyne, M. W. (Glos.) b May 23, 1968

*Allom, M. J. C. (CUCC & Surrey; Pres. MCC 1969-70) b March 23, 1906

*Allott, P. J. W. (Lancs. & Wgtn) b Sept. 14, 1956

Altham, H. S. (OUCC, Surrey & Hants; Pres. MCC 1959-60) b Nov. 30, 1888, d March 11, 1965

*Amalean, K. N. (SL) b April 7, 1965

*Amarnath, Lala (N. Ind., S. Punjab, Guj., Patiala, U. Pradesh & Ind. Rlwys) b Sept. 11, 1911

*Amarnath, M. (Punjab & Delhi; *CY 1984*) b Sept. 24, 1950

*Amarnath, S. (Punjab & Delhi) b Dec. 30, 1948

*Amar Singh, L. (Patiala, W. Ind. & Naw.) b Dec. 4, 1910, d May 20, 1940

*Ambrose, C. E. L. (Leewards & Northants; *CY 1992*) b Sept. 21, 1963

*Amerasinghe, A. M. J. G. (Nomads) b Feb. 2, 1954

*Ames, L. E. G. (Kent; *CY 1929*) b Dec. 3, 1905, d Feb. 26, 1990

**Amir Elahi (Baroda, N. Ind., S. Punjab & B'pur) b Sept. 1, 1908, d Dec. 28, 1980

*Amiss, D. L. (Warwicks.; *CY 1975*) b April 7, 1943

Amre, P. K. (Raja.) b Aug. 14, 1968

Anderson, I. S. (Derbys. & Boland) b April 24, 1960

*Anderson, J. H. (W. Prov.) b April 26, 1874, d March 11, 1926

*Anderson, R. W. (Cant., N. Dist., Otago & C. Dist.) b Oct. 2, 1948

*Anderson, W. McD. (Otago, C. Dist. & Cant.) b Oct. 8, 1919, d Dec. 21, 1979

Andrew, C. R. (CUCC) b Feb. 18, 1963

*Andrew, K. V. (Northants) b Dec. 15, 1929

Andrew, S. J. W. (Hants & Essex) b Jan. 27, 1966

*Andrews, B. (Cant., C. Dist. & Otago) b April 4, 1945

*Andrews, T. J. E. (NSW) b Aug. 26, 1890, d Jan. 28, 1970

Andrews, W. H. R. (Som.) b April 14, 1908, d Jan. 9, 1989

Angell, F. L. (Som.) b June 29, 1922

*Anil Dalpat (Kar. & PIA) b Sept. 20, 1963

*Ankola, S. A. (M'tra & Bombay) b March 1, 1968

*Anurasiri, S. D. (Pan.) b Feb. 25, 1966

*Anwar Hussain (N. Ind., Bombay, Sind & Kar.) b July 16, 1920

*Anwar Khan (Kar., Sind & NBP) b Dec. 24, 1955

*Appleyard, R. (Yorks.; *CY 1952*) b June 27, 1924

*Apte, A. L. (Ind. Us, Bombay & Raja.) b Oct. 24, 1934

*Apte, M. L. (Bombay & Bengal) b Oct. 5, 1932

*Aqib Javed (PACO & Hants) b Aug. 5, 1972

*Archer, A. G. (Worcs.) b Dec. 6, 1871, d July 15, 1935

*Archer, K. A. (Qld) b Jan. 17, 1928

*Archer, R. G. (Qld) b Oct. 25, 1933

*Arif Butt (Lahore & Pak. Rlwys) b May 17, 1944

Arlott, John (Writer & Broadcaster) b Feb. 25, 1914, d Dec. 14, 1991

*Armitage, T. (Yorks.) b April 25, 1848, d Sept. 21, 1922

Armstrong, N. F. (Leics.) b Dec. 22, 1892, d Jan. 19, 1990

Armstrong, T. R. (Derbys.) b Oct. 13, 1909

*Armstrong, W. W. (Vic.; *CY 1903*) b May 22, 1879, d July 13, 1947

Arnold, A. P. (Cant. & Northants) b Oct. 16, 1926

*Arnold, E. G. (Worcs.) b Nov. 7, 1876, d Oct. 25, 1942

*Arnold, G. G. (Surrey & Sussex; *CY 1972*) b Sept. 3, 1944

*Arnold, J. (Hants) b Nov. 30, 1907, d April 4, 1984

Arnott, K. J. (Zimb.) b March 8, 1961

*Arshad Ayub (H'bad) b Aug. 2, 1958

Arshad Pervez (Sargodha, Lahore, Pak. Us, Servis Ind., HBL & Punjab) b Oct. 1, 1952

*Arthurton, K. L. T. (Leewards) b Feb. 21, 1965

*Arun, B. (TN) b Dec. 14, 1962

*Arun Lal (Delhi & Bengal) b Aug. 1, 1955

*Asgarali, N. (T/T) b Dec. 28, 1920

Ashdown, W. H. (Kent) b Dec. 27, 1898, d Sept. 15, 1979

*Ashley, W. H. (W. Prov.) b Feb. 10, 1862, d July 14, 1930

*Ashraf Ali (Lahore, Income Tax, Pak Us, Pak Rlwys & UBL) b April 22, 1958

Ashton, C. T. (CUCC & Essex) b Feb. 19, 1901, d Oct. 31, 1942

Ashton, G. (CUCC & Worcs.) b Sept. 27, 1896, d Feb. 6, 1981

Ashton, Sir H. (CUCC & Essex; *CY 1922*; Pres. MCC 1960-61) b Feb. 13, 1898, d June 17, 1979

Asif Din, M. (Warwicks.) b Sept. 21, 1960
*Asif Iqbal (H'bad, Kar., Kent, PIA & NBP; *CY 1968*) b June 6, 1943
*Asif Masood (Lahore, Punjab U. & PIA) b Jan. 23, 1946
*Asif Mujtaba (Kar. & PIA) b Nov. 4, 1967
Aslett, D. G. (Kent) b Feb. 12, 1958
Aspinall, R. (Yorks.) b Nov. 27, 1918
*Astill, W. E. (Leics.; *CY 1933*) b March 1, 1888, d Feb. 10, 1948
*Atapattu, M. S. (SSC) b Nov. 22, 1972
*Ata-ur-Rehman (Lahore & PACO) b March 28, 1975
*Atherton, M. A. (CUCC & Lancs.; *CY 1991*) b March 23, 1968
*Athey, C. W. J. (Yorks. & Glos.) b Sept. 27, 1957
*Atkinson, C. R. M. (Som.) b July 23, 1931, d June 25, 1991
*Atkinson, D. St E. (B'dos & T/T) b Aug. 9, 1926
*Atkinson, E. St E. (B'dos) b Nov. 6, 1927
Atkinson, G. (Som. & Lancs.) b March 29, 1938
Atkinson, J. C. M. (Som. & CUCC) b July 10, 1968
Atkinson, T. (Notts.) b Sept. 27, 1930, d Sept. 2, 1990
*Attewell, W. (Notts.; *CY 1892*) b June 12, 1861, d June 11, 1927
Austin, Sir H. B. G. (B'dos) b July 15, 1877, d July 27, 1943
Austin, I. D. (Lancs.) b May 30, 1966
*Austin, R. A. (Jam.) b Sept. 5, 1954
Avery, A. V. (Essex) b Dec. 19, 1914
Aworth, C. J. (CUCC & Surrey) b Feb. 19, 1953
Ayling, J. R. (Hants) b June 13, 1967
Aylward, J. (Hants & All-England) b 1741, d Dec. 27, 1827
Aymes, A. N. (Hants) b June 4, 1964
*Azad, K. (Delhi) b Jan. 2, 1959
*Azeem Hafeez (Kar., Allied Bank & PIA) b July 29, 1963
*Azhar Khan (Lahore, Punjab, Pak. Us., PIA & HBL) b Sept. 7, 1955
*Azharuddin, M. (H'bad & Derbys.; *CY 1991*) b Feb. 8, 1963
*Azmat Rana (B'pur, PIA, Punjab, Lahore & MCB) b Nov. 3, 1951

Babington, A. M. (Sussex & Glos.) b July 22, 1963
*Bacchus, S. F. A. F. (Guyana, W. Prov. & Border) b Jan. 31, 1954
*Bacher, Dr A. (Tvl) b May 24, 1942
*Badcock, C. L. (Tas. & S. Aust.) b April 10, 1914, d Dec. 13, 1982
*Badcock, F. T. (Wgtn & Otago) b Aug. 9, 1895, d Sept. 19, 1982
*Baichan, L. (Guyana) b May 12, 1946
*Baig, A. A. (H'bad, OUCC & Som.) b March 19, 1939

Bailey, Sir D. T. L. (Glos.) b Aug. 5, 1918
Bailey, J. (Hants) b April 6, 1908, d Feb. 9, 1988
Bailey, J. A. (Essex & OUCC; Sec. MCC 1974-87) b June 22, 1930
*Bailey, R. J. (Northants) b Oct. 28, 1963
*Bailey, T. E. (Essex & CUCC; *CY 1950*) b Dec. 3, 1923
Baillie, A. W. (Sec. MCC 1858-63) b June 22, 1830, d May 10, 1867
Bainbridge, P. (Glos. & Durham; *CY 1986*) b April 16, 1958
*Bairstow, D. L. (Yorks. & Griq. W.) b Sept. 1, 1951
Baker, R. P. (Surrey) b April 9, 1954
*Bakewell, A. H. (Northants; *CY 1934*) b Nov. 2, 1908, d Jan. 23, 1983
Bakker, P. J. (Hants) b Aug. 19, 1957
*Balaskas, X. C. (Griq. W., Border, W. Prov., Tvl & NE Tvl) b Oct. 15, 1910
*Balderstone, J. C. (Yorks. & Leics.) b Nov. 16, 1940
Baldry, D. O. (Middx & Hants) b Dec. 26, 1931
*Banerjee, S. A. (Bengal & Bihar) b Nov. 1, 1919, d. Sept. 14, 1992
*Banerjee, S. N. (Bengal, Naw., Bihar & M. Pradesh) b Oct. 3, 1911, d Oct. 14, 1980
*Banerjee, S. T. (Bihar) b Feb. 13, 1969
*Bannerman, A. C. (NSW) b March 22, 1854, d Sept. 19, 1924
*Bannerman, Charles (NSW) b July 23, 1851, d Aug. 20, 1930
Bannister, J. D. (Warwicks.) b Aug. 23, 1930
*Baptiste, E. A. E. (Kent, Leewards, Northants & E. Prov.) b March 12, 1960
*Baqa Jilani, M. (N. Ind.) b July 20, 1911, d July 2, 1941
Barber, A. T. (OUCC & Yorks.) b June 17, 1905, d March 10, 1985
*Barber, R. T. (Wgtn & C. Dist.) b June 23, 1925
*Barber, R. W. (Lancs., CUCC & Warwicks; *CY 1967*) b Sept. 26, 1935
*Barber, W. (Yorks.) b April 18, 1901, d Sept. 10, 1968
Barclay, J. R. T. (Sussex & OFS) b Jan. 22, 1954
*Bardsley, W. (NSW; *CY 1910*) b Dec. 7, 1882, d Jan. 20, 1954
Baring, A. E. G. (Hants) b Jan. 21, 1910, d Aug. 29, 1986
Barker, G. (Essex) b July 6, 1931
Barling, H. T. (Surrey) b Sept. 1, 1906, d Jan. 2, 1993
Barlow, A. (Lancs.) b Aug. 31, 1915, d May 9, 1983
*Barlow, E. J. (Tvl, E. Prov., W. Prov., Derbys. & Boland) b Aug. 12, 1940
*Barlow, G. D. (Middx) b March 26, 1950
*Barlow, R. G. (Lancs.) b May 28, 1851, d July 31, 1919

Barnard, H. M. (Hants) b July 18, 1933

Barnes, A. R. (Sec. Aust. Cricket Board 1960-81) b Sept. 12, 1916, d March 14, 1989

*Barnes, S. F. (Warwicks. & Lancs.; *CY 1910*) b April 19, 1873, d Dec. 26, 1967

*Barnes, S. G. (NSW) b June 5, 1916, d Dec. 16, 1973

*Barnes, W. (Notts.; *CY 1890*) b May 27, 1852, d March 24, 1899

Barnett, A. A. (Middx & Lancs.) b Sept. 11, 1970

*Barnett, B. A. (Vic.) b March 23, 1908, d June 29, 1979

*Barnett, C. J. (Glos.; *CY 1937*) b July 3, 1910

*Barnett, K. J. (Derbys. & Boland; *CY 1989*) b July 17, 1960

Barnwell, C. J. P. (Som.) b June 23, 1914

Baroda, Maharaja of (Manager, Ind. in Eng., 1959) b April 2, 1930, d Sept. 1, 1988

*Barratt, F. (Notts.) b April 12, 1894, d Jan. 29, 1947

Barratt, R. J. (Leics.) b May 3, 1942

*Barrett, A. G. (Jam.) b April 5, 1942

Barrett, B. J. (Auck., C. Dist., Worcs. & N. Dist.) b Nov. 16, 1966

*Barrett, J. E. (Vic.) b Oct. 15, 1866, d Feb. 6, 1916

Barrick, D. W. (Northants) b April 28, 1926

*Barrington, K. F. (Surrey; *CY 1960*) b Nov. 24, 1930, d March 14, 1981

Barron, W. (Lancs. & Northants) b Oct. 26, 1917

*Barrow, I. (Jam.) b Jan. 6, 1911, d April 2, 1979

*Bartlett, E. L. (B'dos) b March 18, 1906, d Dec. 21, 1976

*Bartlett, G. A. (C. Dist. & Cant.) b Feb. 3, 1941

Bartlett, H. T. (CUCC, Surrey & Sussex; *CY 1939*) b Oct. 7, 1914, d June 26, 1988

Bartlett, R. J. (Som.) b Oct. 8, 1966

Bartley, T. J. (Umpire) b March 19, 1908, d April 2, 1964

Barton, M. R. (OUCC & Surrey) b Oct. 14, 1914

*Barton, P. T. (Wgtn) b Oct. 9, 1935

*Barton, V. A. (Kent & Hants) b Oct. 6, 1867, d March 23, 1906

Barwick, S. R. (Glam.) b Sept. 6, 1960

Base, S. J. (W. Prov., Glam., Derbys., Boland & Border) b Jan. 2, 1960

Bates, D. L. (Sussex) b May 10, 1933

*Bates, W. (Yorks.) b Nov. 19, 1855, d Jan. 8, 1900

Batty, J. D. (Yorks.) b May 15, 1971

*Baumgartner, H. V. (OFS & Tvl) b Nov. 17, 1883, d April 8, 1938

Baxter, A. D. (Devon, Lancs., Middx & Scotland) b Jan. 20, 1910, d Jan. 28, 1986

*Bean, G. (Notts & Sussex) b March 7, 1864, d March 16, 1923

Bear, M. J. (Essex & Cant.) b Feb. 23, 1934

*Beard, D. D. (C. Dist. & N. Dist.) b Jan. 14, 1920, d July 15, 1982

*Beard, G. R. (NSW) b Aug. 19, 1950

Beauclerk, Lord Frederick (Middx, Surrey & MCC) b May 8, 1773, d April 22, 1850

Beaufort, 10th Duke of (Pres. MCC 1952-53) b April 4, 1900, d Feb. 5, 1984

*Beaumont, R. (Tvl) b Feb. 4, 1884, d May 25, 1958

*Beck, J. E. F. (Wgtn) b Aug. 1, 1934

*Bedi, B. S. (N. Punjab, Delhi & Northants) b Sept. 25, 1946

*Bedser, A. V. (Surrey; *CY 1947*) b July 4, 1918

Bedser, E. A. (Surrey) b July 4, 1918

Beet, G. (Derbys.; Umpire) b April 24, 1886, d Dec. 13, 1946

*Begbie, D. W. (Tvl) b Dec. 12, 1914

Beldham, W. (Hambledon & Surrey) b Feb. 5, 1766, d Feb. 20, 1862

*Bell, A. J. (W. Prov. & Rhod.) b April 15, 1906, d Aug. 2, 1985

Bell, R. V. (Middx & Sussex) b Jan. 7, 1931, d Oct. 26, 1989

*Bell, W. (Cant.) b Sept. 5, 1931

Bellamy, B. W. (Northants) b April 22, 1891, d Dec. 20, 1985

*Benaud, J. (NSW) b May 11, 1944

*Benaud, R. (NSW; *CY 1962*) b Oct. 6, 1930

Benjamin, J. E. (Warwicks. & Surrey) b Feb. 2, 1961

*Benjamin, K. C. G. (Leewards) b April 8, 1967

*Benjamin, W. K. M. (Leewards & Leics.) b Dec. 31, 1964

Bennett, D. (Middx) b Dec. 18, 1933

*Bennett, M. J. (NSW) b Oct. 16, 1956

Bennett, N. H. (Surrey) b Sept. 23, 1912

Bennett, R. (Lancs.) b June 16, 1940

Benson, J. D. R. (Leics.) b March 1, 1967

*Benson, M. R. (Kent) b July 6, 1958

Bernard, J. R. (CUCC & Glos.) b Dec. 7, 1938

Berry, L. G. (Leics.) b April 28, 1906, d Feb. 5, 1985

*Berry, R. (Lancs., Worcs. & Derbys.) b Jan. 29, 1926

*Best, C. A. (B'dos) b May 14, 1959

*Betancourt, N. (T/T) b June 4, 1887, d Oct. 12, 1947

Bhalekar, R. B. (M'tra) b Feb. 17, 1952

*Bhandari, P. (Delhi & Bengal) b Nov. 27, 1935

*Bhat, A. R. (Karn.) b April 16, 1958

Bick, D. A. (Middx) b Feb. 22, 1936, d March 13, 1992

Bicknell, D. J. (Surrey) b June 24, 1967

Bicknell, M. P. (Surrey) b Jan. 14, 1969

Biddulph, K. D. (Som.) b May 29, 1932

*Bilby, G. P. (Wgtn) b May 7, 1941

*Binks, J. G. (Yorks.; *CY 1969*) b Oct. 5, 1935

*Binns, A. P. (Jam.) b July 24, 1929

*Binny, R. M. H. (Karn.) b July 19, 1955

Birch, J. D. (Notts.) b June 18, 1955

Bird, H. D. (Yorks. & Leics.; Umpire) b April 19, 1933

*Bird, M. C. (Lancs. & Surrey) b March 25, 1888, d Dec. 9, 1933

Bird, R. E. (Worcs.) b April 4, 1915, d Feb. 20, 1985

*Birkenshaw, J. (Yorks., Leics. & Worcs.) b Nov. 13, 1940

*Birkett, L. S. (B'dos, BG & T/T) b April 14, 1904

Birrell, H. B. (E. Prov., Rhod. & OUCC) b Dec. 1, 1927

Bishop, G. A. (S. Aust.) b Feb. 25, 1960

*Bishop, I. R. (T/T & Derbys.) b Oct. 24, 1967

*Bisset, Sir Murray (W. Prov.) b April 14, 1876, d Oct. 24, 1931

*Bissett, G. F. (Griq. W., W. Prov. & Tvl) b Nov. 5, 1905, d Nov. 14, 1965

Bissex, M. (Glos.) b Sept. 28, 1944

*Blackham, J. McC. (Vic.; *CY 1891*) b May 11, 1854, d Dec. 28, 1932

*Blackie, D. D. (Vic.) b April 5, 1882, d April 18, 1955

Blackledge, J. F. (Lancs.) b April 15, 1928

Blain, T. E. (C. Dist.) b Feb. 17, 1962

Blair, B. R. (Otago) b Dec. 27, 1957

*Blair, R. W. (Wgtn & C. Dist.) b June 23, 1932

Blake, D. E. (Hants) b April 27, 1925

Blake, Rev. P. D. S. (OUCC & Sussex) b May 23, 1927

Blakey, R. J. (Yorks.) b Jan. 15, 1967

*Blanckenberg, J. M. (W. Prov. & Natal) b Dec. 31, 1893, 'presumed dead'

*Bland, K. C. (Rhod., E. Prov. & OFS; *CY 1966*) b April 5, 1938

Blenkiron, W. (Warwicks.) b July 21, 1942

Bligh, Hon. Ivo (*see* 8th Earl of Darnley)

Blofeld, H. C. (CUCC) b Sept. 23, 1939

Blundell, Sir E. D. (CUCC & NZ) b May 29, 1907, d Sept. 24, 1984

*Blunt, R. C. (Cant. & Otago; *CY 1928*) b Nov. 3, 1900, d June 22, 1966

*Blythe, C. (Kent; *CY 1904*) b May 30, 1879, d Nov. 8, 1917

*Board, J. H. (Glos.) b Feb. 23, 1867, d April 16, 1924

*Bock, E. G. (Griq. W., Tvl & W. Prov.) b Sept. 17, 1908, d Sept. 5, 1961

Bodkin, P. E. (CUCC) b Sept. 15, 1924

Boiling, J. (Surrey) b April 8, 1968

*Bolton, B. A. (Cant. & Wgtn) b May 31, 1935

*Bolus, J. B. (Yorks., Notts. & Derbys.) b Jan. 31, 1934

*Bond, G. E. (W. Prov.) b April 5, 1909, d Aug. 27, 1965

Bond, J. D. (Lancs. & Notts.; *CY 1971*) b May 6, 1932

*Bonnor, G. J. (Vic. & NSW) b Feb. 25, 1855, d June 27, 1912

*Boock, S. L. (Otago & Cant.) b Sept. 20, 1951

*Boon, D. C. (Tas.) b Dec. 29, 1960

Boon, T. J. (Leics.) b Nov. 1, 1961

*Booth, B. C. (NSW) b Oct. 19, 1933

Booth, B. J. (Lancs. & Leics.) b Dec. 3, 1935

*Booth, M. W. (Yorks.; *CY 1914*) b Dec. 10, 1886, d July 1, 1916

Booth, P. (Leics.) b Nov. 2, 1952

Booth, P. A. (Yorks. & Warwicks.) b Sept. 5, 1965

Booth, R. (Yorks. & Worcs.) b Oct. 1, 1926

*Borde, C. G. (Baroda & M'tra) b July 21, 1934

*Border, A. R. (NSW, Glos, Qld & Essex; *CY 1982*) b July 27, 1955

Bore, M. K. (Yorks. & Notts.) b June 2, 1947

Borrington, A. J. (Derbys.) b Dec. 8, 1948

*Bosanquet, B. J. T. (OUCC & Middx; *CY 1905*) b Oct. 13, 1877, d Oct. 12, 1936

Bosch T. (N. Tvl) b March 14, 1966

Bose, G. (Bengal) b May 20, 1947

Boshier, B. S. (Leics.) b March 6, 1932

*Botham, I. T. (Som., Worcs., Durham & Qld; *CY 1978*) b Nov. 24, 1955

*Botten, J. T. (NE Tvl & N. Tvl) b June 21, 1938

Boucher, J. C. (Ireland) b Dec. 22, 1910

Bourne, W. A. (B'dos & Warwicks.) b Nov. 15, 1952

*Bowden, M. P. (Surrey & Tvl) b Nov. 1, 1865, d Feb. 19, 1892

*Bowes, W. E. (Yorks.; *CY 1932*) b July 25, 1908, d Sept. 5, 1987

Bowler, P. D. (Leics., Tas. & Derbys.) b July 30, 1963

*Bowley, E. H. (Sussex & Auck.; *CY 1930*) b June 6, 1890, d July 9, 1974

Bowley, F. L. (Worcs.) b Nov. 9, 1873, d May 31, 1943

Bowman, R. (OUCC & Lancs.) b Jan. 26, 1934

Box, T. (Sussex) b Feb. 7, 1808, d July 12, 1876

*Boyce, K. D. (B'dos & Essex; *CY 1974*) b Oct. 11, 1943

*Boycott, G. (Yorks. & N. Tvl; *CY 1965*) b Oct. 21, 1940

Boyd-Moss, R. J. (CUCC & Northants) b Dec. 16, 1959

Boyes, G. S. (Hants) b March 31, 1899, d Feb. 11, 1973

*Boyle, H. F. (Vic.) b Dec. 10, 1847, d Nov. 21, 1907

*Bracewell, B. P. (C. Dist., Otago & N. Dist.) b Sept. 14, 1959

*Bracewell, J. G. (Otago & Auck.) b April 15, 1958

*Bradburn, G. E. (N. Dist.) b May 26, 1966

*Bradburn, W. P. (N. Dist.) b Nov. 24, 1938

*Bradley, W. M. (Kent) b Jan. 2, 1875, d June 19, 1944

*Bradman, Sir D. G. (NSW & S. Aust.; *CY 1931*) b Aug. 27, 1908

Bradshaw, J. C. (Leics.) b Jan. 25, 1902, d Nov. 8, 1984

Brain, B. M. (Worcs. & Glos.) b Sept. 13, 1940

Bramall, Field-Marshal The Lord (Pres. MCC 1988-89) b Dec. 18, 1923

Brandes, E. A. (Zimb.) b March 5, 1963

*Brann, W. H. (E. Prov.) b April 4, 1899, d Sept. 22, 1953

Brassington, A. J. (Glos.) b Aug. 9, 1954

*Braund, L. C. (Surrey & Som.; *CY 1902*) b Oct. 18, 1875, d Dec. 23, 1955

Bray, C. (Essex) b April 6, 1898

Brayshaw, I. J. (W. Aust.) b Jan. 14, 1942

Brazier, A. F. (Surrey & Kent) b Dec. 7, 1924

Breakwell, D. (Northants & Som.) b July 2, 1948

*Brearley, J. M. (CUCC & Middx; *CY 1977*) b April 28, 1942

*Brearley, W. (Lancs.; *CY 1909*) b March 11, 1876, d Jan. 13, 1937

*Brennan, D. V. (Yorks.) b Feb. 10, 1920, d Jan. 9, 1985

Bridge, W. B. (Warwicks.) b May 29, 1938

Bridger, Rev. J. R. (Hants) b April 8, 1920, d July 14, 1986

Brierley, T. L. (Glam., Lancs. & Canada) b June 15, 1910, d Jan. 7, 1989

Briers, M. P. (Durham) b April 21, 1968

Briers, N. E. (Leics.; *CY 1993*) b Jan. 15, 1955

*Briggs, John (Lancs.; *CY 1889*) b Oct. 3, 1862, d Jan. 11, 1902

*Bright, R. J. (Vic.) b July 13, 1954

*Briscoe, A. W. (Tvl) b Feb. 6, 1911, d April 22, 1941

*Broad, B. C. (Glos. & Notts.) b Sept. 29, 1957

Broadbent, R. G. (Worcs.) b June 21, 1924

Brocklehurst, B. G. (Som.) b Feb. 18, 1922

*Brockwell, W. (Kimberley & Surrey; *CY 1895*) b Jan. 21, 1865, d June 30, 1935

Broderick, V. (Northants) b Aug. 17, 1920

Brodhurst, A. H. (CUCC & Glos.) b July 21, 1916

*Bromfield, H. D. (W. Prov.) b June 26, 1932

*Bromley, E. H. (W. Aust. & Vic.) b Sept. 2, 1912, d Feb. 1, 1967

*Bromley-Davenport, H. R. (CUCC, Bombay Eur. & Middx) b Aug. 18, 1870, d May 23, 1954

*Brookes, D. (Northants; *CY 1957*) b Oct. 29, 1915

Brookes, W. H. (Editor of *Wisden* 1936-39) b Dec. 5, 1894, d May 28, 1955

Brooks, R. A. (OUCC & Som.) b June 14, 1943

*Brown, A. (Kent) b Oct. 17, 1935

Brown, A. S. (Glos.) b June 24, 1936

*Brown, D. J. (Warwicks.) b Jan. 30, 1942

Brown, D. W. J. (Glos.) b Feb. 26, 1942

*Brown, F. R. (CUCC, Surrey & Northants; *CY 1933*; Pres. MCC 1971-72) b Dec. 16, 1910, d July 24, 1991

*Brown, G. (Hants) b Oct. 6, 1887, d Dec. 3, 1964

Brown, J. (Scotland) b Sept. 24, 1931

*Brown, J. T. (Yorks.; *CY 1895*) b Aug. 20, 1869, d Nov. 4, 1904

Brown, K. R. (Middx) b March 18, 1963

*Brown, L. S. (Tvl, NE Tvl & Rhod.) b Nov. 24, 1910, d Sept. 1, 1983

Brown, R. D. (Zimb.) b March 11, 1951

Brown, S. J. E. (Northants & Durham) b June 29, 1969

Brown, S. M. (Middx) b Dec. 8, 1917, d Dec. 28, 1987

*Brown, V. R. (Cant. & Auck.) b Nov. 3, 1959

*Brown, W. A. (NSW & Qld; *CY 1939*) b July 31, 1912

Brown, W. C. (Northants) b Nov. 13, 1900, d Jan. 20, 1986

*Browne, C. R. (B'dos & BG) b Oct. 8, 1890, d Jan. 12, 1964

Bruce, Hon. C. N. (3rd Lord Aberdare) (OUCC & Middx) b Aug. 2, 1885, d Oct. 4, 1957

*Bruce, W. (Vic.) b May 22, 1864, d Aug. 3, 1925

Bryan, G. J. (Kent) b Dec. 29, 1902, d April 4, 1991

Bryan, J. L. (CUCC & Kent; *CY 1922*) b May 26, 1896, d April 23, 1985

Bryan, R. T. (Kent) b July 30, 1898, d July 27, 1970

*Buckenham, C. P. (Essex) b Jan. 16, 1876, d Feb. 23, 1937

Buckingham, J. (Warwicks.) b Jan. 21, 1903, d Jan. 25, 1987

Budd, E. H. (Middx & All-England) b Feb. 23, 1785, d March 29, 1875

Budd, W. L. (Hants) b Oct. 25, 1913, d Aug. 23, 1986

Bull, F. G. (Essex; *CY 1898*) b April 2, 1875, d Sept. 16, 1910

Buller, J. S. (Yorks. & Worcs.; Umpire) b Aug. 23, 1909, d Aug. 7, 1970

Burden, M. D. (Hants) b Oct. 4, 1930, d Nov. 9, 1987

*Burge, P. J. (Qld; *CY 1965*) b May 17, 1932
*Burger, C. G. de V. (Natal) b July 12, 1935
Burgess, G. I. (Som.) b May 5, 1943
*Burgess, M. G. (Auck.) b July 17, 1944
*Burke, C. (Auck.) b March 22, 1914
*Burke, J. W. (NSW; *CY 1957*) b June 12, 1930, d Feb. 2, 1979
*Burke, S. F. (NE Tvl & OFS) b March 11, 1934
*Burki, Javed (Pak. Us, OUCC, Punjab, Lahore, Kar., R'pindi & NWFP) b May 8, 1938
Burmester, M. G. (Zimb.) b Jan. 24, 1968
*Burn, E. J. K. (K. E.) (Tas.) b Sept. 17, 1862, d July 20, 1956
Burnet, J. R. (Yorks.) b Oct. 11, 1918
Burns, N. D. (Essex, W. Prov. & Som.) b Sept. 19, 1965
Burnup, C. J. (CUCC & Kent; *CY 1903*) b Nov. 21, 1875, d April 5, 1960
Burrough, H. D. (Som.) b Feb. 6, 1909
*Burton, F. J. (Vic. & NSW) b Nov. 2, 1865, d Aug. 25, 1929
*Burtt, T. B. (Cant.) b Jan. 22, 1915, d May 24, 1988
Buse, H. F. T. (Som.) b Aug. 5, 1910, d Feb. 23, 1992
Bushby, M. H. (CUCC) b July 29, 1931
Buss, A. (Sussex) b Sept. 1, 1939
Buss, M. A. (Sussex & OFS) b Jan. 24, 1944
Buswell, J. E. (Northants) b July 3, 1909
Butchart, I. P. (Zimb.) b May 9, 1967
*Butcher, A. R. (Surrey & Glam.; *CY 1991*) b Jan. 7, 1954
*Butcher, B. F. (Guyana; *CY 1970*) b Sept. 3, 1933
Butcher, I. P. (Leics. & Glos.) b July 1, 1962
*Butcher, R. O. (Middx, B'dos & Tas.) b Oct. 14, 1953
*Butler, H. J. (Notts.) b March 12, 1913, d July 17, 1991
*Butler, L. S. (T/T) b Feb. 9, 1929
*Butt, H. R. (Sussex) b Dec. 27, 1865, d Dec. 21, 1928
*Butterfield, L. A. (Cant.) b Aug. 29, 1913
*Butts, C. G. (Guyana) b July 8, 1957
Buxton, I. R. (Derbys.) b April 17, 1938
*Buys, I. D. (W. Prov.) b Feb. 3, 1895, dead
Byas, D. (Yorks.) b Aug. 26, 1963
*Bynoe, M. R. (B'dos) b Feb. 23, 1941

Caccia, Lord (Pres. MCC 1973-74) b Dec. 21, 1905, d Oct. 31, 1990
Caddick, A. R. (Som.) b Nov. 21, 1968
Caesar, Julius (Surrey & All-England) b March 25, 1830, d March 6, 1878
Caffyn, W. (Surrey & NSW) b Feb. 2, 1828, d Aug. 28, 1919
Caine, C. Stewart (Editor of *Wisden* 1926-33) b Oct. 28, 1861, d April 15, 1933

*Cairns, B. L. (C. Dist., Otago & N. Dist.) b Oct. 10, 1949
*Cairns, C. L. (N. Dist., Notts. & Cant.) b June 13, 1970
Calder, H. L. (Cranleigh; *CY 1918*) b 1900
*Callaway, S. T. (NSW & Cant.) b Feb. 6, 1868, d Nov. 25, 1923
*Callen, I. W. (Vic. & Boland) b May 2, 1955
*Calthorpe, Hon. F. S. Gough- (CUCC, Sussex & Warwicks.) b May 27, 1892, d Nov. 19, 1935
*Camacho, G. S. (Guyana) b Oct. 15, 1945
*Cameron, F. J. (Jam.) b June 22, 1923
*Cameron, F. J. (Otago) b June 1, 1932
*Cameron, H. B. (Tvl, E. Prov. & W. Prov.; *CY 1936*) b July 5, 1905, d Nov. 2, 1935
*Cameron, J. H. (CUCC, Jam. & Som.) b April 8, 1914
Campbell, A. D. R. (Zimb.) b Sept. 23, 1972
Campbell, G. D. (Tas.) b March 10, 1964
*Campbell, T. (Tvl) b Feb. 9, 1882, d Oct. 5, 1924
Cannings, V. H. D. (Warwicks. & Hants) b April 3, 1919
*Capel, D. J. (Northants & E. Prov.) b Feb. 6, 1963
Caple, R. G. (Middx & Hants) b Dec. 8, 1939
Cardus, Sir Neville (Cricket Writer) b April 3, 1888, d Feb. 27, 1975
*Carew, G. McD. (B'dos) b June 4, 1910, d Dec. 9, 1974
*Carew, M. C. (T/T) b Sept. 15, 1937
*Carkeek, W. (Vic.) b Oct. 17, 1878, d Feb. 20, 1937
*Carlson, P. H. (Qld) b Aug. 8, 1951
*Carlstein, P. R. (OFS, Tvl, Natal & Rhod.) b Oct. 28, 1938
Carpenter, D. (Glos.) b Sept. 12, 1935
Carpenter, R. (Cambs. & Utd England XI) b Nov. 18, 1830, d July 13, 1901
*Carr, A. W. (Notts.; *CY 1923*) b May 21, 1893, d Feb. 7, 1963
*Carr, D. B. (OUCC & Derbys.; *CY 1960*; Sec. TCCB 1974-86) b Dec. 28, 1926
*Carr, D. W. (Kent; *CY 1910*) b March 17, 1872, d March 23, 1950
Carr, J. D. (OUCC & Middx) b June 15, 1963
Carrick, P. (Yorks. & E. Prov.) b July 16, 1952
Carrington, E. (Derbys.) b March 25, 1914
Carse, J. A. (Rhod., W. Prov., E. Prov. & Northants) b Dec. 13, 1958
*Carter, C. P. (Natal & Tvl) b April 23, 1881, d Nov. 8, 1952
*Carter, H. (NSW) b Halifax, Yorks. March 15, 1878, d June 8, 1948
Carter, R. G. (Warwicks.) b April 14, 1933
Carter, R. G. M. (Worcs.) b July 11, 1937

Carter, R. M. (Northants & Cant.) b May 25, 1960

Cartwright, H. (Derbys.) b May 12, 1951

*Cartwright, T. W. (Warwicks., Som. & Glam.) b July 22, 1935

Carty, R. A. (Hants) b July 28, 1922, d March 31, 1984

Cass, G. R. (Essex, Worcs. & Tas.) b April 23, 1940

Castell, A. T. (Hants) b Aug. 6, 1943

Castle, F. (Som.) b April 9, 1909

Catt, A. W. (Kent & W. Prov.) b Oct. 2, 1933

Catterall, R. H. (Tvl, Rhod., Natal & OFS; *CY 1925*) b July 10, 1900, d Jan. 2, 1961

*Cave, H. B. (Wgtn & C. Dist.) b Oct. 10, 1922, d Sept. 15, 1989

Chalk, F. G. H. (OUCC & Kent) b Sept. 7, 1910, d Feb. 17, 1943

*Challenor, G. (B'dos) b June 28, 1888, d July 30, 1947

Chamberlain, W. R. F. (Northants; Chairman TCCB) b April 13, 1925

*Chandrasekhar, B. S. (†Karn.; *CY 1972*) b May 17, 1945

Chandrasekhar, V. B. (TN) b Aug. 21, 1961

*Chang, H. S. (Jam.) b July 22, 1952

*Chapman, A. P. F. (Uppingham, OUCC & Kent; *CY 1919*) b Sept. 3, 1900, d Sept. 16, 1961

*Chapman, H. W. (Natal) b June 30, 1890, d Dec. 1, 1941

*Chappell, G. S. (S. Aust., Som. & Qld; *CY 1973*) b Aug. 7, 1948

*Chappell, I. M. (S. Aust. & Lancs.; *CY 1976*) b Sept. 26, 1943

*Chappell, T. M. (S. Aust., W. Aust. & NSW) b Oct. 21, 1952

*Chapple, M. E. (Cant. & C. Dist.) b July 25, 1930, d July 31, 1985

*Charlton, P. C. (NSW) b April 9, 1867, d Sept. 30, 1954

*Charlwood, H. R. J. (Sussex) b Dec. 19, 1846, d June 6, 1888

*Chatfield, E. J. (Wgtn) b July 3, 1950

*Chatterton, W. (Derbys.) b Dec. 27, 1861, d March 19, 1913

*Chauhan, C. P. S. (M'tra & Delhi) b July 21, 1947

Cheatle, R. G. L. (Sussex & Surrey) b July 31, 1953

*Cheetham, J. E. (W. Prov.) b May 26, 1920, d Aug. 21, 1980

Chester, F. (Worcs.; Umpire) b Jan. 20, 1895, d April 8, 1957

Chesterton, G. H. (OUCC & Worcs.) b July 15, 1922

*Chevallier, G. A. (W. Prov.) b March 9, 1937

*Childs, J. H. (Glos. & Essex; *CY 1987*) b Aug. 15, 1951

*Chipperfield, A. G. (NSW) b Nov. 17, 1905, d July 29, 1987

Chisholm, R. H. E. (Scotland) b May 22, 1927

*Chowdhury, N. R. (Bihar & Bengal) b May 23, 1923, d Dec. 14, 1979

*Christiani, C. M. (BG) b Oct. 28, 1913, d April 4, 1938

*Christiani, R. J. (BG) b July 19, 1920

*Christopherson, S. (Kent; Pres. MCC 1939-45) b Nov. 11, 1861, d April 6, 1949

*Christy, J. A. J. (Tvl & Qld) b Dec. 12, 1904, d Feb. 1, 1971

*Chubb, G. W. A. (Border & Tvl) b April 12, 1911, d Aug. 28, 1982

Clark, D. G. (Kent; Pres. MCC 1977-78) b Jan. 27, 1919

Clark, E. A. (Middx) b April 15, 1937

*Clark, E. W. (Northants) b Aug. 9, 1902, d April 28, 1982

Clark, L. S. (Essex) b March 6, 1914

*Clark, W. M. (W. Aust.) b Sept. 19, 1953

*Clarke, Dr C. B. (B'dos, Northants & Essex) b April 7, 1918

*Clarke, S. T. (B'dos, Surrey, Tvl, OFS & N. Tvl) b Dec. 11, 1954

Clarke, William (Notts.; founded All-England XI & Trent Bridge ground) b Dec. 24, 1798, d Aug. 25, 1856

Clarkson, A. (Yorks. & Som.) b Sept. 5, 1939

Claughton, J. A. (OUCC & Warwicks.) b Sept. 17, 1956

*Clay, J. C. (Glam.) b March 18, 1898, d Aug. 12, 1973

Clay, J. D. (Notts.) b Oct. 15, 1924

Clayton, G. (Lancs. & Som.) b Feb. 3, 1938

Clements, S. M. (OUCC) b April 19, 1956

*Cleverley, D. C. (Auck.) b Dec. 23, 1909

Clift, Patrick B. (Rhod., Leics. & Natal) b July 14, 1953

Clift, Philip B. (Glam.) b Sept. 3, 1918

Clinton, G. S. (Kent, Surrey & Zimb.-Rhod.) b May 5, 1953

*Close, D. B. (Yorks. & Som.; *CY 1964*) b Feb. 24, 1931

Cobb, R. A. (Leics. & Natal) b May 18, 1961

Cobham, 10th Visct (Hon. C. J. Lyttelton) (Worcs.; Pres. MCC 1954) b Aug. 8, 1909, d March 20, 1977

*Cochrane, J. A. K. (Tvl & Griq. W.) b July 15, 1909, d June 15, 1987

Cock, D. F. (Essex) b Oct. 22, 1914, d Sept. 26, 1992

*Coen, S. K. (OFS, W. Prov., Tvl & Border) b Oct. 14, 1902, d Jan. 28, 1967

*Colah, S. M. H. (Bombay, W. Ind. & Naw.) b Sept. 22, 1902, d Sept. 11, 1950

Colchin, Robert ("Long Robin") (Kent & All-England) b Nov. 1713, d April 1750

*Coldwell, L. J. (Worcs.) b Jan. 10, 1933

*Colley, D. J. (NSW) b March 15, 1947
Collin, T. (Warwicks.) b April 7, 1911
*Collinge, R. O. (C. Dist., Wgtn & N. Dist.) b April 2, 1946
*Collins, H. L. (NSW) b Jan. 21, 1889, d May 28, 1959
Collins, R. (Lancs.) b March 10, 1934
*Colquhoun, I. A. (C. Dist.) b June 8, 1924
Coman, P. G. (Cant.) b April 13, 1943
*Commaille, J. M. M. (W. Prov., Natal, OFS & Griq. W.) b Feb. 21, 1883, d July 27, 1956
*Compton, D. C. S. (Middx & Holkar; *CY 1939*) b May 23, 1918
Compton, L. H. (Middx) b Sept. 12, 1912, d Dec. 27, 1984
Coney, J. V. (Wgtn; *CY 1984*) b June 21, 1952
*Congdon, B. E. (C. Dist., Wgtn, Otago & Cant.; *CY 1974*) b Feb. 11, 1938
*Coningham, A. (NSW & Qld) b July 14, 1863, d June 13, 1939
*Connolly, A. N. (Vic. & Middx) b June 29, 1939
Connor, C. A. (Hants) b March 24, 1961
Constable, B. (Surrey) b Feb. 19, 1921
Constant, D. J. (Kent & Leics.; Umpire) b Nov. 9, 1941
*Constantine, Lord L. N. (T/T & B'dos; *CY 1940*) b Sept. 21, 1902, d July 1, 1971
Constantine, L. S. (T/T) b May 25, 1874, d Jan. 5, 1942
*Contractor, N. J. (Guj. & Ind. Rlwys) b March 7, 1934
Conyngham, D. P. (Natal, Tvl & W. Prov.) b May 10, 1897, d July 7, 1979
*Cook, C. (Glos.) b Aug. 23, 1921
*Cook, F. J. (E. Prov.) b 1870, dead
*Cook, G. (Northants & E. Prov.) b Oct. 9, 1951
*Cook, N. G. B. (Leics. & Northants) b June 17, 1956
Cook, S. J. (Tvl & Som.; *CY 1990*) b July 31, 1953
Cook, T. E. (Sussex) b Feb. 5, 1901, d Jan. 15, 1950
*Cooper, A. H. C. (Tvl) b Sept 2, 1893, d July 18, 1963
*Cooper, B. B. (Middx, Kent & Vic.) b March 15, 1844, d Aug. 7, 1914
Cooper, F. S. Ashley- (Cricket Historian) b March 17, 1877, d Jan. 31, 1932
Cooper, G. C. (Sussex) b Sept. 2, 1936
Cooper, H. P. (Yorks. & N. Tvl) b April 17, 1949
Cooper, K. E. (Notts.) b Dec. 27, 1957
*Cooper, W. H. (Vic.) b Sept. 11, 1849, d April 5, 1939
*Cope, G. A. (Yorks.) b Feb. 23, 1947
*Copson, W. H. (Derbys.; *CY 1937*) b April 27, 1908, d Sept. 14, 1971
Cordle, A. E. (Glam.) b Sept. 21, 1940

Cork, D. G. (Derbys.) b Aug. 7, 1971
*Corling, G. E. (NSW) b July 13, 1941
Cornford, J. H. (Sussex) b Dec. 9, 1911, d June 17, 1985
*Cornford, W. L. (Sussex) b Dec. 25, 1900, d Feb. 6, 1964
Cornwallis, Capt. Hon. W. S. (2nd Lord Cornwallis) (Kent) b March 14, 1892, d Jan. 4, 1982
Corrall, P. (Leics.) b July 16, 1906
Corran, A. J. (OUCC & Notts.) b Nov. 25, 1936
*Cosier, G. J. (Vic., S. Aust. & Qld) b April 25,1953
*Cottam, J. T. (NSW) b Sept. 5, 1867, d Jan. 30, 1897
*Cottam, R. M. H. (Hants & Northants) b Oct. 16, 1944
*Cotter, A. (NSW) b Dec. 3, 1884, d Oct. 31, 1917
Cottey, P. A. (Glam. & E. Tvl) b June 2, 1966
Cotton, J. (Notts. & Leics.) b Nov. 7, 1940
Cottrell, G. A. (CUCC) b March 23, 1945
*Coulthard, G. (Vic.) b Aug. 1, 1856, d Oct. 22, 1883
*Coventry, Hon. C. J. (Worcs.) b Feb. 26, 1867, d June 2, 1929
Coverdale, S. P. (CUCC, Yorks., & Northants) b Nov. 20, 1954
Cowan, M. J. (Yorks.) b June 10, 1933
*Cowans, N. G. (Middx) b April 17, 1961
*Cowdrey, C. S. (Kent & Glam.) b Oct. 20, 1957
Cowdrey, G. R. (Kent) b June 27, 1964
*Cowdrey, Sir M. C. (OUCC & Kent; *CY 1956*; Pres. MCC 1986-87) b Dec. 24, 1932
*Cowie, J. (Auck.) b March 30, 1912
Cowley, N. G. (Hants & Glam.) b March 1, 1953
*Cowper, R. M. (Vic. & W. Aust.) b Oct. 5, 1940
Cox, A. L. (Northants) b July 22, 1907, d Nov. 1986
Cox, G., jun. (Sussex) b Aug. 23, 1911, d March 30, 1985
Cox, G. R. (Sussex) b Nov. 29, 1873, d March 24, 1949
*Cox, J. L. (Natal) b June 28, 1886, d July 4, 1971
*Coxon, A. (Yorks.) b Jan. 18, 1916
Craig, E. J. (CUCC & Lancs.) b March 26, 1942
*Craig, I. D. (NSW) b June 12, 1935
Cranfield, L. M. (Glos.) b Aug. 29, 1909
Cranmer, P. (Warwicks.) b Sept. 10, 1914
*Cranston, J. (Glos.) b Jan. 9, 1859, d Dec. 10, 1904
*Cranston, K. (Lancs.) b Oct. 20, 1917
*Crapp, J. F. (Glos.) b Oct. 14, 1912, d Feb. 15, 1981

*Crawford, J. N. (Surrey, S. Aust., Wgtn & Otago; *CY 1907*) b Dec. 1, 1886, d May 2, 1963

*Crawford, P. (NSW) b Aug. 3, 1933

Crawley, A. M. (OUCC & Kent; Pres. MCC 1972-73) b April 10, 1908

Crawley, J. P. (Lancs. & CUCC) b Sept. 21, 1971

Crawley, M. A. (OUCC, Lancs. & Notts.) b Dec. 16, 1967

Cray, S. J. (Essex) b May 29, 1921

*Cresswell, G. F. (Wgtn & C. Dist.) b March 22, 1915, d Jan. 10, 1966

*Cripps, G. (W. Prov.) b Oct. 19, 1865, d July 27, 1943

*Crisp, R. J. (Rhod., W. Prov. & Worcs.) b May 28, 1911

*Croft, C. E. H. (Guyana & Lancs.) b March 15, 1953

Croft, R. D. B. (Glam.) b May 25, 1970

*Cromb, I. B. (Cant.) b June 25, 1905, d March 6, 1984

*Cronje, W. J. (OFS) b Sept. 25, 1969

Crookes, N. S. (Natal) b Nov. 15, 1935

Cross, G. F. (Leics.) b Nov. 15, 1943

*Crowe, J. J. (S. Aust. & Auck.) b Sept. 14, 1958

*Crowe, M. D. (Auck., C. Dist., Som. & Wgtn; *CY 1985*) b Sept. 22, 1962

Crump, B. S. (Northants) b April 25, 1938

Crush, E. (Kent) b April 25, 1917

Cumbes, J. (Lancs., Surrey, Worcs. & Warwicks.) b May 4, 1944

Cummins, A. C. (B'dos) b May 7, 1966

*Cunis, R. S. (Auck. & N. Dist.) b Jan. 5, 1941

*Curnow, S. H. (Tvl) b Dec. 16, 1907, d July 28, 1986

Curran, K. M. (Glos., Zimb. & Natal) b Sept. 7, 1959

*Curtis, T. S. (Worcs. & CUCC) b Jan. 15, 1960

Cuthbertson, G. B. (Middx, Sussex & Northants) b March 23, 1901

Cutmore, J. A. (Essex) b Dec. 28, 1898, d Nov. 30, 1985

*Cuttell, W. R. (Lancs.; *CY 1898*) b Sept. 13, 1864, d Dec. 9, 1929

*Da Costa, O. C. (Jam.) b Sept. 11, 1907, d Oct. 1, 1936

Dacre, C. C. (Auck. & Glos.) b May 15, 1899, d Nov. 2, 1975

Daft, Richard (Notts. & All-England) b Nov. 2, 1835, d July 18, 1900

Dakin, G. F. (E. Prov.) b Aug. 13, 1935

Dale, A. (Glam.) b Oct. 24, 1968

*Dalton, E. L. (Natal) b Dec. 2, 1906, d June 3, 1981

*Dani, H. T. (M'tra & Ind. Serv.) b May 24, 1933

*Daniel, W. W. (B'dos, Middx & W. Aust.) b Jan. 16, 1956

*D'Arcy, J. W. (Cant., Wgtn & Otago) b April 23, 1936

Dare, R. (Hants) b Nov. 26, 1921

*Darling, J. (S. Aust.; *CY 1900*) b Nov. 21, 1870, d Jan. 2, 1946

*Darling, L. S. (Vic.) b Aug. 14, 1909, d June 24, 1992

*Darling, W. M. (S. Aust.) b May 1, 1957

*Darnley, 8th Earl of (Hon. Ivo Bligh) (CUCC & Kent; Pres. MCC 1900) b March 13, 1859, d April 10, 1927

Davey, J. (Glos.) b Sept. 4, 1944

*Davidson, A. K. (NSW; *CY 1962*) b June 14, 1929

Davies, Dai (Glam.) b Aug. 26, 1896, d July 16, 1976

Davies, Emrys (Glam.) b June 27, 1904, d Nov. 10, 1975

*Davies, E. Q. (E. Prov., Tvl & NE Tvl) b Aug. 26, 1909, d Nov. 11, 1976

Davies, H. D. (Glam.) b July 23, 1932

Davies, H. G. (Glam.) b April 23, 1913

Davies, J. G. W. (CUCC & Kent; Pres. MCC 1985-86) b Sept. 10, 1911, d Nov. 5, 1992

Davies, M. (Glam. & Glos.) b April 18, 1969

Davies, T. (Glam.) b Oct. 25, 1960

*Davis, B. A. (T/T & Glam.) b May 2, 1940

*Davis, C. A. (T/T) b Jan. 1, 1944

Davis, E. (Northants) b March 8, 1922

*Davis, I. C. (NSW & Qld) b June 25, 1953

Davis, M. R. (Som.) b Feb. 26, 1962

Davis, P. C. (Northants) b May 24, 1915

Davis, R. C. (Glam.) b Jan. 1, 1946

Davis, R. P. (Kent) b March 18, 1966

*Davis, S. P. (Vic.) b Nov. 8, 1959

*Davis, W. W. (Windwards, Glam., Tas., Northants & Wgtn) b Sept. 18, 1958

Davison, B. F. (Rhod., Leics, Tas. & Glos.) b Dec. 21, 1946

Davison, I. J. (Notts.) b Oct. 4, 1937

Dawkes, G. O. (Leics. & Derbys.) b July 19, 1920

*Dawson, E. W. (CUCC & Leics.) b Feb. 13, 1904, d June 4, 1979

*Dawson, O. C. (Natal & Border) b Sept. 1, 1919

Day, A. P. (Kent; *CY 1910*) b April 10, 1885, d Jan. 22, 1969

*de Alwis, R. G. (SSC) b Feb. 15, 1959

*Dean, H. (Lancs.) b Aug. 13, 1884, d March 12, 1957

*Deane, H. G. (Natal & Tvl) b July 21, 1895, d Oct. 21, 1939

*De Caires, F. I. (BG) b May 12, 1909, d Feb. 2, 1959

*De Courcy, J. H. (NSW) b April 18, 1927

*DeFreitas, P. A. J. (Leics. & Lancs.; *CY 1992*) b Feb. 18, 1966

Delisle, G. P. S. (OUCC & Middx) b Dec. 25, 1934

*Dell, A. R. (Qld) b Aug. 6, 1947

*de Mel, A. L. F. (SL) b May 9, 1959

*Dempster, C. S. (Wgtn, Leics., Scotland & Warwicks.; *CY 1932*) b Nov. 15, 1903, d Feb. 14, 1974

*Dempster, E. W. (Wgtn) b Jan. 25, 1925

*Denness, M. H. (Scotland, Kent & Essex; *CY 1975*) b Dec. 1, 1940

Dennett, E. G. (Glos.) b April 27, 1880, d Sept. 14, 1937

Denning, P. W. (Som.) b Dec. 16, 1949

Dennis, F. (Yorks.) b June 11, 1907

Dennis, S. J. (Yorks., OFS & Glam.) b Oct. 18, 1960

*Denton, D. (Yorks.; *CY 1906*) b July 4, 1874, d Feb. 16, 1950

Deodhar, D. B. (M'tra; oldest living Ranji Trophy player) b Jan. 14, 1892

*Depeiza, C. C. (B'dos) b Oct. 10, 1927

Derrick, J. (Glam.) b Jan. 15, 1963

*Desai, R. B. (Bombay) b June 20, 1939

De Saram, F. C. (OUCC & Ceylon) b Sept. 5, 1912, d April 11, 1983

de Silva, A. M. (CCC) b Dec. 3, 1963

de Silva, D. L. S. (SL) b Nov. 17, 1956, d April 12, 1980

*de Silva, D. S. (SL) b June 11, 1942

*de Silva, E. A. R. (NCC) b March 28, 1956

de Silva, G. N. (SL) b March 12, 1955

*de Silva, G. R. A. (SL) b Dec. 12, 1952

*de Silva, P. A. (NCC) b Oct. 17, 1965

de Smidt, R. (W. Prov.) b Nov. 24, 1883, d Aug. 3, 1986

Devereux, L. N. (Middx, Worcs. & Glam.) b Oct. 20, 1931

de Villiers, P. S. (N. Tvl & Kent) b Oct. 13, 1964

*Dewdney, C. T. (Jam.) b Oct. 23, 1933

*Dewes, J. G. (CUCC & Middx) b Oct. 11, 1926

Dews, G. (Worcs.) b June 5, 1921

*Dexter, E. R. (CUCC & Sussex; *CY 1961*) b May 15, 1935

*Dias, R. L. (CCC) b Oct. 18, 1952

Dibbs, A. H. A. (Pres. MCC 1983-84) b Dec. 9, 1918, d Nov. 28, 1985

*Dick, A. E. (Otago & Wgtn) b Oct. 10, 1936

*Dickinson, G. R. (Otago) b March 11, 1903, d March 17, 1978

*Dilley, G. R. (Kent, Natal & Worcs.) b May 18, 1959

Diment, R. A. (Glos. & Leics.) b Feb. 9, 1927

*Dipper, A. E. (Glos.) b Nov. 9, 1885, d Nov. 7, 1945

*Divecha, R. V. (Bombay, OUCC, Northants, Vidarbha & S'tra) b Oct. 18, 1927

Diver, A. J. D. (Cambs., Middx, Notts. & All-England) b June 6, 1824, d March 25, 1876

Dixon, A. L. (Kent) b Nov. 27, 1933

*Dixon, C. D. (Tvl) b Feb. 12, 1891, d Sept. 9, 1969

Dodds, T. C. (Essex) b May 29, 1919

*Dodemaide, A. I. C. (Vic. & Sussex) b Oct. 5, 1963

*Doggart, G. H. G. (CUCC & Sussex; Pres. MCC 1981-82) b July 18, 1925

*D'Oliveira, B. L. (Worcs.; *CY 1967*) b Oct. 4, 1931

D'Oliveira, D. B. (Worcs.) b Oct. 19, 1960

*Dollery, H. E. (Warwicks. & Wgtn; *CY 1952*) b Oct. 14, 1914, d Jan. 20, 1987

Dollery, K. R. (Qld, Auck., Tas. & Warwicks.) b Dec. 9, 1924

*Dolphin, A. (Yorks.) b Dec. 24, 1885, d Oct. 23, 1942

*Donald, A. A. (OFS & Warwicks.; *CY 1992*) b Oct. 20, 1966

Donelan, B. T. P. (Sussex) b Jan. 3, 1968

*Donnan, H. (NSW) b Nov. 12, 1864, d Aug. 13, 1956

*Donnelly, M. P. (Wgtn, Cant., Middx, Warwicks. & OUCC; *CY 1948*) b Oct. 17, 1917

*Dooland, B. (S. Aust. & Notts.; *CY 1955*) b Nov. 1, 1923, d Sept. 8, 1980

Dorrinton, W. (Kent & All-England) b April 29, 1809, d Nov. 8, 1848

Dorset, 3rd Duke of (Kent) b March 24, 1745, d July 19, 1799

*Doshi, D. R. (Bengal, Notts., Warwicks. & S'tra) b Dec. 22, 1947

*Douglas, J. W. H. T. (Essex; *CY 1915*) b Sept. 3, 1882, d Dec. 19, 1930

Dowding, A. L. (OUCC) b April 4, 1929

*Dowe, U. G. (Jam.) b March 29, 1949

*Dower, R. R. (E. Prov.) b June 4, 1876, d Sept. 15, 1964

Dowling, G. T. (Cant.) b March 4, 1937

*Downton, P. R. (Kent & Middx) b April 4, 1957

*Draper, R. G. (E. Prov. & Griq. W.) b Dec. 24, 1926

Dredge, C. H. (Som.) b Aug. 4, 1954

*Druce, N. F. (CUCC & Surrey; *CY 1898*) b Jan. 1, 1875, d Oct. 27, 1954

Drybrough, C. D. (OUCC & Middx) b Aug. 31, 1938

*D'Souza, A. (Kar., Peshawar & PIA) b Jan. 17, 1939

*Ducat, A. (Surrey; *CY 1920*) b Feb. 16, 1886, d July 23, 1942

*Duckworth, C. A. R. (Natal & Rhod.) b March 22, 1933

*Duckworth, G. (Lancs.; *CY 1929*) b May 9, 1901, d Jan. 5, 1966

Dudleston, B. (Leics., Glos. & Rhod.) b July 16, 1945

Duers, K. G. (Zimb.) b June 30, 1960

*Duff, R. A. (NSW) b Aug. 17, 1878, d Dec. 13, 1911

*Dujon, P. J. L. (Jam.; *CY 1989*) b May 28, 1956

*Duleepsinhji, K. S. (CUCC & Sussex; *CY 1930*) b June 13, 1905, d Dec. 5, 1959

*Dumbrill, R. (Natal & Tvl) b Nov. 19, 1938

*Duminy, J. P. (OUCC, W. Prov. & Tvl) b Dec. 16, 1897, d Jan. 31, 1980

*Duncan, J. R. F. (Qld & Vic.) b March 25, 1944

*Dunell, O. R. (E. Prov.) b July 15, 1856, d Oct. 21, 1929

*Dunning, J. A. (Otago & OUCC) b Feb. 6, 1903, d June 24, 1971

*Du Preez, J. H. (Rhod. & Zimb.) b Nov. 14, 1942

*Durani, S. A. (S'tra, Guj. & Raja.) b Dec. 11, 1934

Durose, A. J. (Northants) b Oct. 10, 1944

*Durston, F. J. (Middx) b July 11, 1893, d April 8, 1965

*Du Toit, J. F. (SA) b April 5, 1868, d July 10, 1909

Dye, J. C. J. (Kent, Northants & E. Prov.) b July 24, 1942

Dyer, D. D. (Natal & Tvl) b Dec. 3, 1946

*Dyer, D. V. (Natal) b May 2, 1914, d June 18, 1990

Dyer, G. C. (NSW) b March 16, 1959

Dyer, R. I. H. B. (Warwicks.) b Dec. 22, 1958

*Dymock, G. (Qld) b July 21, 1945

Dyson, A. H. (Glam.) b July 10, 1905, d June 7, 1978

Dyson, J. (Lancs.) b July 8, 1934

*Dyson, John (NSW) b June 11, 1954

*Eady, C. J. (Tas.) b Oct. 29, 1870, d Dec. 20, 1945

Eagar, E. D. R. (OUCC, Glos. & Hants) b Dec. 8, 1917, d Sept. 13, 1977

Eagar, M. A. (OUCC & Glos.) b March 20, 1934

Eaglestone, J. T. (Middx & Glam.) b July 24, 1923

Ealham, A. G. E. (Kent) b Aug. 30, 1944

Ealham, M. A. (Kent) b Aug. 27, 1969

East, D. E. (Essex) b July 27, 1959

East, R. E. (Essex) b June 20, 1947

Eastman, G. F. (Essex) b April 7, 1903, d March 15, 1991

Eastman, L. C. (Essex & Otago) b June 3, 1897, d April 17, 1941

*Eastwood, K. H. (Vic.) b Nov. 23, 1935

*Ebeling, H. I. (Vic.) b Jan. 1, 1905, d Jan. 12, 1980

Eckersley, P. T. (Lancs.) b July 2, 1904, d Aug. 13, 1940

*Edgar, B. A. (Wgtn) b Nov. 23, 1956

Edinburgh, HRH Duke of (Pres. MCC 1948-49, 1974-75) b June 10, 1921

Edmeades, B. E. A. (Essex) b Sept. 17, 1941

*Edmonds, P. H. (CUCC, Middx & E. Prov.) b March 8, 1951

Edmonds, R. B. (Warwicks.) b March 2, 1941

Edrich, B. R. (Kent & Glam.) b Aug. 18, 1922

Edrich, E. H. (Lancs.) b March 27, 1914

Edrich, G. A. (Lancs.) b July 13, 1918

*Edrich, J. H. (Surrey; *CY 1966*) b June 21, 1937

*Edrich, W. J. (Middx; *CY 1940*) b March 26, 1916, d April 24, 1986

*Edwards, G. N. (C. Dist.) b May 27, 1955

*Edwards, J. D. (Vic.) b June 12, 1862, d July 31, 1911

Edwards, M. J. (CUCC & Surrey) b March 1, 1940

*Edwards, R. (W. Aust. & NSW) b Dec. 1, 1942

*Edwards, R. M. (B'dos) b June 3, 1940

*Edwards, W. J. (W. Aust.) b Dec. 23, 1949

Eele, P. J. (Som.) b Jan. 27, 1935

Eggar, J. D. (OUCC, Hants & Derbys.) b Dec. 1, 1916, d May 3, 1983

*Ehtesham-ud-Din (Lahore, Punjab, PIA, NBP & UBL) b Sept. 4, 1950

Eksteen, C. E. (Tvl) b Dec. 2, 1966

*Elgie, M. K. (Natal) b March 6, 1933

Ellcock, R. M. (Worcs., B'dos & Middx) b June 17, 1965

Elliott, C. S. (Derbys.) b April 24, 1912

*Elliott, H. (Derbys.) b Nov. 2, 1891, d Feb. 2, 1976

Ellis, G. P. (Glam.) b May 24, 1950

Ellis, R. G. P. (OUCC & Middx) b Oct. 20 1960

*Ellison, R. M. (Kent & Tas.; *CY 1986*) b Sept. 21, 1959

Elms, R. B. (Kent & Hants) b April 5, 1949

*Emburey, J. E. (Middx & W. Prov.; *CY 1984*) b Aug. 20, 1952

*Emery, R. W. G. (Auck. & Cant.) b March 28, 1915, d Dec. 18, 1982

*Emery, S. H. (NSW) b Oct. 16, 1885, d Jan. 7, 1967

*Emmett, G. M. (Glos.) b Dec. 2, 1912, d Dec. 18, 1976

*Emmett, T. (Yorks.) b Sept. 3, 1841, d June 30, 1904

*Endean, W. R. (Tvl) b May 31, 1924

*Engineer, F. M. (Bombay & Lancs.) b Feb. 25, 1938

*Evans, A. J. (OUCC, Hants & Kent) b May 1, 1889, d Sept. 18, 1960

Evans, D. G. L. (Glam.; Umpire) b July 27, 1933, d March 25, 1990

*Evans, E. (NSW) b March 6, 1849, d July 2, 1921

Evans, G. (OUCC, Glam. & Leics.) b Aug. 13, 1915

Evans, J. B. (Glam.) b Nov. 9, 1936

Evans, K. P. (Notts.) b Sept. 10, 1963

*Evans, T. G. (Kent; *CY 1951*) b Aug. 18, 1920

Every, T. (Glam.) b Dec. 19, 1909, d Jan. 20, 1990

Eyre, T. J. P. (Derbys.) b Oct. 17, 1939

Faber, M. J. J. (OUCC & Sussex) b Aug. 15, 1950, d Dec. 10, 1991

*Fagg, A. E. (Kent) b June 18, 1915, d Sept. 13, 1977

Fairbairn, A. (Middx) b Jan. 25, 1923

*Fairbrother, N. H. (Lancs.) b Sept. 9, 1963

*Fairfax, A. G. (NSW) b June 16, 1906, d May 17, 1955

Fairservice, C. (Kent & Middx) b Aug. 21, 1909

Fane, F. L. (OUCC & Essex) b April 27, 1875, d Nov. 27, 1960

Fantham, W. E. (Warwicks.) b May 14, 1918

*Farnes, K. (CUCC & Essex; *CY 1939*) b July 8, 1911, d Oct. 20, 1941

*Farooq Hamid (Lahore & PIA) b March 3, 1945

*Farrer, W. S. (Border) b Dec. 8, 1936

*Farrimond, W. (Lancs.) b May 23, 1903, d Nov. 14, 1979

*Farrukh Zaman (Peshawar, NWFP, Punjab & MCB) b April 2, 1956

*Faulkner, G. A. (Tvl) b Dec. 17, 1881, d Sept. 10, 1930

*Favell, L. E. (S. Aust.) b Oct. 6, 1929, d June 14, 1987

*Fazal Mahmood (N. Ind., Punjab & Lahore; *CY 1955*) b Feb. 18, 1927

Fearnley, C. D. (Worcs.) b April 12, 1940

Featherstone, N. G. (Tvl, N. Tvl, Middx & Glam.) b Aug. 20, 1949

'Felix', N. (Wanostrocht) (Kent, Surrey & All-England) b Oct. 4, 1804, d Sept. 3, 1876

*Fellows-Smith, J. P. (OUCC, Tvl & Northants) b Feb. 3, 1932

Feltham, M. A. (Surrey) b June 26, 1963

Felton, N. A. (Som. & Northants) b Oct. 24, 1960

*Fender, P. G. H. (Sussex & Surrey; *CY 1915*) b Aug. 22, 1892, d June 15, 1985

*Ferguson, W. (T/T) b Dec. 14, 1917, d Feb. 23, 1961

*Fernandes, M. P. (BG) b Aug. 12, 1897, d May 8, 1981

Fernando, E. R. (SL) b Feb. 22, 1944

*Fernando, E. R. N. S. (SLAF) b Dec. 19, 1955

Fernando, T. L. (Colts) b Dec. 27, 1962

Ferreira, A. M. (N. Tvl & Warwicks.) b April 13, 1955

Ferris, G. J. F. (Leics. & Leewards) b Oct. 18, 1964

**Ferris, J. J. (NSW, Glos. & S. Aust.; *CY 1889*) b May 21, 1867, d Nov. 21, 1900

*Fichardt, C. G. (OFS) b March 20, 1870, d May 30, 1923

Fiddling, K. (Yorks. & Northants) b Oct. 13, 1917, d June 19, 1992

*Fielder, A. (Kent; *CY 1907*) b July 19, 1877, d Aug. 30, 1949

*Findlay, T. M. (Comb. Is. & Windwards) b Oct. 19, 1943

Findlay, W. (OUCC & Lancs.; Sec. Surrey CCC, Sec. MCC 1926-36) b June 22, 1880, d June 19, 1953

*Fingleton, J. H. (NSW) b April 28, 1908, d Nov. 22, 1981

*Finlason, C. E. (Tvl & Griq. W.) b Feb. 19, 1860, d July 31, 1917

Finney, R. J. (Derbys.) b Aug. 2, 1960

Firth, Rev. Canon J. D'E. E. (Winchester, OUCC & Notts.; *CY 1918*) b Jan. 21, 1900, d Sept. 21, 1957

Fisher, F. E. (Wgtn & C. Dist.) b July 28, 1924

Fisher, P. B. (OUCC, Middx & Worcs.) b Dec. 19, 1954

*Fishlock, L. B. (Surrey; *CY 1947*) b Jan. 2, 1907, d June 26, 1986

Fitton, J. D. (Lancs.) b Aug. 24, 1965

Fitzgerald, R. A. (CUCC & Middx; Sec. MCC 1863-76) b Oct. 1, 1834, d Oct. 28, 1881

*Flavell, J. A. (Worcs.; *CY 1965*) b May 15, 1929

*Fleetwood-Smith, L. O'B. (Vic.) b March 30, 1908, d March 16, 1971

Fleming, M. V. (Kent) b Dec. 12, 1964

Fletcher, D. A. G. (Rhod. & Zimb.) b Sept. 27, 1948

Fletcher, D. G. W. (Surrey) b July 6, 1924

*Fletcher, K. W. R. (Essex; *CY 1974*) b May 20, 1944

Fletcher, S. D. (Yorks. & Lancs.) b June 8, 1964

*Floquet, C. E. (Tvl) b Nov. 3, 1884, d Nov. 22, 1963

Flower, A. (Zimb.) b April 28, 1968

*Flowers, W. (Notts.) b Dec. 7, 1856, d Nov. 1, 1926

Foat, J. C. (Glos.) b Nov. 21, 1952

*Foley, H. (Wgtn) b Jan. 28, 1906, d Oct. 16, 1948

Folley, I. (Lancs. & Derbys.) b Jan. 9, 1963

Foord, C. W. (Yorks.) b June 11, 1924

Forbes, C. (Notts.) b Aug. 9, 1936

*Ford, F. G. J. (CUCC & Middx) b Dec. 14, 1866, d Feb. 7, 1940

Ford, N. M. (OUCC, Derbys. & Middx) b Nov. 18, 1906

Fordham, A. (Northants) b Nov. 9, 1964

Foreman, D. J. (W. Prov. & Sussex) b Feb. 1, 1933

Fosh, M. K. (CUCC & Essex) b Sept. 26, 1957

*Foster, F. R. (Warwicks.; *CY 1912*) b Jan. 31, 1889, d May 3, 1958

Foster, G. N. (OUCC, Worcs. & Kent) b Oct. 16, 1884, d Aug. 11, 1971

Foster, H. K. (OUCC & Worcs.; *CY 1911*) b Oct. 30, 1873, d June 23, 1950

Foster, M. K. (Worcs.) b Jan. 1, 1889, d Dec. 3, 1940

*Foster, M. L. C. (Jam.) b May 9, 1943

*Foster, N. A. (Essex & Tvl; *CY 1988*) b May 6, 1962

Foster, P. G. (Kent) b Oct. 9, 1916

*Foster, R. E. (OUCC & Worcs.; *CY 1901*) b April 16, 1878, d May 13, 1914

*Fothergill, A. J. (Som.) b Aug. 26, 1854, d Aug. 1, 1932

Fotheringham, H. R. (Natal & Tvl) b April 4, 1953

*Fowler, G. (Lancs.) b April 20, 1957

Fowler, W. P. (Derbys., N. Dist. & Auck.) b March 13, 1959

*Francis, B. C. (NSW & Essex) b Feb. 18, 1948

Francis, D. A. (Glam.) b Nov. 29, 1953

*Francis, G. N. (B'dos) b Dec. 7, 1897, d Jan. 12, 1942

*Francis, H. H. (Glos. & W. Prov.) b May 26, 1868, d Jan. 7, 1936

Francke, F. M. (SL & Qld) b March 29, 1941

*Francois, C. M. (Griq. W.) b June 20, 1897, d May 26, 1944

*Frank, C. N. (Tvl) b Jan. 27, 1891, d Dec. 26, 1961

*Frank, W. H. B. (SA) b Nov. 23, 1872, d Feb. 16, 1945

Franklin, H. W. F. (OUCC, Surrey & Essex) b June 30, 1901, d May 25, 1985

*Franklin, T. J. (Auck.) b March 18, 1962

*Fraser, A. R. C. (Middx) b Aug. 8, 1965

*Frederick, M. C. (B'dos, Derbys. & Jam.) b May 6, 1927

*Fredericks, R. C. (†Guyana & Glam.; *CY 1974*) b Nov. 11, 1942

*Freeman, A. P. (Kent; *CY 1923*) b May 17, 1888, d Jan. 28, 1965

*Freeman, D. L. (Wgtn) b Sept. 8, 1914

*Freeman, E. W. (S. Aust.) b July 13, 1944

*Freer, F. W. (Vic.) b Dec. 4, 1915

*French, B. N. (Notts.) b Aug. 13, 1959

Frost, G. (Notts.) b Jan. 15, 1947

Frost, M. (Surrey & Glam.) b Oct. 21, 1962

Fry, C. A. (OUCC, Hants & Northants) b Jan. 14, 1940

*Fry, C. B. (OUCC, Sussex & Hants; *CY 1895*) b April 25, 1872, d Sept. 7, 1956

*Fuller, E. R. H. (W. Prov.) b Aug. 2, 1931

*Fuller, R. L. (Jam.) b Jan. 30, 1913, d May 3, 1987

*Fullerton, G. M. (Tvl) b Dec. 8, 1922

Funston, G. K. (NE Tvl & Griq. W.) b Nov. 21, 1948

*Funston, K. J. (NE Tvl, OFS & Tvl) b Dec. 3, 1925

*Furlonge, H. A. (T/T) b June 19, 1934

Gabriel, R. S. (T/T) b June 5, 1952

*Gadkari, C. V. (M'tra & Ind. Serv.) b Feb. 3, 1928

*Gaekwad, A. D. (Baroda) b Sept. 23, 1952

*Gaekwad, D. K. (Baroda) b Oct. 27, 1928

*Gaekwad, H. G. (†M. Pradesh) b Aug. 29, 1923

Gale, R. A. (Middx) b Dec. 10, 1933

*Gallichan, N. (Wgtn) b June 3, 1906, d March 25, 1969

*Gamsy, D. (Natal) b Feb. 17, 1940

*Gandotra, A. (Delhi & Bengal) b Nov. 24, 1948

Ganguly, S. C. (Bengal) b July 8, 1966

*Gannon, J. B. (W. Aust.) b Feb. 8, 1947

*Ganteaume, A. G. (T/T) b Jan. 22, 1921

Gard, T. (Som.) b June 2, 1957

Gardner, L. R. (Leics.) b Feb. 23, 1934

Garland-Wells, H. M. (OUCC & Surrey) b Nov. 14, 1907

Garlick, R. G. (Lancs. & Northants) b April 11, 1917, d May 16, 1988

*Garner, J. (B'dos, Som. & S. Aust.; *CY 1980*) b Dec. 16, 1952

Garnham, M. A. (Glos., Leics. & Essex) b Aug. 20, 1960

*Garrett, T. W. (NSW) b July 26, 1858, d Aug. 6, 1943

*Gaskin, B. B. MacG. (BG) b March 21, 1908, d May 1, 1979

*Gatting, M. W. (Middx; *CY 1984*) b June 6, 1957

*Gaunt, R. A. (W. Aust. & Vic.) b Feb. 26, 1934

*Gavaskar, S. M. (Bombay & Som.; *CY 1980*) b July 10, 1949

*Gay, L. H. (CUCC, Hants & Som.) b March 24, 1871, d Nov. 1, 1949

Geary, A. C. T. (Surrey) b Sept. 11, 1900, d Jan. 23, 1989

*Geary, G. (Leics.; *CY 1927*) b July 9, 1893, d March 6, 1981

*Gedye, S. G. (Auck.) b May 2, 1929

*Gehrs, D. R. A. (S. Aust.) b Nov. 29, 1880, d June 25, 1953

Ghai, R. S. (Punjab) b June 12, 1960

*Ghavri, K. D. (S'tra & Bombay) b Feb. 28, 1951

*Ghazali, M. E. Z. (M'tra & Pak. Serv.) b June 15, 1924

*Ghorpade, J. M. (Baroda) b Oct. 2, 1930, d March 29, 1978

*Ghulam Abbas (Kar., NBP & PIA) b May 1, 1947

*Ghulam Ahmed (H'bad) b July 4, 1922

*Gibb, P. A. (CUCC, Scotland, Yorks. & Essex) b July 11, 1913, d Dec. 7, 1977

Gibbons, H. H. (Worcs.) b Oct. 10, 1904, d Feb. 16, 1973

*Gibbs, G. L. (BG) b Dec. 27, 1925, d Feb. 21, 1979

*Gibbs, L. R. (†Guyana, S. Aust. & Warwicks.; *CY 1972*) b Sept. 29, 1934

Gibbs, P. J. K. (OUCC & Derbys.) b Aug. 17, 1944

Gibson, C. H. (Eton, CUCC & Sussex; *CY 1918*) b Aug. 23, 1900, d Dec. 31, 1976

Gibson, D. (Surrey) b May 1, 1936

*Giffen, G. (S. Aust.; *CY 1894*) b March 27, 1859, d Nov. 29, 1927

*Giffen, W. F. (S. Aust.) b Sept. 20, 1861, d June 29, 1949

*Gifford, N. (Worcs. & Warwicks.; *CY 1975*) b March 30, 1940

*Gilbert, D. R. (NSW, Tas. & Glos.) b Dec. 29, 1960

*Gilchrist, R. (Jam. & H'bad) b June 28, 1934

Giles, R. J. (Notts.) b Oct. 17, 1919

Gilhouley, K. (Yorks. & Notts.) b Aug. 8, 1934

Gill, A. (Notts.) b Aug. 4, 1940

*Gillespie, S. R. (Auck.) b March 2, 1957

Gilliat, R. M. C. (OUCC & Hants) b May 20, 1944

*Gilligan, A. E. R. (CUCC, Surrey & Sussex; *CY 1924*; Pres. MCC 1967-68) b Dec. 23, 1894, d Sept. 5, 1976

*Gilligan, A. H. H. (Sussex) b June 29, 1896, d May 5, 1978

Gilligan, F. W. (OUCC & Essex) b Sept. 20, 1893, d May 4, 1960

*Gilmour, G. J. (NSW) b June 26, 1951

*Gimblett, H. (Som.; *CY 1953*) b Oct. 19, 1914, d March 30, 1978

Gladstone, G. (*see* Marais, G. G.)

Gladwin, Chris (Essex & Derbys.) b May 10, 1962

*Gladwin, Cliff (Derbys.) b April 3, 1916, d April 10, 1988

*Gleeson, J. W. (NSW & E. Prov.) b March 14, 1938

*Gleeson, R. A. (E. Prov.) b Dec. 6, 1873, d Sept. 27, 1919

Glendenen, J. D. (Durham) b June 20, 1965

*Glover, G. K. (Kimberley & Griq. W.) b May 13, 1870, d Nov. 15, 1938

Glover, T. R. (OUCC) b Nov. 26, 1951

Goddard, G. F. (Scotland) b May 19, 1938

*Goddard, J. D. C. (B'dos) b April 21, 1919, d Aug. 26, 1987

*Goddard, T. L. (Natal & NE Tvl) b Aug. 1, 1931

*Goddard, T. W. J. (Glos.; *CY 1938*) b Oct. 1, 1900, d May 22, 1966

Goel, R. (Patiala & Haryana) b Sept. 29, 1942

Goldsmith, S. C. (Kent & Derbys.) b Dec. 19, 1964

Goldstein, F. S. (OUCC, Northants, Tvl & W. Prov.) b Oct. 14, 1944

*Gomes, H. A. (T/T & Middx; *CY 1985*) b July 13, 1953

Gomez, G. E. (T/T) b Oct. 10, 1919

*Gooch, G. A. (Essex & W. Prov.; *CY 1980*) b July 23, 1953

Goodway, C. C. (Warwicks.) b July 10, 1909, d May 22, 1991

Goodwin, K. (Lancs.) b June 25, 1938

Goodwin, T. J. (Leics.) b Jan. 22, 1929

Goonatillake, F. R. M. de S. (SL) b. Aug. 15, 1951

*Goonatillake, H. M. (SL) b Aug. 16, 1952

Goonesena, G. (Ceylon, Notts., CUCC & NSW) b Feb. 16, 1931

*Gopalan, M. J. (Madras) b June 6, 1909

*Gopinath, C. D. (Madras) b March 1, 1930

*Gordon, N. (Tvl) b Aug. 6, 1911

Gore, A. C. (Eton & Army; *CY 1919*) b May 14, 1900, d June 7, 1990

Gould, I. J. (Middx, Auck. & Sussex) b Aug. 19, 1957

*Gover, A. R. (Surrey; *CY 1937*) b Feb. 29, 1908

*Gower, D. I. (Leics. & Hants; *CY 1979*) b April 1, 1957

Gowrie, 1st Lord (Pres. MCC 1948-49) b July 6, 1872, d May 2, 1955

Grace, Dr Alfred b May 17, 1840, d May 24, 1916

Grace, Dr Alfred H. (Glos.) b March 10, 1866, d Sept. 16, 1929

Grace, C. B. (Clifton) b March 1882, d June 6, 1938

*Grace, Dr E. M. (Glos.) b Nov. 28, 1841, d May 20, 1911

Grace, Dr Edgar M. (MCC) (son of E. M. Grace) b Oct. 6, 1886, d Nov. 24, 1974

*Grace, G. F. (Glos.) b Dec. 13, 1850, d Sept. 22, 1880

Grace, Dr Henry (Glos.) b Jan. 31, 1833, d Nov. 15, 1895

Grace, Dr H. M. (father of W. G., E. M. and G. F.) b Feb. 21, 1808, d Dec. 23, 1871

Grace, Mrs H. M. (mother of W. G., E. M. and G. F.) b July 18, 1812, d July 25, 1884

*Grace, Dr W. G. (Glos.; *CY 1896*) b July 18, 1848, d Oct. 23, 1915

Grace, W. G., jun. (CUCC & Glos.) b July 6, 1874, d March 2, 1905

Graf, S. F. (Vic., W. Aust. & Hants) b May 19, 1957

*Graham, H. (Vic. & Otago) b Nov. 22, 1870, d Feb. 7, 1911

Graham, J. N. (Kent) b May 8, 1943

*Graham, R. (W. Prov.) b Sept. 16, 1877, d April 21, 1946

*Grant, G. C. (CUCC, T/T & Rhod.) b May 9, 1907, d Oct. 26, 1978

*Grant, R. S. (CUCC & T/T) b Dec. 15, 1909, d Oct. 18, 1977

Graveney, D. A. (Glos., Som. & Durham) b Jan. 2, 1953

Graveney, J. K. (Glos.) b Dec. 16, 1924

*Graveney, T. W. (Glos., Worcs. & Qld; *CY 1953*) b June 16, 1927

Graves, P. J. (Sussex & OFS) b May 19, 1946

*Gray, A. H. (T/T & Surrey) b May 23, 1963

*Gray, E. J. (Wgtn) b Nov. 18, 1954

Gray, J. R. (Hants) b May 19, 1926

Gray, L. H. (Middx) b Dec. 16, 1915, d Jan. 3, 1983

Greasley, D. G. (Northants) b Jan. 20, 1926

*Greatbatch, M. J. (C. Dist.) b Dec. 11, 1963

Green, A. M. (Sussex & OFS) b May 28, 1960

Green, D. J. (Derbys. & CUCC) b Dec. 18, 1935

Green, D. M. (OUCC, Lancs. & Glos.; *CY 1969*) b Nov. 10, 1939

*Greenhough, T. (Lancs.) b Nov. 9, 1931

*Greenidge, A. E. (B'dos) b Aug. 20, 1956

*Greenidge, C. G. (Hants & B'dos; *CY 1977*) b May 1, 1951

*Greenidge, G. A. (B'dos & Sussex) b May 26, 1948

Greensmith, W. T. (Essex) b Aug. 16, 1930

*Greenwood, A. (Yorks.) b Aug. 20, 1847, d Feb. 12, 1889

Greenwood, P. (Lancs.) b Sept. 11, 1924

Greetham, C. (Som.) b Aug. 28, 1936

*Gregory, David W. (NSW; first Australian captain) b April 15, 1845, d Aug. 4, 1919

*Gregory, E. J. (NSW) b May 29, 1839, d April 22, 1899

*Gregory, J. M. (NSW; *CY 1922*) b Aug. 14, 1895, d Aug. 7, 1973

*Gregory, R. G. (Vic.) b Feb. 28, 1916, d June 10, 1942

*Gregory, S. E. (NSW; *CY 1897*) b April 14, 1870, d August 1, 1929

*Greig, A. W. (Border, E. Prov. & Sussex; *CY 1975*) b Oct. 6, 1946

*Greig, I. A. (CUCC, Border, Sussex & Surrey) b Dec. 8, 1955

*Grell, M. G. (T/T) b Dec. 18, 1899, d Jan. 11, 1976

*Grieve, B. A. F. (Eng.) b May 28, 1864, d Nov. 19, 1917

Grieves, K. J. (NSW & Lancs.) b Aug. 27, 1925, d Jan. 3, 1992

*Grieveson, R. E. (Tvl) b Aug. 24, 1909

*Griffin, G. M. (Natal & Rhod.) b June 12, 1939

*Griffith, C. C. (B'dos; *CY 1964*) b Dec. 14, 1938

Griffith, G. ("Ben") (Surrey & Utd England XI) b Dec. 20, 1833, d May 3, 1879

*Griffith, H. C. (B'dos) b Dec. 1, 1893, d March 18, 1980

Griffith, K. (Worcs.) b Jan. 17, 1950

Griffith, M. G. (CUCC & Sussex) b Nov. 25, 1943

*Griffith, S. C. (CUCC, Surrey & Sussex; Sec. MCC 1962-74; Pres. MCC 1979-80) b June 16, 1914

Griffiths, B. J. (Northants) b June 13, 1949

Griffiths, Rt Hon. The Lord (W. H.) (CUCC & Glam.; Pres. MCC 1990-91) b Sept. 26, 1923

*Grimmett, C. V. (Wgtn, Vic. & S. Aust.; *CY 1931*) b Dec. 25, 1891, d May 2, 1980

Grimshaw, N. (Northants) b May 5, 1911

*Groube, T. U. (Vic.) b Sept. 2, 1857, d Aug. 5, 1927

*Grout, A. T. W. (Qld) b March 30, 1927, d Nov. 9, 1968

Grover, J. N. (OUCC) b Oct. 15, 1915, d Dec. 17, 1990

Groves, M. G. M. (OUCC, Som. & W. Prov.) b Jan. 14, 1943

Grundy, J. (Notts. & Utd England XI) b March 5, 1824, d Nov. 24, 1873

*Guard, G. M. (Bombay & Guj.) b Dec. 12, 1925, d March 13, 1978

*Guest, C. E. J. (Vic. & W. Aust.) b Oct. 7, 1937

*Guha, S. (Bengal) b Jan. 31, 1946

**Guillen, S. C. (T/T & Cant.) b Sept. 24, 1924

Guise, J. L. (OUCC & Middx) b Nov. 25, 1903, d June 29, 1991

**Gul Mahomed (N. Ind., Baroda, H'bad, Punjab & Lahore) b Oct. 15, 1921, d May 8, 1992

*Gunasekera, Y. (SL) b Nov. 8, 1957

*Guneratne, R. P. W. (Nomads) b Jan. 26, 1962

*Gunn, G. (Notts.; *CY 1914*) b June 13, 1879, d June 29, 1958

Gunn, G. V. (Notts.) b June 21, 1905, d Oct. 14, 1957

*Gunn, J. (Notts.; *CY 1904*) b July 19, 1876, d Aug. 21, 1963

Gunn, T. (Sussex) b Sept. 27, 1935

*Gunn, William (Notts.; *CY 1890*) b Dec. 4, 1858, d Jan. 29, 1921

*Gupte, B. P. (Bombay, Bengal & Ind. Rlwys) b Aug. 30, 1934

*Gupte, S. P. (Bombay, Bengal, Raja. & T/T) b Dec. 11, 1929

Gurr, D. R. (OUCC & Som.) b March 27, 1956

*Gursharan Singh (Punjab) b March 8, 1963
*Gurusinha, A. P. (SSC & NCC) b Sept. 16, 1966
*Guy, J. W. (C. Dist., Wgtn, Northants, Cant., Otago & N. Dist.) b Aug. 29, 1934

Haafiz Shahid (WAPDA) b May 10, 1963
Hacker, P. J. (Notts., Derbys. & OFS) b July 16, 1952
Hadlee, B. G. (Cant.) b Dec. 14, 1941
*Hadlee, D. R. (Cant.) b Jan. 6, 1948
*Hadlee, Sir R. J. (Cant., Notts. & Tas.; *CY 1982*) b July 3, 1951
*Hadlee, W. A. (Cant. & Otago) b June 4, 1915
Hafeez, A. (*see* Kardar)
Hagan, D. A. (OUCC) b June 25, 1966
*Haig, N. E. (Middx) b Dec. 12, 1887, d Oct. 27, 1966
*Haigh, S. (Yorks.; *CY 1901*) b March 19, 1871, d Feb. 27, 1921
Halfyard, D. J. (Kent & Notts.) b April 3, 1931
*Hall, A. E. (Tvl & Lancs.) b Jan. 23, 1896, d Jan. 1, 1964
*Hall, G. G. (NE Tvl & E. Prov.) b May 24, 1938, d June 26, 1987
Hall, I. W. (Derbys.) b Dec. 27, 1939
Hall, J. W. (Sussex) b March 30, 1968
Hall, Louis (Yorks.; *CY 1890*) b Nov. 1, 1852, d Nov. 19, 1915
Hall, T. A. (Derbys. & Som.) b Aug. 19, 1930, d April 21, 1984
*Hall, W. W. (B'dos, T/T & Qld) b Sept. 12, 1937
Hallam, A. W. (Lancs. & Notts.; *CY 1908*) b Nov. 12, 1869, d July 24, 1940
Hallam, M. R. (Leics.) b Sept. 10, 1931
*Halliwell, E. A. (Tvl & Middx; *CY 1905*) b Sept. 7, 1864, d Oct. 2, 1919
*Hallows, C. (Lancs.; *CY 1928*) b April 4, 1895, d Nov. 10, 1972
Hallows, J. (Lancs.; *CY 1905*) b Nov. 14, 1873, d May 20, 1910
Halse, C. G. (Natal) b Feb. 28, 1935
*Hamence, R. A. (S. Aust.) b Nov. 25, 1915
Hamer, A. (Yorks. & Derbys.) b Dec. 8, 1916
Hammond, H. E. (Sussex) b Nov. 7, 1907, d June 16, 1985
*Hammond, J. R. (S. Aust.) b April 19, 1950
*Hammond, W. R. (Glos.; *CY 1928*) b June 19, 1903, d July 1, 1965
*Hampshire, J. H. (Yorks., Derbys. & Tas.; Umpire) b Feb. 10, 1941
*Hands, P. A. M. (W. Prov.) b March 18, 1890, d April 27, 1951
*Hands, R. H. M. (W. Prov.) b July 26, 1888, d April 20, 1918
*Hanif Mohammad (B'pur, Kar. & PIA; *CY 1968*) b Dec. 21, 1934

*Hanley, M. A. (Border & W. Prov.) b Nov. 10, 1918
Hanley, R. W. (E. Prov., OFS, Tvl & Northants) b Jan. 29, 1952
*Hanumant Singh (M. Pradesh & Raja.) b March 29, 1939
Harbord, W. E. (Yorks. & OUCC) b Dec. 15, 1908, d July 28, 1992
Harden, R. J. (Som. & C. Dist.) b Aug. 16, 1965
Hardie, B. R. (Scotland & Essex) b Jan. 14, 1950
*Hardikar, M. S. (Bombay) b Feb. 8, 1936
*Hardinge, H. T. W. (Kent; *CY 1915*) b Feb. 25, 1886, d May 8, 1965
*Hardstaff, J. (Notts.) b Nov. 9, 1882, d April 2, 1947
*Hardstaff, J., jun. (Notts. & Auck.; *CY 1938*) b July 3, 1911, d Jan. 1, 1990
Hardy, J. J. E. (Hants, Som., W. Prov. & Glos.) b Oct. 2, 1960
Harfield, L. (Hants) b Aug. 16, 1905, d Nov. 19, 1985
*Harford, N. S. (C. Dist. & Auck.) b Aug. 30, 1930, d March 30, 1981
*Harford, R. I. (Auck.) b May 30, 1936
Harman, R. (Surrey) b Dec. 28, 1941
*Haroon Rashid (Kar., Sind, NBP, PIA & UBL) b March 25, 1953
*Harper, R. A. (Guyana & Northants) b March 17, 1963
Harris, 4th Lord (OUCC & Kent; Pres. MCC 1895) b Feb. 3, 1851, d March 24, 1932
Harris, C. Z. (Cant.) b Nov. 20, 1969
Harris, David (Hants & All-England) b 1755, d May 19, 1803
Harris, M. J. (Middx, Notts., E. Prov. & Wgtn) b May 25, 1944
*Harris, P. G. Z. (Cant.) b July 18, 1927, d Dec. 1, 1991
*Harris, R. M. (Auck.) b July 27, 1933
*Harris, T. A. (Griq. W. & Tvl) b Aug. 27, 1916
Harrison, L. (Hants) b June 8, 1922
*Harry, J. (Vic.) b Aug. 1, 1857, d Oct. 27, 1919
Hart, G. E. (Middx) b Jan. 13, 1902, d April 11, 1987
Hart, R. T. (C. Dist.) b Nov. 7, 1961
*Hartigan, G. P. D. (Border) b Dec. 30, 1884, d Jan. 7, 1955
*Hartigan, R. J. (NSW & Qld) b Dec. 12, 1879, d June 7, 1958
*Hartkopf, A. E. V. (Vic.) b Dec. 28, 1889, d May 20, 1968
Hartland, B. R. (Cant.) b Oct. 22, 1966
Hartley, A. (Lancs.; *CY 1911*) b April 11, 1879, d Oct. 9, 1918
*Hartley, J. C. (OUCC & Sussex) b Nov. 15, 1874, d March 8, 1963

Hartley, P. J. (Warwicks. & Yorks.) b April 18, 1960

Hartley, S. N. (Yorks. & OFS) b March 18, 1956

Harvey, J. F. (Derbys.) b Sept. 27, 1939

*Harvey, M. R. (Vic.) b April 29, 1918

Harvey, P. F. (Notts.) b Jan. 15, 1923

*Harvey, R. L. (Natal) b Sept. 14, 1911

*Harvey, R. N. (Vic. & NSW; *CY 1954*) b Oct. 8, 1928

Harvey-Walker, A. J. (Derbys.) b July 21, 1944

Hasan Jamil (Kalat, Kar., Pak. Us & PIA) b July 25, 1952

*Haseeb Ahsan (Peshawar, Pak. Us, Kar. & PIA) b July 15, 1939

Hassan, B. (Notts.) b March 24, 1944

*Hassett, A. L. (Vic.; *CY 1949*) b Aug. 28, 1913

*Hastings, B. F. (Wgtn, C. Dist. & Cant.) b March 23, 1940

*Hathorn, C. M. H. (Tvl) b April 7, 1878, d May 17, 1920

Hathurusinghe, U. C. (TU) b Sept. 13, 1968

*Hawke, 7th Lord (CUCC & Yorks.; *CY 1909*; Pres. MCC 1914-18) b Aug. 16, 1860, d Oct. 10, 1938

*Hawke, N. J. N. (W. Aust., S. Aust. & Tas.) b June 27, 1939

Hawker, Sir Cyril (Essex; Pres. MCC 1970-71) b July 21, 1900, d Feb. 22, 1991

Hawkins, D. G. (Glos.) b May 18, 1935

*Hayes, E. G. (Surrey & Leics.; *CY 1907*) b Nov. 6, 1876, d Dec. 2, 1953

*Hayes, F. C. (Lancs.) b Dec. 6, 1946

*Hayes, J. A. (Auck. & Cant.) b Jan. 11, 1927

Hayes, K. A. (OUCC & Lancs.) b Sept. 26, 1962

Haygarth, A. (Sussex; Historian) b Aug. 4, 1825, d May 1, 1903

Hayhurst, A. N. (Lancs. & Som.) b Nov. 23, 1962

*Haynes, D. L. (B'dos & Middx; *CY 1991*) b Feb. 15, 1956

Haynes, R. C. (Jam.) b Nov. 11, 1964

Haysman, M. D. (S. Aust., Leics. & N. Tvl) b April 22, 1961

Hayward, T. (Cambs. & All-England) b March 21, 1835, d July 21, 1876

*Hayward, T. W. (Surrey; *CY 1895*) b March 29, 1871, d July 19, 1939

Haywood, P. R. (Leics.) b March 30, 1947

*Hazare, V. S. (M'tra, C. Ind. & Baroda) b March 11, 1915

Hazell, H. L. (Som.) b Sept. 30, 1909, d March 31, 1990

Hazlerigg, Lord, formerly Hon. A. G. (CUCC & Leics.) b Feb. 24, 1910

*Hazlitt, G. R. (Vic. & NSW) b Sept. 4, 1888, d Oct. 30, 1915

Headley, D. W. (Middx) b Jan. 27, 1970

*Headley, G. A. (Jam.; *CY 1934*) b May 30, 1909, d Nov. 30, 1983

*Headley, R. G. A. (Worcs. & Jam.) b June 29, 1939

Healy, I. A. (Qld) b April 30, 1964

Hearn, P. (Kent) b Nov. 18, 1925

*Hearne, Alec (Kent; *CY 1894*) b July 22, 1863, d May 16, 1952

**Hearne, Frank (Kent & W. Prov.) b Nov. 23, 1858, d July 14, 1949

*Hearne, G. A. L. (W. Prov.) b March 27, 1888, d Nov. 13, 1978

*Hearne, George G. (Kent) b July 7, 1856, d Feb. 13, 1932

*Hearne, J. T. (Middx; *CY 1892*) b May 3, 1867, d April 17, 1944

*Hearne, J. W. (Middx; *CY 1912*) b Feb. 11, 1891, d Sept. 14, 1965

Hearne, Thos. (Middx) b Sept. 4, 1826, d May 13, 1900

Hearne, Thos., jun. (Lord's Ground Superintendent) b Dec. 29, 1849, d Jan. 29, 1910

Heath, G. E. M. (Hants) b Feb. 20, 1913

Heath, M. (Hants) b March 9, 1934

Hedges, B. (Glam.) b Nov. 10, 1927

Hedges, L. P. (Tonbridge, OUCC, Kent & Glos.; *CY 1919*) b July 13, 1900, d Jan. 12, 1933

Hegg, W. K. (Lancs.) b Feb. 23, 1968

*Heine, P. S. (NE Tvl, OFS & Tvl) b June 28, 1928

Hemmings, E. E. (Warwicks. & Notts.) b Feb. 20, 1949

Hemsley, E. J. O. (Worcs.) b Sept. 1, 1943

*Henderson, M. (Wgtn) b Aug. 2, 1895, d June 17, 1970

Henderson, R. (Surrey; *CY 1890*) b March 30, 1865, d Jan. 29, 1931

Henderson, S. P. (CUCC, Worcs. & Glam.) b Sept. 24, 1958

*Hendren, E. H. (Middx; *CY 1920*) b Feb. 5, 1889, d Oct. 4, 1962

Hendriks, J. L. (Jam.) b Dec. 21, 1933

*Hendry, H. S. T. L. (NSW & Vic.) b May 24, 1895, d Dec. 16, 1988

Henry, O. (W. Prov., Boland, OFS & Scotland) b Jan. 23, 1952

Hepworth, P. N. (Leics.) b May 4, 1967

Herman, O. W. (Hants) b Sept. 18, 1907, d June 24, 1987

Herman, R. S. (Middx, Border, Griq. W. & Hants) b Nov. 30, 1946

Heron, J. G. (Zimb.) b Nov. 8, 1948

*Heseltine, C. (Hants) b Nov. 26, 1869, d June 13, 1944

Hever, N. G. (Middx & Glam.) b Dec. 17, 1924, d Sept. 11, 1987

Hewett, H. T. (OUCC & Som.; *CY 1893*) b May 25, 1864, d March 4, 1921

Heyhoe-Flint, Rachael (England Women) b June 11, 1939

Heyn, P. D. (SL) b June 26, 1945

*Hibbert, P. A. (Vic.) b July 23, 1952

*Hick, G. A. (Worcs., Zimb., N. Dist. & Qld; *CY 1987*) b May 23, 1966

*Higgs, J. D. (Vic.) b July 11, 1950

*Higgs, K. (Lancs. & Leics.; *CY 1968*) b Jan. 14, 1937

Hignell, A. J. (CUCC & Glos.) b Sept. 4, 1955

*Hilditch, A. M. J. (NSW & S. Aust.) b May 20, 1956

Hill, Alan (Derbys. & OFS) b June 29, 1950

*Hill, Allen (Yorks.) b Nov. 14, 1843, d Aug. 29, 1910

*Hill, A. J. L. (CUCC & Hants) b July 26, 1871, d Sept. 6, 1950

*Hill, C. (S. Aust.; *CY 1900*) b March 18, 1877, d Sept. 5, 1945

Hill, E. (Som.) b July 9, 1923

Hill, G. (Hants) b April 15, 1913

*Hill, J. C. (Vic.) b June 25, 1923, d Aug. 11, 1974

Hill, L. W. (Glam.) b April 14, 1942

Hill, M. (Notts., Derbys & Som.) b Sept. 14, 1935

Hill, N. W. (Notts.) b Aug. 22, 1935

Hill, W. A. (Warwicks.) b April 27, 1910

Hills, R. W. (Kent) b Jan. 8, 1951

Hill-Wood, C. K. (OUCC & Derbys.) b June 5, 1907, d Sept. 21, 1988

Hilton, C. (Lancs. & Essex) b Sept. 26, 1937

Hilton, J. (Lancs. & Som.) b Dec. 29, 1930

*Hilton, M. J. (Lancs.; *CY 1957*) b Aug. 2, 1928, d July 8, 1990

*Hime, C. F. W. (Natal) b Oct. 24, 1869, d Dec. 6, 1940

*Hindlekar, D. D. (Bombay) b Jan. 1, 1909, d March 30, 1949

Hinks, S. G. (Kent & Glos.) b Oct. 12, 1960

*Hirst, G. H. (Yorks.; *CY 1901*) b Sept. 7, 1871, d May 10, 1954

*Hirwani, N. D. (M. Pradesh) b Oct. 18, 1968

*Hitch, J. W. (Surrey; *CY 1914*) b May 7, 1886, d July 7, 1965

Hitchcock, R. E. (Cant. & Warwicks.) b Nov. 28, 1929

*Hoad, E. L. G. (B'dos) b Jan. 29, 1896, d March 5, 1986

*Hoare, D. E. (W. Aust.) b Oct. 19, 1934

*Hobbs, Sir J. B. (Surrey; *CY 1909, special portrait 1926*) b Dec. 16, 1882, d Dec. 21, 1963

*Hobbs, R. N. S. (Essex & Glam.) b May 8, 1942

*Hodges, J. R. (Vic.) b Aug. 11, 1855, death unknown

Hodgkinson, G. F. (Derbys.) b Feb. 19, 1914, d Jan. 7, 1987

Hodgson, A. (Northants) b Oct. 27, 1951

Hodgson, G. D. (Glos.) b Oct. 22, 1966

Hofmeyr, M. B. (OUCC & NE Tvl) b Dec. 9, 1925

*Hogan, T. G. (W. Aust.) b Sept. 23, 1956

*Hogg, R. M. (S. Aust.) b March 5, 1951

Hogg, W. (Lancs. & Warwicks.) b July 12, 1955

*Hohns, T. V. (Qld) b Jan. 23, 1954

Holder, J. W. (Hants; Umpire) b March 19, 1945

*Holder, V. A. (B'dos, Worcs. & OFS) b Oct. 8, 1945

*Holding, M. A. (Jam., Lancs., Derbys., Tas. & Cant.; *CY 1977*) b Feb. 16, 1954

*Hole, G. B. (NSW & S. Aust.) b Jan. 6, 1931, d Feb. 14, 1990

*Holford, D. A. J. (B'dos & T/T) b April 16, 1940

*Holland, R. G. (NSW & Wgtn) b Oct. 19, 1946

*Hollies, W. E. (Warwicks.; *CY 1955*) b June 5, 1912, d April 16, 1981

Hollingdale, R. A. (Sussex) b March 6, 1906, d Aug. 1989

Holmes, Gp Capt. A. J. (Sussex) b June 30, 1899, d May 21, 1950

*Holmes, E. R. T. (OUCC & Surrey; *CY 1936*) b Aug. 21, 1905, d Aug. 16, 1960

Holmes, G. C. (Glam.) b Sept. 16, 1958

*Holmes, P. (Yorks.; *CY 1920*) b Nov. 25, 1886, d Sept. 3, 1971

Holt, A. G. (Hants) b April 8, 1911

*Holt, J. K., jun. (Jam.) b Aug. 12, 1923

Home of the Hirsel, Lord (Middx; Pres. MCC 1966-67) b July 2, 1903

*Hone, L. (MCC) b Jan. 30, 1853, d Dec. 31, 1896

Hooker, R. W. (Middx) b Feb. 22, 1935

Hookes, D. W. (S. Aust.) b May 3, 1955

*Hooper, C. L. (Guyana & Kent) b Dec. 15, 1966

*Hopkins, A. J. Y. (NSW) b May 3, 1874, d April 25, 1931

Hopkins, J. A. (Glam. & E. Prov.) b June 16, 1953

Hopkins, V. (Glos.) b Jan. 21, 1911, d Aug. 6, 1984

*Hopwood, J. L. (Lancs.) b Oct. 30, 1903, d June 15, 1985

*Horan, T. P. (Vic.) b March 8, 1854, d April 16, 1916

*Hordern, H. V. (NSW & Philadelphia) b Feb. 10, 1884, d June 17, 1938

*Hornby, A. N. (Lancs.) b Feb. 10, 1847, d Dec. 17, 1925

*Horne, P. A. (Auck.) b Jan. 21, 1960

Horner, N. F. (Yorks. & Warwicks.) b May 10, 1926

*Hornibrook, P. M. (Qld) b July 27, 1899, d Aug. 25, 1976

Horton, H. (Worcs. & Hants) b April 18, 1923

Horton, J. (Worcs.) b Aug. 12, 1916

*Horton, M. J. (Worcs. & N. Dist.) b April 21, 1934

Hossell, J. J. (Warwicks.) b May 25, 1914

*Hough, K. W. (Auck.) b Oct. 24, 1928

Houghton, D. L. (Zimb.) b June 23, 1957

*Howard, A. B. (B'dos) b Aug. 27, 1946

Howard, A. R. (Glam.) b Dec. 11, 1909

Howard, B. J. (Lancs.) b May 21, 1926

Howard, K. (Lancs.) b June 29, 1941

*Howard, N. D. (Lancs.) b May 18, 1925, d May 31, 1979

Howard, Major R. (Lancs.; MCC Team Manager) b April 17, 1890, d Sept. 10, 1967

*Howarth, G. P. (Auck., Surrey & N. Dist.) b March 29, 1951

*Howarth, H. J. (Auck.) b Dec. 25, 1943

*Howell, H. (Warwicks.) b Nov. 29, 1890, d July 9, 1932

*Howell, W. P. (NSW) b Dec. 29, 1869, d July 14, 1940

Howland, C. B. (CUCC, Sussex & Kent) b Feb. 6, 1936

*Howorth, R. (Worcs.) b April 26, 1909, d April 2, 1980

*Hudson, A. C. (Natal) b March 17, 1966

Hughes, D. P. (Lancs. & Tas.; *CY 1988*) b May 13, 1947

*Hughes, K. J. (W. Aust. & Natal; *CY 1981*) b Jan. 26, 1954

*Hughes, M. G. (Vic. & Essex) b Nov. 23, 1961

Hughes, S. P. (Middx, N. Tvl & Durham) b Dec. 20, 1959

Huish, F. H. (Kent) b Nov. 15, 1869, d March 16, 1957

Hulme, J. H. A. (Middx) b Aug. 26, 1904, d Sept. 26, 1991

Human, J. H. (CUCC & Middx) b Jan. 13, 1912, d July 22, 1991

Humpage, G. W. (Warwicks. & OFS; *CY 1985*) b April 24, 1954

Humphries, D. J. (Leics. & Worcs.) b Aug. 6, 1953

*Humphries, J. (Derbys.) b May 19, 1876, d May 7, 1946

Hunt, A. V. (Scotland & Bermuda) b Oct. 1, 1910

*Hunt, W. A. (NSW) b Aug. 26, 1908, d Dec. 30, 1983

*Hunte, C. C. (B'dos; *CY 1964*) b May 9, 1932

*Hunte, E. A. C. (T/T) b Oct. 3, 1905, d June 26, 1967

Hunter, David (Yorks.) b Feb. 23, 1860, d Jan. 11, 1927

*Hunter, Joseph (Yorks.) b Aug. 3, 1855, d Jan. 4, 1891

Hurd, A. (CUCC & Essex) b Sept. 7, 1937

*Hurst, A. G. (Vic.) b July 15, 1950

Hurst, R. J. (Middx) b Dec. 29, 1933

*Hurwood, A. (Qld) b June 17, 1902, d Sept. 26, 1982

*Hussain, M. Dilawar (C. Ind. & U. Prov.) b March 19, 1907, d Aug. 26, 1967

*Hussain, N. (Essex) b March 28, 1968

*Hutchings, K. L. (Kent; *CY 1907*) b Dec. 7, 1882, d Sept. 3, 1916

Hutchinson, J. M. (Derbys.) (oldest known living county cricketer) b Nov. 29, 1896

*Hutchinson, P. (SA) b Jan. 26, 1862, d Sept. 30, 1925

*Hutton, Sir Leonard (Yorks.; *CY 1938*) b June 23, 1916, d Sept. 6, 1990

*Hutton, R. A. (CUCC, Yorks. & Tvl) b Sept. 6, 1942

*Hylton, L. G. (Jam.) b March 29, 1905, d May 17, 1955

*Ibadulla, K. (Punjab, Warwicks., Tas. & Otago) b Dec. 20, 1935

*Ibrahim, K. C. (Bombay) b Jan. 26, 1919

*Iddon, J. (Lancs.) b Jan. 8, 1902, d April 17, 1946

*Igglesden, A. P. (Kent & W. Prov.) b Oct. 8, 1964

*Ijaz Ahmed (Gujranwala, PACO & HBL) b Sept. 20, 1968

*Ijaz Butt (Pak. Us, Punjab, Lahore, R'pindi & Multan) b March 10, 1938

*Ijaz Faqih (Kar., Sind, PWD & MCB) b March 24, 1956

*Ikin, J. T. (Lancs.) b March 7, 1918, d Sept. 15, 1984

*Illingworth, R. (Yorks. & Leics.; *CY 1960*) b June 8, 1932

*Illingworth, R. K. (Worcs. & Natal) b Aug. 23, 1963

Ilott, M. C. (Essex) b Aug. 27, 1970

*Imran Khan (Lahore, Dawood, Worcs., OUCC, PIA, Sussex & NSW; *CY 1983*) b Nov. 25, 1952

*Imtiaz Ahmed (N. Ind., Comb. Us, NWFP, Pak. Serv., Peshawar & PAF) b Jan. 5, 1928

*Imtiaz Ali (T/T) b July 28, 1954

Inchmore, J. D. (Worcs. & N. Tvl) b Feb. 22, 1949

*Indrajitsinhji, K. S. (S'tra & Delhi) b June 15, 1937

Ingle, R. A. (Som.) b Nov. 5, 1903, d Dec. 19, 1992

Ingleby-Mackenzie, A. C. D. (Hants) b Sept. 15, 1933

Inman C. C. (Ceylon & Leics.) b Jan. 29, 1936

*Inshan Ali (T/T) b Sept. 25, 1949

*Insole, D. J. (CUCC & Essex; *CY 1956*) b April 18, 1926

*Intikhab Alam (Kar., PIA, Surrey, PWD, Sind & Punjab) b Dec. 28, 1941

*Inverarity, R. J. (W. Aust. & S. Aust.) b Jan. 31, 1944

*Inzamam-ul-Haq (Multan & UBL) b March 3, 1970

*Iqbal Qasim (Kar., Sind & NBP) b Aug. 6, 1953

Iqbal Sikandar (Karachi & PIA) b Dec. 19, 1958

*Irani, J. K. (Sind) b Aug. 18, 1923, d Feb. 25, 1982

*Iredale, F. A. (NSW) b June 19, 1867, d April 15, 1926

Iremonger, J. (Notts.; *CY 1903*) b March 5, 1876, d March 25, 1956

*Ironmonger, H. (Qld & Vic.) b April 7, 1882, d June 1, 1971

*Ironside, D. E. J. (Tvl) b May 2, 1925

*Irvine, B. L. (W. Prov., Natal, Essex & Tvl) b March 9, 1944

*Israr Ali (S. Punjab, B'pur & Multan) b May 1, 1927

*Iverson, J. B. (Vic.) b July 27, 1915, d Oct. 24, 1973

*Jackman, R. D. (Surrey, W. Prov. & Rhod.; *CY 1981*) b Aug. 13, 1945

*Jackson, A. (NSW) b Sept. 5, 1909, d Feb. 16, 1933

Jackson, A. B. (Derbys.) b Aug. 21, 1933

Jackson, Sir A. H. M. (Derbys.) b Nov. 9, 1899, d Oct. 11, 1983

*Jackson, Rt Hon. Sir F. S. (CUCC & Yorks.; *CY 1894*; Pres. MCC 1921) b Nov. 21, 1870, d March 9, 1947

Jackson, G. R. (Derbys.) b June 23, 1896, d Feb. 21, 1966

*Jackson, H. L. (Derbys.; *CY 1959*) b April 5, 1921

Jackson, John (Notts. & All-England) b May 21, 1833, d Nov. 4, 1901

Jackson, P. F. (Worcs.) b May 11, 1911

Jacques, T. A. (Yorks.) b Feb. 19, 1905

Jadeja, A. D. (Haryana) b Feb. 1, 1971

*Jahangir Khan (N. Ind. & CUCC) b Feb. 1, 1910, d July 23, 1988

*Jai, L. P. (Bombay) b April 1, 1902, d Jan. 29, 1968

*Jaisimha, M. L. (H'bad) b March 3, 1939

Jakeman, F. (Yorks. & Northants) b Jan. 10, 1920, d May 18, 1986

*Jalal-ud-Din (PWD, Kar., IDBP & Allied Bank) b June 12, 1959

James, A. E. (Sussex) b Aug. 7, 1924

James, C. L. R. (Writer) b Jan. 4, 1901, d May 31, 1989

James, K. C. (Wgtn & Northants) b March 12, 1904, d Aug. 21, 1976

James, K. D. (Middx, Hants & Wgtn) b March 18, 1961

James, R. M. (CUCC & Wgtn) b Oct. 2, 1934

James, S. P. (Glam. & CUCC) b Sept. 7, 1967

James, W. R. (Zimb.) b Aug. 27, 1965

*Jameson, J. A. (Warwicks.) b June 30, 1941

*Jamshedji, R. J. D. (Bombay) b Nov. 18, 1892, d April 5, 1976

*Jardine, D. R. (OUCC & Surrey; *CY 1928*) b Oct. 23, 1900, d June 18, 1958

Jarman, B. N. (S. Aust.) b Feb. 17, 1936

Jarrett, D. W. (OUCC & CUCC) b April 19, 1952

*Jarvis, A. H. (S. Aust.) b Oct. 19, 1860, d Nov. 15, 1933

Jarvis, K. B. S. (Kent & Glos.) b April 23, 1953

Jarvis, M. P. (Zimb.) b Dec. 6, 1955

Jarvis, P. W. (Yorks.) b June 29, 1965

*Jarvis, T. W. (Auck. & Cant.) b July 29, 1944

*Javed Akhtar (R'pindi & Pak. Serv.) b Nov. 21, 1940

*Javed Miandad (Kar., Sind, Sussex, HBL & Glam.; *CY 1982*) b June 12, 1957

*Jayantilal, K. (H'bad) b Jan. 13, 1948

*Jayasekera, R. S. A. (SL) b Dec. 7, 1957

Jayasinghe, S. (Ceylon & Leics.) b Jan. 19, 1931

Jayasinghe, S. A. (SL) b July 15, 1955

*Jayasuriya, S. T. (CCC) b June 30, 1969

Jean-Jacques, M. (Derbys.) b July 2, 1960

Jefferies, S. T. (W. Prov., Derbys., Lancs. & Hants) b Dec. 8, 1959

Jefferson, R. I. (CUCC & Surrey) b Aug. 15, 1941

*Jeganathan, S. (SL) b July 11, 1951

*Jenkins, R. O. (Worcs.; *CY 1950*) b Nov. 24, 1918

Jenkins, V. G. J. (OUCC & Glam.) b Nov. 2, 1911

*Jenner, T. J. (W. Aust. & S. Aust.) b Sept. 8, 1944

*Jennings, C. B. (S. Aust.) b June 5, 1884, d June 20, 1950

Jennings, K. F. (Som.) b Oct. 5, 1953

Jennings, R. V. (Tvl & N. Tvl) b Aug. 9, 1954

Jepson, A. (Notts.) b July 12, 1915

*Jessop, G. L. (CUCC & Glos.; *CY 1898*) b May 19, 1874, d May 11, 1955

Jesty, T. E. (Hants., Border, Griq. W., Cant., Surrey & Lancs.; *CY 1983*) b June 2, 1948

*John, V. B. (SL) b May 27, 1960

Johnson, C. (Yorks.) b Sept. 5, 1947

*Johnson, C. L. (Tvl) b 1871, d May 31, 1908

Johnson, G. W. (Kent & Tvl) b Nov. 8, 1946

*Johnson, H. H. H. (Jam.) b July 17, 1910, d June 24, 1987

Johnson, H. L. (Derbys.) b Nov. 8, 1927

*Johnson, I. W. (Vic.) b Dec. 8, 1918

Johnson, L. A. (Northants) b Aug. 12, 1936

*Johnson, L. J. (Qld) b March 18, 1919, d April 20, 1977

Johnson, P. (Notts.) b April 24, 1965

Johnson, P. D. (CUCC & Notts.) b Nov. 12, 1949

*Johnson, T. F. (T/T) b Jan. 10, 1917, d April 5, 1985

Johnston, B. A. (Broadcaster) b June 24, 1912

*Johnston, W. A. (Vic.; *CY 1949*) b Feb. 26, 1922

Jones, A. (Glam., W. Aust., N. Tvl & Natal; *CY 1978*) b Nov. 4, 1938

Jones, A. A. (Sussex, Som., Middx, Glam., N. Tvl & OFS) b Dec. 9, 1947

*Jones, A. H. (Wgtn) b May 9, 1959

Jones, A. L. (Glam.) b June 1, 1957

Jones, A. N. (Sussex, Border & Som.) b July 22, 1961

*Jones, A. O. (Notts. & CUCC; *CY 1900*) b Aug. 16, 1872, d Dec. 21, 1914

Jones, B. J. R. (Worcs.) b Nov. 2, 1955

*Jones, C. M. (C. E. L.) (BG) b Nov. 3, 1902, d Dec. 10, 1959

*Jones, D. M. (Vic. & Durham; *CY 1990*) b March 24, 1961

*Jones, Ernest (S. Aust. & W. Aust.) b Sept. 30, 1869, d Nov. 23, 1943

Jones, E. C. (Glam.) b Dec. 14, 1912, d April 14, 1989

Jones, E. W. (Glam.) b June 25, 1942

*Jones, I. J. (Glam.) b Dec. 10, 1941

Jones, K. V. (Middx) b March 28, 1942

*Jones, P. E. (T/T) b June 6, 1917, d Nov. 20, 1991

Jones, P. H. (Kent) b June 19, 1935

*Jones, S. P. (NSW, Qld & Auck.) b Aug. 1, 1861, d July 14, 1951

Jones, W. E. (Glam.) b Oct. 31, 1916

Jordan, J. M. (Lancs.) b Feb. 7, 1932

Jorden, A. M. (CUCC & Essex) b Jan. 28, 1947

Jordon, R. C. (Vic.) b Feb. 17, 1937

*Joshi, P. G. (M'tra) b Oct. 27, 1926, d Jan. 8, 1987

Joshi, U. C. (S'tra, Ind. Rlwys, Guj. & Sussex) b Dec. 23, 1944

Joslin, L. R. (Vic.) b Dec. 13, 1947

Jowett, D. C. P. R. (OUCC) b Jan. 24, 1931

Judd, A. K. (CUCC & Hants) b Jan. 1, 1904, d Feb. 15, 1988

Judge, P. F. (Middx, Glam. & Bengal) b May 23, 1916, d March 4, 1992

Julian, R. (Leics.) b Aug. 23, 1936

*Julien, B. D. (T/T & Kent) b March 13, 1950

*Jumadeen, R. R. (T/T) b April 12, 1948

*Jupp, H. (Surrey) b Nov. 19, 1841, d April 8, 1889

*Jupp, V. W. C. (Sussex & Northants; *CY 1928*) b March 27, 1891, d July 9, 1960

*Jurangpathy, B. R. (CCC) b June 25, 1967

*Kallicharran, A. I. (Guyana, Warwicks., Qld, Tvl & OFS; *CY 1983*) b March 21, 1949

Kalpage, R. S. (NCC) b Feb. 19, 1970

*Kaluperuma, L. W. (SL) b May 25, 1949

*Kaluperuma, S. M. S. (SL) b Oct. 22, 1961

Kaluwitharana, R. S. (SL) b Nov. 24, 1969

Kambli, V. G. (Bombay) b Jan. 18, 1972

*Kanhai, R. B. (†Guyana, T/T, W. Aust., Warwicks. & Tas.; *CY 1964*) b Dec. 26, 1935

*Kanitkar, H. S. (M'tra) b Dec. 8, 1942

*Kapil Dev (Haryana, Northants & Worcs.; *CY 1983*) b Jan. 6, 1959

**Kardar, A. H. (formerly Abdul Hafeez) (N. Ind., OUCC, Warwicks. & Pak. Serv.) b Jan. 17, 1925

Karnain, S. H. U. (NCC & Moors) b Aug. 11, 1962

*Keeton, W. W. (Notts.; *CY 1940*) b April 30, 1905, d Oct. 10, 1980

Keighley, W. G. (OUCC & Yorks.) b Jan. 10, 1925

Keith, H. J. (Natal) b Oct. 25, 1927

Kelleher, H. R. A. (Surrey & Northants) b March 3, 1929

Kellett, S. A. (Yorks.) b Oct. 16, 1967

*Kelleway, C. (NSW) b April 25, 1886, d Nov. 16, 1944

Kelly, J. (Notts.) b Sept. 15, 1930

*Kelly, J. J. (NSW; *CY 1903*) b May 10, 1867, d Aug. 14, 1938

*Kelly, T. J. D. (Vic.) b May 3, 1844, d July 20, 1893

*Kempis, G. A. (Natal) b Aug. 4, 1865, d May 19, 1890

*Kendall, T. (Vic. & Tas.) b Aug. 24, 1851, d Aug. 17, 1924

Kendrick, N. M. (Surrey) b Nov. 11, 1967

Kennedy, A. (Lancs.) b Nov. 4, 1949

*Kennedy, A. S. (Hants; *CY 1933*) b Jan. 24, 1891, d Nov. 15, 1959

*Kenny, R. B. (Bombay & Bengal) b Sept. 29, 1930, d Nov. 21, 1985

*Kent, M. F. (Qld) b Nov. 23, 1953

*Kentish, E. S. M. (Jam. & OUCC) b Nov. 21, 1916

*Kenyon, D. (Worcs.; *CY 1963*) b May 15, 1924

*Kerr, J. L. (Cant.) b Dec. 28, 1910

Kerr, K. J. (Tvl & Warwicks.) b Sept. 11, 1961

*Kerr, R. B. (Qld) b June 16, 1961

Kerslake, R. C. (CUCC & Som.) b Dec. 26, 1942

Kettle, M. K. (Northants) b March 18, 1944

*Khalid Hassan (Punjab & Lahore) b July 14, 1937

*Khalid Wazir (Pak.) b April 27, 1936

*Larkins, W. (Northants, E. Prov. & Durham) b Nov. 22, 1953

Larsen, G. R. (Wgtn) b Sept. 27, 1962

*Larter, J. D. F. (Northants) b April 24, 1940

Larwood, H. (Notts.; *CY 1927*) b Nov. 14, 1904

*Lashley, P. D. (B'dos) b Feb. 11, 1937

Latchman, H. C. [A. H.] (Middx & Notts.) b July 26, 1943

Latham, R. T. (Cant.) b June 12, 1961

Lathwell, M. N. (Som.) b Dec. 26, 1971

*Laughlin, T. J. (Vic.) b Jan. 30, 1951

*Laver, F. (Vic.) b Dec. 7, 1869, d Sept. 24, 1919

*Lawrence, D. V. (Glos.) b Jan. 28, 1964

*Lawrence, G. B. (Rhod. & Natal) b March 31, 1932

Lawrence, J. (Som.) b March 29, 1914, d Dec. 10, 1988

*Lawry, W. M. (Vic.; *CY 1962*) b Feb. 11, 1937

*Lawson, G. F. (NSW & Lancs.) b Dec. 7, 1957

Leadbeater, B. (Yorks.) b Aug. 14, 1943

*Leadbeater, E. (Yorks. & Warwicks.) b Aug. 15, 1927

Leary, S. E. (Kent) b April 30, 1933, d Aug. 21, 1988

Lee, C. (Yorks. & Derbys.) b March 17, 1924

Lee, F. S. (Middx & Som.; Umpire) b July 24, 1905, d March 30, 1982

*Lee, H. W. (Middx) b Oct. 26, 1890, d April 21, 1981

Lee, J. W. (Middx & Som.) b Feb. 1, 1904, d June 20, 1944

Lee, P. G. (Northants & Lancs.; *CY 1976*) b Aug. 27, 1945

*Lee, P. K. (S. Aust.) b Sept. 14, 1904, d Aug. 9, 1980

Lees, W. K. (Otago) b March 19, 1952

*Lees, W. S. (Surrey; *CY 1906*) b Dec. 25, 1875, d Sept. 10, 1924

Leese, Sir Oliver, Bt (Pres. MCC 1965-66) b Oct. 27, 1894, d Jan. 20, 1978

*Legall, R. A. (B'dos & T/T) b Dec. 1, 1925

Legard, E. (Warwicks.) b Aug. 23, 1935

*Leggat, I. B. (C. Dist.) b June 7, 1930

*Leggat, J. G. (Cant.) b May 27, 1926, d March 8, 1973

*Legge, G. B. (OUCC & Kent) b Jan. 26, 1903, d Nov. 21, 1940

Lenham, L. J. (Sussex) b May 24, 1936

Lenham, N. J. (Sussex) b Dec. 17, 1965

*le Roux, F. L. (Tvl & E. Prov.) b Feb. 5, 1882, d Sept. 22, 1963

le Roux, G. S. (W. Prov. & Sussex) b Sept. 4, 1955

*Leslie, C. F. H. (OUCC & Middx) b Dec. 8, 1861, d Feb. 12, 1921

Lester, E. (Yorks.) b Feb. 18, 1923

Lester, G. (Leics.) b Dec. 27, 1915

Lester, Dr J. A. (Philadelphia) b Aug. 1, 1871, d Sept. 3, 1969

Lethbridge, C. (Warwicks.) b June 23, 1961

*Lever, J. K. (Essex & Natal; *CY 1979*) b Feb. 24, 1949

*Lever, P. (Lancs. & Tas.) b Sept. 17, 1940

*Leveson Gower, Sir H. D. G. (OUCC & Surrey) b May 8, 1873, d Feb. 1, 1954

*Levett, W. H. V. (Kent) b Jan. 25, 1908

Lewington, P. J. (Warwicks.) b Jan. 30, 1950

*Lewis, A. R. (CUCC & Glam.) b July 6, 1938

Lewis, C. (Kent) b July 27, 1908

*Lewis, C. C. (Leics. & Notts.) b Feb. 14, 1968

*Lewis, D. M. (Jam.) b Feb. 21, 1946

Lewis, E. B. (Warwicks.) b Jan. 5, 1918, d Oct. 19, 1983

Lewis, E. J. (Glam. & Sussex) b Jan. 31, 1942

*Lewis, P. T. (W. Prov.) b Oct. 2, 1884, d Jan. 30, 1976

Lewis, R. V. (Hants) b Aug. 6, 1947

*Leyland, M. (Yorks.; *CY 1929*) b July 20, 1900, d Jan. 1, 1967

*Liaqat Ali (Kar., Sind, HBL & PIA) b May 21, 1955

Lightfoot, A. (Northants) b Jan. 8, 1936

*Lillee, D. K. (W. Aust., Tas. & Northants; *CY 1973*) b July 18, 1949

*Lilley, A. A. (Warwicks.; *CY 1897*) b Nov. 28, 1866, d Nov. 17, 1929

Lilley, A. W. (Essex) b May 8, 1959

Lilley, B. (Notts.) b Feb. 11, 1895, d Aug. 4, 1950

Lillywhite, Fred (Sussex; Editor of *Lillywhite's Guide to Cricketers*) b July 23, 1829, d Sept. 15, 1866

Lillywhite, F. W. ("William") (Sussex) b June 13, 1792, d Aug. 21, 1854

*Lillywhite, James, jun. (Sussex) b Feb. 23, 1842, d Oct. 25, 1929

*Lindsay, D. T. (NE Tvl, N. Tvl & Tvl) b Sept 4, 1939

*Lindsay, J. D. (Tvl & NE Tvl) b Sept. 8, 1909, d Aug. 31, 1990

*Lindsay, N. V. (Tvl & OFS) b July 30, 1886, d Feb. 2, 1976

*Lindwall, R. R. (NSW & Qld; *CY 1949*) b Oct. 3, 1921

*Ling, W. V. S. (Griq. W. & E. Prov.) b Oct. 3, 1891, d Sept. 26, 1960

*Lissette, A. F. (Auck. & N. Dist.) b Nov. 6, 1919, d Jan. 24, 1973

Lister, J. (Yorks. & Worcs.) b May 14, 1930, d Jan. 28, 1991

Lister, W. H. L. (Lancs.) b Oct. 7, 1911

Livingston, L. (NSW & Northants) b May 3, 1920

Livingstone, D. A. (Hants) b Sept. 21, 1933, d Sept. 8, 1988

*Llewellyn, C. B. (Natal & Hants; *CY 1911*) b Sept. 26, 1876, d June 7, 1964

Llewellyn, M. J. (Glam.) b Nov. 27, 1953

Lloyd, B. J. (Glam.) b Sept. 6, 1953

*Lloyd, C. H. (†Guyana & Lancs.; *CY 1971*) b Aug. 31, 1944

*Lloyd, D. (Lancs.) b March 18, 1947

Lloyd, G. D. (Lancs.) b July 1, 1969

*Lloyd, T. A. (Warwicks. & OFS) b Nov. 5, 1956

Lloyds, J. W. (Som., OFS & Glos.) b Nov. 17, 1954

*Loader, P. J. (Surrey and W. Aust.; *CY 1958*) b Oct. 25, 1929

Lobb, B. (Warwicks. & Som.) b Jan. 11, 1931

*Lock, G. A. R. (Surrey, Leics. & W. Aust.; *CY 1954*) b July 5, 1929

Lockwood, Ephraim (Yorks.) b April 4, 1845, d Dec. 19, 1921

*Lockwood, W. H. (Notts. & Surrey; *CY 1899*) b March 25, 1868, d April 26, 1932

Lockyer, T. (Surrey & All-England) b Nov. 1, 1826, d Dec. 22, 1869

Logan, J. D. (SA) b June 24, 1880, d Jan. 3, 1960

Logie, A. L. (T/T) b Sept. 28, 1960

*Lohmann, G. A. (Surrey, W. Prov. & Tvl; *CY 1889*) b June 2, 1865, d Dec. 1, 1901

Lomax, J. G. (Lancs. & Som.) b May 5, 1925, d May 21, 1992

Long, A. (Surrey & Sussex) b Dec. 18, 1940

Lord, G. J. (Warwicks. & Worcs.) b April 25, 1961

Lord, Thomas (Middx; founder of Lord's) b Nov. 23, 1755, d Jan. 13, 1832

*Love, H. S. B. (NSW & Vic.) b Aug. 10, 1895, d July 22, 1969

Love, J. D. (Yorks.) b April 22, 1955

Lovell, G. B. T. (OUCC) b July 11, 1966

*Lowry, T. C. (Wgtn, CUCC & Som.) b Feb. 17, 1898, d July 20, 1976

*Lowson, F. A. (Yorks.) b July 1, 1925, d Sept. 8, 1984

*Loxton, S. J. E. (Vic.) b March 29, 1921

*Lucas, A. P. (CUCC, Surrey, Middx & Essex) b Feb. 20, 1857, d Oct. 12, 1923

*Luckhurst, B. W. (Kent; *CY 1971*) b Feb. 5, 1939

Lumb, R. G. (Yorks.) b Feb. 27, 1950

*Lundie, E. B. (E. Prov., W. Prov. & Tvl) b March 15, 1888, d Sept. 12, 1917

Lynch, M. A. (Surrey & Guyana) b May 21, 1958

Lyon, B. H. (OUCC & Glos.; *CY 1931*) b Jan. 19, 1902, d June 22, 1970

Lyon, J. (Lancs.) b May 17, 1951

Lyon, M. D. (CUCC & Som.) b April 22, 1898, d Feb. 17, 1964

*Lyons, J. J. (S. Aust.) b May 21, 1863, d July 21, 1927

Lyons, K. J. (Glam.) b Dec. 18, 1946

*Lyttelton, Rt Hon. Alfred (CUCC & Middx; Pres. MCC 1898) b Feb. 7, 1857, d July 5, 1913

Lyttelton, Rev. Hon. C. F. (CUCC & Worcs.) b Jan. 26, 1887, d Oct. 3, 1931

Lyttelton, Hon. C. G. (CUCC) b Oct. 27, 1842, d June 9, 1922

Lyttelton, Hon. C. J. (*see* 10th Visct Cobham)

*McAlister, P. A. (Vic.) b July 11, 1869, d May 10, 1938

*Macartney, C. G. (NSW & Otago; *CY 1922*) b June 27, 1886, d Sept. 9, 1958

*Macaulay, G. G. (Yorks.; *CY 1924*) b Dec. 7, 1897, d Dec. 13, 1940

*Macaulay, M. J. (Tvl, W. Prov., OFS, NE Tvl & E. Prov.) b April 19, 1939

*MacBryan, J. C. W. (CUCC & Som.; *CY 1925*) b July 22, 1892, d July 14, 1983

*McCabe, S. J. (NSW; *CY 1935*) b July 16, 1910, d Aug. 25, 1968

McCague, M. J. (Kent & W. Aust.) b May 24, 1969

McCanlis, M. A. (OUCC, Surrey & Glos.) b June 17, 1906, d Sept. 27, 1991

*McCarthy, C. N. (Natal & CUCC) b March 24, 1929

*McConnon, J. E. (Glam.) b June 21, 1922

*McCool, C. L. (NSW, Qld & Som.) b Dec. 9, 1915, d April 5, 1986

McCorkell, N. T. (Hants) b March 23, 1912

*McCormick, E. L. (Vic.) b May 16, 1906, d June 28, 1991

*McCosker, R. B. (NSW; *CY 1976*) b Dec. 11, 1946

McCurdy, R. J. (Vic., Derbys., S. Aust., E. Prov. & Natal) b Dec. 30, 1959

*McDermott, C. J. (Qld; *CY 1986*) b April 14, 1965

*McDonald, C. C. (Vic.) b Nov. 17, 1928

*McDonald, E. A. (Tas., Vic. & Lancs.; *CY 1922*) b Jan. 6, 1891, d July 22, 1937

*McDonnell, P. S. (Vic., NSW & Qld) b Nov. 13, 1858, d Sept. 24, 1896

McEvoy, M. S. A. (Essex & Worcs.) b Jan. 25, 1956

McEwan, K. S. (E. Prov., W. Prov., Essex & W. Aust; *CY 1978*) b July 16, 1952

*McEwan, P. E. (Cant.) b Dec. 19, 1953

McEwan, S. M. (Worcs. & Durham) b May 5, 1962

McFarlane, L. L. (Northants, Lancs. & Glam.) b Aug. 19, 1952

*McGahey, C. P. (Essex; *CY 1902*) b Feb. 12, 1871, d Jan. 10, 1935

*MacGibbon, A. R. (Cant.) b Aug. 28, 1924

*McGirr, H. M. (Wgtn) b Nov. 5, 1891, d April 14, 1964

*McGlew, D. J. (Natal; *CY 1956*) b March 11, 1929

*MacGregor, G. (CUCC & Middx; *CY 1891*) b Aug. 31, 1869, d Aug. 20, 1919
*McGregor, S. N. (Otago) b Dec. 18, 1931
McHugh, F. P. (Yorks. & Glos.) b Nov. 15, 1925
*McIlwraith, J. (Vic.) b Sept. 7, 1857, d July 5, 1938
Macindoe, D. H. (OUCC) b Sept. 1, 1917, d March 3, 1986
*McIntyre, A. J. W. (Surrey; *CY 1958*) b May 14, 1918
*Mackay, K. D. (Qld) b Oct. 24, 1925, d June 13, 1982
McKechnie, B. J. (Otago) b Nov. 6, 1953
*McKenzie, G. D. (W. Aust. & Leics.; *CY 1965*) b June 24, 1941
*McKibbin, T. R. (NSW) b Dec. 10, 1870, d Dec. 15, 1939
*McKinnon, A. H. (E. Prov. & Tvl) b Aug. 20, 1932, d Dec. 2, 1983
*MacKinnon, F. A. (CUCC & Kent) b April 9, 1848, d Feb. 27, 1947
*MacLaren, A. C. (Lancs.; *CY 1895*) b Dec. 1, 1871, d Nov. 17, 1944
*McLaren, J. W. (Qld) b Dec. 24, 1887, d Nov. 17, 1921
*Maclean, J. A. (Qld) b April 27, 1946
Maclean, J. F. (Worcs. & Glos.) b March 1, 1901, d March 9, 1986
*McLean, R. A. (Natal; *CY 1961*) b July 9, 1930
MacLeay, K. H. (W. Aust. & Som.) b April 2, 1959
*McLeod, C. E. (Vic.) b Oct. 24, 1869, d Nov. 26, 1918
*McLeod, E. G. (Auck. & Wgtn) b Oct. 14, 1900, d Sept. 14, 1989
*McLeod, R. W. (Vic.) b Jan. 19, 1868, d June 14, 1907
McMahon, J. W. (Surrey & Som.) b Dec. 28, 1919
*McMahon, T. G. (Wgtn) b Nov. 8, 1929
*McMaster, J. E. P. (Eng.) b March 16, 1861, d June 7, 1929
McMillan, B. M. (Tvl, W. Prov. & Warwicks.) b Dec. 22, 1963
*McMillan, Q. (Tvl) b June 23, 1904, d July 3, 1948
*McMorris, E. D. A. (Jam.) b April 4, 1935
*McRae, D. A. N. (Cant.) b Dec. 25, 1912
*McShane, P. G. (Vic.) b 1857, d Dec. 11, 1903
McSweeney, E. B. (C. Dist. & Wgtn) b March 8, 1957
McVicker, N. M. (Warwicks. & Leics.) b Nov. 4, 1940
*McWatt, C. A. (BG) b Feb. 1, 1922
*Madan Lal (Punjab & Delhi) b March 20, 1951
*Maddocks, L. V. (Vic. & Tas.) b May 24, 1926
*Madray, I. S. (BG) b July 2, 1934

*Madugalle, R. S. (NCC) b April 22, 1959
*Madurasinghe, A. W. R. (Kurunegala) b Jan. 30, 1961
*Maguire, J. N. (Qld, E. Prov. & Leics.) b Sept. 15, 1956
*Mahanama, R. S. (CCC) b May 31, 1966
Maher, B. J. M. (Derbys.) b Feb. 11, 1958
*Mahmood Hussain (Pak. Us, Punjab, Kar., E. Pak. & NTB) b April 2, 1932, d Dec. 25, 1991
*Mailey, A. A. (NSW) b Jan. 3, 1886, d Dec. 31, 1967
*Majid Khan (Lahore, Pak. Us, CUCC, Glam., PIA, Qld & Punjab; *CY 1970*) b Sept. 28, 1946
*Maka, E. S. (Bombay) b March 5, 1922
*Makepeace, J. W. H. (Lancs.) b Aug. 22, 1881, d Dec. 19, 1952
*Malcolm, D. E. (Derbys.) b Feb. 22, 1963
*Malhotra, A. (Haryana & Bengal) b Jan. 26, 1957
*Mallender, N. A. (Northants, Otago & Som.) b Aug. 13, 1961
*Mallett, A. A. (S. Aust.) b July 13, 1945
Mallett, A. W. H. (OUCC & Kent) b Aug. 29, 1924
*Malone, M. F. (W. Aust. & Lancs.) b Oct. 9, 1950
Malone, S. J. (Essex, Hants & Glam.) b Oct. 19, 1953
*Maninder Singh (Delhi) b June 13, 1965
*Manjrekar, S. V. (Bombay) b July 12, 1965
*Manjrekar, V. L. (Bombay, Bengal, Andhra, U. Pradesh, Raja. & M'tra) b Sept. 26, 1931, d Oct. 18, 1983
*Mankad, A. V. (Bombay) b Oct. 12, 1946
*Mankad, V. (M. H.) (W. Ind., Naw., M'tra, Guj., Bengal, Bombay & Raja.; *CY 1947*) b April 12, 1917, d Aug. 21, 1978
*Mann, A. L. (W. Aust.) b Nov. 8, 1945
*Mann, F. G. (CUCC & Middx; Pres. MCC 1984-85) b Sept. 6, 1917
*Mann, F. T. (CUCC & Middx) b March 3, 1888, d Oct. 6, 1964
Mann, J. P. (Middx) b June 13, 1919
*Mann, N. B. F. (Natal & E. Prov.) b Dec. 28, 1920, d July 31, 1952
Manning, J. S. (S. Aust. & Northants) b June 11, 1924, d May 5, 1988
*Mansell, P. N. F. (Rhod.) b March 16, 1920
*Mansoor Akhtar (Kar., UBL & Sind) b Dec. 25, 1956
Mansoor Rana (ADBP & Lahore) b Dec. 27, 1962
*Mantri, M. K. (Bombay & M'tra) b Sept. 1, 1921
*Manzoor Elahi (Multan, Pak. Rlwys & IDBP) b April 15, 1963
*Maqsood Ahmed (S. Punjab, R'pindi & Kar.) b March 26, 1925
Maqsood Rana (Lahore) b Aug. 1, 1972

*Marais, G. G. ("G. Gladstone") (Jam.) b Jan. 14, 1901, d May 19, 1978

Marie, G. V. (OUCC) b Feb. 17, 1945

*Markham, L. A. (Natal) b Sept. 12, 1924

*Marks, V. J. (OUCC, Som. & W. Aust.) b June 25, 1955

Marlar, R. G. (CUCC & Sussex) b Jan. 2, 1931

Marner, P. T. (Lancs. & Leics.) b March 31, 1936

*Marr, A. P. (NSW) b March 28, 1862, d March 15, 1940

*Marriott, C. S. (CUCC, Lancs. & Kent) b Sept. 14, 1895, d Oct. 13, 1966

Marsden, Tom (Eng.) b 1805, d Feb. 27, 1843

Marsh, F. E. (Derbys.) b July 7, 1920

*Marsh, G. R. (W. Aust.) b Dec. 31, 1958

*Marsh, R. W. (W. Aust.; *CY 1982*) b Nov. 4, 1947

Marsh, S. A. (Kent) b Jan. 27, 1961

Marshal, Alan (Qld & Surrey; *CY 1909*) b June 12, 1883, d July 23, 1915

Marshall, J. M. A. (Warwicks.) b Oct. 26, 1916

*Marshall, M. D. (B'dos & Hants; *CY 1983*) b April 18, 1958

*Marshall, N. E. (B'dos & T/T) b Feb. 27, 1924

*Marshall, R. E. (B'dos & Hants; *CY 1959*) b April 25, 1930, d Oct. 27, 1992

Martin, E. J. (Notts.) b Aug. 17, 1925

*Martin, F. (Kent; *CY 1892*) b Oct. 12, 1861, d Dec. 13, 1921

*Martin, F. R. (Jam.) b Oct. 12, 1893, d Nov. 23, 1967

Martin, J. D. (OUCC & Som.) b Dec. 23, 1941

*Martin, J. W. (NSW & S. Aust.) b July 28, 1931, d July 16, 1992

*Martin, J. W. (Kent) b Feb. 16, 1917, d Jan. 4, 1987

Martin, P. J. (Lancs.) b Nov. 15, 1968

Martin, S. H. (Worcs., Natal & Rhod.) b Jan. 11, 1909, d Feb. 1988

Martindale, D. J. R. (Notts.) b Dec 13, 1963

*Martindale, E. A. (B'dos) b Nov. 25, 1909, d March 17, 1972

Maru, R. J. (Middx & Hants) b Oct. 28, 1962

*Marx, W. F. E. (Tvl) b July 4, 1895, d June 2, 1974

*Mason, J. R. (Kent; *CY 1898*) b March 26, 1874, d Oct. 15, 1958

*Masood Anwar (UBL & Multan) b Dec. 12, 1967

Masood Iqbal (Lahore, Punjab U., Pak. Us & HBL) b April 17, 1952

*Massie, H. H. (NSW) b April 11, 1854, d Oct. 12, 1938

*Massie, R. A. L. (W. Aust.; *CY 1973*) b April 14, 1947

*Matheson, A. M. (Auck.) b Feb. 27, 1906, d Dec. 31, 1985

*Mathias, Wallis (Sind, Kar. & NBP) b Feb. 4, 1935

*Matthews, A. D. G. (Northants & Glam.) b May 3, 1904, d July 29, 1977

*Matthews, C. D. (W. Aust. & Lancs.) b Sept. 22, 1962

Matthews, C. R. (W. Prov.) b Feb. 15, 1965

Matthews, C. S. (Notts.) b Oct. 17, 1929

*Matthews, G. R. J. (NSW) b Dec. 15, 1959

*Matthews, T. J. (Vic.) b April 3, 1884, d Oct. 14, 1943

Mattis, E. H. (Jam.) b April 11, 1957

*May, P. B. H. (CUCC & Surrey; *CY 1952*; Pres. MCC 1980-81) b Dec. 31, 1929

*May, T. B. A. (S. Aust.) b Jan. 26, 1962

Mayer, J. H. (Warwicks.) b March 2, 1902, d Sept. 6, 1981

Mayes, R. (Kent) b Oct. 7, 1921

*Maynard, C. (Warwicks. & Lancs.) b April 8, 1958

*Maynard, M. P. (Glam. & N. Dist.) b March 21, 1966

*Mayne, E. R. (S. Aust. & Vic.) b July 2, 1882, d Oct. 26, 1961

*Mayne, L. C. (W. Aust.) b Jan. 23, 1942

*Mead, C. P. (Hants; *CY 1912*) b March 9, 1887, d March 26, 1958

*Mead, W. (Essex; *CY 1904*) b March 25, 1868, d March 18, 1954

Meads, E. A. (Notts.) b Aug. 17, 1916

*Meale, T. (Wgtn) b Nov. 11, 1928

*Meckiff, I. (Vic.) b Jan. 6, 1935

Medlycott, K. T. (Surrey & N. Tvl) b May 12, 1965

*Meher-Homji, K. R. (W. Ind. & Bombay) b Aug. 9, 1911, d Feb. 10, 1982

*Mehra, V. L. (E. Punjab, Ind. Rlwys & Delhi) b March 12, 1938

*Meintjes, D. J. (Tvl) b June 9, 1890, d July 17, 1979

*Melle, M. G. (Tvl & W. Prov.) b June 3, 1930

Melluish, M. E. L. (CUCC & Middx; Pres. MCC 1991-92) b June 13, 1932

*Melville, A. (OUCC, Sussex, Natal & Tvl; *CY 1948*) b May 19, 1910, d April 18, 1983

Mence, M. D. (Warwicks. & Glos.) b April 13, 1944

Mendis, G. D. (Sussex & Lancs.) b April 20, 1955

*Mendis, L. R. D. (SSC) b Aug. 25, 1952

*Mendonca, I. L. (BG) b July 13, 1934

Mercer, J. (Sussex, Glam. & Northants; *CY 1927*) b April 22, 1895, d Aug. 31, 1987

*Merchant, V. M. (Bombay; *CY 1937*) b Oct. 12, 1911, d Oct. 27, 1987

Merrick, T. A. (Leewards, Warwicks. & Kent) b June 10, 1963

*Merritt, W. E. (Cant. & Northants) b Aug. 18, 1908, d June 9, 1977

*Merry, C. A. (T/T) b Jan. 20, 1911, d April 19, 1964

Metcalfe, A. A. (Yorks. & OFS) b Dec. 25, 1963

Metson, C. P. (Middx & Glam.) b July 2, 1963

*Meuleman, K. D. (Vic. & W. Aust.) b Sept. 5, 1923

Meuli, E. M. (C. Dist.) b Feb. 20, 1926

Meyer, B. J. (Glos.; Umpire) b Aug. 21, 1932

*Meyer, R. J. O. (CUCC, Som. & W. Ind.) b March 15, 1905, d March 9, 1991

Mian Mohammad Saaed (N. Ind. Patiala & S. Punjab; Pak.'s first captain) b Aug. 31, 1910, d Aug. 23, 1979

*Middleton, J. (W. Prov.) b Sept. 30, 1865, d Dec. 23, 1913

Middleton, T. C. (Hants) b Feb. 1, 1964

**Midwinter, W. E. (Vic. & Glos.) b June 19, 1851, d Dec. 3, 1890

*Milburn, B. D. (Otago) b Nov. 24, 1943

*Milburn, C. (Northants & W. Aust.; *CY 1967*) b Oct. 23, 1941, d Feb. 28, 1990

*Milkha Singh, A. G. (Madras) b Dec. 31, 1941

Miller, A. J. T. (OUCC & Middx) b May 30, 1963

*Miller, A. M. (Eng.) b Oct. 19, 1869, d June 26, 1959

*Miller, G. (Derbys., Natal & Essex) b Sept. 8, 1952

*Miller, K. R. (Vic., NSW & Notts.; *CY 1954*) b Nov. 28, 1919

*Miller, L. S. M. (C. Dist. & Wgtn) b March 31, 1923

Miller, R. (Warwicks.) b Jan. 6, 1941

*Miller, R. C. (Jam.) b Dec. 24, 1924

*Milligan, F. W. (Yorks.) b March 19, 1870, d March 31, 1900

*Millman, G. (Notts.) b Oct. 2, 1934

Millmow, J. P. (Wgtn) b Sept. 22, 1967

Millns, D. J. (Notts. & Leics.) b Feb. 27, 1965

*Mills, C. H. (Surrey, Kimberley & W. Prov.) b Nov. 26, 1867, d July 26, 1948

*Mills, J. E. (Auck.) b Sept. 3, 1905, d Dec. 11, 1972

Mills, J. M. (CUCC & Warwicks.) b July 27, 1921

Mills, J. P. C. (CUCC & Northants) b Dec. 6, 1958

Milner, J. (Essex) b Aug. 22, 1937

*Milton, C. A. (Glos.; *CY 1959*) b March 10, 1928

*Milton, W. H. (W. Prov.) b Dec. 3, 1854, d March 6, 1930

*Minnett, R. B. (NSW) b June 13, 1888, d Oct. 21, 1955

"Minshull", John (scorer of first recorded century) b *circa* 1741, d Oct. 1793

*Miran Bux (Pak. Serv., Punjab & R'pindi) b April 20, 1907, d Feb. 8, 1991

*Misson, F. M. (NSW) b Nov. 19, 1938

*Mitchell, A. (Yorks.) b Sept. 13, 1902, d Dec. 25, 1976

*Mitchell, B. (Tvl; *CY 1936*) b Jan. 8, 1909

Mitchell, C. G. (Som.) b Jan. 27, 1929

**Mitchell, F. (CUCC, Yorks. & Tvl; *CY 1902*) b Aug. 13, 1872, d Oct. 11, 1935

*Mitchell, T. B. (Derbys.) b Sept. 4, 1902

*Mitchell-Innes, N. S. (OUCC & Som.) b Sept. 7, 1914

*Modi, R. S. (Bombay) b Nov. 11, 1924

*Mohammad Aslam (N. Ind. & Pak. Rlwys) b Jan. 5, 1920

*Mohammad Farooq (Kar.) b April 8, 1938

*Mohammad Ilyas (Lahore & PIA) b March 19, 1946

*Mohammad Munaf (Sind, E. Pak., Kar. & PIA) b Nov. 2, 1935

*Mohammad Nazir (Pak. Rlwys) b March 8, 1946

*Mohsin Kamal (Lahore, Allied Bank & PNSC) b June 16, 1963

*Mohsin Khan (Pak. Rlwys, Kar., Sind, Pak. Us & HBL) b March 15, 1955

*Moin Khan (Karachi & PIA) b Sept. 23, 1971

Moin-ul-Atiq (UBL, Karachi & HBL) b Aug. 5, 1964

*Moir, A. McK. (Otago) b July 17, 1919

Moir, D. G. (Derbys. & Scotland) b April 13, 1957

*Mold, A. W. (Lancs.; *CY 1892*) b May 27, 1863, d April 29, 1921

Moles, A. J. (Warwicks. & Griq. W.) b Feb. 12, 1961

*Moloney, D. A. R. (Wgtn, Otago & Cant.) b Aug. 11, 1910, d July 15, 1942

Monckton of Brenchley, 1st Lord (Pres. MCC 1956-57) b Jan. 17, 1891, d Jan. 9, 1965

Mongia, N. R. (Baroda) b Dec. 19, 1969

Monkhouse, G. (Surrey) b April 26, 1954

*Moodie, G. H. (Jam.) b Nov. 25, 1915

*Moody, T. M. (W. Aust., Warwicks. & Worcs.) b Oct. 2, 1965

*Moon, L. J. (CUCC & Middx) b Feb. 9, 1878, d Nov. 23, 1916

*Mooney, F. L. H. (Wgtn) b May 26, 1921

Moore, D. N. (OUCC & Glos.) b Sept. 26, 1910

Moore, H. I. (Notts.) b Feb. 28, 1941

Moore, R. H. (Hants) b Nov. 14, 1913

Moores, P. (Worcs., Sussex & OFS) b Dec. 18, 1962

*More, K. S. (Baroda) b Sept. 4, 1962

Morgan, D. C. (Derbys.) b Feb. 26, 1929

Morgan, M. (Notts.) b May 21, 1936

*Morkel, R. W. (Auck.) b Feb. 12, 1941

*Morkel, D. P. B. (W. Prov.) b Jan. 25, 1906, d Oct. 6, 1980

Morley, F. (Notts.) b Dec. 16, 1850, d Sept. 28, 1884

Morley, J. D. (Sussex) b Oct. 20, 1950

Moroney, J. (NSW) b July 24, 1917

*Morris, A. R. (NSW; *CY 1949*) b Jan. 19, 1922

*Morris, H. (Glam.) b Oct. 5, 1963

Morris, H. M. (CUCC & Essex) b April 16, 1898, d Nov. 18, 1974

*Morris, J. E. (Derbys. & Griq. W.) b April 1, 1964

Morris, R. E. (OUCC) b June 8, 1967

*Morris, S. (Vic.) b June 22, 1855, d Sept. 20, 1931

*Morrison, B. D. (Wgtn) b Dec. 17, 1933

*Morrison, D. K. (Auck. & Lancs.) b Feb. 3, 1966

*Morrison, J. F. M. (C. Dist. & Wgtn) b Aug. 27, 1947

Mortensen, O. H. (Denmark & Derbys.) b Jan. 29, 1958

*Mortimore, J. B. (Glos.) b May 14, 1933

Mortlock, W. (Surrey & Utd Eng. XI) b July 18, 1832, d Jan. 23, 1884

*Moseley, E. A. (B'dos, Glam., E. Prov. & N. Tvl) b Jan. 5, 1958

Moseley, H. R. (B'dos & Som.) b May 28, 1948

*Moses, H. (NSW) b Feb. 13, 1858, d Dec. 7, 1938

*Moss, A. E. (Middx) b Nov. 14, 1930

Moss, J. K. (Vic.) b June 29, 1947

*Motz, R. C. (Cant.; *CY 1966*) b Jan. 12, 1940

Moulding, R. P. (OUCC & Middx) b Jan. 3, 1958

*Moule, W. H. (Vic.) b Jan. 31, 1858, d Aug. 24, 1939

*Moxon, M. D. (Yorks. & Griq. W.; *CY 1993*) b May 4, 1960

*Mudassar Nazar (Lahore, Punjab, Pak. Us, HBL, PIA & UBL) b April 6, 1956

*Muddiah, V. M. (Mysore & Ind. Serv.) b June 8, 1929

*Mufasir-ul-Haq (Kar., Dacca, PWD, E. Pak. & NBP) b Aug. 16, 1944, d July 27, 1983

Mukherjee, S. P. (Bengal) b Oct. 5, 1964

Mullally, A. D. (W. Aust., Hants & Leics.) b July 12, 1969

Munden, V. S. (Leics.) b Jan. 2, 1928

*Munir Malik (Punjab, R'pindi, Pak. Serv. & Kar.) b July 10, 1934

*Munton, T. A. (Warwicks.) b July 30, 1965

**Murdoch, W. L. (NSW & Sussex) b Oct. 18, 1854, d Feb. 18, 1911

Murphy, A. J. (Lancs. & Surrey) b Aug. 6, 1962

*Murray, A. R. A. (E. Prov.) b April 30, 1922

*Murray, B. A. G. (Wgtn) b Sept. 18, 1940

*Murray, D. A. (B'dos) b Sept. 29, 1950

*Murray, D. L. (T/T, CUCC, Notts. & Warwicks.) b May 20, 1943

*Murray, J. T. (Middx; *CY 1967*) b April 1, 1935

Murray-Willis, P. E. (Worcs. & Northants) b July 14, 1910

Murrell, H. R. (Kent & Middx) b Nov. 19, 1879, d Aug. 15, 1952

Murrills, T. J. (CUCC) b Dec. 22, 1953

Musgrove, H. (Vic.) b Nov. 27, 1860, d Nov. 2, 1931

*Mushtaq Ahmed (UBL & Multan) b June 28, 1970

*Mushtaq Ali, S. (C. Ind., Guj., †M. Pradesh & U. Pradesh) b Dec. 17, 1914

*Mushtaq Mohammad (Kar., Northants & PIA; *CY 1963*) b Nov. 22, 1943

Mynn, Alfred (Kent & All-Eng.) b Jan. 19, 1807, d Oct. 31, 1861

*Nadkarni, R. G. (M'tra & Bombay) b April 4, 1932

*Nadeem Abbasi (R'pindi) b April 15, 1964

*Nadeem Ghauri (HBL) b Oct 12, 1962

Naeem Ahmed (Kar., Pak. Us, NBP, UBL & PIA) b Sept. 20, 1952

Naeem Ahmed (Sargodha) b April 14, 1971

*Nagel, L. E. (Vic.) b March 6, 1905, d Nov. 23, 1971

*Naik, S. S. (Bombay) b Feb. 21, 1945

*Nanan, R. (T/T) b May 29, 1953

*Naoomal Jaoomal, M. (N. Ind. & Sind) b April 17, 1904, d July 18, 1980

*Narasimha Rao, M. V. (H'bad) b Aug. 11, 1954

Naseer Malik (Khairpair & NBP) b Feb. 1, 1950

*Nash, L. J. (Tas. & Vic.) b May 2, 1910, d July 24, 1986

Nash, M. A. (Glam.) b May 9, 1945

*Nasim-ul-Ghani (Kar., Pak. Us, Dacca, E. Pak., PWD & NBP) b May 14, 1941

*Naushad Ali (Kar., E. Pak., R'pindi, Peshawar, NWFP, Punjab & Pak. Serv.) b Oct. 1, 1943

*Naved Anjum (Lahore, UBL & HBL) b July 27, 1963

*Navle, J. G. (Rajputna, C. Ind., Holkar & Gwalior) b Dec. 7, 1902, d Sept. 7, 1979

*Nayak, S. V. (Bombay) b Oct. 20, 1954

*Nayudu, Col. C. K. (C. Ind., Andhra, U. Pradesh & *CY 1933*) b Oct. 31, 1895, d Nov. 14, 1967

*Nayudu, C. S. (C. Ind., Holkar, Baroda, Bengal, Andhra & U. Pradesh) b April 18, 1914

*Nazar Mohammad (N. Ind. & Punjab) b March 5, 1921

*Nazir Ali, S. (S. Punjab & Sussex) b June 8, 1906, d Feb. 18, 1975

Neale, P. A. (Worcs.; *CY 1989*) b June 5, 1954

*Neblett, J. M. (B'dos & BG) b Nov. 13, 1901, d March 28, 1959

Needham, A. (Surrey & Middx) b March 23, 1957

*Nel, J. D. (W. Prov.) b July 10, 1928

Nevell, W. T. (Middx, Surrey & Northants) b June 13, 1916

*Newberry, C. (Tvl) b 1889, d Aug. 1, 1916

Newell, M. (Notts.) b Feb. 25, 1965

*Newham, W. (Sussex) b Dec 12, 1860, d June 26, 1944

Newland, Richard (Sussex) b *circa* 1718, d May 29, 1791

*Newman, Sir J. (Wgtn & Cant.) b July 3, 1902

Newman, J. A. (Hants & Cant.) b Nov. 12, 1884, d Dec. 21, 1973

Newman, P. G. (Derbys.) b Jan. 10, 1959

*Newport, P. J. (Worcs. & Boland) b Oct. 11, 1962

*Newson, E. S. (Tvl & Rhod.) b Dec. 2, 1910, d April 24, 1988

Newstead, J. T. (Yorks.; *CY 1909*) b Sept. 8, 1877, d March 25, 1952

*Niaz Ahmed (Dacca, PWD, E. Pak. & Pak. Rlwys) b Nov. 11, 1945

Nicholas, M. C. J. (Hants) b Sept. 29, 1957

Nicholls, D. (Kent) b Dec. 8, 1943

Nicholls, R. B. (Glos.) b Dec. 4, 1933

*Nichols, M. S. (Essex; *CY 1934*) b Oct. 6, 1900, d Jan. 26, 1961

Nicholson, A. G. (Yorks.) b June 25, 1938, d Nov. 4, 1985

*Nicholson, F. (OFS) b Sept. 17, 1909, d July 30, 1982

*Nicolson, J. F. W. (Natal & OUCC) b July 19, 1899, d Dec. 13, 1935

*Nissar, Mahomed (Patiala, S. Punjab & U. Pradesh) b Aug. 1, 1910, d March 11, 1963

*Nitschke, H. C. (S. Aust.) b April 14, 1905, d Sept. 29, 1982

Nixon, P. A. (Leics.) b Oct. 21, 1970

*Noble, M. A. (NSW; *CY 1900*) b Jan. 28, 1873, d June 22, 1940

*Noblet, G. (S. Aust.) b Sept. 14, 1916

*Noreiga, J. M. (T/T) b April 15, 1936

Norfolk, 16th Duke of (Pres. MCC 1957-58) b May 30, 1908, d Jan. 31, 1975

Norman, M. E. J. C. (Northants & Leics.) b Jan. 19, 1933

*Norton, N. O. (W. Prov. & Border) b May 11, 1881, d June 27, 1968

*Nothling, O. E. (NSW & Qld) b Aug. 1, 1900, d Sept. 26, 1965

*Nourse, A. D. ("Dudley") (Natal; *CY 1948*) b Nov. 12, 1910, d Aug. 14, 1981

*Nourse, A. W. ("Dave") (Natal, Tvl & W. Prov.) b Jan. 26, 1878, d July 8, 1948

Nugent, 1st Lord (Pres. MCC 1962-63) b Aug. 11, 1895, d April 27, 1973

*Nunes, R. K. (Jam.) b June 7, 1894, d July 22, 1958

*Nupen, E. P. (Tvl) b Jan. 1, 1902, d Jan. 29, 1977

*Nurse, S. M. (B'dos; *CY 1967*) b Nov. 10, 1933

Nutter, A. E. (Lancs. & Northants) b June 28, 1913

*Nyalchand, S. (W. Ind., Kathiawar, Guj. & S'tra) b Sept. 14, 1919

Nye, J. K. (Sussex) b May 23, 1914

Nyren, John (Hants) b Dec. 15, 1764, d June 28, 1837

Nyren, Richard (Hants & Sussex) b 1734, d April 25, 1797

Oakes, C. (Sussex) b Aug. 10, 1912

Oakes, J. (Sussex) b March 3, 1916

*Oakman, A. S. M. (Sussex) b April 20, 1930

Oates, T. W. (Notts.) b Aug. 9, 1875, d June 18, 1949

Oates, W. F. (Yorks. & Derbys.) b June 11, 1929

O'Brien, F. P. (Cant. & Northants) b Feb. 11, 1911, d Oct. 22, 1991

*O'Brien, L. P. (Vic.) b July 2, 1907

*O'Brien, Sir T. C. (OUCC & Middx) b Nov. 5, 1861, d Dec. 9, 1948

*Ochse, A. E. (Tvl) b March 11, 1870, d April 11, 1918

*Ochse, A. L. (E. Prov.) b Oct. 11, 1899, d May 6, 1949

*O'Connor, J. (Essex) b Nov. 6, 1897, d Feb. 22, 1977

*O'Connor, J. D. A. (NSW & S. Aust.) b Sept. 9, 1875, d Aug. 23, 1941

*O'Donnell, S. P. (Vic.) b Jan. 26, 1963

*Ogilvie, A. D. (Qld) b June 3, 1951

O'Gorman, T. J. G. (Derbys.) b May 15, 1967

*O'Keeffe, K. J. (NSW & Som.) b Nov. 25, 1949

*Old, C. M. (Yorks., Warwicks. & N. Tvl; *CY 1979*) b Dec. 22, 1948

*Oldfield, N. (Lancs. & Northants) b April 30, 1911

*Oldfield, W. A. (NSW; *CY 1927*) b Sept. 9, 1894, d Aug. 10, 1976

Oldham, S. (Yorks. & Derbys.) b July 26, 1948

Oldroyd, E. (Yorks.) b Oct. 1, 1888, d Dec. 27, 1964

*O'Linn, S. (Kent, W. Prov. & Tvl) b May 5, 1927

Oliver, P. R. (Warwicks.) b May 9, 1956

*O'Neill, N. C. (NSW; *CY 1962*) b Feb. 19, 1937

Ontong, R. C. (Border, Tvl, N. Tvl & Glam.) b Sept. 9, 1955

Opatha, A. R. M. (SL) b Aug. 5, 1947

Ord, J. S. (Warwicks.) b July 12, 1912

*O'Reilly, W. J. (NSW; *CY 1935*) b Dec. 20, 1905, d Oct. 6, 1992

O'Riordan, A. J. (Ireland) b July 20, 1940

Ormrod, J. A. (Worcs. & Lancs.) b Dec. 22, 1942

O'Shaughnessy, S. J. (Lancs. & Worcs.) b Sept. 9, 1961

Oslear, D. O. (Umpire) b March 3, 1929

Ostler, D. P. (Warwicks.) b July 15, 1970

*O'Sullivan, D. R. (C. Dist. & Hants) b Nov. 16, 1944

Outschoorn, L. (Worcs.) b Sept. 26, 1918

*Overton, G. W. F. (Otago) b June 8, 1919

*Owen-Smith, H. G. O. (W. Prov., OUCC & Middx; *CY 1930*) b Feb. 18, 1909, d Feb. 28, 1990

Owen-Thomas, D. R. (CUCC & Surrey) b Sept. 20, 1948

*Oxenham, R. K. (Qld) b July 28, 1891, d Aug. 16, 1939

*Padgett, D. E. V. (Yorks.) b July 20, 1934

*Padmore, A. L. (B'dos) b Dec. 17, 1946

Page, H. A. (Tvl & Essex) b July 3, 1962

Page, J. C. T. (Kent) b May 20, 1930, d Dec. 14, 1990

Page, M. H. (Derbys.) b June 17, 1941

*Page, M. L. (Cant.) b May 8, 1902, d Feb. 13, 1987

*Pai, A. M. (Bombay) b April 28, 1945

*Paine, G. A. E. (Middx & Warwicks.; *CY 1935*) b June 11, 1908, d March 30, 1978

*Pairaudeau, B. H. (BG & N. Dist.) b April 14, 1931

*Palairet, L. C. H. (OUCC & Som.; *CY 1893*) b May 27, 1870, d March 27, 1933

Palairet, R. C. N. (OUCC & Som.; Joint-Manager MCC in Australia 1932-33) b June 25, 1871, d Feb. 11, 1955

*Palm, A. W. (W. Prov.) b June 8, 1901, d Aug. 17, 1966

*Palmer, C. H. (Worcs. & Leics.; Pres. MCC 1978-79) b May 15, 1919

*Palmer, G. E. (Vic. & Tas.) b Feb. 22, 1860, d Aug. 22, 1910

Palmer, G. V. (Som.) b Nov. 1, 1965

*Palmer, K. E. (Som.; Umpire) b April 22, 1937

Palmer, R. (Som.) b July 12, 1942

*Pandit, C. S. (Bombay) b Sept. 30, 1961

Pardon, Charles Frederick (Editor of *Wisden* 1887-90) b March 28, 1850, d April 18, 1890

Pardon, Sydney H. (Editor of *Wisden* 1891-1925) b Sept. 23, 1855, d Nov. 20, 1925

*Parfitt, P. H. (Middx; *CY 1963*) b Dec. 8, 1936

Paris, C. G. A. (Hants; Pres. MCC 1975-76) b Aug. 20, 1911

Parish, R. J. (Aust. Administrator) b May 7, 1916

*Parkar, G. A. (Bombay) b Oct. 24, 1955

*Parkar, R. D. (Bombay) b Oct. 31, 1946

Parkar, Z. (Bombay) b Nov. 22, 1957

*Parker, C. W. L. (Glos.; *CY 1923*) b Oct. 14, 1882, d July 11, 1959

*Parker, G. M. (SA) b May 27, 1899, d May 1, 1969

Parker, G. W. (CUCC & Glos.) b Feb. 11, 1912

Parker, J. F. (Surrey) b April 23, 1913, d Jan. 27, 1983

*Parker, J. M. (N. Dist. & Worcs.) b Feb. 21, 1951

Parker, J. P. (Hants) b Nov. 29, 1902, d Aug. 9, 1984

*Parker, N. M. (Otago & Cant.) b Aug. 28, 1948

*Parker, P. W. G. (CUCC, Sussex, Natal & Durham) b Jan. 15, 1956

*Parkhouse, W. G. A. (Glam.) b Oct. 12, 1925

*Parkin, C. H. (Yorks. & Lancs.; *CY 1924*) b Feb. 18, 1886, d June 15, 1943

*Parkin, D. C. (E. Prov., Tvl & Griq. W.) b Feb. 18, 1870, d March 20, 1936

Parks, H. W. (Sussex) b July 18, 1906, d May 7, 1984

*Parks, J. H. (Sussex & Cant.; *CY 1938*) b May 12, 1903, d Nov. 21, 1980

*Parks, J. M. (Sussex & Som.; *CY 1968*) b Oct. 21, 1931

Parks, R. J. (Hants) b June 15, 1959

*Parore, A. C. (Auck.) b Jan. 23, 1971

Parr, F. D. (Lancs.) b June 1, 1928

Parr, George (Notts. & All-England) b May 22, 1826, d June 23, 1891

*Parry, D. R. (Comb. Is. & Leewards) b Dec. 22, 1954

*Parsana, D. D. (S'tra, Ind. Rlwys & Guj.) b Dec. 2, 1947

Parsons, A. B. D. (CUCC & Surrey) b Sept. 20, 1933

Parsons, A. E. W. (Auck. & Sussex) b Jan. 9, 1949

Parsons, G. J. (Leics., Warwicks., Boland, Griq. W. & OFS) b Oct. 17, 1959

Parsons, Canon J. H. (Warwicks.) b May 30, 1890, d Feb. 2, 1981

*Partridge, J. T. (Rhod.) b Dec. 9, 1932, d June 7, 1988

Partridge, N. E. (Malvern, CUCC & Warwicks.; *CY 1919*) b Aug. 10, 1900, d March 10, 1982

Partridge, R. J. (Northants) b Feb. 11, 1912

Parvez Mir (R'pindi, Lahore, Punjab, Pak. Us, Derbys., HBL & Glam.) b Sept. 24, 1953

*Pascoe, L. S. (NSW) b Feb. 13, 1950

Pasqual, S. P. (SL) b Oct. 15, 1961

*Passailaigue, C. C. (Jam.) b Aug. 1902, d Jan. 7, 1972

*Patankar, C. T. (Bombay) b Nov. 24, 1930

**Pataudi, Iftikhar Ali, Nawab of (OUCC, Worcs., Patiala, N. Ind. & S. Punjab; *CY 1932*) b March 16, 1910, d Jan. 5, 1952

*Pataudi, Mansur Ali, Nawab of (Sussex, OUCC, Delhi & H'bad; *CY 1968*) b Jan. 5, 1941

Patel, A. (S'tra) b March 6, 1957

*Patel, B. P. (Karn.) b Nov. 24, 1952

*Patel, D. N. (Worcs. & Auck.) b Oct. 25, 1958

*Patel, J. M. (Guj.) b Nov. 26, 1924, d Dec. 12, 1992

*Patel, R. (Baroda) b June 1, 1964

Pathmanathan, G. (OUCC, CUCC & SL) b Jan. 23, 1954

Patiala, Maharaja of (N. Ind., Patiala & S. Punjab) b Jan. 17, 1913, d June 17, 1974

*Patil, S. M. (Bombay & M. Pradesh) b Aug. 18, 1956

*Patil, S. R. (M'tra) b Oct. 10, 1933

*Patterson, B. P. (Jam., Tas. & Lancs.) b Sept. 15, 1961

Pauline, D. B. (Surrey & Glam.) b Dec. 15, 1960

Pawson, A. G. (OUCC & Worcs.) b May 30, 1888, d Feb. 25, 1986

Pawson, H. A. (OUCC & Kent) b Aug. 22, 1921

Payn, L. W. (Natal) b May 6, 1915, d May 2, 1992

*Payne, T. R. O. (B'dos) b Feb. 13, 1957

*Paynter, E. (Lancs.; *CY 1938*) b Nov. 5, 1901, d Feb. 5, 1979

Payton, W. R. D. (Notts.) b Feb. 13, 1882, d May 2, 1943

Pearce, G. (Sussex) b Oct. 27, 1908, d June 16, 1986

Pearce, T. N. (Essex) b Nov. 3, 1905

*Pearse, C. O. C. (Natal) b Oct. 10, 1884, d May 7, 1953

Pearson, D. B. (Worcs.) b March 29, 1937

*Peate, E. (Yorks.) b March 2, 1856, d March 11, 1900

Peck, I. G. (CUCC & Northants) b Oct. 18, 1957

*Peebles, I. A. R. (OUCC, Middx & Scotland; *CY 1931*) b Jan. 20, 1908, d Feb. 28, 1980

*Peel, R. (Yorks.; *CY 1889*) b Feb. 12, 1857, d Aug. 12, 1941

*Pegler, S. J. (Tvl) b July 28, 1888, d Sept. 10, 1972

*Pellew, C. E. (S. Aust.) b Sept. 21, 1893, d May 9, 1981

Penn, C. (Kent) b June 19, 1963

*Penn, F. (Kent) b March 7, 1851, d Dec. 26, 1916

Penney, T. L. (Boland & Warwicks.) b June 11, 1968

Pepper, C. G. (NSW & Aust. Serv.; Umpire) b Sept. 15, 1918

Perera, K. G. (Mor.) b May 22, 1964

Perkins, C. G. (Northants) b June 4, 1911

Perkins, H. (CUCC & Cambs.; Sec. MCC 1876-97) b Dec. 10, 1832, d May 6, 1916

*Perks, R. T. D. (Worcs.) b Oct. 4, 1911, d Nov. 22, 1977

Perrin, P. A. (Essex; *CY 1905*) b May 26, 1876, d Nov. 20, 1945

Perryman, S. P. (Warwicks. & Worcs.) b Oct. 22, 1955

*Pervez Sajjad (Lahore, PIA & Kar.) b Aug. 30, 1942

Petherick, P. J. (Otago & Wgtn) b Sept. 25, 1942

*Petrie, E. C. (Auck. & N. Dist.) b May 22, 1927

Petrie, R. G. (Cant.) b Aug. 23, 1967

*Phadkar, D. G. (M'tra, Bombay, Bengal & Ind. Rlwys) b Dec. 10, 1925, d March 17, 1985

Phebey, A. H. (Kent) b Oct. 1, 1924

Phelan, P. J. (Essex) b Feb. 9, 1938

*Philipson, H. (OUCC & Middx) b June 8, 1866, d Dec. 4, 1935

*Phillip, N. (Comb. Is., Windwards & Essex) b June 12, 1948

Phillips, R. B. (NSW & Qld) b May 23, 1954

*Phillips, W. B. (S. Aust.) b March 1, 1958

*Phillips, W. N. (Vic.) b Nov. 7, 1962

Phillipson, C. P. (Sussex) b Feb. 10, 1952

Phillipson, W. E. (Lancs.) b Dec. 3, 1910, d Aug. 24, 1991

*Philpott, P. I. (NSW) b Nov. 21, 1934

Piachaud, J. D. (OUCC, Hants & Ceylon) b March 1, 1937

Pick, R. A. (Notts. & Wgtn) b Nov. 19, 1963

Pickles, C. S. (Yorks.) b Jan. 30, 1966

Pickles, L. (Som.) b Sept. 17, 1932

Pienaar, R. F. (Tvl, W. Prov., N. Tvl & Kent) b July 17, 1961

Pieris, H. S. M. (SL) b Feb. 16, 1946

*Pierre, L. R. (T/T) b June 5, 1921, d April 14, 1989

Pierson, A. R. K. (Warwicks.) b July 21, 1963

*Pigott, A. C. S. (Sussex & Wgtn) b June 4, 1958

Pilch, Fuller (Norfolk & Kent) b March 17, 1804, d May 1, 1870

Pilling, H. (Lancs.) b Feb. 23, 1943

*Pilling, R. (Lancs.; *CY 1891*) b July 5, 1855, d March 28, 1891

Piper, K. J. (Warwicks.) b Dec. 18, 1969

*Pithey, A. J. (Rhod. & W. Prov.) b July 17, 1933

*Pithey, D. B. (Rhod., OUCC, Northants, W. Prov., Natal & Tvl) b Oct. 4, 1936

Pitman, R. W. C. (Hants) b Feb. 21, 1933

*Place, W. (Lancs.) b Dec 7, 1914

Platt, R. K. (Yorks. & Northants) b Dec. 21, 1932

*Playle, W. R. (Auck. & W. Aust.) b Dec. 1, 1938

Pleass, J. E. (Glam.) b May 21, 1923

*Plimsoll, J. B. (W. Prov. & Natal) b Oct. 27, 1917

Pocock, N. E. J. (Hants) b Dec. 15, 1951

*Pocock, P. I. (Surrey & N. Tvl) b Sept. 24, 1946

Pollard, P. R. (Notts.) b Sept. 24, 1968

*Pollard, R. (Lancs.) b June 19, 1912, d Dec. 16, 1985

*Pollard, V. (C. Dist. & Cant.) b Burnley Sept. 7, 1945

Pollock, A. J. (CUCC) b April 19, 1962

*Pollock, P. M. (E. Prov.; *CY 1966*) b June 30, 1941

*Pollock, R. G. (E. Prov. & Tvl; *CY 1966*) b Feb. 27, 1944

*Ponsford, W. H. (Vic.; *CY 1935*) b Oct. 19, 1900, d April 6, 1991

Pont, K. R. (Essex) b Jan. 16, 1953

Poole, C. J. (Notts.) b March 13, 1921

Pooley, E. (Surrey & first England tour) b Feb. 13, 1838, d July 18, 1907

*Poore, M. B. (Cant.) b June 1, 1930

*Poore, Brig-Gen. R. M. (Hants & SA; *CY 1900*) b March 20, 1866, d July 14, 1938

Pope, A. V. (Derbys.) b Aug. 15, 1909

*Pope, G. H. (Derbys.) b Jan. 27, 1911

*Pope, R. J. (NSW) b Feb. 18, 1864, d July 27, 1952

Popplewell, N. F. M. (CUCC & Som.) b Aug. 8, 1957

Portal of Hungerford, 1st Lord (Pres. MCC 1958-59) b May 21, 1893, d April 22, 1971

Porter, A. (Glam.) b March 25, 1914

Porter, G. D. (W. Aust.) b March 18, 1915

Pothecary, A. E. (Hants) b March 1, 1906, d May 21, 1991

*Pothecary, J. E. (W. Prov.) b Dec. 6, 1933

Potter, G. (Sussex) b Oct. 26, 1931

Potter, L. (Kent, Griq. W., Leics. & OFS) b Nov. 7, 1962

*Pougher, A. D. (Leics.) b April 19, 1865, d May 20, 1926

Pountain, F. R. (Sussex) b April 23, 1941

*Powell, A. W. (Griq. W.) b July 18, 1873, d Sept. 11, 1948

*Prabhakar, M. (Delhi) b April 15, 1963

*Prasanna, E. A. S. (†Karn.) b May 22, 1940

Pratt, R. L. (Leics.) b Nov. 15, 1938

Pressdee, J. S. (Glam. & NE Tvl) b June 19, 1933

Preston, Hubert (Editor of *Wisden* 1944-51) b Dec. 16, 1868, d Aug. 6, 1960

Preston, K. C. (Essex) b Aug. 22, 1925

Preston, Norman (Editor of *Wisden* 1951-80) b March 18, 1903, d March 6, 1980

Pretlove, J. F. (CUCC & Kent) b Nov. 23, 1932

Price, D. G. (CUCC) b Feb. 7, 1965

Price, E. J. (Lancs. & Essex) b Oct. 27, 1918

*Price, J. S. E. (Middx) b July 22, 1937

*Price, W. F. F. (Middx) b April 25, 1902, d Jan. 13, 1969

Prichard, P. J. (Essex) b Jan. 7, 1965

*Prideaux, R. M. (CUCC, Kent, Northants, Sussex & OFS) b July 31, 1939

Pridgeon, A. P. (Worcs.) b Feb. 22, 1954

*Priest, M. W. (Cant.) b Aug. 12, 1961

*Prince, C. F. H. (W. Prov., Border & E. Prov.) b Sept. 11, 1874, d March 5, 1948

Pringle, C. (Auck.) b Jan. 26, 1968

*Pringle, D. R. (CUCC & Essex) b Sept. 18, 1958

Pringle, M. W. (W. Prov.) b June 22, 1966

Pritchard, T. L. (Wgtn, Warwicks. & Kent) b March 10, 1917

*Procter, M. J. (Glos., Natal, W. Prov., Rhod. & OFS; *CY 1970*) b Sept. 15, 1946

Prodger, J. M. (Kent) b Sept. 1, 1935

*Promnitz, H. L. E. (Border, Griq. W. & OFS) b Feb. 23, 1904, d Sept. 7, 1983

Prouton, R. O. (Hants) b March 1, 1926

Pugh, C. T. M. (Glos.) b March 13, 1937

Pullan, D. A. (Notts.) b May 1, 1944

*Pullar, G. (Lancs. & Glos.; *CY 1960*) b Aug. 1, 1935

*Puna, N. (N. Dist.) b Oct. 28, 1929

*Punjabi, P. H. (Sind & Guj.) b Sept. 20, 1921

Pycroft, A. J. (Zimb.) b June 6, 1956

*Qasim Omar (Kar. & MCB) b Feb. 9, 1957

Quaife, B. W. (Warwicks. & Worcs.) b Nov. 24, 1899, d Nov. 28, 1984

*Quaife, William (W. G.) (Warwicks. & Griq. W.; *CY 1902*) b March 17, 1872, d Oct. 13, 1951

*Quinn, N. A. (Griq. W. & Tvl) b Feb. 21, 1908, d Aug. 5, 1934

*Rabone, G. O. (Wgtn & Auck.) b Nov. 6, 1921

*Rackemann, C. G. (Qld) b June 3, 1960

*Radford, N. V. (Lancs., Tvl & Worcs.; *CY 1986*) b June 7, 1957

*Radley, C. T. (Middx; *CY 1979*) b May 13, 1944

*Rae, A. F. (Jam.) b Sept. 30, 1922

Raees Mohammad (Kar.) b Dec. 24, 1932

*Rai Singh, K. (S. Punjab & Ind. Serv.) b Feb. 24, 1922

Rait Kerr, Col. R. S. (Sec. MCC 1936-52) b April 13, 1891, d April 2, 1961

Rajadurai, B. E. A. (SSC) b Aug. 24, 1965

*Rajindernath, V. (N. Ind., U. Prov., S. Punjab, Bihar & E. Punjab) b Jan. 7, 1928, d Nov. 22, 1989

*Rajinder Pal (Delhi, S. Punjab & Punjab) b Nov. 18, 1937

*Rajput, L. S. (Bombay) b Dec. 18, 1961

*Raju, S. L. V. (H'bad) b July 9, 1969

Ralph, L. H. R. (Essex) b May 22, 1920

*Ramadhin, S. (T/T & Lancs.; *CY 1951*) b May 1, 1929

*Raman, W. V. (TN) b May 23, 1965

*Ramanayake, C. P. H. (TU) b Jan. 8, 1965

*Ramaswami, C. (Madras) b June 18, 1896

*Ramchand, G. S. (Sind, Bombay & Raja.) b July 26, 1927

*Ramiz Raja (Lahore, Allied Bank & PNSC) b July 14, 1962

*Ramji, L. (W. Ind.) b 1900, d Dec. 20, 1948

*Ramprakash, M. R. (Middx) b Sept. 5, 1969

Ramsamooj, D. (T/T & Northants) b July 5, 1932

*Ranasinghe, A. N. (BRC) b Oct. 13, 1956

Ranasinghe, S. K. (SL) b July 4, 1962

*Ranatunga, A. (SSC) b Dec. 1, 1963

*Ranatunga, D. (SSC) b Oct. 12, 1962

*Randall, D. W. (Notts.; *CY 1980*) b Feb. 24, 1951

Randhir Singh (Orissa & Bihar) b Aug. 16, 1957

*Rangachari, C. R. (Madras) b April 14, 1916

*Rangnekar, K. M. (M'tra, Bombay & †M. Pradesh) b June 27, 1917, d Oct. 11, 1984

*Ranjane, V. B. (M'tra & Ind. Rlwys) b July 22, 1937

Ranjitsinhji, K. S., afterwards H. H. the Jam Sahib of Nawanagar (CUCC & Sussex; *CY 1897*) b Sept. 10, 1872, d April 2, 1933

*Ransford, V. S. (Vic.; *CY 1910*) b March 20, 1885, d March 19, 1958

Ransom, V. J. (Hants & Surrey) b March 17, 1918

*Rashid Khan (PWD, Kar. & PIA) b Dec. 15, 1959

*Rashid Latif (Kar. & UBL) b Oct. 14, 1968

Ratcliffe, J. D. (Warwicks.) b June 19, 1969

Ratcliffe, R. M. (Lancs.) b Oct. 29, 1951

Ratnayake, N. L. K. (SSC) b Nov. 22, 1968

*Ratnayake, R. J. (NCC) b Jan. 2, 1964

*Ratnayeke, J. R. (NCC) b May 2, 1960

Rawson, P. W. E. (Zimb. & Natal) b May 25, 1957

Rayment, A. W. H. (Hants) b May 29, 1928

*Razdan, V. (Delhi) b Aug. 25, 1969

*Read, H. D. (Surrey & Essex) b Jan. 28, 1910

*Read, J. M. (Surrey; *CY 1890*) b Feb. 9, 1859, d Feb. 17, 1929

*Read, W. W. (Surrey; *CY 1893*) b Nov. 23, 1855, d Jan. 6, 1907

*Reddy, B. (TN) b Nov. 12, 1954

*Redmond, R. E. (Wgtn & Auck.) b Dec. 29, 1944

Reed, B. L. (Hants) b Sept. 17, 1937

*Reedman, J. C. (S. Aust.) b Oct. 9, 1865, d March 25, 1924

Rees, A. (Glam.) b Feb. 17, 1938

*Reeve, D. A. (Sussex & Warwicks.) b April 2, 1963

Reeves, W. (Essex; Umpire) b Jan. 22, 1875, d March 22, 1944

*Rege, M. R. (M'tra) b March 18, 1924

*Rehman, S. F. (Punjab, Pak. Us & Lahore) b June 11, 1935

*Reid, B. A. (W. Aust.) b March 14, 1963

*Reid, J. F. (Auck.) b March 3, 1956

*Reid, J. R. (Wgtn & Otago; *CY 1959*) b June 3, 1928

Reid, K. P. (E. Prov. & Northants) b July 24, 1951

*Reid, N. (W. Prov.) b Dec. 26, 1890, d June 6, 1947

Reid, R. B. (Wgtn & Auck.) b Dec. 3, 1958

Reidy, B. W. (Lancs.) b Sept. 18, 1953

*Reiffel, P. R. (Vic.) b April 19, 1966

*Relf, A. E. (Sussex & Auck.; *CY 1914*) b June 26, 1874, d March 26, 1937

*Renneburg, D. A. (NSW) b Sept. 23, 1942

Revill, A. C. (Derbys. & Leics.) b March 27, 1923

Reynolds, B. L. (Northants) b June 10, 1932

Rhodes, A. E. G. (Derbys.) b Oct. 10, 1916, d Oct. 18, 1983

*Rhodes, H. J. (Derbys.) b July 22, 1936

Rhodes, J. N. (Natal) b July 26, 1969

Rhodes, S. D. (Notts.) b March 24, 1910, d Jan. 7, 1989

Rhodes, S. J. (Yorks. & Worcs.) b June 17, 1964

*Rhodes, W. (Yorks.; *CY 1899*) b Oct. 29, 1877, d July 8, 1973

Rice, C. E. B. (Tvl & Notts.; *CY 1981*) b July 23, 1949

Rice, J. M. (Hants) b Oct. 23, 1949

*Richards, A. R. (W. Prov.) b 1868, d Jan. 9, 1904

*Richards, B. A. (Natal, Glos., Hants & S. Aust.; *CY 1969*) b July 21, 1945

*Richards, C. J. (Surrey & OFS) b Aug. 10, 1958

Richards, G. (Glam.) b Nov. 29, 1951

*Richards, I. V. A. (Comb. Is., Leewards, Som., Qld & Glam.; *CY 1977*) b March 7, 1952

*Richards, W. H. M. (SA) b Aug. 1862, d Jan. 4, 1903

*Richardson, A. J. (S. Aust.) b July 24, 1888, d Dec. 23, 1973

Richardson, A. W. (Derbys.) b March 4, 1907, d July 29, 1983

*Richardson, D. J. (E. Prov. & N. Tvl) b Sept. 16, 1959

*Richardson, D. W. (Worcs.) b Nov. 3, 1934

Richardson, G. W. (Derbys.) b April 26, 1938

*Richardson, P. E. (Worcs. & Kent; *CY 1957*) b July 4, 1931

*Richardson, R. B. (Leewards; *CY 1992*) b Jan. 12, 1962

*Richardson, T. (Surrey & Som.; *CY 1897*) b Aug. 11, 1870, d July 2, 1912

*Richardson, V. Y. (S. Aust.) b Sept. 7, 1894, d Oct. 29, 1969

*Richmond, T. L. (Notts.) b June 23, 1890, d Dec. 29, 1957

*Rickards, K. R. (Jam. & Essex) b Aug. 23, 1923

Riddington, A. (Leics.) b Dec. 22, 1911

*Ridgway, F. (Kent) b Aug. 10, 1923

*Rigg, K. E. (Vic.) b May 21, 1906

Riley, H. (Leics.) b Oct. 3, 1902, d Jan. 24, 1989

*Ring, D. T. (Vic.) b Oct. 14, 1918

Ripley, D. (Northants) b Sept. 13, 1966

Rist, F. H. (Essex) b March 30, 1914

Ritchie, G. M. (Qld) b Jan. 23, 1960

*Rixon, S. J. (NSW) b Feb. 25, 1954

*Rizwan-uz-Zaman (Kar. & PIA) b Sept. 4, 1962

*Roach, C. A. (T/T) b March 13, 1904, d April 16, 1988

*Roberts, A. D. G. (N. Dist.) b May 6, 1947, d Oct. 26, 1989

*Roberts, A. M. E. (Comb. Is., Leewards, Hants, NSW & Leics.; *CY 1975*) b Jan. 29, 1951

*Roberts, A. T. (Windwards) b Sept. 18, 1937

*Roberts, A. W. (Cant. & Otago) b Aug. 20, 1909, d May 13, 1978

Roberts, B. (Tvl & Derbys.) b May 30, 1962

Roberts, The Hon. Sir Denys (Pres. MCC 1989-90) b Jan. 19, 1923

Roberts, S. J. (Cant.) b March 22, 1965

Roberts, W. B. (Lancs. & Victory Tests) b Sept. 27, 1914, d Aug. 24, 1951

*Robertson, G. K. (C. Dist.) b July 15, 1960

*Robertson, J. B. (W. Prov.) b June 5, 1906, d July 5, 1985

*Robertson, J. D. (Middx; *CY 1948*) b Feb. 22, 1917

*Robertson, W. R. (Vic.) b Oct. 6, 1861, d June 24, 1938

Robertson-Glasgow, R. C. (OUCC & Som.; Writer) b July 15, 1901, d March 4, 1965

Robins, D. H. (Warwicks.) b June 26, 1914

Robins, R. V. C. (Middx) b March 13, 1935

*Robins, R. W. V. (CUCC & Middx; *CY 1930*) b June 3, 1906, d Dec. 12, 1968

Robinson, A. L. (Yorks.) b Aug. 17, 1946

Robinson, Emmott (Yorks.) b Nov. 16, 1883, d Nov. 17, 1969

Robinson, Ellis P. (Yorks. & Som.) b Aug. 10, 1911

Robinson, H. B. (OUCC & Canada) b March 3, 1919

Robinson, M. (Glam., Warwicks., H'bad & Madras) b July 16, 1921

Robinson, M. A. (Northants & Yorks.) b Nov. 23, 1966

Robinson, P. E. (Yorks. & Leics.) b Aug. 3, 1963

Robinson, P. J. (Worcs. & Som.) b Feb. 9, 1943

*Robinson, R. D. (Vic.) b June 8, 1946

*Robinson, R. H. (NSW, S. Aust. & Otago) b March 26, 1914, d Aug. 10, 1965

*Robinson, R. T. (Notts.; *CY 1986*) b Nov. 21, 1958

Robson, E. (Som.) b May 1, 1870, d May 23, 1924

Rochford, P. (Glos.) b Aug. 27, 1928, d June 18, 1992

*Rodriguez, W. V. (T/T) b June 25, 1934

Roe, B. (Som.) b Jan. 27, 1939

*Roebuck, P. M. (CUCC & Som.; *CY 1988*) b March 6, 1956

Rogers, N. H. (Hants) b March 9, 1918

Romaines, P. W. (Northants, Glos. & Griq. W.) b Dec. 25, 1955

*Roope, G. R. J. (Surrey & Griq. W.) b July 12, 1946

*Root, C. F. (Derbys. & Worcs.) b April 16, 1890, d Jan. 20, 1954

*Rorke, G. F. (NSW) b June 27, 1938

*Rose, B. C. (Som.; *CY 1980*) b June 4, 1950

Rose, G. D. (Middx & Som.) b April 12, 1964

Roseberry, M. A. (Middx) b Nov. 28, 1966

*Rose-Innes, A. (Kimberley & Tvl) b Feb. 16, 1868, d Nov. 22, 1946

Ross, C. J. (Wgtn & OUCC) b June 24, 1954

Rotherham, G. A. (Rugby, CUCC, Warwicks. & Wgtn; *CY 1918*) b May 28, 1899, d Jan. 31, 1985

Rouse, S. J. (Warwicks.) b Jan. 20, 1949

Routledge, R. (Middx) b July 7, 1920

*Routledge, T. W. (W. Prov. & Tvl) b April 18, 1867, d May 9, 1927

*Rowan, A. M. B. (Tvl) b Feb. 7, 1921

*Rowan, E. A. B. (Tvl; *CY 1952*) b July 20, 1909

*Rowe, C. G. (Wgtn & C. Dist.) b June 30, 1915

Rowe, C. J. C. (Kent & Glam.) b May 5, 1953

Rowe, E. J. (Notts.) b July 21, 1920, d Dec. 17, 1989

*Rowe, G. A. (W. Prov.) b June 15, 1874, d Jan. 8, 1950

*Rowe, L. G. (Jam. & Derbys.) b Jan. 8, 1949

*Roy, A. (Bengal) b June 5, 1945

*Roy, Pankaj (Bengal) b May 31, 1928

*Roy, Pranab (Bengal) b Feb. 10, 1957

*Royle, Rev. V. P. F. A. (OUCC & Lancs.) b Jan. 29, 1854, d May 21, 1929

*Rumsey, F. E. (Worcs., Som. & Derbys.) b Dec. 4, 1935

*Rushmere, M. W. (E. Prov.) b Jan. 7, 1965

*Russell, A. C. [C. A. G.] (Essex; *CY 1923*) b Oct. 7, 1887, d March 23, 1961

Russell, P. E. (Derbys.) b May 9, 1944

*Russell, R. C. (Glos.; *CY 1990*) b Aug. 15, 1963

Russell, S. E. (Middx & Glos.) b Oct. 4, 1937

*Russell, W. E. (Middx) b July 3, 1936

Russom, N. (CUCC & Som.) b Dec. 3, 1958

Rutherford, I. A. (Worcs. & Otago) b June 30, 1957

*Rutherford, J. W. (W. Aust.) b Sept. 25, 1929

*Rutherford, K. R. (Otago) b Oct. 26, 1965

Ryan, M. (Yorks.) b June 23, 1933

*Ryder, J. (Vic.) b Aug. 8, 1889, d April 3, 1977

Saadat Ali (Lahore, UBL & HBFC) b Feb. 6, 1955

*Sadiq Mohammad (Kar., PIA, Tas., Essex, Glos. & UBL) b May 3, 1945

*Saeed Ahmed (Punjab, Pak. Us, Lahore, PIA, Kar., PWD & Sind) b Oct. 1, 1937

*Saeed Anwar (UBL & ADBP) b Sept. 6, 1968

*Saggers, R. A. (NSW) b May 15, 1917, d March 1987

Sainsbury, G. E. (Essex & Glos.) b Jan. 17, 1958

Sainsbury, P. J. (Hants; *CY 1974*) b June 13, 1934

*St Hill, E. L. (T/T) b March 9, 1904, d May 21, 1957

*St Hill, W. H. (T/T) b July 6, 1893, d 1957

Sajid Ali (Kar. & NBP) b July 1, 1963

Sajjad Akbar (PNSC & Sargodha) b March 1, 1961

Sale, R., jun. (OUCC, Warwicks. & Derbys.) b Oct. 4, 1919, d Feb. 3, 1987

*Saleem Altaf (Lahore & PIA) b April 19, 1944

*Saleem Jaffer (Kar. & UBL) b Nov. 19, 1962

*Salim Malik (Lahore, HBL & Essex; *CY 1988*) b April 16, 1963

Salim Pervez (NBP) b Sept. 9, 1947

*Salim Yousuf (Sind, Kar., IDBP, Allied Bank & Customs) b Dec. 7, 1959

*Salisbury, I. D. K. (Sussex; *CY 1993*) b Jan. 21, 1970

Samaranayake, A. D. A. (SL) b Feb. 25, 1962

*Samarasekera, M. A. R. (CCC) b Aug. 5, 1961

Sampson, H. (Yorks. & All-England) b March 13, 1813, d March 29, 1885

*Samuelson, S. V. (Natal) b Nov. 21, 1883, d Nov. 18, 1958

*Sandham, A. (Surrey; *CY 1923*) b July 6, 1890, d April 20, 1982

*Sandhu, B. S. (Bombay) b Aug. 3, 1956

*Sardesai, D. N. (Bombay) b Aug. 8, 1940

*Sarfraz Nawaz (Lahore, Punjab, North-ants, Pak. Rlwys & UBL) b Dec. 1, 1948

*Sarwate, C. T. (CP & B, M'tra, Bombay & †M. Pradesh) b June 22, 1920

*Saunders, J. V. (Vic. & Wgtn) b Feb. 3, 1876, d Dec. 21, 1927

Savage, J. S. (Leics. & Lancs.) b March 3, 1929

Savage, R. Le Q. (OUCC & Warwicks.) b Dec. 10, 1955

Savill, L. A. (Essex) b June 30, 1935

Saville, G. J. (Essex) b Feb. 5, 1944

Saxelby, K. (Notts.) b Feb. 23, 1959

*Saxena, R. C. (Delhi & Bihar) b Sept. 20, 1944

Sayer, D. M. (OUCC & Kent) b Sept. 19, 1936

*Scarlett, R. O. (Jam.) b Aug. 15, 1934

*Schultz, S. S. (CUCC & Lancs.) b Aug. 29, 1857, d Dec. 18, 1937

*Schwarz, R. O. (Middx & Natal; *CY 1908*) b May 4, 1875, d Nov. 18, 1918

*Scott, A. P. H. (Jam.) b July 29, 1934

Scott, Christopher J. (Lancs.) b Sept. 16, 1959

Scott, Colin J. (Glos.) b May 1, 1919

Scott, C. W. (Notts. & Durham) b Jan. 23, 1964

*Scott, H. J. H. (Vic.) b Dec. 26, 1858, d Sept. 23, 1910

Scott, M. E. (Northants) b May 8, 1936

*Scott, O. C. (Jam.) b Aug. 25, 1893, d June 16, 1961

*Scott, R. H. (Cant.) b March 6, 1917

Scott, R. J. (Hants & Glos.) b Nov. 2, 1963

Scott, S. W. (Middx; *CY 1893*) b March 24, 1854, d Dec. 8, 1933

*Scott, V. J. (Auck.) b July 31, 1916, d Aug. 2, 1980

*Scotton, W. H. (Notts.) b Jan. 15, 1856, d July 9, 1893

*Sealey, B. J. (T/T) b Aug. 12, 1899, d Sept. 12, 1963

*Sealy, J. E. D. (B'dos & T/T) b Sept. 11, 1912, d Jan. 3, 1982

Seamer, J. W. (Som. & OUCC) b June 23, 1913

*Seccull, A. W. (Kimberley, W. Prov. & Tvl) b Sept. 14, 1868, d July 20, 1945

*Sekar, T. A. P. (TN) b March 28, 1955

*Selby, J. (Notts.) b July 1, 1849, d March 11, 1894

Sellers, A. B. (Yorks.; *CY 1940*) b March 5, 1907, d Feb. 20, 1981

*Sellers, R. H. D. (S. Aust.) b Aug. 20, 1940

*Selvey, M. W. W. (CUCC, Surrey, Middx, Glam. & OFS) b April 25, 1948

*Sen, P. (Bengal) b May 31, 1926, d Jan. 27, 1970

*Sen Gupta, A. K. (Ind. Serv.) b Aug. 3, 1939

*Senanayake, C. P. (CCC) b Dec. 19, 1962

*Serjeant, C. S. (W. Aust.) b Nov. 1, 1951

Seymour, James (Kent) b Oct. 25, 1879, d Sept. 30, 1930

*Seymour, M. A. (W. Prov.) b June 5, 1936

*Shackleton, D. (Hants.; *CY 1959*) b Aug. 12, 1924

*Shafiq Ahmad (Lahore, Punjab, NBP & UBL) b March 28, 1949

*Shafqat Rana (Lahore & PIA) b Aug. 10, 1943

Shah, A. H. (Zimb.) b Aug. 7, 1959

*Shahid Israr (Kar. & Sind) b March 1, 1950

*Shahid Mahboob (Karachi, Quetta & PACO) b Aug. 25, 1962

*Shahid Mahmoud (Kar., Pak. Us & PWD) b March 17, 1939

Shahid, N. (Essex) b April 23, 1969

*Shahid Saeed (HBFC) b Jan. 6, 1966

Shakil Khan (WAPDA & HBL) b May 28, 1968

*Shalders, W. A. (Griq. W. & Tvl) b Feb. 12, 1880, d March 18, 1917

*Sharma, Ajay (Delhi) b April 3, 1964

*Sharma, Chetan (Haryana) b Jan. 3, 1966

*Sharma, Gopal (U. Pradesh) b Aug. 3, 1960

*Sharma, P. (Raja.) b Jan. 5, 1948

Sharma, R. (Derbys.) b June 27, 1962

Sharma, Sanjeev (Delhi) b Aug. 25, 1965

Sharp, G. (Northants) b March 12, 1950

Sharp, H. P. H. (Middx; Middx scorer) b Oct. 6, 1917

*Sharp, J. (Lancs.) b Feb. 15, 1878, d Jan. 28, 1938

Sharp, K. (Yorks. & Griq. W.) b April 6, 1959

*Sharpe, D. (Punjab, Pak. Rlwys, Lahore & S. Aust.) b Aug. 3, 1937

*Sharpe, J. W. (Surrey & Notts.; *CY 1892*) b Dec. 9, 1866, d June 19, 1936

*Sharpe, P. J. (Yorks. & Derbys.; *CY 1963*) b Dec. 27, 1936

*Shastri, R. J. (Bombay & Glam.) b May 27, 1962

*Shaw, Alfred (Notts. & Sussex) b Aug. 29, 1842, d Jan. 16, 1907

Shaw, C. (Yorks.) b Feb. 17, 1964

Shaw, T. G. (E. Prov.) b July 5, 1959

*Sheahan, A. P. (Vic.) b Sept. 30, 1946

Sheffield, J. R. (Essex & Wgtn) b Nov. 19, 1906

*Shepherd, B. K. (W. Aust.) b April 23, 1937

*Shepherd, D. J. (Glam.; *CY 1970*) b Aug. 12, 1927

Shepherd, D. R. (Glos.; Umpire) b Dec. 27, 1940

*Shepherd, J. N. (B'dos, Kent, Rhod. & Glos.; *CY 1979*) b Nov. 9, 1943

Shepherd, T. F. (Surrey) b Dec. 5, 1889, d Feb. 13, 1957

*Sheppard, Rt Rev. D. S. (Bishop of Liverpool) (CUCC & Sussex; *CY 1953*) b March 6, 1929

*Shepstone, G. H. (Tvl) b April 8, 1876, d July 3, 1940

*Sherwell, P. W. (Tvl) b Aug. 17, 1880, d April 17, 1948

*Sherwin, M. (Notts.; *CY 1891*) b Feb. 26, 1851, d July 3, 1910

*Shillingford, G. C. (Comb. Is. & Windwards) b Sept. 25, 1944

*Shillingford, I. T. (Comb. Is. & Windwards) b April 18, 1944

*Shinde, S. G. (Baroda, M'tra & Bombay) b Aug. 18, 1923, d June 22, 1955

Shine, K. J. (Hants) b Feb. 22, 1969

Shirreff, A. C. (CUCC, Hants, Kent & Som.) b Feb. 12, 1919

*Shivnarine, S. (Guyana) b May 13, 1952

*Shoaib Mohammad (Kar. & PIA) b Jan. 8, 1961

*Shodhan, R. H. (Guj. & Baroda) b Oct. 18, 1928

*Shrewsbury, Arthur (Notts.; *CY 1890*) b April 11, 1856, d May 19, 1903

*Shrimpton, M. J. F. (C. Dist. & N. Dist.) b June 23, 1940

*Shuja-ud-Din, Col. (N. Ind., Pak. Us, Pak. Serv., B'pur & R'pindi) b April 10, 1930

*Shukla, R. C. (Bihar & Delhi) b Feb. 4, 1948

*Shuter, J. (Kent & Surrey) b Feb. 9, 1855, d July 5, 1920

*Shuttleworth, K. (Lancs. & Leics.) b Nov. 13, 1944

Siddons, J. D. (Vic.) b April 25, 1964

*Sidebottom, A. (Yorks. & OFS) b April 1, 1954

*Sidhu, N. S. (Punjab) b Oct. 20, 1963

*Siedle, I. J. (Natal) b Jan. 11, 1903, d Aug. 24, 1982

*Sievers, M. W. (Vic.) b April 13, 1912, d May 10, 1968

*Sikander Bakht (PWD, PIA, Sind, Kar. & UBL) b Aug. 25, 1957

Silk, D. R. W. (CUCC & Som.; Pres. MCC 1992-) b Oct. 8, 1931

*Silva, S. A. R. (NCC) b Dec. 12, 1960

Simmons, J. (Lancs. & Tas.; *CY 1985*) b March 28, 1941

*Simmons, P. V. (T/T) b April 18, 1963

*Simpson, R. B. (NSW & W. Aust.; *CY 1965*) b Feb. 3, 1936

*Simpson, R. T. (Notts. & Sind; *CY 1950*) b Feb. 27, 1920

*Simpson-Hayward, G. H. (Worcs.) b June 7, 1875, d Oct. 2, 1936

Sims, Sir Arthur (Cant.) b July 22, 1877, d April 27, 1969

*Sims, J. M. (Middx) b May 13, 1903, d April 27, 1973

Sinclair, B. W. (Wgtn) b Oct. 23, 1936

*Sinclair, I. McK. (Cant.) b June 1, 1933

*Sinclair, J. H. (Tvl) b Oct. 16, 1876, d Feb. 23, 1913

*Sincock, D. J. (S. Aust.) b Feb. 1, 1942

*Sinfield, R. A. (Glos.) b Dec. 24, 1900, d March 17, 1988

*Singh, Charan K. (T/T) b 1938

Singh, "Robin" [R. R.] (TN) b Sept. 14, 1963

Singh, R. P. (U. Pradesh) b Jan. 6, 1963

Singh, Swaranjit (CUCC, Warwicks., E. Punjab & Bengal) b July 18, 1931

Singleton, A. P. (OUCC, Worcs. & Rhod.) b Aug. 5, 1914

*Sivaramakrishnan, L. (TN) b Dec. 31, 1965

Skelding, A. (Leics.; Umpire) b Sept. 5, 1886, d April 17, 1960

Skinner, D. A. (Derbys.) b March 22, 1920

Skinner, L. E. (Surrey & Guyana) b Sept. 7, 1950

*Slack, W. N. (Middx & Windwards) b Dec. 12, 1954, d Jan. 15, 1989

Slade, D. N. F. (Worcs.) b Aug. 24, 1940

Slade, W. D. (Glam.) b Sept. 27, 1941

*Slater, K. N. (W. Aust.) b March 12, 1935

*Sleep, P. R. (S. Aust.) b May 4, 1957

*Slight, J. (Vic.) b Oct. 20, 1855, d Dec. 9, 1930

Slocombe, P. A. (Som.) b Sept. 6, 1954

*Smailes, T. F. (Yorks.) b March 27, 1910, d Dec. 1, 1970

Smales, K. (Yorks. & Notts.) b Sept. 15, 1927

Small, G. C. (Warwicks. & S. Aust.) b Oct. 18, 1961

Small, John, sen. (Hants & All-England) b April 19, 1737, d Dec. 31, 1826

*Small, J. A. (T/T) b Nov. 3, 1892, d April 26, 1958

*Small, M. A. (B'dos) b Feb. 12, 1964

Smedley, M. J. (Notts.) b Oct. 28, 1941

*Smith, A. C. (OUCC & Warwicks.; Chief Exec. TCCB 1987-) b Oct. 25, 1936

Smith, B. F. (Leics.) b April 3, 1972

*Smith, Sir C. Aubrey (CUCC, Sussex & Tvl) b July 21, 1863, d Dec. 20, 1948

*Smith, C. I. J. (Middx; *CY 1935*) b Aug. 25, 1906, d Feb. 9, 1979

*Smith, C. J. E. (Tvl) b Dec. 25, 1872, d March 27, 1947

*Smith, C. L. (Natal, Glam. & Hants; *CY 1984*) b Oct. 15, 1958

Smith, C. S. (CUCC & Lancs.) b Oct. 1, 1932

*Smith, C. W. (B'dos) b July 29, 1933

*Smith, Denis (Derbys.; *CY 1936*) b Jan. 24, 1907, d Sept. 12, 1979

*Smith, D. B. M. (Vic.) b Sept. 14, 1884, d July 29, 1963

Smith, D. H. K. (Derbys. & OFS) b June 29, 1940

*Smith, D. M. (Surrey, Worcs. & Sussex) b Jan. 9, 1956

*Smith, D. R. (Glos.) b Oct. 5, 1934

Smith, D. V. (Sussex) b June 14, 1923

Smith, Edwin (Derbys.) b Jan. 2, 1934

*Smith, E. J. (Warwicks.) b Feb. 6, 1886, d Aug. 31, 1979

*Smith, F. B. (Cant.) b March 13, 1922

*Smith, F. W. (Tvl) No details of birth or death known

Smith, G. (Kent) b Nov. 30, 1925

Smith, G. J. (Essex) b April 2, 1935

*Smith, Harry (Glos.) b May 21, 1890, d Nov. 12, 1937

*Smith, H. D. (Otago & Cant.) b Jan. 8, 1913, d Jan. 25, 1986

Smith, I. (Glam. & Durham) b March 11, 1967

*Smith, I. D. S. (C. Dist. & Auck.) b Feb. 28, 1957

Smith, K. D. (Warwicks.) b July 9, 1956

Smith, M. J. (Middx) b Jan. 4, 1942

*Smith, M. J. K. (OUCC, Leics. & Warwicks.; *CY 1960*) b June 30, 1933

Smith, N. (Yorks. & Essex) b April 1, 1949

*Smith, O. G. (Jam.; *CY 1958*) b May 5, 1933, d Sept. 9, 1959

Smith, P. A. (Warwicks.) b April 5, 1964

Smith, Ray (Essex) b Aug. 10, 1914

Smith, Roy (Som.) b April 14, 1930

*Smith, R. A. (Natal & Hants; *CY 1990*) b Sept. 13, 1963

Smith, R. C. (Leics.) b Aug. 3, 1935

*Smith, S. B. (NSW & Tvl) b Oct. 18, 1961

Smith, S. G. (T/T, Northants & Auck.; *CY 1915*) b Jan. 15, 1881, d Oct. 25, 1963

*Smith, T. P. B. (Essex; *CY 1947*) b Oct. 30, 1908, d Aug. 4, 1967

*Smith, V. I. (Natal) b Feb. 23, 1925

Smith, W. A. (Surrey) b Sept. 15, 1937

*Smith, W. C. (Surrey; *CY 1911*) b Oct. 4, 1877, d July 16, 1946

*Smithson, G. A. (Yorks. & Leics.) b Nov. 1, 1926, d Sept. 6, 1970

*Snedden, C. A. (Auck.) b Jan. 7, 1918

Snedden, M. C. (Auck.) b Nov. 23, 1958

*Snell, R. P. (Tvl & Som.) b Sept. 12, 1968

Snellgrove, K. L. (Lancs.) b Nov. 12, 1941

*Snooke, S. D. (W. Prov. & Tvl) b Nov. 11, 1878, d April 4, 1959

*Snooke, S. J. (Border, W. Prov. & Tvl) b Feb. 1, 1881, d Aug. 14, 1966

*Snow, J. A. (Sussex; *CY 1973*) b Oct. 13, 1941

Snowden, W. (CUCC) b Sept. 27, 1952

*Sobers, Sir G. S. (B'dos, S. Aust. & Notts.; *CY 1964*) b July 28, 1936

Sohail Fazal (Lahore) b Nov. 11, 1967

*Sohoni, S. W. (M'tra, Baroda & Bombay) b March 5, 1918

Solanky, J. W. (E. Africa & Glam.) b June 30, 1942

Solkar, E. D. (Bombay & Sussex) b March 18, 1948

*Solomon, J. S. (BG) b Aug. 26, 1930

*Solomon, W. R. T. (Tvl & E. Prov.) b April 23, 1872, d July 12, 1964

*Sood, M. M. (Delhi) b July 6, 1939

Southern, J. W. (Hants) b Sept. 2, 1952

*Southerton, James (Surrey, Hants & Sussex) b Nov. 16, 1827, d June 16, 1880

Southerton, S. J. (Editor of *Wisden* 1934-35) b July 7, 1874, d March 12, 1935

*Sparling, J. T. (Auck.) b July 24, 1938

Speak, N. J. (Lancs.) b Nov. 21, 1966

Speight, M. P. (Sussex & Wgtn) b Oct. 24, 1967

Spencer, C. T. (Leics.) b Aug. 18, 1931

Spencer, J. (CUCC & Sussex) b Oct. 6, 1949

Spencer, T. W. (Kent) b March 22, 1914

Sperry, J. (Leics.) b March 19, 1910

*Spofforth, F. R. (NSW & Vic.) b Sept. 9, 1853, d June 4, 1926

*Spooner, R. H. (Lancs.; *CY 1905*) b Oct. 21, 1880, d Oct. 2, 1961

*Spooner, R. T. (Warwicks.) b Dec. 30, 1919

Springall, J. D. (Notts.) b Sept. 19, 1932

*Srikkanth, K. (TN) b Dec. 21, 1959

*Srinath, J. (Karn.) b Aug. 31, 1969

*Srinivasan, T. E. (TN) b Oct. 26, 1950

*Stackpole, K. R. (Vic.; *CY 1973*) b July 10, 1940

Standen, J. A. (Worcs.) b May 30, 1935

Standing, D. K. (Sussex) b Oct. 21, 1963

Stanworth, J. (Lancs.) b Sept. 30, 1960

*Stanyforth, Lt.-Col. R. T. (Yorks.) b May 30, 1892, d Feb. 20, 1964

*Staples, S. J. (Notts.; *CY 1929*) b Sept. 18, 1892, d June 4, 1950

Starkie, S. (Northants) b April 4, 1926

*Statham, J. B. (Lancs.; *CY 1955*) b June 17, 1930

*Stayers, S. C. (†Guyana & Bombay) b June 9, 1937

*Steel, A. G. (CUCC & Lancs.; Pres. MCC 1902) b Sept. 24, 1858, d June 15, 1914

*Steele, D. S. (Northants & Derbys.; *CY 1976*) b Sept. 29, 1941

Steele, J. F. (Leics., Natal & Glam.) b July 23, 1946

Stephens, E. J. (Glos.) b March 23, 1909, d April 3, 1983

Stephenson, F. D. (B'dos, Glos., Tas., Notts., Sussex & OFS; *CY 1989*) b April 8, 1959

Stephenson, G. R. (Derbys. & Hants) b Nov. 19, 1942

Stephenson, H. H. (Surrey & All-England) b May 3, 1832, d Dec. 17, 1896

Stephenson, H. W. (Som.) b July 18, 1920

*Stephenson, J. P. (Essex & Boland) b March 14, 1965

Stephenson, Lt.-Col. J. R. (Sec. MCC 1987-) b Feb. 25, 1931

Stephenson, Lt.-Col. J. W. A. (Essex & Worcs.) b Aug. 1, 1907, d May 20, 1982

Stevens, Edward ("Lumpy") (Hants) b *circa* 1735, d Sept. 7, 1819

*Stevens, G. B. (S. Aust.) b Feb. 29, 1932

*Stevens, G. T. S. (UCS, OUCC & Middx; *CY 1918*) b Jan. 7, 1901, d Sept. 19, 1970

*Stevenson, G. B. (Yorks. & Northants) b Dec. 16, 1955

Stevenson, K. (Derbys. & Hants) b Oct. 6, 1950

Stevenson, M. H. (CUCC & Derbys.) b June 13, 1927

*Stewart, A. J. (Surrey; *CY 1993*) b April 8, 1963

*Stewart, M. J. (Surrey; *CY 1958*) b Sept. 16, 1932

*Stewart, R. B. (SA) b Sept. 3, 1856, d Sept. 12, 1913

Stewart, R. W. (Glos. & Middx) b Feb. 28, 1945

Stewart, W. J. (Warwicks. & Northants) b Oct. 31, 1934

*Stirling, D. A. (C. Dist.) b Oct. 5, 1961

Stocks, F. W. (Notts.) b Nov. 6, 1917

*Stoddart, A. E. (Middx; *CY 1893*) b March 11, 1863, d April 11, 1915

*Stollmeyer, J. B. (T/T) b April 11, 1921, d Sept. 10, 1989

*Stollmeyer, V. H. (T/T) b Jan. 24, 1916

*Storer, W. (Derbys.; *CY 1899*) b Jan. 25, 1867, d Feb. 28, 1912

Storey, S. J. (Surrey & Sussex) b Jan. 6, 1941

Stott, L. W. (Auck.) b Dec. 8, 1946

Stott, W. B. (Yorks.) b July 18, 1934

Stovold, A. W. (Glos. & OFS) b March 19, 1953

*Street, G. B. (Sussex) b Dec. 6, 1889, d April 24, 1924

*Stricker, L. A. (Tvl) b May 26, 1884, d Feb. 5, 1960

Stringer, P. M. (Yorks. & Leics.) b Feb. 23, 1943

*Strudwick, H. (Surrey; *CY 1912*) b Jan. 28, 1880, d Feb. 14, 1970

*Studd, C. T. (CUCC & Middx) b Dec. 2, 1860, d July 16, 1931

*Studd, G. B. (CUCC & Middx) b Oct. 20, 1859, d Feb. 13, 1945

Studd, Sir Peter M. (CUCC) b Sept. 15, 1916

Sturt, M. O. C. (Middx) b Sept. 12, 1940

*Su'a, M. L. (Auck.) b Nov. 7, 1966

*Subba Row, R. (CUCC, Surrey & Northants; *CY 1961*) b Jan. 29, 1932

*Subramanya, V. (Mysore) b July 16, 1936

Such, P. M. (Notts., Leics. & Essex) b June 12, 1964

Sudhakar Rao, R. (Karn.) b Aug. 8, 1952

Sueter, T. (Hants & Surrey) b *circa* 1749, d Feb. 17, 1827

*Sugg, F. H. (Yorks., Derbys. & Lancs.; *CY 1890*) b Jan. 11, 1862, d May 29, 1933

Sullivan, J. (Lancs.) b Feb. 5, 1945

Sully, H. (Som. & Northants) b Nov. 1, 1939

*Sunderram, G. R. (Bombay & Raja.) b March 29, 1930

Sunnucks, P. R. (Kent) b June 22, 1916

*Surendranath, R. (Ind. Serv.) b Jan. 4, 1937

Surridge, W. S. (Surrey; *CY 1953*) b Sept. 3, 1917, d April 13, 1992

*Surti, R. F. (Guj., Raja. & Qld) b May 25, 1936

*Susskind, M. J. (CUCC, Middx & Tvl) b June 8, 1891, d July 9, 1957

*Sutcliffe, B. (Auck., Otago & N. Dist.; *CY 1950*) b Nov. 17, 1923

*Sutcliffe, H. (Yorks.; *CY 1920*) b Nov. 24, 1894, d Jan. 22, 1978

Sutcliffe, S. P. (OUCC & Warwicks.) b May 22, 1960

Sutcliffe, W. H. H. (Yorks.) b Oct. 10, 1926

Suttle, K. G. (Sussex) b Aug. 25, 1928

Swallow, I. G. (Yorks. & Som.) b Dec. 18, 1962

Swamy, V. N. (Ind. Serv.) b May 23, 1924, d May 1, 1983

Swanton, E. W. (Middx; Writer) b Feb. 11, 1907

Swarbrook, F. W. (Derbys., Griq. W. & OFS) b Dec. 17, 1950

Swart, P. D. (Rhod., W. Prov., Glam. & Boland) b April 27, 1946

*Swetman, R. (Surrey, Notts & Glos.) b Oct. 25, 1933

Sydenham, D. A. D. (Surrey) b April 6, 1934

Symington, S. J. (Leics.) b Sept. 16, 1926

*Taber, H. B. (NSW) b April 29, 1940

*Taberer, H. M. (OUCC & Natal) b Oct. 7, 1870, d June 5, 1932

*Tahir Naqqash (Servis Ind., MCB, Punjab & Lahore) b July 6, 1959

Tait, A. (Northants & Glos.) b Dec. 27, 1953

*Talat Ali (Lahore, PIA & UBL) b May 29, 1950

*Tallon, D. (Qld; *CY 1949*) b Feb. 17, 1916, d Sept. 7, 1984

*Tamhane, N. S. (Bombay) b Aug. 4, 1931

*Tancred, A. B. (Kimberley, Griq. W. & Tvl) b Aug. 20, 1865, d Nov. 23, 1911

*Tancred, L. J. (Tvl) b Oct. 7, 1876, d July 28, 1934

*Tancred, V. M. (Tvl) b July 7, 1875, d June 3, 1904

Tanvir Mehdi (Lahore & UBL) b Nov. 7, 1972

*Tapscott, G. L. (Griq. W.) b Nov. 7, 1889, d Dec. 13, 1940

*Tapscott, L. E. (Griq. W.) b March 18, 1894, d July 7, 1934

*Tarapore, K. K. (Bombay) b Dec. 17, 1910, d June 15, 1986

*Tarrant, F. A. (Vic., Middx & Patiala; *CY 1908*) b Dec. 11, 1880, d Jan. 29, 1951

Tarrant, George F. (Cambs. & All-England) b Dec. 7, 1838, d July 2, 1870

*Taslim Arif (Kar., Sind & NBP) b May 1, 1954

*Tate, F. W. (Sussex) b July 24, 1867, d Feb. 24, 1943

*Tate, M. W. (Sussex; *CY 1924*) b May 30, 1895, d May 18, 1956

*Tattersall, R. (Lancs.) b Aug. 17, 1922

*Tauseef Ahmed (PWD, UBL & Kar.) b May 10, 1958

*Tavaré, C. J. (OUCC, Kent & Som.) b Oct. 27, 1954

*Tayfield, H. J. (Natal, Rhod. & Tvl; *CY 1956*) b Jan. 30, 1929

*Taylor, A. I. (Tvl) b July 25, 1925

Taylor, B. (Essex; *CY 1972*) b June 19, 1932

*Taylor, B. R. (Cant. & Wgtn) b July 12, 1943

Taylor, C. W. (Middx) b Aug. 12, 1966

*Taylor, Daniel (Natal) b Jan. 9, 1887, d Jan. 24, 1957

*Taylor, D. D. (Auck. & Warwicks.) b March 2, 1923, d Dec. 5, 1980

Taylor, D. J. S. (Surrey, Som. & Griq. W.) b Nov. 12, 1942

Taylor, G. R. (Hants) b Nov. 25, 1909, d Oct. 31, 1986

*Taylor, H. W. (Natal, Tvl & W. Prov.; *CY 1925*) b May 5, 1889, d Feb. 8, 1973

*Taylor, J. M. (NSW) b Oct. 10, 1895, d May 12, 1971

*Taylor, J. O. (T/T) b Jan. 3, 1932

Taylor, J. P. (Derbys. & Northants) b Aug. 8, 1964

*Taylor, K. (Yorks. & Auck.) b Aug. 21, 1935

Taylor, K. A. (Warwicks.) b Sept. 29, 1916

*Taylor, L. B. (Leics. & Natal) b Oct. 25, 1953

*Taylor, M. A. (NSW; *CY 1990*) b Oct 27, 1964

Taylor, M. N. S. (Notts. & Hants) b Nov. 12, 1942

Taylor, N. R. (Kent) b July 21, 1959

*Taylor, P. L. (NSW & Qld) b Aug. 22, 1956

*Taylor, R. M. (Essex) b Nov. 30, 1909, d Jan. 1984

*Taylor, R. W. (Derbys.; *CY 1977*) b July 17, 1941

Taylor, T. L. (CUCC & Yorks.; *CY 1901*) b May 25, 1878, d March 16, 1960

Taylor, W. (Notts.) b Jan. 24, 1947

Tedstone, G. A. (Warwicks. & Glos.) b Jan. 19, 1961

*Tendulkar, S. R. (Bombay & Yorks.) b April 24, 1973

Tennekoon, A. P. B. (SL) b Oct. 29, 1946

*Tennyson, 3rd Lord (Hon. L. H.) (Hants; *CY 1914*) b Nov. 7, 1889, d June 6, 1951

Terry, V. P. (Hants) b Jan. 14, 1959

Theunissen, N. H. (W. Prov.) b May 4, 1867, d Nov. 9, 1929

Thomas, D. J. (Surrey, N. Tvl & Glos.) b June 30, 1959

*Thomas, G. (NSW) b March 21, 1938

*Thomas, J. G. (Glam., Border, E. Prov. & Northants) b Aug. 12, 1960

Thompson, A. W. (Middx) b April 17, 1916

*Thompson, G. J. (Northants; *CY 1906*) b Oct. 27, 1877, d March 3, 1943

Thompson, J. R. (CUCC & Warwicks.) b May 10, 1918

Thompson, R. G. (Warwicks.) b Sept. 26, 1932

Thoms, G. R. (Vic.) b March 22, 1927

*Thomson, A. L. (Vic.) b Dec. 2, 1945

*Thomson, J. R. (NSW, Qld & Middx) b Aug. 16, 1950

*Thomson, K. (Cant.) b Feb. 26, 1941

*Thomson, N. F. D. (NSW) b May 29, 1839, d Sept. 2, 1896

*Thomson, N. I. (Sussex) b Jan. 23, 1929

*Thomson, S. A. (N. Dist.) b Jan. 27, 1969

Thorne, D. A. (Warwicks & OUCC) b Dec. 12, 1964

Thornton, C. I. (CUCC, Kent & Middx) b March 20, 1850, d Dec. 10, 1929

*Thornton, P. G. (Yorks., Middx & SA) b Dec. 24, 1867, d Jan. 31, 1939

Thorpe, G. P. (Surrey) b Aug. 1, 1969

*Thurlow, H. M. (Qld) b Jan. 10, 1903, d Dec. 3, 1975

Tillekeratne, H. P. (NCC) b July 14, 1967

Tilly, H. W. (Middx) b May 25, 1932

Timms, B. S. V. (Hants & Warwicks.) b Dec. 17, 1940

Timms, J. E. (Northants) b Nov. 3, 1906, d May 18, 1980

Timms, W. W. (Northants) b Sept. 28, 1902, d Sept. 30, 1986

Tindall, M. (CUCC & Middx) b March 31, 1914

Tindall, R. A. E. (Surrey) b Sept. 23, 1935

*Tindill, E. W. T. (Wgtn) b Dec. 18, 1910

Tissera, M. H. (SL) b March 23, 1939

*Titmus, F. J. (Middx, Surrey & OFS; *CY 1963*) b Nov. 24, 1932

Todd, L. J. (Kent) b June 19, 1907, d Aug. 20, 1967

Todd, P. A. (Notts. & Glam.) b March 12, 1953

Tolchard, J. G. (Leics.) b March 17, 1944

*Tolchard, R. W. (Leics.) b June 15, 1946

Tomlins, K. P. (Middx & Glos.) b Oct. 23, 1957

*Tomlinson, D. S. (Rhod. & Border) b Sept. 4, 1910

Tompkin, M. (Leics.) b Feb. 17, 1919, d Sept. 27, 1956

Toogood, G. J. (OUCC) b Nov. 19, 1961

*Toohey, P. M. (NSW) b April 20, 1954

Tooley, C. D. M. (OUCC) b April 19, 1964

Topley, T. D. (Surrey, Essex & Griq. W.) b Feb. 25, 1964

Tordoff, G. G. (CUCC & Som.) b Dec. 6, 1929

*Toshack, E. R. H. (NSW) b Dec. 15, 1914

Townsend, A. (Warwicks.) b Aug. 26, 1921

Townsend, A. F. (Derbys.) b March 29, 1912

*Townsend, C. L. (Glos.; *CY 1899*) b Nov. 7, 1876, d Oct. 17, 1958

*Townsend, D. C. H. (OUCC) b April 20, 1912

*Townsend, L. F. (Derbys. & Auck.; *CY 1934*) b June 8, 1903

*Traicos, A. J. (Rhod. & Zimb.) b May 17, 1947

Travers, J. P. F. (S. Aust.) b Jan. 10, 1871, d Sept. 15, 1942

*Tremlett, M. F. (Som. & C. Dist.) b July 5, 1923, d July 30, 1984

Tremlett, T. M. (Hants) b July 26, 1956

*Tribe, G. E. (Vic. & Northants; *CY 1955*) b Oct. 4, 1920

*Trim, J. (BG) b Jan. 24, 1915, d Nov. 12, 1960

*Trimborn, P. H. J. (Natal) b May 18, 1940

**Trott, A. E. (Vic., Middx & Hawkes Bay; *CY 1899*) b Feb. 6, 1873, d July 30, 1914

*Trott, G. H. S. (Vic.; *CY 1894*) b Aug. 5, 1866, d Nov. 10, 1917

*Troup, G. B. (Auck.) b Oct. 3, 1952

*Trueman, F. S. (Yorks.; *CY 1953*) b Feb. 6, 1931

*Trumble, H. (Vic.; *CY 1897*) b May 12, 1867, d Aug. 14, 1938

*Trumble, J. W. (Vic.) b Sept. 16, 1863, d Aug. 17, 1944

Trump, H. R. J. (Som.) b Oct. 11, 1968

*Trumper, V. T. (NSW; *CY 1903*) b Nov. 2, 1877, d June 28, 1915

*Truscott, P. B. (Wgtn) b Aug. 14, 1941

*Tuckett, L. (OFS) b Feb. 6, 1919

*Tuckett, L. R. (Natal & OFS) b April 19, 1885, d April 8, 1963
*Tufnell, N. C. (CUCC & Surrey) b June 13, 1887, d Aug. 3, 1951
*Tufnell, P. C. R. (Middx) b April 29, 1966
Tuke, Sir Anthony (Pres. MCC 1982-83) b Aug. 22, 1920
Tunnicliffe, C. J. (Derbys.) b Aug. 11, 1951
Tunnicliffe, H. T. (Notts.) b March 4, 1950
Tunnicliffe, J. (Yorks.; *CY 1901*) b Aug. 26, 1866, d July 11, 1948
*Turnbull, M. J. (CUCC & Glam.; *CY 1931*) b March 16, 1906, d Aug. 5, 1944
*Turner, A. (NSW) b July 23, 1950
*Turner, C. T. B. (NSW; *CY 1889*) b Nov. 16, 1862, d Jan. 1, 1944
Turner, D. R. (Hants & W. Prov.) b Feb. 5, 1949
Turner, F. M. (Leics.) b Aug. 8, 1934
Turner, G. J. (W. Prov., N. Tvl & OUCC) b Aug. 5, 1964
*Turner, G. M. (Otago, N. Dist. & Worcs.; *CY 1971*) b May 26, 1947
Turner, R. J. (CUCC & Som.) b Nov. 25, 1967
Turner, S. (Essex & Natal) b July 18, 1943
*Twentyman-Jones, P. S. (W. Prov.) b Sept. 13, 1876, d March 8, 1954
Twining, R. H. (OUCC & Middx; Pres. MCC 1964-65) b Nov. 3, 1889, d Jan. 3, 1979
Twose, R. G. (Warwicks. & N. Dist.) b April 17, 1968
*Tyldesley, E. (Lancs.; *CY 1920*) b Feb. 5, 1889, d May 5, 1962
*Tyldesley, J. T. (Lancs.; *CY 1902*) b Nov. 22, 1873, d Nov. 27, 1930
*Tyldesley, R. K. (Lancs.; *CY 1925*) b March 11, 1897, d Sept. 17, 1943
*Tylecote, E. F. S. (OUCC & Kent) b June 23, 1849, d March 15, 1938
*Tyler, E. J. (Som.) b Oct. 13, 1864, d Jan. 25, 1917
*Tyson, F. H. (Northants; *CY 1956*) b June 6, 1930

Udal, S. D. (Hants) b March 18, 1969
Ufton, D. G. (Kent) b May 31, 1928
*Ulyett, G. (Yorks.) b Oct. 21, 1851, d June 18, 1898
*Umrigar, P. R. (Bombay & Guj.) b March 28, 1926
*Underwood, D. L. (Kent; *CY 1969*) b June 8, 1945
Unwin, F. St G. (Essex) b April 23, 1911, d Oct. 4, 1990

*Valentine, A. L. (Jam.; *CY 1951*) b April 29, 1930
*Valentine, B. H. (CUCC & Kent) b Jan. 17, 1908, d Feb. 2, 1983

*Valentine, V. A. (Jam.) b April 4, 1908, d July 6, 1972
*Vance, R. H. (Wgtn) b March 31, 1955
*van der Bijl, P. G. (W. Prov. & OUCC) b Oct. 21, 1907, d Feb. 16, 1973
van der Bijl, V. A. P. (Natal, Middx & Tvl; *CY 1981*) b March 19, 1948
Van der Gucht, P. I. (Glos. & Bengal) b Nov. 2, 1911
*Van der Merwe, E. A. (Tvl) b Nov. 9, 1904, d Feb. 28, 1971
*Van der Merwe, P. L. (W. Prov. & E. Prov.) b March 14, 1937
van Geloven, J. (Yorks. & Leics.) b Jan. 4, 1934
*Van Ryneveld, C. B. (W. Prov. & OUCC) b March 19, 1928
van Zyl, C. J. P. G. (OFS & Glam.) b Oct. 1, 1961
Varachia, R. (First Pres. SA Cricket Union) b Oct. 12, 1915, d Dec. 11, 1981
Varey, D. W. (CUCC & Lancs.) b Oct. 15, 1961
Varnals, G. D. (E. Prov., Tvl & Natal) b July 24, 1935
Vaulkhard, P. (Notts. & Derbys.) b Sept. 15, 1911
Veivers, T. R. (Qld) b April 6, 1937
*Veletta, M. R. J. (W. Aust.) b Oct. 30, 1963
*Vengsarkar, D. B. (Bombay; *CY 1987*) b April 6, 1956
*Venkataraghavan, S. (†TN & Derbys.) b April 21, 1946
*Venkataramana, M. (TN) b April 24, 1966
*Verity, H. (Yorks.; *CY 1932*) b May 18, 1905, d July 31, 1943
*Vernon, G. F. (Middx) b June 20, 1856, d Aug. 10, 1902
Vigar, F. H. (Essex) b July 7, 1917
*Viljoen, K. G. (Griq. W., OFS & Tvl) b May 14, 1910, d Jan. 21, 1974
*Vincent, C. L. (Tvl) b Feb. 16, 1902, d Aug. 24, 1968
*Vine, J. (Sussex; *CY 1906*) b May 15, 1875, d April 25, 1946
*Vintcent, C. H. (Tvl & Griq. W.) b Sept. 2, 1866, d Sept. 28, 1943
Virgin, R. T. (Som., Northants & W. Prov.; *CY 1971*) b Aug. 26, 1939
*Viswanath, G. R. (†Karn.) b Feb. 12, 1949
*Viswanath, S. (Karn.) b Nov. 29, 1962
*Vivian, G. E. (Auck.) b Feb. 28, 1946
*Vivian, H. G. (Auck.) b Nov. 4, 1912, d Aug. 12, 1983
*Vizianagram, Maharaj Kumar of, Sir Vijay A. (U. Prov.) b Dec. 28, 1905, d Dec. 2, 1965
*Voce, W. (Notts.; *CY 1933*) b Aug. 8, 1909, d June 6, 1984
*Vogler, A. E. E. (Middx, Natal, Tvl & E. Prov.; *CY 1908*) b Nov. 28, 1876, d Aug. 9, 1946
Vonhagt, D. M. (Moors) b March 31, 1965

*Waddington, A. (Yorks.) b Feb. 4, 1893, d Oct. 28, 1959

Waddington, J. E. (Griq. W.) b Dec. 30, 1918, d Nov. 24, 1985

*Wade, H. F. (Natal) b Sept. 14, 1905, d Nov. 22, 1980

Wade, T. H. (Essex) b Nov. 24, 1910, d July 25, 1987

*Wade, W. W. (Natal) b June 18, 1914

*Wadekar, A. L. (Bombay) b April 1, 1941

*Wadsworth, K. J. (C. Dist. & Cant.) b Nov. 30, 1946, d Aug. 19, 1976

*Wainwright, E. (Yorks.; *CY 1894*) b April 8, 1865, d Oct. 28, 1919

*Waite, J. H. B. (E. Prov. & Tvl) b Jan. 19, 1930

*Waite, M. G. (S. Aust.) b Jan. 7, 1911, d Dec. 16, 1985

*Walcott, C. L. (B'dos & BG; *CY 1958*) b Jan. 17, 1926

*Walcott, L. A. (B'dos) b Jan. 18, 1894, d Feb. 27, 1984

Walden, F. I. (Northants; Umpire) b March 1, 1888, d May 3, 1949

Walford, M. M. (OUCC & Som.) b Nov. 27, 1915

Walker, A. (Northants) b July 7, 1962

Walker, A. K. (NSW & Notts.) b Oct. 4, 1925

Walker, C. (Yorks. & Hants) b June 27, 1920, d Dec. 3, 1992

Walker, I. D. (Middx) b Jan. 8, 1844, d July 6, 1898

*Walker, M. H. N. (Vic.) b Sept. 12, 1948

*Walker, P. M. (Glam., Tvl & W. Prov.) b Feb. 17, 1936

Walker, V. E. (Middx) b April 20, 1837, d Jan. 3, 1906

Walker, W. (Notts.) b Nov. 24, 1892, d Dec. 3, 1991

*Wall, T. W. (S. Aust.) b May 13, 1904, d March 25, 1981

Wallace, P. A. (B'dos) b Aug. 2, 1970

*Wallace, W. M. (Auck.) b Dec. 19, 1916

Waller, A. C. (Zimb.) b Sept. 25, 1959

Waller, C. E. (Surrey & Sussex) b Oct. 3, 1948

*Walsh, C. A. (Jam. & Glos.; *CY 1987*) b Oct. 30, 1962

Walsh, J. E. (NSW & Leics.) b Dec. 4, 1912, d May 20, 1980

*Walter, K. A. (Tvl) b Nov. 5, 1939

*Walters, C. F. (Glam. & Worcs.; *CY 1934*) b Aug. 28, 1905, d Dec. 23, 1992

*Walters, F. H. (Vic. & NSW) b Feb. 9, 1860, d June 1, 1922

Walters, J. (Derbys.) b Aug. 7, 1949

*Walters, K. D. (NSW) b Dec. 21, 1945

Walton, A. C. (OUCC & Middx) b Sept. 26, 1933

*Waqar Hassan (Pak. Us, Punjab, Pak. Serv. & Kar.) b Sept. 12, 1932

*Waqar Younis (Multan, UBL & Surrey; *CY 1992*) b Nov. 16, 1971

*Ward, Alan (Derbys., Leics. & Border) b Aug. 10, 1947

*Ward, Albert (Yorks. & Lancs.; *CY 1890*) b Nov. 21, 1865, d Jan. 6, 1939

Ward, B. (Essex) b Feb. 28, 1944

Ward, D. (Glam.) b Aug. 30, 1934

Ward, D. M. (Surrey) b Feb. 10, 1961

*Ward, F. A. (S. Aust.) b Feb. 23, 1909, d March 25, 1974

*Ward, J. T. (Cant.) b March 11, 1937

*Ward, T. A. (Tvl) b Aug. 2, 1887, d Feb. 16, 1936

Ward, T. R. (Kent) b Jan. 18, 1968

Ward, William (MCC & Hants) b July 24, 1787, d June 30, 1849

*Wardle, J. H. (Yorks.; *CY 1954*) b Jan. 8, 1923, d July 23, 1985

*Warnapura, B. (SL) b March 1, 1953

*Warnaweera, K. P. J. (Galle) b Nov. 23, 1960

Warne, F. B. (Worcs., Vic. & Tvl) b Oct. 3, 1906

*Warne, S. K. (Vic.) b Sept. 13, 1969

Warner, A. E. (Worcs. & Derbys.) b May 12, 1959

*Warner, Sir P. F. (OUCC & Middx; *CY 1904, special portrait 1921*; Pres. MCC 1950-51) b Oct. 2, 1873, d Jan. 30, 1963

*Warr, J. J. (CUCC & Middx; Pres. MCC 1987-88) b July 16, 1927

*Warren, A. R. (Derbys.) b April 2, 1875, d Sept. 3, 1951

*Washbrook, C. (Lancs.; *CY 1947*) b Dec. 6, 1914

*Wasim Akram (Lahore, PACO, PNSC, PIA & Lancs.; *CY 1993*) b June 3, 1966

*Wasim Bari (Kar., PIA & Sind) b March 23, 1948

Wasim Haider (Faisalabad & PIA) b June 6, 1967

*Wasim Raja (Lahore, Sargodha, Pak. Us, PIA, Punjab & NBP) b July 3, 1952

Wass, T. G. (Notts.; *CY 1908*) b Dec. 26, 1873, d Oct. 27, 1953

*Wassan, A. S. (Delhi) b March 23, 1968

Wassell, A. (Hants) b April 15, 1940

*Watkin, S. L. (Glam.) b Sept. 15, 1964

*Watkins, A. J. (Glam.) b April 21, 1922

*Watkins, J. C. (Natal) b April 10, 1923

*Watkins, J. R. (NSW) b April 16, 1943

Watkinson, M. (Lancs.) b Aug. 1, 1961

*Watson, C. (Jam. & Delhi) b July 1, 1938

Watson, F. B. (Lancs.) b Sept. 17, 1898, d Feb. 1, 1976

*Watson, G. D. (Vic., W. Aust. & NSW) b March 8, 1945

Watson, G. G. (NSW, W. Aust. & Worcs.) b Jan. 29, 1955

*Watson, W. (Yorks. & Leics.; *CY 1954*) b March 7, 1920

*Watson, W. (Auck.) b Aug. 31, 1965
*Watson, W. J. (NSW) b Jan. 31, 1931
Watson, W. K. (Border, N. Tvl, E. Prov. & Notts.) b May 21, 1955
*Watt, L. (Otago) b Sept. 17, 1924
Watts, H. E. (CUCC & Som.) b March 4, 1922
Watts, P. D. (Northants & Notts.) b March 31, 1938
Watts, P. J. (Northants) b June 16, 1940
*Waugh, M. E. (NSW & Essex; *CY 1991*) b June 2, 1965
*Waugh, S. R. (NSW & Som.; *CY 1989*) b June 2, 1965
*Wazir Ali, S. (C. Ind., S. Punjab & Patiala) b Sept. 15, 1903, d June 17, 1950
*Wazir Mohammad (B'pur & Kar.) b Dec. 22, 1929
*Webb, M. G. (Otago & Cant.) b June 22, 1947
*Webb, P. N. (Auck.) b July 14, 1957
Webb, R. J. (Otago) b Sept. 15, 1952
Webb, R. T. (Sussex) b July 11, 1922
*Webbe, A. J. (OUCC & Middx) b Jan. 16, 1855, d Feb. 19, 1941
Webster, J. (CUCC & Northants) b Oct. 28, 1917
Webster, Dr R. V. (Warwicks. & Otago) b June 10, 1939
Webster, W. H. (CUCC & Middx; Pres. MCC 1976-77) b Feb. 22, 1910, d June 19, 1986
*Weekes, E. D. (B'dos; *CY 1951*) b Feb. 26, 1925
*Weekes, K. H. (Jam.) b Jan. 24, 1912
Weekes, P. N. (Middx) b July 8, 1969
Weeks, R. T. (Warwicks.) b April 30, 1930
*Weerasinghe, C. D. U. S. (TU) b March 1, 1968
*Weir, G. L. (Auck.) b June 2, 1908
*Wellard, A. W. (Som.; *CY 1936*) b April 8, 1902, d Dec. 31, 1980
*Wellham, D. M. (NSW, Tas. & Qld) b March 13, 1959
Wellings, E. M. (OUCC & Surrey) b April 6, 1909, d Sept. 10, 1992
Wells, A. P. (Sussex & Border) b Oct. 2, 1961
Wells, B. D. (Glos. & Notts.) b July 27, 1930
Wells, C. M. (Sussex, Border & W. Prov.) b March 3, 1960
Wells, V. J. (Kent & Leics.) b Aug. 6, 1965
Wenman, E. G. (Kent & England) b Aug. 18, 1803, d Dec. 31, 1879
Wensley, A. F. (Sussex) b May 23, 1898, d June 17, 1970
*Wesley, C. (Natal) b Sept. 5, 1937
**Wessels, K. C. (OFS, W. Prov., N. Tvl, Sussex, Qld & E. Prov.) b Sept. 14, 1957
West, G. H. (Editor of *Wisden* 1880-86) b 1851, d Oct. 6, 1896

*Westcott, R. J. (W. Prov.) b Sept. 19, 1927
Weston, M. J. (Worcs.) b April 8, 1959
*Wettimuny, M. D. (SL) b June 11, 1951
*Wettimuny, S. (SL; *CY 1985*) b Aug. 12, 1956
Wettimuny, S. R. de S. (SL) b Feb. 7, 1949
*Wharton, A. (Lancs. & Leics.) b April 30, 1923
*Whatmore, D. F. (Vic.) b March 16, 1954
Wheatley, K. J. (Hants) b Jan. 20, 1946
Wheatley, O. S. (CUCC, Warwicks. & Glam.; *CY 1969*) b May 28, 1935
Whitaker, Haddon (Editor of *Wisden* 1940-43) b Aug. 30, 1908, d Jan. 5, 1982
*Whitaker, J. J. (Leics.; *CY 1987*) b May 5, 1962
Whitcombe, P. A. (OUCC & Middx) b April 23, 1923
White, A. F. T. (CUCC, Warwicks. & Worcs.) b Sept. 5, 1915
White, C. (Vic. & Yorks.) b Dec. 16, 1969
*White, D. J. (N. Dist.) b June 26, 1961
*White, D. W. (Hants & Glam.) b Dec. 14, 1935
White, E. C. S. (NSW) b July 14, 1913
*White, G. C. (Tvl) b Feb. 5, 1882, d Oct. 17, 1918
*White, J. C. (Som.; *CY 1929*) b Feb. 19, 1891, d May 2, 1961
White, Hon. L. R. (5th Lord Annaly) (Middx & Victory Test) b March 15, 1927, d Sept. 30, 1990
White, R. A. (Middx & Notts.; Umpire) b Oct. 6, 1936
White, R. C. (CUCC, Glos. & Tvl) b Jan. 29, 1941
*White, W. A. (B'dos) b Nov. 20, 1938
Whitehead, J. P. (Yorks. & Worcs.) b Sept. 3, 1925
Whitehouse, J. (Warwicks.) b April 8, 1949
*Whitelaw, P. E. (Auck.) b Feb. 10, 1910, d Aug. 28, 1988
Whitfield, B. J. (Natal) b March 14, 1959
Whitfield, E. W. (Surrey & Northants) b May 31, 1911
Whiting, N. H. (Worcs.) b Oct. 2, 1920
Whitington, R. S. (S. Aust. & Victory Tests; Writer) b June 30, 1912, d March 13, 1984
*Whitney, M. R. (NSW & Glos.) b Feb. 24, 1959
Whittaker, G. J. (Surrey) b May 29, 1916
Whitticase, P. (Leics.) b March 15, 1965
Whittingham, N. B. (Notts.) b Oct. 22, 1940
*Whitty, W. J. (S. Aust.) b Aug. 15, 1886, d Jan. 30, 1974
*Whysall, W. W. (Notts.; *CY 1925*) b Oct. 31, 1887, d Nov. 11, 1930
*Wickremasinghe, A. G. D. (NCC) b Dec. 27, 1965

*Wickremasinghe, G. P. (BRC & SSC) b Aug. 14, 1971

*Wiener, J. M. (Vic.) b May 1, 1955

*Wight, C. V. (BG) b July 28, 1902, d Oct. 4, 1969

*Wight, G. L. (BG) b May 28, 1929

Wight, P. B. (BG, Som., & Cant.) b June 25, 1930

*Wijegunawardene, K. I. W. (CCC) b Nov. 23, 1964

*Wijesuriya, R. G. C. E. (Mor.) b Feb. 18, 1960

Wild, D. J. (Northants) b Nov. 28, 1962

*Wiles, C. A. (B'dos & T/T) b Aug. 11, 1892, d Nov. 4, 1957

*Wilkins, A. H. (Glam., Glos. & N. Tvl) b Aug. 22, 1953

Wilkins, C. P. (Derbys., Border, E. Prov. & Natal) b July 31, 1944

*Wilkinson, L. L. (Lancs.) b Nov. 5, 1916

Wilkinson, P. A. (Notts.) b Aug. 23, 1951

Wilkinson, Col. W. A. C. (OUCC) b Dec. 6, 1892, d Sept. 19, 1983

Willatt, G. L. (CUCC, Notts. & Derbys.) b May 7, 1918

*Willett, E. T. (Comb. Is. & Leewards) b May 1, 1953

Willett, M. D. (Surrey) b April 21, 1933

*Willey, P. (Northants, E. Prov. & Leics.) b Dec. 6, 1949

*Williams, A. B. (Jam.) b Nov. 21, 1949

Williams, C. C. P. (Lord Williams of Elvet) (OUCC & Essex) b Feb. 9, 1933

*Williams, D. (T/T) b Nov. 4, 1963

Williams, D. L. (Glam.) b Nov. 20, 1946

*Williams, E. A. V. (B'dos) b April 10, 1914

*Williams, N. F. (Middx, Windwards & Tas.) b July 2, 1962

Williams, R. G. (Northants) b Aug. 10, 1957

*Williams, R. J. (Natal) b April 12, 1912, d May 14, 1984

Williamson, J. G. (Northants) b April 4, 1936

*Willis, R. G. D. (Surrey, Warwicks. & N. Tvl; *CY 1978*) b May 30, 1949

*Willoughby, J. T. (SA) b Nov. 7, 1874, d *circa* 1955

Willsher, E. (Kent & All-England) b Nov. 22, 1828, d Oct. 7, 1885

Wilmot, K. (Warwicks.) b April 3, 1911

Wilson, A. (Lancs.) b April 24, 1921

Wilson, A. E. (Middx & Glos.) b May 18, 1910

*Wilson, Rev. C. E. M. (CUCC & Yorks.) b May 15, 1875, d Feb. 8, 1944

*Wilson, D. (Yorks. & MCC) b Aug. 7, 1937

*Wilson, E. R. (CUCC & Yorks.) b March 25, 1879, d July 21, 1957

Wilson, J. V. (Yorks.; *CY 1961*) b Jan. 17, 1921

*Wilson, J. W. (Vic. & S. Aust.) b Aug. 20, 1921, d Oct. 13, 1985

Wilson, P. H. L. (Surrey, Som. & N. Tvl) b Aug. 17, 1958

Wilson, R. C. (Kent) b Feb. 18, 1928

*Wimble, C. S. (Tvl) b Jan. 9, 1864, d Jan. 28, 1930

Windows, A. R. (Glos. & CUCC) b Sept. 25, 1942

Winfield, H. M. (Notts.) b June 13, 1933

Wingfield Digby, Rev. A. R. (OUCC) b July 25, 1950

Winn, C. E. (OUCC & Sussex) b Nov. 13, 1926

*Winslow, P. L. (Sussex, Tvl & Rhod.) b May 21, 1929

Wisden, John (Sussex; founder John Wisden and Co. and *Wisden's Cricketers' Almanack*) b Sept. 5, 1826, d April 5, 1884

*Wishart, K. L. (BG) b Nov. 28, 1908, d Oct. 18, 1972

Wolton, A. V. G. (Warwicks.) b June 12, 1919, d Sept. 9, 1990

*Wood, A. (Yorks.; *CY 1939*) b Aug. 25, 1898, d April 1, 1973

*Wood, B. (Yorks., Lancs., Derbys. & E. Prov.) b Dec. 26, 1942

Wood, C. J. B. (Leics.) b Nov. 21, 1875, d June 5, 1960

Wood, D. J. (Sussex) b May 19, 1914, d March 12, 1989

*Wood, G. E. C. (CUCC & Kent) b Aug. 22, 1893, d March 18, 1971

*Wood, G. M. (W. Aust.) b Nov. 6, 1956

*Wood, H. (Kent & Surrey; *CY 1891*) b Dec. 14, 1854, d April 30, 1919

*Wood, R. (Lancs. & Vic.) b March 7, 1860, d Jan. 6, 1915

*Woodcock, A. J. (S. Aust.) b Feb. 27, 1948

Woodcock, John C. (Editor of *Wisden* 1980-86) b Aug. 7, 1926

*Woodfull, W. M. (Vic.; *CY 1927*) b Aug. 22, 1897, d Aug. 11, 1965

Woodhead, F. G. (Notts.) b Oct. 30, 1912, d May 24, 1991

Woodhouse, G. E. S. (Som.) b Feb. 15, 1924, d Jan. 19, 1988

**Woods, S. M. J. (CUCC & Som.; *CY 1889*) b April 13, 1867, d April 30, 1931

Wookey, S. M. (CUCC & OUCC) b Sept. 2, 1954

Wooler, C. R. D. (Leics. & Rhod.) b June 30, 1930

Wooller, W. (CUCC & Glam.) b Nov. 20, 1912

Woolley, C. N. (Glos. & Northants) b May 5, 1886, d Nov. 3, 1962

*Woolley, F. E. (Kent; *CY 1911*) b May 27, 1887, d Oct. 18, 1978

*Woolley, R. D. (Tas.) b Sept. 16, 1954

*Woolmer, R. A. (Kent, Natal & W. Prov.; *CY 1976*) b May 14, 1948

*Worrall, J. (Vic.) b May 12, 1863, d Nov. 17, 1937

*Worrell, Sir F. M. M. (B'dos & Jam.; *CY 1951*) b Aug. 1, 1924, d March 13, 1967

Worsley, D. R. (OUCC & Lancs.) b July 18, 1941

Worsley, Sir W. A. 4th Bt (Yorks.; Pres. MCC 1961-62) b April 5, 1890, d Dec. 4, 1973

*Worthington, T. S. (Derbys.; *CY 1937*) b Aug. 21, 1905, d Aug. 31, 1973

Wright, A. (Warwicks.) b Aug. 25, 1941

Wright, A. J. (Glos.) b July 27, 1962

*Wright, C. W. (CUCC & Notts.) b May 27, 1863, d Jan. 10, 1936

*Wright, D. V. P. (Kent; *CY 1940*) b Aug. 21, 1914

Wright, Graeme A. (Editor of *Wisden* 1986-92) b April 23, 1943

*Wright, J. G. (N. Dist., Derbys., Cant. & Auck.) b July 5, 1954

*Wright, K. J. (W. Aust. & S. Aust.) b Dec. 27, 1953

Wright, L. G. (Derbys.; *CY 1906*) b June 15, 1862, d Jan. 11, 1953

Wyatt, J. G. (Som.) b June 19, 1963

*Wyatt, R. E. S. (Warwicks. & Worcs.; *CY 1930*) b May 2, 1901

*Wynne, O. E. (Tvl & W. Prov.) b June 1, 1919, d July 13, 1975

*Wynyard, E. G. (Hants) b April 1, 1861, d Oct. 30, 1936

Yachad, M. (N. Tvl & Tvl) b Nov. 17, 1960

*Yadav, N. S. (H'bad) b Jan. 26, 1957

*Yajurvindra Singh (M'tra & S'tra) b Aug. 1, 1952

*Yallop, G. N. (Vic.) b Oct. 7, 1952

*Yardley, B. (W. Aust.) b Sept. 5, 1947

*Yardley, N. W. D. (CUCC & Yorks.; *CY 1948*) b March 19, 1915, d Oct. 4, 1989

Yardley, T. J. (Worcs. & Northants) b Oct. 27, 1946

Yarnold, H. (Worcs.) b July 6, 1917, d Aug. 13, 1974

*Yashpal Sharma (Punjab) b Aug. 11, 1954

Yates, G. (Lancs.) b Sept. 20, 1967

Yawar Saeed (Som. & Punjab) b Jan. 22, 1935

*Yograj Singh (Haryana & Punjab) b March 25, 1958

Young, B. A. (N. Dist.) b Nov. 3, 1964

Young, D. M. (Worcs. & Glos.) b April 15, 1924

Young, H. I. (Essex) b Feb. 5, 1876, d Dec. 12, 1964

*Young, J. A. (Middx) b Oct. 14, 1912

*Young, R. A. (CUCC & Sussex) b Sept. 16, 1885, d July 1, 1968

*Younis Ahmed (Lahore, Kar., Surrey, PIA, S. Aust., Worcs. & Glam.) b Oct. 20, 1947

*Yuile, B. W. (C. Dist.) b Oct. 29, 1941

*Zaheer Abbas (Kar., Glos., PWD, Dawood Indust., Sind & PIA; *CY 1972*) b July 24, 1947

Zahid Ahmed (PIA & Peshawar) b Nov. 15, 1961

Zahid Fazal (PACO & PIA) b Nov. 10, 1973

*Zakir Khan (Sind, Peshawar & ADBP) b April 3, 1963

Zesers, A. K. (S. Aust.) b March 11, 1967

*Zoehrer, T. J. (W. Aust.) b Sept. 25, 1961

*Zulch, J. W. (Tvl) b Jan. 2, 1886, d May 19, 1924

*Zulfiqar Ahmed (B'pur & PIA) b Nov. 22, 1926

*Zulqarnain (Pak. Rlwys, Lahore & HBFC) b May 25, 1962

CRICKET ASSOCIATIONS AND SOCIETIES

AUCKLAND, CRICKET SOCIETY OF: J. H. Palmer, Eden Park, PO Box 2860, Auckland 1, New Zealand.

AUSTRALIAN CRICKET SOCIETY: D. Manning, Ravenstone, 240-246 Oban Road, North Ringwood, Victoria 3134.

BLACKLEY CRICKET SOCIETY: D. N. Butterfield, 7 Bayswater Terrace, Halifax, West Yorkshire, HX3 0NB.

CAMBRIDGE UNIVERSITY CRICKET SOCIETY: Ms H. Hackney, St Catharine's College, Cambridge CB2 1RL.

CHELTENHAM CRICKET SOCIETY: P. Murphy, 1 Colesbourne Road, Benhall, Cheltenham, Gloucestershire GL51 6DJ.

CHESTERFIELD CRICKET SOCIETY: J. S. Cook, 44 Morris Avenue, Newbold, Chesterfield, Derbyshire S41 7BA.

COUNCIL OF CRICKET SOCIETIES, THE: B. Rickson, 31 Grange Avenue, Cheadle Hulme, Cheshire SK8 5EN.

CRICKET MEMORABILIA SOCIETY: A. Sheldon, 29 Highclere Road, Crumpsall, Manchester M8 6WS.

CRICKET SOCIETY, THE: E. R. Budd, 16 Storey Court, 39 St John's Wood Road, London NW8 8QX.

CRICKET SOCIETY, THE (Midlands Branch): Dr A. A. Walker, "Sarnia", Hernes Nest, Bewdley, Worcestershire DY12 2ET.

CRICKET STATISTICIANS, ASSOCIATION OF: P. Wynne-Thomas, 3 Radcliffe Road, West Bridgford, Nottingham NG2 5FF.

CRICKET STATISTICIANS AND SCORERS OF INDIA, ASSOCIATION OF: Dr Vasant Naik, 102 B. Madhav Wadi, M.M.G. Road, Dadar, Bombay 400 014, India.

DERBYSHIRE CRICKET SOCIETY: P. J. Peek, 78 Suffolk Avenue, Chaddesden, Derby DE21 6ER.

DUKINFIELD CRICKET LOVERS' SOCIETY: F. Stafford, 17 Clarence Road, Wallasey, Wirral.

EAST RIDING CRICKET SOCIETY: S. J. Clarke, 12 Meadow Lane, Newport, North Humberside HU15 2QN.

ESSEX CRICKET SOCIETY: M. K. Smith, 321 Westbourne Grove, Westcliff-on-Sea, Essex SS0 0PU.

GLOUCESTERSHIRE CRICKET LOVERS' SOCIETY: M. Simpson, 318 Canford Lane, Westbury-on-Trym, Bristol BS9 3PL.

GOOD EGG CRICKET SOCIETY: R. Whitaker, c/o 15 Sunnyfield Avenue, Cliviger, Burnley, Lancashire.

HAMPSHIRE CRICKET SOCIETY: J. Moore, 85 Kingsway, Chandlers Ford, Hants.

HEAVY WOOLLEN CRICKET SOCIETY: G. S. Cooper, 27 Milford Grove, Gomersal, Cleckheaton, West Yorkshire BO19 4BB.

INDIA, THE CRICKET SOCIETY OF: Sander Nakai, 1047 Pocket-B, Sector-A, Vasant Kunj, New Delhi 1120 030 India.

LANCASHIRE AND CHESHIRE CRICKET SOCIETY: H. W. Pardoe, "Crantock", 117a Barlow Moor Road, Didsbury, Manchester M20 8TS.

LINCOLNSHIRE CRICKET LOVERS' SOCIETY: C. Kennedy, 26 Eastwood Avenue, Great Grimsby, South Humberside DN34 5BE.

MERSEYSIDE CRICKET SOCIETY: W. T. Robins, 11 Yew Tree Road, Hunts Cross, Liverpool L25 9QN.

NEEDWOOD CRICKET LOVERS' SOCIETY: J. Snowball, "The Coppers", Sudbury Road, Yoxall, Staffordshire.

NORFOLK CRICKET SOCIETY: D. Lester King, 3 Buckling Court, Recorder Road, Norwich, Norfolk NR1 1NW.

NORTHERN CRICKET SOCIETY: K. Harvey, 5 St Margaret's Drive, Gledhow Lane, Roundhay, Leeds, Yorkshire LS8 1RU.

NOTTINGHAM CRICKET LOVERS' SOCIETY: G. Blagdurn, 2 Inham Circus, Chilwell, Beeston, Nottingham NG9 4FN.

OXFORD UNIVERSITY CRICKET SOCIETY: G. Davies, Jesus College, Oxford OX1 3DW.

PAKISTAN ASSOCIATION OF CRICKET STATISTICIANS: Abid Ali Kazi, 5-A, 11/1 Sunset Lane, Phase 11, Defence Housing Society, Karachi, Pakistan.

ROTHERHAM CRICKET SOCIETY: J. A. R. Atkin, 15 Gallow Tree Road, Rotherham, South Yorkshire S65 3FE.

SCOTLAND, CRICKET SOCIETY OF: A. J. Robertson, 5 Riverside Road, Eaglesham, Glasgow G76 0DQ.

SOMERSET WYVERNS: R. Keeley, 62 Schubert Road, Putney, London SW15 2QS.

SOUTH AFRICA, CRICKET SOCIETY OF: Mrs J. Gleason, PO Box 7840, Sandton, Transvaal 2146, South Africa.

STOURBRIDGE AND DISTRICT CRICKET SOCIETY: R. Barber, 6 Carlton Avenue, Pedmore, Stourbridge, West Midlands DY9 9ED.

SUSSEX CRICKET SOCIETY: B. Rowe, Crofton, Woodlands, Hove, Sussex BN3.

SWISS CRICKET ASSOCIATION: Dr B. Pattison, 9 Ch. du Bois Contens, 1291 Commugny, Switzerland.

WEST LANCASHIRE CRICKET SOCIETY: G. O. Shipton, 9 Breeze Road, Southport, Lancashire PR8 2HG.

WOMBWELL CRICKET LOVERS' SOCIETY: J. Sokell, 42 Woodstock Road, Barnsley, South Yorkshire S75 1DX.

YORKSHIRE CCC SUPPORTERS' ASSOCIATION: R. C. Johnson, 38 Micklebring Lane, Braithwell, Rotherham, Yorkshire S66 7AS.

ZIMBABWE, CRICKET SOCIETY OF: J. B. Stockwell, 6 Howard Close, Mount Pleasant, Harare, Zimbabwe.

OBITUARIES

ARCHER, DAVID MYRTON, who died on October 24, 1992 in hospital in Barbados after a short illness, aged 61, was the most experienced umpire in the West Indies. Unusually, he had the advantage of having played first-class cricket: he represented the Windward Islands in the Shell Shield tournament in 1966-67. Archer was born in Barbados where he once produced an outstanding performance in club cricket, taking 17 wickets in a day, including all ten in an innings. He made his début as a Test umpire in the Bridgetown Test against England in 1980-81 and stood in 28 Tests in all, his last being West Indies' inaugural match against South Africa in April 1992. In 1982 he umpired in ten matches in England and he was chosen as the West Indian representative in the 1987-88 World Cup when the idea of independent umpires received its first major trial. He had a well-deserved reputation as an excellent decision-maker; however, like other West Indian umpires of the period he was content to let the players dictate what constituted fair play in the broadest sense. Archer was also a publican who ran the Umpire's Inn in Barbados, which was popular with cricketers and many others.

BAKER, EDWARD STANLEY, who died at Great Dunmow, Essex, on March 15, 1992, aged 81, was an amateur wicket-keeper who played in 32 matches for Worcestershire in 1933 and 1934. In 1934, he played virtually all season, the idea being to relieve Bernard Quaife from his duties behind the stumps so he could concentrate on his batting. In all Baker had 40 dismissals, five of which were stumpings.

BANERJEE, SUDANGSU ABINASH, who died on September 14, 1992, aged 72, after a long illness, was the first Bengali player to represent India in Test cricket, five weeks before his namesake S. N. Banerjee. He was a right-arm medium-paced line-and-length bowler who played in the Third Test of the 1948-49 series against John Goddard's West Indians in Calcutta, when he opened the bowling, dismissed Denis Atkinson with his fifth ball and finished with first-innings figures of four for 120. He also held three catches and was evidently unlucky not to be picked again. "Montu" Banerjee was born in Calcutta, and played for Bengal, Bihar and Maharashtra in the Ranji Trophy. He took 92 first-class wickets, at an average of 23.28.

BICK, DONALD ALBERT, who died from a heart attack at Ware in Hertfordshire, on January 13, 1992, aged 55, was on the Middlesex staff from 1954 to 1967, where he was happy to stay as Fred Titmus's off-spinning understudy. Almost any other county would have been glad to give a player of his ability regular first-team cricket but he was not an ambitious man and preferred his family and his garden to the possibility of advancement. Early on, there were hopes that he might develop into a genuine batsman but, although he looked sound enough, he could not resist the temptation to attack too soon. In the end he had to settle for a place in the bottom half of the order and he never scored more than the entertaining 85 he made for Colonel L. C. Stevens's XI against Cambridge University at Eastbourne in 1960. His bowling was always steady, but he never developed the spin and guile that might have disturbed the best players. He twice returned figures of five for 22: against Yorkshire at Scarborough in 1959 and in 1965 against the University at Cambridge. That year Bick won a regular place at last, took 61 wickets and was awarded his cap. In all he made 2,221 runs in 147 matches, averaging 13.96, and took 234 wickets at 27.70. He held 35 catches. On leaving Lord's he played for Hertfordshire (1968-74) and, for a number of years, was coach at the City of London School. He was an easy-going, humorous man, remembered by team-mates for the difficulty he found in saying an unkind word about anyone, no matter what the provocation.

BOWLEY, HERRICK BROWETT, who died in December 1991, aged 80, was born at Kirby Muxloe. He played in 13 matches for Leicestershire as a leg-spinner – 11 of them in an extended trial in 1937. He had a minor triumph against Hampshire at Leicester with four for 17 in 13.2 overs, but he was never again able to approach that sort of form. His 17 wickets cost 54.05 each. His elder brother Fred also played for the county.

BUSE, HERBERT FRANCIS THOMAS, the Somerset all-rounder, died in hospital in Bath on February 23, 1992, aged 81. Bertie Buse played in 304 first-class matches between 1929 and 1953. He will be best remembered for the disaster that attended his benefit match at Bath in 1953, which was the last but one first-class match in England to be completed in a day. Somerset were bowled out for 55 and 79 and lost to Lancashire by an innings and 24; Buse helped cause his own misfortune by taking six for 41.

In Somerset Buse will be recalled with enormous affection for his deeds in the preceding seasons when equally heavy defeats were not unknown, though they were rarely quite so spectacular. A right-hand bat with an obdurate defence, he was in his element shoring up his side's innings when it was threatening to disintegrate. His main scoring stroke was a curious and very personal dab/cut which somehow escaped the clutches of the slips and flew off in the direction of third man. He also bowled right-arm at medium pace or a little above and was much more formidable than his neat, fastidious run-up suggested. At the last moment before delivery he would spring into life and send down a late, waspish out-swinger or, as an occasional surprise, an in-swinger. John Arlott likened his approach to that of a butler bringing in the tea, though Buse never took too kindly to this. He did look rather prim on the field, but he was a steely competitor who delighted in tormenting high-class batsmen.

Buse was born in Bristol, but moved to Bath and was working in a solicitor's office there when he made his first-class début as an 18-year-old. Sharing the new ball against Surrey at The Oval with Arthur Wellard, he rose to the occasion with an opening spell of 6-1-22-0 against Hobbs and Sandham and played two determined innings. Thereafter he was given few chances of making an impression until 1938 when he contributed 1,067 runs and 61 wickets and took more catches than anyone except Luckes, the wicket-keeper. His figures were even better in 1939, when he took eight for 41 against Derbyshire. And he quickly rediscovered his touch after the war. He helped Bill Andrews bowl out the 1946 Indian touring team for 64 immediately after they had made 533 for three at Hove. In 1948 he had his best year with the bat, making 1,279 runs, more than any Somerset player except Gimblett. The following year he began the season by taking seven for 26 at Taunton in the second innings of Freddie Brown's first match as Northamptonshire captain when Brown's team, needing 64 to win, scraped home by two wickets.

Though he always looked inscrutable, he was much loved within the county and throughout the game. In all he made 10,623 runs, including seven hundreds, at an average of 22.69. He passed 1,000 runs in a season five times, captured 657 wickets at a cost of 28.77 and held 151 catches. He was a useful rugby full back and an accomplished performer at table tennis and billiards.

CHEGWYN, JOHN WILLIAM, MBE, who died on May 26, 1992, aged 83, was best known for his work spreading cricket to the small towns of rural Australia. He would take along a few stars, play the locals and hold informal coaching clinics. His policy was simple. "On the field we give of our best," he would say, "and off the field we accept your hospitality." Before that, Jack Chegwyn had made his name as a high-class middle-order batsman, but he was only able to play five matches for New South Wales in 1940-41 and 1941-42 before the war intervened. He made 375 first-class runs at an average of 46.87 and scored 103 against a South Australian attack including Clarrie Grimmett. He was appointed MBE for his services to cricket and was a New South Wales selector for a quarter of a century.

CORDNER, LAURENCE OSMASTON, died on July 11, 1992 at Penshurst, Victoria, at the age of 81. Larry Cordner was a leg-break and googly bowler and lower-order batsman who played in three first-class matches for Victoria in the early 1930s. Against the West Indians in 1930-31 he took three wickets for 154, including those of Roach and Headley. Batting No. 10 in the second innings, he made 30 not out, helping his side to a draw when they had nine wickets down.

CORNELIUS, Judge ALVIN ROBERTS, who died in Lahore on December 21, 1991, aged 88, was a founding father of Pakistan cricket. He was a founder member of the Cricket Board of Pakistan and served as vice-president from 1948 to 1953, playing a major role in the negotiations that led to his country being accepted as a full member of the Imperial Cricket Conference in 1952. He formed the Eaglets Society to foster young players, pending a proper structure for first-class cricket in Pakistan, and was honoured with life membership of MCC. He was a former chief justice of Pakistan.

DARLING, LEONARD STUART, the Australian left-handed batsman who played in 12 Test matches between the wars, died at Adelaide on June 24, 1992, aged 82. Len Darling was athletically built and a graceful, dashing player with a fine array of attacking strokes which he used to good effect in the Sheffield Shield for Victoria from 1931-32 to 1936-37. He had few chances to show what he could do at Test level, but looked the part more than once before his sudden retirement at the end of 1936-37.

Darling, who was born at South Yarra in Victoria, played in his first senior match as a 17-year-old in 1926-27, but had to wait until 1928-29 before making his début in the Shield at Sydney in an amazing match. Victoria fought off defeat after New South Wales had declared at 713 for six, leaving Bradman 340 not out. Victoria inevitably followed on but, helped by 96 from Darling, gained an honourable draw. That season he hit 87 at Melbourne against an MCC team containing Larwood, Tate, Freeman and Geary in their attack. He made no showing again until 1931-32 when he made his maiden hundred and averaged 48.88 in the Shield. Next year he came right to the fore, averaging 69.14 in state matches with three hundreds, and was brought in to bolster Australia's beleaguered Test team for the last two Tests of the Bodyline series at Brisbane and Sydney. At Brisbane he was run out for 39 in the second innings; and at Sydney his attacking 85 was top score in a total of 435. Many thought he was less bothered by the onslaught of Larwood and company than anyone else except Stan McCabe. In 1933-34 he made his highest score, 188 against Queensland, and his 93 at Sydney in the final Shield match of the season enabled Victoria to draw and thus take the trophy by a single point.

In England in 1934 the other batsmen were dwarfed by Bradman and Ponsford. Darling played in the first four Tests, but achieved little, and *Wisden* commented on his tendency to flick at balls moving away. In other matches he played some delightful innings and made 1,022 runs on the tour at 34.06. Back at home in 1934-35, he was in brilliant form, hitting three hundreds in successive matches, and was an automatic choice for the 1935-36 tour of South Africa. There he had a much better series and averaged 45.80. Against England in 1936-37, Australia experimented with several young batsman and Darling was only included for the famous New Year Test at Melbourne; in front of a 65,000 crowd he held two brilliant catches to dispose of Hammond and Leyland. At the end of the season, when he was only 27, he suddenly retired and moved to Adelaide; it was believed that marriage played an important part in his decision. He eventually became sales manager of the Adelaide Quarrying Company. In 100 first-class matches he made 5,780 runs for an average of 42.50, which included 16 hundreds. His total in 12 Tests was 474 runs at 27.88. He was a superb fielder in any position and a moderate right-arm medium-pace bowler, whose 32 first-class wickets cost exactly 47. "If ever there has been a better team man than Darls," wrote Bill O'Reilly, "I have not yet had the pleasure of meeting him."

DAVIES, JACK GALE WILMOT, OBE, who died at Cambridge on November 5, 1992, aged 81, was a remarkable man who achieved many distinctions both within cricket and outside it. He had many of the Renaissance Man qualities of C. B. Fry; but he was a shy person and often those who knew him well in one field were quite unaware of his achievements elsewhere. Perhaps his greatest cricketing feat was to cause the dismissals of both Hutton and Bradman for ducks in one week when playing for Cambridge University in May 1934. Against Yorkshire he ran out the young Hutton, who was making his first-class début and had pushed a ball to cover expecting to score his first run. The significance of this only became apparent with the years. But six days later he caused a sensation by clean bowling Bradman for his first-ever nought in England with a ball that went straight on and hit off stump. A large crowd at Fenner's was not entirely pleased with Davies.

The rest of his playing career, though a little anticlimactic, was still very successful, but conducted in the old-fashioned amateur way. He was a stylish and dashing right-hand batsman, mostly in the middle order (though he had a notably successful period as an opener for Kent in 1946), a slow off-break bowler capable of running through an innings and a brilliant cover point. He had an outstanding school career at Tonbridge both inside and outside the classroom. He was a member of the cricket XI for four years, and captain in 1930, when he took 30 wickets and made 780 runs at 45.88; *Wisden* said he was "rather too careless to be really brilliant".

Davies won a Classical Scholarship to St John's College, Cambridge and was all set for a Blue in 1931, but he sprained his ankle before the Lord's match and was forced to drop out. His place went to A. T. Ratcliffe, who scored 201. Davies played little in 1932 but finally earned recognition a year later, due to some steady bowling, and in 1934 he began to fulfil his batting promise with an outstanding 133 against Surrey at The Oval soon after his acts of *lèse majesté* at Fenner's. Davies then took eight wickets in the University match, including five for 43 in the first innings, which might have given Cambridge victory except that his captain, J. H. Human, did not bring him on until he had tried six other bowlers and the score was 318 for three. He also found time to take a first-class honours degree in classics – an unusual achievement for a cricket Blue, especially in that era — play rugby for Blackheath and Kent and win the Syriax Cup, the rugby fives singles championship, three times.

He played occasional matches for Kent before the war, taking seven for 20 against Essex at Tunbridge Wells in 1936, and getting the side out of trouble with 89 against Leicestershire on the same ground a year later. In 1946 he played regularly, was promoted to open, scored three centuries, including 168 at

Worcester when he carried the team to victory, and made 1,246 runs, though he was a colonel at the time and had important War Office duties. He maintained his form well until he finally gave up in 1951; he played his final first-class match when he was almost 50, for MCC in 1961 against, appropriately, Cambridge. In 153 matches he scored 5,982 runs, averaging 23.92, and took 258 wickets at 30.41.

In 1939 Davies took a degree at the National Institute of Industrial Psychology and he became Chief Psychologist, Directorate for the Selection of Personnel, at the War Office. He later served at the United Nations. In 1952 he was appointed Secretary of the Cambridge University Appointments Board, and thereafter he became a father figure to generations of Cambridge cricketers. He was elected Treasurer of the Cambridge Cricket Club in 1958 and for many years Davies and the groundsman Cyril Coote were the embodiment of the continuing traditions of Cambridge cricket. He was also Treasurer (1976-80) and President (1985-86) of MCC and was made an Honorary Vice-President in 1989. From 1969 to 1976 he was an executive director of the Bank of England. As late as 1990, he reported a couple of cricket matches from Fenner's for the *Daily Telegraph*. The sharpness of his mind was obvious to anyone who worked with him in committee, whatever the subject. His engaging laugh prevented his intelligence becoming too intimidating.

DESHON, Major DAVID PETER TOWER, who collapsed and died at Heathrow Airport on January 18, 1992, aged 68, was a cricketer who might have gone far in the first-class game if he had been able to give the time to it. He was a right-handed batsman with a keen eye and quick footwork. At Sherborne School he made 1,570 runs from 1939 to 1941 for an average of 52.33 and he handsomely confirmed his ability in 1941 with a brilliant hundred before lunch at Lord's for South Public Schools against North Public Schools. He dominated a partnership of 173 for the second wicket with Trevor Bailey, who made 63. Deshon captained The Army after the war and played four matches for Somerset between 1947 and 1953 without being able to repeat such form.

DINES, WILLIAM JAMES, who died at Gidea Park, Essex on June 16, 1992, at the age of 75, played as a professional in 20 matches for Essex between 1947 and 1949. He was engaged primarily as a right-arm medium-paced bowler, and in his first Championship match – against Northamptonshire at Ilford in May 1947 – took two wickets in his second over and dismissed Jack Timms soon afterwards. He never again found wickets so easy to come by, but he held on to his place until July by playing a number of important late-order innings. His 15 first-class wickets cost 65.33 each; he made 431 runs at an average of 18.73.

DITCHFIELD, WILLIAM GEORGE, who died at Dunedin, New Zealand, on March 21, 1991, aged 87, was Otago's oldest surviving first-class cricketer. A right-hand opening bat and right-arm medium-pace bowler, he played a single game against Wellington at Carisbrook in 1933-34, not without distinction. He scored 55 and shared an opening stand of 94 with V. G. Cavanagh to help set up a 199-run victory.

DOS SANTOS, Sir ERROL LIONEL, who died in November 1992, at the age of 102, was an influential administrator both in the pre-independence Trinidadian government and in West Indian cricket. He was President of the West Indies Cricket Board of Control from 1954 to 1970 and was particularly involved in the development of Queen's Park Oval in Port-of-Spain into a major arena. He was also instrumental in manoeuvring John Goddard into the captaincy for both the 1950 and 1957 tours of England, ahead of Sir Errol's fellow Trinidadian Jeff Stollmeyer. He was appointed CBE in 1939 and received a knighthood in 1946. A fervent Anglophile, he later moved to England.

EDGAR, ARTHUR JOHN, died on April 21, 1992, aged 67. A right-hand batsman and wicket-keeper, he kept for Wellington in three first-class matches in 1955-56, while T. G. MacMahon was on tour in India and Pakistan. His son Bruce played 39 Tests for New Zealand.

ELLIS, PERCY ARTHUR, who died on April 25, 1992, aged 85, at Lilydale, Victoria, played in three first-class matches for his state in 1930-31 as a batsman. He hit 59 against Tasmania at Hobart, following this with 47 as an opener for a weakened team against the West Indian tourists at Melbourne. His total of 149 runs came at an average of 29.80.

EVEREST, JAMES KERSE, who died in Hamilton on September 28, 1992, aged 74, was a left-handed opening batsman whose first-class career was stunted because Northern Districts were not admitted into the Plunket Shield until 1956. He made 69 in their first game against Auckland and 104 in the fourth against Canterbury. He was named as Batsman of the Year by the 1957 *New Zealand Cricket Almanack*. By this time he was 39. In his three first-class seasons he made 809 runs for an average of 36.77, figures which helped to support earlier complaints that his ability and powers of concentration should have won him consideration for a Test place long before. In a Hawke Cup match for Waikato he hit 264 in 485 minutes against Manawatu, a competition record.

FELL, DESMOND ROBERT, who died on January 22, 1992, aged 79, was a left-handed opening batsman who played 38 times for Natal between 1931-32 and 1949-50 and was considered unlucky by some not to have been chosen for the South African tour of England in 1947. He played one match in England, for the Dominions team led by Learie Constantine against England at Lord's in 1945, which was described by *Wisden* as "one of the finest games ever seen". Fell made 12 and 28. In his career, he made 1,958 first-class runs at 31.58 and scored five centuries. He later became an umpire and stood in the Test between South Africa and New Zealand at Durban in 1961-62.

FERNANDES, JUDE, Saurashtra's former Ranji Trophy player, died on September 22, 1992 at Rajkot after a long illness, aged 44. A right-arm medium-pace bowler, he made his first-class début in 1969-70. In a total of 23 matches he captured 56 wickets. His best performance was against Gujarat when he took five for 48.

FIDDLING, KENNETH, who died in the Royal Halifax Infirmary on June 19, 1992, aged 74, was a wicket-keeper who left Yorkshire to get a first-team place at Northamptonshire. Ken Fiddling was an important member of the team which rose dramatically from the foot of the table under Freddie Brown. He was born at Hebden Bridge and progressed to senior cricket via Todmorden and the Yorkshire Colts. He played in his first match for Yorkshire against Scotland at Harrogate in August 1938, as deputy for Arthur Wood, who was himself deputising for the injured Leslie Ames in "Hutton's match" at The Oval. Next year he made his Championship début against Derbyshire at Sheffield in memorable circumstances when Smailes and the unknown Smurthwaite skittled out the opposition for 20. In 1946, P. A. Gibb was regarded as the first-choice keeper with the ageing Wood and Fiddling as his understudies. J. H. Nash, the Yorkshire secretary, thought Fiddling was "brilliant but inconsistent", not a combination much appreciated in Yorkshire at the time. So in 1947 he moved to Northampton. Herbert Strudwick watched him and said he was the best wicket-keeper in England. He was keeping to an interesting and varied attack, which included Brown's own leg-breaks, and in 1951 he had 59 victims. After that, Fiddling began to be affected by ill health and injury. He missed much of 1952 through appendicitis, and a stress fracture forced him out of the game in 1953. He received a testimonial of £2,028. His batting, at No. 10 or 11, was mainly defensive; he passed fifty just once and scored 1,380 runs at 11.69. In 160 matches, 18 for Yorkshire, the rest for Northamptonshire, he made 302 dismissals, 76 of them stumpings. After retiring he went back to Yorkshire and played in the Bradford League.

FUSSELL, BASIL JOHN, was killed in a road accident on October 13, 1991, aged 55. Fussell was a right-handed batsman who was picked to play for Transvaal in a friendly against Border in 1957-58 and was out for nought in both innings. He did not play another first-class match for six seasons, until he played twice for Transvaal B. In the second game, he spectacularly redeemed his earlier failure by scoring 115 in 144 minutes against Orange Free State.

GHOSH, A. N., who died in Calcutta on November 25, 1991, aged 93, was a former President of the Board of Control for Cricket in India (BCCI). He also served as President and Treasurer of the Cricket Association of Bengal. He was made an honorary life member of MCC.

GRAY, ROGER IBBOTSON, QC, who died in October 1992, aged 71, was a lower-order right-hand bat and a right-arm medium-pace bowler. He appeared in one first-class match for Oxford University against the Free Foresters in 1947. He scored nought and 11 and took no wicket for 57 in the match. He was President of the Oxford Union and was later a Deputy High Court Judge.

GREENSTOCK, JOHN WILFRID, who died in hospital on February 2, 1992, aged 86, was an orthodox slow left-arm bowler who, without doing anything exceptional at Malvern, nevertheless went on to win a Blue at Oxford in 1925, 1926 and 1927. He also played 13 matches for Worcestershire, his father's county. He began with the reputation of being a fine fielder, and soon began to show a slow bowler's temperament by working patiently for his wickets. He was no great spinner of the ball, but was accurate and could flight it subtly. His best figures were five for 36 against The Army at Oxford in 1926. That same year at Lord's he frustrated Cambridge with five for 77 when they were trying to force the pace in the second innings. Greenstock took 139 wickets (113 for the University) at 26.34 and made 507 runs for an average of 9.38.

GRIEVES, KENNETH JOHN, died suddenly at his home in Rawtenstall on January 3, 1992, aged 66. For many years after the war Ken Grieves represented to English cricket followers the epitome of the Australian professional, ferociously hard on the field, delightfully charming off it. He played 452 matches for Lancashire between 1949 and 1964, scoring runs, taking wickets and – above all – snapping up close-to-the-wicket catches. Unusually for an Australian, he also played soccer and made 147 Football League appearances as a goalkeeper for Bury, Bolton and Stockport. Grieves was brought up in Sydney and stepped into the New South Wales team when first-class cricket was resumed in Australia on a non-competitive basis in 1945-46. He made a lively hundred against the Australian Services. However, he was less successful the following year when the Sheffield Shield resumed and in 1947 he accepted an offer to play for Rawtenstall in the Lancashire League. The club had been hoping to sign Keith Miller instead. Two years later Lancashire signed Grieves and he was an immediate success. He made 128 and took five for 64 against the New Zealanders at Old Trafford and it looked as though he might achieve the double. However, the captain, Nigel Howard, like some of his successors, appeared to undervalue and underuse Grieves's leg-spin, and he finished with 1,407 runs and 63 wickets. In the wetter summers that followed 1949, his batting fallibilities began to be exposed. He was no stylist, preferring the cut and pull to anything else, and attacking in general to defence. He still managed to pass 1,000 runs in all but two of his 15 seasons. His bowling was comparatively neglected but he more than made up for this with his close fielding on either side of the wicket, though Lancashire followers of the period recollect most the leg-trap he formed with Jack Ikin and Geoff Edrich when Roy Tattersall was bowling.

He took a record 555 catches for the county, 205 in the four seasons 1950 to 1953, 63 in the 1950 season alone, eight in a match against Sussex in 1951. In the hot summer of 1959 he achieved new batting heights: 2,253 runs, an unbeaten 202 against the Indians at Blackpool and an important innings of exactly 100 at The Oval that helped prevent Surrey winning an eighth consecutive Championship. He passed 1,500 runs again in 1961 but retired and went into business in 1962 when Lancashire, beginning a long period of decline and turmoil, turned to the club cricketer Joe Blackledge as their captain. This anachronistic move was not a success and Grieves came back to lead the side in 1963. Initially, there were signs of improvement but in 1964 the team went backwards again with dissent inside the team and growing anger amongst the members. Lancashire announced that they intended to build a new team who would "pay a proper respect to the captain". Grieves was blamed, sacked as captain and went back to the leagues. He later returned to Old Trafford, served on the committee for 13 years and was elected a vice-president in December 1991. In his full career he compiled 22,454 runs at an average of 33.66, a total boosted by a successful tour of India and Ceylon in 1950-51 with Leslie Ames's Commonwealth Team, hit 29 centuries, held 608 catches and took 242 wickets at a cost of 29.78. His former team-mate Alan Wharton paid tribute to his loyalty, true sporting instincts and a sense of fun which never deserted him, even when the going was roughest.

GUL MAHOMED was one of the small band of cricketers who have represented two countries in Tests. He played eight times for India and once for Pakistan. He was born in Lahore and died there on May 8, 1992, aged 70, after a long illness. Gul Mahomed was a diminutive, dashing left-handed batsman who could bowl steady left-arm seamers at medium pace. Above all, he was an outstandingly brilliant fielder in the cover area; he could gather left-handed and return at great speed at a time when Indian fielding was often very unathletic. It was once said that a fish could not slither out of his hands. As a youth, he played for Islamia College, the nursery of many Test cricketers from Punjab, and made his début in the Ranji Trophy in 1938-39 for Northern India when he was 17. He soon announced his class by hitting 95 for Muslims against Hindus in the Northern India Triangular Tournament. He made real progress in 1942 and scored a forceful hundred for the Rest of India against Western India, facing an attack of Test standard. Meanwhile, the Bombay Pentangular Tournament had provided him with the chance of making two more hundreds and he and Hazare – batsmen of contrasting styles – shared a stand of 302 for a Bengal Cyclone XI against a Bijapur Famine XI in the Brabourne Stadium in Bombay. This was a foretaste of what came later.

Gul Mahomed did well enough in trials to secure a place on the trip to England in 1946 but, in an interview many years later, he was sharply critical of the Nawab of Pataudi's captaincy, maintaining that no one apart from Merchant was given a proper chance to run into consistent form. He played without success at Lord's in the First Test. Back in India, however, he and Hazare shared what remains the largest stand for any wicket in first-class cricket. It was in the final of the Ranji Trophy between Baroda and Holkar. Gul Mahomed came in with the score at 91 for three. When he was out for 319, eight hours 53 minutes later, they had put on 577 for the fourth wicket, part of a total of 784.

Gul was a member of the post-Independence team which toured Australia as pioneers in 1947-48, captained by Lala Amarnath. The team failed dismally and he made only 130 runs in five Tests but fielded brilliantly throughout. He represented India against the newcomers Pakistan in their first two Tests in 1952-53. But he then migrated to Pakistan and in 1956-57 he was chosen for his new country against Ian Johnson's Australians at Karachi, and made the winning hit. Earlier, he had been a great success as a professional in the Lancashire League with Ramsbottom. In his full first-class career he compiled 5,614 runs, including 12 hundreds, for an average of 33.81, besides holding 60 catches and saving countless runs. He picked up 107 wickets in occasional spells, which cost him 27.19 apiece. In his nine Tests he made only 205 runs at 12.81, but he was popular wherever he played and was an early exemplar of the best sub-continental tradition of entertainment and athleticism.

HAINSWORTH, Dr SIDNEY BEETHAM, CBE, who died at Hull on October 24, 1992, aged 93, was chairman of J. H. Fenner & Co, which he transformed into a multi-national group, and a cricket enthusiast who promoted the Fenner Trophy at the Scarborough Festival. He was the prime mover in the erection of the Sutcliffe Memorial Gates at Headingley.

HARBORD, WILLIAM EDWARD, who died at Harrogate on July 28, 1992, aged 83, was the second-last player born outside Yorkshire to play for the county before the club removed its barriers for the 1992 season. Between Harbord's last game in 1935 and Sachin Tendulkar's first appearance 57 years later, there was only W. G. Keighley (1947-51), who was born in Nice. Harbord was born in Rutland, and played 16 games as an amateur between 1929 and 1935. He was educated at Eton and Oxford, where he failed to win a Blue though he made a century in The Parks playing for Yorkshire in 1930. He did not match this form again. However, he was chosen for MCC's tour to the West Indies in 1934-35 under R. E. S. Wyatt. Although this team, like others to the newly-fledged Test-playing countries at the time, was nowhere near full England strength, this remains a mysterious selection. He left the tour in the middle to go on a private trip to Miami, returning in time to escort Wyatt to hospital when his jaw was broken by Martindale in the opening over of England's innings in the fourth and final Test at Kingston. He was employed as twelfth man in the first two Tests and in four matches on tour made 81 runs. Harbord made 512 first-class runs for an average of 18.28; his change bowling was hardly used. He later became chairman of John Smith's Brewery and served for more than 20 years on the Yorkshire committee.

HARTLAND, IAN ROBERT, who died of cancer in Christchurch, New Zealand, in March 1992, aged 52, played as an opening batsman and right-arm medium-pace bowler for Canterbury in 16 matches from 1960-61 to 1965-66. Representing New Zealand Colts in 1960-61 against a young MCC team (almost all of whom became Test players) he hit 62. His most successful season was 1964-65, when he averaged 37.00 and played a major part in Canterbury winning the Plunket Shield. He lost form the following season and did not play again. He finished with 613 career runs at 24.52. Hartland lived to see his son, Blair, open the innings for New Zealand against England on his Test début at Christchurch in January 1992.

HAYGARTH, NIGEL, who died on August 31, 1992, aged 60, was a devoted servant of the Cricket Society for 41 years, as a player for 30 of those years and an administrator for 20. He was elected to the executive committee in 1971 and became chairman in 1983, resigning only when he became seriously ill. He was in the Uppingham XI as a boy, heading the bowling averages in 1950 with 15 wickets at 12.86 and making useful runs.

HAYHURST, ALBERT, who died at Reading on November 8, 1991, aged 86, played in seven first-class matches as a professional for Warwickshire in 1934 and 1935. He was a right-arm fast-medium bowler and lower-order batsman. He played for Buckinghamshire from 1948 to 1953 and for Luton Town and Reading at centre-half in the Football League.

HEATLEY, JOHN, died of cancer on December 8, 1991, aged 56. He was elected to the Nottinghamshire Committee in 1967 when only 32 and gave unbroken service until 1989. He became the youngest chairman in the club's history in 1978, serving for five years. Heatley was a great enthusiast and moderniser who played a major role in the revamping of the county team and ground in the late 1970s and in bringing Phil Carling to Trent Bridge in 1978 with the then novel title of chief executive. He thus helped pioneer the modern pattern of cricket administration. He was well-known locally for his deeds as opening batsman and wicket-keeper for Radcliffe-on-Trent.

HOWA, HASSAN, the South African cricket administrator, died in Cape Town on February 12, 1992, aged 69. Hassan Howa came from a mixture of Indian, Turkish and Scottish stock that ought to have defeated even the South African government. It led to him being classified as "coloured" and forcibly removed from the centre of Cape Town to a distant suburb when the Coloured area, District Six, was demolished. For many years, he led the opposition to sporting apartheid in general and the South African cricket establishment in particular. He was president of the Western Province Cricket Board, the South African Cricket Board and the highly politicised umbrella organisation, the South African Council on Sport (SACOS), which developed the policy of No Normal Sport in An Abnormal Society. When the whites-only South African Cricket Association began talking to Howa's organisation in 1977 he withdrew from an agreement when, he said, it became clear he was required to act as a front man while the whites carried on more or less as before. His enemies, and there were plenty, said personal vanity was more of a factor. Ten years later, when he resumed talks with the head of white-led cricket, Ali Bacher, he was ousted as president of the Western Province Board and SACOS by militants. In his last few years, when he was suffering regular heart attacks and operated mainly from his armchair, he was regarded as a compromiser by left-wingers and as inflexible and outdated by the figures close to the African National Congress who helped South Africa resume its place in world cricket. He withheld his blessing from the new United Cricket Board, which he thought had been put together with indecent haste, and to the end refused to visit the ground at Newlands. He was an enthusiastic cricketer in his youth, but the politics inevitably overshadowed everything else later. He was courageous in the face of both injustice and illness and when the strife has passed into history he will be remembered with far more affection than venom.

INGLE, REGINALD ADDINGTON, who died on December 19, 1992, aged 89, was one of the many amateurs who appeared for Somerset between the wars. Unlike some, he justified his place and he went on to be captain from 1932 to 1937. Reggie Ingle came from a family of lawyers in Bath, was in the XI at Oundle from 1920 to 1922 and, even though he failed to get a Blue at Cambridge, became a Somerset player as a 19-year-old in 1923. He made a fifty in his first match, against Essex, but struggled after that until he made a hundred in each innings –

117 and 100 not out – against Middlesex in the opening game of 1928. He passed 1,000 runs both that year and again in 1932, his first season as captain. R. C. Robertson-Glasgow wrote that he needed to be angry to be at his best, in which case he could be "ripped from a pleasing suggestion of stylishness to the very suburbs of greatness". He was not often angry, however, and though he batted courageously against some of the fastest bowlers of his day, including McDonald and Larwood, never became a consistent run-getter. His easy-going temperament helped make him, among the professionals, a popular captain and, at first, a successful one: Somerset finished seventh in 1932, their highest position since 1919. The team mostly did less well after that and Ingle eventually resigned the captaincy, or was manoeuvred out of it, amid some bitterness. He played a few games in 1938 and 1939 but he rarely returned to the ground thereafter. Ingle made 9,829 runs in his career at 18.75, with ten centuries. He held 129 catches.

JUDGE, PETER FRANCIS, who died on March 4, 1992, aged 75, was a skilful fastish medium right-arm bowler who made a remarkable entry into first-class cricket as a 17-year-old in August 1933, only weeks after he had left St Paul's School. Middlesex gave him a game against Surrey at The Oval; he took five for 77 in 37 overs and four for 62, one of the best first-class débuts a bowler has ever had. In the next game, against Derbyshire at Lord's, he rapidly dismissed the first three batsmen and finished with an analysis of 20–10–27–5. Everything after that was an anticlimax. He only played a handful of matches the following year and then disappeared from the first-class game until 1939 when he became a professional for Glamorgan, taking 69 wickets, including eight for 75 against Yorkshire at Bradford. In the war, he was in the RAF and played some first-class cricket in India. He then returned to Glamorgan and continued to take useful wickets, including seven for 23 on a drying Cardiff pitch against Derbyshire, before injury forced him to retire in 1947. The previous season Judge had the bizarre experience of being dismissed for nought twice inside a minute. In the game against the Indians at Cardiff, he was bowled by C. T. Sarwate at the end of the first innings, at which point Glamorgan followed on. But with little time left, the captain Johnnie Clay decided to give the crowd some entertainment, so he waived the ten minutes between innings, and reversed his batting order. The batsmen then at the crease stayed out there and Sarwate bowled Judge again, first ball.

JULIEN, SHANE WILLAN, who took his own life in Barbados on January 25, 1992, aged 36, was a tall, powerful right-handed batsman and a useful medium-pace bowler. He was born in Grenada and came to England to study at Trent College, near Nottingham, where he had an outstanding season in 1974 with 546 runs (average 54.60) and 37 wickets at 9.56. In the 1980s he represented three different West Indian teams, Barbados in a one-day game, and his native Windward Islands and the Leeward Islands in the Shell Shield. He was also a member of the West Indies B team which toured Zimbabwe in 1983-84.

KAY, EDWIN, JP, who died on March 4, 1991, aged 81, was once described in the *Manchester Guardian* as "the Herbert Sutcliffe of the Lancashire Leagues". He made his début for Middleton when he was 15, against the bowling of S. F. Barnes, and never lost his place until he retired 30 years later; he scored a half-century on every ground in the Central Lancashire League. For some years he opened with his identical twin John, who batted capless; otherwise only the Middleton scorer could tell them apart. In 1959 Edwin succeeded John as secretary of the League and held the post for 31 years. He was asked to play for Worcestershire in the 1930s but declined after being told the pay was £3 10s a week. He was President of Lancashire in 1983 and 1984 and head printer of the *Manchester Evening News*.

LACEY, DONALD P., who died in Kingston, Jamaica, on November 26, 1991, aged 89, was a member of the Jamaica Cricket Board from 1929 to 1977 and President from 1969. He was also Hon. Secretary/Treasurer of the West Indies Cricket Board from 1945 to 1954. In 1948-49 he managed the first and highly successful tour of India by a full West Indies team. He was an honorary life member of MCC.

LOMAX, JAMES GEOFFREY, the Lancashire and Somerset all-rounder, died at Taunton on May 21, 1992, aged 67. Geoff Lomax was a dependable and versatile cricketer. He left first-class cricket in 1962, the year before the start of the one-day game in which he would probably have excelled. He could bat anywhere in the order, bowl right-handed at medium-fast and catch reliably. Lomax was born at Rochdale and started with Lancashire in 1949, making steady progress, was capped in 1952 but unexpectedly released the following year. He moved to the more relaxed cricketing climate of Taunton and in 1954 made a courageous hundred (his only other one was in 1962) against Frank Tyson in spite of an elbow injury. In 1958 he reached 1,000 for the first time and took 50 inexpensive wickets. He dominated the game against Nottinghamshire at Weston-super-Mare, making 80 and 53 as an opener and bringing off the hat-trick. He made 1,298 runs in 1959. The full details of Lomax's career are: 8,672 runs at 19.70, 316 wickets at 34.09 each and 238 catches. But figures cannot illustrate all the in-filling he did and his unselfish response to whatever the situation demanded, or the fact that he was a real gentleman.

McMAHON, NORMAN, who died on December 21, 1991, aged 69, was a long-serving officer of the Queensland Cricket Association. He was Chairman from 1967 to 1987 and a life member. He came to England on the ill-starred tour of 1977 as assistant manager to Len Maddocks.

McNAMARA, LISLE ERNEST, who died on July 21, 1991, aged 73, was an all-rounder and change bowler who played regular Currie Cup cricket for Griqualand West between 1936-37 and 1950-51. The highlight of his 35-match career was 119 out of a total of only 207 against Natal at Kimberley in 1946-47. It was his only hundred, though he made 80 not out against the Australian touring team in 1949-50. He scored a total of 1,387 runs at 23.50 and took 30 wickets at 37.72. His son also played for the province.

MAHMOOD HUSSAIN, the Pakistan fast-medium right-arm bowler, died in hospital at Harrow on December 25, 1991, aged 59. He formed part of a three-pronged seam attack fielded by Pakistan in her early years as a Test-playing country. Fazal Mahmood was the chief wicket-taker but Mahmood Hussain could be relied upon to keep the runs down, even on the most heart-breaking pitches. He was a willing servant but captains, to their cost, were often tempted to overbowl him. It was too much even for a powerful frame and towards the end of his Test career he was plagued by injuries. With the bat, he was a useful tailender and played an important part in two tight finishes, saving Pakistan from a Test defeat on each occasion.

Mahmood first attracted attention in 1949-50 when he took 16 wickets in the Universities final for Punjab against Sind. He was chosen for Pakistan's inaugural tour of neighbouring India in 1952-53. Pakistan won their second-ever Test, Mahmood's first, on a matting wicket at Lucknow and he took four for 92 in 42 overs in the match. He took eight more wickets in the remaining three Tests. He was one of the successes of Pakistan's first tour of England, in 1954, taking 72 wickets, and played an important role in the Pakistanis' improbable win at The Oval, helping Fazal Mahmood wreck England's first innings and, coming in at

No. 11, sharing two stubborn last-wicket stands of 27 and 24 that proved decisive in a game won by 24 runs.

His best Test figures, six for 67, came in Dacca when India visited Pakistan in 1954-55. Academic commitments then kept him busy for most of the next two years but he returned in fine form, taking eight for 93 for Karachi Whites against the Greens in 1956-57 and winning selection for Pakistan's first tour of the Caribbean in 1957-58. In the Third Test at Kingston he broke down after delivering five balls and had to watch Sobers make his 365 not out. But his four for 48 helped ensure victory at Dacca when West Indies returned the tour the following season. By the time he was picked for England in 1962 he needed conserving to bring out his best, but his captain Javed Burki pressed him into service too early too often. He broke down with a groin injury after the Third Test at Leeds and that spelt the end of his Test career. His last two victims were Colin Cowdrey and Ted Dexter.

In 27 Tests, Mahmood's 68 wickets were obtained at a cost of 38.64. In all matches he took 322 wickets at 25.07 and made 1,107 runs for an average of 10.74. A popular figure at Lord's in his retirement, he was much respected for his courage and determination on the field. He was a fine ambassador for his country at a time when Pakistan cricket was less contentious than it later became.

MAHONEY, RICHARD, BEM, died at Ipswich, Queensland, on June 20, 1992, aged 68. Ric Mahoney was the Queensland state junior coach who guided such prominent players as Greg Ritchie and Craig McDermott along the road to success. McDermott warmly acknowledged the help and encouragement he received from him during his long lean spell. Although he was included in the state squad in the 1940s, Mahoney never played a first-class match.

MAPPLEBECK, WALTER OLIVER, who died at Wellington, New Zealand, on April 27, 1992, aged 77, played in one first-class match for Canterbury in 1936-37 and three more in 1940-41 as a fast-medium right-arm bowler. He was not especially tall, but nevertheless generated real pace. He recalled, at his club's centennial celebration, a remark made to him by his captain Ian Cromb, after his first over at the top level: "This is a Plunket Shield match, not a Mothers' Union meeting!" Mapplebeck had the perfect reply, taking six for 43, five bowled. Four years later, he had another success with five for 59 against Wellington. In his four matches he captured 21 wickets at 21.76.

MARSHALL, ROY EDWIN, who died from cancer in a Taunton hospice on October 27, 1992, aged 62, may well have been the finest white batsman to have come from the Caribbean. His fame rests largely upon his 18 seasons with Hampshire from 1955 to 1972, when he made more than 27,000 Championship runs, and did so in a manner that shone like a beacon in a period when cricket was often drab and mean-spirited. He had all the strokes, though he avoided the hook and he always insisted on playing the spinners from the crease. He drove handsomely, and when a ball was short of a length, on or outside the off-stump, he would cut or slash with devastating power, sometimes even testing third man's catching ability.

Marshall was born on April 25, 1930, on a sugar plantation about ten miles outside Bridgetown. He was fortunate to be able to develop his game in Barbados, an island teeming with young cricketers, and in a cricketing family – his elder brother Norman also played Test cricket. Roy progressed so rapidly that he was chosen to represent the island when he was three months short of his 16th birthday. Another chance came in January 1949, when he secured his place. He made 149 against Trinidad at Bridgetown and followed this up in the second match with scores of 110 and 57. After hitting 191 against British Guiana in

February 1950, he was chosen as the third opening batsman and youngest member of John Goddard's team to tour England.

His tour got off to a cruel start: on the boat he contracted measles; then he heard that his father had died suddenly from a heart attack. In the circumstances, his 1,117 runs at an average of 39.89 was highly commendable; he had little chance of making the Test team. The most significant innings he played turned out to be the 135 he scored against Hampshire at Southampton. Desmond Eagar, the Hampshire captain, was impressed enough to send Marshall a contract two years later. By then he had played in four Tests, to no great effect, on West Indies' tour of Australasia in 1951-52. At the time, moving into county cricket meant giving up his Test aspirations; the combination of political uncertainty in the West Indies and the presence of the three Ws in the batting line-up is believed to have assisted his decision.

Marshall qualified for the county in 1955, made 2,115 runs and played the major role in lifting Hampshire to third in the table, at that time their highest ever. He even finished top of their Championship bowling averages, taking 25 wickets with off-spinners which he could have bowled to even greater effect had he been more interested. It took him a while to adjust to damp wickets and he was less successful in the wet summer of 1956, but he was fast acquiring a reputation as one of the most watchable cricketers on the circuit. In 1957 he hit a century in 66 minutes against Kent at Southampton, the fastest for Hampshire since 1927. He was chosen as one of the Five Cricketers of the Year in 1959 and in 1961 he had a stupendous season. He passed 2,000 runs (as he did in 1955 and every year from 1958 and 1962), went on to make 2,607 and Hampshire won their first Championship. "People said we didn't have any stars," said the captain, Colin Ingleby-Mackenzie. "But we had two major stars, Shackleton and Marshall." Sometimes the presence of Marshall was a disadvantage: Ingleby-Mackenzie was anxious to force results from games that were going nowhere but other captains were reluctant to set attainable targets when Marshall was around. With his partner Jimmy Gray providing staider contrast, Hampshire had the best opening partnership in the game.

He remained a highly effective county player for another decade. In 1966 he succeeded Ingleby-Mackenzie as captain and, despite the happy-go-lucky nature of his batting, actually proved a far more cautious leader than his predecessor. But he took an ageing team to fifth position twice and to second place in the Sunday League in its inaugural year, 1969. He had another sparkling season in 1970, his last year as captain, when he was 40. By then he had dropped down the order to accommodate Hampshire's new overseas star, Barry Richards. They had a good deal in common. Both might have played dozens of Tests but actually only played four each. Both were at their best against the most demanding bowlers but could get bored if the challenge was unworthy of them. Marshall had a very keen cricket brain and strong opinions on how the game should be played. It sometimes made him a difficult player to captain. It added depth to his own captaincy, to his coaching later on, and – after he had moved to Taunton – to his contributions as a member of the Somerset committee. He was an affable man and a good companion who for a time ran a pub in Taunton and regularly took the chance to go on the more sociable kind of cricket tours. He scored 35,725 runs, averaging 35.94, 30,303 of them for Hampshire, and 68 centuries. In 1972, he passed 1,000 runs as he had done every year since he qualified and, as a 42-year-old, made his third double-century, an awesome 203 against Derbyshire. He had a brilliant throw from the deep and held 294 catches. He took 176 wickets at 28.93. In his four Tests he made 143 runs and averaged 20.42. This was obviously no reflection of his real merit. Had he played for West Indies in 1963, when he was close to his peak and a mighty team was short only of a reliable opening partner for Conrad Hunte, he might have proved the point.

MARTIN, JOHN WESLEY, the New South Wales and Australian all-rounder, died from a heart attack on July 16, 1992, aged 60. He was one of the most popular post-war Australian first-class cricketers. Johnny Martin bowled left-arm googlies and hit hard and left-handed in the lower order. He played for New South Wales between 1956-57 and 1967-68, except for a single season (1958-59) when he tried his luck with South Australia. Soon after his début he was chosen to go on a short non-Test tour to New Zealand, where he took six for 47 in the third representative match in Auckland. In 1957-58, supported by sympathetic captaincy, he made further progress with the ball, but exceeded all expectations as a batsman by thumping his way to a total of 414 runs in the Sheffield Shield for an average of 51.75, second only to Norman O'Neill. In 1959-60, he took 45 Shield wickets and the following year made the Test team against Frank Worrell's West Indians. He was twelfth man for the Tied Test at Brisbane and was then picked at Melbourne, where he scored an uninhibited 55 batting at No. 10 and removed Kanhai, Sobers and Worrell in four balls in the second innings. He found it difficult to scale such heights in Test cricket again, and his eight Tests were spread over five series, culminating in South Africa in 1966-67. He was picked for the tour to England in 1964 but the wickets were too low and slow for him.

Martin was a country boy, one of ten children whose father ran the post office and general store at Burrell Creek near the northern New South Wales coast. He practised and played endlessly on concrete wickets and eventually joined the Petersham club in Sydney, travelling the 300 miles every weekend for three years on the overnight train until he received the call to play for the state. He took 293 wickets for New South Wales, 17 in Tests and 445 in all at 31.17. He scored 3,970 runs, averaging 23.77. Though he was small, he could give the ball a tremendous clout and was reckoned to have hit more than 160 sixes for Petersham. He was known as "Little Fave" and indeed was everyone's favourite both because of his style of play and his general cheerfulness. He went back to Burrell Creek and took over his father's store.

MINSHULL-FOGG, JOHN, who died on July 30, 1992, aged 71, was a driving force behind the launch of the National Village Cricket Championship in 1972, the final of which has now become a regular and enjoyable part of the Lord's season. He wrote *The Haig Book of Village Cricket*, published in 1972. He continued his involvement and was a regular and valued contributor to both *Wisden* and the *Daily Telegraph* on village, school, youth and club cricket.

MORILD, JENS AKSIL, who died on November 5, 1991, aged 78, was the eldest of five Danish cricketing brothers. He scored more runs than any other Danish batsman in his era – 16,082 with 26 centuries – and played his last match when he was 75. This marked the 25th anniversary of the Danish Forty Club and his own 25 years as president.

MOTT-RADCLYFFE, Sir CHARLES EDWARD, who died in November 1992, aged 80, was an enthusiastic cricketer who turned out regularly for Eton Ramblers and the Free Foresters. He was MP for Windsor from 1942 to 1970 and captained the Lords and Commons XI from 1952 to 1970. His political career peaked with a period as a Conservative Party whip after the war. He always retained his zest for cricket.

NELSON, PETER JOHN MYTTON, who died at Canterbury on January 17, 1992, at the age of 73, was an amateur who played in two first-class matches in 1938 and 1946, batting left-handed and bowling left-arm fast-medium. He played for Northamptonshire against Cambridge in 1938 and had a useful match with scores of 32 and 20 not out. Eight years later, he appeared for Kent against his old county.

NIELSEN, KURT, who died in Aalborg, Denmark, on March 26, 1992, aged 78, founded the Dansk Cricket-Forbund, the Danish Cricket Association, in 1953, was President for 18 years and President-emeritus until his death. His leadership took Denmark to associate membership of ICC in 1966, and he was made an honorary life member of MCC.

O'DALY, GUY NOLAN, who died on September 29, 1991, aged 83, was a right-arm fast-medium bowler. In his only first-class match, for Glamorgan against Cambridge University at Swansea in June 1938, he was out for nine, then broke down after sending down seven overs for 17 runs without taking a wicket. He took no further part in the match. He was sometimes known as Guy Daly.

OLIVER, JOHN ARCHIBALD RALPH, who died on February 24, 1992, aged 73, played in 152 matches for Bedfordshire from 1935 to 1961 and in one first-class match in 1951 for the Minor Counties against Kent at Canterbury, when he made 84 not out. He also appeared several times for Northamptonshire in the non-Championship year of 1945. He was a stylish right-handed opening batsman and dual purpose bowler (medium pace and off-spin) who, like many gifted amateurs, found Minor County cricket exactly to his taste. Oliver made more than 6,000 runs for Bedfordshire and took 230 wickets. He was Chairman of the County Club for 19 years and served on the executive committee of the Minor Counties Cricket Association for more than 30. He also played county hockey and soccer for the Corinthian Casuals.

O'REILLY, WILLIAM JOSEPH, OBE, who died in a Sydney hospital on October 6, 1992, aged 86, was probably the greatest spin bowler the game has ever produced. Bill "Tiger" O'Reilly was unquestionably one of cricket's great figures: as a player, as a character and later as a writer on the game. His cricket was proof that spin bowling was not necessarily a gentle art. He was 6ft 2in tall, gripped the ball in his enormous right hand and released it at a pace that could be almost fast-medium. It would then bounce ferociously on the hard pitches of his time and, on occasion, knock wicket-keepers off their feet. He bowled leg-breaks and, especially, top-spinners and googlies, backed up by an intimidating manner. Jack Fingleton said he was "a flurry of limbs, fire and steel-edged temper". It has been suggested that his action and the general commotion before delivery were born of a deep sense of frustration at not being able to bowl fast enough to knock the batsman down. Off the field, his gruffness was mitigated by his intelligence, erudition, wit and twinkling eyes.

He played 27 Test matches and took 144 wickets – 102 of them Englishmen and the vital wicket of Walter Hammond ten times – averaging 22.59. But his figures have to be judged by the fact that all but one of his Tests came in the 1930s, when other bowlers were dominated by batsmen to an unprecedented extent. No one ever dominated O'Reilly. Even when England made 903 at The Oval in 1938, he bowled 85 overs and finished with figures of three for 178. And before that, he had secured the Ashes by taking five for 66 and five for 56 at Headingley.

O'Reilly was born in White Cliffs in the New South Wales bush into a large Irish family on December 20, 1905. His father was a small-town schoolmaster and young Bill was above average at several sports, including tennis, athletics and rugby. Cricket was harder to arrange. According to Jack Fingleton in *Cricket Crisis*, the four O'Reilly brothers played with a gum-wood bat and a piece of banksia root chiselled down to make a ball. Since the others were older, Bill inevitably bowled more than he batted. The brothers also cuffed him a lot, possibly because he was starting to show them up. In 1917 the family moved to Wingello. When he played his first match for Wingello Juniors, the team walked to the opposition's ground seven miles away in Tallong, with their dogs chasing

Bill O'Reilly in the nets at Trent Bridge, 1938.

rabbits along the way. In 1919, he went to the high school in the larger town of Goulburn, where he concentrated on his athletics as much as his cricket. And when he went to the teachers' college at Sydney University in his late teens he was more interested in such events as the hop, step and jump, in which he held the state record. According to Fingleton's account he would probably have been lost to cricket had he not been asked to make up the numbers in a Sydney junior match and, with a method that at first made everyone giggle, whipped out the opposition.

In the summer of 1925-26, the young O'Reilly, by now an undergraduate at the teachers' college in Sydney University, met the man whose destiny was to be linked with his for ever. O'Reilly's own account of this remains a classic. He was passing through Bowral Station on his way home to Wingello for his summer holiday when he heard his name being called down the platform. He put his head out of the carriage window and was told to get out at once: Wingello were playing at Bowral and needed him.

"How was I to know that I was about to cross swords with the greatest cricketer that ever set foot on a cricket field? He didn't have it all his own way, let me tell you. Well, not for the first couple of overs, anyway." By the close of play, 17-year-old Don Bradman was 234 not out. The match resumed a week later, according to the local custom. "The sun shone, the birds sang sweetly and the flowers bloomed as never before. I bowled him first ball with a leg-break which came from the leg stump to hit the off bail. Suddenly cricket was the best game in the whole wide world."

In 1926-27 O'Reilly was chosen for the New South Wales state practice squad on the strength of one match for North Sydney. A year later he made his first-class début against the New Zealanders. But teachers in New South Wales work for the state rather than an individual school and the newly-qualified O'Reilly was despatched to three different bush towns. This may have cost him the chance of a Test against England in 1928-29 and, very probably, a tour in 1930. He was transferred back to Sydney in time for the 1931-32 season and after four more matches made his début for Australia. He performed quietly in a match in which Bradman scored 299 and Grimmett took 14 wickets, but he had arrived.

In the 1932-33 Bodyline series he took 27 wickets, without anyone noticing much, given what else was happening. In the series in England in 1934 he took 28 wickets, including seven in an innings twice. At Trent Bridge he won the match with seven for 54, achieved by what *Wisden* called "clever variation in flight and pace combined with spin off the worn turf". In blazing heat at Old Trafford, he transformed the game in an over which England began at 68 for no wicket. Walters was caught at forward short leg off the first ball, Wyatt bowled middle stump by the second and Hammond, after glancing a four off the third, was bowled by the fourth. Hendren and Leyland recaptured the initiative and England declared at 627 for nine but O'Reilly finished with seven for 189. He took 109 wickets on the tour, including nine for 38 against Somerset. He went back to Australia and suddenly announced his retirement. He had married in 1933, had a daughter and was anxious about his teaching career. However, Sydney Grammar School offered him a job that enabled him to play on. He toured South Africa in 1935-36 and took 27 wickets again, 25 in the great series against England in 1936-37 and 22 back in England in 1938, despite the unforgiving wickets ("dosed up to the eyeballs", said O'Reilly) of Trent Bridge and The Oval.

He played only one more Test, the one-off game against New Zealand at Wellington in March 1946 when he was already 40. The opposition barely beat his age: they were bowled out for 42 and 54 and O'Reilly took five for 14 and three for 19. It was the 11th time he had taken five in an innings in Tests. O'Reilly then began writing on cricket for the *Sydney Morning Herald* with a muscular, very Australian prose style flavoured with wit and imagery ("You can smell the gumleaves off him", he wrote of one country boy just starting with Queensland). Until he finally retired in 1988, he was as revered in Australian press boxes as he had been on the field. His opinions often came more from the heart than the head, especially if it was a question of attacking the selectors for playing safe and ignoring a young player, most especially a young leg-spinner. But he was consistent, loved quality and hated one-day cricket ("hit-and-giggle") which he generally refused to watch. He was hot-blooded and humorous which perhaps explains why his relationship with the cooler Bradman is believed to have been based on intense mutual respect rather than the profoundest form of Australian mateship. While Sir Donald walked the corridors of cricketing power O'Reilly was the rumbustious backbencher.

His last few years were rendered miserable by illness, including the loss of a leg. But he was blessed with a marriage to Molly that lasted 59 years. In his career he took 774 wickets at 16.60 and was successful at every level: playing for North Sydney and St George, he topped the Sydney Grade averages 12 times and took 962 wickets at 9.44. He took a wicket every 49 balls in his first-class career and it was said he never bowled a wide. His batting was left-handed, hard-hitting and occasionally stubborn (1,655 runs at 13.13); he never quite forgave himself for getting out at Lord's in 1934 when he might have saved the follow-on, in which case he rather than Verity would have had use of a rain-affected wicket. He did save the follow-on by making 30 not out at Old Trafford in the next Test. Future generations will have to judge the greatness of his bowling on the fragments of film that survive and the written descriptions, of which R. C. Robertson-Glasgow's may stand as definitive:

> As with those more florid opponents of legendary heroes, there seemed to be more arms than Nature or the rules allow. During the run-up, a sort of fierce galumph, the right forearm worked like a piston; at delivery the head was ducked low as if to butt the batsman on to his stumps. But it didn't take long to see the greatness; the control of leg-break, top-spinner and googly; the change of pace and trajectory without apparent change in action; the scrupulous length; the vitality; and, informing and rounding all, the brain to diagnose what patient required what treatment.

When O'Reilly died, Bradman said he was the greatest bowler he had ever faced or watched.

PANDOVE, DHRUV MAHENDER, was killed in a car accident near New Delhi on January 31, 1992. He was an attractive left-handed batsman, full of promise, and at 18 was already being tipped for Test honours. The Indian team observed, two minutes' silence for him before the start of play during the Fifth Test match against Australia in Perth. In November 1987, aged only 13, he made 94 for Punjab against Himachal Pradesh on his début in the Ranji Trophy – an astonishing achievement – and a year later he hit 137 against Jammu and Kashmir in his third first-class match. He became the youngest player ever to have reached 1,000 runs in the Ranji Trophy when he scored 170, his second century, against Services a few weeks before his death. His father, M. P. Pandove, was formerly captain of Punjab and is now secretary of the Punjab Cricket Association.

PAYN, LESLIE WILLIAM, who died on May 2, 1992, at Scottburgh, Natal, aged 76, was an all-rounder who played for Natal from 1936-37 to 1952-53 as a hard-hitting right-handed bat and slow-medium left-arm bowler. In his first season at senior level, he took eight for 89 on début against Orange Free State. That season he also made 103 against Transvaal and in doing so helped Dudley Nourse in a seventh-wicket partnership of 240. In 1946-47 he had match figures of seven for 64 in 63.2 overs against Orange Free State, which helped him win him a place on the 1947 tour of England. But he was unsuccessful on tour and though he twice did well against MCC in 1948-49, he never made the Test team. In 51 first-class matches Payn made 657 runs at an average of 14.28 and took 151 wickets at a cost of 25.78. He later became a hard-working organiser of cricket, especially in country areas, and took touring sides to Britain and South America.

PERKINS, ARTHUR LIONEL BERTIE, died on May 6, 1992 in Durban, South Africa, aged 86. Bertie Perkins played in six matches for Glamorgan between 1925 and 1933 as a right-handed amateur batsman. His highest score of 26 not out was made on his first-class début against H. D. G. Leveson Gower's XI at Swansea.

PITCHFORD, LEONARD, who died on May 10, 1992 in a nursing home at Clydach, South Wales, aged 91, was a right-handed batsman who played in two matches for Glamorgan in 1935 as a professional. He scored heavily for Monmouthshire in the Minor Counties championship, making 247 not out against Dorset at Abercarn in 1933, and in 1935 he hit 226 for Glamorgan Second XI against Berkshire, averaging 70.71 for the season.

POORE, EDWARD, who died after being bitten by a rat at Haifa, Israel, on June 29, 1991, aged 42, was a popular and eccentric spectator on the grounds of the county circuit. He spent his time at English cricket grounds when he was not roaming the world's trouble-spots. When he died, he was helping to run a hostel in the Arab quarter of Jerusalem. His ponytail and frequently bare feet successfully disguised the fact that he went to Harrow and was a great-nephew of Brigadier General R. M. Poore, who once scored 304 for Hampshire.

REES-DAVIES, WILLIAM RUPERT, QC, who died in January 1992, aged 75, was the outstanding public school bowler in 1935 and the fastest seen at Eton since G. O. B. Allen. He took 34 wickets at 14.73, reserving his best form for the big occasions. In two games against Harrow and Winchester he had 14 victims and added a further 15 with impressive performances in the representative matches at Lord's. After such high promise, a Blue at Cambridge in 1936 seemed to be a certainty. But the burden of a reputation and the general air of expectancy undermined his confidence. He played seven matches but he was dogged by trouble with his inordinately long run-up. He did not turn out in 1937 and was fortunate to play at Lord's in 1938; Cambridge, with one of the weakest attacks for many years, had conceded a series of huge totals and he did not escape heavy punishment himself. In 15 first-class matches he captured 33 wickets at a cost of 43.42. His batting was negligible and he only managed 37 runs in 23 visits to the crease. Rees-Davies lost an arm in the war and afterwards was often in pain. He became a QC and was a Conservative MP for 30 years. He regularly proposed measures to liberalise gambling and thus became known in the House, with varying degrees of affection, as "the one-armed bandit".

RIMINGTON, STANLEY GARNET, who died on November 23, 1991, aged 99, made 91 in his only first-class appearance at Launceston in February 1922 for Victoria against Tasmania.

ROCHFORD, PETER, collapsed and died in a pub in Stroud on June 18, 1992, aged 63. He had been suffering from cancer. Rochford had a varied career in cricket in which his enthusiasm never matured into sustained success. In the 1950s he showed enormous promise as a wicket-keeper. He played for Yorkshire Second XI in 1950 and 1951, then moved to Gloucestershire where he made his first-class début in 1952. By 1955 he had taken over from Andy Wilson as the regular keeper, even though he was not much of a batsman. He made 60 dismissals in both 1955 and 1956, when he helped the spinners, Sam Cook and "Bomber" Wells, take the county to third place. However, his career came to an abrupt close in 1957 following a clash with authority. He became a successful coach of young wicket-keepers, was a first-class umpire from 1975 to 1977, and wrote whenever he could for a variety of newspapers and cricket magazines. In his all too brief career he had 152 victims, 34 of them stumped.

SIMPSON, Col FRANK WILLIAM, DSO, OBE, died in August 1992, aged 83. He played in two first-class matches, as a right-handed opening batsman. In 1931 he captained The Army at Lord's against MCC, leading his side to victory by four wickets. In 1948 he scored 32 and 40 for Combined Services against Glamorgan at Pontypridd. He served with distinction in Normandy after the D-day landings.

SINGH, RAJA BHALENDRA, was born into Patiala's royal Sikh household on August 9, 1919 and died on April 16, 1992. He was the son of Bhupendra Singh, the legendary Maharaj of Patiala (who reportedly had 300 wives and concubines) and brother of the Yuvraj, Yadavendra Singh, who played in a Test match at Madras against England in 1933-34. Singh was given a trial in the Seniors' Match at Cambridge University in 1939, when his slow right-arm bowling produced a return of five for 40. On the strength of this he was included in the team against Northamptonshire. This was his only first-class match in England but in India he later played 12 matches for Southern Punjab and Patiala. A middle-order right-handed batsman, he made 392 runs for an average of 21.77, including 109 for Southern Punjab against Northern India at Patiala in 1943-44. He took 25 wickets at 27.00 apiece. He later became President of the Indian Olympic Association and was a member of the International Olympic Committee for 45 years.

SINGLETON, Sir EDWARD HENRY SIBBALD, died on September 6, 1992, aged 71. A right-handed all-rounder, "Tim" Singleton was a member of the Shrewsbury XI from 1937 to 1939, doing well enough to suggest that in normal circumstances he would have stood a good chance of a Blue. He did turn in some useful performances at Oxford in 1940, including six for 32 in the Freshmen's Trial and handy runs against an Anti-Aircraft XI. Singleton served as a pilot in the Fleet Air Arm from 1941 to 1945 and qualified as a solicitor in 1949. He was elected to the Council of the Law Society in 1961. In 1974 he became its youngest-ever President and, as was customary, received a knighthood the following year. Two of his brothers played for Worcestershire; his elder brother A.P. (Sandy) was captain in 1946.

SMITH, ARTHUR, who died on October 18, 1991, aged 79, sold scorecards and newspapers on Yorkshire grounds for more than 50 years. He was a much-loved institution at Headingley, where his gravelly voice shouting "Up-to-date scorecards" or "Green Final" was the inevitable background accompaniment to every great moment on the field.

SMITH, JOHN WESTWOOD ROWLEY, who died on December 12, 1991, aged 67, was a wicket-keeper and right-handed bat. Educated at Stoneygate and Repton, he played in two first-class matches for Leicestershire in 1950 and one in 1955. At Grace Road on his début, he had the character-building experience of keeping through a West Indian innings of 682 for two declared (651 on the opening day). There were only 18 byes but not much passed the bat.

SNAPE, MAURICE DESMOND, died on April 17, 1992, aged 68. Desmond Snape was a right-hand batsman who played twice for Derbyshire in 1949 but failed to score a run or take a catch. He was left not out on nought against Sussex at Ilkeston and was then out for a pair against Warwickshire at Edgbaston.

SOMERVILLE, CHARLES ROSS, died in May 1992 in Ontario, aged 88. "Sandy" Somerville was a leading member of the Canadian team which carried out an 11-match tour of England during July and August 1922 – "a delightful holiday", *Wisden* called it – and made 92 against Free Foresters at The Oval, the highest score for the Canadians all tour. He was for many years the best amateur golfer in Canada and won the US Amateur Championship in 1932.

SPITTEL, MALCOLM, who died in 1992 in Australia, aged 76, played as an all-rounder for Ceylon. He captained his school, St Joseph's College, his club, the Nondescripts, and his country – against MCC in 1954-55. When Vijay Merchant took a side to Ceylon in 1945, Spittel scored a sparkling 124 against a top-class attack.

STEVENS, ROY GILBERT, who died on October 6, 1992, at the age of 59, was a left-handed batsman who played regularly for the Royal Navy. His one first-class match was for Combined Services against Ireland at Belfast in 1962. He was secretary of Somerset from 1975 to 1979 and of Sussex from 1980 to 1983. He cut a slightly old-fashioned figure at a time when clubs were starting to appoint marketing-oriented men rather than ex-officers as administrators.

SURRIDGE, WALTER STUART, the famous Surrey captain of the 1950s, died suddenly on April 13, 1992 while visiting his company's factory at Glossop. He was 74. Stuart Surridge was the most successful leader in the history of the County Championship. In 1952 he took control of a side which was rich in talent but needed to feel the smack of firm government to do itself real justice. According to Alec Bedser, Surridge had the nerve to write in his diary after being confirmed as captain: "Surrey will win the Championship for the next five years." The correct figure was seven, the first five under Surridge.

The magnitude of Surridge's achievement can be appreciated by a glance at the county's record between 1952 and 1956. They won 86 games out of 140 and lost 20. Every year except 1953, when they slipped to 13 wins, they won more than half their 28 Championship fixtures. In 1955 they had a record which will probably never be approached – they won 23 games and lost the remaining five, drawing none. It was testament to his insistence on attack at all times, even to the point which cautious men might call recklessness.

Surridge possessed enormous enthusiasm and irrepressible energy, coupled with a strong streak of aggression. He combined something of the qualities of two of his predecessors as Surrey captain, the imaginative Percy Fender and the combative Douglas Jardine. As Sir Neville Cardus put it in a different context, "invisible arrows of antagonism darted across the field" when Surrey were playing and some opponents let it be known that they thought things had gone a bit far. It was significant that Surridge was never chosen to captain the Gentlemen against the Players. Indeed, Surridge fought to avoid losing his players for what he regarded as an irrelevant fixture.

Jardine himself, writing in the 1957 *Wisden*, pinpointed "inspiration" as Surridge's supreme gift. Above all, he insisted on a high standard of catching, setting a magnificent example himself in dangerous positions round the bat. With Peter May as his only high-class batsman, Surridge settled for the principle that bowlers and catches win matches. Collectively the batsmen gave May adequate support but it was the strength of an attack containing Bedser, Laker, Lock and later Loader, playing on helpful wickets at The Oval, that overpowered most teams.

One of the most significant of Surridge's successes was his ten-wicket win over Ian Johnson's team at The Oval in May 1956 – the first by a county over the Australians for 44 years. Laker took ten for 88 in the first innings to foreshadow his more famous triumph at Old Trafford later that summer. Two other extra-ordinary matches illustrated what a bold captain could do on uncovered pitches. Against Warwickshire at The Oval in 1953 play started 30 minutes late. Warwickshire were quickly hustled out for 45. Surrey raced to 146 with Surridge hitting three sixes himself. Then they routed the visitors in 70 minutes for 52. Surridge claimed the extra half-hour and won in a day by an innings and 49. A year later, on another wet pitch, Worcestershire were dismissed for 25 and 40, losing an innings and 27 runs in only five hours' play after Surridge had declared at 92 for three. This declaration was apparently regarded as insane by many of the Surrey players but Surridge had rung up for a weather forecast and was determined to finish the game.

He was never an autocrat, preferring at all times to share his ideas with his players. Before he became captain he had established a long-standing and informal relationship with the younger professionals, some of whom he would pack into his father's substantial Buick when they set off to play in club and ground matches. When captain, he abolished the antiquated accommodation and travel distinctions which then prevailed between amateurs and professionals – in spite of rumblings from the committee.

The name Stuart Surridge was famous in cricket long before he began playing. Surridge's grandfather was a batmaker (he also made violins) who set up his own business in the 1870s; Stuart Surridge bats were used by such players as Herbert Sutcliffe and Duleepsinhji. Surridge captained Emanuel School in 1935, appeared regularly for the Surrey Amateurs and first played for the county Second XI in 1937. He became a very useful bustling type of fast-medium bowler, once Alf Gover had smoothed out an awkward action, and was a hard-hitting tail-end batsman. In 1948, when Alec Bedser was playing in the Tests, he was entrusted with the new ball and took 64 wickets at 28.60 apiece, good enough to make his place secure. In 1951 he achieved his best performances with both bat and ball, 87 against Glamorgan and seven for 49 against Lancashire. In 267 first-class matches Surridge took 506 wickets at 28.89. His batting brought him 3,882 runs, average 12.94, and he held 375 catches (58 in 1952), many of them brilliant. He was chosen as one of the Five Cricketers of the Year in the 1953 *Wisden*. He toured Rhodesia with Surrey in 1959-60 and took a team to Bermuda in 1961. When his playing days were over, Surridge served for many years on Surrey's cricket committee and was President in 1982. His familiar presence round The Oval and the family business will be greatly missed. The company is now in the hands of Surridge's son, also called Stuart.

SWAROOP KISHEN, who died on November 21, 1992, aged 62, was one of the best-known Indian Test umpires and undoubtedly the most distinctive. He was an exceptionally tubby man who looked like Alfred Hitchcock, chewed betel-nut and generally lent an air of jollity to some highly-charged cricket matches. He umpired in 17 Tests, equalling the Indian record held by B. Satyaji Rao, between 1978-79 and 1984-85, and acquired a reputation for exceptional fair-mindedness among touring players. This, however, was dissipated in his last Test, at Bombay in 1984-85, when, often after interminable pauses for thought, he gave out several England batsmen in bizarre circumstances. He had been a wicket-keeper at Delhi University and worked in the Auditor-General's office.

TOOMEY, FRANCIS JOACHIM, who had succeeded Bill Ditchfield (whose death is also recorded in this section) as Otago's oldest surviving first-class cricketer, died on March 14, 1992, aged 88. Frank Toomey was a wicket-keeper who played three games in 1934-35 and 1935-36. Standing up to the stumps, he got a badly cut eye against MCC in 1935-36 when Joe Hardstaff snicked a rising ball into his face. His replacement, G. H. Mills, went on to play 55 times.

TURK, KENNETH, who died on May 3, 1992, aged 67, was President of Hartley Wintney CC in north Hampshire and had played for the club for 40 years. He went out to bat at No. 11 for the club Second XI against Shepherd's Bush, hit a six, then collapsed on the field and died.

VAN ROSSEM, Capt. WILLEM, MVO, who died on December 9, 1991, aged 71, was the Netherlands' representative on the International Cricket Council from 1975 to 1988. He was President of the Flamingos and worked untiringly for the development of Dutch cricket.

VAN TONDER, GIDEON JACOBUS, died on March 8, 1991, aged 84. Gielie van Tonder played two Currie Cup matches for Orange Free State in 1929-30, against Transvaal and Natal. He scored 0, 2, 0 and 0. He bowled against Natal and had figures of 14-1-64-0. He did not take a catch in either game. Free State lost them both, by an innings and 357 and an innings and 173.

VAN WEELDE, WALTER, died on November 20, 1992, aged 68. Wally van Weelde scored 13,920 runs and 27 centuries in Dutch cricket and was the outstanding batsman of his era. He had a reputation as the Dutch Denis Compton: for his prodigious scoring, his apparent insouciance and his zest for life. He played for the Netherlands 32 times and was part of the team that beat the Australians in 1964. He and his son Rob both captained the country and several other members of the family have been prominent in Dutch cricket.

WALTERS, CYRIL FREDERICK, who died on December 23, 1992, aged 87, had an extraordinary career. He began playing insignificantly for Glamorgan, moved to Worcestershire where his cricket was transformed, rose to captain England against Australia and then suddenly left the game forever. He is remembered as one of the game's great stylists; R. E. S. Wyatt, almost certainly the last man alive who could make such a comparison, thought his batting could only be likened to that of R. H. Spooner.

Walters was a doctor's son, born in Bedlinog, Glamorgan on August 28, 1905, and (like the only other Welshman to captain England, Tony Lewis) went to Neath Grammar School. He was picked for Glamorgan as a 17-year-old in 1923 and for the next five seasons played indifferently in a struggling side. He did score two centuries in 1926 and appeared to be establishing himself, but in 1927 he was interviewed by Worcestershire for the post of secretary, which offered clubs one way round the problem of paying amateurs. He was asked what he thought his batting average for Worcestershire could be. He said 50. At the time his career average was 17.

Under the qualification rules of the time, he was not allowed to play for his new county until 1930, but in the meantime he met E. J. "Tiger" Smith, the Warwickshire player who used to go down to Worcester to help with the coaching. Smith told him not to grip the bat so tightly and when Walters re-entered county cricket he was a different player. In 1931 he became captain and started opening regularly. In 1932 he was top of the county's averages and the following year he was able to keep the promise he made at his interview. He scored 2,404 runs and nine Championship centuries, opened in all three Tests against West Indies and was chosen as one of the Five Cricketers of the Year in the 1934 *Wisden*. In the Lord's Test of 1933, his first, he scored 51 and reportedly matched Walter Hammond stroke for stroke. He was even more successful on the tour of India

[*J. M. Wheeler; David Frith Collection*
Cyril Walters at Dean Park, Bournemouth, 1932.

under Jardine that winter, rounding off the series with 102 in the final Test at Madras.

Then, less than a year after his first appearance, he was captain of England against Australia, because he was senior amateur, when Wyatt withdrew from the Nottingham Test with a broken thumb. England lost by 238 runs when O'Reilly and Grimmett bowled them out for 141 on a worn pitch; Walters was the top scorer with 46. At Lord's, Wyatt was back in command and won the toss. Walters scored 82. "He played a pedigree innings," wrote Neville Cardus in the *Manchester Guardian*, "it was by MacLaren out of F. S. Jackson. His strokes were aglow with style; he made them swiftly and late. His wrists gave lustre to every movement of his bat. This was an innings fit for Lord's and a Test match."

Walters maintained form throughout that memorable series, finishing with 401 runs at 50.12; only Leyland scored more for England. He again passed 2,000 in all matches and shared a brilliant stand of 160 with Wyatt to give the Gentlemen their first win over the Players at Lord's in 20 years. Every honour in cricket appeared open to him. The following season he strained a tendon in his hand and missed some cricket. He appeared to be batting as well as ever and made 118 and 94 against Kent at the beginning of August. Then, suddenly, he resigned as Worcestershire's secretary and retired. His brief and glorious ascendancy had finished even more abruptly than it began.

The mystery about this decision has never wholly been unravelled. It is known that Walters had often felt unwell during long innings and had been very sick in India. He was newly married and it was said that his wife did not like cricket. Walters joined a wine business and later owned hotels. In 1986 he told *Wisden Cricket Monthly* that both P. F. Warner and P. A. Perrin, two of the three Test selectors, had pleaded with him to continue playing and hinted that he could captain MCC in Australia in 1936-37 – even that he could take his wife with him. He still refused. "I'd decided I couldn't go on playing forever," he said. However, he admitted the decision had been painful. "I wouldn't go anywhere near cricket because I was afraid if I did, I would start playing again. I never went near a match of any sort."

Though he occasionally went to Lord's later, he hardly ever visited Worcester until a few years ago when he rang the club and shyly asked if he might come and see them. After that, he returned several times, charmed everyone with his courtesy and good humour, and was made president of the club's old players' association. By then he was living back in Neath again, with a picture of himself cover-driving Bill O'Reilly over the mantelpiece. Until he died, he was still an imposing, upright man, immaculate in both his dress and his manners. He was still playing golf in 1992 and drove a Mercedes; he told a friend shortly before he died that he had just been cautioned by the police for driving at a speed well in excess of his age. He made 12,145 runs in first-class cricket at an average of 30.74 including 21 centuries. In his 11 Tests he scored 784 runs at 52.26, an average that stands comparison with the greatest players. When he died, R. E. S. Wyatt said: "Cyril Walters was a great friend of mine. He had tremendous charm, modesty, a sense of humour and enormous cricketing ability. He was a very good timer of the ball, very graceful, and could play every stroke except the hook. He made batting look very easy. The only player I can compare him to is Reggie Spooner. There's no modern player like him."

WELLINGS, EVELYN MAITLAND, died in hospital at Basingstoke on September 10, 1992, aged 83, his ashes by his own request being cast into the Channel. E. M. ("Lyn") Wellings was cricket correspondent of the now-defunct London *Evening News* from 1938 to 1973 and was one of the most idiosyncratic of all writers on the game. He was a very good games player at school and university, and was successful both as a batsman and as a bowler of off-breaks and off-cutters. For Cheltenham against Haileybury at Lord's in 1927, he took seven for 113, bowling unchanged, and then carried his bat through his school's first innings for 44 not out, though Cheltenham still lost. At Oxford he won a golf Blue (he later reached the last 32 of the English Championship). He failed to make much impression as a cricketer in his first year at Oxford but won Blues in 1929 and 1931, taking five for 118 in the first innings of the Varsity match in 1929 and five for 25 in the second innings in 1931. He did not play in 1930 because of loss of form, according to the official history, though it was widely believed, in a year when Oxford was riven by factionalism, that he could not get on with the captain, P. G. T. Kingsley. This sort of falling-out was to be more of a pointer to his future than his successes on the field.

He played four matches for Surrey in 1931 and 36 first-class matches in all, making a century for H. D. G. Leveson Gower's XI against Cambridge in 1933 and finishing with 836 runs at 20.39 and 108 wickets at 30.14. More significantly, he took a job with the *Daily Mirror* and then moved to the *Evening News* and, as Ian Wooldridge put it, "dipped his pen in vitriol". Wellings reported more than 200 Tests with a trenchancy that has never been matched. He attacked inefficiency on or off the field in indignant terms. He hated one-day cricket, overseas players in county teams, South Africa's isolation, faulty technique and, in later years, everything to do with the Test and County Cricket Board. He was right more often than many people cared to admit but the tone of his argument was so forceful that it usually upset more people than it won over. From 1945 to 1972 he also wrote on Public Schools cricket for *Wisden*, which he did with a magisterial sweep that no one else can ever have brought to the subject.

He retired to Spain but returned to live in Hampshire and to write unmellowed articles for *Wisden Cricket Monthly* until shortly before his death. Personally, he was cantankerous and his temper became legendary amongst his colleagues. Once the telephonist who was supposed to send over his reports for successive editions of that day's *Evening News* failed to appear at The Oval. Wellings wrote his reports as usual but let them pile up on the desk and then posted them. A lesser journalist would have been fired instantly. A greater one would have behaved differently.

WESTERMAN, PETER, who played nine matches for Surrey in 1949 to 1951 as an amateur, died in March 1992, aged 71. He was a fastish right-arm bowler and a tail-end batsman. In his first match, against Gloucestershire at The Oval, he took five for 51 in 22 overs. A year later he had figures of five for 49 against Cambridge University, including the wicket of Peter May, bowled for one.

WICKSON, WILLIAM D., died aged 77 on April 15, 1992, only two days after becoming President of Surrey. He was a retired headmaster, who had been much involved with youth cricket and Corinthian Casuals FC.

WRIGHT, RONALD CHARLES BARTON, died on July 3, 1992, aged 89. "Roy" Wright was a left-handed batsman who played ten matches for Northamptonshire as an amateur between 1923 and 1931, scoring 160 runs with a highest score of 56 not out. His brother, A. J. B. Wright, also played for the county but they were not related to the three other Wrights who appeared for Northamptonshire between the wars.

YEATES, SIDNEY FERGUS MACRAE, who died on March 19, 1992, at Auchenflower, Brisbane, aged 79, played in three first-class matches for Queensland, all at Brisbane in 1933-34. Fergus Yeates was a leg-break and googly bowler. He only took six wickets at 60.16, but his three for 47 against South Australia helped Queensland to victory after a run of 12 defeats and a draw in 13 first-class matches.

CRICKET BOOKS, 1992

By J. L. CARR

Publishers of cricket books may have joined house-agents and manufacturers in a continuing decline of trade. There must have been discouraging memos from Accounts to Editorial in 1992 so that only a handful of general publishers have ventured an investment. A couple of brave men, Mr Craven and Mr Cavanagh from Seascale and Manchester, have confidently put hands into pockets to publish their own books – and very worthwhile books they are.

By and large, the publishers have followed well-trodden paths, such as bringing out books about the prowess and performance of individual players, seasoned with a pinch of controversy to excite mention from sports editors – and thus quicken sales – and with a flavouring of family history and hobbies and so on to reassure us that cricketers too are human beings. One player, in fact, admits that, occasionally, he reads a book. There are collections of brief lives of players worthy of resurrection. There are the usual how-to-perform-better books. The largest section can be loosely classified as side-glances or footnotes to cricket history; most of them, whilst re-telling familiar tales of matches won or lost, do add welcome detail that was hitherto unreported. Except for the occasional passage where defective memory has shed its rosy glow or when literature has gone to the author's head, all these are non-fiction. But there are also a couple of novels.

The big sellers are biographies of the currently great. And here publishers are in luck: because a cricketer's prime comes early and they don't need to wait until their man has finished with life or life has finished with him. This has tremendous sales advantages. The biographee might utter some idiotic pronouncement during the book's selling-life or, later on, perform some extraordinary act (preferably of a criminal nature) to warrant a reprint. It is generally agreed that biographies do little more than masquerade as truth. They can be a goulash of conjecture, justification and regret. Best of all, they are a second chance for the chap to be quoted as saying what he should have said first time. As for autobiographies – if one-third lives may be called that – they are unlikely to be of surpassing interest because players are inhibited both by the libel laws and the likelihood of continually running into a verbal victim. In the case of a near-illiterate, there may also be a proper fear of what a ghost might say on his behalf.

However, since the widespread use of tape-recorders, autobiographies can at least sound authentic. And in **Mad Jack**, Don Wilson, the Yorkshire left-arm spinner, who played from the late 1950s to the early 1970s and became chief coach at Lord's, convincingly talks like himself. The book contains the usual tedious obligatory tales of off-the-field fun on overseas tours, an occasional reminder of long-gone *causes célèbres*, like the row between Wardle and his amateur captain, and the familiarities expected by fans – "Illy" and "Closey" (but nearly always "Geoffrey"). And – oh, dear – Peter O'Toole, an actor, has written a Foreword:

> O! Lord love you, this cricketer has yet again transmogrified the elegant loftiness of himself into a white and crook-backed, hilarious and snarling, hugely blue-eyed, gorgeous gargoyle . . .

and continues along these lines for four and a quarter pages.

The superscription on David Gower's **Gower – The Autobiography** is "by David Gower" and, in smaller type, "and Martin Johnson". How much is Gower and how much Johnson we may never know. So much space is given in explanation why he, Gower, is not the Gower many believe him to be that the book could fairly be described as an Apologia. The tone of the book is to ask: Why do I get caught off more wide deliveries than did Boycott? and to reply with other questions. Why can some chaps give up smoking more easily than others? Why are some men more single-minded than others? Why indeed! Surely Gower's 117 Test appearances mean he needs no excuses. Cricket is a game and a good game is a good spectacle. What sort of a game would it be for the rest of us if the batting list was a succession of Boycotts or, for that matter, Gooches?

And so to **Graham Gooch** by Ivo Tennant. This book concludes with 1991, Gooch's Year, his apogee. Under his captaincy and by his example (154 not out and batting through the innings) West Indies are defeated, Essex win the Championship, there is an OBE from the Queen, a Toyota from Toyota and, employed as Graham Gooch Ltd, a safe job in a recession. As Tennant points out, he may be that Essex Man Mrs Thatcher brought about. Here is proof that top ball, dart and cue players were the true economic successes of the era. No wonder that Gooch's father has transferred his vote from the Labour Party. And yet a schoolteacher once reported, "If Graham tried harder he could make a successful office-boy." It doesn't do to look back. At Jimmy Wilde, Wilf Mannion, George Hirst, Captain Webb. How meanly we rewarded our ancient heroes!

In **England Expects**, Mark Peel, head of political studies at Fettes College, reminds us of a batsman with many similarities to Gooch, the same determination and skill but with a more nervously poised temperament: Ken Barrington. This workmanlike book springs from a happy idea. Besides its account of Barrington's career (almost 32,000 runs in first-class cricket and none of them whilst wearing a tin hat), it glances back at Surrey during the great days of May, the Bedsers, Lock, Laker and, of course, Surridge. Like Hutton, Barrington came from a soberly secure family background and his prospective father-in-law insisted that he save £500 before consenting to his marriage to a charming school-teacher. Playing at Adelaide with the temperature over a hundred, Barrington greeted the incoming Titmus with a suggestion that they cut out quick singles. "Okay," said Titmus. "We'll cut out yours."

Apart from some over-narrow margins, **Len Hutton Remembered** is a handsome, well-designed book printed on paper allowing pictures to be integrated with relevant text. The plan of the book's begetter, Donald Trelford, was simple and satisfactory. He enlisted two accomplished writers, Michael and Simon Davie, to provide anecdotal background and an out-standing series of interviews, so that his book has a 30-page long biography, 75 pages of reminiscences by England players, 60 more from Yorkshire contemporaries and, finally, Bishop David Sheppard's eulogy delivered at Hutton's memorial service in York Minster. The photographs are many and telling. The one which told me most was a wartime picture of *Captains* Sutcliffe and Verity, *Sergeant-Major* Smailes and *Sergeants* Leyland and Hutton.

A Wayward Genius, by Greg Growden, is a less happy tale. L. O'B. Fleetwood-Smith, the pre-war Australian spin bowler, survives in the memory of many because of his impressive name, film-star looks, centre-

parting and the hiding he suffered in that 1938 Oval Test – 87 overs and one wicket (Hammond's) for 298 runs. This book tells the unhappy story of his final years, booze-drugged, derelict, barefoot and in rags. It is a startling aside to the brewers' advertisements defacing the apparel of current England players. Mercifully, a determined woman helped him back to decency.

In 1939, I travelled from Calcutta to Karachi, little knowing that I should see the day when a native of the sub-continent need not be a prince to become an international cricket celebrity. Well we all know now. And **Wasim and Waqar** confirms this. Their biography by John Crace looks at the pair's education and teenage years before going into a run-of-the-mill account of their playing careers. Because it does not include the 1992 tour of England, the book's chief interest may be its frank opinions, particularly on umpiring. For instance,

> All of Pakistan's umpires unofficially admit that Imran has been the one captain who has never asked them to "help him out". On one occasion the umpires walked into the Pakistani dressing-room and asked him for instructions. "You do your job, and we'll do ours," was the reply.

Like all players, I have recognised that umpires are wayward, misguided, perverse in their interpretation of the lbw law . . . but necessary, and certainly not calculatingly dishonest. Such a startling statement had a destabilising effect upon me similar to that upon some parsons confronted with the possibility of women priests. But publishers must insist on such astringent seasoning of biographies of men exceptional only in their skills with ball and bat which must yet pay their way in literature's market-place. Years later – and often not too many – unless something extraordinary has befallen them, most players disappear from public memory. And only a small band of ransomed souls, the Graces, Trumpers, Bradmans, Constantines, survive the fell hands of time and accountants. But some, like Alfred Gover, author of **The Long Run**, are saved from limbo by the length of their careers, particularly if, like him, they become proprietors of a cricket school. Almost sixty years after his death, Brigadier General Poore, **The Army's Grace**, is revived by Jeremy Lonsdale largely on the strength of his army career from 1884 (The Wiltshire Militia) to 1921 (The Jhansi Brigade), with its glimpses of the last imperial years. Mind you, he took time off in 1899 to make seven hundreds including a triple-century for Hampshire and to head the English batting averages.

For those cricketers whose fame is less likely to be perpetuated, the best bet is selection for a collection – **The Guinness Book of Test Cricket Captains** by David Lemmon, for example, a large, handsome book which lists and elaborates upon 69 England captains and almost 150 captains of other international cricketing countries. This not only is an informative reference work but bravely comes out with opinions as on Dexter: "he was a surprisingly dull and unenterprising captain. His judgment and handling of men . . . was often poor," and on Hutton, "he must rank with Jardine as among the very best of England captains".

Like local history and religion, cricket is a godsend to small publishers chary of seeking bank loans. The game usually can provide enough purchasers of low-priced books to keep them in business. Of these firms Spellmount of Tunbridge Wells is a prime example. In their series on counties they have ventured upon **Famous Cricketers of Middlesex** by Dean Hayes. And this kind of work usually can be relied upon to unearth nuggets of

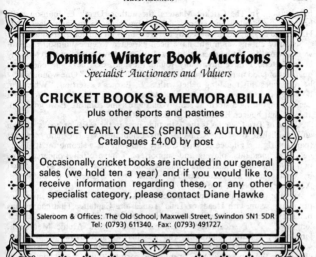

information. In **The Cricket Masters**, the author, Derek L. Johnson, tells how, as a schoolboy, he asked: "May I have your autograph please, Mr Hammond?" and was answered by the great man, "I am not Mr Hammond."

So dusty an answer might have been expected to cure Johnson of hero-worship for life, but he goes on to say: "When I have mixed in the company of cricketers, I have invariably found they possess the same endearing qualities of good nature, courtesy and, above all, modesty." One wonders how he reconciles this touching belief with S. F. Barnes's assertion: "When I'm bowling, there's only one captain. Me." Or A. C. MacLaren's reported declaration during a storm at sea, "Well there's one comfort. If we go down, at least that bugger Barnes will go down with us."

A Tale of Two Counties is the 25th and latest in the series of books written and published by Nico Craven. This celebrates West Country cricket (particularly the Gloucestershire County club) and is welcome for its lively details of incidents, players and supporters. I have often wondered how, in a 1990 three-day match, the immense total of 1,641 runs came to be scored by Glamorgan and Worcestershire – and at Abergavenny of all places. Abergavenny! Now I know.

Another doughty one-man publisher, Roy Cavanagh, has opened up a very promising seam with **Heads or Tails? Lancashire Captains**. That county has had some interesting incumbents like Hornby of "my Hornby and my Barlow long ago", P. T. Eckersley, Washbrook and, again, Archie MacLaren, labelled by Winston Churchill, who was his fag at Harrow, as "a snotty so-and-so". And this last takes one back to those expansive years when, after election to the captaincy, A. C. went off to earn his living as a schoolmaster, returning during his holidays to make 424 v Somerset.

Another exceptionally informative collection, this time targeted at Yorkshire readers, is **Six More Days of Grace**, by G. Derek West – fairly brief playing-biographies of Tom Emmett, Edward Barratt, George Ulyett, W. H. Scotton, Willie Bates and Robert Peel, with their secondary names, "A Joy for Ever", "Happy Jack", "Patience on a Monument", "The Dashing Young Yorkshireman", "A Rare Plucked One" and "The Forgotten Man". These romantic additions, echoing their Age, should encourage some sports editor to offer a small prize for embellishments similar to Ian Botham's "Guy the Gorilla" to attach to Gooch, Gatting and Gower.

Each of these six worthies has a Wanted Description. Robert Peel was short, stocky, 5ft 6in, 11 stone, an Anglo-Saxon type, with his hair parted on the left, falling in a soft cowlick over his forehead, with a neat non-soup-strainer moustache, a dour demeanour. He was unemotional in victory or defeat and did not sign his name on his marriage certificate, probably through modesty. I am an inconstant attender of county games and should welcome similar diverting identifications printed on the scorecards. Anyway, this book with its accompanying 31 steel engravings, and modestly priced at £9.95, is my nomination for Best Buy of the Year.

The appliance of science

In poverty-stricken pre-war days, my sole cricket book was an inheritance from an aunt, a farmer's wife, who annually performed a feat almost unknown at that time – after the corn harvest, she took a week's holiday: always the same week, always the same place – Scarborough for the Festival.

The book was W. G. Grace's *Cricket*. Perhaps because, in that long-gone year of 1891, he had the book field almost to himself, Grace's volume took in everything: the game's history, its records, curiosities, brief biogs., the evolution of bats and fifty pages given over to pronouncements on how to field, bowl and bat better. (The batting section begins, "I should like to say that good batsmen are born, not made; but my long experience comes up before me, and tells me that it is not so.") But nowadays we live in the Age of the Specialist and this year there are individual books on fielding, bowling and **Captaincy**, by Gooch. If you still wonder why Gower was not in the Indian tour party, reading between this last book's lines will answer you. And, by the way, for a book whose author is likely to meet many of those he mentions, this is franker than most offerings. Perhaps, having read once in his Sunday paper that Ted Dexter considered he had the charisma of a dead fish, the iron has lodged in Gooch's soul.

Anyway, he faces up to a problem that has perplexed village and county captains ever since the game was invented – what prime qualities should a captain have? In the dawn of cricket's history, it seems that sheer force of personality plus outstanding skill were the desirable attributes. But then, for a hundred years and more, a right social background ruled the roost. Gooch seems to understand this. He says: "I was well aware that I wasn't the 'right sort'." But then he explains why he is.

The Complete Book of Modern Fielding Practices, by Chris Stone, teaches by numerous diagrams and has suggestions for little games to smarten up stopping, returning and avoiding throwing an arm out. And it has two solemn thoughts: "Every cricketer spends most of his time in the field so he might as well learn to enjoy that" (Kepler Wessels) and "Every catch dropped is an extra batsman for the other side" (Sir Donald Bradman). The author of **The Bowler's Art**, Brian Wilkins, was a lecturer in pharmaceutical chemistry and can give a scientific explanation of what Ian Botham has been doing these many years perhaps without knowing how he did it. His book also has a marvellous cover and one of those evocative sub-titles so favoured by the Victorians – Understanding Spin, Swing and Swerve. And it fulfils one's hope with splendid statements such as "Stitching covers 30 per cent of a ball" and "A cricket ball is a blunt object pushing through air leaving a turbulent wake wider than the ball". Which of these pronouncements are original and which were quarried from the 76 books listed in his bibliography, the author doesn't say. I marvelled how anyone learnt to confound batsmen before its publication. How ever did Laker manage without it? And Rhodes. Need he have spent that rainy winter bowling, bowling, bowling against a haystack? And what would J. M. Barrie have made of it? It is said that his deliveries were so slow that, if one was not to his satisfaction, he had time to reach out and snatch it back.

What *is* a Googly? by Robert Eastaway, a lecturer in Creative Thinking, is for wives and girlfriends with a will to learn and for difficult quibblers like G. B. Shaw who, when told that a Test Match was in progress, asked what they were testing. The book answers questions like "What is the difference between cricket and baseball?" Answer: "Cricketers run in straight lines, not in circles." But it doesn't shy away from impossible speculation: "What goes through the mind of a bowler?" The sequence of the Glossary and Index is alphabetical – flannels/flight (noun)/flight (verb)/flipper/floater/follow on/footmarks/ . . . and so on.

Finally, in this how-to-do-it selection, there is **The Zen of Cricket** by Tony Francis, subtitled Learning from Positive Thought. "Zen" is not in my 1935 Concise Oxford Dictionary. In fact, it must be so new a word and with such hidden meaning that the author himself is reticent. Its gist may be "Briefly becoming someone less usual than oneself". Now, of course, like Horatius on the Bridge, such a transposition happens to most of us sometime or another: we discover ourselves in an abnormal situation and respond briefly with abnormal behaviour. But, as I said before, the book's author is not explicit in his definition and instead cites cases of Zen-in-action. Here are three from many.

> "Before sending down his second ball, Bill O'Reilly looked hard at me. I thought for a moment he was trying to hypnotise me." (Denis Compton) – Zen-inducement.

> Bernie Thomas [the physiotherapist] exhorted Close to put his shirt back on: "The lower-order batsmen were nervous enough without seeing the weals all over the chest." – Zen in reverse.

> "Bob Taylor and I tried to talk to him [Willis] between wickets or at the end of an over . . . We didn't feel we were getting through." (J. M. Brearley) – Zen-somnambulation.

This last took place during the 1981 Test at Headingley when Willis was in the midst of skittling Australia with his eight for 43. As was once said of Hutton whilst he was winning a 1954 Test: "You could speak to him and he wouldn't know you were there." Viva Zen! For my money, Mr Francis makes his case.

Sex and violence

Now, frustratingly for cricket anthologists, there is such a dearth of fiction featuring the game that it is a touching tribute to the tolerance of cricket-book purchasers that no publisher of anthologies has yet been sued for selling outworn material – Charles Dickens's good old Dingley Dell piece from *Pickwick Papers*, for instance, or Hugh de Selincourt's *The Cricket Match* and certainly (yes, certainly) that tiresome knee-capping bull of a blacksmith everlastingly charging over the brow of A. G. Macdonell's *England, Their England*. So what of novels like Mike Seabrook's **Out of Bounds** and John Parker's **The Twelfth Man**? Although both tell entertaining stories, neither is the real thing: cricketing is little more than scenery, their backdrop. The chief concern of *Out of Bounds* is a homosexual relationship between a school-master and a young player. It is a deeply felt story told with restraint but cricket is a sideline pursuit at which both the principal characters are competent practitioners. It has no more than marginal influence on the novel's plot.

Authors, preoccupied with their own problems, often forget that a publisher sinks or swims by his ability to buy manuscripts which he can turn into books which he can sell to booksellers, which booksellers can sell to book-buyers. And Parker's book, apart from its plot and its cricket content, is very interesting as a conscious effort (or so it seems to me) by a writer to give a publisher a book which he can take on as a safe bet. A recipe is scrupulously followed: Use personal experience. Choose a background you

understand. Grip your reader on page one and, preferably, line one. (Kingsley Amis recommended "A shot rang out." Parker goes for "Look Out!"). Keep things happening. Stir in some violence and offer safe sex for dessert. End it with a bang, the louder the better. Mr Parker's hero is a younger Bulldog Drummond serving an apprenticeship in county cricket. The duties of a twelfth man are detailed with feeling. And, now and then, one is reminded that a fair number of professional cricketers talk in a crude sub-language.

Ill-considered strong opinions, cries of rage, violent absurdities also make good reading. They invite dispute, raise hackles, sell newspapers. But their shelf-life is brief and soon we are asking what all the fuss has been about. And I believe that it is for this reason that cricket-book readers ultimately fall back upon facts, on what actually happened. Their pleasure is a personal interpretation of dates, places, names, scorecards of games lost, won or drawn. John Wisden knew this and his enduring *Almanack* is proof of it. And for such enthusiasts, **First-Class Cricket: A Complete Record 1938** cannot be recommended too vigorously. It is a 10in × 9in book, handsome out and in – attractively bound, and with well laid-out pages printed on paper which allows its many pictures to be sensibly integrated with the text. Its editors, the Secretary and Treasurer of the Association of Cricket Statisticians, have reprinted the scorecards of each 1938 (that *annus mirabilis*) game played by counties, universities, MCC, the Australian touring side and the first-class matches in India, New Zealand, South Africa and Australia. And there is a summary of each game's notable action. Does this sound like dollops of suet pudding? Well, these summaries have relieving ingredients. For instance, the outcome of one Test was swayed because "Hardstaff injured his hand with a car-spanner". And, for Middlesex versus Oxford University, "Mr E. W. Swanton made 13 in his first innings and 15 in his second". But shall we ever know why, against Australia, Mr W. H. V. Levett opened the Kent bowling with a bread roll?

Christopher Helm, Publishers, have added **The History of Leicestershire C.C.C.**, by Dennis Lambert, and **The History of Nottinghamshire C.C.C.**, by Peter Wynne-Thomas, to their county series. In the latter county's tale there is a brief aside, nowadays more relevant to the rugby union game:

> T. B. Reddick was asked by the Committee whether he wished to play as amateur or professional. He enquired which paid better. He played as an amateur.

And, in this same book, there is a portrait of a very ordinary-looking E. B. Alletson. Well, we all know of Alletson and his 189 at Hove in 1911. (John Arlott's account, **Alletson's Innings**, has been re-issued in 1992.) His rise to glory was very rapid – 90 minutes – after most of the crowd had left the ground. There is also a photo of a small reporter scarcely out of his teens, with an immense flat-cap, who is allowed on to the 1907 team picture. Now what befell young Mr G. Williamson? Did he rise to be sports editor or did he report the Alletson phenomenon and, muttering "Lord, now lettest thou thy servant depart in peace for mine eyes have seen thy salvation", did he immediately seek a place in a teacher-training college? The book doesn't say and even has left him out of the index.

And that "the spectators had left the ground . . ." I was a schoolboy when Nottinghamshire played Yorkshire at Headingley in 1932. My brother-in-law prophesied rain so we caught an early train back to Sherburn-in-Elmet. It

didn't rain and Hedley Verity took ten wickets for ten runs: this blighted my youth.

Leicestershire, perhaps because they have won the Championship only once, may need all the history they can get. Lambert gives this in great detail, even putting beyond doubt the pronunciation of that Pougher who, against Essex in 1894, made 109 and took 14 wickets for 89 runs. (It is "Puffer".) Those with a perverse taste for unimportant detail will welcome light now shed upon Alexander Skelding, who retired from fast bowling in 1931 but umpired until he was 71. This, of course, was that Mr Skelding who, at Sheffield in 1932 with Horace Fisher bowling left-arm slows, adjudicated in favour of two successive lbws. When the third ball struck the leg of W. T. Luckes of Somerset, he again raised a forefinger and (it is said) in tones of deep solemnity pronounced, "As God is my witness, that is OUT also."

From Minor to Major by Simon Hughes tells the story of Durham's first season in the County Championship from the inside. **Durham: Birth of a First-Class County**, by Ralph Dellor, proclaims the county's coming out and its pre-history. We can now cancel out an inscription once seen on the north border of a map of Yorkshire: "Serious cricket is not played north of this line." Apart from celebrated exiles like Milburn, Stoddart, Willey and Cecil Parkin, the County always had less-known notables who stayed at home. Take A. A. W. Mewburn, captain in Durham's first county match in 1882. Against Northumberland, he took seven for 31 and made 47 not out of a winning total of 75 for six. And Robert Percival's throw of 140 yards 2 feet, circa 1882, is still unsurpassed.

The Illustrated History of County Cricket, by Eric Midwinter, published in association with Bass Brewers, is a big good-looking book which treads already well-mapped ground. Its foreword, entitled Beer, Glorious Beer, lists celebrated players who have retired into hotel and pub management, rhapsodising, "Cricket and its spectacle have, on the whole, found a decent harmony in their pastime and the foaming beverage." That "on the whole"? Can it be a hint of doubt? May perhaps there be another list – of blighted hopes and broken careers because of too enthusiastic attachment to "the foaming beverage"?

It always is cheering to come across a real addition to the game's history like **Cricket at Scarborough** by Ian Hall, which gives the North-Eastern Railway credit for nudging in a future cricket-week by opening its line from York to the fishing port in 1845. Apart from a history of the town's own club and the photographs of hundreds of local, Yorkshire and England players, town notabilities, officials, patrons like Lord Hawke and Leveson Gower, the book has revived an ancient controversy.

In 1945, an Australian, Cec Pepper, struck a ball from Eric Hollies over the roofs of three-storeyed boarding-houses surrounding the ground and into Trafalgar Square. He claimed to be the only man to have done this. *Wisden* said he wasn't and merely repeated a Scarborough President's (Mr C. I. Thornton) 1886 rejection of a ball from I Zingari's A. C. Steel. Mr Pepper said: Not so. Mr Thornton's high-flier flew *between* a gap in the boarding-house terraces.

My aunt was not present on either occasion.

J. L. Carr is a publisher and author whose works include the cricket novel A Season in Sinji *and* Carr's Dictionary of extra-ordinary English Cricketers. *His novels* A Month in the Country *and* The Battle of Pollocks Crossing *were both short-listed for the Booker Prize.*

BOOKS RECEIVED IN 1992

GENERAL

Bannister, Jack **Jack in the Box** (Macdonald/Queen Anne Press, £14.99)

Bryden, Colin **Return of the Prodigal:** South Africa's Cricketing Comeback (Jonathan Ball Publishers, PO Box 2105, Parklands 2121, South Africa, Rand 79.95)

Cotter, Gerry **The Test Match Career of Sir Richard Hadlee** (Robert Hale, £15.95)

Coward, Mike (photographs by Michael Rayner) **Caribbean Odyssey:** Australia and Cricket in the West Indies (Simon and Schuster, Australia, 20 Barcoo Street, East Roseville, NSW 2069, no price given)

Crace, John **Wasim and Waqar:** Imran's Inheritors (Boxtree, £15.99)

Craven, Nico **A Tale of Two Counties** (from the author, The Coach House, Ponsonby, Seascale, Cumberland CA20 1BX, £5.35)

Eagar, Patrick **Caught in the Frame:** 150 Years of Cricket Photography (Collins Willow, £19.99)

Eastaway, Robert **What *is* a Googly?** The Mysteries of Cricket Explained (Robson Books, £6.99)

Francis, Tony **The Zen of Cricket** (Stanley Paul, £14.99)

Gooch, Graham with Patrick Murphy **Captaincy** (Stanley Paul, £15.99)

Gover, Alfred **The Long Run** (Pelham Books, £15.99)

Gower, David with Martin Johnson **Gower – The Autobiography** (Collins Willow, £14.99)

Griffiths, Peter and Wynne-Thomas, Peter **The Australian Tour to England 1948** (Limlow Books, St Peter's Hill, Litlington, Royston, Herts. SG8 0QF, £7.50 + 50p p&p)

Growden, Greg **A Wayward Genius:** The Fleetwood-Smith Story (ABC Enterprises, GPO Box 9994, Sydney, NSW 2000 or 54 Portland Place, London W1N 4DY, $A19.95)

Hall, Ian with John Found **Cricket at Scarborough:** A Social History of the Club and its Festival (Breedon Books, £14.95)

Hignell, Andrew **A 'Favourit' Game:** Cricket in South Wales before 1914 (University of Wales Press, 6 Gwennyth Street, Cathays, Cardiff CF2 4YD, £17.95)

Johnson, Derek L. **The Cricket Masters, 1880-1991** (Spellmount, £4.50)

Johnston, Brian **Someone Who Was** (Methuen, £14.99)

Lemmon, David **The Guinness Book of Test Cricket Captains** (Guinness, £14.99)

Lloyd, David **G'day ya Pommie b......** (Weidenfeld & Nicolson, £10.99)

Lonsdale, Jeremy **The Army's Grace:** The Life of Brigadier General R. M. Poore (Spellmount, £12.95)

Midwinter, Eric **The Illustrated History of County Cricket** (Kingswood Press/Bass, £17.99)

Murphy, Patrick (photographs by Paul Barker) **The Rothmans Book of Village Cricket** (Bloomsbury, £16.99)

Peel, Mark **England Expects:** A Biography of Ken Barrington (Kingswood Press, £14.99)

Pollard, Jack **The Complete Illustrated History of Australian Cricket** (Pelham Books, £20)

Randall, Derek **Rags:** The Autobiography (Sport-in-Print, 3 Radcliffe Road, West Bridgford, Nottingham NG2 5FF, £14.99)

Rayvern Allen, David **More Cricket Extras** (Guinness, £6.99)

Roebuck, Peter **Tangled up in White** (Hodder & Stoughton, £14.99)

Scott, Neville and Cook, Nick **England Test Cricket: The Years of Indecision 1981-92** (Kingswood Press, £14.99)

Tennant, Ivo **Graham Gooch: The Biography** (Witherby, £15.99)

Trelford, Donald **Len Hutton Remembered** (Witherby, £16.99)

West, G. Derek **Six More Days of Grace** (Darf Publishers, £9.95)

Wilson, Don with Stephen Thorpe **Mad Jack** (Kingswood Press, £14.99)

FICTION

Lewis, Simon **One Hell of a Season** (from 1E Severn Road, Diep River, Cape Town, Rand 16)

Parker, John **The Twelfth Man** (Andre Deutsch, £13.99)

Seabrook, Mike **Out of Bounds** (GMP Publishers, PO Box 247, London N17 9QR, £7.95)

COUNTIES

Cavanagh, Roy and Lorimer, Malcolm **Heads or Tails? Lancashire Captains 1865-1991** (from Roy Cavanagh, 20 Hyde Road, Worsley, Manchester M28 5SE, £6 + £1 p&p)

Dellor, Ralph **Durham: Birth of a First-Class County** (Bloomsbury, £14.99)

Hayes, Dean **Famous Cricketers of Middlesex** (Spellmount, £15.95)

Hignell, Andrew **A Who's Who of Glamorgan County Cricket Club 1888-1991** (Breedon Books, £14.95)

Hughes, Simon **From Minor to Major:** Durham's First Year in the Championship (Hodder & Stoughton, £14.99)

Lambert, Dennis **The History of Leicestershire C.C.C.** (Christopher Helm, £17.99)

Lorimer, Malcolm and Ambrose, Don **Cricket Grounds of Lancashire** (ACS, 3 Radcliffe Road, West Bridgford, Nottingham NG2 5FF, £4)

Woodhouse, Tony **A Who's Who of Yorkshire County Cricket Club** (Breedon Books, £14.95)

Wynne-Thomas, Peter **The History of Nottinghamshire C.C.C.** (Christopher Helm, £17.99)

STATISTICAL

Association of Cricket Statisticians **Cricket Matches 1850-1854** (ACS, 3 Radcliffe Road, West Bridgford, Nottingham NG2 5FF, £7.50)

Barnard, Neil **Walter Hammond:** His Record Innings-by-Innings (Famous Cricketers Series – no. 13) (ACS, 3 Radcliffe Road, West Bridgford, Nottingham NG2 5FF, £4.50)

Frindall, Bill **A Tale of Two Captains:** England v West Indies 1991 (Boundary Books, £38 + £2 p&p, limited edition)

Ledbetter, Jim ed. with Peter Wynne-Thomas **First-Class Cricket: A Complete Record 1938** (Limlow Books, St Peter's Hill, Litlington, Royston, Herts. SG8 0QF, £16.95 + £2 p&p)

Semmens, Lee **Frank Tarrant:** His Record Innings-by-Innings (Famous Cricketers Series – no. 11) (ACS, 3 Radcliffe Road, West Bridgford, Nottingham NG2 5FF, £4)

Wilde, Simon **Ranjitsinhji:** His Record Innings-by-Innings (Famous Cricketers Series – no. 12) (ACS, 3 Radcliffe Road, West Bridgford, Nottingham NG2 5FF, £3)

TECHNICAL

Ferguson, Doug **Cricket: Technique, Tactics, Training** (Crowood Press, £8.99)

Mehra, Rajen and Puri, Narottam **Cricket Laws** (Marine Sports, 53 Gokhale Road (North), Dadar, Bombay 400 028, Rs 50)

Sharangpani, Dr R. C. **Fitness Training in Cricket** (Marine Sports, 53 Gokhale Road (North), Dadar, Bombay 400 028, Rs 50)

Stone, Chris **The Complete Book of Modern Fielding Practices** (Robert Hale, £14.95)

Wilkins, Brian **The Bowler's Art** (A&C Black, £12.99)

REPRINTS AND UPDATES

Arlott, John **Alletson's Innings** (J. W. McKenzie, 12 Stoneleigh Park Road, Ewell, Surrey KT19 0QT, no price given) *Reprint of 1957 edition, with supplementary material*

Blofeld, Henry **On the Edge of my Seat** (Stanley Paul, £8.99) *Reminiscences, updated to cover World Cup*

Powell, William **The Wisden Guide to Cricket Grounds** (Stanley Paul, £12.99) *Enlarged and updated to cover Durham*

Ross, Alan ed. **The Kingswood Book of Cricket** (Kingswood, £16.99) *New version of the Cricketer's Companion, first published 1960*

John Wisden's Cricketers' Almanack for 1893 (reprint from Willows Publishing, 17 The Willows, Stone, Staffs. ST15 0DE, £38 plus £1 p&p UK, £3 overseas)

HANDBOOKS AND ANNUALS

Armstrong, David ed. **Minor Counties Cricket Annual and Official Handbook** (ACS, 3 Radcliffe Road, West Bridgford, Nottingham NG2 5FF, £3.75)

Australian Broadcasting Corporation **ABC Australian Cricket Almanac, 1992** (ABC Enterprises, GPO Box 9994, Sydney, NSW 2000 or 54 Portland Place, London W1N 4DY, no price given)

Bader, Nauman and Abid Ali Kazi **Cricket Yearbook 1990-91** (Cricketer International, Asian edition – no price or details)

Bailey, Philip comp. **ACS International Cricket Year Book 1992** (ACS, 3 Radcliffe Road, West Bridgford, Nottingham NG2 5FF, £6.50)

Edwards, Neil ed. **Club Cricket Conference Handbook 1992** (Club Cricket Conference, 361 West Barnes Lane, New Malden, Surrey KT3 6JF, £4 to affiliates)

Frindall, Bill ed. **Playfair Cricket Annual 1992** (Headline/Queen Anne Press, paperback, £2.99)

Hatton, Les comp. **ACS First Class Counties Second Eleven Annual** (ACS, 3 Radcliffe Road, West Bridgford, Nottingham NG2 5FF, £3.50)

League Cricket Conference Handbook (Rob Sproston Sports, Nantwich, £1.50)

Lemmon, David ed. **Benson and Hedges Cricket Year** (Headline, £19.99)

Lockwood, Richard ed. **The Official TCCB Cricket Statistics** (Lennard/Queen Anne Press, £13.99)

Miller, Allan ed. **Allan's Australian Cricket Annual 1992-93** (from Allan Miller, PO Box 974, Busselton, WA 6280, $A30 or Sport-in-Print, 3 Radcliffe Road, West Bridgford, Nottingham NG2 5FF, £14)

National Cricket Association Handbook 1992 (NCA, Lord's Ground, London NW8 8QZ, £4)

Sproat, Iain ed. **The Cricketers' Who's Who 1992** (Lennard, paperback, £10.95)

COUNTY YEARBOOKS, 1992

Glamorgan (Glamorgan CCC, £4)
Hampshire (Hampshire CCC, £5)
Kent (Kent CCC, £4.50)
Northamptonshire (Northamptonshire CCC, £6.50)
Somerset (Somerset CCC, £5)
Surrey (Surrey CCC, £5)
Yorkshire (Yorkshire CCC, £6 + 75p p&p)

SOUVENIRS

Lord's: the Official Pictorial Souvenir (MCC, Lord's Ground, London NW8 8QN, £2.50)
Champions 1991: The rise and rise of Essex CCC (Byline Publishing, 347 Billing Road East, Northampton, £2.50)

PERIODICALS

The Cricketer International (monthly) editorial director Richard Hutton (Beech Hanger, Ashurst, Tunbridge Wells, Kent TN3 9ST, £1.95)
Cricket World (monthly) ed. Bill Frindall (The Club Cricketer, 2a Chelverton Road, London SW15 1RH, £1.95)
The Googly (fanzine, frequency uncertain) (5 The Meades, North Cheam, Surrey)
The Journal of the Cricket Society (twice yearly) ed. Clive W. Porter (from Mr P. Ellis, 63 Groveland Road, Beckenham, Kent BR3 3PX, £3)
Red Stripe Caribbean Quarterly ed. Tony Cozier (Cozier Publishing, PO Box 40W, Worthing, Christ Church, Barbados)
Wisden Cricket Monthly ed. David Frith (25 Down Road, Merrow, Guildford, Surrey GU1 2PY, £1.90)

MISCELLANEOUS

Raiji, Vasant **Parsika:** The Pioneers of Cricket – exhibition notes (K. R. Cama Oriental Institute, Bombay, no price given)

LOCAL HISTORIES

Mayne, P. J. **Godalming Cricket 225 not out** (from Simon Crowther, High Down, South Munstead Lane, Godalming, Surrey GU8 4AG)
Twort, Richard **100 Years of Uphill Castle Cricket Club** (The Uphill Struggle Marketing Co., 7 South Road, Weston-super-Mare, £9.95)
West, Alan **One Hundred Years of the Ribblesdale Cricket League** (from J. Cross, Moorlands, 54 Stoney Bank Road, Earby, Colne, Lancs. BB8 6RX, £4.95)

THE CRICKET SOCIETY LITERARY AWARD

The Cricket Society Literary Award has been presented since 1970 to the author of the cricket book judged as best of the year. The 1992 award, worth £750 and sponsored by the *Daily Telegraph*, went to Mark Peel for **England Expects:** A Biography of Ken Barrington.

THE CRICKET PRESS IN 1992

By MURRAY HEDGCOCK

When the England captain Graham Gooch published a book in 1992 with the anodyne title "Captaincy", his collected thoughts on David Gower's attitude to Test cricket created much fuss. They overshadowed other significant chapters, notably one headed simply: "Dealing with the media". Long before his marriage difficulties got into the papers at the end of 1992, Gooch had made his distrust of the press plainer than any other England captain. But he summed up: "We players shouldn't bleat when we are fairly criticised by the media as long as it's not libellous or untrue. We're there to be shot at and we enjoy the perks when they come along."

This was an unexpected declaration from an honest player, whose rise to become not just a top-class batsman but also an outstanding captain has been one of the cricketing stories of the past decade. It is a story that has been duly recognised and reported, perhaps beyond the expectations of those who thought that by the 1990s cricket would be struggling for space in the newspapers. For years a theory existed that cricket benefited from artificial media attention sponsored by ageing sports editors brought up on football in winter and cricket in summer and geared to split their year between them. Once these old-timers were replaced by a new generation of executives (ran the argument) cricket would slide into the background, to be replaced by squash and golf and fun runs and American football.

It has not happened that way at all. The 1992 Test series between England and Pakistan generated more headlines for a longer period than cricket has received for many years. Whether all the publicity was good for the game was open to question. Although they lost the series, Gooch's England largely escaped criticism for once. Cricket boiled over in the papers when Aqib Javed boiled over at umpire Roy Palmer in the Old Trafford Test. After that, the papers revelled in attacking Pakistan's on-the-field behaviour and attitude to umpiring.

Then Micky Stewart, the England manager, demonstrated at The Oval how not to handle media interest in a delicate question, by hinting at wrong-doing but refusing either to say how he thought Pakistan swung the ball or to defuse interest with a properly diplomatic choice of words. After that, the dispute over alleged ball-tampering by Pakistani bowlers rose in a crescendo. As it did so, Britain's two main sensationalist tabloid papers vied with each other by headlines that kept getting bolder, both in their lettering and their accusations against the Pakistan bowlers. "NAILED" cried *The Sun* after The Oval. Two weeks later, after the ball was changed at the Lord's one-day international it was: "GOT 'EM BY THE BALL".

Two days later the *Daily Mirror* topped this by printing what it claimed was "The story they all wanted – World Exclusive – How Pakistan cheat at cricket" in which the England player Allan Lamb said he was "blowing the whistle . . . Wasim Akram and Waqar Younis have been getting away with murder all summer". Lamb was promptly fined £5,000 (later reduced) by the Test and County Cricket Board. It was cynically assumed that Lamb had been paid considerably more than this by the *Mirror* but the parties denied that any payment had been involved at all. The paper called the

affair "Lambgate" and ran it until "Lambgate: Day 35" by which time the readers must have been bewildered.

The most ferocious attack on the tourists came, however, in the staider *Sunday Telegraph*, written by Simon Heffer, not a cricket correspondent but a regular commentator on the game. Under the headline "The pariahs of cricket", he damned everything to do with the Pakistani game in what was probably the most savage diatribe on the cricketing mores of another country since Bodyline 60 years earlier. Heffer called on the TCCB to "tell the Pakistanis there will be no further tours by or to England . . . until there is clear evidence of a dramatic change of attitude in Pakistani cricket. The alternative is to have cricket continually degraded by the Pakistanis". The Pakistani High Commissioner in London called the piece "odious and objectionable".

Meanwhile, two former England captains defended the Pakistanis in their very different ways. Mike Brearley wrote perceptively in *The Observer* about the way mutual suspicion had developed over many years between Pakistani players and English umpires: "I would defend the English umpires against charges of intentional bias; but I would not be completely sure that there was no trace of subliminal prejudice." Geoff Boycott, in *The Sun*, was blunter on the question of whether Wasim and Waqar cheated: "Quit squealing. These two could have bowled us out with an orange."

However, the nine Pakistani reporters covering the tour awoke on many mornings to attacks on their country. Fareshteh A. Gati of *The News*, Karachi, one of the few top-level women cricket correspondents, said in conversation that at home she criticised her national team freely but on tour found herself responding defensively to or counter-attacking what was in the English papers. "In Pakistan when Border's side had troubles, I spoke out against our umpiring, but here this season, it's my country right or wrong, and I do believe my country is being hard done by."

Ms Gati was capable of counter-attacking fairly vigorously, as in her report from the Headingley Test where she turned round the normal attacks by English touring teams not only on Pakistani umpiring but also on Pakistani food: "The Pakistanis, who cannot stomach the lunches served by the clubs at cricket grounds and often send out for samosas, chicken tikkas and doner kebabs, will now have to send out for lemon lozenges to soothe their sore throats after the appeals turned down by Kitchen and Palmer. They appealed at least 19 times for leg-before decisions and even if you minus some as being very optimistic there were five shouts which would have changed the state of the scoreboard. So much for fair play and integrity."

It took, of all papers, *The New York Times*, to put everything in reasonable perspective. Under the headline "Cricket's hot summer: Where are the gentlemen?" William E. Schmidt wrote: "For a game that has become over the centuries a kind of symbol for the British spirit of fair play, civilised behaviour and good sportsmanship, England and cricket have both seen better seasons than the summer of '92."

Schmidt went on: "Part of the problem is that many of cricket's most enthusiastic supporters regard the game as if it were frozen in time, suspended in a kind of Edwardian panorama . . . but increasingly at the international level cricket has become something of a blood sport, performed by highly-paid athletes before rambunctious crowds whose nationalist passions sometimes get the better of them."

In the year when Germany played at Lord's for the first time, the Munich newspaper *Suddeutsche Zeitung* also carried a lengthy feature on the game and the writer, Gerd Kroncke, displayed a very fair grasp of the subject. Oddly, he had more trouble with names than atmosphere, calling the batsman who complained about ball-tampering "David Lamb" and suggesting that it was all like the Bodyline row sparked by the England captain "Gerald Jardine". Poor Allan; poor Douglas.

CRICKETANA IN 1992

By DAVID FRITH

Despite the assertion by a famous City financier that "with many extreme manias, investors lose about 90 per cent of their investment after the bubble has burst", collectors of cricket books and memorabilia would appear to be on firm ground still. Whatever uncertainty was sensed in the previous *Wisden* survey, in 1981, this particular bubble remains intact. Not only does calculated investment in rare books and ephemera seem sounder than it is in most other areas – even real estate – but the ranks of collectors and indeed of dealers, both up and down-market, are swelling continually.

The "association" factor seems always to guarantee high prices. In 1992, the full set of *Wisdens* owned by the late John Arlott caused a saleroom frenzy when Christie's sold it in London. Broken up to ensure the greatest realisation, and thus inevitably scattered among a wide range of buyers, the run made £22,160, on top of which the customary buyers' premium of ten per cent (subject to VAT) had to be paid. The first three issues, 1864-66, bound together, alone fetched £6,800. Among the residue of the Arlott collection (which he had much reduced when he retired in 1980), letters (1959-61) between him and Basil D'Oliveira, whom the commentator fatefully helped find a new life in England, made as much as £800, their historical significance recognised. Another two-sided gem in this sale was a three-page manuscript tribute to Arlott by Neville Cardus, which fetched £600.

Such sales give the pursuit extra impetus, but nothing in 1992, or any other year, has been as spectacular as MCC's "offloading" in 1987, when, as part of its bicentenary celebrations, the club auctioned off almost 1,000 lots of material considered surplus, raising almost £250,000. The MCC sale attracted buyers who craved some article or other bearing the MCC label, and this fuelled many stupendous bids. The revenue is being used for renovation and the occasional prize acquisition such as the oil of the 9th Earl of Winchilsea, a founder of MCC. The club has a problem familiar to most archivists and collectors: shortage of storage space. Otherwise, it might be seen as a major competitor to big-purse buyers such as Melbourne Cricket Club and the Bradman Museum.

From the vast quantities of cricketana changing hands each year through dealers and auction sales spring some exceptional attractions. Victor Trumper's inscribed silver pocket-watch has sold for almost £1,000. George Hirst's assorted hand-me-downs sparked some determined bidding too, his

1897-98 Australian tour contract making over £700. When Sir George ("Gubby") Allen's effects were put into auction early in 1992, his Bentley motor-car (£8,000) went for £2,000 less than a bundle of 24 very candid letters written by the England amateur fast bowler to his parents during the stormy 1932-33 "Bodyline" tour of Australia. These were bought by the State Library of New South Wales and therefore remain open to public scrutiny. An album containing over 300 snapshots by Allen on that tour extracted a dizzy £8,500 from a private buyer.

Apart from *Wisdens*, standard reference books – *Scores & Biographies* for instance – grow steadily and reliably in value, as do autographs and pictorial delights such as Chevallier Tayler's *The Empire's Cricketers* (1905). *Vanity Fair* caricatures enjoyed raging increases prior to a levelling-off in price, with the print of E. W. Dillon of Kent suddenly emerging as a supreme rarity with a 1992 price-tag of £2,000 or so, up to 25 times the cost of others in the series.

Modern prints and limited editions continue to proliferate, and cricketers are now alert to the potential value of their old bats and caps when their benefit years come along. But old is sought-after and famous association is an assurance of abiding value. For most collectors, there is no bubble to be burst. They are simply aiming to have something meaningful and tangible by which to assert their devotion to cricket. Or, as Australian writer (and collector) Phillip Adams has written: "To hoard anything is to have a feeling of comfort and well-being. Like a squirrel with its nuts, like Kerry with his billions, you are consoled."

CRICKET EQUIPMENT IN 1992

By NORMAN HARRIS

The most recent meaningful innovation in the bat world occurred in 1974, with the arrival of a bat that other manufacturers dismissed as a gimmick. One said it had not got "a cat in hell's chance". That bat was the Gray-Nicolls Scoop. In fact, the Scoop has maintained its popularity and is today the only non-orthodox (if it can still be so described) bat for which there is a substantial demand in the shops.

The rash of innovatory bats which followed has, however, seemed to justify the term gimmick. There was a period when steel or carbon fibre in bat handles was all the rage. One offering was the "Reaper", a bat with many small holes which were supposed to reduce air resistance – and were said to emit a faint whistling noise as the air passed through them. The whistling could, however, have come in hope from the principal user of this bat, Bob Willis. Other efforts were more serious. The Scoop (which applied the principle of perimeter weighting) had cast doubt on how much wood was necessary in the "hump" of the bat, and where exactly that hump should be. Bats emerged with the traditional square shoulders trimmed away so that they resembled an inverted claret glass. Others were "bull-nosed", with the hump concentrated right at the bottom; others "sharky", with the hump higher up.

Such bats are still being made, but the demand is not great. More recently, energetic marketing by Classic Bat of Bristol has created publicity for a bat which seems to have something in common with the Reaper. This is the double-sided bat. Being of the same thickness throughout, it looks more like a plank than a bat. Classic maintains that it has spread the bat's middle, or "percussion point", over the entire surface. Others would argue that it has no middle. Despite the publicity for the bat when it was approved – hesitantly – by MCC during the 1991 season, batsmen in the first-class game have shown little interest in using it. In 1992, Classic produced the "Butterfly" bat. The name comes from the stain that appears in some willow – a mark that, while unattractive to some, does not affect performance. Classic made a virtue of the stain, offering the Butterfly bat at a record recommended retail price of £199.95.

Otherwise, innovation now seems to be focusing on protection. Batting gloves are still not managing to cut the game's high incidence of broken fingers and the idea of a fixed hand guard is increasingly attracting attention. Prototypes for at least three were put forward last year and – like the double-sided bat – gave MCC a problem. The guardians of the game wished to help batsmen avoid injury, but they were worried about allowing unsightly additions to the bat – additions which, possibly, could change the balance of advantage between bat and ball. Another problem was that, while Law 6 is precise about the dimensions and material of the blade, it has almost nothing to say about the handle. In the end, MCC's decision was to withhold approval of a guard which attached to the top of the blade but to allow another that attached to the handle.

All the designs are inspired by sword handles, the approved item, from Duke's, being given the slight misnomer of Scabbard. All, too, effectively increase the area of bat and/or glove off which the batsman may be caught –

especially an item that is a solid wire cage, clipped to the handle, which protects the batsman's hands so completely that he needs no gloves. It therefore comes down to a question of whether hand protection had a higher priority for a batsman than the slightly increased risk of getting out. The use of such guards may well be restricted to batsmen with chronic injury problems, or who are recovering from a hand injury.

Finally, one must put bat prices into perspective by asking what customers actually pay (as opposed to the list price of fancy bats). When *Wisden* last examined this subject, in 1985, the top bat in the shops was selling at £75. Now, the figure is £150 (or £199.95 for the Butterfly bat). If that seems a dramatic jump one should add that in some well-established shops the same top-of-the-range bat may be obtainable at no more than £90. For the grassroots cricketer, a real bargain is more attractive than innovation.

CRICKET GROUNDS IN 1992

Six grounds in Britain were used for first-class cricket for the first time in 1992, the most since 1946. This sudden spurt of growth in the game's geographical spread was entirely due to the promotion of Durham. Pending the construction of their new headquarters at Chester-le-Street, Durham are moving their home games round the county in the manner pioneered by Essex. They used five different grounds in the Championship – Darlington, Durham University, Gateshead Fell, Hartlepool and Stockton-on-Tees – and the existing ground at Ropery Lane, Chester-le-Street for the match against the Pakistanis.

The University ground, also known as the Racecourse, was the first, the largest and the most imposing: like Worcester, it is overlooked by the cathedral; like St John's, Antigua, it is right next to the prison. Stockton Cricket Club's home at Grangefield Road, which served ham and pease pudding sandwiches, was considered the friendliest; Park Drive, Hartlepool the prettiest; and Eastwood Gardens, Gateshead Fell, had the best wicket. The Feethams ground at Darlington had the largest sightscreen in England: the white-painted back end of Darlington Football Club's stand. The only venue used by Durham that had any background in first-class cricket, Northumberland's headquarters at Jesmond, Newcastle-upon-Tyne (which has staged matches between Minor Counties and touring teams), was given just one Benson and Hedges match in 1992 and has been taken off the fixture list for 1993 because the playing area is too small.

There was only one other new venue on the county list in 1992: the tree-lined company ground owned by the Dowty Group at Arle Court, Cheltenham, where Gloucestershire played their two home Benson and Hedges matches while Bristol was being rebuilt. However, 1992 saw the successful return of first-class cricket to Park Avenue, Bradford, a ground that means much to Yorkshire cricket and which had been unused since 1985 when the ancient but soulful pavilion was demolished. Derbyshire took a County Championship match to the Rutland Ground at Ilkeston for the first time since 1980. Folkestone and Hinckley vanished from the scene, both for the foreseeable future. The season saw what appeared to be the last matches at Dean Park, Bournemouth, which had staged first-class games since 1897, because Hampshire were unable to agree financial terms with the owner. Prospects of cricket returning to the town looked bleak.

The general policy of most counties is to concentrate cricket in their main centres. However, despite the reduced fixture list for 1993 caused by the switch to four-day cricket, the effects have been less drastic than some feared. There will be 153 Championship matches in 1993 as opposed to 198 in 1992; they will be played on 52 grounds instead of 58.

Liverpool returns to the list after a year's absence due to Lancashire's rotation of their out-grounds and Bournemouth is the only apparently permanent casualty. The others to lose out are Uxbridge, Coventry and Worksop, which are all expected to return in future; Blackpool and Southport, which are definitely due back in 1994; and Neath, which will stage Glamorgan's match against the Australians rather than Surrey. This will be regarded by the locals as a very fair exchange. Somerset's festival at Weston-super-Mare was unexpectedly reprieved in the autumn following an injection of council cash. However, like most towns which have traditionally staged a full-scale cricket week, Weston's allocation has been cut to one Championship and one Sunday League match. Some have had even worse cutbacks – Chesterfield is down from three matches to one – and in order to keep the rest of Yorkshire happy, Leeds is scheduled to stage only two Championship matches.

Gloucestershire will not be playing a Sunday League match at Swindon in 1993 and Northamptonshire's once-lucrative game at Tring, which was hastily dropped last year because of loss of sponsorship, has also been abolished. There is only one completely new venue on the 1993 fixture list. The annual Glamorgan match sponsored by Taff Ely Council has been switched from Ynysangharad Park, Pontypridd, where there were problems caused by restrictions on car parking as well as pronunciation. It will be staged instead at the cricket and rugby club at Pentyrch between Pontypridd and Cardiff.

WORLD CUP, 1995

The International Cricket Council decided on February 2, 1993, that the sixth World Cup, to be held in 1995, will be staged in India, Pakistan and Sri Lanka. ICC was deadlocked between the sub-continent's bid and one from England, until the Test and County Cricket Board withdrew their bid in exchange for a promise that England would hold the seventh competition in 1998.

INDEX TO CRICKETERS

Note: For reasons of space, certain entries which appear in alphabetical order in sections of the Almanack are not included in this index. These include names that appear in Test Cricketers, Births and Deaths of Cricketers and individual batting and bowling performances in the 1992 first-class season.

c. = catches; *d.* = dismissals; *p'ship* = partnership; *r.* = runs; *w.* = wickets.
* Signifies not out or an unbroken partnership.

Atkins, P. D. (Surrey):– Hundred on début, *98*.

Atkinson, D. St E. (WI):– Test captain, *195*, *209*; Test hundred, *197*; All-round in Test, *155*; 347 for 7th wkt v Australia, *115*, *148*, *198*; Test p'ship records, *198*, *210*.

Attewell, W. (Eng.):– 1,951 w., *124*; 100 w. (10), *123*.

Aymes, A. N. (Hants):– 10 d. in match, *129*.

Azad, K. (Ind.):– Handled the ball, *116*.

Azhar Abbas (B'pur):– 10 d. in match, *129*.

Azharuddin, M. (Ind.):– Test captain, *186*, *201*, *216*, *224*; 3,168 r. in Tests, *143*; 2,000 r. since 1969 (1), *103*; 4 hundreds in succession, *100*; 11 Test hundreds, *138*, *187*, *202*, *217*, *223*, *225*; Hundred on Test début, *136*, *187*; 5 c. in Test innings, *157*; Test p'ship records, *188*, *223*, *224*.

Aziz Malik (Lahore Div.):– Hit the ball twice, *117*.

B

Babington, A. M. (Glos.):– 8 w. in innings, *246*.

Bacchus, S. F. A. F. (WI):– 250 v India, *137*, *212*.

Bacher, A. (SA):– Test captain, *193*.

Badcock, C. L. (Aust.):– 325 v Victoria, *95*; 1 Test hundred, *168*.

Badcock, F. T. (NZ):– Test p'ship record, *209*.

Baichan, L. (WI):– Hundred on Test début, *138*, *215*; Double-hundred and hundred, *99*; 2 hundreds in match (2), *99*.

Baig, A. A. (Ind.):– Hundred on Test début, *138*, *187*.

Bailey, T. E. (Eng.):– All-round, *126*, *127*, *155*; 28,641 r., *107*; 2,290 r. in Tests, *141*; 1,000 r. (17), *104*; 1 Test hundred, *184*; Slow batting in Test, *147*; 2,082 w., *124*; 132 w. in Tests, *151*; 100 w. (9), *123*; 10 w. in innings, *118*; 10 w. or more in Test (1), *182*; Test p'ship record, *191*.

Bairstow, D. L. (Eng.):– 1,099 d., *130*; 255 d. in Sunday League, *764*; 11 c. in match, *128*; 7 c. in innings, *128*.

Baker, R. P. (Surrey):– Highest avge in English season, *105*.

Bakewell, A. H. (Eng.):– 1 Test hundred, *180*; 8 c. in match, *130*.

Bakker, P. J. (Hants):– Career figures, *858-9*.

Balan Pandit, B. (Kerala):– 410 for 4th wkt, *114*.

Balaskas, X. C. (SA):– 1 Test hundred, *208*.

Bali, P. (Jammu & Kashmir):– Handled the Ball, *116*, *930*.

Banerjee, S. N. (Ind.):– 249 for 10th wkt, *115*.

Banks, D. A. (Worcs. and Warwicks.):– Hundred on début, *98*.

Bannerman, C. (Aust.):– Hundred on Test début, *137*, *168*.

Bannister, J. D. (Warwicks.):– 10 w. in innings, *118*.

Baptiste, E. A. E. (WI):– Test p'ship record, *182*.

Barber, R. W. (Eng.):– 1 Test hundred, *166*; Test p'ship record, *191*.

Barbour, E. P. (NSW):– 270 for 8th wkt, *115*.

Bardsley, W. (Aust.):– Test captain, *165*; 2,469 r. in Tests, *142*; 53 hundreds, *102*; 6 Test hundreds, *168*, *194*; 2 hundreds in same Test, *139*, *168*; Carrying bat in Test, *145*; 397 for 5th wkt, *114*; Test p'ship record, *195*.

Barker, G. (Essex):– 1,000 r. (15), *104*.

Barlow, E. J. (SA):– 2,516 r. in Tests, *142*; 43 hundreds, *102*; 6 Test hundreds, *177*, *194*; 341 for 3rd wkt v Australia, *148*, *195*.

Barlow, R. G. (Eng.):– Hit the ball twice, *117*; 4 hat-tricks, *121*.

Barnard, P. H. (N. Tvl):– 264 for 1st wkt, *929*.

Barnes, S. F. (Eng.):– 189 w. in Tests, *151*; 106 w. v Australia, *173*; 104 w. in South African season, *123*; 49 w. and 34 w. in series, *151*, *213*; 17 w. in Test, *119*, *150*; 14 w. in Test, *150*; 10 w. or more in Test (7), *171*, *178*; 9 w. in Test innings, *149*; 8 w. in Test innings (2), *149*.

Barnes, S. G. (Aust.):– 3 Test hundreds, *168*, *201*; 405 for 5th wkt v England, *114*, *148*, *170*; Test p'ship records, *170*, *202*.

Barnes, W. (Eng.):– 1 Test hundred, *166*.

Barnett, C. J. (Eng.):– 25,389 r., *107*; 48 hundreds, *102*; 2 Test hundreds, *166*; 11 sixes in innings, *112*.

Barnett, K. J. (Eng.):– Captain of Derbyshire, *315*; 38 hundreds, *102*; Carrying bat in 1992, *145*; Test p'ship record, *192*.

Barratt, E. (Surrey):– 10 w. in innings, *117*.

Barrett, J. E. (Aust.):– Carrying bat in Test, *145*.

Barrick, D. W. (Northants):– 347 for 5th wkt, *114*.

Barrington, K. F. (Eng.):– 31,714 r., *107*; 6,806 r. (avge 58.67) in Tests, *141*, *144*; 2,111 r. v Australia, *173*; 1,039 Test r. in year, *140*; 1,000 r. (15), *104*; 76 hundreds, *101*; 20 Test hundreds, *144*, *166*, *176*, *180*, *184*, *187*, *190*; 256 v Australia, *137*, *166*; Highest avge in English season (2), *105*; 64 c. in season, *131*; 369 for 2nd wkt

G

Metson, C. P. (Glam.):– 7 d. in innings, *128.*

Michau, M. (E. Prov.):– 258 for 4th wkt, *929.*

Middleton, T. C. (Hants):– First to 1,000 r. in 1992, *245;* 221 in 1992, *244;* 267 for 1st wkt, *245.*

Milburn, C. (Eng.):– 2 Test hundreds, *180, 190;* Test p'ship record, *182.*

Miller, G. (Eng.):– Slow batting in Test, *147.*

Miller, K. R. (Aust.):– 2,958 r. in Tests, *142;* 41 hundreds, *102;* 7 Test hundreds, *169, 197;* 170 w. in Tests, *152;* 10 w. or more in Test (1), *172;* All-round in Tests, *154, 155;* Test p'ship records, *195, 198.*

Mills, J. E. (NZ):– Hundred on Test début, *138, 185;* Test p'ship record, *185.*

Mills, P. T. (Glos.):– 5 w. for 0 r., *119.*

Milton, C. A. (Eng.):– 32,150 r., *106;* Highest aggregate in English season, *105;* 1,000 r. (16), *104;* 56 hundreds, *102;* 2 hundreds in match (2), *100;* Hundred on Test début, *138, 184;* 758 c., *131;* 63 c. in season, *131;* 8 c. in match, *130.*

Milton, W. H. (SA):– Test captain, *175.*

Miran Bux (Pak.):– Test début at 47, *162;* Oldest Pakistan Test player, *163.*

Mitchell, A. (Eng.):– 44 hundreds, *102;* 4 successive hundreds, *100.*

Mitchell, B. (SA):– 3,471 r. in Tests, *142;* 8 Test hundreds, *177, 208;* 2 hundreds in same Test, *139, 176;* 6 c. in Test, *158;* 299 for 7th wkt, *115;* Test p'ship records, *178, 208.*

Mitchell, F. (Eng. and SA):– Test captain, *175, 193.*

Mitchell, T. B. (Eng.):– 100 w. (10), *123;* 10 w. in innings, *118.*

Mitter, J. (Bengal):– 231 for 9th wkt, *115.*

Modi, R. S. (Ind.):– 1 Test hundred, *213;* 410 for 3rd wkt, *114;* 371 for 6th wkt, *114.*

Mohammad Farooq (Pak.):– Test p'ship record, *220.*

Mohammad Hasnain (Kar. Blues):– 12 w. in match and 8 w. in innings, *930.*

Mohammad Ilyas (Pak.):– 1 Test hundred, *219;* Test p'ship record, *219.*

Mohammad Iqbal (Muslim Model HS):– 475* v Islamia HS, *241.*

Mohammad Yusuf (R'pindi):– Handled the ball, *116.*

Mohol, S. N. (M'tra):– 4 w. with consecutive balls, *120.*

Mohsin Kamal (Pak.):– Hat-trick in 1991-92, *930.*

Mohsin Khan (Pak.):– 2,709 r. in Tests, *143;* 1,029 Test r. in year, *140;* 7 Test hundreds, *190, 204, 223, 226;* Handled the ball, *116;* 426 for 2nd wkt, *113;* Test p'ship records, *191, 205, 227.*

Mohsin Mirza (Kar. Whites):– 13 w. in match and 8 w. in innings, *930.*

Mold, A. W. (Eng.):– 1,673 w., *124;* 100 w. (9), *123;* 4 w. with consecutive balls, *120.*

Moles, A. J. (Warwicks):– 10,000 r., *248;* 285 for 1st wkt, *245.*

Moloney, D. A. R. (NZ):– Test p'ship record, *185.*

Moody, T. M. (Aust.):– 917 r. in Sunday League season, *763;* 2 Test hundreds, *202, 206;* Hundred before lunch, *245;* Hundred in 26 min., *109;* Fifty in 11 min., *109;* Test p'ship record, *206.*

Mooney, F. L. H. (NZ):– Test p'ship record, *185.*

Moore, R. H. (Hants):– Highest for Hampshire, *97;* 316 v Warwickshire in day, *96, 97, 110.*

Moores, P. (Sussex):– 251 for 5th wkt, *246.*

More, K. S. (Ind.):– 86 d. in one-day ints, *234;* 18 d. in W. Cup, *238;* 6 st. in Test, *156;* 5 d. in one-day int., *234;* 5 st. in Test innings, *156;* Test p'ship records, *202, 217.*

Morgan, H. E. (Glam.):– 254 v Monmouthshire, *240.*

Moroney, J. R. (Aust.):– 2 hundreds in same Test, *139, 194.*

Morris, A. R. (Aust.):– Test captain, *165, 196;* 12,614 r. (avge 53.67), *108;* 3,533 r. in Tests, *141;* 2,080 r. v England, *171;* 46 hundreds, *102;* 12 Test hundreds, *169, 194, 197, 202;* 2 hundreds in same Test, *139, 169;* 2 hundreds in match (2), *100;* 148 and 111 on début, *98;* 301 for 2nd wkt v England, *148;* Test p'ship record, *202.*

Morris, H. (Eng.):– Captain of Glamorgan, *363;* 2,000 r. since 1969 (1), *103;* 10 hundreds in season, *101;* 2 hundreds in match (2), *100;* 250 for 1st wkt, *245;* Test p'ship record, *192.*

Morris, J. E. (Eng.):– 259 for 2nd wkt, *245.*

Morrison, D. K. (NZ):– Slow scoring, *146.*

Morrison, J. F. M. (NZ):– 1 Test hundred, *200.*

Mortimore, J. B. (Eng.):– All-round, *127;* 1,807 w., *124.*

Moss, A. E. (Cant.):– 10 w. in innings on début, *117.*

Motz, R. C. (NZ):– 100 w. in Tests, *152.*

Moxon, M. D. (Eng.):– Cricketer of the Year, *34;* Captain of Yorkshire, *587;* Hundred on début, *98.*

Mudassar Nazar (Pak.):– 4,114 r. in Tests, *143;* 761 r. in series, *140;* 42 hundreds, *102;* 10 Test hundreds, *190, 219, 223;* Slowest Test hundred, *147;* Carrying bat in Test, *145;* 111 w. in one-day ints, *235;* All-round in one-day ints, *235;* 451 for 3rd wkt, *114, 148, 223;* Test p'ship records, *191, 219, 223.*

R

Rabone, G. O. (NZ):– Test captain, *183, 207;* 1 Test hundred, *208;* Test p'ship record, *209.*

Rackemann, C. G. (Aust.):– 10 w. or more in Test (1), *205;* Test p'ship record, *206.*

Radford, N. V. (Eng.):– Most w. in English season (2), *122;* 100 w. since 1969 (2), *122.*

Radley, C. T. (Eng.):– 26,441 r., *107;* 6,650 r. in Sunday League, *763;* 1,000 r. (16), *104;* 46 hundreds, *102;* 2 Test hundreds, *184, 190;* 91 c. in Sunday League, *765.*

Radley, P. J. L. (OFS):– 7 d. in innings, *128.*

Rae, A. F. (WI):– 4 Test hundreds, *181, 212.*

Raiji, M. N. (Bombay):– 360 for 5th wkt, *114.*

Raja Sarfraz (R'pindi):– 240 for 8th wkt, *115.*

Rajput, L. S. (Ind.):– 239 in 1991-92, *928;* 475 for 2nd wkt, *113, 929.*

Raju, S. L. V. (Ind.):– 6 w. for 12 r. in Test, *150.*

Ramadhin, S. (WI):– Most balls in single innings, *154;* Most balls in Test match, *154;* 188 w. in Tests, *152;* 10 w. or more in Test (1), *182.*

Raman, W. V. (Ind.):– 313 v Goa, *96;* 206 and 226 in 1991-92, *928;* 3 successive hundreds, *928;* Double-hundred and hundred in match, *99, 929;* 12 sixes in innings, *112;* 356 for 6th wkt, *114.*

Ramanamurthy, M. V. (Hyd.):– 244* for 9th wkt, *115.*

Ramanayake, C. P. H. (SL):– Test p'ship records, *193, 206.*

Ramaswami, C. (Ind.):– Test début at 40, *162.*

Ramchand, G. S. (Ind.):– Test captain, *201;* 2 Test hundreds, *202, 217;* Test p'ship record, *217.*

Ramiz Raja (Pak.):– 4,176 r. in one-day ints, *232;* 2,149 r. in Tests, *143;* 7 one-day int hundreds, *232;* 2 Test hundreds, *223, 226;* Slow scoring in Test, *147;* Test p'ship records, *219, 227.*

Ramprakash, M. R. (Eng.):– 233 in 1992, *244.*

Ranasinghe, A. N. (SL):– Test p'ship record, *225.*

Ranatunga, A. (SL):– Test captain, *205, 220, 224;* 33 Tests, *90, 163;* 22 consecutive Tests, *163;* 107 one-day ints, *236;* 2,856 r. in one-day ints, *232;* 1,830 r. in Tests, *144;* 739 r. in Sri Lankan season, *104;* 200* in 1991-92, *928;* 2 Test hundreds, *225, 226;* Test p'ship records, *192, 206, 221, 225, 227.*

Ranatunga, D. (SL):– Test p'ship record, *206.*

Randall, B. (E. Tvl):– 6 d. in innings, *931.*

Randall, D. W. (Eng.):– 28,186 r., *107;* 6,962 r. in Sunday League, *763;* 2,658 r. in B & H Cup, *664;* 2,470 r. in Tests, *141;* 2,000 r. since 1969 (1), *103;* 52 hundreds, *102;* 7 Test hundreds, *167, 184, 187, 190;* Double-hundred and hundred, *99;* Test p'ship record, *188.*

Ranjitsinhji, K. S. (HH the Jam Sahib of Nawanagar) (Eng.):– 24,692 r. (avge 56.37), *108;* 3,159 r. in season, *103;* 1,000 r. in 2 separate months, *111;* 72 hundreds, *102;* 2 Test hundreds, *167;* Hundred on Test début, *137, 167;* 344 for 7th wkt, *115.*

Ransford, V. S. (Aust.):– 1 Test hundred, *169;* Test p'ship records, *195.*

Rao, J. S. (Ind. Serv.):– Double hat-trick, *120;* 3 hat-tricks, *121.*

Rashid Israr (HBL):– 350 v National Bank, *95.*

Rashid Khan (Pak.):– Test p'ship records, *227.*

Ratnayake, R. J. (SL):– 73 w. in Tests, *153;* 9 w. in Test, *149, 225;* Test p'ship records, *193, 206, 221, 225, 227.*

Ratnayeke, J. R. (SL):– 85 w. in one-day ints, *233;* 8 w. in Test innings, *149;* Best bowling v Australia, *206;* Test p'ship records, *193, 206, 225, 227.*

Razdan, V. (Delhi):– 206 for 8th wkt, *930.*

Read, W. W. (Eng.):– Test captain, *165, 175;* 338 v Oxford Univ., *95;* 38 hundreds, *102;* 1 Test hundred, *167;* Test p'ship record, *170.*

Redmond, R. E. (NZ):– Hundred on Test début, *138, 219;* Test p'ship record, *219.*

Redpath, I. R. (Aust.):– 4,737 r. in Tests, *141;* 8 Test hundreds, *169, 197, 199, 204;* Carrying bat in Test, *145;* 32 r. in over, *111.*

Rees, A. (Glam.):– Handled the ball, *116.*

Reeve, D. A. (Eng.):– Captain of Warwickshire, *555;* 3 c. in W. Cup innings, *238.*

Reid, B. A. (Aust.):– 12 w. in match, *930;* 10 w. or more in Test (2), *172, 203;* Hat-trick in one-day int., *234.*

Reid, J. F. (NZ):– 6 Test hundreds, *200, 217, 219, 221;* 106 w. in Tests, *152;* Test p'ship records, *200, 219, 221.*

Reid, J. R. (NZ):– Test captain, *90, 183, 207, 209, 216, 218;* 58 consecutive Tests, *163;* 3,428 r. in Tests, *143;* 2,188 r. in overseas season, *105;* 1,915 r. in South African season, *104;* 39 hundreds, *102;* 6 Test hundreds, *185, 208, 217, 219;* 50 boundaries in innings, *112;* 15 sixes in innings, *112;* Test p'ship records, *209, 217, 219.*

Relf, A. E. (Eng.):– 1,897 w., *124;* 100 w. (11), *123;* All-round, *127.*

S

INDEX OF FILLERS

TEST MATCHES, 1992-93

Full details of these Tests, and others too late for inclusion, will appear in the 1994 edition of *Wisden*.

SRI LANKA v AUSTRALIA

First Test: At Sinhalese Sports Club, Colombo, August 17, 18, 19, 21, 22. Australia won by 16 runs. Toss: Sri Lanka. Australia 256 (M. A. Taylor 42, D. C. Boon 32, I. A. Healy 66 not out, Extras 32; C. P. H. Ramanayake three for 51, U. C. Hathurusinghe four for 66) and 471 (M. A. Taylor 43, D. C. Boon 68, D. M. Jones 57, M. E. Waugh 56, G. R. J. Matthews 64, C. J. McDermott 40, S. K. Warne 35, Extras 58; C. P. H. Ramanayake three for 113, S. D. Anurasiri four for 127); Sri Lanka 547 for eight dec. (R. S. Mahanama 78, A. P. Gurusinha 137, A. Ranatunga 127, R. S. Kaluwitharana 132 not out; G. R. J. Matthews three for 93) and 164 (R. S. Mahanama 39, U. C. Hathurusinghe 36, A. P. Gurusinha 31 not out, P. A. de Silva 37; G. R. J. Matthews four for 76, S. K. Warne three for 11).

Sri Lanka reached 500 for the first time in Tests, with Kaluwitharana the second Sri Lankan to make a century on Test début. They were set a target of 181 in 58 overs, but lost their last eight wickets for 37; Warne took the last three in 11 balls without conceding a run.

Second Test: At Khettarama Stadium, Colombo, August 28, 29, 30, September 1, 2. Drawn. Toss: Sri Lanka. Australia 247 (D. M. Jones 77, G. R. J. Matthews 55, Extras 32; C. P. H. Ramanayake three for 64, D. K. Liyanage three for 66) and 296 for six dec. (T. M. Moody 54, D. M. Jones 100 not out, G. R. J. Matthews 51; S. D. Anurasiri three for 66); Sri Lanka 258 for nine dec. (U. C. Hathurusinghe 67, P. A. de Silva 85; C. J. McDermott four for 53) and 136 for two (R. S. Mahanama 69, U. C. Hathurusinghe 49).

Khettarama Stadium became Test cricket's 66th ground – and Colombo's fourth.

Third Test: At Moratuwa, September 8, 9, 10, 12, 13. Drawn. Toss: Australia. Australia 337 (A. R. Border 106, G. R. J. Matthews 57, I. A. Healy 71; C. P. H. Ramanayake three for 75, D. K. Liyanage four for 56) and 271 for eight (A. R. Border 78, G. R. J. Matthews 96, I. A. Healy 49; C. P. H. Ramanayake three for 75, D. K. Liyanage four for 56); Sri Lanka 274 for nine dec. (R. S. Mahanama 50, P. A. de Silva 58, H. P. Tillekeratne 82, A. Ranatunga 48; C. J. McDermott four for 89, A. I. C. Dodemaide four for 65).

Tyronne Fernando Stadium became the 67th Test ground. Border's 24th Test century was his first for four years, and made him the first Australian to reach 100 against six Test countries. When 25, Ranatunga became the first Sri Lankan to make 2,000 runs in Tests. M. E. Waugh made a pair for the second Test running.

ZIMBABWE v INDIA

Inaugural Test: At Harare, October 18, 19, 20, 21, 22. Drawn. Toss: Zimbabwe. Zimbabwe 456 (K. J. Arnott 40, G. W. Flower 82, A. D. R. Campbell 45, A. J. Pycroft 39, D. L. Houghton 121, A. Flower 59, Extras 35; M. Prabhakar three for 66, J. Srinath three for 89, A. Kumble three for 79) and 146 for four dec. (K. J. Arnott 32, A. J. Pycroft 46, D. L. Houghton 41 not out); India 307 (W. V. Raman 43, S. V. Manjrekar 104, Kapil Dev 60, K. S. More 41; M. G. Burmester three for 78, A. J. Traicos five for 86).

Zimbabwe became the ninth Test nation, and Harare Sports Club the 68th Test ground. Zimbabwe were the first country to avoid defeat in their maiden Test since Australia (against England, in 1876-77); Houghton was the first player to score a century on his country's début since C. Bannerman for Australia. Only Australia (245) and Sri Lanka (218) had had innings totals of 200 or over in their first Tests. Traicos, who played three Tests for South Africa in 1969-70, became the 14th player to appear for two countries, a record interval of 22 years and 222 days since his last Test. Manjrekar took 500 minutes to reach 100, the fourth slowest century in Tests and the slowest for India. Three umpires were used for the first time in Tests; H. D. Bird of England stood in his 48th Test, equalling F. Chester's record, while Zimbabweans K. Kanjee and I. D. Robinson alternated day by day at the other end.

ZIMBABWE v NEW ZEALAND

First Test: At Bulawayo, November 1, 2, 3, 4, 5. Drawn. Toss: New Zealand. New Zealand 325 for three dec. (M. J. Greatbatch 87, R. T. Latham 119, A. H. Jones 67 not out, M. D. Crowe 42) and 222 for five dec. (M. J. Greatbatch 88, R. T. Latham 48, A. H. Jones 39 retired hurt; M. P. Jarvis three for 38); Zimbabwe 219 (K. J. Arnott 30, D. L. Houghton 36, A. Flower 81; D. N. Patel six for 113) and 197 for one (K. J. Arnott 101 not out, G. W. Flower 45, A. D. R. Campbell 48 not out).

Bulawayo Athletic Club became Test cricket's 69th ground. H. D. Bird stood in a record 49th Test. Ten hours' play were lost to rain after a prolonged drought. Off-spinner Patel took the new ball and returned his best figures in Tests.

Second Test: At Harare, November 7, 9, 10, 11, 12. New Zealand won by 177 runs. Toss: New Zealand. New Zealand 335 (M. J. Greatbatch 55, M. D. Crowe 140, K. R. Rutherford 74; D. H. Brain three for 49) and 262 for five dec. (M. D. Crowe 61, K. R. Rutherford 89, D. N. Patel 58 not out); Zimbabwe 283 for nine dec. (K. J. Arnott 68, A. D. R. Campbell 52, A. J. Pycroft 60, M. G. Burmester 30 not out; M. L. Su'a five for 85) and 137 (A. D. R. Campbell 35, G. J. Crocker 33; D. N. Patel six for 50).

Zimbabwe's first defeat came in their third Test, after they were bowled out chasing a target of 315 in 71 overs. They were also beaten in a one-day international at the same venue on November 8, the first such match to interrupt a Test. H. D. Bird became the first umpire to stand in 50 Tests.

SOUTH AFRICA v INDIA

First Test: At Durban, November 13, 14, 15, 16, 17. Drawn. Toss: India. South Africa 254 (K. C. Wessels 118, J. N. Rhodes 41, M. W. Pringle 33; Kapil Dev three for 43) and 176 for three (S. J. Cook 43, A. C. Hudson 55, K. C. Wessels 32); India 277 (M. Azharuddin 36, P. K. Amre 103, K. S. More 55, Extras 31; B. M. McMillan three for 52).

South Africa met India for the first time in Tests in their first home Test since March 1970. Cook was dismissed by the first ball of the match on his Test début, an unprecedented event. Wessels, formerly of Australia, became the first player to score Test centuries for two teams. S. R. Tendulkar of India was the first player to be given out (run out) by a third umpire watching a television replay in the pavilion – K. E. Liebenberg, who alternated with C. J. Mitchley while S. A. Bucknor of West Indies stood throughout at the other end. P. K. Amre became the 58th player to score a century on his Test début. O. Henry was South Africa's first non-white Test player and their oldest on Test début (40 years and 295 days). The fourth day was lost to rain.

Second Test: At Johannesburg, November 26, 27, 28, 29, 30. Drawn. Toss: South Africa. South Africa 292 (J. N. Rhodes 91, B. M. McMillan 98, C. R. Matthews 31; M. Prabhakar four for 90) and 252 (S. J. Cook 31, A. C. Hudson 53, D. J. Richardson 50; A. Kumble six for 53); India 227 (S. R. Tendulkar 111; A. A. Donald three for 78, B. M. McMillan four for 74) and 141 for four (A. D. Jadeja 43, S. V. Manjrekar 32 not out, P. K. Amre 35 not out).

Umpire S. A. Bucknor was criticised for refusing to consult the "television" umpire; he reprieved Rhodes on 28 when the cameras suggested he was run out.

Third Test: At Port Elizabeth, December 26, 27, 28, 29. South Africa won by nine wickets. Toss: South Africa. India 212 (M. Azharuddin 60; A. A. Donald five for 55, B. M. McMillan three for 41) and 215 (Kapil Dev 129; A. A. Donald seven for 84); South Africa 275 (A. C. Hudson 52, W. J. Cronje 135; A. Kumble three for 81, S. L. V. Raju three for 73) and 155 for one (K. C. Wessels 95 not out, A. C. Hudson 33).

South Africa achieved their first Test victory since March 1970, also at Port Elizabeth. Donald's 12 wickets for 139 were the fourth best match figures by any bowler for South Africa, and D. J. Richardson's nine catches were the most in a Test by a South African wicket-keeper. M. Prabhakar was fined 10 per cent of his match fee for dissent when out in the second innings.

Fourth Test: At Cape Town, January 2, 3, 4, 5, 6. Drawn. Toss: South Africa. South Africa 360 for nine dec. (W. J. Cronje 33, D. J. Cullinan 46, J. N. Rhodes 86, B. M. McMillan 52, O. Henry 34; A. Kumble three for 101) and 130 for six dec. (K. C. Wessels 34; J. Srinath four for 33); India 276 (M. Prabhakar 62, S. V. Manjrekar 46, S. R. Tendulkar 73, Kapil Dev 34; C. R. Matthews three for 32) and 29 for one.

The run-rate over five days was 1.83 per over; India scored only 148 in six hours on the third day and took ten and a quarter hours to reach 276. South Africa took the series 1-0.

SRI LANKA v NEW ZEALAND

First Test: At Moratuwa, November 27, 28, 29, December 1, 2. Drawn. Toss: Sri Lanka. New Zealand 288 (A. H. Jones 35, K. R. Rutherford 105, C. Z. Harris 56, Extras 35; D. K. Liyanage four for 82) and 195 for five (B. R. Hartland 52, J. G. Wright 42, K. R. Rutherford 53); Sri Lanka 327 for six dec. (R. S. Mahanama 153, A. P. Gurusinha 43, P. A. de Silva 62, Extras 32).

The series was reduced from three Tests to two after a bomb killed Sri Lankan naval commander Clancy Fernando outside the New Zealanders' hotel in Colombo, prompting five players and the coach, Warren Lees, to go home. Wright, one of their replacements, became the first New Zealander to score 5,000 Test runs when 25 in the second innings.

Second Test: At Sinhalese Sports Club, Colombo, December 6, 7, 8, 9. Sri Lanka won by nine wickets. Toss: Sri Lanka. Sri Lanka 394 (R. S. Mahanama 109, A. Ranatunga 76, H. P. Tillekeratne 93; M. B. Owens four for 101, G. E. Bradburn three for 134) and 70 for one; New Zealand 102 (J. G. Wright 30; K. P. J. Warnaweera four for 25, M. Muralitharan three for 22) and 361 (J. G. Wright 50, M. D. Crowe 107, K. R. Rutherford 38, A. C. Parore 60; M. Muralitharan four for 134).

Sri Lanka's third win in all Tests and their first over New Zealand came with four sessions to spare. Mahanama scored his second Test hundred in successive innings. Tillekeratne's seven catches in the match equalled the Test record for a fielder.

AUSTRALIA v WEST INDIES

First Test: At Brisbane, November 27, 28, 29, 30, December 1. Drawn. Toss: Australia. Australia 293 (D. C. Boon 48, M. E. Waugh 39, D. R. Martyn 36, A. R. Border 73, G. R. J. Matthews 30; C. L. Hooper four for 75) and 308 (D. C. Boon 111, M. A. Taylor 34, M. E. Waugh 60; C. E. L. Ambrose five for 66); West Indies 371 (B. C. Lara 58, K. L. T. Arthurton 157 not out, C. L. Hooper 47; B. A. Reid five for 112) and 133 for eight (R. B. Richardson 66, C. L. Hooper 32; C. J. McDermott four for 35).

Ambrose took his 150th Test wicket in his 35th match. Lara was given out stumped by I. A. Healy, who later claimed he had told umpire T. A. Prue he had hit the wicket only with his glove. ICC referee R. Subba Row fined Border half his match fee and M. G. Hughes 10 per cent for disputing decisions on the last day.

Second Test: At Melbourne, December 26, 27, 28, 29, 30. Australia won by 139 runs. Toss: Australia. Australia 395 (D. C. Boon 46, S. R. Waugh 38, M. E. Waugh 112, A. R. Border 110; C. E. L. Ambrose four for 70, I. R. Bishop three for 84, C. A. Walsh four for 91) and 196 (M. A. Taylor 42, D. R. Martyn 67 not out; I. R. Bishop three for 45); West Indies 233 (B. C. Lara 52, K. L. T. Arthurton 71, J. C. Adams 47; C. J. McDermott four for 66, M. G. Hughes three for 51) and 219 (P. V. Simmons 110, R. B. Richardson 52; S. K. Warne seven for 52).

Border reached his 25th century in his 135th Test. Hughes took his 150th Test wicket in his 39th match. West Indies lost their last nine wickets for 76 – seven of them to Warne for 21.

Third Test: At Sydney, January 2, 3, 4, 5, 6. Drawn. Toss: Australia. Australia 503 for nine dec. (D. C. Boon 76, S. R. Waugh 100, M. E. Waugh 57, A. R. Border 74, G. R. J. Matthews 79, I. A. Healy 36 not out, Extras 30; C. L. Hooper three for 137) and 117 for no wkt (M. A. Taylor 46 not out, D. C. Boon 63 not out); West Indies 606 (R. B. Richardson 109, B. C. Lara 277, K. L. T. Arthurton 47, J. C. Adams 77 not out; M. G. Hughes three for 76).

When 21 in the first innings, Border reached 10,000 runs in his 136th Test – second only to S. M. Gavaskar (10,122). Richardson scored his 15th Test century and Lara his first, going on to the highest score in Australia–West Indies Tests. In the second innings Boon, when nine, reached 5,000 Test runs in his 69th match.

Fourth Test: At Adelaide, January 23, 24, 25, 26. West Indies won by one run. Toss: West Indies. West Indies 252 (D. L. Haynes 45, P. V. Simmons 46, B. C. Lara 52, J. R. Murray 49 not out; M. G. Hughes five for 64) and 146 (R. B. Richardson 72; C. J. McDermott three for 66, T. B. A. May five for nine); Australia 213 (D. C. Boon 39 not out, S. R. Waugh 42, M. G. Hughes 43; C. E. L. Ambrose six for 74) and 184 (J. L. Langer 54, T. B. A. May 42 not out; C. E. L. Ambrose four for 46, C. A. Walsh three for 44).

West Indies secured the narrowest victory in Test history on the fourth day when Walsh had last man McDermott caught behind, when Australia needed two runs to win and secure the series.

Fifth Test: At Perth, January 30, 31, February 1. West Indies won by an innings and 25 runs. Toss: Australia. Australia 119 (D. C. Boon 44; C. E. L. Ambrose seven for 25) and 178 (D. C. Boon 52, D. R. Martyn 31; I. R. Bishop six for 40); West Indies 322 (P. V. Simmons 80, R. B. Richardson 47, K. L. T. Arthurton 77, J. R. Murray 37; C. J. McDermott three for 85, M. G. Hughes four for 71).

West Indies claimed the Frank Worrell Trophy with eight sessions to spare. Ambrose took seven wickets for one run in 32 balls. He finished with 33 in the series, a record in Tests between these teams. A. R. Border made a pair, leaving him still 50 short of overtaking S. M. Gavaskar's Test run record.

NEW ZEALAND v PAKISTAN

Only Test: At Hamilton, January 2, 3, 4, 5. Pakistan won by 33 runs. Toss: New Zealand. Pakistan 216 (Javed Miandad 92, Rashid Latif 32 not out; D. K. Morrison three for 42, M. L. Su'a five for 73) and 174 (Inzamam-ul-Haq 75, Rashid Latif 33; D. K. Morrison five for 41); New Zealand 264 (M. J. Greatbatch 133, B. R. Hartland 43, Extras 33; Wasim Akram three for 66, Waqar Younis four for 59, Mushtaq Ahmed three for 87) and 93 (Wasim Akram five for 45, Waqar Younis five for 22).

K. R. Rutherford captained New Zealand because M. D. Crowe was injured. New Zealand were set 127 in more than two days, but they were bowled out in 43.3 overs halfway through the fourth day (the highest score was Extras, on 22, and Waqar Younis took his 100th Test wicket in his 20th Test). ICC referee P. J. Burge warned both teams for persistent sledging.

FIXTURES, 1993

Indicates Sunday play.   †*Not first-class.*

All County Championship matches are of four days' duration.

Wednesday, April 14

Cambridge	Cambridge U. v Derbys. (3 days)
Oxford	Oxford U. v Durham (3 days)

Saturday, April 17

Cambridge*	Cambridge U. v Yorks. (3 days)
Oxford	Oxford U. v Lancs. (3 days)

Tuesday, April 20

The Oval	†Surrey 2nd XI v England Under-19 (4 days)

Wednesday, April 21

Cambridge	Cambridge U. v Kent (3 days)
Oxford	Oxford U. v Glam. (3 days)

Thursday, April 22

Chelmsford*	Essex v England A (4 days)

Saturday, April 24

Cambridge	†Combined Universities v Middx (1 day)

Sunday, April 25

Cambridge	†Combined Universities v Northants (1 day)

Tuesday, April 27
†Benson and Hedges Cup – Preliminary Round (1 day)

Hartlepool	Durham v Minor Counties
Bristol	Glos. v Derbys.
Southampton	Hants v Combined Universities
Canterbury	Kent v Glam.
Forfar	Scotland v Essex

Thursday, April 29

Cardiff*	Glam. v Sussex
Bristol*	Glos. v Middx
Southampton*	Hants v Somerset
Leicester*	Leics. v Surrey
Nottingham*	Notts. v Worcs.
Birmingham*	Warwicks. v Northants
Leeds	Yorks. v Lancs. (friendly match, 4 days)

Friday, April 30

Radlett	†England Amateur XI v Australians (1 day)

Saturday, May 1

Cambridge*	Cambridge U. v Essex (3 days)

Sunday, May 2

Arundel	†Lavinia, Duchess of Norfolk's XI v Australians (1 day)

Monday, May 3

Lord's	†Middx v Australians (1 day)

Wednesday, May 5

Worcester	Worcs. v Australians (3 days)
Cambridge	Cambridge U. v Glam. (3 days)
Oxford	Oxford U. v Hants (3 days)
Lord's	†MCC v MCC Young Cricketers (1 day)

Thursday, May 6

Chelmsford	Essex v Yorks.
Manchester	Lancs. v Durham
Leicester	Leics. v Notts.
Lord's	Middx v Kent
Northampton	Northants v Glos.
Hove	Sussex v Surrey
Birmingham	Warwicks. v Derbys.

Saturday, May 8

Taunton*	Somerset v Australians (3 days)

Tuesday, May 11

†Benson and Hedges Cup – First Round
(1 day)

Stockton-on-Tees or Jesmond	Durham or Minor Counties v Hants or Combined Universities
Bristol or Derby	Glos. or Derbys. v Middx
Canterbury or Cardiff	Kent or Glam. v Sussex
Leicester	Leics. v Warwicks.
Nottingham	Notts. v Somerset
The Oval	Surrey v Lancs.
Worcester	Worcs. v Scotland or Essex
Leeds	Yorks. v Northants

Thursday, May 13

Hove*	Sussex v Australians (3 days)
Derby	Derbys. v Glam.
Stockton-on-Tees	Durham v Hants
Canterbury	Kent v Warwicks.
Lord's	Middx v Notts.
Taunton	Somerset v Lancs.
The Oval	Surrey v Essex
Bradford	Yorks. v Worcs.

Saturday, May 15

Cambridge*	Cambridge U. v Leics. (3 days)
Oxford	Oxford U. v Northants (3 days)

Sunday, May 16

Northampton	†Northants v Australians (1 day)

Wednesday, May 19

Manchester	†ENGLAND v AUSTRALIA (1st 1-day Texaco Trophy)
Cambridge	Cambridge U. v Lancs. (3 days)
Oxford	Oxford U. v Middx (3 days)

Thursday, May 20

Chelmsford	Essex v Derbys.
Swansea	Glam. v Northants
Bristol	Glos. v Durham
Southampton	Hants v Yorks.
Nottingham	Notts. v Kent
Horsham	Sussex v Leics.
Worcester	Worcs. v Somerset

Friday, May 21

Birmingham	†ENGLAND v AUSTRALIA (2nd 1-day Texaco Trophy)

Sunday, May 23

Lord's	†ENGLAND v AUSTRALIA (3rd 1-day Texaco Trophy)

Tuesday, May 25

†Benson and Hedges Cup – Quarter-finals
(1 day)

The Oval or Leeds‡	Surrey or Yorks. v Australians (3 days)

‡ Or Northants or Notts. if both Surrey and Yorks. in B&H Cup quarter-finals.

Thursday, May 27

Derby	Derbys. v Hants
Darlington	Durham v Kent
Gloucester	Glos. v Worcs.
Liverpool	Lancs. v Warwicks.
Lord's	Middx v Sussex
Taunton	Somerset v Glam.

Saturday, May 29

Leicester*	Leics. v Australians (3 days)
Oxford	Oxford U. v Notts. (3 days)

Thursday, June 3

Manchester*	ENGLAND v AUSTRALIA (1st Cornhill Test, 5 days)
Chelmsford	Essex v Somerset
Tunbridge Wells	Kent v Glos.
Leicester	Leics. v Durham
Lord's	Middx v Derbys.
Northampton	Northants v Worcs.
Nottingham	Notts. v Hants
The Oval	Surrey v Lancs.
Birmingham	Warwicks. v Sussex
Middlesbrough	Yorks. v Glam.

Tuesday, June 8

†Benson and Hedges Cup – Semi-finals
(1 day)

Wednesday, June 9

| Birmingham or Nottingham‡ | Warwicks. or Notts. v Australians (3 days) |

‡ *Or Somerset if both Warwicks. and Notts. in B&H Cup semi-finals.*

Thursday, June 10

Chesterfield	Derbys. v Yorks.
Gateshead Fell	Durham v Middx
Basingstoke	Hants v Kent
Manchester	Lancs. v Essex
The Oval	Surrey v Glam.
Hove	Sussex v Northants
Worcester	Worcs. v Leics.

Saturday, June 12

Bristol*	Glos. v Australians (3 days)
Cambridge*	Cambridge U. v Notts. (3 days)
Oxford	Oxford U. v Warwicks. (3 days)
Eglinton*	Ireland v Scotland (3 days)

Thursday, June 17

Lord's*	ENGLAND v AUSTRALIA (2nd Cornhill Test, 5 days)
Colwyn Bay	Glam. v Durham
Canterbury	Kent v Derbys.
Manchester	Lancs. v Sussex
Northampton	Northants v Hants
Nottingham	Notts. v Essex
Bath	Somerset v Middx
Birmingham	Warwicks. v Surrey
Sheffield	Yorks. v Glos.

Friday, June 18

| Worcester* | Worcs. v Oxford U. (3 days) |

Tuesday, June 22

†NatWest Bank Trophy – First Round
(1 day)

Marlow	Bucks. v Leics.
Warrington	Cheshire v Notts.
Exmouth	Devon v Derbys.
Swansea	Glam. v Oxon.
Bristol	Glos. v Herts.
Canterbury	Kent v Middx
Lakenham	Norfolk v Warwicks.
Northampton	Northants v Lancs.
Edinburgh (Myreside)	Scotland v Worcs.
Telford (St Georges)	Salop v Somerset
Stone	Staffs. v Hants
Bury St Edmunds	Suffolk v Essex
The Oval	Surrey v Dorset
Hove	Sussex v Wales
Trowbridge	Wilts. v Durham
Leeds	Yorks. v Ireland

Wednesday, June 23

| Oxford | Combined Universities v Australians (3 days) |
| Lord's | †MCC v Melbourne CC (1 day) |

Thursday, June 24

Derby	Derbys. v Lancs.
Stockton-on-Tees	Durham v Worcs.
Ilford	Essex v Warwicks.
Swansea	Glam. v Notts.
Leicester	Leics. v Glos.
Lord's	Middx v Surrey
Luton	Northants v Somerset
Leeds	Yorks. v Kent

Saturday, June 26

| Southampton* | Hants v Australians (3 days) |
| Hove* | Sussex v Cambridge U. (3 days) |

Tuesday, June 29

| Lord's | †Eton v Harrow (1 day) |

Wednesday, June 30

| Lord's | Oxford U. v Cambridge U. (3 days) |

Thursday, July 1

Nottingham	ENGLAND v AUSTRALIA (3rd Cornhill Test, 5 days)
Cardiff	Glam. v Middx
Bristol	Glos. v Hants
Maidstone	Kent v Essex
Leicester	Leics. v Lancs.
Northampton	Northants v Notts.
Taunton	Somerset v Sussex
The Oval	Surrey v Durham
Birmingham	Warwicks. v Yorks.
Kidderminster	Worcs. v Derbys.

Wednesday, July 7

†NatWest Bank Trophy – Second Round
(1 day)

Marlow or Leicester	Bucks. or Leics. v Surrey or Dorset
Warrington or Nottingham	Cheshire or Notts. v Salop or Somerset
Cardiff or Oxford (Christ Church)	Glam. or Oxon. v Wilts. or Durham
Bristol or Hitchin	Glos. or Herts. v Yorks. or Ireland
Lakenham or Birmingham	Norfolk or Warwicks. v Kent or Middx
Glasgow (Titwood) or Worcester	Scotland or Worcs. v Devon or Derbys.
Bury St Edmunds or Chelmsford	Suffolk or Essex v Northants or Lancs.
Hove or Colwyn Bay	Sussex or Wales v Staffs. or Hants

Thursday, July 8

Stone	†Minor Counties v Australians (1 day)

Friday, July 9

Oxford	†MCC Schools Festival (4 days)

Saturday, July 10

Lord's	†BENSON AND HEDGES CUP FINAL (1 day)
Dublin (Clontarf)	†Ireland v Australians (1 day)

Monday, July 12

Harrogate	†Tilcon Trophy (3 days)

Tuesday, July 13

Derby	Derbys. v Australians (3 days)
Jesmond	†England XI v Rest of the World XI (1 day)
Lord's	†MCC v MCC Schools (1 day)

Wednesday, July 14

Jesmond	†England XI v Rest of the World XI (1 day)
Canterbury	†Kent v Surrey (Seeboard Trophy, 1 day)
Lord's	†MCC Schools v NAYC (1 day)

Thursday, July 15

Southend	Essex v Leics.
Portsmouth	Hants v Worcs.
Manchester	Lancs. v Glam.
Nottingham	Notts. v Somerset
Guildford	Surrey v Glos.
Arundel	Sussex v Kent
Birmingham	Warwicks. v Middx
Harrogate	Yorks. v Northants
Lord's	†NCA Young Cricketers v Combined Services (1 day)

Saturday, July 17

Durham Univ.*	Durham v Australians (3 days)

Thursday, July 22

Leeds*	ENGLAND v AUSTRALIA (4th Cornhill Test, 5 days)
Derby	Derbys. v Sussex
Chelmsford	Essex v Durham
Manchester	Lancs. v Notts.
Leicester	Leics. v Warwicks.
Lord's	Middx v Hants
Northampton	Northants v Surrey
Taunton	Somerset v Kent
Worcester	Worcs. v Glam.

Tuesday, July 27

†NatWest Bank Trophy – Quarter-finals
(1 day)

Wednesday, July 28

Northampton or Manchester	Northants or Lancs. v Australians (3 days)

Thursday, July 29

Durham Univ.	Durham v Sussex
Chelmsford	Essex v Worcs.
Cheltenham	Glos. v Derbys.
Southampton	Hants v Warwicks.
Canterbury	Kent v Leics.
Taunton	Somerset v Yorks.
The Oval	Surrey v Notts.

Saturday, July 31

Neath*	Glam. v Australians (3 days)

Sunday, August 1

Lord's	†Women's World Cup Final (1 day)

Wednesday, August 4

Hove	†Sussex v Kent or Surrey (Seeboard Trophy, 1 day)

Thursday, August 5

Birmingham*	ENGLAND v AUSTRALIA (5th Cornhill Test, 5 days)
Durham Univ.	Durham v Derbys.
Cardiff	Glam. v Warwicks.
Cheltenham	Glos. v Lancs.
Canterbury	Kent v Surrey
Lord's	Middx v Leics.
Northampton	Northants v Essex
Nottingham	Notts. v Yorks.
Hove	Sussex v Worcs.
Leicester	†England Under-19 v West Indies Under-19 (1st 1-day)

Saturday, August 7

Chelmsford	†England Under-19 v West Indies Under-19 (2nd 1-day)

Tuesday, August 10

†NatWest Bank Trophy – Semi-finals (1 day)

Wednesday, August 11

Canterbury‡	Kent v Australians (3 days)

‡ *To be played as a 1-day match on Friday, August 13 if Kent in NatWest semi-finals.*

Thursday, August 12

Derby	Derbys. v Somerset
Southampton	Hants v Lancs.
Leicester	Leics. v Glam.
Northampton	Northants v Durham
Eastbourne	Sussex v Notts.
Birmingham	Warwicks. v Glos.
Worcester	Worcs. v Surrey
Scarborough	Yorks. v Middx
Nottingham*	†England Under-19 v West Indies Under-19 (1st "Test", 4 days)

Saturday, August 14

Chelmsford*	Essex v Australians (3 days)

Sunday, August 15

Lord's	†MCC v Ireland (2 days)

Monday, August 16

†Bain Clarkson Trophy Semi-finals (1 day)

Tuesday, August 17

†Bain Clarkson Trophy Semi-finals (1 day) (if not played on August 16)

Thursday, August 19

The Oval*	ENGLAND v AUSTRALIA (6th Cornhill Test, 5 days)
Ilkeston	Derbys. v Surrey
Darlington	Durham v Warwicks.
Swansea	Glam. v Hants
Bristol	Glos. v Essex
Manchester	Lancs. v Middx
Lord's	Middx v Northants
Weston-super-Mare	Somerset v Leics.
Worcester	Worcs. v Kent

Wednesday, August 25

†Minor Counties Knockout Final (1 day)

Thursday, August 26

Colchester	Essex v Middx
Abergavenny	Glam. v Glos.
Portsmouth	Hants v Sussex
Lytham	Lancs. v Kent
Northampton	Northants v Leics.
Nottingham	Notts. v Derbys.
The Oval	Surrey v Somerset
Birmingham	Warwicks. v Worcs.
Leeds	Yorks. v Durham
Hove*	†England Under-19 v West Indies Under-19 (2nd "Test", 4 days)

Friday, August 27

Lord's	†National Club Championship Final (1 day)

Sunday, August 29

Lord's	†National Village Championship Final (1 day)

Tuesday, August 31

Chester-le-Street	Durham v Notts.
Canterbury	Kent v Northants
Leicester	Leics. v Yorks.
Taunton	Somerset v Glos.

The Oval	Surrey v Hants
Hove	Sussex v Essex
Worcester	Worcs. v Lancs.

Saturday, September 4

Lord's	†NATWEST BANK TROPHY FINAL (1 day)

Sunday, September 5

Brecon (to be confirmed)	†Glam. v Zimbabweans (1 day)

Monday, September 6

†Bain Clarkson Trophy Final (1 day)

Scarborough	†Joshua Tetley Festival Trophy (3 days)

Tuesday, September 7

Birmingham	†Warwicks. v Zimbabweans (1 day)

Wednesday, September 8

The Oval	Surrey v Zimbabweans (3 days)

Thursday, September 9

Derby	Derbys. v Northants
Cardiff	Glam. v Essex
Bristol	Glos. v Notts.
Southampton	Hants v Leics.
Lord's	Middx v Lancs.
Birmingham	Warwicks. v Somerset
Scarborough	Yorks. v Sussex

Friday, September 10

Manchester*	†England Under-19 v West Indies Under-19 (3rd "Test", 4 days)

Saturday, September 11

Canterbury	Kent v Zimbabweans (3 days)

Thursday, September 16

Hartlepool	Durham v Somerset
Chelmsford	Essex v Hants
Canterbury	Kent v Glam.
Manchester	Lancs. v Northants
Leicester	Leics. v Derbys.
Nottingham	Notts. v Warwicks.
The Oval	Surrey v Yorks.
Hove	Sussex v Glos.
Worcester	Worcs. v Middx

AUSTRALIAN TOUR, 1993

APRIL

30 Radlett	†v England Amateur XI (1 day)

MAY

2 Arundel	†v Lavinia, Duchess of Norfolk's XI (1 day)
3 Lord's	†v Middx (1 day)
5 Worcester	v Worcs.
8 Taunton*	v Somerset
13 Hove*	v Sussex
16 Northampton	†v Northants (1 day)
19 Manchester	†v ENGLAND (1st 1-day Texaco Trophy)
21 Birmingham	†v ENGLAND (2nd 1-day Texaco Trophy)
23 Lord's	†v ENGLAND (3rd 1-day Texaco Trophy)
25 The Oval or Leeds‡	v Surrey or Yorks.

‡ *Or Northants or Notts. if both Surrey and Yorks. in B&H Cup quarter-finals.*

29 Leicester*	v Leics.

JUNE

3 Manchester*	v ENGLAND (1st Cornhill Test, 5 days)
9 Birmingham or Nottingham‡	v Warwicks. or Notts.

‡ *Or Somerset if both Warwicks. and Notts. in B&H Cup semi-finals.*

12 Bristol*	v Glos.
17 Lord's*	v ENGLAND (2nd Cornhill Test, 5 days)
23 Oxford	v Combined Universities
26 Southampton*	v Hants

JULY

1 Nottingham	v ENGLAND (3rd Cornhill Test, 5 days)
8 Stone	†v Minor Counties (1 day)

10 Dublin   †v Ireland (1 day)
   (Clontarf)
13 Derby   v Derbys.
17 Durham   v Durham
   Univ.*
22 Leeds*   v ENGLAND (4th
                        Cornhill Test, 5 days)
28 Northampton or   v Northants or Lancs.
   Manchester
31 Neath*   v Glam.

AUGUST

5 Birmingham*   v ENGLAND (5th
                       Cornhill Test, 5 days)
11 Canterbury‡   v Kent

   ‡ *To be played as a 1-day match on Friday,
   August 13 if Kent in NatWest semi-finals.*

14 Chelmsford*   v Essex
19 The Oval*   v ENGLAND (6th
                       Cornhill Test, 5 days)

†AXA EQUITY & LAW LEAGUE, 1993

MAY

9–Essex v Yorks. (Chelmsford); Lancs. v Durham (Manchester); Leics. v Notts. (Leicester); Middx v Kent (Lord's); Northants v Glos. (Northampton); Sussex v Surrey (Hove); Warwicks. v Derbys. (Birmingham).

16–Derbys. v Glam. (Derby); Durham v Hants (Stockton-on-Tees); Kent v Warwicks. (Canterbury); Middx v Notts. (Lord's); Somerset v Lancs. (Taunton); Surrey v Essex (The Oval); Yorks. v Worcs. (Leeds).

23–Essex v Derbys. (Chelmsford); Glam. v Northants (Pentyrch); Glos. v Durham (Bristol); Hants v Yorks. (Southampton); Notts. v Kent (Nottingham); Sussex v Leics. (Horsham); Worcs. v Somerset (Worcester).

30–Derbys. v Hants (Checkley); Durham v Kent (Darlington); Glos. v Worcs. (Gloucester); Lancs. v Warwicks. (Manchester); Middx v Sussex (Lord's); Somerset v Glam. (Taunton).

JUNE

6–Essex v Somerset (Chelmsford); Kent v Glos. (Tunbridge Wells); Leics. v Durham (Leicester); Middx v Derbys. (Lord's); Northants v Worcs. (Northampton); Notts. v Hants (Nottingham); Surrey v Lancs. (The Oval); Warwicks. v Sussex (Birmingham); Yorks. v Glam. (Middlesbrough).

13–Derbys. v Yorks. (Chesterfield); Durham v Middx (Gateshead Fell); Hants v Kent (Basingstoke); Lancs. v Essex (Manchester); Surrey v Glam. (The Oval); Sussex v Northants (Hove); Worcs. v Leics. (Worcester).

20–Glam. v Durham (Colwyn Bay); Kent v Derbys. (Canterbury); Lancs. v Sussex (Manchester); Northants v Hants (Northampton); Notts. v Essex (Nottingham); Somerset v Middx (Bath); Warwicks. v Surrey (Birmingham); Yorks. v Glos. (Sheffield).

27–Derbys. v Lancs. (Derby); Durham v Worcs. (Stockton-on-Tees); Essex v Warwicks. (Ilford); Glam. v Notts. (Swansea); Leics. v Glos. (Leicester); Middx v Surrey (Lord's); Northants v Somerset (Luton); Yorks. v Kent (Leeds).

JULY

4–Glam. v Middx (Cardiff); Glos. v Hants (Bristol); Kent v Essex (Maidstone); Leics. v Lancs. (Leicester); Northants v Notts. (Northampton); Somerset v Sussex (Taunton); Surrey v Durham (The Oval); Warwicks. v Yorks. (Birmingham); Worcs. v Derbys. (Worcester).

11–Glam. v Sussex (Llanelli); Glos. v Middx (Moreton-in-Marsh); Hants v Somerset (Southampton); Leics. v Surrey (Leicester); Notts. v Worcs. (Nottingham); Warwicks. v Northants (Birmingham). *Note: Matches involving B&H Cup finalists to be rearranged.*

18–Essex v Leics. (Southend); Hants v Worcs. (Portsmouth); Lancs. v Glam. (Manchester); Notts. v Somerset (Nottingham); Surrey v Glos. (Guildford); Sussex v Kent (Hove); Warwicks. v Middx (Birmingham); Yorks. v Northants (Leeds).

25–Derbys. v Sussex (Derby); Essex v Durham (Chelmsford); Lancs. v Notts. (Manchester); Leics. v Warwicks. (Leicester); Middx v Hants (Lord's); Northants v Surrey (Northampton); Somerset v Kent (Taunton); Worcs. v Glam. (Worcester).

AUGUST

1–Durham v Sussex (Durham Univ.); Essex v Worcs. (Chelmsford); Glos. v Derbys. (Cheltenham); Hants v Warwicks. (Southampton); Kent v Leics. (Canterbury); Somerset v Yorks. (Taunton); Surrey v Notts. (The Oval).

8–Durham v Derbys. (Durham Univ.); Glam. v Warwicks. (Neath); Glos. v Lancs. (Cheltenham); Kent v Surrey (Canterbury); Middx v Leics. (Lord's); Northants v Essex (Northampton); Notts. v Yorks. (Nottingham); Sussex v Worcs. (Hove).

15–Derbys. v Somerset (Derby); Hants v Lancs. (Southampton); Leics. v Glam. (Leicester); Northants v Durham (Northampton); Sussex v Notts. (Eastbourne); Warwicks. v Glos. (Birmingham); Worcs. v Surrey (Worcester); Yorks. v Middx (Scarborough).

22–Derbys. v Surrey (Ilkeston); Durham v Warwicks. (Darlington); Glam. v Hants (Swansea); Glos. v Essex (Bristol); Lancs. v Yorks. (Manchester); Middx v Northants (Lord's); Somerset v Leics. (Weston-super-Mare); Worcs. v Kent (Worcester).

29–Essex v Middx (Colchester); Glam. v Glos. (Ebbw Vale); Hants v Sussex (Portsmouth); Lancs. v Kent (Manchester); Northants v Leics. (Northampton); Notts. v Derbys. (Nottingham); Surrey v Somerset (The Oval); Warwicks. v Worcs. (Birmingham); Yorks. v Durham (Leeds).

SEPTEMBER

5–Durham v Notts. (Chester-le-Street); Kent v Northants (Canterbury); Leics. v Yorks. (Leicester); Somerset v Glos. (Taunton); Surrey v Hants (The Oval); Sussex v Essex (Hove); Worcs. v Lancs. (Worcester). *Note: Matches involving NatWest Trophy finalists to be rearranged.*

12–Derbys. v Northants (Derby); Glam. v Essex (Cardiff); Glos. v Notts. (Bristol); Hants v Leics. (Southampton); Middx v Lancs. (Lord's); Warwicks. v Somerset (Birmingham); Yorks. v Sussex (Scarborough).

19–Durham v Somerset (Hartlepool); Essex v Hants (Chelmsford); Kent v Glam. (Canterbury); Lancs. v Northants (Manchester); Leics. v Derbys. (Leicester); Notts. v Warwicks. (Nottingham); Surrey v Yorks. (The Oval); Sussex v Glos. (Hove); Worcs. v Middx (Worcester).

†MINOR COUNTIES CHAMPIONSHIP, 1993

All matches are of two days' duration.

MAY

30–Lincs. v Herts. (Sleaford); Northumb. v Beds. (Jesmond); Oxon. v Salop (Pressed Steel, Oxford); Wales v Herefords. (Ebbw Vale); Wilts. v Devon (Westbury).

JUNE

1–Berks. v Salop (Kidmore End); Bucks. v Staffs. (Aylesbury); Cumb. v Beds. (Barrow); Suffolk v Herts. (Framlingham).

2–Cambs. v Norfolk (Wisbech).

13–Beds. v Suffolk (Henlow); Cumb. v Lincs. (Carlisle); Dorset v Wales (Sherborne); Herts. v Northumb. (St Albans); Oxon. v Berks. (Christ Church, Oxford).

14–Cheshire v Cornwall (Stalybridge).

15–Bucks. v Northumb. (Beaconsfield); Staffs. v Cambs. (Brewood).

16–Salop v Cornwall (Bridgnorth).

17–Dorset v Herefords. (Weymouth).

27–Beds. v Bucks. (Leighton Buzzard); Dorset v Devon (Dorchester); Northumb. v Lincs. (Jesmond); Oxon. v Wilts. (Challow and Chidrey); Salop v Cheshire (Wellington); Wales v Berks. (Pontarddulais).

28–Herts. v Staffs. (Radlett).

29–Herefords. v Cheshire (Colwall).

30–Suffolk v Cambs. (Ransome's, Ipswich).

JULY

4—*Lincs. v Bucks. (Burghley Park). *Note: to be rearranged if either Lincs. or Bucks. in Holt Cup semi-finals.*

5—Norfolk v Cumb. (Lakenham).

7—Suffolk v Cumb. (Bury St Edmunds).

8—Wilts. v Herefords. (Marlborough).

11—Beds. v Lincs. (Bedford Town); Dorset v Cornwall (Canford); Herefords. v Oxon. (Hereford City); Wales v Cheshire (Colwyn Bay).

12—Cambs. v Herts. (Cambridge).

13—Staffs. v Northumb. (Wolverhampton); Wilts. v Cornwall (Trowbridge).

18—Cornwall v Wales (Falmouth); Herts. v Cumb. (Hertford); Lincs. v Norfolk (Cleethorpes); Oxon. v Dorset (St Edward's School, Oxford); Salop v Devon (Shifnal).

20—Beds. v Staffs. (Luton); Bucks. v Cumb. (Marlow); Cheshire v Devon (Bowdon); Northumb. v Norfolk (Jesmond).

25—Cornwall v Berks. (Truro); Herefords. v Salop (Leominster); Northumb. v Cambs. (Jesmond); Staffs. v Lincs. (Meir Heath); Suffolk v Bucks. (Copdock CC).

27—Cumb. v Cambs. (Netherfield); Devon v Berks. (Torquay); Norfolk v Bucks. (Lakenham); Wilts. v Salop (Trowbridge).

29—Norfolk v Suffolk (Lakenham).

AUGUST

1—Cumb. v Northumb. (Millom); Herts. v Beds. (St Albans); Oxon. v Cheshire (Banbury CC); Wales v Wilts. (Swansea).

2—Norfolk v Staffs. (Lakenham).

3—Berks. v Cheshire (Reading).

4—Cambs. v Lincs. (March); Suffolk v Staffs. (Mildenhall).

5—Norfolk v Beds. (Lakenham).

8—Berks. v Wilts. (Finchampstead); Bucks. v Cambs. (Slough); Salop v Dorset (Shrewsbury); Wales v Oxon. (Northop Hall).

10—Cheshire v Dorset (Boughton Hall).

15—Berks. v Dorset (Falkland CC); Cornwall v Oxon. (St Austell); Devon v Herefords. (Exmouth); Lincs. v Suffolk (Lincoln Lindum); Staffs. v Cumb. (Leek).

16—Herts. v Norfolk (Hertford).

17—Cornwall v Herefords. (Camborne); Devon v Oxon. (Bovey Tracey); Northumb. v Suffolk (Jesmond).

18—Cambs. v Beds. (Cambridge).

22—Cheshire v Wilts. (Neston); Devon v Cornwall (Sidmouth); Salop v Wales (Oswestry).

29—Bucks. v Herts. (Amersham); Devon v Wales (Instow); Dorset v Wilts. (Weymouth); Herefords. v Berks. (Brockhampton).

SEPTEMBER

12—Final at Worcester.

†HOLT CUP KNOCKOUT COMPETITION, 1993

All matches are of one day's duration.

Preliminary Round

May 23 Bucks. v Oxon. (Chesham); Herts. v Berks. (Bishop's Stortford); Norfolk v Beds. (Lakenham); Suffolk v Cambs. (Bury St Edmunds).

First Round

June 6 Cheshire v Cumb. (Warrington); Dorset v Devon (Sherborne); Herefords. v Staffs. (Hereford City); Herts. or Berks. v Bucks. or Oxon. (Shenley Park or Maidenhead & Bray); Norfolk or Beds. v Suffolk or Cambs. (Lakenham or Bedford School); Northumb. v Lincs. (Jesmond); Wales v Salop (Usk); Wilts. v Cornwall (Trowbridge).

Quarter-finals to be played on June 20.

Semi-finals to be played on July 4.

Final to be played on August 25 at Lord's (reserve day August 26).

†RAPID CRICKETLINE SECOND ELEVEN CHAMPIONSHIP, 1993

All matches are of three days' duration.

APRIL

28—Derbys. v Hants (Derby); Lancs. v Surrey (Manchester); Middx v Glos. (Uxbridge); Sussex v Durham (Hove); Warwicks. v Notts. (Coventry & North Warwicks.); Worcs. v Leics. (Worcester).

MAY

2—Somerset v Glos. (Bath).

5—Derbys. v Warwicks. (Ilkeston); Glam. v Northants (Cardiff); Glos. v Surrey (Bristol); Leics. v Kent (Oakham); Middx v Sussex (Harrow); Notts. v Worcs. (Nottingham); Yorks. v Essex (Leeds).

12—Derbys. v Durham (Chesterfield); Essex v Sussex (Chelmsford); Glam. v Notts. (Ammanford); Hants v Glos. (Southampton); Kent v Warwicks. (Maidstone); Lancs. v Leics. (Manchester); Middx v Northants (Harrow); Worcs. v Somerset (Old Hill).

19—Glam. v Hants (Cardiff); Kent v Essex (Canterbury); Leics. v Notts. (Leicester); Northants v Somerset (Northampton); Worcs. v Lancs. (Kidderminster); Yorks. v Middx (Leeds).

26—Derbys. v Leics. (Heanor); Essex v Somerset (Colchester); Glam. v Kent (Swansea); Hants v Yorks. (Portsmouth); Middx v Durham (Lensbury); Northants v Worcs. (Oundle School); Warwicks. v Lancs. (Walmley).

JUNE

2—Durham v Surrey (Felling); Glam. v Yorks. (Swansea); Middx v Leics. (Harrow); Notts. v Derbys. (Worthington Simpson, Newark); Somerset v Lancs. (Taunton); Sussex v Warwicks. (Hove).

9—Essex v Warwicks. (Southend); Glam. v Surrey (Pontymister); Glos. v Worcs. (Dowty Arle Court, Cheltenham); Kent v Sussex (Gore Court, Sittingbourne); Lancs. v Durham (Southport); Leics. v Hants (Leicester); Northants v Notts. (Old Northamptonians); Yorks. v Derbys. (Harrogate).

16—Durham v Notts. (Shildon); Essex v Leics. (Chelmsford); Glos. v Northants (Bristol); Hants v Kent (Southampton);

Middx v Glam. (RAF Vine Lane, Uxbridge); Surrey v Warwicks. (The Oval).

23—Derbys. v Glam. (Abbotsholme School, Rocester); Lancs. v Kent (Manchester); Notts. v Yorks. (Worksop CC); Somerset v Durham (Taunton); Surrey v Essex (Oxted); Worcs. v Sussex (Worcester).

30—Derbys. v Somerset (Derby); Durham v Leics. (Chester-le-Street); Lancs. v Glam. (Manchester); Middx v Hants (Uxbridge); Northants v Kent (Luton); Sussex v Surrey (Hove); Yorks. v Warwicks. (Sheffield).

JULY

3—Hants v Notts. (Southampton).

7—Durham v Glam. (Boldon CC); Kent v Worcs. (Dartford); Middx v Notts. (Southgate); Northants v Essex (Northampton); Somerset v Sussex (Taunton); Surrey v Derbys. (The Oval); Yorks. v Lancs. (Todmorden).

11—Somerset v Hants (Taunton).

14—Glos. v Kent (King's School, Gloucester); Leics. v Glam. (Leicester); Northants v Derbys. (Bedford School); Surrey v Somerset (The Oval); Sussex v Hants (Hove); Warwicks. v Middx (Old Edwardians); Worcs. v Essex (Halesowen).

21—Derbys. v Lancs. (Chesterfield); Durham v Kent (Seaton Carew); Glos. v Essex (Bristol); Hants v Worcs. (Southampton); Northants v Yorks. (Wellingborough School); Notts. v Somerset (Nottingham); Surrey v Middx (The Oval); Warwicks. v Leics. (Griff and Coton, Nuneaton).

28—Glam. v Glos. (Cardiff); Kent v Derbys. (Folkestone); Leics. v Surrey (Leicester); Notts. v Essex (Steetley, Shireoaks); Sussex v Northants (Horsham); Warwicks. v Hants (Leamington Spa); Worcs. v Middx (Worcester); Yorks. v Durham (Marske-by-Sea).

AUGUST

3—Hants v Northants (Southampton).

4—Essex v Middx (Chelmsford); Glos. v Derbys. (Bristol); Kent v Somerset (Maidstone); Lancs. v Notts. (Manchester); Surrey v Yorks. (The Oval); Sussex v Leics. (Horsham); Warwicks. v Glam. (Moseley); Worcs. v Durham (Barnt Green).

11—Durham v Northants (Sunderland CC); Essex v Derbys. (Southend); Glam. v Worcs. (Usk); Lancs. v Hants (Blackpool); Notts. v Surrey (Worksop College); Somerset v Leics. (Clevedon); Warwicks. v Glos. (Studley); Yorks. v Sussex (Elland).

15—Durham v Glos. (South Shields).

18—Essex v Lancs. (Chelmsford); Leics. v Glos. (Hinckley); Northants v Surrey (Northampton); Notts. v Kent (Nottingham); Somerset v Middx (Taunton); Sussex v Glam. (Hove); Warwicks. v Durham (Birmingham); Yorks. v Worcs. (York).

25—Derbys. v Middx (Derby); Glos. v Notts. (Bristol); Hants v Essex (Southampton); Kent v Yorks. (Folkestone); Leics. v Northants (Kibworth); Somerset v Glam. (Taunton); Sussex v Lancs. (Eastbourne); Worcs. v Warwicks. (Worcester).

SEPTEMBER

1—Essex v Durham (Colchester); Hants v Surrey (Basingstoke); Kent v Middx (British Gas, Eltham); Lancs. v Glos. (Manchester); Notts. v Sussex (Nottingham); Warwicks. v Northants (Birmingham); Yorks. v Somerset (Bradford).

8—Durham v Hants (Boldon CC); Essex v Glam. (Chelmsford); Leics. v Yorks. (Leicester); Middx v Lancs. (RAF Vine Lane, Uxbridge); Somerset v Warwicks. (Taunton); Surrey v Kent (Banstead); Sussex v Glos. (Hove); Worcs. v Derbys. (Worcester).

15—Derbys. v Sussex (Chesterfield); Glos. v Yorks. (Bristol); Lancs. v Northants (Northern, Crosby); Surrey v Worcs. (Banstead).

†BAIN CLARKSON TROPHY, 1993

All matches are of one day's duration.

MAY

3—Surrey v Kent (The Oval); Warwicks. v Northants (Birmingham).

4—Derbys. v Leics. (Ilkeston); Middx v Sussex (Harrow); Yorks. v Notts. (Bingley).

10—Glos. v Worcs. (Bristol); Lancs. v Yorks. (Southport); Leics. v Durham (Hinckley); MCC Young Cricketers v Middx (Southgate).

11—Derbys. v Durham (Chesterfield); Essex v Sussex (Newbury Park); Hants v Glos. (Southampton); Lancs. v Leics. (Manchester); Warwicks. v Somerset (Birmingham).

17—Glos. v Somerset (Bristol); Leics. v Derbys. (Leicester); Middx v MCC Young Cricketers (Lensbury); Sussex v Kent (Hove).

18—Glam. v Hants (Cardiff); Glos. v Warwicks. (Bristol); Kent v Essex (Canterbury); Lancs. v Durham (Northern, Crosby); Leics. v Notts. (Leicester); Northants v Somerset (Northampton).

24—Hants v Glam. (Portsmouth); Notts. v Derbys. (Farnsfield); Somerset v Worcs. (Taunton); Warwicks. v Glos. (Solihull).

25—Derbys. v Yorks. (Chesterfield); Essex v Middx (Newbury Park); Glam. v Warwicks. (Bridgend); Sussex v MCC Young Cricketers (Eastbourne).

JUNE

1—Hants v Worcs. (Southampton); Kent v Middx (Tunbridge Wells); Leics. v Lancs. (Leicester); Somerset v Glos. (Taunton).

7—Durham v Derbys. (Durham City CC); Middx v Kent (Shenley); Somerset v Hants (Taunton).

8—Essex v Surrey (Southend); Hants v Warwicks. (Finchampstead); Kent v Sussex (Gore Court, Sittingbourne); Yorks. v Derbys. (Bradford).

14—Glam. v Northants (Merthyr Tydfil); Kent v Surrey (Maidstone); MCC Young Cricketers v Sussex (Southgate).

15–Durham v Notts. (Norton CC); Glos. v Northants (Bristol); Sussex v Essex (Lewes Priory); Worcs. v Somerset (Worcester).

21–Hants v Northants (Southampton); Lancs. v Derbys. (Blackpool); Notts. v Leics. (Collingham); Somerset v Glam. (Taunton); Worcs. v Glos. (Worcester).

22–Hants v Somerset (Southampton); Notts. v Yorks. (Worksop College); Surrey v Essex (Oxted); Warwicks. v Worcs. (Birmingham).

28–Notts. v Durham (Worthington Simpson, Newark); Somerset v Northants (Taunton); Surrey v MCC Young Cricketers (The Oval); Worcs. v Warwicks. (Worcester).

29–Derbys. v Notts. (Knypersley); Durham v Leics. (Philadelphia CC); Essex v MCC Young Cricketers (Wickford); Northants v Glos. (Tring); Sussex v Surrey (Hove); Worcs. v Glam. (Worcester).

JULY

5–Durham v Lancs. (Durham School); Glam. v Somerset (Bridgend); Kent v MCC Young Cricketers (Canterbury); Middx v Essex (Harrow).

6–Northants v Hants (Northampton); Somerset v Warwicks. (Taunton); Yorks. v Lancs. (Bingley).

9–Glos. v Hants (Bristol).

12–Essex v Kent (Wickford); Glam. v Glos. (Cardiff); Northants v Worcs. (Northampton); Notts. v Lancs. (Nottingham); Surrey v Sussex (The Oval).

13–Glos. v Glam. (King's School, Gloucester); Leics. v Yorks. (Leicester); MCC Young Cricketers v Essex (Southgate); Northants v Warwicks. (Northampton).

19–MCC Young Cricketers v Surrey (Slough); Sussex v Middx (Hove); Warwicks. v Glam. (Coventry & North Warwicks.); Worcs. v Northants (Worcester); Yorks. v Leics. (Bradford).

20–Derbys. v Lancs. (Leek); Northants v Glam. (Banbury CC); Surrey v Middx (Guildford).

26–Durham v Yorks. (Bishop Auckland); MCC Young Cricketers v Kent (Slough); Middx v Surrey (Harrow); Worcs. v Hants (Ombersley).

27–Glam. v Worcs. (Panteg); Lancs. v Notts. (Wigan); Warwicks. v Hants (Knowle & Dorridge); Yorks. v Durham (Marske-by-Sea).

Semi-finals to be played on August 16 or 17.

Final to be played on September 6 (reserve day September 7).

Second Eleven fixtures were still subject to confirmation when Wisden *went to press.*

†WOMEN'S CRICKET, 1993

MAY

9–National Club Knockout.

22–National League.

29–Area Championship (Wellingborough School and Kimbolton School; 5 days).

JUNE

5–National League.

6–National League.

19–National Club Knockout.

26–National League.

JULY

3–Junior Outdoor Six-a-Side Tournament.

AUGUST

14–National Club Knockout.

15–National League.

21–National Club Knockout.

28–Territorial Tournament (Westminster Coll., Oxford; 3 days).

SEPTEMBER

4–National Club Knockout Final (Sussex).

†WOMEN'S WORLD CUP, 1993

JULY

20–Australia v Netherlands (Warrington); Caribbean Federation v India (John Player Sports Ground, Nottingham); Denmark v England (Banstead); Ireland v New Zealand (Shenley, Herts.).

21–Australia v India (Collingham, Yorks.); Caribbean Federation v Netherlands (West Bromwich Dartford, Birmingham); Denmark v Ireland (Christ Church, Oxford); England v New Zealand (Lloyds Bank, Beckenham).

24–Australia v Caribbean Federation (Tunbridge Wells); Denmark v New Zealand (Wellington Coll., Berks.); England v Ireland (Reading); India v Netherlands (Beaconsfield).

25–Australia v Ireland (Bank of England, Roehampton); Caribbean Federation v Denmark (Lloyds Bank, Beckenham); England v India (Finchampstead); Netherlands v New Zealand (Lindfield, Sussex).

26–Australia v England (Guildford); Caribbean Federation v New Zealand (Civil Service Sports Ground, Chiswick); Denmark v Netherlands (Wellington Coll., Berks.); India v Ireland (Wellington Coll., Berks.).

28–Australia v Denmark (Honor Oak, Dulwich); Caribbean Federation v England (Horsham, Sussex); India v New Zealand (Ealing, Middx); Ireland v Netherlands (Marlow, Bucks.).

29–Australia v New Zealand (Midland Bank, Beckenham); Caribbean Federation v Ireland (Dorking); Denmark v India (Slough); England v Netherlands (Ealing).

AUGUST

1–WORLD CUP FINAL (Lord's) (reserve day August 2).